RHS PLANT FINDER 2011-2012

DEVISED BY CHRIS PHILIP
AND REALISED BY TONY LORD

EDITOR-IN-CHIEF
JANET CUBEY

RHS EDITORS
JAMES ARMITAGE DAWN EDWARDS
NEIL LANCASTER CHRISTOPHER WHITEHOUSE

COMPILER
JUDITH MERRICK

CONSULTANT EDITOR
TONY LORD

Royal
Horticultural
Society

Published by
The Royal Horticultural Society
80 Vincent Square
London SW1P 2PE

First edition April 1987
Twenty-fifth edition April 2011

British Library Cataloguing Publication Data.
A Catalogue record for this book is available from the British Library.

ISBN 978-1-907057-18-2

Compiled by
The Royal Horticultural Society
80 Vincent Square,
London SW1P 2PE
Registered charity no: 222879/SC038262

www.rhs.org.uk

Illustrations by Sarah Young
Maps by Alan Cooper

Produced for The Royal Horticultural Society by
COOLING BROWN

Printed and bound in England by Clays Ltd, St Ives Plc

The Compiler and the Editors of the *RHS Plant Finder* have taken every care, in the time available, to check all the information supplied to them by the nurseries concerned. Nevertheless, in a work of this kind, containing as it does hundreds of thousands of separate computer encodings, errors and omissions will, inevitably, occur. Neither the RHS, the Publisher nor the Editors can accept responsibility for any consequences that may arise from such errors.

If you find mistakes we hope that you will let us know so that the matter can be corrected in the next edition.

Front cover photographs: *Aster novi-belgii* 'Professor Anton Kippenberg' (RHS/Carol Sheppard)
Spine: *Streptocarpus* 'Harlequin Blue' (RHS/Carol Sheppard)
Back cover from left to right: *Aquilegia* 'Florida' (State Series) (RHS), *Dahlia* 'Ryecroft Jan' (RHS/Leigh Hunt), *Viola* 'Étain' (RHS/Christopher Whitehouse), *Callicarpa americana* (RHS/Carol Sheppard)

www.rhs.org.uk

Contents

INTRODUCTION

The *RHS Plant Finder* exists to put enthusiastic gardeners in touch with suppliers of plants. The book is divided into two related sections – **PLANTS** and **NURSERIES. PLANTS** includes an A–Z Plant Directory of about 70,000 plant names, against which are listed a series of nursery codes. These codes point the reader to the full nursery details contained in the **NURSERIES** section towards the back of the book.

The *RHS Plant Finder* is comprehensively updated every year and provides the plant lover with the richest source of suppliers known to us.

As you will see from the entries in the **NURSERY DETAILS BY CODE** many nurseries do not now publish a printed catalogue but produce an online version only. This is a growing trend, fuelled by the cost of printing a full catalogue.

It is important to remember when ordering that many of the nurseries listed in the book are small, family-run, businesses that propagate their own material. They cannot therefore guarantee to hold large stocks of the plants they list. Some will, however, propagate to order.

NEW IN THIS EDITION

In this edition's topical essay RHS Horticultural Adviser, Helen Bostock, explains how the RHS has become involved in a research project which will contribute to the debate on the impact of gardens as a wildlife habitat.

The changes made to genera used in the book this year, which reflect the decisions of the RHS Advisory Committee on Nomenclature and Taxonomy (ACONAT), include: the separation of *Morella* as being distinct from *Myrica*; the adoption of *Argyrocytisus* as being distinct from *Cytisus*; inclusion of *Calopsis* and *Ischryolepis* within *Restio.* Following the decision to accept Goldblatt and Manning, *The Iris Family: Natural History and Classification* (2008) as the standard reference for genera in the *Iridaceae*, the following changes were also made: recognition of *Afrocrocus* as being distinct from *Romulea*; inclusion of *Phalocallis* within *Cypella;* inclusion of *Anomatheca* within *Freesia*; inclusion of *Schizostylis* within *Hesperantha*; inclusion of *Belamcanda*, *Hermodactylus* and *Pardanthopsis* within *Iris;* inclusion of *Galaxia*, *Gynandriris*, *Hexaglottis* and *Homeria* within *Moraea*

If there is a botanical issue that you wish to bring to the attention of the editors, or that you wish ACONAT to discuss, please contact us.

AVAILABLE FROM THE COMPILER

APPLICATION FOR ENTRY

Nurseries appearing in the *RHS Plant Finder* for the first time this year are printed in bold type in the *Nursery Index by Name* starting on p.936.

If you wish your nursery to be considered for inclusion in the next edition of the *RHS Plant Finder* (2012-2013), contact the Compiler at the address below. Entries to the book are free.

PLANTS LAST LISTED IN EARLIER EDITIONS

Plants cease to be listed for a variety of reasons. For more information turn to *How to Use the Plant Directory* on p.18. A listing of the 50,000 or so plants listed in earlier editions, but for which we currently have no known supplier, is available online at www.rhs.org.uk/rhsplantfinder/documents.asp.

LISTS OF NURSERIES FOR PLANTS WITH MORE THAN 30 SUPPLIERS

To prevent the book from becoming too big, we do not print the nursery codes where more than 30 nurseries offer the same plant. The plant is then listed as being "Widely available". This is detailed more fully in *How to Use the Plant Directory* on p.18.

If any readers have difficulty in finding such a plant, we will be pleased to send a full list of all the nurseries that we have on file as stockists. All such enquiries must include the full name of the plant being sought, as shown in the *RHS Plant Finder*, together with an A5 size SAE.

The above may be obtained from:
The Compiler, *RHS Plant Finder*, RHS Garden Wisley, Woking, Surrey GU23 6QB
Email: plantfinder@rhs.org.uk

This information is also available online.

The RHS Plant Finder Online

The *RHS Plant Finder* is available on the Internet. Visit the Royal Horticultural Society's website **www.rhs.org.uk** and search the *RHS Plant Finder Online.*

Acknowledgements

Judith Merrick, helped by June Skinner, compiled this edition. Richard Sanford managed the editing of the plant names on the database. Rupert Wilson and Julia Barclay administered the Horticultural Database, using the BG-Base™ Collection Management Software.

RHS Botanists James Armitage, Dawn Edwards, Neil Lancaster and Christopher Whitehouse have undertaken the task of editing the new plant names in this edition of the book.

As always, we are greatly indebted to Peter Cooling of Cooling Brown Ltd, for his skill in enabling us to turn our mass of raw data into a published format.

We should also like to acknowledge the help of Simon Maughan, RHS Editor, John David, RHS Chief Scientist, Tony Lord, Consultant Editor, Carol Sheppard, RHS Images Co-ordinator (Science and Advice), Louise Bowering, RHS Special Publications Manager, Kerry Walter of BG-BASE (UK) Ltd., Max Phillips of Strange Software Ltd. and Alan Cooper.

Our colleagues on the RHS Advisory Committee on Nomenclature and Taxonomy, along with the RHS International Cultivar Registrars, have all provided valuable guidance and information. Many nurseries have supplied helpful information on plants, which has proved useful in verifying some of the more obscure names, and have suggested corrections to existing entries. Some of these remain to be checked and will be entered in the next edition, although those that contravene the Codes of Nomenclature may have to be rejected. We appreciate your patience while these checks are made. We are also grateful to all our regular correspondents and to the many readers who have made comments and suggestions.

Clematis	D. Donald, Int. Cultivar Registrar, RHS
Chrysanthemum	J. Barker (2007–08)
Conifers	S. McDonald, Int. Cultivar Registrar, RHS
Dahlia	R. Hedge, S. McDonald, RHS Wisley
Dianthus	Dr A.C. Leslie, Int. Cultivar Registrar, RHS
Geranium	D.X. Victor (2003), Int. Cultivar Registrar
Heathers	Dr E.C. Nelson, Int. Cultivar Registrar
Ilex	S. Andrews (2006)
Iris	J. Hewitt (2005, 2007–08)
Lavandula	S. Andrews (2003 & 2005)
Lilium	D. Donald, Int. Cultivar Registrar, RHS
Meconopsis	Dr E. Stevens (2003,'05 & 2007)
Narcissus	S. McDonald, Int. Cultivar Registrar, RHS
Nerine	Dr J.C. David (2009)
Quercus	P. Trehane, Int. Cultivar Registrar (2009)
Rhododendron	Dr A.C. Leslie, Int. Cultivar Registrar, RHS
Sorbus	Dr H. McAllister
Thymus	M. Easter (2003–09)
Viburnum	C. Sanders

Janet Cubey
RHS Chief of Horticultural Informatics
February 2011

Conservation and the Environment

Invasive Plants

As the *RHS Plant Finder* demonstrates, gardens in Britain have been greatly enriched by the diversity of plants introduced to cultivation from abroad. While the vast majority of those introduced have enhanced our gardens, a few have proved to be highly invasive and to threaten native habitats. Once such plants are established it is very difficult, costly and potentially damaging to native ecosystems to eradicate or control the invasive "alien" species. Gardeners can help by choosing not to buy or distribute non-native invasive plants and by taking steps to prevent them escaping into the wild and by disposing of them in a responsible way.

Ten of the most serious invasive non-native species are no longer listed in the *RHS Plant Finder*. Any cultivars or varieties of them that are listed are believed to be less invasive than the species themselves. These 10 plants are:

Azolla filiculoides – fairy fern
Crassula helmsii – New Zealand pygmy weed
Elodea nuttalli – Nuttall's waterweed
Fallopia japonica – Japanese knotweed
Heracleum mantegazzianum – giant hogweed
Hydrocotyle ranunculoides – floating pennywort
Impatiens glandulifera – Himalayan balsam
Lagarosiphon major – curly waterweed
Ludwigia grandiflora – water primrose
Myriophyllum aquaticum – parrot's feather

It is expected that at least half of these will be banned from sale under recent UK legislation in autumn 2011 or spring 2012. Further species are considered to present a threat to UK habitats and gardeners are encouraged to grow alternative plants. Guidance on this can be found in three booklets:

Gardening without harmful invasive plants
Landscaping without harmful invasive plants
Keeping ponds and aquaria without harmful invasive plants

These are available on the Plantlife website (www.plantlife.org.uk) or by post from Plantlife. For further information on non-native invasive species see the GB non-native species secretariat website (www.nonnativespecies.org)

Bringing plants back from abroad

Travelling can be a great source of inspiration for gardeners and often provides an opportunity to encounter new and interesting plants. Anyone wishing to bring plants back into Britain from overseas must realise, however, that this is a complex matter. Various regulations are in force that apply to amateur gardeners as well as to commercial nurseries. The penalties for breaking these can be serious.

Some of the most important regulatory instruments are listed below.

Plant Health regulations are in place to control the spread of pests and diseases. Plants are divided into the categories of prohibited, controlled and unrestricted, but there are also limits that vary according to the part of the world you are travelling from. For full details contact the Food and Environment Research Agency, (www.fera.defra.gov.uk/plants/plantHealth/index.cfm).

The Convention on International Trade in Endangered Species (CITES) affects the transport of animal and plant material across international boundaries. Its aim is to prevent exploitative trade and thereby to prevent harm and the ultimate extinction of wild populations. A tighter regime on trade in species of wild fauna and flora exists in the EU that requires export permits for any plants listed in Appendices A, B & C and import permits for Appendices A & B. There is a further Appendix D for non-CITES listed species that the EU consider to be endangered. A broad range of plants is covered in these Appendices, including *Cactaceae* and *Orchidaceae* and, although species are mentioned in the convention title, the restrictions cover all cultivars and hybrids of listed species too, except for specific exclusions, where there are annotations in the Appendices. Details of the plants listed in the Appendices can be found on the website of the UK's CITES Management Authority, Animal Health, (www.defra.gov.uk/animalhealth/cites/legislation.html).

The Convention on Biological Diversity (CBD or the "Rio Convention") recognises the property rights of individual countries in relation to their own biodiversity. It exists to enable access to that biodiversity, but equally to ensure the sharing of any benefit derived from it. In principle it is possible to collect plant material from other countries that have asserted their rights under the CBD, by ensuring that you have obtained documentary evidence of prior informed consent on the basis of mutually agreed terms for any uses that the material will be put to in the future. In practice the legal requirements for collecting plant material varies from country to country and it is advisable to contact the National Focal Point for further information. These details and other information on the Convention can be found on the CBD website (www.cbd.int).

European Habitats Directive. The full implementation of this Directive into UK law in 2007 extended protection to all of the European

Protected Species (EPS) listed in the Appendices of that Directive (these are Appendices II(b) and IV(b) for plants) whether they are native to the UK or not. This requires a licence for material of any of these species collected in the wild after 1994. These are issued by Natural England (for England), the Countryside Council for Wales (in Wales) and Scottish Natural Heritage (for Scotland), (www.jncc.gov.uk/page-1374).

Contact addresses:
Plantlife
14 Rollestone Street
Salisbury
Wiltshire
SP1 1DX
Tel: (01722) 342730

Wildlife Licensing and Registration Service (WRLS)
Animal Health
1/17 Temple Quay House
2 The Square
Temple Quay
Bristol
BS1 6EB
Tel: 0117 372 8774

Plant Health
Room 10GA01
The Food and Environment Research Agency
Sand Hutton
York
YO41 1LZ
Tel: (01904) 465625

Joint Nature Conservation Committee
Monkstone House
City Road
Peterborough
PE1 1JY
Tel: (01733) 562626

Department for Environment, Food & Rural Affairs (Defra)
Nobel House
17 Smith Square
London
SW1P 3JR
Email for general biodiversity queries:
biodiversity@defra.gsi.gov.uk

RHS Research into Plants for Biodiversity

Wildlife gardening has only recently gained acceptance as a topic for serious scientific study. This is not before time, since the impact of gardens as a habitat is quite substantial, with the number of domestic gardens in the UK estimated at over 16 million, equating to hundreds of millions of plants.

Frustration at the lack of recognition is expressed by ecologists such as Dr Ken Thompson, a senior research Fellow at the University of Sheffield and lead scientist in the Biodiversity in Urban Gardens Sheffield (BUGS) project. "I know it's a heretical thing to say," he wrote in 2009, "but most farmland would be improved by having a housing estate built on it from a biodiversity point of view. If you're comparing gardens with the equivalent area of modern intensive farmland, gardens are much better." [*The Times*, September 8th 2009].

Certainly, if we are to maximise the potential of gardens for reducing biodiversity loss, we must begin to take the topic a little more seriously. This means asking questions; finding out which practices work and which don't; investigating the impact of one approach over another; offering gardeners, whether professional or amateur, good evidence for the advice on offer rather than relying on assumptions. The world of horticulture has never held back from investing in research. It is now time, therefore, for serious research into biodiversity horticulture.

Over the last 10 years or so, momentum has been gathering with a growing number of projects and studies into all aspects of wildlife gardening being undertaken by universities, conservation bodies and keen individuals such as Jennifer Owen, who in 2010 was awarded the RHS Veitch Memorial Medal for her 30-year study into the wildlife in her Leicester garden. Many of these studies focus on the conservation of individual plant and animal species, though some look at specific habitats such as garden ponds and a number of researchers have taken the bold step of investigating the rich biodiversity of gardens individually or collectively.

I say 'bold step' because of the complex nature of studying gardens. Rarely identified in the UK Government's Local Biodiversity Action Plans (BAPS), gardens tend to be relatively small pockets of privately owned land difficult to access for scientific research (although some work has been done using aerial imagery) and typified by a myriad of styles, features and plant combinations. Studying them is made doubly difficult by the fact that they are subject to regular changes of ownership and management. It is little wonder that they have been under-studied and consequently undervalued in their role in supporting wildlife.

In 2008, the Science team at RHS Wisley recognised that there was a particular gap in horticultural understanding that warranted investigation: does the geographical origin of a plant in a garden have a bearing on its wildlife value?

The plant-focused basis of the work struck a chord with the RHS. Here was something that would be of direct relevance to its members and to gardeners in general but, as with all studies into garden biodiversity, the topic was not going to lend itself easily to investigation. In fact, some in the scientific community were so sure that this topic either couldn't be studied or that the outcome would simply prove them right, that they felt it was a waste of time to undertake it in the first place.

The debate is centred on the role of garden plants in supporting wildlife. The botanical composition of gardens differs significantly from that of more natural habitats. Of plants in an average garden, only around 30%[1] are native (i.e. indigenous to Britain). Since gardens tend to be relatively rich in biodiversity, this leaves a big question mark over the part the 70% non-native plants have to play.

Invertebrates – 'bugs' to most people – are at the heart of garden ecology and much misunderstood. Admittedly, some inflict unsightly damage on a range of garden plants, but the majority are simply getting on with eating and being eaten.

Using in-house entomological expertise, the RHS devised a three-year field trial to investigate the impact of different planting schemes on invertebrate abundance and diversity. As with any project seeking to capture the imagination, a snappy title was required: hence Plants for Bugs.

During 2008/9, work was undertaken at RHS Garden Wisley to construct a trials plot consisting of 18 3×3m beds. The entire plot was replicated at a second site nearby in Wisley Village. Each bed is separated by a 1-m wide path and planted with 14 different species of plants, from bulbs, ferns, grasses and herbaceous perennials to shrubs and a climber.

It would take decades of research to cover every plant in cultivation so, instead of looking at plants as individual species, the approach has been to assess

---

[1] Loram, A., Thompson, K., Warren, P.H. & Gaston, K.J. 2008. Urban domestic gardens (XII): the richness and composition of the flora in five cities. *Journal of Vegetation Science*, 19, 321–330

how specific groups of plants performed. This involved growing native and non-native plants alongside each other and studying any differences in the fauna associated with them. The hypothesis was that no differences would be found.

To test this hypothesis, plants from one of three different geographical regions were planted in each bed: Britain (i.e. native plants), the rest of the northern hemisphere (i.e. non-native but with some botanical and ecological similarities to British natives) and the southern hemisphere (i.e. non-native plants that are often remote, in botanical and ecological terms, from native British flora). For example, in the native bed one of the 14 plant species is hemp agrimony (*Eupatorium cannabinum*); in the equivalent position in the northern hemisphere bed, the North American Joe-pye weed (*Eupatorium maculatum*) and South American *Verbena bonariensis* in the southern hemisphere bed.

The beds are planted to imitate a mini garden border and, with the exception of zero pesticide use (for obvious reasons), are being managed very much as any gardener would manage an ordinary plot, so weeded, fed and watered when necessary, cut back in spring, etc. A botanist or astute visitor might spot the distinction between the plantings but would the bugs be as discerning?

By the start of 2010 – coincidentally the UN International Year of Biodiversity – the plots were prepared and the scientific team was ready to begin the first of three years of monitoring. Recording protocols, created with the help of consultants and research establishments such as Rothamsted Research in Hertfordshire, were put into practice.

A total of four separate monitoring methods were developed:

1. **Observation of flower-visiting insects**
   During calm, sunny conditions, each bed is observed for flying insects such as bees and butterflies visiting or resting on the flowers. These insects are particularly important as they include some of the pollinators which are vital for the production of many crops. Many species are of conservation concern but, since it is these insects that most gardeners consider attractive, they are usually actively encouraged into their gardens.
2. **Vortis suction sampler**
   One level below the flowers is the foliage layer. Herbivores such as caterpillars, aphids, leaf beetle larvae and leafhoppers abound in this zone. They are captured using a vacuum-style piece of equipment called a Vortis suction sampler. The nozzle is swept slowly over each plant; the insect matter captured by this method is then identified in the laboratory. The survival of such herbivores is directly dependent on suitable plant availability and, although not generally regarded as "the gardener's friend", they in turn support many organisms higher up the food chain.
3. **Pitfall traps**
   At ground level, pitfall trapping is a standardised method that monitors the activity of insects such as ground beetles. The trap, a plastic cup, is set in the soil in the centre of each plot and left in place for a fortnight. Small creatures crawling over the soil are captured when they tumble into the cup.
4. **Slug and snail (gastropod) traps**
   Although not encouraged in most gardens, slugs and snails are also monitored in this project. The trap consists of chicken feed used as bait, placed under an upturned plastic saucer to provide slugs and snails with shelter. Traps are set during damp weather conditions when molluscs are more likely to be active.

This 'top-to-toe' approach to data collection ensures we maximise the number and diversity of species found using plants or other resources within each bed. This recording method is repeated around five times between the months of March and October.

By the end of the first year (2010), over 14000 invertebrates had been counted and identified. This promising start gives confidence in the recording methods and suggests that by the end of the three year study sufficient data will be available to analyse.

Some figures from 2010 include:

- Over 2300 flying insects were observed visiting the plots, including seven species of bumblebee and twelve species of butterfly.
- From the pitfall traps over 6000 ground-dwelling insects and other invertebrates have been counted and over 160 species identified, including 30 species (630 specimens) of ground beetle and four species of woodlice (437 specimens).
- The Vortis suction sampler has captured over 3000 invertebrates off the foliage and 115 species have been identified.
- A mere 45 slugs and snails were caught, possibly due to the dry summer.

With two years still to run, meaningful conclusions cannot yet be drawn from the data. But that does not prevent us from looking ahead at some of the possibilities opened up by the Plants for Bugs research. We need to be cautious, however. A single study into this complex topic will almost certainly fuel yet more debate and further research. Without a pioneer study such as Plants for Bugs, the debate surrounding planting for wildlife remains scientifically uncharted territory, leaving gardeners floundering for direction. So where might the findings take us?

One potential outcome is that there is a marked richness of invertebrates in the native beds as compared to the non-native beds. This is certainly the expectation of many plant and animal conservationists. It will strengthen the trend towards the increased use of British native plants in gardens and ensure RHS advice to wildlife gardeners has a strong emphasis on incorporating wild flowers into planting schemes.

Another possibility is that results might reveal that the northern hemisphere near-native group of plants performs on a par with the British natives. If this were the case, wildlife gardeners could rely heavily on this plant group without necessarily feeling they have to augment it with many pure natives. Certainly plants originating from Northern Europe, North America, China and Japan are relatively well adapted to the UK climate (e.g. fully hardy) and are already extremely popular with British gardeners.

It is also possible that few tangible differences will be discernible across all three plant groups. This certainly would be a headline story since it would suggest that it really doesn't matter what you plant, so long as you plant as wide a range of plants as possible.

Whatever the outcome, we mustn't lose sight of the fact that wildlife gardening is still gardening.

With the exception of a handful of invasive plants, it would be hard to argue that any plant is actually bad for wildlife but with 70,000 plants listed in the current *RHS Plant Finder* and with the average garden size getting ever smaller, the need for evidence-based advice to help gardeners make well-informed decisions on choosing plants has never been more important.

Helen Bostock
RHS Horticultural Adviser

To learn more about the project visit www.rhs.org.uk/plants4bugs

EXTENDED GLOSSARY

This glossary combines some of the helpful introductory sections from older editions in an alphabetical listing. A fuller, more discursive account of plant names, *Guide to Plant Names*, and a detailed guide to the typography of plant names, *Recommended Style for Printing Plant Names*, are both available as RHS Advisory Leaflets. To request a copy of either please send an A4 SAE to The Compiler at the contact address given on page 4.

ADVISORY COMMITTEE ON NOMENCLATURE AND TAXONOMY

This Panel advises the RHS on individual problems of nomenclature regarding plants in cultivation and, in particular, use of names in the *RHS Horticultural Database*, reflected in the annual publication of the *RHS Plant Finder*.

The aim is always to make the plant names in the *RHS Plant Finder* as consistent, reliable and stable as possible and acceptable to gardeners and botanists alike, not only in the British Isles but around the world. Recent proposals to change or correct names are examined with the aim of creating a balance between the stability of well-known names and botanical and taxonomic correctness. In some cases the Panel feels that the conflicting views on the names of some groups of plants will not easily be resolved. The Panel's policy is then to wait and review the situation once a more obvious consensus is reached, rather than rush to rename plants only to have to change them again when opinions have shifted.

The Panel is chaired by Dr Alan Leslie (RHS) with Dr Janet Cubey (RHS) (Vice-Chair) and includes: Dr Crinan Alexander (RBGE), Susyn Andrews, Chris Brickell, Dr James Compton, Dr John David (RHS), Mike Grant (RHS Publications), John Grimshaw, Dr Stephen Jury (University of Reading), Dr Tony Lord, Prof David Mabberley (corresponding member, RBGKew), Dr Charles Nelson, Chris Sanders, Julian Shaw (RHS), with Dr Christopher Whitehouse (RHS) as Secretary.

AUTHORITIES

In order that plant names can be used with precision throughout the scientific world, the name of the person who coined the name of a plant species (its author, or authority) is added to the plant name. Usually this information is of little consequence to gardeners, except in cases where the same name has been given to two different plants or a name is commonly misapplied. Although only one usage is correct, both may be encountered in books, so indicating the author is the only way to be certain about which plant is being referred to. This can happen equally with cultivars. Authors' names, where it is appropriate to cite them, appear in a smaller typeface after the species or cultivar name to which they refer and are abbreviated following Brummitt and Powell's *Authors of Plant Names*.

🏆 AWARD OF GARDEN MERIT

The Award of Garden Merit (AGM) is intended to be of practical value to the ordinary gardener and is therefore awarded only after a period of assessment by the Society's Standing and Joint Committees. An AGM plant:

- must be available
- must be of outstanding excellence for garden decoration or use
- must be of good constitution
- must not require highly specialist growing conditions or care
- must not be particularly susceptible to any pest or disease
- must not be subject to an unreasonable degree of reversion

The AGM symbol is cited in conjunction with the **hardiness** rating. A full list of AGM plants may be found on the RHS website at www.rhs.org.uk/plants/plant-trials-and-awards/plant-awards.

BOTANICAL NAMES

The aim of the botanical naming system is to provide each different plant with a single, unique, universal name. The basic unit of plant classification is the species. Species that share a number of significant characteristics are grouped together to form a genus (plural **genera**). The name of a species is made up of two elements; the name of the genus followed by the specific epithet, for example, *Narcissus romieuxii*.

Variation within a species can be recognised by division into subspecies (usually abbreviated to subsp.), varietas (or variety abbreviated to var.) and forma (or form abbreviated to f.). Whilst it is

unusual for a plant to have all of these, it is possible, as in this example, *Narcissus romieuxii* subsp. *albidus* var. *zaianicus* f. *lutescens*.
The botanical elements are always given in italics, with only the genus taking an initial capital letter. The rank indications are never in italics. In instances where the rank is not known it is necessary to form an invalid construction by quoting a second epithet without a rank. This is an unsatisfactory situation, but requires considerable research to resolve.

In some genera, such as *Hosta*, we list the cultivar names alphabetically with the species or **hybrid** to which they are attributed afterwards in parentheses. For example, *Hosta* 'Reversed' (*sieboldiana*). In other situations where the aim is not to create a list alphabetically by cultivar name we would recommend styling this as *Hosta sieboldiana* 'Reversed'.

CLASSIFICATION OF GENERA

Genera that include a large number of species or with many cultivars are often subdivided into informal horticultural classifications or more formal Cultivar Groups, each based on a particular characteristic or combination of characteristics. Colour of flower or fruit and shape of flower are common examples and, with fruit, whether a cultivar is grown for culinary or dessert purposes. How such groups are named differs from genus to genus.

To help users of the *RHS Plant Finder* find the plants they want, the classifications used within cultivated genera are listed using codes and plants are marked with the appropriate code in brackets after its name in the Plant Directory. To find the explanation of each code, simply look it up under the genus concerned in the **Classification of Genera** starting on p.29. The codes relating to edible fruits are also listed here, but these apply across several genera.

COLLECTORS' REFERENCES

Abbreviations (usually with numbers) following a plant name refer to the collector(s) of the plant. These abbreviations are expanded, with a collector's name or expedition title, in the section **Collectors' References** starting on p.20.

A collector's reference may indicate a new, as yet unnamed range of variation within a species. The inclusion of collectors' references in the *RHS Plant Finder* supports the book's role in sourcing unusual plants.

The Convention on Biological Diversity calls for conservation of biodiversity, its sustainable use and the fair and equitable sharing of any derived benefits. Since its adoption in 1993, collectors are required to have prior informed consent from the country of origin for the acquisition and commercialisation of collected material.

COMMON NAMES

In a work such as this, it is necessary to refer to plants by their botanical names for the sake of universal comprehension and clarity. However, at the same time we recognise that with fruit and vegetables most people are more familiar with their common names than their botanical ones. Cross-references are therefore given from common to botanical names for fruit, vegetables and the commoner culinary herbs throughout the Plant Directory.

CULTIVAR

Literally meaning cultivated variety, cultivar names are given to denote variation within species and that generated by hybridisation, in cultivation. To make them easily distinguishable from botanical names, they are not printed in italics and are enclosed in single quotation marks. Cultivar names coined since 1959 should follow the rules of the International Code of Nomenclature for Cultivated Plants (**ICNCP**).

DESCRIPTIVE TERMS

Terms that appear after the main part of the plant name are shown in a smaller font to distinguish them. These descriptive elements give extra information about the plant and may include the **collector's reference**, **authority**, or what colour it is. For example, *Fritillaria thessala* SBEL 443, *Penstemon* 'Sour Grapes' M.Fish, *Lobelia tupa* dark orange.

FAMILIES

Genera are grouped into larger groups of related plants called families. Most family names, with the exception of eight familiar names, end with the same group of letters, *-aceae*. While it is still acceptable to use these eight exceptions, the modern trend adopted in the *RHS Plant Finder* is to use alternative names with *–aceae* endings. The families concerned are *Compositae* (*Asteraceae*), *Cruciferae* (*Brassicaceae*), *Gramineae* (*Poaceae*), *Guttiferae* (*Clusiaceae*), *Labiatae* (*Lamiaceae*), *Leguminosae* (split here into *Caesalpiniaceae*, *Mimosaceae* and *Papilionaceae*), *Palmae* (*Arecaceae*) and *Umbelliferae* (*Apiceae*).

Apart from these exceptions we now follow (from 2010) *Mabberley's Plant Book* (3rd edition).

GENUS (plural – GENERA)

Genera used in the *RHS Plant Finder* are almost always those given in Brummitt's *Vascular Plant*

Families and Genera. For spellings and genders of generic names, Greuter's *Names in Current Use for Extant Plant Genera* has also been consulted. See **Botanical Names.**

GREX

Within orchids, hybrids of the same parentage, regardless of how alike they are, are given a grex name. Individuals can be selected, given cultivar names and propagated vegetatively. For example, *Pleione* Versailles gx 'Bucklebury', where Versailles is the grex name and 'Bucklebury' is a selected **cultivar.**

GROUP

This is a collective name for a group of cultivars within a genus with similar characteristics. The word Group is always included and, where cited with a cultivar name, it is enclosed in brackets, for example, *Actaea simplex* (Atropurpurea Group) 'Brunette', where 'Brunette' is a distinct cultivar in a group of purple-leaved cultivars.

Another example of a Group is *Rhododendron polycladum* Scintillans Group. In this case *Rhododendron scintillans* was a species that is now botanically 'sunk' within *R. polycladum*, but it is still recognised horticulturally as a Group.

Group names are also used for swarms of hybrids with the same parentage, for example, *Rhododendron* Polar Bear Group. These were formerly treated as **grex** names, a term now used only for orchids. A single clone from the Group may be given the same cultivar name, for example, *Rhododendron* 'Polar Bear'.

HARDINESS

Hardiness ratings are shown for **Award of Garden Merit** plants. The categories used are as follows:

H1 = plants requiring heated glass in the British Isles
H2 = plants requiring unheated glass in the British Isles
H3 = plants hardy outside in some regions of the British Isles or in particular situations, or which, while usually grown outside in summer, need frost-free protection in winter (eg. dahlias)
H4 = plants hardy throughout the British Isles
H1-2, H2-3, H3-4 = plants intermediate between the two ratings given
H1+3 = requiring heated glass; may be grown outside in summer

HYBRIDS

Some species, when grown together, in the wild or in cultivation, are found to interbreed and form hybrids. In some instances a hybrid name is coined, for example hybrids between *Primula hirsuta* and *P. minima* are given the name *Primula × forsteri*, the multiplication sign indicating hybrid origin. Hybrid formulae that quote the parentage of the hybrid are used where a unique name has not been coined, for example *Rhododendron calophytum × R. praevernum*. In hybrid formulae you will find parents in alphabetical order, with the male (m) and female (f) parent indicated where known. Hybrids between different genera are also possible, for example × *Mahoberberis* is the name given to hybrids between *Mahonia* and *Berberis*.

There are also a few special-case hybrids called graft hybrids, where the tissues of two plants are physically rather than genetically mixed. These are indicated by an addition rather than a multiplication sign, so *Laburnum* + *Cytisus* becomes + *Laburnocytisus*.

ICNCP

The ICNCP is the International Code of Nomenclature for Cultivated Plants. First published in 1959, the most recent (8th) edition was published in 2009.

Cultivar names that do not conform to this Code, and for which there is no valid alternative, are flagged I (for invalid). This code states that the minimum requirement is for a cultivar name to be given in conjunction with the name of the genus. However, in the *RHS Plant Finder* we choose to give as full a name as possible to give the gardener and botanist more information about the plant, following the Recommendation in the Code.

NOTES ON NOMENCLATURE AND IDENTIFICATION

The **Notes on Nomenclature and Identification**, starting on p.24, give further information for names that are complex or may be confusing. See also **Advisory Committee on Nomenclature and Taxonomy.**

PLANT BREEDERS' RIGHTS

Plants covered by an *active* grant of Plant Breeders' Rights (PBR) are indicated throughout the Plant Directory. Grants indicated are those awarded by both UK and EU Plant Variety Rights offices. Because grants can both come into force and lapse at any time, this book can only aim to represent the situation at one point in time, but it is hoped that this will act as a useful guide to growers and gardeners. UK grants represent the position as of the end of December 2010 and EU grants as of the end of December 2010. We do not give any indication where PBR grants may be pending.

To obtain PBR protection, a new plant must be registered and pass tests for distinctness, uniformity and stability under an approved name. This approved name, under the rules of the **ICNCP**, established by a legal process, has to be regarded as the cultivar name. Increasingly however, these approved names are a code or "nonsense" name and are therefore often unpronounceable and meaningless, so the plants are given other names designed to attract sales when they are released. These secondary names are often referred to as selling names but are officially termed **trade designations**.

For further information on UK PBR contact:
Plant Variety Rights Office, Whitehouse Lane, Huntingdon Road, Cambridge CB3 0LF
Tel: (01223) 342350
Website: www.fera.defra.gov.uk/plants/plantVarieties/

For details of plants covered by EU Community Rights contact:
Community Plant Variety Office (CPVO),
3 Boulevard Maréchal Foch, BP 10121
FR-49101 Angers, Cedex 02, France
Tel: 00 33 (02) 41 25 64 00
Fax: 00 33 (02) 41 25 64 10
Website: www.cpvo.europa.eu

The *RHS Plant Finder* takes no responsibility for ensuring that nurseries selling plants with PBR are licensed to do so.

Reverse Synonyms

It is likely that users of this book will come across names in certain genera that they did not expect to find. This may be because species have been transferred from another genus (or **genera**). In the list of **Reverse Synonyms** on p.34, the name on the left-hand side is that of an accepted genus to which species have been transferred from the genus on the right. Sometimes all species will have been transferred, but in many cases only a few will be affected. Consulting **Reverse Synonyms** enables users to find the genera from which species have been transferred. Where the right-hand genus is found in the Plant Directory, the movement of species becomes clear through the cross-references in the nursery code column.

Selling Names

See **Trade Designations**

Series

With seed-raised plants and some popular vegetatively-propagated plants, especially bedding plants and pot plants such as *Petunia* or *Impatiens*, Series have become increasingly popular. A Series contains a number of similar cultivars, but differs from a **Group** in that it is a marketing device, with cultivars added to create a range of flower colours in plants of similar habit. Individual colour elements within a series may be represented by slightly different cultivars over the years.

The word Series is always included and, where cited with a cultivar name it is enclosed in brackets, for example *Aquilegia* 'Robin' (Songbird Series). The Series name usually follows the rest of the plant name, but sometimes in this book we list it before the cultivar name in order to group members of a series together when they occur next to one another on the page.

Species

See under **Botanical Names**

Subspecies

See under **Botanical Names**

Synonyms

Although the ideal is for each species or cultivar to have only one name, anyone dealing with plants soon comes across a situation where one plant has received two or more names, or two plants have received the same name. In each case, only one name and application, for reasons of precision and stability, can be regarded as correct. Additional names are known as synonyms. Further information on synonyms and why plants change names is available in *Guide to Plant Names*. See the introduction to this glossary for details of how to request a copy.

See also **Reverse Synonyms**.

Trade Designations

A **trade designation** is the name used to market a plant when the cultivar name is considered unsuitable for selling purposes. It is styled in a different typeface and without single quotation marks.

In the case of **Plant Breeders' Rights** it is a legal requirement for the cultivar name to appear with the trade designation on a label at the point of sale. Most plants are sold under only one trade designation, but some, especially roses, are sold under a number of names, particularly when cultivars are introduced from other countries. Usually, the correct cultivar name is the only way to ensure that the same plant is not bought unwittingly under two or more different trade designations. The *RHS Plant Finder* follows the recommendations of the **ICNCP** when dealing with trade designations and PBR. These are always to quote the cultivar name and trade designation together and to style the trade designation in a different typeface, without single quotation marks.

TRANSLATIONS

When a cultivar name is translated from the language of first publication, the translation is regarded as a **trade designation** and styled accordingly. We endeavour to recognise the original cultivar name in every case and to give an English translation where it is in general use.

VARIEGATED PLANTS

Following a suggestion from the Variegated Plant Group of the Hardy Plant Society, a (v) is cited after those plants which are "variegated". The dividing line between variegation and less distinct colour marking is necessarily arbitrary and plants with light veins, pale, silver or dark zones, or leaves flushed in paler colours, are not shown as being variegated unless there is an absolutely sharp distinction between paler and darker zones.

For further details of the Variegated Plant Group, please write to:

Jerry Webb, Esq.,
17 Heron Way, Minster Heights,
Ilminster TA19 0BX

VARIETY

See under **Botanical Names** and **Cultivar**

'The question of nomenclature is always a vexed one. The only thing certain is, that it is impossible to please everyone.'

W.J. BEAN – PREFACE TO FIRST EDITION OF *Trees & Shrubs Hardy in the British Isles*

HORTAX
The Horticultural Taxonomy Group

If you have an interest in the names of garden plants and wish to learn more or would like to make a comment about the International Code of Nomenclature for Cultivated Plants (ICNCP) visit the HORTAX website: www.hortax.org.uk

Symbols and Abbreviations

Symbols Appearing to the Left of the Name

- * Name not validated. Not listed in the appropriate International Registration Authority checklist nor in works cited in the Bibliography. For fuller discussion see p.11
- I Invalid name. See *International Code of Botanical Nomenclature 2006* and *International Code of Nomenclature for Cultivated Plants 2009*. For fuller discussion see p.11
- N Refer to Notes on Nomenclature and Identification on p.24
- § Plant listed elsewhere in the Plant Directory under a synonym
- × Hybrid genus
- \+ Graft hybrid genus

Symbols Appearing to the Right of the Name

- ✿ Plant Heritage (NCCPG) National Plant Collection® exists for all or part of this genus. Provisional Collections appear in brackets. Full details of the Plant Heritage Collections are found in the *2010 National Plant Collections® Directory* available from: www.plantheritage.com or Plant Heritage, 12 Home Farm, Loseley Park, Guildford, Surrey GU3 1HS
- ♀H4 The Royal Horticultural Society's Award of Garden Merit, see p.11
- (d) double-flowered
- (F) Fruit
- (f) female
- (m) male
- (v) variegated plant, see p.15
- PBR Plant Breeders Rights see p.13
- **new** New plant entry in this edition

For abbreviations relating to individual genera see **Classification of Genera** p.29

For **Collectors' References** see p.20

For symbols used in the **Nurseries** section see p.839

Symbols and Abbreviations Used as Part of the Name

- × hybrid species
- aff. affinis (akin to)
- agg. aggregate, a single name used to cover a group of very similar plants, regarded by some as separate species
- ambig. ambiguous, a name used by two authors for different plants and where it is unclear which is being offered
- cf. compare to
- cl. clone
- f. forma (botanical form)
- gx grex
- sensu lato in the broadest sense
- sp. species
- subsp. subspecies
- subvar. subvarietas (botanical subvariety)
- var. varietas (botanical variety)

It is not within the remit of this book to check that nurseries are applying the right names to the right plants or to ensure nurseries selling plants with Plant Breeders' Rights are licensed to do so.

Please, never use an old edition

Plants

Whatever plant you are looking for, maybe an old favourite or a more unusual cultivar, search here for a list of the suppliers that are closest to you.

How to Use the Plant Directory

Nursery Codes

Look up the plant you require in the alphabetical Plant Directory. Against each plant you will find one or more four-letter codes, for example WCru, each code represents one nursery offering that plant. The first letter of each code indicates the main area of the country in which the nursery is situated. For this geographical key, refer to the **Nursery Codes and Symbols** on p.838.

Turn to the **Nursery Details by Code** starting on p.842 where, in alphabetical order of codes, you will find details of each nursery which offers the plant in question. If you wish to visit any nursery, you may find its location on one of the maps (following p.945). Please note, however, that not all nurseries, especially mail order only nurseries, choose to be shown on the maps. For a fuller explanation of how to use the nursery listings please turn to p.839. **Always check that the nursery you select has the plant in stock before you set out.**

Plants with more than 30 Suppliers

In some cases, against the plant name you will see the term 'Widely available' instead of a nursery code. If we were to include every plant listed by all nurseries, the *RHS Plant Finder* would become unmanageably bulky. We therefore ask nurseries to restrict their entries to those plants that are not already well represented. As a result, if more than 30 nurseries offer any plant the Directory gives no nursery codes and the plant is listed instead as being 'Widely available'.

You should have little difficulty in locating these in local nurseries or garden centres. However, if you are unable to find such plants, we will be pleased to send a full list of all the nurseries that we have on file as stockists. To obtain a list, please see the Introduction on p.4 or go to www.rhs.org.uk/rhsplantfinder/.

Finding Fruit, Vegetables and Herbs

You will need to search for these by their botanical names. Common names are cross-referenced to their botanical names in the Plant Directory.

If you have Difficulty Finding your Plant

If you cannot immediately find the plant you seek, look through the various species of the genus. You may be using an incomplete name. The problem is most likely to arise in very large genera such as *Phlox* where there are a number of possible species, each with a large number of cultivars. A search through the whole genus may well bring success. Please note that, for space reasons, the following are not listed in the Plant Directory: annuals, orchids, except hardy terrestrial orchids; cacti, except hardy cacti.

Cross-references

It may be that the plant name you seek is a synonym. Our intention is to list nursery codes only against the correct botanical name. Where you find a synonym you will be cross-referred to the correct name. Occasionally you may find that the correct botanical name to which you have been referred is not listed. This is because it was last listed in an earlier edition as explained below.

Plants Last Listed in Earlier Editions

It may be that the plant you are seeking has no known suppliers and is thus not listed.

The loss of a plant name from the Directory may arise for a number of reasons – the supplier may have gone out of business, or may not have responded to our latest questionnaire and has therefore been removed from the book. Such plants may well be still available but we have no current knowledge of their whereabouts. Alternatively, some plants may have been misnamed by nurseries in previous editions, but are now appearing under their correct name.

To obtain a listing of plants last listed in earlier editions please see the Introduction on p.4 or go to our website where it is available as a pdf.

Please, never use an old edition

USING THE PLANT DIRECTORY

The main purpose of the Plant Directory is to help the reader correctly identify the plant they seek and find its stockist. Each nursery has a unique identification code which appears to the right of the plant name. Turn to Nursery Details by Code on p.842 for the address, opening times and other details of the nursery. The first letter of each nursery code denotes its geographical region. Turn to the map on p.838 to find your region code and then identify the nurseries in your area.

Another purpose of the Directory is to provide more information about the plant through the symbols and other information. For example, if it has an alternative names, is new to this edition or has received the RHS Award of Garden Merit.

ABBREVIATIONS
To save space a dash indicates that the previous heading is repeated. If written out in full the name would be Euonymus alatus *'Fire Ball'.*

NEW
Plant new to this edition.

DESCRIPTIVE TERM
See p.12.

SYMBOLS TO THE LEFT OF THE NAME
Provides information about the name of the plant. See p.16 for the key.

SYMBOLS TO THE RIGHT OF THE NAME
Tells you more about the plant itself, e.g. (v) *indicates that the plant is variegated,* (F) = *fruit. See p.16 for the key.*

SELLING NAMES
See p.14.

Euonymus (*Celastraceae*)

	Name	Nursery codes
	B&L 12543	EPla EWes
	B&SWJ 4457	WPGP
	CC 4522	CPLG
	alatus ♈H4	Widely available
	- B&SWJ 8794	WCru
	- var. ***apterus***	EPfP
	- Chicago Fire	see *E. alatus* 'Timber Creek'
	- 'Ciliodentatus'	see *E. alatus* 'Compactus'
§	- 'Compactus' ♈H4	Widely available
§	- 'Fire Ball'	EPfP
	- Little Moses = 'Odom'	MBlu
*	- 'Macrophyllus'	EPfP
	- 'Rudy Haag'	CPMA EPfP
	- 'Select'	see *E. alatus* 'Fire Ball'
	- 'Silver Cloud' **new**	EPfP
§	- 'Timber Creek'	CPMA EPfP MBlu MBri NLar
	americanus	EPfP GIBF MBlu NLar
	- 'Evergreen' **new**	EPfP
	- narrow-leaved	EPfP NLar
	atropurpureus	EPfP
	'Benkomoki' **new**	MGos
	bungeanus	CMCN EPfP EPla NLar
	- 'Dart's Pride'	CPMA EPfP NLar
	- 'Fireflame'	EPfP NLar
*	- var. ***mongolicus***	EPfP
	- 'Pendulus'	EPfP MBlu SIFN
	- var. ***semipersistens***	CPMA EPla
	carnosus	EPfP NLar
	'Copper Wire'	EMil SPoG
	cornutus var. ***quinquecornutus***	CPMA EPfP LPan MBlu NBhm NLar SIFN SPoG WPGP WPat
	'Den Haag'	EPfP MBri
	echinatus	EPfP EPla
	- BL&M 306	SLon
	europaeus	Widely available
	- f. ***albus***	CPMA CTho EPfP LTwo NLar
	- 'Atropurpureus'	CMCN CTho EPfP MBlu MBri NLar SIFN
	- 'Atrorubens'	CPMA
	- 'Aucubifolius' (v)	EPfP
*	- 'Aureus'	CNat
	- 'Brilliant' **new**	EPfP
*	- f. ***bulgaricus***	EPfP
	- 'Chrysophyllus'	EPfP MBlu NLar
	- 'Howard'	EPfP
	- var. ***intermedius***	ENot EPfP MAsh MBlu NLar
	- 'Miss Pinkie'	CEnd CMCN
	- 'Pumilis' **new**	EPfP
	- 'Red Cascade' ♈H4	Widely available
	- 'Scarlet Wonder'	CPMA EPfP MBri NLar
	- 'Thornhayes'	CTho EPfP
I	- 'Variegatus' **new**	EPfP
	farreri	see *E. nanus*
	fimbriatus	EPfP
	fortunei Blondy = 'Interbolwi' PBR (v)	Widely available

♈H4
This plant has received the RHS Award of Garden Merit. See p.11.

CROSS-REFERENCES
Directs you to the correct name of the plant and the nursery codes. See p.18.

NURSERY CODE
A unique code identifying each nursery. Turn to p.842 for details of the nurseries.

WIDELY AVAILABLE
Indicates that more than 30 Plant Finder nurseries supply the plant, and it may be available locally. See p.18.

PBR
Plant Breeders' Rights. See p.13.

Supplementary Keys to the Directory

Collectors' References

Abbreviations following a plant name, refer to the collector(s) of the plant. These abbreviations are expanded below, with a collector's name or expedition title. For a fuller explanation, see p.12.

A&JW Watson, A. & J.
A&L Ala, A. & Lancaster, Roy
AB&S Archibald, James; Blanchard, John W. & Salmon, M.
AC Clark, Alan J.
AC&H Apold, J.; Cox, Peter & Hutchison, Peter
AC&W Albury; Cheese, M. & Watson, J.M.
ACE AGS Expedition to China (1994)
ACL Leslie, Alan C.
AER Robinson, Allan
AGS/ES AGS Expedition to Sikkim (1983)
AGSJ AGS Expedition to Japan (1988)
AH Hoog, A.
AIM Avent, Tony Mexico (1994)
Airth Airth, Murray
Akagi Akagi Botanical Garden
AL&JS Sharman, Joseph L. & Leslie, Alan C.
APA Cox, K.; Hootman, S.; Hudson, T.; et al, Expedition to Arunchal Pradesh (2005)
ARG Argent, G.C.G.
ARJA Ruksans, J. & Siesums, A.
B Blanchard, John
B&F MA Brown, Robert & Fisher, Rif & Middle Atlas (2007)
B L. Beer, Len
B&L Brickell, Christopher D. & Leslie, Alan C.
B&M & BM Brickell, Christopher D. & Mathew, Brian
B&S Bird P. & Salmon M.
B&SWJ Wynn-Jones, Bleddyn & Susan
B&V Burras, K. & Vosa, C.G.
BB Bartholomew, B.
BC Chudziak, W.
BC&W Beckett; Cheese, M. & Watson, J.M.
Beavis Beavis, Derek S.
Berry Berry, P.
Berry & Brako Berry, P. & Brako, Lois
BKBlount Blount, B.K.
BL&M University of Bangor Expedition to NE Nepal
BM Mathew, Brian F.
BM&W Binns, David L.; Mason, M. & Wright, A.
BOA Boardman, P.
Breedlove Breedlove, D.
BR Rushbrooke, Ben
BS Smith, Basil
BSBE Bowles Scholarship Botanical Expedition (1963)
BSSS Crûg Expedition, Jordan (1991)
Bu Bubert, S.
Burtt Burtt, Brian L.
C Cole, Desmond T.
C&C Cox, P.A. & Cox, K.N.E.
C&Cu Cox, K.N.E. & Cubey, J.
C&H Cox, Peter & Hutchison, Peter
C&K Chamberlain & Knott
C&R Christian & Roderick
C&S Clark, Alan & Sinclair, Ian W.J.
C&V K.N.E. Cox & Vergera, S.
C&W Cheese, M. & Watson, J.M.
CC Chadwell, Christopher
CC&H Chamberlain, David F.; Cox, Peter & Hutchison, P.
CC&McK Chadwell, Christopher & McKelvie, A.
CC&MR Chadwell, Christopher & Ramsay
CCH&H Chamberlain, D.F.; Cox, P.; Hutchison, P. & Hootman, S.
CCH&H Chamberlain, Cox, Hootman & Hutchison
CD&R Compton, J.; D'Arcy, J. & Rix, E.M.
CDB Brickell, Christopher D.
CDC Coode, Mark J.E.; Dockrill, Alexander
CDC&C Compton; D'Arcy; Christopher & Coke
CDPR Compton; D'Arcy; Pope & Rix
CE&H Christian, P.J.; Elliott & Hoog
CEE Chengdu Edinburgh Expedition China (1991)
CGV Vosa, Canio
CGW Grey-Wilson, Christopher
CH Christian, P. & Hoog, A.

CH&M Cox, P.; Hutchison, P. & Maxwell-MacDonald, D.
CHP&W Kashmir Botanical Expedition
CL Lovell, Chris
CLD Chungtien, Lijiang & Dali Exped. China (1990)
CM&W Cheese M.; Mitchel J. & Watson, J.
CN&W Clark; Neilson & Wilson
CNDS Nelson, C. & Sayers D.
Cooper Cooper, R.E.
Cox Cox, Peter A.
CPC Cobblewood Plant Collection
CPN Compton, James
CS Stapleton, Christopher
CSE Cyclamen Society Expedition (1990)
CT Teune, Carla
CWJ Colley, Finlay; Wynn-Jones, Bleddyn, Taiwan (2007)
Dahl Dahl, Sally
DBG Denver Botanic Garden, Colorado
DC Cheshire, David
DF Fox, D.
DG Green, D.
DHTU Hinkley, D.; Turkey (2000)
DJH Hinkley, Dan
DJHC Hinkley, China
DJHV Hinkley, Dan, Vietnam
DM Millais, David
Doleshy Doleshy, F.L.
DS&T Drake, Sharman J. & Thompson
DWD Rose, D.
DZ Zummell, D.
ECN Nelson, E. Charles
EDHCH Hammond, Eric D.
EGM Millais, T.
EKB Balls, Edward K.
EM East Malling Research Station
EMAK Edinburgh Makalu Expedition (1991)
EMR Rix, E.Martyn
EN Needham, Edward F.
ENF Fuller, E. Nigel
ETE Edinburgh Taiwan Expedition (1993)
ETOT Kirkham, T.S.; Flanagan, Mark
F Forrest, G.
F&M Fernandez & Mendoza, Mexico
F&W Watson, J. & Flores, A.
Farrer Farrer, Reginald
FK Kinmonth, Fergus W.
FMB Bailey, F.M.
G Gardner, Martin F.
G&K Gardner, Martin F. & Knees, Sabina G.
G&P Gardner, Martin F. & Page, Christopher N.
GDJ Dumont, Gerard
GG Gusman, G.
GS Sherriff, George
Green Green, D.
Guitt Guittoneau, G.G.
Guiz Guizhou Expedition (1985)
GWJ Goddard, Sally; Wynne-Jones, Bleddyn & Susan
G-W&P Grey-Wilson, Christopher & Phillips
H Huggins, Paul
H&B Hilliard, Olive M. & Burtt, Brian L.
H&D Howick, C. & Darby
H&M Howick, Charles & McNamara, William A.
H&W Hedge, Ian C. & Wendelbo, Per W.
Harry Smith Smith, K.A.Harry
Hartside Hartside Nursery
HCM Heronswood Expedition to Chile (1998)
HECC Hutchison; Evans; Cox, P.; Cox, K.
HEHEHE Zetterlund, H. et al, Gothenburg Botanic Gardens Expedition to northern China
Hird Hird
HH&K Hannay, S & S & Kingsbury, N.
HLMS Springate, L.S.
HM&S Halliwell, B.; Mason, D. & Smallcombe
HOA Hoog, Anton
Hummel Hummel, D.
HW&E Wendelbo, Per; Hedge, I. & Ekberg, L.
HWEL Hirst, J.Michael; Webster, D.
HWJ Crûg Heronswood Joint Expedition
HWJCM Crûg Heronswood Expedition
HWJK Crûg Heronswood Expedition, East Nepal (2002)
HZ Zetterlund, Henrik
ICE Instituto de Investigaciónes Ecológicas Chiloé & RBGE
IDS International Dendrological Society
ISI Int. Succulent Introductions
J&JA Archibald, James & Jennifer
J. Jurasek Jurasek, J.
JCA Archibald, James
JE Jack Elliott
JJ Jackson, J.
JJ&JH Halda, J. & Halda, J.
JJH Halda, Joseph J.
JLS Sharman, J.L.
JM-MK Mahr, J.; Kammerlander, M.
JMT Mann Taylor, J.
JN Nielson, Jens
JR Russell, J.
JRM Marr, John
JW Watson, J.M.
K Kirkpatrick, George
K&LG Gillanders, Kenneth & Gillanders, L.
K&Mc Kirkpatrick, George & McBeath, Ronald J.D.
K&P Josef Kopec & Milan Prasil
K&T Kurashige, Y. & Tsukie, S.
KC Cox, Kenneth
KEKE Kew/Edinburgh Kanchenjunga Expedition (1989)
KGB Kunming/Gothenburg Botanical Expedition (1993)

KM	Marsh, K.
KR	Rushforth, K.D.
KRW	Wooster, K.R. (distributed after his death by Kath Dryden)
KW	Kingdon-Ward, F.
KWJ	Crûg-World of Ferns Joint Expedition, Vietnam (2007)
L	Lancaster, C. Roy
L&S	Ludlow, Francis & Sherriff, George
LA	Long Ashton Research Station clonal selection scheme
LB	Bird P.; Salmon, M.
LEG	Lesotho Edinburgh/Gothenburg Expedition (1997)
Lismore	Lismore Nursery, Breeder's Number
LM&S	Leslie, Mattern & Sharman
LP	Palmer, W.J.L.
LS&E	Ludlow, Frank; Sherriff, George & Elliott, E. E.
LS&H	Ludlow, Frank; Sherriff, George & Hicks, J. H.
LS&T	Ludlow, Frank; Sherriff, George & Taylor, George
M&PS	Mike & Polly Stone
M&T	Mathew & Tomlinson
Mac&W	McPhail & Watson
McB	McBeath, R.J.D.
McLaren	McLaren, H.D.
MDM	Myers, Michael D.
MECC	Scottish Rock Garden Club, Nepal (1997)
MESE	Alpine Garden Society Expedition, Greece (1999)
MF	Foster, Maurice
MH	Heasman, Matthew T.
MK	Kammerlander, Michael
MP	Pavelka, Mojmir
MPF	Frankis, M.P.
MS	Salmon, M.
MS&CL	Salmon, M. & Lovell, C.
MSF	Fillan, M.S.
NAPE	Hootman, S.; et al, Expedition to Naglaland and Arunachal Pradesh (2003)
NICE	North India Expedition (1997)
NJM	Macer, N.J.
NN	Nielsen & Nielsen (2009)
NNS	Ratko, Ron
NS	Turland, Nick
NVFDE	Northern Vietnam First Darwin Expedition
Og	Ogisu, Mikinori
OS	Sonderhousen, O.
P. Bon	Bonavia, P.
P&C	Paterson, David S. & Clarke, Sidney
P&W	Polastri & Watson, J. M.
PAB	Barney, P.A.
PB	Bird, Peter
PC&H	Pattison, G.; Catt, P. & Hickson, M.
PD	Davis, Peter H.
PF	Furse, Paul
PJC	Christian, Paul J.
PJC&AH	P.J. Christian & A. Hogg
PNMK	Nicholls, P.; Kammerlander, M.
Polunin	Polunin, Oleg
Pras	Prasil, M.
PS&W	Polunin, Oleg; Sykes, William & Williams, John
PW	Wharton, Peter
R	Rock, J.F.C.
RB	Brown, R.
RBS	Brown, Ray, Sakharin Island
RCB AM	Brown, Robert, Expedition to Armenia
RCB/Arg	Brown, Robert, Argentina, (2002)
RCB E	Brown, Robert, Expedition to Spain (Andalucia)
RCB/Eq	Brown, Robert, Ecuador, (1988)
RCB RA	Brown, Robert
RCB RL	Brown, Robert, Expedition to Lebanon
RCB/TQ	Brown, Robert, Turkey (2001)
RE	Evans, Ron
RH	Hancock, R.
RKMP	Ruksans, J.; Krumins, A.; Kitts, M.; Paivel, A.
RM	Ruksans, J. & Kitts, M.
RMRP	Rocky Mountain Rare Plants, Denver, Colorado
RS	Suckow, Reinhart
RSC	Richard Somer Cocks
RV	Richard Valder
RWJ	Crûg Farm-Rickards Ferns Expedition to Taiwan (2003)
S&B	Blanchard, J.W. & Salmon, M.
S&F	Salmon, M. & Fillan, M.
S&L	Sinclair, Ian W.J. & Long, David G.
S&SH	Sheilah & Spencer Hannay
Sandham	Sandham, John
SB&L	Salmon, Bird & Lovell
SBEC	Sino-British Expedition to Cangshan
SBEL	Sino-British Lijiang Expedition
SBQE	Sino-British Expedition to Quinghai
Sch	Schilling, Anthony D.
SD	Sashal Dayal
SDR	Rankin, Stella & David
SEH	Hootman, Steve
SEP	Swedish Expedition to Pakistan
SF	Forde, P.
SG	Salmon, M. & Guy, P.
SH	Hannay, Spencer
Sich	Simmons, Erskine, Howick & Mcnamara
SJ	Johansson, Stellan
SLIZE	Swedish-Latvian-Iranian Zagros Expedition to Iran (May 1988)
SOJA	Kew/Quarryhill Expedition to Southern Japan

SS&W	Stainton, J.D. Adam; Sykes, William & Williams, John
SSNY	Sino-Scottish Expedition to NW Yunnan (1992)
T	Taylor, Nigel P.
T&K	Taylor, Nigel P. & Knees, Sabina
TH	Hudson, T.
TS&BC	Smythe, T. & Cherry, B.
TSS	Spring Smyth, T.L.M.
TW	Tony Weston
USDAPI	US Department of Agriculture Plant Index Number
USDAPQ	US Dept. of Agriculture Plant Quarantine Number
USNA	United States National Arboretum
VHH	Vernon H. Heywood
VV	Victor, David
W	Wilson, Ernest H.
WM	McLewin, William
Woods	Woods, Patrick J.B.
Wr	Wraight, David & Anke
WWJ	Wharton, Peter; Wynn-Jones, Bleddyn & Susan
Yu	Yu, Tse-tsun

Notes on Nomenclature and Identification

These notes refer to plants in the Plant Directory that are marked with a 'N' to the left of the name. 'Bean Supplement' refers to W.J. Bean *Trees & Shrubs Hardy in the British Isles* (Supplement to the 8th edition) edited by D L Clarke 1988.

Acer davidii **'Ernest Wilson' and *A. davidii* 'George Forrest'**
These cultivars should be grafted in order to retain the characteristics of the original clones. However, many plants offered under these names are seed-raised.

Acer palmatum **'Sango-kaku' / 'Senkaki'**
Two or more clones are offered under these names. *A. palmatum* 'Eddisbury' is similar with brighter coral stems.

Achillea ptarmica **The Pearl Group / *A. ptarmica* (The Pearl Group) 'Boule de Neige' / *A. ptarmica* (The Pearl Group) 'The Pearl'**
In the recent trial of achilleas at Wisley, only one of the several stocks submitted as 'The Pearl' matched the original appearance of this plant according to Graham Stuart Thomas, this being from Wisley's own stock. At rather less than 60cm (2ft), this needed little support, being the shortest of the plants bearing this name, with slightly grey, not glossy dark green, leaves and a non-invasive habit. This has been designated as the type for this cultivar and only this clone should bear the cultivar name 'The Pearl'. The Pearl Group covers all other double-flowered clones of this species, including seed-raised plants which are markedly inferior, sometimes scarcely double, often invasive and usually needing careful staking. It has been claimed that 'The Pearl' was a re-naming of Lemoine's 'Boule de Neige' but not all authorities agree: all plants submitted to the Wisley trial as 'Boule de Neige' were different from each other, not the same clone as Wisley's 'The Pearl' and referrable to The Pearl Group.

Anemone nemorosa **'Alba Plena'**
This name is used for several double white forms including *A. nemorosa* 'Flore Pleno' and *A. nemorosa* 'Vestal'.

Artemisia ludoviciana **subsp. *ludoviciana* var. *latiloba* / *A. ludoviciana* 'Valerie Finnis'**
Leaves of the former are glabrous at maturity, those of the latter are not.

Artemisia stelleriana **'Boughton Silver'**
This was thought to be the first validly published name for this plant, 'Silver Brocade' having been published earlier but invalidly in an undated publication. However, an earlier valid publication for the cultivar name 'Mori' has subsequently been found for the same plant. A proposal to conserve 'Boughton Silver' has been tabled because of its more widespread use.

Aster amellus Violet Queen
It is probable that more than one cultivar is sold under this name.

Aster dumosus
Many of the asters listed under *A. novi-belgii* contain varying amounts of *A. dumosus* blood in their parentage. It is not possible to allocate these to one species or the other and they are therefore listed under *A. novi-belgii*.

Aster* × *frikartii **'Mönch'**
The true plant is very rare in British gardens. Most plants are another form of *A.* × *frikartii*, usually 'Wunder von Stäfa'.

Aster novi-belgii
See note under *A. dumosus*. *A. laevis* is also involved in the parentage of most cultivars.

Berberis buxifolia **'Nana' misapplied / 'Pygmaea'**
See explanation in Bean Supplement.

Betula utilis **var. *jacquemontii***
Plants are often the clones *B. utilis* var. *jacquemontii* 'Inverleith' or *B. utilis* var. *jacquemontii* 'Doorenbos'

Brachyscome
Originally published as *Brachyscome* by Cassini who later revised his spelling to *Brachycome*. The original spelling has been internationally adopted.

Calamagrostis* × *acutiflora **'Karl Foerster'**
C. × *acutiflora* 'Stricta' differs in being 15cm taller, 10–15 days earlier flowering with a less fluffy inflorescence.

Calceolaria integrifolia sensu lato
Christine Ehrhart (*Systematic Botany*. (2005. 30(2):383–411) has demonstrated that this is a complex involving nine distinct species (*C. andina*, *C. angustifolia*, *C. auriculata*, *C. georgiana*, *C. integrifolia sensu stricto*, *C. rubiginosa*, *C. talcana*, *C. verbascifolia* and *C. viscosissima*). However, it is not yet clear to which species plants in cultivation belong or whether they are hybrids.

Caltha polypetala
This name is often applied to a large-flowered variant of *C. palustris*. The true species has more (7–10) petals.

Camassia leichtlinii **'Alba'**
The true cultivar has blueish-white, not cream flowers.

Camassia leichtlinii **'Plena'**
This has starry, transparent green-white flowers; creamy-white 'Semiplena' is sometimes offered under this name.

Campanula lactiflora **'Alba'**
This refers to the pure white-flowered clone, not to blueish- or greyish-white flowered plants, nor to seed-raised plants.

Canna
Species names marked 'N' are among those sometimes included within *Canna indica* L. See *Blumea* 53:247–318 for a complete list.

Carex morrowii **'Variegata'**
C. oshimensis 'Evergold' is sometimes sold under this name.

Carya illinoinensis
The correct spelling of this name is discussed in *Baileya*, **10**(1) (1962).

Cassinia retorta
Now included within *C. leptophylla*. A valid infra-specific epithet has yet to be published.

Ceanothus **'Italian Skies'**
Many plants under this name are not true to name.

Chamaecyparis lawsoniana **'Columnaris Glauca'**
Plants under this name might be *C. lawsoniana* 'Columnaris' or a new invalidly named cultivar.

Clematis chrysocoma
The true *C. chrysocoma* is a non-climbing erect plant with dense yellow down on the young growth, still uncommon in cultivation.

Clematis montana
This name should be used for the typical white-flowered variety only. Pink-flowered variants are referable to *C. montana* var. *rubens*.

Clematis **'Victoria'**
Raised by Cripps (1867). There is also a Latvian cultivar of this name with petals with a central white bar in the collection of Janis Ruplēns which is probably, though not certainly, of his own raising.

Colchicum **'Autumn Queen'**
Entries here might refer to the slightly different *C.* 'Prinses Astrid'.

Cornus **'Norman Hadden'**
See note in Bean Supplement, p.184.

Cotoneaster dammeri
Plants sold under this name are usually *C. dammeri* 'Major'.

Cotoneaster frigidus **'Cornubia'**
According to Hylmø this cultivar, like all other variants of this species, is fully deciduous. Several evergreen cotoneasters are also grown under this name; most are clones of *C.* × *watereri* or *C. salicifolius*.

Crataegus coccinea
C. intricata, *C. pedicellata* and *C. biltmoreana* are occasionally supplied under this name.

Crocus cartwrightianus **'Albus'**
The plant offered is the true cultivar and not *C. hadriaticus*.

Dianthus **fringed pink**
D. 'Old Fringed Pink' and *D.* 'Old Fringed White' are also sometimes sold under this name.

Dianthus **'Musgrave's Pink' (p)**
This is the registered name of this white-flowered cultivar.

Epilobium glabellum **misapplied**
Plants under this name are not *E. glabellum* but are close to *E. wilsonii* Petrie or perhaps a hybrid of it.

Erodium glandulosum
Plants under this name are often hybrids.

Erodium guttatum
Doubtfully in commerce; plants under this name are usually *E. heteradenum*, *E. cheilanthifolium* or hybrids.

Fagus sylvatica **Atropurpurea Group / Cuprea Group**
It is desirable to provide a name, Cuprea Group, for less richly coloured forms, used in historic landscapes before the purple clones appeared.

Fagus sylvatica **'Pendula'**
This name refers to the Knap Hill clone, the most common weeping form in English gardens. Other clones occur, particularly in Cornwall and Ireland.

Fuchsia loxensis
For a comparison of the true species with the hybrids 'Speciosa' and 'Loxensis' commonly grown under this name, see Boullemier's Check List (2nd ed.) p.268.

Geum **'Borisii'**
This name refers to cultivars of *G. coccineum* Sibthorp & Smith, especially *G.* 'Werner Arends' and not to *G.* × *borisii* Kelleper.

Halimium halimifolium
Plants under this name are sometimes *H.* × *pauanum* or *H.* × *santae.*

Hebe **'Carl Teschner'**
See note in Bean Supplement, p.264.

Hedera helix **'Caenwoodiana' / 'Pedata'**
Some authorities consider these to be distinct cultivars while others think them different morphological forms of the same unstable clone.

Hedera helix **'Oro di Bogliasco'**
Priority between this name and 'Jubiläum Goldherz' and 'Goldheart' has yet to be finally resolved.

Helleborus **×** ***hybridus*** **/** ***H. orientalis*** **misapplied**
The name *H.* × *hybridus* for acaulescent hellebore hybrids does not seem to follow the *International Code of Botanical Nomenclature* Article H.3.2 requiring one of the parent species to be designated and does not seem to have been typified, contrary to Article 7 of the Code. However, the illustration accompanying the original description in Vilmorin's *Blumengärtnerei* 3(1): 27 (1894) shows that one parent of the cross must have been *H. guttatus*, now treated as part of *H. orientalis.* Taking this illustration as the type for this hybrid species makes it possible to retain *H.* × *hybridus* formally as a hybrid binomial (rather than *H. hybridus* as in a previous edition), as the Code's requirement to distinguish one parent is now met.

***Hemerocallis fulva* 'Kwanso', 'Kwanso Variegata', 'Flore Pleno' and 'Green Kwanso'**
For a discussion of these plants see *The Plantsman*, 7(2).

***Heuchera villosa* 'Palace Purple'**
This cultivar name refers only to plants with deep purple-red foliage. Seed-raised plants of inferior colouring should not be offered under this name.

Hosta montana
This name refers only to plants long grown in Europe, which differ from *H. elata*.

***Hydrangea macrophylla* Teller Series**
This is used both as a descriptive common name for Lacecap hydrangeas (German *teller* = plate, referring to the more or less flat inflorescence) and for the series of hybrids raised by Wädenswil in Switzerland bearing German names of birds. It is not generally possible to link a hydrangea described by the series name plus a colour description (e.g. Teller Blau, Teller Rosa, Teller Rot) to a single cultivar.

Hypericum fragile
The true *H. fragile* is probably not available from British nurseries.

Ilex* × *altaclerensis
The argument for this spelling is given by Susyn Andrews, *The Plantsman*, 5(2) and is not superseded by the more recent comments in the Supplement to Bean's Trees and Shrubs.

Iris
Apart from those noted below, cultivar names marked 'N' are not registered. The majority of those marked 'I' have been previously used for a different cultivar.

***Iris histrioides* 'Major'**
Two clones are offered under this name, the true one pale blue with darker spotting on the falls, the incorrect one violet-blue with almost horizontal falls.

Juniperus* × *media
This name is illegitimate if applied to hybrids of *J. chinensis* × *J. sabina*, having been previously used for a different hybrid (P.A. Schmidt, *IDS Yearbook 1993*, 47–48). Because of its importance to gardeners, a proposal to conserve its present use was tabled but subsequently rejected.

Lavandula spica
This name is classed as a name to be rejected (*nomen rejiciendum*) by the *International Code of Botanical Nomenclature*.

Lavatera olbia* and *L. thuringiaca
Although *L. olbia* is usually shrubby and *L. thuringiaca* usually herbaceous, both species are very variable. Cultivars formerly ascribed to one species or the other have been shown to be hybrids and are referable to the recently-named hybrid species *L.* × *clementii*.

***Lobelia* 'Russian Princess'**
This name, originally for a pink-flowered, green-leaved cultivar, is now generally applied to a purple-flowered, dark-leaved cultivar that seems to lack a valid name.

***Lonicera periclymenum* 'Serotina'**
See note in Bean Supplement, p.315.

Lonicera sempervirens* f. *sulphurea
Plants in the British Isles usually a yellow-flowered form of *L. periclymenum*.

***Malus domestica* 'Dummellor's Seedling'**
The phonetic spelling 'Dumelow's Seedling' contravenes the ICBN ruling on orthography, i.e. that, except for intentional latinisations, commemorative names should be based on the original spelling of the person's name (Article 60.11). The spelling adopted here is that used on the gravestone of the raiser in Leicestershire.

***Meconopsis* Fertile Blue Group**
This Group comprises seed-raised and intrinsically perennial tall blue poppies of as yet indeterminate origin. The only cultivars so far established are 'Lingholm' (synonyms 'Blue Ice' and 'Correnie') and 'Kingsbarns'.

***Meconopsis napaulensis* misapplied**
In his revision of the evergreen monocarpic species, Dr C. Grey-Wilson has established that *M. napaulensis* DC., a dwarfish yellow-flowered species not usually more than 1.1m tall and endemic to C Nepal, is not currently in cultivation. The well-known plants of gardens which pass for *M. napaulensis* are hybrids, for the present to be known as *M. napaulensis* misapplied. The parents of the hybrids are *M. staintonii* (from W Nepal) and *M. paniculata* (a yellow-flowered species with a purple stigma) or *M. staintonii* and *M. regia* or a complex mixture of all three species. *M. staintonii*, newly described by C. Grey-Wilson (*Bot. Mag.* (2006) 23(2):176–209), is a tall (to 2.5m), robust species with red or pink flowers and a dark green stigma, near in appearance to *M. napaulensis* of gardens, but less so to true *M. napaulensis*. As *M. staintonii*, like its near relatives, readily hybridises in cultivation, it is rarely seen in an unadulterated form.

***Melissa officinalis* 'Variegata'**
The true cultivar of this name has leaves striped with white.

***Osmanthus heterophyllus* 'Gulftide'**
Probably correctly *O.* × *fortunei* 'Gulftide'.

***Pelargonium* 'Lass o' Gowrie'**
The American plant of this name has pointed, not rounded leaf lobes.

Pelargonium quercifolium
Plants under this name are mainly hybrids. The true species has pointed, not rounded leaf lobes.

***Penstemon* 'Taoensis'**
This name for a small-flowered cultivar or hybrid of *P. isophyllus* originally appeared as 'Taoense' but must be corrected to agree in gender with *Penstemon* (masculine). Presumably an invalid name (published in Latin form since 1958), it is not synonymous with *P. crandallii* subsp. *glabrescens* var. *taosensis.*

Pernettya
Botanists now consider that *Pernettya* (fruit a berry) is not separable from *Gaultheria* (fruit a capsule) because in some species the fruit is intermediate between a berry and a capsule. For a fuller explanation see D. Middleton, *The Plantsman*, 12(3).

Pinus ayacahuite
P. ayacahuite var. *veitchii* (syn. *P. veitchii)* is occasionally sold under this name.

***Pinus nigra* 'Cebennensis Nana'**
A doubtful name, possibly a synonym for *P. nigra* 'Nana'.

Polemonium archibaldiae
Usually sterile with lavender-blue flowers. A self-fertile white-flowered plant is sometimes sold under this name.

***Prunus laurocerasus* 'Castlewellan'**
We are grateful to Dr Charles Nelson for informing us that the name 'Marbled White' is not valid because although it has priority of publication it does not have the approval of the originator who asked for it to be called 'Castlewellan'.

Prunus serrulata* var. *pubescens
See note in Bean Supplement, p.398.

***Prunus* × *subhirtella* 'Rosea'**
Might be *P. pendula* var. *ascendens* 'Rosea', *P. pendula* 'Pendula Rosea', or *P.* × *subhirtella* 'Autumnalis Rosea'.

Rheum* × *hybridum
The name *R.* × *cultorum* was published without adequate description and must be abandoned in favour of the validly published *R.* × *hybridum.*

***Rhododendron* (azaleas)**
All names marked 'N', except for the following, refer to more than one cultivar.

Rhus hirta and R. typhina
Linnaeus published both *R. typhina* and *R. hirta* as names for the same species. Though *R. hirta* has priority, it has been proposed that the name *R. typhina* should be conserved.

Rosa gentiliana
Plants under this name are usually the cultivar 'Polyantha Grandiflora' but might otherwise be *R. multiflora* 'Wilsonii', *R. multiflora* var. *cathayensis, R. henryi* or another hybrid.

***Rosa* 'Jacques Cartier' misapplied**
For a discussion on the correct identity of this rose see *Heritage Rose Foundation News*, Oct. 1989 & Jan. 1990.

***Rosa* 'Kazanlik'**
For a discussion on the correct identity of this rose see *Heritage Roses,* Nov. 1991.

***Rosa* Sweetheart**
This is not the same as the Sweetheart Rose, a common name for *R.* 'Cécile Brünner'.

Rosa wichurana
This is the correct spelling according to the ICBN 1994 Article 60.11 (which enforces Recommendation 60C.1c) and not *wichuraiana* for this rose commemorating Max Wichura.

***Rubus fruticosus* L. agg.**
Though some cultivated blackberries do belong to *Rubus fruticosus* L. *sensu stricto,* others are more correctly ascribed to other species of *Rubus* section *Glandulosus* (including *R. armeniacus, R. laciniatus* or *R. ulmifolius)* or are hybrids of species within this section. Because it is almost impossible to ascribe every cultivar to a single species or hybrid, they are listed under *R. fruticosus* L. agg. (i.e. aggregate) for convenience.

Salvia microphylla* var. *neurepia
The type of this variety is referable to the typical variety, *S. microphylla* var. *microphylla.*

***Salvia officinalis* 'Aurea'**
S. officinalis var. *aurea* is a rare variant of the common sage with leaves entirely of gold. It is represented in cultivation by the cultivar 'Kew Gold'. The plant usually offered as *S. officinalis* 'Aurea' is the gold variegated sage *S. officinalis* 'Icterina'.

***Sambucus nigra* 'Aurea'**
Plants under this name are usually not *S. nigra.*

***Skimmia japonica* 'Foremanii'**
The true cultivar, which belongs to *S. japonica* Rogersii Group, is believed to be lost to cultivation. Plants offered under this name are usually *S. japonica* 'Veitchii'.

***Spiraea japonica* 'Shirobana'**
Shirobana-shimotsuke is the common name for *S. japonica* var. *albiflora.* Shirobana means white-flowered and does not apply to the two-coloured form.

Staphylea holocarpa* var. *rosea
This botanical variety has woolly leaves. The cultivar 'Rosea', with which it is often confused, does not.

***Tricyrtis* Hototogisu**
This is the common name applied generally to all Japanese *Tricyrtis* and specifically to *T. hirta.*

Tricyrtis macropoda
This name has been used for at least five different species.

Uncinia rubra
This name is also misapplied to *U. egmontiana* and *U. uncinata*.

***Viburnum opulus* 'Fructu Luteo'**
See note below.

***Viburnum opulus* 'Xanthocarpum'**
Some entries under this name might be the less compact *V. opulus* 'Fructu Luteo'.

Viburnum plicatum
Entries may include the 'snowball' form, *V. plicatum* f. *plicatum* (syn. *V. plicatum* 'Sterile'), as well as the 'lacecap' form, *V. plicatum* f. *tomentosum*.

Viola labradorica
See Note in *The Garden*, **110(2)**: 96.

***Vitis* 'Fragola'**
This appears to refer to *uva fragola*, the strawberry grape, and therefore plants under this name may be found to be either *V. labrusca* or *V.* × *labruscana*.

***Wisteria floribunda* 'Violacea Plena' and *W. floribunda* 'Yae-kokuryū'**
We are grateful to Yoko Otsuki, who has established through Engei Kyokai (the Horticultural Society of Japan) that there are two different double selections of *Wisteria floribunda*. 'Violacea Plena' has double lavender/lilac flowers, while 'Yae-kokuryū' has more ragged and tightly double flowers with purple/indigo centres. Each is distinctive but it is probable that both are confused in the British nursery trade. 'Yae-fuji' might be an earlier name for 'Violacea Plena' or a Group name covering a range of doubles but, as *fuji* is the Japanese common name for the species, it would not be a valid name under the ICNCP.

CLASSIFICATION OF GENERA

Genera including a large number of species, or with many cultivars, are often subdivided into informal horticultural classifications, or formal cultivar groups in the case of *Clematis* and *Tulipa*. The breeding of new cultivars is sometimes limited to hybrids between closely-related species, thus for *Saxifraga* and *Primula*, the cultivars are allocated to the sections given in the infrageneric treatments cited. Please turn to p.12 for a fuller explanation.

ACTINIDIA

(s-p) Self-pollinating

BEGONIA

(C) Cane-like
(R) Rex Cultorum
(S) Semperflorens Cultorum
(T) × *tuberhybrida* (Tuberous)

CHRYSANTHEMUM

(By the National Chrysanthemum Society)
(1) Indoor Large (Exhibition)
(2) Indoor Medium (Exhibition)
(3a) Indoor Incurved: Large-flowered
(3b) Indoor Incurved: Medium-flowered
(3c) Indoor Incurved: Small-flowered
(4a) Indoor Reflexed: Large-flowered
(4b) Indoor Reflexed: Medium-flowered
(4c) Indoor Reflexed: S mall-flowered
(5a) Indoor Intermediate: Large-flowered
(5b) Indoor Intermediate: Medium-flowered
(5c) Indoor Intermediate: Small-flowered
(6a) Indoor Anemone: Large-flowered
(6b) Indoor Anemone: Medium-flowered
(6c) Indoor Anemone: Small-flowered
(7a) Indoor Single: Large-flowered
(7b) Indoor Single: Medium-flowered
(7c) Indoor Single: Small-flowered
(8a) Indoor True Pompon
(8b) Indoor Semi-pompon
(9a) Indoor Spray: Anemone
(9b) Indoor Spray: Pompon
(9c) Indoor Spray: Reflexed
(9d) Indoor Spray: Single
(9e) Indoor Spray: Intermediate
(9f) Indoor Spray: Spider, Quill, Spoon or Any Other Type
(10a) Indoor, Spider
(10b) Indoor, Quill
(10c) Indoor, Spoon
(11) Any Other Indoor Type
(12a) Indoor, Charm
(12b) Indoor, Cascade
(13a) October-flowering Incurved: Large-flowered
(13b) October-flowering Incurved: Medium-flowered
(13c) October-flowering Incurved: Small-flowered
(14a) October-flowering Reflexed: Large-flowered
(14b) October-flowering Reflexed: Medium-flowered
(14c) October-flowering Reflexed: Small-flowered
(15a) October-flowering Intermediate: Large-flowered
(15b) October-flowering Intermediate: Medium-flowered
(15c) October-flowered Intermediate: Small-flowered
(16) October-flowering Large
(17a) October-flowering Single: Large-flowered
(17b) October-flowering Single: Medium-flowered
(17c) October-flowering Single: Small-flowered
(18a) October-flowering Pompon: True Pompon
(18b) October-flowering Pompon: Semi-pompon
(19a) October-flowering Spray: Anemone
(19b) October-flowering Spray: Pompon
(19c) October-flowering Spray: Reflexed
(19d) October-flowering Spray: Single
(19e) October-flowering Spray: Intermediate
(19f) October-flowering Spray: Spider, Quill, Spoon or Any Other Type
(20) Any Other October-flowering Type
(21a) Korean: Anemone
(21b) Korean: Pompon
(21c) Korean: Reflexed
(21d) Korean: Single
(21e) Korean: Intermediate
(21f) Korean: Spider, Quill, Spoon, or any other type
(22a) Charm: Anemone
(22b) Charm: Pompon
(22c) Charm: Reflexed
(22d) Charm: Single
(22e) Charm: Intermediate
(22f) Charm: Spider, Quill, Spoon or Any Other Type
(23a) Early-flowering Outdoor Incurved: Large-flowered

(23b)	Early-flowering Outdoor Incurved: Medium-flowered
(23c)	Early-flowering Outdoor Incurved: Small-flowered
(24a)	Early-flowering Outdoor Reflexed: Large-flowered
(24b)	Early-flowering Outdoor Reflexed: Medium-flowered
(24c)	Early-flowering Outdoor Reflexed: Small-flowered
(25a)	Early-flowering Outdoor Intermediate: Large-flowered
(25b)	Early-flowering Outdoor Intermediate: Medium-flowered
(25c)	Early-flowering Outdoor Intermediate: Small-flowered
(26a)	Early-flowering Outdoor Anemone: Large-flowered
(26b)	Early-flowering Outdoor Anemone: Medium-flowered
(27a)	Early-flowering Outdoor Single: Large-flowered
(27b)	Early-flowering Outdoor Single:Medium-flowered
(28a)	Early-flowering Outdoor Pompon: True Pompon
(28b)	Early-flowering Outdoor Pompon: Semi-pompon
(29a)	Early-flowering Outdoor Spray: Anemone
(29b)	Early-flowering Outdoor Spray: Pompon
(29c)	Early-flowering Outdoor Spray: Reflexed
(29d)	Early-flowering Outdoor Spray: Single
(29e)	Early-flowering Outdoor Spray: Intermediate
(29f)	Early-flowering Outdoor Spray: Spider, Quill, Spoon or Any Other Type
(30)	Any Other Early-flowering Outdoor Type

Clematis

(Cultivar Groups as per Matthews, V. (2002) *The International Clematis Register & Checklist 2002*, RHS, London.)

(A)	Atragene Group
(Ar)	Armandii Group
(C)	Cirrhosa Group
(EL)	Early Large-flowered Group
(F)	Flammula Group
(Fo)	Forsteri Group
(H)	Heracleifolia Group
(I)	Integrifolia Group
(LL)	Late Large-flowered Group
(M)	Montana Group
(T)	Texensis Group
(Ta)	Tangutica Group
(V)	Viorna Group
(Vb)	Vitalba Group
(Vt)	Viticella Group

Dahlia

(Classification according to The International Dahlia Register (1969), 20th Supp. (2009) formed through consultation with national dahlia societies.)

(Sin)	1 Single
(Anem)	2 Anemone-flowered
(Col)	3 Collerette
(WL)	4 Waterlily (unassigned)
(LWL)	4B Waterlily, Large
(MWL)	4C Waterlily, Medium
(SWL)	4D Waterlily, Small
(MinWL)	4E Waterlily, Miniature
(D)	5 Decorative (unassigned)
(GD)	5A Decorative, Giant
(LD)	5B Decorative, Large
(MD)	5C Decorative, Medium
(SD)	5D Decorative, Small
(MinD)	5E Decorative, Miniature
(SBa)	6D Small Ball
(MinBa)	6E Miniature Ball
(Pom)	7 Pompon
(C)	8 Cactus (unassigned)
(GC)	8A Cactus, Giant
(LC)	8B Cactus, Large
(MC)	8C Cactus, Medium
(SC)	8D Cactus, Small
(MinC)	8E Cactus, Miniature
(S-c)	9 Semi-cactus (unassigned)
(GS-c)	9A Semi-cactus, Giant
(LS-c)	9B Semi-cactus, Large
(MS-c)	9C Semi-cactus, Medium
(SS-c)	9D Semi-cactus, Small
(MinS-c)	9E Semi-cactus, Miniature
(Misc)	10 Miscellaneous
(Fim)	11 Fimbriated
(SinO)	12 Single Orchid (Star)
(DblO)	13 Double Orchid
(B)	Botanical
(DwB)	Dwarf Bedding
(Lil)	Lilliput (in combination)

Dianthus

(By the RHS)

(b)	Carnation, border
(M)	Carnation, Malmaison
(pf)	Carnation, perpetual-flowering
(p)	Pink
(p,a)	Pink, annual

Fruit

(B)	Black (*Vitis*), Blackcurrant (*Ribes*)
(Ball)	Ballerina (*Malus*)
(C)	Culinary (*Malus, Prunus, Pyrus, Ribes*)
(Cider)	Cider (*Malus*)

(D)	Dessert (*Malus, Prunus, Pyrus, Ribes*)
(F)	Fruit
(G)	Glasshouse (*Vitis*)
(O)	Outdoor (*Vitis*)
(P)	Pinkcurrant (*Ribes*)
(Perry)	Perry (*Pyrus*)
(R)	Red (*Vitis*), Redcurrant (*Ribes*)
(S)	Seedless (*Citrus, Vitis*)
(W)	White (*Vitis*), Whitecurrant (*Ribes*)

Fuchsia

(E)	Encliandra
(T)	Variants and hybrids of F. *triphylla*

Gladiolus

(B)	Butterfly
(E)	Exotic
(G)	Giant
(L)	Large
(M)	Medium
(Min)	Miniature
(N)	Nanus
(P)	Primulinus
(S)	Small
(Tub)	Tubergenii

Hepatica nobilis

(Adapted from the International Hepatica Society classification for *Hepatica nobilis*)

(1)	Hyoujun (normal)
(2)	(degenerated anther)
(3)	Otome (degenerated stamen)
(4)	Henka (petal deformity)
(5/d)	Herashibe (semi-double, primitive)
(5A/d)	Choji (semi-double, primitive)
(6/d)	Nidan (semi-double, advanced)
(7/d)	Sandan (double, primitive)
(8/d)	Karako (double, advanced)
(9/d)	Sene-e (double, completed)

Hydrangea macrophylla

(H)	Hortensia
(L)	Lacecap

Iris

(By the American Iris Society)

(AB)	Arilbred
(BB)	Border Bearded
(Cal-Sib)	Series *Californicae* × Series *Sibiricae*
(CH)	Californian Hybrid
(DB)	Dwarf Bearded (not assigned)
(Dut)	Dutch
(IB)	Intermediate Bearded
(J)	Juno (subgenus *Scorpiris*)
(La)	Louisiana Hybrid
(MDB)	Miniature Dwarf Bearded
(MTB)	Miniature Tall Bearded
(Rc)	Regeliocyclus (Section *Regelia* × Section *Oncocyclus*)
(SDB)	Standard Dwarf Bearded
(Sino-Sib)	Series *Sibiricae*, chromosome number 2n=40
(SpH)	Species Hybrid
(Spuria)	Spuria
(TB)	Tall Bearded

Lilium

(Classification according to *The International Lily Register* (ed. 4, 2007))

(I)	Asiatic hybrids derived from *L. amabile, L. bulbiferum, L. callosum, L. cernuum, L. concolor, L. dauricum, L. davidii, L. × hollandicum, L. lancifolium, L. lankongense, L. leichtlinii, L. × maculatum* and *L. pumilum, L. × scottiae, L. wardii* and *L. wilsonii.*
(II)	Martagon hybrids derived from *L. dalhansonii, L. hansonii, L. martagon, L. medeoloides and L. tsingtauense*
(III)	Euro-Caucasian hybrids derived from *L. candidum, L. chalcedonicum, L. kesselringianum, L. monadelphum, L. pomponium, L. pyrenaicum* and *L. × testaceum.*
(IV)	American hybrids derived from *L. bolanderi, L. × burbankii, L. canadense, L. columbianum, L. grayi, L. humboldtii, L. kelleyanum, L. kelloggii, L. maritimum, L. michauxii, L. michiganense, L. occidentale, L. × pardaboldtii, L. pardalinum, L. parryi, L. parvum, L. philadelphicum, L. pitkinense, L. superbum, L. vollmeri, L. washingtonianum* and *L. wigginsii.*
(V)	Longiflorum lilies derived from *L. formosanum, L. longiflorum, L. philippinense and L. wallichianum.*
(VI)	Trumpet and Aurelian hybrids derived from *L. × aurelianense, L. brownii, L. × centigale, L. henryi, L. × imperiale, L. × kewense, L. leucantheum, L. regale, L. rosthornii, L. sargentiae, L. sulphureum* and *L. sulphurgale* (but excluding hybrids of *L. henryi* with all species listed in Division VII).
(VII)	Oriental hybrids derived from *L. auratum, L. japonicum, L. nobilissimum, L. × parkmanii, L rubellum* and *L. speciosum* (but excl. all hybrids of these with *L. henryi*).
(VIII)	Other hybrids not covered by any of the previous divisions (I-VII)
(IX)	Species and cultivars of species

a/	upward-facing flowers
b/	outward-facing flowers
c/	downward-facing flowers
/a	trumpet-shaped flowers
/b	bowl-shaped flowers
/c	flat flowers (or with only tepal tips recurved)
/d	recurved flowers

Malus *see* Fruit

Narcissus

(By the RHS, revised 1998)

(1)	Trumpet
(2)	Large-cupped
(3)	Small-cupped
(4)	Double
(5)	Triandrus
(6)	Cyclamineus
(7)	Jonquilla and Apodanthus
(8)	Tazetta
(9)	Poeticus
(10)	Bulbocodium
(11a)	Split-corona: Collar
(11b)	Split-corona: Papillon
(12)	Miscellaneous
(13)	Species

Nymphaea

(H)	Hardy
(D)	Day-blooming
(N)	Night-blooming
(T)	Tropical

Papaver

(SPS)	Super Poppy Series

Paeonia

(S)	Shrubby

Pelargonium

(A)	Angel
(C)	Coloured Foliage (in combination)
(Ca)	Cactus (in combination)
(d)	Double (in combination)
(Dec)	Decorative
(Dw)	Dwarf
(DwI)	Dwarf Ivy-leaved
(Fr)	Frutetorum
(I)	Ivy-leaved
(Min)	Miniature
(MinI)	Miniature Ivy-leaved
(R)	Regal
(Sc)	Scented-leaved
(St)	Stellar (in combination)
(T)	Tulip (in combination)
(U)	Unique
(Z)	Zonal

Primula

(Classification by Section as per Richards. J. (2002) *Primula* (2nd edition). Batsford, London)

(Ag)	*Auganthus*
(Al)	*Aleuritia*
(Am)	*Amethystinae*
(Ar)	*Armerina*
(Au)	*Auricula*
(A)	Alpine Auricula
(B)	Border Auricula
(S)	Show Auricula
(St)	Striped Auricula
(Bu)	*Bullatae*
(Ca)	*Capitatae*
(Cf)	*Cordifoliae*
(Ch)	*Chartaceae*
(Co)	*Cortusoides*
(Cr)	*Carolinella*
(Cu)	*Cuneifoliae*
(Cy)	*Crystallophlomis*
(Da)	*Davidii*
(De)	*Denticulatae*
(Dr)	*Dryadifoliae*
(F)	*Fedtschenkoanae*
(G)	*Glabrae*
(Ma)	*Malvaceae*
(Mi)	*Minutissimae*
(Mo)	*Monocarpicae*
(Mu)	*Muscarioides*
(Ob)	*Obconicolisteri*
(Or)	*Oreophlomis*
(Pa)	*Parryi*
(Pe)	*Petiolares*
(Pf)	*Proliferae*
(Pi)	*Pinnatae*
(Pr)	*Primula*
(Poly)	Polyanthus
(Prim)	Primrose
(Pu)	*Pulchellae*
(Py)	*Pycnoloba*
(R)	*Reinii*
(Si)	*Sikkimenses*
(So)	*Soldanelloides*
(Sp)	*Sphondylia*
(Sr)	*Sredinskya*
(Su)	*Suffrutescentes*
(Y)	*Yunnanenses*

Prunus *see* Fruit

Pyrus *see* Fruit

Rhododendron

(A)	Azalea (deciduous, species or unclassified hybrid)
(Ad)	Azaleodendron
(EA)	Evergreen azalea
(G)	Ghent azalea (deciduous)

(K) Knap Hill or Exbury azalea (deciduous)
(M) Mollis azalea (deciduous)
(O) Occidentalis azalea (deciduous)
(R) Rustica azalea (deciduous)
(V) Vireya rhododendron
(Vs) Viscosa azalea (deciduous)

RIBES *SEE* FRUIT

ROSA

(A) Alba
(Bb) Bourbon
(Bs) Boursault
(Ce) Centifolia
(Ch) China
(Cl) Climbing (in combination)
(D) Damask
(DPo) Damask Portland
(F) Floribunda or Cluster-flowered
(G) Gallica
(Ga) Garnette
(GC) Ground Cover
(HM) Hybrid Musk
(HP) Hybrid Perpetual
(HT) Hybrid Tea or Large-flowered
(Min) Miniature
(Mo) Moss (in combination)
(N) Noisette
(Patio) Patio, Miniature Floribunda or Dwarf Cluster-flowered
(Poly) Polyantha
(Ra) Rambler
(RH) Rubiginosa hybrid (Hybrid Sweet Briar)
(Ru) Rugosa
(S) Shrub
(SpH) Spinosissima Hybrid
(T) Tea

SAXIFRAGA

(Classification by Section from Gornall, R.J. (1987). *Botanical Journal of the Linnean Society,* 95(4): 273-292)

(1) *Ciliatae*
(2) *Cymbalaria*
(3) *Merkianae*
(4) *Micranthes*
(5) *Irregulares*
(6) *Heterisia*
(7) *Porphyrion*
(8) *Ligulatae*
(9) *Xanthizoon*
(10) *Trachyphyllum*
(11) *Gymnopera*
(12) *Cotylea*
(13) *Odontophyllae*
(14) *Mesogyne*
(15) *Saxifraga*

TULIPA

(Classification by Cultivar Group from *Classified List and International Register of Tulip Names* by Koninklijke Algemeene Vereniging voor Bloembollencultuur 1996)

(1) Single Early Group
(2) Double Early Group
(3) Triumph Group
(4) Darwin Hybrid Group
(5) Single Late Group (including Darwin Group and Cottage Group)
(6) Lily-flowered Group
(7) Fringed Group
(8) Viridiflora Group
(9) Rembrandt Group
(10) Parrot Group
(11) Double Late Group
(12) Kaufmanniana Group
(13) Fosteriana Group
(14) Greigii Group
(15) Miscellaneous

VERBENA

(G) Species and hybrids considered by some botanists to belong to the separate genus *Glandularia.*

VIOLA

(C) Cornuta Hybrid
(dVt) Double Violet
(ExVa) Exhibition Viola
(FP) Fancy Pansy
(PVt) Parma Violet
(SP) Show Pansy
(T) Tricolor
(Va) Viola
(Vt) Violet
(Vtta) Violetta

VITIS *SEE* FRUIT

REVERSE SYNONYMS

The following list of reverse synonyms is intended to help users find from which genus an unfamiliar plant name has been cross-referred. For a fuller explanation see p.14.

Abelmoschus – Hibiscus
Abronia – Verbena
Abutilon – Corynabutilon
Acacia – Racosperma
Acca – Feijoa
× *Achicodonia – Eucodonia*
Achillea – Anthemis
Achillea – Tanacetum
Acinos – Calamintha
Acinos – Clinopodium
Acinos – Micromeria
Acis – Leucojum
Acmella – Spilanthes
Actaea – Cimicifuga
Actaea – Souliea
Adlumia – Dicentra
Aethionema – Eunomia
Agapetes – Pentapterygium
Agarista – Leucothoe
Agastache – Cedronella
Agathosma – Barosma
Agave – Manfreda
Agave – × *Mangave*
Ageratina – Eupatorium
Agrostis – Eragrostis
Aichryson – Aeonium
Ajania – Chrysanthemum
Ajania – Dendranthema
Ajania – Eupatorium
Albizia – Acacia
Alcea – Althaea
Allardia – Waldheimia
Allocasuarina – Casuarina
Aloysia – Lippia
Althaea – Malva
Alyogyne – Anisodontea
Alyogyne – Hibiscus
Alyssum – Ptilotrichum
Amana – Tulipa
× *Amarygia – Amaryllis*
Amaryllis – Brunsvigia
Amberhoa – Centaurea
Amomyrtus – Myrtus
Amsonia – Rhazya
Anacamptis – Orchis
Anaphalis – Gnaphalium
Anchusa – Lycopsis
Androsace – Douglasia
Androstoma – Cyathodes
Anemanthele – Oryzopsis
Anemanthele – Stipa
Anemone – Eriocapitella
Anisodontea – Malvastrum
Anisodus – Scopolia
Anomatheca – Freesia
Anomatheca – Lapeirousia
Anredera – Boussingaultia
Antirrhinum – Asarina
Aphanes – Alchemilla
Arctanthemum – Chrysanthemum
Arctostaphylos – Arbutus
Arctotis – Venidium
Arctotis – × *Venidioarctotis*
Arenga – Didymosperma
Argyranthemum – Anthemis
Argyranthemum – Chrysanthemum
Armoracia – Cochlearia
Arnoglossum – Cacalia
Arundinaria – Pseudosasa
Asarina – Antirrhinum
Asarum – Hexastylis
Asparagus – Myrsiphyllum
Asparagus – Smilax
Asperula – Galium
Asphodeline – Asphodelus
Asplenium – Camptosorus
Asplenium – Ceterach
Asplenium – Phyllitis
Asplenium – Scolopendrium
Aster – Crinitaria
Aster – Doellingeria
Aster – Erigeron
Aster – Microglossa
Aster – Symphyotrichum
Astilboides – Rodgersia
Asyneuma – Campanula
Athanasia – Hymenolepis
Atropanthe – Scopolia
Aurinia – Alyssum
Austrocedrus – Libocedrus
Austromyrtus – Myrtus
Azorella – Bolax
Azorina – Campanula

Bambusa – Arundinaria
Barnadesia- Mutisia
Bashania – Arundinaria
Bassia – Kochia
Beaucarnea – Nolina
Bellevalia – Muscari
Bellis – Erigeron
Bignonia – Campsis
Blechnum – Lomaria
Blechnum – Struthiopteris
Blepharocalyx – Temu
Bolax – Azorella
Bolboschoenus – Scirpus
Bonia – Indocalamus
Borago – Anchusa
Bothriochloa – Andropogon
Bouteloua – Chondrosum
Boykinia – Telesonix
Brachychiton – Sterculia
Brachyglottis – Senecio
Brimeura – Hyacinthus
Brodiaea – Triteleia
Brugmansia – Datura
Brunnera – Anchusa
Buglossoides – Lithospermum
Bulbine – Bulbinopsis

Cacalia – Adenostyles
Caladium – Xanthosoma
Calamagrostis – Stipa
Calamintha – Clinopodium
Calamintha – Thymus
Calibrachoa – Petunia
Callisia – Phyodina
Callisia – Tradescantia
Calocedrus – Libocedrus
Calomeria – Humea
Caloscordum – Nothoscordum
Calylophus – Oenothera
Calytrix – Lhotzkya
Camellia – Thea
Campanula – Symphyandra
Cardamine – Dentaria
Carmichaelia – × *Carmispartium*
Carmichaelia – Chordospartium
Carmichaelia – Corallospartium
Carpobrotus – Lampranthus
Cedronella – Agastache
Centaurium – Erythraea
Centella – Hydrocotyle
Centranthus – Kentranthus
Centranthus – Valeriana

Cephalaria – Scabiosa
Ceratostigma – Plumbago
Chaenomeles – Cydonia
Chaenorhinum – Linaria
Chamaecytisus – Cytisus
Chamaedaphne – Cassandra
Chamaemelum – Anthemis
Chamerion – Chamaenerion
Chamerion – Epilobium
Chasmanthium – Uniola
Cheilanthes – Notholaena
Chiastophyllum – Cotyledon
Chimonobambusa – Arundinaria
Chimonobambusa – Qiongzhuea
Chionohebe – Parahebe
Chionohebe – Pygmea
× *Chionoscilla – Scilla*
Chlorophytum – Diuranthera
Chromolaena – Eupatorium
Chrysanthemum – Dendranthema
Chrysopsis – Heterotheca
Cicerbita – Lactuca
Cionura – Marsdenia
Cissus – Ampelopsis
Cissus – Parthenocissus
× *Citrofortunella – Citrus*
Clarkia – Eucharidium
Clarkia – Godetia
Clavinodum – Arundinaria
Claytonia – Calandrinia
Claytonia – Montia
Clematis – Atragene
Clematis – Clematopsis
Cleyera – Eurya
Clinopodium – Calamintha
Clytostoma – Bignonia
Clytostoma – Pandorea
Cnicus – Carduus
Conoclinium – Eupatorium
Codariocalyx – Desmodium
Codonopsis – Campanumoea
Collospermum – Astelia
Colobanthus – Arenaria
Consolida – Delphinium
Cordyline – Dracaena
Cornus – Chamaepericlymenum
Cornus – Dendrobenthamia
Coronilla – Securigera
Cortaderia – Gynerium
Corydalis – Capnoides
Corydalis – Fumaria
Corydalis – Pseudofumaria
Cosmos – Bidens
Cotinus – Rhus
Cotula – Leptinella

Crassula – Rochea
Crassula – Sedum
Crassula – Tillaea
× *Crataegosorbus – Sorbus*
Cremanthodium – Ligularia
Crinodendron – Tricuspidaria
Crocosmia – Antholyza
Crocosmia – Curtonus
Crocosmia – Montbretia
Cruciata – Galium
Ctenanthe – Calathea
Ctenanthe – Stromanthe
Cupressus – Chamaecyparis
× *Cuprocyparis – Chamaecyparis*
× *Cuprocyparis – Cupressocyparis*
Cyclosorus – Pneumatopteris
Cylindropuntia – Opuntia
Cymbalaria – Linaria
Cymophyllus – Carex
Cyperus – Mariscus
Cypripedium – Criogenes
Cyrtanthus – Anoiganthus
Cyrtanthus – Vallota
Cyrtomium – Phanerophlebia
Cyrtomium – Polystichum
Cytisophyllum – Cytisus
Cytisus – Argyrocytisus
Cytisus – Genista
Cytisus – Lembotropis
Cytisus – Spartocytisus

Daboecia – Menziesia
Dacrycarpus – Podocarpus
Dactylicapnos – Dicentra
Dactylorhiza – Orchis
Dalea – Petalostemon
Danae – Ruscus
Darmera – Peltiphyllum
Datura – Brugmansia
Davallia – Humata
Delairea – Senecio
Delosperma – Lampranthus
Delosperma – Mesembryanthemum
Dendrocalamus – Bambusa
Desmodium – Lespedeza
Deuterocohnia – Abromeitiella
Dicentra – Corydalis
Dichelostemma – Brodiaea
Dicliptera – Barleria
Dicliptera – Justicia
Diervilla – Weigela
Dietes – Moraea
Diplazium – Athyrium
Dipogon – Dolichos
Disporopsis – Polygonatum

Dolichothrix – Helichrysum
Dracaena – Pleomele
Dracunculus – Arum
Dregea – Wattakaka
Drepanostachyum – Bambusa
Drepanostachyum – Chimonobambusa
Drepanostachyum – Gelidocalamus
Drepanostachyum – Thamnocalamus
Drimys – Tasmannia
Duchesnea – Fragaria
Dypsis – Chrysalidocarpus
Dypsis – Neodypsis

Echeveria – Cotyledon
Echinacea – Rudbeckia
Echinospartum – Genista
Edraianthus – Wahlenbergia
Egeria – Elodea
Elatostema – Pellionia
Eleutherococcus – Acanthopanax
Elliottia – Botryostege
Elliottia – Cladothamnus
Elymus – Agropyron
Elymus – Leymus
Ensete – Musa
Epipremnum – Philodendron
Epipremnum – Scindapsus
Episcia – Alsobia
Eranthis – Aconitum
Eremophila – Myoporum
Erepsia – Semnanthe
Erigeron – Haplopappus
Erysimum – Cheiranthus
Eucalyptus – Corymbia
Eupatorium – Ageratina
Eupatorium – Ayapana
Eupatorium – Bartlettina
Euphorbia – Poinsettia
Euryops – Senecio
Eustachys – Chloris
Eustoma – Lisianthus
Euthamia – Solidago

Fallopia – Bilderdykia
Fallopia – Polygonum
Fallopia – Reynoutria
Farfugium – Ligularia
Fargesia – Arundinaria
Fargesia – Borinda
Fargesia – Semiarundinaria
Fargesia – Sinarundinaria
Fargesia – Thamnocalamus
Fatsia – Aralia
Felicia – Agathaea
Felicia – Aster

Fibigia – Farsetia
Filipendula – Spiraea
Ficinia – Isolepis
Foeniculum – Ferula
Fortunella – Citrus
Frangula – Rhamnus

Galium – Asperula
Gaultheria – Chiogenes
Gaultheria – Pernettya
Gaultheria – × Gaulnettya
Gelasine – Sisyrinchium
Genista – Chamaespartium
Genista – Cytisus
Genista – Echinospartum
Genista – Teline
Gethyum – Ancrumia
Geum – Sieversia
Gladiolus – Acidanthera
Gladiolus – Anomalesia
Gladiolus – Homoglossum
Gladiolus – Petamenes
Glebionis – Chrysanthemum
Glebionis – Xanthophthalmum
Glechoma – Nepeta
Gloxinia – Seemannia
Gloxinia – Sinningia
Gomphocarpus – Asclepias
Gomphocarpus – Asclepias
Goniolimon – Limonium
Goniophlebium – Polypodium
Graptopetalum – Sedum
Graptopetalum – Tacitus
Greenovia – Sempervivum
Gymnadenia – Nigritella
Gymnospermium – Leontice

Habranthus – Zephyranthes
Hacquetia – Dondia
× Halimiocistus – Cistus
× Halimiocistus – Halimium
Halimione – Atriplex
Halimium – Cistus
Halimium – Helianthemum
Halimium – × Halimiocistus
Halocarpus – Dacrydium
Hanabusaya – Symphyandra
Harrimanella – Cassiope
Hedychium – Brachychilum
Helianthella – Helianthus
Helianthemum – Cistus
Helianthus – Coreopsis
Helianthus – Heliopsis
Helichrysum – Gnaphalium
Helicodiceros – Dracunculus
Helictotrichon – Avena
Helictotrichon – Avenula
Hepatica – Anemone
Herbertia – Alophia
Hermodactylus – Iris
Heterocentron – Schizocentron
Heteromeles – Photinia
Heterotheca – Chrysopsis
× Heucherella – Heuchera
× Heucherella – Tiarella
Hibbertia – Candollea
Hieracium – Andryala
Himalayacalamus – Arundinaria
Himalayacalamus – Chimonobambusa
Himalayacalamus – Drepanostachyum
Himalayacalamus – Drepanostachyum
Himalayacalamus – Thamnocalamus
Hippocrepis – Coronilla
Hippolytia – Achillea
Hippolytia – Tanacetum
Hoheria – Plagianthus
Homalocladium – Muehlenbeckia
Howea – Kentia
Hyacinthoides – Endymion
Hyacinthoides – Scilla
Hydrangea – Schizophragma
Hylomecon – Chelidonium
Hymenocallis – Elisena
Hymenocallis – Ismene
Hymenoxys – Dugaldia
Hymenoxys – Helenium
Hyophorbe – Mascarena
Hypoxis – Rhodohypoxis

Ichthyoselmis – Dicentra
Incarvillea – Amphicome
Indocalamus – Sasa
Iochroma – Acnistus
Iochroma – Cestrum
Iochroma – Dunalia
Iostephane – Coreopsis
Ipheion – Tristagma
Ipheion – Triteleia
Ipomoea – Calonyction
Ipomoea – Mina
Ipomoea – Pharbitis
Ipomopsis – Gilia
Ischyrolepis – Restio
Isolepis – Scirpus
Isotoma – Laurentia
Isotoma – Solenopsis

Jamesbrittenia – Sutera
Jeffersonia – Plagiorhegma
Jovibarba – Sempervivum
Juncus – Scirpus
Junellia – Verbena
Jurinea – Jurinella
Justicia – Beloperone
Justicia – Duvernoia
Justicia – Jacobinia
Justicia – Libonia

Kadsura – Schisandra
Kalanchoe – Bryophyllum
Kalanchoe – Kitchingia
Kalimeris – Aster
Kalimeris – Asteromoea
Kalimeris – Boltonia
Kalopanax – Acanthopanax
Kalopanax – Eleutherococcus
Keckiella – Penstemon
Keckiella – Penstemon
Kitagawia – Peucedanum
Knautia – Scabiosa
Kniphofia – Tritoma
Kohleria – Isoloma
Krascheninnikovia – Ceratoides
Kunzea – Leptospermum

Lablab – Dolichos
Lagarosiphon – Elodea
Lagarostrobos – Dacrydium
Lamium – Galeobdolon
Lamium – Lamiastrum
Lampranthus – Mesembryanthemum
Lamprocapnos – Dicentra
Laserpitium – Siler
Lavatera – Malva
Ledebouria – Scilla
× Ledodendron – Rhododendron
Ledum – Rhododendron
Leontodon – Microseris
Lepechinia – Sphacele
Lepidothamnus – Dacrydium
Leptecophylla – Cyathodes
Leptinella – Cotula
Leptodactylon – Gilia
Leucanthemella – Chrysanthemum
Leucanthemella – Leucanthemum
Leucanthemopsis – Chrysanthemum
Leucanthemum – Chrysanthemum
Leucochrysum – Helipterum
Leucocoryne – Beauverdia
Leucophyta – Calocephalus
Leucopogon – Cyathodes
Leucopogon – Styphelia

× *Leucoraoulia – Raoulia*
Leymus – Elymus
Ligularia – Senecio
Ligustrum – Parasyringa
Lilium – Nomocharis
Limonium – Statice
Linanthus – Linanthastrum
Lindelofia – Adelocaryum
Ligularia – Cacalia
Lindera – Parabenzoin
Lindernia – Ilysanthes
Liriope – Ophiopogon
Lithodora – Lithospermum
Lobelia – Monopsis
Lophomyrtus – Myrtus
Lophospermum – Asarina
Lophospermum – Maurandya
Lophostemon – Tristania
Lotus – Dorycnium
Lotus – Tetragonolobus
Ludwigia – Jussiaea
Luma – Myrtus
× *Lycene – Lychnis*
Lychnis – Agrostemma
Lychnis – Silene
Lychnis – Viscaria
Lycianthes – Solanum
Lytocaryum – Cocos
Lytocaryum – Microcoelum

Macfadyena – Bignonia
Macfadyena – Doxantha
Machaeranthera – Xylorhiza
Machaerina – Baumea
Mackaya – Asystasia
Macleaya – Bocconia
Maclura – Cudrania
Macropiper – Piper
Magnolia – Manglietia
Magnolia – Michelia
Magnolia – Parakmeria
Mahonia – Berberis
Maianthemum – Smilacina
Mandevilla – Dipladenia
Mandragora – Atropa
Marrubium – Ballota
Matricaria – Tripleurosperum
Maurandella – Asarina
Maurandya – Asarina
Melanoselinum – Thapsia
Melicytus – Hymenanthera
Melinis – Rhynchelytrum
Mentha – Preslia
Merremia – Ipomoea
Merwilla – Scilla

Mimulus – Diplacus
Minuartia – Arabis
Minuartia – Arenaria
Moltkia – Lithodora
Moltkia – Lithospermum
Monochoria – Pontederia
Monopsis – Lobelia
Morina – Acanthocalyx
Morina – Acanthocalyx
Mukdenia – Aceriphyllum
Muscari – Hyacinthus
Muscari – Leopoldia
Muscari – Muscarimia
Muscari – Pseudomuscari
Myrteola – Myrtus

Naiocrene – Claytonia
Naiocrene – Montia
Nectaroscordum – Allium
Nematanthus – Hypocyrta
Nemesia – Diascia × Linaria
Neolitsea – Litsea
Neopanax – Pseudopanax
Neopaxia – Claytonia
Neopaxia – Montia
Neoregelia – Nidularium
Nepeta – Dracocephalum
× *Niduregelia – Guzmania*
Nipponanthemum – Chrysanthemum
Nipponanthemum – Leucanthemum
Nolina – Beaucarnea
Notospartium – Carmichaelia
Nymphoides – Villarsia

Ochagavia – Fascicularia
Oemleria – Osmaronia
Oenothera – Chamissonia
Olsynium – Sisyrinchium
Onixotis – Dipidax
Onoclea – Matteuccia
Ophiopogon – Convallaria
Orbea – Stapelia
Orchis – Anacamptis
Orchis – Dactylorhiza
Oreopteris – Thelypteris
Orostachys – Sedum
Oscularia – Lampranthus
Osmanthus – Phillyrea
Osmanthus – × *Osmarea*
Othonna – Hertia
Othonna – Othonnopsis
Oxygraphis – Ranunculus
Oziroë – Fortunatia
Ozothamhus – Helichrysum

Pachyphragma – Cardamine
Pachyphragma – Thlaspi
Pachystegia – Olearia
Packera – Senecio
Paederota – Veronica
Pallenis – Asteriscus
Papaver – Meconopsis
Parahebe – Derwentia
Parahebe – Hebe
Parahebe – Veronica
Parasenecio – Cacalia
Paraserianthes – Albizia
Paris – Daiswa
Parthenocissus – Ampelopsis
Parthenocissus – Vitis
Passiflora – Tetrapathaea
Paxistima – Pachystema
Pecteilis – Habenaria
Pelargonium – Geranium
Peltoboykinia – Boykinia
Penstemon – Chelone
Penstemon – Nothochelone
Penstemon – Pennellianthus
Pentaglottis – Anchusa
Pericallis – Cineraria
Pericallis – Senecio
Persea – Machilus
Persicaria – Aconogonon
Persicaria – Antenoron
Persicaria – Bistorta
Persicaria – Polygonum
Persicaria – Tovara
Petrocoptis – Lychnis
Petrophytum – Spiraea
Petrorhagia – Tunica
Petroselinum – Carum
Phalocallis – Cypella
Phegopteris – Thelypteris
Phlebodium – Polypodium
Phoenicaulis – Parrya
Photinia – Stransvaesia
Photinia – × *Stravinia*
Phuopsis – Crucianella
Phyla – Lippia
Phymatosorus – Microsorum
Phymosia – Sphaeralcea
Physoplexis – Phyteuma
Physostegia – Dracocephalum
Pieris – Arcterica
Pilosella – Hieracium
Platycladus – Thuja
Plecostachys – Helichrysum
Plectranthus – Coleus
Plectranthus – Solenostemon
Pleioblastus – Arundinaria

Pleioblastus – Sasa
Podophyllum – Dysosma
Podranea – Tecoma
Polianthes – Bravoa
Polygonum – Persicaria
Polypodium – Phlebodium
Polyscias – Nothopanax
Polyspora – Gordonia
Poncirus – Aegle
Potentilla – Comarum
Pratia – Lobelia
Prenanthes – Nabalus
Pritzelago – Hutchinsia
Prumnopitys – Podocarpus
Prunus – Amygdalus
Pseudocydonia – Chaenomeles
Pseudogynoxys – Senecio
Pseudopanax – Metapanax
Pseudopanax – Neopanax
Pseudosasa – Arundinaria
Pseudotsuga – Tsuga
Pseudowintera – Drimys
Pterocephalus – Scabiosa
Pteryxia – Cymopterus
Ptilostemon – Cirsium
Pulicaria – Inula
Pulsatilla – Anemone
Purshia – Cowania
Puschkinia – Scilla
Pycreus – Cyperus
Pyrrocoma – Aster
Pyrrocoma – Haplopappus

Reineckea – Liriope
Retama – Genista
Retama – Lygos
Rhapis – Chamaerops
Rhodanthe – Helipterum
Rhodanthemum – Argyranthemum
Rhodanthemum – Chrysanthemopsis
Rhodanthemum – Chrysanthemum
Rhodanthemum – Leucanthemopsis
Rhodanthemum – Leucanthemum
Rhodanthemum – Pyrethropsis
Rhodiola – Clementsia
Rhodiola – Rosularia
Rhodiola – Sedum
Rhododendron – Azalea
Rhododendron – Azaleodendron
Rhododendron – Rhodora
Rhododendron – Therorhodion
Rhododendron – Tsusiophyllum
Rhodophiala – Hippeastrum
× Rhodoxis – Rhodohypoxis
Rhus – Toxicodendron
Rhyncospora – Dichromena
Rosularia – Cotyledon
Rosularia – Sempervivella
Rothmannia – Gardenia
Ruellia – Dipteracanthus

Saccharum – Erianthus
Sagina – Minuartia
Sanguisorba – Dendriopoterium
Sanguisorba – Poterium
Sasa – Arundinaria
Sasaella – Arundinaria
Sasaella – Pleioblastus
Sasaella – Sasa
Sauromatum – Arum
Saussurea – Jurinea
Scadoxus – Haemanthus
Schefflera – Brassaia
Schefflera – Dizygotheca
Schefflera – Heptapleurum
Schizachyrium – Andropogon
Schizostachyum – Arundinaria
Schizostachyum – Thamnocalamus
Schizostylis – Hesperantha
Schoenoplectus – Scirpus
Scilla – Oncostema
Scirpoides – Scirpus
Securigera – Coronilla
Sedum – Cotyledon
Sedum – Hylotelephium
Sedum – Sedastrum
Semiaquilegia – Aquilegia
Semiaquilegia – Paraquilegia
Semiarundinaria – Arundinaria
Semiarundinaria – Oligostachyum
Senecio – Cineraria
Senecio – Kleinia
Senecio – Ligularia
Senna – Cassia
Seriphidium – Artemisia
Shortia – Schizocodon
Sibbaldiopsis – Potentilla
Sieversia – Geum
Silene – Lychnis
Silene – Melandrium
Silene – Saponaria
Sinacalia – Ligularia
Sinacalia – Senecio
Sinningia – Gesneria
Sinningia – Rechsteineria
Sinobambusa – Pleioblastus
Sinobambusa – Pseudosasa
Siphocranion – Chamaesphacos
Sisymbrium – Hesperis
Sisyrinchium – Phaiophleps
Smallanthus – Polymnia
Solanum – Syphomandra
Soleirolia – Helxine
Solenostemon – Coleus
Solidago – Aster
Solidago – × Solidaster
× Solidaster – Aster
× Solidaster – Solidago
Sophora – Styphnolobium
Sorbaria – Spiraea
Sparaxis – Synnotia
Sphaeralcea – Iliamna
Sphaeromeria – Tanacetum
Spirodela – Lemna
Spraguea – Calyptridium
Stachys – Betonica
Stemmacantha – Centaurea
Stemmacantha – Leuzea
Stenomesson – Urceolina
Stenotus – Haplopappus
Stewartia – Stuartia
Stipa – Achnatherum
Stipa – Agrostis
Stipa – Calamagrostis
Stipa – Lasiagrostis
Stipa – Nassella
Strobilanthes – Parachampionella
Strobilanthes – Pteracanthus
Styphnolobium – Sophora
Succisa – Scabiosa
Sutera – Bacopa
Syagrus – Arecastrum
Syagrus – Cocos
Syncarpha – Helipterum
Syzygium – Caryophyllus

Talbotia – Vellozia
Tanacetum – Achillea
Tanacetum – Balsamita
Tanacetum – Chrysanthemum
Tanacetum – Matricaria
Tanacetum – Pyrethrum
Tanacetum – Spathipappus
Tecoma – Tecomaria
Telanthophora – Senecio
Telekia – Buphthalmum
Tetradium – Euodia
Tetraneuris – Actinella
Tetraneuris – Actinella
Tetraneuris – Hymenoxys
Tetrapanax – Fatsia
Thamnocalamus – Arundinaria
Thlaspi – Hutchinsia
Thlaspi – Noccaea
Thlaspi – Vania

Thuja – Thujopsis
Thymus – Origanum
Tiarella – × Heucherella
Tigridia – Rigidella
Tonestus – Haplopappus
Toona – Cedrela
Trachelium – Diosphaera
Trachycarpus – Chamaerops
Tradescantia – Rhoeo
Tradescantia – Setcreasea
Tradescantia – Zebrina
Trichopetalum – Anthericum
Trichophorum – Scirpus
Tripetaleia – Elliottia
Tripleurospermum – Gentiana
Tripleurospermum – Matricaria
Tripogandra – Tradescantia
Tristaniopsis – Tristania
Triteleia – Brodiaea
Tritonia – Crocosmia
Tritonia – Montbretia
Trochiscanthes – Angelica
Tropaeolum – Nasturtium hort.
Tupistra – Campylandra
Tutcheria – Pyrenaria
Tweedia – Oxypetalum

Ugni – Myrtus
Utricularia – Polypompholyx
Uvularia – Oakesiella

Vaccaria – Melandrium
Vaccinium – Oxycoccus
Verbascum – Celsia
Verbascum – × Celsioverbascum
Verbena – Glandularia
Verbena – Lippia
Veronicastrum – Veronica
Vigna – Phaseolus
Viola – Erpetion
Vitaliana – Androsace
Vitaliana – Douglasia

Wedelia – Zexmenia
Weigela – Diervilla
Weigela – Macrodiervilla

Xanthocyparis – Cupressus
Xanthorhiza – Zanthorhiza
Xerochrysum – Bracteantha
Xerochrysum – Helichrysum

Yushania – Arundinaria
Yushania – Sinarundinaria
Yushania – Thamnocalamus

Zantedeschia – Calla
Zauschneria – Epilobium
Zephyranthes – × Cooperanthes
Zephyranthes – Cooperia

THE PLANT DIRECTORY

A

Abelia ✿ (*Caprifoliaceae*)

	Auderose = 'Minaud'[PBR]	SBfd
	chinensis misapplied	see *A.* × *grandiflora*
§	***chinensis*** R.Br.	CBcs CMac CPLG EBee ELan EPfP EWTr LRHS MAsh MMuc SBfd SEND SKHP SPer SPoG SRms WGrn WPat
	'Edward Goucher'	CBar CDoC CDul CWSG CWib EBee ECrN ELan EPfP EWTr LBMP LRHS LSRN LTen MAsh MGos MRav MSwo NBir SBfd SEND SGol SPer SPlb SWvt WFar WPat WSHC
	engleriana	CPLG EBee EPfP LRHS MAsh MBlu NLar SEND SLon WFar
	floribunda ♀H3	CBcs CDul CMac CPLG CSBt CWib EBee ECre ELan ELon EPfP EWTr IDee LHop LRHS MRav NLar SEND SGol SKHP SPer SPoG SRms SSpi WAbe WPat
§	× ***grandiflora*** ♀H4	Widely available
	- 'Aurea'	see *A.* × *grandiflora* 'Gold Spot'
	- 'Compacta'	LRHS WFar
	- Confetti = 'Conti'[PBR] (v)	CBcs CDoC CMac CSBt CSPN CWSG EBee ECrN ELan EPfP LAst LRHS LSRN LTen MAsh MGos MRav MSwo NEgg NLar SBfd SGol SLim SPer SPoG SWvt WCot WFar WGob
	- dwarf	CDoC
§	- 'Francis Mason' (v)	Widely available
§	- 'Gold Spot' (v)	CWSG EBee EPfP LRHS MAsh MGos MWat SGol WGob WPat
	- 'Gold Strike'	see *A.* × *grandiflora* 'Gold Spot'
	- Golden Panache = 'Minpan'	MRav
	- 'Goldsport'	see *A.* × *grandiflora* 'Gold Spot'
	- 'Hopleys'[PBR] (v)	CBcs CDoC CDul CMac CSBt CTri CWib EBee ELan EPfP LHop LRHS MAsh MGos MRav NHol SEND SLim SLon SPoG SWvt WCot WFar WGrn WHar
	- 'Kaleidoscope'[PBR] (v)	CAbP CDoC CMac CWGN EBee EHoe ELan EPPr EPfP EShb LAst LRHS LSRN MAsh MGos MPkF SBfd SGol SHil SLim SPoG SPtl SSta SWvt WCot WFar WGob WGrn
	- 'Panache' (v)	CDoC LLHF LTen WCot
	- 'Prostrate White'	EBee LRHS NLar
	- 'Semperflorens'	EBee EMil LRHS SBfd
	- 'Sherwoodii'	EBee EMil EPfP LRHS MAsh SLim WPat
	- 'Sunrise' (v)	ELan EPfP NLar SLim
	- Sunshine Daydream = 'Abelops' (v) **new**	EPPr MPkF
	- 'Variegata'	see *A.* × *grandiflora* 'Francis Mason'
	mosanensis	EBee ELan EPfP LLHF LRHS MBlu NCGa NLar SLon SPoG SSpi WSHC
	parvifolia 'Bumblebee'	EBee SPoG
	Petite Garden = 'Minedward' **new**	SBfd
	rupestris misapplied	see *A.* × *grandiflora*
	rupestris Lindl.	see *A. chinensis* R.Br.
	schumannii ♀H4	CAbP CBcs CMHG CMac CPLG CSBt CTri EBee ECrN ELan EPfP LHop LRHS LSRN MAsh MBri MMuc MRav NLar SHil SKHP SLim SLon SPer SWvt WFar WGrn WPat
	spathulata	WFar
	triflora	CAbP CPLG CWib ECre EPfP LAst LHop LRHS MMuc NLar SEND SKHP SPhx WFar WGob WSHC

Abeliophyllum (*Oleaceae*)

distichum	CBcs CDoC CWib EBee ECrN ELan ELon EPfP EWTr LAst LBMP LRHS MAsh MBlu MBri MGos SBfd SGol SPer SSpi SWvt WCFE WFar WSHC
- Roseum Group	CBcs CDoC CJun CPLG EBee ELan ELon EPfP LHop LRHS MAsh MGos MMuc MRav SKHP SLon SPoG

Abelmoschus (*Malvaceae*)

	esculentus	SVic
§	***manihot***	XDel

Abies (*Pinaceae*)

alba	CDul NWea
- 'Bystricka'	NLar
- 'Compacta'	CKen
- 'Green Spiral'	NLar
- 'King's Dwarf'	CKen
- 'Microphylla'	CKen
- 'Münsterland'	CKen NLar
- 'Nana' misapplied	see *Picea glauca* 'Nana'
- 'Nana' ambig.	CKen
- 'Pendula'	CKen
- 'Pyramidalis' **new**	NLar
amabilis	GLin WEve
- 'Spreading Star'	SLim
arizonica	see *A. lasiocarpa* var. *arizonica*
balsamea	CDul GKin NWea
- 'Cook's Blue'	CKen
- Hudsonia Group ♀H4	CDoC CKen EHul EPot LRHS NLar NWad SLim SPoG WEve
- 'Jamie'	CKen MAsh NLar
- 'Le Feber'	CKen
- 'Nana'	CKen EHul MAsh NPCo NWad WFar WGor
- var. ***phanerolepis*** 'Bear Swamp'	CKen NLar

	Name	Suppliers
	- 'Piccolo'	CDoC CKen EHul LRHS NLar WEve WFar WGor
	- 'Prostrata'	EHul WEve
	- 'Renswoude'	CKen
	- 'Tyler Blue'	CKen NLar
	- 'Verkade's Prostrate'	CKen
*	***borisii-regis*** 'Pendula'	CKen
	brachyphylla dwarf	see *A. homolepis* 'Prostrata'
	cephalonica	CDul CKen CMCN NWea
	- 'Greg's Broom'	CKen
§	- 'Meyer's Dwarf'	EHul LRHS NLar NPCo SLim SPoG WEve
	- 'Nana'	see *A. cephalonica* 'Meyer's Dwarf'
	cilicica 'Spring Grove'	CKen
	colimensis NJM 09.074	WPGP
	concolor ♀H4	CBcs CDul CTho LMaj LTen MMuc NWea SEND WEve
	- 'Archer's Dwarf'	CKen MGos NLar SLim
	- 'Argentea' Niemetz, 1903	CKen
	- 'Aurea'	MGos NLar WEve
	- 'Birthday Broom'	CKen
	- 'Blue Sapphire'	CKen NLar
	- 'Blue Spreader'	CKen
§	- 'Compacta' ♀H4	CDoC CKen LRHS MGos NLar NWea SCoo SLim SPoG WEve WFar
	- 'Fagerhult'	CKen
	- 'Gable's Weeping'	CKen
	- 'Glauca'	see *A. concolor* Violacea Group
	- 'Glauca Compacta'	see *A. concolor* 'Compacta'
	- 'Hillier Broom'	see *A. concolor* 'Hillier's Dwarf'
§	- 'Hillier's Dwarf'	CKen
	- 'Husky Pup'	CKen
	- (Lowiana Group) 'Creamy'	CKen NLar
	- 'Masonic Broom'	CKen
	- 'Mike Stearn'	CKen
	- 'Mora'	CKen
	- 'Ostrov nad Ohri'	CKen
	- 'Piggelmee'	CKen NLar
	- 'Pygmy'	CKen
	- 'Scooter'	CKen NLar
*	- 'Swift's Silver'	WEve
§	- Violacea Group	CKen MAsh MGos SLim WEve WFar
	- - prostrate	LRHS
	- 'Wattez Prostrate'	LRHS WFar
	- 'Wattezii'	CKen
	- 'Wintergold'	CKen MGos NLar NPCo SLim WEve
	delavayi	CDul EPfP MGos NWea
	- var. ***delavayi*** Fabri Group	see *A. fabri*
I	- 'Nana'	CKen
	- 'Nana Headfort'	see *A. fargesii* 'Headfort'
§	***fabri***	CDul CKen
	fargesii	CKen NLar
§	- 'Headfort'	NLar
	forrestii	CKen
	- var. ***georgei***	NWea
	fraseri	CTho MMuc NWea WEve
	- 'Blue Bonnet'	CKen NLar
	- 'Piglet's' witches' broom	NLar
	- 'Raul's Dwarf'	CKen
	grandis	CBcs CDul CJun EPfP MMuc NWea
	- 'Compacta'	CKen
	- 'Van Dedem's Dwarf'	CKen NLar SLim WEve
	holophylla	NLar
	homolepis	CKen NLar NWea
§	- 'Prostrata'	CKen
	kawakamii	CKen
	koreana	Widely available
	- 'Alpin Star'	CKen MAsh NLar
	- 'Aurea'	see *A. koreana* 'Flava'
	- 'Blaue Zwo'	CKen NLar
	- 'Blauer Eskimo'	CKen MAsh NLar SLim
	- 'Blauer Pfiff'	CKen
	- 'Blinsham Gold'	CKen
	- 'Blue Emperor'	CKen NLar
	- 'Blue Magic'	CKen NLar
	- 'Blue 'n' Silver'	NLar WEve
	- 'Bonsai Blue'	IVic
	- 'Cis'	CDoC CKen LRHS NHol NLar SLim SPoG
	- 'Compact Dwarf'	MGos NLar WEve
	- 'Crystal Globe'	CKen NLar
	- 'Dark Hill'	NLar
	- 'Doni-tajuso'	CKen NLar WGor
	- 'Eisregen'	CKen
	- 'Festival'	NLar
§	- 'Flava'	CKen MGos NPCo WEve
	- 'Fliegender Untertasse'	IVic
	- 'Frosty'	SLim SPoG
	- 'Gait'	CKen NLar
	- 'Golden Glow'	NLar SLim WFar
	- 'Goldener Traum'	CKen
	- 'Green Carpet'	CKen LRHS
	- 'Horstmann'	CKen
	- 'Ice Breaker'	MAsh SLim
	- 'Inverleith'	CKen
	- 'Kleiner Prinz'	NLar
	- 'Kohout'	CKen
	- 'Kohout's Icebreaker' **new**	CKen
	- 'Lippetal'	CKen
	- 'Luminetta'	CKen LRHS MGos NLar
	- 'Nadelkissen'	CKen
	- 'Nisbet'	LRHS NHol NLar NPCo SCoo SLim WEve
	- 'Oberon'	CDoC CKen MAsh NHol NLar NWad SLim
	- 'Piccolo'	CKen
	- 'Pinocchio'	CDoC CKen MGos NLar
	- 'Prostrata'	see *A. koreana* 'Prostrate Beauty'
§	- 'Prostrate Beauty'	WEve WFar
	- 'Ry' **new**	NLar
	- 'Scherenbach'	NLar
	- 'Schweden König'	NLar
	- 'Sherwood Compact'	CKen
	- 'Silberkugel'	CKen CMen NLar NWad SLim
	- 'Silberlocke' ♀H4	CDoC CDul CKen GKin LRHS MAsh MBlu MBri MGos NEgg NLar SCoo SLim SPer SPoG WEve WFar WHar
	- 'Silbermavers'	CKen
	- 'Silberperl'	CKen CMen LRHS NLar
	- 'Silberschmelze'	MGos
	- 'Silberzwerg'	NHol NLar
	- 'Silver Show'	CDoC CDul CKen NLar
	- 'Threave'	CKen NLar
	- 'Tundra'	NLar
	- 'Verdener Dom'	NLar
	- 'Winter Goldtip'	WEve
	lasiocarpa	CDul NWea
	- 'Alpine Beauty'	CKen NLar
§	- var. ***arizonica***	CDul
§	- - 'Argentea'	WEve
	- - 'Compacta' Hornibr. ♀H4	CDoC CKen CMac EHul ELan LRHS MBri MGos SLim SPoG WFar WGor

	- - 'Kenwith Blue'	CKen MGos SLim WEve WFar
	- 'Compacta' Beissn.	LRHS MAsh NHol WEve WFar
	- 'Day Creek'	CKen NLar
	- 'Duflon'	CKen
	- 'Elaine'	CKen
	- 'Glauca'	see *A. lasiocarpa* var. *arizonica* 'Argentea'
	- 'Green Globe'	CKen LRHS NLar WEve
	- 'Joe's Alpine'	CKen
*	- 'King's Blue'	CKen
	- 'Logan Pass'	CKen NLar
	- 'Mulligan's Dwarf'	CKen
	- 'Prickly Pete'	CKen NLar
I	- 'Prostrata'	CMac
	- 'Stevens Blue'	MAsh NLar
	- 'Toenisvorst'	CKen
	- 'Utah'	CKen
I	***magnifica*** 'Nana'	CKen
	- witches' broom	CKen
	nebrodensis	CKen
	nobilis	see *A. procera*
	nordmanniana ♀H4	CCVT CDul CJun CMac CTri EHul EPfP LMaj LTen MGos MMuc NEgg NWea SBfd SEND SPoG WEve WMou
	- 'Arne's Dwarf'	CKen
	- 'Barabits' Compact'	MBri MGos NLar
	- 'Barabits' Spreader'	CKen
	- 'Dahlheim'	MAsh
	- subsp. ***equi-trojani***	CDul NWea
	- - 'Archer'	CKen NPCo
	- 'Golden Spreader' ♀H4	CDoC CKen CMac LRHS MAsh MBri MGos NLar NPCo SCoo SLim SPoG WEve WFar WThu
	- 'Hasselt'	CKen
	- 'Jakobsen'	CKen
	- 'Silberspitze'	CKen
	numidica	CKen
	- 'Glauca'	CKen
	- 'Lawrenceville'	NPCo WFar
	pinsapo	CDul SEND
	- 'Atlas'	MAsh NLar
	- 'Aurea'	CKen LRHS MGos MPkF NLar SLim SPoG WEve WFar
I	- 'Aurea Nana'	CKen
	- 'Fastigiata'	MPkF SGol
	- 'Glauca' ♀H4	CDoC CDul CKen CTho EHul ELan LMaj LRHS MBlu NLar SLim SPoG WEve
	- 'Hamondii'	CKen
I	- 'Horstmann'	CKen NHol NLar NPCo SLim WEve
	- 'Kelleriis'	NLar
	- 'Marokko' **new**	NLar
	- 'Pendula'	CKen MGos NLar WEve
	- 'Quicksilver'	CKen
§	***procera*** ♀H4	CBcs CDul NWea WEve
	- 'Bizarro'	NLar WEve
	- 'Blaue Hexe'	CKen IVic LRHS MAsh NLar SLim SPoG WFar
	- Glauca Group	CDoC CDul CTho GKin LRHS LTen MAsh MBlu MBri MGos SLim WEve WFar
	- - 'Glauca Prostrata'	GKin MGos SLim WEve WFar
	- 'La Graciosa'	NLar
	- 'Noble's Dwarf'	SLim
	- 'Obrighofen'	NLar
	- 'Sherwoodii'	CKen SLim
	recurvata	NLar
	Rosemoor hybrid	CKen
	sachalinensis	CKen
	veitchii	CDul CTho
	- 'Heddergott'	CKen MGos SLim
	- 'Heine'	CKen
	- 'Kramer'	CKen NLar
I	- 'Pendula'	CKen IVic
	- 'Rumburk'	CKen
	- 'Syców'	CKen

Abromeitiella see *Deuterocohnia*

Abrotanella (*Asteraceae*)

sp.	ECho

Abutilon ✿ (*Malvaceae*)

'Amiti'	ELar
'Apricot Belle'	SMDP WTcb
'Ashford Red'	CBcs CCCN EBee ELan LRHS MAsh SAga SBfd SKHP SMDP WCot WFar WKif WTcb
'Boule de Neige'	SMrm WTcb
'Canary Bird' ♀H2	CBcs CCCN CHEx CHll SMDP SUsu WKif WTcb
'Cannington Carol' (v) ♀H2	CCCN CHll ELan LLHF LSRN SEND SLim WTcb
'Cannington Peter' (v) ♀H2	CCCN LSRN
'Cannington Sonia' (v)	SMDP
'Cloth of Gold'	CMac WTcb
'Cynthia Pike' (v)	LRHS
'Flamenco'	CWGN LRHS NEgg SLim
'Heather Bennington'	SMDP
'Henry Makepeace'	ELar SMDP
'Hinton Seedling'	CCCN CRHN WTcb
× ***hybridum*** apricot-flowered	CHEx WTcb
- red-flowered	CHEx
indicum	CCCN
'Ines'	IVic WPGP
'Jacqueline Morris'	LRHS MAsh SMrm
'John Thompson'	CCCN CWGN EBee LSRN
'Kentish Belle' ♀H2-3	Widely available
'Kreutzberger'	ELar
'Lemon Queen'	ELar
'Linda Vista Peach' ♀H2	ELar SMDP
'Louis Marignac'	ELar
'Marion' ♀H2	CRHN ELar LRHS LSRN SMDP SMrm
'Master Michael'	CMac GKin SEND
megapotamicum ♀H3	Widely available
- 'Variegatum' (v)	CBcs CCCN CMac EBee ELan ELar EPfP LRHS MAsh MGos MOWG MSCN NEgg SBfd SKHP SLim SLon SPer SPoG SWvt WGrn WTcb XLum
- 'Wisley Red'	CRHN CSBt CSPN GKin LRHS SKHP SMDP
× ***milleri*** ♀H2	CMac CRHN WCot WWlt
- 'Variegatum' (v)	CCCN CHEx CMac LRHS NEgg WCot
- 'Ventnor Gold'	SBfd
'Millie Houghton'	WTcb
'Nabob' ♀H2	CCCN CDoC CHGN CPLG CRHN EBee EUJe LRHS MOWG SBfd SMDP SMrm SPoG WFar WTcb
'Old Rose Belle'	SMDP
'Orange Hot Lava'	CPLG IVic WPGP
'Orange Vein'	EShb SMDP

	'Patrick Synge'	CCCN CHGN CHll CMHG EBtc EShb IVic MOWG SBfd SPhx WPGP WTcb
	pictum 'Thompsonii' (v)	CHEx EShb SBfd WTcb
I	- 'Variegatum' (v)	EShb
	'Pink Lady'	SMDP
	'Red Bells'	ELar
	'Red Queen'	ELar
	'Russels Dwarf'	CCCN
	'Satin Pink Belle'	SMDP
	'Savitzii' (v) ♀H2	MSCN SBfd
	'Simcox White'	CCCN
	'Snow Boy'	ELar
	'Snowfall'	SMDP
	'Sophia Jackson'	WTcb
	'Souvenir de Bonn' (v) ♀H2	CHll ELar EShb LSou SBfd SMDP SMrm WTcb
	× ***suntense***	CBcs CCCN CHll CMHG CSBt ELan EPfP ESwi LHop LRHS MNrw MOWG MSCN NPer SChF SEND
	- 'Jermyns' ♀H3	CAbP CPLG EBee ELan EPfP GCra LRHS LSRN MAsh MBri MGos SCoo SHil SKHP SPoG SSpi SWvt WCot
	- Ralph Gould seedling	MAsh
	'Tango'	CWGN EUJe LRHS SEND SLim
	variegated, salmon-flowered (v)	LAst SEND
	'Victory'	CCCN CWGN SKHP SLim
	vitifolium	CBcs CCCN CDTJ CWib EPfP EShb MAvo NBid NEgg SPad WBor WHil WKif
	- 'Album'	CBcs CDul CHll CPLG ELan GCal GQui LHop MWat NChi SEND SPer SSpi WFar WSpi
	- 'Buckland'	CGHE
	- 'Tennant's White' ♀H3	CAbP CCCN CPLG EBee EPfP LRHS MAsh MBri SHil SKHP WTcb
	- 'Veronica Tennant' ♀H3	CPLG GQui IVic SMrm WKif
	'Waltz'	CWGN EUJe LLHF LRHS SBfd SEND SLim
	'Westfield Bronze'	CRHN SMDP

Acacia (*Mimosaceae*)

	sp.	LSRN
	acinacea	IDee SPlb
	adunca	SPlb
	angustissima new	SPlb
	armata	see *A. paradoxa*
	axillaris	SPlb
	baileyana ♀H2	CBcs CCCN CDul CEnt CGHE CMac CSBt CTsd EBee EHoe ELan EPfP IVic LRHS LSRN MAsh MGos MOWG MWat SBfd SBig SCoo SEND SGar SLim SPer SPlb SWvt WFar WPat
	- var. ***aurea***	SPlb
	- 'Purpurea' ♀H2	Widely available
	- 'Songlines' new	MBri SHil
	boormanii	SBrt SPlb WPGP
	brachybotrya	CDTJ
	cardiophylla	SEND
	caven NJM 08.0021	WPGP
	covenyi	CTrC WPGP
	cultriformis	CCCN CTsd ESwi SBfd SEND
	dealbata ♀H2	Widely available
	- 'Argentea' new	MGos SHil
	- 'Gaulois Astier'	CSBt EBee ELon LRHS LSRN MAsh MBri MGos MREP SBfd SHil SPoG SSpi SWvt WPGP
	- subsp. ***subalpina***	EGFP WPGP
	'Exeter Hybrid'	CDoy CSBt
	fimbriata	CRHN
	floribunda 'Lisette'	LRHS SHil
	gregorii new	SPlb
	implexa new	SBrt
	julibrissin	see *Albizia julibrissin*
	juniperina	see *A. ulicifolia*
	karroo	CArn CCCN CDTJ CTrC SPlb
	kybeanensis	EBee
	longifolia	CBcs CCCN CDTJ EPfP LRHS SHil SPer
	- subsp. ***sophorae***	CCCN
	macradenia	SPlb
	mearnsii	CCCN EBee SEND
	melanoxylon	CBcs CDTJ CTsd ESwi IGor MTPN SEND SLim SPlb
§	***paradoxa*** ♀H2	ECou ELon ESwi IDee LRHS SEND
	pataczekii	CSBt EPfP EWes WPGP
	pendula	SPlb
	podalyriifolia	CAbb CCCN ETod SPlb
	pravissima ♀H2-3	Widely available
	- 'Bushwalk Baby'	MOWG
	retinodes ♀H2	CBcs CCCN CDTJ CDoC CRHN CTsd EAmu EBee EPfP ESwi ETod IDee LRHS LSRN MTPN SBfd SEND SLim SPad SWvt WCFE
	- blue-leaved	ESwi
	riceana	CCCN CTsd SBrt
	rubida	IDee MREP SPlb
	sentis	see *A. victoriae*
	spectabilis	CCCN SEND SPlb
	suaveolens	SPlb
§	***ulicifolia***	CSBt
	verticillata	CBcs CCCN CDTJ CHGN CHll CTsd EPfP MOWG MTPN
	- riverine form	CPLG CTrC EBee EPfP LRHS SEND
§	***victoriae***	SPlb

Acaena (*Rosaceae*)

	adscendens misapplied	see *A. affinis*, *A. saccaticupula* 'Blue Haze'
	adscendens ambig. 'Glauca'	EHoe NBir
§	***affinis***	EBee ECha SDix
	anserinifolia misapplied	see *A. novae-zelandiae*
	buchananii	CTri EBee ECho EDAr EHoe GAbr MBrN MMuc NLar SRms WFar WPer
	caerulea hort.	see *A. caesiiglauca*
§	***caesiiglauca***	CTri EBee EDAr GAbr GQue MLHP SGar
	eupatoria	EBee
	fissistipula	EDAr
	inermis	SPlb
	- 'Purpurea'	CSam EBee ECha EHoe ETod GAbr GBin GKev GQue LRHS NDov NHol NLar SPlb WHoo WMoo WPtf
	magellanica	EBee GCal GKev
	microphylla ♀H4	CMea CSam CTri EBee ECho EDAr LRHS MBel MBrN NLar NMen SPlb SRms WFar WMoo
	- 'Braune Feder'	EBee
	- Copper Carpet	see *A. microphylla* 'Kupferteppich'
	- 'Dichte Matte'	EBee
	- 'Glauca'	see *A. caesiiglauca*
§	- 'Kupferteppich'	CSam EBee ECho ECtt EHoe EPPr ETod GAbr GCal GQue LHop MBri MMuc MRav NBir NBro NDov NLar WMoo WPat WPer WPtf WWEG

	Name	Suppliers
	myriophylla	ECho EDAr
§	***novae-zelandiae***	CTri EBee SDix WMoo
	'Pewter'	see *A. saccaticupula* 'Blue Haze'
	'Purple Carpet'	see *A. microphylla* 'Kupferteppich'
	'Purple Haze'	CSpe
§	***saccaticupula*** 'Blue Haze'	EBee ECha ECho EDAr EHoe ETod LHop LRHS MBrN MRav NChi NRHS SPer SPlb SRms WFar WHoo WMoo WPtf WWEG
	splendens	SPlb

Acalypha (*Euphorbiaceae*)

	Name	Suppliers
	pendula	see *A. reptans*
§	***reptans***	CCCN

Acanthocalyx see *Morina*

Acantholimon (*Plumbaginaceae*)

	Name	Suppliers
	acerosum	XSen
	androsaceum	see *A. ulicinum*
	armenum	XSen
	glumaceum	LLHF
	trojanum	XSen
§	***ulicinum***	GKev WAbe XSen

Acanthopanax see *Eleutherococcus*

	Name	Suppliers
	ricinifolius	see *Kalopanax septemlobus*

Acanthus ✿ (*Acanthaceae*)

	Name	Suppliers
	balcanicus misapplied	see *A. hungaricus*
	'Candelabra'	WHil
	caroli-alexandri	see *A. spinosus*
	dioscoridis	GCal MAvo SMHy WHil
	- var. ***perringii***	CDes CRDP ECha LRHS MAvo MNrw WCot WFar WHil XLum
	- smooth-leaved	WCot WHil
	eminens	WCot
	hirsutus	CMea EPri IFoB MAvo SBig WCot WHil
	- f. ***roseus***	WFar
	- subsp. ***syriacus***	EHrv GCal NLar WCot WFar WHil
	- - JCA 106500	WHil
	'Hollande du Nort'	EBee GBin WHil
§	***hungaricus***	CArn CHid CMHG CMac EBee ECtt ELan EShb GBBs IBoy LRHS MBel MMuc MRav NLar NRHS SDix SPer SPhx SWat WCot WFar WHil WMnd WWEG XLum
	- AL&JS 90097YU	WHil
	- MESE 561	EPPr WHil
	longifolius Host	see *A. hungaricus*
	mollis	Widely available
	- from Turkey	GCal
	- 'Fielding Gold'	see *A. mollis* 'Hollard's Gold'
	- free-flowering	GCal MAvo XLum
§	- 'Hollard's Gold'	CBct CCon CHEx CMac CPLG EAEE EBee ECha ECtt ELan EPPr EPfP GBuc GKin GMaP LHop LRHS MBri NCGa NEgg NLBP NOrc SBfd SPoG SWat WCot WFar WHil WWEG XLum
	- 'Jefalba'	see *A. mollis* (Latifolius Group) 'Rue Ledan'
	- Latifolius Group	EBee EPfP MRav SRms WHil WHoo WTin
§	- - 'Rue Ledan'	EBee ECtt EShb GBin IPot LHop LRHS MAvo MDKP NGdn NLar SMHy SPhx WCot WFar WHil WTin WWEG XLum
	- 'Long Spike'	GCal WHil
	- 'Niger'	LRHS NRHS
	- 'Tasmanian Angel' (v)	WCot
	'Morning's Candle'	EBee ECtt MBri NGdn WHil
	sennii	CCse CDes EBee LHop SMad SPhx WSHC XLum
	spinosus misapplied	see *A. spinosus* Spinosissimus Group
§	***spinosus*** L. ♀H4	Widely available
	- Ferguson's form	MAvo WCot WHil XLum
	- 'Lady Moore' (v)	NLar WHil XLum
	- 'Royal Haughty'	EWes MAvo XLum
§	- Spinosissimus Group	CBct CCon CMHG ECha ELan ELon GBin GCal GCra LEdu MRav SBfd SWat WCot WFar WMnd WTin
	'Summer Beauty'	EBee ECtt EWes GBin LHop MAvo WCot WFar WHil WWEG XLum
	'Whitewater' (v) **new**	CWGN EBee NLar WCot

Acca (*Myrtaceae*)

	Name	Suppliers
	sellowiana (F)	CBcs CDTJ CDul CMHG CMac CPLG EBee ECrN ELan EPfP ERom EWTr LAst LHop LRHS MGos MREP NPla SBfd SLPl SLim SPer SPlb SPoG SVic SWvt WCot WFar WSHC XSen
	- 'Apollo' (F)	EBee LRHS
	- 'Coolidge' (F)	CAgr
	- 'Gemini' (F)	LRHS
	- 'Mammoth' (F)	CAgr CBcs CCCN EBee
	- 'Triumph' (F)	CAgr CBcs CCCN
	- 'Unique' (F)	CAgr EUJe
	- 'Variegata' (F/v)	CCCN ELan LAst

Acer ✿ (*Sapindaceae*)

	Name	Suppliers
	albopurpurascens CWJ 12361	WCru
	amoenum B&SWJ 10916	WCru
	- 'Firecracker'PBR	see *A. palmatum* var. *dissectum* 'Firecracker'
	barbinerve	EPfP
	buergerianum	CBcs CDul CJun CMCN CMen LMaj MMuc MPkF NEgg NLar SEND SGol
	- var. ***formosanum*** B&SWJ 7032	WCru
	- - CWJ 12477	WCru
	- 'Himcode'	NLar
	- 'Mino-yatsubusa'	MPkF
	- 'Miyasama-yatsubusa'	MPkF
	- 'Naruto'	CMCN MPkF
	calcaratum	CMCN
	campbellii B&SWJ 7685	WCru
	- subsp. ***campbellii*** GWJ 9360 **new**	WCru
	- 'Exuberance'	CJun
	campestre ♀H4	Widely available
	- 'Carnival' (v)	CCVT CDul CJun EBee ECrN ELon MAsh MBlu MBri MPkF NLar NPCo SGol SMad SPer SPoG SWvt WHar
	- 'Elsrijk'	CCVT CLnd LMaj SCoo SGol
	- 'Evelyn'	see *A. campestre* 'Queen Elizabeth'
	- 'Evenly Red'	WPGP
	- 'Pendulum'	ECrN
	- 'Postelense'	CJun CMCN EBee MBlu
	- 'Pulverulentum' (v)	CJun CMCN NPCo
§	- 'Queen Elizabeth'	MGos SGol SKHP
	- 'Red Shine'	SGol

	- 'Royal Ruby'	CJun CWSG MGos SKHP WFar
*	- 'Ruby Glow'	ECrN
	- 'Schwerinii'	CDul
I	- 'Silver Celebration' (v)	CJun
	- 'William Caldwell'	CTho EBee ECrN MBri
	capillipes ♀H4	CBcs CDul CLnd CMCN CTho CWib EBee ECrN GKin LMaj MGos MMuc NWea SEND SPer SPlb SPoG WFar WHCr WHar WPGP
	- 'Antoine' **new**	MBri
	- 'Candy Stripe'	see *A.* × *conspicuum* 'Candy Stripe'
	- 'Honey Dew'	CJun
	aff. ***capillipes*** **new**	MWat
	cappadocicum	CCVT CDul CMCN ECrN LMaj MMuc MSnd NWea SEND WMou
	- 'Aureum' ♀H4	CBcs CCVT CDoC CDul CLnd CMCN CTho EBee ECrN ELan EPfP GBin GKin IArd MAsh MBlu MBri MGos MRav NLar SGol SLim SPer SPoG SSpi SWvt WFar WHar
	- var. ***mono***	see *A. pictum*
	- 'Rubrum' ♀H4	CBcs CDul CLnd CMCN EBee ECrN EPfP GKin IDee LMaj MBlu MGos MRav SGol SLim SPer WFar WHar WHer
	- var. ***sinicum***	EPfP GBin WFar
	- var. ***tricaudatum***	CPLG
	carpinifolium	IArd MBlu MPkF NLar
	- B&SWJ 10955	WCru
	- B&SWJ 11124	WCru
§	***caudatifolium***	CMCN
	- CWJ 12403	WCru
	- RWJ 9843	WCru
§	***caudatum*** CWJ 12403	WCru
	- GWJ 9279	WCru
	- GWJ 9317	WCru
	- HWJK 2240	WCru
	- HWJK 2338	WCru
	- subsp. ***ukurunduense***	MPkF
	- - B&SWJ 8658	WCru
	circinatum	CBcs CCVT CDoC CDul CJun CLnd CMCN EBee ECrN EPfP GBin IVic MBlu MMuc MSnd NLar NWea SEND SPlb SSta WFar WMou WPat
	- B&SWJ 9565	WCru
	- 'Burgundy Jewel'	CJun
	- 'Little Gem'	CJun
	- 'Monroe'	CJun
	- 'Pacific Fire'	CJun
	- 'Sunglow'	CJun NLar
	circinatum* × *palmatum	SBig
	cissifolium	CMCN EPfP IArd NLar
	- B&SWJ 10801	WCru
§	× ***conspicuum*** 'Candy Stripe'	CBcs CJun NLar SLim WPGP
	- 'Elephant's Ear'	CJun EPfP NLar
	- 'Mozart'	CJun MBlu MPkF SSta
	- 'Phoenix'	CBcs CJun CMCN CTho EPfP GKin IVic MAsh MBlu MBri NLar SSta WHar WPGP WPat
	- 'Silver Ghost'	MPkF
§	- 'Silver Vein'	CDoC CJun CMCN EPfP NLar WPGP
	crataegifolium B&SWJ 11036	WCru
	- B&SWJ 11355	WCru
	- 'Ittai-san-nishiki'	SSta
	- 'Meuri-keade-no-fuiri' (v)	MPkF
	- 'Meuri-no-ōfu' (v)	MPkF
	- 'Veitchii' (v)	CJun CMCN EBee EPfP MBri MPkF SBig SSpi SSta
	creticum misapplied	see *A. sempervirens*
	dasycarpum	see *A. saccharinum*
	davidii	CBcs CDoC CDul CLnd CMCN CPLG CPne ECrN LMaj LTen MBlu MGos MRav SEND SGol SLim SPer SSta WFar WPat
§	- 'Canton'	CJun
	- 'Cantonspark'	see *A. davidii* 'Canton'
	- 'Cascade'	CJun SSta
	- 'Chinese Temple'	SBir
N	- 'Ernest Wilson'	CBcs NLar
N	- 'George Forrest' ♀H4	CCVT CDoC CDul CJun CLnd CMCN CMac CPLG CTho CWSG EBee ECrN ELan EPfP GBin LAst MMuc NLar NWea SBfd SEND SLim SPer SPoG WFar WHa
	- 'Hagelunie'	SBir
	- 'Hansu-suru' (v)	SSta
	- 'Karmen'	CBcs CDul CGHE CJun WPGP
	- 'Madeline Spitta'	CMCN MBri
	- 'Purple Bark'	CJun CPLG MBri NLar SBir
	- 'Rosalie'	CBcs CJun EPfP MBlu MBri SBir
	- 'Serpentine' ♀H4	CBcs CDoC CDul CJun CMCN EBee ELan EPfP GBin MBlu MBri NEgg NLar SMad SSta WFar WPGP
	- 'Silver Vein'	see *A.* × *conspicuum* 'Silver Vein'
	discolor	CMCN
	distylum	CMCN
	elegantulum	CDoC CJun CPLG GBin IDee WPGP
	erianthum	CMCN
	erythranthum B&SWJ 11733	WCru
	- DJHV 06147	WCru
	fabri	CPLG
	- WWJ 11614	WCru
	flabellatum	CMCN
	- var. ***yunnanense***	EBee MSnd
	forrestii	CMCN CPLG EPfP MBri
	- BWJ 7515	WCru
	- 'Alice'	CJun
	- 'Sirene'	CJun
	- 'Sparkling'	CJun
	× ***freemanii***	CMCN
	- 'Armstrong'	CCVT SGol WFar
	- Autumn Blaze = 'Jeffersred'	CBcs CCVT CDoC CDul CMCN EBee EPfP LMaj MBlu MGos MMuc SBir SCoo SEND SGol SMad SPer SPoG WFar WHar
	- Celebration = 'Celzam'	CCVT CDul MGos WFar
	- 'Indian Summer'	see *A.* × *freemanii* 'Morgan'
§	- 'Morgan'	CJun SBir
	fulvescens	see *A. longipes*
	ginnala	see *A. tataricum* subsp. *ginnala*
	globosum	see *A. platanoides* 'Globosum'
	grandidentatum	see *A. saccharum* subsp. *grandidentatum*
	griseum ♀H4	Widely available
	grosseri	CDul CMCN CTri IGor SGol
	- var. ***hersii*** ♀H4	CBcs CDoC CDul CLnd CMac CWib EBee ECrN ELan EPfP LRHS MBri MMuc MRav NLar NWea SEND SLim SPer SPoG SWvt WFar WHar

	Name	Suppliers
	- 'Leiden'	EPfP
	heldreichii	CMCN EGFP
	henryi	CBcs CDul EPfP LMaj NEgg NLar
	heptaphlebium B&SWJ 11695	WCru
	- B&SWJ 11713	WCru
	- DJHV 06063	WCru
	japonicum	CMCN MMuc SEND SEWo WHCr
	- B&SWJ 8417	WCru
§	- 'Aconitifolium' Υ^{H4}	Widely available
	- 'Ao-jutan'	CJun
	- 'Attaryi'	CMen LRHS MPkF NLar
	- 'Aureum'	see *A. shirasawanum* 'Aureum'
	- 'Emmit's Pumpkins' **new**	CJun
	- 'Ezo-no-momiji'	see *A. shirasawanum* 'Ezo-no-momiji'
	- 'Fairy Lights'	NLar
	- 'Filicifolium'	see *A. japonicum* 'Aconitifolium'
	- 'Green Cascade'	CJun CMCN CMac CMen IVic LRHS MPkF NLar NPCo SBig WPGP WPat
	- 'Kalmthout'	NLar
	- 'King's Copse'	CJun LRHS
	- 'Laciniatum'	see *A. japonicum* 'Aconitifolium'
	- f. ***microphyllum***	see *A. shirasawanum* 'Microphyllum'
	- 'Ogurayama'	see *A. shirasawanum* 'Ogurayama'
	- 'Ō-isami'	EPfP MPkF NLar SBig
	- 'Ō-taki'	CJun
	- 'Vitifolium' Υ^{H4}	CDoC CDul CJun CMCN CMac CSBt ELan EPfP GBin LRHS LTen MBlu MBri MGos MPkF NEgg NLar NPCo SBig SGol SPer SSta WCFE WPGP
	kawakamii	see *A. caudatifolium*
	laevigatum	CMCN
	- B&SWJ 11684	WCru
§	- var. ***reticulatum*** B&SWJ 11698	WCru
	laxiflorum HWJK 2249	EBee WCru
	lobelii Bunge	see *A. turkestanicum*
§	***longipes***	CMCN
	macrophyllum	CMCN EPfP MBlu
	mandschuricum	CDul MBlu
§	***maximowiczianum***	CBcs CMCN CTho ELan MMuc MPkF SEND SGol WFar
	maximowiczii	MPkF WHCr
	metcalfii GWJ 9360	WCru
	micranthum	CDoC CGHE CMCN EPfP GKin MBlu NLar SSpi WHar WPGP
	miyabei	MPkF
	mono	see *A. pictum*
*	- f. ***ambiguum*** B&SWJ 8806	WCru
	monspessulanum	CDul CLnd CMCN SEND
	morifolium	EBee
	- B&SWJ 11473	WCru
	morrisonense	see *A. caudatifolium*
	negundo	CDul CMCN CTho CWib ECrN LMaj NWea
	- 'Auratum'	CMCN SGol
	- 'Aureomarginatum' (v)	ECrN LMaj SGol
	- 'Aureovariegatum' (v)	CBcs
§	- 'Elegans' (v)	CDul CMCN ECrN SCoo WFar WHar
	- 'Elegantissimum'	see *A. negundo* 'Elegans'
	- 'Flamingo' (v)	CBcs CCVT CDoC CDul CMac CWSG CWib ECrN ELan ELon EPfP LHop LRHS MAsh NLar NRHS NWea SBfd SGol SHil SLim SMad SPer SPoG SWvt WFar WHar
	- 'Kelly's Gold'	CBcs CTho NLar NWea SBfd SGol SLim SPoG WFar WHar
	- 'Variegatum' (v)	ECrN SGol WFar
	- var. ***violaceum***	CMCN
	- 'Winter Lightning'	CJun CTho
	nikoense	see *A. maximowiczianum*
	'Norwegian Sunset' **new**	CCVT
	oblongum	CMCN
	- KWJ 12232	WCru
	- var. ***concolor*** HWJ 869	WCru
	- - WWJ 11851	WCru
	oliverianum	CPLG EPfP
	- subsp. ***formosanum*** CWJ 12437	WCru
	- - RWJ 9912	WCru
	opalus	CMCN MMuc SEND
	orientale misapplied	see *A. sempervirens*
	orizabense	EBee
	palmatum	CBar CBcs CCVT CDoy CDul CMCN CMHG CMen CSBt CTri CWib EPfP GKin MBlu MGos NEgg NWea SEWo SGol SPlb SWvt WFar WHar WPat
	- 'Akane'	CMen
§	- 'Aka-shigitatsu-sawa'	CBcs CJun CMCN CMac CMen LRHS MGos MPkF NLar SGol WFar
	- 'Akegarasu'	CMen NLar
	- 'Akita-yatsubusa'	MPkF
	- 'Alpenweiss'	CJun
	- 'Alpine Sunrise'	MPkF
	- 'Amagi-shigure'	CJun
	- 'Amber Ghost'	CJun
	- 'Aoba-jo'	CJun CMen MPkF NLar NPCo
	- 'Ao-kanzashi' (v)	MPkF NLar
	- 'Aoshime-no-uchi'	see *A. palmatum* 'Shinobuga-oka'
	- 'Aoyagi'	CDul CJun CMCN CMen EPfP LRHS MGos MPkF NHol NLar NPCo SSta WPat
§	- 'Arakawa'	CMCN CMac CMen MPkF NLar NPCo
	- 'Arakawa-ukon'	CJun NLar
	- 'Aratama'	CBty CJun CMen LRHS MGos MPkF NLar
	- 'Ariake-nomura'	CMen MPkF
	- 'Asahi-zuru' (v)	CBcs CDoC CJun CMCN CMen LRHS MBri MGos MPkF NLar NPCo SBod SHil SPer WFar
	- 'Ashurst Wood'	SBig
	- 'Atrolineare'	CMen MPkF NLar WPat
	- 'Atropurpureum'	Widely available
	- 'Atropurpureum Novum'	MPkF NLar SGol
	- 'Attraction'	CMCN CMen NPCo
	- 'Aureum'	CMCN CMac CMen CWib EBee ELan EPfP LAst LMil LRHS MAsh MGos MPkF NHol NLar NPCo SPoG SSpi WCFE WFar
	- Autumn Glory Group	CJun CMac CMen
	- 'Autumn Red'	CMen NPCo
*	- 'Autumn Showers'	CJun
	- 'Azuma-murasaki'	CJun CMen MPkF NLar
	- 'Beni-chidori'	CMen NLar
	- 'Beni-gasa'	CJun MPkF WPat
	- 'Beni-hime'	MBri MPkF NLar WPat
	- 'Beni-hoshi'	MPkF
	- 'Beni-kagami'	CJun CMCN EPfP MPkF NLar SGol
	- 'Beni-kawa'	CJun CMen LRHS MPkF NPCo SBig WPat

	Name	Suppliers
	- 'Beni-komachi'	CBcs CBty CJun CMCN CMen ELon EPfP LRHS MBri MGos MPkF NLar SSta WPat
	- 'Beni-maiko'	CJun CMCN CMen CWib EBee EPfP LRHS MBri MGos MPkF NLar NPCo NPri SBig SCoo SHil SWvt WPat
	- 'Beni-musume'	MPkF NLar
	- 'Beni-otake'	CBcs CBty CJun CMen ELan EPfP EUJe IVic LRHS MBri MGos MPkF NLar NPCo SBig SBod SChF
	- 'Beni-otome'	MPkF
	- 'Beni-schichihenge' (v)	CBcs CBty CJun CMCN CMen CWCL CWGN GKin LMil LRHS MAsh MBri MGos MPkF NHol NPCo SBfd SBig SBod SCoo SHil SSta WPat
	- 'Beni-shi-en'	CJun MPkF NLar WPat
	- 'Beni-shigitatsu-sawa'	see *A. palmatum* 'Aka-shigitatsu-sawa'
	- 'Beni-tsukasa' (v)	CJun CMen EBee EPfP LRHS MAsh MPkF NLar NPCo SChF SSpi SSta
	- 'Beni-tsuru'	MPkF
	- 'Beni-ubi-gohon'	CJun MPkF NLar
	- 'Beni-zuru'	WPat
	- 'Berry Broom'	MPkF NLar
	- 'Berry Dwarf'	CJun MPkF
	- 'Bi Hō'	CJun IVic NLar SGol
	- 'Bloodgood' 🏆^{H4}	Widely available
	- 'Bonfire' misapplied	see *A. palmatum* 'Seigai'
	- 'Bonfire' ambig.	CJun
	- 'Bonnie Bergman'	CJun
	- 'Brandt's Dwarf'	WPat
	- 'Burgundy Lace' 🏆^{H4}	CBcs CBty CDoC CJun CMCN CMen CWib EBee ELan ELon EPfP EUJe GKin LMil LRHS LSRN MAsh MBri MGos MPkF MWat NPCo SBig SBod SCoo SGol SPoG SSta WFar WPat
	- 'Butterfly' (v)	Widely available
	- 'Calico'	CJun
	- 'Caperci Dwarf'	MPkF
	- 'Carlis Corner'	CJun MPkF
	- 'Carminium'	see *A. palmatum* 'Corallinum'
	- 'Chikuma-no'	CMen MPkF
	- 'Chirimen-nishiki' (v)	MPkF
	- 'Chitose-yama' 🏆^{H4}	CBty CJun CMCN CMac CMen CWCL EBee EPfP GKin LMil LRHS MAsh MBri MGos MPkF MRav NHol NLar NPCo SHil SLim SSpi SSta WFar WPat
§	- 'Chiyo-hime'	ELan EPfP MGos NLar NPCo
	- 'Coonara Pygmy'	CBty CCVT CJun CMCN CMac CMen GKin LRHS MGos MPkF NLar NPCo SCoo WFar
	- 'Coral Pink'	CJun CMen MPkF SSta
§	- 'Corallinum'	CDul CJun CMCN CMen MPkF NLar NPCo WCFE WPat
	- var. ***coreanum*** B&SWJ 8606	WCru
	- - 'Korean Gem'	CJun CMen MPkF NPCo
	- 'Crimson Prince'	CJun LTen MPkF SCoo
	- 'Crippsii'	CBcs CBty CMac CMen EUJe GBin LRHS MGos MPkF SCoo WFar WPat
	- 'Curtis Strapleaf'	MPkF
	- 'Deshōjō'	CBty CMCN CMen CWSG CWib GKin MBlu MGos MPkF NLar SCoo SGol
	- 'Diana'	CMen MPkF NLar SGol
	- 'Diane Verkade'	MPkF
	- var. ***dissectum*** 🏆^{H4}	Widely available
	- - 'Ao-shidare'	CJun LRHS
	- - 'Ariadne' (v)	CJun CWib MBri MGos MPkF NLar SBig SCoo SPoG WPat
	- - 'Autumn Fire'	CJun
	- - 'Baby Lace'	CJun CWGN IVic NLar SSta
	- - 'Balcombe Green'	SBig
	- - 'Baldsmith'	CJun CLnd EUJe LMil LRHS MPkF NLar WPat
	- - 'Barrie Bergman'	CJun WPat
	- - 'Beni-fushigi'	MPkF WPat
	- - 'Beni-shidare Tricolor' (v)	CMen MPkF NLar
	- - 'Beni-shidare Variegated' (v)	CJun CMCN
	- - 'Berrima Bridge'	CJun
	- - 'Bewley's Red'	CJun
	- - 'Brocade'	CJun IVic MPkF WPat
	- - 'Bronzewing'	CJun
	- - 'Chantilly Lace'	CJun MPkF
	- - 'Crimson Princess'	CBcs LBuc LMil LRHS MPkF SBod
	- - 'Crimson Queen' 🏆^{H4}	Widely available
	- - Dissectum Atropurpureum Group	CBcs CCVT CJun CMac CTri ELan EPfP LRHS MGos NLar NWea SBig SCoo SLim SReu SSta WFar
	- - 'Dissectum Flavescens'	CJun CMac CMen LMil MBlu MPkF NPCo
§	- - 'Dissectum Nigrum'	CJun CMac CMen LRHS MPkF NLar NPCo WPat
	- - 'Dissectum Palmatifidum'	CDoC CMen LRHS MPkF NPCo SCoo SGol SPer WFar
	- - 'Dissectum Rubrifolium'	MPkF
§	- - 'Dissectum Variegatum' (v)	CJun MPkF NPCo
	- - Dissectum Viride Group	CBcs CJun CLnd CMCN CMac CMen CSBt ELan ELon EPfP LAst LMil LRHS MAsh MBlu MGos MSwo NEgg NPCo NWea SBfd SBod SLim SPer SSta WFar
	- - 'Ellen'	CJun MPkF WPat
	- - 'Emerald Lace'	CJun GKin LBuc LRHS MBri MPkF NLar SBfd SHil SSta WCFE
	- - 'Felice'	CJun MPkF WPat
	- - 'Filigree' (v)	CJun CMCN CMen EPfP MAsh MGos MPkF NLar NPCo SBig SSta WCFE WPat
§	- - 'Firecracker'^{PBR} **new**	MPkF
	- - 'Garnet' 🏆^{H4}	Widely available
	- - 'Goshiki-shidare' (v)	CJun CMen MPkF
	- - 'Green Globe'	CJun LRHS NLar
	- - 'Green Hornet'	CJun WPat
	- - 'Green Lace'	CMen LRHS MPkF
	- - 'Green Mist'	CJun SSta WPat
	- - 'Hanzel'	WPat
	- - 'Inaba-shidare' 🏆^{H4}	Widely available
	- - 'Jeddeloh Orange'	MPkF
I	- - 'Kawaii'	CJun
	- - 'Kiri-nishiki'	CJun CMen LRHS MPkF NLar NPCo
*	- - 'Lionheart'	CJun CMen CWGN LRHS MGos MPkF NLar SBod SCoo WFar
	- - 'Nomura-nishiki' (v)	CMen
	- - 'Octopus'	CJun NLar
	- - 'Orangeola'	CBcs CBty CJun CLnd CMen CSBt EUJe IVic LRHS MAsh MGos MPkF NHol NLar NPCo SBfd SBig SBod SCoo SSta WPat
	- - 'Ornatum'	CMCN CMen CWCL CWib EPfP LAst LRHS LSRN LTen MGos MPkF NEgg NPCo NPri SBfd SCoo WCFE WFar

- - 'Otto's Dissectum' CJun
- - 'Pendulum Julian' CMCN EUJe LRHS MPkF NLar
- - 'Pink Ballerina' (v) CJun
- - 'Pink Filigree' CJun CMen MPkF NLar
- - 'Raraflora' CJun
- - 'Red Autumn Lace' CJun WPat
- - 'Red Dragon' CDoC CJun CMen CWGN LMil LRHS MPkF NLar NPCo SBig WPat
- - 'Red Feather' CJun
- - 'Red Filigree Lace' CJun CMCN CMen CWGN MGos MPkF NPCo SBig WPat
- - 'Red Select' CBty LRHS MPkF
- - 'Seiryū' ♀H4 Widely available
§ - - 'Shōjō-shidare' CJun CMen LRHS MPkF NLar
- - 'Shu-shidare' CJun
- - 'Spring Delight' CJun MPkF NLar
- - 'Suisei' (v) MPkF
- - 'Sunset' CJun MPkF WPat
- - 'Tamukeyama' CBcs CBty CJun CMCN CMen EBee ELan EUJe LMil LRHS MBri MGos MPkF NLar NPCo SBod SCoo SGol SLau WFar WHar WPat
- - 'Toyama-nishiki' (v) CMCN CMen CWGN LRHS MPkF NLar NPCo
- - 'Waterfall' CJun CMCN
- - 'Watnong' CJun LRHS MPkF
- - 'Zaaling' CMen NPCo
- 'Doctor Tilt' MPkF
- 'Donzuru-bo' CJun
- 'Dormansland' SBig
- 'Dragon's Fire' CJun
- 'Earthfire' LRHS MPkF WPat
I - 'Ebbingei' CMac
- 'Eddisbury' CJun CMen CSBt GBin MBlu MPkF NLar SSta WPGP WPat
- 'Edna Bergman' CJun
- 'Effegi' see *A. palmatum* 'Fireglow'
- 'Eimini' MPkF
- 'Elegans' CMen EPfP MPkF NLar NPCo
- 'Elizabeth' CJun MPkF
- Emperor 1 see *A. palmatum* 'Wolff'
- 'Englishtown' MPkF WPat
- 'Enkan' CJun CMen CWGN MBri MGos MPkF NLar NPri SGol WPat
- 'Eono-momiji' CMen
- 'Ever Red' see *A. palmatum* var. *dissectum* 'Dissectum Nigrum'
- 'Fairy Hair' CJun
- 'Fall's Fire' CJun NLar
- 'Fascination' CJun
- 'Fior d'Arancio' CJun IVic MPkF NLar NPCo WPat
- 'Fireball' CJun
§ - 'Fireglow' CBcs CBty CDoC CJun CMCN CMen CSBt CWCL CWib LMaj LMil LRHS MBri MGos MPkF NEgg NLar NPCo SBod SCoo SPer WFar WPat
- 'First Ghost' CJun
- 'Fjellheim' CJun MPkF
- 'Frederici Guglielmi' see *A. palmatum* var. *dissectum* 'Dissectum Variegatum'
- 'Garyū' MPkF
- 'Geisha' CJun MPkF
- 'Geisha Gone Wild' (v) CJun MPkF
- 'Genshu-yama-momiji' NLar
- 'Gentaku' CJun
- 'Germaine's Gyration' CJun
- 'Ghost' CJun
- 'Gibbsii' CMen NPCo
I - 'Globosum' MPkF
- 'Glowing Embers' CJun MPkF WPat
- 'Golden Pond' CJun
- 'Goshiki-kotohime' (v) CBty CJun CMCN MPkF NLar SBod
- 'Goten-nomura' NLar
- 'Grace' CJun
- 'Grandma Ghost' CJun
- 'Green Flag' CJun
- 'Green Star' WPat
- 'Green Trompenburg' CJun CMen MGos MPkF NEgg NLar NPCo
- 'Groundcover' MPkF
§ - 'Hagoromo' CMac CMen MPkF NPCo SCoo WFar
- 'Hamano-maru' MPkF
- 'Hana-matoi'PBR (v) CMCN MPkF
- 'Hanami-nishiki' CMen MPkF NEgg WPat
- 'Haru-iro' CJun
- 'Harusame' (v) MPkF NLar
- 'Hazeroino' (v) CMen MPkF
- 'Heartbeat' CJun LRHS MPkF
- 'Heffner's Red' CJun MPkF
- 'Helena' see *A. shirasawanum* 'Helena'
- var. ***heptalobum*** CMCN
§ - 'Heptalobum Elegans' LRHS
- 'Heptalobum Elegans Purpureum' see *A. palmatum* 'Hessei'
- 'Heptalobum Rubrum' NLar
- 'Herbstfeuer' CJun MPkF
§ - 'Hessei' CCVT CMen MPkF NLar
- 'Higasayama' (v) CBcs CJun CMCN CMen CWGN IVic LRHS MGos MPkF NLar NPCo WPat
- 'Hino-tori-nishiki' CMen NLar SGol
- 'Hōgyoku' CJun CMCN CMen LRHS MPkF WPat
- 'Hondoshi' NLar
- 'Honō-o' MPkF NLar
- 'Hoshi-kuzu' MPkF NLar
- 'Hupp's Dwarf' CJun MPkF
- 'Hupp's Red Willow' **new** NLar
- 'Ibo-nishiki' CMen MPkF
- 'Ichigyōji' CJun CMen IVic MAsh NLar NPCo SBig SChF WPGP WPat
- 'Ightham Gold' SSta
- 'Iijima-sunago' CMen MPkF
- 'Inazuma' CBcs CDoC CJun CMCN CMen LMil LRHS MGos MPkF NLar SBod SCoo SLau WFar WPat
- 'Irish Lace' CJun MPkF
- 'Iso-chidori' MPkF
- 'Issai-nishiki' CMen MPkF NLar NPCo
* - 'Issai-nishiki-kawazu' MPkF
- 'Jane' MPkF NLar
- 'Japanese Sunrise' CJun EUJe LRHS MPkF WPat
- 'Jerre Schwartz' MGos MPkF NLar WPat
- 'Jirō-shidare' CJun EPfP MPkF NLar SBig
- 'JJ' CJun
- 'Julia D.' CJun NLar
- 'Kaba' CMen IVic MPkF
- 'Kagero' (v) MPkF WFar
§ - 'Kagiri-nishiki' (v) CBcs CJun CMCN CMac CMen CWGN IVic LRHS LTen MPkF NEgg NLar WFar
- 'Kamagata' CBty CJun CMCN CMen EPfP GKin IVic LMil LRHS MAsh MGos MPkF NLar NPCo SCoo SPer WPGP WPat

	Cultivar	Suppliers
	- 'Kandy Kitchen'	CJun CMen LRHS MBri
	- 'Karaori-nishiki' (v)	CMen MPkF NLar
	- 'Karasugawa' (v)	CJun CMen CWGN MGos MPkF NLar NPCo
	- 'Kasagiyama'	CJun CMen LRHS MGos MPkF
	- 'Kasen-nishiki'	CMen MPkF
	- 'Kashima'	CJun CMCN CMen LRHS MPkF NLar NPCo WFar WPat
	- 'Kashima-yatsubusa'	MPkF
	- 'Katja'	CJun CMen MPkF
	- 'Katsura' ♀H4	Widely available
	- 'Katsura-nishiki'	MPkF
	- 'Kawahara Rose'	MPkF NLar
	- 'Ki-hachijō'	CJun CMCN CMen MPkF NLar WPat
	- 'Killarney'	CJun
	- 'Kingsville Variegated' (v)	MPkF
	- 'Kinky Krinkle'	CJun MPkF
	- 'Kinran'	CMen LRHS MPkF NPCo WPat
	- 'Kinshii'	CBty CJun CMCN CMen EPfP IVic LRHS MPkF NHol NLar NPCo WHar WPat
	- 'Kiyohime'	CDoC CMCN CMen MPkF WFar WPat
	- 'Koba-shōjō'	MPkF
	- 'Kogane-nishiki'	CMen NLar SBfd SGol
	- 'Kogane-sakae'	CJun MPkF
	- 'Kokobunji-nishiki' (v)	MPkF
	- 'Komache-hime'	CJun CMen MPkF WPat
*	- 'Komaru'	NLar
	- 'Komon-nishiki' (v)	CJun CMen MPkF
	- 'Koriba'	CJun MPkF NLar
	- 'Koshibori-nishiki'	MPkF
§	- 'Koshimino'	CJun
	- 'Kotohime'	CJun CMCN CMen EBee GKin IVic LRHS MGos MPkF NLar SBig SCoo SPoG SSta
	- 'Koto-ito-komachi'	CJun CMen ELon EPfP MPkF NLar NPCo WPat
	- 'Koto-maru'	MPkF NLar
	- 'Koto-no-ito'	CMCN EUJe LMil LRHS MGos MPkF NLar SGol WPat
	- 'Koya-san'	CMen MPkF NLar
	- 'Kurabu-yama'	CMen MPkF NLar
	- 'Kuro-hime' **new**	WPat
	- 'Kurui-jishi'	MGos MPkF
	- 'Kyōryū'	MPkF
	- 'Kyra'	CMen MPkF
	- 'Leather Leaf'	MPkF
§	- 'Linearilobum'	CBcs CDoC CMen EPfP IVic LMil LRHS MGos MPkF NLar NPCo SBod SCoo SLau WFar
	- 'Little Princess'	see *A. palmatum* 'Chiyo-hime'
	- 'Lozita'	NLar WPat
	- 'Lutescens'	CMen MPkF NPCo
	- 'Lydia'	MPkF NLar
	- 'Maiko'	CMen MPkF
	- 'Mama'	CMen NPCo
	- 'Mapi-no-machihime'	CJun CMCN CMen EBee ELan LRHS MAsh MGos MPkF NHol WPGP WPat
	- 'Marakumo'	MPkF
	- 'Marasaki-yama'	MPkF
	- 'Mardi Gras'	CJun
	- 'Margaret'	MPkF WPat
	- 'Margaret Bee'	CJun MPkF
	- 'Marjan'	CJun MPkF NLar
	- 'Marlo' PBR	MAsh MRav NPri
	- 'Masamurasaki'	CMen MPkF
	- 'Masukagami' (v)	CJun MPkF NLar
	- 'Matsuga-e' (v)	CMen MPkF NPCo
	- 'Matsukaze'	CJun CMCN CMen
	- var. ***matsumurae*** B&SWJ 11100	WCru
	- 'Matsuyoi'	CJun MPkF NLar
	- 'Meihō-nishiki'	CJun
	- 'Melanie'	CJun SBig
	- 'Meoto'	CJun
	- 'Midori-no-teiboku'	CJun MPkF
	- 'Mikawa-yatsubusa'	CMCN CMac CMen EUJe IVic MGos MPkF NLar NPCo WPat
	- 'Mikazuki' (v)	CJun
	- 'Mimaye'	CJun
	- 'Mini Mondo'	MPkF
	- 'Mino-gasa'	NLar
	- 'Mirte'	CJun CMen MPkF SBig SBod WFar WPat
	- 'Mizuho-beni'	CJun CMen NLar NPCo
	- 'Mizu-kuguri'	MPkF NLar
	- 'Momoiro-koya-san'	CJun MPkF NLar SGol WPat
	- 'Mon Papa'	CJun CMen NLar
	- 'Monzukushi'	CJun MPkF
	- 'Moonfire'	CJun CMCN ELan EPfP LRHS MAsh MGos MPkF NLar SBod WPat
	- 'Mr Sun'	CJun
*	- 'Muncaster'	SBig
	- 'Murasaki-hime'	MPkF
	- 'Murasaki-kiyohime'	CBty CJun CMCN CMen LRHS MPkF NLar NPCo SChF WPGP WPat
	- 'Mure-hibari'	CJun CMen MPkF
	- 'Murogawa'	CJun CMen NPCo
	- 'Musashino' **new**	CJun
	- 'Nakata'	NLar
	- 'Nanase-gawa'	MPkF
	- 'Nicholsonii'	CMen IVic MPkF NLar NPCo WFar WPat
	- 'Nigrum' ♀H4	CMCN CTri WPat
	- 'Nishiki-gasane' (v)	CMen MPkF
§	- 'Nishiki-gawa'	CJun CMen MPkF NPCo
	- 'Nishiki-momiji'	CMen
	- 'Nishiki-yamato'	NLar
	- 'Nomura'	CJun CMen
	- 'Nomurishidare' misapplied	see *A. palmatum* var. *dissectum* 'Shōjō-shidare'
	- 'Nomurishidare' Wada	SSpi
	- 'Nuresagi'	CJun MPkF WPat
	- 'Ōgi-nagashi' (v)	MPkF NLar
	- 'Ōgi-no-sen'	MPkF
	- 'Ōgon-sarasa'	CJun MPkF
	- 'Ojishi'	CMen MPkF
	- 'Ō-kagami'	CBcs CBty CDoC CJun CMac CMen CSBt ELon EPfP LMil LRHS MAsh MGos MPkF NLar NPCo SCoo WPat
	- 'Okukuji-nishiki'	CJun
	- 'Okushimo'	CJun CMCN CMen IVic LRHS MPkF NHol NLar NPCo SSta
	- 'Omato'	CJun MAsh MPkF SBig WFar
	- 'Omurayama'	CBcs CBty CDoC CJun CMCN CMen EPfP LMil LRHS MGos MPkF NLar NPCo SBod SCoo SPer SSta WFar
	- 'Orange Dream'	Widely available
	- 'Oranges and Lemons'	CJun NLar
	- 'Oregon Sunset'	CJun LBuc MPkF NLar
	- 'Oridono-nishiki' (v)	CBcs CDoC CDul CJun CMCN CMac CMen CWCL CWGN EBee ELan ELon EPfP LAst LRHS LTen MAsh MBlu MGos MPkF NEgg NLar

		NPCo SBfd SLim SPer SPoG SSta WFar
	- 'Oriental Mystery' **new**	CJun
	- 'Ōsakazuki' ♀H4	Widely available
	- 'Ōshio-beni'	CJun CMen NPCo
	- 'Ōshū-shidare'	CJun CMen MPkF WFar
	- 'Oto-hime'	CJun CMen LRHS MPkF NPCo
	- 'Otome-zakura'	CJun CMen LRHS MPkF WPat
	- 'Peaches and Cream' (v)	CBcs CJun CMen LRHS MPkF NLar NPCo SPer SSta WPat
	- 'Peve Chameleon'	MPkF NLar
	- 'Peve Dave'	MPkF NLar
	- 'Peve Multicolor'	CJun MPkF NLar
	- 'Peve Ollie' PBR	GKin MPkF NLar
	- 'Peve Stanley'	MPkF NLar
	- 'Peve Starfish' **new**	NLar
	- 'Phoenix'	CJun EBee MBri MPkF NPri
	- 'Pine Bark Maple'	see *A. palmatum* 'Nishiki-gawa'
	- 'Pixie'	CBty CJun CMen EUJe IVic LRHS MGos MPkF NLar WPat
	- 'Pung-kil'	IVic MPkF
	- 'Purple Ghost'	CJun NLar SLim
	- 'Red Baron'	CJun
	- 'Red Blush'	CJun
	- 'Red Cloud'	CJun MPkF NLar
	- 'Red Crusader'	NLar
	- 'Red Elf'	MPkF
	- 'Red Emperor'	ELan EUJe LMil LRHS MBri MPkF NLar WPat
	- 'Red Flame'	NLar
	- 'Red Flash'	CJun CMen MPkF
	- 'Red Jonas'	MPkF NLar
	- 'Red Pygmy' ♀H4	CDoC CJun CMCN CMac CMen CWCL CWGN CWib EBee EPfP GKin IVic LMil LRHS MAsh MBlu MBri MGos NHol NLar NPCo NPri SCoo SGol SPer SPoG SSpi SSta WFar WPat
	- 'Red Spider'	CJun
	- 'Red Wood'	CBcs CCVT CDoC CJun MPkF SGol SLau SPer
	- 'Redwine' **new**	MPkF
	- 'Renjaku-maru'	MPkF
	- 'Reticulatum'	see *A. palmatum* 'Shigitatsu-sawa'
	- 'Ribesifolium'	see *A. palmatum* 'Shishigashira'
	- 'Rising Sun'	CJun NLar
	- 'Rokugatsu-en-nishiki'	WPat
	- 'Roseomarginatum'	see *A. palmatum* 'Kagiri-nishiki'
	- 'Rough Bark Maple'	see *A. palmatum* 'Arakawa'
	- 'Royle'	CJun
	- 'Rubrum'	CMen
I	- 'Rubrum Kaiser'	CJun
	- 'Ruby Ridge'	CJun
	- 'Ruby Star'	CJun MPkF NLar
	- 'Rufescens'	MPkF
	- 'Ryokū-ryū'	CMen MPkF
	- 'Ryusen'	CJun
	- 'Ryuzu'	CJun MPkF WPat
	- 'Sagara-nishiki' (v)	CJun CMen LRHS MPkF NPCo
	- 'Sai-ho'	MPkF
	- 'Saint Jean'	MPkF
	- 'Samidare'	CJun MPkF NLar
	- 'Sandra'	CMen MPkF
N	- 'Sango-kaku' ♀H4	Widely available
	- 'Saoshika'	CJun CMen MPkF NLar
	- 'Sa-otome'	CMen MPkF
	- 'Satsuki-beni'	CJun CMen MPkF NPCo
	- 'Sazanami'	CDoC CJun CMen MPkF NLar WPat
	- 'Scolopendriifolium'	see *A. palmatum* 'Linearilobum'
§	- 'Seigai'	CJun MPkF WCFE
	- 'Seigen'	CJun CMCN CMen MPkF NPCo
I	- 'Seigen Aureum'	CJun
	- 'Seiun-kaku'	CJun CMen MPkF WPat
	- 'Sekimori'	CJun NLar SBig
	- 'Sekka-yatsubusa'	CMCN CMen MPkF NLar
	- 'Semi-no-hane'	CJun NLar
N	- 'Senkaki'	see *A. palmatum* 'Sango-kaku'
	- 'Septemlobum Elegans'	see *A. palmatum* 'Heptalobum Elegans'
	- 'Septemlobum Purpureum'	see *A. palmatum* 'Hessei'
	- 'Sessilifolium' dwarf	see *A. palmatum* 'Hagoromo'
	- 'Sessilifolium' tall	see *A. palmatum* 'Koshimino'
	- 'Shaina'	CBcs CDoC CJun CMen CSBt CWGN CWib EBee EPfP IVic LRHS LTen MBlu MBri MGos MPkF NLar NPCo SCoo SGol SLim WFar WHar WMou
	- 'Sharon' **new**	WPat
	- 'Sharp's Pygmy'	CBty CJun CMen LRHS MPkF NPCo WPat
	- 'Sherwood Flame'	CDoC CJun CMen CWib LRHS MAsh MBlu MGos MPkF NLar NPCo SCoo WFar WPat
	- 'Shichigosan'	CMen
	- 'Shidava Gold'	CJun MPkF WPat
	- 'Shi-en'	MPkF
	- 'Shigarami'	CJun CMen MPkF
§	- 'Shigitatsu-sawa' (v)	CBcs CBty CJun CMCN CMac CMen LRHS MGos MPkF NLar NPCo SBig
	- 'Shigure-bato'	CJun MPkF
	- 'Shigurezome'	MPkF NLar
	- 'Shikageori-nishiki'	CJun CMen MPkF
	- 'Shime-no-uchi'	CJun MPkF SBig
	- 'Shimofuri-nishiki'	MPkF
	- 'Shin-chishio' **new**	CJun
	- 'Shindeshōjō'	Widely available
§	- 'Shinobuga-oka'	CBcs CJun CMCN CMen EUJe LRHS MPkF SLau
	- 'Shinonome'	CJun CMen MPkF NLar
	- 'Shirazz' (v)	CBty CDoC CWGN EUJe LMil LRHS MBri MGos MPkF NLar SPoG
§	- 'Shishigashira'	CDoC CJun CMCN CMac CMen EPfP EUJe GKin IArd IVic LRHS MBlu MBri MGos MPkF NLar NPCo SBfd SCoo SGol SPoG WFar WPat
	- 'Shishio'	CBcs CBty CMCN CMen LMil LRHS MPkF NPCo SBig SSpi WPat
	- 'Shishio Improved'	CJun CMCN CMac CMen ELon EPfP LRHS MAsh MGos MPkF NHol NLar NPCo SBig SChF SWvt
	- 'Shishio-hime'	MPkF
	- 'Shishi-yatsubusa'	CJun MPkF
	- 'Shōjō'	CJun CMCN NLar WFar
	- 'Shōjō-no-mai'	CJun
	- 'Shōjō-nomura'	CMen MGos MPkF NLar WPat
	- 'Sister Ghost'	CJun
	- 'Skeeter's Broom'	CBcs CBty CJun CMen EBee ELan EPfP LBuc LMil LRHS MBri MGos MPkF NPCo SBig SBod SCoo WPGP WPat
*	- 'Sode-nishiki'	CJun MPkF NLar
	- 'Stella Rossa'	CJun LRHS MPkF NLar WPat
	- 'Sumi-nagashi'	CBcs CBty CDoC CMen CWCL GBin LMil LRHS MGos MPkF NLar

		NPCo SBod SCoo SGol SLau WHar WPat
I	- 'Summer Gold'	CJun MBri MPkF SWvt
*	- 'Sunago'	NLar
	- 'Sunshine'	LBuc MPkF
	- 'Susan'	MPkF
	- 'Taiyō-nishiki'	CJun MPkF
	- 'Takao'	CMen
	- 'Tama-hime'	CJun CMen MPkF NPCo
	- 'Tana'	CJun CMCN CMen EPfP MPkF NLar WFar WPat
	- 'Tarō-yama'	CJun MPkF WPat
	- 'Tatsuta'	CMen MPkF WHar
	- 'Taylor'[PBR] (v)	CWGN EBee EPfP IVic LRHS MAsh MGos MPkF NLar NPri SCoo SHil WPat
	- 'Tennyo-no-hoshi'	CMen MPkF NLar NPCo
	- 'Tiger Rose'	CJun NLar
	- 'Tiny Tim'	CJun MPkF
	- 'Tobiosho'	CJun
	- 'Trompenburg' 𝕐[H4]	Widely available
	- 'Tsuchigumo'	CJun CMen MPkF NLar
	- 'Tsukasa Silhouette'	CJun
	- 'Tsukuma-no'	MPkF
	- 'Tsukushigata'	MPkF SGol WPat
	- 'Tsuma-beni'	CMCN CMen EPfP LRHS MPkF NPCo
	- 'Tsuma-gaki'	CDoC CJun CMen MBri MGos MPkF NLar NPCo WPat
	- 'Tsuri-nishiki'	CJun CMen MPkF NLar
	- 'Twombly's Red Sentinel'	CJun MBlu MPkF
	- 'Ueno-homare'	CMen MPkF WPat
	- 'Ueno-yama'	CBcs CJun MGos MPkF SBfd SBod WPat
	- 'Ukigumo' (v)	CBcs CJun CLnd CMCN CMac CMen CWib ELan GKin LMil LRHS MGos MPkF MRav NHol NLar NPCo SBfd SBig SCoo SPer SPoG SSta WFar WPat
	- 'Ukon'	CCVT CJun CMen LMil LRHS MPkF NPCo SCoo
	- 'Umegae'	CJun
	- 'Uncle Ghost'	CJun
	- 'Usu-midori'	CJun
	- 'Utsu-semi'	CJun MPkF
	- 'Van der Akker'	CJun
	- 'Versicolor' (v)	CJun CMCN MPkF
	- 'Vic Pink'	CJun
	- 'Villa Taranto'	CBty CDoC CJun CMCN CMen EBee ELon EPfP EUJe IVic LRHS MAsh MBri MGos MPkF NHol NLar NPCo SChF SCoo SGol SSpi SSta WPGP WPat
	- 'Volubile'	CMCN CMen MPkF NPCo
	- 'Wabito'	CJun CMen MPkF
	- 'Waka-midori'	CMen
	- 'Waka-momiji' (v)	CJun
	- 'Wakehurst Pink' (v)	CMCN MPkF WPat
	- 'Wendy'	CJun CMen IVic MPkF NLar SGol WPat
	- 'Wetumpka Red'	CJun
	- 'Whitney Red'	CMen
	- 'Wildgoose'	MPkF
	- 'Will D'	CJun
	- 'Wilson's Pink Dwarf'	CJun CMen CWib EBee GKin IVic LRHS MBri MGos MPkF NLar NPCo SChF SCoo SLim SPoG WPGP
	- 'Winter Flame'	CJun GBin LMil LRHS MPkF NHol NLar WPat
§	- 'Wolff'	MPkF
	- 'Wolff's Broom'	MPkF WPat
	- 'Wou-nishiki'	CMCN CMen MPkF NPCo
	- 'Yana-gawa'	CMen
	- 'Yasemin'	CJun CMen CWGN IVic MPkF NLar NPCo SBig
	- 'Yatsubusa'	MPkF NLar
	- 'Yezo-nishiki'	CMen LRHS MPkF WFar
	- 'Yūba-e'	MPkF NLar WFar WPat
	- 'Yūgure'	IVic MPkF NLar WFar
	- 'Yuri-hime'	MPkF
	papilio	see *A. caudatum*
	pauciflorum 'Blaze Away' **new**	CJun
	pectinatum GWJ 9354	WCru
	- subsp. ***pectinatum*** B&SWJ 8270	WCru
	- - HWJ 569	WCru
	- - HWJ 944	WCru
	pensylvanicum 𝕐[H4]	CBcs CDul CLnd CMCN CTho ECrN ELan EPfP LMaj MGos MMuc MRav NWea SEND SLim SPer SSpi SSta WFar WPat
	- 'Erythrocladum'	CJun CMCN EPfP MAsh MBri NEgg NHol NLar SBig SLim WFar WPGP
	pentaphyllum	SBig
*	***phlebanthum*** B&SWJ 9751	WCru
§	***pictum***	CMCN
	- subsp. ***okamotoanum***	CMCN
	- - B&SWJ 8516	WCru
	- 'Shufu-nishiki'	CMCN
	- 'Usugomo'	WPat
	aff. ***pictum*** MCN0931 **new**	CMCN
	- MCN0951 **new**	CMCN
	platanoides 𝕐[H4]	CBcs CCVT CDoC CDul CLnd CMCN CSBt CTri CWib ECrN ELan EPfP MGos MMuc MSwo NWea SBfd SEND SEWo SGol SPer WFar WHar WMou
	- 'Charles Joly'	LMaj
	- 'Cleveland'	CBcs CCVT
	- 'Columnare'	CCVT CDul CMCN CWib SCoo
	- 'Crimson King' 𝕐[H4]	Widely available
	- 'Crimson Sentry'	CCVT CDoC CDul CLnd CTri EBee ELan EPfP IArd IVic LAst LTen MAsh MGos MRav SBfd SEWo SGol SPoG WFar WHar
	- 'Deborah'	CBcs CDul CTho LMaj SGol
	- 'Drummondii' (v)	Widely available
	- 'Emerald Queen'	CCVT ECrN LMaj
	- 'Faassen's Black'	CJun
§	- 'Globosum'	CMCN ECrN LBuc LMaj NLar SWvt
	- 'Goldsworth Purple'	CLnd NEgg
	- 'Laciniatum'	CMCN
	- 'Marit'	WPat
	- Princeton Gold = 'Prigo'[PBR]	CBcs CDoC CDul ELan EMil LBuc LRHS MAsh MBri MGos SBfd SCoo SEWo SGol SLim SPer SPoG WHar
	- 'Reitenbachii'	CDul LMaj
	- 'Royal Red'	CDul CWib ECrN LMaj MRav NLar SBfd SCoo SEWo
	- 'Schwedleri' 𝕐[H4]	CDul CMCN EPfP SGol
	pseudoplatanus	CBcs CCVT CDul CLnd CMCN CSBt CTri ECrN ELan LBuc MGos NWea SBfd SGol SPer WFar WHar WMou
§	- 'Atropurpureum'	CDoC CDul ECrN NWea SEWo WHar

	Name	Suppliers
	- 'Brilliantissimum' ♀H4	Widely available
	- 'Erectum'	WFar
	- 'Erythrocarpum'	CMac
	- 'Gadsby'	CDul EBee
	- 'Leopoldii' misapplied	see *A. pseudoplatanus* f. *variegatum*
	- 'Prinz Handjéry'	CBcs CDul CMCN CTri CWib MAsh MGos NHol NLar NWea SGol SPer WHar
	- 'Spaethii' misapplied	see *A. pseudoplatanus* 'Atropurpureum'
§	- f. ***variegatum*** (v)	NEgg
	- - 'Esk Sunset' (v)	CBcs CLnd EBee LRHS MGos MPkF NLar SMad SPoG WHar
	- - 'Leopoldii' ambig. (v)	CBcs CCVT CDul CLnd CMCN ECrN ELan LAst MMuc SEND SPer SWvt WFar
	- - 'Simon-Louis Frères' (v)	CBcs CCVT CDul CLnd CMCN CWSG CWib EBee ECrN LAst MAsh MGos MMuc NEgg NLar SBfd SBod SCrf SEND SGol SPer SPoG SWvt WFar WHar
	- 'Worley'	CBcs CDul CLnd CMCN CMac ECrN MMuc MRav NWea SBfd SEND SGol SLim SPer
	pseudosieboldianum	CJun CMCN IArd MBlu MPkF
	- B&SWJ 8468	WCru
	- B&SWJ 8746	WCru
	- B&SWJ 8769	WCru
	- var. ***microsieboldianum*** B&SWJ 8766	WCru
	pycnanthum	EPfP
	'Red Flamingo' (v)	CJun CWSG LRHS MBri MGos MPkF NLar SGol SSta WPat
	reticulatum	see *A. laevigatum* var. *reticulatum*
	rubescens	CJun
	- B&SWJ 6735	WCru
	- CWJ 12438	WCru
	- RWJ 9840	WCru
	- variegated (v)	CJun WPGP
	rubrum	Widely available
	- Autumn Flame	see *A. rubrum* 'Pete's Red'
	- 'Autumn Flame'	CLnd
	- 'Autumn Spire'	CJun
	- 'Bowhall'	SBir
	- 'Brandywine'	CDul CJun CTho EBee LRHS MAsh MBlu MBri NLar NWea SBir SCoo SPoG WHar
	- 'Candy Ice' (v)	CJun
	- 'Columnare'	EPfP
	- 'Embers'	CJun NLar
	- Fairview Flame	see *A. rubrum* 'Pete's Fairview'
	- Fireball = 'Firzam'	CJun
	- 'Firedance'	CJun
	- 'New World'	NLar SCoo
	- 'Northwind'	CJun
	- 'Northwood'	CJun
	- 'October Glory' ♀H4	Widely available
§	- 'Pete's Fairview'	SPer
§	- 'Pete's Red'	MPkF
	- 'Red King'	CJun
	- Red Sunset = 'Franksred'	CCVT CDul CJun CLnd CMCN CTho EBee EPfP LMaj LTen NLar SBir SCoo SGol SLim SSta
	- 'Scanlon'	CBcs CDul CJun CMCN CTho ELan EPfP LAst LMaj MBlu SPer
	- 'Schlesingeri'	CJun CMCN CMac EPfP
	- 'Somerset'	CJun CTho CTri EBee LRHS NLar SCoo SLim WHar
	- Summer Red = 'Hosr'	CJun SCoo SLim
	- 'Sun Valley'	CJun EBee MAsh SCoo SLim WHar
	- 'Tilford'	CJun SCoo SSta
§	***rufinerve*** ♀H4	CBcs CCVT CDoC CDul CLnd CMCN CTho CTri EBee ECrN ELan EPfP EWTr LMaj LRHS MBri MMuc NEgg NLar NWea SCoo SEND SGol SPer WHar
	- B&SWJ 10845	GKin WCru
	- B&SWJ 10924	WCru
	- B&SWJ 10959	WCru
	- B&SWJ 11571	WCru
	- 'Albolimbatum'	see *A. rufinerve* 'Hatsuyuki'
	- 'Erythrocladum'	CJun EBee SKHP
§	- 'Hatsuyuki' (v)	CJun CMCN SBig SSta
	- 'Ko-fuji-nishiki'	SSta
	- 'Winter Gold'	CJun EPfP NLar SSta
	- 'Yakushima-nishiki'	SSta
§	***saccharinum***	CBcs CCVT CDoC CDul CLnd CMCN CTri CWib EBee ECrN ELan EPfP MGos MMuc MSnd NWea SCoo SEND SGol SPer WFar WHar
	- 'Born's Gracious'	CJun
	- 'Fastigiatum'	see *A. saccharinum* f. *pyramidale*
	- f. ***laciniatum***	CCVT EBee MBlu MGos MMuc SEND SGol SPer
	- 'Laciniatum Wieri'	CDul CMCN SGol
	- f. ***lutescens***	CDul
§	- f. ***pyramidale***	CDoC CLnd ECrN LMaj NWea SPer
	saccharum	CAgr CDoC CDul CLnd CMCN CTho ECrN EPfP MBlu NWea SPer
	- 'Brocade'	CJun
	- 'Fiddlers Creek'	CJun
§	- subsp. ***grandidentatum***	EPfP NLar
§	***sempervirens***	CJun EBee EPfP LEdu MPkF SChF WPGP
	'Sensu'	CJun
	serrulatum CWJ 12437	WCru
	- RWJ 9912	WCru
	shirasawanum	CMCN
§	- 'Aureum' ♀H4	Widely available
	- 'Autumn Moon'	CBcs CBty CJun CMCN CMen CWGN EPfP LRHS MBri MPkF NLar NPCo NPri SBfd SCoo SGol SHil SLim WPat
§	- 'Ezo-no-momiji'	CJun CMen MPkF NLar NPCo
	- 'Gloria'	LRHS
§	- 'Helena'	MPkF NLar WPat
	- 'Jordan'[PBR]	CWGN EBee MBri MGos MPkF NLar
	- 'Lovett'	CJun
§	- 'Microphyllum'	MPkF
§	- 'Ogurayama'	CJun CMen NPCo
	- 'Palmatifolium'	CJun
	- 'Red Dawn'	CJun
	- 'Susanne'	CJun CMen MPkF
	- var. ***tenuifolium*** B&SWJ 11073	WCru
	sieboldianum	CDul CMen CTho CTri ECrN MAsh MMuc SEND SGol WHCr WHar WMou WPat
	- B&SWJ 10849	WCru
	- B&SWJ 11049	WCru
	- B&SWJ 11090	WCru
	- 'Sode-no-uchi'	CJun CMen MPkF NPCo
	- var. ***tsushimense*** B&SWJ 10962	WCru
	sikkimense B&SWJ 11613	WCru

- B&SWJ 11689	WCru
- B&SWJ 11703	WCru
- DJHV 06152	WCru
- WWJ 11601	WCru
- WWJ 11613	WCru
- WWJ 11853	WCru
'Silver Cardinal' (v)	CBcs CJun CMCN EPfP MGos MPkF NLar WHar
'Silver Vein'	see *A.* × *conspicuum* 'Silver Vein'
spicatum	EPfP NLar
§ ***stachyophyllum***	GQui
- BWJ 8101	WCru
sterculiaceum subsp. ***franchetii***	NLar
- subsp. ***sterculiaceum*** GWJ 9317	WCru
takesimense B&SWJ 8500	WCru
- B&SWJ 8540	WCru
tataricum	CCVT CMCN
- subsp. ***aidzuense*** B&SWJ 10958	WCru
§ - subsp. ***ginnala***	CBcs CCVT CLnd CMCN CTri GKin LMaj MBlu MGos MMuc NLar NWea SEND SPer
- - 'Flame'	CDul CJun EBee ELan EPfP MGos MMuc MSnd NLar NWea
- - 'Red Wing'	CJun EBee
tegmentosum	CBcs CJun CMCN EPfP MBlu
- B&SWJ 8421	WCru
- subsp. ***glaucorufinerve***	see *A. rufinerve*
- 'Joe Witt' **new**	NLar
tetramerum	see *A. stachyophyllum*
tonkinense subsp. ***liquidambarifolium*** DJHV 06173	WCru
trautvetteri	CMCN EPfP
triflorum ♀H4	CBcs CCVT CDul CJun CMCN EPfP LMaj MBlu NLar SSpi WFar
truncatum	MBlu MPkF
- B&SWJ 8914	WCru
- 'Akikaze-nishiki' (v)	CJun MPkF
tschonoskii subsp. ***koreanum***	MPkF
§ ***turkestanicum***	SSta WFar
velutinum	CMCN
'White Tigress'	CDoC CDul CJun CTho LRHS MBri NLar NWea WPGP WPat
× ***zoeschense***	CMCN MPkF
- 'Annae'	SGol

Aceriphyllum see *Mukdenia*

× *Achicodonia* (*Gesneriaceae*)

'Dark Velvet'	WDib

Achillea (*Asteraceae*)

ageratifolia ♀H4	CMea ECho ECtt EDAr EWTr LBee LRHS NGdn SRms WFar
§ ***ageratum***	CArn CPrp ECho EGHP ELau ENfk EOHP GPoy LEdu MHer MNHC SIde SRms WGwG WHer WJek WPer XLum
'Alabaster'	EBee NDov SAga SPhx
aleppica	WCot
Anthea = 'Anblo' [PBR]	CKno CWCL EBee ECtt GBBs IBoy LBMP LRHS LSRN MRav NChi NLar SRGP SRms SWvt WFar
§ 'Apfelblüte' (Galaxy Series)	CWCL EBee ECha ECtt ELan EPfP EWTr GKin LRHS LSRN MBel MMuc MRav MSpe NDov NGdn NHol NLBP NSti NWad SEND SPer WFar WMnd WPer WPtf WWEG
Appleblossom	see *A.* 'Apfelblüte' (Galaxy Series)
'Apricot Beauty'	EBee ECtt GBBs GMaP GQue LSRN SBod
'Apricot Delight' (Tutti Frutti Series)	EBee MNrw NCGa
argentea misapplied	see *A. clavennae*, *A. umbellata*
argentea Lamarck	see *Tanacetum argenteum*
argentea ambig.	NMen
I ***argentifolia*** hort.	WKif
aurea	see *A. chrysocoma*
'Bahama'	GBin GQue NBro
'Belle Epoque' ♀H4	WWEG
biebersteinii	XLum
brachyphylla	EHoe
'Breckland Bouquet'	ECtt EWes
'Breckland Ruby'	EWes
'Carmina Burana'	CMea
'Christine's Pink' ♀H4	MSpe MTis
§ ***chrysocoma***	ECho EDAr MMuc MWat WMoo
- 'Grandiflora'	ECha LPla MMuc NGdn
§ ***clavennae***	ECho EDAr MWat SBch SMrm SRms WAbe
clypeolata Sibth. & Sm.	EBee EPPr LRHS NLar SMad SPlb SRms
coarctata	NBir WPer XSen
Colorado Group	CWCL LRHS NChi SPav
'Coronation Gold' ♀H4	CDoC CPrp CWCL EBee ECtt ELan EPfP GBuc LAst LRHS MNFA MRav MWat NChi NDov SAga SDys SPer SWvt WCAu WCot WFar WWEG XLum
'Credo' ♀H4	CPrp EBee ECha ECtt ELon EPPr EPfP EWTr LPla LRHS MBel MCot MNFA MRav MSpe NGdn NHol NLar NSti NWad SMad SMrm SPer SPhx SUsu SWat WMnd WPtf WWEG
crithmifolia	XLum
decolorans	see *A. ageratum*
erba-rotta	WPer
- subsp. ***moschata***	NBro
§ 'Fanal'	Widely available
'Faust'	ELon MNrw SMrm SUsu
'Federsee'	MArl
'Feuerland'	CMac CSam EBee ECha ECtt ELon EPPr EPfP GKin LRHS MRav MSpe NBir NDov NGdn NSti SMad SMrm SPer SPoG WFar WPer WWEG
filipendulina	WHrl
- 'Cloth of Gold' ♀H4	Widely available
- 'Gold Plate' ♀H4	Widely available
- 'Parker's Variety' ♀H4	EBee GQue NBre WMoo
'Fleur van Zonneveld'	MSpe MTis NDov
Flowers of Sulphur	see *A.* 'Schwefelblüte'
(Forncett Series) 'Forncett Beauty'	SWvt WPtf
- 'Forncett Bride'	NBre
- 'Forncett Candy'	WWEG
- 'Forncett Citrus'	MAvo
- 'Forncett Fletton'	CCon CWCL EBee ECtt ELon EPPr EPfP EShb GKin LHop MAsh MNFA MNrw MRav MSpe MTis NCGa NGdn NHol NWad WPtf WWEG WWlt
- 'Forncett Ivory'	EPPr MAvo WPtf

	Name	Suppliers
	fraasii	MCot MDKP XSen
	(Galaxy Series) red-flowered	WSpi
	'Gloria Jean'	SHar SPhx SUsu
	'Gold and Grey'	SMrm WWEG
	'Goldstar'	EBee
	grandifolia misapplied	see *Tanacetum macrophyllum* (Waldst. & Kit.) Sch.Bip.
§	***grandifolia*** Friv.	CElw COIW CSam LPla MRav NBro SPhx SSvw SUsu WAul WBor WFar WHer WMnd WMoo WOut
	'Gravat'	MArl
	'Great Expectations'	see *A.* 'Hoffnung'
	'Heidi' ♀H4	CCVN WPtf WWEG
	'Heinrich Vogeler'	EBee
	'Helios' ♀H4	EBee
	'Hella Glashoff' ♀H4	CMea CWCL CWan EBee ELon GBin LRHS NRHS SAga WCot WFar
§	'Hoffnung'	CPrp CWCL EBee MRav MSpe WMnd WPer WWEG
	× ***huteri***	ECho ECtt EDAr EPfP EPot LRHS MAsh MRav NGdn SEND SRms WAbe WFar WNew WPer
	'Inca Gold'	CWCL EBee ECGP ECha ECtt EHrv EPPr EShb GBuc GQue LRHS MRav MSpe MTis NHol NSti NWad WCFE WFar WGwG WHoo WWEG
	'Jacqueline'	EWll MSpe MTis WPer
	'Judity'	WOut
	× ***kellereri***	XSen
	'King Alfred'	CMea EPfP
	× ***kolbiana***	MWat NMen SRms
§	'Lachsschönheit' (Galaxy Series) ♀H4	Widely available
	× ***lewisii***	NMen
	- 'King Edward' ♀H4	ECho EDAr EPfP GMaP NBir SBch SRms WAbe WFar WIce WPer
	ligustica	WCot
	'Lucky Break' ♀H4	MSpe MTis SDix SUsu WCot
	macrophylla	MBNS NBre
	'Marie Ann'	EBee ECtt GQue LSRN MNrw NLar SPhx SRGP
	'Marmalade'	MTis NDov SMrm WMnd WPGP WWEG
	'Martina' ♀H4	CDoC CPrp EBee ECtt EPPr GBuc GKin IPot LAst LBMP LHop MAsh MBNS MBel MBri MCot MRav NCGa NDov NGdn NHol NOrc NWad SRGP WWEG
	'McVities'	CWCL ECtt EPPr MSpe MTis WMnd WPtf WWEG
	millefolium	CArn CHab CWan EHrv ELau ENfk GPoy MNHC NLan NMir SPlb WHer WJek WSFF XLum
	- 'Bloodstone'	EBee ECtt EWes MRav WPtf
	- 'Carla Hussey'	WFar
	- 'Cassis'	CCVN CSpe ETod GQue LDai LRHS MNHC NGBl NLar SGar SPav SPet SWal WBrk WFar WMoo WPtf
§	- 'Cerise Queen'	Widely available
	- 'Chamois' **new**	MNrw
	- 'Cherry King'	NBir
	- 'Christel'	CCVN EWes GBin SUsu
	- 'Christine'	GBee GBin
	- 'Circus'	XLum
	- 'Dark Lilac Beauty'	EWTr
	- 'Harlekin'	EBee
	- 'Kelwayi' ♀H4	WPtf
	- Kirschkönigin	see *A. millefolium* 'Cerise Queen'
	- 'Lansdorferglut' ♀H4	LPla LRHS MTis SPhx WWEG
	- 'Laura'	CSam CWGN EBee LSou MAsh MBri MNrw NCGa
	- 'Lavender Beauty'	see *A. millefolium* 'Lilac Beauty'
§	- 'Lilac Beauty'	CBar COIW CPrp EBee ECha ELon EPfP GBin GBuc IBoy IPot LBMP LRHS LSRN MRav MSpe NBir NDov NEgg NWad SBfd SHil SRms WFar WHoo WPer WPtf WWEG XLum
*	- 'Lilac Queen'	MArl
	- 'Little Suzie'	MAsh MBri
	- 'Lollypop'	LDai
	- 'Oertels Rose'	WFar
	- 'Old Brocade'	EShb MTis WPtf WWEG
	- Pastel Shades	IFoB
	- 'Peggy Sue'	CWGN EBee MAsh MBri NCGa
	- 'Pomegranate' (Tutti Frutti Series)	CWGN EBee LHop LLHF MAsh MNrw MTis NCGa SHar
	- 'Pretty Woman'	CSam EBee MAsh MBri NCGa
	- 'Raspberry Ripple'	GBin
	- 'Red Beauty'	CWCL EPfP GBin MAsh MBNS MSpe SRms WWEG XLum
	- 'Red Salmon'	EWes
	- 'Red Velvet'	Widely available
	- 'Rose Madder'	CPrp CWCL EBee ECtt EGHP EHoe EPPr GKin GMaP LPla LRHS MAsh MBri MNrw MSpe NBir NCGa NGdn NHol NLar NSti SMrm SPav SWvt WCot WGwG WHoo WPtf XLum
	- 'Ruby Port'	WFar
	- 'Salmon Pink'	ITim WFar
	- 'Salmon Queen'	EGHP NHol
	- 'Sammetriese'	CWan LRHS MNrw NCGa SMad SPhx WWEG
	- 'Schneetaler'	EBee GBin
	- 'Serenade'	EBee ECtt MAsh MSpe WFar
	- 'Sue's Pink'	CSam MSpe
	- 'Summertime'	LAst
	- 'Tickled Pink'	WPer
	- 'White Queen'	EBee SBod
	- 'Wonderful Wampee' **new**	EBee MNrw MTis
	'Mondpagode' ♀H4	CPrp EBee EPPr EWTr LPla LRHS LSRN MAvo MBNS MCot MNFA MRav NGdn SMHy SPhx SSvw WFar WKif
*	'Moonbeam'	GKin SEND
	'Moonshine' ♀H3	Widely available
	'Moonwalker'	CAbP EBee EPfP NBre NGBl SIde SPav WBrk WCot WFar WPer
	nana	GEdr
	nobilis	WOut
	- subsp. ***neilreichii***	EBee ECGP EHoe EHrv EWTr GCal GQue IKil LAst LRHS MNrw NSti SPer SWvt WHal WTin WWEG
*	***odilis***	LRHS
	'Paprika' (Galaxy Series)	Widely available
	'Peardrop'	NBre
	pindicola subsp. ***integrifolia***	EWes
	pink-flowered from Santa Cruz Island	CKno CWCL
	'Pink Grapefruit' (Tutti Frutti Series)	EBee MAsh MNrw MTis NCGa
	'Pink Lady'	GBBs
	'Pretty Belinda'	EBee ECtt EPfP LPla LRHS LSRN LSou MBNS MCot MSpe NLar NPri NSti SBea SKHP SPoG STes WWlt
	'Prospero'	WCot WWEG

	ptarmica	CArn CBre ELau MHer NMir NPri SIde XLum
*	- 'Ballerina'	MBNS MWhi NBre NDov NGdn NLar
	- Innocence	see *A. ptarmica* 'Unschuld'
	- 'Nana Compacta'	CSpe EBee ECha EPPr GBin IBoy LRHS NBir NCGa SPlb SUsu WCFE WFar WWEG
	- 'Perry's White' (d)	CBcs CBre EBee ECha IPot MNrw NDov NGdn SRGP WCot
	- 'Stephanie Cohen'	see *A. sibirica* 'Stephanie Cohen'
N	- The Pearl Group seed-raised (d)	CTri ELan MMuc SPlb SWat WMoo WPer WTin
N	- - 'Boule de Neige' (clonal) (d)	GKin MRav MSpe NBre NPer NSti SPer SPet WFar XLum
N	- - 'The Pearl' (clonal) (d) ♀H4	CMac CSBt CWCL EBee ECha EPfP IBoy IFoB LAst LHop LPot LRHS LSRN MBel MLHP MRav MWat NBid NBir NBro SRms SWal WBor WBrk WCot WFar WHer WHil WJek
§	- 'Unschuld'	NBir
	pyrenaica	XLum
	'Rougham Salmon'	WPtf
	'Safran' **new**	LRHS
	salicifolia 'Silver Spray'	GQue NLar SPav WOut
	'Sally'	EPPr MSpe
	Salmon Beauty	see *A.* 'Lachsschönheit'
	'Sandstone'	see *A.* 'Wesersandstein'
	'Saucy Seduction' (Tutti Frutti Series)	EBee LLHF MAsh MTis NCGa
§	'Schwefelblüte'	EBee MRav NBir SBch SMrm
	'Schwellenburg'	CDes NBre WCot
	sibirica	WPtf
	subsp. ***camschatica***	
	- - 'Love Parade'	EBee EPfP ITim LRHS MBNS MMuc MNFA MNrw MRav NGdn NLar SAga SPer WFar WMoo WWEG XLum
§	- 'Stephanie Cohen'	CPrp GBee GBin WFar WWEG
	'Smiling Queen'	IBoy
	'Stephanie'	ECtt EPPr EWes LSRN MSpe
	Summer Berries Group	CSpe LRHS
	Summer Pastels Group	EPfP IBoy IFro LRHS NLar NOrc SBfd SPav SPoG SRms SWal
	'Summerwine' ♀H4	Widely available
	'Sunbeam'	SHar
	'Sunny Seduction' **new**	NCGa
I	'Taygetea'	EBee ECtt ELan EPPr EPfP MBNS NPnk SDix SPer SPet SRkn WCot WPer WSHC WWEG
	'Terracotta'	Widely available
	'The Beacon'	see *A.* 'Fanal'
	'Tissington Flame' **new**	MTis
	'Tissington Old Rose'	MAvo MNrw MSpe MTis WBrk
	tomentosa ♀H4	CTri ECha ECho ECtt MAsh WCot
§	- 'Aurea'	EBee ECho LRHS NBre NBro SPhx
	- 'Goldie'	EDAr
	- 'Maynard's Gold'	see *A. tomentosa* 'Aurea'
	'Tri-colour'	NGdn NWad
§	***umbellata***	WAbe WBrk XSen
	'W.B. Childs'	ECha ELan MCot MNrw MRav NDov SHar WCot
	'Walther Funcke'	Widely available
§	'Wesersandstein'	CWCL EBee ECtt EPPr ETod GMaP LPla LRHS MNrw NBir NPro STes WCot WFar WPer WWEG
	'Wilczekii'	SRms
	'Yellowstone'	EWes LDai

× *Achimenantha* (*Gesneriaceae*)

'Aries'	EABi WDib
'Himalayan Sunrise'	GHim LAma
'Inferno' ♀H1	EABi GHim WDib
'Sagittarius' **new**	GHim
'Texas Spotted Leopard' **new**	EABi
'Tyche'	EABi

Achimenes (*Gesneriaceae*)

'Addano'	WDib
'Ambroise Verschaffelt' ♀H1	EABi LAma WDib
'Ami Van Houtte'	WDib
'Aphrodite' **new**	GHim
'Apricot Glow'	EABi
'Aquamarine'	WDib
'Ballerina'	WDib
'Bloody Marie' **new**	EABi
'Blue David'	EABi
'Blue Sparkles'	EABi GHim SDeJ
'Boy David'	EABi
'Caligula' **new**	EABi
'Camille Brozzoni'	EABi
'Cascade Fashionable Pink'	WDib
'Cascade Rose Red'	WDib
'Cascade Violet Night'	WDib
'Cattleya'	LAma
'Charity'	WDib
'Charm'	GHim SDeJ
'Cherry Blossom' **new**	EABi
'Claret'	EABi WDib
'Clouded Yellow'	EABi
'Clouded Yellow Stone' **new**	GHim
'Coral Cameo Mix'	EABi
'Cornell Favourite'	EABi
'Côte d'Ivoire' **new**	EABi
'Crackerjack'	WDib
'Crummock Water'	EABi WDib
'Dazzler' **new**	EABi
'Derwentwater'	EABi
'Donna'	EABi
'Dot'	EABi
'Double Pink Rose' (d)	WDib
'Electra'	EABi
'English Waltz'	EABi GHim
erecta	EABi WDib
'Erlkönig'	WDib
'Extravaganza'	WDib
'Flamenco'	WDib
'Flaming Embers' **new**	EABi
'Freckle Face' **new**	EABi
'Glory'	EABi WDib
grandiflora 'Robert Dressler'	EABi
'Grape Wine'	EABi
'Hard to Get'	EABi
'Harry Williams'	EABi GHim LAma WDib
'Hilda Michelssen' ♀H1	EABi WDib
'Himalayan Angel' **new**	GHim
'Jay Dee Coral'	WDib
'Jay Dee Large White'	WDib
'Jay Dee Pink'	WDib
'Jay Dee Purple'	WDib
'Jennifer Goode'	EABi WDib
'Johanna Michelssen'	WDib
'Jubilee Gem'	EABi
'Just Divine'	EABi WDib
'Kim Blue'	WDib

	'Light Lilac'	WDib
	'Little Beauty'	WDib
	longiflora	EABi
§	- var. ***alba***	GHim
	- 'Alba'	see *A. longiflora* var. *alba*
	- 'Major'	WDib
	'Luneberg'	EABi
	'Maxima'	LAma
	'Menuett'	WDib
	mexicana new	GHim SDeJ
	'Mozelle'	EABi
	'Opal'	WDib
	'Orange Delight'	EABi WDib
	'Orange Queen'	EABi
	(Palette Series) 'Palette Lilac'	EABi
	- 'Palette Red'	EABi
	- 'Palette Salmon'	EABi
	- 'Palette White'	EABi
	'Pally'	WDib
	'Patens Major'	EABi WDib
	'Peach Blossom'	GHim LAma WDib
	'Peach Glow'	EABi GHim WDib
	'Pearly Queen'	EABi
	pedunculata new	EABi
	'Petite Fadette'	EABi
	'Pink Beauty'	EABi
	'Pink Rose' (d)	EABi
	'Platinum'	EABi
	'Primadonna'	SDeJ WDib
	'Pulcherrima'	GHim SDeJ
I	'Purple Hybrid'	EABi
	'Purple King'	WDib
	'Purple Queen'	WDib
	'Purple Triumph'	WDib
	'Queen of Queens'	WDib
	'Rainbow'	EABi WDib
	'Red Diamond' new	EABi
	'Red Elfe'	EABi
	'Red Giant'	EABi
	'Red Hilda Michelssen'	WDib
	'Rhino' new	EABi
	'Rosa Charm'	EABi
	'Rose Dream'	EABi
	'Rosy Doll'	GHim
	'Sergé Saliba'	EABi
	'Show-off'	WDib
	'Snow Princess'	SDeJ
	'Spring Time' new	GHim
	'Stan's Delight' (d) ♀H1	EABi GHim WDib
	'Sterntaler'	WDib
	'Summer Sunset'	EABi
	'Sweet & Sour'	EABi
	'Tarantella'	EABi WDib
	'Teresa'	EABi
	(Tetra Series) 'Tetra Himalayan Orange' new	GHim
	- 'Tetra Himalayan Purple' new	GHim
	- 'Tetra Verschaffelt'	EABi
	- 'Tetra Wine Red Charm'	EABi
	'Tiger Eye'	WDib
	'Trailing Yellow'	EABi
	'Vie-en-Rose'	EABi
	'Violacea Semiplena'	WDib
	'Vivid'	EABi GHim WDib
	'Weinrot Elfe'	WDib
	'Wetterlow's Triumph'	EABi WDib
	'Yellow Beauty'	WDib

Achlys (*Berberidaceae*)

	japonica	GEdr WCru
	triphylla	WCru

Achnatherum see *Stipa*

Achyranthes (*Amaranthaceae*)

	bidentata	CArn

Acidanthera see *Gladiolus*

Acinos (*Lamiaceae*)

§	***alpinus***	EDAr GJos ITim LLHF MHer MMuc WJek XLum
§	***corsicus***	NMen WHoo WKif

Aciphylla (*Apiaceae*)

	aurea	EBee GBin GCal GKev SMad SPlb
	dieffenbachii	CBrP EUJe GBin
	glacialis new	EBee
	glaucescens	ECou GBin SPlb
	kirkii	EBee
	'Lomond'	EBee GBin GKev
	montana	EPot GLin
	pinnatifida	EBee EPot

Acis (*Amaryllidaceae*)

§	***autumnalis*** ♀H4	CAvo CBro CDes CElw CTca CTri EBee ECha ECho EHrv EPot EWes GEdr GKev ITim LAma LEdu LRHS NBir NMen SMrm SRms SRot WAbe WHil WHoo WPGP
	- 'Cobb's Variety'	EBee ECho WCot
	- var. ***oporantha***	CWCL CYeo EPri LWSt
	- - from Morocco	ECho
	- - f. ***dispathaceous***	LWSt
	- var. ***pulchella***	ECho GKev
	- 'September Snow'	GKev LWSt
§	***longifolia***	ECho
	nicaeensis ♀H2-3	ECho EPot GCal GKev LLHF LRHS SCnR WAbe WCot WThu
	- PJC 277	LWSt
§	***rosea***	ECho LLHF MAvo NMen WAbe WThu
§	***tingitana***	ECho
§	***trichophylla***	ECho LLHF SCnR WCot
	- J&JA 630.501	LWSt
	- f. ***purpurascens***	ECho WCot
§	***valentina***	ECho EPot SCnR SRot WCot

Acmella (*Asteraceae*)

§	***oleracea***	CArn

Acmena (*Myrtaceae*)

	smithii	EShb

Acnistus (*Solanaceae*)

	australis	see *Iochroma australe*

Aconitum (*Ranunculaceae*)

	B&SWJ 2954 from Nepal	WCru
	CNDS 036 from Burma	WCru
	GWJ 9417 from northern India	WCru
	KR 7589	CDes
	alboviolaceum	LLHF WCot
	- var. ***alboviolaceum***	WCru
	f. ***albiflorum*** B&SWJ 4105	

	- - B&SWJ 8444	WCru
	- var. ***purpurascens*** B&SWJ 8477	WCru
	altissimum	see *A. lycoctonum* subsp. *vulparia*
	anglicum	see *A. napellus* subsp. *napellus* Anglicum Group
§	***anthora***	CArn EBee EPfP EWTr IKil LRHS SBfd
	anthora* × *carmichaelii Arendsii Group **new**	EHrv
	arcuatum	see *A. fischeri* var. *arcuatum*
	austroyunnanense	WSHC
	- BWJ 7902	WCru
	autumnale misapplied	see *A. carmichaelii* Wilsonii Group
	autumnale Rchb.	see *A. fischeri* Rchb.
	× ***bicolor***	see *A.* × *cammarum* 'Bicolor'
	'Blue Lagoon'^{PBR}	CWGN
	'Blue Opal'	CDes EBee ECtt EWes WPGP
	'Blue Sceptre'	GBin LDai LRHS
	'Bressingham Spire' Y^{H4}	Widely available
	bulbilliferum HWJK 2120	WCru
§	× ***cammarum*** 'Bicolor' Y^{H4}	Widely available
	- 'Eleanora'	CCon EBee ECtt EPfP EWes GBuc GCra LHop LRHS LSou MNrw NLar SPer SPoG SRms WCot WWEG
	- 'Grandiflorum Album'	LPla MNrw
	- 'Pink Sensation'^{PBR}	CCon EBee EPfP GQue LLHF MBNS MBel NBre NCGa NDov NLar NPnk NSti
§	***carmichaelii***	Widely available
	- Arendsii Group	ECtt GKev LAst LRHS SPhx SRot
	- - 'Arendsii' Y^{H4}	Widely available
	- - 'Cloudy'^{PBR} **new**	NRHS
	- 'Redleaf'^{PBR}	see *A. carmichaelii* 'Royal Flush'
	- 'River Arrow'	WCot
	- 'River Avon'	WCot
	- 'River Dee'	WCot
	- 'River Devon'	WCot
	- 'River Finn'	WCot
	- 'River Lugg'	WCot
	- 'River Lune'	WCot
	- 'River Medway'	WCot
	- 'River Nene'	WCot
	- 'River Ouse'	WCot
	- 'River Severn'	WCot
	- 'River Spey'	WCot
	- 'River Tees'	WCot
	- 'River Teifi'	WCot
	- 'River Trent'	WCot
	- 'River Welland'	WCot
§	- 'Royal Flush'^{PBR}	CWGN EBee ECtt EPfP GAbr IBoy MAvo MBNS MBri MNrw NLar SUsu WCot WHil
	- var. ***truppelianum*** HWJ 732	EBee WCru
§	- Wilsonii Group	CPrp EBee ECGP GMaP LPla LRHS MCot MRav MWat NCGa NDov NEgg SPhx WFar WPer
	- - 'Barker's Variety'	CCon CKno EBee ECtt ELon EPfP GBuc GCal GQue LHop LRHS NGdn NHol NLar NSti WSpi
	- - 'Kelmscott' Y^{H4}	ECtt EWes MCot MRav SAga SDix SMHy WFar WRHF WSpi
	- - 'Spätlese'	CAbP CSam CWGN EBee ECtt ELon EPfP GCal IBoy LEdu LRHS LSou MCot MNFA NBir NDov NGdn SMHy SMrm SPer SUsu WCot WWEG
	chasmanthum	LRHS
	chiisanense B&SWJ 4446	WCru
	cilicicum	see *Eranthis hyemalis* Cilicica Group
	'Cloudy'	CPrp EBee ECtt NGdn WCot
	compactum	see *A. napellus* subsp. *vulgare*
	confertiflorum	see *A. anthora*
	delphiniifolium	CPLG
	elliotii	EBee
	elwesii	EBee LRHS NBre
	episcopale	WCru
	aff. ***episcopale***	WWEG
	- CLD 1426	GBuc
	excelsum	see *A. lycoctonum* subsp. *lycoctonum*
	ferox	EBee ELon EWes LLHF
	- HWJK 2217	WCru
	fischeri misapplied	see *A. carmichaelii*
§	***fischeri*** Rchb.	CWib EBee MMuc MSCN NCGa SEND WCot WHil
	- B&SWJ 8809	WCru
§	- var. ***arcuatum*** B&SWJ 774	WCru
	formosanum	LEdu
	- B&SWJ 3057	WCru
	fukutomei B&SWJ 337	MRav WCru
	gammiei GWJ 9418	WCru
	gmelinii	see *A. lycoctonum* subsp. *lycoctonum*
	grossedentatum	LPla
§	***hemsleyanum***	CMea CPLG CRHN CWGN ECtt EPfP GCra GQue NBid NHol SGar WCru
	- 'Red Wine'	CCon GHim LRHS WWEG
	hyemale	see *Eranthis hyemalis*
	incisofidum	WCot
	'Ivorine'	CRow CTri EBee ECha ELan EPfP GBuc GCra GMaP LAst LEdu LRHS LSRN MCot NGdn NPri NRHS NSti SMad SPer SUsu WFar WGwG WPnP WTin
	jaluense B&SWJ 8741	WCru
	japonicum	EBee GCal LRHS
	- var. ***hakonense***	CPLG
	- var. ***montanum*** B&SWJ 5507	WCru
§	- subsp. ***napiforme***	EWes SAga
	- - B&SWJ 943	CDes EBee ELon WCru
§	- subsp. ***subcuneatum*** B&SWJ 6228	WCru
	krylovii	WCot
	laciniatum GWJ 9254	WCru
	- GWJ 9324	WCru
	lamarckii	see *A. lycoctonum* subsp. *neapolitanum*
	lasianthum	see *A. lycoctonum* subsp. *vulparia*
	loczyanum B&SWJ 11529	WCru
	longecassidatum B&SWJ 4277	WCru
	- B&SWJ 8486	WCru
	- B&SWJ 8488	WCru
	lycoctonum	LRHS NLar SBfd WSpi
	- 'Darkeyes'	CAbP LRHS WCot WFar
	- 'Graupe'	WCot
	- 'Langhuso'	WCot
§	- subsp. ***lycoctonum***	SRms WCot
	- - var. ***rubicundum***	LRHS
§	- subsp. ***moldavicum***	LRHS WCot

§ - subsp. ***neapolitanum*** ECtt ELan GCal GMaP MBel MMuc NLar SEND WFar WWEG
- 'Russian Yellow' EWld GCal

§ - subsp. ***vulparia*** CArn CCon CMac CPrp GPoy MNFA MNrw MRav NEgg NGdn WAul WCot WPer

mairei see *A. vilmorinianum*

moldavicum see *A. lycoctonum* subsp. *moldavicum*

nagarum WCot
- KR 7589 WPGP

napellus Widely available
- 'Bergfürst' CMea LPla LRHS MBri MNFA SPhx
- 'Blue Valley' EBee EPfP EWes NPro SBfd SPoG WHil
- subsp. ***fissurae*** LRHS
- 'Gletschereis' GBin
- subsp. ***napellus*** SRms

§ - - Anglicum Group CSev CWan EBee MCot NLar WCot
- 'Rubellum' EBee ECtt ELan IBoy LRHS MCot MMuc NBir NBro NEgg NPri SMrm SPoG WMnd
- 'Schneewittchen' EBee EWes IPot SSvw
- 'Sphere's Variety' NOrc

§ - subsp. ***vulgare*** WFar
- - 'Albidum' CMea CPrp EBee EHrv ELan ELon EPfP GAbr GMaP LEdu LRHS MBel MHoo MSCN NBid NHol NLar NPri SMrm SPer SPet WAul WBor WPer
- - 'Carneum' GCra LRHS MHoo WHer WKif

napiforme see *A. japonicum* subsp. *napiforme*

neapolitanum see *A. lycoctonum* subsp. *neapolitanum*

'Newry Blue' EBee ELan EPfP GBuc LRHS MHoo NBir NHol NLar SBfd SGar SMad SRms WFar WPer WSpi WWEG

orientale misapplied see *A. lycoctonum* subsp. *vulparia*

orientale ambig. NPro

paniculatum misapplied see *A. variegatum* subsp. *paniculatum*

piepunense GKev

proliferum B&SWJ 4107 WCru

pseudohuiliense CPLG

pseudolaeve EWld
- B&SWJ 8663 WCru
- var. ***erectum*** B&SWJ 8466 WCru

pubiceps white-flowered GCal

pyramidale see *A. napellus* subsp. *vulgare*

pyrenaicum misapplied see *A. lycoctonum* subsp. *neapolitanum*

ranunculifolius see *A. lycoctonum* subsp. *neapolitanum*

senanense var. ***incisum*** B&SWJ 11032 **new** WCru

seoulense B&SWJ 694 WCru
- B&SWJ 864 WCru

septentrionale see *A. lycoctonum* subsp. *lycoctonum*

'Spark's Variety' ♀ H4 Widely available

spicatum GWJ 9393 WCru
- GWJ 9394 WCru

'Stainless Steel' Widely available

subcuneatum see *A. japonicum* subsp. *subcuneatum*

× ***tubergenii*** see *Eranthis hyemalis* Tubergenii Group

uchiyamae B&SWJ 1005 WCru
- B&SWJ 1216 ELon EPPr WCru
- B&SWJ 4446 NLar

variegatum GCal

§ - subsp. ***paniculatum*** MBri WCot

§ ***vilmorinianum*** BWJ 8055 WCru

volubile misapplied see *A. hemsleyanum*

volubile Pall. CCon GCal

vulparia see *A. lycoctonum* subsp. *vulparia*

yamazakii WCru

yezoense GCal

zigzag var. ***ryohakuense*** B&SWJ 8906 WCru

Aconogonon see *Persicaria*

Acorus ✿ (*Acoraceae*)

calamus CArn CBen CKno CWat EHon ELau GPoy LPBA MSKA NPer SWat WHer WMAq
- subsp. ***angustatus*** GPoy
- 'Argenteostriatus' (v) CBen CRow CWat EBee ECha ECtt EHon LPBA MCot MMuc MWts NOrc SRms SWat WMAq WWEG

* ***christophii*** ELon EPPr EWes SApp WMoo

gramineus ELau GPoy LPBA MSKA NPer SWat WHer WMoo
- 'Golden Edge' (v) ELon EWes
- 'Hakuro-nishiki' (v) EBee ECtt EHoe EHul EPPr EPot EShb LPBA MGos MMoz NBid NHol SBfd SRms SWvt WMoo XLum
- 'Kinchinjunga' (v) IFro
- 'Licorice' EBee EPPr GBin GCal MBNS MDKP SPoG WGrn WMoo
- 'Masamune' (v) EWes GBin GCal SApp WMoo WTin
- 'Minimus Aureus' CBre GCal
- 'Oborozuki' misapplied see *A. gramineus* 'Ōgon'
- 'Oborozuki' (v) EBee EHoe

§ - 'Ōgon' (v) Widely available
- var. ***pusillus*** NBro WWEG
- 'Variegatus' (v) Widely available

'Intermedius' NPer

Acradenia (*Rutaceae*)

frankliniae CBcs CMHG CMac CTrC CTsd IDee MBlu SKHP SPlb WHor WPGP WSHC

Actaea (*Ranunculaceae*)

alba misapplied see *A. pachypoda*, *A. rubra* f. *neglecta*

arizonica EBee GCal LPla LRHS WCru

asiatica CDes EBee
- B&SWJ 616 WCru
- B&SWJ 6351 from Japan WCru
- B&SWJ 8694 from Korea WCru
- BWJ 8174 from China WCru

biternata B&SWJ 5591 WCru
- B&SWJ 8917 WCru
- B&SWJ 11190 WCru

'Chocoholic' EBee ECtt MAsh NCGa

§ ***cimicifuga*** CLAP GCal GPoy LRHS
- B&SWJ 2657 WCru

§ ***cordifolia*** EBee GBin GMaP LHop LPBA LRHS MSCN NGdn SMrm WBor WCot
- 'Blickfang' CLAP
- variegated (v) LRHS

dahurica EBee GQue LRHS NLar SWat WCot
- B&SWJ 8426 WCru

	- B&SWJ 8573	WCru
	- tall	GBin GCal
	erythrocarpa	see *A. rubra*
	frigida B&SWJ 2966	WCru
	heracleifolia B&SWJ 8843	WCru
§	***japonica***	CLAP GCal WFar
	- B&SWJ 5828	WCru
	- B&SWJ 11136	WCru
	- var. ***acutiloba*** B&SWJ 6257	WCru
	- compact	GBin
	- - B&SWJ 8758A	WCot WCru
I	- 'Minima'	LRHS
	mairei	GCal LRHS
	- BWJ 7635	WCru
	- BWJ 7939	WCru
§	***matsumurae***	CPLG
	- B&SWJ 11187	WCru
	- B&SWJ 11528	WCru
	- 'Elstead Variety' ♀H4	CPLG GCal MBri MRav
	- 'Frau Herms'	LRHS
	- 'White Pearl'	Widely available
§	***pachypoda*** ♀H4	CBro CPLG EBee ECGP EPfP GCal GPoy IGor LRHS NBid NLar WCot WCru
	- 'Misty Blue' new	EBee LSou MBel SHar SPoG WCot WHil
	- f. ***rubrocarpa***	GCal
§	***podocarpa***	SPlb SRms WCru
	racemosa ♀H4	CArn CMac EBee ELan EPfP GCal GPoy LRHS MHoo NBid NGdn NSti SPer SWvt WFar WMnd
	- 'Washfield'	WCot
§	***rubra*** ♀H4	CBro CHid CMHG EBee ECha ELan GCal LRHS MCot MMHG NBid SMad WCru
	- B&SWJ 9555	WCru
	- ***alba***	see *A. pachypoda*, *A. rubra* f. *neglecta*
§	- f. ***neglecta***	CDes EBee GAbr GCal GQue SKHP WCot WCru
	simplex	EBee ECha GCra LRHS NEgg SEND SWat WCot
	- B&SWJ 8653	WCru
	- B&SWJ 8664	WCru
	- B&SWJ 10957	WCru
	- B&SWJ 11133	WCru
§	- Atropurpurea Group	Widely available
	- - 'Bernard Mitchell'	CCon
	- - 'Black Negligee'	CLAP CPLG CWGN EBee ECtt GEdr GQue IBoy LLHF LPla LRHS LSou NCGa NMyG NPri SBfd SPad SPoG SWat WCot WWEG
	- - 'Brunette' ♀H4	Widely available
	- - 'Carbonella'	EBee ECtt
	- - 'Hillside Black Beauty'	CCVN CLAP EBee ECtt GBin GMaP LRHS MNrw NBir NLar NPnk WCot
	- - 'James Compton'	Widely available
	- - 'Mountain Wave'	CLAP EBee ECtt WCot WPGP
	- 'Hugo'	CSpe
	- 'Pink Spike'	Widely available
§	- 'Prichard's Giant'	CLAP ECha GBin LRHS MBri MRav MSpe NDov WFar
	- ***ramosa***	see *A. simplex* 'Prichard's Giant'
	- 'Silver Axe'	GCal LRHS NBre NGdn
	- variegated (v)	CDes WCot
	spicata	EPPr GBin GCra GPoy LRHS NLar WCru
	- from England	GCal WCru
	- var. ***leucocarpa*** new	ECtt
	taiwanensis B&SWJ 3413	WCru
	- RWJ 9996	WCru
	yesoensis B&SWJ 6355	WCru
	- B&SWJ 10860	WCru
	yunnanensis	GCal

Actinella see *Tetraneuris*

Actinidia (*Actinidiaceae*)

	BWJ 8161 from China	WCru
	arguta new	CPne
	- (f/F)	CAgr NLar
	- 74-32 (m)	CAgr
	- B&SWJ 4455 from Jejudo, South Korea	WCru
	- B&SWJ 4823 from Japan	WCru
	- B&SWJ 8529 from Ulleungdo, South Korea	WCru
	- 'Ananasnaya' (f/F)	CAgr
	- var. ***cordifolia*** (f/F)	CAgr
	- 'Geneva 2' (f/F)	CAgr
	- 'Issai' (s-p/F)	CAgr CBcs CCCN EPfP EPom EUJe LBuc LRHS LSRN MGos NLar SVic
	- 'Jumbo' new	SVic
	- 'Ken's Red' (F)	CAgr SVic
	- 'Kiwai Vert' (f/F)	CAgr
	- LL#1 (m)	CAgr
	- LL#2 (f/F)	CAgr
	- LL#3 (m)	CAgr
	- 'Meader' (m)	CAgr
	- 'MSU' (F)	CAgr
	- 'Shoko' (f)	WCru
	- 'Unchae' (m)	WCru
	- 'Weiki'	SVic
	chinensis misapplied	see *A. deliciosa*
	chinensis ambig.	CDoy
§	***deliciosa***	ERom MGos MRav SBfd WFar WSHC
	- 'Atlas' (m)	CAgr NLar
*	- 'Boskoop'	ELan EUJe MCoo MGos
	- 'Hayward' (f/F)	CAgr CBcs CCCN CDoC CHEx CMac EBee EPfP LHop LRHS LSRN MCoo MREP NLar SPer SWvt WFar
	- hermaphrodite (F)	ELan SBfd
	- 'Jenny' (s-p/F)	CAgr CHEx CMac CSut CTri EBee EPfP EPom LAst LBuc LRHS MBri MGos SBfd SLim SPoG SVic
	- 'Solo'	CCCN CDoC CMac CMam CSBt EBee ECrN EPfP LRHS LSRN MCoo NLar SBfd SLim SPer SPoG SWvt WPGP
	- 'Tomuri' (m)	CBcs CCCN CDoC CHEx CMac EBee EPfP LRHS LSRN MCoo NLar SPer SWvt
	hypoleuca B&SWJ 5942	WCru
	kolomikta ♀H4	Widely available
	- (m)	MBlu NPla
	- B&SWJ 4243	LSRN WCru
	- 'Red Beauty' (F)	CAgr
	- 'Tomoko' (f/F)	WCru
	- 'Yazuaki' (m)	WCru
	latifolia B&SWJ 3563	WCru
	melanandra	SPlb
	petelotii HWJ 628	WCru
	pilosula misapplied	see *A. tetramera* var. *maloides*
	polygama	GCal
	- B&SWJ 5444	WCru

- B&SWJ 8525 from Korea WCru
- B&SWJ 8923 from Japan WCru
rufa B&SWJ 3525 WCru
aff. ***strigosa*** HWJK 2367 WCru
tetramera B&SWJ 3564 WCru
§ - var. ***maloides*** CBcs CCCN CPLG CRHN CSPN CWGN EBee ELon EPfP EWTr GCal LHop LRHS LSRN LTen MBri MGos NRHS SBfd SBrt SCoo SHil SKHP SPoG WCru WPGP WSHC

Adansonia (*Malvaceae*)

grandidieri SPlb
gregorii SPlb
madagascariensis new SPlb
rubrostipa SPlb
za new SPlb

Adelocaryum see *Lindelofia*

Adenia (*Passifloraceae*)

glauca LToo

Adenium (*Apocynaceae*)

obesum ♀H1 LToo
- subsp. ***boehmianum*** LToo
- subsp. ***swazicum*** LToo

Adenocarpus (*Papilionaceae*)

decorticans SPlb

Adenophora (*Campanulaceae*)

BWJ 7696 from China WCru
'Afterglow' see *Campanula rapunculoides* 'Afterglow'
'Amethyst' EDif
asiatica see *Hanabusaya asiatica*
aurita CCon CRDP WCot
bulleyana CCon ELan GCra GJos IKil LRHS NBid NGdn SPav SPlb WCot WFar
capillaris subsp. ***leptosepala*** BWJ 7986 WCru
coelestis CPLG NBid
- B&SWJ 7998 WCru
confusa LDai LHop MDKP WFar WHer WSHC
* ***cymerae*** LDai WTcb
forrestii WFar
grandiflora B&SWJ 8555 WCru
jasionifolia BWJ 7946 WCru
khasiana CPLG LLHF MDKP NLar
lamarkii B&SWJ 8738 WCru
latifolia misapplied see *A. pereskiifolia*
latifolia ambig. white-flowered MMuc
latifolia Fischer WFar
liliifolia EBee ELan EPfP GCal LRHS MMuc NPer WFar XLum
maximowicziana B&SWJ 11008 new WCru
morrisonensis RWJ 10008 WCru
§ ***nikoensis*** ECtt NBid
§ ***pereskiifolia*** EBee EWes SHar SPlb WCot WTcb
polyantha EHrv NLar SRms WFar
polymorpha see *A. nikoensis*
potaninii CCon EBee EHrv ELan MMuc SEND WFar WHal WPtf
- pale-flowered LPla MMuc SEND WHal
remotiflora B&SWJ 11016 WCru
- B&SWJ 8714 WCru
takedae B&SWJ 11424 WCru
- var. ***howozana*** MLHP
tashiroi CPrp EPfP XLum
trachelioides B&SWJ 8614 new WCru
triphylla NBir SPav
- B&SWJ 8608 WCru
- B&SWJ 10916 WCru
- var. ***hakusanensis*** LLHF
- var. ***japonica*** LDai
- - B&SWJ 8835 WCru
- - B&SWJ 10933 WCru
uehatae GEdr
- B&SWJ 126 SKHP WCru

Adiantum ✿ (*Pteridaceae*)

sp. CMac
aethiopicum CHVG XBlo
§ ***aleuticum*** ♀H4 CLAP MMoz NBid NBro NLar WFib WPGP
- 'Imbricatum' CBty CElw CHVG CLAP CMea ECha EHrv ELon GEdr IKil ISha IVic LRHS MAvo MGos NBid NLar NMyG SBfd SDix WCot WFar WFib
§ - 'Japonicum' CDes EBee LRHS NBir WFar WHal WPGP
- 'Miss Sharples' CDTJ CLAP ELan GEdr LBMP LRHS MGos NBid NLar NMyG SRms SUsu WFar
§ - 'Subpumilum' ♀H4 CLAP LRHS NBid NMyG WAbe WFib
bonatianum CPLG
capillus-veneris CBty ISha WFib
- 'Mairisii' see *A.* × *mairisii*
chilense WCot
hispidulum CBty CCCN ISha LRHS
- 'Bronze Venus' CCCN EBee GBin LRHS
§ × ***mairisii*** ♀H3 CBty ISha
pedatum misapplied see *A. aleuticum*
pedatum ambig. CBty EBee ISha
pedatum L. ♀H4 CBcs CHEx CLAP ECha EFer ELan ELon EPfP GEdr GMaP LAst LPBA LPot LRHS MBri SApp SPer SWat WFar WPGP
- Asiatic form see *A. aleuticum* 'Japonicum'
- 'Japonicum' see *A. aleuticum* 'Japonicum'
- 'Roseum' see *A. aleuticum* 'Japonicum'
- var. ***subpumilum*** see *A. aleuticum* 'Subpumilum'
raddianum 'Fragrans' see *A. raddianum* 'Fragrantissimum'
§ - 'Fragrantissimum' EShb
venustum ♀H4 CBty CGHE CHEx CLAP EFer EPot ISha IVic MCot MWat SChr SKHP SRms SWat WAbe WCot WFar WFib WHal WIvy WPGP

Adina (*Rubiaceae*)

rubella NLar

Adlumia (*Papaveraceae*)

fungosa CSpe LRHS

Adonis (*Ranunculaceae*)

amurensis misapplied see *A.* 'Fukujukai', *A. multiflora*
amurensis ambig. CMea EBee EPot GEdr LAma LEdu LLHF LRHS LWst SCnR WCot WFar

	- 'Pleniflora'	see *A. multiflora* 'Sandanzaki'
	brevistyla	WAbe
	'Chichibu-beni'	GEdr
	dahurica	LWst
§	'Fukujukai'	ECha GEdr LWst WFar
§	***multiflora***	EHrv SRot
	- 'Hakuju' new	GEdr
	- 'Hanazono' (d) new	GEdr
§	- 'Sandanzaki' (d)	EBee EPot EWes GEdr LRHS WCot
	vernalis	EBee GPoy LRHS MHoo NLar

Adoxa (*Adoxaceae*)

	moschatellina	CRWN NMen NRya WHer WSFF WShi

Aechmea (*Bromeliaceae*)

	sp.	XBlo
	caudata var. ***variegata***	CHEx
	fasciata ♀H1	XBlo
	ramosa	XBlo
	victoriana	XBlo

Aegle (*Rutaceae*)

	sepiaria	see *Poncirus trifoliata*

Aegopodium (*Apiaceae*)

	podagraria 'Dangerous' (v)	CHid
	- gold-margined (v)	EPPr
	- 'Variegatum' (v)	Widely available

Aeonium (*Crassulaceae*)

	sp.	CArn
	arboreum ♀H1	CAbb CDTJ CHEx EShb GCal SBfd SEND SMrm WNew
	- 'Atropurpureum' ♀H1	CAbb CHEx EAmu EShb LAst MAsh NEgg NPer SBfd SEND SPer SPoG SWal WCot WNew
I	- 'Magnificum'	ESwi ETod
	- 'Variegatum' (v)	NPer
	balsamiferum	CCCN CDTJ CHEx SBfd SChr
	'Black Cap'	CCCN
	'Blushing Beauty'	CAbb MAsh WCot
	canariense	CCCN CDTJ CHEx ETod
	castello-paivae	EShb SChr
	ciliatum	SPlb
	cuneatum	SEND
	decorum	SEND
*	- 'Variegatum' (v)	MAsh WCot
	'Dinner Plate'	CHEx
	'Dinner Plate' × ***haworthii***	CHEx
	haworthii ♀H1	CHEx SBHP SEND
	- 'Variegatum' (v)	EOHP EShb SChr
	hierrense	SPlb
	holochrysum Webb & Berth.	CAbb
	lindleyi	SChr
	nobile	CBrP
	percarneum	EShb
	simsii variegated (v)	EShb
	tabuliforme ♀H1	CCCN CDTJ CSpe EUJe SMad WCot
	urbicum	CHEx
	'Voodoo'	EAmu ETod
	'Zwartkop' ♀H1	Widely available

Aeschynanthus (*Gesneriaceae*)

	'Big Apple'	WDib
	Black Pagoda Group	WDib
	buxifolius KR 7798	WAbe
	'Fire Wheel'	WDib
	hildebrandii	WDib
	'Hot Flash'	WDib
	'Little Tiger'	WDib
	longicalyx	WDib
§	***longicaulis*** ♀H1	WDib
	marmoratus	see *A. longicaulis*
	radicans ♀H1	WDib
	'Scooby Doo'	WDib
	speciosus ♀H1	WDib

Aesculus ✿ (*Sapindaceae*)

	arguta	see *A. glabra* var. *arguta*
	× ***arnoldiana***	CDul CMCN
	- 'Autumn Splendor'	EPfP
	assamica WWJ 11886	WCru
§	× ***bushii***	CDul CMCN NLar
	californica	CBcs CDul CMCN CMac EPfP ERod SKHP WPGP
	× ***carnea***	CDul CTri SGol WHar
	- 'Aureomarginata' (v)	ERod LLHF WHar WPat
	- 'Briotii' ♀H4	CBcs CCVT CDoC CDul CLnd CMac CSBt CTho CTri CWib EBee ECrN ELan EPfP LBuc LRHS MBri MGos MMuc NLar NWea SCoo SEND SEWo SLim SPer SPoG WFar WHar
	- 'Plantierensis'	CDul ECrN MBri
*	- 'Variegata' (v)	CDul CMCN MGos
	chinensis	CMCN EGFP MBri
	flava ♀H4	CCVT CDul CLnd CMCN CTho EBee ECrN ELan EPfP EWTr LMaj MBri MMuc SEND SLim SSpi WFar
	- f. ***vestita***	CDul MBlu MBri NLar
	georgiana	see *A. sylvatica*
	glabra	CDul CMCN CTho
	- 'April Fire'	MBlu
§	- var. ***arguta***	CMCN
	- 'Autumn Blaze'	EPfP MBlu
	- 'October Red'	EPfP MBlu MBri
	glaucescens	see *A.* × *neglecta*
	hippocastanum ♀H4	CBcs CCVT CDul CLnd CMac CRWN CSBt CTho CTri CWib EBee ECrN ELan EPfP GAbr LAst LBuc MBri MGos MMuc MSwo NWea SBfd SEND SEWo SGol SLim SPer WFar WHar
	- 'Aureomarginata' (v)	CMac
§	- 'Baumannii' (d) ♀H4	CDoC CDul CLnd CMCN ECrN ELan EPfP ERod LMaj MGos MSwo NWea SPer WFar
	- 'Digitata'	CDul CMCN WPat
	- 'Flore Pleno'	see *A. hippocastanum* 'Baumannii'
	- 'Hampton Court Gold'	CBcs CDul CMCN CMac
	- f. ***laciniata***	CDul CMCN ERod IArd MAsh MBlu NLar SMad WCot WPat
	- 'Monstrosa'	WPat
	- 'Wisselink'	CDul CMCN ECrN MBlu SMad WPat
	indica	CDul CHEx CLnd CMCN ECrN ELan EPfP IDee LMaj MMuc SEND SGol
	- 'Sydney Pearce' ♀H4	CBcs CDul CJun CMCN EBee EPfP ERod EWTr GKin MBlu MBri MGos NLar SBrt SLim WPat
	× ***marylandica***	CDul WPat
	× ***mississippiensis***	see *A.* × *bushii*
	× ***mutabilis*** 'Harbisonii'	NLar WPat
	- 'Induta'	CDul CMCN EBee EPfP GBin IArd LRHS MBri NLar NSti SKHP WFar

§	- 'Penduliflora'	CDul
§	× ***neglecta***	CMCN
	- 'Autumn Fire'	EBee MBlu MBri SLim WPat
	- 'Erythroblastos' ♀H4	CBcs CDul CJun CMCN EPfP ERod MAsh MBlu MBri MRav SCoo SMad SPoG SSpi WCot WPat
	parviflora ♀H4	CBcs CDul CLnd CMCN CMac CTri EBee ELan EPfP EUJe EWTr GKin LMaj MBlu MGos MPkF MRav NEgg SEND SGol SLPl SLim SMad SPer SSpi SWvt WFar WHar
§	***pavia*** ♀H4	CBcs CDul CLnd CMCN EPfP
	- 'Atrosanguinea'	CLnd CMCN EPfP ERod MBlu MBri SKHP SMad
I	- 'Biltmore Buckeye'	MPkF
	- var. ***discolor*** 'Koehnei'	CDul CMCN EPfP MBlu MBri NLar
	- 'Penduliflora'	see *A.* × *mutabilis* 'Penduliflora'
	- 'Purple Spring'	MBri WPat
	- 'Rosea Nana'	CMCN LLHF WPat
	splendens	see *A. pavia*
§	***sylvatica***	CMCN
	turbinata	CBcs CDul
	wilsonii	CDul CPLG

Aethionema (*Brassicaceae*)

	armenum	EDAr GKev LLHF
	capitatum	EDAr
§	***grandiflorum*** ♀H4	EDAr GKev LRHS NBro SRms WFar
	- Pulchellum Group ♀H4	CSpe GKev
	iberideum	MDKP MWat SRms
*	***kotschyi*** hort.	WAbe
	membranaceum	CPBP EDAr WFar
	oppositifolium	LLHF MWat
	pulchellum	see *A. grandiflorum*
	schistosum	EDAr LLHF
	spicatum	WFar
	stylosum new	GKev
	'Warley Rose' ♀H4	ECho ELan EPot GJos GMaP LHop LRHS MAsh MSCN NBir NMen NRHS SBch SRms WFar WIce WThu
	'Warley Ruber'	CMea NBir NMen SBch WAbe WFar

Aethusa (*Apiaceae*)

cynapium	CSpe

Aextoxicon (*Aextoxicaceae*)

punctatum	CBcs

Afrocarpus (*Podocarpaceae*)

falcatus	ECou

Afrocrocus (*Iridaceae*)

unifolius from Roggeveld	ECho

Agapanthus ✿ (*Agapanthaceae*)

	sp.	XPde
	from Johannesburg	ECha
	'Aberdeen'	XPde
	'Adonis'	CPrp IBlr
	'African Moon'	CPen CPne CPrp
	'African Skies' new	CPne
	africanus misapplied	CElw CPLG CWCL CWib EBee EHrv ELan EPfP EUJe GAbr GHim LEdu LRHS MNHC MWat SChr SCob SPav SPer SRot SVic WBor WFar WPer WSpi WWEG XLum
	- 'Albus' misapplied	CBcs CDoC CPLG CWCL EBee ELan EPfP LSRN LRHS LTen MGos SDeJ SEND SPav SPer WBor WFar WHil WPer WWEG XLum
	'Aimee'	CBro
	'Albatross'	CPne
	'Albus' ambig.	GKev GMaP MGos MHer MWat SPad
	'Alice Gloucester' new	CPrp
	'Amsterdam'	CPen CPne EBee NHoy XPde
	'Angela'	CPen CPne CPrp CYeo ELon IBal NHoy XPde
	'Anthea'	XPde
	'Aphrodite'	IBlr
	'Apple Court'	XPde
	'Aquamarine'	CAvo NHoy
	'Arctic Star'	CCCN CKno CPLG CPen CPne CPou CPrp CTca CWCL CYeo ELon IBal LRHS LSou NHoy SDys SFai XPde
	Ardernei hybrid	CAvo CPLG CPrp ECha ECtt EWes EWoo GAbr GCal IBal IBlr LSou MAvo NEgg SMrm WCot WGwG WPGP WWEG XPde
§	'Argenteus Vittatus' (v) ♀H1	CPen CPrp NHoy
	'Atlas'	IBlr
	'Aureovittatus' (v)	IBal NHoy
	'Baby Blue'	see *A.* 'Blue Baby' Rom.
	'Baby Pete'	CPen SFai
	Back in Black = 'B in B'PBR	CPLG CWCL EBee ELan EPfP EWes MBNS MBri NBid NHoy NOrc NSti SMrm SPtl WFar
	'Ballerina'	CPne
	'Ballyrogan'	IBlr
	'Balmoral'	CPne
	'Bangor Blue'	IBlr
	'Barnfield Blue'	CPne
	'Barnsley'	NHoy
	'Basutoland'	LRHS
	'Beatrice'	CPne XPde
	'Beeches Dwarf'	ELan NHoy
	'Beloved'	NHoy
	'Ben Hope'	CBro IBal IBlr NHoy WCot XPde
	'Beth Chatto'	see *A. campanulatus* 'Albovittatus'
	'Bethlehem Star'	CPne
	'Bianco'	XPde
	'Bicton Bell'	IBal IBlr
	'Big Blue'	CMac CPrp EBee EPfP GKev LSRN LSou SBfd SEND SRkn
	Birr hybrids	WCot
	'Black Beauty' new	WSpi
	'Black Buddhist'	CPen CPrp EBee ECtt EPri GBuc LSou MAvo MGos NGdn NHoy NPri SPer SPtl WHil
	'Black Magic'	CPne
	'Black Pantha'PBR	Widely available
§	'Blue Baby' Rom.	CCCN CPen ELan ELon IBlr LRHS NHoy XPde
	'Blue Bird'	CPne LRHS NRHS SHil XPde
	'Blue Boy'	XPde
	'Blue Brush'	CMac CPen CPrp CSBt EBee EPfP IBal LRHS LSou NHoy SCoo SEND SFai WCot
	'Blue Cascade'	IBlr
	'Blue Companion'	CPne CPrp IBal IBlr NHoy WMnd
	'Blue Diamond' ambig.	CMac NHoy
	'Blue Dot'	CPrp EBee ECtt LLHF LRHS LSou NGdn SDys
	'Blue Dragon'	NHoy

	Name	Suppliers
	'Blue Formality'	IBal IBlr
	'Blue Giant'	CBro CCCN CKno CPen CPrp EBee EPfP IBlr LRHS MGos NHoy SWat WCFE WPGP WWEG
	'Blue Globe'	CHid CPen EPri GMaP LRHS MSCN WWEG
	'Blue Gown'	CSam
	'Blue Haze'	XPde
	'Blue Heaven'[PBR]	CPne EBee EWoo LHop MBri NHoy NPnk
	'Blue Horizons' **new**	EBee
	'Blue Ice'	CPen CPne CPou
	'Blue Imp'	CBro IBlr SApp
	'Blue Jay'	CPen
	'Blue Lakes'	XPde
	'Blue Méoni'	XPde
	'Blue Moon'	CAbP CAvo CBro CPen CYeo EBee ECha ECtt EWoo IBlr LRHS MAvo MNrw NHoy NLar SFai SPer WCot
	'Blue Nile'	CPne XPde
	'Blue Prince'	CPen LRHS NHoy
	'Blue Ribbon'	XPde
	'Blue Skies' ambig.	NCGa NHoy XPde
I	'Blue Skies' Dunlop	IBlr
	'Blue Sparkler'	CPne
	'Blue Spear'	CPen
	'Blue Triumphator'	CTca EBee EPfP EWTr EWll GMaP IBlr LRHS MHer NHoy NPla WSpi WWEG XPde
	'Blue Umbrella'	EBee NHoy
	'Blue Velvet'	CPne XPde
	blue-flowered	WCFE
	Bluestorm = 'Atiblu'[PBR]	EPfP NHoy
	'Bluety'[PBR]	CPen NHoy XPde
	'Bray Valley' **new**	CPne
	'Bressingham Blue'	CBro CPne CPrp CTri EWes GCal IBal IBlr LRHS MRav NHoy NRHS SFai SMHy SWat WSpi XPde
	'Bressingham Bounty'	IBal LRHS SFai XPde
	'Bressingham White'	CPne EBee ECGP EHrv LRHS MBri MRav NCGa NHoy SWat WSpi XPde
	'Bristol'	XPde
	'Brody'	CPne
	'Buckingham Palace'	CBro CDes CPrp EWes GAbr IBlr NHoy WCot WPGP XPde
	'Cally Blue'	GAbr GCal IBal NHoy
	'Cally Longstem'	EBee GCal
	'Cally Pale Blue'	GCal IBal
	'Cambridge'	XPde
	campanulatus	CMac CPrp EBee ELan EPfP EWTr GKin IBal IBlr IGor LRHS MCot MMuc MRav NEgg NHoy NSti SEND SWat WCot WPGP
	- var. ***albidus***	CYeo EBee ECha ELan EPfP EShb GKin IBlr LHop LRHS MMuc NBid NGdn NHol NHoy NMRc NSti SEND SPer WGwG WHoo WPGP XPde
§	- 'Albovittatus' (v)	CPrp ECho IBal LRHS LSou NHoy
	- bright blue-flowered	GCal
	- 'Buckland'	IBlr
	- 'Cobalt Blue'	CPrp EBee GBin GKin LRHS LSou MAsh MMuc NGdn NHoy SEND
	- dark blue-flowered	WSpi XPde
	- 'Oxford Blue'	CPrp IBal IBlr LRHS NHoy WSpi XPde
	- subsp. ***patens*** ♀H3	CPrp EBee EPfP IBal LRHS MRav SWat WPGP WSpi
	- - deep blue-flowered	CCon IBlr LRHS NHoy WWEG XPde
	- 'Profusion'	CBro CPne CPrp EBee ECha IBal IBlr LRHS NHoy XPde
	- variegated (v)	EBee ECha NPer
	- 'Wedgwood Blue'	CPrp EBee IBal IBlr LRHS NHoy NRHS WHil WSpi XPde
	- 'Wendy'	CPne EBee IBal IBlr LRHS NHoy NRHS XPde
	- 'White Hope'	IBal IBlr
	'Carefree'	CPrp IBal
	'Castle of Mey'	CBro CPLG CPen CPrp GAbr IBal IBlr LPla LRHS NHoy SMrm WPGP XPde
	'Catharina'	XPde
§	***caulescens*** ♀H1	EBee IBlr LRHS SMHy WPGP XPde
	- subsp. ***angustifolius***	CHid CPrp ELon IBlr SEND SPer WCot WPGP
	- subsp. ***caulescens***	IBlr SWat
	'Cedric Morris'	CPen IBlr NHoy XPde
	'Celebration'	CPne
	'Chandra'	IBlr
	'Charlotte'[PBR]	CMac CPen EBee EPfP LRHS NHoy SPoG XPde
	'Cherry Holley'	ELon XPde
	'Chika's Blue'	MAvo
	'Clarence House'	CBro CPen CPrp XPde
	'Cloudy Days'	CPne
	coddii	CPLG CPne EWes IBlr SMrm WCot XPde
	'Colin Edward'	NHoy
	'Columba'	CPen CYeo EBee ELon IBal LAma LDai NBid NHoy XPde
	comptonii	see *A. praecox* subsp. *minimus*
	'Congratulations'	NHoy
	'Cool Blue'	CPne XPde
	'Corina'	EBee
	'Cornish Sky'	CPne
	'Crystal Drop'	CPLG CPen CPne CPou CPrp EPri SWat WPGP
	'Dainty Lady'	NHoy
	Danube	see *A.* 'Donau'
	'Dartmoor'	CPne
	'Dawn Star'	CPne XPde
	'Debbie'	XPde
	'Delft'	CPrp IBal IBlr
	Dell Garden hybrids	LRHS
	'Density'	IBlr
	'Devon Dawn'	CPne
	'Diana'	XPde
	'Dnjepr'	XPde
	'Dokter Brouwer'	CCVN CPen CYeo EBee ECtt IBal IKil LRHS LSRN MCot MDKP NBid NHoy XPde
§	'Donau'	CBro CDoC CPen CYeo EBee EPri EShb GKev IBal LSou NBir NHoy NOrc SWat WHil XPde
	'Dorothy Edwards' **new**	SFai
	'Dorothy Kate'	CPne
	Double Diamond = 'Rfdd'	CPen CPne CWCL CWGN EBee EPri EWes IBal LBMP LRHS LSRN LSou NHoy SFai SPoG SUsu WSpi
	'Dream'	NHoy
	'Duivenbrugge Blue'	CPne XPde
	'Duivenbrugge White'	CPne EBee XPde
	dyeri	see *A. inapertus* subsp. *intermedius*
	'Early Blue' **new**	EWTr
	'Ed Carman' (v)	LSou

	'Eggesford Sky'	CPne
	'Elaine Anne'	NHoy
	'Elisabeth'	CPne XPde
	'Elizabeth Salisbury'	CPne
	'Enigma'	CAbb CBro CCCN CPLG CPen CPne CWCL CWGN CYeo EBee ECha EPri EShb EWoo IBal LRHS LSRN NHoy SBfd SFai SLon SPoG SRkn SWat WCot WSpi
	'Essence of Summer'	WCot
	'Ethel's Joy'	CPen
	'Eve'	IBlr XPde
	'Evening Star'	CPne ECha XPde
	'Exmoor'	CPne
	'Findlay's Blue'	SMHy WHil
	'Finnline' (v)	CPen CPne CPrp
	'Flanders Giant'	XPde
	'Flore Pleno' (d)	Widely available
	'Forget-me-not'	NHoy
	'Gayle's Lilac'	CBcs CElw CPLG CPen CPne CPrp CSam CYeo EBee ECtt ELan ELon EPfP EWoo GKin IBal LRHS LSRN LSou MAsh MRav NGdn NHoy NSti SApp SBfd SEND SMrm WWEG
	'Gem'	CPne ELon
I	'Giganteus Albus'	XPde
	'Glacier Stream'	CBro CPen EBee ECtt EHrv EPri GBuc IKil NHoy
	'Glen Avon'	CAbb CBro CCon CPLG CPen CPne CPrp CYeo EBee EWoo GBin IBal LRHS LSRN NHoy NLar SApp SCoo SFai SLon WSpi XPde
	'Golden Rule' (v)	CPrp EHoe GBuc IBal IBlr XPde
	'Goldfinger' (v)	CPne
	'Goliath'	CPne
	'Grey Ruler'	LSou
	'Hanneke'	CPen
	'Happy Birthday'	NHoy
	'Harvest Blue'	XPde
§	Headbourne hybrids	Widely available
	Headbourne hybrids dark blue-flowered	GBuc LRHS
	Headbourne hybrids dwarf	GBuc LRHS
	'Headbourne White'	CAvo EPri
	'Heather Gail'	NHoy
	'Heavenly Blue'	CCCN CPne
	'Helen'	IBlr
	'Holbeach'	CPen XPde
	'Holbrook'	CSam XPde
	'Holly Ann'	NHoy
	'Hoyland'	NHoy
	'Hyacinth'	NHoy
	'Hydon Mist'	XPde
	'Ice Blue Star'	CPne XPde
	'Ice Lolly'	CBro CPen IKil XPde
	inapertus	CAvo CBro CPrp CSpe EWes SAga SMHy SMrm SWat WCot WPGP WSpi XPde
	- dwarf	IBlr
	- subsp. ***hollandii***	CPom GCal IBal IBlr NHoy SWat WCot XPde
	- - 'Zealot'	IBlr
	- 'Ice Cascade'	CPen EBee IBal LSou NHoy SBfd SWat
	- 'Icicle'	GCal
	- subsp. ***inapertus***	IBlr SWat
I	- - 'Albus'	EPPr IBlr LRHS
	- - 'Cyan'	IBlr

	- - 'White'	CPne CPrp
§	- subsp. ***intermedius***	CBro CPrp EBee EPfP IBlr NHoy SWat
	- - 'Long Tom'	CPLG EPri WPGP
	- - white-flowered	CPen CPou
	- large	IBal
	- 'Little Black Number'	CPen
	- 'Margaret'	EBee
	- 'Midnight Cascade'	CPLG CPar CPen CPne EBee IBal IPot LSou NBid NHoy SBfd SWat
I	- 'Nigrescens'	CPen
	- subsp. ***parviflorus***	IBlr
	- subsp. ***pendulus***	CCon CPne IBlr LRHS WPGP
	- - 'Graskop'	CAbb CBcs CCCN CCon CPLG CPen CPne CSpe CYeo EBee ELon EPfP EPri EWoo GBin IBal IBlr LRHS LSou NHoy SBfd SFai SKHP SPoG WPGP XPde
	- - 'Violet Dusk'	IBlr
	- 'Sapphire Cascade'	CPen CYeo IBal LSou NHoy SBfd SWat
	'Indigo Dreams' **new**	CPne
	'Inkspots'	CAbb CCCN CMac CPen CSpe CWCL EBee IBal LRHS LSou SBfd SFai SPoG SUsu
	'Innocence'	IBlr
	'Intermedius' Leichtlin	IBal XPde
I	'Intermedius' van Tubergen	EBee NBid
	'Isis'	CAvo CBro CCon CPne CPrp CSam CTri EBee ECha GBuc IBal IBlr LRHS MAvo NHoy WSpi XPde
	'Jack Elliott'	MAvo
	'Jack's Blue'	Widely available
	'James' **new**	CPne
	'Jersey Giant'	NHoy XPde
	'Jodie'	CPne ELon XPde
	'Johanna'	CPen EBee XPde
	Johannesberg hybrids	EPfP
	'Jolanda'	CPrp ELon
	'K. Wiley'	SUsu WSHC
	'Kalmthout Blue'	CSpe
	'Kingston Blue'	IBal IBlr IGor NBid NHoy WSHC WWEG XPde
	'Kobaltglocke'	EBee
	'Kobold'	CBro NHoy
	'Lady Edith'	IBlr
§	'Lady Grey'	IBlr
	'Lady Moore'	CBro CSpe IBlr IGor SMHy XPde
	'Lapis'	CPne IBal
	'Latent Blue'	IBlr
	'Lavender Haze'	CPen CPne EBee EPfP IBal LRHS LSou NHoy SFai WSpi
	'Leicester'	CPen CPne XPde
	'Liam's Lilac'	CPLG CPar CPen CPne CPou EBee ELon EWoo IBal LRHS SFai WCot
	'Lilac Flash'	CPen CPne
	'Lilac Time'	CPLG CPne CPrp IBlr SAga SFai WCot XPde
	'Lilliput'	CBcs CBro CMac CMea CPrp CSpe EBee ECha ECtt ELan EPfP GBuc GKev GMaP IBal LHop LRHS MAvo MRav NGdn SApp SMrm SUsu WCFE WFar XPde
	'Limoges'	XPde
	'Little Beauty'	NHoy
	'Little White'	CPen
	'Littlecourt'	CBro
	'Loch Hope' ♀^{H3}	CAvo CBro CDoC CPne CSam EBee ELon EPfP EWoo GAbr

Name	Suppliers
	GCal IBal LRHS LSou MRav NHoy NRHS SApp SFai WCot WGwG WHoo XPde
'Lowland Nursery'	XPde
'Luly'	CPen CPrp EPfP IBal LRHS NHoy SHil SWat XPde
'Luna' **new**	EBee
'Lydenburg'	CPen CPne CPrp EPri IBal IBlr NHoy
'Lyn Valley'	CPne
'Mabel Grey'	see *A.* 'Lady Grey'
'Magnifico'	IBal IBlr
'Malaga'	XPde
'Malvern Hills'	XPde
'Marchants Cobalt Cracker'	SMHy
'Marcus'	CPne
'Margaret'	EBee IBal NHoy
'Maria' **new**	CPne
'Marianne'	XPde
'Mariètte'	CPen EBee XPde
'Marjorie'	CPne SApp XPde
'Martine'	CPen EBee
'Maureen'	CPne
'May Snow' (v)	WCot
'Megan's Mauve'	CPne CPou ELon EPri SFai
'Meibont' (v)	CPne IBal WCot XPde
'Mercury'	IBlr
'Metalica'	NHoy
Midknight Blue = 'Monmid'	LRHS NHoy
'Midnight'	CPen EWes SAga WSHC WSpi
'Midnight Blue' ambig.	CMea CPen CPne EBee ELan IBal IGor MGos MHer SFai
'Midnight Blue' P. Wood	GCal IBlr
'Midnight Dream' **new**	CPen
§ 'Midnight Star'	Widely available
'Miniature Blue'	SWat
'Misty Dawn' (v)	EBee IBal WCot
mixed seedlings	CPne EPfP IBal MGos NHoy NOrc WHil XPde
mixed white-flowered	WCFE
'Montreal'	XPde
'Mood Indigo'	CPne
'Moonshine'	CPen
I 'Mooreanus' misapplied	EBee EPfP IBal IGor NBid XPde
'Morning Star'	CPne
'Mount Stewart'	IBal IBlr
'My Love'	NHoy
'Navy Blue'	see *A.* 'Midnight Star'
'New Love'	EBee
'New Orleans'	XPde
'Newa'	XPde
'Night Sky'	CPne
'Nikki'	CPne
'Norman Hadden'	IBlr
'Northern Light'	CPen EBee LLHF
'Northern Star' PBR	CAbb CKno CPLG CPen CPne CPrp CYeo EBee ELon EWes EWoo GBin IBal LBMP LRHS LSou SBfd SFai SLon SPoG WPGP WWlt
nutans	see *A. caulescens*
'Nyx'	IBlr
'NZ Blue'	XPde
'NZ White'	XPde
'Oslo'	CPne NHoy XPde
'Oxbridge'	IBlr
'Pacific Blue' **new**	EBee
Palmer's hybrids	see *A.* Headbourne hybrids
'Paris'	CPen XPde
'Patent Blue'	CPrp IBlr
'Patriot'	CYeo EPfP LRHS MBri NRHS SHil
'Pauline'	NHoy
'Penelope Palmer'	CPrp IBlr
'Penny Slade'	SAga XPde
'Peter Franklin' **new**	CPne
'Peter Pan' ambig.	Widely available
'Peter Pan White' **new**	EBee
'Petite White' **new**	CPne
'Phantom'	CDes CPne GCal IBal IBlr SFai XPde
'Pinchbeck'	XPde
Pine Cottage hybrids	CPne
'Pinky'	XPde
'Pinocchio'	CPen CWib EBee NHol NHoy XPde
'Plas Merdyn Blue'	CPrp IBlr
'Plas Merdyn White'	CPne CPrp IBlr NHoy XPde
'Podge Mill'	CPne IBlr SMHy XPde
'Polar Ice'	CCon CPen CPne CYeo EBee ECtt ELon EPri GAbr IBal IBlr IBoy LRHS SMad WCAu WSpi XPde
'Polar White'	NHoy
'Porcelain'	IBal IBlr
praecox	CPrp EShb GAbr IBal IBlr LRHS NHoy
- 'Albiflorus'	CBro CPne CPou CPrp CTri EPri ERom IBal LRHS NEgg NHoy SEND WSpi XPde
- 'Floribundus'	SWat
- 'Maximus Albus'	CPou IBal IBlr
§ - subsp. ***minimus***	CElw CPne CPou EWTr GAbr IBal IBlr NHoy SWat WCot XPde
- - 'Adelaide'	CPrp
- - blue-flowered	SWat
- - white-flowered	CPne SWat
- 'Neptune'	IBlr
§ - subsp. ***orientalis***	CBro CCCN CPne CSut IBlr IBoy SBfd SWat
- - 'Cape Blue'	CPrp
- - 'Mount Thomas' **new**	CPrp
- - 'Silver Star' (v)	CPen NHoy
- subsp. ***praecox***	IBlr
- - azure-flowered	CPrp SWat
- - 'Variegatus'	see *A.* 'Argenteus Vittatus'
- 'Saturn'	IBlr
- Slieve Donard form	IBlr
- 'Uranus'	IBlr
- 'Venus'	IBlr
- 'Vittatus' (v)	NHoy
'Premier'	CPrp EBee IBal IBlr LRHS NHoy NRHS
'Pride of Bicton'	CPne
'Princess Margaret'	CPne XPde
'Proteus'	XPde
§ 'Purple Cloud'	Widely available
'Purple Haze'	CPen
'Purple Star'	CCCN CKno
'Queen Anne'	NHoy
'Queen Mother'	LRHS XPde
Queen Mum = 'Pmn06'	CPen CPne EBee IBal MBri SFai SHil
'Quink Drops'	SMHy
'Radiant Star'	EBee IBal NHoy
'Raveningham Hall'	XPde
'Regal Beauty'	CPar CPen CPne CSBt CSev EBee EShb EWoo IBal LRHS LSRN LSou NBid NHoy NLar SBfd SFai SRkn WSpi
'Remembrance'	NHoy
'Rhapsody in Blue' **new**	CPne

	Name	Suppliers
	'Rhone'	IBlr XPde
	rich blue-flowered	XPde
	'Rosemary'	SAga XPde
	'Rosewarne'	CBcs CCCN CKno CMac CPLG EBee EPfP GBin IBal IBlr LRHS NHoy NLar SFai XPde
	'Rotterdam'	CPen EBee NHoy XPde
	'Royal Blue'	CBro GMaP NHol NHoy SBfd
	'Royal Lodge'	XPde
	'Royal Purple'	XPde
	'Sally Anne'	CPne
	'San Gabriel' (v)	CPne XPde
	'Sandringham'	CDes CPen CPne CPrp EWes IBlr WPGP XPde
	'Sapphire'	IBlr XPde
	'Sarah'[PBR]	CPen LSou NHoy
	'Sea Coral'	CCCN CCon CMac CPne CPrp EBee GAbr LRHS MAsh MAvo NHoy NSti SHom WGwG
	'Sea Foam'	CMac CPen CPne EBee IBal NLar SBfd XPde
	'Sea Mist'	CCCN CPne IBal
	'Sea Spray'	CCCN CKno IBal LRHS LSRN NHoy XPde
	'Selma Bock'	CPen
	'Senna'[PBR]	CPLG EBee IBal LRHS LSou NHoy
	'Septemberhemel'	CPen XPde
	'Sevilla'	XPde
	'Silver Anniversary'	NHoy
	'Silver Baby'	CKno CPen CPne CPrp CWGN CYeo ELon EPfP LRHS MAvo MNrw NHoy WHil
	'Silver Jubilee'	XPde
	'Silver Lining'	EBee ECtt IBal NHoy
	'Silver Mist'	CPen CPne EBee IBlr LRHS SWat XPde
	Silver Moon = 'Notfred'[PBR] (v)	CPen CPne ELan EPfP EWes EWoo GBin IBal LBMP LRHS LSou MGos NHoy NSti SFai SPer SPoG XPde
	'Silver Sceptre'	IBlr
	'Silver Stream'	NHoy
	'Sky'	CAbb CPar CPne CSBt CYeo EBee EWoo GBin IBal IBlr LRHS LSRN LSou NBid SBfd SFai SKHP SPoG SRkn SRms SWat WCot WSpi XPde
	'Sky Rocket'	IBal IBlr
	'Sky Star'	IBal XPde
	'Slieve Donard'	IBlr
	'Sneeuwwitje'	XPde
	'Snow Cloud'	CAbb CBro CPLG CPen CPne CSBt EBee EPfP IBal LRHS NEgg NHoy SBfd SFai SLon XPde
	'Snow Pixie'	CBro CSpe CWGN EBee IBal LSRN LSou NHoy SFai WSpi
	'Snow Princess'	CPen EPfP IBal LRHS
	'Snow Shadows'	CBro
	'Snow White'	GBin
	'Snowball'	CBcs CDoC COlW CPLG CPen CPne CYeo EBee LRHS LSou NHoy SBfd WWEG XPde
	'Snowdrops'	CCCN IBal LHop LSRN MNrw SApp SKHP SMrm
	'Sofie'	CPen EWoo NHoy
	'Southern Star'	CPne
	'Spokes'	IBlr
	'Starburst'	IBlr
	'Stars and Stripes'	EBee IBal LBuc LRHS SFai
	'Stéphanie'	XPde

	Name	Suppliers
	'Stéphanie Charm'	CPen XPde
	'Stockholm' **new**	CPrp SMad
	'Storm Cloud' Reads	see *A.* 'Purple Cloud'
	'Storm Cloud' (d)	CBro CCon
	'Streamline'	Widely available
	'Summer Clouds'	CPne ELan NHoy
	'Summer Delight' **new**	CPne
	'Summer Skies'	CPne IBal NHoy
	'Sunfield'	CKno CPen CPrp EBee EPfP IBal LAma LRHS LSRN NHoy NPer XPde
	'Sunset Dreams' **new**	CPne
	'Sunset Skies' **new**	CPne
	'Super Star'	CPne XPde
I	'Supreme'	IBal IBlr
	'Suzan'	XPde
	'Sylvia'[PBR]	NHoy
	'Sylvine'	CPen CPne XPde
	'Tall Boy'	IBal IBlr
	'Tarka'	CPLG CPen CPne CPrp CWCL CYeo EBee ELon IBal LSou NLar SDys SFai
	'Taw Valley'	CKno CPen CPne CPrp CYeo ELon SFai SLon WPGP
	'Thumbelina'	CBro CKno CMac CPne CSev CWCL EBee EPfP EWoo IBal LSou NHoy SFai
	'Timaru'	Widely available
	'Tinkerbell' (v)	Widely available
	'Tiny Tim'	EBee XPde
	'Titan'	IBlr
	'Tom Thumb'	CAvo COlW CPLG ECtt EPfP IBal LRHS LSou NHoy SFai SRot WGor
	'Torbay'	CPne CPrp CYeo EAEE EBee ECtt ELon EShb GCal GKin IBlr LRHS NCGa NEgg WHoo WWEG XPde
	'Tornado'	CPen EBee ECGP ECtt ELon GBin IBal LPla LRHS MNrw NHoy WCot
	'Tranquil'	NHoy
	Tresco hybrid	CHEx
	'Tresco Select'	NHoy
	'Triangle'	CPen CPne
	'Trudy'	XPde
	'Twilight'	IBlr
	umbellatus L'Hérit.	see *A. africanus*
	umbellatus Redouté	see *A. praecox* subsp. *orientalis*
	'Underway'	EWes GCal GKev IBal IBlr XPde
	'Vague Bleue'	XPde
	'Velvet Night'	CPen
	'Violetta'	CPne
	'Virginia'	XPde
	'Wavy Navy'	CPen
	'Wedding Day'	CPne
	'Wembworthy'	CPne
	'White Avon' **new**	CPen
	'White Dragon'	NHoy
	'White Dwarf'	see *A.* white dwarf hybrids
§	white-flowered, dwarf	CBro CPen CPne ECha ECtt EPfP EShb GBuc IBal LRHS MAsh NBir NGdn SEND SHil WFar
	'White Heaven'[PBR]	CHVG CKno CPen CPne CSev CSpe EBee ECtt ELon EWoo GAbr IBal LHop LPla LRHS LSou MAvo MBel MBri MNrw NHoy NPnk SEND SFai SMrm SUsu SWat WCot WWEG XPde
	'White Ice'	CBcs CPen LRHS SApp
	'White Orb'	NHoy

'White Smile' EPri
'White Star' XPde
'White Starlet' NHoy XPde
'White Superior' CPen GMaP LAst SPet WCAu WHil XPde
'White Triumphator' WCot WSpi
'White Umbrella' LRHS NHoy
white-flowered CHEx
'Whitestorm' NHoy
'Whitney'PBR CPen IBlr
'Windlebrooke' CCCN CPne ECha EPri XPde
'Windsor Castle' CPen CPrp IBal IBlr XPde
'Windsor Grey' Widely available
'Winsome' IBlr
'Winter Sky' XPde
'Wolga' CBro EWll
'Wolkberg' Kirstenbosch IBlr
'Yellow Tips' CPne XPde
'Yolande' LAma
'Yves Klein' CPrp IBlr
'Zachary' CPen CPne CPou CPrp CYeo ELon IBal LRHS
'Zebra' NHoy
'Zella Thomas' EBee XPde
'Zomba' CPne

Agapetes (*Ericaceae*)

'Ludgvan Cross' ♀H1-2 CCCN CDoC CTsd EBee SSpi
serpens ♀H1 CCCN CHEx CWib EShb SLon
- 'Scarlet Elf' CCCN EBee LRHS WCot
smithiana var. ***major*** GGGa

Agastache (*Lamiaceae*)

'After Eight' EBee NCGa NDov
anethiodora see *A. foeniculum* (Pursh) Kuntze
anisata see *A. foeniculum* (Pursh) Kuntze
aurantiaca CMea NLar SEND SPhx
- 'Apricot Sprite' EBee EPfP LDai MBri MHer MNHC MSCN NEgg NGdn SGar SRkn SUsu
'Black Adder' Widely available
'Blue Delight' SBch
'Blue Fortune' ♀H3-4 CBcs EBee LHop MBri MCot NDov SMrm SPer SPhx SWvt WWEG
§ ***cana*** LDai SPhx
- 'Purple Pygmy' CSpe EPfP LHop SMrm SPer SRot
'Cotton Candy' EBee
'Firebird' EAEE EBee ECtt ELan GKin LHop LSou MBri SMrm SPer SWat SWvt WAul WWEG
foeniculum misapplied see *A. rugosa*
§ ***foeniculum*** (Pursh) Kuntze CArn CMea EBee ECha EGHP ELan ENfk GMaP GPoy MCot MHer MHoo MNHC SPav SPhx SRms WJek WPer WWEG
- 'Alabaster' CBcs EBee NLar
- 'Alba' EGHP NBre SBfd SHDw SPav
'Giant' SUsu
'Globetrotter' EBee
'Glowing Embers' ECtt
'Heatwave' EBee NCGa WCot
'Kolibri' EBee
'Linda' EBee NDov
§ ***mexicana*** LDai SMrm SPav
- 'Marchants Pink' SMrm
- 'Red Fortune'PBR CWGN EAEE EBee ECtt EPPr LHop LSou MBel MBri NEgg NSti SMrm SPad SUsu WCot
- 'Rosea' see *A. cana*
- 'Sangria' EBee EDif ELon LHop NDov NGdn SBch SBfd SPad SPhx
nepetoides SPav
'Painted Lady' CSpe ECtt SAga WTcb
pallidiflora **new** SPhx
- var. ***neomexicana*** 'Lavender Haze' EPfP MRav
'Pink Perfume'PBR **new** EBee
'Pink Pop' EBee EPfP SPhx
'Purple Candle' EWes
'Purple Haze' EBee NDov
'Raspberry Summer'PBR EBee ECtt LSou NCGa NDov NLar SBfd
'Rose Mint' CSpe
§ ***rugosa*** CArn ELau GPoy LEdu LHop MHoo MNHC NEgg SPav SPhx SWat WHfH WJek WMoo WPer
- B&SWJ 4187 from Korea WCru
- f. ***albiflora*** NBre NEgg
- - 'Liquorice White' EPfP MBel MHoo NLar SMrm SPer SPlb
- 'Golden Jubilee'PBR CSpe EAEE EBee ECha ECtt ELan ELon EPfP IBoy LDai LHop MHer MNHC MSpe MWat NLar NOrc NSti SBea SBfd SPoG SUsu WFar WHil WJek WMoo WPer WWEG XLum
- 'Korean Zest' WCru
- 'Liquorice Blue' EPfP MBel NEgg NGBl NGdn NLar NOrc SBfd SPer SPoG SWvt WFar WHrl WMoo WPer
- pink-flowered CEnt
rupestris CSpe EDif NLar SBch SPhx
- 'Apache Sunset' ELon MBri SBch SPlb
'Serpentine' EBee NDov SPhx
'Summer Fiesta' **new** LSou NCGa SUsu
'Summer Glow' CWGN EBee ECtt LSou NCGa SUsu
'Summer Love'PBR EBee LSou NCGa NDov NLar SUsu
'Summer Sky' **new** EBee NCGa NDov
'Tangerine Dreams' ♀H3 CDoC EBee ECtt EDif EPfP LHop LSou NCGa NEgg NGdn SBch SCoo SMrm SPoG SUsu WWlt
'Tutti-frutti' EBee ECtt NCGa SPhx
urticifolia CSpe
- 'Alba' CSpe WPer

Agathaea see *Felicia*

Agathis (*Araucariaceae*)

australis CBrP CDoC

Agathosma (*Rutaceae*)

ovata CCCN

Agave ✿ (*Asparagaceae*)

albomarginata CDTJ EGri
americana ♀H1 CAbb CBcs CBen CDoC CHEx CTrC EAmu EGri EPfP EShb EUJe IBlr LRHS MWat SBfd SBod SBst SChr SEND SMad SPer SPlb SPoG STrG SWvt
- 'Marginata' (v) ♀H3-4 CBrP CDTJ CHll IBlr MAvo MREP NLBP SEND WCot WSFF
- 'Mediopicta' misapplied see *A. americana* 'Mediopicta Alba'
- 'Mediopicta' (v) ♀H1 CDTJ CHEx ETod SBig
§ - 'Mediopicta Alba' (v) ♀H1 CBrP CDTJ EAmu EShb ESwi SBfd SChr SEND WCot
- 'Mediopicta Aurea' (v) WCot

- subsp. ***protamericana***	EGri
- - blue **new**	EBee
- subsp. ***protamericana*** × ***scabra*** F&M 310	WPGP
- 'Striata' (v)	EShb WCot
- 'Variegata' (v) ♀H1	CAbb CBcs CBen CCse CDoC CHEx EAmu EGri EPfP EShb EUJe EWes LEdu LHop LRHS MBel MGos MRav MWat NPer NPla SBfd SBst SChr SMad SPer SPlb SPoG SWvt WCot
angustifolia	see *A. vivipara* var. *vivipara*
- var. ***marginata*** hort.	SBig WCot
applanata	EGri WPGP
× ***arizonica***	EGri
asperrima	CDTJ EGri
§ - subsp. ***maderensis***	SPlb
atrovirens **new**	WCot
- var. ***mirabilis***	EGri
- - F&M 245	WPGP
attenuata	CAbb CBrP EAmu SBig SPlb WPGP
avellanidens	EGri
beauleriana	EAmu EGri SBig
boldinghiana	WCot
bovicornuta	WCot
bracteosa	CCCN EGri SChr
celsii	see *A. mitis* var. *mitis*
chiapensis	EGri
chrysantha	CCCN CTrC EBee EGri ETod WCot WGrn WPGP
- 'Black Canyon'	WCot
chrysoglossa	WPGP
colimana	see *A. ortgiesiana*
colorata	CCCN CDTJ WCot
'Cornelius'	WCot
cupreata	EGri ETod
datylio	EGri
de-meesteriana	EAmu
- var. ***marginata*** (v)	EAmu
deserti	CDoC LRHS WCot
difformis	EGri ETod
- NJM 05.034	WPGP
durangensis	SPlb
elongata	see *A. vivipara* var. *vivipara*
felgeri	CDTJ
ferdinandi-regis	see *A. victoriae-reginae*
ferox	see *A. salmiana* var. *ferox*
filifera ♀H1	CCCN CDTJ CHEx EAmu ETod SChr SEND SPlb WCot
flexispina	EGri ETod SPlb
garciae-mendozae	CDTJ
- NJM 05.073	WPGP
geminiflora	CCCN CDTJ EAmu EShb WCot
gentryi	CDTJ EGri ETod
- F&M 213A	WPGP
ghiesbreghtii	EAmu EGri
gigantea	see *Furcraea foetida*
goldmaniana	see *A. shawii* subsp. *goldmaniana*
× ***gracilipes***	WPGP
guadalajarana	CDTJ EGri WCot WPGP
havardiana	CTrC EAmu EGri EUJe WCot WPGP XSen
- DJH 1326	WCot
horrida	EGri ETod SBig
- subsp. ***horrida***	SPlb
- 'Perotensis'	EGri EShb
hurteri	CDTJ EGri
impressa	WCot
kerchovei	WCot
lechuguilla	CDTJ EGri SChr WPGP XSen
lophantha	see *A. univittata*
- var. ***caerulescens***	see *A. univittata*
§ 'Macha Mocha'	WCot
macroacantha	CDTJ
maculosa	WCot WPGP
marmorata	WCot
maximilliana	SPlb
mitis var. ***albidior***	EGri
§ - var. ***mitis***	CDoC EAmu EGri
- var. ***mitis*** × ***variegata***	WCot
mitriformis	EGri
montana	CDTJ CGHE EAmu EBee EGri ETod EUJe SBst SChr SMad SPlb WCot
- F&M 221	WPGP
- F&M 289	WPGP
neomexicana	CCCN EAmu EBee EGri ETod EUJe WPGP
- S&B 948	WCot
× ***nigra*** hort.	EAmu EGri
nizandensis	CHEx
§ ***obscura***	CDTJ EGri ETod
ocahui	EGri ETod
oroensis	WCot
§ ***ortgiesiana***	EGri
ovatifolia	EGri SKHP SPlb
- NJM 09.002	WPGP
palmeri	CCCN CTrC EBee WPGP
panamana	see *A. vivipara* var. *vivipara*
parrasana	EAmu EGri EUJe SChr WPGP
parryi	CDTJ CDoC EAmu EGri ETod GKev MDev SBst SChr SPlb WPGP XSen
- var. ***couesii***	SKHP XSen
- 'Cream Spike' (v)	WCot
- var. ***huachucensis***	CDTJ WCot
- 'Ohi-kissho-ten-nishiki' (v)	WCot
- subsp. ***parryi***	CDTJ WCot WPGP
- - JCA 1.035.000	WPGP
- small **new**	EGri
- small, variegated (v) **new**	EGri
- var. ***truncata***	EAmu EGri
parviflora ♀H1	EGri WCot
pendula	EGri
polyacantha F&M 120	WPGP
- var. ***xalapensis***	see *A. obscura*
potatorum ♀H1	EGri ETod
- var. ***verschaffeltii***	EAmu
rzedowskiana **new**	EGri
salmiana	CDTJ EAmu EGri SBig SPlb
- F&M 290	WPGP
- subsp. ***crassispina***	SPlb
§ - var. ***ferox***	CDTJ CDoC CTrC EAmu EGri ETod MDev MREP SBig WCot
scabra	CCCN CDoC EBee EGri
- subsp. ***maderensis***	see *A. asperrima* subsp. *maderensis*
schidigera	EGri ETod WCot
- 'Shira-ito-no-ohi' (v)	WCot
schottii	CDTJ EGri WCot
'Sharkskin'	WCot
§ ***shawii*** subsp. ***goldmaniana***	EGri
shrevei	ETod
- subsp. ***magna***	EGri SPlb
sileri	WCot
sisalana	EAmu ETod

- 'Variegata' (v) EAmu
stictata WCot
striata EAmu EGri ETod WCot
* - ***rubra*** CDTJ SPlb
stricta ♀H1 CCCN CDTJ EAmu EGri ETod MREP WCot
- blue-leaved ETod
- dwarf CBrP
- 'Nana' CDTJ
tequilana variegated (v) WCot
titanota EAmu
toumeyana CAbb EGri WCot
- var. ***bella*** CDTJ
triangularis CDTJ EGri ETod
§ ***univittata*** CDTJ EGri WCot
- 'Quadricolor' (v) WCot
utahensis ♀H1 EGri ETod SEND XSen
- var. ***eborispina*** EGri
- var. ***nevadensis*** EGri
variegata WCot
- B&SWJ 10234 WCru
§ ***victoriae-reginae*** ♀H1 CBrP CCCN CDTJ EAmu EGri EShb SWal
- variegated (v) EGri
virginica WCot
§ ***vivipara*** var. ***vivipara*** EGri SBig WCot
vizcainoensis EGri
weberi EAmu
wocomahi EGri
xylonacantha EGri ETod SChr SPlb WCot
- blue-leaved **new** EGri
zebra EGri

Ageratina (*Asteraceae*)

§ ***altissima*** CHid CMac EBee ELan EPfP LRHS MCot WHfH WTin
- 'Braunlaub' CPrp EBee ECtt LPla LRHS NBir NBre SEND SWat WHrl WMnd WPtf
- 'Chocolate' ♀H4 Widely available
§ ***aromatica*** CFis EBee MRav NBro SWat WSFF
§ ***ligustrina*** ♀H3 CMHG CPLG CRHN CTri EBee ECha EHoe ELan EPfP GCal LHop LRHS MBlu NCGa SAga SDix SEND SLim SPer SPoG SRkn SUsu WMnd WPGP WPat WSFF WSHC
§ ***occidentalis*** NNS 94-53 WCot

Ageratum (*Asteraceae*)

'Blue Champion' **new** NPri
corymbosum CHII CSpe EShb
houstonianum 'High Tide Blue' **new** NPri

Agonis (*Myrtaceae*)

flexuosa CCCN

Agrimonia (*Rosaceae*)

eupatoria CArn CHab CRWN EBee ENfk GPoy MHer MHoo MNHC NMir SIde SWat WHer WHfH
* - var. ***alba*** NLar
grandiflora EBee
odorata misapplied see *A. procera*
odorata (L.) Mill. see *A. repens*
pilosa CArn EBee
§ ***procera*** EBee
§ ***repens*** WMoo

Agropyron (*Poaceae*)

glaucum see *Elymus hispidus*
magellanicum see *Elymus magellanicus*
pubiflorum see *Elymus magellanicus*

Agrostemma (*Caryophyllaceae*)

coronaria see *Lychnis coronaria*
githago CHab MNHC SBch
- 'Ocean Pearl' CSpe

Agrostis (*Poaceae*)

calamagrostis see *Stipa calamagrostis*
§ ***canina*** 'Silver Needles' (v) EWes LRHS NBir WWEG
capillaris CHab
§ ***montevidensis*** NWsh SMad
nebulosa CKno SPhx
- 'Fibre Optics' see *Panicum* 'Fibre Optics'
stolonifera 'Julia Ann' (v) WCot

Aichryson (*Crassulaceae*)

× ***aizoides*** EBak WCot
var. ***domesticum*** 'Variegatum' (v) ♀H1

Ailanthus (*Simaroubaceae*)

§ ***altissima*** CBcs CCVT CDul CHEx CMac CPLG EBee EPfP EUJe IDee LEdu MBlu NWea SEND SPer SPlb SWvt
- var. ***tanakae*** CWJ 12452 WCru
- - RWJ 9906 WCru
glandulosa see *A. altissima*

Ainsliaea (*Asteraceae*)

acerifolia B&SWJ 4795 WCru
- var. ***subapoda*** B&SWJ 11537 **new** WCru
apiculata B&SWJ 11397 WCru
- var. ***acerifolia*** B&SWJ 6059 **new** WCru
chapaensis B&SWJ 11720 WCru
aff. ***elegans*** WWJ 11720 WCru
nervosa B&SWJ 11344 WCru
petelotii B&SWJ 11732 WCru
tonkinensis B&SWJ 11819 WCru
uniflora GEdr
- B&SWJ 11336 WCru

Ajania (*Asteraceae*)

§ ***pacifica*** EBee
- 'Mimosa White' **new** EBee
- 'Silver Edge' XLum

Ajuga (*Lamiaceae*)

ciliata var. ***villosior*** CCon MAvo
genevensis LRHS SPhx
- 'Tottenham' WOut
incisa EBee GCal
- 'Bikun' (v) CLAP LRHS SRGP WCot
- 'Blue Enigma' CLAP CPLG EBee EWes NCGa
- 'Blue Ensign' LDai
'Little Court Pink' see *A. reptans* 'Purple Torch'
lupulina EBee
metallica hort. see *A. pyramidalis*
'Pink Spires' EBee NCot
§ ***pyramidalis*** CArn LRHS
- 'Metallica Crispa' CBct EBee ECho ECtt ELan EPPr EPfP EPri EWes GKin LRHS NBir NHol NLar SRms SWvt WCot WFar

reptans	CArn CHab CRWN CTri CWan EBee ECtt ENfk GKev GPoy LPBA LRHS MCot MHer MHoo MNHC NMir SGar WFar WJek
- f. ***albiflora***	CBar CRow LRHS WHfH
- - 'Alba'	CArn CBre EBee ECtt EPfP MRav NBro SBfd SRms WCAu WFar WMoo
- - 'Sanne'	EBee
- 'Arctic Fox' (v)	EBee ECho LSou MRav MSCN NRya SWvt WFar WHer
- 'Argentea'	see *A. reptans* 'Variegata'
§ - 'Atropurpurea'	CBar CWan EBee ECha ECho ELan EPfP GAbr LPBA LRHS MGos MLHP MSpe SGol SPer SPlb SRms SWvt WBrk WFar WJek WPer WWEG
- Black Scallop = 'Binblasca'PBR	Widely available
- 'Braunherz'	Widely available
- 'Bronze Beauty' **new**	EBee
- 'Burgundy Glow' (v)	Widely available
§ - 'Catlin's Giant' ♀H4	Widely available
- 'Chocolate Chip'	see *A. reptans* 'Valfredda'
- 'Delight' (v)	ECho
- 'Dixie Chip'	EBee EPfP NLar
- 'Ebony'	LSRN
- 'Evening Glow'	WMoo
- 'Flisteridge'	CNat
- 'Golden Beauty'	EBee ECho ECtt LAst
- 'Golden Glow' (v) **new**	LRHS SHil
- 'Grey Lady'	GBuc
- 'Harlequin' (v)	SWvt
- 'Jumbo'	see *A. reptans* 'Jungle Beauty'
§ - 'Jungle Beauty'	EAEE EBee EPfP GKin MRav WFar
- 'Macrophylla'	see *A. reptans* 'Catlin's Giant'
§ - 'Multicolor' (v)	CBcs CBct EBee ECho ELan LRHS MAsh MRav SPer SPlb SPoG SRms SWvt WFar WMoo WNew WWEG
- 'Palisander'	NEgg NLar
- 'Party Colours'	CLAP EBee
- 'Pink Elf'	CMHG ECho GCra MRav NBro SWat WBrk WFar WRHF WWEG
- 'Pink Splendour'	NBre
- 'Pink Surprise'	ECtt EHoe EPri MHer MLHP NRya WFar WGwG WWEG
- 'Purple Brocade'	EBee EHoe LRHS
§ - 'Purple Torch'	EBee NBir NLar SRms WWFP
- 'Purpurea'	see *A. reptans* 'Atropurpurea'
- 'Rainbow'	see *A. reptans* 'Multicolor'
- 'Rosea'	EAEE EBee NPnk WCAu WFar WMoo
- 'Rowden Amethyst'	CRow
- 'Rowden Appleblossom'	CRow
- 'Rowden Royal Purple'	CRow EBee
- 'Silver Queen'	EBee
- 'Stölzle'	EBee
- 'Sugar Plum'	ECtt ELon EPPr EShb NLar
- 'Toffee Chip'PBR (v)	LSou SGol
- 'Tricolor'	see *A. reptans* 'Multicolor'
§ - 'Valfredda'	CEnt EBee ECho ECtt EPfP GKev LAst LRHS NEgg NLar SHar WCot WFar WGwG WMoo WPer WWEG
§ - 'Variegata' (v)	CBct EBee ECho ECtt EPfP SEND SPer SPoG SRms SWat WFar

Akebia ✿ (*Lardizabalaceae*)

longeracemosa	NLar
- B&SWJ 3606	CPLG LEdu WCot WCru WPGP
× ***pentaphylla***	ELan EPfP LRHS MAsh MRav NLar NRHS SEND SPer
- B&SWJ 2829	WCru
quinata	Widely available
- B&SWJ 4425	WCru
- 'Alba'	CBcs CHll CSPN CSpe CWGN NLar SMDP WPat
- 'Amethyst'	EBee SKHP
- 'Amethyst Glow'	EPfP NLar SPer SPoG
- cream-flowered	EBee EPfP EWld LRHS LSRN MRav SBfd SKHP SPer SPoG SSta SWvt WCru WPGP
- 'Shirobana' **new**	MBlu
- variegated (v)	CBcs LLHF SMad WCot WCru WPat
- 'White Chocolate'	ESwi NLar WCru WSHC
trifoliata	CBcs EBee ELan EPfP MBlu SLim SLon WOld
- B&SWJ 2829	WCru
- B&SWJ 5063	WCru

Alangium (*Cornaceae*)

platanifolium	CAbP CBcs CPLG NLar SBrt WPGP
- var. ***macrophyllum***	EPfP SEND SPoG WBor
- var. ***platanifolium***	NLar

Albizia (*Mimosaceae*)

chinensis	EBee EPfP LRHS
distachya	see *Paraserianthes lophantha*
§ ***julibrissin***	CArn CDTJ CTrC CWib EAmu EPfP LMaj NEgg
- 'Ernest Wilson'	EBee MTPN WCFE WGrn
- Ombrella = 'Boubri'PBR	ELan EMil LRHS MBri SCoo SPoG WHar
- f. ***rosea*** ♀H2-3	Widely available
I - 'Rouge Selection'	LRHS SLim
- 'Summer Chocolate'	CBcs CTrC CWGN EBee ELan EPfP LRHS MPkF NRHS SCoo SHil SMad SPoG WHar
kalkora	SBrt SPlb
lophantha	see *Paraserianthes lophantha*

Albuca ✿ (*Hyacinthaceae*)

sp.	WCot
JCA 15856	CTca WHil
from Lesotho	GCal
angolensis	CPou
aurea	CTca EBee WCot
* ***batliana***	ECho
batteniana	CCon EBee ECho
canadensis (L.) F.M. Leight.	CPou MAvo
cooperi	ECho
'Dirk Wallace'	CPLG
fastigiata	ECho
- f. ***floribunda***	WCot
flaccida	WHil
fragrans	EBee
glauca	EBee ECho
humilis	CDes CPLG EBee ECho LLHF NMen NRya WAbe WCot WHil
longifolia	ECho
nelsonii	CAvo CPne CPrp CTca EBee ECho
setosa	CTca ECho
shawii	CBro CPne CPou CTca EBee ECho EHrv EPot EPri GKin LAst LRHS MHer NCGa SAga SEND SGar SPet SPoG SUsu WAbe WCot WHil
trichophylla	ECho

× *Alcalthaea* (*Malvaceae*)

suffrutescens 'Parkallee' (d)	CAbP CDes EBee ECtt ELan ELon GAbr LDai LHop LPla LRHS

	MAvo MNrw NGdn NLar NSti SPad SPhx SUsu WBrk WCot WHoo WOut
- 'Parkfrieden' (d)	CSpe EBee ECtt ELon MAvo SPhx
- 'Parkrondell' (d)	EBee ECha ECtt ELan ELon LHop LPla MAvo MNrw WOut

Alcea (*Malvaceae*)

'Apple Blossom' (d)	EPfP
'Arabian Nights'	SPav
'Blackcurrant Whirl'	SPav
ficifolia	NChi SPav WFar WHil WMoo
'Peaches and Cream'	ELan
'Peaches 'n' Dreams'	EPfP LHop NGBl
§ ***rosea***	SVic WFar
- 'Blacknight' (Spotlight Series) new	NPri
- Chater's Double Group (d)	ECtt EPfP MBri SBfd SPoG SRms WRHF
- - chamois (d)	EPfP
- - chestnut brown-flowered (d)	EPfP
- - pink-flowered (d)	ELan EPfP
- - purple-flowered (d)	EPfP LAst SPoG
- - red-flowered (d)	ELan EPfP SPoG
- - salmon pink-flowered (d)	ELan EPfP
- - scarlet-flowered (d)	EPfP SPoG
- - violet-flowered (d)	EPfP
- - white-flowered (d)	ELan EPfP MWat SPoG
- - yellow-flowered (d)	EPfP SPoG
- 'Crème de Cassis'	ELan EPfP LPot LRHS NGBl SPav
- double pink-flowered (d)	MHer
- double red-flowered (d)	MHer
- double rose-flowered (d)	EBee
- double white-flowered (d)	MHer
- double yellow-flowered (d)	EBee MHer
- 'Mars Magic' (Spotlight Series) new	EBee MWat NPri
- 'Nigra'	CSpe EBee ECtt ELan EPfP LAst LBMP LHop LRHS LSRN MHer MNHC MSpe MWat NGBl NGdn NPri SBfd SPer WCAu WFar WWEG XEll
- 'Polarstar' (Spotlight Series) new	EBee NPri
- Summer Carnival Group	CWib SRms
- 'Sunshine' (Spotlight Series) new	EBee MWat NPri
§ ***rugosa***	MSpe SHar SPav SWal XSen

Alcea × *Althaea* see × *Alcalthaea*

Alchemilla ✿ (*Rosaceae*)

abyssinica	EBee WHrl
alpina misapplied	see *A. conjuncta*
alpina ambig.	MCot
alpina L.	CEnt CMea EBee ECho EHoe ELan EPfP LHop LRHS MMuc MRav NChi SBch SEND SRms SWat WFar WMoo WNew WPer WSHC
aroanica	EBee
caucasica new	EBee
§ ***conjuncta***	Widely available
ellenbeckii	EBee ECho EPfP GAbr NChi WPGP WWFP
epipsila	EBee ELan EShb EWTr LRHS NLar SPhx WPer
erythropoda ♀H4	Widely available
faeroensis	EBee LRHS NRHS WMoo WPer WPtf
- var. ***pumila***	GEdr NMen WAbe
§ ***fulgens***	EWTr
glaucescens	CNat
hoppeana (Reichenb.) Dalla Torre	EBee
iniquiformis	EBee WPGP
lapeyrousei	EBee NChi
mollis ♀H4	Widely available
* - 'Robusta'	MMuc SEND SPlb SWat WFar WMoo WPnP
- 'Thriller'	EPfP LRHS WFar
monticola	WPer
'Mr Poland's Variety'	see *A. venosa*
pedata	NChi
peristerica	EBee
psilomischa	LRHS
pumila	NBre
saxatilis	IFoB LRHS
sericata 'Gold Strike'	MWhi WHil
speciosa	EBee LRHS SBch
splendens misapplied	see *A. fulgens*
straminea	MRav NBre
§ ***venosa***	LRHS SMHy
vetteri	EBee WHrl
vulgaris misapplied	see *A.* × *xanthochlora*
§ ***xanthochlora***	CArn EBee GPoy NLar SRms WHer

Aldrovanda (*Droseraceae*)

vesiculosa	EFEx

alecost see *Tanacetum balsamita*

Alectryon (*Sapindaceae*)

excelsus	CBcs ECou

Aletris (*Melanthiaceae*)

farinosa	CArn

Alisma (*Alismataceae*)

lanceolatum	MSKA
plantago-aquatica	CBen CHab CRow CSpe EHon LPBA MSKA NPer SWat WMAq XBlo
- var. ***parviflorum***	CBen LPBA MSKA MWts SPlb SWat WMAq

Alkanna (*Boraginaceae*)

tinctoria	CArn CHab

Allamanda (*Apocynaceae*)

cathartica	CCCN
- 'Silver Dwarf'	LRHS

Allardia (*Asteraceae*)

tridactylites CC 5993 new	GKev

Alliaria (*Brassicaceae*)

petiolata	CArn CHab GPoy NLan WHer WSFF

Allium (*Alliaceae*)

RCB UA 5	WCot
SSSE 250	GEdr
aciphyllum	WCot
§ ***acuminatum***	CPom EBee ECho GBin NBir NMen
I - 'Album'	ECho LRHS
acutiflorum	LAma
aflatunense misapplied	see *A. hollandicum*
aflatunense ambig.	ECho LRHS LSRN SDeJ SEND WCot WFar WWEG

	aflatunense B. Fedtsch.	SApp
I	- 'Alba'	ECho
	'Akbulak'	EBee ECho LAma
	albopilosum	see *A. cristophii*
	altaicum	ECho
	altissimum	LAma
	- 'Goliath'	CGrW CTca EBee GKev LRHS NRHS WCot
	amabile	see *A. mairei* var. *amabile*
	'Ambassador'	CBro CMea CTca EBee ECho ERCP GBin LAma LRHS MNrw SHar SPhx WCot
	ampeloprasum	CPrp ECha ECho LAma SEND SPlb SVic WHer WShi
	- var. ***babingtonii***	CAgr CArn CPom CPrp CTca GPoy LEdu WHer WHil WShi
	amphibolum	ECho LAma
	amplectens	ECho LAma LLHF
§	***angulosum***	CAvo CMea CTca EBee ECho LAma LPla WCot
	aschersonianum	EBee ERCP SDeJ
	atropurpureum	EBee ECha EHrv ELan EPfP ERCP LAma LEdu LRHS MWat NRHS SDeJ SPer SPhx
	atropurpureum* × *schubertii	LSRN
	atroviolaceum	ECho
	azureum	see *A. caeruleum*
	backhousianum	LAma
	balansae	ECho
	barszczewskii	ECho
	'Beau Regard' ♀H4	CTca CWCL EBee ECho ELan ERCP GBin LAma NLar
	beesianum misapplied	see *A. cyaneum*
	beesianum W.W. Smith	CDes CPne CPom GEdr LRHS NBir NRya
	- SDR 4771	GKev
	- 'Album'	ECho
	blandum	see *A. carolinianum*
	bodeanum	see *A. cristophii*
	bolanderi	ECho
	'Bolero' **new**	ECho
	brevicaule	ECho
	bucharicum	ECho
	bulgaricum	see *Nectaroscordum siculum* subsp. *bulgaricum*
§	***caeruleum*** ♀H4	Widely available
	- ***azureum***	see *A. caeruleum*
	caesium ♀H4	ECho ERCP
	- tall	LWst
	caespitosum	ECho
	callimischon	CBro
	- subsp. ***callimischon***	ECho
	- subsp. ***haemostictum***	CDes ECho NMen WAbe WCot
	canadense	CArn ECho
§	***carinatum***	ECho
§	- subsp. ***pulchellum*** ♀H4	CBro EBee ECha ECho ELon EPot LAma LHop LLWP LRHS MHer MNrw MWat SMrm SPhx WHil WPer
	- - f. ***album*** ♀H4	CBro EBee ECha ECho ELon LEdu LLWP MNrw SBch SMrm SPhx WPtf
	- - 'Tubergen'	ECho
	'Carlito'	LAma
§	***carolinianum***	ECho LAma
	cepa	SVic
	- Aggregatum Group	ELau GPoy
	- - 'Golden Gourmet' ♀H3 **new**	SVic
	- - 'Matador' ♀H3 **new**	SVic
	- - 'Pikant' ♀H3 **new**	SVic
	- 'Kew White'	WCot
	- 'Perutile'	CArn CHby EOHP GPoy LEdu MHer SBfd SHDw
	- Proliferum Group	CArn CHab CHby CPrp CSev CWan EGHP EOHP EWhm GPoy LEdu MHer MHoo MNHC SBfd SIde WGwG WHer WJek
	- 'Red Brunswick' **new**	SVic
	- var. ***viviparum***	ECho LAma
	- 'White Lisbon' ♀H4	SVic
	cernuum	CAvo CBro CDes CMea CTca CYeo EBee ECha ECho EHrv EPfP EPot ERCP IFoB LAma LEdu LHop LRHS MBel MLHP MNrw NMen NRHS SDeJ SHom SKHP SPhx SRms WPer
§	- 'Hidcote' ♀H4	CSam WKif
	- 'Major'	see *A. cernuum* 'Hidcote'
	- var. ***obtusum***	ECho WPer
	- pink-flowered	NBir
	- 'White Dwarf'	EBee ECho
	chinense	GPoy
	cirrhosum	see *A. carinatum* subsp. *pulchellum*
	commutatum	ECho
	cowanii	see *A. neapolitanum* Cowanii Group
	crenulatum	CPom ECho LAma
§	***cristophii*** ♀H4	Widely available
	cupanii	EBee ECho
	cupuliferum	ECho
	curtum RCB RL 13	WCot
§	***cyaneum*** ♀H4	CPBP CPom ECho GEdr LAma LBee LRHS MHer NMen NRya WCot
*	- ***album***	ECho
	- 'Cobalt Blue'	ECho
	cyathophorum	CYeo ECho EWld LRHS
§	- var. ***farreri***	CArn CAvo CBre CBro EBee ECho EPot GEdr LEdu LLWP LRHS MLHP MNrw MRav NChi NRya SBch SSvw WCot WPer
	darwasicum	ECho
	- RM 8274	ECho
	decipiens	ECho LAma
	dichlamydeum	ECho LWst
§	***drummondii***	ECho LRHS
	'Early Emperor'	CBro CWCL EBee ERCP LAma
	elatum	see *A. macleanii*
	'Emir'	CAvo CBro
	ericetorum	ECho WCot
	falcifolium	EBee ECho EPot LAma LLHF NMen NMin WCot
	farreri	see *A. cyathophorum* var. *farreri*
	fasciculatum	LAma
	fimbriatum	ECho
	- var. ***abramsii***	ECho
	- var. ***purdyi***	ECho
	'Firmament'	CAvo CBro EBee ECha ECho ERCP GBin LAma LRHS NLar SDeJ SHar SPhx
	fistulosum	CArn CHby CWan ECho EGHP ELau ENfk GPoy LAma LEdu MHer MHoo MMuc MNHC NPri SEND SIde SVic WGwG WJek WPer
	- 'Red Welsh'	CPrp WJek
	- red-flowered	CHby

	flavidum	LRHS
	flavum ♀H4	CArn CBro CTca ECha ECho EPot ERCP GKev LAma MRav NSla SDeJ WGwG WThu WWEG
§	- 'Blue Leaf'	ECho LEdu NBir SMrm
	- subsp. ***flavum***	EBee ECho MMHG WPer
	- - var. ***minus***	ECho
	- 'Glaucum'	see *A. flavum* 'Blue Leaf'
	- var. ***nanum***	CYeo ECho EPot GEdr
	- subsp. ***tauricum***	CSpe EBee ECho SPhx
	'Forelock'	CAvo CBro CTca EBee ERCP LAma LRHS MNrw WCot
	forrestii	EBee ECho MDKP WCot
	geyeri	EBee ECho LLHF WCot
	giganteum ♀H4	CAvo CBcs CTca CWCL EBee ECtt EHrv ELan EPfP ERCP GKev GPoy IBoy LAma LRHS LSRN MBri MNHC MWat NLar NOrc SDeJ SMrm SPer SPoG SRms SWat SWvt WFar WWEG
	'Gladiator' ♀H4	CAvo CCon CTca CWCL EBee ECho ECtt ERCP GMaP LAma LRHS LSRN MNrw MRav NOrc SBfd SDeJ SPad WWEG
	glaucum	see *A. senescens* subsp. *glaucum*
	'Globemaster' ♀H4	CAvo CBro CMea CTca CWCL EBee ECho ECtt EHrv ELan EPfP EPot ERCP LAma LEdu LRHS LSRN MAvo MBri MMHG MNrw NLar NRHS SBfd SDeJ SPer SPhx WCot WFar WWEG
	globosum	ECho
	'Globus'	CTca LAma
	goodingii	EBee ECho
	guttatum subsp. ***dalmaticum***	ECho
	- - HOA 9114	ECho
	- subsp. ***sardoum***	ECho
	- - CH 859	ECho
	haemanthoides	WCot
	haematochiton	ECho WCot
	'Hair'	see *A. vineale* 'Hair'
	heldreichii	ECho
*	***hirtifolium*** var. ***album***	EBee ECho LAma LRHS
	'His Excellency'	CCon EBee ERCP LAma LRHS NRHS
§	***hollandicum*** ♀H4	CAvo CBro CTca CWCL EBee ECha ECtt EPfP GKev LAma MWat NEgg NOrc SPer SPlb WFar
	- 'Purple Sensation' ♀H4	Widely available
	hookeri	LEdu
	- ACE 2430	EBee WCot
	- var. ***muliense***	GEdr LEdu
	humile	ECho GEdr
	hyalinum pink-flowered	EBee WCot
	hymenorrhizum	ECho
	inconspicuum	LAma
§	***insubricum*** ♀H4	CDes ECho GEdr GKev LWst MNrw NBir NMen WAbe
	jajlae	see *A. rotundum* subsp. *jajlae*
	jesdianum 'Michael Hoog'	see *A. rosenorum* 'Michael H. Hoog'
	- 'Purple King'	EBee LAma LRHS MNrw
	- 'White Empress'PBR	CAvo EBee SPhx
	kansuense	see *A. sikkimense*
	karataviense ♀H3	CAvo CBro CElw CMea CTca EBee ECha EHrv ELan EPfP EPot EWTr GAbr GBin GKev LAma LRHS MBri MCot NBir NLar NRHS SBfd SDeJ SMrm SWvt WFar
	- 'Ivory Queen'	CAvo CBro CMea CTca EBee ECha ECtt EPfP ERCP GAbr GKev LAma LRHS LSRN NLar SBfd SDeJ SMrm SPad SPlb WFar
	komarovianum	see *A. thunbergii*
	komarovii	CPom
	ledebourianum	EBee ECho LAma
	lenkoranicum	CAvo EBee ECho LAma WCot
	libani	WPer
§	***lineare***	ECho
	litvinovii	ECho LAma LWst
	longicuspis	ECho
	loratum	LAma
	'Lucy Ball'	EBee ERCP LAma LRHS NBir NLar SDeJ
§	***lusitanicum***	CBro CTca ECha ECho ERCP LAma NBre NMen SDix SMHy WAbe WCot
§	***macleanii***	EBee ECho LAma LRHS
	macranthum	CPom EBee ECho EPot GEdr LAma LRHS WCot
	macrochaetum	ECho
	macropetalum	ECho
	mairei	CYeo ECho LHop LLWP LRHS NMen NRHS NRya WTin
§	- var. ***amabile***	CYeo ECho GEdr NChi NRHS NRya NSla WThu
	- - pink-flowered	ECho
	- - red-flowered	ECho
	maximowiczii	EBee ECho
	- white-flowered	LAma NMen
	'Mercurius'PBR	EBee ERCP LAma LRHS MNrw SPhx WCot
	moly	CArn CWCL EBee ECho GKev LAma LRHS MBri MMuc MRav NRHS NRya SBfd SDeJ SEND SRms SWal XLum
	- 'Jeannine' ♀H4	CBro CTca EBee ECho EPot GAbr GBin LAma LRHS MMHG NRHS WShi
	'Mont Blanc'	CMea EBee ELan ERCP GBin GQue LAma LRHS MNrw NLar WWEG
	multibulbosum	see *A. nigrum*
	murrayanum misapplied	see *A. unifolium*
	murrayanum Regel	see *A. acuminatum*
	myrianthum	ECho LAma
	narcissiflorum misapplied	see *A. insubricum*
§	***narcissiflorum*** Vill.	CRDP CSpe ECho LWst MNrw
	neapolitanum	EBee ECho EPot LAma MBri MCot SEND SPer SRms WGwG
§	- Cowanii Group	CBro ECho LHop LRHS SDeJ WCot
	- 'Grandiflorum'	ECho
	nevskianum	EBee ECho LAma SKHP
§	***nigrum***	CAvo CBro EBee ECho EHrv EPfP EPot ERCP LAma LRHS MCot MRav NBir SDeJ SPhx WCot
	nutans	CPrp EBee ECho EGHP LAma LEdu MHer SHDw WHal WHil WJek
	nuttallii	see *A. drummondii*
§	***obliquum***	CArn CAvo CBro CPom ECha ECho ERCP SPhx WCot WTin
	ochotense	WCot
	odorum L.	see *A. ramosum* L.
	oleraceum	EBee ECho WHer
	olympicum	CDes ECho LWst
§	***oreophilum***	CSam EBee ECha ECho EPfP GAbr LAma LRHS MLHP SMrm SPer SRms WCot WHoo

- 'Agalik'	ECho
- 'Zwanenburg' ♀H4	ECho EPot
oreoprasum	ECho
oschaninii	LAma
ostrowskianum	see *A. oreophilum*
ovalifolium	WCot
var. ***leuconeurum***	
palentinum	LAma
pallasii	ECho
pallens	CBre ECho NBir
§ ***paniculatum***	EBee SCnR
* - var. ***minor***	ECho LAma
paradoxum	ECho LEdu NBir
- var. ***normale***	CBro CDes CPom CRDP EBee ECho EPot ERCP EWld MRav NBir NMen WCot
pedemontanum	see *A. narcissiflorum* Villars
pendulinum	ECho
'Pinball Wizard'	CBro CTca EBee ERCP LAma LRHS
'Pink Jewel' **new**	ERCP WCot
platycaule	ECho LAma SKHP WCot
platyspathum	ECho
plummerae	EBee ECho SKHP
plurifoliatum	ECho LAma
polyphyllum	see *A. carolinianum*
polyrrhizum	ECho
porrum	NPri
'Musselburgh' **new**	
przewalskianum	LAma
pskemense	ECho LAma WCot
pulchellum	see *A. carinatum* subsp. *pulchellum*
'Purple Rain'	ERCP LAma
pyrenaicum misapplied	see *A. angulosum*
pyrenaicum Costa & Vayr.	SEND
ramosum Jacq.	see *A. obliquum*
§ ***ramosum*** L.	EBee ECho EGHP LAma LEdu MHoo WPer
'Rien Poortvliet'	ECho LAma
robustum	ECho
rosenbachianum misapplied	see *A. stipitatum*
rosenbachianum Regel	CBro EBee LRHS
- 'Album'	EBee ERCP GBin LAma LRHS WCot
- 'Michael Hoog'	see *A. rosenorum* 'Michael H. Hoog'
- 'Shing'	EBee IBal LAma MNrw
§ ***rosenorum*** 'Michael H. Hoog'	EBee ECho EPot LAma LRHS
roseum	CMea EBee ECho EPfP EPot LAma MDKP SDeJ
- f. ***albiflorum***	ECho
§ - var. ***bulbiferum***	ECho
- 'Grandiflorum'	see *A. roseum* var. *bulbiferum*
rotundum	ECho
§ - subsp. ***jajlae***	ECho LLWP
- subsp. ***rotundum***	ECho
'Round and Purple'	EBee ECho ERCP LAma LRHS MAvo NRHS
sanbornii var. ***sanbornii***	ECho
sarawschanicum	ECho
- 'Bright Boy'	ECho
sativum	CArn ECho ENfk MHer NPri SIde SPoG
- var. ***ophioscorodon***	EBee ECho GPoy LAma SPlb
saxatile	ECho
schmitzii	ECho SSvw
schoenoprasum	Widely available
- f. ***albiflorum***	CArn CPbn CPrp ECha ECho LEdu MHer NBir NCGa SIde WCot WHer
- 'Black Isle Blush'	CDes CPbn CTca EBee GPoy LEdu LPla MHer SMHy
- 'Corsican White'	LEdu
- fine-leaved	ELau
- 'Forescate'	CPrp CTca EBee ECha EWes LAma LHop LRHS MRav NBir NGdn SIde SPet SSvw XLum
- medium-leaved	ELau
- 'Netherbyres Dwarf'	CArn
- 'Pink Perfection'	GPoy LEdu LPla MHer SMHy
- 'Polyphant'	CBre
- var. ***sibiricum***	SDix WShi
- 'Silver Chimes'	CAvo CDes CWan EBee EWhm MRav SBfd SHDw
- thick-leaved	ECho ELau NPri
- 'Wilau'	ELau
schubertii	CAvo CBro CElw CSpe CTca CWCL EBee ECtt EHrv ELan EPfP EPot ERCP GBin GKev LAma LRHS MBri MNrw NRHS SDeJ SPer SPhx WCot WFar
scorodoprasum	EBee ECho SIde
- subsp. ***jajlae***	see *A. rotundum* subsp. *jajlae*
- 'Passion' **new**	ECho
- subsp. ***scorodoprasum***	ECho LAma LEdu
semenowii	ECho
senescens	CArn CBro CDes CTca CTri CYeo EBee ECGP EPot EWTr LAma LEdu LRHS MRav SApp SBch SBfd SEND SMrm SRms SSvw WTin XLum XSen
§ - subsp. ***glaucum***	CArn CAvo CMea CPBP CPom CPrp CSpe EAEE EBee ECha ECho GEdr LAst LEdu LRHS NGdn NRHS NRya SPet SUsu SWat WCot WPer WTin
- subsp. ***senescens***	EBee ECho LEdu NMRc SAga
serra	WCot
sessiliflorum	ECho
setifolium	ECho
sewerzowii	ECho
sibthorpianum	see *A. paniculatum*
siculum	see *Nectaroscordum siculum*
§ ***sikkimense***	CCon CPom CWCL CYeo EBee ECho EPot EWTr GEdr LEdu LRHS MDKP NMen NRHS NSla SMHy SPet SSvw WCot WPer
'Silver Spring'	EBee ECho GBin LAma LRHS MNrw SDeJ WCot
siskiyouense	ECho
sphaerocephalon	Widely available
'Spider' **new**	EBee
splendens	ECho GAbr
stellatum	LRHS WGwG
stellerianum	WPer
- var. ***kurilense***	CPBP WAbe WThu
§ ***stipitatum***	ECho ERCP LAma LRHS SPhx WCot
- 'Album'	CBro ECho LRHS
- 'Mars'	CCon EBee EPfP ERCP LAma LRHS NLar NRHS
- 'Mount Everest'	CAvo CBro CCon CHid CTca EBee EPfP EPot ERCP GKev GMaP LAma LRHS MNrw MWat NLar SDeJ SMrm SPer SPhx WCot WShi

	- 'Violet Beauty'	CCse CWCL EBee LAma MWat SBfd WCot
	- 'White Giant'	CTca EBee ERCP LAma LRHS MNrw NRHS
	stracheyi	WCot
	'Stratos'	EBee ERCP LAma LRHS NRHS
	strictum Ledeb.	see *A. szovitsii*
	strictum Schrad.	see *A. lineare*
	subhirsutum	CPom EBee XLum
	subvillosum	WCot
	'Summer Beauty'	see *A. lusitanicum*
	'Summer Drummer'	CMea CTca EBee ERCP
	'Sweet Discovery'	EBee ECho LAma LRHS
§	***szovitsii***	ECho
	tanguticum	LRHS
	taquetii	see *A. thunbergii*
	tauricola	ECho
	texanum	ECho LAma
§	***thunbergii*** ♀H4	EBee ECho EPot LAma NBir NRya SCnR SPhx WAbe WWEG
	- 'Album'	ECho WAbe
	- 'Ozawa'	CDes EBee ECho NMen WAbe WCot
	tibeticum	see *A. sikkimense*
	togashii	ECho
*	***tournefortii***	ECho
	triquetrum	ECho ELan ELau EPfP EPot IBlr LAma LEdu NBir NLar SEND WCot WHer WMoo XLum
	tschimganicum	LAma SKHP
	tuberosum	Widely available
	- B&SWJ 8881	WCru
	- purple/mauve-flowered	CHby ECho ELau
	tubiflorum	ECho
	turkestanicum	ECho
	umbilicatum	ECho
§	***unifolium*** ♀H4	CAvo CPom CSam EBee ECho EPfP EPot ERCP GAbr GKev LAma MRav NBir NLBP SDeJ SEND WFar WPer
	ursinum	CArn CHab CHby CWan EBee ECho EOHP EWTr GPoy LAma LRHS MHoo MWat NMir WJek WSFF WShi
	'Valerie Finnis'	CPBP
	validum	SPhx
	- NNS 06-41	WCot
	victorialis	CDes ECho
	- 'Cantabria'	EBee
	vineale	CArn NMir WHer
	- 'Dready' **new**	ECho
§	- 'Hair'	CTca EBee EPfP ERCP GKev LAma LRHS MCot NBir
	violaceum	see *A. carinatum*
	virgunculae	CMea CPBP NRya WAbe
	wallichii	ECho EWes GMaP LEdu MBNS NBir NChi SKHP WCot WTin XLum
	- ACE 2458	WCot
	- dark-flowered	CDes CPne CPom ECho GKev WCot
	zaprjagajevii	WCot
	zebdanense	EBee ECho LAma

almond see *Prunus dulcis*

Alnus ✿ (*Betulaceae*)

	cordata ♀H4	CBcs CCVT CDoC CDul CLnd CMCN CMac CSBt CSto CTho CTri EBee ECrN ELan EPfP LBuc LMaj MGos MMuc NEgg NLar NWea SEND SEWo SGol SPer SPlb WFar WMou
	cremastogyne	CMCN EBtc EGFP NLar
	crispa	see *A. viridis* subsp. *crispa*
	fauriei from Niigata, Japan	CSto
	firma	CMCN CSto
	glutinosa	CBcs CCVT CDoC CDul CHab CLnd CMac CRWN CSBt CTho CTri EBee ECrN EPfP EWTr LBuc LMaj MGos NWea SEWo SGol SPer WHar WMou WSFF
	- 'Aurea'	CDul CTho CWib MBlu MGos
	- var. ***barbata***	CSto
	- 'Imperialis' ♀H4	CCVT CDoC CDul CLnd CTho ECrN ELan EPfP EWTr LHop MBlu MBri MMuc MPkF NBro NLar NWea SBfd SEND SEWo SGol SKHP SPer WHar
	- 'Laciniata'	CCVT CDoC CDul CMac CTho ECrN MBlu MGos WFar
	hirsuta	CSto NWea
	incana	CCVT CDoC CDul CLnd CMCN CTho CWib ECrN LBuc MGos MMuc NLar NWea SGol SPer WHar WMou
	- 'Aurea'	CBcs CDul CLnd CMac CTho EBee ECrN ELan EPfP IArd LMaj MBlu MBri MGos MRav NBro NEgg NLar NWea SBfd SEWo SGol SPer WFar WHar
	- 'Laciniata'	CTho MGos SCoo WFar WMou
	- 'Pendula'	CTho
	japonica	CSto NLar
	aff. ***jorullensis*** NJM 09.070 **new**	WPGP
	maximowiczii	CSto
	- from Ulleungdo **new**	WCru
	oregana	see *A. rubra*
	pendula	CSto
	- B&SWJ 10895	WCru
	rhombifolia	EBtc
§	***rubra***	CCVT CDoC CDul CLnd CMCN CTho ECrN ELan NWea
	- f. ***pinnatisecta***	CMCN CTho MBlu
	sieboldiana	WCru
	× ***spaethii***	MBlu MMuc SEND
	subcordata	CSto
	viridis	CAgr CSto EBtc NWea
§	- subsp. ***crispa***	CSto
	- subsp. ***sinuata***	CAgr CSto NWea

Alocasia ✿ (*Araceae*)

× ***amazonica*** ♀H1	XBlo
'Aurora'	EAmu
'Black Stem'	EAmu IBoy
'Calidora'	CDTJ SPlb
cucullata	XBlo
gageana	CDTJ
lauterbachiana	EAmu
macrorrhiza	CCon CDTJ EAmu SBig SBst
- 'Variegata' (v) ♀H1	GHim
- 'Violacea' **new**	GHim
'Mayan Mask' **new**	EAmu
odora	CDTJ EAmu GHim SPlb XBlo
plumbea	XBlo
'Portodora'	EAmu
'Stingray'	EAmu
wentii	CDTJ EAmu SPlb WCot
- 'Aline'PBR (v)	EAmu
- 'Victory' (v)	EAmu

Aloe ✿ (*Asphodelaceae*)

aculeata	CAbb EShb
africana	CAbb
ammophila	LToo
arborescens	CAbb CBrP CDTJ CDoC CHEx EAmu EShb EUJe SBst SEND SPlb
aristata ♀H1	CHEx EGri ETod EUJe SBfd SChr SEND SPlb WPGP
barbadensis	see *A. vera*
barberae	CCCN
betsileensis new	LToo
brevifolia ♀H1	CAbb CBrP EAmu EShb EUJe SBst
broomii	CAbb CCCN CDoC EPfP LToo SPlb
camperi 'Maculata'	SEND
castanea	CAbb
ciliaris	CHll EShb
comptonii	CAbb EShb
cooperi	CCCN CDTJ CDoC EShb
dawei	EShb
descoingsii ♀H1	LToo
dichotoma	CAbb SPlb
distans	SEND
ecklonis	CCCN CTrC SPlb
elegans new	LToo
ferox	CAbb CBrP CCCN CDTJ CDoC CTrC EAmu GPoy MDev SBfd SBig SEND
fosteri	CDTJ
greatheadii var. ***davyana***	SChr
humilis	CBrP CTrC SChr SEND
juvenna	EShb
kedongensis	SEND
krapohliana	CAbb
lineata new	CAbb
littoralis	CAbb
lutescens new	CAbb
maculata	CDTJ MDev
marlothii	CAbb CCCN EShb SPlb
melanacantha ♀H1	CAbb
microstigma	CCCN MDev
mitriformis	CBrP EPfP SChr SEND
mutabilis	CHEx SChr SEND
peglerae	CAbb
petricola	CAbb
plicatilis	CCCN CDTJ EShb
pluridens	CAbb
polyphylla	CAbb EAmu WPGP
pratensis	CCCN CDTJ SChr
reitzii	CAbb SPlb
speciosa	CAbb
spicata	CAbb
× ***spinosissima***	CDoC SChr
striata	CAbb CCCN EShb LToo
striatula	CAbb CBrP CDTJ CDoC CGHE CHEx CSam CTca CTrC EAmu EBee EGri EShb EUJe IBlr LTen SBHP SBig SChr SEND SKHP SPlb WCot WPGP
- var. ***caesia***	IBlr
succotrina	CAbb
suprafoliata	CAbb
thraskii	CAbb
tomentosa new	LToo
variegata (v) ♀H1	EShb
§ ***vera*** ♀H1	CArn CCCN CDoC CHab CHby CSpe EOHP EUJe GPoy MHoo MNHC NPer NPla NPri SBch SBfd SEND SIde SMad SPlb SVic SWal WJek
wickensii	CAbb LToo
yavellana new	SPlb

Alonsoa (*Scrophulariaceae*)

'Bright Spark'	CSpe WKif
incisifolia	CCCN CSpe
meridionalis	CCCN SBfd
- 'Rebel'	LAst LSou MSCN SBfd SRkn WBor
* - 'Salmon Beauty'	LRHS
'Pink Beauty'	CSpe
'Scarlet Lucky Lips' new	LSou
warscewiczii	CCCN
- 'Peachy-keen'	CSpe

Alopecurus (*Poaceae*)

alpinus	see *A. borealis*
§ ***borealis***	LRHS
- subsp. ***glaucus***	EBee ELan EPPr SPer
geniculatus	CRWN
pratensis	CHab NOrc
- 'Aureovariegatus' (v)	CWan EBee EHoe EPPr GMaP NBid SApp SLim SPer WFar XLum
- 'Aureus'	ECha LRHS MRav NBro SPlb WWEG
- 'No Overtaking' (v)	EPPr

Alophia (*Iridaceae*)

lahue	see *Herbertia lahue*

Aloysia (*Verbenaceae*)

citriodora	see *A. citrodora*
§ ***citrodora*** ♀H2	Widely available
gratissima	WJek
triphylla	see *A. citrodora*

Alpinia (*Zingiberaceae*)

formosana	LEdu
galanga	CArn
japonica	CPLG LEdu
- B&SWJ 8889	WCru
nutans misapplied	see *A. zerumbet*
officinarum	CArn CDTJ
speciosa	see *A. zerumbet*
§ ***zerumbet***	EAmu
- B&SWJ 11512	WCru
- 'Variegata' (v)	CDTJ EAmu EUJe XBlo

Alsobia see *Episcia*

Alstroemeria (*Alstroemeriaceae*)

'Adonis' PBR	LRHS WViv
'Aimi'	CCon ELan SPer SWal SWvt WViv
'Alexis' PBR	WViv
'Angelina'	LRHS SWvt
'Apollo' ♀H4	CBcs CTsd ELan MBNS MNrw NBre SPer SWal SWvt WViv
'Athena'	LRHS WViv
aurantiaca	see *A. aurea*
§ ***aurea***	MRav NLar SRms XLum
- 'Apricot'	GCal
- 'Dover Orange'	IGor
- 'Lutea'	SDeJ SPlb
- 'Orange King'	CTsd ELan EPfP NLar SDeJ SMrm
'Blushing Bride'	CCon ELon MBNS SWvt
'Bolero'	WViv
'Bonanza'	SLon SPer WViv

brasiliensis	CTsd GCal MNrw WCot WSHC WViv XLum
- 'Cally Star' (v) **new**	GCal
Butterfly hybrids	SWal
'Cahors'	LBuc LRHS MBri SHil
'Candy Floss'	EBee EPfP
'Celine'	WViv
'Charm'	LRHS WViv
'Chi Chi'	WCot
§ 'Christina'PBR	LRHS MBNS NPri SLon SWvt WViv
'Coronet' ΨH4	MBNS WViv
'Dandy Candy'	CAbP ELon EWll IBoy ITim LAst MAvo MNrw NGdn NLar SPoG SUsu WBrk WCot
'Dayspring Delight' (v)	CRDP
'Diana' **new**	SWal
diluta subsp. ***chrysantha*** F&W 8700	WCot
Doctor Salter's hybrids	SRms
'Douceur d'Automne'	LBuc LRHS MBri SHil
'Elvira'	LRHS SPer WViv
'Eternal Love'	IBoy
'Evening Song'	CCon LRHS MBNS SLon SPer SWal SWvt WViv
exserens	WCot
'Flaming Star'	CBcs WViv
'Frances' (v)	CAvo CBro
'Freedom'	CWGN EBee ECtt ELon LAst LSou MAvo MBNS NEgg NLar SMad SPoG SUsu WCot
'Friendship' ΨH4	CBcs CTsd ELan NBre SPlb SWal SWvt WViv
'Gloria'	MBNS SWvt WViv
'Glory of the Andes' (v)	CWGN NLar
'Golden Delight'	ELan LRHS SPer WViv
haemantha	MDKP
I 'Hatch Hybrid'	GCal
'Hawera'	GCal SMrm
hookeri	ECho GBin GCal SCnR
- subsp. ***cummingiana***	LLHF WCot
Inca Adore = 'Koadore'PBR	CPLG EBee MBri NPri SPoG
Inca Avanti = 'Koncavanti'	LBuc WViv
Inca Azure = 'Konazur'	ELon SPoG SUsu WViv
Inca Birdy = 'Konirdy'	WViv
Inca Classic = 'Konclassic'	EBee WHlf WViv
Inca Coral = 'Konocoral'	WViv
Inca Desert = 'Konesert'PBR	WViv
Inca Devotion = 'Konevotio'PBR	EBee MBri NMir
Inca Exotica = 'Koexotica'PBR	EBee LHop LRHS MBri MGos NMir NPri SPoG WViv
Inca Ginger	WViv
Inca Glow = 'Koglow'PBR	CPLG EBee ELon MGos SDeJ WViv
Inca Ice = 'Koice'	CWGN EBee GBin LHop LRHS MGos NLar NPri SPoG WViv
Inca Joli = 'Koncajoli'	LBuc WViv
Inca Lake = 'Koncalake'	LBuc WViv
Inca Mambo **new**	WViv
Inca Milk = 'Koncamilk' **new**	WHlf WViv
Inca Moonlight = 'Komolight'	WViv
Inca Obsession = 'Koobsion'	LRHS WViv
Inca Pride = 'Kopride'	WViv
Inca Pulse = 'Konpulse'PBR	EBee ELon GBin LHop LRHS MBri SDeJ SPoG WViv
Inca Serin = 'Koserin'PBR	EBee LHop LRHS WViv
Inca Tropic = 'Kotrop'	CPLG EBee LRHS MBri MGos NPri SPoG WHlf WViv
Inca Yuko = 'Koncayuko' **new**	LBuc WViv
Inticancha Creamy Dark Pink = 'Tescreda'	SDeJ WViv
Inticancha Dark Purple = 'Tesdarklin'	WViv
Inticancha Machu = 'Tesmach' **new**	WViv
Inticancha Maya = 'Tesmaya' **new**	WViv
Inticancha Navayo = 'Tesnava' **new**	WViv
Inticancha Purple = 'Tespurplin'PBR	EBee WViv
Inticancha Red = 'Tesrobiri'	EBee WViv
Inticancha Sunday = 'Tessunday'	WViv
Inticancha Sunlight = 'Tessunlight'	WViv
Inticancha White Pink Blush = 'Tesblushin'PBR	WViv
Inticancha White Pink Heart = 'Tesheartin'	WViv
Inticancha White = 'Teswhitin'PBR	WViv
Isabella = 'Stalis'	LSRN
'Laguna'	WViv
ligtu hybrids	CAvo CBcs ECha ELan EPfP LAst LHop MNrw NLar NPer SDeJ SRms SWal SWvt WBrk WHoo WWEG
- var. ***ligtu***	SMHy WCot
'Little Eleanor'	SWal WFar WViv
'Little Miss Charlotte'	WFar
'Little Miss Christina'PBR	see *A.* 'Christina'
'Little Miss Davina'	LBuc LRHS NPri WViv
'Little Miss Gina'	NPri WViv
'Little Miss Isabel'	LRHS WViv
'Little Miss Lucy'	LRHS NPri WViv
'Little Miss Matilda'	WViv
'Little Miss Natalie'PBR	see *A.* 'Natalie'
'Little Miss Rosanna'	SWal WViv
'Little Miss Roselind'	see *A.* 'Roselind'
'Little Miss Sophie'PBR	see *A.* 'Sophie'
'Little Miss Tara'PBR	see *A.* 'Tara'
'Little Miss Veronica'	MBNS WViv
'Louise'	LSRN
'Lucinda'	CBcs SWvt
'Maestro'PBR	WViv
magnifica	WCot
- subsp. ***maxima***	WCot
'Marina'	MBNS
'Marissa'	GMaP IBoy
'Mars'	LRHS SUsu SWal
'Mauve Majesty'	EBee ECtt ELon IBoy ITim LSou MAvo MNrw NLar SPoG SUsu WCot
'Moulin Rouge'	ELan LRHS MBNS SLon WViv
§ 'Natalie'PBR	LBuc NPri WViv
'Neptune'	LBuc LRHS MBri SHil
'Orange Gem' ΨH4	MBNS
'Orange Glory' ΨH4	ELon GMaP MBNS SWvt WViv WWlt
'Orange Supreme'	LRHS WViv
'Oriana'	ELan SWvt WViv

	patagonica	WAbe
§	***paupercula*** F&W 10560	WCot
	pelegrina	ECho
	'Perfect Blue'	WViv
	'Perfect Love'	MNrw
	philippii	WCot
	'Phoenix' (v)	CCon LRHS SLon SUsu SWal SWvt WCot WViv
	'Pink Lady' **new**	WViv
	'Pink Perfection'	NLar
	'Pink Sensation'	WViv
	'Polka'	MBNS SWal WViv
	presliana RB 94103	WCot
	- subsp. ***australis***	SMrm
	Princess Angela = 'Staprilan'	CBcs ELan MBNS NLar
	Princess Anouska = 'Zaprinous'PBR	MNrw NLar SLon SPer WViv
	Princess Ariane = 'Zapriari'PBR	LRHS WViv
	Princess Camilla = 'Stapricamil'PBR	CBcs LRHS SLon SPer SPoG
	Princess Daniela = 'Stapridani'PBR	SCoo SPoG
	Princess Diana = 'Zapridapal'PBR	WViv
	Princess Eliane = 'Zaprielia' **new**	WViv
	Princess Ella = 'Staprirange'	NLar
	Princess Emma = 'Zaprimma'PBR	WViv
	Princess Fabiana = 'Zaprifabi'PBR	ELan LRHS MGos SPoG WViv
	Princess Felicia = 'Zapricia'PBR	LRHS SPer
	Princess Isabella = 'Zapribel'PBR	LRHS LSRN NLar WViv
	Princess Ivana = 'Staprivane'PBR	LRHS NLar SPoG
	Princess Juliana = 'Staterpa'	SPoG
	Princess Julieta = 'Zaprijul'PBR	LRHS NLar SPoG WViv
	Princess Letizia = 'Zaprilet'PBR	LRHS MNrw
	Princess Leyla = 'Stapriley'PBR	CBcs LRHS MBNS SLon SPer SPoG
	Princess Lilian = 'Zaprilian'	WViv
	Princess Louise = 'Zaprilou'PBR	LRHS LSRN WViv
	Princess Margaret	NLar
	Princess Marilene = 'Staprilene'PBR	LRHS MBNS WViv
	Princess Mary = 'Zaprimary'PBR	LRHS NLar
	Princess Mathilde = 'Zaprimat'PBR	LRHS WViv
	Princess Monica = 'Staprimon'PBR	LRHS MBNS SPoG
	Princess Oxana = 'Staprioxa'PBR	LRHS NLar
	Princess Paola = 'Stapripal'PBR	MBNS MNrw SCoo WViv
	Princess Ragna	see *A.* Princess Stephanie
	Princess Sara = 'Staprisara'PBR	SPoG WViv
	Princess Sarah = 'Stalicamp'	MBNS
	Princess Sissi = 'Staprisis'	SPoG
§	Princess Sophia = 'Stajello'	SPoG
§	Princess Stephanie = 'Stapirag'	NLar
	Princess Susana = 'Staprisusa'PBR	NLar SCoo SPoG
	Princess Theresa = 'Zapriteres'PBR	LRHS NLar
	Princess Zavina = 'Staprivina'PBR	CBcs CCon LRHS MBNS NLar SPer
	pseudospathulata	WCot
§	***psittacina***	CAvo CBro CGHE CHll CSam ECha EHrv ELan EPfP GBin GBuc GCal GCra LHop MCot MHer NChi SRms SWal WFar WSHC WViv XLum
	- 'Mona Lisa'	EWll GBuc LLHF LSou NLar WCot
	- 'Royal Star' (v)	CBro CPLG CWCL EAEE EBee ELan ELon EPPr EPfP GBuc GCal LHop LRHS LSou MAvo NLar SHar SPoG SRms WCot WFar WHoo WSHC WWEG WWlt XLum
	pulchella Sims	see *A. psittacina*
	'Purple Rain'	ELan LRHS MNrw SLon SWvt WViv
	'Red Beauty' (v)	see *A.* 'Spitfire'
	'Red Beauty'	ELan GMaP LRHS MBNS SPer SWvt WCot
	'Red Coat'	EBee NLar
	'Red Elf'	IBoy MBNS SUsu SWvt WViv
	'Rhubarb and Custard'	EBee EPfP
§	'Roselind'	CCon ELan LRHS MBNS NPri SWal SWvt WViv
	'Saturne'	EPfP LBuc LRHS MBri NRHS SHil
	'Selina'	LRHS MBNS NBre SWal WViv
	'Serenade'	CBcs CCon ELan WViv
	'Short Purple'	ELon LSou WCot
	'Sonata'	WViv
§	'Sophie'PBR	ELan MBNS NPri SLon SWvt WViv
§	'Spitfire' (v)	CRDP EPfP IBoy LRHS SHil SLon SWvt WViv
	'Spring Delight' (v)	CRDP WCot
	'Strawberry Lace'	EBee EPfP
	'Sunrise'	WWlt
	'Sunstar'	GMaP
	'Sweet Laura'PBR	CAbP EBee ECtt ELon LAst LLHF LSRN MAvo MBNS NEgg NGdn NLar SMad SPoG WCot
	'Tanya'	LRHS WViv
§	'Tara'PBR	MBNS NPri SPlb SWvt WViv
	'Tessa'	LRHS MBNS NBre SLon WViv
	'Turkish Delight'	EBee EPfP
	'Uranus'	LBuc LRHS MBri SHil
	'Ventura'	WViv
	violacea	see *A. paupercula*
	'White Apollo'	WCot
	'Yellow Friendship' ♀H4	MBNS NLar SWvt WViv
	Yellow King	see *A.* Princess Sophia

Althaea (*Malvaceae*)

	armeniaca	LPla NLar WCot WOut
	cannabina	CArn CFis CSpe ELan GCal GQui LPla MHer MNrw NGBl SUsu WBor WHal WOld WSHC
	officinalis	CArn CHab CPrp CSev CWan EBee ELan ENfk GPoy MHer MHoo MNHC SIde WHfH WJek XLum
	- ***alba***	LSou NLar
§	- 'Romney Marsh'	EBee GCal MRav SEND WFar WKif WSHC

rosea	see *Alcea rosea*
rugosostellulata	see *Alcea rugosa*

Altingia (*Hamamelidaceae*)

poilanei B&SWJ 11756	WCru

× *Alworthia* (*Asphodelaceae*)

'Black Gem'	EBee EPfP EShb

Alyogyne (*Malvaceae*)

'Attraction'	ECou
hakeifolia	ECou
- 'Elle Maree'	CSpe ECou MOWG
- 'Melissa Anne'	ECou MOWG
§ ***huegelii***	CCCN CSpe ECou SRkn SUsu
- 'Lavender Lass'	ECou
- 'Santa Cruz'	CCCN CHll CSpe EBee ECou LHop MOWG SEND SLon WPGP
- 'White Delight' **new**	ECou
'Joy'	ECou
Magic Moments = 'Hutwow'	LBuc
'Shepherds Delight'	ECou

Alyssoides (*Brassicaceae*)

utriculata	NBre XSen

Alyssum (*Brassicaceae*)

aizoides Boiss. **new**	GKev
argenteum	NBre
corymbosum	see *Aurinia corymbosa*
montanum	ECha ECho MWat SPlb SRms
§ - 'Berggold'	ECtt EPfP LRHS MMuc
- Mountain Gold	see *A. montanum* 'Berggold'
obovatum	WIce
repens	NBre
saxatile	see *Aurinia saxatilis*
- 'Summit'	EDAr
spinosum	EPot
- 'Roseum' ♀H4	CMea CTri ECha ELan GMaP MLHP MWat NMen SBch WAbe
- 'Strawberries and Cream'	WAbe
stribrnyi	LLHF
tortuosum	SEND
wulfenianum	EDAr GAbr IFoB LLHF NBre SEND WIce

Amaranthus (*Amaranthaceae*)

'Autumn Palette' **new**	CSpe
hypochondriacus 'Pygmy Torch' ♀H3	CSpe

× *Amarcrinum* (*Amaryllidaceae*)

'Dorothy Hannibal'	GCal WCot
memoria-corsii	CPrp ECho
- 'Howardii'	CCon CDes EBee ECho EShb LEdu SDeJ WCot

× *Amarine* (*Amaryllidaceae*)

tubergenii	CAvo
- 'Zwanenburg'	EBee WCot

× *Amarygia* (*Amaryllidaceae*)

parkeri	ECho
§ - 'Alba'	CAvo CBro CPrp EBee ECho WCot

Amaryllis (*Amaryllidaceae*)

§ ***belladonna*** ♀H2-3	CBcs CBro CHEx CPne CPrp CTca EBee ECho EPfP ERCP EShb LAma SChr SDeJ SEND SMrm SPav SPer WCot
- 'Johannesburg'	WCot
- 'Kimberley'	CPne
- 'Parkeri Alba'	see × *Amarygia parkeri* 'Alba'
- 'Purpurea'	WCot
- white-flowered	ECho SDeJ WCot

Amberboa (*Asteraceae*)

§ ***moschata***	WCot

Ambrosina (*Araceae*)

bassii from Tunisia	ECho

Amelanchier ✿ (*Rosaceae*)

alnifolia	CTho
- 'Forestburg'	NLar
- 'Obelisk' PBR	CDoC CDul EBee GKin LBuc LHop LLHF LRHS MAsh MBri MGos NCGa SCoo SSta WHar
- pink-fruited	NLar
§ - var. ***pumila***	LHop MMHG WTin
- 'Regent' (F)	NLar
- var. ***semi-integrifolia***	NLar
- 'Smokey'	CDul
§ ***arborea***	CTho SBfd
asiatica	LSRN
bartramiana	CTho SSta
- 'Eskimo'	NLar
canadensis K. Koch	see *A. lamarckii*
canadensis Sieb. & Zucc.	see *A. arborea*
canadensis ambig.	CDul NPri SBfd SBod SEWo SGol SPoG WHar
canadensis (L.) Medik.	CAgr CDoC CJun CLnd CMac CSBt CSam CTho CTri CWSG CWib EBee ECrN ELan EPfP LEdu LHop LRHS MGos MRav MSwo NCGa NWea SPer WFar WMoo WPat
- 'Prince William'	CAgr MCoo SSta
- Rainbow Pillar = 'Glenn Form'	EBee LRHS MAsh MBlu MBri MGos SGol SLim SPoG SSta WHar
× ***grandiflora*** 'Autumn Brilliance'	CJun NHol NLar SGol
- 'Ballerina' ♀H4	Widely available
- 'Cole's Select'	EBee LRHS SKHP
- 'Forest Prince' **new**	NLar
- 'Princess Diana'	MBlu NLar SCoo
- 'Robin Hill'	CBcs CCVT CDul CMac EBee ECrN EMil LAst LBuc MAsh MBlu MGos MRav NEgg NLar NWea SBfd SCoo SEWo SGol SHil SLim SMad SPoG WFar WHar
- 'Rubescens'	CDul CJun EBee EPfP NLar SLon
'La Paloma'	EBee EPfP LRHS MAsh MBri SCoo WHar
laevis	CBcs CDul CTri EPfP MGos MSwo NLar
- 'Cumulus'	NLar
- 'Prince Charles'	NLar
- 'R.J. Hilton'	MBri MWat SCoo WHar
- 'Snow Cloud'	CDoC
- 'Snowflakes'	CJun EBee EMil LRHS MAsh MGos MWat NHol NLar SEWo SLim SPer SPoG WHar
§ ***lamarckii*** ♀H4	Widely available
ovalis misapplied	see *A. spicata* (Lam.) K. Koch.
ovalis Medik.	SGar SPlb
- 'Edelweiss'	CJun IArd MBlu NEgg NLar SCoo

- 'Helvetia' NLar
pumila see *A. alnifolia* var. *pumila*
rotundifolia ambig. MCoo
sanguinea 'Chimney Rock' new NLar
sinica CBcs NLar
§ ***spicata*** (Lam.) K. Koch MCoo SSta
stolonifera new CTri

× *Amelasorbus* (*Rosaceae*)

raciborskiana MBlu MBri

Amicia (*Papilionaceae*)

zygomeris CAbb CCse CHEx CHGN CHll CPom CSpe ELon EWes EWld EWll GBin GCal LHop MCot SDix SEND SMad SMrm SPoG WCot WSHC
- 'John's Big Splash' (v) new WCot

Ammi (*Apiaceae*)

majus CArn CSpe MNHC SDix SMrm SPhx WJek
visnaga CArn CBre CHby CSpe ELau MNHC SPhx WHal WJek

Ammobium (*Asteraceae*)

calyceroides ECou

Ammocharis (*Amaryllidaceae*)

coranica ECho WCot

Ammophila (*Poaceae*)

arenaria CKno CRWN EBee SMea XLum
breviligulata SPhx

Amomum (*Zingiberaceae*)

subulatum GHim

Amomyrtus (*Myrtaceae*)

§ ***luma*** CAgr CBcs CDoC CDul CHEx CTri EBee ELan GQui IDee WCot WJek

Amorpha (*Papilionaceae*)

canescens EBee LRHS SPlb
fruticosa CBcs EBee EBtc EWTr MBlu MMuc SEND SPlb
herbacea NLar
paniculata NLar

Amorphophallus ✿ (*Araceae*)

Chen Yi A-102 WCot
albus CDTJ LEdu SChr WCot
bulbifer CDTJ EAmu EBee GHim LAma SBig SBst SDeJ
dunnii CDTJ
kerrii CPLG WCot
kiusianus WCot
- B&SWJ 4845 WCru
konjac CCon CDTJ CDes CGHE CHEx CPLG CSpe EAmu EBee EUJe LEdu SChF WCot WPGP
nepalensis CDTJ EAmu EBee GHim SBst
rivieri CPom EBee GCal LRHS SDeJ WCot
stipitatus WCot

Ampelocalamus (*Poaceae*)

§ ***mocrophyllum*** ERod WJun WPGP
scandens WPGP

Ampelocissus (*Vitaceae*)

sikkimensis HWJK 2066 WCru

Ampelodesmos (*Poaceae*)

mauritanica CHid CKno COlW CSam CTrC EBee ECha EHoe EShb EWes LRHS MWhi SEND SMHy SMad SPlb WCot WWEG XLum

Ampelopsis (*Vitaceae*)

aconitifolia NLar
- 'Chinese Lace' EBee LRHS MRav NLar WPGP
arborea WCru
brevipedunculata ELan MMHG SCoo SGar SKHP SLim SPer SPhx SPoG WFar
- var. ***maximowiczii*** 'Elegans' (v) CBcs CHEx CMac CWib EBee ELan EPfP EShb LAst LBMP LHop LRHS MGos MMuc MRav NBro SAga SPer SPoG SWvt WCot WPat WSHC
delavayana MMuc
henryana see *Parthenocissus henryana*
megalophylla CHEx ELan EShb GCal MMuc NCGa NLar SKHP SPer WCru WFar
sempervirens hort. ex Veitch see *Cissus striata*
tricuspidata 'Veitchii' see *Parthenocissus tricuspidata* 'Veitchii'

Amphicome see *Incarvillea*

Amsonia (*Apocynaceae*)

'Blue Ice' new EBee IPot
ciliata EBee ELan IKil SKHP SUsu XLum
§ ***elliptica*** LRHS
hubrichtii CCon CCse CEnt CSpe EBee ECha ELon EPPr LEdu LHop LRHS NLar SMad SMrm SPad SPhx WHoo WPer WPtf WSHC
illustris CAbP CEnt CSpe EBee EPPr GCal LRHS NLar SHar SMHy SPhx SUsu WHoo WHrl WPer WSHC WTin
jonesii SMHy
§ ***orientalis*** Widely available
sinensis see *A. elliptica*
tabernaemontana Widely available
- var. ***salicifolia*** CEnt CSpe EBee EWll WCAu WTin
- 'Stella Azul' EBee IPot

Amygdalus see *Prunus*

Anacamptis (*Orchidaceae*)

coriophora NLAp
fragrans NLAp
§ ***laxiflora*** NLAp
longicornu new NLAp
§ ***morio*** NLAp
morio* × *papilionacea NLAp
papilionacea new NLAp
pyramidalis EFEx NLAp WHer
sancta NLAp

Anacyclus (*Asteraceae*)

pyrethrum GPoy
- var. ***depressus*** CTri EBee ECho ELan EPfP GMaP LRHS MAsh MMuc SPlb SRot WCFE WHoo WPer WWFP
- - 'Garden Gnome' CTri ECho SRms WHil
- - 'Silberkissen' EDAr NSla

Anagallis (Primulaceae)

monellii ♀H4	MNrw
- Blue Compact	LSou
= 'Wesanacomp'	
- subsp. ***linifolia*** 'Blue Light'	CSpe
- 'Skylover'	CCCN LAst NPri
- 'Sunrise'	SUsu
tenella 'Studland'	CEnt EPot GAbr WAbe

Ananas (Bromeliaceae)

comosus (F)	CCCN
- 'Champaca' (F)	CCCN
lucidus	LRHS

Anaphalioides (Asteraceae)

§ ***bellidioides***	CTri ECou

Anaphalis (Asteraceae)

alpicola	EBee EPot NBre NMen
margaritacea	CBcs EBee ECha ECtt GMaP NBid SBfd SRms WFar WMoo WPtf
§ - 'Neuschnee'	CTri EBee EPfP NBre NGdn WFar WPer WWEG XLum
- New Snow	see *A. margaritacea* 'Neuschnee'
- var. ***yedoensis*** ♀H4	CTri MCot MLHP NBre SDix SGar SPer
§ ***nepalensis*** var. ***monocephala***	ELan MCot NBre NSti
nubigena	see *A. nepalensis* var. *monocephala*
subumbellata	LRHS
transnokoensis	EBee EWes
§ ***trinervis***	CPLG GCra XLum
triplinervis ♀H4	EHoe ELan EPfP GAbr GMaP IBoy IFoB LRHS MCot MRav NBid NLar NPri SEND SPer WCot WHoo WMoo WWEG
- CC 1620	EBee NBir
- 'Silberregen'	EBee
§ - 'Sommerschnee' ♀H4	CMac EBee ECha ECtt EHoe EPfP IBoy LBMP LPot LRHS MCot MRav NEgg NLar SPer WMnd WPer
- Summer Snow	see *A. triplinervis* 'Sommerschnee'

Anchusa (Boraginaceae)

sp.	CHab
§ ***azurea***	NLar
- 'Dropmore'	CTri EBee ELan EPfP LAst MNHC NEgg NLar NOrc SBfd SRms WWEG
- 'Feltham Pride'	EBee EPfP LRHS SRms SWvt WFar WHoo WTcb
- 'Little John'	EBee SRms
- 'Loddon Royalist' ♀H4	Widely available
- 'Opal'	ECtt EPfP GCal LRHS MMHG
capensis 'Blue Angel'	LRHS MNHC SWvt WFar
cespitosa Lam.	ECho ELan EWes LLHF WAbe
italica	see *A. azurea*
laxiflora	see *Borago pygmaea*
myosotidiflora	see *Brunnera macrophylla*
officinalis	CArn MNHC
sempervirens	see *Pentaglottis sempervirens*

Ancylostemon (Gesneriaceae)

convexus B&SWJ 6624	WCru

Andrachne (Phyllanthaceae)

colchica	EBee WCot

Androcymbium (Colchicaceae)

cuspidatum 'Karoopoort'	ECho
dregei 'Loeriesfontein'	ECho
eucomoides 'Varsputs'	ECho
gramineum	ECho
- from Morocco	ECho
melanthioides	ECho
volutare 'Tanqua'	ECho

Andromeda (Ericaceae)

glaucophylla f. ***latifolia***	IVic
polifolia	ECho MAsh WFar
- 'Alba'	EBee ECho LRHS MAsh SPer SPlb SWvt WFar WThu
- 'Blue Ice'	EBee ELan EPfP IDee LRHS MAsh NHar NLar NMen SLim SPer SPoG SSpi WAbe WFar WPat
- 'Compacta' ♀H4	CDoC CMac EBee ECho EPfP EPot GEdr LSRN LTen MAsh NMen NWad SBfd SPoG SRms SWvt WGwG WSHC
- 'Compacta Alba' ♀H4	ECho
- 'Grandiflora'	ECho GEdr
- 'Hayachine'	ITim
- 'Kirigamine'	EBee LRHS MAsh NHar
- 'Macrophylla' ♀H4	ECho EPot GEdr NHar WAbe WPat WThu
- 'Nana'	CSBt ELan EPfP LRHS MAsh NMen
- 'Nikko'	CMac
- 'Shibutsu'	NHar NMen

Andropogon (Poaceae)

gerardii	CKno CRWN EBee EHoe EPPr LEdu MWhi NWsh SApp SPhx WWEG
scoparius	see *Schizachyrium scoparium*
ternarius	EBee

Androsace (Primulaceae)

CC 6619	GKev
CC 6625	GKev
albana	GKev
alpina	WAbe
armeniaca new	GKev
- var. ***macrantha***	GKev
* ***bayanharshanensis*** new	GKev
bisulca var. ***aurata***	EPot
brachystegia new	GKev
bulleyana	GKev WAbe
caduca	WAbe
cantabrica	EPot
carnea	ECho
- SDR 6357	GKev
- subsp. ***brigantiaca***	GKev NRHS NRya NSla WAbe WHoo
- var. ***halleri***	see *A. carnea* subsp. *rosea*
- subsp. ***laggeri*** ♀H4	ECho GKev LLHF NRHS NSla WAbe WFar
- - 'Andorra'	NHar
§ - subsp. ***rosea*** ♀H4	CPBP ECho WAbe
carnea × ***pyrenaica***	CYeo ECho EPot LLHF NMen
chamaejasme	ECho EPot GKev
- subsp. ***carinata*** new	GKev
ciliata	WAbe
cylindrica	ECho LRHS NMen NRHS
cylindrica × ***hirtella***	ECho LLHF LRHS NRHS WAbe
delavayi	WAbe
- ACE 1786	EPot WAbe
elatior new	WAbe

	foliosa	GKev
	geraniifolia	EBee ECha GKev SRms WAbe
	globifera	EPot WAbe
	gracilis PB 99/20	EPot
	halleri	see *A. carnea* subsp. *rosea*
	hausmannii	CPBP
	hedraeantha	CPBP EPot WAbe
	himalaica	CPBP EPot GEdr NMen WAbe
	hirtella	LLHF WAbe
	idahoensis	WAbe
	idahoensis × ***laevigata***	WAbe
	incana	WAbe
	integra new	WAbe
	jacquemontii	see *A. villosa* var. *jacquemontii*
	kosopoljanskii	EPot GJos WAbe
	lactea	WAbe
	laevigata	CPBP ITim NMen WAbe
	- 'Gothenburg'	WAbe WPat
	- 'Saddle Mount'	CPBP WAbe
	lanuginosa ♀H4	CMea CSpe ECho ECtt EDAr EHoe EPot GEdr MMuc MWat NHar NHol NMen SBch SRms SRot WAbe WIce
	lehmanniana	WAbe
	- 'Gotëborg Yellow'	WAbe
	limprichtii	see *A. sarmentosa* var. *watkinsii*
	mariae	WAbe
	× ***marpensis***	EPot NMen WAbe
	mathildae	NMen
	microphylla	see *A. mucronifolia* G.Watt
	'Millstream'	GKev
	minor	EPot WAbe
	montana	WAbe
	mucronifolia misapplied	see *A. sempervivoides*
§	***mucronifolia*** G.Watt	WAbe
	mucronifolia × ***sempervivoides***	EPot NHar
	muscoidea	GKev WAbe
	- SEP 132	CPBP WAbe
	- 'Breviscapa'	EPot
	- f. ***longiscapa***	WAbe
	- Schacht's form	EPot WAbe
	nivalis Chumstick form	LLHF
	ochotensis	WAbe
	× ***pedemontana***	GKev
	primuloides	see *A. studiosorum*
	pubescens	ECho LLHF LRHS NMen NRHS WAbe
	pyrenaica	ECho LLHF LRHS NMen NRHS WAbe
	rigida	EPot LLHF WAbe
	robusta subsp. ***purpurea***	WAbe
	- - 'Dolpo Dwarf'	WAbe
	rotundifolia	EBee GEdr GKev
	- stoloniferous	GEdr
	sarmentosa misapplied	see *A. studiosorum*
	sarmentosa ambig.	EDAr GJos GKev
	sarmentosa Wall.	SRms WHoo
	- from Namche, Nepal	EPot EWld WAbe
	- Galmont's form	see *A. studiosorum* 'Salmon's Variety'
	- 'Sherriffii'	ECho EPot GKev SRms WIce
§	- var. ***watkinsii***	EPot NMen
	- var. ***yunnanensis*** misapplied	see *A. studiosorum*
	selago	WAbe
	- 'Red Eye'	WAbe
§	***sempervivoides*** ♀H4	CYeo ECho EDAr EPot GEdr GJos GKev GMaP LHop LRHS NHol NMen NRHS SPlb SRms WAbe WIce WPat
	- CC 4622	GKev
	- CC 4631	GKev
	- CC 5299	GKev
	- CC 5317	GKev
	- 'Susan Joan'	EPot GEdr GKev WAbe
	septentrionalis	GKev
	sericea	WAbe
	spinulifera	GKev
	- SDR 6733	GKev
	strigillosa	WAbe
§	***studiosorum*** ♀H4	EPot GEdr GKev NSla WAbe
	- 'Chumbyi'	GEdr LLHF SHar SRms WIce WPat WThu
	- 'Doksa'	CPBP EPot GEdr NMen SHar WAbe WIce WPat
§	- 'Salmon's Variety'	CMea CTri WAbe
	tangulashanensis	GKev WAbe
	tapete ACE 1725	WAbe
	vandellii	WAbe
	villosa SDR 5445	GKev
	- var. ***arachnoidea***	GKev
§	- var. ***jacquemontii***	CPBP NHar SHar
	- - lilac-flowered	EPot WAbe
	- - pink-flowered	EPot WAbe
	- subsp. ***taurica***	WAbe
	vitaliana	see *Vitaliana primuliflora*
	wardii	GKev WAbe
	watkinsii	see *A. sarmentosa* var. *watkinsii*
	yargongensis	GKev WAbe
	zambalensis	WAbe

Androstoma (*Epacridaceae*)

§	***empetrifolia***	WThu

Andryala (*Asteraceae*)

	lanata	see *Hieracium lanatum*

Anemanthele (*Poaceae*)

§	***lessoniana*** ♀H4	Widely available
	- 'Gold Hue'	CKno

Anemarrhena (*Asparagaceae*)

	asphodeloides	CArn WCot

Anemone ✿ (*Ranunculaceae*)

	Chen Yi T49	WCot
	aconitifolia Michx.	see *A. narcissiflora*
	altaica	EBee GHim GKev LWSt NLar SRms
	amurensis	CPLG
	apennina ♀H4	CAvo CLAP ECGP ECho EHrv LWSt WShi WTin
	- var. ***albiflora***	CLAP EBee ECho EPPr EPot MAvo
	- double white-flowered (d)	LRHS
	- double-flowered (d)	ECho EHrv EPPr MAvo WCru
	- 'Petrovac'	CLAP EBee EPot LLHF LWSt SPhx WCot
	baicalensis	WSHC
	baissunensis	LWSt
	baldensis	ECho EDAr GBuc GKev IGor SRms WPtf
	barbulata	CPLG EBee EWes GBuc GEdr GKev NLar WSHC
	blanda ♀H4	ECho LAma LRHS MAsh MAvo MBri MLHP MNHC MWat NLar SBfd SEND SWal WBor WCot WFar WShi
I	- 'Alba'	LRHS
	- 'Blue Star'	ECho

	- blue-flowered	CAvo CBro CMea CSam CTri ECGP ECho ELan EPfP EPot ERCP GAbr GKev GMaP IGor LAma LRHS MBri MNFA SDeJ SMrm SPer SPhx SPoG SRms WFar WHoo
	- 'Charmer'	CGrW ECho EPot NMen SDeJ SMrm
	- 'Ingramii'	LWst WCot
	- var. ***rosea*** ♀H4	ECho ELan EPfP GKev LAma LRHS SBch SDeJ SPer SPoG WFar
	- - 'Pink Charmer'	ECho NLar
	- - 'Pink Star'	CAvo ECho ERCP GKev LAma LEdu NBir
	- - 'Radar' ♀H4	CAvo CMea ECho EPot ERCP LAma LRHS MNrw NBir SDeJ WAbe
	- 'Violet Star'	ECGP ECho GKev NLar SDeJ SPhx WCot
	- 'White Charmer'	ECho
	- 'White Splendour' ♀H4	CAvo CBro CMea CSam CTri ECho ELan EPfP EPot ERCP GAbr GKev LAma LPot LRHS NBir NLar NMen SDeJ SMrm SPer SPhx SPoG SRms WCot WFar
	blue-flowered from China	CDes
	caerulea	LWst
	canadensis	CSpe EBee ELon EPPr GBuc LRHS WCot
	caroliniana	ECho LRHS
	caucasica	ECho LWst
	chapaensis HWJ 631	WCru
	coronaria	SVic
	- De Caen Group	CHid EPfP GKev LAma LRHS SPoG WFar
	- - 'Bicolor'	CHid GKev SDeJ WRHF
§	- - 'Die Braut'	ERCP NBir SDeJ WFar
	- - 'His Excellency'	see *A. coronaria* (De Caen Group) 'Hollandia'
§	- - 'Hollandia'	CSpe LPot SDeJ
	- - 'Mister Fokker'	CTca ERCP LAma SDeJ WFar
	- - The Bride	see *A. coronaria* (De Caen Group) 'Die Braut'
	- - 'The Governor'	CTca GKev SDeJ WFar
	- Jerusalem hybrids	WFar
	- Saint Bridgid Group (d)	EPfP GKev LAma WFar
	- - 'Lord Lieutenant' (d)	CMea EPfP ERCP GKev NBir SDeJ WFar
	- - 'Mount Everest' (d)	ERCP GKev NBir SDeJ
	- - 'Saint Bridgid' (d)	CHid
	- - 'The Admiral' (d)	EPfP GKev NBir SDeJ WFar
	- 'Sylphide' (Mona Lisa Series)	ERCP LPot NBir SDeJ WCot WFar
	cylindrica	EBee MDKP NBre NLar XEll
	'Danish Flag' **new**	MNrw
	decapetala	GBuc MHer
	demissa	WCot
	- SDR 3307	EBee
	- SDR 4306	GKev
	- var. ***major*** **new**	GKev
	dichotoma	SSvw
	drummondii	GKev LRHS NChi WHrl
	eranthoides	ECho LWst
	fanninii	GCal
	fasciculata	see *A. narcissiflora*
	flaccida	CLAP EBee ECho EHrv EPPr GEdr LRHS MAvo MMHG MNFA MNrw NRHS SBch WCot WCru WFar WHal WSHC
	globosa	see *A. multifida* Poir.
	gortschakowii	LWst
	'Guernica'	ECho EWes
	'Hatakeyama Double' (d)	GCal WSHC
	'Hatakeyama Single'	WCot
	hepatica L.	see *Hepatica nobilis*
§	***hortensis***	EBee ECho
§	***hupehensis***	CPLG EBee GMaP NOrc WFar WPer
	- BWJ 8190	WCru
	- f. ***alba***	CLAP CPLG CSpe IFro WPGP
§	- 'Bowles's Pink' ♀H4	CDes CElw CPLG EBee ECho SPet WCru WPGP WTin
	- 'Crispa'	see *A.* × *hybrida* 'Lady Gilmour' Wolley-Dod
	- 'Eugenie'	EBee ECtt GBuc LRHS NBir NHol
	- 'Hadspen Abundance' ♀H4	Widely available
	- var. ***hupehensis*** **new**	WSpi XLum
§	- var. ***japonica***	CPou XLum
	- - B&SWJ 4886	WCru
	- - 'Bodnant Burgundy'	EBee LRHS WPGP
§	- - 'Bressingham Glow'	CMHG CMac CPLG CSam EBee ECtt ELan EPfP EPot GKin LRHS MBri MRav NBir NHol NOrc SPet WAbb WBrk WFar WWEG
§	- - 'Pamina' ♀H4	Widely available
	- - Prince Henry	see *A. hupehensis* var. *japonica* 'Prinz Heinrich'
§	- - 'Prinz Heinrich' ♀H4	Widely available
§	- - 'Rotkäppchen'	EBee ECtt GKin GQue IVic LRHS LSou MAvo NGdn NHol NLBP NLar SEND SMrm SWvt WCot WSHC
	- - 'Splendens'	CMHG EBee EPfP GBBs LAst LHop LRHS MAsh MCot MMuc NEgg NGdn SHil SPer SUsu SWvt WAbb WHal WWEG XLum
	- 'Little Princess'PBR	EBee ECtt
	- 'Ouvertüre'	EBee ECtt GBuc GQue MAvo WCot WPGP
	- 'Praecox'	CMea EBee EPfP GBBs LRHS LSou MBNS NBir NCGa NHol NSti SBfd SHil SWvt WAbb WFar WHal WMnd WWEG
	- 'September Charm'	see *A.* × *hybrida* 'September Charm'
	- 'Superba'	EBee GBin WKif
§	× ***hybrida***	ECho LRHS NChi NEgg SEND SGar WFar WMoo
	- 'Alba' misapplied (UK)	see *A.* × *hybrida* 'Honorine Jobert'
	- 'Alba Dura'	see *A. tomentosa* 'Albadura'
	- 'Albert Schweitzer'	see *A.* × *hybrida* 'Elegans'
	- 'Alice'	LRHS
	- 'Andrea Atkinson'	Widely available
	- 'Bowles's Pink'	see *A. hupehensis* 'Bowles's Pink'
	- 'Bressingham Glow'	see *A. hupehensis* var. *japonica* 'Bressingham Glow'
	- 'Coupe d'Argent'	EBee IKil
§	- 'Elegans' ♀H4	CSam EBee ECtt GMaP LHop LRHS MMuc NBir NGdn SEND SWat SWvt WSpi
§	- 'Géante des Blanches'	EBee MAvo SMrm
§	- 'Honorine Jobert' ♀H4	Widely available
§	- 'Königin Charlotte' ♀H4	Widely available
	- 'Lady Gilmour' misapplied	see *A.* × *hybrida* 'Montrose'
	- 'Lady Gilmour' ambig.	GAbr GMaP MBel SMrm SPad
§	- 'Lady Gilmour' Wolley-Dod	CSam EBee ECtt EPfP GCra LEdu LRHS LSou MBri MRav NBir NEgg WCot WCru WWEG XLum
	- 'Loreley'	CMea EBee EPfP GBuc LRHS NLar SBfd SWvt WWEG
	- 'Luise Uhink'	CPou LRHS

	- 'Märchenfee'	EBee MAvo
	- 'Margarete' Kayser & Seibert	CPLG CPar EBee ECtt ELan EPfP LRHS MBri MGos NGdn SBfd WCru
	- 'Max Vogel'	see *A.* × *hybrida* 'Elegans'
	- 'Monterosa'	see *A.* × *hybrida* 'Montrose'
§	- 'Montrose'	CPou EBee ECha EHrv EWes GCal GMaP LRHS LSou NBir NLar SRms SWat
	- 'Pamina'	see *A. hupehensis* var. *japonica* 'Pamina'
	- (Pretty Lady Series) 'Pretty Lady Diana' **new**	ECtt
	- - 'Pretty Lady Emily' **new**	ECtt SHar
	- - 'Pretty Lady Susan' **new**	ECtt SHar
	- Prince Henry	see *A. hupehensis* var. *japonica* 'Prinz Heinrich'
	- 'Profusion'	CTri LBuc LRHS NRHS WHal
	- Queen Charlotte	see *A.* × *hybrida* 'Königin Charlotte'
	- 'Richard Ahrens'	EBee ECtt EPfP GBuc GCal GMaP LAst LHop LRHS MGos MLHP NEgg NGdn NHol NLar NOrc SBfd SPad SWat WCru WFar WMnd WWEG
§	- 'Robustissima'	EBee ECtt EPfP GBBs GMaP LRHS LSRN MCot MGos MNrw MRav NBir NDov NGdn NRHS NSti SEND SPer SWat SWvt WAbb WFar WMnd WMoo WWEG
	- 'Rosenschale'	EBee LRHS WCru
	- 'Rotkäppchen'	see *A. hupehensis* var. *japonica* 'Rotkäppchen'
§	- 'September Charm' ♀H4	Widely available
	- 'Serenade'	CSam EBee ECtt EPau EPfP GBBs LRHS LSRN MAsh MRav NBir NCGa NLar SMrm SPoG SRkn WCAu WMoo WWEG
	- Tourbillon	see *A.* × *hybrida* 'Whirlwind'
§	- 'Whirlwind'	Widely available
	- 'White Queen'	see *A.* × *hybrida* 'Géante des Blanches'
	- Wirbelwind	see *A.* × *hybrida* 'Whirlwind'
	japonica	see *A.* × *hybrida*, *A. hupehensis*, *A. hupehensis* var. *japonica*
	keiskeana	GEdr LWSt WCru
§	× ***lesseri***	CBro CCon CSpe EBee ECha ECho EDAr EHrv ELan GKev LHop MHer SPhx SRms WHil
	leveillei	Widely available
	- BWJ 7919	WCru
§	× ***lipsiensis***	CBro CDes ECho EHrv EPfP EPot EShb GBBs GEdr GMaP IFro MAvo MMoz MNrw NLar NMen NRya SMrm WCot WCru WHal WPGP WSHC
	- 'Pallida' ♀H4	CSam CSpe EBee ECho ELon GBuc GEdr GKev IGor LEdu LLWP LWSt MAvo NLar SKHP SSvw WCot WShi XEll
	- 'Schwefelfeuer' **new**	GHim
	- 'Vindobonensis'	WCot
	***lithophila* new**	LLHF
	lyallii	EBee GKev
	magellanica hort. ex Wehrh.	see *A. multifida* Poir.
	matsudae B&SWJ 1452	WCru
	multifida misapplied, red-flowered	see *A.* × *lesseri*
§	***multifida*** Poir.	EBee ECha ECho EPfP EWTr GJos IFoB LHop LRHS NBir NSti SPoG SRms WHoo
	- Annabella Series	EPfP GAbr GKev
	- - 'Annabella Deep Rose'	WHrl
	- 'Major'	CCon CMea CPrp CSpe EPfP NPro SMrm WFar WIce
	- f. ***polysepala***	NEgg
	- 'Rubra'	CBro CMea EAEE EBee EDAr EHrv EPfP GAbr GEdr GKev LRHS MCot NBir NEgg NLar SMrm SPoG STes WHoo
	- white-flowered	LRHS
	- yellow-flowered	CBro GBBs MCot NSum
§	***narcissiflora***	CSpe EBee ECho EHrv GKev LRHS MMHG NBir NChi
	- SDR 5496	GKev
	- var. ***citrina***	LRHS
	nemorosa ♀H4	Widely available
N	- 'Alba Plena' (d)	CSam EBee ECha ECho EPPr GBuc GEdr LWSt MAvo NGdn NPnk WAbb WFar WSHC
	- 'Allenii' ♀H4	CBro EBee ECha ECho EHrv ELon EPot GBuc GEdr GMaP ITim LRHS MAvo MMoz MNFA MRav NMen NRya WFar WShi
	- 'Amy Doncaster'	CLAP ECho
	- 'Atley'	EBee GEdr LWSt MAvo
	- 'Atrocaerulea'	CLAP GBuc IBlr NLar WFar
	- 'Ballyrogan Blue'	MNrw
	- 'Bill Baker's Pink'	CDes CLAP LEdu
	- 'Blue Beauty'	CLAP EBee ELon GBuc GMaP IBlr LWSt MAvo NMen SBch
	- 'Blue Bonnet'	CElw ECho GBuc IGor MAvo MNrw
	- 'Blue Eyes' (d)	CDes CElw CLAP EBee GBuc GEdr GMaP IBlr IGor LWSt MAvo MMoz NBir NMyG WCot WFar WSHC
	- 'Blue Queen'	GAbr
	- 'Bowles's Purple'	ECho ELon GBBs GBuc GMaP IBlr LRHS MAvo MNrw NBid NHar NMyG NRHS NRya SKHP WBor WCot WFar WPnP WTin
	- 'Bracteata'	CBro CFis ECho GBuc GEdr LRHS MMHG MMoz NMen
	- 'Bracteata Pleniflora' (d)	CLAP ECho EHrv ELon GBuc GMaP IBlr IGor LHop LWSt MAvo MNrw NBir NMen NMyG NPnk WCot WFar WHal
	- 'Buckland'	CFwr CLAP EBee EPfP IBlr LWSt SKHP WFar
	- 'Caerulea'	EPot ITim
	- 'Cedric's Pink'	CLAP EPPr IBlr LLHF MMHG MNrw WFar
	- 'Celestial'	EBee ECho ELan EPPr GBuc MAvo
	- 'Dee Day'	CLAP EBee EHrv GBuc MAvo MNrw SCnR WFar
	- 'Dell Garden'	EPPr
	- 'Evelyn Meadows' ♀H4	CLAP
	- 'Flore Pleno' (d)	CDes ECho GAbr IFro MMoz NBir NMen NMyG WBor
	- 'Frühlingsfee'	NLar
	- 'Gerda Ramusen'	CDes CLAP ECho ELan ELon EWes GBuc LLHF
I	- 'Gigantea Rubra'	WCot
	- 'Green Fingers'	CLAP EBee ECho EHrv EPPr EPot GBuc GEdr GMaP LWSt MAvo MMHG MNrw WCot WSHC
	- 'Hakumane Senjuizaki'	WCot
	- 'Hannah Gubbay'	CLAP IBlr MAvo MNrw
	- 'Hilda'	EBee ECho EPot GBuc GEdr MNrw NBir NMen NPnk NRHS NRya
	- 'Ice and Fire'	SSvw

- 'Jack Brownless' CLAP
- 'Kassari Kirju' LWst
- 'Kentish Pink' GBBs GMaP NPnk
- 'Knightshayes Vestal' (d) CLAP CPLG MRav NHol WCot
- 'Kyffhäuser Rote' **new** WCot
- 'Lady Doneraile' CDes CLAP EPot GBuc MDKP NBir NLar WFar
- 'Latvian Pink' EBee ECho EPot GEdr LWst MAvo
- 'Leeds' Variety' CLAP EPot GAbr GBuc GMaP ITim LWst MAvo MNrw NMen NMyG NPnk
- 'Lionel Bacon' LWst
- 'Lismore Blue' EBee ECho EPPr EPot
- 'Lismore Pink' GEdr
- 'Lucia' EBee EPot GEdr LWst
- 'Lychette' EBee ECho EHrv EPPr EPot GAbr GBuc IBlr ITim LWst MAvo MNrw NMyG WFar
- 'Marie Rose' EPot
- 'Mart's Blue' CDes EBee GBuc
- 'Miss Eunice' CDes CLAP
- 'Monstrosa' ECho GBuc
- 'New Pink' CLAP IBlr
- 'Parlez Vous' CPLG EBee ECho EHrv EPPr GEdr MAvo MNrw NMen NPnk SCnR SSvw WFar
- 'Pat's Pink' WShi
- 'Pentre Pink' EPot IBlr MCot MNrw MSSP WFar
- 'Picos Pink' EHrv GBuc LWst SCnR
- 'Pink Carpet' GEdr
- pink-flowered CLAP ECho
- 'Polar Star' CLAP
- 'Robinsoniana' ♀H4 Widely available
- 'Rosea' CLAP EBee ECho GEdr MNrw SMrm
- 'Royal Blue' CBro CLAP ECho EHrv EPPr GAbr GEdr GMaP LAma LWst MAvo NHol NMen NPnk NRHS WCot WFar WPnP WTin
- 'Rubra' EPot MNrw
- 'Slack Top Pink' MAvo
- 'Stammheim' (d) CLAP EPPr
- 'Super Allenii' GBuc MAvo
- 'Tinney's Blush' CLAP
- 'Tomas' CLAP EBee ECho ELon EPot GBuc GEdr NHar
- 'Vestal' (d) ♀H4 Widely available
- 'Virescens' ♀H4 CAvo CLAP CWCL EBee ECho EHrv ELon EPPr EPot GAbr GBuc GEdr GMaP LWst MAvo MMoz NBir NHar NRHS WPtf WShi
- 'Viridiflora' CFwr CLAP CPLG ECho EPfP GAbr GBuc LHop MNrw NBir NSti SSvw WCot WFar WSHC
- 'Westwell Pink' CLAP ECho EPPr LLHF MAvo MNrw MSSP SPhx WCot WShi
- white-flowered NRHS
- 'Wilks' Giant' MAvo WFar
- 'Wilks' White' ELon EPPr GEdr WFar
- 'Wisley Pink' EPot MAvo
- 'Wyatt's Pink' CFis CLAP ELon LWst MAvo NCGa WFar WTin
- 'Yerda Ramusem' EBee ECho EPPr GBuc MAvo

nemorosa* × *ranunculoides see *A.* × *lipsiensis*
nikoensis EBee ECho LWst
obtusiloba CLAP GBuc GEdr SRms WAbe
- CLD 1549 GEdr
- 'Alba' WAbe
- blue-flowered **new** WAbe

I - 'Sulphurea' CDes GEdr NMen WCot
- yellow-flowered WAbe

palmata EDAr EWTr EWes LDai LEdu MDKP NBre NPnk SBea SMad WBor WCru
parviflora ECho
patens see *Pulsatilla patens*
pavonina CMea CSpe EBee ECha LRHS NBir SLon SMHy SPoG SUsu WAbe WCot
- lilac-flowered NBir SUsu
- pink-flowered NBir SUsu

petiolulosa LWst
polyanthes CSpe
prattii CLAP CPLG EPPr GEdr WCot WHal
pseudoaltaica GEdr LWst WCru
- blue-flowered GEdr LWst
- 'Yuki-no-sei' (d) GEdr

pulsatilla see *Pulsatilla vulgaris*
quinquefolia WCot
raddeana ECho LWst
ranunculoides ♀H4 Widely available
- 'Frank Waley' WCot
- 'Grandiflora' **new** EBee MAvo

* - ***laciniata*** CLAP GBuc NMen WCot
- 'Pleniflora' (d) CLAP EBee ECha ECho EPot GBBs GBuc LEdu LWst MAvo NLar NMen WCot WFar
- subsp. ***ranunculoides*** ECho GKev WHil
- 'Semi Plena' ECho
- subsp. ***wockeana*** CDes CSam EBee ECho GBuc MAvo

reflexa EBee GKev LLHF
riparia see *A. virginiana* var. *alba*
rivularis CAvo CLAP CMea CPar EBee ECha GAbr GBuc GKev GPoy IPot LEdu LHop LRHS NBir NChi NHar NLar NPnk NRHS NWad SMad WCru WFar WHoo WKif WMoo WTin
- BWJ 7611 WCru
- CC 4587 GKev
- CC 4588 CPLG
- 'Blue Back' GCal
- 'Glacier' NEgg WPer WSpi

aff. ***rivularis*** WPtf WSpi
rupicola IGor NBir
× ***seemannii*** see *A.* × *lipsiensis*
stellata Lam. see *A. hortensis*
stolonifera double-flowered (d) CElw EBee GEdr MAvo WCot WSHC
sulphurea misapplied see *Pulsatilla alpina* subsp. *apiifolia*
sumatrana B&SWJ 11265 WCru
sylvestris Widely available
- 'Elise Fellmann' (d) CSpe EBee EPfP GBin GBuc IPot WHal WHil
- 'Flore Pleno' (d) NMen
- 'Macrantha' EPfP GAbr NGdn SMrm WCot

tetrasepala WCot
§ ***tomentosa*** EBee ECha LRHS NBre SDix SRms SWat
§ - 'Albadura' EBee
- 'Robustissima' see *A.* × *hybrida* 'Robustissima'

trifolia L. EPPr GBuc NBid SCnR SRms WCot WPat
trullifolia CDes GBee GBin GCra GEdr NSla WAbe
vernalis see *Pulsatilla vernalis*

virginiana	EBee GAbr LDai LEdu LPla MDKP NBid NPnk SPhx WHrl WWEG
§ - var. ***alba***	NSti
vitifolia misapplied	see *A. tomentosa*

Anemonella (*Ranunculaceae*)

thalictroides	Widely available
- 'Alba Plena' (d)	ECho
- 'Amelia'	CLAP EPPr GEdr NHar SCnR WAbe
- 'Babe'	LWst
- 'Betty Blake' (d)	GEdr WCot
- 'Big'	LWst
- 'Cameo'	CLAP EFEx EPPr GEdr LWst NHar SCnR WCot WCru WFar
- 'Diamante'	WCot
- 'Double Green' (d)	CLAP EFEx GEdr LWst
- 'Flore Pleno' (d)	GBuc
- 'Full Double White' (d)	EFEx GEdr LWst
- 'Green Hurricane' (d)	EFEx GEdr LWst
- 'Jade Feather'	CElw
- f. ***rosea***	CElw CLAP CRDP ECho ELan GBuc IPot LLHF WAbe WCru WFar
- - 'Oscar Schoaf' (d)	CLAP GEdr ITim LWst WAbe
- - semi-double (d)	CElw CLAP CRDP EHrv LWst MAvo NLar
- semi-double white-flowered (d)	CElw CLAP CRDP EPPr NMen WAbe WCot
- 'Tairin'	GEdr LWst
- 'XXL' **new**	WCot

Anemonopsis (*Ranunculaceae*)

macrophylla	CLAP CPBP CPLG CRDP CSpe EBee ECha ECho EWes GCal GEdr LRHS MNrw MRav NLar SBea SMad SPhx WAbe WCru WFar WPGP WSHC
- 'White Swan'	GEdr WCru WSHC

Anemopsis (*Saururaceae*)

californica	EBee EWay IFoB MSKA MWts NLar WCot WPGP

Anethum (*Apiaceae*)

graveolens	CArn ENfk GPoy MHer MHoo MNHC NPri SBfd SIde SVic SWal
- 'Dukat'	CSev EGHP ELau MHoo
- fern-leaved	MHoo

angelica see *Angelica archangelica*

Angelica (*Apiaceae*)

sp.	CHab
acutiloba	CSpe MMHG NLar
- var. ***iwatensis*** B&SWJ 11197	WCru
anomala B&SWJ 10886	WCru
archangelica	Widely available
arguta	MHer
atropurpurea	CArn EBee ECtt EPfP GKev GQue LRHS MHer MHoo MNrw MRav NCGa NSti SWat WFar WJek WMnd WWEG WWlt
dahurica	MHoo SPhx WOut XLum
- B&SWJ 8603	WCru
decursiva	CArn
- B&SWJ 5746	WCru
'Ebony'	CBre EBee GAbr LEdu LHop MDKP MHer NCGa SBfd SMrm SPad SPoG WBor WCot
edulis B&SWJ 10968	LEdu WCru
gigas	Widely available
- B&SWJ 4170	WCru
hispanica	see *A. pachycarpa*
japonica B&SWJ 11480	WCru
- B&SWJ 8816a	WCru
montana	see *A. sylvestris*
morii RWJ 9802	WCru
§ ***pachycarpa***	CArn CSpe EBee EGHP ELan EPri GKev GMaP LHop LRHS MHer MHoo MSpe NBir NPnk NRHS SBfd SGar SIde SMrm SPhx SPoG WJek WOut WWEG XLum
pubescens B&SWJ 11129	WCru
- B&SWJ 5593	WCru
- var. ***matsumurae*** B&SWJ 6387	WCru
sachalinensis	CSpe
sinensis	CArn GPoy MHoo
'Summer Delight'	see *Ligusticum scoticum*
§ ***sylvestris***	CArn CHab CRWN EGHP
* - 'Purpurea'	CSpe EWes WPGP
- 'Vicar's Mead'	CDes CSev LEdu LPla LRHS LSRN MDKP NBir NChi NLar NPnk SPhx WBor WCot WJek WPtf WSpi
taiwaniana	CArn CDTJ ELan LRHS MDKP SGar WTcb
ursina B&SWJ 10829	WCru

Angelonia (*Plantaginaceae*)

(Angelface Series) Angelface Blue Improved **new**	NPri
- Angelface Wedgwood Blue = 'Anwedg'	NPri

Anigozanthos (*Haemodoraceae*)

'Bush Ranger' (Bush Gems Series)	CCCN
flavidus	EAmu ECre EOHP SPlb
- 'Ember'	CCCN
- 'Illusion'	CCCN
- 'Opal'	CCCN
- 'Pearl'	CCCN
- red-flowered	SPlb
- 'Splendour'	CCCN
- 'Yellow Gem'	CCCN
manglesii ♀H1	SPlb

Anisacanthus (*Acanthaceae*)

quadrifidus var. ***wrightii***	WCot

anise see *Pimpinella anisum*

Anisodontea (*Malvaceae*)

§ ***capensis***	CCCN CHGN CHll ELan EPri GBee LAst MCot MOWG NBir SBfd SChF SLim SMrm SPlb SRkn SRms SWvt
- 'Pink Pearl'	LRHS
- 'Tara's Pink'	CSpe EWes SAga SMrm
'El Royo'	EBee ECtt LSou SPad WCot
elegans	SAga
'Elegant Lady'	CSpe SUsu
huegelii	see *Alyogyne huegelii*
× ***hypomadara*** misapplied	see *A. capensis*
§ × ***hypomadara*** (Sprague) D.M. Bates	SEND
julii	SPlb
Lady in Pink = 'Nuanilaninp'	LHop
'Large Magenta'	EBee LSou

	malvastroides	LHop WWlt
	'Orchard Pink'	SEND
	scabrosa	CSev

Anisodus (*Solanaceae*)

	carnioliciodes BWJ 7501	WCru
§	***luridus***	EWld GCal

Annona (*Annonaceae*)

	cherimola (F)	CCCN XBlo

Anoiganthus see *Cyrtanthus*

Anomalesia see *Gladiolus*

Anomatheca (*Iridaceae*)

	cruenta	see *Freesia laxa*

Anopterus (*Escalloniaceae*)

	glandulosus	IBlr WSHC

Anredera (*Basellaceae*)

§	***cordifolia***	CRHN ECho EShb LEdu

Antennaria (*Asteraceae*)

	aprica	see *A. parvifolia*
	dioica	CArn CTri ECtt EDAr GAbr GJos GPoy NRHS NSla SPlb SRms WFar
	- 'Alba'	EHoe
	- 'Alex Duguid'	EPot GEdr LRHS
	- 'Aprica'	see *A. parvifolia*
	- 'Minima'	ECho EPot GEdr ITim MWat NBro NHar NMen WAbe
	- 'Nyewoods Variety'	EPot
	- red-flowered	ECho
	- var. ***rosea***	see *A. rosea*
	- 'Rotes Wunder'	CMea EPot SBch WAbe
*	- 'Rubra'	ECha ECho ECtt EDAr LRHS MHer NMen WIce
	'Joy'	EPot GEdr WAbe
	macrophylla hort.	see *A. microphylla*
§	***microphylla***	SRms
§	***parvifolia***	CTri ECho NPri SRms SRot
	- var. ***rosea***	see *A. microphylla*
	plantaginifolia	EBee
§	***rosea*** ♀H4	ECho GMaP LBMP LRHS MAsh NMen SPlb SRms WFar WHoo WIce WPer

Antenoron see *Persicaria*

Anthemis ✿ (*Asteraceae*)

	from Turkey	ECtt EWes LLWP
	arvensis	CHab
§	'Beauty of Grallagh'	GBuc GCal SDix
	'Cally Cream'	GCal NCGa SMHy SMrm SUsu
	'Cally White'	GCal
	carpatica	LRHS NBro
	- compact	NSla
	- 'Karpatenschnee'	EBee LRHS NBre NRHS WWEG
	cretica subsp. ***columnae***	WAbe
	- subsp. ***pontica*** new	NLar
	'Daisy Bee'	EBee MAvo
	frutescens Hort. & Siebert & Voss.	see *Argyranthemum frutescens*
	'Grallagh Gold' misapplied, orange-yellow	see *A.* 'Beauty of Grallagh'
	'Grallagh Gold'	ECtt EWes LDai MWat NPer
§	***marschalliana***	CMea EBee ECha ECho ECtt EDAr EPot LBee LRHS NRHS SAga SMrm SPlb WCot
	nobilis	see *Chamaemelum nobile*
	punctata	WNew
	- subsp. ***cupaniana*** ♀H3-4	Widely available
	- - 'Nana'	NPer SHar
	rudolphiana	see *A. marschalliana*
	sancti-johannis	CMHG CWib EAEE EBee EPfP LDai LRHS LSou NPer SBfd SMrm SPer SRms WMoo
	'Sauce Béarnaise'	WMnd
	Susanna Mitchell = 'Blomit'	CMea EBee ECtt ELon EPfP EWll GMaP LRHS LSRN MLHP MNrw NBir NDov NPnk NRHS SMrm SRGP SWvt WMnd WPer WSHC WWEG XLum
	'Tetworth'	CElw EBee ECha ECtt EHrv ELan EPfP LSRN SMad SUsu WFar WWEG
	tinctoria	CArn CHby CMac ENfk GPoy LRHS MHer NPer SWvt WHfH WJek WSFF
	- 'Alba'	EBee LRHS NLar NRHS WFar WWEG
	- 'Charme'PBR	EBee LAst LHop LRHS NLar NRHS SPoG SWvt WCot
	- 'Compacta'	EWes GCal MNrw XLum
	- dwarf	SBri SUsu
	- 'E.C. Buxton'	Widely available
	- 'Eva'	NBre NDov WWEG
I	- 'Golden Rays'	MDKP SBfd SDix WWEG
	- 'Kelwayi'	CSBt CTri EBee EPfP LRHS NBro NLar NPer SBfd SGar SPer SRms SWat WMoo WWEG
	- 'Lemon Ice'	GMaP
	- 'Lemon Maid'	CCon ELon EPfP GBin LRHS NBre SMrm
	- 'Sauce Hollandaise'	Widely available
	- subsp. ***tinctoria***	SMrm
	- 'Wargrave Variety'	CElw CMac COlW CSam CWCL EBee ECha ECtt EHrv ELan EPfP LBMP LRHS LSou MNFA NBir NBro NCGa NChi NEgg NGdn NHol NPnk SDix SPhx SWvt WFar WMnd WTin
	'Tinpenny Sparkle'	CAbP CSam EBee ECtt EWll GMaP LSou MAvo MBel NDov NLar NSti WAul WBrk WCot WFar WHoo WRHF WTin
	triumfettii	NPer NPnk
	tuberculata	NChi SAga SBch
	'White Water'	WAbe

Anthericum (*Asparagaceae*)

	algeriense	see *A. liliago*
*	***bovei***	CBro
§	***liliago***	EBee ECho ELan GCal GMaP IFoB LHop LRHS MBel MCot MRav NCGa NLar WAul WPer WWEG
	- 'Major' ♀H4	CAvo CBro CDes ECGP ECha ECho EHrv IGor MLHP WPGP
	plumosum	see *Trichopetalum plumosum*
	ramosum	CDes CSpe ECha ECho ELan EPot EWTr EWes GCal GKev LRHS MBrN NBid NBir NCGa NLar SMrm SPhx WPGP WPer

Antholyza (*Iridaceae*)

	coccinea	see *Crocosmia paniculata*
	× ***crocosmioides***	see *Crocosmia* × *crocosmioides*
	paniculata	see *Crocosmia paniculata*

Anthoxanthum (*Poaceae*)

odoratum CHab CRWN ELau GPoy XLum

Anthriscus (*Apiaceae*)

cerefolium CArn CHby ELau ENfk EPfP GPoy MHer MHoo MNHC SBfd WJek
sylvestris CHab NMir SPhx WSFF
- 'Broadleas Blush' CNat
- 'Moonlit Night' EHoe
- 'Ravenswing' Widely available

Anthurium (*Araceae*)

andraeanum 'Glowing Pink' XBlo
- 'Red Heart' XBlo
- 'Tivolo' XBlo
'Aztec' XBlo
Baleno = 'Anthauf4'PBR XBlo
'Caribo' XBlo
crenatum XBlo
'Crimson' XBlo
'Magenta' XBlo
'Mikra' XBlo
'Octavia' XBlo
'Pico Bello' XBlo
'Pink Champion' XBlo
'Porcelaine White' XBlo
Red Champion = 'Anthbnena'PBR XBlo
'Vitara' XBlo
White Champion = 'Anthefaqyr'PBR XBlo

Anthyllis (*Papilionaceae*)

aurea new LLHF
barba-jovis CSpe LRHS
hermanniae 'Compacta' see *A. hermanniae* 'Minor'
§ - 'Minor' EPot NLar NMen WAbe
montana LRHS NRHS
subsp. **atropurpurea**
- 'Rubra' ♀H4 ECho EDAr EPot EWes LHop LLHF NLar NMen
- 'Rubra Compacta' WAbe
vulneraria CHab NMir NRya SEND WSFF
- var. **coccinea** CSpe EBee EDAr ELan GAbr MBel NLar NRHS NSla SEND WCFE WHal WHil WIce

Antirrhinum (*Plantaginaceae*)

asarina see *Asarina procumbens*
barrelieri SEND
braun-blanquetii GCra SEND WCot WMoo XLum
'Eternal' new LRHS
Florini Series new NPri
hispanicum 'Avalanche' ECtt
- subsp. **hispanicum** 'Roseum' CMea CSpe
majus WCot
- 'Black Prince' CSpe ECtt LHop SPhx
- Liberty Classic Series new NPri
- - 'Liberty Classic Bronze' new NPri
- - 'Liberty Classic Rose Pink' new NPri
- - 'Liberty Classic Scarlet' new NPri
- - 'Liberty Classic White' new NPri
- - 'Liberty Classic Yellow' new NPri
- 'Night and Day' CSpe WMoo
- (Sonnet Series) 'Sonnet Pink' new NPri
- - 'Sonnet White' new NPri
- - 'Sonnet Yellow' new NPri
molle CSpe ECtt GKev MCot NPer NRHS NSla SChF WAbe
- pink-flowered WAbe
- white-flowered new GKev
pulverulentum WAbe
sempervirens MHer WAbe XLum
siculum WCot

añu see *Tropaeolum tuberosum*

Aphelandra (*Acanthaceae*)

squarrosa 'Citrina' XBlo

Aphyllanthes (*Asparagaceae*)

monspeliensis ECho XLum

Apios (*Papilionaceae*)

§ **americana** CAgr CPom EBee ECho EWes GBin LEdu NBir NSti WCot WCru WSHC
tuberosa see *A. americana*

Apium (*Apiaceae*)

graveolens CArn CHab CPrp ELau ENfk GPoy MHer MNHC SBfd SIde SVic WJek
- var. **rapaceum** 'Prinz' ♀H3 new SVic
- (Secalinum Group) 'Par-cel' EGHP MHer

Apium × Petroselinum (*Apiaceae*)

hybrid, misapplied see *A. graveolens* Secalinum Group

Apocynum (*Apocynaceae*)

cannabinum CArn GPoy

Apodolirion (*Amaryllidaceae*)

macowanii ECho

Aponogeton (*Aponogetonaceae*)

desertorum new EWay
distachyos CBen CRow CWat EHon EWay LPBA MSKA MWts NPer SCoo SVic SWat WMAq XLum

apple see *Malus domestica*

apricot see *Prunus armeniaca*

Aptenia (*Aizoaceae*)

cordifolia ♀H1-2 CCCN NPer SChr SEND SPet
- 'Variegata' (v) CCCN SEND

Aquilegia ✿ (*Ranunculaceae*)

sp. SVic
akitensis misapplied see *A. flabellata* var. *pumila*
* **alba variegata** (v) ECho
alpina CMea CPrp EBee ECho ECtt EPfP IPot MAsh MNHC NGdn SBfd SPer SRms WCAu WFar WMoo WPer WTou XLum

	'Alpine Blue'	SPet
	amaliae	see *A. ottonis* subsp. *amaliae*
	amurensis	CLAP
	'Apple Blossom'	NBir WTou
	aragonensis	see *A. pyrenaica*
§	***atrata***	CLAP CPou EBee ECho LRHS MDKP WPer WTou
	aurea misapplied	see *A. vulgaris* golden-leaved
	aurea Janka	WTou
	bertolonii ♀H4	CMea ECho GKev LHop LRHS MAsh NMen NRHS NRya NSla SRms WHoo WIce
	Biedermeier Group	EBee ECho EPfP GAbr LRHS NGdn NNor NOrc SBfd SPoG SRot WFar WTou
	'Blackcurrant' **new**	CWCL
	'Blue Jay' (Songbird Series)	LRHS MHer
	'Blue Star' (Star Series)	EAEE EBee ELan EPfP EWTr LRHS NDov NEgg NPnk WCot WPer WTou
	'Bluebird' (Songbird Series) ♀H2	LBuc LRHS NBir NPer NPri
	brevistyla	EBee NNor
	'Fruit and Nut Chocolate'	EBee IBoy MBNS MBel NMyG SUsu WCot
	buergeriana	GEdr MDKP SPhx WPer WTou
	- 'Calimero'	EBee LRHS MBNS MDKP NLar SBea WFar
	- f. ***flavescens***	WTou
	- var. ***oxysepala***	see *A. oxysepala*
	'Bunting' (Songbird Series) ♀H2	CWGN NLar NPri WFar
	canadensis ♀H4	CLAP CSpe EBee EHoe ELan LRHS MSpe NBir NBro SBfd SGar SRms SUsu WPer WTou XLum
	- 'Corbett'	GEdr MDKP WAbe
	- 'Little Lanterns'	EBee ECtt EPPr LHop LRHS MDKP MPnt NLar WFar WHil WIce
	- 'Nana'	GEdr SBch WThu
	- 'Pink Lanterns'	LRHS
	'Cardinal' (Songbird Series)	LBuc LRHS MHer NLar WFar
	chaplinei	NBir SBch
	chrysantha	EHrv GKev NBre SRms WKif WPer WTou
	- var. ***hinckleyana***	WTou
	- 'Yellow Queen'	CPLG CPrp CWCL EBee EPPr EPfP GAbr GMaP LBMP LHop LRHS MAvo MBri MDKP MWat NBre NGdn NLar NPri SBea SMrm SPad STes WCFE WHil XLum
	clematiflora	see *A. vulgaris* var. *stellata*
	coerulea ♀H4	EBee GKev MDKP NNor SRms
	- var. ***alpina***	GKev
	- var. ***coerulea***	GKev
	- 'Himmelblau'	NBre
	'Colorado' (State Series)	MBri
	'Crimson Star'	EBee ELan EPfP GJos LRHS MDKP SPer SPoG WMoo WTou WWEG
	'Debutante'	MDKP
	desertorum	MDKP WTou
	dichroa **new**	WPGP
	discolor	EPot GKev LLHF NRHS WThu WTou
	'Double Rubies' (d)	ELan LSRN WMoo
	'Dove' (Songbird Series) ♀H2	CWGN EWll LRHS MHer NLar NPri SMrm WFar
I	'Dragonfly'	CBcs CWib ELan EPfP LRHS NGdn SBfd SPer SPet SPoG WFar WTou WWEG
	ecalcarata	see *Semiaquilegia ecalcarata*
	einseleana	LLHF
	'Elegance'	WTou
	'Elegant Moonstone' **new**	WTou
	'Elegant Opal' **new**	WTou
	'Elegant Ruby' **new**	WTou
	flabellata ♀H4	EBee GCra WTou
	- f. ***alba***	CTri ECho ELan WTou
	- - 'White Jewel' (Jewel Series)	GKev
	- 'Blackcurrant Ice'	EPfP LRHS MBri MHer SHil
	- Cameo Series	EDAr GMaP LRHS WFar WGor
	- - 'Cameo Blue and White'	CWib NCGa SRot WFar
	- - 'Cameo Blush'	WFar
	- - 'Cameo Pink and White'	MHer NCGa SRot WFar
	- - 'Cameo White'	SRot
	- 'Georgia' (State Series) ♀H3-4	MBri SMrm
	- Jewel Series	ECho
	- 'Ministar'	ECho WFar WHil
	- 'Nana Alba'	see *A. flabellata* var. *pumila* f. *alba*
§	- var. ***pumila*** ♀H4	CCon CWCL ECha ECho EDAr EPot GKev LHop LRHS MDKP NGdn NRHS WAbe WFar WTou
§	- - f. ***alba*** ♀H4	ECha ECho GKev LHop LRHS NRHS SRms WTou
	- - 'Atlantis'	EPPr GAbr LRHS
	- - 'Flore Pleno' (d)	ECho
I	- - f. ***kurilensis*** 'Rosea'	CCon GKev WAbe
	'Flamboyant'	WTou
	formosa	CMea EBee MDKP NChi SMHy WKif WTou
§	***fragrans***	CLAP CTsd EBee ELan EPfP GEdr GJos LRHS SMrm SPad WGwG WHoo WTou
	glandulosa	LLHF NLar WTou
	glauca	see *A. fragrans*
	'Golden Guiness'	WPnP WTou
	'Goldfinch' (Songbird Series)	CWGN ELon LBuc LRHS MHer NBir WPer
	grata	MDKP
	'Heavenly Blue'	LRHS SMrm SPhx WTou
	'Hensol Harebell' ♀H4	SRms
	'Honeydew'	WTou
	'Iceberg' (*fragrans* hybrid)	WTou
	japonica	see *A. flabellata* var. *pumila*
	jonesii × ***saximontana***	GKev
	June Blake's giant yellow strain **new**	WCot
	June Blake's good yellow and orange strain **new**	WCot
	'Kansas' (State Series)	MBri
	karelinii	EBee GKev
	'Koralle'	MDKP NBre WTou
	'Kristall'	EBee LSRN MDKP NBre SPhx SSvw XLum
	laramiensis	CPBP WAbe
	'Leprechaun Gold' (v)	EPfP LAst NGdn
	'Lime Sorbet'	WTou
	longissima ♀H4	CMea EBee GKev MDKP MHer NPnk SHar WHoo WTou
	'Louisiana' (State Series) ♀H2	MBri
	'Magpie'	see *A. vulgaris* 'William Guiness'
	'Maxi'	MDKP NBre WHil
	McKana Group	Widely available
	'Milk and Honey'	WTou
	'Montana' (State Series)	MBri

moorcroftiana	EBee
Mrs Scott-Elliot hybrids	CSBt EPfP GAbr SGar SPet WFar WHil
Music Series ♀H4	SRms
nigricans	see *A. atrata*
nivalis	LLHF
olympica	EWes
'Oranges and Lemons'	WCot WTou
Origami Series	WFar
- 'Origami Red and White' ♀H2 **new**	NPri
- 'Origami Rose and White' ♀H2 **new**	NPri
- 'Origami Yellow' ♀H3-4	NPri
§ ***ottonis*** subsp. ***amaliae***	CPBP LLHF WAbe
§ ***oxysepala***	CPLG EBee GCal WTou
- B&SWJ 4775	WCru
Perfumed Garden Group	LRHS WTou
'Pink Star' (Star Series) **new**	NPnk
pleated burgundy-flowered	LRHS
'Port Wine' **new**	CWCL
'Purple Emperor' PBR	EPfP LRHS
§ ***pyrenaica***	GKev WTou
* - f. ***alba***	WTou
- dwarf **new**	GKev
'Red Hobbit'	CBct CSBt CSpe EAEE EBee ELan EPfP IBoy LHop LRHS LSou MDKP MHer MSpe NBre NEgg NGdn SBea SHil WFar WGwG WHil WHoo
'Red Star' (Star Series)	CPrp EAEE EBee EPfP LRHS NDov NEgg WFar WHil WPer WTou
'Robin' (Songbird Series)	CWGN MHer SMrm WFar
rockii	CCon CLAP EWes GCal GJos GKev MDKP SBrt WTou
- B&SWJ 7965	WCru
'Roman Bronze'	see *Aquilegia* × *Semiaquilegia* 'Roman Bronze'
'Rose Queen'	EBee EPfP MDKP NBre NNor WHoo WTou
saximontana	GKev NLar NSla WTou
§ 'Schneekönigin'	CWCL GMaP LRHS WCFE
scopulorum	EBee GKev LLHF WAbe
shockleyi	CDes WTou
Shooting Stars **new**	WTou
sibirica	CCon GKev LLHF WTou
'Silver Queen'	EBee ELan MDKP
skinneri	CPLG CSpe EBee ELan IFro LRHS WMnd WTou
- 'Tequila Sunrise'	CSpe CWCL CWib EBee ELan LSRN LSou MHer NNor SPad
Snow Queen	see *A.* 'Schneekönigin'
Songbird Series	WFar
'Spitfire'	LRHS NCGa NPri SPoG
Spring Magic Series	LRHS
- 'Spring Magic Blue and White'	LRHS WTou
- 'Spring Magic Pink and White'	WTou
- 'Spring Magic Rose and Ivory'	WTou
State Series **new**	WWEG
stellata	see *A. vulgaris* var. *stellata*
'Sunburst Ruby'	LRHS MDKP WMoo WTou
triternata	NNor
'Virginia' (State Series)	MBri SGar
viridiflora	CFis CLAP EBee ELan EPfP GAbr GCal MBel SGar WAbe WCot WFar WHil WMnd WPer WTou
- 'Chocolate Soldier'	CSpe CWCL EDif
Volcano! **new**	WTou
vulgaris	CArn CHab CMHG CRWN CWCL EPfP GKev GPoy LLWP LRHS MHer MMuc MNHC NBro NGdn NMir SEND SPlb WMoo WShi WTin WWEG
- 'Adelaide Addison'	ECha LRHS SUsu WFar WHoo WTou
- var. ***alba***	CMea EPPr LRHS NDov SEND WTou
- 'Altrosa'	NBre
- 'Aureovariegata'	see *A. vulgaris* Vervaeneana Group
- 'Blackbird' (d) **new**	CWCL
- ***clematiflora***	see *A. vulgaris* var. *stellata*
- Clementine Series	EPfP LRHS
- - 'Clementine Blue' **new**	EPfP NPri WCot
- - 'Clementine Dark Purple' (d)	EPfP SPoG
- - 'Clementine Red' (d)	EPfP NPri SPoG
- - 'Clementine Salmon Rose' (d)	EPfP LRHS SPoG
- - 'Clementine White' (d)	EPfP SPoG
- 'Crystal Star'	LRHS
- var. ***flore-pleno*** (d)	LLWP WTou
- - bicolour	WTou
- - black-flowered (d)	LRHS LSou MBel SEND WCot WTou
- - blue-flowered (d)	WTou
- - 'Dorothy Rose' (Dorothy Series) (d)	EBee LSRN SPad
- - 'Double Pleat' (d)	EPfP SEND
- - 'Double Pleat' blue/white-flowered (d)	CPrp
- - 'Double Pleat' pink/white-flowered (d)	CPrp
- - 'Jane Hollow' (d)	CPou
- - pale blue-flowered (d)	WCot WTou
- - pink-flowered (d)	WTou
- - purple-flowered (d)	WTou
- - red-flowered (d)	WTou
- - 'Strawberry Ice Cream' (d)	NBro NNor
* - - 'White Bonnet' (d)	CWCL SMrm
- - white-flowered (d)	WTou
- 'Foggy Bottom Blues'	LRHS
§ - golden-leaved	ECho WTou
- Grandmother's Garden Group	WTou
- 'Heidi'	NBre
- 'Mellow Yellow'	CTsd EBee LRHS MDKP SDix WMoo
- 'Miss Coventry'	SMHy
- 'Miss M. J. Huish'	WTou
- Munstead White	see *A. vulgaris* 'Nivea'
§ - 'Nivea' ♀H4	CPou CSpe EBee ECha ELan EPfP MBri NChi SPoG
- 'Pink Spurless'	see *A. vulgaris* var. *stellata* pink-flowered
- 'Pom Pom Crimson' (Pom Pom Series)	NBro WCot
- scented	WTou
- 'Sorcery'	WTou
§ - var. ***stellata***	EHrv ELan GKev LEdu LRHS LSou MWhi NBir NBro NNor WKif WMoo WTou
- - Barlow Series (d)	WFar WTou WWEG
- - - 'Black Barlow' (d)	Widely available
- - black-flowered	WTou

	Name	Suppliers
	- - 'Blue Barlow' (Barlow Series) (d)	CSpe EBee ECtt EPfP GMaP LRHS LSRN MWat NBre NPri NRHS SHil SPer WCot WMnd WTou WWEG
	- - 'Blue Fountain'	WTou
	- - blue-flowered	LRHS WTou
	- - 'Bordeaux Barlow' (Barlow Series)	EBee LRHS WTou WWEG
	- - 'Christa Barlow' (Barlow Series) (d)	EBee EPfP LRHS NBre NGdn SPer WHlf WTou
	- - double-flowered (d)	WTou
	- - 'Firewheel'	WMoo WTou
	- - 'Greenapples' (d)	CAbP CBre CPrp CWCL EBee ELan GKev GQue IBoy LAst LBMP LPla LRHS MBel MPie MWat NDov NGdn SMrm WCot WTou WWEG WWFP
*	- - 'Iceberg'	LRHS
	- - 'Nora Barlow' (Barlow Series) (d) ♀H4	Widely available
§	- - pink-flowered	LRHS WTou
	- - red-flowered	WTou
	- - 'Rose Barlow' (Barlow Series) (d)	EPfP GBin LRHS LSRN WMnd WTou
	- - 'Royal Purple' (d)	NBro NNor WMoo WTou
	- - 'Ruby Port' (d)	Widely available
	- - 'Ruby Port' crimped (d)	WPnP
	- - 'Touchwood Dreamtime' **new**	WTou
	- - (Vervaeneana Group) 'Sweet Dreams' (v/d)	WTou
	- - 'White Barlow' (Barlow Series) (d)	EBee EPfP LRHS SHil SPer WTou
	- - white-flowered	CSpe GCra LRHS NBro WFar WTou
	- variegated foliage	see *A. vulgaris* Vervaeneana Group
§	- Vervaeneana Group (v)	CMHG CWCL ECtt EHrv ELan EPfP LRHS NBir NPer SBfd SPlb SRms SWat WFar WMoo WTou
	- - 'Lime Frost' (v)	WTou
	- - 'Woodside Blue' (v)	LRHS WTou WWEG
	- - 'Woodside White' (v)	NBir WBrk WTou
§	- 'William Guiness'	Widely available
	- 'William Guiness Doubles' (d)	WMoo WTou
	'White Star' (Star Series)	CPrp EBee ELan EPfP EWTr LAst LRHS MRav NEgg NPnk WHil WTou WWEG
	white-flowered	WTou
	Winky Series	ELan NCGa NNor WHil WRHF
	- 'Winky Blue-White Double' (d) **new**	WTou
	- 'Winky Blue-White'	GBin LRHS NLar NPri SMrm WCFE WFar WTou
	- 'Winky Double Red-White' (d) **new**	LRHS
	- 'Winky Purple-White'	NLar NPri WFar
	- 'Winky Red-White'	LRHS NLar NPri SRot SWvt WFar WTou
	- 'Winky Rose-Rose'	LRHS SMrm
	'Winky Wooh' **new**	CBct WBor
	yabeana	EWld GKev MWhi WCot WMoo
	'Yellow Star' (Star Series) ♀H3-4	EPfP WWEG

Aquilegia × Semiaquilegia ✿ (*Ranunculaceae*)

	Name	Suppliers
	hybrid, blue-flowered	NGdn WCru
§	'Roman Bronze'	LRHS WMoo WTou

Arabis (*Brassicaceae*)

	Name	Suppliers
	albida	see *A. alpina* subsp. *caucasica*
	alpina	MAsh SPlb
§	- subsp. ***caucasica***	ECho SEND WFar
	- - 'Corfe Castle'	ECtt
	- - 'Douler Angevine' (v)	ECtt ELon MPnt NPri SPoG WFar WIce
	- - 'Flore Pleno' (d) ♀H4	CElw CSpe CTri CWCL ECho ECtt ELan GAbr GJos GMaP MAvo SBch SRms WFar WHoo WNew
	- - 'Pinkie'	ECho
	- - 'Pixie Cream'	LBMP NGdn SBch
	- - 'Rosea'	GJos LRHS NBir SEND SRms WFar
§	- - 'Schneehaube' ♀H4	CTri CWib ECho ECtt EPfP GMaP LRHS NBir NGdn SPhx SPoG SRms SWal
	- - Snowcap	see *A. alpina* subsp. *caucasica* 'Schneehaube'
	- - 'Snowdrop'	WFar
	- - 'Variegata' (v)	ECho ECtt ELan ELon GMaP LAst LRHS NPri SPoG SRms WFar
	androsacea	SRms
	× ***arendsii*** 'Compinkie'	GJos LBMP SPlb SRms
	blepharophylla	EPfP WFar WSHC
	- 'Alba'	ELan
§	- 'Frühlingszauber' ♀H4	CTri ELan EPfP GJos LRHS NBir NGdn NPri SPoG SRms WCot
	- 'Rose Delight'	LRHS
	- 'Rote Sensation'	ELan NGdn
	- Spring Charm	see *A. blepharophylla* 'Frühlingszauber'
	bryoides	NMen
	carduchorum	XLum
	caucasica	see *A. alpina* subsp. *caucasica*
	ferdinandi-coburgi	ECho MWat NHol WNew XLum
	- 'Aureovariegata' (v)	CMea CTri ECho ECtt EDAr ELan SPet SWvt
	- 'Old Gold'	ECho EDAr EHoe EPfP LBee LRHS MAsh MHer NHol SPoG SRms SRot SWvt WCFE WFar WHil WRHF
	- 'Variegata'	see *A. procurrens* 'Variegata'
§	***procurrens*** 'Variegata' (v) ♀H4	CTri ECho ECtt EHoe ELan EPfP EWes GEdr LBee LRHS MAsh MBrN MHer SPlb SRms SRot WFar WNew
§	***scabra***	CNat
	Snow Cap	see *A. alpina* subsp. *caucasica* 'Schneehaube'
	stelleri	NBre
	stricta	see *A. scabra*
	× ***wilczekii***	EPot

Arachniodes (*Dryopteridaceae*)

	Name	Suppliers
	davalliaeformis	GBin ISha LRHS
	miqueliana **new**	ISha
	simplicior (v)	CBty CCCN CKel GBin ISha LRHS WCot WPat
	standishii	CBty ISha

Araiostegia (*Davalliaceae*)

	Name	Suppliers
	faberiana	CPLG
	hymenophylloides	SKHP WCot
	parvipinnata	see *A. perdurans*
§	***perdurans***	WCot WPGP
	- B&SWJ 1608	WCru
	pulchra HWJ 1007 **new**	WCru

Aralia ✿ (*Araliaceae*)

	Name	Suppliers
	apioides EDHCH 9720	WCru
	armata B&SWJ 6719	WCru
	- RWJ 10060	WCru
	cachemirica	CDTJ CLAP EWes GAbr GCal MBrN NBid NLar SDix SMad SPlb WCru WHal

californica	EBee GCal GPoy IGor LEdu NLar SDix SKHP WCru
castanopsidicola CWJ 12411 **new**	WCru
chapaensis B&SWJ 11812	WCru
- HWJ 723	WCru
chinensis misapplied	see *A. elata*, *A. stipulata*
chinensis L. BWJ 8102	WCru
continentalis	CLAP IGor NLar
- B&SWJ 4152	WCru
- B&SWJ 8524	WCru
cordata	EBee EWes GCal GKev LEdu NLar
- B&SWJ 5511	CDes WCru
- B&SWJ 5596	WCru
- 'Sun King' **new**	NLar
decaisneana B&SWJ 6828	WCru
- RWJ 9910	WCru
§ ***elata*** ♀H4	CBcs CCVT CDoC CDul CHEx CHll CMac CPLG EBee ELan EPfP GKev IDee LRHS LSRN MBlu MGos MMuc NBid SCoo SGol SHil SLim SPer SPoG SWvt WFar
- B&SWJ 5480	WCru
- 'Albomarginata'	see *A. elata* 'Variegata'
- 'Aureo-marginata' (v)	CMac EUJe
- 'Aureovariegata' (v)	CBcs CDoC ELan EWes NLar SCoo
- 'Golden Umbrella' (v)	LSRN NLar
- 'Silver Umbrella' (v)	CDoC NLar
§ - 'Variegata' (v) ♀H4	CBcs CDoC ELan EPfP EUJe MGos NLar SCoo
foliolosa B&SWJ 8360	WCru
kansuensis BWJ 7650	WCru
- CD&R 2289	WCru
leschenaultii B&SWJ 9515	WCru
- B&SWJ 11789	WCru
montana	WPGP
- RWJ 10101	WCru
papyrifera	see *Tetrapanax papyrifer*
racemosa	CArn EBee GPoy GQue LEdu LPla MNrw NLar SRms WFar
- B&SWJ 9570	WCru
searelliana B&SWJ 11736	WCru
sieboldii de Vriese	see *Fatsia japonica*
spinifolia B&SWJ 11745	WCru
spinosa L.	CArn GKev LEdu MBlu NLar SPlb
§ ***stipulata***	NLar
subcordata HWJK 2385	WCru
verticillata B&SWJ 11797	WCru
vietnamensis B&SWJ 12349E	WCru

Araucaria (*Araucariaceae*)

angustifolia	WPGP
angustifolia × ***araucana*** **new**	WPGP
§ ***araucana***	Widely available
bidwillii	CTrC
cunninghamii	ECou
excelsa misapplied	see *A. heterophylla*
§ ***heterophylla*** ♀H1	CCCN CDoC MBri SEND
imbricata	see *A. araucana*

Araujia (*Apocynaceae*)

sericifera	CHll CMac CRHN CSpe GEdr SGar SPav WCot WSHC

Arbutus ✿ (*Ericaceae*)

andrachne	EPfP
× ***andrachnoides*** ♀H4	CAbP CHGN CJun CTri EBee ELan EPfP LRHS LSRN MAsh MRav SMad SPer SPoG SSta WPGP WPat
'Marina'	CAbP CDoC CJun CTrC EBee ELan EPfP IVic LHop LRHS MAsh MBlu SBfd SEND SLPl SPer SPoG SReu SSpi SSta WFar WPGP WPat
menziesii ♀H3	CBcs CDoC CMCN CTho EBee EPfP IGor LRHS LSRN MGos MMuc SMad SPer WFar
unedo ♀H4	Widely available
- 'Atlantic'	CCCN CJun EBee ECrN EPfP IVic LRHS LSRN MAsh MGos SBfd SBig SHil SLim SPtl SWvt WPGP WPat
- 'Compacta'	CBcs CCCN CDoC EBee IArd LRHS MAsh MGos NLar SGol SLon SWvt WCFE
- 'Elfin King'	EBee ELan EPfP LRHS MAsh NLar SLon SPoG
- 'Quercifolia'	CAbP CHll CJun EBee ELan LLHF MAsh MMHG NLar WPat
- Roselily = 'Minlily'PBR	SBig
- f. ***rubra*** ♀H4	Widely available
xalapensis	SPlb
- NJM 09.026	WPGP

Archontophoenix (*Arecaceae*)

alexandrae	EAmu
cunninghamiana ♀H1	CBrP EAmu XBlo

Arctanthemum (*Asteraceae*)

§ ***arcticum***	CKno ECha LBMP NLar WPer
- 'Polarstern' **new**	EBee
- 'Roseum'	EBee
- 'Schwefelglanz'	NCGa

Arcterica see *Pieris*

Arctium (*Asteraceae*)

lappa	CArn GPoy SIde SVic WSFF
- 'Takinogawa Long'	MNHC
minus	NMir

Arctostaphylos (*Ericaceae*)

uva-ursi	GPoy NLar NMen SPlb
- 'Massachusetts'	EBee NLar
- 'Snowcap'	MAsh
- 'Vancouver Jade'	CDoC EBee GKin LRHS LSRN MAsh SBfd SCoo SLon SPer SPoG SReu SRms SSta SWvt

Arctotis (*Asteraceae*)

Hannah = 'Archnah'PBR	CSpe ECtt MBNS WHil
Hayley = 'Archley'PBR	CCCN ECtt MBNS NPri WHil
'Hello'	SMrm
'Holly' **new**	LAst
× ***hybrida*** hort. 'Apricot'	CCCN CHEx ECtt LAst NPri SAga SMrm
- cream-flowered	CHEx SAga
- 'Flame' ♀H1+3	CCCN ECtt LAst MBNS SAga SCoo SMrm SRms SUsu
- 'Midday Sun'	ECtt
- 'Red Devil'	CCCN LAst LSou MBNS SAga SCoo SMrm SUsu
- 'Wine'	CCCN CHEx LAst LSou MBNS NPri SCoo SMrm SRkn SUsu
'Prostrate Raspberry'	SAga

Ardisia (*Primulaceae*)

japonica B&SWJ 1032	WCru
- var. ***angusta***	WCot
- var. ***minor*** B&SWJ 1841	WCru
- - B&SWJ 3809	WCru
- 'Miyo-nishiki' (v)	WCot
pusilla	GBin

Areca (*Arecaceae*)

triandra	XBlo

Arecastrum see *Syagrus*

Arenaria (*Caryophyllaceae*)

aggregata subsp. ***erinacea***	GKev
alfacarensis	see *A. lithops*
balearica	CWCL ECho EWes MAsh NSla SPlb SRms
capillaris	CTri
globiflora	WAbe
- CC 4827	GKev
grandiflora	WAbe XLum
kansuensis **new**	ITim WAbe
ledebouriana	EDAr MWat NLar
§ ***lithops***	EPot
montana ♀H4	CMea ECha ECho ECtt EDAr EPfP GMaP ITim LHop LRHS MAsh MGos MLHP NMen NPri SPet SPhx SPlb SRms WAbe WFar WIce WWFP
- 'Avalanche'	ECtt
- 'Blizzard'	EPfP
pseudacantholimon	WAbe
pulvinata	see *A. lithops*
purpurascens	CMea CYeo ECho EPot EWes LLHF MAsh NLar NMen SRms SRot WAbe
- 'Elliott's Variety'	NMen WPat
tetraquetra subsp. ***amabilis***	EPot NMen NSla WAbe
tmolea	NMen
verna	see *Minuartia verna*

Arenga (*Arecaceae*)

engleri	EAmu

Argania (*Sapotaceae*)

spinosa	WPGP

Argemone (*Papaveraceae*)

grandiflora	CSpe SBch
mexicana	ELan

Argyranthemum ✿ (*Asteraceae*)

'Beth'	GBee
Butterfly = 'Ulyssis' ♀H1+3	LAst
canariense hort.	see *A. frutescens* subsp. *canariae*
Cherry Harmony = 'Supa532' (Daisy Crazy Series) (d)	MCot
Cherry Love = 'Supacher' PBR (Daisy Crazy Series)	CCCN EPfP
'Cornish Gold' ♀H1+3	CBcs CCCN CWCL SBfd
'Donington Hero' ♀H1+3	MHom
'Flamingo'	see *Rhodanthemum gayanum*
§ ***foeniculaceum*** misapplied	CTri ELan
- pink-flowered	see *A.* 'Petite Pink'
§ ***foeniculaceum*** (Willd.) Webb & Sch.Bip.	MCot
- 'Royal Haze' ♀H1+3	CCCN CHll NPer
§ ***frutescens***	CHEx SEND WKif
- Beauty Yellow = 'Wesaryel' PBR **new**	LAst
§ - subsp. ***canariae*** ♀H1+3	CCCN
'Gill's Pink'	MHom WPnn
'Glory White' **new**	LAst
gracile	CHll
- 'Chelsea Girl' ♀H1+3	CCCN CHEx MCot MHom WKif
'Guernsey Pink'	MHom
Gypsy Rose = 'M9/18d'	CCCN
'Jamaica Primrose' ♀H1+3	CHEx CSpe CTri ECtt MAsh MHom SAga SDix WPnn
'Jamaica Snowstorm'	see *A.* 'Snow Storm'
'Julieanne'	CBcs CWCL MBNS
'Levada Cream' ♀H1+3	MHom
Madeira Cherry Red = 'Bonmadcher' PBR **new**	SGar
§ ***maderense*** ♀H1+3	CHll GCal
'Mary Wootton' (d)	ECtt
mawii	see *Rhodanthemum gayanum*
Meteor Red = 'Supa742' **new**	MBNS
ochroleucum	see *A. maderense*
Pacific Gold = 'Pacargone' PBR (d)	CBcs
§ 'Petite Pink' ♀H1+3	CCCN ECtt
Ping-Pong = 'Innping' PBR (d)	CCCN
'Pink Australian' (d)	CCCN MHom
'Pink Delight'	see *A.* 'Petite Pink'
Polly = 'Innpolly' PBR	SBfd
Pomponette Pink = 'Supa392' PBR (d)	CBcs
'Powder Puff' (d)	ECtt
'Silver Queen'	see *A. foeniculaceum* misapplied
§ 'Snow Storm' ♀H1+3	LAst MHom WPnn
Sole Mio = 'Supa3047' (d)	CWCL
'Starlight Red' (Daisy Crazy Series)	LAst
Strawberry Pink = 'Suparosa' (Daisy Crazy Series)	EPfP
'Sugar and Ice' (d)	CCCN
'Sugar Baby' PBR (d)	CCCN
Sultan's Dream = 'Supadream' (Daisy Crazy Series)	EPfP
Sultan's Lemon = 'Supalem' PBR (Daisy Crazy Series)	EPfP
'Summer Melody' PBR (d)	CBcs CCCN
'Summer Pink'	CCCN
Summit Pink = 'Cobsing' PBR (Daisy Crazy Series)	EPfP
'Vancouver' (d) ♀H1+3	CCCN CHll CWCL ECtt LAst SBHP
* 'Vera'	CCCN
'White Spider'	CCCN ELan MHom
'Yellow Empire' **new**	WGor

Argyrocytisus (*Papilionaceae*)

§ ***battandieri*** ♀H4	Widely available
- 'Yellow Tail' ♀H4	CDul EPfP LRHS MBri SHil SKHP SSta

Ariopsis (*Araceae*)

peltata **new**	GHim

Arisaema ✿ (*Araceae*)

	Name	Suppliers
	C&H 7026	LWst
	CC 2792	WCot
	CC 4904	CPLG
	CC 5511	CPLG
	Chen Yi 97	WCot
	amurense	CElw CLAP ECho GBuc GCal LAma MMoz
§	- subsp. ***robustum***	ECho WCot
*	***angustatum*** var. ***amurense***	GEdr LAma
	asperatum	LAma WCot
	biauriculatum	see *A. wattii*
	brachyspathum	see *A. heterophyllum*
	brevipes	CPLG GEdr
	candidissimum ♀H4	Widely available
	- from Yunnan	WCot
	- white-flowered	GEdr LAma WCot
	ciliatum	CDes ELon GBuc GEdr LAma LEdu MMoz MNrw NHar NLar SRot WCot
	- var. ***liubaense***	CFwr CGHE CWCL EPfP EWld GBuc GHim MMoz WIvy
	- - CT 369	CLAP CPLG EBee EPfP LWst SCnR SDys SKHP WCot WPGP WSHC
	- variegated (v)	WCot
	aff. ***ciliatum***	WCot
	concinnum	CCon EAmu EBee EWld GBin GEdr GHim LAma NHol NLar SBst WPnP XLum
	consanguineum	CDes CFwr CGHE CHEx CLAP CPLG EPfP GBin GCal GEdr GHim LAma LWst MBel MMoz NHar NLar NSla SMrm WCot WPGP WPnP XLum
	- B&SWJ 071	WCru
	- CC 3635	EBee
	- CLD 1519	ECho GBuc
	- GG 84193	WCot
	- PJ 277	WCot
	- dark-flowered	WCot
	- 'J. Balis'	WCot
	- subsp. ***kelung-insulare*** B&SWJ 256	WCru
	- 'Qinling'	WCot
	- variegated (v)	WCot
	cf. ***consanguineum*** NJM 09.098	WPGP
	costatum	CCCN CHEx EAmu EBee ECho EPfP EPot EUJe GBin GEdr GHim LAma LRHS MMoz NHol SBst WCot WPGP XLum
	dilatatum	LAma
	dracontium	ECho LAma NLar XLum
	ehimense	LWst
	elephas	ECho LAma LWst WCot
	erubescens	NLar
	- marbled-leaved	GEdr
	- white-lined-leaved	WCot
	exappendiculatum	CDes GHim MMoz
	fargesii	CPLG EBee ECho GEdr LAma LWst MMoz SChF SKHP WCot
	flavum	CDes CGHE CLAP CPom CWCL EBee ECho ELon EPfP EPot EWld GBuc GCal LAma LWst MMoz NHar NHol NLar SPlb SWal WCot
	- CC 6303	ITim

	Name	Suppliers
	- subsp. ***abbreviatum***	GBuc
	- - CC 6300	ITim
	- tall	ECho
	formosanum B&SWJ 280	WCru
	- var. ***bicolorifolium*** B&SWJ 3528	WCru
	- f. ***stenophyllum*** B&SWJ 1477	WCru
§	***franchetianum***	CPLG EBee GEdr LAma WCot
	fraternum	LWst WCot
	galeatum	EBee ECho EPot GHim LAma NHol WCot XLum
	grapsospadix B&SWJ 7000	WCru
§	***griffithii***	CBro CPne EBee ECho EUJe GEdr GHim LAma LRHS MMoz NHol SDeJ XLum
	- 'Numbuq'	GCra
	- var. ***pradhanii***	EBee GHim LWst XLum
	helleborifolium	see *A. tortuosum*
§	***heterophyllum***	GEdr LWst
	intermedium	EBee ECho GBin GEdr GHim LAma MMoz MNrw NHol
	iyoanum subsp. ***nakaianum***	GEdr
	jacquemontii	CLAP ECho EWld GBin GCra GEdr GHim NLar WCot
	- CC 5184	ITim
	japonicum Komarov	see *A. serratum*
	jinshajiangense	CPLG
	kishidae	GEdr LWst
	kiushianum	EFEx GEdr LAma LWst MMoz WCot
	leschenaultii	EBee LAma LWst WCot
	lichiangense	LAma WCot
§	***lobatum***	CPLG EBee LAma
	maximowiczii	GEdr
	meleagris	LAma
§	***nepenthoides***	CBcs EAmu EBee ECho EPot EUJe GEdr GHim ITim LAma LRHS MMoz MNrw NHol NLar WPnP XLum
	ochraceum	see *A. nepenthoides*
	onoticum	see *A. lobatum*
	petelotii B&SWJ 9706	WCru
	polyphyllum B&SWJ 3904	WCru
	propinquum	CLAP EBee ECho GBin GHim LAma NHol WCot
	purpureogaleatum	see *A. franchetianum*
	rhizomatum	LAma
	rhombiforme	LAma LWst
	ringens misapplied	see *A. amurense* subsp. ***robustum***
	ringens ambig.	GKev SKHP
	ringens (Thunberg) Schott	EFEx GEdr LAma LEdu LWst
	- f. ***praecox*** B&SWJ 1515	WCru
	- f. ***sieboldii*** B&SWJ 551	WCru
	robustum	see *A. amurense* subsp. ***robustum***
	saxatile	LAma WCot
	sazensoo	GEdr LAma LWst
§	***serratum***	ECho LAma MMoz MNrw
	sikokianum	CBcs CBro EBee ECho EFEx EHrv EPot GEdr LAma LRHS SKHP WPnP
	- var. ***serratum***	CCon
	- variegated (v)	GEdr LWst
	speciosum	CHEx CPLG EAmu EBee ECho EWld GAbr GEdr GHim LAma LRHS MMoz NHol NLar SDeJ SPlb WCot WPnP XLum

	- CC 3100	WCot
*	- var. ***magnificum***	EBee EHrv EWld GEdr GHim NHol WCot WPnP
	- var. ***mirabile***	EBee GEdr GHim
*	- var. ***sikkimense***	LAma
	taiwanense	CLAP SKHP WCot
	- B&SWJ 269	WCru
	- B&SWJ 356	WCot
	- var. ***brevipedunculatum*** B&SWJ 1859	WCru
	- f. ***cinereum*** B&SWJ 19121	WCru
	- silver-leaved	WCot
	tashiroi	GEdr
	ternatipartitum	GEdr LWst
	thunbergii	EFEx LRHS WCot
	- subsp. ***autumnale*** B&SWJ 1425	WCru
	- subsp. ***urashima***	EBee EFEx GEdr LAma LWst WCot
§	***tortuosum***	CPLG CPne EAmu EBee ECha ECho EHrv EUJe EWld GBin GBuc GEdr GHim LAma LEdu LWst MAvo MNrw NEgg NLar SChF WCot WPGP WPnP XLum
	- CC 1760	WCot
	- SDR 3987	GKev
	triphyllum	CElw CLAP CPLG EBee ECho EPot GPoy LAma LRHS MMoz NLar SPlb WCot WPnP
	- subsp. ***stewardsonii***	LWst
	- subsp. ***triphyllum*** var. ***atrorubens***	CLAP
§	***utile***	EBee ECho EPot GBin GEdr GHim LAma XLum
	verrucosum	see *A. griffithii*
	- var. ***utile***	see *A. utile*
§	***wattii***	LAma
	yamatense	LWst
	- subsp. ***sugimotoi***	LAma
	yunnanense	CLAP LAma

Arisarum (*Araceae*)

	proboscideum	Widely available
	vulgare	ECho WCot
	- from Crete	ECho
*	- f. ***maculatum***	ECho
	- subsp. ***simorrhinum***	ECho
	- subsp. ***vulgare***	ECho

Aristea (*Iridaceae*)

	africana 'Worcester'	ECho
	angolensis	EBee
§	***capitata***	CHll CPrp CSpe SGar
	- pink-flowered	CPrp EPri
	ecklonii	CHEx CPLG CPou CPrp CTca CTrC CTsd EBee EPri EShb IGor SGar SHom WCot
	- GWJ 9469	WCru
	ensifolia	ELan SAga WSHC
	grandis	CCon WCot
	spiralis 'Paarl'	ECho
	thyrsiflora	see *A. capitata*
	woodii 'Clarens'	ECho

Aristolochia (*Aristolochiaceae*)

	baetica	CArn CPLG
	californica	LEdu SKHP
	chilensis	CCCN
	clematitis	CArn EBee ECho GPoy LEdu LPla
	cucurbitifolia B&SWJ 7043	WCru
	delavayi	CHEx
	durior	see *A. macrophylla*
	gigantea	CCCN CHll
	grandiflora	CCCN CHll
	griffithii B&SWJ 2118	WCru
	heterophylla	see *A. kaempferi* f. *heterophylla*
	kaempferi	CCCN
	- B&SWJ 293	WCru
§	- f. ***heterophylla*** B&SWJ 3109	WCru
	× ***kewensis***	CCCN
	liukiuensis B&SWJ 4960	WCru
§	***macrophylla***	CArn CBcs CCCN CHEx CMac EBee EPfP MRav NEgg SLim
	manshuriensis B&SWJ 962	WCru
	moupinensis BWJ 8181	WCru
	onoei B&SWJ 4960	WCru
	rotunda	SKHP
	sempervirens	SBrt SKHP WCru WSHC
	sipho	see *A. macrophylla*
	tomentosa	SKHP

Aristotelia (*Elaeocarpaceae*)

§	***chilensis***	IVic LEdu
	- 'Variegata' (v)	CCCN CMac CWib EBee GQui MAsh SBod SEND SPlb
	fruticosa	IGor
	- (f)	ECou
	- (m)	ECou
	- black-fruited (f)	ECou
	- white-fruited (f)	ECou
	macqui	see *A. chilensis*
	peduncularis	CPLG
	serrata	ECou
	- (f)	ECou
	- (m)	ECou

Armeria (*Plumbaginaceae*)

§	***alliacea*** (Cav.) Hoffmanns. & Link	ECha LRHS
	- f. ***leucantha***	SRms WMoo
	alpina	MWat
	'Bees' Ruby'	EBee
	'Bloodgood'	ECho ECtt
	'Brutus'	CDes MAvo SUsu
	caespitosa	see *A. juniperifolia*
	Joystick Series	GJos MMuc SEND
	- 'Joystick Lilac Shades'	EBee EDAr EPfP EShb LRHS NLar
	- 'Joystick Pink'	EDAr SWal
	- 'Joystick Red'	EBee EDAr EPfP EShb EWll LRHS WHil
	- 'Joystick White'	EPfP EWll LRHS NLar
§	***juniperifolia*** ♀H4	CMea ECho ELan EPfP GMaP LBee LRHS MAsh MHer NMen NRHS NSla SPoG SRms WIce XLum
	- 'Alba'	CMea CYeo ECho ELan EPfP EPot GMaP LRHS MAsh MHer MMuc NMen SBch SPoG SRms WAbe WFar WHoo WThu
§	- 'Bevan's Variety' ♀H4	CYeo ECha ECho ECtt ELan EPfP EPot GMaP LEdu MMuc MWat NLar NMen NRya SEND SPoG SRms SRot WAbe WFar WHoo WNew WPat
	- 'Brookside'	GJos

	- dark-flowered	WAbe
	- 'New Zealand Form'	see *A. juniperifolia* 'Sugar Baby'
	- rose-flowered	ITim
§	- 'Sugar Baby'	CSpe
	juniperifolia* × *maritima	SBch
§	***maritima***	CArn CHab ECho EPfP GJos LAst LPot LRHS MNHC MSCN NEgg NRHS SBfd SPet WCFE WFar WHfH WJek WMoo WNew
	- from Patagonia	GKev
	- 'Alba'	CBcs COlW CTri ECha ECho ELan EPfP GJos GMaP LBMP LEdu LRHS MCot MLHP MMuc NRya SBfd SEND SPet SPlb SPoG SWal WCFE WFar WMoo WNew
	- 'Armada Rose'	LRHS
	- 'Bloodstone'	CTri ECho ECtt ELan MAsh MWat
	- 'Corsica'	CTri ECha MMuc NBir SBch SEND
	- Düsseldorf Pride	see *A. maritima* 'Düsseldorfer Stolz'
§	- 'Düsseldorfer Stolz'	CElw COlW ECha ECho ECtt EDAr ELan EPfP GKev GMaP LHop LRHS MCot MLHP NDov NMen NPri SPoG WNew XLum
	- 'Laucheana'	SBch WHoo WMoo
	- 'Nifty Thrifty' (v)	CFis CMea CTri EBee ECho ECtt EHoe EPot EWes LRHS MHer SIde SPoG SRot WFar
*	- 'Pink Lusitanica'	LBMP LRHS
	- 'Rosa Stolz'	NDov
I	- 'Rubrifolia'	Widely available
	- 'Ruby Glow'	CTri SBch
	- 'Schöne von Fellbach'	XLum
	- 'Splendens'	CBcs COlW CTri CYeo ECho EDAr EPfP GMaP LAst LRHS MAsh MGos MMuc NMir NRya SBch SBfd SEND SPoG SWal WFar WMoo WPer XLum
	- 'Splendens Alba'	XLum
	- 'Vindictive' ♀H4	CMea CTri EPfP
	morisii	SBch
	'Ornament'	SBfd
	plantaginea	see *A. alliacea* (Cav.) Hoffmanns. & Link
	pseudarmeria	EBee ECho ELan EPfP GCal LPot MWhi XLum
	- 'Alba'	SSvw
	- 'Drumstick White'	WPer
	- hybrids	CTri ELan
	pungens SDR 5622	GKev
	'Vesuvius'	NDov WCot XLum
	vulgaris	see *A. maritima*
	welwitschii	IFoB SRms
	'Westacre Beauty'	EWes

Armoracia (*Brassicaceae*)

§	***rusticana***	CArn CHby CPrp CSev CTri ELau ENfk EPfP GAbr GPoy MHer MHoo MMuc MNHC NPer NPri SBfd SEND SIde SVic WHer WJek
	- 'Variegata' (v)	ELau EWhm GCal IFoB LEdu LHop MAvo NSti SMad WHer WJek WMoo

Arnica (*Asteraceae*)

	angustifolia subsp. ***alpina***	SRms
	- subsp. ***iljinii***	NBir
	chamissonis Schmidt	see *A. sachalinensis*
	chamissonis Less.	CHby EBee ENfk MNHC NLar WJek XLum
	montana	CArn EBee EOHP GPoy MHer MHoo MNHC SRms SWat
	- SDR 6939	GKev
§	***sachalinensis*** RBS 0206	EPPr

Arnoglossum (*Asteraceae*)

	atriplicifolium	LRHS

Aronia (*Rosaceae*)

	arbutifolia	CBcs CTri EPfP EWTr LSRN MBlu NWea SGol SLon SPlb
	- 'Erecta'	CDul EBee ELan EPfP GBin LHop LRHS MBlu MBri MMuc NLar SBfd SEND SLPl SPoG SRms SSpi
	melanocarpa	CDul CMCN CSpe CTsd CWib ELan EPfP GKin IGor LEdu LRHS MAsh MMuc NRHS SEND WFar WGrn
	- 'Autumn Magic'	CBcs CDoC CJun EBee ELan EPfP EWTr GBin IVic LAst LHop LRHS MAsh MMuc NLar SCoo SLPl SLon
	- var. ***grandifolia***	CJun
	- 'Hugin'	CAgr CJun NLar
	× ***prunifolia***	CDoC GAbr LEdu WGrn
	- 'Aron' (F)	CJun
	- 'Brilliant'	CDoC CDul CTri EBee EMil EPfP GKin LRHS NEgg NLar SGol SPer
	- 'Nero' (F)	CAgr GBin NLar
	- 'Serina' (F)	CJun NLar
	- 'Viking' (F)	CAgr CJun EBee ECrN EPfP EPom LBuc LHop LRHS MBlu MMuc NBro NLar SEND SGol SLim

Arracacia (*Apiaceae*)

	B&SWJ 9023 from Guatemala	WCru

Arrhenatherum (*Poaceae*)

	elatius	CHab
	- var. ***bulbosum*** 'Variegatum' (v)	EBee EHoe ELan EPPr GBin GMaP LBMP MMoz MMuc MWhi NBid NOak NOrc NWad SEND SWal WMoo WPtf WWEG

Artemisia ✿ (*Asteraceae*)

	RBS 0207	CPLG
	from Taiwan	WHer
§	***abrotanum*** ♀H4	Widely available
	- 'Courson' **new**	EBee
	absinthium	CArn CEls CHab CPbn CSev CWan ELan ENfk GPoy MHer MHoo MNHC NLar NSti SIde SVic WJek XSen
	- 'Lambrook Giant'	CEls
	- 'Lambrook Mist' ♀H3-4	CEls CFis CMac CPrp CSev EBee ECtt ELan EPfP GCal GQue LRHS MRav NDov SWat WMnd WWEG XLum
	- 'Lambrook Silver' ♀H4	Widely available
	- 'Silver Ghost'	CEls
	afra	CArn CEls IFro XSen
§	***alba***	CEls EOHP GPoy MHer SIde WJek WPer XSen
§	- 'Canescens' ♀H4	CEls CSam CTri EBee ECha ECtt ELan EPfP GMaP LAst LBMP LRHS MAsh MHer MRav SDix SEND SMrm SPer WAul WCFE WCot WMnd WPer WWEG
	annua	CArn CEls SIde

	anomala	CArn CEls
	arborescens 🏆H3	CArn CEls LRHS NEgg SDix SPer WKif
	- 'Brass Band'	see *A.* 'Powis Castle'
	- 'Faith Raven'	CEls EBee EPfP GBin MBNS NLar SMad WFar
	- 'Little Mice'	CEls EBee WWEG
	- 'Porquerolles'	CEls
	argyi	CEls
§	***armeniaca***	CEls ECho XSen
	assoana	see *A. caucasica*
	atrata	CEls
	barrelieri	CEls
	californica	CEls
	- 'Canyon Gray'	CEls
	campestris	XLum XSen
	- subsp. ***borealis***	CEls
	- subsp. ***campestris***	CEls
	- subsp. ***maritima***	CEls
	- - from Wales	CEls
	camphorata	see *A. alba*
	cana	see *Seriphidium canum*
	canariensis	see *A. thuscula*
	canescens misapplied	see *A. alba* 'Canescens'
	canescens Willd.	see *A. armeniaca*
	capillaris	CArn CEls XLum
§	***caucasica*** 🏆H3-4	CEls CFis ECho EPot EWes MHer SChF SPhx SRms SRot WPer XSen
	- var. ***caucasica***	CEls
	chamaemelifolia	CEls MHer NBre WJek XSen
	cretacea	see *Seriphidium nutans*
	discolor Dougl. ex Besser	see *A. michauxiana*
	douglasiana	CEls XLum
	- 'Valerie Finnis'	see *A. ludoviciana* 'Valerie Finnis'
	dracunculus	ECha MNHC MRav SBfd SPlb SWal WBrk WHfH WPer
	- French	CArn CEls CHby CSev CWan EGHP ELau ENfk EWhm GPoy LEdu MHer MHoo NPri SBfd SEND SIde WGwG WJek XLum
	- Russian	CEls ENfk SVic
	ferganensis	see *Seriphidium ferganense*
	filifolia	CEls XSen
	fragrans Willd.	see *Seriphidium fragrans*
	frigida 🏆H3-4	CEls
	genipi	CEls MHoo
	glacialis	CEls
	gmelinii	CEls
	gnaphalodes	see *A. ludoviciana*
	gorgonum	CEls EWes SEND
	gracilis hort.	see *A. scoparia*
	'Hausserman'	XLum
	herba-alba	CEls XSen
	'Huntington'	CEls
	japonica	CEls
	kawakamii B&SWJ 088	WCru
	kitadakensis	CEls
	- 'Guizhou'	see *A. lactiflora* Guizhou Group
	laciniata	CEls
	lactiflora 🏆H4	CDoy CEls CPrp EBee ECha ECtt ELan GAbr GBee GMaP MHoo MRav NGdn NOrc SDix SMrm SPer SRms WFar WHfH WMoo WTin XLum
	- 'Elfenbein'	EBee GCal LHop LPla SMHy
§	- Guizhou Group	Widely available
	- - 'Dark Delight'	ECtt EWes
	- 'Jim Russell'	CDes CElw EBee ECtt EWes MAvo NBre SPhx WWFP
	- ***purpurea***	see *A. lactiflora* Guizhou Group
	- 'Stonyford'	MSCN
	- 'Weisses Wunder'	EBee
	lanata Willd.	see *A. caucasica*
	lanata Lam. **new**	XSen
	laxa	see *A. umbelliformis*
§	***ludoviciana***	CEls ELan ETod GBee IFoB NLar NOrc NPer SBch SRms WCFE XLum
	- var. ***latifolia***	see *A. ludoviciana* subsp. *ludoviciana* var. *latiloba*
	- subsp. ***ludoviciana*** var. ***incompta***	CEls LAst
N	- - var. ***latiloba***	CEls EHoe LHop NBro NPnk SWvt WCot WHoo WPer
	- subsp. ***mexicana*** var. ***albula***	CEls SMrm
	- 'Silver Queen' 🏆H4	Widely available
N	- 'Valerie Finnis' 🏆H4	Widely available
	maritima	see *Seriphidium maritimum*
	mauiensis	CEls
§	***michauxiana***	CEls EBee NSti XSen
	molinieri	CEls XSen
	mutellina	see *A. umbelliformis*
	niitakayamensis	CEls
	nitida	CEls
	nutans	see *Seriphidium nutans*
	palmeri hort.	see *A. ludoviciana*
	pamirica	CEls
	aff. ***parviflora*** CLD 1531	CEls
	pedemontana	see *A. caucasica*
	pontica	CArn CEls CWan EBee ECha EHoe ELan GMaP GPoy LRHS MBNS MHer MNHC MRav NBro NSti SPer SSvw WCAu WFar WHfH WHil WHoo WJek WPer WWEG XSen
§	'Powis Castle' 🏆H3	Widely available
	princeps	CArn CEls ELau SIde
	procera Willd.	see *A. abrotanum*
	purshiana	see *A. ludoviciana*
	pycnocephala	CEls
	- 'David's Choice'	CEls SMad
	ramosa	CEls
	'Rosenschleier'	EWes LPla MAvo NBre WFar WPGP WTin WWEG
	schmidtiana 🏆H4	CEls CFis ECha MWat NOrc SRms WKif
	- 'Nana' 🏆H4	Widely available
	- 'Nana Attraction'	LRHS
§	***scoparia***	MHoo
	'Sea Foam'	EPfP LRHS
	selengensis	CEls
	spinescens **new**	XSen
	splendens misapplied	see *A. alba* 'Canescens'
	splendens Willd.	SPhx
	- var. ***brachyphylla***	MAsh
	stelleriana	CArn CEls CTri ECha GBee IFoB LHop MCot MHer NBro NPri SPer SRms
	- RBS 0207	CEls NLar
N	- 'Boughton Silver'	CEls EBee ECtt EHoe ELan EPfP GBBs GMaP IKil LDai LRHS MAsh MCot MRav NSti NWad SBfd SMrm SPer SRms SWvt WMnd WWEG
N	- 'Mori'	see *A. stelleriana* 'Boughton Silver'
	- 'Nana'	CEls SWvt
	- 'Prostrata'	see *A. stelleriana* 'Boughton Silver'

- 'Silver Brocade'	see *A. stelleriana* 'Boughton Silver'
taurica	CEls
§ ***thuscula***	CEls
tridentata	see *Seriphidium tridentatum*
§ ***umbelliformis***	CEls
vallesiaca	see *Seriphidium vallesiacum*
verlotiorum	CEls
vulgaris L.	CArn CEls ELau GPoy MHer MHoo MNHC WHer
- 'Cragg-Barber Eye' (v)	EBee NBid SAga
- Oriental Limelight = 'Janlim' (v)	CEls COIW EBee ECtt EHoe EPfP GAbr LEdu LHop LRHS MNHC MWhi NBir NEgg NLar SBfd SBod SWal SWvt WFar WHer WJek
- 'Variegata' (v)	CEls EBee EPfP NBir WHer WMoo XLum
× ***wurzellii***	CEls

Arthropodium (*Asparagaceae*)

candidum	ECGP ECho ECou EHoe ITim MPie
- 'Cappucino'	CBcs
- 'Capri'	LPot
- 'Maculatum'	ECho GEdr LEdu SBrt SPlb
- ***purpureum***	EBee ECho IKil
cirratum	CHEx CSpe ECho ECou IKil MHer SBch SWal
- 'Matapouri Bay'	CAbb CBcs CHEx EBee ECre WPGP
milleflorum	SBrt
minus	CPLG ECou

Arthrostylidium (*Poaceae*)

naibuense	CDTJ

artichoke, globe see *Cynara cardunculus* Scolymus Group

artichoke, Jerusalem see *Helianthus tuberosus*

Arum (*Araceae*)

alpinum	see *A. cylindraceum*
besserianum	ECho LWst
byzantinum	ECho LWst
'Chameleon'	EPPr MNrw NBir NLar SEND SKHP SMad SPer WCot WCru WHil WHoo WPGP WWEG
§ ***concinnatum***	EBee ECho SChr SKHP
- black-spotted	ECho
- 'Mount Ida'	ECho EWld SKHP
- purple	ECho
- variegated (v)	WCot
concinnatum* × *cyrenaicum	ECho GKev
- - from Crete	LWst
cornutum	see *Sauromatum venosum*
creticum	CBro CCon CMea CSpe ECha ECho GCal LRHS MNrw MRav SCnR SEND SKHP SRot SUsu WBor
- MS 696	MNrw
- VV CR741	GKev
- FCC form	see *A. creticum* 'Karpathos'
§ - 'Karpathos'	CPLG ECho GKev LAma LWst MMoz SKHP WAbe WCot WPGP
- 'Marmaris White'	SCnR WCot
- yellow-spotted	NBir WIvy
§ ***cylindraceum***	ECho
cyrenaicum	EBee ECho LEdu LWst WCot
- MS 696 from Crete	WCot
- from Crete	ECho
dioscoridis	CPom EBee ECho EWes GCra GKev MMoz WCot
- JCA 195.197	WCot
- var. ***cyprium***	ECho GKev LWst
§ - var. ***dioscoridis*** JCA 5396A	LWst
- var. ***liepoldtii***	see *A. dioscoridis* var. *dioscoridis*
- var. ***philistaeum*** HKEP 9263	LWst
- var. ***smithii***	see *A. dioscoridis* var. *dioscoridis*
- var. ***syriacum***	LWst
dracunculus	see *Dracunculus vulgaris*
elongatum	CPom LWst
- RS 274/87	EBee LWst
euxinum	ECho
hygrophilum	CPom LWst
italicum	CArn CLAP CTri ECho GAbr IBoy LAma LBMP NLar SDeJ SWat WCot WFar WShi
- subsp. ***albispathum***	EBee ECho MMoz WCot WPGP
- 'Black Spot'	EPPr
- black-spotted	ECho SCnR WFar
- 'Edward Dougal'	WCot
- giant	ECho WHil
- 'Green Marble'	SEND WFar WWEG
- subsp. ***italicum***	ECho EShb WBrk
- - 'Cyclops'	CHid WWEG
§ - - 'Marmoratum' ♀H4	Widely available
- - 'Sparkler'	WCot
- - 'Spotted Jack'	MNrw WCot WCru WWEG
- - 'Tiny'	CCon CPLG GCal SCnR SMHy SWvt WWEG
§ - - 'White Winter'	CElw WBrk WCot WWEG
- 'Nancy Lindsay'	MMoz
- subsp. ***neglectum***	SChr
- - 'Miss Janay Hall' (v)	CAvo EWes LLHF MDKP MMoz WCot
- 'Pictum'	see *A. italicum* subsp. *italicum* 'Marmoratum'
jacquemontii	ECho
korolkowii	LWst WCot
maculatum	CArn CRWN EBee ECho EPot GKev GPoy LAma MHer MRav NLar NMir WHer WShi
- 'Painted Lady' (v)	WCot
- 'Pleddel'	MRav
- Tar Spot Group	SEND
nickelii	see *A. concinnatum*
§ ***nigrum***	CPom ECho EWes LLHF WCot WGwG
- 'Trebinje' **new**	LWst
orientale	EPot
- VV RR.55	LWst
palaestinum	EBee LWst
petteri misapplied	see *A. nigrum*
pictum	CLAP CMac CPLG ECho EWes LEdu LLHF WCot
- from Majorca	WCot
- 'Taff's Form'	see *A. italicum* subsp. *italicum* 'White Winter'
purpureospathum	CPom EBee ECho EPPr GKev WCot
- VV CR.543	LWst
rupicola var. ***rupicola***	ECho LWst
- var. ***virescens***	ECho LWst

Aruncus ✿ (*Rosaceae*)

aethusifolius ♀H4	Widely available
- 'Little Gem'	ECho WCru

	asiaticus B&SWJ 8624	WCru
	dioicus	Widely available
§	- (m) ♀H4	CDoC CMac CRow ECha ELan MBNS MRav MWts NBro NSti SBfd SMad SPer SRms SWat WMoo WPer
	- var. ***acuminatus***	EBee
	- Child of Two Worlds	see *A. dioicus* 'Zweiweltenkind'
	- 'Glasnevin'	CSev ECtt GBee LRHS MRav WFar
	- var. ***kamtschaticus***	EWes LRHS MGos NBre NLar WHrl
	- - RBS 0208	NGdn
	- 'Kneiffii'	Widely available
§	- 'Zweiweltenkind'	CEnt EBee EHrv GCal LRHS NBre NLar SMad WCot
	'Guinea Fowl'	EBee GQue MAvo MBri NCGa NGdn NHar WHil
	'Horatio'	CSam EBee GBin IPot LHop LPla MPie NDov SAga SMHy SMad SPhx SUsu WCot
	'Johannifest'	CDes EBee ECtt IPot WCot
	'Misty Lace'	EBee GBin MAvo NCGa NGdn NHar NLar SMrm SPoG
	'Noble Spirit'	CEnt EBee MBel NGdn NLar NMRc SPoG SWat
	'Perlehuhn'	CDes
	plumosus	see *A. dioicus*
	sinensis	NBre
	sylvestris	see *A. dioicus*
	'Woldemar Meier'	EBee GBin WCot

Arundinaria (*Poaceae*)

	amabilis	see *Pseudosasa amabilis* (McClure) Keng f.
	anceps	see *Yushania anceps*
	angustifolia	see *Pleioblastus chino* 'Murakamianus'
	auricoma	see *Pleioblastus viridistriatus*
	disticha	see *Pleioblastus pygmaeus* 'Distichus'
	falconeri	see *Himalayacalamus falconeri*
	fargesii	see *Bashania fargesii*
	fastuosa	see *Semiarundinaria fastuosa*
	fortunei	see *Pleioblastus variegatus*
	funghomii	see *Schizostachyum funghomii*
§	***gigantea***	CDTJ MWht
	- subsp. ***tecta***	CBcs
	hindsii	see *Pleioblastus hindsii*
	hookeriana misapplied	see *Himalayacalamus falconeri* 'Damarapa'
	hookeriana Munro	see *Himalayacalamus hookerianus*
	humilis	see *Pleioblastus humilis*
	japonica	see *Pseudosasa japonica*
	jaunsarensis	see *Yushania anceps*
	maling	see *Yushania maling*
	marmorea	see *Chimonobambusa marmorea*
	murielae	see *Fargesia murielae*
	nitida	see *Fargesia nitida*
	oedogonata	see *Clavinodum oedogonatum*
	palmata	see *Sasa palmata*
	pumila	see *Pleioblastus argenteostriatus* f. *pumilus*
	pygmaea	see *Pleioblastus pygmaeus*
	quadrangularis	see *Chimonobambusa quadrangularis*
	simonii	see *Pleioblastus simonii*
	spathiflora	see *Thamnocalamus spathiflorus*
	tessellata	see *Thamnocalamus tessellatus*
	vagans	see *Sasaella ramosa*
	variegata	see *Pleioblastus variegatus*
	veitchii	see *Sasa veitchii*
	viridistriata	see *Pleioblastus viridistriatus*
	'Wang Tsai'	see *Bambusa multiplex* 'Floribunda'

Arundo (*Poaceae*)

	donax	Widely available
	- 'Golden Chain' (v)	CEnt CKno EBee ELan EPPr EShb EWes LRHS SBfd SMad WFar
	- 'Macrophylla'	CHGN CKno ETod LEdu SApp WPGP
	- 'Peppermint Stick' (v) **new**	EBee
	- 'Variegata'	see *A. donax* var. *versicolor*
§	- var. ***versicolor*** (v)	Widely available
I	- - 'Aureovariegata' (v)	CDTJ MDKP NRHS
	formosana	CKno EPPr
	- 'Golden Showers'	EBee ESwi EUJe GBin SBfd SEND

Asarina (*Plantaginaceae*)

	barclayana	see *Maurandya barclayana*
	erubescens	see *Lophospermum erubescens*
	lophantha	see *Lophospermum scandens*
	lophospermum	see *Lophospermum scandens*
§	***procumbens***	CEnt CTri ECho EDAr LBMP NBir NRya SGar SPhx SRms WBrk WKif
	- 'Alba'	IFro

Asarum (*Aristolochiaceae*)

	Chen Yi 5	WCot
	albomaculatum	ECho
	- B&SWJ 1726	WCru
	arifolium	EHrv EPPr GBBs
	asaroides	LWst
	campaniflorum	ECho LAma LWst WCot WCru
	canadense	CArn EBee ECho EHrv EPfP EWld GBBs GEdr GPoy LEdu MMoz NLar WCru WWEG
	caudatum	CDes CHEx CLAP EBee ECha ECho EPfP GEdr LEdu NBro NLar SRms WCot WCru WFar WPGP
	- deciduous	WCru
	- white-flowered	EHrv SKHP WCru
	caudigerum	WCot
	- B&SWJ 1517	WCru
	- HWJ 641 from Vietnam **new**	WCru
	caulescens	EBee ECho EPPr LAma LWst WCru
	- B&SWJ 5886	WCru
	delavayi	EBee ECho LAma LWst WCot WCru
	epigynum B&SWJ 3443	WCru
	- 'Kikko'	GEdr
	- 'Silver Web'	WCru
	europaeum ♀H4	Widely available
	fauriei	WCru
	forbesii	EBee ECho LWst MMoz NLar
	fudsinoi **new**	GEdr
	geophilum	MMoz
	hartwegii	CLAP IGor LWst NLar WCru WThu
	- NNS 05-85	WCot
	hatsushimae	GEdr
	himalaicum GWJ 9341	WCru
	hypogynum B&SWJ 3628	WCru
	infrapurpureum B&SWJ 1994	WCru

- 'Taroko Web'	WCru
kumageanum	WCot
lemmonii	LEdu LRHS
leptophyllum B&SWJ 1983	WCru
longirhizomatosum	WCru
macranthum	WCot
- B&SWJ 1691	WCru
maculatum B&SWJ 1114	WCru
magnificum	LAma LWst MMoz WCru
maximum	CCon CLAP ECho LAma MMoz NMen WCot WCru
- 'Silver Panda'	CBct CDes CMil CPLG EBee ECtt EHrv ESwi GEdr LRHS LSou MBel NPnk SKHP SMad SPoG WCot
megacalyx	GEdr
naniflorum 'Eco Decor'	CLAP EHrv GEdr LRHS LSou MCot WCot
nipponicum	GEdr
- B&SWJ 2839	WCru
petelotii HWJ 1043	WCru
pulchellum	EHrv LWst WCot WCru
rigescens	EHrv
satsumense	GEdr
savatieri	GEdr
sieboldii	GEdr GPoy WCru
simile	GEdr
splendens	CBct CBro CDes EBee ECho EHrv EPfP GBBs GCal GEdr GMaP LAma LEdu MBel MRav NGdn NLar NPnk NSti SKHP SMad WCot WCru WFar WPGP XLum
taipingshanianum B&SWJ 1688	WCot WCru
- 'Elfin Yellow'	WCru
taitonense	LWst
takasago-saishin **new**	NLar
unzen	GEdr
viridiflorum	GEdr LWst
wulingense	CPLG WCru

Asclepias (*Apocynaceae*)

'Cinderella'	EBee ECtt
curassavica	CCCN EShb SRkn XLum
- 'Red Butterfly'	SLon
- 'Silky Gold' **new**	SPet
- 'Silky Red'	SPet
exaltata **new**	SBrt
§ ***fascicularis***	SBrt
fasciculata	see *A. fascicularis*
incarnata	ELan IFoB LRHS MRav NBre SBrt SMrm SPlb WPer XLum
- 'Alba'	CPom
- 'Ice Ballet'	CAbP CPrp EBee ELan IFoB LHop LRHS NLar SAga SPer SPet SPoG WPer
- 'Soulmate'	ELan EPfP LPot MMuc NGdn SPer SPet WHil WKif
- 'White Superior'	EBee
physocarpa	see *Gomphocarpus physocarpus*
purpurascens	CArn CPom EBee
speciosa	NBre WPGP
sullivantii	EBee NBre SBrt
syriaca	CArn CPom EBee LRHS MBel NBre XLum
tuberosa	CArn CBcs CPom CPrp CWib EBee ECtt GPoy LSou MHer MNHC NEgg SMad SPoG XLum XSen
- Gay Butterflies Group	LRHS SMrm
- 'Hello Yellow'	EBee

Asimina (*Annonaceae*)

triloba (F)	CBcs CDTJ MBlu NLar SGol SPlb
- 'Davis' (F)	CAgr
- 'Nc-1' (F)	CAgr
- 'Pennsylvania Golden' (F)	CAgr
- 'Prolific' (F)	CAgr
- 'Sunflowers'	CCCN

Asparagus (*Asparagaceae*)

RCB AM 23	WCot
from Malawi, hardy	SKHP
asparagoides ♀H1	EShb
cochinchinensis	WPGP
densiflorus 'Mazeppa'	EShb
- 'Myersii' ♀H1	EShb SEND
- Sprengeri Group ♀H1	SEND
falcatus	SEND
filicinus **new**	XBlo
- var. ***giraldii***	WCot
aff. ***meioclados*** B&SWJ 8309 **new**	WCru
officinalis 'Argenteuil'	LEdu
- 'Backlim' ♀H4	ECrN EMil EPom
- 'Connover's Colossal' ♀H4	CSBt CWan LSRN MNHC SEND SVic
- 'Crimson Pacific'	SVic
- 'Dariana'	EMil
- 'Franklim'	WFar
- 'Gijnlim' ♀H4	ECrN EMil EPom SEND WFar
- 'Guelph Millennium'	EPom
- 'Jersey Knight'	SVic
- 'Mary Washington'	LEdu
- 'Pacific 2000'	EPom LSRN SPoG
- 'Pacific Purple'	EPom SPoG
- var. ***prostratus*** from Britain	GCal
- 'Stewart's Purple'	EPom
pseudoscaber 'Spitzenschleier'	CDes EShb SDix SMad WCot
schoberioides	LEdu
- B&SWJ 8814	WCru
suaveolens	EShb
virgatus	EShb WCot WPGP

Asperula (*Rubiaceae*)

§ ***arcadiensis*** ♀H3	ECho WAbe WPat WThu
aristata subsp. ***scabra***	CSpe ECha ELan WCot
- subsp. ***thessala***	see *A. sintenisii*
boissieri	ECho EPot WThu
daphneola	ECho EWes WAbe
gussonei	CMea ECho MWat NMen WAbe
lilaciflora	ECho
- var. ***caespitosa***	see *A. lilaciflora* subsp. *lilaciflora*
§ - subsp. ***lilaciflora***	ECho NMen
nitida	ECho
- subsp. ***puberula***	see *A. sintenisii*
- subsp. ***subcapitellata*** **new**	CPBP
odorata	see *Galium odoratum*
§ ***sintenisii*** ♀H2-3	CMea ECho NMen WAbe WHoo WPat WThu
suberosa misapplied	see *A. arcadiensis*
taurina subsp. ***caucasica***	NLar WBor
tinctoria	CArn GPoy MHer SRms

Asphodeline (*Asphodelaceae*)

§ ***brevicaulis***	WCot XSen
liburnica	CBro CSam EBee ECha ELan GAbr SEND SSvw WCot WHoo WPer XLum XSen

§	***lutea***	Widely available
§	- 'Gelbkerze'	EBee EPfP LRHS NRHS
	- Yellow Candle	see *A. lutea* 'Gelbkerze'
	taurica	ECho MBNS SMHy WCot
	tenuior new	XSen

Asphodelus (*Asphodelaceae*)

	acaulis	ECho LLHF WAbe WCot XLum
	- SF 37	WCot
§	***aestivus***	EBee EWes GCal MBel SPhx SSvw
	- Cally Spear strain	GCal
	albus	CArn CAvo CSpe ECha EPPr GBin IFoB LRHS MCot NBid SPer SPlb SRms WAul WWEG XLum
	brevicaulis	see *Asphodeline brevicaulis*
	cerasiferus	see *A. ramosus*
	fistulosus	LEdu SAga SPhx
	lusitanicus	see *A. ramosus*
	luteus	see *Asphodeline lutea*
	microcarpus	see *A. aestivus*
§	***ramosus***	CPar ECho GCal MNrw WCot

Aspidistra (*Asparagaceae*)

	Chen Yi 135	WCot
	from China	WCot
	attenuata	IBlr
	- B&SWJ 377	WCru
	caespitosa 'Jade Ribbons'	EShb IBlr WCot
	'China Star'	CHEx IBlr WCot
	daibuensis	IBlr
	- B&SWJ 312b	WCru
	- 'Totally Dotty' (v) new	WCru
	elatior ♀H1	CBct CHEx CTsd EBak EShb IBlr LEdu MRav NLar NPla SEND SMad WCot WWFP
	- 'Akebono' (v)	WCot
	- 'Asahi' (v)	IBlr WCot
	- 'Hoshi-zora' (v)	IBlr WCot
	- 'Lennon's Song' (v)	WCot
	- 'Milky Way' (v)	CBct CHid EShb IBlr MMoz SEND WCot
	- 'Morning Frost' (v)	IBlr
	- 'Okame' (v)	IBlr WCot
	- 'Variegata' (v) ♀H1	CBct CHEx IBlr IFoB NBir SEND WCot
	- 'Variegata Exotica' (v)	XBlo
	leshanensis (v)	IBlr
	linearifolia 'Leopard'	IBlr WCot
	lurida	CBct EBee EShb
	- 'Irish Mist' (v)	IBlr
	minutiflora	WCot
	mushaensis B&SWJ 1953	WCru
	aff. ***mushaensis*** 'Spotty Dotty' (v)	WCru
	aff. ***omeiensis***	WCot
	aff. ***patentiloba***	WCot
	saxicola 'Uan Fat Lady'	see *A. zongbayi* 'Uan Fat Lady'
	sutepensis B&SWJ 5216	WCru
	typica 'China Sun'	IBlr WCot
	zongbayi	WCot
§	- 'Uan Fat Lady'	WCot WCru

Asplenium ✿ (*Aspleniaceae*)

	adiantum-nigrum	CBty WAbe
	antiquum	CBty
	australasicum	EShb
	bulbiferum misapplied	see *A.* × *lucrosum*
	bulbiferum ambig. × ***oblongifolium***	GBin
	bulbiferum Forst.f.	ESwi GBin
§	***ceterach***	CBty EFer WAbe WHer
	difforme × ***dimorphum***	CBty
	× ***ebenoides***	CBty NMyG WCot
§	× ***lucrosum*** ♀H1-2	CBty CDTJ CKel EOHP ESwi
	'Maori Princess'	WFib
	nidus ♀H1	XBlo
	oblongifolium	GBin
	ruta-muraria	EFer
§	***scolopendrium*** ♀H4	Widely available
	- 'Angustatum'	CBty CLAP EBee ECha ELon EPPr EPfP ERod EShb GBin GKev LAst LRHS MBri MGos MMoz NEgg NHol NLar NPri NWad SEND SPoG SRms WFar WMoo WPat WPnP WPtf WWEG
	- Crispum Group	CLAP EFer ELan MRav MWat NBid NHol SApp SRms SRot WFib WPGP WPtf
	- - 'Crispum Bolton's Nobile' ♀H4	WFib
	- - 'Golden Queen'	CLAP
	- Crispum Cristatum Group	CLAP LTen MMuc
	- Crispum Fimbriatum Group	CLAP EBee GQui
	- Cristatum Group	Widely available
	- Fimbriatum Group	CLAP
	- 'Furcatum'	CBty CDTJ CLAP EBee GBin GEdr LRHS NHol NLar SEND
	- 'Kaye's Lacerated' ♀H4	CLAP EFer WFib
	- Laceratum Group	CLAP
	- Marginatum Group	EFer
	- 'Muricatum'	CLAP ELan GBin MRav MWhi NBid NHol WFib WTin
	- 'Ramocristatum'	CLAP
	- Ramomarginatum Group	CLAP ELan WFar
	- 'Sagittatoprojectum Sclater'	WFib
	- Undulatum Group	CBty CDTJ CLAP EAEE EBee ECha EPfP EUJe LRHS MMoz MMuc NBir NEgg NHol NLar SBfd SEND SRms WIvy WPnP
	- Undulatum Cristatum Group	CLAP
	trichomanes ♀H4	Widely available
	- Cristatum Group	SRms WFar
	- Incisum Group	EFer NOrc SRms WAbe

Astelia (*Asteliaceae*)

	alpina	IBlr
	banksii	CBcs CDoC CHEx CHll CSpe CTrC EBee IBal LRHS LSRN LTen MGos NRHS SBfd SCoo SHil SLim WCot
§	***chathamica*** ♀H3	Widely available
	- 'Silver Spear'	see *A. chathamica*
	chathamica × ***fragrans***	ECou
	cunninghamii	see *A. solandri*
	fragrans	CBcs CCon EBee ECou GCal IBlr LEdu
	graminea	GCal
	grandis	CBcs IBlr LEdu
	nervosa	CTsd ECou IBlr LEdu LSRN
	- 'Alpine Ruby'	IBlr
	- 'Bronze Giant'	IBlr
	- 'Silver Sabre'	IBlr
	- 'Westland'	CBcs CDoC CKno COlW CSpe CTrC CTsd EBee EUJe GCal IBlr LEdu LHop LRHS LSRN MGos MPie

		MRav SBfd SEND SHil SLim SMrm SPad SPlb SPoG SWvt WCot
	nivicola 'Golden Gem'	IBlr
	- 'Red Gem'	GCal LEdu
	petriei	IBlr
	'Red Devil'	CBcs CDoC CSpe CTrC IBoy LRHS SHil WHer
	'Silver Mound'	EPfP
§	***solandri***	ECou IBlr
	trinervia	GCal IBlr

Aster ✿ (*Asteraceae*)

	acris	see *A. sedifolius*
	ageratoides	CPou CPrp LRHS WOld
	- 'Ashvi'	WCot
	- 'Asran'	CWan EBee ECtt EHoe EPPr EWes LSou MMuc MPie SEND SSvw WCot WOld XLum
	- 'Harry Smith'	EBee NDov
	- 'Starshine' PBR	EPPr NSti WCot
§	***albescens***	LRHS
	alpigenus var. ***alpigenus***	LLHF
	- var. ***haydenii***	LLHF
	alpinus ♀H4	ECho EPfP GJos GKev LPot MAsh SRms WFar XSen
	- var. ***albus***	EBee EDAr EPfP LRHS NBro NLar SPoG
	- 'Antje' **new**	EBee
	- Dark Beauty	see *A. alpinus* 'Dunkle Schöne'
§	- 'Dunkle Schöne'	EBee EDAr LDai LRHS SPoG SRms WPer
	- 'Goliath'	EBee EPfP LRHS NBre NBro NLar SPlb WFar WPer
	- 'Happy End'	ECho NBre NLar SPoG SRms
	- 'Pinkie'	EBee EDAr EPfP LRHS NLar
	- 'Trimix'	ECho NBir SRms
	- 'White Beauty'	SRms
	amelloides	see *Felicia amelloides*
	amellus	CArn LRHS LSou WMoo
	- 'Blue King'	EBee GBuc MAvo NWsh SMrm SWvt
	- 'Breslau'	EBee LRHS MAvo
	- 'Brilliant'	CPrp EBee ECtt EPPr GBuc LAst LRHS LSou MAvo MBNS MNFA MRav MWat SMrm SMrs SPer SRGP WHoo WOld
	- 'Doktor Otto Petschek'	EBee
	- 'Forncett Flourish'	WCot WOld
	- 'Framfieldii' ♀H4	NDov SMHy WCot WOld
	- 'Gründer'	LRHS MAvo WHil WOld
	- 'Jacqueline Genebrier' ♀H4	ELon GBuc NDov
	- 'Jubilee'	LRHS
	- 'King George' ♀H4	Widely available
	- 'Kobold'	LRHS
	- 'Lac de Genève'	LRHS
	- 'Lady Hindlip'	CSam
	- 'Louise'	LRHS MBrN SBch SUsu
	- 'Mira'	EBee
	- 'Moerheim Gem'	LRHS WOld
	- 'Nocturne'	WCot WOld
	- 'Peach Blossom'	EBee
	- Pink Zenith	see *A. amellus* 'Rosa Erfüllung'
§	- 'Rosa Erfüllung'	CMac EBee ECtt ELan ELon EPPr EPfP GBuc GMaP IVic LAst LHop LRHS LSou MCot MRav NDov NWsh SAga SPhx SRGP SWvt WCAu WCot WMnd WOld
	- 'Rotfeuer'	ELon GQue WCot
	- 'Rudolph Goethe'	EBee ECtt ELan EMil EPPr EPfP GBee LAst LRHS NRHS SBHP SRGP WMoo WOld WSpi WWEG
	- 'Silbersee'	CSam LRHS NDov
	- 'Sonia'	GBuc LRHS MNFA MRav SUsu
	- 'Sonora'	EBee LPla SAga SMrm SPhx SRGP SUsu WKif WOld
	- 'Sternkugel'	WOld
	- 'Vanity'	LRHS WOld
§	- 'Veilchenkönigin' ♀H4	Widely available
N	- Violet Queen	see *A. amellus* 'Veilchenkönigin'
	- 'Weltfriede'	WOld
	× ***amethystinus*** **new**	WCot
	'Anita Pfeiffer'	LRHS
	'Anja's Choice'	EBee LHop WOld
	asper	see *A. bakerianus*
	asperulus misapplied	see *A. peduncularis*
§	***bakerianus***	WFar
	'Blue Autumn'	EBee NCGa
	capensis 'Variegatus'	see *Felicia amelloides* variegated
	'Carmen' **new**	EBee
§	***carolinianus***	EShb XEll
	'Cassandra'	NCGa
	'Cheavers'	LRHS
	'Chesters Star'	WOld
	ciliolatus	LRHS
	'Climax' misapplied	see *A. laevis* 'Arcturus', *A. laevis* 'Calliope'
	'Climax' ambig.	CElw ELan GCal GQue MMuc MRav NBid SEND SMrm XLum
	'Climax' Vicary Gibbs	WOld
	coelestis	see *Felicia amelloides*
	coloradoensis	CPBP LLHF NSla XSen
	'Connecticut Snow Flurry'	see *A. ericoides* f. *prostratus* 'Snow Flurry'
	conspicuus	EBee
	'Coombe Fishacre' ♀H4	COIW CSam EBee ELan GBuc GCal LPla MCot MNFA MRav NCGa NLar SBfd SMrm SMrs SSvw SUsu WFar WHoo WOld WSpi WTin
	cordifolius	LRHS
	- 'Aldebaran'	NDov WOld
	- 'Blutenregen'	EBee
	- 'Chieftain' ♀H4	MNrw SPhx WOld
	- 'Elegans'	CSam LRHS WMnd WOld
	- 'Ideal'	EBee NLar WOld XLum
	- 'Silver Spray'	CKno CPrp EBee ECtt GMaP GQue MHom MWat NBre SRGP WOld WPer XLum
	- 'Sweet Lavender' ♀H4	SBfd WOld
	- 'White Chief'	WOld
	corymbosus	see *A. divaricatus*
	'Cotswold Gem'	WCot WOld
	delavayi	SUsu
	diffusus	see *A. lateriflorus*
	diplostephioides	EBee EDAr EPPr EPfP GBin GBuc GCal IKil LBMP LRHS MBNS MMHG NBre NLar SPlb WAul WPer WPtf
§	***divaricatus***	Widely available
§	- 'Eastern Star'	NCGa WCot WOld
	- Raiche form	see *A. divaricatus* 'Eastern Star'
N	***dumosus***	CPLG WPer
	- 'Biteliness'	NBre NLar
	- Sapphire = 'Kiesapphire' PBR	CPrp ELon LHop LRHS LSRN MBri NEgg SRGP SWvt
	'Dwarf Barbados'	EPfP LRHS
	ericoides	CKno MCot NBre NOrc WWEG

	- 'Blue Star' ♀H4	CPrp CSam EBee LRHS NLar SPer WMnd WOld WWEG
	- 'Blue Wonder'	XLum
	- 'Brimstone' ♀H4	MRav NBre WOld
	- 'Cinderella'	CPrp GBee LRHS NMRc NRHS NSti WOld WWEG
	- 'Constance'	WOld
	- 'Erlkönig'	ECGP EPri EShb GCal GQue LAst LRHS NGdn NLar NPnk SWat WCot WMnd WOld WPer XLum
	- 'Esther'	CPrp EBee ECha ELan NCGa SMrm WOld
	- 'Golden Spray' ♀H4	EBee EPfP GMaP GQue NLar SPer WMnd WOld
	- 'Herbstmyrte'	CSam LRHS
	- 'Hon. Edith Gibbs'	WOld
	- 'Monte Cassino'	see *A. pilosus* var. *pringlei* 'Monte Cassino'
	- 'Pink Cloud' ♀H4	CHVG COIW CPrp EBee ECtt EPfP EPri EShb GBuc GCal LAst LRHS MNFA MSpe NCGa NHol NLar NOrc SPer SRGP SWat WFar WMnd WOld WPer WSpi WWEG
	- f. ***prostratus***	EPot GBuc GQue SGar WFar XSen
§	- - 'Snow Flurry' ♀H4	CMea EBee ECha ECtt GBuc LEdu LPla MAvo MNFA MNrw NLar SAga SMrm WCot WMnd WOld WOut WPer XLum
	- 'Rosy Veil'	MHom NBir NGdn
	- 'Schneegitter'	EBee LRHS WCot
	- 'Schneetanne'	NBre
	- 'Star Shower'	LRHS
	- 'Sulphurea'	MWat
	- 'Vimmer's Delight'	WCot
	- 'White Heather'	CPrp NLar WMnd WOld WPer WRHF WSpi
	- 'Yvette Richardson'	MHom SMHy WOld WWEG
	falcatus	WCot
	- var. ***commutatus***	WCot
	'Fanny's Fall'	see *A. oblongifolius* 'Fanny's'
§	***flaccidus***	LRHS
	foliaceus from Montana	EPPr
	- var. ***parryi***	EBee
	× ***frikartii***	CMac EBee ELan EPfP EShb LRHS MRav SMrm SWvt WOld
	- 'Eiger'	WOld
	- 'Flora's Delight'	GCal LRHS NDov NLar NRHS WOld WWEG
	- 'Jungfrau'	CWGN EBee EPPr GBuc GMaP GQue LRHS MRav NLar SPhx WOld WWEG
N	- 'Mönch' ♀H4	Widely available
	- Wonder of Stafa	see *A.* × *frikartii* 'Wunder von Stäfa'
§	- 'Wunder von Stäfa' ♀H4	CKno CPLG EBee ECtt ELan ELon EPfP EWTr GBuc GMaP LHop LRHS LSRN LSou MBNS MCot MRav NBir NDov NLar SWvt WCot WMnd WOld WWEG XLum
	furcatus	XLum
	glehnii 'Aglenii'	EBee
	'Glow in the Dark'	MAvo WCot WOld
	greatae	EBee
	hayatae	SBrt
	- B&SWJ 8790	WCru
	'Herfstweelde'	CPrp EBee SMad SUsu WOld
§	× ***herveyi***	CCon CPrp CSam EBee ECtt ELan EPfP GCal LLWP LRHS MMuc MNFA MSpe NLar NSti NWsh SAga SDix SPer SPhx SPoG SRGP WBor WCot WMnd WOld WPtf

	'Hon. Vicary Gibbs' (*ericoides* hybrid)	MNFA WOld WOut
	hybridus luteus	see *Solidago* × ***luteus***
	'Ivy House'	ECtt
	'Kylie' ♀H4	CDes CHVG CPrp EBee ECtt LRHS LSRN MHom NCGa SPhx SRGP SUsu WBor WBrk WCot WFar WHil WOld WTin
	laevis	LEdu NBre NLar WPer
	- 'Anneke Van der Jeugd'	EBee
§	- 'Arcturus'	CCon LRHS MHom MNrw NBir NCGa NSti SSvw WCot WOld WWlt XLum
	- 'Blauhügel'	LPla NDov
	- 'Blauschleier' **new**	EBee
	- 'Blue Bird'	SUsu
§	- 'Calliope'	Widely available
	- 'Cally Compact'	GQue NLar
	- var. ***geyeri***	MNrw
	- 'Nightshade'	MAvo MNrw WBrk WOld
	- 'Vesta'	WOld
	- white-flowered	WOld
	lanceolatus Willd.	EPPr NCGa
	- 'Edwin Beckett'	CBre MHom MNrw WOld
§	***lateriflorus***	MAvo WOld WPer
	- 'Bleke Bet'	WCot WOld
	- 'Buck's Fizz'	NLar SBfd WOld
	- 'Chloe'	CSam EBee NCGa SPhx
	- 'Datschi'	XLum
	- var. ***horizontalis*** ♀H4	Widely available
	- 'Jan'	WOld
	- 'Lady in Black'	Widely available
	- 'Lovely'	CSam EBee LRHS NBre SRGP WCot
	- 'Prince'	Widely available
	laterifolius 'Snow Flurry'	see *A. ericoides* f. *prostratus* 'Snow Flurry'
	'Les Moutiers'	MHom MNrw WOld
§	***linosyris***	EBee EPfP EWes GBin GQue LRHS MAvo NLar SMrm WHer WOld XLum
	- 'Goldilocks'	see *A. linosyris*
	'Little Carlow' (*cordifolius* hybrid) ♀H4	Widely available
	'Little Dorrit' (*cordifolius* hybrid)	ECtt NWsh WOld
	maackii	SMrm
	macrophyllus	ELan GBee LRHS MSpe NLar WOld
	- 'Albus'	EBee EPPr WFar WOld
	- 'Twilight'	see *A.* × ***herveyi***
	mongolicus	see *Kalimeris mongolica*
	'Mrs Dean'	ECtt
	natalensis	see *Felicia rosulata*
	'Natasha'	LSRN
	'Noreen'	MAvo
	novae-angliae	CArn WOld
	- 'Alex Deamon'	MAvo WOld
	- 'Anabelle de Chazal'	ECtt MAvo SMrs WOld
	- 'Andenken an Alma Pötschke'	Widely available
	- 'Andenken an Paul Gerber'	EBee ECtt LHop MAvo MHom MNrw WOld
	- 'Augusta'	MAvo WBrk WOld
	- Autumn Snow	see *A. novae-angliae* 'Herbstschnee'
	- 'Barr's Blue'	CMac EBee ELon EPfP GCra MAvo MHom MMuc MWat NLar NWsh SEND SMrs SPer SRms WBrk WMoo WOld

	- 'Barr's Pink'	CBre CMac EBee ECtt ELon EPfP MAvo MCot MHer MHom MLHP MMuc MPie MWat NLar SEND WBrk WFar WOld WPer WSFF WSpi
*	- 'Barr's Purple'	ECtt WBrk WCFE WOld
	- 'Barr's Violet'	ECtt MAvo MHom SRms WBrk WCot WHal WHoo WHrl WMoo WOld WPer WTin WWEG
	- 'Brockamin'	MNrw WBrk
	- 'Christopher Harbutt'	LEdu SRGP WOld
	- 'Colwall Century'	MAvo WOld
	- 'Colwall Constellation'	MAvo WOld
	- 'Colwall Galaxy'	MAvo WHrl WOld
	- 'Colwall Orbit'	MAvo WOld
	- 'Crimson Beauty'	MAvo MHer MHom MNrw MWat WBrk WOld
	- 'Dapper Tapper'	WCot
	- 'Evensong'	ECtt MAvo WBrk WOld
	- 'Festival'	WBrk
	- 'Foxy Emily'	MAvo WOld
	- 'Harrington's Pink' ♀H4	Widely available
	- 'Helen Picton'	CSam ECtt ELon MAvo MBrN MHer MHom MWat WBrk WOld
§	- 'Herbstschnee'	Widely available
	- 'James Ritchie'	EWes LLHF WHoo WOld
	- 'John Davies'	MAvo MNrw WHil WOld
	- 'Kate Deamon' **new**	WOld
	- 'Lachsglut'	ELon MAvo SMrm WCot
	- 'Ladies Day'	WOld
	- 'Lou Williams'	ECtt ELon MAvo MNrw MWat SMrs WHil WOld
I	- 'Lucida'	MAvo WHal WOld
	- 'Lye End Beauty'	CKno ECtt ELon LLWP MAvo MHom MNFA MNrw MWat SMrs WBrk WCot WHoo WMoo WOld WTin
	- 'Marina Wolkonsky'	EBee ECtt ELon EWes LHop MAvo MNrw MWat SMrs SPhx SUsu WBrk WCot WKif WOld
	- 'Millennium Star'	MAvo WOld
	- 'Miss K.E. Mash'	MAvo MHom SRGP WBrk WOld WWEG
	- 'Mrs S.T. Wright'	CPrp CTri ECtt EWes MAvo MBrN MHom MNFA MNrw SMrs SRGP WFar WOld WWEG
	- 'Mrs S.W. Stern'	WOld
	- 'Naomi'	MAvo WOld
	- 'Pink Parfait'	CSam ECtt LRHS MAvo NBre NGdn SMrs SRms WBrk WCot WOld
	- 'Pink Victor'	CTri MAvo SRms WMoo
	- 'Pride of Rougham'	EWes
	- 'Primrose Upward'	MAvo MNrw NWsh WCot WOld
	- 'Purple Cloud'	CSam LHop MAvo MHer MHom MWat NBre NGdn WBrk WHal WOld WWEG
I	- 'Purple Dome'	Widely available
	- 'Quinton Menzies'	CSam ELon MAvo WBrk WOld WWEG
	- 'Red Cloud'	NBre SMrm WBrk WOld
	- 'Rosa Sieger' ♀H4	CBre CPrp CSam EBee ECtt GMaP GQue MAvo MHom MNrw NGdn SPhx SUsu WBor WBrk WOld WWEG XLum
	- 'Rose Williams'	MAvo WOld WOut
	- 'Roter Stern'	ECtt MAvo WBrk WOld
	- 'Rougham Purple'	EWes
	- 'Rubinschatz'	EBee MAvo MHom MWat NBre SRms WOld XLum
	- 'Rudelsburg'	MAvo NDov
	- 'Saint Michael's'	WOld
	- 'Sayer's Croft'	ELon LRHS MHom MWat WCot WHil WHoo WOld WOut WTin
	- September Ruby	see *A. novae-angliae* 'Septemberrubin'
§	- 'Septemberrubin'	CMea EBee ECtt ELon EPfP IFoB LEdu LHop LSou MBel MMuc MNFA MRav NWsh SEND SMrs SPhx SRGP SUsu WFar WOld WSpi XLum
	- 'Treasure'	CBre EBee ECtt ELon EWes LRHS MAvo NBre NRHS SMrm SMrs SRGP WBrk WMoo WOld
	- 'Vibrant Dome'PBR	MAvo NLar
	- 'Violet Haze'	CMea
	- 'Violetta'	EBee ECtt ELon LRHS LSou MAvo MHom MNFA MNrw NMRc SMrs SPhx WFar WHoo WKif WOld WTin
	- 'W. Bowman'	WOld
	- 'Wow'	ELon SMrm
N	***novi-belgii***	WHer
	- 'Ada Ballard'	CMac EBee LDai LHop LRHS LSRN NBre NEgg SBfd SMrm SMrs SPer SRGP WMoo WOld WSpi WWEG
	- 'Albanian'	WOld
	- 'Alderman Vokes'	WOld
	- 'Alex Norman'	WOld
	- 'Algar's Pride'	ECtt WOld WWEG
	- 'Alice Haslam'	CMac EBee ECtt LRHS NEgg NLar NOrc SBfd SRGP SRms WCAu WOld WPer WWEG
	- 'Alpenglow'	WOld
	- 'Angela Peel'	LRHS
	- 'Anita Ballard'	WOld
	- 'Anita Webb'	NBir WOld
	- 'Anneke'	LRHS NLar SRGP SRkn WOld
	- 'Apollo'	LRHS MWat NEgg NLar WFar WOld
	- 'Apple Blossom'	WOld
	- 'Arctic'	WOld
	- 'Audrey'	CEnt CFis CMac EBee ECtt GMaP LRHS LSRN MBNS NEgg NGdn NOrc SRGP SRms WFar WOld
	- 'Autumn Beauty'	WOld
	- 'Autumn Days'	WOld
	- 'Autumn Glory'	WOld
	- 'Autumn Rose'	SMrs WOld
	- 'Baby Climax'	WOld
	- 'Bahamas' (Island Series)	EPfP EWll LRHS LSou NLar NWsh SBfd SGar SHil SRms SWvt WCot WHil
	- 'Barbados' (Island Series)	EPfP LRHS LSou MBri NLar SHil SWvt WCot
	- 'Beauty of Colwall'	WOld
	- 'Beechwood Challenger'	WOld
	- 'Beechwood Charm'	WOld
	- 'Beechwood Rival'	CTri EBee LRHS MBri WOld
	- 'Blandie'	CTri EBee EPfP SRGP WOld
	- 'Blauglut'	WOld
	- 'Blue Baby'	CMac WPer
	- 'Blue Bouquet'	CTri SRms WOld
	- 'Blue Boy'	WOld WWEG
	- 'Blue Danube'	SMrs WHrl WOld
	- 'Blue Eyes'	SMrs SUsu WOld
	- 'Blue Gown'	CCse GCal GQue WOld WOut
	- 'Blue Lagoon'	CFis CMea ELan MBri MMuc SMrs SRGP WBrk WOld

- 'Blue Patrol'	WOld
- 'Blue Radiance'	WOld
- 'Blue Spire'	WOld
- 'Bonanza'	WOld
- 'Boningale Blue'	WOld
- 'Boningale White'	NDov WOld
- 'Bridesmaid'	WOld
- 'Bridgette'	NPnk
- 'Bright Eyes'	SRGP
- 'Brightest and Best'	WOld
- 'Brigitte'	NLar
- 'Cameo'	WOld
- 'Cantab'	WOld
- 'Carlingcott'	WOld
- 'Carnival'	CMac EBee ECtt IVic LDai LRHS MMHG NEgg NOrc SMrs SRGP WOld
- 'Cecily'	WOld WWEG
- 'Charles Wilson'	WOld
- 'Chatterbox'	ELan EPfP LPot LRHS MRav MWat NEgg NLar WOld
- 'Chelwood'	WOld
- 'Chequers'	EBee MBNS NEgg SMrs SRGP WOld
- 'Christina'	see *A. novi-belgii* 'Kristina'
- 'Christine Soanes'	WOld
- 'Cliff Lewis'	WOld
- 'Climax Albus'	see *A.* 'White Climax'
- 'Cloudy Blue'	WOld
- 'Colonel F.R. Durham'	WOld
- 'Coombe Gladys'	WOld
- 'Coombe Margaret'	WOld WOut
- 'Coombe Radiance'	WOld
- 'Coombe Ronald'	MWat WOld
- 'Coombe Rosemary'	ECtt LRHS NLar WBor WOld
- 'Coombe Violet'	MWat WOld
- 'Countess of Dudley'	CFis WOld WPer
- 'Court Herald'	WOld
- 'Crimson Brocade'	CCon EBee ECtt ELan EPfP LRHS MBri NDov NLar SBfd SPoG SRGP WSpi
- 'Dandy'	CMac EBee ELan LRHS NBir NEgg NGdn SRGP WFar WOld
- 'Daniela'	SRms WBrk WOld
- 'Daphne Anne'	WOld
- 'Dauerblau'	GBin WOld
- 'Davey's True Blue'	CTri SMrs WOld XLum
- 'David Murray'	WOld
- 'Dazzler'	WOld WWEG
- Debbie = 'Dasdebi' (Mystery Lady Series) (d)	LRHS
- Demi = 'Dasdem' (Mystery Lady Series) (d)	LRHS
- 'Destiny'	WOld
- 'Diana'	NWsh
- 'Diana Watts'	WOld
- 'Dietgard'	MWat WOld WWEG
- 'Dolly'	NBir SRms WOld WWEG
- 'Dora Chiswell'	WOld
- 'Dusky Maid'	WOld
- 'Dwarf Ibiza'	LRHS
- 'Elizabeth'	CElw WOld
- 'Elizabeth Hutton'	WOld
- 'Elsie Dale'	WOld
- 'Elta'	WOld
- 'Erica'	CElw MWat WOld
- 'Ernest Ballard'	WOld
- 'Eva'	SRms WOld
- 'Eventide'	CElw CTri EBee LSRN WOld WRHF

- 'Fair Lady'	LRHS MWat WOld
- 'Faith'	WOld
- 'Farncombe Lilac'	NCot
- 'Farrington'	WOld
- 'Fellowship' ♀H4	CCon CDes COlW EBee ECtt ELon LEdu MAvo MBri MMuc MNrw NCGa NDov SEND SHar SMrs SPer SRGP SRms SUsu WBrk WCot WOld WWEG
- 'Flamingo'	EBee LRHS WOld
- 'Fontaine'	WOld
- 'Freda Ballard'	CFis ECtt GMaP LHop LRHS LSRN MWat SMrs SRGP WCAu WNew WOld WWEG
- 'Freya'	LSRN WOld WSHC
- 'Fuldatal'	WOld
- 'Gayborder Blue'	WOld
- 'Gayborder Royal'	CCon WOld
- 'Glory of Colwall'	WOld
- 'Goliath'	WOld
- 'Grey Lady'	WOld WWEG
- 'Guardsman'	WOld
- 'Gulliver'	WOld WWEG
- 'Gurney Slade'	WOld
- 'Guy Ballard'	WOld
- 'Harrison's Blue'	MWat SMrs WOld WPer
- 'Heinz Richard'	CFis COlW EBee ECha LRHS MHer NBir NBre NGdn SBch SMrs SRGP SRms WOld WWEG
- 'Helen'	WOld
- 'Helen Ballard'	SRms WBrk WOld
- 'Herbstgruss vom Bresserhof'	NBre NLar WOld
- 'Herbstpurzel'	WOld
- 'Hilda Ballard'	WOld
- 'Ibiza'	CYeo LRHS WCot
- 'Ilse Brensell'	WOld WWEG
- Ingrid = 'Dasing' (Mystery Lady Series) (d)	LRHS
- 'Irene'	WOld
- 'Janet Watts'	WOld
- 'Jean'	ELon MWat SBfd SRms WOld WPer
- 'Jean Gyte'	WOld
- 'Jeanette'	SRms WOld
- 'Jenny'	COlW CSBt EBee ECtt EPPr EPfP GBin GMaP LHop LRHS LSRN MBri MRav MWat NBir NDov NEgg NGdn SBfd SPer SPoG SRGP SRkn SRms WFar WMnd WOld WWEG
- Jessica = 'Dasjes' (Mystery Lady Series) (d)	LRHS
- 'Jollity'	WOld
- 'Julia'	WOld
- 'Karminkuppel'	NBre WOld
- 'Kassel'	SRms WOld
- Katharine = 'Daskat' (Mystery Lady Series) (d)	LRHS
- 'King of the Belgians'	WOld
§ - 'Kristina'	COlW CWan EBee ECha EPPr ITim LRHS MRav NBir WCot WOld WWEG
- 'Lady Frances'	EBee SRms WOld
- 'Lady in Blue'	CSBt EBee ECtt ELan EPPr EPfP LAst LEdu LHop LRHS MBNS MBri MLHP MWat NEgg NGdn NRHS NWad SBfd SPer SPoG SRGP SRms SWat SWvt WFar WOld WTin WWEG

- 'Lassie' CElw MWat WOld
- 'Lavender Dream' WOld
- 'Lawrence Chiswell' WOld
- 'Lederstrumpf' NDov
- 'Lilac Time' WOld
- 'Lisa Dawn' ECtt SMrs WOld
- 'Little Boy Blue' LRHS NBre SRms WOld XLum
- 'Little Man in Blue' WOld WWEG
- 'Little Pink Beauty' CEnt COlW EBee ECtt ELan EPfP ITim LAst LHop LRHS MBNS NEgg NGdn NWad SGar SPer SRGP SRms STes WFar WOld WWEG
- 'Little Pink Lady' LRHS SRms WOld
- 'Little Pink Pyramid' SRms WOld WWEG
- 'Little Red Boy' WOld
- 'Little Treasure' WOld
- 'Madge Cato' MAvo SRms WOld
- 'Mammoth' WOld
- 'Margery Bennett' WOld
- 'Marie Ballard' CMac COlW CSBt EBee GMaP LEdu LRHS MBri MHer MRav MWat MWhi NBre NCGa NGdn NLar NOrc NPer SBfd SMrm SPer SRGP SRms SWat WBrk WCAu WNew WOld WPer WWEG
- 'Marie's Pretty Please' WOld
- 'Marjorie' LSRN SBfd SPoG SRGP WOld XLum
- 'Martonie' WPer
- 'Mary Ann Neil' SMrs SRms WOld
- 'Mary Deane' WOld WPer
- 'Mauve Magic' MWat SRms WOld WWEG
- 'Melbourne Belle' WOld
- 'Melbourne Magnet' WOld
- 'Michael Watts' WOld
- 'Midget' WOld
- 'Mistress Quickly' MCot SMrs WOld WWEG
- 'Mittelmeer' XLum
- 'Mount Everest' LHop NCGa SPhx WOld WPer WWEG
- 'Mrs Leo Hunter' WOld
- 'Neron' NDov
- 'Nesthäkchen' WOld
- 'Newton's Pink' WOld
- 'Niobe' CMac WOld
- 'Nobilis' WOld
- 'Norman's Jubilee' EBee EPfP LRHS NBir NEgg SMrs WOld WWEG
- 'Nursteed Charm' WOld
- 'Oktoberschneekuppel' WOld
- 'Orlando' WOld
- 'Pamela' WOld
- 'Patricia Ballard' CBcs CCon CHab CMac CSBt EBee GCra GMaP LRHS MHer MWat MWhi NBir NLar NPer NWad SBfd SMrs SPer SRGP WFar WNew WOld WPer WWEG
- 'Peace' WOld
- 'Percy Thrower' ECtt SMrs WOld
- 'Peter Chiswell' SRms WOld
- 'Peter Harrison' EBee GMaP NBir WMnd WOld WPer XLum
- 'Peter Pan' GBee LRHS NLar SHar WOld
- 'Picture' NBre
- 'Pink Lace' MBNS WOld WPer
- 'Plenty' WOld
- 'Porzellan' CElw CFis COlW EBee ECtt MAvo MBNS NDov NGdn SMrs SRGP WCot WOld
- 'Pride of Colwall' SRms WOld
- 'Priory Blush' WOld
- 'Professor Anton Kippenberg' CEnt CFis CWan EBee EPfP GMaP LLWP LRHS MRav NBre NLar SHil SPer SRGP SRms SWvt WMnd WOld XLum
- 'Prosperity' NBre WOld
- 'Purple Dome' CFis ECha LEdu LSRN MHer MWat SHar SRkn WOld WOut
- 'Queen Mary' WOld
- 'Queen of Colwall' WOld
- 'Ralph Picton' WOld
- 'Raspberry Ripple' WOld
- 'Rector' see *A. novi-belgii* 'The Rector'
- 'Red Robin' MSpe MWat
- 'Red Sunset' SRms WOld

* - 'Reitlinstal' EBee
- 'Rembrandt' EBee ECtt LDai NEgg NGdn SHar SMrs SRGP
- 'Remembrance' MWat SRms WBrk WOld WWEG
- 'Reverend Vincent Dale' WOld
- 'Richness' MAvo WOld
- 'Roland Smith' WOld
- 'Rose Bonnet' CSBt SPlb WOld
- 'Roseanne' WOld
- 'Rosebud' ambig. WOld WWEG
- 'Rosenquartz' NLar
- 'Rosenwichtel' LRHS NLar WOld WWEG
- 'Royal Ruby' EBee ECtt LRHS NLar WOld WWEG
- 'Royal Velvet' WOld
- 'Rozika' WOld
- 'Rufus' WOld
- 'Sailor Boy' NCGa WOld
- 'Saint Egwyn' WOld
- 'Sam Banham' MNrw WOld
- 'Samoa' (Island Series) EPfP EUJe EWll LRHS LSou MBri NLar NPri SBfd SHil SRms WCot WHil
- 'Sandford White Swan' GBuc MHom WBrk WOld WWEG
- 'Sarah Ballard' LRHS SHil SRGP WOld

§ - 'Schneekissen' EBee ECtt EPfP EWTr GMaP LRHS MBNS MHer MMuc NWsh SBfd SPer SRGP SWvt WFar WOld WWEG XLum
- 'Schöne von Dietlikon' CKno MAvo MWat WOld XLum
- 'Schoolgirl' WOld WWEG
- 'Sheena' WOld
- 'Silberblaukissen' GBin WOld
- Snow Cushion see *A. novi-belgii* 'Schneekissen'
- 'Snowdrift' WOld
- 'Snowsprite' CBcs CSBt ELan LRHS MWat NEgg NLar NOrc NPro SMrs SRGP SRms SWat WOld
- 'Sonata' GMaP WOld
- 'Sophia' MWat SMrs WOld
- 'Starlight' EBee ECtt NLar WFar WOld WRHF
- 'Steinebrück' WOld
- 'Sterling Silver' WOld
- 'Sunset' WOld
- 'Susan' WOld
- 'Sweet Briar' CElw WOld
- 'Tapestry' WOld
- 'Terry's Pride' EBee SRGP WOld WWEG
- 'The Archbishop' ECtt WOld
- 'The Bishop' WOld
- 'The Cardinal' WOld
- 'The Dean' WOld

	Name	Suppliers
§	- 'The Rector'	WOld
	- 'The Sexton'	WOld
	- 'Thundercloud'	MWat WOld
	- 'Timsbury'	SRms WBrk WOld WWEG
	- 'Tovarich'	WOld
	- 'Trudi Ann'	NBir WOld
	- 'Twinkle'	WOld
	- 'Victor'	WOld
	- 'Vignem'	NSti
	- 'Violet Lady'	WOld
	- 'Violetta'	SMrs
	- 'Waterperry'	MWat WBrk WOld
	- 'Weisses Wunder'	WOld
	- 'White Ladies'	CBcs CHab ECtt GCra GMaP LRHS MMuc MWat NLar NOrc SBfd SEND SHil SPer SRGP XLum
	- 'White Swan'	ECtt WOld
	- 'White Wings'	MWat WOld
	- 'Winston S. Churchill'	CEnt CTri EBee ELan EPfP GMaP LRHS MWat SBfd SPlb SPoG SRGP WOld WSpi
	novii-belgii 'Farncombe Wine Red' **new**	NCot
	oblongifolius	WOld WPer XSen
§	- 'Fanny's'	CPrp EBee ECtt GCal GQue SPoG SRGP WCot WFar WOld
	'Ochtendgloren' (*pringlei* hybrid) Ψ^{H4}	CDes CPrp CSam EBee ECtt EPPr EWes GBuc MHom MNrw MSpe NCGa SMrm WCot WFar WHal WOld WOut
	Octoberlight	see *A.* 'Oktoberlicht'
§	'Oktoberlicht'	EBee LRHS NCGa SMrm WOld
	oolentangiensis	LRHS WPer
	'Orchidee'	EBee EPri EWes
	'Orpheus'	MNrw
	pappei	see *Felicia amoena*
	'Pearl Star'	WOld
§	***peduncularis***	EBee EPPr LPla LRHS MBri NRHS SUsu WCot
	petiolatus	see *Felicia petiolata*
	'Photograph' Ψ^{H4}	CHVG CSam EBee LRHS MAvo MHom NPnk SMrm WMnd WOld
§	***pilosus*** var. ***demotus*** Ψ^{H4}	ECha EWes MRav WOld WTin
§	- var. ***pringlei*** 'Monte Cassino' Ψ^{H4}	CHid CSBt EBee ECtt EPfP GQue IPot LHop LPot LRHS MBNS MRav MWat SMrm SPer SPhx SRGP WOld WSpi WWEG XLum
	- - 'October Glory'	CCse NDov WPer
	- - 'Phoebe'	WOld
	- - 'Pink Cushion'	WCot
	'Pink Star'	CMea EBee ECtt GMaP LRHS MNFA MRav MWat NDov NSti SBfd SPhx WFar WHoo WOld WOut WTin XLum
	'Pixie Dark Eye' (*ericoides* hybrid)	CDes EBee SMHy WCot
	'Pixie Red Eye' (*ericoides* hybrid)	WCot
	'Plowden's Pink'	WOld
	'Prairie Lavender'	WOld
	'Prairie Pink'	WOld
	'Prairie Purple'	WOld
	'Prairie Violet'	WOld
	'Primrose Path'	EBee MNrw NCGa WCot
	ptarmicoides	see *Solidago ptarmicoides*
	puniceus	EBee NBre XLum
	purdomii	see *A. flaccidus*
	pyrenaeus 'Lutetia'	CPrp EBee ECha GAbr GBuc GCal GMaP MAvo MHom MNFA MWat NCGa NDov NLar SPoG SRGP WCot WFar WKif WOld WWEG XLum
	radula	CSam EBee EPPr EWes LPla MAvo MNrw NBre NLar WOld WSHC
	'Ringdove' (*ericoides* hybrid) Ψ^{H4}	CKno CPrp MAvo MCot MHom MNFA NCGa NSti SRGP WCot WOld
	'Rosa Star'	WOld
	'Rose Queen'	MAvo
	rotundifolius 'Variegatus'	see *Felicia amelloides* variegated
	rugulosus 'Asrugo'	EBee
	sagittifolius Wed.	XLum
	× ***salignus***	WOld
	- Scottish form	WOld
*	***sativus atrocaeruleus***	LRHS
§	***scaber***	EBee NWsh WCot
	scandens	see *A. carolinianus*
	schreberi	CCon EBee EPPr EWes MAvo MSpe NBre NCGa NWsh WBor WCot WOld
§	***sedifolius***	EBee ECtt ELan GQue LEdu MAvo MDKP MWat NBid NSti SDix SEND SPoG SUsu WCot WFar WMnd WOld WPer WWlt
	- RCB AM -5	WCot
	- 'Nanus'	CPLG ELan GCal LRHS MHom MNFA MRav NBir NLar NWsh SPer WAbe WCot WFar WMnd WOld WSpi WTin XLum
	- 'Roseus'	LRHS
§	***sibiricus***	NBre NLar WOld
	'Snow Flurry'	see *A. ericoides* f. *prostratus* 'Snow Flurry'
	'Snow Star'	WOld
	spathulifolius	XLum
	spectabilis	EBee LRHS WOld
	stracheyi	EDAr
	subcaeruleus	see *A. tongolensis*
	'Sunhelene'	CDes EBee WCot
	'Sunqueen'	WCot
	tataricus	LPla
	- 'Jindai'	EBee WFar
	thomsonii	WFar WOld
	- 'Nanus'	EBee GBee GMaP LRHS MCot SBch WCot WOld WSHC WSpi
	tibeticus	see *A. flaccidus*
	'Tina'	NDov
	Tonga = 'Dasfour'	CYeo EPfP EWTr LRHS LSou NBir NLar NPri SHil SRms SWvt WCot WHil
§	***tongolensis***	GKev SBHP
	- 'Berggarten'	EBee LDai LRHS WOld
	- 'Dunkleviolette'	SRms
	- 'Napsbury'	EBee LRHS WOld
	- 'Wartburgstern'	CCon EBee EPfP NGdn STes WPer WWEG
	tradescantii misapplied	see *A. pilosus* var. *demotus*
	tradescantii L.	ELan MBNS MRav NSti SMad WBrk WCot WOld WTin
	trinervius var. ***harae***	WOld
	tripolium	WHer
	'Triumph'	WCot
	turbinellus misapplied Ψ^{H4}	CKno EPfP GCal IKil LPla NGdn NWsh SMHy SPhx SRkn SUsu WOld WPtf WTin
	turbinellus Lindl.	CSam EBee EPfP EWTr GBee LRHS MWat NCGa NDov NLBP NLar WOld WSpi

- hybrid	WFar WOld
umbellatus	CBre CKno EBee ECha GQue NBir NDov NLar WCot WOld WTin
- 'Weisser Schirm' **new**	EBee
'Vasterival'	EBee MAvo MSpe NCGa NDov SMHy SSvw WBrk
vimineus Lam.	see *A. lateriflorus*
- 'Ptarmicoides'	see *Solidago ptarmicoides*
§ 'White Climax'	MHom WBrk WCot
'Wood's Pink'	EBee WHil
'Wood's Purple' **new**	WHil
'Yvonne'	CBre

Asteranthera (*Gesneriaceae*)

ovata	CGHE EBee EPfP GGGa LRHS LSou MAsh SLon WAbe WPGP WSHC

Asteriscus (*Asteraceae*)

'Gold Coin'	see *Pallenis maritima*
maritimus	see *Pallenis maritima*

Asteromoea (*Asteraceae*)

mongolica	see *Kalimeris mongolica*
pinnatifida	see *Kalimeris pinnatifida*

Asteropyrum (*Ranunculaceae*)

cavaleriei	GEdr WCot WCru

Asterotrichion (*Malvaceae*)

discolor	ECou SPlb

Astilbe ✿ (*Saxifragaceae*)

CC 5201	CPLG
'Alive and Kicking'	MBri
'Amerika' (× *arendsii*)	CMHG CSBt
'Amethyst' (× *arendsii*)	CMHG CMac EBee ELon EPfP LRHS MRav NBir NBre SApp SPer SPoG WHoo WMoo WWEG
'Angel Wings' (× *arendsii*)	NPro
'Anita Pfeifer' (× *arendsii*)	CMHG ELon GBin IBoy LPBA NLar
'Aphrodite' (*simplicifolia* hybrid)	CBcs CWCL GCal LRHS MDKP MLHP NBre NPro WGor WWEG
× ***arendsii***	EPfP IFoB NBre WMoo WPer
'Astary White' (× *arendsii*) (Astary Series) **new**	LRHS
astilboides	CMHG SWvt
'Atrorosea' (*simplicifolia* hybrid)	LRHS NCot SRms
'Avalanche'	GBin NHol SPad WMnd WWEG
§ 'Beauty of Ernst' (× *arendsii*)	EBee LPBA LSou MSCN SPoG SRms WHil WMoo
§ 'Beauty of Lisse' (× *arendsii*)	EBee LRHS LSou MAsh MSCN SPoG WHil
Bella Group (× *arendsii*)	NBre SPet WMnd
'Bergkristall' (× *arendsii*)	CMHG
'Betsy Cuperus' (*thunbergii* hybrid)	CMHG EBee GBin MRav NBre SApp
'Bonn' (*japonica* hybrid)	CWCL CWat LRHS NLBP SCoo SRms
'Boogie Woogie' PBR (× *arendsii*)	MAsh
§ 'Brautschleier' (× *arendsii*) ♀H4	CMHG CMac CPLG CPrp CTri ECtt EPfP GCra GKev LRHS LSRN MSCN NGdn NLBP NLar WPnP WPtf XLum
'Bremen' (*japonica* hybrid)	CMHG GBin LPBA LRHS
'Bressingham Beauty' (× *arendsii*)	CMHG CPLG CPrp CSam CWCL ECtt ELan EPfP GKev GMaP LAst LHop LPBA LRHS MRav MWhi NHol NPro SPer SWvt WBor WFar WMoo WWEG
Bridal Veil (× *arendsii*)	see *A.* 'Brautschleier'
§ 'Bronce Elegans' (*simplicifolia* hybrid) ♀H4	CCon CMHG CPrp EBee ECha EPfP GBin GBuc GMaP LRHS MRav NHol NOrc NPro WFar WMoo WOut WWEG
* ***bumalda*** 'Bronze Pygmy'	MMoz NHol
'Bumalda' (× *arendsii*)	CCon CFis CSBt CWCL GBin GMaP IBoy LRHS MWts NChi NGdn NOrc NPro SPlb WFar WMoo
'Burgunderrot' (× *arendsii*)	CWCL EPfP MBri MNrw NLar SMrm
'Carnea' (*simplicifolia* hybrid)	CMHG
'Catherine Deneuve'	see *A.* 'Federsee'
'Cattleya Dunkel' (× *arendsii*)	CMHG
'Cattleya' (× *arendsii*)	CMHG CSam EBee GBuc LRHS NLar NRHS WMoo
'Ceres' (× *arendsii*)	CMHG
'Cherry Ripe'	see *A.* 'Feuer'
chinensis	CMHG ECho LRHS NBre NRHS WFar WSHC
- B&SWJ 8178	WCru
- from Russia	GCal
- 'Brokat'	GBin
- 'Christian'	GBin
- var. ***davidii***	CMHG
- - B&SWJ 8583	WCru
- - B&SWJ 8645	WCru
- 'Diamonds and Pearls' PBR	CWGN GAbr LSou MAvo MBri WFar WHil
- 'Finale'	COlW NHol NPro SPer WFar WOut
- 'Frankentroll'	CMHG
- 'Intermezzo'	GCal GMaP LRHS NLar
- 'Little Vision in Pink'	WHil
- 'Love and Pride'	LSou MBri
- 'Milk and Honey' PBR	ECtt LSou MBNS WFar
§ - var. ***pumila*** ♀H4	Widely available
- - 'Serenade'	CMac NGdn WFar
- 'Purple Glory'	CMHG EWll IKil
- 'Spätsommer'	CMHG
- var. ***taquetii***	CMac EBee EPfP LRHS NBre NSti SRms
- - Purple Lance	see *A. chinensis* var. *taquetii* 'Purpurlanze'
§ - - 'Purpurlanze'	Widely available
§ - - 'Superba' ♀H4	CMHG CMac CRow CTri ECha GBin IBoy LRHS MLHP NBro SDix SPer SRms WFar WMoo
- 'Troll'	GBin
- 'Veronika Klose'	CMHG EBee NLar NPro WWEG
- 'Vision in Pink' PBR	CWCL EWll LSou MBNS NPri SBfd WFar WHil
- 'Vision in Red' PBR	CMil CWCL CWat ECtt EWll LRHS LSou MBNS MBri MNrw NLar NPri SBfd SPoG WCAu WFar WHil
- 'Vision in White'	MAsh NPri SBfd SPoG WFar WHil
- 'Visions'	CMHG CMac CWCL EBee IBoy LRHS LSou MBNS MBri NBro NGdn NPro NRHS SBfd WFar
Cologne	see *A.* 'Köln'
Color Flash	see *A.* 'Beauty of Ernst'
Color Flash Lime	see *A.* 'Beauty of Lisse'
'Country and Western' PBR (× *arendsii*)	LSou

	Name	Suppliers
	'Crimson Feather'	see *A.*'Gloria Purpurea'
	× ***crispa***	ECho WCFE
	- 'Gnom'	NHar SAga
	- 'Lilliput'	ECtt GBee NBir NHar NLar NPro NRya
§	- 'Perkeo' ♀H4	CBcs CCon ECha ECho ECtt ELan EPfP GMaP LRHS NBir NHar NLar NMen NMyG NPro SRms WAul WCot WFar WMoo WWEG
	- 'Peter Pan'	see *A.* × *crispa* 'Perkeo'
	- 'Red Rog' **new**	NPro
	- 'Snow Queen'	NBir NHar NMen NPro
	'Darwin's Dream'	EBee GAbr IBoy NLar NPri NPro WFar
	'Darwin's Favourite' (× *arendsii*)	CWCL
	'Delft Lace' **new**	EBee
	'Deutschland' (*japonica* hybrid)	Widely available
§	'Diamant' (× *arendsii*)	CMHG EBee LRHS LSRN MMuc NGdn NHol SEND WFar
	Diamond	see *A.*'Diamant'
	'Drayton Glory' (× *arendsii*)	see *A.* × *rosea* 'Peach Blossom'
	'Drum and Bass' PBR	LSou MAsh NLar
	'Dunkelachs' (*simplicifolia* hybrid)	EBee LRHS MSCN NMyG WFar
	'Dusseldorf' (*japonica* hybrid)	CMHG CSam CWCL LRHS NHol
	'Eden's Odysseus'	GBin IBoy NHol
	'Elegans' (*simplicifolia* hybrid)	CMHG CMac WFar
	Elizabeth Bloom = 'Eliblo' PBR (× *arendsii*)	EBee ELon LRHS MRav NDov NEgg NGdn NHol NRHS WFar
	'Elizabeth' (*japonica* hybrid)	CMHG
	'Ellie' (× *arendsii*)	CMHG CMac CWCL GQue LRHS LSRN LSou MAsh MBNS MBri NGdn NHol NLar SMrm WFar WPtf
	'Else Schluck' (× *arendsii*)	ECha
	'Erica' (× *arendsii*)	CMHG CPLG CTri EWll NLar NPnk NPro WFar WMnd WMoo WWEG
	'Etna' (*japonica* hybrid)	CBcs CMHG CSam EBee IBoy LRHS NEgg NGdn NHol NLar SMrm SRms WPnP
	'Europa' (*japonica* hybrid)	CMHG CMac EBee ECtt LRHS MGos NGdn NRHS SBfd SPoG WFar WMoo
	'Fanal' (× *arendsii*) ♀H4	Widely available
	'Fata Morgana' (× *arendsii* hybrid)	CMHG
§	'Federsee' (× *arendsii*)	CBcs CMHG ECha ECtt ELan LRHS MBNS NBre NBro NGdn NPro SMrm WFar XLum
§	'Feuer' (× *arendsii*)	CMHG CMac CPrp EBee ECtt ELan EPfP GBuc LBMP LRHS NEgg NGdn NHol NLar NOrc NPro WBor WMoo
	Fire	see *A.*'Feuer'
	'Fireberry' PBR (Short 'n' Sweet Series)	LSou MAsh NLar
	'Flamingo' PBR (× *arendsii*)	EBee GBin MBNS SMrm
§	***formosa*** B&SWJ 10946	WCru
	'Gertrud Brix' (× *arendsii*)	CBcs CWat MMuc NBir NGdn NPro XLum
§	***glaberrima***	NBid NMen
§	- var. ***saxatilis*** ♀H4	CRow EBee EPfP GBin GEdr IFro NHar NSla WAbe WHal WThu
	- ***saxosa***	see *A. glaberrima* var. *saxatilis*
	'Gladstone' (× *arendsii*)	see *A.*'W.E. Gladstone'
§	'Gloria Purpurea' (× *arendsii*)	CMHG NLBP WMoo
	'Gloria' (× *arendsii*)	CMHG CMac CTri ECtt LPBA MRav NRHS WFar
	Glow	see *A.*'Glut'
§	'Glut' (× *arendsii*)	CCon CMHG CWCL EBee ECtt LRHS MMuc NGdn NHol NRHS SRms WFar WHil
	'Granat' (× *arendsii*)	CFis CMHG CMac GBuc NBir NBre NDov NEgg NGdn NHol WFar WMoo
*	Grande Group (× *arendsii*)	LRHS NBre
	grandis	CMHG GBee WHer
	'Grete Püngel' (× *arendsii*)	ECha GBin WWEG
	'Harmony' (× *arendsii*)	CMHG
	'Heart and Soul' PBR	EPfP LSou MAvo MBri
	'Hennie Graafland' (*simplicifolia* hybrid)	CBcs CMHG CWCL EBee GAbr GBin GQue LRHS LSou NLar SHar
	'Henry Noblett'	GBin
	'Holden Clough' (*japonica* hybrid)	NHol NWad
	Hyacinth	see *A.*'Hyazinth'
§	'Hyazinth' (× *arendsii*)	CMHG CPLG CPrp EBee GBin GMaP LBMP LRHS LSou NHol WFar
	'Inshriach Pink' (*simplicifolia* hybrid)	CBcs CCVN CMHG CPrp CYeo EBee EHoe ELan LRHS MBri NBir NHar NHol SAga SBch WFar WHal WOut
	'Irrlicht' (× *arendsii*)	CMHG CMac EBee ELan EPfP EShb GBuc IBoy LHop LPBA LRHS NWad SMrm SPer SWat WAul WWEG
	japonica	CPLG
*	- 'Pumila'	NBir NGdn
	- var. ***terrestris***	see *A. glaberrima*
	'Jo Ophorst' (*davidii* hybrid)	CMHG ECtt GBuc LRHS NEgg NGdn NHol NLar WFar
	'Jump and Jive' PBR	LSou MAsh WFar
	'Koblenz' (*japonica* hybrid)	CMHG CWCL MDKP
§	'Köln' (*japonica* hybrid)	CMHG CWat GBin LPBA LRHS NMyG WFar
	koreana	WCot WPGP
	- B&SWJ 8611	WCru
	- B&SWJ 8680	WCru
	'Kriemhilde'	CMHG MSCN
	'Kvële' (× *arendsii*)	CMHG WMoo
§	'Lachskönigin' (× *arendsii*)	CMHG
	'Lilli Goos' (× *arendsii*)	CMHG GBin GCal
	'Lollipop'	MAsh MBNS NPro SRms
	longicarpa B&SWJ 6711	WCru
	macroflora	GCal
	'Maggie Daley'	EBee IBoy NBro NPro WMoo
	'Mainz' (*japonica* hybrid)	CHVG CMHG ECtt ELan LPBA
	'Mars' (× *arendsii*)	CMHG
	microphylla	CMHG
	- B&SWJ 11085	WCru
	- pink-flowered	CMHG
	'Mighty Pip' (× *arendsii*) **new**	WHlf
	'Moerheim Glory' (× *arendsii*)	GBin IBoy NBre NGdn NLar
	'Moerheimii' (*thunbergii* hybrid)	CMHG
	'Mont Blanc' (× *arendsii*)	CMHG
	'Montgomery' (*japonica* hybrid)	CMHG CWCL CWGN EBee EShb GAbr GBin IKil LBMP LRHS LSRN MAvo MBNS MBri MCot MMuc NBro NCGa NEgg NGdn NHol SAga SBfd SMrm
	'Nikki'	NCGa NLar NPro
§	***okuyamae*** B&SWJ 10975	WCru
	Ostrich Plume	see *A.*'Straussenfeder'

	'Paul Gaärder' (× *arendsii*)	CMHG
	'Peaches and Cream'	EBee MMHG NBro NLar NMRc NPnk
	'Peter Barrow' (*glaberrima* hybrid)	GBin SRms
	'Pink Fanal'	LRHS
	'Pink Lightning' PBR (*simplicifolia* hybrid)	CWCL EBee MAvo MBNS MBri NLar NOrc SMrm
	Pink Pearl (× *arendsii*)	see *A.* 'Rosa Perle'
	'Poschka'	CCon NPro
I	'Poschka Alba'	CCon NPro
	'Professor van der Wielen' (*thunbergii* hybrid)	CCon CMHG EBee GQue LRHS NHol NLar SPer SRms WWEG
	pumila	see *A. chinensis* var. *pumila*
*	'Queen'	LPBA
	'Radius'	LPBA MAsh NGdn NLar WHil WPnP
	'Red Baron'	SPad
	Red Light	see *A.* 'Rotlicht'
	'Red Sentinel' (*japonica* hybrid)	CBcs CWCL CWat EBee EPfP GBin GMaP IBoy LRHS MAsh MBri NBro NCGa NGdn NHol NPro SBfd WFar WHrl
	'Rheinland' (*japonica* hybrid) ♀H4	CBcs CMHG CWCL CYeo GBin LPBA LRHS MBel MMuc NGdn NRHS SEND SHil SRot WHoo WPnP
	'Rhythm and Blues' PBR	EBee ECtt NLar
	rivularis	CMHG WCot
	- CC 4547	EBee
	- GWJ 9366	WCru
I	- 'Grandiflora' **new**	EBee
§	- var. ***myriantha***	NBre
	- - BWJ 8076a	WCru
	- - SICH 757	CPLG
	'Robinson's Pink'	NGdn
	'Rock and Roll' PBR	EBee LPBA LSRN MSCN WHil
§	'Rosa Perle' (× *arendsii*)	CMHG CSam NHol
§	× ***rosea*** 'Peach Blossom'	CBcs CMHG ELon GCra IBoy LPBA LRHS NBir NGdn NPro SBfd SPoG WFar WHoo WMoo
	'Rosea' (*simplicifolia* hybrid)	NHol WFar
§	'Rotlicht' (× *arendsii*)	CMHG CMac LRHS NGdn NHol NPro SBfd WFar WGor
	'Salland'	LRHS
	Salmon Queen	see *A.* 'Lachskönigin'
	'Salmonea' (*simplicifolia* hybrid)	CMHG
	'Saxosa'	see *A. glaberrima* var. *saxatilis*
	Showstar Group (× *arendsii*)	LRHS MSnd WHil
	simplicifolia ♀H4	CRow SKHP WFar
	- 'Alba'	CMHG NPro
	- Bronze Elegance	see *A.* 'Bronce Elegans'
	- 'Darwin's Snow Sprite'	CMac NHol NLar WFar
	- 'Jacqueline'	LSou NHol
*	- 'Nana Alba'	NPro
	- 'Praecox Alba'	GBin NEgg WWEG
	- 'Rose of Cimarron'	NPro
	- 'Sheila Haxton'	LRHS NHar
	- 'White Sensation' PBR	LRHS NLar
	'Snowdrift' (× *arendsii*)	CHid CMHG CWat GMaP IKil LBMP LRHS MBNS MBel MDKP MMuc MWat NBir NEgg NOrc NPro SPer SWat WFar WWEG
	'Solferino' (× *arendsii*)	CMHG
	'Spartan' (× *arendsii*)	see *A.* 'Rotlicht'
	'Spinell' (× *arendsii*)	CWCL EBee LRHS NBre NMRc WPnP WWEG
	'Sprite' (*simplicifolia* hybrid) ♀H4	Widely available
	'Stand and Deliver' PBR	ECtt
§	'Straussenfeder' (*thunbergii* hybrid) ♀H4	CMHG CMac CTri ECtt EPfP GBin GMaP LBMP LHop LRHS NBid NBir NBro NGdn NHol NLar NOrc SPer SPoG WAul WCAu WMoo WPtf WWEG
	'Sugar Plum' (*simplicifolia* hybrid)	NGdn
	'Sugarberry' PBR (Short 'n' Sweet Series)	NLar
	'Superba'	see *A. chinensis* var. *taquetii* 'Superba'
	thunbergii	CEnt CPLG LRHS
	- var. ***congesta*** B&SWJ 10961	WCru
	- var. ***formosa***	see *A. formosa*
	- var. ***hachijoensis*** B&SWJ 5622	WCru
	- var. ***okuyamae***	see *A. okuyamae*
	- var. ***sikokumontanum*** B&SWJ 11164	WCru
	- var. ***terrestris*** B&SWJ 6125	WCru
	'To Have and To Hold'	LSou
	'Venus' (× *arendsii*)	ECha ECtt GMaP LPBA LRHS MBNS MCot NGdn NHol NOrc NRHS SPer SWat WFar WMoo
	'Vesuvius' (*japonica* hybrid)	CBcs LRHS MDKP NBro NLar
	virescens	see *A. rivularis* var. *myriantha*
§	'W.E. Gladstone' (*japonica* hybrid)	CWat WGor
	'Walküre' (× *arendsii*)	CMHG
	'Walter Bitner'	GBin LRHS MBNS NBre NHol SRGP
	'Washington' (*japonica* hybrid)	EBee LAst MDKP NBre NGdn WPnP
§	'Weisse Gloria' (× *arendsii*)	CMHG CMac CPrp ECha GBin GBuc LPBA LRHS NBro NDov NEgg NHol NMyG NOrc NPro NRHS SBfd SCoo SHil SMrm WBor WMoo
	White Gloria	see *A.* 'Weisse Gloria'
	'White Wings' PBR (*simplicifolia* hybrid)	NLar
	'William Reeves' (× *arendsii*)	CMHG NHol
	'Willie Buchanan' (*simplicifolia* hybrid)	CBcs CHid CMHG CPrp CYeo EHoe GAbr GMaP LBMP LRHS NEgg NGdn NHar NHol NMen SApp SPer SRms WAbe WFar WMoo WNew WWEG
	Younique Carmine = 'Verscarmine' PBR	LSou WHil
	Younique Pink = 'Verspink' PBR	WHil
	Younique Silvery Pink = 'Versilverypink' PBR	WHil
	Younique White = 'Verswhite' PBR **new**	NCGa
	'Zuster Theresa' (× *arendsii*)	CMHG LPBA LRHS MBNS MNrw NBro NRHS WFar

Astilboides (*Saxifragaceae*)

§	***tabularis***	Widely available

Astragalus (*Papilionaceae*)

	canadensis	LRHS SPhx
	glycyphyllos	CArn SPhx
	lusitanicus	WCot
	membranaceus	CArn

	neglectus new	SPhx
	purshii	ECho
	vexilliflexus new	SPhx

Astrantia ✿ (Apiaceae)

	'Atomic Sunburst'	GQue
	bavarica	GCal MFie SMrm
	'Berendien Stam'	EBee MAvo MFie
	'Bloody Mary'	ELan GBuc LSRN MAvo MFie NGdn NLar NPnk
	'Bradfield Rose' new	EHrv
	'Buckland'	Widely available
	'Bury Court'	NDov
	carniolica	NEgg
	- ***major***	see *A. major*
	- 'Rubra'	CBcs EBee GMaP MFie MPkF
	- 'Variegata'	see *A. major* 'Sunningdale Variegated'
	'Clear Pink'	NDov
	'Dark Shiny Eyes'	CLAP CPLG CWCL EBee ECtt IBoy LLHF MBNS NCGa NGBo NGdn NLar NSti SPoG SWvt
	'Hadspen Blood'	Widely available
	'Helen'	NLar
	helleborifolia misapplied	see *A. maxima*
	'Larch Cottage Clear Pink'	NLar
	'Larch Cottage Magic'	MAvo NLar
	'Madeleine'	see *A. major* 'Madeleine van Bennekom'
§	***major***	Widely available
	- 'Abbey Road'PBR	CBct CKno CLAP CPLG CSev CWCL EBee ECtt LHop LSou MAvo MFie NEgg NLar SCob SMrm SPoG SPtl WWlt
I	- 'Alba'	CBcs CMHG CWCL EBee ECha EHrv IBal IKil LRHS MCot MFie MRav NBir NGdn NPer WGwG WMnd WMoo
	- subsp. ***biebersteinii***	LRHS MFie NBir
	- 'Bo-Ann'	CWCL IBoy MFie NLar WAul WFar
	- 'Celtic Star'	CSpe EBee MFie SWvt
	- 'Claret'	Widely available
	- Cliff's form	MFie
	- 'Cottage Herbery'	MAvo
	- 'Elmblut'	MAvo MFie WHil
	- 'Florence'PBR	CWCL EBee ECtt GBin LRHS MTis NCGa NDov SPoG
	- 'Gill Richardson'	Widely available
	- 'Gracilis'	EBee
	- 'Greenfingers'	EWes
	- 'Gwaun Valley'	WFar
	- subsp. ***involucrata***	EBee LRHS MBel MFie SWat
	- - 'Barrister'	CSam CWCL GBuc LRHS MAvo MFie NLar
	- - 'Canneman'	EBee EWes LPla MFie NLar WCot
	- - 'Jumble Hole'	NDov
	- - 'Margery Fish'	see *A. major* subsp. *involucrata* 'Shaggy'
	- - 'Moira Reid'	CBct CKno CLAP CPLG CSam EBee ECrc ECtt ELan EShb GCal GMaP LRHS LSRN MAvo MCot MFie MRav MWhi NDov NPnk
	- - 'Orlando'	CLAP EBee MFie
§	- - 'Shaggy' ♀H4	Widely available
	- - 'Snape Cottage' new	CDes
	- 'Jade Lady'	WFar
	- 'Jitse'	EBee MAvo
	- 'Lars'	CPLG CWib EBee ECtt ELan ELon EPfP GAbr GCra IBal IFoB LSRN LTen MBri MFie MNrw MWhi NBid NGdn NLar NPnk SBfd SPer SPet SPoG SRot SWal SWvt WCAu WFar
	- 'Little Snowstar'	IBal
	- 'Lola'	CBcs EBee GBuc NCGa SMrm
§	- 'Madeleine van Bennekom'	CLAP EBee GBin MAvo NCGa
	- 'Paper Moon'	WFar
	- 'Penny's Pink'	EBee EWTr MFie NPnk WCot
	- 'Percy Picton'	MAvo
	- 'Pink Pride'	EBee IFro LSou NCGa
	- 'Pink Sensation'	EBee
	- 'Primadonna'	CYeo EBee EHrv EPri GMaP MFie NHol NLar SPlb WFar WPer WWEG
	- 'Princesse Sturdza'	EBee LSou NCGa WHil WWlt
	- 'Reverse Sunningdale Variegated' (v)	LSou MAvo MFie
	- 'Rosa Lee'	CWCL EBee MAvo MFie NPnk WAul
	- var. ***rosea***	CBre CWCL EBee EHrv EPfP GKev LHop LRHS LSRN MFie MRav MWat MWhi NGdn SAga SPer WCAu WFar WMoo WWEG
	- - George's form	CBct CKno CLAP CPrp CWCL EAEE EBee ECtt LHop LRHS LSRN MFie NCGa NDov NEgg NPnk SMrm SPoG WGwG
	- 'Rosensinfonie'	EBee GMaP MFie NBro NGdn NPnk NPro WFar WMnd
§	- 'Rubra'	CSBt CSpe CWCL EBee ECtt ELan EPfP IBoy LAst LRHS MBel MFie MGos MSpe NBir NChi NPer NPnk SPad SRms SWat WBor WCAu WCru WFar WHal WMnd WMoo WWEG
	- 'Ruby Cloud'	CHid CPrp CWCL EBee ECtt EPri IBal LBMP LRHS MFie MNHC MNrw NBro NGdn NSti SBod SHar SRot WFar WMnd
	- 'Ruby Glow'	LRHS MFie
	- 'Ruby Star'	CLAP CMil ECGP ECtt ELon GMaP IBoy LRHS MAvo MBel MFie NDov NLar SUsu SWvt WCot WHoo
	- 'Ruby Wedding'	Widely available
	- 'Silver Glow'	ECtt IBal WFar
	- 'Star of Billion'PBR	CLAP ECtt MBri
	- 'Star of Fire'PBR	EBee LSou MBel MBri NCGa
	- 'Star of Summer'	EBee LSou
	- 'Starburst'	MFie WFar
	- 'Sue Barnes' (v)	EBee GCal MAvo MFie
§	- 'Sunningdale Variegated' (v) ♀H4	Widely available
	- 'Titoki Point'	MFie WCot
	- 'Venice'PBR	CLAP CWCL CWGN ECtt LRHS LSou MAvo MTis NCGa NDov NLar NSti SMrm SPoG STes WFar WHil WWlt
§	***maxima*** ♀H4	Widely available
	- 'Mark Fenwick'	MFie NBir
*	- ***rosea***	ECtt MDKP MNrw MWhi NBir NGdn WWEG
	minor	WCru
	'Moulin Rouge'PBR	Widely available
	'Pink Crush'	LRHS
	'Queen's Children'	EBee GBuc
	'Rainbow'	MFie NLar
	'Roma'PBR	Widely available
	rubra	see *A. major* 'Rubra'

'Sheila's Red'	LRHS LSRN NDov
'Snow Star'PBR	CWCL CWib EBee EHrv EPfP GBin LRHS MBNS MFie NCGa NLar NPnk NRHS SHil SPoG
'Star of Beauty'PBR	CLAP CWCL ECtt LSou MBri MFie MMHG MSCN NCGa NGdn NLar NSti SMrm WFar WHil
'Star of Heaven'	NLar
'Star of Royals'PBR	CLAP ECtt LSou MBri SBfd
'Superstar'	CMea CMil CYeo ECGP ECtt ELon IBoy IPot LRHS MAvo MBNS MBel MTis NDov NLar SMrm SWvt WCot
'Warren Hills'	CCVN CLAP GMaP MFie NLar NPnk
'Washfield'	CYeo MTis NCGa NDov

Astrodaucus (*Apiaceae*)

orientalis	SPhx

Asyneuma (*Campanulaceae*)

canescens	CEnt LRHS LSou NBre SGar
§ ***prenanthoides***	SMrm
- 'Cambell Blue'	LRHS
pulvinatum	WAbe

Asystasia (*Acanthaceae*)

bella	see *Mackaya bella*
§ ***gangetica***	CSev
violacea	see *A. gangetica*

Athamanta (*Apiaceae*)

turbith	CSpe
- subsp. ***haynaldii***	EBee
vestina	SPhx

Athanasia (*Asteraceae*)

§ ***parviflora***	SPlb

Atherosperma (*Atherospermataceae*)

moschatum	CBcs CDoC CHII CPne IRar SKHP WSHC

Athrotaxis (*Cupressaceae*)

cupressoides	CDoC CDul CKen WThu
laxifolia	CDoC CKen MGos WThu
selaginoides	CDoC IGor

Athyrium ✿ (*Woodsiaceae*)

'Branford Beauty'	CBty CCCN CDes CLAP GBin ISha LRHS NLar WPGP
'Branford Rambler'	CLAP ISha
filix-femina ♀H4	Widely available
§ - subsp. ***angustum***	CBty CLAP ELan GBin MMoz NGdn WMoo
- - f. ***rubellum***	CCCN CDes CElw CKel CLAP
'Lady in Red'	CWCL EBee ELon ESwi ISha LRHS LSRN LTen MGos NBid NLar SPoG WMoo WWEG
- 'Corymbiferum'	SRms
- 'Crispum Grandiceps Kaye'	NGdn SRms
- Cristatum Group	CLAP EBee EFer ELan LSRN MMoz NGdn SWat WFib
- 'Dre's Dagger'	NLar SBod
- 'Fieldii'	CLAP SRms
- 'Frizelliae' ♀H4	Widely available
- 'Frizelliae Capitatum'	CLAP WFib WPGP
- 'Frizelliae Cristatum'	SRms
- 'Grandiceps'	CLAP EBee SRms
- 'Lady Victoria' **new**	CLAP
- 'Lady-in-Lace'	CBty CLAP WCot
- 'Minutissimum'	CBty CDes CGHE CLAP EBee ECha ELan ISha MMoz SUsu
* - 'Nudicaule'	SRms
- Plumosum Group	CLAP WFib
- 'Plumosum Axminster'	CBty CLAP EFer NLar NMyG WFar
- 'Plumosum Divaricatum'	SRms
- 'Plumosum Druery'	CLAP
- Red Stem	see *A. filix-femina* 'Rotstiel'
§ - 'Rotstiel'	CDTJ CLAP EBee MMoz SBfd WMoo WPnP WWEG
- 'Vernoniae' ♀H4	CBty CDTJ CLAP ELan LPBA MMoz NLar
- 'Vernoniae Cristatum'	CLAP WFib
- 'Victoriae'	CBty CCCN CDTJ CDes CPrp CWCL EBee EFer GEdr GMaP ISha LPBA LRHS LTen MMuc NBid NGdn NLar NMyG SHil WMoo WPat WWEG XLum
- Victoriae Group	see *A. filix-femina* subsp. *angustum*
- 'Victoriae' seedling	MBri WPtf
'Ghost'	CBty CCCN CDes CKel CLAP ISha LRHS LSou LTen MAvo MGos NCGa NLar NMyG NSti WPat WPtf
goeringianum 'Pictum'	see *A. niponicum* var. *pictum*
niponicum	NMyG WHal
- f. ***metallicum***	see *A. niponicum* var. *pictum*
§ - var. ***pictum*** ♀H3	Widely available
- - 'Apple Court'	CBty CCCN ISha LRHS NLar
- - 'Burgundy Lace'PBR	CBty CLAP MNrw NLar NMyG NPri SMrm WCot WPat WPtf
* - - 'Cristatoflabellatum'	CLAP EBee
- - 'Pewter Lace'PBR	CBty NLar
- - 'Red Beauty'	CBty CDTJ CEnt CLAP EBee ECha EPfP GBin LRHS LSRN LTen NHol NLar SBfd SGol SPad SPoG WMoo WPat WPnP
- - 'Regal Red'	CBty ISha LRHS
- - 'Silver Falls'	CBty CLAP EAmu EShb NMyG WCot WHal WPGP
- - 'Soul Mate'	CLAP
- - 'Ursula's Red'	CBcs CBty CCVN CElw CLAP CTrC EShb LHop LRHS LSRN LSou MAvo NBid NBir NEgg NLar NPnk SMrm SPer WCot WFar WPGP
- - 'Wildwood Twist'	CBty CLAP NMyG
'Ocean's Fury'	CLAP
otophorum ♀H4	ISha MRav NBid SRms WIvy WPGP
- var. ***okanum***	Widely available
vidalii	CDTJ CLAP EBee ISha LRHS LSou MAvo MMoz NEgg NLar NMyG SMrm WFib WWEG

Atractylodes (*Asteraceae*)

japonica	EFEx
macrocephala	CArn EFEx

Atragene see *Clematis*

Atriplex (*Amaranthaceae*)

canescens	NLar
cinerea	CTrC ECou
halimus	CArn CBcs ECha ECre EHoe ELau EPPr LTen MBri MRav NLar SDix SEND SLon SPer SPlb WCot
hortensis	ENfk

- var. ***rubra*** CArn CEnt CSpe EGHP ELan LSou MHer MNHC SHDw SIde SMrm WCot WJek

Atropa (*Solanaceae*)

acuminata CArn
bella-donna CArn GPoy SEND
mandragora see *Mandragora officinarum*

Aubrieta (*Brassicaceae*)

'Alba' see *A.* 'Fiona'
albomarginata see *A.* 'Argenteovariegata'
'Alix Brett' CMea CPBP LRHS
'Ann Kendall' ECtt
§ 'Argenteovariegata' (v) ♀H4 ECho ELan LRHS WFar
'Astolat' (v) ECho
§ 'Aureovariegata' (v) ♀H4 CMea ECho ELan MAsh NPer WAbe XLum
Axcent Series **new** LPot
- 'Axcent Antique Magenta' WGor
- 'Axcent Antique Rose' WGor
bicolour CMea
Blaue Schönheit see *A.* 'Blue Beauty'
'Blaumeise' LRHS WSpi
§ 'Blue Beauty' CMea ECtt EPfP GAbr MAsh WHil WHoo WNew WSpi
'Blue Chip' ECtt
'Blue Emperor' WSpi
'Blue Whale' ECtt ELon LHop SRot SWvt
§ 'Bob Saunders' (d) CFis CMea ECho LRHS NCGa
'Bressingham Pink' (d) ♀H4 CMea ECtt ELan EPfP SPoG
'Bressingham Red' ECho ECtt ELan EPfP LHop SPoG
'Bubble Purple' EPfP
canescens XSen
- subsp. ***cilicica*** EPot
Cascade Series GJos SEND SPoG
- 'Blue Cascade' EPfP MBNS SBfd SPlb SPoG WGor
- 'Lilac Cascade' SPoG
- 'Purple Cascade' CTri CWib EPfP LSRN MAsh MBNS MWat SPlb SPoG SRms WFar WGor
- 'Red Cascade' ♀H4 CTri CWib ECtt EPfP LSRN MBNS SPlb SPoG SWal
deltoidea SVic XSen
* - 'Gloria' CMea CWCL SRot
- Variegata Group (v) ECtt NPri NSla
- - 'Nana Variegata' (v) CMea WGor
'Doctor Mules' ♀H4 ECtt LRHS SRms WAbe
'Doctor Mules Variegata' (v) CTri ECho ECtt ELan ELon EPfP LAst MAsh MHer NPri SPoG SWvt WHoo
double pink-flowered (d) **new** EPfP
Double Stock-flowered Group pink-flowered (d) NPri
'Downers Variegata' (v) EPot
'Elsa Lancaster' NMen NSla WAbe
§ 'Fiona' ECtt
glabrescens CPBP WAbe
'Gloria' ECtt EPot GAbr WIce
'Gloriosa' MAsh
'Golden Emperor' **new** MHer
'Golden King' see *A.* 'Aureovariegata'
gracilis EPot GEdr NMen WAbe
- ZE&S 51630 GKev
- 'Kitte Rose' ECtt LRHS
'Greencourt Purple' ♀H4 CFis CMea ECho ELan MHer MWat
'Hamburger Stadtpark' CWCL ECho ECtt ELan EPfP LHop MAsh SRot
'Hemswell Purity'PBR see *A.* 'Snow Maiden'
'Kati' NCGa
'Kitte' ECho ECtt ELan EPfP LRHS NLar NPri SPoG
'Kitte Blue' ELan LRHS
'Kitte Purple' ELan LRHS
'Leichtlinii' XLum
macedonica EPot WAbe
'Mars' MAsh
pinardii WAbe XSen
'Pink Beauty' ECtt WIce
'Purple Charm' SRms
'Red Carpet' ECho ECtt ELan MAsh MHer SRms
'Red Carpet Variegated' (v) CMea
'Rose Queen' CMea
Royal Series ♀H4 COIW
- 'Royal Blue' EPfP EPot LRHS NEgg WFar WMoo XLum
- 'Royal Lavender' WFar
- 'Royal Lilac' WFar
- 'Royal Red' EPfP LRHS SBch WFar WGor WMoo
- 'Royal Rose' LRHS NBre WFar
- 'Royal Violet' CTri EPfP LRHS WFar WMoo XLum
'Schofield's Double' see *A.* 'Bob Saunders'
'Silberrand' ECha
§ 'Snow Maiden'PBR ECtt
'Somerfield Silver' ELan EPfP
'Somerford Lime' (v) ECtt ELan EPfP LSou WIce
'Swan Red' (v) ECtt ELon EPot LAst LRHS MHer NEgg NSla WHil WHoo
'Triumphante' ECtt
'Valerie' (v) EPot
'Whitewell Gem' WMoo

Aucuba ✿ (*Garryaceae*)

japonica CCVT CDul MSCN SEWo
- 'Crassifolia' (m) EBtc GBin
- 'Crotonifolia' (f/v) ♀H4 Widely available
- 'Crotonifolia' (m/v) CMac MAsh SGol SRms WRHF
- 'Dentata' CHEx WCru
- 'February Star' (f/v) SDix
- 'Golden King' (m/v) ♀H4 CDoC CMac CWib EBee ELan ELon EPfP LRHS LSRN MAsh MGos MWat NLar SGol SLim SPer SPoG
- 'Golden Spangles' (f/v) CBcs CDoC IVic NLar SLim SWvt
- 'Goldstrike' (v) EBee LRHS LSRN MAsh NEgg SMad
- 'Hillieri' (f) EBtc
- f. ***longifolia*** ♀H4 CMac NLar SDix WCot WCru
- - 'Salicifolia' (f) CHEx ESwi LAst MRav NLar WCru WFar WPGP
- 'Maculata' hort. see *A. japonica* 'Variegata'
- 'Marmorata' LRHS MBri MGos NRHS SHil
- 'Mr Goldstrike' (m/v) EPfP LRHS SBfd SLim
- Pepper Pot = 'Shilpot' (m/v) CHEx EBee EPfP LRHS MAsh SLon SPoG
- 'Picturata' (m/v) CDul CHEx CMac CSBt EBee ELan LRHS MAsh MGos NHol NLar SEND SLim SPer WFar
- 'Rozannie' (f/m) ♀H4 CBar CBcs CDoC CDul CMac CSBt EBee ECrN ELan ELon EPfP IVic LRHS LSRN MAsh MBlu MGos MRav NLar NPri SBfd SLim SPer SPoG SWvt WFar
- 'Sulphurea Marginata' (f/v) CBcs CMac CTri EBee ECrN EPfP ESwi LRHS NLar SPer
§ - 'Variegata' (f/v) Widely available
omeiensis CPLG

- B&SWJ 2864	WCru
- BWJ 8048	WCru
- L 614	WPGP

Aulax (*Proteaceae*)

cancellata	SPlb

Aurinia (*Brassicaceae*)

§ ***corymbosa***	ECho
§ ***saxatilis*** ♀H4	ECho EDAr EPfP MAsh NPri SPlb WFar WNew
- 'Argentea'	ECho
- 'Citrina' ♀H4	ECha ECtt MWat SBch SRms
- 'Compacta'	CTri ECtt GJos WIce
- 'Dudley Nevill Variegated' (v)	ECho ECtt ELon EWes MHer WFar
- Gold Ball	see *A. saxatilis* 'Goldkugel'
- 'Gold Dust'	ECho ECtt SRms
- 'Golden Queen'	ECtt MHer
§ - 'Goldkugel'	ECho EPfP NPri SPoG
- 'Variegata' (v)	NPri SPoG

Austrocedrus (*Cupressaceae*)

§ ***chilensis***	CKen CMen IGor SBig
- 'Thornhayes Ghost'	CTho

Avena (*Poaceae*)

candida	see *Helictotrichon sempervirens*

Avenula see *Helictotrichon*

Averrhoa (*Oxalidaceae*)

carambola (F)	CCCN

avocado see *Persea americana*

Azalea see *Rhododendron*

Azara ✿ (*Salicaceae*)

sp.	NEgg
dentata	CBcs CHll CMac LAst WFar
- 'Variegata'	see *A. integrifolia* 'Variegata'
* ***integerrima***	GQui
integrifolia	CBcs CCCN GBin
- 'Uarie'	CCCN
§ - 'Variegata' (v)	CWib EBee IRar LRHS NEgg
lanceolata	CDul CMCN CPLG CPne CTri EBee GBin LEdu NSti WFar WGrn
microphylla ♀H3	CBcs CDoy CDul CMCN CMac CPLG CTri EBee ELon EPfP IVic LAst LRHS MAsh MGos MMuc NSti SBfd SDix SEND SHil SLim SPer SPlb SSpi WFar WPGP WSHC
- 'Gold Edge' (v)	EBee EPfP LRHS WFar
- 'Variegata' (v)	CBcs CDoC CJun CMac CPLG CWib EBee EHoe EPfP GQui LAst LBMP LRHS MAsh MMuc MRav NLar NSti SEND SLon SPoG SSpi WFar WPat WSHC
* ***patagonica***	MBlu
petiolaris	CMCN CTri GBin LEdu
serrata ♀H3	CBcs CDul CEnt CMCN CWib EBee EPfP LHop LRHS MSCN NCGa NLar SBfd SDix SEND SGar SGol SPer SPoG SRms WBor WFar WHar WKif WSHC
- 'Maurice Mason'	CDoC EBee
uruguayensis	CCCN CPLG EBtc

Azorella (*Apiaceae*)

filamentosa	ECou
glebaria misapplied	see *A. trifurcata*
glebaria A. Gray	see *Bolax gummifer*
gummifer	see *Bolax gummifer*
lycopodioides	GEdr WAbe
patagonica	EPot
§ ***trifurcata***	CPar CSpe CTri ECho ECtt EPot GAbr GEdr MMuc NBir SPlb WPer
- 'Nana'	ECho MWat WPat WThu XLum

Azorina (*Campanulaceae*)

§ ***vidalii***	SGar

B

Babiana (*Iridaceae*)

angustifolia	ECho
'Blue Gem'	ECho
fragrans 'Porterville'	ECho
- 'Rawsonville'	ECho
pygmaea	WCot
rubrocyanea	SBir
stricta ♀H1-2	CCCN ECho SDeJ
- 'Purple Star'	CPLG ECho
- 'Tubergen's Blue'	ECho
villosa	ECho WCot
- 'Tulbagh'	ECho
'Zwanenburg's Glory'	CPrp ECho

Baccharis (*Asteraceae*)

halimifolia	CBcs CTrC GLin LRHS SEND XLum
patagonica	LRHS MMuc SEND SPhx
sphaerocephala	IDee

Backhousia (*Myrtaceae*)

citriodora	CArn

Bacopa (*Plantaginaceae*)

'Snowflake'	see *Sutera cordata* 'Snowflake'

Baeckea (*Myrtaceae*)

gunniana	CPLG
linifolia	SPlb
virgata	CTrC ECou SPlb

Baeometra (*Colchicaceae*)

uniflora 'Malmesbury'	ECho

Balbisia (*Ledocarpaceae*)

peduncularis	CCCN SEND

Baldellia (*Alismataceae*)

ranunculoides	CRow WMAq

Ballota ✿ (*Lamiaceae*)

acetabulosa ♀H3-4	CMHG ECha EWes WCot XSen
'All Hallow's Green'	see *Marrubium bourgaei* var. *bourgaei* 'All Hallows Green'
hirsuta	XSen
nigra	CArn GPoy MHer MHoo MNHC NMir

§ - 'Archer's Variegated' (v) LDai
- 'Variegata' see *B. nigra* 'Archer's Variegated'
pseudodictamnus ♀H3-4 CBcs CTri EBee ECha EHoe ELan EPfP GMaP LHop LRHS LSRN MCot MRav NPer SDix SEND SLon SMrm SPer SPoG WCFE WSHC XLum XSen
- B&M 8119 WCot
- from Crete ECha SEND
rupestris 'Frogswell Carolyn' (v) IFro

Balsamita see *Tanacetum*

Balsamorhiza (*Asteraceae*)

incana SBrt
sagittata ECho

Bambusa (*Poaceae*)

glaucescens see *B. multiplex*
§ ***multiplex*** XBlo
- 'Alphonso-Karrii' CEnt ERod SBig
- 'Elegans' see *B. multiplex* 'Floribunda'
- 'Fernleaf' see *B. multiplex* 'Floribunda'
§ - 'Floribunda' CHEx EShb XBlo
- 'Golden Goddess' XBlo
- 'Silverstripe' see *B. multiplex* 'Variegata'
§ - 'Variegata' (v) XBlo
- 'Wang Tsai' see *B. multiplex* 'Floribunda'
pubescens see *Dendrocalamus strictus*
ventricosa SBig XBlo
vulgaris XBlo
- 'Vittata' ERod XBlo

banana see *Ensete*, *Musa*

Banksia (*Proteaceae*)

aemula MOWG
canei SPlb
ericifolia CDTJ
- var. ***ericifolia*** CCCN CTrC
- var. ***macrantha*** SPlb
grandis CBcs CCCN LTen MOWG
integrifolia CBcs CCCN CDTJ CTrC EAmu MOWG SPlb WPGP
marginata CTrC SPlb
media SPlb
oblongifolia SPlb
paludosa CTrC SPlb
robur CBcs CCCN SPlb
serrata MOWG SPlb
speciosa SPlb
spinulosa CTrC
- var. ***collina*** CTrC SPlb
- var. ***spinulosa*** CBcs CCCN
violacea SPlb

Baptisia (*Papilionaceae*)

§ ***alba*** EBee EPfP GBBs NLar
- var. ***alba*** 'Wayne's World' EBee IPot
§ - var. ***macrophylla*** CCse EBee EWes LPla LRHS NBir SPhx WCot
australis ♀H4 Widely available
- 'Caspian Blue' CPLG CWCL LEdu LHop WSHC
- 'Exaltata' ELan LHop LRHS
- var. ***minor*** EBee NLar SPhx WPGP WSHC
- 'Nelson's Navy' SMHy
× ***bicolor*** 'Starlite' (Prairieblues Series) EBee SKHP SPoG
bracteata LRHS
- var. ***leucophaea*** EBee LRHS LSou SPhx
- - 'Butterball' **new** EBee
'Carolina Moonlight' EBee IPot LHop SKHP SPoG
lactea see *B. alba* var. *macrophylla*
leucantha see *B. alba* var. *macrophylla*
megacarpa LRHS SKHP
pendula see *B. alba*
'Purple Smoke' CAbP CPLG CSpe EBee ECtt EPPr GBuc LEdu LRHS MAvo MMuc MNrw NBre NSti SEND SMHy SPhx SUsu WCot WKif
sphaerocarpa EBee SPhx
- 'Screamin' Yellow' LRHS
tinctoria CArn MHoo SPhx
× ***varicolor*** 'Twilite' (Prairieblues Series) EBee SKHP SPoG

Barbarea (*Brassicaceae*)

praecox see *B. verna*
rupicola 'Sunnyola' EDAr
§ ***verna*** EGHP GPoy MHer SVic
vulgaris 'Variegata' (v) LDai NBro WMoo

Barleria (*Acanthaceae*)

micans CCCN
repens MOWG
suberecta see *Dicliptera sericea*

Barosma see *Agathosma*

Bartlettina (*Asteraceae*)

§ ***sordida*** CCCN EBee EUJe IRar

Basella (*Basellaceae*)

rubra SHDw SVic

Bashania (*Poaceae*)

§ ***fargesii*** CDoC ENBC ERod MMuc MRav MWht SEND WJun
I ***qingchengshanensis*** ERod MWht WJun

basil see *Ocimum basilicum*

Bauera (*Cunoniaceae*)

rubioides WAbe

Bauhinia (*Caesalpiniaceae*)

galpinii SPlb
* ***lutea*** CCCN
natalensis SPlb
purpurea L. CCCN SPlb
tomentosa CCCN
variegata 'Candida' CSpe
'White Lady' CCCN
yunnanensis EDif

Baumea see *Machaerina*

bay see *Laurus nobilis*

Beaucarnea (*Dracaenaceae*)

recurvata ♀H1 CTrC EGri LRHS SEND SPlb

Beaufortia (*Myrtaceae*)

sparsa IRar MOWG
squarrosa SPlb

Beauverdia see *Leucocoryne*

Beckmannia (*Poaceae*)

eruciformis	XLum

Bedfordia (*Asteraceae*)

linearis	SPlb

Beesia (*Ranunculaceae*)

calthifolia	CBct CCon CLAP CMHG CSpe EHrv EPfP GEdr IGor LLHF WCru WPGP WSHC
- DJHC 98447	CDes CLAP CPLG
deltophylla	EBee EWld WCot

Begonia ✿ (*Begoniaceae*)

B&SWJ 2692 from Sikkim, India	WCot
B&SWJ 10279 from Mexico	CHEx WCru
B&SWJ 10442 from Guatemala	WCru
BWJ 7840 from China	WCru
Chen Yi 5	WCot
Chen Yi 7	WCot
DJHC 580	WCot
from Vietnam	ERhR
'Abel Carrière' (R)	ERhR WDib
acida	ERhR
aconitifolia (C)	ERhR EShb
acutifolia Jacq.	ERhR
'Aladdin'	ERhR
'Alamo III'	ERhR
albopicta (C)	EBak ERhR
- 'Rosea' (C)	CDoC EShb WDib
alice-clarkiae	ERhR
'Alleryi'	ERhR
Allure (Million Kisses Series) **new**	LAst SPoG
alnifolia	ERhR
'Alto Scharff' 🏆H1	ERhR
'Alzasco' (C)	ERhR
'Amazon Delta' (R)	SBrm
'Amigo Pink' (C)	ERhR
Amour = 'Yamour' (Million Kisses Series) **new**	SPoG
'Anita Roseanna' (C)	ERhR
'Ann Anderson' (C)	ERhR
'Anna Christine' (C)	ERhR
§ ***annulata***	ERhR
- HWJK 2424	ESwi WCru
- 'Himalayan Velvet' **new**	GHim
'Aquarius'	ERhR
'Arabian Sunset' (C)	ERhR
arborescens var. ***arborescens***	ERhR
'Argentea' (R)	EBak
'Argenteo-guttata'	ERhR EShb
'Aries'	ERhR
'Arthur Mallet' (Mallet Series) (C)	ERhR
'Aruba'	ERhR
'Autumn Glow' (T)	ERhR
'Avalanche' (T)	ERhR
'Axel Lange' (R)	SBrm
'Aya' (C)	WDib
'Bahamas'	ERhR
'Bantam Delight'	ERhR
'Barbara Ann' (C)	ERhR
'Barbara Hamilton' (C)	ERhR
'Barbara Parker' (C)	ERhR
'Barclay Griffiths'	ERhR
'Beatrice Haddrell'	ERhR WDib
(Belleconia Series) Belleconia Apricot Blush = 'Innbellab' **new**	ESwi
- Belleconia Rose = 'Innbellro'PBR **new**	ESwi
- Belleconia Soft Orange = 'Innbellpea' **new**	ESwi LAst
'Benitochiba' (R)	CDes CLAP ERhR ESwi EUJe IBoy LRHS LSou MAvo MNrw SEND WCot WDib
'Benitsubomi' **new**	LSou
'Bess'	ERhR
'Bessie Buxton'	ERhR
'Bethlehem Star'	ERhR WDib
§ 'Bettina Rothschild' (R)	ERhR SBrm WDib
'Beverly Jean'	ERhR
'Big Mac'	ERhR
'Bill's Beauty'	ERhR
'Black Jack' (C)	ERhR
'Black Raspberry'	ERhR
'Blackberry Swirl' (R)	WDib
'Blanc de Neige'	ERhR
'Blue Vein'	ERhR
'Bokit'	ERhR WDib
'Bokit' × ***imperialis***	WDib
boliviensis (T)	CDes CDoC EBee ESwi ETod GCal WCot WCru
- 'Firecracker'	WDib
Bonfire Choc Pink = 'Nzcfive' **new**	LAst
Bonfire = 'Nzcone'PBR	EPfP ERhR LBuc SPoG
'Boomer' (C)	ERhR
'Bouton de Rose' (T)	SDeJ
bowerae	ERhR
§ - var. ***nigramarga***	ERhR
'Boy Friend'	ERhR
bracteosa	ERhR
bradei	ERhR
brevirimosa	ERhR
- subsp. ***exotica***	ERhR
'Brown Twist'	WDib
'Bunchii'	ERhR
'Burgundy Velvet'	ERhR WDib
'Burle Marx' 🏆H1	ERhR EShb SDix WDib
'Calico Kew'	ERhR
'Calla Queen' (S)	ERhR
'Can-can'	see *B.* 'Herzog von Sagan'
'Candy Floss'	WCru
'Captain Nemo' (R)	ERhR SBrm
cardiocarpa	ERhR
'Carol Mac'	ERhR
'Carolina Moon' (R) 🏆H1	ERhR
carolineifolia	WCot WDib
carrieae	ERhR
'Casey Corwin' (R)	SBrm WDib
'Cathedral'	CDoC ERhR WDib
'Chantilly Lace'	ERhR
I ***chapaensis*** HWJ 642	WCru
'Charles Chevalier'	ERhR
'Charles Jaros'	ERhR
'Charm' (S)	ERhR
'Cherry Sundae' (S)	ERhR
'Chesson'	ERhR
'China Curl' (R) 🏆H1	ERhR WDib
chitoensis B&SWJ 1954	WCru
chloroneura	ERhR WDib
'Chocolate Box'	ERhR
'Chocolate Chip'	ERhR

'Christmas Candy' ERhR
'Chumash' ERhR
'Cistine' ERhR
'Cleopatra' ♀H1 ERhR GHim WDib
'Clifton' ERhR
coccinea (C) ERhR WDib
'Coconut Ice' EShb
conchifolia ERhR
  f. ***rubrimacula***
'Concord' ERhR
'Connee Boswell' ERhR WDib
convolvulacea ERhR
cooperi ERhR
'Cora Anne' ERhR
'Cora Miller' (R) ERhR
§ ***corallina*** (C) EBak
- 'Lucerna Amazon' (C) ERhR
'Corbeille de Feu' ERhR
'Cowardly Lion' (R) ERhR
'Cracklin' Rosie' (C) ERhR
crassicaulis ERhR
'Crestabruchii' ERhR
'Crystal Brook' ERhR
§ ***cubensis*** ERhR
cucullata (S) ERhR
- var. ***arenosicola*** (S) CSpe EBee EShb ESwi ETod SEND SKHP WCot
'Curly Fireflush' (R) ERhR MSCN SBrm WDib
'Dales' Delight' (C) ERhR
'Dancin' Fred' ERhR
'Dancing Girl' ERhR
'D'Artagnan' ERhR
'David Blais' (R) ♀H1 WDib
'Dawnal Meyer' (C) ERhR WDib
I 'De Elegans' ERhR WDib
'Decker's Select' ERhR
'Deco Diamond Dust' ERhR
decora ERhR
deliciosa ERhR
Devil Series (S) **new** NPri
- 'Devil Red' (S) LAst
- 'Devil Rose' (S) LAst
- 'Devil White' (S) LAst
'Dewdrop' (R) ♀H1 ERhR WDib
diadema ERhR
'Di-anna' (C) ERhR
'Dibleys Pink Showers'PBR WDib
dichotoma ERhR
dichroa (C) ERhR
'Dielytra' ERhR
'Di-erna' (C) ERhR
dietrichiana ERhR
'Digswelliana' ERhR
dipetala ERhR
discolor see *B. grandis* subsp. *evansiana*
domingensis ambig. ERhR
'Don Miller' (C) ERhR WDib
(Doublet Series) 'Doublet Pink' (S/d) ERhR
- 'Doublet Red' (S/d) ERhR
- 'Doublet White' (S/d) ERhR
'Douglas Nisbet' (C) ERhR
Dragon Wing Red = 'Bepared'PBR ♀H1+3 LAst
§ ***dregei*** (T) ♀H1 ERhR GCal
- var. ***dregei*** (T) ERhR
- 'Glasgow' (T) ERhR
'Druryi' ERhR
'Dwarf Houghtonii' ERhR
'Earl of Pearl' ERhR
'Ebony' (C) ERhR
echinosepala ERhR
edmundoi (C) ERhR
egregia ERhR
'Elaine' ERhR
'Elaine Ayres' (C) ERhR
§ 'Elaine Wilkerson' ERhR
'Elaine's Baby' see *B.* 'Elaine Wilkerson'
'Elda' ERhR
'Elda Haring' (R) ERhR SBrm
Elegance = 'Yagance'PBR (Million Kisses Series) LSou SPoG
'Elizabeth Hayden' ERhR
'Elsie M. Frey' ERhR
emeiensis CSpe ERhR SKHP
'Emerald Beauty' (R) ♀H1 ERhR SBrm
'Emerald Giant' (R) ERhR WDib
'Emma Watson' ERhR
'Enchantment' ERhR
'Enech' ERhR
'English Knight' ERhR
'English Lace' ERhR
epipsila ERhR
'Erythrophylla' EShb
'Erythrophylla Bunchii' ERhR
§ 'Erythrophylla Helix' ERhR
'Escargot' (R) ♀H1 WDib
'Essie Hunt' ERhR
'Esther Albertine' (C) ♀H1 ERhR
'Etna' (R) SBrm
'Evening Star' ERhR
'Fairy' ERhR
feastii 'Helix' see *B.* 'Erythrophylla Helix'
fernando-costae ERhR
ferruginea B&SWJ 10479 from Costa Rica WCru
§ 'Feuerkönigin' (S) ERhR
'Filigree' (R) ERhR
Fimbriata Group (T) SDeJ
'Fire Flush' see *B.* 'Bettina Rothschild'
'Fireworks' (R) ♀H1 ERhR WDib
'Five and Dime' ERhR
'Flamboyant' (T) ERhR WGor
Flaming Queen see *B.* 'Feuerkönigin'
'Flamingo' (C) ERhR
'Flamingo Queen' (C) ERhR
'Flo 'Belle Moseley' (C) ERhR WDib
'Florence Carrell' ERhR
'Florence Rita' (C) ERhR
'Flying High' ERhR
foliosa ERhR
- var. ***amplifolia*** see *B. boltonis* var. *boltonis*
§ - var. ***miniata*** ♀H1 CDoC CHll CSpe EBak ERhR EShb MArl SDix WDib
- - pink-flowered CCCN CDTJ
- - red-flowered CCCN CDTJ
- - 'Rosea' CDoC
'Frances Lyons' (C) ERhR
'Frau Helene Harms' (T) ERhR
'Freckles' (R) ERhR
'Fred Bedson' ERhR
friburgensis ERhR
'Friendship' ERhR
'Frosty Fairyland' ERhR
'Frosty Knight' ERhR
'Fuchsifoliosa' ERhR
fuchsioides see *B. foliosa* var. *miniata*
fusca ERhR

	Name	Suppliers
	'Fuscomaculata'	ERhR
	gehrtii	ERhR
	geranioides (T)	ERhR
	glabra	ERhR
	glandulosa misapplied	see *B. multinervia*
	glandulosa ambig.	ERhR
	glaucophylla	see *B. radicans* Vell.
	'Gloire de Sceaux'	ERhR
	'Glowing Embers'	LBuc SPoG
	goegoensis	ERhR
	'Good 'n' Plenty'	ERhR
	gracilis (T) F&M 266	WPGP
	- F&M 337	WPGP
	'Granada'	ERhR
	grandis (T)	XLum
§	- subsp. ***evansiana*** ♀H3-4	CHEx CSam CSpe CTsd EBee ERhR EShb ETod EUJe GCal LAst LEdu LPla NMRc SBch SDix SEND SKHP SPlb WCot WCru WFar WMoo
	- - B&SWJ 11188	WCru
	- - var. ***alba*** hort.	CLAP CSpe ERhR EShb ESwi EWld EWll GCal LEdu LPla LRHS SBch SKHP SPoG SSpi WCot WMoo WPGP XLum
	- - 'Claret Jug'	CPLG EBee EShb ESwi ETod WCot WGrn WPGP WWEG
	- - 'Pink Parasol'	CLAP ESwi WCru
	- - 'Sublime' **new**	LEdu
	- 'Sapporo'	EBee EPPr ESwi GCal WCru
§	- subsp. ***sinensis***	ERhR WCot
I	- - 'Red Undies'	CLAP EBee ESwi WCru
	aff. ***grandis*** subsp. ***sinensis*** (T)	SKHP
	- - BWJ 8133	WCru
*	'Great Beverly'	ERhR
	'Green Acres'	ERhR
	'Green Gold' (R)	SBrm WDib
	'Green Lace'	ERhR
	'Grey Feather'	ERhR
	griffithii	see *B. annulata*
	'Gryphon' **new**	LAst
	'Gustav Lind' (S)	ERhR
	haageana hort. ex W. Watson	see *B. scharffii*
	handelii	ERhR
*	'Happy Heart'	ERhR
*	'Harry's Beard'	ERhR
	'Hastor'	ERhR
	hatacoa	ERhR
	- silver-leaved	ERhR EShb WDib
	- spotted-leaved	ERhR
	'Hazel's Front Porch' (C)	ERhR
	Heaven Series (S) **new**	NPri
	'Helen Lewis' ♀H1	ERhR
	'Helen Teupel' (R)	ERhR WDib
	'Helene Jaros'	ERhR
	'Her Majesty' (R)	ERhR
§	***heracleifolia***	ERhR
	- var. ***longipila***	see *B. heracleifolia*
	- var. ***nigricans***	see *B. heracleifolia*
§	'Herzog von Sagan' (R)	ERhR
	'Hilo Holiday' (R) ♀H1	WDib
	hispida var. ***cucullifera***	ERhR
	'Holmes Chapel'	ERhR
§	***holtonis*** var. ***holtonis***	ERhR
	homonyma	see *B. dregei*
	Honeymoon (Million Kisses Series) **new**	LAst
	'Honeysuckle' (C)	ERhR
	'Hot Tamale'	ERhR
	hydrocotylifolia	ERhR
	hypolipara	see *B. sericoneura*
	(Illumination Series) 'Illumination Apricot' (T/d)	SCoo WGor
	- 'Illumination Orange' (T/d) ♀H2-3	WGor
	- 'Illumination Rose' (T/d)	SCoo WGor
	- 'Illumination Salmon Pink' (T/d) ♀H2-3	SCoo
	- 'Illumination Scarlet' (T/d)	WGor
	- 'Illumination White' (T/d)	SCoo WGor
	imperialis	ERhR
	incarnata	ERhR
	- 'Metallica'	see *B. metallica*
	'Ingramii'	ERhR
	'Interlaken' (C)	ERhR
	× ***intermedia*** Veitch ex Van Houtte 'Bertinii' (T)	SDeJ
	'Ivy Ever'	ERhR
	'Jelly Roll Morton'	ERhR
	'Joe Hayden'	ERhR
	'John Tonkin' (C)	ERhR
	johnstonii	ERhR
	josephii (T) **new**	GHim
	'Jubilee Mine'	ERhR
	juliana	ERhR
	'Jumbo Jeans'	ERhR
	'Jumbo Jet' (C)	ERhR
	'Kagaribi' (C)	ERhR
	kellermanii	ERhR
	'Kentwood' (C)	ERhR
	kenworthyae	ERhR
	'Kit Jeans'	ERhR
	'Kit Jeans Mounger'	ERhR
	'La Paloma' (C)	WDib
	'Lacewing'	ERhR
	'Lady Clare'	ERhR
*	'Lady France'	ERhR
	Large-flowered Double Group (T/d) **new**	SDeJ
	'Laurie's Love' (C)	ERhR
	'Lawrence H. Fewkes'	ERhR
	leathermaniae (C)	ERhR
	'Legia'	ERhR
	'Lenore Olivier' (C)	ERhR
	'Leopard'	ERhR
	'Lexington'	ERhR
	'Libor' (C)	ERhR
	'Lime Swirl'	ERhR WDib
	'Limeade'	WDib
	limmingheana	see *B. radicans* Vell.
	'Linda Dawn' (C)	ERhR
	'Linda Harley'	ERhR
	'Linda Myatt'	ERhR
	lindeniana	ERhR
	listada ♀H1	ERhR WDib
	'Lithuania'	ERhR
	'Little Brother Montgomery' ♀H1	ERhR EShb SDix WDib
	'Little Darling'	ERhR
	'Lois Burks' (C)	ERhR WDib
	'Loma Alta'	ERhR
	'Looking Glass' (C)	ERhR WDib
	'Lospe-tu'	ERhR

Name	Suppliers
'Lubbergei' (C)	ERhR
'Lucerna' (C)	EBak ERhR
'Lucky Colours' (R)	SBrm
'Lulu Bower' (C)	ERhR
luxurians ♀H1	CHEx CHll CSpe ERhR WCot
- 'Ziesenhenne'	ERhR
lyman-smithii	ERhR
'Mabel Corwin'	ERhR
macduffieana	see *B. corallina*
'Mac's Gold'	ERhR
maculata (C) ♀H1	ERhR
- 'Wightii' (C)	CSpe ERhR WDib
'Mad Hatter'	ERhR
'Madame Butterfly' (C)	ERhR
'Magic Carpet'	ERhR
'Magic Lace'	ERhR
'Magma' (R)	SBrm
'Manacris'	ERhR
manicata	ERhR
'Margaritae'	ERhR
'Marmaduke' ♀H1	WDib
'Marmorata' (T)	SDeJ
'Martha Floro' (C)	ERhR
'Martin Johnson' (R) ♀H1	ERhR WDib
'Martin's Mystery'	ERhR
masoniana ♀H1	ERhR GHim WDib WSFF
'Maurice Amey'	ERhR
'Maverick'	ERhR
mazae	ERhR
'Medora' (C)	ERhR
'Merry Christmas' (R) ♀H1	ERhR WDib
metachroa	ERhR
'Metallic Mist'PBR	ESwi EUJe LSou NSti WCot
§ ***metallica*** ♀H1	ERhR EShb
'Michaele'	ERhR
'Midnight Sun'	ERhR
'Midnight Twister'	ERhR
'Mikado' (R) ♀H1	ERhR
Million Kisses Series	ERhR
minor	ERhR
'Mirage' ♀H1	ERhR
'Mishmi Silver'	GCal
mollicaulis	ERhR
'Moon Maid'	ERhR
'Mrs Hashimoto' (C)	ERhR
'Mrs Hatcher' (R)	ERhR
§ ***multinervia***	ERhR
'Munchkin' ♀H1	ERhR WDib
'My Best Friend'	WDib
* 'Mystic'	ERhR
'Mystique'	ERhR
'Namur' (R) ♀H1	WDib
'Nancy Cummings'	ERhR
natalensis	see *B. dregei*
'Nelly Bly'	ERhR
nelumbiifolia	ERhR
nigramarga	see *B. bowerae* var. *nigramarga*
nigritarum	ERhR
'Nokomis' (C)	ERhR
Nonstop Series (T/d) ♀H2-3 **new**	LAst SDeJ
'Norah Bedson'	ERhR
'Northern Lights' (S)	ERhR
§ ***obliqua*** L.	ERhR
obscura	ERhR
'Obsession' (C)	ERhR
odorata	see *B. obliqua* L.
'Odorata Alba'	ERhR
olbia	ERhR

Name	Suppliers
'Old Gold' (T)	ERhR
'Oliver Twist'	ERhR
'Orange Dainty'	ERhR
'Orange Pinafore (C)'	ERhR
'Orange Rubra' (C) ♀H1	ERhR
'Organdy' (mixed) **new**	LAst
'Orient' (R)	ERhR
'Orpha C. Fox' (C)	ERhR
'Orrell' (C)	ERhR
'Othello'	ERhR
paleata	ERhR
palmata	CDTJ CHEx CPLG EShb GCal SKHP WCot WPGP
- B&SWJ 2692 from Sikkim	WCot
'Palomar Prince'	ERhR
'Panasoffkee'	ERhR
'Panther'	ERhR
'Papillon' (T)	ERhR
paranaënsis	ERhR
parilis	ERhR
partita	see *B. dregei*
'Passing Storm'	ERhR
Passion = 'Yabos'PBR (Million Kisses Series)	LBuc LSou WBor
'Patricia Ogdon'	ERhR
'Paul Bee'	ERhR
'Paul Harley'	ERhR
paulensis	ERhR
'Peach Parfait' (C)	ERhR
pearcei (T)	ERhR
'Pearl Ripple'	ERhR
'Pearls' (C)	ERhR
pedatifida	CCon SKHP
- DJHC 98473	WCru
aff. ***pedatifida*** **new**	CDes
'Peggy Stevens' (C)	ERhR
peltata	ERhR
Pendula Group (T)	SDeJ
* 'Penelope Jane'	ERhR
'Persian Brocade'	ERhR
'Petite Marie' (C)	ERhR
'Piccolo'	ERhR
'Pickobeth' (C)	ERhR
'Picotee' (T)	CSut SDeJ
'Pinafore' (C) ♀H1	ERhR
'Pink Champagne' (R) ♀H1	WDib
I 'Pink Lady'	WCru
'Pink Nacre'	ERhR
'Pink Parade' (C)	ERhR
'Pink Spot Lucerne' (C)	ERhR
'Pink Taffeta'	ERhR
plagioneura	see *B. cubensis*
'Plum Rose'	ERhR
plumieri	ERhR
'Pollux'	WDib
polyantha	ERhR
polygonoides	ERhR
popenoei	ERhR
'Potpourri'	ERhR
'Président Carnot' (C)	ERhR
'Pretty Rose'	ERhR
'Preussen'	ERhR
'Princess of Hanover' (R) ♀H1	ERhR WDib
* 'Princessa Rio de Plata'	ERhR
prismatocarpa	ERhR
procumbens	see *B. radicans* Vell.
pustulata 'Argentea'	ERhR
putii B&SWJ 7245	WCru

'Queen Mother' (R) ERhR
'Queen Olympus' ERhR WDib
'Quinebaug' ERhR
§ ***radicans*** Vell. ♀H1 ERhR
'Raquel Wood' ERhR
'Raspberry Swirl' (R) ♀H1 ERhR WDib
ravenii (T) CHEx SKHP
- B&SWJ 1954 GCal WCot
'Raymond George Nelson' ♀H1 ERhR
'Razzmatazz' (R) WDib
'Red Berry' (R) ERhR
'Red Dragon' (R) WDib
'Red Kiss' (R) SBrm
'Red Planet' ERhR
'Red Reign' ERhR
'Red Robin' (R) SBrm WDib
'Red Spider' ERhR
'Red Undies' (*grandis*) see *B. grandis* subsp. *sinensis* 'Red Undies'
'Regal Minuet' (R) SBrm WDib
reniformis ERhR
'Richmondensis' (S) ERhR EShb
'Ricinifolia' ERhR EShb GCal
'Ricky Minter' ♀H1 ERhR
'Rip van Winkle' ERhR
'Robin' (R) ERhR
'Robin's Red' (C) ERhR
'Rocheart' (R) ♀H1 SBrm WDib
'Roi de Roses' (R) ♀H1 ERhR
Romance = 'Yamance'PBR (Million Kisses Series) LAst
'Rose with Bronze Leaf' (Big Series) LSou
roxburghii ERhR
'Royal Lustre' ERhR
'Rubacon' ERhR
rubella **new** GHim
rubro-setulosa ERhR
'Sabre Dance' (R) ERhR
'Sachsen' ERhR
'Sal's Comet' (R) ♀H1 WDib
'Sal's Moondust' WDib
sanguinea ERhR
'Scarlett O'Hara' (R) ERhR
§ ***scharffii*** EBak ERhR SDix
'Scherzo' ERhR WDib
'Secpuoc' ERhR
§ ***sericoneura*** ERhR
'Serlis' ERhR
serratipetala EBak ERhR WDib
'Shamus' ERhR
* ***sheperdii*** WDib
'Sherbet Bon Bon' LBuc
'Shiloh' (R) ERhR
* 'Shinihart' ERhR
'Sierra Mist' (C) ERhR
sikkimensis GCal
- B&SWJ 2692 WCru
silletensis subsp. ***mengyangensis*** GCal
'Silver Cloud' (R) ♀H1 ERhR WDib
'Silver Dawn' (R) ERhR
'Silver Giant' (R) ERhR
'Silver Jewell' WDib
'Silver Lace' WDib
'Silver Mist' (C) ERhR
'Silver Points' ERhR
'Silver Splendor' **new** CLAP CSpe EUJe WCot
'Silver Spray' (R) **new** SBrm
'Silver Sweet' (R) ERhR
'Silver Wings' ERhR
'Sinbad' (C) ERhR
sinensis see *B. grandis* subsp. *sinensis*
* 'Sir Charles' ERhR
'Sir John Falstaff' ERhR
sizemoreae WDib
Skeezar Group ERhR
- 'Brown Lake' ERhR
'Snow Storm' WDib
* 'Snowcap' (C) ♀H1 ERhR EShb WDib
socotrana (T) ERhR
solananthera A. DC. ♀H1 ERhR EShb WDib
soli-mutata WDib
sonderiana (T) GCal
'Speculata' (R) ERhR
'Spellbound' ERhR
'Spindrift' ERhR
'Splotches' ERhR
'Stained Glass' WDib
'Stichael Maeae' ERhR
stipulacea ambig. ERhR
subvillosa ERhR
'Sugar Plum' ERhR
(Summerwings Series) Summerwings Orange = 'Innbolora'PBR **new** ESwi
- Summerwings White = 'Innbolwhi'PBR **new** ESwi
Super Olympia Series ♀H2-3 **new** LAst
- 'Super Olympia Red' (S) LAst
- 'Super Olympia Rose' (S) LAst
- 'Super Olympia White' (S) LAst
(Superba Group) 'Irene Nuss' (C) ♀H1 ERhR
- 'Lana' (C) ERhR
- 'Sophie Cecile' (C) ♀H1 ERhR
sutherlandii (T) ♀H1 CCCN CPom EABi EBak ERhR EWld IGor LAst LRHS MDev NBir NPer SBch SDix SEND WCot WDib WFar WPGP
- 'Papaya' (T) CSpe
'Swan Song' ERhR
'Sweet Magic' ERhR
'Swirly Top' (C) ERhR
'Switzerland' (T) SDeJ
'Sylvan Triumph' (C) ERhR
taliensis SKHP
- EDHCH 042 WCru
- 'White-boned Demon' SKHP
'Tapestry' ERhR
'Tar Baby' (T) ERhR
'Tea Rose' ERhR
teuscheri ERhR
'Texastar' ERhR WDib
'The Wiz' ERhR
thelmae ERhR
'Thumotec' ERhR
'Thunderclap' ERhR
'Thurstonii' ♀H1 ERhR EShb
'Tiger Paws' ♀H1 ERhR EShb
'Tim Anderson' (R) SBrm
'Tingley Mallet' (Mallet Series) (C) ERhR
'Tiny Bright' (R) ERhR
'Tiny Gem' ERhR
'Tom Ment' (C) ERhR

	'Tom Ment II' (C)	ERhR
	'Tomoshiba'	ERhR
	'Tondelayo'	ERhR
	'Tribute'	ERhR
	'Trinidad'	ERhR
*	***tripartita*** (T)	ERhR WDib
	'Twilight'	ERhR
	'Two Face'	ERhR WDib
	ulmifolia	ERhR
	undulata (C)	ERhR
	'Universe'	ERhR
	'Venetian Red' (R)	ERhR
	venosa	ERhR
	'Venus'	ERhR
	'Verschaffeltii'	ERhR
	versicolor	ERhR
	'Vesuvius' (R)	WDib
	'Viaudii'	ERhR
	'Viau-Scharff'	ERhR
	'Weltonensis'	ERhR
	'Weltoniensis Alba' (T)	ERhR
	'White Cascade'	ERhR
	'Wild Swan'	WCru
	williamsii Rusby & Nash	see *B. wollnyi*
	'Witchcraft' (R)	ERhR
	'Withlacoochee'	ERhR
§	***wollnyi***	ERhR
	'Wood Nymph' (R)	ERhR
	'Zuensis'	ERhR

Beilschmiedia (*Lauraceae*)

	berteroana	IDee

Bellevalia (*Asparagaceae*)

	atroviolacea	ECho
	brevipedicellata	ECho
	ciliata	ECho
	'Cream Pearl'	ECho WCot
	desertorum JCA 0.227.690	WCot
	dubia	CDes CPom ECho WCot
	- subsp. ***hackelii***	ECho
	forniculata	ECho LWst
	hyacinthoides	ECho WCot
	longipes	ECho
	longistyla J&JA 227.950	LWst
*	***maura***	ECho
§	***paradoxa***	CHid CMea EBee ECho EHrv ERCP LLHF MNrw SDeJ WCot
	- white-flowered	ECho
	pycnantha misapplied	see *B. paradoxa*
	romana	CPom EBee ECho ERCP GKev SDeJ WCot WHil
	sarmatica	ECho
	sessiliflora	ECho
	tabriziana	CDes ECho WCot
	trifoliata	ECho
	webbiana	ECho

Bellis (*Asteraceae*)

§	***caerulescens***	GAbr
	perennis	CArn
	- 'Alice'	WCot
	- 'Dresden China'	EWes GAbr
	- 'Galaxy White' (Galaxy Series)	EPfP
	- Hen and Chickens	see *B. perennis* 'Prolifera' single-flowered
	- 'Parkinson's Great White'	GAbr
§	- 'Prolifera' single-flowered	GAbr LRHS WHer
	- 'Rusher Rose'	EPfP
	- 'Single Blue'	see *B. caerulescens*
	- 'The Pearl'	GAbr WCot
	- 'White Pearl'	LRHS
	rotundifolia 'Caerulescens'	see *B. caerulescens*
	sylvestris	CArn WCot

Bellium (*Asteraceae*)

*	***crassifolium canescens***	WPer

Beloperone see *Justicia*

	guttata	see *Justicia brandegeeana*

Bensoniella (*Saxifragaceae*)

	oregona	CPLG

Benthamiella (*Solanaceae*)

	nordenskjoldii	WAbe
	patagonica	WAbe
	- F&W 9345	ITim WAbe
	- white-flowered **new**	WAbe
	- yellow-flowered **new**	WAbe

Berberidopsis (*Berberidopsidaceae*)

	corallina	Widely available

Berberis ✿ (*Berberidaceae*)

	CC 4730	CPLG
	NJM 09.165	WPGP
	aggregata	MMuc NBir SEND SPer SRms
	amurensis var. ***latifolia*** B&SWJ 8539	WCru
	aquifolium	see *Mahonia aquifolium*
	- 'Fascicularis'	see *Mahonia × wagneri* 'Pinnacle'
	aristata ambig.	CArn
	asiatica	CPLG GPoy
	'Baby Bear'	CJun
	bealei	see *Mahonia japonica* Bealei Group
	× ***bristolensis***	SRms
N	***buxifolia*** 'Nana' misapplied	see *B. microphylla* 'Pygmaea'
	calliantha	WFar
	candidula C.K. Schneid.	CDul EBee EPfP LRHS MMuc MSwo NLar SLon SPer
	- 'Jytte'	see *B.* 'Jytte'
	× ***carminea*** 'Pirate King'	CSBt EPfP LRHS MAsh SPoG SWvt WPat
	darwinii ♀H4	Widely available
I	- 'Compacta'	CDoC CMac EBee ECrN EPfP LAst LBuc LHop LRHS LTen MAsh NEgg NLar NRHS SHil SLim SPoG WCot WFar
	dictyophylla ♀H4	CJun EBee EMil EPfP LHop LRHS MGos MMuc NLar SKHP SPer SPoG SSpi WPat WSHC WSpi
	dulcis 'Nana'	see *B. microphylla* 'Pygmaea'
	dumicola	MSnd
	empetrifolia	LEdu
	× ***frikartii*** 'Amstelveen' ♀H4	CCVT CDoC EBee ELan EPfP LAst LRHS MBNS MMuc MRav NLar SBfd SEND WMoo
	- 'Telstar'	EBee EBtc EWTr LBuc MRav NLar NPro SLim WMoo
	gagnepainii misapplied	see *B. gagnepainii* var. *lanceifolia*
	gagnepainii C.K. Schneid.	CDul CMac SLPl
§	- var. ***lanceifolia***	CTri MGos MMuc NWea SEND SGol SLim WFar
	- - 'Fernspray'	EPfP MRav SRms
	- 'Purpurea'	see *B.* × *interposita* 'Wallich's Purple'

	Name	Suppliers
	'Georgei' 🏆[H4]	CMHG CWib EPfP GQui LRHS
	'Goldilocks'	CJun EPfP LAst LSRN MBlu
	goudotii B&SWJ 10769	WCru
	heterophylla **new**	GKev
	× ***hybridogagnepainii*** 'Chenaultii'	EBee
	hypokerina	CMac
	insignis	GCal IDee
	- subsp. ***insignis*** var. ***insignis***	WPat
	- - B&SWJ 2432	WCru
§	× ***interposita*** 'Wallich's Purple'	CCVT EBee EPfP MRav MSwo SPer WMoo
	jamesiana	WPat
	julianae 🏆[H4]	CBar CBcs CDul CHab CMac EBee ECrN ELan EPfP LAst MGos MMuc MSwo NWea SBfd SEND SGol SLPl SPer SRms SWvt WFar WHar WSHC
§	'Jytte'	EBee EMil
	kawakamii	SLPl
	koreana	CDul EBee EPfP NLar
	- 'Rubin'	CAgr
	linearifolia 'Orange King'	CBcs CMac CTri EBee ELan EPfP LRHS MAsh MBlu MGos NEgg NLar SCoo SPer SPoG WFar WHar WPat
	'Little Favourite'	see *B. thunbergii* f. *atropurpurea* 'Atropurpurea Nana'
	× ***lologensis*** 'Apricot Queen' 🏆[H4]	CBcs CMac EBee EPfP LRHS MAsh MGos MRav NLar SCoo SPer SPoG WPat
	- 'Mystery Fire'	EBee MAsh MBri MGos NHol NLar SGol SPoG SWvt WHar WMoo
	- 'Stapehill'	CMac EBee ELan EPfP LRHS MAsh SPoG
	× ***media*** Park Jewel	see *B.* × *media* 'Parkjuweel'
§	- 'Parkjuweel'	CBcs CMac EBee IArd MRav WFar WMoo
	- 'Red Jewel' 🏆[H4]	CDoC CMac EBee ECrN EPfP LRHS MAsh MGos MMuc MRav NRHS SCoo SEND SPer SPoG WCFE WFar WMoo
	microphylla	EPfP WCFE
§	- 'Pygmaea'	CAbP CBcs CSBt EBee EPfP EWTr LRHS MAsh MGos MRav SLim SPer SPoG WFar
	mitifolia	NLar
	montana	WPGP WPat
	morrisonensis	GBin
	× ***ottawensis*** 'Auricoma'	LTen SEND SGol SWvt
	- f. ***purpurea***	CCVT CMac CWib LRHS MGos WHar
§	- - 'Superba' 🏆[H4]	Widely available
§	- 'Silver Miles' (v)	EHoe MRav NLar WFar WPat
§	***panlanensis***	LEdu
	- 'Cally Rose'	GCal
	poiretii	CPLG NLar
	polyantha	CTri
	var. ***polyantha*** **new**	
	'Red Tears'	CJun MMHG MRav NLar SPer WFar WMoo
	'Rubrostilla'	EBee
	× ***rubrostilla*** 'Cherry Ripe'	CMac
	- 'Rubrostilla'	EBee
	- 'Wisley'	LRHS
	sanguinea misapplied	see *B. panlanensis*
	sargentiana	SLPl
	sieboldii	LLHF MAsh MRav WPat WSpi
§	***soulieana***	EPfP LRHS
	stenophylla Hance	see *B. soulieana*
	× ***stenophylla*** Lindl. 🏆[H4]	CCVT CDoC CDul CSBt CTri EBee EPfP LBuc LTen MBri MRav NWea SBfd SEND SGol SPer WHar WMoo
	- 'Claret Cascade'	EBee MGos MMuc MRav NLar SPer WFar
	- 'Corallina Compacta' 🏆[H4]	CMac CMea EBee ECho ELan ELon EPfP EPot LHop LRHS MAsh NMen SPer SPoG SRms WAbe WPat WThu
	- 'Crawley Gem'	EBee NLar WFar
	- 'Etna'	EBee ELan LRHS MAsh SCoo SPoG
	- 'Irwinii'	CMac EBee LRHS MGos SPer WFar
	- 'Nana'	LRHS SRms
	- 'Pink Pearl' (v)	CMHG
	taliensis	CPLG
	temolaica 🏆[H4]	CGHE CJun EBee EBtc EPfP MAsh MGos MRav MSnd NEgg NLar NWea SMad SPer SSta WCFE WCot WPGP WPat WSpi
	- SF 95186	NSti
	thunbergii 🏆[H4]	CBar CBcs CDoC CDul CMac ECrN EPfP LBuc NLar NWea SPer SWvt WFar WMou
	- f. ***atropurpurea***	CBar CBcs CCVT CMac CSBt CTri EBee EPfP LAst LBuc LTen MAsh MGos MRav MSwo NEgg NLar NWea SCoo SGol SPer SPlb WFar WMoo WMou
	- - 'Admiration'[PBR]	CBcs CDoC CSBt ELan EPfP LBMP LBuc LLHF LRHS LSRN LSqu MAsh MBri MGos MMHG NEgg NHol NLar SBfd SCoo SLim SLon SPer SPoG SPtl SWvt WPat
§	- - 'Atropurpurea Nana' 🏆[H4]	Widely available
	- - 'Aurea'	CBcs CDoC CDul CMac EBee EHoe ELan EPfP EPot LRHS LSRN MAsh MBlu MGos MRav MWat NPri SBod SLim SPlb SSpi SWvt WFar WMoo WSHC
	- - 'Bagatelle' 🏆[H4]	CDoC EBee ELan EPfP EPot IArd IVic LAst LBMP LHop LRHS LSRN MAsh MBri MGos MRav NEgg NLar SLim SPer SPoG SWvt WCFE WMoo WPat
	- - 'Concorde'	LRHS MBlu
	- - 'Dart's Red Lady'	CJun CPLG CSBt CWib EBee EHoe ELan EPfP LRHS LSRN MAsh NLar NPro SLim SPer SPoG SWvt WFar WPat
	- - 'Erecta'	CMac EPfP MRav SPer SPoG WCFE
	- - 'Golden Ring' (v) 🏆[H4]	CBcs CDoC CDul CMac EBee EHoe ELan EPfP LBMP LHop LRHS LSRN MAsh MGos MMuc MRav NEgg NHol SBfd SLim SPer SPoG SWvt WFar WMoo WPat
	- - 'Harlequin' (v)	CBcs CDoC EBee ELan EPfP LRHS LSRN MAsh MBri MGos NEgg SBfd SGol SHil SLim SPer SPoG SWvt WFar WHar WPat
	- - 'Helmond Pillar'	Widely available
	- - 'Pink Queen' (v)	CDul EBee ELan EMil EPfP LHop LRHS MAsh NLar WFar WMou WPat
	- - 'Red Chief' 🏆[H4]	CBcs CMac EBee EHoe ELan EPfP LRHS LSRN MAsh MGos MMuc

	MSwo NEgg NRHS SBfd SGol SHil SLim SLon SPer SPoG SWvt WFar WHar WMoo WPat
- - 'Red Pillar'	CDoC CMac EBee EHoe ELan EPfP IVic LAst LRHS MAsh MBri MGos MWat NEgg SHil SLim SWvt WFar WPat
- - 'Red Rocket'	EPfP LBuc LRHS NLar WMoo
- - 'Rose Glow' (v) ♀H4	Widely available
- - 'Rosy Rocket'PBR (v)	CWGN ECrN LRHS MAsh MBri SPer SPoG
- 'Atropurpurea Superba'	see *B.* × *ottawensis* f. *purpurea* 'Superba'
- Bonanza Gold = 'Bogozam'PBR	CBcs CDoC EBee ELan EPfP LBMP LRHS MAsh MRav NLar SLim SPer SPoG WFar WPat
- 'Boum'	EHoe
- 'Carpetbagger'	WHar
- 'Crimson Pygmy'	see *B. thunbergii* f. *atropurpurea* 'Atropurpurea Nana'
- 'Diabolic'	LBuc LRHS MAsh NHol SHil SPer SPoG WGrn
- 'Fireball'	LRHS MAsh
- 'Golden Rocket'PBR	EPfP LHop LLHF LRHS MAsh MGos MWat SBfd SPer
- 'Golden Torch'	CSBt EBee ELan EMil EPfP LRHS LSRN MAsh MBri MRav NEgg SBfd SHil SLim SWvt WPat
- 'Green Carpet'	CDul CMac LHop LRHS MBlu NLar SGol SPoG
- 'Green Mantle'	see *B. thunbergii* 'Kelleriis'
- 'Green Marble'	see *B. thunbergii* 'Kelleriis'
- 'Green Ornament'	NHol
§ - 'J.N. Variegated' (v)	MWat
§ - 'Kelleriis' (v)	LHop LRHS MGos MMuc MRav NHol NLar SLon WFar
- 'Kobold'	CMac EBee EPfP LHop LRHS MAsh MGos NEgg NLar NRHS SLim SPer SPoG WFar WMoo
- 'Maria'PBR	CWGN ELon EMil LLHF LRHS LSou MBri MGos NCGa NEgg NHol NLar SHil SLim SPoG WHar WMoo
- 'Orange Rocket'PBR	EPfP LRHS MAsh MBri NHol SPer SPoG WCot
- 'Pow-wow'	CDoC EBee LRHS MAsh MBri MGos NEgg NLar SCoo SLim SPoG SWvt WPat
- 'Silver Beauty' (v)	CBcs CMHG EBee ELan MGos MSwo
- 'Silver Mile'	see *B.* × *ottawensis* 'Silver Miles'
- 'Somerset'	CMac
- 'Starburst'PBR (v)	CBcs CDoC CDul CSBt EPfP LRHS LSRN MAsh MBri MGos MWat NEgg NPri NRHS SBfd SCoo SHil SLim SLon SPoG SWvt
- Stardust	see *B. thunbergii* 'J.N. Variegated'
- 'Tiny Gold'PBR	GBin LAst LBuc LRHS LSRN MAsh MGos NPro SLim SLon SPoG SWvt
* - 'Tricolor' (v)	CMac MRav WFar WPat
valdiviana	CBcs CDul CGHE CJun CMHG CPLG EBee EPfP IArd IDee SKHP SMad SSpi WPGP WPat
verruculosa ♀H4	CBcs CDoy CDul EBee EPfP EWTr LAst LHop LRHS MGos NLar NWea SCoo SPer SRms SWvt WFar
- 'Hard's Rob'	NLar
aff. ***verticillata*** B&SWJ 10672	WCru
virescens B&SWJ 2646D	WCru
vulgaris	CArn CHab CNat EPfP GPoy MCoo NWea
- 'Wiltshire Wonder' (v)	CNat
wilsoniae	CBcs CDoy CDul CMac CTri EBee ELan EPfP LHop MMuc NLar NWea SPer WCFE WFar
- L 650	CGHE
- SDR 4219	GKev
- blue-leaved	MAsh WFar WPat
- var. ***guhtzunica***	EWes

Berchemia (*Rhamnaceae*)

racemosa	CMen NLar WSHC

Bergenia ✿ (*Saxifragaceae*)

'Abendglocken'	CMac ECGP ECha ECtt EPfP GQue LRHS NSti WCot WFar
§ 'Abendglut'	Widely available
'Admiral'	CBct ECha MLHP MNFA WCot
afghanica	XLum
* ***agavifolia***	CBct XLum
'Andrea'	WCot
'Autumn Magic'	CBct COlW CTrC GQue LAst LHop LRHS LSou NEgg NPri SPoG
'Baby Doll'	Widely available
'Bach'	EBee LSou NLar WCot
§ 'Ballawley' clonal ♀H4	ECha GCal IBlr IGor LRHS MLHP MRav NEgg WCot WFar WMnd WWEG XLum
§ Ballawley hybrids	SDix
'Ballawley Red'	NEgg
'Ballawley' seed-raised	see *B.* Ballawley hybrids
'Bartók'	CDes EBee MAvo NLar WCot
beesiana	see *B. purpurascens*
'Beethoven'	CBct CDes EBee ECha GCra IGor MRav NBir NBre SUsu WCot WPGP
Bell Tower	see *B.* 'Glockenturm'
'Biedermeier'	ECha
'Bizet'	CBct XLum
'Borodin'	CBct
'Brahms'	CBct EBee WCot
'Bressingham Bountiful'	CBct
'Bressingham Ruby'PBR	CBcs CBct CLAP EBee ECha ECtt ELon IPot LRHS LSRN MBel MGos MRav NBir NEgg WCot WPGP
'Bressingham Salmon'	EBee ECtt ELan ELon GMaP LRHS LSRN MRav NLar WCot WMnd
'Bressingham White' ♀H4	Widely available
'Britten'	WCot
ciliata	CBct CDes CHEx CLAP CMac CTca EShb GCra LEdu LRHS MLHP MRav NBir NHol NLar SDix SUsu WKif WPGP WSHC WTin XLum
- f. ***ligulata***	see *B. pacumbis*
- 'Patricia Furness'	CLAP
- 'Wilton'	CBct CDes CLAP EBee WCot WWEG
ciliata × ***crassifolia***	see *B.* × *schmidtii*
'Claire Maxine'	EBee GBin GCal NLar WCot
cordifolia	Widely available
- 'Lunar Glow'	CBct EBee ECtt LHop NPri SPoG
- 'Purpurea' ♀H4	CBcs CDoC EBee ECha ECrN ELan EPfP LBuc LRHS MLHP MRav NBir NEgg SPer SRms WFar XLum

	- 'Rosa Schwester'	ECha GBin
	- 'Rosa Zeiten'	EBee GBin
	- 'Rose'	LRHS SEND
	- 'Tubby Andrews' (v)	CBct EBee EShb GEdr LEdu LRHS MAvo MBel MBrN MBri MDKP NEgg NLar NPro SBfd WHrl WWEG
	- 'Vinterglöd'	CTrC EBee ELan ELon EPfP GMaP GQue IFoB LRHS MWat NBre NGdn NLar SWvt WFar WHil WPnP XLum
	crassifolia	EBee EPfP GKev NBre SRms WWEG XLum
	- 'Autumn Red'	CBct ECha
	- 'Orbicularis'	see *B.* × *schmidtii*
I	- var. ***pacifica***	XLum
	- - 'Cally Gem'	EBee GCal
*	***cyanea***	CLAP WCot
	'David'	ECha EWes WWEG
	'Delbees'	see *B.* 'Ballawley' clonal
	'Doppelgänger'	EBee SUsu
	'Eden's Dark Margin'	CBct CMil EBee ECtt ELon GBin LAst LDai LRHS LSou MSCN NCGa NMyG NPro SPoG WCot
	'Eden's Magic Giant'	CBct CCon CMil EBee ECGP ELon EWll GBin IBoy LPla LRHS MBNS NCGa SPoG WCot
	emeiensis	CDes CLAP GCal IGor SUsu WCot WPGP
	- hybrid	CBct
	'Eric Smith'	CBct EBee ECha GCal GCra MBri MNFA WCAu WCot WMnd
	'Eroica'	CBct COlW CSpe CTrC EBee ECha ECtt ELan EPfP EUJe GBin GEdr LHop LRHS LSou MBri MMuc MRav NBre NRHS NSti SCob SPer WHoo WMnd WPtf WSpi
	'Evening Glow'	see *B.* 'Abendglut'
	'Frau Holle'	MBri
§	'Glockenturm'	CBct NEgg
	'Harzkristall'	CBct COlW CTrC GBin LHop LRHS SPoG
	'Hellen Dillon'	see *B. purpurascens* 'Irish Crimson'
	'Herbstblute'	EBee WCAu
	'Jo Watanabe'	CBct MRav
	'Kashmir'	XLum
	'Lambrook'	see *B.* 'Margery Fish'
§	'Margery Fish'	CBct CFis ECha SPer
	milesii	see *B. stracheyi*
§	'Morgenröte' ♀^{H4}	CBcs CBct EBee ECha ELon EPfP GMaP LAst LHop LRHS LSRN MGos MNFA MRav NHol NLar NRHS NSti SBfd SPer SRms SWvt WCFE WCot WWEG
	'Morning Light'	EBee ECtt NPro
	Morning Red	see *B.* 'Morgenröte'
	'Mrs Crawford'	CBct ECha
	'Oeschberg'	CBct GBin GCal
	'Opal'	CBct EBee GBin
	'Overture'	Widely available
§	***pacumbis***	CHEx CLAP EBee GBin GCal NBid NBre NSti
	- B&SWJ 2693	WCru
	- CC 1793	SBch WCot
	- CC 3616	CBct CDes GEdr WCot WPGP
	'Perfect'	EBee WMnd
	'Pink Dragonfly'	CDes CMac CMil EBee ECtt ELon GBin LBMP LRHS MBri SPoG WCAu WCot
	'Pinneberg'	GBin
	'Pugsley's Pink'	CBct
	'Purple Queen'	LRHS
§	***purpurascens*** ♀^{H4}	CMac EBee EPfP GMaP IGor LRHS MBrN SBfd SPer WTin WWEG
	- SDR 4548	GKev
	- var. ***delavayi*** ♀^{H4}	LRHS MBri NBre NLar SRms
§	- 'Irish Crimson'	CDes CGHE WCot
	aff. ***purpurascens***	NGdn
	- ACE 2175	WCot
	'Purpurglocken'	EBee ECtt GCal LRHS WAul WCAu
	'Red Beauty'	EHoe EPfP LRHS MSnd SBfd
	'Red Rush' **new**	EBee
	'Rietheim'	EBee GBin
	'Rosi Klose'	CDes CLAP EBee ECha ECtt EHoe EHrv ELon EWes GCra LHop LRHS MBri MNFA MRav MWat NBre NGdn SUsu WCot WFar WGwG WHoo WWEG
	'Rosi Ruffles'	EBee MBNS
	'Rotblum'	CBct EBee ECtt EHoe ELon EPfP GMaP MSCN NBir NGdn NOrc WFar WWEG
§	× ***schmidtii*** ♀^{H4}	CBct CMac GBin LRHS MRav NBir NBre NLar WCot WWEG
	'Schneekissen'	CBct CMac CPrp EBee ECGP ECtt LRHS MRav WCAu
§	'Schneekoenigin'	CBct ECha GBin GCal MRav
§	'Silberlicht' ♀^{H4}	Widely available
	Silverlight	see *B.* 'Silberlicht'
	'Simply Sweet'	WCot
	Snow Queen	see *B.* 'Schneekoenigin'
§	***stracheyi***	CBct CCon CPLG ECha GCal MLHP NBid NLar SApp SDix WCot
	- CC 4609	EBee
	- CC 5225	GKev
	- Alba Group	EBee ECha GCal SMHy SUsu WPGP
	- 'Ice Queen'	WCot
	'Sunningdale'	CBcs CMac EBee ECha ELan EPfP GCra GMaP LHop LRHS MRav NBir NGdn SPer SWvt WMnd WWEG
	tianquanensis	EBee WPGP
	'Walter Kienli'	EBee GBin
	Winter Fairy Tales	see *B.* 'Wintermärchen'
§	'Wintermärchen'	CBct EBee ECha ECtt ELan ELon EPfP GBin GCra LAst LRHS MGos MLHP MMuc MRav NHol NPro SBfd WCAu WCot WMnd WWEG

Bergeranthus (*Aizoaceae*)

multiceps	SChr
vespertinus	XLum

Berkheya (*Asteraceae*)

multijuga	EPfP LRHS SBHP
- 'Golden Spike'	LSou WHil
purpurea	CBcs CCVN CSpe EBee ELon EPfP EPri GKev LEdu LRHS MDKP MNrw MPie NEgg SBch SBea SGar SMrm SPet SPlb WCot WHer WKif WSHC
- 'Pink Sensation'	WCot
- 'Silver Spike'	EPfP GKev LHop LSRN NGdn
- 'Zulu Warrior'	CMac NGBl SBHP SRkn

Berlandiera (*Asteraceae*)

lyrata	CArn EBee

Berneuxia (*Diapensiaceae*)

thibetica	IBlr

Berula (Apiaceae)

erecta EBee NPer

Berzelia (Bruniaceae)

galpinii SPlb

Beschorneria (Asparagaceae)

albiflora CSpe EBee WPGP
septentrionalis CAbP CCon CDTJ CGHE CSpe CTrC EBee EGri ESwi GAbr IBoy LRHS LSou MBNS MBel SBfd SEND SMrm SPad WCot WGrn WPGP
septentrionalis × yuccoides CHll WPGP
tubiflora CDTJ CHEx
yuccoides ♀H3 CAbb CBcs CHEx CPLG CPne CTrC EAmu EBee EGri EMil ESwi EUJe IBlr LEdu SEND
- 'Quicksilver' CBcs CCCN CDoC CKno CMHG CPLG CSBt CTrC EBee EPfP EUJe IVic LHop LRHS MBri MGos MPkF SBfd SHil SLim SSpi WGrn WPGP

Bessera (Asparagaceae)

elegans CAvo CCon CGrW EBee ECho EPot LAma MHer MNrw SDeJ WCot

Beta (Amaranthaceae)

trigyna WCot
vulgaris SHDw SVic WHer
- 'Bull's Blood' CSpe WJek
- subsp. **cicla** SVic
var. **flavescens** Bright Lights ♀H3
- - - 'Rhubarb Chard' ♀H3 WJek
- subsp. **maritima** CAgr

Betonica see *Stachys*

Betula ✿ (Betulaceae)

alba L. see *B. pendula*, *B. pubescens*
albosinensis misapplied see *B. utilis*
albosinensis Burkill ♀H4 CDul CLnd CMCN EBee EPfP WFar
- W 4106 CSto
- from Gansu, China CSto
- 'Bowling Green' CJun CPLG MBlu WPGP
- 'China Ruby' CJun CSto SSpi SSta WPGP
- 'Chinese Garden' CJun
- clone F see *B. albosinensis* 'Ness'
- 'Fascination' CCVT CMCN EBee IDee LMaj LTen MBlu MGos NLar SKHP WHar
- 'Hergest' CJun ECrN EPfP LRHS MBri MGos SCoo SLau WHar
- 'K.Ashburner' CJun CTho
§ - 'Ness' CJun CTho
- 'Pink Champagne' CJun CSto WPGP
- 'Red Panda' new CJun
- 'Rhinegold' MBlu
- 'Sable' SLim
- var. **septentrionalis** ♀H4 CBcs CCVT CDoC CDul CLnd CSto CTho CWib EBee ECrN ELon EPfP EWTr GBin GKin LAst MAsh MBlu MGos MRav MSwo NWea SBfd SCoo SGol SLim SPer WMou WPGP
- - 'Kansu' CJun EBee LRHS MBri NLar NWea SBig SCoo SMad SSpi SSta WHar
- - 'Purdom' CJun SBig

§ **alleghaniensis** CCVT CDul CMCN CSto EBee ECrN EPfP GBin MMuc NLar NWea SEND SGol WCru
apoiensis 'Mount Apoi' CJun SBig
§ **× caerulea** CSto
caerulea-grandis see *B.* × *caerulea*
chichibuensis CSto WHer
chinensis CMCN
'Conyngham' CJun CTho MBlu SLau
cordifolia see *B. papyrifera* var. *cordifolia*
costata misapplied see *B. ermanii* 'Grayswood Hill'
costata ambig. CMCN ECrN MMuc SEND SGol
costata Trautv. CLnd CTho EBee ELan MSwo
* - 'Fincham Cream' CJun SBig
'Crimson Frost' new EBee
cylindrostachya EBee
dahurica Pall. CSto IDee
- 'Maurice Foster' CJun CTho WPGP
- 'Stone Farm' CJun
delavayi EBee
divaricata CJun
ermanii CBcs CCVT CDoC CDul CLnd CMCN CMac CSBt CTri ECrN ELan GQui LAst LMaj LRHS MAsh MBlu MGos MMuc MRav NEgg NLar NWea SBfd SEND SGol WFar WMou
- B&SWJ 8801 from South Korea WCru
- from Hokkaido, Japan CSto
- 'Blush' CJun MBlu SBig SCoo WHCr
- var. **ermanii** LSRN
- - MSF 825 EBee
- - MSF 865 WPGP
§ - 'Grayswood Hill' ♀H4 CJun CMCN CMHG CSBt CTho CTri EBee EPfP GQui MAsh MBlu MGos NLar SCoo SLim SMad SPer WPGP
- 'Hakkoda Orange' CJun CTho MBri MWat SCoo WHar WPGP
- 'Holland' IArd IDee LMaj NLar
- 'Moonbeam' WHar
- 'Mount Zao' CJun CSto IVic WPGP
* - 'Pendula' CJun EBee LLHF MAsh MBlu SBig SBir SCoo
- 'Polar Bear' CJun EBee MBlu MBri NLar SCoo SSta
- 'Zao Purple' CDul
'Fetisowii' CDul CJun EBee EBtc ECrN MBlu SBig WHar
globispica CJun
insignis CSto
- B&SWJ 11751 WCru
'Inverleith' see *B. utilis* var. *jacquemontii* 'Inverleith'
jacquemontii see *B. utilis* var. *jacquemontii*
§ **kenaica** SSta
lenta CDul CMCN CSto EPfP IArd MBlu MMuc NWea SEND
luminifera CJun EBee EBtc NLar
lutea see *B. alleghaniensis*
§ **mandshurica** CSto NEgg WHCr
§ - var. **japonica** MMuc MSnd NWea
- - 'Whitespire Senior' CDul
maximowicziana CDul CMCN CSto CWib EPfP IDee LHop SGol
medwedewii CDul CJun CLnd CMCN CSto EBee EPfP NWea
- 'Gold Bark' CJun CMCN EPfP MBlu

	Name	Suppliers
	michauxii	NLar WCru
	nana	CDul EBee MGos MRav NHar NHol NWea SSta
	- 'Glengarry'	EPot GBin GEdr NLar
	nigra	CBcs CCVT CDoC CDul CLnd CMCN CSBt CTho CTri EBee ECrN LMaj MAsh MBri SEWo SGol SHil WFar WMou
	- Dura-Heat = 'Bnmtf'	MGos NLar
	- Heritage = 'Cully' ♀H4	CDul CLnd CTho EBee LHop LRHS LTen MGos MRav NWea SBfd SBig SCoo SGol WMou
	- 'Little King'	CJun MGos MPkF NLar SKHP
	- 'Peter Collinson'	CJun
	- 'Summer Cascade'	EBee MAsh NLar SBfd SKHP SLon
	- Tecumseh Compact = 'Studetec'	MBlu MPkF SGol
	- Wakehurst form	EPfP SPer SPoG
	papyrifera	Widely available
	- 'Belle Vue' **new**	WPGP
§	- var. ***cordifolia***	CSto
	- - 'Clarenville'	CJun WPGP
	- var. ***kenaica***	see *B. kenaica*
	- 'Saint George'	CJun CTho
	- 'Vancouver'	CJun CTho MBlu
§	***pendula*** ♀H4	Widely available
	- 'Bangor'	CJun CLnd SSta
	- f. ***crispa***	see *B. pendula* 'Laciniata'
	- 'Dalecarlica' misapplied	see *B. pendula* 'Laciniata'
	- 'Dalecarlica' ambig.	CBcs CCVT CSBt ECrN MRav SCrf SHil SLim
	- 'Dark Prince'	CJun
	- 'Fastigiata'	CCVT CDul CLnd CSBt CTho EBee ECrN ELan LMaj MGos NEgg NWea SCoo SGol SPer SPoG
*	- 'Golden Beauty'	CDoC CDul CMac MAsh MGos MWat NLar SBfd SCoo SLim SPer SPoG SSpi WFar WHar
	- 'Golden Cloud'	GKin
§	- 'Laciniata' ♀H4	CDul CMCN CMac CTho CWib EBee ELan EPfP IDee LAst LMaj MBlu MGos MRav MSwo NWea SBfd SCoo SGol SPer WCFE WHar WMou WPat
	- 'Long Trunk'	CDul EBee ECrN LAst LLHF LSRN MBlu SGol SLim WHar
	- 'Purpurea'	CCVT CDul CLnd CMCN CMac CSBt CWib EBee ECrN ELan ELon EPfP EWTr GKin LAst LSRN MGos MSwo NLar NWea SBfd SCoo SGol SPer SPoG WFar
	- 'Silver Grace'	CJun EBee ECrN LSRN SKHP
	- 'Swiss Glory'	LMaj
	- 'Tristis' ♀H4	CBcs CCVT CDoC CDul CJun CLnd CMCN CMac CSBt CTho CTri EBee ECrN EPfP LAst LSRN MGos MRav MSwo NLar NWea SBfd SGol SLim SPer SSpi WFar WHar WMou
	- 'Youngii'	Widely available
	- 'Zwitsers Glorie'	SKHP
§	***pendulata*** 'Spider Alley'PBR	LRHS
	platyphylla misapplied	see *B. mandshurica*
	platyphylla (Regel) V.N.Voroschilov subsp. ***kamtschatica***	see *B. mandshurica* var. *japonica*
	platyphylla Sukaczev Dakota Pinnacle = 'Fargo'	EBee SCoo WHar
	- subsp. ***platyphylla***	MSnd
	populifolia	CSto
	pseudomiddendorffii	GKev
§	***pubescens***	CCVT CDul CHab CLnd CSto CTri ECrN GQue NWea SLPl WFar WMou
	- var. ***pumila*** **new**	CSto
	raddeana	EBtc
	'Royal Frost'	CDul CJun EBee IArd IDee MAsh MBlu MWat NLar SLim SPoG WHar
	'Silver Trestles'PBR	see *B. pendulata* 'Spider Alley'
	szechuanica	NEgg NPCo WPGP
	- W 983	WPGP
	- 'Liuba White'	CJun CTho
	- 'Moonlight'	SLau
	'Trost Dwarf'	GBin
§	***utilis***	CDul CMCN CSBt CSto ECrN EMil LMaj MAsh MMuc SEND SSta WFar
	- BL&M 100 from central Nepal	CSto
	- GWJ 9259	WCru
	- H&M 1480 from Sichuan, China	CSto
	- HWJK 2250	WCru
	- HWJK 2345	WCru
	- SCH 2168	EBee
	- SICH 667 from Sichuan, China	CSto
	- S&L from Nepal	CDul
	- Yu 10163 from Yunnan, China	CSto
	- from eastern Nepal	CSto
	- 'Buckland'	ECrN
	- 'China Bronze' **new**	WPGP
	- 'Darkness'	SLon
	- 'Fascination'	CDul CJun EPfP IArd MBri MGos NWea SCoo SLim SSpi SSta WHCr WSpi
*	- 'Fastigiata'	CJun SBig SSta
	- 'Forrest's Blush'	CDul CJun CSto EBee LSRN MBri SBig WHar WPGP
N	- var. ***jacquemontii***	Widely available
	- - Polunin	WPGP
	- - 'Doorenbos' ♀H4	Widely available
	- - 'Grayswood Ghost' ♀H4	CDul CJun CMCN CMHG CTho CTri EPfP LRHS MAsh MBlu MBri NWea SBig SBir SLau SLim SSta WHar WPGP WSpi
§	- - 'Inverleith'	CDul CJun CLnd EBee MAsh SBig SBir SCoo SLim WPGP
	- - 'Jermyns' ♀H4	CDul CJun CMHG CMac CTri EPfP IVic LRHS LSRN MAsh MBlu MBri SCoo SLau SMad SPer SSta WHCr WHar
	- - 'McBeath'	SLau
	- - 'Silver Shadow' ♀H4	CDul CJun CTho EBee EPfP LRHS LSRN MBlu NWea SBig SBir SCoo SKHP SLau SLim SPer SPoG SSta WSpi
	- - 'Trinity College'	CDul CJun CTri EBee MBri SBig SBir SSpi SSta WHCr WHar
	- 'Khumbii'	SSta
	- 'Knightshayes'	CTho
	- 'Moonbeam'	CDul CJun EBee LRHS MBri SBig SCoo SPoG WHar
	- 'Mount Luoji' **new**	WPGP
	- 'Nepalese Orange' **new**	WPGP
	- var. ***occidentalis*** 'Kyelang'	CJun CTho IVic
	- 'Polar Bear'	LRHS

- var. ***prattii***	CJun CTho
- - Park Wood 1123	CSto EBee WPGP
- 'Ramdana River'	CLnd CMHG WPGP
- 'Schilling'	CJun
- 'Silver Queen'	SPoG
- 'Wakehurst Place Chocolate'	CDul CJun CSBt CTho EBee MBlu MBri NWea SBig SCoo SLim SSpi SSta WHCr WHar WSpi
* - var. ***yunnanensis*** new	CSto
cf. ***utilis***	CTri SGol
verrucosa	see *B. pendula*

Biarum (*Araceae*)

S&L 604	WCot
SB&L 597	WCot
bovei	ECho WCot
- LB 351	WCot
carratracense	WCot
- from Spain	WCot
davisii	ECho EPot LWst WCot
dispar	WCot
- SB&L 294	WCot
- SB&L 564	WCot
- S&L 290/2	WCot
ditschianum	WCot
- from Turkey	WCot
marmarisense	ECho LWst WCot
ochridense hort.	see *B. tenuifolium* subsp. *abbreviatum* autumn-flowering
tenuifolium	EBee ECho WCot
- LB 223	WCot
- LB 295	WCot
- PB 357	WCot
- S&L 174	WCot
- subsp. ***abbreviatum***	LWst
- - MS 974	WCot
- - from Greece	ECho
§ - - autumn-flowering	WCot
- subsp. ***arundanum***	WCot
- subsp. ***galianii*** PB 435	WCot
- subsp. ***idomenaeum*** MS 738	WCot
- subsp. ***zelebori***	ECho WCot
- - CRL 502	WCot
- - LB 300	WCot
- - PB 224	WCot
- - PB 334	WCot

Bidens (*Asteraceae*)

B&SWJ 10276 from Mexico	WCru
atrosanguinea	see *Cosmos atrosanguineus*
§ ***aurea***	CEnt ECtt EWes GCal LAst LEdu MDKP MNrw MSpe NPer SAga SMrm SPet WBor WFar WOld
- B&SWJ 9049 from Guatemala	WCru
- 'Cream Streaked Yellow'	GCal GQue
- cream-flowered	MNrw
- 'Golden Drop'	EWes LSou
- 'Hannay's Lemon Drop'	CCVN CEnt CKno EBee ECtt ELon EPfP EShb LHop LPla LSou MDKP MNrw MSpe SAga SPoG SSvw SUsu WBor WHlf WMoo WPGP
- 'Rising Sun'	EBee EWes
- white-flowered	GCal
ferulifolia ♀H1+3	ECtt MBel NPer
- Golden Flame = 'Samsawae'	NPri
- Peter's Gold Rush = 'Topteppich'PBR	LSou
- Solaire = 'Bidtis 1'PBR	WGor
- 'Yellow Charm'	LSou
heterophylla Ortega	see *B. aurea*
heterophylla misapplied	CEnt CPrp ECtt MCot MRav MWat WFar WHal WMoo XLum
- CD&R 1515	LPla
humilis	see *B. triplinervia* var. *macrantha*
integrifolia	SMad
'Pirate's Treasure' new	LAst
'Southon Star'	SUsu
triplinervia B&SWJ 10413	WCru
- B&SWJ 10696	WCru
§ - var. ***macrantha***	ELon LHop

Bignonia (*Bignoniaceae*)

capreolata	CCCN CRHN EBee WCot WSHC
- 'Dragon Lady'	SKHP WCot
lindleyana	see *Clytostoma calystegioides*
tweedieana	see *Macfadyena unguis-cati*
unguis-cati	see *Macfadyena unguis-cati*

Bilderdykia see *Fallopia*

Billardiera (*Pittosporaceae*)

cymosa	MOWG WSHC
longiflora ♀H3	CBcs CHid CMac CSBt CTri CWib EBee ECou ELan EPfP GEdr IArd ITim LRHS LSRN MAsh MGos MOWG MRav NLar SEND SLim SPer SPoG SWvt WKif WPGP WPat WSHC
- 'Cherry Berry'	CBcs CMac EBee ELan EPfP LRHS LSRN NLar SLim SPer SPoG SRms SWvt WSHC
- ***fructu-albo***	CBcs EBee ELan EWes SLon SPer SWvt

Billbergia (*Bromeliaceae*)

nutans	CBen CHEx CHll EBak ESwi EUJe IBlr LEdu MRav SChr SEND SPlb WGwG WSFF
- var. ***schimperiana***	EShb
* - 'Variegata' (v)	CCon CHll EShb EUJe SChr WCot
pyramidalis ♀H1	XBlo
I - 'Variegata' (v)	IBlr
× ***windii*** ♀H1	CCon CHEx EBak

Biserrula (*Papilionaceae*)

pelecinus new	WCot

Bismarckia (*Arecaceae*)

nobilis	CCCN EAmu

Bistorta see *Persicaria*

Bituminaria (*Papilionaceae*)

bituminosa	WTcb
- HH&K 174	WSHC

blackberry see *Rubus fruticosus*

blackcurrant see *Ribes nigrum*

Blackstonia (*Gentianaceae*)

perfoliata	CRDP

Blechnum (*Blechnaceae*)

alpinum	see *B. penna-marina* subsp. *alpinum*
brasiliense ♀H1	ISha
§ ***chilense*** ♀H3	CBcs CBty CDTJ CDes CGHE CHEx CLAP EAmu EBee EPfP GCal GCra GKev IArd IBlr IDee LEdu LRHS MMoz MMuc SBig SDix SKHP WCot WCru WMoo WPGP
discolor	CLAP CTrC
fluviatile	CBcs CDTJ CLAP CTrC MMoz
gibbum	CBty
- 'Silver Lady'	ISha
magellanicum misapplied	see *B. chilense*
magellanicum (Desv.) Mett.	CKel EAmu SBig SKHP WPGP
minus	CBty
§ ***niponicum***	GBin
novae-zelandiae	CBcs CDTJ CTrC EUJe
nudum	CBty CDTJ CKel EAmu ESwi LTen
penna-marina ♀H4	CBty CCCN CElw CKel CLAP CPLG EFer GAbr GCal GMaP LEdu LRHS MRav NBir WFib WMoo WOut WWEG XLum
§ - subsp. ***alpinum***	CLAP EBee ECha GEdr SKHP WMoo
- 'Cristatum'	CLAP GAbr
punctulatum	ISha
spicant ♀H4	Widely available
tabulare misapplied	see *B. chilense*
tabulare (Thunb.) Kuhn ♀H1	CBcs CDTJ CKel EAmu EPfP WPGP
wattsii	CDes EAmu

Blepharocalyx (*Myrtaceae*)

§ ***cruckshanksii***	CCCN CPLG EBee ELon IArd IDee LHop LRHS NLar WBor
- 'Heaven Scent'	see *B. cruckshanksii*

Blephilia (*Lamiaceae*)

ciliata	SPhx

Bletilla ✿ (*Orchidaceae*)

sp.	NDav
Brigantes gx	CDes EBee
formosana	NLAp
hyacinthina	see *B. striata*
ochracea	CPLG NLAp WCot
Penway Pixie gx	NLAp
Penway Sunset gx	WCot
sinensis	CPLG
§ ***striata***	CBct CDes CPLG CPom CTri EBee ECho EPot LAma LEdu LRHS MNrw NLAp NMen SAga SDeJ SPer WCot WFar WPGP
- ***alba***	see *B. striata* f. *gebina*
- 'Albostriata'	CBct CPLG EBee ECho ELan LAma LRHS NLAp WCot
§ - f. ***gebina***	CCse CDes CPLG CTri EBee ECho EPot LAma LEdu LRHS NLAp NLar SDeJ WCot WFar WPGP
- - variegated (v)	EPot LEdu NMen WCot
- var. ***japonica***	IGor
- 'Junpaku'	LWst
- 'Kuchi-beni' new	LWst
- 'Lips'	LWst
- 'Murasaki Shikibu'	LWst
- 'Soryu'	LWst
- variegated (v)	LRHS
szetschuanica	LWst

Bloomeria (*Asparagaceae*)

crocea	EBee ECho GKev
- var. ***aurea***	ECho GKev GLin
- var. ***montana***	ECho

blueberry see *Vaccinium corymbosum*

Blumea (*Asteraceae*)

balsamifera	CHab

Bocconia (*Papaveraceae*)

cordata	see *Macleaya cordata* (Willd.) R. Br.
frutescens F&M 358	WPGP
microcarpa	see *Macleaya microcarpa*

Boehmeria (*Urticaceae*)

nipononivea 'Kogane-mushi' (v)	WCot
nivea	WCot
sylvatica	NLar

Boenninghausenia (*Rutaceae*)

albiflora	CRDP
- B&SWJ 1479	WCru
- BWJ 8141 from China	WCru
- pink-flowered B&SWJ 3112	WCru
japonica B&SWJ 11186	WCru

Bolax (*Apiaceae*)

glebaria	see *B. gummifer*
§ ***gummifer***	ECho WAbe

Bolboschoenus (*Cyperaceae*)

§ ***maritimus***	CRWN LPBA SMea

Boltonia (*Asteraceae*)

asteroides	EHrv GCra LRHS MMuc SMrm SPer SWat WRHF XLum
- var. ***latisquama***	EBee GMaP GQue LSou MAvo MRav MWat NCGa NLar SHar SMad SSvw WBor WFar WHal WHil
- - 'Nana'	MRav NBre WFar
- - 'Snowbank'	EBee ELan GCal LHop LRHS MSpe NDov
- 'Pink Beauty'	LHop MSpe
decurrens	EBee GCal NBre WBor
incisa	see *Kalimeris incisa*

Bolusanthus (*Papilionaceae*)

speciosus	SPlb

Bomarea (*Alstroemeriaceae*)

F&M 130	WPGP
acutifolia	SKHP
- B&SWJ 9094	WCru
- B&SWJ 9130	WCru
- B&SWJ 10388	WCru
aff. ***andreana*** B&SWJ 10617	WCru
boliviensis	WCru
caldasii	see *B. multiflora*
costaricensis B&SWJ 10467	WCru
distichifolia	WCot
§ ***edulis***	CGHE CRHN CWGN EWld MHer WCot WKif WPGP
- B&SWJ 9017	LEdu WCru

	- F&M 104	WPGP
	frondea	see *B. multiflora*
	aff. ***frondea*** B&SWJ 10681	WCru
	hirsuta B&SWJ 10774	WCru
	hirtella	see *B. edulis*
§	***multiflora*** ♀H1	CBcs CCCN CCon CHEx EBee EShb GCal IKil SKHP WBor WCot WCru WPGP WSHC
	patacocensis	WCot
	salsilla	CAvo CCCN SKHP WCot WPGP WSHC

Bombax (*Malvaceae*)

	ceiba	SPlb

Bongardia (*Berberidaceae*)

	chrysogonum	CAvo ECho LLHF LRHS WCot WHal

Bonia (*Poaceae*)

§	***solida***	CHEx ERod MMoz MMuc MWht SEND WJun

borage see *Borago officinalis*

Borago (*Boraginaceae*)

	alba	MNHC
	laxiflora	see *B. pygmaea*
	officinalis	CArn CHby CSev CWan EGHP ELau ENfk EPfP GPoy MHer MHoo MNHC NBir NPri SBch SBfd SVic WJek
	- 'Alba'	CBre CSev EGHP ELau ENfk MHoo SBch SBfd SIde WJek WTou
	- 'Bill Archer' (v)	CNat
§	***pygmaea***	CArn CHid CPLG CSpe EGHP ELan MHer MHoo MNrw NSti WGwG WJek WMoo

Borinda (*Poaceae*)

	KR 4558	ERod
	KR 5950	ERod
	albocerea	EPfP ERod MWht WJun
	- Yunnan 1	ERod WJun WPGP
	- Yunnan 2	CDTJ CEnt ERod MMoz WJun WPGP
	- Yunnan 3a	CDTJ CEnt ERod WJun WPGP
	- Yunnan 3b	ERod WJun
	- Yunnan 4	CDTJ CEnt WPGP
	boliana	SBig WJun
	edulis	WJun
	frigida	CDTJ CEnt WJun WPGP
	- KR 4059	ERod MWht
	fungosa	EAmu ESwi WJun WPGP
	grossa KR 5931	MWht
	lushuiensis	WJun
	macclureana KR 5050	WJun
	- KR 5051	MWht
	- KR 5177 from Gyala, Nepal	ERod ESwi MWht WJun
	- KR 5602	ERod
	- KR 5950	ERod
	- KR 6236	ESwi
	- KR 6243	ERod WJun
	- KR 6400 from Show La	ESwi
	- KR 6438 from Pasm Tso	ESwi
*	***muliensis***	WJun
	papyrifera	CEnt ERod WJun WPGP
	- CS 1046	WJun
	- KR 3968	WJun
	- KR 7613	MWht WJun
	scabrida	CDTJ CEnt ERod ETod MMoz MWht WJun WPGP
	- 'Asian Wonder'	LRHS MBlu MGos NLar SPoG

Boronia (*Rutaceae*)

	heterophylla	CBcs CCCN CTsd EBee EPfP IDee IVic LRHS MOWG WAbe
	- 'Ice Charlotte'	CBcs CCCN IDee

Bossiaea (*Papilionaceae*)

	riparia	SPlb

Bothriochloa (*Poaceae*)

§	***bladhii***	CKno EPPr
	caucasica	see *B. bladhii*

Bougainvillea (*Nyctaginaceae*)

	'Alexandra'	LRHS
	'Brilliant' misapplied	see *B.* × *buttiana* 'Raspberry Ice'
§	× ***buttiana*** 'Raspberry Ice' (v)	EShb
	glabra ♀H1	CMen LRHS
§	- 'Sanderiana'	LRHS
	'Hawaiian Scarlet'	see *B.* 'San Diego Red'
	'Purple Robe'	MREP
§	'San Diego Red' ♀H1	EShb
	'Sanderiana'	see *B. glabra* 'Sanderiana'
	Scarlett O'Hara	see *B.* 'San Diego Red'
	spectabilis 'Vera Deep Purple'PBR	LRHS
	'Tropical Rainbow'	see *B.* × *buttiana* 'Raspberry Ice'

Boussingaultia (*Basellaceae*)

	baselloides Hook.	see *Anredera cordifolia*

Bouteloua (*Poaceae*)

	curtipendula	CRWN EBee LRHS
§	***gracilis***	EBee EHoe LEdu MWhi NWsh SMad SMea SMrm SUsu SWal WPGP WWEG XLum

Bouvardia (*Rubiaceae*)

	ternifolia	CSpe CWGN ESwi GAbr LSou SPad SUsu WCot

Bowiea (*Asparagaceae*)

	volubilis	EBee EShb GHim

Bowkeria (*Stilbaceae*)

	sp.	CCCN
	cymosa	SPlb
	verticillata	CHll WBor

Boykinia (*Saxifragaceae*)

	aconitifolia	CMac EWld LRHS MRav NLar NRya SMad WCru WMoo
	elata	see *B. occidentalis*
	heucheriformis	see *B. jamesii*
§	***jamesii***	GEdr GKev LRHS
	lycoctonifolia	EBee NLar
	major	EBee
§	***occidentalis***	MMHG WCru WMoo WPtf XLum
	rotundifolia	EBee EWld GJos GKev NBir WCru WMoo
	tellimoides	see *Peltoboykinia tellimoides*

boysenberry see *Rubus* 'Boysenberry'

Brachychilum see *Hedychium*

Brachychiton (*Malvaceae*)

acerifolius	CHEx SPlb
populneus	SPlb

Brachyelytrum (*Poaceae*)

japonicum	EPPr LRHS NLar

Brachyglottis ✿ (*Asteraceae*)

§ ***bidwillii***	CBcs IRar IVic WHor
- 'Basil Fox'	WAbe
§ ***buchananii***	WSHC
§ ***compacta***	EBee ECou ELan EPfP LRHS MAsh SLon SPer SPoG
compacta × ***monroi***	ECou
'County Park'	ECou ELon
(Dunedin Group) 'Drysdale'	EBee ELan EPfP LRHS MAsh SBfd SBod SKHP SLon SRGP SWvt
§ - 'Moira Reid' (v)	CPLG CTsd
§ - 'Sunshine' ♀H4	CBar CDoC CDul CSBt CTri CWib EBee ECrN ELan EPfP IVic LRHS MGos MRav MSwo MWat NPer NPri NWea SBfd SCob SEND SLim SPer SPlb SPoG SRGP SRms SWvt WFar
'Frosty'	EBee ECou ECrN
greyi misapplied	see *B.* (Dunedin Group) 'Sunshine'
§ ***greyi*** (Hook. f.) B. Nord.	CMac EBee EPfP MWhi SGol
greyi × ***repanda***	CDoC EShb
huntii × ***stewartii***	SEND
laxifolia misapplied	see *B.* (Dunedin Group) 'Sunshine'
'Leith's Gold'	CBcs CTrC
§ ***monroi*** ♀H4	CBcs CMac CSBt CWib EBee ECou EHoe ELan EPfP IVic LRHS MRav SGol SKHP SLon SPoG
- 'Clarence'	ECou
repanda	CBcs
- 'Purpurea'	CBcs
- var. ***rangiora***	CTsd
§ ***rotundifolia***	CCCN CDoC SEND
'Silver Waves'	ECou
I 'Sunshine Improved'	CBcs EHoe
'Sunshine Variegated'	see *B.* (Dunedin Group) 'Moira Reid'
Walberton's Silver Dormouse = 'Walbrach'PBR	EPfP LBuc LRHS SPoG SRkn WFar WHil

Brachypodium (*Poaceae*)

pinnatum	EHoe EPPr
sylvaticum	CHab GCal MMuc SEND

Brachyscome (*Asteraceae*)

N 'Blue Mist'	SPet
iberidifolia 'Brachy Blue' **new**	LAst
Mauve Mystique = 'Pacimamy'PBR	LHop
'Metallic Blue'	NPri
'Pink Mist'	SPet
rigidula	CPBP ECou
'Strawberry Mousse'	LAst SPet
Surdaisy Strawberry Pink = 'Bonbrapi'	LAst NPri

Brachystachyum (*Poaceae*)

densiflorum	ERod NLar

Brachystelma (*Asclepiadaceae*)

circinatum	LToo

Bracteantha see *Xerochrysum*

Brahea (*Arecaceae*)

armata	CBrP CDTJ CPHo EAmu EPfP EShb ESwi ETod EUJe MGos MREP SBfd SBst SChr SPlb
edulis	CBrP EAmu EGri SChr
'Super Silver'	WCot

Brassaia see *Schefflera*

Brassica (*Brassicaceae*)

japonica	see *B. juncea* var. *crispifolia*
§ ***juncea*** var. ***crispifolia***	MNHC
nigra	CArn
oleracea	SVic WHer
- 'Nine Star Perennial'	CAgr SVic
- 'Palmifolia' **new**	SVic
* ***rapa*** var. ***japonica***	SHDw

Bravoa (*Agavaceae*)

geminiflora	see *Polianthes geminiflora*

Briggsia (*Gesneriaceae*)

aurantiaca × ***speciosa*** **new**	GKev

Brighamia (*Campanulaceae*)

insignis	CCCN

Brillantaisia (*Acanthaceae*)

kirungae	CCCN

Brimeura (*Asparagaceae*)

§ ***amethystina*** ♀H4	CPLG CPom ECho GBin GKev LEdu LRHS NMRc SPhx WCot
- 'Alba'	ECho GKev SDeJ SMrm SPhx WCot
§ ***fastigiata***	SCnR

Briza (*Poaceae*)

maxima	CEnt CKno CTri EHoe LEdu LHop NGdn NSti SPhx WHal WHer WTou
media	Widely available
- 'Golden Bee'	CKno EHoe ELon EPPr EPfP MMHG NLar NRHS
- 'Limouzi'	CCon CElw CKno EBee EHoe ELon EPPr EPfP GCal LEdu MAvo NSti SMad SMea XLum
- 'Russells'PBR	CHid CKno EBee EHoe EPPr EPfP LHop LPot LRHS MAvo MBri NCGa NRHS NWsh SBfd SEND SHil SMea SPer SPoG SWvt WGrn
subaristata	EBee EPPr GCal LRHS MWhi WHrl
triloba	EWes MMHG NWsh SMea

Brodiaea (*Asparagaceae*)

§ ***californica***	EBee ECho GKev NMen WCot
- NNS 00-108	WCot
- NNS 02-65	GKev
- NNS 06-102	WCot
coronaria	WCot
'Corrina'	see *Triteleia* 'Corrina'
elegans	EBee ECho
ida-maia	see *Dichelostemma ida-maia*
laxa	see *Triteleia laxa*

pallida	WCot
peduncularis	see *Triteleia peduncularis*
stellaris	ECho

Bromus (*Poaceae*)

erectus	CHab
inermis 'Skinner's Gold' (v)	EBee EHoe EPPr EWes NLar NMRc SMea WCot WWEG

Broussonetia (*Moraceae*)

kazinoki	CArn LHop NLar
papyrifera	CAbP CBcs CDul EBtc EGFP ELan GBin IVic LMaj WPGP
- 'Billardii'	NLar
- 'Laciniata'	EBee IDee NLar SMad

Browallia (*Solanaceae*)

from Sikkim	CSpe

Bruckenthalia see *Erica*

Brugmansia ✿ (*Solanaceae*)

§ ***arborea***	CDTJ SEND SRms
§ - 'Knightii' (d) ♀H1	CDTJ ELan
aurea	CCCN CHEx EUJe
× ***candida***	CCCN CHEx
- 'Blush'	EUJe
§ - 'Grand Marnier' ♀H1	CDTJ CHEx CHll ELan
- 'Plena'	see *B. arborea* 'Knightii'
§ - 'Variegata' (v)	CCCN CDTJ CHll CSam
§ ***chlorantha***	CBcs
× ***cubensis*** 'Charles Grimaldi'	CSam
'Flowerdream' (d)	EUJe
§ × ***insignis***	CHll
§ - pink-flowered	CHEx SEND
rosei	see *B. sanguinea* subsp. *sanguinea* var. *flava*
§ ***sanguinea***	CBcs CCCN CHEx CHll EShb EUJe IDee IRar SEND SPlb
- red-flowered	CHEx
- 'Rosea'	see *B.* × *insignis* pink-flowered
§ - subsp. ***sanguinea*** var. ***flava***	CHEx
§ ***suaveolens*** ♀H1	CHEx CHll ELan EUJe
- pink-flowered	EShb
- ***rosea***	see *B.* × *insignis* pink-flowered
- 'Variegata' (v)	EShb
- yellow-flowered	EShb
suaveolens × ***versicolor***	see *B.* × *insignis*
'Variegata Sunset'	see *B.* × *candida* 'Variegata'
versicolor misapplied	see *B. arborea*
§ ***versicolor*** Lagerh.	CCCN
yellow-flowered	LRHS

Brunfelsia (*Solanaceae*)

americana	CCCN MOWG
calycina	see *B. pauciflora*
jamaicensis	MOWG
lactea	CCCN
§ ***pauciflora*** ♀H1	CCCN ELan
- 'Floribunda'	MOWG

Brunia (*Bruniaceae*)

albiflora	SPlb

Brunnera ✿ (*Boraginaceae*)

§ ***macrophylla*** ♀H4	Widely available
- 'Agnes Amez'	CLAP
- 'Alba'	see *B. macrophylla* 'Betty Bowring'
§ - 'Betty Bowring'	Widely available
- 'Blaukuppel'	CLAP EBee EWes LRHS NBir WFar
- 'Dawson's White' (v)	Widely available
- 'Diane's Gold' **new**	ECtt MPnt
- 'Emerald Mist' (v)	EBee ECtt EPfP MAsh NLar NSti SBfd SWvt
- 'Gordano Gold' (v)	EHoe EPPr NBir WCot
- 'Green Gold' (v)	EBee NLar NSti
- 'Hadspen Cream' (v) ♀H4	Widely available
- 'Hopley's Gold' **new**	LHop
- 'Inspector Morse' **new**	SWvt
- 'Jack Frost' PBR ♀H4	Widely available
- 'King's Ransom' (v)	EBee ECtt MAsh NLar NSti WFar
- 'Langford Hewitt' (v)	MNrw
- 'Langtrees'	CBct CMac EBee ECha ECtt EHoe GBuc GCal GCra IBal LHop LRHS MCot MMuc MRav MWhi NBir NGdn NOrc SEND SPer SWat WFar WKif WPtf WWEG
- 'Looking Glass' PBR	Widely available
- 'Marley's White'	CAbP CLAP EBee LLHF NDov NEgg NLar SBch SBfd SUsu WCot
§ - 'Mister Morse' PBR (v)	Widely available
- 'Silver Wings'	CElw EAEE EBee ECtt EPfP EWll GEdr LRHS MBri MWhi MWts NBir NGdn NLar NSti SHar SPoG SWat WCAu
- 'Spring Yellow'	EBee ECtt NLar
'Mrs Morse' PBR	see *B. macrophylla* 'Mister Morse'
sibirica	CLAP EBee EPPr EWes NBid

Brunsvigia (*Amaryllidaceae*)

bosmaniae	ECho
marginata	ECho
pulchra	ECho WCot
radula 'Vanrhynsdorp'	ECho
radulosa	ECho
rosea 'Minor'	see *Amaryllis belladonna*
striata	ECho

Bryonia (*Cucurbitaceae*)

dioica	CArn GPoy NMir

Bryophyllum see *Kalanchoe*

Buchloe (*Poaceae*)

dactyloides	CRWN

Buddleja ✿ (*Scrophulariaceae*)

HCM 98.017 from Chile	WPGP
agathosma	CPLG MOWG SLon WKif WLav WPGP WSHC
albiflora	SLon WLav
alternifolia ♀H4	Widely available
- 'Argentea'	CBcs CDoC EBee ELan EMil EPfP EWTr LBMP LRHS MBNS MRav NLar SKHP SRGP WCot WLav WPat WSHC XSen
asiatica ♀H2	EShb MOWG SLon WLav
- B&SWJ 11278	WCru
auriculata	CBcs CDul CHid CPLG CWib EBee ELan EPfP EShb LRHS MOWG MRav SDix SKHP SLon SPlb SPoG WCru WLav WPat
'Autumn Surprise'	SLon
'Blue Chip'	EBee EPfP LBuc LRHS MAsh MGos SLim SLon
* 'Blue Trerice'	CPLG

Buzz Series **new**	LBMP LBuc
- 'Buzz Ivory' **new**	CBct SMDP WHil
- 'Buzz Lavender' **new**	CBct LRHS
- 'Buzz Lilac' **new**	LRHS
- 'Buzz Magenta' **new**	CBct LRHS WHil
- 'Buzz Sky Blue' **new**	SMDP
caryopteridifolia	GQui SEND SLon WCot
colvilei	CBcs CDoC CDul ECre ELan EPfP GCal GKin IArd IDee LAst SBrt SLon WBor WPat WSpi
- B&SWJ 2121	WCru
- GWJ 9399	WCru
- 'Kewensis'	CHGN CHid CPLG EBee EWes GCal NLar SLon WCFE WCru WLav WPat WSHC WSpi
cordata	SLon
- B&SWJ 10433	WCru
- F&M 220	WPGP
coriacea	SLon WSpi
§ ***crispa***	CHid CPLG CSpe EBee ECha ELan EMil EPfP LRHS MOWG SEND SLon SPer SRkn WKif WPGP WSHC WSpi XSen
- var. ***farreri***	CHGN CHid SLon
crotonoides subsp. ***amplexicaulis***	SLon
curviflora f. ***venenifera***	SLon
- - B&SWJ 6036	WCru
'David Griffin' **new**	LRHS
davidii	CArn CCVT NWea
- B&SWJ 8083	WCru
- Adonis Blue = 'Adokeep'[PBR]	CBcs EBee LBuc LRHS NPri SLon
- 'African Queen'	CAni LRHS SLon SRGP WLav
- var. ***alba***	CWib
§ - 'Autumn Beauty'	CAni SLon WLav
- 'Bath Beauty'	CAni
- 'Beijing'	see *B. davidii* 'Autumn Beauty'
- 'Bishop's Velvet'	CAni
- 'Black Knight' ♀H4	Widely available
- 'Blue Horizon'	CAni NLar SLon SRGP WCot WLav WMoo WRHF
- 'Border Beauty'	CAni SLon WLav
- 'Boskoop Beauty'	CAni
- 'Brown's Beauty'	CAni
- Camberwell Beauty = 'Camkeep' (English Butterfly Series)	CHll CSBt LBuc LRHS NHol SLon
- 'Car Wash'	CAni
- 'Castle Blue'	SLon
- 'Castle School'	CAni CSam
§ - 'Charming'	CDul WMoo WSHC WWlt
- 'Clive Farrell'	see *B. davidii* 'Autumn Beauty'
- 'Corinne Tremaine'	WHer
- 'Dartmoor' ♀H4	CAni CDul CHll CMHG CMac CPLG CTri EBee ECre ECtt ELan EPfP GCal LRHS MAsh MGos MRav NLar NPer SDix SIde SLim SPer SPlb SPoG WFar WSHC
- 'Dart's Ornamental White'	MRav SLon WLav
- 'Dart's Papillon Blue'	CAni SLon WLav
- 'Dart's Purple Rain'	CAni SLon WLav
- 'Dubonnet'	CAni SLon WLav
- 'Dudley's Compact Lavender'	CAni
- 'Ecolonia'	CAni SLon WLav
- 'Ellen's Blue' **new**	LRHS NRHS
- 'Empire Blue' ♀H4	CAni CBar CBcs CDoC CDul CHab CSBt EBee ECtt EPfP GKin LRHS LSRN MGos MRav NBir NPer NWea SBfd SEND SPer SPlb SPoG SRGP SRms SWat SWvt WFar WWlt
- 'Fascinating'	CAni GCal MRav NBir SLon WLav
- 'Flaming Violet'	CAni SLon WLav
- 'Florence'	EBee LLHF LRHS LSRN LSou MWat NEgg NLar NWad SLon SRGP WFar WHar WMoo
- 'Fortune'	CAni
- 'Glasnevin Hybrid'	CAni LRHS NSti SDix SLon WLav
- 'Gonglepod'	CAni SLon WLav
- 'Greenway's River Dart'	CAni SLon
- 'Grey Dawn'	WLav
- 'Gulliver'[PBR]	EBee NLar SGol SLon WFar
- 'Harlequin' (v)	Widely available
- 'Heath'	SPhx
- 'Ile de France'	CAni CBcs CWib NWea SLon SRms WLav
- 'Leela Kapila'	MGos SLon
- 'Les Kneale'	CAni SLon WLav
- 'Lyme Bay'	CAni
- Marbled White = 'Markeep'[PBR]	CSBt LBuc SLon WMoo
- Masquerade = 'Notbud'[PBR] (v)	MRav SLon WGor
§ - Nanho Blue = 'Mongo' ♀H4	CAni CMHG CMac CSBt EBee ECrN ECtt ELan EPfP GKin LAst LRHS MAsh MGos MLHP MMuc MRav MSwo MWat NBir NLar NRHS SGol SLim SPoG SRGP WFar WHar WMoo XSen
- 'Nanho Petite Indigo'	see *B. davidii* Nanho Blue
- 'Nanho Petite Plum'	see *B. davidii* Nanho Purple
- 'Nanho Petite Purple'	see *B. davidii* Nanho Purple
§ - Nanho Purple = 'Monum' ♀H4	CAni CDoC CMHG CMac CTri CWib EBee ELan EPfP LAst LRHS LSRN MGos MRav NLar SGol SLim SLon SPer SPlb SPoG SRGP WHar XSen
- Nanho White = 'Monite'	EBee EHoe ELan EPfP LRHS NRHS SGol SLon SPer SPoG SRms
- var. ***nanhoensis***	CAni CDul MAsh SEND SGol SIde WLav
- - blue-flowered	NHol NWad SLon SPer
- 'Orchid Beauty'	CAni SLon WLav
- 'Orpheus'	CAni SLon WLav
- 'Panache'	EPfP LRHS SLon
- 'Peace'	CMac CTri EPfP LSRN MRav NLar SLon SPoG WLav
- Peacock = 'Peakeep'[PBR] (English Butterfly Series)	CBcs
- 'Persephone'	SLon WLav
- 'Petite Indigo'	see *B. davidii* Nanho Blue
- 'Pink Beauty'	LAst LSRN SRGP
- 'Pink Charming'	see *B. davidii* 'Charming'
- 'Pink Pearl'	CAni SEND SLon WLav
- 'Pink Spreader'	CAni LRHS SLon WLav
- 'Pixie Blue'	CAni LBMP LBuc LRHS MAsh SGar SLon WLav
- 'Pixie Red'	CAni LBMP LBuc LRHS MAsh NEgg NLar SEND WLav
- 'Pixie White'	LBuc LRHS MAsh NLar SEND WLav
- Purple Emperor = 'Pyrkeep' (English Butterfly Series)	CBcs LBuc NBir SLon
- 'Purple Friend'	CAni SLon WLav
- 'Purple Prince'	CAni
- 'Red Admiral'	CAni LLHF LRHS MAsh SLon SPoG SRGP

Plant	Suppliers
- Rêve de Papillon Blue = 'Minpap3' **new**	EMil
- Rêve de Papillon = 'Minpap'	EMil LRHS NRHS
- Rêve de Papillon White	EMil
- 'Royal Purple'	CAni SLim SWvt
- 'Royal Red' ♀H4	Widely available
- 'Saith Ffynnon Early'	WSFF
- 'Santana' (v)	CAni CDul CMac EBee EHoe ELon EPfP EWes LAst LRHS LSou MRav NEgg NHol NLar SBfd SWvt WCFE WCot WHar WMoo WPat WSpi
- 'Shapcott Blue'	CAni
- 'Shire Blue'	WLav
- 'Southcombe Splendour'	CAni
- 'Summer Beauty'	CAni CWib LRHS MGos MRav SLon WLav
- 'Summer House Blue'	LBuc LRHS SLon WLav
- 'Twotones'	WLav
- 'Variegata' (v)	CAni LRHS MAsh SLon SWvt WLav
- 'White Ball'	EHoe ELan EPfP NLar SLon WLav
- 'White Bouquet'	CAni CCVT CDul CSBt EPfP EWTr GKin LAst LRHS MHer MSwo MWat NWea SEND SPer SRGP SWvt WLav
- 'White Cloud'	CAni ECrN GQui MGos SRms WGwG
- 'White Harlequin' (v)	SLon WCFE
- 'White Profusion' ♀H4	CAni CBar CBcs CDul CHab CSam CWCL EBee ECtt ELan EPfP LPot LRHS MGos MRav NBir NEgg NLar NPri NWea SBfd SGol SLim SWat SWvt WCFE WFar WHar
- 'White Wings'	SLon WLav
- 'Widecombe'	CAni
§ ***delavayi***	CPLG ECre SEND WCru
fallowiana misapplied	see *B.* 'West Hill'
fallowiana Balf. f. & W.W. Sm	ELan GQui LRHS WLav WSpi
- ACE 2481	LRHS
- BWJ 7803	WCru
- var. ***alba*** ♀H3	CDoC CHGN CHid CMac EBee ECrN ECre ELan EPfP LRHS MAsh MRav NChi NLar NSti SLon SPer SPoG WFar WPGP WSHC
'Flower Power'	see *B.* × *weyeriana* 'Bicolor'
forrestii	WCru
globosa ♀H4	Widely available
- RCB/Arg C-11	WCot
- 'Cally Orange'	GCal WGwG
- 'Lemon Ball'	MBlu NPer SLon WLav
glomerata	EShb SLon WPGP
- 'Silver Service'	ELan LRHS SKHP
heliophila	see *B. delavayi*
indica	SLon WBor
japonica	SLon
- B&SWJ 8912	WCru
× ***lewisiana*** 'Margaret Pike'	MOWG SLon
limitanea	SLon
lindleyana	Widely available
aff. ***lindleyana***	EWTr WSpi
- B&SWJ 11478	WCru
'Lochinch' ♀H3-4	Widely available
longifolia	SLon XSen
'Longstock'	SLon
'Longstock Silver'	SLon
loricata	CHGN CPLG CTsd CWib EBee GBin GQui LRHS MOWG SEND SGar SKHP SLon SPlb WLav WPGP
macrostachya	GLin
- HWJ 602	WCru
- WWJ 12016	WCru
§ ***madagascariensis*** ♀H1	CBcs CRHN MOWG NLar SGar SLon SPlb WHar
* 'Malvern Blue' (English Butterfly Series)	CAni
megalocephala B&SWJ 9106	WCru WPGP
§ 'Morning Mist'PBR	CDoC CMHG CPLG CWGN EBee EHoe ELan EPfP LAst LBMP LLHF LRHS LSRN LSou MOWG NBir NEgg NHol NLar NPri SBfd SLon SPoG SRms WCot WHar WPGP
myriantha	CPLG SLon XSen
nappii	SLon
nicodemia	see *B. madagascariensis*
nivea	CHid CMHG CPLG MOWG SLon WLav XSen
- B&SWJ 2679	WCru
- pink-flowered	SLon
officinalis ♀H2	CPLG MOWG SLon
paniculata	SLon
parvifolia	SLon
- MPF 148	WLav
× ***pikei*** 'Hever'	GCal XSen
'Pink Delight' ♀H4	Widely available
'Pink Perfection'	CAni
'Pride of Hever'	MOWG SDys
'Pride of Longstock'	LBuc LRHS SLon
saligna	SLon
'Salmon Spheres'	SLon
salviifolia	CBcs CHid CPLG CRHN CTsd EBee ELan IDee LRHS MBlu NSti SEND SPlb SWal WGwG WHer WLav WPGP
- white-flowered	SLon WPGP
Silver AnniversaryPBR	see *B.* 'Morning Mist'
'Silver Surprise'	EMil
stachyoides	MOWG
stenostachya	CPLG SLon
sterniana	see *B. crispa*
'Sugar Plum'	LBuc SLon
tibetica	see *B. crispa*
tubiflora	MOWG SLon WLav
venenifera B&SWJ 895	WCru
§ 'West Hill'	SLon WLav
× ***weyeriana***	CDul ECtt EPfP GQui MMuc MNrw MSwo NBir SBfd SGar SPad SPlb SWvt WGwG
§ - 'Bicolor'	LRHS MNrw
- 'Golden Glow' (v)	CEnt CTri ECrN EPfP GBin LSRN NLar SLon WLav WSFF
- 'Honeycomb'	NLar
- 'Lady de Ramsey'	SEND
- 'Moonlight'	CBcs CPLG ELan GBin IFro LAst SBfd SLon WCot WLav WSpi
- 'Pink Pagoda'	SLon
- 'Sungold' ♀H4	Widely available
'Winter Sun'	SLon
yunnanensis	CBcs GCal NLar SLon
- B&SWJ 8146	WCru

Buglossoides (*Boraginaceae*)

Plant	Suppliers
§ ***purpurocaerulea***	CEnt CHll CPom CSpe EBee ECha ELan EPfP LHop MLHP MWhi NBid NChi WCot WSHC XLum

Bukiniczia (*Plumbaginaceae*)

cabulica	CSpe GKev WAbe

Bulbine (*Asphodelaceae*)

SH 74	CCse
abyssinica	ECho
alooides	ECho
annua misapplied	see *B. semibarbata*
bulbosa misapplied	see *B. semibarbata*
capitata 'Bloemfontein'	ECho
caulescens	see *B. frutescens*
§ ***frutescens***	CDoC CHll EShb MHer SGar WBrk WJek
- 'Hallmark'	CCCN
latifolia	CCCN EShb
narcissifolia 'Ladybrand'	ECho
§ ***semibarbata***	CCCN

Bulbinella (*Asphodelaceae*)

angustifolia	ECho
cauda-felis	WCot
- 'Tulbagh'	ECho
eburnifolia	CDes ECho WCot
gibbsii var. ***balanifera***	ECho
graminifolia 'Clanwilliam'	ECho
hookeri	CPLG CPom EBee ECho ECou EWld GBee GBin GEdr GKev ITim LRHS MHer SRms WHal WThu
latifolia	ECho
- subsp. ***doleritica***	ECho
- subsp. ***latifolia***	IBlr
nutans	ECho WPGP
punctulata 'Piketberg'	ECho

Bulbinopsis see *Bulbine*

Bulbocodium (*Colchicaceae*)

vernum	ECho EPot GKev LAma LLHF LRHS NMin SDeJ

bullace see *Prunus insititia*

Bunias (*Brassicaceae*)

orientalis	CAgr ELau

Bunium (*Apiaceae*)

bulbocastanum	CSpe LEdu SBfd SHDw XLum

Buphthalmum (*Asteraceae*)

salicifolium	CSam EBee ELan EPfP MMuc MNFA NBro NGdn SEND SPer SRms SWat WCot WFar WPer WWEG XLum
- 'Alpengold'	CFis ECha GMaP LRHS NBre NLar
- 'Dora'	CSam ECtt LRHS WCot
- 'Sunwheel'	LRHS SRms
speciosum	see *Telekia speciosa*

Bupleurum (*Apiaceae*)

angulosum	CSpe LRHS NBir WTcb
- copper-leaved	see *B. longifolium*
falcatum	ECGP ECha LRHS NDov WCot
fruticosum	CBcs CSpe EBee EPfP LPla LRHS MAsh SDix SEND SKHP SLon SMad SPer SPoG SSpi WCot WPGP WPat XSen
* ***griffithii***	SPhx
§ ***longifolium***	CElw CMea CPom CSpe EBee EWes LEdu LRHS MDKP MNrw NChi SKHP SMrm
- subsp. ***aureum***	SPhx
ranunculoides	XLum
rotundifolium 'Copper'	WCot
spinosum	CSpe SMad WHil XSen
tenue	CArn

Burchellia (*Rubiaceae*)

capensis	SPlb

Bursaria (*Pittosporaceae*)

spinosa	CCCN CHll EBee ECou NLar

Butia (*Arecaceae*)

capitata	CAbb CBcs CBrP CCCN CDTJ CHEx CPHo CTrC EAmu EGri ESwi ETod EUJe LMaj LTen MGos MREP MWat SBfd SBst SChr
§ - var. ***odorata***	EAmu SPlb
eriospatha	CDTJ EAmu SChr
odorata	see *B. capitata* var. *odorata*
yatay	CDTJ EAmu SBig

Butomus (*Butomaceae*)

umbellatus ♀H4	CBen CRow CWat ECha EHon EPfP EWay GQue LPBA MNrw MRav MSKA MWts NBir NPer SWat WMAq WTin XLum
- f. ***albiflorus***	MSKA
- 'Rosenrot'	CRow EWay
- 'Schneeweisschen'	CRow EWay GQue MNrw MWts NLar

butternut see *Juglans cinerea*

× *Butyagrus* (*Arecaceae*)

nabonnandii	EAmu

Buxus ✿ (*Buxaceae*)

aurea 'Marginata'	see *B. sempervirens* 'Marginata'
balearica ♀H4	MBlu
'Green Gem'	NHol NWad
'Green Mound'	LBMP
'Green Velvet'	EPfP WSpi
harlandii hort.	CMen SRiv
japonica 'Nana'	see *B. microphylla*
§ ***microphylla***	MHer NWad NWea SGol
- 'Asiatic Winter'	see *B. microphylla* var. *japonica* 'Winter Gem'
§ - 'Compacta'	CMen LLHF MHer NMen NWad SRiv WCot WPat WThu
- 'Curly Locks'	MHer NWad
- 'Faulkner'	CCVT ELan EPfP LBuc LHop LRHS LSRN MAsh MBNS MGos MREP SBfd SEWo SGol SHil SPoG SRiv WMoo
- Golden Dream = 'Peergold'PBR	NLar
- 'Golden Triumph'PBR	EPfP
- 'Green Pillow'	EPfP MHer SRiv WSpi
- 'Herrenhausen'	WSpi
- var. ***insularis***	see *B. sinica* var. *insularis*
- var. ***japonica*** 'Green Jade'	WSpi
- - 'Morris Midget'	IArd NWad
- - 'National'	WSpi
§ - - 'Winter Gem'	MHer MRav NLar SLPl WSpi
- 'John Baldwin'	SRiv

	- var. ***microphylla*** **new**	WSpi
	sempervirens ♀H4	Widely available
§	- 'Angustifolia'	MHer MRav NWad SMad
	- 'Argentea'	see *B. sempervirens* 'Argenteo-variegata'
§	- 'Argenteo-variegata' (v)	EPfP IFoB NEgg SGol WFar
	- 'Aurea'	see *B. sempervirens* 'Aureovariegata'
	- 'Aurea Maculata'	see *B. sempervirens* 'Aureovariegata'
	- 'Aurea Marginata'	see *B. sempervirens* 'Marginata'
	- 'Aurea Pendula' (v)	CJun
§	- 'Aureovariegata' (v)	EPfP EShb LRHS MGos MHer MRav NSti SBod SPer SRiv WFar WMoo
	- 'Bentley Blue'	NWea
	- 'Blauer Heinz'	ELan IVic MHer MRav SRiv WSpi
I	- 'Brilliantissima'	WMoo WSpi
	- clipped ball	CWib EPfP LSRN MGos NLar SGol SLim SRiv WFar
	- clipped bird	SRiv
	- clipped cone	LSRN SGol SRiv
	- clipped pyramid	CWib EPfP LSRN MGos NLar SGol SLim SRiv
	- clipped spiral	LSRN SGol SLim SRiv
	- 'Elegans'	IFoB LRHS
§	- 'Elegantissima' (v) ♀H4	Widely available
	- 'Gold Tip'	see *B. sempervirens* 'Notata'
	- 'Golden Frimley' (v)	LHop
§	- 'Graham Blandy'	IVic MHer SGol SRiv WSpi
	- 'Green Balloon'	EPfP LBuc
	- 'Greenpeace'	see *B. sempervirens* 'Graham Blandy'
	- 'Handsworthiensis'	CLnd CTri NHol NLar NWea SEND SPer SRms WMoo WSpi
	- 'Japonica Aurea'	see *B. sempervirens* 'Latifolia Maculata'
	- 'Kensington Gardens'	WSpi
	- 'King Midas'	IVic
	- 'Kingsville'	see *B. microphylla* 'Compacta'
	- 'Kingsville Dwarf'	see *B. microphylla* 'Compacta'
	- 'Krakow'	NLar
	- 'Lace'	NSti
	- 'Latifolia Aurea Maculata' **new**	WSpi
	- 'Latifolia Macrophylla'	SLon
§	- 'Latifolia Maculata' (v) ♀H4	CAbP CDoC CWib EBee EPfP LRHS NPer SEND SPoG SRiv WJek
	- 'Longifolia'	see *B. sempervirens* 'Angustifolia'
§	- 'Marginata' (v)	CArn CPne IFoB LHop LRHS LTen SGol SLon WHar WSpi
	- 'Memorial'	MHer NWad SMHy SRiv WSpi
	- 'Myosotidifolia'	NPro SRiv WCot WSpi
	- 'Myrtifolia'	MHer
§	- 'Notata' (v)	IFoB MAsh SBfd SBod WMoo
	- 'Parasol'	MHer
	- 'Prostrata'	NWad NWea
*	- 'Pygmaea'	WAbe
	- 'Pyramidalis'	SEND WFar
	- 'Rosmarinifolia'	MHer MRav
	- 'Rotundifolia'	ELan SEND SIde WMoo
	- 'Silver Beauty' (v)	NEgg
	- 'Silver Variegated'	see *B. sempervirens* 'Elegantissima'
	- 'Suffruticosa' ♀H4	Widely available
*	- 'Suffruticosa Covent Garden' **new**	MREP
	- 'Suffruticosa Variegata' (v)	EOHP SRms SWvt
	- 'Twisty'	WFar
	- 'Vardar Valley'	NPro SRiv WSpi
*	- 'Variegata' (v)	ECrN ELan MSwo WRHF
	- 'Waterfall'	MHer
	- 'Wisley Blue'	WSpi
§	***sinica*** var. ***insularis***	MAsh
	- - 'Justin Brouwers'	MHer SRiv
	- - 'Tide Hill'	MHer SRiv WFar WSpi

C

Cachrys (*Apiaceae*)

	alpina	SPhx

Caesalpinia (*Caesalpiniaceae*)

	gilliesii	CBcs CSpe EBee EGri EUJe LSRN SBrt SPlb
	- RCB/Arg N-1	SEND
	pulcherrima	CCCN SPlb
	spinosa	CBcs SPlb WSHC

Caiophora (*Loasaceae*)

	coronata	SPlb

Caladium (*Araceae*)

§	***bicolor*** (v)	GHim
	'Candidum' (v)	SDeJ
	'Florida Cardinal' (v)	SDeJ
	'Fred Bause' **new**	GHim
	'Freida Hemple'	SDeJ
	× ***hortulanum***	see *C. bicolor*
	'White Christmas' (v)	SDeJ

Calamagrostis (*Poaceae*)

	from Korea	NDov
	× ***acutiflora***	XLum
	- 'Avalanche'	CKno EBee EHoe EPPr EWes LRHS MWhi NRHS NWsh
	- 'Eldorado' (v)	WCot
N	- 'Karl Foerster'	Widely available
	- 'Overdam' (v)	Widely available
	- 'Stricta'	EBee EPPr NWsh
	- 'Waldenbuch'	CKno EBee NDov
	argentea	see *Stipa calamagrostis*
	arundinacea	CElw CMac COIW CPLG CSpe ECou LEdu SDix SGar SPlb WFar WMoo WPGP XLum
	'Avalanche'	CKno GBin GQue MAsh NOak
§	***brachytricha*** ♀H4	Widely available
	canadensis	EPPr
	emodensis	CCVN CEnt CKno CSpe CWCL EBee ECha EHoe LEdu MAvo MMoz MWhi NOak NWsh SMad WCot WGrn WMoo WPGP
	epigejos	CKno EBee LEdu WHrl
	nutkaensis	EPPr
	splendens misapplied	see *Stipa calamagrostis*
	splendens Trin.	LPla NDov
	varia	CKno EHoe SMrm WHrl

Calamintha (*Lamiaceae*)

	alpina	see *Acinos alpinus*
§	***ascendens***	CArn EBee SGar SPhx WMoo
	clinopodium	see *Clinopodium vulgare*
	cretica	EBee WPer
*	'Fritz Kuhn'	WWEG
§	***grandiflora***	CArn EBee ECha EDAr ELan GJos GPoy LEdu LRHS MHer MNHC

		MRav MWat MWhi NBir NPer SEND SMrm SPer SPlb SSvw WCAu WFar WJek WMoo WTin XLum
	- 'Elfin Purple'	EBee EPfP SBfd
	- 'Variegata' (v)	CPrp EBee ECtt ELan ENfk EPPr EPfP LAst NPri SBfd SPoG WFar WGrn
	'Harrogate' new	NDov
§	***menthifolia***	MHoo NBre NLar WJek XLum
§	***nepeta***	CArn CHab CMea CWan EBee ECha ECtt ENfk GMaP LAst LRHS MHer MNFA MNHC NBro SBch SEND SMrm SPhx SPlb SPoG SWal SWat WCAu WJek WMoo WOut WPer
	- subsp. ***glandulosa***	CEnt ECGP WMoo
	- - ACL 1050/90	EBee WHoo
	- - 'White Cloud'	CSpe EBee ECGP EHrv ELan GQue LLWP MRav NBir SPoG WCAu WMoo
	- 'Gottfried Kuehn'	EBee LPla MRav
§	- subsp. ***nepeta***	CPrp ELan ELon EPfP MCot MHer MLHP MRav MWat NDov NSti SPer SUsu WHal WTin XLum
	- - 'Blue Cloud'	CFis CMea CSam CSpe EBee ECha EHrv EPfP LRHS MAvo MSpe NBir NCGa NDov SPhx SUsu WCAu WFar WMoo
	- 'Weisse Riese'	EBee SPhx
	nepetoides	see *C. nepeta* subsp. *nepeta*
	officinalis misapplied	see *C. ascendens*
	sylvatica	see *C. menthifolia*
I	- 'Menthe'	EBee LPla
	vulgaris	see *Clinopodium vulgare*

calamondin see × *Citrofortunella microcarpa*

Calandrinia (*Portulacaceae*)

	grandiflora	LLHF
*	***ranunculina***	CPBP
	sibirica	see *Claytonia sibirica*
	umbellata	EDAr LBMP MAsh WIce WPer
	- 'Ruby Tuesday'	NPri

Calanthe (*Orchidaceae*)

	alismifolia	EBee EFEx
	arcuata	EFEx
	arisanenesis	EFEx
	aristulifera	EFEx GEdr LWst NLAp
	bicolor	see *C. striata*
	discolor	CDes EBee EFEx GEdr LAma LWst NLAp WCot
	- subsp. ***amamiana***	EFEx
	- var. ***flava***	see *C. striata*
	- subsp. ***tokunoshimensis***	EFEx
	fargesii	LWst WCot
	graciliflora	EFEx
	Hizen gx	GEdr
	Kozu gx	GEdr LEdu LWst
	- red-flowered	LWst
	mannii	EFEx
	nipponica	CBct EBee EFEx GEdr LAma LWst NLAp
	reflexa	EBee EFEx GEdr LAma LWst NLAp
	sieboldii	see *C. striata*
§	***striata***	CBct EBee EFEx GEdr LAma LWst NLAp WCot
	sylvatica	EBee NLAp
	Takane gx	GEdr LWst NLAp
	tricarinata	CBct EFEx GEdr LAma LWst NLAp
	triplicata	EBee

Calathea (*Marantaceae*)

	argyrophylla 'Exotica'	XBlo
	louisae 'Maui Queen'	XBlo
§	***majestica*** ♀H1	XBlo
	makoyana ♀H1	XBlo
	oppenheimiana	see *Ctenanthe oppenheimiana*
	ornata	see *C. majestica*
	picturata 'Argentea' ♀H1	XBlo
	roseopicta ♀H1	XBlo
	rufibarba	XBlo
*	***stromata***	XBlo
	zebrina ♀H1	XBlo
	'Zoizia'	XBlo

Calceolaria (*Calceolariaceae*)

	acutifolia	see *C. polyrhiza* Cav.
	arachnoidea	EBee SKHP SPlb
§	***biflora***	ECho EPfP GKev MAsh NLar WPer
	- 'Goldcap'	ECho SMrm
	- 'Goldcrest Amber'	SPlb
	corymbosa	GKev
	falklandica	ECho GKev SRms
	fothergillii	GKev WAbe
	'Goldcrest'	ECho LRHS SRms
N	***integrifolia*** ♀H3	CAbb CDTJ CPLG CRHN CSpe CTri ECtt ELan EPfP MSCN SEND SGar SPer SRms WAbe WWlt
	- bronze	MSCN SPer
	- 'Gaines' Yellow'	EBee GCal
	'John Innes'	ECho
	'Kentish Hero'	CSpe GCal WAbe
	aff. ***pavonii***	CRHN
	perfoliata B&SWJ 10638	WCru
	plantaginea	see *C. biflora*
§	***polyrhiza*** Cav.	ECho
	rugosa	see *C. integrifolia*
	tenella	NRHS NSla WAbe
	uniflora	CPBP
	- var. ***darwinii***	ECho GKev NSla WAbe
	'Walter Shrimpton'	ECho EPot EWes WAbe

Calendula (*Asteraceae*)

	arvensis	CCCN
	'Bronze Beauty' new	CSpe
	officinalis	CArn ELau ENfk GPoy MHer MHoo MNHC SBfd SIde SPav SVic SWvt WJek WSFF
	- (Calypso Series) 'Calypso Orange' new	MHoo
	- - 'Calypso Yellow' new	MHoo
	- Fiesta Gitana Group ♀H4	CPrp WJek
	- 'Touch of Red Buff' (Touch of Red Series) new	CSpe
	'Tarifa'	SEND

Calibanus (*Asparagaceae*)

	hookeri	EShb

Calibrachoa (*Solanaceae*)

	(Cabaret Series) Cabaret Apricot = 'Balcabapt'	NPri
	- Cabaret Blue	NPri
	- Cabaret Hot Pink = 'Balcabhopi' PBR	NPri

- Cabaret Mango Tango = 'Balcabango' **new** LAst
- Cabaret Purple Glow = 'Balcabplo'[PBR] **new** LAst
- Cabaret Red Improved = 'Balcabimred' NPri
- Cabaret Rose = 'Balcabrose'[PBR] LAst
- Cabaret Scarlet = 'Balcabscar'[PBR] LAst
- Cabaret White Improved = 'Balcabwitim' NPri
- Cabaret Yellow = 'Balcabyelow'[PBR] NPri
- Cabaret Yellow Improved LAst
(Can-can Series) Can-can Mocha = 'Balcanoa' LAst
- Can-can Orange = 'Balcanoran' **new** LAst
- Can-can Strawberry = 'Balcanerry' LAst
(Million Bells Series) Million Bells Cherry = 'Sunbelchipi'[PBR] WGor
- Million Bells Pink Terracotta = 'Sunbelrikist' LAst
- Million Bells Trailing Blue = 'Sunbelkubu'[PBR] LAst
- Million Bells Trailing Ice = 'Sunbelkuriho'[PBR] LAst
- Million Bells Trailing Lavender Vein = 'Sunbelbura'[PBR] LSou
- Million Bells Trailing Lemon **new** LSou
- Million Bells Trailing Pink Morn = 'Sunbelkupapi'[PBR] LAst
- Million Bells Trailing Plum **new** LSou
(Superbells Series) Superbells Apricot Punch = 'Uscali41308' **new** LAst
- Superbells Candy White = 'Uscali48'[PBR] LSou
- Superbells Imperial Purple = 'Uscali100'[PBR] LSou WGor
- Superbells Orange = 'Uscali41109' LSou WGor
- Superbells Pink = 'Uscali11'[PBR] ♀H3 LSou
- Superbells Red = 'Uscali28'[PBR] LSou WGor
- Superbells Yellow = 'Uscali53002' WGor

Calibrachoa × *Petunia* see × *Petchoa*

Calla (*Araceae*)

aethiopica see *Zantedeschia aethiopica*
palustris CRow CWat EHon EWay LPBA MSKA MWts NPer SWat WMAq

Calliandra (*Mimosaceae*)

'Dixie Pink' CCCN
eriophylla SPlb
haematocephala MOWG
portoricensis CCCN
surinamensis CCCN
tweediei CCCN MOWG

Callianthemum (*Ranunculaceae*)

anemonoides LLHF WAbe WCot
kernerianum WAbe
miyabeanum LWst

Callicarpa (*Lamiaceae*)

americana CPLG NLar
- var. ***lactea*** CMCN
bodinieri NBir
- var. ***giraldii*** GBin MRav NLar SGol
- - 'Profusion' ♀H4 Widely available
cathayana NLar
dichotoma CBcs CPLG ELan NLar WPat
- 'Issai' LLHF NLar SBfd WPat
- 'Shirobana' NLar
- 'Variegata' (v) **new** CJun
japonica CMen CPLG NLar
- f. ***albibacca*** NLar
- 'Koshima-no-homate' NLar
- 'Leucocarpa' CBcs CMac CPLG ELan EPfP MRav NLar SPer SPoG WFar
- var. ***luxurians*** B&SWJ 8521 WCru
kwangtungensis CBcs EPfP NLar
mollis CPLG NLar
shikokiana NLar
× ***shirasawana*** NLar
aff. ***tikusikensis*** B&SWJ 7127 WCru
yunnanensis NLar

Callirhoe (*Malvaceae*)

involucrata ELon SMad WHrl
- var. ***tenuissima*** **new** GCal

Callisia (*Commelinaceae*)

fragrans EShb

Callistemon (*Myrtaceae*)

acuminatus CCCN
'Awanga Dam' ECou
'Burgundy' MOWG
'Candy Pink' MOWG
citrinus CHll CTri CWSG EBee ECou EPfP EPri ERom EShb MREP SEND SGar SPlb SRms WHar
- 'Albus' see *C. citrinus* 'White Anzac'
- 'Angela' MOWG
- 'Firebrand' CDoC LRHS MAsh
- 'Splendens' ♀H3 Widely available
§ - 'White Anzac' CDoC CHll CMac ELan EPfP MOWG SEND SPoG SSta
comboynensis CCCN
'Eureka' MOWG
glaucus see *C. speciosus*
'Hannah's Child' MOWG
'Happy Valley' MOWG
'Havering Gold' ECou
'Havering Pink' ECou
'Havering Red' ECou
'Inferno' LRHS
'Injune' MOWG
'Kings Park Special' MOWG
laevis hort. see *C. rugulosus*
linearifolius LSRN
linearis ♀H3 CBcs CMac CTrC CTri ECou ECrN ELan EPfP IVic LRHS LSRN MAsh

	MHer MOWG SEND SLim SLon SPlb SRms SWal SWvt WSHC
macropunctatus	SPlb
'Masotti'PBR	LRHS NRHS SHil SLim
'Mauve Mist'	CCCN CDoC ELan ELon EPfP EPri GBin LRHS MAsh MOWG SPoG WGrn
'Millie Marsden' **new**	MOWG
pachyphyllus	ECou MOWG
- var. ***viridis***	MOWG
pallidus	CBcs CCCN CHEx CMHG CMac CTrC CWib EBee ECou ELan EPfP LRHS MAsh MHer MOWG MRav SDys SEND SPer SPlb SPoG SSta
- 'Candle Glow'	MOWG
- 'Father Christmas'	MOWG
paludosus	see *C. sieberi* DC.
pearsonii 'Rocky Rambler'	MOWG
'Perth Pink'	CBcs CCCN CDoC ELan EPfP LHop LRHS MOWG SLim
phoeniceus	ECou MOWG
- 'Pink Ice'	MOWG
pinifolius	SPlb
- 'Sockeye'	MOWG
'Pink Champagne'	MOWG
§ ***pityoides***	CPLG ECou IRar MOWG SPoG
- from Brown's Swamp, Australia	ECou
recurvus	MOWG
'Red Clusters'	CDoC CMac CTsd EBee ELan EPfP EUJe IArd LRHS MAsh MOWG NEgg NPri SBfd SWvt
'Reeve's Pink'	MOWG
rigidus	CBcs CDoC CEnt CHEx CMHG CTri CWib ELan EPfP EPri IArd LRHS LSRN LTen MGos MRav NLar SBfd SPer SWvt
'Rose Opal'	CTrC EUJe
§ ***rugulosus***	CBcs CCCN IDee MOWG SBfd SWvt
salignus ♀H3	CBcs CCCN CDoC CDul CEnt CHEx CMac CTrC CTri EPfP GLin LRHS MHer MOWG MRav NEgg NLar SLim SPer
- Flaming Fire = 'Flaipp'	NLar
sieberi misapplied	see *C. pityoides*
§ ***sieberi*** DC.	CBcs CDoC CMHG CTrC ECou ELan EPfP IVic LRHS MMuc MOWG NBir NLar SEND SLim SPlb WFar
- purple-flowered	MOWG
§ ***speciosus***	CDul CTrC EBee IDee MOWG NLar SPlb
subulatus	CDoC CHEx CTrC EBee ECou MOWG NLar SPlb WMoo
- 'Crimson Tail'	EBee MMuc NLar SBfd SEND
I - 'Packer's Selection'	ECou MOWG
'Taree Pink'	MOWG
viminalis	CBcs CCCN MOWG SPlb
- 'Captain Cook'	CMac ECou IDee LBuc LRHS LSRN MAsh MGos MOWG NLar SBfd SRms SWvt
- 'Endeavor'	CCCN SLim
- 'Hannah Ray'	MOWG
- Hot Pink = 'Kkho1'PBR	LRHS MPkF SCoo SLim
- 'Little John'	CSBt CWSG LRHS LSRN MAsh MOWG SBfd SEND SPad SWvt
- 'Malawi Giant'	MOWG
'Violaceus'	IRar SPlb
viridiflorus	CTrC ECou IRar LRHS SEND SPlb SWal WGwG
- 'County Park Dwarf'	ECou
'White Anzac'	see *C. citrinus* 'White Anzac'

Callistephus (*Asteraceae*)

chinensis **new**	SVic

Callitriche (*Plantaginaceae*)

sp.	WSFF
§ ***palustris***	MSKA MWts
stagnalis	WMAq
verna	see *C. palustris*

Callitris (*Cupressaceae*)

rhomboidea	IGor

Calluna ✿ (*Ericaceae*)

vulgaris	SWhi WOut
- 'Aberdeen'	GHeS
- 'Adrie'	GHeS SWhi
- 'Alba Argentea'	GHeS
- 'Alba Aurea'	GHeS
- 'Alba Carlton'	GHeS
- 'Alba Dumosa'	GHeS
- 'Alba Elata'	GHeS
- 'Alba Elegans'	GHeS
- 'Alba Elongata'	see *C. vulgaris* 'Mair's Variety'
- 'Alba Erecta'	GHeS
- 'Alba Jae'	GHeS
- 'Alba Minor'	GHeS
- 'Alba Multiflora'	GHeS
- 'Alba Pilosa'	GHeS
§ - 'Alba Plena' (d)	GHeS
- 'Alba Praecox'	GHeS
- 'Alba Pumila'	GHeS
§ - 'Alba Rigida'	GHeS MAsh
- 'Alec Martin' (d)	GHeS
- 'Alex Warwick'	GHeS
- 'Alexandra'PBR (Garden Girls Series) ♀H4	GHeS IVic NHol SCoo SPoG
- 'Alice Knight'	GHeS
- 'Alicia'PBR (Garden Girls Series) ♀H4	CBcs CHab GHeS NHol SCoo SPoG SWhi
- 'Alieke'	GHeS
- 'Alina'	GHeS
- 'Alison Yates'	GHeS
- 'Allegretto'	GHeS
- 'Allegro' ♀H4	EPfP GHeS MMuc SCoo SEND SWhi
- 'Alportii'	GHeS
- 'Alportii Praecox'	GHeS
- 'Alys Sutcliffe'	GHeS
- 'Amanda Wain'	GHeS
- 'Amethyst'PBR (Garden Girls Series)	CBcs GHeS MMuc NHol SPoG SWhi
- 'Amilto'	CFst GHeS
- 'Andrew Proudley'	GHeS
- 'Anette'PBR (Garden Girls Series) ♀H4	GHeS SCoo SWhi
- 'Angela Wain'	GHeS MAsh
- 'Anna'	GHeS
- 'Annabel' (d)	GHeS
- 'Anne Dobbin'	GHeS
- 'Annegret'	see *C. vulgaris* 'Marlies'
- 'Anneke'	GHeS
- 'Annemarie' (d) ♀H4	CFst CSBt EPfP GHeS MAsh NHol SCoo SPlb SWhi
- 'Anne's Goldzwerg' **new**	CFst

Cultivar	Suppliers
- 'Anne's Zwerg'	CFst GHeS
- 'Anthony Davis' ♀H4	GHeS NHol
- 'Anthony Wain'	GHeS
- 'Anton'	GHeS
- 'Antrujo Gold'	GHeS
- 'Aphrodite'PBR (Garden Girls Series)	CHab GHeS SWhi
- 'Apollo'	GHeS
- 'Applecross' (d)	GHeS
- 'Arabella'PBR	GHeS
- 'Argentea'	GHeS
- 'Ariadne'	GHeS
- 'Arina'	GHeS MAsh SCoo
- 'Arran Gold'	GHeS
- 'Ashgarth Amber'	GHeS
- 'Ashgarth Amethyst'	GHeS
- 'Ashgarth Shell Pink'	GHeS
- 'Asterix'	GHeS
- 'Atalanta'	GHeS
- 'Atholl Gold'	GHeS
- 'August Beauty'	GHeS
- 'Aurea'	GHeS
- 'Aurora'	GHeS
- 'Autumn Glow'	GHeS
- 'Babette'	GHeS
- 'Baby Ben'	CFst GHeS
- 'Baby Wicklow'	GHeS
- 'Barbara'	GHeS
- 'Barbara Fleur'	GHeS
- 'Barja'	GHeS
- 'Barnett Anley'	GHeS
- 'Battle of Arnhem'	GHeS
- 'Bayport'	GHeS
- 'Beechwood Crimson'	GHeS
I - 'Bella Rosa'	GHeS
- 'Ben Nevis'	GHeS
- 'Bennachie Bronze'	GHeS
- 'Bennachie Prostrate'	GHeS
- 'Beoley Crimson'	GHeS MAsh SCoo
- 'Beoley Crimson Variegated' (v)	GHeS
- 'Beoley Gold' ♀H4	CSBt CTri EPfP GHeS NHol SCoo SWhi
- 'Beoley Silver'	GHeS SCoo SWhi
- 'Bernadette'	GHeS
- 'Betty Baum'	GHeS
- 'Bispingen'	GHeS
- 'Blazeaway'	CTri EPfP GHeS MAsh NHol SCoo SWhi
- 'Blueness'	GHeS
- 'Bognie'	GHeS
- 'Bonfire Brilliance'	CSBt GHeS NHol
- 'Bonita'PBR (Garden Girls Series)	CFst GHeS SWhi
- 'Bonne's Darkness'	GHeS
- 'Bonsaï'	GHeS
- 'Boreray'	GHeS
- 'Boskoop'	GHeS IVic MAsh NHol SWhi
- 'Bradford'	GHeS
- 'Braemar'	GHeS
- 'Braeriach'	GHeS
- 'Branchy Anne'	GHeS
- 'Bray Head'	GHeS
- 'Brita Elisabeth' (d)	GHeS
- 'Bronze Beauty'	GHeS
- 'Bud Lyle'	GHeS
- 'Bunsall'	GHeS
- 'Buxton Snowdrift'	GHeS
- 'C.W. Nix'	CSBt GHeS
- 'Caerketton White'	GHeS
- 'Caleb Threlkeld'	GHeS
- 'Calf of Man'	GHeS
- 'Californian Midge'	GHeS NHol
- 'Camla Variety'	GHeS
- 'Carl Röders' (d)	GHeS
- 'Carmen'	GHeS
- 'Carngold'	GHeS
- 'Carole Chapman'	GHeS
- 'Carolyn'	GHeS
- 'Cassa'	GHeS
- 'Catherine'	GHeS
- 'Catherine Anne'	GHeS
- 'Celtic Gold'	GHeS
- 'Charles Chapman'	GHeS
§ - 'Chernobyl' (d)	GHeS MAsh NHol
- 'Chindit'	GHeS
I - 'Christin'	GHeS
- 'Christina'	GHeS
- 'Cilcennin Common'	GHeS
- 'Clare Carpet'	GHeS
- 'Coby'	GHeS
- 'Coccinea'	GHeS
- 'Colette'	GHeS
- 'Con Brio'	CFst GHeS SCoo SWhi
- 'Connemara Colleen' **new**	CFst
- 'Copper Glow'	GHeS
- 'Coral Island'	GHeS
- 'Corbett's Red'	GHeS
- 'Corrie's White'	GHeS
- 'Cottswood Gold'	GHeS NHol SCoo
- 'County Wicklow' (d) ♀H4	CBcs CFst CTri EPfP GHeS MAsh MMuc NHol SBfd SCoo SEND SWhi
- 'Craig Rossie'	GHeS
- 'Crail Orange'	GHeS
- 'Cramond' (d)	GHeS
- 'Cream Steving'	GHeS
- 'Crimson Glory'	GHeS MAsh
- 'Crimson Sunset'	GHeS
- 'Crinkly Tuft'	GHeS
- 'Crowborough Beacon'	GHeS
- 'Cuprea'	EPfP GHeS MAsh NHol SBfd SCoo SWhi
- 'Dainty Bess'	GHeS
- 'Dapiali'	GHeS
- 'Dark Alicia'	GHeS
- 'Dark Beauty'PBR (d) ♀H4	CBcs CFst EPfP GHeS IVic MAsh NHol SCoo SWhi
- 'Dark Star' (d) ♀H4	CFst EPfP GHeS MAsh MMuc NHol SCoo SWhi
- 'Darkness' ♀H4	CBcs CFst CTri EPfP GHeS MAsh NHol SCoo SWhi
- 'Darleyensis'	GHeS
- 'Dart's Amethyst'	GHeS
- 'Dart's Beauty'	GHeS
- 'Dart's Brilliant'	GHeS
- 'Dart's Flamboyant'	GHeS
- 'Dart's Gold'	GHeS MAsh NHol
- 'Dart's Hedgehog'	GHeS
- 'Dart's Parakeet'	GHeS
- 'Dart's Parrot'	GHeS
- 'Dart's Silver Rocket'	GHeS
- 'Dart's Squirrel'	GHeS
- 'David Eason'	GHeS
- 'David Hagenaars'	GHeS SWhi
- 'David Hutton'	GHeS
- 'David Platt' (d)	GHeS
- 'Denkewitz'	GHeS

- 'Denny Pratt' GHeS
- 'Desiree' GHeS
- 'Devon' (d) GHeS
- 'Diana' GHeS
- 'Dickson's Blazes' GHeS
- 'Dirry' GHeS NHol
- 'Doctor Murray's White' see *C. vulgaris* 'Mullardoch'
- 'Doris Rushworth' GHeS
- 'Drum-ra' GHeS
- 'Dunnet Lime' GHeS SPlb
- 'Dunnydeer' GHeS
- 'Dunwood' GHeS

§ - 'Durford Wood' GHeS
- 'Dwingeloo Delight' GHeS
- 'E.F. Brown' GHeS
- 'E. Hoare' GHeS
- 'Easter-bonfire' GHeS NHol SCoo SWhi
- 'Eckart Miessner' GHeS
- 'Edith Godbolt' GHeS
- 'Elaine' GHeS
- 'Elegant Pearl' GHeS
- 'Elegantissima' GHeS MAsh MMuc SEND
- 'Eleonore' (d) GHeS
- 'Elkstone White' GHeS
- 'Ellen' GHeS
- 'Ellie Barbour' GHeS
- 'Elly' GHeS
- 'Else Frye' (d) GHeS
- 'Elsie Purnell' (d) ♀H4 CFst EPfP GHeS MAsh NHol SBfd SCoo SPlb
- 'Emerald Jock' GHeS
- 'Emma Louise Tuke' GHeS
- 'Eric Easton' GHeS
- 'Eskdale Gold' GHeS
- 'Eurosa' GHeS
- 'Fairy' GHeS
- 'Falling Star' GHeS
- 'Feuerwerk' GHeS SCoo

§ - 'Finale' GHeS
- 'Findling' GHeS
- 'Fire King' GHeS
- 'Fire Star' GHeS
- 'Firebreak' GHeS NHol
- 'Firefly' ♀H4 CBcs CFst CSBt EPfP GHeS MAsh MMuc NHol NWea SCoo SWhi
- 'Flamingo' GHeS MAsh MMuc NHol SCoo SEND SWhi
- 'Flatling' GHeS
- 'Flore Pleno' (d) GHeS
- 'Floriferous' GHeS
- 'Florrie Spicer' GHeS
- 'Fokko' (d) GHeS
- 'Forest Fire' **new** CFst SWhi
- 'Fort Bragg' GHeS
- 'Fortyniner Gold' GHeS
- 'Foxhollow Wanderer' GHeS
- 'Foxii' GHeS
- 'Foxii Floribunda' GHeS
- 'Foxii Lett's Form' see *C. vulgaris* 'Velvet Dome', 'Mousehole'
- 'Foxii Nana' CFst GHeS NHol SWhi
- 'Foya' GHeS
- 'Fraser's Old Gold' GHeS
- 'Fred J. Chapple' GHeS MAsh SWhi
- 'Fréjus' GHeS
- 'French Grey' GHeS
- 'Fritz Kircher'PBR GHeS
- 'Gaia' GHeS
- 'Gerda' GHeS
- 'Ginkel's Glorie' GHeS
- 'Glasa' GHeS
- 'Glen Mashie' GHeS
- 'Glencoe' (d) GHeS
- 'Glendoick Silver' GHeS
- 'Glenfiddich' CSBt GHeS MAsh NHol
- 'Glenlivet' GHeS
- 'Glenmorangie' GHeS
- 'Gloucester Boy' GHeS
- 'Gnome' GHeS
- 'Gold Charm' GHeS
- 'Gold Finch' GHeS
- 'Gold Flame' GHeS
- Gold Hamilton see *C. vulgaris* 'Chernobyl'
- 'Gold Haze' ♀H4 CTri GHeS MAsh NHol SCoo SWhi
- 'Gold Knight' EPfP GHeS MAsh SCoo
- 'Gold Kup' GHeS
- 'Gold Mist' GHeS
- 'Gold Spronk' GHeS
- 'Goldcarmen' GHeS
- 'Golden Blazeaway' GHeS
- 'Golden Carpet' CSBt GHeS MAsh NHol
- 'Golden Dew' GHeS
- 'Golden Dream' (d) GHeS
- 'Golden Feather' GHeS
- 'Golden Fleece' CFst GHeS
- 'Golden Max' GHeS
- 'Golden Rivulet' GHeS
- 'Golden Turret' GHeS MAsh NHol
- 'Golden Wonder' (d) GHeS
- 'Goldsworth Crimson' GHeS
- 'Goldsworth Crimson Variegated' (v) GHeS
- 'Goscote Wine' GHeS
- 'Grasmeriensis' GHeS
- 'Green Cardinal' GHeS
- 'Grey Carpet' CFst GHeS
- 'Grijsje' GHeS
- 'Grizabella' GHeS
- 'Grizzly' GHeS
- 'Grönsinka' GHeS
- 'Guinea Gold' GHeS MAsh

§ - 'H.E. Beale' (d) CTri EPfP GHeS NHol SCoo
- 'Hamlet Green' GHeS
- 'Hammondii' GHeS
- 'Hammondii Aureifolia' GHeS MAsh SPlb SWhi
- 'Hammondii Rubrifolia' GHeS SWhi
- 'Harlekin' GHeS
- 'Harry Gibbon' (d) GHeS
- 'Harten's Findling' GHeS
- 'Hatje's Herbstfeuer' (d) GHeS
- 'Hayesensis' GHeS
- 'Heidberg' GHeS
- 'Heidepracht' GHeS
- 'Heidesinfonie' GHeS
- 'Heideteppich' GHeS
- 'Heidezwerg' GHeS
- 'Heike' (d) GHeS
- 'Herbert Mitchell' GHeS
- 'Hester' GHeS
- 'Hetty' GHeS
- 'Hibernica' GHeS
- 'Hiemalis' GHeS
- 'Hiemalis Southcote' see *C. vulgaris* 'Durford Wood'
- Highland Cream see *C. vulgaris* 'Punch's Dessert'
- 'Highland Rose' GHeS SPlb
- 'Highland Spring' GHeS

	- 'Hilda Turberfield'	GHeS
	- 'Hillbrook Limelight'	GHeS
	- 'Hillbrook Orange'	GHeS
	- 'Hillbrook Sparkler'	GHeS
	- 'Hinton White'	GHeS
	- 'Hirsuta Albiflora'	GHeS
	- 'Hirsuta Typica'	GHeS
	- 'Hollandia'	GHeS
	- 'Holstein'	GHeS
	- 'Hookstone'	GHeS
	- 'Hoyerhagen'	GHeS
§	- 'Hugh Nicholson'	GHeS
	- 'Humpty Dumpty'	GHeS NHol
	- 'Hypnoides'	GHeS
	- 'Ide's Double' (d)	GHeS
	- 'Inchcolm'	GHeS
	- 'Inchkeith'	GHeS
	- 'Ineke'	GHeS
	- 'Inge'	GHeS
	- 'Ingrid Bouter' (d)	GHeS
	- 'Inshriach Bronze'	GHeS
	- 'Iris van Leyen'	GHeS
	- 'Islay Mist'	GHeS
	- 'Isle of Hirta'	GHeS
	- 'Isobel Frye'	GHeS
	- 'Isobel Hughes' (d)	GHeS
	- 'J.H. Hamilton' (d) ♀H4	CTri GHeS MAsh NHol SCoo SWhi
	- 'Jan'	GHeS
	- 'Jan Dekker'	GHeS MAsh NHol SWhi
	- 'Janice Chapman'	GHeS
	- 'Japanese White'	GHeS
	- 'Jenny'	GHeS
	- 'Jill'	GHeS
	- 'Jimmy Dyce' (d)	GHeS
	- 'Joan Sparkes' (d)	GHeS
	- 'Jochen'	GHeS
	- 'Johan Slegers'	GHeS
	- John Denver	see *C. vulgaris* 'Marleen Select'
	- 'John F. Letts'	GHeS NHol
	- 'Johnson's Variety'	GHeS SCoo
	- 'Jos' Lemon'	GHeS
	- 'Jos' Whitie'	GHeS
	- 'Josefine'	GHeS SWhi
	- 'Joseph's Coat'	GHeS
	- 'Joy Vanstone' ♀H4	CFst EPfP GHeS MAsh NHol
	- 'Julia'	GHeS
	- 'Julie Ann Platt'	GHeS
	- 'Juno'	GHeS
	- 'Kaiser'	GHeS
	- 'Karin Blum'	GHeS
	- 'Kermit'	GHeS
	- 'Kerstin' ♀H4	CFst GHeS NHol SCoo SPlb SWhi
	- 'Kerstin Jacke'	NHol
	- 'Kinlochruel' (d) ♀H4	CBcs CFst CSBt CTri EPfP GHeS MAsh MMuc NHol SEND SPlb SWhi
	- 'Kir Royal'	GHeS
	- 'Kirby White'	GHeS MAsh NHol SPlb SWhi
	- 'Kirsty Anderson'	GHeS
	- 'Kit Hill'	GHeS
	- 'Klaudine' PBR	CFst IVic
	- 'Knaphill'	GHeS
I	- 'Kontrast'	GHeS
	- 'Kuphaldtii'	GHeS
	- 'Kuppendorf'	GHeS
	- 'Kynance'	GHeS
	- 'Lady Maithe'	GHeS
	- 'Lambstails'	GHeS
	- 'L'Ancresse'	GHeS
	- 'Larissa' PBR (Garden Girls Series)	GHeS
	- 'Lemon Gem'	GHeS
	- 'Lemon Queen'	CFst GHeS
	- 'Leprechaun'	NHol SWhi
	- 'Leslie Slinger'	GHeS NHol SCoo SWhi
	- 'Lewis Lilac'	GHeS
	- 'Liebestraum'	GHeS
	- 'Lilac Elegance'	GHeS
	- 'Lime Glade'	GHeS
	- 'Lime Gold'	GHeS
	- 'Little John'	GHeS LSRN
	- 'Llanbedrog Pride' (d)	GHeS
	- 'Loch Turret'	GHeS
	- 'Loch-na-Seil'	GHeS
	- 'Long White'	CFst GHeS SWhi
	- 'Loni'	GHeS
	- 'Lüneberg Heath'	GHeS
	- 'Lyle's Late White'	GHeS
	- 'Lyle's Surprise'	GHeS
	- 'Lyndon Proudley'	GHeS
	- 'Macdonald of Glencoe'	GHeS
	- 'Madonna' PBR **new**	CFst SWhi
§	- 'Mair's Variety' ♀H4	GHeS SBfd SCoo
	- 'Mallard'	GHeS
	- 'Manitoba'	GHeS
	- 'Manuel'	GHeS
	- 'Marianne'	GHeS
	- 'Marie'	GHeS
	- 'Marion Blum'	GHeS
	- 'Marleen'	GHeS MAsh NHol SWhi
§	- 'Marleen Select'	GHeS
§	- 'Marlies'	GHeS SWhi
	- 'Martha Hermann'	GHeS
	- 'Martine Langenberg'	GHeS
	- 'Masquerade'	GHeS
	- 'Matita'	GHeS
	- 'Mauvelyn'	GHeS
	- 'Mazurka'	GHeS
	- 'Melanie' (Garden Girls Series)	GHeS MAsh NHol SCoo SWhi
	- 'Mick Jamieson' (d)	GHeS
	- 'Mies'	GHeS
	- 'Minima'	GHeS
	- 'Minima Smith's Variety'	GHeS
	- 'Miniöxabäck'	GHeS
	- 'Minty'	GHeS
	- 'Mirato'	GHeS
	- 'Mirelle'	GHeS
	- 'Miss Muffet'	GHeS NHol
	- 'Molecule'	GHeS
	- 'Monika' (d)	GHeS
	- 'Moon Glow'	GHeS
	- 'Mountain Snow'	GHeS
§	- 'Mousehole'	GHeS NHol
	- 'Mrs Alf'	GHeS
	- 'Mrs E. Wilson' (d)	GHeS
	- 'Mrs Pat'	GHeS MAsh NHol
	- 'Mrs Pinxteren'	GHeS
	- 'Mrs Ronald Gray'	GHeS
	- 'Mullach Mor'	GHeS
§	- 'Mullardoch'	GHeS
	- 'Mullion' ♀H4	GHeS
	- 'Multicolor'	GHeS MAsh NHol
	- 'Murielle Dobson'	GHeS
§	- 'My Dream' (d) ♀H4	CSBt EPfP GHeS NHol SCoo
	- 'Nana'	GHeS
	- 'Nana Compacta'	GHeS

	- 'Natasja'	GHeS
	- 'Naturpark'	GHeS
	- 'Nele' (d)	GHeS
	- 'Nico'	GHeS
	- 'Nofretete'	GHeS
	- Nordlicht	see *C. vulgaris* 'Skone'
	- 'October White'	GHeS
	- 'Odette'	GHeS
	- 'Oiseval'	GHeS
	- 'Old Rose'	GHeS
	- 'Olive Turner'	GHeS
	- 'Olympic Gold'	GHeS
	- 'Orange and Gold'	GHeS
	- 'Orange Carpet'	GHeS
	- 'Orange Max'	GHeS NHol
	- 'Orange Queen'	CSBt GHeS
	- 'Öxabäck'	GHeS
	- 'Oxshott Common'	GHeS
	- 'Pallida'	GHeS
	- 'Parsons' Gold'	GHeS
	- 'Parsons' Grey Selected'	GHeS
	- 'Pastell' (d)	GHeS
	- 'Pat's Gold'	GHeS
	- 'Peace'	GHeS
	- 'Pearl Drop'	GHeS
	- 'Peggy'	GHeS
	- 'Penhale'	GHeS
	- 'Penny Bun'	GHeS
	- 'Pennyacre Gold'	GHeS
	- 'Pennyacre Lemon'	GHeS
	- 'Pepper and Salt'	see *C. vulgaris* 'Hugh Nicholson'
	- 'Perestrojka'	GHeS
	- 'Peter Sparkes' (d) ♀H4	CBcs CFst CHab CSBt EPfP GHeS MAsh MMuc NHol SCoo SEND SWhi
	- 'Petra'	GHeS
	- 'Pewter Plate'	GHeS
	- 'Pink Alicia' PBR (Garden Girls Series)	GHeS
	- 'Pink Beale'	see *C. vulgaris* 'H.E. Beale'
	- 'Pink Dream' (d)	GHeS
	- 'Pink Gown'	GHeS
	- 'Pink Spreader'	GHeS
	- 'Pink Tips'	GHeS
	- 'Plantarium'	GHeS
	- 'Platt's Surprise' (d)	GHeS
	- 'Polly'	GHeS
	- 'Poolster'	GHeS
	- 'Porth Wen White'	GHeS
	- 'Prizewinner'	GHeS
*	- 'Procumbens'	GHeS
	- 'Prostrata Flagelliformis'	GHeS
	- 'Prostrate Orange'	GHeS MAsh
§	- 'Punch's Dessert'	GHeS
	- 'Purple Passion'	EPfP SBfd SCoo
	- 'Pygmaea'	GHeS
	- 'Pyramidalis'	GHeS
	- 'Pyrenaica'	GHeS
	- 'R.A. McEwan'	GHeS
	- 'Radnor' (d) ♀H4	CSBt GHeS MAsh
	- 'Radnor Gold' (d)	GHeS
	- 'Raket'	GHeS
	- 'Ralph Purnell'	GHeS SBfd SCoo
	- 'Ralph Purnell Select'	GHeS
	- 'Ralph's Pearl'	GHeS
	- 'Ralph's Red'	GHeS
	- 'Randall's Crimson'	GHeS
	- 'Rannoch'	GHeS
	- 'Rebecca's Red'	GHeS
	- 'Red Beauty' **new**	CFst SWhi
	- 'Red Carpet'	GHeS
	- 'Red Favorit' (d)	CFst GHeS SWhi
	- 'Red Fred'	GHeS NHol SCoo
	- 'Red Haze'	EPfP GHeS NHol SCoo
	- 'Red Max'	GHeS
	- 'Red Pimpernel'	EPfP GHeS NHol SBfd SCoo SWhi
	- 'Red Rug'	GHeS
	- 'Red Star' (d)	CBcs GHeS MAsh NHol
	- 'Red Wings'	GHeS
	- 'Redbud'	GHeS
	- 'Redgauntlet'	GHeS
	- 'Reini'	GHeS SWhi
	- 'Rica'	GHeS
	- 'Richard Cooper'	GHeS
	- 'Rieanne'	GHeS
	- 'Rigida Prostrata'	see *C. vulgaris* 'Alba Rigida'
	- 'Rivington'	GHeS
	- 'Robber Knight'	GHeS
	- 'Robert Chapman' ♀H4	CFst CSBt CTri GHeS MAsh NHol SWhi
I	- 'Rock Spray'	GHeS
	- 'Röding'	GHeS
	- 'Rokoko'	GHeS
	- 'Roland Haagen' ♀H4	GHeS
	- 'Roma'	GHeS
	- 'Romina'	GHeS NHol
	- 'Ronas Hill'	CFst GHeS
	- 'Roodkapje'	GHeS
	- 'Rosalind' ambig.	EPfP
	- 'Rosalind, Crastock Heath'	GHeS
	- 'Rosalind, Underwood's'	EPfP GHeS NHol
	- 'Ross Hutton'	GHeS
	- 'Roswitha'	CFst GHeS
	- 'Roter Oktober'	GHeS SWhi
	- 'Rotfuchs'	GHeS
	- 'Ruby Slinger'	GHeS NHol SWhi
	- 'Rusty Triumph'	GHeS
	- 'Ruth Sparkes' (d)	GHeS NHol
	- 'Sabrina' (d)	GHeS
	- 'Saima'	GHeS
	- 'Saint Nick'	GHeS
	- 'Salland'	GHeS
	- 'Sally Anne Proudley'	GHeS
	- 'Salmon Leap'	GHeS NHol
	- 'Sam Hewitt'	GHeS
	- 'Sampford Sunset'	GHeS
	- 'Sandhammaren'	GHeS
	- 'Sandwood Bay'	GHeS
	- 'Sandy' PBR (Garden Girls Series)	CFst GHeS NHol SPoG SWhi
	- 'Sarah Platt' (d)	GHeS
	- 'Saskia'	GHeS
	- 'Schneewolke'	GHeS
	- 'Scholje's Jimmy'	GHeS
	- 'Scholje's Rubin' (d)	GHeS
	- 'Scholje's Super Star' (d)	GHeS
	- 'Schurig's Sensation' (d)	GHeS IVic
	- 'Schurig's Wonder' (d)	GHeS
	- 'Scotch Mist'	GHeS
	- 'Sedloňov'	GHeS
	- 'Sellingsloh'	GHeS
	- 'September Pink'	GHeS
	- 'Serlei'	GHeS
	- 'Serlei Aurea' ♀H4	CSBt EPfP GHeS MAsh NHol
	- 'Serlei Grandiflora'	GHeS
	- 'Serlei Purpurea'	GHeS
	- 'Serlei Rubra'	GHeS

	- 'Sesam'	GHeS
	- 'Sesse'	GHeS
	- 'Shirley'	GHeS MAsh
	- 'Silberspargel'	GHeS
	- 'Silver Cloud'	GHeS
	- 'Silver Fox'	CFst GHeS
	- 'Silver King'	GHeS
	- 'Silver Knight'	CSBt EPfP GHeS MAsh NHol SCoo SPlb SWhi
	- 'Silver Pearl'	GHeS
	- 'Silver Queen' ♀H4	CFst GHeS MAsh NHol SWhi
	- 'Silver Rose' ♀H4	GHeS
	- 'Silver Sandra'	GHeS
	- 'Silver Spire'	GHeS
	- 'Silver Stream'	GHeS
	- 'Silvie'	GHeS
	- 'Simone'	GHeS
	- 'Sir Anthony Hopkins'	GHeS
	- 'Sir John Charrington' ♀H4	CSBt EPfP GHeS MAsh NHol SWhi
	- 'Sirsson'	GHeS
	- 'Sister Anne' ♀H4	CFst CSBt EPfP GHeS MAsh MMuc NHol SCoo SWhi
	- 'Skipper'	GHeS NHol
§	- 'Skone' (v)	GHeS
	- 'Snowball'	see *C. vulgaris* 'My Dream'
	- 'Snowflake'	GHeS
	- 'Soay'	GHeS
	- 'Sonja' (d)	GHeS IVic
	- 'Sonning' (d)	GHeS
	- 'Sonny Boy'	GHeS
	- 'Sophia' (d)	GHeS
	- 'Sparkling Stars'	GHeS NHol
	- 'Sphinx'	GHeS
	- 'Spicata'	GHeS
	- 'Spicata Aurea'	GHeS
	- 'Spicata Nana'	GHeS
	- 'Spider'	GHeS
	- 'Spitfire'	GHeS MAsh NHol
	- 'Spook'	GHeS
	- 'Spring Cream' ♀H4	CFst GHeS MAsh MMuc NHol SCoo SPoG SWhi
	- 'Spring Glow'	GHeS
	- 'Spring Torch'	CFst CSBt GHeS MAsh NHol SCoo SPoG SWhi
	- 'Springbank'	GHeS
	- 'Stag's Horn'	GHeS
I	- 'Startler'	GHeS
	- 'Stefanie'	GHeS NHol SWhi
	- 'Stranger'	GHeS
	- 'Strawberry Delight' (d)	EPfP GHeS SBfd SCoo
	- 'Summer Elegance'	GHeS
	- 'Summer Orange'	GHeS NHol
	- 'Summer White' (d)	GHeS
	- 'Sunningdale'	see *C. vulgaris* 'Finale'
	- 'Sunrise'	EPfP GHeS
	- 'Sunset' ♀H4	CFst GHeS MAsh SWhi
	- 'Sunset Glow'	GHeS
	- 'Talisker'	GHeS
	- 'Tenella'	GHeS
	- 'Tenuis'	GHeS
	- 'Terrick's Orange'	GHeS
	- 'The Pygmy'	GHeS
	- 'Theresa' (Garden Girls Series)	CFst GHeS
	- 'Tib' (d) ♀H4	CFst CSBt GHeS MAsh NHol SWhi
	- 'Tijdens Copper'	GHeS
	- 'Tino'	GHeS
	- 'Tom Thumb'	GHeS
	- 'Tomentosa Alba'	GHeS
	- 'Torogay'	GHeS
	- 'Torulosa'	GHeS
	- 'Tremans'	GHeS
	- 'Tricolorifolia'	EPfP GHeS MAsh NHol SCoo SWhi
	- 'Underwoodii'	GHeS
	- 'Unity'	GHeS
	- 'Valorian'	GHeS
	- 'Van Beek'	GHeS
§	- 'Velvet Dome'	GHeS
	- 'Velvet Fascination' ♀H4	EPfP GHeS NHol SBfd SCoo SWhi
	- 'Violet Bamford'	GHeS
	- 'Visser's Fancy'	GHeS
	- 'Walter Ingwersen'	GHeS
	- 'Waquoit Brightness'	GHeS
	- 'Westerlee Gold'	GHeS
	- 'Westerlee Green'	GHeS
	- 'Westphalia'	GHeS
	- 'White Bouquet'	see *C. vulgaris* 'Alba Plena'
	- 'White Carpet'	GHeS
	- 'White Coral' (d)	EPfP GHeS IVic SCoo
	- 'White Gold'	GHeS
	- 'White Gown'	GHeS
	- 'White Lawn' ♀H4	CFst GHeS MAsh MMuc NHol SWhi
	- 'White Mite'	GHeS
	- 'White Pearl' (d)	GHeS
	- 'White Princess'	see *C. vulgaris* 'White Queen'
§	- 'White Queen'	GHeS
	- 'White Star' (d)	GHeS
	- 'Whiteness'	GHeS
	- 'Wickwar Flame' ♀H4	CBcs CFst CHab CSBt EPfP GHeS MMuc NHol SCoo SPlb SWhi
	- 'Wilma'	GHeS
	- 'Wingates Gem'	GHeS
	- 'Wingates Gold'	GHeS
	- 'Winter Chocolate'	CSBt EPfP GHeS MAsh NHol SCoo SWhi
	- 'Winter Fire'	GHeS
	- 'Winter Red'	GHeS
	- 'Wollmer's Weisse' (d)	GHeS
	- 'Wood Close'	GHeS
	- 'Yellow Basket'	GHeS
	- 'Yellow Beauty'[PBR]	GHeS
	- 'Yellow Globe'	GHeS
	- 'Yellow One'	GHeS
	- 'Yvette's Gold'	CFst GHeS
	- 'Yvette's Silver'	CFst GHeS
	- 'Yvonne Clare'	GHeS

Calocedrus (*Cupressaceae*)

§	***decurrens*** ♀H4	CBcs CDoC CDul CLnd CMac CMen CTho EHul EPfP LRHS MBlu MGos NPCo NWea SBfd SLim SPer SPoG WEve
	- 'Aureovariegata' (v)	CBcs CWib EHul LRHS MBlu MBri NLar SCoo SPoG WEve
	- 'Berrima Gold'	CDoC CKen LRHS MGos NLar SLim SPoG WEve
	- 'Columnaris'	LMaj
§	- 'Depressa'	CKen
	- 'Intricata'	CKen NLar SLim
	- 'Maupin Glow' (v)	NLar SLim
	- 'Nana'	see *C. decurrens* 'Depressa'
	- 'Pillar'	CKen NLar

Calocephalus (*Asteraceae*)

	brownii	see *Leucophyta brownii*
	'Silver Sand'	LAst LSou

Calochortus (*Liliaceae*)

albus ECho
- var. ***rubellus*** ECho
aureus **new** ECho
caeruleus ECho
'Cupido'[PBR] CPLG ECho GKev LAma
invenustus ECho
luteus Douglas ex Lindl. EPot
- 'Golden Orb'[PBR] CGrW CPLG ECho GKev LAma SDeJ
splendens LAma
- 'Violet Queen' CGrW ECho GKev LAma
superbus ECho EPot GKev SDeJ
'Symphony'[PBR] CPLG ECho EPot GKev LAma SDeJ
venustus CGrW ECho EPot GKev LAma SDeJ

Calomeria (*Asteraceae*)

§ ***amaranthoides*** WJek

Calonyction see *Ipomoea*

Calopogon (*Orchidaceae*)

tuberosus NLAp

Caloscordum (*Alliaceae*)

§ ***neriniflorum*** WAbe

Calothamnus (*Myrtaceae*)

quadrifidus ECou
- yellow-flowered MOWG
validus SPlb

Calotropis (*Apocynaceae*)

procera **new** SPlb

Calpurnia (*Papilionaceae*)

aurea SPlb

Caltha ✿ (*Ranunculaceae*)

howellii see *C. leptosepala* subsp. *howellii*
introloba SWat
laeta see *C. palustris* var. *palustris*
leptosepala CLAP CRow EBee EWTr EWay GEdr LLHF NLar
§ - subsp. ***howellii*** NNS 02-92 GKev
- - NNS 07-87 GKev
natans EWay
palustris 🏆H4 Widely available
- var. ***alba*** Widely available
- 'Auenwald' CDes CLAP CRow EBee
- var. ***barthei*** GEdr
- - f. ***atrorubra*** GEdr
- 'Flore Pleno' (d) 🏆H4 Widely available
- 'Honeydew' CDes CLAP CRow EWay LRHS WSHC
- 'Marilyn' CLAP
- 'Multiplex' (d) EBee ECtt GBuc GKev SRot
§ - var. ***palustris*** CBen CBre CRow ECha EHon ELan EWay LPBA SWat WFar
- - 'Plena' (d) CRow CWat EPfP EWay LRHS MCot MSKA SPoG WFar
- var. ***radicans*** CRow GEdr
- - 'Flore Pleno' (d) CRow
- 'Stagnalis' CRow MSKA MWts
- 'Yellow Giant' MSKA
N ***polypetala*** misapplied see *C. palustris* var. *palustris*
N ***polypetala*** Hochst. ex Lorent CCon CWat EBee EWll GCal MSCN MSKA NPer SMad SWat WMAq
sagittata WSHC

Calycanthus (*Calycanthaceae*)

fertilis see *C. floridus* var. *glaucus*
floridus CAgr CArn CBcs CDul CJun CMCN CPom CTri CWib EBee ELan EPfP EWTr IDee LAst LEdu LRHS MBNS MBlu MBri MMuc NLar SEND SPer SPlb SPoG SSpi WCFE WSHC
- 'Athens' CBcs CJun NLar
§ - var. ***glaucus*** EPfP LRHS MAsh MGos NLar SHil WSHC
- - 'Purpureus' CBcs CJun MBlu MBri NLar
- var. ***laevigatus*** see *C. floridus* var. *glaucus*
- 'Michael Lindsay' CJun MBri NLar
mohrii **new** NLar
occidentalis CAgr CArn CBcs CDul CMCN CSpe CWib EBee EPPr MBlu MMuc SEND SGar SSpi WCFE

Calystegia (*Convolvulaceae*)

'Angel's Trumpets' SKHP
§ ***hederacea*** 'Flore Pleno' (d) SMad WCot
japonica 'Flore Pleno' see *C. hederacea* 'Flore Pleno'
soldanella NNS 99-85 WCot

Calytrix (*Myrtaceae*)

tetragona SPlb

Camassia ✿ (*Asparagaceae*)

biflora F&W 8669 EBee
'Blue Heaven' **new** EBee ERCP SDeJ
cusickii Widely available
- white-flowered IFoB
- 'Zwanenburg' CTca EBee ERCP GKev NRHS WCot
esculenta Lindl. see *C. quamash*
leichtlinii misapplied see *C. leichtlinii* subsp. *suksdorfii*
N - 'Alba' hort. see *C. leichtlinii* subsp. *leichtlinii*
* ***leichtlinii*** (Baker) S.Watson 'Alba Plena' MNrw MWat NBir
I - 'Atrocaerulea' **new** STes
- 'Blue Wave' ERCP NHol NWad SBch
§ - subsp. ***leichtlinii*** 🏆H4 Widely available
- 'Magdalen' CAvo
N - 'Plena' (d) ECha
- 'Sacajawea' CAvo CMea CTca EBee ECtt ERCP LRHS SBch SDeJ
- 'Semiplena' (d) CAvo CBro CMea CRDP CTca EBee ECtt ERCP IPot LRHS MBel MCot MNrw NSti SDix SPhx WAul WCot WHoo WShi
- 'Sky Blue' CMea EBee LRHS
§ - subsp. ***suksdorfii*** CSam EBee GCra WCot
- - 'Alba' LRHS
- - Caerulea Group Widely available
- - 'Electra' CAvo ECha SMHy SUsu
- - 'Lady Eve Price' SMHy
§ ***quamash*** CArn CAvo CBro CTca CWCL EBee ECha EPfP EPot ERCP GKev ITim LAma LEdu LRHS MBel MBri MCot NBir NCGa NMen NRHS SDeJ SGar SRms WShi XLum
- 'Blue Melody' (v) CAvo CBro CSam CTca EBee ECtt EPot ERCP GKev GMaP LEdu LRHS NMRc NMen SDeJ WRHF
- subsp. ***maxima*** NNS 06-119 **new** GKev

- 'Orion' CBro EBee GKev WAul WCot

Camellia ✿ (*Theaceae*)

'Adorable' (*pitardii* hybrid) LRHS LSRN
'Alpen Glo' MPkF
'Annette Carol' CDoC
'April Blush' SCog
'Ariel's Song' CDoC
'Auburn White' see *C. japonica* 'Mrs Bertha A. Harms'
'Baby Bear' CDoC MPkF SCam
'Barbara Clark' (*saluenensis* × *reticulata*) CDoC LRHS LSRN MGos SCog SCoo
'Bertha Harms Blush' see *C. japonica* 'Mrs Bertha A. Harms'
'Bett's Supreme' CDoC
'Black Lace' ♀H4 CTrh CTri EPfP LBuc LRHS LSRN MAsh MBri MMuc NLar SCam SCog SCoo SEND SHil WGob
'Blissful Dawn' CBcs
'Bonnie Marie' CDoC MGos SCam SCog
'Canterbury' CDoC
'Champêtres Spring Awakening' MPkF
'China Lady' (*granthamiana* × *reticulata*) SCam
'Cinnamon Cindy' CDoC LRHS SCog
'Cinnamon Sensation' SCog
'Confucius' (*reticulata* hybrid) SCam
'Congratulations' CSBt LBuc LSRN
'Contessa Lavinia Maggi' see *C. japonica* 'Lavinia Maggi'
'Cornish Snow' (*cuspidata* × *saluenensis*) ♀H4 CBcs CDoC CSBt CTri ELan EPfP MGos SCam SCog SPer SSpi
'Cornish Spring' (*cuspidata* × *japonica*) ♀H4 CCCN CDoC CSBt CTrh CTsd ELan EPfP LRHS MAsh MGos SCam SCog
'Crimson Candles' LRHS MPkF SCam
cuspidata SCam SCog
'Dainty Dale' CDoC SCam
'Delia Williams' see *C.* × *williamsii* 'Citation'
'Den Burton' (*japonica* × *reticulata*) SCam
'Diamond Head' (*japonica* × *reticulata*) CBcs
'Diana's Charm' CDoC LSRN
'Doctor Clifford Parks' (*japonica* × *reticulata*) ♀H2 CDoC SCam SCog
'Donckelaeri' see *C. japonica* 'Masayoshi'
edithae LRHS
'El Dorado' (*pitardii* × *japonica*) CDoC
'Elizabeth Bolitho' SCam
'Extravaganza' (*japonica* hybrid) CBcs CTrh IArd SCam SCog
'Fairy Blush' CDoC MPkF
'Fairy Wand' CDoC MPkF
'Felice Harris' (*reticulata* × *sasanqua*) CDoC SCam SCog
'Festival of Lights' **new** MPkF
'Fiesta Grande' SCam
'Fire 'n' Ice' CDoC SCam
forrestii NLar
'Forty-niner' (*reticulata* × *japonica*) CBcs
'Fox's Fancy' CDoC
'Fragrant Pink' (*japonica* subsp. *rusticana* × *lutchuensis*) CTrh SCam
'Francie L' (*reticulata* × *saluenensis*) ♀H3-4 CDoC CDul EPfP SCam SCog SSta
'Frau Minna Seidel' see *C. japonica* subsp. *rusticana* 'Otome'
'Free Spirit' **new** CTrh
'Freedom Bell' ♀H4 CDoC CMHG CTrh EPfP GKin LRHS MAsh MPkF SCam SCog SCoo
'Gael's Dream' (*reticulata* hybrid) SCam
'Gay Baby' CDoC
'Golden Anniversary' see *C. japonica* 'Dahlohnega'
grijsii CPLG CTrh SCam
handelii CPLG
'Happy Anniversary' CSBt LBuc LSRN
§ ***hiemalis*** 'Bonanza' MPkF SCam
- 'Chansonette' CDoC ELon SCam SCog
§ - 'Dazzler' CBcs SCam SCog
- 'Interlude' MPkF
- 'Kanjirō' CDoC SCam
- 'Shōwa-no-sakae' CDoC LRHS MPkF SCog
§ - 'Sparkling Burgundy' ♀H3 CBcs CDoC ELon EPfP LRHS MGos NPri SCam SCog SMDP
'High Fragrance' LRHS MPkF
'Hooker' CDoC
'Ice Follies' SCam
'Imbricata Rubra' see *C. japonica* 'Imbricata'
'Inspiration' (*reticulata* × *saluenensis*) ♀H4 CDoC CMac CSam CTrh CWSG EPfP GKin LSRN MBri MGos NLar SCam SCog SPer SSpi
'Invitation' NHim
japonica CBcs MWat SEWo
- 'Aaron's Ruby' CDoC ELon LRHS SCog
- 'Ada Pieper' CTrh
- 'Adelina Patti' ♀H4 CBcs CDoC CMHG CTrh ELon SCam SCog
- 'Adolphe Audusson' ♀H4 Widely available
- 'Adolphe Audusson Special' LSRN
§ - 'Akashigata' ♀H4 CBcs CDoC CMac ELon EPfP LRHS LSRN MGos SCam SCog SLim SPer SPoG SSta
- 'Alba Plena' ♀H4 CTrh MGos SCog SPer WFar
- 'Alba Simplex' CDoC CMac CTrh ELan EPfP IVic MGos SCam SCog SPer SSta
- 'Alexander Hunter' ♀H4 CDoC LRHS SCog
- 'Alison Leigh Woodroof' CDoC
§ - 'Althaeiflora' CBcs CDoC ELon LRHS MGos SCam SCog
- 'Amazing Graces' CDoC
- 'Anemoniflora' CDoC ELan EPfP LRHS SCam SCog WFar
- 'Angel' LSRN SCam WBor
- 'Angello' CWSG WGob
- 'Ann Sothern' CBcs
- 'Annette Gehry' CBcs
- 'Annie Wylam' ♀H4 CTrh SCog
- 'Apollo' ambig. CBcs CDoC LRHS MBri MGos NPri WGob
§ - 'Apollo' Paul, 1911 MGos MSwo SCam SCog
§ - 'Apple Blossom' ♀H4 CBcs ELan
- 'Arajishi' misapplied see *C. japonica* subsp. *rusticana*
* - 'Augustine Supreme' CMac
- 'Australis' ♀H4 SCam
- 'Ave Maria' ♀H4 CDoC CTrh MAsh
- 'Baby Pearl' LSRN SCam
- 'Baby Sis' CDoC LRHS
- 'Ballet Dancer' ♀H4 CDoC ELon LSRN MGos SCam SCog

	Cultivar	Suppliers
	– 'Bambino'	CDoC
	– 'Barbara Woodroof'	CBcs
	– 'Baron Gomer'	see *C. japonica* 'Comte de Gomer'
	– 'Baronne Leguay'	SCam
	– 'Beau Harp'	CDoC LRHS SCam
	– 'Bella Romana'	SCam
	– 'Benten-kagura' (v)	CDoC
§	– 'Berenice Boddy' ♀H4	CDoC LRHS
	– 'Berenice Perfection'	CDoC SCog
	– 'Betty Foy Sanders'	CTrh
	– 'Betty Robinson'	CDoC LRHS
	– 'Betty Sheffield'	CDoC MAsh MGos SCog
	– 'Betty Sheffield Pink'	LRHS SCam
	– 'Betty Sheffield Supreme'	CBcs
	– 'Betty's Beauty'	LRHS
	– 'Billie McCaskill'	SCam
	– 'Black Magic'	CTrh
	– 'Black Tie'	CDoC ELan ELon EUJe LRHS MAsh MGos SCam SCog
	– 'Blackburnia'	see *C. japonica* 'Althaeiflora'
	– 'Blaze of Glory'	SCog
§	– 'Blood of China'	CBcs CDoC CSBt ELan LBuc LRHS LSRN MBri MGos MMuc SCam SCog SCoo SEND SHil SPer WFar WGob WMoo
	– 'Bob Hope' ♀H4	CBcs CDoC CTrh CTri LRHS MAsh MGos
	– 'Bob's Tinsie' ♀H4	CDoC CMHG CSBt CTrh EPfP LRHS LSRN MAsh MPkF NLar
§	– 'Bokuhan' ♀H4	CDoC MPkF
	– 'Bright Buoy'	CDoC
	– 'Brushfield's Yellow' ♀H4	CBcs CDoC CMHG CSBt CWSG ELan ELon EPfP IArd LMil LRHS LSRN MAsh MBri MGos NEgg NHim NLar SBfd SCam SCog SCoo SPer SSta WFar WGob
	– 'Bush Hill Beauty'	see *C. japonica* 'Lady de Saumarez'
§	– 'C.M. Hovey' ♀H4	CMHG CMac LRHS MAsh
	– 'C.M. Wilson'	CDoC CMac SCog
	– 'Campsii Alba'	CDoC CTsd
	– 'Can Can'	CDoC ELon SCam SCog
	– 'Candy Apple'	CTrh
	– 'Candy Stripe'	CDoC SCam
	– 'Captain Blood'	CDoC
	– 'Cara Mia'	CBcs CDoC CTsd SCam
	– 'Carter's Sunburst' ♀H4	CBcs CDoC ELan EPfP SCog
	– 'Cassandra'	EPfP LRHS SHil
	– 'Chandleri Elegans'	see *C. japonica* 'Elegans'
	– 'Charlotte de Rothschild'	CTrh CTri EPfP
	– 'Cheryll Lynn'	CDoC
	– 'Christmas Beauty'	SCam
	– 'Cinderella'	CDoC SCog SSta
	– 'Clarke Hubbs'	CDoC
	– Classique = 'Kerguelen'PBR	LRHS MPkF
	– 'Colonel Firey'	see *C. japonica* 'C.M. Hovey'
	– 'Commander Mulroy' ♀H4	CDoC CTrh SCam
§	– 'Comte de Gomer'	CDoC ELan ELon EPfP LRHS MBri NPri SCog
	– 'Conspicua'	CBcs
	– 'Contessa Samailoff'	CDoC
§	– 'Coquettii' ♀H4	CBcs CDul LRHS MAsh SCam
	– 'Coral Pink Lotus'	CDoC
	– 'Coral Queen'	CDoC SCam
	– 'Cornish Excellence'	CDoC SCam
	– 'Curly Lady'PBR	MPkF NPri WMoo
§	– 'Dahlohnega'	CDoC CSBt CTrh ELon LBuc LRHS LSRN MAsh MPkF SCam
	– 'Daikagura'	CBcs CDoC
	– 'Dainty'	CBcs
	– 'Daitairin'	see *C. japonica* 'Dewatairin'
	– 'Dark of the Moon'	CDoC
	– 'Dear Jenny'	CBcs
	– 'Debutante'	CBcs CDoC CMac ELon MAsh SCam SCog
	– 'Deep Secret' ♀H4	CDoC SCog
	– 'Desire' ♀H4	CBcs CDoC CMHG CSBt CTrh CTsd CWSG EPfP GEdr LRHS LSRN MAsh MPkF SBfd SCam SCog SCoo SPoG WGob
	– 'Devonia'	CBcs SCog
§	– 'Dewatairin' (Higo)	CBcs CDoC MGos SCam SCog
	– 'Dixie Knight'	CBcs CDoC LRHS MGos SCam SCog
	– 'Dobreei'	CMac
	– 'Doctor Burnside'	CDoC CTrh LRHS SCam SCog
	– 'Doctor King'	GEdr
	– 'Doctor Tinsley' ♀H4	CDoC LRHS MAsh NPri SCoo
	– 'Dolly Dyer'	CDoC MPkF
	– 'Dona Herzilia de Freitas Magalhaes'	CDoC ELon SCam SCog
	– 'Dona Jane Andresson'	SCam
	– 'Donckelaeri'	see *C. japonica* 'Masayoshi'
	– 'Donnan's Dream'	CTrh
	– 'Drama Girl' ♀H2	CBcs CDoC EPfP MGos SBod SCam SCog
	– 'Dream Time'	CBcs
	– 'Duc de Bretagne'	SCog
	– 'Ed Combatalade'	CDoC
	– 'Edelweiss'	CDoC MGos SCam SCog
	– 'Effendee'	see *C. sasanqua* 'Rosea Plena'
	– 'Eleanor Hagood'	CBcs
§	– 'Elegans' ♀H4	CBcs CDoC ELon EPfP LMil LRHS NEgg SBfd SCam SCog SCoo SLim SPer SPoG WFar
	– 'Elegans Champagne'	EPfP
	– 'Elegans Splendor'	CDoC
	– 'Elisabeth'	CDoC
	– 'Elizabeth Cooper'	CTrh LSRN
	– 'Elizabeth Dowd'	CBcs SCog
	– 'Elizabeth Hawkins'	CTrh LRHS MMuc NCGa SEND
	– 'Emily Wilson'	CDoC
	– 'Emmett Barnes'	SCam
	– 'Emmett Pfingstl'	SCam
	– 'Emperor of Russia'	CBcs CDoC
	– 'Eric Baker'	CDoC SCam
	– 'Erin Farmer'	CBcs
	– 'Eugène Lizé'	SCam
	– 'Eximia'	EPfP LRHS SCam SCog
	– 'Fanny'	SCog
	– 'Fashionata'	CDoC
	– 'Feast Perfection'	CDoC
	– 'Finlandia Variegated'	CDoC ELon SCam SCog
	– 'Fire Dance'	CDoC
	– 'Fire Falls' ♀H4	CDoC CMHG
	– 'Firebird'	CBcs
	– 'Flame'	CBcs
	– 'Flamingo'	CDoC
	– 'Flashlight'	CDoC EPfP MAsh
§	– 'Fleur Dipater'	SCam WGob
	– 'Flowerwood'	SCog
	– 'Forest Green'	CDoC MAsh
	– 'Fortune Teller'	CBcs
	– 'Frans van Damme'	CBcs
	– 'Fred Sander'	CBcs CDoC ELon MGos SCam SCog
	– 'Frizzle White'	SApp

Cultivar	Suppliers
- 'Frosty Morn'	CBcs CDoC ELan
- 'Furo-an'	CBcs MAsh
- 'Geisha Girl'	SCog
- 'Général Lamoricière'	LRHS
§ - 'Gigantea'	LRHS SCam
- 'Giuditta Rosani'	CDoC
- 'Gladys Wannamaker'	SCog
- 'Glen 40'	see *C. japonica* 'Coquettii'
- 'Gloire de Nantes' ♀H4	CTrh SCam SCog
- 'Gold Tone'	CDoC MGos SCam
* - 'Golden Wedding' (v)	SCog
- 'Goshozakura'	CDoC
- 'Grace Bunton'	CBcs CDoC ELon MGos SCam SCog
- 'Granada'	SCog
- 'Grand Prix' ♀H4	CDoC ELon LSRN MGos SCam SCog
- 'Grand Slam' ♀H2	CBcs CDoC CDul MAsh SCam
- 'Grand Sultan'	CDoC
- 'Guest of Honor'	CBcs CDoC
- 'Guilio Nuccio' ♀H4	CBcs CDoC CTri ELan ELon EPfP IArd LMil LRHS LSRN MGos NEgg NPri SBfd SCam SCog SCoo SLim SPer
- 'Gus Menard'	SCam
- 'Gwenneth Morey'	CBcs CDoC
- 'H.A. Downing'	CDoC SCam
§ - 'Hagoromo' ♀H4	CBcs CDoC CTrh ELan SBfd SCam SCog SPer
- 'Hakugan'	EPfP NLar
§ - 'Hakurakuten' ♀H4	CDoC CTri IArd NHim SCog
- 'Hanafūki'	CDoC MAsh MGos SCam SCog
- 'Happy Birthday'	LBuc LSRN
- 'Haru-no-utena'	CTrh
- 'Hatsuzakura'	see *C. japonica* 'Dewatairin'
- 'Hawaii'	CDoC CMac CTrh MGos SCog
- 'Her Majesty Queen Elizabeth II'	CDoC
- Herme	see *C. japonica* 'Hikarugenji'
- 'High Hat'	CBcs SCog
- 'High, Wide 'n' Handsome'	CDoC
§ - 'Hikarugenji'	CDoC MGos SCog
- 'Hinomaru'	CDoC CMac
- 'Holly Bright'	CTrh
- 'Honeyglow'	CDoC
- 'Ichisetsu'	SCog
§ - 'Imbricata'	LBuc LRHS MMuc SCog SEND
- 'Incarnata'	SCam
- 'Italiana Vera'	LBuc LRHS MAsh
- 'J.J. Whitfield'	CMac SCam
- 'Jack Jones Scented'	CMHG
- 'Janet Waterhouse'	SCam WFar
§ - 'Japonica Variegata' (v)	CDoC LRHS SCam
- 'Jean Clere'	CDoC MGos SCog
- 'Jennifer Turnbull'	CDoC
- 'Jessie Katz'	CDoC
- 'Jingle Bells'	CBcs
- 'Jitsugetsusei'	CDoC
- 'Joseph Pfingstl' ♀H4	CDoC CTri EPfP LRHS MMuc NPri SCam SCog SEND
- 'Joshua E. Youtz'	SCog
- 'Jovey Carlyon'	CBcs LRHS
- 'Joy Sander'	see *C. japonica* 'Apple Blossom'
§ - 'Julia Drayton'	MAsh
- 'Julia France'	SCog
- 'June McCaskill'	CDoC
- 'Juno'	CBcs LRHS SCam SCoo
- 'Jupiter' Paul, 1904 ♀H4	CBcs CDoC CMac CTri EPfP LMil LSRN MGos SCam SCog SPer
- 'Kellingtoniana'	see *C. japonica* 'Gigantea'
- 'Kentucky'	LRHS SCam
- 'Kick-off'	CBcs CTrh SCog
- 'Kimberley'	CBcs CDoC LSRN SCog
- 'King Size'	CDoC MGos
- 'King's Ransom'	CDoC CMac LRHS
- 'Kingyoba-shiro-wabisuke'	CDoC CHll
- 'Kingyo-tsubaki'	CDoC SCam SSta
- 'Kitty Berry'	CTrh
- 'Kokinran'	CDoC SCam
§ - 'Konronkoku' ♀H4	CBcs CDoC LRHS SCog
- 'Kouron-jura'	see *C. japonica* 'Konronkoku'
- 'Kramer's Supreme'	CBcs CCCN CDoC CDul ELon LBuc LRHS LSRN MGos NHim SCog SCoo SHil SPer WFar
§ - 'Kumasaka'	CTri
- 'La Pace Rubra'	SCam
- 'Lady Campbell'	CTri GEdr NLar NPri SCam SPad
- 'Lady Clare'	see *C. japonica* 'Akashigata'
§ - 'Lady de Saumarez'	CBcs CDoC CMac
- 'Lady Erma'	CBcs
- 'Lady Loch'	CTrh MAsh MGos SCam
- 'Lady Mackinnon'	MAsh
- 'Lady Marion'	see *C. japonica* 'Kumasaka'
- 'Lady McCulloch'	LRHS
- 'Lady Saint Clair'	CDoC
- 'Lady Vansittart'	CDoC CTrh ELan EPfP LRHS LSRN MAsh MBri MGos MPkF SBfd SCam SCog SCoo SLim SPer SPoG SSta WGob
§ - 'Lady Vansittart Pink'	CMac SBfd
- 'Lady Vansittart Red'	see *C. japonica* 'Lady Vansittart Pink'
- 'Lady Vansittart Shell'	see *C. japonica* 'Yours Truly'
- 'Lady Vere de Vere' (d)	CDoC
- 'Latifolia'	SCam
- 'Laurie Bray'	SCog
§ - 'Lavinia Maggi' ♀H4	CBcs CDoC CTri ELan ELon EPfP LBuc LMil LRHS LSRN MAsh MBri MGos NPri SCam SCog SCoo SHil SPoG SReu SRms SSta WGob
- 'L'Avvenire'	SCog
§ - 'Le Lys'	SCam
- 'Lemon Drop'	CTrh
- 'Leonora Novick'	CDoC SCog
- 'Lillian Rickets'	CDoC
- 'Lily Pons' ♀H4	CDoC CTrh
- 'Little Bit'	CBcs CDoC CMHG CTrh ELon MGos SCam SCog SSta
- 'Little Red Riding Hood'	CDoC
- 'Little Slam'	CDoC
- 'Lovelight' ♀H4	CTrh LRHS MAsh
- 'Lucy Hester'	CDoC
- 'Ludgvan Red'	LRHS
- 'Lulu Belle'	SCog
- 'Mabel Blackwell'	SCam
- 'Madame de Strekaloff'	CMac CSBt SCam
- 'Madame Hahn'	CDoC
- 'Madame Lebois'	CDoC SCam
- 'Madame Martin Cachet'	SCog
- 'Madge Miller'	MAsh
- 'Magic Moments'	SCog
- 'Magnoliiflora'	see *C. japonica* 'Hagoromo'
- 'Maiden's Blush'	CMac
- 'Man Size'	CDoC
- 'Manuroa Road'	LRHS MPkF
- 'Margaret Davis'	CCCN CDoC CSBt ELan ELon EPfP LBuc LRHS LSRN MAsh MBri MGos

	MPkF NEgg NPri SBfd SCam SCoo SHil SLim SPoG WGob
– 'Margaret Davis Picotee' $\mathbb{Y}^{H4}$	CBcs CMHG CTrh SCog SPer
– 'Margaret Rose'	SCam
– 'Margaret Short'	CDoC
– 'Marguérite Gouillon'	CBcs CDoC SSta
– 'Marian Mitchell'	SCam
– 'Mariana'	CDoC SCog
– 'Marie Bracey'	CBcs
– 'Marjorie Magnificent'	LBuc LRHS MAsh SCoo
– 'Mark Alan'	CDoC LRHS LSRN MPkF
– 'Maroon and Gold'	CDoC LRHS LSRN SCog
– 'Mars' $\mathbb{Y}^{H4}$	CBcs LMil MGos SCam SCog SPer WFar
– 'Mary Alice Cox'	CDoC
– 'Mary Costa'	CBcs CDoC CTrh
– 'Mary J. Wheeler'	LSRN
§ – 'Masayoshi' $\mathbb{Y}^{H4}$	CBcs CSBt LRHS SCam SCog
– 'Mathotiana Alba' $\mathbb{Y}^{H4}$	CDoC CMac CTri ELan EPfP LSRN MGos MMuc SCam SCog SEND SPer
– 'Mathotiana Purple King'	see *C. japonica* 'Julia Drayton'
§ – 'Mathotiana Rosea' $\mathbb{Y}^{H4}$	CMac SCam
– 'Mathotiana Supreme'	CDoC SCam SCog
– 'Matterhorn'	CTrh MAsh
– 'Mattie Cole'	CDoC SCam
– 'Maui'	CDoC
– 'Mercury' $\mathbb{Y}^{H4}$	CBcs CMac EPfP GGGa SCog
– 'Mercury Variegated' (v)	CMHG
– 'Mermaid'	CDoC
– 'Midnight'	CBcs CDoC CMHG LBuc LRHS MAsh SCoo
– 'Midnight Magic'	CTrh CTri
– 'Midnight Serenade'	CDoC LRHS
– 'Midsummer's Day'	CBcs
§ – 'Mikenjaku'	CBcs CDoC EPfP LBuc LRHS MAsh SCog WGob
– 'Miriam Stevenson'	SCam
– 'Miss Charleston'	SCog
– 'Miss Lyla'	NLar
– 'Modern Art'	MPkF
– 'Momiji-gari'	CDoC SCam
– 'Monstruosa Rubra'	see *C. japonica* 'Gigantea'
– 'Monte Carlo'	CDoC SCam SCog
– 'Moonlight'	CDoC
– 'Moonlight Bay'	CTrh
– 'Moshe Dayan'	CDoC CWSG LBuc LRHS MAsh SCog SCoo WGob
– 'Moshio'	CDoC
§ – 'Mrs Bertha A. Harms'	CDoC LRHS MAsh MGos SCam SCog
– 'Mrs Charles Cobb'	LRHS
– 'Mrs D.W. Davis'	CBcs CDoC EPfP SCam
– 'Mrs Lyman Clarke'	CDoC
– 'Mrs William Thompson'	SCam
§ – 'Mystic'	CDoC
– 'Nagasaki'	see *C. japonica* 'Mikenjaku'
– 'Nigra'	see *C. japonica* 'Konronkoku'
– 'Nina Avery'	CDoC
– 'Nioi-fubuki' (Higo)	CDoC
– 'Nobilissima'	CDoC CMac CTrh CTri EPfP EUJe MBlu MMuc NLar SCam SCog SCoo SEND SPer SPoG
– 'Nokogiriba-tsubaki'	MPkF SCam
– 'Nuccio's Amigo'	MAsh
– 'Nuccio's Cameo'	CDoC CTrh LRHS MAsh SCoo
– 'Nuccio's Carousel'	MPkF
– 'Nuccio's Gem' $\mathbb{Y}^{H4}$	CDoC CMHG ELan EPfP LRHS MGos SCoo SSta
– 'Nuccio's Jewel' $\mathbb{Y}^{H4}$	CDoC CSBt CTrh CWSG ELon EPfP GEdr LBuc LRHS LSRN MAsh MPkF NPri SCam SCog SPer WGob WMoo
– 'Nuccio's Pearl'	CBcs CDoC EPfP LRHS LSRN MAsh MBri MMuc NEgg SCam SCog SCoo SEND WGob
– 'Nuccio's Pink Lace'	CDoC CTri
– 'Olga Anderson'	CDoC MGos
– 'Onetia Holland'	CBcs CDoC EPfP LSRN MGos SBfd SCam SCog SLim
– 'Oo-La-La'	CTrh LRHS MPkF
– 'Optima'	CBcs CDoC ELon LRHS SCam SCog SCoo
– 'Optima Rosea'	SPoG
– 'Orandakō'	LRHS MBri SHil
– 'Paeoniiflora Alba'	SCam
– 'Patricia Ann'	LSRN
– 'Paul Jones Supreme'	CDoC
– 'Paulette Goddard'	SCam
– 'Paul's Apollo'	see *C. japonica* 'Apollo' Paul, 1911
– 'Peachblossom'	see *C. japonica* 'Fleur Dipater'
– 'Pearl Harbor'	SCam
– 'Pensacola Red'	CDoC
– 'Pink Champagne'	NPri
– 'Pink Perfection'	see *C. japonica* subsp. *rusticana* 'Otome'
– 'Preston Rose'	CDoC
– 'Primavera'	CTrh SCam SCog
– 'Prince Murat'	CDoC LRHS
– 'Princess Baciocchi'	CBcs SCam
– 'Princess du Mahe'	CMac
– 'Purple Emperor'	see *C. japonica* 'Julia Drayton'
– 'R.L. Wheeler' $\mathbb{Y}^{H4}$	CBcs CDoC CSBt CTri EPfP LRHS LSRN MBri NPri SBfd SCog SCoo
– 'Raspberry Ripple' **new**	MPkF
– 'Red Dandy'	CDoC MGos SCam SCog
– 'Red Red Rose'	CDoC LRHS
– 'Reg Ragland'	CDoC MGos SCam SCog
– 'Roger Hall'	CBcs CDoC CTrh LRHS LSRN MPkF SCog SCoo SPoG
– 'Roman Soldier'	CBcs
– 'Rosa Mundi'	LRHS
– 'Rosularis'	CDoC SCam SCog
– 'Royal Velvet'	CDoC CTrh
– 'Rubescens Major' $\mathbb{Y}^{H4}$	CBcs
– 'Ruddigore'	CTrh
§ – subsp. ***rusticana***	CBcs CDoC SCog
– – 'Arajishi' misapplied	see *C. japonica* subsp. *rusticana*
– – 'Arajishi' Ko'emon	SCam
§ – – 'Otome'	SBod
– – 'Reigyoku' (v)	CBcs CDoC
– 'Sabiniana'	LRHS
– 'Saint André'	CMac LRHS SCoo
– 'Sally Harrell'	SCam
– 'San Dimas' $\mathbb{Y}^{H4}$	CDoC CTrh SCam SCog
– 'Saturnia'	CDoC ELon LBuc LRHS WBor WMoo
– 'Sawada's Dream'	CDoC SCog
– 'Scented Red'	CDoC
– 'Scentsation' $\mathbb{Y}^{H4}$	CDoC CMHG CTri MBri SCog SHil
– 'Sea Foam'	LRHS
– 'Sea Gull'	CTrh
– 'Senator Duncan U. Fletcher'	CDoC

– 'Shikibu'	CTrh
– 'Shiragiku'	CBcs CDoC EPfP SCog
– 'Shiro Chan'	CDoC ELon MGos SCog
– 'Shirobotan'	CDoC ELon LRHS MAsh MGos SCam SCog SCoo
– 'Silver Anniversary'	CBcs CDoC CMHG CSBt CTrh CTri ELan ELon EPfP LBuc LMil LRHS LSRN MAsh MGos NEgg NLar NPri SBfd SCam SCog SCoo SLim SPer SPoG SReu WGob
– 'Silver Ruffles'	CDoC
– 'Something Beautiful'	CDoC
– 'Souvenir de Bahuaud-Litou' ♀H4	CBcs CDoC SCam SCog
– 'Spencer's Pink'	CDoC
– 'Splendens Carlyon'	LRHS SCoo
– 'Spring Fever'	SCam
– 'Spring Fling'	CTrh
– 'Spring Formal'	CTrh
– 'Spring Frill'	SCam SCog
– 'Stacy Susan' **new**	MPkF
– 'Stardust'	SCam
– 'Strawberry Blonde'	SCog
– 'Strawberry Parfait'	CDoC
– 'Strawberry Swirl'	SCog
– 'Sugar Babe'	CDoC CTrh LRHS MAsh SCam SCog SCoo
– 'Sunset Glory'	SCam
– 'Sweetheart'	SCog
– 'Sylva' ♀H4	GGGa SBod SSpi
– 'Sylvia'	CMac
– 'Takanini'	CDoC
– 'Tama-no-ura'	CDoC
– 'Tammia'	CDoC LRHS MAsh
– 'Tarō'an'	CDoC
– 'Teresa Ragland'	CDoC SCam
– 'Teringa'	CDoC
– 'The Mikado'	CDoC LRHS SCog
– 'Tickled Pink'	CDoC
– 'Tiffany'	CBcs CDoC LRHS MAsh MGos SCam SCog SCoo
– 'Tinker Bell'	CDoC SCam SCog
– 'Tom Pouce'	MPkF
– 'Tom Thumb' ♀H4	CDoC CTrh LRHS MAsh SRms SSta
– 'Tomorrow'	CDoC CWSG MAsh MMuc NEgg SCam SCog
– 'Tomorrow Park Hill'	SCog
§ – 'Tomorrow Variegated' (v)	MGos SCam
– 'Tomorrow's Dawn'	CDoC
– 'Touchdown'	SCam
– 'Trewithen White'	CDoC
§ – 'Tricolor' ♀H4	CBcs CDoC CMHG CMac CSBt ELon LRHS MAsh MGos MMuc SBfd SCam SCog SCoo SEND SPer WFar
– 'Tricolor Red'	see *C. japonica* 'Lady de Saumarez'
– 'Trinkett'	CDoC
– 'Valtevareda'	CDoC
– variegated (v)	SCog
– 'Victor de Bisschop'	see *C. japonica* 'Le Lys'
– 'Victor Emmanuel'	see *C. japonica* 'Blood of China'
– 'Ville de Nantes'	LRHS MGos
– 'Virginia Carlyon'	CDoC
– 'Virginia Robinson'	SCam
– 'Virgin's Blush'	SCam
– 'Vittorio Emanuele II'	CDoC CTrh LBuc LRHS MAsh MGos SCoo
– 'Volcano'	CDoC MPkF

– 'Vosper's Rose'	CDoC
– 'Warrior'	CDoC SCog
– 'White Nun'	CBcs SCog
– 'White Swan'	CSBt LRHS MAsh SCoo
– 'Wilamina' ♀H4	CDoC CMHG
– 'Wildfire'	LRHS SCam
– 'William Bartlett'	CTrh
– 'William Honey'	CTrh
– 'Wisley White'	see *C. japonica* 'Hakurakuten'
– 'Witman Yellow'	CTrh
§ – 'Yours Truly'	CBcs CDoC CMac CTrh CTsd LRHS LSRN MAsh SCog
– 'Yukimi-guruma'	CDoC
'John Tooby'	CDoC
'Jury's Yellow'	see *C.* × *williamsii* 'Jury's Yellow'
'Larry Piet' (*reticulata* hybrid)	SCam
'Lasca Beauty' (*japonica* × *reticulata*)	CBcs SCam
'Lavender Queen'	see *C. sasanqua* 'Lavender Queen'
'Leonard Messel' (*reticulata* × (× *williamsii*)) ♀H4	CBcs CDoC CDul CMHG CMac CTri EPfP LRHS MAsh MGos MPkF NLar SCam SCog SCoo SPer SPoG SReu
'Liz Henslowe'	CDoC
'Madame Victor de Bisschop'	see *C. japonica* 'Le Lys'
'Magic Mum'	LSRN
'Mandalay Queen' (*reticulata* hybrid)	SCam
'Maud Messel' (× *williamsii* × *reticulata*)	SCam
'Milo Rowell'	CDoC
'Mimosa Jury'	CDoC
'Monticello'	CDoC
'Mystique'	see *C. japonica* 'Mystic', *C. reticulata* 'Mystique'
'Nicky Crisp' (*japonica* × *pitardii*)	CDoC MPkF
'Nijinski' (*reticulata* hybrid)	CDoC
'Nonie Haydon' (*pitardii* hybrid)	CDoC
oleifera	CPLG NLar SCog
'Phyl Doak' (*reticulata* × *saluenensis*)	CDoC
'Pink Goddess' **new**	MPkF
'Pink Spangles'	see *C. japonica* 'Mathotiana Rosea'
pitardii	CDoC
– 'Snippet'	CDoC
'Polar Ice' (*oleifera* hybrid)	CDoC SCog
'Polyanna'	CDoC SCog
'Portuense'	see *C. japonica* 'Japonica Variegata'
'Quintessence' (*japonica* × *lutchuensis*)	CDoC CTrh LRHS SCam SCog
reticulata 'Captain Rawes'	SCam
– 'Jean Morel'	SCam
– 'Les Jury'	LMil
– 'Mary Williams'	LMil NLar SCoo
– 'Miss Tulare'	CDoC
§ – 'Mystique'	CDoC
– 'Simpatica'	SCam
– 'Songzilin'	SCam
'Rose du Steir' (*reticulata* hybrid)	MPkF SCam
rosiflora 'Roseaflora Cascade'	CDoC
'Royalty' (*japonica* × *reticulata*) ♀H3	CBcs
rusticana	see *C. japonica* subsp. *rusticana*

	'Salutation' (*reticulata* × *saluenensis*)	SCam
I	***sasanqua*** 'Alba'	CTri
I	- 'Apple Blossom'	MAsh
	- 'Baronesa de Soutelinho'	ELon SCam SCog
	- 'Bettie Patricia'	SCog
	- 'Bonanza'	see *C. hiemalis* 'Bonanza'
	- Borde Hill form	SCam
	- 'Brocéliande' **new**	MPkF
	- 'Cleopatra'	EPfP MAsh
	- 'Cotton Candy'	CDoC
	- 'Crimson King' ♀H3	CDoC SCam
	- 'Dazzler'	see *C. hiemalis* 'Dazzler'
	- 'Early Pearly'	CDoC
I	- 'Exquisite'	CDoC
	- 'Flamingo'	see *C. sasanqua* 'Fukuzutsumi'
	- 'Fragrans'	ELon SCam SCog SMDP
	- 'Fuji-no-mine'	ELon SCam SCog
§	- 'Fukuzutsumi'	CSBt SCam
	- 'Gay Sue'	CDoC CTrh
	- 'Hiryū'	SCam
	- 'Hugh Evans' ♀H3	CAbP CBcs CDoC CTrh ELan ELon EPfP LRHS SCam SCog SCoo SMDP SSta
	- 'Jean May' ♀H3	CDoC ELan ELon EPfP LRHS SCam SCog SCoo SSta
	- 'Kenkyō'	ELon SCam SCog SSta
§	- 'Lavender Queen'	SCam
	- 'Maiden's Blush'	LRHS SCam SCog
	- 'Narumigata'	CAbP CBcs CDoC CDul CHll CMac CTrh ELon EPfP LRHS MBlu SCam SSta
	- 'New Dawn'	SCam SCog
	- 'Nyewoods'	CMac
	- 'Papaver'	SCam SCog
	- 'Paradise Audrey'	LRHS
	- 'Paradise Belinda' PBR	CDoC LRHS MWat
	- 'Paradise Blush'	CDoC LRHS MWat NRHS SCog
	- 'Paradise Glow'	CBcs CDoC LMil LRHS NRHS SCam SCog SPoG
	- 'Paradise Helen'	LRHS SCam
	- 'Paradise Hilda'	CDoC LRHS SCam
	- 'Paradise Joan'	CDoC
	- 'Paradise Little Liane' PBR	CDoC SCam SCog
	- 'Paradise Pearl'	CDoC LRHS NRHS SCam SCog
	- 'Paradise Petite' PBR	SCog
	- 'Paradise Sayaka'	CDoC
	- 'Paradise Venessa' PBR	CBcs CDoC EPfP LRHS SCam SCog SPoG
	- 'Peach Blossom'	CBcs
	- 'Plantation Pink'	CWSG ELan EPfP LRHS NPri SCam SCog SPoG SRkn
	- 'Rainbow'	CAbP CBcs CDoC CTrh CWSG ELan ELon EPfP LRHS MPkF SCam SCoo SSta WFar
	- 'Rosea'	ELon SCam SCog
§	- 'Rosea Plena'	CBcs CMac SCam
	- 'Sasanqua Rubra'	CMac SCam SCog SMDP
	- 'Sasanqua Variegata' (v)	MPkF SCam SCog
	- 'Setsugekka'	CDoC SCog
	- 'Shishigashira' Nihon Engei Kai Zasshi, 1894	SCog
	- 'Silver Dollar'	CDoC
	- 'Snowflake'	SCam SSta
	- 'Souvenir de Claude Brivet'	CDoC
	- 'Sparkling Burgundy'	see *C. hiemalis* 'Sparkling Burgundy'
	- 'Tanya'	CDoC
	- 'Versicolor'	EPfP MPkF
	- 'Winter's Joy'	CBcs
	- 'Winter's Snowman'	CBcs CDoC EPfP LRHS SCam SCog
	'Satan's Robe' (*reticulata* hybrid)	CDoC MGos SCog
	'Scented Gem'	MPkF SCam
	'Scented Sun'	CTrh
	'Scentuous' (*japonica* × *lutchuensis*)	CDoC CTrh
	'Show Girl' (*reticulata* × *sasanqua*)	SCam SCog
§	***sinensis***	CBcs CCCN CTrh GPoy LRHS SCam SPlb WCot
	- var. ***assamica*** **new**	CCCN
	- var. ***sinensis*** **new**	CCCN
	'Sir Victor Davis'	CDoC
	'Snow Flurry' (*oleifera* hybrid)	CBcs LRHS SCam SCog
	'Spring Festival' (*cuspidata* hybrid) ♀H4	CDoC CMHG CTrh MMuc MPkF NLar SCog SPoG WMoo
	'Spring Mist' (*japonica* × *lutchuensis*)	CDoC CMHG CTrh
	'Sugar Dream'	CDoC CTrh SCam
	'Superscent'	CTrh
	'Survivor'	MPkF SCam
	'Swan Lake'	NPri SCog
	'Sweet Emily Kate' (*japonica* × *lutchuensis*)	CDoC MPkF
	'Sweet Jane'	LRHS MPkF SBfd SCam SCog
	'Tarōkaja' (wabisuke)	SCam
	thea	see *C. sinensis*
	'Tinsie'	see *C. japonica* 'Bokuhan'
	'Tiny Princess' (*fraterna* × *japonica*)	CBcs CMac
	'Tom Knudsen' (*japonica* × *reticulata*) ♀H3	CDoC SCam
	'Tomorrow Supreme'	see *C. japonica* 'Tomorrow Variegated'
	transnokoensis	CMac CPLG CTrh MPkF SCam
	'Tricolor Sieboldii'	see *C. japonica* 'Tricolor'
	'Tristrem Carlyon' (*reticulata* hybrid) ♀H4	CDoC CTri EPfP SCam WGob
	tsaii	CDoC CHEx
	'Usu-ōtome'	see *C. japonica* subsp. *rusticana* 'Otome'
	'Valley Knudsen' (*reticulata* × *saluenensis*)	SCog
	× ***vernalis***	SCam
	- 'Ginryû'	SCam
	- 'Star Above Star'	CMHG
	- 'Yuletide'	CDoC CTrh LRHS LSRN MAsh MPkF MWat SCam SCog
	'Volcano'	CDoC
	'White Retic' (*japonica* × *reticulata*)	SCam
	× ***williamsii*** 'Angel Wings'	LRHS
	- 'Anticipation' ♀H4	Widely available
	- 'Anticipation Variegated'	MAsh
	- 'Ballet Queen'	CBcs CDoC CSBt MGos SCam
	- 'Ballet Queen Variegated'	CDoC SCog
	- 'Bartley Number Five'	CMac
	- 'Beatrice Michael'	CMac
	- 'Blue Danube'	CBcs
	- 'Bow Bells'	CDoC CTri ELan SCam SSta
	- 'Bowen Bryant' ♀H4	GGGa SCog
	- 'Brigadoon' ♀H4	CBcs CDoC CTrh CTri EPfP GGGa GKin MGos SCam SCog
	- 'Burncoose'	CBcs

– 'Burncoose Apple Blossom'	CDoC
– 'Buttons 'n' Bows'	CDoC MPkF SCog
– 'C.F. Coates'	CDoC SCam SCog
– 'Caerhays'	CBcs SCam
– 'Carnation'	MAsh
– 'Carolyn Williams'	CBcs SCam
– 'Celebration'	CBcs CSBt LSRN
– 'Charlean'	CDoC SCam
– 'Charles Colbert'	CDoC LRHS
– 'Charles Michael'	CBcs
– 'China Clay' ♀H4	CBcs CDoC EPfP
§ – 'Citation'	CBcs CMac SCog
– 'Clarrie Fawcett' ♀H4	CDoC
– 'Contribution'	CTrh
– 'Coral Delight'	MPkF
– 'Crinkles'	CDoC SCam
– 'Daintiness' ♀H4	CDoC SCog
– 'Dark Nite'	CMHG
– 'Debbie' ♀H4	Widely available
– 'Debbie's Carnation'	CDoC CMHG
– 'Donation' ♀H4	Widely available
– 'Dream Boat'	CBcs CDoC LRHS
– 'E.G. Waterhouse'	CDoC CTrh CTri ELan ELon EPfP GKin LRHS MAsh MGos MMuc SCam SCog SEND SPoG SSta WGob
– 'E.T.R. Carlyon' ♀H4	CDoC CTrh CTri ELan EPfP LBuc LRHS MAsh MPkF NLar SCog SCoo SLim SPoG
– 'Elegant Beauty' ♀H4	CDoC ELon SCam SCog
– 'Elizabeth Anderson' ♀H4	CTrh SCam
– 'Elizabeth de Rothschild'	GGGa
– 'Ellamine'	CBcs
– 'Elsie Jury' ♀H3	CBcs CDoC CMac CTri ELan GKin MGos SCam SCog SPer
– 'Exaltation'	CDoC SCam SCog
– 'Fiona Colville'	CDoC
– 'Francis Hanger'	CDoC CDul CTrh SCam SCog SPer
– 'Galaxie' ♀H4	CBcs CDoC SCog
– 'Gay Time'	SCog
– 'George Blandford' ♀H4	CBcs CMac
– 'Glenn's Orbit' ♀H4	CDoC SCam SCog
– 'Golden Spangles' (v)	CBcs CDoC CMac ELan EPfP GKin LRHS MGos MMuc NLar SBfd SCam SCog SEND SLim SPer
– 'Grand Jury'	LRHS
– 'Gwavas'	CBcs CCCN CDoC LRHS MAsh SCam SCog SCoo
– 'Hilo'	CDoC SCam
– 'Hiraethlyn'	CBcs
– 'Holland Orchid'	SCog
– 'J.C. Williams' ♀H4	CBcs CMac CTri EPfP MMuc SCog SEND
– 'Jamie'	CDoC
– 'Jean Claris'	CDoC SCog
– 'Jenefer Carlyon'	CDoC
– 'Jill Totty'	SCog
– 'Joan Trehane' ♀H4	SCam
– 'Julia Hamiter' ♀H4	CBcs CDoC
§ – 'Jury's Yellow' ♀H4	Widely available
– 'Lady's Maid'	CBcs
– 'Laura Boscawen'	CDoC SCam
– 'Les Jury' ♀H4	CDoC CGHE CMHG CSBt CTrh LMil LSRN NEgg NLar SBfd SCog SLim
– 'Little Lavender'	CDoC
– 'Margaret Waterhouse'	CBcs CDoC SCam SCog
– 'Marjorie Waldegrave'	LRHS
– 'Mary Christian' ♀H4	CBcs SCam SSta
– 'Mary Jobson'	CBcs
– 'Mary Larcom'	CBcs
– 'Mary Phoebe Taylor' ♀H4	CBcs CDoC LRHS MPkF NLar SCam SCog SCoo SLim
– 'Mildred Veitch'	CDoy
– 'Mirage'	CDoC SCam
– 'Moira Reid'	CDoC
– 'Monica Dance'	CBcs CDoC
– 'Muskoka' ♀H4	CBcs
– 'Night Rider'	CDoC MPkF
– 'November Pink'	CBcs
– 'Palaxie'	SCam
– 'Phillippa Forward'	CBcs CMac
– 'Pink Dahlia'	SCam
– 'Rendezvous'	CDoC MGos SCam SCog
– 'Rose Bouquet'	CDoC
– 'Rosemary Williams'	CBcs
– 'Ruby Bells'	CMHG
– 'Ruby Wedding' (d)	CDoC CMHG CSBt CTrh EPfP LBuc LMil LRHS LSRN MAsh NEgg NLar NPri SBfd SCog SCoo SLim SPoG
– 'Saint Ewe' ♀H4	CBcs CDoC CSBt CTri ELan EPfP LBuc LRHS MBri MGos NHim NLar NPri SCam SCog SCoo SPer
– 'Saint Michael'	CBcs CDoC
– 'Sayonara'	SCam SCog
– 'Senorita' ♀H4	CDoC ELon GKin MBri SCam SCog
– 'Simon Bolitho'	SCog
– 'Sun Song'	SCog
– 'Taylor's Perfection'	SCam
– 'The Duchess of Cornwall'	CDoC SCam
– 'Tiptoe'	CDoC GKin
– 'Tulip Time'	MPkF
– 'Waltz Time'	CDoC SCam
– 'Water Lily' ♀H4	CBcs CDoC CTri ELan ELon EPfP MGos SCam
– 'Wilber Foss' ♀H4	CBcs CDoC ELon GKin LRHS MGos MMuc SCog SEND
– 'Winton' (*cuspidata* × *saluenensis*)	CBcs CDoC
– 'Wynne Rayner'	CDoC SCam
'Winter's Charm' (*oleifera* × *sasanqua*)	SCog
'Winter's Dream' (*biemalis* × *oleifera*)	SCog
'Winter's Interlude' (*oleifera* × *sinensis*)	CBcs CDoC SCam SCog
'Winter's Joy'	SCog
'Winter's Toughie' (*sasanqua* hybrid)	CBcs CDoC SCam SCog
'Wirlinga Belle'	SCog
'Yoimachi' (*fraterna* × *sasanqua*)	CDoC CTrh
yunnanensis	IDee

Camissonia (*Onagraceae*)

bistorta 'Sunflakes' **new**	CSpe

Campanula ✿ (*Campanulaceae*)

sp.	WCot
RCB AM 13	WCot
RCB UA 15	WCot
abietina	see *C. patula* subsp. *abietina*
alaskana	see *C. rotundifolia* var. *alaskana*
§ ***alliariifolia***	Widely available

- DHTU 0126 WCru
- 'Ivory Bells' see *C. alliariifolia*
alpina MDKP
americana EWTr XLum
arvatica EACa ECho EDAr EPot GMaP LRHS MDKP NHar NMen NRHS
- 'Alba' GMaP
aucheri see *C. bellidifolia* subsp. *aucheri*
autraniana ITim
barbata CCon EACa EBee ECho EDAr EPfP MWat WAbe WMoo
- SDR 6365 GKev
'Belinda' CMea CPBP
bellidifolia EPot LLHF NBir
§ - subsp. ***aucheri*** EBee EDAr EPfP EPot ITim
- subsp. ***saxifraga*** ITim NMen
besenginica EPot
§ ***betulifolia*** ♀H4 CSam EACa NSla
'Birch Hybrid' ♀H4 CFis EACa EBee ECho ECtt EDAr ELan EPfP LRHS MMuc WFar WRHF XLum
bononiensis EACa LLHF SRms XLum
'Bumblebee' WAbe
'Burghaltii' ♀H4 EHrv ELan GBee GCal LRHS NLar SHar SMrm WFar WMnd WOut WPer
'Cantata' EPot WAbe
§ ***carnica*** ECho WTcb
carpatica ♀H4 ECho EPfP MLHP NBre NBro NGdn SPlb SRms SWat XLum
- f. ***alba*** ECho LRHS NBre NGdn NRHS SPlb SWat XLum
§ - - 'Weisse Clips' CBar EAEE EBee ECho ECtt ELan EPfP GKin LAst LHop LRHS MAsh NEgg NGdn NHol NPri SBfd SPer SPoG SRms SWvt WFar WGwG
§ - 'Blaue Clips' CBar CBcs EBee ECho ECtt ELan EPfP GKin GMaP IFoB LAst LHop LRHS MAsh MGos NEgg NGdn NPri SBfd SPer SPoG SRms SWvt WFar
- Blue Clips see *C. carpatica* 'Blaue Clips'
- 'Blue Moonlight' EACa ECho LHop LRHS NRHS
- 'Chewton Joy' CTri ECho LLHF LRHS NRHS
- dwarf EPot
- 'Karpatenkrone' EACa EBee GBin NBre
- 'Kathy' GBuc
* - var. ***pelviformis*** SMHy
- 'Silberschale' NBre
- 'Suzie' IPot
- var. ***turbinata*** ECho SRms WAbe
- - 'Foerster' EACa EBee ECho LRHS XLum
- - 'Isabel' ECho LLHF LRHS NRHS
- - 'Jewel' ECho LHop LRHS NRHS
- White Clips see *C. carpatica* f. *alba* 'Weisse Clips'
cashmeriana 'Blue Cloud' CWib
cephallenica see *C. garganica* subsp. *cephallenica*
§ ***chamissonis*** ECho EPot GEdr LLHF NWad WPat
- 'Alba' GEdr
- 'Major' CYeo EWes GKev LBee
- 'Oyobeni' EACa
§ - 'Superba' ♀H4 ECho ELan NMen NRya WAbe
§ ***cochlearifolia*** ♀H4 CEnt CSpe CTri EBee ECho EDAr EPfP GEdr GJos GMaP LRHS MAsh MMuc SBch SBfd SPoG SVic WFar WHoo WSpi XLum
- SDR 5318 GKev
- var. ***alba*** CSpe CTri EDAr MHer MMuc NMen NRya SBch SRms WHoo WPer XLum
- - 'Bavaria White' ECho
- - 'White Baby' (Baby Series) CYeo ECho ECtt ELon EPfP EPot GJos LRHS SPet SPoG
- 'Annie Hall' ECho
- 'Bavaria Blue' ECho ELon GJos NHol SPet
- 'Blue Baby' (Baby Series) ECho ECtt EPfP GJos LRHS MHer SPoG SRms SRot
- 'Blue Wonder' ITim
- 'Cambridge Blue' EACa
- 'Elizabeth Oliver' (d) CCon CTri CWGN ECho ECtt EDAr GCal GMaP LHop LRHS MAsh MHer NBir NRHS SPlb SRms WAbe WFar WHil WHoo WRHF
- 'Oakington Blue' LLHF WAbe
- var. ***pallida*** 'Silver Chimes' ECho
- 'R.B. Loder' (d) LRHS MHer
- 'Tubby' ECho EPot GJos GKev LLHF LRHS MHer SRms
- 'Warleyensis' see *C.* × *haylodgensis* W. Brockbank 'Warley White'
collina CTri EACa LLHF
'Covadonga' CMea EACa ECho LHop LLHF LRHS NRHS SBch WAbe
cretica ITim
'Crystal' ECtt MAvo MNrw MSpe SMHy SUsu
dasyantha see *C. chamissonis*
dolomitica EACa EBee GKev LLHF NMen
'E.K. Toogood' CCon CElw CPBP EACa ECho ECtt GJos MWat SRms XLum
elatines LRHS
ephesia GKev
- SDR 1111 GKev
eriocarpa see *C. latifolia* 'Eriocarpa'
'Faichem Lilac' GCra LLHF NPro STes WCot
fenestrellata EACa NMen SRms WAbe
finitima see *C. betulifolia*
foliosa EACa WPer
fragilis ECho IFoB
- 'Hirsuta' ECho
garganica ♀H4 EACa ECho EPfP GKev GMaP LAst LRHS MAsh MDKP MMuc MRav NEgg SBfd SEND SPet SWvt WFar WMoo XLum
- 'Aurea' see *C. garganica* 'Dickson's Gold'
- 'Backhouse' LRHS
- 'Blue Diamond' ECho IVic LHop MAsh WAbe WFar
§ - subsp. ***cephallenica*** CElw EACa NBro
§ - 'Dickson's Gold' Widely available
- 'Erinus Major' EACa IVic XLum
- 'Hirsuta' ECho
- 'Major' ECho LAst SPoG WFar WRHF
- 'Mrs Resholt' ECtt ESwi LAst SDix SWvt WFar WGor
- 'W.H. Paine' ♀H4 ECho ECtt IFoB IGor MDKP NMen WAbe WHoo
'Glandore' EACa XLum
glomerata CEnt CPLG CRWN GAbr GJos LSRN MNHC NBir NBro NLan NMir WBrk WFar XSen
- var. ***acaulis*** EACa EBee EPfP GKev LRHS NLar SBfd SPet WFar WPer WSpi XLum
- var. ***alba*** CBcs CCon CSpe EACa EAEE EBee ECtt ELan EPfP GJos GMaP LBMP

	LRHS MLHP MRav SBfd SPer SPlb SPoG SWat WCAu WFar WMnd WPer WWEG XLum
§ - - 'Schneekrone'	ECha LRHS NBre SMrm WFar
- Bellefleur Series **new**	EBee
- 'Caroline'	CSpe CWGN EBee ECha ECtt ELan ELon EPPr EPri EShb EWll GBuc GMaP LEdu LRHS LSRN MAvo MBel MCot MNrw MRav NCGa NSti WAul WCAu WCot WFar WHil WMnd
- Crown of Snow	see *C. glomerata* var. *alba* 'Schneekrone'
- var. ***dahurica***	CCon ELon LRHS NBre NLar SMrm SPet WPer
- 'Emerald'	EACa EBee ECtt LRHS MBri MHer NRHS SHil WFar WHlf
- 'Joan Elliott'	EBee ECGP ECha ECtt EShb GBuc LEdu LSRN MNFA MWat WAul WSpi
- 'Purple Pixie'	LRHS
- 'Superba' ♀^{H4}	Widely available
grossekii	CCon LLHF LRHS WHrl WTcb
hakkiarica	EBee GEdr WCot
'Hannah'	ECho LHop LRHS
× ***haylodgensis*** misapplied	see *C.* × *haylodgensis* 'Plena'
§ × ***haylodgensis*** W. Brockbank 'Marion Fisher' (d)	CPBP ECtt EDAr EPot NMen WAbe WCot WHoo
§ - 'Plena' (d)	ECho ECtt EDAr ELan EPot LBee LHop LRHS NMen NPri SRms WAbe WCot WFar WHoo WKif
§ - 'Warley White' (d)	EACa ECho NMen XLum
- 'Yvonne'	ECtt LHop WFar WHil WNew
'Hemswell Starlight'	WAbe
hercegovina 'Nana'	ITim NMen WAbe
hierapetrae	WAbe
'Hilltop Snow'	NMen WAbe
hofmannii	EBee EDAr ELan GKev ITim MBNS NLar
§ ***incurva***	CSpe EACa EBee ELan GJos GKev WMoo
- 'Alba'	GKev
× ***innesii***	see *C.* 'John Innes'
isophylla ♀^{H2}	ECho
- 'Alba' ♀^{H2}	ECho
- Starina Bicolor Star = 'Camp Bulewhit'^{PBR}	LRHS
Jenny = 'Harjen'^{PBR}	CWGN EBee EPPr SHar
'Joe Elliott' ♀$^{H2-3}$	CPBP ECho NSla WAbe
§ 'John Innes'	CPBP
kemulariae	LLHF
- 'Alba'	ITim
'Kent Belle' ♀^{H4}	Widely available
khasiana	EBee GKev
lactiflora	CElw CMac EBee ECha EPfP GAbr GCra IFoB ITim LRHS MCot MLHP MSCN MWhi NEgg SPer WFar WHoo WMoo WPer WSpi WWEG XLum
- ***alba***	see *C. lactiflora* white-flowered
N - 'Alba' ♀^{H4}	EBee EPfP GMaP IVic MDKP MSCN WFar WMnd
- 'Avalanche'	EACa EBee ECtt LRHS SPoG WHil
- 'Blue Cross'	EBee LRHS
- 'Dixter Presence'	IPot SMHy SUsu
- dwarf pink-flowered	EACa EBee EPfP MBNS WSpi
- 'Favourite'	CCon CSpe EBee ECtt MNrw NGdn
- hybrids	GJos

- 'Loddon Anna' ♀^{H4}	Widely available
- 'Macrantha' **new**	WSpi
- 'Moorland Rose'	WMoo
- 'Pouffe'	CHid CPrp EACa EAEE EBee ECtt ELan ELon EPfP EWTr GMaP IVic LRHS MDKP MRav NBro NGdn NLar SMrm SPer SWat SWvt WFar
- 'Prichard's Variety' ♀^{H4}	Widely available
- 'Superba' ♀^{H4}	ECtt EHrv IVic WSpi
- 'Violet'	SWat WPer WSpi
- 'White Pouffe'	CPrp EACa EBee ECtt ELan ELon EPfP GMaP IVic LRHS LSRN MDKP MLHP NLar SPer SPoG SWat WFar
§ - white-flowered	ECha GBin MBNS NBir SMrm SPer SWat WFar WPer WSpi
latifolia	ECha GJos LPot LRHS MCot NBid NOrc SEND SPer SRms WCot WFar WMoo
- var. ***alba***	EBee ELan EPfP EWTr GCra GJos LRHS MAvo MMuc MTis NGdn SEND SPav SPer SRms WHal WPer WSpi WWEG
- - 'White Ladies'	LRHS
* - 'Amethyst'	CPrp WSpi
- blue-flowered	WSpi
- 'Brantwood'	CFis GAbr LRHS MRav SPav SRms SWat WCot WMnd WSpi
§ - 'Eriocarpa'	LRHS
- 'Gloaming'	ECtt LRHS NPnk
- var. ***macrantha***	EBee ELan ELon EPfP GMaP IPot LHop LRHS MAvo MBri MWat NGdn NSti SBfd SPav SPer SWat SWvt WCot WMoo WPer WSpi WWEG
- - 'Alba'	EBee ECha ECtt EHrv GMaP LHop MRav SBfd WCot WMoo WPer WWEG
- - 'Peter Lewis' **new**	EBee
- 'Misty Dawn'	MAvo WCot
latiloba	CElw CMHG SBch SGar WBrk WCot WFar WKif WSpi
§ - 'Alba' ♀^{H4}	CElw EBee ELan GCal GCra MCot MDKP MMuc NEgg NLar SBch SEND SGar WBrk WKif WSpi
- 'Hidcote Amethyst' ♀^{H4}	CSpe CWGN EBee ECtt EHrv ELan ELon EPfP EWll GAbr GBuc GCal LRHS MCot MMuc MRav MWhi NBid NBir NGdn NLar SEND SGar WCot WFar WKif WMnd WSpi WWEG
- 'Highcliffe Variety' ♀^{H4}	CPrp EBee ECtt ELan EPfP EShb GBuc GCra IBoy LRHS MDKP MMuc MRav NLar SEND SMrm SPoG WCot WHlf WKif WMnd WSpi WWEG
* - 'Highdown'	GBuc
- 'Percy Piper' ♀^{H4}	EACa EBee ECtt ELan GBuc LRHS MRav NBre NBro NLar WSpi
- 'Splash'	MAvo
'Linda'	LSRN
linifolia	see *C. carnica*
'Lynchmere'	CMea WAbe
makaschvilii	CEnt CSpe EACa EBee GEdr GKev LRHS MHer NLar SMad SMrm WCot WHrl WPer
'Marion Fisher'	see *C.* × *haylodgensis* W. Brockbank 'Marion Fisher'

medium	LAst
§ - var. ***calycanthema*** hort.	EPfP
- 'Cup and Saucer'	see *C. medium* var. *calycanthema* hort.
'Mevr. V. Vollenhove'	EBee IBoy WCot
'Monic'	EPfP
muralis	see *C. portenschlagiana*
nitida	see *C. persicifolia* var. *planiflora*
'Norman Grove'	EPot
ochroleuca	CMea CPom CSpe GBin SWat WCFE WCot WHrl
- 'White Beauty'	CWib
- 'White Bells'	MWhi
odontosepala	EBee
- from Iran	EPPr NLar
'Oliver's Choice'	WHrl
olympica misapplied	see *C. rotundifolia* 'Olympica'
ossetica	EBee ECtt EWTr MLHP
- hybrids **new**	EWTr
patula	GJos NLar WKif XLum
§ - subsp. ***abietina***	NLar
'Paul Furse'	EBee ECtt EHrv LRHS MDKP MSpe NBre NCGa NPro NSti WWEG
pelviformis	MNrw
pendula	EPfP EWes GBee MBNS NLar
persicifolia	CBcs CMac CSBt CTri EBee EHon EPfP GAbr GJos GMaP LRHS MLHP MMuc NBro NEgg NMir NPri SBfd SDix SPer SPoG WCot WHoo WMoo WPer WTin XLum
- var. ***alba***	Widely available
§ - 'Alba Coronata' (d)	GAbr WFar WSpi
- 'Alba Plena'	see *C. persicifolia* 'Alba Coronata'
- 'Azure Beauty'	CSpe EBee ECtt ELan NCGa NLar WCot WSpi
- 'Beau Belle'	EPfP LSou NLar
§ - 'Bennett's Blue' (d)	EHrv ELan EPfP MRav SPer SRms SWat
- 'Best China' (d)	MAvo
- 'Blue Bloomers' (d)	CElw CLAP ECtt EPri EWes IKil LRHS MAvo MBel MNFA MRav NLBP NRHS NWad SMrm WBrk WCot WHal WPer WSpi XLum
- blue cup-in-cup (d)	ELon MDKP MTis WFar WPtf
- 'Blue-eyed Blonde'[PBR] (v)	ECtt LSou NDov
- blue-flowered	IFoB LAst SEND SPlb WFar WSpi
- 'Boule de Neige' (d)	ECtt LRHS WCFE WSpi WWEG
- 'Caerulea Coronata'	see *C. persicifolia* 'Coronata'
§ - 'Chettle Charm'[PBR] ♀H4	Widely available
- 'Cornish Mist'	CCon CDes CPLG EBee ECtt EHrv ELan EPfP LPla MCot NLar WCot
§ - 'Coronata' (d)	GCra LRHS NLar
- cup and saucer blue (d)	GCra
- double blue-flowered (d)	NBro
- double white-flowered (d)	ELan
- 'Fleur de Neige' (d) ♀H4	NBre WCot WWEG
- 'Frances' (d)	CLAP WCot
- 'Gawen'	CMac EBee ECtt GBee GMaP MCot MTis NBre NDov SMrm WCot
- 'George Chiswell'[PBR]	see *C. persicifolia* 'Chettle Charm'
- 'Grandiflora'	SMrm
- 'Grandiflora Alba'	NLar NWad SMrm XLum
- 'Grandiflora Caerulea'	NLar
§ - 'Hampstead White' (d)	EWhm GCal NBro WHil WMnd WSpi WWEG
- 'Hetty'	see *C. persicifolia* 'Hampstead White'
- Irish double white-flowered (d)	MAvo
- 'Kelly's Gold'	CCon ELon EPfP LAst LRHS NBir NLar WBor WWEG
- 'La Belle'	CWGN EBee ECtt LSou MNrw NLar
- 'La Bello'[PBR]	CWGN EBee ECtt MNrw
- 'La Bonne Amie'	EBee ECtt IKil NDov NLar XEll
- 'Moerheimii' (d)	EPfP
- 'Perry's Boy Blue'	NPer
§ - var. ***planiflora***	CPBP EPot MWat
- - f. ***alba***	MWat
- 'Powder Puff' (d)	EBee GBin LSou MBel MCot NEgg SMrm WCot
- 'Pride of Exmouth' (d)	EHrv ELan EShb MHer WCFE WMnd WPer WSpi WWEG
- subsp. ***sessiliflora*** 'Alba'	see *C. latiloba* 'Alba'
- 'Snowdrift'	ELan SRms
- Takion Series	CSpe
- - 'Takion Blue'	EBee LRHS MSCN
- - 'Takion White'	EBee EPfP LRHS
- 'Telham Beauty' misapplied	CSBt CWCL EBee ELan EPfP LRHS MRav SMrm SPer SRms SWvt WMnd WPer
- 'Telham Beauty' ambig.	LAst LRHS MCot MSCN NEgg NGBl SBfd SPad SRkn SWvt WWEG XLum
- 'Telham Beauty' D. Thurston	NLar
- 'Tinpenny Blue'	WTin
- 'White Queen' (d)	WMnd
- 'Wortham Belle' misapplied	see *C. persicifolia* 'Bennett's Blue'
- 'Wortham Belle' ambig.	CWCL CWGN WHoo
- 'Wortham Belle' Blooms	ECtt LRHS MBNS MCot NDov NEgg WGwG
petrophila	WAbe
pilosa	see *C. chamissonis*
- 'Superba'	see *C. chamissonis* 'Superba'
'Pink Octopus'[PBR]	CCVN CSev CWGN EBee ECtt EHrv GBin IBoy IPot LLHF LRHS MBNS MBel MMoz MTis NCGa NGdn NLar NPnk SMrm SPad SRkn WCot WSpi
planiflora	see *C. persicifolia* var. *planiflora*
§ ***portenschlagiana*** ♀H4	Widely available
- 'Biokovo'	XLum
- 'Catharina'	EBee ECtt LRHS
- 'Lieselotte'	CElw CPBP LLHF SBch
- 'Major'	LAst LBMP WFar WMoo
- 'Resholdt's Variety'	CBar CMea CSam EBee ECho ECtt EDAr EPfP EPot GMaP LHop LRHS MMuc MRav NPri SEND WMoo WPer XLum
poscharskyana	Widely available
- 'Blauranke'	EACa EBee EWes
- 'Blue Gown'	EACa GMaP MNFA
- 'Blue Waterfall'	CWCL CWGN EACa EBee LRHS MBNS NCGa NDov NRHS SPoG WCot WFar
- 'E.H. Frost'	CElw EACa EBee ECho ECtt EDAr EPPr EPfP GMaP LHop MAsh MBri MCot MMuc MWat NBro NRya SAga SEND SRGP SRms SWvt WBrk WFar WMoo WPer XLum
- 'Freya'	XLum
- 'Lilacina'	EPPr
- 'Lisduggan Variety'	CElw EACa EBee ECtt EDAr EPPr EWes GMaP LHop LRHS MAsh MBri MHer MNFA NBro WCot WFar WIce WMoo WPer XLum
- 'Nana Alba'	EACa EPPr
- 'Pinkins'[PBR]	EACa
- 'Stella' ♀H4	EBee ECha ECho ECtt EPPr EPfP LRHS LSRN MAsh MAvo MRav

		NBro NDov SPer SRGP SWvt WFar WMoo WRHF XLum
	- 'Trollkind'	EBee EPPr
	- variegated (v)	EHoe
	- white-flowered	CTri ECho ELan WFar
	prenanthoides	see *Asyneuma prenanthoides*
	primulifolia	ELan LRHS MNrw NBir SRms SWat WMoo XLum
	- 'Blue Oasis'	LSRN
	× ***pseudoraineri*** hort.	EACa EWes LRHS NMen NRHS
	pulla	CPBP CSpe CWCL EACa ECho ECtt EDAr ELon GMaP LRHS MAsh NRHS NSla SPoG SRot WAbe WHoo WIce
	- 'Alba'	EACa ECho ECtt EDAr EPot LRHS MAsh NRHS WAbe
	× ***pulloides*** hort.	EACa EBee ECho ECtt EPot SRkn
	'G.F. Wilson' ♀H4	WFar
	- 'Jelly Bells'	EBee IPot NDov NLar
	punctata	CMHG CSpe GJos GKev LEdu LRHS MCot NBro NSti SBfd SPer SWat WFar WGwG WMoo WPer
	- f. ***albiflora***	MNrw WFar WMnd
	- - 'Alba'	CCVN
	- 'Alina's Double' (d)	MBel MNrw MSpe WCot WWEG
	- 'Cherry Pie'	EPfP LRHS
	- dwarf	CPBP GKev
	- 'Einhorn JP'	IVic
	- 'Golddrache JP'	IVic
	- 'Hexe JP'	IVic
	- var. ***hondoensis***	MLHP
	- - 'Bossy Boots'	SMrm
	- hose-in-hose (d)	MMHG NLar WFar WGwG
	- 'Hot Lips'	CMac ELan EPPr EPfP LRHS LSRN NPnk NPro SBfd SPet SRGP WWEG
*	- var. ***howozana***	GKev
	- var. ***microdonta*** B&SWJ 5553	WCru
	- 'Milky Way'	EPPr
	- 'Milly'	IVic LLHF
	- 'Moorgeist JP'	IVic
*	- 'Nana'	CCVN
	- 'Nasachtal'	IVic
	- 'Pantaloons' (d)	CMac CSpe EBee ECtt EDif LRHS LSRN MDKP NLar SMrm WCot
	- 'Pink Chimes'[PBR]	EBee GKev IVic LSou MBNS
	- 'Plum Wine'	MSpe
	- 'Pumpernickel JP'	IVic
	- 'Reifrock'	IVic SMrm
	- 'Rosea'	SRms
	- f. ***rubriflora***	CCVN ECtt EHrv ELan EPfP GCra GJos LBMP LHop LRHS MCot MNrw MWat MWhi NEgg NOrc SBfd SGar SPer WFar WMnd WPat WPer WTcb WWEG XLum
	- - 'Beetroot'	EBee ECtt EHrv GKev IKil IVic LAst MHer MTis NLar WHrl WPer
	- - 'Bowl of Cherries'[PBR]	CSpe EBee ECtt EPPr EPfP ESwi IVic LLHF LRHS LSRN LSou MMHG NLar NPnk SRkn SRot
	- - 'Cherry Bells'	EBee ECtt EPfP IVic LSRN MNrw NLar SPoG
	- - 'Vienna Festival'	CSBt LSou NLar WCot
	- - 'Wine 'n' Rubies'	ECtt GBee LSRN LSou MAvo MDKP MNrw MSCN WCot
	- 'Seejungfrau JP'	IVic
	- 'Troll JP'	IVic
	- 'Twilight Bells'	NBre
	- 'Wedding Bells'	EACa ECtt EHrv ELan EPri GKev LAst LDai LRHS LSRN MHer MSpe MTis NCGa NLar NSti SPet SPoG SRkn WCAu WHil WWEG
	- 'Weisser Schwan JP'	IVic
	- 'Weisser Turm JP'	IVic
I	- 'White Bells'	ELan EPPr MDKP
	- white hose-in-hose (d)	MNrw WBrk
	'Purple Sensation'[PBR]	CSpe EBee ECtt EPfP IBoy LSou MBel MDev MNrw MTis NCGa NPnk NSti WCot
	pusilla	see *C. cochlearifolia*
	pyramidalis	CSpe EBee ELan EPfP GJos LRHS NGBl NOrc SBfd SEND SPav SPlb WSpi WTcb WWEG XLum
	- 'Alba'	CSpe CWib EBee ELan EPfP GJos LRHS NLar SBfd SEND SPav SPlb WSpi WWEG XLum
	- lavender blue-flowered	CWib
	raddeana	EACa EBee MDKP WBrk
	raineri ♀H4	ECho EPot NMen NSla WAbe
*	- 'Alba'	ECho NMen WAbe
	- 'Nettleton Gold'	ECho EPot LRHS
§	***rapunculoides***	EBee GJos GKev NBre SWat WCFE XLum
§	- 'Afterglow'	MAvo MSpe WCot
	- 'Alba'	EACa MAvo XLum
	rapunculus	CArn WBor WCot XLum
	recurva	see *C. incurva*
	rhomboidalis Gorter	see *C. rapunculoides*
	rhomboidalis L.	XLum
	rigidipila	WHer WOut
	rotundifolia	CArn CRWN EACa ECho EPfP GJos MCot MHer MNHC NBre NGBl NLan SIde SPlb SWat WAbe WBrk WPer WPtf XLum
§	- var. ***alaskana***	LRHS
	- var. ***alba***	CElw EWes WAbe
§	- 'Olympica'	IGor MMuc NLar SEND WFar WHoo
	- 'Superba'	ECho
	- 'White Gem'	CHVG CMea EBee EPfP GJos LBMP LRHS NBre WPtf
	'Royal Wave'	CAbP EBee ECtt IPot MAvo NDov NLar WCot
	rupestris	LLHF WPat
	rupicola	WAbe
	'Samantha'	EBee ECtt LHop LRHS LSRN SMrm SRGP XEll
	'Sarastro'	Widely available
	sarmatica	EPfP GAbr GKev LRHS MNFA NBid SRms WKif
	- 'Hemelstraling'	EBee NLar
	'Senior'	EPPr IVic SHar
	'Serafinental'	IVic
	speciosa	EBee MWhi NBre
	'Stansfieldii'	CPBP ECho LLHF LRHS NMen NRHS
	'Summer Nights' **new**	NCGa
	'Summer Pearl'	CPBP ECtt SBfd
	'Summertime Blues'[PBR]	ECtt NDov NLar
§	'Swannables'	CPou EBee LLHF MNFA NCGa NChi WOut
	takesimana	Widely available
	- B&SWJ 8499	WCru
I	- 'Alba'	LBMP MDKP NBre WMoo
	- 'Beautiful Trust'	CCVN CLAP LHop MCot MSpe NPnk WCot WCru WSpi
	- 'Elizabeth'	Widely available
	- 'Elizabeth II' (d)	ECtt MDKP WCot WSpi

thyrsoides	SPav WAbe
'Timsbury Chimes' new	CPBP
'Timsbury Perfection'	NHar WAbe
'Tiny Bells'	LLHF
tommasiniana ♀H4	WAbe
trachelium	CEnt CMHG CMea EBee ELon GJos LRHS MRav NLan NMir SWat WCot WFar WHer WMoo WOut WPer WWEG
- var. ***alba***	CLAP CMea EWTr GKev LRHS MNrw NLar SWat WCot WFar WMoo WPer
- - 'Alba Flore Pleno' (d)	CLAP LEdu SMHy
- 'Bernice' (d)	Widely available
- lilac-blue-flowered	SWat
- 'Snowball'	CMac EShb LSRN
'Tymonsii'	CPBP ECho LLHF NBir NMen
'Van-Houttei'	CDes EWes SAga SUsu WCot WFar WPer WSpi
versicolor	CSpe
vidalii	see *Azorina vidalii*
waldsteiniana	WAbe
wanneri	EPfP NLar
'Warley White'	see *C.* × *haylodgensis* W. Brockbank 'Warley White'
'Warleyensis'	see *C.* × *haylodgensis* W. Brockbank 'Warley White'
× ***wockei*** 'Puck'	EACa ECho ECtt EPot LHop LLHF LRHS WAbe
zangezura	EBee EDAr EPfP GKev IKil NGdn SBfd
zoysii	NMen

Campanula × *Symphyandra* see *Campanula*

Campanumoea see *Codonopsis*

Campsis (*Bignoniaceae*)

grandiflora	CArn CBcs CSBt CSPN CWGN EBee ELan EPfP LRHS LSRN SPer SRms SWvt WCFE
radicans	CArn CBcs CDul CMac CRHN CWib EBee ECrN ELan EPfP LRHS LSRN MSwo SBfd SLon SPer SPlb
- 'Atrosanguinea'	SBfd
- 'Flamenco'	CBcs CDoC CMac CSPN CWCL EBee ELan EUJe LRHS LSRN MAsh NLar SBfd SCoo SLim SPoG SWvt WFar
§ - f. ***flava*** ♀H4	CBcs CDoC CHEx CMac CTri EBee ELan ELon EPfP LHop LRHS MAsh MBlu MGos NLar NPla NSti SBfd SLim SPer SPoG SWvt WSHC
- 'Indian Summer'	CBcs CSBt CSPN CWGN EBee EPfP LRHS LSRN LSou MBlu MBri MGos MREP NLar SBfd SCoo SPoG WHar
- 'Stromboli'	EPfP
- 'Yellow Trumpet'	see *C. radicans* f. *flava*
× ***tagliabuana*** Dancing Flame = 'Huidan'PBR	CWGN EBee LRHS SGol SPoG
- 'Madame Galen' ♀H4	Widely available

Camptosema (*Papilionaceae*)

praeandinum	WPGP

Camptosorus see *Asplenium*

Camptotheca (*Nyssaceae*)

acuminata	WPGP

Campylandra see *Tupistra*

Campylotropis (*Papilionaceae*)

macrocarpa	EPfP NLar

Canarina (*Campanulaceae*)

canariensis ♀H1	CCCN ECho MOWG WPGP

Candollea see *Hibbertia*

Canna ✿ (*Cannaceae*)

	'Adam's Orange'	CDTJ CHEx XBlo
	'Alaska' ♀H3	EAmu
N	***altensteinii***	CDTJ SHaC SPlb XBlo
	'Ambassador'	LAma SCan SDeJ
	'Ambassadour'	SCan SHaC
	'Annaeei' ♀H3	EAmu
	'Annei-Rubra' new	SCan
	'Anthony and Cleopatra' (v)	WCot
	'Argentina'	SCan
	'Assaut'	SCan SHaC
	'Atlantis'	XBlo
	'Australia'	CDTJ EAmu EPfP SCan SHaC WCot XBlo
	'Austria'	SCan
	'Bethany'	SCan
	'Black Knight'	CCon ECGP LAma LSRN MSCN SCan SEND XBlo
	'Bonfire'	CDTJ CHEx GHim
	brasiliensis	CCon CHll CRHN SCan SHaC WTcb XBlo
	'Brillant'	LAma SCan SDeJ SHaC
	'Caballero'	XLum
	'Canary'	XBlo
	'Centenaire de Rozain-Boucharlat'	SCan SHaC XLum
	'Centurion'	LAma
	'Chinese Coral' Schmid	CHEx LAma
I	'Citrina'	XBlo
§	'City of Portland'	LAma
§	'Cleopatra'	CCCN EAmu LAma SCan XBlo
*	'Cléopâtre'	NGdn
§	'Colibri'	LAma
	'Confetti'	see *C.* 'Colibri'
	'Corrida'	XLum
	'Corsica' (Island Series)	SCan
	'Creamy White'	CHEx SHaC XBlo
	'Crimson Beauty'	LAma
	'Délibáb'	LAma
	'Di Bartolo'	XBlo
	'Durban' Hiley, orange-flowered	see *C.* 'Phasion'
	'Durban' ambig.	CWGN EBee EPfP LAma LSRN MNrw
	'E. Neubert'	SCan SHaC
N	***edulis***	CDTJ CHEx EUJe
§	× ***ehemanii*** ♀H3	CAvo CDTJ CRHN ETod EUJe SCan SDix SHaC WPGP
	'En Avant'	CHEx LAma SPlb
	'Endeavour'	CHEx EUJe MSKA SCan
	'Erebus' ♀H3	MSKA SCan SDix SHaC
	'Ermine'	WCot
	'Étoile du Feu'	XBlo
	'Eureka'	SCan
	'Evening Star'	LAma
	'Fatamorgana'	LAma
	'Felix Ragout'	LAma
	Firebird	see *C.* 'Oiseau de Feu'

	flaccida	SHaC
	'Flame'	XBlo
§	'Florence Vaughan'	SCan
	'General Eisenhower' ♀H3	EAmu SCan
	generalis* × *indica	SHaC
	glauca	SDix SHaC
	'Gnom'	SCan SDeJ
*	'Gold Ader'	LAma
	'Gold Dream'	LAma
	'Golden Lucifer'	ELan LAma
	'Golden Orb'	SCan
	'Gran Canaria'	SCan
	'Grande'	CCon SCan SHaC
	'Heinrich Seidel'	CHEx CHll SCan
	Henlade hybrids	CDTJ
	'Henlade Pink' **new**	SCan
	'Henlade Red' **new**	SCan
	'Hercule'	CHEx SCan
	'Hungaria'	SCan
	hybrids	SHaC
	'Ibis'	EAmu EPfP
	'Ibiza' (Island Series) **new**	SCan
	indica	CAbb CDTJ LTen SCan SGar SHaC SPlb
	- 'Kreta' (Island Series)	SCan
	- 'Purpurea'	CDTJ CHEx EAmu EUJe SCan SDix SHaC SMrm SPlb WPGP
	- 'Red King Rupert'	CCCN
	- 'Russian Red' ♀H3	SHaC
	- Tropicanna Gold = 'Mactro'PBR	CCCN EPfP SCan SPoG
	'Ingeborg' ♀H3	LAma
	'Intrigue'	SCan
	iridiflora misapplied	see *C.* × *ehemanii*
	iridiflora Ruiz & Pav.	CDTJ CHEx CSpe
	'Italia'	SCan
	jacobiniflora	SCan SHaC
	'Kalimpong'	CDTJ SCan
I	'King Humbert' (blood-red)	CBcs CDTJ CHEx EPfP LAma XBlo
	King Humbert (orange-red)	see *C.* 'Roi Humbert'
	'King Midas'	see *C.* 'Richard Wallace'
	'Königin Charlotte'	SCan SDeJ SHaC
	'La Bohème' (Grand Opera Series)	LAma
	latifolia	SHaC
	'Lesotho Lil'	CHll SCan
	'Libération'	XLum
	'Liberté'	see *C.* 'Wyoming'
	'Louis Cayeux' ♀H3	SDix
	'Louis Cottin'	CBcs CCCN CDTJ CHEx EPfP LAma
	'Lucifer'	CCCN CHEx LAma NEgg NPer XLum
N	***lutea***	CHEx SHaC XBlo
	'Madame Angèle Martin'	XBlo
	'Madeira' (Island Series)	EUJe SCan
	'Malawiensis Variegata'	see *C.* 'Striata'
	'Marabout'	SBst SCan
	'Marvel'	LAma
	'Maudie Malcolm'	EPfP
	'Montaigne'	XLum
	'Moonshine'	CCCN
	'Mrs Alfred F. Conard' **new**	SCan
	'Mrs Oklahoma'	LAma SCan
	'Musifolia' ♀H3	CDTJ CHEx EAmu ETod EUJe EWes SCan SDix SHaC XBlo
	'Mystique' ♀H3	EWes SCan SDix
	'Ointment Pink'	XBlo
§	'Oiseau de Feu'	LAma XLum
	'Oiseau d'Or'	XLum
	'Orange Beauty'	SCan
	'Orange Perfection'	CCon LAma SCan SMrm
	'Orange Punch'	EAmu WCot
	'Orchid'	see *C.* 'City of Portland'
	'Osric'	CSpe
	'Panache'	CDTJ CHEx CRHN SCan WCot
	paniculata	SHaC
	'Park Princess' **new**	SHaC
	'Peach Pink'	XBlo
	'Pearlescent Pink'	XBlo
	'Perkeo'	LAma
§	'Phasion' (v) ♀H3	CCCN CHEx CHll CSpe ELan EPfP EUJe EWes LRHS LSRN MSCN NPer NPla SBst SCan SDix SEND SHaC SPoG WCot XBlo
	'Picasso' ♀H3	CBcs CCCN CDTJ CHEx CPLG LAma SEND XBlo
	'Pink Champagne'	XBlo
	'Pink Futurity' (Futurity Series)	CCCN
	'Pink Sunburst' (v)	CDTJ SCan
	'Plaster Pink'	XBlo
	'President'	LAma SCan SHaC XBlo XLum
	'Pretoria'	see *C.* 'Striata'
	'Pretoria Variegata'	see *C.* 'Striata'
	'Pringle Bay' (v)	SCan
	'Professor Lorentz'	see *C.* 'Wyoming'
	'Ra' ♀H3	MSKA SHaC
	'Red Futurity' (Futurity Series)	SCan
§	'Richard Wallace'	CPLG LAma SCan SHaC SPlb XBlo
§	'Roi Humbert'	SCan SHaC
	'Roi Soleil' ♀H3	LAma XLum
	'Roitelet'	CHEx
	'Roma'	SCan SHaC
	'Rose Futurity' (Futurity Series)	SCan
	'Rosemond Coles'	CHEx LAma SCan SHaC XBlo
	'Saladin'	XLum
	'Sémaphore'	EBee EUJe SCan SPad WCot XBlo
	'Shenandoah' ♀H3	SCan
	'Singapore Girl'	SCan
	'Snow-white'	XBlo
	'Soudan'	CDTJ SCan
N	***speciosa***	CDTJ GHim XBlo
	'Statue of Liberty'	SCan
	'Strasbourg'	LAma NPer SCan XLum
	'Strawberry Pink'	XBlo
	'Striata' misapplied	see *C.* 'Stuttgart'
§	'Striata' (v) ♀H3	CCCN CDTJ CHEx CSpe CWGN EBee EPfP EUJe GHim LSRN MREP NPla SCan SEND SHaC SMad WCot XBlo XLum
	'Striped Beauty' (v)	CCCN CDTJ EUJe GHim SCan
§	'Stuttgart' (v)	CDTJ CSpe EAmu EWes SCan SHaC WCot
	'Summer Gold'	XBlo
	'Summer Joy'	SHaC
	'Sunset'	WCot
	'Tali' **new**	SCan
	'Talisman'	LAma XBlo
	'Taney'	EUJe MSKA SHaC
	'Taroudant'	XLum
	'Tenerife'	SCan
	'Tirol'	SCan
	'Tricarinata'	CHEx
	(Tropical Series) 'Tropical Bronze Scarlet' **new**	SCan

- 'Tropical Red'	SCan SHaC
- 'Tropical Rose'	SCan SHaC SRms
- 'Tropical Salmon'	SCan SHaC
- 'Tropical White'	SCan SHaC
- 'Tropical Yellow'	SCan SGar SHaC
Tropicanna	see *C.* 'Phasion'
Tropicanna Black = 'Lon01' PBR new	SCan
tuerckheimii	SCan SHaC
'Valentine'	EAmu EBee WCot
'Vanilla Pink'	XBlo
* 'Variegata' (v)	LAma LSou
'Verdi' ♀H3	CSpe LAma SCan SHaC
N ***warscewiczii***	CDTJ CPLG SCan SHaC
'Weymouth'	CDTJ
'Whithelm Pride' ♀H3	SCan SDeJ SHaC
'Wintzer's Colossal'	SCan
'Woodbridge Pink'	XBlo
§ 'Wyoming' ♀H3	CBcs CCCN CDTJ CHEx ECGP ETod EUJe LAma SCan SDeJ SEND SHaC XBlo
'Yara'	SCan SDeJ SHaC
'Yellow Humbert' misapplied	see *C.* 'Richard Wallace', *C.* 'Cleopatra', *C.* 'Florence Vaughan'
'Yellow Humbert'	LAma SCan

Cantua (*Polemoniaceae*)

buxifolia ♀H2-3	CAbb CBcs CCCN CPLG EBee ECre IRar LRHS MOWG WPGP
- 'Alba'	CCCN EBee
- 'Dancing Oaks'	WCot

Cape gooseberry see *Physalis peruviana*

Capnoides see *Corydalis*

Capparis (*Capparaceae*)

spinosa	CCCN
- subsp. ***rupestris***	SPlb

Capsicum (*Solanaceae*)

annuum	CCCN
- var. ***annuum*** (Longham Group) cayenne	CCCN
- - 'Prairie Fire' ♀H2	CCCN
- 'Apache' ♀H2	CCCN SEND

Caragana (*Papilionaceae*)

CC 3945	CPLG
arborescens	CAgr CArn CDul CMCN ELan EPfP NWea SEND SPer SPlb
- 'Lorbergii'	MBlu SPer
- 'Pendula'	CMac CWib ELan ESwi LAst MAsh NEgg NLar SCoo SLim SPer
- 'Walker'	CMac CWib EBee ELan EPfP MAsh MBlu MBri MGos NHol NLar NWea SCoo SLim SPer
pygmaea	NLar

carambola see *Averrhoa carambola*

caraway see *Carum carvi*

Cardamine ✿ (*Brassicaceae*)

angustata	WCru
asarifolia misapplied	see *Pachyphragma macrophyllum*
asarifolia L.	LRHS
bulbifera	CLAP EBee ELon EPPr GEdr LEdu NRya WCru WSHC
bulbosa new	GBuc
californica	EPPr NRya WCru WMoo
concatenata	WCru
digitata	EBee NCGa
diphylla	CDes CLAP LEdu NLar SKHP WCot WCru
- 'American Sweetheart'	CPLG WCot
- 'Eco Cut Leaf'	CDes CPLG EBee WCot WCru
- 'Eco Moonlight'	WCru
enneaphylla	CLAP NDov NLar
glanduligera	ECha ELon EPPr GBuc GEdr LEdu MMoz MNrw NSla SMrm WCot WCru WSHC
§ ***heptaphylla***	CAvo CLAP ECha ECho ELon IGor WSHC
- 'Big White'	GBuc GCal NCGa
- Guincho form	CLAP EPPr WCot
- white-flowered	CLAP GMaP
§ ***kitaibelii***	CLAP LEdu WCru
latifolia Vahl	see *C. raphanifolia*
macrophylla	CLAP EBee EHrv LEdu SWat WCot WFar WSHC
- CD&R 561	NCGa
- 'Bright and Bronzy'	CPLG GEdr WCru
maxima	LEdu WCru
microphylla	WAbe
pachystigma	GBuc
pentaphylla ♀H4	CBro CSpe EBee ECho ELan ELon EPPr GAbr GBuc GEdr GMaP IFro IGor MCot NBir NLar WCot
- bright pink-flowered	CLAP WCot
pratensis	CArn CRWN CWat EBee EHon LRHS MCot MHer MNHC MSKA NLan NMir NPri SIde SWat WHer WMoo WSFF WShi
- 'Diane's Petticoat'	MAvo MHer MNrw WHoo
- 'Edith' (d)	CLAP LRHS MMoz MNrw
- 'Flore Pleno' (d)	CBct CBre EBee ECha ELan EPfP GBuc GMaP IFro MHer MNrw NBid NBir NBro NCGa NLar NPnk NPri NSla SBch SWat WCot WFar WSFF
- 'William' (d)	MAvo MNrw WMoo
quinquefolia	CDes CElw CLAP CMea CPom ECha EHrv ELon GBuc LEdu MCot MMoz NCGa NLar NMyG SDys SMrm WBrk WCot WCru WFar WOut WPGP
§ ***raphanifolia***	CBre CDes CPLG CRow EBee GAbr GBin GCal IFro LEdu LRHS NBid NBro NSti SKHP SWat WMoo WOut WPGP WTin
trifolia	CMac ECha EHrv ELon EPPr GBin GCal GEdr GMaP IFro LRHS MRav NBir NBro NLar NRya SWat WCot WCru WFar WMoo
waldsteinii	CDes CElw CLAP CPLG CSpe EBee ECho EHrv GBuc GEdr LEdu NCGa SBch SCnR SUsu WCru WSHC WTcb
yezoensis B&SWJ 4659	WCru

cardamon see *Elettaria cardamomum*

Cardiandra (*Hydrangeaceae*)

alternifolia	LLHF
- B&SWJ 5719	WCru
- B&SWJ 5845	WCru
- B&SWJ 6177	WCru

- B&SWJ 6354 WCru
- subsp. ***moellendorffii*** WPGP
- 'Pink Geisha' WCru

amamiohshimensis WCru
formosana CGHE CPLG WPGP
- B&SWJ 2005 WCru
- 'Crûg's Abundant' WCru
- 'Hsitou' WCru
- 'Hsitou Splendour' WCru

Cardiocrinum ✿ (*Liliaceae*)

cathayanum EBee GEdr WCot
cordatum ECho LWst
- B&SWJ 2812 WCru
- B&SWJ 4841 WCru
- B&SWJ 5427 WCru
- B&SWJ 6336 WCru
- var. ***glehnii*** CCCN ECho GBuc GEdr
- - B&SWJ 4722 WCru
- - B&SWJ 4758 WCru
- red-veined GEdr MNrw

giganteum Widely available
- B&SWJ 2419 WCru
- GWJ 9219 from Sikkim WCru
- HWJK 2158 from Nepal WCru
- var. ***yunnanense*** ECho EPfP GAbr GBuc GEdr GGGa GLin LRHS NBid WCot WCru WPGP

cardoon see *Cynara cardunculus*

Carduus (*Asteraceae*)

benedictus see *Cnicus benedictus*

Carex (*Cyperaceae*)

from Uganda SApp
acuta MSKA
- 'Variegata' (v) CBen CMac CRow EHoe EHon EShb GMaP IFro LPBA MMoz MWts NBro NOak SApp SBfd SEND WCot WHal WMoo

acutiformis CRWN NMir
alba EPPr WCot
'Amazon Mist' EBee EPPr LHop NWsh WNew
appalachica EPPr
appressa SApp
arenaria CKno GBin
atrata EBee EHoe WHrl
§ - subsp. ***pullata*** GCal
aurea EPPr IFoB
baccans CPLG GCal
bebbii EPPr
berggrenii EBee ECou EHoe ELan EPPr LPBA LPot LRHS NLar SPlb WTin
binervis CRWN
boottiana EWes
brunnea CMac EWes SBfd SHDw
- 'Jenneke' (v) EBee EPfP LRHS MAsh MBri SBfd SHDw SLim SWvt WCot
- 'Variegata' (v) CEnt EHoe SApp SBfd SHDw

buchananii ♀H4 Widely available
- 'Green Twist' CKno LPla
- 'Viridis' ELan EPPr GBin XLum

§ ***canescens*** subsp. ***canescens*** CRWN
chathamica EBee LRHS SApp SGar
'China Blue' MMoz SApp
ciliatomarginata 'Treasure Island' (v) EPPr
comans CPne EPPr EPfP NBro
- from Dunedin, New Zealand EPPr
- 'Bronze Perfection' SMea WFar XLum
- bronze-leaved Widely available
- 'Bronzita' EPPr LRHS
- 'Copper Green' SMea
- 'Dancing Flame' CWCL EBee ELon MBri NWsh
- 'Frosted Curls' Widely available
- red-leaved CBcs CWCL NLar SRms
- 'Small Red' see *C. comans* 'Taranaki'

§ - 'Taranaki' EPPr EPfP MBNS SCoo SWal
conica MWat
- 'Hime-kan-suge' see *C. conica* 'Snowline'
- 'Kiku-sakura' (v) EPPr

§ - 'Snowline' (v) CMac EBee ECha EHoe ELan EPfP GAbr GKev GMaP LEdu LLWP LPBA LRHS LTen MMoz NBro NLar NWsh SBfd SGol SWal SWvt WPer XLum

crinita EPPr
cristatella EPPr
curta see *C. canescens* subsp. *canescens*
dallii EWes WHrl
davalliana new EBee
davisii EPPr
demissa see *C. viridula* subsp. *oedocarpa*
depauperata CRWN EHoe
digitata CRWN
dioica CRWN
dipsacea CKno CMac CWCL EBee EHoe EPPr EShb GMaP MAsh MMoz MNrw NRHS NWsh SBch SBea SBfd SEND WHal WMoo WPer WWEG
- 'Dark Horse' CKno EBee EHoe EPPr ETod LLHF LRHS SBfd SEND SMea WPtf

divulsa CKno
- subsp. ***divulsa*** CRWN
- subsp. ***leersii*** EPPr

§ ***dolichostachya*** 'Kaga-nishiki' (v) CSBt EBee EPPr LEdu LHop LRHS SLim
duthiei see *C. atrata* subsp. *pullata*
ebenea LRHS
echinata CRWN
§ ***elata*** 'Aurea' (v) ♀H4 Widely available
- 'Bowles's Golden' see *C. elata* 'Aurea'
- 'Knightshayes' ♀H4 CKno EWes MWhi NLar WCot

'Evergold' see *C. oshimensis* 'Evergold'
firma 'Variegata' (v) GEdr MWat NMen WAbe WThu
flacca CHab CKno CRWN EHoe EPPr GBin XLum
- 'Bias' (v) EBee MMoz
- 'Blue Zinger' CKno WWEG

§ - subsp. ***flacca*** EBee EWes MMoz NSti SMea
flagellifera CBcs CHEx CMac CSpe CTri CWCL EBee EHoe EPPr EPfP EShb GCal GMaP LRHS LSRN MBrN MLHP MMuc MWhi NBir SEND SMrm SPlb WFar WWEG XLum
- 'Auburn Cascade' EBee LHop LRHS NWad SApp SBfd
- 'Coca-Cola' NOak
- 'Rapunzel' EBee EPPr

flava CKno EHoe EPPr
folliculata new EBee
fortunei see *C. morrowii* Boott
fraseri see *Cymophyllus fraserianus*
fraserianus see *Cymophyllus fraserianus*

	glauca Bosc. ex Boott	see *C. glaucescens*
	glauca Scop.	see *C. flacca* subsp. *flacca*
§	***glaucescens***	CWCL EPPr SBfd
	'Gold Fountains'	see *C. dolichostachya* 'Kaga-nishiki'
	granularis	EPPr
I	'Grayassina'	EPPr
	grayi	CDes CWCL EBee EHoe LEdu LRHS
		MBlu MSKA NCGa NLar NOak
		NPnk XLum
	'Happy Wanderer'	SLPl
	hirta	CRWN
	hostiana	CRWN
	hystricina	LRHS
	'Ice Dance' (v)	CKno EBee EHon EPPr EPfP GKev
		GQue LEdu LPot LRHS MAsh MBri
		MMoz MSCN NHol NOak NOrc
		NRHS SBch SBfd SGol SHil SWvt
		WCot WWEG
	kaloides	EBee EHoe EPPr LRHS XLum
	'Kan-suge'	see *C. morrowii* Boott
*	***leformeri***	XLum
§	***leporina***	CRWN
	lupulina	GBin NOak
	lurida	EPfP MBNS
	- 'Silver'	EPPr MBNS
	maritima Gunnerus	CRWN
	mertensii NNS 07-98	EPPr
	Milk Chocolate = 'Milchoc'^{PBR} (v)	EBee EPfP SApp
	morrowii misapplied	see *C. oshimensis*
§	***morrowii*** Boott	CWCL EPPr NWad
I	- 'Fisher's Form' (v)	CKno CTri EBee ELan EPPr
		LHop MMoz MRav NGdn NHol
		NLar NWsh SApp SBfd SEND
		SWvt WFar WGrn WPer WWEG
	- 'Gilt' (v)	EBee EHoe EPPr MBNS NHol
	- 'Nana Variegata' (v)	CTri NBir
	- 'Pinkie'	WPtf
	- var. ***temnolepis*** 'Silk Tassel' (v)	EPPr
N	- 'Variegata' (v)	EHoe EHrv ELan EPPr GCal GMaP
		LAst LPBA MMoz MMuc NBir NSti
		SEND SGol SLPl SRms WFar XLum
	muehlenbergii	EPPr
	muricata	EPPr
	muskingumensis	Widely available
	- 'Ice Fountains' (v)	EPPr WWEG
	- 'Little Midge'	CKno CMac EBee EPPr GBin GCal
		LEdu MAsh NOak WCot WWEG
	- 'Little Titch' **new**	SMHy
	- 'Oehme' (v)	CKno CWCL EBee EPPr EShb GBin
		GCal LEdu NBid NHol NRHS NWad
		WPtf WTin WWEG
	- 'Silberstreif' (v)	CKno EBee EPPr GBin LEdu MMuc
		NLar SApp SEND XLum
	nigra (L.) Reichard	CRWN EHon EPPr XLum
§	- 'On-line' (v)	CKno EBee EHrv EPPr MBNS MMoz
		NRHS NWsh SApp
	- 'Variegata'	see *C. nigra* 'On-line'
	No 1, Nanking (Greg's broad leaf)	MMoz
	No 4, Nanking (Greg's thin leaf)	EPPr MMoz SApp
	normalis	EPPr
	obnupta	CKno EPPr
	ornithopoda 'Aurea'	see *C. ornithopoda* 'Variegata'
§	- 'Variegata' (v)	EBee ECtt EPPr NBro NGdn
		NHol NOak NWsh SBch WMoo
		WWEG
§	***oshimensis***	EPPr MMoz
	- Everest = 'Fiwhite' (v)	CKno EBee LRHS SBfd SPoG WCot
§	- 'Evergold' (v) Ψ^{H4}	Widely available
	- 'Everillo' **new**	WCot
	- 'J.S. Greenwell' **new**	EBee
	- 'Variegata' (v)	NBir
	otrubae	CHab CRWN
	ovalis	see *C. leporina*
	panicea	CKno CRWN CSBt CWCL EBee
		EHoe EPPr MMoz MSKA SApp
		WGrn WMoo
	paniculata	CRWN XLum
	parviflora	SMea
	pendula	Widely available
	- 'Cool Jazz' (v)	EPPr MSKA
	- 'Moonraker' (v)	CWCL EHoe EPPr ESwi MBNS
		MSKA NOak SApp SLPl WCot
		WWEG
	petriei	CWCL ECha ELon ETod EWes LLWP
		MBNS WCot WFar
	phyllocephala	EShb
	- 'Sparkler' (v)	EBee ECtt EHoe ELon EPfP LAst
		LEdu LRHS NSti SBfd SPad SWvt
		XLum
	plantaginea	EBee EHoe EPPr GBin LEdu SApp
		WCot WMoo WWEG
	praegracilis	CKno EPPr
	Pritchard's selection (v)	IFro
	projecta	EPPr
	pseudocyperus	CBen CPom CRWN EHoe EHon
		GBin LPBA MMoz MSKA NPer
		NWsh SWat WMoo WPnP
	pulicaris	CRWN
	punctata	XLum
	'Red Rooster'	EBee MWat WNew
	remota	CKno CRWN EHoe EPPr SMea
	riparia	CRWN LPBA MMoz MSKA NPer
		SEND SMea SWat WShi
	- 'Bowles's Golden'	see *C. elata* 'Aurea'
	rostrata	CRWN SEND
	sabynensis	see *C. umbrosa* subsp. *sabynensis*
	secta	CKno CTrC ECou EPPr GBin GMaP
		MNrw NRHS SHDw WMoo WPer
	- from Dunedin, New Zealand	EPPr
	siderosticha	SLPl
	- 'Banana Boat'	see *C. siderosticha* 'Golden Falls'
	- 'Echigo-nishiki' (v)	EPPr
§	- 'Golden Falls' (v)	LEdu LRHS NOak NOrc SMad
	- 'Golden Fountains'	WCot
	- 'Kisokaido' (v)	EPPr LEdu
	- 'Old Barn'	EBee
	- 'Shima-nishiki' (v)	CJun EBee ECtt EPPr EPfP LAst
		LRHS MBNS NOak NPro SAga
		WWEG
	- 'Shiro-nakafu' **new**	EBee
	- 'Variegata' (v)	CHEx CPrp EBee EHoe ELan ELon
		EPPr EPfP EShb GCal LAst LEdu
		LHop LRHS NBir NBro NLar NOak
		NSti NWsh SApp SBfd SLim WBor
		WTin WWEG
	'Silver Sceptre' (v)	EBee ECtt EHoe EPPr EShb GMaP
		LRHS LTen MBNS MGos NHol NPro
		NSti NWsh SBfd SEND SLim SPlb
		SWal SWvt WBrk WMoo
	'Silver Sparkler'	NBir
	'Silver Streams'	WWEG
	solandri	CKno LEdu LPla NWsh SApp SBfd
		SHDw WPtf

spissa MNrw
stricta 'Bowles's Golden' see *C. elata* 'Aurea'
sylvatica CRWN EBee EHoe
tenuiculmis CWCL EBee EPPr EShb LHop MAsh NOak NSti NWad NWsh SBfd WCot WTin WWEG
- 'Cappucino' CKno
testacea Widely available
- 'Autumn Gold' SBfd
- dark-leaved EPfP
- 'Old Gold' ELan EPPr EWes LRHS NOak SBfd SMad SPlb WFar WGrn WMoo
- 'Prairie Fire' EBee EPPr LHop LRHS
texensis EPPr
'The Beatles' EHoe EPPr NBir
trifida CHEx CKno EHoe MNrw NWsh
- 'Chatham Blue' CHid GBin LRHS MMoz SEND
* - 'Glauca' **new** CWCL
- 'Rekohu Sunrise'^{PBR} (v) CBct CKno EBee ELon EPfP ESwi LRHS MBri SBfd SLon SPoG
umbrosa subsp. ***sabynensis*** 'Thinny Thin' (v) EPPr EShb
§ ***viridula*** CRWN
subsp. ***oedocarpa***
- subsp. ***viridula*** CRWN
vulpina EPPr LRHS
vulpinoidea EPPr LRHS

Carica (*Caricaceae*)

papaya (F) XBlo
- 'Babaco' CCCN

Carissa (*Apocynaceae*)

grandiflora see *C. macrocarpa*
§ ***macrocarpa*** (F) CCCN

Carlina (*Asteraceae*)

acaulis CArn ECho ELan GEdr SPlb WFar
- subsp. ***acaulis*** GPoy
- bronze-leaved LDai
- var. ***caulescens*** see *C. acaulis* subsp. *simplex*
§ - subsp. ***simplex*** EBee ECha NPri
- - bronze-leaved EBee SMad SPhx
vulgaris 'Silver Star' SPhx

Carmichaelia (*Papilionaceae*)

'Abundance' ECou
'Angie' ECou
angustata 'Buller' ECou
appressa ECou
- 'Ellesmere' ECou
astonii ECou
- 'Ben More' ECou
- 'Chalk Ridge' ECou
australis WSHC
'Charm' ECou
'Clifford Bay' ECou
corrugata ECou
curta ECou
enysii LLHF
fieldii 'Westhaven' ECou
flagelliformis 'Roro' ECou
glabrata WCot
'Hay and Honey' ECou
kirkii ECou WThu
'Lilac Haze' ECou
monroi ECou
- 'Rangitata' ECou
- 'Tekapo' ECou
odorata CPLG ECou
- 'Lakeside' ECou
- 'Riverside' ECou
ovata 'Calf Creek' ECou
'Parson's Tiny' ECou
petriei ECou SMad
- 'Aviemore' ECou
- 'Lindis' ECou
- 'Pukaki' ECou
'Porter's Pass' ECou
'Spangle' ECou
stevensonii EPfP
'Tangle' ECou
uniflora ECou
- 'Bealey' ECou
williamsii ECou

× *Carmispartium* see *Carmichaelia*

Carpenteria (*Hydrangeaceae*)

californica $\mathbb{Y}^{H3}$ CJun CSBt CTri EBee ELan EPfP EWTr LAst LRHS MBri MGos MWat NLar NPri SEND SGar SSpi SWvt WPat WSpi
- 'Bodnant' CDul EBee ELan LRHS MBri MGos NLar NRHS SHil SWvt WPGP WSpi
- 'Elizabeth' CAbP CBcs CJun CSBt CWGN EBee ELan EPfP LRHS LSRN MAsh SPoG SSpi SSta WPGP WPat
- 'Eskimo' EBee WCot
- 'Ladhams' Variety' CBcs CDul CJun EBee EPfP LRHS MGos MRav NLar SRkn SWvt WSpi

Carpinus ✿ (*Betulaceae*)

sp. CMen LSRN
betulus $\mathbb{Y}^{H4}$ Widely available
- 'Columnaris' CDul CLnd CTho EBee
* - 'Columnaris Nana' LLHF MPkF WPat
§ - 'Fastigiata' $\mathbb{Y}^{H4}$ CBcs CCVT CDoC CDul CLnd CMCN CMac CSBt CTho CWib EBee ECrN ELan EPfP LAst LBuc LHop LMaj LRHS MGos NEgg NPri NWea SBfd SCoo SEWo SGol WFar WHar WMou
- 'Frans Fontaine' CCVT CDoC CDul CLnd CMCN CTho EBee EPfP IArd LHop LMaj MBlu MBri MGos NLar NWea SCoo SEWo SLim SPer SPoG WHar
- 'Globus' MBlu
- 'Incisa' WMou
- 'Lucas' **new** SSta
- 'Monument' MPkF
- 'Pendula' CDul CTho EBee MBlu SPoG
- 'Purpurea' MBlu MGos NLar
- 'Pyramidalis' see *C. betulus* 'Fastigiata'
- 'Quercifolia' CDul
caroliniana CDul CLnd CMCN EPfP SBir SMad WMou
- 'Sentinel Dries' MBlu MBri
cordata MBlu SSta
coreana EGFP IArd SBir SSta
eximia **new** SSta
fangiana CBcs CDul CPLG CTho EBee EPfP IVic SKHP SMad SSta WPGP
fargesiana EGFP
fargesii see *C. viminea*

henryana CMen CPLG SBir
japonica ♀[H4] CDul CLnd CMCN CMen EBee EGFP EPfP LLHF MBlu MBri NLar SBir SCoo SEWo SMad SSta
- B&SWJ 10803 WCru
- B&SWJ 11072 WCru
kawakamii CWJ 12412 WCru
- CWJ 12449 WCru
laxiflora CMen CPLG WPGP
- B&SWJ 10809 WCru
- B&SWJ 11035 WCru
- var. ***longispica*** B&SWJ 8772 WCru
- var. ***macrostachya*** see *C. viminea*
orientalis SBir
polyneura SBir SSta
pubescens WPGP
- 'Abbotsbury' **new** SSta
rankanensis SSta
- RWJ 9839 WCru
× ***schuschaensis*** EBtc SBir
shensiensis CDul
tschonoskii B&SWJ 10800 WCru
turczaninowii ♀[H4] CDul CMCN CMen EGFP NLar SBir SSta WPGP
§ ***viminea*** CPLG SBir SSta

Carpobrotus (*Aizoaceae*)

§ ***edulis*** CCCN CDTJ CDoC EShb SEND WHer XLum
- var. ***edulis*** CHEx
- var. ***rubescens*** CCCN CHEx
muirii CCCN
sauerae CCCN

Carpodetus (*Rousseaceae*)

serratus CBcs IVic

Carrierea (*Salicaceae*)

calycina IVic WPGP

carrot see *Daucus carota*

Carthamus (*Asteraceae*)

tinctorius CArn MNHC SPav

Carum (*Apiaceae*)

carvi CArn CWan ELau ENfk GPoy MHer MHoo MNHC SIde SVic WJek
petroselinum see *Petroselinum crispum*

Carya ✿ (*Juglandaceae*)

cordiformis CTho MBlu
N ***illinoinensis*** (F) CAgr CBcs MBri
- 'Carlson No 3' seedling (F) CAgr
- 'Colby' seedling (F) CAgr
- 'Cornfield' (F) CAgr
- 'Lucas' (F) CAgr
laciniosa (F) CTho EPfP
- 'Henry' (F) CAgr
- 'Keystone' seedling (F) CAgr
ovata (F) CAgr CBcs CMCN CTho EPfP MBlu SSpi
- 'Grainger' seedling (F) CAgr
- 'Neilson' seedling (F) CAgr
- 'Weschcke' seedling (F) CAgr
- 'Yoder no 1' seedling (F) CAgr
tomentosa EPfP

Caryophyllus see *Syzygium*

Caryopteris ✿ (*Lamiaceae*)

× ***clandonensis*** CMac ECtt MWat NBir WFar
- 'Arthur Simmonds' ♀[H4] CTri ECha ELan EPfP LHop LSRN SBod SPer WGor
- 'Dark Knight' CMea CSpe ECtt ELan EPfP LAst LBuc LRHS MAsh MBri MWat NPnk SBfd SHar SPoG SPtl SWvt WHoo
- 'Ferndown' CDoC CWib ELon EPfP NLar SEND SPoG SRms
- 'First Choice' ♀[H3-4] CDul CMac EBee ECtt ELan EPPr EPfP EShb LAst LHop LRHS LSRN LSqu MAsh MGos SDys SLim SPer SPoG SRkn SWvt
- 'Gold Giant' EBee LRHS MAsh SPer SPoG
- Grand Bleu = 'Inoveris'[PBR] CDul CMac CSBt EBee ELan EPfP EShb LRHS LSRN MGos MSwo NLar NRHS SGol SHil SWvt WPat WRHF
- 'Heavenly Baby' ♀[H3-4] EBee EPfP LRHS MAsh NRHS SKHP SLon SPoG
- 'Heavenly Blue' Widely available
- Hint of Gold = 'Lisaura'[PBR] ♀[H3-4] EBee ELan EPfP LRHS MAsh NRHS SBfd SPoG
- 'Kew Blue' Widely available
- 'Longwood Blue' CCse EBee ELan EPfP LRHS MAsh NRHS SRms
- Sterling Silver = 'Lissilv'[PBR] EBee EPfP LRHS MAsh NRHS SPer SPoG
- 'Summer Gold' MAsh MRav
- 'Summer Sorbet'[PBR] (v) ♀[H3-4] CDoC CWGN EBee EHoe ELan EPfP EWes LHop LRHS MAsh MGos MTPN MWat NEgg NPnk NRHS SBfd SCoo SEND SLim SPad SPer SPoG SWvt WHar
- 'White Surprise'[PBR] CWGN EBee ELan EMil EPfP EWTr LRHS MPkF SPoG
- 'Worcester Gold' ♀[H3-4] Widely available
divaricata CMCN WHil
- 'Electrum' LSou
- 'Jade Shades' EBee LSou
§ ***incana*** EBee EPfP SPer
- 'Autumn Pink'[PBR] ECrN ELan EPfP LSRN SEND
- 'Blue Cascade' EBee EBtc ELan GQue MRav NLar SRms WGrn WPat
§ - 'Jason'[PBR] EBee ECrN ELon EPPr EPfP MBri MPkF NEgg SPoG
- Sunshine Blue[PBR] see *C. incana* 'Jason'
mastacanthus see *C. incana*

Caryota (*Arecaceae*)

mitis ♀[H1] CCCN EAmu
- 'Himalaya' EAmu
obtusa EAmu

Cassandra see *Chamaedaphne*

Cassia (*Caesalpiniaceae*)

corymbosa Lam. see *Senna corymbosa*
marilandica see *Senna marilandica*

Cassinia (*Asteraceae*)

fulvida CBcs ECou EHoe
leptophylla CBcs SPer
- 'Avalanche Creek' ECou
- subsp. ***vauvilliersii*** EBee SEND SPer
- - var. ***albida*** SPer
'Ward Silver' CTrC ECou EHoe EWes SEND

Cassinia × *Helichrysum* (*Asteraceae*)

hybrid WKif

Cassiope ✿ (*Ericaceae*)

'Askival Freebird' see *C.* Freebird Group
'Askival Snowbird' ITim NHar
'Askival Snow-wreath' see *C.* Snow-wreath Group
'Badenoch' ECho EPot GBin GEdr
'Edinburgh' ♀H4 ECho EPot GBin GEdr NHar NWad WIce WThu
fastigiata WAbe
§ Freebird Group NHar
lycopodioides 'Beatrice Lilley' GBin GEdr NHar WThu
- 'Jim Lever' NHar WAbe
mertensiana ECho EPot GEdr
- 'California Pink' GKev NHar NWad
- var. ***californica*** ITim NWad WThu
- var. ***gracilis*** ITim NHar NWad WThu
'Muirhead' ♀H4 ECho NHar WThu
'Randle Cooke' ♀H4 ECho EPot GEdr NHar WIce WThu
selaginoides GBin
- LS&E 13284 WAbe WThu
§ Snow-wreath Group ITim
tetragona ITim WAbe

Castanea ✿ (*Fagaceae*)

'Bouche de Bétizac' (F) CAgr CMam
crenata CAgr CDul
henryi EGFP
'Maraval' (F) CAgr CTho MBlu MBri MCoo MWat SGol WHar
'Maridonne' (F) CAgr CMam
'Marigoule' (F) CAgr CMam EPom MCoo WHar
'Marlhac' (F) CAgr CMam
'Marsol' (F) CAgr MCoo SGol
mollissima CBcs EGFP
'Précoce Migoule' (F) CAgr
sativa ♀H4 CBcs CCVT CDoC CDul CLnd CSBt CTho CTri CWib ECrN ELan EPfP EWTr LAst LBuc MAsh MBri MGos MMuc NPri NWea SBfd SEND SEWo SGol SLim SPer WFar WHar WMou
§ - 'Albomarginata' (v) ♀H4 CDoC CDul EBee EPfP LHop MAsh MBlu MBri MGos
- 'Anny's Red' MBlu
- 'Anny's Summer Red' CDul
- 'Argenteovariegata' see *C. sativa* 'Albomarginata'
- 'Aspleniifolia' CDul
- 'Aureomarginata' see *C. sativa* 'Variegata'
- 'Belle Epine' (F) CAgr
- 'Bournette' (F) CAgr CMam
* - 'Doré de Lyon' CAgr
- 'Marron Comballe' (F) CAgr
- 'Marron de Goujounac' (F) CAgr
- 'Marron de Lyon' (F) CAgr CDul EPfP EPom IVic MBri SVic
- 'Regal' (F) new EPom
§ - 'Variegata' (v) CBcs CDul CLnd CMCN ELan LMaj MGos

Castanopsis (*Fagaceae*)

eyrei CMCN
sclerophylla CBcs LEdu WPGP
sieboldii new CMCN

Castanospermum (*Papilionaceae*)

australe CArn

Castilleja (*Orobanchaceae*)

miniata WAbe
unalaschcensis new GKev

Catalpa ✿ (*Bignoniaceae*)

bignonioides ♀H4 CBcs CCVT CDul CHEx CHab CLnd CMCN CSBt CTho CTri EBee ECrN ELan EPfP EWTr GKin LEdu MBri MSwo NWea SBfd SEND SGol SPad SPer SPlb WFar
- 'Aurea' ♀H4 Widely available
* - 'Aurea Nana' MBri
- 'Nana' EBee LMaj MBri MWat SLim WHar WPat
- 'Purpurea' see *C.* × *erubescens* 'Purpurea'
- 'Variegata' (v) ELon EPfP LHop LRHS MAsh MGos NWea WPat
bungei EGFP MBlu SGol
§ × ***erubescens*** 'Purpurea' ♀H4 CBcs CDoC CDul CLnd CMac CTho EAmu EBee ELan ELon EPfP EWTr LRHS LTen MAsh MBlu MBri MGos MRav NLar SBfd SHil SLim SPer SPoG WHar WPGP WPat
fargesii f. ***duclouxii*** CBcs CDul EPfP IVic MBlu MBri NLar WPGP
ovata CTho EGFP
- 'Slender Silhouette' NLar
speciosa CBcs CDul CTho EWTr SEND
- 'Frederik' NLar
- 'Pulverulenta' (v) CDoC CMCN EBee MGos SBig WPat
* ***szechuanica*** NLar

Catananche (*Asteraceae*)

caerulea Widely available
- 'Alba' EBee ECha EPfP IFoB LBMP LRHS NBir NPri SBfd SMrm SPer SPoG SWvt WMoo WPer
- 'Amor Blue' LRHS
- 'Bicolor' MHer MSpe WHoo WMoo
- 'Major' ♀H4 EBee LDai LRHS SHil SRms WHlf

Catha (*Celastraceae*)

edulis CArn GPoy WHfH WJek

Catharanthus (*Apocynaceae*)

roseus ♀H1 GPoy

Caulokaempferia (*Zingiberaceae*)

petelotii B&SWJ 11818 WCru
sikkimensis new GHim

Caulophyllum (*Berberidaceae*)

thalictroides EBee EPPr GEdr IPot LEdu SRot WCru WFar WMoo WPnP WSHC
- subsp. ***robustum*** WCru

Cautleya ✿ (*Zingiberaceae*)

cathcartii CPLG LEdu
- 'Tenzing's Gold' LWst WCru
§ ***gracilis*** CDTJ CPLG EBee EPfP ETod EUJe GCal GHim IBlr MMoz MNrw SBig XLum
- B&SWJ 7186 LEdu WCru
- NJM 09.105 WPGP
- 'Edinburgh Lemon' IBlr
lutea see *C. gracilis*

spicata	CBct CCCN CDTJ CDoC CHEx CSpe CTsd EBee ECho EUJe GHim IBlr MMoz SBHP SBig SBst XLum
- CC 3676	CPLG EPPr WCot
- 'Arun Flame'	LEdu WCru
- 'Crûg Canary'	LEdu WCru
- 'Livia' **new**	GHim
* - var. ***lutea***	CBct CHEx ETod LEdu WBor
- 'Robusta'	CAvo CGHE CHEx CPLG CPrp EAmu EBee GCal GCra IBlr LEdu LRHS MNrw NRHS SChF SMad WBor WCru WPGP WSHC

Cavendishia (*Ericaceae*)

bracteata **new**	LRHS

Cayratia (*Vitaceae*)

japonica B&SWJ 6636	WCru
§ ***thomsonii*** BWJ 8123	WCru

Ceanothus ✿ (*Rhamnaceae*)

'A.T. Johnson'	ECrN SGol SPer SRms
americanus	CArn
arboreus 'Trewithen Blue' ♀H3	CBcs CDul CMac CSBt CWib EBee ELan EPfP LAst LHop LRHS LSRN MAsh MBri MGos MRav MSwo NRHS SBfd SCoo SEND SHil SLim SPer SPlb SPoG SWvt WSHC
'Autumnal Blue' ♀H3	Widely available
'Blue Cushion'	CBcs CDoC CTri EBee LRHS MAsh MGos MRav NHol SLim SLon SWvt WFar
'Blue Diamond'PBR	LSRN NLar
'Blue Jeans'	EBee ELan IArd LRHS MAsh MMuc NLar
'Blue Mound' ♀H3	Widely available
'Blue Sapphire'PBR	CBcs CDoC CMac CWGN EBee ELan ELon EPfP LAst LRHS LSRN MAsh MGos MRav NEgg NLar NPri SPer SPoG SWvt
'Burkwoodii' ♀H3	CBcs CDoC CDul CHab CSBt EBee EPfP LAst LRHS LSRN MAsh MGos MRav NEgg SBfd SLim SPer SPoG SWvt WFar
'Cascade' ♀H3	CBcs CHab CWSG EBee LRHS LSRN MAsh MGos MWat SLim SLon SPer SPlb
'Centennial'	MRav
'Concha' ♀H3	Widely available
'Cynthia Postan'	EBee EPfP LRHS MAsh MWat NLar SCoo
'Dark Star' ♀H3	CBcs CDoC CMHG CSPN CTri CWGN EBee EPfP LBMP LRHS LSRN MAsh MGos MOWG NHol SCoo SLim SPoG SPtl SSta SWvt
'Delight'	CBcs EBee EPfP WFar
× ***delileanus*** 'Gloire de Versailles' ♀H4	CBcs CDoC CDul CTri CWib EBee ELan ELon EPfP EWTr LAst LBMP LHop LRHS MGos MRav MSwo NLar NRHS SGol SPer SWvt WSHC
- 'Henri Desfossé'	EBee ELan EPfP LRHS LSRN MRav MSwo NLar SPer SPoG
- 'Indigo'	EBee EPfP
- 'Topaze' ♀H4	CDul EBee ELan EPfP LPot LRHS MOWG MRav NLar SGol SLon WHar WKif
dentatus misapplied	see *C.* × *lobbianus*
dentatus Torr. & A.Gray	SPlb
- var. ***floribundus***	SDix
- 'Prostratus'	SBfd
'Diamond Heights'	see *C. griseus* var. *horizontalis* 'Diamond Heights'
'Edinburgh' ♀H3	CWSG EPfP WFar
El Dorado = 'Perado' (v)	LRHS MAsh NLar
gloriosus	EBee EWes
- 'Anchor Bay'	EBee EPfP LRHS MAsh
- 'Emily Brown'	CBcs CDoC CSPN CTrC ELan LAst LRHS LSRN MRav NLar SBfd SHil
griseus	MAsh
§ - var. ***horizontalis***	CMac EPfP LSRN MAsh MBri SPer
'Diamond Heights' (v)	WFar
- - 'Silver Surprise'PBR (v)	CSPN EBee ELan EPfP LBuc LRHS LSRN MAsh MGos NEgg NLar SLim
- - 'Yankee Point'	CBcs CDoC CMac CSBt CWib EBee ECrN EPfP LRHS LSRN LTen MAsh MGos MRav MSwo MWat NLar SBfd SCoo SEND SLim SPlb SPoG SWvt
- 'Kurt Zadnik'	LRHS MAsh
impressus	CTri EBee EPfP LRHS MAsh SEND SHil SLPl SPer SWvt WFar
- 'Victoria'	EBee LSRN MGos MWat NLar SBfd SRGP
N 'Italian Skies' ♀H3	CBcs CDoC CHab CSBt CWSG CWib EBee ELan EPfP LAst LBMP LHop LRHS LSRN MAsh MGos MSwo NEgg NLar SCoo SGol SLim SLon SPer SPlb SPoG SWvt WFar
'Lemon and Lime'	LRHS
§ × ***lobbianus***	CDul CTri
'Madagascar'	EBee ELon EPfP LRHS SCoo SPoG
× ***pallidus*** 'Marie Simon'	CBcs CWib EBee ELan EPfP LAst LRHS LSRN MAsh MGos SPer SPoG SRms SWvt WCFE WHar WKif
- 'Perle Rose'	CBcs CDul EBee EPfP LLHF LRHS MGos MOWG NLar SPer SPoG WKif WSHC
§ 'Pershore Zanzibar'PBR (v)	CBcs CMac CSBt CSPN CWSG EBee EHoe ELan EPfP EShb LAst LBuc LRHS LSRN MGos MRav MSwo NEgg NLar NPri SCoo SGar SGol SLim SPer SPoG SWvt
'Pin Cushion'	CWSG CWib EBee EPfP LRHS MAsh NHol
'Point Millerton'	see *C. thyrsiflorus* 'Millerton Point'
'Popcorn'	EBee LRHS
prostratus	MAsh SMad
'Puget Blue' ♀H4	Widely available
'Ray Hartman'	NLar
repens	see *C. thyrsiflorus* var. *repens*
'Snow Flurries'	see *C. thyrsiflorus* 'Snow Flurry'
'Snow Showers'	CBcs CWSG
'Southmead' ♀H3	CDoC CTri EBee ECrN ELan EPfP LBMP LRHS MAsh MGos MSwo MWat SHil SLim
thyrsiflorus	CTri CWib MAsh SPer SRms SWvt WHar
§ - 'Millerton Point'	EBee EPfP LAst LRHS MAsh MGos NLar SBfd SCoo SLim SPoG
§ - var. ***repens*** ♀H3	Widely available
- 'Skylark' ♀H3	CBar CBcs CDoC CMac CWCL EBee ELan EPau EPfP EWTr LHop LPot LRHS LSRN LTen MAsh MBri MGos MLHP NLar NPri SDix SEND SGol SHil SLim SSpi WPat XSen

§ – 'Snow Flurry'	CWib EPfP LBMP MSwo
'Tilden Park'	EBee LRHS MAsh
'Tuxedo'PBR	LBuc LRHS MAsh MSCN WCot
× ***veitchianus***	CDoy CSBt EBee ELan EPfP LRHS MAsh SEND SPer
'Zanzibar'PBR	see *C.*'Pershore Zanzibar'

Cedrela (*Meliaceae*)

sinensis	see *Toona sinensis*

Cedronella (*Lamiaceae*)

§ ***canariensis***	CArn CPrp EBee EGHP ENfk GPoy MHer MNHC SIde SWat WJek
mexicana	see *Agastache mexicana*
triphylla	see *C. canariensis*

Cedrus (*Pinaceae*)

atlantica	CDul CJun CLnd CMac CMen EHul NWea SEND SGol WEve WMou
– 'Aurea'	CDul MBri MGos NLar NPCo NWea SSta WHar
– 'Fastigiata'	CDul EHul LRHS MAsh MGos NLar SCoo SLim WEve
– Glauca Group ♀H4	Widely available
– – 'Glauca Fastigiata'	CKen CMen WEve
– – 'Glauca Pendula'	CCVT CDoC CDul CMen EHul EPfP LMaj LRHS MBlu MBri MGos NEgg NPCo NWea SGol SLim SPoG SSta WEve WFar WHar
– – 'Silberspitz'	CKen
– 'Pendula'	MAsh SMad
– 'Sahara Frost'	NLar
– 'Saphir Nymph'	MAsh SLim
brevifolia	LTen MGos NLar SBfd WEve
– 'Epstein'	NLar
– 'Hillier Compact'	CKen NLar
– 'Kenwith'	CKen NLar
deodara ♀H4	Widely available
– 'Albospica' (v)	MAsh SWvt
– 'Aurea' ♀H4	CDoC CKen CTho EHul EPfP LMaj LRHS MAsh MBri MGos NEgg NLar SGol SLim WEve WFar WHar
– 'Blue Dwarf'	CKen WEve
* – 'Blue Mountain Broom'	CKen
– 'Blue Snake'	CKen IVic
– 'Blue Surprise'	SLim
– 'Bush's Electra'	CJun NHol
– 'Cream Puff'	MGos
– 'Devinely Blue'	CKen LRHS SLim SPoG
– 'Feelin' Blue'	CDoC CDul CKen EHul LRHS MAsh MBri MGos NEgg NLar NPCo SCoo SLim SWvt WEve WFar
– 'Gold Cascade'	SLim
– 'Gold Mound'	CKen WEve
– 'Golden Horizon'	CDoC CKen CMac CMen EHul LRHS MAsh MBri MGos NEgg NPCo SCoo SLim SPoG WEve WFar
– 'Karl Fuchs'	EWTr LTen NLar WGor
– 'Kelly Gold'	WEve
– 'Klondyke'	MAsh
– 'Lime Glow'	SLim
– 'Miles High'	CJun
– 'Mountain Beauty'	CKen
– 'Nana'	CKen
– 'Nivea'	CKen
– 'Pendula'	CKen EHul LMaj MGos NWea SLim WEve WGor
– 'Pygmy'	CKen
– 'Raywood's Prostrate'	CKen
– 'Robusta'	WEve
– 'Roman Candle'	NPCo WEve WFar
– 'Scott'	CKen
– 'Silver Mist'	CKen MGos
– 'Silver Spring'	NLar
libani ♀H4	CCVT CDoC CDul CLnd CMCN CTho ECrN EHul ELan EPfP EWTr LRHS MAsh MBlu MBri MMuc NLar NWea SBfd SEND SGol SLim SPer SPlb SWvt WEve WFar WHar WMou
– 'Blue Angel'	NLar SLim
– 'Comte de Dijon'	EHul NLar
– 'Fontaine'	NLar
– 'Green Prince'	NLar
– 'Hedgehog'	NLar
– 'Home Park'	CKen NLar
– 'May'	NLar
– Nana Group	CKen NPCo
– 'Sargentii'	CKen EHul MGos NPCo WEve

Ceiba (*Malvaceae*)

pentandra new	SPlb

Celastrus (*Celastraceae*)

dependens CWJ 12478	WCru
flagellaris B&SWJ 8572	WCru
hookeri B&SWJ 11667	WCru
kusanoi CWJ 12445	WCru
orbiculatus	CBcs CDoC CMac ELan EPPr IGor LHop LRHS MRav NSti SLon SPer WBor
– 'Diana' (f)	CMac
– 'Hercules' (m)	CMac
– Hermaphrodite Group ♀H4	EBee SDix SEND SKHP WSHC
– var. ***papillosus*** B&SWJ 591	WCru
– var. ***punctatus*** CWJ 12439	WCru
scandens	CMac SPhx SPlb
stephanotiifolius B&SWJ 4727	WCru

Celmisia (*Asteraceae*)

allanii	IBlr WAbe
angustifolia	IBlr
argentea	WAbe
Ballyrogan hybrids	IBlr
bellidioides	EPot EWes MDKP NHar NSla WAbe
bonplandii	IBlr
brevifolia	EPot IBlr
coriacea misapplied	see *C. semicordata*
coriacea Raoul	see *C. mackaui*
'David Shackleton'	IBlr
densiflora	IBlr
– silver-leaved	IBlr
discolor	IBlr
'Eggleston Silver'	NBir NEgg
glandulosa	GCra IBlr
gracilenta	WAbe
haastii	IBlr
'Harry Bryce'	IBlr
hectorii	IBlr WAbe
hectorii × ***ramulosa***	WAbe
hookeri	IBlr
Inshriach hybrids	IBlr

latifolia IBlr
- large-leaved IBlr
longifolia large-leaved IBlr
- small-leaved IBlr
lyallii EPot
§ ***mackaui*** IBlr
monroi EPot IBlr
prorepens IBlr
ramulosa var. ***tuberculata*** IBlr NSla
§ ***semicordata*** GCra IBlr NSla WAbe
- subsp. ***aurigans*** IBlr
- subsp. ***stricta*** IBlr
sessiliflora WAbe
spectabilis subsp. ***magnifica*** EPot
verbascifolia IBlr
§ ***walkeri*** IBlr
webbiana see *C. walkeri*

Celosia (*Amaranthaceae*)

argentea var. ***cristata*** Plumosa Group Kimono Series **new** LAst
- - - 'Smart Look Red' ♀H3 **new** NPri

Celsia see *Verbascum*

× *Celsioverbascum* see *Verbascum*

Celtica see *Stipa*

Celtis (*Cannabaceae*)

australis CBcs EBtc MGos MMuc SEND
biondii EGFP
bungeana NLar
caucasica EGFP NLar
ehrenbergiana **new** EGFP
julianae NLar
occidentalis CDul ELan SGol
reticulata EGFP
sinensis CMen
tenuifolia EGFP

Cenolophium (*Apiaceae*)

denudatum CDes CSpe EBee ECha NChi WPGP

Centaurea ✿ (*Asteraceae*)

HH&K 271 NBid
RCB AM -6 WCot
RCB UA 18 WCot
alba LDai
alpestris EBee MSpe NLar SPhx WPGP WPer
'Amethyst on Ice' LRHS
athoa EBee
§ ***atropurpurea*** CDes CSpe EBee EPfP EWes GQue LDai LRHS MAvo MSpe NBid NLar NRHS SHar SMrm SPhx SPlb SUsu WHrl WPGP
bagadensis EBee GKev
bella CDes CPrp EAEE EBee ECtt ELon GCal LBMP LHop LPla LRHS MBel MCot MLHP MRav MSpe NBro NMRc NSti SEND SMHy SPet SPhx SPoG SWat WKif WMnd XLum XSen
- 'Katherine' (v) MSpe
benoistii misapplied see *C. atropurpurea*
benoistii ambig. CSpe EBee
benoistii × ***orientalis*** ambig. SPhx
'Blewit' CDes EBee MAvo MSpe WPGP
cana see *C. triumfettii* subsp. *cana*
candidissima misapplied see *C. cineraria*
'Caramia' CDes EBee MAvo
carniolica SDR 5443 EBee GKev MSpe
cheiranthifolia CDes EPPr MAvo MNrw MSpe NBid NBir NLBP WFar WPGP XSen
- var. ***purpurascens*** CDes
§ ***cineraria*** ECre ELon LDai SPhx WHil
- subsp. ***cineraria*** ♀H3 CSpe SEND WCot
cyanus CHab MHer MNHC SVic WJek
- 'Black Ball' CSpe MNHC
- 'Blue Ball' CSpe
cynaroides see *Stemmacantha centaureoides*
dealbata CMac COIW CPrp CWib EBee EPfP EWTr GJos IFoB LRHS LTen MLHP MSpe NBro NLar NMir NOrc NPri SBfd SEND SMrm WCot WFar WMoo WPer WWEG XLum
- 'Steenbergii' CMac EBee ELan GCal LEdu LLWP MSpe NBid NBir NGdn NPer NSti SPer SPoG WAbb WCot WFar WMnd
- 'Steenbergii' variegated (v) LDai
debeauxii subsp. ***nemoralis*** LDai NLar
fischeri Willd. MSpe WPGP
glastifolia EBee GCal LRHS MSpe WPGP
gymnocarpa see *C. cineraria*
hypoleuca NBid
jacea EShb GKev GQue MSpe NBid NLar WCot WPer
'John Coutts' Widely available
'Jordy' EBee ECtt GBin GBuc IPot LDai MAvo MSpe NCGa NLar SPhx SSvw WCAu WKif
karabaghensis EBee GCal WPGP
kotschyana CDes EBee WPGP
macrocephala Widely available
mollis NBid
montana Widely available
- 'Alba' Widely available
- 'Amethyst Dream' PBR **new** IPot
- 'Amethyst in Snow' EBee ECtt GBin IPot MAvo NLar SBfd SPoG
- 'Black Sprite' **new** EBee NDov NLar
§ - 'Carnea' CCVN CDes CElw CPom CSam EBee GCra GMaP MAvo MCot MSpe NBir NChi NLBP NLar SAga SPhx WCAu WMoo WWEG
- 'Elworthy Glacier' **new** CElw
- 'Gold Bullion' CPrp CSpe EBee ECtt ELan ELon EPfP EWes GMaP LDai LRHS MAvo MRav MSpe NBid NBir NLar NPro NRHS SAga SMad SMrm WSHC WWEG
- 'Grandiflora' EBee MBri MSpe
- 'Joyce' CElw CPom LDai MAvo MSpe NBid NLar WSHC
- 'Lady Flora Hastings' CBre CCse CDes CElw CKno CPom CSam CSpe EBee LDai MAvo MSpe NBid WPGP WWEG
- 'Lilac Heart' **new** EBee
- lilac-flowered MAvo NBid
- 'Ochroleuca' CDes CElw EBee LDai MSpe NBid NBre WPGP

- 'Parham'	CPrp CSev EBee ECtt ELan ELon GCal LBMP LLWP LRHS LSRN MBel MBri MCot MMuc MNrw MRav MSpe MWat NDov NEgg NSti SEND SPer SPlb SPoG WMnd WSHC
- 'Purple Heart'	CDes EBee ECtt ELon IPot LSou MAvo MBel MHer MNrw MSpe NLar NPri SMrm SRot WCAu
- 'Purple Prose'	CElw MAvo
- 'Purpurea'	CDes CElw CPom MSpe SUsu
- 'Rosea'	see *C. montana* 'Carnea'
* - ***violacea***	NBid
- 'Violetta'	EBee MAvo NBid NBir WFar WMoo
montana × ***triumfettii*** new	EBee
moschata	see *Amberboa moschata*
nervosa	see *C. uniflora* subsp. *nervosa*
nigra	CArn CHab CRWN EBee EPfP GJos MNHC MSpe NBre NLan NMir SMrm WMoo WOut WSFF XLum
- var. ***alba***	CBre NBid
- 'Elstead'	MSpe
- subsp. ***rivularis***	ECha LDai MMuc NBid NBre SEND XLum
nogmovii	EBee MAvo MSpe
orientalis	CFis CSpe EBee ECGP EWes GCal LRHS MSpe NBre NLar SEND SPhx SPoG WHoo
pannonica	NBid WSHC
subsp. ***pannonica*** HH&K 259	
phrygia	COIW MSpe NBre WPer
pulcherrima	EBee LRHS MSpe NBre SPhx
'Pulchra Major'	see *Stemmacantha centaureoides*
rupestris	EPfP MSpe NBre SGar SPhx WPer
ruthenica	EBee LRHS NLar SKHP SMad SPer SPhx SPlb WCot
salicifolia	MSpe NBir
salonitana RCB AM 1	WCot
scabiosa	CArn CHab CRWN CWib MHer MNHC MSpe NBid NBir NBre NLan NLar NMir SGar SPhx WPer
- f. ***albiflora***	GQue LRHS MSpe
simplicicaulis	CSam LRHS MAsh MSpe SBch SMrm SRms WHoo WSHC XSen
thracica	CDes EBee WCot
'Totnes Fat Lemon'	CDes
triumfettii	CPBP
- 'Blue Dreams'	CDes LDai MSpe
§ - subsp. ***cana***	XSen
I - - 'Rosea'	WBrk
- 'Hoar Frost'	CDes MSpe NDov WPGP
- subsp. ***stricta***	CPrp MSpe
uniflora	EBee XSen
§ - subsp. ***nervosa***	MSpe NBid NBre NBro NLar WPer XLum
woronowii	MAvo MSpe

Centaurium (*Gentianaceae*)

erythraea	CArn GPoy MHer MHoo MNHC
scilloides	CPBP NMen NSla WAbe

Centella (*Apiaceae*)

§ ***asiatica***	CArn EOHP GPoy LEdu WJek

Centradenia (*Melastomataceae*)

inaequilateralis	CCCN
- 'Cascade'	LAst MBri SPet

Centranthus (*Caprifoliaceae*)

§ ***lecoqii***	ECtt EWes LPla SPhx WCot
§ ***ruber***	Widely available
§ - 'Albus'	Widely available
- 'Atrococcineus'	ECha MAvo MMuc WPer
- 'Clair'	CNat
- var. ***coccineus***	CBcs CHab EBee ELan EPfP GAbr GBin GKin GMaP LBMP LRHS MCot MNHC MRav MWat NPri SBfd SEND SHil SMrm SPer SPhx SRot SWat WCot WFar WGwG WWEG
- mauve-flowered misapplied	see *C. lecoqii*
- mauve-flowered	NBir
- 'Nettleton' new	CNat
- 'Roseus'	EPfP WMoo
- 'Rosy Red'	SBfd
- 'Snowcloud'	ECtt ENfk EPfP MNHC WHil
'White Cloud'	WJek

Centropogon (*Campanulaceae*)

§ ***ayavacensis*** subsp. ***ayavacensis*** B&SWJ 10663	WCru
cordifolius B&SWJ 10282	WCru
costaricae B&SWJ 10455	WCru
ferrugineus B&SWJ 10665	WCru
hirsutus B&SWJ 10657	WCru
aff. ***valerii*** B&SWJ 10341	WCru
willdenowianus	see *C. ayavacensis* subsp. *ayavacensis*

Cephalanthera (*Orchidaceae*)

falcata	EFEx
longibracteata	EFEx NLAp
longifolia new	NLAp

Cephalanthus (*Rubiaceae*)

occidentalis	CWib EBee ELon GBin IVic LRHS LSou MAsh MBNS MBlu MBri MGos MMuc NLar SEND SHil SLim SPoG WBor WCFE WGob

Cephalaria (*Caprifoliaceae*)

§ ***alpina***	COIW EBee EPPr EPfP LBMP LRHS MHer MNrw MRav NLar SPhx SRms SWat WCot WPer XLum
ambrosioides MESE 503	EBee
anatolica KM T-04-72	EBee
caucasica	see *C. gigantea*
dipsacoides	CEnt ECha LPla MSpe NLar SKHP SMHy SPhx WMoo WTcb
§ ***flava***	EBee LRHS NBre
galpiniana	SPlb
- subsp. ***simplicior***	EBee
§ ***gigantea***	Widely available
graeca	see *C. flava*
leucantha	CArn CFis EBee GBin NBid NBre SMrm SPhx WMoo
litvinovii	CElw SPhx
tatarica hort.	see *C. gigantea*
tchihatchewii	EBee

Cephalaria × *Scabiosa* (*Caprifoliaceae*)

C. alpina × ***S. cinerea***	LRHS

Cephalotaxus (*Taxaceae*)

fortunei	CDul
- 'Prostrate Spreader'	SLim WEve

harringtonia	ERom LEdu
- var. ***drupacea***	CDoC NWea
- 'Fastigiata'	CBcs CDoC EHul IArd IDee LRHS MAsh MBri MDev MGos NLar NWea SCoo SPoG WFar
- 'Gimborn's Pillow'	NWea
- 'Korean Gold'	CKen LRHS MDev NLar SPoG
- 'Prostrata'	LRHS SPoG
sinensis	CMCN

Cerastium (*Caryophyllaceae*)

alpinum	ECho IFoB SRms
- var. ***lanatum***	ECho EDAr EWes
arvense	XLum
candidissimum	EWes
fontanum	CHab
tomentosum	CBar ECho EPfP MMuc NPri SEND SPer SPet SPlb SPoG WFar
- var. ***columnae***	ECha ECho EHoe EWes XLum
- 'Yo Yo'	WFar

Ceratonia (*Caesalpiniaceae*)

siliqua	CBcs GPoy SPlb

Ceratophyllum (*Ceratophyllaceae*)

demersum	CBen CWat EHon EWay MSKA MWts SWat WMAq WSFF

Ceratostigma ✿ (*Plumbaginaceae*)

abyssinicum	ELan SEND
asperrimum B&SWJ 7260	WCru
'Autumn Blue'	EPfP LRHS
capensis	CMac
griffithii	Widely available
- wild-collected	GCal
§ ***plumbaginoides*** ♀H3-4	Widely available
willmottianum ♀H3-4	Widely available
- BWJ 8140	WCru
- Desert Skies = 'Palmgold'PBR	CBcs EBee ELan EPfP LAst MBlu MGos NLar SGol SLim SPer SWvt
- Forest Blue = 'Lice'PBR	CDoC CMac CSBt CSpe CWSG EBee ELan EPPr EPfP LAst LRHS LSRN MBri MGos MRav NLar NPri SBfd SCoo SHil SLim SPer SPoG SPtl SReu SWvt WPat

Cercidiphyllum ✿ (*Cercidiphyllaceae*)

japonicum ♀H4	Widely available
- HEHEHE 316	GKev
- 'Boyd's Dwarf'	CJun EBee LLHF LRHS MAsh NLar SPoG SSta WAbe WCot
- 'Herkenrode Dwarf'	NLar
- 'Heronswood Globe'	CJun EPfP MBlu NLar SSta WSpi
- 'Kreukenberg Dwarf'	CJun SSta
- f. ***miquelianum*** new	SSta
- 'Morioka Weeping'	CJun CTho EBee MPkF NLar SChF SMad SSta WPGP
- 'Peach'	CJun NLar
§ - f. ***pendulum*** ♀H4	CDul CJun CLnd CMCN CMHG CMac CPLG CTri EBee ELan EPfP GBin GKin LRHS MAsh MBlu MGos NEgg NLar NRHS SCoo SHil SLim SPoG SSpi SSta WHar
- - 'Amazing Grace'	CTho MBlu NLar SSta
- 'Raspberry'	CJun NLar SSta
- Red Fox	see *C. japonicum* 'Rotfuchs'
§ - 'Rotfuchs'	Widely available
- 'Ruby'	CJun EBee MBlu NLar SChF WPGP
- 'Strawberry'	CBcs CJun EBee LHop MBlu NLar SSta
- 'Tidal Wave'	CJun NLar SSta
- 'Titania' new	SSta
magnificum	CDoC CMCN CPLG EPfP IDee MBlu MPkF NEgg NLar SSta WPGP
- f. ***pendulum***	see *C. japonicum* f. *pendulum*

Cercis (*Caesalpiniaceae*)

canadensis	CBcs CDul CLnd CMCN CWGN EPfP MGos MMuc NEgg NLar NWea SCoo SEND SLim SPer WPat WRHF
- 'Ace of Hearts'PBR	MPkF SSta
- f. ***alba***	ESwi LSRN WMou
- - 'Royal White'	CJun EPfP IArd LRHS MBlu
- 'Appalachian Red'	CJun LSRN MBlu MGos NLar SGol SKHP
- 'Cascading Hearts'	CBcs ESwi NLar
- 'Flame'	CJun NLar SKHP SSta WPGP WPat
- 'Forest Pansy' ♀H4	Widely available
- 'Hearts of Gold'PBR	CTho CWGN EBee EWTr LRHS MAsh MBlu MBri MGos MPkF MRav NLar SBfd SHil SKHP SLim SLon SPoG WHar WMou
- Lavender Twist = 'Covey'	CBcs EBee ESwi LAst LRHS LSRN MAsh MBlu MBri MGos NLar SBfd SGol SKHP SLim SLon SPoG WHar WMou
- Little Woody = 'Litwo'PBR	MPkF NLar SGol
- 'Melon Beauty' new	NLar SKHP WPat
- var. ***mexicana*** 'Sanderson' NJM 09.024	WPGP
§ - var. ***occidentalis***	LEdu NLar SSta
- 'Pauline Lily'	NLar
- 'Pink Heartbreaker'	SGol
- 'Rubye Atkinson'	CJun NLar SSpi
- 'Tennessee Pink'	CJun NLar
- var. ***texensis*** 'Oklahoma'	CJun EBee ESwi LSRN MGos MPkF NLar NPCo SKHP WHar WMou
- - 'Texas White'	CBcs CJun EBee MAsh MBri MPkF NLar SGol SKHP SLim SPoG WHar WPat
- - 'Traveller'	SGol
- 'The Rising Sun' new	MBlu
chinensis	LLHF NLar SPer
- f. ***alba***	CTho MGos
- 'Avondale'	Widely available
- 'Don Egolf'	CJun LSRN MBlu MGos MPkF NLar SGol SKHP SSta
chingii	CPLG WPGP
gigantea	NLar
griffithii	LLHF NLar SSta
occidentalis	see *C. canadensis* var. *occidentalis*
racemosa	CPLG IDee NLar WPGP
siliquastrum ♀H4	Widely available
- f. ***albida***	CTho ECrN ELan EPfP EPri EWes LRHS SEND SHil SKHP SSpi WCFE WSpi
- 'Bodnant'	CTho EBee EPfP EWes LAst LLHF LRHS LSRN MBlu MBri MGos NLar NRHS SHil SSta WHar WPat
- 'White Swan'	CJun CTho EWes
yunnanensis	NLar

Cereus (*Cactaceae*)

repandus new	SPlb

Cerinthe (*Boraginaceae*)

glabra	LBMP SPlb

major SWvt
- 'Kiwi Blue' CHll MDKP
- 'Purpurascens' CMea CSpe ELan EPfP LBMP LRHS MNHC SEND SMrm SPer SPhx SPoG WKif WWEG
- 'Yellow Gem' ELan
retorta LDai

Ceropegia (*Apocynaceae*)

§ **linearis** subsp. **woodii** ♀H1 EShb SRms
pubescens GWJ 9441 WCru
woodii see *C. linearis* subsp. *woodii*

Cestrum (*Solanaceae*)

aurantiacum EShb
auriculatum MOWG
× **cultum** CHll EShb
- 'Cretan Pink' CCCN MOWG
- 'Cretan Purple' CBcs CCCN CHGN CHll CRHN EBee ELan ELon EPfP EShb LHop LRHS MOWG SEND SPoG WKif WSHC
diurnum × **nocturnum** EShb
§ **elegans** CDoC CHEx CHll CPLG CRHN CTsd EBee ELan ELon EPfP EUJe LRHS MOWG NEgg SEND SLon
fasciculatum EShb MOWG
'Newellii' ♀H2 CBcs CCCN CMHG CPLG CWCL CWib EBak EBee ELan ELon EPfP EShb EUJe LRHS MOWG SEND SGar WKif WSHC
nocturnum CCCN CHll EBak EOHP EShb IDee MOWG
parqui ♀H3 CAbb CBcs CCCN CHll CTsd CWib EBee ELan EPfP IDee LHop LRHS MOWG SDix SEND SGar SLon SMad SUsu WJek WKif WSHC
psittacinum CPLG
purpureum (Lindl.) Standl. see *C. elegans*
roseum CPLG
- B&SWJ 10255 from Oaxaca State, Mexico WCru
- 'Ilnacullin' EBee
* **splendens** MOWG

Ceterach (*Aspleniaceae*)

officinarum see *Asplenium ceterach*

Chaenomeles (*Rosaceae*)

cathayensis CAgr CTho LEdu NLar
§ **japonica** EBee MMuc SEND WFar
- 'Chojubai' CMen
- 'Cido' CAgr LBuc MCoo
- 'Orange Beauty' LRHS NHol SPer WFar
- 'Sargentii' CMac EPfP MGos NBro SGol
'John Pilger' NHol
lagenaria see *C. speciosa*
Madame Butterfly = 'Whitice' CDoC EBee EPfP LAst LRHS LSRN MAsh MMuc MRav NEgg SBfd SBod SEND SLim SPoG
maulei see *C. japonica*
'Orange Star' EBee LRHS NLar
sinensis see *Pseudocydonia sinensis*
§ **speciosa** NWea SMrm
- 'Apple Blossom' see *C. speciosa* 'Moerloosei'
- 'Brilliant' EPfP
- 'Cardinalis' CMac
- 'Contorta' LBMP LRHS MAsh WFar
- 'Eximia' LRHS LTen
- 'Falconnet Charlet' (d) EBee LRHS MRav SBfd WFar
- 'Flocon Rose' EPfP LRHS
- 'Friesdorfer' LRHS
- 'Geisha Girl' (d) ♀H4 CBcs CDoC CMac CSBt CWSG EBee EPfP LAst LHop LPot LRHS LSRN MAsh MGos MRav MSwo MWat NPri SAga SBfd SGol SHil SLim SMrm SPer SPoG SRms SWvt WFar
- 'Grayshott Salmon' NPro WFar
- Hot Fire = 'Minvesu' EBee EMil EPfP
- 'Kinshiden' EPfP LRHS
- 'Knap Hill Radiance' SLim
§ - 'Moerloosei' ♀H4 CDoC CDul CJun CMac CSBt EBee ELan EPfP EWTr GBin LAst LRHS LSRN MAsh MBlu MGos MMuc MRav MSwo NRHS SAga SEND SLim SPer SPoG SRms SSta SWvt WFar WMoo
- 'Nivalis' Widely available
- 'Rubra Grandiflora' ECrN LRHS WBor
- 'Simonii' (d) CBcs EBee EPfP MGos MRav NWea SPer WFar
- 'Snow' LBMP MAsh MSwo SRms
- 'Umbilicata' MBlu NLar SPer SRms
- 'Yukigotan' CDoC EBee LRHS MBri MMuc NLar SBfd SEND SGol SHil WPat
× **superba** IBoy
- 'Boule de Feu' CTri CWib ECtt MCoo
- 'Cameo' (d) EBee ELon EPfP LHop LRHS MBNS MRav MWat NLar SGol SLPl
- 'Clementine' CWib
- 'Coquelicot' LRHS
- 'Crimson and Gold' ♀H4 Widely available
- 'Elly Mossel' CMac CWib NLar WFar
- 'Fascination' NLar
- 'Fire Dance' CDul CHll CWib EBee ECtt LRHS MSwo NLar SGol SPer WRHF
- 'Fusion' CAgr
- 'Hever Castle' CJun
- 'Hollandia' SRms
- 'Issai White' MRav
- 'Jet Trail' CBcs CMac CSBt EBee ECtt ELan EPfP LAst LRHS LSRN MAsh MBri MGos MRav MSwo NLar NRHS SGol SHil SLPl SLim SPoG SWvt WFar
- 'Knap Hill Scarlet' ♀H4 CDoC CDul EBee ECtt EPfP LPot LRHS MAsh MGos MMuc SEND SLim SPer SPoG SRms SWvt
- 'Lemon and Lime' ELan EPfP LRHS MAsh MGos MRav SLon SRms
- 'Nicoline' ♀H4 CBcs CDoC CDul EBee EPfP IBoy LRHS MGos NEgg SLim WFar
- 'Pink Lady' ♀H4 Widely available
- 'Red Joy' EBee EPfP LRHS NLar WGrn
- 'Red Trail' MRav
- 'Rowallane' ♀H4 CHll EBee ELan EPfP MRav SPer
- 'Salmon Horizon' EPfP MGos NLar
- 'Tortuosa' EBee LHop WGrn
'Toyo-nishiki' MBlu NLar

Chaenorhinum (*Plantaginaceae*)

§ **origanifolium** ECho SBch SPlb
- 'Blue Dream' CSpe ECho EPfP EWTr GKev IPot MAsh SPoG SWvt WMoo WPer WRHF

- 'Dreamcatcher' EPfP
- 'Summer Skies' NPri SPet

Chaerophyllum (*Apiaceae*)

hirsutum CRow
- 'Roseum' Widely available

Chamaecyparis ✿ (*Cupressaceae*)

formosensis CKen
funebris see *Cupressus funebris*
lawsoniana CDul EHul NWea WMou
- SIN 1820 GLin
- 'Albospica' (v) WFar
- 'Allumii Aurea' see *C. lawsoniana* 'Alumigold'
- 'Allumii Magnificent' CDul
§ - 'Alumigold' MAsh MGos SCoo
- 'Alumii' EHul MAsh MGos NWea
- 'Aurea' CDul
- 'Aurea Densa' ♀H4 CKen CMac CSBt CTri EHul EPfP MAsh MGos NEgg WEve WGor
- 'Barry's Silver' WEve
- 'Bleu Nantais' CKen CMac EHul LBee LRHS MAsh MGos SCoo SLim SPoG WCFE WEve WFar WGor
- 'Blom' CKen EHul
§ - 'Blue Gown' EHul
- 'Blue Surprise' CKen EHul WFar
- 'Brégéon' CKen NLar
- 'Broomhill Gold' CDoC CSBt EHul LRHS MAsh MGos NPri SCoo SLim SPer SPoG WBor WEve
- 'Caudata' CKen NLar
- 'Chantry Gold' EHul WEve
§ - 'Chilworth Silver' ♀H4 CSBt EHul LBee LRHS MAsh SCoo SLim SPer SPoG SRms WFar
- 'Columnaris' CBcs CDoC EPfP LAst LBee LMaj LRHS MBri MGos NEgg NWea SCoo SPoG WFar
- 'Columnaris Aurea' see *C. lawsoniana* 'Golden Spire'
N - 'Columnaris Glauca' CMac CWib EHul MAsh MGos NEgg NWea SCoo SPer WFar
- 'Crawford's Compact' CMac
- 'Cream Crackers' EHul SPoG
- 'Cream Glow' CKen CSBt LRHS MAsh MGos NLar SCoo SLim SPoG WFar WGor
- 'Croftway' EHul
- 'Dik's Weeping' CDoC NLar NWea SLim WEve
- 'Duncanii' EHul
- 'Dutch Gold' EHul MAsh
- 'Dwarf Blue' see *C. lawsoniana* 'Pick's Dwarf Blue'
- 'Eclipse' CKen
- 'Elegantissima' ambig. CKen
- 'Ellwoodii' ♀H4 CDul CMac CSBt CTri CWib EHul EPfP LAst LRHS MGos NPri NWea SCoo SLim SPer SPoG SRms WFar
I - 'Ellwoodii Glauca' SPlb
- 'Ellwood's Empire' EHul
- 'Ellwood's Gold' ♀H4 CBcs CDoC CSBt CWib EHul ELan EPfP EPot LBee LRHS MAsh MBri MGos MWat NPri NWea SPer SPlb SPoG SRms WEve WFar WMoo
- 'Ellwood's Gold Pillar' EHul LBee LRHS MAsh MGos NHol SLim SPoG WBor WFar WGor
§ - 'Ellwood's Nymph' CKen LRHS MAsh SCoo SLim WFar
- Ellwood's Pillar = 'Flolar' CDoC CMac EHul EPot LAst LBee LRHS MBri MGos NHol NLar SCoo SLim WCFE WFar
- 'Ellwood's Pygmy' CMac
- 'Ellwood's Silver' MAsh WFar
- 'Ellwood's Silver Threads' CMac
- 'Ellwood's Variegata' see *C. lawsoniana* 'Ellwood's White'
§ - 'Ellwood's White' (v) CKen CSBt EHul EPfP SPoG WFar
I - 'Emerald' CKen
- 'Emerald Spire' MAsh
- 'Empire' WFar
- 'Erecta Aurea' EHul
- 'Erecta Viridis' CBcs NEgg NWea WFar
- 'Ericoides' EHul
- 'Filiformis Compacta' EHul
- 'Filip's Golden Tears' MAsh SLim
- 'Fleckellwood' CWib EHul MAsh
- 'Fletcheri' ♀H4 CMac EHul NWea WFar
- 'Fletcheri Aurea' see *C. lawsoniana* 'Yellow Transparent'
- 'Fletcher's White' EHul
- 'Forsteckensis' CKen EHul NLar NWea WFar
I - 'Forsteckensis Aurea' CDoC NLar
- 'Fraseri' NWea
- 'Gimbornii' ♀H4 EHul LBee SCoo SLim WFar
- 'Glauca' CDul
- 'Gnome' CDoC CKen CMac EHul GEdr LAst LRHS MGos SCoo SLim SPoG WEve WGor WThu
§ - 'Golden Pot' CDoC CMac CSBt CWib EHul LBee LRHS MGos SCoo WFar
§ - 'Golden Queen' EHul
- 'Golden Showers' EHul
§ - 'Golden Spire' MAsh NLar WFar
- 'Golden Triumph' EHul
- 'Golden Wonder' EHul MAsh MGos NEgg NLar NWea SCoo WEve WFar
- 'Goldfinger' NLar
- 'Grayswood Feather' CDoC EHul LBee LRHS MAsh MGos MWat SCoo SPlb WEve
- 'Grayswood Gold' EHul WEve
- 'Grayswood Pillar' ♀H4 CDul EHul MGos
- 'Green Globe' CDoC CKen CMen CSBt EHul LBee MAsh MGos NLar SLim WEve WThu
§ - 'Green Hedger' ♀H4 CDul CSBt NWea WFar
§ - 'Green Pillar' CDul CWib LAst LBee NEgg SCoo
- 'Green Spire' see *C. lawsoniana* 'Green Pillar'
- 'Hogger's Blue Gown' see *C. lawsoniana* 'Blue Gown'
- 'Imbricata Pendula' CDoC CKen NLar SLim SMad
- 'Intertexta' ♀H4 WEve
- 'Ivonne' EHul MGos WEve
- 'Jackman's Green Hedger' see *C. lawsoniana* 'Green Hedger'
- 'Jackman's Variety' see *C. lawsoniana* 'Green Pillar'
- 'Jeanette' CKen
- 'Kelleriis Gold' EHul
- 'Killarny Salmon' CMac
- 'Kilmacurragh' ♀H4 CMac MAsh MGos NWea WCFE
- 'Kilworth Column' CDoC MGos NLar NWea
- 'Kingswood' CDoC
- 'Knowefieldensis' CMac
- 'Lane' misapplied see *C. lawsoniana* 'Lanei Aurea'
- 'Lane' den Ouden CWib MGos MRav NEgg SCoo WFar
§ - 'Lanei Aurea' ♀H4 EHul MGos SPoG WFar
- 'Lemon Pillar' WEve
- 'Lemon Queen' CDul EHul LBee WEve
- 'Little Spire' ♀H4 CDoC LRHS MBri MGos NHol NLar SBfd SCoo SLim SPoG WEve WGor
- 'Lombartsii' WFar
- 'Lutea' ♀H4 CMac EHul MGos

§ – 'Lutea Nana' ♀H4 CMac EHul MAsh MGos NLar
§ – 'Lutea Smithii' NWea
– 'Luteocompacta' LBee
* – 'MacPenny's Gold' CMac
– 'Minima Argentea' see *C. lawsoniana* 'Nana Argentea'
– 'Minima Aurea' ♀H4 CDoC CDul CKen CMac CWib EHul EPfP EPot LAst LBee LRHS MAsh MBri MGos NEgg NWea SLim SPer SPoG WBor WCFE WEve WFar WMoo
– 'Minima Glauca' ♀H4 CMac EHul EPfP GEdr LAst LRHS MGos MWat NEgg NWea SCoo SLim SPer SRms WEve WFar
* – 'Moonsprite' CKen EHul LAst LRHS NLar SCoo SLim SPoG WGor
– 'Nana' CMac
– 'Nana Albospica' (v) EHul LBee SCoo SPoG WFar WGor
§ – 'Nana Argentea' CKen CMac EHul SCoo SPoG WFar WGor
– 'Nana Lutea' see *C. lawsoniana* 'Lutea Nana'
– 'Nicole' EHul LAst MAsh NWea SCoo WGor
– 'Nidiformis' EHul
– 'Nyewoods' see *C. lawsoniana* 'Chilworth Silver'
– 'Nymph' see *C. lawsoniana* 'Ellwood's Nymph'
– 'Pagoda' MAsh
§ – 'Pelt's Blue' ♀H4 CBcs CDoC CDul CKen CSBt EHul LBee LRHS MGos NLar SBfd SCoo SLim SPoG WFar
– 'Pembury Blue' ♀H4 CDoC CDul CWib EHul EPfP LBee LRHS MAsh MGos MRav NEgg NLar NWea SCoo SLim SPer SPoG WFar
§ – 'Pick's Dwarf Blue' LRHS MGos WEve
– Pot of Gold see *C. lawsoniana* 'Golden Pot'
– 'Pottenii' CMac EHul LBee MAsh MGos NWea WFar
– 'Pygmaea Argentea' (v) ♀H4 CKen CMac CSBt CWib EHul ELan LBee MAsh MBri MGos NEgg NHol NWea SLim SPer SPoG WBor WCFE WFar
– 'Pygmy' EHul LRHS NHol NLar NWea SCoo SLim WEve
– 'Rijnhof' EHul LBee
– 'Rimpelaar' CDoC
– 'Rock Gold' WEve
– 'Rogersii' WFar
– 'Royal Gold' EHul
– 'Silver Queen' (v) CKen
– 'Silver Threads' (v) EHul ELan LBee MAsh SPoG WFar
– 'Silver Tip' (v) EHul LRHS SCoo SLim
– 'Smithii' see *C. lawsoniana* 'Lutea Smithii'
– 'Snow Flurry' (v) CKen EHul SPoG WFar WGor
– 'Snow White' PBR (v) CKen EHul LBee LRHS MAsh MBri MGos NHol SCoo SLim SPoG WFar WGor
– 'Springtime' PBR CSBt EHul LBee MAsh SCoo SLim
– 'Stardust' ♀H4 CBcs CDoC CDul CSBt CWib EHul ELan LRHS MAsh NEgg NPri NWea SCoo SLim SPoG
– 'Stewartii' CDul NEgg NWea SCoo
* – 'Summer Cream' EHul
– 'Summer Snow' (v) CDoC EHul EPfP LBee LRHS MGos MWat NHol NPri SCoo SLim WFar
– 'Sunkist' LRHS SCoo SLim WFar
– 'Tamariscifolia' CDoC EHul WCFE WFar
– 'Tharandtensis Caesia' WFar
– 'Tilford' EHul
– 'Treasure' (v) CSBt EHul LRHS MAsh SCoo SLim WFar
– 'Van Pelt' see *C. lawsoniana* 'Pelt's Blue'
– 'Westermannii' (v) CMac
– 'White Spot' (v) EHul NPri WFar
– 'Winston Churchill' MGos NWea
– 'Wisselii' ♀H4 CDoC CKen CMac EHul NLar NWea SCoo SRms WCFE WFar
– 'Wisselii Nana' CKen EHul
– 'Wissel's Saguaro' CDoC CKen IVic MGos NLar SLim
– 'Witzeliana' CDul MGos NLar
– 'Yellow Queen' see *C. lawsoniana* 'Golden Queen'
– 'Yellow Success' see *C. lawsoniana* 'Golden Queen'
§ – 'Yellow Transparent' CMac
– 'Yvonne' CDoC CDul LRHS MAsh MBri MGos MWat NEgg NLar SCoo SLim SPoG WEve

leylandii see × *Cuprocyparis leylandii*
obtusa 'Albovariegata' (v) CKen
– 'Arneson's Compact' CKen
– 'Aurea' CDoC SCoo WEve
– 'Aurora' CKen ELan MAsh MGos SLim WEve
– 'Bambi' CDoC CKen MGos NLar WAbe WEve WThu
– 'Barkenny' CKen
– 'Bartley' CKen
– 'Bassett' CKen
– 'Bess' CKen
– 'Brigitt' CKen
– 'Buttonball' CKen
– 'Caespitosa' WAbe
– 'Chabo-yadori' CDoC EHul LRHS MGos SLim WFar
– 'Chilworth' CDoC CKen MGos NLar
– 'Chima-anihiba' CKen
– 'Chirimen' CDoC CKen MGos NLar NWad SLim
– 'Clarke's Seedling' CDoC NLar
– 'Confucius' CDoC EHul MGos
§ – 'Crippsii' ♀H4 CBcs CDoC CDul CMac LRHS MGos SCoo SLim
– 'Crippsii Aurea' see *C. obtusa* 'Crippsii'
– 'Dainty Doll' CDoC CKen MGos NLar
– 'Densa' see *C. obtusa* 'Nana Densa'
– 'Draht' CDoC MGos NLar
– 'Draht Hexe' CKen
– 'Elf' CKen
– 'Ellie B' CKen
– 'Ericoides' CKen
– 'Fernspray Gold' CDoC CDul CKen CTri EHul LRHS MAsh NEgg SBfd SCoo SLim SPer SPoG WFar
– 'Flabelliformis' CKen
– 'Gnome' CKen CMen
– 'Gold Fern' CKen MGos WFar
– 'Golden Fairy' CDoC CKen MGos WEve
– 'Golden Filament' (v) CKen
– 'Golden Nymph' CDoC CKen MGos NLar
– 'Golden Sprite' CDoC CKen MGos NLar WAbe WEve WThu
– 'Goldilocks' EHul
– 'Gracilis Aurea' CKen CMac
– 'Green Diamond' CKen
– 'Hage' CKen
– 'Hannah' NLar
– 'Hypnoides Nana' CKen
– 'Intermedia' CDoC CKen MGos WAbe
– 'Ivan's Column' CKen

	Name	Suppliers
	- 'Junior'	CKen
	- 'Juniperoides'	CKen WThu
	- 'Juniperoides Compacta'	WAbe
	- 'Kamarachiba'	CDoC CKen CSBt EHul LAst LBee LRHS MAsh NLar SCoo SLim SPoG WEve WFar WGor
	- 'Kerdalo'	NLar SLim SPoG
	- 'Konijn'	EHul
	- 'Kosteri'	CDoC CKen CMac EHul ELan EPot LBee LPot MAsh NEgg NHol SCoo WEve WGor
	- 'Kyoto Creeper'	CKen
	- 'Leprechaun'	NLar WAbe
	- 'Limerick'	CKen
	- 'Little Markey'	CKen
	- 'Lucas'PBR	CDoC NLar SLim
	- 'Marian'	CKen MGos NLar
§	- 'Mariesii' (v)	CKen
	- 'Melody'	CKen NLar
	- 'Meroke'	NLar
	- 'Minima'	CKen MGos
	- 'Nana' ♀H4	CDoC CKen CMac CMen LBee MGos NHol NWad WEve
	- 'Nana Aurea' ♀H4	CDoC CMac CMea CSBt EHul EPfP MAsh MGos NHol WEve WFar
§	- 'Nana Densa'	CDoC CKen CMac NLar
	- 'Nana Gracilis' ♀H4	CDoC CDul CKen CMen CSBt EHul ELan EPfP GEdr IVic LAst LRHS MAsh MBri MGos NEgg NWad NWea SCoo SLim SPoG WEve WFar
I	- 'Nana Gracilis Aurea'	CMen EHul WEve
I	- 'Nana Lutea'	CDoC CKen EHul EPfP EPot LBee LRHS MAsh MGos NHol SCoo SLim SPoG
	- 'Nana Rigida'	see *C. obtusa* 'Rigid Dwarf'
	- 'Nana Variegata'	see *C. obtusa* 'Mariesii'
	- 'Pygmaea'	CSBt EHul LRHS MGos SCoo SLim WEve
	- 'Rashahiba'	SLim
§	- 'Rigid Dwarf'	CDoC CKen EHul LBee LPot NLar SCoo SPoG WEve
	- 'Saffron Spray'	LRHS SLim
	- 'Snowflake' (v)	CDoC CKen NWad SBfd WEve WFar
	- 'Snowkist' (v)	CKen
	- 'Spiralis'	CKen
	- 'Stoneham'	CKen
	- 'Suirova-hiba'	SLim
	- 'Tempelhof'	CKen EHul LRHS MAsh MGos NEgg NLar SCoo SLim WEve
	- 'Tetragona Aurea'	CBcs CMac EHul LRHS MGos NLar SCoo SLim WEve
	- 'Timothy'	CMac
	- 'Tonia' (v)	CKen EHul LRHS NHol NLar SLim WEve WGor
	- 'Topsie'	CKen NLar
	- 'Tsatsumi'	CDoC EMil
	- 'Tsatsumi Gold'	CDoC CKen EHul LRHS MPkF NLar SCoo SLim SPoG
	- 'Verdon'	CKen
	- 'Winter Gold'	WEve
	- 'Wissel'	CKen
	- 'Wyckoff'	CKen
	- 'Yellowtip' (v)	CKen MAsh MGos WEve
	pisifera 'Aurea' **new**	LAst
	- 'Aurea Nana' misapplied	see *C. pisifera* 'Strathmore'
	- 'Avenue'	EHul
	- 'Baby Blue'	EHul ELan EPfP LRHS MGos SCoo SLim WGor

	Name	Suppliers
	- 'Blue Globe'	CKen
	- 'Boulevard' ♀H4	CBcs CDoC CDul CJun CMac CSBt CWib EHul ELan EPfP EPot LAst LBee LRHS MAsh MGos NEgg NPri NWea SBfd SLim SPer WEve WFar WMoo
	- 'Compacta Variegata' (v)	MAsh NEgg NHol
	- 'Curly Tops'	CSBt EHul LRHS MGos SCoo SLim WEve WGor
	- 'Devon Cream'	MGos NEgg SCoo WFar
	- 'Filifera'	CMac CSBt LRHS SCoo WFar
	- 'Filifera Aurea' ♀H4	CKen CMac CWib EHul EPfP LBee MAsh MGos NEgg NHol NWea SCoo SPer WCFE WEve WFar
	- 'Filifera Aureovariegata' (v)	EHul LRHS SCoo
	- 'Filifera Nana'	EHul ELan LRHS SLim SPoG WFar
	- 'Filifera Nana Aurea'	see *C. pisifera* 'Golden Mop'
	- 'Filifera Sungold'	see *C. pisifera* 'Sungold'
	- 'Fuiri-tsukomo'	CKen
	- 'Gold Cushion'	CKen
	- 'Gold Dust'	see *C. pisifera* 'Plumosa Aurea'
	- 'Gold Spangle'	CKen EHul WFar
§	- 'Golden Mop' ♀H4	CKen EHul NLar
	- 'Green Pincushion'	CKen CMen
	- 'Hime-himuro'	CKen
	- 'Hime-sawara'	CKen CMen
	- 'Margaret'	CKen
	- 'Nana'	CKen CMen EHul MAsh MGos NHol WFar
I	- 'Nana Albovariegata' (v)	CDoC MAsh WFar WThu
	- 'Nana Aureovariegata' (v)	CDoC CSBt EHul LBee LRHS SCoo SLim SPer WEve WFar
I	- 'Nana Compacta'	CMac SRms
	- 'Nana Variegata' (v)	CMac LBee NWad SLim WFar
I	- 'Parslorii'	CKen
	- 'Pici'	CKen
§	- 'Plumosa Aurea'	CKen EHul MAsh NWea WFar
	- 'Plumosa Aurea Compacta'	CKen
	- 'Plumosa Aurea Nana'	MAsh MGos WFar
I	- 'Plumosa Aurea Nana Compacta'	CMac
	- 'Plumosa Aurescens'	CDoC CMac
§	- 'Plumosa Compressa'	CDoC CKen EHul EUJe NWad SCoo SLim WEve WFar WGor WThu
	- 'Plumosa Densa'	see *C. pisifera* 'Plumosa Compressa'
	- 'Plumosa Flavescens'	EHul
I	- 'Plumosa Juniperoides'	CKen EHul EPot SCoo SLim WFar WGor
I	- 'Plumosa Pygmaea'	EPot
§	- 'Plumosa Rogersii'	EHul NHol
I	- 'Pygmaea Tsukumo'	NLar
	- 'Rogersii'	see *C. pisifera* 'Plumosa Rogersii'
	- 'Silver and Gold' (v)	EHul
	- 'Silver Lode' (v)	CKen
	- 'Snow' (v)	CKen
	- 'Snowflake'	CKen EHul MGos NHol
	- 'Spaan's Cannon Ball'	CKen
§	- 'Squarrosa'	MWat WFar
	- 'Squarrosa Dumosa'	CKen EHul
I	- 'Squarrosa Lombarts'	CSBt EHul
	- 'Squarrosa Lutea'	CKen
	- 'Squarrosa Sulphurea'	CSBt EHul EPfP LRHS SLim WFar
	- 'Squarrosa Veitchii'	see *C. pisifera* 'Squarrosa'
§	- 'Strathmore'	CKen EHul NWad
§	- 'Sungold'	CDoC CKen CSBt EHul LAst LRHS MAsh SCoo SLim SPoG WEve
	- 'Tama-himuro'	CKen
	- 'Teddy Bear'	MBri NLar
	- 'True Blue'	EHul LAst MGos NLar

	- 'Winter Beauty'	LRHS
	thyoides 'Andelyensis'	CMac CSBt EHul LAst NEgg SCoo WFar
	- 'Andelyensis Nana'	CKen
	- 'Aurea'	EHul
	- 'Conica'	CKen MAsh
	- 'Ericoides' ♀H4	CKen CTri EHul LBee SPlb WFar
	- 'Little Jamie'	CKen
	- 'Red Star'	see *C. thyoides* 'Rubicon'
§	- 'Rubicon'	CMac CSBt EHul EPfP EPot LBee LRHS MGos NEgg SBfd SLim SPoG WFar
	- 'Top Point'	LBee LRHS MAsh MGos SCoo SLim SPoG
	- 'Variegata' (v)	EHul

Chamaecytisus (*Papilionaceae*)

§	***albus*** (Hacq.) Rothm.	GQui
§	***hirsutus***	WPGP
	prolifer	CPLG
§	***purpureus***	CWCL EBee ELan EPfP LHop MRav NWea SPer WFar WPat
	- f. ***albus***	EBee EPfP
§	- 'Atropurpureus' ♀H4	CWCL EBee NWea
	- 'Incarnatus'	see *C. purpureus* 'Atropurpureus'
§	***supinus***	CPLG IRar SRms

Chamaedaphne (*Ericaceae*)

	calyculata	CBcs
	- 'Nana'	NHar

Chamaedorea (*Arecaceae*)

	metallica misapplied	see *C. microspadix*
§	***microspadix***	CPHo EAmu SChr
	radicalis	CBrP CPHo EAmu SChr

Chamaemelum (*Asteraceae*)

§	***nobile***	CArn CHby CPrp CSev CTri CWan EGHP ELau ENfk EPfP GPoy MBri MHer MHoo MNHC NGdn NPri SBfd SEND SPlb SRms SVic WJek WPer
	- dwarf	SMor SVic
	- dwarf, double-flowered (d)	LEdu
	- 'Flore Pleno' (d)	Widely available
	- 'Treneague'	Widely available

Chamaenerion see *Chamerion*

Chamaepericlymenum see *Cornus*

Chamaerops (*Arecaceae*)

	excelsa misapplied	see *Trachycarpus fortunei*
	excelsa Thunb.	see *Rhapis excelsa*
	humilis ♀H3	CAbb CBcs CBrP CHEx CTrC CWSG EGri EPfP ESwi EUJe LRHS MGos MMuc MREP NPla NPri SBfd SChr SEND SHil SPlb SPoG STrG WCot WPGP
§	- var. ***argentea***	CBrP CDTJ CPHo CTrC EAmu ETod LRHS MGos SBfd SHil SPlb WCot
	- var. ***cerifera***	see *C. humilis* var. *argentea*
	- 'Vulcano'	CDTJ EAmu MBri MGos SChr

Chamaespartium see *Genista*

Chamaesphacos (*Lamiaceae*)

	ilicifolius misapplied	see *Siphocranion macranthum*

Chambeyronia (*Arecaceae*)

	macrocarpa	EAmu

Chamelaucium (*Myrtaceae*)

	uncinatum	CCCN EShb MOWG
	- 'Snowflake'	LRHS

Chamerion (*Onagraceae*)

§	***angustifolium***	SEND SWat WSFF XLum
§	- 'Album'	Widely available
	- 'Isobel'	MRav WCot
	- 'Stahl Rose'	CElw CHid CMea EBee EPfP EWes LPla MCot NPri NSti SMrm SPhx SPoG SSvw SWat WCot WSHC
§	***dodonaei***	CFis ELan EWes LPla MMuc SPhx WCot WFar

Chasmanthe (*Iridaceae*)

	bicolor	CDes CPLG CPrp CTca IDee
	floribunda	CAbb CHEx CPrp CTca EBee
	- var. ***duckittii***	CCon CPrp ECho EPfP

Chasmanthium (*Poaceae*)

§	***latifolium***	CKno EBee ECha EHoe ELan ELon EPPr EPfP EShb LRHS MBrN MMoz MSCN NRHS SGol SMrm SPoG WAul WBor WCot WFar WWEG WWFP XLum
	- 'Golden Spangles' **new**	CKno
	- 'River Mist' (v) **new**	CAbP EBee ELon IBoy SPoG
	- 'Variegatum' (v)	WCot
	laxum	CKno EPPr SMea

Cheilanthes (*Pteridaceae*)

	argentea	ISha
	distans	ISha SRms
	lanosa	CBty CCCN CHid CLAP EBee EFer EWes GCal GEdr ISha LRHS WCot
	siliquosa NNS 05-92	WCot
	sinuata	ISha
	tomentosa	CBty CCCN CLAP ISha LRHS
	wootonii	WAbe
	wrightii **new**	ISha

Cheiranthus see *Erysimum*

Cheirolophus (*Asteraceae*)

	benoistii misapplied	see *Centaurea atropurpurea*
	benoistii (Humb.) Holub	CSpe EBee MRav SKHP WSHC
	teydis	SPlb

Chelidonium (*Papaveraceae*)

	japonicum	see *Hylomecon japonica*
	majus	CArn CRWN GPoy GQui MHer NMir WHer WSFF
	- 'Flore Pleno' (d)	CBre NBid NBro WCFE WHer WTou
	- var. ***laciniatum***	NBir WCot

Chelone (*Plantaginaceae*)

	barbata	see *Penstemon barbatus*
§	***glabra***	Widely available
	lyonii	ELan MDKP NBre NLar SPad SPhx WMoo WPer WShi
	- 'Hot Lips'	EBee LHop WCAu
	- 'Pink Temptation'	EBee GEdr SPet

obliqua Widely available
- var. ***alba*** see *C. glabra*
- 'Forncett Foremost' GQui
- 'Forncett Poppet' NBre
- 'Ieniemienie' EBee
- 'Pink Sensation' EBee NBre WFar
* - ***rosea*** MMuc SEND WGwG

Chelonopsis (*Lamiaceae*)

moschata CLAP EBee GBin LEdu SMad WMoo WPGP
yagiharana CDes MDKP NBid NPnk SHar WMoo WPer

Chengiopanax (*Araliaceae*)

sciadophylloides B&SWJ 4728 WCru

Chenopodium (*Amaranthaceae*)

ambrosioides CArn
bonus-henricus CAgr CArn CHab CHby CWan ENfk GPoy LPot MCoo MHer MNHC SBfd SIde WHer WJek
giganteum MNHC SHDw WJek

cherimoya see *Annona cherimola*

cherry, Duke see *Prunus × gondouinii*

cherry, sour or morello see *Prunus cerasus*

cherry, sweet see *Prunus avium*

chervil see *Anthriscus cerefolium*

chestnut, sweet see *Castanea sativa*

Chiastophyllum (*Crassulaceae*)

§ ***oppositifolium*** ♀H4 CBcs CSam CTri EBee ECha ECho EDAr ELan EPfP GAbr GEdr GJos GKev LAst LRHS MAsh MLHP MRav MSCN NBid NMen NRHS SPlb SRms WAbe WKif WMoo WSHC XLum
- 'Frosted Jade' see *C. oppositifolium* 'Jim's Pride'
- 'Jane's Reverse' (v) EBee WCot
§ - 'Jim's Pride' (v) CMea EBee ECha ECho EHoe EWes GAbr GBuc GEdr GKev GMaP LAst LRHS MHer MRav NHar NMen NPer NPri SPlb SPoG SRGP SRms SRot WAbe WFar WMoo WSHC WWEG
simplicifolium see *C. oppositifolium*

Chiliotrichum (*Asteraceae*)

diffusum (G. Forst.) Kuntze CWib
- 'Siska' CBcs SMad

Chilopsis (*Bignoniaceae*)

linearis (Cav.) Sweet CArn

Chimonanthus ✿ (*Calycanthaceae*)

fragrans see *C. praecox*
nitens CBcs CMCN NLar
§ ***praecox*** Widely available
- 'Brockhill Goldleaf' NLar
- 'Grandiflorus' ♀H4 CJun EBee EPfP LRHS MAsh SPoG SSta WPGP WPat
- 'Luteus' ♀H4 CJun EBee ELan EPfP LRHS LSRN MAsh MGos SPoG SSpi SSta WPGP WPat
- 'Sunburst' CJun
- 'Trenython' CJun WPGP
yunnanensis IArd NLar

Chimonobambusa (*Poaceae*)

KR 7592 MWht
hookeriana misapplied see *Himalayacalamus falconeri* 'Damarapa'
§ ***marmorea*** CDTJ CEnt EAmu ERod MMoz MMuc MWht SBig SEND
- 'Variegata' (v) CDTJ ERod ESwi MMoz SLPl
§ ***quadrangularis*** CBcs CDTJ CDoC CEnt CHEx EPfP ERod ESwi MMoz MWht SBig WJun WPGP
- 'Nagaminei' (v) ERod WJun
- 'Suow' (v) CDTJ WPGP
- 'Tatejima' ERod WJun
tumidissinoda CDTJ CEnt EPfP ERod ESwi EUJe MMoz MMuc MWhi MWht SBig SEND SGol WJun WPGP

Chinese chives see *Allium tuberosum*

Chiogenes see *Gaultheria*

Chionanthus (*Oleaceae*)

retusus CBcs CDul CMCN EBee EPfP LRHS MBri MPkF NLar SHil SKHP SPer SSpi
- 'Tokyo Tower' **new** CJun
virginicus CBcs CDoC CDul CJun CMCN EBee ECrN ELan EPfP GBin GKin IArd IDee LHop LRHS MBlu MBri MMuc MRav NEgg SEND SKHP SPer SPlb SSpi WPGP

Chionochloa (*Poaceae*)

conspicua CGHE CKno EBee GBee GBin GCal NBid NBir SMea WPGP
- 'Rubra' see *C. rubra*
flavescens EHoe GAbr GBin LRHS
flavicans CTrC GAbr LRHS SGar SMad SMea
§ ***rubra*** CBcs CElw CGHE CKno CSpe EBee EHoe ELan EWes GCal GMaP LEdu LHop LRHS MAsh MAvo MMoz MRav NChi SApp SGar SMad SMrm WCot WMoo WPGP WTin WWEG
- subsp. ***cuprea*** EBee GBin SMad

Chionodoxa ✿ (*Hyacinthaceae*)

cretica see *C. nana*
§ ***forbesii*** CBro CWCL ECGP ECho EPfP EPot GKev NBir SDeJ SMrm SPer SRms WFar WRHF WShi
- 'Alba' ECho LAma
- 'Blue Giant' ECho ELan EPot ERCP
- 'Rosea' ECho LAma
- Siehei Group see *C. siehei*
- 'Tmoli' ECho
- 'Violet Beauty' ECho GKev SDeJ
- 'Zwanenburg' ECho LWst
gigantea see *C. luciliae* Gigantea Group
lochiae LWst
luciliae misapplied see *C. forbesii*

	luciliae ambig.	CAvo ECho SEND
	luciliae Boiss. ♀H4	CBro EPfP LAma LRHS MBri MMuc SPer
	- 'Alba'	ECho LRHS MCot SDeJ SMrm SPer
§	- Gigantea Group	ECho GKev LAma
	- - 'Alba'	EPot GKev
§	***nana***	ECho
	'Pink Giant'	CAvo CBro CMea ECho ELan EPfP EPot ERCP GKev LAma LRHS MCot SBch SDeJ SMrm WCot XLum
	sardensis ♀H4	CBro CPrp ECho EPot ERCP GKev LAma LRHS SDeJ SPhx WBor WCot WShi
§	***siehei*** ♀H4	CBro

Chionographis (*Melanthiaceae*)

japonica	EFEx GEdr WCru

Chionohebe (*Plantaginaceae*)

§	***densifolia***	EPot
	pulvinaris	NSla

× *Chionoscilla* (*Hyacinthaceae*)

§	***allenii***	ECho SPhx WCot

Chirita (*Gesneriaceae*)

	'Aiko'	WDib
	'Candy'	WDib
	'Chastity'	WDib
	'Diane Marie'	WDib
	'Erika'	WDib
	flavimaculata	WDib
	heterotricha	WDib
	'Keiko'	WDib
*	***latifolia* × *linearifolia***	WDib
	linearifolia	WDib
	linearifolia* × *sinensis	WDib
	longgangensis	WDib
	'New York'	WDib
	sinensis ♀H1	WDib
	- 'Hisako'	WDib
	speciosa 'Crûg Cornetto'	WCru
	'Stardust'	WDib
	'Sweet Dreams'	WDib
	tamiana	WDib

Chironia (*Gentianaceae*)

baccifera	SPlb

× *Chitalpa* (*Bignoniaceae*)

tashkentensis	CBcs EBee EPfP MTPN WPGP
- 'Morning Cloud'	MBlu
- 'Pink Dawn'	ESwi LRHS MBlu MBri SPad
- Summer Bells = 'Minsum'	CDoC LHop MAsh MGos NPri SBig SEND WCot

chives see *Allium schoenoprasum*

Chlidanthus (*Amaryllidaceae*)

fragrans	CCCN ECho EShb SDeJ SEND XLum

Chloranthus (*Chloranthaceae*)

fortunei	CDes CLAP WPGP
- 'Domino'	EBee IBoy WCot
japonicus	GBuc GEdr WCru
oldhamii	GEdr
- B&SWJ 2019	LEdu WCru
serratus	GEdr WCru

Chloris (*Poaceae*)

distichophylla	see *Eustachys distichophylla*

Chlorophytum (*Asparagaceae*)

comosum	EShb SEND SVic
- 'Aureomarginata'	SEND
- 'Variegatum' (v) ♀H1+3	CDTJ EShb SEND SRms
- 'Vittatum' (v) ♀H1+3	EShb SRms
krookianum	CCon EBee WCot
macrophyllum	EShb
majus	WCot
nepalense B&SWJ 2393	WCru
- B&SWJ 2528	WCru
orchidastrum 'Green Orange' **new**	WCot
saundersiae	CPLG

Choisya (*Rutaceae*)

	× ***dewitteana*** 'Aztec Pearl' ♀H4	Widely available
	- Golden Gift = 'Lismarty'PBR	EBee LRHS LSqu MAsh SSpi
	- Goldfingers = 'Limo'PBR	Widely available
	- White Dazzler = 'Londaz'PBR	CSBt CWGN EBee ELan ELon EPfP GBin LBuc LHop LRHS LSRN MAsh MBel MBri MGos MPkF NPri NRHS SBfd SHil SLim SLon SRkn WCot WGrn
	dumosa	LHop
	- var. ***arizonica***	WCot
	ternata ♀H4	Widely available
	- Moonshine = 'Walcho'PBR	EBee NHol NLar WCot
	- MoonsleeperPBR	see *C. ternata* Sundance
	- Snow Flurries = 'Lisflurry'PBR	EBee ELan EPfP LRHS LSqu MAsh SPoG
§	- Sundance = 'Lich'PBR ♀H3	Widely available

Chondrosum (*Poaceae*)

gracile	see *Bouteloua gracilis*

Chordospartium see *Carmichaelia*

Chorisia (*Bombacaceae*)

speciosa	CCCN EShb

Chorizema (*Papilionaceae*)

cordatum ♀H1	ECou
dicksonii	SPlb

Chromolaena (*Asteraceae*)

arnottiana RCB/Arg L2	CDes

Chronanthus see *Cytisus*

Chrysalidocarpus see *Dypsis*

Chrysanthemopsis see *Rhodanthemum*

Chrysanthemum ✿ (*Asteraceae*)

'Action Bronze' (22)	EPfP
'Agnes Ann' (21d)	EWoo MNrw
'Alan Foxall Yellow' (3b) **new**	MCms
'Albert's Yellow' (21d)	EWoo
'Alec Bedser' (25a)	NHal
'Alehmer Rote' (21)	LDai MNrw WWEG

	Name	Suppliers
	'Alex Young' (25b)	MCms NHal
	'Aline' (21)	EWoo MNrw
	'Alison' (29c)	EWoo MNrw
	'Alison's Dad'	MNrw
	'Allouise' (25b) ♀H3	NHal
	'Allouise Pink' (25b)	MCms
	'Allyson Peace' (14a)	MCms NHal
	alpinum	see *Leucanthemopsis alpina*
	'Amber Gigantic' (1)	NHal
	'Amber Matlock' (24b)	MCms
	'American Beauty Lemon' (5b)	MCms
	'American Beauty White' (5b)	MCms
	'Anastasia' (21c)	CHid EBee ECtt ELon LDai LRHS MNrw MRav NSti SPhx WHoo WWEG
	'Angela Blundell' (19b)	WCot
	'Angela Cosimini' (25b) **new**	MCms
	'Angelic' (28)	EWoo
	'Anja's Bouquet'	see *C.* 'Mei-kyō'
	'Anne Ratsey' (21)	CSam MNrw
	'Anne, Lady Brocket' (21d)	ECtt EWoo MNrw NWsh SSvw
	'Anthony Peace' (25b)	NHal
	'Antigua' PBR	MCms
	'Apollo' H. Shoesmith	EWoo LLHF MNrw WCot WTin
	'Apollo' (21)	EBee EWll LDai NCGa SMrs SPhx SSvw WHoo
	'Apricot'	see *C.* 'Cottage Apricot'
	'Apricot Chessington' (25a)	NHal
	'Apricot Courtier' (24a)	MCms NHal
	'Apricot Enbee Wedding'	see *C.* 'Bronze Enbee Wedding'
	arcticum L.	see *Arctanthemum arcticum*
	argenteum	see *Tanacetum argenteum*
	'Astro' (25b)	NHal
	'Aunt Millicent' (21d) ♀H4	EWoo LLHF MNrw NHal SPhx WCot
	'Balcombe Perfection' (5a)	NHal
	balsamita	see *Tanacetum balsamita*
	Barbara = 'Yobarbara' (22)	NHal
	'Beacon' (5a) ♀H2	NHal
	'Belle' (21d)	EWoo MNrw
	'Beppie Bronze' (29e)	MCms
	'Beppie Purple' (29e)	MCms
	'Beppie Red' (29e)	MCms
	'Beppie Rose' (29e)	MCms
	'Beppie Yellow' (29e)	MCms
	'Bernadette Wade' (23a)	NHal
	'Best Man' (29e)	MCms
	'Betty' (21)	EWoo
	'Bill Holden' (14a)	MCms NHal
	'Bill Wade' (25a)	NHal
	'Billy Bell' (15a)	MCms NHal
	'Blanche Poitevene' (5b)	EMal
	'Bob Green' (13b) **new**	MCms
	'Bobby Swinburn' (13b)	NHal
	Bravo = 'Yobra' (22c) ♀H3	NHal
*	'Breitner's Supreme'	MNrw WWEG
	'Brennpunkt'	EWoo SMrs
	'Bretforton Road' **new**	WCot
	'Brierton Violet' (17b)	NHal
	'Bright Eye' (21b)	LRHS WMnd
	'Brightness' (21)	EWoo SSvw
	'Bronze Cassandra' (5b) ♀H2	NHal
	'Bronze Dee Gem' (29c)	NHal
§	'Bronze Elegance' (28b)	CTri EBee EWoo LDai LRHS MNrw NBir NGdn NSti NWsh SMrs SRms SSvw WBor WMnd WPer
§	'Bronze Enbee Wedding' (29d) ♀H3	NHal
	'Bronze Gigantic' (1) **new**	NHal
	'Bronze Matlock' (24b)	NHal
	'Bronze Max Riley' (23b) ♀H3	NHal
	'Bronze Mayford Perfection' (5a) ♀H2	NHal
	'Bronze Mei-kyo'	see *C.* 'Bronze Elegance'
	'Bronze William Florentine' (15a)	MCms
	'Brown Eyes' (21)	EWoo
	'Bunty' (28)	SMad
	burnt orange-flowered	MNrw
	'Burnwood Belle' (3b)	NHal
	'Buxton Ruby' **new**	EWoo
	'Capel Manor'	EBee EWoo MNrw WCot
	'Carmine Blush' (21) ♀H4	EBee EWoo MNrw SMrs SPhx SSvw WCot
	'Cassandra' (5b) ♀H2	NHal
	'Caukeel Copper' (29c) ♀H3	NHal
	'Charles Tandy Yellow' (15b) **new**	MCms
	'Chelsea Physic Garden'	EBee EWoo GBee IGor LLHF MNrw SMrs SPhx SSvw SUsu WCot WWEG
	'Chempak Rose' (14b) **new**	MCms
	'Cherry Chessington' (25a)	NHal
	'Cherry Riley's Dynasty' (14a)	MCms
	Chesapeake = 'Yochesapeake' PBR (10a)	NHal
	'Chestnut Talbot Maid'	MCms
	'Chestnut Talbot Parade' (29c) ♀H3	MCms
	'Christopher Lawson' (24b)	NHal
	'Cinderella'	WMnd
	cinerariifolium	see *Tanacetum cinerariifolium*
	'Clapham Delight' (23a)	MCms NHal
	'Clara Curtis' (21d)	Widely available
	'Clare Louise' (24b)	MCms
	'Clarksdale' (15b) **new**	MCms
	'Clive Skinner' (25b)	NHal
	'Colsterworth' **new**	MNrw
	'Columbine' (21d)	EWoo
	'Contralto' (22)	EWoo
	'Coral Reef' (10b)	NHal
	'Cornetto' (25b)	MCms NHal
	corymbosum	see *Tanacetum corymbosum*
§	'Cottage Apricot' (21)	CPrp EBee ECGP EWoo LDai LRHS MBNS MLHP MNrw MRav
	'Cottage Bronze'	MNrw
	'Cottage Lemon'	MNrw
	'Cottage Pink'	see *C.* 'Emperor of China'
	'Cottage Yellow'	EWoo SMrs SSvw WHoo
	'Coup de Soleil'	WCot
	'Courtier' (24a)	NHal
	'Cousin Joan'	EBee EWoo LDai LLHF MNrw NCGa SUsu WCot
	'Cream Duke of Kent' (1)	NHal
	'Cream Elegance' (9c)	NHal
	'Cream Patricia Millar' (14b)	NHal
	'Cream Talbot Maid'	MCms
	'Cream West Bromwich' (14a)	MCms
	Dana = 'Yodana' (25b) ♀H3	NHal
	Dance = 'Fidance' PBR	MCms
	Dance Salmon = 'Fidancesal' PBR	MCms

	'Dance Sunny'	MCms
	'Dance White'	MCms
	'Daniel Cooper' (21)	EWoo MNrw
	'Daphne' (21d)	EWoo
	'Darren Pugh' (3b)	NHal
	'Dee Gem' (29c) ♀H3	NHal
	'Delta' (5b)	NHal
	'Delta Copper Bronze'	NHal
	'Delta Crimson' (29d)	NHal
	'Delta Yellow' (29)	NHal
	'Denise' (28b) ♀H3	EWoo
	'Dennis Gill' (25b) **new**	MCms
	'Deva Glow' (25a)	MCms
	'Dezianne'	MCms
	'Dezianne Yellow'	MCms
	'Dixter Orange' **new**	GCal
§	'Doctor Tom Parr' (21c)	CPLG ELan EWoo GCal LHop MNrw
	'Don't Start' (7a) **new**	MCms
	'Doreen Statham' (4b)	NHal
	'Doris Ozols' (25a)	NHal
	'Dorothy Stone' (25b)	NHal
	'Dorridge Crystal' (24a)	MCms NHal
	'Dublin'	MCms
	'Duchess of Edinburgh' (21d)	CFis CPrp EBee ECtt ELan EPfP EShb EWoo GBin LRHS MNrw SBfd SDys SMrs SPhx SSvw WMnd XLum
	'Duke of Kent' (1)	NHal
	'Dulwich Pink' **new**	EWoo
	'Dutchy' PBR	MCms
	'Early Yellow'	EWoo MNrw WCot
	'Edelweiss' (21)	EWoo
	'Edward Shaw' (5a) **new**	MCms
	'Egret' (23b)	MCms NHal
	'Elegance' (9c)	NHal
	'Elizabeth Lawson' (5b)	NHal
	'Elizabeth Shoesmith' (1)	NHal
	'Ellen' (29c)	NHal
§	'Emperor of China' (21)	CElw EBee ECtt EWoo IGor MNrw MRav NHal SMrs SPhx SSvw SUsu WBor WCot WMnd WWEG XLum
	'Enbee Wedding' (29d) ♀H3	MCms NHal
	'Energy' PBR	MCms
	'Esther' (21d)	EWTr EWoo MNrw NCGa SMrs
	'Ethel Edwards' (25b)	NHal
	'Eva Allen' (25b) **new**	MCms
	'Fairweather' (3b)	MCms NHal
	'Fairweather Peach' (3b) **new**	MCms
	'Feeling Green Dark' PBR	MCms
	foeniculaceum misapplied	see *Argyranthemum foeniculaceum* misapplied
	foeniculaceum (Willd.) Desf.	see *Argyranthemum foeniculaceum* (Willd.) Webb & Sch. Bip.
	'Fondant'	NHal
	'Froggy' PBR	MCms
	frutescens	see *Argyranthemum frutescens*
	'Gala Burgundy'	EPfP NLar
	'Gambit' (24a)	NHal
	'Geoff Amos' (3b)	NHal
	'Geoff Bradey' (15a)	MCms NHal
	'Geoff Sylvester' (25a)	NHal
	'George Griffiths' (24b) ♀H3	NHal
	'Gigantic' (1)	NHal
	'Gillette' (23b) **new**	MCms
	'Ginger Nut' (25b) **new**	MCms
	'Ginger Nut Yellow' (25b) **new**	MCms
I	'Gladys' (12a)	EBee
	'Gladys Emerson' (3b)	NHal
	'Gold Enbee Wedding' (29d) ♀H3	MCms
	'Gold Marianne' **new**	XLum
	'Golden Cassandra' (5b) ♀H2	NHal
	'Golden Chalice' (12a)	NHal
	'Golden Courtier' (24a)	MCms NHal
	'Golden Gigantic' (1)	NHal
	'Golden Mayford Perfection' (5a) ♀H2	NHal
	'Golden Plover' (22)	NHal
	'Golden Rain' (10a) ♀H2	NHal
	'Golden Wedding' (21)	MNrw
	'Golden Woolman's Glory' (7a)	NHal
	'Goldengreenheart' (21)	EShb EWoo LLHF MNrw SMrs WHoo
	'Goldmarianne' (21)	GBin
	'Grandchild' (21c) ♀H4	EWoo LLHF MNrw NHal SMrs
§	× ***grandiflorum***	SRms
	– 'Corinna'	GBin
	'Hanenburg'	NHal
	haradjanii	see *Tanacetum haradjanii*
	'Harold Lawson' (5a)	NHal
	'Harry Gee' (1)	NHal
	'Harry Tolley' (14b)	MCms
*	'Hazel' (21)	EWoo
	'Heather James' (3b)	NHal
	'Hebe' (21d)	EBee
	'Heide' (29c) ♀H3	NHal
	'Herbstbrokat'	GBin XLum
	'Hesketh Knight' (5b) ♀H2	NHal
	Holly = 'Yoholly' (22b) ♀H3	NHal
	'Honey Enbee Wedding' (29d)	NHal
	'Horningsea Pink' (19d)	ECGP WBor
	'Imp' (21e)	EWoo
	'Innocence' (21)	ECtt ELan EWoo GBee IGor MNrw MRav NGdn NSti SAga SSvw WHoo
	'Isabellrosa' (21) **new**	EWoo
	'Janet South'	EWoo MNrw
	'Jante Wells' (21b)	EWoo MNrw WBor WWEG
	'Jenny Wren' (12a)	NHal
	'Jessie Cooper' misapplied	see *C.* 'Mrs Jessie Cooper' (21)
	'Jessie Habgood' (1)	NHal
	'Jimmy Tranter' (14b)	NHal
	'John Harrison' (25b)	MCms NHal
	'John Hughes' (3b)	NHal
	'John Lowry' (24a)	MCms NHal
	'John Riley' (14a)	NHal
	'John Wingfield' (14b)	MCms NHal
	'John Wingfield Honey' (14b) **new**	MCms
	'John Wingfield Pearl' (14b) **new**	MCms
	'Joyce Fountain' (24a)	MCms NHal
	'Joyce Frieda' (13b)	MCms NHal
	'Julia' (28)	EPfP EWoo
	'Julia Peterson'	MHer WCot WHoo WTin
	'Julie Lagravère' (28)	EWoo MNrw SMrs WPtf XLum
	'Juweeltja'	NHal
	'Karen Taylor' (29c) ♀H3	NHal
	'Kath Stephenson' (7b)	MCms NHal
	'Kath Stephenson Honey' (7b) **new**	MCms
	'Kath Stephenson Peach' (7b) **new**	MCms

Name	Suppliers
'Kath Stephenson Primrose' (7b)	MCms
'Kath Stephenson Rose' (7b)	MCms NHal
'Kath Stephenson Salmon' (7b) **new**	MCms
'Katie Jane' (7b)	NHal
'Kay Woolman' (13b)	MCms NHal
'Kay Woolman Yellow' (13b) **new**	MCms
'Kenny Buglass' (25b)	NHal
'Kiyominomeisui'	NHal
'Kleiner Bernstein'	WCot
× ***koreanum***	see *C.* × *grandiflorum*
§ 'Lady in Pink' (21)	EWoo LDai LRHS MNrw
'Lady Manito' **new**	EWoo
'Lakelanders' (3b)	NHal
'Leo' (21b)	EWoo
leucanthemum	see *Leucanthemum vulgare*
'Lexy'PBR	MCms
'Lexy Red'PBR	MCms
'Lilac Chessington' (25a)	NHal
Linda = 'Lindayo'PBR (22c) ♀H3	NHal
'Lindie' (28)	WHil
'Little Dorrit' (21f)	EWoo
'Lollipop'PBR	MCms
'Lorna Wood' (13b)	MCms NHal
'Louise' (25b)	EWoo MNrw
'Lucy' (29a) ♀H3	NHal
'Lucy Simpson' (21d)	EWoo SBch
'Lundy' (2)	NHal
'Lydia Mannion' (7b) **new**	MCms
'Lynn Johnson' (15a)	NHal
Lynn = 'Yolynn' (22c) ♀H3	NHal
macrophyllum	see *Tanacetum macrophyllum* (Waldst. & Kit.) Sch.Bip.
'Malcolm Perkins' (25a)	MCms
'Mancetta Comet' (29a)	NHal
'Mancetta Symbol' (5a)	MCms NHal
'Mandarin' **new**	EWoo
maresii	see *Rhodanthemum hosmariense*
'Margaret' (29c) ♀H3	NHal WCot
'Marion' (25a)	LDai MNrw WCot
'Mark Woolman' (1)	NHal
'Mary' (21f)	EWoo LDai MNrw NHal
'Mary Stoker' (21d)	CPrp EBee ECtt ELan EPfP EWoo LRHS MNrw MRav NCGa NHal NLar NSti SSvw SUsu WAul WCAu WMnd WWEG
'Matador' (14a)	NHal
'Matlock' (24b)	NHal
'Mauve Gem' (21f) ♀H3	EWoo MNrw NHal
'Mavis' (21) ♀H3	EWoo
mawii	see *Rhodanthemum gayanum*
'Max Riley' (23b) ♀H3	MCms NHal
maximum misapplied	see *Leucanthemum* × *superbum*
maximum Ramond	see *Leucanthemum maximum* (Ramond) DC.
'Maxine Johnson' (25b)	NHal
'May Shoesmith' (5a) ♀H2	NHal
'Mayford Perfection' (5a) ♀H2	NHal
§ 'Mei-kyō' (28b)	CFis CMea CTri EBee ECtt EWoo IGor MNrw SMrs SRms SSvw WBor WHil WPer WWEG
'Membury' (24b)	NHal
'Michelle Preston' (13b)	NHal
'Millennium' (25b) ♀H3	MCms NHal
'Misty Cream' (25b)	MCms
'Misty Golden' (25b)	MCms
'Misty Lemon' (25b)	MCms
'Moira' (21d)	EWoo
'Moonlight' (29d/K)	MRav
'Morning Star' (12a)	NHal
§ 'Mrs Jessie Cooper' (21)	CHGN ELan EWoo GBee GQue LDai MNrw NBir NLar SDys SMrs SSvw SUsu WCot WHil WHoo WPtf WTin
'Mrs Jessie Cooper No 1'	NCGa NWsh
'Mrs Jessie Cooper No 2'	MNrw
'Muriel Odell' (7b)	MCms
'Music' (23b)	NHal
'Muxton Sable' (10a)	NHal
'Myss Carol' (29c) ♀H3	NHal
'Myss Debbie' (29e)	NHal
'Myss Goldie' (29c)	MCms
'Myss Jem' (29e)	NHal
'Myss Jem Red' (29e)	NHal
'Myss Marion' (29c) ♀H3	EWoo NHal
'Myss Saffron' (29c) ♀H3	NHal
'Nancy Perry' (21d)	CSam EWoo GBee MNrw MRav SSvw XLum
'Nantyderry Sunshine' (28b) ♀H4	CPrp EBee LLHF LRHS MNrw SPhx SSvw WBor WCot WMnd WPer WWEG
'Naru' (9c)	NHal
'Natalie Sarah' (29d) ♀H3 **new**	MCms NHal
'Nell Gwynn' (21d) ♀H3	EWoo MNrw NHal
Nicole = 'Yonicole' (22c) ♀H3	NHal
nipponicum	see *Nipponanthemum nipponicum*
'Olwyn' (4b)	NHal
'Orange Allouise' (25b)	MCms NHal
'Orange Enbee Wedding' (29d)	NHal
pacificum	see *Ajania pacifica*
parthenium	see *Tanacetum parthenium*
'Patricia Millar' (14b)	MCms NHal
'Patricia Millar Cerise' (14b) **new**	MCms
'Patricia Millar Coral' (14b) **new**	MCms
'Patricia Millar Orange' (14b) **new**	NHal
'Patricia Millar Yellow' (14b) **new**	NHal
'Paul Boissier' (30Rub)	CFis ECtt EWoo LDai MNrw NSti SMrs SPhx SSvw WCot WMnd
'Pauline White' (15a)	MCms
'Peach Courtier' (24a)	NHal
'Peach Enbee Wedding' (29d) ♀H3	NHal
'Peach John Wingfield' (14b)	MCms NHal
'Peach Patricia Millar' (14b)	MCms
'Pearl Celebration' (24a)	MCms
'Pennine Bullion'	NHal
'Pennine Gift' (29c)	NHal
'Pennine Marie' (29a) ♀H3	NHal
'Pennine Oriel' (29a) ♀H3	MCms NHal
'Pennine Point' (19c)	NHal
'Pennine Polo' (29d) ♀H3	NHal
'Pennine Ranger' (29d)	NHal
'Pennine Swan' (29c)	NHal
'Pennine Toy' (19d)	NHal
'Penny's Yellow'	LLHF
'Perry's Peach' (21a) ♀H4	EWoo LDai LLHF MNrw NCGa NHal NPer SPhx SSvw

'Peter Rowe' (23b)	NHal
'Peter Sare' (21d)	LRHS
'Peterkin'	CMac ECtt ELon EWoo LRHS WWEG
'Pink Anemone' **new**	EWoo
'Pink Duke of Kent' (1)	NHal
'Pink John Wingfield' (14b)	NHal
'Pink Progression'	see *C.* 'Lady in Pink'
'Polar Gem' (3a)	NHal
'President Osaka'	MNrw
'Primrose Allouise' (24b) ♀H3	NHal
'Primrose Chessington' (25a)	MCms
'Primrose Courtier'	see *C.* 'Yellow Courtier'
'Primrose Dorothy Stone' (25b)	NHal
'Primrose Enbee Wedding' (29d) ♀H3	MCms NHal
'Primrose Fairweather' (3b) **new**	MCms
'Primrose Jessie Habgood' (1)	NHal
'Primrose John Hughes' (3b)	NHal
'Primrose Mayford Perfection' (5a) ♀H2	NHal
'Primrose Sam Vinter' (5a)	NHal
'Primrose West Bromwich' (14a)	MCms NHal
'Prince Charles' **new**	EWoo
'Princess' (21d)	LLHF
'Promise' (25a)	NHal
ptarmiciflorum	see *Tanacetum ptarmiciflorum*
'Purleigh White' (28b)	ECtt ELon EWoo LDai MNrw NSti SMrs SSvw WCot WWEG
'Purple Chempak Rose' (14b)	MCms NHal
'Ralph Lambert' (1)	NHal
'Raquel' (21)	MNrw
'Red Balcombe Perfection' (5a)	NHal
'Red Chempak Rose' (14b)	MCms
'Red Mayford Perfection' (5a)	NHal
'Red Pennine Gift' (29c)	NHal
'Red Regal Mist' (25b)	MCms
'Red Shirley Model' (3a)	NHal
'Redbreast' (12a)	NHal
'Regal Mist Purple' (25b)	MCms NHal
'Richmond' (3b)	NHal
'Riley's Dynasty' (14a)	MCms
'Ringdove' (12a)	NHal
'Rita McMahon' (29d) ♀H3	NHal
'Robeam' (9c) ♀H2	NHal
Robin = 'Yorobi' (22c)	NHal
'Roen Sarah' (29c)	NHal
'Romantika'	EWoo
'Rose Enbee Wedding' (29d)	MCms NHal
'Rose Madder'	EWoo MNrw WCot
'Rose Mayford Perfection' (5a) ♀H2	NHal
'Rose Patricia Millar' (14b)	NHal
'Rosetta'	WCot
'Rosy Yoigloo'PBR **new**	SHar
'Roy Bevan' (29d) **new**	MCms
'Royal Command' (21a)	MNrw NGBo SMrs WCot
'Royal Sport' **new**	EWoo
rubellum	see *C. zawadskii*
'Ruby Enbee Wedding' (29d) ♀H3	MCms NHal
'Ruby Glow' (7b) **new**	MCms
'Ruby Mound' (21c) ♀H3	EWoo LLHF MNrw NHal SDys SMrs SPhx SSvw SUsu
'Ruby Raynor' (21) ♀H4	EWoo MNrw NHal SDys SMrs SUsu WCot
'Rumpelstilzchen' (21d)	CMea ECtt EWoo MNrw NWsh SMrs WPer
'Salhouse Joy' (10a)	NHal
'Salmon Allouise' (25b)	NHal
'Salmon Enbee Wedding' (29d) ♀H3	NHal
'Salmon Fairweather' (3b) **new**	MCms
'Salmon John Wingfield' (24b)	MCms
'Salmon Pauline White' (15a)	MCms
'Salmon Talbot Maid'	MCms
'Salmon Talbot Parade' (29c) ♀H3 **new**	MCms
'Sam Vinter' (5a)	NHal
'Sarah Louise' (25b)	NHal
'Savanna Charlton' (25a) **new**	MCms
'Sea Urchin' (21f) ♀H3	MNrw NHal SDys
'Sheena' (9f/10)	NHal
'Sheffield' **new**	EWoo
'Sheila Coles' (7b)	MCms NHal
'Shenley Orange' **new**	EWoo LLHF
'Shining Light' (21f)	EWoo LLHF MNrw
'Shirley Primrose' (1)	NHal
sinense	see *C.* × *grandiflorum*
'Sonnenschein'	LHop
'Sound'	MCms
'Southway Sheba' (29d) ♀H3	MCms NHal
'Southway Sheba Bronze' (29d) **new**	MCms
'Southway Shimmer' (29d)	NHal
'Southway Shiraz' (29d)	NHal
'Southway Snoopy' (29d)	NHal
'Southway Strontium' (29d)	NHal
'Southway Sunkissed' (29d)	NHal
'Spartan Canary'	EWoo SWal
'Spartan Display'	EWoo SWal
'Spartan Fire'	SWal
'Spartan Glory' (25b)	SWal
'Spartan Linnet'	EWoo SWal
'Spartan Raspberry' (21d)	EWoo SWal
'Spartan Seagull' (21d)	EWoo MNrw SMrs SSvw SWal
'Spartan Star' (29d)	SWal
'Stallion'PBR	MCms
'Starlet' (21f)	EWoo LLHF NHal
'Stockton' (3b) ♀H2	NHal
'Stratford Pink' (21d) **new**	EWoo
'Suffolk Pink'	EShb EWoo MNrw
'Sundae'PBR (22c)	EPfP
Sundoro = 'Yosun' (22d)	NHal
'Sunny Yoigloo'PBR **new**	SHar
Swan = 'Fiswan'PBR	MCms
'Syllabub' ♀H3	ECtt
'Symphony' (10a)	NHal
'Talbot Maid' (29c)	MCms
'Talbot Parade' (29c) ♀H3	MCms
'Talbot Parade Pink' (29c) **new**	MCms
'Tapestry Rose' (21d)	CMea EWoo LDai MNrw NCGa SPhx SSvw WBor

'Terry Brook' (29e) new — NHal
'Terry Morris' (7b) new — MCms
'Thoroughbred' (24a) — NHal
'Tom Parr' — see *C.* 'Doctor Tom Parr'
'Tom Snowball' (3b) — NHal
'Topsy' (21c) — EWoo
'Tracy Waller' (24b) — NHal
Triumph = 'Yotri' (22) — NHal
uliginosum — see *Leucanthemella serotina*
'Uri' — EWoo SAga SPhx
'Vagabond Prince' — EWoo MNrw NCGa WBor WHoo
'Venice' (24b) — NHal
'Venus' (21) — NCGa WCot
'Venus One' — EWoo LDai MNrw NHal SPhx
'Vibrant' (9c) ♀H2 — NHal
'Vulcano Dark' — MCms
'Warm Yoigloo' PBR new — SHar
'Wedding Day' (29k) — EWoo MNrw WTin
'Wedding Sunshine' (21) — LDai MNrw
welwitschii — see *Glebionis segetum*
'Wembley' (24b) — NHal
'Wendy Tench' (21d) — ECtt EWoo NWsh
'West Bromwich' (14a) — NHal
weyrichii — EBee ECho LEdu NLar NRHS SRms WWEG
'White Allouise' (25b) ♀H3 — MCms NHal
'White Beppie' (29e) — MCms
'White Cassandra' (5b) — NHal
'White Enbee Wedding' (29d) — MCms NHal
'White Fairweather' (3b) — MCms NHal
'White Gem' (21f) — NHal
'White Gloss' (21e) — LLHF MNrw SSvw
'White Pearl Celebration' (24a) — MCms
'White Tower' (27) — EWoo MNrw
'Wilder Charms' — WHil
'William Florentine' (15a) — MCms NHal
'Wills Wonderful' (21d) new — EWoo
'Win' (9c) — NHal
'Winning's Red' (21) — EWoo LHop NCGa SMad SSvw WCot
'Wizard' PBR — EPfP
'Woolman's Glory' (7a) — NHal
'Woolman's Glory Red' (7a) new — MCms
'Woolman's Star' (3a) — NHal
'Woolman's Venture' (14b) — MCms NHal
'Yellow Allouise' (25b) — MCms
'Yellow American Beauty' (5b) ♀H2 — MCms
'Yellow Billy Bell' (15a) — NHal
'Yellow Clapham Delight' (23a) — MCms NHal
§ 'Yellow Courtier' (24a) — MCms NHal
'Yellow Duke of Kent' (1) — NHal
'Yellow Egret' (23b) — NHal
'Yellow Ellen' (29c) — NHal
'Yellow Enbee Wedding' (29d) — MCms NHal
'Yellow Harold Lawson' (5a) — NHal
'Yellow Heide' (29c) ♀H3 — NHal
'Yellow John Hughes' (3b) ♀H2 — NHal
'Yellow John Wingfield' (14b) — MCms NHal
'Yellow May Shoesmith' (5a) — NHal
'Yellow Mayford Perfection' (5a) ♀H2 — NHal
'Yellow Pennine Oriel' (29a) ♀H3 — MCms NHal
'Yellow Starlet' (21f) — EWoo LLHF MNrw
'Yellow Woolman's Glory' (7a) new — MCms
yezoense ♀H4 — ELan LRHS MNrw SRms SSvw WPer
- B&SWJ 10872 — WCru
- 'Roseum' — ECtt
'Yonashville' new — SRms
§ ***zawadskii*** — CMac

Chrysogonum (*Asteraceae*)

australe — EBee
virginianum — CMea CPrp EBee ECha EWes LRHS MRav SBch SPer WFar WWEG
- var. ***australe*** 'Andre Viette' — EBee

Chrysolepis (*Fagaceae*)

chrysophylla new — CMCN

Chrysopogon (*Poaceae*)

gryllus — EBee SApp WPGP

Chrysopsis (*Asteraceae*)

§ ***mariana*** — WOld
villosa (Pursh) Nutt. ex DC. — see *Heterotheca villosa*

Chrysosplenium (*Saxifragaceae*)

alternifolium — GEdr
davidianum — CBre CSam CSpe EBee ECha EPot EWld GCal GEdr GJos GKev LRHS NBir NLar NRHS NSla WBor WCot WCru WMoo WPtf
- SBEC 233 — CPLG
flagelliferum — GEdr
- B&SWJ 8902 — WCru
hebetatum — GEdr
- B&SWJ 9835 — WCru
lanuginosum — GEdr
var. ***formosanum***
- - B&SWJ 6979 — ESwi WCru
macrophyllum — CDes CPLG CSpe EWld GCal GMaP IGor MMHG MPie MTPN NLar SHar WBor WCot WCru WSHC
macrostemon var. ***shiobarense*** B&SWJ 6173 — WCru
oppositifolium — EBee NMir WSFF WShi

Chusquea (*Poaceae*)

breviglumis misapplied — see *C. culeou* 'Tenuis'
culeou ♀H4 — CAbb CBcs CDoC CEnt CHEx CHid EAmu ENBC EPfP EUJe IDee LAst LEdu MAvo MGos MMoz MWht SBig SPlb SSta WJun
- 'Breviglumis' — see *C. culeou* 'Tenuis'
- 'Purple Splendour' — WJun
§ - 'Tenuis' — ERod WJun
- weeping — CDTJ
cumingii — CBcs GBin WJun WPGP
gigantea — CDTJ CEnt CPLG EPfP ERod ESwi MMoz MWht SBig WJun WPGP
montana — CBcs CDTJ
mulleri F&M 104A from Mexico — WPGP

quila	MMoz
valdiviensis	WJun

Cicerbita (*Asteraceae*)

BWJ 7891 from China	WCru
§ ***alpina***	GAbr NBid SPlb
bourgaei	LRHS
plumieri	EWes GAbr IFro WCot WFar WMoo WPtf
- 'Blott' (v)	WCot

Cichorium (*Asteraceae*)

intybus	CArn CHby CPom CPrp EBee EGHP ELan ELau ENfk GPoy LHop MBel MHoo MNHC NBir NCGa NMir NPri SBfd SGar SIde SPer SPlb SPoG SVic WFar WHrl WJek WMoo WSHC
- f. ***album***	CPrp EBee ECha ECtt GKin LHop LRHS MBel MCot NBir NCGa SBea SPer SWat
- 'Roseum'	CPrp EBee ECha ECtt ELan EWTr GKin LHop LRHS MBel MCot NBir NCGa SBea SPer SPoG SWat WHrl

Cimicifuga see *Actaea*

acerina	see *Actaea japonica*
americana	see *Actaea podocarpa*
cordifolia (DC.) Torrey & A.Gray	see *Actaea cordifolia*
cordifolia Pursh	see *Actaea podocarpa*
foetida	see *Actaea cimicifuga*
racemosa var. ***cordifolia***	see *Actaea cordifolia*
- 'Purpurea'	see *Actaea simplex* Atropurpurea Group
ramosa	see *Actaea simplex* 'Prichard's Giant'
rubifolia	see *Actaea cordifolia*
simplex var. ***matsumurae***	see *Actaea matsumurae*

Cineraria (*Asteraceae*)

maritima	see *Senecio cineraria*

Cinnamomum (*Lauraceae*)

camphora	CBcs CHEx CPLG IGor IRar LRHS SPlb
parthenoxylon	EGFP

Cionura (*Asclepiadaceae*)

oreophila	CRHN EBee ELan GCal SKHP WPGP WSHC

Circaea (*Onagraceae*)

alpina	EBee
lutetiana	WHer
- 'Caveat Emptor' (v)	NBid WCot

Cirsium (*Asteraceae*)

anartiolepis F&M 252	EBee WPGP
arvense	WSFF
* ***atroroseum***	SWat
ciliatum	EBee
diacantha	see *Ptilostemon diacantha*
eriophorum	LDai
helenioides	see *C. heterophyllum*
§ ***heterophyllum***	CHid CPom EBee EWld LDai LEdu MAvo NChi NLar SHar WHil WPGP
japonicum 'Early Pink Beauty'	LDai
- 'Pink Beauty'	SPhx WWEG
- 'Rose Beauty'	EBee IPot LRHS
- variegated (v)	WCot
'Mount Etna'	CMHG CPrp EBee EWhm GKin LHop LRHS MBNS MMuc MSpe NGdn SEND WPGP WWEG
oleraceum	LEdu LRHS NBid NLar
purpuratum	WPGP
rivulare 'Atropurpureum'	Widely available
tuberosum	SKHP SPhx
vulgare	WSFF

Cissus (*Vitaceae*)

antarctica ♀H1	CCCN EShb SEND
pedata B&SWJ 2371	WCru
quadrangularis	SBfd
rhombifolia ♀H1	EOHP SEND
§ ***striata***	CBcs CDoC CHEx CMac CTrC CWCL EBee ELon EShb IBoy LRHS MRav SBfd SEND SLim SWvt WCFE WSHC

Cistus ✿ (*Cistaceae*)

acutifolius misapplied	see *C. × pulverulentus*
× ***aguilarii***	CBcs CHEx CSBt CTri LAst MRav WSHC
- 'Maculatus' ♀H3	CDoC CDul CPLG CSam CTrC EBee ELan EPfP LRHS LSRN MAsh MMuc NLar SBfd SCoo SEND SLPl SPer SPoG SWvt WKif WPGP WSpi
albidus	CArn WKif XSen
algarvensis	see *Halimium ocymoides*
'Ann Baker'	SLPl
'Anne Palmer'	see *C. × fernandesiae* 'Anne Palmer'
× ***argenteus*** 'Blushing Peggy Sammons'	CDoC NLar XSen
- Golden Treasure = 'Nepond' (v)	SWvt
- 'Paper Moon'	EWTr LSRN NLar
§ - 'Peggy Sammons' ♀H3	CDoC EBee ECha ELan EPfP LBMP LPot LRHS LSRN MAsh MGos MNHC NLar SCoo SEND SLim SPer SWvt WHar WSHC XSen
- 'Silver Ghost'	EBee EPfP LRHS SLim
- 'Silver Pink' ambig.	CBar CBcs CDoC CDul CWib EBee ECtt ELan EPfP LRHS LTen MAsh MBri MGos MRav MSwo MWat NBir NLar NPri SBfd SHil SLim SPer SPoG SSta WFar
- 'Stripey'	XSen
'Blanche'	see *C. ladanifer* 'Blanche'
× ***bornetianus*** 'Jester'	CSBt EBee EPfP LRHS MAsh MBri SHil
× ***canescens*** f. ***albus***	CWib WKif XSen
§ ***clusii***	NLar
- subsp. ***multiflorus***	XSen
× ***corbariensis***	see *C. × hybridus*
creticus	CDoC CMac CPLG CSam ELau LAst LRHS MBri MGos NLar SBfd SGar SHil SLon SPoG SRms WKif WPGP WSpi
- subsp. ***corsicus***	XSen
§ - subsp. ***creticus***	EBee ELan ELon EPfP LRHS MRav SCoo SPer
§ - subsp. ***incanus***	NRHS
× ***crispatus***	XSen
§ - 'Warley Rose'	GMaP WKif XLum
crispus misapplied	see *C. × pulverulentus*, *C. × purpureus*

§	***crispus*** L.	ELan LRHS SEND SGol
	- 'Prostratus'	see *C. crispus* L.
	- 'Sunset'	see *C.* × *pulverulentus* 'Sunset'
§	× ***cyprius*** ♀H4	CArn ELan EPfP GBin LRHS MGos MNHC MRav MWat SDix SEND SPer SRms WSpi
§	- var. ***ellipticus*** 'Elma' ♀H3	EBee ELan EPfP LRHS MAsh NLar SPer XSen
§	× ***dansereaui***	CMHG CMac CSBt CWib LRHS MGos NLar SWvt
	- 'Decumbens' ♀H4	CDul CMHG CTri EBee ELan EPfP LHop LRHS MAsh MBNS MBri MRav MSwo NLar SBfd SCoo SGar SHil SPer SPoG SWvt WPGP
	- 'Jenkyn Place'	CDoC EBee GMaP IVic LSRN MBNS MGos SEND SLPl SPer SPoG SUsu WKif
	'Elma'	see *C.* × *cyprius* var. *ellipticus* 'Elma'
	'Enigma'	CDoC
§	× ***fernandesiae*** 'Anne Palmer'	EBee EPfP LLHF LRHS LSRN MAsh MNHC NLar SEND SPoG SRGP
	× ***florentinus*** misapplied	see × *Halimiocistus* 'Ingwersenii'
	× ***florentinus*** ambig.	XLum
§	× ***florentinus*** Lam.	CAbP GMaP XSen
	- 'Fontfroide'	MMuc SEND
*	- 'Tramontane'	XSen
	'Gordon Cooper'	LSRN SEND SPoG
	× ***heterocalyx*** 'Chelsea Bonnet'	EPfP GMaP LRHS MBNS SCoo SEND SLim SPoG XSen
§	× ***hybridus***	Widely available
	- 'Gold Prize' (v)	CMHG CWGN CWSG ELan MGos NEgg NLar SBfd SWvt WFar WGrn WHar
	- Little Miss Sunshine = 'Dunnecis' (v)	EBee EMil LBMP LBuc LRHS MAsh MBri SHil SPer SPoG
	- Rospico = 'Rencis'PBR (v)	EBee LBuc LRHS
	incanus	see *C. creticus* subsp. *incanus*
	ingwerseniana	see × *Halimiocistus* 'Ingwersenii'
	'Jessamy Beauty'	SLPl WIce
	'Jessamy Bride'	SLPl
	ladanifer misapplied	see *C.* × *cyprius*
	ladanifer ambig.	CMac WKif
	ladanifer L. ♀H3	CDoC CDul CSBt CTri ECha ELan EPfP GPoy MRav MSwo SBfd SGar SPer SWvt WFar WHar WSpi
§	- 'Blanche'	EBee EWTr LLHF LSRN SEND SSpi WKif WSpi
§	- 'Paladin'	SBfd
	- Palhinhae Group	see *C. ladanifer* var. *sulcatus*
	- 'Pat'	EBee ELan EPfP LRHS LSRN MAsh NBir SPoG SSpi
§	- var. ***sulcatus***	CDoC EBee ELan EPfP LHop LRHS WCot
	lasianthus	see *Halimium lasianthum*
	laurifolius ♀H4	CDoC CDul EBee EPfP MGos NBir NEgg NLar SEND SKHP SLPl SPer WSpi XLum XSen
	- subsp. ***atlanticus***	XSen
	× ***laxus*** 'Snow White'	CDoC CTrC CWGN EPfP LAst LRHS MGos NPer NPro SLPl SLim SLon SUsu
	× ***ledon***	SLPl
§	× ***lenis*** 'Grayswood Pink' ♀H4	CDoC CMHG CPLG CTrC CTri CWSG EBee ECrN ELan EPfP EWTr LHop LRHS LSRN MAsh MCot MGos MMuc MSwo NLar SEND SLim SPer SPlb SWvt WKif XLum
	libanotis 'Major' **new**	WSpi XSen
	× ***longifolius***	see *C.* × *nigricans*
	× ***loretii*** misapplied	see *C.* × *dansereaui*
	× ***loretii*** Rouy & Foucaud	see *C.* × *stenophyllus*
	× ***lucasii***	XSen
	× ***lusitanicus*** Maund	see *C.* × *dansereaui*
	'Merrist Wood Cream'	see × *Halimiocistus wintonensis* 'Merrist Wood Cream'
	monspeliensis	CAbP CMac EBee EPfP LRHS MAsh MBNS MMuc SEND SLon SPer XSen
	- 'Vicar's Mead'	CCCN CDoC ELan EPfP LRHS MBNS MMuc SEND
	monspeliensis × ***salviifolius***	see *C.* × *florentinus* Lam.
§	× ***nigricans***	CTrC XSen
	× ***oblongifolius***	XSen
	× ***obtusifolius*** misapplied	see *C.* × *nigricans*
	× ***obtusifolius*** ambig.	EBee LRHS MRav SKHP WNew
	× ***obtusifolius*** Sweet	EPfP EWes SLPl
§	- 'Thrive'	EPfP LRHS MBri MGos NRHS SCoo SHil
	ocymoides	see *Halimium ocymoides*
	'Paladin'	see *C. ladanifer* 'Paladin'
	palhinhae	see *C. ladanifer* var. *sulcatus*
	parviflorus misapplied	see *C.* × *lenis* 'Grayswood Pink'
	parviflorus Lam.	WSHC
*	× ***pauranthus*** 'Natacha'	XSen
	'Peggy Sammons'	see *C.* × *argenteus* 'Peggy Sammons'
	× ***platysepalus***	SLPl
	populifolius	CMHG CMac EBee ECha EPfP LLHF LRHS NLar SGol SPer
	- var. ***lasiocalyx***	see *C. populifolius* subsp. *major*
§	- subsp. ***major*** ♀H3	EBee EPfP LRHS LSRN SKHP WPGP WSpi
§	× ***pulverulentus***	CPLG CTri EBee ECha EPfP MMHG SWal WSHC XSen
*	- Delilei Group	XSen
	- - 'Fiona'	XSen
§	- 'Sunset' ♀H3	Widely available
	- 'Warley Rose'	see *C.* × *crispatus* 'Warley Rose'
§	× ***purpureus*** ♀H3	Widely available
	- 'Alan Fradd'	Widely available
	- var. ***argenteus*** f. ***stictus***	EPfP LRHS LSRN XSen
	- 'Betty Taudevin'	see *C.* × *purpureus*
	× ***rodiaei*** 'Jessabel'	EBee EPfP LRHS MAsh SCoo SEND SPoG
	- 'Jessica'	NLar WSpi
	rosmarinifolius	see *C. clusii*
	'Ruby Cluster'	CCCN LRHS LSRN MMuc NLar SEND
	sahucii	see × *Halimiocistus sahucii*
	salviifolius	CAbP CArn CCCN XSen
	- 'Avalanche'	LRHS MRav WAbe
	- 'Gold Star'	LRHS
	- 'May Snow'	LBuc LRHS
	- 'Prostratus'	EBee ELan EPfP IRar LRHS WPGP WSpi
	'Silver Pink' misapplied	see *C.* × *lenis* 'Grayswood Pink'
	'Silver Pink' ambig.	CMac CWSG EBee SMad WKif
	× ***skanbergii*** ♀H3	CHEx CMac CSBt CTri CWib ELan EPfP LHop LRHS MGos MLHP MMuc MRav MWat NBir NLar SDix SEND SMrm SPer SPoG XLum XSen
	'Snow Fire' ♀H4	CCCN CDoC CTrC EBee EPfP LRHS LSRN MAsh MGos MMuc MWat NLar NPro SBfd SCoo SEND SLPl SPoG WGrn

§	× ***stenophyllus***	CWib EBee EPfP SPer
	'Summer Snow'	LRHS
	× ***tephreus***	XSen
	'Thornfield White'	LRHS
	'Thrive'	see *C.* × *obtusifolius* 'Thrive'
	tomentosus	see *Helianthemum nummularium* subsp. *tomentosum*
	× ***verguinii***	LHop SDix
	villosus	see *C. creticus* subsp. *creticus*
	wintonensis	see × *Halimiocistus wintonensis*

Citharexylum (*Verbenaceae*)

	spicatum	CPLG WBor WPGP

× *Citrofortunella* (*Rutaceae*)

	sp.	CCCN
§	***microcarpa*** (F) ♀H1	CCCN CDoC EPfP LRHS NLar SEND SHil
	mitis	see × *C. microcarpa*

Citrullus (*Cucurbitaceae*)

	colocynthis	CArn

Citrus (*Rutaceae*)

	aurantiifolia (F)	CCCN EPfP EUJe SVic
	aurantium	SPlb
	- 'Bouquet de Fleurs' (F)	CCCN
	- 'Seville' (F)	LSRN
	calamondin	see × *Citrofortunella microcarpa*
	'Fukushu' (F)	CCCN
	hystrix	CCCN CDoC LSRN NPla
	jambhiri 'Otaheite' (F)	CCCN
	japonica	see *Fortunella japonica*
	'Kulci' (F)	CCCN
	kumquat	see *Fortunella margarita*
	'La Valette' (F)	CCCN LSRN
	× ***latifolia*** (F/S)	CCCN CDoC EPfP LRHS MREP
	limetta	CCCN
	limettoides (F)	CArn
	limon (F)	CHEx EPfP EUJe LRHS LSRN MREP SEND SHil
	- 'Eureka' (F)	CCCN
	- 'Fino' (F)	CCCN
	- 'Four Seasons' (F)	CCCN LSRN NLar
§	- 'Garey's Eureka' (F)	CDoC EPfP
	- 'Quatre Saisons'	see *C. limon* 'Garey's Eureka'
	- 'Variegata' (F/v) ♀H1	CCCN
	- 'Verna' (F)	CCCN
	- 'Villa Franca' (F)	SVic
	'Lipo' (F)	CCCN NLar
	madurensis	see *Fortunella japonica*
	× ***meyeri***	CHEx
	- 'Meyer' (F) ♀H1	CBcs CCCN CHll CTri EPfP LRHS LSRN NLar SPer
	microcarpa Philippine lime	see × *Citrofortunella microcarpa*
	mitis	see × *Citrofortunella microcarpa*
	× ***nobilis*** Ortanique Group (F)	CCCN
	× ***paradisi*** (F)	CCCN EUJe MREP SVic
	- 'Golden Special' (F)	SVic
	- 'Star Ruby' (F/S)	CCCN
	'Pursta' (F)	CCCN
	reticulata (F)	CCCN LRHS MREP SVic
	- 'Hernandina' (F)	CCCN
	- Mandarin Group (F)	CDoC EPfP
	- - 'Clementine' (F)	CDoC LRHS
	- - 'Esbal' (F)	CCCN
	- - 'Nules' (F/S)	CCCN
	- 'Nova'	see *C.* × *tangelo* 'Nova'
	- 'Suntina'	see *C.* × *tangelo* 'Nova'
	sinensis (F)	CCCN LRHS SHil SVic
	- 'Fukumoto' (F)	CCCN
	- 'Lane Late' (F)	CCCN
	- 'Navelina' (F/S)	CCCN CDoC
	- 'Sanguinelli' (F)	CCCN
	- 'Valencia' (F)	CCCN SVic
§	× ***tangelo*** 'Nova' (F/S)	CCCN
	unshiu 'Miyagawa'	CCCN
	- 'Okitsu' (F/S)	CCCN

Cladium (*Cyperaceae*)

	mariscus	XLum

Cladrastis (*Papilionaceae*)

§	***kentukea***	CBcs CDul CLnd CMCN ELan EPfP EUJe LRHS MBlu MBri MRav NLar SSpi WHar
§	- 'Perkins Pink'	MBlu MBri SSpi
	- 'Rosea'	see *C. kentukea* 'Perkins Pink'
	lutea	see *C. kentukea*
	sinensis	CGHE CPLG EBee EPfP MBlu SKHP WPGP

Clarkia (*Onagraceae*)

*	***repens***	CSpe

Clavinodum (*Poaceae*)

§	***oedogonatum***	MWht

Claytonia (*Portulacaceae*)

	alsinoides	see *C. sibirica*
	caroliniana	EBee
§	***perfoliata***	CArn GPoy WHer
§	***sibirica***	CAgr CArn CElw EBee LSou MMoz WPtf XLum
	- f. ***albiflora***	CElw MMoz MPie WCot WMoo
	virginica	EBee LAma LRHS MMoz WFar WMoo

Clematis ✿ (*Ranunculaceae*)

	BWJ 7630 from China	WCru
	BWJ 8169 from China	WCru
	CC 711	CPLG
	CC 4710	CPLG
	CC 5904	GKev
	SDR 6151	GKev
	'Abigail' (Vt) **new**	NHaw
	Abilene = 'Evipo027' **new**	LBuc LSqu NPri SWCr
	'Abundance' (Vt) ♀H4	CDoC CRHN CSPN CWCL EBee ETho LRHS LSRN MAsh MBri NHol NTay SBfd SDix SPer SPet
	acuminata var. ***sikkimensis*** B&SWJ 7202	WCru
	addisonii	CBcs CSPN NHaw
	afoliata	ECou WThu
	afoliata × ***forsteri***	ECou
	'Ai-Nor' (EL)	ETho
	'Akaishi' (EL)	ETho NTay
	akebioides	NHaw
	- SDR 5966	GKev
	- SDR 6110	GKev
	Alabast = 'Poulala'PBR (EL) ♀H4	CLng CSPN EBee ETho LRHS NHaw NTay SCoo SPoG
	'Alba Luxurians' (Vt) ♀H4	CBcs CDoC CDoy CElw CRHN CSPN CTri CWCL EBee ELan ELon EPfP ETho LRHS LSRN MAsh MBri MGos MRav NHol

	Name	Suppliers
		NTay SDix SLim SPer SPet SPoG SWCr WFar WPGP
	'Albatross' (EL)	LSRN
	'Albert' (A)	NTay
	'Albiflora' (A)	CLng CSPN NTay
	'Albina Plena' (A/d)	ETho LRHS MGos SLon
	'Aleksandrit' (EL)	NHaw
	'Alice Fisk' (EL)	CSPN EBee ETho LRHS LSRN MSwo NHaw SLim WGor
	'Alionushka' (I) ΨH4	CRHN EBee ELan ELon EPfP ETho LRHS LSRN MAsh MBri MGos NLar NRHS SLim SPer SPet SPoG SWCr
	'Allanah' (LL)	EBee ETho LRHS LSRN MAsh MGos NHaw SCoo SLim SPoG WFar
	alpina ΨH4	GKin IBoy LSRN MAsh MRav MWhi NHaw NPer SEWo SPlb WFar
	- 'Albiflora'	see *C. sibirica*
	- 'Columbine White'	see *C.* 'White Columbine'
I	- 'Odorata'	CSPN NHaw
§	- 'Pamela Jackman' ΨH4	CDoC CMac CSPN CWSG EBee ELan IBal LRHS LSRN MAsh MBri MMuc NEgg NRHS NTay SCoo SDix SEND SLim SPer SPet SPoG SWCr SWvt WFar
	- pink-flowered	GKev
	- 'Stolwijk Gold' (A)	CSPN ETho MBlu MGos NHaw NTay SRms
	alternata	CWGN ETho
	'Amelia' (I) **new**	SMDP
	'Amelia Joan' (Ta)	MWat
	'Ameshisuto' (EL)	ETho
	'Amethyst Beauty' (A)	EPfP LRHS
	Amethyst Beauty = 'Evipo043'	ETho LSqu NPri NRHS NTay SLon
	'Andromeda' (EL)	CSPN EBee ETho LRHS NHaw NTay SWCr WFar
	Angelique = 'Evipo017' (EL)	CLng CSPN EPfP ETho LBuc LRHS LSqu NPri NRHS NTay SCoo SLon SPer SWCr
	'Anita' (Ta)	ETho LSRN NHaw NTay SLim SMDP
	'Anna Karolina' (EL)	NTay
	Anna Louise = 'Evithree'PBR (EL) ΨH4	CLng CSPN CWCL EBee EPfP ETho LBuc LRHS LSRN LSqu MBri NTay SCoo SLim SLon SPer SWCr
	'Annabel' (EL)	CSPN LSRN MAsh
	Anniversary = 'Pynot' (EL)	LSRN SCoo
	'Aotearoa' (LL)	EBee NHaw
	'Aphrodite Elegafumina'	CCon CRHN CWGN LRHS NHaw SWCr
	apiifolia B&SWJ 4838	WCru
	'Apple Blossom' (Ar) ΨH4	Widely available
	'Arabella' (I) ΨH4	CRHN CSPN CSam CWCL EBee ELan ELon EPfP EShb ETho LRHS LSRN MAsh MBri NLar NPri NRHS NTay SEND SLim SPer SPoG SWCr SWvt WFar WSHC
§	Arctic Queen = 'Evitwo'PBR (EL) ΨH4	CLng CSPN CWCL EBee EPfP ETho LBuc LRHS LSRN LSqu MAsh MBri MWat NPri NTay SCoo SLon SPer SPoG SWCr WFar
	armandii	Widely available
	- 'Enham Star'	LRHS MBri MGos SHil
§	- 'Little White Charm'	CBcs EBee LRHS SBfd SKHP SMDP
	- 'Meyeniana'	see *C. armandii* 'Little White Charm'
I	- 'Snowdrift'	CBcs CSBt CSPN CWSG EBee ELan EPfP ETho LRHS LSRN LTen MAsh MGos MSwo NEgg NLar NTay SBfd SKHP SPer SPoG SRms SWCr
	× ***aromatica***	CBcs CCon CPrp CSPN CWGN EAEE EBee ELan ELon EPfP ETho LRHS MAsh MRav NTay SCoo SPoG WGwG
§	'Asagasumi' (EL)	ETho
	'Asao' (EL)	CLng EBee ELan EPfP ETho IBoy LRHS MGos MRav NTay SCoo SEND SPer SPoG SWCr
	'Ascotiensis' (LL)	CLng CRHN CSPN EBee EPfP ETho LRHS MAsh NHaw NTay SCoo SLim SLon SPoG SWCr WFar
	'Aureolin' (Ta)	CSPN EBee
	Avant-garde = 'Evipo033'PBR (Vt)	CLng CSPN CWGN EBee EPfP ETho LSqu NTay SLon SPoG
§	'Bagatelle' (LL)	CLng CSPN LRHS LSRN NHaw SGol SMDP WFar
	'Bal Maiden' (Vt)	CRHN NHaw
§	'Ballerina in Blue' (A/d)	IPot NHaw
	'Ballet Skirt' (A/d) ΨH4	NHaw
	'Barbara' (LL)	ETho LSRN MRav NHaw NTay
	'Barbara Dibley' (EL)	CLng CTri CWSG LRHS MAsh NHaw SCoo SDix SLim SPet
	'Barbara Harrington'PBR (LL)	CLng LRHS LSRN MAsh NHaw SLon SWCr
	'Barbara Jackman' (EL)	CMac EBee ETho LRHS LSRN MAsh MRav MSwo NTay SCoo SLon SPer SWCr
	'Basil Bartlett' (Fo)	ECou
	'Beata' (LL)	MGos NHaw
	'Beauty of Worcester' (EL)	CCon CMac CSPN CWSG EBee ELan ELon EPfP ETho LRHS LSRN MAsh MSwo NHaw NTay SCoo SDix SEND SGol SLim SPer SPet WFar WSpi
	'Bees' Jubilee' (EL)	CBcs CMac CWSG EBee ELan ETho LRHS LSRN MAsh MGos MRav MSwo NBir NLar NTay SDix SLim SPer SPet SPoG SWvt WFar
	'Bella' (EL)	LSRN NHaw NTay
	'Belle Nantaise' (EL)	NTay SCoo SPet SRms
	'Belle of Woking' (EL)	CSPN CWSG EBee ELan ELon ETho LRHS LSRN MAsh MRav NTay SCoo SGol SLim SPoG SWCr
	'Bells of Emei Shan'	EBee ETho WCru
	'Berry Red' (A)	CWGN
§	'Beth Currie' (EL)	CLng CSPN EPfP LRHS SWCr
	'Betina'	see *C.* 'Red Beetroot Beauty'
	'Betty Corning' (Vt) ΨH4	CRHN CSPN CWGN EBee ELan ELon EPfP ETho LRHS LSRN MBel MBri NTay SCoo SLon SRms SWCr WFar
	'Betty Risdon' (EL)	ETho MAsh NTay
	BijouPBR	see *C.* Thumbelina
	'Bill MacKenzie' (Ta) ΨH4	Widely available
	'Black Prince' (Vt)	CRHN CWGN EBee ELan ETho LRHS LSRN MGos NHaw NLar NTay SLim SLon SMDP SRms
	'Black Tea' (LL)	CSPN LRHS LSRN NHaw NTay SLim SLon SWCr
§	'Błękitny Anioł' (LL) ΨH4	CLng CMac CRHN CSPN ELon ETho LRHS MAsh MGos NLar NTay SCoo SPer SPet SPoG SWCr WBor WFar
	Blue Angel	see *C.* 'Błękitny Anioł'
	'Blue Belle' (Vt)	CRHN ELan NHol SLon WFar
	'Blue Bird' (A/d)	CBcs CWCL EBee LRHS NTay SMDP SPer SPoG SRms

Name	Suppliers
Blue Blood	see *C.*'Königskind'
'Blue Boy' (EL)	see *C.* 'Elsa Späth'
'Blue Boy' (I)	see *C.* × *diversifolia* 'Blue Boy' (I)
'Blue Dancer' (A)	CBcs CLng EBee EPfP ETho LRHS MAsh MBri MGos NLar NTay SWCr
'Blue Eclipse' (A)	CSPN CTri CWGN MBri MGos NHaw NTay
'Blue Eyes' (EL)	CSPN ELon ETho LSRN NHaw NTay SLim
§ 'Blue Light' PBR (EL/d)	CSPN ELan LRHS MGos NLar NTay WFar
Blue Moon = 'Evirin' PBR (EL)	CLng EPfP ETho LRHS LSRN NLar NTay SCoo SLon SPoG SWCr WFar
Blue Pirouette = 'Zobluepi' PBR (I)	NLar SMDP
Blue Rain	see *C.*'Sinii Dozhd'
'Blue Ravine' (EL)	EBee EPfP LRHS MGos NLar NTay SCoo
Blue River = 'Zoblueriver' PBR	ELan
'Blue Tapers' (A)	NHaw
Bonanza = 'Evipo031' PBR	CLng EBee EPfP ETho LRHS LSqu MWat NLar NTay SCoo SDix SLon SPer SPoG SWCr
× ***bonstedtii*** 'Crépuscule' (H)	LRHS MCot SMDP
'Boskoop Beauty' (EL)	NHaw
Bourbon = 'Evipo018' PBR	EPfP ETho LBuc LRHS LSqu NRHS SCoo SLon SPer SPoG SWCr
brachyura B&SWJ 8854	WCru
'Brocade' (Vt)	CRHN CSPN NHaw
'Broughton Bride' (A)	CLng CSPN CTri CWGN ETho MAsh MBri NHol NTay SMDP
'Broughton Star' (M/d) ΨH4	CMac CRHN CSBt CSPN CWib EBee ELan EPfP ETho IBoy LRHS LSRN LTen MAsh MBlu MBri MGos MRav MSwo NBir NHol NTay SBfd SLim SLon SPet SPoG SRms WBor WFar
'Brunette' (A)	CSPN EBee ELan EPfP ETho IPot LRHS MAsh MBri MGos NHaw NLar NTay SLon SPoG SWCr
buchananiana Finet & Gagnep.	see *C. rehderiana*
buchananiana DC. B&SWJ 8333a	WCru
'Buckland Beauty' (V)	CLng CSPN CWGN NTay SMDP
'Buckland Cascade'	SMDP
'Buckland Longshanks' (H)	SMDP
'Burford Bell' (V)	NHaw
'Burford Princess' (Vt)	CRHN NHaw
'Burford White' (A)	CSPN EBee MBri NLar
'Burma Star' (EL)	CWGN ETho LRHS NHaw NTay
Caddick's Cascade = 'Semu'	CSPN CWGN ETho NHaw
calycina	see *C. cirrhosa* var. *balearica*
campaniflora	see *C. viticella* subsp. *campaniflora*
'Candleglow' (A)	MBri NHaw
'Candy Stripe'	CLng LRHS NTay SCoo SPoG SWCr
'Capitaine Thuilleaux'	see *C.* 'Souvenir du Capitaine Thuilleaux'
'Cardinal Wyszynski'	see *C.*'Kardynał Wyszyński'
'Carmencita' (Vt)	CRHN CSPN EBee LRHS LSRN NHaw SCoo SLon SPet WFar
'Carnaby' (EL)	CBcs CSPN CWCL EBee ELan ELon EPfP ETho LRHS LSRN MAsh MBri MGos NPri NTay SCoo SLim SPoG SWCr
'Carnival Queen'	CSPN MAsh
'Carol Leeds' (Vt)	NHaw
'Caroline' (LL)	CSPN CWGN EBee ETho LSRN NHaw NTay SMDP
× ***cartmanii*** hort. 'Avalanche' PBR (Fo/m) ΨH3	CSPN ELan EPfP ETho GBin LBuc LRHS MWat NLar NPri NTay SBfd SCoo SLim SLon SPoG
- 'Joe' (Fo/m)	CBcs EBee ELan EPfP ETho EWes ITim LRHS LSRN MGos NTay SBfd SCoo SPer SPoG SWCr WIce
- 'Joe' × ***marmoraria*** (Fo)	ECho MGos SWCr
- 'Joe' × 'Sharon'	LSRN
- 'White Abundance' PBR (Fo/f)	ETho LRHS NLar SPoG
× ***cartmanii*** hort. × ***petriei*** (Fo)	ECho
Cassis = 'Evipo020' PBR	CSPN CWGN EBee EPfP ETho LBuc LRHS LSRN LSqu NTay SCoo SLon SPer SPoG SWCr
'Celebration' PBR Godfrey	LBuc NTay SLim
Cezanne = 'Evipo023' PBR (EL)	CLng CSPN EPfP ETho LBuc LRHS LSqu MWat NPri NRHS NTay SCoo SLon SPer SWCr
'Chacewater' (Vt)	CRHN
'Chalcedony' (EL)	CSPN CWGN EBee ETho MGos NTay
Chantilly = 'Evipo021' PBR	CSPN EPfP ETho LBuc LRHS LSRN LSqu NPri NTay SCoo SLon SPer SWCr
'Charissima' (EL)	CSPN CWGN EPfP LRHS MAsh MGos NLar SCoo SPet SWCr WFar
'Charlie Brown' (LL)	CRHN
'Chatsworth' (Vt)	CRHN EPfP LRHS SLon SWCr
Cherokee	see *C.* Ooh La La
Chevalier = 'Evipo040'	EPfP ETho LRHS SLon SPer SPoG SWCr
chiisanensis	WSHC
- B&SWJ 4560	WCru
- B&SWJ 8706	WCru
- B&SWJ 8800	WCru
- 'Lemon Bells' (A)	ELan EPfP LRHS MAsh SCoo SLon SPoG SWCr
- 'Love Child' (A)	ELan NTay
chinensis misapplied	see *C. terniflora*
chinensis Osbeck RWJ 10042	WCru
Chinook = 'Evipo013' PBR	CLng LRHS SLim
chrysantha	see *C. tangutica*
chrysocoma misapplied	see *C. spooneri*
N ***chrysocoma*** Franch.	SMDP
'Cicciolina' (Vt)	CRHN ETho NHaw
cirrhosa	CTri ELan LRHS MAsh MGos MWhi SWCr
§ - var. ***balearica***	Widely available
- 'Jingle Bells'	CLng CMac CRHN EBee EPfP ETho LRHS LSRN MAsh MBri MWat NTay SCoo SLim SLon SPoG SWCr WFar WSpi
- 'Ourika Valley'	EBee EPfP ETho LRHS MAsh MBri MWat NLar NTay WFar
- var. ***purpurascens*** 'Freckles' ΨH3	Widely available
- - 'Lansdowne Gem'	CMac CSPN CWGN CWib LRHS NTay SKHP SMDP SPoG WSpi
- 'Wisley Cream' ΨH3	CBcs CDul CMac CSPN CWCL CWib EBee ELan EPfP ETho LRHS LSRN MAsh MBri MGos

	MSwo MWat NTay SCoo SEND SKHP SLim SPer SPoG SRms SWCr SWvt WFar
clarkeana misapplied	see *C. urophylla* 'Winter Beauty'
columbiana var. ***tenuiloba*** 'Ylva' (A)	WAbe
'Columbine' (A)	CWSG EBee ETho LRHS MAsh MSwo NTay SDix SPer
'Columella' (A)	ETho MGos NHaw NLar
'Comtesse de Bouchaud' (LL) ♀H4	CDoC CMac CSPN CTri CWCL CWSG EBee ELan EPfP EShb ETho LRHS LSRN MAsh MBri MGos MRav NPri NRHS NTay SDix SEND SLim SPer SPet SPoG SWCr WBor WFar
Confetti = 'Evipo036'PBR	CLng EBee EPfP ETho LRHS LSRN NTay SLim SLon
'Congratulations' (EL)	EBee ELon LRHS LSRN NTay SLim
connata	GQui
- GWJ 9386	WCru
- HWJCM 132	WCru
aff. ***connata*** GWJ 9431 from West Bengal	WCru
- HWJK 2176 from Nepal	WCru
'Constance' (A) ♀H4	CMac CSPN CWCL EBee EPfP ETho LRHS LSRN NHaw NLar NTay SCoo SPer SRms SWCr
'Continuity' (M)	CWGN
'Cora' (I)	CWGN
'Cornish Spirit' (Vt)	CRHN
'Corona' (EL)	CLng CSPN EPfP MAsh NHaw SCoo WFar
'Corry' (Ta)	NLar NTay
'Côte d'Azur' (H)	CBcs CCse CMac CPLG GCal LRHS MNrw NTay
'Countess of Lovelace' (EL)	CBcs CSPN CWSG EBee ELan EPfP ETho LRHS LSRN MAsh MBri MGos NTay SCoo SPet WFar
County Park hybrids (Fo)	ECou
'Cragside' (A)	EBee ETho MMuc SEND
§ 'Crimson King' (LL)	EBee MAsh NHaw NLar WGor
'Crinkle'PBR (M)	CCCN CLng SLim
§ ***crispa***	CElw NHaw SBrt
§ Crystal Fountain = 'Evipo038'PBR (EL)	CLng CSPN CWCL CWGN EBee EPfP ETho LBuc LRHS LSRN LSqu MBri MWat NTay SCoo SLim SLon SPer SPoG SWCr
§ 'Daihelios' (Ta)	CSPN ETho LRHS MGos NTay SCoo
'Danae' (Vt)	CRHN NHaw
Dancing Dorien = 'Zodado' (EL) **new**	WCot
Dancing King = 'Zodaki'PBR (EL) **new**	NTay
Dancing Queen = 'Zodaque'PBR (EL)	ETho NTay WSpi
'Daniel Deronda' (EL) ♀H4	CDoC CSPN CWCL CWSG ELan ELon ETho IBoy LRHS LSRN MAsh MGos NBir NTay SCoo SDix SEND SLim SPoG SWCr WFar
'Dark Eyes' (Vt)	CSPN CWGN ETho
'Dark Secret' (A)	MBri NHaw NTay
'Dawn' (EL)	CCCN CLng CSPN ELon ETho LRHS LSRN MAsh NTay SCoo SPer SWCr
'Débutante' (EL)	NHaw
'Denny's Double' (EL/d)	CSPN CWGN CWSG ETho LRHS MAsh NTay
Diamantina = 'Evipo039'PBR	EPfP ETho LRHS LSqu NPri NRHS NTay SLon SPer SPoG SWCr
'Diana' (LL)	ETho LSRN NTay
Diana's Delight = 'Evipo026'	EPfP ETho LRHS LSRN LSqu NTay SLon SPer SPoG SWCr
dioscoreifolia	see *C. terniflora*
§ × ***diversifolia***	CRHN EBee MGos NHaw SDix
§ - 'Blue Boy' (I)	CRHN CSPN EBee MGos NHaw SLon
- 'Heather Herschell' (I)	CRHN CSPN EBee ELon NHaw SMDP
§ - 'Hendersonii' (I)	EAEE EBee ELan ELon EPfP ETho GBuc LHop LRHS LSRN MAsh MCot MRav MSwo NBir NTay SDix SPer SWat WKif
§ - 'Olgae' (I)	CPLG CSPN EBee NHaw SMDP WGwG
'Doctor Ruppel' (EL)	CDul CMac CSPN CWCL CWSG ELon EPfP ETho IBoy LRHS LSRN MAsh MBri MGos MRav MSwo NBir NPri NTay SDix SGol SLim SPer SWCr WFar
'Dominika' (LL)	NHaw
'Dorath'	ELon LRHS NHaw NTay
'Dorothy Tolver' (EL)	ETho
'Dorothy Walton'	see *C.* 'Bagatelle'
'Double Cross'	ECou
'Double Delight' (M) **new**	CWGN
'Duchess of Albany' (1882) (LL) **new**	MBri
'Duchess of Albany' (1897) (T)	CSPN CTri CWSG CWib EBee ELan EPfP ETho IBal LRHS LSRN MAsh MGos NEgg NHol SGol SPer SWCr WFar
'Duchess of Edinburgh' (EL)	CBcs CMac CWSG EBee ELan EPfP IBoy LRHS LSRN MAsh MGos MSwo NEgg NHol NTay SDix SEND SGol SLim SPet SPoG SWCr WFar
'Duchess of Sutherland' (EL)	MAsh MGos NHaw SDix
'Dulcie'	NHaw
× ***durandii*** ♀H4	CBcs CRHN CSPN CWCL EBee ELan EPfP ETho LRHS LSRN MAsh MBri MRav NPri NTay SCoo SPer SPoG SWCr WFar
'Dutch Sky' (LL)	ETho MBri
'Early Sensation' (Fo/f)	CBcs CSPN CTri CWSG CWib EBee ELan ELon EPfP ETho EUJe LRHS LSRN MAsh MBri MGos NHol NTay SBfd SCoo SLim SPer SPoG SWCr SWvt WFar
'East Malling' (M)	NHaw
East River = 'Zoeastri' (I) **new**	ELan
'Eclipse' (H)	NHaw SMDP
'Edith' (EL) ♀H4	ETho LSRN MAsh NHaw NLar NTay WGor
'Edouard Desfossé' (EL)	CLng
'Edward Prichard'	CSPN EBee ELon MAsh MGos NHaw NTay SDix SMDP
'Eetika' (LL)	CRHN ETho NHaw
'Ekstra' (LL)	NHaw
'Eleanor' (Fo/f)	ECou GEdr
'Elf' (Vt)	SMDP
'Elfin' (Fo/v)	ECou
'Elizabeth' (M) ♀H4	Widely available
§ 'Elsa Späth' (EL)	CMac CPLG CSPN CTri EBee ELan EPfP ETho LRHS LSRN MAsh MBri MGos NRHS NTay SLim SPer SPoG SWCr WFar
'Elten' (M)	CSPN SMDP
'Elvan' (Vt)	CRHN IPot NHaw NLar SPet

Name	Suppliers
'Emilia Plater' (Vt)	CRHN EBee ETho LRHS MGos NHaw SLon
Empress = 'Evipo011'PBR (EL)	CSPN EBee ELan EPfP ETho LBuc LRHS LSqu MWat NTay SLon SWCr
'Entel' (Vt)	CRHN NHaw
× ***eriostemon***	see *C.* × *diversifolia*
'Ernest Markham' (LL) 🏆H4	CBcs CDoC CMac CSPN CWCL EBee ELan EPfP ETho IBoy LRHS LSRN LTen MAsh MBri MGos MSwo NEgg NPri NTay SDix SGol SLim SPer SPoG SWCr SWvt WFar
'Essex Star' (Fo)	ECou
'Étoile de Malicorne' (EL)	MAsh WGor
'Étoile de Paris' (EL)	EBee
'Étoile Rose' (Vt)	CMac CRHN CSPN CTri CWCL ELan EPfP ETho LRHS LSRN MAsh MGos NHol NTay SCoo SDix SLim SLon SPer SWCr WBor WFar
'Étoile Violette' (Vt) 🏆H4	Widely available
Evening Star = 'Evista' (EL)	EPfP WFar
'Eximia'	see *C.* 'Ballerina in Blue'
'Fair Rosamond' (EL)	EBee EPfP MAsh MGos NHaw NLar NTay
'Fairy' (Fo/f)	ECou
Fairy BluePBR	see *C.* Crystal Fountain
× ***fargesioides***	see *C.* 'Paul Farges'
fasciculiflora	CMHG
- KWJ 12160	WCru
- L 657	WCru WPGP
'Fascination'PBR (I)	CWGN IPot NHaw NTay SMDP
fauriei	WSHC
Filigree = 'Evipo029'PBR	CSPN LBuc LRHS NTay SWCr
'Fireworks' (EL)	CSPN CWGN EBee ELon EPfP ETho IBoy LRHS LSRN MAsh MBri MGos MRav NEgg NLar NPri NTay SLim SPer SPoG SWCr WFar WGor
'Flamingo' (EL)	CWCL CWSG
flammula	CMac CSPN CWib EBee ELan EPfP LRHS LSRN MAsh MBlu MRav NRHS NTay SDix SPer SPoG SWCr SWvt WFar WSHC WSpi XLum
- 'Rubra Marginata'	see *C.* × *triternata* 'Rubromarginata'
Fleuri = 'Evipo042' (EL)	CSPN EPfP ETho LBuc LRHS NPri NTay SCoo SLon SPoG SWCr
florida	CWGN
- 'Bicolor'	see *C. florida* var. *florida* 'Sieboldiana'
- var. ***flore-pleno*** (d)	CCCN CSPN CWCL EBee ELan EPfP ETho LRHS LSRN MAsh NEgg NTay SPoG SWCr WFar
§ - var. ***florida*** 'Sieboldiana' (d)	CBcs CSPN CWCL CWSG EBee ELan EPfP ETho LRHS LSRN MAsh MBri MGos NTay SLim SPer SPoG SRkn SWCr WFar WPGP
- var. ***normalis*** Pistachio = 'Evirida'PBR (LL)	CCCN CLng CSPN CWCL CWGN EBee EPfP ETho LRHS LSRN LSqu MAsh NLar NTay SLim SLon SPoG SWCr WFar
- - 'Thorncroft' (LL)	ETho
'Floris V' (I)	IPot NHaw NLar
'Flutter' (M)	LRHS
foetida × 'Lunar Lass' (Fo)	ECho ECou
foetida × ***petriei***	ECho ECou
'Fond Memories' (EL)	EBee EPfP ETho LSRN NLar NTay SLon
Forever Friends = 'Zofofri'	ETho
I 'Forget-me-not'	LSRN NLar
forrestii	see *C. napaulensis*
§ ***forsteri***	CBcs CSPN WSHC
'Foxtrot' (Vt)	CRHN NHaw
'Foxy' (A) 🏆H4	CLng EBee LRHS MBri NHaw NLar NTay SLon
'Fragrant Joy' (Fo/m)	ECou
'Fragrant Oberon' (Fo)	ECou NTay SMDP WHlf WSpi
'Fragrant Spring' (M)	CSBt CSPN CWGN EBee ETho IBoy LRHS MGos NHaw NLar SEND SLim SMDP WFar WSpi
'Frances Rivis' (A) 🏆H4	CMac CSPN CSam CWCL EBee ELan EPfP ETho LRHS LSRN MAsh MBlu MBri MGos MMuc MRav MSwo NLar NTay NWea SAga SDix SEND SGol SPer SPoG SRms SWCr WSpi
'Francesca' (A)	LSRN
'Frankie' (A) 🏆H4	CLng CSPN ELan EPfP ETho LRHS LSRN MAsh MBri NTay SCoo SWCr
Franziska Maria = 'Evipo008' (EL)	CLng EPfP LBuc LRHS LSqu MAsh NTay SCoo SLon SWCr
'Frau Mikiko' (EL)	ETho MGos
'Frau Susanne' (EL)	ETho
'Freda' (M) 🏆H4	CRHN CTri CWGN CWSG EBee ELan EPfP ETho LRHS LSRN MBlu MBri MGos MRav NHol NTay SDix SLim SPer SWCr
fruticosa **new**	SBrt
'Fryderyk Chopin' (EL)	CSPN EBee NHaw NLar
'Fujimusume' (EL) 🏆H4	CSPN CWGN EBee ETho IPot LRHS MAsh NHaw NTay SPoG SWCr WFar
fujisanensis B&SWJ 11370	WCru
'Fukuzono'	ETho LRHS LSRN NHaw NRHS NTay SWCr
fusca misapplied	see *C. japonica*
fusca Turcz.	GBin MAsh SBrt WIvy
- dwarf	CWGN NHaw
§ - var. ***fusca***	ETho
- var. ***kamtschatica***	see *C. fusca* Turcz. var. *fusca*
'Fuyu-no-tabi' (EL)	ETho
'Gabrielle' (EL)	EBee LSRN NHaw
GalorePBR	see *C.* Vesuvius
Gazelle = 'Evipo014'PBR	CLng LRHS NTay SKHP
'Gemini' (EL)	MGos
'Generał Sikorski' (EL)	CBcs CMac CSPN CWSG EBee ELan EPfP ETho LRHS LSRN MAsh MBri MGos NTay SCoo SLim SPer SWCr
gentianoides	LSRN SBrt WAbe WCot
'Geoffrey Tolver' (LL)	ETho
'Georg' (A/d)	NHaw
Giant Star = 'Gistar'PBR (M)	CLng IBoy LAst LRHS MGos NEgg NLar NPer SLim SPoG WMoo
'Gillian Blades' (EL) 🏆H4	CLng CSPN EBee ELan EPfP ETho LRHS LSRN MAsh NHaw SCoo SPer SPoG SWCr
§ 'Gipsy Queen' (LL) 🏆H4	CBcs CMac CSPN CWCL CWSG EBee ELan EPfP ETho IBoy LRHS LSRN LTen MAsh NTay SDix SGol SLim SPer SPoG SWCr WFar
'Gladys Picard' (EL)	EBee NHaw WFar
glauca Turcz.	see *C. intricata*
glaucophylla	WCru
'Gojōgawa' (EL)	ETho
'Golden Harvest' (Ta)	NLar WFar
Golden Tiara = 'Kugotia'PBR (Ta) 🏆H4	CSPN CWGN EBee ETho GBin LSRN MAsh MGos NLar NTay SRms

	Name	Suppliers
	'Gothenburg' (M)	EBee NHaw WFar
	'Grace' (Ta)	CRHN NHaw NLar NTay
	grandiflora new	SLim SRms
I	'Grandiflora' (F)	LRHS WFar
	'Grandiflora Sanguinea' Johnson	see *C.* 'Södertälje'
	'Grandiflora Sanguinea' (Vt)	NTay
	grata misapplied	see *C.* × *jouiniana*
	grata Wall. B&SWJ 6774	WCru
	'Gravetye Beauty' (T)	CMac CRHN CSPN EBee ELan EPfP ETho LAst LRHS LSRN MAsh MBri MGos NHol NTay SDix SLon SPer SRkn SRms SWCr WCot WSpi
§	'Grażyna'	ETho NTay
	'Green Velvet' (Fo/m)	ECou
	grewiiflora B&SWJ 2956	WCru
	'Guernsey Cream' (EL)	CCon CSPN CWCL CWSG EBee EPfP ETho LRHS LSRN MAsh MBri MGos NLar NTay SCoo SDix SLim SWCr WFar
	Guiding Promise = 'Evipo053'	LRHS NTay
	'Guiding Star' (EL)	NHaw
	'H.F. Young' (EL)	CSPN CWSG EBee ELan EPfP ETho LRHS LSRN MAsh MBri MGos NLar NTay SCoo SDix SPer SWCr
	haenkeana	NHaw
	'Hagley Hybrid' (LL)	CDoC CDul CMac CSPN CWCL EBee ELan EPfP ETho LRHS LSRN LTen MAsh MBri MGos MRav NEgg NLar NTay SBfd SDix SEND SGol SLim SPer SPet SPoG SRms SWCr WFar
	'Hakuōkan' (EL)	CSPN EBee EPfP ETho IPot LRHS LSRN MAsh NLar SCoo
	'Hakuree' ambig.	LRHS
	'Hakuree' (I)	ETho SMDP
	'Hanaguruma' (EL)	CSPN EBee ETho LRHS LSRN NHaw WFar
	'Hanajima' (I)	ETho SMDP WAbe
	'Hania' (EL)	ETho
	'Happy Anniversary' (EL)	EBee LBuc LSRN NLar NTay
§	Happy Birthday = 'Zohapbi' (LL) new	NTay
	Harlow Carr = 'Evipo004' PBR	CLng CMac EBee EPfP LRHS MBri NTay SCoo SDix SLim SRms SWCr
	'Haru Ichiban' (EL)	ETho
	Havering Hybrids (Fo)	ECou
	'Helen Cropper' (EL)	ETho MAsh
	'Helios'	see *C.* 'Daihelios'
	'Helsingborg' (A) ♀H4	CLng CSPN EBee ELan EPfP ETho LRHS MAsh MBri NPri NTay SCoo SPoG SRms SWCr
	hendersonii Koch	see *C.* × *diversifolia* 'Hendersonii'
	hendersonii Stand.	see *C.* × *diversifolia*
I	'Hendersonii' (I)	GBuc LSRN MWat SRkn
I	'Hendersonii Rubra' (Ar)	CSPN NLar
	'Hendryetta' PBR (I)	EBee EPfP SMDP SRkn
	henryi	EShb LSRN MAsh NTay
	- B&SWJ 3402	WCru
	- var. ***morii*** B&SWJ 1668	WCru
	'Henryi' (EL) ♀H4	CMac CSPN CTri CWCL CWSG EBee ELan EPfP ETho LRHS LSRN MBri MGos MRav MSwo NEgg SDix SPer SPet SPoG SWCr WFar
	heracleifolia	CCon CMac CPou ECtt LRHS MAsh NLar NRHS SBfd WWEG XLum

	Name	Suppliers
	- Alan Bloom PBR	see *C. tubulosa* Alan Bloom
	- 'Blue Dwarf'	ETho MGos SMDP WAbe
	- 'Cassandra'	CSpe CWGN EAEE ECtt ELon EPfP EShb ETho GCal LHop LRHS LSRN MGos NBro NCGa NLar NOrc SAga SChF SMDP WCot WGwG
	- 'China Purple'	CPLG LRHS LSou MSCN NLar SMDP WHoo
	- var. ***davidiana***	see *C. tubulosa*
	- 'Pink Dwarf' (H)	CWGN ETho NLar NTay SMDP WAbe
	- 'Roundway Blue Bird' (H)	LHop NHaw SMDP
	'Herbert Johnson' (EL)	MAsh
	hexapetala Forster	see *C. forsteri*
	hexasepala	see *C. forsteri*
	'Hikarugenji' (EL)	NHaw
	hirsutissima	WAbe
	'Honora' (LL)	CSPN CWGN LRHS MAsh NTay SCoo
	'Horn of Plenty' (EL)	LRHS NHaw
	'Huldine' (LL) ♀H4	CBcs CRHN CSPN EBee ELan EPfP ETho LRHS LSRN MAsh MRav NTay SDix SLon SPet SWCr
	'Huvi' (LL)	CWGN ETho NHaw
	'Hybrida Sieboldii' (EL)	SCoo
	Hyde Hall = 'Evipo009' PBR (EL)	CLng CMac CSPN CWGN EBee ELan EPfP IBal LRHS LSqu MAsh NTay SCoo SLim SLon SPer SWCr
	'Hythe Egret' (Fo)	ECho LLHF
	I Am a Little Beauty = 'Zolibe' (Vt)	CRHN NHaw NTay
	I Am Lady Q = 'Zoiamladyq' PBR (Vt)	CRHN CWGN NTay
	I Am Red Robin = 'Zorero' PBR (A)	CSPN IPot NTay WIce
	I am Stanislaus = 'Stanislaus'	SMDP
	ianthina	SMDP
	- var. ***kuripoensis*** B&SWJ 700	WCru
	'Ibi' (EL)	CWGN
	Ice Blue = 'Evipo003' PBR (Prairie Series) (EL)	CLng EPfP ETho LBuc LRHS LSqu NTay SCoo SLim SLon SPer SPoG SWCr
	'Ice Crystal'	NLar
	'Ice Maiden' (EL)	NTay
	'Ice Queen' (EL)	MAsh
	'Imperial' (EL)	NHaw
	'Ingrid Biedenkopf' (Vt) new	NHaw
	Inspiration = 'Zoin' PBR (I)	CSPN EBee ELan EPfP ETho MGos NLar SCoo
	integrifolia	CElw CPLG CPou CSpe EBee EHrv EPfP IFoB LHop MAsh MBel MBri MGos MHer MWat NLar NPer NTay SGar SPer SRms WCot WHoo WPer WWEG
	- RCB UA 10	WCot
I	- 'Alba'	CBcs CSPN EBee ECtt ELon EWTr LRHS LSRN MBNS MCot MDKP NBir NHaw NSti NTay SCoo WWlt
	- blue-flowered	ITim
	- 'Budapest' (I)	NHaw
	- 'Hendersonii' Koch	see *C.* × *diversifolia* 'Hendersonii'
	- 'Olgae'	see *C.* × *diversifolia* 'Olgae'
	- 'Ozawa's Blue' (I)	CWGN EAEE ETho LRHS MBNS MCot

	– white-flowered	see *C. integrifolia* 'Alba'
§	***intricata***	CBcs CPLG MGos
	'Iola Fair' (EL)	NHaw NTay
I	'Ishobel' (EL)	NTay
	ispahanica	SGar
	'Ivan Olsson' (EL)	ETho MGos NTay
	'Jackmanii' (LL) ♀H4	CBcs CMac CTri EBee EPfP ETho IBoy LRHS LSRN MAsh MGos NWea SBfd SCoo SEND SLim SPer SPet SPoG SWCr WFar
	'Jackmanii Alba' (EL)	ELan ELon EPfP ETho LRHS LSRN MAsh SCoo SLim SPet SPoG WSpi
	Jackmanii Purpurea = 'Zojapur'PBR	ETho
	'Jackmanii Rubra' (EL)	ETho
	'Jackmanii Superba' misapplied	see *C.* 'Gipsy Queen'
	'Jackmanii Superba' ambig. (LL)	CMac CSPN CWCL CWSG ELan EPfP ETho LAst LRHS MAsh MBri MGos MRav MSwo NEgg NPer NPri NTay SDix SLim SPer SPoG SWCr WFar WSpi
	'Jacqueline du Pré' (A) ♀H4	CBcs CMac CSPN CWCL EBee ELan EPfP ETho LRHS MGos NHaw NLar NTay SMDP
	'Jacqui' (M/d)	ETho MGos NHaw NLar
	'James Mason' (EL)	CSPN EBee ETho LSRN NHaw
	'Jan Fopma'PBR (I)	CWGN ETho NTay SMDP
	'Jan Lindmark' (A/d)	CLng EBee ETho LRHS MAsh MGos NLar NTay SCoo WFar
§	'Jan Paweł II' (EL)	EBee ELan ETho LRHS MAsh NTay SBfd SCoo SPer
§	***japonica***	NHaw SMDP
	– B&SWJ 11204	WCru
§	– var. ***obvallata*** B&SWJ 8900	WCru
	'Jenny' (M/d)	ETho LSRN MGos NHaw NLar NTay SMDP SPoG SWCr
	'Jenny Caddick' (Vt)	ETho NHaw SMDP
	'Jerzy Popiełuszko' (EL)	ETho
I	'Jessica' **new**	NTay
	Jewel of Merk	see *C.* Happy Birthday
	'Jim Hollis' (EL)	MAsh
	'Joan Baker' (Vt)	CRHN
	'Joan Picton' (EL)	MAsh
	John Howells = 'Zojohnhowells'PBR (Vt)	EBee ETho LSRN NTay SLon
	'John Huxtable' (LL) ♀H4	CLng EPfP ETho LRHS MAsh NHaw NTay SWCr WGor
	John Paul II	see *C.* 'Jan Paweł II'
	'John Treasure' (Vt)	CRHN LRHS NHaw NLar SMDP
	'John Warren' (EL)	CWSG EBee LRHS MAsh NHaw NTay SCoo SLim SWCr WFar
	Jolly Good = 'Zojogo'PBR (LL)	ETho NTay
	Josephine = 'Evijohill'PBR (EL) ♀H4	CLng CSPN CWCL EBee EPfP ETho LRHS LSRN LSqu MAsh MBri MWat NLar NPri NRHS NTay SCoo SLim SPer SPoG SWCr WFar
§	× ***jouiniana***	MAsh MRav SEND SWCr WSHC
	– 'Chance' (H)	NHaw NTay
	'Julka' (EL)	EBee ETho NHaw NTay
	'June Pyne' (EL)	EBee ETho
	'Justa' (Vt)	NHaw
	'Juuli' (I)	LRHS LSRN
	'Kaaru' (LL)	CRHN CSPN
	'Kacper' (EL)	ETho MGos NHaw
	'Kaen' (EL)	ETho NTay
	'Kaiu' (V)	CSPN CWGN EBee LRHS NHaw SLim SMDP SWCr
§	'Kakio' (EL)	CLng ETho LRHS LSRN MGos NTay SDix SLim SPer SPoG SWCr WFar
	'Kalina' (EL)	ETho NHaw
I	'Kamilla' (EL)	CWGN NTay
§	'Kardynał Wyszyński' (EL)	ETho MAsh MGos SMDP
§	'Kasmu' (Vt)	NHaw
	'Kathleen Dunford' (EL)	LSRN MAsh NHaw NTay SCoo
	'Kathleen Wheeler' (EL)	MAsh
	'Kathryn Chapman' (Vt)	CRHN NHaw
	'Ken Donson' (EL) ♀H4	EBee MGos NTay SCoo
	'Kermesina' (Vt) ♀H4	CCon CRHN CWCL EBee ELan EPfP ETho IBoy LRHS MAsh MBri MGos MHer SBfd SCoo SDix SLim SPoG SRms SWCr
	'Kiev' (Vt)	NHaw
	'Killifreth' (Vt)	CRHN NHaw
	'King Edward VII' (EL)	EBee NTay WGor
	Kingfisher = 'Evipo037'PBR (EL)	CSPN ELan EPfP ETho LBuc LRHS LSqu NPri NRHS NTay SCoo SLon SPer SPoG SWCr
	'Kinju Atarashi' (LL)	ETho WHlf
	'Kiri Te Kanawa' (EL)	CSPN EBee ELon ETho LRHS LSRN MAsh MGos NHaw NLar NTay SMDP
	'Kommerei' (LL)	ETho NHaw
§	'Königskind' (EL)	CSPN ETho MGos NLar
	koreana	MAsh WCru
	'Küllus' (LL)	CWGN NTay
	ladakhiana	CElw GQui NHaw SMDP WPGP WPtf
	'Lady Betty Balfour' (LL)	CLng CMac CSPN CWSG ETho LRHS LTen MAsh NTay SCoo SDix SPet SPoG WFar
	'Lady Bird Johnson' (T)	EBee ELon EPfP IPot LRHS LSRN NTay SCoo SLim
	'Lady Caroline Nevill' (EL)	MAsh
	'Lady Londesborough' (EL)	EBee EPfP MAsh NHaw NTay SCoo SDix SEND
	'Lady Northcliffe' (EL)	CLng CSPN CTri CWSG EPfP ETho LRHS MAsh NTay SDix SPet WSpi
	'Lambton Park' (Ta) ♀H4	CCon CRHN ETho LRHS LSRN NHaw NLar NTay SMDP
	lasiandra	NHaw
	'Last Dance' (Ta)	CRHN
	Lasting Love	see *C.* 'Grażyna'
	'Lasurstern' (EL) ♀H4	CBcs CMac CPLG CSPN CTri EBee ELan EPfP ETho LRHS LSRN MAsh MBri NTay SDix SPoG SWCr WFar
	'Laura' (LL)	NHaw
	'Laura Denny' (EL)	ETho MAsh
	'Lavender Lace' (EL)	MAsh
	'Lavender Twirl' **new**	CRHN
	'Lawsoniana' (EL)	CMac EBee MAsh WSpi
	'Lech Wałęsa' (EL)	ETho
	'Lemon Chiffon' (EL)	CLng CSPN EBee ETho LRHS NHaw NTay SPoG SWCr
	Liberation = 'Evifive'PBR (EL)	CLng EBee LRHS MAsh NLar SCoo SLim SLon SPoG SWCr
§	***ligusticifolia***	NHaw
	'Lilacina Floribunda' (EL)	NHaw
	'Lilactime' (EL)	NHaw
	'Lincoln Star' (EL)	CLng CMac EBee ELon LRHS MAsh MGos SDix SLim SPer SPet SPoG
	'Little Bas' (Vt)	CRHN EBee MBri NHaw NLar NTay SLon

	Name	Suppliers
	'Little Butterfly' (Vt)	CRHN MGos NHaw
	'Little Mermaid' (EL)	ETho
	'Little Nell' (Vt)	CCCN CRHN CSPN EBee ELan EPfP ETho LSRN MAsh NTay SCoo SDix SLon SPer SPet WFar WSpi
	'Lord Herschell'	CSPN CWGN ETho LRHS SMDP
	'Lord Nevill' (EL)	CWSG EPfP LRHS MAsh SPer WFar
	'Louise Pummell' (Fo)	ECou
	'Louise Rowe' (EL)	CLng EBee ELan ETho LRHS LSRN MGos NHaw NTay SDix SWCr
	loureiroana HWJ 663	WCru
	'Love Jewelry' (EL)	ETho NHaw NTay
	'Loving Memory'	ETho
I	'Lucey' (LL)	NTay
	'Lunar Lass' (Fo/f)	ECho ETho ITim LRHS SBfd WAbe WIce
I	'Lunar Lass Variegata' (Fo/v)	ECho LLHF
	'Luxuriant Blue' (Vt)	CRHN NHaw NTay
	'M. Koster' (Vt)	CDoC CRHN EBee EPfP ETho MAsh NHaw SLon SRms
	macropetala (d)	CBcs CDoy CSBt EBee ELan EPfP ETho LAst LRHS MAsh MGos MRav MWhi NTay SDix SPer SWCr WFar
	- 'Blue Lagoon'	see *C. macropetala* 'Lagoon' Jackman 1959
	- 'Lagoon' Jackman 1956	see *C. macropetala* 'Maidwell Hall' Jackman
	- 'Lagoon' ambig.	LSRN SLim SWCr
§	- 'Lagoon' Jackman 1959 (A/d) ♀H4	CSPN EBee ETho LRHS LSRN MAsh MSwo NTay SCoo SPoG
§	- 'Maidwell Hall' Jackman (A/d)	CSPN CTri CWSG EBee EPfP ETho IPot LSRN MGos NTay WSpi
	- 'Maidwell Hall' O.E.P. Wyatt (A)	MRav SCoo SPer
	- 'Wesselton' (A/d) ♀H4	CSPN CTri EPfP ETho LRHS MAsh MBri NHaw NTay SWCr WFar
	- 'White Moth'	see *C.* 'White Moth'
	'Madame Baron-Veillard' (LL)	CLng LRHS NEgg SCoo WFar
	'Madame Edouard André' (LL)	CLng CSPN EPfP LRHS MAsh NTay SCoo SPet SPoG SWCr WFar
	'Madame Grangé' (LL) ♀H4	CSPN EPfP LRHS MAsh NHaw NTay SCoo SPoG
	'Madame Julia Correvon' (Vt) ♀H4	Widely available
	'Madame le Coultre'	see *C.* 'Mevrouw Le Coultre'
	'Majojo' (Fo)	EPot GEdr LLHF
	mandschurica	ETho GCal NHaw NLar XLum
	marata	WThu
	'Margaret Hunt' (LL)	CSPN ELan ETho IBoy LSRN MAsh NHaw NTay SBfd SGol
	'Margaret Jones' (M/d)	NHaw
	'Maria Cornelia'PBR (Vt)	CRHN CWGN ETho NTay
	'Marie Boisselot' (EL) ♀H4	CBcs CMac CSPN CTri CWCL CWSG EBee ELan EPfP ETho IBoy LRHS LSRN MAsh MBri MGos MRav MSwo NPri NTay SDix SEND SPer SPet SPoG SWCr
	'Marjorie' (M/d)	CBcs CDoC CSPN CTri CWSG ELan EPfP ETho GKin IBoy LRHS LSRN MAsh MGos MRav NEgg NHol NTay SGar SLim SPer SPet SPoG SRms SWCr WFar WSHC
	'Markham's Pink' (A/d) ♀H4	CCon CSBt CSPN CTri CWCL CWSG EBee ELan EPfP ETho LBMP LRHS LSRN MAsh MBri MRav MSwo NEgg NPri NTay SDix SEND SLim SPer SPet SPoG SWCr WFar WSHC WSpi

	Name	Suppliers
	marmoraria ♀H2-3	ECho LHop LRHS NRHS WFar
	- hybrid (Fo)	NSla
	marmoraria × petriei	ECho
	'Marmori' (LL)	CWGN ETho NHaw SWCr
	'Mary Rose'	see *C. viticella* 'Flore Pleno'
	'Mary Whistler' (A)	MGos
I	'Masquerade' (EL)	MBri
	'Matka Siedliska' (EL)	MAsh
	'Maureen' (LL)	CSPN CWGN CWSG MAsh
	maximowicziana	see *C. terniflora*
	'Mayleen' (M) ♀H4	CPou CSBt CTri CWSG EBee EPfP ETho IBoy LRHS MAsh MBri MGos MRav NEgg NTay SBfd SCoo SLim SPer SPoG SRms SWCr WFar
	'Mazury' (LL)	ETho
	Medley = 'Evipo012'PBR	CLng LRHS
	'Melodie' (Vt) **new**	NHaw
§	'Mevrouw Le Coultre' (EL)	IBoy SGol
	meyeniana var. ***insularis*** B&SWJ 6700	WCru
	microphylla	ECou
	Mienie Belle = 'Zomibel'PBR (T)	CWGN ETho
	'Mikelite' (Vt)	NHaw
	'Miniseelik' (LL)	NTay
	'Minister' (EL)	EBee
	'Minuet' (Vt) ♀H4	CRHN CSPN EBee ELon EPfP ETho LRHS MAsh MSwo NTay SCoo SDix SLon SPer WSpi
	'Miranda' (I) **new**	SMDP
	'Miriam Markham' (EL)	NHaw
	'Miss Bateman' (EL) ♀H4	CDoC CMac CSPN CTri CWCL CWSG EBee ELan EPfP ETho LRHS LSRN MAsh MBri NTay SDix SEND SGol SLim SPer SPet SPoG SWCr WBor
	'Miss Christine' (M)	EBee ETho LSRN NTay SMDP WFar
	'Miss Crawshay' (EL)	NHaw
	'Moniuszko' (EL)	CWGN
N	***montana***	CPLG CSBt MAsh MGos SBfd SDix SEWo SPet WFar
	- B&SWJ 6724 from Taiwan	WCru
	- B&SWJ 6930	WCru
	- BWJ 8189b from China	WCru
	- HWJK 2156 from Nepal	WCru
	- var. ***alba***	see *C. montana* var. *montana*
	- 'Alexander' (M)	CPou CWSG EPfP LRHS SWCr
	- var. ***grandiflora*** (M) ♀H4	CDoy CMac CSam CWSG EBee ELan EPfP ETho GKin LBuc LHop LPot LRHS MAsh MBri MMuc MWat NBir NPri NRHS NTay SBfd SEND SLim SPer SPet SPoG SRms SWCr WFar
§	- var. ***montana***	CBar CDoy MAsh NRHS SPoG
I	- 'Peveril'	CSPN
	- var. ***rubens*** misapplied	see *C. montana* var. *montana*
	- var. ***rubens*** E.H. Wilson	CDoC CSBt CTri ELan EPfP ETho LRHS LTen MBri MSwo NHol NWea SDix SPlb WFar
I	- - 'Odorata' (M)	EBee ETho GKin LRHS MRav SCoo SLim SPoG WGor
	- - 'Pink Perfection' (M)	CDoC CMac CWSG EBee ELan EPfP GKin LRHS LSRN MAsh NEgg NRHS NTay SCoo SLim SPer SPoG SWCr WFar
	- - 'Tetrarose' (M) ♀H4	Widely available
I	- 'Rubens Superba' (M)	CTri CWSG GKin NPri SGol SRms SWCr WFar

	Name	Suppliers
	- var. ***sericea***	see *C. spooneri*
§	- var. ***wilsonii***	CSPN CSam EBee ELan EPfP ETho GKin LRHS LSRN MAsh MGos MNHC MRav MSwo NTay SDix SMDP SPer SPoG SRms SWCr WFar
	'Monte Cassino' (EL)	CSPN CWGN EBee LRHS MAsh NTay SMDP
	'Moonbeam' (Fo)	CJun CMHG EAEE ECou ELan EPot EWTr GEdr ITim LRHS MGos MRav NOrc WGwG
	Moonfleet = 'Evipo046' **new**	CLng NTay SLim
§	'Moonlight' (EL)	MAsh
	'Moonman' (Fo)	ECou LLHF
	Morning Cloud	see *C.* 'Yukikomachi'
	'Morning Heaven' (Vt) **new**	NHaw
	Morning Star = 'Zoklako'^{PBR} (EL)	CWGN ETho
	Morning Yellow = 'Cadmy'^{PBR} (M)	CCCN CLng EBee IBoy LRHS NEgg
	'Mrs Cholmondeley' (EL) $\mathbb{Y}^{H4}$	CMac CSPN CWSG EBee ELan ELon EPfP ETho LRHS LSRN MAsh MBri MGos MSwo NPri NTay SLim SPer SWCr WFar
	'Mrs George Jackman' (EL) $\mathbb{Y}^{H4}$	CLng CSPN ETho LRHS LTen MAsh MGos NLar NTay SCoo
	'Mrs Hope' (EL)	MAsh
	'Mrs James Mason' (EL)	NHaw
	'Mrs N.Thompson' (EL)	CMac CSPN CTri CWCL EBee ELan ETho IBoy LRHS LSRN MAsh MBri NBir NEgg NHol NPer NTay SDix SGol SLim SPer SPoG SWCr WFar
	'Mrs P.B.Truax' (EL)	LRHS MAsh NTay SMDP
	'Mrs Robert Brydon' (H)	ECtt LSRN MBNS NLar NTay SRms WCot WFar WHil
	'Mrs Spencer Castle' (EL)	CSPN ETho MAsh
	'Mrs T. Lundell' (Vt)	CRHN CSPN MGos NHaw
	'Multi Blue' (EL)	CBcs CWSG EBee ELan ELon EPfP ETho IBoy LAst LRHS LSRN MAsh MBri MGos MRav NTay SGol SLim SPer SPoG SRms SWCr WFar
	'My Angel'^{PBR} (Ta)	CSPN ELan NHaw NLar NTay
	'Myōjō' (EL)	EBee
	'Nadezhda' (LL)	SMDP
§	***napaulensis***	CSPN CTri CWCL EBee EPfP ETho MNrw NTay SMDP WCru WFar WSHC
I	'Natacha' (EL)	EBee NHaw NTay SCoo
	'Natascha' (EL)	CLng CSPN LRHS LSRN NPri
	'Negritianka' (LL)	CSPN EBee EPfP LRHS LSRN NHaw
	'Negus' (LL)	MGos
	'Nelly Moser' (EL) $\mathbb{Y}^{H4}$	CBcs CDoC CMac CSPN CTri CWCL EBee ELan EPfP ETho IBoy LRHS LSRN MAsh MBri MRav MSwo NBir NEgg NPri SBfd SDix SEND SLim SPer SPoG SRms SWCr WBor WFar
	'Nelly Moser Neu' (EL)	NTay
	'New Dawn' (M)	CSPN NHaw SBfd
	'New Love'^{PBR} (H)	CSPN ETho LSRN NHaw NLar NTay
	New Zealand hybrids (Fo)	ECou
	'Night Veil' (Vt)	ETho
	'Nikolai Rubtsov' (LL)	SMDP
	'Niobe' (EL) $\mathbb{Y}^{H4}$	CBcs CMac CSPN CWCL CWSG EBee ELan EPfP EShb ETho IBoy LRHS LSRN MAsh MBri MGos MSwo NHol NPri NTay SDix SEND SLim SPer SPet SPoG SRms SWCr WFar
	'North Star' (EL)	LRHS MAsh NTay
	North Star (LL)	see *C.* 'Põhjanael'
	'Nunn's Gift' (Fo)	ETho
	nutans var. ***thyrsoidea***	see *C. rehderiana*, *C. veitchiana*
	obvallata	see *C. japonica* var. *obvallata*
	'Ocean Pearl' (A)	EBee ETho LSRN MBri NLar NTay
	ochotensis	SDys
	Octopus = 'Zooct'^{PBR} (A)	NTay
	'Odoriba' (V)	CRHN CWGN ETho NHaw SMDP
	'Omoshiro' (EL)	CWGN ETho LRHS NHaw NTay
§	Ooh La La = 'Evipo041' (EL)	CSPN EPfP ETho LBuc LRHS MWat NPri NRHS NTay SCoo SLim SPoG SWCr
	'Oonagare Ichigoo' (Vt)	MGos
	Opaline	see *C.* 'Asagasumi'
	orientalis misapplied	see *C. tibetana* subsp. *vernayi*
	orientalis L.	CElw GCra SCoo WFar
	- 'Orange Peel'	see *C. tibetana* subsp. *vernayi* var. *vernayi* 'Orange Peel'
	'Paddington' (EL)	ETho
	'Pagoda' (Vt) $\mathbb{Y}^{H4}$	CBcs CDoC CRHN EBee EPfP MAsh MBri MRav SCoo SLon SMDP SRms
	Palette = 'Evipo034'^{PBR} (Vt)	CLng LRHS MBri NTay SLon
	'Pamela' (F)	ETho NHaw NTay
	'Pamela Jackman'	see *C. alpina* 'Pamela Jackman'
	'Pamiat Serdtsa' (I)	ETho NHaw
	'Pamina' (EL)	ETho
	'Pangbourne Pink' (I) $\mathbb{Y}^{H4}$	CSPN CWCL EBee EPfP ETho LRHS NHaw NTay SCoo SWCr
	paniculata Thunb.	see *C. terniflora*
	paniculata J.G. Gmel. (f)	ETho
	'Paradise Queen' (EL)	EBee LBuc NLar WFar
	'Parasol' (EL)	MBri
	Parisienne = 'Evipo019'^{PBR}	CSPN EPfP ETho LRHS LSqu NPri NTay SCoo SLon SPer SPoG SWCr
	parviflora DC.	see *C. viticella* subsp. *campaniflora*
	parviloba var. ***bartlettii*** B&SWJ 6788	WCru
	'Pastel Blue' (I)	ETho SMDP
	'Pastel Pink' (I)	SMDP
	'Pastel Princess' (EL)	NHaw NTay
	'Pat Coleman' (EL)	ETho
	patens	CElw
	- 'Korean Moon' (EL)	WCru
§	- 'Manshuu Ki' (EL)	CSPN EBee ELon EPfP ETho LRHS MAsh NTay SPer
	- 'Yukiokoshi' (EL)	ETho
	Patricia Ann Fretwell = 'Pafar' (EL)	SMDP
§	'Paul Farges' (Vb) $\mathbb{Y}^{H4}$	CSPN CWGN ETho MAsh NHaw NTay SMDP
	'Pauline' (A/d) $\mathbb{Y}^{H4}$	CBcs CLng CWSG EBee LRHS LSRN MGos NTay SCoo SLim SWCr
	'Pearl Rose' (A/d)	CWSG
	'Pendragon' (Vt)	CRHN NHaw
	'Pennell's Purity' (LL)	NHaw NTay
	Peppermint = 'Evipo005'^{PBR}	CSPN EBee EPfP LBuc LRHS LSqu NTay SCoo SLon SPoG SWCr
	'Percy Picton' (EL)	MAsh
	'Perida' (LL) **new**	ETho
	'Perle d'Azur' (LL)	Widely available
	'Perrin's Pride' (Vt)	CLng LRHS MGos NLar NTay SCoo SWCr
	Petit Faucon = 'Evisix'^{PBR} (I) $\mathbb{Y}^{H4}$	CLng EBee EPfP ETho LAst LRHS LSRN LSqu MAsh MBri NLar SCoo SDix SLim SPer SPoG SWCr
	petriei	ECou WThu

	- 'Princess' (Fo/f)	ECou
	- 'Steepdown' (Fo/f)	ECou
	'Peveril Pearl' (EL)	ETho NTay
	'Peveril Pristine' (Vt)	SMDP
	'Peveril Profusion' (T)	SMDP
	'Phoenix' (EL)	NTay
	Picardy = 'Evipo024'PBR (EL)	CLng CSPN EPfP ETho LBuc LRHS LSqu NPri NTay SCoo SLim SPer SPoG SWCr
I	'Picton's Variety' (M)	CSPN CTri MBri NHaw WFar
	'Piilu' (EL)	CSPN CWGN EBee ELan ETho LBuc LRHS LSRN LSou MAsh MBNS MBri MGos NHaw NLar NTay SCoo SGol SLim SMDP SPoG SWCr
	'Pink Celebration' (EL)	ETho
	Pink Champagne	see *C.* 'Kakio'
	'Pink Fantasy' (LL)	CLng CRHN CSPN CTri EBee ETho LRHS MAsh MGos NLar NTay SCoo SLim SRkn SWCr
	'Pink Flamingo' (A) ♀H4	CLng CSPN CWCL EBee ELan EPfP ETho LRHS MAsh NTay SCoo SLim SPoG SRkn SWCr WBor
	'Pink Ice' (I)	CSPN EBee LRHS NHaw
	'Pirko' (Vt)	NHaw
§	***pitcheri***	GKev NHaw SBrt SMDP
	'Pixie' (Fo/m)	CSPN ECou ELan ELon EPfP ETho LRHS MGos MWat NHaw NLar NTay SCoo SLim SPoG
I	'Pleniflora' (M/d)	NHaw
§	'Plum Beauty' (A)	NHaw
§	'Põhjanael' (LL)	CSPN EBee NLar
	Polar BearPBR	see *C.* Arctic Queen
	'Poldice' (Vt)	CRHN
	'Polish Spirit' (LL) ♀H4	CBar CDoC CMac CRHN CSPN CTri CWCL EBee ELan EPfP ETho LAst LRHS LSRN LTen MAsh MMuc NHol NTay SBfd SEND SGol SLon SPer SPoG SRkn SWCr WFar
	potaninii	CCon GCra NChi WPtf WSHC
	- 'Summer Snow'	see *C.* 'Paul Farges'
	'Praecox' (H) ♀H4	CRHN CWCL EAEE EBee ELan EPfP ETho LHop LRHS MAsh MBri MWhi NBir NSti NTay SDix SPer SPoG SWCr WGwG
	'Primrose Star'PBR	see *C.* 'Star'
	'Prince Charles' (LL) ♀H4	CPou CRHN CSPN CTri EBee ELan EPfP ETho LRHS LSRN MAsh MBri MGos NLar NTay SCoo SDix SEND SGol SLim SPer SPet SPoG SWCr WFar WGwG
	'Prince Philip' (EL)	WFar
§	'Princess Diana' (T) ♀H4	CRHN CSPN CSam CWGN CWSG EBee ELan ETho LBuc LRHS LSRN MAsh MBel MBlu MGos MSwo NHol NTay SCoo SEND SGol SLim SPer SPoG SRkn SRms SWCr
§	'Princess of Wales' (1875) (EL)	EPfP LSRN NLar SLon WFar
	'Prins Hendrik' (EL)	WGor
	'Prinsesse Alexandra'PBR (EL)	ETho NTay
	'Propertius' (A)	CSPN CWGN ETho LRHS MGos NHaw NTay SMDP
	'Prosperity' (M)	ETho
	'Proteus' (EL)	CLng CSPN EBee ELan EPfP ETho LRHS MAsh MGos MWat NTay SCoo SLim SWCr
	'Pruinina'	see *C.* 'Plum Beauty'
	psilandra CWJ 12377	WCru
	'Purple Haze' (Vt)	CRHN NHaw
	'Purple Princess' (H)	CMac NTay
	'Purple Rain' (A)	CTri
	'Purple Spider' (A/d)	CMac CSPN EBee ETho IPot MAsh MBlu MBri NHaw NHol NLar NTay SCoo
	'Purpurea Plena Elegans' (Vt/d) ♀H4	CBcs CMac CRHN CSam CTri CWCL CWSG EBee ELan ELon EPfP ETho IBoy LAst LRHS LSRN MAsh MBri MRav MSwo NEgg NHol NTay SDix SLim SPer SPoG SWCr WBor WFar
	quadribracteolata	NHaw
	'Ragamuffin' (EL/d)	MGos
	'Rahvarinne' (LL)	ETho
	'Ramona' (LL)	CLng LRHS LSRN NHaw SWCr
	ranunculoides	GKev
	'Rapture' (T) **new**	MBri
	'Rasputin' (LL) **new**	ETho
	Rebecca = 'Evipo016'PBR (EL)	CSPN CWCL EPfP LBuc LRHS LSRN LSqu MBri NTay SCoo SDix SLon SPer SPoG SWCr
	recta	CSPN ECtt MNrw MWhi NLar WHil WTin
I	- 'Peveril' (F)	LRHS
	- 'Purpurea' (F)	CBcs CSpe EBee EHoe ELan EPfP LHop LRHS MAsh MNrw MSCN NBir NSti NTay SChF SDix SEND SPer SWCr WHoo WTin XLum
	- 'Velvet Night' (F)	CSpe EAEE ECtt ESwi ETho GBuc LRHS MAvo MBNS MBel NEgg NLar SMDP WCot WGwG
§	'Red Beetroot Beauty' (A)	CSPN MAsh
	'Red Cooler'	see *C.* 'Crimson King'
	'Red Pearl' (EL)	EBee ETho LRHS LSRN MGos NTay SLim SPoG SWCr
I	'Red Star' (d) **new**	EPfP NTay WCot
	Reflections = 'Evipo035'	EPfP ETho LRHS LSqu MWat NPri NRHS NTay SLon SWCr
§	***rehderiana*** ♀H4	CCon CRHN CSPN CSam EBee ELan EPfP ETho LRHS MAsh MBlu MRav NBir NTay SChF SDix SPer WPGP WSHC
	- BWJ 7700	WCru
	'Remembrance' (LL)	EBee EPfP ETho LSRN
	repens Finet & Gagn.	see *C. montana* var. *wilsonii*
	'Rhapsody' ambig.	CLng EBee EPfP ETho LRHS MAsh NTay SCoo SWCr WFar
	'Rhapsody' B. Fretwell (EL)	CSPN LSRN NHaw
	'Richard Pennell' (EL) ♀H4	EBee LRHS MAsh SDix SLim SWCr
	'Rising Star'	LRHS NHaw
	'Robud'PBR (M/d)	CLng NPer
	'Roelie' (Vt) **new**	NHaw
	'Roko-Kolla' (LL)	EBee ETho
	'Romance' (Vt) **new**	NTay
	'Romantika' (LL)	CSPN EBee ELan ELon ETho IBoy IPot LRHS LSRN MAsh NHaw NTay SCoo SGol
	'Rooguchi' (I)	CLng CWGN EBee ETho LRHS NHaw SMDP SPoG SWCr
	'Rosa Königskind' (EL)	EBee ETho
	'Rosamunde' (LL) **new**	ETho
	'Rose Supreme' (EL)	ETho
I	'Rosea' (I) ♀H4	CPrp CSPN EAEE EPfP ETho LHop LRHS LSRN MCot NTay WGwG

I	'Rosea' (Vt)	NHaw
	Rosemoor = 'Evipo002'[PBR] (EL)	CLng CSPN CWCL CWGN EBee EPfP ETho IBal LBuc LRHS LSqu MAsh MBri NTay SCoo SDix SLim SLon SWCr
	'Rosy O'Grady' (A) ♀H4	CWCL EBee ELan MAsh MBri NLar NTay SRms
	'Rosy Pagoda' (A)	EBee ELan LRHS MBri NBir NHaw NLar SLim
	'Rouge Cardinal' (LL)	CMac CSPN CWSG EBee ELan EPfP ETho IBoy LRHS LSRN MAsh MBri MGos NEgg NTay SDix SEND SGol SLim SPer SPet SPoG SRms SWCr WFar
	'Royal Velours' (Vt) ♀H4	CDoC CRHN CSPN CTri EBee ELan EPfP ETho LRHS LSRN MAsh MBri MGos NHol SCoo SDix SEND SLim SPer SPoG SWCr
	Royal Velvet = 'Evifour'[PBR] (EL)	CLng CSPN CWCL EPfP IBal LRHS LSRN MBri NTay SCoo
	'Royalty' (EL) ♀H4	CLng CSPN ELan EPfP IBal LRHS LSRN MAsh NBir NTay SCoo SPer SPoG SWCr
	'Rubens Superba'	see *C. montana* 'Rubens Superba'
	'Rubra' (Vt)	MBlu
	'Ruby' (A)	CSPN CWSG EBee EPfP ETho LRHS LSRN MAsh NTay SCoo SPer SRms
	'Ruby Glow' (EL)	CLng EPfP LRHS LSRN NTay SCoo SPoG SWCr
	'Ruby Wedding' (T)	LBuc LSRN MBri NTay
	'Rüütel' (EL)	ETho LRHS MAsh MGos NHaw SCoo SMDP
	'Sally Cadge' (EL)	NHaw NTay
	'Samantha Denny' (EL)	CSPN MAsh NHaw
	'Sander' (H)	ETho SMDP
	Saphyra Indigo = 'Cleminov 51'[PBR] (I)	CLng
	Savannah = 'Evipo015'[PBR] (Vt)	CLng LRHS NTay SLim
	'Scartho Gem' (EL)	CLng LRHS SCoo SWCr
	'Sealand Gem' (EL)	MAsh NHaw
	'Serenata' (EL)	NTay
	serratifolia	ETho GLog MDKP MWhi SDix SPlb SWal WFar
	- B&SWJ 8458 from Korea	WCru
	'Sheila Thacker' (EL)	ETho
	Shimmer = 'Evipo028'	EPfP ETho LRHS LSqu MWat NPri NTay SLon SWCr
	'Shin-shigyoku' (EL)	NTay
	'Shirayukihime' (EL)	NLar NTay
§	'Shiva' (A)	MBri
	'Sialia' (A/d)	CSPN
§	***sibirica***	EPfP
	'Signe' (Vt)	see *C.* 'Kasmu'
	'Signe' (EL)	NTay
	'Silver Moon' (EL)	CLng CSPN EPfP ETho LRHS MAsh NLar NTay SCoo
	simensis **new**	LEdu
	'Simplicity' (A)	CSPN MBri
	simsii Small	see *C. pitcheri*
	simsii Sweet	see *C. crispa*
	'Sinee Plamia' (LL)	NHaw
§	'Sinii Dozhd' (I)	CWCL NHaw
	'Sir Eric Savill' (M)	ETho
	'Sir Garnet Wolseley' (EL)	SDix
	'Sir Trevor Lawrence' (T)	CSPN EBee ETho LRHS MAsh NHaw NTay WFar
	'Sizaia Ptitsa' (I)	ETho
	'Snow Bells'[PBR]	LRHS
	'Snow Queen' (EL)	CCon CLng CSPN EBee ELon EPfP ETho LRHS MBri NTay SLim SPet SPoG SRms SWCr
	'Snowbird' (A/d)	CSPN EBee EPfP LRHS MAsh NHaw NTay SPoG
	'Snowdrift'	see *C. armandii* 'Snowdrift'
§	'Södertälje' (Vt)	CRHN EBee EPfP ETho LRHS MAsh SCoo WFar
	'Solidarność' (EL)	ETho
	songarica	EBee
	'Southern Cross' (Fo)	ECou
	'Souvenir de J.L. Delbard' (EL)	NTay
§	'Souvenir du Capitaine Thuilleaux' (EL)	LRHS MAsh NTay
	'Special Occasion' (EL)	CLng CSPN CWGN EBee ETho LRHS LSRN NHaw NLar NPri NTay SCoo SPoG SWCr WFar
§	***spooneri***	CTri EBee MAsh SCoo SLim WSpi
	'Sputnik' (I)	CWGN MAsh NHaw
	stans	CElw CPLG CPou EBee EPfP IFro LRHS NLar SMDP
	- B&SWJ 5073	WCru
	- B&SWJ 6345	WCru
§	'Star'[PBR] (M/d)	CSPN EPfP LRHS MSwo NLar NTay SPer SPoG WFar
	'Star of India' (LL)	CLng EBee EPfP ETho LRHS MAsh MGos NTay SCoo SLim SPoG SWCr WBor WFar
	Star River = 'Zostarri'[PBR]	EBee
I	'Starfish' (EL)	MGos NHaw
	'Starlight' (M)	EBee ELon LRHS NTay SLim
	'Stasik' (LL)	NHaw
	'Stephanie' (A)	CSPN
	Still Waters = 'Zostiwa'[PBR] (EL)	CSPN CWGN ETho NTay
	Sugar Candy = 'Evione'[PBR] (EL)	CLng IBal LRHS MAsh MBri NTay SCoo SLim
	Summer Dream = 'Zosumdre'[PBR]	ETho NTay
	Summer Snow	see *C.* 'Paul Farges'
	'Sundance' (Ta)	CSPN SMDP
	Sunny Sky = 'Zosusk' (Vt) **new**	NTay
	'Sunrise'[PBR] (M/d)	CSPN CWGN EBee ETho LRHS MSwo NHaw NLar NTay WFar
	'Sunset' (EL) ♀H4	CLng EBee ELon LRHS LSRN MAsh MBri NLar NTay SCoo SLim SPoG SWCr WFar
	'Swedish Bells' (I)	ETho
	'Sweet Scentsation' (F)	EPfP NLar
	'Sylvia Denny' (EL)	CWSG EBee ELan ETho NTay SPet
	'Sympatia' (LL)	NHaw
	'Syrena' (LL)	NHaw
	szuyuanensis B&SWJ 6791	WCru
	- CWJ 12455	WCru
	'Tae' (EL)	ETho
	'Tage Lundell' (A)	CLng CSPN EBee EPfP NLar NTay SMDP
	'Tango' (Vt)	CRHN NHaw NTay
§	***tangutica***	Widely available
	'Tapestry' (I)	NHaw SMDP
	'Tartu' (EL)	ETho
	tashiroi purple-flowered B&SWJ 7005	WCru
	- 'Yellow Peril'	WCru
	'Tateshina' (EL)	NTay
	'Teksa' (LL)	NHaw

	Temptation = 'Zotemp'PBR (EL)	CSPN ETho NTay
§	***terniflora***	CBcs EBee EPfP ETho NHaw SKHP
	- B&SWJ 5751	WCru
	'Teshio' (EL)	IPot NHaw
	texensis	WSHC
	- 'The Princess of Wales'	see *C.* 'Princess Diana'
	'The Bride' (EL)	CSPN CWGN EBee ETho LRHS LSRN MGos NHaw NTay
	'The First Lady' (EL)	CSPN ETho MAsh
	'The President' (EL) ♀H4	Widely available
	'The Princess of Wales' (EL)	see *C.* 'Princess of Wales' (1875) (EL)
	'The Princess of Wales' (T)	see *C.* 'Princess Diana' (T)
	'The Vagabond' (EL)	CSPN ELan ELon EPfP ETho LRHS LSRN MAsh NHaw NLar NTay SCoo SLim SPet SPoG SWCr
§	Thumbelina = 'Evipo030'PBR (EL)	LRHS NRHS NTay
	thunbergii misapplied	see *C. terniflora*
	'Tibetan Mix' (Ta)	MAsh SMDP
	tibetana	MAsh NHaw
	- 'Black Tibet' (Ta)	SMDP
§	- subsp. ***vernayi***	CMHG
§	- - var. ***vernayi***	CBcs CDoC ETho MRav SEND SGar
	'Orange Peel'	WFar
	LS&E 13342 (Ta)	
	'Tie Dye' (LL)	ELan EPfP ETho NTay WCot
	Timpany NZ hybrids (Fo)	ITim
	'Tinkerbell'	see *C.* 'Shiva'
	'Toki' (EL)	CWGN
	tongluensis GWJ 9358	WCru
	- HWJK 2368	WCru
	'Treasure Trove' (Ta)	CSPN MAsh SMDP
	'Triinu' (Vt)	NHaw
	× ***triternata***	LSRN
§	- 'Rubromarginata' ♀H4	CCon CDoC CMac CRHN CSPN CSam CWGN EBee ELan ELon EPfP ETho LRHS LSRN MBri MGos MRav NTay SDix SLim SLon SPer SPoG SRkn SRms SWCr
	'Tsuzuki' (EL)	CSPN
§	***tubulosa***	CSPN ETho SMDP
§	- Alan Bloom = 'Alblo'PBR (H)	LRHS NRHS
	- 'Wyevale' (H) ♀H4	CMac CPrp CSPN EAEE ELan ELon EPfP LHop LRHS MAsh MCot MRav NSti NTay SAga SCoo SDix SMDP SPoG WCot WWlt
	'Twilight' (EL)	CLng CSPN EPfP LRHS MAsh NTay SWCr WFar
	Twinkle Bell = 'Wer01' **new**	NTay
	uncinata B&SWJ 11368	WCru
	- CWJ 12373	WCru
§	***urophylla*** 'Winter Beauty'	CDoC EBee ETho LSRN MBri NTay SBrt SMDP SPoG
	urticifolia B&SWJ 8651	WCru
	- B&SWJ 8852	WCru
	'Utopia' (EL) **new**	CSPN NTay
	'Valge Daam' (LL)	CWGN ETho NHaw
	'Vanessa' (LL)	CRHN MAsh NTay
	'Vanilla Cream' (Fo)	ECou
	'Vanso'PBR	see *C.* 'Blue Light'
	× ***vedrariensis*** 'Hidcote' (M)	NHaw SMDP
	- 'Highdown' (M)	EBee
§	***veitchiana***	NHaw
	'Venosa Violacea' (Vt) ♀H4	CMac CRHN CSPN CSam EBee ELan ELon EPfP ETho LRHS LSRN MAsh MRav NHol NTay SCoo SDix SPer SPoG SRms SWCr WFar
	'Vera' (M)	CSPN LRHS LSRN MBel NTay SCoo SLim WFar
	vernayi	see *C. tibetana* subsp. *vernayi*
	'Veronica's Choice' (EL)	CSPN EBee ELan LRHS MGos MRav NHaw NTay SPet
	Versailles = 'Evipo025'PBR (EL)	LRHS NTay SLim
§	Vesuvius = 'Evipo032'PBR (Vt)	CLng EPfP LRHS LSqu NTay SCoo SLim SLon
	'Vetka'PBR (LL)	NHaw
	Victor Hugo = 'Evipo007'PBR (LL)	CLng EBee EPfP IBal LBuc LRHS NLar NTay SCoo SDix SWCr
N	'Victoria' (LL) ♀H4	CRHN CSPN ETho LRHS LSRN MAsh MRav NHaw NTay SCoo SDix SPoG SWCr
	Viennetta = 'Evipo006'PBR	CSPN EPfP ETho LRHS LSqu NRHS NTay SCoo SLon SPer SPoG SRms SWCr
	'Vilhelm ne'	NTay
	'Ville de Lyon' (LL)	CBcs CMac CRHN CSPN CWCL EBee ELan EPfP IBoy LRHS LSRN MAsh MBri MGos NEgg NTay SBfd SDix SEND SGol SLim SPer SPet SPoG SWCr WFar
	'Vince Denny' (Ta)	EBee NHaw SMDP
	Vino = 'Poulvo'PBR (EL)	CLng EBee IBal LRHS NHaw NTay SCoo SLim SWCr
I	'Viola' (LL)	CSPN CWGN EBee ELon ETho LRHS LSRN MAsh MBri MGos NHaw NTay SMDP WFar
	'Violet Charm' (EL)	MAsh
	'Violet Elizabeth' (EL)	MRav NTay
I	'Violet Purple' (A)	NHaw
	viorna	NHaw NTay WCru
	virginiana misapplied	see *C. vitalba*
	virginiana Hook.	see *C. ligusticifolia*
	virginiana L.	CElw
§	***vitalba***	CArn CRWN ECrN ETho NHaw NTay NWea WHer WSFF
	- SDR 6610	GKev
	viticella ♀H4	CRHN CWib ETho GKev MBri NHaw SWal WSHC
§	- subsp. ***campaniflora***	CSPN EShb ETho GCal NHaw
§	- 'Flore Pleno' (Vt/d)	CRHN CSPN EBee ELon EPfP ETho IPot LRHS LSRN NHaw NTay SLon SWCr WCot
	- 'Hågelby Blue' (Vt) **new**	NHaw
	- 'Hågelby Pink' (Vt)	CRHN CWGN NHaw
	- 'Hågelby White' (Vt)	CWGN NHaw SMDP
	- 'Hanna' (Vt)	CRHN LSRN NHaw
	- 'Mary Rose'	see *C. viticella* 'Flore Pleno'
	'Vivienne'	see *C.* 'Beth Currie'
	'Vivienne Lawson' (LL)	MAsh
	'Voluceau' (Vt)	CLng CPou CRHN EBee ELan LRHS LSRN MAsh MRav SRms SWCr
	'Vostok' (LL)	MGos NTay
	'Vyvyan Pennell' (EL)	CBcs CMac CSPN CTri EBee ELan EPfP ETho IBoy LRHS LSRN MAsh MBri MGos MSwo NEgg NLar NTay SGol SLim SPer SPet SPoG SWCr WFar
	'W.E. Gladstone' (EL)	ETho LRHS MAsh SDix SPer
	Wada's Primrose	see *C. patens* 'Manshuu Ki'
	'Walenburg' (Vt)	CRHN CWGN ETho NHaw SLon
	'Walter Pennell' (EL)	CBcs CLng CWSG EBee IBal LRHS MAsh SCoo WGor
	'Warsaw' (Ta)	NLar SWCr

'Warszawska Nike' (EL) ♀H4	CLng CMac CRHN EBee ELan EPfP ETho LRHS MAsh MBri MGos NTay SCoo SGol SLim SPer SPet SPoG
'Warszawska Olga' (EL)	ETho
'Warwickshire Rose' (M)	CLng CRHN CSPN CTri CWGN CWSG ETho LRHS LSRN MAsh MWat NHaw NTay SLim SPoG SWCr WFar WSHC
'Waterperry Star' (Ta)	MWat
'Wedding Day' (EL)	ETho LSRN NLar NTay
'Wee Willie Winkie' (M)	LRHS SCoo
'Westerplatte' (EL)	CLng CRHN CSPN CWGN EBee EPfP ETho LRHS MAsh MGos NHaw NTay SLim SMDP SPoG SWCr WFar
'Whirligig' (A)	CSPN
§ 'White Columbine' (A) ♀H4	ETho LRHS MBri MGos NTay SDix SGol SLim SPet
'White Lady' (A/d)	NHaw NTay
'White Magic'PBR (Vt)	CRHN ETho
§ 'White Moth' (A/d)	CSPN ELan ETho LSRN MAsh MGos MRav NHaw NTay SLim SPer SPoG WSpi
'White Satin' (A)	SWCr
'White Swan' (A/d)	CSPN MAsh MBri NHol NLar NPri SCoo
'White Wings' (A/d)	LSRN SPet
'Will Goodwin' (EL) ♀H4	CBcs CLng CMac CWCL ELan EPfP LRHS MAsh MBri SLim SRms SWCr
'William Kennett' (EL)	CLng CWSG ELan EPfP ETho IBoy LTen MAsh MBri MGos SDix
'Willy' (A)	CBcs CSPN EBee ELan EPfP ETho LRHS MAsh MBri MSwo NLar NTay SDix SEND SLim SPer SPet SPoG SRms SWCr
Wisley = 'Evipo001'PBR (Vt)	CBcs CLng CSPN EPfP LRHS MAsh MBri NLar NTay SLim SLon SWCr
'Xerxes' misapplied	see *C.* 'Elsa Späth'
'Yatsuhashi'	CCon LRHS
'Yellow Queen' Holland	see *C. patens* 'Manshuu Ki'
'Yellow Queen' Lundell/Treasures	see *C.* 'Moonlight'
§ 'Yukikomachi' (EL)	CSPN ETho NHaw NTay
'Yvette Houry' (EL)	NHaw NLar NTay
'Yvonne Hay'	SMDP
'Zephyr' (Vt)	NHaw SMDP

Clematopsis see *Clematis*

Clementsia see *Rhodiola*

Cleome (*Cleomaceae*)

hassleriana 'Helen Campbell' ♀H3	CSpe SPhx
'Odyssee Deep Rose' **new**	NPri
'Odyssee White' **new**	NPri
Senorita Rosalita = 'Inncleosr'PBR	NPri

Clerodendrum (*Lamiaceae*)

bungei	Widely available
- 'Pink Diamond' (v)	CCCN CDoC CWGN EBee ELan EPfP EThi EUJe EWes LBuc LHop LRHS LSRN MGos MPkF NLar NPri SBfd SEND SKHP SLim SPer SPoG SPtl WFar
§ ***chinense***	CCCN CHII
var. ***chinense*** (d) ♀H1	
- 'Pleniflorum'	see *C. chinense* var. *chinense*
fragrans var. ***pleniflorum***	see *C. chinense* var. *chinense*
* ***mutabile*** B&SWJ 6651	WCru
myricoides	CCCN CHII CRHN ELan MOWG
'Ugandense' ♀H1	SMrm WSFF
philippinum	see *C. chinense* var. *chinense*
aff. ***subscaposum*** WWJ 11735	WCru
thomsoniae ♀H1	ELan MBri WSFF
trichotomum	CBcs CCVT CDul CElw CLnd CMCN CPLG CSam CSpe CTho CTri CWib EBee EPfP ERom EUJe IArd IVic LRHS MGos SLPl SLim SLon SPer SSta WBor WHar
- 'Carnival' (v)	CAbP CBcs CCCN CDul CJun CLnd CMac CPLG EBee ELan EPfP EWes LRHS MAsh MBri NLar NRHS SBfd SKHP SLim SMad SPer SPoG WCot WPat
- var. ***fargesii*** ♀H4	Widely available
- 'Purple Blaze'	EPfP
- 'Purple Haze'	CJun MBri NLar
- 'Shiro'	WCru
wallichii	CSpe EShb

Clethra ✿ (*Clethraceae*)

acuminata	EPfP GKin
alnifolia	CBcs CDul CMHG CPLG CTrC EBee MPkF SRms WCFE WCot WFar
- 'Anne Bidwell'	EWTr MBlu NLar
- 'Creel's Calico' (v)	NLar
- 'Fern Valley Pink'	CCCN CMac EBee ELon GKin LLHF LRHS NLar
- 'Hokie Pink'	GKin NLar
- 'Hummingbird'	CCCN CDoC CMac CPLG CWib EBee ELan EPfP GKin IDee LRHS MAsh MBlu MGos MWat NPCo NRHS SLim SPad SPoG SSpi SWvt WFar WSHC
- 'Paniculata' ♀H4	CDoC EPfP LRHS MMuc MNHC SAga WBor
- 'Pink Spire'	CDoC CPLG ECrN EPfP EWTr GKin MMHG MMuc MRav NEgg NLar SCoo WFar
- 'Rosea'	CTri GKin GQui MGos MMHG MPkF SPer WFar
- 'Ruby Spice'	CBcs CCCN CMac CPLG CWib EBee ELan ELon EPfP GBin GGGa GKin IDee LAst LRHS LSRN MAsh MBlu MGos NCGa NEgg NLar NRHS SLim SPer SPoG SWvt WFar WGob
- 'September Beauty'	MBri NLar
- 'Sixteen Candles'	GGGa GKin NLar
arborea	CBcs CHEx CMHG CTrC NLar
barbinervis ♀H4	CBcs CDoC CPLG EBee EPfP GGGa GKin IDee IVic LRHS MBlu NLar SPer SSpi WFar WSHC
- B&SWJ 11562	WCru
delavayi Franch.	CCCN CDoC EBee EPfP EWes GGGa GQui IDee NLar SKHP SSpi
- SBEC 1513	CPLG
- Stone's hardy strain	SKHP
fargesii	CPLG EPfP GKin MGos NLar
monostachya	CPLG GGGa NLar
pringlei	NLar WSHC

tomentosa 'Cottondale'	NLar

Cleyera (*Pentaphylacaceae*)

fortunei	see *C. japonica* 'Fortunei'
- 'Variegata'	see *C. japonica* 'Fortunei'
§ ***japonica*** 'Fortunei' (v)	CCCN CMHG CMac CWib IArd LRHS SHil SSta
- var. ***japonica***	CGHE EBee WPGP
- 'Tricolor' (v)	CBcs MPkF
- var. ***wallichii***	EBee WPGP

Clianthus ✿ (*Papilionaceae*)

maximus	CTrC
§ ***puniceus*** ♀H2	CAbb CDoy CHEx CHll CMHG CPLG CPom CSBt CTsd CWib EBee EGri EPfP IBoy LHop LRHS MOWG SEND SPer SPlb SPoG WCot WPGP WSHC
§ - 'Albus' ♀H2	CBcs CHEx CHGN CHll CPLG CWib EBee EPfP IBoy IDee LRHS MOWG SGar SPer SPoG WCot WPGP
- 'Flamingo'	see *C. puniceus* 'Roseus'
- 'Kaka King'	CBcs EWes MREP SPoG
- 'Red Admiral'	see *C. puniceus*
- 'Red Cardinal'	see *C. puniceus*
§ - 'Roseus'	CBcs CPLG EBee EPfP EUJe IVic LRHS SPer SPoG WCot WPGP
- 'White Heron'	see *C. puniceus* 'Albus'

Clinopodium (*Lamiaceae*)

ascendens	see *Calamintha ascendens*
calamintha	see *Calamintha nepeta*
grandiflorum	see *Calamintha grandiflora*
§ ***vulgare***	CArn CHab CRWN EBee EGHP MHer MNHC NMir SIde WMoo WOut WPtf

Clintonia (*Liliaceae*)

andrewsiana	CLAP ECho EHrv EWes MNrw WCru
borealis	EBee
- SDR 6503	GKev
udensis	WCru
- HWJK 2339 from Nepal	WCru
umbellulata	CLAP GCal LRHS WCru
uniflora	CLAP ECho EHrv EWes MNrw

Clitoria (*Papilionaceae*)

ternatea double-flowered (d)	WCot

Clivia ✿ (*Amaryllidaceae*)

caulescens	WCot
gardenii	WCot
gardenii* × *miniata	WCot
miniata ♀H1	CAbb CBcs CTca CTsd ECho EWoo GHim SMrm SRms WCot
- 'Aurea' ♀H1	CSpe EWoo
- 'Beverley's Delight'	WCot
- broad-leaved **new**	EWoo
- - dark orange-flowered **new**	EWoo
- var. ***citrina*** ♀H1	CTca ECho LAma WCot
- 'Citrina Spider'	CFwr
- Daruma Group	WCot
- green-centred	EWoo WCot
- hybrids	SEND
- 'Light of Buddha' (v)	WCot
- 'Orange Spider'	CFwr
- pastel shades	CFwr EWoo WCot
- 'Vico Yellow'	EWoo
- 'Viscy Yellow'	CTsd
- 'Wide Leaf Monk'	WCot
nobilis ♀H1	WCot
'San Marcus Yellow' × 'Solomone Yellow'	WCot

Clusia (*Clusiaceae*)

rosea	CCCN

Clypeola (*Brassicaceae*)

jonthlaspi	WCot

Clytostoma (*Bignoniaceae*)

§ ***calystegioides***	CCCN CHll CRHN EShb

Cneorum (*Rutaceae*)

tricoccon	SKHP WPat WSHC

Cnicus (*Asteraceae*)

§ ***benedictus***	CArn SIde

Cnidium (*Apiaceae*)

officinale	GPoy

Coaxana (*Apiaceae*)

purpurea B&SWJ 9028	WCru

Cobaea (*Polemoniaceae*)

lutea B&SWJ 9142A	WCru
pringlei	CRHN WPGP WSHC
- CD&R 1323	WCot
scandens ♀H3	CCCN CDTJ CSpe ELan NPri SBfd SGar SPer
- f. ***alba*** ♀H3	CSpe SPer

cobnut see *Corylus avellana*

Cocculus (*Menispermaceae*)

laurifolius	EUJe
§ ***orbiculatus***	CPLG
- B&SWJ 535	WCru
trilobus	see *C. orbiculatus*

Cochlearia (*Brassicaceae*)

armoracia	see *Armoracia rusticana*
officinalis	CArn ELau MHer WHer

Cocos (*Arecaceae*)

plumosa	see *Syagrus romanzoffiana*
weddelliana	see *Lytocaryum weddellianum*

Codonanthe (*Gesneriaceae*)

gracilis	WDib
'Paula'	WDib

× *Codonatanthus* (*Gesneriaceae*)

'Golden Tambourine'	WDib
'Sunset'	WDib
'Tambourine'	WDib

Codonopsis (*Campanulaceae*)

HWJK 2105 from Nepal	WCru
affinis HWJCM 70	WCru
- HWJK 2151	WCru
benthamii GWJ 9352	WCru
bhutanica	NEgg
cardiophylla	EWld GCal
celebica HWJ 665	WCru

clematidea CSpe EBee ECha ECho EPfP EPot EWld GCal LRHS MNrw NEgg NLar NSum SPhx SPlb SRms SWvt WWEG
convolvulacea misapplied see *C. grey-wilsonii*
convolvulacea Kurz NSla
- 'Alba' see *C. grey-wilsonii* 'Himal Snow'
- Forrest's form see *C. forrestii* Diels
- var. ***hirsuta*** B&SWJ 7812 WCru
'Dangshen' see *C. pilosula*
dicentrifolia HWJCM 267 WCru
forrestii misapplied see *C. grey-wilsonii*
§ ***forrestii*** Diels ECho NHar WTcb
- BWJ 7776 WCru
- BWJ 7847 WCru
§ ***grey-wilsonii*** ♀H4 CBro CCon ECho EWld GEdr WIvy
- B&SWJ 7532 WCru
§ - 'Himal Snow' ECho EWld GEdr GKev MDKP NCGa
handeliana see *C. tubulosa*
inflata GWJ 9442 WCru
kawakamii B&SWJ 1592 WCru
- RWJ 10007 WCru
§ ***lanceolata*** EWld SBrt
- B&SWJ 562 WCru
meleagris ambig. CCon
mollis ECho NLar NSum
nepalensis Grey-Wilson see *C. grey-wilsonii*
obtusa EWld
ovata NBro SPhx SRms
§ ***pilosula*** EWld GPoy SPhx
- BWJ 7910 WCru
§ ***rotundifolia*** var. ***angustifolia*** EWld MDKP WCru
- var. ***grandiflora*** EWld
silvestris see *C. pilosula*
subsimplex BWJ 7502 WCru
tangshen misapplied see *C. rotundifolia* var. *angustifolia*
tangshen Oliv. CArn
§ ***tubulosa*** LRHS
ussuriensis see *C. lanceolata*
vinciflora CPBP CPne ECho GEdr GKev WIvy
viridiflora WCru
viridis HWJK 2435 WCru

Coffea (Rubiaceae)

arabica CArn CCCN

coffee see *Coffea*

Coincya (Brassicaceae)

wrightii PJL 20098 CHid

Colchicum ✿ (Colchicaceae)

agrippinum ♀H4 CAvo CBro CTca ECha ECho EPot GBin GKev LWst MRav NBir NMen NRya WHoo WTin
'Antares' ECha NBir
asteranthum LWst
atropurpureum ECho LAma
- Drake's form ECho
'Attlee' LAma
'Autumn Herald' ECho GKev LAma
N 'Autumn Queen' CTca ECho GKev LAma
§ ***autumnale*** CArn CAvo CBro CHab ECho EPot GKev GPoy LAma NMen NRya SDeJ WShi
- CH 871 LWst
* - 'Albopilosum' NBir
- 'Alboplenum' CTca ECho EPot ERCP GKev LAma LRHS LWst WTin
- 'Album' CAvo CBro CTca ECho EPot ERCP GKev LAma LRHS NBir SPer WHoo WShi WTin
- 'Atropurpureum' ECho
- 'Karin Persson' LWst
- var. ***major*** hort. see *C. byzantinum* Ker Gawl.
- var. ***minor*** hort. see *C. autumnale*
§ - 'Nancy Lindsay' ♀H4 CBro ECho EPot LLHF LRHS SCnR WCot WShi
- 'Pannonicum' see *C. autumnale* 'Nancy Lindsay'
§ - 'Pleniflorum' (d) ECho EPot GAbr GKev LAma
* - ***roseum*** ECho
- 'Roseum Plenum' see *C. autumnale* 'Pleniflorum'
baytopiorum ECho GKev LWst
- from Turkey ECho
§ ***bivonae*** ECho EPot
- HOA 9139 LWst
- 'Apollo' ECho GKev LWst
- 'Petrovac' LWst
- 'Vesta' LWst
Blom's hybrid WTin
§ ***boissieri*** ECho EPot LWst SCnR
bornmuelleri misapplied see *C. speciosum* var. *bornmuelleri* hort.
bornmuelleri Freyn CBro ECho EPot GKev LAma
bowlesianum see *C. bivonae*
brachyphyllum OS 1030 LWst
§ ***byzantinum*** Ker Gawl. ♀H4 CBro EPot GKev LAma NBir SDeJ WTin
- ***album*** see *C. byzantinum* 'Innocence'
§ - 'Innocence' CBro ECho EPot GKev
chalcedonicum subsp. ***punctatum*** LWst
cilicicum ECho EPot LAma
- Bowles's form ECho
- 'Purpureum' CTca ECho GKev LAma LLHF
'Conquest' see *C.* 'Glory of Heemstede'
corsicum ECho GKev LWst NMen WThu
cupanii ECho
- var. ***pulverulentum*** ECho
davisii ECho
'Dick Trotter' ECho EPot
'Disraeli' ECho GKev
falcifolium ECho LWst
§ ***giganteum*** ECho LAma LRHS
§ 'Glory of Heemstede' ECho GKev
graecum ECho
- HOA 9141 LWst
'Harlekijn' ECho ERCP
hungaricum ECho EPot LWst
- f. ***albiflorum*** ECho EPot GKev LWst
- 'Valentine' LWst
- 'Velebit Star' ECho GKev LWst
illyricum see *C. giganteum*
'Janis' LWst
'Jochem Hof' ECho GKev LEdu
'Jolanthe' LWst
kesselringii ECho GKev LWst
kotschyi LWst
laetum misapplied see *C. parnassicum*
'Lilac Bedder' ECho
'Lilac Wonder' ECho EPfP GKev LAma MRav SDeJ SEND SPer WCot
longifolium see *C. neapolitanum*
lusitanum LAma
luteum ECho LWst

macrophyllum	ECho LAma
- HOA 9806	LWst
micranthum	ECho
minutum	ECho LWst
munzurense	LWst
§ ***neapolitanum***	LWst
parlatoris	ECho LWst
§ ***parnassicum***	ECha ECho LWst
- CH 835	LWst
'Pink Goblet' ΨH4	CBro LAma
'Poseidon'	ECho
procurrens	see *C. boissieri*
pusillum VV CR.441	LWst
'Rosy Dawn' ΨH4	CBro CTca ECha ECho GKev NRya
sanguicolle new	LWst
sfikasianum	ECho LWst
sibthorpii	see *C. bivonae*
speciosum ΨH4	CAvo CBro ECho EPot GKev LAma NBir
- 'Album' ΨH4	CAvo CBro ECha ECho EPfP EPot ERCP GKev LAma LRHS MBri NBir SDeJ
- 'Atrorubens'	ECha ECho MBri
I - var. ***bornmuelleri*** hort.	ECho LWst
- var. ***illyricum*** hort.	see *C. giganteum*
- 'Ordu'	ECho
- 'Rubrum'	ECho
szovitsii Fisch. & B. Mey.	ECho
- pink-flowered	LWst
- 'Snow White'	LWst
- 'Tivi'	ECho LWst
- white-flowered	ECho LWst
tenorei ΨH4	ECho EPot GKev LAma LLHF NBir
'The Giant'	CBro CTca ECho EPfP EPot GKev LAma SDeJ WCot
triphyllum	ECho LWst
troodi ambig.	ECho
variegatum	ECho LAma LWst
'Violet Queen'	ECho GAbr GKev LAma
'Waterlily' (d) ΨH4	CAvo CBro CTca ECho ELan EPfP EPot ERCP GBin GKev LAma LRHS NBir SDeJ WCot WHoo
'William Dykes'	ECho
'Zephyr'	ECho LAma

Coleonema (*Rutaceae*)

album	CSpe
'Mellow Yellow'	SPtl
§ ***pulchellum***	CCCN CHEx CSpe
pulchrum misapplied	see *C. pulchellum*
'Sunset Gold'	CSpe CTrC SAga SPlb

Coleus see *Solenostemon*

Colignonia (*Nyctaginaceae*)

ovalifolia B&SWJ 10644	WCru

Colletia (*Rhamnaceae*)

armata	see *C. hystrix*
cruciata	see *C. paradoxa*
§ ***hystrix***	CBcs CMac CTri CTsd ELon IVic NLar SMad WSHC
- RCB RA S-3	WCot
- 'Rosea'	CMac CTrC GCal MBlu SKHP
§ ***paradoxa***	CBcs CCCN CTrC CWib ELan EPfP GCal LAst SKHP SMad SPoG
paradoxa* × *spinosissima	SMad

Colliguaja (*Euphorbiaceae*)

integerrima new	IRar

Collinsonia (*Lamiaceae*)

canadensis	CArn ELan

Collomia (*Polemoniaceae*)

grandiflora	WCot

Colobanthus (*Caryophyllaceae*)

canaliculatus	CPBP

Colocasia (*Araceae*)

affinis var. ***jeningsii***	CCon CDTJ EAmu GHim
antiquorum	see *C. esculenta*
§ ***esculenta*** ΨH1	CBct CCon CDTJ CHEx EAmu EUJe GHim MSKA SPlb XBlo
- 'Black Beauty'	EAmu
- 'Black Magic'	CAbb CBct CDTJ CHEx CHll EAmu EBee ECtt EUJe GHim IBoy IKil LRHS MSKA SBfd SBig SBst SDix SEND SPad WCot XBlo
- 'Black Ruffles'	CDTJ
- 'Blue Hawaii'	LRHS WCot
- burgundy-stemmed	CAbb CDTJ EBee GHim IBoy SBig SBst
- 'Chicago Harlequin'	CDTJ EAmu
- 'Diamond Head'	CWGN EAmu EBee ESwi EUJe IBoy LRHS MBel SPad WCot
- 'Emerald' new	GHim
- 'Fontanesii'	CDTJ CHEx EAmu GHim MPkF SBst WCot
- 'Hawaiian Eye'	LRHS WCot
- 'Hilo Bay'	ESwi IBoy LRHS WCot
- 'Hilo Beauty'	EAmu EBee XBlo
- 'Hilo High Colour' new	GHim
- 'Illustris'	CDTJ GHim WCot
- 'Jack's Giant'	EAmu
- 'Mojito' (v)	EAmu
- 'Nancy's Revenge'	EAmu
- 'Nigrescens'	EAmu
- 'Pineapple Princess' (v)	LRHS WCot
- 'Pink China'	EAmu
- 'Ruffles'	EUJe
- 'Sangria' new	EAmu
- 'Tea Cup'	EAmu
fallax	CCon CHEx EAmu
formosana B&SWJ 6909	WCru
gaoligongensis	CCon
gigantea	CDTJ EAmu
'Himalayan Dragon'	SKHP

Colquhounia (*Lamiaceae*)

coccinea	CArn CHll CMHG CTrC EShb MBlu MRav NLar SBrt SGar SLon WSHC
- Sch 2458	WPGP
§ - var. ***mollis*** B&SWJ 7222	WCru
- var. ***vestita*** misapplied	see *C. coccinea* var. *mollis*
- var. ***vestita*** ambig.	CBcs CTsd EBee EPfP LRHS SEND XLum

Columnea (*Gesneriaceae*)

'Aladdin's Lamp'	WDib
× ***banksii*** ΨH1	EOHP WDib
§ 'Broget Stavanger' (v)	WDib
'Chanticleer' ΨH1	WDib
I 'Firedragon'	WDib

	'Gavin Brown'	WDib
	gloriosa	EBak
	'Inferno'	WDib
	'Katsura'	WDib
	'Merkur'	WDib
I	'Midnight Lantern'	WDib
	'Rising Sun'	WDib
	schiedeana	EOHP WDib
	'Sherbert'	WDib
	'Stavanger' ♀H1	WDib
	'Stavanger Variegated'	see *C.* 'Broget Stavanger'

Colutea (*Papilionaceae*)

	arborescens	CBcs CPLG CWib EBee ELan LRHS MBlu MGos MMuc NWea SEND SPer SPlb SPoG
	× ***media***	CPom MBlu SGar
	- 'Copper Beauty'	CBcs EBee LRHS MGos NLar SPer
	orientalis	CCCN

Colvillea (*Caesalpiniaceae*)

	racemosa new	SPlb

Comarum see *Potentilla*

Combretum (*Combretaceae*)

	fruticosum	CCCN

Commelina (*Commelinaceae*)

	coelestis	see *C. tuberosa* Coelestis Group
	dianthifolia	GCal SRms WPer WPtf
	- 'Electric Blue'	EPfP LRHS SHil SVic
	robusta	CSpe WCot
	tuberosa	ELan NWad XLum
	- B&SWJ 10353	WCru
	- 'Alba'	ELan GCal WPer
	- 'Axminster Lilac'	WPer
	- blue-flowered new	SDeJ
§	- Coelestis Group	CSpe EBee ECha IGor LHop LRHS SDys SRms WKif WPer WSHC
	- - 'Sleeping Beauty'	MSpe

Comptonia (*Myricaceae*)

	peregrina	IVic WCru

Conandron (*Gesneriaceae*)

	ramondoides B&SWJ 8929	WCru
	- 'Akabana'	GEdr

Coniogramme (*Pteridaceae*)

	japonica	WFib

Conium (*Apiaceae*)

	maculatum	CArn

Conoclinium (*Asteraceae*)

§	***coelestinum***	EBee EWes LHop LRHS SBrt XLum

Conopodium (*Apiaceae*)

	majus	CRWN WShi

Conostylis (*Haemodoraceae*)

	candicans	ECou

Consolida (*Ranunculaceae*)

§	***ajacis***	MNHC
	ambigua	see *C. ajacis*

Convallaria ✿ (*Asparagaceae*)

	japonica	see *Ophiopogon jaburan*
	keiskei	EPPr MAvo WWEG
	majalis ♀H4	Widely available
	- 'Albostriata' (v)	CBct CFwr CLAP CRDP CRow EBee ECho EHoe EHrv ELan EPPr EPfP GMaP LRHS LWst MAvo MCot MNrw MRav NBir NPnk NSti WCot WFar WHer WPnP WWFP
	- 'Berlin Giant'	MAvo NBre NRya SDeJ
	- 'Blush'	CAvo
	- 'Bordeaux'	CHid CPLG EBee EPPr EWhm MHer WCot
	- 'Bridal Choice'	EBee GBin NLar WCAu
	- 'Dorien'	CBct CBre EPPr MAvo
	- 'Flore Pleno' (d)	EBee WWEG
	- 'Géant de Fortin'	CAvo CBct CBro CCon CLAP CPLG CRow ECho EPot GCal GEdr MMoz MRav NBir NBre NLar NMyG SBch WCot WFar WWEG
	- 'Gerard Debureaux'	see *C. majalis* 'Green Tapestry'
§	- 'Green Tapestry' (v)	CBct CLAP CRow MAvo
	- 'Haldon Grange' (v)	CDes CLAP EPPr
	- 'Hardwick Hall' (v)	CBct CCse CLAP CPLG CRow ECha ECho EHoe EHrv EPot MAvo NBre NMyG WAul WCot WFar WTin WWEG
	- 'Hofheim' (v)	CLAP CRow MAvo WCot WWEG
	- 'Prolificans'	CBct CCon CCse CLAP CRDP EBee ECho EHrv EPPr EPfP GAbr LSou MAvo MRav NBir NLar NPnk NSti WCot WFar WHil WPnP
	- var. ***rosea***	Widely available
	- 'Variegata' (v)	CAvo EBee EPot LHop LRHS MLHP NMyG SBch SMad WHil WThu WWEG
	- 'Vic Pawlowski's Gold' (v)	CBct CDes CLAP CMac CPLG CRow ELon EPPr LWst MAvo MMoz NSla

Convolvulus (*Convolvulaceae*)

	althaeoides	CFis CMea ECho ELan EPri NBir SEND SPhx WAbb
§	- subsp. ***tenuissimus***	CSpe ECtt EWes WCFE WCot
§	***boissieri***	WAbe
	cantabricus	LRHS MDKP XLum XSen
	chilensis	CCCN
	cneorum ♀H3	Widely available
	- 'Snow Angel'	EBee LRHS LSou SWvt WCot
	elegantissimus	see *C. althaeoides* subsp. *tenuissimus*
	humilis	ECho
	lineatus	ECho EWes NMen
	mauritanicus	see *C. sabatius*
	nitidus	see *C. boissieri*
§	***sabatius*** ♀H3	CCCN CHEx CSam CTri ECho ECtt ELan EPfP LAst LHop LRHS MCot SBfd SEND SGar SLim SPer SPlb SPoG WCFE XLum
	- dark-flowered	CCCN CSpe ECho GCal SMrm
	- 'Moroccan Beauty' PBR	LSou

× *Cooperanthes* see *Zephyranthes*

Cooperia see *Zephyranthes*

Copernicia (*Arecaceae*)

	alba	EAmu

Coprosma (*Rubiaceae*)

acerosa	CTrC
- 'Hawera'	CBcs
- 'Live Wire' (f)	ECou
- 'Red Rocks'	CTrC
atropurpurea (f)	ECou
- (m)	ECou
'Autumn Orange' (f)	ECou
'Autumn Prince' (m)	ECou
baueri misapplied	see *C. repens*
'Beatson's Gold' (f/v)	CBcs CDTJ CHGN CHll CPLG CTrC CTsd EBee ELan EPfP EShb IVic LRHS SEND SLim SWvt WGrn WSHC
'Black Cloud'	CTrC EBee LRHS
'Blue Pearls' (f)	ECou
'Blue Skies'	NHar WThu
brunnea	ECou WThu
- (f) **new**	WThu
- (m) **new**	WThu
- 'Blue Beauty' (f)	ECou
- 'Violet Fleck' (f)	ECou
'Bruno' (m)	CTrC ECou
'Cappuccino'	CBcs LSou
cheesemanii (f)	ECou
- (m)	ECou
- 'Hanmer Red' (f)	ECou
- 'Mack' (m)	ECou
- 'Red Mack' (f)	ECou
'Clearwater Gold'	CTrC
'Coppershine'	CPLG CTrC
crassifolia × ***repens*** (m)	ECou
× ***cunninghamii*** (f)	ECou
× ***cunninghamii*** × ***macrocarpa*** (m)	ECou
'Cutie' (f)	CTrC ECou
'Dark Purple' **new**	LRHS
'Dark Spire'	CTrC
depressa	ECou WThu
- 'Orange Spread' (f)	ECou
'Evening Glow'[PBR] (f/v)	CCCN CDTJ CDoC CSBt EBee ELan EPfP EShb IVic LBMP LBuc LRHS LSRN LSou MAsh MPie MPkF SEND SHil SLim
'Fire Burst'[PBR]	CBcs CCCN CDoC EBee ELan EPfP EShb EUJe LBuc LRHS LSou MAsh MBri MPkF MRav SHil SLim SLon SPtl
grandifolia	ECou
'Green Girl' (f)	ECou
'Green Globe'	CHll
'Hinerua' (f)	ECou
'Indigo Lustre' (f)	ECou
'Jewel' (f)	ECou
'Karo Red'[PBR] (v)	CBcs CDoC CTrC EBee ELan ELon EPfP LBuc MPkF SLim
× ***kirkii*** 'Gold Edge'	ECou
I - 'Kirkii' (f)	CHll ECou
I - 'Kirkii Variegata' (f/v)	CBcs CDoC CTrC CTsd EBee ECou EPfP EShb LRHS SEND SLim
'Kiwi' (m)	ECou
'Kiwi-gold' (m/v)	ECou
'Lemon and Lime'[PBR] (v)	CTrC EBee ELan EPfP EUJe LRHS MAsh MBri MPkF SHil SPoG
'Lemon Drops' (f)	ECou
linariifolia (m)	ECou
lucida **new**	IDee
macrocarpa (f)	ECou
- (m)	CTrC ECou
nitida (f)	ECou
parviflora (m)	ECou
- red-fruited (f)	ECou
- white-fruited (f)	ECou
'Pearl Drops' (f)	ECou
'Pearl's Sister' (f)	ECou
'Pearly Queen' (f)	ECou
petriei	ECou WThu
- 'Don' (m)	ECou
- 'Lyn' (f)	ECou
- 'White Pearls'	WThu
'Pride'	CDoC
propinqua (f)	ECou
- (m)	ECou
- var. ***latiuscula*** (f)	ECou
- - (m)	ECou
'Prostrata' (m)	ECou
pseudocuneata (m)	ECou
quadrifida	ECou
'Rainbow Surprise'[PBR] (v)	CCCN CDoC CPLG CSBt EBee ELan LRHS LSou MBri MPkF MRav SHil SLim WFar
§ ***repens***	CBcs CPLG EShb SPlb
- (f)	ECou
- (m)	ECou
- 'County Park Plum' (v)	CBcs ECou ELon
- 'County Park Purple' (f)	ECou ELon
- 'County Park Red'	ECou ELon
- 'Exotica' (f/v)	ECou
- 'Marble King' (m/v)	ECou
- 'Marble Queen' (m/v) ♀H1-2	CBcs ECou
- 'Orangeade' (f)	ECou
- 'Pacific Lady'	EBee ECou
- Pacific Night = 'Hutpac'[PBR]	CDoC CSBt CTrC ECou ELan EPfP EUJe IVic LBuc LRHS MAsh MBri MGos MPkF SHil SLon SPoG WFar
- Pacific Sunset = 'Jwncopps' (v)	EPfP LBuc LRHS MAsh SLon
- 'Painter's Palette' (m)	EBee ECou EShb
- 'Picturata' (m/v) ♀H1-2	ECou EShb SEND
- 'Pink Splendour' (m/v)	CBcs ECou
- 'Rangatiri' (f)	ECou
- 'Silver Queen' (m/v)	ECou
- 'Variegata' (m/v)	ECou
rigida	ECou
- 'Ann' (f)	ECou
- 'Tan' (m)	ECou
robusta	CBcs ECou
- 'Sally Blunt' (f)	ECou
- 'Steepdown' (f)	ECou
- 'Tim Blunt' (m)	ECou
- 'Variegata' (m/v)	ECou
- 'William' (m)	ECou
- 'Woodside' (f)	ECou
'Roy's Red' (m)	CDoC EBee EShb LRHS LSRN SEND SPoG
rugosa	CPLG
- (f)	ECou
'Snowberry' (f)	ECou
'Taiko'	CTrC
'Translucent Gold' (f)	ECou
'Violet Drops' (f)	ECou
virescens (f)	ECou
'Walter Brockie'	CHGN CHll SEND
'White Lady' (f)	ECou
'Winter Bronze' (f)	ECou

Coptis (*Ranunculaceae*)

japonica	WCru
- var. ***dissecta***	WCru
- var. ***major***	CDes EBee WCru WSHC
omeiensis	WCru
quinquefolia B&SWJ 1677	WCru
ramosa B&SWJ 6000	WCru
- B&SWJ 6030	WCru
trifolia	WCru

Corallospartium see *Carmichaelia*

Cordyline ✿ (*Asparagaceae*)

australis ♀H3	Widely available
- 'Albertii' (v) ♀H3	CCCN CTrC MBri SEND
- 'Atlantic Green' **new**	SHil
- 'Atropurpurea'	CCCN CDoC EUJe MWat SEND WFar
- 'Black Night'	CCCN ESwi LRHS
- 'Black Tower'	CDoC
- Burgundy Spire = 'Jel01'PBR	LBuc LRHS SPoG
- 'Claret'	CBcs CTrC
- 'Coffee Cream'	CCCN ELan EPfP SBfd SPer
- 'Olive Fountain'	CCCN
- 'Peko'PBR	CCCN
- 'Pink Champagne'	CCCN EBee ELon LBuc LRHS LSRN MGos NEgg SBfd SLim SPoG
- Pink Passion = 'Seipin'PBR	CTrC EBee ELon EPfP LBuc LRHS NPri SBfd SEND
- 'Pink Stripe' (v)	CCCN CDoC ELan EPfP ESwi LRHS LSRN MBri SLim SWvt
- 'Purple Heart'	CCCN MSwo
- Purpurea Group	CBcs CDTJ CTrC CWSG EBee ELan ELon EPfP LRHS MGos SEND SPer SPlb WFar
- 'Red Sensation'	CCCN CHEx CTrC SWvt
- 'Sparkler'	CCCN EPfP ESwi LRHS MBri MGos SHil
- 'Sundance' ♀H3	CBcs CDoC CMac CWSG CWib EBee EPfP LRHS MAsh MBri MGos MSwo NPer SBfd SEND SLim SPoG SRms SWvt WFar
- 'Torbay Dazzler' (v) ♀H3	CAbb CBcs CDoC CHEx COlW CSBt CWSG EBee ELan ELon EPfP EUJe IVic LRHS LSRN MAsh MBri MGos MREP NEgg NPla NPri SBfd SEND SHil SLim SPer SPoG SWvt
- 'Torbay Red' ♀H3	CCCN CDoC CMac CWSG EBee ELan ELon EPfP LRHS LSRN MAsh MBri NPri SBfd SPer SWvt WFar
- 'Torbay Sunset'	CCCN CDoC CTrC
- 'Variegata' (v)	MWat
'Autumn'	CCCN
banksii	CPne CTsd GCal
'Candy Cane'	EAmu ESwi
'Cardinal'PBR	CBcs
congesta	SPlb
'Dark Star'	CBcs CCCN CDTJ CDoC CMac COlW SLim
Electric Pink = 'Sprilecpink' **new**	LBuc
'Eurostar'	CTrC
'Eurostripe'PBR **new**	LRHS MBri SHil
Festival Grass = 'Jurred'	LRHS
'Firecracker'	LRHS MBri SHil
fruticosa 'Red Edge' ♀H1	XBlo
'Green Goddess'	SBfd SLim
§ ***indivisa***	CBcs CDTJ CTrC CTsd EAmu EBak ELon IDee LMaj SPlb WPGP
kaspar	CCCN CHEx CTsd
obtecta	CCCN CTsd
- bronze-leaved	CTsd
pumilio	LRHS
'Purple Sensation'	CBcs CCCN CTrC EUJe LRHS MAsh NPri
'Purple Tower' ♀H3	CDoC CHEx MGos SLim
'Red Bush'	XBlo
'Red Fountain'PBR	ESwi
'Red Star'	CAbb CBar CBcs CCCN CDoC COlW CSBt CTrC CWGN CWSG CWib EBee ELan EPfP IVic LRHS LTen MBri MSwo NPer SHil SPoG SWvt WFar
Renegade = 'Tana'PBR	LRHS
'Southern Splendour'	CCCN EAmu ELan ELon EPfP ESwi LBuc LRHS MBri MGos SHil
§ ***stricta***	CHEx
'Sunrise' (v)	CTrC CWGN EAmu EBee EUJe LRHS MBri SHil
terminalis	see *C. fruticosa*

Coreopsis (*Asteraceae*)

'Astolat'	EAEE EBee LSou MRav SPer
auriculata Cutting Gold	see *C.* 'Schnittgold'
- 'Elfin Gold'	EBee EDAr LBMP SBfd
- 'Nana'	EBee MNrw NBre WFar
- 'Superba'	LRHS MRav
- 'Zamphir'	EBee EPfP MNrw WCot
'Autumn Blush'	EBee LHop LSou NLar SBfd
'Baby Gold'	see *C. lanceolata* 'Sonnenkind' (unblotched)
Baby Sun	see *C.* 'Sonnenkind' (red-blotched)
'Calypso' (v)	ECtt EWes LBuc LRHS SMad
'Cosmic Eye' (Big Bang Series) **new**	NCGa
'Cranberry Ice' **new**	CWGN
'Cutting Edge'	CEnt
'Dream'	SRkn
'Full Moon'PBR (Big Bang Series)	EBee
'Gold Nugget'PBR	SBfd
'Golden Pompom'PBR (d)	EBee LRHS LSou
grandiflora	EHrv NEgg
- 'Badengold'	EBee
- 'Bernwode' (v)	CMac EBee LSou NLar SWvt
- 'Domino'	EBee LRHS NBre
- 'Early Sunrise' ♀H4	CSBt EBee ECtt EPfP LBMP LDai LPot LRHS MAsh MBri NBir NGBl NPer SAga SBfd SGar SPet SPhx SPoG SWvt WFar WWEG XLum
- Flying Saucers = 'Walcoreop'PBR	EBee EPfP LBuc LRHS SCoo SPoG
- 'Heliot'	LPot SPhx
- 'Mayfield Giant'	CSBt EBee EShb LHop MNrw NPri SPer SRms SWvt WHrl
- 'Presto' (d)	ELon LBuc SBfd
- 'Rising Sun'	EBee MBri NPri SBfd SPhx WPer
- 'Sunburst'	EBee ELon EPfP LTen NBre WPer XLum
- 'Sunfire'	LRHS MAsh MBri MHer SHil SPhx
- 'Sunray'	CBcs CDoC CSBt CWib EBee ECtt ELon EPfP EShb LRHS LSRN MAvo MBri MGos NGdn NPri NRHS SBfd SHil SPad SPlb SPoG SRms SWvt WMoo XLum

	- 'Tetra Riesen'	NBre
	integrifolia	LRHS
	'Jethro Tull'	EBee SPoG
	'Jive' (Coloropsis Series)	CSpe CWGN
	lanceolata	NBre
	- 'Goldfink'	LRHS MRav SRms
	- 'Goldteppich'	LRHS
	- 'Little Sundial'	EBee LSou
§	- 'Sonnenkind' (unblotched)	GMaP MAsh XLum
	- 'Walter'	EBee ECtt LRHS LSou MAsh NDov NEgg SPoG WCot WWEG XLum
	'Limerock Passion' PBR	EBee EPfP LRHS LSou NPnk SBfd SHar SRkn
	'Limerock Ruby' PBR	CSev EBee ECtt EPfP GMaP LHop LRHS LSou NEgg NPnk SBfd SMrm SPer SRkn SWvt WCot WSpi
	major	CSam EBee
	'Mango Punch' **new**	CSpe
	maximiliani	see *Helianthus maximiliani*
	'Moonlight' **new**	CSev
	palmata	EBee
	'Pink Lady' PBR	LHop
	'Pinwheel'	LSou
	pubescens	LSou
	- 'Sunshine Superman'	EBee LSou
	pulchra	LRHS
	'Redshift'	EBee NDov
	rosea	CPom WFar WPer
	- 'American Dream'	CSBt EBee ELan EPfP GMaP LAst LRHS LSRN MHer NBir NGdn SBfd SPer SPlb SRms SWvt WFar WRHF XLum
	- 'Heaven's Gate' PBR	EBee ELan MAvo
	- 'Nana'	XLum
	- 'Sweet Dreams' PBR	CSev EBee LHop LRHS LSRN SPer SRkn SUsu
	'Rum Punch' PBR	CSpe LHop SUsu WHil
	'Sangria' PBR	LHop SPoG
§	'Schnittgold'	CWan EBee LSou NBre WPer
	'Snowberry'	EBee ECtt LRHS NLar SBfd
I	'Sonnenkind' (red-blotched)	EBee ECtt LRHS NBre WPer
	'Sterntaler'	CCon CMea EBee ECtt EPPr EPau EPfP EShb LHop LRHS MAsh MBri NPri SBfd SMrm SPad SPet SPoG SWvt WPer WWEG XLum
	Sun Child	see *C.* 'Sonnenkind' (red-blotched)
	'Tequila Sunrise' (v)	ELan NLar
	tinctoria	CArn
	tripteris	EPfP IPot LPla LRHS MMuc NBre SEND SMad SPhx WMoo
	- 'Mostenveld'	EBee
	verticillata	CMac EBee ECha GCal LRHS MBrN MGos MHer MWat NPer SBfd SDix SRms WFar WHal
	- Crème Brûlée = 'Crembru' PBR	EBee ECtt EWes LRHS NEgg NPnk SCoo SMrm SPer SRkn SUsu WCot WSpi
I	- 'Golden Gain'	EBee ECtt LHop LRHS MArl NGdn SBfd WFar WMnd WWEG
	- 'Golden Shower'	see *C. verticillata* 'Grandiflora'
§	- 'Grandiflora' 𝕐H4	CBcs CPrp CTca EAEE EBee ELan EPfP GMaP LRHS MRav NCGa NGdn NHol NRHS SPer WFar WMnd XLum
	- 'Limerock Dream' PBR	EBee LRHS LSou SBfd SHar
	- 'Moonbeam' 𝕐H4	Widely available
	- 'Old Timer' 𝕐H4	SDix SUsu
	- 'Ruby Red'	CAbP EBee LRHS MAvo MBri NRHS SUsu
	- 'Sunbeam' **new**	EBee
	- 'Zagreb' 𝕐H4	Widely available

coriander see *Coriandrum sativum*

Coriandrum (*Apiaceae*)

*	***citratus***	ELau
	sativum	CArn ENfk GPoy MHer MHoo MNHC NPri SBfd SIde SPoG
	- 'Confetti'	MHoo
	- 'Leisure'	MHoo SVic
	- 'Santo'	EGHP ELau
	- 'Slobolt'	EGHP ELau

Coriaria ✿ (*Coriariaceae*)

	arborea	WCru
	intermedia B&SWJ 019	WCru
	japonica	EWld NLar WCru
	- B&SWJ 2833	WCru
	- subsp. ***intermedia*** B&SWJ 3877	WCru
	kingiana	WCru WPGP
§	***microphylla***	WCru
	- B&SWJ 8999	WCru
	myrtifolia	EWld NLar WCru
	nepalensis	NLar WCru
	- BWJ 7755	WCru
	pteridoides	WCru
	ruscifolia	WCru
	- HCM 98178	WCru
	sarmentosa	WCru
	terminalis	GCal
	f. ***fructu-rubro***	
	- var. ***xanthocarpa***	EPfP GCal WCot WCru
	- - GWJ 9204	WCru
	- - HWJK 2112c	WCru
	thymifolia	see *C. microphylla*

Cornus ✿ (*Cornaceae*)

	alba L.	CBar CCVT CDoC CDul CLnd ECrN MHer MRav NWea SEWo SRms WMou
	- 'Alleman's Compact'	CJun
	- 'Argenteovariegata'	see *C. alba* 'Variegata'
	- 'Aurea' 𝕐H4	Widely available
	- Baton Rouge = 'Minbat' PBR	EBee EMil EPfP LRHS SBfd
	- 'Cream Cracker' PBR (v)	EBee MRav
	- 'Elegantissima' (v) 𝕐H4	Widely available
	- 'Gouchaultii' (v)	CBcs CJun CMac EBee GKin LRHS LTen MAsh MRav NLar NRHS SBfd SGol SHil SLim SPer SRms WFar WMoo
	- 'Hessei' misapplied	see *C. sanguinea* 'Compressa'
	- 'Hessei' Hesse	CJun WPat
	- Hutchinson's form **new**	WCot
	- Ivory Halo = 'Bailhalo' PBR	EBee EMil EPfP LSRN MAsh MGos MRav NLar NWea SLim SPer SPoG
	- 'Kesselringii'	Widely available
	- Red Gnome = 'Regnzam'	ELon LLHF MAsh WPat
	- 'Ruby'	CJun
	- 'Siberian Pearls'	CBcs CJun EBee ELan GKin MBlu NLar
§	- 'Sibirica' 𝕐H4	Widely available
	- 'Sibirica Variegata' (v)	CDoC CJun CMac EBee ELon EPfP GCra GKin LRHS LSRN MAsh MBlu MGos NCGa NEgg NRHS SBfd SHil

Name	Suppliers
	SLim SPer SPoG SSpi SWvt WCFE WFar WHar WMoo
- 'Snow Pearls'	CJun
- 'Spaethii' (v) ♀H4	Widely available
§ - 'Variegata' (v)	CBcs LAst MGos SEND
- 'Westonbirt'	see *C. alba* 'Sibirica'
alternifolia	CBcs CCVT CMCN CTho ELan
§ - 'Argentea' (v) ♀H4	Widely available
- 'Brunette'	CJun NLar
- 'Golden Surprise'	CJun
- 'Silver Giant' (v)	CJun NLar
- 'Variegata'	see *C. alternifolia* 'Argentea'
- 'Yellow Spring'	CJun NLar
amomum	CAbP EBee EBtc NLar WFar
- 'Blue Cloud'	CJun
- 'Lady Jane'	NLar
angustata	CMCN SKHP SSpi
- 'Full Moon'	CJun
'Ascona'	CBcs CJun ELan EPfP NLar SSta WPat
Aurora = 'Rutban' (Stellar Series)	CJun MBlu NLar SGol
canadensis ♀H4	Widely available
candidissima Marshall	see *C. racemosa*
capitata	CBcs CDoC CDul CJun CMac CTsd EBee EPfP EWTr GKev IDee LHop LRHS MGos SEND SGar SKHP SPoG SSpi WCru WFar WPGP
- ACE 2033	SSpi
- subsp. ***emeiensis***	CJun
- 'Foreness Fog' **new**	SEND
§ Celestial = 'Rutdan' (Stellar Series)	CJun LRHS NLar SGol SKHP
'Celestial Shadow'	MGos MPkF SGol
'Centennial'	LRHS
chinensis	SSta SWvt
'Constellation' (Stellar Series)	CJun EBee MAsh SGol
controversa	CBcs CCVT CDul CLnd CMCN CTri ECrN ELan EPfP EWTr MBlu MMuc MWat NLar SEND SEWo SGol SLPl SLim SSpi SSta SWvt WFar WHar
- 'Candlelight'	EBee MBlu NLar
§ - 'Frans Type' (v)	CJun ERom LSRN SReu SSta
I - 'Marginata Nord'	NLar
- 'Pagoda'	CJun EPfP MBlu NLar
- 'Troya Dwarf'	CJun NLar
- 'Variegata' (v) ♀H4	Widely available
- 'Variegata' Frans type	see *C. controversa* 'Frans Type'
- 'Winter Orange'	CJun NLar
'Dorothy'	CJun NLar
'Eddie's White Wonder' ♀H4	Widely available
florida	CDul CLnd CMCN CTho LAst MMHG MMuc NWea SEND SPer WHCr WHar
- 'Alba Plena' (d)	CJun NLar
- 'Apple Blossom'	CJun CMac CMen NPCo
- 'Aurea' × ***kousa***	MPkF
- 'Autumn Gold'	SSta
- Cherokee Brave = 'Comco No 1'	CBcs CJun CMen ESwi LMil LRHS MAsh MGos NPCo SBfd SGol SPoG SSta WGob
- 'Cherokee Chief' ♀H4	CBcs CDul CJun CMac CMen CTri GKin IVic LSRN MGos MPkF NPCo SBfd SLim WGob WHar
- 'Cherokee Daybreak'	see *C. florida* 'Daybreak'
- 'Cherokee Princess'	CJun LRHS MAsh SGol SPoG SSta
- 'Cherokee Sunset'	see *C. florida* 'Sunset'
- 'Cloud Nine'	CBcs CDoC CJun CMac CMen EBee MGos MPkF NLar NPCo WGob WHar
- 'Daniela' (v)	NLar
§ - 'Daybreak' (v)	CBcs CJun EBee ESwi LRHS LSRN MAsh MBri MGos MPkF SBfd SPoG SSta WHar
- 'Eternal Dogwood' (d)	ESwi LSRN MGos SGol
- 'First Lady' (v)	CBcs CJun CMac CMen NPCo WGob
- 'G.H. Ford' (v)	NLar
- 'Golden Nugget' (v)	CJun
- 'Granary Gold'	SSta
- 'Moonglow'	CJun
- 'Pendula'	CJun
- 'Pink Flame' (v)	CJun NLar SSta
- f. ***pluribracteata*** (d)	NLar
- var. ***pringlei***	CJun
- 'Purple Glory'	CBcs CJun LRHS NLar
- 'Pygmaea'	NLar
- 'Rainbow' (v)	CAbP CBcs CJun CMac CWib EBee GKin LRHS MAsh MBri MGos MPkF SBfd SLim SPoG SSpi WHar
- 'Red Giant'	CAbP CBcs CJun NLar
- f. ***rubra***	CBcs CDul CTri CWib ELan GKin LMaj LRHS MGos MRav NPCo SEND SPer
- 'Spring Day'	CMac CMen NPCo WGob
- 'Spring Song'	CJun CMac CMen NPCo WGob
- 'Springtime'	CJun NLar
- 'Stoke's Pink'	CJun CMac CMen NPCo WGob
§ - 'Sunset' (v)	CJun CMen CWib LRHS MAsh MBri MGos NLar NPCo SBfd SHil SPer SSta SWvt WGob WHar
- 'Sweetwater'	CJun
- 'Tricolor'	see *C. florida* 'Welchii'
§ - 'Welchii' (v)	CMac
- 'White Cloud'	CJun
'Gloria Birkett'	CAbP CJun EBee EPfP LMil LRHS MAsh NPCo SSpi WGob
hemsleyi	SKHP
hessei misapplied	see *C. sanguinea* 'Compressa'
hongkongensis	NLar
- B&SWJ 11700	WCru
- subsp. ***gigantea*** KWJ 12225	WCru
- subsp. ***melanotricha***	WPGP
- subsp. ***tonkinensis*** B&SWJ 11791	WCru
'Jerry Mundy' **new**	CMac IVic
'Kelsey Dwarf'	see *C. sericea* 'Kelseyi'
'Kenwyn Clapp'	CJun
kousa	CCVT CDoC CMCN CMHG CMac CTho ELan EPfP ERom GKin LMaj MSnd NEgg NLar SBfd SPer SPlb WFar WHar
- 'Akabana'	CJun
- 'Akatsuki'	MPkF SSta
- 'All Summer'	CJun
- 'Angyo Issai'	NLar
- 'Autumn Rose'	CJun EPfP NLar
- 'Beni-fuji'	CJun NLar
- 'Big Apple'	CJun LRHS MAsh NLar SSpi
- 'Blue Shadow'	CJun MBri NLar SSta
- 'Boldre Beauty'	SSpi
- 'Bonfire' (v)	CJun
- 'Bultinck's Beauty'	NLar
- 'Bultinck's Giant'	NLar

- 'Bush's Pink' CJun
- 'Cherokee' CJun
- 'China Dawn' (v) CJun SSta
- var. ***chinensis*** ♀H4 Widely available
- - 'Bodnant Form' CJun CMac NLar NPCo SSta
- - 'China Girl' CDul CJun EBee ELan EPfP EWTr GKin IArd LAst LMil LRHS LSRN MAsh MBlu MBri MGos MRav MSwo NLar SHil SLim SPoG SSpi SSta WPat
- - 'Claudia' IVic NLar SSta
- - 'Great Star' MAsh
- - 'Greta's Gold' (v) CJun SSta
- - 'Ikone' IVic
- - 'Milky Way' CJun CMCN EBee LSRN MBlu MGos MPkF NLar NPCo SGol SSpi WPat
- - 'Snowflake' CJun
- - 'Spinners' CJun
- - 'Summer Stars' CJun NLar
- - 'White Dusted' (v) CJun EPfP MBlu NLar
- - 'White Fountain' CWSG LRHS MBri MPkF MPnt NLar WHar
- - 'Wieting's Select' CJun IArd IDee IVic MBri MPkF NLar
- - 'Wisley Queen' CAbP CJun CMHG LRHS SSpi SSta
- 'Claudine' CJun
- 'Doctor Bump' CJun
- 'Doubloon' CJun LRHS WPat
- 'Dwarf Pink' CJun
- 'Ed Mezitt' CJun NLar SSpi
- 'Eline'PBR **new** MBlu
- 'Elizabeth Lustgarten' CJun MBlu MPkF SSta
- 'Eurostar' IVic NLar
- 'Eva'PBR **new** MBlu MWat
- 'Fanfare' CJun NLar
- 'Fernie's Favourite' CJun
- Galilean = 'Galzam' CJun MGos MPkF
- 'Gay Head' CJun
I - 'Girard's Nana' CJun
- 'Gold Cup' (v) CJun MPkF SSta
- 'Gold Star' (v) CBcs CJun CMac CWGN ELan EPfP LMil MAsh MBri MGos MPkF NLar NPCo SPoG SSta WGob
- 'Greensleeves' CJun LRHS SSta
- 'Heart Throb' CBcs CJun MGos NLar SGol
- 'Highland' CJun
- 'John Slocock' CJun MBri NLar
- 'Kim' NLar
- 'Kreutzdame' CJun MBlu MBri NLar
- 'Laura'PBR SSta
- 'Little Beauty' CJun
- 'Lustgarten Weeping' CJun NLar
- 'Madame Butterfly' CJun LRHS MBlu MBri NLar NPCo
- 'Marwood Dawn' CMHG SSta
- 'Marwood Twilight' **new** CMHG
- 'Melanie'PBR **new** MBlu
- 'Milky Way' CDul ESwi GBin SGol
- 'Milky Way Select' CBcs CJun LMaj LRHS MGos
- 'Minuma' NLar
- 'Miss Petty' CJun MPkF NLar
- 'Miss Satomi' ♀H4 Widely available
- 'Moonbeam' CJun MBri NLar WPat
- 'Mount Fuji' CJun CMHG MBlu MBri NLar SSta
- 'National' CJun EBee EPfP LMil LRHS MAsh MGos MPkF NLar SSta WPat
- 'Nicole' CDoC EBee LRHS NLar WGob WPat
- 'Ohkan' CJun
- 'Pevé Limbo' (v) CJun NLar
- 'Pevé Satomi Compact' NLar
- 'Polywood' CJun NLar
- 'Radiant Rose' CJun MBri MPkF NLar SSpi SSta
- 'Rasen' CJun NLar
- 'Rel Whirlwind' CJun NLar
- 'Rosea' CJun
- Samaratin = 'Samzam' (v) CBcs CJun LSRN MBri MGos MPkF SGol SKHP SSta
- 'Satomi Akatuki' (v) **new** NLar
- 'Schmetterling' CJun MBlu NLar WPat
- 'Silver Pheasant' (v) NLar
- 'Snowbird' CJun
- 'Snowboy' (v) CBcs CDul CJun CMac MBlu NPCo SMad
- 'Snowflurries' CJun
- 'Southern Cross' CJun GBin
- 'Square Dance' CJun
- 'Steeple' CJun
- 'Summer Fun' CJun LRHS SPoG SSpi SSta
- 'Summer Gold' (v) MPkF
- 'Summer Majesty' CJun
- 'Sunsplash' (v) CJun NLar SSta
- 'Temple Jewel' (v) CJun
- 'Teutonia' CJun IDee IVic MBri MGos NLar SSta
- 'Trinity Star' CJun SSpi
- 'Triple Crown' CJun WPat
- 'Tsukubanomine' CJun NLar
- 'Vale Milky Way' (v) NLar
- 'Weaver's Weeping' CJun MPkF NLar
- 'Weisse Fontäne' CJun NLar
- 'White Dream' CJun NLar
- 'White Giant' CJun
- 'Wolf Eyes' (v) CJun EBee MAsh MBlu MPkF NLar SGol SSpi SSta

macrophylla Wall. EPfP NLar
- MSF 821 WPGP

mas Widely available
- 'Aurea' (v) CAbP CJun EBee ELan ELon EPfP LRHS MAsh MBlu MBri MGos MRav NEgg NLar NPCo NRHS SGol SLim SPer SPoG SSpi SSta WPat
§ - 'Aureoelegantissima' (v) CGHE CJun CMac EBee LRHS MAsh MBri NEgg NLar SPer SPoG SSpi WPat
- 'Devin' NLar
- 'Elegant' CAgr
- 'Elegantissima' see *C. mas* 'Aureoelegantissima'
- 'Golden Glory' ♀H4 CJun EPfP MBri NLar SKHP
- 'Gourmet' CAgr
- 'Happy Face' NLar
- 'Hillier's Upright' CJun
- 'Jolico' CJun LRHS MBlu NLar SKHP
- 'Kasanlaker' NLar
- 'Pioneer' CJun
- 'Redstone' CJun
- 'Schönbrunner Gourmet Dirndl' **new** MCoo
- 'Spring Glow' CJun NLar
- 'Titus' NLar
- 'Variegata' (v) ♀H4 CAbP CBcs CJun CMCN CMac EBee EPfP LRHS MAsh MBlu MBri MGos NLar NPCo SKHP SPer SPoG SSpi
- 'Xanthocarpa' CJun NLar
- 'Yellow' CAgr

N 'Norman Hadden' ♀H4 Widely available

nuttallii	CDul CTho CTri CWib EBee ELan EPfP GLin MGos MMuc SEND SPer SWvt WFar
- 'Colrigo Giant'	CJun
- 'Gold Spot' (v)	CJun CMac MGos NPCo NWea
- 'Monarch'	CJun CTho NLar SKHP SSpi WPat
- 'North Star'	CJun NLar
- 'Pink Blush'	NLar
- 'Portlemouth'	CJun WGob
- 'Zurico'	CJun MPkF NLar
officinalis	CAgr CDul CMCN CMac EPfP LRHS NLar SKHP
- 'Ellen'	NLar
- 'Kintoki'	SKHP
'Ormonde'	CJun CWGN NLar NPCo SSpi SSta WGob
'Pink Blush'	CJun
'Porlock' ♀H4	CDul CJun CMCN EPfP ITim LRHS LSRN MAsh MBri NLar SHil WPat
pumila	CJun NLar
§ ***racemosa***	NLar
rugosa	EBtc NLar
I × ***rutgersiensis*** **new**	LRHS
- Galaxy	see *C.* Celestial
Ruth Ellen = 'Rutlan' (Stellar Series)	CJun NLar WPat
sanguinea	CBcs CCVT CDul CHab CLnd CRWN CTri ECrN EPfP LBuc LMaj MMuc MRav MSwo NWea SEWo SGol SPer SVic WHar WMou
- 'Anny'	CJun MAsh MBlu WCot WPat
- 'Anny's Winter Orange'	CJun
§ - 'Compressa'	EPfP MRav NLar
- 'Magic Flame'	CJun EBee ELon EPfP NLar WPat
- 'Midwinter Fire'	Widely available
- 'Winter Beauty'	CJun CSBt CWib EBee ELon EPfP LBMP MAsh MBlu NEgg NLar NWea SLon SWvt WCFE WHar WPat
§ ***sericea***	MSCN SRms WMoo
- 'Bud's Yellow'	EBee LRHS MAsh MBlu MBri MGos SHil
- 'Cardinal'	CHGN EPfP LRHS MAsh MBri NLar NRHS SHil
- 'Coral Red'	CJun
- 'Flaviramea' ♀H4	Widely available
- 'Hedgerows Gold' (v)	CJun CSBt EBee ELan EMil EPfP LHop LRHS MAsh MBri MGos NRHS SBfd SHil SPoG WPat
- 'Isanti'	CJun
§ - 'Kelseyi'	CJun CMac EBee EPfP LTen MBrN MRav NLar SLPl SPer WFar WMoo
- Kelsey's Gold = 'Rosco'	MAsh WPat
- subsp. ***occidentalis*** 'Sunshine'	CJun NLar NPro
§ - 'White Gold' (v) ♀H4	CDoC CJun EBee EHoe ELon EPfP MBri MRav MSwo NLar NPro SLon SPer SPoG WFar WMoo
- 'White Spot'	see *C. sericea* 'White Gold'
Stardust = 'Rutfan' (Stellar Series)	CJun
Stellar Pink = 'Rutgan' (Stellar Series)	CBcs CJun IVic LRHS MAsh MBri MGos MPkF NLar SGol SKHP WGob
stolonifera	see *C. sericea*
× ***unalaschkensis***	EBee LLHF
- NNS 08-101	GKev
Venus = 'Kn30 8'PBR	CJun ELan LBuc LRHS MAsh MBlu MBri MPkF SPoG SSta
walteri B&SWJ 8776	WCru

Corokia (*Argyrophyllaceae*)

buddlejoides	CBcs CDoC CHGN CMHG CTrC CTsd ECou NPnk SEND WFar
'Coppershine'	CMHG
cotoneaster	CAbP CBcs CDul CMac CTrC CTri EBee ECho ECou ELan EPfP EPot LRHS MAsh MGos MPkF NLar SBfd SMad SPer SPoG SPtl SWvt WCot WFar WGrn WHar WPat
- 'Boundary Hill'	ECou
- 'Brown's Stream'	ECou
- 'Geenty's Ghost'	CTrC
- 'Hodder River'	ECou
- 'Ohau Scarlet'	ECou
- 'Ohau Yellow'	ECou
- 'Swale Stream'	ECou
- 'Wanaka'	ECou
* ***daphnoides***	NPnk
macrocarpa	CDoC ECou
* ***parviflora***	CTrC
× ***virgata***	CAbP CDoC CMHG CTrC CTri ECou ELan EPfP GBin IDee LRHS NLar SPer SWvt WHar WSHC
- 'Bronze King'	CDoC EBee EPfP LRHS MOWG MPkF SPer
- 'Bronze Lady'	ECou MGos
- 'Cheesemanii'	ECou
- 'County Park Lemon'	ECou
- 'County Park Orange'	ECou
- 'County Park Purple'	ECou
- 'County Park Red'	ECou
- 'Frosted Chocolate'	CBcs CDoC CMHG CTrC CTsd EBee ECou ELan EPfP ETod IVic LHop LLHF LRHS MAsh MGos MOWG MPkF MWat SEND SKHP SLim SPoG SWvt WCot WFar WGrn WHar
- 'Geenty's Green'	CTrC EBee ECou LRHS
- 'Havering'	ECou
- 'Mangatangi'	CTrC
- 'Pink Delight'	CDoC EBee ECou EPfP ESwi MAsh MRav
- 'Red Wonder'	CDoC CMHG CMac CTrC EBee ELan EPfP IVic LRHS MMHG MPkF SEND SLim SPoG WGrn WHar
- 'Sandrine'	ECou
- 'Silver Ghost'	CDoC ECou
- 'Sunsplash' (v)	CBcs CDoC CMac CTrC CTsd EBee ECou EPfP ESwi LBMP LHop LLHF LRHS MAsh MGos MPkF NLar NPnk SBfd SEND SPoG SWvt WFar WGrn WHar
I - 'Virgata'	ECou
- 'Wingletye'	ECou
- 'Yellow Wonder'	CBcs CDoC CMHG CTrC EBee ESwi LRHS MGos NLar SEND SLim SPoG SWvt

Coronilla (*Papilionaceae*)

comosa	see *Hippocrepis comosa*
coronata	WCot
emerus	see *Hippocrepis emerus*
glauca	see *C. valentina* subsp. *glauca*
valentina	CDoC CRHN CSPN EBee LHop SDix WSHC XLum
- 'Creamed Corn'	WCot
§ - subsp. ***glauca*** ♀H3	CDul CMac CSBt CTri CWib EBee ELan ELon EPfP LRHS

	LSRN SBfd SEND SGar SLim SPer SPoG SRms SWvt WAbe WFar WPat WWlt XSen
- - 'Brockhill Blue'	EBee IVic LRHS WCot
- - 'Citrina' 𝕐H3	Widely available
* - - 'Pygmaea'	LRHS WCot
- - 'Variegata' (v)	CBcs CDoC CMac CSPN CTri CWib EBee EHoe ELan ELon EPfP LRHS MAsh MCot SBfd SEND SLim SLon SMad SMrm SPer SPoG WCot WFar
varia	see *Securigera varia*

Correa (*Rutaceae*)

alba	CCCN CDoC CPLG CTrC ECou EPfP WGwG WHar
- 'Pinkie' 𝕐H2	CBcs CPLG ECou MOWG SAga WCot
alba* × *backhouseana	MOWG
backhouseana 𝕐H2	CAbb CBcs CDoC CHll CMac CPLG CTrC CTri EBee ECou ELan EPfP EWld IDee IVic LHop LPot LRHS MOWG NLar SAga SBrt SEND SGar WHar WSHC
- 'Peaches and Cream'	CSBt IVic SRkn
decumbens	CAbb CTrC ECou
'Dusky Bells' 𝕐H2	CBcs CCCN CDoC CHll CTri EBee ECou ECre EPfP IVic LBMP LHop LRHS MAsh MOWG SAga SEND SHil SLim SMrm SPlb SPoG SPtl SRkn
'Dusky Maid'	CCCN CPLG
'Federation Belle'	CDoC ECou MOWG
glabra	MOWG
'Gwen'	CDoC ECou
'Harrisii'	see *C.* 'Mannii'
'Inglewood Gold'	ECou
'Ivory Bells'	ECou EPfP SBrt
lawrenceana	CTrC ECou IRar SEND WAbe
§ 'Mannii' 𝕐H2	CBcs CDoC CPLG CPom EBee ECre ELan ELon EPfP IVic LRHS MOWG SEND SPoG WSHC
'Marian's Marvel' 𝕐H2	CCCN CDoC CPLG CTrC EBee ECou ECre EPfP EWld IDee LBMP MAsh MOWG SBrt SEND SGar SPoG SRkn WAbe
'Peachy Cream'	CDoC EBee EPfP LRHS
'Pink Mist'	CDoC ECou
'Poorinda Mary'	ECou MOWG
pulchella 𝕐H2	CDoC CPLG CTri IRar
- orange-flowered	MOWG
- 'Pink Mist'	MOWG
reflexa 𝕐H2	CDoC CPLG ECou SBrt
- var. ***nummulariifolia***	ECou IRar LBMP MAsh MOWG SBrt WAbe
- var. ***reflexa***	CPLG
- - 'Mary's Choice'	CDoC
* - ***virens***	CPLG
schlechtendalii	ECou

Cortaderia ✿ (*Poaceae*)

argentea	see *C. selloana*
fulvida misapplied	see *C. richardii* (Endl.) Zotov
§ ***fulvida*** (Buchanan) Zotov	CKno EBee EWes GBin IArd IDee MNrw NWsh SEND SMad
jubata 'Candy Floss'	CKno
richardii misapplied	see *C. fulvida* (Buchanan) Zotov
richardii ambig.	CCon CPLG CTrC EHoe GBin MMuc NBir SMad WHrl WWEG
§ ***richardii*** (Endl.) Zotov 𝕐H3-4	CBcs CKno EBee EPPr ESwi EWes GMaP IBlr MAvo MWhi SEND WCru WMnd WPGP
- Brown's strain **new**	WCot
§ ***selloana***	CBcs CDul CHEx CTri CWib EHul IBoy MGos MRav NBir NGBl SBfd SGol SPlb WFar
§ - 'Albolineata' (v)	CBcs CBct ELon EWes MWht NOak NWsh SBfd SEND SLim SPer SPoG SWvt
§ - 'Aureolineata' (v) 𝕐H3-4	CBcs CBct CDoC CMac CWCL EHoe ELan EPfP IVic LRHS MGos NBid NOak NWsh SBfd SEND SLim SPer SPoG SWvt WPat
- 'Evita' PBR	CKno EPPr SMad SPer WCot
- 'Gold Band'	see *C. selloana* 'Aureolineata'
- 'Golden Goblin' PBR **new**	EBee EPPr
- 'Icalma'	EPPr
- 'Monstrosa'	SEND SMad
- 'Patagonia'	EHoe EPPr
- 'Petite Plumes' (v)	LBuc SBfd
- 'Pink Feather'	EPfP LTen SApp SEND
- 'Pumila' 𝕐H4	Widely available
- 'Rendatleri'	CBcs CDoC ELan LSRN SCoo SLim SPer SPoG
- 'Rosea'	EBee EPfP MAsh MGos NGdn NLar SBfd SGol WFar WWEG
- 'Silver Comet'	EWes
- Silver Feather = 'Notcort' (v)	MGos SLim
- 'Silver Fountain' (v)	ELan EPfP LRHS
- 'Silver Stripe'	see *C. selloana* 'Albolineata'
- 'Splendid Star' PBR (v)	CBcs CDoC EBee EHoe EUJe GBin LBuc LHop LRHS LTen MBri MGos MREP NLar NOak SBfd SLim SMad SPoG SWvt WCot
- 'Sunningdale Silver' 𝕐H3-4	CDoC CMac EBee ECha ECtt EHoe EHul ELan ELon EPfP LRHS LSRN MBri MGos SBfd SEND SLim SMad SPer SPoG SWvt WFar
* - 'White Feather'	NGdn NWsh SApp SLim WFar WWEG
Toe Toe	see *C. richardii* (Endl.) Zotov

Cortia (*Apiaceae*)

depressa	EBee

Cortiella (*Apiaceae*)

aff. ***hookeri*** HWJK 2291	WCru

Cortusa (*Primulaceae*)

brotheri	EBee ECho GKev
* ***caucasica***	EBee GKev
* - 'Alba'	GKev
matthioli	EBee ECho EPfP GKev NMen SRms
- 'Alba'	CCon ECho GEdr NMen SRms WCot
- subsp. ***pekinensis***	CCon EBee ECho EDAr GEdr MLHP NBid NLar NMen SPet SRms WFar WPnP WSHC XLum
- - var. ***sachalinensis*** **new**	GKev
turkestanica	ECho LLHF

Corydalis ✿ (*Papaveraceae*)

from Sichuan, China	MDKP
× ***allenii*** 'Enno'	LWst
ambigua misapplied	see *C. fumariifolia*
anthriscifolia	CLAP EWes MDKP SSvw WCot

	'Blackberry Wine'	CPLG EBee ECtt EPfP GBuc MDKP MPnt NLar NPnk
	'Blue Panda'	see *C. flexuosa* 'Blue Panda'
	'Bronze Beauty'	WMoo
	bulbosa misapplied	see *C. cava*
	bulbosa (L.) DC.	see *C. solida*
	buschii	CLAP CPBP EBee ECho GBin GBuc GEdr GKev NHar NMyG SCnR
	'Canary Feathers'[PBR]	EBee ECtt LLHF MBNS NLar NMyG NPnk NPri SPoG WCot
	cashmeriana	GEdr LRHS NBid NHar NMen NRHS WAbe WHal
	- 'Kailash'	LRHS
	cashmeriana* × *flexuosa	CBro CLAP ECho LHop LRHS WAbe
	caucasica	ECho GBuc LWst NMen
	- var. ***alba*** misapplied	see *C. malkensis*
§	***cava***	CLAP EBee ECho EPot LAma LWst SPhx WShi
	- 'Albiflora'	CLAP ECho SPhx
	- subsp. ***cava***	ECho
	chaerophylla	IBlr
	cheilanthifolia	CDoy CPLG CRow CSpe EBee EHrv EPfP LEdu LPla LRHS SGar SPhx SRms WFar WTin XLum
	- 'Manchu'	SPtl
	'Craigton Blue'	CLAP EBee GBuc GEdr GKev IPot ITim NHar WAbe
	curviflora subsp. ***rosthornii***	CPLG EWes
	- - 'Blue Heron'	NLar
	darwasica	LWst
	davidii	CPLG
	decipiens Schott, Nyman & Kotschy	see *C. solida* subsp. *incisa*
I	***decipiens*** misapplied Ψ[H4]	CPom ECho EPot
I	- purple-flowered	EBee ECho LWst
	densiflora	LWst
	'Early Bird'	ECtt EWes
	elata	CLAP CSpe CYeo EBee EWes GBuc GEdr GKev IBlr IFro LHop LRHS LSou MArl MCot MNrw NBid NBir SPhx SPoG WCot WCru WHal WMnd WPtf WSHC
	- 'Blue Summit'	CLAP EBee ECtt EPPr LRHS
	elata* × *flexuosa clone 1	CCse CLAP CPLG GEdr
	flexuosa Ψ[H4]	CSpe EBee ECho EPfP GBin MArl MLHP MNrw NSla WAbe WBor WFar WSHC XLum
	- CD&R 528	IFro NRya
	- 'Balang Mist'	CLAP CPLG NHar
	- 'Blue Dragon'	see *C. flexuosa* 'Purple Leaf'
§	- 'Blue Panda'	CPLG EBee EPPr EPot EWes GBuc GMaP NHar WCru WFar
	- 'China Blue'	Widely available
	- 'Golden Panda'[PBR] (v)	CBct EBee ECtt ITim MBNS NPnk WCot
	- 'Hale Cat'	EBee ECtt EPPr
	- 'Hidden Purple'	CHid
	- 'Nightshade'	CPLG CYeo ECtt LLHF LRHS NBid WCot WHoo
I	- 'Norman's Seedling'	EBee EPPr IVic WPGP
	- 'Père David'	CMac CSBt CSpe EBee ECha ECho ELan EPfP EPPr ITim LRHS MHer MSpe MWat NBir NCGa SBfd SPer SPlb SPoG SWvt WCru WFar WSHC WWEG XLum
§	- 'Purple Leaf'	Widely available
	'Foundling'	LWst
§	***fumariifolia***	GKev
	glaucescens	LWst
	- 'Early Beauty'	LWst
	'Golden Spinners'	IVic
	haussknechtii	LWst
	'Heavenly Blue'	NMen
	henrikii	LWst NMen
	incisa	ECho ERCP LAma NMen
	- B&SWJ 4417	WCru
	integra	LWst
	'Kingfisher'	CDes CHid CLAP EWes GEdr LRHS NHar NLar NSla SBch WAbe
	kusnetzovii	LWst
	ledebouriana	EPot LWst
	leucanthema DJHC 752	CDes CLAP CPLG
	- 'Silver Spectre' (v)	CPLG EBee ECtt LLHF LRHS WMoo
	linstowiana	CSpe LRHS
	- CD&R 605	CLAP CPLG
§	***lutea***	CBcs CRWN EBee EPfP IBlr IFoB IFro MMuc NBir NPer NPri NWad SEND SRms WCot WMoo
	macrocentra	LWst
	magadanica	LLHF LRHS MMoz
§	***malkensis*** Ψ[H4]	CWCL EBee ECho EHrv EPot GBin GBuc LLHF LRHS LWst NBir NMen NRya SCnR WCot WThu
	maracandica	LWst
	'Maya' (v)	XLum
	moorcroftiana	CPLG
	'New Contender'	LWst
	nobilis	CPom CSpe ECho IFoB LLHF SPhx
	ochotensis	LRHS
§	***ochroleuca***	CElw CPom CRow CSpe GCal LPla LRHS NMRc WMoo
	ophiocarpa	CSpe EHoe ELan GCal IBlr SWal WHil WMoo
	ornata	LWst
	pachycentra	CPLG WAbe
	paczoskii	CPBP ECho GBuc GKev LRHS LWst MNrw NMen
	paschei	LWst
	popovii	LWst SCnR
	pseudofumaria alba	see *C. ochroleuca*
	pumila	ECho
	'Rainier Blue'	IVic
	rosea 'American Dream'	CWCL
	scandens	see *Dactylicapnos scandens*
	schanginii	LWst
	subsp. ***ainii*** Ψ[H2]	
	- - from Sjasu Valley, Kazakhstan **new**	LWst
	- subsp. ***schanginii***	LWst
	scouleri	NBir
	shimienensis	CPom
	- 'Berry Exciting'[PBR]	CBct CHid CLAP CWCL CWGN ECtt ELon EPPr EPfP GBuc LHop LSou MBNS MTis NPnk NPri SPoG WBor
	siamensis	IFoB
	- B&SWJ 7200	WCru
§	***solida***	CAvo CBro CPom EBee ECho ECtt ELan EPfP EPot GAbr IBlr ITim LAma LEdu LRHS MRav NLar NMen NPnk NRHS NRya SDeJ SMrm SPhx WCot WFar WHil WShi WTin
	- 'Fire Bird' **new**	GEdr LWst
	- 'Firecracker'	CBro ECho LLHF LRHS SPhx

- 'Frodo' LAma
- 'Ice Pink' NMen
§ - subsp. ***incisa*** ♀H4 EBee ECho GKev MNrw SPhx WCot
- - white-flowered LWst
- 'Kissproof' LWst
- lilac-flowered IFoB
- 'Maxima' NMen
- 'Moonlight Shade' ECho
- Nettleton seedlings EPot
- 'Night Heron' LWst
- 'Pink Discovery' LWst
- 'Pipit' **new** LWst
- 'Purple Beauty' ECho GEdr GKev LWst MNrw SPhx
- 'Purple Bird' LWst
- 'Quiet Elegance' LAma
- 'Redwing' LWst
§ - subsp. ***solida*** CLAP ECho EPot GBin GKev NBir NRya SPhx WCot
- - from Penza, Russia LAma LLHF LWst NCot NMen
- - 'Beth Evans' Widely available
- - 'Blushing Girl' ECho LAma
- - 'Dieter Schacht' ♀H4 EBee GKev ITim LAma LLHF NLar NMen WAbe WCot
- - 'Evening Shade' ECho LAma
- - 'George Baker' ♀H4 Widely available
- - 'Lahovice' WAbe WCot
- - Prasil Group GKev LWst SPhx WBor
- - 'White Knight' LAma WCot
- 'Spoonbill' LWst
- f. ***transsylvanica*** see *C. solida* subsp. *solida*
- 'White Swallow' GEdr LLHF LWst NMen
- 'Zwanenberg' LWst
aff. ***solida*** subsp. ***incisa*** LAma
'Spinners' CDes CElw CFis CLAP EBee ECha ECtt EPPr GCal GKev IVic MDKP SBch SSvw WSHC XLum
stipulata B&SWJ 2951 WCru
taliensis CPLG GLog SBfd
tauricola EPot GEdr LWst NMen
temulifolia CFis CWGN EBee ECtt GBin GEdr
'Chocolate Stars' LEdu LHop LLHF LPla LSou MBNS NCGa NSti WCot WSHC
tomentella GEdr
'Tory MP' CBct CDes CEnt CHid CLAP CPLG CPne CPom CSam CSpe EBee EPPr GAbr GEdr IFro LRHS MDKP MNrw MSpe NBid NCGa NHar WHoo WMnd WPGP
transsylvanica hort. see *C. solida* subsp. *solida*
turtschaninovii GHim LWst SKHP
- 'Gorin' LWst
vittae IFoB
- 'Goliath' LWst
wendelboi IFoB
- LS&T 05-73 LWst
- subsp. ***congesta*** LWst
- Jonus form NMen
- subsp. ***wendelboi*** LWst
'Wildside Blue' CLAP
wilsonii CPLG GEdr IFoB IGor
zetterlundii LWst

Corylopsis ✿ (*Hamamelidaceae*)

glabrescens CHGN CJun LRHS
- var. ***gotoana*** CJun EBee EPfP LRHS MAsh NLar SPoG SSpi SSta WPat
- - 'Chollipo' CAbP CBcs LRHS NLar SSta
- - 'Lemon Drop' NLar
glandulifera NLar SSpi
himalayana WAbe
multiflora SSpi
pauciflora ♀H4 Widely available
platypetala see *C. sinensis* var. *calvescens*
- var. ***laevis*** see *C. sinensis* var. *calvescens*
sinensis GBin
§ - var. ***calvescens*** CBcs CJun NLar
§ - - f. ***veitchiana*** ♀H4 CDoy CJun CSam ELan EPfP LRHS NLar SSpi
§ - var. ***sinensis*** ♀H4 CDoC CJun EBee ELon EPfP IDee IVic LAst LRHS MAsh NLar SLon SReu WAbe
- - 'Spring Purple' CAbP CBcs CGHE CJun CMac EBee EPfP IVic LRHS NLar SChF SHil SKHP SSpi SSta WPGP WPat
- 'Veitch's Purple' CJun NLar
spicata CBcs CDoy CDul CJun EBee IDee IGor LRHS LTen MGos MRav NEgg NLar SGol SLim SSpi WPat
* - 'Aurea' **new** GGGa
- 'Golden Spring' EPfP NLar
- 'Red Eye' IVic NLar
veitchiana see *C. sinensis* var. *calvescens* f. *veitchiana*
willmottiae see *C. sinensis* var. *sinensis*
'Winterthur' **new** SSta

Corylus ✿ (*Betulaceae*)

avellana (F) CBcs CCVT CDoC CDul CHab CLnd CMac CRWN CTho CTri ECrN EPfP EPom EWTr GAbr LAst LBuc MAsh MBri MGos NEgg NLar NWea SBfd SBod SEWo SPer SVic WHar WMou
- 'Anny's Red Dwarf' IArd
- 'Aurea' CBcs CDul CSBt CTho CTri EBee ECrN ELan EPfP EWTr GBin LBuc LRHS MBlu MBri MGos MRav NLar NWea SLim SPer SSta SWvt WFar
- 'Bollwylle' see *C. maxima* 'Halle'sche Riesennuss'
§ - 'Butler' (F) CAgr CMac CMam CTho CTri GTwe IArd MBri SKee SPoG WHar
- 'Casina' (F) CAgr CTho
- 'Contorta' Widely available
- 'Corabel' (F) CAgr CMam MBri MCoo
- 'Cosford' (F) CAgr CCVT CDul CMac CSBt CTho CTri ECrN EPom GTwe IArd LBuc LRHS MBlu MBri MGos NLar SEWo SKee SPer WHar
- Emoa Series MCoo
§ - 'Ennis' (F) CAgr CMam GTwe LRHS MBri SKee WHar
- 'Fortin' (F) ECrN
§ - 'Fuscorubra' (F) CJun EPom MRav NLar
- 'Gustav's Zeller' (F) CAgr MCoo
§ - 'Heterophylla' CDul EBee EPfP MBri NLar SSta WHar WPat
- 'Laciniata' see *C. avellana* 'Heterophylla'
§ - 'Lang Tidlig Zeller' (F) CAgr LRHS MBri MCoo NWea
- 'Louis Berger' (F) **new** NLar
- 'Merveille de Bollwyller' see *C. maxima* 'Halle'sche Riesennuss'
- 'Nottingham Prolific' see *C. avellana* 'Pearson's Prolific'
- 'Pauetet' (F) CAgr
§ - 'Pearson's Prolific' (F) CAgr CSBt GTwe LBuc MMuc NLar SEND SKee

- 'Pendula' — EBee MAsh MBlu SCoo SLim WHar WPat
- 'Purpurea' — see *C. avellana* 'Fuscorubra'
- 'Red Dwarf' **new** — NLar
- 'Red Majestic'PBR — Widely available
- 'Tonda di Giffoni' (F) — CAgr MCoo
- 'Webb's Prize Cob' (F) — CAgr CDul ECrN GTwe IArd MBlu MMuc NLar SEND SKee SVic WMou

colurna ♀H4 — CCVT CDul CLnd CMCN CMac EBee ECrN EPfP EWTr IArd MBlu MGos NLar NWea SCoo SGol SPer WHar WMou
- 'Te-Terra Red' — CJun CMCN EBee MAsh MBlu MBri NLar SLon SMad SSpi WHar

× ***colurnoides*** 'Chinoka' (F) — MCoo WHar
- 'Freeoka' (F) — MCoo WHar
- 'Laroka' (F) — ECrN

Early Long Zeller — see *C. avellana* 'Lang Tidlig Zeller'

maxima (F) — CMac CTri EPom GTwe MSwo NWea
- 'Butler' — see *C. avellana* 'Butler'
- 'Ennis' — see *C. avellana* 'Ennis'
- 'Fertile de Coutard' — see *C. maxima* 'White Filbert'
- 'Frizzled Filbert' (F) — ECrN
- 'Frühe van Frauendorf' — see *C. maxima* 'Red Filbert'
- 'Garibaldi' (F) — NLar
- 'Grote Lambertsnoot' — see *C. maxima* 'Kentish Cob'
- 'Gunslebert' (F) — CAgr CCVT CMac CMam CSBt CTho CTri ECrN GTwe LRHS MBri SKee SPoG WHar
- Halle Giant — see *C. maxima* 'Halle'sche Riesennuss'
- § 'Halle'sche Riesennuss' (F) — CAgr CMam ECrN GTwe MBri MMuc NLar SEND SKee WHar
- § 'Kentish Cob' (F) — CAgr CBcs CDul CMac CSBt CTho CWSG ECrN ELan EPfP EPom GTwe IArd LBuc LRHS MBlu MBri MGos MWat NLar SEWo SKee SLim SPer SPoG SRms WHar
- 'Lambert's Filbert' — see *C. maxima* 'Kentish Cob'
- 'Longue d'Espagne' — see *C. maxima* 'Kentish Cob'
- 'Monsieur de Bouweller' — see *C. maxima* 'Halle'sche Riesennuss'
- 'Purple Filbert' — see *C. maxima* 'Purpurea'
- § 'Purpurea' (F) ♀H4 — Widely available
- § 'Red Filbert' (F) — CTho CWSG EPom GTwe IArd MAsh MBlu MBri NLar SCoo SGol SKee SLim SSta WHar WPat
- 'Red Zellernut' — see *C. maxima* 'Red Filbert'
- 'Spanish White' — see *C. maxima* 'White Filbert'
- § 'White Filbert' (F) — GTwe SKee WHar
- 'White Spanish Filbert' — see *C. maxima* 'White Filbert'
- 'Witpit Lambertsnoot' — see *C. maxima* 'White Filbert'

'Nottingham Early' (F) — NLar

Corymbia see *Eucalyptus*

Corynabutilon see *Abutilon*

Corynephorus (*Poaceae*)

canescens — EBee NBir WWEG

Corynocarpus (*Corynocarpaceae*)

laevigatus — CBcs CHEx ECou MBri

Cosmos (*Asteraceae*)

§ ***atrosanguineus*** — Widely available
- Chocamocha = 'Thomocha'PBR — CAvo CBcs CCCN CHid CSpe CWCL CWGN EBee ECtt EPfP EUJe IBoy LHop LSRN LSou NCGa NDov NLar NPri SBfd SMrm SPer SRot SUsu

bipinnatus 'Antiquity' **new** — NPri SPhx
- 'Double Click' **new** — SPhx
- 'Purity' — CSpe SPhx
- Sensation Series **new** — SPhx
- (Sonata Series) 'Sonata Carmine' — LSou NPri SPoG
- - 'Sonata Pink' — LSou NPri SPoG
- - 'Sonata White' — CSpe LAst LSou NPri SPoG

caudatus **new** — WJek

peucedanifolius — CSpe
- 'Flamingo' — CGrW EBee EPfP ERCP LSou SDeJ SPer WHil

sulphureus Bright Lights mixed **new** — CSpe

Cosmos × *Dahlia* (*Asteraceae*)

'Mexican Black' — EBee ECtt ERCP IBoy MBNS MBel WCot

costmary see *Tanacetum balsamita*

Cotinus ✿ (*Anacardiaceae*)

americanus — see *C. obovatus*

§ ***coggygria*** ♀H4 — CArn CBcs CDoC CMCN CMac CSBt CWSG ECrN ELan EPfP LHop MBri MMuc MRav MSwo MWat NWea SBfd SEND SGol SPer SWvt WFar WHar
- Golden Spirit = 'Ancot'PBR — Widely available
- Green Fountain = 'Kolcot'PBR — EBee
- 'Kanari' — CJun NLar WPat
- 'Nordine' — NLar WPat
- 'Notcutt's Variety' — ELan MRav
- 'Old Fashioned' — MGos MPkF WMou
- 'Pink Champagne' — CBcs CJun EPfP MAsh NLar SSta WPat
- Purpureus Group — EPfP SEND SGol
- 'Red Beauty' — CJun NLar
- Red Spirit = 'Firstpur' — NLar
- 'Royal Purple' ♀H4 — Widely available
- Rubrifolius Group — CBcs EBee EPfP SGol SPer SWvt WFar
- Smokey Joe = 'Lisjo'PBR — EBee EPfP LRHS MAsh NCGa NRHS SLon SPoG SPtl SSta SWvt WHar
- 'Smokey Joe Purple' — LSou
- 'Velvet Cloak' — CAbP CJun ELan EPfP GKin LRHS MGos MPkF MRav NLar SGol SLon SWvt WHar WMou
- 'Young Lady'PBR — Widely available

Dusky Maiden = 'Londus'PBR — ELon EPfP GBin LRHS MAsh MBri MGos MWat NLar NRHS SHil SLon WPat

'Flame' ♀H4 — CDul CJun EBee ELan EPfP EWTr LRHS MAsh MBri MGos MRav SBfd SHil SKHP SLim SPer SPoG SWvt WPat

'Grace' — Widely available

§ ***obovatus*** ♀H4 — CJun CMCN EBtc ELon EPfP IArd LLHF LRHS MBlu MPkF MRav SSpi SSta WPat

Cotoneaster ✿ (*Rosaceae*)

SDR 5804 — GKev

acuminatus — SRms

adpressus ♀H4 — MSwo

§	– 'Little Gem'	EBee ECho NHar NLar
	– var. ***praecox***	see *C. nanshan*
	– 'Tom Thumb'	see *C. adpressus* 'Little Gem'
	affinis	SRms
	albokermesinus	SRms
	amoenus	SLPl SRms
	– 'Fire Mountain'	NPro
§	***apiculatus***	SRms
§	***ascendens***	SRms
	assamensis	SRms
§	***astrophoros***	CMac EBee MBlu NHar
	atropurpureus	SRms
§	– 'Variegatus' (v) ♀H4	Widely available
	boisianus	SRms
	bradyi	SRms
§	***bullatus*** ♀H4	CDul CTri EPfP IGor MGos MMuc NLar SPer SRms
	– 'Firebird'	see *C. ignescens*
	– f. ***floribundus***	see *C. bullatus*
	– var. ***macrophyllus***	see *C. rehderi*
	– 'McLaren'	SRms
	bumthangensis	SRms
	buxifolius blue-leaved	see *C. lidjiangensis*
	– 'Brno'	see *C. marginatus* 'Brno'
	– f. ***vellaeus***	see *C. astrophoros*
	camilli-schneideri	SRms
	canescens	SRms
§	***cashmiriensis*** ♀H4	MGos
	cinnabarinus	SRms
§	***cochleatus***	CDul LAst MGos NMen SRms
§	***congestus***	CSBt CWib EBee MGos MSwo MWat SPlb SRms WHar XLum
	– 'Nanus'	CMea ELan GEdr MGos
	conspicuus	CBcs LAst SRms
	– 'Decorus' ♀H4	CDoC CDul CSBt CWSG EBee EPfP LAst LHop LRHS MBri MGos MMuc MSwo NEgg NLar NWea SBfd SGol SHil SLim SPer SPlb SPoG SWvt WHar WMoo
	– 'Leicester Gem'	SRms
	– 'Red Glory'	CMac WWau
	cooperi	SRms
	cordifolius	MBlu SRms
	cornifolius	SRms
	cuspidatus	MBlu
N	***dammeri*** ♀H4	Widely available
§	– 'Major'	CBar LBuc SPoG
§	– 'Mooncreeper'	SEND
	– 'Oakwood'	see *C. radicans* 'Eichholz'
	– var. ***radicans*** misapplied	see *C. dammeri* 'Major'
	– var. ***radicans*** C.K.Schneid.	see *C. radicans*
	dielsianus	NLar NWea SRms
	distichus var. ***tongolensis***	see *C. splendens*
	divaricatus	EPfP NLar NWea SPer SRms WFar
	duthieanus 'Boer'	see *C. apiculatus*
	elatus	SRms
	elegans	SRms
	emeiensis	SRms
	'Erlinda'	see *C.* × *suecicus* 'Erlinda'
	'Exburiensis'	CBcs CCVT CDoC CDul EBee EPfP LAst MAsh MBri MGos MMuc MRav MWat NLar SEND SGol WFar WHar
	falconeri	SRms
	fastigiatus	SRms
	flinckii	SRms
	floccosus	NWea
	floridus	SRms
	forrestii	SRms
	franchetii	Widely available
	– var. ***cinerascens***	SRms
	frigidus	SRms
N	– 'Cornubia' ♀H4	Widely available
	– 'Saint Monica'	MBlu
	gamblei	SRms
	ganghobaensis	SRms
	glabratus	SLPl SRms
	glacialis	SRms
	glaucophyllus	IArd SEND SRms
§	***glomerulatus***	SRms
	gracilis	SRms
	granatensis	SRms
	harrovianus	NLar SLPl SRms
I	***hedegaardii*** 'Fructu Luteo'	SRms
	henryanus	SRms
	– 'Corina'	SRms
	'Herbstfeuer'	see *C. salicifolius* 'Herbstfeuer'
	'Highlight'	see *C. pluriflorus*
§	***hjelmqvistii***	EBee LBuc SRms
	– 'Robustus'	see *C. hjelmqvistii*
	– 'Rotundifolius'	see *C. hjelmqvistii*
	hodjingensis	SRms
	horizontalis ♀H4	Widely available
	– 'Tangstedt'	SGol
	– 'Variegatus'	see *C. atropurpureus* 'Variegatus'
	– var. ***wilsonii***	see *C. ascendens*
	hualiensis	SRms
	humifusus	see *C. dammeri*
	hummelii	SRms
	hunanensis B&SWJ 3143	WCru
§	'Hybridus Pendulus'	Widely available
§	***hylmoei***	SLPl SRms
	hypocarpus	SRms
	ignavus	SLPl SRms
§	***ignescens***	NWea SRms
	ignotus	SRms
	induratus	SLPl SRms
	insculptus	SRms
	integerrimus	SRms
§	***integrifolius*** ♀H4	EBee MAsh NMen NRHS SPoG SRms WMoo
	– 'Silver Shadow'	NLar
	kangdingensis	SRms
	lacteus ♀H4	Widely available
	lancasteri	SRms
	langei	SRms
	laxiflorus	SRms
§	***lidjiangensis***	SRms WWau
§	***linearifolius***	GCra
	lucidus	CDul NLar SRms
	– 'Mini'	SLPl
	ludlowii	SRms
	magnificus	SRms
§	***mairei***	NWea SRms
	marginatus Lindl. ex Loudon	SRms
§	– 'Blazovice'	SRms
§	– 'Brno'	SRms
	marquandii	SRms
§	***meiophyllus***	MBlu
	meuselii	SRms
	microphyllus misapplied	see *C. purpurascens*
	microphyllus ambig.	CBcs
	microphyllus Wall. ex Lindl.	CDul CTri EBee LRHS MGos NWea SDix SPer SPoG WMoo
	– NICE 004	WCFE
	– var. ***cochleatus*** misapplied	see *C. cashmiriensis*

	- var. ***cochleatus*** (Franch.) Rehd. & Wils.	see *C. cochleatus*
	- var. ***cochleatus*** ambig.	EPot NSla
	- 'Donard Gem'	see *C. astrophoros*
	- 'Ruby'	SRms
	- 'Teulon Porter'	see *C. astrophoros*
	- var. ***thymifolius*** misapplied	see *C. linearifolius*
	- var. ***thymifolius*** (Lindl.) Koehne	see *C. integrifolius*
	- var. ***thymifolius*** ambig.	LRHS
	milkedandaensis	SRms
	miniatus	SRms
	mirabilis	SRms
	monopyrenus	SRms
	'Mooncreeper'	see *C. dammeri* 'Mooncreeper'
	morrisonensis	SRms
	moupinensis	SRms
	- BWJ 8167	WCru
	mucronatus	SRms
	multiflorus Bunge	NLar SRms
§	***nanshan***	CAbP NLar NWea SRms
	- 'Boer'	see *C. apiculatus*
	naoujanensis	EPfP LRHS MBri
	- 'Berried Treasure' **new**	LBuc SHil
	newryensis	SRms
	nitens	SRms
	nitidifolius	see *C. glomerulatus*
	nohelii	SRms
	notabilis	SRms
	nummularioides	SRms
	nummularius	SRms
	obscurus	SRms
	obtusus Wall. ex Lindl.	SRms
	pangiensis	SRms
	pannosus	SLPl SRms
	- 'Speckles'	SRms
	paradoxus	SRms
	parkeri	SRms
	pekinensis	SRms
	permutatus	see *C. pluriflorus*
	perpusillus	SRms WFar
§	***pluriflorus***	CDul SRms
	poluninii	SRms
	polycarpus	SRms
	praecox 'Boer'	see *C. apiculatus*
	procumbens	SRms
	- 'Queen of Carpets'	CDoC CDul EBee ELan EPfP LHop LRHS LSRN MAsh MBri MGos MRav MWat MWhi NRHS SBfd SCoo SHil SLim SPoG SRms SWvt WMoo
	- 'Streib's Findling'	see *C.* 'Streib's Findling'
	prostratus	SRms
	przewalskii	SRms
	pseudo-obscurus	SRms
§	***purpurascens***	CSBt
	pyrenaicus	see *C. congestus*
	qungbixiensis	SRms
	racemiflorus	SRms
§	***radicans***	SBfd
§	- 'Eichholz'	EBee MGos NHol NWad SBfd SPoG
§	***rehderi***	CMHG NLar SRms
	roseus	SRms
	'Rothschildianus' ♀H4	Widely available
	rugosus	SRms
	salicifolius	MSwo NLar NWea SEND SRms WFar
	- Autumn Fire	see *C. salicifolius* 'Herbstfeuer'
§	- 'Avonbank'	CDoC LTen NLar WHar
	- 'Brno Orangeade'	SRms
	- 'Gnom'	CDul CMac EBee ELan EPfP LRHS MAsh MGos MRav NBir NEgg SEND SPer SPoG SRms WHar WMoo
§	- 'Herbstfeuer'	MRav MSwo SRms
	- Park Carpet	see *C. salicifolius* 'Parkteppich'
§	- 'Parkteppich'	NWea
	- 'Pendulus'	see *C.* 'Hybridus Pendulus'
	- 'Repens'	CDoC CWib EPfP MWhi NHol NPla NPri NWad NWea SGol SLim SPer SPoG SRms WFar WHar
	- var. ***rugosus*** (E.Pritzel) Rehder & E.H.Wilson	see *C. hylmoei*
	- 'Scarlet Leader'	CMac
	salwinensis	SLPl SRms
	sandakphuensis	SRms
	scandinavicus	SRms
	schantungensis	SRms
	schlechtendalii 'Blazovice'	see *C. marginatus* 'Blazovice'
	- 'Brno'	see *C. marginatus* 'Brno'
	schubertii	SRms
	serotinus misapplied	see *C. meiophyllus*
	serotinus Hutchinson	NLar SLPl SRms
	shannanensis	SRms
	shansiensis	SRms
	sherriffii	SRms
	sikangensis	SRms
	simonsii ♀H4	CBcs CCVT CDoC CDul CLnd CMac EBee ECrN ELan EPfP LBuc LPot LRHS MGos MMuc NHol NLar NWad NWea SEND SGol SPer SPoG SRms WFar WHar WWau
§	***splendens***	SRms WFar
	- 'Sabrina'	see *C. splendens*
	spongbergii	SRms
	staintonii	SRms
	sternianus ♀H4	EBee EPfP SLPl SRms
	- ACE 2200	EPot
§	'Streib's Findling'	MAsh NLar SGol
	suavis	SRms
	subacutus	SRms
	subadpressus	SRms
	× ***suecicus*** 'Coral Beauty'	Widely available
§	- 'Erlinda' (v)	NLar SRms
	- 'Ifor'	SLPl SRms
	- 'Juliette' (v)	EHoe LRHS LSRN MAsh NLar SCoo SLim WFar WHar
	- 'Skogholm'	CBcs CDul CWib EBee EPfP LRHS MAsh MGos NWea SPer SRms WHar
	taoensis	SRms
	tardiflorus	SRms
	tauricus	SRms
	teijiashanensis	SRms
	tengyuehensis	SRms
	thimphuensis	SRms
	tomentellus	WCFE
	tomentosus	SRms
	turbinatus	SLPl SRms
	'Valkenburg'	SRms
	vandelaarii	SLPl SRms
	veitchii	NLar SRms
	verruculosus	SRms
	villosulus	SRms
	vilmorinianus	SRms
	wardii misapplied	see *C. mairei*
	wardii W.W.Sm.	SRms

× ***watereri***	CCVT CWib ELon LRHS MMuc MSwo NWea SBfd SEND SHil WJas
- 'Avonbank'	see *C. salicifolius* 'Avonbank'
- 'Cornubia'	see *C. frigidus* 'Cornubia'
- 'John Waterer' ♀H4	EPfP MGos SPoG WFar
- 'Notcutt's Variety'	EPfP
- 'Pendulus'	see *C.* 'Hybridus Pendulus'
- 'Pink Champagne'	CMac MRav
wilsonii	SRms
yalungensis	SRms
yinchangensis	SRms
zabelii	SRms

Cotula (*Asteraceae*)

atrata	see *Leptinella atrata*
coronopifolia	CWat LPBA NPer SWat
hispida ambig.	EBee
§ ***hispida*** (DC.) Harv.	CMea CTri ECho EDAr EHoe EPot GMaP ITim MAsh MHer MSCN MWat NPer SPoG SRms WIce WJek WPat WPer XLum
lineariloba (DC.) Hilliard	ECha ECho EWes LRHS
minor	see *Leptinella minor*
'Platt's Black'	see *Leptinella squalida* 'Platt's Black'
potentilloides	see *Leptinella potentillina*
pyrethrifolia	see *Leptinella pyrethrifolia*
rotundata	see *Leptinella rotundata*
serrulata	see *Leptinella serrulata*
squalida	see *Leptinella squalida*

Cotyledon (*Crassulaceae*)

chrysantha	see *Rosularia chrysantha*
gibbiflora var. ***metallica***	see *Echeveria gibbiflora* var. *metallica*
oppositifolia	see *Chiastophyllum oppositifolium*
orbiculata	CHEx ETod SDix SPlb
- var. ***oblonga***	EShb
- var. ***orbiculata***	EShb
- 'Silver Waves'	MCot
simplicifolia	see *Chiastophyllum oppositifolium*

Cowania see *Purshia*

Crambe (*Brassicaceae*)

cordifolia ♀H4	Widely available
maritima ♀H4	CArn CSev CSpe EBee ECha EPfP GKev GMaP GPoy LRHS MCoo MCot MRav NEgg NLar NPnk NSti SEND SPer SWat WCot WFar WJek WMnd WPGP WPer WWEG XLum
- 'Lilywhite'	CAgr CArn EBee SVic
tatarica	NLar WPer XLum

cranberry see *Vaccinium macrocarpon, V. oxycoccos*

Crassula (*Crassulaceae*)

arborescens	EShb EUJe SChr SRms
argentea	see *C. ovata*
atropurpurea	SEND
subsp. ***arborescens*** 'Blue Mist'	
coccinea	EShb SPlb
multicava	CHEx
muscosa	SChr SRot
obtusa	SRot
orbicularis	WCot
§ ***ovata*** ♀H1	CDoC CHEx EBak EOHP EPfP NPer NPla SChr SEND SPlb SWal WThu
- 'Blue Bird'	LToo
- 'Gollum'	SWal
- 'Hummel's Sunset' (v) ♀H1	SWal
- 'Variegata' (v)	EBak WCot
perfoliata	EShb EUJe SRot WCot
var. ***falcata*** ♀H1	
perforata	EUJe
- 'Variegata' (v)	SRot
portulacea	see *C. ovata*
§ ***sarcocaulis***	CBcs CHEx CTri ECho ELan ELon GEdr GMaP MAsh MSCN NMen SEND SGar SPlb SPoG SRms SRot SWal WAbe WIce WSHC XSen
I - 'Alba'	GEdr
sedifolia	see *C. setulosa* 'Milfordiae'
sediformis	see *C. setulosa* 'Milfordiae'
setulosa	SPlb
§ - 'Milfordiae'	CTri ECho EPot NBir
socialis	WAbe
- 'Major'	SChr
tetragona	SEND
* ***tomentosa*** 'Variegata' (v)	EShb

+ *Crataegomespilus* (*Rosaceae*)

'Jules d'Asnières'	NLar

× *Crataegosorbus* (*Rosaceae*)

miczurinii 'Ivan's Belle'	CAgr

Crataegus (*Rosaceae*)

F&M 196	WPGP
arnoldiana	CAgr CDul CLnd CTri EBee ECrN EPfP MCoo MMuc MWat NWea SCoo SEND SLPl SPer
'Autumn Glory'	CLnd EBee ECrN
azarolus	EPfP
champlainensis	CLnd
chrysocarpa	EPfP
chungtienensis	SSpi
- SDR 5104	GKev
N ***coccinea*** misapplied	see *C. intricata*
N ***coccinea*** ambig.	NWea
§ ***coccinea*** L.	CAgr CLnd CTho EBee SCoo
coccinioides	EPfP
cordata	see *C. phaenopyrum*
crus-galli misapplied	see *C. persimilis* 'Prunifolia'
crus-galli L.	CCVT CDoC CDul CLnd CTho EBee ECrN EPfP IGor LAst MBri NWea SPer WJas
dahurica	EPfP
× ***dippeliana***	EPfP
dsungarica	EPfP
× ***durobrivensis***	CAgr CDul CLnd EPfP MBri NLar
ellwangeriana	CAgr ECrN EPfP SDix
- 'Fire Ball'	MBlu
gemmosa	NLar NWea SSpi
greggiana	EPfP IGor
× ***grignonensis***	CBcs CDul CLnd CTho ECrN LMaj MAsh MBri SEND SPer WJas
§ ***intricata***	EPfP NWea
irrasa	EPfP
jonesiae	EPfP
korolkowii	IGor
laciniata Ucria	see *C. orientalis*
§ ***laevigata***	CCVT CDul NWea
- 'Coccinea Plena'	see *C. laevigata* 'Paul's Scarlet'
- 'Crimson Cloud'	Widely available

- 'Gireoudii' CDul CWib LAst MGos NLar NSti WJas
- 'Mutabilis' CTri SGol
§ - 'Paul's Scarlet' (d) ♀H4 Widely available
- 'Pink Corkscrew' EPfP LLHF MBlu SMad WPat
- 'Plena' (d) CBcs CDoC CDul CLnd CMac CSBt CTri CWib ECrN EPfP LAst MGos MRav MSwo MWat NWea SBfd SCrf SEWo SGol SLim SPer WFar WHar
- 'Rosea' GKin SEND
- 'Rosea Flore Pleno' (d) ♀H4 Widely available
× ***lavalleei*** CCVT CDul CLnd CTri ECrN ELan EPfP LAst LMaj MAsh MMuc MRav MSwo NWea SCoo SEND SLon SPer
- 'Carrierei' ♀H4 CDoC CDul CTho EBee EPfP EWTr IVic LHop LMaj MAsh MBri NWea SCoo SEWo WCot WMou
lobulata EPfP
mexicana see *C. pubescens* f. *stipulacea*
mollis CAgr CTho ECrN EPfP WSpi
monogyna Widely available
§ - 'Biflora' CDul CLnd CTho CTri EBee ECrN LRHS MAsh MCoo MGos NWea SLim
- 'Compacta' MBlu WPat
- 'Praecox' see *C. monogyna* 'Biflora'
- 'Stricta' CCVT CDul CSBt EBee ECrN EPfP IDee LMaj MMuc SEND SGol
- 'Variegata' (v) ECrN
× ***mordenensis*** 'Toba' (d) CDul CLnd EPfP SGol
nigra EPfP IGor
§ ***orientalis*** CCVT CDul CLnd CMCN CTho CTri EBee ECrN EPfP IArd IDee MAsh MBlu MBri MCoo MGos MWat NLar NWea SCoo SLim SMad SSpi WHar WJas WMou
oxyacantha see *C. laevigata*
pedicellata see *C. coccinea* L.
pentagyna EPfP
§ ***persimilis*** 'Prunifolia' ♀H4 Widely available
- 'Prunifolia Splendens' CCVT EBee EWTr GBin LBuc LRHS MBri MCoo SCoo WPat
§ ***phaenopyrum*** CDul CLnd CTho EBee EPfP IDee MBri MGos SLPl
pinnatifida EPfP
- var. ***major*** CDul EPfP MBri MCoo NWea
- - 'Big Golden Star' CAgr CLnd CTho ECrN EPfP LRHS MBlu MCoo NLar SCoo
'Praecox' see *C. monogyna* 'Biflora'
prunifolia see *C. persimilis* 'Prunifolia'
pseudoheterophylla EPfP
§ ***pubescens*** f. ***stipulacea*** CDul CTho ECrN EPfP
punctata CTho SLPl
- f. ***aurea*** EPfP
sanguinea EPfP
schraderiana CAgr CDul CLnd CTho EBtc EPfP IVic MBri NLar NWea SCoo WHar
sorbifolia EPfP
submollis IGor
succulenta EPfP
- 'Jubilee' PBR **new** EBee
- var. ***macracantha*** CMCN EPfP
suksdorfii EPfP
tanacetifolia CAgr CDul CTho EPfP MBlu MBri SPer
tracyi MBri
turkestanica EPfP
viridis 'Winter King' EPfP SLim
wattiana CLnd EBee ELan EPfP

× *Crataemespilus* (*Rosaceae*)

grandiflora CDul CLnd WSpi

Craterocapsa (*Campanulaceae*)

***congesta* new** CPBP

Crawfurdia (*Gentianaceae*)

pasquieri B&SWJ 8264 WCru
speciosa B&SWJ 2138 WCru

Cremanthodium (*Asteraceae*)

CC 6525 GKev
arnicoides EBee GKev

Cremastra (*Orchidaceae*)

variabilis LWst

× *Cremnosedum* (*Crassulaceae*)

§ 'Little Gem' NMen WAbe

Crenularia see *Aethionema*

Crepis (*Asteraceae*)

aurea ECho
incana ♀H4 CMea ECho ECtt MAsh MAvo NChi NMen NRHS NSla NWad SPhx SRms WPat
- 'Pink Mist' NLar

Crinitaria see *Aster*

Crinodendron (*Elaeocarpaceae*)

hookerianum ♀H3 Widely available
- 'Ada Hoffmann' CBcs CDoC CMac CPLG CTrC EBee ELan ELon EPfP GAbr GCal GKev GKin IVic LRHS LSRN MBlu MBri MGos MPkF MREP NLar SBfd SChF SKHP SLim SPoG WBor WPat
patagua CBcs CCCN CDoy CHid CPLG CTri CWib EBee ELon EPri ESwi IArd IVic LRHS MMuc NEgg NLar SEND SPlb SPoG WFar WSHC

Crinum (*Amaryllidaceae*)

amoenum CCCN EBee ECho GHim WCot
asiaticum WCot
- DJHC 970606 WCot
- var. ***sinicum*** WCot
§ ***bulbispermum*** CCon CPrp EBee ELan GCal LRHS WCot
campanulatum WCot
capense see *C. bulbispermum*
'Carolina Beauty' WCot
'Cintho Alpha' **new** SDeJ SPer
'Elizabeth Traub' WCot
'Ellen Bosanquet' CCCN CCon CDes CTca EBee ELan GBin GHim WCot
'Emma Jones' WCot
'Hanibal's Dwarf' EBee WCot WPGP
moorei CAvo CBro CCon CDes CRHN CTca ECho IVic LEdu SChr WPGP
- f. ***album*** CCCN CTca EBee GBin GHim
'Ollene' WCot
§ × ***powellii*** ♀H3 Widely available
- 'Album' ♀H3 CAvo CBro CDes CHEx CPrp CTca CTri EBee ECha ECho ELan ELon EPfP EWes GCra LAma LEdu

	LRHS MNrw MRav SDeJ SEND SMad SPer SRms SSpi WCot WFar WHil WPGP
- 'Longifolium'	see *C. bulbispermum*
- 'Roseum'	see *C.* × *powellii*
'Sangria'	WCot
'Summer Nocturne'	WCot
variabile	EBee WCot
'White Queen'	WCot
yemense misapplied	WCot

Criogenes see *Cypripedium*

Crithmum (*Apiaceae*)

maritimum	CArn GPoy MHoo MNHC SPlb WJek XLum
- 'Isleta del Moro' new	GPoy

Crocosmia ✿ (*Iridaceae*)

'Alistair'	ECtt
'Anniversary'	IBlr
'Apricot'	CTca ECrc IBal
'Apricot Surprise'	ELon
aurea misapplied	see *C.* × *crocosmiiflora* 'George Davison' Davison
aurea ambig.	EShb GCal
aurea (Pappe ex Hook.f.) Planch.	CPou ECtt IBlr
- subsp. ***aurea***	CTca IBlr
- - 'Maculata'	IBlr
- subsp. ***pauciflora***	IBlr
'Auricorn'	EBee IBlr NCot NHol
'Auriol'	EBee IBlr NCot
'Aurora'	NGdn
'Baywalker' new	MAvo
'Beth Chatto'	CTca CYeo ECrc ECtt IBal MAvo
Bressingham Beacon = 'Blos'	CPrp IBlr LRHS MSpe WRHF
'Bressingham Blaze'	CBre CMHG CTca ECrc ECtt IBlr LRHS NGdn NHol WCot WHil
Bridgemere hybrid	ECrc NHol
Bright Eyes = 'Walbreyes'PBR	EPfP LRHS
'Buttercups' new	CMea
'Cadenza'	IBal IBlr NHol
'Carnival'	ECtt IBlr
'Cascade'	EBee IBal IBlr NCot
'Chinatown'	IBal IBlr NCot NHol WHil
'Chrome' new	CSam
'Citronella' misapplied	see *C.* × *crocosmiiflora* 'Honey Angels'
'Comet' Knutty	CTca EBee ECrc GCal IBlr MAvo WMoo
'Cornish Copper' new	CTca
× ***crocosmiiflora***	CHEx CTca CTri EBee IBlr MCot NHol SEND SPlb SRms WBrk WCot WFar WMoo WShi
- 'A.E.Amos'	ECrc ECtt
- 'A.J. Hogan'	CTca CYeo IBal IBlr NHol
- 'African Glow'	CDes CTca ECrc IBal
- 'Amber Sun'	IBlr
- 'Amberglow'	CBgR CElw CPLG IBal IBlr NHol NPer
- 'Apricot Queen'	CTca IBlr NHol
- 'Autumn Gold'	IBlr
- 'B.A.Walker' new	ECrc
- 'Baby Barnaby'	CBre CDes CTca ECtt IBlr NHol
- 'Babylon'	Widely available
- 'Bicolor'	CTca IBal IBlr MAvo SUsu WHil
- 'Burford Bronze'	CTca IBal IBlr MAvo NHol
- 'Burnt Umber' new	EBee
- 'Buttercup'	CSam CTca EBee ECrc ECtt EPfP ERCP EWll GAbr IBal IBlr IKil MAvo MCot NBre NHol SBfd SRkn STes WMoo WWEG
- 'Canary Bird'	CBro CSam CYeo ECtt GAbr IBal IBlr LRHS NGdn NHol WBrk WRHF WSpi
- 'Cardinale'	IBlr
§ - 'Carmin Brillant' ♀H3-4	Widely available
- 'Carminea'	STes
- 'Challa'	CTca ECrc ECtt
- 'Citrina'	CTca MNrw SMrm WSpi
- 'Citronella' J.E. Fitt	CBgR CBro CPLG CPrp CSam CTri EBee ECha ECrc EPfP GMaP GQue LRHS MBel MRav NGdn NHol SPer WCot WGwG
§ - 'Coleton Fishacre'	Widely available
§ - 'Columbus'	CAvo CPar CPrp CSam CTca EBee ECrc ELon EPPr EPfP EPri IBal IBlr LHop LRHS LSou MAvo MSCN NHol SGar SPer WHil WMnd WWEG
- 'Colwall'	IBal IBlr NCot
- 'Comet' new	LRHS
- 'Constance'	CBgR CBro CSam CTca ECrc ECtt IBal IBlr LRHS MAvo MBri NBid NGdn NHol WBrk
- 'Corona'	CTca IBal IBlr MAvo NHol
- 'Corten'	IBlr
§ - 'Croesus'	CTca ECrc IBal IBlr MRav
- 'Custard Cream'	CPrp CSpe CTca ECrc IBlr LRHS NHol
- 'D.H. Houghton'	IBlr
- 'Debutante'	CDes CHVG CTca CYeo ECrc EPri IBal IBlr LRHS NHol SHar SUsu WHoo WSHC
§ - 'Diadème'	CSam CTca CWCL NHol
- 'Dusky Maiden'	Widely available
- 'Dwarf Gold'	IBal
§ - 'E.A. Bowles'	CPou CTca EBee ECrc IBlr LRHS WCot
- 'Eastern Promise'	CBre CPrp CTca ELon IBal IBlr WHil
- 'Eclatant'	IBlr
- 'Elegans'	ECrc ECtt IBal IBlr LRHS NRHS
§ - 'Emily McKenzie'	Widely available
- 'Etoile de Feu'	IBlr
- 'Fantasie'	CBgR ECrc IBal
- 'Festival Orange'	ECrc IBlr
- 'Fire Jumper'	CDes CTca EBee MAvo WPGP
- 'Firebrand'	EBee IBlr NCot
- 'Fireglow'	CTca EBee ECtt IBal IBlr NCot WPer
- 'Flamethrower'	IBlr
- 'George Davison' misapplied	see *C.* × *crocosmiiflora* 'Golden Glory' ambig., 'Sulphurea'
§ - 'George Davison' Davison	Widely available
- 'Gillian' new	ECrc
- 'Gloria'	CTca ECrc IBal IBlr MAvo
- 'Golden Glory' misapplied	see *C.* × *crocosmiiflora* 'Diadème'
§ - 'Golden Glory' ambig.	CPLG CWCL EHrv ELan GBuc IBal IBlr MSwo MWat NBir NHol SPlb WCot
- 'Goldfinch'	EBee ECrc IBlr NCot NHol WHil WWEG
- 'Goldie'	CTca ECrc MAvo
- 'Hades'	IBlr MAvo

	- 'Harvest Sun'	IBlr
	- 'Heligan'	EPfP
	- 'His Majesty'	CBro CPne CSam CSpe CTca CYeo ECrc ECtt IBal IBlr LRHS NHol WHil
	- 'Hoey Joey'	ECrc NGdn
§	- 'Honey Angels'	Widely available
	- 'Honey Bells'	ECrc LRHS WBrk
	- 'Irish Dawn'	ECrc IBal IBlr NBre NHol
§	- 'Jackanapes'	CDes CPrp CTca CWCL ECtt ELan ELon GCal IBal IBlr LRHS MBri MGos MLHP SBfd SUsu WPGP
	- 'Jackanapes VI'	IBal
	- 'James Coey' misapplied	see *C.* × *crocosmiiflora* 'Carmin Brillant'
	- 'James Coey' J.E. Fitt	EAEE EBee ECha EHoe EPfP GKin IFoB MLHP NDov NGdn NHol SMrm WMoo
	- 'Jesse van Dyke'	IBlr
§	- 'Jessie'	CTca ECrc IBlr LRHS
	- 'Judith'	CTca EBee ECrc IBlr NCot
	- 'Kapoor'	IBlr
	- 'Kiautschou'	CTca CWCL EBee IBal IBlr LRHS NGdn NHol WHil
	- 'Lady Hamilton'	CBro CCon CElw CPLG CSam CTca ECtt GCal GCra IBal IBlr LRHS MAvo MBri MRav NCGa NHol NLar SBfd WCot WHil WHoo WMoo WWEG
	- 'Lady McKenzie'	see *C.* × *crocosmiiflora* 'Emily McKenzie'
	- 'Lady Oxford'	CTca CYeo ECrc IBlr LRHS NHol WHil
	- 'Lambrook Gold'	CAvo ECrc IBlr
	- 'Lemon Fleece' **new**	CCVN
	- 'Lord Nelson'	CPLG CTca IBal NHol
	- 'Loweswater'	CYeo ECrc MAvo SUsu
	- 'Lutea'	ECtt IBal IBlr LRHS NHol
	- 'Marjorie'	ECrc
	- 'Mars'	CElw EBee ECrc ECtt EWes EWll GAbr IBal IBlr IFoB LRHS MAvo NGdn NHol NSti SBfd SPlb SRkn WWEG
	- 'Mephistopheles'	CHVG CTca IBlr MAvo NHol WHil
	- 'Merryman'	CTca ECrc GAbr IBal MAvo
	- 'Météore'	CBgR EBee EPPr EPfP EPot GAbr GQue LRHS MBNS NBre NHol NRHS SBfd SHil WWEG
	- 'Morgenlicht'	CTca ECtt IBlr NHol WBrk WCot
	- 'Moses'	CTca ECrc
	- 'Mount Usher'	CCon CCse CPrp CTca ECrc GAbr GCal IBal IBlr NHol SGar
	- 'Mrs David Howard'	SApp
§	- 'Mrs Geoffrey Howard'	CDes CSam CTca CWCL ECtt IBal IBlr LEdu LRHS NHol SHar SUsu WBrk WCru WPGP
	- 'Mrs Morrison'	see *C.* × *crocosmiiflora* 'Mrs Geoffrey Howard'
	- 'Newry Seedling'	see *C.* × *crocosmiiflora* 'Prometheus'
	- 'Nimbus'	CTca IBal IBlr WHil
§	- 'Norwich Canary'	CBgR CHVG CMHG COIW CTca EBee ECha EPPr EPfP EPri GBuc GCra IBal IBlr LRHS MRav NBir NGdn NHol NSti WBrk WCot WHil WMoo WOut WWEG
	- 'Olympic Fire'	CTca ECrc IBlr MAvo NCot NHol
	- 'Olympic Sunrise'	CTca
	- 'Pepper'	IBlr
	- 'Ping Pong'	CTca
	- 'Plaisir'	CTca IBal IBlr LRHS MAvo NBid NHol WWEG
	- 'Polo'	CBgR CSam CTca CWCL
	- 'Princess'	see *C. pottsii* 'Princess'
§	- 'Princess Alexandra'	IBlr
	- 'Prolificans'	ECrc IBlr
§	- 'Prometheus'	CTca IBal IBlr NHol
	- 'Queen Alexandra' misapplied	see *C.* × *crocosmiiflora* 'Princess Alexandra'
§	- 'Queen Alexandra' J.E. Fitt	CTca ECha IBlr LEdu NHol SPer WHal WMoo WPer
	- 'Queen Charlotte'	CTca ECrc IBal IBlr
	- 'Queen Mary II'	see *C.* × *crocosmiiflora* 'Columbus'
	- 'Queen of Spain'	CTca EBee IBal IBlr LRHS MDKP WHil WWEG
	- 'Rayon d'Or'	CDes EBee ECrc IBlr WPGP
	- 'Red King'	EBee EPfP IBal IBlr LHop LRHS MPnt NRHS SBfd WHil WMoo WRHF WWEG
	- 'Red Knight'	GAbr IBlr NHol
	- 'Rheingold' misapplied	see *C.* × *crocosmiiflora* 'Diadème'
	- 'Rose Queen'	IBlr MNrw
	- 'Saint Clements'	CTca EBee IBlr NCot NHol
	- 'Saracen'	CMac CSpe CTca EAEE EBee ECtt ELon GBuc GCal GKin IBal IBlr LAst LEdu LRHS LSou MBNS MCot NBre NGdn NLar SKHP SMrm WCot WMoo
	- 'Severn Seas'	ECrc ECtt WSpi
	- 'Sir Mathew Wilson'	CDes EBee IBal IBlr LRHS WCot WPGP
	- 'Solfatare' ♀H3	Widely available
	- 'Solfatare Coleton Fishacre'	see *C.* × *crocosmiiflora* 'Coleton Fishacre'
	- 'Star of the East' ♀H3	Widely available
	- 'Starbright'	IBlr
	- 'Starfire'	ECrc
	- 'Sultan'	CDes CPLG ECrc IBlr WMoo
	- 'Tiger's Eye'	CTca
	- 'Venus'	CBgR CBre CPou CTca ECtt ELon EPPr EShb IBal IBlr LPla LRHS MAvo MCot MPnt NBre NHol NLar WHil WMoo
	- 'Vesuvius'	ECrc GCal IBlr LRHS NCGa WSHC
	- 'Vic's Yellow'	ECrc SGar
	- 'Voyager'	EBee ECtt ELon EPot ERCP IBal IBlr LHop LRHS MBri NHol NLar SDeJ WHil
	- Wasdale strain	ECrc
	- 'Zeal Tan'	CElw CMHG CPLG CSam CTca CWCL EBee ECtt EHrv ELan ELon EPri GCal IBal IBlr LEdu MAvo MBNS MCot MNFA NEgg NLar NWsh SBfd SUsu WBrk WCot
§	× ***crocosmioides***	CTca IBlr WHil
	- 'Castle Ward Late'	CPou CTca CYeo EAEE ECha ECrc ECtt GAbr GCal GCra GQue IBal IBlr LHop LRHS MAvo NHol SMrm SUsu WMoo
	- 'Mount Stewart Late'	IBlr
§	- 'Vulcan' Leichtlin	CMac CTca IBlr LRHS WHil
	'Cylvia'	ECrc
	'Darkleaf Apricot'	see *C.* × *crocosmiiflora* 'Coleton Fishacre'
	'Devil's Advocate'	CTca
	'Doctor Marion Wood'	CYeo EBee ECrc
	'Eldorado'	see *C.* × *crocosmiiflora* 'E.A. Bowles'

	'Elegance'	IBlr
	'Ellenbank Canary'	CBgR CTca MAvo
	'Ellenbank Firecrest'	CBgR CDes CTca EBee MAvo NCGa WPGP
	'Ellenbank Skylark'	CBgR MAvo
	'Emberglow'	Widely available
	'Fandango'	IBal IBlr NCot NHol
	'Fernhill'	ECrc IBlr
*	'Feuerser'	ECtt
	'Fire King' misapplied	see *C.* × *crocosmiiflora* 'Jackanapes'
	'Fire King' ambig.	EBee ECrc ERCP GAbr IBal LRHS NSti SWvt WHil
	'Fire Sprite'	IBlr
	'Firefly'	IBlr
	'Fireworks'	EBee NCot
	'Flaire'	IBlr
	'Fleuve Jaune'	CTca ECrc ECtt LRHS
	'Forest Fire'	EBee IBal LLHF LSou
	fucata	IBlr
	- 'Jupiter'	see *C.* 'Jupiter'
	fucata* × *paniculata	CTca IBal NHol
	'Fugue'	IBlr NCot
	'Fusilade'	IBlr
	'Gold Sprite'	IBlr NCot
	'Golden Ballerina'^PBR	CPrp EBee ECtt EWes GBin IBal LRHS LSou NCGa SPoG SRkn WWlt
	'Golden Dew'	CTca EBee ECrc ECtt EPfP GAbr GQue IBal MBNS NCGa NEgg SBfd SKHP WCot
	Golden Fleece *sensu* Lemoine	see *C.* × *crocosmiiflora* 'Coleton Fishacre'
	'Harlequin'	CElw CTca CYeo MAvo WHlf
	'Harmonia'	CDes CTca
	'Hellfire'	CBgR CMea CPar CSam CSpe CTca EBee ECtt ELon EWhm GAbr IBal IBoy LEdu LLHF LRHS MAvo MBNS MBel MNrw MTis NDov NGdn SMad SPer WCot WWlt
	'Highlight'	ECrc IBal IBlr MAvo NHol
	'Irish Flame'	NHol
	'Irish Sunset'	NHol
	'Jennine'	EBee ECrc IBal LRHS NHol
	'Jenny'	MAvo
	Jenny Bloom = 'Blacro'^PBR	ECrc LRHS NChi SMrs
	'John Boots'	EBee ECtt ELon GAbr GBuc IBal IBlr LRHS MCot MDev NBid NHol WHil
§	'Jupiter'	CBre CHVG CPou CPrp CSam CTca CWCL EBee GCal IBal IBlr LRHS MAvo MRav NCGa NHol SApp SEND WHil
	'Kathleen'	ECrc LRHS
	'King George'	CTca
	'Krakatoa'	CHll CPrp CTca EBee ECrc GBee GBin IBal LLHF MAvo SKHP SPoG SRkn SWvt WMoo
	'Lady Wilson' misapplied	see *C.* × *crocosmiiflora* 'Norwich Canary'
	'Lana de Savary'	CPrp CTca EBee EWes GCal IBal IBlr LRHS NBid NHol
	'Late Cornish'	see *C.* × *crocosmiiflora* 'Queen Alexandra' J.E. Fitt
	'Late Lucifer'	CHEx CTca CTri GCal IBlr LSRN SDix SMHy
	× ***latifolia***	see *C.* × *crocosmioides*
	'Limpopo'	CBgR CCVN CMac CMea CPar CTca CYeo EAEE EBee ECha ECtt ELon EPri GAbr GQue IBal LRHS MAvo MBNS MNrw MSCN NEgg NLar NPnk SBfd SMrm SPer WCot WWFP
	'Lucifer' ♀H4	Widely available
	'Malahide Castle Red'	SMad
	'Mandarin'	ECrc IBlr
	'Marcotijn'	CHVG CTca IBal IBlr IGor LRHS NHol
	masoniorum ♀H3	Widely available
	- from Satan's Nek, South Africa	CTca
	- 'African Dawn'	CTca ECrc ECtt
	- 'Amber'	IBlr
	- 'Dixter Flame'	ECtt IBlr IFoB SDix WOut
	- 'Firebird'	CTca GCra IBlr IGor LRHS NBre NHol NRHS WSpi
	- 'Flamenco'	IBlr
	- 'Golden Swan'	ECtt
	- Holehird strain	ECrc ECtt
	- 'Kiaora'	ECrc IBlr
	- 'Moira Reid'	ECrc IBlr NHol
	- red-flowered	IBlr
	- 'Rowallane Apricot'	IBlr
	- 'Rowallane Orange'	CPrp CTca GAbr GBin IBlr MAvo NHol
	- 'Rowallane Yellow' ♀H3-4	CPrp CTca ECtt GAbr GCal IBlr IGor LRHS MBri MMuc NCGa NHol SEND SMHy WCot WSHC
	- Slieve Donard selection	CTca ECrc IBal
	- 'Tropicana'	IBlr
	mathewsiana	IBlr
	mathewsiana* × *paniculata	CTca
	'Mex'	WCot
	'Minotaur'	IBlr
	'Miss Scarlet'	EPfP LRHS
	'Mistral'	CBgR CCCN CMea CTca EBee ECtt EPPr EPfP EPot GAbr GBuc GKev IBal IBlr LAst LRHS NBre NHol NRHS SBfd WMoo
	'Moorland Blaze'	WMoo
	'Mount Stewart'	see *C.* × *crocosmiiflora* 'Jessie'
	'Mr Bedford'	see *C.* × *crocosmiiflora* 'Croesus'
	'Mullard Pink'	CTca ECrc
	'Okavango'^PBR	CBgR CBre CBro CMac CTca CYeo EBee ECtt ELon EPri GAbr GQue IBal MAvo MBNS MCot MNrw NGdn NLar SKHP WCot WHil
	Old Hat	see *C.* 'Walberton Red'
	'Orange Devil'	CBre EBee ECtt EHrv GKin IBal IBlr LLHF MAvo MBNS MBri WHil
	'Orange Lucifer'	NBre
	'Orange River'	MAvo WCot
	'Orangeade'	CTca ECtt IBal IBlr LRHS NHol
	'Out of the West'	WOut
	'Pageant'	ECrc
§	***paniculata***	CMac CPou CTca ECtt GAbr MNFA NBid NHol NOrc SBfd SPet WBrk WCot WMoo WOut WShi
	- from Howick	CTca
	- from Kologha	CTca
	- brown/orange-flowered	IBlr
	- 'Cally Greyleaf'	EWld GCal
	- 'Cally Sword'	GCal
	- 'Major'	CTri IBlr
	- 'Natal'	CPrp CTca ECtt IBal NHol WFar
	- red-flowered	CTca IBlr LRHS SWvt
	- triploid	IBlr
	aff. ***paniculata***	ECtt IBlr

'Paul's Best Yellow'	CDes CSam CTca EBee ECGP ECtt ELon EWes GAbr IBal LLHF LRHS MAvo MBNS MTis NSti SHar SMad SMrm SPer SUsu SWvt WCot
pearsei	CTca IBlr
'Phillipa Browne'	CTca EBee ECtt GBin IBal LSou NEgg NLar WCot WMoo
pottsii	CBgR CTca ECtt GBin IBal IBlr LRHS NHol NLar WPtf WWEG
- CD&R 109	CPou
- 'Culzean Pink'	COlW CPLG CPrp CTca EBee GAbr GBin GCal IBal IBlr LPla LRHS MLHP MSpe NBid NBir NCot NHol WCot WOut
- deep pink-flowered	IBlr IGor WMoo
- 'Grandiflora'	IBlr
§ - 'Princess'	ECrc IBal
- tall	CTca
'Quantreau'	EBee IBlr NCot
'Queen Alexandria' **new**	LRHS
'R.W. Wallace'	CTca IBal NHol
'Red Devils'	NHol
'Red Star'	IBal
'Roman Gold'	IBlr
rosea	see *Tritonia disticha* subsp. *rubrolucens*
'Rowden Bronze'	see *C.* × *crocosmiiflora* 'Coleton Fishacre'
'Rowden Chrome'	see *C.* × *crocosmiiflora* 'George Davison' Davison
'Ruby Velvet'	IBlr
'Rubygold'	CPrp IBlr
'Saffron Queen'	IBlr
'Salsa'	WCot
'Saturn'	see *C.* 'Jupiter'
'Scarlatti'	CTca GAbr IBal IBlr NHol
'Severn Sunrise' ♀H3-4	Widely available
'Shocking'	EBee ECrc IBlr NCot NHol
'Sonate'	CTca NHol SPlb
'Spitfire'	CHVG CPLG CPrp CSam CTca CWCL ECha ECtt ELan GAbr IBal IBlr LHop LRHS MArl MAvo MRav NHol SWvt
§ 'Sulphurea'	CHVG CPLG CPou CPrp CSam ECtt EPfP IBal IBlr MAvo MSpe NHol SDix WBrk WCot WHal WPer
'Sunzest'	CTca ECrc MAvo
'Tamar Glow'	CTca
'Tamar New Dawn'	CTca
'Tamar Peace'	CTca
'Tangerine'	ECrc
'Tangerine Queen'	CTca CYeo ECrc ECtt GAbr IBal IBlr LRHS NHol SUsu WHil WMoo
'Tiger'	CElw CTca ECrc IBlr MAvo
'Vulcan' Leichtlin	see *C.* × *crocosmioides* 'Vulcan' Leichtlin
I 'Vulcan' A. Bloom	CTca CYeo ECtt GAbr IBal IBlr MAvo NHol SAga WCot
§ 'Walberton Red'	CTca ECrc EWes IBal IBlr LRHS MAvo MBri SAga SApp SKHP SMad SUsu WCot
Walberton Yellow = 'Walcroy'[PBR]	EPfP LRHS MAsh SApp SMHy SUsu WCot
with reflexed petals **new**	MAvo
'Zambesi'[PBR]	CDes CMac CTca CYeo EBee ECtt EHrv ELon GAbr GQue IBal LHop MBNS MBri MCot MNrw MTis NCGa NLar SBfd SKHP SPer WCot WHil WPGP
'Zeal Giant'	CRow CTca ECrc ECtt IBlr MAvo NHol
'Zeal Remembrance'	CTca
'Zeal Unnamed'	CPrp CTca EBee ECrc GBee IBal IBlr NHol WFar

Crocus ✿ (*Iridaceae*)

abantensis	ECho
'Advance'	CBro ECho EPot ERCP LAma MBri SDeJ WShi
alatavicus	ECho
albiflorus	see *C. vernus* subsp. *albiflorus*
ancyrensis	ECho EPot GKev LAma SDeJ
- 'Golden Bunch'	ECho SDeJ WShi
§ ***angustifolius*** ♀H4	ECho EPot GKev SDeJ
- 'Berlin Gold'	ECho
- bronze-tinged	NMin
- 'Minor'	ECho EPot
- 'Oreanda'	LWst
antalyensis	ECho LWst
- white-flowered	LWst
- yellow-flowered	LWst
'Ard Schenk'	ECho GKev LAma LRHS
asturicus	see *C. serotinus* subsp. *salzmannii*
asumaniae	ECho
'Aubade'	ECho EPot GKev
aureus	see *C. flavus* subsp. *flavus*
banaticus ♀H4	ECho EPot GKev LLHF LWst NHar NMen
- 'Snowdrift' **new**	NHar
baytopiorum	ECho NMen
biflorus	ECho
- subsp. ***adamii***	ECho
- subsp. ***biflorus***	ECho
- subsp. ***crewei***	ECho
- subsp. ***isauricus***	ECho
- subsp. ***melantherus***	ECho LWst
- 'Miss Vain'	ECho EPot ERCP GKev LAma MBri
- subsp. ***pulchricolor*** MP 8102	LWst
- subsp. ***punctatus*** **new**	ECho
- 'Serevan'	LWst NMin
- subsp. ***stridii***	LWst
- subsp. ***tauri***	ECho LWst
- subsp. ***weldenii***	ECho
- - 'Albus'	ECho EPot LAma
- - 'Fairy'	ECho LAma
'Blue Bird'	CBro ECho EPot LAma SPhx
'Blue Pearl' ♀H4	CAvo CBro ECho EPfP EPot GKev LRHS MBri NBir SDeJ SPer SPhx WShi
boryi	ECho WCot
- VV GR.1410	LWst
cambessedesii	ECho
§ ***cancellatus*** subsp. ***cancellatus***	ECho EPot GKev LAma LLHF
- var. ***cilicicus***	see *C. cancellatus* subsp. *cancellatus*
- subsp. ***lycius***	ECho EPot LWst
- subsp. ***mazziaricus***	EPot
- - large-flowered	LWst
- - 'Menalo'	LWst
- - 'Parnassus'	LWst
- - 'Pilion'	LWst
- - 'Rendina'	LWst
- subsp. ***pamphylicus***	ECho
candidus	ECho
- 'Lune'	ECho LWst

	Name	Suppliers
	- var. ***subflavus***	see *C. olivieri* subsp. *olivieri*
	cartwrightianus ♀H4	ECho GKev LLHF LRHS SPhx
	- CE&H 613	LWst
	- 'Albus' misapplied	see *C. hadriaticus*
N	- 'Albus' Tubergen ♀H4	ECho EPot GKev SDeJ
	- 'Halloween'	LWst
	- white-flowered clone	LWst
	chrysanthus ♀H4	CHab
	- 'Afyon'	LWst
	- 'Blue Peter'	ECho LWst
	- 'Cream Beauty' ♀H4	CAvo CBro CMea ECho EPfP EPot GKev LAma LRHS MBri NBir SDeJ SPhx WShi
	- 'E.A. Bowles' ♀H4	ECho
	- 'E.P. Bowles'	LAma MBri
	- 'Early Gold'	ECho LWst
	- var. ***fuscotinctus***	ECho EPfP EPot LAma MBri SDeJ
	- late-flowering VV GB.235	LWst
	- 'Milea'	LWst
	- 'Moonlight'	LAma
	- 'Uschak Orange'	ECho
	- 'Warley'	ECho
	- 'Zwanenburg Bronze' ♀H4	ECho EPfP GKev LAma
	'Cloth of Gold'	see *C. angustifolius*
	clusii	see *C. serotinus* subsp. *clusii*
	corsicus ♀H4	ECho EPot LWst
	cvijicii	LWst
	dalmaticus	EPot
	- 'Petrovac'	LWst
	danfordiae	ECho
	'Dorothy'	ECho EPot GKev LAma
	'Dutch Yellow'	see *C.* × *luteus* 'Golden Yellow'
	'Ego'	ECho LWst
	etruscus ♀H4	ECho LWst
	- 'Rosalind'	ECho
	- 'Zwanenburg' ♀H4	ECho EPot GKev LAma LRHS SDeJ
	flavus	ECho
§	- subsp. ***flavus*** ♀H4	ECho EPot LAma WShi
	fleischeri	ECho EPot LAma
	gargaricus subsp. ***herbertii***	LWst
	'Gipsy Girl'	CAvo ECho EPot ERCP LAma MBri SPhx
	'Golden Mammoth'	see *C.* × *luteus* 'Golden Yellow'
	'Goldilocks' ♀H4	ECho GKev LAma SDeJ WShi
	goulimyi ♀H4	CBro ECho EPot GKev LAma LLHF SDeJ WCot
	- 'Albus'	see *C. goulimyi* subsp. *goulimyi* 'Mani White'
§	- subsp. ***goulimyi*** 'Mani White' ♀H4	CAvo SCnR
	- subsp. ***leucanthus*** HOA 0183	LWst
§	***hadriaticus*** ♀H4	ECho EPot GKev LAma LLHF
	- 'Alepohori'	LWst
	- var. ***chrysobelonicus***	see *C. hadriaticus*
	- subsp. ***hadriaticus*** f. ***lilacinus***	EPot LWst
	- 'Jumbo'	LWst
	'Herald'	CAvo ECho LAma
	imperati subsp. ***imperati*** var. ***albus*** new	WAbe
	- subsp. ***suaveolens***	ECho EPot
	- - 'De Jager'	ECho ERCP LAma
	'Janis Ruksans'	CAvo LWst
	'Jeanne d'Arc'	CAvo CBro ECho EPfP EPot GKev LAma MBri NBir SDeJ WShi
	'Jeannine'	ECho EPot SDeJ
	× ***jessoppiae***	ECho LWst
	karduchorum	ECho LAma
	korolkowii	CGrW ECho GKev LAma LWst
	- 'Golden Nugget'	EPot
	- 'Kiss of Spring'	ECho EPot
	kosaninii	ECho EPot NMin
	- CH 801	LWst
	- 'April View'	EPot NMin
	kotschyanus ♀H4	ECho NRya
	- 'Albus'	ECho SDeJ
§	- subsp. ***kotschyanus***	ECho EPot LAma SDeJ
	- 'Reliance'	ECho LWst
	kotschyanus × ***ochroleucus***	ECho
	'Ladykiller' ♀H4	CAvo CBro ECho EPot ERCP GKev LAma MBri NMin SPhx WShi
	laevigatus ♀H4	ECho WCot
	- CE&H 612	LWst
	- HOA 0138	LWst
	- HOA 0153	LWst
	- 'Fontenayi'	CBro ECho EPot ERCP GKev
	- white-flowered	ECho
	'Large Yellow'	see *C.* × *luteus* 'Golden Yellow'
	ligusticus	ECho
	'Little Amber'	LWst
	longiflorus ♀H4	CBro ECho GEdr LLHF
§	× ***luteus*** 'Golden Yellow' ♀H4	CAvo EPfP EPot GKev LAma WShi
§	- 'Stellaris' ♀H4	ECho
	malyi ♀H4	ECho NMin
	- 'Ballerina'	ECho LWst
	- 'Sveti Roc'	EPot LWst
	mathewii	ECho EPot WCot
	- HKEP 9291	LWst
	- 'Dream Dancer'	LWst
	medius ♀H4	CBro EPot LAma
	minimus	ECho EPot ERCP LAma LLHF
	niveus	CBro ECho EPot GKev LAma LLHF
	- VV GR.1410	LWst
	- VV KA.2312	LWst
	nudiflorus	ECho EPot GKev LAma LLHF NMen
	ochroleucus ♀H4	ECho EPot GKev LLHF SDeJ
	olivieri	ECho
	- subsp. ***balansae***	ECho
	- - 'Zwanenburg'	ECho EPot
	- subsp. ***istanbulensis***	LWst
§	- subsp. ***olivieri***	ECho
	- - HOA 0156	LWst
	- - 'Little Tiger'	ECho LWst
	oreocreticus	ECho
	pallasii	ECho
	- VV KR.75	LWst
	- subsp. ***pallasii***	ECho
	- subsp. ***turcicus*** VV TW.855	LWst
	- white-flowered	LWst
	paschei HKEP 9034	LWst
	pelistericus	LWst
	pestalozzae	ECho
	- var. ***caeruleus***	ECho
	- - CRO 401	LWst
	'Prins Claus'	ECho EPfP EPot ERCP LAma MBri SBch SDeJ
	'Prinses Beatrix'	ECho NMin
	pulchellus ♀H4	ECho EPot ERCP GKev LAma NRHS
	- 'Albus'	ECho EPot
	- 'Inspiration'	ECho

- 'Michael Hoog' ECho
'Purple Heart' LWst
'Purpureus' see *C. vernus* 'Purpureus Grandiflorus'
reticulatus ECho
- VVYY.306 LWst
- subsp. ***reticulatus*** ECho EPot
robertianus HOA 9856 LWst
'Romance' CAvo EPot GKev LAma MBri SDeJ SPer
'Ruby Giant' CAvo CBro ECho EPfP EPot GKev LAma MBri NBir SDeJ SPer SPhx WShi
rujanensis ECho LWst
salzmannii see *C. serotinus* subsp. *salzmannii*
sativus CArn CAvo CBro CPrp CTca ECho ELan EOHP EPot ERCP GKev GPoy LAma NBir SDeJ SVic
'Saturnus' EPot LAma
scardicus LWst
scepusiensis see *C. vernus* subsp. *vernus*
§ ***serotinus*** subsp. ***clusii*** ECho LAma
§ - subsp. ***salzmannii*** ECho LAma LLHF
- - HOA 9911 LWst
- - KPW 9425 LWst
- - KPW 9432 LWst
- - 'Atropurpureus' WCot
sibiricus see *C. sieberi*
§ ***sieberi*** ♀H4 EPot
§ - 'Albus' ♀H4 CAvo CBro ECho EPot GKev SDeJ
- subsp. ***atticus*** ECho LAma
- - 'Firefly' ECho EPot GKev LAma SDeJ SPhx
- - 'Stunner' LWst
- 'Bowles' White' see *C. sieberi* 'Albus'
- 'Hubert Edelsten' ♀H4 ECho LAma
- 'Ronald Ginns' EPot
- subsp. ***sublimis*** 'Tricolor' ♀H4 CAvo CBro CTca ECho EPfP EPot GKev LAma MBri NBir SDeJ SPer
- 'Vardousia' LWst
- 'Violet Queen' ECho LAma
'Snow Bunting' ♀H4 CAvo CBro CTca ECho EPfP EPot GKev LAma NBir SDeJ SPer SPhx WShi
speciosus ♀H4 CAvo CBro CTca LAma MLHP NBir SDeJ SPer WCot WShi
- 'Aino' ECho LWst
- 'Aitchisonii' ECho EPot GKev LAma LRHS NRHS
- 'Albus' ♀H4 CAvo CBro ECho EPot ERCP GKev
- 'Artabir' ECho EPot GKev LRHS SDeJ
- 'Cassiope' ECho EPot GKev LAma LRHS NRHS SDeJ
- 'Conqueror' CBro ECho EPot ERCP GKev LAma LRHS SDeJ WBor
- 'Lithuanian Autumn' LWst
- 'Oxonian' ECho EPot GKev LAma LWst SPhx
- subsp. ***speciosus*** ECho EPot SDeJ
- subsp. ***xantholaimos*** LWst
'Spring Beauty' **new** CAvo EPfP SDeJ
× ***stellaris*** see *C.* × *luteus* 'Stellaris'
susianus see *C. angustifolius*
suterianus see *C. olivieri* subsp. *olivieri*
tommasinianus ♀H4 CAvo CBro CGrW CHab CMea CTca ECho EPot LAma LLWP MBri MRav NBir SDeJ SPhx SRms WShi
- 'Albus' CMea ECho EPot LAma WShi
- 'Barr's Purple' ECho EPot GKev LAma SDeJ
- 'Claret' ECho
- 'Lilac Beauty' ECho EPfP EPot LAma SPer
- 'Pictus' ECho EPot LAma LLHF WShi
- 'Roseus' CAvo ECho EPot ERCP GKev LAma NMin SPhx WCot WShi
- 'Whitewell Purple' CAvo CBro ECho EPot ERCP GKev LAma MBri NBir SDeJ WShi
tournefortii ♀H2-4 ECho EPot SCnR
* - 'Albus' ECho
vallicola LWst
'Vanguard' ♀H4 CAvo CBro ECho EPfP EPot LAma SBch SDeJ
veluchensis ECho
veneris ECho
§ ***vernus*** subsp. ***albiflorus*** ECho EPot
- 'Fantasy' ECho WShi
- 'Flower Record' ECho GKev LAma NBir
- 'Graecus' ECho EPot
- 'Grand Maître' CAvo LAma MBri SDeJ
- 'Haarlem Gem' ECho EPot
- 'King of the Striped' ECho LAma SPer
- 'Krasno Polje' LWst
- 'Michael's Purple' ECho
- 'Negro Boy' ECho EPot GKev LAma
- 'Pickwick' CAvo ECho EPfP EPot LAma MBri NBir SDeJ WShi
§ - 'Purpureus Grandiflorus' CBro EPot SDeJ
- 'Queen of the Blues' CBro EPot GKev WShi
- 'Remembrance' CAvo CBro ECho EPfP EPot GKev LAma NBir SDeJ WShi
- 'Tatra Shades' ECho
- 'Twilight' EPot
- Uklin strain ECho
§ - subsp. ***vernus*** ECho
- - 'Grandiflorus' see *C. vernus* 'Purpureus Grandiflorus'
- - Heuffelianus Group ECho EPot
- - var. ***neapolitanus*** LWst
versicolor ECho
- 'Picturatus' CMea ECho EPot ERCP LAma LLHF NMin SDeJ
vitellinus ECho EPot LWst
- white-flowered **new** LWst
'White Triumphator' LAma
'Yalta' ECho ERCP GKev SPhx
'Yellow Giant' **new** SDeJ
'Yellow Mammoth' see *C.* × *luteus* 'Golden Yellow'
'Zenith' ECho EPot
'Zephyr' ♀H4 CBro ECho EPot LAma
zonatus see *C. kotschyanus* subsp. *kotschyanus*

Croomia (*Stemonaceae*)

heterosepala WCru

Crotalaria (*Papilionaceae*)

laburnifolia CCCN

Crowea (*Rutaceae*)

exalata × ***saligna*** CPLG

Crucianella (*Rubiaceae*)

stylosa see *Phuopsis stylosa*

Cruciata (*Rubiaceae*)

§ ***laevipes*** NMir

Crusea (*Rubiaceae*)

coccinea SBrt
- 'Crûg Crimson' WCru

Cryptanthus (*Bromeliaceae*)

Black Mystic Group **new**	EAmu

Cryptocarya (*Lauraceae*)

alba	CBcs GBin IArd

Cryptogramma (*Pteridaceae*)

crispa	WHer

Cryptomeria ✿ (*Cupressaceae*)

	fortunei	see *C. japonica* var. *sinensis*
	japonica ΨH4	CDul CMen CTho ELau EPfP MBlu MMuc SEND WEve
	- Araucarioides Group	EHul NLar
	- 'Atawai'	NLar
	- 'Aurea'	ELan
	- 'Bandai'	LBuc
	- 'Bandai-sugi' ΨH4	CKen CMac CMen EHul EPfP EPot GKin LRHS MGos NHol NLar SCoo SLim WGor
	- 'Barabits Gold'	MGos WEve
	- 'Birodo'	CKen
	- 'Black Dragon'	SLim
	- 'Compressa'	CDoC CKen EHul EPfP LBee MGos SCoo SLim WGor WThu
§	- 'Cristata'	CBcs CDoC CMac ELan LRHS MGos MPkF SLim SPoG
	- 'Dacrydioides'	CDoC GKin NLar SLim
	- Elegans Group	CBcs CDoy CDul CMac CSBt ECrN EHul ELan EPfP LAst LRHS MBri MGos MMuc NEgg NLar NWea SBfd SCoo SEND SLim SPer SPoG WFar
	- 'Elegans Aurea'	EHul ELan WEve
	- 'Elegans Compacta' ΨH4	CDoC CMac CSBt CWib EHul ELan LBee LRHS MBri MMuc NLar NWea SCoo SEND SLim SPoG WEve
	- 'Elegans Nana'	LBee LRHS NEgg SRms WBor
	- 'Elegans Viridis'	ELan LRHS NEgg SBod SLim SPer SPoG
	- 'Globosa Nana' ΨH4	EHul EPfP ERom LAst LBee LRHS MGos NEgg SCoo SLim SPoG WFar WGor
	- 'Golden Promise'	LRHS NWad SCoo SLim WEve WGor
	- Gracilis Group	CDoC
	- 'Jindai-sugi'	GKin NLar
	- 'Karl Fuchs'	SLim
	- 'Kilmacurragh'	CKen EHul NWea SLim
	- 'Knaptonensis' (v)	CDoC WEve
	- 'Kohui-yatsubusa'	CKen
*	- 'Konijn-yatsubusa'	CKen
	- 'Koshyi'	CKen
	- 'Little Champion'	CDoC CKen LRHS NLar SLim
	- 'Little Diamond'	CKen
	- 'Little Sonja' **new**	SLim
	- 'Littleworth Dwarf'	see *C. japonica* 'Littleworth Gnom'
§	- 'Littleworth Gnom'	NLar
	- 'Lobbii Nana' hort.	see *C. japonica* 'Nana'
§	- 'Mankichi-sugi'	WEve
	- 'Monstrosa Nana'	see *C. japonica* 'Mankichi-sugi'
	- 'Mushroom'	WFar
§	- 'Nana'	CDoC CMac EHul EPfP WFar
	- 'Osaka-tama'	CKen
	- 'Pipo'	CKen
	- 'Pygmaea'	MGos NHol NWad SRms
	- 'Rasen'	ELan
	- 'Rasen-sugi'	GKin IVic LRHS MGos SCoo SLim SMad SPoG
	- 'Rein's Dense Jade'	SLim
	- 'Sekkan-sugi'	CBcs CDoC CDul CMac EHul EPfP ESwi GBin GKin IArd LAst LBee LRHS MGos NLar SBfd SCoo SLim SPoG WBor WEve WFar
	- 'Sekka-sugi'	see *C. japonica* 'Cristata'
§	- var. ***sinensis***	CMCN
*	- - 'Vilmoriniana Compacta'	MAsh
§	- 'Spiralis'	CDoC CKen CMac EHul ELan EPfP GKin LAst LBee LRHS MGos NEgg NHol NWad NWea SCoo SLim SPer SPoG WEve WFar
§	- 'Spiraliter Falcata'	CDoC NLar
§	- 'Tansu'	CDoC CKen
	- 'Tenzan-sugi'	CDoC CKen MGos NWad SLim WThu
	- 'Tilford Cream'	MAsh
	- 'Tilford Gold'	EHul EPot MGos NEgg NHol WEve WFar WGor
	- 'Toda'	CKen
	- 'Top Gold' (v)	NLar
	- 'Vilmorin Gold'	CKen MGos NHol WFar
	- 'Vilmoriniana' ΨH4	CDoC CKen CMen CTri EHul EPfP EPot GKin LBee MBri MGos NEgg NHol SCoo SLim SPer SPoG WEve WFar WMoo
	- 'Winter Bronze'	CKen
	- 'Yatsubusa'	see *C. japonica* 'Tansu'
	- 'Yore-sugi'	see *C. japonica* 'Spiralis', 'Spiraliter Falcata'
	- 'Yoshino'	CKen LRHS SLim
	sinensis	see *C. japonica* var. *sinensis*

Cryptostegia (*Apocynaceae*)

grandiflora	CCCN

Cryptotaenia (*Apiaceae*)

japonica	CHby CPou MHer MNHC WHer WJek
- f. ***atropurpurea***	CSpe EBee EHoe LEdu MBel MNrw SDix SPhx WFar

Ctenanthe (*Marantaceae*)

	lubbersiana ΨH1	XBlo
§	***oppenheimiana***	XBlo

Cucubalus (*Caryophyllaceae*)

baccifer	EWld NLar WPer

Cudrania see *Maclura*

cumin see *Cuminum cyminum*

Cuminum (*Apiaceae*)

cyminum	CArn ELau MNHC SIde SVic

Cunninghamia (*Cupressaceae*)

	konishii	CPLG
	- 'Coolyns Compact'	WThu
§	***lanceolata***	CBcs CDTJ CDoC CDul CGHE CKen CMCN CMac CTho EPfP GKin LRHS MBlu SBfd SLim SMad SSpi SSta WBor WEve WPGP
	- 'Glauca'	CJun CPLG CTho IVic
	- 'Little Leo'	CKen LRHS
	sinensis	see *C. lanceolata*
	unicaniculata	see *C. lanceolata*

Cunonia (*Cunoniaceae*)

	capensis	CPLG

Cuphea (*Lythraceae*)

	caeciliae	SGar WWlt
	cyanea	CMHG SDix WWlt
	'Firecracker'	NPri
	hyssopifolia ♀H1	CHll SBfd SWvt
	- 'Alba'	CCCN SBfd SWvt
	- pink-flowered	CCCN SBfd
	- red-flowered	CCCN
	- 'Rosea'	SEND SWvt
§	***ignea*** ♀H1	SVic WWlt
§	***llavea*** 'Georgia Scarlet'	CCCN LAst LSou WWlt
	- 'Tiny Mice'	see *C. llavea* 'Georgia Scarlet'
I	***macrophylla*** hort.	CHll WWlt
	maculata	CCCN
	platycentra	see *C. ignea*
	'Torpedo'	LSou
	'Vienco Lavender'	LSou
	viscosissima	CSpe MCot

× *Cupressocyparis* see × *Cuprocyparis*

Cupressus (*Cupressaceae*)

	arizonica var. ***arizonica*** 'Arctic'	CDoC SLim
§	- var. ***glabra***	SEND
	- - 'Angaston'	SLim
	- - 'Aurea'	CMac EHul LRHS MAsh MGos NPCo SGol SLim WBor WFar
	- - 'Blue Ice' ♀H3	CBcs CDoC CDul CMac CTho EHul LRHS MAsh MGos NPCo SCoo SLim SPer SPoG SWvt WFar
	- - 'Compacta'	CKen
	- - 'Conica'	CKen
I	- - 'Fastigiata'	CCVT CDoC ECrN EHul EPfP LMaj SBfd
	- - 'Glauca'	EPfP MBlu
*	- - 'Lutea'	SPoG
	- 'Pyramidalis' ♀H3	ECrN EPfP SEND SGol
	atlantica	LRHS SLim
	cashmeriana ♀H2	CBcs CDTJ CDoC CTho ELan IGor IVic LRHS NPCo SLim WFar
§	***funebris***	IArd
	glabra	see *C. arizonica* var. *glabra*
	lusitanica 'Brice's Weeping'	CKen LRHS SLim
	- 'Brookhall'	IArd
	- 'Glauca Pendula'	CDoC CKen
	- 'Pygmy'	CKen
	macrocarpa	CBcs CCVT CDoC CDul CTho EHul SEND
	- 'Compacta'	CKen
	- 'Conybearii Aurea'	NPCo
	- 'Gold Spread'	EHul LRHS SLim WFar
	- 'Goldcrest' ♀H3	CBcs CCVT CDoC CDul CMac ECrN EHul ELan LBee LRHS MBri MGos NBir NPri NWea SBfd SEND SEWo SGol SLim SPer SPoG SWvt WCFE WEve WFar
	- 'Golden Cone'	CKen NPCo SEND
	- 'Golden Pillar' ♀H3	CDoC CMac EHul SWvt WFar
	- 'Golden Spire'	WFar
	- 'Greenstead Magnificent'	LRHS SLim
	- 'Horizontalis Aurea'	EHul
	- 'Lohbrunner'	CKen
	- 'Lutea'	CDoC NPCo WFar
I	- 'Pendula'	SLim
	- 'Pygmaea'	CKen
	- 'Sulphur Cushion'	CKen
	- 'Wilma'	CSBt EHul LAst LBee LRHS MAsh MGos NEgg SBfd SCoo SGol SLim SPoG SWvt
	- 'Woking'	CKen
	sempervirens	CDul CMCN CPne EAmu EHul ELan ERom LRHS MAsh NPri SBfd SHil SPlb WEve WFar
	- 'Bolgheri'	SBig
	- 'Garda'	CDoC
	- 'Green Pencil'	CKen WEve
	- 'Northdown Column' **new**	SEND
	- 'Pyramidalis'	see *C. sempervirens* Stricta Group
	- var. ***sempervirens***	see *C. sempervirens* Stricta Group
§	- Stricta Group ♀H3	CBcs CCVT CDul CKen CMCN CTho EHul EPfP EWTr MREP NLar SBfd SEND SEWo SGol WCFE WEve
	- 'Swane's Gold'	CBcs CDoC CDul CKen EHul EPfP LRHS NPCo SLim SPoG WCFE WEve WFar
	- 'Totem Pole'	CCVT CKen CSBt CTho CTri EHul EPfP EUJe LBee LRHS MGos NEgg SCoo SEND SHil SLim SPoG SWvt WEve

× *Cuprocyparis* (*Cupressaceae*)

§	***leylandii*** ♀H4	CBcs CCVT CDoC CDul CMac CTri ECrN EHul EPfP LBuc LRHS LSRN MAsh MBri MGos MMuc NEgg NPri NWea SBfd SEND SGol SLim SPer SPoG SWvt WEve WHar WMou
I	- '2001'	CCVT CDoC SGol SLim WMou
	- 'Blue Jeans' PBR	SEND
§	- 'Castlewellan'	CBcs CCVT CDoC CDul CMac CTri EHul EPfP ERom LBuc LRHS LSRN MAsh MBri MGos MMuc NPri NWea SBfd SEND SGol SLim SPer SPoG SWvt WEve WFar WHar WMou
	- Excalibur Gold = 'Drabb' PBR	CDoC
	- 'Ferngold'	MAsh
	- 'Galway Gold'	see × *C. leylandii* 'Castlewellan'
	- 'Gold Rider' ♀H4	CDoC EHul LBuc LTen MAsh MGos MMuc NEgg NWea SCoo SEND SMad SPer SPoG SWvt WEve WHar
	- 'Haggerston Grey' **new**	SEND
§	- 'Harlequin' (v)	CMac SEND SWvt
	- 'Herculea'	CDoC NPri
	- 'Leighton Green'	WMou
	- 'Naylor's Blue'	CMac
	- 'Olive's Green'	EHul SWvt
	- 'Robinson's Gold' ♀H4	CMac EHul GQui LRHS NWea SEND SLim WFar WMou
	- 'Silver Dust' (v)	WFar
	- 'Variegata'	see × *C. leylandii* 'Harlequin'
	- 'Winter Sun'	WCFE
	ovensii	EHul

Curculigo (*Hypoxidaceae*)

	capitulata	XBlo
	crassifolia B&SWJ 2318	WCru

Curcuma ✿ (*Zingiberaceae*)

	aeruginosa 'Indian Surprise' **new**	GHim

alismatifolia	EPfP SDeJ
longa	CArn WHer
roscoeana	GHim LAma SDeJ
zedoaria	LAma
- 'Bicolor Wonder'	CCCN GHim SBst
- 'Pink Wonder'	CCCN GHim
- 'White Wonder'	CCCN GHim SDeJ

Curtonus see *Crocosmia*

Cussonia (*Araliaceae*)

paniculata	CDTJ CWGN EAmu EShb EUJe WCot
spicata	CDTJ

custard apple see *Annona cherimola*

Cyananthus (*Campanulaceae*)

integer misapplied	see *C. microphyllus*
lobatus ♀H4	LLHF
- 'Albus'	EPot EWes WAbe
- dark	WAbe
- giant	EPot GEdr NHar WAbe
- 'Midnight'	GEdr
lobatus × microphyllus	EPot WAbe
§ ***microphyllus*** ♀H4	EPot GEdr GJos GMaP NSla WAbe
sherriffii	EPot GJos IFoB WAbe
spathulifolius	WAbe

Cyanotis (*Commelinaceae*)

somaliensis ♀H1	EShb

Cyathea (*Cyatheaceae*)

australis	CBty CDTJ CKel EAmu ESwi ETod LRHS MGos
brownii	ISha
cooperi	CDTJ CKel EAmu ESwi LRHS WFib
* - 'Brentwood'	ISha
cunninghamii	EAmu
dealbata	CDTJ CKel EAmu MGos
dregei	SPlb
medullaris	CKel EAmu LRHS MGos
milnei	CDTJ
smithii	CDTJ CKel EAmu
tomentosissima	CDTJ CKel EAmu

Cyathodes (*Ericaceae*)

colensoi	see *Leucopogon colensoi*
empetrifolia	see *Androstoma empetrifolia*
fraseri	see *Leucopogon fraseri*
juniperina	see *Leptecophylla juniperina*
parviflora	see *Leucopogon parviflorus*

Cybistetes (*Amaryllidaceae*)

longifolia	WCot

Cycas (*Cycadaceae*)

circinalis	EAmu
panzhihuaensis	CBrP SPlb
revoluta ♀H1	CAbb CBrP CCCN CDoC CHEx CTrC EAmu EPfP EUJe MBri MREP NLar SBfd SBst SChr SEND SMad STrG WCot XBlo
revoluta × taitungensis	CBrP
§ ***rumphii***	CBrP
taitungensis	CBrP
thouarsii	see *C. rumphii*

Cyclamen ✿ (*Primulaceae*)

africanum	CBro ECho EJWh EPot GKev LAma LRHS LWst MAsh NRHS WCot
africanum × hederifolium	ECho
§ ***alpinum***	CBro ECho EJWh EPot GKev LAma LLHF LRHS LWst MAsh NRHS SDeJ
- 'Nettleton White'	MAsh
balearicum	CBro ECho EJWh EPot LAma LRHS LWst MAsh NMen
cilicium ♀H2-4	CBro ECho EJWh EPfP ERCP GBuc LAma LRHS LWst MAsh MHer MWat NMen NRHS WHoo WIvy WPat WShi
- f. ***album***	CBro ECho EJWh GBuc LAma LLHF LRHS LWst MAsh NMen NRHS WCot
- patterned-leaved	ECho NBir
colchicum	ECho MAsh
§ ***coum*** ♀H4	Widely available
- var. ***abchasicum***	see *C. coum* subsp. *caucasicum*
§ - subsp. ***caucasicum***	LWst MAsh
- subsp. ***coum***	CBro ECho LEdu MAsh
- - f. ***albissimum***	GBuc
- - - 'George Bisson'	MAsh
- - - 'Golan Heights'	MAsh WIvy
- - f. ***coum*** Nymans Group	MAsh
- - - Pewter Group ♀H2-4	ECho GBuc GKev MAsh WIvy
- - - - bicoloured	EJWh
- - - - 'Blush'	GBuc
- - - - 'Maurice Dryden'	CBro CLAP ECho LAma LHop LRHS LWst MAsh NRHS WHoo
- - - - red-flowered	LAma WPat
- - - - 'Tilebarn Elizabeth'	GEdr MAsh NBir WHoo
- - - - white-flowered	MAsh
- - - 'Roseum'	CAvo GBuc LRHS
- - - Silver Group	CAvo CBro ECho GEdr LHop LRHS LWst NPnk NRya WHoo
- - - - red-flowered	EPot WHoo
- - magenta-flowered	CWCL WHoo
- - f. ***pallidum*** 'Album'	CAvo ECho EPot GKev LAma LWst MAsh NMen SDeJ SMrm SPer WHoo WPat
- dark pink-flowered	CAvo CLAP ECho WHoo
- hybrid	ERCP
- marble-leaved	ECho LHop WHoo
- plain-leaved	CLAP
- red-flowered	CLAP ECho NWad
I - 'Rubrum'	GKev LWst
- silver speckled leaf **new**	EHrv NRHS
- 'Tilebarn Graham'	MAsh
creticum	ECho EJWh MAsh NRHS
cyprium	CBro ECho EJWh LRHS LWst MAsh
- 'E.S.'	ECho MAsh
- 'Galaxy'	MAsh
elegans	EJWh MAsh
europaeum	see *C. purpurascens*
fatrense	see *C. purpurascens* subsp. *purpurascens* from Fatra, Slovakia
graecum	CBro ECho EJWh LLHF LRHS MAsh NMen NRHS WCot WIvy WThu XEll
- subsp. ***anatolicum***	MAsh
- subsp. ***candicum***	EPot MAsh
- subsp. ***graecum*** f. ***album***	CBro ECho EJWh LRHS LWst MAsh
- - f. ***graecum*** 'Glyfada'	MAsh

§ ***hederifolium*** ΨH4	Widely available
- S&L 175/1	WCot XLum
- arrow-head	CLAP ECho SBea
- var. ***confusum***	MAsh WCot
- var. ***hederifolium*** f. ***albiflorum***	CAvo CBro CTri ECho EHrv EPot GKev LAma LEdu LRHS NMen NPnk NWad SDeJ WCot WHoo WPat WPnP XLum
- - - 'Album'	MAsh
- - - Bowles's Apollo Group	GBuc
§ - - - - 'Artemis'	MAsh
- - - - 'White Bowles's Apollo'	see *C. hederifolium* var. *hederifolium* f. *albiflorum* (Bowles's Apollo Group) 'Artemis'
- - - 'Daley Thompson'	WCot
- - - 'Linnett Stargazer'	WCot
- - - 'Nettleton Silver'	see *C. hederifolium* var. *hederifolium* f. *albiflorum* 'White Cloud'
- - - 'Perlenteppich'	GMaP
- - - silver-leaved **new**	SDys
§ - - - 'White Cloud'	CLAP ECho MAsh WCot WHoo WIvy
- - f. ***hederifolium*** Bowles's Apollo Group	CHid CLAP ECGP GBuc MAsh
- - - 'Fairy Rings'	MAsh
- - - 'Ruby Glow'	GBuc LRHS MAsh NBir WCot WPat WThu
- - - Silver Cloud Group	CBro CHid CLAP EHrv GBuc MAsh NBir WCot WHoo WIvy WPat
- - - 'Silver Shield'	MAsh
- - - 'Stargazer'	LLHF MAsh WCot
- - 'Tilebarn Silver Arrow'	MAsh
- island scented strain	WCot
- 'Pewter Mist'	LAma
- 'Rose Pearls'	SRot
- 'San Marino Silver'	GEdr
- scented	NWad
- Silver-leaved Group	ECho EPot LHop MAsh SBea SRot WFar
× ***hildebrandii***	EWld LLHF
ibericum	see *C. coum* subsp. *caucasicum*
intaminatum	CBro ECho EJWh LAma LLHF LRHS LWst MAsh NMen NRHS WIvy
- patterned-leaved	EJWh MAsh
- pink-flowered	MAsh NMen
- plain-leaved	MAsh WThu
latifolium	see *C. persicum*
libanoticum	CBro ECho EJWh EPot LAma LRHS LWst MAsh NMen NRHS XEll
mirabile ΨH2-3	CBro ECho EJWh EPot GBuc GKev LAma LLHF LRHS LWst MAsh NMen NRHS SDeJ WIvy WThu
- f. ***mirabile*** 'Tilebarn Anne'	MAsh
- - 'Tilebarn Nicholas'	ECho MAsh
- f. ***niveum***	EJWh
- - 'Tilebarn Jan'	ECho MAsh
neapolitanum	see *C. hederifolium*
orbiculatum	see *C. coum*
parviflorum	EJWh MAsh
§ ***persicum***	CBro CWCL ECho EJWh GBuc LRHS MAsh NRHS
- white-flowered	ECho MAsh
pseudibericum ΨH2-3	CBro ECho EJWh EPot GKev LAma LHop LLHF LRHS LWst MAsh NMen NRHS SDeJ WThu
- AC&W 664	NMen
- f. ***roseum***	MAsh NMen
§ ***purpurascens*** ΨH4	CBro ECho EJWh GBuc LLHF MAsh NMen WHoo WIvy WPat
- var. ***fatrense***	see *C. purpurascens* subsp. *purpurascens* from Fatra, Slovakia
- 'Lake Garda'	MAsh
§ - subsp. ***purpurascens*** from Fatra, Slovakia	MAsh
repandum	CAvo CBro ECho EHrv EJWh LAma LLHF LRHS LWst MAsh NMen SCnR WHer
- 'Pelops' misapplied	see *C. rhodium* subsp. *peloponnesiacum*
- subsp. ***repandum*** f. ***album***	EJWh MAsh
rhodium ΨH2-3	EJWh LWst MAsh WCot
§ - subsp. ***peloponnesiacum***	ECGP
- subsp. ***rhodium***	MAsh
- subsp. ***vividum***	MAsh
rohlfsianum	CBro ECho EJWh LLHF LRHS MAsh
× ***saundersiae***	EJWh MAsh
× ***schwarzii***	MAsh
trochopteranthum	see *C. alpinum*
× ***wellensiekii***	MAsh

Cyclea (*Menispermaceae*)

polypetala KWJ 12157	WCru

Cydonia ✿ (*Rosaceae*)

japonica	see *Chaenomeles speciosa*
oblonga (F)	ECrN ERom LMaj
- 'Agvambari' (F)	SKee
- 'Champion' (F)	CAgr CBcs CMam ECrN GTwe LBuc MCoo NEgg NLar SKee SVic WHar
- 'Early Prolific' (F)	MMuc SEND
- 'Ekmek' (F)	SKee
- 'Isfahan' (F)	SKee
- 'Krymsk' (F)	CAgr
- 'Leskovac' (F)	CAgr EPom NLar
§ - 'Lusitanica' (F)	CAgr ECrN GTwe MCoo SKee SPer WHar
- 'Meech's Prolific' (F)	CAgr CDul CLnd CTho CTri ECrN EMil EPom GTwe LRHS MBlu MBri MGos MRav MWat NLar NWea SBfd SEWo SFam SKee SLim SPer SPoG WHar
- pear-shaped (F)	ECrN NEgg SPer
- Portugal	see *C. oblonga* 'Lusitanica'
- 'Rea's Mammoth' (F)	NLar
- 'Seibosa' (F)	SKee
- 'Serbian Gold' (F)	CTho EPom GTwe LRHS MBri WHar
- 'Shams' (F)	SKee
- 'Sobu' (F)	SKee
- 'Vranja' (F) ΨH4	Widely available

Cymbalaria (*Plantaginaceae*)

§ ***hepaticifolia***	WPer
§ ***muralis***	ECho ECtt GAbr LBMP MHer NPri WGor WIce XLum
- 'Albiflora'	see *C. muralis* 'Pallidior'
- 'Kenilworth White'	WMoo
- 'Nana Alba'	MSCN WPer
§ - 'Pallidior'	ECho
§ ***pallida***	CPBP MMuc NSla SBch SEND SPlb WMoo WPer
- 'Alba'	MMuc SEND WMoo
§ ***pilosa***	ECtt NLar

Cymbopogon (Poaceae)

citratus	CArn CCCN EGHP ENfk GPoy MHoo MNHC SBfd SHDw SIde SVic WJek
flexuosus	CCCN ELau MHer MHoo WJek
martini	CArn
nardus	CArn GPoy

Cymophyllus (Cyperaceae)

§ ***fraserianus***	CDes CHEx GBin

Cynanchum (Apocynaceae)

acuminatifolium	GBin GCal
ascyrifolium	EBee

Cynara (Asteraceae)

§ ***baetica*** subsp. ***maroccana***	LDai SBrt
cardunculus ♀H3-4	Widely available
- ACL 380/78	SWat
I - 'Cardy'	EBee LRHS NCGa
- dwarf	SMHy
I - 'Florist Cardy'	IGor NLar
- 'Gobbo di Nizza'	ELau LEdu SVic WHer
- 'Porto Spineless'	LEdu
§ - Scolymus Group	CBcs CHEx CWan EBee EHoe EWes GPoy IGor LEdu LRHS LSRN MBri MNHC NPri SBfd SEND SMrm SPav SPer SPhx SPoG SVic WHer WWEG
- - 'Carciofo Violetto Precoce'	WHer
- - 'Gigante di Romagna'	WHer
- - 'Gros Camus de Bretagne'	MAvo WCot
- - 'Gros Vert de Lâon'	CBcs ELan ELau LRHS WCot
- - 'Imperial Star'	ELau LEdu SVic
- - 'Large Green'	NLar
- - 'Monica Lynden-Bell'	WCot
- - 'Purple Globe'	CArn CPrp ELau SMrm
- - 'Romanesco'	ELau SVic
- - 'Vert Globe'	CSBt CSev ELau ENfk LEdu MRav MWat NPer NPri SMrm SPad SVic SWal
- - 'Violet de Provence'	CSBt ELau SWal
- - 'Violetto di Chioggia'	CSev ELau LEdu WHer
hystrix misapplied	see *C. baetica* subsp. *maroccana*
scolymus	see *C. cardunculus* Scolymus Group
syriaca new	XSen

Cynodon (Poaceae)

aethiopicus	EBee EHoe LEdu SBfd SHDw SWal WCot

Cynoglossum (Boraginaceae)

dioscoridis	SPhx
grande	SBrt
nervosum	EBee ELan EPfP GAbr LAst LHop LRHS MLHP MMuc MRav NChi NEgg SEND SPer SPhx WCot WWEG
officinale	CArn MHer WSFF

Cynosurus (Poaceae)

cristatus	CHab NMir
- viviparous	CNat

Cypella (Iridaceae)

§ ***coelestis***	WPGP
herbertii	CDes CPom
plumbea	see *C. coelestis*

Cyperus (Cyperaceae)

§ ***albostriatus***	CCCN CHEx EShb IDee
alternifolius misapplied	see *C. involucratus*
alternifolius L.	CBen EAmu EBee EPfP EUJe LPBA MSKA WMAq
- 'Compactus'	see *C. involucratus* 'Nanus'
'Chira'	MBNS NWsh WGwG
diffusus misapplied	see *C. albostriatus*
§ ***eragrostis***	CArn EHoe GCal MWts NSti SDix SPlb SWat WAbb WGrn WMAq WMoo WTcb
esculentus	CArn LEdu
fuscus	MDKP WFar WHal WMoo WTcb
glaber	IBoy LDai MAsh MBNS
haspan misapplied	see *C. papyrus* 'Nanus'
haspan L.	MSKA
§ ***involucratus*** ♀H1	CHEx EBak EShb EWay LPBA MSKA MWts SEND SMad SWat WMnd WMoo
- 'Gracilis'	EBak
§ - 'Nanus'	EShb LPBA SEND
longus	CBen CWat EBee EHoe EHon EPPr GCal LPBA MMuc MWts NPer NWsh SEND SWal SWat WHal WMAq XLum
papyrus ♀H1	CDTJ CHEx CKno EAmu EUJe MSKA SBig XBlo
§ - 'Nanus' ♀H1	CHEx XBlo
ustulatus	CKno MDKP
vegetus	see *C. eragrostis*

Cyphanthera (Solanaceae)

tasmanica	ECou

Cyphomandra see Solanum

Cypripedium (Orchidaceae)

acaule	NLAp
Achim gx new	XFro
Aki gx	GEdr LWSt NLAp XFro
- 'Pastel'	GEdr LWSt NLAp XFro
× ***alaskanum***	NLAp
× ***andrewsii***	GEdr LWSt
Barbel Schmidt gx new	NLAp
× ***barbeyi***	see *C.* × *ventricosum*
Bernd gx new	GEdr
Birgit gx pastel-flowered new	LWSt NLAp XFro
calceolus	CCon LRHS LWSt NLAp
californicum	GEdr LRHS NLAp
Carol Ilene gx new	GEdr
Cleo Pinkepank gx new	NLAp
× ***columbianum***	LWSt NLAp
corrugatum	see *C. tibeticum*
debile	GEdr
Dietrich gx	GEdr LWSt NLAp
Emil gx	GEdr LWSt NLAp XFro
fargesii	GEdr
fasciolatum	GEdr LWSt NLAp
flavum	GBin GEdr LRHS NLAp
- S008-1 from Hengduan Mts, China new	NLAp
- white-flowered	GEdr LRHS NLAp
- white-flowered × ***reginae***	GEdr
- yellow-flowered	GEdr NLAp

flavum 'Yellow Ball' × *reginae* new	GEdr
Florence gx	NLAp
formosanum	GEdr LAma LWst NLAp SKHP
franchetii	GEdr NLAp
Gabriela gx new	NLAp
Gidget gx new	NLAp
Gisela gx	GEdr LAma LWst NLAp XFro
- 'Pastel'	GEdr LWst NLAp
- 'Yellow'	CAvo LAma
guttatum	GEdr LWst
- var. *yatabeanum*	see *C. yatabeanum*
Hank Small gx	GEdr LWst NLAp XFro
Hans Erni gx	NLAp
henryi	GEdr LAma NLAp
henryi × *montanum* new	NLAp
himalaicum	NLAp
Inge gx	GEdr LWst NLAp XFro
Ingrid gx	GEdr LWst XFro
Irene gx	LWst
japonicum	GEdr NLAp
Judith gx	GEdr
kentuckiense	CCCN CCon GEdr LRHS LWst NLAp
kentuckiense × *macranthos* 'Red Russian' new	GEdr
Kristi Lyn gx	GEdr LWst NLAp XFro
lichiangense	GEdr
lichiangense × *reginae*	GEdr
Lothar Pinkepank gx new	NLAp
Lucy Pinkepank gx new	GEdr
macranthos	GEdr LRHS LWst NLAp
- 'Hotei' new	NLAp
- var. *hotei-atsumorianum* Sadovsky	NLAp
Maria gx	GEdr LWst NLAp XFro
Memoria Gerd Kohls gx	NLAp
Michael gx	GEdr LWst XFro
Michael Pastel gx	GEdr LWst NLAp
parviflorum	NLAp
- var. *makasin*	NLAp
- subsp. *parviflorum* var. *planipetalum* new	NLAp
§ - var. *pubescens*	GEdr LAma LRHS LWst NLAp
- var. *pubescens* × *reginae*	GEdr
Paul gx	GEdr LWst NLAp XFro
Peter gx new	LWst XFro
Philipp gx	GEdr LWst NLAp XFro
plectrochilum	GEdr
Pluto gx new	XFro
pubescens	see *C. parviflorum* var. *pubescens*
Rascal gx	GEdr LWst NLAp
reginae	CCCN EBee EHrv EWes GEdr GKev LAma LRHS NLAp SKHP
- f. *album*	GEdr LRHS NLAp
- 'Red Pouch'	GEdr
Renate gx	LWst
- pastel-flowered	LWst XFro
Sabine gx	GEdr LWst NLAp XFro
- pastel-flowered	GEdr LWst NLAp XFro
Sebastian gx	GEdr LWst NLAp XFro
segawae	LAma
shanxiense S015-1 from Hengduan Mts, China new	NLAp
- S015-2 from Hengduan Mts, China new	NLAp
Sunny gx	GEdr NLAp
§ *tibeticum*	NLAp
- S028-1 from Hengduan Mts, China new	NLAp
- S028-2 from Hengduan Mts, China new	NLAp
Tilman gx new	GEdr XFro
Tower Hill gx new	GEdr
Ulla Silkens gx	GEdr LAma LWst NLAp XFro
Ursel gx	GEdr LWst NLAp XFro
§ × *ventricosum*	GEdr LRHS LWst NLAp XFro
- 'Pastel'	LWst NLAp XFro
- white-flowered	GEdr
Victoria gx	GEdr LWst NLAp XFro
Warren gx new	GEdr
Werner Frosch gx new	GEdr
§ *yatabeanum*	GEdr
yunnanense	GEdr NLAp

Cyrilla (*Cyrillaceae*)

racemiflora	CMac

Cyrtanthus (*Amaryllidaceae*)

sp.	WHil
from high altitude	WCot
'Alaska'	ECho
§ *brachyscyphus*	ECho EPot EShb
breviflorus	ECho NMen WPGP
'Edwina'	CCCN ECho
§ *elatus* ♀H1	CSpe ECho EWll LAma LEdu LRHS SEND WCot
- 'Cream Beauty'	ECho
- pink-flowered	ECho
- 'Pink Diamond'	ECho WCot
'Elizabeth'	CCCN ECho
mackenii	ECho EShb WPGP
- cream white-flowered	CCCN ECho GHim
- 'Himalayan Pink'	CCCN EBee ECho
- orange-flowered new	GHim
- pink-flowered	GHim
- red-flowered	CCCN EBee ECho GHim
- white-flowered	EBee
montanus	ECho WCot
obliquus	WCot
parviflorus	see *C. brachyscyphus*
purpureus	see *C. elatus*
rhodesianus	GCal
sanguineus	ECho WCot
smithiae	ECho
speciosus	see *C. elatus*

Cyrtomium (*Dryopteridaceae*)

§ *caryotideum*	CBty CLAP ISha WWEG
§ *falcatum* ♀H3	CBty CCon CHEx CHVG CLAP CMHG EBee EFer ELan ELon EPfP EUJe GMaP IVic LRHS NOrc SBfd SEND SHil SPoG SRms SRot WCot WFar WMoo XBlo XLum
- 'Rochfordianum'	CBty CCCN GBin ISha LRHS LTen MWat WFib
§ *fortunei* ♀H4	CHid CLAP EBee EFer ELan ELon EPfP EUJe IDee LRHS LTen MGos MRav NBid NGdn SBfd SPad SPer SPoG SRms WCFE WFib WMoo WPat WPnP WWEG
- var. *clivicola*	CBty CEnt CKel CPrp CWCL EBee EPfP EShb ISha LPot LRHS LTen MGos MMoz MRav NLar SBfd WPat
macrophyllum	CLAP GLin

Cystopteris ✿ (*Woodsiaceae*)

	bulbifera	CLAP MNFA
	dickieana	CLAP GBin WFib
	fragilis	EBee EFer WFib
	moupinensis B&SWJ 6767	WCru

Cytisus (*Papilionaceae*)

	albus misapplied	see *C. multiflorus*
	albus Hacq.	see *Chamaecytisus albus* (Hacq.) Rothm.
	'Amber Elf' PBR	MBri SRms
	'Andreanus'	see *C. scoparius* f. *andreanus*
	'Apricot Gem'	LRHS NLar
	battandieri	see *Argyrocytisus battandieri*
	× ***beanii*** ♀H4	CDul ELan EPfP LRHS MAsh SLon SRms WFar
	'Boskoop Glory'	NLar
	'Boskoop Ruby' ♀H4	CDoC CMac CSBt EBee EPfP LBMP LPot LRHS LSRN MAsh MNHC NEgg NPri SBfd SHil SPer SWvt WBor WFar WHar WRHF
	'Burkwoodii' ♀H4	CBcs CDoC CDul EBee ELan EPfP LAst LRHS LSRN MSwo MWat NEgg SBfd SPoG WFar
	canariensis	see *Genista canariensis*
	'Compact Crimson'	CDoC LRHS SBfd
	'Cottage'	GEdr
	'Daisy Hill'	CWCL
§	***decumbens***	MAsh
	'Donard Gem'	CDoC LRHS SBfd
	'Firefly'	CBcs CMac NBro
	'Golden Cascade'	CBcs CDoC CWCL ELan LBMP LRHS MAsh NEgg SBfd SLim
	'Golden Sunlight'	CSBt EPfP MSwo
	'Golden Tears'	NPri
	'Goldfinch'	CDoC CSBt CWCL EBee ELan LRHS MAsh MBri MSwo NLar SPad
	hirsutus	see *Chamaecytisus hirsutus*
	'Hollandia' ♀H4	CBcs CDoC CSBt EPfP EWTr GAbr LBMP MAsh MGos MMuc MRav NHol SEND SGol WFar
	× ***kewensis*** ♀H4	CMac EBee ELan EPfP LRHS MAsh MGos MRav NHol NWea SEND SPer SRms
	- 'Niki'	EPfP LRHS MAsh MMuc SEND SPer WRHF
	'Killiney Red'	ELan MBri
	'Killiney Salmon'	LSRN MMuc MRav
	'La Coquette'	CDoC EBee EPfP LRHS MAsh SBfd SPlb
	'Lena' ♀H4	CDoC CMac CSBt EPfP LRHS LSRN LTen MAsh MBri MGos MMuc MWat NBir NEgg NHol NLar NPri NRHS SEND SGol SHil SLim SPoG WBor WFar WHar
	leucanthus	see *Chamaecytisus albus* (Hacq.) Rothm.
	'Luna'	MGos SHil
	maderensis	see *Genista maderensis*
	'Maria Burkwood'	NLar
	'Minstead'	CDoC EBee ELan LBuc NEgg SLim SPer
	'Moonlight'	NBro
	'Moyclare Pink'	CMHG EBee
	'Mrs Norman Henry'	NLar
§	***multiflorus*** ♀H4	SRms
	'Newry Seedling'	CMac
	nigricans 'Cyni'	EBee ELan ELon IArd LAst LRHS MAsh MMuc SEND SPer SPoG SSpi
	'Palette'	MMuc
	'Porlock'	see *Genista* 'Porlock'
	× ***praecox***	CMac CWCL LAst LRHS MAsh NEgg SGol SPlb SPoG WFar WHar
	- 'Albus'	CBcs CDoC CDul CMac ELan EPfP GAbr LAst LRHS LSRN MAsh MGos MRav NHol SBfd SHil SPer WFar WHar
	- 'Allgold' ♀H4	CBcs CDoC CDul CMac CSBt CTri CWCL EBee EPfP LRHS LSRN MAsh MBri MMuc MRav NEgg NHol NPri NRHS NWea SBfd SEND SGol SHil SLon SPer SPoG SRms SWvt WFar
	- 'Canary Bird'	see *C.* × *praecox* 'Goldspeer'
	- 'Frisia'	NBro
§	- 'Goldspeer'	MNHC MWat
	- 'Lilac Lady'	EBee LRHS MWat
	- 'Warminster' ♀H4	EBee EPfP MBri MMuc MRav NWea SBfd SEND SPer SRms
	purpureus	see *Chamaecytisus purpureus*
	- 'Atropurpureus'	see *Chamaecytisus purpureus* 'Atropurpureus'
	racemosus	see *Genista* × *spachiana*
	Red Favourite	see *C.* 'Roter Favorit'
	'Red Wings'	MMuc
§	'Roter Favorit'	EPfP LTen MWat WGor
	scoparius	CArn CDul CRWN NWea SRms
§	- f. ***andreanus*** ♀H4	CDoC CTri EPfP NWea SPer
	- 'Cornish Cream'	CDoC CDul CSBt EPfP LRHS SPer
	- 'Firefly' **new**	CBcs
	- 'Fulgens'	CMac CWCL EPfP
§	- subsp. ***maritimus***	MCoo SLPl
	- Monarch strain	GJos SWal
	- var. ***prostratus***	see *C. scoparius* subsp. *maritimus*
	× ***spachianus***	see *Genista* × *spachiana*
	supinus	see *Chamaecytisus supinus*
	'White Lion' **new**	CMac
	'Windlesham Ruby'	CDoC CPLG EBee ELan EPfP LRHS LSRN NLar SBfd SLim SPer WFar
	'Zeelandia' ♀H4	CMac EBee ELon EPfP LRHS LTen MWat NEgg NHol SPer

Daboecia ✿ (*Ericaceae*)

§	***cantabrica***	MMuc SEND
§	- f. ***alba***	CSBt GHeS MBri NWad SPer SRms SWhi
	- - 'Alba Globosa'	GHeS
	- - 'Bellita'	GHeS
	- - 'Creeping White'	GHeS
	- - 'David Moss' ♀H4	GHeS MMuc SEND
I	- - 'Early Bride'	GHeS
	- - 'Snowdrift'	GHeS
	- - 'White Carpet'	GHeS
	- 'Alberta White' **new**	IVic
	- 'Amelie' PBR	CFst IVic SWhi
	- 'Arielle' ♀H4	CFst GHeS
	- 'Atropurpurea'	CSBt GHeS MAsh NWad SPer SWhi
	- 'Barbara Phillips' ♀H4	GHeS

	- 'Bicolor' ♀H4	GHeS
	- 'Blueless'	GHeS
	- f. ***blumii*** 'Pink Blum'	CFst GHeS
	- - 'Purple Blum'	CFst GHeS
	- - 'White Blum'	CFst GHeS SWhi
	- 'Bubbles'	CFst GHeS
	- 'Celtic Star'	GHeS
	- 'Chaldon'	CFst GHeS
	- 'Charles Nelson' (d)	CFst GHeS
	- 'Cherub'	GHeS
	- 'Cinderella'	GHeS IVic
	- 'Cleggan'	GHeS
	- 'Clifden'	GHeS
	- 'Covadonga'	GHeS
	- 'Cupido'	CTsd GHeS IVic
§	- 'Donard Pink'	GHeS
	- 'Ellen Norris' new	CFst
	- 'Eskdale Baron'	GHeS
	- 'Eskdale Blea'	GHeS
	- 'Eskdale Blonde'	GHeS
	- 'Glamour'	CFst GHeS
I	- 'Globosa Pink'	GHeS
	- 'Harlequin'	GHeS
	- 'Heather Yates'	CFst GHeS MAsh
	- 'Heraut'	GHeS
	- 'Hookstone Purple'	GHeS NWad
	- 'Irish Shine'	GHeS
	- 'Johnny Boy'	GHeS
	- 'Lilac Osmond'	GHeS
	- 'Pink'	see *D. cantabrica* 'Donard Pink'
	- 'Pink Lady'	GHeS
	- 'Polifolia'	GHeS SRms
	- 'Porter's Variety'	GHeS
	- 'Praegerae'	CTri GHeS SWhi
	- 'Purpurea'	GHeS
	- 'Rainbow' (v)	GHeS SWhi
	- 'Rodeo' ♀H4	GHeS
	- 'Rosea'	GHeS
	- 'Rubra'	GHeS
	- subsp. ***scotica*** 'Bearsden'	GHeS
	- - 'Ben'	GHeS
	- - 'Cora'	CFst GHeS
	- - 'Golden Imp'	CFst GHeS SWhi
	- - 'Goscote'	GHeS MGos
	- - 'Jack Drake' ♀H4	CFst GHeS MBri SWhi
	- - 'Katherine's Choice'	CBcs CFst GHeS
	- - 'Red Imp'	GHeS
	- - 'Robin'	CFst GHeS
	- - 'Silverwells' ♀H4	CBcs CFst GHeS MAsh MBri NHol SWhi
	- - 'Tabramhill'	GHeS
	- - 'William Buchanan' ♀H4	CFst GHeS GJos MAsh MBri NHol NWad SCoo SWhi
	- - 'William Buchanan Gold' (v)	GHeS MBri
	- 'Tinkerbell'	CFst GJos SWhi
	- 'Vanessa' PBR new	IVic
	- 'Waley's Red' ♀H4	CFst GHeS NHol NWad SWhi
	- 'Wijnie'	GHeS

Dacrycarpus (Podocarpaceae)

§	***dacrydioides***	CBrP ECou LEdu
	- 'Dark Delight'	ECou

Dacrydium (Podocarpaceae)

	bidwillii	see *Halocarpus bidwillii*
	cupressinum	CBcs CDoC CTrC SMad SPlb
	franklinii	see *Lagarostrobos franklinii*
	laxifolium	see *Lepidothamnus laxifolius*

Dactylicapnos (Papaveraceae)

§	***lichiangensis***	WCru WSHC
	macrocapnos	CCon EPfP GCal IFro MDKP WCru WTou
§	***scandens***	CRHN EPfP GCal IRos MNrw MSCN
	- GWJ 9438	WCru
	- 'Shirley Clemo'	CPLG
	torulosa	WTou
	- B&SWJ 7814	WCru
§	***ventii*** GWJ 9376	WCru

Dactylis (Poaceae)

	glomerata	CHab WSFF
	- 'Variegata' (v)	EBee LTen MMuc NBid SBfd SEND SHDw WFar

Dactylorhiza (Orchidaceae)

	sp.	NDav
	alpestris	CCon CLAP EBee NLAp SKHP WCot
	aristata	EFEx LWst
	× ***braunii***	ECha EHrv
§	***elata*** ♀H4	GAbr IBlr LAma NLAp SUsu WCot
	- Duguid's	NLAp WThu
§	***foliosa*** ♀H4	CCCN CTsd GCra IBlr MNrw NLAp WFar WOld
§	***fuchsii***	CCCN CMil EBee EPot LEdu LRHS MMoz MNrw NLAp NMen NRya NSla SKHP SUsu WCot WHer
	- 'Bressingham Bonus'	LRHS
	- subsp. ***okellyi*** new	NLAp
	- pink-flowered	CCon
	× ***grandis***	CLAP IBlr SCnR
	- Blackthorn hybrid	CLAP LWst
	incarnata	CPrp NBid NLAp
	- subsp. ***ochroleuca***	NLAp
	lapponica	NLAp
§	***maculata***	CCon CHid EBee EHrv ELan EPfP LAma NLAp NMen WBor WCot WHer
	- subsp. ***ericetorum***	LRHS NLAp
	- 'Madam Butterfly'	LRHS
	maderensis	see *D. foliosa*
§	***majalis***	CLAP EBee EPot LAma LRHS LWst MNrw NLAp WSFF
	- subsp. ***occidentalis***	NLAp
	- subsp. ***sphagnicola***	CLAP
	mascula	see *Orchis mascula*
	praetermissa	CCCN CCon CLAP EBee LRHS NLAp NMen SKHP WCot
	- subsp. ***praetermissa*** hybrid	SKHP
	purpurella	CLAP CPrp EBee GAbr GJos LRHS NLAp NMen NRya
	saccifera	NLAp
	sambucina	NLAp
	'Valerie Finnis'	GKev

Dahlia ✿ (Asteraceae)

'A la Mode' (LD)	CWGr
'Abacus Sol' new	WAba
'Abba' (SD)	ECtt
'Abbie' (SD)	NHal
'Abingdon Ace' (SD)	CWGr
'Abridge Alex' (SD)	CWGr
'Abridge Ben' (MinD)	CWGr

	'Abridge Natalie' (SWL)	CWGr
	'Abridge Primrose' (SWL)	CWGr
I	'Acapulco' (S-c)	ERCP
	'Adelaide Fontane' (LD)	CWGr
	'Admiral Rawlings' (SD)	CWGr WHal WWlt
	'Aimie' (MinD)	CWGr
	'Aitara Caress' (MinC)	NHal
	'Aitara Cloud' (MinC)	CWGr NHal
	'Akita' (Misc)	CSut CWGr EPfP WAba
	'Alauna Clair-Obscur' (Fim)	ERCP
	'Albert Schweitzer' (MS-c)	CWGr
	'Alden Regal' (MinC)	CWGr
	'Alfred C' (GS-c)	CWGr
	'Alfred Grille' (MS-c)	CWGr SDeJ SMrm SPer
	'Alf's Mascot' (MD)	WAba
	'Aljo' (MS-c)	CWGr
	'All Triumph' (MinS-c)	CWGr
	'Allan Snowfire' (MS-c)	LAyl NHal WAba
	'Allan Sparkes' (SWL) ♀H3	CWGr
	'Alloway Candy'	ERCP
	'Alloway Cottage' (MD)	CWGr NHal
	'Alltami Apollo' (GS-c)	CWGr
	'Alltami Corsair' (MS-c)	CWGr
	'Alltami Ruby' (MS-c)	CWGr
	'Almand's Climax' (GD) ♀H3	CWGr WAba
	'Almand's Supreme' (GS-c)	CWGr
	'Alpen Beauty' (Col)	CWGr
	'Alpen Fern' (Fim)	CWGr
	'Alpen Mildred' (SS-c)	CWGr
	'Alpen Sun' (MinS-c)	CWGr
	'Alstergruss' (Col)	CBgR
	'Alva's Doris' (SS-c) ♀H3	LAyl WAba
	'Alva's Regalia' (MD)	LRHS
	'Alva's Supreme' (GD) ♀H3	CWGr LAyl NHal WAba
	'Amanda Jarvis' (SC)	CWGr
	'Amanjanca' (MinS-c)	CWGr
	'Amaran Guard' (LD)	CWGr
	'Amaran Pico' (MD)	CWGr
	'Amaran Relish' (LD)	CWGr
	'Amaran Return' (GD)	CWGr
	'Amaran Troy' (SWL)	CWGr
	'Amber Banker' (MC)	CWGr
	'Amber Festival' (SD)	NHal
	'Amber Quartz' **new**	SMrm
	'Amber Vale' (MinD)	CWGr
	'Amberglow' (MinBa)	CWGr LAyl
	'Amberley Joan' (SD)	CWGr
	'Amberley Victoria' (MD)	CWGr
	'Ambition' (SS-c)	CWGr ERCP
	'Amelia's Surprise' (LD)	CWGr
	'American Copper' (GD)	CWGr
	American Pie = 'Vdtg26'PBR (Dark Angel Series) (Sin)	LRHS
	'Amgard Coronet' (MinD)	CWGr
	'Amgard Delicate' (LD)	CWGr
	'Amgard Rosie' (SD)	CWGr
	'Amira' (SBa)	CWGr NHal WAba
	'Amorangi Joy' (SC)	CWGr
	'Amy Cave' (SBa)	NHal
*	'Anaïs'	CWGr
	'Ananta Patel' (SD)	CWGr
	'Anchorite' (SD)	CWGr
	'Andrea Clark' (MD)	NHal
	'Andrea Lawson'	GBin NHal
	'Andrew Mitchell' (MS-c)	CWGr NHal
	'Andries' Amber' (MinS-c)	CWGr
	'Andries' Orange' (MinS-c)	ECtt LRHS LYaf
	'Anelog' (MinBa) **new**	NHal
	'Anita Summerhayes' (Misc) **new**	CWGr
	'Anja Doc' (MS-c)	CWGr
	'Ann Breckenfelder' (Col) ♀H3	CWGr EBee ECtt EHrv ERCP EUJe GBin LRHS MBNS NEgg NHal SDix SMrm WCot
	'Anniversary Ball' (MinBa)	CWGr LAyl
	'Apache' (MS-c/Fim)	ERCP SPer WAba
	'Apache Blauw'	ERCP
I	'Appleblossom' (Col)	CWGr
	'Apricot Honeymoon Dress' (SD)	CWGr
	'April Heather' (Col)	NHal
	'Arabian Night' (SD)	CAvo CBcs CBgR CSpe CSut CWGr EBee ECtt EHrv ELan ERCP GBin LAyl LRHS LSRN MBri MNrw NHal SBfd SDeJ SMrm SPer SWal WCot WWEG
	'Aranka' (Col) **new**	CWGr
	'Arc de Triomphe' (MD)	CWGr
	'Arlequin' (LD)	CWGr
	'Arnhem' (SD)	CWGr
	'Art Act' **new**	ERCP
	'Arthur Godfrey' (GD)	CWGr
	'Arthur Hankin' (SD)	CWGr
	'Arthur Hills' (SC)	CWGr
	'Arthur's Delight' (GD)	CWGr
	'Asahi Chohje' (Anem) ♀H3	CWGr
	'Athalie' (SC)	CWGr
	'Athelston John' (SC)	CWGr
	'Atilla' (SD)	CWGr
	'Atlantic City' (MinD) **new**	CWGr
	'Aubrey Keys' (SD) **new**	CWGr
	'Audacity' (MD)	CWGr LAyl
	'Audrey R' (SWL)	CWGr
	'Aurora's Kiss' (MinBa)	NHal
	'Aurwen's Violet' (Pom)	CHVG LAyl NHal
	australis	CWGr WPGP
	- B&SWJ 10208	WCru
	- B&SWJ 10358	WCru
	- B&SWJ 10389	WCru
	'Autumn Fairy' (D)	ERCP SDeJ
	'Autumn Lustre' (SWL) ♀H3	CWGr
	'Avignon' (Jumbo Collection) **new**	SDeJ
	'Avoca Amanda' (MD) **new**	NHal WAba
	'Avoca Comanche' (SS-c)	NHal
	'Avoca Salmon' (MD)	NHal
	'Awaikoe' (Col)	CWGr
	'B.J. Beauty' (MD)	CWGr LAyl NHal
	'Babette' (S-c)	LYaf SMrm
	'Baby Fonteneau' (SS-c)	CWGr
	'Baby Royal' (SD)	CWGr
	'Babylon Bronze'	CSut WAba
	'Babylon Paars' (MD)	LRHS SDeJ
	'Babylon Pink' (MD) **new**	SDeJ
	'Babylon Rose' (GD)	LRHS
	'Bagley Blush' (MinD)	WAba
	'Bahama Lemon'	see *D.* 'Lemon Cane'
	'Balcombe' (SD)	CWGr
	'Ballego's Glory' (MD)	CWGr
	'Bambino' (Lil)	CWGr
	'Banker' (MC)	CWGr
	'Bantling' (MinBa)	CWGr ECtt ERCP
	'Baret Joy' (MD)	WAba
	'Barbara Schell' (GD)	CWGr
	'Barbara's Pastelle' (MS-c)	CWGr
	'Barbarry Ball' (SBa)	CWGr
	'Barbarry Banker' (MinD)	LAyl

	Cultivar	Suppliers
	'Barbarry Bluebird' (MinD)	NHal
	'Barbarry Cadet' (MinD)	CWGr
	'Barbarry Carousel' (SBa)	CWGr
	'Barbarry Challenger' (MinD)	CWGr
	'Barbarry Chevron' (MD)	CWGr
	'Barbarry Dominion' (MinD)	CWGr
	'Barbarry Gem' (MinBa)	CWGr
	'Barbarry Ideal' (MinD)	CWGr
	'Barbarry Melody' (SD) **new**	NHal
	'Barbarry Monitor' (MinBa)	CWGr
	'Barbarry Noble' (MinD)	CWGr
	'Barbarry Oracle' (SD)	CWGr
	'Barbarry Pimpernel' (SD)	CWGr
	'Barbarry Pinky' (SD)	CWGr
	'Barbarry Red' (MinD)	CWGr
	'Barbarry Triumph' (MinD)	CWGr
	'Barberry Maverick'	GBin
	'Barbetta' (MinD)	CWGr
	'Barbette' (MinD)	CWGr
	'Baret Joy' (LS-c)	NHal
	'Bargaly Blush' (MD)	NHal
	'Baron Ray' (SD)	CWGr
	'Barry Williams' (MD)	CWGr
	'Bart' (SD)	CWGr
	'Bassingbourne Beauty' (SD)	CWGr
I	'Bea' (SWL)	WAba
	'Beacon Light' (SD)	CWGr
I	'Beatrice' (MinBa)	CWGr
	'Beatrice' (MinD)	CWGr
	'Bednall Beauty' (Misc/DwB) ♀[H3]	CBgR CHll CSpe CWCL CWGr EBee ECtt EHrv ELan EUJe EWes LHop LRHS LSRN MRav NEgg SBfd WAba WCot WWEG
	'Bell Boy' (MinBa)	ECtt
	'Bella S' (GD)	CWGr
	'Belle Epoque' (MC)	CWGr
	'Belle Moore' (SD)	CWGr
	'Berger's Rekord' (S-c)	CWGr ERCP
	'Berliner Orange' (MD)	ERCP
	'Bernice Sunset' (SS-c)	CWGr
	'Berolina' (MinD)	CWGr
	'Berwick Banker' (SBa)	CWGr
	'Berwick Wood' (MD)	CWGr NHal
	'Bess Painter' (SD)	CWGr
	'Beth's Chaplet'	WCot
	'Betty Ann' (Pom)	CWGr
	'Betty Bowen' (SD)	CWGr
	'Bicentenary' (SD) **new**	CWGr
	'Biddenham Sunset' (MS-c)	CWGr
	'Big Orange' (GD)	CWGr
	'Bill Homberg' (GD)	CWGr
	'Bingo' (MinD)	CWGr
	'Bishop of Auckland'[PBR] (Misc)	CSpe CWGN CWGr EBee ECtt EHrv ERCP LRHS MBri MCot NEgg SDeJ SHil SPoG WCot WWEG WWlt
	'Bishop of Cambridge' (Sin) **new**	SDeJ
	'Bishop of Canterbury'[PBR] (Misc)	CPrp CWGr EBee ECtt EPfP LRHS LSou MBri MTis NHal NRHS SDeJ SHil SPoG
	'Bishop of Dover'	CWGr EBee SDeJ
	'Bishop of Lancaster' (Misc)	CWGr EBee
	'Bishop of Leicester' (Misc)	CSpe CWGr ECtt EPfP EPot LRHS LSou MBri MNrw SDeJ SMrm SPet
	'Bishop of Llandaff' (Misc) ♀[H3]	Widely available
	'Bishop of Oxford' (Misc)	COIW CPrp CSpe EBee ECtt ELan EPfP LRHS LSou MBri MTis SDeJ SHil SPet SPoG WFar
	'Bishop of York' (Misc)	CAvo CPrp CSpe CWGr EBee ECtt EPfP EPot LRHS LSou MBri MTis NGdn SDeJ SHil SPet SPoG WFar
	'Bishop Peter Price' (Sin)	CWGr
	'Bishop's Children'	SBod
	'Bitsa' (MinBa)	CWGr SMrm
	'Bitter Lemon' (SD)	CWGr
	'Black Beauty'	CSpe SPhx
	'Black Fire' (SD)	CWGr ECtt
	'Black Monarch' (GD)	CWGr NHal
	'Black Narcissus' (MC)	CWGr EPfP SMrm SPer WWlt
	'Black Spider' (SS-c)	CWGr ECtt
	'Black Star' (Sin)	EPfP
	'Black Touch'	ERCP
	'Black Wizard' (MS-c)	EPfP
	'Blackberry Ripple' (S-c)	CWGr ERCP
	'Blaze' (MD)	CWGr
	'Blewbury First' (SWL)	CWGr
	'Bliss' (SWL)	CWGr
	'Bloodstone' (SD)	CWGr
	'Bloom's Amy' (MinD)	CWGr
	'Bloom's Graham' (SS-c)	CWGr
	'Blue Beard' (SS-c)	CWGr
	'Blue Boy' (SD)	ERCP SMrm SPer
	'Blue Diamond' (MC)	CWGr
	'Bluesette' (SD)	CWGr
	'Blyton Lady in Red' (MinD)	NHal
	'Blyton Softer Gleam' (MinD)	NHal
	'Bob Fitzjohn' (GS-c)	CWGr
	'Bokay' (SWL)	CWGr
	'Bonanza' (SD)	CWGr
	'Bonaventura' (C)	LRHS
	'Bonaventure' (GD)	NHal
	'Bonesta' (MinD)	CWGr
	'Bonne Espérance' (Sin/Lil)	CWGr
	'Bonny Blue' (SBa)	CWGr
	'Bonny Brenda' (MinD)	CWGr
	'Boogie Woogie' (Anem)	CWGr
	'Border Princess' (SC/DwB)	CWGr
	'Border Triumph' (DwB)	CWGr
	'Boy Scout' (MinBa)	CWGr
	'Brackenhill Flame' (SD)	CWGr
	'Brackenridge Ballerina' (SWL)	CWGr LAyl NHal WAba
	'Brandaris' (MS-c)	CWGr
	'Brandon James' (MinD) **new**	SDeJ
	'Brandysnap' (SD)	CWGr
	'Brantwood' (Sin)	CSam CWGr
	Braveheart = 'Vdtg67'[PBR] (Dark Angel Series) (Sin)	LRHS
	'Brian's Dream' (MinD)	LAyl NHal
	'Bride's Bouquet' (Col)	CWGr ERCP
	'Bridge View Aloha' (MS-c) ♀[H3]	CWGr
	'Bridgette' (SD)	CWGr
	'Bronze Glints' (MS-c)	WAba
	'Brookfield Delight' (Sin/Lil) ♀[H3]	CWGr SUsu
	'Brookfield Rene' (MinD)	CWGr
	'Brookfield Snowball' (SBa)	CWGr
	'Brookfield Sweetie' (DwB/Lil)	CWGr
	'Brookside Cheri' (SC)	CWGr

'Brookside Snowball' (SB) CWGr
'Bryn Terfel' (GD) NHal WAba
'Butch' (MD) **new** CWGr
'Butterball' (MinD/DwB) SDeJ
* 'Buttercup' (Pom) CWGr
'Buttermere' (SD) CWGr
'By George' (GD) CWGr
'Caballero' (SWL) **new** CWGr
'Café au Lait' (GD) CWGr IPot SDeJ SEND SMrm SPer WAba
'Calgary' (SD) CWGr
'Camano Passion' (MS-c) CWGr
'Camano Regal' (MS-c) CWGr
'Camano Sitka' (MS-c) **new** WAba
'Cameo' (WL) CWGr LAyl NHal
campanulata **new** CWGr
'Campos Philip M' (GD) CWGr
'Canary Fubuki' (MD) CWGr ERCP SDeJ
I 'Candlelight' (GD) NHal
I 'Candy' (SD) CWGr
'Candy Cane' (MinBa) CWGr
'Candy Cupid' (MinBa) ♀H3 WAba
Candy Eyes = 'Zone Ten'PBR (Sin/DwB) CWGN CWGr EBee EPfP GBin LRHS LSRN LSou MBri MGos SHar SPoG SUsu WBor
'Candy Hamilton Lilian' (SD) CWGr
'Candy Keene' (LS-c) CWGr NHal
'Caproz Jerry Garcia' (MD) CWGr
'Capulet' (SBa) CWGr
'Careless' (SD) CWGr
'Caribbean Fantasy' CWGr EBee SPet WAba
'Carole Melville' (MinBa) CWGr
'Carolina Moon' (SD) CWGr LAyl NHal
'Carstone Firebox' (Col) **new** NHal
'Carstone Ruby' (SD) NHal
'Carstone Sunbeam' (SD) CWGr
'Carstone Suntan' (MinC) CWGr NHal
'Carstone Valliant' (MinBa) NHal
'Cascade Ken' (Col) ♀H3 **new** WAba
'Catherine Deneuve' (Misc) CWGN CWGr
'Cerise Prefect' (MS-c) CWGr
'Cha Cha' (SS-c) CWGr
'Charles Dickens' (SBa) CWGr
'Charlie Briggs' (SBa) NHal
'Charlie Dimmock' (SWL) ♀H3 LAyl NHal WAba
'Charlie Two' (MD) CWGr NHal
'Chat Noir' (MS-c) CAvo CWGr ECtt ERCP LRHS
'Chee' (SWL) CWGr
'Cheerio' (SS-c) CWGr EBee LRHS
'Cherokee Beauty' (GD) CWGr
'Cherry Wine' (SD) CWGr
'Cherrywood Millfield' (MS-c) CWGr
'Cherrywood Wilderness' (MD) CWGr
'Cherubino' (Col) CWGr
'Cherwell Goldcrest' (SS-c) CWGr NHal
'Cherwell Siskin' (MD) WAba
'Cherwell Skylark' (SS-c) ♀H3 NHal
'Chessy' (Sin/Lil) ♀H3 CWGr WAba
'Cheyenne' (MinD) WAba
'Chic' (MinBa) ECtt
'Chic en Rouge' LSou
'Chilson's Pride' (SD) CWGr
'Chiltern Amber' (SD) CWGr
'Chiltern Herald' (MS-c) CWGr
'Chimborazo' (Col) CWGr LAyl SDix
'Chinese Lantern' (SD) CWGr
'Chloe's Keene' (LS-c) CWGr
'Chorus Girl' (MinD) CWGr
'Christine' (SD) SPer
I 'Christine' (SWL) CWGr WAba
'Christmas Carol' (Col) CWGr ECtt GBin WAba
'Christmas Star' (Col) CWGr
'Christopher Nickerson' (MS-c) CWGr
'Christopher Taylor' (SWL) NHal WAba
'Clair de Lune' (Col) ♀H3 CWCL CWGr EBee ECtt EHrv ERCP LRHS NHal NSti SMrm WAba WCot
'Claire Diane' (SD) CWGr
'Claire Louise Kitchener' (MWL) CWGr
'Clara May' (MS-c/Fim) CWGr
'Clarion' (MS-c) CWGr LRHS
'Clarion 79' (DwB) SUsu
'Classic A.1' (MC) CWGr
'Classic Rosamunde'PBR (Misc) CBgR NHal
'Classic Summertime' (Misc) CBgR
'Classic Swanlake'PBR (Misc) CWGr ERCP
'Classic Thaïs'PBR (Misc) CBgR
'Claudette' (D) ECtt
'Clearview Irene' (MS-c) CWGr NHal
'Clearwater David' (SD) GBin
coccinea (B) CBgR CGHE CHll CSpe CWGr EHrv EPfP GBin GCal MCot SDix SMHy WCot WPGP
- B&SWJ 9126 WCru
- NJM 05.072 WPGP
- hybrids WHil
- var. ***palmeri*** CAvo WPGP XEll
coccinea* × *merckii (B) EWes
'Color Spectacle' (LS-c) CWGr
'Colour Magic' (LS-c) CWGr
'Coltness Gem' (Sin/DwB) CWGr
'Comet' (Misc/Anem) CWGr
'Como Polly' (LD) CWGr
I 'Concordia' (SD) CWGr
'Confection' (MinD) NHal
'Contessa' (SWL) CWGr SDeJ
'Coral Jupiter' (GS-c) CWGr NHal
'Cornel' (SBa) CWGr ERCP LAyl LYaf NHal WAba
'Cornel Brons' (MinBa) ERCP WAba
'Cornish Minx' (Pom) CWGr
'Cornish Ruby' CCon EBee EPfP
'Corona' (SS-c/DwB) SDeJ
'Coronella' (MD) CWGr
'Corrine' (SWL) WAba
'Cortez Silver' (MD) CWGr
'Cortez Sovereign' (SS-c) CWGr
'Corton Bess' (SD) CWGr
'Corton Olympic' (GD) CWGr
'Corydon' (SD) CWGr
'Cottesmore' (MD) CWGr
'Cottonrail' (Col) ECtt
'Country Boy' (MS-c) CWGr
'Craigowan' (MS-c) NHal
'Crazy Legs' (MinD) CWGr
'Crazy Love' (SD) WAba
'Cream Alva's' (GD) ♀H3 CWGr

'Cream Elegans' (SS-c)	CWGr
'Cream Moonlight' (MS-c)	CWGr
'Cream Reliance' (SD)	CWGr
'Crichton Honey' (SBa)	CWGr
'Croesus' (GS-c)	CWGr
'Crossfield Anne' (MinD)	CWGr
'Crossfield Ebony' (Pom)	CWGr
'Crossfield Festival' (LD)	CWGr
'Croydon Jumbo' (GD)	CWGr
'Croydon Snotop' (GD)	CWGr
'Cryfield Jane' (MinBa)	CWGr
'Cryfield Keene' (LS-c)	CWGr
'Cryfield Max' (SC)	CWGr
'Curate' (Misc)	CWGr
'Curiosity' (Col)	CWGr
'Currant Cream' (SBa)	CWGr
'Cycloop' (SS-c)	CWGr
'Czardas'	GCal
'D. Day' (MS-c)	CWGr
'Daddy's Choice' (SS-c)	CWGr
'Daily Mail' (GD) **new**	CWGr
'Daleko Gold' (MD)	CWGr
'Daleko Jupiter' (GS-c)	CWGr NHal WAba
'Daleko National' (MD)	CWGr
'Daleko Tangerine' (MD)	CWGr
(Dali Series) 'Dali Orange' **new**	LSou
- 'Dali Pink' **new**	LSou
- 'Dali Scarlet' **new**	LSou
'Dana Audrey' (MinC)	CWGr
'Dana Dream' (MinS-c)	CWGr
'Dana Iris' (SS-c)	CWGr
'Dana Sunset' (SC)	CWGr
'Danum Belle' (SD)	CWGr
'Danum Chippy' (SD)	CWGr
'Danum Gail' (LD)	CWGr WAba
'Danum Hero' (LD)	CWGr
'Danum Meteor' (GS-c)	CWGr WAba
'Danum Rebel' (LS-c)	CWGr
'Danum Rhoda' (GD)	CWGr
'Danum Torch' (Col)	CWGr ECtt
'Dark Desire'^{PBR} (Sin/DwB)	CCon CSpe CWCL CWGN CWGr EBee ECtt LHop NSti WCot
'Dark Spirit' (MinD) **new**	ECtt WAba
'Dark Splendour' (MC)	CWGr
'Dark Stranger' (MC) ♀H3	CWGr
'Darkarin' **new**	SPer
'Darlington Diamond' (MS-c)	CWGr
'Darlington Jubilation' (SS-c)	CWGr
'Davar Jim' (SS-c) ♀H3	CWGr
'Davenport Honey' (MinD)	CWGr
'Davenport Sunlight' (MS-c)	CWGr
'Dave's Snip' (MinD)	CWGr WAba
'David Digweed' (SD)	NHal
'David Howard' (MinD) ♀H3	Widely available
'David's Choice' (MinD)	CWGr
'Dawn Chorus' (MinD)	CWGr
'Dawn Sky' (SD)	LAyl
'Deborah's Kiwi' (SC)	CWGr NHal
'Debra Anne Craven' (GS-c)	CWGr NHal WAba
'Decorette' (DwB/SD)	CWGr
'Decorette Bronze' (MinD/DwB)	CWGr
'Decorette Rose' (MinD/DwB)	CWGr
'Deepest Yellow' (MinBa)	CWGr SDeJ
'Demi Schneider' (Col) **new**	CWGr
'Denise Willow' (Pom)	WAba
'Dentelle de Venise' (MC)	CWGr
'Deuil du Roi Albert' (MD)	CWGr
'Deutschland' (MD)	CWGr
I 'Devon Elegans'	CWGr
'Devon Joy' (MinD)	CWGr
'Devon Liam' (LS-c) **new**	CWGr
'Devon Temptation' (Sc) **new**	CWGr
'Diamond Rose' (Anem/DwB)	CWGr
'Diana Gregory' (Pom)	CWGr
'Dick Westfall' (GS-c)	CWGr
'Dikara Jodie' (MD)	NHal
'Dikara Moon' (MD)	NHal
'Director' (SD)	CWGr
dissecta	CWGr EBee
- F&M 191	WPGP
'Doc van Horn' (LS-c)	CWGr
'Doctor Anne Dyson' (SC)	CWGr
'Doctor Arnett' (GS-c)	CWGr
'Doctor Caroline Rabbitt' (SD)	CWGr
'Doctor John Grainger' (MinD)	CWGr EBee LRHS
'Doktor Hans Ricken' (SD)	WAba
'Don Hill' (Col) ♀H3	CWGr NHal WAba WCot
'Doris Bacon' (SBa)	CWGr
'Doris Day' (SC)	CWGr LYaf NHal
'Doris Knight' (SC)	LYaf
'Doris Rollins' (SC)	CWGr
'Dottie D.' (SBa)	CWGr
'Double Dream Fantasy' (Misc)	LRHS
'Dovegrove' (Sin)	CSam CWGr SUsu
'Downham Royal' (MinBa)	ERCP
Dracula = 'Vdtg17'^{PBR} (Dark Angel Series) (Sin)	EPfP LRHS
Dragon Ball = 'Vdtg31'^{PBR} (Dark Angel Series) (Sin)	EPfP LRHS
'Dream Fantasy' (Dream Series) (Misc)	EUJe WBor
'Dreamy Inspire' **new**	NLar
'Dreamy Moonlight' **new**	NLar WHil
'Drummer Boy' (LD)	CWGr
'Duddon Grace' (WL)	NHal
'Duet' (MD)	CWGr ECtt GBin
'Dusky Harmony' (SWL)	CWGr
'Dutch Explosion' (SS-c) **new**	GBin
'Dutch Triumph' (LD)	CWGr
'Easter Sunday' (Col)	CWGr
'Eastwood Moonlight' (MS-c)	CWGr NHal WAba
'Eastwood Star' (MS-c)	CWGr WAba
'Edge of Joy'	SPer
'Edgeway Joyce' (MinBa)	CWGr
'Edinburgh' (SD)	CWGr ERCP SDeJ SWal
'Edith Jones' (Col) **new**	WAba
'Edith Mueller' (Pom)	CWGr
'Eileen Denny' (MS-c)	CWGr
'El Cid' (SD)	CWGr
'El Paso' (SD)	CWGr
'Elga'	ERCP
'Elgico Leanne' (MC)	CWGr
'Elizabeth Snowden' (Col)	CWGr
'Ella Britton' (MinD)	LRHS
'Ellen Huston' (Misc/DwB) ♀H3	CBgR CWGr ECtt ERCP LRHS NHal SBfd WCot
'Elma E' (LD)	CWGr LAyl NHal WAba
'Elmbrook Chieftain' (GD)	CWGr

'Elmbrook Rebel' (GS-c)	CWGr
'Embrace' (SC)	LAyl NHal WAba
'Emma's Coronet' (MinD)	CWGr WAba
'Emmie Lou' (MD)	CWGr
'Emory Paul' (LD)	CWGr ERCP
'Emperor' (MD)	CWGr
'Enfield Salmon' (LD)	CWGr
'Engadin' (MD)	CWGr
'Engelhardt's Matador' (MD)	CBgR CHll EBee ECtt ERCP LAst LRHS NSti SBfd SMrm WCot
'Enid Adams' (SD)	CWGr
'Eric's Choice' (SD)	CWGr
'Ernie Pitt' (SD)	CWGr
'Etheral' (Sin) **new**	CWGr
'Eugina Huston' (GD)	CWGr
'Eunice Arrigo' (LS-c)	CWGr
'Eveline' (SD)	CWGr ERCP MBri
'Evelyn Rumbold' (GD)	CWGr
'Evening Lady' (MinD)	CWGr
excelsa (B)	CHll WPGP
- B&SWJ 10238	WCru
- 'Penelope Sky'	WCru
'Excentrique' (Misc)	CWGr ECtt
'Exotic Dwarf' (Sin/Lil) ♀H3	CWGN EBee ECtt EHrv LRHS NHal WCot
'Explosion' (SS-c)	CWGr
'Extase' (MD)	CWGr
'Eye Candy'	LRHS
'Fabula' (Col)	CWGr LRHS
'Fairfield Frost' (Col)	NHal
'Fairway Pilot' (GD)	CWGr
'Fairway Spur' (GD)	NHal WAba
'Fairy Queen' (MinC)	CWGr
'Famoso' (Col)	ERCP
'Fantastico' (Col)	ERCP LRHS
I 'Fascination' (Misc) ♀H3	CBcs CHVG COIW CSam CWGr EBee ECtt ERCP LAyl MCot MSCN NEgg NGdn NLar SBfd SDeJ SMrm SPet SUsu WHoo WWEG
'Fascination Aus' (Col)	CWGr
'Fashion Monger' (Col)	CWGr ECtt EHrv NEgg NHal
'Ferncliffe Illusion' (LD)	CWGr ERCP LRHS
'Festivo' (Col)	CWGr LRHS
'Feu Céleste' (Col)	CWGr
'Fidalgo Blacky' (MinD)	CWGr
'Fidalgo Bounce' (SD)	CWGr
'Fidalgo Climax' (LS-c/Fim)	CWGr
'Fidalgo Magic' (MD)	CWGr WAba
'Fidalgo Snowman' (GS-c)	CWGr
'Fidalgo Splash' (MD)	CWGr
'Fidalgo Supreme' (MD)	CWGr LAyl
'Fiesta' (Pom) **new**	SDeJ
Figaro Series ♀H3 **new**	NPri
'Figurine' (SWL) ♀H3	CWGr WAba
'Fille du Diable' (LS-c)	CWGr
'Finchcocks' (SWL) ♀H3	LAyl
'Fiona Stewart' (SBa)	CWGr
'Fire and Ice'	CWGr ERCP WAba
'Fire Mountain' (MinD)	NHal
'Firebird' (MS-c)	see *D.* 'Vuurvogel'
'Firebird' (Sin)	CWGr
'Firebrand' ambig. (S-c)	CWGr
'Firepot' **new**	ERCP SMrm
'Fleur' (MinD/Fim)	SMrm SPer
'Fleur Mountjoy' (Col)	CWGr
'Fleurel' PBR	ERCP LRHS SDeJ
'Floorinoor' (Anem)	WAba
* 'Florence Vernon' (MinBa)	CWGr

'Flutterby' (SWL)	CWGr
'Forrestal' (MS-c)	CWGr
'Fortuna' (Col)	ERCP
'Frank Holmes' (Pom)	CWGr WAba
'Frank Hornsey' (SD)	CWGr
'Frank Lovell' (GS-c)	CWGr
'Franz Kafka' (Pom)	CWGr ERCP SDeJ
'Frau Louise Mayer' (SS-c)	CWGr
'Freak of Nature'	WAba
'Fred Wallace' (SC)	CWGr
'Freelancer' (LC)	CWGr
'Freestyle' (SC)	CWGr WAba
§ 'Freya's Paso Doble' (Anem) ♀H3	LAyl
'Freya's Sweetheart' (Sin)	CWGr
'Freya's Thalia' (Sin/Lil) ♀H3	CWGr
'Friendship' (LC)	CWGr
'Frigoulet'	CSut CWGr ERCP WAba
'Fringed Star' (MS-c)	CWGr
'Funfair' (MD)	CWGr
'Funny Face' (Misc)	CWGr WAba
'Fusion' (MD) ♀H3	CWGr SHar WCot
'Fuzzy Wuzzy' (MD)	CSut WAba
'G.F. Hemerik' (Sin)	CWGr LRHS
'Gainesville' (MinD)	EPfP
'Gala Parade' (SD)	CWGr
'Gale Lane' (Pom)	CWGr
(Gallery Series) 'Gallery Art Deco' PBR (SD) ♀H3	ERCP LRHS MBri NHal NRHS SBfd SHil
- 'Gallery Art Fair' PBR (MinD) ♀H3	CWGr LRHS MBri NHal SDeJ SHil
- 'Gallery Art Nouveau' PBR (MinD) ♀H3	CWGr ERCP LRHS MBri NHal SBfd SHil WCot
- 'Gallery Bellini' PBR (SD) **new**	SDeJ
- 'Gallery Cézanne' PBR (MinD)	CWGr LRHS MBri NRHS SHil
- 'Gallery La Tour' PBR (MinD) **new**	SDeJ
- 'Gallery Leonardo' PBR (SD) ♀H3	CWGr LRHS SDeJ
- 'Gallery Matisse' PBR (SD)	CWGr LRHS
- 'Gallery Pablo' PBR (SD) ♀H3 **new**	CWGr MBri
- 'Gallery Rembrandt' PBR (MinD) ♀H3	CWGr LRHS
- 'Gallery Renoir' PBR (SD) ♀H3	CWGr LRHS MBri NHal NRHS SHil
- 'Gallery Rivera' PBR	MBri SDeJ SHil
- 'Gallery Salvador' PBR (SD)	CWGr ERCP
- 'Gallery Singer' PBR (MinD) ♀H3	CWGr LRHS
- 'Gallery Vermeer' PBR (MinD)	CWGr LRHS
- 'Gallery Vincent' PBR (MinD) ♀H3	CWGr LRHS
'Gamelan' (Anem/DwB)	CWGr
'Garden Festival' (SWL)	CWGr ERCP WAba
'Garden Party' (MC/DwB) ♀H3	CWGr LAyl
'Garden Princess' (SC/DwB)	CWGr
'Garden Wonder' (SD)	CWGr SBfd SDeJ SMrm
'Gargantuan' (GS-c)	CWGr
'Garnet Quartz' **new**	EBee
Gateshead Festival	see *D.* 'Peach Melba' (SD)
'Gay Mini' (MinD)	CWGr
'Gay Princess' (SWL)	CWGr LAyl
'Gay Triumph' (GS-c)	CWGr

Name	Suppliers
'Geerlings' Cupido' (SWL)	CWGr WAba
'Geerlings' Moonlight' (MD)	CWGr
'Geerlings' Yellow' (SS-c)	CWGr
'Gemma Darling' (GD)	CWGr
'Gemma's Place' (Pom)	CWGr
'Genova' (MinBa) **new**	ERCP
'Geoffrey Kent' (MinD) ♀H3	NHal
'Gerrie Hoek' (SWL)	CWGr ECtt ERCP IPot LRHS LYaf SDeJ
'Gilt Edge' (MD)	CWGr
'Gilwood Pip' (SD)	CWGr
'Gina Lombaert' (MS-c)	CWGr SEND WAba
'Gipsy Night'	ERCP SDeJ SWal
'Giraffe' (DblO)	CWGr ERCP LRHS WAba
'Giselle'	SPet
'Gitty' (SBa)	CWGr
'Glad Huston' (DwSS-c)	CWGr
'Glenafton' (Pom)	CWGr
'Glenbank Paleface' (Pom)	CWGr
'Glenbank Twinkle' (MinC)	CWGr
'Globular' (MinBa)	CWGr
'Glorie van Heemstede' (SWL) ♀H3	CWGr ERCP LAyl LYaf NHal SDeJ SEND
'Glorie van Naardwijk' (SD)	SWal
'Glorie van Noordwijk' (MinS-c)	CWGr ERCP SDeJ WAba
'Glory' (LD)	CWGr
'Glow Orange' (MinBa)	CWGr
'Go American' (GD)	NHal
'Gold Crown' (LS-c)	SDeJ
'Golden Charmer' (SC)	CWGr
'Golden Emblem' (MD)	ECtt SDeJ SWal
'Golden Fizz' (MinBa)	CWGr
'Golden Glitter' (MS-c)	CWGr
'Golden Heart' (MS-c)	CWGr
'Golden Impact' (MS-c)	CWGr
'Golden Leader' (SD)	CWGr
'Golden Scepter' (MinD)	CWGr WAba
'Golden Turban' (MD)	CWGr
'Goldilocks' (S-c)	CWGr
'Good Earth' (MC)	CWGr SDeJ SMrm
'Good Hope' (MinD)	CWGr
'Goshen Beauty' (SWL)	CWGr
'Goya's Venus' (SS-c)	CWGr
'Grace Nash' (SD)	CWGr
'Grace Rushton' (SWL)	CWGr
'Gracie S' (MinC)	CWGr NHal
'Grand Prix' (GD)	CWGr SDeJ
'Grand Willo' (Pom)	WAba
'Grayval Gem' (Pom) **new**	NHal
'Grenadier' (SD) ♀H3	CWGr EBee ECtt ERCP LRHS SDix WAba WCot WWEG
'Grenidor Pastelle' (MS-c)	CWGr NHal WAba
'Gretchen Heine' (SD)	CWGr
'Grock' (Pom)	CWGr
'Gunyuu' (GD)	CWGr
'Gurtla Twilight' (Pom)	CWGr NHal
'Gute Laune' (MinS-c)	CWGr
'Gwyneth' (SWL)	CHVG WAba
'Gypsy Boy' (LD)	LAyl
'Gypsy Girl' (SD)	CWGr
'Hallwood Satin' (MD)	CWGr
'Hallwood Tiptop' (MinD)	CWGr
'Hamari Accord' (LS-c) ♀H3	CWGr LAyl
'Hamari Bride' (MS-c) ♀H3	CWGr
'Hamari Girl' (GD)	CWGr NHal
'Hamari Gold' (GD) ♀H3	CWGr NHal WAba
'Hamari Katrina' (LS-c)	WAba
'Hamari Rosé' (MinBa) ♀H3	CWGr NHal
'Hamari Sunshine' (LD) ♀H3	NHal
'Hamilton Amanda' (SD)	CWGr
'Hamilton Lillian' (SD) ♀H3	WAba
'Hans Radi' (Misc)	WAba
'Hans Ricken' (SD)	CWGr
'Happy Caroline' (MinD)	CWGr
'Happy Days Red' **new**	EPfP
'Happy Halloween' (SD) **new**	CWGr
(Happy Single Series)	CWGr ERCP SDeJ
Happy Single Date = 'HS Date'^{PBR} (Sin) **new**	
- Happy Single First Love = 'HS First Love'^{PBR} (Sin)	CWGr ERCP LSou SDeJ
- Happy Single Flame = 'HS Flame'^{PBR} (Sin)	CWGr SGar
- Happy Single Juliet = 'HS Juliet'^{PBR} (Sin)	CWGr ERCP LRHS SDeJ
- Happy Single Kiss = 'HS Kiss'^{PBR} (Sin)	LRHS MBri
- Happy Single Party = 'HS Party'^{PBR} (Sin)	CWGr ERCP LRHS
- Happy Single Princess = 'HS Princess' (Sin)	ERCP
- Happy Single Romeo = 'HS Romeo'^{PBR} (Sin)	CWGr LRHS MBri NPri SDeJ SGar
- Happy Single Wink = 'HS Wink'^{PBR} (Sin)	CWGr EPfP ERCP LRHS LSou MBri NPri SDeJ
'Happy Tip Purple' **new**	LSou
'Haresbrook' (Sin)	NGdn WAba
'Harvest' (LS-c/Fim)	CWGr
'Harvest Amanda' (Sin/Lil) ♀H3	CWGr
'Harvest Brownie' (Sin/Lil)	CWGr
'Harvest Dandy' (Sin/Lil)	CWGr
§ 'Harvest Imp' (Sin/Lil)	CWGr
§ 'Harvest Samantha' (Sin/Lil) ♀H3	CWGr NHal
'Haseley Bridal Wish' (MC)	CWGr
'Haseley Goldicote' (SD)	CWGr
'Haseley Miranda' (SD)	CWGr
'Hawai'^{PBR}	CSut
'Hayley Jayne' (SC)	CWGr ERCP WAba
'Heather Huston' (MD)	CWGr
'Heather Jones' (MinD) **new**	CWGr
'Helga' (MS-c)	ECtt
'Hello There' (MS-c) **new**	CWGr
'Henri Lewii' (SC)	CWGr
'Henriette' (MC)	CWGr
'Herbert Smith' (D)	SEND
'Hexton Copper' (SBa)	CWGr
'Higherfield Champion' (SS-c)	CWGr
'Highgate Lustre' (MS-c)	CWGr
'Highgate Torch' (MS-c)	CWGr
'Hildepuppe' (Pom)	CWGr
'Hillcrest Albino' (SS-c)	CWGr
'Hillcrest Amour' (SD)	CWGr
'Hillcrest Camelot' (GS-c)	CWGr
'Hillcrest Contessa' (MinBa)	CWGr
'Hillcrest Delight' (MD)	NHal
'Hillcrest Desire' (SC) ♀H3	LAyl WAba
'Hillcrest Embers' (LD) **new**	WAba
'Hillcrest Fiesta' (MS-c)	CWGr
'Hillcrest Hannah' (MinD)	NHal
'Hillcrest Heights' (LS-c)	CWGr WAba
'Hillcrest Jake' (MS-c) **new**	NHal
'Hillcrest Jessica J' (MC) **new**	CWGr

'Hillcrest Kismet' (MD)	LAyl NHal
'Hillcrest Regal' (Col) ♀[H3]	CWGr WAba
'Hillcrest Royal' (MC) ♀[H3]	CWGr LAyl NHal SDix SUsu
'Hill's Delight' (MS-c)	CWGr
'Hockley Maroon' (SD)	CWGr
'Holland Festival' (GD)	CWGr LRHS
'Hollyhill Bewitched' (SD) **new**	WAba
'Hollyhill Cotton Candy' (MC) **new**	WAba
'Hollyhill Flamingo' (MS-c) **new**	WAba
'Home Run' (Sin) **new**	CWGr
'Homer T' (LS-c)	CWGr
'Honest John' (LD)	CWGr
'Honeymoon Dress' (SD)	CWGr
'Honka' (SinO) ♀[H3]	CBgR CSpe CWGr EBee ECtt ERCP LAyl LRHS MCot NHal NSti WAba WCot
'Honka Red' (Misc)	ERCP NHal
'Honka Surprise' (Misc)	CWGr ECtt EPfP ERCP NHal WCot
'Honka White' (Misc)	CWGr ERCP
'Honor Francis'	WCot WWEG
'Horst Athalie' (SC) **new**	CWGr
'Hot Chocolate' (MinD)	CWGr
'Hugh Mather' (MWL)	CWGr GBin
'Hugs and Kisses'	EPfP
'Hulin's Carnival' (MinD)	CWGr
'Hy Clown' (SD)	CWGr
'Icarus' (SS-c)	WAba
'Ice Cube' (MD) **new**	ERCP
'Ice Queen' (SWL)	CWGr
'Ida Gayer' (LD)	CWGr
'I-lyke-it' (SS-c)	CWGr
'Imagion'	EPfP
'Imp'	see *D.* 'Harvest Imp'
imperialis (B)	CCon CDTJ CHEx CHll CWGr EWes LEdu LRHS SBig SDix WAba WHal
- B&SWJ 8997	WCru
- 'Alba' (B)	CCon CWGr WPGP
- pink double-flowered (B)	WPGP
'Impression Famosa'	LRHS
'Impression Fantastico'	CWGr
'Impression Fortuna' (Col/DwB)	CWGr
'Inca' (Anem)	WAba
'Inca Dambuster' (GS-c)	CWGr NHal
'Inca Matchless' (MD)	CWGr
'Inca Panorama' (MD)	CWGr
'Inca Royale' (LD)	CWGr
'Inca Vanguard' (GD)	CWGr
'Inca Vulcan' (GS-c)	CWGr
'Indian Summer' (SC)	CWGr NHal WAba
'Inglebrook Jill' (Col)	CWGr
'Inland Dynasty' (GS-c)	CWGr
'Inn's Gerrie Hoek' (MD)	CWGr
'Invader' (SC)	CWGr
'Iris' (Pom)	CWGr
'Irisel' (MS-c)	CWGr
'Islander' (LD)	CWGr
'Ivanetti' (MinBa)	CWGr EPfP NHal WAba
'Ivy Della' (SD)	CWGr
'Jackie Magson' (SS-c)	CWGr WAba
'Jackie's Baby' (MinD)	WAba
'Jacqueline Tivey' (SD)	CWGr
'Jaldec Jerry' (GS-c)	CWGr
'Jaldec Joker' (SC)	CWGr
'Jaldec Jolly' (SC)	CWGr
'Jamaica' (MinWL)	CWGr
'Jamaica' (SD) **new**	WAba
'Jamie' (SS-c)	CWGr
'Jan Carden'	CWGr
'Jan Lennon' (MS-c)	CWGr
I 'Jan van Schaffelaar' (Pom)	ERCP SDeJ
'Janal Amy' (GS-c)	CWGr NHal WAba
'Jane Cowl' (LD)	CWGr
'Jane Horton' (Col)	CWGr
'Janet Beckett' (LC)	CWGr
'Janet Clarke' (Pom)	CWGr
'Janet Howell' (Col)	CWGr
'Japanese Waterlily' (SWL)	CWGr
'Jason' (SS-c)	WAba
'Jazzy' (Col)	CWGr
'Je Maintiendrai' (GD)	CWGr
'Jean Fairs' (MinWL) ♀[H3]	CWGr LYaf
'Jean Marie'[PBR] (MD)	CWGr ERCP
'Jean Melville' (MinD)	CWGr
'Jeanne d'Arc' (GC)	CWGr EPfP
'Jeannie Leroux' (SS-c/Fim)	CWGr
'Jennie' (MS-c/Fim)	CWGr
'Jescot Buttercup' (SD)	CWGr
'Jescot India' (MinD)	CWGr
'Jescot Jess' (MinD)	CWGr LYaf
'Jescot Jim' (SD)	CWGr
'Jescot Julie' (DblO)	ERCP GBin LAyl
'Jescot Lingold' (MinD)	CWGr ECtt
'Jescot Redun' (MinD)	CWGr
'Jessica' (S-c)	CWGr
'Jessica Willows' (SWL)	NHal
'Jessie G' (SBa)	CWGr
'Jessie Ross' (MinD/DwB)	CWGr
'Jet' (SS-c)	CWGr
'Jill Day' (SC)	CWGr LYaf
'Jill Doc' (MD)	CWGr
'Jill's Delight' (MD)	CWGr
'Jim Branigan' (LS-c)	CWGr NHal WAba
'Joan Walker' (SD) **new**	CWGr
'Jocondo' (GD)	CWGr NHal
'Joe Swift' (Misc) **new**	CWGr
'Johann' (Pom)	CWGr NHal
'John Street' (SWL) ♀[H3]	CWGr
'John's Champion' (MD)	CWGr
'Jomanda' (MinBa) ♀[H3]	CWGr GBin LYaf NHal
'Jo's Choice' (MinD)	LYaf
'Joy Donaldson' (MC)	CWGr
'Joyce Green' (GS-c)	CWGr
'Juanita' (MS-c)	CWGr
'Jules Dyson' (Misc)	SDys
'Julie One' (DblO)	CWGr
'Jura' (SS-c)	CWGr EPfP ERCP
'Just Jill' (MinD)	CWGr
'Juul's Allstar' (Misc) ♀[H3]	CWGr
'Kaiser Wilhelm' (SBa)	CWGr
'Kaiserwalzer' (Col)	CWGr
'Karenglen' (MinD) ♀[H3]	CWGr LYaf NHal
'Kari Quill' (SC)	CWGr
'Karma Amanda'[PBR] (SD)	CWGr LRHS WAba
'Karma Bon Bini'[PBR] (SC)	WAba
'Karma Choc'[PBR] (SD)	CWGr EPfP ERCP IPot LRHS MSCN NHal NRHS SMrm SPer SWal WAba
'Karma Corona'[PBR] (SC)	CWGr WAba
'Karma Fuchsiana' (SD)	CWGr ERCP LRHS SBfd WAba
'Karma Irene'[PBR] (SD)	ERCP
'Karma Lagoon'[PBR] (SD)	CWGr ERCP LRHS SBfd WAba
'Karma Maarten Zwaan'[PBR] (SWL)	CWGr WAba

	Name	Suppliers
	'Karma Naomi'PBR (SD)	ERCP LRHS SMrm WAba
	'Karma Pink Corona'PBR (SC)	WAba
	'Karma Prospero'PBR (SD)	ERCP LRHS MSCN SBfd SMrm WAba
	'Karma Red Corona'PBR (SC)	SDeJ WAba
	'Karma Royal Sea'PBR (SD)	CWGr
	'Karma Sangria'PBR (SC)	CWGr LRHS SDeJ WAba
	'Karma Serena'PBR	SDeJ WAba
	'Karma Yin Yang' (SD)	WAba
	'Karras 150' (SS-c)	CWGr
	'Kasasagi' (Pom)	CWGr
	'Kate Mountjoy' (Col)	CWGr
	'Kate's Pastelle' (MS-c)	WAba
	'Kathryn's Cupid' (MinBa) ♀H3	CWGr
I	'Katie' (SD) **new**	NHal
	'Katie Dahl' (MinD)	NHal
	'Katisha' (MinD)	CWGr
	'Kea Magic' (GD)	WAba
	'Keith's Choice' (MD)	NHal WAba
	'Keith's Pet' (Sin)	CWGr
	'Kelsea Carla' (SS-c) ♀H3	CWGr WAba
	'Kelvin Floodlight' (GD)	CWGr SMrm SPer
	'Kenn Emerland' (MS-c)	EPfP
	'Kenora Canada' (MS-c)	CWGr
	'Kenora Challenger' (LS-c)	CWGr NHal WAba
	'Kenora Christmas' (SBa)	CWGr
	'Kenora Clyde' (GS-c)	CWGr
	'Kenora Jubilee' (LS-c)	NHal
	'Kenora Lisa' (MD)	WAba
	'Kenora Macop-B' (MC/Fim)	CSut CWGr IPot LRHS WAba
	'Kenora Moonbeam' (MD)	CWGr
	'Kenora Sunburst' (LS-c)	CWGr
	'Kenora Sunset' (MS-c) ♀H3	LAyl LYaf NHal
	'Kenora Superb' (LS-c)	CWGr NHal
	'Kenora Valentine' (LD) ♀H3	CWGr LAyl NHal
	'Ken's Flame' (SWL)	CWGr
	'Key West' (LD)	CWGr
	'Kidd's Climax' (GD) ♀H3	CWGr ERCP WAba
	'Kilburn Fiesta' (MS-c) **new**	NHal
	'Kilmorie' (SS-c)	NHal
	'Kim Willo' (Pom)	CWGr
	'Kingston' (MinD)	CWGr
	'Kismet' (SBa)	CWGr
	'Kiss' (MinD)	CWGr
	'Kiss Me' (SD)	EPfP
	'Kit Kat' (LC)	CWGr
	'Kiwi Brother' (SS-c)	CWGr
	'Kiwi Cousin' (SC)	CWGr
	'Kiwi Gloria' (SC)	CWGr GBin NHal
	'Klondike' (MS-c)	ERCP WAba
I	'Knockout' (Sin)PBR	EBee EPfP GBin LRHS LSRN LSou MBri MGos SHar SPoG
	'Kochelsee' (MinD)	CWGr
	'Kogane Fubuki' (Fim) **new**	CWGr WAba
	'Kotare Jackpot' (SS-c)	CWGr
	'Kung Fu' (SD)	CWGr
I	'Kyoto' (SWL)	CWGr
	'L.A.T.E.' (MinBa)	GBin NHal WAba
	'La Gioconda' (Col)	CWGr
	'La Recoleta' (D)	ERCP WAba
	'La Rouvre' (SS-c)	GBin
	'Lady Kerkrade' (SC)	CWGr
	'Lady Linda' (SD)	CWGr LYaf NHal WAba
	'Lady Orpah' (SD)	CWGr
	'Lakeland Sunset' (SC) ♀H3 **new**	CWGr

	Name	Suppliers
	'L'Ancresse' (MinBa)	GBin LAyl NHal WAba
	'Last Dance' (MD)	CWGr
	'Laura's Choice' (SD)	CWGr
	'Lauren's Moonlight'	see *D.* 'Pim's Moonlight'
	'Lavender Freestyle' (SC)	CWGr
	'Lavender Leycett' (GD)	CWGr
	'Lavender Line' (SS-c)	NHal
	'Lavengro' (GD)	CWGr
	'Le Baron' (SD)	ERCP
	'Le Castel' (SWL) ♀H3	CWGr SDeJ
	'Le Patineur' (MD)	CWGr
	'Le Vonne Splinter' (GS-c)	CWGr
	'Leander' (GS-c)	CWGr
	'Lemon Cane' (Misc)	CWGr WAba
§	'Lemon Cane' (SD) **new**	ECtt
	'Lemon Elegans' (SS-c) ♀H3	CWGr LYaf NHal
	'Lemon Meringue' (SD)	CWGr ECtt
*	'Lemon Puff' (Anem)	CWGr
	'Lemon Zing' (MinBa)	LAyl NHal
	'Lexington' (Pom)	CWGr
	'Libretto' (Col)	CWGr
	'Life Force' (GD)	CWGr
	'Life Style' (Anem)	SPer
	'Light Music' (MS-c)	CWGr
	'Lilac Athalie' (SC)	CWGr
	'Lilac Bull' (MinD)	LRHS
	'Lilac Marston' (MinD) ♀H3	NHal
	'Lilac Taratahi' (SC) ♀H3	CSam CWGr LAyl
	'Lilac Time' (MD)	CWGr ERCP SDeJ
	'Lilac Willo' (Pom)	CWGr
	'Lilian Alice' (Col)	CHVG NHal
	'Lillianne Ballego' (MinD)	CWGr
	'Linda's Baby' (MinBa) **new**	WAba
	'Linda's Chester' (SC)	CWGr LYaf
	'Lisa'	CWGr
	'Lismore Canary' (SWL)	WAba
	'Lismore Carol' (Pom)	CWGr NHal
	'Lismore Moonlight' (Pom)	LAyl NHal
	'Lismore Robin' (MinD)	NHal
	'Lismore Willie' (SWL) ♀H3	CWGr LYaf WAba
	'Little Dorrit' (Sin/Lil) ♀H3	CWGr
	'Little Fawn' (SS-c) **new**	CWGr
	'Little Glenfern' (MinC)	CWGr
	'Little John' (Sin/Lil)	CWGr
	'Little Laura' (MinBa)	CWGr
	'Little Matthew' (Pom)	CWGr
	'Little Robert' (MinD)	EPfP
	'Little Sally' (Pom)	CWGr
	'Little Scottie' (Pom)	CWGr
	'Little Snowdrop' (Pom)	CWGr
	'Little Tiger' (MinD)	CWGr
	'Little Treasure'	EPfP
	'Liz' (LS-c)	CWGr
	'Lloyd Huston' (GS-c)	CWGr
	'Lois Walcher' (MD)	CWGr
	'Lorona Dawn' (SinO)	ERCP NHal WAba
	'Loud Applause' (SC)	CWGr
	'Lucky Number' (MD)	CWGr ERCP
	'Ludwig Helfert' (S-c)	CWGr ERCP SEND WAba
	'Lupin Dixie' (SC)	CWGr
	'Lyn Mayo' (SD)	CWGr
	'Mabel Ann' (GD)	CWGr LAyl NHal WAba
	'Madame de Rosa' (LS-c)	LAyl NHal
	'Madame Simone Stappers' (WL)	CWGr EBee ECtt ETod LRHS
	'Madame Vera' (SD)	CWGr LYaf
	'Madelaine Ann' (GD)	CWGr
	'Mafolie' (GS-c)	CWGr
	'Magenta Magic' (Sin/DwB)	NHal

	'Magenta Star' (Sin) ♀H3	GBin SUsu
	'Maggie C' (MS-c)	NHal
	'Magic Moment' (MS-c)	CWGr
	'Magnificat' (MinD)	CWGr
	'Majestic Athalie' (SC)	CWGr
	'Majjas Symbol' (MS-c)	CWGr
	'Malham Portia' (SWL)	WAba
	'Maltby Fanfare' (Col)	CWGr
I	'Mambo'	ERCP
	'Mandy' (MinD)	CWGr
	'Manhattan Island' (SD) **new**	ERCP
	'Marble Ball' (MinD)	ERCP SDeJ
	'Margaret Ann' (MinD)	CWGr
	'Margaret Haggo' (SWL)	NHal
	'Marie' (SD)	CWGr
	'Marie Schnugg' (Misc) ♀H3	CWGr
	'Mariposa' (Col)	CWGr
	'Marissa' (SWL)	CWGr
	'Mark Damp' (LS-c)	CWGr
	'Mark Hardwick' (GD)	CWGr
	'Mark Lockwood' (Pom)	CWGr
	'Market Joy' (SS-c)	CWGr
	'Marla Lu' (MC)	CWGr
	'Marlene Joy' (MS-c/Fim)	CWGr WAba
	'Mars' (Col)	CWGr
	'Marshmello Sky' (Col)	CWGr
	'Martina' (SD)	NHal
	'Martin's Yellow' (Pom)	NHal
	'Mary Eveline' (Col)	ECtt LAyl NHal
	'Mary Evelyn' (SC) **new**	SMrm SPer
	'Mary Layton' (Col)	CWGr
	'Mary Lunns' (Pom)	CWGr
	'Mary Partridge' (SWL)	CWGr
	'Mary Pitt' (MinD)	CWGr
	'Mary Richards' (SD)	CWGr
	'Mary's Jomanda' (SBa) ♀H3	CWGr GBin NHal
	'Master Michael' (Pom)	CWGr
	'Matador' (D)	EPfP
	'Matchless' (C) **new**	CWGr
	'Matilda Huston' (SS-c)	CWGr LAyl NHal
	'Maureen Hardwick' (GD)	CWGr
	(Maxi Series) 'Maxi Romero' **new**	MBri
	- 'Maxi Tampico' **new**	MBri
	'Maxine Bailey' (SD)	CWGr
	'Maya' (SD)	IPot
	'Megan Dean' (MinBa)	NHal WAba
	'Meiro' (SD)	CWGr
	'Melanie Jane' (MS-c)	CWGr
	'Melody Dixie' PBR (MinD)	CWGr
	'Melody Dora' PBR (SD)	CWGr
	'Melody Harmony' PBR (SD)	EPfP
	merckii (B)	CBgR CCon CGHE CSpe CWGr EBee EWes LRHS MNrw MRav NRHS WAba WPGP WSHC
	- F&M 222	WPGP
	- 'Alba' (B)	CSpe SUsu WCru
	- compact (B)	WPGP
	'Mermaid of Zennor' (Sin)	CCon
	'Mevrouw Clement Andries' (MS-c/Fim)	CWGr ERCP
	'Miami' (SD)	CWGr
	'Michael J' (MinD)	CWGr
	'Michigan' (MinD)	CWGr
	'Mick' (SC)	CWGr
	'Mick's Peppermint' (MS-c)	CWGr
	'Midnight' (Pom)	CHVG CWGr
	'Mies' (Sin)	CWGr
	'Mingus Alex' (MS-c/Fim)	CWGr
	'Mingus Kyle D' (SD)	CWGr
	'Mingus Nichole' (LD)	CWGr
	'Mingus Randy' (LS-c)	SPer
	'Mingus Wesley' (LD) **new**	WAba
	'Mingus Whitney' (GS-c)	CWGr
	'Mini' (Sin/Lil)	CWGr
	'Mini Red' (MinS-c)	CWGr
	'Minley Carol' (Pom) ♀H3	CWGr LAyl NHal WAba
	'Minley Iris' (Pom)	CWGr
	'Mish-Mash' (Fim/MS-c)	CWGr
	'Miss Blanc' (SD)	CWGr
	'Miss Ellen' (Misc) ♀H3	CWGr
	'Miss Swiss' (SD)	CWGr
	'Misterton' (MD)	CWGr
	'Mistill Beauty' (SC)	CWGr
	'Mistral' (MS-c/Fim)	ECtt
	'Mom's Special' (LD)	CWGr LRHS
I	'Mon Trésor' (MinS-c)	CWGr
	'Monk Marc' (SC)	CWGr
	'Monkstown Diane' (SC)	CWGr
	'Moonfire' (Misc/DwB) ♀H3	CSam CWCL CWGN CWGr EBee ECtt EHrv ELan EPfP ERCP EUJe LAyl LRHS MBri NEgg NHal NPri NRHS SBfd SDix SMrm SPer WAba WCot WHil WHoo WWEG
	'Moonglow' (LS-c)	CWGr ERCP
	'Moor Place' (Pom)	NHal WAba WWEG
	'Moray Susan' (SWL)	CWGr WAba
	'Moret' (SS-c)	CWGr
	'Morley Lass' (SS-c)	CWGr
	'Motto' (LD)	CWGr
	'Mount Noddy' (Sin)	CWGr
	'Mr Optimist' (SD) **new**	SPer
	'Mrs A. Woods' (MD)	CWGr
	'Mrs Black' (Pom)	CWGr
	'Mrs Eileen' (GD)	ERCP
	'Mrs George Le Boutillier' (LD)	CWGr
	'Mrs McDonald Quill' (LD)	CWGr
	'Mrs Silverston' (SD)	CWGr
	'Mum's Lipstick' (Fim) **new**	CWGr
	'München' (MinD)	CWGr NGdn
	'Murdoch'	CBgR EBee ECtt EHrv LRHS SMrm WCot
	'Murillo'	LAyl
	'Murray May' (LD)	CWGr
	'Murray Petite' (SS-c)	CWGr
	'Musette' (MinD)	CWGr
	'My Beverley' (Fim)	LAyl NHal
	'My Love' (SS-c)	CSut CWGr ERCP SEND SMrm WAba
	'Myama Fubuki' (MS-c)	ERCP
	'Myrtle's Folly' (Fim) **new**	ERCP
	'Mystery Day' (MD)	CWGr ECtt SBfd SMrm
	Mystic Desire	see *D.* 'Scarlet Fern'
	Mystic Mars	see *D.* 'Scarlet Fern'
	'Nagano' (MinD)	CWGr SDeJ
	'Nancy H' (MinBa)	CWGr
	'Nargold' (Fim)	CWGr LAyl
	'Narrow's Tricia' (MS-c)	WAba
	'Natal' (MinBa)	ECtt ERCP
	'Nathalie's Wedding' (SWL)	ERCP SUsu
	'Nationwide' (SD)	CWGr
	'Nellie Geerlings' (Sin)	CWGr
	'Nenekazi' (Fim)	CWGr
	'Nepos' (SWL)	CWGr GBin
	'Nescio' (Pom)	CWGr ERCP SDeJ
	'New Baby' (MinBa)	ERCP

'New Dimension' (SS-c) CWGr
'Newsham Wonder' (SD) CWGr
'Nicola' (SS-c) CWGr
'Nicolette' (MWL) CWGr
I 'Night Queen' (MinBa) ERCP
'Nina Chester' (SD) CWGr
'Nippon' (Sin) EBee LRHS
'Nonette' (SWL) CBgR CWGN CWGr EBee ECtt LRHS NEgg WCot
'Norbeck Dusky' (SS-c) CWGr
'Noreen' (Pom) CWGr NHal
'Norman Lockwood' (Pom) CWGr
'North Sea' (MD) CWGr
'Northland Primrose' (SC) CWGr
'Northwest Cosmos' (Sin) ♀H3 CWGr
* 'Nuit d'Eté' (MS-c) CAvo CSpe CWGr EPfP ERCP LRHS SEND SPad SWal WAba
Nunton form (SD) CWGr
'Nunton Harvest' (SD) CWGr
'Nymphenburg' (SD) CWGr
'Oakwood Diamond' (SBa) CWGr
'Oakwood Goldcrest' (SS-c) CWGr NHal
'Old Boy' (SBa) CWGr
'Omo' (Sin/Lil) ♀H3 WAba
'Onesta' (SD) CWGr ERCP SDeJ
'Onslow Michelle' (SD) CWGr
'Opal' (SBa) CWGr
'Optic Illusion' (SD) CWGr
'Opus' (SD) CWGr
'Orange Cushion' (MinD) CWGr
'Orange Fubuki' (SD) ERCP
'Orange Keith's Choice' (MD) CWGr
'Orange Nugget' (MinBa) CWGr SDeJ
I 'Orange Queen' (MC) CWGr
'Oranjestad' (SWL) CWGr
'Orchid Princess' (MS-c) ERCP
'Orel' (Col) CWGr WAba
'Oreti Bliss' (SC) LAyl NHal
'Oreti Classic' (MD) NHal
'Orfeo' (MC) CHVG CWGr ECtt ERCP MNrw SDeJ SWal
'Oriental Dream' (D) LRHS
'Ornamental Rays' (SC) CWGr
'Osaka' (SD) CWGr
'Osirium' (SD) ERCP SPer
'Othello' (MS-c) CWGr
'Otto's Thrill' (LD) ERCP SMrm
'Pablo' LRHS SHil
'Pacific Argyle' (SD) NHal
'Paint Box' (MS-c) CWGr
'Painted Girl' (D) ERCP
'Pam Howden' (SWL) NHal
'Pamela' (SD) CWGr
'Pari Taha Sunrise' (MS-c) CWGr
'Park Princess' (SC/DwB) CWGr LAyl NGdn NHal SDeJ SMrm
'Parkflamme' (MinD) CWGr
'Parkland Rave' (SS-c) **new** CWGr
'Paroa Gillian' (SC) CWGr
'Party' SDeJ
'Paso Doble' misapplied see *D.* 'Freya's Paso Doble'
'Pat Knight' (Col) CHVG CWGr WAba
'Pat Mark' (LS-c) CWGr LAyl
'Pat 'n' Dee' (SD) CWGr
'Patricia' (Col) CHVG NHal
'Paul Chester' (SC) CWGr
'Paul Critchley' (SC) CWGr
'Paul Smith' (SBa) CWGr
'Peace Pact' (SWL) CWGr WAba
'Peach Athalie' (SC) CWGr
'Peach Brandy' (MinWL) SMrm
'Peach Cupid' (MinBa) ♀H3 CWGr
§ 'Peach Melba' (SD) NHal
'Peaches and Cream'PBR (MinD) SBfd
'Peachette' (Misc/Lil) ♀H3 CWGr
'Pearl Hornsey' (SD) CWGr
'Pearl of Heemstede' (SD) ♀H3 CWGr LAyl NHal
'Pearl Sharowean' (MS-c) CWGr WAba
'Pearson's Benn' (SS-c) CWGr
'Pearson's Mellanie' (SC) CWGr
'Pembroke Levenna' (MinBa) NHal
'Pembroke Pattie' (Pom) CWGr NHal
'Pennsclout' (GD) CWGr
'Pennsgift' (GD) CWGr
'Pensford Marion' (Pom) CWGr
'Perfect Partner' (Sin) **new** CWGr
'Perfectos' (MC) CWGr
'Peter' (MinD) CWGr ECtt
'Peter Nelson' (SBa) CWGr
'Petit Byoux' (DwCol) CWGr
'Pfitzer's Joker' WAba
I 'Phoenix' (MD) WAba
'Pianella' (SS-c) CWGr
§ 'Pim's Moonlight' (MS-c) NHal
'Pinelands Morgenster' (Fim) CWGr
'Pinelands Pam' (Fim) CWGr
'Pinelands Pixie' (Fim) NHal
'Pinelands Princess' (Fim) **new** ERCP
'Pink Attraction' (MinD) CWGr
'Pink Giraffe' (O) ♀H3 CWGr ERCP LRHS
'Pink Jupiter' (GS-c) CWGr NHal
'Pink Katisha' (MinD) CWGr
'Pink Leycett' (GD) CWGr
'Pink Loveliness' (SWL) CWGr
'Pink Newby' (MinD) CWGr
'Pink Pastelle' (MS-c) ♀H3 NHal WAba
'Pink Preference' (SS-c) CWGr
'Pink Risca Miner' (SBa) CWGr
'Pink Robin Hood' (SBa) CWGr
'Pink Sensation' (SC) ♀H3 CWGr
'Pink Shirley Alliance' (SC) CWGr LAyl
'Pink Skin' (MD) ECtt ERCP LRHS SDeJ
'Pink Sylvia' (MinD) CWGr
'Pink Symbol' (MS-c) CWGr
pinnata WAba
\- B&SWJ 10240 WCru
'Piperoo' (MC) CWGr
'Piper's Pink' (SS-c/DwB) CWGr ECtt LAyl LRHS
I 'Pippa' (MinWL) CWGr
'Playboy' (GD) CWGr
'Polar Sight' (GC) CWGr
'Pollyanna' (MD) **new** CWGr
'Polventon Supreme' (SBa) CWGr
'Pontiac' (SC) CWGr LAyl
'Pooh' (Col) see *D.* 'Pooh - Swan Island'
§ 'Pooh - Swan Island' (Col) CHVG CWGr ERCP GBin LAyl NHal WCot
'Poppet' (MinD) WAba
'Popular Guest' (MS-c/Fim) CWGr
'Pot Black' (MinBa) CWGr
'Potgeiter' (MinBa) CWGr ERCP

	Name	Suppliers
	'Prefere' (Sin)	CWGr
	'Preference' (SS-c)	CWGr ERCP
	'Preston Park' (Sin/DwB) ♀H3	CWGr LAyl NHal
	Pretty Woman = 'Vdtg43'PBR (Dark Angel Series) (Sin)	LRHS
	Pride of Berlin	see *D.* 'Stolz von Berlin'
	'Prime Minister' (GD)	CWGr
	'Primeur' (MS-c)	CWGr
	'Primrose Diane' (SD)	CWGr
	'Primrose Pastelle' (MS-c)	NHal
	'Primrose Rustig' (MD)	CWGr
	'Prince Valiant' (SD)	CWGr
I	'Princess' (Col) **new**	SDeJ
	'Princess Beatrix' (LD)	CWGr
	'Princess Marie José' (Sin)	CWGr
	'Princesse Elisabeth' (MinD)	ERCP
	'Princesse Gracia' (MinD)	ERCP
	'Princesse Laetitia' (MinD)	ERCP
	'Prinzessin Irene von Preussen' (SD)	CWGr
	'Procyon' (SD)	CWGr WAba
	'Prom' (Pom)	CWGr
	'Promise' (MS-c/Fim)	CWGr ECtt ERCP WAba
	aff. ***pteropoda*** F&M 312	WPGP
	'Pumpkin Pie'	CBgR
	'Punky' (Pom)	CWGr
	'Purbeck Lydia' (LS-c)	CWGr
	'Purity' (SS-c)	CWGr
	'Purpinca' (Anem)	CWGr
	'Purple Cottesmore' (MWL)	CWGr
	'Purple Gem' (SS-c)	CWGr ERCP SMrm WAba
	'Purple Haze' (Misc) **new**	ERCP
	'Purple Splash' (SWL) **new**	CWGr
	aff. ***purpusii*** B&SWJ 10321	WCru
	'Pussycat' (SD)	CWGr
	'Que Sera' (Misc) **new**	WAba
	'Quel Diable' (LS-c)	CWGr
	'Rachel de Thame' (Sin) **new**	CWGr
	'Rachel's Place' (Pom)	CWGr
	'Radfo' (SS-c)	WAba
	'Radiance' (MC)	CWGr ERCP
	'Raffles' (SD)	CWGr LAyl
	'Ragged Robin' (Misc)	CBgR CSpe CWGN ECtt EHrv ETod LRHS
	'Raiser's Pride' (MC)	NHal
	'Raymond Guernsey'	ECtt LRHS
	'Rebecca Lynn' (MinD)	CWGr
	'Red Alert' (LBa)	CWGr
	'Red and White' (SD)	CWGr
	'Red Arrows' (SD)	CWGr
	'Red Balloon' (SBa)	CWGr
	'Red Cap' (MinD)	CWGr
	'Red Carol' (Pom)	CWGr NHal
	'Red Diamond' (MD)	CWGr NHal
	'Red Fubuki' (SD)	SDeJ SWal
	'Red Highlight' (LS-c)	CWGr
	'Red Majorette' (SS-c)	CWGr SDeJ SWal
	'Red Pimpernel' (SD)	CWGr
	'Red Pygmy' (SS-c)	CWGr
	'Red Riding Hood' (MinBa)	CWGr
	'Red Velvet' (SWL)	CWGr
	'Reddy' (DwLil)	CWGr
	'Regal Boy' (SBa)	CWGr
	'Reginald Keene' (LS-c)	CWGr NHal
	'Renato Tozio' (SD)	CWGr
	'Reputation' (LC)	CWGr
	'Requiem' (SD)	ECtt ERCP
	'Reverend P. Holian' (GS-c)	CWGr
	'Revive' **new**	CWGr
	'Rhonda' (Pom)	NHal
	'Richard Marc' (SC)	CWGr
	'Richard S' (LS-c)	NHal
	'Ridlings Annette' **new**	WAba
	'Ridlings Salmon Wheels' (Col) **new**	WAba
	'Ridlings Wicked' (SWL) **new**	WAba
	'Riisa' (MinBa)	CWGr WAba
	'Rip City' (SS-c)	CSpe CWGr ERCP MCot WCot
	'Rita Easterbrook' (LD)	CWGr
	'Rita Shrimpton' (Misc) **new**	CWGr WAba
	'Roan' (MinD)	CWGr
	'Robbie Huston' (LS-c)	CWGr
	'Rocco' (MinBa)	ERCP
	'Rosalinde' (S-c)	CWGr
	'Rose Jupiter' (GS-c)	NHal
	'Rose Quartz' (Misc) **new**	SMrm
	'Rose Tendre' (MS-c)	CWGr
	'Rosella' (MD)	SDeJ SWal
	'Rosemary Webb' (SD)	CWGr
	'Rossendale Lewis' (MinD) **new**	NHal
	'Rossendale Luke' (SD)	CWGr
	'Rossendale Natasha' (MinBa)	NHal
	'Rossendale Peach' (SD)	WAba
	'Rosy Cloud' (MD)	CWGr
	'Rothesay Castle' (MinD/DwB)	CWGr
	'Rothesay Herald' (SD/DwB)	CWGr
	'Rothesay Reveller' (MD)	CWGr
	'Rothesay Robin' (SD)	GBin
	'Rothesay Rose' (SWL)	CWGr
	'Rotonde' (SC)	CWGr
I	'Roxy' (Sin/DwB)	CBcs CBgR CWGr EBee ECtt EHrv ELan EPfP ERCP EUJe LAst LAyl LRHS LSRN MAvo MNrw NEgg NGdn NHal NRHS SBfd SMrm WCot WHoo WWEG
	'Royal Amethyst' (MD) **new**	CWGr
	'Royal Visit' (SD)	CWGr
	'Royal Wedding' (LS-c)	CWGr
	'Ruby Red' (MinBa)	CWGr
	'Ruby Wedding' (MinD)	CWGr
	rudis **new**	CWGr WPGP
	'Ruskin Amanda' (MS-c) **new**	WAba
	'Ruskin Andrea' (SS-c)	NHal
	'Ruskin Bride' (MS-c)	NHal WAba
	'Ruskin Buttercup' (MinD)	CWGr
	'Ruskin Charlotte' (LS-c)	CWGr LAyl WAba
	'Ruskin Diana' (SD)	CWGr NHal
	'Ruskin Emil' (SS-c)	CWGr
	'Ruskin Gypsy' (SBa)	CWGr
	'Ruskin Harmony' ambig. **new**	CWGr NHal WAba
	'Ruskin Limelight' (MC) **new**	NHal WAba
	'Ruskin Marigold' (SS-c)	CWGr LAyl NHal WAba
	'Ruskin Michelle' (MS-c)	GBin WAba
	'Ruskin Myra' (SS-c)	CWGr LAyl NHal WAba
	'Ruskin Petite' (MinBa)	CWGr
	'Ruskin Respectable' (SS-c) **new**	WAba
	'Ruskin Sensation' (MS-c) **new**	NHal
	'Ruskin Splendour' (MS-c)	NHal

	Name	Suppliers
	'Ruskin Tangerine' (SBa)	NHal
	'Russell Turner' (SS-c)	CWGr
	'Rusty Hope' (MinD)	CWGr
	'Ryecroft Brenda T' (SD)	NHal
	'Ryecroft Claire' (MinD)	NHal
	'Ryecroft Crystal' (SS-c)	NHal
	'Ryecroft Delight' (MinBa)	NHal
	'Ryecroft Dream' (S-c)	CWGr
	'Ryecroft Gem' (MinBa)	NHal
	'Ryecroft Ice' (LD) **new**	NHal
	'Ryecroft Jan' (MinBa) ♀H3	CWGr NHal
	'Ryecroft Jim' (Anem)	NHal
	'Ryecroft Laura' (MinBa)	NHal
	'Ryecroft Magnum' (MD)	CWGr NHal
	'Ryecroft Rebel' (MD)	NHal
	'Ryecroft Sparkler' (MinC)	NHal
	'Ryecroft Zoe' (SS-c)	NHal
	'Ryedale Pinky' (SD)	CWGr
	'Ryedale Rebecca' (GS-c)	CWGr
	'Safe Shot' (MD)	CWGr
	'Saint-Saëns' (S-c)	ERCP SDeJ SEND WAba
	'Sakura Fubuki' (Fim)	ERCP
	'Salmon Carpet' (MinD)	CWGr
	'Salmon Keene' (LS-c)	WAba
	'Salmon Symbol' (MS-c)	WAba
	'Sam Hopkins' (SD)	LAyl NHal
	'Sam Huston' (GD)	CWGr
	'Samantha'	see *D.* 'Harvest Samantha'
	'Sandra' ambig.	ERCP
	'Sans Souci' (GC)	CWGr
	'Santa Claus' (MD)	CWGr SPer
	'Sarabande' (MS-c)	CWGr
	'Sarah' (MinS-c)	CWGr ECtt LRHS
	'Sarah G' (LS-c)	CWGr EBee
	'Sarah Louise' (SWL)	CWGr
	'Sarah Thomas' (Col) **new**	CWGr
	'Sascha' (SWL) ♀H3	LAyl NHal
	'Scarborough Ace' (MD)	CWGr
	'Scarborough Fair' (MS-c)	NHal
	'Scarlet Comet' (Anem)	CWGr
§	'Scarlet Fern' (Sin)	LRHS LSRN
	'Scarlet Kokarde' (MinD)	CWGr
	'Scarlet Rotterdam' (MS-c)	CWGr
	'Scarlett Claire' (Col) **new**	CWGr WAba
	'Scaur Swinton' (MD)	CWGr LAyl NHal
	'Schweitzer's Kokarde' (MinD)	CWGr
	'Scura' (DwSin)	CWGr ERCP
	'Sean C' (Col)	NHal
	'Seattle' (SD)	CSut CWGr
	'Seduction' (MinD)	EPfP ERCP
	'Seikeman's Feuerball' (MinD)	WAba
	'Senzoe Ursula' (SD)	CWGr
	'Serano' (MC) **new**	CAvo
	'Shandy' (SS-c)	CWGr LAyl NHal
	'Shannon' (SD)	CWGr
	'Sheila Mooney' (LD)	WAba
	'Shep's Memory' (SWL) ♀H3 **new**	CWGr
	sherffii	CWGr
	'Sherwood Monarch' (GS-c)	CWGr
	'Sherwood Titan' (GD)	CWGr
	'Shining Star' (SC)	CWGr
	'Shirley Pillman' (Misc) **new**	CWGr
	'Shooting Star' (LS-c)	CSut CWGr WAba
	'Show 'n' Tell' (Fim)	ERCP
	'Shy Princess' (MC)	CWGr
	'Siedlerstolz' (SD)	CWGr
	'Silver City' (LD)	CWGr NHal
	'Silver Years' (MD)	CWGr
	'Sir Alf Ramsey' (GD)	CWGr LAyl NHal
	'Sisa' (SD)	CWGr
	'Skipley Spot' (SD)	CWGr
	'Skipper Rock' (GD)	CWGr
	'Sky High' (SD)	CWGr
	'Small World' (Pom) ♀H3	CWGr LAyl NHal WAba
	'Smokey' (MD)	CWGr SEND WAba
	'Smoky O' (MS-c)	CWGr
	'Sneezy' (Sin)	CWGr LRHS
	'Snip' (MinS-c)	WAba
	'Snow Cap' (SS-c)	SDeJ
	'Snow Fairy' (MinC)	CWGr
	'Snow White' (DwSin)	CWGr
	'Snowflake' (SWL)	CWGr ERCP SDeJ WAba
	'Snowstorm' (MD)	CWGr SBfd
	'So Dainty' (MinS-c) ♀H3	CWGr LAyl
	'Song of Olympia' (SWL)	CWGr
	'Sonia'	CWGr
	'Sonia Henie' (SBa)	CWGr
	'Sorbet' (DwB)	LRHS
I	'Sorbet' (MS-c)	LAyl NHal
	sorensenii	CWGr
	'Sorrento Fiesta' (SS-c)	WAba
	'Sorrento Flush' (SD) **new**	WAba
	'Soulman' (Anem)	CSpe CWGr
	'Sourire de Crozon' (SD)	CWGr
	'Souvenir d'Eté' (Pom)	SDeJ
	'Sparkler' (SS-c)	CWGr
	'Spartacus' (LD)	CWGr LAyl NHal
	'Spassmacher' (MS-c)	CWGr
	'Spectacular' (SD)	CWGr
	'Spencer' (SD)	CWGr
	'Spennythorn King' (SD)	CWGr
	'Spikey Symbol' (MS-c)	CWGr
	'Staleen Condesa' (MS-c) ♀H3	NHal
	'Star Child' (SinO)	CWGr WAba
	'Star Elite' (MC)	CWGr
	'Star Surprise' (SC)	CWGr SDeJ
	Star Wars (Dark Angel Series)	EPfP LRHS
	'Starburst'	LRHS
	'Starlight Keene' (LS-c)	CWGr
	'Starry Night' (MinS-c)	CWGr
	'Star's Favourite' (MC)	ERCP
	'Star's Lady' (SC)	CWGr
	'Stefan Bergerhoff' (MinD)	CWGr
	'Stella J' (SWL)	CWGr
	'Stellyvonne' (LS-c/Fim)	CWGr
	'Steven's Vanda' (MinD) **new**	WAba
	'Stevie D' (SD) ♀H3	CWGr
§	'Stolz von Berlin' (MinBa)	ERCP
	'Stoneleigh Cherry' (Pom)	LAyl
	'Stoneleigh Joyce' (Pom)	CWGr
	'Storm Warning' (GD)	CWGr
	'Stylemaster' (MC)	CWGr
	'Sue Mountjoy' (Col)	CWGr
	'Sue Willo' (Pom)	CWGr
	'Suffolk Fantasy' (SD)	CWGr
	'Suffolk Punch' (MD)	CWGr LAyl
	'Suitzus Julie' (Misc)	CWGr
	'Summer Festival' (SD)	CWGr
I	'Summer Night' (SC)	ECGP LAyl MCot NHal
	'Summer's End' (SWL)	CWGr
	'Sunlight' (SBa)	CWGr
	'Sunlight Pastelle' (MS-c)	CWGr WAba
	'Sunny' (MinBa) **new**	WAba

	'Sunray Glint' (MS-c)	CWGr WAba
	'Sunray Silk' (MS-c)	CWGr
	'Sunset' (WL) **new**	WAba
I	'Sunshine' (Sin)	CHVG ECtt LAyl LRHS WAba
	'Super Trouper' (SD)	CWGr
	'Superfine' (SC)	CWGr WAba
	'Susan Carey' (LS-c) **new**	WAba
	'Susan Gilliott' (MS-c)	NHal
	'Suzette' (SD/DwB)	CWGr
	'Swallow Falls' (SD)	CWGr
	'Swan Lake' (SD)	SPet
	'Swanvale' (SD)	CWGr
	'Sweet Content' (SD)	CWGr
	'Sweet Sensation' (MS-c)	CWGr
	'Swiss Miss' (MinBa)	CWGr
I	'Sylvia' (SBa)	CWGr SMrm WAba
	'Sylvia's Desire' (SC)	CWGr
	'Sympathy' (SWL)	CWGr
	'Syston Harlequin' (SD)	CWGr
	'Syston Sophia' (LBa)	CWGr
	'Tahiti Sunrise' (MS-c)	CWGr
	'Tahoma Moonshot' (SinO) **new**	CWGr
	'Tahoma Star' (SinO) **new**	SMrm
	'Tahoma Tom Tom' (MS-c)	NHal
	'Tally Ho' (Misc) ♀H3	EBee ECGP ECtt EHrv EPfP LRHS MRav NRHS SDys SMrm WCot WFar
	'Tam Tam' (MinBa)	EPfP SPer
	'Tapestry' (Sin) **new**	CWGr
	'Taratahi Ruby' (SWL) ♀H3	CWGr ERCP GBin LAyl LYaf NHal WAba
	'Tartan' (MD)	CWGr
	Taxi Driver = 'Vdtg57'PBR (Dark Angel Series) (Sin)	EPfP LRHS
	'Teesbrooke Audrey' (Col)	CHVG CWGr ECtt LAyl NHal WAba
	'Teesbrooke Red Eye' (Col) ♀H3	CWGr ERCP GBin NHal WAba
	'Temptress' (SS-c)	CWGr
	'Tender Moon' (SD)	CWGr
	tenuicaulis	CCon CDTJ CWGr SBig
	- F&M 99	WPGP
	- F&M 257	WPGP
	- F&M 355	WPGP
	- F&M 369	WPGP
	'Terracotta' (DwB)	NHal
	'Thames Valley' (MD)	CWGr
	'That's It!' (SD)	CWGr
	'The Phantom' (Anem)	ERCP
	'Thelma Clements' (LD)	CWGr
	'Theo Sprengers' (MD)	CWGr
	'Thika' (SD)	CWGr
	'Thomas A. Edison' (MD)	CWGr ERCP SDeJ
	'Thoresby Jewel' (SD)	CWGr
I	'Tiara' (SD)	CWGr
	'Tiger Eye' (MD)	CWGr
	'Tina B' (SBa)	CWGr
	'Tinker's White' (SD)	CWGr
	'Tioga Spice' (Fim)	NHal
I	'Tiptoe' (MinD)	LAyl NHal
	'Toga' (SWL)	CWGr
	'Tohsuikyoh' (Misc)	CWGr WAba
	'Tommy Doc' (SS-c)	CWGr WAba
	'Tommy Keith' (MinBa)	CWGr
	'Tomo' (SD)	LAyl NHal
	'Top Affair' (MS-c)	CWGr
	'Top Choice' (GS-c)	CWGr
	'Top Totty' (MinD)	NHal
	'Topmix' (Sin) **new**	SDeJ
	'Toto' (Anem)	CWGr ERCP WAba
	'Treby Dainty' (MinBa)	NHal
	'Trelawny' (GD)	CWGr
	'Trelyn Daisy' (Col) ♀H3 **new**	CWGr
	'Trelyn Kiwi' (SS-c) ♀H3	CWGr GBin NHal WAba
	'Trelyn Rebecca' (Col) **new**	NHal
	'Trelyn Rhiannon' (SC) ♀H3 **new**	CWGr
	'Trelyn Seren' (SinO) **new**	NHal
	'Trengrove Autumn' (MD)	CWGr
	'Trengrove Millennium' (MD)	CWGr NHal
	'Trengrove Tauranga' (MD)	CWGr
	'Trevor' (Col)	CWGr
	'Tricolor' **new**	MSCN
	'Trotter's Jo-Anne' (MS-c) **new**	CWGr
	'Troy Dyson' (Misc)	SDys
	'Tsuki-yorine-shisha' (MC)	CWGr
	'Tu Tu' (MS-c)	CWGr
	'Tudor 1' (Misc/DwB)	NHal
	'Tui Avis' (MinC)	CWGr
	'Tui Orange' (SS-c)	CWGr WAba
	'Tula Rosa' (Pom)	CWGr
	'Tutankhamun' (Pom)	CWGr
	'Twiggy' (SWL)	CWGr
	'Twilight Time' (MD)	CWGr SDeJ
	'Twyning's After Eight' (Sin) ♀H3	CPLG CSpe CWCL CWGN CWGr EBee ECtt EHrv ELan EPfP ERCP ETod GBin LRHS MAvo MCot MMHG NEgg NHal NSti SDix SDys SMrm SPer SUsu WBor WCot WHoo
	'Twyning's Aniseed' (Sin)	CWGr EPfP ETod
	'Twyning's Black Cherry' (MinD) **new**	CWGr
	'Twyning's Candy' (Sin) ♀H3	CWGr
	'Twyning's Chocolate' (Sin) ♀H3	CWGr
	'Twyning's Peppermint' (Sin)	CWGr
	'Twyning's Pink Fish' (Col) ♀H3	CWGr ETod
	'Twyning's Revel' (Sin) **new**	CSam CWGr SUsu
	'Twyning's Smartie' (Sin) ♀H3	CWGr GBin SMrm
	'Twyning's White Chocolate' (Sin)	CWGr
	'Tyrell'	EPfP
	'Uchuu' (GD)	CWGr
	'United' (SD)	CWGr
	'Usugesho' (LD)	CWGr
	'Vader Abraham' (MinD)	CWGr
	'Val Saint Lambert' (MC)	CWGr
	'Vancouver' (Misc)	CSut ERCP SDeJ SMrm WAba
	'Variace' (MinBa)	CWGr
	'Velda Inez' (MinD)	CWGr
	'Vera's Elma' (LD)	CWGr
	'Vicky Crutchfield' (SWL)	WCot
	'Victory Day' (LC)	CWGr
	'Vino' (Pom) **new**	CWGr
	'Violet Davies' (MS-c)	CWGr
	'Vivex' (Pom)	CWGr
	'Volkskanzler' (Sin)	CWGr
	'Vulcan' (LS-c)	CWGr
	'Vulkan' (MS-c)	ERCP
§	'Vuurvogel' (MS-c)	CWGr ERCP LRHS SDeJ WAba
	'Walter Hardisty' (GD)	CWGr
	'Walter James' (SD)	CWGr
	'Waltzing Mathilda' (Misc)	CAvo ERCP

'Wanborough Gem' (SBa) CWGr
'Wanda's Aurora' (GD) NHal
'Wanda's Capella' (GD) CWGr WAba
'Wandy' (Pom) ♀H3 CWGr WAba
'War of the Roses' (SD) SGar SWal WHer
'Warkton Willo' (Pom) CWGr
'Waveney Pearl' (SD) CWGr
'Welcome Guest' (MS-c) CWGr WAba
'Wendy' (MinBa) CWGr
'Wendy's Place' (Pom) CWGr
'Weston Dove' (MinS-c) WAba
'Weston Miss' (MinS-c) CHVG CWGr
'Weston Nugget' (MinC) CWGr WAba
'Weston Pirate' (MinC) ♀H3 CWGr NHal WAba
'Weston Princekin' (MinS-c) CWGr
'Weston Spanish Dancer' (MinC) ♀H3 CWGr LAyl LYaf NHal WAba
'Weston Teatime' (DwfC) CWGr
'Weston Torero' (MinC) **new** CWGr
'Wheels' (Col) CWGr WAba
'White Alva's' (GD) ♀H3 LAyl NHal
'White Aster' (Pom) CWGr
'White Ballerina' (SWL) LAyl NHal
'White Ballet' (SD) ♀H3 CWGr LAyl
'White Cameo' (SWL) CWGr
'White Charlie Two' (MD) NHal
'White Hunter' (SD) CWGr
'White Katrina' (LS-c) WAba
'White Klankstad' (SC) CWGr
'White Knight' (MinD) NHal
'White Linda' (SD) CWGr NHal
'White Magenta Star' (Sin) **new** CSam CWGr
'White Moonlight' (MS-c) LAyl NHal WAba
'White Nettie' (MinBa) CWGr
'White Pastelle' (MS-c) CWGr WAba
'White Perfection' (LD) CWGr ECtt EPfP ERCP SDeJ
'White Rustig' (MD) CWGr
'White Star' (MS-c) CWGr ERCP SDeJ WAba
'White Swallow' (SS-c) NHal
'Who Dun It' (LD) **new** ERCP
'Wicky Woo' (SD) CWGr
'William B' (GD) CWGr
'Willo's Borealis' (Pom) NHal
'Willo's Night' (Pom) CWGr
'Willo's Surprise' (Pom) CWGr NHal
'Willo's Violet' (Pom) CWGr NHal WAba
'Willowfield Matthew' (MinD) NHal
'Willowfield Mick' (LD) CWGr
'Wine & Roses' (SWL) CWGr
'Winholme Diane' (SD) NHal WAba
'Winkie Colonel' (GD) CWGr
'Winnie' (Pom) CWGr
'Winsome' (SWL) CWGr
'Winston Churchill' (MinD) LYaf
'Winter Springs' (S-Sc) ERCP
'Wishes and Dreams' (Sin) **new** SPer
'Wisk' (Pom) CWGr
'Wittem' (MD) CWGr
'Witteman's Best' (LS-c) ERCP
'Witteman's Superba' (SS-c) ♀H3 CWGr NHal SDix
'Wizard of Oz' (MinBa) **new** CWGr
'Woodbridge' (Sin) ♀H3 CSpe CWGr
'Woodside Finale' (MinD) NHal
'Wootton Carnival' (SC) **new** CWGr
'Wootton Cupid' (MinBa) ♀H3 CWGr
'Wootton Impact' (MS-c) ♀H3 NHal
'Wootton Tempest' (MS-c) CWGr
'Wootton Windmill' (Col) CWGr
'Worton Blue Streak' (SS-c) CWGr ERCP
'Worton Revival' (MD) CWGr
'Worton Superb' (SD) CWGr
'Yellow Baby' (Pom) CWGr
I 'Yellow Bird' (Col) CWGr
'Yellow Galator' (MC) CWGr
'Yellow Hammer' (Sin/DwB) ♀H3 CWGr LAyl NHal
'Yellow Linda's Chester' (SC) CWGr
'Yellow Pages' (SD) CWGr
'Yellow Passions' (MD) **new** ERCP
'Yellow Pet' (SD) CWGr
'Yellow Sneezy' (Sin/Lil) LRHS
'Yellow Spiky' (MS-c) CWGr
'Yellow Star' (MS-c) CWGr ERCP SDeJ
'Yellow Vulcan' (GS-c) **new** CWGr
'Yelno Enchantment' (SWL) CWGr LAyl
'Yelno Firelight' (SWL) CWGr
'Yelno Harmony' (SD) ♀H3 CWGr
'Yelno Petite Glory' (MinD) CWGr
'York and Lancaster' (MD) CBgR CWGr
'Young Bees' (MD) CWGr
'Yukino' (Col) CWGr
I 'Yvonne' (MWL) WAba
'Zagato' (MinD) CWGr
* 'Zakuro-fubuki' (MD) CWGr
'Zakuro-hime' (SD) CWGr
I 'Zelda' (LD) CWGr
'Zest' (MinD) CWGr
'Zorro' (GD) ♀H3 CWGr ERCP NHal WAba
'Zurich' (SS-c) CWGr

Daiswa see *Paris*

Dalea (*Papilionaceae*)

sp. **new** EWll
candida EBee
purpurea EBee SPhx
- 'Stephanie' EBee EWll

Dalechampia (*Euphorbiaceae*)

dioscoreifolia CCCN
spathulata CCCN

damson see *Prunus insititia*

Danae (*Asparagaceae*)

§ ***racemosa*** CBcs CPne CTri EBee ELan EPfP ERom MGos MRav SEND SRms SSpi SWvt WCot WCru WPGP WPat

Daphne ✿ (*Thymelaeaceae*)

DJHC 98164 from China WCru
acutiloba CJun GKev WSpi
- 'Fragrant Cloud' CJun CPLG EWes SChF
albowiana CJun EWes LLHF LRHS WSpi
alpina CJun GKev NEgg NHol WAbe
altaica CJun
arbuscula ♀H4 CJun EPot LLHF MWat NMen WThu

	- subsp. ***arbuscula*** f. ***albiflora***	CJun
	- 'Diva'	CJun
	- 'Muran Pride'	CJun
	- f. ***radicans***	CJun
	arbuscula × ***cneorum*** var. ***verlotii***	CJun
	arbuscula × 'Leila Haines'	see *D.* × *schlyteri*
	arisanensis B&SWJ 6983	WCru
	bholua	CAbP CHll CJun EPfP LRHS MGos SReu SSpi WAbe
I	- 'Alba'	CBcs CJun CLAP CMac EPfP LRHS MGos WPGP WSpi
	- 'Darjeeling'	CBcs CHll CJun CLAP CPLG CWSG EPfP GBin LRHS SKHP SLim WPGP WSpi
	- var. ***glacialis*** 'Gurkha'	CGHE CJun CPLG ELan EPfP IRar SChF SKHP WPGP
	- 'Jacqueline Postill' ♀H3	Widely available
	- 'Limpsfield'	CJun LRHS SCoo SSta
	- 'Peter Smithers'	CJun CLAP CPLG LRHS LSRN SChF SReu SSta WPGP
	- 'Wisley Purple'	CJun
	blagayana	CJun ECho NBir SRms WThu
	- 'Brenda Anderson'	CJun NMen WAbe
	'Bramdean'	see *D.* × *napolitana* 'Bramdean'
	× ***burkwoodii*** ♀H4	LSRN
	- 'Albert Burkwood'	CJun
	- 'Astrid' (v)	CBcs CJun CWSG LRHS MGos NLar SHil SLon
	- 'Briggs Moonlight' (v)	MAsh
§	- 'Carol Mackie' (v)	CJun LRHS NLar
	- 'G.K.Argles' (v) ♀H4	CJun
I	- 'Gold Sport'	CJun SChF
	- 'Gold Strike' (v)	CJun
	- 'Golden Treasure'	CJun MAsh SChF
	- 'Jan Dekker'	NLar
	- 'Lavenirei'	CJun
	- 'Somerset'	CBcs CJun CWSG ELan MRav MSwo NWea WThu
§	- 'Somerset Gold Edge' (v)	CJun
§	- 'Somerset Variegated' (v)	WThu
	- 'Variegata' broad cream edge	see *D.* × *burkwoodii* 'Somerset Variegated'
	- 'Variegata' broad gold edge	see *D.* × *burkwoodii* 'Somerset Gold Edge'
	- 'Variegata' narrow gold edge	see *D.* × *burkwoodii* 'Carol Mackie'
	calcicola 'Gang-ho-ba'	CJun WAbe
	- 'Sichuan Gold'	CJun
	caucasica	CJun
	circassica	CJun SChF
	cneorum	CBcs CJun EBee GBin GEdr IVic MGos MWat NMen
	- f. ***alba***	CJun
	- 'Benaco'	CJun
	- 'Blackthorn Triumph'	CJun WAbe
	- 'Eximia' ♀H4	CJun GKev WAbe WThu
	- 'Klaus Patzner'	CJun
	- 'Lac des Gloriettes'	CJun
	- 'Puszta'	CJun WAbe
	- var. ***pygmaea***	CJun EPot WAbe
	- - 'Alba'	CJun
	- 'Rubra'	LRHS
	- 'Ruby Glow'	CJun
	- 'Variegata' (v)	CJun GEdr
	- 'Velký Kosir'	CJun MWat SChF WAbe
	- var. ***verlotii***	EPot
	collina	see *D. sericea* Collina Group
	domini	GKev
	× ***eschmannii*** 'Jacob Eschmann'	CJun
	'Forarch'	CJun
	genkwa	CJun SKHP WCru WThu
	giraldii	CJun
	gnidioides	CJun
	'Guardsman'	CJun MAsh SChF
	× ***hendersonii***	CJun
	- 'Appleblossom'	CJun SChF WAbe
	- 'Aymon Correvon'	CJun WThu
	- 'Blackthorn Rose'	CJun
	- 'Ernst Hauser'	CJun WAbe WIce WThu
	- 'Fritz Kummert'	CJun WAbe WThu
	- 'Jeanette Brickell'	CJun WAbe
	- 'Kath Dryden'	CJun SChF WAbe
	- 'Marion White'	CJun WAbe
	- 'Rosebud'	CJun WThu
	- 'Solferino'	CJun
	'Hinton'	CJun
	× ***houtteana***	CJun
	× ***hybrida***	CJun
	japonica 'Striata'	see *D. odora* 'Aureomarginata'
	jasminea	CJun ECho NMen WAbe
	jezoensis	CJun LRHS SSta
	× ***jintyae*** 'Pink Cascade'	CJun
	juliae	CJun WAbe
	kamtschatica	CJun
	'Kilmeston Beauty'	CJun
	kosaninii	CJun
	× ***latymeri*** 'Spring Sonnet'	CJun SChF
	laureola	CBcs CJun EPfP GPoy MMHG NBir NPer WAbe WCFE WSpi
	- 'Kingsley Green'	CJun
	- 'Margaret Mathew'	CJun EPfP SChF
	- subsp. ***philippi***	CJun CMac EBee ELan EPfP EWTr LHop LRHS MAsh MBlu NLar NMen SKHP WPat WSpi
	'Leila Haines'	CJun
	× ***mantensiana*** 'Audrey Vockins'	CJun SChF
	- 'Manten'	CJun MAsh
	× ***mauerbachii*** 'Perfume of Spring'	CJun ECho SChF
	'Meon'	see *D.* × *napolitana* 'Meon'
	mezereum	CTri EBee ECho GAbr GPoy IFoB ITim LRHS MBri MGos NChi NPri NWea SChF SGol SLim SWvt WCFE WFar WHar WPGP
	- f. ***alba***	CBcs CJun CLAP ECho GKev MGos NChi SChF SRms SWvt WAbe WCFE
	- - 'Bowles's Variety'	CJun EPot
	- 'Rosea'	ECho SRms
	- var. ***rubra***	CBcs CJun CMac CWSG CWib ELan GKin LRHS MGos MRav MSwo SPer WAbe WFar
	× ***napolitana*** ♀H4	CJun EPfP SChF
§	- 'Bramdean'	CJun WThu
§	- 'Meon'	CJun NHol WAbe WPat WThu
	odora	CJun CWSG EPfP GBin LRHS LSRN MSwo NMen SLim
§	- f. ***alba***	CCCN CJun CMac
	- - 'Sakiwaka'	CCCN CJun CLAP CPLG EWes SKHP
§	- 'Aureomarginata' (v) ♀H3-4	Widely available
	- 'Clotted Cream' (v)	CJun
	- 'Geisha Girl' (v)	CJun MGos
	- var. ***leucantha***	see *D. odora* f. *alba*
	- 'Limelight'	CJun

- 'Mae-jima' (v)	CJun CPLG EBee ELan EPfP LLHF LRHS MAsh NLar SCoo SLon SMad SPoG
- 'Marginata'	see *D. odora* 'Aureomarginata'
- 'Rebecca' (v)	LBuc LRHS SPoG
- var. ***rubra*** (v)	CCCN CCon CJun CLAP LLHF
- 'Walberton' (v)	EPfP LRHS
oleoides	CJun GKev NLar
papyracea	CPLG
petraea	CJun WAbe
- 'Cima Tombea'	CJun
- 'Corna Blacca'	CJun
- 'Garnet'	CJun WAbe
- 'Grandiflora'	CJun WAbe
- 'Lydora'	CJun WAbe
- 'Persebee'	CJun
- 'Punchinello'	CJun
- 'Tuflungo'	CJun
'Pink Star'	CJun
pontica ♀H4	CBcs CGHE CJun CWSG EBee EOHP EPfP LRHS MAsh MBri NLar SDix SKHP SPer SPoG SSpi WPGP WSpi
pseudomezereum	WCru
retusa	see *D. tangutica* Retusa Group
'Richard's Choice'	CJun
× ***rollsdorfii*** 'Arnold Cihlarz'	CJun MAsh WAbe
- 'Wilhelm Schacht'	CAbP CJun EPot IVic MAsh SChF WAbe WThu
'Rossetii'	CJun
'Rosy Wave'	CJun SChF
§ × ***schlyteri***	CJun EPot
- 'Lovisa Maria'	CJun WAbe
sericea	CJun NLar
§ - Collina Group	CAbP CJun EPfP IRar MAsh WIce WThu
'Spring Beauty'	CJun
'Spring Herald'	CJun
'Stasek' (v)	CJun
striata **new**	GKev
× ***suendermannii*** 'Franz Suendermann'	WAbe
× ***susannae*** 'Anton Fahndrich'	CJun GKev NLar WAbe
- 'Cheriton'	CJun EPfP EPot LRHS NHol NMen WAbe WThu
- 'Tage Lundell'	CJun IVic
- 'Tichborne'	CAbP CJun EPot NMen SChF WAbe WThu
tangutica ♀H4	CBcs CJun CPLG CTri CWSG EBee ECho ELan EPfP EPot GAbr GKev LRHS LSRN MAsh MGos NBir NHol NMen NPCo SCoo SEND SKHP SPoG SRkn SRms SSpi SSta WKif WSpi
§ - Retusa Group ♀H4	CJun CPLG ECho ELan ELon EPot GAbr GBin GEdr GMaP LHop LRHS NBir NMen NRya NSla SPer SRms WSpi
× ***transatlantica*** 'Beulah Cross' (v)	CAbP CJun EBee ELan LLHF LRHS MAsh SChF SCoo SLon
- Eternal Fragrance = 'Blafra'PBR	CAbP CCCN CLAP CPLG CWGN EBee ELan ELon EPfP GEdr LLHF LRHS LSqu MAsh MBri MGos SCoo SKHP SLim SLon SPer SPoG SSpi WPGP
- 'Jim's Pride'	SChF
'Valerie Hillier'	CJun IRar LRHS SChF SHil
velenovskyi	CJun
× ***whiteorum*** 'Beauworth'	CJun WAbe
- 'Kilmeston'	CJun NMen WAbe
- 'Warnford'	CJun
wolongensis 'Kevock Star'	CPLG GKev

Daphniphyllum (*Daphniphyllaceae*)

KWJ 12244 from northern Vietnam **new**	WCru
aff. ***angustifolium*** B&SWJ 8225	WCru
- B&SWJ 11804	WCru
- WWJ 12020	WCru
calycinum B&SWJ 4058	WCru
glaucescens	WCru
subsp. ***oldhamii*** var. ***kengii*** B&SWJ 6872	
- - - B&SWJ 7119	WCru
- - var. ***oldhamii*** B&SWJ 7056	WCru
- - - CWJ 12351	WCru
humile	see *D. macropodum* var. *humile*
aff. ***longeracemosum*** B&SWJ 11788	WCru
macropodum	CBcs CCCN CGHE CHEx CWib EBee EPfP LRHS NLar SDix SKHP SMad SSpi WCru WPGP
- B&SWJ 581	WCru
- B&SWJ 2898	WCru
- B&SWJ 6809 from Taiwan	WCru
- B&SWJ 8507 from Ulleungdo, South Korea	WCru
- B&SWJ 8763 from Cheju-do, Korea	WCru
- B&SWJ 11489 from Yakushima, Japan	WCru
- dwarf	WCru
§ - var. ***humile*** B&SWJ 11232	WCru
majus B&SWJ 11744	WCru
paxianum B&SWJ 9755	WCru
pentandrum B&SWJ 6888	WCru
- B&SWJ 7056	WCru
- CWJ 12393	WCru
- RWJ 9836	WCru
teijsmannii B&SWJ 11110 from Japan	WCru
- B&SWJ 11112	WCru
- B&SWJ 11358 from Japan	WCru
aff. ***teijsmannii*** CWJ 12350 from Taiwan	WCru

Darlingtonia (*Sarraceniaceae*)

californica ♀H1	CSWC EFEx NChu WSSs

Darmera (*Saxifragaceae*)

peltata ♀H4	Widely available
- 'Nana'	CHEx EBee ECha GBuc LRHS LSou NBid NHol NLar NMyG SLPl SWat WFar WMoo

Dasylirion (*Asparagaceae*)

§ ***acrotrichum***	CDTJ CPLG EGri EShb
berlandieri	CPLG
- NJM 05.048	WPGP
cedrosanum	CDTJ
durangense **new**	EGri
glaucophyllum	EAmu MREP SBfd
gracile Planchon	see *D. acrotrichum*
leiophyllum	WPGP

longissimum	CAbb CBrP CTrC EAmu EShb ETod EUJe SChr
lucidum new	EGri
miquihuanense	EAmu EBee SMad
- F&M 301A	WPGP
- F&M 321	WPGP
- NJM 05.062	WPGP
quadrangulatum	EGri SPlb
- NJM 05.064	WPGP
serratifolium	EAmu ERom EUJe SBfd SChr
texanum	CTrC EGri IDee LEdu
wheeleri ♀H1	CBrP CTrC EAmu EGri SPlb

date see *Phoenix dactylifera*

Datisca (*Datiscaceae*)

cannabina	CArn CDTJ CSpe EBee ECha EPPr GBin GCal LPla NChi NLar SDix SMHy SMad SMrm SPhx WMoo WPGP WPer

Datura (*Solanaceae*)

arborea	see *Brugmansia arborea*
chlorantha	see *Brugmansia chlorantha*
cornigera	see *Brugmansia arborea*
ferox	CArn
rosea	see *Brugmansia* × *insignis* pink-flowered
rosei	see *Brugmansia sanguinea*
sanguinea	see *Brugmansia sanguinea*
stramonium	CArn
suaveolens	see *Brugmansia suaveolens*
versicolor	see *Brugmansia versicolor* Lagerh.
- 'Grand Marnier'	see *Brugmansia* × *candida* 'Grand Marnier'

Daubenya (*Asparagaceae*)

alba	ECho
aurea	ECho
- var. ***coccinea***	ECho
marginata	ECho
namaquensis	ECho

Daucus (*Apiaceae*)

carota	CArn CHab CRWN NMir SVic WSFF

Davallia (*Davalliaceae*)

canariensis ♀H1	CMen SEND
mariesii ♀H3	CMen ISha WCot
- B&SWJ 4448	WCru
- var. ***stenolepis***	CMen
tasmanii	CMen
trichomanoides	CBty CMen
- f. ***barbata***	CMen

Davidia (*Nyssaceae*)

involucrata ♀H4	Widely available
- 'Sonoma'	MBlu
- var. ***vilmoriniana*** ♀H4	CBcs CDoC CWCL ELan EPfP LRHS MAsh MBlu MGos SBfd SLim SPer

Daviesia (*Papilionaceae*)

cordata	SPlb
* ***ovalifolia***	SPlb
pectinata	SPlb

Debregeasia (*Urticaceae*)

longifolia WWJ 11686	WCru

Decaisnea (*Lardizabalaceae*)

fargesii	Widely available
- B&SWJ 8070	WCru

Decumaria (*Hydrangeaceae*)

barbara	CBcs CMac NLar NSti SEND SLim WCru WSHC
- 'Vicki'	NLar
sinensis	EBee EPfP LRHS SEND SKHP SLon SPoG SSpi WCru WSHC

Degenia (*Brassicaceae*)

velebitica	GKev

Deinanthe (*Hydrangeaceae*)

bifida	CDes CMil CPLG EBee EPfP EWes LRHS NRHS WCru WPGP
- B&SWJ 5436	EWld GEdr SBig WCru
- B&SWJ 5551	WCru
- 'Pink-Kii'	WCru
- 'Pink-Shi'	EWld GEdr LEdu NLar WCru
bifida* × *caerulea	CLAP GEdr WCru
'Blue Blush'	WCru
caerulea	CLAP CMil EBee GCra GEdr IGor LEdu LHop LRHS NLar NPnk SKHP WCru WPGP WSHC
- 'Blue Wonder'	CLAP CPLG EBee LLHF

Delonix (*Caesalpiniaceae*)

decaryi	SPlb
regia	SPlb

Delosperma (*Aizoaceae*)

from Graaf Reinet, South Africa	EPot NSla
from Sani Pass, South Africa	EPot WAbe
§ ***aberdeenense*** ♀H1	CHEx XLum
alpinum new	EPot
ashtonii	CCCN GEdr
basuticum	NSla
'Basutoland'	see *D. nubigenum*
congestum	CCCN CMea ECho EDAr EPot EWll GEdr SAga WAbe WIce
- 'Gold Nugget'	ECho LRHS NRHS
- white-flowered	EDAr
cooperi	CCCN CTri ECho ECtt EDAr EPfP EPot GBin GEdr GKev ITim LRHS LSou MSCN NHol NRHS SBfd SEND SPlb WIce WPer WPnn XLum XSen
floribundum 'Starburst'	EDAr EWll
kofleri* × *nubigenum	XLum
lavisiae	SPlb
lineare	XLum
Mesa Verde = 'Kelaidis'	ECtt
§ ***nubigenum***	CTri ECho ECtt ELan EPot GAbr GEdr GKev ITim MSCN SEND SPlb SPoG SWal WPer
'Ruby Coral'	EPot
sphalmanthoides	CPBP EPot GEdr WAbe
sutherlandii	ECho EDAr GAbr GBin SBfd SEND XLum
- 'Peach Star'	CCCN EDAr LRHS SBfd WIce
Table Mountain = 'John Proffitt'	CCCN EDAr GKev XLum

Delphinium ✿ (*Ranunculaceae*)

sp.	SVic
'After Midnight'	CNMi

'Ailsa'	CNMi
'Alice Artindale' (d)	CDes CNMi EBee EWes EWld IFoB MAvo WCot
ambiguum	see *Consolida ajacis*
'Ann Woodfield'	CNMi
'Apollo'	WSpi
'Ariel' ambig.	LRHS
Astolat Group	CBcs CSBt CTri CWCL CWib EBee ELan EPfP GMaP LBMP LRHS MBri MGos MLHP MWat NBir NHol NLar SBfd SPer SPoG SWvt WCAu WFar WPer XLum
'Atholl' ♀H4	CNMi ELar
'Augenweide'	EBee
(Aurora Series) 'Aurora Dark Blue'	LRHS
- 'Aurora Deep Purple'	LRHS
- 'Aurora Lavender'	LRHS
'Bambi' **new**	CNMi
'Basil Clitheroe'	LRHS
Belladonna Group	ELan EPfP
- 'Atlantis' ♀H4	EBee ECha ELar LRHS NLar SMrm WCot WSpi
- 'Balaton'	ELar
- 'Blue Bees'	LRHS
- 'Capri'	EBee
- 'Casa Blanca'	EBee ELar EPfP GMaP LRHS NLar SBfd WSpi XLum
- 'Cliveden Beauty'	EBee EPfP GMaP LHop LRHS MAvo NLar SBfd SMrm XLum
- 'Delft Blue' PBR	EBee
§ - 'Janny Arrow' PBR	LRHS
- 'Moerheimii'	LRHS WSpi
- 'Peace'	LRHS
- 'Piccolo'	ECha LRHS NLar
- 'Pink Sensation'	see *D.* × *ruysii* 'Pink Sensation'
- 'Völkerfrieden' ♀H4	ELar GQue LRHS MNrw MRav WCot WSpi
× ***bellamosum***	EPfP GMaP LRHS MAvo NLar SBfd XLum
'Berghimmel'	LRHS
'Beryl Burton'	CNMi
'Black Arrow' **new**	WCot
Black Knight Group	Widely available
'Black Pearl'	ECtt
'Black Velvet'	CBcs
'Blackbird' **new**	CWCL
'Blue Arrow'	see *D.* 'Blue Max Arrow', *D.* (Belladonna Group) 'Janny Arrow', *D.* 'Kings Blue Arrow'
Blue Bird Group	CBcs CSBt CTri EBee ELan EPfP GMaP LRHS MGos MWat NLar NMir SBfd SPer SPoG WCAu WFar WHoo XLum
'Blue Butterfly'	see *D. grandiflorum* 'Blue Butterfly'
'Blue Dawn' ♀H4	CNMi ELar
Blue Fountains Group	CSBt EPfP LRHS LSRN SPer SPet SPoG SRms
'Blue Jay'	CBcs CTri EBee ECtt EPfP LRHS LSRN MWat NBir NHol SBfd SPer WPer WSpi XLum
'Blue Lace'	LRHS WSpi WWEG
§ 'Blue Max Arrow'	LRHS
'Blue Mirror'	SRms
'Blue Nile' ♀H4	CNMi
'Blue Oasis'	CNMi
Blue River	CBcs
'Blue Skies'	ECtt NLar
Blue Springs Group	NGdn
'Blue Tit'	CNMi
'Bob Geldof' **new**	CNMi
'Boudicca' **new**	CNMi
'Bruce' ♀H4	CNMi ELar
brunonianum	WThu
'Butterball'	CNMi ELar WSpi
Cameliard Group	CBcs CSBt EBee ECtt ELan EPfP LBMP LHop LRHS MWat NLar SPer SPoG
'Can-Can' ♀H4	CNMi ELar
cardinale	SPlb
cashmerianum	WAbe
ceratophorum	WCru
var. ***ceratophorum*** BWJ 7799	
'Chelsea Star'	CNMi LRHS
'Cher'	CNMi
'Cherry Blossom'	EPfP
'Cherub' ♀H4	ELar
chinense	see *D. grandiflorum*
'Christel'	EBee LRHS LSRN
'Christine Harbutt'	ELar
'Clack's Choice'	CNMi
'Claire' ♀H4	CNMi ELar
'Clifford Sky' ♀H4	ELar LRHS NRHS
'Conspicuous' ♀H4	CNMi ELar
'Constance Rivett' ♀H4	ELar
'Coral Sunset' PBR (d)	MBri WFar
'Crown Jewel'	ELar
'Cupid'	ELar
'Darling Sue'	CNMi
'Darwin's Blue Indulgence' PBR	MBri WFar
'Darwin's Pink Indulgence' PBR	MBri WFar
'Darwin's Purple Indulgence' **new**	WFar
delavayi	LRHS
'Desante Blue'	LRHS
'Diamant' PBR	EWll LRHS
'Dreaming Spires'	SRms SWal
drepanocentrum HWJK 2263	WCru
'Dunsden Green'	CNMi
Dusky Maidens Group	CMea IFoB LRHS WSpi WWEG
dwarf, dark blue-flowered	LRHS
elatum	GCal SRms
- SDR 6374	GKev
- SDR 6391	GKev
- 'Dasante Blue' **new**	NPri
- 'Double Innocence' (New Millennium Series) (d)	IPot LRHS SMrm
- 'Morning Lights' (New Millennium Series)	CMea
'Elisabeth Sahin' ♀H4	ELar
'Elizabeth Cook' ♀H4	CNMi ELar
'Elmfreude'	LRHS WSpi
'Emily Hawkins' ♀H4	CNMi
'Etonian'	LRHS
exaltatum	LBMP LPla
'Fanfare'	CNMi ELar
'Faust' ♀H4	CNMi ELar EWll LRHS
'Fenella' ♀H4	CNMi ELar LRHS
'Finsteraarhorn'	LRHS MAvo WSpi
'Florestan'	CNMi
'Foxhill Nina' ♀H4	CNMi ELar
'Franjo Sahin'	CNMi ELar

	Galahad Group	CBcs CSBt CTri CWCL CWib EBee ECtt EHrv ELan EPfP GMaP LHop LRHS MBri MWat NBir NGdn NHol NLar NMir NPri SBfd SMrm SPer SPlb SPoG WCAu WFar WHoo WPer
	'Galahad' (Pacific Hybrids Series)	MGos XLum
	'Galileo' ♀H4	CNMi
	'Garden Party'	WSpi
	'Gemini' **new**	CNMi
	'Gemma'	CNMi
	'Gillian Dallas' ♀H4	EBee ELar
	glaciale HWJK 2299	WCru
	'Gossamer'	CNMi ECtt IKil
§	***grandiflorum***	GKev
§	- 'Blauer Zwerg'	SPoG
§	- 'Blue Butterfly'	CSpe EPfP LBMP LHop LRHS SPlb SPoG WSHC
	- Blue Dwarf	see *D. grandiflorum* 'Blauer Zwerg'
	- 'Delfix'	LRHS
	- pale blue-flowered **new**	GKev
	- (Summer Series) 'Summer Blues'	LRHS MBri NRHS SHil SRot
	- - 'Summer Nights'	EPfP LRHS MBri SHil
	- - 'Summer Stars'	LRHS MBri SHil
*	- 'Tom Pouce'	EPfP
	'Green Twist' (New Millennium Series)	EWll LRHS WSpi WWEG
	(Guardian Series) 'Guardian Blue'	LRHS NPri
	- 'Guardian Lavender'	LRHS NPri
	- 'Guardian White'	LRHS NPri
	Guinevere Group	CBcs CSBt CWCL CWib EBee ECtt EPfP LRHS MBri NBir NLar SBfd SPer SPoG WFar XLum
	- 'Lady Guinevere'	IBoy
	'Guy Langdon'	CNMi
	halteratum **new**	CSpe
	hansenii	LLHF
	'Highlander Blueberry Pie' **new**	WHlf
	'Highlander Crystal Delight' **new**	WHlf
	'Highlander Morning Sunrise' **new**	WHlf
	'Holly Cookland Wilkins' ♀H4	CNMi
	'Honey Pink' **new**	CNMi
I	'Independence'	LRHS
	'Innocence' **new**	CMea
	Ivory Towers Group	ECtt
	'Jenny Agutter'	CNMi
	'Jill Curley' ♀H4	ELar LRHS
	'Joan Edwards'	CNMi
	'Kathleen Cooke'	CNMi
	'Kestrel' ♀H4	CNMi ELar
	King Arthur Group	CBcs CSBt CWCL EBee ECtt ELan EPfP LBMP LHop LPot LRHS LSRN MGos MWat NLar SBfd SPer SPoG WFar WPer XLum
§	'Kings Blue Arrow' PBR	LRHS
	'La Bohème'	WCot
§	'Langdon's Royal Flush' ♀H4	ELar LRHS
	'Lanzenträger'	LRHS
	'Layla'	CNMi
	'Leonora'	CNMi ELar
	'Lillian Basset'	CNMi
	'Lily Radley'	ELar
	'Loch Leven' ♀H4	CNMi
	'Lord Butler' ♀H4	CNMi ELar LRHS
	'Lucia Sahin' ♀H4	CNMi
	maackianum	CPom EWld GCal LLHF WCot
	Magic Fountains Series	CSam IFoB LRHS SGar SPlb SPoG WFar WGor
	- 'Magic Fountains Cherry Blossom'	EPfP SBfd SPoG WFar
	- 'Magic Fountains Dark Blue'	EPfP GMaP LSRN NEgg NLar SBfd SPoG WFar
	- 'Magic Fountains Deep Blue'	NLar SBfd
	- 'Magic Fountains Lavender'	EPfP SBfd
	- 'Magic Fountains Lilac Pink'	EPfP SBfd SPoG
	- 'Magic Fountains Lilac Rose'	NLar WFar WGor
	- 'Magic Fountains Pure White'	EPfP NEgg NLar SBfd WFar
	- 'Magic Fountains Sky Blue'	EPfP SBfd SPoG WFar
	'Margaret' ♀H4	CNMi ELar
	'Marilyn Clarissa' **new**	CNMi
	'Merlin' ambig.	LRHS LSRN
	'Michael Ayres' ♀H4	CNMi ELar
	micropetalum CNDS 031	WCru
	'Mighty Atom'	CNMi EWll IPot
	'Min' ♀H4	CNMi ELar
	'Misty Mauves' (New Millennium Series) (d)	LRHS SMrm WSpi
	'Molly Buchanan'	CNMi
	'Moonbeam'	ELar
	'Morgentau'	EBee LRHS
	'Mother Teresa'	CNMi
	'Mrs Newton Lees'	EWll IKil LRHS
	'Ned Wit'	IKil
	New Century hybrids	CBcs
	'Nobility'	ELar WSpi
	nudicaule 'Laurin'	LRHS WFar
	'Olive Poppleton' ♀H4	CNMi
	'Oliver' ♀H4	CNMi ELar
	'Our Deb' ♀H4	ELar
	oxysepalum	LLHF
	Pacific hybrids	EPfP LHop LSRN MHer MLHP NLar SBfd SPet SRms SWal SWvt WFar
	'Pagan Purples' (New Millennium Series) (d)	IFoB WSpi
	'Patricia Johnson'	CNMi ELar
	Percival Group	LRHS NLar
	'Pericles'	CNMi LRHS
	'Pink Punch' (New Millennium Series) **new**	IPot
	Pink River = 'Barfourtythree' PBR	CBcs
	'Pink Ruffles'	CNMi ELar
	'Plagu Blue' PBR	WCot WSpi
	Princess Caroline = 'Odabar' PBR	CBcs
	'Purple Passion' (New Millennium Series)	EPfP IPot LRHS WWEG
	'Purple Velvet' ♀H4	CNMi ELar
	pylzowii	EWld
	'Red Caroline'	CBcs
	requienii	CSpe EWld NSti
	'Rona'	CNMi
	'Rosemary Brock' ♀H4	ELar
	Round Table Mixture	CTri

'Royal Aspirations' (New Millennium Series) CMea IPot LRHS MAvo WWEG
'Royal Flush' see *D.* 'Langdon's Royal Flush'
'Ruby' CNMi
'Ruby Tuesday' **new** CNMi
§ × ***ruysii*** 'Pink Sensation' CWCL LRHS NGBo NLar WSpi
'Sandpiper' ♀H4 CNMi
'Sarita' SUsu
'Schönbuch' LRHS
'Secret'PBR LRHS
'Silver Jubilee' CNMi ELar
'Snow Crown' WSpi
'Snow Queen Arrow' LRHS
'Sommerabend' LRHS
'Sooty' **new** CNMi
'Spindrift' ♀H4 CNMi ELar
stapeliosmum B&SWJ 2954 WCru
- HWJK 2179 WCru
staphisagria CArn EOHP
'Stardust' WSpi
'Starlight'PBR LRHS
'Strawberry Fair' LRHS
Summer Skies Group CBcs CSBt CTri CWCL EBee ECtt ELan EPfP LHop LRHS MBri MWat NBir NLar SBfd SMrm SPer SPoG WCAu WFar WHoo XLum
'Summer Wine' ELar
'Summerfield Diana' CNMi
'Summerfield Oberon' CNMi ELar WCot
'Sungleam' ♀H4 EBee ECtt ELar IKil IPot WSpi
'Sunkissed' ♀H4 CNMi ELar
'Sunny Skies' (New Millennium Series) CMea LRHS
'Susan Edmunds'PBR (d) ♀H4 CNMi
sutchuenense CPom EWTr EWld WWlt
- BWJ 7867 WCru
tatsienense IFoB SRms WAbe
tenii BWJ 7693 WCru
'Tiddles' ♀H4 ELar
'Tiger Eye' CNMi ELar
'Trudy' **new** CNMi
'Vanessa Mae' CNMi
vestitum EWld
'Walton Benjamin' CNMi
'Walton Gemstone' ♀H4 ELar
White River = 'Barfourtyfive'PBR CBcs
'White Swan' EPfP
'Wishful Thinking'PBR MBri WFar
Woodfield strain WHrl
'Yvonne' LRHS LSRN
'Zauberflöte' LRHS

Dendranthema see *Chrysanthemum*

pacificum see *Ajania pacifica*

Dendriopoterium see *Sanguisorba*

Dendrobenthamia see *Cornus*

Dendrocalamus (*Poaceae*)

asper XBlo
calostachys SPlb
giganteus XBlo
§ ***strictus*** XBlo

Dendromecon (*Papaveraceae*)

rigida CBcs EBee EPfP LRHS NLar SAga SKHP WPGP WSHC

Dendropanax (*Araliaceae*)

trifidus B&SWJ 11230 WCru

Dennstaedtia (*Dennstaedtiaceae*)

punctilobula CLAP WCot

Dentaria see *Cardamine*

pinnata see *Cardamine heptaphylla*
polyphylla see *Cardamine kitaibelii*

Deparia (*Woodsiaceae*)

okuboana **new** ISha

Dermatobotrys (*Scrophulariaceae*)

saundersii ECre

Derwentia see *Parahebe*

Deschampsia (*Poaceae*)

cespitosa CKno COIW CRWN CWib EPPr EPfP LBMP LPot LRHS MWat SMrm SPlb WCFE WCot WGwG WMnd WMoo WTin WWEG XLum
- subsp. ***alpina*** LEdu
- Bronze Veil see *D. cespitosa* 'Bronzeschleier'
§ - 'Bronzeschleier' CMea CPrp CWCL EAEE EBee EHoe ELan EPPr EPfP GMaP LEdu LRHS MAsh MAvo MBrN NGdn NOak NRHS NWsh SApp SPer SPhx SRms SSvw WMoo WPtf WWEG XLum
- brown-leaved SApp
- subsp. ***cespitosa*** **new** CTrC
- 'Coral Cloud' GQue
- 'Fairy's Joke' see *D. cespitosa* var. *vivipara*
- 'Fose' SApp
- Gold Dust see *D. cespitosa* 'Goldstaub'
- Golden Dew see *D. cespitosa* 'Goldtau'
- Golden Pendant see *D. cespitosa* 'Goldgehänge'
- Golden Shower see *D. cespitosa* 'Goldgehänge'
- Golden Veil see *D. cespitosa* 'Goldschleier'
§ - 'Goldgehänge' CSam EHoe EHul MMHG NBir NPro WWEG
§ - 'Goldschleier' CPrp CSam EBee ECha EPPr EPfP GCal GMaP GQue LEdu LRHS NGdn NRHS NWsh SApp SBfd SPhx WMoo WPGP XLum
§ - 'Goldstaub' EPPr
§ - 'Goldtau' Widely available
- 'Mill End' **new** CKno
- 'Morning Dew' WFar
- 'Northern Lights' (v) CWCL EBee ELan EPfP LEdu LRHS MBel MBri MMuc NBro NSti SApp SBfd SEND SLim SPoG SRms SWvt WPGP WPtf WWEG
- 'Pixie Fountain' CKno EBee EDAr EPPr WWEG
- 'Schottland' CKno EBee EPPr GBin NDov
- 'Tardiflora' EBee
- 'Tauträger' EBee
§ - var. ***vivipara*** EHoe EPPr GBin LRHS NBro
- 'Waldschatt' EBee
- 'Willow Green' GCal SCoo
flexuosa COIW EHoe NBir NWsh SMrm
- 'Tatra Gold' Widely available
holciformis 'Marin' **new** CKno
media EHoe

Desfontainia (*Loganiaceae*)

§ ***spinosa*** ♀H3 Widely available

- 'Harold Comber' CMac GKin WCru WHor
- f. ***hookeri*** see *D. spinosa*

Desmodium (*Papilionaceae*)

callianthum CMac EBee LRHS SBrt WSHC
canadense CDes CPom EBee LRHS NLar
§ ***elegans*** ♀H4 CBcs CHEx CPLG EBee ELan EPfP LRHS MBri NLar SBrt SKHP WCot WHer WKif WPGP WSHC
- f. ***albiflorum*** SBrt
paniculatum CPom
praestans see *D. yunnanense*
tiliifolium see *D. elegans*
§ ***yunnanense*** CHEx CPLG EBee WSHC

Deuterocohnia (*Bromeliaceae*)

brevifolia ♀H1 EBee WCot WPGP
longipetala RCB/Arg L-5 WCot

Deutzia ✿ (*Hydrangeaceae*)

CC 4548 CPLG
CC 4550 CPLG
calycosa GQui
- B&SWJ 7742 WPat
- BWJ 8007 WCru
- 'Dali' CDoC CPLG SDys
aff. ***calycosa*** SIN 1878 GLin
chunii see *D. ningpoensis*
compacta CMCN SLon WFar WPGP
- GWJ 9202 WCru
- GWJ 9203 WCru
- GWJ 9339 WCru
- 'Lavender Time' CDoC CMac CPLG EBee EWTr NLar WCFE WPat
cordatula B&SWJ 3720 WCru
- B&SWJ 6917 WCru
corymbosa CDoC
crenata B&SWJ 8886 WCru
- B&SWJ 8896 WCru
- B&SWJ 8924 WCru
- 'Flore Pleno' see *D. scabra* 'Plena'
- var. ***heterotricha*** B&SWJ 5805 WCru
- - B&SWJ 8879 WCru
- var. ***nakaiana*** WPat
- - B&SWJ 11184 WCru
- - 'Nikko' see *D. gracilis* 'Nikko'
§ - 'Pride of Rochester' (d) CBcs CMCN CWib EBee ECrN GKin LRHS LSou LTen MGos MMuc MRav NLar SBod SEND SGol SLim SPoG SWvt WGrn
discolor 'Major' CPLG WPat
× ***elegantissima*** IVic SRms
- 'Fasciculata' EBee EPfP LRHS SPer
- 'Rosealind' ♀H4 CBar CBcs CDul CPLG CTri EBee EPfP EWTr GKin LHop LRHS LSRN MGos MMuc MRav SEND SLim SRms SWvt WCFE WKif WPat WSHC
glabrata B&SWJ 617 GQui WCru
- B&SWJ 8427 WCru
glomeruliflora BWJ 7742 WCru
gracilis CDoC CDoy CSBt EBee ELan EPfP EWTr GKin GQui LPot LTen MAsh MGos MRav MSwo SPad SPer SPoG WFar WSpi
- B&SWJ 8927 WCru
- 'Aurea' CBcs EPfP NLar
- 'Carminea' see *D.* × *rosea* 'Carminea'
§ - 'Marmorata' (v) SLon WCot
§ - 'Nikko' CBcs CMCN CMac CPLG CTri EBee ECho EShb EWes GKin LRHS MGos MHer MWhi NHol NLar NPro SGol SHil SPlb SPoG WKif WSHC
- var. ***ogatae*** B&SWJ 8911 WCru
- 'Rosea' see *D.* × *rosea*
- 'Variegata' see *D. gracilis* 'Marmorata'
grandiflora NChi WPGP
hookeriana LBuc LLHF LRHS NRHS SHil WFar
× ***hybrida*** 'Contraste' CMac SPer
- 'Joconde' CPLG WFar WKif
- 'Magicien' Widely available
- 'Mont Rose' ♀H4 CBar CDoC CDul CPLG EBee ELan ELon EPfP GKin LBuc LRHS MAsh MBri MGos MMuc MRav MSwo MWhi NLar NPri SEND SGol SLim SPer SPoG SWvt WFar WKif WSpi
§ - 'Strawberry Fields' ♀H4 CBcs CGHE CMCN CPLG CTri EBee ELan ELon EPfP GKin IArd LAst LBMP LBuc LHop LRHS LSRN LSou MAsh MBlu MGos NEgg NLar SLon SPad SPoG WFar WKif WPGP
'Iris Alford' CGHE EBee LBuc LRHS MBri MGos NRHS SHil SLon WFar WPGP
× ***kalmiiflora*** CJun CMac CPLG CSBt CTri EBee GKin GQui LRHS MAsh NLar SLPl SPer SRms
longifolia WPGP WPat
- 'Veitchii' ♀H4 CDoy CSBt GQui MRav WCFE
- 'Vilmoriniae' MRav
× ***magnifica*** CBcs CDul EBee ELan GQui SRms
- 'Nancy' GKin
- 'Rubra' see *D.* × *hybrida* 'Strawberry Fields'
maximowicziana B&SWJ 11567 WCru
monbeigii CDoC CPLG EBee LRHS MRav WKif
- BWJ 7728 WCru
multiradiata WPGP
§ ***ningpoensis*** ♀H4 CPLG EPfP GQui SLPl SMrm SPer WPGP
paniculata B&SWJ 8592 WCru
parviflora var. ***barbinervis*** B&SWJ 8478 WCru
'Pink Pompon' see *D.* 'Rosea Plena'
prunifolia B&SWJ 8588 WCru
pulchra CAbP CDoC CMCN CPom EBee EPfP IDee LRHS MRav NPro SLon SMrm SPer SSpi WFar WPGP WPat WSpi
- B&SWJ 3870 WCru
- B&SWJ 6908 WCru
purpurascens BWJ 7859 WCru
§ × ***rosea*** CDul CWib EPfP LAst LRHS MAsh SRms WFar WKif WRHF
- 'Campanulata' CPLG EPfP MSwo
§ - 'Carminea' MAsh SPlb SRms WFar WPat
§ 'Rosea Plena' (d) CDoC CMac CPLG CSBt CWib EBee EPfP EWTr GKin IVic LBuc LRHS MAsh MGos MMuc NEgg NLar SLim WFar WPat
rubens WPat
scabra CDul CTri
- B&SWJ 11127 WCru
- B&SWJ 11168 WCru

- B&SWJ 11178	WCru
§ - 'Candidissima' (d)	CDul CMac GQui MRav NLar SPer WPat WRHF
- 'Codsall Pink'	MRav
§ - 'Plena' (d)	CPLG EBee ECrN ECtt ELan EPfP GKin SPer WCFE
- 'Pride of Rochester'	see *D. crenata* 'Pride of Rochester'
- 'Punctata' (v)	EHoe MAsh MMuc SEND SRms WFar
- 'Robert Fortune'	SPlb
- 'Variegata' (v)	CDul CMac
setchuenensis	CMac GQui SSpi WPat WSHC
- var. ***corymbiflora*** ♀H4	CBcs CDoC CDul CGHE CPLG CSam CTri EBee EPfP EWTr IArd IDee LHop LRHS MBri MSwo SPoG WFar WKif WPGP
staminea HWJK 2180	WCru
taiwanensis	SGol WPat
- B&SWJ 6858	EBee WCru
- CWJ 12443	WCru
- CWJ 12459	WCru
'Tourbillon Rouge'	EBee EPfP LRHS LSRN NLar SBfd
× ***wellsii***	see *D. scabra* 'Candidissima'
× ***wilsonii***	SRms

Dianella (*Hemerocallidaceae*)

brevicaulis	ECou LEdu
caerulea	CMac ECha ECou ELan EPri IGor LEdu MNrw MOWG NBir SMrm
- Breeze = 'Dcnco'PBR	ELan NOak
- Cassa Blue = 'Dbb03'PBR	EBee ELan EPPr EPfP EWes GEdr LAst LHop LRHS MMHG NOak SPer SPoG
- 'Kulnura'	ECou
- Little Jess = 'Dcmp01'PBR	CPLG GEdr MMHG NOak SPoG
- 'Variegata'	see *D. tasmanica* 'Variegata'
ensifolia	LEdu
intermedia	CTrC IBlr
- 'Variegata' (v)	IBlr
nigra	CBcs CPLG CPou CTrC ECou IFro LEdu
- 'Margaret Pringle' (v)	CBcs CPLG CTrC ECou NOak
revoluta	CCon ECou
- Baby Bliss = 'Dtn03'PBR	CKno EBee NOak WCot
- 'Hartz Mountain'	ECou
- Little Rev = 'Dr5000'PBR	EBee ELan EPfP ESwi GEdr MMHG NOak SMrm
tasmanica	Widely available
- from Logan	GCal
- 'Emerald Arch'	ELan ESwi NOak SPer
- 'Prosser'	ECou
- Tasred = 'Tr20'PBR	CPLG EBee ELan EPPr EPfP ESwi GBin GEdr LHop MCot MMHG NOak SPer SPoG
§ - 'Variegata' (v)	CCCN CCon CDTJ CPLG CSpe EBee ECou ELan EPfP LHop SEND WCot

Dianthus ✿ (*Caryophyllaceae*)

sp.	SVic
AC&W 2116	ECtt GEdr
'Admiral Crompton' (pf)	CNMi
'Aicardi' (pf) **new**	CNMi
'Alan Titchmarsh' (p)	EBee ECtt ELan EPfP LRHS LSRN LSou MGos MTis NCGa NEgg SHar SPoG SWvt
'Albert Hill' (p)	SAll
'Aldridge Yellow' (b)	SAll
'Alfriston' (b) ♀H4	SAll
'Alice' (p)	LSRN SAll
'Alice Lever' (p)	WAbe
§ 'Allen's Maria' (p)	SAll
'Allspice' (p)	MRav WHoo
Allwoodii Group (p)	NNor
Allwoodii Alpinus Group (p)	NGdn SRms WFar XLum
'Allwood's Celebration' (p)	SAll
'Allwood's Crimson' (pf)	SAll
'Allwood's Delight' (p)	SAll
alpinus ♀H4	GJos NMen NSla WFar WNew
- 'Albus'	NWad
- 'Joan's Blood' ♀H4	ECho ELon EPot GBuc LSRN NMen WAbe WFar
'Alyson' (p)	SAll
amurensis	ECho EDAr EPPr GCal MLHP NDov NNor SPhx SSvw WSHC
- 'Andrey' (p)	NNor WHrl
anatolicus	CTri ECho EDAr MHer NGdn WPer XLum
'Anders Apollo' (p) **new**	CNMi
'Anders Cream Princess' (pf)	CNMi
'Anders Dora Bryant' (p) **new**	CNMi
'Anders Emily Elizabeth' (p) **new**	CNMi
'Anders Faith' (p) **new**	CNMi
'Anders Gypsy' (p) **new**	CNMi
'Anders Irene Ann' (pf) **new**	CNMi
'Anders Kath Phillips' (pf) ♀H4 **new**	CNMi
'Anders Melody' (p) **new**	SAll
'Anders Patricia Griffiths' (p) **new**	CNMi SAll
'Anders Royal Purple' (pf) **new**	CNMi
'Anders Sundance' (pf)	CNMi
'Anders Wendy Derrick' (pf) **new**	CNMi
'Andrew Morton' (b)	SAll
'Angela Carol' (pf) **new**	CNMi
'Angelo' (b)	SAll
'Ann Franklin' (pf) ♀H1	CNMi
'Anne Jones' (b)	EPfP
'Annette' (p)	ECho EDAr EPot GKev LRHS LSRN MAsh NGdn NRHS SRGP SWvt
'Annie Claybourne' (pf)	CNMi
'Antique'	SAll
'Apple Tea' (pf)	SAll
'Apricot Sue' (pf)	CNMi SAll
Arctic Star = 'Devon Arctic Star' (p)	CMea CTri ECho ELan ELon GMaP NEgg SPoG SRms SRot SWvt WFar
arenarius	CCon EDAr GKev LEdu NGdn SPlb XLum
- 'Little Maiden'	EDif NCGa NGdn SBch SPhx WIce
- 'Snow Flurries'	ITim
'Argus'	IGor
armeria	CFis WHer WOut
arpadianus	GEdr NGdn
- var. ***pumilus***	EPot LLHF
'Arthur Leslie' (b)	SAll
'Artu' (pf)	SAll
§ × ***arvernensis*** (p) ♀H4	ECha ECho EPot SBch
- 'Albus'	ECho
'Audrey Robinson' (pf)	CNMi
'Aurora' (b)	SAll
'Auvergne'	see *D.* × *arvernensis*
'Averiensis'	see *D.* 'Berlin Snow'
'Baby Treasure' (p)	ECtt
'Badenia' (p)	ECha

	Name	Suppliers
	'Bailey's Celebration' (p)	EAEE ECtt EPfP LRHS LSou MTis NCGa NDov SRGP WGwG
§	'Bailey's Daily Mail' (p) ♀H4	CBcs
	'Barbara Norton' (p)	ECtt
	barbatus	MNrw SVic
	- SDR 6404	GKev
	- Barbarini Series	WGor
	- 'Black Adder'	CSpe
I	- 'Darkest of All'	CSpe
	- Nigrescens Group (p,a) ♀H4	CBre CMea CSpe MNHC SPhx WHil
I	- 'Sooty' (p,a)	EBee EDAr ELan SHar WCFE WFar
	- 'Super Parfait Strawberry' (Super Parfait Series) ♀H3	LRHS
	- 'Tuxedo Black'	WMoo
§	'Bat's Double Red' (p/d)	SAll
	'Becky Robinson' (p) ♀H4	CNMi SAll
	'Belmont Ruby Wedding' (p) **new**	CNMi
§	'Berlin Snow' (p)	CPBP ELan EPot EWes ITim LRHS
	'Betty Miller' (b)	SAll
	'Betty Morton' (p) ♀H4	ECtt IFoB WKif
	'Betty's Choice' (pf)	CNMi
	'Betty's Delight' (pf)	CNMi
	'Bill Smith' (pf)	CNMi
	'Black Baccara' (pf)	SAll
	'Blue Hedgehog'	ECtt
	'Blue Hills' (p)	ECho GKev
	'Blue Ice' (b)	SAll
	'Blush'	see *D.* 'Souvenir de la Malmaison'
	'Bobby' (p)	SAll
	'Bob's Highlight' (pf)	CNMi
	'Bombardier' (p)	ECtt
	'Bookham Gleam' (b)	SAll
	'Bookham Grand' (b)	SAll
	'Bookham Heroine' (b)	SAll
	'Bookham Lad' (b)	SAll
	'Border Special' (b)	SAll
	'Bouquet Purple' (p)	CSpe
	'Bovey Belle' (p) ♀H4	CBcs SAll
	'Bressingham Pink' (p)	ECtt
	brevicaulis	WAbe
	- subsp. ***brevicaulis*** **new**	LLHF
	'Brian Tumbler' (b) ♀H4	SAll
	'Bridal Veil' (p)	SAll SBch WHer
	'Brigadier' (p)	ECtt
	'Brilliance' (p)	MSCN WMoo
	'Brilliant'	see *D. deltoides* 'Brilliant'
	'Brilliant Star' (p) ♀H4	ECho ECtt LRHS MWat NRHS SEND SPet SWvt WIce WWFP
	'Brympton Red' (p)	CFis ECha SAll
	'Bryony Lisa' (b) ♀H4	SAll
	caesius	see *D. gratianopolitanus*
	callizonus	EPot LLHF NMen
	'Calypso' (pf)	CTri
	'Calypso Star' (p) ♀H4	ECho ECtt NGdn SPet SPoG
	'Camilla' (b)	CNMi
	'Can-can' (pf)	ECho ECtt
	'Candy Clove' (b)	SAll
	Candy Floss = 'Devon Flavia'PBR (Scent First Series) (p) ♀H4	ECtt ELan LAst LBMP LRHS MTis NEgg NPri SBfd SEND SHil SMrm SPoG WHil
	'Candy Spice' (p)	MRav
	Capri = 'Kocapri' (pf) **new**	SAll
§	'Carmine Letitia Wyatt'PBR (p) ♀H4	ECtt LRHS NCGa SPoG
	carthusianorum	CArn CKno LDai LPla MCot MNFA NDov NGdn SAll SGar SPhx SPlb SSvw SWat WKif WPGP WPer WWFP
I	- 'Rupert's Pink'	NGdn SBch
	caryophyllus	CArn ELau ENfk
	'Casser's Pink' (p)	SBch
	'Charles' (p)	SAll
	'Charles Edward' (p)	SAll
	'Charles Musgrave'	see *D.* 'Musgrave's Pink'
	Charlie = 'Hilcharly' (pf)	SAll
	'Chastity' (p)	LLHF SAll WHoo
	Cheddar pink	see *D. gratianopolitanus*
	'Cherly'	LSRN
	'Cherry Clove' (b)	SAll
	'Cherry Pie' (p)	ECtt LRHS SPoG WMnd
	'Cheryl'	see *D.* 'Houndspool Cheryl'
	'Chetwyn Hannah Scholes' (p) **new**	CNMi
	'Chetwyn Ruth Gillies' (pf) **new**	CNMi
	'Chianti Double' (p)	SAll
	chinensis 'Black and White'	CSpe
	'Chris Crew' (b) ♀H4	SAll
	'Citrien'PBR (pf) **new**	LRHS SWal
	'Clara' (pf)	CNMi
	'Clara's Lass' (pf)	CNMi
	'Clare' (p)	SAll
	'Claret Joy' (p) ♀H4	CBcs EBee ECtt EPfP LRHS MMuc NEgg SAll SEND
§	'Cockenzie Pink' (p)	SAll SBch WHer
	Coconut Sundae = 'Wp05 Yves' (p)	ECtt ELan ELon EWTr EWll LAst LHop LRHS LSRN MSCN NCGa NNor NPri SBfd SMrm SRot WBor WHil
	'Colin Short' (pf) **new**	CNMi
	'Constance' (p)	SAll
	'Constance Finnis'	see *D.* 'Fair Folly'
	'Consul' (b)	SAll
	'Conwy Silver'	WAbe
	'Conwy Star'	CPBP NMen WAbe
	'Coquette' (pf)	SAll
	'Coral Reef'PBR (p)	ECtt ELan GAbr MWat NNor SPoG
	'Coronation Ruby' (p) ♀H4	SAll
	'Cosmic Swirl Red' (p)	WHil
	'Coste Budde' (p)	WSHC
	Cracker = 'Wp10 Sab06' (Early Bird Series) (p)	ECho GAbr
	'Cranmere Pool' (p) ♀H4	CBcs EBee ECtt ELan EPfP LRHS NGdn NNor SBfd SPoG SWvt WMnd WRHF WWEG
	'Cream Sue' (pf)	CNMi
	'Crimson Chance' (p)	NSla
	'Crimson Warrior' (pf) **new**	CNMi
	'Crock of Gold' (b)	SAll
	'Crompton Bride' (pf)	CNMi
	'Crompton Classic' (pf)	CNMi
	'Crompton Princess' (pf)	CNMi
	cruentus	NDov SPhx WPer WWEG
	'Crystal White' (pf) **new**	SWal
	'D.D.R.'	see *D.* 'Berlin Snow'
	'Dad's Favourite' (p)	CEnt CFis SAll WHer
	'Daily Mail'	see *D.* 'Bailey's Daily Mail'
	'Dainty Dame' (p) ♀H4	CSpe CTri EBee ECho EPfP LRHS MNHC NRHS SAll SBch SPoG SRot WFar
	'Dancing Queen'PBR (p)	MTis MWat NNor WWFP
	'Daphne' (p)	SAll
	'Dark Star' (p)	ECho
	'Dark Tempo' (pf)	SAll

	'Dartington Double' (p)	ECho SEND
	'David' (p)	EBee EPfP LSRN SAll SBch
	'David Russell' (b) ♀H4	SAll
	'David Saunders' (b) ♀H4	SAll
	'Dawlish Joy' (p)	SPoG
	'Dawn' (b)	SAll
	'Dawn' (pf)	ECho
	'Dedham Beauty'	MPie SEND WCot WWEG
	deltoides ♀H4	CArn CEnt ECha ECho ENfk EPfP LEdu MAsh MMuc SPlb SRms WFar WJek WNew WPtf
	- 'Albus'	ECha EPfP GKev MNHC NGdn WMoo
	- 'Arctic Fire'	CWib ECho EPfP NGdn NHol WFar WMoo
	- 'Bright Eyes' (p)	ECho LRHS MTis MWat
§	- 'Brilliant'	CTri ECho EPau GJos LAst MBNS MNHC NGdn NSla SAll SRms WFar WGor WWEG
	- 'Canta Libra'	SWal
	- 'Dark Eyes' (p)	EWes
	- 'Erectus'	EPfP
	- Flashing Light	see *D. deltoides* 'Leuchtfunk'
§	- 'Leuchtfunk'	CMea ECho ECtt EPfP LAst LRHS MWat NNor SBch SPoG WMoo WWEG
I	- 'Luneburg Heath Maiden Pink'	NGdn SSvw
	- 'Microchip'	WFar WMoo
	- 'Nelli' (p)	ECho NGdn SSvw WMoo
	- red-flowered	SVic
	- 'Shrimp'	NGdn
	- 'Vampir'	GAbr
	'Dennis' (p)	LSRN SAll
	'Desert Song' (b)	SAll
	'Desmond'	EBee EPfP LHop
	'Devon Blush' (p)	ECtt
	'Devon Cream'PBR (p)	EBee ECtt ELan GAbr LAst LRHS LSou MWat NEgg WHil WMnd
	'Devon Dove'PBR (p) ♀H4	CMea CSBt CTri EBee ECtt ELan EPfP LHop LRHS LSou MRav MWat NCGa NDov NEgg SBfd
	'Devon General'PBR (p)	CTri SBfd
	'Devon Glow' (p) ♀H4	EPfP
	'Devon Magic'PBR (p)	ECtt ELan WFar
	'Devon Pearl'PBR (p)	WMnd
	'Devon Wizard'PBR (p) ♀H4	CSBt EBee ECtt EPfP LRHS MRav MSpe NCGa NDov NEgg NNor SBfd SEND WFar
	'Dewdrop' (p)	CMea CTri EBee ECho ECtt EPfP MAsh MHer NBir NGdn NPro SAga SAll SBch SEND WFar
	'Diamond Scarlet' (Diamond Series)	LRHS
	'Diana'	see *D.* Dona
	'Diane' (p) ♀H4	EBee ELan EPfP LRHS NEgg SAll SPoG SWvt WMnd
*	'Diane Cape'	SAll
	'Diplomat' (b)	SAll
§	Dona = 'Brecas' (pf)	LSRN SRGP
	'Dora' (p)	ECho LRHS
	'Doris' (p) ♀H4	Widely available
	'Doris Allwood' (pf)	CNMi CSBt EMal SAll
	'Doris Elite' (p)	SAll
	'Doris Galbally' (b)	SAll
	'Doris Majestic' (p)	SAll
	'Doris Ruby'	see *D.* 'Houndspool Ruby'
	'Doris Supreme' (p)	SAll
	'Double Lace' **new**	LRHS
	'Double North'	ELon
	'Dubarry' (p)	CTri CWan ECtt WPer
	'Duchess of Fife' (p)	EBee ECtt EPfP
	'Duchess of Roxburghe' (pf)	EMal SAll
	'Duchess of Westminster' (M)	EMal SAll
	'Duke of Norfolk' (pf)	EMal SAll
	'Dunkirk Spirit' (pf) ♀H1	CNMi
	'Dusky' (p)	CNMi
	'Dusky Janelle' (pf) **new**	CNMi
	'Earl of Essex' (p)	SAll
	'Edenside Scarlet' (b)	SAll
	'Edenside White' (b)	SAll
	'Edna' (p)	SAll
	'Edward Allwood' (pf)	SAll
	'Edwin Cross' (b)	SAll
	'Eileen' (p)	SAll
	'Eileen Lever' (p)	CPBP IFoB ITim MWat WAbe
	'Eileen Neal' (b) ♀H4	SAll
	'Eileen O'Connor' (b) ♀H4	SAll
	'Eleanor Parker' (p)	WAbe
	'Eleanor's Old Irish' (p)	CAbP EBee ELon LRHS MPie MWhi SEND WCot WHoo WTin WWEG
	'Elfin Star' (p)	ECho SPet
	'Elizabeth' (p)	CEnt
	'Elizabethan' (p)	CFis CSpe MCot SDys
*	'Elizabethan Pink' (p)	SAll
	'Ellen Ladd' (pf) **new**	CNMi
	'Elsie Ketchen' (pf) **new**	CNMi
	Emma = 'Barmane' (pf) **new**	SAll
	'Emma West' (pf) **new**	CNMi
	'Emperor'	see *D.* 'Bat's Double Red'
	erinaceus	ECho GJos WAbe WPat
	- var. ***alpinus***	EPot
	- Duguid's	WThu
	'Erycina' (b)	SAll
	'Ethel Hurford' (p)	WHoo
	'Eva Humphries' (b)	SAll
	'Evening Star' (p) ♀H4	CTri ECho GAbr LRHS MAsh NEgg NRHS SPet SPoG SWvt WIce
	'Exquisite' (b)	SAll
§	'Fair Folly' (p)	IGor SAll SBch WHer
	'Fanal' (p)	NBir
	'Farnham Rose' (p)	SAll
	'Fenbow Nutmeg Clove' (b)	SDix WMnd
	Festival Tessino = 'Hiltesval' (pf) **new**	SAll
	'Fettes Mount' (p)	LPla MWhi WCot
	'Feuerhexe' (p)	EPot
	'Fimbriatus' (p)	WHoo
	'Fiona' (p)	SAll
	Fire Star = 'Devon Xera' (p) ♀H4 **new**	ECho MWat SHil SRms
	'Firestar' (p)	CTri ELan EPot LRHS MAsh MWat SPet SRot SWvt
	'First Lady' (b)	SAll
	Fizzy = 'Wp08 Ver03'PBR (Early Bird Series) (p/d)	CMea ECho EDAr LBMP SBfd
	'Flanders' (b) ♀H4	SAll
	'Fleur' (p)	SAll
	'Floristan Mix' (p,a)	NNor
	'Forest Princess' (b)	SAll
	'Forest Sprite' (b)	SAll
	'Forest Treasure' (b)	SAll
	'Forest Violet' (b)	SAll
	'Forge Pink' **new**	LLHF
	'Fortuna' (p)	SAll
	'Fountain's Abbey' (p)	IGor
	'Fragrant Ann' (pf) ♀H1	CNMi

	Plant	Suppliers
	'Fragrant Phyllis' (pf)	CNMi
	'Frances Isabel' (p)	SAll
	'Frank Bruno' (pf)	CNMi
	'Freda' (p)	SAll
	'Freda Woodliffe' (p)	EPot NMen WAbe
	'Freya' (pf) **new**	SAll
	freynii	ECho EPot EWes GKev WAbe
*	- var. ***nana***	GKev
*	'Frilly'	LBMP
	Frilly = 'Wp08 Ulr03'[PBR]	ECho
	(Early Bird Series) (p) **new**	
N	fringed pink	see *D. superbus*
	furcatus	GKev
	'Fusilier' (p)	CElw CTri ECho ECtt EDAr EPfP
		GBuc GMaP LHop LRHS MAsh SAll
		SEND SHar SRot SWvt WFar
	'Gail Graham' (b)	SAll
	'Gail Tilsley' (b)	SAll
	'Garland' (p)	CMea CTri SAga
	'Gaydena' (b)	SAll
	giganteus	WSHC
	'Gingham Gown' (p)	ECtt EPot NBir SAll
	glacialis subsp. ***gelidus***	EPot
	'Gold Dust'	SAll
	'Gold Flake' (p)	SBch
	'Gold Fleck'	ECtt EPot EWTr
	'Golden Cross' (b) ♀H4	SAll
	'Grandma Calvert' (p)	SAll SBch
	graniticus	EPot
	'Gran's Favourite' (p) ♀H4	Widely available
§	***gratianopolitanus*** ♀H4	CArn CTri ENfk EPfP EPot GJos
		GKev LEdu MHer MNHC MRav
		NBid SEND WGwG
	- 'Albus'	EPot MHer
	- dwarf	WAbe
*	- 'Karlik' (p)	GJos GKev
§	- 'Tiny Rubies' (p)	SDys WAbe
	'Green Lane' (p)	CHll
	'Greensides' (p)	SAll
	'Grey Dove' (b) ♀H4	SAll
	'Greytown' (b)	GCal
	Gucci = 'Hilgucci' (pf) **new**	SAll
	'Gypsy Star' (p)	ECho SPoG
	haematocalyx	EPot NMen
	- 'Alpinus'	see *D. haematocalyx*
		subsp. *pindicola*
§	- subsp. ***pindicola***	LLHF NMen NRHS WAbe
	'Hannah Gertsen' (p/d)	SAll
	'Harkell Special' (b)	SAll
	'Harlequin' (p)	WPer
	'Haytor Rock' (p) ♀H4	EBee EPfP LRHS NCGa NNor
	'Haytor White' (p) ♀H4	CBcs CTri CWib EPfP MRav MWhi
		SAll WWEG
	'Hazel Ruth' (b) ♀H4	SAll
	'Heath' (b)	SAll
	'Helen' (p)	ELon LSRN SAll
	'Helena Hitchcock' (p)	SAll
	'Hereford Butter Market' (p)	EBee
	'Hidcote' (p)	CTri LLHF LRHS MAsh WFar
	'Hidcote Red'	ECho MWat
	'Highland Fraser' (p)	WKif
	'Hope' (p)	SAll SBch
	'Hot Spice' (p) ♀H4	SPoG
§	'Houndspool Cheryl' (p) ♀H4	CTri EBee EPfP SAll SBfd SRGP
		WFar
§	'Houndspool Ruby' (p) ♀H4	CBcs EPfP LBMP LSRN MAsh SAll
		SBfd
	hyssopifolius	CArn GJos
	'Ian' (p)	LSRN SAll WWEG

	Plant	Suppliers
	Iced Gem = 'Wp06 Fatima'[PBR]	ELon EPfP LBMP LHop LRHS LSRN
	(Scent First Series) (p/d)	MWat NNor SBfd SHil SPoG SRot
	'Icomb' (p)	WHoo WPer
	'Inchmery' (p)	SAll SBch WHer WHoo
	'India Star'[PBR] (p) ♀H4	CTri EBee ECho EPPr EPfP LBMP
		LRHS MAsh MWat NEgg SEND
		SRms SRot WIce
	'Inferno' (b) **new**	EBee
	'Inglestone' (p)	CTri WPer
	Inka = 'Barinka'[PBR] (pf)	SAll
	'Inshriach Dazzler' (p) ♀H4	CPBP CYeo ECho ECtt EPot GMaP
		LRHS MAsh MHer NEgg NGdn
		NHar NHol SRot WAbe
	'Inshriach Startler' (p)	CMea WNew
	'Ipswich Pink' (p)	MNHC
	× ***isensis***	CSpe EDif
	'Jack's Lass' (pf) **new**	CNMi
	'Jacqueline Ann' (pf) ♀H1	CNMi
	'James Portman' (p)	EBee ELon WMnd
	'Jane Austen' (p)	WPer
	'Janelle Welch' (pf)	CNMi
	'Janet Walker' (p)	GMaP
	'Jess Hewins' (pf)	CNMi SAll
*	'Jewel'	ECtt
	'Joan Schofield' (p)	SBch
	'Joanne' (pf)	CNMi
	'Joanne's Highlight' (pf)	CNMi
	'Joe Vernon' (pf)	CNMi
	'Johnny' (pf) **new**	SAll
	'Joy' (p) ♀H4	EBee EPfP LAst SAll SPoG WWEG
	'Julian' (p)	SAll
	'Julie Ann Davis' (b)	SAll
	'Kahori' (p) **new**	NPri
	'Kathleen Hitchcock'	SAll
	(b) ♀H4	
	'Kessock Charm'	MNrw
	'Kesteven Chamonix' (p)	WPer
	'Kesteven Kirkstead'	MNrw SAll
	(p) ♀H4	
	'Kim' (p)	NDov
	kitaibelii	see *D. petraeus* subsp. *petraeus*
	'Kiwi Fast Lane'	SWal
	(Kiwi Series) **new**	
	knappii	CFis EBee GKev LDai SPhx WHer
		WMoo WPer
	'Kristina' (pf) ♀H1	SAll
	'La Bourboule' (p) ♀H4	CMea CTri ECho ECtt EDAr GAbr
		LRHS MAsh MWat NMen SBch
		WFar WPat WRHF
	'La Bourboule Alba' (p)	CTri ECho ECtt EDAr EPot MAsh
		WFar WGor
	'Laced Joy' (p)	SAll
	'Laced Monarch' (p)	CBcs EBee ECtt ELan EPfP GCra
		LHop LRHS MMuc NCGa NEgg
		NNor SAll SEND SMrm SPlb SPoG
		WWEG
	'Laced Mrs Sinkins' (p)	CNMi SAll
	'Laced Prudence'	see *D.* 'Prudence'
	'Laced Romeo' (p)	SAll
	'Laced Treasure' (p)	SAll
	'Lady Granville' (p)	IGor SAll SBch
	Lady in Red = 'Wp04	CSBt EAEE EBee ECtt ELan EPfP
	Xanthe'[PBR] (p)	LRHS LSou MTis NNor
	Lady Madonna = 'Wp04	MTis MWat
	Opal'[PBR] (p) ♀H4	
	'Lady Wharncliffe' (p)	SBch
	'Lady Windermere' (M)	EMal
	'Lancing Monarch' (b)	SAll
	'Lancing Supreme' (p/d)	SAll

Name	Suppliers
'Laura' (p)	SAll
'Lavender Lady' (pf)	CNMi
'Leatham Pastel' (pf)	CNMi
'Lemsii' (p) Υ^{H4}	ECtt NGdn NMen WPer
'Leslie Rennison' (b)	SAll
'Letitia Wyatt' (p) Υ^{H4}	CMea EPfP LRHS MRav MWat SBch SBfd SPoG SRGP
'Leuchtkugel'	CPBP ECho LLHF NMen
leucophaeus var. ***leucophaeus***	LLHF
'Lily Lesurf' (b)	SAll
Lily the Pink = 'Wp05 Idare'^{PBR} (p)	LRHS MTis
'Linfield Annie's Fancy' (pf)	CNMi
'Linfield Doreen Ashmore' (p)	SAll
'Linfield Dorothy Perry' (p) Υ^{H4}	SAll
'Linfield Frances Clarke' (p) **new**	CNMi
'Linfield Isobel Croft' (p)	SAll
'Linfield Julie' (p)	SAll
'Linfield Kathy Booker' (p) Υ^{H4}	SAll
'Linfield Pink Margaret' (p) **new**	CNMi SAll
Lion King = 'Hillik'^{PBR} (pf)	SAll
'Little Ben' (p)	SAll
'Little Jock' (p/d)	ECho ECtt EDAr LRHS MAsh MHer MWat NRHS SAll SBch SPlb SPoG WFar WRHF
'Little Miss Muffet' (p)	CHll
'Liz Rigby' (b)	SAll
'London Brocade' (p)	CNMi SAll
'London Glow' (p)	CNMi SAll SBch
'London Lovely' (p)	SAll
'London Poppet' (p)	CNMi SAll
'Lord Nuffield' (b)	SAll
lumnitzeri	GKev LLHF NGdn NMen WPer
'Lustre' (b)	SAll
Luxor = 'Barxorlu' (pf) **new**	SWal
'Madonna' (pf)	EPfP WHer
'Madras' (pf) **new**	SAll
'Maggie' (p)	LSRN
'Maisie Neal' (b) Υ^{H4}	SAll
'Mambo' (pf) Υ^{H4}	SAll
'Mandy' (p)	SAll
'Manon des Sources' (pf) **new**	CNMi
'Margaret Taylor' (p) **new**	CNMi
'Maria'	see *D.* 'Allen's Maria'
'Marjery Breeze'	SAll
'Marmion' (M)	EMal SAll
'Mars' (p)	ECho ECtt
'Ma's Choice' (p) **new**	SAll
'Matthew' (p)	WHoo
'Maudie Hinds' (b)	SAll
'Max Hellewell' (pf) **new**	CNMi
'Maybole' (b)	SAll
'Mendip Hills' (b)	SAll
Mendlesham Minx = 'Russmin'^{PBR} (p)	EBee ECho EDAr ELan EPPr LRHS MWat NRHS SAll SBfd SRms SWvt
'Merlin' Υ^{H4}	NEgg
'Messines Pink' (p)	SAll
'Michael Saunders' (b) Υ^{H4}	SAll
Michelle = 'Komichel' (pf) **new**	SAll
microlepis	ECho EDAr GKev NGdn NSla WAbe
– f. ***albus***	GKev NSla WAbe
– ED 791562	NGdn
– 'Leuchtkugel'	ECho WAbe
– var. ***musalae***	ECho ITim LLHF NMen
'Milky Way' (pf)	SAll
'Mike Briggs' (b)	SAll
'Miss Sinkins' (p)	CTri IFoB SPet
'Monica Wyatt' (p) Υ^{H4}	CBcs EBee ECtt EPfP LRHS NCGa NEgg SPoG WGwG WWEG WWFP
'Montrose Pink'	see *D.* 'Cockenzie Pink'
'Monty Allwood' (p)	SAll
'Moor Corbeth' (p) **new**	CNMi
'Moor Editha' (p) **new**	CNMi
'Moor Hazel-eye' (p) **new**	CNMi
'Mother of Pearl' (Perfume Pinks Series)	EWll MTis MWat SBfd
'Moulin Rouge' (p) Υ^{H4}	CTri EAEE EBee ECtt ELan EPfP GAbr GCra LHop LRHS LSou MSpe MTis MWat NDov SPhx SPoG WWEG
'Mrs Clark'	see *D.* 'Nellie Clark'
'Mrs Gumbly' (p)	CNMi
'Mrs Macbride' (p)	SAll
'Mrs Roxburgh' (p)	CSam
'Mrs Sinkins' (p)	Widely available
'Murray's Laced Pink' (p)	MWhi
N 'Musgrave's Pink' (p)	CFis CHid ECha MRav SAll SBch
'Musgrave's White'	see *D.* 'Musgrave's Pink'
myrtinervius	CCon CPBP ECho EDAr GKev MHer NGdn WHoo
Mystic Star = 'Devon Sapphire' (p) Υ^{H4}	CMea ECho ELan EPPr MAsh MAvo SBfd WIce
'Napoleon III' (p)	SAll
'Napoli' **new**	WHil
'Natalie Saunders' (b) Υ^{H4}	SAll
'Nautilus' (b)	SAll
neglectus misapplied	see *D. pavonius*
§ 'Nellie Clark' (p)	MWat
'Neon Star'^{PBR} (p) Υ^{H4}	CTri EBee ECho EDAr ELan GBuc GKev LRHS MAsh MWat NRHS SHil SPoG SRms SRot WFar
'Night Star' (p) Υ^{H4}	ECho ELan EPfP GKev GMaP LHop LPot LRHS MAsh NEgg NRHS SBch SEND SPet SRot WFar WHil WPtf
'Nika' (pf)	SAll
nitidus	NBir
noeanus	see *D. petraeus* subsp. *noeanus*
'Northland' (pf)	CNMi EMal SAll
'Nyewoods Cream' (p)	CMea CTri ECho EPot MHer NGdn NMen NPri WPer
§ 'Oakington' (p)	CTri MRav
'Oakington Rose'	see *D.* 'Oakington'
'Oakwood Billy Boole' (p) **new**	CNMi
'Oakwood Candy' (p) **new**	CNMi
'Oakwood Erin Mitchell' (p)	CNMi
'Oakwood Romance' (p) Υ^{H4}	CNMi
'Oakwood Sweetheart' (p) **new**	SAll
'Old Blush'	see *D.* 'Souvenir de la Malmaison'
'Old Clove Red' (b)	EBee SEND
'Old Crimson Clove' (b)	SBch
'Old Dutch Pink' (p)	SBch
'Old French Red' (pf)	EMal

	Name	Suppliers
	'Old Mother Hubbard' (p)	CHII
	'Old Red Clove' (p)	WCot
§	'Old Square Eyes' (p)	MNrw SAll
	'Old Velvet' (p)	CNMi GCal MNrw SAll
	'Oliver' (p)	SAll
	'Onix' (pf) **new**	SAll
	'Orange Maid' (b)	SAll
	oschtenicus	GKev
	'Owston Third Avenue' (p) **new**	SAll
	'Oxford Magic' (p)	SAll
	'Paddington' (p)	CNMi
	'Painted Lady' (p)	SAll
	'Paisley Gem' (p)	SAll SBch
	'Pamela Flett' (p) **new**	CNMi
	Passion = 'Wp Passion'[PBR] (Scent First Series) (p)	EBee ECtt ELan EPfP EWll GBin LBMP LRHS LSou MAvo MBel MPie MTis NNor NRHS SBfd SHil SPoG WCot WHil
§	***pavonius*** ♀H4	EWes NGdn NMen SBch WPer
	'Pax' (pf)	SAll
	'Peach' (p)	SEND
	'Pendle Mrs Riley' (p) **new**	CNMi
	'Peter Wood' (b) ♀H4	SAll
§	***petraeus***	EWes NGdn WThu XLum
§	- subsp. ***noeanus***	LHop LLHF WHal WPer
§	- subsp. ***petraeus***	WPer
	'Petticoat Lace' (p)	SAll
	'Phantom' (b)	SAll
	'Pheasant's Eye' (p)	SAll WHer
	'Picaro' (pf) **new**	SAll
*	'Picton's Propeller' (p)	GBuc
	Pierrot = 'Kobusa' (pf)	CNMi
	'Pike's Pink' (p) ♀H4	CSpe CTri EBee ECho ECtt EDAr ELan EPfP LHop LRHS MAsh MHer MMuc MRav MWat NBir NGdn NMen SAll SBch SEND SPet WAbe
	pindicola	see *D. haematocalyx* subsp. *pindicola*
	pinifolius	IFro
	'Pink Devon Pearl'[PBR]	LPot
	'Pink Doris' (pf)	CNMi
	'Pink Dover' (pf)	SAll
	'Pink Fantasy' (b)	SAll
	'Pink Fizz'	LRHS
	'Pink Jacqueline Ann' (pf)	CNMi
	'Pink Jewel' (p)	CMea CPBP ECtt GKev MAsh NMen SAll SBch
	'Pink Mrs Sinkins' (p)	ECha MHer MLHP MNrw SAll
	'Pink Pearl' (b)	SAll
	'Pixie' (b)	EPot NGdn
	'Pixie Star'[PBR] (p) ♀H4	ECho EPPr EPfP LBMP MAsh MWat SPoG SRot WIce
	plumarius	CArn MLHP SAll WHer
	- 'Ipswich Pinks'	GJos
	- 'Sonata'	GJos
	Popstar = 'Wp04 Esther' (p)	ECho EWll SRms
	'Pretty' (p)	SAll
	Pretty Flamingo[PBR]	see *D.* 'Carmine Letitia Wyatt'
	'Prince Charming' (p)	ECho ECtt MAsh
	'Princess of Wales' (M)	EMal SAll
	'Priory Pink' (p)	SAll
§	'Prudence' (p)	SAll
	'Pudsey Prize' (p)	CPBP EPot WAbe
	'Pummelchen' (p)	ITim
	'Purple Jenny' (p)	SAll
	'Queen of Hearts' (p)	CTri ECho SEND
§	'Queen of Henri' (p)	EBee ECho ECtt LRHS MHer WFar
	'Queen of Sheba' (p)	IGor SAll SBch WHer WKif
	'Raggio di Sole' (pf)	CNMi
	'Rainbow Loveliness' (p,a)	SAll
	'Ralph Gould' (p)	ECho
	'Raspberry Parfait'	LRHS
	'Raspberry Sundae' (p)	ECtt ELan EPfP LBMP LRHS LSRN NCGa SBfd SEND SHil SPoG WBor WHil
	Rebekah = 'Wp09 Mar05' (Early Bird Series) (p)	EPPr LBMP
	'Red Star'[PBR] (p) ♀H4	ECho ELan GJos LRHS SRot WIce
	Reina = 'Lonreina'[PBR] (pf)	SAll
	'Reine de Henri'	see *D.* 'Queen of Henri'
	'Richard Pollak' (b)	SAll
	'Rivendell' (p)	ECho NMen WAbe
	'Robert Allwood' (pf)	SAll
	'Robin Ritchie' (p)	CNMi WHoo
	'Robina's Daughter'	GAbr
	Romance = 'Wp09 Wen04' (Scent First Series) (p) **new**	LBMP LRHS MTis MWat SBfd SHil
	'Rose de Mai' (p)	CNMi CSam SAll SBch WHoo
	'Rose Devon Pearl'[PBR]	EPfP
	'Rose Joy' (p) ♀H4	EBee EPfP MWat
§	'Rose Monica Wyatt'[PBR] (p) ♀H4	EAEE LRHS NCGa NDov
	Rosebud = 'Wp08 Ros03'[PBR] (Early Bird Series) (p) **new**	EDAr EPPr
	'Roysii' (p)	WPer
	'Ruby'	see *D.* 'Houndspool Ruby'
	'Ruby Doris'	see *D.* 'Houndspool Ruby'
	'Ruby Wedding' (p)	LSRN
	'Russian Skies' **new**	EWld
	'Sam Barlow' (p)	SAll SBch
	sanguineus	NDov
	'Santa Claus' (b)	SAll
	scopulorum perplexans	ITim
	'Seren Wen' **new**	WAbe
	serotinus	EPot WCot
	Shandy = 'Barshandy' (pf) **new**	SAll
	Sherbet = 'Wp08 Ros03'[PBR] (Early Bird Series) (p) **new**	GAbr
	Shooting Star = 'Wp04 Flores'[PBR] (p)	ECho LRHS SRms
	'Shot Silk' (pf)	SAll
	'Show Aristocrat' (p)	SAll
	'Show Beauty' (p)	ECtt SAll
	Show Girl = 'Hilshow' (pf)	LRHS MTis SBfd
	Show Girl = 'Wp08 Uni02'[PBR] (Scent First Series) (p) **new**	ELan EWll
	'Show Glory' (p)	SAll
	'Show Harlequin' (p)	SAll
	'Show Satin' (p)	ECtt SAll
	'Shrimp' (b)	CWib
	Silver Star = 'Wp10 Hel01' (p) **new**	ECho EPPr
	'Singapore Girl' (Kiwi Series)	CWGN SGar
	Slap 'n' Tickle = 'Wp05 Pp22'[PBR] (Scent First Series) (p)	ECtt LHop LRHS LSRN MTis NCGa NPri NRHS SBfd SHil SPoG SRot
	'Snowshill Manor' (p)	WPer
	'Solomon' (p)	IGor SAll
	Sonia = 'Lonsonia'[PBR] (pf) **new**	SAll
	'Sops-in-wine' (p)	CSam ECha ECtt MSCN SAll
	'Sorbetto'[PBR] (pf) **new**	SAll

§	'Souvenir de la Malmaison' (M)	EMal SAll
	'Spangle' (b)	SAll
	'Spencer Bickham' (p)	MNrw
	spiculifolius	CFis EDAr EPot SBch WFar
	'Spirit' (pf)	SAll
	'Spring Star' (p)	ECtt SRot WJek
	'Square Eyes'	see *D.* 'Old Square Eyes'
	squarrosus	ECho EPot GEdr WAbe
*	- ***alpinus***	ECho
	- 'Nanus'	see *D.* 'Berlin Snow'
	'Starburst'PBR (p)	CMea ECho ELon EPPr EWll GAbr NCGa SBfd SHil
	Stardust = 'Wp07 Opr04'PBR (Early Bird Series) (p) **new**	EBee ECho EPPr WIce
	Starlight = 'Hilstar'	CMea LRHS NCGa SRms
	Starlight = 'Wp 06Parnia'PBR (p) **new**	ECho
	'Starry Eyes' (p) ♀H4	CSam ECho ELan EPPr GMaP LRHS NEgg NPri NRHS SBch SRms SRot SWvt WAbe WFar
	'Storm' (pf)	CNMi EMal SAll
	stramineus **new**	GKev
	'Strawberries and Cream' (p)	CBcs EBee ECtt LRHS NEgg NOrc SPoG WMnd
	subacaulis	EDAr GAbr IFoB NGdn
	- subsp. ***brachyanthus***	GJos NMen WAbe
	- - 'Murray Lyon'	CPBP NMen WThu
	suendermannii	see *D. petraeus*
	Sugar Plum = 'Wp08 Ian04'PBR (Scent First Series) (p)	ELan EPfP EWll LBuc MTis MWat SBfd
	'Summerfield Adam' (p)	SAll
	'Summerfield Amy Francesca' (p)	SAll
	'Summerfield Blaze' (p)	SAll
	'Summerfield Daniel' (b)	SAll
	'Summerfield Debbie' (p)	SAll
	'Summerfield Emma Louise' (p)	SAll
	'Summerfield Rebecca' (p)	SAll
	SummertimePBR	see *D.* 'Rose Monica Wyatt'
	'Sunburst' (p)	ELon
	(Sunflor Series) 'Sunflor Bianca' **new**	WHil
	- 'Sunflor Citrien' **new**	WHil
	- 'Sunflor Odessa Purple'	SWal
	- 'Sunflor Odessa Red'	SGar SWal
	'Sunray' (b)	SAll
	'Sunstar' (b)	SAll
§	***superbus***	CMHG EDAr EWTr GBBs LHop MNFA MNrw NNor SBch SPhx WMoo
	- 'Crimsonia'	MBrN SBch
I	- 'Primadonna'	GQue
	'Susan' (p)	SAll
	'Susannah' (p)	SAll
*	'Susan's Seedling' (p)	SAll
	'Sutton Brierley Grace' (p) **new**	CNMi
	'Sutton Pamela Flett Supreme' (p) **new**	CNMi
	'Swanlake' (p)	SAll
	'Sway Lass' (p)	SEND
	'Sweet Sophie' (pf)	CNMi
	'Sweet Sue' (b)	SAll
	'Sweetheart Abbey' (p)	CNMi IGor
I	'Sweetness Mix' (p)	GJos
	sylvestris	GEdr
	- dwarf	EPot
	'Tamsin Fifield' (b) ♀H4	SAll
	'Tatra Blush' (p)	GCal
	'Tatra Fragrance' (p)	CCse GCal SAll
	'Tatra Ghost' (p)	SAll SBch SDys
	'Tayside Red' (M)	EMal SAll
	'Terranova' (pf)	CNMi
	'Thomas' (p)	SBch
	'Thora' (M)	EMal SAll
	Tickled Pink = 'Devon Pp 11' (Scent First Series) (p)	ECtt ELan ELon EWll GAbr LBMP LRHS LSRN MTis MWat NPri SBfd SHil SPoG WHil
	'Tiny Rubies'	see *D. gratianopolitanus* 'Tiny Rubies'
	'Tolima' (pf) **new**	SAll
	'Tony's Choice' (pf)	CNMi
	'Tracy Jardine' (pf)	CNMi
	'Treasure' (p)	SAll
	'Trevor' (p)	SAll
	'Tropic Butterfly' (p) **new**	LPot
	'Tudor'	MNrw
	turkestanicus	NBir NNor WPtf
	Tyrolean trailing carnations	SAll
	'Uncle Teddy' (b) ♀H4	SAll
	'Unique' (p)	IGor SAll SBch
	'Ursula Le Grove' (p)	WHer
	'Valda Wyatt' (p) ♀H4	CBcs EAEE EBee ELan EPfP LAst LRHS MWat NCGa NEgg NNor SAll SBfd SEND SPoG SWvt WGwG WMnd
	Vega = 'Kovega' (pf) **new**	SAll
	Viana = 'Kovian'PBR (pf) ♀H1 **new**	CNMi
	'Vic Masters'	SBch
	'Violet Clove' (b)	SAll
	'W.A. Musgrave'	see *D.* 'Musgrave's Pink'
	'Waithman Beauty' (p)	CTri ECtt GEdr GMaP SAll WHoo WPer WTin
	'Waithman's Jubilee' (p)	MWhi SAll
	'Warden Hybrid' (p)	CTri EBee ECho ECtt EPfP GAbr GMaP LAst LRHS NGdn NRHS NWad SBch SPoG SWvt WAbe WFar
	'Waterloo Sunset'PBR (p)	CMea CSBt GAbr LRHS MTis SBfd
	'Weetwood Double' (p)	MWhi SBch
	'Welton Mandy' (p) **new**	CNMi
	'Welton Raspberry Ice' (p) **new**	SAll
	'Welton Star' (p) **new**	CNMi
	weyrichii	ECho EPot
	'Whatfield Anona' (p)	SAll
	'Whatfield Beauty' (p)	ECho ECtt ELan
	'Whatfield Brilliant' (p)	ECho
	'Whatfield Cancan' (p) ♀H4	CMea ECho ECtt EPot EWTr GMaP LHop LRHS MAsh MNHC MWat NEgg NGdn NPri SAll SBch SPoG SWvt WJek WNew WWFP
	'Whatfield Cyclops' (p)	ECho SAll
	'Whatfield Dawn' (p)	ECho
	'Whatfield Dorothy Mann' (p)	ECho SAll SBch
	'Whatfield Fuchsia Floss' (p)	SAll
	'Whatfield Gem' (p)	EBee ECho ECtt ELan EPfP GAbr GEdr LRHS MWat NGdn NMen SAll SPoG SWvt WFar WHoo WNew WPer WRHF
	'Whatfield Joy' (p)	EBee ECho ECtt ELan EPfP EPot LRHS MAsh MHer NGdn NMen SAll WFar WHoo

'Whatfield Magenta' (p) ♀H4	CSam ECho ECtt ELan EPfP EPot LHop LRHS MAsh MWat NMen NRHS SAll SPoG WAbe
'Whatfield Mini' (p)	SAll WPer
'Whatfield Miss' (p)	SAll
'Whatfield Misty Morn' (p)	ECho SAll
'Whatfield Nine Star' (p) **new**	ECho
'Whatfield Peach' (p)	SAll SBch
'Whatfield Polly Anne' (p)	EWld
'Whatfield Pretty Lady' (p)	ECho SAll
'Whatfield Rose' (p)	ECho
'Whatfield Ruby' (p)	ECho ELan GJos SAll WFar
'Whatfield Supergem' (p)	ECho ECtt EPot
'Whatfield White' (p)	ECho ECtt SAll
'Whatfield White Moon' (p)	ECho
'Whatfield Wisp' (p)	CPBP CTri ECho EPfP EPot GEdr MRav NBir NMen WNew
'White and Crimson' (p)	SAll
'White Joy' PBR (p) ♀H4	MRav
'White Ladies' (p)	ELan MRav SAll
'White Liberty' PBR (pf)	SAll
'Whitehill' (p) ♀H4	ECho MHer NMen
'Whitesmith' (b) ♀H4	SAll
'Widecombe Fair' (p) ♀H4	CTri ECtt ELan EPfP SAll SBfd SPoG
'William Brownhill' (p)	CNMi
'Zebra' (b)	SAll

Diapensia (*Diapensiaceae*)

lapponica var. ***obovata***	NHar WAbe

Diarrhena (*Poaceae*)

japonica	MMoz

Diascia (*Scrophulariaceae*)

'Alice Cap'	SBch
'Andrew'	SBch
'Appleby Appleblossom'	SBch
'Appleby Apricot'	NDov
'Aquarius'	SBch
barberae 'Belmore Beauty' (v)	ECtt EWes WPer
- 'Blackthorn Apricot' ♀H3-4	CBar EAEE EBee ECha ECtt ELan EPfP GMaP LRHS LSRN NDov SMrm SPer SPlb SPoG SWvt WWEG XEll
§ - 'Fisher's Flora' ♀H3-4	EPyc NDov
§ - 'Ruby Field' ♀H3-4	CBar CMea EBee ECha ECtt ELan EPfP LHop LRHS LSRN NEgg SPer SPoG SWvt WWEG
Blue Bonnet = 'Hecbon'	GBee SBch SWvt
'Blush'	see *D. integerrima* 'Blush'
Breezee Apricot = 'Diaspritwo' PBR	LHop
Breezee Snow = 'Inndiabzsno' PBR	LHop SMrm
'Candy Floss'	SBch
Coral Belle = 'Hecbel' PBR ♀H3-4	ECtt EPot EWes GBin LHop LRHS LSou SBfd SMrm
cordata misapplied	see *D. barberae* 'Fisher's Flora'
cordifolia	see *D. barberae* 'Fisher's Flora'
'Denim Blue'	CSpe EPfP LAst NLar SPoG WPer
elegans misapplied	see *D. fetcaniensis, D. vigilis*
'Elizabeth' ♀H3-4	WHrl
'Emma'	SMHy SWvt
felthamii	see *D. fetcaniensis*
§ ***fetcaniensis***	CMHG CMea CPrp EBee EShb GMaP LRHS MHer NEgg WBrk WCFE WHal WKif
- 'Daydream'	LBuc SBch WHrl
flanaganii misapplied	see *D. vigilis*
(Flying Colours Series) Flying Colours Appleblossom = 'Diastara'	EPfP SPoG
- Flying Colours Apricot = 'Diastina'	EPfP
- Flying Colours Red = 'Diastonia' PBR	EPfP SPoG
'Frilly' ♀H3-4	ECtt
'Hector Harrison'	see *D.* 'Salmon Supreme'
Ice Cracker = 'Hecrack'	CMea ELan LHop LRHS SBch
Ice Cream = 'Icepol'	SCoo
Iceberg = 'Hecice' PBR	SWvt
§ ***integerrima*** ♀H3-4	ECha ELon NDov
- from Lesotho	SMrm
- 'Alba'	see *D. integerrima* 'Blush'
§ - 'Blush'	CSpe
- 'Ivory Angel'	see *D. integerrima* 'Blush'
integrifolia	see *D. integerrima*
'Jacqueline's Joy'	CMea NPer SBch
'Joyce's Choice' ♀H3-4	EWes LRHS
Juliet Pink With Eye = 'Baljulpiney' **new**	LAst
Juliet White = 'Baljalite' **new**	LAst
'Katherine Sharman' (v)	EWes
'Lady Valerie' ♀H3-4	EWes WPer
'Lilac Belle' ♀H3-4	CMea EBee ECtt ELan LHop LRHS NBir NEgg NRHS SBch SPlb SPoG
'Lilac Gem'	SBch
'Lilac Mist' ♀H3-4	NPer
lilacina × ***rigescens***	GBee
Little Dancer = 'Pendan' PBR	EPot LSou MSCN NLar SBfd SCoo SLon SMrm
'Little Dazzler'	WRHF
Little Dreamer = 'Pender' PBR	NLar SBfd
Little Drifter = 'Pendrif' PBR	LSou NLar WRHF
Little Maiden = 'Penmaid' PBR	NLar WGor
Little Tango = 'Pentang' PBR	CPrp LHop LSou NLar SBfd WCot
'Marilyn'	NDov SBch
(Miracle Series) 'Miracle Carmine'	LSou
- 'Miracle Rose-Pink'	LSou
- 'Miracle White'	LSou
patens	CHll
personata	CHVG CHll CMea CPrp CSpe CTri EBee ECtt ELon LLHF LPla LSou MCot SAga SMHy SPer SUsu WCot WPer WSHC
- 'Hopleys'	EWes LHop MAvo NCGa SHar
'Peter'	NDov
Pink Panther = 'Penther'	ECtt NLar SCoo SWvt
'Pitlochrie Pink'	GBin
Red Ace = 'Hecrace' PBR	EPfP GBin LAst LHop NPer SWvt
Redstart = 'Hecstart'	ECtt NGdn SWvt
rigescens ♀H3	CHEx COlW CPrp CSpe CWCL ECtt ELan EPot GEdr LHop MHer MRav NPer SPlb SPoG SWvt WBor WCFE WSHC WSpi
§ - 'Anne Rennie'	EBee LRHS MCot SWvt
- pale-flowered	see *D. rigescens* 'Anne Rennie'
(Romeo Series) Romeo Bright Pink = 'Balromink' **new**	LAst
- Romeo Orange = 'Balromor' **new**	LAst NPri

'Ruby Field'	see *D. barberae* 'Ruby Field'
'Rupert Lambert' ♀H3-4	EWes NDov SBri WPer
§ 'Salmon Supreme'	EBee ECtt ELan LRHS NGdn NPer SPoG WPer
tetcaniensis 'African Queen' new	EDif
'Twinkle' ♀H3-4	ECtt LRHS NBir NPer NRHS
* 'Twins Gully'	EWes GCal SMrm
§ ***vigilis*** ♀H3	CMHG CMea CPLG EPfP EPot GBee LHop LRHS NBro SAga SBch WHal WPnn WRHF
- 'Jack Elliott'	MRav WCFE
(Whisper Series) Whisper Apricot Improved = 'Balwhisaptim'PBR	SCoo
- Whisper Cranberry Red = 'Balwhiscran'PBR	SCoo
- Whisper Pumpkin = 'Balwhispum'	SGar
Wink White = 'Balwinwite'PBR (Wink Series)	LAst

Dicentra ✿ (*Papaveraceae*)

CC 4452	CPLG
'Adrian Bloom'	CPLG EBee ECtt EPfP LAst LHop LRHS LSRN SMrm SWvt WFar WMoo
'Aurora'	EBee ECtt ELon EPfP GBuc LAst LRHS LSou MRav NGdn NLar NSti SBfd SPer SPoG SWvt WFar WMoo
'Boothman's Variety'	see *D.* 'Stuart Boothman'
'Bountiful'	CMac EBee LSou MRav NGdn SWvt WGwG
'Brownie'	GBuc
'Burning Hearts'	CWCL CWGN EBee IPot LHop LLHF LSou MAsh MBri MPnt NCGa NGBo SPer WHil
canadensis	CLAP EBee GBuc GHim MAvo NLar WAbe WCru WHal
'Candy Hearts'PBR	EBee ECtt ELan EPfP LHop LRHS MBri NBro NGdn NLar WFar WHil
cucullaria	CElw CLAP CMea CPBP CWCL EBee ECho ELon EPot GBuc ITim LRHS MNrw MRav NLar NMen WAbe WCru WFar
- 'Pittsburg'	CRDP EBee EPPr GBuc MNrw SCnR
eximia misapplied	see *D. formosa*
eximia (Ker Gawl.) Torr.	EBee
- 'Alba'	see *D. eximia* 'Snowdrift'
§ - 'Snowdrift'	CLAP EBee ECtt ELan EPfP LAst MCot SRms WFar WMoo
'Fire Island'	EBee
'Firecracker'	EBee
§ ***formosa***	CBcs CTri EBee ECha EHrv ELan EPfP GKev IFro LAma LAst LRHS MLHP NBro NGdn NMen NOrc NPri SPlb SRms WFar WMoo WWEG
- f. ***alba***	ECha GAbr GCra GMaP NBir SRms WCru WFar WKif
- 'Bacchanal' ♀H4	Widely available
- 'Coldham'	ELon WSHC
- 'Cox's Dark Red'	CLAP CPLG EBee EWes GBuc LLHF LWst NMen SKHP WOut
- 'Langtrees' ♀H4	CMac CRow CSam EBee ECha EHrv EPau EPfP GBuc LHop LRHS MLHP MRav NBro SGar SRms SWvt WCru WFar WMoo WOut WPtf WSHC
- subsp. ***oregana***	CLAP EBee EPPr IGor LWst NBre NChi NMen SKHP WHal
- - NNS 00-233	CLAP
- - 'Rosea'	EPPr
- Snowflakes = 'Fusd'	EWes LRHS MRav
- 'Spring Gold'	ECha ELon EPPr LBuc LRHS NLar WMoo
- 'Spring Magic'	EPPr LBuc LRHS NLar
'Ivory Hearts'PBR	CWGN EBee ECtt ELan EPfP LHop LRHS LSRN MAsh MAvo MBri MCot NBro NCGa NGdn NLar NPnk NRHS NSti SMrm SPer SPoG SPtl WHil
§ 'Katie'	EPPr
'Katy'	see *D.* 'Katie'
'King of Hearts'	Widely available
lichiangensis	see *Dactylicapnos lichiangensis*
'Luxuriant' ♀H4	CBcs CMea CSBt EBee ECtt ELan EPfP GBuc LAst LHop LRHS MCot MGos MRav SBfd SMrm SPad SPer SPoG SRms SRot SWvt WFar WMoo WPnP WWEG
macrantha	see *Ichthyoselmis macrantha*
'Pearl Drops'	CRow EBee ELan GMaP LRHS MCot MMoz MRav NBid NMen SRms WAbb WHil WMoo
peregrina	GEdr WAbe
- ***alba***	GEdr
'Red Fountain'	CWCL EBee IPot LHop LRHS MBri NCGa NGBo NPnk NSti SMad WHil
scandens	see *Dactylicapnos scandens*
'Silver Beads'	ELon
spectabilis	see *Lamprocapnos spectabilis*
'Spring Morning'	CElw CMHG CSam EAEE EBee ECtt EPPr LBMP LRHS LSou NOrc
§ 'Stuart Boothman' ♀H4	Widely available
thalictrifolia	see *D. scandens*
'Valentine'	EBee MAsh MBri MSCN NLar
ventii	see *Dactylicapnos ventii*

Dichelachne (*Poaceae*)

crinita	SMea

Dichelostemma (*Asparagaceae*)

congestum	CAvo EBee ECho LRHS SDeJ
§ ***ida-maia***	CAvo CGrW ECho EPot LRHS MCot SDeJ
- 'Pink Diamond'	CGrW EBee ECho SDeJ WCot
multiflorum	WCot
volubile	CTca ECho WCot
- 'Pink Giant' new	SDeJ

Dichocarpum (*Ranunculaceae*)

§ ***dicarpon*** B&SWJ 11555	WCru

Dichondra (*Convolvulaceae*)

argentea 'Silver Falls'	CSpe EShb ESwi LSou LSqH NPri SCoo SPoG
§ ***micrantha***	EShb
repens misapplied	see *D. micrantha*

Dichopogon (*Anthericaceae*)

strictus	ECou WSFF

Dichorisandra (*Commelinaceae*)

thyrsiflora Blue Bamboo = 'Bodine'	LRHS

Dichroa (*Hydrangeaceae*)

febrifuga CAbb CBcs CDoC CHEx CHGN CHll CMil CPLG CTsd CWib EBee ELan EWes LRHS WCru WPGP
- B&SWJ 2367 WCru
- HWJK 2430 WCru
- pink-flowered CHEx
hirsuta B&SWJ 8207 from Vietnam WCru
aff. ***hirsuta*** B&SWJ 8371 from Lao WCru
versicolor B&SWJ 6565 WCru
- B&SWJ 6605 from Thailand WCru
aff. ***yunnanensis*** B&SWJ 9734 WCru

Dichromena see *Rhynchospora*

Dichrostachys (*Mimosaceae*)

cinerea new SPlb

Dicksonia ✿ (*Dicksoniaceae*)

antarctica ♀H3 CAbb CBcs CDoC CHEx CSBt CSam CTrC EPfP ERod EUJe EWTr EWes GAbr IBal LEdu LRHS LSRN MGos MREP SBfd SChr SEND SHil SPad SPoG SWvt WCot WFib WMoo WPGP
fibrosa ♀H3 CBcs CDTJ CKel CTrC EAmu EExo GBin ISha LTen MDev
sellowiana CDTJ CKel
squarrosa ♀H2 CBcs CBty CCCN CDTJ CKel CTrC EAmu MGos

Dicliptera (*Acanthaceae*)

§ ***sericea*** CHll EShb IKil LHop MSCN SBch SEND SGar SMrm SRkn WCot WHil WPGP WTcb
suberecta see *D. sericea*

Dicoma (*Asteraceae*)

anomala SPlb

Dictamnus ✿ (*Rutaceae*)

albus Widely available
- var. ***albus*** ♀H4 MAvo NPnk SEND
§ - var. ***purpureus*** ♀H4 Widely available
* - ***turkestanicus*** GCal
fraxinella see *D. albus* var. *purpureus*

Didymochlaena (*Dryopteridaceae*)

lunulata see *D. truncatula*
§ ***truncatula*** XBlo

Dierama ✿ (*Iridaceae*)

sp. WHil
adelphicum EBee
ambiguum EBee EWld IGor SBfd XLum
'Aphrodite' NFir
argyreum CCCN CElw CMac CMea CTsd CWCL EBee EPri GBin GEdr NFir NLar SBfd SBrt SPoG SRot XLum
'Ariel' IBlr
'Ballyrogan Red' IBlr
'Black Knight' CPLG IBlr
'Blackberry Bells' new CWCL SPoG
'Blue Belle' CMac CPen CWCL EBee GBin IBal IVic LBMP LBuc LRHS LSou SPtl
'Blush' IBlr
'Buckland White' WPGP
'Candy Stripe' CBcs CWCL IBal
'Carmine' new CWCL
'Cherry Chimes' EPfP
'Cinnamon Fairy' new EBee
cooperi CElw CPou CTca EBee IBlr NBir WWEG
'Coral Bells' CDes EBee GCal
'Cosmos' CPLG CWCL EDAr EOHP EPri GAbr LRHS MHer MWhi SBfd SMad
'Dark Angel' NCGa
'Delicacy' IBlr
'Desire' IBlr
dissimile EBee IGor NFir
'Donard Legacy' IBlr NLar
§ ***dracomontanum*** Widely available
- JCA 3.141.100 WPGP
- dwarf, pale pink-flowered LRHS
- Wisley Princess Group MBri
dracomontanum* × *pulcherrimum SMad
dubium EBee IBlr
ensifolium see *D. pendulum*
erectum CBcs CCCN CHid CMac CWCL EBee EPri GEdr IBlr LRHS NLar SBfd SRot
'Fairy Bells' CPen
floriferum IBlr
formosum CCon CGHE EBee WPGP
galpinii CCCN CGHE CWCL CYeo EBee ELan EPri GBin GEdr IGor LLHF LRHS NFir NLar WPGP
grandiflorum CPou CYeo IBlr IGor
'Guinevere' Widely available
igneum Widely available
- CD&R 278 CPLG CPou GBuc
insigne CCCN CHid CWCL EBee LRHS
'Iris' IBlr
jucundum CWCL EBee GBuc
'Knee-high Lavender' CDes SAga WPGP
'Lancelot' CBcs CCon CElw CPLG CYeo EBee ECtt EHrv GEdr IBal IBlr LRHS MBNS MRav NBir NCGa NEgg NFir NGdn NPnk NSti SPer SWvt WCot WKif
latifolium CGHE CHid IBlr MNrw
luteoalbidum EWld
'Mandarin' IBlr
medium CGHE CSpe EBee ELon SUsu SWat WPGP WWEG
'Milkmaid' CPLG IBlr NCot
'Miranda' CAbP EBee ECtt EPri GEdr IBal LRHS MBNS MBel NEgg NGdn NPnk NSti SPad WCot WFar
mossii CBcs CCCN CCon CHid CMHG CMac CMea CPLG CWCL CYeo EBee ELan EPri GEdr IBlr IGor LHop LRHS SBfd SPlb SRot WHer WPGP XLum
nixonianum IBlr
'Painted Lady' CPen CWCL LBuc LRHS SBfd SKHP SLon
pallidum SGar
'Pamina' CPLG CPrp IBlr
'Papagena' IBlr
'Papageno' IBlr
pauciflorum CCCN CCon CGHE CHid CPLG CPrp CWCL CWib CYeo EBee EDAr

	EPri GEdr MHer MNrw NBir NFir NLar SMrm SRot SWat WPGP WSHC WWEG
- CD&R 197	CPBP MDKP
§ ***pendulum***	CBro EBee ELan EPfP GBBs GEdr IBlr LRHS LSRN MGos MNrw MRav SMrm SWvt WCot WFar WWEG
'Petite Fairy'	CPen
pictum	IBlr
'Pink Rocket'	MHer
Plant World hybrids	ELon SEND
Plant World Jewels	CWCL
'Pretty Flamingo'	CPLG CPrp IBlr
'Puck'	CDes EBee GCal IBlr IGor MRav WHil WPGP
pulcherrimum	Widely available
- var. ***album***	CCCN CGHE CSpe CWCL CYeo ELan GEdr IBlr LRHS MHer MNrw MWhi WPGP WWEG
- 'Blackbird'	CBcs CCCN CCon CDes CKno CMac CPLG CSam CSpe CWCL CWGN EBee ECtt ELan EPri GEdr IBlr IBoy LAst LHop LRHS LSRN MHer NPnk SKHP SUsu SWvt WHil WPGP WWEG
- dark pink-flowered	IBoy
- dwarf	ELon
- 'Falcon'	IBlr
- 'Flamingo'	IBlr
- lilac-flowered	LHop
- 'Merlin'	CElw CMea CPLG CPou CSpe CWCL CYeo EBee ECtt EHrv ELon GAbr GEdr GMaP IBal IBlr IBoy LRHS MBel MNrw MWhi NBir NGdn NPnk NSti SUsu SWvt WCot WGwG WHoo
- pale-flowered	ECha
- 'Pearly Queen'	EBee
- 'Peregrine'	IBoy
- purple-flowered	LRHS
- 'Redwing'	IBlr
- Slieve Donard hybrids	EBee ECtt EDAr GBuc ITim LAst LRHS NEgg SBfd SMad SPet WFar WHil WHrl WMnd WWEG
pumilum misapplied	see *D. dracomontanum*
'Queen of the Night'	IBlr
reynoldsii	Widely available
robustum	CGHE CPLG CPou CWCL EBee IBlr LRHS MNrw NFir NLar SBfd SMad WHer WPGP
'Sarastro'	CPLG IBlr
'September Charm'	IBlr
sertum	EBee
'Spring Dancer'	EHoe NHol
'Tamino'	IBlr
'Tiny Bells'	EBee EDAr GCal SMHy
'Titania'	GCal IBlr
trichorhizum	CCCN CCon CGHE CPLG CPrp CWCL CYeo EBee ELan EPri IBlr LHop LRHS NFir NLar SBfd WPGP WWEG
'Tubular Bells'	IBlr
tyrium	EBee
'Violet Ice'	IBlr
'Westminster Chimes'	IBlr
'Zulu Bells'	ELon

Diervilla ✿ (*Caprifoliaceae*)

middendorffiana	see *Weigela middendorffiana*
rivularis 'Troja Black'	EPPr NLar
§ ***sessilifolia***	CBcs CHGN CMac EBee EPPr IDee LAst MRav NLar NMRc SGar SLon WCot WFar WMoo
- 'Butterfly'	CMac EPPr NLar WMoo
- Cool Splash = 'Lpdc Podaras' (v)	CWGN EBee ELan EMil EPPr EPfP LBuc LRHS MAsh NPri SPoG
× ***splendens***	CMHG CPLG CWib EBee EHoe ELan EPPr EPfP IDee LHop LRHS MBNS MBlu MGos MRav MSwo SEND SLPl SPer SPoG SPtl

Dietes (*Iridaceae*)

bicolor	CAbb CHEx CPLG CPrp CTca EPri LEdu LSou SChr SHom WSHC
butcheriana	CDes
grandiflora	CAbb CArn CCse CPLG CPne CPrp CTca EBee ECho GBin SBch WSHC
§ ***iridioides***	CPne CPrp CTca EBee ECho WCot
robinsoniana	CSpe

Digitalis ✿ (*Plantaginaceae*)

sp.	SVic
RCB/TQ 059 from İkizdere	WCru
'Albino'	EPfP LRHS
ambigua	see *D. grandiflora*
apricot hybrids	see *D. purpurea* 'Sutton's Apricot'
cariensis	GAbr
davisiana	CPLG GAbr MNHC WMoo
dubia	EPfP NBir
'Elsie Kelsey'	ECtt NBir SWvt WHil
eriostachya	see *D. lutea*
ferruginea ♀H4	Widely available
- subsp. ***ferruginea*** new	WSpi
- 'Gelber Herold'	CLAP EBee GMaP NBre NLar SMrm SPhx WFar
- 'Gigantea'	CLAP EBee ECtt ELan ETod GKev GQue LAst LRHS MBNS NChi SCob SWat WAul WCot WFar WWEG
* ***floribunda***	NBir
fontanesii	CEnt NBir
'Foxtrot'	EPfP LBuc LRHS MBri SHil
× ***fulva***	NBir
'Glory of Roundway'	CDes CLAP EBee ECtt IBoy LEdu LSou MHer MTis NLar SPer WCot
§ Goldcrest = 'Waldigone'	EBee LBuc LRHS SPoG
§ ***grandiflora*** ♀H4	Widely available
- 'Carillon'	EBee ELan EPfP IFoB LAst LBMP LDai LRHS NBir NLar SRot
- 'Cream Bell'	EPfP LRHS
- 'Dwarf Carillon'	EWld
heywoodii	see *D. purpurea* subsp. *heywoodii*
'Illumination'	LRHS
kishinskyi	see *D. parviflora*
laevigata	CCon EBee EPfP LRHS MCot NBro SBfd SEND SPav SPet WMnd WMoo WPer
- white-flowered	WCot
lamarckii misapplied	see *D. lanata*
§ ***lanata***	CArn EBee ECtt EGHP ELan EPfP GKev LAst LRHS MBNS MNHC NGdn NOrc SBfd SPav SPer SPlb SRms WFar WMnd WPer WWEG
- 'Café Crème'	CLAP SPet
§ ***lutea***	Widely available

	- SDR 6377	GKev
	- SDR 6413	GKev
I	- 'Aurea' **new**	LPla
§	- subsp. ***australis***	LDai
	- 'Flashing Spires' (v)	SPad
	× ***mertonensis*** ♀H4	Widely available
	- 'Raspberry' **new**	CLAP
	- 'Summer King'	ECtt ELan LSRN NBre NLar NPri SMrm
	micrantha	see *D. lutea* subsp. *australis*
	obscura	CFis EBee ECho EHrv GKev IFoB LRHS MHer NBir SIde SPet SPlb WMnd
*	- 'Dusky Maid'	LRHS SPet
	orientalis	see *D. grandiflora*
§	***parviflora***	CCVN CDes CEnt CSam EBee ECha ECtt ELan EPPr EPfP GAbr GCra GJos GKev LRHS MAvo MBNS MSCN MWhi NBro NChi SBea SEND SPav SWal WMnd WMoo WPGP WPer WWEG
	- 'Milk Chocolate'	CBcs CLAP CMHG CSpe ECtt ELan EPfP GBin GBuc GJos GQue LHop LRHS LSRN LSou MCot MNHC MWat NBir NBre NEgg SBHP SIde SKHP SMrm SPet SSvw WFar
	'Pink Chapel'	EBee ECtt WCot
	'Polkadot Pippa' **new**	WHlf
	purpurea	CArn CHab EBee EGHP ELan ENfk EPfP GPoy LRHS MHer MLHP MMuc MNHC NLan NMir NPri SBfd SEND SIde SPlb SPoG WBrk WJek WMoo WSFF WWFP
	- 'Alba'	see *D. purpurea* f. *albiflora*
§	- f. ***albiflora***	Widely available
	- - 'Anne Redetzky'PBR	CSpe ELan LRHS WMnd
	- - unspotted	CWan
	- Camelot Series	LRHS WRHF
	- - 'Camelot Cream'	EBee EPfP LRHS MCot NLar NPri SWvt
	- - 'Camelot Lavender'	EBee EPfP LRHS MBri NEgg NLar NPri NRHS SWvt
	- - 'Camelot Rose'	EBee EPfP LRHS MBri NEgg NLar NPri NRHS SWvt
	- - 'Camelot White'	EBee EPfP LRHS NEgg NLar NRHS
*	- 'Campanulata Alba'	MBel
	- 'Chedglow' (v)	CNat
	- 'Dalmatian Purple'	LRHS MBri NRHS SHil
	- 'Dalmatian White'	MBri NPri SHil
	- Excelsior Group	CBcs CMac CSBt CTri EAEE ECtt EHrv EPfP GJos GMaP IBoy LAst LHop LRHS MBri MWat NHol NMir SBfd SPer SPoG SRms SWvt WFar WGor WWEG XLum
	- - (Suttons; Unwins) ♀H4	ECtt MRav
	- Foxy Group	CMac CWib EPfP LRHS SBfd SPet SPoG WWEG
	- - 'Foxy Apricot'	CLAP SWvt
	- - 'Foxy Pink'	CLAP
	- Giant Spotted Group	ECtt EPfP LRHS SPoG
	- Glittering Prizes Group	SWat
	- Gloxinioides Group	ELan
	- - 'The Shirley' ♀H4	SGar WMoo
§	- subsp. ***heywoodii***	ELan WMoo WWEG
	- - 'Silver Fox'	ECtt LRHS LSRN WCot
	- subsp. ***mariana***	EBee GKev
	- 'Pam's Choice'	CCVN CHid CLAP CPLG CSpe EBee ECtt EPfP GJos GKev LAst LHop LRHS LSRN MBel MBri MGos MWat NEgg NGBl NLar SBfd SMrm SPer SRGP WGwG WMnd WMoo WWEG WWlt
	- 'Pam's Split'	CHid
	- 'Primrose Carousel'	ECtt NEgg NLar NPri
	- 'Snow Thimble'	CLAP EBee LHop LRHS MAvo MBri MTis NLar NRHS WBor WCAu WWEG
§	- 'Sutton's Apricot' ♀H4	Widely available
	- white cen-type mutant	NChi
	purpurea × ***thapsi***	WWEG
	'Red Skin'	CPom SPad WMoo
	'Saltwood Summer'	LBuc LRHS MBri NRHS SHil
	'Serendipity'	EPfP LBuc LRHS MBri SHil
	'Spice Island'PBR	CLAP EBee ECtt ELon ESwi GBin IBoy LRHS LSou MAvo MBel MTis NCGa NDov NLar NSti SPer SPoG SUsu WCot WWlt
*	***stewartii***	ECtt ELan EWes GCra LDai WHil WMoo
	'Strawberry Fayre'	GJos
	thapsi	ECtt EDif ELan EPfP LRHS SIde WMoo WPer WWEG XLum
	- 'Spanish Peaks'	CHid LRHS LSou
	trojana	EBee ECtt GKev IFoB SGar SPhx
	- 'Helen of Troy'	ECtt ELan SKHP WSpi
	viridiflora	CPLG ECtt NBro SGar WFar
	'Walberton's Goldcrest'	see *D.* Goldcrest

dill see *Anethum graveolens*

Diocirea (*Scrophulariaceae*)

violacea	ECou

Dionaea ✿ (*Droseraceae*)

muscipula	CHew CSWC EECP NChu SKHP SPlb WSSs
- 'Akai Ryu'	CSWC EECP NChu WSSs
- 'B52'	CSWC EECP WSSs
- 'Big Mouth'	CSWC
- (Dentate Traps Group) 'Dentate Traps' **new**	WSSs
- 'Red Piranha'	NChu
- 'Royal Red'	CHew CSWC NChu WSSs
- 'Sawtooth'	EECP WSSs
- shark-toothed	CSWC EECP NChu
- 'Spider'	CSWC EECP NChu

Dionysia (*Primulaceae*)

'Annielle'	WAbe
archibaldii	WAbe
- 'Tora'	WAbe
aretioides ♀H2	WAbe
- 'Bevere'	WAbe
- 'Phyllis Carter'	ECho
'Bernd Wetzel'	WAbe
bryoides	WAbe
- 'Esselmont'	WAbe
'Charleson Thomas'	WAbe
'Charlson Emma'	WAbe
'Charlson Gem'	WAbe
'Charlson Jake'	WAbe
'Charlson Moonglow'	WAbe
'Charlson Petite'	WAbe
'Charlson Primrose'	WAbe
'Chris Grey-Wilson'	WAbe
curviflora	WAbe
'Emmely'	WAbe
'Eric Watson'	WAbe
'Ewesley Iota'	WAbe

'Ewesley Kappa'	WAbe
'Ewesley Theta'	WAbe
janthina	WAbe
'Judith Bramley'	WAbe
'Lycaena'	WAbe
'Manuela'	WAbe
'Monika'	WAbe
'Pascal'	WAbe
'Schneeball'	WAbe
tapetodes	WAbe
- 'Brimstone'	WAbe
- 'Peter Edwards'	WAbe
'Tess'	WAbe

Dioon (*Zamiaceae*)

califanoi	CBrP
caputoi	CBrP
edule ♀H1	CBrP SBst SChr SPlb
- var. ***angustifolium***	CBrP
mejiae	CBrP
merolae	CBrP
rzedowskii	CBrP
spinulosum	CBrP SBig

Dioscorea (*Dioscoreaceae*)

CC 5622	EWld
araucana	LSou
batatas	CAgr CArn LEdu
caucasica new	EBee
deltoidea	CPLG
japonica	CAgr EShb LEdu
quinqueloba	WCru
villosa	CArn

Diosma (*Rutaceae*)

ericoides	SEND SWvt
- 'Pink Fountain'	CAbb EBee LBuc LRHS SEND SPoG
- 'Sunset Gold'	CWGN EBee LBuc LRHS MAsh SCoo SEND SPoG
hirsuta 'Silver Flame'	EBee SEND

Diosphaera (*Campanulaceae*)

asperuloides	see *Trachelium asperuloides*

Diospyros (*Ebenaceae*)

austroafricana	SPlb
* ***hyrcanum***	EGFP NLar
kaki (F)	CBcs CMCN EPfP ERom MREP NPla WPGP
- 'Fuyu'	CAgr
- 'Kostata'	CAgr
- 'Mazelii'	CAgr WPGP
lotus	CAgr CBcs CMCN LEdu NLar SPlb
- (f)	CAgr
- (m)	CAgr
lycioides	SPlb
'Nikita's Gift'	CAgr
rhombifolia	CBcs
'Russian Beauty'	CAgr
virginiana (F)	CAgr CBcs CMCN NLar SPlb SSpi
- 'Early Golden'	CAgr
- 'Meader'	CAgr

Dipcadi (*Hyacinthaceae*)

ciliare	CLak
marlothii 'Bloemfontein'	ECho
serotinum	ECho
- subsp. ***lividum***	WPGP
viride	CLak
white-flowered	CLak

Dipelta (*Caprifoliaceae*)

floribunda ♀H4	CBcs CDoy CDul CJun CMCN CMac CPLG ELan EPfP LRHS MBlu MBri NLar SKHP WPGP WPat
ventricosa	CAbP CBcs CGHE CJun CPLG EBee ELan EPfP LRHS MAsh MBlu NLar SChF SSpi WPGP WPat
yunnanensis	CBcs CJun CPLG EBee ELan EPfP LRHS NLar SKHP SSpi WPGP WPat

Diphylleia (*Berberidaceae*)

cymosa	CLAP EBee ECha GCal GEdr MRav SPhx WCot WCru WTin
- red-marked	CDes
grayi	CLAP GEdr WCru
sinensis	CPLG GEdr WCru

Dipidax see *Onixotis*

Diplacus see *Mimulus*

Dipladenia see *Mandevilla*

Diplarrena (*Iridaceae*)

§ ***latifolia***	CWri GBBs GCal IBlr IGor LRHS WKif WPtf
- Helen Dillon's form	IBlr
moraea	CAbP CAbb CMac CWCL EBee ECho ELon GAbr GBBs GBin GCal IBlr IFoB IKil LRHS MCot NCGa NLBP WAbe WPGP WSHC
- ***minor***	IBlr
- 'Slieve Donard'	IBlr
- West Coast form	see *D. latifolia*

Diplotaxis (*Brassicaceae*)

muralis	CArn ELau WJek
tenuifolia	ELau ENfk MNHC

Dipogon (*Papilionaceae*)

§ ***lignosus***	CSpe

Dipsacus (*Caprifoliaceae*)

§ ***fullonum***	CArn CHab CMac CWan ENfk EPfP GAbr GKev MBri MHer MNHC NMir NPri SBch SEND SIde WHer WJek WSFF
inermis	CElw CSam ECha NBid NLar WFar
japonicus	SKHP
- HWJ 695	SPhx WCru
pilosus	CPom
sativus	NLar
strigosus	SPhx
sylvestris	see *D. fullonum*

Dipteracanthus see *Ruellia*

Dipteronia (*Aceraceae*)

sinensis	CBcs CMCN MBri NLar WPGP

Disanthus (*Hamamelidaceae*)

cercidifolius ♀H4	CAbP CBcs CJun CMCN CMac EBee EPfP GKin IArd IDee LRHS MAsh MBlu MPkF NLar SPoG SSpi WPGP
- 'Ena-nishiki' (v)	NLar

Discaria (Rhamnaceae)

	chacaye	LEdu WPGP

Diselma (Cupressaceae)

	archeri	CDoC CKen SCoo SLim
	- 'Read Dwarf'	CKen

Disphyma (Aizoaceae)

	crassifolium	SChr

Disporopsis (Asparagaceae)

	B&SWJ 229 from Taiwan	WCru
	B&SWJ 1864 from Taiwan	WCru
	aspersa	CAvo CLAP CSpe EBee ECho EPPr EWld LEdu MAvo NBir WCru WPGP
	- tall	CBct CPLG WCru
	fuscopicta	CBct CLAP EBee EHrv EPPr MAvo WCru WTin WWEG
	longifolia	CLAP
	- B&SWJ 5284	WCru
*	**luzoniensis** B&SWJ 3891	CBct CPLG GEdr LEdu WCru
	'Min Shan'	CPLG ELon
*	**nova**	EPPr
§	**pernyi**	Widely available
	- B&SWJ 1864	CBct EPPr
	- 'Bill Baker'	LEdu MAvo
	aff. **pernyi** new	WWlt
	taiwanensis	CAvo
	- B&SWJ 3388	CBct WCru
	undulata	LEdu NBid WCru

Disporum (Colchicaceae)

	austrosinense B&SWJ 9777	LEdu WCru
	bodinieri	CPLG EBee LEdu WPnP
	- BWJ 8128	WCru
	- DJHC 765	WCru
	cantoniense	CCon CPom EBee EPPr EPri GEdr GHim IFoB LEdu LWst MPie WBor WCru WFar
	- B&L 12512	CDes CLAP CPLG
	- B&SWJ 1424	WCru
	- B&SWJ 9715	WCru
	- DJHC 98485	CDes CLAP EBee LEdu MMoz SKHP
I	- 'Aureovariegata'	CBct CDes EBee LEdu WCot
	- var. **cantoniense** f. **brunneum** B&SWJ 5290	WCru
	- var. **kawakamii** B&SWJ 350	WCru
	- - RWJ 10103	CBct WCru
	- var. **multiflorum** B&SWJ 11252	WCru
	- - B&SWJ 11291	WCru
	- 'Night Heron'	CBct CDes CLAP CPLG EBee EHrv IFoB LEdu LWst WCot WFar WPnP
	- var. **sikkimense** B&SWJ 2337	WCru
	- - B&SWJ 2358	WCru
*	- var. **y-tiense** HWJ 1045 new	WCru
*	**flavum**	CAvo CBct ECho EHrv MMHG SUsu WPnP
	hookeri	CLAP CPom EBee ECho LWst MNrw NMen WCru
	- var. **oreganum**	EBee EPPr IBlr IFoB LRHS WCru
	lanuginosum	CBct EBee EPPr GEdr LRHS MAvo WCot WCru
	leschenaultianum B&SWJ 9484	WCru
	- B&SWJ 9505	WCru
	leucanthum	WCru WFar
	- B&SWJ 2389	WCru
	longistylum	LEdu
	- B&SWJ 2859	WCru
	- L 1564	CBct WCru
	- 'Green Giant'	CBct CDes CLAP CPLG EBee EPfP IFoB LEdu LSou LWst NMyG WFar WHil WPnP
	lutescens	EBee EPot WCru
	maculatum	CBct CDes CLAP EHrv IFoB LEdu MNrw WCru
	megalanthum	CBct CLAP CPLG IFoB MMoz WCru
	- CD&R 2412B	CLAP CPLG EBee EHrv EPPr
	nantouense	LEdu WCot
	- B&SWJ 359	CBct WCru WFar
	- B&SWJ 6812	WCru
	sessile	EBee ECho LEdu WCru
	- AGSJ 146	GBuc NMen
	- B&SWJ 2824	WCru
I	- 'Aureovariegatum' (v)	ECho MAvo WCru
	- 'Cricket'	GEdr
	- 'Kinga' (v)	EBee GEdr
	- f. **macrophyllum** B&SWJ 4316	WCru
I	- 'Robustum Variegatum'	EBee MAvo
	- 'Variegatum' (v)	CAvo CHEx CPLG EBee ECho EHrv ELan ELon EPPr EPfP EPot GBBs GEdr GMaP LEdu LRHS MBel MRav NLar SPhx WBor WCot WCru WFar WHil WPGP WPnP
	- var. **yakushimense**	ECho LEdu
	- yellow-margined (v)	CBct
	shimadae B&SWJ 399	WCru
	smilacinum	LWst NLar WCru WFar
	- B&SWJ 713	WCru
*	- 'Aureovariegatum' (v)	LEdu MAvo WCru
	- pink-flowered	WCru
	smithii	CBct CPom EBee ECho EPfP GAbr GEdr GKev LEdu NBir NMen SUsu WCot WCru WFar WPGP
	taiwanense B&SWJ 1513	WCru
	- B&SWJ 2018	WCru
	tonkinense B&SWJ 11672	WCru
	- B&SWJ 11814	WCru
	- HWJ 882	WCru
	trabeculatum	CBct WCru
	- 'Nakafu'	LEdu WCru
	trachycarpum	CLAP
	uniflorum	CBct CGHE CLAP CPom EBee ECho EPfP LEdu LRHS MNrw NBid NMyG SMHy WFar WSHC
	- B&SWJ 651	CBct LEdu WCot WCru
	- B&SWJ 872	WCru
	- B&SWJ 4100	WCru
	viridescens	CBct EBee EHrv LEdu SKHP WCru
	- B&SWJ 4598	WCru

Distylium (Hamamelidaceae)

	myricoides	CMCN NLar WFar
	racemosum	CBcs CMac EPfP GKin IGor IVic MBlu NLar SLPl SSta WSHC

Diuranthera see Chlorophytum

Dizygotheca see *Schefflera*

Dobinea (*Anacardiaceae*)

vulgaris B&SWJ 2532 WCru

Dodecatheon (*Primulaceae*)

alpinum NHar SRms
- subsp. ***alpinum*** EBee
- - NNS 02-132 GKev
amethystinum see *D. pulchellum*
'Aphrodite'PBR NLar WFar
austrofrigidum EBee GKev NCGa NHar
clevelandii GKev MDKP
- subsp. ***insulare*** LLHF
- subsp. ***patulum*** ECho LRHS NRHS
conjugens LLHF
cusickii see *D. pulchellum* subsp. *cusickii*
dentatum ♀H4 CElw CPBP GEdr GKev LEdu MDKP NHar WAbe WFar
- subsp. ***ellisiae*** GKev
- subsp. ***utahense*** new NHar
frigidum WAbe
§ ***hendersonii*** ♀H4 EPot GKev NMen SRms
integrifolium see *D. hendersonii*
§ ***jeffreyi*** EBee ECho EPPr GBuc GEdr GKev LEdu LRHS MDev MNrw NCGa NLar NMen NPnk WAbe WBor
- NNS 07-168 GKev
- NNS 08-120 GKev
- subsp. ***pygmaeum*** GKev
- 'Rotlicht' EBee SRms WTcb
* × ***lemoinei*** WAbe
§ ***meadia*** ♀H4 Widely available
- from Cedar County, USA WAbe
- f. ***album*** ♀H4 CBro EBee ECho ELan EPfP EPot GEdr GKev LAma LEdu LHop LRHS MBel MMoz MNrw NCGa NHol NLar NMen NMyG NPnk NRHS SKHP SPer SRms SWvt
- 'Aphrodite' EPfP GEdr LSou WBor
* - 'Goliath' CFis
- membranaceous WAbe
- 'Queen Victoria' EBee ECho GBuc GEdr LEdu NLar NPnk SKHP WFar
- red shades GBuc SMrm
pauciflorum misapplied see *D. pulchellum*
pauciflorum (Dur.) E. Greene see *D. meadia*
poeticum CPBP
- NNS 00-259 EBee NCGa
§ ***pulchellum*** ♀H4 CBro EBee ECho EDAr GEdr GKev LHop LRHS MNrw NMen NRHS SBfd WIce WTcb
§ - subsp. ***cusickii*** LEdu SRms
- subsp. ***pulchellum*** 'Red Wings' EBee ECho EPot LLHF LRHS MDKP NBir NHar NLar NMen NPnk SKHP WFar
- ***radicatum*** see *D. pulchellum*
- 'Sooke Variety' WAbe
radicatum see *D. pulchellum*
redolens EBee GBuc WAbe
tetrandrum see *D. jeffreyi*

Dodonaea (*Sapindaceae*)

viscosa CBcs ECou SPlb
- (f) ECou
- (m) ECou
- 'Purpurea' CAbb CBcs CDoC CHGN CPLG CTrC CTsd EAmu EBee ECre EHoe ELon EUJe IVic LRHS LTen SLim

Doellingeria (*Asteraceae*)

scabra see *Aster scaber*

Dolichandra (*Bignoniaceae*)

cynanchoides RCB RA Q-4 WCot

Dolichos (*Papilionaceae*)

lignosus see *Dipogon lignosus*
purpureus see *Lablab purpureus*

Dombeya (*Malvaceae*)

burgessiae IDee
calantha CCCN
wallichii CCCN

Dondia see *Hacquetia*

Doodia (*Blechnaceae*)

media CBty EBee GBin ISha LRHS

Doronicum (*Asteraceae*)

austriacum NBid
caucasicum see *D. orientale*
§ ***columnae*** CBcs
cordatum see *D. columnae*
§ × ***excelsum*** 'Harpur Crewe' CPrp EBee LEdu LRHS MRav NPer
'Finesse' GCal LRHS SRms
§ 'Frühlingspracht' (d) LRHS
'Little Leo' EBee ELan EPfP GJos LRHS LSRN MBrN NLar NPri SBfd SPet SPoG SRGP
§ ***orientale*** CWan EBee EPfP GJos LRHS SEND SPer SPoG SWat
- 'Goldzwerg' EBee
- 'Leonardo' LBuc
- 'Leonardo Compact' LBuc LPot
- 'Magnificum' CSBt EPfP GMaP LRHS MBNS MBri NEgg NGBl NMir SMrm SPoG SRms WCot WFar
pardalianches CFis CMea ECha MMuc SEND WRHF
- 'Goldstrauss' EBee
plantagineum 'Excelsum' see *D.* × *excelsum* 'Harpur Crewe'
Spring Beauty see *D.* 'Frühlingspracht'

Doryanthes (*Doryanthaceae*)

excelsa CHEx CTrC
palmeri CBrP CHEx

Dorycnium see *Lotus*

Douglasia see *Androsace*

vitaliana see *Vitaliana primuliflora*

Dovyalis (*Salicaceae*)

caffra (F) XBlo

Doxantha see *Macfadyena*

Draba (*Brassicaceae*)

acaulis WAbe
aizoides ECho LRHS MAsh SPlb SRms XLum
aizoon see *D. lasiocarpa*
athoa EDAr

	borealis	XLum
	bruniifolia	EWes XLum
	bryoides	see *D. rigida* var. *bryoides*
	'Buttermilk' new	WAbe
	cretica	NMen
	cusickii	GKev
	cuspidata	GKev
	dedeana	EWes
	dubia	EDAr
	fladnizensis	LLHF
	var. ***pattersonii*** new	
	glacialis	EDAr
	hispanica	EDAr
	imbricata	see *D. rigida* var. *imbricata*
	'John Saxton' new	WAbe
§	***lasiocarpa***	XLum
	longisiliqua ♀H2	CPBP LLHF WAbe
	- EMR 2551	EPot
	mollissima	EPot WAbe
	- 'Göteborg'	EPot
	oligosperma	EDAr
	ossetica	WAbe
	parnassica	EDAr
	polytricha	WAbe
§	***rigida*** var. ***bryoides***	WThu
§	- var. ***imbricata***	NSla
	- - f. ***compacta***	EPot
	rosularis	EDAr
	× ***salomonii***	EPot
	scardica	see *D. lasiocarpa*
	ventosa	WAbe
	yunnanensis	CPBP WAbe

Dracaena ✿ (*Asparagaceae*)

	cochinchinensis	SPlb
	draco ♀H1	CTrC EShb SPlb WCot XBlo
	fragrans Deremensis Group	XBlo
	indivisa	see *Cordyline indivisa*
	'Lemon Lime Tips'	XBlo
	marginata (v) ♀H1	XBlo
	- 'Tricolor' (v) ♀H1	XBlo
	stricta	see *Cordyline stricta*

Dracocephalum (*Lamiaceae*)

	argunense	SBch SPhx SRms
*	- 'Album'	GKev
	- 'Blue Carpet'	NLar
	- 'Fuji Blue'	CEnt CPLG EBee EDAr EPfP EWes GKev LRHS LSRN NBre SPoG WIce
	- 'Fuji White'	CEnt CPLG EBee LSRN SPhx SPoG
	austriacum	SBrt
	botryoides	LLHF SPhx
	calophyllum	EBee GKev
	forrestii	GKev MAvo
	aff. ***forrestii***	LLHF
	grandiflorum	GJos LLHF MMHG SBHP SBch SPhx XLum
	- 'Altai Blue'	LRHS
	hemsleyanum	LLHF
	isabellae	LRHS
	mairei	see *D. renatii*
	moldavica	SIde
	nutans	LRHS
	peregrinum	SBrt
	- 'Blue Dragon'	SPhx
	prattii	see *Nepeta prattii*
§	***renatii***	LLHF SPhx
	rupestre	EBee
	ruyschiana	ELan EWes GEdr LRHS MRav SPhx
	- 'Blue Moon'	NLar
	sibiricum	see *Nepeta sibirica*
*	***tataricum***	LRHS
	virginicum	see *Physostegia virginiana*
	wendelboi	LLHF NBir

Dracunculus (*Araceae*)

	canariensis	WCot
	muscivorus	see *Helicodiceros muscivorus*
§	***vulgaris***	CHid CPom EBee ECho EHrv EPfP EPot ERCP ESwi EUJe GKev LRHS MMoz MRav NRHS SDix SEND SMad SPlb WCot

Dregea (*Apocynaceae*)

	sinensis	CCCN CHll CRHN ELan EPfP EShb EWes LRHS MOWG MRav SEND SKHP WPGP WSHC
	- 'Brockhill Silver'	SKHP
	- 'Variegata' (v)	EWes WCot

Drepanostachyum (*Poaceae*)

	falconeri	see *Himalayacalamus falconeri*, *Himalayacalamus falconeri* 'Damarapa'
	hookerianum	see *Himalayacalamus hookerianus*
§	***khasianum***	CDTJ CPLG WPGP

Drimia (*Asparagaceae*)

	angustifolia ambig.	ECho
	anomala	CLak
	basutica new	CLak
	elata	CLak
	involuta	CLak
	mzimvubuensis	CLak
	sphaerocephala	CLak
	uniflora	CLak

Drimiopsis (*Hyacinthaceae*)

	maculata	LToo WCot

Drimys (*Winteraceae*)

	andina	CPLG EPfP SEND
	aromatica	see *D. lanceolata*
	colorata	see *Pseudowintera colorata*
	granadensis	WCru
	var. ***grandiflora*** B&SWJ 10777	
§	***lanceolata***	Widely available
	- (f)	CTrC ECou EUJe SPer
	- (m)	CDoC CTrC ECou SPer
	- 'Mount Wellington'	GCal
	- 'Red Spice' new	ESwi SPtl
	- 'Suzette' (v)	LRHS MBlu
*	***latifolia***	CBcs CHEx IDee
	winteri ♀H4	Widely available
§	- var. ***chilensis***	CPLG EPfP LRHS SSpi WCru WPGP
	- Latifolia Group	see *D. winteri* var. *chilensis*

Drosanthemum (*Aizoaceae*)

	hispidum	ECho ELan EPfP LRHS MAsh NMen NRHS SBHP SPlb SPoG WAbe WNew
	speciosum	ECho
*	***sutherlandii***	ECho

Drosera ✿ (*Droseraceae*)

admirabilis	CHew CSWC
aliciae	CHew CSWC EECP NChu
andersoniana	EFEx
androsacea	CHew
anglica	CSWC NChu
ascendens	CHew
binata	CHew EECP
- var. ***binata***	CSWC
§ - subsp. ***dichotoma***	CHew CSWC
- 'Extrema'	CHew
- 'Multifida'	CHew
browniana	EFEx
bulbigena	EFEx
bulbosa subsp. ***bulbosa***	EFEx
- subsp. ***major***	EFEx
callistos	CHew
capensis	CHew CSWC NChu SPlb SWal
- 'Albino'	CHew EECP SWal
- red	CSWC NChu SWal
dichotoma	see *D. binata* subsp. *dichotoma*
dichrosepala	CHew EECP
echinoblastus	CHew
enodes	CHew
ericksoniae	CHew
erythrorhiza	EFEx
- subsp. ***collina***	EFEx
- subsp. ***erythrorhiza***	CHew EFEx
- subsp. ***magna***	EFEx
- subsp. ***squamosa***	EFEx
filiformis	NChu SWal
- var. ***filiformis***	CHew CSWC EECP
gigantea	EFEx
graniticola	EFEx
helodes	CHew
heterophylla	EFEx
× ***hybrida***	CSWC
intermedia	CSWC
lasiantha	CHew
leioblastus	CHew
loureiroi	EFEx
macrantha	EFEx
- subsp. ***macrantha***	EFEx
macrophylla subsp. ***macrophylla***	EFEx
mannii	CHew
marchantii subsp. ***prophylla***	EFEx
menziesii subsp. ***basifolia***	EFEx
- subsp. ***menziesii***	EFEx
- subsp. ***thysanosepala***	EFEx
modesta	EFEx
nidiformis	CHew
orbiculata	EFEx
paleacea subsp. ***trichocaulis***	CHew
peltata	EFEx
platypoda	EFEx
pulchella	CHew
pycnoblasta	CHew
pygmaea	CHew
ramellosa	EFEx
roseana	CHew
rosulata	EFEx
rotundifolia	CSWC WHer
salina	EFEx
sargentii	CHew
scorpioides	CHew CSWC EECP
slackii	CHew NChu
spatulata	CSWC
stelliflora	CHew
stolonifera	EFEx
subsp. ***compacta***	
- subsp. ***humilis***	EFEx
- subsp. ***porrecta***	EFEx
- subsp. ***rupicola***	EFEx
- subsp. ***stolonifera***	EFEx
tubaestylus	EFEx
zonaria	EFEx

Drosophyllum (*Drosophyllaceae*)

lusitanicum	CHew

Dryandra (*Proteaceae*)

formosa	LTen SPlb WCot

Dryas (*Rosaceae*)

drummondii	ECho LLHF WAbe
§ ***integrifolia***	NMen
- 'Greenland Green'	WAbe
octopetala ♀H4	CMea EBee ECho GJos GKev LHop LRHS MAsh MWat NChi NRHS SPoG SRms WAbe
§ - dwarf	EPot
- subsp. ***hookeriana***	LLHF
- 'Minor' ♀H4	NMen WAbe
× ***suendermannii*** ♀H4	CMea CYeo EBee EPfP EPot GEdr GMaP NHar NMen WAbe
tenella misapplied	see *D. octopetala* dwarf
tenella Pursh	see *D. integrifolia*

Dryopteris ✿ (*Dryopteridaceae*)

aemula	EFer SRms
§ ***affinis*** ♀H4	CBty CLAP CMac EBee ECha EPfP ERod GMaP LBuc LPBA LRHS LTen MCot MGos MMoz NPri SPer SPoG SRms WCot WFib WShi WWEG
- subsp. ***affinis*** **new**	WSpi
§ - subsp. ***borreri***	SRms
- subsp. ***cambrensis***	ISha
- - 'Crispa Barnes'	WPGP
- - 'Insubrica'	EFer
- 'Congesta'	CLAP EBee WWEG
- 'Congesta Cristata'	CLAP EFer GMaP LPBA SRot
§ - 'Crispa Gracilis' ♀H4	CKel CLAP ELan ERod GBin ISha LTen MMoz NBir NEgg NHol NMyG WWEG
* - 'Crispa Gracilis Congesta'	CBty GEdr NGdn NWad SBfd WFib WPat WRHF
- Crispa Group	CLAP EHon GBBs MMoz WSpi WWEG
§ - 'Cristata' ♀H4	Widely available
- 'Cristata Angustata' ♀H4	CBty CLAP EFer ELan EPfP ETod LTen MMoz NBid NGdn NHol NRHS SRms WBor WFib WMoo WPGP
- 'Cristata The King'	see *D. affinis* 'Cristata'
- 'Grandiceps Askew'	EFer SRms WFib
- 'Pinderi'	CBty CLAP EBee ELan GBin ISha NMyG SRms WWEG
- Polydactyla Group	CLAP WFar WSpi
- - 'Polydactyla Dadds'	CBty CLAP LLHF NLar NMyG SEND WWEG
- - 'Polydactyla Mapplebeck' ♀H4	CLAP LPBA NBid SRms WFib

	- 'Revolvens'	CLAP EFer
	atrata misapplied	see *D. cycadina*
	atrata (Wall. ex Kunze) Ching	CDTJ CKel CWCL EWTr SBfd SPoG XLum
	× ***australis***	CLAP ISha LTen
	austriaca	see *D. dilatata*
	bissetiana	ISha
	blanfordii	WPGP
	- from Kashmir **new**	ISha
	borreri	see *D. affinis* subsp. *borreri*
	buschiana	CBty CDTJ CLAP EBee MRav NLar WWEG
	carthusiana	CLAP EBee EFer GBin NLar WPtf WSpi
	- 'Cristata'	EFer
	celsa	ISha
	championii	CCCN CLAP ISha LRHS
	clintoniana	CLAP EFer GBin LRHS MMoz NMyG WPGP
	× ***complexa***	CBty ISha
	- 'Stablerae'	CLAP EFer GBin MWhi WFib WPGP
	- 'Stablerae' crisped	NMyG WFib
	crassirhizoma	CCCN CKel CLAP EBee GBin ISha LRHS MMoz MMuc NMyG WSpi
	cristata	CLAP CWCL EBee EPfP WMoo WSpi XLum
§	***cycadina*** ♀H4	CHEx CLAP EBee EFer ELan EPPr EPfP ERod EShb EUJe GBin ISha LPBA LRHS LTen MBri MGos MMoz MWat NBid NBir NMyG SBfd WFib WMoo WPnP
§	***dilatata*** ♀H4	CRWN ECha EFer ELan EPfP ERod LRHS MMuc MRav SRms WFib WHal WShi WSpi
	- 'Crispa Whiteside' ♀H4	CBty CLAP CWCL EBee EFer EPfP ERod LBMP LRHS LTen MBri MMoz MWhi NLar SBfd SPlb WFib WMoo WPGP WPat WSpi WWEG
	- 'Cristata' **new**	WSpi
	- 'Grandiceps'	CLAP CMac EFer WFib
	- 'Jimmy Dyce'	CLAP ISha
	- 'Lepidota Crispa Cristata'	CLAP EBee
	- 'Lepidota Cristata' ♀H4	CBty CLAP CWCL ELan EPPr ERod GBin LTen MMuc NGdn NMyG SEND SRms WFar WFib WMoo WRHF
	- 'Lepidota Grandiceps'	CLAP
*	- 'Recurvata'	CBty CLAP ISha LLHF NLar
	erythrosora ♀H4	Widely available
	- 'Brilliance'	CCCN CLAP GQue ISha LRHS LSou NLar SMrm
	- var. ***koidzumiana*** **new**	ISha
	- var. ***prolifica*** ♀H4	CBty CKel CLAP EBee ELan GMaP ISha LRHS LTen MGos MMoz NBir NEgg NLar NPri SPoG WFib WSpi WWEG
	filix-mas ♀H4	Widely available
	- 'Angustata Cristata' **new**	WSpi
	- 'Barnesii'	CLAP CWCL EBee EFer ERod GBin ISha LTen MMuc NLar SEND SGol SPlb SPoG WWEG
	- 'Crispa'	CBty CLAP EBee EHon LRHS LTen SGol SRms WFib WSpi
	- 'Crispa Congesta'	see *D. affinis* 'Crispa Gracilis'
	- 'Crispa Cristata'	CBty CLAP CWCL EBee EFer ELan EPfP ERod EUJe GMaP IKil LHop LRHS LTen MBri NBid NBir SEND SPoG SRms WFib WGor WWEG
	- 'Cristata' ♀H4	CLAP EBee EFer ELan EPfP LPot LTen MMoz NMyG NOrc SRms WMoo
	- Cristata Group	EFer
*	- - 'Cristata Grandiceps'	EFer
	- - 'Cristata Jackson'	CLAP SPlb
	- - 'Cristata Martindale'	CLAP NBid SRms WFib
	- - 'Fred Jackson'	CLAP WFib
	- 'Depauperata'	CLAP WPGP
	- 'Euxinensis'	CLAP
	- 'Furcans'	CLAP
	- 'Grandiceps Wills' ♀H4	NBid WFib
	- 'Linearis'	EBee EFer EHon ELan ISha LAst LPBA MCot MGos SRms WFib
	- 'Linearis Congesta'	WPGP
	- 'Linearis Polydactyla'	CBty CDes CLAP CMac CWCL EBee EFer ELan EPPr EPfP LRHS LTen MMoz MMuc MRav NGdn NHol NMyG SBod SEND SPoG WFar WIvy WMoo WPnP WPtf WSpi XLum
	- 'Parsley'	CLAP ISha
*	- Polydactyla Group	ECha MGos MRav MWat NEgg
I	- 'Revolvens'	WFib
	- 'Rich Beauty'	LTen
	goldieana	CDTJ CLAP EBee EFer EWTr GBin GMaP ISha LRHS MMuc NBid NBir NLar NMyG SUsu WCot WFar WFib WMoo WPnP WSpi WWEG
	hirtipes misapplied	see *D. cycadina*
	intermedia	ISha
	labordei	CBty GBin ISha LRHS
	lacera	ISha
	lepidopoda	CBty GLin
	ludoviciana	CBty ISha
	marginalis	CDTJ CKel CLAP EBee GBin LRHS MMoz NLar NMyG SBfd SEND WMoo WSpi
	pacifica	CLAP
	paleacea	CLAP
	pseudofilix-mas	ISha
	pseudomas	see *D. affinis*
	× ***remota***	ISha
	× ***separabilis***	ISha
	sieboldii	CBty CCon CEnt CHEx CLAP CWCL EBee EFer ELan ERod EShb EUJe GEdr ISha LRHS LTen MMuc NBid NBir NCGa NGdn NLar NMyG SBfd SRms WMoo WPGP WWEG
	stewartii	CLAP GBin LLHF LTen NLar NMyG WWEG
	tokyoensis	CDTJ CKel CLAP EBee GBin ISha LRHS MMoz NLar NMyG WPGP WSpi
	uniformis	CLAP EFer
	wallichiana ♀H4	Widely available
	- F&M 107	WPGP

Duchesnea (*Rosaceae*)

	chrysantha	see *D. indica*
§	***indica***	LEdu MRav SEND WMoo WOut XLum
§	- 'Harlequin' (v)	CPLG
*	- 'Snowflake' (v)	WMoo
	- 'Variegata'	see *D. indica* 'Harlequin'

Dugaldia (*Asteraceae*)

	hoopesii	see *Hymenoxys hoopesii*

Dulichium (*Cyperaceae*)

arundinaceum	LSRN

Dunalia (*Solanaceae*)

australis	see *Iochroma australe*
- blue-flowered	see *Iochroma australe* 'Bill Evans'
- white-flowered	see *Iochroma australe* 'Andean Snow'

Duranta (*Verbenaceae*)

§ ***erecta***	CCCN CHll EShb
§ - 'Geisha Girl'	CCCN EShb
- 'Sapphire Swirl'	see *D. erecta* 'Geisha Girl'
- 'Variegata' (v)	CCCN EShb
plumieri	see *D. erecta*
repens	see *D. erecta*
serratifolia	CCCN

Duvernoia see *Justicia*

Dyckia (*Bromeliaceae*)

frigida	EGri WCot WGrn
leptostachya	WCot WGrn
marnier-lapostollei	WCot
'Morris Hobbs'	WCot
remotiflora	CBrP EGri SChr
velascana	CHEx EGri

Dymondia (*Asteraceae*)

margaretae	WAbe
* ***repens***	WHil

Dypsis (*Arecaceae*)

§ ***decaryi***	CCCN EAmu XBlo
decipiens	CBrP
lutescens ♀H1	MBri XBlo

Dysosma see *Podophyllum*

E

Ebracteola (*Aizoaceae*)

wilmaniae new	CPBP

Ecballium (*Cucurbitaceae*)

elaterium	CArn CDTJ LEdu SGar SIde WPGP

Eccremocarpus (*Bignoniaceae*)

scaber	CBcs CRHN EBee ELan EPfP LBMP LHop LRHS MBri MNrw NPer SBfd SEND SGar SLim
- 'Aureus'	EPfP
- 'Carmineus'	EPfP EWld SGar
- orange-flowered	SPoG
- red-flowered new	NRHS SPoG
I - 'Roseus'	NLar
- 'Tresco Cream'	CSpe

Echeandia (*Asparagaceae*)

formosa B&SWJ 9147	WCru

Echeveria ✿ (*Crassulaceae*)

affinis	EUJe SRot
agavoides ♀H1	MRav WCot
albicans new	SPlb
amoena new	CDoC
* 'Black Knight'	CDoC
* 'Black Prince'	CAbb CBcs CDes CDoC EBee ELan MSCN NPer SPlb SRot WCot WPGP
'Blue Boy' new	CDoC
'Blue Prince'	CDoC
'Blue Waves'	WCot
* ***cana***	CDoC EBee EWll SRot
cante new	SPlb
carnicolor RE 37 new	CDoC
'Chrissy 'n' Ryan' new	CDoC
coccinea	ELan
colorata	WCot
- f. ***brandtii*** new	CDoC
colorata × ***peacockii*** RE 240 new	CDoC
'Corymbosa'	WCot
'Crûg Ice'	WCru
'Curly Locks'	WCot
'Derenceana' new	CDoC
× ***derosa***	EPfP
'Doris Taylor'	MSCN
'Duchess of Nuremberg'	CDoC EUJe SMrm SPlb SRot
elegans ♀H1	CDoC CHEx EPfP EUJe LSou SEND SPlb WGwG WNew
'Galaxy Mars' (Galaxy Hybrids Series) new	CDoC
'Giant Mexican Firecracker' new	CDoC
§ ***gibbiflora*** var. ***metallica*** ♀H1	EPfP
× ***gilva*** RE 133 new	CDoC
* - 'Red' ♀H1	WCot
glauca Baker	see *E. secunda* var. *glauca*
'Golden Torch' new	CDoC
harmsii ♀H1	CDoC WGwG
'Hens and Chicks'	CHEx
hyalina RE 614 new	CDoC
'Ileen' new	CDoC
'J. van Keppel' new	CDoC
lilacina	CDoC EUJe SMrm SPlb SRot
lutea RE 502 new	CDoC
'Mahogany'	CDoC SUsu WCot WGrn
'Mauna Loa'	CAbb CDoC EBee MCot WCot WGrn
maxonii B&SWJ 10396	WCru
'Meridian'	CHEx
'Mexico City'	CDoC
montana B&SWJ 10277	WCru
- RE 376 new	CDoC
- RE 431 new	CDoC
multicaulis	MSCN
nodulosa	WCot
peacockii	EOHP MHer MSCN SMrm SPet SPlb WNew
'Perle d'Azur'	CHEx WCot
'Perle von Nürnberg' ♀H1	CAbb SMad SPet
pulidonis ♀H1	CDoC EPfP MHer WCot
purpusorum RE 63A new	CDoC
quitensis RE 529 new	CDoC
- 'Laguna de Chicola' new	CDoC
'Ron Evans' new	CDoC
runyonii 'Topsy Turvy'	CDoC CHEx EOHP EPfP SPet SRot
secunda	CAbb SPlb SWal
§ - var. ***glauca*** ♀H1	CDTJ CDes CDoC CHEx EAmu EBee ELan EShb ETod GAbr NBir SEND WPGP

* - - 'Gigantea'	NDov NPer WPGP
setosa ♀H1	EPfP
- var. ***ciliata***	EShb
- var. ***deminuta***	SPlb
shaviana	EBee EUJe SRot WCot
- RE 581 **new**	CDoC
'Son of Pearl' **new**	CDoC
subsessilis **new**	WCot
- RE 163 **new**	CDoC
'Violet Queen'	CDoC

Echinacea ✿ (*Asteraceae*)

§ 'Adam Saul' **new**	EBee
§ 'After Midnight'[PBR] (Big Sky Series)	CBcs CHab CPar ECtt EBee EGHP IPot LRHS LSou NLar NRHS
'Amber Mist' (Mistical Series) **new**	EBee
angustifolia	CArn EBee EGHP EHrv ENfk EPfP GPoy LRHS MHer MHoo SEND SPhx WJek
§ 'Art's Pride'[PBR]	CHab EBee EHrv EPfP LRHS LSRN LSou MGos MRav NBir NEgg NPnk NPri SBfd SMrm SUsu WFar
'Coral Reef'	EBee SBfd
Crazy Pink	see *E.* 'Adam Saul'
'Emily Saul'	see *E.* 'After Midnight' (Big Sky Series)
'Evan Saul'[PBR]	see *E.* 'Sundown'
'Firebird'	EBee ECtt LRHS SBfd
'Flame Thrower'	CWGN EBee ECtt LRHS NLar SBfd SHar
'Green Envy'[PBR]	CBcs CWGN EBee ECtt ELan EPfP EWll GQue LRHS LSou MBNS MBel MBri MNrw NEgg NLar NPnk NSti SBfd SKHP SMrm SPer SPoG SUsu WAul WCot WWEG
'Green Jewel'	EUJe LRHS NDov WCot
'Gum Drop' **new**	EBee
§ 'Harvest Moon'[PBR] (Big Sky Series)	Widely available
'Heavenly Dream' **new**	EBee WWEG
'Hot Lava'	CWGN EBee NDov SPoG
'Hot Papaya' (d)	EBee ECtt EWll IBoy IPot LRHS LSou MBNS MBri MTis SUsu WCot WWEG
'Hot Summer'	CPar EBee ECtt IPot LRHS MBri NCGa SPoG WHlf
'Irresistible' (d)	CWGN EBee IPot
'Katie Saul'[PBR]	see *E.* 'Summer Sky'
'Mac 'n' Cheese'	EBee LRHS LSou NDov WCot WWEG
'Mama Mia' **new**	EBee
Mango Meadowbrite ='CBG Cone3'	EBee EPfP LRHS NRHS SPoG
'Matthew Saul'[PBR]	see *E.* 'Harvest Moon'
'Maui Sunshine'	EBee NDov SBfd SHar
Orange Meadowbrite[PBR]	see *E.* 'Art's Pride'
pallida	CArn CKno CMea CPrp CWib EBee EGHP ELan EPfP EPri EShb GPoy LEdu LHop LRHS MHoo MNFA MWhi NDov NGdn NPri SKHP SPer SPhx SWvt WJek WMoo WPtf WWEG XLum
- 'Hula Dancer'	CMea EBee EPfP MCot NGdn NPri SPhx SSvw WWEG
paradoxa	CArn CPou EBee ECtt EGHP EHrv ELan EPfP EPri GPoy LAst LDai LHop LRHS LSRN MCot NGdn NPri SMrm SPav SPer SPhx SPlb SWvt WFar WWEG XLum
- var. ***paradoxa*** **new**	MHoo
- 'Yellow Mellow'	EPfP LSRN
'Piccolino' **new**	EBee WCot
'Pink Mist' (Mistical Series) **new**	EBee
Pixie Meadowbrite ='CBG Cone 2'	CAbP CDes CWGN EBee ECtt IKil LRHS WCot WPGP
§ ***purpurea***	Widely available
- 'Alaska'[PBR]	EBee IBoy LRHS LSou NGdn NLar NRHS
- 'Alba'	EPfP LBMP LRHS MNHC SHil SMrm WCot XLum
- 'Augustkönigin'	CKno EBee EHrv NBir
- 'Avalanche'[PBR]	EBee ELon LSou SBfd
- 'Baby Swan Pink' **new**	SPhx
- 'Baby Swan White'	CSam ELon LBMP LRHS NLar NRHS STes WCot WWEG
- Bressingham hybrids	LRHS MRav MWat NRHS SMrm SPer SPhx WFar WGwG
- 'Coconut Lime'[PBR]	CWGN EBee ECtt EGHP EPfP LRHS LSou MTis NPnk SPer SRkn SUsu WCot
- Doppelganger	see *E. purpurea* 'Doubledecker'
§ - 'Doubledecker'	CWCL EBee EGHP EPfP LLHF LRHS NGdn NPri SBfd STes SWat XLum
- Elton Knight ='Elbrook'[PBR] ♀H3	EBee ECtt IPot LRHS LSRN MBri SDix SKHP SRkn SWvt
- 'Fancy Frills'	ECtt LSou
- 'Fatal Attraction'[PBR]	Widely available
- 'Fragrant Angel'[PBR]	CHid CKno CMac EBee ECtt EPfP LHop LRHS LSRN LSou MBel MCot NLar SKHP SPoG SUsu SWat SWvt WCot
- 'Green Jewel'[PBR]	LSou
- 'Hope'[PBR]	CPar LRHS LSou NLar SUsu
- 'Jade'	CAbP EBee ECtt EHrv GQue LRHS LSRN LSou MBNS MCot NDov NEgg NGdn NLar NPnk SMrm SUsu SWat WCot
- 'Kim's Knee High'[PBR]	CKno CMac CMea EBee ECtt EHrv ELan EPfP GMaP LRHS LSRN LSou MAsh MCot MRav NBir NGdn NLar NPnk NRHS SApp SPer SRkn STes SWat SWvt WCot WFar WPGP WWEG
- 'Kim's Mop Head'	CKno EBee ECtt EHrv ELan ELon EPfP EWes LRHS LSou MAsh MCot MRav NGdn NLar NOrc NPnk WCot WFar WWEG
§ - 'Leuchtstern'	CKno EBee EGHP EPfP LRHS NBir NGdn SWat WMnd WWEG XLum
- 'Lilliput'[PBR]	NLar
- 'Little Magnus'[PBR]	EBee LRHS
- 'Lucky Star'	EBee EPfP LRHS NCGa SBea SPhx WCFE
- 'Magnus' ♀H4	Widely available
- 'Magnus Superior' **new**	EBee LRHS NRHS SBea SPhx
- 'Maxima'	CAbP EBee ECtt EHrv LRHS MNrw NDov WCot WWEG
- 'Meringue'[PBR] **new**	EBee
- 'Merlot'[PBR]	LSou SUsu
- 'Mistral'	LRHS NRHS
- 'Mount Hood' **new**	WHlf
- 'Pica Bella'	CWGN EBee ECtt EPfP LAst LRHS LSou NLar NRHS
- 'Pink Double Delight'[PBR]	EGHP LHop LRHS MRav NGdn SWat WHlf

- 'Pink Glow'	NDov
- 'Pink Poodle'	EBee EPri IBoy LSou SBfd
- 'Prairie Frost' (v)	EGHP
- 'Prairie Splendor'	EPfP LRHS SPhx
- 'Primadonna Deep Rose'	EBee IFro LEdu NBre NGBl SRot SVic
- Primadonna mixed **new**	ELon
- 'Primadonna White'	LEdu LRHS NPri SRot
- 'Profusion' **new**	EBee
- 'Purity'	LRHS
- 'Razzmatazz'PBR (d)	CAbP CMac CWGN EBee ECtt EGHP EHrv ELan EUJe EWes IBoy LHop LRHS LSRN MBri MGos MNrw MRav NEgg NGdn NPnk NSti SPer SUsu SWat SWvt WCot
- 'Red Knee High'	EBee ECtt LRHS MBri
- 'Robert Bloom'	CAbP EBee ECtt GQue LHop LRHS MCot MRav NBir SWvt
- 'Rubinglow'	CElw ECtt EGHP EHrv LBMP LSou MDKP NBir NLar SBfd SUsu SWvt WCot
- 'Rubinstern' ♀H4	Widely available
- 'Ruby Giant' ♀H4	CCon CKno CWGN EBee ECtt EGHP EHrv ELan EUJe GMaP LAst LHop LRHS LSRN LSou MBel MCot MDKP MGos MNFA MTis NEgg NLar SBfd SMad SPer SPoG SUsu WCot WWEG
- 'The King'	EBee EGHP NGdn
- 'Verbesserter Leuchtstern'	EGHP NLar
- 'Vintage Wine'PBR	CKno CMac CWGN EBee ECtt EGHP EHrv ELan ELon EPfP GMaP GQue IBoy IKil LPla LRHS LSou MBel MNrw MTis NEgg NLar NPnk NSti SPer SPoG SWvt WCot WWEG
- 'Virgin'PBR	IPot NCGa NDov
- 'White Lustre'	ECha EPfP NBre SRms WFar
- White Natalie = 'Norwhinat'PBR	EBee
- 'White Swan'	Widely available
'Raspberry Tart'	EBee LRHS LSou
ritro 'Blue Cloud'	LRHS
'Secret Lust' (d) **new**	EBee
'Secret Passion' **new**	CWGN EBee
simulata	EBee SPhx
'Starlight'	see *E. purpurea* 'Leuchtstern'
'Strawberry Shortcake' **new**	WHlf
'Summer Cocktail' **new**	EBee MSCN NCGa
'Summer Salsa' **new**	WCot
§ 'Summer Sky'PBR (Big Sky Series)	ECtt EGHP IPot LRHS LSou MBNS NDov NLar NPnk SPhx SUsu WCot
'Summer Sun' **new**	EBee NCGa
§ 'Sundown'PBR (Big Sky Series)	CBcs CCVN CHab CMac CPar CSev CWCL ECtt EGHP EHrv EPfP ETod IPot LBMP LPot LRHS LSou MBNS MRav MWhi NLar NOrc NPnk NRHS SBfd SPoG SRkn SUsu WWlt
'Sunrise'PBR (Big Sky Series)	Widely available
'Sunset'PBR (Big Sky Series)	CAbP EBee ECtt EGHP EHrv EWes LAst LDai LLHF LRHS LSRN LSou MBNS MBri MGos MSCN NEgg NGdn NPnk NRHS SBfd SMrm SPer SPoG SUsu SWat SWvt WWEG
'Tangerine Dream'	EBee LSou NLar
tennesseensis	CArn SPhx WPGP
- 'Rocky Top'	CBcs CMea EBee EGHP EHrv EPfP LRHS LSRN MNFA SBfd SKHP SPhx WCot
'Tiki Torch'PBR	CMea CPar CWGN ECtt EWes GMaP LBMP LRHS LSou MAvo MBel MCot NDov NLar SBfd SPer SPoG WCot WWEG WWlt
'Tomato Soup'	CMea CPar CWGN EBee ECtt GMaP LBMP LLHF LRHS LSou MAvo MBNS MBel MCot MNrw NDov NLar SBfd SPoG SUsu WCAu WCot WWEG
'Twilight'PBR (Big Sky Series)	EBee ECtt EGHP LBMP LRHS LSou MNrw NOrc NPnk SRkn SUsu WCot
'White Mist' (Mistical Series) **new**	EBee

Echinops (Asteraceae)

RCB AM -14	WCot
RCB/TQ H-2	WCot
albus	see *E.* 'Nivalis'
babatagensis	EBee
§ ***bannaticus***	CBcs CHab CSBt EBee NBid WWEG
* - 'Albus'	EBee NGdn
- 'Blue Globe'	CBct CMHG CSev EBee EHoe ELon EPfP EShb GCal IBoy LRHS LSRN MCot MGos NCGa NChi NGdn SBfd SMrm SPhx SPoG WFar WMnd WWEG
- 'Star Frost'	EBee EPfP GQue LRHS NLar SBfd SPhx
- 'Taplow Blue' ♀H4	Widely available
commutatus	see *E. exaltatus*
§ ***exaltatus***	LPla NBir
maracandicus	EBee GCal WCot
§ 'Nivalis'	CBre SEND
* ***perringii***	GCal
'Real Stone'	LSou
ritro misapplied	see *E. bannaticus*
§ ***ritro*** L. ♀H4	Widely available
- subsp. ***ruthenicus*** ♀H4	ELan MNFA MRav
- - 'Platinum Blue'	EBee ECtt LRHS NEgg NLar SBfd SPet SPhx WMnd WPer
- 'Veitch's Blue' misapplied	see *E. ritro* L.
- 'Veitch's Blue'	Widely available
sphaerocephalus	NBir SMrm SPlb
- 'Arctic Glow'	CMHG CMac CPou EBee ECha ECtt EHoe EHrv ELan EPfP GMaP LRHS MBel MBri MCot MWhi NDov NGdn NLar SBfd SMrm SPer SPlb SPoG SWvt WCAu WFar WMnd WWEG
terscheckii	EAmu
tjanschanicus	CMea LDai LRHS WWEG

Echinospartum (Papilionaceae)

sp.	CArn

Echium (Boraginaceae)

acanthocarpum	XPde
aculeatum	XPde
- 'Bicolor'	XPde
- 'Rosea'	XPde
boissieri	CCCN ELan XPde
brevirame	XPde
callithyrsum	XPde
§ ***candicans*** ♀H2-3	CAbb CBcs CCCN CCon CHEx CSpe CTrC EBee ECre ELan EShb IBoy IDee SPad XPde
- 'Ciel'	XPde
- 'Marine'	XPde

§	– 'Rouge'	XPde
	decaisnei subsp. ***decaisnei***	XPde
	famarae	XPde
	fastuosum	see *E. candicans*
	– 'Rouge'	see *E. candicans* 'Rouge'
	gentianoides	SPlb XPde
	– 'Dark Globe'	XPde
	– 'Maryvonne'	XPde
	– 'Pablina'	XPde
	giganteum	XPde
	handiense	XPde
	italicum	CCCN NLar SIde XPde
	lusitanicum	CCCN
	– subsp. ***polycaulon***	XPde
	onosmifolium	XPde
	pininana ♀H2-3	CAbb CBcs CDoC CHEx CTrC CTsd EAmu EBee ECre EGri ELan EUJe EWll IDee LRHS SBfd SBst SChr SEND SGar SIde SPav WKif WSFF XPde
	– 'Snow Tower'	CCCN CDTJ CTrC EAmu ELan SBst XPde
	'Pink Fountain'	CCCN CDTJ CTrC ECre ELan NLar SBst XPde
	plantagineum	XPde
	rosulatum	CCCN XPde
	russicum	CCCN CSpe EBee EWll IDee LHop LRHS MHoo NLar SIde SPad SPav SPhx SPlb WCot WPer XPde
	simplex	XPde
	strictum	CCCN XPde
	sventenii	XPde
	tuberculatum	SPhx WMoo XPde
	vulgare	CArn CCCN CHab ELan ENfk MHer MHoo MNHC NLar NMir NPri SBch SIde WHer WHfH WJek WOut WSFF
	– 'Blue Bedder'	WSFF
	– Drake's form	SPhx
	webbii	MMHG XPde
	wildpretii ♀H2-3	CCCN CDTJ ELan EUJe SPlb XPde
	– subsp. ***wildpretii***	SPav

Edgeworthia (*Thymelaeaceae*)

§	***chrysantha***	CBcs CHGN CJun CPLG CWib EBee ELan EPfP GBin GKin IDee LRHS MGos MTPN NLar NRHS SBig SHil SPer SPoG WSHC
I	– 'Grandiflora'	CJun GBin LRHS MBri MGos NLar
§	– 'Red Dragon'	CJun
	– f. ***rubra*** hort.	see *E. chrysantha* 'Red Dragon'
	papyrifera	see *E. chrysantha*

Edraianthus (*Campanulaceae*)

	croaticus	see *E. graminifolius*
	dinaricus	EPot NMen
§	***graminifolius***	CPBP NMen WPat XLum
	owerinianus	CPBP WAbe
	parnassicus	CPBP
§	***pumilio*** ♀H4	EPot GKev NMen SRms WAbe
§	***serpyllifolius***	NMen WPat
	– 'Major'	NMen WAbe
	wettsteinii	CPBP EPot

Egeria (*Hydrocharitaceae*)

§	***densa***	CBen

Ehretia (*Boraginaceae*)

	anacua	CBcs
	dicksonii	CBcs CHEx IArd IVic WPGP

Ehrharta (*Poaceae*)

	thunbergii	EPPr

Eichhornia (*Pontederiaceae*)

	crassipes	CBen CWat LPBA MSKA MWts SCoo
	– 'Major'	NPer

Elaeagnus (*Elaeagnaceae*)

	angustifolia	CAgr CBcs CDul EPfP LMaj MCoo MGos NLar NWea SPer SRms WFar
	– Caspica Group	see *E.* 'Quicksilver'
	argentea	see *E. commutata*
§	***commutata***	CBcs CMac EBee ECrN EHoe EPfP LHop MBlu MWhi NLar SPer
§	× ***ebbingei***	Widely available
	– 'Coastal Gold' (v)	CAbP CBcs CDoC CDul CTrC EBee EPfP LBMP LRHS LSRN MAsh MGos NRHS SGol SLim SRms
I	– 'Compacta' **new**	SHil
	– 'Gilt Edge' (v) ♀H4	Widely available
*	– 'Gold Flash'	LAst
	– Gold Splash = 'Lannou' (v)	CDoC CMac CTrC CWSG EBee EPfP LRHS SPoG SWvt
	– 'Lemon Ice' (v)	NLar
	– 'Limelight' (v)	Widely available
	– 'Moonlight'	EBee LRHS MAsh
	– 'Salcombe Seedling'	CCCN NLar
	– 'Viveleg' PBR (v) **new**	LRHS MBri SEWo SHil
	glabra 'Reflexa'	see *E.* × ***reflexa***
	macrophylla	CMac WMoo
	multiflora	CDul EBee NLar SPer
	parvifolia	CCCN ELan
	pungens	ERom EWTr NBir
	– 'Argenteovariegata'	see *E. pungens* 'Variegata'
	– 'Aureovariegata'	see *E. pungens* 'Maculata'
	– 'Dicksonii' (v)	CWib EBee LRHS NLar SLon SPer SRms
	– 'Forest Gold' (v)	EBee ELan EPfP LRHS MAsh
	– 'Frederici' (v)	CBcs CDoC CMHG CMac CTrC EBee ECrN EHoe ELan EPfP LAst LBMP LHop LRHS MAsh MRav NLar SPer SPoG SWvt WPat
	– 'Goldrim' (v) ♀H4	EPfP WMoo
	– 'Hosuba-fukurin' (v)	EBee ELan GKin LBuc LLHF LRHS MAsh SLon
§	– 'Maculata' (v)	Widely available
§	– 'Variegata' (v)	CBcs CMac NBir SPer
§	'Quicksilver' ♀H4	Widely available
§	× ***reflexa***	CBcs WPGP
	× ***submacrophylla***	see *E.* × ***ebbingei***
	umbellata	CBcs CDul CPLG EPfP MAsh MBlu NLar SPer WPat WSHC
	– 'Big Red' (F)	CAgr
	– var. ***borealis*** 'Polar Lights'	NLar
	– 'Brilliant Rose' (F)	CAgr
	– 'Garnet'	CAgr
	– 'Hidden Springs' (F)	CAgr
	– 'Jewel' (F)	CAgr
	– 'Newgate' (F)	CAgr
	– 'Red Cascade' (F)	CAgr
	– 'Ruby'	CAgr
	– 'Sweet 'n' Tart' (F)	CAgr

Elaeocarpus (*Elaeocarpaceae*)

	sylvestris	LEdu
	var. ***ellipticus*** **new**	

Elatostema (*Urticaceae*)

rugosum CHEx

elderberry see *Sambucus nigra*

Elegia (*Restionaceae*)

capensis CAbb CCCN CCon CDTJ CDoC CHEx CPLG CTrC EAmu ESwi ETod GBin LTen SPlb SPoG WPGP
elephantina CCon LTen
hookeriana NEgg
macrocarpa CCCN SPlb
mucronata CTrC
spathacea CCon
tectorum CAbb CCon CDoC CHEx CPrp CSpe CTrC EAmu EBee EPfP EUJe GBin LRHS LSRN MGos NOak NPla SApp SBfd SHDw SPer SPlb SPoG
- dwarf CDes

Eleocharis (*Cyperaceae*)

sp. SEND
acicularis CWat MSKA
palustris CRWN

Eleorchis (*Orchidaceae*)

japonica LWst NLAp

Elettaria (*Zingiberaceae*)

cardamomum CArn EOHP EShb GPoy LEdu SBfd SHDw WJek

Eleutherococcus (*Araliaceae*)

hypoleucus B&SWJ 5532 WCru
nakaianus B&SWJ 5027 WCru
pictus see *Kalopanax septemlobus*
senticosus GPoy
- B&SWJ 4568 WCru
septemlobus see *Kalopanax septemlobus*
sessiliflorus B&SWJ 4528 WCru
- B&SWJ 8457 WCru
sieboldianus CBcs MRav SEND
- 'Variegatus' (v) CBcs CSpe EBee EHoe ELan ELon EPfP EUJe GBin LAst LRHS MRav NEgg NLar WHer WSHC
trifoliatus RWJ 10108 WCru

Elingamita (*Primulaceae*)

johnsonii ECou

Elisena (*Amaryllidaceae*)

longipetala see *Hymenocallis longipetala*

Ellisiophyllum (*Plantaginaceae*)

pinnatum B&SWJ 197 CDes EBee EWld WCot WCru WPGP

Elmera (*Saxifragaceae*)

racemosa WPtf

Elodea (*Hydrocharitaceae*)

canadensis MSKA NBir WMAq
densa see *Egeria densa*

Elsholtzia (*Lamiaceae*)

fruticosa CArn
stauntonii CArn CBcs EBee ECha GBin GPoy IVic LRHS MHer NLar SBch SEND SPer SPoG WBor WSHC XLum

Elymus (*Poaceae*)

arenarius see *Leymus arenarius*
canadensis CRWN EHoe EPPr
- f. ***glaucifolius*** CCon GCal
cinereus from Washington State, USA WPGP
elongatus SApp
glaucus misapplied see *E. hispidus*
§ ***hispidus*** EHoe EPPr MBlu MBri MLHP SPer WCFE WCot
§ ***magellanicus*** Widely available
- 'Blue Sword' LRHS MBri MGos SHil SLon SRms WPtf
riparius EPPr
sibiricus EPPr
solandri EHoe EWes
villosus EPPr
- var. ***arkansanus*** EPPr
virginicus EBee EPPr

Embothrium ✿ (*Proteaceae*)

coccineum CBcs CDoy CGHE EBee EPfP GKev GKin SPlb WPGP WPat
- Lanceolatum Group CDoC CDul CHid CTsd ECre ELan ELon EPfP EUJe GKin LRHS MBlu MMuc MPkF SBfd SEND SLim SMad SPer SSpi SSta WAbe WBor
- - 'Inca Flame' CCCN CDoC EBee ELan EPfP LRHS MAsh SBfd SPoG SWvt
- - 'Ñorquinco' ♀H3 CBcs CDoC
- Longifolium Group CCCN IBlr WPGP

Eminium (*Araceae*)

regelii new LWst
spiculatum LB 374/5 WCot

Emmenopterys (*Rubiaceae*)

henryi CBcs CDul CGHE EPfP IArd IDee MBlu NLar SMad WCot WPGP

Empetrum (*Ericaceae*)

nigrum GPoy

Enantiophylla (*Apiaceae*)

B&SWJ 10318 from Guatemala WCru
heydeana B&SWJ 9114 WCru

Encephalartos ✿ (*Zamiaceae*)

altensteinii CBrP
caffer CBrP
cycadifolius CBrP
ferox CBrP
horridus CBrP
lanatus CBrP
lebomboensis CBrP
lehmannii CBrP
natalensis CBrP
umbeluziensis CBrP
villosus CBrP

Endymion see *Hyacinthoides*

Enkianthus ✿ (*Ericaceae*)

campanulatus ♀H4 Widely available
- var. ***campanulatus*** f. ***albiflorus*** CBcs GKin IVic LTen NLar

I - 'Hollandia' CBcs GKin
- var. ***palibinii*** EBee EPfP GGGa GKin LRHS MAsh SSpi SSta
- 'Red Bells' CDoC CMac EBee EPfP GBin GKin LRHS MAsh NLar SSpi SSta SWvt WFar
- 'Red Velvet' CBcs GKin NLar
- 'Ruby Glow' CBcs IVic NLar
- var. ***sikokianus*** EPfP GGGa GKin NLar
- 'Tokyo Masquerade' GKin NLar
* - 'Variegatus' (v) EBee LRHS MAsh SPoG
- 'Venus' CBcs GKin NLar
- 'Victoria' CBcs NLar
- 'Wallaby' LRHS NLar WAbe
cernuus f. ***rubens*** ♀H4 CBcs CMac EPfP GBin GGGa GKin NLar
chinensis CBcs CPne EBee EPfP GGGa LRHS MAsh
deflexus CMCN EBee GGGa LRHS MAsh SSpi WPGP
perulatus ♀H4 CMac EBee GBin GKin LRHS MGos MRav NLar SEND SHil SSpi WFar
serrulatus new GGGa

Ensete (*Musaceae*)

gilletii XBlo
- from Malawi XBlo
- from Mozambique XBlo
glaucum CDTJ CDoC EAmu EUJe GCal GHim SBst
§ ***ventricosum*** ♀H1+3 CCCN CDTJ CDoC CHll EAmu EUJe LSou SEND XBlo
§ - 'Maurelii' CBct CBrP CCCN CDTJ CDoC CHEx CHll CSpe EAmu ESwi EUJe LRHS NPla SDix SEND SPer SPoG WCot WPGP
- 'Rubrum' see *E. ventricosum* 'Maurelii'
- 'Tandarra Red' CAbb CBct CDoC ESwi LSou

Entelea (*Malvaceae*)

arborescens CHEx ECou EShb

Eomecon (*Papaveraceae*)

chionantha CCon CDes CHEx CPLG CSam CSpe CWCL EBee ECho EHrv GAbr GBuc GCal GCra LEdu LRHS MLHP MRav NBid WCru WFar WHer WMoo WPGP WPtf WWEG XLum

Epacris (*Ericaceae*)

impressa new WAbe
serpyllifolia WThu

Ephedra (*Ephedraceae*)

chilensis XLum
- 'Mellow Yellow' EBee
- 'Quite White' EBee
distachya GPoy
equisetina CArn IFro
fedtschenkoi XSen
gerardiana EBee GEdr IFro LRHS
- var. ***sikkimensis*** WOld XLum
intermedia RCB/TQ K-1 WCot
minuta CKen MSCN
monosperma GEdr WThu XLum
nevadensis CArn GPoy
sinica CArn GEdr GPoy
viridis CArn

Epigaea (*Ericaceae*)

asiatica WAbe
gaultherioides GGGa

Epilobium (*Onagraceae*)

angustifolium see *Chamerion angustifolium*
- f. ***leucanthum*** see *Chamerion angustifolium* 'Album'
californicum misapplied see *Zauschneria californica*
canum see *Zauschneria californica* subsp. *cana*
dodonaei see *Chamerion dodonaei*
garrettii see *Zauschneria californica* subsp. *garrettii*
N ***glabellum*** misapplied CMea MSCN NSla NRHS SUsu WCFE WKif WWlt
microphyllum see *Zauschneria californica* subsp. *cana*
rosmarinifolium see *Chamerion dodonaei*
septentrionale see *Zauschneria septentrionalis*
villosum see *Zauschneria californica* subsp. *mexicana*

Epimedium ✿ (*Berberidaceae*)

Chen Yi 8 from Jian Xi, China WCot
from Yunnan, China CDes CLAP CPom
acuminatum CCon CElw CGHE CLAP EFEx GEdr LEdu MNrw SUsu WMoo WPGP WSHC
- L 575 CDes CElw CPLG EBee EHrv
- 'Galaxy' CDes CJun CLAP CMil CPLG WPGP
'Akakage' CLAP CPLG GBuc
'Akebono' CDes CJun CLAP CMil CSpe EBee EPPr GAbr GEdr IFoB LSou NCGa NLar SBfd SDix WCot
alpinum CFis CMac EBee EPPr GEdr LEdu WMoo XLum
'Amanogawa' CDes CJun CLAP CMil CPom EHrv IFoB LEdu MAvo SUsu WPGP
'Amber Queen'PBR CLAP EBee EPPr EPfP EWTr GEdr LLHF MMHG NCGa NHar NLar NPnk SBfd SMHy SPhx WCAu WCot WFar
'Anju' GEdr
'Arctic Wings'PBR CLAP EBee EWTr GEdr MBNS NGdn SBfd WCot
'Asiatic Hybrid' CJun CLAP WHal
'Autumn Raspberry' CJun
'Beni-kujaku' CDes CJun CLAP EBee GEdr
'Beni-yushima' GEdr
'Black Sea' CJun CLAP CSpe EBee EPPr LHop MAvo MNrw NCGa NLar
brachyrrhizum CDes CJun CLAP CMil CPLG CPom GEdr LLHF NMyG WPGP
brevicornu CLAP CPom WPGP
- Og 82.010 CJun CLAP
- Og 88.010 CJun CLAP GEdr
'Buckland Spider' CDes CLAP EBee EPPr GEdr MNrw WPGP
campanulatum CGHE LLHF
- Og 93087 CJun
× ***cantabrigiense*** CBro CMac ECtt ESwi GBuc GEdr GMaP MRav NBre SRms WWEG
chlorandrum CLAP EHrv IFoB LEdu SUsu WPGP
- Og 94.003 CDes EBee
creeping yellow EBee LSou MBri WHil
cremeum see *E. grandiflorum* subsp. *koreanum*

davidii	CDes CGHE CMil EPPr GEdr LEdu MNrw SKHP WFar WHal WPGP WSHC
- CPC 960079	CPLG EBee
- EMR 4125	CElw CJun CLAP CPLG EHrv NCGa
- dwarf	CPLG
diphyllum	CDes CGHE CPLG CPom EBee EHrv ELan IVic WHal WPGP
- 'White Splash'	GEdr
dolichostemon	CElw CLAP
- Og 81-010	CJun
ecalcaratum	CDes CLAP CPom EBee LEdu MNrw WPGP
- Og 93.082	CJun CPLG
elongatum	CLAP
'Emperor'	see *E.* 'Phoenix'
'Enchantress'	CDes CElw CJun CLAP CMil CPom ECha EHrv EWld IFoB MNrw SAga WHal
epsteinii	CDes CFis CLAP CMil CPom EBee EPPr GEdr LEdu LLHF MNrw SMad WCot WPGP
- CPC 940347	CJun CPLG IVic
fangii	CPLG
fargesii	CDes CMil CPLG EBee EHrv LEdu MAvo NCGa WCot WPGP
- 'Pink Constellation'	CDes CJun CLAP CPom GEdr LEdu LHop SBch WPGP
'Fire Dragon'PBR	CLAP CWCL EPfP GEdr LLHF MAvo MBNS NHar SMrm WCAu WHil
flavum	EBee SKHP WPGP
- Og 92.036	CDes CJun CLAP EHrv
'Flowers of Sulphur'PBR	CLAP GEdr
franchetii	CCon CGHE CPLG SKHP
- 'Brimstone Butterfly'	CDes CFis CJun CLAP CMil CPLG EBee EPPr GEdr LHop WCot WHoo WPGP
'Fukujuji'	CLAP GEdr
'Golden Eagle'	CDes CJun CLAP CPLG CPom EWes EWld MNrw
§ ***grandiflorum*** ♀H4	CBcs CElw COlW CTri CYeo EBee EHrv ELan ELon EPfP EWTr GBuc GEdr NBir NLar NMen NMyG NPnk SPer WFar WPnP WPtf WSpi WWEG
- 'Album'	CLAP
- 'Beni-chidori'	CJun CLAP EBee GEdr
- 'Crimson Beauty'	CJun CLAP MRav WHal WHoo WSHC WSpi
- 'Crimson Queen'	CDes IFoB LEdu WPGP
- 'Freya'	CDes WSHC
§ - var. ***higoense***	CDes CJun EBee EHrv GEdr WHal WPGP
- 'Jennie Maillard'	SUsu
- 'Koji'	CLAP EBee NLar WSHC
§ - subsp. ***koreanum***	CLAP ECha EFEx NMyG
- 'La Rocaille'	CLAP EBee EHrv
- lilac-flowered	CLAP EHrv WFar WHal
- 'Lilacinum'	EBee
- lilac-pink-flowered	SMHy
- 'Lilafee'	Widely available
- 'Mount Kitadake'	CLAP WAbe
- 'Nanum' ♀H4	CDes CJun CMil CPBP CPom EBee ECho EPot EWTr GBuc GEdr MNrw NMen NMyG SKHP WAbe WPGP WThu
- purple-flowered **new**	EHrv
- 'Purple Prince'	CDes CLAP CPLG EHrv WPGP
- 'Queen Esta'	CDes CJun CLAP CMil EBee LEdu MNrw SBch WPGP WSHC
- 'Red Beauty'	CLAP EBee ELon GEdr LSou MCot NLar SBfd WGrn WSpi
- 'Rose Queen' ♀H4	CSam EBee ECha EHrv ELan ELon EPfP EThi GEdr GMaP LRHS MAvo MBri MRav NBir NMyG NSti SUsu SWvt WMoo WWEG
- 'Roseum'	CLAP CMac CMil EBee ESwi NMen SWvt WSpi
- 'Rubinkrone'	EBee GBuc GEdr GMaP MNrw NMyG
- 'Sirius'	CJun CLAP EBee MNrw
- f. ***violaceum***	CJun CLAP ECha LRHS WCFE WSHC
- 'White Beauty'	WSHC
- 'White Queen' ♀H4	CCon CElw CJun EBee EHrv EPPr LLHF SMHy WCot WHal
- 'Wildside Red'	CJun
- 'Yellow Princess'	CDes CElw CJun CLAP
- 'Yubae'	GEdr IFoB LWst
'Hagoromo'	GEdr
'Hakubai'	GEdr
'Harugasumi'	GEdr
'Heavenly Purple'	CJun
higoense	see *E. grandiflorum* var. *higoense*
ilicifolium	CDes CJun CMil EBee LEdu SUsu WPGP
'Jean O'Neill'	CDes CLAP EBee LEdu WCot WPGP
'Jenny Pym'	EBee
'Kaguyahime'	CJun CLAP CMil EHrv EPPr IFoB WSHC
'Koki'	GEdr
'Kotobuki'	GEdr
latisepalum	CDes CLAP CMil CPom EBee EHrv LEdu MNrw NCGa NLar WCot WPGP
- Og 91.002	CJun
'Lemon Meringue Pie'	CJun
leptorrhizum	CDes CElw CGHE CJun CLAP CPLG EBee EHrv EPPr EWTr EWld GBuc IVic LEdu MNFA MNrw NCGa NHar NMyG SBch SKHP SUsu WCot WHal
- Og Y44	CPLG WSHC
- 'Mariko'	CDes CJun CLAP CPLG CPom WPGP
lishihchenii	CDes CJun CLAP EHrv WPGP
- Og 96024	GEdr
'Little Shrimp'	CJun CTri EBee GMaP LLHF LRHS MNFA MNrw NLar SUsu
macranthum	see *E. grandiflorum*
'Madame Butterfly'PBR	GEdr
membranaceum	CCon CGHE CLAP CMil EBee LEdu LLHF NCGa SUsu WHal WPGP
- Og 93.047	CJun EPPr GEdr
mikinorii	CPom GEdr
myrianthum	CDes CJun LEdu WPGP
ogisui	CDes CLAP CMil CPom SMHy WPGP WThu
- Og 91.001	CJun CPLG EBee EHrv MNrw SKHP
§ × ***omeiense*** 'Akame'	CDes CGHE CJun CLAP CMil CPLG EBee EPPr WPGP
- 'Emei Shan'	see *E.* × *omeiense* 'Akame'
- 'Myriad Years'	CLAP
- 'Pale Fire'	EWld
- 'Pale Fire Sibling'	CDes CJun CPom
- 'Stormcloud'	CDes CGHE CJun CLAP CMil CPLG CPom EPPr MNrw WPGP
pauciflorum	CHid EBee EPPr EWTr GEdr LEdu NHar NMyG SMad WPGP

- Og 92.123 CJun CLAP
× ***perralchicum*** ♀H4 CBro CJun CMac CTri ECha GKev LRHS MLHP NLar SGar SLPl WPnP WSHC
- 'Fröhnleiten' Widely available
- 'Lichtenberg' CDes SUsu
- 'Wisley' CElw CJun CSam EHrv EWes
perralderianum CHEx CMac CSam ELan EPot GEdr GMaP MBel MCot MNrw SRms WHal WPnP WSpi XLum
- 'Weihenstephan' MMoz WPnP
aff. ***perralderianum*** **new** WSpi
§ 'Phoenix' CDes WPGP
'Pink Champagne' EBee EPfP MBri NCGa
'Pink Elf'PBR CLAP EBee EPfP EWTr GEdr LLHF MBel NCGa NLar NOrc NPnk NSti SBfd SRms WCot WHil
pinnatum ECho GMaP WHal WSpi
§ - subsp. ***colchicum*** ♀H4 CJun CLAP CMac CPom CWCL EBee ELan EPfP EWTr GBBs GBuc GEdr LEdu LRHS MCot MRav NGdn NLar SBfd SDix WCAu WCot WFar WHoo WPnP WSpi WTin WWEG
- - L 321 CDes WPGP
- ***elegans*** see *E. pinnatum* subsp. *colchicum*
platypetalum CLAP SUsu WCot WPGP
- Og 93.085 CJun
pubescens EBee EHrv IFoB SAga
- Og 91.003 CJun WPGP
pubigerum CJun CSam EBee ECha EHrv EWTr GAbr GBuc GEdr LEdu MNFA NHol NLar NMRc NMyG SBfd SWvt WHal WPtf WSpi WTcb WWEG
rhizomatosum CLAP EPPr GEdr GMaP LLHF NMyG WPGP WSHC
- Og 92.114 CJun EBee EHrv WCot
× ***rubrum*** ♀H4 Widely available
sagittatum CLAP EFEx
'Sakura-maru' GEdr
'Sasaki' CLAP EBee EWTr GBin GBuc GEdr NHar NLar NMyG WSpi XEll
sempervirens CJun CLAP EBee WHal
- 'Cream Sickle' GEdr
- 'Okuda's White' CDes EBee WPGP
- var. ***sempervirens*** CLAP
× ***setosum*** CJun CPom ECha EHrv NLar WHal
'Shiho' GBin GEdr
'Starcloud' **new** NCGa
stellulatum 'Wudang Star' CDes CGHE CJun CLAP CMil CPLG CPom EHrv EWes GEdr IFoB IVic WPGP WSpi
sutchuenense CLAP
'Suzuka' GEdr LEdu
'Tama-no-genpei' CDes CJun CPom
'Tanima-no-yuki' GEdr
'Tokiwa-gozen' GEdr
× ***versicolor*** CPLG LRHS
- 'Cherry Tart' CLAP
- 'Cupreum' CJun CLAP EBee GBuc SBfd WCAu
§ - 'Discolor' CDes CElw CFis CLAP CPom EHrv EPPr EWld NBir SMHy
- 'Neosulphureum' CBro CDes CLAP EBee EHrv EPPr SLPl WPGP WThu
- 'Sulphureum' ♀H4 Widely available
- 'Versicolor' see *E.* × *versicolor* 'Discolor'
× ***warleyense*** Widely available
- 'Orangekönigin' CElw CWCL EBee ELon EPfP GBBs GMaP LAst LBMP LHop LRHS LSRN MBri MNFA MNrw MRav MSCN NBro NLar NMyG NSti SBfd SEND WBor WCAu WFar WHal WHil WKif WPnP
'William Stearn' CDes CJun CLAP CPLG
wushanense CLAP CMil EHrv EPPr LEdu
- Og 93.019 CJun
- 'Caramel' CDes CJun CLAP CMil CPLG CPom EBee EHrv GEdr LEdu SKHP WPGP WSHC
'Yachimata-hime' **new** GEdr
'Yokihi' GEdr
× ***youngianum*** CMac NEgg
- 'Merlin' CJun CLAP CMil EBee ECha EPfP EPot GBuc GEdr IFoB MBri NHar NLar NSti WHal WSHC
- 'Niveum' ♀H4 Widely available
- 'Roseum' Widely available
- 'Shikinomai' CJun CLAP CPLG EPPr EPot
- 'Tamabotan' CDes CLAP GEdr MAvo MNrw MRav
§ - 'Typicum' CLAP EWTr GBuc LRHS WSHC
- white-flowered NMen
- 'Yenomoto' CJun CLAP EHrv
- 'Youngianum' see *E.* × *youngianum* 'Typicum'
zhushanense GEdr LEdu

Epipactis (*Orchidaceae*)

Barbarossa gx LWst
Catalina gx LWst
gigantea CAvo CBro CCon EBee ECha ECho EHrv ELan EPot GBin GEdr GKev LRHS LWst MAvo MNrw MRav NCGa NChi NDav NLAp NMen WPGP
gigantea × ***veratrifolia*** see *E.* Lowland Legacy gx
gigantea × ***mairei*** LWst
helleborine WHer
Lizzy Lou gx LWst
§ **Lowland Legacy gx** NLAp
- 'Irène' LWst
mairei LWst
palustris EBee ECho EHrv GEdr LRHS NDav NLAp NLar NPnk WHer WPnP
Renate gx LWst
royleana GEdr NLAp
Sabine gx GEdr LWst WFar
- 'Frankfurt' CDes EWld MNrw NMen
thunbergii EFEx GEdr LWst NLAp
- yellow-flowered GEdr
veratrifolia LWst

Epipremnum (*Araceae*)

pinnatum 'Marble Queen' (v) XBlo

Episcia (*Gesneriaceae*)

dianthiflora SRms WDib
'San Miguel' WDib

Equisetum ✿ (*Equisetaceae*)

arvense CArn
'Bandit' (v) CDes CNat SMad WMoo
× ***bowmanii*** CNat
* ***camtschatcense*** CDes ETod EWay SBig SMad SPlb XLum
× ***dycei*** CNat
fluviatile CNat MSKA NLar

hyemale	CBen CKno CTrC EHoe EPfP MSCN MSKA MWts NOak NPer NSti SPlb WCot WFar WMoo XLum
§ - var. ***affine***	CNat CRow ELan EWll LEdu LSou MBlu MSKA NPnk WMAq WOld
- var. ***robustum***	see *E. hyemale* var. *affine*
pratense	CNat
ramosissimum	LEdu LPBA NPla SWat
var. ***japonicum***	CTrC
robustum	CTrC
scirpoides	EBee EFer EHoe EWay LPBA MSCN MSKA MWts NLar NPer NWad SPlb SWat WMAq WMoo WPnP XLum
telmateia	LEdu SMad
variegatum	EBee EFer

Eragrostis (*Poaceae*)

RCB/Arg S-7	EBee WCot
airoides misapplied	see *Agrostis montevidensis*
airoides ambig.	GAbr WMnd WMoo
chloromelas	EPPr
curvula	CElw CKno CMea CWCL EBee ECha EHoe EPPr GAbr GCal LEdu LRHS MAvo MRav MWat MWhi NBir NChi NGdn NOak NRHS NWsh SEND SMrm SPhx WMoo XLum
- S&SH 10	CDes CElw CKno EPPr SMHy WPGP
- 'Totnes Burgundy'	CDes CKno CPLG CWCL EBee ECha EHoe EPPr MAvo MNrw NOak NRHS SMea SPhx SRms SUsu WCot WMoo WPGP
elliottii	CKno EBee ECha EPPr LBMP LHop LRHS MAvo NWsh SBfd SEND SHDw SMea SMrm WFar WWEG
- 'Wind Dancer'	EPPr LRHS
'Silver Needles'	see *Agrostis canina* 'Silver Needles'
spectabilis	CCon CKno CSBt CTrC EBee EPfP LBMP LDai LRHS MDKP MMHG MWhi NGdn NLar NWsh SBfd SEND SMea SMrm WFar WMoo WWEG
trichodes	CCon CKno EBee EHoe LDai LEdu NWsh SMad SMea SMrm SUsu WCot WHrl WPer

Eranthemum (*Acanthaceae*)

pulchellum ♀H1	ECre

Eranthis (*Ranunculaceae*)

cilicica	see *E. hyemalis* Cilicica Group
§ ***hyemalis*** ♀H4	CBro CMea CSpe CTca CWCL ECho EHrv ELan ELon EPfP GKev LAma LRHS MAvo MBel MCot MRav MWat NLar NRHS SDeJ SMrm SPer SPhx WBor WCot WFar WGwG WHoo WShi
§ - Cilicica Group	CBro ECho EHrv ELan ELon EPot GEdr GKev GMaP LAma LRHS MBel NLar NRHS SDeJ SPhx WCot WShi
- 'Flore Pleno' (d)	ECho LWst WCot
- 'Grünling'	CAvo LWst WCot
- 'Orange Glow'	WCot
- 'Pauline' **new**	WCot
- 'Schwefelglanz'	CAvo CBro EPot LWst NMRc WCot
§ - Tubergenii Group	ECho EPot LWst
- - 'Guinea Gold' ♀H4	CMea CTca ECho GEdr LWst
pinnatifida	EFEx GEdr LWst WCru
× ***tubergenii***	see *E. hyemalis* Tubergenii Group

Ercilla (*Phytolaccaceae*)

volubilis	CPLG CRHN CWGN EBee EWes IDee LHop LRHS NSti SEND WCru WSHC

Eremophila (*Scrophulariaceae*)

§ ***debilis***	ECou
'Kilbara Carpet'	ECou
longifolia	SPlb
maculata	ECou
- 'Peaches and Cream'	MOWG
'Yellow Trumpet'	ECou

Eremostachys (*Lamiaceae*)

laciniata	XSen

Eremurus (*Asphodelaceae*)

altaicus JCA 0.443.809	WCot
'Brutus'	EBee LAma SPhx
bungei	see *E. stenophyllus* subsp. *stenophyllus*
cristatus JCA 0.444.029	WCot
'Disco'	EBee
'Emmy Ro'	EBee LAma LRHS WCot
'Foxtrot' **new**	EBee
fuscus JCA 0.444.043	WCot
'Grace'	LAma
'Helena'	EBee LAma LRHS
himalaicus	CAvo CBro CTca EBee EHrv ELan EPot ERCP LAma LRHS MHer NLar SDeJ SPer SPhx WWEG
'Image'	EBee LRHS
× ***isabellinus*** 'Cleopatra'	CAvo EBee EHrv EPot ERCP GMaP LAma LRHS MBNS MBel MGos MHer SDeJ SPhx SPoG WHlf WWEG
- 'Obelisk'	EBee ELan LAma
- 'Pinokkio'	CAvo EBee EPot LAma LRHS MBNS MHer SDeJ
- Ruiter hybrids	CMea EBee ELan EPfP GKev GMaP LAma LAst LRHS MGos MNrw SEND SPer SPet SPhx SPoG WFar
- Shelford hybrids	CAvo CBcs EBee ELan GKev LAma SDeJ SPhx
- 'Tropical Dream'	EBee
'Jeanne-Claire'	EBee LAma LRHS NLar
'Joanna'	EBee LAma LRHS LSRN NLar
lactiflorus	EBee WCot
'Line Dance'	EBee ELon LAma
'Luca Ro'	EBee NLar
'Moneymaker'	EBee LAma
'Oase'	EBee EHrv ELan LAma SDeJ
'Paradiso'	EBee
regelii JCA 444.083	WCot
'Rexona'	EBee LAma MBNS SDeJ
robustus ♀H4	CAvo CBcs CBro CMea EBee EHrv ELan EPot ERCP LAma LRHS MAvo MHer MNrw NLar SDeJ SPhx SPlb WWEG
'Roford'	EBee LAma MNrw
'Romance'	EBee ELon EPot ERCP LAma MBNS MBel MNrw NLar NMRc SDeJ SPhx WWEG
'Rumba'	EBee LAma
'Samba'	EBee LAma
sogdianus JCA 0.444.090	WCot
stenophyllus ♀H4	CBro CTri CWib EPot ERCP LHop LRHS MPkF MWat NLar SDeJ SEND

	SMrm SPhx SPoG WCot WFar WWEG
§ - subsp. ***stenophyllus***	CAvo CBcs EBee EHrv EPfP GMaP LAma MHer MNrw NLBP NPer NPri SPer WFar
'Tap Dance'	EBee LAma
'White Beauty Favourite'^{PBR}	EBee ERCP SPhx
'Yellow Giant'	EBee
zenaidae JCA 0.444.409	WCot

Erepsia (*Aizoaceae*)

lacera	SPlb

Erianthus see *Saccharum*

Erica ✿ (*Ericaceae*)

aestiva	SPlb
'African Fanfare'	GHeS
× ***afroeuropaea***	GHeS
alopecurus	SPlb
arborea	CBcs IRar SPlb
- var. ***alpina*** $\mathbb{Y}^{H4}$	CDoC CTri EPfP GHeS SPer SPoG SWhi
§ - - f. ***aureifolia*** 'Albert's Gold' $\mathbb{Y}^{H4}$	CSBt CTri ELan EPfP GAbr GHeS MAsh MBri NHol NRHS SCoo SPer SPoG SWhi WFar
- 'Arbora Gold'	see *E. arborea* var. *alpina* f. *aureifolia* 'Albert's Gold'
- 'Arnold's Gold'	see *E. arborea* var. *alpina* f. *aureifolia* 'Albert's Gold'
- 'Estrella Gold' $\mathbb{Y}^{H4}$	CBcs CDoC CSBt CTri ELan ELon EPfP GHeS MAsh SCoo SPer SPoG SWhi
- 'Great Star'	SBfd
- 'Picos Pygmy'	GHeS
- 'Spanish Lime'	GHeS
- 'Spring Smile'	GHeS
× ***arendsiana*** **new**	CFst
- 'Charnwood Pink' **new**	CFst
australis $\mathbb{Y}^{H4}$	ELon
- f. ***albiflora*** 'Mr Robert' $\mathbb{Y}^{H3}$	CFst GCal GHeS
- 'Castellar Blush'	GHeS
- 'Holehird'	GHeS
- 'Riverslea' $\mathbb{Y}^{H4}$	CFst CTri GCal GHeS SPoG SWhi
- 'Trisha' **new**	CFst
bauera	CFst
caffra	GHeS SPlb
canaliculata $\mathbb{Y}^{H3}$	CFst GHeS
carnea 'Accent'	GHeS
- 'Adrienne Duncan' $\mathbb{Y}^{H4}$	GHeS MAsh NHol SCoo SRms
- 'Alan Coates'	GHeS
I - 'Alba'	GHeS
- f. ***alba*** 'C.J. Backhouse'	GHeS SRms
- - 'Cecilia M. Beale'	GHeS
- - 'Golden Starlet' $\mathbb{Y}^{H4}$	CFst CHab CSBt CTri EPfP GHeS MAsh NHol NWea SCoo SRms SWhi
- - 'Ice Princess' $\mathbb{Y}^{H4}$	EPfP GHeS MAsh NHol NPri SCoo SRms SWhi
- - 'Isabell' $\mathbb{Y}^{H4}$	CFst EPfP GHeS IVic MAsh NPri SCoo SRms SWhi
- - Madame Seedling	see *E. carnea* f. *alba* 'Weisse March Seedling'
- - 'Romance'	GHeS
- - 'Rosalinde Schorn'	GHeS SRms
- - 'Schneekuppe'	GHeS SWhi
- - 'Schneesturm'	GHeS SRms
- - 'Snow Prince'	GHeS
- - 'Snow Queen'	GHeS MAsh SRms
- - 'Springwood White' $\mathbb{Y}^{H4}$	CFst CSBt CTri ELan EPfP GHeS MAsh NHol SEND SLon SRms SWhi
§ - - 'Weisse March Seedling'	GHeS
- - 'Whitehall'	CFst GHeS MAsh NHol SBfd SCoo SRms SWhi
- - 'Winter Snow'	CFst CSBt ELan GHeS MAsh SCoo SRms
- 'Amy Doncaster'	see *E. carnea* 'Treasure Trove'
- 'Ann Sparkes' $\mathbb{Y}^{H4}$	CFst CSBt CTri ELan EPfP GHeS MAsh NHol SCoo SRms SWhi
- 'Atrorubra'	GHeS SWhi
- f. ***aureifolia*** 'Altadena'	GHeS
- - 'Aurea'	GHeS NHol SCoo SRms
- - 'Barry Sellers'	GHeS MAsh SRms
§ - - 'Bell's Extra Special'	CFst EPfP GHeS SBfd SRms
- - 'Foxhollow' $\mathbb{Y}^{H4}$	CBcs CFst CTri EPfP GHeS IArd MAsh NHol SCoo SRms SWhi
- - 'Gelber Findling'	GHeS SRms
- - 'Gelderingen Gold'	GHeS
- - 'Hilletje'	CFst GHeS SRms
- - 'January Sun'	GHeS SRms
- - 'Moonlight'	GHeS
- - 'Netherfield Orange'	GHeS
- - 'Sunshine Rambler' $\mathbb{Y}^{H4}$	GHeS
- - 'Tybesta Gold'	GHeS
- - 'Westwood Yellow' $\mathbb{Y}^{H4}$	CSBt GHeS MAsh NHol SRms SWhi
- - 'Winter Gold'	GHeS
- 'Beoley Pink'	GHeS SRms
I - 'Carnea'	GHeS
- 'Catherine Kolster'	GHeS
- 'Challenger' $\mathbb{Y}^{H4}$	EPfP GHeS MAsh NHol SCoo SLon SRms SWhi
- 'Christine Fletcher'	GHeS
- 'Clare Wilkinson'	GHeS SRms
- 'Claribelle' **new**	CFst
- 'David's Seedling'	GHeS
- 'December Red'	CFst ELan EPfP GHeS MAsh MMuc NHol SCoo SRms SWhi
- 'Diana Young'	SCoo SWhi
- 'Dømmesmoen'	GHeS SRms
- 'Dorset Sunshine' **new**	CFst
- 'Dwingeloo Pride'	GHeS
- 'Early Red'	GHeS SRms
- 'Eileen Porter'	CFst GHeS MAsh NHol SEND
- 'Eva'	CBcs CFst CHab GHeS IVic SRms
- 'Foxhollow Fairy'	CHab GHeS SRms
- 'Gracilis'	GHeS SRms
- 'Hamburg'	GHeS
- 'Heathwood'	CBcs GHeS MAsh NHol SRms SWhi
- 'Jack Stitt'	GHeS
- 'James Backhouse'	CTri GHeS
- 'Jason Attwater'	GHeS SRms
- 'Jean'	GHeS
- 'Jennifer Anne'	GHeS SRms
- 'John Kampa'	GHeS NHol SRms
- 'John Pook'	GHeS SCoo SRms
- 'King George'	CTri GHeS MAsh NHol SRms SWhi
§ - 'Kramer's Rubin'	CFst ELan GHeS SRms
- 'Lake Garda'	GHeS
- 'Late Pink'	GHeS
- 'Lena'	see *E.* × *darleyensis* 'Lena'
- 'Lesley Sparkes'	CFst GHeS
- 'Little Peter'	GHeS
- 'Lohse's Rubin'	GHeS NHol NWea SRms SWhi
- 'Lohse's Rubinfeuer'	GHeS
- 'Lohse's Rubinschimmer'	GHeS
- 'Loughrigg' $\mathbb{Y}^{H4}$	CTri GHeS MAsh NHol SCoo SRms SWhi

	– 'March Seedling'	CFst EPfP GHeS MAsh NHol SCoo SLon SRms SWhi
	– 'Margery Frearson'	GHeS SRms
I	– 'Martin'	GHeS SRms
	– 'Memory' **new**	SWhi
	– 'Mrs Sam Doncaster'	GHeS
	– 'Myretoun Ruby' ♀H4	CBcs CFst CSBt CTri EPfP GHeS MAsh NHol NPri SBfd SCoo SRms SWhi
	– 'Nathalie' ♀H4	CFst CSBt GHeS IVic MAsh NHol SCoo SRms SWhi
	– 'Oriënt'	GHeS MAsh
	– 'Pallida'	GHeS
	– 'Pink Beauty'	see *E. carnea* 'Pink Pearl'
	– 'Pink Cloud'	GHeS
	– 'Pink Mist'	GHeS MAsh SRms SWhi
§	– 'Pink Pearl'	GHeS
	– 'Pink Spangles' ♀H4	CBcs CFst CHab CSBt CTri GHeS MAsh NHol SBfd SCoo SRms SWhi
	– 'Pirbright Rose'	GHeS SRms
	– 'Polden Pride'	GHeS SRms
	– 'Porter's Red'	GHeS
	– 'Praecox Rubra' ♀H4	EPfP GHeS NHol SCoo SRms
	– 'Prince of Wales'	GHeS
	– 'Queen Mary'	GHeS SRms
	– 'Queen of Spain'	GHeS MAsh SRms
	– 'R.B. Cooke' ♀H4	EPfP GHeS MAsh SCoo SRms
	– 'Red Rover'	GHeS
	– 'Robert Jan'	GHeS SRms
	– 'Rosalie' ♀H4	CFst EPfP GHeS IArd MAsh MMuc SCoo SEND SRms SWhi
	– 'Rosantha'	CFst CHab GHeS SRms
	– 'Rosea'	SPlb
	– 'Rosy Gem'	GHeS
	– 'Rosy Morn'	GHeS SRms
	– 'Rotes Juwel'	GHeS SRms
	– 'Rubinteppich'	GHeS SRms
	– 'Ruby Glow'	GHeS NHol
	– 'Scatterley'	GHeS SRms
	– 'Schatzalp'	GHeS SRms
	– 'Sherwood Creeping'	GHeS SRms
	– 'Smart's Heath'	GHeS SRms
	– 'Sneznik'	GHeS
	– 'Snow White'	ELan
	– 'Spring Cottage Crimson'	GHeS
	– 'Spring Day'	GHeS
	– 'Springwood Pink'	CSBt CTri GHeS MAsh NHol NPri SRms SWhi
I	– 'Startler'	GHeS MAsh NHol
	– 'Tanja'	SWhi
	– 'Thomas Kingscote'	GHeS
§	– 'Treasure Trove'	CFst GHeS SWhi
	– 'Viking'	GHeS MAsh NHol
	– 'Vivellii' ♀H4	CBcs CTri GHeS MAsh NHol SCoo SRms SWhi
	– 'Vivellii Aurea'	GHeS
	– 'Walter Reisert'	GHeS SRms
	– 'Wanda'	GHeS
	– 'Wentwood Red'	GHeS SRms
	– Whisky	see *E. carnea* f. *aureifolia* 'Bell's Extra Special'
	– 'Winter Beauty'	GHeS MAsh NHol
	– 'Winter Melody'	GHeS
	– Winter Rubin	see *E. carnea* 'Kramer's Rubin'
	– 'Winter Sport'	GHeS
	– 'Winterfreude'	GHeS
	– 'Wintersonne'	CBcs CFst CHab EPfP GHeS MMuc SRms SWhi
	cerinthoidies 'Roohartje' **new**	CFst
	ciliaris f. ***albiflora*** 'Stoborough' ♀H4	CFst GHeS
	– – 'White Wings'	GHeS
	– f. ***aureifolia*** 'Aurea'	GHeS
	– 'Bretagne'	GHeS SWhi
	– 'Camla'	GHeS
	– 'Corfe Castle'	CFst GHeS
	– 'David McClintock'	CFst GHeS SWhi
	– 'Fada das Serras'	GHeS
	– 'Globosa'	GHeS SWhi
	– 'Mawiana'	GHeS
	– 'Mrs C.H. Gill' ♀H4	GHeS
	– 'Ram'	GHeS
	– 'Rotundiflora'	GHeS
	– 'Stapehill'	GHeS
	– 'Wych'	GHeS
	cinerea	SWhi
	– f. ***alba*** 'Alba Major'	GHeS
	– – 'Alba Minor' ♀H4	CFst GHeS MAsh NHol SWhi
	– – 'Celebration'	GHeS NHol SWhi
	– – 'Doctor Small's Seedling'	GHeS
	– – 'Domino'	GHeS MAsh
	– – 'Geke'	GHeS
	– – 'Godrevy'	GHeS
	– – 'Honeymoon'	GHeS
	– – 'Hookstone White' ♀H4	GHeS SWhi
	– – 'Jos' Honeymoon'	GHeS
	– – 'Marina'	GHeS
	– – 'Nell'	GHeS
	– – 'Snow Cream'	GHeS
	– – 'White Dale'	GHeS
	– 'Alette'	GHeS
	– 'Alfred Bowerman'	GHeS
	– 'Angarrack'	GHeS
	– 'Anja Bakker'	GHeS
	– 'Anja Blum'	GHeS
	– 'Anja Slegers'	GHeS
	– 'Apple Blossom'	GHeS
	– 'Aquarel'	GHeS
	– 'Ashdown Forest'	GHeS
	– 'Ashgarth Garnet'	GHeS
	– 'Atropurpurea'	GHeS MAsh
	– 'Atrorubens'	GHeS
	– 'Atrorubens, Daisy Hill'	GHeS
	– 'Atrosanguinea Reuthe's Variety'	GHeS
	– 'Atrosanguinea Smith's Variety'	GHeS
I	– 'Aurea'	MMuc
	– f. ***aureifolia*** 'Alice Ann Davies'	GHeS
	– – 'Ann Berry'	GHeS
	– – 'Apricot Charm'	CSBt GHeS
	– – 'Constance'	GHeS
	– – 'Fiddler's Gold' ♀H4	GHeS MAsh NHol SWhi
	– – 'Golden Charm'	GHeS NHol SWhi
	– – 'Golden Drop'	CFst CSBt GHeS MAsh NHol
	– – 'Golden Hue' ♀H4	GHeS MAsh NHol
	– – 'Golden Sport'	GHeS
	– – 'Golden Striker'	GHeS
	– – 'Golden Tee'	GHeS
	– – 'Goldilocks'	CFst GHeS
	– – 'Jack London'	GHeS
	– – 'John Eason'	GHeS
	– – 'Jos' Golden'	GHeS
	– – 'Robert Michael'	GHeS
	– – 'Rock Pool'	GHeS NHol

- - 'Screel'	GHeS
- - 'Summer Gold'	GHeS SWhi
- - 'Windlebrooke' ♀H4	GHeS NHol
- 'Baylay's Variety'	GHeS
- 'Bemmel'	GHeS
- 'Blossom Time'	GHeS
- 'Bucklebury Red'	GHeS
- 'C.D. Eason' ♀H4	CBcs CSBt CTri EPfP GHeS IVic MAsh NHol SCoo SWhi
§ - 'C.G. Best' ♀H4	GHeS
- 'Cairn Valley'	GHeS
- 'Caldy Island'	GHeS
- 'Cevennes'	GHeS GJos MAsh SWhi
- 'Champs Hill' ♀H4	GHeS
- 'Cindy' ♀H4	GHeS MAsh NHol
- 'Coccinea'	GHeS
- 'Colligan Bridge'	GHeS
- 'Contrast'	GHeS
- 'Crimson Glow'	GHeS
- 'Discovery'	CFst GHeS
- 'Duncan Fraser'	GHeS
- 'Eden Valley' ♀H4	GHeS MAsh NHol SCoo
- 'Eline'	GHeS
- 'England'	GHeS
- 'Felthorpe'	GHeS
- 'Flamingo'	GHeS
- 'Foxhollow Mahogany'	GHeS
- 'Frances'	GHeS
- 'Frankrijk'	GHeS
- 'Fred Corston'	GHeS
- 'G. Osmond'	GHeS
- 'Glasnevin Red'	GHeS IVic
- 'Glencairn'	GHeS MMuc NHol SEND SWhi
- 'Graham Thomas'	see *E. cinerea* 'C.G. Best'
- 'Grandiflora'	GHeS
- 'Guernsey Lime'	GHeS
- 'Guernsey Pink'	GHeS
- 'Guernsey Plum'	GHeS
- 'Guernsey Purple'	GHeS
- 'Hardwick's Rose'	GHeS
- 'Harry Fulcher'	GHeS
- 'Heatherbank'	GHeS
- 'Heathfield'	GHeS
- 'Heidebrand'	GHeS
- 'Hermann Dijkhuizen'	GHeS
- 'Hookstone Lavender'	GHeS
- 'Hutton's Seedling'	GHeS
- 'Iberian Beauty'	GHeS
- 'Janet'	GHeS
- 'Jersey Wonder'	GHeS
- 'Jiri'	GHeS
- 'John Ardron'	GHeS
- 'Joseph Murphy'	CFst GHeS
- 'Josephine Ross'	GHeS
- 'Joyce Burfitt'	CFst GHeS
- 'Katinka'	CBcs CFst GHeS GJos IVic NHol SWhi
- 'Kerry Cherry'	GHeS
- 'Knap Hill Pink' ♀H4	GHeS
- 'Lady Skelton'	GHeS
- 'Lavender Lady'	GHeS
- 'Lilac Time'	GHeS
- 'Lilacina'	GHeS
- 'Lime Soda' ♀H4	GHeS
- 'Lorna Anne Hutton'	GHeS
- 'Michael Hugo'	GHeS
- 'Miss Waters'	GHeS
- 'Mrs Dill'	GHeS
- 'Mrs E.A. Mitchell'	GHeS NHol SPlb
- 'Mrs Ford'	GHeS
- 'My Love'	CFst GHeS SWhi
- 'Neptune'	GHeS
- 'Newick Lilac'	GHeS
- 'Next Best'	GHeS
- 'Novar'	GHeS
- 'Old Rose'	GHeS
- 'P.S. Patrick' ♀H4	GHeS SWhi
- 'Pallas'	GHeS
- 'Pallida'	GHeS
- 'Paul's Purple'	GHeS
- 'Peñaz'	GHeS
- 'Pentreath' ♀H4	GHeS MMuc SEND
- 'Pink Foam'	GHeS
- 'Pink Ice' ♀H4	CTri EPfP GHeS MAsh NHol SWhi
- 'Plummer's Seedling'	GHeS
- 'Promenade'	GHeS
- 'Prostrate Lavender'	GHeS
- 'Providence'	CFst GHeS
- 'Purple Beauty'	GHeS MAsh SWhi
- 'Purple Robe'	GHeS SWhi
- 'Purple Spreader'	GHeS
- 'Purpurea'	GHeS
- 'Pygmaea'	GHeS
- 'Red Pentreath'	GHeS
- 'Rock Ruth'	GHeS
- 'Romiley'	GHeS MAsh
- 'Rose Queen'	GHeS
- 'Rosea'	GHeS
I - 'Rosea Splendens'	GHeS
- 'Rosita' **new**	CFst
- 'Rosy Chimes'	GHeS
- 'Roter Kobold'	SWhi
- 'Rozanne Waterer'	GHeS
- 'Ruby'	GHeS
- 'Sandpit Hill'	CFst GHeS
- 'Schizopetala'	GHeS
- 'Sea Foam'	GHeS
- 'Sherry'	GHeS MAsh NHol SWhi
- 'Smith's Lawn'	GHeS
- 'Spicata'	GHeS
- 'Splendens'	GHeS
- 'Startler'	GHeS MAsh
- 'Stephen Davis' ♀H4	GHeS MAsh NHol SCoo SWhi
- 'Strawberry Bells'	GHeS
- 'Sue Lloyd'	GHeS
- 'Ted Oliver' **new**	CFst
- 'Tilford'	GHeS
- 'Tom Waterer'	GHeS
- 'Underwood Pink'	GHeS
- 'Uschie Ziehmann'	GHeS
- 'Velvet Night' ♀H4	CSBt GHeS MAsh MMuc NHol SWhi
- 'Victoria'	GHeS
- 'Violacea'	GHeS
- 'Violetta'	GHeS
- 'Vivienne Patricia'	CFst GHeS SWhi
- 'W.G. Notley'	GHeS
- 'West End'	GHeS
- 'Wine'	GHeS
- 'Yvonne'	GHeS
cooperi	SPlb
cruenta	CFst
- 'Straw Hill' **new**	CFst
curviflora	GHeS SPlb
× ***darleyensis*** 'Alba'	see *E.* × *darleyensis* f. *albiflora* 'Silberschmelze'
- f. ***albiflora*** 'Ada S. Collings'	GHeS MAsh SRms

-- 'Dunreggan' GHeS
-- 'N.R.Webster' GHeS MAsh SRms
§ -- 'Silberschmelze' CSBt CTri EPfP GHeS MAsh MMuc NHol NPri SCoo SEND SRms SWhi
-- 'White Glow' CTri GHeS MAsh SRms
-- 'White Perfection' Υ^{H4} CBcs CFst CSBt EPfP GHeS IArd IVic MAsh NHol NPri SBfd SCoo SPoG SRms SWhi
- 'Archie Graham' GHeS SRms
- 'Arthur Johnson' Υ^{H4} CFst CSBt CTri GHeS MAsh NHol SRms SWhi
§ - f. ***aureifolia*** 'Eva Gold'[PBR] CFst GHeS MAsh NHol SWhi
-- 'Jack H. Brummage' CSBt CTri GHeS IArd MAsh NHol SRms SWhi
-- 'Mary Helen' CSBt EPfP GHeS MAsh NHol SBfd SCoo SRms SWhi
-- 'Moonshine' CFst NHol SRms SWhi
-- 'Tweety' CBcs CFst GHeS SRms
- 'Aurélie Brégeon' CFst GHeS MAsh SRms
- 'Bert' CFst SBfd SCoo
- 'Bing' CFst SBfd SCoo
- 'Cherry Stevens' see *E.* × *darleyensis* 'Furzey'
§ - 'Darley Dale' CFst CSBt ELan EPfP GHeS MAsh MMuc NHol NPri SBfd SCoo SEND SLon SPer SPoG SRms SWhi
- 'Epe' CFst GHeS SRms
- 'Erecta' GHeS
- 'Eva'[PBR] see *E.* × *darleyensis* f. *aureifolia* 'Eva Gold'
§ - 'Furzey' Υ^{H4} CSBt EPfP GHeS MAsh NHol NWea SCoo SPer SRms SWhi
- 'George Rendall' CSBt CTri EPfP GHeS MAsh NHol SCoo SRms
- 'Ghost Hills' Υ^{H4} CSBt EPfP GHeS MAsh NHol NPri SBfd SCoo SPer SPoG SRms SWhi
- 'Golden Perfect' **new** CFst
- 'Irish Treasure' **new** CFst
- 'J.W. Porter' Υ^{H4} CFst EPfP GHeS MMuc SCoo SEND SLon SRms SWhi
- 'James Smith' GHeS SRms
- 'Jenny Porter' Υ^{H4} CSBt ELan EPfP GHeS MAsh SCoo SLon SWhi
- 'Katia'[PBR] (Winter Belles Series) **new** CFst MAsh SWhi
- 'Kramer's Rote' Υ^{H4} CBcs CFst CSBt CTri ELan EPfP GHeS MAsh MMuc NHol NPri SBfd SCoo SEND SPoG SRms SWhi
§ - 'Lena' CFst GHeS
- 'Lucie'[PBR] (Winter Belles Series) CFst MAsh SWhi
- 'Margaret Porter' CFst EPfP GHeS MAsh SCoo SPer SWhi
- Molten Silver see *E.* × *darleyensis* f. *albiflora* 'Silberschmelze'
- 'Mrs Parris' Red' GHeS
- 'Phoebe'[PBR] **new** CFst MAsh SWhi
- 'Pink Perfection' see *E.* × *darleyensis* 'Darley Dale'
- 'Spring Surprise'[PBR] CFst EPfP GHeS SCoo SWhi
- 'W.G. Pine' GHeS SRms
- 'White Fairy' GHeS
- 'White Spring Surprise' **new** SWhi
- 'Winter Surprise' SWhi
- 'Winter Treasure' **new** CFst
discolor CFst GHeS
erigena f. ***alba*** 'Alba' GHeS
-- 'Brian Proudley' CFst GHeS
-- 'Ivory' GHeS
-- 'Mrs Parris' White' GHeS
-- 'Nana Alba' GHeS
-- 'Nana Compacta' GHeS
-- 'W.T. Rackliff' Υ^{H4} CBcs CFst CSBt EPfP GHeS MAsh NHol SCoo SRms SWhi
-- 'W.T. Rackliff Variegated' (v) GHeS
- f. ***aureifolia*** 'Golden Lady' Υ^{H4} CFst CSBt GHeS MAsh NHol SCoo SRms SWhi
-- 'Thing Nee' CFst GHeS SRms SWhi
- 'Brightness' CSBt EPfP GHeS MAsh NHol SCoo
- 'Coccinea' GHeS
- 'Ewan Jones' GHeS
- 'Glauca' GHeS
- 'Hibernica' GHeS
- 'Hibernica Alba' GHeS
- 'Irish Dusk' Υ^{H4} CBcs CFst CSBt CTri EPfP GHeS MAsh MMuc NHol NWea SCoo SEND SRms SWhi
- 'Irish Salmon' GHeS
- 'Irish Silver' GHeS
- 'Maxima' GHeS
- 'Mrs Parris' Lavender' GHeS
- 'Nana' GHeS
- 'Rosea' GHeS
- 'Rosslare' CFst GHeS
- 'Rubra' GHeS
- 'Superba' CFst GHeS MAsh SRms SWhi
× ***garforthensis*** 'Tracy Wilson' GHeS
'Ghislaine' GHeS
glauca var. ***elegans*** CDes
- var. ***glauca*** SPlb
gracilis SPoG
× ***griffithsii*** 'Ashlea Gold' GHeS
- 'Elegant Spike' GHeS
§ - 'Heaven Scent' GHeS SWhi
- 'Jacqueline' CFst GHeS NHol SWhi
- 'Valerie Griffiths' CFst GHeS MAsh NHol SWhi
haematosiphon **new** CFst
'Heaven Scent' see *E.* × *griffithsii* 'Heaven Scent'
'Hélène' GHeS
× ***krameri*** 'Otto' GHeS
- 'Rudi' GHeS IVic
leucantha **new** CFst
lusitanica Υ^{H3} CFst GHeS SPoG
- f. ***aureifolia*** 'George Hunt' CFst ELan EPfP GHeS MAsh NHol SLon SPer SPoG
- 'Sheffield Park' CFst ELan EPfP GHeS MAsh SPer SPoG
lutea white-flowered **new** CDes
mackayana GHeS
subsp. ***andevalensis***
-- f. ***albiflora*** CFst GHeS
- 'Donegal' GHeS
- f. ***eburnea*** 'Doctor Ronald Gray' GHeS
-- 'Shining Light' CFst GHeS
- 'Errigal Dusk' CFst GHeS
- 'Galicia' GHeS
- 'Lawsoniana' GHeS
- f. ***multiplicata*** 'Ann D. Frearson' (d) GHeS
-- 'Maura' (d) GHeS
-- 'Plena' (d) CFst GHeS WHer
- 'William M'Calla' GHeS
mammosa CFst SPlb

Name	Suppliers
manipuliflora 'Aldeburgh'	GHeS
§ - 'Cascades'	GHeS
- 'Corfu'	GHeS
- 'Don Richards'	GHeS
- 'Ian Cooper'	GHeS
- 'Korçula'	GHeS
- 'Toothill Mustard'	GHeS
- 'Waterfall'	see *E. manipuliflora* 'Cascades'
mediterranea	see *E. erigena*
multiflora f. ***alba*** 'Formentor'	GHeS
× ***oldenburgensis*** 'Ammerland'	CFst GHeS SCoo SRms
- 'Oldenburg'	GHeS
patersonii	SPlb
perspicua	CDes SPlb
quadrangularis **new**	CFst
racemosa	CFst GHeS
rubens **new**	CFst
scoparia subsp. ***azorica***	GHeS
- subsp. ***maderincola***	CFst
f. ***aureifolia*** 'Levada Gold' **new**	GHeS
- - - 'Madeira Gold'	GHeS
§ - 'Minima'	GHeS
- subsp. ***platycodon***	GHeS
- 'Pumila'	see *E. scoparia* 'Minima'
§ ***senilis*** var. ***australis*** **new**	CFst
spiculifolia	WPat WThu
- f. ***albiflora***	GHeS
- 'Balkan Rose'	GCal GHeS
'Spring Field White'	MMuc
straussiana	SPlb
I × ***stuartii*** 'Charles Stuart'	GHeS
- 'Connemara'	GHeS
- 'Irish Lemon' ♀H4	CFst CSBt EPfP GHeS MAsh NHol SWhi
- 'Irish Orange'	CSBt GHeS MAsh NHol SWhi
- 'Irish Rose'	GHeS
- 'Nacung'	GHeS
- 'Pat Turpin'	GHeS
subdivaricata	CFst GHeS
tegetiformis	see *E. senilis* var. *australis*
terminalis ♀H4	GHeS
- 'Golden Oriole'	GHeS
- 'Thelma Woolner'	GHeS
tetralix 'Alba'	GHeS
- f. ***alba*** 'Bartinney'	GHeS
- - 'Dee'	GHeS
- - 'Hailstones'	GHeS
- - 'Melbury White'	GHeS
- 'Alba Mollis' ♀H4	CFst CSBt GHeS MAsh NHol SWhi
- 'Alba Praecox'	GHeS
§ - f. ***alba*** 'Ruby's Variety'	GHeS
- 'Allendale Pink'	GHeS
- 'Ardy'	GHeS
- f. ***aureifolia*** 'Renate'	GHeS
- - 'Ruth's Gold'	GHeS MAsh NHol
- - 'Swedish Yellow'	GHeS
- 'Bala'	GHeS
- 'Con Underwood' ♀H4	CSBt GHeS MAsh NHol SWhi
- 'Curled Roundstone'	GHeS
- 'Dänemark'	GHeS
- 'Daphne Underwood'	GHeS
- 'Darleyensis'	GHeS
- 'Delta'	GHeS
- 'Foxhome'	GHeS
- 'George Fraser'	GHeS
- 'Gratis'	GHeS
- 'Hookstone Pink'	GHeS
- 'Humoresque'	GHeS
- 'Jos' Creeping'	GHeS
- 'Ken Underwood'	GHeS
- 'L.E. Underwood'	GHeS NHol
- 'Mary Grace'	GHeS
- 'Morning Glow'	see *E.* × *watsonii* 'F. White'
- 'Pink Glow'	GHeS
- 'Pink Pepper' (v)	GHeS
- f. ***racemosa*** 'Terschelling'	GHeS
- 'Riko'	CFst GHeS
- 'Rosea'	GHeS
- 'Rubra'	GHeS
- 'Ruby's Velvet'	see *E. tetralix* f. *alba* 'Ruby's Variety'
- 'Salmon Seedling'	GHeS
- 'Samtpfötchen'	CFst GHeS
- 'Silver Bells'	CSBt GHeS
- f. ***stellata*** 'Helma'	GHeS
- - 'Helma Variegated' (v)	GHeS
- - 'Pink Star' ♀H4	CFst GHeS MAsh NHol SWhi
- 'Stikker'	GHeS
- 'Tina'	GHeS
- 'Trixie'	GHeS
- 'White House'	GHeS
tumida **new**	CDes
umbellata	GHeS
- f. ***albiflora*** 'Anne Small'	GHeS
- 'David Small'	GHeS
vagans f. ***alba***	MMuc
- f. ***alba*** 'Bianca'	GHeS
- - 'Cornish Cream' ♀H4	EPfP GHeS MAsh NHol SWhi
- - 'Cream'	GHeS MAsh
- - 'Diana's Gold'	GHeS SRms
- - 'French White'	GHeS
- - 'Golden Triumph'	CFst GHeS SWhi
- - 'Kevernensis Alba' ♀H4	GHeS NWad SEND
- - 'Leucantha'	GHeS
- 'Alba Nana'	see *E. vagans* f. *alba* 'Nana'
§ - f. ***alba*** 'Nana'	GHeS
- - 'White Lady'	GHeS
- - 'White Rocket'	GHeS
- - 'White Spire'	GHeS
- f. ***aureifolia*** 'Valerie Proudley' ♀H4	CFst CSBt GHeS MAsh NHol
- - 'Yellow John'	CFst GHeS SRms SWhi
- 'Birch Glow' ♀H4	EPfP GHeS MAsh SWhi
- 'Carnea'	GHeS
- 'Charm'	GHeS
- 'Chittendenii'	GHeS
- 'Diana Hornibrook'	GHeS
- 'Fiddlestone'	GHeS
- 'George Underwood'	GHeS
- 'Grandiflora'	GHeS
- 'Holden Pink'	GHeS MAsh
- 'Hookstone Rose'	GHeS
- 'Ida M. Britten'	GHeS
- 'J.C. Fletcher'	GHeS
- 'Keira'	CFst SRms SWhi
- 'Lilacina'	GHeS
- 'Lyonesse' ♀H4	GHeS MAsh MMuc NHol SEND SWhi
- 'Miss Waterer'	GHeS
- 'Mrs D.F. Maxwell' ♀H4	CBcs CFst CSBt GHeS MAsh NHol SWhi
- 'Mrs Donaldson'	CFst GHeS
- 'Pallida'	GHeS

- 'Peach Blossom' GHeS
- 'Pyrenees Pink' GHeS MAsh
- 'Rosea' GHeS
- 'Rubra' GHeS
- 'Saint Keverne' CSBt GHeS IArd IVic MAsh NHol SWhi
- 'Summertime' CFst GHeS
- 'Valerie Smith' GHeS
- 'Viridiflora' GHeS

× ***veitchii*** MMuc SEND
- 'Brockhill' GHeS
- 'Exeter' ♀H3 CDoy CSBt ELan EPfP GAbr GHeS MAsh NHol NRHS SWhi
- 'Gold Tips' ♀H4 CSBt EPfP GHeS NHol SWhi
- 'Pink Joy' GHeS SWhi

versicolor CFst SPlb

verticillata CFst GHeS
- 'Ruby Lace' **new** CFst
- 'Violet Grey' **new** CFst

viridescens GHeS

× ***watsonii*** 'Cherry Turpin' GHeS
- 'Claire Elise' **new** CFst
- 'Dawn' ♀H4 GHeS SWhi
- 'Dorothy Metheny' GHeS
- 'Dorset Beauty' GHeS
- § 'F. White' GHeS
- 'Gwen' GHeS
- 'H. Maxwell' GHeS SWhi
- 'Mary' GHeS SWhi
- 'Pink Pacific' CFst GHeS
- 'Rachel' GHeS
- 'Truro' GHeS

× ***williamsii*** 'Cow-y-Jack' GHeS
- 'Croft Pascoe' GHeS
- 'David Coombe' GHeS
- 'Gew Graze' GHeS
- 'Gold Button' GHeS
- 'Gwavas' GHeS
- 'Jean Julian' GHeS
- 'Ken Wilson' CFst GHeS
- 'Lizard Downs' GHeS
- 'Marion Hughes' GHeS
- 'P.D. Williams' ♀H4 GHeS

× ***willmorei*** **new** CFst
- 'Linton's Red' **new** CFst

I 'Winter Fire' (*oatesii* hybrid) GHeS

woodii SPlb

Erigeron ✿ (*Asteraceae*)

from Big Horn, USA NMen

acris subsp. ***angulosus*** **new** GKev

'Adria' EBee ECtt LLHF LRHS MBNS SPer WBrk WFar WMnd WWEG

annuus CSpe NDov

aurantiacus EBee EPfP NBre NBro NPri SWal WPer

aureus 'Canary Bird' ♀H4 EPfP EPot NBir NMen NSla WAbe
- 'The Giant' WAbe

'Azure Beauty' EBee EPfP SBfd

Azure Fairy see *E.* 'Azurfee'

§ 'Azurfee' CSBt EBee ELan EPfP GMaP MBNS NBir NLar NPri SPer SPhx SPoG SWvt WMoo WPer WWEG

Black Sea see *E.* 'Schwarzes Meer'

'Blue Beauty' CMac EPfP LRHS

caespitosus **new** EDAr

'Charity' MRav WBrk

chrysopsidis var. ***brevifolius*** LLHF
- subsp. ***chrysopsidis*** NNS 08-147 **new** GKev
- 'Grand Ridge' ECho LHop LLHF LRHS NRHS WAbe

compositus CTri SRms
- § var. ***discoideus*** EDAr NMen NSla SPlb WPer
- 'Rocky' ECho

Darkest of All see *E.* 'Dunkelste Aller'

deep pink-flowered CHEx

'Dignity' EBee ELan GBuc LHop LLHF LRHS MBrN MRav SMrm SPet SUsu WBrk WCot WFar WWEG

'Dimity' CMea ECha NBir NBre SAga WAbe WBrk WFar WHal WSFF

divergens **new** EBee

'Dominator' EBee

I 'Dunkelste Aller' ♀H3 CMea CSam EBee ELan EPfP GMaP LBMP LHop LRHS LSou MAvo MRav MSpe MWat NDov NMRc NPri SPer SPoG SRms SWvt WCAu WFar WWEG

elegantulus CMea

* ***ereganus*** NBre WBrk

flettii ECho EDAr

'Foersters Liebling' ♀H4 EBee GBin MBel WCot WWEG

formosissimus GBin

'Four Winds' CAbP EBee ECho ECtt ELan EWes GKev LRHS MRav NGdn NMen WPer WWEG

'Gaiety' LRHS NBre WBrk

glaucus CCCN CSBt ECho GBee GJos LRHS MAsh MBNS MRav NBre NGdn SEND SMad WBrk WFar WHoo
- 'Albus' CFis LHop LRHS MBNS WFar WPer
- 'Elstead Pink' CTri EBee ECtt ELan LRHS WFar
- 'Roger Raiche' CMea MRav SMrm
- 'Rose Purple' **new** CFis
- 'Roseus' CBcs SEND
- 'Sea Breeze' CCCN COIW CPrp EBee ECtt EWll GJos GMaP LAst LHop LRHS MBNS MBri NDov NPri SBfd SHil SPoG STes WBor WNew
- 'Viewpoint Blue' LRHS

howellii NBre

humilis EDAr

§ ***karvinskianus*** ♀H3 Widely available
- 'Stallone' NPri

leiomerus GKev LBee LLHF

linearis LLHF NMen

'Mrs F.H. Beale' ECtt LSou MSpe SRGP

mucronatus see *E. karvinskianus*

multiradiatus GCal

'Nachthimmel' ECtt NBre NGdn

ochroleucus var. ***scribneri*** LLHF

'Offenham Excellence' WCot

oreganus LRHS

philadelphicus CElw IGor MNrw NBir NBro

'Pink Beauty' SKHP

Pink Jewel see *E.* 'Rosa Juwel'

Pink Triumph see *E.* 'Rosa Triumph'

pinnatisectus CPBP GKev NMen

poliospermus var. ***poliospermus*** **new** LLHF

'Profusion' see *E. karvinskianus*

'Prosperity' EBee

pumilus CDes

	Name	Suppliers
	pygmaeus	LLHF
	pyrenaicus Rouy	see *Aster pyrenaeus*
	'Quakeress'	CElw CPrp EBee ECtt EPfP EShb GBuc GMaP IKil LHop LRHS MNrw MRav MSpe NGdn SBfd SMrm SUsu WBrk WFar WWEG
§	'Rosa Juwel'	CSBt CTri EBee ECtt ELan EPfP GMaP LRHS MBNS MRav NBir NPri SPer SPoG SRms SWal SWvt WMnd WMoo WPer
§	'Rosa Triumph'	EBee WCAu
	'Rosenballett'	LRHS WCot
	'Rotes Meer'	CMac ELan MRav MSpe WFar
	rotundifolius 'Caerulescens'	see *Bellis caerulescens*
	salsuginosus misapplied	see *Aster sibiricus*
§	'Schneewittchen'	EBee ELan EPfP LHop MBNS MBel MPie MRav MSpe MWat NCGa SBfd SHar SPet SPoG SWvt WWEG
§	'Schwarzes Meer'	EBee LPla MBel MNrw SMrm SPer SPoG WCot WFar
	scopulinus	CPBP ITim LLHF WAbe WPat
	'Serenity'	LRHS
	simplex	ECho LRHS
	'Sincerity'	WBrk WFar
	'Snow Queen'	WFar
	Snow White	see *E.* 'Schneewittchen'
	'Sommerneuschnee'	EBee ECha GBin LPla NDov SPhx WCAu WCot WMnd
	speciosus	EBee
	'Strahlenmeer'	EBee MSpe NBre
	trifidus	see *E. compositus* var. *discoideus*
	uniflorus	LLHF MAsh SRms
	'Unity'	LRHS
	'Wayne Roderick'	EBee LRHS SRGP
	'White Quakeress'	CMea EBee MRav WBrk WCot
	'Wuppertal'	NGdn

Erinacea (*Papilionaceae*)

	Name	Suppliers
§	***anthyllis*** ♀H4	WThu
	pungens	see *E. anthyllis*

Erinus (*Plantaginaceae*)

	Name	Suppliers
	alpinus ♀H4	CTri ECho ECtt EDAr GAbr GJos GKev MAsh MLHP MWat NBir NHol NRHS NSla SRms WCot WFar WPer XLum
	- var. ***albus***	ECho GJos NMen SRms WHoo WPer XLum
	- 'Doktor Hähnle'	ECho EDAr GMaP NMen NRya SRms WFar WHoo XLum
	- 'Mrs Charles Boyle'	NMen

Eriobotrya (*Rosaceae*)

	Name	Suppliers
	'Coppertone'	see × *Rhaphiobotrya* 'Coppertone'
	deflexa	CBcs CHEx
	japonica (F) ♀H3	Widely available
	- 'Baffico' (F)	CAgr
	- 'BB' (F)	CAgr
	- 'Gold Nugget' (F)	XBlo
	- 'Mrs Cookson' (F)	MBri
	- 'Oliver' (F) new	MBri
	- 'Ottaviana' (F)	CAgr

Eriocapitella see *Anemone*

Eriocephalus (*Asteraceae*)

	Name	Suppliers
	africanus	SPlb WJek

Eriogonum (*Polygonaceae*)

	Name	Suppliers
	alleni new	WCot
	cespitosum	LLHF WAbe
	- NNS 03-254	GKev
	jamesii	WPat
	umbellatum	ECho GKev
	- var. ***humistratum***	WPat
	- var. ***torreyanum***	CMea

Eriophorum (*Cyperaceae*)

	Name	Suppliers
	angustifolium	CBen CRWN CWat EHoe EHon ELon LPBA MSKA MWts SPlb SWat WMAq WPer WPnP XLum
	chamissonis new	MWts
	latifolium	LPBA MSKA MWts XLum
	rousseauianum	MSKA
	vaginatum	CRow EBee EHoe EWay MSKA XLum

Eriophyllum (*Asteraceae*)

	Name	Suppliers
	lanatum	CFis EBee ECha EPfP MDKP NBid NBre NGBl WWEG XLum

Erodium (*Geraniaceae*)

	Name	Suppliers
	absinthoides	LRHS NSla XSen
	- var. ***amanum***	see *E. amanum*
§	***acaule***	LLHF WFar
§	***amanum***	CSpe EWes
	'Ardwick Redeye'	IPot
	balearicum	see *E.* × *variabile* 'Album'
	'Bidderi'	GJos IPot NChi XSen
	'Candy Store'	LRHS
	'Carmel'	XSen
	'Caroline'	CMea WHoo
	carvifolium	WFar
§	***castellanum***	EBee LLHF NBro NMen SMrm
	'Catherine Buñuel'	NMen
	celtibericum	EPot XSen
	- 'Javalambre'	XSen
	- 'Peñagolosa'	XSen
	'Cézembre'	XSen
	chamaedryoides	see *E. reichardii*
	- 'Roseum'	see *E.* × *variabile* 'Roseum'
	cheilanthifolium 'David Crocker'	EPot IGor NMen
	chrysanthum	CElw CSam CTri CYeo EBee ECha ECho ECtt EDAr EPfP EPot EWTr GBuc GJos GMaP LHop LRHS MRav NLar NMen NRya SEND SMrm SRot WFar WTin XLum XSen
	- pink-flowered	CSpe EHrv EPot LHop NMen SEND SMrm SRot XLum
	corsicum	ECho NMen WAbe
	- 'Album'	ECho LLHF NMen WAbe
	'County Park'	CMea EBee ECha MLHP SRms XSen
	daucoides misapplied	see *E. castellanum*
	daucoides Boiss.	EBee
	foetidum	NMen
	- 'Couvé'	NMen
	'Fran's Delight'	CMea ECtt EPot GJos GMaP NMen SBch SUsu WHoo
	'Freedom' new	CSpe EBee NDov NLar WHil XEll
	'Fripetta'	WAbe WIce XSen
	'Gini's Choice'	WCot
N	***glandulosum*** ♀H4	CMea EBee ECho EPfP MMuc SBch SEND SRms SRot WFar WPat XSen
	- 'Marie Poligné'	XSen

	'Grey Blush'	SMHy WKif
	gruinum	SPhx SWal
	guicciardii	XSen
	guttatum misapplied	see *E.* 'Katherine Joy'
N	***guttatum*** (Desf.) Willd.	EPot EWTr LHop MAsh MWat NMen SRms WNew
	hymenodes L'Hér.	see *E. trifolium*
	'Isabel' **new**	SUsu
	'Julie Ritchie'	CMea WHoo
§	'Katherine Joy'	EWes MHer SBch SRGP SRot WAbe XSen
	× ***kolbianum***	SMHy WAbe WCot WFar WHoo WPnn XSen
	- 'Natasha'	CFis CMHG EBee ECtt EHoe EPot EWes GBuc GMaP MHer NMen NSla SPoG SRGP WAbe WFar WIce WKif XSen
	'Las Meninas'	CRDP EBee NLar SUsu WCot
	× ***lindavicum***	ECha NChi WPnn XSen
	macradenum	see *E. glandulosum*
	manescavii	Widely available
	'Marchants Mikado'	WKif
	'Maryla'	CMea NMen WIce
	'Merstham Pink'	GMaP SRms XLum XSen
	'Mesquita'	CMea
	'Norse Pink'	GJos
	'Pallidum'	CSam
	pelargoniiflorum	CHid CSpe EBee ELan EPfP EWTr LRHS MCot NBro SEND SMrm SRms WFar WHil WKif WPer WPnn WSHC
	'Peter Vernon'	XSen
	petraeum subsp. ***petraeum***	EPot MSpe
	'Pickering Pink'	NMen SEND
	'Pippa Mills'	CMea
	'Princesse Marion'	MLHP XSen
*	'Purple Haze'	EBee MSCN SMrm SRms SRot WFar
§	***reichardii***	CTri ECho ECtt LRHS MBrN MHer NRHS SPet SPoG SRms WCFE WPnn
	- 'Album'	CEnt ECho EPPr GEdr MAsh NMen NRHS SGar SMrm SPet SPoG WFar WHoo WPnn
*	- 'Rubrum'	CElw ECho
	'Robertino'	NMen WAbe
	rodiei	EWes MAsh WKif
	romanum	see *E. acaule*
§	***rupestre***	ECho ECtt MAsh SRms SRot
	'Sarck'	XSen
	sibthorpianum	XSen
	'Spanish Eyes'	EBee ECtt IBoy IPot LRHS MBel NEgg NPri SRot SUsu WCot WFar WHlf WKif
	'Stephanie'	CFis CMHG ECho ELan EPot EWes GMaP LRHS LSRN NMen SWal WAbe WIce XSen
	supracanum	see *E. rupestre*
	'Tiny Kyni'	WFar XSen
	trichomanifolium L'Hér.	EWes LRHS
§	***trifolium***	ECho ELan EPfP EWld LRHS MHer NRHS NSla
	× ***variabile***	ECtt
§	- 'Album'	CMea EBee ECho EPfP EPot LAst LRHS MHer MMuc NEgg NPri NRHS NSla SRms SRot WAbe WBrk WFar WPer
I	- 'Bishop's Form'	Widely available
	- 'Candy'	ELon GEdr MHer
	- 'Derek'	ECho SRGP
	- 'Flore Pleno' (d)	CFis ECho ELan EPfP EWes LRHS MHer NMen SPoG SRms WBrk WFar WPer
	- 'Red Rock'	CTri
§	- 'Roseum' 🏆H4	ECho ECtt ELan ELon EPfP MMuc MSCN NSla SEND SPlb SRms WBrk WFar WPer
I	'Westacre Seedling'	EWes
	'Whitwell Superb'	XSen

Erpetion see *Viola*

Eruca (*Brassicaceae*)

vesicaria	CWan ENfk
- subsp. ***sativa***	CSpe EGHP ELau GPoy MHer MHoo MNHC SIde SVic

Eryngium ✿ (*Apiaceae*)

	NJM 09.072	WPGP
	from Roger Grounds **new**	MAvo
§	***agavifolium***	Widely available
	alpinum 🏆H4	CBcs CHab CSpe EBee ECha ECho ELan ELon GKev GMaP LAst LHop LRHS MGos MSCN NBir SEND SKHP SMrm SPer SPet SRms SRot WFar
	- 'Amethyst'	IPot LRHS LSRN NBro SMrm
	- 'Blue Jacket'	NSti
	- 'Blue Star'	CPLG CSpe EBee ECtt EHrv ELan ELon EPfP GBuc LRHS MTis NGBl NLar SPtl WCFE WPer WWEG
	- 'Holden Blue'	MAvo
	- 'Slieve Donard'	see *E.* × *zabelii* 'Donard Variety'
	- 'Superbum'	CSpe ECtt EHrv GJos GLog LRHS MNrw SRms SWat
	amethystinum	CCse CMac EBee EPfP EPri LRHS MAvo MCot SMrm SPoG WHoo WPer WWEG XLum
	biebersteinianum	see *E. caeruleum*
	'Blue Jackpot'	EWes MAvo NCGa SMrm WFar
	'Blue Steel'	EWTr LLHF MDKP NChi SBfd SEND
	bourgatii	Widely available
	- Graham Stuart Thomas's selection	Widely available
	- 'Oxford Blue' 🏆H4	CRDP EBee EHrv GMaP MHer NLar SAga SGar SKHP SWvt
	- 'Picos Amethyst'	CBcs CMac CWCL EBee LHop LRHS LSRN LSou MGos NCGa NLar NSti SCoo SKHP
	- 'Picos Blue' PBR	Widely available
	- 'Silver Blue'	LRHS
	bromeliifolium misapplied	see *E. agavifolium*, *E. eburneum*
	bromeliifolium ambig.	EBee LRHS
§	***caeruleum***	MNrw
	campestre	CArn MDKP NLar WPer WWEG
	caucasicum	see *E. caeruleum*
	'Cobalt Star'	MAvo MDKP
	creticum	NBro
	cymosum B&SWJ 10267	WCru
	decaisneanum misapplied	see *E. pandanifolium*
	deppeanum	SSvw
	- F&M 54	WPGP
	- NJM 05.031	EBee LEdu
	Dove Cottage hybrid	NDov NLar
	ebracteatum	MAvo
	- var. ***poterioides***	LPla SMHy SMad SPhx SUsu
§	***eburneum***	CCon EBee ECha EPfP EWes GCal GMaP LRHS MAvo MSpe NBro NChi SBfd SKHP SMad

aff. ***eburneum***	CMac
'Electric Haze'	EBee ECtt LRHS LSou MCot MWhi SPoG
elegans var. ***elegans*** CDPR 3076	WPGP
foetidum	CArn
§ ***giganteum*** 🏆H4	Widely available
- 'Silver Ghost' 🏆H4	CMea CPLG CSam CSpe EBee ECtt EWll LHop LPot LRHS MAvo NChi NDov NGdn NSti SBfd SKHP SMrm SPer SWat SWvt WCot WWEG
gracile B&SWJ 10205	WCru
- B&SWJ 10351	WCru
- B&SWJ 10441	WCru
'Green Jade'	LRHS
guatemalense B&SWJ 8989	WCru
- B&SWJ 10322	WCru
- B&SWJ 10420	WCru
horridum misapplied	see *E. eburneum*
horridum ambig.	EWes MNrw NChi WMnd
horridum Malme	CCVN WCot
humile B&SWJ 10464	WCru
'Lapis Blue'	MAvo
leavenworthii	LRHS
maritimum	CArn CPom CPou EBee GPoy MDKP MHer MNHC NLar SMrm SPhx SPlb WAbe
Miss Willmott's ghost	see *E. giganteum*
monocephalum	EBee
× ***oliverianum*** 🏆H4	CMea EBee ECha ECtt EHrv ELan EPfP GAbr GBuc GCal LAst LHop LRHS MAvo MBel MLHP MNFA MRav NBir NChi NLar SDix SPoG SUsu SWat WCot WHoo
palmatum	NChi
§ ***pandanifolium*** 🏆H4	CCon CHEx CMHG EBee ELan EPfP EUJe EWes LEdu LHop LPot MNrw SEND SKHP SMad SPlb SPoG SUsu SWvt WCot WCru WMnd WPGP WWEG
- 'Physic Purple'	CSpe
planum	Widely available
- 'Bethlehem' 🏆H4	NLar SUsu SWat
§ - 'Blauer Zwerg'	CKno EBee
- 'Blaukappe'	CMea COIW CPLG EBee EHrv ELon EPfP LDai LRHS NLar SEND SKHP SMrm SPet SPhx WAul WTcb WWEG
* - 'Blue Candle'	EBee NLar
- Blue Dwarf	see *E. planum* 'Blauer Zwerg'
- 'Blue Glitter'	CSpe ELon LRHS NLar SPhx WWEG
- 'Blue Hobbit'	CMea CPLG EAEE EBee ELon EPfP LBuc LRHS LSqH MHer NGdn NLBP NLar NRHS NSla SPet SPoG WFar
- 'Blue Ribbon'	LAst LRHS LSou
- 'Flüela'	CBct EBee EWes GBuc LRHS LSRN MBel NEgg SWat WCAu
- 'Jade Frost'PBR (v)	CAbP CPLG CWGN EBee ELon EPfP EWes LAst LHop LLHF LRHS LSou MAvo MBNS MBel MNrw MPnt MRav MTis NLar NSti SKHP SPad SPoG SUsu WCot
- 'Little Blue Wonder'PBR **new**	CBct
- 'Naughty Jackpot' (v) **new**	NLar
- 'Paradise Jackpot'PBR	LSou MSCN SPer WHil
- 'Seven Seas'	CCon EBee ECtt LRHS MBNS MBel NEgg WPer
- 'Silver Salentino' **new**	SPhx
- 'Silver Stone'	EBee ECtt GMaP LDai LRHS NLar WHil
- 'Sunny Jackpot'PBR	NLar NSti
- 'Tetra Blau'	LRHS
- 'Tetra Petra'	LHop LRHS NEgg WPer
- 'Tiny Jackpot' **new**	EBee NLar NPnk
- 'Violet Blue'	GCal
- 'White Glitter' **new**	SPhx WWEG
proteiflorum	EBee EPfP GCal IGor LRHS MDKP NLar SKHP SPhx SPlb
- F&M 224	WPGP
serbicum	GCal SMHy WCot
serra	EWes LDai LRHS SEND
- RB 90454	EBee MAvo MDKP
strotheri B&SWJ 9109	WCru
- B&SWJ 10392	WCru
tricuspidatum	ECtt LRHS WPer WWEG
× ***tripartitum*** 🏆H4	CTri EAEE EBee ECha ECtt EHrv ELan EPPr EPfP EWTr GMaP LAst LHop LRHS LSRN MBri MNFA MRav MWat NBro NEgg SEND SGar SPhx SPoG SRkn SWat SWvt WFar WWlt
* ***umbelliferum***	GCal LAst MBNS MDKP NPri SKHP
variifolium	Widely available
- 'Miss Marbel'	EPfP
venustum	EBee LRHS MCot NLar SBfd SMrm
yuccifolium	EBee EPfP EWes GCal LEdu LRHS MAvo NLar SBfd SDix SMrm SPhx SPlb SWvt WHoo XLum
× ***zabelii***	CRDP ECha MAvo NBir NChi
- 'Big Blue'	CSpe EBee LRHS NCGa NLar SMad SUsu WCot
- 'Blaue Ritter'	EBee SKHP SWat
§ - 'Donard Variety'	EBee ECtt GBuc GCal IPot LRHS MAvo MDKP MTis NLar SWat
- 'Forncett Ultra'	GCal
- 'Jewel'	MAvo SApp SWat
- 'Jos Eijking'PBR	Widely available
- 'Violetta'	IGor NLar SWat WFar WHoo

Erysimum ✿ (*Brassicaceae*)

amoenum	LLHF WAbe
'Andy's Oranges and Lemons' (v) **new**	WCot
'Anne Marie'	EPfP
'Anthony Hicks'	CHll
'Apricot Delight'	see *E.* 'Apricot Twist'
§ 'Apricot Twist'	Widely available
arkansanum	see *E. helveticum*
asperum	GJos IFro
'Audrey's Pink' **new**	CSev WHoo
'Bowles's Mauve' 🏆H3	Widely available
'Bowles's Purple'	SRms SWvt
'Bowles's Yellow'	WCot
'Bredon' 🏆H3	EPfP NPer
'Butterscotch'	MMHG WHoo WTin
caricum **new**	WAbe
cheiri	CArn MHer
- 'Bloody Warrior' (d)	CElw ECtt
- 'Harpur Crewe' (d)	CHll ECtt ELan ELon EPfP GMaP NPer SRms SUsu WCot
- 'Orange Bedder' (Bedder Series)	NBir
'Chelsea Jacket'	EPfP
'Constant Cheer'	CBar CMea CPrp CSBt CSpe CWCL ECtt ELan ELon EPfP GMaP IFoB MCot NPer SAga SBfd SEND SPer

	SPoG SRGP SUsu SWal SWvt WCAu WHil WKif XLum
'Cotswold Gem' (v)	ECtt EHoe ELan EPfP LDai LSou MAsh MHer NPer SBfd SBri SLim SWvt WCot
'Dawn Breaker'	ECtt EWes LRHS MAsh MTis WCot
'Devon Sunset'	MBrN SAga
'Dorothy Elmhirst'	see *E.* 'Mrs L.K. Elmhirst'
dwarf, lemon-flowered	WHoo
'Ellen Willmott'	CEnt
'Emm's Variety'	EPot
'Gold Rush'	GJos
'Gold Shot'	GJos
'Golden Gem'	ECho EPfP
'Golden Jubilee'	ECho ECtt ELon GBuc WFar WIce
'Hector's Gatepost'	CWCL EWTr LSRN SRGP
§ ***helveticum***	ECho IFro LRHS SRms XLum
'Jacob's Jacket'	ECha ECtt MBNS MHer NPer
'Jenny Brook'PBR	EBee NCGa
'John Codrington'	GBin LHop NPer SAga SUsu WKif
'Jubilee Gold'	EBee WWEG
'Julian Orchard'	SAga
kotschyanum	ECho EPot GEdr LRHS NMen NSla SRms WAbe WIce
linifolium	SRms WFar WGor
- 'Little Kiss Lilac'	GJos
§ - 'Variegatum' (v)	CCCN CSBt CWCL CWan EBee ECtt ELan ELon EPfP LPot LRHS NEgg NLar NPer NPri SEND SGar SPer SPoG SRot WCAu XLum
- 'Variegatum' peach-flowered (v)	NLBP
'Moonlight'	EBee EPot GBuc GMaP MHer MRav NBir SRms WHoo
§ 'Mrs L.K. Elmhirst'	ECtt ELon MMHG NPer WHoo
mutabile	CTri EBee EPfP MAsh MRav SIde SPhx WHal
'My Old Mum'	CWGN EAEE EBee ECtt EWTr LRHS LSRN LSou MAsh MBNS MRav SEND WGwG
'Orange Flame'	CMea ECha ECho ELon EPot LHop MHer NPer WHoo WNew WPer
'Orange King' **new**	WIce
'Parish's'	CCse CElw CSpe MRav SAga SUsu WWFP
'Parkwood Gold'	CYeo ECho EDAr GJos GKev
'Pastel Patchwork'	CSpe LRHS LSou SBfd SUsu SWal
Perry's hybrid	NPer
'Perry's Peculiar'	NPer
'Perry's Surprise'	NPer
'Perry's Variegated' (v)	NPer
'Plant World Lemon'	CHGN ELon MTis NLar NPri SPoG
'Poppet'	CSpe
'Poppet Heaton'	CHll
§ ***pulchellum***	ECha
pumilum DC.	see *E. helveticum*
pusillum	WAbe
'Roddy's Own'	EDif
rupestre	see *E. pulchellum*
'Ruston Royal'	ECha
Rysi Bronze = 'Innrysibro'PBR	LHop LSou NLar SPoG WHil
Rysi Gold = 'Innrysigol'PBR	EBee SPoG WCot
Rysi Moon **new**	CWGN WHil
scoparium	ECha
'Sissinghurst Variegated'	see *E. linifolium* 'Variegatum'
'Spice Island' **new**	NCGa
'Sprite'	CMea CTri EPot NPer SEND
'Starbright'	CWCL LRHS
'Stars and Stripes' (v)	EPfP LRHS LSou SBfd SRkn
Sunburst = 'Listrace'	CMea CWGN EBee ECtt ELon LSou MTis SPoG WCot WHil WWlt
'Sunshine'	SWal
'Sweet Sorbet'	ELon EPfP GMaP MTis NEgg NLar SRkn SWal SWvt WHil
'Walberton's Fragrant Star' (v)	LBuc LRHS SPoG
Walberton's Fragrant Sunshine = 'Walfrasun'	CHll EPfP LRHS SBfd SCoo SPoG
'Wenlock Beauty'	CFis LDai SRms
'Winter Joy'	ELon LLHF LSou MBNS NLar WCot WHil
Winter Orchid **new**	CWGN NDov WCot
Winter Rouge **new**	CMea CWCL
Winter Sorbet = 'Inneryws' PBR	ELon EPfP LBMP MTis NPri SPoG
'Yellow Flame'	WPer

Erythraea see *Centaurium*

Erythrina (*Papilionaceae*)

abyssinica	SPlb
amazonica	SPlb
arborescens	SPlb
× ***bidwillii***	CCCN WPGP
crista-galli	CBcs CCCN CDTJ CHll CPom CSpe EAmu EBee ELan EPfP ESwi EUJe LEdu LRHS SPlb WCot WPGP
guatemalensis	SPlb
herbacea	SPlb
§ ***humeana***	CDTJ SPlb
latissima	CDTJ SPlb
lysistemon	SPlb
princeps	see *E. humeana*
rubrinervia **new**	SPlb
speciosa **new**	SPlb
vespertilio	SPlb

Erythronium ✿ (*Liliaceae*)

albidum	CLAP EBee ECho GBuc GEdr IBlr LAma LWst MMoz NMen
americanum	CArn CLAP ECho EPot IBlr LAma LWst MMoz MNrw NMen WAbe
'Apple Blossom'	ECho LWst
'Beechpark'	IBlr
'Blush'	ECho IBlr
'Bronze Beauty'	IBlr
'Californian Star'	IBlr
californicum ♀H4	CCon CLAP ECho GBuc GEdr IBlr LWst SCnR
- J&JA 13216	CLAP
- JCA 1.350.200	LWst
- 'Brimstone'	IBlr
- 'Bronze Edge'	IBlr
- 'Dark Delight'	IBlr
- 'Harvington Snowgoose'	CAvo CLAP EBee EHrv LLHF LRHS LWst MBri SKHP
- Plas Merdyn form	IBlr
- 'Purple Heart' × ***revolutum*** **new**	IBlr
- 'White Beauty' ♀H4	Widely available
californicum × ***hendersonii***	EBee IBlr
caucasicum	CLAP LWst
citrinum	GBuc LLHF NMen
- J&JA 13462	CLAP

- subsp. ***citrinum***	GBuc
citrinum* × *hendersonii	IBlr
'Citronella'	CBro CCon CLAP EPot GBuc GEdr GKev IBlr LWst NMen WAbe
cliftonii hort.	see *E. multiscapideum* Cliftonii Group
'Craigton Cover Girl'	IBlr
'Craigton Cream'	LWst
'Delicacy'	IBlr
dens-canis ♀H4	CAvo CBcs CBro CElw CTca CTri ECha ECho EHrv ELan EPot ERCP GKev GMaP IBlr IFro LAma LEdu LPot MNrw NBir NEgg NHol NRya SPer WAbe WBor WFar WPnP WShi
- JCA 470.001	CLAP
- from Slovenia	CLAP
- 'Charmer'	ECho GEdr MNrw
- 'Frans Hals'	CLAP EBee ECho EPot GBuc GCra GEdr GKev IPot MNrw SKHP WHal
- large-flowered **new**	IBlr
- 'Lilac Wonder'	EBee ECho EPot GBuc GEdr GKev GMaP IPot LAma LEdu MAvo MNrw SDeJ
* - 'Moerheimii' (d)	EBee ECho EPot GEdr GKev IBlr
- var. ***niveum***	IBlr LWst NEgg
- 'Old Aberdeen'	CLAP EBee EHrv IBlr LWst MNrw
- 'Pink Perfection'	EBee ECho EPot GEdr GKev LEdu MNrw NMin SDeJ
- 'Purple King'	EBee ECGP ECho EPot GBuc GEdr GKev GMaP IPot LAma LWst MMoz MNrw NHol NWad SDeJ
- 'Rose Queen'	CAvo CCon EBee ECho EHrv EPot GBuc GEdr GKev GMaP IPot LAma MAvo MNrw NMin NWad SDeJ SPhx WHal
* - 'Semi-plenum' (d)	IBlr
- 'Snowflake'	CAvo CLAP CTca EBee ECha ECho EPot GBuc GEdr GKev IPot LAma MMoz MNrw NBir NMen NMin NWad SDeJ SKHP SPhx WAbe
- 'White Splendour'	ECho IBlr LWst MNrw
- white-flowered, from Serbia	ECho
elegans	ECho GBuc LLHF LWst
'Flash'	IBlr
§ ***grandiflorum***	CLAP ECho NMen
- M&PS 007	CLAP NMen
- M&PS 96/024	NMen
- subsp. ***chrysandrum***	see *E. grandiflorum*
helenae	CLAP ECho IBlr
hendersonii	CLAP EBee ECho EHrv EPot GBuc LWst MSSP SKHP WAbe
- J&JA 12945	CLAP
howellii	CLAP
- J&JA 13441	CLAP
'Janice'	LWst
japonicum	CBcs EBee ECho EFEx EPot GEdr LAma LWst MBel MNrw NMen WFar
'Jeanette Brickell'	CLAP GBuc IBlr LWst
'Jeannine'	GBuc GEdr IBlr LWst
'Joan Wiley'	LWst
'Joanna'	GBuc IBlr LWst MNrw NMen
'John Brookes'	LWst
'Keith'	LWst
'Kinfauns Pink'	CWCL GBuc LLHF LWst
klamathense	EPot
'Kondo'	CCon CTri EBee ECho EPfP EPot GEdr GKev GMaP IBlr LAma LWst NBir NHol NLar NMen NWad SPer WAbe WCot WHil
'Margaret Mathew'	CLAP IBlr LWst WAbe
'Minnehaha'	GBuc LWst
montanum	ECho EHrv
§ ***multiscapideum***	CLAP CMea ECho GBuc LLHF LWst MSSP WCot
- NNS 02-166	WCot
§ - Cliftonii Group	CLAP GBuc LWst SKHP WCot
'Oregon Encore'	IBlr
oregonum	CLAP EBee ECha ECho EHrv EPot GBuc GEdr IBlr LLHF LRHS LWst MNrw MSSP SKHP
- subsp. ***leucandrum***	CLAP LWst
- subsp. ***oregonum*** NNS 01-202	WCot
I - 'Sulphur Form'	CLAP
'Pagoda' ♀H4	Widely available
purdyi	see *E. multiscapideum*
revolutum ♀H4	CBro CLAP CWCL EBee ECho EHrv EPot GBuc GEdr GKev GMaP IBlr LAma LRHS LWst MNrw MSSP NMen NRHS SCnR SKHP SRot WCru
- from God's Valley	MNrw
- 'Dark Dapple'	IBlr
- 'Guincho Splendour'	IBlr
I - 'Inshriach Form'	IBlr
- Johnsonii Group	ECho LWst WCru
- 'Knightshayes'	CAvo EBee GBuc LRHS MBri NRHS SKHP SPtl
- 'Knightshayes Pink'	CLAP EHrv IBlr LLHF LWst NBir WShi
- 'Pink Beauty'	GKev LWst
- Plas Merdyn form	IBlr
- 'Rose Beauty'	ECho NMen
- 'Wild Salmon'	CLAP EHrv LLHF LRHS LWst MBri
'Rippling Waters'	IBlr
'Rosalind'	IBlr LWst SCnR
sibiricum	ECho NMen
'Sundisc'	ECha ECho GBuc GEdr IBlr LWst NMen WAbe
'Susannah'	IBlr LWst
taylorii	LWst
tuolumnense ♀H4	CBro CCon CLAP CTca CWCL EBee ECho EHrv EPot GBuc GEdr GKev GMaP IBlr LAma MCot MMoz MNrw NMen SDeJ SPhx WCot WRHF
- EBA clone 2	IBlr LWst
- EBA clone 3	IBlr
- 'Edgar Klein'	LWst
- Plas Merdyn form	IBlr
- 'Spindlestone'	EBee GBuc GEdr IBlr LRHS LWst
umbilicatum	EBee GEdr IBlr LWst MSSP

Escallonia ✿ (*Escalloniaceae*)

'Alice'	SLPl SPer
'Apple Blossom' ♀H4	Widely available
§ ***bifida*** ♀H3	CDoC CDul CHGN LRHS SDix WCot WSFF WSHC
'C.F. Ball'	CBcs CSBt CTri ELan GKin LBMP LBuc LRHS MAsh MSwo NEgg NPla NWea SEND SGol SRms WFar WMoo
'Compacta Coccinea'	LRHS
'Dart's Rosy Red'	LBMP SLPl WMoo
'Donard Beauty'	NEgg SRms
'Donard Brilliance'	SGol

'Donard Radiance' ♀H4	CBcs CDoC CDul CMac CSBt CWib EBee ELan EPfP EShb LHop LRHS LSRN NLar NWad NWea SGol SLim SPer SPoG SRms SWvt WFar WMoo
'Donard Seedling'	CBcs CCVT CDoC CDul CHab EBee ECrN ELan EPfP GKin LAst LBuc LRHS MAsh MGos MSwo NPer NWea SBfd SGol SLPl SLim SPer SRms SWvt WFar WMoo
'Donard Star'	CWib EPfP NLar NWad NWea SLPl WCFE
'Donard White'	SPoG
'Edinensis'	EBee EPfP MGos NLar SLim WMoo
'Everest'	EBee EPfP LAst LBuc LRHS MAsh NEgg SLon
× ***exoniensis***	SRms
'Gwendolyn Anley'	SLPl
'Hopleys Gold'PBR	see *E. laevis* 'Gold Brian'
illinita	EBee GQui NLar
'Iveyi' ♀H3	Widely available
'Jamie'PBR	EBee EShb LLHF LSRN WMoo
§ ***laevis***	LRHS
§ - 'Gold Brian'PBR	CDul CMac EBee EHoe ELan EPau EPfP LRHS LSRN MAsh MGos MWat SCoo SGol SPer WFar WHar
- 'Gold Ellen' (v)	CSBt CTri CWSG EBee EHoe ELan ELon EPfP LRHS LSRN MAsh MBri MGos MRav MSwo NEgg NHol NLar NWad SAga SBfd SCoo SEND SHil SLim SPer SPoG SRms SWvt WMoo
'Langleyensis' ♀H4	CDoy CHab CMac CTri CWib NWea SGol WFar WHar
montevidensis	see *E. bifida*
organensis	see *E. laevis*
'Peach Blossom' ♀H4	CBar CDoC CDul CWib EBee ELan ELon EPfP GKin LHop LRHS MAsh MLHP MMuc MSwo NBir NHol SBfd SCoo SEND SGol SLPl SLim SPer SPoG SRms WFar
'Pink Elf'	MSwo
'Pink Pyramid'	LRHS
'Pride of Donard' ♀H4	CDoC CHab CSBt EBee EPfP GKin LRHS LTen MGos SRms
punctata	see *E. rubra*
Red Carpet = 'Loncar'PBR	EBee ELon LAst LRHS NHol SLon WHar WMoo
'Red Dream'	CSBt CWSG EBee EPfP LBMP LRHS MAsh MBlu MBri MGos MSwo NLar NWad SAga SBfd SCoo SEWo SHil SPoG SRms SWvt
'Red Elf'	CMac EBee ELan EPfP GKin LAst LRHS MBri MGos MSCN MWat NEgg SCoo SGar SHil SLPl SPer SPlb SPoG SRms SWvt WFar
'Red Hedger'	CDoC CHab CSBt CTsd CWib ELan EShb MRav SBfd SCoo SRms WMoo
'Red Knight' **new**	MAsh
'Red Robin'	SPoG
resinosa	CPLG IRos SPlb WJek
revoluta	CTri
§ ***rubra***	MLHP
- SDR 7052	GKev
- 'Crimson Spire' ♀H4	Widely available
- 'Ingramii'	CWib NWea SEND
- var. ***macrantha***	Widely available
* - - ***aurea***	NPla
- 'Pygmaea'	see *E. rubra* 'Woodside'
§ - 'Woodside'	ECho EPfP LLHF MLHP NWad SGol SRms
'Silver Anniversary'	MSwo
'Slieve Donard'	CMac EPfP MRav NEgg NWad NWea SLPl SLim SLon SRms WFar
tucumanensis	SPlb
'Ventnor'	WPGP

Eschscholzia (*Papaveraceae*)

californica ♀H4	MBel SEND
- 'Alba' **new**	CSpe
- 'Fire Bush' (Thai Silk Series) **new**	SPhx
- 'Gini's Cream'	CSpe
- 'Ivory Castle'	SPhx
- 'Jersey Cream'	CSpe
- subsp. ***mexicana*** 'Sun Shades' **new**	SPhx
- 'Mission Bells' **new**	WHil
- 'Red Chief' **new**	SPhx

Espeletia (*Asteraceae*)

aff. ***summapacis*** B&SWJ 10766	WCru

Esterhuysenia (*Aizoaceae*)

alpina	CPBP

Eucalyptus ✿ (*Myrtaceae*)

alpina	SPlb
amygdalina	SPlb
archeri	CCVT CDTJ CDoC CDul CTho CTrC CWCL ELan EPfP LRHS MBri MGos MWhi NLar SBfd SHil WCot
§ ***bridgesiana***	CCVT
caesia	SPlb
camaldulensis	SPlb
camphora	CCCN CTsd EBee ESwi SEND
cinerea	ELan SBig SPlb
citriodora	EOHP MHer SPlb
coccifera	CBcs CCVT CDoC CSBt CTsd EBee ELan EPfP EUJe LMaj LRHS LTen NEgg NPer SBig SEND SEWo SPlb WCot WWau
cordata	CCVT CDul ELan WWau
crucis subsp. ***crucis***	SPlb
curtisii	SPlb
cypellocarpa	SPlb
dalrympleana ♀H3	CDoC CDul CMHG CMac CWCL ELan EPfP EUJe EWes LRHS LSRN MGos MSwo NLar NPer SBig SEND SHil SLim SPer SPlb SRms WCot WPGP WWau
debeuzevillei	see *E. pauciflora* subsp. *debeuzevillei*
delegatensis	CMHG GLin NPer
divaricata	see *E. gunnii* subsp. *divaricata*
erythrocorys	SPlb
eximia	SPlb
* - 'Nana'	SPlb
ficifolia	CBcs CDTJ
fraxinoides	SPlb
gamophylla	SPlb
glaucescens	CMHG CWCL ELan EPfP ETod EWes LRHS SBfd SEWo SHil SPer
globulus	MNHC SPlb

	goniocalyx	EPfP
§	***gregsoniana***	CDoC CTrC EPfP SPlb
	gunnii ♀H3	Widely available
	- Azura = 'Cagire'PBR	LRHS LSRN MPkF SBfd SEWo SLon
§	- subsp. ***divaricata***	CCVT EPfP MBri
	- 'Silbertropfen'	EUJe
	johnstonii	CCVT NLar SEND SPer WWau
	kitsoniana	ELan
	kruseana	SPlb
	kybeanensis	WCot
	leucoxylon subsp. ***megalocarpa***	SPlb
	'Little Boy Blue'	CWib LSRN
	macrocarpa	SPlb
*	***moorei nana***	CDTJ
	nicholii	CBcs CCVT CDul EBee EHoe ELan EPfP EUJe EWes LAst LRHS MGos NLar SCoo SEND SLim SMad SPoG WCot WWau
	niphophila	see *E. pauciflora* subsp. *niphophila*
	nitens	CDTJ CTsd SBig SEND SPlb
	parvifolia ♀H4	CCCN CCVT CDoC CMac EPfP LRHS LTen MWhi NLar SCoo SEND
	pauciflora	CCCN CDoC CSBt CTsd ELan EUJe MGos NLar SPer
§	- subsp. ***debeuzevillei***	CDoC CDul EPfP EWes LMaj MGos SBig
	- var. ***nana***	see *E. gregsoniana*
§	- subsp. ***niphophila*** ♀H4	Widely available
	- subsp. ***pauciflora***	SEND
	perriniana	CBcs CCCN CCVT CDul CMHG CSBt CWCL EBee ELan EPfP EUJe LRHS MBri MGos MWat MWhi NEgg SBfd SBig SCoo SHil SLim SPer SPlb SPoG SWvt WFar
	pulverulenta	CMac ETod SPlb
	- 'Baby Blue'	EBee LHop NLar SPer SPoG SWvt
	rodwayi	WWau
	rossii	SPlb
	rubida	CCCN CMHG
	sideroxylon	SPlb
	- 'Rosea'	SPlb
	stuartiana	see *E. bridgesiana*
	subcrenulata	CTrC ELan EPfP GLin
	tetraptera	SPlb
	torquata	SPlb
	urnigera	CDoC LHop
	viminalis	LRHS WWau

Eucharidium see *Clarkia*

Eucharis (*Amaryllidaceae*)

§	***amazonica*** ♀H1	CCCN ECho GHim LAma SDeJ SPav
	grandiflora misapplied	see *E. amazonica*

Eucodonia (*Gesneriaceae*)

	'Adele'	EABi

Eucomis ✿ (*Asparagaceae*)

	AlohaPBR	see *E.* 'Leia'
	autumnalis misapplied	see *E. zambesiaca*
§	***autumnalis*** (Mill.) Chitt. ♀H2-3	CAvo CBro CDes CHEx CTsd EBee ECho EPot ERCP LAma LRHS SDeJ SPav SPer SPlb SWal WHil WTin
	- subsp. ***autumnalis*** 'Peace Candles'	CTca
	bicolor ♀H2-3	Widely available
	- 'Alba'	CAvo CPLG CTca EAmu EBee ECho EPot LAma LRHS
	- 'Stars and Stripes'	WCru
	'Cabernet Candles'	CTca
§	***comosa***	CAvo CBro CHEx CHll CPrp CSam CTca EBee ERCP EShb LAma LEdu LRHS NRHS SDeJ SMad SPav WHil WTin WWEG
	- 'Cornwood'	CAvo CTca WHil
	- 'First Red'	CDes WPGP
	- green-leaved	CTca
	- 'Kilimanjaro'	CTca
	- 'Lotte'	CTca
	- 'Oakhurst'	CBct ECtt ESwi GBin LBuc LHop WHil
	- purple-leaved	CAvo EShb
	- 'Sparkling Burgundy'	Widely available
	- 'Sparkling Rosy' **new**	EBee WFar
	- var. ***striata***	CDes
	'Frank Lawley'	CDes
	humilis	CTca
	- 'Twinkle Stars'	EBee
	hybrid	SDix
	'John Huxtable' **new**	GCal
	'John Treasure'	SMHy WHil
	'Joy's Purple'	CBro CPar CTca EPri LRHS
§	'Leia'PBR	CTca LRHS
	montana	CBro CPar CPrp CTca EBee LAma WCot WPGP
	- hybrids	CTca
	pallidiflora ♀H4	CAvo CGHE CHEx LEdu SMHy WPGP
	'Pink Gin' **new**	CAvo
	pole-evansii	CBro CCon CDes CPLG CPar CPne CTca CTrC EAEE EAmu EBee ELan EPri ERCP EUJe IGor IVic LAma LHop LRHS MMHG MRav SDeJ SMrm WCru WHil WTin WWEG
	- 'Burgundy'	GBin
I	- 'Purpurea'	CPLG EBee GCal
	punctata	see *E. comosa*
	regia	CTca
	- JCA 3.230.709	WCot
*	***reichenbachii***	CDTJ
	'Swazi Pride'	CTca WHil
	undulata	see *E. autumnalis* (Mill.) Chitt.
	vandermerwei	CAvo CBro CDes CFwr CTca EBee EPot ERCP LAma LWst SDeJ SKHP WPGP
	- 'Octopus'	CCCN CJun CKno CPLG CPrp CTca EAmu EBee ELan EPfP ESwi EUJe LRHS LSou LWst MAvo MGos SBfd SMad SPad SPer WCot WFar WWEG
§	***zambesiaca***	CPrp CTca GCal SMHy WHil WWEG
	- JCA 3.230.709	WCot
	- 'White Dwarf'	ECho EShb LBMP SPer WFar
	'Zeal Bronze'	CGHE CMHG CTca ELan EPfP GCal GCra LRHS NSti WHrl

Eucommia (*Eucommiaceae*)

	ulmoides	CCCN CDul CMCN EBtc EPfP IArd IDee NLar WPGP

Eucrosia (*Amaryllidaceae*)

	bicolor	LAma

Eucryphia ✿ (*Cunoniaceae*)

	cordifolia	CAbP CBcs CGHE CMac CWib GKin LAst MBlu

- Crarae hardy form GGGa
§ ***cordifolia* × *lucida*** CBcs CCCN ELan MSnd SLdr SPer
glutinosa ♀H4 CBcs CCCN EPfP GGGa GKev GKin LRHS MAsh SPer SSpi WFar
- 'Miniature' EBee EPfP SChF WPGP
× ***hillieri*** WSpi
- 'Winton' CMHG GQui
× ***intermedia*** CMac CPLG CTrC CWSG ELan EPfP GKin LRHS NLar SLdr SRms SSpi WFar
- 'Rostrevor' ♀H3 CBcs CDul CMHG CMac CPLG CTho EBee ELan EPfP GBin GGGa GQui IVic LRHS LSRN MAsh MBlu MGos NHim NLar NRHS SReu SSta WFar WSHC WSpi
'Leatherwood Cream' GKin WSpi
lucida CCCN CDoC CTho CTrC ELan IArd NHim NLar WFar WSpi
- 'Ballerina' CMHG CMac CTho EBee ELon GKin LRHS MAsh MGos SCoo SPoG SSpi SSta WFar WPGP
- 'Dumpling' CGHE CPLG WPGP
- 'Gilt Edge' (v) CBcs CTrC CWGN GKin LLHF LRHS
- 'Pink Cloud' CBcs CDoC CDul CGHE CMac CPLG CTho CTrC EBee ELan EPfP EWTr GGGa GKin GQui IVic LHop LRHS LSRN MBlu NLar SLdr SLim SPer SSpi SSta SWvt WFar WPGP
- 'Pink Whisper' see *E. milliganii* subsp. *pubescens* 'Pink Whisper'
- 'Spring Glow' (v) CTrC CWGN EBee LLHF LRHS MAsh NHim SPoG
milliganii CAbP CDoC CMac CTrC EBee ELan EPfP GGGa GQui IVic LHop LRHS MBlu SBrt SRms SSpi WPGP
§ - subsp. ***pubescens*** 'Pink Whisper' NHim WPGP
moorei CBcs CCCN CMac CPLG GGGa GQui IVic MMuc NHim SSpi
× ***nymansensis*** CHab CWib LSRN SReu SRms SSpi
- 'George Graham' CMHG GGGa
- 'Nymans Silver' (v) EBee ELan GGGa LLHF LRHS MAsh NHim SPoG SSpi WPat
- 'Nymansay' ♀H3 Widely available
'Penwith' misapplied see *E. cordifolia* × *lucida*
'Penwith' ambig. CDoC CTsd GKin GQui MMuc SEND SPer

Eugenia (*Myrtaceae*)

uniflora CCCN

Eunomia see *Aethionema*

Euodia (*Rutaceae*)

daniellii see *Tetradium daniellii*
hupehensis see *Tetradium daniellii* Hupehense Group

Euonymus ✿ (*Celastraceae*)

B&L 12543 EWes
CC 4522 CPLG
alatus ♀H4 Widely available
- B&SWJ 8794 WCru
- var. ***apterus*** EPfP SPoG WGrn
- - B&SWJ 11051 WCru
- Chicago Fire see *E. alatus* 'Timber Creek'
- 'Compactus' ♀H4 Widely available
§ - 'Fire Ball' CJun EPfP
* - 'Macrophyllus' CJun EPfP
- 'Rudy Haag' CJun EPfP NLar
- 'Select' see *E. alatus* 'Fire Ball'
- 'Silver Cloud' CJun EPfP
§ - 'Timber Creek' CJun EPfP LLHF MBlu NLar WPat
americanus EPfP MBlu NLar
- 'Evergreen' EPfP
- narrow-leaved CJun EPfP
atropurpureus EPfP
bungeanus EPfP WPat
- 'Dart's Pride' CJun EPfP NLar
- 'Fireflame' CJun EPfP WPat
* - var. ***mongolicus*** EPfP
- 'Pendulus' CJun EPfP MBlu SCoo
- var. ***semipersistens*** CJun
carnosus CJun EPfP
chibae B&SWJ 11159 WCru
'Copper Wire' EHoe
cornutus CDul CJun CMCN ELan EPfP GKev
var. ***quinquecornutus*** IDee IGor MBlu MMHG NLar WPGP WPat
'Den Haag' CJun EPfP NLar
echinatus EPfP
europaeus Widely available
- from Slovakia **new** WCru
- f. ***albus*** CJun CTho EPfP NLar
- 'Atropurpureus' CMCN CTho EPfP
- 'Atrorubens' CJun
- 'Aucubifolius' (v) CMac
* - 'Aureus' CNat
- 'Brilliant' CJun EPfP NLar
* - f. ***bulgaricus*** EPfP
- 'Chrysophyllus' EPfP MBlu
- 'Howard' EPfP
- var. ***intermedius*** CJun EPfP MBlu MBri NLar
- 'Red Cascade' ♀H4 Widely available
- 'Scarlet Wonder' CJun EPfP
- 'Thornhayes' CTho EPfP NLar
I - 'Variegatus' (v) EPfP
europeaus 'Pumilis' EPfP
farreri see *E. nanus*
fimbriatus CJun EPfP SEND
fortunei LEdu NWad
- Blondy = 'Interbolwi'PBR (v) CDoC CDul CTri CWSG CWib EBee ECrN ELan EPfP LAst LRHS MAsh MBri MGos MRav MSwo NEgg NHol NLar NPri NWad SBfd SCoo SEND SGol SLim SPer SPoG
- 'Canadale Gold' (v) EBee EPfP LRHS MAsh NHol NPri SLon SPoG WFar
- 'Coloratus' CMac EBee EPfP MBlu MSwo SEND SPer
- 'Dart's Blanket' CDul EBee ELan EPPr MRav SEND
- 'Emerald Cushion' CDul
- 'Emerald Gaiety' (v) ♀H4 Widely available
- 'Emerald 'n' Gold' (v) ♀H4 Widely available
- 'Emerald Surprise' (v) ♀H4 EPfP SRGP
- 'Gold Spot' see *E. fortunei* 'Sunspot'
- 'Gold Tip' see *E. fortunei* 'Golden Prince'
- 'Golden Harlequin' (v) CSBt LRHS MAsh NWad SPoG
§ - 'Golden Pillar' (v) EHoe
§ - 'Golden Prince' (v) CMac EHoe MRav MSwo SRms
- Goldy = 'Waldbolwi'PBR LRHS MGos NLar SGol SHil
- 'Harlequin' (v) CBar CBcs CDul CMac CSBt CWGN CWSG EBee EHoe ELan ELon EPfP EShb LBuc LRHS LSRN MAsh MBlu

		MGos MRav NBir NPro SBfd SGol SLim SPer SRms SWvt WFar
	- 'Hort's Blaze'	EPPr
	- 'Kewensis'	CDoC CHid CMac CWib EBee EUJe GCal GEdr LRHS MWhi SPoG WCru
	- 'Longwood' **new**	EBee
	- 'Minimus'	CDul CTri EPPr NPro XLum
*	- 'Minimus Variegatus' (v)	ECho EPPr EShb SPlb
§	- var. ***radicans***	EWld
	- 'Sheridan Gold'	CMac CTri MRav NWad SBod
	- 'Silver Gem'	see *E. fortunei* 'Variegatus'
	- 'Silver Pillar' (v)	EHoe WFar
	- 'Silver Queen' (v)	Widely available
	- 'Silverstone' PBR (v)	EPfP LRHS NPro SPoG
	- 'Sunshine' (v)	ELan EPfP LRHS MAsh NWad SLon SPoG
§	- 'Sunspot' (v)	CBcs CMac ELan MGos MSwo SEND SRms WFar WHar WRHF
	- 'Tustin' ♀H4	EPPr LTen
§	- 'Variegatus' (v)	SRms
	- 'Wolong Ghost'	CDoC CPLG EBee EMil GKin IArd IDee LRHS MBlu MGos NRHS SGol SKHP WCot
	frigidus	EPfP
	grandiflorus	CJun EPfP NLar SCoo WFar
	- 'Red Wine'	CJun CTho ELon EMil EPfP LHop LRHS SEND SKHP WPGP WPat
	- f. ***salicifolius***	CJun EPfP
	hamiltonianus	CMCN EBee EBtc ECrN EPfP SEND SSpi
	- 'Fiesta'	CJun EPfP
	- subsp. ***hians***	see *E. hamiltonianus* subsp. *sieboldianus*
	- 'Indian Summer'	CJun ELon EPfP LRHS MBri MMHG NLar SCoo SKHP SPoG SSpi WPGP WPat
	- 'Koi Boy'	CJun
	- 'Miss Pinkie'	CDul CJun EPfP IVic MGos NLar SCoo WPat
	- 'Pink Delight'	CJun
	- 'Poort Bulten'	CJun EPfP NLar
	- 'Popcorn'	CJun EPfP WPat
	- 'Rainbow'	CJun EPfP
	- 'Red Chief'	CJun EPfP NLar
	- 'Red Elf'	CJun EPfP NLar
	- 'Rising Sun'	CJun EBee EPfP MBri NLar
§	- subsp. ***sieboldianus***	CDul CJun CMen CPLG CTho EPfP MRav NPCo SLPl WFar WPat
	- - B&SWJ 10941	WCru
	- - 'Calocarpus'	CJun EPfP SCoo
	- - 'Coral Charm'	CJun EPfP NLar
	- - var. ***sanguineus*** B&SWJ 11140	WCru
	- - - B&SWJ 11386	WCru
	- - Semiexsertus Group	EPfP
*	- - var. ***yedoensis*** f. ***koehneanus***	EPfP
	- 'Snow'	CJun EPfP WPat
	- 'Winter Glory'	CJun MMHG NLar WPat
	- var. ***yedoensis***	see *E. hamiltonianus* subsp. *sieboldianus*
	japonicus	CBcs CCVT CDoC CDul CMac CTri ECrN EPfP SBfd SBod SEND SEWo SPer
	- 'Albomarginatus'	CBcs CDul CTri EHoe EPfP LRHS SEND SRms
§	- 'Aureomarginatus' **new**	CWCL LRHS
	- 'Aureopictus'	see *E. japonicus* 'Aureus'

	- 'Aureovariegatus'	see *E. japonicus* 'Ovatus Aureus'
§	- 'Aureus' (v)	CBcs CDoC CSBt CWib EBee LAst LRHS LTen NPri SCoo SLon SPer WHar
	- 'Benkomasaki'	EPfP
	- 'Bravo'	CDoC CDul EBee EHoe EPfP IVic LRHS LTen MAsh MGos NLar NRHS SBfd SCoo SEWo SHil SLim SPer SPoG SWvt WFar
	- 'Chollipo' ♀H4	EBee ELan EPfP LRHS MAsh SBfd SEND SHil SPoG
	- 'Compactus'	SCoo
	- 'Duc d'Anjou' misapplied	see *E. japonicus* 'Viridivariegatus'
	- 'Duc d'Anjou' Carrière (v)	CBcs EBee EHoe ELan EPfP EWes MRav SBfd SEND SPoG
	- 'Elegantissimus Aureus'	see *E. japonicus* 'Aureomarginatus'
	- Exstase = 'Goldbolwi' PBR (v)	SPoG WCot
	- 'Francien' (v)	LBuc LRHS SHil
	- 'Gold Queen' PBR	LRHS
	- 'Golden Maiden'	ELan EPfP LRHS MAsh SLim SLon SPoG SWvt
	- 'Golden Pillar'	see *E. fortunei* 'Golden Pillar'
	- 'Green Rocket'	EBee EPfP EShb LRHS MBri SBfd SGol SHil SPoG
	- 'Green Spider'	SPoG
	- 'Grey Beauty'	ELon EShb NLar
	- 'Hibarimisake'	EPfP
	- 'Kathy' PBR	EPfP LRHS NLar SHil SPoG SRGP
§	- 'Latifolius Albomarginatus' (v)	ELan EPfP MRav MSwo SBfd SPer
	- 'Luna'	see *E. japonicus* 'Aureus'
	- 'Macrophyllus Albus'	see *E. japonicus* 'Latifolius Albomarginatus'
	- 'Maiden's Gold'	CSBt EBee
	- 'Marieke'	see *E. japonicus* 'Ovatus Aureus'
	- 'Mediopictus'	SEND
	- 'Microphyllus'	CDoC MRav SBfd WFar
§	- 'Microphyllus Albovariegatus' (v)	CBcs CDoC CDul CMac CMea CSBt CTri CWSG ELan EPfP LAst LBMP LRHS MGos SBfd SEND SHil SLim SPoG SRms SWvt WFar
§	- 'Microphyllus Aureovariegatus' (v)	CDoC ELan EPfP LRHS MAsh NLar SBfd SEND
	- 'Microphyllus Aureus'	see *E. japonicus* 'Microphyllus Pulchellus'
§	- 'Microphyllus Pulchellus' (v)	CBcs CDoC CMac CSBt EBee ECrN EPfP LRHS LTen MAsh MGos SBfd SHil SWvt
	- 'Microphyllus Variegatus'	see *E. japonicus* 'Microphyllus Albovariegatus'
§	- 'Ovatus Aureus' (v) ♀H4	CBar CDoC CDul CMac CPLG CSBt CTri CWSG EBee ELon EPfP LAst LRHS MGos MNHC MRav NLar SBfd SEND SGol SHil SLim SPer SPlb SPoG SRms SWvt WFar
	- 'Président Gauthier' (v)	CBar CDoC EBee LTen MGos SBfd SCoo SLim SPer SWvt WCFE
	- 'Pulchellus Aureovariegatus'	see *E. japonicus* 'Microphyllus Aureovariegatus'
I	- 'Pyramidatus'	EPfP
	- 'Robustus'	EPfP
	- 'Rokujo'	GEdr
	- 'Silver King'	CMac
	- 'Silver Krista' (v)	NLar SPoG
	- 'Susan' (v)	CDoC CMac EShb MAsh SRGP
§	- 'Viridivariegatus' (v)	LRHS
	kachinensis B&SWJ 11668	WCru

kiautschovicus EPfP
- 'Berry Hill' EPfP NLar
- 'Manhattan' EPfP NLar
latifolius CJun CMCN EPfP WPat
lucidus CHll CPLG IRar SSpi WFar
maackii GKin NWea
macropterus CJun EPfP
maximowiczianus EPfP WCot WPat
morrisonensis EPfP
- B&SWJ 3700 WCru
myrianthus CJun EPfP EWes MAsh MBlu NLar
§ ***nanus*** CJun CWib EPfP NLar WRHF WThu
- var. ***turkestanicus*** EBee EPfP GKin LHop LRHS SLon SRms WOld
obovatus EPfP NLar
occidentalis EPfP
oresbius EPfP
oxyphyllus CDul CJun CMCN CTho EPfP IArd NLar SEND WCru WPat
- 'Angyo Elegant' (v) EPfP
- 'Waasland' CJun EPfP
pauciflorus EPfP
phellomanus ΨH4 CTho EBee EPfP EWTr GKin IDee LHop LRHS MBlu MGos MPkF MRav NLar SCoo SEND SKHP WFar WPGP
- 'Silver Surprise' (v) CJun ELon EPfP WPat
Pierrolino = 'Heespierrolino'PBR LRHS MRav NWad SCoo
§ ***planipes*** ΨH4 Widely available
- 'Dart's August Flame' CJun EPfP
- 'Gold Ore' EPfP
- 'Sancho' CJun EPfP WPat
quelpaertensis EPfP
radicans see *E. fortunei* var. *radicans*
'Rokojō' LLHF WPat
'Rokojō Variegated' (v) WCot
rongchuensis CJun EPfP
rosmarinifolius see *E. nanus*
sachalinensis misapplied see *E. planipes*
sachalinensis (F. Schmidt) Maxim. B&SWJ 10835 **new** WCru
sacrosanctus CJun EPfP NLar
sanguineus CJun EPfP NLar SSpi
spraguei EPfP
- CWJ 12446 WCru
theifolius GWJ 9377 WCru
tingens CJun EPfP NLar
trapococcus EPfP
vagans EPfP WCot
verrucosus CJun NLar
vidalii EPfP
yedoensis see *E. hamiltonianus* subsp. *sieboldianus*

Eupatoriadelphus see *Eupatorium*

Eupatorium ✿ (*Asteraceae*)

B&SWJ 9052 from Guatemala WCru
album misapplied see *Ageratina altissima*
album L. NBid SWat
altissimum SRms
aromaticum see *Ageratina aromatica*
atrorubens see *Bartlettina sordida*
cannabinum CArn CHab CWan EBee EGHP EHon ELan EShb GPoy IFoB LPBA MBNS MHer MMuc MNHC MRav NBir NMir NPer SEND SPav SWat WHfH WPer WSFF
§ - f. ***albiflorum*** SPhx
- 'Album' see *E. cannabinum* f. *albiflorum*
- f. ***cannabinum*** 'Flore Pleno' (d) CMac CPrp CSev EBee ECha ECtt ELan ELon EPfP LHop LRHS MBel MHer MRav NBir NDov NEgg NGdn SAga SPhx SWat WAul WCot WFar WMnd WPtf WSFF WTin XLum
- - 'Spraypaint' (v) WSFF
capillifolium ΨH3 CSpe EBee ECtt ESwi EWes LHop LSou SAga SDix SHar SMad SMrm SUsu WCot WWEG
chinense CSpe
coelestinum see *Conoclinium coelestinum*
dubium 'Baby Joe'PBR CWGN EBee NPnk
- 'Little Joe' CKno EBee EPPr NPnk
fistulosum f. ***albidum*** 'Bartered Bride' CKno EBee ECtt EWes GCal LRHS WHil
- - 'Ivory Towers' **new** WWEG
- - 'Massive White' ΨH4 CCon GCal NBir NSti
- 'Berggarten' EBee GCal
- 'Carin' WSFF
fortunei CArn
- 'Fine Line' (v) CKno EPPr LSou MHer WSFF WWEG
- 'Pink Elegance' (v) EBee EShb LRHS SPoG
- 'Pink Frost' (v) NLar
hyssopifolium LRHS
japonicum GPoy
ligustrinum see *Ageratina ligustrina*
lindleyanum CKno
maculatum MDKP NGdn NLar NPnk WHrl
- Atropurpureum Group ΨH4 Widely available
- - 'Gateway' EBee GCal LRHS NBre NLar WHil WHoo WPtf WSFF WTin
- - 'Glutball' CKno EBee ELon GCal LBMP LPla LRHS MNrw NChi NRHS SMad
- - 'Little Red' GBin WSFF
- - 'Orchard Dene' ΨH4 SMHy
- - 'Phantom'PBR EBee ECtt GQue IPot LRHS MBri MWts NCGa NLar SSvw WPtf
- - 'Purple Bush' ΨH4 CKno EBee ECha ECtt ELon EPPr GBee GBin GCal GQue LRHS MDKP NBre NEgg NPnk SPad SPhx SSvw WCAu WSFF WWEG
- - 'Red Dwarf' **new** MSCN NOrc WHil
- - 'Riesenschirm' ΨH4 Widely available
makinoi var. ***oppositifolium*** B&SWJ 8449 WCru
micranthum see *Ageratina ligustrina*
occidentale see *Ageratina occidentalis*
perfoliatum CArn CKno EBee GPoy LRHS MNrw NBre NLar SPav SPhx WSFF
purpureum Widely available
- 'Album' CTri MBel SPhx
rugosum see *Ageratina altissima*
variabile 'Golders Green' (v) EWes WWEG
weinmannianum see *Ageratina ligustrina*

Euphorbia ✿ (*Euphorbiaceae*)

'Abbey Dore' WCot
ambovombensis LToo
amygdaloides ECtt SWat SWvt
- 'Bob's Choice' EWes
- 'Craigieburn' CDes EWes GBuc GCra LRHS MAsh MGos MRav NDov SUsu WPGP WWEG

	Name	Suppliers
	- 'Frosted Flame'[PBR] **new**	CSpe MPnt WCot
§	- 'Purpurea'	Widely available
§	- var. ***robbiae*** ♀H4	Widely available
	- - dwarf	EWes
	- - 'Pom Pom'	EBee LSou WPGP
	- - 'Redbud'	EWes LSou SLPl
	- 'Rubra'	see *E. amygdaloides* 'Purpurea'
	- 'Winter Glow'	CSpe
	- yellow-leaved	WCot
	baselicis	CPom CSpe WPer
	biglandulosa Desf.	see *E. rigida*
	Blackbird = 'Nothowlee'[PBR]	Widely available
	'Blue Dome'	CSpe
	'Blue Haze'	CDes CPom EBee LRHS MAvo MGos NWit WCot WPGP
	caerulescens	LToo
	canariensis	EPfP
	capitulata	EPot EWes
	cashmeriana	NWit WCot
	- CC&McK 607	EWes
	ceratocarpa	CGHE CSpe EBee ECtt EWes GMaP LPla LRHS LSou NEgg NWit SEND SMad WCot WPGP WSHC
	characias	CBcs CHEx CMac CWCL EBee ECtt EHrv EPfP LRHS MCot MLHP MRav NPer SBfd SMrm SPer SRms SWvt WBrk WCot WMnd WPer WWEG XLum XSen
	- 'Black Pearl'	CBcs CWCL EBee ECtt EHrv EPfP LAst LHop LRHS MBri MGos MPnt NEgg NLBP NPnk NRHS SBfd SBod SHil SMrm SPer SPoG SPtl SWvt WFar WSpi WWEG
	- 'Blue Wonder'	CMac CPLG EBee ECtt EHrv ELan EPfP GAbr GMaP LRHS LSou MAvo MCot MGos NCGa NEgg NGdn NLar NSti NWit SPad WCot WWEG
	- subsp. ***characias***	GMaP SEND
	- - 'Blue Hills'	ECtt WWEG
	- - 'Burrow Silver' (v)	CCon EBee LDai LHop LSRN MRav NEgg SMrm SPer SWvt WFar
	- - 'Humpty Dumpty'	CPLG CSev EBee ECtt EHrv ELan EPfP GMaP LBMP LRHS LSRN MBri MGos MWat NDov NGdn NLar NPer SBfd SPer SRms SWvt WCot WFar WWEG
	- 'Dwarf Black Pearl'	ECtt WWEG
	- 'Forescate'	CMac CSev EBee EPfP GBin LHop LRHS LSRN SBfd WWEG
	- 'Glacier Blue'	LRHS
	- 'Goldbrook'	CWCL ECtt EHoe GBin LRHS MRav NCGa NDov NGdn WSpi
	- 'Kestrel' (v)	MAvo WCot
	- 'Portuguese Velvet' ♀H4	Widely available
	- Silver Swan = 'Wilcott'[PBR] (v)	Widely available
	- 'Spring Splendour'	EWes LRHS
	- 'Starbright'	EBee
	- 'Tasmanian Tiger'[PBR] (v)	CMac CSpe CWCL CWGN EUJe EWes LHop LRHS LSou MAsh MAvo MGos MPnt NBir NRHS NWit SBfd SKHP SPoG SRkn SWvt WCot
	- 'Variegata' (v)	MAvo
	- subsp. ***wulfenii*** ♀H3-4	Widely available
	- - 'Bosahan' (v)	CBcs CPLG
	- - 'Emmer Green' (v)	CPLG EBee EHrv ELon EPfP EWes GAbr GMaP LRHS LSou MAvo MBel MMHG NPnk NSti NWit SMrm WCot WWEG
	- - 'Jimmy Platt'	SRms WCot
§	- - 'John Tomlinson' ♀H3-4	EHrv EWes LSRN MRav SUsu WSpi
	- - Kew form	see *E. characias* subsp. *wulfenii* 'John Tomlinson'
	- - 'Lambrook Gold' ♀H3-4	CSam CWCL EPfP GCra LRHS MRav NLar NPer SMad WCot WMnd WWEG
	- - 'Lambrook Gold' seed-raised	see *E. characias* subsp. *wulfenii* Margery Fish Group
	- - 'Lambrook Yellow'	EBee WSpi
§	- - Margery Fish Group	CMac CWCL EBee LRHS NBir NCGa SPer
	- - 'Perry's Tangerine'	EWes NPer NWit
§	- - 'Purple and Gold'	EWes GMaP MAvo NLar NWit SWvt WWEG
	- - 'Purpurea'	see *E. characias* subsp. *wulfenii* 'Purple and Gold'
	- - 'Silver Shadow'	WCot
	- - 'Thelma's Giant'	MAvo NWit
	- - 'Westacre Giant'	EWes
	clavarioides var. ***truncata***	WCot
	'Copton Ash'	CSpe EBee EPPr EWes MAvo SKHP XSen
	corallioides	EBee ECha GAbr GKev IFro LRHS NPer NSti SPav WHer
§	***cornigera*** ♀H4	ECha EPfP GBuc LRHS MCot MMuc MRav MSpe NBid NGdn NSti NWit SEND SPhx SWat WAul WCru
	- 'Goldener Turm'	EAEE EBee ECtt ESwi GAbr GBin GBuc GCal LPla LRHS LSou MBNS MNrw NDov NWit SDix SMrm SPer WCot
	corollata	EBee
	croizatii	LToo
	cylindrifolia var. ***tubifera***	LToo
	cyparissias	CBcs EBee ECha ELan LRHS MLHP MRav NBir NGdn NLar NMen SBfd SPav SRms WBrk WCot WFar WPer XLum XSen
	- 'Baby'	WFar
	- 'Betten'	see *E. × gayeri* 'Betten'
	- 'Bushman Boy'	SMrm
	- 'Clarice Howard'	see *E. cyparissias* 'Fens Ruby'
§	- 'Fens Ruby'	Widely available
	- 'Orange Man'	CTca EBee ECtt EPfP EWes LBMP LRHS LSou NBro NEgg NGdn NLar SMrm SPoG SWat SWvt WBrk WFar WWEG
	- 'Purpurea'	see *E. cyparissias* 'Fens Ruby'
	- 'Red Devil'	NWit SMrm WWEG
	- 'Tall Boy'	EWes SMrm
	decaryi var. ***spirosticha***	LToo
	deflexa	CDes EBee EWes MAvo
	'Despina'[PBR]	LRHS
§	***donii***	EWes MAvo NWit SDix
	- HWJK 2405	WCru
	- 'Amjillasa'	SAga SBrt SDix SMHy
	dulcis	CBre ECtt NBro NWit
	- 'Chameleon'	Widely available
	'Efanthia'[PBR]	CKno CSev EBee EPfP EWes LAst LHop LRHS LSou NLar NPri SMrm SRot
	enopla	EPfP
	enormis	LToo
	epithymoides	see *E. polychroma*
	esculenta	LToo
	esula Baker's form	NWit

	Excalibur = 'Froeup'PBR ♀H4	CKno CMac CPLG CWCL EBee ELan ELon EPPr GBin IVic LHop LRHS MBNS MBri MMuc MNrw MRav NBir NEgg NLar SBfd SEND SPer SPoG WSpi
	flavicoma	GCal WSHC
	fragifera	NWit
§	× ***gayeri*** 'Betten'	EBee LPla
	glauca	ECou NWit SKHP
	'Golden Foam'	see *E. stricta*
	griffithii	CHll IFoB NBro SPav SWat WFar WMoo
	- 'Dixter' ♀H4	Widely available
	- 'Dixter Flame'	IFoB NWit
	- 'Fern Cottage'	CElw EWes MSpe WMnd WWEG
	- 'Fireglow'	Widely available
	- 'King's Caple'	ELon EWes NLar SPoG WCru WSpi
	- 'Wickstead'	COlW GBin MLHP NLar WSpi
	groenewaldii	LToo
	'Helena'PBR (v)	CPLG EPPr EPfP LHop LRHS LSRN NLar NPnk SRot SWvt WHil
	horrida ♀H1	SPlb
	hyberna	NMen SWat
	hypericifolia Diamond Frost = 'Inneuphe'PBR	CCVN CSpe ESwi LHop LSou SRkn WCot
	ingens	CAbb SPlb
	jacquemontii	IFoB NChi NLar NWit
	'Jade Dragon'	EBee LRHS SBfd SWvt WWEG
	'Jessie'	NCGa
	jolkinii	CPLG
	Kalipso = 'Innkalff'	NLar SRot
	knuthii	LToo
	'Lambrook Silver'	SRkn
	lathyris	CArn CBre LRHS MHer MLHP NLar NPer NWit SRms SVic
	longifolia misapplied	see *E. cornigera*
	longifolia D. Don	see *E. donii*
	longifolia Lam.	see *E. mellifera*
	margalidiana	EWes MAvo NWit
	× ***martini*** ♀H3	Widely available
	- 'Aperitif'PBR	EPfP EUJe MNHC SMrm
	- 'Ascot Rainbow'	EBee EPfP EWes LBuc LRHS MAsh MBri NCGa SHar SHil SPoG WSpi
	- 'Baby Charm'	CTrC CWCL EAEE EBee EWll GKin IPot LRHS LSRN MAvo MBri NDov NGdn NPnk NPri SMrm
	- 'Cherokee'	WCot
	- dwarf	CCon
	- 'Helen Robinson'	MAvo WCot WPGP
	- Helena's Blush = 'Inneuphhel' (v)	EPfP EWll
	- 'Kolibri'	EBee EPfP NLar SPoG SWvt
	- 'Little John'	LBuc LRHS MBri SHil
	- Rudolph = 'Waleuphrud'	EPfP LRHS
	- 'Tiny Tim'	EBee ELon EPPr EPfP GBin LRHS LSRN MAsh SBfd SPoG SWvt
§	***mellifera*** ♀H3	Widely available
	meloformis ♀H1	LToo
	milii ♀H1	EBak
	moratii	LToo
	myrsinites ♀H4	Widely available
	- red-tinged	see *E. myrsinites* 'Washfield'
§	- 'Washfield' **new**	SBrt
	nereidum	EWes NWit
	nicaeensis	EBee GCal LPla LRHS MSpe SEND SPer SPhx XSen
	- subsp. ***glareosa***	NWit
	obesa ♀H1 **new**	LToo
	oblongata	EWes LRHS NWit SEND
	palustris ♀H4	Widely available
	- 'Walenburg's Glorie'	CMHG CWCL EBee ECha ELan EWTr GQue IBoy MAvo MBri MNrw MRav NMRc NSti NWit SMad SWat WKif
	- 'Zauberflöte'	SRms
	× ***paradoxa***	NWit
	paralias	GCal WCot WHer
	× ***pasteurii***	CCon CDTJ EUJe EWes LSou MAvo MNrw MSpe NBir NWit SDix SMad SPhx WCot WPGP WTou
	- 'Devil's Honey'	CHid
	- 'John Phillips'	CGHE CMHG CPLG CPom EBee EPfP IVic LRHS SBfd SChF WPGP WSpi
	- 'Phrampton Phatty'	WPGP
	pekinensis	SKHP
	perangusta	LToo
	persistens	LToo
	pilosa 'Major'	see *E. polychroma* 'Major'
	pithyusa	CSpe EBee ECha ELan EPfP MRav SEND WCot WPer WSHC XSen
	platyclada	LToo
§	***polychroma*** ♀H4	Widely available
	- 'Bonfire'PBR	EBee ECtt LRHS MBri NCGa NLar
§	- 'Candy'	EBee ECha ECtt EPfP LRHS WMnd
	- compact	NWit
	- 'First Blush' (v)	EBee EWes NWit
	- 'Golden Fusion'	EPfP LBuc LRHS MAsh MAvo MBri NRHS SHil WFar
§	- 'Lacy' (v)	CDoC EBee EWes GCal LRHS NBir NGdn NWit SKHP
§	- 'Major' ♀H4	CPLG LRHS WCot WKif
	- 'Midas'	CWCL MAvo MNrw NWit SDix SMrm
	- 'Purpurea'	see *E. polychroma* 'Candy'
*	- 'Senior'	LRHS MAvo NWit
	- 'Sonnengold'	EWes LRHS
	- 'Variegata'	see *E. polychroma* 'Lacy'
	portlandica	NWit WHer
§	× ***pseudovirgata***	NWit
	pulvinata	LToo
	'Red Flush'	EPfP LRHS
	Redwing = 'Charam'PBR ♀H4	CBcs CMac EBee ELan EPfP IKil LBuc LRHS LSou MAsh MAvo MBri MGos MRav NDov NLar NWit SCoo SLim SPer SPoG SWvt
	reflexa	see *E. seguieriana* subsp. *niciciana*
§	***rigida*** ♀H4	CBro CFis EHoe EHrv ELan EPfP EUJe EWes LPla LRHS MAvo MSpe SMrm SPhx WFar WPGP WPer WSpi WWEG XSen
	- 'Sardis'	NWit
	robbiae	see *E. amygdaloides* var. *robbiae*
	rothiana GWJ 9479a	WCru
	'Roundway Titan'	EBee LRHS SSpi WSHC
	sarawschanica	ECha GQue LPla LRHS NWit SMad SPhx
	schillingii ♀H4	EBee EHoe ELan EPfP GCra GMaP LHop LRHS MAvo MBri MRav SBod SDix SMrm SPer SPhx SPlb SPoG SUsu SWvt WCru WFar WSpi WWEG
	schoenlandii	LToo
	seguieriana	ECha NLar WPer
§	- subsp. ***niciciana***	EBee GBin WHoo
	serrulata Thuill.	see *E. stricta*

	sikkimensis ♀H4	CMHG CPLG CPom CWCL EBee ECha ELan EWTr GCal LRHS NEgg NLar NPer SMrm SRms WCru WFar
	- 'Crûg Contrast'	WCru
	soongarica	NWit
	spinosa	NWit SPlb XSen
§	***stricta***	CPom LRHS MAvo SGar
	stygiana	CCon CPLG CSam CSpe ELon EShb EWes GBin GCal LRHS MAvo SMrm SPlb WCru
	- subsp. ***stygiana***	CGHE EBee WPGP
	symmetrica	LToo
	Thalia = 'Innthal'	EPfP LTen
	tirucalli	EShb
	tortirama	LToo
	umfoloziensis	LToo
	uralensis	see *E.* × *pseudovirgata*
	valdevillosocarpa	SPhx WPer
	'Velvet Ruby'	CSev EBee EWes LSRN LSou MAvo NWit SWvt WCot
	viguieri ♀H1	LToo
	villosa Waldst. & Kit. ex Willd.	NWit
§	***virgata***	EWes NWit
	× ***waldsteinii***	see *E. virgata*
	wallichii misapplied	see *E. donii*
	wallichii Kohli	see *E. cornigera*
	wallichii ambig.	CSam MRav NPnk
	wallichii Hook. f.	CPLG EBee EPfP GCal MNrw NOrc SKHP
	- 'Lemon and Lime'	CWib
	'Whistleberry Garnet'	CMac CWCL EBee EPfP LBMP LLHF LRHS LSou NGdn NSti NWit SDix SKHP SPoG WWlt

Euptelea (*Eupteleaceae*)

	franchetii	see *E. pleiosperma*
§	***pleiosperma***	IArd IDee NLar SSpi
	polyandra	EPfP NLar SBrt

Eurya (*Pentaphylacaceae*)

japonica	WPGP
- 'Variegata' misapplied	see *Cleyera japonica* 'Fortunei'

Euryops (*Asteraceae*)

	abrotanifolius	CCCN
§	***acraeus*** ♀H4	CMea CSBt ECho EPfP EPot EWes GEdr LRHS MAsh MWat NMen SAga WAbe
§	***chrysanthemoides***	CCCN CDoC CHEx CTrC EShb SEND
	- 'Sonnenschein'	SPet
	evansii	see *E. acraeus*
	lateriflorus	SPlb
	linearis	SEND
	pectinatus ♀H2	CBcs CCCN CDTJ CDoC CHEx CPLG CTca CTrC CTri EBee EPfP EShb IVic LAst LRHS MNrw MOWG MRav SEND SGar SWvt WCFE WHer
	tysonii	CTca CTrC EWes GEdr SPlb WAbe
	virgineus	CCCN CDoC CPLG CTrC SPlb

Euscaphis (*Staphyleaceae*)

japonica	EGFP

Eustachys (*Poaceae*)

§	***distichophylla***	NWsh WTcb

Eustrephus (*Philesiaceae*)

latifolius	ECou

Eutaxia (*Papilionaceae*)

obovata	ECou

Euterpe (*Arecaceae*)

edulis	EAmu

Euthamia (*Asteraceae*)

gymnospermoides	EWes

Eutrochium see *Eupatorium*

Ewartia (*Asteraceae*)

planchonii	GEdr NRHS NSla WAbe

Exochorda (*Rosaceae*)

	alberti	see *E. korolkowii*
	giraldii var. ***wilsonii***	CMac CPLG EBee EPfP LHop LRHS MBlu MRav NLar SLim SSta SWvt
§	***korolkowii***	LRHS MAsh NLar
	× ***macrantha***	LRHS
	- 'Irish Pearl'	CPLG
	- 'The Bride' ♀H4	Widely available
	racemosa	EPfP MMuc NLar SPer
	serratifolia	CBcs EPfP LRHS SPoG
	- 'Snow White'	CJun EBee EWes GKin IArd MBlu NLar SBfd SLon SPoG

F

Fabiana (*Solanaceae*)

imbricata	CAbP ELon EPfP LLHF LRHS SLon SPer SPlb
- 'Prostrata'	CBcs EBee EPfP LRHS SSpi WRHF
- f. ***violacea*** ♀H3	CPLG CSBt CTri EBee EPfP LLHF LRHS MMuc SEND SPer WKif

Fagopyrum (*Polygonaceae*)

	cymosum	see *F. dibotrys*
§	***dibotrys***	EBee ECha ELan EWld

Fagus ✿ (*Fagaceae*)

§	***crenata***	CMen
	- 'Mount Fuji'	CMen LLHF SBir
	engleriana	CMCN CPLG SBir
	grandifolia	SBir
	subsp. ***mexicana***	
	japonica	SBir
	- var. ***multinervis***	SBir
	longipetiolata	CPLG
	lucida	CPLG
	orientalis	CMCN SBir
	- 'Iskander'	IArd MBlu
	sieboldii	see *F. crenata*
	sylvatica ♀H4	Widely available
§	- 'Albomarginata' (v)	CMCN
	- 'Albovariegata'	see *F. sylvatica* 'Albomarginata'
	- 'Ansorgei'	EBee LLHF MBlu MPkF NLar
	- 'Arcuata'	SBir
N	- Atropurpurea Group	Widely available
	- 'Aurea Pendula'	CMCN MBlu SBir WPat

	- 'Bicolor Sartini'	MBlu
	- 'Black Swan'	CLnd CMCN EBee ECrN IArd LLHF MAsh MBlu MGos NEgg NLar NPCo SBir SLon
	- 'Cochleata'	CMCN
	- 'Cockleshell'	MBlu MBri SBir
	- 'Cristata'	MBlu
N	- Cuprea Group	NWea
§	- 'Dawyck' ♕H4	CBcs CDoC CDul CLnd CMac CSBt CTho EBee ECrN ELan EPfP LAst LMaj MBri MGos NEgg NLar NPCo NWea SBir SGol SLau SLim SPer
	- 'Dawyck Gold' ♕H4	CBcs CDoC CDul CLnd CMCN CMac CTho CTri EBee GKin IVic LAst LMaj MAsh MBlu MBri MGos MSwo NEgg NPCo NWea SBir SGol SLau SLim SPer WFar
	- 'Dawyck Purple' ♕H4	CBcs CDoC CDul CLnd CMCN CMac CTho CTri CWib EBee EPfP EWTr GKin IVic LHop LSRN MAsh MBlu MBri MGos NEgg NLar NWea SBfd SBir SGol SLim SPer SPoG WFar
	- 'Eugen'	SBir
	- 'Fastigiata' misapplied	see *F. sylvatica* 'Dawyck'
	- 'Felderbach'	MBlu SBir
	- 'Franken' (v)	LLHF MBlu SBir
	- 'Greenwood'	LLHF MBlu
	- var. ***heterophylla***	CLnd CSBt CTho NWea
	- - 'Aspleniifolia' ♕H4	CBcs CDoC CDul CMCN CMac EBee ECrN ELan EPfP GKin MAsh MBlu MBri MGos NPCo SBir SCoo SLau SPer SPoG WFar WMou
	- - f. ***laciniata***	MBlu
	- 'Horizontalis'	MBlu
	- 'Incisa'	MBlu
	- 'Luteovariegata' (v)	CMCN
	- 'Mercedes'	CDoC CMCN LLHF MBlu NPCo WPat
N	- 'Pendula' ♕H4	CBcs CDoC CDul CLnd CMCN CSBt CTho EBee ECrN ELan EPfP LMaj MGos MSwo NEgg NPCo NWea SGol SLau SPer WHar WMou
	- 'Prince George of Crete'	CDul CMCN SBir
	- 'Purple Fountain' ♕H4	CDoC CDul CMCN EBee ELan LAst LHop LTen MAsh MBlu MBri MGos MWat NLar SBir SLau SLim WFar
	- Purple-leaved Group	see *F. sylvatica* Atropurpurea Group
	- 'Purpurea Latifolia'	EWTr LMaj
	- 'Purpurea Pendula'	CBcs CCVT CDul CMCN CSBt CTri CWib ELan EPfP GKin IVic LAst MAsh MBri MGos MSwo NEgg NPCo NWea SCoo SGol SLau SLim SPer SPoG WFar WHar
§	- 'Purpurea Tricolor' (v)	CDul CMCN ECrN MAsh MBlu MGos NWea SBir SCoo
	- 'Quercifolia'	MBlu
	- 'Red Obelisk'	see *F. sylvatica* 'Rohan Obelisk'
	- 'Riversii' ♕H4	CBcs CDoC CDul CLnd CMCN CTho CTri CWib ECrN ELan EPfP GKin LAst MAsh MBri MGos NEgg NWea SLim SPer SPoG WFar WHar
	- 'Rohan Gold'	CDul CMCN EBee MBlu
§	- 'Rohan Obelisk'	CDul CMCN CTho ELan EWTr GBin IArd MBlu NLar SBir
	- 'Rohan Trompenburg'	CMCN MBlu
	- 'Rohan Weeping'	MBlu SBir
	- 'Rohanii'	CBcs CDoC CDul CLnd CMCN CTri EBee ELan EPfP GKin LHop MGos NPCo SBir SLau SPer WFar WHar WMou
	- 'Roseomarginata'	see *F. sylvatica* 'Purpurea Tricolor'
	- 'Rotundifolia'	CDoC CDul MBlu
	- 'Spaethiana'	GKin
	- 'Striata'	LLHF NPCo SBir
	- 'Sychrov'	SBir
	- f. ***tortuosa***	MPkF
	- 'Tortuosa Purpurea'	CDul MBlu
	- 'Tricolor' misapplied	see *F. sylvatica* 'Purpurea Tricolor'
	- 'Tricolor' ambig. (v)	SLau
	- 'Tricolor' (v)	CBcs CLnd CMac CSBt CWib EBee ELan LLHF NEgg
	- 'Viridivariegata' (v)	CMCN
	- 'Zlatia'	CBcs CDul CLnd CMCN CSBt CWib ELan EPfP MBlu MGos MPkF MSwo NWea SBir SGol SLau SPer

Falkia (*Convolvulaceae*)

	repens	CSpe

Fallopia (*Polygonaceae*)

	aubertii	see *F. baldschuanica*
§	***baldschuanica***	CBcs CMac CSBt CTri CWib EBee ELan EPfP LBuc LRHS MAsh MGos MSwo NEgg NPri NWea SBfd SEND SLim SLon SPer SPlb SPoG SWvt WFar WHar
	- Summer Sunshine = 'Acofal'PBR	ELan
§	***japonica*** var. ***compacta***	NLar WMoo
	- - 'Fuji Snow'	see *F. japonica* var. *compacta* 'Milk Boy'
§	- - 'Milk Boy' (v)	EShb LRHS NGBo
	- - f. ***rosea*** hort.	LRHS
	- - 'Variegata' misapplied	see *F. japonica* var. *compacta* 'Milk Boy'
§	***multiflora***	CArn NPri
	- var. ***hypoleuca***	SCoo SLim
	- - B&SWJ 120	EBee WCru
	sachalinensis	NLar

Farfugium (*Asteraceae*)

§	***japonicum***	CHEx LRHS MBel
	- B&SWJ 884	WCru
	- 'Argenteum' (v)	CCon SMad WCot
§	- 'Aureomaculatum' (v) ♕H1	CCon CHEx CHII EPfP LEdu LRHS
	- 'Bumpy Ride'	WCot
	- 'Crispatum'	CAbP CCon ECtt ELan EPfP LAst LEdu NSti SMad WCot WFar WWEG
	- double-flowered (d)	WCru
	- var. ***formosanum*** B&SWJ 7125	WCru
	- - CWJ 12356	WCru
	- var. ***giganteum***	CHEx
	- 'Kagami-jishi' (v)	WCot
	- 'Kaimon Dake'	WCot
I	- 'Nanum'	CHEx
	- 'Ryuto'	WCot
I	- 'Tsuwa-buki'	WCot
	'Last Dance' **new**	MAsh
	tussilagineum	see *F. japonicum*

Fargesia (*Poaceae*)

	from Jiuzhaigou, China	CDTJ CEnt EPfP ERod ETod EUJe GBin MBri MMoz MMuc

	MWht NLar NWsh SBig SEND WJun WPGP
adpressa	WJun
angustissima	CDTJ CEnt ENBC EPfP ERod MMuc MWht SBig SEND WJun
confusa	CDTJ
denudata	CDTJ CEnt ENBC ERod SBig WJun
- L 1575	MMoz MWht
- Xian 1	CDTJ MMoz WPGP
dracocephala	CAbb CDoC CEnt EPfP ERod ESwi GBin LEdu LRHS MAvo MBrN MDev MMoz MMuc MWht SBig SEND SLPl WJun WMoo WPGP
- 'White Dragon' **new**	WPGP
ferax	WJun
§ ***murielae*** ♀H4	CDoC CEnt CHEx EHul ELan ENBC EPau EPfP ERod MGos MMoz MMuc MWhi MWht NGdn SBfd SEND SPlb SPoG WFar WJun WMoo WPGP
- 'Amy'	NLar
- 'Bimbo'	CEnt EPfP ERod ESwi ETod GBin LAst LRHS MWht NLar WJun WMoo WPGP
- 'Dana Jumbo'	LRHS
- 'Grüne Hecke'	ERod MWht SBig
- 'Harewood'	MMoz MWht SWvt WFar WPGP
- 'Joy'	GBin NLar WMoo
- 'Jumbo'	CEnt CHEx CSBt EAmu ELan ELon ENBC EPfP ERod ESwi EUJe GBin LRHS MAvo MBri MDev MGos MMoz MWht NGdn NWsh SBig SPer SPoG SRms SWvt WFar WJun
- 'Kranich'	NLar
- 'Lava'	MBri
- 'Mae'	CDTJ MWht
- 'Pinocchio'	MBri
- 'Simba' ♀H4	Widely available
- 'Vampire'	ERod EUJe LRHS MBri SBig
- 'Willow'	MBri
* ***nepalensis***	ESwi
§ ***nitida***	Widely available
- 'Eisenach'	MMoz WFar
- 'Great Wall'	EAmu GBin MBlu MBri MGos MWhi MWht
- Jiuzhaigou 1	see *F.* Red Panda
- 'Jiuzhaigou 2'	WJun
- 'Jiuzhaigou 4'	WPGP
- 'Jiuzhaigou 8'	WPGP
- 'Jiuzhaigou Genf'	WPGP
- 'Nymphenburg' ♀H4	MBri MMoz NLar SBig SEND WFar
- 'Wakehurst'	NLar
perlonga	WJun
- Yunnan 6	ERod MMoz WPGP
§ Red Panda = 'Jiu'	LRHS WJun
robusta	CAbb CDTJ CEnt ENBC EPfP ERod ETod GCal MAvo MBrN MBri MMoz MMuc MWhi MWht NGdn NLar SBig SEND SLPl WJun
- 'Campbell' **new**	EAmu
- 'Ming Yunnan'	LEdu WJun
- 'P. King' **new**	ERod
- 'Pingwu'	CDTJ CEnt ERod ETod GBin MGos MWht NLar SBig WJun
- 'Red Sheath'	CEnt ERod MMoz MWht WJun WPGP
- 'Wolong'	CDoC ERod ETod GBin MMoz MWht WJun WPGP
rufa	CAbb CEnt EAmu ENBC EPPr EPfP ERod GCal LRHS LSRN MAvo MBrN MDev MGos MMoz MMuc MWat MWhi MWht NLar SBig SEND WJun WPGP
spathacea misapplied	see *F. murielae*
utilis	CEnt ERod ETod LEdu MMoz MMuc MWht NLar SEND WJun
yulongshanensis	ERod MWht WJun
yunnanensis **new**	EAmu

Farsetia (*Brassicaceae*)

clypeata	see *Fibigia clypeata*

Fascicularia (*Bromeliaceae*)

andina	see *F. bicolor*
§ ***bicolor***	Widely available
§ - subsp. ***bicolor***	CMac CPne EGri SMad
§ - subsp. ***canaliculata***	CHEx EBee IBlr LEdu SBfd SChr SKHP SPad WCot WPGP
kirchhoffiana	see *F. bicolor* subsp. *canaliculata*
litoralis	see *Ochagavia litoralis*
pitcairniifolia misapplied	see *F. bicolor* subsp. *bicolor*
pitcairniifolia (Verlot) Mez	see *Ochagavia litoralis*

× *Fatshedera* (*Araliaceae*)

lizei ♀H3	CBcs CDoC CDul CHEx CMac CTri EBee ECrN ELon EPfP LRHS MAsh MBel MRav NEgg SBfd SDix SEND SPer SPlb SPoG SWvt
§ - 'Annemieke' (v) ♀H3	CBcs CDoC CHEx CMac CRHN EBee ELan EPfP LHop LRHS MAsh MRav NEgg SBfd SEND SMad SPer SPoG WBor
- 'Lemon and Lime'	see × *F. lizei* 'Annemieke'
- 'Maculata'	see × *F. lizei* 'Annemieke'
- 'Variegata' (v) ♀H3	CHEx CMac EBee EBtc ELan EPfP LAst LRHS LTen MAsh MBel MGos NEgg SBfd SEND SPer SWvt WCFE

Fatsia (*Araliaceae*)

§ ***japonica*** ♀H4	Widely available
- 'Moseri'	CPLG CSam CTrC ECtt ELan ESwi EUJe LHop NGdn NLar SWvt WCot
- 'Spider's Web' (v)	CAbb CHid CPLG CWGN EAmu ECtt ELan ELon ESwi EUJe LSou MRav NGBo SBfd SPer SPoG WCot WGrn
- 'Variegata' (v) ♀H3	CBcs CMac EAmu ELan EPfP LRHS MBri MGos MRav SEND SLim SPer WCot
oligocarpella	CHEx
papyrifera	see *Tetrapanax papyrifer*
polycarpa	CDTJ CPLG EAmu WPGP
- B&SWJ 7144	CPLG WCru
- RWJ 10133	WCru

Faucaria (*Aizoaceae*)

felina	SWal
tigrina ♀H1	EPfP EUJe

Fauria see *Nephrophyllidium*

Fedia (*Valerianaceae*)

cornucopiae	CArn

Feijoa see *Acca*

Felicia (*Asteraceae*)

§	***amelloides***	CCCN CHEx LAst MCot NPri SBfd SEND SGar SPlb
	- 'Santa Anita' ♀H3	CTri
§	- variegated (v)	CCCN ECtt LSou MBri MCot NPer SBfd SEND SPet
§	***amoena***	CTri
	- 'Variegata' (v)	CCCN CTri
	capensis	see *F. amelloides*
	coelestis	see *F. amelloides*
	echinata	CCCN
	filifolia	SPlb
	fruticosa	CHII
	natalensis	see *F. rosulata*
	pappei	see *F. amoena*
§	***petiolata***	CMea CTri EWes NSti WOut WWFP
§	***rosulata***	CMea CPBP ECho MBrN MHer NBro NLar SFgr SRot WIce
	uliginosa	EWes GEdr WAbe

Fenestraria (*Aizoaceae*)

	rhodalophylla subsp. ***aurantiaca*** ♀H1 **new**	LToo

fennel see *Foeniculum vulgare*

fenugreek see *Trigonella foenum-graecum*

Ferraria (*Iridaceae*)

	LP 18095	WCot
§	***crispa***	ECho WCot
	- var. ***nortieri***	WCot
	divaricata **new**	WCot
	schaeferi	WCot
	undulata	see *F. crispa*

Ferula (*Apiaceae*)

	assa-foetida	CArn EOHP LDai
	chiliantha	see *F. communis* subsp. *glauca*
§	***communis***	CArn CMea CSpe EBee ECGP ECha ELan EPfP GCra IBoy NLar SDix SEND SPav SPhx SPlb WBor WCot WJek
	- 'Gigantea'	see *F. communis*
§	- subsp. ***glauca***	CArn EWes SDix SGar WCot WPGP
*	- Purpurea Group **new**	ELan
	'Giant Bronze'	see *Foeniculum vulgare* 'Giant Bronze'
	tingitana 'Cedric Morris'	ECha GCra SDix

Ferulago (*Apiaceae*)

	sylvatica	SPhx

Festuca (*Poaceae*)

	actae	XLum
	amethystina	CKno CWCL CWib EHoe LEdu LRHS NGdn SEND SMea SRot WMoo WTin WWEG XLum
	- 'Aprilgrün'	EPPr XLum
	arundinacea	CHab CRWN MMoz SEND
	californica	CKno EPPr
	coxii	CHid WCot
	curvula subsp. ***crassifolia***	EShb
	'Eisvogel'	EBee
	elegans	EPPr XLum
	eskia	EAEE EBee EHoe EPPr LRHS XLum
	filiformis	CHab
	'Fromefield Blue'	EHul
§	***gautieri***	EBee EPPr GBin SMea XLum
	- 'Pic Carlit'	GBin
	gigantea	CHab EBee SEND XLum
	glacialis	XLum
	glauca Vill.	CBar CBcs CWib EBee ELan EPfP EShb GMaP LPot MBNS MGos MRav MWat NGdn NOak SBfd SLim SPer SPlb SRms SWal WTin WWEG
I	- 'Auslese'	CPLG EPPr NGdn
	- 'Azurit'	EBee EHoe EPPr EWes NWad NWsh SPad SPoG
§	- 'Blaufuchs' ♀H4	EAEE EBee EHon EHrv EPfP EWes GMaP LRHS MAsh MAvo MBlu MGos MRav NRHS NWad SBfd SLim SPer SPlb SWvt WFar WWEG XLum
§	- 'Blauglut'	EBee EPfP LRHS MBri MRav
	- Blue Fox	see *F. glauca* 'Blaufuchs'
	- Blue Glow	see *F. glauca* 'Blauglut'
	- 'Elijah Blue'	Widely available
	- 'Euchre'	LSRN
	- 'Golden Toupee'	EBee ECha EHoe ELan EPfP EWes LAst LRHS MAsh MBlu MGos NBir NEgg NHol SLim SPer SPlb SWvt WFar WWEG
	- 'Harz'	EHoe EHul SApp
	- 'Intense Blue'	CKno EWes SMad SPoG
*	- ***minima***	CCCN WGrn WWEG
	- 'Pallens'	see *F. longifolia*
	- Sea Urchin	see *F. glauca* 'Seeigel'
§	- 'Seeigel'	EHoe EPPr LRHS NWad
	- Select	see *F. glauca* 'Auslese'
	- 'Seven Seas'	see *F. valesiaca* 'Silbersee'
	- 'Silberreiher'	EPPr WWEG
	- 'Solling'	XLum
	- 'Uchte'	CWCL EPPr LHop WPtf
	'Hogar'	EBee EPPr
	idahoensis	EShb
	- 'Tomales Bay'	CKno
§	***longifolia***	EPPr
	mairei	CKno CTrC ECha EHoe EPPr SPhx WCAu XLum
	novae-zelandiae	CWCL
	ovina	CHab CWan EPfP GBin WSFF
	- var. ***gallica***	NWsh
	- 'Söhrewald'	EHoe EPPr
*	- 'Tetra Gold'	SWvt
	paniculata	CKno EHoe EPPr XLum
	pratensis	CHab
	punctoria	EBee MMuc SEND SMea
	rubra	CHab CKno CRWN WSFF XLum
	- subsp. ***rubra***	CRWN
	scoparia	see *F. gautieri*
	'Siskiyou Blue'	CKno EBee EPPr WWEG
	tatrae	GBin SEND WCot
	tolucensis NJM 09.071 **new**	WPGP
	valesiaca	SMea
	- var. ***glaucantha***	CWib EPPr NGdn NLar SEND WWEG XLum
§	- 'Silbersee'	EAEE EBee EHoe EPPr GBin LRHS NWsh SRms
	- Silver Sea	see *F. valesiaca* 'Silbersee'
	violacea	EPPr SWal
	vivipara	CPrp EHoe LEdu NBid
*	'Willow Green'	SPlb

Fibigia (*Brassicaceae*)

§	***clypeata***	LDai
I	- 'Select'	CSpe

Ficus ✿ (*Moraceae*)

	benjamina 'Alii'	WCot
	carica (F)	CCCN ETod EUJe LMaj MBri MNHC MREP SEWo SLon SPad
	- 'Adam' (F)	CCCN SEND
	- 'Beall' (F)	CCCN
	- 'Bellone' (F)	CCCN
	- 'Black Ischia' (F)	CCCN
	- 'Black Mission' (F)	EAmu
	- 'Black Neck Lady' (F)	MGos NRHS SHil
	- 'Bornholm' (F)	LSRN NLar
	- 'Bourjassotte Grise' (F)	CAgr
	- 'Brogiotto' (F)	CCCN
	- 'Brown Turkey' (F) ♀H3	Widely available
	- 'Brunswick' (F)	CAgr CCCN CHll CRHN ELan ELon EPfP EPom GTwe LRHS MCoo NLar SEND SLim WCot WHar
	- 'Castle Kennedy' (F)	CCCN GTwe
	- 'Celeste' (F)	CBcs CCCN SPer
	- 'Colummaro Black Apulia' (F)	CCCN
	- 'Colummaro White Apulia' (F)	CCCN
	- 'Continental' (F)	LRHS SHil
	- 'Dalmatie' (F)	CAgr CCCN ELan EPfP LRHS MCoo MGos SEND WPGP
I	- 'Digitata' (F)	MBlu
	- 'Digredo' (F) **new**	CCCN
	- 'Dorée de Porquerolles' (F) **new**	CCCN
	- 'Filacciano' (F)	CCCN
	- 'Flanders' (F) **new**	CCCN
	- 'Goutte d'Or' (F)	CAgr CCCN EPfP
	- 'Green Ischia' (F) **new**	CCCN
	- 'Grise de Marseille' (F) **new**	CCCN
	- 'Grise de Saint Jean' (F)	CCCN
	- 'Ice Crystal' (F)	LBuc LRHS MBlu SPoG WHar WPGP
	- 'Jordan' (F) **new**	IDee
	- 'Kadota' (F)	CCCN IDee SBfd
*	- 'Laciniata' (F)	MBri
	- 'Malta' (F)	GTwe
	- 'Marseillaise' (F)	GTwe
	- 'Melanzana' (F)	CCCN
	- 'Moscatel' (F) **new**	CCCN
	- 'Neck Lady White' (F)	MGos SHil
	- 'Negrétte de Porquerolles' (F) **new**	CCCN
	- 'Nero' (F)	ELon SGol
	- 'Newlyn Harbour' (F)	ELon
	- 'Noire de Caromb' (F)	CAgr CCCN EPfP LRHS MCoo
	- 'Noire de Provence'	see *F. carica* 'Reculver'
	- 'Osborn's Prolific' (F)	ECrN EMil EPfP SEND SGol SWvt WPGP
	- 'Panachée' (F)	CCCN EPom
	- 'Pied de Boeuf' (F)	CCCN
	- 'Pinet' (F)	LRHS MGos SHil
	- 'Porthminster' (F)	CHEx
	- 'Précoce de Dalmatie' (F)	NLar
	- 'Précoce Ronde de Bordeaux' (F)	SEND
	- 'Quinta' (F) **new**	CCCN
§	- 'Reculver' (F)	SEND
	- 'Ronde de Bordeaux' (F) **new**	CCCN
	- 'Rouge de Bordeaux' (F)	CCCN SPlb
	- 'Safi' (F) **new**	CCCN
	- 'Sultane' (F)	CAgr
	- 'Verte d'Argenteuil' (F)	CCCN
	- 'Violetta'PBR (F)	LRHS MBri NLar NRHS WHar
	- 'Violette Dauphine' (F)	EPfP
	- 'Violette Normande' (F)	SEND
	- 'White Adriatic' (F) **new**	CBcs
	- 'White Genoa'	see *F. carica* 'White Marseilles'
§	- 'White Marseilles' (F)	CAgr CCCN CWib ECrN LRHS MBri MCoo SEND WPGP
	- 'Zidi' (F) **new**	CCCN
	pubigera	CPLG
	pumila ♀H1	CHEx
	- 'Variegata' (v)	CHEx EShb

fig see *Ficus carica*

filbert see *Corylus maxima*

Filipendula ✿ (*Rosaceae*)

	alnifolia 'Variegata'	see *F. ulmaria* 'Variegata'
	camtschatica	CCon CRow EBee ECha ELan LEdu LRHS MCot NBid NLar WFar WPGP
	- B&SWJ 10987	WCru
	- 'Rosea'	LHop MRav SMad
	digitata 'Nana'	see *F. multijuga*
	formosa B&SWJ 8707	WCru
	hexapetala	see *F. vulgaris*
	- 'Flore Pleno'	see *F. vulgaris* 'Multiplex'
	'Kahome'	CPrp CRow EBee ELon EShb GMaP IFoB IPot LRHS NBir NGdn NLar NMir NOrc SPer SPet SPhx SWat WMoo WPnP WWEG
	kiraishiensis B&SWJ 1571	WCru
§	***multijuga***	CRow EBee EWhm GCal IFoB LRHS NHol WMoo
	- var. ***yezoensis*** B&SWJ 10828	SMrm WCru
	palmata	EBee ECha MLHP NBre SWat WMoo
	- 'Digitata Nana'	see *F. multijuga*
	- dwarf	CDes CLAP MLHP
	- 'Elegantissima'	see *F. purpurea* 'Elegans'
	- 'Göteborg'	EBee
	- 'Nana'	see *F. multijuga*
	- 'Rosea'	CMac NBir
	- 'Rubra'	CTri GCra MRav NGdn
	purpurea ♀H4	CKno CRow CSBt ECha ELon EPfP IBlr LPBA LRHS MBri MMuc SBod SEND WCru WFar WMoo
	- f. ***albiflora***	EBee MBri NPri WMoo
§	- 'Elegans'	CRow EBee ECha ELon MLHP NBid NHol NSti SPer SPet SWat WMoo WPnP
	- 'Nephele'	EBee
	- 'Pink Dreamland'	SPhx
*	- 'Plena' (d)	NLar
*	- ***splendens*** **new**	GBin
	'Queen of the Prairies'	see *F. rubra*
	'Red Umbrellas' **new**	EBee LSou MSCN SPoG WHil
§	***rubra***	CRow IFro LSRN MCot WSFF
§	- 'Venusta' ♀H4	Widely available
	- 'Venusta Magnifica'	see *F. rubra* 'Venusta'
	rufinervis B&SWJ 8611	WCru
§	***ulmaria***	CArn CBen CHab CHby CRWN CWan CWat EBee EHon ELau ENfk GMaP GPoy MCot MHer MHoo MMuc MNHC NLan NMir SEND SIde SWat WHfH WJek WMoo WPnP WSFF WShi XLum
	- 'Aurea'	CMac CRow CTri EBee ECha ECtt EHoe ELan GAbr GMaP LRHS

		MLHP MRav NBid NLar NRHS SMad SPer SRms WCot WFar WMoo WSHC WTin WWEG
	- 'Flore Pleno' (d)	CBre EBee LHop LRHS MRav NBid NBre SIde SPer SWat WCot WFar
	- 'Rosea'	CDes EBee IBlr MBel MHer
§	- 'Variegata' (v)	CBen CPrp EBee ECtt EHoe ELan GBuc IFoB LBMP LRHS NBid NGdn NLar NMRc SPer WFar WHfH WMoo WPGP WPnP WTin WWEG WWFP
§	***vulgaris***	CArn CHab CRWN CWan LRHS MBel MLHP MMuc MNHC NBro NLBP NMir SBfd SEND SWat WHfH WJek WPer WWEG
	- 'Flore Pleno'	see *F. vulgaris* 'Multiplex'
	- 'Grandiflora'	CBre EBee
§	- 'Multiplex' (d)	CMac EBee ECha ELan GMaP LRHS MHer MMuc MRav MWts NBid NBir NPri NRya SEND SPer SRms WAul WFar WMoo WTin XLum
	- 'Plena'	see *F. vulgaris* 'Multiplex'
	- 'Rosea'	NBre

Firmiana (*Malvaceae*)

simplex	CHEx EShb EUJe IDee WPGP

Fitzroya (*Cupressaceae*)

cupressoides	CBcs CDoC CMac CTho GBin IArd IDee LRHS SCoo SLim WThu

Foeniculum (*Apiaceae*)

	vulgare	Widely available
	- 'Bronze'	see *F. vulgare* 'Purpureum'
	- var. ***dulce***	CSev ENfk SIde
§	- 'Giant Bronze'	EBee ELan SPhx WGrn WSpi
§	- 'Purpureum'	Widely available
	- 'Smokey'	ECha MRav
	- 'Sweet Florence' **new**	SVic

Fontanesia (*Oleaceae*)

phillyreoides	CBcs

Fontinalis (*Fontinalaceae*)

sp.	LPBA

Forsythia (*Oleaceae*)

	'Arnold Dwarf'	ECrN NBir NLar SRms
	'Beatrix Farrand' ambig.	CTri EBee MWat NWea SEND SRms
	'Beatrix Farrand' K. Sax	MMuc NLar
	'Fiesta' (v)	CJun EBee EPfP LAst LRHS MAsh MGos MRav MSwo SBfd SPer SPoG WCot WFar
	giraldiana	MSwo SLon SRms
	Gold Tide PBR	see *F.* Marée d'Or
	'Golden Bells'	WHar
	'Golden Nugget'	CMac ELan EPfP LBuc LRHS MAsh SCoo SLon SPoG WCFE
	'Golden Times' (v)	CMac EWes LAst LBuc LPot LSRN MAsh MGos NLar NWea SCoo SPoG SWvt WFar
	× ***intermedia*** 'Arnold Giant'	MBlu
	- 'Goldrausch'	EBee LRHS MAsh NLar
	- 'Goldzauber'	NWea
	- 'Josefa' (v)	WPat
	- 'Lynwood Variety' ♀H4	Widely available
	- 'Lynwood Variety' variegated (v)	CWib
	- Minigold = 'Flojor'	CMac CSBt EBee MSwo MWat NLar SRms
	- 'Spectabilis'	CDul EBee EPfP LBuc NWea SCoo SGol SLim WFar
	- 'Spectabilis Variegated' (v)	CMHG MBNS NPro
	- 'Spring Glory'	MHer WSpi
	- 'Variegata' (v)	WGwG
	- Week End = 'Courtalyn' PBR ♀H4	CWSG EBee EPfP LBuc LRHS LSou MAsh MBri MMuc NHol NLar NPri SEND SGol SLPl SLon SPlb WFar
§	Marée d'Or = 'Courtasol' PBR ♀H4	IVic LRHS MAsh MGos MRav NLar NWea SLon SPer SPoG
	Mêlée d'Or = 'Courtaneur'	SCoo SGol
	Melissa = 'Courtadic'	NLar NWea
	ovata 'Tetragold'	EBee NWea
	'Paulina'	NLar WAbe
*	'Spring Beauty'	WSpi
	suspensa	CMac CTri CWib EOHP EPfP NWea SPlb SRms
	- f. ***atrocaulis***	NWea
	- 'Nymans'	MBri MRav NSti SEND
§	- 'Taff's Arnold' (v)	CJun CPLG EBee WSpi
	- 'Variegata'	see *F. suspensa* 'Taff's Arnold'
	'Tremonia'	NEgg NLar WGwG
	viridissima	NWea
	- 'Bronxensis'	CMac ECho GEdr LHop LLHF MAsh NBir NLar WAbe WCot WPat
	- Citrus Swizzle = 'Mckcitrine' PBR **new**	EMil
	- var. ***koreana*** 'Kumsom' (v)	EBee MAsh SLim SPoG
	- 'Weber's Bronx'	NLar WAbe

Fortunatia see *Oziroë*

Fortunella (*Rutaceae*)

§	***japonica*** (F)	EPfP
§	***margarita*** (F)	CDoC LRHS LSRN SHil

Fothergilla (*Hamamelidaceae*)

gardenii	CBcs CJun EBee ELan EPfP LRHS MBlu MGos MRav NLar SPer SWvt
- 'Blue Mist'	CAbP CDoC CJun CPLG EBee ELan ELon EPfP GKin GQue IVic LRHS MAsh MPkF NLar SBfd SKHP SPer SPoG SReu SSta WPat
- 'Harold Epstein'	NLar
- 'Suzanne'	NLar
- 'Zundert'	NLar
'Huntsman'	CCCN EBee
× ***intermedia*** Beaver Creek = 'Klmtwo'	NLar
- 'Blue Shadow'	CBcs CJun EBee LSRN MGos MPkF MRav NLar SGol SKHP
- 'Mount Airy'	CJun CMCN EBee EPfP GBin LRHS MBri MPkF NLar SKHP SPtl SSpi SSta
- 'Red Licorice'	CJun NLar
- 'Sea Spray'	CJun
- 'Windy City'	CJun MBri NLar
major ♀H4	CBcs CDul CJun CWib EBee ELan EPfP GKin IDee LRHS LSRN MAsh MBlu MGos NEgg NLar NPri SHil SPer SPoG SReu SWvt WFar WPat
- 'Bulkyard'	CJun
- Monticola Group	CDoC CDul CJun EBee ELan EPfP LRHS MAsh MGos SBfd SEND SLim SPer SSpi SSta

Fouquieria (*Fouquieriaceae*)

Plant	Suppliers
splendens **new**	SPlb

Fragaria (*Rosaceae*)

Plant	Suppliers
from Taiwan	WHer
alpina	see *F. vesca* 'Semperflorens'
– 'Alba'	see *F. vesca* 'Semperflorens Alba'
× ***ananassa*** 'Albion'PBR (F)	CSBt CSut LSRN MCoo SPer
– 'Alice'PBR (F) ♀H4	CMac EPom LBuc LRHS MCoo WWFS
– 'Aromel' (F) ♀H4	CAgr EPfP GTwe LBuc LRHS
– 'Bogota' (F)	LRHS
– 'Bolero' (F)	LRHS MBri
– 'Calypso'PBR (F)	CAgr CSBt LBuc LRHS SEND
– 'Cambridge Favourite' (F) ♀H4	CAgr CMac CSBt CTri CWCL EMil EPfP EPom GPri GTwe LBuc LRHS MBri MCoo MGos NEgg NPri SEND SPlb WWFS
– 'Cambridge Vigour' (F)	LRHS
– 'Christine' (F)	CSut EMil EPom GPri LRHS WWFS
– 'Darselect'PBR (F)	EPom
– 'Elegance' (F)	CSut EPom WWFS
– 'Elsanta' (F)	CSBt CTri CWCL EMil EPfP EPom GPri GTwe IArd LBuc LEdu LRHS NEgg NPri SBfd SEND SPer
– 'Elvira' (F)	EPfP LRHS
* – 'Emily' (F)	CAgr GPri
– 'Eros'PBR (F)	LBuc
– 'Fenella' (F) **new**	CMac EPom MCoo WWFS
– 'Flamenco'PBR (F)	CSut EPom LRHS
– 'Florence'PBR (F)	CSBt CTri EMil EPfP EPom GTwe LBuc LRHS MBri SPer WWFS
– Fraise des Bois	see *F. vesca*
– 'Fruitful Summer' (F)	LRHS
– 'Hapil' (F) ♀H4	CTri EMil EPfP EPom GPri GTwe LBuc LEdu LRHS WWFS
– 'Honeoye' (F) ♀H4	CAgr CSBt EMil EPfP EPom GAbr GPri GTwe LBuc LEdu LRHS MBri MCoo NWad SBfd SEND SPer WWFS
– 'Judibell'PBR (F)	LRHS WWFS
– 'Korona'PBR (F)	CMac EPom
– 'Loran' (F)	LRHS
– 'Lucy' (F)	CSut
– 'Malling Opal'PBR (F)	EPom GTwe
– 'Malling Pearl' (F)	EMil GTwe
– 'Malwina'PBR (F) **new**	CSut SVic
– 'Mount Everest' (F) **new**	EMil
– 'Pandora' (F)	LEdu LRHS
– 'Pegasus'PBR (F) ♀H4	CSBt EPfP EPom GPri GTwe LBuc LRHS NPri WWFS
– Pink Panda = 'Frel'PBR (F)	CMac CTri EAEE EBee ELan LHop LRHS MGos MRav NDov NEgg NLar SPer SPoG WCAu WJek WWFP
– pink-flowered (F)	LPot MBel
– 'Rabunda' (F)	LRHS
– Red Ruby = 'Samba'PBR (F)	CMac EAEE EBee LHop LRHS MBel MNrw MWat NEgg NGdn NLar SPer SPoG
– 'Redgauntlet' (F)	EPfP GPri GTwe LBuc LRHS
– 'Rhapsody' (F) ♀H4	GTwe LRHS LSRN
– 'Royal Sovereign' (F)	CMac CTri EPom GTwe LEdu LRHS NBir SVic
– 'Sasha' (F)	GPri
– 'Senga Sengana' (F)	SVic
– 'Sonata'PBR (F)	CSut EPom LRHS
– 'Sophie'PBR (F)	EMil LEdu LRHS WWFS
– 'Sweetheart' (F) **new**	LRHS
– 'Symphony'PBR (F) ♀H4	CAgr CSBt EPfP EPom LBuc LRHS LSRN MBri SPer WWFS
– 'Totem' (F)	GTwe LRHS
§ – 'Variegata' (v)	CTri EAEE EBee EHrv LDai LHop MHoo MRav SPer SPoG WMoo XLum
'Bowles's Double'	see *F. vesca* 'Multiplex'
chiloensis (F)	LEdu
– 'Chaval' (F)	CHid ECha EPPr MRav NChi WMoo
– 'Variegata' misapplied	see *F.* × *ananassa* 'Variegata'
daltoniana	GCra
'Delican' **new**	SHar
indica	see *Duchesnea indica*
'Lipstick'	EBee NLar
moschata	CAgr
nubicola	CAgr GPoy
– 'Mount Omei'	EBee
'Roman'	LRHS
'Variegata'	see *F.* × *ananassa* 'Variegata'
§ ***vesca*** (F)	CAgr CArn CBcs CRWN CWan EGHP EPfP GPoy MHer MNHC NMir NPri SEND SIde SPlb SVic WGwG WJek WPer WSFF WShi
– 'Alexandra' (F)	CArn CPrp ELau ENfk EPPr SBfd SHar SIde
– 'Alpina Scarletta' (F) **new**	ENfk
– 'Baron Solemacher' (F)	SBfd SHDw SPhx WHer WRHF
– 'Flore Pleno'	see *F. vesca* 'Multiplex'
– 'Fructu Albo' (F)	CAgr CArn CBre CRow CWan GLin NLar WMoo
– 'Golden Alexandra'	EBee ECha EHoe ELau EWes MHer NPro WCot WHer WOut
– 'Golden Surprise'	SBfd SHDw
– 'Mara des Bois'PBR (F)	EPom
– 'Mignonette'	NDov SHar
– 'Monophylla' (F)	CRow SIde WHer
§ – 'Multiplex' (d)	CRow EGHP MRav NChi NLar WBor WHer WOut
§ – 'Muricata'	CBre CRow LEdu
– 'Pineapple Crush' (F)	WHer
– 'Plymouth Strawberry'	see *F. vesca* 'Muricata'
§ – 'Semperflorens' (F)	SWal
§ – 'Semperflorens Alba' (F)	CAgr
– 'Variegata' misapplied	see *F.* × *ananassa* 'Variegata'
* – 'Variegata' ambig. (v)	EGHP EHoe LRHS NEgg WFar WWEG
virginiana	CAgr
– subsp. ***glauca***	EPPr
viridis	CAgr

Francoa (*Francoaceae*)

Plant	Suppliers
appendiculata	CAbP GAbr GQui NBir SGar WHer WMoo
– red-flowered	LHop
Ballyrogan strain	IBlr
'Confetti'	CAbP CKno CPLG ELan ELon LRHS MAvo SWal WCot
'Purple Spike'	see *F. sonchifolia* Rogerson's form
ramosa	CCVN CCon CTri EHrv EWld IBlr LRHS MNrw NBro SDix WKif WMoo
* – 'Alba'	CSpe EDif
sonchifolia	Widely available
– 'Alba'	GKev SUsu WMoo
– 'Cally Dwarf Purple'	MAvo
– 'Culm View Lilac'	CCVN MAvo
– dark-flowered **new**	GKev

- 'Doctor Tom Smith' WCot
- 'Lynda Windsor' CRDP MAvo
- 'Molly Anderson' MAvo SUsu
- 'Pink Bouquet' CKno CMac EBee MPnt SHar WOut
- 'Pink Giant' GBin GKev ITim MAvo MHer SMrm WCot WHil WMoo

§ - Rogerson's form CCVN CElw CEnt CRDP CSam CTri EBee EHrv ELon ITim IVic LBMP LHop LRHS MAvo MBel MBri MNHC NBir NChi SAga SDix SGar SMrm SUsu WCot WHil WMoo WWEG

Frangula (*Rhamnaceae*)

§ ***alnus*** CArn CCVT CDul CHab CRWN CTri ECrN EShb LBuc MBlu MWat NWea SEWo WFar WMou WSFF
- 'Aspleniifolia' CWSG EBee EPfP LRHS MBlu MMuc MPkF NLar WPat
- 'Columnaris' SLPl
- 'Fine Line' new NLar
- 'Ron Williams' LBuc MBlu WCot

Frankenia (*Frankeniaceae*)

laevis SRms
thymifolia CTri CYeo ECho MAsh MHer MWat NPri SEND SPlb WFar WTin XLum

Franklinia (*Theaceae*)

alatamaha CBcs IVic MBlu MBri SEND WPGP

Fraxinus ✿ (*Oleaceae*)

americana CDul CMCN EPfP EWTr NEgg
- 'Autumn Purple' CDul CMCN CTho EBee ECrN EPfP MAsh MBlu WMou

angustifolia CMCN

§ - subsp. ***oxycarpa*** SEND
- 'Raywood' ♀H4 Widely available

bungeana EGFP
caroliniana EGFP
chinensis CDul CLnd CMCN EGFP
excelsior CBcs CCVT CDoC CDul CHab CLnd CMac CRWN CSBt CTho CTri CWib ECrN EPfP LAst LBuc MBri MGos MMuc NWea SBfd SEND SEWo SGol SLim SPer WMou
- 'Aurea Pendula' CCVT CDul CMac CWib MBlu MGos SPoG
- 'Crispa' MBlu NLar
- f. ***diversifolia*** CDul MBri
- 'Jaspidea' ♀H4 Widely available
- 'Nana' LLHF LMaj WPat
- 'Pendula' ♀H4 CCVT CDoC CDul CLnd CMac EBee ECrN ELan LAst LMaj MBlu NEgg NWea SGol SLim SPer WMou
- 'R.E. Davey' CDul CNat
- variegated (v) CMac
- 'Westhof's Glorie' ♀H4 CCVT CDoC CDul CLnd EBee ECrN LMaj SBfd WFar

hopeiensis MBlu
insularis var. ***henryana*** CDul CMCN
lanuginosa new EGFP
latifolia CMCN MBlu
mariesii see *F. sieboldiana*
nigra CMCN
ornus ♀H4 CArn CCVT CDul CLnd CMCN CMac CTri EBee ECrN ELan EPfP EWTr LAst LEdu MMuc MSnd MSwo NWea SEND SPer WFar WMoo WMou
- 'Arie Peters' CDul
- 'Mecsek' MBlu
- 'Obelisk' EBee EBtc MAsh MBlu MBri NLar SPoG

oxycarpa see *F. angustifolia* subsp. *oxycarpa*
paxiana EGFP
pennsylvanica CDul CLnd CMCN
- Cimmaron = 'Cimmzam' CDul MAsh
- 'Variegata' (v) CLnd EBee

quadrangulata CDul
richardi CDul

§ ***sieboldiana*** CDoC CDul CMCN EPfP MBri SSpi

velutina CDul CLnd SLPl
xanthoxyloides CDul MBlu NEgg
- var. ***dumosa*** EBee

Freesia (*Iridaceae*)

sp. CWCL
alba Foster see *F. lactea*
double mixed (d) CWCL SWal
'Fragrant Sunburst' new LBuc
fucata ECho
grandiflora CHll CPLG ECho WCot
grandiflora* × *laxa CDes

§ ***lactea*** CDes ECho

§ ***laxa*** ♀H2-3 CAvo CPLG CRHN CSev CSpe CTri CYeo ECha ECho EHrv ELan EPot EPri GKev LEdu LRHS MCot NMen SHom WAbe WBrk WCot WPat WPer
- var. ***alba*** ♀H2-3 CPLG CPom CRHN CSev CSpe ECho ELan EPri MCot NMen WAbe WBrk
- blue-flowered ECho WAbe WBrk
- 'Joan Evans' CRHN CSpe CYeo ECho ELan LLHF NMen SBch SHom WAbe WBrk
- red-spotted CPLG ECho
- ***viridiflora*** ECho

Rainbow mixture SWal
refracta 'Worcester' ECho
viridis CDes CPLG ECho
xanthospila WCot

Fremontodendron (*Malvaceae*)

'California Glory' ♀H3 CBcs CDoC CDul CMac CWSG EBee ELon EPfP EUJe LAst LBMP LHop LRHS LSRN MAsh MBlu MGos MWat NEgg NPla NPri NRHS SBfd SBod SHil SMad SPer SPoG SWvt WHar
californicum CDoy CTri CWib ELan MBri NLar SEND SLim SPlb WFar
'Dara's Gold' LRHS
'Pacific Sunset' EBee EPfP LSRN MGos MRav NEgg SGol WFar
'Tequila Sunrise' CBcs CDoC CJun CWGN EUJe LHop LLHF NLar SBfd WPGP

Freylinia (*Scrophulariaceae*)

cestroides see *F. lanceolata*

§ ***lanceolata*** CBcs CCCN CTrC CWib EBee SPlb

tropica CHll
visseri MOWG

Fritillaria ✿ (*Liliaceae*)

acmopetala ♀H4 CAvo CBro CCon CHid CWCL ECho EPot ERCP GBuc GKev ITim

		LAma LRHS MBel MNrw MSSP NMen NMin SDeJ SPhx WCot
	- 'Brunette'	EPot
	- subsp. ***wendelboi***	ECho EPot GKev LAma WCot
	- - 'Zwanenburg'	LWst
	affinis	CWCL ECho EPot GBin GBuc ITim LAma LWst NMen
	- NNS 00-336	WCot
§	- var. ***gracilis***	LWst
	- 'Sunray'	EPot GEdr
§	- var. ***tristulis***	CWCL ITim NMen
	- 'Vancouver Island'	ECho
	amana	CTca CWCL ECho EPot ERCP GKev ITim LAma LLHF MSSP NMen NMin WCot
	- 'Cambridge' ΨH4	WCot
	- yellow-flowered	EPot
	arabica	see *F. persica*
	armena MP 8146	LWst
	assyriaca	EPfP EPot GBuc
	aurea	NMen
	- 'Golden Flag'	ECho EPot GKev LLHF SPhx
	biflora	ECho EPot
	- 'Martha Roderick'	ECho GKev LAma NMen SDeJ
§	***bithynica***	ECho EPot GKev ITim LAma LWst MSSP
	- from Turkey	WCot
	brandegeei	LWst
	bucharica	ECho EPot GKev LWst NMin
	- 'Nurek Giant'	ECho LWst
	camschatcensis	CAvo CBro CPom CWCL ECha ECho EFEx EPfP EPot ERCP GBuc GEdr GHim GKev GMaP LAma LRHS MSSP NBir NHar NLar NMen NSla SDeJ SPhx WAbe WCot WCru
	- from Alaska	NHar
	- 'Aurea'	ECho GBuc LWst NMen SPhx
	- black-flowered	ECho NHar
	- double-flowered (d)	CCon ECho GBuc GEdr LAma LWst NMen
	- f. ***flavescens***	EFEx GEdr LAma
	- green-flowered	MSSP NMen
	- yellow-flowered	GBuc
	carduchorum	see *F. minuta*
	carica	ECho EPot NMen
	- brown-flowered	ECho
	- tall clone	LWst
	caucasica	ECho NMen
	cirrhosa	GEdr LWst
	- brown-flowered	GEdr LWst NMen
	- green-flowered	GEdr LWst NMen
	citrina	see *F. bithynica*
	conica	LWst NMen
	crassifolia	LAma
§	- subsp. ***kurdica***	GKev ITim LWst NMen
	davidii	SCnR
	davisii	ECho EPot GEdr GKev LAma LLHF LRHS NMen WCot
	delphinensis	see *F. tubiformis*
	eduardii	ECho EPot GKev LRHS LWst NRHS WCot
	elwesii	ECho EPot ERCP GEdr ITim LLHF LRHS LWst NMen SDeJ SPhx
	ferganensis	see *F. walujewii*
	glauca	LAma
*	- 'Golden Flag'	ECho
	- 'Goldilocks'	ECho NMen SDeJ
	graeca	ECho EPot GBuc GKev ITim NMen NMin SDeJ
	- subsp. ***graeca***	GBuc
	- subsp. ***ionica***	see *F. graeca* subsp. *thessala*
§	- subsp. ***thessala***	NMen WCot
	- - 'Milea' **new**	LWst
	gussichiae	NMen SPhx
	hermonis	LWst
	hispanica	see *F. lusitanica*
	imperialis	ECGP MBri
	- 'April Flame'	LAma
	- 'Aureomarginata' (v)	ELon LAma LRHS NRHS
	- 'Aurora'	EHrv EPot ERCP GKev LAma LRHS MBri NLar NPer SDeJ SPhx WFar
	- 'Garland Star'	GKev LAma LRHS NLar
	- 'Grenadier'	LAma
	- var. ***inodora***	GKev LAma LRHS
	- 'Lutea'	CAvo CTca EHrv ELan EPfP ERCP GKev LRHS SPhx SPoG WFar
	- 'Maxima'	see *F. imperialis* 'Rubra Maxima'
	- 'Maxima Lutea' ΨH4	CBro ELan EPfP EPot ERCP LAma MBri NLar SDeJ SPer SPoG
	- 'Orange Brilliant'	GKev LAma
	- 'Prolifera'	GKev LAma NLar SDeJ
	- 'Rubra'	CTca ERCP GAbr GKev LAma NLar SPer WFar
§	- 'Rubra Maxima'	CBro CTca EHrv ELan EPfP EPot ERCP GKev LAma LRHS SDeJ SPhx
	- 'Slagzwaard'	GKev
	- 'Striped Beauty'	CTca GKev LAma SDeJ
	- 'Sulpherino'	LAma
	- 'The Premier'	GKev LAma LRHS NRHS SDeJ
	- 'William Rex'	CAvo EPfP EPot ERCP GKev LAma LRHS SDeJ SPhx SPoG
	involucrata	WCot
	ionica	see *F. graeca* subsp. *thessala*
	japonica var. ***koidzumiana***	EFEx GEdr LWst
	karadaghensis	see *F. crassifolia* subsp. *kurdica*
	kotschyana	ECho EPot GEdr LWst NMen WCot
	- subsp. ***grandiflora***	WCot
	lanceolata	see *F. affinis* var. *tristulis*
	latakiensis	ECho EPot GEdr LWst
§	***latifolia***	GEdr NMen
	- var. ***nobilis***	see *F. latifolia*
§	***lusitanica***	ITim MSSP NMen
	meleagris	Widely available
	- 'Artemis' **new**	GBuc
	- var. ***unicolor*** subvar. ***alba*** ΨH4	CBro ECho ERCP GBuc GKev LAma MBel MBri MMHG MSSP MWat SDeJ SMrm SPer SPhx WAul WPnP WShi
	- - - 'Aphrodite'	EPot NBir
	messanensis subsp. ***gracilis***	LWst MSSP
	michailovskyi ΨH2	CHid CTri CWCL ECho EPfP EPot ERCP GBuc GEdr GKev LAma LHop LRHS MNrw NMen NRHS SDeJ SRms WFar
	minima	ECho
§	***minuta***	ECho EPot ERCP LAma LWst NMen NMin
	montana	NMen WCot
	nigra Mill.	see *F. pyrenaica*
	obliqua	LWst
	olivieri GBK 82	LWst
§	***orientalis***	LWst MSSP
	pallidiflora ΨH4	CBro CLAP CTca CWCL ECho EPot ERCP GBuc GCra GKev LAma MBri MSSP NBir NMen SDeJ SPhx

§	***persica***	CAvo ECha ECho EHrv ELon EPfP EPot ERCP GKev LAma LHop LRHS MBri MNrw NMen NRHS SPhx
	- 'Adiyaman' ♀H4	CBro ELan LRHS SDeJ
	- 'Chocolate'	CWCL
	- 'Ivory Bells'	CAvo EPot ERCP LAma LRHS NLar SDeJ SKHP SPhx
	- 'Ivory Queen'	CBro
*	- 'Senkoy'	LRHS
	phaeanthera	see *F. affinis* var. *gracilis*
	pinardii	ECho EPot NMen
	pontica ♀H4	CAvo CBro CLAP CWCL ECho EPot ERCP GBuc GEdr GKev ITim LAma LWst MBel MNrw MSSP NMen SDeJ SPhx WCru
	pudica	ECho GEdr GKev LAma LWst MSSP NMen SPhx WCot
*	- 'Fragrant'	ECho NMen
	- 'Giant'	ECho EPot GKev NMin SDeJ
	- 'Richard Britten'	NMen
	purdyi	ECho
§	***pyrenaica*** ♀H4	CLAP CTca CWCL ECho EPot GCra GEdr LAma LLHF LWst MSSP NMen SPhx WCru WTin
	- 'Cedric Morris'	MSSP WCot
	raddeana	ECho EPot ERCP GKev LAma LRHS LWst NLar SDeJ SPhx WCot
	recurva HZ 95-037	LWst
	regelii	LWst
	rhodocanakis	GKev NMen NMin WCot
	- subsp. ***argolica***	NMen
	rubra major	see *F. imperialis* 'Rubra Maxima'
	ruthenica	ECho LWst NMen
	sewerzowii	ECho EPot LAma
	- 'Black Bear'	LWst
	- 'Brown Eyes'	LWst
	- 'Gulliver'	LWst
	sinica	LLHF WCot
	stenanthera	ECho EPot LAma NMen
	stribrnyi	LWst
	tachengensis	see *F. yuminensis*
	tenella	see *F. orientalis*
	thunbergii	ECho GEdr GKev LLHF NMen SPhx WCot
	tortifolia	NMen
§	***tubiformis***	MSSP
	tuntasia subsp. ***tuntasia***	WCot
	uva-vulpis	CCon CMea CTca ECtt ELon EPfP EPot ERCP GEdr GKev LAma LHop LRHS MNrw NBir NMen NRHS SDeJ SPhx SWal WCru WFar
	verticillata	CBro ECha EPot GEdr GKev LAma LWst NMen SPhx WCru
§	***walujewii***	MSSP WCot
	whittallii	ECho EPot GKev MSSP NMen
	- PW 72-64B	LWst
	- 'Green Light'	NMin
§	***yuminensis***	WCot

Fuchsia ✿ (*Onagraceae*)

	'A.M. Larwick'	CSil EBak
	'A.W. Taylor'	EBak
	'Abbé Farges' (d)	CDoC CLoc CSil CWVF EBak EPts MWat SVic
	'Abigail' ambig.	CWVF
	'Abigail Storey'	CSil
	'Abundance'	CSil
	'Achievement' ♀H4	CDoC CLoc CSil LCla MJac SVic
	'Adalbert Bogner' (d)	CDoC
	'Adinda' (T) ♀H1	CDoC EPts LCla
	'Admiration'	CSil
	'Ailsa Garnett' (d)	EBak
	'Aintree'	CTsd CWVF
	'Airedale'	CWVF
	'Aladna's Sander' (d)	CWVF
	'Alan Ayckbourn'	CWVF
	'Alan Titchmarsh'	CDoC EPts LCla SLBF
	'Alaska' (d)	CLoc EBak SVic
	'Albertina'	SVic
	'Albertus Schwab'	LCla
	'Alde'	CWVF
	'Alderford'	SLBF
	'Alf Thornley' (d)	CTsd CWVF
	'Alfred Rambaud' (d)	CDoC CSil
	'Alice Ashton' (d)	EBak
	'Alice Blue Gown' (d)	CWVF
	'Alice Doran'	CDoC CSil LCla MWat
	'Alice Hoffman' (d) ♀H3-4	Widely available
	'Alice Mary' (d)	EBak
	'Alice Sweetapple' (d)	CWVF
	'Alice Travis' (d)	EBak
	'Alipat'	EBak
	'Alison Ewart'	CLoc CWVF EBak MJac SPet SVic
	'Alison Patricia' ♀H3	CWVF EBak LAst MJac SLBF SVic
	'Alison Reynolds' (d)	CWVF
	'Alison Ruth Griffin' (d)	MJac
	'Alison Ryle' (d)	EBak
	'Alison Sweetman' ♀H1+3	CSil CWVF MJac
	'Allure' (d)	CWVF
	Aloha = 'Sanicomf'PBR (Sunangels Series)	SLBF
	alpestris	CDoC CSil EBak GCal LCla SVic
	'Alwin' (d)	CWVF
	'Alyce Larson' (d)	CWVF EBak MJac SVic
	'Amazing Grace' (d)	MJac
	'Amazing Maisie' (d)	SLBF
	'Ambassador'	CTsd EBak SVic
	'Amelie Aubin'	CLoc CWVF EBak SVic
	'America'	CWVF
	'Amethyst Fire' (d)	CSil
	'Amigo' ambig.	EBak
§	***ampliata***	CDoC LCla
	'Amy'	MJac
	'Amy Lye'	CLoc CSil EBak SVic
	'Amy Ruth'	CWVF
§	'Andenken an Heinrich Henkel' (T)	CDoC CLoc CWVF EBak
	'André Le Nostre' (d)	CWVF EBak SVic
	'Andreas Schwab'	LCla
	andrei	CDoC LCla
	'Andrew'	EBak
	'Andrew Carnegie' (d)	CLoc
	'Andrew George'	MJac
	'Andrew Hadfield'	CWVF SVic
	'Andromeda' De Groot	CSil
	'Angela Leslie' (d)	CLoc CWVF EBak SVic
	'Angela Rippon'	CWVF MJac
	'Angel's Flight' (d)	EBak
	'Angel's Kiss' (E)	CDoC LCla SLBF
	'Anita' (d)	CLoc CWVF EPts LAst MJac SLBF SVic WGor
	'Anjo' (v)	CWVF
	'Ann Howard Tripp'	CDoC CLoc CWVF MJac SVic
	'Ann Lee' (d)	EBak
	'Ann Marie McManus'	CSil
	'Anna of Longleat' (d)	CWVF EBak LAst MJac SPet
	'Anna Silvena'	LSou

	'Annabel' (d) 🏆H3	CCCN CDoC CLoc CTri CWVF EBak EPts LAst MJac SLBF SPet SVic
	'Anneke de Keijzer'	CDoC LCla
	'Annie Geurts'	CDoC
	'Annie M.G. Schmidt'	EPts
	'Another Storey'	CSil
	'Ant and Dec' (d/v)	MJac
	'Anthea Day' (d)	CLoc
	'Antigone'	SLBF
	'Aphrodite' (d)	CLoc CWVF EBak
	'Applause' (d)	CLoc CWVF EBak EPts SPet SVic
	aprica misapplied	see *F.* × *bacillaris*
	aprica Lundell	see *F. microphylla* subsp. *aprica*
	'Apricot Ice'	CLoc SVic
	'Arabella'	CWVF
	'Arabella Improved'	CWVF SVic
	arborea	see *F. arborescens*
§	***arborescens***	CDoC CHEx CHll CLoc CSil CWVF EBak EWld LCla MCot SDys SVic WWlt
	- B&SWJ 10475	WCru
	'Arcadia Gold' (d)	CWVF SVic
	'Arcady'	CLoc CWVF
	'Ariel' (E)	CDoC CSil LRHS SVic
	'Arkie'	MJac
	'Arlendon' (d)	CWVF
	'Army Nurse' (d) 🏆H4	CDoC CLoc CSil CWVF ELan ELon EPfP EPts LAst LPot LRHS MGos NBir NLar SEND SHil SLBF SLim SPet SVic
	'Arthur Baxter'	EBak
	'Ashley'	CDoC LCla
	'Ashley and Isobel'	CWVF
	'Ashtede'	SLBF
	'Ashville' **new**	SLBF
	'Atahualpa' (T)	CDoC
	'Athela'	EBak
	'Atlantic Star'	CWVF MJac
	'Atlantis' (d)	CWVF MJac
	'Atomic Glow' (d)	EBak SVic
	'Aubergine'	see *F.* 'Gerharda's Aubergine'
	'Audrey Hepburn'	CWVF
	'Auenland'	MJac
	'Aunt Hilda'	CSil
	'Aunt Juliana' (d)	EBak
	'Auntie Jinks'	CDoC CWVF EBak LAst MJac SLBF SPet SVic
	'Aurora Superba'	CLoc CWVF EBak SLBF
	'Australia Fair' (d)	CWVF EBak
§	***austromontana***	EBak
	'Autumnale' 🏆H1+3	CDoC CHEx CLoc CWVF EBak EPts LAst SBfd SLBF SMrm SPet SPoG SVic WHil
	'Avalanche' ambig. (d)	CDoC CLoc EBak LRHS SLBF
	'Avocet'	CLoc EBak
	'Avon Celebration' (d)	CLoc
	'Avon Gem'	CLoc CSil
	'Avon Glow' (d)	CLoc
	'Avon Gold'	CLoc
	ayavacensis	CDoC LCla
	'Azure Sky' (d)	MJac
	'Baby Blue Eyes' 🏆H3-4	CDoC CSil CWVF ELon EPfP LRHS LSRN MAsh MBri SHil
	'Baby Blush'	CSil
	'Baby Bright'	CWVF LCla
	'Baby Pink' (d)	CWVF
	'Baby Thumb' (v)	EPts
	'Babyface' Tolley (d)	SVic

§	× ***bacillaris*** (E)	CAbb CDoC CEnt CHGN CSil EBak EBee EWes GCal NLar SBfd SLBF SPoG
§	- 'Cottinghamii' (E)	CDoC CSil EWld IRar SPlb WSHC
	- 'Oosje'	see *F.* 'Oosje'
§	- 'Reflexa' (E)	CAbP CCCN CTrC LSou
	'Baden Powell' (E)	SVic
	'Bagworthy Water'	CLoc
	'Baker's Tri' (T)	EBak
	'Balkonkönigin'	CLoc CWVF EBak
	'Ballerina'	CDoC
	'Ballerina Dreams' **new**	LAst
	'Ballerina Girl' (E)	SLBF
	'Ballet Girl' (d) 🏆H1+3	CLoc CWVF EBak SLBF
	'Bambini'	CWVF EPts
	'Banks Peninsula'	GBin GQui
	'Barbara'	CLoc CSil CTsd CWVF EBak EPts MJac SPet SVic
	'Barbara Evans'	SLBF
	'Barbara Pountain' (d)	CWVF
	'Barbara Windsor'	CWVF MJac
	'Barry's Queen'	see *F.* 'Golden Border Queen'
	'Bartje'	SLBF
	'Bashful' (d)	CDoC CSil EPts LCla SPet SVic
	'Beacon'	CDoC CLoc CMac CSil CWVF EBak EPfP EPts LAst LCla LRHS MJac MWat SLBF SPet SPoG SVic
	'Beacon Rosa'	CDoC CLoc CSil CWVF ELon EPts LAst LCla LRHS MJac SLBF SPet SPoG SVic
	'Beacon Superior'	CSil
	'Bealings' (d)	CWVF SVic
	'Beau Nash'	CLoc
	'Beauty of Bath' (d)	CLoc EBak
	'Beauty of Clyffe Hall' Lye	CSil EBak
	'Beauty of Exeter' (d)	CWVF EBak
	'Beauty of Meise' (d)	CDoC
	'Beauty of Prussia' (d)	CLoc CSil CWVF
	'Beauty of Swanley'	EBak
	'Beauty of Trowbridge'	CWVF LCla
	'Becky Jane'	CSil
	'Bella Forbes' (d) 🏆H1+3	CSil EBak
	'Bella Rosella' (California Dreamers Series) (d)	EPts LAst MJac SCoo SLBF
	'Belsay Beauty' (d)	CWVF MJac SVic
	'Belvoir Beauty' (d)	CLoc
	'Ben de Jong'	CDoC LCla SLBF
	'Ben Jammin'	CLoc CSil CWVF EPfP EPts LAst LRHS MJac SEND SPoG SVic
	'Béranger' Lemoine, 1897 (d)	CSil EBak
	'Berba's Happiness' (d)	CWVF
	'Berliner Kind' (d)	CSil CWVF EBak
	'Bermuda' (d)	CWVF
	'Bernadette' (d)	CWVF
	'Bernie's Big-un' (d)	MJac
	'Bernisser Hardy' 🏆H3-4	CDoC CSil EPts LCla LRHS SEND SLBF SLim
	'Beryl Clarke' (v)	EPts
	'Bessie Kimberley' (T)	CDoC LCla
	'Beth Robley' (d)	CWVF
	'Betsy Huuskes'	SLBF
	'Betsy Ross' (d)	EBak
	Betty = 'Shabetty'PBR (Shadowdancer Series)	LAst
	'Beverley'	CWVF EBak EPts
	'Beverley Sisters' (d)	MJac
	'Bewitched' (d)	EBak
	'Bianca' (d)	CWVF SVic

	Name	Suppliers
	'Bicentennial' (d)	CLoc CWVF EBak EPts LAst MJac SPet SVic
	'Big Slim'	SLBF
	'Bill Stevens' (d)	CTsd
	'Billy' PBR	CDoC
	'Billy Green' (T) ♀H1+3	CDoC CLoc CWVF EBak EPts LCla MHer MJac SVic
	'Billy P'	LAst
	'Bilton'	CSil
	'Bishop's Bells' (d)	CWVF SVic
	'Bits' (d)	CTsd
	'Bittersweet' (d)	SVic
	'Black Beauty' (d)	CWVF
	'Black Country 21'	SLBF
	'Black Prince'	CDoC CWVF SVic
	'Blackmore Vale' (d)	CWVF
	'Blacky' (d)	CCCN EBak GBin LAst LSou MSCN NPri SBfd SDys SEND SGar SMrm SPet SVic
I	'Blanche Regina' (d)	CWVF MJac
	'Bland's New Striped'	EBak EPts LAst LSou SLBF
	'Blaze Away' (d)	LAst MJac WGor
	'Blood Donor' (d)	MJac
	'Blowick'	CWVF MJac SPet
	'Blue Beauty' (d)	CSil EBak
	'Blue Bush'	CSil CWVF EPts MJac SVic
	'Blue Butterfly' (d)	CWVF EBak SVic
	'Blue Eyes' (d)	CDoC SPet
	'Blue Gown' (d)	CDoC CLoc CSil CWVF EBak MGos SVic
	'Blue Lace' (d)	CSil
	'Blue Lagoon' ambig. (d)	CWVF
	'Blue Lake' (d)	CWVF
	'Blue Mink'	EBak
	'Blue Mirage' (d)	CLoc CWVF LAst SVic
	'Blue Mist' (d)	EBak
	'Blue Pearl' (d)	CWVF EBak
	'Blue Pinwheel'	CWVF EBak
	'Blue Satin' (d)	LAst
	'Blue Tit'	CSil LCla
	'Blue Veil' (d)	CLoc CWVF MJac SCoo SVic
	'Blue Waves' (d)	CLoc CSBt CWVF EBak MJac SVic
	'Blush o' Dawn' (d)	CLoc CTsd CWVF EBak EPts SVic
	'Bob Bartrum'	EPts SLBF
	'Bob Pacey'	CWVF
	'Bobby Boy' (d)	EBak
	'Bobby Dazzler' (d)	CWVF
	'Bobby Shaftoe' (d)	EBak
	'Bobby Wingrove'	EBak
	'Bobby's Girl'	EPts
	'Bobolink' (d)	EBak
	'Bob's Best' (d)	CWVF EPts MJac
	'Boerhaave'	EBak
	boliviana Britton	see *F. sanctae-rosae*
	boliviana ambig.	CBcs CTsd
§	***boliviana*** Carrière	CDoC CHEx CHll CLoc CWVF EBak LCla
§	- var. ***alba*** ♀H1+3	CDoC CHll CLoc EBak EPts LCla MREP SVic
	- var. ***boliviana***	CRHN SVic
	- var. ***luxurians*** 'Alba'	see *F. boliviana* Carrière var. *alba*
	- f. ***puberulenta*** Munz	see *F. boliviana* Carrière
	'Bon Accorde'	CLoc CWVF EBak EPts SLBF SVic
	'Bon Bon' (d)	CWVF EBak SVic
	'Bonita' (d)	CWVF SVic
	'Bonnie Lass' (d)	EBak
	'Bora Bora' (d)	CWVF EBak SVic
	'Borde Hill' (d)	EPts
	'Border Princess'	EBak
	'Border Queen' ♀H3-4	CDoC CLoc CSil CWVF EBak EPts EWes MJac MSCN SLBF SPet SVic
	'Border Reiver'	CWVF EBak SVic
	'Börnemann's Beste'	see *F.* 'Georg Börnemann'
	'Bouffant'	CLoc SVic
	'Bountiful' Munkner (d)	CLoc CWVF
	'Bouquet' (d)	CDoC CSil
	'Bow Bells'	CDoC CLoc CWVF MJac SPet SVic
	'Boy Marc' (T) ♀H1	LCla
	'Braamt's Glorie'	CDoC
	bracelinae	CDoC CSil
	'Brandt's 500 Club'	CLoc EBak
	'Breckland'	EBak
	'Breeders' Delight'	CSil CWVF
	'Breeder's Dream' (d)	EBak
	'Breevis Minimus'	SLBF
	'Brenda' (d)	CLoc CWVF EBak
	'Brenda White'	CDoC CLoc CWVF EBak SVic
	'Brentwood' (d)	EBak
	brevilobis	CSil
	'Brian C. Morrison' (T)	LCla
	'Brian G. Soanes'	EBak
	'Brian Kimberley' (T)	LCla
	'Bridal Veil' (d)	EBak
	'Bridesmaid' (d)	CWVF EBak SPet SVic
	'Brigadoon' (d)	EBak
	'Brighton Belle' (T)	CDoC CWVF
	'Brilliant' ambig.	CWVF
	'Brilliant' Bull, 1865	CDoC CLoc CSil EBak LCla
	'Briony Caunt'	CSil
	'British Jubilee' (d)	CWVF SVic
	'Brixham Orpheus'	CWVF
	'Brodsworth'	CSil
	'Bronze Banks Peninsula'	CDoC CSil
	'Brookwood Belle' (d)	CTsd CWVF EPts LCla MJac SLBF
	'Brookwood Joy' (d)	CWVF
	'Brutus' ♀H4	CDoC CLoc CSil CWVF EBak EPfP EPts LRHS MAsh MBri MGos MSCN MWat SCoo SHil SLBF SPet SPoG SVic
	'Bryan Breary' (E)	LCla
	'Buddha' (d)	EBak
	'Bugle Boy'	LCla
	'Bunny' (d)	CWVF EBak SLBF SVic
	'Burstwick'	CSil
	'Burton Brew'	MJac
	'Buster' (d)	LCla
	'Buttercup'	CLoc CWVF EBak SVic
	'C.J. Howlett'	CSil EBak
	'Caballero' (d)	EBak
	'Caesar' (d)	CWVF EBak
	'Caledonia'	CSil EBak
	'Callaly Pink'	CWVF
	'Cambridge Louie'	CWVF EBak SPet
	campos-portoi	CDoC CSil CTsd LCla WHil WPGP
	'Candlelight' (d)	EBak
	'Candy Bells' (d)	CSBt
	canescens misapplied	see *F. ampliata*
	'Canny Bob'	MJac
	'Canopy' (d)	CWVF
	'Capri' (d)	CWVF EBak
	'Cara Mia' (d)	CLoc CTsd SPet
	'Caradela' (d)	CLoc MJac
	'Cardinal'	CLoc
	'Cardinal Farges' (d)	CLoc CWVF SLBF SVic
	'Careless Whisper'	CDoC LCla SLBF
	'Carioca'	EBak

	'Carl Drude' (d)	CSil CTsd SVic
	'Carla Johnston' ♀$^{H1+3}$	CDoC CLoc CWVF EPts MJac SVic
	'Carl's Brummagem Beauty'	MJac
	'Carmel Blue'	CCCN CDoC CLoc LAst LRHS SBfd SVic WGor
	'Carmen' Lemoine (d)	CDoC CSil
	'Carmine Bell'	CSil
	'Carnea'	CSil CWib
	'Carnoustie' (d)	EBak
	'Carol Grace' (d)	CLoc
	'Carol Nash' (d)	CLoc
	'Caroline'	CLoc CWVF EBak EPts SLBF SVic
	'Caroline's Joy'	LAst MJac SBfd SCoo SPet
	'Cascade'	CDoC CLoc CWVF EPts LBMP MJac SLBF SPet
	'Caspar Hauser' (d)	CWVF SLBF SVic
	'Catharina' (T)	CDoC
	'Catherine Bartlett'	CWVF
	'Cathie MacDougall' (d)	EBak
	'Cecile' (d)	CCCN CDoC CWVF EPts LAst MJac SLBF SVic
	'Celadore' (d)	CWVF SVic
	'Celebration' (d)	CLoc CWVF
	'Celia Smedley' ♀^{H3}	CDoC CLoc CWVF EBak EPts LAst LCla MJac SLBF SPet SVic
	'Centerpiece' (d)	EBak
	'Ceri'	CLoc
	'Cerrig'	SVic
	'Champagne Celebration'	CLoc
	'Chancellor' (d)	CWVF
	'Chandleri'	CWVF SLBF SVic
	'Chang' ♀$^{H1+3}$	CDoC CLoc CWVF EBak LCla SLBF SVic
	'Chantelle Garcia' (d)	CDoC SLBF
	'Chantry Park' (T)	LCla
	'Charisma'	SVic
	'Charles Edward' (d)	CSil
	'Charles Welch'	EPts
	Charlie Dimmock = 'Foncha'^{PBR} (d)	CLoc LAst
	'Charlie Gardiner'	CWVF EBak
	'Charlie Girl' (d)	EBak SVic
	'Charming'	CDoC CLoc CSil CWVF EBak LRHS MAsh MJac SVic
	'Chase Delight' (v)	SLBF
	'Chatt's Delight'	SLBF
	'Checkerboard' ♀^{H3}	CLoc CWVF EBak EPts LAst LCla MJac MSCN SLBF SPet SVic
	'Cheers' (d)	CWVF
	'Chelsea Louise'	EPts
	'Cherry'^{PBR} Götz	LAst
	'Chessboard'	CLoc MBri
	'Chillerton Beauty' ♀^{H3}	CLoc CSil CTri CWVF ELan ELon EPfP EPts LAst LCla LRHS MJac NLar SEND SLBF SPet SVic WMnd
	'China Doll' (d)	CWVF EBak SVic
	'China Lantern'	CLoc CSil CWVF EBak SVic
	'Chor Echo'	CDoC
	'Chris Nicholls' (d)	CSil
	'Chris Tarrant' (d)	EPts
	'Christina Becker'	SVic
	'Christine Bamford'	CDoC CSil CTsd CWVF
	'Christine Rogers'	CDoC
	'Churchtown'	CWVF
	cinerea	CDoC LCla
	'Cinnabarina' (E)	CLoc
	'Cinque Port Liberty' (d)	SLBF
	'Cinvenu'	LCla
	'Cinvulca'	LCla
	'Circe' (d)	CWVF EBak SVic
	'Circus'	EBak
	'Circus Spangles' (d)	CLoc LAst
	'Citation'	CLoc CWVF EBak SVic
	'City of Adelaide' (d)	CLoc
	'City of Leicester'	CWVF MHer SPet
	'Clair de Lune'	CDoC CWVF EBak SVic
	'Claire Evans' (d)	CWVF
	'Claire Oram'	CLoc
	'Claudia' (d)	CDoC LAst LCla MJac SLBF
	'Cliantha' (d)	CDoC
	'Clifford Gadsby' (d)	EBak
	'Cliff's Hardy'	CDoC CSil LCla
	'Cliff's Own'	SVic
	'Cliff's Unique' (d)	CWVF EPts
	'Clifton Beauty' (d)	CWVF MJac
	'Clifton Belle' (d)	CWVF
	'Clifton Charm'	CSil EPts LCla MJac SVic
	'Clipper'	CSil CWVF
	'Cloth of Gold'	CLoc CWVF EBak MHer MJac SPet SVic
	'Cloverdale Jewel' (d)	CDoC CWVF EBak SPet SVic
	'Cloverdale Joy'	EBak
	'Cloverdale Pearl'	CDoC CWVF EBak SPet SPoG SVic
	'Coachman' ♀^{H4}	CLoc CWVF EBak EPts LAst LCla SLBF SPet SVic
	coccinea	CDoC CSil CTsd
	'Codringtonii'	CSil
	× ***colensoi***	CDoC CSil ECou LCla
	'Collingwood' (d)	CLoc CWVF EBak
	'Colne Fantasy' (v)	CDoC
	'Come Dancing' (d)	CDoC CWVF SPet SVic
	'Comet' Banks	CWVF
I	'Comet' Tiret (d)	CDoC CLoc EBak
	'Comperen Lutea' (d)	CDoC
	'Conchilla' (d)	EBak
	'Connie' (d)	EBak SVic
	'Connor's Cascade'	SLBF
	'Conspicua' ♀$^{H3-4}$	CDoC CSil CWVF EBak ELon SLBF SVic
	'Constable Country' (d)	CWVF
	'Constance' (d)	CDoC CLoc CSil CWVF LCla MJac SLBF SPet SVic
	'Constance Comer'	MJac
	'Constellation' ambig.	CWVF
	'Constellation' Schnabel, 1957 (d)	CLoc EBak
	'Contraste' (d)	SBfd
	'Coombe Park'	MJac
	'Copycat'	CSil
	'Coquet Bell'	CWVF EBak
	'Coquet Dale' (d)	CWVF EBak
	'Coral Baby' (E)	LCla
	'Coral Rose' (d)	SVic
	'Coral Seas'	EBak
	'Coralle' (T)	CCCN CDoC CLoc CWVF EBak EPts LCla MHer MJac MSCN SLBF SVic
	'Corallina' ♀$^{H3-4}$	CDoC CLoc CSil CTsd EBak ELon SBfd SVic WFar WPnn
I	'Corallina Variegata' (v)	CSil
*	***cordata*** B&SWJ 9095	WCru
	- B&SWJ 10325	WCru
	cordifolia misapplied	see *F. splendens*
	'Core'ngrato' (d)	CLoc CWVF EBak
	'Cornelia Smith' (T)	CDoC LCla

'Cornwall Calls' (d) EBak
'Corsage' (d) CWVF SVic
'Corsair' (d) EBak SVic
corymbiflora misapplied see *F. boliviana* Carrière
corymbiflora Ruíz & Pav. CDoC EBak SVic
'Cosmopolitan' (d) EBak
'Costa Brava' CLoc EBak
'Cotta Bright Star' CDoC CWVF LCla
'Cotta Carousel' LCla
'Cotta Christmas Tree' CDoC LCla SLBF
'Cotta Fairy' CWVF
'Cotta Vino' SVic
'Cottinghamii' see *F.* × *bacillaris* 'Cottinghamii'
'Cotton Candy' (d) CLoc CWVF SVic
'Countdown Carol' (d) EPts
'Countess of Aberdeen' CWVF EBak SLBF
'Countess of Maritza' (d) CLoc CWVF
'County Park' ECou
'Court Jester' (d) CLoc EBak
'Cover Girl' (d) EBak EPts
'Coxeen' EBak
'Crackerjack' CLoc EBak
'Creampuff' (d) CTsd
'Crescendo' (d) CLoc CWVF
'Crinkley Bottom' (d) EPts MJac SLBF
'Crinoline' (d) EBak
'Crosby Serendipity' CLoc
'Crosby Soroptimist' CWVF MJac
'Cross Check' CWVF
'Crusader' (d) CWVF
'Crystal Blue' EBak SVic
'Crystal Stars' (d) SVic
'Cupid' EBak
'Curly Q' EBak SVic
'Curtain Call' (d) CWVF EBak SVic
cylindracea misapplied see *F.* × *bacillaris*
cylindracea Lindl. (E) CSil LCla
- (E/f) B&SWJ 10294 WCru
'Cymon' (d) CWVF
'Cymru' (d) SVic
cyrtandroides CSil
'Dainty' EBak
'Dainty Lady' (d) EBak
'Daisy Bell' CDoC CLoc CTsd CWVF EBak LCla MJac SPet SVic
'Dalton' EBak
'Dana Samantha' EPts
'Dancing Bloom' EPts
'Dancing Flame' (d) ♀H1+3 CLoc CWVF EBak EPts LAst LBMP MJac SLBF SVic
'Daniel Pfaller' (d) MJac
'Danish Pastry' CWVF SPet
'Danny Boy' (d) CLoc CWVF EBak SVic
'Dark Eyes' (d) ♀H4 CCCN CLoc CSil CWVF EBak LAst LBMP MJac SBfd SLBF SPet SVic
'Dark Night' (d) CSil
'Dark Secret' (d) EBak
'Dark Treasure' (d) CDoC CTsd
'Daryn John Woods' CDoC LCla
'David' ♀H3-4 CDoC CLoc CSil CWVF ELon EOHP EPfP EPts LAst LCla LSRN MAvo SLBF SLPl WGor WHil
'David Alston' (d) CLoc CWVF EBak
'David Lockyer' (d) CLoc CWVF SVic
'David Savage' (d) LCla
'David Ward' (d) NEgg
'Dawn' EBak
'Dawn Fantasia' (v) CLoc EPts
'Dawn Redfern' (d) CWVF
'Dawn Sky' (d) EBak
'Dawn Star' (d) CLoc CWVF MJac SVic
'Dawn Thunder' (d) SVic
'Day by Day' CSil
'Day Star' EBak
'De Groot's Floriant' LCla
'De Mijnlamp' (d) CDoC
'Debby' (d) EBak
'Deben Petite' (E) LCla
'Deborah Jane' SLBF
'Deborah Street' (d) CLoc
§ ***decussata*** Ruíz & Pav. EBak
'Dee Copley' (d) EBak
'Dee Star' (d) SVic
'Deep Purple' (d) CDoC CLoc CWVF LAst LBMP MJac SCoo SGar SLBF
'Delia Smith' (d) EPts
'Delilah' (d) CWVF
'Delta's Bride' SLBF
'Delta's Dream' CTsd CWVF
'Delta's Drop' SVic
'Delta's Groom' LCla SLBF
'Delta's Ko' (d) SVic
'Delta's Parade' (d) CDoC
'Delta's Rien' SVic
'Delta's Sara' CDoC CSil LAst LRHS MBri MJac SHil SLim SPoG
'Delta's Symphonie' (d) CWVF
'Delta's Wonder' CSil SVic
§ ***denticulata*** CDoC CLoc CWVF EBak EPts LAst LCla MHer SEND SLBF SVic
'Derby Imp' CWVF
'Desperate Daniel' EPts
'Devonshire Dumpling' (d) CCCN CDoC CLoc CTsd CWVF EBak EPts LAst MJac SLBF SPet SVic
'Diablo' (d) EBak
'Diamond Wedding' SVic
'Diana' (d) EBak
'Diana Wills' (d) CWVF
'Diana Wright' CDoC CSil LPla
Diana, Princess of Wales = 'Fucdpw'PBR LAst MJac SBfd
'Diane Brown' CWVF
'Diane Stephens' SLBF
§ 'Die Schöne Wilhelmine' SLBF SVic
'Dilly-Dilly' (d) CWVF
'Dimples' (d) CSil
'Dipton Dainty' (d) CLoc EBak SVic
'Display' ♀H4 CDoC CLoc CSil CWVF EBak EPfP EPts LAst LCla LRHS MJac NPer SLBF SPet SPoG SVic WFar
'Doc' CDoC CSil EPts SPet SVic
'Docteur Topinard' CLoc EBak
'Doctor' see *F.* 'The Doctor'
'Doctor Foster' ♀H4 CDoC CLoc CSil CTri EBak EPfP SVic
'Doctor Mason' CWVF
'Doctor Olson' (d) CLoc EBak
'Doctor Robert' CWVF EPts MJac SVic
'Dodo' LCla SLBF
§ 'Dollar Prinzessin' (d) ♀H4 CDoC CLoc CMac CSil CTsd CWVF EBak EPfP EPts LAst LCla LRHS MAsh MBri MGos MJac MWat NPer SHil SLBF SLim SMrm SPet SPlb SVic WFar
'Dominyana' EBak LCla
'Don Peralta' EBak
'Dopy' (d) CDoC EPts SPet SVic

'Doreen Redfern'	CLoc CWVF MJac SPet SVic
'Doreen Stroud' (d)	CWVF
'Doris Deaves'	SLBF
'Doris Joan'	SLBF
'Dorothea Flower'	CLoc CWVF EBak
'Dorothy'	LCla SLBF SPet
'Dorothy Ann'	LCla SLBF
'Dorothy Cheal'	CWVF
'Dorothy Day' (d)	CLoc
'Dorothy Hanley' (d)	CCCN CLoc EPts LAst LRHS LSRN LSou MAsh MJac SEND SLBF SPet SVic
'Dorothy Oosting' (d)	CDoC
'Dorothy Shields' (d)	CWVF MJac
'Dorrian Brogdale' (T)	LCla
'Dorset Abigail'	CWVF
'Dorset Delight' (d)	CWVF
'Dotti' (d) **new**	SLBF
'Drake 400' (d)	CLoc
'Drama Girl' (d)	CWVF
'Drame' (d)	CDoC CSil CWVF EBak SVic
'Drum Major' (d)	EBak
'Du Barry' (d)	EBak
'Duchess of Albany'	CLoc EBak
'Duchess of Cornwall' (d)	EPts
'Duet' (d)	SVic
'Duke of Wellington' Haag, 1956 (d)	CLoc
'Dulcie Elizabeth' (d)	CWVF EBak MJac SPet
'Dunrobin Bedder'	CSil
'Dusky Beauty'	CWVF SVic
'Dusky Rose' (d)	CLoc CWVF EBak MJac SVic
'Dutch Mill'	CLoc CWVF EBak
'Duyfken'	CWVF
'Dying Embers'	CLoc MSCN
'Dymph Werker van Groenland' (E)	LCla
'East Anglian'	CLoc EBak
'Easter Belle'	LRHS
'Easter Bonnet' (d)	CLoc CWVF
'Ebb 'n' Flow'	EBak
'Ebbtide' (d)	CLoc EBak
'Echo'	CWVF
'Ed Largarde' (d)	EBak
'Eden Lady'	CDoC CLoc SPet
'Eden Princess'	CWVF MJac
'Eden Rock' (d)	WGor
'Edith' ambig.	EPts
'Edith' Brown (d)	CSil LCla SLBF
'Edith Emery' (d)	SPet
'Edna May'	CWVF
'Edna W. Smith'	CWVF
'Eileen Drew'	SLBF
'Eileen Raffill'	EBak
'Eileen Saunders'	CSil EBak
'El Camino' (d)	CWVF
'El Cid'	CLoc CSil EBak SVic
'Elaine Ann'	EPts MJac
'Elaine Taylor' (d)	MJac
'Eleanor Leytham'	CWVF EBak SVic
'Eleanor Rawlins'	CSil EBak
'Elf'	CSil
'Elfin Glade'	CLoc CSil CWVF EBak
'Elfrida' (d)	CSil
'Elfriede Ott' (T) ♀H1	CLoc EBak LCla
'Elizabeth' ambig.	CTsd
'Elizabeth' Whiteman, 1941	EBak
'Elizabeth Honnorine'	SVic
'Elizabeth Travis' (d)	EBak

	'Ellen Morgan' (d)	CWVF EBak
	'Elma'	LCla
	'Elsa' (d)	CWVF SVic
	'Elsie Maude' (d)	CWVF
	'Elsie Mitchell' (d)	CTsd CWVF SPet
	'Elysée'	CSil
§	'Emile de Wildeman' (d)	CWVF EBak SPet
	'Emile Zola'	CSil
	'Emily Austen'	CWVF
	'Emma Alice' (d)	CWVF
	'Emma Margaret'	SLBF
	'Empress of Prussia' ♀H4	CDoC CLoc CSil CWVF EBak EPts SLBF SVic WMnd
	'Enchanted' (d)	CWVF EBak
	encliandra	CDoC
	subsp. ***encliandra*** (E)	
*	- var. ***gris*** (E)	CSil
§	'Enfant Prodigue' (d)	CDoC CLoc CSil SDix SLBF SMrm SVic WMnd
	'English Rose' (d)	CWVF
	'Enstone'	see *F. magellanica* var. *molinae* 'Enstone'
	'Eric's Hardy' (d)	CDoC
	'Eric's Majestic' (d)	MJac
	'Erika Köth' (T)	LCla
	'Ernest Rankin'	CSil SVic
	'Ernie'[PBR]	LAst SLBF
	'Ernie Bromley'	CSil CWVF
	'Ernie Wise' (d)	MJac SCoo
	'Eroica'	SVic
	'Eruption'	CDoC CLoc LAst MCot
	'Esmerelda'	MJac
	'Estelle Marie'	CLoc CWVF EBak SPet SVic
	'Eternal Flame' (d)	CWVF EBak EPts SVic
	'Ethel May' (d)	MJac
	'Ethel Wilson'	CSil
	'Eusebia' (d)	CTsd SVic
	'Eva Boerg'	CCCN CLoc CSil CTri CWVF EBak LAst SPet SVic WKif
	'Evelyn Stanley' (d)	CWVF
§	'Evelyn Steele Little'	EBak
	'Evening Sky' (d)	EBak
	'Evensong'	CLoc CWVF EBak SVic
	excorticata	CAbb CBcs CDoC CPLG CSil CTsd MCot SPlb
	'Exmoor Paths'	CSil
	'Exmoor Pearl'	CSil
	'Exmoor Rose'	CSil
	'Exmoor Silver'	CSil
	'Exmoor Woods'	CSil
	'Fabian Franck' (T)	CDoC LCla
	'Fairy Floss'	SLBF
	'Falklands' (d)	CSil SLBF
	'Falling Stars'	CLoc CWVF EBak SVic
	'Fan Dancer' (d)	EBak
	'Fancy Pants' (d)	CLoc CWVF EBak SVic
	'Fanfare'	CDoC EBak LCla SVic
	'Fascination'	see *F.* 'Emile de Wildeman'
	'Fashion' (d)	EBak
	'Favourite'	EBak
	'Felicity Kendal' (d)	MJac SCoo
	'Feltham's Pride'	CWVF
	'Fenman'	CWVF SVic
	'Festival Lights' (E)	SLBF
	'Festoon'	EBak
	'Fey' (d)	CWVF
	'Ffion'	CDoC EPts
	'Fiery Spider'	EBak SVic
	'Finn'	CDoC CWVF EPts

'Fiona'	CDoC CLoc CWVF EBak SPet SVic
'Fiorelli Flowers' (d)	CDoC
'Fire Mountain' (d)	CLoc SVic
'Firecracker'PBR	see *F.* 'John Ridding'
'Firefly'	SVic
'Firelite' (d)	EBak
'Firenza' (d)	CWVF
'First Kiss' (d)	CWVF
'First Lady' (d)	CWVF
'First Lord'	CWVF
'First Success' (E)	CDoC CWVF LCla SVic
'Flair' (d)	CLoc CWVF
'Flame'	EBak
'Flamenco Dancer' (California Dreamers Series) (d)	CLoc
'Flamingo' (d)	SVic
'Flash' ♀H3-4	CLoc CSil CTri CWVF EBak EPfP EPts LCla MJac SLBF SPet SPoG SVic
'Flashlight'	CDoC CSil CWVF EPfP EWld LAst LCla LRHS MAvo MJac SCoo WFar
'Flashlight Amélioré'	CSil
'Flat Jack o' Lancashire' (d)	CSil SLBF
'Flavia' (d)	EBak
'Fleur de Picardie'	SLBF
'Flirtation Waltz' (d)	CLoc CWVF EBak MJac SVic
'Flocon de Neige'	CSil EBak
'Flogman'	LCla
'Floral City' (d)	CLoc EBak
'Florence Taylor' (d)	CWVF
'Florence Turner'	CSil EBak
'Florentina' (d)	CLoc CWVF EBak SVic
'Florrie's Gem' (d)	SLBF
'Flowerdream' (d)	CWVF
'Flyaway' (d)	EBak
'Fly-by-night' (d)	CWVF
'Flying Cloud' (d)	CDoC CLoc CSil CWVF EBak SVic
'Flying Scotsman' (d)	CDoC CLoc CWVF EBak EPts MJac SCoo SVic
'Folies Bergères' (d)	EBak
'Foline'	SVic
'Foolke'	CSil EBak
'Forfar's Pride' (d)	CSil
'Forget-me-not'	CLoc CWVF EBak SVic
'Fort Bragg' (d)	CWVF EBak
'Fountains Abbey' (d)	CWVF
'Four Farthings' (d)	EPts
'Foxgrove Wood' ♀H3-4	CSil CWVF EBak EPts SLBF
'Foxtrot' (d)	CWVF
'Foxy Lady' (d)	CWVF
'Frances Haskins'	CSil
'Frank Saunders'	CWVF LCla SLBF
'Frank Unsworth' (d)	CWVF EPts MJac SPet
'Frankfurt 2006'	MJac
'Frankie's Magnificent Seven' (d)	EPts
'Franz von Zon'	LCla SLBF
'Frau Hilde Rademacher' (d)	CDoC CSil CWVF EBak EPts SLBF SVic
'Frauke'	SVic
'Fred Hansford'	CDoC CSil CWVF
'Fred's First' (d)	CDoC CSil
'Freefall'	EBak
'Friendly Fire' (d)	CLoc
'Frosted Flame'	CLoc CTsd CWVF EBak LAst LCla MJac SLBF SPet
'Frühling' (d)	CSil EBak
'Fuchsiade '88'	CLoc CSil CWVF EBak SLBF
'Fuchsiarama '91' (T) ♀H1	CWVF
'Fuji-san'	CDoC ELon EPts
'Fuksie Foetsie' (E)	CDoC CSil
fulgens (T) ♀H1+3	CDoC GCal LCla LRHS
* - 'Variegata' (T/v)	CDoC CLoc EPts LCla
'Fulpila'	LCla SLBF
'Für Elise' (d)	EBak
'Gala' (d)	EBak
'Galadriel'	ECtt
'Garden News' (d) ♀H3-4	CDoC CLoc CSil CWVF EPfP EPts LAst LCla LRHS MAsh MAvo MBri MJac MSCN NPer SLBF SPet SVic WFar WMnd
'Garden Week' (d)	CDoC CWVF SVic
'Gartenmeister Bonstedt' (T) ♀H1+3	CDoC CLoc CWVF EBak EWld LCla SVic
'Gary Rhodes' (d)	EBak MJac SBfd SCoo
'Gay Fandango' (d)	CLoc CTsd CWVF EBak
'Gay Parasol' (d)	LAst MJac SVic
'Gay Paree' (d)	EBak
'Gay Senorita'	EBak
'Gay Spinner' (d)	CLoc
gehrigeri	EBak
'Gemma Fisher' (d)	EPts
Gene = 'Goetzgene'PBR (Shadowdancer Series)	LAst LSou SCoo
'Général Monk' (d)	CDoC CSil CWVF EBak EPts LAst SVic
'Général Voyron'	CSil
'General Wavell' (d)	SVic
'Genii' ♀H4	Widely available
'Geoff Oke'	CDoC SLBF
'Geoffrey Smith' (d)	CSil EPts
§ 'Georg Börnemann' (T)	CLoc EBak
'George Allen White' (d)	CWVF
'George Barr'	EPfP LRHS
'George Johnson'	CDoC
'George Travis' (d)	EBak
'Gerald Drewitt'	CSil
§ 'Gerharda's Aubergine'	CLoc CSil CWVF
'Gesneriana'	CLoc EBak
'Ghislaine' (d)	CDoC
'Giant Pink Enchanted' (d)	CLoc EBak
'Gilda' (d)	CWVF MJac SVic
'Gillian Althea' (d)	CWVF
'Gilt Edge' (v)	CLoc
'Gina Bowman' (E)	CDoC LCla SLBF
Ginger = 'Goetzginger'PBR (Shadowdancer Series)	LAst LSou SCoo
'Gipsy Princess' (d)	CLoc
'Girls' Brigade'	CWVF
'Gladiator' (d)	CMac EBak SVic
'Gladys Godfrey'	EBak
'Gladys Lorimer'	CDoC CWVF EPts LRHS
'Gladys Miller'	CLoc
glazioviana	CDoC CSil CWVF EPts GCal LCla MHer SLBF WGwG
'Glenby' (d)	CWVF
'Glendale'	CWVF
'Glitters'	CWVF EBak
§ 'Globosa'	CAgr CSil EBak
'Glow'	CSil EBak
'Glowing Embers'	EBak
'Glowing Lilac' (d)	EPts
'Gold Brocade'	EPfP
'Gold Crest'	EBak
'Gold Leaf'	CWVF

'Golden Anniversary' (d) CLoc CWVF EBak MJac SVic
'Golden Arrow' (T) LCla SVic
§ 'Golden Border Queen' CLoc EBak SPet
'Golden Dawn' CLoc CWVF EBak SVic
'Golden Girl' SLBF
'Golden Herald' CSil SLBF
'Golden la Campanella' (d/v) CLoc
'Golden Lena' (d/v) CSil CWVF
'Golden Marinka' (v) ♀H3 CLoc EBak LSou SPet SVic
'Golden Swingtime' (d) MJac SPet SVic
'Golden Treasure' (v) CLoc CSil CWVF
'Golden Vergeer' (v) SLBF
'Golden Wedding' SVic
'Goldsworth Beauty' CSil
'Golondrina' CSil CWVF EBak
'Goody Goody' EBak SVic
'Gordon Boy' (d) CSil
'Gordon Thorley' CSil
'Gordon's China Rose' LCla
'Gota' CDoC SLBF
'Göttingen' (T) EBak
'Governor Pat Brown' (d) EBak
'Grace Darling' CWVF EBak
gracilis see *F. magellanica* var. *gracilis*
'Graf Witte' CDoC CSil CWVF SPet SVic
'Grand Duke' (T/d) CWVF
'Grand Prix' (d) SVic
'Grand Slam' (d) SVic
'Grandad Hobbs' (d) LCla SLBF
'Grandma Sinton' (d) CLoc CWVF
'Grandpa Jack' (d) SLBF
'Granny Charlton' WCFE
'Grayrigg' CDoC CSil CTsd ELon EPts LCla LSRN SLBF SUsu
'Great Ouse' (d) EPts
'Great Scott' (d) CLoc
'Green 'n' Gold' EBak
'Greenpeace' CDoC SVic
'Grey Lady' (d) CSil SVic
'Groene Kan's Glorie' CTsd SVic
'Grumpy' CWVF EPts SPet SVic
'Gruss aus dem Bodethal' CLoc CWVF EBak EPts SLBF
'Guinevere' CWVF EBak
'Gustave Doré' (d) CSil EBak
'Guy Dauphine' (d) EBak
'Gwen Dodge' SVic
'Gypsy Girl' (d) CWVF
'H.G. Brown' CSil EBak
'Hampshire Blue' CDoC CWVF SVic
'Hanna' (d) LRHS
'Hannah Louise' (d) EPts
'Hannah Rogers' SLBF
'Hans Callaars' LCla
'Happiness' (d) SVic
'Happy' CDoC CSil CTsd CWVF EPts LCla MSCN SPet SVic
'Happy Anniversary' CLoc SVic
'Happy Fellow' CDoC CLoc CSil EBak
'Happy Wedding Day' (d) CLoc CWVF EPts LAst MJac SCoo SLBF SPet SVic
'Hapsburgh' EBak
'Harbour Lites' SLBF
'Harlow Car' CDoC CWVF EPts
'Harlow Perfection' CDoC
'Harmony' Niederholzer, 1946 EBak
'Harry Dunnett' (T) EBak
'Harry Gray' (d) CLoc CWVF EBak EPts LAst MJac SLBF SPet SVic
'Harry Pullen' EBak
'Harry Taylor' (d) EPts
'Harry's Sunshine' SLBF
'Harti's Olivia' CDoC
hartwegii CDoC CSil GCal LCla MHer
'Harvey's Reward' SLBF
'Hathersage' (d) EBak
hatschbachii CDoC CSil CTsd ECre ELon EWes GCal LCla LRHS MCot MHer SDix SLon SPlb SPoG WPnn
'Haute Cuisine' (d) CLoc SVic
'Hawaiian Sunset' (d) CLoc CWVF EPts SLBF
'Hawkshead' ♀H3-4 Widely available
'Hayley Jay' (d) CDoC SLBF
'Hazel' (d) CWVF SVic
'Heart Throb' (d) EBak
'Heavenly Hayley' (d) SLBF
'Hebe' EBak
'Heidi Ann' (d) ♀H3 CDoC CLoc CSil CWVF EBak EPts LAst LRHS MAsh SLBF SPet SVic
'Heidi Blue' (d) SLBF
'Heidi Joy' CSil
§ 'Heidi Weiss' (d) CDoC CLoc CSil CWVF SPet
'Heinrich Henkel' see *F.* 'Andenken an Heinrich Henkel'
'Helen Clare' (d) CLoc CWVF EBak
'Helen Gair' (d) CWVF
'Helen Lang' EPts
'Hellen Devine' CWVF
'Hemsleyana' see *F. microphylla* subsp. *hemsleyana*
'Henning Becker' ♀H3 CWVF ELan ELon
'Henri Poincaré' EBak
'Henrieke Dimi' (d) CDoC
'Herald' ♀H4 CDoC CSil CWVF EBak EPfP LRHS LSou MAsh SLBF SVic
'Herbé de Jacques' see *F.* 'Mr West'
'Heri Shusui' (d) CDoC
'Heritage' (d) CLoc CSil EBak
'Herman de Graaff' (d) SLBF
'Hermiena' CLoc CWVF EPts SLBF SVic
'Heron' CSil EBak
'Herps Pierement' SLBF
'Hessett Festival' (d) CWVF EBak
'Heston Blue' (d) CWVF
'Heydon' CWVF
'Hi Jinks' (d) EBak SVic
hidalgensis see *F. microphylla* subsp. *hidalgensis*
'Hidcote Beauty' CLoc CWVF EBak LCla SLBF SPet SVic
'Highland Pipes' LCla SVic
'Hilda May Salmon' CWVF
'Hindu Belle' EBak
'Hinnerike' (E) CSil CWVF LCla SVic
'Hiroshige' (T) LCla
'His Excellency' (d) EBak
'Hobo' (d) CSil
'Hobson's Choice' (d) CWVF SLBF
'Holly's Beauty' (d) CDoC CLoc EPts LAst
'Hollywood Park' (d) EBak
'Hot Coals' CWVF EPts MCot MJac SVic
'Howerd Hebden' CDoC
'Howlett's Hardy' ♀H3-4 CDoC CLoc CSil CWVF EBak NLar SVic WMnd
'Huet's Kwarts' CDoC
'Huet's Turkoois' CDoC
'Hula Girl' (d) CDoC CWVF EBak MJac SPet
'Huntsman' (d) CCCN CDoC
'Ian Leedham' (d) EBak

	Cultivar	Suppliers
	'Ian Storey'	CDoC CSil
	'Ice Cream Soda' (d)	EBak
	'Iceberg'	CWVF EBak SVic
	'Icecap'	CWVF SVic
	'Iced Champagne'	CLoc CWVF EBak MJac
	'Ichiban' (d)	CLoc
	'Ida' (d)	EBak
	'Igloo Maid' (d)	CLoc CWVF EBak SVic
	'Imogen Faye' (d) **new**	SLBF
	'Impala' (d)	CWVF
	'Imperial Fantasy' (d)	CWVF
	'Impudence'	CLoc CWVF EBak
	'Impulse' (d)	CLoc
	'Independence' (d)	SVic
	'Indian Maid' (d)	CDoC CWVF EBak
	'Insulinde' (T)	CDoC CWVF EPts LCla MHer MJac SLBF
	'Interlude' (d)	EBak
	'Iolanthe' (T)	CWVF
	'Irene L. Peartree' (d)	CWVF LCla
	'Irene Sinton' (d)	MJac
	'Iris Amer' (d)	CLoc CWVF EBak
	'Irving Alexander' (d)	CDoC
	'Isabel Ryan'	CSil
	'Isis' Lemoine	CSil
	'Isle of Mull'	CSil
	'Isle of Purbeck'	SVic
	'Italiano' (d)	CWVF MJac SVic
	'Ivy Grace'	CSil
	'Jack Acland'	CWVF
	'Jack Shahan' ♀H3	CCCN CDoC CLoc CSil CWVF EBak LAst LCla MJac SLBF
	'Jack Stanway' (v)	CDoC CWVF
	'Jack Wilson'	CSil
	'Jackie Bull' (d)	CWVF EBak
	'Jackpot' (d)	EBak
	'Jackqueline' (T)	CWVF
	'Jamboree' (d)	EBak
	'James Lye' (d)	CWVF EBak
	'James Travis' (E/d)	CDoC CSil EBak LCla SLBF
	'Jan Bremer'	SVic
	'Jandel'	CWVF
	'Jane Humber' (d)	CWVF
	'Jane Lye'	EBak
	'Janice Ann'	LCla
	'Janice Perry's Gold' (v)	CLoc MJac SLBF
	'Janie' (d)	EPfP MAsh
	'Jap Vantveer' (T)	LCla
	'Jasper's Triphy White' (T) **new**	SLBF
	'Jaunty Jack'	SLBF
	'Javelin'	CDoC
	'Jean Baker'	CDoC
	'Jean Campbell'	EBak
	'Jean Frisby'	CLoc
	'Jean Taylor'	EPts
	'Jean Webb' (v)	WCot
	'Jennifer'	EBak MJac
	'Jennifer Ann'	SLBF
	'Jennifer Lister' (d)	CSil
	'Jenny May'	CLoc EPts
	'Jenny Sorensen'	CWVF
	'Jess'	LCla SLBF
	'Jessie Pearson'	CWVF
	'Jessimae'	CWVF SPet
	'Jester' Holmes (d)	CLoc CSil
	'Jet Fire' (d)	EBak
	'Jezebel' (d)	SVic
	'Jiddles' (E)	LCla
	'Jill Holloway' (T)	SLBF
	'Jill Whitworth'	CDoC WPnn
	'Jim Coleman'	CWVF SVic
	'Jim Dodge' (d)	EPts
	'Jim Hawkins'	EBak
	'Jim Muncaster'	CWVF
	'Jim Watts'	CDoC CTsd
	jimenezii	CDoC
	'Jimmy Cricket' (E)	CDoC SLBF
	'Joan Barnes' (d)	CWVF
	'Joan Cooper'	CLoc CSil CWVF EBak SLBF SVic
	'Joan Goy'	CWVF MJac SVic
	'Joan Knight'	CLoc
	'Joan Margaret' (d)	MJac
	'Joan Morris'	SLBF
	'Joan Pacey'	CDoC CWVF EBak
	'Joan Smith'	EBak
	'Joan Waters' (d)	CWVF
	'Joanna Lumley' (d)	EPts MJac
	'Jo-Anne Fisher' (d)	EPts
	'Joe Kusber' (d)	CWVF EBak
	'John Bartlett'	CLoc
	'John Grooms' (d)	CLoc SVic
	'John Lockyer'	CLoc CWVF EBak
	'John Maynard Scales' (T)	CDoC CWVF LCla MJac
§	'John Ridding'[PBR] (T/v)	CLoc EPts LAst SPoG
	'John Suckley' (d)	EBak
	'John Wright'	LCla
	'Jomam' ♀H3	CWVF
	'Jon Oram'	CLoc CWVF
	'Jonny Wilkinson'	MJac
	'Jose's Joan' (d)	CWVF SVic
	'Joy Patmore'	CLoc CTsd CWVF EBak SLBF SPet
	'Joyce Adey' (d)	CWVF
	'Joyce Sinton'	CLoc CWVF
	'Joyce Wilson' (d)	EPts
	'Judith Coupland'	CWVF
	'Jülchen'	CWVF
	'Jules Daloges' (d)	EBak
	'Julie Marie' (d)	CWVF MJac
	'June Gardner'	CWVF
	'Jungle'	LCla SLBF
I	'Juno' Kennett	EBak
	'Jupiter Seventy'	EBak
	'Jus' For You'	MJac
	'Just Pilk' **new**	SLBF
	'Just Pink' (E)	CDoC
	'Justin's Pride'	CDoC CSil
	'Kaleidoscope' (d)	EBak
	'Karen Isles' (E)	CDoC LCla SLBF
	'Karen Louise' (d)	CLoc
	'Karin de Groot'	SVic
	'Kate Taylor' (d)	SLBF
	'Kath van Hanegem'	CLoc SLBF
	'Kath Wilson' **new**	LAst
	'Kathryn Maidment'	SVic
	'Katie Rogers'	EPts
	'Katie Susan'	SLBF
	'Katinka' (E)	CDoC CWVF LCla SLBF
	'Katjan'	CSil LCla SLBF
	'Katrina' (d)	CLoc EBak
	'Katrina Thompsen'	CLoc CWVF EPts SLBF
	'Katy Flynn'	CLoc CWVF SLBF
	'Keepsake' (d)	EBak
	'Kegworth Carnival' (d)	CWVF
	'Ken Goldsmith' (T)	CWVF
	'Ken Jennings'	CWVF
	'Kenny Dalglish' (d)	CSil
	'Kenny Holmes'	CWVF

	'Kenny Walkling'	LCla SLBF
	'Kernan Robson' (d)	CLoc CWVF EBak
	'Keystone'	EBak
	'Kimberly' (d)	EBak
	'King of Bath' (d)	EBak
	'King of Hearts' (d)	EBak
	'King's Ransom' (d)	CLoc CWVF EBak SPet SVic
	'Kiss 'n'Tell'	CWVF MJac
	'Kit Oxtoby' (d)	CDoC CWVF LCla MJac
	'Kiwi' (d)	EBak
	'Knockout' (d)	CWVF SVic
	'Kobold'	SLBF
	'Kolding Perle'	CWVF SLBF
	'Komeet'	CDoC SBfd
	'Kon-Tiki' (d)	SPet
	'Kuniko Atarashi' (d)	EPts
	'Kwintet'	CWVF EBak MJac SPet
	'La Bianca'	EBak
	'La Campanella' (d) 𝕐^{H3}	CCCN CDoC CLoc CWVF EBak EPts LAst MJac MSCN SBfd SLBF SPet SVic
	'La Fiesta' (d)	EBak
	'La France' (d)	EBak
	'La Neige' ambig.	CTsd CWVF
	'La Neige' Lemoine (d)	EBak
	'La Porte' (d)	CLoc CWVF
	'La Rosita' (d)	EBak
I	'La Traviata' Blackwell (d)	EBak
	'Lace Petticoats' (d)	EBak SVic
	'Lady Beth' (d)	SVic
	'Lady Boothby'	Widely available
	'Lady Framlingham' (d)	EPts
	'Lady in Grey' (d)	MJac SVic
	'Lady Isobel Barnett'	CLoc CWVF EBak MJac SPet SVic
	'Lady Kathleen Spence'	CWVF EBak SPet SVic
	'Lady Patricia Mountbatten'	CWVF SVic
	'Lady Ramsey'	EBak
	'Lady Rebecca' (d)	CLoc
	'Lady Thumb' (d) 𝕐^{H3}	Widely available
	'Laing's Hybrid'	CWVF EBak
	'Lakeland Princess'	EBak
	'Lakeside'	EBak
	'Lambada'	LAst SLBF
	'Lancambe'	CSil
	'Lancashire Lass'	CWVF
	'Lancelot'	EBak
	'Lapshead White'	CPLG
	'Lark' (T)	CWVF
	'Lassie' (d)	CDoC CLoc CWVF EBak
	'Last Chance' (E)	SLBF
	'Laura' ambig.	CWVF SPet SVic
I	'Laura' (Dutch)	CLoc EPts LCla SLBF
	'Laura Cross' (E)	CDoC SLBF
	'Lauren'	CDoC
	'Lavender Kate' (d)	CWVF EBak
	'Lazy Lady' (d)	CWVF EBak
	'Lechlade Apache'	CDoC LCla
	'Lechlade Bullet'	LCla
	'Lechlade Chinaman'	CDoC SVic
	'Lechlade Debutante'	CDoC LCla
	'Lechlade Fire-eater' (T)	CDoC
	'Lechlade Gorgon'	CDoC CWVF LCla SLBF
	'Lechlade Magician'	CDoC CSil EPts LCla SLBF SPet SVic
	'Lechlade Maiden'	CDoC CWVF LCla
	'Lechlade Martianess'	LCla SVic
	'Lechlade Potentate'	LCla
	'Lechlade Tinkerbell' (E)	CDoC LCla
	'Lechlade Violet' (T)	CSil LCla SVic
	lehmanii	LCla
	'Len Bielby' (T)	CDoC CWVF LCla
	'Lena' (d) 𝕐^{H3}	CDoC CLoc CMac CSil CTri CWVF EBak EPts MJac SLBF SMrm SPer SPlb SVic
	'Lena Dalton' (d)	CLoc CWVF EBak SVic
	'Leonora'	CDoC CLoc CWVF EBak SLBF SPet SVic
	'Lesley' (T)	CWVF LCla
	'Lesley's Wonder'	MJac
	'Leslie Bowman'	LCla
	'Lett's Delight' (d)	CWVF EPts
	'Letty Lye'	EBak
	'Leverhulme'	see *F.* 'Leverkusen'
§	'Leverkusen' (T)	CDoC CLoc EBak LCla MJac
I	'Liebesträume' Blackwell (d)	EBak
	'Liebriez' (d) 𝕐$^{H3-4}$	CSil EBak SPet SVic
	'Liemers Lantaern'	CWVF
	'Likalin'	CWVF
	'Lilac'	EBak
	'Lilac Dainty' (d)	CSil
	'Lilac Lustre' (d)	CLoc CWVF EBak SPet SVic
	'Lilac Mist' **new**	SLBF
	'Lilac Queen' (d)	EBak
	'Lillian Annetts' (d)	CDoC CWVF MJac SLBF
	'Lillibet' (d)	CLoc CWVF EBak
	'Lime Lite' (d)	MJac
I	'Limelight' Weston	SLBF
	'Linda Goulding'	CTsd CWVF EBak SVic
	'Linda Grace'	MJac
	'Linda Hinchliffe' **new**	MJac
	'Linda Rosling' (d)	CDoC
	'Lindisfarne' (d)	CLoc CWVF EBak MJac SPet
	'Lindsey Victoria' (d)	SVic
	'Lionel'	CSil
	'Lipstick'	SLBF
	'Lisa' (d)	EPts SPet
	'Little Beauty'	CDoC CSil CWVF SVic
	'Little Boy Blue'	EPts
	'Little Brook Gem'	SLBF
	'Little Catbells' (E)	SLBF
	'Little Gene'	EBak
	'Little Nan'	SLBF
	'Little Ouse' (d)	CWVF
	'Little Scamp'	SLBF
	'Liz' (d)	CSil EBak
	Liza = 'Goetzliza'^{PBR} (Shadowdancer Series)	LAst LSou
	'Lochinver' (d)	CWVF
	'Loeky'	CDoC CLoc CWVF EBak SVic
	'Logan Garden'	see *F. magellanica* 'Logan Woods'
	'Lolita' (d)	CWVF EBak
	'London 2000'	CDoC LCla MJac SLBF
	'London in Bloom'	SLBF
	'Lonely Ballerina' (d)	CLoc CWVF
	'Long Distance' (T)	CDoC LCla
	'Long Wings'	LCla SVic
	'Lord Byron'	CLoc EBak
	'Lord Derby'	CSil
	'Lord Jim'	CDoC LCla
	'Lord Lonsdale'	CWVF EBak EPts LCla SVic
	'Lord Roberts'	CLoc CWVF SLBF
	'Lore Ritscka' (d)	MJac
	'Lorelei'	CDoC
	'Lorna Fairclough'	MJac
	'Lorna Florence'	SLBF
	'Lorna Swinbank'	CWVF SVic
	'Lorraine's Delight' (d)	SVic

	'Lottie Hobby' (E) ♀H1+3	CDoC CLoc CMac CSil CTrC CTsd CWVF EPfP EPts LCla MLHP SVic
	'Louise Emershaw' (d)	CWVF EBak MJac SVic
	'Louise Nicholls'	MJac
	'Loulabel'	SVic
	'Lovable' (d)	EBak
	'Loveliness'	CLoc CWVF EBak SVic
	'Lovely Linda'	SLBF
	'Love's Reward' ♀H1+3	CLoc CWVF MJac SLBF SVic
	'Lower Raydon'	EBak
I	'Loxensis'	CDoC CWVF EBak SVic
N	***loxensis*** misapplied	see *F.* 'Speciosa', *F.* 'Loxensis'
	'Loxhore Herald'	CSil
	'Loxhore Lullaby' (E)	CSil LCla
	'Loxhore Minuet' (T)	CDoC LCla
	'Loxhore Posthorn' (T)	CDoC LCla
	'Lucinda'	CWVF
	'Lucky Strike' (d)	EBak
	Lucy = 'Goetzlucy' (Shadowdancer Series)	EBak
	'Lucy Locket'	MJac
	'Lustre'	CWVF EBak SVic
I	'Lycioides'	LCla
	lycioides misapplied	see *F.* 'Lycioides'
§	***lycioides*** Andrews	EBak
	'Lye's Excelsior'	EBak
	'Lye's Own'	EBak SLBF SPet
	'Lye's Unique' ♀H1+3	CDoC CLoc CWVF EBak EPts LCla MJac SLBF SPet SVic
	'Lynette' (d)	CLoc
	'Lynn Cunningham'	CDoC
	'Lynn Ellen' (d)	CDoC CWVF EBak
	'Lynne Patricia' (d)	EPts SLBF
	'Mabel Greaves' (d)	CWVF
	'Machu Picchu'	CLoc CWVF EPts LCla SVic
	macrophylla	CDoC WMoo
	'Madame Aubin'	CSil
	'Madame Butterfly' (d)	CLoc
	'Madame Cornélissen' (d) ♀H3	CDoC CLoc CMac CSBt CSil CTri CWVF EBak EBee EPfP EPts LAst LRHS MAsh MBri MRav SBod SCoo SHil SLBF SLim SPer SPet SPoG SVic WFar WHil
	'Madame Eva Boye'	EBak
	'Maes-y-Groes'	CSil
	magellanica	CDoC CSil CTsd CWib GKev MLHP MMuc NPer NWea SPer SVic WFar WMoo WPnn
	- 'Alba'	see *F. magellanica* var. *molinae*
I	- 'Alba Aureovariegata' (v)	CDoC CMac CTrC EPfP LRHS SPer SVic WFar
	- 'Alba Variegata' (v)	CSil
	- 'Americana Elegans'	CDoC CSil
	- 'Angel's Teardrop'	CDoC
	- 'Comber'	CSil
	- var. ***conica***	CDoC CSil
	- var. ***discolor***	CSil
	- 'Duchy of Cornwall'	CDoC
	- 'Exmoor Gold' (v)	CSil
§	- var. ***gracilis*** ♀H3	CAgr CDoC CHEx CLoc CSil CTri CWVF EPfP EUJe LRHS MLHP NBro SCoo SVic WGwG WMoo WPnn
	- - 'Aurea' ♀H3-4	CBcs CDoC CMac CSil CTsd CWVF EBee ELan EPfP GQui LCla LRHS MHer MRav SAga SCoo SDix SLBF SPer SPet SPoG WFar WMoo WSpi
	- - 'Purple Mountain'	EPfP LRHS
§	- - 'Tricolor' (v) ♀H3	CDoC CSil CTsd EPfP EPts EWes LBMP LCla LRHS NLar SEND SLBF SRms WCFE WPnn
	- - 'Variegata' (v) ♀H3	CDoC CSil CTsd EBak EPfP LCla LRHS MGos MRav SBfd SDix SPer SPet WPnn WSpi
	- 'Guiding Star'	CDoC
	- 'Lady Bacon'	CDoC CSil ELon EPts EWes GCal LHop MCot SDys SEND SHom SLBF SMHy SUsu WSHC
§	- 'Logan Woods'	CDoC CSil ELon GKin SLBF SMrm
	- 'Longipedunculata'	CDoC CSil SLPl
	- 'Lyonesse Lady'	CDoC
	- var. ***macrostema***	CSil
	- var. ***magellanica*** **new**	WSpi
§	- var. ***molinae***	Widely available
§	- - 'Enstone' (v)	ELon LAst
	- - 'Golden Sharpitor' (v)	CCCN LAst MDKP SBfd
§	- - 'Sharpitor' (v)	CDoC CSil CTsd EBak EBee EHoe ELan ELon EPfP IFro LRHS MAsh NPer SAga SBch SBfd SVic WFar WKif WMoo WSHC
	- var. ***myrtifolia***	CDoC CSil CTsd
*	- var. ***prostrata***	CSil
	- 'Pumila'	CDoC CEnt CSil EWes GCal ITim LRHS MHer MLHP SAga SCoo SMHy SRot SVic WAbe
	- ***purpurea***	LRHS SBch
	- 'Red Mountain'	EWes
	- 'Sea King'	CDoC
	- 'Sea Spray'	CDoC
	- 'Seahorse'	CDoC
§	- 'Thompsonii' ♀H3-4	CDoC CSil ECGP SBch SMHy
	- 'Threave' **new**	CDoC
§	- 'Versicolor' (v)	Widely available
	'Magenta Flush'	CDoC CWVF
	'Magic Flute'	CLoc CWVF MJac SVic
	'Maharaja' (d)	EBak
	'Major Heaphy'	CWVF EBak
	'Malibu Mist' (d)	CWVF
	'Mama Bleuss' (d)	EBak
	'Mancunian' (d)	CWVF
I	'Mandarin' Schnabel	EBak
	'Mandi Oxtoby' (T)	LCla
	'Mantilla' (T)	CDoC CLoc CWVF EBak LCla MJac SVic
	'Marbled Sky'	SVic
	'Marcel Michiels' (d)	CDoC
	'Marcia' PBR (Shadowdancer Series)	CLoc LAst LSou
	'Marcus Graham' (d)	CLoc CTsd CWVF EBak SCoo SVic
	'Marcus Hanton' (d)	CWVF
	'Mardi Gras' (d)	EBak
	'Margaret' (d) ♀H4	CDoC CLoc CSil CTri CTsd CWVF EBak EPts SEND SLBF SPet SVic WFar
	'Margaret Bird'	LCla
	'Margaret Brown' ♀H4	CDoC CLoc CSil CTri CWVF EBak LCla LRHS MWat SLBF SMrm SPet SVic
	'Margaret Davidson' (d)	CLoc
	'Margaret Pilkington'	CTsd CWVF SVic
	'Margaret Roe'	CSil CWVF EBak MJac SPet
	'Margaret Susan'	EBak
	'Margarite Dawson' (d)	CSil
	'Margery Blake'	CSil EBak
	'Maria Landy'	CWVF MJac
	'Maria Mathilde' (d)	SLBF

	'Marilyn Olsen'	CWVF
	'Marin Belle'	EBak
	'Marin Glow' ♀H3	CLoc CWVF EBak SLBF SVic
	'Marinka' ♀H3	CLoc CWVF EBak EPts LAst LBMP LCla MJac SLBF SPet SVic WHil
	'Mark Kirby' (d)	CWVF EBak
	'Marlies de Keijzer' (E)	CDoC LCla SLBF
	Martha = 'Goetzmart'[PBR] (Shadowdancer Series)	LAst LHop WBor
	'Martina'	SLBF
	'Martin's Inspiration'	CDoC LCla
	'Martin's Little Beauty'	CDoC
	'Martin's Yellow Surprise' (T)	LCla SLBF SVic
	'Marty' (d)	EBak
	'Mary' (T) ♀H1+3	CDoC CLoc CWVF EPts LCla SLBF SVic
	'Mary Lockyer' (d)	CLoc EBak
	'Mary Poppins'	CWVF SVic
	'Mary Reynolds' (d)	CWVF
	'Mary Thorne'	CSil EBak
	'Mary's Millennium'	CWVF
	'Masquerade' (d)	EBak SVic
	'Mauve Beauty' (d)	CSil CWVF SLBF
	'Mauve Lace' (d)	CSil
	'Mauve Wisp' (d)	SVic
	'Mavis Enderby' **new**	SLBF
	'Max Jaffa'	CWVF
I	'Maxima'	CDoC EPts LCla SLBF
	'Maxima's Baby'	CDoC
	'Mayblossom' (d)	CWVF
	'Mayfayre' (d)	CLoc
	'Mayfield'	CWVF
	'Mazda'	CWVF
	'Meadowlark' (d)	CWVF EBak
	'Medard's Botsaert' (d)	CDoC
	'Meditation' (d)	CLoc CSil
	'Melanie'	CTsd SVic
	'Melissa Heavens'	CWVF
	'Melody'	EBak SPet SVic
	'Melody Ann' (d)	EBak
	'Melting Moments' (d)	SCoo
	'Mendocino Rose'	SVic
	'Mephisto'	CSil CWVF
	'Mercurius'	CSil
	'Merlin'	CDoC CSil LCla
	'Merry Mary' (d)	CWVF EBak
I	'Mexicali Rose' Machado	CLoc
	'Michael' (d)	CWVF EPts
	'Michael Wallis' (T)	CDoC LCla SLBF
	'Michelle Wallace'	SLBF SVic
	michoacanensis misapplied	see *F. microphylla* subsp. *aprica*
	michoacanensis Sessé & Moç. (E) B&SWJ 9027	WCru
	- B&SWJ 9148	WCru
	'Micky Goult' ♀H1+3	CLoc CWVF EPts MJac SLBF SPet SVic
	'Microchip' (E)	CSil LCla
	microphylla (E)	CBcs CDoC CElw CLoc CPLG CSil CWVF EBak EBee ELon GCal IDee NBro NLar SBch SVic WBor
	- B&SWJ 10331	WCru
§	- subsp. ***aprica*** (E)	CDoC LCla
	- - 'Dolly's Dress'	WCru
	- 'Cornish Pixie'	CDoC
§	- subsp. ***hemsleyana*** (E)	CDoC CPLG CSil LCla
	- - B&SWJ 10478	WCru
	- - 'Silver Lining'	LHop WCru WSHC
§	- subsp. ***hidalgensis*** (E)	CDoC CSil LCla
	- subsp. ***microphylla*** (E)	CSil
§	- subsp. ***minimiflora*** (E)	SVic
	- subsp. ***quercetorum*** (E)	CDoC CSil CTsd
	- 'Variegata' (E/v)	EWes
	'Midas'	CWVF
	'Midnight Sun' (d)	CWVF EBak
	'Midwinter'	CWVF SVic
	'Mieke Meursing' ♀H1+3	CDoC CLoc CWVF EBak MJac SPet
	'Miep Aalhuizen'	CDoC LCla SVic
	'Mike Oxtoby' (T)	CWVF
	'Millennium'	CLoc EBak EPts MJac SCoo
	'Millie Butler'	CWVF
	'Ming'	CLoc
	'Miniature Jewels' (E)	SLBF
	minimiflora misapplied	see *F.* × ***bacillaris***
	minimiflora Hemsl.	see *F. microphylla* subsp. *minimiflora*
	'Minirose'	CDoC CWVF EPts SLBF
	'Minnesota' (d)	EBak
	'Miramere'	EPts
	'Mischief'	SVic
	'Miss California' (d)	CDoC CLoc CWVF EBak LAst
	'Miss Great Britain'	CWVF
	'Miss Lye'	CSil
	'Miss Muffett' (d)	CSil EPts
	'Miss Vallejo' (d)	EBak
	'Mission Bells'	CDoC CLoc CWVF EBak EPts SPet
	'Misty Blue' (d)	SVic
	'Misty Haze' (d)	CWVF SVic
	'Molesworth' (d)	CWVF EBak MJac
	'Money Spinner'	CLoc EBak
	'Monsieur Thibaut' ♀H4	CSil SPer
	'Monte Rosa' (d)	CWVF
	'Montevideo' (d)	CWVF
	'Monument' (d)	CSil
	'Mood Indigo' (d)	CWVF SLBF SVic
	'Moody Blues'	SLBF
	'Moonbeam' (d)	CLoc
	'Moonglow'	CTsd MJac
	'Moonlight Sonata'	CLoc CWVF EBak SPet
	'Moonraker' (d)	CWVF SVic
	'More Applause' (d)	CLoc
	'Morning Light' (d)	CLoc EBak SVic
	'Morning Mist'	EBak
	'Morrells' (d)	EBak
	'Moth Blue' (d)	CWVF EBak
	'Mother's Day'	SVic
	'Mountain Mist' (d)	CWVF SVic
	'Moyra' (d)	CWVF
	'Mr A. Huggett'	CLoc CSil CWVF EPts SLBF
	'Mr W. Rundle'	EBak SVic
§	'Mr West' (v)	LRHS LSou MBri MCot WMoo
	'Mrs Churchill'	CLoc
	'Mrs John D. Fredericks'	CSil
	'Mrs Lawrence Lyon' (d)	EBak
	'Mrs Lee Belton' (E)	CDoC LCla SLBF
	'Mrs Lovell Swisher' ♀H4	CWVF EBak LCla SVic
	'Mrs Marshall'	CWVF EBak SLBF
	'Mrs Popple' ♀H3	Widely available
	'Mrs W. Castle'	CDoC CSil SVic
	'Mrs W.P. Wood' ♀H3	CDoC CLoc CSil CWVF ELon LRHS MSCN SVic
	'Mrs W. Rundle'	CLoc CWVF EBak SLBF
	'Muriel' (d)	CLoc CWVF EBak
	'Murru's Pierre Marie' (d)	SLBF
	'My Delight'	CWVF
	'My Fair Lady' (d)	CLoc CWVF EBak
	'My Little Cracker'	CDoC

'My Little Sparkler'	SLBF
'My Mum'	LCla SLBF
'My Pat'	SLBF
'My Reward' (d)	CWVF
'Nancy Lou' (d)	CDoC CLoc CWVF LAst MJac SLBF SPet SVic
'Nanny Ed' (d)	CWVF
'Natasha Sinton' (d)	CCCN CLoc CWVF LAst MJac SPet
'Native Dancer' (d)	CWVF EBak
'Nautilus' (d)	EBak
'Neapolitan' (d)	CDoC SLBF
'Neck' **new**	LCla
'Nell Gwyn'	CLoc CWVF EBak SVic
'Nellie Nuttall' ♀H3	CLoc CWVF EBak EPts SPet SVic
'Neopolitan' (E)	CLoc CSil EPts SVic
'Nettala'	CDoC SVic
'Neue Welt'	CSil CWVF EBak
'New Fascination' (d)	EBak
'New Millennium'	CDoC
'Nice 'n' Easy' (d)	LRHS MJac
'Nicki Fenwick-Raven' (E)	LCla
'Nicki's Findling'	CDoC CTsd CWVF EPts LCla MJac
'Nicola'	EBak
'Nicola Jane' (d)	CDoC CSil CWVF EBak EPts LCla MJac SHar SLBF SPet SVic
'Nicolette'	CWVF MJac
'Nightingale' (d)	CLoc EBak
§ ***nigricans***	CDoC
- B&SWJ 10664	WCru
'Nina Wills'	EBak
'Niobe' (d)	EBak
'Niula'	CDoC LCla
'No Name' (d)	EBak
'Nonchalance' (T)	LCla
'Norman Welton'	SLBF
'Normandy Bell'	EBak SVic
'Northern Jewel' **new**	SLBF
'Northilda'	SVic
'Northumbrian Belle'	EBak
'Northumbrian Pipes'	LCla
'Northway'	CLoc CWVF MJac SPet SVic
'Norvell Gillespie' (d)	EBak
'Novato'	EBak
'Novella' (d)	CWVF EBak
'Nuance'	LCla
'Nunthorpe Gem' (d)	CDoC CSil
'O Sole Mio'	SVic
obconica (E)	CDoC CSil
'Obcylin' (E)	CDoC LCla
'Obergärtner Koch' (T) ♀H1	CDoC
'Ocean Beach'	CDoC EPts
'Oetnang' (d)	CTri SCoo
'Oh Carol' (E) **new**	LCla
'Old Somerset' (v)	CCCN CDoC SVic
'Olga Storey'	CDoC
'Olive Smith'	CWVF EPts LCla MJac
'Olympic Lass' (d)	EBak
'Olympic Sunset'	SVic
'Onward'	CSil
§ 'Oosje' (E)	CDoC CSil LCla SLBF SVic
'Opalescent' (d)	CLoc CWVF SVic
'Orange Crush'	CLoc CWVF EBak LAst MJac SPet
'Orange Crystal'	CWVF EBak MJac SLBF SVic
'Orange Drops'	CLoc CWVF EBak EPts SVic
'Orange Flare'	CLoc CWVF EBak SLBF SVic
'Orange Heart'	LCla
'Orange King' (d)	CLoc CWVF
'Orange Mirage'	CLoc CWVF EBak LAst SLBF SPet SVic
'Orange Star' (E)	CDoC
'Orangeblossom'	SLBF
'Oranje van Os'	CWVF
'Orient Express' (T) ♀H1	CDoC CLoc CWVF MJac SVic
'Oriental Sunrise'	CWVF
'Ornamental Pearl' (v)	CLoc CWVF EBak
'Orwell' (d)	CWVF
'Oso Sweet'	CWVF
'Other Fellow'	CWVF EBak EPts LCla MJac SLBF SPet SVic
'Oulton Empress' (E)	LCla SLBF
'Oulton Fairy' (E)	SLBF
'Oulton Red Imp' (E)	LCla SLBF
'Oulton Travellers Rest' (E)	SLBF
'Our Carol' **new**	SLBF
'Our Darling'	CWVF
'Our Hilary'	SLBF
'Our Joy' (d)	SLBF
'Our Nan' (d)	MJac
'Our Pamela'	MJac
'Our Spencer'	SLBF
'Our Ted' (T)	EBak EPts
'Our William'	SLBF
'Overbecks'	see *F. magellanica* var. *molinae* 'Sharpitor'
'P.E. King' (d)	SLBF
'Pabbe's Wikwief'	CDoC
'Pacemaker'	MGos
'Pacific Grove' Greene	see *F.* 'Evelyn Steele Little'
'Pacific Grove' Niederholzer (d)	EBak
'Pacific Queen' (d)	EBak
'Pacquesa' (d)	CWVF EBak SPet SVic
'Padre Pio' (d)	CWVF EBak MJac
'Pallas'	CSil
'Pam Plack'	CDoC CSil LCla SLBF
'Pamela Knights' (d)	EBak
'Pamela Wallace'	SLBF
'Pam's People'	LCla
'Pan America' (d)	EBak
'Panache' (d)	LCla
'Pangea' (T)	LCla
paniculata (T) ♀H1+3	CCCN CDoC CRHN CWVF EBak EPts IDee LCla MCot MHer MREP SLBF WCru
'Panique'	CDoC LCla
'Pantaloons' (d)	EBak
'Pantomine Dame' (d)	CWVF
'Panylla Prince'	CDoC LCla SLBF
'Papa Bleuss' (d)	CWVF EBak
'Papoose' (d)	CDoC CSil EBak LCla SEND SLBF SVic
'Parkstone Centenary' (d)	CWVF
'Party Frock'	CDoC CLoc CWVF EBak
parviflora misapplied	see *F.* × ***bacillaris***
parviflora Lindl.	see *F. lycioides* Andrews
'Pastel'	EBak
'Pat Meara'	CLoc EBak
'Pathétique' (d)	CLoc
'Patience' (d)	CDoC CWVF EBak SLBF
'Patio King'	EBak
'Patio Princess' (d)	CLoc CWVF EPts LAst
'Patricia' ambig.	LAst
'Patricia' Wood	EBak
'Pat's Smile'	SLBF
'Patty Evans' (d)	CWVF EBak
'Paul Cambon' (d)	EBak
'Paul Fisher'	CDoC
'Paul Roe' (d)	MJac

'Paul Storey' CDoC CSil
'Paula Jane' (d) CDoC CTsd CWVF LAst MJac SLBF SVic WGor
'Pauline Rawlins' (d) CLoc EBak
'Peace' (d) EBak
'Peachy' (California Dreamers Series) (d) CDoC CLoc LAst SCoo
'Peachy Keen' (d) EBak
'Peacock' (d) CLoc
'Pee Wee Rose' CSil EBak SVic
'Peggy Burford' (T) LCla
Peggy = 'Goetzpeg'[PBR] (Shadowdancer Series) LAst LHop LSou SCoo
'Peggy King' CDoC CSil EBak SPet SVic
'Peloria' (d) CLoc EBak
'People's Princess' MJac
'Peper Harow' EBak
'Pepi' (d) CWVF EBak
'Peppermint Candy' (d) CDoC CWVF MJac
'Peppermint Stick' (d) CDoC CLoc CWVF EBak SPet SVic
'Perky Pink' (d) CWVF EBak EPts
'Perry Park' CWVF EBak MJac SVic
'Perry's Jumbo' NPer
perscandens CBcs CPLG CSil LCla WGwG
'Personality' (d) EBak
'Peter Bielby' (d) CWVF
'Peter Crookes' (T) CWVF
'Peter Grange' EBak
'Peter James' (d) CSil
'Peter Meredith' MJac
'Peter Pan' CSil CWVF
petiolaris CDoC LCla
– B&SWJ 10675 WCru
'Petit Four' CWVF
'Petite' (d) EBak
'Phaidra' CDoC LCla
'Pharaoh' CLoc
'Phénoménal' (d) CSil CWVF EBak
'Phillip Taylor' MJac
'Phil's Pill' SLBF
'Phryne' (d) CSil EBak SVic
'Phyllis' (d) ♀H4 CAgr CDoC CLoc CSil CWVF EBak ELon EPts LCla LRHS MJac SEND SHil SLBF SPet SVic WFar
'Piet van der Sande' CDoC LCla
'Piggelmee' CDoC
'Pinch Me' (d) CWVF EBak SPet SVic
'Pink Aurora' CLoc
'Pink Ballet Girl' (d) CLoc EBak SVic
'Pink Bon Accord' CLoc CTsd CWVF SVic
'Pink Cloud' CLoc EBak
'Pink Cornet' LCla
'Pink Darling' CLoc EBak
'Pink Dessert' EBak
'Pink Domino' (d) CSil
'Pink Fairy' (d) EBak SPet
'Pink Fandango' (d) CLoc
'Pink Fantasia' CDoC CLoc CWVF EBak EPts LAst LCla MJac SLBF SVic
'Pink Flamingo' (d) EBak
'Pink Galore' (d) CLoc CWVF EBak LAst MJac SLBF SPet SVic
'Pink Goon' (d) CDoC CSil LCla SLBF SVic
'Pink Haze' CSil SVic
'Pink Jade' CWVF EBak
'Pink la Campanella' CWVF EBak SLBF WGor
'Pink Lace' (d) SPet
'Pink Marshmallow' (d) ♀H1+3 CDoC CLoc CWVF EBak MJac SLBF SPet SVic
'Pink Panther' (d) SVic
'Pink Pearl' Bright (d) CSil EBak
'Pink Profusion' EBak
'Pink Quartet' (d) CLoc CWVF EBak
'Pink Rain' CWVF MJac
'Pink Slippers' CLoc
'Pink Spangles' CWVF SVic
'Pink Surprise' (d) CTsd
'Pink Temptation' CLoc CWVF EBak LAst SVic
'Pinwheel' (d) CLoc EBak
'Piper' (d) CDoC CWVF
'Piper's Vale' (T) CDoC MJac SLBF
'Pirbright' CWVF
'Pixie' CDoC CLoc CSil CWVF EBak MJac SLBF SPet SVic
'Playboy' (d) SVic
'Playford' CWVF EBak
'Plenty' EBak SVic
'Plumb Bob' (d) CWVF
'Pole Star' CSil
'Polskie Fuksji' CDoC
'Pop Whitlock' (v) CWVF MCot SPet SVic
'Poppet' CWVF
'Popsie Girl' CDoC SLBF
'Port Arthur' (d) CSil EBak
'Postiljon' CWVF EBak
'Postman' CDoC
'Powder Puff' ambig. CWVF SPet
'Powder Puff' Hodges (d) CLoc SVic
I 'Powder Puff' Tabraham (d) CSil
'Prelude' ambig. SVic
'Prelude' Blackwell CLoc CSil
I 'Prelude' Kennett (d) EBak
'President' CDoC CSil EBak LRHS
'President B.W. Rawlins' EBak
'President Barrie Nash' CLoc
§ 'President Elliot' CSil
'President George Bartlett' (d) CDoC CLoc CSil EPts MJac SLBF
'President Jim Muil' SLBF
'President Joan Morris' (d) SLBF
'President John Porter' SLBF
'President Leo Boullemier' CWVF EBak MJac SPet SVic
'President Margaret Slater' CLoc CWVF EBak SPet SVic
'President Moir' (d) SLBF
'President Norman Hobbs' CWVF
'President Roosevelt' (d) CDoC
'President Stanley Wilson' (d) CWVF EBak EPts
'President Wilf Sharp' (d) SVic
'Preston' **new** CMac
'Preston Guild' ♀H1+3 CDoC CLoc CSil CWVF EBak NPer SDys SLBF SPet SVic
'Pride of the West' EBak
'Prince of Orange' CLoc CWVF EBak SVic
'Princess Dollar' see *F.* 'Dollar Prinzessin'
'Princess Pamela' (d) SLBF
'Princessita' CWVF EBak SPet
procumbens CBcs CCCN CDoC CLoc CPLG CSil CTrC CWVF EBak ECou EPfP EPts GCal IDee LCla MCot MHer SLBF SWal
– 'Argentea' see *F. procumbens* 'Wirral'
– 'Variegata' see *F. procumbens* 'Wirral'
§ – 'Wirral' (v) CBcs CDoC CLoc CSil CTrC CTsd WBor
'Prodigy' see *F.* 'Enfant Prodigue'
'Profusion' ambig. SVic

'Prosperity' (d) ♀H3	CDoC CLoc CSil CWVF EBak EBee EPfP EPts LCla LRHS MJac SLBF SPet SVic
'Pumila'	CMac CPLG CWib EBee ELan EPfP EPts LRHS SDix SPet SVic
'Purbeck Mist' (d)	CWVF
'Purperklokje'	CSil CWVF EBak SVic
'Purple Emperor' (d)	CLoc
'Purple Heart' (d)	CLoc EBak
'Purple Lace'	CSil SVic
'Purple Rain'	EPts
'Purple Splendour' (d)	CDoC CSil
'Pussy Cat' (T)	CLoc CWVF EBak SVic
'Putney Pride'	EPts
'Put's Folly'	CWVF EBak MJac SPet
putumayensis	CSil EBak
'Quasar' (d)	CCCN CDoC CLoc CWVF EPts LAst MJac SLBF SVic
'Queen Mabs'	EBak
'Queen Mary'	CLoc CSil EBak
'Queen of Bath' (d)	EBak SVic
'Queen of Derby' (d)	CSil CWVF
'Queen of Hearts' Kennett (d)	SVic
'Queen's Park' (d)	EBak
'Query'	CSil EBak SVic
'R.A.F.' (d)	CLoc CWVF EBak EPts SLBF SPet SVic
'Radcliffe Bedder' (d)	CSil
'Radings Gerda' (E)	LCla SLBF
'Radings Inge' (E)	CDoC
'Radings Karin'	CDoC
'Radings Michelle'	CSil CWVF
'Rahnee'	CWVF
'Rainbow'	CWVF
'Ralph's Delight' (d)	CWVF
'Rambling Rose' (d)	CLoc CWVF EBak MJac
'Rams Royal' (d)	CDoC CWVF
'Raspberry' (d)	CLoc CWVF EBak SVic
'Raspberry Sweet' (d)	CWVF
'Ratae Beauty'	CWVF
'Ratatouille' (d)	SVic
ravenii	CSil
'Ravensbarrow'	CSil
'Ravenslaw'	CSil
'Ray Redfern'	CWVF
'Razzle Dazzle' (d)	EBak
'Reading Show' (d)	CSil CWVF EPts SLBF
'Rebecca Williamson' (d)	CWVF MJac
'Rebeka Sinton' (v)	CLoc EBak
'Red Ace' (d)	CSil
'Red Imp' (d)	CSil
'Red Jacket' (d)	CWVF EBak
'Red Petticoat'	CWVF
'Red Rain'	CWVF
'Red Ribbons' (d)	EBak
'Red Rum' (d)	SPet
'Red Shadows' (d)	CLoc CWVF EBak
'Red Spider'	CCCN CLoc CWVF EBak LAst SCoo SPet SVic
'Red Wing'	CLoc
'Reflexa'	see *F.* × *bacillaris* 'Reflexa'
'Reg Gubler'	SLBF
'Regal'	CLoc
'Regal Robe' (d)	CDoC
regia	CSil
- var. ***radicans***	CSil
- subsp. ***regia***	CSil CTsd LCla
- subsp. ***reitzii***	CDul CSil EWes LCla
- subsp. ***serrae***	CDoC CSil

'Remember Eric'	CDoC CSil
'Remembrance' (d)	CSil EPts LCla SLBF
'Remus' (d)	SVic
'Rene Schwab'	LCla
'Requiem'	CLoc
'Reverend Doctor Brown' (d)	EBak
'Reverend Elliott'	see *F.* 'President Elliot'
'Rhapsody' ambig.	SVic
I 'Rhapsody' Blackwell (d)	CLoc
'Rhombifolia'	CSil
'Riccartonii' ♀H3	Widely available
'Richard John' (v)	SVic
'Richard John Carrington'	CSil
'Ridestar' (d)	CLoc CWVF EBak
'Rigoletto'	SVic
'Rijs 2001' (E)	CDoC SLBF
'Rina Felix'	CDoC
'Ringwood Gold'	SVic
'Ringwood Market' (d)	CSil CWVF EPts MJac SCoo SLBF SPet SVic
'Rivendell'	EPts
'Riverdancer Claire'	CDoC
'Robert Lutters'	SVic
'Robin Hood' (d)	CSil
'Rocket Fire' (California Dreamers Series) (d)	MJac
'Roesse Blacky'	CDoC SBfd
'Roesse Callisto'	CDoC
'Roesse Juliet'	CDoC
'Roesse Peacock' (d)	CDoC
'Roger de Cooker' (T)	CLoc EPts LCla
'Rohees Lava'	SLBF
'Rohees Leada' (d)	SLBF
'Rohees New Millennium' (d)	SLBF
'Rohees Tethys' (d)	SLBF
'Rolla' (d)	CWVF EBak
'Rolt's Ruby' (d)	CSil CWVF SVic
'Roman City' (d)	CLoc SVic
'Romance' (d)	CWVF
'Romany Rose'	CLoc
'Ronald L. Lockerbie' (d)	CLoc CWVF SVic
'Rondo'	MJac
'Ronnie Barker' (d)	MJac
'Ron's Ruby'	CSil
'Roos Breytenbach' (T)	CCCN CDoC LAst LCla MJac
'Rosamunda' (d)	CLoc
'Rose Aylett' (d)	EBak
'Rose Bradwardine' (d)	EBak
'Rose Churchill' (d)	MJac
'Rose Fantasia'	CDoC CLoc CWVF EPts LAst MJac SLBF
'Rose of Castile'	CDoC CLoc CSil EBak LCla MJac MWat SLBF SVic WWlt
'Rose of Castile Improved' ♀H4	CSil CWVF EBak LCla MJac SPet
'Rose of Denmark'	CCCN CLoc CSil CWVF EBak MBri MJac SCoo SLBF SPet WGor
'Rose Reverie' (d)	EBak
'Rose Winston' (d)	LAst SCoo
rosea misapplied	see *F.* 'Globosa'
rosea Ruíz & Pav.	see *F. lycioides* Andrews
'Rosebud' (d)	EBak
'Rosecroft Beauty' (d)	CSil CWVF EBak SVic
Rosella = 'Goetzrose'PBR (Shadowdancer Series)	LAst
'Rosemarie Higham'	LAst MJac SCoo
'Rosemary Day'	CLoc
'Ross Lea' (d)	CSil

'Roswitha'	SLBF
'Rosy Bows'	CWVF
'Rosy Frills' (d)	CWVF MJac SVic
'Rosy Morn' (d)	CLoc EBak
'Rough Silk'	CLoc CWVF EBak
'Roy Castle' (d)	CWVF
'Roy Walker' (d)	CWVF
'Royal Academy' (d)	EPts
'Royal and Ancient'	CWVF
'Royal Mosaic' (California Dreamers Series) (d)	CDoC MJac
'Royal Orchid'	EBak
'Royal Purple' (d)	CSil EBak
'Royal Serenade' (d)	CWVF
'Royal Touch' (d)	EBak
'Royal Velvet' (d) ♀H3	CCCN CLoc CWVF EBak EPts LRHS MAsh MJac SLBF SPet SVic
'Rubra Grandiflora'	CWVF EBak LCla SDys SLBF
'Ruby Wedding' (d)	CWVF SLBF
'Ruddigore'	CWVF
'Ruffles' (d)	CWVF EBak
'Rufus' ♀H3-4	CDoC CLoc CMac CSil CWVF EBak ELan EPfP EPts LCla MJac MSCN SLBF SPet SVic WFar
'Ruth'	CSil SVic
'Ruth Brazewell' (d)	CLoc
'Ruth King' (d)	CWVF EBak
'Rutland Water'	CDoC
'S'Wonderful' (d)	CLoc EBak
'Sailor'	EPts SVic
'Sally Bell'	CSil
'Salmon Cascade'	CWVF EBak EPts LCla MJac SLBF
'Salmon Glow'	CWVF MJac SVic
'Sam Sheppard'	SLBF
'Samba' (d)	LAst
'Samson' (d/v)	EBak
'San Diego' (d)	CWVF
'San Francisco'	EBak
'San Leandro' (d)	EBak
'San Mateo' (d)	EBak
§ ***sanctae-rosae***	CDoC EBak LCla
'Sandboy'	CWVF EBak
'Sanguinea'	CSil
'Sanrina'	CDoC
'Santa Cruz' (d)	CMac CSil CWVF EBak SLBF SVic
'Santa Lucia' (d)	CLoc EBak
'Santa Monica' (d)	EBak
'Sapphire' (d)	EBak
'Sara Helen' (d)	CLoc EBak
'Sarah Brightman' (d)	MJac
'Sarah Eliza' (d)	SCoo
'Sarah Jane' (d)	CSil EBak SVic
'Sarah Louise'	CWVF
'Sarong' (d)	EBak
'Satellite'	CLoc CWVF EBak
'Saturnus'	CSil CWVF EBak ELon LRHS MAsh SLBF SPet SPoG
'Saxondale Sue'	SVic
'Scabieuse'	CSil
scabriuscula	CDoC LCla
scandens	see *F. decussata* Ruíz & Pav.
'Scarcity'	CDoC CSil CWVF EBak SVic
'Schneeball' (d)	CDoC CSil EBak SVic
'Schneewitcher'	CDoC CSil EPts
'Schneewittchen' Klein	CSil EBak
'Schönbrunner Schuljubiläum' (T)	EBak
'Schone Hanaurin'	SLBF
'Schöne Wilhelmine'	see *F.* 'Die Schöne Wilhelmine'
'Scotch Heather' (d)	CWVF
'Sea Shell' (d)	CWVF EBak
'Seaforth'	EBak
'Sealand Prince'	CDoC CSil CTsd CWVF LCla SVic
'Sebastopol' (d)	CLoc
'Selma Lavrijsen'	CDoC
serratifolia Hook.	see *F. austromontana*
serratifolia Ruíz & Pav.	see *F. denticulata*
'Seventh Heaven' (d)	CLoc CTsd CWVF LAst MJac SCoo SVic
'Shady Blue'	CWVF
'Shangri-La' (d)	EBak
'Shanley'	CWVF SVic
'Sharon Allsop' (d)	CWVF
'Sharon Caunt' (d)	CSil
'Sharpitor'	see *F. magellanica* var. *molinae* 'Sharpitor'
'Shawna Ree' (E)	CDoC
'Sheila Crooks' (d)	CDoC CWVF EBak
'Sheila Kirby'	CWVF
'Sheila Steele' (d)	CWVF
'Sheila's Love'	MJac
'Shelford'	CDoC CLoc CWVF EBak EPts MJac SLBF SVic
'Shell Pink'	SVic
'She's a Beauty'	MJac
'Shirley Halladay' (d)	LCla
'Shirley'PBR (Shadowdancer Series)	LAst LSou SCoo
'Shooting Star' (d)	EBak
'Showfire'	EBak
'Showtime' (d)	CWVF
'Shrimp Cocktail'	CLoc MBri MSCN
'Shuna Lindsay'	LCla
'Siberoet' (E)	CDoC LCla SLBF
'Sierra Blue' (d)	CDoC CLoc CWVF EBak
'Silver Anniversary' (d)	SVic
'Silver Dollar'	SVic
'Silver Pink'	CSil
'Silverdale'	CDoC CSil EPts
'Simon J. Rowell'	LCla
simplicicaulis	CDoC EBak LCla
- pale-flowered	GCal
'Sincerity' (d)	CLoc
'Siobhan'	CWVF
'Siobhan Evans' (d)	SLBF
'Sir Alfred Ramsey'	CWVF EBak
'Sir David Attenborough' (d)	MJac
'Sir David Jason'	MJac
'Sir Ian Botham' (d)	MJac
'Sir Matt Busby' (d)	EPts LAst MJac
'Sir Thomas Allen'	SLBF
'Siren' Baker (d)	EBak
'Sister Ann Haley'	EPts
'Sister Sister' (d)	SLBF
'Sleepy'	CDoC CSil CTsd EPts SPet SVic
'Sleigh Bells'	CLoc CWVF EBak SVic
'Small Pipes'	CWVF
'Smokey Mountain' (d)	SVic
'Sneezy'	EPts SVic
'Snow Burner' (California Dreamers Series) (d)	CDoC CLoc LAst
'Snow White' (d)	SVic
'Snowbird' (d)	SLBF
§ 'Snowcap' (d) ♀H3-4	CCCN CDoC CLoc CSil CWVF EBak EPfP EPts GKin LAst LCla LRHS MAsh MBri MGos MJac MWat NPer SBfd SCoo SHil SLBF SLim SPet SPoG SVic WFar

	'Snowdon' (d)	CWVF
	'Snowdrift' Colville (d)	CLoc
	'Snowdrift' Kennett (d)	EBak
	'Snowfall'	CWVF
	'Snowfire' (d)	CLoc CWVF SCoo SVic
	'Snowflake' (E)	CDoC EPts LCla SLBF WBor
	'Son of Thumb' ♀H4	CDoC CLoc CSil CWVF EPfP EPts LAst LBMP LRHS MAsh MGos MJac SLBF SLim SPet SVic WFar
	'Sonata' (d)	CLoc CWVF EBak SVic
	'Sophie Louise'	CWVF EPts SLBF
	'Sophisticated Lady' (d)	CLoc CWVF EBak EPts SPet SVic
	'South Gate' (d)	CLoc CWVF EBak EPts LAst LBMP SPet SVic
	'South Lakeland'	CSil
	'South Seas' (d)	EBak SVic
	'Southern Pride'	SLBF
	'Southlanders'	EBak
	'Space Shuttle'	CLoc LCla SLBF
	'Sparky' (T)	CLoc CWVF EPts LCla
§	'Speciosa'	CDoC EBak LCla
	'Spion Kop' (d)	CCCN CDoC CWVF EBak LAst SPet WGor
§	***splendens*** ♀H1+3	CCCN CDoC CLoc CSil EBak IDee LCla MCot NPer SLBF SMrm
	- B&SWJ 10469	WCru
	- 'Karl Hartweg'	CDoC
	'Squadron Leader' (d)	CWVF EBak EPts
	'Stanley Cash' (d)	CLoc CWVF SPet SVic
	'Star Wars'	CDoC CLoc EPts MJac
	'Stardust'	CDoC CWVF EBak
	'Steeley' (d)	SVic
	'Stella Ann' (T)	CWVF EBak EPts LCla
	'Stella Marina' (d)	EBak
	'Straat Cumberland'	LCla
	'Straat Fiji'	LCla
	'Straat Fuknoka'	CDoC LCla
	'Straat Futami' (E)	CDoC EPts LCla
	'Straat Kobe' (T)	CDoC LCla
	'Straat La Plata'	LCla
	'Straat Magelhaen'	LCla
	'Straat Messina'	LCla
	'Straat of Plenty'	CDoC LCla
	'Strawberry Delight' (d)	CLoc CWVF EBak MJac SPet SVic
	'Strawberry Sundae' (d)	CLoc CWVF EBak
	'Strawberry Supreme' (d)	CSil
	'String of Pearls'	CLoc CWVF MJac SLBF SPet SVic
	'Stuart Joe'	CWVF
	'Sue'	SLBF
	'Suffolk Splendour' (d)	EPts
	'Sugar Almond' (d)	CWVF
	'Sugar Blues' (d)	EBak
	'Sugar Plum Fairy' (E) **new**	SHom
	'Sunkissed' (d)	EBak
	'Sunningdale' (T)	CWVF
	'Sunny Jim'	SVic
	'Sunny Smiles'	CSil CWVF
	'Sunray' (v)	CDoC CLoc COlW CWVF EBak ELon LBuc LRHS MAsh MGos MWat NEgg NRHS SBfd SCoo SEND SHil SLim SPoG WCot
	'Sunset'	CLoc CWVF EBak SPer
	'Supersport' (d)	SVic
	'Superstar'	CWVF EPts SVic
	'Susan Ford' (d)	CWVF SPet
	'Susan Green'	CSil CWVF EBak MJac
	'Susan McMaster'	CLoc
	'Susan Olcese' (d)	CWVF EBak
	'Susan Travis'	CLoc CSil CWVF EBak SVic
	'Swanley Gem' ♀H3	CLoc CWVF EBak SLBF SPet SVic
	'Swanley Pendula'	CLoc
	'Swanley Yellow'	CWVF EBak SVic
	'Sweet Leilani' (d)	EBak
	'Sweet Sarah' (E)	EPts
I	'Sweetheart' van Wieringen	EBak
	'Swingtime' (d) ♀H3	CCCN CLoc CWVF EBak EPts LAst LCla MGos MJac SLBF SPet SVic
	sylvatica misapplied	see *F. nigricans*
	sylvatica Benth.	CDoC
	'Sylvia Barker'	CWVF LCla SLBF
	'Sylvia Rose' (d)	CWVF
	'Sylvia's Choice'	EBak
	'Symphony'	CLoc CWVF EBak
	'T.S.J.' (E)	CDoC LCla
	'Taco'	CDoC LCla
	'Taddle'	CWVF SLBF
	'Taffeta Bow' (d)	CLoc SVic
	'Taffy' (d)	EBak
	'Tamworth'	CLoc CWVF EBak MJac SVic
	'Tangerine'	CLoc CWVF EBak SVic WCot
	'Tanya Bridger' (d)	EBak
	'Tarra Valley'	LCla SVic
	'Task Force'	CWVF SVic
	'Tausendschön' (d)	CLoc
	'Ted Perry' (d)	CWVF
	'Temptation' ambig.	CWVF
	'Temptation' Peterson	CLoc EBak
	'Tennessee Waltz' (d) ♀H3	CDoC CLoc CSil CWVF EBak EPts SLBF SPet SVic
	'Tessa Jane'	CSil
	tetradactyla misapplied	see *F.* × *bacillaris*
	'Texas Longhorn' (d)	CLoc CWVF EBak SVic
	'Thalia' (T) ♀H1+3	CCCN CDoC CHEx CLoc CWVF EBak EPfP EPts EUJe LAst LCla LSRN MBri MCot MHer MJac NEgg NPri SGar SLBF SMrm SPer SPlb SPoG SVic WWlt
	'Thamar'	CDoC CLoc CWVF EPts SVic
	'That's It' (d)	EBak SVic
	'The Aristocrat' (d)	CLoc EBak
§	'The Doctor'	CLoc CSil CWVF EBak
	'The Jester' (d)	EBak
	'The Madame' (d)	CWVF EBak
	'The Tarns'	CSil CWVF EBak SVic
	'Thelma Vint'	CDoC
	'Therese Dupois'	CSil
	'Théroigne de Méricourt'	EBak
	'Thilco'	CDoC CSil
	'Thistle Hill' (d)	CDoC CSil
	'Thomas' (d)	EPts
	'Thompsonii'	see *F. magellanica* 'Thompsonii'
	'Thornley's Hardy'	CSil MRav SVic
	'Three Cheers'	CLoc EBak
	'Three Counties'	EBak
	'Thunderbird' (d)	CLoc CWVF EBak
	thymifolia (E)	CWVF EBee GCra LRHS MHer SBch SDys SMHy WKif
	- subsp. ***minimiflora*** (E)	CSil
	- subsp. ***thymifolia*** (E)	CDoC CSil CTsd
	'Tiara' (d)	EBak
	'Tiffany' Reedstrom (d)	EBak
	'Tillingbourne' (d)	CSil SLBF
	'Time After Time'	CLoc
	'Timlin Brened' (T)	CWVF EBak
	'Timothy Titus' (T) ♀H1	LCla
	'Ting-a-ling'	CLoc CWVF EBak SPet SVic
	'Tinker Bell' Hodges	EBak SVic
	'Tintern Abbey'	CWVF

'Tjinegara' CDoC LCla
'Toby Bridger' (d) CLoc EBak
'Toby Foreman' SLBF
'Tolling Bell' CWVF EBak SPet
'Tom Goedeman' LCla
'Tom H. Oliver' (d) EBak
'Tom Knights' EBak SPet
'Tom Thorne' EBak
'Tom Thumb' ♀H3 Widely available
'Tom West' misapplied see *F.* 'Mr West'
'Tom West' Meillez (v) CDoC CHEx CLoc CMHG CSBt CSil CTsd CWVF CWib EBak EHoe EPts LAst LCla LHop LRHS LSRN MAsh MAvo MHer MJac MSCN SAga SBfd SDix SLBF SLim WFar WHil
'Tom Woods' CWVF
'Ton Ten Hove' CDoC LCla
'Tony Talbot' **new** MJac
'Tony's Treat' (d) EPts
'Toos' SVic
'Topaz' (d) CLoc EBak
'Topper' (d) CWVF
'Torch' (d) CLoc CWVF EBak SVic
'Torchlight' CWVF EPts LCla
'Torvill and Dean' (d) CLoc CWVF EPts LAst MJac SLBF SPet WGor
'Tosca' CWVF
'Town Crier' SLBF
'Tracid' (d) CSil
'Trail Blazer' (d) CLoc CWVF EBak MJac
'Trailing Queen' EBak MJac
'Trase' (d) CDoC CSil CWVF CWib EBak SVic
'Traudchen Bonstedt' (T) ♀H1 CDoC CLoc CWVF EBak LCla SVic
'Traviata' see *F.* 'La Traviata' Blackwell
'Treasure' (d) EBak
'Tresco' CSil
'Tricolor' see *F. magellanica* var. *gracilis* 'Tricolor'
'Trientje' LCla SLBF
'Trimley Bells' EBak
'Trio' (d) CLoc
triphylla (T) EBak MHer
'Trish's Triumph' EPts
'Tristesse' (d) CLoc CWVF EBak
'Troika' (d) EBak
'Troon' CWVF
'Tropicana' (d) CLoc CWVF EBak SVic
'Troubador' Waltz (d) CLoc
'Troutbeck' CSil
'Trudi Davro' LAst MJac SCoo
'Trudy' CDoC CSil CWVF EBak SVic
'Truly Treena' (d) SLBF
'Trumpeter' ambig. CDoC CWVF
'Trumpeter' Fry SVic
'Trumpeter' Reiter (T) CLoc EBak EPts LCla MJac
'Tubular Bells' (T) LCla
'Tuonela' (d) CLoc CWVF EBak
'Tutti-frutti' (d) CLoc
'Twinkling Stars' CWVF MJac SVic
'Twinny' CWVF EPts
'Two Tiers' (d) CSil CWVF
'U.F.O.' CTsd CWVF SVic
'Ullswater' (d) CWVF EBak
'Ultramar' (d) EBak
'Uncle Charley' (d) CDoC CSil EBak SVic
'Uncle Jinks' SPet
'Uncle Steve' (d) EBak SVic
'University of Liverpool' CLoc MJac
'Upward Look' EBak
'Valda May' (d) CWVF
'Valentine' (d) EBak
'Valerie Ann' (d) EBak SPet SVic
'Valerie Bradley' EPts
'Valiant' EBak
'Vanessa Jackson' CLoc CWVF MJac SVic
'Vanity Fair' (d) CLoc EBak
'Variegated Lottie Hobby' (E/v) CSil
'Variegated Pixie' (v) CSil
'Variegated Procumbens' see *F. procumbens* 'Wirral'
'Variegated Swingtime' (v) EBak LAst SLBF
'Variegated Waveney Sunrise' (v) MBri
'Veenlust' EBak
'Velvet Crush' LAst
'Vendeta' CDoC LCla
'Venus Victrix' CSil EBak
venusta CDoC EBak LCla
'Vera Garcia' **new** SLBF
'Versicolor' see *F. magellanica* 'Versicolor'
'Victorian' (d) SVic
'Victory' Reiter (d) EBak
'Vielliebchen' CDoC CSil
'Vintage Dovercourt' LCla
'Violet Bassett-Burr' (d) CLoc EBak
'Violet Gem' (d) CLoc
'Violet Lace' (d) CSil
'Violet Rosette' (d) CWVF EBak SVic
Violetta = 'Goetzviol' (Shadowdancer Series) CDoC LAst LSou SCoo
'Viva Ireland' EBak
'Vivien Colville' CLoc
'Vobeglo' CWVF
'Vogue' (d) EBak
'Voltaire' CSil EBak
'Voodoo' (d) CCCN CDoC CLoc CTsd CWVF EBak EPts LAst SBfd SCoo SLBF SVic
vulcanica CDoC LCla
'Vyvian Miller' CWVF
'W.P. Wood' CDoC CSil
'Wagtails White Pixie' CSil EBak EPfP
'Waldfee' (E) CCVN CDoC CSil LCla
'Waldis Alina' SLBF
'Waldis Billy' **new** SLBF
'Waldis Junella' (d) SLBF
'Waldis Ovambo' SLBF
'Waldis Spezi' CDoC LCla
'Waldis Speziella' SLBF
'Walsingham' (d) CWVF EBak
'Walton Jewel' EBak
'Walz Bella' LCla
'Walz Blauwkous' (d) CDoC CWVF
'Walz Fluit' MJac
'Walz Freule' CWVF MJac
'Walz Harp' CWVF SVic
'Walz Jubelteen' CDoC CLoc CWVF ELon EPts LCla MJac SLBF SVic
'Walz Lucifer' CWVF LCla SLBF
'Walz Mandoline' (d) CWVF SVic
'Walz Panfluit' LCla
'Walz Polka' CDoC LCla SLBF
'Walz Sprietje' CDoC
'Walz Triangel' (d) SVic
'Walz Tuba' CDoC

'Wapenveld 150' LCla
'Wapenveld's Bloei' CDoC LCla SLBF
'War Paint' (d) CLoc EBak
'Warton Crag' CWVF SVic
'Water Nymph' CLoc SLBF SVic
'Wattenpost' SLBF
'Wave of Life' CWVF
'Waveney Gem' CDoC CLoc CWVF EBak LCla MJac SLBF
'Waveney Queen' CWVF SVic
'Waveney Sunrise' CWVF MJac SPet SVic
'Waveney Unique' CWVF
'Waveney Valley' CWVF EBak
'Waveney Waltz' CWVF EBak
'Wedding Bells' ambig. SVic
'Welsh Dragon' (d) CLoc CWVF EBak
'Wendy' Catt see *F.* 'Snowcap'
'Wendy's Beauty' (d) CLoc EBak EPts MJac
'Wentworth' CWVF SVic
'Wessex Belle' (d/v) CWVF
'Wessex Hardy' CSil
'Westham' LCla
'Westminster Chimes' (d) CLoc CWVF SPet SVic
'Wharfedale' ♀H3 CSil ELon MJac SLBF SVic
'Whickham Blue' CWVF
'Whirlaway' (d) CLoc CWVF EBak SVic
'White Ann' see *F.* 'Heidi Weiss'
'White Clove' CDoC CSil SVic
'White Galore' (d) CWVF EBak SVic
'White Général Monk' (d) CDoC CSil
'White Gold' (v) EBak
'White Haven' SVic
'White Heidi Ann' (d) CSil
'White Joy' EBak
'White King' (d) CLoc CWVF EBak LAst SVic
'White Lace' CSil
'White Pixie' ♀H3-4 CDoC CSil EPts MJac SLBF SPer SPet SVic
'White Queen' ambig. CWVF EPfP
'White Queen' Doyle EBak
'White Spider' CLoc CWVF EBak SVic
'White Veil' (d) CWVF
'Whiteknights Amethyst' CDoC CSil
'Whiteknights Blush' CCse CDoC CPLG CSil EBee EPfP EWes GCal GQui LRHS NLar SMrm
'Whiteknights Cheeky' (T) CWVF EBak EPts LCla SVic
'Whiteknights Green Glister' CSil EPfP
'Whiteknights Pearl' ♀H1+3 CSil CTsd CWVF ECha EPfP EPts LAst LCla LRHS SDys SEND SLBF SMHy SPet SVic
'Whitton Starburst' CDoC LCla
'Wicked Queen' (d) CSil SVic
'Widnes Wonder' new SLBF
'Widow Twanky' (d) CWVF
'Wigan Pier' (d) EPts MJac SLBF
'Wight Magic' (d) MJac
'Wild and Beautiful' (d) CTsd CWVF SVic
'Wilf Langton' SLBF
'Wilhelmina Schwab' CDoC LCla
'Willow Tinsdale' LAst LSou SLim
'Wilma van Druten' CDoC LCla
'Wilson's Colours' EPts
'Wilson's Joy' MJac
'Wilson's Pearls' (d) CTsd CWVF SLBF SPet
'Wilson's Sugar Pink' EPts LCla MJac
'Win Oxtoby' (d) CWVF
'Windhapper' LCla SLBF
'Windmill' CWVF
'Wine and Roses' (d) EBak
'Wingrove's Mammoth' (d) SVic
'Wings of Song' (d) CWVF EBak
'Winston Churchill' (d) ♀H3 CLoc CWVF EBak LAst LRHS MJac SBfd SCoo SPet SVic
'Witchipoo' SLBF
'Woodnook' (d) CWVF
'Woodside' (d) CSil SVic
'Ymkje' EBak
'Yolanda Franck' CDoC LAst
'York Manor' CDoC
'Yvonne Schwab' CDoC LCla
'Zeebrook' SVic
'Zellertal' CDoC
'Zets Bravo' CDoC
'Ziegfield Girl' (d) EBak SVic
'Zifi' SLBF
'Zulu King' CDoC CSil SVic
'Zulu Queen' SVic
'Zwarte Snor' (d) CWVF

Fumaria (*Papaveraceae*)

capreolata new WSFF
lutea see *Corydalis lutea*
officinalis CArn

Furcraea (*Asparagaceae*)

bedinghausii see *F. parmentieri*
§ ***foetida*** CCCN SBig
§ – var. ***mediopicta*** (v) SBig
– 'Variegata' see *F. foetida* var. *mediopicta*
gigantea see *F. foetida*
longaeva misapplied see *F. parmentieri*
macdougalii SPlb
§ ***parmentieri*** CAbb CBcs CCCN CCon CDTJ CHEx CHGN CHll CPLG CPne CTrC CTsd EAmu EBee EGri GBin LEdu SBst SPlb WCot WPGP
– NJM 05.081 WPGP
selloa var. ***marginata*** (v) CDoC CHEx EAmu

Gahnia (*Cyperaceae*)

sieberiana SPlb

Gaillardia (*Asteraceae*)

aristata 'Maxima Aurea' EPfP MSpe NBre NPri SPhx
'Arizona Sun' EBee ECtt LRHS MHer NPri SGar SHil SPad SPet SVic WCAu
'Bijou' EBee LRHS NBre NLar SWvt
'Candy Corn' new EBee
'Dwarf Goblin' NGBl SPet
§ 'Fackelschein' EBee MSpe NBre XLum
'Fanfare' PBR CMac CWGN EBee ECtt ELon LHop LRHS LSou MGos NPri SCoo SMrm SPer SPoG
'Frenzy' (Commotion Series) new EBee
* giant hybrids WFar
Goblin see *G.* × *grandiflora* 'Kobold'
'Golden Queen' XLum
× ***grandiflora*** 'Amber Wheels' EBee EPfP NDov NGdn NPri SBfd SPhx WWEG
– 'Bremen' EBee XLum

- 'Burgunder' CPrp CSBt CSpe EBee ECtt ELan EPfP EShb LAst LHop LRHS LSRN LSou MBri MSpe NGBl NLar NPri SBfd SPer SPhx SPoG SWvt WCAu WWEG XLum
- 'Dazzler' ♀H4 CSBt EAEE EBee ECtt ELan EPfP LAst LRHS NLar SPer SPoG WMoo WWEG XLum
§ - 'Goldkobold' XLum
- 'Granada' LRHS
§ - 'Kobold' CBcs CMac CSBt EBee ECtt ELon EPfP GMaP LAst LRHS MBri NBre NEgg NHol NLar NPri SPer SPlb SPoG SWvt WWEG XLum
- 'Mesa Yellow' **new** NPri
- (Sunburst Series) Sunburst Burgundy **new** SPet
- - Sunburst Burgundy Picotee = 'Granretip' **new** LRHS
- 'Tizzy' **new** EBee
- 'Tokajer' EBee EPfP LRHS NBre NLar SPhx XLum
'Naomi Sunshine' **new** SHar
§ 'Oranges and Lemons'PBR CPrp EBee ECtt ELon LAst LHop LRHS LSou MSpe NLar SHar SMrm SPoG WCAu
Saint ClementsPBR see *G.* 'Oranges and Lemons'
Torchlight see *G.* 'Fackelschein'
Yellow Goblin see *G.* × *grandiflora* 'Goldkobold'

Galax (*Diapensiaceae*)

aphylla see *G. urceolata*
§ ***urceolata*** ECho IBlr

Galactites (*Asteraceae*)

tomentosa EHoe EHrv ELan EPfP EPyc EWTr LDai SGar SPav

Galanthus ✿ (*Amaryllidaceae*)

'Acton Pigot No. 3' **new** CAvo
'Alison Hilary' **new** CAvo
× ***allenii*** CAvo CBro WIvy
§ ***alpinus*** var. ***alpinus*** NMen
'Anne of Geierstein' WCot
'Annette' LAma LRHS NMyG
'Armine' CAvo CElw IFoB
'Atkinsii' ♀H4 CAvo CBgR CBro CElw CLAP CWCL ECha ECho EPot EWoo GAbr GEdr IFoB IGor LAma LRHS MAsh MHom MRav MWat NBir NMyG WCot WFar WHoo WShi WTin
'Autumn Beauty' CBro LRHS
'Barbara's Double' (d) CAvo CBgR CLAP WFar
'Benhall Beauty' CAvo EWoo WTin
'Benton Magnet' EWoo
'Bertram Anderson' EWoo WCol
'Bess' CAvo CElw CSna IFoB
'Bill Bishop' CAvo ECha EWoo IPot LRHS MAsh WFar
'Blewbury' **new** LRHS
'Brenda Troyle' CBro CElw CLAP ECha ELon EPot GAbr GEdr IGor IPot LRHS MHom NMyG WCot WFar WIvy
'Byfield Special' **new** CAvo
byzantinus see *G. plicatus* subsp. *byzantinus*
'Castlegar' CAvo IFoB
caucasicus misapplied see *G. elwesii* var. *monostictus*
caucasicus (Bak.) Grossh. see *G. alpinus* var. *alpinus*
caucasicus ambig. GAbr IFoB
- 'Comet' see *G. elwesii* 'Comet'
- var. ***hiemalis*** Stern see *G. elwesii* var. *monostictus* Hiemalis Group
'Chequers' **new** LRHS
'Cicely Hall' **new** WFar
'Clare Blakeway-Phillips' CLAP LRHS
corcyrensis spring-flowering see *G. reginae-olgae* subsp. *vernalis*
- winter-flowering see *G. reginae-olgae* subsp. *reginae-olgae* Winter-flowering Group
'Cordelia' (d) CLAP IFoB IPot LRHS NMyG
'Curly' CDes EWoo
'Daglingworth' CElw
'Desdemona' (d) CBgR CBro CLAP EPot LRHS NMyG WCot WFar WIvy
'Ding Dong' CAvo CDes WCol
'Dionysus' (d) CBgR CBro CLAP CPLG ECha EPot EWoo GEdr IGor LLHF LRHS LWst MHom NBir NMyG WBrk WCol WFar WShi WTin
'Drummond's Giant' IFoB
§ ***elwesii*** ♀H4 CBro CTri CWCL ECho ELan ELon EPfP EPot ERCP GKev IFoB IGor ITim LAma LRHS MAsh MWat NBir NRHS SDeJ SPoG SRms WCot WHoo WShi
- 'Abington Green' CSna
- 'Broadleigh Gardens' LRHS
- 'Cedric's Prolific' ECha EWoo IFoB IGor LRHS NMyG WFar
§ - 'Comet' CElw ELon EWoo GBuc IFoB WCol
- cf. 'Comet' WFar
- 'Daphne's Scissors' CBgR CSna NCot
- 'David Shackleton' CAvo EWoo IFoB LRHS MAsh
- 'Early Twin' **new** WCot
- 'Echoes' **new** WCot
- Edward Whittall Group CLAP
- var. ***elwesii*** 'Fenstead End' EWoo
- - 'Fred's Giant' WFar
- - 'Kite' EWoo LRHS
- - 'Magnus' CLAP NBir
- - 'Maidwell L' CBro CSna LRHS MAsh
- - 'Sibbertoft Magnet' CAvo IFoB
- 'Godfrey Owen' **new** CDes
- 'Green Brush' **new** CAvo WCol
- (Hiemalis Group) 'Barnes' WCot
- 'J. Haydn' ECho LAma MAsh NMyG WCol
- 'Jessica' **new** CAvo
- 'Kyre Park' CDes NCot
- 'Long 'drop' IFoB
- 'Mandarin' **new** WCol
- 'Marielle' EPPr
- 'Marjorie Brown' CFis LRHS NMyG WCol
- var. ***maximus*** see *G. elwesii* 'Yvonne Hay'
- 'Milkwood' see *G. elwesii* 'Mrs Macnamara'
§ - var. ***monostictus*** ♀H4 CAvo ECho EWoo IFoB LLHF LRHS MAsh WBrk WCol WFar WIvy
- - 'G. Handel' ECho LAma LRHS NMyG WFar
- - 'Green Tips' CAvo
- - 'H. Purcell' ECho LAma LRHS
§ - - Hiemalis Group CBro CDes ECha EPot LRHS LWst MHom WCot
- - late-flowering LWst
- - 'Miller's Late' **new** CAvo
- - 'Rogers Rough' SDys
- - 'Warwickshire Gemini' CDes
§ - 'Mrs Macnamara' CAvo CDes EWoo IFoB LRHS WCol WFar

– 'Penelope Ann'	LRHS
– 'Selborne Green Tips'	CAvo
– 'Sickle'	CAvo CDes CSna LRHS
– 'Sir Edward Elgar'	LAma LRHS
– 'Spring Pearl' **new**	LWst
– 'Washfield Colesbourne'	see *G.* 'Washfield Colesbourne'
§ – 'Yvonne Hay' **new**	WCol
aff. ***elwesii*** var. ***monostictus***	WFar
'Erway'	CAvo MHom
'F63'	IFoB
'Falkland House'	WCol
'Faringdon Double' (d)	CAvo LRHS WCol
'Fieldgate Prelude' **new**	CAvo
fosteri	CBro ECho LRHS SCnR
'G71' (d)	IFoB
'Galatea'	CBro CLAP CSna ECha EWoo LRHS MAsh MHom SDys WFar WIvy
'George Elwes' **new**	CAvo WCol
'Ginns'	CDes CLAP ELon EWoo IFoB
§ ***gracilis***	CAvo CBro CLAP CPLG LRHS
– 'Highdown'	CElw CLAP IFoB LWst MHom
– 'Vic Horton'	WThu
graecus misapplied	see *G. gracilis*
graecus Orph. ex Boiss.	see *G. elwesii*
'Grande Juge'	IFoB
'Grayling'	see *G. plicatus* 'Percy Picton'
Greatorex double (d)	CLAP
'Green Man' **new**	CAvo
'Greenfields'	CBgR CSna IFoB IGor
'Heffalump' (d)	CAvo CDes
'Hill Poë' (d)	CBro CDes CElw CLAP EPot IFoB IPot LRHS MHom MWat NMyG WCol
'Hippolyta' (d)	CAvo CBro CElw CLAP ECha ELon EPot EWoo GAbr GEdr IFoB IGor LAma LRHS MAsh MHom NMyG SKHP SMrm WCol WCot WFar WIvy WShi
'Hobson's Choice'	LRHS
'Honeysuckle Cottage' **new**	CAvo
× ***hybridus*** 'Merlin'	CAvo CBro CElw IFoB IGor LRHS MHom NMyG WCot WIvy WTin
– 'Robin Hood'	CAvo CLAP IFoB LRHS WFar
'Icicle'	CAvo
§ ***ikariae*** Bak.	CBgR CElw EPfP LWst WFar
– 'Georgia'	LRHS
– Latifolius Group	see *G. platyphyllus*
– subsp. ***snogerupii***	see *G. ikariae* Bak.
'Imbolc'	CAvo
'Irish Green' **new**	CAvo
'Jacquenetta' (d)	CAvo CBro CElw CLAP CSna EWoo IFoB IGor ITim LRHS MHom NMyG WTin
'James Backhouse'	CElw ECha LRHS WCol WHoo WShi
'John Gray'	CAvo CBro CSna EWoo IFoB MAsh WCol
'Ketton'	CBro CElw CSna EWoo LRHS NRya WCol WIvy
'Kildare'	WCol
'Kingston Double' (d)	CAvo CBgR CLAP
'Lady Beatrix Stanley' (d)	CAvo CBro CElw CLAP ECha EPot GAbr GEdr IFoB LLWP LRHS MAsh MHom NMyG WCol WCot WFar WTin
lagodechianus	LRHS MPhe
'Lapwing'	CAvo WCol
latifolius Rupr.	see *G. platyphyllus*
'Lavinia' (d)	CAvo CElw CLAP LRHS MHom WFar
'Lerinda'	IFoB
'Limetree'	CBgR CElw CLAP EPri EWoo LRHS MHom NCot
'Little Ben'	CAvo
'Little John'	LRHS WBrk
'Little Magnet' **new**	CAvo
'Lord Lieutenant' **new**	WCol
lutescens	see *G. nivalis* Sandersii Group
'Lyn'	CBro LRHS NBir
'Magnet' ♀H4	CAvo CBgR CBro CElw CLAP ECha ECho ELon EPot EWoo GAbr GEdr IGor ITim LAma LRHS LWst MAsh MHom MWat NBir NMyG SKHP WBrk WCol WCot WFar WHoo WShi
aff. 'Magnet' **new**	SMrm WFar
'Maidwell'	IFoB
'Martha MacLaren' **new**	WCol
'Melanie Broughton' **new**	CAvo
'Mighty Atom'	CDes CLAP WBrk
'Moccas'	CBgR CElw CSna
'Modern Art'	CAvo CDes EWoo IFoB WFar
'Mrs Backhouse No 12'	LRHS
'Mrs Thompson'	CAvo CDes CElw ECha LRHS WCol WIvy
'Natalie Garton' **new**	CAvo
'Neill Fraser'	LRHS MHom
nivalis ♀H4	Widely available
– 'Anglesey Abbey'	CAvo EHrv EWoo IFoB MHom
– 'April Fool'	MHom WTin
– 'Bitton'	CLAP
– 'Blonde Inge'	CAvo IFoB
– 'Chedworth'	CElw WBrk
– 'Cornwood' **new**	CAvo EWoo
– 'Dreycott Greentip'	IFoB
– 'Elfin'	CElw
– 'Fuzz' **new**	CAvo
– 'Gloucester Old Spot' **new**	WCol
– 'Greenish'	CDes EWoo LRHS WCol
– subsp. ***imperati***	CPLG
– 'Lutescens'	see *G. nivalis* Sandersii Group
– 'Major Pam'	IFoB
– 'Maximus'	LRHS WShi
– 'Melvillei'	EWoo
– f. ***pleniflorus*** (d)	CTca ECha GKev SPoG WFar
– – 'Bagpuize Virginia' (d)	CAvo
– – 'Blewbury Tart' (d)	CAvo CBro CElw CFis CLAP CSna EWoo IFoB LRHS WBrk WCol WFar
– – 'Flore Pleno' (d) ♀H4	CBro CPLG CWCL EPfP EPot ERCP IFoB ITim LAma LHop LLWP LRHS MMuc NCot NRya SDeJ SEND SMrm SPer SRms WBrk WCot WFar WHoo WPnP WShi
– – 'Lady Elphinstone' (d)	CAvo CBro CDes CLAP CRow CSna IFoB LLHF LRHS MAsh MHom NMyG NRya WCol WCot WIvy
– – 'Octopussy' (d) **new**	WCol
– – 'Pusey Green Tips' (d)	CAvo CBro CElw CLAP EPot GEdr IFoB IPot LRHS NMyG WCol WCot WTin
§ – – 'Wonston Double' (d)	CAvo IFoB
– Poculiformis Group	CLAP
– – 'Angelique' **new**	CAvo
§ – Sandersii Group	CDes CRDP IFoB WFar
§ – Scharlockii Group	CAvo CBgR CElw IGor LRHS MHom WBrk
– 'Tiny'	MHom NBir WFar
– 'Tiny Tim'	ITim LRHS NRya WCol

- 'Virescens'	CLAP IFoB WFar
- 'Viridapice'	CAvo CBgR CBro CElw CPLG ECha ECho EPot GEdr GKev IFoB IGor LAma LRHS MAsh MWat NBir NMen SDeJ SKHP WCol WCot WFar WHoo WShi WTin
- 'White Dream' **new**	WShi
'Ophelia' (d)	CAvo CBro EPot EWoo GAbr IGor LRHS MHom MWat NMyG SKHP WBrk WCol WFar WHoo
'Orion'	CDes
'Peg Sharples'	CAvo IFoB MHom NCot
peshmenii	EPot LLHF WCol
§ ***platyphyllus***	CPLG LRHS
plicatus ♀H4	CAvo CBro CElw EPot GAbr GEdr LRHS MCot MHom NMen NMyG WBrk WCol WCot WFar WHoo WShi WTin
- 'Augustus'	CAvo CBro CElw ELon GEdr IFoB IGor ITim LRHS MAsh MHom NMyG WCot WFar WIvy WTin
- 'Baxendale's Late'	CAvo CLAP EWoo
- 'Bill Clark' **new**	CDes
- 'Bolu Shades'	LWst
- 'Bowles's Large'	CElw
§ - subsp. ***byzantinus***	CBro LRHS MHom WThu
- 'Colossus'	CBro IFoB WCol WFar
- 'Diggory'	WCol
- 'Gerard Parker'	CAvo IFoB WCol
- 'Green Hayes' **new**	CAvo
- 'Greenpeace'	CSna
- 'Lambrook Greensleeves' **new**	CAvo
- late flowering	LWst
- 'Limey' **new**	EWoo
- - 'Oreanda'	IPot
§ - 'Percy Picton'	CAvo
- 'Sally Pasmore'	CAvo
- 'Sophie North'	CLAP IFoB
- 'The Pearl'	IFoB
- 'Three Ships'	CAvo EWoo
- 'Trym'	WCol WFar
- 'Warham'	CBro EPot GAbr GEdr IFoB IGor LRHS MHom NMyG WCot
- 'Warham Rectory'	LRHS
- 'Wendy's Gold'	CBro CDes CSna EWld IFoB LRHS WCol WFar
'Pride o' the Mill' **new**	CAvo
'Primrose Warburg'	CAvo CDes IFoB
reginae-olgae	CAvo CBro GKev LRHS WThu
§ - subsp. ***reginae-olgae*** Winter-flowering Group	CBro
§ - subsp. ***vernalis***	EPot IFoB NMyG WCot
'Reverend Hailstone'	LRHS
'Richard Ayres' (d)	CAvo IFoB LRHS WCol
rizehensis	CAvo CLAP IFoB LLHF LRHS LWst MHom NMyG
- Baytop 34474	IFoB LRHS
'Rodmarton' **new**	MAsh
'S.Arnott' ♀H4	CAvo CBro CElw CLAP CPLG ECha ECho ELon EPot EWoo GAbr GBuc GEdr IFoB IGor LAma LRHS MAsh MWat NBir NMen NRHS NRya SDeJ WBrk WCol WCot WFar WHoo WTin
'Saint Anne's'	CAvo CDes CElw CSna IFoB MAsh WCol WIvy
'Scharlockii'	see *G. nivalis* Scharlockii Group
'Seagull'	CAvo
'Sentinel' **new**	CAvo
'Shaggy'	LRHS
'Silverwells'	CSna GEdr IFoB LRHS
'Spindlestone Surprise'	CAvo EWoo GEdr
§ 'Straffan'	CAvo CBro CElw EPot GEdr IFoB IGor LRHS MHom NMyG WBrk WCol WCot WFar
'Sutton Courtenay'	CAvo CDes CSna LRHS
'The O'Mahoney'	see *G.* 'Straffan'
'Titania' (d)	CBro ELon IFoB IGor LRHS MHom WCol WFar
'Tubby Merlin'	CDes CElw CLAP EWoo IFoB LRHS MAsh WCol WIvy
'Uncle Dick' **new**	CAvo
× ***valentinei*** 'Compton Court'	CBro
§ 'Washfield Colesbourne'	EWoo
'Washfield Warham'	CAvo ECha EWoo ITim LRHS NMyG
'Wasp' **new**	WCol
'Welshway' **new**	WCol
'White Admiral'	SKHP
'White Dreams'	LRHS WFar
'White Swan' Ballard (d)	CElw LRHS
'William Thomson'	CSna
'Winifrede Mathias'	CElw CLAP LRHS
'Wisley Magnet'	LRHS
'Wonston Double'	see *G. nivalis* f. *pleniflorus* 'Wonston Double'
woronowii ♀H4	CAvo CBro CElw CLAP CTca CTri ECho EPfP EPot GKev IFoB ITim LAma LRHS MAsh MBri MHom MWat NBir NMyG NRHS SDeJ WBrk WCot WFar

Galega (*Papilionaceae*)

bicolor	NBir NBre NChi SRms SWat
'Duchess of Bedford'	EBee GBin
× ***hartlandii***	CPLG LRHS
- 'Alba' ♀H4	EBee EHrv ELon EWes IBlr LRHS MArl MCot SMHy SWat WCot WHoo WSHC WTcb
- 'Candida'	NBir
- 'Lady Wilson' ♀H4	CPom EBee ECtt ELon EWes EWld MArl MLHP WAul WCot WOut WTcb
- 'Spring Light' (v)	EWes LSou
'Her Majesty'	see *G.* 'His Majesty'
§ 'His Majesty'	CDes CKno EBee ECtt IFro MCot MDKP MLHP MRav SMrm WCot WPGP
officinalis	Widely available
- 'Alba' ♀H4	CPom CPrp ECtt ELan EPfP LEdu LPot MAvo MBrN MHer MNHC NPnk SMrm SPer SWal WHer WHrl WKif WMoo
- Coconut Ice = 'Kelgal' (v)	CAbP SPer
- 'Lincoln Gold'	MTPN
orientalis	CDes ECha ECtt EWes LEdu LRHS MArl MCot SPhx WAbb WCot WMoo WPGP WSHC

Galeobdolon see *Lamium*

Galeopsis (*Lamiaceae*)

tetrahit	WSFF

Galium (*Rubiaceae*)

cruciata	see *Cruciata laevipes*

mollugo CArn CHab CRWN SIde
§ ***odoratum*** Widely available
verum CArn CHab CRWN ENfk GJos GPoy MCoo MHer NLan NMir SIde

Galtonia (*Hyacinthaceae*)

candicans ♀H4 Widely available
- 'Moonbeam' (d) CRDP EBee
princeps CBro CDes CSam CTca ECha GBin GCra LRHS SGar WHil WPGP
regalis CPLG CTca WPGP
viridiflora CAvo CBro CTca EBee ECha ELan EPot ERCP GBin GCal LEdu LRHS MNrw NChi SDeJ WFar WPer XLum

Galvezia (*Plantaginaceae*)

speciosa SUsu

Gamblea (*Araliaceae*)

pseudoevodiifolia B&SWJ 11707 WCru

Garcinia (*Clusiaceae*)

mangostana CCCN

Gardenia (*Rubiaceae*)

augusta see *G. jasminoides*
florida L. see *G. jasminoides*
grandiflora see *G. jasminoides*
§ ***jasminoides*** ♀H1 CArn CBcs CCCN EBak MBri
- 'Kleim's Hardy' Widely available
magnifica MOWG
'Perfumed Petticoats' **new** WHlf
thunbergia SPlb

garlic see *Allium sativum*

Garrya ✿ (*Garryaceae*)

congdonii NLar
elliptica CBcs CDul CMac EBee ECrN EPfP LRHS LSRN MBri MGos NPri NWea SBfd SEND SPlb WFar WHar WPat
- (f) MSwo SWvt
- (m) CDoC CTri ELon LAst MAsh MBlu NLar SGol SLim
- 'James Roof' (m) ♀H4 Widely available
× ***issaquahensis*** 'Glasnevin Wine' CAbP CDul CJun EBee ELan ELon EPfP IArd LRHS MAsh MBri MGos NLar SCoo SLim SPer SPoG
- 'Pat Ballard' (m) EPfP NLar
× ***thuretii*** CBcs CDul MBri MGos NLar

Gasteria ✿ (*Asphodelaceae*)

bicolor var. ***liliputana*** SPlb
carinata var. ***verrucosa*** EShb MSCN
ellaphieae **new** LToo
excelsa LToo
nitida var. ***armstrongii*** ♀H1 LToo
- var. ***nitida*** variegated (v) WCot
'Smokey' EShb

× *Gaulnettya* see *Gaultheria*

Gaultheria ✿ (*Ericaceae*)

sp. LSRN
adenothrix NMen WThu
antarctica WThu
antipoda 'Adpressa' WThu
cardiosepala GEdr
- CLD 1351 GEdr
crassa 'John Saxton' **new** WAbe
cuneata ♀H4 EBee ECho GEdr LRHS MAsh NHar WThu
- 'Pinkie' ECho
depressa var. ***novae-zelandiae*** NWad
forrestii CPLG
§ ***fragrantissima*** GKev
hispidula ECho
itoana ECho GEdr GJos GKev NHar
miqueliana WThu
§ ***mucronata*** CDul EPfP MAsh NWea
- (m) CBcs CDoC CMac CSBt CTri CWSG EBee EPfP LRHS MGos NEgg NWad SPer SRms WFar
- 'Bell's Seedling' (f/m) ♀H4 CBcs CDoC CDul CTri CWSG EBee EPfP LRHS MAsh MMuc NBir NEgg SPer SPoG
- 'Cherry Ripe' (f) CMac MMuc
- 'Crimsonia' (f) ♀H4 CBcs CMac EPfP SPer SRms
- 'Indian Lake' NWad
- 'Lilacina' (f) CBcs CMac
- 'Lilian' (f) CSBt NWad
- Mother of Pearl see *G. mucronata* 'Parelmoer'
- 'Mulberry Wine' (f) ♀H4 CDul CSBt CTri NEgg NHol SPer
§ - 'Parelmoer' (f) CSBt NEgg SPer
- 'Pink Pearl' (f) ♀H4 MAsh SRms
§ - 'Signaal' (f) CBcs EBee EPfP MAsh NEgg NWad SPer
- Signal see *G. mucronata* 'Signaal'
§ - 'Sneeuwwitje' (f) CBcs CDul EPfP MAsh NBir SPer
- Snow White see *G. mucronata* 'Sneeuwwitje'
- 'Thymifolia' (m) EPfP
- white-berried (f) MMuc
- 'Wintertime' (f) ♀H4 CMac SRms
§ ***myrsinoides*** WThu
nana Colenso see *G. parvula*
nummularioides GEdr NHar NLar
ovalifolia see *G. fragrantissima*
§ ***parvula*** WThu
'Pearls' NHar WAbe WThu
'Pilgrim' LSRN
'Pink Champagne' ITim
procumbens ♀H4 CAgr CBcs CDoC CMac CWSG EBee ECho EPfP GJos GMaP GPoy LRHS MAsh MBlu MBri MGos MWat NEgg NRHS NWea SLim SPer SPlb SPoG SReu SRms SWvt WFar
- 'Very Berry' EShb NHol NWad WFar
prostrata see *G. myrsinoides*
pumila GAbr LEdu NHar
schultesii WThu
shallon CAgr CBcs CDul CSBt EBee EPfP MGos SPer SRms SWvt WFar
sinensis NHar
- lilac-berried NHar WThu
tasmanica ECou
tetramera CPLG
trichophylla NHar
× ***wisleyensis*** LRHS SLon SRms SSta
- 'Pink Pixie' EBee LRHS MAsh NLar NMen SSta
- 'Ruby' CMac
- 'Wisley Pearl' CBcs IBlr IRar NLar SCoo WFar
yunnanensis CPLG

Gaura (*Onagraceae*)

lindheimeri ♀H4 CMea COlW CSBt CSpe CWib EBee ECha ELan EPfP EShb EWTr LAst

	LHop LRHS MCot MHer NEgg NRHS SBch SPer SPhx SUsu WFar WHoo WMnd WMoo WPer XLum XSen
- 'Ballerina Blush'	LAst
- 'Ballerina Rose'	LAst SGar SPet
- Belleza Series	CWCL LRHS MBri SHil WGor
- 'Blaze'PBR **new**	LHop
- Cherry Brandy = 'Gauchebra'PBR	EBee ECtt EPfP EWes LRHS MBri NRHS SHil SWvt WFar
- 'Corrie's Gold' (v)	EAEE EBee ECha ECtt EHoe ELan EPfP LRHS MHer SBfd SGar SPer SPet WCFE WMnd WWEG
- 'Crimson Butterflies'PBR	EBee EPfP LRHS WCot
§ - 'Heather's Delight'	MRav
- In the Pink	see *G. lindheimeri* 'Heather's Delight'
- 'Jo Adela' (v)	ELan EPfP
- Karalee Petite = 'Gauka'	CWCL EPfP
- Karalee Petite ImprovedPBR	see *G. lindheimeri* Lillipop Pink
- Karalee Pink	LSRN MBri
- Karalee White = 'Nugauwhite'PBR	CSpe CWCL EPfP LAst LHop LRHS LSRN LSou MBri NLar NRHS SBfd SCoo SHil SPoG
§ - Lillipop Pink = 'Redgapi'PBR	CPrp CWCL ELon EPfP LAst LBMP LHop LRHS LSou MBrN MBri NEgg NLar SBfd SMrm SPoG
- 'Madonna' (v)	EBee
- 'My Melody'PBR (v)	CWCL EBee LPot SBfd
- 'Occitania' (v)	XLum
- Papillon = 'Nugaupapil'	ELon LHop SMrm
- 'Passionate Blush'PBR	CBcs CMac CWCL EBee EPfP LRHS LSRN LSou SLon SPoG SRms
- 'Passionate Rainbow'PBR (v)	CWCL EBee EHoe EPfP LRHS LSou SPoG SRms
- 'Pink Dwarf'	EPfP LRHS
- 'Rosyjane'	CKno CSpe CWCL EBee EHoe EPPr EPfP LAst LBMP LHop LRHS LSRN LSou MBri MRav NRHS SHar SHil SLon SMrm SPad SPer SPoG SRms SUsu
- 'Ruby Ruby' **new**	SHar
- 'Siskiyou Pink'	CBcs CSBt CWCL EBee ECha EHoe EHrv ELan EPfP LRHS LSRN MWat SBfd SMad SPer SWat SWvt WCFE WFar WGwG WMnd WWEG XLum
- Snow Fountain = 'Walsnofou'	EBee LRHS
- 'Snowstorm'	EBee
- 'Summer Breeze'	EBee EDif SBea SBfd SPhx
- 'The Bride'	CEnt CTri EBee ECtt EHrv EPfP LRHS LSRN LSou MMuc MPie MRav MWat SEND SPav SPet SWal SWvt WHil WMnd
- 'Tutti Frutti'PBR	EBee LBuc LRHS LSou SPoG SUsu
- 'Vanilla'PBR	CWCL EBee LBMP LBuc LRHS LSou SPoG SUsu
I - 'Variegata' (v)	CWCL LRHS SHil SRms
- 'Whirling Butterflies'	CKno CSpe CWCL EBee ELan ELon EPfP GMaP LRHS MWat SMad SPav SPer SWat SWvt WMnd WWEG
- 'White Dove'	EBee EPfP
- 'White Heron'	MNrw
sinuata	SHar

Gazania (*Asteraceae*)

'Aztec' ♀H1+3	CCCN SUsu
'Bicton Orange'	CCCN COlW ECtt SCoo
'Big Kiss White Flame' (Kiss Series)	SPoG
'Big Kiss Yellow Flame' (Kiss Series)	SPoG
'Blackberry Ripple'	CCCN COlW LAst SCoo SMrm
'Blackcurrant Ice'	MCot
'Christopher'	SCoo
'Christopher Lloyd'	CCCN COlW ECtt LAst NPri SMrm SUsu
'Cookei' ♀H1+3	CSpe
'Cornish Pixie'	CCCN
'Cream Beauty'	MCot
Daybreak Series	WFar
- 'Daybreak Rose Stripe'	NGBl
- 'Daybreak Red Stripe'	NGBl
Gazoo Series	SPoG
'Jamaica Ginger'	SMrm
Kiss Series **new**	SGar
krebsiana	CCCN
'Lemon Beauty'	ECtt
linearis	COlW
'Magic'	CCCN NPri SCoo
Nahui = 'Suga119' (Sunbathers Series)	CCCN
'Orange Beauty'	CHEx ELan
'Red Velvet'	CHEx
rigens 'Variegata' (v) ♀H1+3	CCCN ELan
Rumi = 'Suga116' (Sunbathers Series)	CCCN
Sunset Jane Lemon Spot = 'Sugajale' (Sunbathers Series)	CCCN
Sunset Jane = 'Sugaja'PBR (Sunbathers Series)	CCCN
'Talent'	SEND
Tiger Eye = 'Gazte'PBR (v)	CCCN CWGN LAst LSou
Toptokai = 'Suga407' (Sunbathers Series)	CCCN
'Torbay Silver'	CHEx
Totonaca = 'Suga212' (Sunbathers Series)	CCCN

Geissorhiza (*Iridaceae*)

aspera	ECho
bracteata	ECho
brehmii 'Rawsonville'	ECho
darlingensis	ECho
imbricata	ECho
- subsp. ***bicolor***	ECho
inequalis	ECho
inflexa	ECho
monanthos	ECho
ornithogaloides	ECho
- subsp. ***marlothii***	ECho
radians	ECho
rosea	ECho
splendidissima	ECho

Gelasine (*Iridaceae*)

§ ***coerulea***	WSHC

Gelidocalamus (*Poaceae*)

fangianus	see *Ampelocalamus mocrophyllum*

Gelsemium (*Gelsemiaceae*)

rankinii	EBee LRHS
sempervirens ♀H1-2	CArn CCCN CHll CRHN EBee EShb LRHS LSRN MOWG SBrt SLim SPoG

Genista (*Papilionaceae*)

	aetnensis ♀H4	CDul ELan EPfP EWTr NLar SEND SPer SRms WPat
§	***canariensis***	CPLG CSBt CWib
	cinerea	WCFE
	decumbens	see *Cytisus decumbens*
	delphinensis	see *G. sagittalis* subsp. *delphinensis*
	'Emerald Spreader'	see *G. pilosa* 'Yellow Spreader'
	fragrans	see *G. canariensis*
	hispanica	CBcs CDul CSBt CTri EBee ELan EPfP MGos NLar SEND SLim SPer SRms SWvt WCFE WHar
	humifusa	see *G. pulchella*
	lydia ♀H4	Widely available
§	***maderensis***	EWes LBuc LRHS SHil
	pilosa	MAsh NMen
	- 'Goldilocks'	EBee LRHS MMuc SEND
	- 'Lemon Spreader'	see *G. pilosa* 'Yellow Spreader'
	- var. ***minor***	NLar NMen SBch WAbe
	- 'Procumbens'	MDKP MHer
	- 'Vancouver Gold'	CBcs CMac EBee ELan EPfP MAsh MGos MRav SMad SPer SRms WGor
§	- 'Yellow Spreader'	CBcs MAsh MSwo
§	'Porlock' ♀H3	CDoC CDul CMac CPLG CSBt CTri CWSG CWib EBee ELon EPfP LRHS MAsh MBri MNHC MRav SBfd SEND SHil SLim
§	***pulchella***	CTri
	sagittalis	CTri EBee LRHS MMuc NBir SPer WWFP
§	- subsp. ***delphinensis*** ♀H4	NMen
	- ***minor***	see *G. sagittalis* subsp. *delphinensis*
§	× ***spachiana*** ♀H1	CTri LRHS SBfd SPoG
	tenera 'Golden Shower'	SLPl
	tinctoria	CArn CHab EOHP GPoy MHer SIde WHer
§	- 'Flore Pleno' (d) ♀H4	ECho GEdr NMen NPro
	- 'Humifusa'	EPot GEdr
	- 'Moesiaca'	WAbe
	- 'Plena'	see *G. tinctoria* 'Flore Pleno'
	- 'Royal Gold' ♀H4	CWib EPfP MRav NWad SPer SPlb
	villarsii	see *G. pulchella*

Gentiana ✿ (*Gentianaceae*)

§	***acaulis*** ♀H4	ECho ELan EPfP EPot GEdr GKev GMaP ITim LHop LRHS MAsh MWat NGdn NHar NMen NRHS NSla SPlb SRms WAbe WPat
	- f. ***alba***	WThu
	- - 'Snowstorm'	GKev
	- 'Belvedere'	EPot NMen WAbe
	- 'Coelestina'	WThu
	- 'Dinarica'	see *G. dinarica*
	- 'Holzmannii'	IVic NMen WAbe
	- 'Krumrey'	EPot GEdr GKev
	- 'Max Frei'	NHar
	- 'Rannoch'	GEdr NMen
	- 'Stumpy'	EPot GEdr
	- 'Trotter's Variety'	EPot WAbe
	- 'Undulatifolia'	EPot
	- 'Velkokvensis'	EPot IVic
	affinis	LHop
	'Alex Duguid'	GEdr IVic NHar
	'Amethyst'	EPot GEdr GMaP LRHS SPoG WAbe
	andrewsii	SPhx
	angulosa misapplied	see *G. verna* L. 'Angulosa' hort.
	angustifolia	GKev WAbe
I	- 'Alba'	EPot GKev
	- Frei hybrid	GKev
	'Ann's Special'	GEdr
	asclepiadea ♀H4	Widely available
	- 'Alba'	CLAP EBee GCal GEdr GKev IGor LEdu MDKP MNrw NBid SPer SRms WCFE WHoo WTin
	- 'Knightshayes'	CLAP EBee GKev LLHF NLar
	- 'Phyllis'	EBee NLar
	- 'Pink Cascade'	EBee GEdr
	- 'Pink Swallow'	CLAP EBee GAbr GBBs GEdr GQue NLar WWEG
	- 'Rosea'	GMaP MDKP MNrw
	atuntsiensis	EPot
	'Balmoral' PBR	GMaP
	'Barbara Lyle'	WAbe
	bavarica var. ***subacaulis***	SPlb
	× ***bernardii***	see *G.* × *stevenagensis* 'Bernardii'
	'Berrybank Dome'	CSam GEdr GMaP
	'Berrybank Sky'	GEdr GMaP NCGa
	'Berrybank Snowflakes' **new**	GMaP
	'Berrybank Star'	GEdr GMaP
	bisetaea	GKev SRms
	'Blauer Stern'	IVic
	'Blue Heaven'	GEdr
	'Blue Magic' PBR **new**	LRHS
	'Blue Sea'	LRHS
	'Blue Silk'	EPot EWes GEdr GKev IVic LRHS NHar SPoG WAbe
	brachyphylla	WAbe
	- subsp. ***favratii***	WAbe
	'Braemar' PBR	GMaP NHar
	'Cairngorm'	GAbr GEdr LRHS NHar
	'Carmen'	GEdr NHar
	× ***caroli***	WAbe
	clusii	NMen WAbe
	coelestis	NHar
	'Compact Gem'	EPot GEdr NHar NHol WAbe
§	***cruciata***	EBee LHop MMHG NLar
	- SDR 6406	GKev
§	***dahurica***	EBee ECho GEdr GKev NGdn NLar
	depressa	EPot WAbe
	'Devonhall'	GEdr IVic NHar NHol NWad
	'Diana' PBR	LRHS
§	***dinarica***	ECho EPot NHar NMen
	- 'Colonel Stitt'	GEdr WThu
	divisa	GKev
	'Dumpy'	GEdr
	'Elehn'	NHar
	'Elizabeth'	CSam GEdr
	'Ettrick'	GEdr IVic NHar NHol
	'Eugen's Allerbester' (d)	GEdr GKev GMaP IVic LRHS NHar NHol NWad SPer SPoG WAbe
	'Eugen's Bester'	NHar
	farreri	GKev
	- 'Duguid'	GEdr
	- Silken Star Group **new**	WAbe
	fetissowii	see *G. macrophylla* var. *fetissowii*
	'Gellerhard'	GEdr NHar
	'Gewahn'	GEdr IVic NHar
I	'Glamis Strain'	GEdr LRHS NHar
	'Glen Isla'	EWes
	'Glen Moy'	GEdr
	'Glendevon'	GEdr WAbe
§	***gracilipes***	GEdr GKev MWat SPlb SRms
	- 'Yuatensis'	see *G. macrophylla* var. *fetissowii*
	'Henry'	GEdr WAbe
	Inshriach hybrids	LRHS

	Name	Suppliers
	'Inverleith' ♀H4	EWes GAbr GEdr LRHS NHol SPlb
	'Iona'PBR	GMaP NCGa NHar
	'Joan Ward'	LRHS SPer SPoG
	'John Aitken'	GEdr
	'Juwel'	GEdr
	'Kirriemuir'	EWes
	kochiana	see *G. acaulis*
	kurroo	LHop
	- var. ***brevidens***	see *G. dahurica*
	lagodechiana	see *G. septemfida* var. *lagodechiana*
	cf. ***lawrencei*** SSSE 237	NHar
	'Little Diamond'PBR	LRHS NLar
	'Lucerna'	EPfP GEdr GKev LRHS NHol
	lutea	EBee EWTr GKev GPoy LLHF LRHS NBid NChi SMad SRms WPer
	- SDR 3502	GKev
	× ***macaulayi*** 'Blue Bonnets'	GEdr
	- 'Elata'	IVic NWad
	- 'Kidbrooke Seedling'	CTri EWes GEdr GKev GMaP LRHS WAbe
	- 'Kingfisher'	CTri GKev IVic LRHS NBir WAbe
§	- 'Praecox'	GEdr
§	- 'Wells's Variety'	LRHS
§	***macrophylla*** var. ***fetissowii***	ECho GKev LLHF
	makinoi 'Marsha'PBR	CHll EBee LRHS NCGa SPoG WCot WHlf
	- 'Royal Blue'	GCal LRHS WWEG
	- 'Sensation'PBR	GEdr NHar
	'Margaret'	GEdr WAbe
	'Maryfield'	GEdr
	'Melanie'	GEdr NHol
	microdonta	GEdr
	'Multiflora'	LRHS
	occidentalis	EPot
	olgae	LHop
	olivieri	LLHF
	paradoxa	GKev LLHF NSla WAbe WPat
	- 'Blauer Herold'	MWat
	phlogifolia	see *G. cruciata*
	pneumonanthe	LRHS SPlb
	prolata	NHar
	pumila subsp. ***delphinensis***	WAbe WPat
	purdomii	see *G. gracilipes*
	'Saphir Select'	GEdr
	saxosa	EPfP GKev ITim LRHS NBir NMen NSla WAbe
	scabra	LRHS
	- 'Zuikorindo'	EBee NLar
	'Selektra'	IVic
	septemfida ♀H4	GEdr GKev LBee LHop LRHS MAsh MBri MWat NBir NRHS SPlb SRms WGwG WHoo WKif
	- 'Alba'	LLHF
	- var. ***kolakovskyi*** new	LLHF
§	- var. ***lagodechiana*** ♀H4	LLHF LRHS NMen SRms XLum
	'Serenity'	EPot GEdr IVic LRHS NWad WAbe
	'Shot Silk'	CSam CTri EPot EWes GEdr GJos GMaP LRHS MGos NBir NCGa NHar NHol SPoG WAbe
	'Silken Giant'	GEdr WAbe
	'Silken Night'	GEdr WAbe
	'Silken Seas'	GEdr NHar NHol WAbe
	'Silken Skies'	GEdr NHar WAbe
	'Silken Surprise'	WAbe
	sino-ornata ♀H4	CTri ECho GKev GMaP LSRN MAsh MBri NCGa NMen SRms WAbe
	- CLD 476B	GEdr
	- SDR 5127	GKev LRHS MGos
	- 'Angel's Wings'	GEdr LRHS
	- 'Bellatrix'	GEdr IVic NHar
	- 'Blautopf'	IVic
	- 'Brin Form'	SRms
	- 'Downfield'	GKev LRHS
	- 'Edith Sarah'	GEdr IVic
	- 'Mary Lyle'	GEdr
	- 'Oha'	IVic
	- 'Praecox'	see *G.* × *macaulayi* 'Praecox'
	- 'Purity'	GEdr LRHS WAbe
	- 'Starlight'	NHar
I	- 'Trotter's Form'	EWes
	- 'Weisser Traum'	GEdr IVic LRHS NHol NLar SPoG
	- 'White Wings'	EWes
	siphonantha	WAbe
	'Sir Rupert'	IVic NHar
	'Soutra'	GEdr
	'Sternschuppe' new	GKev
	× ***stevenagensis*** ♀H4	CTri LRHS
§	- 'Bernardii'	GEdr NHar WAbe
	- dark-flowered	WAbe
	stipitata subsp. ***tizuensis***	WAbe
	straminea	LLHF MDKP
	'Strathmore' ♀H4	CSam CTri EWes GAbr GEdr GKev GMaP LRHS NBir NCGa NHar NHol SPlb WAbe
	'Suendermannii'	GKev
	syringea	WAbe
	ternifolia 'Cangshan'	GEdr WAbe
	- 'Dali'	GEdr GKev NBir NHar
	tianschanica	LHop
	tibetica	CArn EBee GEdr GPoy LEdu LRHS WAul WPer XLum
	triflora	GKev LHop LRHS
	- 'Alba'	GKev LRHS
	- f. ***horomuiensis***	GCal
	- var. ***japonica***	NLar WWEG
	- 'Royal Blue'	EBee LRHS
	veitchiorum	GKev WAbe
	verna	ECho EPfP EWes ITim LHop LRHS LSRN NMen NPri NRHS NSla SPoG WAbe WPat
	- 'Alba'	GKev ITim NSla WAbe WPat
§	- 'Angulosa' hort. ♀H4	ITim MAsh
	- subsp. ***angulosa*** (Bieb.) V.E.Avet. new	WIce
	- subsp. ***balcanica***	WPat
	- subsp. ***oschtenica***	WAbe
	- subsp. ***tergestina***	WAbe
	villosa	LHop
	'Violette'	GEdr LRHS NHar NHol SPer
	waltonii	EWes
	wellsii	see *G.* × *macaulayi* 'Wells's Variety'
	wutaiensis	see *G. macrophylla* var. *fetissowii*
	zekuensis	EBee GKev

Geranium ✿ (*Geraniaceae*)

Name	Suppliers
from Bambashata Altai Mountains	NCot
aconitifolium misapplied	see *G. palmatum*
aconitifolium L'Hér.	see *G. rivulare*
'Alan Mayes'	CElw CMac CSev EBee ECtt EPPr EWoo GBin GBuc GKin LRHS LSou NGdn SRGP WFar WPtf
'Alan's Blue'	EBee NChi
albanum	CElw EPPr GAbr LLWP MMuc MNrw SDix SEND SRGP WMoo WPtf
albiflorum	ELan NCot WSpi
anemonifolium	see *G. palmatum*

	'Ann Folkard' ♀H4	Widely available
	'Ann Folkard' × ***psilostemon***	LSRN
	'Anne Thomson' ♀H4	CElw CSpe CWCL EBee ECtt EPPr GBuc GKin GMaP LAst LHop LRHS LSRN LSou MBel MNFA MNrw NBid NBir NChi NDov NLar SRGP SUsu WBrk WCru WGwG WMoo WPnP WSpi
	× ***antipodeum*** 'Black Ice'	SBch
	- 'Chocolate Candy'PBR	EPfP LBuc LRHS
	- 'Elizabeth Wood'	SMrm
	- (*G. sessiliflorum* subsp. *novae-zelandiae* 'Nigricans' × *G. traversii* var. *elegans*)	SRms
	- 'Kahlua'	EPfP
	- 'Pink Spice'PBR	EBee EWoo GKin LBuc LRHS MGos SRms
	- 'Sea Spray'	CMHG ECtt MCot NBro WMnd
	- 'Stanhoe'	ECtt MAvo
	antrorsum	ECou
	aristatum	CDes EPPr EWes GCal MNFA MNrw MRav NBir SRGP WCru WMoo
	armenum	see *G. psilostemon*
	'Arnoldshof'	EPPr
	asphodeloides	CBre CElw CHid CSev IFro LLWP MBNS MNrw MWhi NBid NBir NCot SPav SRGP WBrk WFar WMnd WMoo WPnP WTin
	- subsp. ***asphodeloides*** white-flowered	SRGP WMoo
	- 'Starlight'	NBid
	atlanticum Hook. f.	see *G. malviflorum*
	'Aussie Gem'	EBee
	'Baby Blue'	see *G. himalayense* 'Baby Blue'
	'Benjamin Browne'	CSev
	'Bertie Crûg'	COlW EBee ECtt EHoe EHrv ELon GKev LLHF NBir NDov SBfd SMrm SPoG SRms SRot SWat SWvt WBor WCru
	'Bill Baker'	EWoo
	biuncinatum	IFro
	'Blue Boy'	NLar
	'Blue Cloud' ♀H4	Widely available
	'Blue Pearl'	EBee EPPr NBir NSti SRGP WMoo
§	Blue Sunrise = 'Blogold'PBR ♀H4	CSev EBee ECtt ELan ELon EPPr EPfP GAbr LAst LRHS LSRN MAsh MAvo MBel MNrw NCGa NEgg NLar NMyG NSti SMrm SPoG SRms SRot WCot WFar WHil WPGP WSpi
	'Bob's Blunder'	EBee ECtt EPfP LRHS LSRN MBNS MBel MNrw NLar SMrm SPoG SRGP SWvt WCot WFar WHoo
	bohemicum	SRGP WHer
	- 'Orchid Blue'	EPfP SWvt
	'Brookside' ♀H4	Widely available
	'Buckland Beauty'	CDes CElw CPLG CYeo WBor
	'Buxton's Blue'	see *G. wallichianum* 'Buxton's Variety'
	caeruleatum	EPPr GCal
	caespitosum	LLHF
	caffrum	IFro SPlb SRGP
	canariense	see *G. reuteri*
	candicans misapplied	see *G. lambertii*
§	× ***cantabrigiense***	CMac CSBt ECtt IFro LRHS MHer MNrw NBir NBro NPer NSti SGar SMrm SRms WBrk WCru WFar WMoo
	- 'Berggarten'	EBee EPPr GBin SBch SRGP WPtf
	- 'Biokovo'	Widely available
	- 'Cambridge'	CBcs CMHG CPrp EBee ECha ECtt EHrv ELan EPPr EPfP GAbr GKin LHop LRHS MCot MRav MSwo MWhi NCot SPer SWal SWat WBrk WFar WMnd WMoo WPnP WPtf
	- 'Harz'	EPPr
	- 'Karmina'	CFis EBee EPPr EPfP LRHS MWhi SHil SWat WBrk WHoo WMoo WPtf WWEG XLum
	- 'Rosalina'	EPPr
	- 'St Ola'	Widely available
	- 'Vorjura'	EBee EPPr SMHy
	- 'Westray'PBR	CHVG CMac COlW EBee ECtt EPPr EPfP EShb GAbr GBuc LAst LBMP LRHS LSou MMuc NGdn NLar NSti SBfd SEND SMrm SRkn SRms SWvt WBrk
	'Catherine Deneuve' **new**	EBee
	'Chantilly'	CFis CSev EBee ECGP ECtt EPPr LRHS MAvo MNrw NBir NCGa NChi SBch WCru WGwG WMoo WPtf
	'Chipchase Castle' **new**	NChi
	christensenianum B&SWJ 8022	WCru
	cinereum	ECho WSpi
	cinereum 'Apple Blossom'	see *G.* × *lindavicum* 'Apple Blossom'
	- 'Elizabeth'	ECtt GBuc LSRN
	- 'Sateene'PBR	CFis CYeo EBee EPPr GMaP LRHS MDev NDov SPoG SRot
	- 'Souvenir de René Macé'	EPPr
	(Cinereum Group) 'Alice'PBR	CYeo EBee EPPr GMaP IPot LLHF LSRN MBNS NHar NLar NSti SRot
	- 'Ballerina' ♀H4	Widely available
	- 'Carol'	CWGN CYeo EAEE EBee EPPr EWes GKin LRHS LSRN LSou MAsh MAvo MBNS MSpe NCGa NHar NLar NSti SRkn SWvt WFar WSpi
I	- 'Heather'	EPPr
	- 'Lambrook Helen'	CFis CPLG
	- 'Laurence Flatman'	CElw CKno CPLG CSam CYeo EBee ECtt EPfP EPri GBuc GMaP LAst LBMP LRHS LSou MGos NBid NEgg NHar NRHS NRya NSla SRms SRot SWat WAbe WFar WHoo WMnd WPat
	- 'Lizabeth'PBR	EPPr GBin LSou NHar WHil
	- 'Penny Lane'PBR	EPPr MAsh
	- 'Prima Ballerina'	NLar
	- 'Purple Pillow'	Widely available
	- René Macé = 'Progera'	LRHS SRkn
	- Rothbury Gem = 'Gerfos'PBR ♀H4	CMac CWGN EBee EPPr IPot LLHF LRHS NChi SKHP SUsu SWvt
	- 'Signal'	EBee EPPr MAsh MSCN NCGa NHar NLar
	- Thumping Heart = 'Thumbling Hearts'	EBee EPPr MAsh
	'Claridge Druce'	see *G.* × *oxonianum* 'Claridge Druce'
	clarkei **new**	ELan
	- Raina 82.83	MNrw
	- 'Kashmir Pink'	Widely available
§	- 'Kashmir White' ♀H4	Widely available
	- 'Mount Stewart'	CPLG EBee WCru WPGP
	- (Purple-flowered Group) 'Kashmir Purple'	Widely available

clarum B&SWJ 10246	WCru
collinum	EPPr NBir NCot SRGP WCru
'Colour Carousel'	EBee GBin
'Coombland White'	CCon CPLG CSev EBee ECtt EPPr EWoo GBuc LSou MAvo MBel MCot MNrw NLar NSti SBfd SKHP SRGP WCot WMoo WPnP
'Criss Canning'	EPPr
'Cyril's Blue'	EBee NChi
'Cyril's Fancy'	EBee EPPr MAvo WPtf
dahuricum	WCru
dalmaticum ♀H4	Widely available
- 'Album'	CYeo EBee ECho ECtt ELan EPPr EPot GBuc LRHS MRav NDov NMen NRya SBch SRGP SRms SWat WAbe WCru WFar
- 'Bressingham Pink'	ECtt EPPr
- 'Bridal Bouquet'	LLHF NChi NCot NMen NSla
- 'Croftlea'	NMen
- 'Stades Hellrosa'	EPPr
dalmaticum* × *macrorrhizum	see *G.* × *cantabrigiense*
delavayi misapplied	see *G. sinense*
delavayi Franch.	WSpi
'Devon Pride'	CElw EBee
'Dilys' ♀H4	CElw CPrp EBee ELan EPPr GBuc MCot MLHP MNFA MNrw NBir NChi NDov NGdn NLar SBfd SRGP SUsu WCru WHal WMoo WPnP
dissectum	CHll
'Distant Hills'	EBee EPPr NCot SRGP SUsu WPtf
'Diva'	CSam EBee EPPr EPfP LLHF SRGP WCru
'Double Jewel'	see *G. pratense* 'Double Jewel'
Dragon Heart = 'Bremdra'PBR	CLAP CMac CSev EBee ECtt EPPr EWoo LSRN MBri MPnt NCGa NSti SKHP SPoG SUsu WHil WPtf
'Dusky Crûg'	Widely available
'Dusky Gem'	MAvo
'Dusky Rose'	CLAP CPrp CSpe ECtt ELan EPfP EWoo LAst MBri MGos NCGa NLar SRGP SRot WFar WSpi
'Elizabeth Ross'	MAvo WCru
'Elke'	Widely available
'Ella'	CWGN
'Elworthy Dusky'	CElw
'Elworthy Eyecatcher'	CDes CElw CLAP EBee EPPr MAvo MNrw NCot SRGP SUsu WPGP
'Elworthy Tiger'	CElw MAvo
'Emily'	SRGP
endressii ♀H4	CBre CElw CSev EBee ECha ECho EPfP GAbr GLog GMaP LPot MBNS MCot MHer NBro NPer SEND SPlb SRGP SRms SWvt WFar WMoo WPtf WSpi WWEG XLum
- 'Album'	see *G.* 'Mary Mottram'
- 'Castle Drogo' ♀H4	EBee EPPr SRGP
- 'Prestbury White'	see *G.* × *oxonianum* 'Prestbury Blush'
- 'Rose'	MAvo WPer
- 'Wargrave Pink'	see *G.* × *oxonianum* 'Wargrave Pink'
erianthum	GMaP MLHP SRGP WCru WMoo WSHC
- 'Axeltree'	SUsu WCot
- 'Cally Pearl'	GCal
- 'Calm Sea'	SUsu WCru WMoo WPtf
- f. ***leucanthum*** 'Undine'	SUsu
- 'Neptune'	MNFA WCru WPtf WWEG
eriostemon Fischer	see *G. platyanthum*
'Eureka Blue' **new**	MTis WHlf
'Eva'	EBee WPnP
'Expression'PBR	see *G.* 'Tanya Rendall'
'Extravaganza'	EBee
'Farncombe Cerise Star'	CElw GCal
§ ***farreri***	CPLG ECho LHop LLHF LRHS NBir NRHS
'Fay Anna' **new**	MAsh MBri NCGa WFar WHil
'Foundling'	MAvo NDov
fremontii	EWld
goldmannii	SKHP
gracile	CFis GMaP LRHS LSou MNrw NBir NBre SRGP WBrk WCru WMoo
- 'Blanche'	EPPr
- 'Blush'	CElw EPPr LPla MNFA
- 'Golden Gracile' **new**	MNrw
grandiflorum	see *G. himalayense*
'Grasmere'	ECtt
'Gwen Thompson'	WOut
gymnocaulon	CMac EPPr GKin LRHS NLar SRGP WCru
gymnocaulon* × *platypetalum	NCot
'Harmony'	EBee EPPr WPtf
harveyi	CMea ELan EWes GCal LRHS NChi SPhx SRGP WKif WPat WSpi
hayatanum	WSpi
- B&SWJ 164	WCru WMoo
§ ***himalayense***	Widely available
- CC 1957 from Tibetan border	CPLG EPPr
- ***alpinum***	see *G. himalayense* 'Gravetye'
§ - 'Baby Blue'	CElw EBee EPPr GBuc GCal GCra IFro LRHS MAvo MNFA MNrw NCot NGdn NLar NRHS NSti SBch SMrm SRGP WBrk WCAu WCru WMoo WPnP WPtf
- 'Birch Double'	see *G. himalayense* 'Plenum'
- 'Derrick Cook'	CDes CElw CLAP EBee EPPr GBuc MAvo MNFA MWhi SUsu WBrk WPtf
- 'Devil's Blue'	EPPr SRGP WPtf
§ - 'Gravetye' ♀H4	Widely available
- 'Irish Blue'	CElw EBee EPPr GBee GBuc GCal GCra IGor MSpe NLar NSti SRGP WCru WMoo WPnP WPtf WTin
- ***meeboldii***	see *G. himalayense*
- 'Pale Irish Blue'	GCal NCot
§ - 'Plenum' (d)	Widely available
ibericum misapplied	see *G.* × *magnificum*
ibericum Cav.	CSBt CTri NBre NLar SPav SRGP WFar
- 'Blue Springs'	ECtt
- subsp. ***ibericum***	CMac EBee EPPr
- subsp. ***jubatum***	EPPr LRHS MNFA MNrw SRms WCru WSpi
- - 'White Zigana'	CDes CFis CPrp EAEE EBee ECGP ECtt EPPr EPfP EWTr EWoo LRHS MAvo MNFA SBch SBfd SPoG WPtf
- subsp. ***jubatum* × *renardii***	SWvt
- var. ***platypetalum*** misapplied	see *G.* × *magnificum*
- var. ***platypetalum*** Boiss.	see *G. platypetalum* Fisch. & C.A.Mey.

	Name	Suppliers
§	– 'Ushguli Grijs'	EBee NLar WCot WPtf
	ibericum* × *libani	CDes EBee
	incanum	CAbP CMHG EBee ELon EShb EWes NBir NHol SBrt SRGP WSpi
	– white-flowered	SRGP
	'Ivan' ♀H4	CElw CEnt CFis CLAP EBee ECtt EPPr LRHS NChi NCot NLar SRGP WCru WMoo WPnP
	'Jean Armour'	CDes EAEE EBee ECtt EPPr GBuc LRHS NGdn SPoG SRGP WFar WPGP
	'Johnson's Blue' ♀H4	Widely available
	'Jolly Bee'PBR	see *G.* Rozanne = 'Gerwat'
	'Joy'	CLAP COIW CPrp EBee ECtt ELon EPPr GBuc LRHS LSou MAvo MCot MNrw MRav NBir NCGa NDov NEgg NLar NSti NWad SBfd SRGP SRms WMoo WPnP
	'Karen Wouters'	EBee
	'Kashmir Blue'	CPLG EBee ECtt ELan EPPr EPfP GMaP LRHS MAvo NGdn NLar NPnk SWat WCAu WFar WKif WMoo WPnP WPtf WWEG
	'Kashmir Green'	CLAP EBee ECtt EPPr GBin LAst LLHF MAvo WMoo WPnP
§	'Kate'	WCru
	'Kate Folkard'	see *G.* 'Kate'
§	'Khan'	CFis EBee EPPr IFro IPot LRHS MAvo NCot NPro SDys SMHy SRGP SUsu WBrk WCru
	'Kirsty'	EBee
	kishtvariense	GCal LRHS MNrw MRav NCot NSti WCru
	koraiense	NBre WMoo WPtf
	– B&SWJ 797	WCru
	– B&SWJ 878	CPLG WCru
	koreanum ambig.	EBee NLar WMoo
	– B&SWJ 602	CPLG WCru
	krameri	NLar
	– B&SWJ 1142	CPLG WCru
	'Lakwijk Star'	MAsh MBri
§	***lambertii***	EWes GBuc GCal LRHS NBir
	– 'Swansdown'	GBuc WCru
	lanuginosum	LRHS
I	***libani***	ELon EPPr LLWP LRHS MCot NBid NChi NSti WBrk WCot WSHC WTin
	– RCB RL B-2	WCot
	libani* × *peloponnesiacum	EBee WPGP
	'Libretto'	WCru
	'Light Dilys'	EBee EPPr NDov
§	× ***lindavicum*** 'Apple Blossom'	CMea LRHS MSCN NMen
	– 'Gypsy' ♀H4	SBch
	linearilobum subsp. ***transversale***	EBee SRot WCru WPnP
I	– – 'Laciniatum'	LWst
	– – 'Rose Foundling'	LWst
§	'Little David'	EBee NLar SUsu
	'Little Devil'	see *G.* 'Little David'
	'Little Gem'	CMea EBee EPPr LRHS MAvo NChi NLar WMoo
	lucidum	NCot WPtf WSFF
	'Luscious Linda'	EBee MAvo NLar WPnP
	'Lydia'	SRGP
§	***macrorrhizum***	CArn CSBt CTca EBee ECrN EDAr ELon EPfP GKev GKin IFro LEdu MBNS MCot MRav MWat MWhi NBro NCGa NPnk SRms SWat WCAu WFar WHil WSpi WWEG XLum
	– AL & JS 90179YU	CHid EPPr
	– 'Album' ♀H4	Widely available
	– 'Bevan's Variety' ♀H4	Widely available
	– 'Bulgaria'	EPPr WBrk
	– 'Cham-ce'	EPPr WBrk
	– 'Czakor'	Widely available
I	– 'De Bilt'	EBee EWes WBrk
	– 'Freundorf'	EBee EPPr EWes GCal NCot WBrk
	– 'Ingwersen's Variety' ♀H4	Widely available
	– 'Lohfelden'	EBee EPPr EWes GBuc GCal SRGP WCru
	– 'Mount Olympus'	see *G. macrorrhizum* 'White-Ness'
	– 'Mytikas' ♀H4	EBee EPPr WPtf
	– 'Pindus'	CPrp CYeo EBee EPPr GAbr GBuc LRHS MBNS NBre NDov NSti SPoG SRGP WCru WFar WPtf
	– 'Prionia'	EPPr NCot
	– 'Purpurrot'	WBrk WWEG
	– 'Ridsko'	EPPr GCal LPla LRHS NBro SRGP WBrk WCru
	– ***roseum***	see *G. macrorrhizum*
	– 'Rotblut'	EPPr SRGP WBrk
	– 'Sandwijck'	EPPr SBch WBrk
	– 'Snow Sprite'	CEnt EPPr EPyc LLHF NPro WBrk WHrl
	– 'Spessart'	CBar CSev EBee ELan ELon EPPr EPfP EWoo GMaP LAst LHop LRHS MBri MGos MMuc NLar SBfd SEND SPer WBrk WRHF WSpi WWEG XLum
	– 'Variegatum' (v)	CFis EHrv ELan GMaP LEdu NBir SRGP SRms WBrk WCot WFar WMnd WWEG
	– 'Velebit'	EPPr SRGP WCru XLum
§	– 'White-Ness' ♀H4	Widely available
	– 'Witoscha'	EBee LRHS
	macrostylum	WCot WCru WPer
I	– 'Caeruleum'	WPtf
	– 'Leonidas'	EPPr WCot WPnP
	– 'Talish'	EPPr
	– 'Uln Oag Triag'	EPPr
	maculatum	CArn CElw CSev EPfP LLWP LRHS MAvo MMHG MNrw MRav NSti SRGP SWat WCru WHal WPnP WSpi
	– from Kath Dryden	EPPr
	– f. ***albiflorum***	CLAP EBee ELan EPPr EPfP EWoo LRHS MNFA MNrw MTis MWhi NChi NLar NSti SMrm SRGP WBrk WCru WMoo WPnP
	– 'Beth Chatto'	Widely available
	– 'Elizabeth Ann'PBR ♀H4	Widely available
	– 'Espresso'	Widely available
	– 'Putnam County' **new**	EPPr
	– 'Shameface'	EPPr WMoo
	– 'Silver Buttons'	CDes EBee
	– 'Smoky Mountain'	EBee EPPr
	– 'Spring Purple'	CElw EBee EPPr MAvo NChi NLar
	– 'Sweetwater'	EPPr
	– 'Vickie Lynn'	CLAP EBee EPPr MAvo NChi
	maderense ♀H2	CAbb CBcs CCon CHEx CSpe CTrC EBee ECre ELan EPfP EShb EWes LRHS NBir NPer SDix SEND SPav SRGP SRkn WCru
	– 'Guernsey White'	CCon CTrC IBoy IDee SMrm WCot WOut
	– white-flowered	CSpe LDai

	maderense* × *palmatum	CHll
§	**× *magnificum*** ♀H4	Widely available
	- 'Blue Blood'	CElw CLAP CSev EBee ECtt EPPr GAbr IBoy IPot LRHS LSou MBNS MBel MCot NGdn NPnk NSti SBch SMrm WCot WPtf WWEG
	- 'Ernst Pagels'	NCot
	- 'Hylander'	EPPr
	- 'Peter Yeo'	EPPr MNFA SRGP
	- 'Rosemoor'	CElw CHid EBee ECtt EHrv ELan EPPr EPfP GCal IKil LHop LRHS MWhi NPro SBfd SMrm SPer WCot WMnd WPtf XLum
	- 'Vital'	EBee
	magniflorum	EWes EWoo NBid NGdn WSpi
	'Maître Hugo'	EBee
§	***malviflorum***	CFis CMHG ECha ELan EPPr LRHS NCot SBch SPhx WAul WCot WCru WPer
	- from Spain	EWes WSHC
	- pink-flowered	EPPr
§	'Mary Mottram'	CElw EPPr LDai NBir WCot
	'Mavis Simpson' ♀H4	Widely available
	maximowiczii	SBch WPtf
	'Melinda'PBR	EBee EPPr EWoo IPot NDov NMir
	'Mellow Yellow'	SUsu
	'Memories'PBR	EBee ECtt EPPr LRHS LSRN MBNS
	'Meryl Anne'	SRGP WPtf
	microphyllum	see *G. potentilloides*
	'Midnight Clouds' new	EBee MAvo NCGa NSti WFar WHlf WWlt
	molle	NBir WSFF
	× *monacense*	CPrp EBee ELan IFoB LEdu LRHS MBNS MWat SRGP SWat WCru WMoo WPnP WPtf
	- var. ***anglicum***	CCon ECtt EPPr GMaP LRHS MRav MTis MWhi WMoo
	- 'Anne Stevens'	WPtf
	- 'Claudine Dupont'	CElw EBee EPPr IFro MAvo NChi NWad WCot WPtf
	- dark-flowered	WMoo
	- 'Emma White'	EPPr NChi SBch
	- var. ***monacense***	NEgg WSpi
	- - 'Breckland Fever'	EBee EPPr NChi SRGP
§	- - 'Muldoon'	EBee EPPr EPfP LRHS MBel NBir SRGP WMoo WPnP
*	'Money Peniche'	XEll
	'Mourning Widow'	see *G. phaeum* 'Lady in Mourning'
	'Mrs Jean Moss'	EBee EPPr EWes NCot
	'Mrs Judith Bradshaw'	EBee NChi NCot
	napuligerum misapplied	see *G. farreri*
	napuligerum Franch.	NSla
	'Natalie'	EBee EPPr LRHS LSRN MAvo NChi SUsu
	nepalense	SRGP SRms
	'Nicola'	CElw EBee EPPr IFro MAvo MNFA NLar SBch SRGP
	'Nimbus' ♀H4	Widely available
	nodosum	Widely available
	- 'Blueberry Ice'	CElw MAvo
	- 'Clos du Coudray'	EBee EWoo NLar
	- dark-flowered	see *G. nodosum* 'Swish Purple'
	- 'Darkleaf'	MAvo
	- 'Hexham Big Eyes'	CElw EWes MAvo
	- 'Hexham Freckles'	EBee
	- 'Hexham Lace'	CElw
	- 'Julie's Velvet'	CDes LEdu SBch WBor WHoo WPGP WTin
	- pale-flowered	see *G. nodosum* 'Svelte Lilac'
	- 'Pascal'	EPPr
	- 'Saucy Charlie'	SBch
	- 'Silverwood'	CElw CLAP EBee EPPr EWoo LSou MAvo MNFA NChi SBch SUsu WCot WHoo WWFP
	- 'Simon'	EBee MAvo SRGP
§	- 'Svelte Lilac'	CElw EAEE EBee EPPr EPfP LAst LBMP LRHS LSou MNFA MNrw NBro NDov NHol SPoG SRGP SWat WBrk WCAu WCru WFar WMoo WPnP
§	- 'Swish Purple'	CElw EBee EPPr NLar SRGP WCru WMoo WPGP WPnP
	- 'Whiteleaf'	CElw CMac EBee EPPr GCal MNFA NChi NPro SBch SMrs SRGP WCru WFar WHal WMoo WPGP WPnP
	'Nora Bremner'	SUsu
	'Nunnykirk Pink'	EWes SUsu
	'Nunwood Purple'	EBee EPPr MAvo MNFA WPtf
	ocellatum	IFro
	'Old Rose'	LRHS MNFA SRGP WCru
§	***orientalitibeticum***	CCon CMHG CPLG CSpe ECtt EPPr GAbr GKev IFro LEdu MCot MHer MMuc NBid NLar SEND SKHP SMad WCot WFar WMoo WSpi WWEG
	'Orion' ♀H4	Widely available
	'Orkney Blue'	CElw EPPr WCru
	Orkney Cherry = 'Bremerry'PBR	CMac EBee ECtt EPPr EPfP LLHF MAvo NDov NLar NSti SPoG SRkn SRms WMoo
	'Orkney Dawn'	WCru WPnP
	'Orkney Pink'	EBee ECtt EPPr EPfP LAst LHop LSRN MLHP NSti SBfd SPoG SRGP SRkn SWat WFar
	'Out of the Blue'	WOut
	× *oxonianum*	LRHS NCot WMoo
	- 'A.T. Johnson' ♀H4	CBcs EBee ECtt ELan EPfP GKin LAst LHop LRHS MRav MWat MWhi NBir NEgg NGdn NRHS NSti SBfd SPer SRGP SRms SWat WCru WMnd WMoo WPtf WWEG
	- 'Andy's Star'	EBee NCot
	- 'Ankum's White'	CLAP
	- 'Anmore'	SRGP
	- 'Beholder's Eye' ♀H4	CHid CPrp EBee EPPr GAbr NLar SBch SRGP WPnP WPtf WWEG
	- 'Breckland Sunset'	EPPr SBch SRGP
	- 'Bregover Pearl'	CBre CElw EBee EPPr SRGP WMoo
	- 'Bressingham's Delight'	ECtt SRGP
	- 'Buttercup'	EBee EPPr SRGP
I	- 'Cally Seedling'	EBee EWes GCal
	- 'Chocolate Strawberry'	EBee EPPr EWes
§	- 'Claridge Druce'	Widely available
	- 'Coronet'	CCon GCal SRGP WMoo
	- 'David Rowlinson'	EPPr
	- 'Diane's Treasure'	SBch
	- 'Dirk Gunst'	CElw
	- 'Elworthy Misty'	CElw EPPr SBch SRGP
	- 'Frank Lawley'	LLWP NBid NChi SBch SRGP WBrk WMoo
§	- 'Fran's Star' (d)	SRGP WBrk WCru
	- 'Frilly Gilly'	EBee
	- 'Hexham Pink'	EPPr EWes NChi SRGP
	- 'Hollywood'	EBee ELan EPPr EPfP NLar NPer SRGP SRms WBrk WMoo WPtf WWEG

- 'JS Anne-Marie' EBee
- 'Julie Brennan' GAbr SMrs
- 'Kate Moss' EBee EPPr EWes NSti SRGP
- 'Katherine Adele' EBee ECtt EPPr EPfP EWes GCal LPla LSou MAvo MSpe NCot NLar NSti SBfd SEND SRGP SRms WFar
§ - 'Kingston' CElw EPPr
- 'Königshof' EPPr EWes
- 'Kurt's Variegated' see *G.* × *oxonianum* 'Spring Fling'
- 'Lace Time' CBre CCon CPrp CSev EBee ECtt EPPr GBuc GKin LRHS LSRN MBri MSpe NCot NEgg NHol SBch SBfd SPer SRGP SRms WMnd WMoo
- 'Lady Moore' LRHS NBro NCot SRGP WMoo WPtf
- 'Lambrook Gillian' CFis EBee EPPr SBch SRGP WBrk WPtf
- 'Lasting Impression' EPPr SRGP
- 'Laura Skelton' CElw NCot
- 'Little John' EWes
- 'Maid Marion' EWes
- 'Maurice Moka' **new** EBee MAsh
- 'Miriam Rundle' CElw EPPr LRHS SRGP WCru WMoo WWEG
- 'Moorland Jenny' CElw WMoo
- 'Moorland Star' WMoo
- 'Music from Big Pink' EPPr EWes
- 'Pale Walter's Gift' GCal
- 'Pat Smallacombe' EBee NCot WMoo
- 'Patricia Josephine' WCAu
- 'Pearl Boland' EBee EPPr SRGP
- 'Phantom' EBee EPPr
- 'Phoebe Noble' CBre CElw CFis CPrp EPPr LRHS MNrw NCot NLar NRHS SMrm SRGP WMoo
- 'Phoebe's Blush' EPPr GCal GQue SRGP
- 'Pink Cluster' CLAP
- 'Pink Lace' LSou
§ - 'Prestbury Blush' CBre CElw EPPr SRGP
- 'Prestbury White' see *G.* × *oxonianum* 'Prestbury Blush'
- 'Raspberry Ice' EWes
- 'Rebecca Moss' CPrp EBee ECtt ELan EPPr GAbr GCra LRHS LSRN NCot NRHS NSti SBch SMrm SRGP WCru WFar WOut WWEG
- 'Robin's Ginger Nut' EBee EWes
- 'Rodbylund' EBee
- 'Rose Clair' CCon CTca EBee ELan EPPr EPfP LRHS MWhi NBir NLar SBfd SGar SRGP WCru WMnd WMoo WPtf WWEG
- 'Rosemary' SBch
- 'Rosemary Verey' SBch
- 'Rosenlicht' CPrp EPPr GKin LRHS MRav NLar SRGP WCru WMnd WMoo WPtf XLum
- 'Sandy' EWes
§ - 'Spring Fling' (v) ECtt EPPr EWes LPla NSti NWad SRGP WFar
- 'Stillingfleet Keira' EBee NSti SRGP
- 'Summer Surprise' EPPr EWes WCru
- 'Susan' EPPr EWes
- 'Susie White' EPPr SRGP WCru
§ - f. ***thurstonianum*** Widely available
- - 'Armitageae' EPPr SRGP
- - 'Breckland Brownie' CElw EBee EPPr EWes MAvo SRGP
- - 'Crûg Star' WCru
- - 'David McClintock' SBch SRGP WMoo
- - 'Peter Hale' CMea
- - 'Red Sputnik' EPPr SRGP
- - 'Sherwood' EBee ECtt EPPr GCal GQue MBel MSpe NBro NEgg NSti SApp SMrm SRGP WFar WMoo
- - 'Southcombe Double' (d) CLAP CWCL ECtt ELan EPPr EPfP GCra LRHS LSou MBri SBea SPer SPoG SRGP SRms WCru WFar WMoo WPtf WWEG
§ - - 'Southcombe Star' EBee EPPr GAbr GCal LRHS NBro NGdn SRGP WCru WFar WMoo WPer WWEG
- - 'Sue Cox' EPPr
- 'Trevor's White' CLAP EPPr LLWP LRHS MNFA SBch SRGP WCru
- 'Wageningen' ♀H4 CBre EBee EPPr EWTr GCal LPla LRHS LSou MBri MNFA NGdn NRHS SBfd SEND SMrm SRGP SRms WCot WCru WMoo WPtf
- 'Walter's Gift' CYeo EBee ECtt EPPr EPri EShb EWoo LLWP LRHS LSou MAvo MRav MWhi NBir NBro NCGa NLar NPer SMrm WBrk WCru WFar WHoo WMoo
§ - 'Wargrave Pink' ♀H4 Widely available
- 'Waystrode' EBee EPPr SRGP
- 'Westacre White' EWes
- 'Whitehaven' SRGP
- 'Whiter Shade of Pale' EPPr
- 'Winscombe' EBee EPfP GCal SRGP WFar WMnd WMoo WWEG

§ ***palmatum*** ♀H3 CAbb CBcs CHEx CMac CPLG CSpe CTrC EBee EHoe EHrv EWoo GAbr GBuc IFro IKil LRHS MPie NBro NPer SDys SGar SMad SMrm SPhx SRkn WCru WKif WMoo WPGP

palustre CElw EBee EPPr LRHS MMuc MNrw NCot SEND SRGP WMoo WPtf

Patricia = 'Brempat' ♀H4 Widely available

peloponnesiacum EAEE EBee EPPr EWes GQue LRHS MAsh MNFA NOrc NWad WFar WMoo WPtf

'Perfect Storm' CLAP CWGN ECtt LLHF NCGa NLar SMrm

phaeum Widely available
- 'Advendo' **new** EBee EPPr NCot
- 'Album' Widely available
- 'Alec's Pink' EBee EPPr LLWP NCot SBch SHar WOut WPtf
- 'All Saints' EPPr LEdu SRGP
- 'Angelina' EPPr NCot WPtf
- 'Aureum' see *G. phaeum* 'Golden Spring'
- 'Blauwvoet' EBee EPPr LBMP NChi NCot
- 'Blue Shadow' CDes CElw EBee EPPr LEdu LLWP SRGP WPtf
- 'Caborn Lilac' LLWP
- 'Calligrapher' CElw EPPr LLHF NChi NCot SMrs SRGP SUsu WMoo WPtf
- 'Chocolate Chip' EPPr NCot
- 'Conny Broe' (v) CLAP SBch
- 'Countess of Grey' SMrs
- 'Dark Dream' NCot
- dark-flowered NCot
- 'David Bromley' NCot WCru WPtf
- 'David Martin' EBee EPPr NCot

	- 'Enid'	EPPr
	- 'George Stone'	EBee EPPr LLHF WPtf
	- 'Golden Samobor'	CElw EPPr NCot
§	- 'Golden Spring'	EBee EPPr MAvo NCot NPro SRGP
	- 'Hannah Perry'	EPPr LLWP MTis WPtf
	- 'Hector's Lavender'	NCot SRGP
	- var. ***hungaricum***	EBee EPPr LLWP SRGP WPtf
	- 'James Haunch'	EPPr
	- 'Judith's Blue'	EBee NChi NCot
	- 'Klepper'	EBee EPPr GBin WPtf
	- 'Lady in Black'	NCot
§	- 'Lady in Mourning'	CPLG EBee EPPr GCal MNFA NChi SRGP SRms SWat WCru WMoo
	- 'Lavender Pinwheel'	EBee EPfP MBri SPer SPoG WHil
	- 'Lilacina' **new**	WPtf
	- 'Lily Lovell'	Widely available
	- 'Lisa' (v)	CFis CLAP EBee EPPr MNrw NCot SMHy WCot
	- 'Little Boy'	EPPr
	- var. ***lividum***	CBre CPrp EBee GMaP LLWP MRav NCot SRGP SRms WFar WPnP XLum
	- - 'Joan Baker'	CBre CSam EBee EPPr LPla MNFA NChi NCot NGdn NSti SBch SDys SRGP WCru WMoo WPnP WWEG
	- - 'Majus'	EBee ECtt EPPr EPfP EPyc LLWP LPla LRHS SBch WFar WMoo
	- 'Maggie's Delight' (v)	SRGP
	- 'Marchant's Ghost'	IFro NGdn SMHy
	- 'Margaret Hunt'	NLar
	- 'Margaret Wilson' (v)	Widely available
	- 'Mierhausen'	EBee EPPr NCot WPtf
	- 'Mojito' (v) **new**	EBee
	- 'Moorland Dylan'	WMoo WPtf
	- 'Mottisfont Rose'	SBch
	- 'Mourning Widow'	see *G. phaeum* 'Lady in Mourning'
	- 'Mrs Charles Perrin'	CElw CFis EPPr WPtf
	- 'Mrs Withey Price'	EPPr
	- 'Night Time'	EBee EPPr SBch WPtf
	- 'Nightshade'	NCot WPtf WSpi
	- 'Our Pat' ♀H4	CDes EBee EPPr NChi NCot WCot
	- var. ***phaeum***	NMRc SGar WPtf WSpi
	- - 'Langthorns Blue'	CSev CWCL EBee ELan EPPr EWes LEdu LRHS MNrw SRGP SWvt WPtf
	- - 'Samobor'	Widely available
	- 'Phantom of the Opera' (v)	EPPr NChi
I	- 'Ploeger de Bilt'	EPPr WPtf
	- purple-flowered	NCot NPnk
	- 'Rachel's Rhapsody'	CElw EBee EPPr MAvo NCot SRGP WPtf
	- 'Raven'	EBee EPPr EWoo MAvo MTis NChi NCot SUsu WHlf WPtf
	- red-flowered	MRav
	- 'Rise Top Lilac'	NCot WPGP WPtf
	- 'Rose'	LRHS
	- 'Rose Air'	EPPr SRGP WMoo
	- 'Rose Madder'	CCon CElw COlW EBee EPPr EPyc GBuc GCal LEdu LLWP LPla MNrw NChi NCot NMRc SBch SRGP SUsu WCru WMoo
	- 'Saturn'	EPPr
	- 'Séricourt'	CDes WCot
	- 'Shadowlight' **new**	EBee MTis
	- 'Slatina'	EPPr WPtf
	- 'Small Grey'	EPPr
	- 'Springtime' PBR	EPPr EPfP LLHF MBNS NChi NCot NGdn WCAu
	- 'Stillingfleet Ghost'	EBee EPPr LEdu LRHS MNrw NChi NCot NSti
	- 'Taff's Jester' (v)	EBee EWes LPla NHol SApp SRGP WCot
§	- 'Variegatum' (v)	CBre CMac EHoe ELan EPPr GMaP IFro LRHS MCot MRav NBir NBro NCot NEgg NPro SRGP WAbb WCru WHer WMoo WTin
	- 'Vintage Dave'	WOut
	- 'Walküre'	CSev EBee EPPr EWes EWoo MAvo NLar WPtf
	'Philippe Vapelle'	Widely available
	'Pink Carpet'	EBee NDov SBfd
	'Pink Delight'	CElw CMea MAvo MNrw SBch
	'Pink Penny'	CLAP EBee EPPr EPfP IPot LRHS NCGa NGBo SMrm SRGP WMoo WPtf
	'Pink Splash'	LSou WPtf
§	***platyanthum***	EPPr MNrw MWhi SRGP WCru WPtf
	- var. ***reinii***	WCru
	- 'Russian Giant'	EPPr
	platypetalum misapplied	see *G.* × *magnificum*
	platypetalum Franch.	see *G. sinense*
§	***platypetalum*** Fisch. & C.A. Mey.	EPPr LRHS NBir SRGP WCru XLum
	- 'Genyell'	EBee
	- 'Georgia Blue'	WCru WPtf
	- 'Turco'	EBee EPPr
§	***pogonanthum***	GLog NBir
§	***potentilloides***	GCal NBir SRGP WMoo
	pratense	Widely available
	- 'Algera Double'	EBee
	- 'Bittersweet'	EBee EPPr
	- Black Beauty = 'Nodbeauty' PBR	CBcs CPLG CPar CSBt CSev CWCL CWGN EBee ECtt EPPr EPfP EWes LRHS LSRN LSou MGos NCGa NLar NPri SBfd SPer SPoG SRkn SRot SWat WCot WFar WSpi
	- 'Blue Lagoon'	EPPr
*	- 'Blue Skies'	LSou WSpi
	- 'Cluden Sapphire'	EPPr MWhi NChi NGdn NHol NPro WCru WSpi
§	- 'Double Jewel' (d)	CWCL CWGN EPfP IPot LLHF LRHS MAsh MBNS MBri NCGa NLar NMRc WBor WPtf
	- 'Else Lacey' (d)	EBee
	- 'Flore Pleno'	see *G. pratense* 'Plenum Violaceum'
I	- 'Himalayanum'	NLar
	- 'Hocus Pocus'	EBee ECtt EHrv ELan EPfP EWoo LRHS MAvo MBNS MBri MDev NBro NLar NSti SBfd
	- 'Ilja'	EBee
	- 'Janet's Special'	WHoo
	- 'Midnight Blues'	EBee GBin MAsh NCGa SMrm
	- Midnight Reiter strain	CBcs CBct CPLG CSev CSpe CWGN EBee ELan EPfP GBuc IFoB LRHS MAvo MBel NBro NChi NGdn NLBP NLar NPnk SDys SPhx SWat SWvt WCru WFar WPnP
	- 'Mrs Kendall Clark' ♀H4	Widely available
	- 'New Dimension'	CBcs EBee ELan EPfP NSti
	- 'Okey Dokey'	EBee MAsh
	- 'Pennine Cloud' **new**	CSev
	- 'Picotee'	EBee
	- 'Plenum Album' (d)	CLAP ECtt ELan EPPr EWes LLHF MNrw NEgg NGdn NLar SPer WPtf WWEG
	- 'Plenum Caeruleum' (d)	CMHG ECtt EPPr GCra MRav NBid NEgg NGdn NLar SWat WFar WSHC

§	- 'Plenum Violaceum' (d) ♀H4	Widely available
	- var. ***pratense*** f. ***albiflorum***	CElw CSam EPPr EWTr EWoo GCra GMaP IFro LRHS MNrw NBid NCot NOrc SBfd WMnd WMoo
	- - - 'Galactic'	CLAP COIW EBee ECGP EPPr IBoy LRHS MBel MTis NBir NLar SMrm SPhx WCot WCru WMoo WPnP WSpi
	- - - 'Laura'PBR (d)	CPLG CWCL EPPr EWes LRHS LSRN LSou MAsh NSti SKHP SMrm SPoG
	- - - 'Plenum Album' (d)	CDes EBee EPPr EWoo MTis NSti STes WCot WPnP
	- - - 'Silver Queen'	EBee ECtt EPPr LRHS LSou MBel NBir NBre SRGP WMoo WPGP WPtf
	- 'Purple Heron'	CDes EHrv LSRN WFar
*	- 'Purple-haze'	CTca MCot NLar WHrl WMoo WTou
	- 'Rectum Album'	see *G. clarkei* 'Kashmir White'
§	- 'Rose Queen'	EPPr MRav NBir NHol NLar SRGP WCru
	- 'Roseum'	see *G. pratense* 'Rose Queen'
	- 'Splish-splash'	see *G. pratense* 'Striatum'
	- 'Stanton Mill'	NBid
	- var. ***stewartianum***	MRav
	- - 'Elizabeth Yeo'	CLAP EBee ECGP ECtt EPPr EWTr EWoo NLar NWad WCru
	- - 'Purple Silk'	EPPr
§	- 'Striatum'	Widely available
	- 'Striatum' dwarf	WCru
	- 'Striatum' pale-flowered	CBre
	- variegated, white-flowered (v)	WCot
§	- Victor Reiter Junior strain	CElw CPrp CSev CSpe EBee ELan LEdu LRHS MLHP MMHG MNFA NBir NGdn SMrm SPoG SRot WCot WCru WFar WPtf
	- 'Wisley Blue'	EBee EPPr SBch SRGP WHal
	- 'Yorkshire Queen'	EPPr NGdn NSti WCru
	'Prelude'	CBre CDes CElw CSev EBee ELon EPPr NBir NCot NLar NPro SRGP SUsu WPtf
	procurrens	CBre CElw COIW CTri EPPr EShb GAbr GCal GCra LLWP LRHS WBor WBrk WCru WMoo WPtf
§	***psilostemon*** ♀H4	Widely available
	- 'Bressingham Flair'	CCon CLAP CPrp EBee EPfP GAbr GBuc GCra LRHS MRav NBid SPer SRms WCru WFar WMoo
	- 'Coton Goliath'	EPPr EWes NCot
	- 'Fluorescent'	SMrm
	- 'Jason Bloom'	EPPr LRHS NRHS
	- 'Madelon'	CElw EBee MAvo NCot
	- 'Moorland Jack'	WMoo
	'Midnight Star'	EWes
	pulchrum	CHid CSpe EWes EWld LRHS SRGP WCot WPGP WPer
	punctatum hort.	see *G.* × *monacense* var. *monacense* 'Muldoon'
	- 'Variegatum'	see *G. phaeum* 'Variegatum'
	'Purple Rain'	EBee EPPr NChi
	pylzowianum	MRav NBid NRya SBch WFar WMoo
	pyrenaicum	CRWN GAbr NBre NSti WTou
	- f. ***albiflorum***	GAbr IFro MNrw NBir SRGP WBrk WCot WPer WTou
	- 'Barney Brighteye'	SRGP
	- 'Bill Wallis'	Widely available
	- 'Bright Eyes'	LLWP NCot
	- 'Isparta'	CFis EPPr IFro LPla NCot SBch SPhx SRGP WBrk WTou
	- 'Summer Sky'	GBin SPav SRGP
	- 'Summer Snow'	CCon NLar
	'Rainbow'PBR	EPPr EWoo MBNS
	Rambling Robin Group	ECre EHoe EPri EWes NLBP
	rectum	EPPr NBre WCru
	- 'Album'	see *G. clarkei* 'Kashmir White'
	'Red Admiral'	EBee ECtt EPPr GBuc GCal LRHS LSou MAvo NCot NLar NSti SRGP SUsu WFar
	reflexum	CFis CPrp EPPr WCru
	- 'Katara Pass'	EPPr NChi
	refractoides	WCot
	refractum	CPLG
	regelii	EPPr LRHS WCru WMoo WPtf
	renardii ♀H4	Widely available
	- 'Beldo'	MAvo
	- blue-flowered	see *G. renardii* 'Whiteknights'
	- 'Tcschelda'	CMHG EAEE EBee ECha ECtt EPPr EShb GBuc LRHS NBir SBfd SMrm SRms SUsu WFar WMoo XLum
§	- 'Whiteknights'	EBee NBir WCru
	- 'Zetterlund'	CFis CPrp EAEE EBee EHrv ELan EPPr EPfP EPri LHop LRHS MWat NEgg NSti SBfd WBrk WFar WMnd WMoo WPtf
§	***reuteri***	CBcs LDai SGar SRGP WCru
	'Richard Nutt'	EBee
	richardsonii	CSpe EBee EPPr EPfP EWTr GCal LRHS MCot MNrw NBir NBre NDov NWad SRGP WCru WPtf
	- pink-flowered	MAvo
	- white-flowered **new**	NChi
	'Rise and Shine' **new**	EBee NDov
	× ***riversleaianum*** 'Russell Prichard' ♀H4	Widely available
§	***rivulare***	NBre NLar WMnd WPtf
	robertianum	CArn ENfk EPPr LLHF MHer SRms WSFF
§	- 'Album'	EPPr SHar SRGP SRms
	- f. ***bernettii***	see *G. robertianum* 'Album'
	- 'Celtic White'	CBre EPPr GCal IFro MHer SPav SRGP
	robustum	ECre EPri LRHS MGos MNrw NBir NBro SKHP SPav SPlb SRGP WFar WKif WSHC
	'Rosetta'PBR	EBee LRHS NCGa NRHS
	'Rosie Crûg'	SWvt
	rosthornii	WCru
	'Rothbury Red'	EBee LLHF NChi
§	Rozanne = 'Gerwat'PBR ♀H4	Widely available
	rubescens	see *G. yeoi*
	rubifolium	MNFA WCru
§	'Ruprecht'	LRHS
	ruprechtii misapplied	see *G.* 'Ruprecht'
	ruprechtii (Grossh.) Woronow	EPPr MNrw NBre SRGP WPer WPtf
	Sabani Blue = 'Bremigo'PBR	CAbP CLAP CMac CSev CSpe EBee ECtt EPPr EWes EWoo LBMP LPla MTis NChi NLar NSti SMHy SPer SPoG SRkn WCot WHil
	'Salome'	Widely available
	'Sandrine'PBR	CBcs CLAP CSev CWCL CWGN EBee EPfP GQue IPot LLHF LRHS LSou MNrw NDov NSti SMrm SPoG SRms WCot WHil WPnP

	sanguineum	Widely available
	– Alan Bloom = 'Bloger'PBR	EPPr LRHS
	– 'Album' ♀H4	Widely available
	– 'Alpenglow'	EPPr SBch SRGP WBrk
	– 'Ankum's Pride' ♀H4	CElw CPrp EAEE EBee EPPr LRHS LSou MNFA MTis NCGa NDov NGdn NHar NLar NSti SBch SMrs SRGP SUsu SWat WBrk WCru WFar WMoo WPnP WPtf
	– 'Apfelblüte'	EBee EPPr GJos IPot MAsh NLar SSvw WFar
	– 'Aviemore' ♀H4	CElw CFis EBee EPPr GCal SBch
	– 'Barnsley'	CElw CPrp EPPr NBro NPro WHrl
	– 'Belle of Herterton'	EPPr MAvo NBid NPro SUsu WBrk WCru
	– 'Bloody Graham'	EBee EPPr MAvo SBch WBrk WMoo
	– 'Candy Pink'	EPPr
	– 'Canon Miles'	CElw EBee EPPr LRHS MTis SRGP
	– 'Catforth Carnival'	EPPr
	– 'Cedric Morris'	CElw CYeo ECha ELon EPPr GCra LRHS MAvo MNFA NBid SBch SMrs SRGP WBrk WCru
	– 'Compactum'	EBee WMoo XLum
§	– 'Droplet'	SRGP
	– 'Elsbeth'	CElw CPrp EBee ECha ECtt EPPr EWes GCal LRHS NGdn NLar NSti SBfd SMrm SPoG SRGP WBrk WCru WHal WMoo WPnP WWEG XLum
	– 'Feu d'Automne'	EBee EPPr
	– 'Fran's Star'	see *G.* × *oxonianum* 'Fran's Star'
	– 'Glenluce'	CElw CMea CPrp EBee ECtt EPPr EPfP GBuc GCal LHop LRHS MNFA MRav MSpe NDov NOrc SRGP SRms SWat WBrk WFar WHal WMnd WPer WSpi WTin
	– 'Hampshire Purple'	see *G. sanguineum* 'New Hampshire Purple'
	– 'Holden'	CElw EPPr WBrk
	– 'Inverness'	EBee EPPr
	– 'Joanna'	CFis MAvo
	– 'John Elsley'	CPrp EAEE EBee ECtt EHoe EPPr LAst LLWP LRHS LSou MAsh MNFA MSpe MWhi NBro NGdn SRGP SWat WMnd WPer WPnP WWEG
	– 'John Innes'	EPPr
	– 'Jubilee Pink'	GCal WCru
	– 'Kristin Jacob'	EPPr
	– var. ***lancastrense***	see *G. sanguineum* var. *striatum*
	– 'Leeds Variety'	see *G. sanguineum* 'Rod Leeds'
§	– 'Little Bead' ♀H4	EBee ECho EDAr NWad WBrk XLum
	– 'Max Frei'	Widely available
	– 'Minutum'	see *G. sanguineum* 'Droplet'
	– 'Nanum'	see *G. sanguineum* 'Little Bead'
§	– 'New Hampshire Purple'	CLAP CPrp EBee ECtt EPPr IPot MAvo MNFA NBro NGdn NLar NSti SSvw
	– 'Nyewood'	CPrp EAEE EBee ECGP ECtt EPPr LRHS MBel SEND SRGP WBrk WCru
I	– 'Plenum' (d)	EPPr
	– 'Prado' **new**	XLum
	– 'Pride of Coombland'	SMrs
	– var. ***prostratum*** (Cav.) Pers.	see *G. sanguineum* var. *striatum*
	– 'Purple Flame'	see *G. sanguineum* 'New Hampshire Purple'
§	– 'Rod Leeds'	CFis CLAP EBee NPro SRGP
	– 'Sara'	MAvo
	– 'Shepherd's Warning' ♀H4	CMea CTri EBee ECtt EPPr GCal MMuc NBir NLar SEND SRGP SUsu SWat WCru WFar WHoo WIce WTin
	– 'Shooting Star'	NCot
	– 'South Nutfield'	CElw MAvo NCot
§	– var. ***striatum*** ♀H4	Widely available
	– – deep pink-flowered	CSBt MSwo SWvt
	– – 'Mottisfont'	SBch
	– – 'Reginald Farrer'	WCru
	– – 'Splendens' ♀H4	CElw CSev CWib ELan EPPr GCal LBee LHop LRHS NBid NChi NCot WCru WTin
	– 'Vision Light Pink'	EPPr
	– 'Vision Violet'	EBee EPPr IFoB MAvo SGar SWvt WBrk WPer
	– 'Westacre Poppet'	EPPr EWes
	'Sanne'	EBee EWoo MAvo WCot
	saxatile	EPPr
	'Scapa Flow'	EBee GCal
	schlechteri	EWes
	'Sea Pink'	EDAr
	'Sellindge Blue'	MNFA
	sessiliflorum	ECou
I	– subsp. ***novae-zelandiae*** 'Nigricans'	CFis ECha ECho EHrv ELan GAbr GKev MCot MHer NLar SBch SRGP
§	– – 'Porters Pass'	EBee ECho EHoe EWes MNrw NBir SBch SPlb WHoo
	– – red-leaved	see *G. sessiliflorum* subsp. *novae-zelandiae* 'Porters Pass'
	'Sheilah Hannay'	CSpe
	shikokianum	CLAP EBee GKev NLar SRGP WHrl WPtf
	– var. ***kaimontanum***	WCru
	– var. ***quelpaertense***	CFis
	– – B&SWJ 1234	WCru
	– var. ***yoshiianum*** B&SWJ 6147	WCru
	'Shocking Blue'	EBee EPPr NSti
	'Silva'	CElw ECtt EPPr MNFA MNrw MRav SWat WCru
*	'Silver Shadow'	MCot SPhx
§	***sinense***	CCon CPLG EBee ECtt EPfP GBuc GCal LRHS MCot MNrw NGdn NLar NMyG SMrs SRGP WGwG WMnd XLum
	'Sirak' ♀H4	Widely available
	soboliferum	ELan EPPr LRHS NBir SBch SMad SRGP WCru WMoo WPtf
	– Cally strain	CDes GCal MAvo
	– var. ***kiusianum***	CElw
	– 'Starman'	EBee ECtt EPPr EPfP EWoo LRHS LSou MBri MDev MSwo NCGa NGBo NLar SKHP SPoG SUsu WMoo
	'Solitaire'	CDes CGHE EBee
	'Southcombe Star'	see *G.* × *oxonianum* f. *thurstonianum* 'Southcombe Star'
	'Southease Celestial'	SMHy
	'Spinners'	CElw CHid CMac COIW CSam CWCL EBee ECtt EPPr EPfP GCal GMaP LHop LRHS LSRN MAsh MAvo MNFA MRav MWhi NBid NBir NGdn NHol NSti SPer SWat WCru WMnd WMoo
	stapfianum var. ***roseum***	see *G. orientalitibeticum*

'Stephanie' CDes CElw CSev EBee EPPr EPfP EWes LRHS MAvo MBNS MNFA MSpe NGdn NLar NSti WPnP
'Storm Chaser' CLAP CMac CSpe GBin LRHS NSti SPoG
'Strawberry Frost' LLHF
subcaulescens ♀H4 Widely available
- 'Giuseppii' ♀H4 CPLG CYeo EAEE EBee ECtt ELon EPot GBuc LSou MHer MRav NDov NLar NPnk NPri SBfd SMrm SRGP SRot SWvt WFar
- 'Splendens' ♀H4 CSpe CTri EAEE EBee ECtt EPPr GBuc LHop LRHS LSou MCot MHer NEgg NPri NRHS NSla SRms SWat WFar WGwG WSpi
'Sue Crûg' CPrp EBee ECtt ELan EPfP EShb GCra LAst LLWP LRHS LSou MWhi NDov NEgg NGdn NLar NSti SBch SPer SPoG SRGP SRkn WAul WCru WMoo WTin
'Sue's Sister' WCru
'Summer Cloud' EPPr MNFA SRGP WOut
Summer Skies = 'Gernic'PBR (d) CMac CPLG CSev CWCL EBee ECtt ELan EPPr EPfP EWoo GAbr GMaP LRHS LSou MSCN MWat NBro NEgg NLar SBfd SMrs SPer SWvt WCAu WCot WFar WPnP WPtf WSHC
suzukii WPtf
- B&SWJ 016 CPLG WCru
'Sweet Heidy'PBR CSev EBee ECtt EPPr LBMP LLHF LRHS MSwo NCGa NLar NSti SPoG WBor WFar WHil
sylvaticum CRWN NBid NGdn NMir WMoo WPtf WShi
- 'Afrodite' EPPr
- f. ***albiflorum*** CBre CElw EBee ELan EWoo NSti WCru
- 'Album' ♀H4 Widely available
- 'Amanda' EPPr
- 'Amy Doncaster' Widely available
- 'Angulatum' CElw EBee EPPr MNFA SMrm WMoo WPtf
- 'Birch Lilac' CElw CLAP EBee EPPr EPri GBuc GCal LRHS MAvo NPnk WFar WMoo
- 'Birgit Lion' EBee
- 'Caeruleum' GCal
- 'Coquetdale Lilac' EBee NChi
- 'Ice Blue' EPPr MNFA NChi
- 'Immaculée' EPPr MRav
- 'Kanzlersgrund' CElw EPPr
- 'Lilac Time' EPPr
- 'Mayflower' ♀H4 Widely available
- 'Meran' EPPr LRHS
- 'Nikita' CLAP EPPr
- f. ***roseum*** CFis EPPr NBre NLar WPtf
- - 'Baker's Pink' CElw CLAP EPPr GCra MNFA MNrw MRav NBir SBch SRGP WCru WFar WMoo WPtf
- subsp. ***sylvaticum*** var. ***wanneri*** EBee EPPr WCru
§ 'Tanya Rendall'PBR CMHG CSam CYeo EBee ECtt EHrv ELan ELon EPPr IPot LRHS MBri NDov SPer SPoG SRms WCot WFar WPnP WWEG
'Terre Franche' EBee EPPr NLar SBch SMrs SSvw WWEG XLum
§ ***thunbergii*** CCon CHid EWes LSou SRGP WMoo WPnP XLum
- 'Jester's Jacket' (v) CFis EBee LRHS MGos MNrw SGar SRGP WCot WFar WHrl WSpi
- pink-flowered SRGP
- white-flowered EPPr SRGP
thurstonianum see *G.* × *oxonianum* f. *thurstonianum*
'Tinpenny Mauve' WHoo WTin
'Tiny Monster' CDes CFis EBee ECtt EPPr EWes GBin IKil MAvo MNFA MNrw MWhi NGdn NSti SBfd SPhx WBrk WCot WFar
transbaicalicum EBee EPPr LRHS XLum
traversii CWib
- var. ***elegans*** CSpe CWib ECtt LRHS
tuberosum CElw CHid ECha ECho ELan EShb MRav NBir NBro NCot NGdn NLBP SBch SKHP WRHF WSpi
- subsp. ***linearifolium*** WCru
- 'Rosie's Mauve' new MAvo
'Ushguli Grijs' see *G. ibericum* Cav. 'Ushguli Grijs'
'Vera May' SUsu
'Verguld Saffier'PBR see *G.* Blue Sunrise
versicolor CMac CMea COIW CRWN EBee EPPr EPfP GAbr LRHS MHer MMuc MNrw SEND SRms WFar WMoo
- 'Kingston' see *G.* × *oxonianum* 'Kingston'
§ - 'Snow White' ECtt EPPr MNrw SRGP WCru WMoo
- 'The Bride' CMea ECtt
- 'White Lady' see *G. versicolor* 'Snow White'
'Victor Reiter' see *G. pratense* Victor Reiter Junior strain
violareum see *Pelargonium* 'Splendide'
viscosissimum SRGP WMnd
- var. ***incisum*** LRHS
- rose pink-flowered NBir
wallichianum CFis CMac CPou EBee IFro NBir NSti WMoo
§ - 'Buxton's Variety' ♀H4 Widely available
- 'Chris' EWes SRGP SUsu
- 'Crystal Lake'PBR CWGN EBee ECtt EPfP EWoo IPot LAst LSou MBNS NBir NSti SMrm WPtf
- 'Havana Blues' new EBee EPPr EWoo MBri
- magenta-flowered GBuc
- pale blue-flowered CElw
- 'Pink Buxton' EBee EWes NLar
- pink-flowered CFis CLAP GBuc GCal WCru
- 'Rosetta' new EPPr
- 'Rosie' LRHS SRGP
- 'Syabru' LRHS MNrw NLar SMHy WMoo
- 'Sylvia's Surprise'PBR LRHS
'Wednesday's Child' WFar
wilfordii misapplied see *G. thunbergii*
Wisley hybrid see *G.* 'Khan'
wlassovianum Widely available
- 'Blue Star' IPot MRav NPro SRGP WFar
§ ***yeoi*** CSpe EPPr NBir NBro NSti SEND SRGP WCru WOut
yesoense EBee EPPr NBir NSti SRGP
- var. ***nipponicum*** WCru
yoshinoi misapplied see *G. thunbergii*
yoshinoi Makino LRHS
yunnanense misapplied see *G. pogonanthum*
yunnanense ambig. CCon

Gerbera (*Asteraceae*)

'Brandy' (Garvinea Series) WHlf
(Everlast Series) Everlast Carmine = 'Amgerbcar' ELon EUJe LBuc LHop LRHS LSou MBNS SBfd SMrm SPoG WHil

- Everlast Orange = 'Amgerbora' LRHS SPoG

- Everlast Pink = 'Amgerbpink' ELon LAst LBuc LRHS LSou MBNS SBfd SHar SPoG WHil

- Everlast White = 'Amgerbwhi' ELon LBuc LHop LRHS SBfd SHar SMrm SPoG WHil

- Everlast Yellow LHop LSou MBNS SBfd SPoG WHil

'Fleurie'^{PBR} (Garvinea Series) **new** MBNS WHil

(Garvinea Series) Garvinea Jilly WHlf

- Garvinea Lisa = 'Garlisa'^{PBR} **new** WHlf

- Garvinvea Rachel = 'Garrachel'^{PBR} EBee IBoy MBNS WCot WHlf

- Garvinea Sylvana = 'Garsylvana' **new** EBee MBNS WCot

- Garvinea Valerie **new** WHlf

'Orangina'^{PBR} (Garvinea Series) EBee ELon WHlf

'Pam'^{PBR} (Garvinea Series) EBee WHlf

Gesneria (*Gesneriaceae*)

cardinalis see *Sinningia cardinalis*

Gethyllis (*Amaryllidaceae*)

afra 'Paarl' ECho

barkerae ECho

- 'Nardouwsberg' ECho

- subsp. ***paucifolius*** ECho

britteniana 'Rietputs' ECho

ciliaris ECho

- 'Porterville' ECho

grandiflora ECho

gregoriana ECho

hallii 'Komiesberg' ECho

linearis 'Piketburg' ECho

oligophylla 'Moedverloor' ECho

transkarooica 'Waboomsberg' ECho

verticillata ECho

- 'Pikenierskloof' ECho

villosa ECho

Geum ✿ (*Rosaceae*)

'Abendsonne' CDes CElw EBee MAvo MSpe NPro SBri WWEG

aleppicum NBre XLum

alpinum see *G. montanum*

andicola NBre

'Apricot Beauty' CWCL

'Apricot Delight' **new** LLHF NPro

'Baby Tangerine' NMen

'Beech House Apricot' CElw CLAP EBee ECtt EPri GCra LRHS MAvo MNFA MNrw MRav NCGa NChi NHol NLar NPro SApp SBri SPoG WMoo WPnP WTin WWEG XLum

'Bell Bank' Widely available

'Birkhead's Creamy Lemon' CElw EBee MAvo NBir SBri WHrl

'Blazing Sunset' (d) Widely available

'Blood Orange' MAvo NPro

N 'Borisii' Widely available

'Bremner's Gold' SBri

'Bremner's Nectarine' CElw MAvo MNrw MSpe NChi NPro WWEG

'Broomrigg Beauty' **new** MAvo NPro

bulgaricum CElw EBee MRav NBir NLar NPro NRya WTin XLum

'Butterscotch' EBee MAvo SBri

calthifolium EPPr LRHS MRav NBre NBro

capense NBre NPro SPlb

- JJ&JH 9401271 EBee

§ ***chiloense*** LEdu

- 'Farncombe' NCot

- 'Red Dragon' CBre CWCL EBee ELon LLHF LSRN NBre SWvt

'Chipchase' MAvo NChi NPro SBri SHar WHoo WWEG

coccineum misapplied see *G. chiloense*

coccineum ambig. NCGa

coccineum Sibth. & Sm. 'Ann' EPri MSpe

- 'Cooky' CElw ECrc EPfP GJos LRHS MMuc MSCN NGBl NLar NPro SHil SPad SPoG SRms SWal SWvt WFar WPer WWEG

- 'Eos' CDes CElw CSpe CWCL EBee ECtt ELon EWes LEdu LHop MAsh MAvo MNrw MPnt NGdn NLar NPri NPro SPoG WCot WMoo WWEG

- 'Koi' **new** EBee LBuc

- 'Queen of Orange' CBre CEnt NPro WRHF

- 'Werner Arends' CMHG EBee GAbr GCal MAvo MBri MNrw MRav NDov SBri WCot WFar WMoo WWEG

'Copper Pennies' **new** NPro

'Coppertone' CElw CLAP ECtt EHrv ELan EPri LRHS MAvo MRav MSpe NBir NBro NCGa NChi NRya SBri WAul WTin

'Cotton Candy' **new** MAvo NPro

'Cream Crackers' NPro

'Custard Pie' NPro

'Dawn' **new** SBri

'Deano's Delight' **new** NPro

'Diana' EBee MNrw NPro SBri WWEG

'Dingle Apricot' CElw ECtt GAbr GBin MNrw MRav MSpe NBir WWEG

'Dolly North' (d) CCVN EBee ECrc EPyc GAbr MArl MAvo MCot MNrw MRav MSpe NBro NGdn SBri WHal WWEG

'Elizabeth' **new** SBri

'Elworthy Amber' **new** MAvo

'Emory Quinn' **new** NPro

'Fancy Frills' MDKP

'Farmer John Cross' CBre CDes CElw CLAP EBee ECtt EPri GJos LPla MAvo MNrw MSpe MTis NCGa NCot NLar SBri WHal WMoo WWEG

'Feuermeer' CElw EBee MAvo MSpe NLar NPro SBri

'Fire Opal' (d) ♀^{H4} CDes CElw CWCL EBee EWes LPla MAvo NBir NBre NPro SBri WMoo WWEG

'Fireball' LRHS LSou MAvo NBre

'Flame' NPro SBri

'Flames of Passion'^{PBR} CCVN CHVG CWCL CWGN CYeo EBee ECrc ECtt ELon GQue IBoy ITim LHop LPla LSou MAvo MBNS MBel NBir NDov NLar SPad SPoG SRGP WCAu WCot WFar WWEG

'Fresh Woods' WWEG

'Georgenberg' Widely available

'Glencoe' CElw

'Golden Joy' **new** WHoo

'Hannay's' MAvo MSpe NPro SBri SUsu

'Herterton Primrose' CCon CDes CElw CLAP CWCL EBee ECtt EPPr GBuc GCal LLHF

		MAvo MSpe MTis NCGa NSti SBri SUsu WHal WHoo WWEG
	'Hilltop Beacon' (d)	CElw LLHF MAvo NPro SBri WHoo
*	***hybridum luteum***	NSti SBri
	× ***intermedium***	CBre EPPr NGdn NLar NPro SBri WMoo WWEG
	- 'Diane'	CDes GJos MAvo MSpe NBre NChi SBri SUsu WHoo
	'Ivorine' **new**	MAvo
	'Jolly Roger'	NPro
	'Karlskaer'	CDes CElw CWCL EBee ECtt EPri EWes GBin GBuc GQue LHop LRHS MAsh MAvo MBri MNrw MSpe MTis NGdn NLar SAga SBea SBri SMrm WCot WFar WMoo WNew WPtf WWEG
	'Kashmir'	SBri
	'Kath Inman'	SBri WWEG
	'Kathryn' **new**	CDes MAvo
	'Lady Stratheden' (d) ♀H4	Widely available
	'Lemon Delight'	CElw
	'Lemon Drops'	Widely available
	'Lionel Cox'	Widely available
	'Lisanne'	CElw CSam EBee IPot MAsh MAvo MSpe NCGa NCot NDov SBri SMHy SUsu
	'Little Lottie' **new**	NPro
	'Little Twister'	NPro
	macrophyllum	EBee
	magellanicum	EWes NBre NLar WPtf
	'Magic Toybox' **new**	NPro
	'Mai Tai' **new**	WHlf
	'Mandarin' (d)	CCon CDes CElw GAbr GCal MAvo SBri
	'Mango' **new**	SBri
	'Mango Lassi'	MAvo WCAu
	'Marmalade'	CSev EBee ECrc ECtt ELon EPri EWTr GAbr GJos MAvo MNrw MSpe MTis NBre NCGa NLar NMRc NPnk NPro SMHy SUsu WHrl WKif WMoo WOut WWEG
	'Midnight Serenade' **new**	MAvo
§	***montanum*** ♀H4	CEnt EBee ECho EDAr GCra GKev LRHS MAsh MMuc NBir NBro NPri NRya SEND SPet SRms WWEG
	- SDR 5495	GKev
	'Moonlight Serenade'	EBee NPro
	'Moorland Sorbet'	NPro SBri WFar WMoo WPtf WWEG
	'Mrs J. Bradshaw' (d) ♀H4	Widely available
	'Mrs W. Moore'	CBre CDes CElw CLAP CWCL EBee ECtt EPPr EShb GAbr GJos LDai MAvo MHer MNrw MTis NBir NCGa NChi NLBP NLar NPnk NPro SBri SRGP WHoo WMoo WWEG
	'Nordek'	EBee ECtt GAbr GBuc GCal GJos LAst LRHS MNFA MNrw MRav NEgg NGdn SBri WPtf WWEG
	'Norwell Yellow Lamp' **new**	MAvo
	'Octavie'	SBri
	'Orangeman'	MAvo MNrw
	parviflorum	NBre NBro
	'Paso Doble'	CElw
	'Peachy Proud' **new**	NPro
	pentapetalum	see *Sieversia pentapetala*
	- 'Flore Pleno' (d)	WAbe
	'Pink Frills'	CElw CWCL EBee ECtt EHrv EPPr EPri EWTr EWes GAbr GQue LPla MAvo MRav MSpe NCGa NLar SBri SMHy SMrm STes SUsu WWEG
	'Poco'	EBee MAvo NPro SBri
	'Pomelos'	SBri
	'Present'	CElw EBee ECrc ECtt MAvo NBre NCGa NChi NPro SBri WWEG
	'Primrose'	GAbr GJos GQue NGdn NLar NPro SBri
	'Prince of Orange' (d)	CElw GAbr LRHS MAvo MNrw MRav NBre SBri WFar WHrl WWEG
	'Prinses Juliana'	Widely available
	pyrenaicum	EBee NBre NCGa
	quellyon	see *G. chiloense*
I	'Rearsby Hybrid'	LLHF MAvo MRav MSpe NPro SPlb SUsu WHoo WWEG
	'Red Wings' (d)	EBee EPPr GBuc GCal GMaP GQue LRHS MRav NBir NCGa NPro SBri SHar SMHy SUsu WGwG WWEG
§	***reptans***	GBin
	rhodopeum	LLHF
	'Rijnstroom'	EBee ELan EPPr LDai MAvo MNrw MSpe WCAu WPtf
	rivale	CArn CBen CHab COIW EBee EHon EPfP MCot MHer MNHC NBro NLan NMir NPer SPet SPlb SRms SWat WFar WMAq WMoo WPer WWEG
	- 'Album'	Widely available
	- 'Apricot'	SBri
	- 'Barbra Lawton'	MAvo MDKP MSpe SBri WWEG
	- 'Cream Drop'	CElw MAvo MCot MSpe NCGa NChi NPnk NPro SBri SMrm WWEG
	- 'Leonard's Double' (d)	CPrp CSev WNew WWEG
	- 'Leonard's Variety'	Widely available
	- 'Marika'	CCVN CHid CRow EBee EPri LRHS MAvo MSpe NBre NCGa SBri SMrm SRGP WMoo WPtf WWEG
	- 'Marmalade'	CBre CElw CWCL IPot NChi NPro SApp SBri SUsu WPtf
	- 'Snowflake'	MAvo MSpe NPro
	'Rubin'	CElw ECtt EPPr EPyc GCra IPot NBre NBro NDov SBri SUsu
	'Rusty Young'	MAvo NPro
	'Savanna Sunset'	MAvo NPro
	'Sigiswang'	CDes CElw EBee EWes GAbr GJos MNrw MRav NBre NPro SBri SMrm WCAu WWEG
	'Stacey's Sunrise'	NPro SBri
	'Star of Bethlehem' **new**	NPro
I	'Starker's Magnificum'	WCot
	'Strawberries and Cream'	NPro
	'Sunrise' (d)	ELon WHil
	'Sweet Angel Dar' **new**	NPro
	'Tangerine'	EPri LSou MRav MSpe NPro SBri WWEG
	'Tango Dream' **new**	MAvo
	'Terracotta'	MTis
	'Tinpenny Orange'	CElw MAvo NPro SBri WTin WWEG
	× ***tirolense***	EBee MAvo NBre NCGa NPro
	'Totally Tangerine'	LBuc LRHS SHar
	'Trevor's Lemon' **new**	MAvo
	triflorum	CElw EBee EHrv EShb MNrw NLar NPnk SPhx WFar WTin
	- var. ***campanulatum***	CCon NPro WWEG
	'Turbango' **new**	NPro
	'Turnpike Troubadour' **new**	NPro
	urbanum	CArn CHab ENfk GJos NLan SWat WHer WHfH WMoo
	- from Patagonia	MDKP
	'Wallace's Peach'	SBri SWal

Gevuina (*Proteaceae*)

avellana	CBcs CHEx EBee WPGP

Gilia ✿ (*Polemoniaceae*)

achilleifolia	SPhx
aggregata	see *Ipomopsis aggregata*
californica	see *Leptodactylon californicum*

Gillenia (*Rosaceae*)

stipulata	CLAP EBee LEdu MNrw SPhx SUsu
trifoliata ♀H4	Widely available

Ginkgo (*Ginkgoaceae*)

biloba ♀H4	Widely available
- B&SWJ 8753	WCru
- 'Anny's Dwarf'	MAsh SBig
- 'Autumn Gold' (m)	CBcs CDul CMCN EBee ECrN LAst LLHF MBlu MGos MPkF NLar SBig SLim
I - 'Barabits Nana'	SBig
- 'Beijing Gold'	IVic MBlu MPkF NLar SBig SMad
- 'California Sunset'	MBlu NLar SBig SMad
- 'Chase Manhattan'	MPkF
- 'Chi-chi'	MPkF SBig SLim
- 'Chotek'	SBig
- 'Chris' Dwarf'	NLar
- 'Doctor Causton' (f)	CAgr
- 'Doctor Causton' (m)	CAgr
- 'Eastern Star' (f)	CAgr
- 'Elmwood'	NLar
- 'Elsie'	SBig
- 'Everton Broom' **new**	SLim
- 'Fairmount' (m)	MBlu SBig
- 'Fastigiata' (m)	CMCN EBee EPfP ESwi MBlu MGos SBig
- 'Globosa' **new**	MBlu
- 'Gnome'	ESwi LSRN MGos MPkF
- 'Golden Globe'	ESwi MPkF NLar
- 'Gresham'	MPkF
- 'Horizontalis'	MBlu SBig SLim
- 'Jade Butterflies'	CBcs GBin MBlu MBri MPkF NLar SBig SLim
- 'Jerry Vercade'	MPkF
- 'King of Dongting' (f)	CAgr ESwi MBlu SBig
- 'Lakeview' (m)	MPkF SBig
- 'Mariken'	ELan EPfP ESwi GKin LRHS MGos MPkF NLar SBig SLim SLon SMad SPoG
- 'Mayfield' (m)	SBig
- 'Menhir' **new**	MPkF
- 'Montezuma' **new**	SBig
- Ohazuki Group (f)	CAgr SBig
- Pendula Group	CMCN ECrN ESwi MAsh MBlu MPkF NPri SBig SGol
- - 'Pendula Gruga' **new**	SBig
- 'Pixie'	SBig
- 'Princeton Sentry' (m)	CDoC EBee IVic SBig
- 'Robbie's Twist'	MPkF SBig
- 'Santa Cruz' **new**	SBig
- 'Saratoga' (m)	CAgr CBcs CDoC CJun CMCN EBee ECrN EPfP ESwi LRHS MBri MGos MPkF SBig SLim SMad SSpi
- 'Shangri-La' (m) **new**	MBlu
- 'Sinclair'	MPkF
- 'Tit'	CMCN EPfP ESwi MGos NLar SBig
- 'Tremonia'	CMCN EPfP MBlu MPkF NLar SBig SLim
- 'Troll'	CDoC MAsh MBlu NLar SBig SCoo SLim SMad
- 'Tubifolia'	CMCN ESwi MBlu MPkF NLar SBig
- 'Umbrella'	SBig
- Variegata Group (v)	CBcs CJun CMen ESwi MGos MPkF NLar SBig SLim SPoG
- 'W.B.'	MPkF
- 'Weeping Wonder' (f) **new**	SBig
- 'Witches Broom' **new**	SBig

ginseng see *Panax ginseng*

Gladiolus (*Iridaceae*)

sp.	MNrw
abyssinucus	GCal
acuminatus	WCot
'Akuta' (M/E)	CGrW
alatus	ECho
- 'Rawsonville'	ECho
'Alba' (N)	CGrW
'Alexandra' (P)	WCot
'Allosius' (S)	CGrW
'Amanda Mahy' (N)	LAma
'Amsterdam' (G)	CGrW
'Andre Viette'	LLHF WCot
angustus	CDes WCot
antakiensis	CPou
'Anyu S' (L)	CGrW
'Atom' (S/P)	CAvo CBro CGrW ECho LAma WCot
aureus	WCot
Barnard hybrids	CGrW
'Beautiful Angel'	CGrW
'Beauty Bride' (L)	CGrW
'Beauty of Holland'PBR (L)	CGrW
'Big Boss' (G)	CGrW
'Black Star'	EPfP ERCP SPer
'Blackbird' (S)	CGrW
'Blue Frost' (L)	SDeJ
'Blue Tropic'	CSut
'Bonfire' (G)	CGrW
'Boone'	SMrm WCot
'Break of Dawn'	SDeJ
× ***brenchleyensis***	CPen
brevifolius 'Somerset West'	ECho
- 'Villiersdorp'	ECho
'Buhler's Humor' **new**	CGrW
byzantinus	see *G. communis* subsp. *byzantinus*
caeruleus	WCot
- 'Saldanha'	ECho
callianthus	see *G. murielae*
cardinalis	CDes CPne CRDP GBin GCal IBlr LEdu SKHP WCru
carinatus	CDes CGrW ECho WCot
carinatus* × *orchidiflorus	WCot
carinatus* × *huttonii 'Purple Spray'	WCot
'Carine' (N)	GKev LAma SDeJ
carmineus	CGrW ECho LWst WCot
carneus	CGrW ECho EPot GCal SDeJ
caryophyllaceus	CGrW ECho
'Charm' (N/Tub)	CBro LAma LEdu SDeJ
'Charming Beauty' (Tub)	ECho LAma SDeJ
'Charming Lady' (Tub)	ECho LAma
'Cherry Berry' (S) **new**	CGrW
'Cindy' (B)	ECho
citrinus	see *G. trichonemifolius*
'Claudia' (N)	CGrW

'Columbine' (P) SDeJ
× ***colvillii*** CPne IBlr
- 'Albus' ERCP
- 'The Bride' ♀H3 CAvo CBro CElw EBee EPot GKev LAma LDai LEdu LSRN SDeJ SPhx
§ ***communis*** Widely available
subsp. ***byzantinus*** ♀H4
'Coral Dream' (L) CGrW
'Côte d'Azur' (G) CGrW
'Cotton Queen' (L) CGrW
crassifolius ECho
'Cream Perfection' (L) CGrW SDeJ
'Creamy Yellow' (S) CGrW
'Cristabel' WCot
§ ***dalenii*** CGrW CPou ECho IBlr
- 'Apricot Delight' **new** IBlr
- 'Citrone Spectrum' **new** IBlr
- subsp. ***dalenii*** CPrp IBlr
- 'Guardsman' **new** IBlr
- green-flowered IBlr
* - f. ***rubra*** IBlr
- yellow-flowered EBee
'Dawn Boy' (S) **new** CGrW
'Daydreamer' (L) CGrW
'Delirium' **new** CGrW
densifolius ECho
'Dion' (M) **new** CGrW
'Dixon' (L) **new** CGrW
ecklonii ECho
- 'Mount Thomas' ECho
'Elvira' (N) CAvo ECho GKev LAma
'Emerald Spring' (S) CGrW WCot
'Esta Bonita' (G) CGrW
'Excel' (L) **new** CGrW
'Extasy'PBR (L) CGrW
'Farondole' **new** SDeJ
'Felicita' (L) **new** CGrW
'Fidelio' (L) SDeJ
'Finishing Touch'PBR (L) CGrW
'Flame Eye' (M) **new** CGrW
flanaganii CDes CMea CPBP CPLG CSpe ECho EPot GCal GHim ITim LLHF LWSt NRHS NSla SChr WAbe WCot
- JCA 261.000 SKHP
'Flevo Cosmic' (Min) CGrW
'Flevo Dancer' (S) CGrW
'Flevo Eclips'PBR (G) CGrW
'Flevo Frizzle' CGrW
'Flevo Junior' (S) CGrW
'Flevo Libre'PBR (L) CGrW
'Flevo Primo'PBR (S) CGrW
'Flevo Shine' (M) **new** CGrW
'Flevo Smile' (S) CGrW WCot
'Flevo Souvenir'PBR (L) CGrW
'Flevo Spirit' **new** CGrW
'Flevo Sunset'PBR (L) CGrW
floribundus hort. ECho
- subsp. ***fasciatus*** CGrW
fourcadei CGrW ECho
'Frangine' (L) CGrW
'French Silk' (L) CGrW
'Frosty White' (L) **new** CGrW
garnieri CDes EBee WCot
geardii WCot
'Gold Struck' (L) CGrW
'Good Luck' (N) CBro
gracilis ECho WCot
grandis see *G. liliaceus*
'Green Star' (L) CGrW ERCP SDeJ
gueinzii 'Mossel Bay' ECho
'Halley' (N) CGrW ECho LAma
'Happy Weekend' (L) SDeJ
hirsutus CGrW ECho
'Holland Pearl' (B) ERCP SDeJ
'Huron County' (L) CGrW
'Huron Jewel' (M) CGrW
'Huron Pleasure' CGrW
'Huron Silk' (L) CGrW
huttonii CDes CGrW ECho WCot
huttonii* × *liliaceus **new** CDes
huttonii* × *tristis CPou
huttonii* × *tristis CDes WCot
var. ***concolor***
hyalinus CGrW
'Ibadan'PBR (L) CGrW
'Ice Cream' SPer
illyricus CGrW CSam ECho GCal WShi
imbricatus CGrW ECho GHim
- RS 0572 LWSt
'Impressive' (N) CBro LAma MAvo SDeJ
'Indian Summer'PBR **new** CGrW
inflatus CGrW ECho
- 'Ceres' ECho
involutus CGrW
- 'Mossel Bay' ECho
§ ***italicus*** CGrW CHid EBee ELan EPfP GBin GCal GKev MWat SKHP WHil XLum
'Jacksonville Gold' (L) SDeJ
'Jayvee' (S) CGrW
'Jester' (L) CSut
'Jim S' (G) CGrW
'Jolie Julie' (L) **new** CGrW
kotschyanus ECho
'Kristin' (L) CGrW
'Kuki-oki' (L) **new** CGrW
'Lady Lucille' (M) CGrW
'Lavender Flare' (S) CGrW
'Lavy Linda' (L) **new** CGrW
'Lemon Drop' (S) CGrW
leptosiphon CGrW SGar
- 'Molenaars River' ECho
§ ***liliaceus*** CGrW ECho WCot
- 'Caledon' ECho
'Little Rainbow' (P) WCot
'Little Wiggy' (P) CGrW
longicollis ECho
'Loulou' (G) CGrW
'Lowland Queen' (L) CGrW
'Mademoiselle de Paris' ERCP
'Marj S' (L) CGrW
'Match Point' (L) SDeJ
meliusculus ECho
'Melodrame' **new** CGrW
'Mexico' CSut SDeJ
miniatus CDes
'Mirella' (N) CAvo LAma MRav
'Mon Amour'PBR CGrW
mortonius GCal
'Mr Chris' (S) CGrW
§ ***murielae*** ♀H3 CAvo CBro CGrW CMea EBee ECho EPfP ERCP EWll LAma LEdu LRHS MCot NRHS SCoo SDeJ SHil SPer SPet SPhx SPlb STes WHal WHoo WPtf
natalensis see *G. dalenii*

'Nathalie' (N)	CGrW SDeJ
'Nori' (M)	ERCP
'Nova Lux' (L)	SDeJ
'Nymph' (N)	CAvo EPot LAma LDai LEdu SDeJ
'Oasis'PBR (G)	CGrW
'Of Singular Beauty' (G)	CGrW
§ ***oppositiflorus***	CPou IBlr SChr WHil
- subsp. ***salmoneus***	see *G. oppositiflorus*
orchidiflorus	CGrW ECho
'Oscar' (G)	ERCP
palustris	CDes CRDP
papilio	Widely available
- 'David Hills'	CDes NCGa WCot WHal
§ - Purpureoauratus Group	CBro CSam EBee IBlr SRms
- 'Ruby'	CAvo CDes CMea CPen CPne CPou CPrp CTca EPri IPot LEdu LSRN NCGa NChi SMad SUsu WCot WHil WHoo
- yellow-flowered	CCse CMea
'Parade' (G)	CGrW
'Passos'PBR	ERCP
'Peach Blossom' (N)	WCot
'Peach Melba' (L) **new**	CGrW
'Perseus' (P/Min)	ERCP
'Perth Pearl' (M)	CGrW
'Peter Pears' (L)	SDeJ
'Phyllis M' (L)	CGrW
Pilbeam hybrids	CGrW WCot
'Plum Tart' (L)	ERCP
'Pop Art'	SDeJ
primulinus	see *G. dalenii*
'Prins Claus' (N)	CBro CGrW CTca GKev LAma
'Prinses Margaret Rose' (Min)	CSut SDeJ
priorii 'Dasberg'	ECho
'Priscilla' (L)	MLHP SDeJ
pritzelii	CGrW
- 'Quaggasfontein'	ECho
'Purple Flora'	ERCP SPer
'Purple Prince' (M)	CGrW WCot
purpureoauratus	see *G. papilio* Purpureoauratus Group
quadrangularis	CGrW ECho
'Rasmin' (L)	CGrW
'Raspberry Swirl' (L/E)	CGrW
recurvus	CGrW ECho
'Red Deer' (L)	CGrW
'Robinetta' (*recurvus* hybrid) ♀H3	ECho LAma LDai MAvo SDeJ
'Roma' (L)	CGrW
'Rose Flame' (L)	CGrW
'Royal Spire'	CGrW
'Rusty Red' (P)	CGrW
'Ruth Ann'	CGrW
'San Remo'PBR (L)	CGrW
saundersii	CDes GCal
'Scarlet Lady' (P)	CGrW
scullyi	CGrW
- 'Ceres Karoo'	ECho
'Secret Lady' (M) **new**	CGrW
segetum	see *G. italicus*
sericeovillosus	IBlr
'Sharkey' (G)	CGrW
'Show Star' (L)	CGrW
'Show Stopper' (G)	CGrW
'Sirael' (L/E)	CGrW
'Slick Chick' (S) **new**	CGrW
'Smoke 'n' Mirrors' **new**	CGrW
'Smoke Stack' (L)	CGrW
'Snowdon'	CGrW
'Solveiga' (L/E)	CGrW
'Sophie'PBR	CGrW
'Spic and Span' (L)	SDeJ
'Spinners'	IBlr
splendens	CDes CGrW WCot WPGP
- 'Roggeveld'	ECho
'Stiena' (L)	CGrW
'Tan Royale' (P)	CGrW
'Tante Ann' (M)	CGrW
'Tarryn' (L) **new**	CGrW
'Teamwork' (L) **new**	CGrW
'Terry' (G)	CGrW
'Trader Horn' (G)	SDeJ
'Traderhorn' (G) **new**	CGrW
§ ***trichonemifolius***	CGrW ECho
tristis	CAvo CBro CDes CElw CGHE CGrW CPne CPou CPrp ECha ECho EHrv ELan ELon GBin GCal GKev SAga SDix WFar WHal WHil WPGP
- var. ***concolor***	CGrW CPou CPrp
undulatus	CDes CGrW ECho WCot
uysiae	CGrW ECho
- 'Gannaga'	ECho
vandermerwei	CGrW ECho
'Velvet Eyes' (M)	SDeJ
venustus	CGrW ECho
'Video' (L)	CGrW
'Violetta' (M)	CGrW
virescens	CGrW
- 'Ceres'	ECho
watermeyeri	CGrW
watsonioides	CPou SKHP WCot
'Wax Ruffles' (L/E)	CGrW
'White Prosperity' (L)	CSut ERCP SDeJ
'White Willie' (S)	CGrW
'Yellow Gem' **new**	SDeJ
'Zamora' (L) **new**	CGrW

Glandularia see *Verbena*

Glaux (*Primulaceae*)

maritima	WPer

Glaucidium (*Ranunculaceae*)

palmatum ♀H4	CPLG CWCL EBee EFEx EPot GBuc GEdr GKev NSla WCru WHal
- 'Album'	see *G. palmatum* var. *leucanthum*
§ - var. ***leucanthum***	EFEx GEdr GKev

Glaucium (*Papaveraceae*)

§ ***corniculatum***	CAbP CSpe LRHS SPhx
flavum	CArn CSpe ECha ELan MHer NMRc SEND SPav XSen
- ***aurantiacum***	see *G. flavum* f. *fulvum*
- f. ***flavum*** **new**	LLHF
§ - f. ***fulvum***	ECha LRHS SDix WCot XSen
- orange-flowered	see *G. flavum* f. *fulvum*
- red-flowered	see *G. corniculatum*
phoenicium	see *G. corniculatum*

Glebionis (*Asteraceae*)

coronaria	MNHC
§ ***segetum***	CHab

Glechoma (*Lamiaceae*)

hederacea	CArn GPoy MHer NMir WHer
- 'Barry Yinger Variegated' (v)	EBee
§ - 'Variegata' (v)	SPer SPet XLum

Gleditsia (*Caesalpiniaceae*)

caspica	CArn LEdu
japonica	EPfP LEdu NLar
triacanthos	CDul CWib IDee LEdu SEND SPlb
- 'Calhoun'	CAgr
- 'Elegantissima' (v)	SPer
- 'Emerald Cascade'	CBcs EBee
- f. ***inermis*** Spectrum = 'Speczam'	EBee LRHS MAsh MBri
- 'Millwood'	CAgr
- 'Rubylace'	CBcs CCVT CDul CLnd CMCN CMac CSBt EBee ECrN ELan EPfP EWTr IVic LAst LSRN MBlu MBri MGos MRav MSwo NLar SGol SKHP SLim SMad SPer
- 'Skyline'	LMaj
- 'Sunburst' ♀H4	Widely available

Globba ✿ (*Zingiberaceae*)

marantina	GHim LAma
'Mount Everest'	GHim
racemosa new	GHim
- var. ***hookeri*** HWJCM 471	WCru
winitii 'Mount Everest'	LAma

Globularia (*Plantaginaceae*)

bellidifolia	see *G. meridionalis*
bisnagarica	GKev
cordifolia ♀H4	ECho EDAr EPot GEdr LRHS NBir NMen WCot WPat
- 'Alba'	NHar
× ***indubia***	IRar
§ ***meridionalis***	EPot EWes GMaP MWat NMen WPat
- 'Blue Bonnets'	GEdr NHar
- 'Hort's Variety'	NMen NSla WAbe WPat
nana	see *G. repens*
nudicaulis	GEdr GKev
punctata	CCon CSpe GKev SRms
pygmaea	see *G. meridionalis*
§ ***repens***	EPot GEdr NHar NMen WAbe WPat
stygia	GKev
trichosantha	SRms
valentina	GEdr GKev

Gloriosa (*Colchicaceae*)

lutea	see *G. superba* 'Lutea'
rothschildiana	see *G. superba* 'Rothschildiana'
superba ♀H1	ERCP GHim SDeJ
- 'Carsonii'	ERCP LAma
- 'Greenii'	ERCP LAma LWSt SDeJ
§ - 'Lutea'	GHim LAma LRHS SDeJ
§ - 'Rothschildiana'	CBcs CGrW GHim LAma LRHS SDeJ SRms WCot
- 'Simplex'	CLak
- 'Verschuurii'	CLak

Glottiphyllum (*Aizoaceae*)

sp. new	WHil

Gloxinia (*Gesneriaceae*)

sp.	EABi
nematanthodes 'Evita'	SUsu
sylvatica 'Bolivian Sunset'	WDib

Glumicalyx (*Scrophulariaceae*)

flanaganii	GKev

Glyceria (*Poaceae*)

aquatica variegata	see *G. maxima* var. *variegata*
maxima	CRWN MMuc MSKA NMir NPer SEND SPlb
§ - var. ***variegata*** (v)	CWCL CWat EBee ECha EHoe EHon ELan EPfP GCra GMaP IBoy LHop LPBA LRHS MBlu MMuc MWhi NGdn NOrc NWsh SEND SMrm SPer SRms SVic SWat WMAq WMoo WWEG XLum
notata	SVic
spectabilis 'Variegata'	see *G. maxima* var. *variegata*

Glycyrrhiza (*Papilionaceae*)

echinata	CArn
§ ***glabra***	CArn CCCN CHby EBee ELau ENfk GPoy MHer MHoo MNHC SDix SIde WJek
glandulifera	see *G. glabra*
uralensis	CArn EBee ELau GPoy MHer SPhx
yunnanensis	CSpe

Glyptostrobus (*Cupressaceae*)

pensilis	CGHE CPLG WPGP

Gmelina (*Lamiaceae*)

hystrix	CCCN

Gnaphalium (*Asteraceae*)

'Fairy Gold'	see *Helichrysum thianschanicum* 'Goldkind'
trinerve	see *Anaphalis trinervis*

Godetia see *Clarkia*

goji berry see *Lycium barbarum*

Gomphocarpus (*Apocynaceae*)

§ ***physocarpus***	CArn CDTJ SBfd

Gomphostigma (*Scrophulariaceae*)

virgatum	CPLG CTrC EPPr IDee LSou SAga SMad SMrm SPlb SSvw WCFE WCot WHrl
- 'White Candy'	EBee NLar

Gomphrena (*Amaranthaceae*)

globosa	CCCN

Goniolimon (*Plumbaginaceae*)

collinum 'Sea Spray'	CMea EBee EDAr MBNS WHil
incanum 'Blue Diamond'	WCot
speciosum	EDAr GKev LLHF
§ ***tataricum***	EBee NLar
§ - var. ***angustifolium***	EBee SRms WPer
- 'Woodcreek'	NLar

Goodia (*Papilionaceae*)

lotifolia	CCCN

Goodyera (*Orchidaceae*)

biflora	EFEx
pubescens	EFEx
schlechtendaliana	EFEx

gooseberry see *Ribes uva-crispa*

Gordonia (*Theaceae*)

axillaris	see *Polyspora axillaris*

Grafia (*Apiaceae*)

golaka new	EBee

granadilla see *Passiflora quadrangularis*

granadilla, purple see *Passiflora edulis*

granadilla, sweet see *Passiflora ligularis*

grape see *Vitis*

grapefruit see *Citrus* × *paradisi*

Graptopetalum (*Crassulaceae*)

filiferum	CDoC EUJe SPlb
§ ***paraguayense***	CDoC SEND
'Superbum' new	CDoC

× *Graptoveria* (*Crassulaceae*)

'Acaulis' new	CDoC
'Caerulescens' new	CDoC
'Mrs Richards' new	CDoC
'Ron Ginns' new	CDoC
'Titubans' new	CDoC
'Van Keppel' new	CDoC

Gratiola (*Plantaginaceae*)

officinalis	CArn CWan EHon MHer MHoo MSKA

Greenovia (*Crassulaceae*)

§ ***aurea***	NMen SPlb
diplocycla 'Gigantea'	SPlb

Greigia (*Bromeliaceae*)

sphacelata	IDee

Grevillea (*Proteaceae*)

alpina 'Olympic Flame'	CBcs CCCN CDoC CPLG CSBt CWib EBee EPfP LRHS MMuc MOWG SCoo SEND SGar SPoG SRms WGrn
australis	ECou
banksii 'Canberra Hybrid'	see *G.* 'Canberra Gem'
- var. ***forsteri***	SPlb
barklyana	MOWG
'Bronze Rambler'	MOWG
§ 'Canberra Gem' ♀H3-4	Widely available
'Clearview David'	CCCN CMac CTrC CWGN EUJe LRHS LSRN MAsh MOWG SCoo SLim SSpi WPat
'Cranbrook Yellow'	CDoC EPfP
crithmifolia	SPlb
'Elegance' red-flowered	MOWG
'Evelyn's Coronet'	MOWG
johnsonii	CMac CWSG EUJe MOWG
juniperina	CBcs CCCN CMac CPLG EBee EPfP LRHS MGos SLim
- f. ***sulphurea***	CCCN CDoC CHll CPLG CTrC CTsd ELon EPfP LRHS MAsh MOWG SEND SPlb SPoG WGrn WPat WSHC
lanigera	EUJe
I - 'Lutea'	MOWG
- 'Mount Tamboritha'	CBcs CCCN CDoC CDul CMac CPLG CTrC EBee EPfP IDee LAst LRHS SLim SPoG WFar
- prostrate	MOWG WCot WGrn WPat
leucopteris	SPlb
'Mason's Hybrid'	MOWG
olivacea	LRHS
- 'Apricot Glow'	MOWG
paniculata	SPlb
'Pink Lady'	CWGN ECou ELon EPfP LRHS MOWG SCoo WFar
'Poorinda Constance'	MOWG
'Red Dragon' (v)	LRHS SLim SPtl
robusta ♀H1+3	EShb EUJe MOWG SPlb SSta WCot
'Robyn Gordon'	MOWG
'Rondeau'	CCCN LRHS MGos
rosmarinifolia ♀H3	CAbb CBcs CDoC CHll CMac CPLG CSBt CTrC CTri CWib EBee EPfP EShb GKin IDee MOWG MWat SBod SCoo SLim SLon SPer SPlb SPoG SSta WFar
- 'Desert Flame'	CPLG
- 'Jenkinsii'	CDoC CMac CPLG CSBt EBee EPfP EUJe SBfd SLim SSpi
'Scarlet Sprite'	MOWG
§ × ***semperflorens***	CTrC CWib LRHS MOWG SEND SPlb WGrn
'Spider Man'	LRHS
'Splendour'	MOWG
thelemanniana Spriggs' form	MOWG
tolminsis	see *G.* × *semperflorens*
victoriae	CDoC CTsd EBee EPfP IVic MOWG SCoo WCot WPGP
- subsp. ***victoriae***	CPLG
- yellow-flowered	LRHS
williamsonii	ECou LRHS MAsh SCoo WGrn WPat

Grewia (*Malvaceae*)

occidentalis	CDoC MOWG

Greyia (*Melianthaceae*)

sutherlandii	CTrC MOWG SGar SPlb

Grindelia (*Asteraceae*)

§ ***camporum***	CWCL SPlb WPer
chiloensis	CAbb SMad XLum
- F&W 9390	WCot
integrifolia	XLum
robusta	see *G. camporum*
stricta	CArn

Griselinia ✿ (*Griseliniaceae*)

littoralis ♀H3	Widely available
- 'Bantry Bay' (v)	CAbP CCCN CDoC CTsd CWSG EBee EHoe ELan ESwi LRHS MAsh NCGa SEND SLim SPer SPoG SWvt WFar
- 'Brodick Gold'	CPLG GKin
- 'Dixon's Cream' (v)	CBcs CCCN CMac CSBt EBee EPfP GQui IArd LRHS SGol SLim SLon SPoG
- Green Horizon = 'Whenuapai' PBR new	LBuc SLim
- 'Green Jewel' (v)	CCCN CTrC CWib ESwi NLar
- 'Luscombe's Gold'	EBee
- 'Variegata' (v) ♀H3	Widely available
ruscifolia	CMac
scandens	CCCN WSHC

guava, common see *Psidium guajava*

guava, purple or strawberry see *Psidium littorale* var. *longipes*

Gunnera ✿ (*Gunneraceae*)

chilensis see *G. tinctoria*
cordifolia CPne
dentata CPne
hamiltonii ECha EWld GAbr NBir
magellanica Widely available
- 'Muñoz Gamero' WShi
- 'Osorno' EBee MMoz
manicata ♀H3-4 Widely available
aff. ***monoica*** purple-leaved CPne
perpensa CBcs CCCN CDes EBee EWTr
prorepens CMac CPLG EBee ECha GEdr NBir SBfd WGwG WWEG
scabra see *G. tinctoria*
§ ***tinctoria*** ♀H4 CCCN CHEx CMHG CMac CPLG CWib EBee ECha EHon ELan EPfP EUJe GBin IVic LRHS NCot NLar SBfd SDix SEND SWat SWvt WFar WPGP

Gymnadenia (*Orchidaceae*)

* ***camtschatica*** f. ***alba*** LWst
conopsea ECho EFEx LWst NLAp
× ***densiflora*** NLAp
odoratissima NLAp

Gymnocarpium (*Woodsiaceae*)

dryopteris ♀H4 CLAP EFer GKev GMaP ISha LEdu MMoz MMuc NLar WAbe WFib WPtf WShi
- 'Plumosum' ♀H4 CBty CKel CLAP EBee EPfP ERod LRHS NHar NLar WFib WHal WMoo WWEG
oyamense CLAP EFer SKHP
robertianum EFer EWld

Gymnocladus (*Caesalpiniaceae*)

dioica CBcs CDul CLnd CMCN EBtc ELan EPfP LRHS MBlu MBri SHil SPer SSpi WPGP

Gymnospermium (*Berberidaceae*)

§ ***albertii*** LWst
sylvaticum LWst

Gynandriris (*Iridaceae*)

* ***sisyrinchium purpurea*** ECho

Gynerium (*Poaceae*)

argenteum see *Cortaderia selloana*

Gynostemma (*Cucurbitaceae*)

pentaphyllum CAgr
- B&SWJ 570 WCru

Gypsophila (*Caryophyllaceae*)

acutifolia EBee
aretioides ECho EPot LHop LRHS NMen NRHS
§ - 'Caucasica' CPBP ECho EPot GEdr LLHF
- 'Compacta' see *G. aretioides* 'Caucasica'
cerastioides CMea CTri ECho ECtt EDAr EPfP EWTr GAbr LBMP LHop LRHS MRav NGdn NLar NMen SMad SPlb SRms SWvt WAbe WHoo WIce WNew WPat WPer
dubia see *G. repens* 'Dubia'
fastigiata 'Silverstar' EBee LRHS LSou SHil
(Festival Series) 'Festival'PBR ECtt
- 'Festival Pink' ECtt GBee LRHS SPoG WFar
gracilescens see *G. tenuifolia*
'Jolien' (v) EBee ELan WIce
muralis 'Garden Bride' SWvt
- 'Gypsy Deep Rose' EPfP LRHS
- 'Gypsy Pink' (d) EPfP SWvt
- 'Pink Sugardot' SBch
'Pacific Rose' MRav
pacifica NBre NLar SBfd SEND WPer
paniculata EBee EPfP NBre NEgg SMrm SRms XLum
- 'Bristol Fairy' (d) ♀H4 CSBt EBee ECha ECtt ELan EPfP GMaP LRHS NLar SPoG SWvt WCAu WFar WWEG XLum
- 'Compacta Plena' (d) EBee ECtt ELan EPfP GMaP LHop MRav NDov NEgg NGdn SRms
- double white-flowered (d) XLum
- 'Fairy Perfect' EBee
- Festival Star = 'Danfestar'PBR (Festival Series) LAst
- 'Flamingo' (d) CBcs EBee ECha LHop NLar SWvt XLum
- My Pink = 'Dangypink' EBee
- 'Pacific Pink' EBee
- 'Perfekta' CBcs SPer
§ - 'Schneeflocke' (d) EBee EPfP GMaP LRHS NBre NLar SPhx SRms WWEG
- Snowflake see *G. paniculata* 'Schneeflocke'
- Summer Sparkles = 'Esm Chispa'PBR LBuc
repens ♀H4 ECtt EPfP GJos MAsh MWat SBch SPlb SWvt WFar WPer XLum
- 'Dorothy Teacher' CMea ECho ECtt LBee LRHS MAsh SBch WGor
§ - 'Dubia' ECha ECho ECtt EDAr EPot MAsh MHer MMuc NLar SEND SPoG SRms WPer WSHC
- 'Fratensis' ECho ECtt LLHF MAsh NMen WIce
- Pink Beauty see *G. repens* 'Rosa Schönheit'
§ - 'Rosa Schönheit' EBee ECha EPot LRHS NDov SPer XLum
- 'Rosea' CPBP CTri CWib EBee ECho ECtt EDAr EPfP GJos GMaP LBMP MAsh MWat NGdn SEND SPoG SRms SWvt WFar WHoo WIce XLum
- 'Silver Carpet' (v) WPer
- white-flowered CMea CWib ECho ELan EPfP LRHS NGdn SWvt WPer
§ 'Rosenschleier' (d) ♀H4 CMea EBee ECha ECtt ELan EPfP LAst MAvo MBel MCot MRav NCGa NDov NEgg NGdn SBch SPer SPoG SRms SRot SWvt WHoo WSHC WWEG XLum
I 'Rosenschleier Variegata' (v) MAvo WWEG
'Rosy Veil' see *G.* 'Rosenschleier'
§ ***tenuifolia*** EPot GMaP LBee MWat NMen
Veil of Roses see *G.* 'Rosenschleier'
'White Festival'PBR (Festival Series) (d) EBee LRHS SPoG WFar

Gyptis (*Asteraceae*)

commersonii LHop

H

Haberlea (*Gesneriaceae*)

	ferdinandi-coburgii	CLAP ECho NMen
	- 'Connie Davidson'	GEdr GKev NMen
	rhodopensis ♀H4	CDes CElw EBee ECho EDAr GEdr GKev MWat NMen NRHS NSla SRms WAbe WPGP
	- 'Virginalis'	CElw CLAP NMen NSla WThu

Habranthus ✿ (*Amaryllidaceae*)

	andersonii	see *H. tubispathus*
	brachyandrus	GCal SRms
	gracilifolius	ECho WThu
	'Hortensis' **new**	GHim
	howardii	ECho
	martinezii	CPBP ECho EPot WCot
	mexicanus **new**	ECho
§	***robustus*** ♀H1	CCCN CPLG CPne EBee ECho EPot EShb ITim LAma LHop SEND WCot WHil WPGP
§	***tubispathus*** ♀H1	CYeo EBee ECho EDif EPot GCal WCot WHil

Hacquetia (*Apiaceae*)

	epipactis ♀H4	Widely available
§	- 'Thor' (v)	CLAP EHrv EWes GEdr LLHF MAvo NChi NMen SUsu WAbe WCot WFar WPGP
	- 'Variegata'	see *H. epipactis* 'Thor'

Haemanthus (*Amaryllidaceae*)

	albiflos ♀H1	CHEx CPne CPrp CSpe CTca ECho EOHP EShb LAma SRms SWal WCot
	amarylloides subsp. ***polyanthes***	ECho
	barkerae	ECho
	carneus	ECho
	coccineus ♀H1	CLak ECho
	crispus	ECho
	humilis	ECho
	kalbreyeri	see *Scadoxus multiflorus* subsp. *multiflorus*
	katherinae	see *Scadoxus multiflorus* subsp. *katherinae*
	lanceifolius	ECho
	montanus	ECho
	natalensis	see *Scadoxus puniceus*
	pauculifolius	ECho
	pubescens subsp. ***leipoldtii***	ECho
	sanguineus	ECho

Hagenia (*Rosaceae*)

	abyssinica **new**	LEdu

Hakea (*Proteaceae*)

§	***drupacea***	CBcs CTrC
	epiglottis	CTrC ECou
	laurina	SPlb
	lissocarpha	CTrC
§	***lissosperma***	CDoC ECou EPfP SPlb WPGP
	microcarpa	ECou
	nodosa	CCCN
	platysperma	SPlb
§	***salicifolia***	CCCN SPlb WCot
	- 'Gold Medal' (v)	CTrC
	saligna	see *H. salicifolia*
	sericea misapplied	see *H. lissosperma*
	sericea Schrad. & J.C.Wendl.	ECou WCot
	- pink-flowered	SPlb WCot
	suaveolens	see *H. drupacea*
	teretifolia	CTrC
	victoriae **new**	SPlb

Hakonechloa ✿ (*Poaceae*)

	macra	CEnt CGHE CKno CMac CSam EBee EHoe EPPr EShb GCal MAsh MAvo MMoz MRav NDov NOak SApp SMad SPhx SPoG WPGP WSHC
§	- 'Alboaurea' (v) ♀H4	CBcs CHVG CKno CPLG CWGN EBee ELan EPfP LAst LRHS LSRN MGos MMuc NCGa NPla NRHS SAga SApp SEND SHil SUsu WFar
	- 'Albovariegata' (v)	CKno CWan EPPr GCal LEdu MAsh MAvo
	- 'All Gold'	CKno EBee EPPr EWes LEdu MAsh SMad SPoG WCot
	- 'Aureola' ♀H4	Widely available
*	- 'Mediopicta' (v)	SApp
	- 'Mediovariegata' (v)	CGHE CWCL EBee EPPr WPGP
	- 'Naomi' (v)	EBee EPfP LRHS SPer
	- 'Nicolas'	CSam CSpe EBee ECtt ELon EPfP EWes GBin IBoy LLHF LRHS LSRN LSou MAvo MBel MCot NLBP SMad SMrm SPad SPer SPoG WCot WWEG
	- 'Samurai' (v) **new**	CKno
	- 'Stripe It Rich' (v)	EWes MAsh SBfd SGol
	- 'Variegata'	see *H. macra* 'Alboaurea'

Halesia (*Styracaceae*)

§	***carolina***	Widely available
	- Monticola Group	CBcs CCVT CDul CMCN EBee ELan EPfP GBin IVic LRHS MAsh MMuc NLar NRHS SEND SPer SPoG SSpi SWvt WMou
I	- - 'Variegata' (v) **new**	SSta
	- UConn = 'Wedding Bells'	CJun MBlu SKHP
	- Vestita Group ♀H4	CDoC CDul CJun CTho EBee EPfP LRHS MAsh MBlu MGos MRav NLar SPer SPoG SSpi SSta WGob WPat
	- - 'Rosea'	CBcs CJun EPfP MBlu SKHP
	diptera	MBlu NEgg SKHP
	- Magniflora Group	CJun EPfP MBlu
	tetraptera	see *H. carolina*

× *Halimiocistus* (*Cistaceae*)

	algarvensis	see *Halimium ocymoides*
§	'Ingwersenii'	CBcs CDoC ECho ELan EWes LRHS SBfd SPer SRms
	revolii misapplied	see × *H. sahucii*
§	***sahucii*** ♀H4	CBcs CDoC CSBt CTri EBee ECha ELan EPfP EUJe LBMP LRHS LTen MAsh MBNS MRav MSwo MWat NPri NRHS SBfd SEND SPer SPoG SPtl SRms SWvt WFar
	- Ice Dancer = 'Ebhals'PBR (v)	CDoC EBee EPfP LAst MAsh SBfd SPer SWvt
	'Susan'	see *Halimium* 'Susan'
§	***wintonensis*** ♀H3	CBcs CDoC EBee ELan EPfP GMaP LRHS MAsh SLon SPer SRms WHar WSHC

§	– 'Merrist Wood Cream' ♀H3	CBcs CDoC CMac CSBt EBee ELan EPfP LAst LRHS LSRN MAsh MRav MSwo NBir SBfd SEND SLim SPer SPoG SSpi SWvt WFar WPat WSHC

Halimium (Cistaceae)

§	***calycinum***	CDoC EBee ELan EPfP IVic LRHS MAsh MBri MMuc NPri SBfd SCoo SEND SHil SLim SPer SPoG SWvt WAbe WCFE WGob
	commutatum	see *H. calycinum*
N	***halimifolium*** misapplied	see *H.* × *pauanum*
§	***lasianthum*** ♀H3	CBcs CMac CSBt CWib ELan EPfP LPot LRHS MRav SBfd SLim WKif
	– 'Concolor'	CWib EBee LRHS MAsh MSwo SWvt
	– subsp. ***formosum*** 'Sandling'	EBee ELan EPfP LRHS MAsh MMuc SLon SRms
	libanotis	see *H. calycinum*
§	***ocymoides*** ♀H3	CBcs CDoC CWib ELan EPfP IVic LRHS MSwo WHar WKif
§	× ***pauanum***	LRHS MMuc SEND
§	'Susan' ♀H3	CDoC ELan EPfP GKev LRHS MMHG SCoo SLim SPer SPoG WAbe
§	***umbellatum***	EPfP LHop MMuc SEND SPer
	wintonense	see × *Halimiocistus wintonensis*

Halimodendron (Papilionaceae)

halodendron	CArn CBcs CDul EBee MBlu SPer

Halleria (Stilbaceae)

lucida	CCCN EBee

Halocarpus (Podocarpaceae)

§	***bidwillii***	CDoC ECou

Haloragis (Haloragaceae)

erecta	SPlb XLum
– 'Rubra'	WCot WPer
– 'Wellington Bronze'	CEnt CPLG CSpe EBee ECtt EHoe LEdu LRHS MLHP WHer WMoo XLum

Hamamelis ✿ (Hamamelidaceae)

	'Amethyst'	CJun NLar SGol SPtl
	'Brevipetala'	CBcs CJun NLar
	'Danny'	CJun NLar
	'Dishi'	CJun
	'Doerak'	CJun MBlu
	'Fire Blaze'	CJun
	'Girard Orange'	EPfP
	× ***intermedia*** 'Advent'	CJun NLar
	– 'Angelly' ♀H4	CJun IVic MBlu MBri NLar SBir SGol
	– 'Aphrodite' ♀H4	CJun EPfP IVic LRHS MAsh MBlu MBri MGos MRav NCGa NLar SBir SEND SHil
	– 'Arnhem' **new**	NLar
	– 'Arnold Promise' ♀H4	Widely available
	– 'Aurora' ♀H4	CJun LRHS MBlu MBri MMuc NHol NLar NRHS SEND
	– 'Barmstedt Gold' ♀H4	CJun EBee EPfP IVic LRHS LSRN MAsh MGos NLar SHil SPoG SReu
	– 'Bernstein'	CJun IVic
	– 'Birgit'	NLar
	– 'Carmine Red'	CJun CMac NLar
	– 'Copper Beauty'	see *H.* × *intermedia* 'Jelena'
	– 'Cyrille' **new**	MMuc NLar SEND
	– 'Diane' ♀H4	Widely available
§	– 'Feuerzauber'	CMac CSBt CTri EBee LBuc NLar SPer SPtl
	– Fire Cracker	see *H.* × *intermedia* 'Feuerzauber'
	– 'Frederic'	CJun EPfP LRHS MAsh SBir
	– 'Gimborn's Perfume'	NLar
	– 'Gingerbread'	CJun EBee EPfP LRHS MAsh MWat NLar SPtl
	– 'Glowing Embers'	CJun LRHS MAsh
	– 'Harlow Carr'	LRHS
	– 'Harry'	CJun IVic LRHS MAsh MBri NLar SBir
	– 'Heinrich Bruns'	CJun
§	– 'Jelena' ♀H4	Widely available
	– 'Limelight'	CJun MBlu NLar
	– 'Livia'	CJun EPfP LRHS MAsh MBri NLar SBir SCoo SSpi
	– Magic Fire	see *H.* × *intermedia* 'Feuerzauber'
	– 'Moonlight'	CJun NLar
	– 'Nina'	EPfP LRHS MAsh MWat NHol NLar SBir
	– 'Ninotchka'	CJun
	– 'Old Copper'	NLar
	– 'Orange Beauty'	CBcs EBee LRHS MBlu SBod SCoo SGol
	– 'Orange Peel'	CJun EPfP LLHF LRHS MAsh MBri NLar SBir SSta
	– 'Ostergold'	CJun NLar
	– 'Pallida' ♀H4	Widely available
	– 'Primavera'	CJun CWSG IArd NLar NPCo
	– 'Ripe Corn'	CJun EBee EPfP LRHS MAsh MBri SPoG
	– 'Robert'	CJun EPfP LRHS MAsh MBri
	– 'Rubin'	CJun EPfP LRHS MAsh MBri MGos NLar NRHS SCoo SPoG
	– 'Rubinstar'	CJun
	– 'Ruby Glow'	CBcs CMac CWGN CWib EBee LSRN MGos NLar NPCo NWea SBfd SCoo SLim SPer
	– 'Savill Starlight'	CJun
	– 'Spanish Spider'	MBlu NLar
	– 'Strawberries and Cream'	CJun NLar
	– 'Sunburst'	CJun LRHS NLar SGol SHil
	– 'Twilight'	CJun NLar
	– 'Vesna' ♀H4	CJun CMac EPfP LRHS MAsh MBlu MGos MWat NLar NRHS SBir SCoo SPoG
	– 'Westerstede'	CJun CWSG EBee EPfP IArd LSRN MGos NHol NLar NPla NWea SBfd SCoo SEWo SGol SLim WHar
	– 'Wiero'	CJun NLar
	– 'Zitronenjette'	CJun
	japonica	WFar
	– 'Pendula'	CJun MBlu NLar
	– 'Rubra'	NPCo
	– 'Zuccariniana'	NLar
	mollis ♀H4	Widely available
	– 'Boskoop'	CJun NLar
	– 'Coombe Wood'	CJun
	– 'Goldcrest'	CJun
	– 'Imperialis'	CJun
	– 'Iwado'	CJun
	– 'Jermyns Gold' ♀H4	CJun LRHS SHil
	– 'Kort's Yellow'	CJun
	– 'Wisley Supreme'	CJun ELan EPfP LLHF LRHS MAsh MBri NRHS SGol SSpi
	'Rochester'	CJun NLar NPCo
	vernalis 'Lombarts' Weeping'	NLar

	- purple	MBlu NLar
	- 'Sandra' ♀H4	CBcs CMCN ELan EPfP LRHS MAsh MBlu MGos MRav MWat NLar SLon SPer SPoG SReu
	virginiana	CAgr GPoy IDee MMuc NWea SEND
	- 'Mohonk Red'	CJun

Hamelia (*Rubiaceae*)

	patens	CCCN

Hanabusaya (*Campanulaceae*)

§	***asiatica***	EWTr NCGa NChi

Haplocarpha (*Asteraceae*)

	rueppellii	NBro SRms SRot

Haplopappus (*Asteraceae*)

	coronopifolius	see *H. glutinosus*
§	***glutinosus***	ECha ECho ECtt GEdr MMuc NLar SPlb SRms
	lyallii	see *Tonestus lyallii*
	prunelloides	NGBo
	var. ***mustersii***	
	- - F&W 9384	WCot
	rehderi	EBee GJos MWat

Hardenbergia (*Papilionaceae*)

	comptoniana ♀H1	CPLG WCot
	- shrubby	CSpe
	violacea ♀H1	CCCN CHll CRHN CSpe ELan IDee LRHS MHer SEND SHil SLim SPer WCot
	- f. ***alba***	CHll ECou LRHS SEND
	- - 'White Crystal'	SPer
	- - 'White Wanderer'	CCCN
	- dwarf	ECou
	- 'Happy Wanderer'	CCCN EBee LRHS MOWG SChF SPoG
	- f. ***rosea***	CCCN EBee LRHS SPer

Harpephyllum (*Anacardiaceae*)

	caffrum (F)	XBlo

Hastingsia (*Asparagaceae*)

	alba	WSHC

Haworthia ✿ (*Asphodelaceae*)

	attenuata	EShb
	'Black Prince'	EPfP EShb SBch
	cymbiformis	EPfP
	fasciata	EPfP SEND SWal
	glabrata var. ***concolor***	EPfP EShb
	pumila ♀H1	SEND
	radula	EPfP
	tesselata	see *H. venosa* subsp. *tesselata*
§	***venosa***	SEND
	subsp. ***tesselata*** ♀H1	

hazelnut see *Corylus*

Hebe ✿ (*Plantaginaceae*)

	albicans ♀H4	CMac ELan EPfP GKin LAst LPot LRHS LSRN MAsh MBri MGos MRav NPri NWea SBfd SCoo SHil SLim SPer SPoG SRms SWal SWvt WFar XLum
	- prostrate	see *H. albicans* 'Snow Cover'
*	- 'Snow Carpet'	CCCN LRHS
§	- 'Snow Cover'	EWes LRHS
	- 'Snow Drift'	see *H. albicans* 'Snow Cover'
	- 'Snow Mound'	SHea
§	'Alicia Amherst'	CDoy LRHS SHea SPer SRms SWal WCFE
	'Amanda Cook' (v)	NPer SGol SPoG
	'Amethyst'	SBfd SHea
§	'Amy'	ELon LRHS NPer SCoo SLim SPer SWvt
	× ***andersonii***	EPfP LRHS SHea
§	- 'Andersonii Variegata' (v)	LRHS SBfd SRms
	- 'Argenteovariegata'	see *H.* × *andersonii* 'Andersonii Variegata'
	'Andressa Paula'	CCCN LRHS
	'Anna'	EPfP
	anomala misapplied	see *H.* 'Imposter'
	anomala (Armstr.) Cockayne	LRHS SHea
§	***armstrongii***	ECho
	'Arthur'	ECou
	'Autumn Glory'	CSBt CWSG ELan EPfP LAst LRHS MAsh MGos MLHP MSwo NBir NPri SBfd SCob SGol SLim SPer SPlb SPoG SWvt XLum
	'Autumn Joy'	SWvt
	azurea	see *H. venustula*
	'Azurens'	see *H.* 'Maori Gem'
	'Baby Blush' PBR	LRHS SLim
	'Baby Boo' (v) **new**	LRHS SLon
	'Baby Marie'	CAbP CAbb CSBt ECho ECou ELan ELon EPfP GKin LBMP LBuc LRHS LSRN MGos MSwo NLar NMen NPer SBfd SCoo SLim SPoG SRGP SRms SRot SWvt
	'Beatrice'	SHea
	'Beverley Hills' PBR	CSBt ECrN LRHS WHar
	'Bicolor Wand'	CCCN CTsd LRHS SHea
	bishopiana	ECou EPfP
	'Black Beauty'	LBuc LRHS SLim
	'Black Knight' **new**	LRHS SLim
	'Black Panther'	ELon
	'Blue Clouds' ♀H3	LAst LHop LLHF LRHS MSwo SPer WCFE
§	'Blue Gem'	CTrC SBfd SLim
	'Blue Shamrock'	SWvt
	Blue Star = 'Vergeer 1' PBR	EPfP LRHS MAsh NLar SLon SPoG
	'Bluebell'	SHea
	'Blush Wand'	SHea
	'Blushing Bride' (v)	LRHS SLim
	bollonsii	SHea
	'Boscawenii'	ECre SHea WHer
	'Bouquet' PBR	NEgg
§	'Bowles's Hybrid'	CCCN LRHS MRav MSwo SBod SEND SHea SRms
	brachysiphon	CTrC CTri MRav SEND SHea SPer SRms
	'Bracken Hill' **new**	SHea
	brevifolia	LRHS SLim
	breviracemosa	SHea
	Bronze Glow = 'Lowglo'	LRHS
	'Bronzy Baby' PBR (v)	SPoG
	buchananii	ECho EPot MHer NPer
§	- 'Fenwickii'	ECho
	- 'Minima'	ECho EPot
	- 'Minor' Hort N.Z.	ECho GBin NBir
	buxifolia misapplied	see *H. odora*
	buxifolia (Benth.) Andersen	CMac ELan LHop MMuc NWea SEND SWal WHar XLum
	'C.P. Raffill'	SHea

§	'Caledonia' 🏆H3	CCCN CSBt EPfP GKev LBMP LRHS LSRN MAsh MBri MGos NPer NPri SBfd SCoo SHea SLim SPoG SRms SWvt WHoo XLum
	'Candy'	SHea
§	***canterburiensis***	ECou
N	'Carl Teschner'	see *H.* 'Youngii'
	'Carnea'	SHea
	'Carnea Variegata' (v)	EPfP EShb LRHS MSCN SLim SPer SPoG
	carnosula	NBir SPer WHar
	catarractae	see *Parahebe catarractae*
	'Celine'	LBuc LRHS SBfd SRGP
	'Champagne'	CCCN EPfP LAst LPot LRHS LSRN NLar NWad SBfd SCoo SEND SLim XLum
	Champion = 'Champseiont' PBR	LRHS LTen MSwo SCoo
	'Charming White'	LRHS LSRN SBfd
	chathamica	ECou LRHS
	'Christabel'	LRHS
	'Clear Skies' PBR	ECou LRHS NEgg SLim
	'Colwall'	ECho
	'Conwy Knight'	SRms WAbe
	corriganii	SHea
	corstorphinensis	SHea
	'County Park'	ECou EWes SWal
	'Cranleighensis'	CTsd SBfd SHea
	'Cupins'	SWal
	cupressoides	IRar LRHS MSCN SEND
	- 'Boughton Dome'	CTri ECho EPfP MAsh MCot MGos MHer NMen SWal WAbe WHoo WPer
	darwiniana	see *H. glaucophylla*
	'Dazzler' (v)	CAbP
	decumbens	EWes
	'Denise'	LRHS
	'Diamond'	LRHS LSRN SLon
	dieffenbachii	SHea
	diosmifolia	CAbb CDoC EPfP LRHS SHea SLim
	- 'Wairua Beauty' **new**	SLim
	divaricata	ECou SHea
*	- 'Marlborough'	ECou
	- 'Nelson'	ECou
	'Dorothy Peach'	see *H.* 'Watson's Pink'
	'E.B. Anderson'	see *H.* 'Caledonia'
	'Eclipse' **new**	LAst
	'Edington'	LRHS SPer WCFE
	'Ellie'	LRHS
	elliptica	ECou SBfd SHea
	- 'Anatoki'	SHea
	- 'Charleston'	SHea
	- 'Kapiti'	ECou
	- 'Variegata'	see *H.* 'Silver Queen'
	'Emerald Dome'	see *H.* 'Emerald Gem'
§	'Emerald Gem' 🏆H3	CMac CTrC CTri ECho EPfP EShb LRHS LSRN MAsh MBri MGos MHer MMuc MSwo NLar SBfd SEND SHil SPer SPlb SPoG
	'Emerald Green'	see *H.* 'Emerald Gem'
	epacridea	EWes
§	'Eveline'	CSBt CTri LRHS NBir SLim SPer
	evenosa	SHea
	'Eversley Seedling'	see *H.* 'Bowles's Hybrid'
	'Fairfieldii'	EOHP IRar WPat
	'First Light' PBR	CWSG LRHS NPri SGol SRms WHar
	'Fragrant Jewel'	CAbP CWib LRHS SEND SLim SPhx
	× ***franciscana***	ECou SHea
	- 'Blue Gem' ambig.	ELan EPfP LRHS MRav NBir NPer SBfd SEND SGol SPer SPlb SPoG SRms SWal WHar
	- 'Lavender Queen'	LRHS SHea
	- 'Purple Tips' misapplied	see *H. speciosa* 'Variegata'
	- 'Variegata'	see *H.* 'Silver Queen'
I	- 'White Gem'	SRms
	- yellow-variegated (v)	SPer
	'Franjo'	ECou
	'Frozen Flame' (v)	ELan LBuc LRHS SPoG
	Garden Beauty Blue = 'Cliv' PBR	LBuc LRHS SLim SRms
	Garden Beauty Pink = 'Lowink'	LBuc SLim SRms
	Garden Beauty Purple = 'Nold' PBR	LBuc LRHS SLim
	'Garden Elegance Blue'	LBuc LRHS NPri SLim
	'Garden Elegance Blush'	LRHS
	'Garden Elegance Pastel'	LBuc SLim
	'Garden Elegance Pink'	LBuc NPri SLim
	'Garden Elegance Purple'	LBuc SLim
	'Garden Elegance Rose'	LBuc SLim
	'Gauntlettii'	see *H.* 'Eveline'
	'Gibby'	LRHS
§	***glaucophylla***	SHea
	- 'Clarence'	ECou
	- 'Joan Hunwick' **new**	SHea
I	'Glaucophylla Variegata' (v)	CTri EPfP LRHS NBir SCoo SLim SPer
	'Gnome'	LRHS
	'Godefroyana'	see *H. pinguifolia* 'Godefroyana'
	'Goethe'	SEND
	'Gold Beauty' (v)	LBuc LRHS NPri SLim SPoG
	'Golden Nugget'	LRHS
	'Goldrush' PBR (v)	LBuc SPoG
	gracillima	SHea
	'Gran's Favourite'	LRHS LSRN
	'Great Orme' 🏆H3	CDul CSBt CWib ECou ECrN ELan EPfP LAst LRHS LSRN MAsh MGos MRav MSwo NPer SBfd SEND SLim SPer SPlb SPoG SRms SWvt WAbe WSFF
	'Green Globe'	see *H.* 'Emerald Gem'
	'Greensleeves'	LRHS
	'Grethe'	SPoG
	'Hadspen Pink'	LRHS
	'Hagley Park'	LRHS SAga SWal
§	'Hartii'	EPfP LRHS MRav SBfd SLim
	'Headfortii'	SHea
	'Heartbreaker' PBR (v)	CWSG ELan EPfP LAst LBuc LRHS MAsh MGos NLar NPri SBfd SCoo SLim SPoG SPtl SWvt
	'Heidi'	SHea
	'Hidcote'	LRHS SLim
	'Hielan Lassie'	LRHS SHea
	'Highdown Pink' **new**	SHea
	'Highdownensis'	LRHS
	'Hinderwell'	NPer
	hulkeana 🏆H3	LRHS LSou MHer SAga SUsu WAbe WKif
§	'Imposter'	SRms
	'Inspiration'	LRHS SHea
	insularis	ECou
	'James Stirling'	see *H. ochracea* 'James Stirling'
	'Jane Holden'	LRHS
	'Joanna'	ECou
§	'Johny Day'	LRHS
	'Judy'	LRHS

	Name	Suppliers
	'Karo Golden Esk'	EPfP LRHS
	'Kirkii'	CDul EPfP LAst NLar SBfd SHea SPer SWal XLum
	'Knightshayes'	see *H.* 'Caledonia'
	'La Favorite' **new**	SHea
	'La Séduisante'	CTri ECou LRHS SEND SHea SRms
	'Lady Ann' PBR (v)	CSBt CWSG EPfP LRHS NEgg NLar NPri SPoG WHar
	'Lady Ardilaun'	see *H.* 'Amy'
	laevis	see *H. venustula*
	latifolia	see *H.* 'Blue Gem'
	'Lavender Spray'	see *H.* 'Hartii'
	leiophylla	SHea
	Leopard = 'Lowand' **new**	LRHS
	'Lewisii'	SHea
	'Lilac Wand'	CTsd SHea
	'Lindsayi'	ECou LRHS SHea
	'Lisa'	EPfP
	'Lopen' (v)	ECou
	lyallii	see *Parahebe lyallii*
	lycopodioides	EWes
	- 'Aurea'	see *H. armstrongii*
	'Lynash'	LRHS
	mackenii	see *H.* 'Emerald Gem'
	macrantha ♀H3	LRHS SDix SPer SRms WAbe
	macrocarpa	ECou LRHS
	- var. ***latisepala***	ECou LRHS SLim
	- var. ***macrocarpa***	SLim
	'Magic Summer'	LBuc LRHS
§	'Maori Gem'	SBfd
	'Margery Fish'	see *H.* 'Primley Gem'
	'Margret' PBR ♀H4	CSBt CWCL EPfP LAst LBMP LRHS LSRN MAsh MBrN MGos NPri SBfd SCoo SHea SLim SPer SPoG SRGP SRms
	'Marie Antoinette'	LRHS
	'Marjorie'	CDul CMac CTrC ELan EPfP LAst LRHS LSRN MGos MSwo NLar NPer NWea SBfd SBod SPer SPoG SRms SWvt
	matthewsii	MAsh
	'Mauve Queen'	LRHS
	'Mauvena'	SPer
	'McKean'	see *H.* 'Emerald Gem'
	'Megan'	ECou
	'Mercury'	ECou
	'Mette'	LLHF
	Midnight Sky = 'Lowten' PBR	LBuc LRHS NPri SCoo SLim SPoG SPtl
	'Midsummer Beauty' ♀H3	CWCL ECou EPfP LAst LRHS LSRN MGos MLHP MRav NBir SBfd SEND SHea SLim SPer SPlb SPoG SRms SWvt WHar WSFF XLum
	'Milmont Emerald'	see *H.* 'Emerald Gem'
	'Miss Fittall'	SHea
§	'Mohawk' PBR	SWal
*	'Moppets Hardy'	SPer
	'Mrs E. Tennant' **new**	SHea
§	'Mrs Winder' ♀H4	Widely available
	'Mystery'	ECou SWal
	'Nantyderry'	LRHS SGar SHea
§	'Neil's Choice' ♀H4	ECou ELon LRHS SHea SWal
	'Neopolitan'	LRHS SLim
	'New Zealand'	XLum
	'Nicola's Blush' ♀H4	CCVN CSBt ECou ELon EPfP EShb LAst LRHS LSRN MCot MGos MMuc MRav MWat NBir NCot NLar NWad SBfd SCoo SEND SGol SPer SPoG SRGP SRms SWvt WGwG WKif

	Name	Suppliers
	ochracea	LRHS SWal
§	- 'James Stirling' ♀H4	CBcs CMac CSBt ECho ELan EPfP EShb GKin LRHS LSRN LTen MAsh MBri MGos MSwo NBir NLar NPri NWad SBfd SCoo SLim SPer SPlb SPoG SWvt
	'Oddity'	LRHS
§	***odora***	CTrC ECou EPfP
I	- 'Nana'	EPfP
	- 'New Zealand Gold'	LRHS MAsh MMuc SCoo SEND SWal
	- 'Summer Frost'	LRHS
	'Oratia Beauty' ♀H4	LRHS MRav NLar SEND SLim
	'Orphan Annie' PBR (v)	CWSG LRHS LSRN SPoG
	parviflora misapplied	see *H.* 'Bowles's Hybrid'
	parviflora (Vahl) Cockayne	see *H. stenophylla*
	& Allan var. ***angustifolia***	
	- 'Holdsworth'	LRHS
	- 'Palmerston'	SHea
	'Pascal' ♀H4	ELan EPfP LRHS LSRN MBri MGos SBfd SCoo SLim SLon SPer SPoG SRms SWvt
	'Pastel Elegance'	LRHS
	'Patti Dossett'	see *H. speciosa* 'Patti Dossett'
	pauciramosa	GCal SRms
	'Pearl of Paradise' PBR	SPoG
	perfoliata	see *Parahebe perfoliata*
	'Perry's Rubyleaf'	NPer
	'Petra's Pink'	CCCN LRHS SLim
	'Pewter Dome' ♀H4	CMac CSBt ECou EHoe EPfP LHop LRHS MGos MRav SBfd SDix SHea SPer SRms SWal SWvt WPer
	pimeleoides	ECou
	- 'Glauca'	NPer SGol
	- 'Glaucocaerulea'	ECou
	- 'Quicksilver' ♀H4	CAbP CSBt CTri ECou EDAr ELan EPfP LAst LRHS LSRN MGos MMuc MRav MSwo NBir NPer SBfd SCoo SLim SPer SWal WHar WPat
	pinguifolia	ECou SPlb
	- 'Dobson'	LRHS
§	- 'Godefroyana'	SWal
	- 'Golden Fleece' **new**	LBuc
	- 'Pagei' ♀H4	Widely available
	- 'Sutherlandii'	CBcs CDoC CDul ECho LRHS LSRN LTen MGos NWea SCoo SHea SWvt WFar
	'Pink Elegance'	LRHS
	'Pink Elephant' (v) ♀H3	ELan LBMP LBuc LRHS MAsh MWat NLar NPri SBfd SLim SPoG
	'Pink Fantasy'	LRHS MRav
	'Pink Goddess'	LRHS SRGP
	'Pink Lady' PBR	SGol SPoG
	'Pink Paradise' PBR	CAbP ELan EPfP LRHS SPoG SRms
	'Pink Payne'	see *H.* 'Eveline'
	'Pink Pixie'	LBuc MBri MGos SCoo
	'Pink Princess'	LRHS
	'Pink Wand'	CTsd SHea
	'Porlock Purple'	see *Parahebe catarractae* 'Delight'
	'Pretty in Pink'	LRHS
§	'Primley Gem'	LRHS
	propinqua	NMen
I	'Prostrata'	CSBt
	'Purple Elegance'	LRHS
	'Purple Emperor'	see *H.* 'Neil's Choice'
	'Purple Paradise' PBR	LRHS MBri NEgg SPoG
	'Purple Picture'	ELon
	'Purple Pixie' PBR	see *H.* 'Mohawk'

	Name	Suppliers
	'Purple Princess'	LRHS SGol
	'Purple Queen'	ELan EPfP EShb LRHS MCot SPoG
	Purple Shamrock = 'Neprock'PBR (v)	EPfP LAst LBuc LRHS LSRN MBri MGos MWat NEgg NLar SBfd SCoo SLim SPer SPoG SRms SWvt WHar
	'Purple Tips' misapplied	see *H. speciosa* 'Variegata'
	'Rachel'	LRHS LSRN SLon
§	***rakaiensis*** ♀H4	Widely available
	- 'Golden Dome'	see *H. rakaiensis*
	raoulii	WAbe
	Raspberry Ripple = 'Tullyraspb'PBR **new**	LBuc
	'Raven'	LRHS
	recurva	CSam CTri EPfP LPot LRHS MCot MGos MMuc SHea SRms SWal
	- 'Boughton Silver' ♀H3	ELan LRHS SEND SLim
	'Red Edge' ♀H4	Widely available
	'Red Ruth'	see *H.* 'Eveline'
	'Reine des Blanches' **new**	SHea
	rigidula	LRHS MMuc SEND SWal
	'Ronda'	ECou
	'Rose Elegance'	LRHS
	'Rosie'PBR	CSBt LAst LRHS LSRN NMen SCoo SPer SWvt
	'Royal Blue'	LRHS SLim
	'Royal Purple'	see *H.* 'Alicia Amherst'
	salicifolia	CCCN CMac CTca ECou ELan EPfP LAst LRHS MGos MRav NWad SBfd SEND SPer SPlb SRms WGwG XLum
	'Sandra Joy'	LRHS
	'Sapphire' ♀H4	ECou EPfP LRHS MAsh MGos NPri SBfd SCoo SHea SLim SRms SWal SWvt
	'Sarana'	LRHS
	'Shiraz'	LRHS
	'Silver Dollar' (v)	CAbP CCCN CMac CSBt ELan LRHS LTen MGos MMuc NEgg NWad SLim SPer SPoG SRms SWal
§	'Silver Queen' (v) ♀H2	CSBt ECou ELan EPfP EShb LRHS MAsh MGos MRav NEgg NLar NPer SBfd SEND SPer SPoG SRms
	'Simon Délaux'	ECou LRHS SEND SLim
I	'Southlandii'	ECho LAst MWhi SGol
	speciosa	SHea
	- 'Johny Day'	see *H.* 'Johny Day'
§	- 'Patti Dossett'	LRHS
	- 'Rangatira'	ECou
§	- 'Variegata' (v)	LRHS NPer
	'Spender's Seedling' misapplied	see *H. stenophylla*
	'Spender's Seedling' ambig.	MCot MMuc MSCN
	'Spender's Seedling' Hort.	ECou LRHS MRav SEND SHea SPoG SRms
	'Spring Glory'	LRHS
§	***stenophylla***	EShb SBfd SDix SEND
	stricta	ECou LRHS
	- var. ***egmontiana***	LRHS
	- var. ***macroura***	SHea
	- var. ***stricta*** **new**	SHea
	'Stuart Fraser'	SWal
	subalpina	CSBt ECho LTen SHea
	'Summer Blue'	LRHS MRav
	'Super Red'	CSBt LRHS SBfd SLim
	'Sweet Kim' (v)	CMac LBuc LRHS SLim SPoG
	'Tina'	ECou
	'Tom Marshall'	see *H. canterburiensis*
	topiaria ♀H4	CAbP CSBt CSam ECho ECou EPfP GCal LAst LHop LRHS LTen MBrN MMuc MRav MSwo NBir SBfd SCoo SEND SPer SPoG SWal WGwG
	- 'Doctor Favier'	LRHS SRms
	townsonii	ECou LHop LRHS
	traversii	ECou SHea SRms
	- 'Mason River'	ECou
	- 'Woodside'	ECou
	'Tricolor'	see *H. speciosa* 'Variegata'
	'Trixie'	ECou LRHS
	'Twisty'	ELan LRHS
	'Valentino'PBR	LHop LRHS NEgg SCoo SLim
	'Veitchii'	see *H.* 'Alicia Amherst'
§	***venustula***	ECou IArd LRHS MMuc SEND
	- 'Patricia Davies'	ECou
	vernicosa ♀H3	CDul ECho EPfP LRHS MGos MHer NWad SBfd SCoo SPer SPlb SRot SWvt WAbe
	'Violet Wand'	LRHS SHea
	'Vogue'	LRHS
	'Waikiki'	see *H.* 'Mrs Winder'
§	'Warley'	LRHS
	'Warley Pink'	LRHS
	'Warleyensis'	see *H.* 'Warley'
§	'Watson's Pink'	LRHS SHea SPer WKif
	'White Gem' (*brachysiphon* hybrid) ♀H4	CWCL LRHS NPer SEND SHea SPer SWal WFar
	'White Heather'	EPfP LRHS NBir SBfd SHea
	'White Paradise'PBR	SPoG
	'Wild Romance' **new**	LBuc
	'Willcoxii'	see *H. buchananii* 'Fenwickii'
	'Wingletye' ♀H3	CCCN ECou LRHS WAbe WGwG WPer XLum
	'Winter Glow'	CCCN LRHS SBfd SCoo
	'Wiri Blush'	LRHS SLim SWvt
	'Wiri Charm'	CAbP CBcs CMac CSBt ECrN ELon EPfP LAst LHop LRHS MGos MSwo NEgg SBfd SEND SHea SLim SPoG SWal
	'Wiri Cloud' ♀H3	CBcs CMac EPfP LRHS MGos MMuc MSwo SBfd SEND
	'Wiri Dawn' ♀H3	ELan EPfP EWes LRHS MGos SBfd SLim SWvt
	'Wiri Desire'	CCCN LRHS
	'Wiri Gem'	LRHS SLim
	'Wiri Icing Sugar'	LRHS
	'Wiri Image'	CBcs CSBt EPfP LRHS MRav SEND SPoG
	'Wiri Joy'	LRHS SEND SPoG
	'Wiri Mist'	CBcs CTrC LRHS SBfd SCoo SPoG SWal XLum
	'Wiri Prince'	CTrC LRHS
	'Wiri Splash'	CTrC EPfP LRHS SGol SPoG
	'Wiri Vision'	CSBt LRHS SEND
	'Wiri Vogue' **new**	LRHS SLim
§	'Youngii' ♀H3-4	CMac CSBt CTri ELan EPfP GKin LAst LBMP LPot LRHS MAsh MGos MHer MRav MWat NBir NMen NPri SBfd SEND SGol SLim SPer SPlb SPoG SRms SWvt WCFE WHoo

Hebenstretia (*Scrophulariaceae*)

	Name	Suppliers
	dura	CPBP
	- 'Jeanie'	SGar
*	***quinquinervis***	LSou

Hechtia (*Bromeliaceae*)

	Name	Suppliers
	texensis **new**	EGri

Hedeoma (*Lamiaceae*)

	Name	Suppliers
	ciliolata new	WAbe
	hyssopifolia	SPhx

Hedera ✿ (*Araliaceae*)

	Name	Suppliers
§	***algeriensis***	CDoC WFib
	- 'Bellecour'	WFib XLum
§	- 'Gloire de Marengo' (v) ♀H3	Widely available
§	- 'Gloire de Marengo' arborescent (v)	SPer
	- 'Marginomaculata' (v) ♀H3	CDoC EPfP EShb LRHS MAsh SBfd SMad WCot WFib
	- 'Montgomery'	LRHS LSRN MWht SBfd
	- 'Ravensholst' ♀H3	CMac EShb MRav SGol WFib
§	***azorica***	EShb WFar WFib
	- 'Pico'	EShb WFib
	- 'Variegata' (v)	WCot
	canariensis misapplied	see *H. algeriensis*
	- var. ***azorica***	see *H. azorica*
	- 'Cantabrian'	see *H. maroccana* 'Spanish Canary'
	- 'Gloire de Marengo'	see *H. algeriensis* 'Gloire de Marengo'
	- 'Variegata'	see *H. algeriensis* 'Gloire de Marengo'
	chinensis	see *H. sinensis* var. *sinensis*
	- typica	see *H. sinensis* var. *sinensis*
§	***colchica*** ♀H4	CDul NWea SPer WCFE WFar WFib
	- 'Batumi'	MBNS WFib
	- 'Dentata' ♀H4	CHEx MRav MWhi NEgg SGol WFib
	- 'Dentata Aurea'	see *H. colchica* 'Dentata Variegata'
§	- 'Dentata Variegata' (v) ♀H4	Widely available
	- 'My Heart'	see *H. colchica*
	- 'Paddy's Pride'	see *H. colchica* 'Sulphur Heart'
§	- 'Sulphur Heart' (v) ♀H4	Widely available
	- 'Variegata'	see *H. colchica* 'Dentata Variegata'
	cristata	see *H. helix* 'Parsley Crested'
§	***cypria***	CDoC EWld WFib
	helix	CArn CCVT CMac CRWN CTri MGos NWea WSFF XLum
	- 'Adam' (v)	CWib EBee LAst LSRN MAsh MBri WFib
	- 'Amberwaves'	MBri WFib
	- 'Angularis Aurea' ♀H4	EPfP NBir WFib
	- 'Anita'	GBin WFib
§	- 'Anna Marie' (v)	CMac MBri SRms WFib
	- 'Anne Borch'	see *H. helix* 'Anna Marie'
	- 'Arborescens'	EBee WSFF XLum
	- 'Ardingly' (v)	MWhi WFib
	- 'Atropurpurea'	EBee EPPr GBin WFib
	- 'Baden-Baden'	EShb
	- var. ***baltica***	WFib
	- 'Bill Archer'	GBin WFib
	- 'Bird's Foot'	see *H. helix* 'Pedata'
	- 'Boskoop'	WFib
	- 'Bredon'	MRav
	- 'Brimstone' (v)	WFib
§	- 'Brokamp'	SLPl WFib
	- 'Buttercup'	CBcs CDul CMac CTri EBee EHoe ELan EPfP EShb LAst LRHS LSRN MAsh MBri MGos MWhi NBid NWad SBfd SLim SPer SPoG SRms WCFE WFar WFib
	- 'Buttercup' arborescent	SPoG
	- 'Caecilia' (v) ♀H4	EPfP LRHS MSwo SPer SWvt WCot WFib
N	- 'Caenwoodiana'	see *H. helix* 'Pedata'
	- 'Caenwoodiana Aurea'	WFib
	- 'Calico' (v)	WFib
	- 'Calypso'	WFib
	- 'Carolina Crinkle'	MWhi
	- 'Cathedral Wall'	WFib
§	- 'Cavendishii' (v)	SRms WFib
	- 'Cavendishii Latina'	WCot
§	- 'Ceridwen' (v) ♀H4	MBri SDys SPlb WFib
	- 'Cheeky'	WFib
	- 'Cheltenham Blizzard' (v)	CNat
	- 'Chester' (v)	LRHS WFib
	- 'Chicago'	CWib WFib
	- 'Chicago Variegated' (v)	WFib
	- 'Chrysophylla'	MSwo
	- 'Clotted Cream' (v)	CMac EBee ECGP ELon LBMP LRHS MAsh WFib
	- 'Cockle Shell'	WFib
	- 'Colin'	GBin
§	- 'Congesta' ♀H4	CMac GCra NBir SRms WFib
	- 'Conglomerata'	CBcs ELan MMoz NBir SRms WFib
	- 'Conglomerata Erecta'	WCFE WFib
	- 'Courage'	WFib
	- 'Crenata'	WFib
	- 'Crispa'	MRav
	- 'Cristata'	see *H. helix* 'Parsley Crested'
	- 'Curleylocks'	see *H. helix* 'Manda's Crested'
	- 'Curley-Q'	see *H. helix* 'Dragon Claw'
	- 'Curvaceous' (v)	WCot WFib
	- 'Cyprus'	see *H. cypria*
	- 'Dainty Bess'	CWib
	- 'Dead Again'	GBin WCot
§	- 'Dealbata' (v)	CMac WFib
	- 'Deltoidea'	see *H. hibernica* 'Deltoidea'
	- 'Discolor'	see *H. helix* 'Minor Marmorata', *H. helix* 'Dealbata'
§	- 'Donerailensis'	MBlu WFib
	- 'Don's Papillon'	CNat
§	- 'Dragon Claw'	SDys WFib
	- 'Duckfoot' ♀H4	CDoC EShb GBin MWhi WFib
	- 'Eileen' (v)	WFib
	- 'Elfenbein' (v)	WFib
	- 'Erecta' ♀H4	CDul CTca EPPr EPfP GCal LAst LRHS MBlu MGos NHol NWad SBfd SDys SHil SPer SPlb WFar WFib XLum
	- 'Erin'	see *H. helix* 'Pin Oak'
	- 'Ester' (v)	CBar LAst MAsh SRGP
§	- 'Eva' (v)	WFib
	- 'Fantasia' (v)	EShb MBri WFib
	- 'Feenfinger'	SDys WFib
	- 'Ferney'	WFib
	- 'Filigran'	WFib
	- 'Flashback' (v)	WFib
	- 'Flavescens'	WFib
	- 'Fluffy Ruffles'	WFib
I	- 'Francis Ivy'	WFib
	- 'Frizzle'	WFib
	- 'Frosty' (v)	WFib
	- 'Funny Girl'	WFib
	- 'Garland'	WFib
	- 'Gavotte'	WFib
	- 'Gilded Hawke'	WFib
	- 'Glache' (v)	MRav WFib
	- 'Glacier' (v) ♀H4	Widely available
	- 'Glymii'	EBee WFar WFib WTin
	- 'Gold Harald'	see *H. helix* 'Goldchild'
	- 'Gold Ripple'	NLar SEND
§	- 'Goldchild' (v) ♀H3-4	CBar CBcs CDoC CMac EBee EHoe ELon EPfP EShb LAst LRHS LTen

		MAsh MGos MRav MSwo MWat NBir NEgg NHol NRHS SBfd SLim SPer SPoG SWvt WFib
	- 'Golden Ann'	see *H. helix* 'Ceridwen'
*	- 'Golden Arrow'	ELan LRHS MAsh
	- 'Golden Curl' (v)	CMac EPfP LRHS
	- 'Golden Ester'	see *H. helix* 'Ceridwen'
	- 'Golden Gate' (v)	LAst
	- 'Golden Girl'	SDys WFib
	- 'Golden Ingot' (v) ♀H4	ELan EShb MWhi SBfd SDys WFib
	- 'Golden Jytte' (v)	WFib
	- 'Golden Kolibri'	see *H. helix* 'Midas Touch'
	- 'Golden Mathilde' (v)	GBin
	- 'Goldfinch'	MBri WFib
	- 'Goldfinger'	EShb MBri WFib
	- 'Goldheart'	see *H. helix* 'Oro di Bogliasco'
	- 'Goldstern' (v)	MRav MWhi WFib
	- 'Gracilis'	see *H. hibernica* 'Gracilis'
	- 'Green Finger'	see *H. helix* 'Très Coupé'
	- 'Green Ripple'	CBcs CTri EBee EShb LRHS MGos MSwo MWht NBro NPri NRHS SEND SLim SPer SPlb SRms WFar WFib
	- 'Greenman'	SDys WFib
	- 'Halebob'	EShb MBri SDys WFib
	- 'Hamilton'	see *H. hibernica* 'Hamilton'
	- 'Harald' (v)	CTri CWib MAsh WFib
*	- 'Hazel' (v)	WFib
	- 'Heise' (v)	WFib
	- 'Heise Denmark' (v)	WFib
	- 'Helvig'	see *H. helix* 'White Knight'
	- 'Henrietta'	WFib
	- 'Hispanica'	see *H. iberica*
	- 'Hite's Miniature'	see *H. helix* 'Merion Beauty'
	- 'Holly'	see *H. helix* 'Parsley Crested'
	- 'Hullavington'	CNat
	- 'Humpty Dumpty'	CPLG
	- 'Imp'	see *H. helix* 'Brokamp'
	- 'Itsy Bitsy'	see *H. helix* 'Pin Oak'
	- 'Ivalace' ♀H4	CBcs EBee ECha EPfP EShb LTen MGos MSwo MWhi MWht SDys SRms WFib WTin XLum
	- 'Jake'	EShb MBri WFib
	- 'Jasper'	WFib
	- 'Jersey Doris' (v)	WFib
	- 'Jerusalem'	see *H. helix* 'Schäfer Three'
	- 'Jester's Gold'	ELan EPfP MBri SBfd
	- 'Jubilee' (v)	WFib
	- 'Kaleidoscope'	WFib
	- 'Kevin'	WFib
	- 'Kolibri' (v)	CDoC EBee EPfP EShb LAst MBri MGos SBfd WFib
§	- 'Königer's Auslese'	EShb WFib
	- 'Lalla Rookh'	MRav WFib
	- 'Leo Swicegood'	MWhi WFib
	- 'Light Fingers'	EPfP LRHS MAsh SDys WFib WHrl
	- 'Limey'	WFib
	- 'Little Diamond' (v)	CDoC CMac CTri EBee ELan EPfP LBuc LRHS LTen MAsh MBri SLon SWvt WFib WHrl WTin
	- 'Little Luzii'	EShb WFib
	- 'Liz'	see *H. helix* 'Eva'
	- 'Luzii' (v)	WFib
	- 'Maculata'	see *H. helix* 'Minor Marmorata'
§	- 'Manda's Crested' ♀H4	NLar WFib
	- 'Maple Leaf' ♀H4	EShb SDys WFib
	- 'Maple Queen'	MBri
	- 'Marginata Elegantissima'	see *H. helix* 'Tricolor'
	- 'Marginata Minor'	see *H. helix* 'Cavendishii'
I	- 'Marmorata' Fibrex	WFib
	- 'Masquerade' (v)	EBee WGor
	- 'Mathilde' (v)	SBfd WFib
	- 'Melanie' ♀H4	ECha SRGP WFib
	- 'Meon'	WFib
§	- 'Merion Beauty'	WFib
§	- 'Midas Touch' (v) ♀H3-4	CWib EPPr EPfP MBri WFib
	- 'Minature Needlepoint' **new**	EBee
	- 'Mini Ester' (v)	MBri
	- 'Mini Heron'	MBri
	- 'Minikin' (v)	WCot
	- 'Minima' misapplied	see *H. helix* 'Spetchley'
	- 'Minima' Hibberd	see *H. helix* 'Donerailensis'
	- 'Minima' M.Young	see *H. helix* 'Congesta'
§	- 'Minor Marmorata' (v) ♀H4	CWan XLum
	- 'Mint Kolibri'	EHoe MBri
	- 'Minty' (v)	WFib
	- 'Misty' (v)	WFib
	- 'Needlepoint'	XLum
	- 'Niagara Falls'	LRHS
	- 'Nigra Aurea' (v)	WFib
	- 'Obovata'	WFib
N	- 'Oro di Bogliasco' (v)	CDul CMac CTri EBee EPfP EShb GKin LRHS MBri MRav MSwo NPri NRHS NWad NWea SBfd SEND SLim SPer SPlb SPoG SRms SWvt WFar WFib
	- 'Ovata'	WFib
§	- 'Parsley Crested' ♀H4	CMac EBee EPfP EShb LRHS MGos NBid SGol WFib
	- 'Patent Leather'	WFib
N	- 'Pedata'	CDul MSwo SDys WFib
	- 'Perkeo'	WFib
	- 'Peter' (v)	WFib
§	- 'Pin Oak'	EBee
	- 'Pink 'n' Curly'	WCot WFib
	- 'Pink 'n' Very Curly'	WCot
§	- 'Pittsburgh'	EShb LTen SBfd WFib
	- 'Plume d'Or'	WFib
§	- f. ***poetarum***	MBlu WCot WFib
	- - 'Poetica Arborea'	ECha SDix
	- 'Poetica'	see *H. helix* f. *poetarum*
	- 'Raleigh Delight' (v)	WCot
	- 'Ray's Supreme'	see *H. helix* 'Pittsburgh'
	- subsp. ***rhizomatifera***	WFib
	- 'Richard John'	WFib
	- 'Ritterkreuz'	WFib
	- 'Romanze' (v)	WFib
	- 'Russelliana'	WFib
	- 'Sagittifolia' misapplied	see *H. helix* 'Königer's Auslese'
	- 'Sagittifolia' Hibberd	see *H. hibernica* 'Sagittifolia'
	- 'Sagittifolia' ambig.	ECrN LRHS MAsh
	- 'Sagittifolia Variegata' (v)	MBri WFib WRHF
	- 'Saint Agnes'	LRHS
	- 'Sally' (v)	WFib
	- 'Salt and Pepper'	see *H. helix* 'Minor Marmorata'
§	- 'Schäfer Three' (v)	CWib WFib
	- 'Seabreeze'	WFib
	- 'Shadow'	WFib
	- 'Shamrock'	EPfP WFib
	- 'Shannon'	WFib
	- 'Silver Ferny'	WFib
	- 'Silver King' (v)	MRav MWht WFib
	- 'Silver Queen'	see *H. helix* 'Tricolor'
§	- 'Spetchley' ♀H4	CMac EBee GCal GEdr GKev MAsh MRav MWhi NPer NWad WCot WFib WHrl WPtf WTin
	- 'Spinosa'	SDys

- 'Splashes' WFib
- 'Stuttgart' WFib
- 'Sunrise' WFib
- 'Suzanne' see *H. nepalensis* 'Suzanne'
- 'Tanja' WFib
- 'Teardrop' WFib
- 'Telecurl' WFib
- 'Temptation' (v) WFib
- 'Tenerife' (v) WFib
- 'Topazolite' (v) WFib

§ - 'Très Coupé' CDoC EShb LRHS MAsh SEND
§ - 'Tricolor' (v) CMac CTri EBee EPfP EShb LRHS MAsh MCot WCFE WFib
- 'Trinity' (v) WFib
- 'Tripod' SDys WFib
- 'Triton' EPfP WFib
- 'Troll' WFib
- 'Ursula' (v) EShb WFib
- 'Very Merry' SDys WFib

* - 'Vitifolium' WFib
§ - 'White Knight' (v) ♀H4 WFib
- 'White Mein Herz' (v) WFib
- 'White Ripple' (v) WFib
- 'Williamsiana' (v) WFib
- 'Woerneri' NLar WFib
- 'Yellow Ripple' EShb MBri SDys WFib
- 'Zebra' (v) WFib

hibernica ♀H4 CCVT CDul CSBt EPfP LBuc LRHS MRav MSwo MWhi NWea SBfd SCob SEWo SGol SPer WFib
- 'Anna Marie' see *H. helix* 'Anna Marie'
- 'Aracena' SLPl

I - 'Arbori Compact' EPfP
- 'Betty Allen' WFib

§ - 'Deltoidea' ♀H4 MWht WCFE WFib
I - 'Digitata Crûg Gold' WCot WCru
- 'Ebony' WFib
- 'Glengariff' WFib

§ - 'Gracilis' WFib
§ - 'Hamilton' WFib
- 'Lobata Major' SRms
- 'Maculata' (v) SLPl WSHC
- 'Palmata' WFib
- 'Rona' WFib

§ - 'Sagittifolia' CTri EPfP SBfd
- 'Sulphurea' (v) WFib
- 'Variegata' (v) WFib

§ ***iberica*** WFib
maderensis WFib
maroccana 'Morocco' WFib

§ - 'Spanish Canary' WFib
nepalensis WFib
- 'Marble Dragon' see *H. sinensis* var. *sinensis* 'Marble Dragon'

§ - 'Suzanne' WFib
pastuchovii CDoC EShb WFib
- from Troödos, Cyprus see *H. cypria*
- 'Ann Ala' CDoC EBee EPfP GBin WCot WFib WGwG
- 'Lagocetti' WFib

§ ***rhombea*** WCot WFib
- 'Eastern Dawn' WFib
- 'Japonica' see *H. rhombea*

I - f. ***pedunculata*** 'Maculata' CWib
- var. ***rhombea*** 'Variegata' (v) WFib

§ ***sinensis*** var. ***sinensis*** WFib
§ - - 'Marble Dragon' WFib

Hedychium ✿ (*Zingiberaceae*)

CC 6412 EWld
'Anne Bishop' SEND
aurantiacum CBcs CBct CHEx EAmu EBee LAma LEdu NPla SBig XLum
brevicaule B&SWJ 7171 WCru
'C.P. Raffill' see *H.* 'Raffillii'
chrysoleucum CCCN CRHN LAma LTen SBst

* 'Clarkei' **new** GHim
coccineum ♀H1 CDTJ EAmu EBee ECho EPfP EUJe IKil MNrw SBig XLum
- B&SWJ 5238 WCru
- var. ***angustifolium*** CGHE CRHN EPfP WPGP
- 'Disney' CDTJ EAmu
'Corelli' CHll
coronarium CAbb CAvo CBct CCCN CDTJ CDes CHll EAmu EBee EPfP EUJe GHim IKil SBig WPGP XBlo XLum
- B&SWJ 3745 WCru
- 'Gold Spot' EUJe GHim SKHP
- 'Orange Spot' EAmu
- var. ***urophyllum*** IBlr
- - HWJ 604 WCru
'Daniel Weeks' EBee
densiflorum CAbb CBct CCCN CDTJ CDes CHEx CHll CPLG CSpe EAmu EBee ECha EPfP EUJe GHim IBlr LEdu NPla SDix SSpi WCru WPGP XLum
- EN 562 CPLG
- LS&H 17393 CPLG WPGP
- 'Assam Orange' CAvo CBct CDoC CGHE CHEx CPLG CPne CRHN CSam CTrC EAmu EBee EPPr GCal IBlr IDee LEdu MNrw SBfd SBig SChr SDix SEND SMad SPlb WCru WPGP WSHC
- 'Sorung' CPLG LEdu SChr WPGP
- 'Stephen' CBct CCCN CCon CDTJ CDes CGHE CHEx CPLG CSam EAmu EBee EPfP EUJe LEdu MNrw SChr SPlb WPGP
'Devon Cream' CCCN CDTJ CHll CPLG EAmu SChr
'Doctor Moy' (v) CDTJ EAmu EBee EUJe
'Elizabeth' CDes EAmu EBee
ellipticum CAbb CDTJ CHEx EAmu EBee EUJe GCal LAma MNrw SBig XLum
- B&SWJ 8354 WCru
'Filigree' CPLG EBee

§ ***flavescens*** CBct CDTJ EAmu EBee EPfP EUJe LAma MNrw SChr WCru
flavum misapplied. see *H. flavescens*
flavum Roxb. CAbb CBcs EBee XLum
forrestii misapplied CTrC EUJe
forrestii Diels CPLG EAmu EBee ETod GCal IBlr IDee MNrw MREP SPlb WPGP
gardnerianum ♀H1 CAbb CBcs CBct CCon CGHE CHEx CHll CPLG CPne CRHN EBee EPfP EUJe IDee IKil LAma LEdu MNrw NBir NPla SBfd SChr SDeJ SMad WCru WPGP XLum
'Gold Flame' CDes EBee MNrw SChr
gracile EAmu EUJe WCru
greenii CBcs CBct CCon CDoC CHEx CHll CPne CRHN EBee ECho EPfP EUJe GHim LEdu MNrw NPla SBfd SBig SChr SDix WBor WCru XLum
griffithianum CSpe EAmu EBee EPfP GHim IKil MNrw SBig XLum

	Name	Suppliers
	- white-flowered	CCCN
	'Hardy Exotics 1'	CHEx
	'Luna Moth'	EAmu WPGP
	maximum	EAmu SChr SKHP WPGP
	- B&SWJ 8261A	WCru
	- HWJ 810	WCru
	× ***moorei*** 'Tara' ♀H3	CAbb CAvo CBct CDes CDoC CGHE CHEx CHll CPLG CPne CRHN CSam EAmu EBee EPfP EUJe IBlr LBMP LEdu MNrw SBfd SBst SChr SPlb SPoG WCru WPGP
	'Pink Flame'	EBee
	'Pink V'	CCon EAmu EBee
	'Pradhan'	CCon
§	'Raffillii'	MNrw SBig WCru
	'Saint Martin's'	CCCN
	'Samsheri'	CHll
	'Shamshiri'	CCCN
	spicatum	CAbb CCon CDTJ CHEx CPLG CRHN EUJe GCal GHim GPoy IBlr LEdu MNrw SGar WCFE WPGP
	- B&SWJ 7231	WCru
	- CC 1705	CPLG
	- CC 3249	EBee
	- P. Bon. 57188	CPLG EBee WPGP
	- from Salween Valley, China	CPLG
	- var. ***acuminatum***	GHim
	- 'Liberty'	WCru
	- 'Singalila'	CDes EBee WCru
	stenopetalum B&SWJ 7155	WCru
	'Tahitian Flame' (v)	EUJe
	'Tai Pink Princess' (Tai Series) **new**	GHim
	thyrsiforme	EAmu EBee EUJe GHim SBig WCru XLum
	villosum	CDTJ EBee ECho
	wardii	CHEx CPLG EUJe WPGP
	× ***wilkeanum***	SPer
	yunnanense	CCon CDes CHll CRHN EBee LEdu MNrw SBig WPGP
	- B&SWJ 9717	WCru
	- BWJ 7900	WCru
	- L 633	CPLG IBlr
	- from Cally Gardens	GCal

Hedysarum (*Papilionaceae*)

Name	Suppliers
coronarium	CSpe ELan MCot WCot WKif WWFP
hedysaroides	IKil
multijugum	CBcs EBee MBlu SPer
tauricum	SPhx

Heimia (*Lythraceae*)

Name	Suppliers
salicifolia	CArn ECre EOHP SEND SGar

Helenium ✿ (*Asteraceae*)

	Name	Suppliers
	'Adios' **new**	MAvo MSpe
	autumnale	CSBt CTri LDai LPot LSRN MLHP MNHC NChi SBod SMrm SPet SWvt WFar WGwG WMoo
	- 'All Gold'	SWvt
I	- 'Cupreum'	SBch
§	- Helena Series	LRHS SWvt
§	- - 'Helena Gold'	EBee EPfP LRHS NBre SBfd WPer
	- - 'Helena Rote Töne'	EBee EPfP LBMP LRHS MWhi SBfd SGar SWal WPer
	- 'Pumilum' **new**	EHrv
	'Baronin Linden'	CSam MAvo MSpe
	'Baudirektor Linne' ♀H4	CSam EBee LRHS MSpe MTis
	'Beatrice' **new**	MSpe MTis
	'Biedermeier'	CSam CWCL EBee ECtt EShb LRHS MRav MSpe NEgg SAga
	bigelovii	XLum
	'Blanche Royale' **new**	MSpe
	'Blütentisch' misapplied	see *H.* 'Riverton Beauty'
	'Blütentisch' Foerster ♀H4	CHVG COIW CSam EBee GMaP LRHS MSpe MTis NCGa NLar SUsu WMnd WWEG
	'Bressingham Gold'	LRHS MNrw MSpe WHrl WWEG
	'Bruno'	CWCL EBee ELan ELon LRHS MArl MSpe NLar NRHS SMrm
	'Butterpat' ♀H4	EBee ECtt EHrv GBee GCra GMaP LRHS MArl MRav MSpe NRHS NSti SBfd SMrm WWEG
	'Can Can'	CSam EBee IPot LSou MAsh MAvo MSpe MTis
	'Chelsey'	CPrp EBee ELan EPfP IBal LHop LRHS LSRN LSou MSpe NLar NPri NSti WWlt
	'Chesney'	LSou
	'Chipperfield Orange'	CElw CSam ECtt MArl MRav MSpe MTis NBre NGdn WOld WWEG XLum
	'Coppelia'	EBee ECtt LRHS MAsh MRav NBir NGdn NRHS
	Copper Spray	see *H.* 'Kupfersprudel'
	'Cremsicle' **new**	NLar
	'Crimson Beauty'	ECtt ELan LRHS
	Dark Beauty	see *H.* 'Dunkle Pracht'
	'Dauerbrenner'	CSam MAvo MSpe MTis
	'Die Blonde'	MSpe NBre SMHy SPhx
	'Double Trouble' PBR	EBee EHrv EPfP IKil LLHF LRHS LSou MBNS MBri MSCN MSpe NGdn NPri NRHS SBfd SPoG STes WCAu WCot WHil
§	'Dunkle Pracht'	CHVG CPrp CSam EBee ECtt EHrv LSRN MCot MSpe NDov NEgg NLar WCAu WCot WFar WWEG
	'El Dorado'	CSam MAvo MSpe MTis NCGa WCot
	'Fata Morgana'	EBee ECtt LEdu LHop LLHF MSpe MTis NBre WCAu
	'Feuersiegel' ♀H4	CSam EBee ECtt EHrv MSpe MTis NBre SUsu WOld WWEG
	'Fiesta'	CSam EBee MAvo MSpe MTis NDov WHoo
	'Flammendes Käthchen'	CSam EBee IPot LRHS MAsh MSpe NBre NCGa NDov NRHS SAga SHar SMrm SUsu
	'Flammenrad'	CSam EBee MSpe
	'Flammenspiel'	EBee ECtt LRHS MAsh MCot MNrw MSpe MTis NLar NRHS
	flexuosum	SPhx
	'Françoise' **new**	CSam
	'Gartensonne' ♀H4	CSam MSpe SMrm WWEG
	'Gay-go-round'	CSam MSpe
	'Gelbe Waldtraut' **new**	MSpe MTis
	Gold Fox	see *H.* 'Goldfuchs'
	'Gold Intoxication'	see *H.* 'Goldrausch'
	Golden Youth	see *H.* 'Goldene Jugend'
§	'Goldene Jugend'	CMea ECtt ELan LRHS MSpe WCot WWEG
§	'Goldfuchs'	CWCL LRHS MSpe WCot
	'Goldkogel' **new**	EBee
§	'Goldlackzwerg'	EBee LRHS MSpe NBre
§	'Goldrausch'	CMac CSam CWCL EBee ECtt EPfP GBee GCra LRHS LSou MDKP

		MSpe MTis MWat NBre NGdn NSti SPhx WMoo WOld WWEG
	'Goldreif'	MSpe
	'Goldriese' **new**	MSpe
	'Hartmut Rieger'	CSam MSpe
	'Helena' misapplied	see *H. autumnale* 'Helena Gold'
	'Helena' Foerster	MSpe NLar WPer
	'Herbstgold' **new**	MSpe
	hoopesii	see *Hymenoxys hoopesii*
	'Indianersommer'	CCVN CElw CSam EBee ECtt EHrv GMaP LDai LRHS MSpe NDov NLar NMRc NOrc SMrm SPer SUsu WFar WHoo WWEG
	'Jam Tarts'	MSpe WCot
	'Julisamt' **new**	MTis
	'July Sun'	NBir
	'Kanaria'	CHVG CPrp EBee EWll GKev GQue LHop LRHS MAsh MAvo MSpe MTis NDov NEgg NLar NRHS SAga SMrm WMnd WOld
	'Karneol' ♀H4	CSam LRHS MSpe SUsu
	'Kleine Aprikose' **new**	MSpe
	'Kleiner Fuchs'	CSam EHrv MSpe MTis NLar WWEG
	'Kokarde'	CSam MAvo MSpe WWEG
	'Königstiger'	CSam EBee ECtt GQue LRHS LSou MAsh MNrw MSpe NBre NDov NRHS SMrm WFar
	'Kugelsonne'	EBee EHrv MSpe NBre
§	'Kupfersprudel'	CSam LRHS MSpe MTis
	'Kupferziegel'	CSam MSpe MTis
	'Kupferzwerg'	CWCL EBee ELan IPot MSpe NBre NDov SPhx SUsu
	'Lambada'	EBee IPot MSpe
	'Lemon Queen'	SAga
	'Loysder Wieck'	EBee ECtt EPfP MSpe MTis NDov NGdn SPet WHil
	'Luc'	MSpe MTis WCot
§	'Mahagoni'	CSam MSpe NRHS
	Mahogany	see *H.* 'Mahagoni'
	'Mahogany'	see *H.* 'Goldlackzwerg'
	'Mardi Gras'	CMac EBee ECtt LRHS LSou MTis NCGa NDov SPoG SUsu
	'Margot'	CSam CWCL MSpe MTis NBre SUsu
	'Marion Nickig'	CSam MSpe NDov
	'Meranti'	CMea MAvo MSpe NDov WCot
	'Mien Ruys'	MTis
	'Moerheim Beauty' ♀H4	Widely available
	'Moth'	MSpe
	'Oldenburg' **new**	MSpe
	'Orange Beauty'	EBee GQue MSpe
	'Patsy'	MSpe
	Pipsqueak = 'Blopip'	EBee ECtt LLHF LRHS MAvo MSpe NBre NPri SPoG
	'Potter's Wheel'	CSam MSpe MTis NDov WWEG
	puberulum	EBee LRHS NBir NLar WHil
	'Puck'	MSpe
	'Pumilum Magnificum'	CWCL EBee EPfP GQue LEdu LHop LRHS MSpe MTis SMad WFar WPGP XLum
	'Ragamuffin'	CSam MSpe SUsu WCot
	'Rauchtopas'	CSam EBee GQue IPot LSou MAvo MSpe MTis NCGa NDov SMrm SPoG SUsu WPGP
	Red and Gold	see *H.* 'Rotgold' Foerster
	'Red Army'	CHVG CPrp EBee ELan IPot LRHS LSou MAvo MBri MNrw MSpe MTis NCGa NGdn NRHS SPet
	'Red Glory'	EHrv MAsh MSpe
	'Red Jewel'	CMea EBee ECtt ELon IPot LLHF LPla LRHS LSou MAvo MNrw MPie MSpe MTis NDov NEgg NGdn NLar NPnk NSti SKHP SMad SMrm WCot WMoo WPGP WWEG
	'Ring of Fire' ♀H4	IPot MSpe SMHy
§	'Riverton Beauty'	CSam LLHF MSpe MTis SUsu WCot WHoo
	'Riverton Gem'	CSam ECtt EHrv LLHF MNrw MSpe MTis NChi WHoo
	'Rotgold' misapplied	see *H. autumnale* Helena Series
§	'Rotgold' Foerster	CMea ECtt LSRN MSpe NBre NChi SRms WFar WMoo WPer
	'Rotkäppchen'	MSpe
	'Rubinkuppel'	LRHS NCGa
	'Rubinzwerg' ♀H4	Widely available
§	'Ruby Thuesday'	EBee ECtt EHrv EPfP IKil LLHF LRHS LSRN LSou MBNS MHer MNrw MSpe MTis NEgg NGdn NLar NOrc NSti SBfd SMad WCot
	'Ruby Tuesday'	see *H.* 'Ruby Thuesday'
	'Sahin's Early Flowerer' ♀H4	Widely available
	'Samtjuwel'	MSpe MTis
	'Schokoladenkönigin' **new**	MSpe
	'Septemberfuchs'	LEdu LPla MCot MSpe MTis NDov SPhx WWEG
	'Septembergold'	EBee MSpe
	'Sonnenkringel'	MSpe
	'Sonnenwunder'	EBee ECha MLHP MSpe NBre
	'Sophie zur Linden'	CSam MSpe MTis
	'Sunshine'	MSpe
	'The Bishop'	COIW CPrp CSam EBee ECtt ELon EPfP GCra LAst LHop LRHS MBri MRav MSCN MSpe NPri SPer SPet SWvt WFar WHil WMnd WWEG
	'Tijuana Brass' **new**	ECtt
	'Tip Top'	SBfd
	'Tresahor Red'	MSpe
	'Two Faced Fan' **new**	MSpe MTis
	'Vicky'	MAvo MSpe
	'Vivace'	LEdu MSpe
	'Wagon Wheel'	MSpe WCot
	'Waldhorn'	LRHS MSpe MTis
	'Waltraut' ♀H4	Widely available
	'Wesergold' ♀H4	EBee EHrv GBBs GQue LLHF LSou MHer MSpe MTis NDov NLar
	'Westerstede' **new**	MSpe
	'Wonnadonga'	EBee MSpe MTis
	'Wyndley'	Widely available
	'Zimbelstern'	CCse CElw EBee ECha ECtt ELon LHop LRHS MAsh MCot MNFA MSpe MTis NLar SMrm SPhx WAul WCot WFar WPGP WWEG
	'Zonnedam'	SBea

Helianthella (*Asteraceae*)

§	***quinquenervis***	CDes EBee GCal LLHF LRHS MHer NLar SPer

Helianthemum ✿ (*Cistaceae*)

	sp.	SVic
	'Alice Howorth'	WHoo WIce
	alpestre serpyllifolium	see *H. nummularium* subsp. ***glabrum***
	'Amabile Plenum' (d)	GAbr GCal
	'Amy Baring' ♀H4	CTri ECho ECtt GAbr LRHS NRHS NWad WPer
	'Annabel' (d)	ECho ECtt GAbr LHop LRHS SSvw WPer

	apenninum	LLHF SRms
	'Apricot'	CTri ECtt
	'Apricot Blush'	WAbe
	'Baby Buttercup'	CMea GAbr
	'Beech Park Red'	CTri EPot MHer SDix WAbe WHoo WIce WKif
	'Ben Afflick'	ECho ECtt LHop LRHS NRHS SRms
	'Ben Alder'	ECtt GAbr MHer
	'Ben Dearg'	CMea ECho ECtt SRms
	'Ben Fhada'	CBcs CMea COIW CSam CTri ECho ECtt ELan ELon EPfP GEdr GMaP LBee LHop LRHS MAsh MHer NEgg SAga SBfd SEND SPer SPoG SRGP SRms WAbe WPer XLum
	'Ben Heckla'	CSam ECho ECtt EPfP GAbr LHop LPot LRHS MAsh NRHS WPer XLum
	'Ben Hope'	CTri ECho ECtt ELan EPfP EWTr MAsh SGol SPer SRGP XLum
§	'Ben Ledi'	CBcs CEnt COIW ECho ECtt ELan EPfP GAbr GEdr GMaP LHop MAsh MHer MSCN NSla SBfd SEND SPoG SRms SRot WAbe WNew WPer
	'Ben Lomond'	GAbr
	'Ben Macdhui'	ECtt GAbr
	'Ben More'	CBcs CEnt CMea COIW ECho ECtt ELan ELon EPfP GAbr GJos GMaP LHop LRHS MAsh MSwo NBir SBfd SEND SPoG SRGP SRms SRot WHoo WIce
	'Ben Nevis'	CTri ECho ECtt GAbr GEdr SRms
	'Ben Vane'	ECho ECtt GAbr LRHS
	'Boughton Double Primrose' (d)	ECho ECtt GMaP WAbe WHoo WSHC
	'Bronzeteppich'	LLHF
	'Broughty Beacon'	ECtt WGor
	'Broughty Sunset'	CSam ECtt GAbr NBir
	'Bunbury'	ECtt ELon GAbr MBrN MSpe MWat NBir NPri SDix SPoG SRms
	canum subsp. ***balcanicum***	WAbe
	'Captivation'	ECtt GAbr
	'Cathy' **new**	CMea
	'Cerise Queen' (d)	CTri ECha ECtt EPfP GAbr GKev LAst LHop MAsh MMHG MSwo SDix SEND SRms WHoo WRHF
	chamaecistus	see *H. nummularium*
	'Cheviot'	CMea ECtt GAbr NBir WHoo WSHC XLum
I	'Chloe's Variegata' (v)	EWes
	'Chocolate Blotch'	ECho GAbr GCra LHop LRHS NWad SAga SEND SRms WPer
	'Cornish Cream'	ECtt GAbr LBee
	croceum	LLHF
	cupreum	ECtt GAbr
	'David Ritchie'	LLHF WHoo
	'Diana'	CMea SAga
	double apricot-flowered (d)	GAbr
	- orange-flowered (d)	LHop
	- primrose-flowered (d)	GAbr
	- red-flowered (d)	NChi
	'Ellen' (d)	CMea
	'Everton Ruby'	see *H.* 'Ben Ledi'
	'Fairy'	ELan EPfP GAbr LLHF
§	'Fire Dragon' ♡H4	CMea ECho ECtt ELan EPfP GAbr GMaP GQue LRHS NBir NRHS SRms WAbe WRHF XLum XSen
	'Fireball'	see *H.* 'Mrs C.W. Earle'
	'Firegold' (v)	WAbe
	'Georgeham'	CMea ECtt ELon EPfP GAbr NBir SRms WGor WHoo WPer XLum
§	'Golden Queen'	ECtt EPfP GAbr LAst MAsh MSwo WPer
	'Hampstead Orange'	CTri
	'Hartswood Ruby'	GMaP MBNS
	'Henfield Brilliant' ♡H4	CHVG CPLG CSam ECho ECtt ELan EPfP GAbr GEdr LHop LRHS MRav NBir NHol SBfd SDix SMad SRms WHoo WPer XLum XSen
	'Highdown'	GAbr SRms
	'Highdown Apricot'	ECho ECtt LHop LLHF LRHS MAsh NMRc SPoG
	'Honeymoon'	ECtt EPfP GAbr NWad WPer
	'Jeanie' (d) **new**	ECho
	'Jubilee' (d) ♡H4	CTri ECho ECtt ELan EPfP GAbr LHop MAsh MBNS NBir NChi SPoG SRms WHil WKif
I	'Jubilee Variegatum' (v)	ECtt
	'Karen's Silver'	WAbe
	'Kathleen Druce' (d)	ECho ECtt EWes GAbr NWad WHoo
	'Kathleen Mary'	CMea
	'Lawrenson's Pink'	ECho ECtt GAbr LHop LRHS MCot SAga SRGP WPer
	'Lemon Queen'	NWsh SBea WPer
	'Lucy Elizabeth'	ECtt
	lunulatum	CMea ECho LLHF LRHS NMen NWad WAbe WPat
	'Magnificum'	MWat
§	'Mrs C.W. Earle' (d) ♡H4	COIW CTri ECho ECtt ELan EPfP GCra LRHS MAsh MBNS MWat NEgg NHol SBfd SRms WPer
	'Mrs Clay'	see *H.* 'Fire Dragon'
	'Mrs Hays'	ECtt
	'Mrs Lake'	GAbr
	'Mrs Moules'	SRms
	mutabile	SPhx SPlb
§	***nummularium***	ECho ENfk GPoy MHer MNHC NMir WAbe WIce WSFF XSen
§	- subsp. ***glabrum***	GAbr WPat
§	- subsp. ***tomentosum***	GAbr MWat
	oelandicum	SRms WAbe
	- subsp. ***alpestre***	NMen
	- subsp. ***piloselloides***	WAbe
	'Old Gold'	ECtt GAbr SRms WAbe
	'Orange Phoenix' (d)	ECtt EPfP GAbr MBNS NPri NWad
	'Ovum Supreme'	GAbr
	pilosum	LLHF
	'Pink Angel' (d)	ECtt MBNS MWat WPer
	'Pink Glow'	WPer
	'Praecox'	CMea CTri ECho GAbr SRms WHoo
	'Prima Donna'	ELan EPfP NBir
	'Prostrate Orange'	SRms
	'Raspberry Ripple'	ECho ECtt ELan EPfP EPot GBin LRHS MAsh NHol NRHS SBfd SGol SPoG SRms
	'Razzle Dazzle' (v)	ECtt ELon GKev LLHF NHol SLon SRms
	'Red Dragon'	ECtt EPot MSCN WAbe
	'Red Orient'	see *H.* 'Supreme'
	'Regenbogen' (d)	CPBP GCal SEND
§	'Rhodanthe Carneum' ♡H4	Widely available
§	'Rosakönigin'	ECtt GAbr MHer WAbe
	'Rose of Leeswood' (d)	CMea CTri ECtt LBee NChi NEgg SAga SPoG SRms WHoo WKif WSHC
	Rose Queen	see *H.* 'Rosakönigin'
	'Roxburgh Gold'	SRms
	'Ruth'	SEND

	'Saint John's College Yellow'	CSam ECho LRHS
	'Salmon Beauty'	ECtt
	'Salmon Queen'	ECho ECtt GAbr LHop LRHS MAsh SEND SRms WPer
*	***scardicum***	CMea
	serpyllifolium	see *H. nummularium* subsp. *glabrum*
	'Shot Silk'	ECtt EWes
	'Snow Queen'	see *H.* 'The Bride'
	'Sterntaler'	GAbr LLHF SRms
	'Sudbury Gem'	CTri ECha ECho LRHS SEND SGol
	'Sulphur Moon'	ECho LHop LLHF LRHS NRHS
	'Sulphureum Plenum' (d)	SGol
	'Sunbeam'	CSam ECho SRms
§	'Supreme'	ECho ELan EPfP EWes LHop MAsh SRms
	'Tangerine'	ECtt GAbr
§	'The Bride' ♀H4	Widely available
	'Tigrinum Plenum' (d)	ECho EWes
	'Tomato Red'	NSla SEND XLum XSen
	tomentosum	see *H. nummularium* subsp. *tomentosum*
	umbellatum	see *Halimium umbellatum*
	'Voltaire'	ECtt EPfP GAbr LLHF NWad XLum
	'Watergate Rose'	MWat NBir
	'Welsh Flame'	WAbe
	'Wisley Pink'	see *H.* 'Rhodanthe Carneum'
	'Wisley Primrose' ♀H4	Widely available
	'Wisley Rose'	NRHS
	'Wisley White'	CTri ECha ECho ECtt ELan EPfP MAsh
	'Wisley Yellow'	ECtt ELan SAga
	'Yellow Queen'	see *H.* 'Golden Queen'

Helianthus (*Asteraceae*)

	sp.	SVic
	RCB/Arg CC-3	WCot
	atrorubens	LHop MRav NBro
	- 'Giganteus'	MAvo
	'Bitter Chocolate'	MAvo WCot
	'Capenoch Star' ♀H4	CElw CPrp EBee ECtt GMaP IBoy LEdu LRHS MBri MRav MSpe MTis NBro NLar SDix SLPl SMrm WCAu WWEG
	'Capenoch Supreme'	ECtt LRHS
	'Carine'	MAvo MLHP MNrw MTis WCot
	'Cosmic Whisper' **new**	EBee MAvo
	decapetalus	MBel
	- Morning Sun	see *H.* 'Morgensonne'
	'Dorian Roxburgh'	WCot
	× ***doronicoides***	LRHS
	giganteus	SHar
	- 'Sheila's Sunshine'	CBre CElw EBee LHop LRHS NDov SHar SMHy WOld
	'Gullick's Variety' ♀H4	CBre EBee ECtt LLWP NBro NChi NLar WOld WWEG XLum
	'Happy Days'	CBre EBee ECtt ELon LSou MAvo MBel MTis NCGa NSti SPoG WCot WFar
	'Hazel's Gold'	EBee ECtt LRHS NBre
	hirsutus	EBee
	× ***kellermanii***	EBee MTis NBre NDov SAga SPhx
§	× ***laetiflorus***	EBee MWhi NBre NLar NOrc WPer
	- 'Grandiflora'	LRHS
§	'Lemon Queen' ♀H4	Widely available
	'Limelight'	see *H.* 'Lemon Queen'
	'Loddon Gold' ♀H4	ECtt ELan EPfP LRHS MAvo MBel MRav MSCN MSpe MTis NBir SMrm SRGP WBrk WCot WFar WWEG
§	***maximiliani***	ELon EWll LDai LRHS MDKP SPav SPhx WPer WPtf
	microcephalus	CSam EBee ELon MTis NDov
	- 'JS Straffe Prairie Gast'	EBee
	'Miss Mellish' ♀H4	EBee MSCN WBrk WCot WHoo WWEG
	mollis	CSam EBee LRHS SBrt SPav WPer
	'Monarch' ♀H4	CMea CSam EBee GBee MAvo MBel MDKP MRav MSpe NBre NCGa NLar SMad SMrm WCot WOld WWEG
§	'Morgensonne'	CPrp ECtt MAvo MTis MWat NDov WCot
	× ***multiflorus*** 'Meteor'	ECtt LRHS NBre WWEG
	'O Sole Mio' **new**	WCot
	occidentalis	EBee LRHS WPer
	orgyalis	see *H. salicifolius*
	quinquenervis	see *Helianthella quinquenervis*
	rigidus misapplied	see *H.* × *laetiflorus*
§	***salicifolius***	Widely available
	- 'Low Down'PBR	EBee LRHS
	- 'Table Mountain'PBR	EBee MAvo WCot
	scaberrimus	see *H.* × *laetiflorus*
	'Soleil d'Or'	EBee ECtt EWll WHal WWEG
	strumosus	WCot
	tomentosus	LRHS
	'Triomphe de Gand'	EBee IPot LRHS MTis MWat NDov
	tuberosus	CArn EBee GPoy SVic
	- 'Fuseau'	SVic
	- 'Garnet'	LEdu
	- 'Sugarball'	LEdu

Helichrysum (*Asteraceae*)

	from Drakensberg Mountains, South Africa	GAbr
	adenocarpum	SPlb
	alveolatum	see *H. splendidum*
	ambiguum	EPfP
	amorginum 'Pink Sapphire'PBR	LRHS
	- Ruby Cluster = 'Blorub'PBR	EPfP IRar LRHS NPri SPer WCot
	angustifolium	see *H. italicum*
	- from Crete	see *H. microphyllum* (Willd.) Cambess.
§	***arwae***	EPot IRar WAbe
	basalticum	WAbe
	bellidioides	see *Anaphalioides bellidioides*
	'Coco'	see *Xerochrysum bracteatum* 'Coco'
	confertum	SPlb
	coralloides	see *Ozothamnus coralloides*
	'County Park Silver'	see *Ozothamnus* 'County Park Silver'
	'Dargan Hill Monarch'	see *Xerochrysum bracteatum* 'Dargan Hill Monarch'
	'Elmstead'	see *H. stoechas* 'White Barn'
	frigidum	CPBP
	hookeri	see *Ozothamnus hookeri*
§	***hypoleucum***	SDix
	'Icicles' **new**	GBin
§	***italicum*** ♀H3	CPrp CWan ECha ENfk EPfP GPoy LPot MHer MNHC NPri SBfd SEND SPet SPoG SRms WGwG WHfH WJek XLum
	- 'Dartington'	CSpe ENfk EOHP GBin SIde WJek
I	- 'Glaucum'	CWib
	- 'Korma'PBR	EBee EHoe ELan EPfP EWTr GBin LRHS LSRN LSou MGos NPri SIde SLon SPoG SRms WJek

	- subsp. ***microphyllum***	see *H. microphyllum* (Willd.) Cambess.
	- 'Nanum'	see *H. microphyllum* (Willd.) Cambess.
§	- subsp. ***serotinum***	CBcs CHVG EHoe EPfP EPot GPoy LRHS MCot MHoo MRav SBfd SLim SPer SRms SWal SWvt WPer XSen
	lanatum	see *H. thianschanicum*
	ledifolium	see *Ozothamnus ledifolius*
	marginatum misapplied	see *H. milfordiae*
	microphyllum misapplied	see *Plecostachys serpyllifolia*
	microphyllum ambig.	SPer
§	***microphyllum*** (Willd.) Cambess.	ENfk EPot MNHC SEND SIde WJek
§	***milfordiae*** ♀H2-3	EPot GEdr NRHS NSla SRms WAbe
	orientale	EPot IRar XSen
	pagophilum	CPBP EPot ITim WAbe
	petiolare ♀H2	EBak ECtt LAst MCot SBfd SGar SPer SPoG
	- 'Aureum'	see *H. petiolare* 'Limelight'
	- 'Goring Silver' ♀H2-3	SPet SPoG
§	- 'Limelight' ♀H2	ECtt LAst MCot NPri SBfd SPer SPet SPoG
	- 'Variegatum' (v) ♀H2	ECtt LAst MCot NPri SBfd SPet SPoG
	plumeum	EPot
	populifolium misapplied	see *H. hypoleucum*
	rosmarinifolium	see *Ozothamnus rosmarinifolius*
§	'Schwefellicht'	EBee ECha EPfP EShb MLHP MRav SPer WCAu WKif WSHC WWEG
	selago	see *Ozothamnus selago*
	serotinum	see *H. italicum* subsp. *serotinum*
	serpyllifolium	see *Plecostachys serpyllifolia*
	sessilioides	EPot WAbe
§	***sibthorpii***	WAbe
	'Skynet'	see *Xerochrysum bracteatum* 'Skynet'
§	***splendidum*** ♀H3	EPfP LRHS NBro SEND SKHP SLon WPer XSen
	stoechas	CArn
§	- 'White Barn'	CSpe NGBo WCot XLum
	Sulphur Light	see *H.* 'Schwefellicht'
§	***thianschanicum***	EDAr SRms XLum XSen
	- Golden Baby	see *H. thianschanicum* 'Goldkind'
§	- 'Goldkind'	NBir
	trilineatum	see *H. splendidum*
	tumidum	see *Ozothamnus selago* var. *tumidus*
	virgineum	see *H. sibthorpii*
	wightii B&SWJ 9503	WCru
	witbergense	WAbe
	woodii	see *H. arwae*

Helicodiceros (*Araceae*)

§	***muscivorus***	CHid EBee WCot

Heliconia ✿ (*Heliconiaceae*)

	caribaea 'Burgundy'	see *H. caribaea* 'Purpurea'
§	- 'Purpurea'	XBlo
	'Golden Torch'	XBlo
	hirsuta 'Halloween' **new**	SPlb
	indica 'Spectabilis'	XBlo
	latispatha 'Orange Gyro'	XBlo
*	- 'Red Gyro'	XBlo
	metallica	XBlo
	psittacorum	CCCN
	rostrata	CCCN SBst XBlo
	schiedeana	CHll
	- 'Fire and Ice'	EAmu

Helictotrichon (*Poaceae*)

	pratense	CHab EHoe
§	***sempervirens*** ♀H4	Widely available
I	- 'Pendulum'	EBee GBin MAvo MSpe
	- 'Saphirsprudel'	CCse EBee LRHS MBri SHil WCot WPGP WWEG

Heliophila (*Brassicaceae*)

	coronopifolia	CSpe

Heliopsis (*Asteraceae*)

	Golden Plume	see *H. helianthoides* var. *scabra* 'Goldgefieder'
	helianthoides	LRHS MLHP NBre
	- 'Limelight'	see *Helianthus* 'Lemon Queen'
	- Loraine Sunshine = 'Helhan'PBR (v)	CWGN EBee LRHS LSou NSti SPoG WCot WFar
	- var. ***scabra***	MCot MDKP SRot WMnd XLum
	- - 'Asahi'	EBee ECtt ELan EWll MBri MDev NLar NPri SPoG WHil WHoo
	- - Ballerina	see *H. helianthoides* var. *scabra* 'Spitzentänzerin'
	- - 'Benzinggold' ♀H4	LSou MRav
	- - 'Bressingham Doubloon' (d)	EBee ECtt LRHS
	- - 'Desert King'	LRHS
	- - 'Gigantea' **new**	LRHS
	- - Golden Plume	see *H. helianthoides* var. *scabra* 'Goldgefieder'
§	- - 'Goldgefieder' ♀H4	EBee EPfP LRHS NBre WFar
	- - Goldgreenheart	see *H. helianthoides* var. *scabra* 'Goldgrünherz'
§	- - 'Goldgrünherz'	EBee LRHS
	- - 'Hohlspiegel'	EBee LRHS
	- - 'Jupiter' **new**	LRHS
	- - 'Lohfelden'	LRHS
	- - 'Patula'	EBee
	- - 'Prairie Sunset'PBR	EBee ECtt MBri WWlt
§	- - 'Sommersonne'	CSBt EBee ECtt EPfP EWll LRHS MSpe MWhi NGBl NLar NPer SHil SMrm SPer SRms WMnd WWEG XLum
§	- - 'Spitzentänzerin' ♀H4	EBee
	- - 'Summer Nights'	CMea EBee LBMP LDai LRHS LSou MBri MDKP MPie MSpe SBea SMrm SPhx WFar
	- - 'Summer Stripe' **new**	MBri
	- - Summer Sun	see *H. helianthoides* var. *scabra* 'Sommersonne'
	- - 'Sunburst'	LRHS
	- - 'Venus'	EBee ECtt EWll LRHS LSou MBri NLar WFar
	- 'Summer Pink'	WHil
	- 'Super Dwarf'	LSou
	- 'Tuscan Sun'	EBee ECtt MBri WHil
	orientalis	LLHF

Heliotropium ✿ (*Boraginaceae*)

§	***amplexicaule***	SDys
	anchusifolium	see *H. amplexicaule*
§	***arborescens***	CArn ENfk EPfP EShb MCot MHom
	- 'Chatsworth' ♀H1	CCCN CSpe ECre ECtt MHom WFar
	- 'Dame Alice de Hales'	ECtt MHom
	- 'Gatton Park'	MHom SMrm
	- 'Lord Roberts'	ECtt MHom WWlt
	- 'Marine'	ECtt WGor
	- 'Mary Fox'	MHom

– 'Mrs J.W. Lowther'	MHom
– 'President Garfield'	MHom WFar
– 'Princess Marina' 🏆H1	EPfP LAst LSou NLar
– 'Reva'	ECtt MHom
– 'The Queen'	ECtt
– 'The Speaker'	MHom
– 'White Lady'	CCCN CSpe ECtt MHom NLar
– 'White Queen'	ECtt MHom
– 'Woodcote'	MHom
'Baby Blue'	NPri
'Butterfly Kisses'	EPfP SPoG
peruvianum	see *H. arborescens*

Helipterum see *Syncarpha*

anthemoides	see *Rhodanthe anthemoides*

Helleborus ✿ (*Ranunculaceae*)

abruzzicus WM 0227	MPhe
abschasicus	see *H. orientalis* Lam. subsp. *abchasicus*
'Amber Gem' (Winter Jewels Series) (d) **new**	MPnt
'Angel Glow'	LRHS
§ ***argutifolius*** 🏆H4	Widely available
– 'Janet Starnes' (v)	MAsh
– 'Little 'Erbert'	MAsh
– mottled-leaved	see *H. argutifolius* 'Pacific Frost'
§ – 'Pacific Frost' (v)	EWes LRHS MAsh
– 'Red Riding Hood'	LRHS
– 'Silver Lace'	CCon EBee ELan EPfP GKev LDai LRHS LSRN MBel MGos NBir NLar NSti SKHP SPer SPoG SUsu
atrorubens misapplied	see *H. orientalis* Lam. subsp. *abchasicus* Early Purple Group
atrorubens Waldst. & Kit.	CDes MRav
– WM 9028 from Slovenia	MPhe
– WM 9805 from Croatia	GBuc MPhe
– WM 9825	LWst
– from Slovenia	EHrv
– spotted form	MPhe
× ***ballardiae***	CLAP MAsh
– 'Candy Love'PBR	LRHS MBri NLar NRHS SHil
– 'HGC Cinnamon Snow'	EBee ESwi LRHS
– 'HGC Pink Frost'	EBee LRHS
'Blue Moon' **new**	MWat
bocconei	LWst
– subsp. ***bocconei***	see *H. multifidus* subsp. *bocconei*
'Briar Rose'	MAsh
colchicus	see *H. orientalis* Lam. subsp. *abchasicus*
corsicus	see *H. argutifolius*
croaticus	LWst
– WM 9313	MPhe
– WM 9810 from Croatia	MPhe
cyclophyllus	GEdr GKev GMaP MPhe NLar SPer
– HOA 8934	LWst WSpi
– HOA 9144	LWst
dumetorum	EHrv GBuc WSpi
– WM 0023	LWst
– WM 9209 from Slovenia	MPhe
– WM 9627 from Croatia	GBuc MPhe
– WM 9832	LWst
§ × ***ericsmithii***	Widely available
– 'Bob's Best'	CHid CLAP CPLG CYeo ESwi LPla LRHS MBNS MBel MNrw NPnk SEND SHar SKHP SMrm SPoG SWvt WCot
– 'HGC Silvermoon'PBR	IBoy LRHS MAsh NLar SPoG
– 'Ruby Glow'	EPfP LRHS
– 'Snow Love'PBR	LRHS MBri NLar NRHS SHil
– 'Winter Moonbeam'PBR	CLAP EHrv EPfP LRHS MAsh MCot NCGa SKHP SLon SPoG
– 'Winter Sunshine'PBR	CLAP EHrv EPfP LBuc LRHS SKHP SPoG
foetidus 🏆H4	Widely available
– 'Chedglow'	CNat EBee
– 'Gold Bullion'	MAsh SBfd SPoG WFar WWEG
– 'Harvington Pewter'	CLAP EHrv LRHS MAsh SPoG
– 'Pewter'	CLAP
– 'Ruth'	MAsh
– 'Sopron'	CLAP NLar
– sweet-scented	MHom
– Wester Flisk Group	CPLG EBee EPfP GBuc IFoB LAst LHop LRHS MAsh MBri MGos MRav MSwo NPer NPnk WFar WPGP
– 'Yorkley'	LSRN
Gold Collection	see *H.* cultivars with names starting HGC
'Golden Sunrise' (Winter Jewels Series) **new**	MPnt NCGa
'Harlequin Gem' (Winter Jewels Series) (d) **new**	MPnt
'HGC Jericho'PBR	IVic
N × ***hybridus***	Widely available
– 'Albin Otto'	LRHS
– 'Amber Queen' (Queen Series)	SBfd WSpi
– anemone-centred	CHid CLAP GBin IFoB LHel MNrw SHil SPoG WFar
– 'Antique Shades'	WFar
– 'Apple Blossom'	WFar
– apricot-flowered	CLAP EPfP GBuc LBMP WFar WSpi WTin
– Ashwood Garden hybrids	EPPr EPfP LRHS MAsh MGos MRav SEND SLon SRms WSpi WWEG
– – anemone-centred	MAsh
– – double-flowered (d)	MAsh
– Ballard's Group	CLAP GEdr LRHS MWat NCGa SPer WFar WMnd WPnP
– 'Black Beauty'	NEgg NHol NPnk WSpi
– black-flowered	CLAP GBuc GKev GMaP NChi WFar WHoo WTin
– 'Blue Lady' (Lady Series)	CBcs EPfP GAbr GBin GEdr IFoB LRHS MBNS MGos NGdn SMad SMrm SPer WSpi
– 'Blue Metallic Lady' (Lady Series)	CPLG CWCL EAEE EPfP GAbr GEdr GKev LAst LBMP LHop LRHS MBNS MWat MWhi NEgg NGdn NPnk SPer WGwG WSpi WWEG
– blue-grey-flowered	SEND
– Bradfield hybrids	MCot
– – anemone-centred	EHrv MCot
– – double-flowered (d)	EHrv MCot
– – picotee	EHrv MCot
– Bradfield Star Group	EHrv
– Caborn hybrids	LLWP
– 'Cherry Blossom' (Winter Jewels Series) **new**	MPnt NCGa
– 'Cinderella' (d)	LRHS
– 'Clare's Purple'	LSRN WSpi
– 'Cosmos'	MBNS SEND
– cream-flowered	CLAP IFro SEND WFar WTin
– dark purple-flowered	LHel SBfd
– dark red-flowered	LHel
– dark-flowered **new**	WSpi
– 'David's Star' (d)	CCon
– deep red-flowered	CLAP GBuc NChi NHol WFar WTin

- double (d) CAvo CLAP CMea CSpe GBuc LHop MNrw NPnk WFar WTin
- - pink-flowered (d) LHel
- - black-flowered (d) CPLG IFoB
- - green-flowered (d) LHel
- - purple-flowered (d) LHel
- - red-flowered (d) CPLG
- - white-flowered (d) CPLG IFoB LHel WSpi
- - yellow-flowered (d) CPLG IFoB IFro LHel
- 'Double Ellen Picotee' (d) GBin WHlf
- 'Double Ellen Red' (d) GBin WHlf
- 'Double Ellen White' (d) GBin WHlf
- Double Ladies, mixed (d) GAbr WCot
- 'Double Vision' (d) EPPr
- Elizabeth Town anemone-centred **new** IFro
- - double (d) **new** IFro
- - picotee **new** IFro
- - red IFro
- 'Emerald Queen' (Queen Series) GBin GQue WSpi
- Farmyard anemone-centred WFar
- - apricot WFar
- - black WFar
- - cream WFar
- - cream, dark-eyed WFar
- - cream, spotted WFar
- - dark pink WFar
- - double apricot (d) WFar
- - - black (d) WFar
- - - cream (d) WFar
- - - cream spotted (d) WFar
- - - pink (d) WFar
- - - pink spotted (d) WFar
- - - primrose (d) WFar
- - - primrose spotted (d) WFar
- - - red (d) WFar
- - - slate-grey (d) WFar
- - - white (d) WFar
- - - white spotted (d) WFar
- - green WFar
- - green spotted WFar
- - picotee WFar
- - pink WFar
- - pink spotted WFar
- - plum WFar
- - primrose WFar
- - primrose dark-eyed WFar
- - primrose spotted WFar
- - red WFar
- - slate spotted WFar
- - slate-grey WFar
- - veined WFar
- - white WFar
- - white dark-eyed WFar
- - white splash WFar
- - white spotted WFar
- 'Farmyard Appleblossom' WFar
- 'Farmyard Woodland' WFar
- 'Gala Queen' (Queen Series) ELon SBfd
- 'Golden Lotus' (d) MPnt NPnk WHlf
- 'Green Ripple' WFar
- green-flowered WFar
- 'Günther Jürgl' (d) WFar
- Harvington double chocolate (d) **new** CLAP SPoG
- - - dark purple (d) LRHS
- - - pink (d) CLAP EBee LRHS NRHS SKHP SLon SPoG
- - - pink speckled (d) **new** SPoG
- - - purple (d) CLAP EBee LRHS NBir NLar SKHP SPoG
- - - red (d) CLAP EBee LRHS NBir NLar NRHS SLon SPoG
- - - speckled (d) LRHS SPoG
- - - white (d) CLAP EBee LRHS NBir NLar NRHS SKHP SLon SPoG
- - - yellow (d) CLAP EBee LRHS NBir NLar NRHS SKHP SLon SPoG
- - - apricot-flowered (d) LRHS SPoG
- - - lime-green (d) CLAP LRHS
- - picotee CLAP EBee LRHS MGos NBir NLar NRHS SKHP SLon SPoG
- - pink EBee LRHS MGos NLar SLon SPoG
- - pink speckled EBee LRHS MGos NLar SLon SPoG
- - red EBee LRHS MGos MHer NLar SLon SPoG
- - speckled EBee LRHS MHer NRHS SLon
- - speckled white EBee SKHP SLon SPoG
- - white EBee LRHS MGos MHer NLar NRHS SKHP SLon SPoG
- - yellow EBee LRHS MGos MHer NLar SKHP SLon SPoG
- - yellow speckled EBee LRHS MGos MHer NLar NRHS SLon SPoG
- 'Harvington Apricots' EBee LRHS NBir NLar SKHP SLon SPoG
- 'Harvington Shades of the Night' EBee LRHS MGos MHer NLar NRHS SKHP SLon SPoG
- 'Harvington Smokey Blues' LRHS NRHS SKHP SLon SPoG
- 'Harvington Smokey Double' (d) EBee NRHS
- 'Helen Ballard' GKev NHol
- Hillier hybrids clear-white LRHS SHil
- - double (d) **new** SHil
- - double pink (d) LRHS
- - pink and white LRHS
- - single **new** SHil
- - slate LRHS NRHS SHil
- - spotted, double-pink (d) LRHS
- - - green LRHS
- - - pink LRHS MBri
- - - white LRHS MBri NRHS
- - yellow MBri
- - anemone-centred MBri SHil
- - burgundy LRHS MBri NRHS SHil
- Homelea hybrids, anemone-centred CRDP
- - double (d) CRDP
- 'Ice Queen' (Queen Series) SBfd WSpi
- ivory-flowered WFar
- Kaye's garden hybrids LRHS WMnd
- Kochii Group LRHS
- 'Lady Macbeth' EWes
- Lady Series NSum
- large, pink-flowered IFro WTin
- maroon-flowered WFar
- mauve freckled, double (d) **new** IFro
- 'Mrs Betty Ranicar' (d) CBro EPfP EWes GEdr IFoB LHop LRHS MBNS MGos NCGa NSum WFar
- 'Onyx Odyssey' CSpe MPnt NCGa
- 'Pale Picotee' **new** GBuc
- pale pink-flowered GBuc

– 'Pamina'	IFoB
§ – Party Dress Group (d)	CHid ELan ELon GBin IFoB LRHS LSRN NLar STes WFar
– – 'Party Dress Pink' (d) **new**	CWCL
– Picotee Group	NLar WTin
– – 'Picotee'	CLAP GBuc IFoB LHel WCru WFar WHoo
– – 'Picotee' double-flowered (d)	CWCL LHel
– pink freckled, double (d) **new**	IFro
– 'Pink Lady' (Lady Series)	CBcs EPfP GQue MGos NEgg NGdn NPri SMrm SPer
– 'Pink Upstart'	IFoB
– pink-flowered	CLAP GAbr GBuc LHel MBNS WFar WHoo WTin
– pink-red-flowered	LHel
– plum-flowered	CLAP GBuc SEND WFar WTin
– 'Pluto'	WFar
– primrose-flowered	CLAP ECGP ELan EWTr GBuc MCot NEgg SBfd SEND WFar WTin
– 'Purple Haze'	NPnk
– purple-flowered	CLAP NHol WBor WFar WHoo
– '(Queen Series) Queen of Hearts'	SBfd WSpi
– – 'Queen of Spades'	SBfd SMad WSpi
– – 'Queen of the Night'	CLAP CPLG CWCL EPfP IBal MWhi STes WSpi
– 'Red Lady' (Lady Series)	CBcs CPLG EAEE EPfP EPot GAbr IBal LAst LHop LRHS LSRN MBNS MGos MWhi NEgg NOrc SMrm SPer WGwG
– 'Red Spotted'	EPfP GEdr LRHS MWhi WWEG
– 'Red Upstart'	IFoB
– red-flowered	GBuc
– slaty blue-flowered	CLAP GBuc IFoB LHel WFar
– slaty purple-flowered	GBuc WFar
– 'Smokey Blue'	EWTr LRHS NPnk WSpi
– smokey purple-flowered	ELan LSRN WFar
– 'Speckled Draco'	CPLG
§ – spotted	CLAP EPfP GBuc GMaP NEgg SBfd SWal WCot WCru WHoo WTin WWEG
– – cream	CLAP NBir WTin
– – double, pink (d)	LHel
– – – white (d)	LHel
– – – yellow (d) **new**	WHlf
– – green	CLAP WFar WTin
– – ivory	CLAP
– – pink	CLAP IFro LHel LRHS MBNS NBir SEND SHil WFar WHoo WTin
– – primrose	CLAP ELan WFar WTin
– – white	GBuc IFro LHel NBir SHil WFar WTin WWEG
– – yellow	LHel SHil
– 'Spotted Lady'	GBin
– Sunshine selections	GKev IBal
– 'Tricastin'	IBoy SPad
– 'Tutu'[PBR]	CWCL EBee EHrv EPfP LBuc LRHS NCGa SPoG
– 'Ushba'	CLAP
– Washfield double-flowered (d)	CSpe EPfP EWTr MGos NCGa SBfd SPer SRkn SWal WBor WRHF WSpi
– – – white (d)	IFoB
– 'White Lady' (Lady Series)	CPLG GEdr IFoB LAst LHop MBNS MGos MWat NEgg NPri SDix SMrm SPer WSpi
– 'White Lady Spotted' (Lady Series)	CHVG ELon EPfP GBin GEdr GQue NEgg SDix SPer
– white-flowered	GBuc LHel WCFE WFar WHoo WTin
– white-veined	WFar

– Winter Queen strain	WWEG
– yellow freckled, double (d) **new**	IFro
– 'Yellow Lady' (Lady Series)	CBcs EPfP EPot GEdr LHop LRHS MBNS MWhi NEgg SMrm SPer WSpi WWEG
– yellow-flowered	GMaP IFoB LHel WFar WHoo WTin
§ 'Ivory Prince'[PBR]	EPfP LBuc LRHS MAsh SPoG
'Jade Star' (Winter Jewels Series) **new**	MPnt
'Kiwi Black Velvet'	IBal
liguricus WM 0230	MPhe
Linnet Series **new**	LBuc
lividus ♀H2-3	CBro CEnt CLAP CSpe EPfP EWes LHop LRHS NBir NRHS SDeJ SKHP SWal SWat
– subsp. ***corsicus***	see *H. argutifolius*
– 'Silver Edge'	EPfP
– 'White Marble'	LRHS SKHP
'Moonshine'[PBR]	CLAP ELon NLar SLon
multifidus	EBee EPPr NBir
§ – subsp. ***bocconei***	EHrv GCal LWSt NLar
– – WM 9719 from Italy	MPhe
– – WM 9905 from Sicily	MPhe
– subsp. ***hercegovinus*** WM 0020	MPhe
– – WM 0622	MPhe
– subsp. ***istriacus***	CBro MAsh
– – WM 9322	MPhe
– – WM 9324	MPhe
– subsp. ***multifidus*** WM 9529	MPhe
– – WM 9748 from Croatia	MPhe
– – WM 9833	MPhe
niger ♀H4	Widely available
– Ashwood strain	CLAP MAsh
– Blackthorn Group	CDes CLAP EHrv NLar
– 'David'	IVic
– 'Double Fashion'[PBR] **new**	LRHS
– double-flowered (d)	CDes ELan MAsh
– 'Eifelturm'	IVic
– Harvington hybrids	CLAP EHrv LRHS MAsh MBri MHer SPoG
– 'HGC Jacob'[PBR]	IVic LBuc LRHS LSRN
– 'HGC Josef Lemper'[PBR]	IVic LRHS LSRN
– 'HGC Joshua'[PBR]	IVic
– 'Ivory Prince'[PBR]	see *H.* 'Ivory Prince'
– Lynda Windsor Group	CRDP
– 'Marion' (d)	IFoB
– 'Maximus'	CLAP EBee EWes
– 'Potter's Wheel'	CLAP ELan EPfP LRHS NBir NLar
– 'Praecox'	EBee EPPr EPfP EWes LRHS
– 'Schneeball'	IVic
– Sunset Group	NLar
– 'White Christmas'	LRHS MBri NRHS SHil
– 'White Magic'	MNrw WSpi
× ***nigercors*** ♀H4	CDes CSpe CYeo ECha ECtt EHrv GMaP LHop LPla LRHS MAsh MCot WCot WFar WPGP
– double-flowered (d)	CYeo GBin LSou MAvo MBNS SMrm WCot
– 'HGC Green Corsican'[PBR]	EBee LRHS
– 'Morning's Pride'[PBR]	EBee LRHS
– 'Pink Beauty'	LBuc NLar SPoG
× ***nigristern***	see *H.* × *ericsmithii*
odorus	EHrv EWes GMaP IFoB MPhe NLar NPnk SPer WSpi XLum
– WM 0312 from Bosnia	MPhe

	- WM 9415	MPhe
	- WM 9728 from Hungary	MPhe
N	***orientalis*** misapplied	see *H.* × *hybridus*
	orientalis ambig.	CBar CHab ECho EHrv LAst LRHS MWat NPri WPtf
	orientalis Lam.	CBcs EWes LRHS MPhe MSwo XLum
§	- subsp. ***abchasicus*** (A. Braun) B. Mathew	GEdr LRHS NLar SRms WFar
	- - WM 9607	LWst
§	- - Early Purple Group	CTri GCal MRav WFar
	- subsp. ***guttatus*** misapplied	see *H.* × *hybridus* spotted
	- subsp. ***guttatus*** (A. Braun & Sauer) B. Mathew	CWCL NChi SRkn
	- - IBT 9401-7	CWCL SEND
	- subsp. ***orientalis*** from the Caucasus	LWst
	'Pink Beauty'PBR	EPfP LRHS MBri NCGa NLar SLon SPoG
	'Pink Ice'	MAsh
	'Pirouette'PBR	CLAP EPfP LRHS MAsh
	purpurascens	EBee EHrv EPPr EPfP GBuc GEdr GMaP IFoB LRHS MAsh MMuc MRav MWat NBir SPer WSpi WWEG XEll
	- WM 0815 from Romania	MPhe
	- WM 9211 from Hungary	MPhe
	- WM 9412	MPhe
	- WM 9922	LWst
	(Rodney Davey Marbled Group) 'Anna's Red' **new**	CRDP
	- 'Penny's Pink' **new**	CRDP
	'Silver Dollar'	EBee EWes LRHS LSRN MAsh SPoG
	'Snow White'	MAsh
	× ***sternii***	CBcs CSpe CTri CWCL ELan EPfP EWTr GMaP IFro LRHS MCot MGos MMoz MNrw MWat NEgg NLar NMRc NRHS SGar SPer WFar WMnd WMoo WTin
	- Aberconwy strain	CLAP
	- Ashwood strain	MAsh NLar
	- 'Beatrice le Blanc'	MAsh
	- Blackthorn Group ♀H3-4	EHrv ELon EPfP GAbr IFoB LHop LRHS MCot MRav SBfd SPer SWvt WBrk WFar WPGP
	- Blackthorn dwarf strain	CLAP EBee
	- Boughton Group	MRav
	- 'Boughton Beauty'	CLAP EBee ELan GBuc LRHS MAsh WSpi
	- pewter-flowered	CSpe
	thibetanus	CCon CLAP CPLG EFEx EHrv EWes GEdr LAma MAsh MCot MPhe NPnk WAbe
	torquatus	CBro EHrv GBuc LRHS MAsh MPhe SPer WFar WTin
	- HOA 9115	LWst
	- LD 308 from Serbia	LWst
	- WM 0609 from Montenegro	MPhe
	- WM 0617 from Serbia	MPhe
	- WM 9106 from Montenegro	GBuc MPhe
	- WM 9820 from Bosnia	MPhe
	- Caborn hybrids	LLWP
	- 'Dido' (d)	CPLG WFar
	- double-flowered, WM 0620 from Montenegro (d)	MPhe
	- hybrids	WFar
	- Party Dress Group	see *H.* × *hybridus* Party Dress Group
	- semi-double-flowered (d)	WFar
	- Wolverton hybrids	WFar
	'Verboom Beauty'	LRHS
	vesicarius	EWes MAsh
	viridis	EBee GPoy IFoB LRHS MCot NLar SRms WFar WTin
	- WM 0444	MPhe
	- subsp. ***occidentalis***	CBro EHrv
	- - WM 9401	MPhe
	- - WM 9502 from Germany	MPhe
	- subsp. ***viridis*** WM 9723 from Italy	MPhe
	Walberton's Rosemary = 'Walhero'	EPfP LBuc LRHS MAsh SHar SPoG
	'Washfield Queen' (Queen Series) **new**	CWCL
	'White Beauty'PBR	EPPr EPfP EWes LBuc LRHS MBri MGos NCGa NLar SPoG

Helonias (*Melanthiaceae*)

	bullata	EBee GEdr LRHS

Heloniopsis (*Melanthiaceae*)

	acutifolia B&SWJ 218	GEdr WCru
	- B&SWJ 6817	WCru
	- B&SWJ 6836	WCru
	japonica	see *H. orientalis*
§	***kawanoi***	CDes CSpe EBee GEdr NMen SKHP WCot WCru
	koreana B&SWJ 4173	WCru
	leucantha B&SWJ 11148 **new**	WCru
§	***orientalis***	CBro CLAP ECho GCal GEdr NMen WCot WCru
	- B&SWJ 6278	WCru
	- B&SWJ 6327	WCru
	- B&SWJ 6380 from Japan	WCru
	- from Korea	CDes EBee EPfP GEdr SChF SKHP SMad
	- var. ***breviscapa***	EBee EPfP LEdu SChF SMad WCru WPGP
	- - B&SWJ 5635	WCru
	- - B&SWJ 5873	WCru
	- - B&SWJ 5938	WCru
	- - 'A-so'	LEdu WCru
	- var. ***flavida*** B&SWJ 11400	WCru
	- variegated (v)	WCru
	- var. ***yakusimensis***	see *H. kawanoi*
	tubiflora B&SWJ 822	WCru
	- 'Temple Blue'	CLAP WCru WPGP
	umbellata	CDes EBee EPfP GEdr SKHP SMad WMoo
	- B&SWJ 1839	CLAP WCru
	- B&SWJ 3732	WCru
	- B&SWJ 6836	WCru
	- B&SWJ 6846	WCru
	- B&SWJ 7117	WCru

Helwingia (*Helwingiaceae*)

	chinensis	ESwi NLar SSpi WBor WPGP
	himalaica	CGHE ESwi WPGP
	japonica	CHGN EFEx

Helxine see *Soleirolia*

Hemerocallis ✿ (*Hemerocallidaceae*)

	'Aabaa'	EWoo
	'Aabachee'	SApp
	'Above the Clouds'	EWoo
	'Absolute Treasure'	CFwr SBrk
	'Absolute Zero'	CFwr SBrk SPol WAul

'Adah'	SDay
'Added Dimensions'	SApp
'Addie Branch Smith'	SDay
'Adeline Goldner'	CFwr
'Admiral's Braid'	EWoo
'Adoration'	SPer
'Africa'	SBrk
'African Chant'	ELan
'Age of Miracles'	SPol
'Ah Youth'	SApp
'Ahoya'	CBgR SPol
'Airs and Graces' **new**	SDay
'Alabama Jubilee'	WNHG
'Alakazam'	EWoo
'Alan'	EBee ECtt LRHS MRav NRHS
'Alaqua'	CCon GBuc LRHS MBNS SApp SBrk WFar
'Alec Allen'	SBrk SDay
'Alejandro Pavlos'	SApp
'Alexander the Great' **new**	WHrl
'Alien Encounter'	SPol
'Alien's Eye'	CFwr
'All American Baby'	CWat MBNS MSpe SBrk SPol
'All American Chief'	SBrk
'All American Magic'	SPol
'All American Plum'	CWCL EPfP MBNS MSpe SBrk WAul WHrl
'All American Tiger'	MSpe SBrk
'All American Windmill'	CFwr EWoo
'All Fired Up'	SBrk SPol
'Allegiance'	WNHG
'Almost Paradise'	SPol
'Alpine Mist'	SDay
'Alpine Rhapsody'	SPol
'Alpine Snow'	EWoo SBrk
altissima	CHEx EBee LPla MNrw SPhx
'Always Afternoon'	CKel EBee EWoo GBuc MBNS MNrw MSpe NCGa SApp SBrk SPol WAul WCAu WHrl WWEG XSen
'Amadeus'	GBuc SApp
'Ambassador'	CBgR
'Amber Classic'	ELon SApp
'American Freedom'	EWoo
'American Revolution'	Widely available
'Amersham'	MNFA SApp
'Amerstone Amethyst Jewel'	SApp
'Amethyst Squid'	EWoo
'Amy'	WWEG
'Anastasia'	SBrk
'Anatomically Correct'	EWoo
'Andrew Christian'	SPol
'Andy Candy'	CFwr
'Angel Artistry'	SApp SDay
'Angel Rodgers'	SApp
'Angel Unawares'	SApp WTin
'Aniakchak'	EWoo
'Ann Kelley'	SApp SBrk SDay
'Anna Warner'	ELon MMuc SEND
'Annabelle's Ghost'	CBgR
'Annie Welch'	ELon EPfP MBNS NBre
'Antarctica'	SApp SPol
'Antique Rose'	CKel SBrk SDay
'Anzac'	COlW ECha ECtt EHrv LHop LRHS MBNS MBel NBre NGdn SAga SApp SPav SWvt WMoo
'Apache Bandana'	EWoo
'Apache Beacon'	EWoo
'Apache Uprising'	SBrk
'Apache War Feather'	EWoo
'Apollo'	XSen
'Apollodorus'	SBrk SDay
'Apple Court Chablis'	SApp SPol
'Apple Court Champagne'	SApp SPol
'Apple Court Damson'	SApp SPol
'Apple Court Ruby'	SApp SPol
'Apple Crisp'	SApp
'Apple Of My Eye'	EWoo
'Apple Tart'	SDay
'Applique'	CFwr
'Après Moi'	MBNS NLar
'Apricot Angel'	SApp
'Apricot Beauty' (d)	CPrp LHop MBNS
'Apricotta'	WCot WPnP
'Apron Strings'	CFwr
'Aquamarine Seedling'	SApp
'Arachnephobia'	EWoo
'Arctic Snow'	CBgR CBro CMac EBee ECrc ECtt ELon EWoo LRHS MBNS MNrw NLar SBrk SPol SUsu WAul WPnP
'Arms to Heaven'	EWoo
'Arpeggio'	WHrl
'Arriba'	MNFA NBro
'Arthur Moore'	SDay
'Artistic Gold'	WTin
'Asian Artistry'	WNHG
'Asiatic Pheasant'	SPol
'Asterisk'	SDay
'Astral Voyager'	CFwr
'Aten'	SBfd SDay WAul
'Athlone'	EWoo
'Atlanta Bouquet'	SBrk
'Atlanta Fringe Benefit'	SApp SDay
'Augusto Bianco'	SApp
'Aunt Wimp'	EWoo
'Authur Vincent'	SPol
'Autumn Jewels'	EWoo
'Autumn Minaret'	EWoo
'Autumn Prince'	EWoo
'Autumn Red'	CBcs GKin LRHS MBNS MMuc MNrw NBir SEND SPol WCot
'Ava Michelle'	SApp SDay
'Avant Garde'	SApp SPol WCAu
'Avon Crystal Rose'	WNHG
'Awakening Dream'	SBrk
'Awesome Blossom'	GBin LSou MBNS MNrw SMrm WCAu WHrl
'Awesome Candy'	EWoo LSRN
'Aztec Firebird'	CFwr EWoo
'Aztec Furnace'	CBro SDay
'Baby Blues'	SDay SPol
'Baby Red Eyes'	CFwr
'Baby Talk'	CCon
'Badge of Honor'	SApp
'Baja'	MNFA WFar
'Bald Eagle'	WWEG
'Bali Hai'	COlW GBee LRHS MBNS MSCN SRms WHrl
'Ballerina Girl'	SBrk
'Bamboo Blackie'	CBgR EWoo SPol
'Banbury Cinnamon'	MBNS MSpe
'Bangkok Belle'	CWat
'Banned in Boston'	EWoo MSpe
'Banzai'	CFwr
'Barbara Mitchell'	EWoo GBuc MBNS MNFA SApp SBrk SDay WAul XSen
'Barbaresco'	SPol

Cultivar	Suppliers
'Barbary Corsair'	MSpe SApp SDay
'Bark At Me'	CFwr
'Barnegat Orange Twister'	CFwr
'Baronet's Badge'	SPol
'Baroni'	ECha
'Bat Signal'	CFwr EWoo
'Bathsheba'	SBrk SPol
'Battle Hymn'	WCAu
'Beat the Barons'	SBrk SPol
'Beautiful Edgings'	CFwr EWoo SBrk SDay SPol
'Beauty Bright'	MSpe
'Beauty to Behold'	SApp SBrk SDay
'Becky Lynn'	ECtt MBNS SApp
'Bees Rose'	XSen
'Beijing'	SBrk
'Bejeweled'	SApp SBrk WTin
'Bela Lugosi'	Widely available
'Believe It'	WNHG
'Bellini'	SBrk
'Ben Lee'	SDay
'Benchmark'	SApp SBrk
'Benedict'	SBrk
'Bengal Bay'	EWoo
'Bengal Fire' **new**	WNHG
'Berlin Lemon' ♀H4	MNFA
'Berlin Maize'	SApp
'Berlin Oxblood'	WAul
'Berlin Red' ♀H4	CPrp EBee ECha GBee GKin LBMP LRHS MNFA MNrw SApp WFar
'Berlin Red Velvet' ♀H4	MNFA
'Berlin Tallboy'	SApp SBrk
'Berlin Watermelon'	MBNS
'Bernard Thompson'	SApp
'Bertie Ferris'	EWoo MSpe NLar SDay
'Bess Ross'	CMHG MNFA XSen
'Bess Vestal'	MWat
'Best Kept Secret'	EWoo SPol
'Bette Davis Eyes'	CBgR CWat SApp SBrk SPol
'Betty Benz'	SBrk
'Betty Jenkins'	SBrk
'Betty Lyn'	SApp
'Betty Warren Woods'	SBrk SDay
'Betty Woods' (d)	SBrk SDay
'Betty's Pick'	EWoo
'Beware the Wizard'	CFwr
'Beyond 2000'	CFwr SApp
'Big Apple'	SApp SBrk SDay SPol
'Big Bird'	EWoo LSRN MBNS MSCN SApp SBrk WAul
'Big Bird's Friend'	CFwr
'Big City Eye'	MBNS SApp SBrk
'Big Golden'	WWEG
'Big Kiss' (d)	SPol
'Big Smile'	CWCL CWGN MBNS MNrw NBro SBrk SDeJ SMrm WFar
'Big Snowbird'	CFwr SBrk
'Big Time Happy'	LRHS MBNS SBfd SBrk SPoG
'Big World'	CBgR
'Bill Norris'	SApp SBrk SDay
'Bird Bath Pink'	SPol
'Birdwing Butterfly'	EWoo SPol
'Bitsy'	ELon LRHS SPet WCot WMnd WWEG
'Black Ambrosia'	SPol
'Black Emanuelle'	CPLG EBee IKil LAst LDai MBNS MNrw MWhi SBch
'Black Eye'	SDay WNHG
'Black Eyed Stella'	CKel MBNS WCot
'Black Eyed Susan'	ECtt MBNS MSpe SBrk
'Black Friar'	EWoo
'Black Ice'	CFwr EWoo SPol
'Black Knight'	EWoo NLar SRms
'Black Magic'	CBro CTri CWat EBee ELan EPfP GKin GMaP IPot LEdu LHop LRHS LSRN MBel MHer MRav MSpe MWhi NBir NEgg NGdn SAga SPer WHer WHrl WMoo
'Black Plush'	EWoo SPol
'Black Prince'	CCon EBee EWll EWoo IBoy LRHS MBNS NBre NBro WAul
'Black Stockings'	EBee EWes IPot SDeJ
'Blackberry Candy'	CSam ECtt GKin MBNS MNrw MSpe NWad SBrk WAul WCAu
'Blackeye Belle' **new**	EWoo
'Blackthorne'	CFwr
'Blessing'	SBrk SDay SPol
'Blonde is Beautiful'	SBrk SDay
'Blue Happiness'	SDay
'Blue Moon'	SApp
'Blue Ridge Shepherd Boy'	CFwr
'Blue Sheen'	CCon CMac EBee ECtt GMaP MBNS WFar WMoo
'Blueberry Candy'	ECtt EWoo IBoy MBNS SApp SBrk WAul
'Blueberry Cream'	CWCL EPfP MBNS MMHG MNrw MSpe SBrk
'Blueberry Frost' **new**	CBgR
'Blueberry Sundae'	CWat EBee
'Blue-eyed Butterfly'	SPol
'Blue-eyed Curls'	CFwr
'Blushing Belle'	MBNS NBro NEgg SApp
'Blutorange'	CFwr
'Bobo Anne'	CWat
'Bogie and Becall'	SPol
'Bold Encounter'	CFwr
'Bold One'	CMHG SPol
'Bold Ruler'	SPol
'Bonanza'	Widely available
'Boney Maroney'	CBgR CFwr EWoo SApp SBrk
'Bonheur'	WHrl
'Bonnie Boy'	XLum
'Booger'	SBrk
'Boogie my Woogie Baby'	CFwr EWoo
'Booroobin Magic'	EWoo
'Border Baby'	ECtt SBrk
'Border Lord'	EWoo
'Born Yesterday'	SApp
'Boulderbrook Serenity'	SDay
'Bourbon Kings'	EBee MBNS MSpe NBre SDeJ SPav WHrl
'Bowl of Roses'	SApp
'Bradley Bernard'	SPol
'Braided Edgings'	CFwr
'Brand New Lover'	SApp SDay
'Brass Buckles'	see *H.* 'Puddin'
'Brasstown' **new**	SPol
'Breed Apart'	SPol
'Brenda Newbold'	SDay SPol
'Brer Rabbit's Baby'	EWoo
'Bridget'	ELan
'Bright Beacon'	SDay SPol
'Bright Spangles'	MSpe SApp
'Brilliant Circle'	ECtt SApp
'Bristol Fashion'	SApp
'Broadway Bold Eyes'	SPol
'Broadway Image'	SBrk
'Broadway Valentine'	SApp SBrk XSen
'Brocaded Gown'	ELan SApp SBrk SDay

'Brookwood Wow'	SApp
'Brown Billows'	EWoo
'Brown Exotica'	EWoo
'Brown Witch'	EWoo
'Brunette'	SApp
'Bruno Müller'	MNFA SApp
'Brushed with Bronze'	SPol
'Bubbly'	SApp SDay
'Bud Producer'	SPol
'Buddha'	WCAu
'Buffy's Doll'	MBNS SApp SBrk
'Bugs Ear'	SDay
'Bumble Bee'	CWat ECtt MBNS NBre SApp
'Burlesque'	SDay SPol WCot
'Burning Daylight' ♀H4	CBgR EBee ECtt EHrv EPfP LAst LRHS MNFA MNrw MRav MWat NBre NEgg SPer SRms WAul WCFE WCot WFar WPtf
'Burning Embers'	SApp
'Bus Stop'	SApp SPol
'Butterfly Ballet'	SBrk
'Butterfly Charm'	CWat
'Butterpat'	SDay
'Butterscotch'	WFar
'Butterscotch Ruffles'	SDay
'Button Box'	SDay
'Buzz Bomb'	CWat ECrc ECtt GBee GKin LRHS LSRN MBNS NEgg NGdn NHol SApp SPer WFar WWEG
'Cabbage Flower'	XSen
'Cage'	SBrk
'Cajun Christmas'	CFwr
'Calico Spider'	SBrk
'California Sunshine'	SApp SPol
'Call Girl'	SDay
'Calypso' **new**	EWoo
'Camden Ballerina'	SDay
'Camden Glory'	SApp
'Camden Gold Dollar'	SApp SBrk SDay
'Camelot Green'	WNHG
'Cameron Quantz'	SApp
'Cameroons'	SDay
'Canadian Border Patrol'	CWCL IBal IPot MBNS MNrw NLar SApp SBrk SPer SPol WCAu WFar WHrl
'Canary Feathers'	SApp
'Canary Glow'	CTri SMrm WFar
'Canary Wings'	CBgR
'Candide'	SApp SDay
'Candied Popcorn Perfection'	CFwr
'Cantique'	SApp SDay SPol
'Capernaum Cocktail'	SPol
'Captain Ahab'	SApp
'Captive Audience'	SBrk
'Capulina'	CFwr EWoo
'Cara Mia'	CBgR MBNS NBir SPol WFar
'Caribbean Jack Dolan'	EWoo
'Carlotta' **new**	SDay
'Carolicolossal'	ELon SDay SPol
'Carolina Cranberry'	ELan
'Carolina Low Country'	CFwr
'Caroline Taylor'	WHrl
'Carolipiecrust'	SApp
'Carrick Wildon'	CFwr EBee
'Carrot'	CFwr
'Cartwheels' ♀H4	EBee EHrv EPfP EShb GBuc GKin GMaP LRHS MBNS MBel MSpe NBro SBch SPer WCAu WFar WMoo WTin
'Casino Gold'	SBrk
'Castile' **new**	SDay
'Castle Strawberry Delight'	SPol
'Catherine Neal'	SBrk SDay SPol
'Catherine Woodbery'	Widely available
'Cathy's Sunset'	CKel CSam EBee ECtt GKin LRHS LSRN MBNS MSpe MWat NBre NBro NEgg NGdn NWad SMrm SRGP
'Cat's Cradle'	SDay
'Caviar'	SDay
'Cedar Waxwing'	MNrw
'Cedric Morris'	LRHS
'Cee Tee'	SBrk
'Celebration of Angels'	SApp
'Celestial City'	SDay
'Celtic Christmas'	CFwr SPol
'Cenla Crepe Myrtle'	EWoo
'Cerulean Star'	EWoo SApp SPol
'Challenger'	EWoo
'Champagne Memory'	SApp
'Chance Encounter'	MBNS NHol SPol
'Changing Latitudes' **new**	SPol
'Charlene Moore' **new**	SPol
'Charles Johnston'	CBgR CKel EWoo MBNS SApp SBrk WAul
'Charlie Pierce Memorial'	MSpe SBrk SPol
'Charon the Ferryman'	CFwr
'Chartreuse Magic'	CMHG
'Chartwell'	EWoo
'Chasing the Sun'	CFwr
'Château Lafite'	SPol
'Cheerful Note'	WNHG
'Cherokee Patterns'	SPol
'Cherry Candy' **new**	MSpe
'Cherry Cheeks'	CCon EBee ECtt ELan ELon EPfP LRHS MBNS MBri MNrw MRav NHol NRHS SApp SBrk SPol WAul WCAu WCot WFar WMoo WWEG
'Cherry Eyed Pumpkin'	EWoo SBrk WCAu
'Cherry Kiss'	IVic SBrk
'Cherry Ripe'	MNFA
'Cherry Smoke'	SApp
'Cherry Tiger'	MBNS MSpe
'Cherry Valentine'	CBcs EBee MBNS MSpe SApp SBrk
'Chesières Lunar Moth'	ELon SApp SPol
'Chesnut Lane'	SApp SBrk SDay
'Chester Cyclone'	SDay
'Chevron Spider'	SDay
'Chicago Antique Tapestry'	SDay
'Chicago Apache'	CCon EPfP EWoo MBNS MNFA NBir NCGa SApp SBch SBrk SMad SPer SPol SUsu WAul
'Chicago Blackout'	CCon CWat ECtt EPfP IPot SApp WCot
'Chicago Brave'	WAul
'Chicago Cattleya'	CCon SApp WAul
'Chicago Cherry'	WNHG
'Chicago Fire'	EBee EPfP MBNS SDay
'Chicago Firecracker'	XLum XSen
'Chicago Heirloom'	CCon MBNS WAul
'Chicago Jewel'	CCon ELon NSti WAul
'Chicago Knobby'	MBNS MNrw SDay
'Chicago Knockout'	CCon ELan EPfP EWoo SPer WAul WWEG
'Chicago Mist'	WNHG
'Chicago Peach'	NBir
'Chicago Petticoats'	SApp WAul

Cultivar	Suppliers
'Chicago Picotee Lace'	SApp WWEG
'Chicago Picotee Memories'	EBee LRHS MBNS
'Chicago Picotee Promise'	WNHG
'Chicago Picotee Queen'	SApp
'Chicago Princess'	EWoo
'Chicago Queen'	SDay WMnd WNHG
'Chicago Rainbow'	CBgR MBNS WAul
'Chicago Royal Crown'	ECtt LRHS MSpe
'Chicago Royal Robe'	CWCL CWat ELon EWll LRHS MBNS NBid NCGa SPer SUsu SWat WCot WTin
'Chicago Ruby'	SApp SBrk
'Chicago Silver'	CCon COlW MBNS WAul
'Chicago Star'	WNHG
'Chicago Sugarplum'	SDay
'Chicago Sunrise'	CBgR EBee GMaP IBoy LRHS MBNS MBri MRav NGdn NOrc NRHS SApp SBrk SPet SWvt WCot WPer WWEG
'Chief Four Fingers'	EWoo
'Chief Sarcoxie' $\mathbb{Y}^{H4}$	SApp
'Child of Fortune'	SApp SDay
'Children's Festival'	CMac EBee ECtt GMaP LPBA LRHS MBNS MRav MSpe NLar SApp SBrk SWvt WFar WMoo
'China Bride'	EWoo SApp SBrk SDay SPol
'China Grove Plantation'	CFwr
'Chinese Autumn'	SApp SBrk
'Chinese Cloisonne'	SApp
'Chinese Coral'	EWoo
'Chinese Imp'	NLar SDay
'Chocolate Candy'	CWGN EBee EPfP IPot MBNS
'Chocolate Cherry Truffle'	SApp
'Choctaw Chick'	CFwr
'Chokecherry Mountain'	EWoo
'Chorus Line'	SApp SBrk SDay SPol WNHG
'Chorus Line Kid'	SPol
'Chosen Love'	SApp
'Christine Lynn'	WNHG
'Christmas Carol'	SApp
'Christmas Is'	CBgR CMac COlW CWGN EBee ELon GBin GKin LPot LRHS LSou MBNS MBel MCot MNrw MSpe NBre NCGa NHol SApp SBrk SDay SPav SPol WAul WCot WHrl WWEG XSen
'Christmas Tidings'	SApp
'Chute Libre'	CFwr
'Ciao'	SApp SDay
'Ciarra Vonnie' **new**	SDay
'Cimarron Knight'	EWoo SBrk SPol WCAu
'Cindy's Eye'	WCot
'Cinnamon Pleasure'	WCAu
'Circle of Beauty'	SBrk SPol
'Circles and Stripes'	CFwr
citrina	CBgR CHid CMac CPLG EBee EWTr EWoo GQue LRHS MCot NGdn WCot WHrl WRHF WTin XLum
citrina × (× ***ochroleuca***)	SMHy WCot
'Civil Law'	SDay
'Civil Rights'	SBrk SDay
'Classic Caper'	WNHG
'Classic Spider'	SApp
'Claudine'	SApp
'Cleo'	EWoo
'Cleopatra'	ELon EWoo SPol WAul
'Clockwork'	SBrk
'Clothed in Glory'	CWCL EWoo MBNS SApp WCot WWEG
'Coburg Fright Wig'	EWoo
'Cocktail Party'	MBri
'Colonel Joe'	EWoo
'Colonial Dame'	WTin
'Colour Me Yellow'	SApp
'Comanche Eyes'	SApp SDay
'Comet Flash'	SPol
'Coming Up Roses'	CPar ELon SApp SBrk SDay
'Concorde Nelson'	CFwr
'Condilla' (d)	SApp SBrk SPol
'Conspicua'	SMHy SPol
'Contessa'	CBro GBin LRHS NRHS SPer
'Cool It'	CKel EBee LHop LRHS MBNS NBre NCGa SApp SDeJ WHrl
'Cool Jazz'	SApp SBrk SDay SPol
'Copper Dawn'	NChi SApp
'Copper Windmill'	SDay SPol
'Copperhead'	SPol
'Coral Crab'	EWoo SApp
'Coral Eye Shadow'	EWoo
'Coral Mist'	ECrc MBNS NBre
'Coral Sparkler'	WNHG
'Coral Spider'	SPol
'Coral Taco'	EWoo
'Corky' $\mathbb{Y}^{H4}$	Widely available
'Corryton Pink'	SPol
'Corsican Bandit'	SDay
'Cosmic Hummingbird'	MSpe SApp SDay
'Cosmopolitan'	MBNS MCot SBrk
'Côte d'Azur'	CFwr
'Country Club'	GMaP MBNS NHol SApp SPol WWEG
'Country Melody'	SDay
'Court Cavalcade'	SBrk
'Court Magician'	EWoo SApp SBrk
'Court Troubadour'	SPol
'Coyote Moon'	SDay
'Cranberry Baby'	CWan SBrk SDay WHoo WNHG WTin
'Cranberry Coulis'	CWat MBNS
'Crawleycrow'	XSen
'Crazy Pierre'	EWoo SPol WHrl XSen
'Cream Drop'	CPrp EBee ECtt GMaP IBoy LRHS MCot MHer MRav NBro NGdn NLar NSti SApp SBrk SPav SPer WAul WCot WHrl WMoo WTin
'Creation'	EWoo
'Creative Edge'	WAul
'Creature of the Night'	SApp
'Crimson Flood'	EWoo
'Crimson Icon'	SDay WTin
'Crimson Pirate'	CBgR CBre CFwr CMac EBee ECrc ELon EPfP EWoo IBoy LHop LSRN MBNS MSpe NBir NHol NOrc NPro SApp SBfd SBrk SPer SPlb SPol SWat WAul WCAu WHrl WMoo WTin
'Crimson Wind'	SApp
'Crintonic Shadowlands'	SPol
'Cripple Creek'	EWoo
'Croesus'	SRms
'Crystal Pinot'	IPot
'Crystalline Pink'	SBrk
'Cupid's Gold'	SBrk SDay
'Curls'	MBNS SDay
'Curly Cinnamon Windmill'	SDay SPol
'Curly Pink Ribbons'	EWoo
'Curly Ripples'	SApp
'Curly Rosy Posy'	SDay

'Custard Candy'	CWCL CWGN EWoo GKin MBNS MBri MSpe NHol SApp SBfd SBrk SUsu WAul WCAu WNHG
'Cynthia Mary'	ECtt GKin LHop MBNS MSpe NBro SRGP WFar
'D.R. McKeithan'	CFwr
'Dad's Best White'	WTin
'Daggy'	SBrk
'Daily Dollar'	LRHS MBNS MSpe NGdn SApp
'Dallas Spider Time'	MNFA SDay
'Dallas Star'	SApp SPol
'Dan Mahony'	MBNS
'Dan Tau'	CKel SDay
'Dance Among the Stars'	CFwr
'Dance Ballerina Dance'	EBee SBrk SDay
'Dancing Crab'	EWoo SPol
'Dancing Dwarf'	SApp SDay
'Dancing Lions'	SDay
'Dancing Shiva'	SApp SBrk SDay SPol
'Dancing Summerbird'	SApp SPol
'Daring Deception'	CCon CKel ECtt ELon IPot LRHS MBNS MNrw MSpe SApp SPad WFar WHrl
'Daring Dilemma'	MSpe SPol
'Daring Reflection'	MSpe SDay
'Darius'	WNHG
'Dark and Handsome'	MBNS
'Dark Angel'	MSpe
'Dark Avenger'	EBee MBNS MSpe SBrk SHar
'Dark Elf'	SApp SDay
'Dark Sprite'	MSpe
'Darker Shade'	SBrk
'Darkest Night'	SApp SBrk
'Darla Anita'	NGBo SBrk
'Date Book' **new**	EWoo
'David Holman'	WNHG
'David Kirchhoff'	IPot SApp WAul
'Davidson Update'	WNHG
'Dazzle'	SApp
'Dazzling Spider'	CFwr
'Debary Canary'	EWoo
'Debussy'	EWoo
'Decatur Ballerina'	WNHG
'Decatur Captivation'	WNHG
'Decatur Cherry Smash'	SDay
'Decatur Dictator'	WNHG
'Decatur Elevator'	EWoo
'Decatur Imp'	WHrl
'Decatur Jewel'	WNHG
'Decatur Rhythm'	WNHG
'Decatur Supreme'	WNHG
'Decatur Treasure Chest'	WNHG
'Dee Dee Mac'	SApp
'Delicate Design'	SApp SPol
'Delightsome'	SBrk SDay
'Demetrius'	CWat MNFA SApp
'Dena Marie's Sister'	CFwr
'Denali'	SBrk
'Derrick Cane'	SPol
'Desdemona'	SPol XLum
'Desert Bandit'	SApp
'Desert Dreams'	WCot
'Desert Icicle'	CFwr EWoo
'Designer Gown'	SApp SDay
'Designer Jeans'	SBrk SPol
'Destined to See'	Widely available
'Devil's Footprint'	SDay SPol
'Devon Cream'	SPer
'Devonshire'	SApp SBrk
'Dewberry Candy'	MSpe
'Diabolique'	CFwr EWoo
'Diamond Dust'	CKel EBee ECtt GBee LRHS MBNS MSpe NLar SApp SMrm SPer WTin
'Dick Kitchingman' **new**	SPol
'Dido'	CTri
'Dipped in Ink'	SPol
'Distant Star'	EWoo
'Diva Assoluta'	SApp
'Divertissment'	CBgR ELon EWoo SApp SDay WHrl
'Do the Twist' **new**	EWoo
'Do You Know Doris'	SDay
'Doll House'	SBrk
'Dominic'	CBgR COIW CPar EWoo IBoy MSpe SApp SBrk SPol WCot WMoo
'Donnie Delight'	SBrk
'Dont Mess with Me'	CFwr
'Dorethe Louise'	SBrk SDay SPol
'Dorothy McDade'	COIW EWoo MNrw
'Dot Paul'	ELan
'Double Action' (d)	SPol
'Double Coffee' (d)	SApp SPav SPol
'Double Corsage' (d)	SApp SPol
'Double Cream' (d)	WCot
'Double Cutie' (d)	NBre NLar SDay WAul
'Double Delicious' (d)	WCot
'Double Doubloon' (d)	XLum
'Double Dream' (d)	MDev WHrl
'Double Firecracker' (d)	CCVN CWat EBee IBal MBNS NBro NLar SBrk XSen
'Double Grapette' (d)	SApp
'Double Layer' (d)	CFwr
'Double Oh Seven' (d)	ELon SApp SPol
'Double Passion' (d)	MBNS
'Double Peach Schnapps' (d)	SBrk
'Double Red Royal' (d)	XSen
'Double River Wye' (d)	CBgR CCon COIW CWat EBee ECtt EPfP EShb IBoy MBNS MHer MNrw NGdn NMRc SApp SMrm SPol SWat WAul WBrk WCot WHoo WHrl WMnd WTin WWEG
'Doublecious'	CWGN
§ 'Doubloon' (d)	COIW LRHS NHol
'Dover Plantation'	CFwr
'Dragon Dreams'	SApp SPol
'Dragon Fire Breath'	CFwr
'Dragon Heart'	EWoo
'Dragon King'	SPol
'Dragon Lore'	MBNS SBrk
'Dragon's Eye'	CWat EWoo MSpe SDay SPol
'Dragon's Orb'	CKel SDay
'Dream Baby'	NBre
'Dream Catcher'	EWoo
'Dream Keeper'	EWoo
'Dreamy Cream'	SBrk
'Dresden Doll'	EBee SPer
'Driven Snow'	SApp
'Druid's Chant'	EWoo LRHS MSpe
'Duke of Durham'	EWoo MBNS MNFA MSpe SApp SPhx
dumortieri	CBro ECha EHrv ELan LRHS MCoo MCot MRav NBid NBir NSti SPer WCot WHrl WTin WWEG
- B&SWJ 1283	WCru
'Dune Needlepoint'	SPol WHrl
'Dutch Beauty'	WFar
'Dutch Gold'	LRHS MNrw NBro
'Dynasty Pink'	SApp
'Earl of Warwick'	CBgR SPol

'Earlianna'	SPol
'Early to Bed'	SBrk
'Earth Angel'	SApp SPol
'Easy Ned'	EWoo SBrk SDay SPol WTin
'Easy Street' **new**	SDay
'Eat Our Wake Pintaheads'	CFwr
'Ebony Prince'	EWoo
'Echo Canyon'	EWoo
'Ed Murray'	GBin MNFA WAul WCAu
'Edgar Brown'	MBNS SBrk SDay
'Edge Ahead'	CMac ECtt GKin LRHS MBNS MSpe NHol SBrk SMrm
'Edge of Darkness'	CKel CWGN EPfP MBNS NBro NLar NSti SApp WAul WFar
'Edge of Heaven'	CWat
'Edna Spalding'	LRHS NRHS SApp SDay
'Eenie Allegro'	CBro ECtt IBal MBNS SPer WMnd
'Eenie Fanfare'	MBNS NBir WAul WWEG
'Eenie Weenie'	CBro ECtt GKev IBal LRHS MBNS NBro SApp SRms WPer WWEG
'Eenie Weenie Non-stop'	ECha EPPr
'Eggplant Ecstasy'	CFwr
'Eggplant Electricity'	EWoo
'Eggplant Escapade'	CBgR MSpe SPol
'Egyptian Ibis'	EWoo MSpe SPol WMnd WNHG
'Egyptian Queen'	CBgR
'El Desperado'	CBcs CBgR CPar CSam EBee ECtt ELon EWoo GBin GBuc IPot LHop LRHS LSRN MBNS MNrw NCGa NEgg SApp SBrk SPav SUsu WAul WCAu WCFE WCot WWEG
'El Glorioso'	CWat
'El Padre'	SApp
'Elaine Strutt'	MBNS MNFA MNrw SApp SDay SWvt WCot
'Eleanor Marcotte'	SDay
'Elegant Candy'	CBgR CKel CMac EBee MBNS MSpe NCGa SApp SBrk WCAu
I 'Elegantissima' **new**	SPol
'Eleonor'	EPfP MBNS SApp SMrm WFar
'Elfin Daydream'	SPol
'Elf's Cap'	SDay
'Elijah Sain'	SPol
'Elizabeth Anne Hudson'	SBrk SDay
'Elizabeth Salter'	CWCL MBNS NLar SApp SBrk SPol SUsu WCAu
'Elmore James' **new**	EWoo
'Eloquent Cay'	CFwr
'Elva White Grow'	SDay
'Elve's Watermark' **new**	SPol
'Emerald Enchantment'	SApp
'Emerald Eye'	SDay
'Emerald Lady'	SPol
'Emily Anne'	SApp SPol
'Emily Jaye'	SApp
'Emmaus'	SApp
'Emperor Butterfly'	SApp
'Enchanted April'	SPol
'Enchanted Circle' **new**	SDay
'Enchanter's Spell'	SDay
'English Cameo'	SPol
'English Toffee'	SApp
'Enjoy'	SBrk
'Entransette'	SApp SBrk SDay
'Entrapment'	IBoy MBNS MBel MSpe SBrk SDeJ
'Envy Me' **new**	SPol
'Erica Nichole Gonzales'	SDay
'Erin Prairie'	SApp
esculenta	SMad
'Eskimo Kisses'	CFwr
'Etched Eyes'	EWoo MSpe SPol
'Eternal Blessing'	SPol
'Ethel Smith'	SApp
'Etruscan Tomb'	SBrk SPol
'Evelyn Claar'	CMac
'Evelyn Lela Stout'	SApp SDay
'Evening Bell'	SApp
'Evening Enchantment'	SBrk
'Evening Glow'	SApp
'Evening Gown'	SPol
'Evening Tulip'	CFwr
'Ever So Ruffled'	SBrk SDay
'Exotic Dancer'	CFwr
'Exotic Love'	MSpe SDay
'Eye Catching'	EWoo
'Eye of Round'	CFwr
'Eye on America'	EBee WCAu
'Eyes Wide Shut'	CFwr
'Eye-yi-yi'	SPol
'Ezekiel'	WHrl XSen
'Fabergé'	SApp SBrk SDay
'Fabulous Prize'	MSpe SApp
'Fairest Love'	EBee LDai MBNS MNrw MSpe
'Fairest of Them' **new**	CBgR
'Fairy Charm'	SApp SDay
'Fairy Finery'	SBrk
'Fairy Frosting'	SDay
'Fairy Summerbird'	SApp SBrk
'Fairy Tale Pink'	EWoo MNFA SApp SBrk SDay SPol
'Fairy Wings'	SPer
'Faith Nabor'	SBrk SPol
'Falcon'	SPol
'Fall Farewell'	WNHG
'Fall Guy'	SApp
'Fama'	SBrk
'Fandango'	LPla SPer
'Fantasia'	EWoo
'Farmer's Daughter'	CBgR EWoo SApp SBrk
'Fashion Model'	SApp WPer
'Feather Down'	SPol
'Feathered Fascination'	SApp
'Feelings'	SApp
'Femme Osage'	SBrk
'Ferengi Gold'	CFwr
'Ferris Wheel'	CBgR EWoo SApp
'Festive Art'	MSpe SBrk SPol
'Final Touch'	CBgR LTen MBNS NBro NGBo SBrk SPol
'Finlandia'	MNFA
'Fire and Fog'	CFwr EPfP MBNS
'Fire and Wind'	CFwr
'Fire from Heaven'	SApp WHrl
'Fire Tree'	SPol
'Fireborn'	CFwr
'Firestorm'	EWoo SApp SPol
'First Formal'	SMrm SPer
'Flaming Sword'	NHol WBrk WRHF
flava	see *H. lilioasphodelus*
'Fleeting Fancy'	SBrk
'Fleishel's Black'	CFwr
'Flight of the Dragon'	SApp
'Flower Pavilion'	SDay SPol
'Floyd Cove'	SBrk SDay
'Fly Catcher'	CBgR SBrk
'Flyaway Home'	SPol
'Flying Saucer'	EWoo
'Foggy London Town'	CFwr

	Name	Suppliers
	'Fol de Rol'	EWoo
	'Fooled Me'	EBee MBNS MBri MSpe NCGa SBrk SPad SPol
	'Foolscap'	EWoo
	'For the Good Times'	EWoo
	'Forbidden Dreams'	EWoo
	'Forgotten Dreams'	EBee MBNS MSpe SBrk
	forrestii	CPLG
	'Forsyth Ace of Hearts' **new**	CBgR
	'Forsyth Frostbound' **new**	SPol
	'Forsyth Lemon Drop'	SDay
	'Forsyth White Sentinel'	CFwr SBrk
	'Forty Second Street'	CCon EBee LHop LRHS MBNS SApp WFar
	'Fox Ears'	EWoo
	'Fragrant Bouquet'	MSpe SBrk
	'Fragrant Pastel Cheers'	SDay
	'Fragrant Treasure'	ERCP
	'Frances Fay'	SPol WAul
	'Frances Joiner'	EWoo
	'Francis of Assisi'	CFwr EWoo
	'Francois Verhaert'	EWoo SBrk
	'Frandean'	MNFA
	'Frank Gladney'	MNFA SApp SBrk
	'Frans Hals'	Widely available
	'Fred Ham'	SBrk XSen
	'Free Wheelin''	MBri
	'French Cavalier'	CFwr
	'French Connection' **new**	SDay
	'French Doll'	SApp
	'French Porcelain'	MSpe SDay
	'Fresh Air'	MNrw
	'Frills and Furbelows' **new**	SDay
	'Fritz Schroer'	CFwr
	'Frosted Encore'	SApp SDay
	'Frosted Pink Ice'	SPol
	'Frosted Vintage Ruffles' **new**	NCGa
	'Frosty White'	SDay
	'Frozen Jade'	SBrk
	'Fuchsia Beauty'	SPol
	'Fuchsia Fashion'	SApp
	'Fuchsia Four' **new**	SPol
	fulva	CTri ELan LPot NBir NBre SGar SPol SRms WBrk WHrl XSen
	- B&SWJ 8647	WCru
N	- 'Flore Pleno' (d)	CDoy CMHG CMac EBee ECtt EHon ELan EPfP GHim LHop LRHS MCot MHer MRav MSpe NBir NBro NGdn NSti SBfd SPav SPer SRms SWat WBrk WCAu WMoo WWEG XSen
N	- 'Green Kwanso' (d)	CAvo CBgR CPLG ECGP ECha LRHS MMHG WAul WFar WPnP WTin
	- var. ***kwanso*** B&SWJ 6328	WCru
	- 'Kwanso' ambig. (d)	LRHS NOrc SBrk
	- var. ***littorea***	CMac
	- var. ***rosea***	LRHS SPol WCot
§	- 'Variegated Kwanso' (d/v)	CRow CWCL EWoo GCal GCra LBMP MRav NBir SMad SUsu WBor WCot WFar WHer WHoo WHrl
	'Fun Fling'	SDay SPol
	'Funky Fuchsia'	SPol
	'Gadsden Firefly'	CFwr
	'Gadsden Goliath'	CFwr SPol
	'Gadsden Light'	SDay SPol
	'Gala Gown'	SApp
	'Gale Storm'	WNHG
	'Garden Portrait'	EWoo SDay SPol
	'Gaucho'	MNFA
	'Gay Music'	MBNS
	'Gay Octopus'	SPol
	'Gay Rapture'	SPer
	'Gay Troubadour'	EWoo
	'Gemini'	SBrk
	'Geneva Firetruck'	CFwr
	'Gentle Country Breeze'	SApp SBrk SPol
	'Gentle Rose'	SBrk SDay
	'Gentle Shepherd'	Widely available
	'George Cunningham'	ECtt EHrv ELan LRHS MRav NBir SMrs SPol WFar
	'George David'	WHrl
	'George Jets On'	SBrk
	'Georgette Belden'	ECGP ECtt GKin LRHS MBNS MBri MSpe MWat NHol SPol WTin
	'Georgia Cream' (d)	NLar
	'German Ballerina'	SPol
	'Get All Excited'	SPol
	'Giant Moon'	CBgR CMHG EBee ECtt ELan LRHS MBNS SPer SRms WFar WHal
	'Giddy Go Round'	EWoo SPol
	'Gingerbread Man'	SApp SBrk
	'Girl Scout'	SApp
	'Give Me Eight'	SPol
	'Glacier Bay'	CBgR CWat MBNS
	'Glacier Gleam'	MSpe
	'Glazed Heather Plum'	SApp SBrk
	'Gleber's Top Cream'	SApp
	'Glittering Treasure'	LRHS
	'Glomunda'	SApp
	'Glory's Legacy'	SBrk
	'Glowing Heart'	SApp SDay
	'Going Bananas' PBR	WCot
	'Gold Elephant'	CFwr SDay
	'Gold Imperial'	NBre
	'Golden Bell'	NGdn
	'Golden Change'	CFwr
	'Golden Chimes' ♀H4	Widely available
	'Golden Empress'	SApp
	'Golden Ginkgo'	MBri MSpe SApp
	'Golden Marvel'	EWoo
	'Golden Orchid'	see *H.* 'Doubloon'
	'Golden Peace'	SBrk
	'Golden Prize'	EWoo GQue NGdn SApp SBrk WCot WFar
	'Golden Scroll'	SApp SBrk SDay
	Golden Zebra = 'Malja' PBR (v)	CWGN ELan EPfP IBoy LRHS MBNS MGos MRav NLar NSti SMad WCot
	'Goldeneye'	SApp
	'Golliwog'	CBgR SDay
	'Grace and Favour'	SPol
	'Grace and Grandeur'	EWoo
	'Graceful Eye'	SApp SBrk SDay
	'Graceland'	SDay
	'Grand Masterpiece'	NGdn SDay SPet WAul
	'Grand Palais'	SApp SBrk SDay
	'Grandiose'	SBrk
	'Grandma Kissed Me'	SPol
	'Granite City Towhead'	CFwr
	'Grape Harvest'	WNHG
	'Grape Magic'	WCot WTin
	'Grape Velvet'	CPar CSpe EWoo MNFA NBre NSti SApp SBch SBrk SPol SRms WAul WCAu WMnd WWEG
	'Great Northern'	SApp
	'Green Canary' **new**	SPol
	'Green Dolphin Street'	SBrk SDay

'Green Dragon'	SPol
'Green Drop'	WFar
'Green Eyed Giant'	MNFA
'Green Eyed Lady'	SDay
'Green Flutter' ♀H4	CBgR CFwr EBee EWoo GCal GQue LPla LSRN MBNS MBri MNFA NBir NBre NGdn NSti SApp SPhx SPol WCot WWEG
'Green Goddess'	XLum
'Green Gold'	CMHG
'Green Mystique' **new**	EBee MBri
'Green Puff'	NBir SDay
'Green Spider'	CBgR SDay
'Green Spill'	CFwr
'Green Valley'	MNFA
'Green Warrior'	EWoo
'Green Widow'	EWoo SDay
'Grey Witch' **new**	SPol
'Greywoods Nautical Nellie'	CFwr
'Grumbly'	ELan WPnP
'Guardian Angel'	WCFE WTin
'Guinea Jubilee'	CFwr
'Gypsy Ballerina'	SApp
'Gypsy Cranberry'	SPol
'Gypsy Prince'	MNFA
'Hail Mary'	SDay
'Hamlet'	SDay WNHG
'Happy Hopi'	SApp
'Happy Returns'	CHid CSBt CTri EBee ECha ELan EWoo GBuc IBal LPot LRHS LSRN MBNS MBel MBri NEgg NGdn NHol NRHS SApp SBrk SRGP SRms WCAu WTin WWEG
'Harbor Blue'	SApp SDay
'Harry Barras'	XLum
'Havana Banana'	SApp
'Hawaiian Nights'	EWoo
'Hawk'	ELon SApp SDay SPol
'Heady Wine'	MSpe SDay
'Heat Wave'	CFwr
'Heather Green'	SApp
'Heavenly Curls' **new**	SPol
'Heavenly Mr Twister'	EWoo
'Heavenly Starfire'	EWoo
'Heavenly Treasure'	SApp SBrk SPol
'Heidi Eidelweiss'	CPLG
'Heirloom Lace'	WFar
'Helaman'	CFwr
'Helix'	CFwr
'Helle Berlinerin' ♀H4	EBee MNFA SApp SPol
'Helter Skelter'	SDay SPol
'Her Majesty's Wizard'	CBgR ELan EWoo MBNS SPol
'Hercules'	NBre
'Heron's Cove'	EWoo
'Hesperus' **new**	EWoo
'Hey There'	SBrk SDay
'High Energy'	SApp
'High Tor'	GQui MNFA SPol WHrl WTin
'Highland Belle'	SApp
'Highland Lord' (d)	EPfP MBNS MSCN SApp XSen
'Highland Summerbird'	SApp
'Hightower'	CFwr
'Hillbilly Heart'	CFwr
'Hint of Blue'	SPol
'His Majesty's Wizard'	SBrk
'Holiday Delight'	MBNS
'Holiday Mood'	ELan SApp
'Holly Dancer'	EWoo SPol
'Honey Jubilee'	SPol
'Honky Tonk Blues'	CFwr
'Hope Diamond'	SDay
'Hornby Castle'	CBro LRHS NHol NRHS
'Hot Cakes'	SBrk
'Hot Chocolate' PBR	EBee SRGP
'Hot Ticket'	SApp SBrk
'Hot Town'	ELan
'Hot Wheels'	SBrk
'Hot Wire'	SBrk
'Houdini'	MSpe WMnd
'House of Bluelights' **new**	SPol
'House of Orange'	SApp SPol
'Howard Goodson'	MNFA
'Howdy'	CFwr
I 'How's the Weather up There?'	EWoo
'Hubbles Buddy'	EWoo
'Humdinger'	SBrk WCot
'Hyperion'	CBgR CMac COlW CPrp CTri EBee ECha ECtt EPfP EWoo GKin LAst LEdu LRHS MNFA MRav MSpe NBid NGdn SApp SMrs SPer SPoG SUsu WCot WWEG
'Ice Carnival'	CKel ELon EPfP LDai LHop MBNS NBre NGdn NOrc SApp SHar SPet
'Ice Castles'	CTri SApp SBrk SDay WHrl
'Ice Cool'	SApp
'Icecap'	WAul WFar WMoo
'Icy Lemon'	SBrk SDay
'Ida Duke Miles'	SBrk SDay
'Ida's Magic'	SApp SBrk WFar
'Igor'	CFwr
'Imperator'	CBen LPBA NHol
'Imperial Lemon'	SApp
'Imperial Wizard'	CFwr
'Impromptu'	SDay
'In Depth' (d)	EPfP EWoo MBNS NBro NLar WCot WHrl
'In Search of Angels'	CFwr
'In Strawberry Time'	WNHG
'Indian Fandango'	EWoo
'Indian Fires'	CFwr
'Indian Giver'	SPol
'Indian Paintbrush'	EWoo MBri NBir SBfd SPol WAul
'Indigo Moon'	SApp SPol
'Indy Envy'	CFwr
'Inky Fingers'	SApp
'Inner View'	ECtt EWoo MBNS NLar SApp WMnd
'Inspired Word'	SBrk
'Invitation to Immortality'	EWoo
'Iowa Greenery'	SPol
'Iridescent Jewel'	SDay
'Irish Elf'	ELon SApp SDay SHar WTin
'Iron Gate Glacier'	EBee MBNS XLum
'Isle of Dreams'	SPol
'Isleworth'	EWoo
'Isolde'	MSpe
'Itsy Bitsy Spider'	CBgR CFwr EWoo
'Ivelyn Brown'	SDay SPol
'Jake Russell'	MBNS MNFA
'Jamaican Jammin"	SPol
'Jamaican Me Crazy'	SBrk
'Jamaican Me Happy'	CFwr
'James Clark'	EWoo
'James Marsh'	CBgR EPfP EWes EWoo MBNS MBri MNrw MSpe NSti SApp WAul WCAu WCot WMnd
'Jan Kay'	SDay
'Janet Gordon'	SBrk SPol

	'Janice Brown'	CKel CWCL CWGN EWoo LAst LSou MBNS MNFA MSpe NCGa NLar NMRc SApp SBrk SDay SPol
	'Jan's Twister'	MNrw SApp SBrk SPol
	'Jason Salter'	NCGa SApp SBrk SDay WAul
	'Jay Turman'	SApp SDay
	'Jazz at the Wool Club'	CFwr
	'Jean'	SDay
	'Jean Swann'	MBNS SBrk
	'Jedi Dot Pierce'	CFwr MSpe SApp SBrk
	'Jedi Irish Spring'	SApp
	'Jedi Rose Frost'	SApp
	'Jedi Tequila Sunrise'	CFwr
	'Jellyfish Jealousy'	EWoo
	'Jenny Wren'	EPPr ETod EWoo MBNS NBre NBro SRGP WAul WWEG
	'Jersey Spider'	EWoo SDay SPol
	'Jerusalem'	SBrk SDay
	'Jesse James'	SApp SPol
	'Jessica Lilian'	SBrk
	'Jewel Case'	WNHG
	'Joan Senior'	Widely available
	'Jocelyn's Oddity'	SApp
	'Jockey Club' (d)	ECtt MBNS
	'Joe Marinello'	SPol
	'John Allen'	CFwr
	'John Bierman'	SBrk
	'John Robert Biggs'	SApp
	'Johnny Come Lately'	SPol
	'Joie de Vivre'	EWoo
	'Jolly Red Giant'	EWoo
	'Jolly White Giant'	CFwr
	'Jolyene Nichole'	SApp SBrk
	'Jordan'	LSRN
	'Journey to Oz'	EWoo
	'Journey's End'	SDay
	'Jovial'	SApp SBrk SDay
	'Judah'	SApp
	'Judge Roy Bean'	EWoo SPol
	'Julie Newmar'	IPot
	'June Melody'	WNHG
	'Jungle Beauty'	CBgR SPol
	'Just Kiss Me' **new**	SPol
	'Justin George'	SPol
	'Justin June'	WHrl
	'Kachina Firecracker'	CFwr EWoo
	'Kansas City Kicker' **new**	IPot
	'Kansas Kitten'	EWoo
	'Karateake'	CFwr
	'Karen's Curls'	EWoo SBrk SPol
	'Kasia'	WHrl
	'Katahdin'	EWoo
	'Kate Carpenter'	SBrk SDay SPol
	'Katherine Harris'	CFwr
	'Kathleen Salter'	EWoo
	'Kathryn June Wood'	EWoo
	'Kathy Macartney'	EWoo
	'Katie Elizabeth Miller'	SBrk
	'Kazuq'	SApp SBrk
	'Kecia'	MNFA
	'Keene'	EWoo
	'Kelly's Girl'	SBrk SPol
	'Kent's Favorite Two'	SBrk
	'Kenyan Sun'	EWoo
	'Kevin Michael Coyne'	EWoo SPol
	'Key to my Heart'	CBgR
	'Key West'	CFwr
	'Kien Mill'	CFwr
	'Kindly Light'	EWoo MNFA SPol

	'King Haiglar'	SApp SBrk
	'King James'	EWoo
	'King's Throne'	WNHG
	'Kiowa Sunset'	MSpe
	'Kisses for Cinderella'	CFwr
	'Kiwi Claret'	MSpe
N	'Kwanso Flore Pleno'	see *H. fulva* 'Green Kwanso'
N	'Kwanso Flore Pleno Variegata'	see *H. fulva* 'Variegated Kwanso'
	'La Peche'	SDay
	'Lace Cookies'	EWoo
	'Lacy Doily'	LLHF MBri WCAu
	'Lacy Marionette'	EWoo SApp SDay SPol
	'Lady Cynthia'	CKel
	'Lady Fingers'	CBgR MNFA SDay SPol
	'Lady Hillary'	SApp
	'Lady Inma'	SApp
	'Lady Liz'	MNFA
	'Lady Mischief'	SApp SDay
	'Lady Neva'	CBgR EWoo SApp SBrk SDay
	'Ladykin'	SApp SBrk SDay SPol
	'Lake Effect'	EWoo
	'Lake Norman Spider'	EWoo MNFA SApp
	'Lake Norman Sunset'	CFwr
	'Lark Song'	LRHS NRHS WFar WHrl
	'Laughing Feather'	EWoo
	'Laughton Tower'	SMHy
	'Laura Lambert'	SPol
	'Lauradell' **new**	SDay
	'Laurena'	SPol
	'Lavender Arrowhead'	SApp
	'Lavender Blue Baby' **new**	SPer
	'Lavender Deal'	EBee LRHS MNrw WNHG
	'Lavender Flushing'	SApp
	'Lavender Green'	CFwr
	'Lavender Handlebars'	SBrk
	'Lavender Illusion'	CSev SApp
	'Lavender Light'	EWoo
	'Lavender Memories'	SDay
	'Lavender Plicata'	SPol
	'Lavender Showstopper'	WCAu
	'Lavender Silver Cords'	SPol
	'Lavender Spider'	CBgR SApp SPol
	'Lavender Tonic'	SDay SPol
	'Legs Limmer'	EWoo
	'Lemon Bells' ♀H4	CWat EBee ECGP ECha EPfP EWoo GKin GMaP LRHS MBNS NBro NCGa SApp SDay WCAu
	'Lemon Dessert'	SBrk
	'Lemon Fellow'	EWoo
	'Lemon Madeline'	EWoo
	'Lemon Meringue Twist'	EWoo
	'Lemon Mint'	SBrk
	'Lemon Starfish'	SApp
	'Lemonora'	SDay
	'Lenox'	SBrk SDay
	'Leonard Bernstein'	EWoo SApp SBrk SPol
	'Leslie Renee'	CFwr
	'Let It Rip'	EWoo
	'Lexington Avenue'	SPol
	'Licorice Candy'	SBrk
	'Licorice Twist' **new**	EWoo
	'Light the Way'	ECha GBin
	'Light Years Away'	ELon MBNS MNrw NBro SApp
	'Lil Ledie'	SApp
§	***lilioasphodelus*** ♀H4	Widely available
	- 'Rowden Golden Jubilee' (v)	CRow
	'Lilly Dache'	EWoo
	'Lilting Belle'	SBrk SPol

'Lilting Lady'	SApp SDay SPol
'Lilting Lady Red'	SApp
'Lilting Lavender'	SDay WCAu WCot
'Lime Frost'	CBgR SBrk SDay SPol
'Limited Edition'	EWoo
'Limoncello'	SApp
'Lin Wright'	EWoo MSpe
'Linda'	MRav NHol
'Linda Agin'	EWoo
'Lines of Splendor'	EWoo
'Lipstick Print'	SBrk
'Little Angel'	SApp
'Little Audrey'	SApp
'Little Bee'	NBre
'Little Big Man'	SDay
'Little Bugger'	ELon NLar WWEG
'Little Bumble Bee'	CCon COIW LRHS MBNS SApp WWEG
'Little Business'	COIW MBNS MNFA SApp SDay WAul
'Little Cadet'	XLum
'Little Carpet'	MBNS SPer SPet
'Little Dart'	ECha
'Little Deeke'	MNFA SApp SBrk SDay WHrl
'Little Dream Red'	SDay
'Little Fat Cat'	CBgR SApp
'Little Fat Dazzler'	SApp SBrk SPol
'Little Fellow'	MBNS
'Little Fruit Cup'	SApp
'Little Grapette'	COIW EPfP ERCP GCra GQue LPla LRHS MBNS MSpe NLar NSti SApp SBrk WAul WBrk WCAu WTin WWEG
'Little Greenie'	SDay
'Little Gypsy Vagabond'	CWat SBrk SDay
'Little Heavenly Angel'	COIW SPol
'Little Judy' **new**	SPol
'Little Kiki' **new**	SDay
'Little Maggie'	SApp SDay SPol
'Little Missy'	CBgR COIW CWat LAst MBNS NBre SPet WHoo
'Little Monica'	SApp SDay
'Little Orange Slices'	CFwr
'Little Pumpkin Face'	CWat
'Little Rainbow'	WWEG
'Little Red Hen'	CSam ECGP GKin LRHS MBNS MSpe NBir NBro NEgg NGdn SUsu WFar
'Little Show Stopper'	EWoo MBNS MSpe NBro NLar NMRc
'Little Swain' **new**	SDay
'Little Sweet Sue'	MNFA
'Little Sweet Talk'	SBrk
'Little Tawny'	ELon
'Little Toddler'	SApp SDay
'Little Violet Lace'	SDay
'Little Wart'	SDay WHrl
'Little Wine Cup'	Widely available
'Little Wine Spider'	SApp
'Little Women'	MBNS SDay
'Little Zinger'	SDay
'Littlest Angel'	SDay
'Littlest Clown'	SDay
'Living in Amsterdam' **new**	EBee
'Lizard's Purple Fashion'	CFwr
'Lochinvar'	GBuc MRav
'Lois Burns'	CFwr EWoo SBrk SDay
'Lonesome Dove'	SBrk SPol
'Long John Silver'	CFwr

'Long Stocking'	CFwr EWoo SPol WCot
'Longfields Anwar'	EWoo
'Longfield's Bandit'	EWoo
'Longfield's Beauty'	EWoo MBNS MSpe NCGa SBrk
'Longfield's Glory'	MBNS MSpe NBre
'Longfield's Mandy'	MSpe
'Longfield's Maxim' (d)	MBNS
'Longfield's Pearl'	SBrk
'Longfield's Pride'	ECho IBoy MBNS SRms WBor
'Longfield's Purple Eye'	NLar
'Longfield's Tropica'	MBNS
'Longfield's Twins'	EBee MBNS WCot
longituba AIK 284	WCot
– B&SWJ 4576	WCru
'Look at Me'	ELan
'Look Lucky'	CFwr
'Lord Camden'	MNFA
'Lori Goldston'	EWoo MBNS
'Loth Lorien'	CFwr
'Louis Burnes' **new**	SPol
'Louis McHargue'	SDay
'Louise Lemly'	CFwr
'Love Glow'	CCon
'Love or Else'	EWoo
'Loving Memories'	SApp
'Lowenstine'	SApp
'Lucille Lennington'	WNHG
'Lucretius'	MNFA
'Luke Senior Junior'	SApp
'Lullaby Baby'	CWat ELan EWoo MBNS NLar SApp SDay SPol
'Lurch'	CFwr
'Luscious Honeydew'	WNHG
'Lusty Lealand'	MBNS MNFA SBrk SDay
'Luverne'	SBrk
'Luxury Lace'	CPrp CWat ECtt ELan EPfP GKin LRHS LSRN MSpe NBir NGdn NHol NWad SPer SPol WAul WFar WHrl WMoo WPnP WTin XLum XSen
'Lydia Bechtold'	SBrk
'Lynn Hall'	ECtt EMil MBNS NLar
'Mabel Fuller'	MRav SPer WHrl
'Macbeth'	MBNS SBrk
'Mad Max'	EWoo MSpe SPol
'Mae Graham'	SApp
'Maestro Puccini'	SDay
'Maggie Fynboe'	CBgR SPol
'Magic Amethyst'	CBgR
'Magic Carpet Ride'	SBrk SPol
'Magic Lace'	EWoo SBrk
'Magic of Oz'	CFwr
'Magnificent Eyes'	SPol
'Magnificent Rainbow'	CBcs SApp
'Mahogany Magic'	SBrk
'Malachite Prism'	CWGN
'Malaysian Masquerade'	SApp
'Malaysian Monarch'	SBrk WMnd WNHG
'Malaysian Spice'	WNHG
'Maleny Bright Eyes'	MSpe
'Maleny Mite'	EWoo
'Maleny Piecrust'	EWoo
'Maleny Tapestry'	MSpe
'Maleny Think Big'	EWoo
'Mallard'	CBgR CWat ECGP ECtt EHrv LLWP LRHS MBNS MNFA MRav MSpe NBir SApp SBrk SPer SWat WCot
'Man on Fire'	MBNS
'Manchurian Apricot'	SBrk SDay

'Mandalay Bay Music' EWoo
'Marble Faun' SApp SBrk SDay
'Margaret Perry' CPrp ECrc MNrw WAul
'Marilyn Siwik' EWoo
'Marion Caldwell' SPol
'Marion Vaughn' ♀H4 CSev EBee ECtt EHrv ELan EPfP EWoo GBuc GKin GMaP LBMP LHop LRHS MBel MNFA MSpe NSti SBch SBrk SDix SPer SRGP SSpi WCot WFar WHoo WPtf WWEG
'Mariska' EWoo SApp SBrk SDay WNHG
'Mark My Word' SApp
'Marked by Lydia' CFwr SPol
'Marse Connell' MSpe
'Martha Adams' SDay
'Martie Everest' EWoo
'Martina Verhaert' CWGN EBee
'Mary Ethel Anderson' EWoo MSpe
'Mary Todd' EBee MBNS SApp WMnd XSen
'Mary's Gold' SBrk SDay SPol
'Mask Ball' SBrk
'Mata Hari' SDay SPol
'Matisse' **new** SPol
'Matt' SBrk
'Mauna Loa' CSBt EBee GQue LRHS MBNS MNFA MNrw MSpe NBre SApp SBrk WAul WCAu WCot
'May May' SApp SPol
'Meadow Mist' CBgR
'Meadow Sprite' SBrk SDay WCot
'Medicine Feather' CFwr EWoo
'Medieval Guild' SApp
'Medusa's Glance' EWoo
'Mega Stella' SApp
'Megatrend' CFwr
'Memory Jordan' CFwr
'Mephistopheles' EWoo
'Merlot Rouge' WAul
'Merry Maker's Serenade' MSpe
'Merry Moppet' EWoo
'Metaphor' SApp SBrk XSen
'Michele Coe' ECtt GKin LPla LRHS MBNS MNFA MSpe NBre NBro NEgg NGdn SApp SRGP WHrl WMoo
middendorffii CMac GMaP LPla LRHS MCoo NSti SMrm WFar WHrl WPnP WThu
'Midnight Dynamite' MBNS SBrk
'Midnight Love' EWoo
'Midnight Magic' EWoo
'Midnight Mantis' SPol
'Midnight Raider' CBgR EWoo
'Mighty Highty Tighty' CFwr
'Mighty Mogul' MNFA
'Mikado' CBgR CMac
'Milady Greensleeves' EWoo SBrk SPol
'Milanese Mango' EWoo MSpe
'Mildred Mitchell' CBgR CFwr CWat EBee MBNS NLar NMRc SApp SBrk
'Millie Schlumpf' SApp SBrk SPol
'Mimosa Umbrella' SPol
'Ming Lo' MSpe SDay
'Ming Porcelain' SApp SBrk SPol
'Mini Pearl' COlW ELon LRHS MBNS MBri MSpe SApp SBrk SPer WPer
'Mini Stella' CBro ECtt IBal MBNS NBre NOrc SBrk SPet WAul WFar
miniature hybrids SRms
'Minnie Wildfire' SPol
minor CBro EBee EDAr EPPr EWTr GKev LRHS NGdn NRHS SRms
- B&SWJ 8841 WCru
'Miracle Maid' WNHG
'Miss Jessie' EWoo MNFA SDay SPol
'Missenden' ♀H4 CBgR MNFA MNrw SApp
'Missouri Beauty' IBoy MBNS SApp SPol
'Missouri Memories' SBrk SPol
'Misty Twisty' CFwr
'Moment of Truth' NBre
'Monica Marie' SBrk
'Mont Royal Demitasse' SPol
'Moon Witch' SBrk SDay SPol
'Moonbeam' SApp
'Moonlight Masquerade' CBgR CWat EBee ECtt EPfP GBuc MMuc NLar SApp SRms SUsu
'Moonlight Mist' SApp SBrk SDay SPol
'Moonlit Caress' CBgR EBee MBNS NBro SApp SBrk WFar
'Moonlit Crystal' SApp SPol
'Moonlit Masquerade' CPar CWGN EWoo GBin MBNS MBel MBri MNrw MSCN MSpe NCGa SBch SBrk SEND SPer SPet SPol WAul WCAu WHrl
'Moonlit Pirouette' SApp
'Moonlit Summerbird' SDay SPol
'Moonstruck Madness' CFwr
'Moontraveller' WCot
'Mormon Spider' MSpe SApp SPol
'Morning Dawn' WWEG
'Morning Sun' MBNS NBre NLar WCot
'Morocco' CFwr SPol
'Morocco Red' CBro CCse CTri ELan NBre WWEG
'Morrie Otte' SPol
'Mosel' SDay
'Moses' Fire' ECtt EPfP MBNS NLar
'Mount Echo Sunrise' EWoo
'Mount Joy' SPer
'Mountain Laurel' ECGP ECtt GKin LDai LRHS LSRN MBNS MCot MRav NEgg SApp SBrk SPol WFar
'Mountain Top Experience' SDay
'Mountain Violet' SApp
'Mrs David Hall' CCse SMrm
'Mrs Hugh Johnson' EBee GCra NHol WHrl
* 'Mrs Lester' SDay
'Muffet's Little Friend' SPol
'Mulberry Frosted Edge' EWoo
multiflora LRHS MNFA NHol
'My Belle' SBrk SDay
'My Darling Clementine' SBrk SDay
'My Hope' SPol
'My Melinda' MSpe SDay
'My Sweet Rose' SBrk
'Mynelle's Starfish' CPar SBrk SPol WHrl
'Nairobi Dawn' SBrk
nana CCon
'Nanuq' EBee SApp SBrk
'Naomi Ruth' MBNS MSpe SApp WTin
'Nashville' CBro ELan WHrl
'Nashville Lights' CBgR SPol
'Nathan Sommers' EWoo
'Natural Veil' SPol
'Navajo Princess' CWat MBNS MNrw SBrk
'Navajo Rodeo' EWoo
'Neal Berrey' SApp SBrk SDay
'Nefertiti' CBgR ELon MBNS NBir NCGa SPer WAul WCAu WTin
'Neon Rose' GKin MWat SBrk

'Netsuke'	SApp SMrm
'New Direction'	CFwr EWoo
'New Swirls'	SApp
'New York Follies'	SBrk
'Newberry Borrowed Time'	CFwr
'Neyron Rose' ♀H4	COlW EPfP GBuc GKin GQue LHop LRHS MBNS MCot NBre NEgg NGdn WMoo
'Nick's Faith'	WHrl
'Nicole Joyce' **new**	SPol
'Night Beacon'	CBgR ECho ECtt ELon EWes EWoo GKin IBal LHop LPot MBNS MBri MNFA MNrw MSpe NLar SApp SBrk SDay SDeJ SPol WCAu WHrl
'Night Embers'	EWoo MBri
'Night Raider'	SApp SBrk SDay
'Night Wings'	EWoo SApp
'Nigrette'	CBen LPBA NHol
'Nile Crane'	CBgR MBNS MNrw MSpe SApp SBrk SDay SHar SPer WAul
'Nile Plum'	EWoo SApp
'Ninth Millennium'	CFwr
'Nivia Guest'	SApp
'Nob Hill'	CCse GBin LRHS SApp SPol WHrl XLum
'Noble Warrior'	MSpe
'Nona's Garnet Spider'	ELon SApp SPol
'Noonday Dreams'	CFwr
'Nordic Night'	CBgR SDay SPol
'North Star'	SApp
'North Wind Dancer'	EWoo
'Northbrook Star'	MNFA
'Norton Beauté'	WCot
'Norton Eyed Seedling'	WNHG
'Norton Orange'	MNFA WFar
'Nosferatu'	SDay SPol
'Not Forgotten' **new**	WNHG
'Nouveau Riche' **new**	SPol
'Nova' ♀H4	CPrp SApp
'Nuclear Meltdown'	EWoo
'Nuka'	XLum
'Numinous Moments'	SDay
'Nutmeg Elf'	CBgR EWoo SBrk SPol
'Oakes Love' **new**	MNrw
'Ocean Rain'	SApp SBrk SDay SPol
'Octopus Hugs'	SBrk
'Official Curse'	SPol
'Ojo de Dios'	EWoo
'Oklahoma Kicking Bird'	SDay
'Old Tangiers'	EWoo SBrk
'Olive Bailey Langdon'	SApp SBrk SPol WCot
'Oliver Billingslea'	EWoo
'Olympic Showcase'	SBrk
'Omomuki'	SApp SBrk
'On and On'	GQue LHop MBNS NCGa
'On Pointe'	EWoo
'On Silken Thread'	SPol
'On the Web'	CFwr SApp
'Oodles' **new**	WHrl
'Oom Pah Pah'	ECha
'Open Hearth'	CFwr SBrk SDay SPol
'Open my Eyes'	EWoo
'Orange Dream'	SDay
'Orange Exotica'	CBgR
'Orange Velvet'	SApp SBrk
'Orangeman' misapplied	LRHS MBNS NGdn
'Orchard Sprite'	SApp
'Orchid Beauty'	ECha MLHP WMoo
'Orchid Candy'	EWoo MBNS NBir SBrk SPol WAul
'Orchid Corsage'	SApp
'Orchid Lady Slipper'	EWoo
'Orchid Moonrise'	EWoo
'Oriental Ruby'	SDay
'Orion's Band'	EWoo
'Ostrich Plume'	SDay
'Ottis Leonard'	CFwr
'Ouachita Beauty'	SPol
'Our Kirsten'	SDay
'Out of Darkness'	EWoo
'Outrageous'	SApp SBrk WNHG
'Outrageous Ramona' **new**	WNHG
'Over the Top'	MBNS
'Paige's Pinata'	CFwr MBNS SApp SBrk
'Paint Your Wagon'	SApp
'Painted Lady'	MNFA SApp
'Painted Pink'	SDay
'Painting the Roses Red'	CFwr
'Palace Garden Beauty'	EWoo SApp
'Palace Guard'	MNFA
'Palantir'	SApp
'Pale Moon Windmill'	CFwr
'Panama Hattie'	SBrk
'Pandora's Box'	Widely available
'Pantaloons'	SApp
'Pantherette'	SApp SPol
'Paper Butterfly'	SBrk SDay SPol
'Papoose'	XLum
'Pardon Me'	CBro CMHG ELan ELon EWoo GKin GMaP LRHS MBNS MBel MNFA MSpe NCGa NGdn NHol SApp SBrk SDeJ SPol SRGP WAul WBor WCAu WFar
'Pardon Me Boy'	SPol
'Parfait'	CBgR EWoo SPol
'Pas de Deux'	SApp
'Passion for Red' **new**	SDay
'Pastel Ballerina'	SBrk SDay
'Pastel Classic'	SApp SBrk
'Pastilline'	SPol
'Pat Mercer'	SApp XSen
'Patchwork Puzzle'	EWoo SBrk SPol
'Patricia'	MBNS
'Patricia Fay'	SApp
'Patricia Gentzel Wright'	EWoo
'Patsy Bickers'	EWoo SApp
'Patterns'	SPol
'Paul Weber'	SApp
'Pawn of Prophecy'	SDay
'Peace be Still'	EWoo
'Peach Float'	EWoo
'Peach Jubilee'	SPol
'Peach Petticoats'	SBrk
'Peach Yum Yum'	CFwr
'Peacock Curls'	EWoo
'Peacock Maiden'	EWoo SApp SBrk SPol XSen
'Pear Ornament'	SBrk SDay
'Pearl Lewis'	SBrk SPol
'Pearl Sherwood'	EWoo
'Peggy Jeffcoat'	CFwr SBrk
'Penelope Vestey'	GBuc MBNS MNFA NBir SApp SPol SRGP
'Penny's Worth'	LEdu LRHS MBNS NOrc WAul WCot WFar WHoo XLum
'Perfect Pleasure'	MBNS
'Persian Melon Plus'	WCAu
'Persian Ruby'	SPol
'Persian Shrine'	SPol
'Petite Ballerina'	SDay

Cultivar	Suppliers
'Phyllis Cantini'	SPol
'Piano Man'	MBNS NLar SBrk WAul WNHG
'Piccadilly Princess'	SBrk SDay WAul
'Picket Fences'	CFwr
'Pink Ambrosia'	EWoo
'Pink Attraction'	SApp
'Pink Charm'	CBen CMac COlW EBee ECha ECtt EPPr GKin GMaP LPBA LRHS MBNS NBro NHol SPol
'Pink Circle'	SDay
'Pink Cotton Candy'	EWoo SBrk SDay SPol
'Pink Crinkles'	SBrk
'Pink Damask' ♀H4	Widely available
'Pink Dazzler' **new**	WNHG
'Pink Dream'	MBNS NBir NBre SPol
'Pink Flirt'	SDay
'Pink Grace'	SPol
'Pink Lady'	MNrw MRav SRms
'Pink Monday'	SDay WNHG
'Pink Pajamas'	CFwr
'Pink Picotee Deluxe'	SBrk
'Pink Picotee Elite'	SBrk
'Pink Prelude'	GBee MBNS MWat NBro SMrm
'Pink Puff'	MBNS NBir NBre NLar
'Pink Rain Dance' **new**	SPol
'Pink Ruffled Love'	CFwr
'Pink Spider'	SDay
'Pink Sundae'	ECha WHrl
'Pink Super Spider'	EWoo MNFA SBrk SDay SPol
'Pink Windmill'	EWoo SPol
'Pinocchio'	SMHy
'Piping Rock'	CFwr
'Pirate Treasure'	MBNS
'Pirate's Patch'	EWoo SBrk SPol WCot
'Pixie Parasol'	WMnd WNHG
'Pixie Pipestone'	SApp SPol
'Pixie Pleasure'	CFwr
'Pizza'	SDay
'Platinum and Gold'	CFwr
'Plinko'	CFwr
'Plum Beauty'	NLar
'Plum Candy'	EWoo
'Pocket Size'	SApp
'Poetic Dance'	EWoo
'Point of Honor'	EWoo
'Pojo'	CFwr SDay
'Pony'	CWat SBrk SPol
'Pookie Bear'	SApp
'Prague Spring'	CFwr MNFA MSpe SDay SPol WCAu
'Prairie Belle'	MBNS NBre NLar SApp SPol WFar
'Prairie Blossoms'	CFwr
'Prairie Blue Eyes'	ECtt IBoy MBNS NPri SApp SPlb SPol WAul WCot WHrl WMnd WWEG
'Prairie Charmer'	MMuc SEND WHrl
'Precious d'Oro'	EBee GQue
'Pretty Miss'	ECtt EWTr LRHS MBri
'Pretty Peggy'	MNFA
'Preview Party'	WNHG
'Primal Scream'	CFwr SApp SBrk SPol WCot
'Primrose Mascotte'	NBir
'Prince Redbird'	SBrk SDay
'Princess Blue Eyes'	SPol
'Princess Ellen'	SApp
'Princess Lilli'	MBNS
'Princeton Eye Glow'	SDay
'Princeton Point Lace'	SApp
'Prissy Frills'	SPol
'Prize Picotee Deluxe'	SPol
'Prize Picotee Elite'	SDay SPol WTin
'Promising Future'	CFwr
'Prophetess'	CFwr
'Protocol'	MSpe SDay SPol
'Proud Mary'	SDay
§ 'Puddin''	CWat SDay WAul
'Pudgie'	SApp
'Pueblo Dreamer'	EWoo
'Pug Yarborough'	SPol
'Pumpkin Kid'	SApp SDay SPol
'Pumpkin Prince'	CFwr
'Puppet Lady'	SApp
'Puppet Show'	SDay
'Pure and Simple'	CFwr SPol
'Pure Country'	CFwr
'Purple Arachne' **new**	SPol
'Purple Bicolor'	WHrl
'Purple Corsage'	SApp
'Purple Grasshopper'	EWoo
'Purple Oddity'	EWoo SPol
'Purple Pinwheel'	EWoo SPol
'Purple Rain'	CWat LRHS MBNS SApp SPol SWvt
'Purple Rain Dance'	SPol
'Purple Waters'	MBNS NBre NOrc SPol WPnP
'Pursuit of Excellence'	SBrk
'Pyewacket'	SApp
'Pygmy Plum'	SBrk SDay
'Queen Empress'	WNHG
'Queen Lily'	WNHG
'Queen of May'	MNrw SApp WCot
'Queens Delight'	SBrk
'Queens Fancy'	SApp
'Queen's Gift'	SApp
'Queensland'	SApp
'Quick Results'	SApp SBrk SDay
'Quinn Buck'	SDay
'Ra Hansen'	SApp SBrk SDay
'Racing Stripes'	CFwr
'Radiant'	CBcs
'Radiant Greetings'	MNFA XSen
'Radiation Biohazard'	CFwr SPol
'Rags to Riches'	CFwr
'Rainbow Candy'	CWGN LLHF MBNS SBrk SPad
'Rainbow Drive'	CFwr
'Raining Violets'	EWoo
'Rajah'	CBgR CMac MBNS MSpe NBro SPer WHrl
'Randall Moore'	SPol
'Rander's Pride'	EWoo
'Rapid Eye Movement'	CFwr
'Raspberry Butterflies'	EWoo
'Raspberry Candy'	CBro GCra IBoy MBNS MNrw MSpe NBro NCGa NHol NOrc SApp SBrk SRms WHrl
'Raspberry Masquerade'	CFwr
'Raspberry Pixie'	SDay SPol
'Raspberry Star'	EWoo
'Raspberry Wine'	ECha
'Rave On'	SApp SBrk WFar
'Raven Woodsong'	EWoo
'Real Wind'	CFwr SApp SBrk SPol
'Red Admiral'	LRHS
'Red Butterfly'	SPol
'Red Eyed Shocker'	CFwr
'Red Flag'	CFwr
'Red Hill'	EWoo
'Red Joy'	SApp

'Red Pennant' CFwr
'Red Precious' ♀H4 MNFA MNrw SApp SMHy WCot
'Red Rain' EWoo
'Red Resplendence' **new** EWoo
'Red Ribbons' EWoo SDay SPol
'Red Ruby' ERCP
'Red Rum' EWll MSpe NBro SBfd SMrm WMoo
'Red Skeletons' CFwr
'Red Suspenders' ECtt MBNS
'Red Thrill' CFwr
'Red Twister' SBrk SDay SPol
'Red Volunteer' SBrk SDay SPol
'Reflections in Time' EWoo
'Regal Giant' EWoo
'Regal Vision' SApp
'Regency Dandy' SApp SDay SPol
'Renee' MNrw
'Respighi' SApp SBrk
'Return Trip' SPol
'Revolute' SDay
'Rhode Island Red' CFwr
'Ribbonette' EBee MBNS MSpe
'Rigamarole' SPol
'Right on Red' CFwr
'Riley Barron' SDay
'Riptide' SApp
'Robespierre' **new** SDay
'Rocket City' ELan SPol WNHG
'Rocky Horror' CFwr
'Rococo' SBrk SDay
'Rodeo Sweetheart' CFwr
'Roger Grounds' CBgR SApp SPol
'Roman Toga' CBgR
'Romanian Rendevous' EWoo
* 'Romantic Rose' EBee MBNS NLar WHrl
'Ron Rousseau' SApp SPol
'Root Beer' WHrl WTin
'Rose Claire' LPla
'Rose Corsage' EWoo
'Rose Emily' SApp SBrk SDay SPol
'Rose Fever' EWoo
'Rose Roland' NBre
'Roseate Spoonbill' EWoo
'Rosella Sheridan' SBrk
'Roses in Snow' IBoy MBNS SBrk SPol
'Roswitha' CWat SApp SPol
'Rosy Lights' CFwr EWoo SPol
'Rosy Returns' LRHS MBNS NLar SBrk SHar
'Round Midnight' SPol
'Royal Braid' EPfP MBNS MNrw MSpe NLar SApp SBrk SPer WAul WCot
'Royal Celebration' WCot
'Royal Corduroy' SBrk
'Royal Elk' EWoo
'Royal Hunter' CFwr
'Royal Parade' SDay
'Royal Prestige' SApp XSen
'Royal Robe' CTri
'Royal Saracen' SDay
'Royal Thornbird' CBgR
'Royal Trophy' **new** WNHG
'Royalty' GCra
'Ruby Moon' CFwr
'Ruby Sentinel' SDay
'Ruby Spider' ELon EWoo SBrk SDay SPol
'Rue Madelaine' SPol
'Ruffled Apricot' CKel MBNS MNFA MSpe SBrk SDay WNHG

'Ruffled Carousel' WNHG
'Rumble Seat Romance' WNHG
'Russian Easter' SBrk
'Russian Rhapsody' CKel SApp SBrk SPol
'Sabie' SApp
'Sabine Baur' CWat EBee EWoo IBal IPot LRHS MBNS MNrw MSpe NLar SApp SBrk WAul WFar
'Sabra Salina' EWoo SBrk SDay
'Sachsen Little Gold' CFwr
'Sachsen Pink Ball' CFwr
'Sachsen Purple Eye' CFwr
'Sachsen Rustic' CFwr
'Sachsen White Giant' CFwr
'Saffron Glow' SDay
* 'Sagamore' SApp
'Saintly' EWoo MSpe
'Salmon Pagoda' **new** EWoo
'Salmon Sheen' SDay SPer
'Sammy' SDay
'Sammy Russell' Widely available
'Samuel Bell' EWoo
'San Luis Halloween' CFwr
'Sanford Code Red' CFwr
'Sanford Star Search' CFwr
'Sangre de Cristo' CFwr
'Santa's Little Helper' CFwr
'Santiago' SPol
'Saratoga Pinwheel' SPol
'Satin Glass' LRHS MNFA
'Satin Glow' ECha MLHP
'Scapes from Hell' EWoo
'Scarlet Butterfly' **new** SPol
'Scarlet Flame' ECha WMoo
'Scarlet Oak' MBri SBrk WAul
'Scarlet Orbit' EWoo SApp SBrk SPol
'Scarlet Prince' WNHG
'Scarlet Ribbons' SPol
'Scatterbrain' CKel SPol
'Schnickel Fritz' EBee
'School Girl' LRHS
'Scorpio' CBgR SPol
'Scotland' IBal SApp
'Screaming Demon' SPol
'Sea Siren' CWat
'Seal of Approval' **new** EBee
'Sebastian' MNFA SApp SBrk
'Secret Splendor' SPol
'Secretary's Sand' EWoo
'Segramoor' SApp
'Seminole Blood' SBrk SPol
'Seminole Wind' EWoo SBrk SPol
'Serena Sunburst' CFwr SBrk SPol
'Serenade' EWoo
'Serene Madonna' CCon EBee GBin SBfd SPoG
'Serenity Bay' CFwr
'Serenity Morgan' EPfP MBNS
'Serge Rigaud' CFwr
'Sergeant Major' EWoo
'Shadowed Pink' WNHG
'Shady Lady' SDay
'Shake the Mountains' CFwr
'Shaman' SApp SBrk SDay SPol
'Shangri La Truffle' CFwr
'She Devil' CFwr
'Shelly Victoria' SDay
'Sherry Lane Carr' SDay SPol
'Sherwood Gladiator' WNHG
'Shibui Splendor' **new** SPol

'Shimek September Morning' SPol
'Shimmering Elegance' CFwr
* 'Shocker' EWoo
'Shogun' MBNS
'Shotgun' SPol
'Show Amber' SApp
'Show Girl' LRHS
'Shuffle the Deck' EWoo
'Significant Other' SApp
'Sigudilla' WNHG
'Silent Sentry' SApp
'Silken Fairy' SDay
'Silken Touch' CBgR SApp SBrk SPol
'Siloam Amazing Grace' SApp SBrk
'Siloam Baby Doll' SDay
'Siloam Baby Talk' ELon GBuc NBir SApp WAul WHoo WMoo WPnP WTin
'Siloam Bertie Ferris' MBNS
'Siloam Bo Peep' SApp SDay WAul
'Siloam Button Box' MBNS SDay WAul WHrl
'Siloam Bye Lo' EWoo MSpe SBrk SDay
'Siloam Cinderella' SBrk SDay SPol
'Siloam David Kirchhoff' MBNS MSpe SDay XSen
'Siloam Doodlebug' CBgR CWat MSpe SBrk
'Siloam Double Classic' (d) SBrk SPol
'Siloam Dream Baby' MBNS MSpe NCGa
'Siloam Ethel Smith' SApp SBrk SDay SPol
'Siloam Fairy Tale' CWat SDay
'Siloam Flower Girl' SDay
'Siloam French Doll' MBNS NLar SApp
'Siloam French Marble' SBrk SDay
'Siloam Frosted Mint' SApp SBrk SPol
'Siloam Gold Coin' SApp SDay
'Siloam Grace Stamile' CCon MBNS SApp SDay
'Siloam Harold Flickinger' SBrk
'Siloam Helpmate' WNHG
'Siloam Jim Cooper' MSpe SBrk
'Siloam Joan Senior' MBNS
'Siloam John Yonski' SDay
'Siloam June Bug' CBgR ELan SApp WCot
'Siloam Justine Lee' MBNS
'Siloam Little Angel' SApp SPol
'Siloam Little Girl' CWat ECtt SBrk SDay
'Siloam Mama' SApp SBrk SDay
'Siloam Merle Kent' EWoo MSpe SApp SBrk SPol
'Siloam Nugget' SApp
'Siloam Orchid Jewel' SDay
'Siloam Paul Watts' EUJe SApp SBrk SPol
'Siloam Penny' SApp
'Siloam Pink Glow' SWat WAul
'Siloam Plum Tree' SApp SPol
'Siloam Pocket Size' SApp SDay
'Siloam Powder Pink' SApp
'Siloam Prissy' SApp
'Siloam Queen's Toy' SPol
'Siloam Ra Hansen' SApp
'Siloam Red Toy' SMHy
'Siloam Ribbon Candy' SApp SDay WNHG
'Siloam Rose Dawn' SApp SBrk SDay SPol
'Siloam Rose Queen' SDay
'Siloam Royal Prince' EPfP MSpe SApp
'Siloam Show Girl' CWGN EWoo GKin MBNS SApp WFar
'Siloam Spizz' SBrk SDay
'Siloam Theresa Moore' **new** SDay
'Siloam Tiny Mite' SDay WHrl
'Siloam Tom Thumb' MBNS MSpe WCAu
'Siloam Ury Winniford' CBro CMac CWan EMil MBNS MSpe NBre NLar SApp SBrk WAul WHoo WHrl WPnP WTin
'Siloam Virginia Henson' EWoo NCGa SApp SBrk WWEG
'Silver Ice' EWoo SApp SBrk SPol
'Silver Lance' SDay SPol
'Silver Quasar' SBrk SDay SPol
'Silver Trumpet' WWEG
'Silver Veil' SDay WFar
'Simply Divine' CFwr
'Sinbad Sailor' NLar
'Singing in the Sunshine' EWoo
'Sir Blackstem' ELon GCal SApp SBrk
'Sir Modred' SPol WNHG
'Sirius' NHol
'Sirocco' WTin
'Sixth Sense' ELon MBNS SBrk WHrl
'Skinwalker' EWoo
'Slapstick' ELon SDay SPol
'Slender Lady' CFwr SBrk SDay
'Small Town' **new** EWoo
'Small World Tornado' EWoo
'Smith Brothers' SPol
'Smoky Mountain Autumn' EWoo SApp SBrk SPol
'Smoky Mountain Bell' SApp
'Smuggler's Gold' ECtt SApp
'Smuggler's Temptation' **new** SPol
'Snappy Rhythm' MNFA
'Snowed In' EWoo SBrk
'Snowy Apparition' ECrc ECtt GKin LHop LRHS MBNS MBri MNFA MWhi NWad SApp SPol WFar
'Snowy Eyes' CHid GKin MBNS NCGa NHol SApp SWat WAul WHrl
'So Excited' SBrk SDay
'So Lovely' EWoo SApp XLum
'So Many Stars' CFwr
'Soft Cashmere' XLum
'Solano Bull's Eye' MLHP
'Sombrero Way' SDay
'Someone Special' SBrk SDay SPol
'Someplace Special' SBrk
'Song In My Heart' EWoo
'Song Sparrow' CBro SApp WPer
'Sorcerer's Song' **new** SDay
'South Seas' LRHS
'Southern Charmer' SBrk
'Southern Prize' SDay
'Sovereign Queen' WNHG
'Spacecoast Dragon Prince' EWoo
'Spacecoast Gator Eye' IPot
'Spacecoast Peach Fringe' CFwr
'Spacecoast Scrambled' CBcs CWGN EPfP MBNS NLar SBrk SMrm
'Spacecoast Starburst' CBcs EBee MBNS NBro SApp SBrk WCAu WCot WFar
'Spanish Fandango' SPol
'Spanish Glow' SBrk SPol
'Sparkling Dawn' SBrk
'Speak of Angels' SApp SBrk
'Spice Hunter' CFwr
'Spider Breeder' EWoo SApp
'Spider Man' CFwr MNFA SApp SBrk SDay SPol WCAu XSen
'Spider Miracle' MNFA SBrk SDay SPol
'Spider Red' CWGN EWoo
'Spider Web' SDay
'Spilled Milk' SPol

'Spindazzle' CBgR CFwr SPol
'Spinne in Lachs' SBrk SPol
'Spiral Charmer' SApp
'Spirit of Sapelo' EWoo
'Spock's Sun' CFwr
'Spode' SApp
'Spooner' CBgR
'Spring Ballerina' SApp
'Spring Willow Song' SDay
'Squash Dolly' EWoo
'Stafford' Widely available
'Staghorn Sumac' GKin LEdu LRHS MBNS NHol WCAu
'Star of Fantasy' CFwr
'Star Twister' CFwr
'Starling' COlW CPar EWoo MNFA SApp WAul WWEG
'Starman's Quest' SPol
'Stars and Stripes' MNFA
'Starstruck' WNHG
'Startle' ELon EPfP MBNS MNrw SApp SBrk WCot WHrl
'Statuesque' EWoo WFar
'Stella de Oro' Widely available
'Stella in Red' EPfP
'Steve Trimmer' CFwr
'Stinnette' WCot
'Stoke Poges' $\mathbb{Y}^{H4}$ CAvo CBgR CBro EBee EPfP GBin LAst LBMP LHop LPot LRHS LSRN MBNS MNFA MSpe NPri SApp SPer STes SWat WFar WHrl
'Stoplight' CBgR ELon LRHS SApp SDay SPol
'Storm of the Century' MNrw
'Storm Over Toledo' CFwr
'Strasbourg' **new** CMac
'Strawberry Candy' CMac COlW CSBt ECtt ELon EWll EWoo IBoy LSRN MBNS MBri MSCN MSpe NGdn SApp SBfd SBrk SPer SPet STes WAul WCAu WHoo WHrl WMoo WWEG
'Strawberry Fields Forever' EWoo MBNS MBri NLar SBrk SHar SPol
'Strawberry Swirl' MNFA
I 'Streaker' B. Brown (v) WCot XSen
'Street Urchin' SPol
'Streets of Heaven' EWoo
'Strider Spider' SApp
'Strutter's Ball' EWoo LPla MBNS MNFA MSCN MSpe NGdn SApp SBfd SBrk SDay SPer SPol SWat WAul WCAu WHrl WMnd
'Sugar Cookie' EWoo SApp SBrk SDay SPol
'Summer Dragon' MBNS SBrk
'Summer Fireworks' EWoo
'Summer Interlude' WMoo
'Summer Jubilee' SApp
'Summer Wine' Widely available
'Sun King' SBrk
'Sunday Gloves' SBrk SPol WNHG
'Sungold Candy' SApp
'Sunray Brilliance' EWoo
'Super Purple' CKel SApp
'Superlative' SApp SBrk SDay SPol
'Susan Weber' EWoo SApp SBrk SPol
'Suzie Wong' MNFA
'Svengali' SDay SPol
'Sweet Charlotte' **new** SPol
'Sweet Hot Chocolate' LRHS MBNS
'Sweet Pea' SDay
'Sweet Sugar Candy' ECtt EWoo SDeJ
'Swirling Spider' CBgR EWoo
'Swirling Water' SDay
'Tahitian Waterfall' CFwr
'Tail Feathers' CFwr
'Taj Mahal' ELon EWoo SApp WFar
'Tall Boy' SApp
'Tang' CHid MBNS MMuc NOrc
'Tangerine Tango' EWoo
'Tango Noturno' SApp SPol
'Tani' SDay
'Tapestry of Dreams' MSpe
'Tarantula' ELon SApp SPol
'Taruga' EWoo SDay
'Tasmania' SPer
'Tchao Pantin' CFwr XSen
'Technical Knockout' EWoo
'Techny Breeze' SBrk
'Techny Spider' SBrk
'Tejas' CElw ELon NBre SPer
'Ten to Midnight' SApp
'Tennessee Flycatcher' EWoo SPol
'Tennessee Williams' SPol
'Tennyson' CFwr
'Tet Set' WNHG
tetraploid hybrid **new** GHim
'Tetraploid Stella de Oro' SDay
'Tetrina's Daughter' $\mathbb{Y}^{H4}$ CBgR LRHS NHol SApp SBrk
'Texas Sunlight' WAul
'Thanks a Bunch' SBrk SPol
'The Tingler' EWoo
'Theresa Hall' WFar
'Thin Man' CFwr
'Third Witch' CFwr EWoo
'Three Diamonds' SPol
'Thumbelina' ECha WMoo XLum
§ ***thunbergii*** ECha GCal MCoo
- 'Ovation' MBNS
'Thundering Ovation' CWGN SBrk
'Thy True Love' SApp SDay
'Tigereye Spider' EWoo
'Tigerling' EWoo MSpe SPol
'Tiger's Eye' SBrk
'Tigger' CFwr SPol
'Time Lord' SApp SDay XSen
'Time to Believe' SPol
'Timeless Fire' SApp SBrk
'Tiny Talisman' SApp SDay
'Tiny Temptress' SDay
'Tirade' CFwr
'Tis Midnight' WNHG
'Tom Collins' SBrk SDay
'Tom Wise' SBrk SPol
'Tomorrow's Song' SApp SPol
'Tone Poem' WNHG
'Tonia Gay' SApp SBrk SDay SPol
'Too Much Fun' CFwr
'Toodleloo Kangaroo' EWoo
'Toothpick' EWoo MSpe SPol
'Tootsie' SDay
'Tootsie Rose' SBrk SDay SPol
'Top Honors' SPol
'Topaz Gem' **new** SPol
'Torpoint' GBee MBNS MRav NEgg SBfd
'Total Eclipse' SBrk
'Totally Tropical' SBrk
'Touched by Magic' CFwr
'Towhead' MRav SDay WCot
'Toyland' EPfP MBNS NBir NGdn NLar SPol

'Trahlyta'	CBgR EWoo MSpe SApp SBrk SDay SPol WHrl WTin
'Treasure of Love'	EWoo
'Tremor'	CFwr
'Trevi Fountain'	EWoo
'Trond'	SDay
'Tropic Sunset'	SBrk
'Tropical Depression'	EWoo
'Tropical Heat Wave'	SApp
'Tropical Toy'	SDay
'Troubled Sleep'	EWoo
'Truchas Sunrise'	EWoo
'True Glory'	SApp
'True Grit'	SApp SBrk
'True North'	CFwr
'True Pink Beauty'	EWoo
'Truffle Heritage'	CFwr
'Tune the Harp'	SPol
'Tuolumne Fairy Tale'	SPol
'Turkish Turban'	SDay SPol
'Tuscawilla Blackout'	SApp SBrk XSen
'Tuscawilla Tigress'	GKin IKil MBNS MNrw NCGa SBrk SMad WAul WHrl
'Tutti Frutti Truffle'	CFwr
'Tuxedo'	SApp SPol
'Twenty Third Psalm'	WHal
'Twiggy'	CFwr MSpe
'Twilight Secrets'	LRHS MBNS
'Twirling Pinata'	EWoo
'Twist and Shout'	CFwr
'Twist of Lemon'	CFwr EWoo SDay
'Twister Time'	CFwr
'Two Faces of Love'	SPol
'Two Part Harmony'	CFwr
'Tylwyth Teg'	CFwr SPol
'Ultimate Destiny'	CWat
'Unchartered Waters'	MBNS SBrk
'Unforgetable Fire'	EWoo
'Unique Purple' **new**	SPol
'Uniquely Different'	SPol
'Upper Class Peach'	SBrk
'Uptown Girl'	SBrk
'Valiant'	EWoo MBNS WHrl
'Vanessa Arden'	SApp
'Vanilla Candy'	MSpe SBrk
'Vanilla Fluff'	WHlf
'Variegated Woottens' **new**	EWoo
'Varsity'	CPLG CWat LRHS NBir NRHS SBrk SPer
'Veins of Truth'	CBgR
'Velvet Shadows'	SDay
'Velvet Widow'	CFwr
'Vendetta'	WNHG
'Vera Biaglow'	MSpe SApp SBrk SPol
'Very Berry Ice'	SPol
'Vespers'	CAbP WFar WPnP
vespertina	see *H. thunbergii*
'Veuve Joyeuse'	XSen
'Vi Simmons'	SBrk
'Victoria Aden'	CBro
'Victoria Elizabeth Barnes'	WNHG
'Victorian Collar'	SApp SBrk
'Victorian Lace'	EWoo
'Victorian Ribbons'	CFwr SPol
'Victorian Violet'	SDay
'Video'	SApp SBrk SDay
'Vintage Bordeaux'	ELan SApp WAul
'Vintage Burgundy'	CBgR WNHG
'Violet Hour'	SDay
'Viracocha'	SApp WMnd WNHG
'Virgin's Blush'	SPer
'Vision of Beauty'	SApp
'Vohann'	SApp SBrk SDay
'Waiting in the Wings'	SBrk
'Walking on Sunshine'	SApp SBrk WCot
'Wally Nance'	SApp
'Walt Disney'	GKin
'War Paint'	SDay
'Warrior Victorious'	CFwr
'Watchyl Christmas Widow'	CFwr
'Watchyl Cyber Spider'	CFwr
'Watchyl Dancing Spider'	CFwr
'Watchyl Digital Scream'	CFwr
'Watchyl Digital Spider'	CFwr
'Watchyl Lavender Blue'	CFwr
'Water Witch'	CWat SApp SDay STes
'Watermelon Man'	EWoo
'Watership Down'	EWoo
'Wayside Green Imp'	MNrw SApp
'We Love'	EWoo
'Weaver's Art'	CFwr SPol
'Web Browser'	CFwr
'Web Dancer'	SPol
'Wedding Band'	SBrk
'Wee Willie Wonka' **new**	WNHG
'Wekiwa'	EWoo
'Welchkins'	SDay WAul
'Welfo White Diamond'	SApp SPol
'Wendy Glawson'	SApp
'Westward Wind'	CFwr EWoo
'What a Day for a Daydream'	CFwr
'When Fortune Smiles'	SBrk
'When I Dream'	SBrk
'Whichford' ♀^{H4}	CBgR CBro CSam EBee ECha ECrc ECtt ELan EWoo GBuc GKin LRHS MBNS MNFA MSpe NEgg SPhx WAul WFar WHrl WPtf
'Whirling Fury'	EWoo SApp
'Whiskey on Ice'	SApp
'White Coral'	LRHS LSRN MBNS MNFA NBro WFar
'White Edged Madonna'	SBch WHrl
'White Lemonade'	SApp
'White Pansy'	SBrk
'White Perfection'	EWoo
'White Temptation'	CCon EPfP IBoy MNFA NCGa NGdn SApp SBrk WAul WHoo WMnd WNHG XSen
'White Tie Affair'	EWoo SApp SBrk SDay
'White Zone'	EWoo
'Whooperee'	SBrk SDay
'Wideyed'	GBin XLum
'Wild about Sherry'	CFwr SPol
'Wild and Wonderful'	EPfP EWoo MSCN NCGa WWlt
'Wild Horses'	CFwr CWGN EBee EPfP EWes LRHS MNrw SBrk SPad SPol WHrl
'Wild Mustang'	MBNS MSpe SBrk
'Wild One'	SApp
'Wild Rose Fandango'	EWoo
'Wild Winter Wine'	CFwr
'Wild Wookie'	CFwr
'Wildest Dreams'	EWoo
'Wildfire Tango'	SApp
'Wilson Spider'	SApp SPol
'Wind Beneath My Sails'	EWoo
'Wind Frills'	SApp SBrk SDay SPol
'Wind Song'	SApp SBrk

'Windmill Yellow'	EWoo SBrk
'Window Dressing'	EWoo SBrk
'Winds of Love'	EWoo
'Windsor Castle'	SApp
'Wine Bubbles'	SApp
'Wine Delight'	SDay
'Wineberry Candy'	EWoo LHop MBNS MSpe NLar SApp WAul
'Winged Migration'	EWoo
'Wings on High'	EWoo SApp
'Winnie the Pooh'	SDay
'Winsome Lady'	ECGP ECha ECtt GKin MBNS MSpe WHrl
'Wisest of Wizards'	MBNS MNrw NCGa SPol WHrl
'Wishing Well'	WCot
'Witch Stitchery'	SDay
'Witches Wink'	EWoo MSpe
'Without Warning'	CBgR
'Women's Work'	SApp
'Wood Duck'	SApp
'Woodside Ruby'	WNHG
'Wounded Heart' **new**	SDay
'Xia Xiang'	EWoo SBrk
'Xochimilco'	WNHG
'Ya Ya Girl'	EWoo
'Yabba Dabba Doo'	MNrw SApp SPol
'Yazoo Green Octopus'	EWoo
'Yearning Love'	SApp
'Yellow Angel'	ELon SApp SPol WCot
'Yellow Explosion'	SApp
'Yellow Lollipop'	SApp SBrk SDay
'Yellow Rain'	WCot
'Yellow Ribbon'	SPol
'Yellow Spider'	SApp
'Yellow Submarine'	MBNS SBrk
'Yesterday Memories'	SBrk SDay
yezoensis	EBtc
'You Angel You'	MBNS MSpe SApp SBrk
'Yuma'	WNHG
'Zagora'	WCAu
'Zampa'	CBgR SDay
'Zara'	SPer
'Zuni Thunderbird'	EWoo

Hepatica ✿ (*Ranunculaceae*)

acutiloba	CBro CRDP EBee ECho EPot GBBs GBuc GEdr LAma MHom MMoz NBir NMen WAbe XEll
- blue-flowered	MAsh
- white-flowered	MAsh NLar
americana	EBee ECho ELan EPot LHop MAsh NBir NPnk
angulosa	see *H. transsilvanica*
(Forest Series) 'Forest Pink' **new**	EBee ELan
- 'Forest Purple' **new**	EBee XEll
- 'Forest Red' **new**	EBee ELan
- 'Forest White' **new**	EBee ELan XEll
henryi	GEdr LAma MAsh NSla
insularis	MAsh
- B&SWJ 859	WCru
maxima	GBuc GEdr MAsh
- B&SWJ 4344	WCru
× ***media*** 'Ballardii'	GBuc GEdr IBlr MNFA
- 'Harvington Beauty'	CLAP EBee EHrv IBlr IFoB LRHS MAsh MHom NBir WSHC
§ ***nobilis*** ♀H4	Widely available
- SDR 5301	GKev
- var. ***asiatica***	MAsh NPnk
- blue-flowered	ECho GEdr IFoB MAsh NSla WAbe WGwG
- 'Cobalt'	CLAP ECho NSla WAbe
- 'Cremar'	MAsh
- dark-blue-flowered	CLAP
- dwarf white-flowered	IFoB
- var. ***japonica***	EPfP EWes IFoB LAma LHop MAsh NBir NSla
- - 'Akabuku' **new**	GEdr
- - 'Akane' (1)	ECho GEdr
- - 'Akanezora' (6/d)	GEdr
- - 'Akebono' (9/d)	GEdr
- - 'Anjyu' (9/d)	GEdr
- - 'Asahi' (7/d)	GEdr
- - 'Asahizuru' (6/d)	GEdr
- - 'Benikanzan'	GEdr
- - 'Benioiran'	GEdr
- - 'Benisuzume' (1)	GEdr
- - 'Benitaiko' (9/d) **new**	GEdr
- - 'Bojyou' (5A/d)	GEdr
- - 'Dewa' (9/d)	GEdr
- - 'Echigobijin'	GEdr
- - 'Ensyu' (9/d)	GEdr
- - 'Fujimusume' (9/d)	GEdr
- - 'Fukujyu' **new**	GEdr
- - 'Gosho-zakura' (5A/d)	GEdr
- - 'Gyousei' (1)	ECho GBuc GEdr
- - 'Hakurin' (6/d)	GEdr
- - 'Haruka' (2)	GEdr
- - 'Harukaze' (5A/d)	GEdr
- - 'Haruno-awajuki' (9/d)	GEdr
- - 'Hatsune' **new**	GEdr
- - Herashibe Group	GBuc
- - 'Hohobeni' (9/d)	GEdr
- - 'Hokutosei' (7/d) **new**	GEdr
- - 'Houkan' (9/d)	GEdr
- - 'Isaribi' (1)	ECho GEdr
- - 'Izayoi' **new**	IFoB
- - 'Junissen' (6/d) **new**	GEdr
- - 'Kagura' (5A/d)	GEdr
- - 'Kasumino'	ECho GEdr
- - 'Kiko' (9/d) **new**	GEdr
- - 'Kimon' (9/d)	GEdr
- - 'Koshi-no-maboroshi'	GEdr
- - 'Kuetsu' (9/d)	GEdr
- - 'Kougyoku' (9/d)	GEdr
- - 'Kousei' (9/d)	GEdr
- - 'Koushirou'	GEdr
- - 'Kuukai' (8/d)	GEdr
- - f. ***magna***	MAsh
- - - 'Murasaki-shikibu' (9/d)	GEdr
- - - 'Seizan'	GEdr
- - - 'Taeka'	GEdr
- - 'Manazuru' (9/d) **new**	GEdr
- - 'Mangekyou'	GEdr
- - 'Miwaku' (1)	GEdr
- - 'Miyuki' (9/d)	GEdr
- - 'Murasaki-sakama' (9/d)	GEdr
- - 'Odoriko' (9/d)	GEdr
- - 'Okina' (9/d)	GEdr
- - 'Ō-murasaki' (1)	ECho GEdr
- - 'Orihime' (9/d)	GEdr
- - 'Reeka' (1) **new**	GEdr
- - 'Ryokurei' (5A/d)	GEdr
- - 'Ryokusetsu' (9/d)	GEdr
- - 'Ryokuun' (9/d)	GEdr
- - 'Ryougetsu' (1)	GEdr
- - 'Sadobeni' (1)	GEdr
- - 'Saichou' (7/d)	GEdr

- - 'Sakuragari' GEdr
- - Sandan Group (7/d) GEdr
- - 'Sansetsu' (7/d) GEdr
- - 'Sawanemidori' (6/d) GEdr
- - 'Sayaka' (1) GEdr
- - 'Seikai' (5A/d-8d) new GEdr
- - 'Seizan' (9/d) new GEdr
- - 'Senhime' (9/d) GEdr
- - 'Setsudo' (d) new GEdr
- - 'Shikouden' (9/d) GEdr
- - 'Shikouryuu' (9/d) GEdr
- - 'Shirayuki' (9/d) GEdr
- - 'Shirin' (d) GEdr
- - 'Shiun' (9/d) GEdr
- - 'Shoujyouno-homare' (9/d) GEdr
- - 'Sougetsu' (6/d) ECho GEdr
- - 'Subaru' (9/d) GEdr
- - 'Suien' (9/d) GEdr
- - 'Tae' (5A/d) GEdr
- - 'Taeka' (9/d) new GEdr
- - 'Takumi' (9/d) new GEdr
- - 'Tamahime' (8/d) GEdr
- - 'Tamakujyaku' (6/d) GEdr
- - 'Tamamushi' (9/d) GEdr
- - 'Tamao' (1) GEdr
- - 'Tamasaburou' (1) GEdr
- - 'Tenjinbai' (1) GEdr
- - 'Tensei' (9/d) GEdr
- - 'Toki' (9/d) GEdr
- - 'Touhou' (9/d) GEdr
- - 'Touryoku' (9/d) GEdr
- - 'Toyama-chiyoiwai' GEdr
- - 'Usugesyou' (9/d) GEdr
- - 'Wakakusa' (9/d) GEdr
- - 'Yahiko' GEdr
- - 'Yahikomuasaki' GEdr
- - 'Yoshinosato' (9/d) GEdr
- - 'Yukishino' GEdr
- - 'Yumegokochi' GEdr
- - 'Yuunami' (1) GEdr
- - 'Yuzuru' (9/d) GEdr
- large, pale blue-flowered NSla
- 'Lilac Picotee' NSla
- mottled leaf ECho
- patterned leaf NSla
- pink-flowered CLAP ECho MAsh NMen
- var. ***pubescens*** MAsh
* - var. ***pyrenaica*** GBuc LEdu MAsh NSla WThu
* - - 'Apple Blossom' GBuc MAsh NBir WAbe
- 'Pyrenean Marbles' CLAP NMen
- red-flowered ECho NMen
- Rene's form WFar
- var. ***rubra*** CLAP ECho NMen NSla
- 'Rubra Plena' (d) ELan GEdr MHom NHar NSla SCnR WPnP
- white-flowered CLAP ECho EHrv MAsh NMen
'Sakaya' ECho
'Shunrin' (d) CRDP
§ ***transsilvanica*** ♀H4 CBro CLAP EBee ECho EHrv EPot GAbr LAma MAsh MCot MMoz NMen NPnk SMrm WPnP WTin
- 'Ada Scott' GEdr
- 'Blue Eyes' EBee ECho EPot GEdr LWst MHom NCGa
- 'Blue Jewel' CCon CLAP EBee ECho ELan EPot GBBs GEdr LWst MCot MHom NCGa NMen WCot WPnP
- blue-flowered IBlr IFoB MAsh
- 'Buis' CLAP EBee ECho GEdr GKev IFoB LRHS MHom NLar WPnP
- 'Eisvogel' CLAP ECho GEdr NMen
- 'Elison Spence' (d) GEdr IBlr MCot
- 'Lilacina' ECho GEdr MAsh NSla
- 'Loddon Blue' IBlr
- pink-flowered CLAP ECho MAsh
- 'Sieben Bergen' IBlr
- white-flowered ECho MAsh
triloba see *H. nobilis*
'Wakana' GEdr
aff. ***yamatutai*** MAsh

Heptacodium (*Caprifoliaceae*)

jasminoides see *H. miconioides*
§ ***miconioides*** Widely available

Heptapleurum see *Schefflera*

Heracleum (*Apiaceae*)

lehmannianum WCot
maximum 'Washington Limes' (v) EWes

Herbertia (*Iridaceae*)

§ ***lahue*** CDes ECho

Hereroa (*Aizoaceae*)

glenensis ECho LRHS NRHS SPlb

Hermannia (*Malvaceae*)

ciliaris new EDif
flammea SPlb
pinnata NMen
stricta WAbe WPat

Herniaria (*Caryophyllaceae*)

glabra CArn GPoy XLum

Hertia see *Othonna*

Hesperaloe (*Asparagaceae*)

F&M 311.1 WPGP
parviflora CTrC EAmu LEdu SBig SPlb WCot XSen

Hesperantha (*Iridaceae*)

§ ***baurii*** ECho EPot EWld GBuc GLin LLHF NMen WAbe
coccinea Widely available
- from Giants Castle CTca
- f. ***alba*** Widely available
- 'Ballyrogan Giant' CCon CDes CTca CYeo ECtt GBuc IBlr MAvo NCot NHol WFar WHer WPGP WSHC
- 'Big Moma' CPrp CYeo MAvo WWEG
- 'Brick Red' MAvo WWEG
- 'Cardinal' NHol WMoo
- 'Cindy Towe' CYeo EBee MAvo
- 'Countesse de Vere' CYeo EBee
- early-flowering CPrp
- 'Elburton Glow' CPrp CYeo MAvo NLar WFar
- 'Fenland Daybreak' Widely available
- 'Good White' CYeo NBir NCGa SUsu WCot
- 'Hilary Gould' CPrp GBuc MAvo NCGa SUsu WFar WHal
- 'Hint of Pink' WOld
- 'Jack Frost' EBee ECtt MAvo NCGa WMoo WWEG

	- 'Jennifer' ♀H4	CBro CTca CTri CYeo EBee EHrv ELon EPfP EShb GAbr GBin GBuc LPot LRHS LSou MAvo MRav NCGa SApp SBfd SRms SUsu SWvt WFar WMoo WOld WWEG XLum
	- late-flowering	NCot
	- 'Maiden's Blush'	CPrp CYeo EBee ECtt EHrv LRHS LSou MAvo MCot MDKP NHol NLar NRHS SBfd SPet SRms WFar
§	- 'Major' ♀H4	Widely available
	- 'Marietta'	CYeo
	- 'Mollie Gould'	CPrp CTca CYeo EAEE EBee ECtt EHrv ELon EShb GBuc GCra LBMP LHop LSou MAvo MHer MMHG NBre NCGa NHol NLar SCoo SPoG SRms WHil WMoo WOld WTin WWEG
	- 'Mrs Hegarty'	Widely available
	- 'November Cheer'	CMac CPrp CTca CYeo IBlr LLHF NBir NLar WFar WWEG XLum
	- 'Oregon Sunset'	CPrp MAvo MDKP
	- 'Pallida'	CSam CYeo ECha ECtt EHrv ELan MLHP MRav NBir WFar
	- 'Pink Marg'	CPrp MAvo
	- 'Professor Barnard'	CCCN CPrp CSpe CTca CYeo EBee ECho ECtt ELon EPfP EPri EShb GAbr MAvo MBNS MSpe NBir NEgg SApp SRot WMoo WOld WWEG
	- 'Red Dragon'	CYeo ECtt GAbr GBuc LLHF NCGa NCot NHol WHoo
I	- 'Rosea'	MBel
	- 'Salmon Charm'	ECtt GBin GBuc LLHF LRHS NCGa WFar WMoo
	- salmon-flowered	NCot
	- 'Silver Pink'	IBlr
	- 'Snow Maiden'	CDes CElw ECtt GAbr
	- 'Strawberry'	CPrp NCot
§	- 'Sunrise' ♀H4	Widely available
	- 'Tambura'	CCse CPou CPrp CSam EBee EHrv GAbr GBuc LHop MAvo SApp SMrm WAbb XLum
	- 'The Bride'	CTri
	- 'Viscountess Byng'	CBcs CBro CTca CTri CWCL CYeo EBee ELon EPau IBlr LRHS NBir SPav SPer WFar WPer WWEG
§	- 'Wilfred H. Bryant'	Widely available
	- 'Zeal Salmon'	CBro CCon CPou CPrp CYeo ECha GAbr GBin MAvo NBir NCGa SApp SMHy WFar
	cucullata	ECho
	falcata	ECho
	grandiflora	ECho
	huttonii	ECho EWld LLHF MHer NBir
	mossii	see *H. baurii*
	oligantha 'Kamiesberg'	ECho
	pauciflora	ECho

Hesperis (*Brassicaceae*)

	dinarica	LRHS
	lutea	see *Sisymbrium luteum*
	matronalis	Widely available
	- ***alba***	see *H. matronalis* var. *albiflora*
§	- var. ***albiflora***	CSpe CTri EBee EGHP ELau EPfP LRHS MCot MMuc NGdn NPnk SIde SPer SPhx SWat WBrk WFar WMnd WMoo
	- - 'Alba Plena' (d)	CAbP EBee ELan ELon LRHS MBel MCot MNrw MPie NBir NCGa NPri WCot WHer WSHC
	- 'Cally Dwarf' (d) **new**	GCal
	- 'Lilacina'	SWat

Hessea (*Amaryllidaceae*)

	breviflora	ECho
	incana 'Pendoornhoek'	ECho
	mathewsii	ECho
	pulcherrima	ECho
	speciosa	ECho
	stellaris	ECho

Heteromeles (*Rosaceae*)

	arbutifolia	see *H. salicifolia*
§	***salicifolia***	WWau

Heteromorpha (*Apiaceae*)

	arborescens	CPLG SPlb

Heteropyxis (*Myrtaceae*)

	natalensis	EShb

Heterotheca (*Asteraceae*)

	camporum	LHop
	var. ***glandulissimum***	
	mariana	see *Chrysopsis mariana*
§	***villosa***	EPPr WCot
	- 'Golden Sunshine'	CPrp

Heuchera ✿ (*Saxifragaceae*)

	sp. **new**	NPri
	'Alan Davidson'	MPnt
	'Alison' **new**	MPnt
	'Amber Waves'PBR	CPLG EHrv ELan EPfP LRHS LSRN MPkF MPnt NBir NBro NGdn NHol SBfd SGol SRGP SWvt WFar
§	***americana***	CEnt ECha MNFA MRav NBir SWvt
	- var. ***americana***	MPnt
	- Dale's strain	EHoe IFoB MPnt NLar SPlb SWvt WMnd WPnP
	- 'Eco-magnififolia'	CLAP EBee
	- 'Harry Hay'	CDes CLAP EBee EPPr LPla MPnt SUsu WPGP WSHC
	- 'Ring of Fire'	EBee ECtt LHop LRHS LSRN MPkF NPri SApp SBfd SPav SWvt WFar
	'Amethyst Myst'	CLAP COlW EBee ECtt EPfP GKev LHop LRHS LSRN MAsh MPkF MPnt NPla SBfd SGol SHeu SLim SPer SRkn WFar WWEG
	'Apple Crisp' **new**	MPnt SHeu
	'Apple Souffle' **new**	SHeu
	'Autumn Haze'PBR	MPnt NHol SHeu
	'Autumn Leaves'	CLAP CMea CWCL EBee ECtt ESwi EWll LBMP LRHS LSou MAsh MPkF MPnt NCGa NDov NHol NLar NPri NWad SBfd SHeu SMrm SPoG WCot
	'Baby's Breath'	ECho MPnt
	'Bardot'	MPnt
	'Beaujolais'PBR	CAbP CLAP ECGP ECtt ELon ESwi LSou MAsh MBNS MNrw MPnt NBir NCGa NLar NSti SEND SHeu SUsu WBrk WCot
	'Beauty Colour'	CAbP CLAP CMac CWCL EBee ECha ECtt ELan ELon EPfP GMaP LHop LRHS LSRN MBri MPie MRav NGdn NHol NWad SBfd SHeu SHil SPer SPoG SWvt WFar WMnd

Name	Suppliers
'Berry Marmalade' **new**	LSou MPnt SHeu
'Berry Smoothie'	Widely available
'Big Top Gold' (Big Top Series) **new**	MAsh
'Binoche'	EBee ECtt MPnt SHeu
'Birkin'	MPnt SHeu
* 'Black Velvet'	CLAP
'Blackberry Crisp' **new**	MPnt SHeu
'Blackberry Jam'	CLAP CSev CSpe EBee ECha ECtt ELan ELon ESwi GCai LBMP LRHS MPnt MTis NBir NHol SFai SHeu SWvt WGor
'Blackbird' ♀H4	CLAP CMac EBee LRHS MPnt MWat SApp SFai SHeu SWvt WMnd
'Blackout'	CAbP ECtt ESwi MAsh MCot MNrw MPnt SEND SHeu WBrk WCot
'Blood Red'	CLAP EBee LSou MAsh MPkF MPnt NWad SBfd SHeu SLim SPoG
'Blood Vein'	MPnt NHol SHeu
'Bouquet' **new**	MPnt
bracteata	MPnt XLum
'Bressingham Glow'	MPnt
Bressingham hybrids	CWib GJos IFoB MLHP MMuc NBir SBfd SPer SRms WFar WPer WWEG
'Bronze Beauty'	MPnt SHeu
'Brown Sugar' **new**	EBee MPnt SHeu
'Brownfinch'	SMHy SUsu
'Brownies'	CAbP CLAP ECtt ESwi LPla MBNS MPnt SHeu SUsu WCot
'Café Olé' PBR	CLAP GCai LSou MPnt SBfd SHeu WHer
'Can-can' ♀H4	Widely available
'Canyon Duet'	EAEE LHop MBNS MPnt NOrc SHeu
'Canyon Pink'	NSti
'Cappuccino'	CLAP EAEE EBee ECtt ELan EPfP IBoy MPnt MRav NBro NGdn SBfd SHeu SWvt WFar
'Caramel' PBR	Widely available
'Carmen'	MPnt
'Cascade Dawn'	CLAP CWCL EBee ECtt EPfP LAst LRHS LSRN LSou MPnt NBir NHol SBfd SPer SWvt WFar
'Champagne Bubbles'	SHeu
Charles Bloom = 'Chablo'	MPnt
'Chatterbox'	MPnt
'Checkers'	see *H.* 'Quilter's Joy'
'Cherries Jubilee' PBR	CAbP CCon CLAP EBee ELon EPfP GMaP LRHS LSRN LSou MAsh MPnt NHol NWad SBfd SLim WFar
'Cherry Cola'	LSou MPnt SHeu
* 'Cherry Red'	CLAP
'Chiqui'	MPnt SMHy
chlorantha	MPnt
'Chocolate Ruffles' PBR	Widely available
'Chocolate Veil' ♀H4	EBee EPfP LSRN MPnt WWEG
'Christa'	EBee MPnt SHeu
'Cinnabar Silver' PBR	CLAP EBee LSou MAsh MPkF MPnt NBir NCGa NDov NHol SBfd SHeu
'Citronelle'	CLAP CSev CWGN EBee ECtt ELon GAbr LSou MBNS MPnt NDov NPnk SHeu WCot
'City Lights'	LSou SHeu
'Color Dream' PBR	MAsh
coral bells	see *H. sanguinea*
'Coral Bouquet'	MPnt SHar SHeu
'Coral Cloud'	MPnt
Crème Brûlée = 'Tnheu041' (Dolce Series)	Widely available
'Crème Caramel'	CPLG IFoB MPnt SBfd SHar
'Crimson Curls'	CLAP EBee LBuc LRHS LSou MAsh MPnt SBfd SFai SHeu SRms SWvt
'Crispy Curly'	SHeu
cylindrica	EPfP LLWP LRHS MPnt WWEG
- var. ***alpina***	GKev
- 'Chartreuse'	SUsu
- 'Francis'	EBee
- 'Greenfinch'	CFis CWan EBee ELan EPfP GKev GMaP LSRN MPnt MRav NBir NOrc SHeu SWat WFar WMnd
- 'Hyperion'	MPnt
'Damask'	MPnt
'Dark Beauty' PBR	CCVN CLAP EBee ECtt ELon GKev LBMP LRHS LSRN LSou MAsh MBNS MPkF NHol NLar NPri NRHS NWad SBfd SHeu SRot WCot
'Dark Mystery' **new**	MAsh
'Dark Secret' PBR	EBee MAsh MPnt SHeu
'David'	MPnt WBrk
'Dennis Davidson'	see *H.* 'Huntsman'
'Dingle Mint Chocolate'	ECtt
Ebony and Ivory = 'E and I' PBR	CAbP CLAP EBee ECtt EPfP EShb GKev GMaP LBMP LHop LRHS LSRN LSou MBri MGos MPnt NBir NHol NLar NRHS SHar SHil SRot SUsu SWvt WFar WWEG
'Eden's Aurora'	WMnd
'Electra'	Widely available
'Electric Lime'	CLAP EBee ECtt ESwi LBMP MPnt NDov NPri SHeu
elegans NNS 05-372	WCot
'Elworthy Rusty'	CElw
'Emperor's Cloak'	ELon LEdu MWhi NLar SHeu SPad SWvt WMoo
'Encore' PBR	EBee MNrw MPnt SHeu
Eton Mess = 'Raspberry' (Fox Series) **new**	MPnt
'Fantasia' PBR	NHol SHeu
'Fire Chief'	CLAP CWCL CWGN EBee ECtt ELon ESwi EWll LBMP LRHS LSou MAsh MBri MPkF MPnt MTis NHol NLar NPri NWad SBfd SFai SHeu SMrm SPoG SRot
'Firebird'	MPnt NBir
Firefly	see *H.* 'Leuchtkäfer'
'Fireworks' PBR ♀H4	CAbP ECtt LAst LRHS MBNS MBri MPnt NLar NPri SBfd SHil SLim SPer SRot WFar
'Florist's Choice'	MNFA
'French Quarter'	MPnt SHeu
'Frosted Violet' PBR	see *H.* 'Frosted Violet Dream'
§ 'Frosted Violet Dream' PBR	CLAP EBee ECtt EPfP LRHS LSRN LSou MAsh MPnt NCGa SBfd SHeu WWEG
'Georgia Peach' PBR	Widely available
'Ginger Ale' PBR	Widely available
'Ginger Peach'	CLAP LSou MPnt NDov NPnk SHeu SUsu
glabra	MPnt
glauca	see *H. americana*
'Gloire d'Orléans'	MPnt XLum
'Green Ivory'	EAEE EBee MPnt MRav SBch WBrk XLum
'Green Spice'	Widely available
'Green Spire'	CLAP
grossulariifolia	GMaP
'Guardian Angel'	CLAP CMac EBee LSou MPnt SFai SHeu SPoG SRGP SRkn SUsu

Name	Suppliers
'Gypsy Dancer'PBR (Dancer Series)	CLAP ECtt EPfP LSou MAsh MGos MPkF MPnt NGdn NHol NWad SBfd SHeu
'Hailstorm' (v)	MPnt
hallii	MPnt
'Havana'	GCai MPnt SHeu
'Helen Dillon' (v)	EBee EShb GMaP LAst MAsh MPnt NBir NPnk SRGP SWvt WFar WWEG
'Hercules'PBR	EBee ECtt MPnt SHeu
hispida	MPnt
'Hollywood'PBR	CMHG CWCL EBee ECtt ELon EPPr EPfP ESwi LAst LBMP LHop LRHS LSRN LSou MBri MPnt MTis NBir NDov NHol NWad SBfd SHeu SPoG SRot WFar
§ 'Huntsman'	MBNS MPnt MRav WFar WMnd
'Jade Gloss'PBR	CLAP EBee EPfP LRHS MAsh MBri MPnt NRHS SBfd SHeu SHil WWEG
'Jubilee'	EBee
'Kassandra'	EBee LRHS MPnt SFai SHeu
Key Lime Pie = 'Tnheu042'PBR (Dolce Series)	CBcs CBct CLAP CPLG CWGN EBee ECtt EPfP EWll GCai LHop LRHS LSRN LSou MAsh MBri MGos NBir NBro NLar NPla NPri SBfd SHeu SHil SPer SRot SWvt WFar WGor
'Lady in Red'	NBre
'Lady Romney'	XLum
'Lemon Chiffon'PBR **new**	MPnt NDov SHeu
§ 'Leuchtkäfer'	Widely available
Licorice = 'Tnheu044'PBR (Dolce Series)	CLAP CWCL ECtt ELon ESwi EUJe EWll LRHS MBNS MBri MGos MPnt NBir NLar NPri SBfd SHeu SHil SLim SRot SWvt WFar WHoo WWEG
'Lime'	CLAP
'Lime Marmalade'	CLAP CSev EBee ECtt ELan ELon ESwi EWll GCai LBMP LRHS LSou MAsh MBNS MBri MPkF MPnt NDov NHol NLar NPnk NPri NWad SBfd SFai SHeu SMrm SPad SPoG WWEG
'Lime Rickey'PBR	Widely available
'Lipstick'	CWGN EBee ELon MAsh MPkF MPnt NDov SBfd SHeu
'Lune Rousse' **new**	SHeu
'Magic Color'PBR	WCot
'Magic Wand' ΥH4	CAbP ECtt ELon MBNS NEgg SHeu
'Magnum' **new**	CWGN EBee ESwi MPnt SHeu
'Mahogany'PBR	CLAP CWCL EBee EPfP EUJe GCai LRHS LSou MAsh MPkF MPnt MTis NBir NGdn NPri SBfd SFai SHeu SLim SWvt
'Malachite'	EBee LRHS MPnt
'Marmalade'PBR	Widely available
'Mars'	EBee EPfP LRHS MPnt SHeu WFar
'Melting Fire'	EBee ETod GJos LRHS LSou MPkF MPnt MWhi NLar SBfd SHeu
'Mercury'	MAsh MAvo
'Metallic Shimmer' (Fox Series) **new**	MPnt
'Metallica'	NGBl SHeu SWal WMoo
micans	see *H. rubescens*
micrantha	GCal MLHP MNFA MPnt SHeu SRms
- var. ***diversifolia*** misapplied	see *H. villosa*
- 'Martha's Compact'	MPnt WCot
§ - 'Ruffles'	ECha MPnt
'Midas Touch'	CLAP CWGN EBee ECtt ELon GCai LSou MAsh MPkF MPnt NCGa SFai SHeu
'Midnight Bayou'	CLAP EBee ECtt ELon ESwi EWll LAst LBMP LHop LRHS MAsh MBri MPnt MTis NPer SFai SHeu SRot SWvt
'Midnight Rose'	Widely available
'Milan'	EBee MPnt SHeu
'Mini Mouse'	EWes LRHS MPnt SHeu
'Mint Frost'PBR	EBee ECtt ELan EPfP LHop LPot LRHS LSou MPnt MRav NBir NCGa NHol SHeu SPoG SWvt WFar WWEG
'Mint Julep'	EBee ECtt LSou MPkF MPnt SBfd SHeu STes
'Miracle'PBR	CLAP EBee ECtt EPfP MAsh MPnt NDov SHeu
'Mocha'PBR	CLAP EBee MBNS MNrw MPnt SBfd SHeu SMrm STes SWvt
'Molly Bush' ΥH4	EBee ECtt LRHS MPnt SHeu
'Mother of Pearl'	MPnt
'Muscat' **new**	MPnt SHeu
'Mysteria'	CLAP LSou MAsh MPkF MPnt SBfd SHeu
'Mystic Angel'	EBee MPnt SHeu
'Neptune'	EBee LRHS MAvo MPnt SHeu
'Oakington Jewel'	LRHS
'Obsidian'PBR	Widely available
'Orphée'	MPnt
'Paris'PBR	CLAP CWCL ECtt GBin LRHS LSou MBri MPkF MPnt NDov SBfd SHeu SHil WWEG
parishii NNS 93384	MPnt
parvifolia var. ***utahensis***	MPnt
'Peach Crisp' **new**	CWGN SHeu
'Peach Flambé'PBR	Widely available
'Peach Pie'	ECtt MPnt
'Peachy Keen'	SHeu
'Pear Crisp' **new**	MPnt
'Peppermint Spice'PBR (21st Century Collection Series)	EBee MPnt NPnk SGol SHeu
'Persian Carpet'	CHEx CWCL ECtt EHrv GMaP LRHS MPnt NBir SHeu SWvt WFar WPtf
(Petite Series) 'Petite Marbled Burgundy'	EBee ECtt EHoe LLHF LRHS MPnt NDov SHeu SWvt WAul WFar
- 'Petite Pearl Fairy'	CAbP EHoe ELan MPnt SHeu SWvt WFar
- 'Petite Pink Bouquet'	EBee EHoe MPnt SHeu
'Pewter Moon'	CBcs EBee ELan GMaP LAst LTen MGos MRav MSpe NBir SEND SHeu WFar WTin XLum
'Pewter Veil'PBR	LRHS SHeu WFar WMnd WWEG
pilosissima	XLum
'Pink Lipstick'	NWad
'Pinot Bianco'	SHeu
'Pinot Gris'PBR	CLAP CWGN EBee ECtt ESwi LRHS LSou MAsh MNrw MPkF MPnt SHeu SUsu WCot
'Pinot Noir'	CLAP MPnt SHeu WOut
'Pistache'	CAbP EBee ECtt ELon LSou MBNS MPkF MPnt NPnk SHeu SPer WBrk WCot
§ 'Pluie de Feu'	CCon CWCL EBee ECtt EPPr GBuc LRHS MPnt MRav NRHS SMrm WFar XLum

'Plum Pudding' PBR	Widely available
'Plum Royale'	Widely available
'Pretty Perinne' new	MPnt SHeu
'Pretty Polly'	MPnt
'Prince'	CWCL EBee ELan EPfP GCai LRHS LSRN MAsh MBNS MBel MPnt NMRc NRHS SApp SBfd SFai SHeu SPoG SWvt
'Prince of Orange' new	EBee WCot
'Prince of Silver'	EBee LRHS MBNS MPnt SHeu WCot
pringlei	see *H. rubescens*
pubescens	ECho MPnt SHeu XLum
pulchella	EBee LLHF MHer MPnt MWat SHeu SRms
- JCA 9508	NMen
'Purple Mountain Majesty'	WFar
'Purple Petticoats' ♀H4	CBcs EBee ECtt EPfP LRHS LSou MLHP MNFA MPkF MPnt NBre NHol NLar NPnk NPri SHar SHeu SLim SRot WFar
'Quick Silver'	LRHS MNFA MPnt NBir SHeu SWvt WFar
§ 'Quilter's Joy' ♀H4	LRHS
'Rachel'	CAbP CWCL EAEE EBee ELan EPfP GBuc GCal GMaP IFoB LRHS LSRN MPnt MRav NBir NGdn NHol NPnk NRHS SBfd SRGP SWvt WAul WBrk WFar XLum
Rain of Fire	see *H.* 'Pluie de Feu'
'Raspberry Regal' ♀H4	ECtt MPnt MRav NBir NSti SHeu SWvt WAul WCot WFar
'Rave On' PBR	Widely available
'Red Spangles'	EBee EPfP LRHS NBir WWEG
'Regina' ♀H4	CAbP EBee EPfP LHop LSRN MPnt NBro SBfd SHeu SWvt WFar
'Rhapsody'	LRHS
richardsonii	MNrw MPnt
'Rickard'	MPnt
'Robert'	MPnt
'Root Beer'	MPnt NDov SHeu
Rosemary Bloom = 'Heuros' PBR	EBee LRHS NRHS
§ ***rubescens***	CAbP ECho NBro NMen WPer WThu
'Ruffles'	see *H. micrantha* 'Ruffles'
'Sanbrot' new	MPnt
§ ***sanguinea***	CMac CSBt MPnt MRav NBir SBfd WPer
- 'Alba' ♀H4	EPPr EWTr LPla MPnt NMRc SMHy SUsu
- 'Geisha's Fan'	CWCL EBee LSou MPkF MPnt MSpe NEgg NHol SBfd SHeu SPer SWvt
- 'Monet' (v)	MLHP MPnt SHeu
- var. ***pulchra***	CPBP
- 'Ruby Bells'	CCVN CMea EBee EPPr EPfP LRHS LSRN MCot MPnt NLar SHeu
- 'Sioux Falls'	EWes MBNS NBre SHeu
- 'Snow Storm' (v)	ELan EPfP MPnt SHeu SPlb WFar WMnd
- 'Splendens'	MPnt XLum
- 'Taff's Joy' (v)	EWes MPnt
- 'White Cloud' (v)	EBee EPfP MPnt NBre SHeu SRms WPer XLum
'Sashay' ♀H4	CLAP ELon LSou MAsh MPkF MPnt NLar SBfd SGol SHeu
'Saturn'	LRHS MAsh MDev MPnt SHeu SWvt WFar
'Schneewittchen'	EBee EPfP MPnt MRav
'Scintillation' ♀H4	MPnt NBre
'Shamrock'	NBre
'Shanghai'	EBee ECtt EPfP LRHS LSou MAsh MPnt SBfd SHeu SUsu
'Silver Indiana'	EBee LRHS LSRN MPnt SHeu
'Silver Light' PBR	EPfP LRHS MPnt SHeu
'Silver Lode' PBR	EBee MPnt SBfd SHeu
'Silver Scrolls' PBR	Widely available
'Silver Shadows'	MBrN MPnt SHeu
'Silver Streak'	see × *Heucherella* 'Silver Streak'
'Sioux Falls'	MPnt
'Smoothie'	MAsh
'Snow Angel'	EPfP MPnt SHeu WCot
'Snowfire' (v)	MPnt SHeu
'Southern Comfort' PBR	CLAP CWCL CWGN EBee ECtt ELon EPPr ESwi LRHS LSou MBNS MPkF MPnt NCGa NDov NHol NLar NPer NPri NWad SBfd SGol SHeu SLim SPoG SWvt WCot
'Sparkling Burgundy'	CLAP EBee ECtt EPfP LSou MPkF MPnt NDov NPri SBfd SHeu SMrm SWvt
'Starry Night' PBR	MPnt SBfd WFar
'Steel City'	MPnt SHeu
'Stormy Seas'	EAEE EBee ELan EPfP GCra LRHS MLHP MPkF MPnt MRav NBir SBfd SHeu SWvt WFar
'Strawberries and Cream' (v)	EHrv MPnt
'Strawberry Candy' PBR	CMac CWCL CWGN ELon GJos LAst LBMP LHop LRHS LSRN LSou MBNS MPnt NBir NLar NWad SBfd SHeu SLim SPer SRkn
'Strawberry Swirl'	EBee ECtt EPfP EWTr GMaP LRHS MGos MPnt MRav NBir NLar NPri NSti SBfd SHeu SWal SWvt WFar
Sugar Frosting = 'Pwheu0104' PBR	ECtt GKev LAst LHop LRHS MBri MPnt NCGa NPri SHeu SHil SRot SWvt WFar
'Sugar Plum'	EBee ECtt EUJe LRHS MBNS MPkF MPnt SHeu
'Swirling Fantasy' PBR	EShb GJos LSou MAsh MDev MPnt SHeu SMrm
'Tangerine Wave' (Fox Series) new	MPnt
'Tara'	EBee MAsh MPnt SHeu
'Tiramisu' PBR	CAbP CHid CLAP CWCL CWGN EBee ECtt ELon ESwi GCai LHop LRHS MBNS MNrw MPnt NBir NPnk NSti SFai SHeu SPer SPoG SRkn SUsu SWvt WCot
'Van Gogh'	SHeu
'Vanilla Spice'	MPnt NHol SHeu
'Veil of Passion'	NBre
'Velvet Night'	EPfP LRHS LSou MPnt NBir NHol SHeu SPlb WFar WMnd WWEG
'Venus'	CMea CWGN ECtt EPfP EShb LRHS MBNS MBel MNrw MPie MPnt NGdn NMRc NSti SEND SHeu SPer WBrk WCot WHoo
'Vesuvius' PBR	MPnt NCGa SHeu
'Vienna' new	MPnt
§ ***villosa***	ECha LRHS MPnt MRav SVic XLum
- 'Autumn Bride'	EBee ECtt MPnt SHeu
- Bressingham Bronze = 'Absi' PBR	EAEE EBee LRHS MPnt NRHS SHeu SPer WFar
- 'Chantilly'	EBee MPnt
- var. ***macrorhiza***	EShb LBMP MPnt NBre WMnd WPnP XLum

N	- 'Palace Purple'	Widely available
	- 'Palace Purple Select'	CBcs CMac CTri CWat CWib LAst MCot NEgg SBfd SEND SLim SWvt WFar
	'Virginale' new	MPnt
	'White Marble'	MPnt
	'White Spires'	EBee LRHS MPnt NRHS
	'White Swirls'	MPnt
	'William How'	MPnt
	'Winter Red'	EAEE EBee LRHS MBNS MPnt NEgg
	'Zabeliana'	MPnt

× *Heucherella* ✿ (*Saxifragaceae*)

	'Alabama Sunrise'PBR	CLAP CMHG EBee ECtt ELon EPPr ESwi ETod LHop LSou MBri MPkF MPnt MTis NCGa NHol NPer NPnk NPri NWad SBfd SGol SHeu SPoG SRot SWvt WBor WGor
	alba 'Bridget Bloom'	EBee ECha ELan EPfP EWTr GMaP LRHS MNFA MPnt MRav NOrc SBfd SPer SRms WFar
§	- 'Rosalie'	EBee ECha LRHS MPnt MRav NBir NBro NPnk NPro SHeu SPlb WFar WSHC
	'Berry Fizz' new	SHeu
	'Birthday Cake'	MPnt SHeu
	'Brass Lantern'	EBee ECtt LSou MPnt NPnk SHeu SUsu
	'Burnished Bronze'PBR	ECtt ELon GKev LRHS LSou MBri MPkF MPnt NBro NEgg NHol NLar NPla NWad SBfd SHeu SRot SWvt WCot WFar
	'Chocolate Lace'PBR	MPnt SHeu
	'Cinnamon Bear'	MPnt SHeu
	'Citrus Shock' new	MPnt
	'Dayglow Pink'PBR	CLAP EBee ECtt EShb GKev GMaP LSRN MPkF MPnt NBro NHol NLar NPnk SHar SHeu STes WFar
	'Fan Dancer'	CLAP MPnt SHeu
	Gold Strike = 'Hertn041'PBR	CLAP ECtt GJos LRHS MBNS MPnt NPnk SHeu
	'Golden Zebra'	CAbP CLAP CSpe CWCL CWGN EBee ECtt ELan GAbr LSou MAsh MBNS MNrw MPkF MPnt MTis NDov NHol NLar NPnk NWad SBfd SHeu SMrm STes WCot WWlt
	'Gunsmoke'	CLAP ECtt LSou MPkF MPnt NPnk SHeu SUsu
	'Heart of Darkness'PBR	CLAP MPnt SBfd SHeu
	'Kimono'PBR ♀H4	Widely available
	'Ninja'PBR	see *Tiarella* 'Ninja'
	'Party Time'PBR	SHeu
	'Persian Carpet'	MPnt
	Pink Whispers = 'Hertn042'PBR	LPot MPnt SHeu WFar
	'Quicksilver'	CBcs EBee EHrv GMaP MPnt SWvt WFar
	'Redstone Falls' new	MPnt SHeu
	'Ring of Fire'	CMac SWvt WFar
§	'Silver Streak'	GAbr LRHS MPnt NBro SHeu SWvt WFar
	'Solar Eclipse' new	SHeu
	'Solar Power'	CWGN EBee MPnt SHeu
	'Stoplight'PBR	Widely available
	'Sunspot'PBR (v)	CLAP EBee ECtt EPfP MGos NBro NSti SGol SHeu WHer
	'Sweet Tea'	Widely available
	'Tapestry'PBR	Widely available
	tiarelloides ♀H4	CMac EBee EPfP WMnd
§	'Viking Ship'PBR	CSev EAEE EBee ECha ECtt GKev LRHS MPnt MRav MTPN NBir NRHS SHeu SUsu WFar
	'Yellowstone Falls' new	MPnt SHeu

Hexastylis see *Asarum*

Hibanobambusa (*Poaceae*)

	'Kimmei'	MMuc SEND
	tranquillans	CEnt ERod MBrN MMoz MMuc MWht SEND WJun
	- 'Shiroshima' (v) ♀H4	CAbb CDTJ CDoC CEnt EAmu ENBC EPfP ERod EUJe MBrN MBri MMoz MMuc MWhi MWht SApp SBfd SBig SEND WJun

Hibbertia (*Dilleniaceae*)

	aspera	CBcs CCCN CRHN EBee ECre IVic LRHS WCFE WCot WSHC
§	***cuneiformis***	CCCN
	obtusifolia	EPot
	pedunculata	WAbe
	procumbens	WAbe
§	***scandens*** ♀H1	CBcs CCCN CHll CRHN ECou ECre ELan MOWG SEND
	'Spring Sunshine'	LHop
	tetrandra	see *H. cuneiformis*
	volubilis	see *H. scandens*

Hibiscus ✿ (*Malvaceae*)

	acetosella 'Red Shield'	CSpe
	coccineus	EBee EShb SBrt SMad
	- 'Texas Star'	XDel
	- 'Texas Star' white-flowered	XDel
	coccineus × ***moscheutos***	SBrt
	dasycalyx	XDel
	'Fantasia'PBR	CWGN XDel
	'Fireball'PBR	EUJe XDel
	grandiflorus	XDel
	hamabo	ELan
	huegelii	see *Alyogyne huegelii*
	'Jazzberry Jam'	XDel
	'Kopper King'PBR	CWGN EUJe MAsh XDel
	'Lady Baltimore'	XDel
	lasiocarpus	XDel
	leopoldii	SRms
	'Lord Baltimore'	XDel
	manihot	see *Abelmoschus manihot*
	militaris	SBrt XDel
	moscheutos	CArn CCon EBee SBrt SMad SVic XDel XLum
	- 'Blue River II'	XDel
	- 'Cranberry Crush'	XDel
	- 'Galaxy'	XLum
	- Luna Series	XDel
	- - 'Luna Blush' new	XDel
	- - 'Luna Pink Swirl' new	XDel
	- - 'Luna Red' new	XDel
	- - 'Luna Rose' new	XDel
	- - 'Luna White' new	XDel
	- 'Moy Grandé' new	XDel
	- 'Old Yella' PBR	CWGN XDel
	- 'Peppermint Schnapps' new	XDel
	- 'Robert Fleming'PBR new	EUJe XDel
	- 'Royal Gems'PBR new	XDel
	- Southern Belle Group	CHEx
	mutabilis	LEdu XDel
	- double-flowered (d)	XDel
	Newbiscus Series	XDel

paramutabilis EWes SMad
'Plum Crazy'PBR XDel
rosa-sinensis EBak MOWG SPlb
– 'Arcadian Spring' new MOWG
– 'Big Tango' MOWG
– 'Blues Man' new MOWG
– 'Byron Metts' MOWG
– 'Candy Floss' (d) new MOWG
– 'Carmen Keene' MOWG
– 'Cloud Nine'PBR new MOWG
– 'Cockatoo' MOWG
– 'Courier Mail' MOWG SPlb
– 'Dorothy Brady' MOWG
– 'Enid Lewis' (d) MOWG
– 'Erin Rachael' new MOWG
– 'Expo' MOWG
– 'Gwen Mary' MOWG
– 'Helene' LSRN
– 'Holly's Pride' MOWG
– 'Hot Bikini' new MOWG
– 'Jambalaya' new MOWG
– 'June's Joy' MOWG
– 'Key West Thunderhead' (d) new MOWG
– 'Lady Bug' new MOWG
– 'Lady Flo' MOWG
– 'Lemon Chiffon' MOWG
– 'Linda Pear' (d) MOWG
– 'Madame DuPont' new MOWG
– 'Mrs Andreasen' (d) MOWG
– 'Rhinestone' MOWG
– 'Soft Shoulders' new MOWG
– 'Spanish Lady' MOWG
– 'Sprinkle Rain' MOWG
– 'Tarantella' MOWG
– 'The Path' MOWG
– 'Vermillion Queen' new MOWG
– 'Weekend' MOWG
– 'White Swan' new MOWG
schizopetalus ♀H1 CCCN MOWG
sinosyriacus 'Lilac Queen' CPLG LRHS SKHP WPGP
– 'Ruby Glow' CPLG LRHS LSRN MGos SKHP WPGP
'Summer Storm' XDel
'Sweet Caroline' XDel
syriacus LEdu MNHC
– 'Admiral Dewey' (d) EBee
– 'Aphrodite' EPfP
– 'Ardens' (d) CSBt EBee ELon LAst MGos NLar
– Blue Bird see *H. syriacus* 'Oiseau Bleu'
– Blue Chiffon = 'Notwood3'PBR LBuc LRHS MGos SPoG
– 'Boule de Feu' (d) EBee ELan
– China Chiffon = 'Bricutts' LRHS MAsh SPoG
– 'Diana' ♀H4 EBee EPfP LRHS LSRN MAsh MGos MRav SCoo SKHP SLon
– 'Dorothy Crane' EBee LRHS SKHP
– 'Duc de Brabant' (d) CSBt EBee ELon EPfP MBlu SPer
– 'Elegantissimus' see *H. syriacus* 'Lady Stanley'
– 'Hamabo' ♀H4 CDul CSBt CTri EBee EMil EPfP EUJe LAst LRHS LSRN MBri MGos MWat NLar NPri SBfd SCoo SEND SGol SHil SLim SPer SPoG SWvt
– 'Helene' EBee ELan LSRN MBlu
– 'Jeanne d'Arc' (d) EMil SGol
§ – 'Lady Stanley' (d) CMac CSBt EBee SCoo SPer SSta
– Lavender Chiffon = 'Notwoodone'PBR ♀H4 EBee ELan EPfP EWes LRHS LSRN MBri MGos NLar SCoo SEND SHil SPer SPoG
– 'Leopoldii' EBee SBfd SKHP
– 'Marina' EBee EPfP EUJe MBlu MRav NLar SBfd SGol
– 'Mauve Queen' new SSta
– 'Meehanii' misapplied see *H. syriacus* 'Purpureus Variegatus'
– 'Meehanii' (v) ♀H4 CSBt EBee EMil EPfP LRHS SCoo SKHP SPer
– 'Monstrosus' EBee NLar
§ – 'Oiseau Bleu' ♀H4 Widely available
– Pink Giant = 'Flogi' CDul EBee ELan EPfP LAst LRHS MAsh MGos MWat SPad SPer
– Purple Ruffles = 'Sanchoyo' (d) EPfP LRHS MBri SHil SPoG
§ – 'Purpureus Variegatus' (v) CMac CSBt LAst LRHS SPoG
– 'Red Heart' ♀H4 CMac CSBt CTri EBee ELan EPfP LAst LRHS MAsh MBri MRav NLar NRHS SEND SHil SKHP SLim SPad SPer SPoG SRms SWvt WCFE
– Rosalbane = 'Minrosa' EMil SGol
– Russian Violet = 'Floru' EBee ELan EMil EPfP LAst LRHS MGos SKHP
– 'Speciosus' SPer
– 'Totus Albus' CMac CSBt
– Ultramarine = 'Minultra'PBR EBee EMil EPfP LRHS SKHP
– 'Variegatus' see *H. syriacus* 'Purpureus Variegatus'
– 'Violet Clair Double' (d) CMac
– White Chiffon = 'Notwoodtwo'PBR (d) ♀H4 EBee ELan EMil EPfP EWes LRHS LSRN LTen MAsh MBri MGos MRav NLar SCoo SHil SPer SPoG
– 'William R. Smith' ♀H4 CDul EBee ELan LAst LRHS MBri MSwo SBfd SEND SHil SPer
– 'Woodbridge' ♀H4 Widely available
trionum CSpe SBch WKif WTou
– 'Sunny Day' ELan
'XXL Eye Catcher' (Newbiscus Series) new XDel
'XXL Fancy Eye' (Newbiscus Series) new XDel
'XXL Mauvelous' (Newbiscus Series) new XDel
'XXL Red Hot' (Newbiscus Series) new XDel

hickory, shagbark see *Carya ovata*

Hieracium (*Asteraceae*)

aurantiacum see *Pilosella aurantiaca*
brunneocroceum see *Pilosella aurantiaca* subsp. *carpathicola*
§ **lanatum** ECho MDKP NBir
maculatum see *H. spilophaeum*
pilosella see *Pilosella officinarum*
× **rubrum** LRHS
scullyi EPPr
§ **spilophaeum** EHoe MMuc NBid NPer WOut
– 'Blue Leaf' WCot
– 'Leopard' CEnt
umbellatum WOut
villosum CPBP EBee ECho EHoe LRHS NBro WHer
waldsteinii MDKP
welwitschii see *H. lanatum*

Hierochloe (*Poaceae*)

odorata EPPr GPoy MBNS WHfH XLum

hildaberry see *Rubus* 'Hildaberry'

Himalayacalamus (*Poaceae*)

asper	CDTJ ERod
cupreus	WJun
§ ***falconeri***	CDTJ CEnt SDix
§ - 'Damarapa'	CDTJ CEnt EPfP MMoz WJun
§ ***hookerianus***	CPLG EAmu EPfP SBst WJun
- 'Himalaya Blue'	CDTJ CTrC MGos
porcatus	CDTJ WJun WPGP

Himantoglossum (*Orchidaceae*)

adriaticum new	NLAp
hircinum	NLAp

× *Hippeasprekelia* (*Amaryllidaceae*)

'Durga Pradhan' new	GHim
'Red Beauty'	WCot
'Red Star'	CCCN

Hippeastrum (*Amaryllidaceae*)

× ***acramannii***	GCal WCot
advenum	see *Rhodophiala advena*
'Alasca'PBR	WHlf
'Alfresco'PBR	LAma
'Amputo'	LAma
'Apple Blossom'	LAma SDeJ SGar
'Baby Star'	SDeJ
'Benfica'	CSpe LAma
bifidum	see *Rhodophiala bifida*
'Black Beauty'	LAma
'Blossom Peacock' (d)	LAma
'Bogota'	LAma
'Bolero'	LAma
'Bouquet'	LAma
'Britney'PBR	LAma
'Chico'	LAma
'Christmas Gift'	LAma
'Dancing Queen'	LAma
'Emerald'	LAma WCot
'Estella'	LAma
'Fairytale'	SDeJ
'Ferrari'	LAma
'Flaming Peacock'	LAma
gracile 'Pamela'	LAma
'Gracilis' new	GHim
'Grandeur'	LAma
'Green Goddess'	LAma
'Helios'PBR	WHlf
'Inca'	LAma
× ***johnsonii*** hort.	CPLG WCot
'La Paz'	LAma
'Lemon Lime'	LAma
'Liberty'	SDeJ
'Lima'	LAma
'Lollypop'	WHlf
'Lovely Garden'	LAma
'Loyalty'PBR	LAma
'Merengue'	LAma
'Misty'	LAma
'Mont Blanc' new	SDeJ
'Mrs Garfield'	GHim LAma
'Naughty Lady'	LAma
papilio ♀H1	CTca GHim LAma MMHG
'Picotee'	LAma SDeJ
'Pink Floyd'	LAma
puniceum	LAma
'Quito'	LAma
'Rebecca'	LAma
'Red Lion'	LAma
'Red Peacock' (d)	LAma
'Rembrandt van Rijn'	LAma
'Rilona'	LAma SDeJ
'Rosario'	LAma
'Royal Velvet'	LAma
'Ruby Meyer'	LAma
'San Antonio Rose'	EBee WCot WPGP
'Santiago'	LAma
striatum	WCot
stylosum	GHim
'Swan Lake'PBR	WHlf
'Sweet Surrender'	LAma
'Tango'	LAma
'Toughie'	CDes EBee LLHF WPGP
vittatum	GHim LAma
'White Christmas'	LAma
'White Dazzler'	LAma

Hippocrepis (*Papilionaceae*)

§ ***comosa***	CRWN EDAr SPhx SSpi
§ ***emerus***	CBcs CCCN CMHG CPLG EBee ELan EPfP LAst LHop MGos MMuc NLar SEND WSHC

Hippophae (*Elaeagnaceae*)

rhamnoides ♀H4	CArn CBcs CCVT CDul CHab CLnd CMac CRWN CSpe CTri EBee ECrN EHoe ELan EPfP LBuc MBlu MCoo MMuc NWea SBfd SEND SEWo SGol SPlb WFar
- (m) new	EPom
- 'Frugna' (f)	CAgr
- 'Hergo' (f)	CAgr MCoo
- 'Juliet' (f)	CAgr
- 'Leikora' (f)	CAgr ELan EPfP IVic MBlu MCoo MGos NLar SPer
- 'Orange Energy' (f/F)	CAgr MCoo
- 'Pollmix' (m)	CAgr ELan EPfP IVic MBlu MCoo MGos NLar SPer
- 'Pollmix 3' (m)	MCoo
- 'Sirola'	MCoo
salicifolia	CAgr
- GWJ 9221	WCru

Hippuris (*Plantaginaceae*)

vulgaris	CBen CWat EHon EWay MSKA NPer WMAq XLum

Hirpicium (*Asteraceae*)

armerioides	SPlb

Hoheria ✿ (*Malvaceae*)

'Ace of Spades'	CMHG EBee EMil EPfP EWTr LHop LRHS SKHP
§ ***angustifolia***	ECou EPfP WPGP
angustifolia × ***sexstylosa***	WPGP
'Borde Hill'	CDul CJun CMHG CMac CTho EBee ECou EPfP IVic LHop LRHS MAsh SKHP SLim SPer SSpi WCFE WPGP WPat
'County Park'	ECou
glabrata	CMac ECou EPfP GBin GGGa IDee NBir SKHP WPGP
'Glory of Amlwch' ♀H3	CAbb CBcs CDul CJun CSam CTho EBee ECou EPfP GGGa GQui SChF SKHP SMad SSpi WKif WPGP

'Hill House' CHll
§ *lyallii* ♀H4 CCCN CDoC CDul CPLG EBee ECou ELan EPfP GCra IArd IDee LRHS LSRN SPer SSpi
- 'Chalk Hills' ECou
- 'Swale Stream' ECou
microphylla see *H. angustifolia*
populnea CBcs CCCN IArd
- 'Alba Variegata' (v) ECou
- 'Holbrook' CSam
- 'Moonlight' CHGN
- 'Purple Shadow' ECou
- 'Variegata' (v) ECou
'Purple Delta' ECou
sexstylosa CAbb CDoC CDul CHEx CHid CMHG CTho CTri CWSG ECou ELan EPfP EWTr LHop LRHS LSRN MGos NEgg SEND SKHP SPer SWvt
- 'Crataegifolia' CAbb GBin
- 'Pendula' CBcs CMac
- 'Stardust' ♀H4 CAbP CBcs CCCN CDul CGHE CJun CMCN CMHG CSBt CTho EBee ECou ELan ELon EPfP IVic LRHS LSRN MAsh MBlu MBri MGos NLar SMad SPer SPoG SSpi WFar WPGP WSHC

Holboellia (*Lardizabalaceae*)

angustifolia NLar WCru
- subsp. *linearifolia* BWJ 8004 WCru
- subsp. *obtusa* DJHC 506 WCru
brachyandra HWJ 1023 WCru
aff. *chapaensis* B&SWJ 7250 WCru
coriacea CBcs CCCN CHll CRHN CSPN CSam ELan EPfP EWld IDee LRHS MGos MOWG MRav NLar SEND SKHP SPer WCFE WCru
- B&SWJ 2818 WCru
fargesii LRHS SKHP WCot WCru
latifolia CBcs CCCN CHEx CHll CMac CSam CTri EBee ELan EPfP GCal LRHS MOWG NLar SBfd SEND SKHP SLPl SLim SPer SPoG WCFE WCot WCru WPGP
- HWJCM 008 WCru
- HWJK 2014 WCru
- HWJK 2213 WCru
- SF 95134 EPfP
- dark-flowered HWJK 2213 WCru

Holcus (*Poaceae*)

lanatus WSFF
mollis 'Albovariegatus' (v) CWCL EBee ECha EHoe ELan EPPr EPfP GMaP LBMP MAsh MWhi NBid NBro NGdn NPer NSti SPlb SRms WFar WPtf WTin WWEG
- 'Jackdaw's Cream' (v) EPPr
- 'White Fog' (v) EBee EPPr MMuc NWad SApp SEND WFar

Holmskioldia (*Lamiaceae*)

* *lutea* CCCN
sanguinea CCCN

Holodiscus (*Rosaceae*)

discolor CBcs CDul EBee ELan EPfP EWTr EWes GCal IDee LRHS MBlu MBri MMHG MMuc MRav NLar SCoo SEND SHil SKHP SLon SPer SPlb SSpi
- var. *ariifolius* EPfP LRHS
dumosus EBee

Homalocladium (*Polygonaceae*)

§ *platycladum* EShb

Homeria (*Iridaceae*)

breyniana var. *aurantiaca* see *Moraea collina*

Homoglossum see *Gladiolus*

Hordeum (*Poaceae*)

chilense EBee
jubatum CKno CSpe CWCL EHoe EWes MSCN MWhi NChi NGdn SApp SEND SPhx SUsu
- from Ussuri NGBl
- 'Early Pink' NDov
secalinum CHab

Horkeliella (*Rosaceae*)

purpurascens NNS 98-323 WCot

Horminum (*Lamiaceae*)

pyrenaicum CPom CPrp EBee ECho LBMP MMuc SEND SRms WFar WMoo WPer WPtf WTin
I - f. *alboviolaceum* EDAr
- dark-flowered ECho GCal
- pale blue-flowered MDKP
- 'Rubrum' EDif

horseradish see *Armoracia rusticana*

Hosta ✿ (*Asparagaceae*)

AGSJ 302 CDes WPGP
'A Many-Splendored Thing' EMic IBal
'Abba Dabba Do' (v) COIW EBee ECtt EGol ELon EMic IBal LBuc LPla NEgg NHol SApp
'Abba Showtime' IBal
'Abby' (v) EGol EMic EPGN IBal SApp WWEG
'Abiqua Ariel' EMic IBal SApp
'Abiqua Blue Crinkles' EMic IBal NBir SApp
'Abiqua Blue Edger' EMic
'Abiqua Delight' (v) IBal
'Abiqua Drinking Gourd' EBee EGol EMic EPGN GMaP IBal MHom SApp WWEG
'Abiqua Ground Cover' EGol IBal
'Abiqua Moonbeam' (v) CCon EMic EPGN IBal MSwo NGdn NMyG SApp
'Abiqua Recluse' EGol EMic IBal SApp
'Abiqua Trumpet' EGol EMic IBal NGdn NLar NNor SApp
'Abraham Lincoln' new IBal
'Academy Blushing Recluse' (v) IBal
'Academy Devon Moor' new IBal
'Academy Fire' (v) IBal
'Ada Reed' IBal
aequinoctiiantha EGol
'Aksarben' EMic
'Alakazaam' (v) new EGol EMic
'Alan Titchmarsh' EPGN
albomarginata see *H. sieboldii* 'Paxton's Original'
§ 'Albomarginata' (*fortunei*) (v) CBcs CMac EGol EHrv GKev IBal LRHS MNrw NBir NGdn SEND SPoG SWvt

'Alex Summers'	EMic IBal WFar
'All That Jazz' (v)	EMic IBal
'Allan P. McConnell' (v)	EGol EMic EPGN GCra IBal LRHS MHom SPoG WHal WWEG
'Allegan Emperor' (v)	IBal
'Allegan Fog' (v)	EGol EMic EPGN IBal LRHS
'Alligator Shoes' (v)	EGol EMic IBal
'Alpine Aire'	EMic
'Alpine Dream'	IBal
'Alternative'	IBal
'Alvatine Taylor' (v)	EGol EMic IBal LAst NGdn
'Amanuma'	EGol EMic IBal MHom
'Amazing Grace' (v)	EMic
'Amber Maiden' (v)	IBal
'Amber Tiara'	EMic IBal
'American Dream' (v)	EGol EMic EPGN IBal LRHS
'American Great Expectations' (v) **new**	NRHS
'American Halo'	EMic IBal LRHS NLar NMRc
'American Hero' (v) **new**	EMic
'American Icon'	EMic IBal
'American Sweetheart'PBR	EMic IBal SApp
'Americana' (v)	EMic IBal
'Amethyst Gem'	EGol IBal
'Amy Elizabeth' (v)	EMic IBal
'Andorian' **new**	IBal
'Andy Taylor'	LRHS
'Angel Feathers' (v)	IBal
'Anglo Saxon' (v)	IBal
'Ann Kulpa' (v)	EMic EPGN IBal NGdn
'Anne' (v)	EMic IBal LRHS LSRN NMyG
'Anne Arett' (*sieboldii*) (v)	EPGN
'Ansly' (v)	IBal
'Antioch' (*fortunei*) (v)	EGol EMic EUJe IBal MRav NLar WFar
'Aoba Tsugaru'	IBal
'Aoki' (*fortunei*)	EMic IBal
'Aphrodite' (*plantaginea*) (d)	IBal LRHS LSou MBNS MCot NGdn NLar SApp SMrm WCot WGwG WWEG
'Apollo'	NNor
'Apple Court'	SApp
'Apple Green'	EMic GKev IBal
'Apple Pie'	SApp
'Aqua Velva'	EGol IBal
'Arc de Triomphe'	EMic IBal SApp
'Archangel'	EGol IBal
'Arctic Blast'	EMic IBal
'Argentea Variegata' (*undulata*)	see *H. undulata* var. *undulata*
'Aristocrat' (Tardiana Group) (v)	EGol EMic EPGN IBal LRHS SApp WFar
'Asian Beauty'	EGol
'Asian Pearl' (v) **new**	IBal
'Aspen Gold' (*tokudama* hybrid)	EMic SApp
'Athena' (v)	IBal
'Atlantis'PBR (v)	EMic IBal NGdn
'August Beauty'	EMic IBal
'August Moon'	Widely available
'Aureoalba' (*fortunei*)	see *H.* 'Spinners'
'Aureomaculata' (*fortunei*)	see *H. fortunei* var. *albopicta*
'Aureomarginata' ambig. (v)	LRHS SCoo
'Aureomarginata' (*montana*) (v)	CMac EGol EHoe ELan EMic EPGN GCal GMaP IBal MMuc NCGa NEgg NGdn NHol NLar SApp WFar WTin WWEG
'Aureomarginata' (*rohdeifolia*) (v)	EMic
§ 'Aureomarginata' (*ventricosa*) (v) ♀H4	ECha EGol EMic EPfP IBal MWat NGdn NMyG SApp WFar WTin
'Aureostriata' (*tardiva*)	see *H.* 'Inaho'
'Aurora Borealis' (*sieboldiana*) (v)	EGol
'Austin Dickinson' (v)	EGol EMic IBal LBuc LRHS NEgg
'Avalanche'	IBal
'Avocado'	ELon EMic IBal
'Azure Mediterranean'	IBal
'Azure Snow'	EGol IBal
'Babbling Brook'	EGol IBal
'Baby Blue' (Tardiana Group)	EMic
'Baby Blue Eyes'	IBal
'Baby Bunting'	EGol EMic EPGN IBal IFoB NBro NLar NNor NPro
'Bali-Hai'	IBal
'Ballerina'	EGol IBal
'Banana Boat' (v)	EGol IBal
'Banana Muffins'	IBal
'Band of Gold'	EMic IBal
'Banyai's Dancing Girl'	EGol EMic IBal
'Barbara Ann' (v)	EMic EPGN IBal MHom NGdn NMyG WWEG
'Barbara May'	IBal
'Barbara White'	IBal
'Barney Fife' **new**	IBal
'Battle Star' (v) **new**	EMic
'Bea's Colossus'	IBal
'Beauty Little Blue'	EGol IBal
'Beauty Substance'	EGol EMic EPGN IBal NNor
'Beckoning'	IBal
'Bedford Blue'	EMic IBal
'Bedford Rise and Shine' (v)	EGol EMic IBal
'Bedford Wakey-Wakey'	EGol
'Bell Bottom Blues'	IBal
bella	see *H. crassifolia*
'Bells of Edinburgh' **new**	IBal
'Bennie McRae'	EGol IBal
'Betcher's Blue'	EGol EMic IBal
'Betsy King'	CMac EBee EGol MRav NMyG
'Bette Davis Eyes'	EGol IBal
'Betty'	EGol IBal
'Bianca'	SApp
'Biddy's Blue'	IBal
'Big Boy' (*montana*)	EGol IBal
'Big Chance'	IBal
'Big Daddy' (*sieboldiana* hybrid) (v)	Widely available
'Big John' (*sieboldiana*)	IBal
'Big Mama'	EBee EGol EMic IBal MBNS MNrw NGdn NLar NPnk SApp
'Big Top'	IBal
'Bigfoot'	EGol IBal
'Biggie'	IBal SApp
'Bill Brinka' (v)	EGol EMic IBal
'Bill Dress's Blue'	IBal
'Birchwood Blue'	EGol
'Birchwood Blue Beauty'	IBal NMyG
'Birchwood Elegance'	NMyG SApp
'Birchwood Gem'	IBal
§ 'Birchwood Parky's Gold'	CCon EBee EGol EMic EPfP EWTr GMaP IBal LBMP LRHS MBNS NGdn NHol NNor SApp
'Birchwood Ruffled Queen'	EGol EMic IBal
'Bitsy Gold'	EGol EMic IBal
'Bitsy Green'	EGol
'Bix Blues'	IBal

'Bizarre' EMic IBal
'Black Beauty' EGol IBal
'Black Hills' EGol EMic IBal
'Black Pearl' IBal
'Blackfoot' EGol EMic IBal
'Blackjack' (*sieboldiana*) IBal SApp
'Blaue Venus' EGol IBal
'Blauspecht' IBal
'Blaze of Glory' IBal
'Blazing Saddles' (v) EMic IBal MBNS
'Blonde Elf' EGol EMic IBal MPnt NEgg NGdn NHol NMyG NNor SApp WWEG
'Blue Angel' misapplied see *H. sieboldiana* var. *elegans*
'Blue Angel' (*sieboldiana*) ♀H4 Widely available
'Blue Arrow' EGol IBal NNor SApp
'Blue Baron' EMic IBal
'Blue Beard' IBal
'Blue Belle' (Tardiana Group) EGol EMic IBal NGdn NPro WTin WWEG
'Blue Blush' (Tardiana Group) EGol EMic IBal NGdn
'Blue Boy' EGol EMic EWes IBal NMyG NNor
'Blue Cadet' CBcs CMac EGol EMic EShb GQue IBal IFoB LPBA LRHS MLHP MWhi NBir NGdn NLar NMyG SApp SMrm SPoG WFar WMnd WWEG
'Blue Canoe' EMic IBal SApp
'Blue Cascade' **new** EMic
'Blue Chip' EMic EPGN IBal SApp
'Blue Clown' IBal
'Blue Cup' (*sieboldiana*) EMic MRav
'Blue Danube' (Tardiana Group) EGol EMic IBal MHom NMyG
'Blue Diamond' (Tardiana Group) EGol EMic NNor WFar WWEG
'Blue Dimples' (Tardiana Group) ECtt EGol EMic IBal
'Blue Edger' EMic IBal NBir
'Blue Eyes' IBal
'Blue Flame' EMic IBal
'Blue Frost' IBal
'Blue Haired Lady' IBal
'Blue Hawaii' EMic IBal
'Blue Heart' (*sieboldiana*) ECha EMic IBal
'Blue Ice' (Tardiana Group) EGol IBal
'Blue Impression' EMic
'Blue Ivory' (v) CBcs EBee EPGN IBal LRHS NMyG
'Blue Jay' (Tardiana Group) EGol EMic IBal SApp
'Blue Lady' EMic IBal
'Blue Mammoth' (*sieboldiana*) EGol EMic IBal SApp
'Blue Maui' EMic IBal
'Blue Monday' EMic IBal
'Blue Moon' (Tardiana Group) CMea EGol EMic EPfP GKev IBal NGdn NNor WAul
'Blue Mountains' IBal LBuc
'Blue Mouse Ears' EGol EMic EPGN EPfP GBin GEdr IBal LRHS MBNS MDev MHom MPnt NGdn NHar NMen NMyG NNor NSla SApp SPoG WFar WWEG
'Blue Plate Special' **new** IBal
'Blue River' (v) EMic IBal SApp
'Blue Seer' (*sieboldiana*) EGol EMic
'Blue Shadows' (*tokudama*) (v) EMic ESwi IBal NLar SApp WFar
'Blue Skies' (Tardiana Group) EGol MHom SApp
'Blue Splendor' (Tardiana Group) IBal
'Blue Umbrellas' (*sieboldiana* hybrid) EGol ELan EMic EPGN EPfP GMaP IBal LRHS MHom NGdn NLar NMyG NNor SApp SMrm
'Blue Veil' EGol IBal
'Blue Vision' EMic EPGN SApp
'Blue Wedgwood' (Tardiana Group) EBee EGol ELan EMic GQue LPBA LRHS MGos MMuc NGdn NMyG SApp SEND WWEG
'Blue Wonder' IBal
'Blueberry à la Mode' **new** EMic
'Blueberry Muffin' **new** EMic
'Blueberry Tart' IBal
'Blütenwunder' SApp
'Bob Deane' (v) EMic IBal
'Bob Olson' (v) EGol IBal
'Bobbie Sue' (v) EGol IBal
'Bogie and Bacall' (v) **new** IBal
'Bold Edger' (v) EGol EMic IBal
'Bold Intrigue' (v) IBal
'Bold Ribbons' (v) EGol EMic GAbr IBal WTin
'Bold Ruffles' (*sieboldiana*) EGol SApp
'Bolt out of the Blue' EMic
'Bonanza' EMic
'Border Bandit' (v) EGol IBal
'Border Favorite' EMic
'Border Street' (v) IBal
§ 'Borwick Beauty' (*sieboldiana*) (v) EGol EMic EPGN IBal LSou MSCN NCGa NGdn NLar NMyG NPnk SApp SPer WAul WWEG
'Bottom Line' (v) IBal
'Bountiful' EGol EMic IBal
'Bouquet' EGol
'Boyz Toy' EMic
'Brandywine' IBal
'Brash and Sassy' IBal
'Brave Amherst' (v) IBal
'Brenda's Beauty' (v) EGol EMic IBal
'Bressingham Blue' EBee ECtt EGol EMic GQue IBal LRHS MRav NLar NMyG NNor SApp SWvt WFar WMnd
'Bridal Veil' EMic IBal
'Bridegroom' EGol EMic IBal
'Bridgeville' IBal
'Brigadier' EGol IBal
'Brigham Blue' IBal
'Bright Glow' (Tardiana Group) EGol EMic IBal
'Bright Lights' (*tokudama*) (v) EGol EMic EPGN GBBs IBal NGdn SApp WFar
'Brim Cup' (v) EBee EGol ELon EPGN GAbr GBuc IBal LAst LSou MBNS NBro NGdn NNor NOrc SApp SBfd SMrm WWEG
'Brooke' EGol EMic IBal NMyG WWEG
'Brother Ronald' (Tardiana Group) EGol EMic IBal SApp
'Brother Stefan' EMic IBal SApp
'Bruce's Blue' EGol
'Bubba' IBal
'Buckshaw Blue' EGol EPGN IBal MDKP NBir NGdn NPro WHrl
'Buckwheat Honey' IBal
'Bulletproof' **new** IBal
'Bunchoko' IBal NNor
'Burke's Dwarf' IBal
'Butter Rim' (*sieboldii*) (v) EGol IBal
'Cadillac' (v) EMic
'Caliban' SApp
'Cally Atom' GCal IBal

'Calypso' (v)	EGol EMic EPGN IBal LBuc WWEG
'Camelot' (Tardiana Group)	EGol EMic IBal LRHS NGdn
'Cameo'	EMic IBal SApp
'Camouflage'	EMic IBal
'Canadian Blue'	EMic MWhi
'Candy Dish'	IBal
'Candy Hearts'	CSam EGol EMic IBal MHom NNor WTin
capitata	NNor
- B&SWJ 588	WCru
'Captain Kirk' (v)	EBee EMic IBal NGdn NMyG SApp
'Captain's Adventure' (v) **new**	EMic NGdn NMyG WFar
caput-avis	see *H. kikutii* var. *caput-avis*
'Carder Blue'	EMic
'Carnival' (v)	EGol EMic EPGN IBal NEgg SApp
'Carol' (*fortunei*) (v)	EGol EMic IBal NEgg NGdn NLar NMyG NNor SApp
'Carolina Blue'	IBal
'Carousel' (v)	EGol IBal
'Carrie' (*sieboldii*) (v)	EGol
'Cascades' (v)	EGol EMic IBal SPoG
'Cat and Mouse'	EGol IBal
'Cathedral Windows' (v)	EMic IBal
'Catherine'	IBal
'Cat's Eyes' (*venusta*) (v)	EGol EMic EPGN IBal NNor SApp
'Cavalcade' (v)	EMic
'Celebration' (v)	EGol ELan EMic IBal LRHS MDKP WWEG
'Celestial'	IBal
'Celtic Uplands'	EMic
'Center of Attention'	EMic IBal NGdn NMyG SApp
'Cha Cha Cha'	IBal
'Chain Lightning' (v)	EMic IBal
'Challenger'	EMic
'Chameleon' (v) **new**	EMic
'Change of Tradition' (*lancifolia*) (v)	EMic
'Chantilly Lace' (v)	EGol EMic SApp WTin WWEG
'Chariots of Fire' (v)	IBal
'Chartreuse Waves'	EGol
'Chartreuse Wiggles' (*sieboldii*)	EGol IBal
'Cheatin' Heart'	EGol EMic IBal WWEG
'Chelsea Babe' (*fortunei*) (v)	EGol
'Cherish'	EGol EMic EPGN IBal NGdn
'Cherry Berry' (v)	EBee EGol EMic EPGN EPfP GBin IBal LRHS MBNS MBel MMuc MNrw NBro NCGa NEgg NGdn NLar NMyG NPro NWad SApp SBfd SPoG WAul WBor WCAu WFar WWEG
'Cherry Tart'	EMic IBal
'Cherub' (v)	EGol IBal
'Chesapeake Bay'	EMic IBal
'Chesterland Gold'	IBal
'China Girl' **new**	EMic
'Chinese Gold' **new**	IBal
'Chinese Sunrise' (v)	CWCL EGol EMic EPGN GBin IBal LBuc MHom NMyG NNor SRms
'Chionea' (v)	IBal
'Chiquita'	EGol IBal
'Chi-town Classic' (v) **new**	IBal
'Chodai Ginba'	IBal
§ 'Chōkō-nishiki' (*montana*) (v)	EGol EMic EPGN IBal LRHS NGdn NMyG NNor SApp SBfd
'Choo Choo Train'	EGol EMic SApp
'Chopsticks'	EMic IBal
'Christmas Candy'PBR	EMic EPGN GAbr IBal LRHS NMyG
'Christmas Cookies'	IBal
'Christmas Lights' (v)	IBal
'Christmas Pageant' (v)	EMic IBal
'Christmas Tree' (v)	EGol EMic EPGN IBal IFoB LPla LRHS NEgg NGdn NMyG SApp WMoo WWEG
'Cinderella'	EMic IBal
'Cinnamon Sticks'	IBal
'Citation' (v)	EGol IBal
'City Lights'	EGol EMic IBal NEgg
'City Slicker' (v)	IBal
'Claudia'	IBal
clausa	EMic
- var. ***normalis***	GQui IBal NBir NGdn NLar
'Clear Fork River Valley'	EMic IBal
'Cleopatra' (v)	IBal
'Clifford's Forest Fire'	EBee EMic EPGN IBal LRHS NLar WFar
'Clifford's Stingray' (v)	EMic IBal LRHS
'Climax' (v)	EMic IBal
'Cloudburst'	EMic IBal
'Clovelly'	EMic IBal
'Clown's Collar' (v)	EMic
'Coconut Custard' **new**	EMic
'Cody'	EGol IBal
'Cold Heart' **new**	EMic
'Collector's Banner'	EGol IBal
'Collector's Choice'	EGol IBal
'Color Festival' (v)	EMic IBal
'Color Glory'	see *H.* 'Borwick Beauty'
'Colossal'	EGol EMic IBal
'Columbus Circle' (v)	EGol EMic IBal
'Confused Angel' (v)	IBal
'Cookie Crumbs' (v)	EGol EMic EPGN IBal SApp
'Cool Hand Luke' (*tokudama*) (v)	IBal
'Coquette' (v)	EGol EMic GAbr IBal
'Corkscrew'	EMic SApp
'Corn Belt' (v)	EMic IBal
'Corn Muffins' **new**	EMic
'Cotillion' (v)	EGol EMic IBal SApp
'Count Your Blessings' (v) **new**	EMic
'Country Mouse' (v)	EGol EMic IBal
'County Park'	EGol EMic IBal
'Cowrie' (v)	IBal
'Cracker Crumbs' (v)	EGol EMic EPGN GEdr GKev IBal MHom NHar NMyG NNor NSla SApp WWEG
'Craig's Temptation'	IBal
§ ***crassifolia***	EMic LRHS XLum
'Cream Cheese' (v)	EGol IBal
'Cream Delight' (*undulata*)	see *H. undulata* var. *undulata*
'Crepe Soul' (v)	EGol IBal
'Crepe Suzette' (v)	EGol EPGN IBal NNor
'Crested Reef'	EGol EMic IBal NMyG
'Crested Surf' (v)	EGol EMic EPGN IBal
'Crinoline Petticoats'	EGol IBal
§ ***crispula*** (v) ♀H4	EGol EMic EPfP IBal MCot MHom MRav NChi NMyG
'Crown Jewel' (v)	EPGN
'Crown Prince' (v)	EGol IBal
'Crown Royalty' **new**	EMic
§ 'Crowned Imperial' (*fortunei*) (v)	CWat EMic NHol
'Crumples' (*sieboldiana*)	EGol IBal

'Crusader' (v)	EGol ELon EMic EPGN IBal LRHS NMyG SApp WFar WWEG
'Crystal Chimes'	IBal
'Crystal Dixie'	EGol EMic IBal SApp
'Cupboard Love'	SApp
'Curlew' (Tardiana Group)	EGol IBal
'Curls'	EMic IBal
'Curtain Call'	IBal
'Cutting Edge'	EMic IBal
'Cuyahoga' (v) **new**	IBal
'Dab a Green'	IBal
'Daisy Doolittle' (v)	EMic IBal SApp
'Dance with Me' (v)	EMic IBal
'Dancing in the Rain' (v)	CWGN EMic EPGN LRHS NBro NGdn SApp WFar
'Dancing Queen'	IBal
'Dark Shadows'	EMic EPGN NGdn NSti
'Dark Star' (v)	EGol EMic EPGN IBal SApp
'Dark Victory'	IBal
'Dawn'	EGol EMic IBal NMyG
'Dawn's Early Light'	EMic
'Dax'	IBal
'Daybreak'	EGol EMic EPGN IBal MBri NBro SApp
'Day's End' (v)	EGol EMic IBal
'Deane's Dream'	EMic IBal
decorata	EGol EMic
'Deep Blue Sea'	EMic IBal SApp
'Deep Pockets'	IBal
'Dee's Golden Jewel' **new**	EMic
'Déjà Blu' (v)	EMic IBal
'Delia' (v)	EPGN
'Deliverance' **new**	IBal
'Delta Dawn' (v)	EMic IBal LRHS NGdn
'Delta Desire'	IBal
'Deluxe Edition'	IBal
'Designer Genes'	EMic IBal SApp
'Devon Blue' (Tardiana Group)	EGol EMic NMyG NNor
'Devon Desire' (*montana*)	NLar
'Devon Discovery'	IBal
'Devon Giant'	EMic IBal NNor SApp
'Devon Gold'	EMic GAbr IBal
'Devon Green'	ELan EMic EPGN GBin IBal IPot LRHS MBel MHom MMuc NBro NEgg NGdn NLar NMyG NPro SApp SBfd SEND WAul WFar WHal WHoo WWEG
'Devon Mist'	IBal NNor
'Devon Tor'	IBal
'Dew Drop' (v)	EMic WWEG
'Dewed Steel'	IBal
'Diamond Tiara' (v)	EGol EMic EPGN IBal LRHS NBir NGdn NMyG WWEG
'Diana Remembered'	EGol EMic EPGN IBal NGdn WBor
'Dick Ward'	EMic EPGN IBal
'Dilithium Crystal'	IBal
'Dillie Perkeo'	IBal
'Dilys'	EMic MNrw
'Dimple'	EMic IBal
'Dinky Donna'	EMic IBal
'Dinner Jacket'	IBal LRHS SBfd
'Dixie Chick' (v)	EGol EMic IBal NNor SApp
'Dixie Chickadee' (v)	EGol EMic
'Dixieland Heat'	IBal
'Doctor Fu Manchu'	IBal
'Domaine de Courson'	EMic EPGN SApp WFar
'Don Stevens' (v)	EGol IBal
'Dorothy'	EMic
'Dorset Blue' (Tardiana Group)	EMic EPGN IBal SApp SBfd
'Dorset Charm' (Tardiana Group)	EGol EMic
'Dorset Flair' (Tardiana Group)	EGol EMic IBal
'Doubloons'	EGol EMic
'Dragon Tails'	EGol EMic IBal LRHS
'Dream Queen' (v)	ECtt EMic LRHS
'Dream Weaver' (v)	EGol EMic EPGN IBal IPot LRHS MHom MNrw NBro NGdn NMyG SApp SPer SPoG WFar WWEG
'Dress Blues'	CMac EMic IBal
'Drummer Boy'	EGol EMic IBal WWEG
'Duchess' (*nakaiana*) (v)	IBal
'Duke of Cornwall' (v)	IBal
'DuPage Delight' (*sieboldiana*) (v)	EGol EMic IBal NGdn NLar
'Dust Devil' (*fortunei*) (v)	EGol IBal
'Earth Angel'PBR (v)	EMic EPGN IBal NGdn SApp SHeu
'Ebb Tide' (*montana*) (v)	IBal
'Ebony Towers' **new**	EMic
'Edge of Night'	EGol EMic IBal
'Edwin Bibby'	EMic
'El Capitan' (v)	EGol EMic EPGN IBal LRHS
'El Niño'PBR (Tardiana Group) (v)	CWGN EGol EMic EPGN IBal IPot LRHS MHom MNrw NBro NCGa NGdn NMyG SApp WFar WWEG
§ 'Elata'	EGol EMic IBal SApp
'Elatior' (*nigrescens*)	EMic IBal
'Eldorado'	see *H.* 'Frances Williams'
'Eleanor Lachman' (v)	EGol EMic IBal
'Eleanor Roosevelt'	IBal
'Elegans'	see *H. sieboldiana* var. *elegans*
'Elfin Power' (*sieboldii*) (v)	EGol
'Elisabeth'	EMic GBin IBal LSRN
'Elizabeth Campbell' (*fortunei*) (v)	EGol EMic
'Elkheart Lake'	EMic
'Ellen'	EMic
'Ellerbroek' (*fortunei*) (v)	EMic IBal
'Ellie Bee'	IBal
'Elsley Japan' **new**	IBal
'Elsley Runner'	EGol IBal WWEG
'Elvis Lives'	EGol EMic EPGN GBin IBal LAst NEgg NGdn NLar NMyG NNor NPro
'Embroidery' (v)	EPGN
'Emerald Carpet'	EGol IBal
'Emerald Crown'	IBal
'Emerald Necklace' (v)	EGol
'Emerald Ruff Cut'	EMic IBal SApp
'Emerald Tiara' (v)	EGol EMic EPGN LRHS MLHP NLar NMyG SApp SBfd WTin WWEG
'Emeralds and Rubies'	EGol EMic IBal
'Emily Dickinson' (v)	EBee EGol EMic IBal LRHS MMuc NNor SApp SEND WWEG
'Empress Wu'	EBee EMic EUJe IBal NGdn
'Encore'	IBal
'English Sunrise' (Tardiana Group)	IBal
'Enterprise'	EBee EMic NGdn SApp
'Eola Sapphire' **new**	EMic
'Eos'	NLar
'Eric Smith' (Tardiana Group)	EGol EMic IBal MHom NMyG WFar
'Eric's Gold'	EPGN IBal

'Erie Magic' (v)	EGol IBal
'Eskimo Pie' (v)	EBee EMic NGdn SApp SMrm WFar
'Essence of Summer'	EMic EPfP IBal SApp
'Eternal Flame'	EMic IBal
'Evelyn McCafferty' (*tokudama* hybrid)	EGol IBal
'Eventide' (v)	EGol IBal
'Everlasting Love' (v)	EGol
'Excitation'	EGol EMic IBal
'Extasy' (v)	EMic IBal NGdn
'Eye Candy' (v)	IBal
'Eye Catcher'	EMic
'Eye Declare' (v)	IBal
'Fair Maiden' (v)	IBal NMyG
'Faith'	EMic
'Faithful Heart' (v)	IBal
'Fall Bouquet' (*longipes* var. *hypoglauca*)	EGol
'Fall Emerald'	EMic
'Fallen Angel'	IBal
'Fan Dance' (v)	EGol EMic IBal
'Fantabulous' (v)	EPGN IBal
'Fantastic' (*sieboldiana* hybrid)	EGol
'Fantasy Island' (v)	EGol EMic IBal
'Fat Boy' **new**	IBal
'Fatal Attraction'	IBal
'Feather Boa'	EGol EMic IBal NHar NMyG WWEG
'Fenman's Fascination'	EMic IBal
'Fiesta' (v)	IBal
'Final Summation' (v) **new**	EMic
'Fire and Ice' (v)	Widely available
'Fire Island'	ECtt EGol EMic EPGN GBin IBal LRHS MHom MNrw NGdn NMyG SApp
'Fireworks' (v)	EBee EGol EMic EPGN EPfP GBin IBal LRHS MBNS MDev NBro NGdn NMyG SApp SMrm SPoG
'First Frost' (v)	EMic EPGN IBal LRHS MAvo MBri MDev NCGa NGdn SApp WWEG
'First Love' (*montana*) **new**	EMic
'First Mate' (v)	EMic IBal
'First Moon'	IBal
'Five O'Clock Shadow' (v)	IBal
'Five O'Clock Somewhere' (v)	IBal
'Flame Stitch' (*ventricosa*) (v)	IBal
'Flapjack' (v) **new**	IBal
'Fleet Week'	EMic IBal
'Flemish Angel' (v) **new**	IBal
'Flemish Gold'	IBal
'Flemish Sky'	EBee EMic IBal NGdn SApp
'Floradora'	EGol EMic IBal NMyG
'Flower Power'	EGol NNor
'Fluted Fountain' **new**	EMic
'Fool's Gold' (*fortunei*)	EMic IBal
'Forest Fireworks' (v)	IBal
'Forest Shadows'	IBal
'Formal Attire' (*sieboldiana* hybrid) (v)	EGol EMic IBal LRHS
'Forncett Frances' (v)	EGol IBal
'Fortis'	see *H. undulata* var. *erromena*
fortunei	EGol EMic NHol NNor WFar
§ - var. ***albopicta*** (v) ♀H4	CSam EBee ECha EGol EHoe ELan EMic EPGN EPfP GBin GMaP LEdu LPot LRHS MRav NEgg NGdn NHol NMyG NNor SApp SBod SPer WBrk WFar WHoo WMnd WTin WWEG
- - f. ***aurea*** ♀H4	CMac ECha EGol EHoe ELan EMic GBin NEgg NLar SRms WFar WHal
- - - dwarf	EMic
- - f. ***viridis***	EHrv NNor
§ - var. ***aureomarginata*** (v) ♀H4	Widely available
- var. ***gigantea***	see *H. montana*
- var. ***hyacinthina*** ♀H4	EGol EMic EPfP LRHS MRav NGdn NLar SApp WPtf XLum
- - variegated (v)	see *H.* 'Crowned Imperial'
- var. ***rugosa***	EMic
- 'Shaman'	SApp
- var. ***stenantha***	EMic
'Fountain of Youth' (*kikutii*)	IBal
'Fourteen Carats' **new**	EMic
'Fourth of July'	EGol IBal
'Fragrant Blue'	EBee EGol EMic GBBs IBal LRHS NBro NGdn NMyG SApp SPoG XLum
'Fragrant Bouquet' (v)	EGol ELan EMic EPGN GAbr IBal LAst LRHS LSRN MMuc NCGa NGdn NHol NLar NMyG SEND WPtf WWEG
'Fragrant Dream'	EGol EMic EPfP IBal NLar WWEG
'Fragrant Fire'	EMic IBal SApp
'Fragrant Gold'	EGol EMic
'Fragrant King'	IBal
'Fragrant Queen'PBR (v) **new**	EMic
'Fragrant Star'	EMic IBal SApp
'Fragrant Surprise' (v)	IBal
'Fran Godfrey'	EMic EPGN IBal NMyG
'Francee' (*fortunei*) (v) ♀H4	Widely available
§ 'Frances Williams' (*sieboldiana*) (v) ♀H4	Widely available
'Frances Williams Improved' (*sieboldiana*) (v)	EGol EPfP GBuc MWat
'Francheska' (v) **new**	EMic
'Fresh' (v)	EGol EMic EPGN IBal SApp
'Fried Bananas'	EGol EMic MBri SApp WWEG
'Fried Green Tomatoes'	EGol EMic IBal NLar NMyG NNor SApp
'Friends' (v) **new**	EMic
'Fringe Benefit' (v)	EGol EMic GAbr IBal SApp WWEG
'Frost Giant' (v)	IBal
'Frosted Dimples'	EMic EPGN IBal
'Frosted Frolic' (v)	EMic
'Frosted Jade' (v)	EBee EGol EMic EPGN IBal NLar SApp SBfd WTin
'Frosted June'	EMic IBal
'Frosted Mouse Ears'	EGol EMic IBal
'Frozen Margarita'	EMic IBal
'Frühlingsgold' (v)	IBal
'Fruit Punch' **new**	EMic
'Fujibotan' (v)	EGol EMic IBal SApp
'Fulda'	EMic IBal
'Funky Monkey' **new**	EMic
'Gaiety' (v)	EGol EMic EPGN IBal
'Gaijin' (v)	EGol IBal SApp
'Garden Party' (v)	IBal
'Garden Treasure'	EGol
'Garnet Prince'	EGol IBal
'Gay Blade' (v)	EGol IBal LRHS SApp
'Gay Feather' (v)	EMic SApp
'Gay Search' (v)	EPGN IBal
'Geisha' (v)	EGol IBal LRHS NGdn NMyG NNor NPro SApp WWEG
'Geisha Satin Ripples'	IBal
'Gemini Moon' (v)	IBal
'Gemstone'	IBal
'Gene's Joy'	EPGN IBal

'Gentle Giant' **new**	IBal
'Gentle Spirit' (v) **new**	IBal
'George M. Dallas' (v) **new**	IBal
'Georgeous George' **new**	IBal
'Ghost Spirit'	IBal SApp WFar
'Ghostmaster' (v)	EMic LRHS WWlt
'Gig Harbor'	IBal
'Gigantea' (*sieboldiana*)	see *H.* 'Elata'
'Gilt by Association'	IBal
'Gilt Edge' (*sieboldiana*) (v)	CWat EMic NMyG WWEG
'Gingee'	IBal
'Ginko Craig' (v)	CMac EBee ECha EGol EHoe ELan EMic EPGN EPfP GKev GMaP IBal LPBA LRHS MRav NBir NGdn NLar NMyG NNor NSti SApp SBfd SPer SPoG WFar WMnd WWEG
'Ginrei'	IBal
'Ginsu Knife' (v)	EMic IBal
'Glad Rags' (v)	IBal
'Glass Hearts'	EMic IBal
glauca	see *H. sieboldiana* var. *elegans*
'Glitter'	EMic IBal
'Glockenspiel'	EGol EMic
I 'Gloriosa' (*fortunei*) (v)	EGol IBal LRHS WFar
'Glory'	EGol IBal
'Glory Hallelujah' **new**	EMic
'Goblin' **new**	EMic
'Goddess of Athena' (*decorata*) (v)	EGol
'Gold Drop' (*venusta* hybrid)	EGol EMic NHol WWEG
'Gold Edger'	CBcs CMac CPrp EGol EHoe ELan EMic EPfP GMaP IBal MRav NBir NGdn NLar NMyG NNor NSti SApp WFar WTin WWEG
'Gold Edger Surprise' (v)	EMic
'Gold Flush' (*ventricosa*)	EMic
§ 'Gold Haze' (*fortunei*)	EGol EMic EPGN IBal MHom NBir NCGa NMyG WWEG
'Gold Leaf' (*fortunei*)	EGol IBal
'Gold Pressed Latinum' **new**	IBal
'Gold Regal'	EGol EMic EPGN IBal LRHS MHom NMyG WFar WMnd
'Gold Rush'	NMyG
'Gold Standard' (*fortunei*) (v)	Widely available
'Goldbrook' (v)	EGol EMic IBal WTin
'Goldbrook Galleon'	EGol IBal
'Goldbrook Gayle' (v)	EGol
'Goldbrook Gaynor'	EGol IBal
'Goldbrook Genie'	EGol IBal
'Goldbrook Ghost' (v)	EGol
'Goldbrook Girl'	EGol IBal
'Goldbrook Glamour' (v)	EGol IBal
'Goldbrook Gleam' (v)	EGol
'Goldbrook Glimmer' (Tardiana Group) (v)	EGol IBal LRHS
'Goldbrook Glory'	EGol EMic IBal
'Goldbrook Gold'	EGol IBal
'Goldbrook Good Gracious' (v)	EGol IBal
'Goldbrook Grace'	EGol
'Goldbrook Gratis' (v)	EGol IBal
'Goldbrook Grayling'	EGol EMic IBal
'Goldbrook Grebe'	EGol IBal
'Goldbrook Greenheart'	IBal
'Golden Age'	see *H.* 'Gold Haze'
'Golden Anniversary'	EGol
'Golden Ben'	ITim
'Golden Essence' **new**	IBal
'Golden Fascination'	EGol
'Golden Fountain'	EMic
'Golden Friendship'	EGol IBal
'Golden Gate'	EGol
'Golden Goal'	IBal
'Golden Guernsey' (v)	EMic
'Golden Isle'	EGol EMic IBal
'Golden Meadows'^{PBR} (*sieboldiana*)	EMic EPGN IBal NGdn SMrm
'Golden Medallion' (*tokudama*)	ECtt EGol ELan EMic IBal LRHS NEgg NGdn NMyG WFar
'Golden Nakaiana'	see *H.* 'Birchwood Parky's Gold'
'Golden' (*nakaiana*)	see *H.* 'Birchwood Parky's Gold'
'Golden Oriole'	EGol EMic IBal NNor WWEG
'Golden Prayers' (*tokudama*)	EBee ECtt EHoe ELan LRHS MRav NBir NBro NEgg NGdn NLar WFar WHal WSHC
'Golden Scepter'	EGol EMic EPGN IBal LRHS NMyG NNor SApp WFar
'Golden Sculpture' (*sieboldiana*)	EGol EMic IBal
'Golden Spider'	EGol EMic IBal WWEG
'Golden Sunburst' (*sieboldiana*)	CPrp EGol ELan IBal NEgg NGdn NLar WFar XLum
'Golden Tiara' (v) ♀^{H4}	Widely available
'Golden Tusk'	IBal
'Golden Waffles'	EMic IBal NEgg
'Goldsmith'	EGol SApp
'Goober'	IBal
'Good as Gold'	EMic EPGN IBal NMyG
'Gorgon'	IBal
'Gosan Leather Strap'	IBal
'Gosan' (*takahashii*)	EGol
gracillima	EPGN IBal NRya WWEG
'Granary Gold' (*fortunei*)	EGol EPGN MHom
'Grand Canyon'	EMic SApp
'Grand Finale'	IBal
'Grand Forks'	IBal
'Grand Marquee' (v)	EMic EPGN GBin IBal NGdn NLar SApp WFar WWEG
'Grand Master'	EGol IBal MDKP SApp
'Grand Prize' (v)	IBal
'Grand Rapids' **new**	EMic IBal
'Grand Slam'	EGol EMic IBal
'Grand Tiara' (v)	EGol EMic EPGN IBal SApp
'Grand Total'	IBal
'Grant Park'	IBal
'Gray Cole' (*sieboldiana*)	EGol EMic IBal NMyG
'Great Arrival'	EMic IBal
'Great Escape'^{PBR} (v)	EMic IBal
'Great Expectations' (*sieboldiana*) (v)	CBar CHid CMac EBee EGol EMic EPGN EPfP IBal IVic LRHS LSRN MBNS MHer MNrw MWhi NBro NCGa NGdn NHol NLar NMyG NNor NSti SAga SApp SHil SMrm WAul WWEG
'Great Lakes Gold'	IBal
'Green Acres' (*montana*)	EMic IBal LEdu WFar
'Green Angel' (*sieboldiana*)	EGol IBal
'Green Blade' **new**	IBal
'Green Dwarf'	WFar
'Green Eyes' (*sieboldii*) (v)	EGol EMic IBal
'Green Fountain' (*kikutii*)	EGol EMic IBal NMyG WWEG
'Green Gold' (*fortunei*) (v)	EMic
'Green Lama'	IBal
'Green Mouse Ears'	EGol EMic IBal
'Green Piecrust'	EGol IBal NNor
'Green Power' **new**	IBal
'Green Sheen'	EGol EMic EPGN
'Green Summer Fragrance'	IBal

'Green Velveteen'	EGol IBal
'Green with Envy' (v)	EGol EMic EPGN IBal NNor SApp WWEG
'Greensleeves' (v)	IBal
'Grey Ghost'	EMic IBal
'Grey Piecrust'	EGol
'Groo Bloo'	IBal
'Ground Cover Trompenburg'	SApp
'Ground Master' (v)	CMac EBee ECtt EGol ELan EPfP GCra GMaP IBal IFoB LPBA MRav MSwo NBro NGdn NNor NSti WFar WMoo WPtf WWEG
'Ground Sulphur'	EGol EMic IBal
'Grover Cleveland' **new**	IBal
'Grünherz'	IBal
'Grunspecht' (Tardiana Group)	IBal
'Guacamole' (v)	CBcs ECha ECtt EGol EMic EPGN EPfP GBin IBal IPot LRHS MBri NGdn NLar NMyG NNor NPnk SApp WAul WHoo WTin WWEG
'Guardian Angel' (*sieboldiana*)	EGol EMic EPGN IBal NLar
'Gum Drop'	EMic NNor
'Gun Metal Blue'	EGol IBal
'Gypsy Rose'	EPGN EPfP IBal MBri NGdn NMyG SApp WFar
'Hacksaw'	EMic IBal
'Hadspen Blue' (Tardiana Group)	Widely available
'Hadspen Hawk' (Tardiana Group)	IBal NMyG SApp
'Hadspen Heron' (Tardiana Group)	EGol EMic MHom MWat NMyG WCot XLum
'Hadspen Nymphaea'	EGol IBal
'Hadspen Rainbow'	EMic IBal
'Hadspen Samphire'	EGol EMic EPGN IBal LRHS MHom NBir NBro
'Hadspen White' (*fortunei*)	EMic IBal NLar
'Haku-chu-han' (*sieboldii*) (v)	IBal
'Hakujima' (*sieboldii*)	EGol IBal
'Hakumuo' (v)	IBal
§ 'Halcyon' (Tardiana Group) ♀H4	Widely available
'Half and Half' **new**	EMic
'Halo'	EGol
'Hampshire County' (v)	EMic IBal
'Hanky Panky' (v)	EMic IBal LRHS NCGa NGdn NMyG NSti WFar
'Hannibal Hamlin' (v) **new**	IBal
'Happily Ever After' (v)	IBal
'Happiness' (Tardiana Group)	EGol EHoe EMic IBal MHom MRav NMyG
'Happy Camper' (v)	IBal
'Happy Hearts'	EGol EMic
'Happy Valley' (v)	IBal
'Harlequin'	SApp
'Harmony' (Tardiana Group)	EGol EMic
'Harpoon' (v)	EMic IBal
'Harriette Ward'	IBal
'Harry van de Laar'	EMic IBal IPot SApp
'Harry van Trier'	EMic GBin
'Hart's Tongue'	IBal
'Harvest Delight' **new**	EMic
'Harvest Glow'	EGol IBal
'Hawkeye' (v)	IBal
'Hazel'	EMic IBal
'Heart Ache'	EGol IBal
'Heart and Soul' (v)	EGol EMic SApp
'Heart Broken'	IBal
'Heart of Chan'	IBal
'Heart Throb'	EMic
'Heartbeat' (v)	IBal
'Heartleaf'	EMic
'Heart's Content' (v)	EGol IBal
'Heartsong' (v)	EGol EMic IBal NMyG
'Heat Wave'PBR (v)	EMic EPGN IBal SApp
'Heavenly Beginnings' (v)	IBal
'Heavenly Tiara' (v)	IBal
'Heideturm'	EBee EGol IBal
'Helen Doriot' (*sieboldiana*)	EGol EMic IBal
'Helen Field Fischer' (*fortunei*)	CPrp IBal
helonioides misapplied f. ***albopicta***	see *H. rohdeifolia* f. ***albopicta***
'Herifu' (v)	EGol EMic
'Herkules'	IBal
'Hertha' (v)	EMic
'Hidden Cove' (v)	EGol IBal
'High Kicker'	EGol
'High Society' (v)	CBcs EBee EMic EPGN EPfP IBal LRHS MHom MNrw NGdn NMyG NNor SApp
'High Tide'	IBal
'Hi-ho Silver' (v)	EMic EPGN IBal WWEG
'Hilda Wassman' (v)	EGol IBal
'Hillbilly Blues' (v)	IBal
'Hippodrome' (v)	EMic IBal
'Hirao Elite'	EMic IBal
'Hirao Majesty'	EGol IBal
'Hirao Splendor'	EGol NMyG
'Hirao Supreme'	EGol EMic IBal
'His Honor' (v)	EMic IBal
'Holly's Honey'	EGol IBal
'Hollywood Lights' (v)	EMic EPfP IBal NGdn NMyG
'Holstein'	see *H.* 'Halcyon'
'Holy Molé' (v)	EMic IBal
'Holy Mouse Ears'	EGol EMic IBal
'Honey Moon'	EGol NNor
'Honeybells' ♀H4	CBcs CMac CTri EBee ECha EGol ELan EMic EPGN EPfP IBal LHop LPBA LRHS MCot MRav NBid NGdn NNor NSti SApp SPer WCAu WFar WPtf WWEG XLum
'Honeysong' (v)	EBee EGol EMic EPGN IBal NNor
'Hoosier Dome'	EMic
'Hoosier Harmony' (v)	EGol EMic
'Hoosier Homecoming'	SApp
'Hope' (v)	EGol IBal SApp
'Hotcakes'	IBal
'Hotspur' (v)	EMic SApp
'Hush Puppie'	EGol EMic IBal
'Hyacintha Variegata' (*fortunei*) (v)	CMac NNor
'Hydon Gleam'	EGol EMic IBal
'Hydon Sunset'	EBee ECtt EGol EMic EPGN GCra IBal LRHS NBir NHol NMyG NNor NRHS NRya NSti SApp SBch WHal WMnd WPtf WTin WWEG
hypoleuca	EGol EMic IBal
'Hyuga-urajiro' (v)	EMic IBal SApp
'Ice Age Trail' (v)	IBal
'Ice Cream' (*cathayana*) (v)	EGol IBal
'Ice Prancer'	EMic
'Iced Lemon' (v)	EGol EMic IBal NNor
'Illicit Affair'	EGol EMic IBal SApp
'Imp' (v)	EMic IBal
§ 'Inaho'	EGol LRHS

'Inca Gold'	EGol IBal
'Independence' (v)	EBee EMic EPGN IBal MBri NBro NMyG SApp SPoG WFar
'Independence Day' (v)	EMic
'Indigo'	IBal
'Innisjade'	IBal
'Inniswood' (v)	CWCL ECtt EMic EPGN EPfP IBal IPot LRHS MBNS NBro NGdn NLar NSti SApp WFar WMnd WWEG
'Invincible'	EBee EGol EMic GBin IBal LAst LPot NBid NEgg NGdn NLar NMyG NNor SApp SPoG WPtf WTin WWEG
'Invincible Spirit' **new**	IBal
'Iona' (*fortunei*)	EGol EMic EPGN NMyG NNor
'Irische See' (Tardiana Group)	EGol IBal
'Irish Eyes' (v)	EMic IBal
'Irish Luck' **new**	EMic
'Iron Gate Delight' (v)	NNor
'Iron Gate Glamour' (v)	EGol
'Iron Gate Special' (v)	EMic
'Iron Gate Supreme' (v)	EMic
'Island Charm' (v)	EGol EMic EPGN IBal LRHS NHar NLar NMyG SApp
'Island Forest Gem'	IBal
'Itsy Bitsy Spider'	EGol
'Ivory Coast' (v)	EMic
'Ivory Necklace' (v)	IBal
'Iwa Soules'	EGol
'Jack of Diamonds'	IBal
'Jade Cascade'	CCon EGol ELan EMic GBin IBal NBir NEgg NLar SApp SMrm WWEG
'Jade Scepter' (*nakaiana*)	EGol EMic
'Jadette' (v)	EGol GBin
'Janet Day' (v)	EMic IBal SApp
'Janet' (*fortunei*) (v)	EBee EGol EMic IBal LRHS NGdn NNor
'Japan Girl'	see *H.* 'Mount Royal'
'Jaws'	IBal
'Jaz'	IBal
'Jerry Landwehr'	IBal
'Jester'	SApp
'Jewel of the Nile' (v)	EMic IBal SApp
'Jim Mathews'	IBal
'Jimmy Crack Corn'	EGol EMic IBal LRHS SApp
'Jingle Bells'	IBal
'John Wargo'	EGol IBal
'Johnny Angel'	EMic
'Joker' (*fortunei*) (v)	NNor
'Jolly Green Giant' (*sieboldiana* hybrid)	EMic
jonesii **new**	EMic
'Joseph'	EGol EMic IBal
'Josephine' (v)	NNor
'Journeyman'	EGol EMic IBal LRHS
'Journey's End' (v)	EMic IBal SApp
'Joyce Trott' (v)	EMic IBal
'Joyful' (v)	IBal
'Jubilee' (v)	IBal
'Judy Rocco'	IBal
'Juha' (v)	EMic IBal SApp
'Jules'	EPGN
'Julia' (v)	EGol EMic IBal
'Julie Morss'	EGol EMic EPGN GMaP IBal MHom NEgg SApp WWEG
'June' PBR (Tardiana Group) (v) ♀H4	Widely available

	'June Fever' PBR (Tardiana Group)	EMic ESwi IBal LRHS MDev NBro NGdn NLar SApp WFar
	'Jurassic Park'	EBee EMic GBin IBal MDev MNrw
	'Just So' (v)	EGol EMic IBal
	'Justine' **new**	EMic
	'Kabitan'	see *H. sieboldii* var. *sieboldii* f. *kabitan*
	'Kabuki'	IBal
	'Kalamazoo' (v)	EMic
	'Kaleidochrome' (v) **new**	IBal
	'Karin'	EGol EMic IBal
	'Katherine Lewis' (Tardiana Group) (v)	ECtt EMic IBal LRHS LSRN NHol
	'Kath's Gold'	EMic
	'Katie Q' (v)	EMic IBal
	'Katsuragawa-beni' (v)	EMic IBal
	'Kelsey'	EGol EMic
	'Kenzie' (v) **new**	EMic
	'Key Lime Pie'	EMic IBal SApp
	'Key West' **new**	EMic
	'Ki-nakafu-otome' (*venusta*)	IBal
§	'Kifukurin-hyuga' (v)	IBal
	'Kifukurin' (*kikutii*)	see *H.* 'Kifukurin Hyuga'
	'Kifukurin-ko-mame' (*gracillima*) (v)	EMic
	'Kifukurin' (*pulchella*) (v)	EGol
	'Kifukurin-ubatake' (*pulchella*) (v)	EGol EMic EPGN IBal
	'Kifukurin' (*venusta*) (v)	EMic
	kikutii	EGol EMic WTin
§	- var. ***caput-avis***	EGol EMic
	- var. ***kikutii*** f. ***leuconota***	SApp
	- var. ***polyneuron***	SApp
	- var. ***pruinosa***	SApp
§	- var. ***yakusimensis***	CPBP GBin IBal SMad
	'Kinbotan' (v)	EGol EMic
	'King James'	IBal
	'King of Spades'	IBal
	'King Tut'	EMic
	'Kingfisher' (Tardiana Group)	EGol
§	'Kirishima'	EMic NSla
	'Kisuji'	see *H.* 'Mediopicta'
	'Kitty Cat'	EMic EPGN IBal SApp
	'Kiwi Black Magic'	EGol IBal
	'Kiwi Blue Baby'	EGol EMic IBal
	'Kiwi Blue Ruffles'	IBal
	'Kiwi Blue Sky'	IBal
	'Kiwi Canoe'	IBal
	'Kiwi Cream Edge' (v)	EMic IBal
	'Kiwi Forest'	IBal
	'Kiwi Fruit'	SApp
	'Kiwi Full Monty' (v)	EBee EMic IBal LRHS
	'Kiwi Gold Rush'	IBal
	'Kiwi Hippo'	EGol IBal
	'Kiwi Jordan'	IBal
	'Kiwi Kaniere Gold'	IBal
	'Kiwi Minnie Gold'	IBal
	'Kiwi Parasol'	IBal
	'Kiwi Skyscraper'	IBal
	'Kiwi Sunlover'	IBal
	'Kiwi Sunshine'	IBal
	'Klopping Variegated' (v)	EGol EMic
	'Knight's Journey'	IBal
	'Knockout' (v)	EGol IBal MBNS MNrw MRav NBro NEgg NGdn NLar NMyG NNor SApp
	'Komodo Dragon'	EMic IBal SKHP WTin

	Name	Suppliers
	'Kong'	IBal
	'Konkubine'	EMic
	'Korean Snow'	IBal
I	'Koreana Variegated' (*undulata*)	EMic
	'Koriyama' (*sieboldiana*) (v)	EMic IBal
	'Krossa Cream Edge' (*sieboldii*) (v)	IBal
	'Krossa Regal' 𝕐H4	Widely available
	'Krugerrand'	IBal
	'Lacy Belle' (v)	CSBt EBee EGol EMic EPfP IBal NBro NGdn NPro SBfd
	'Lady Godiva'	IBal
	'Lady Guineverre'	EMic IBal
	'Lady Helen'	EMic
	'Lady in Red' **new**	IBal
	'Lady Isobel Barnett' (v)	EMic IBal NMyG SApp
	laevigata	EGol IBal SApp
	'Lahn' **new**	IBal
	'Lake Hitchock'	EGol IBal
	'Lake Huron' **new**	IBal
	'Lakeside Accolade'	EGol IBal
	'Lakeside Alex Andra' (v) **new**	IBal
	'Lakeside April Snow' (v)	EMic
	'Lakeside Baby Face' (v)	EGol EMic IBal
	'Lakeside Banana Bay' (v)	IBal
	'Lakeside Beach Captain' (v)	EMic
	'Lakeside Black Satin'	EMic IBal NMyG SApp
	'Lakeside Blue Cherub'	EMic IBal
	'Lakeside Breaking News' (v)	EMic IBal
	'Lakeside Butter Ball'	IBal SApp
	'Lakeside Cha Cha' (v)	EGol EMic IBal MWhi NMyG
	'Lakeside Cindy Cee' (v)	IBal
	'Lakeside Coal Miner'	EMic IBal
	'Lakeside Color Blue' **new**	IBal
	'Lakeside Contender'	IBal
	'Lakeside Cupcake' (v)	EMic IBal LRHS
	'Lakeside Cupid's Cup' (v) **new**	IBal
	'Lakeside Dimpled Darling' (v)	EGol
	'Lakeside Dividing Line' (v)	IBal
	'Lakeside Doodad' (v)	IBal
	'Lakeside Down Sized' (v)	EGol EMic IBal
	'Lakeside Dragonfly' (v)	EMic EPfP IBal IPot LRHS NMyG
	'Lakeside Elfin Fire'	EGol EMic IBal
	'Lakeside Fancy Pants' (v) **new**	IBal
	'Lakeside Feather Light' (v)	IBal
	'Lakeside Foaming Sea' **new**	IBal
	'Lakeside Hazy Morn' (v) **new**	IBal
	'Lakeside Hoola Hoop' (v)	IBal
	'Lakeside Iron Man'	IBal
	'Lakeside Jazzy Jane' (v) **new**	IBal
	'Lakeside Kaleidoscope'	EGol EMic IBal
	'Lakeside Keepsake' (v) **new**	IBal
	'Lakeside Legal Tender'	IBal
	'Lakeside Lime Time'	IBal
	'Lakeside Little Gem'	IBal
	'Lakeside Little Tuft' (v)	EGol EMic IBal NMyG
	'Lakeside Lollipop'	EGol EMic EPGN IBal SApp
	'Lakeside Looking Glass'	EMic IBal
	'Lakeside Love Affaire'	EGol EMic WFar
	'Lakeside Maestro'	IBal NLar
	'Lakeside Meadow Ice' (v)	IBal
	'Lakeside Meter Maid' (v)	IBal
	'Lakeside Midnight Miss' **new**	IBal
	'Lakeside Miss Muffett' (v)	EGol EMic IBal
	'Lakeside Neat Petite'	EGol IBal
	'Lakeside Ninita' (v)	EGol EMic EPGN IBal NMyG
	'Lakeside Old Smokey'	IBal
	'Lakeside Paisley Print' (v) **new**	IBal
	'Lakeside Pebbles' **new**	IBal
	'Lakeside Premier'	EGol EMic IBal
	'Lakeside Prophecy Fulfilled' (v) **new**	IBal
	'Lakeside Rhapsody' (v)	EMic IBal
	'Lakeside Ring Master' (v)	IBal
	'Lakeside Ripples'	IBal
	'Lakeside Rocky Top' (v)	IBal
	'Lakeside Roy El' (v)	IBal
	'Lakeside Sassy Sally' **new**	IBal
	'Lakeside Scamp' (v)	EGol EMic
	'Lakeside Shadows' (v)	IBal
	'Lakeside Shoremaster' (v)	IBal
	'Lakeside Sir Logan'	IBal
	'Lakeside Slick Chick' (v) **new**	IBal
	'Lakeside Sparkle Plenty' (v)	IBal
	'Lakeside Spellbinder' (v)	IBal
	'Lakeside Spruce Goose' (v)	EMic IBal
	'Lakeside Storm Watch'	EMic IBal
	'Lakeside Symphony' (v)	EGol EMic
	'Lakeside Tee Ki' (v) **new**	IBal
	'Lakeside Tycoon'	IBal
	'Lakeside Zesty Zeno' (v) **new**	IBal
	'Lakeside Zinger' (v)	EMic IBal
	lancifolia 𝕐H4	CMac EBee ECha EGol ELan EMic GMaP LRHS MRav NGdn NMyG NSti SApp SBod SRms WAul WKif WSHC WTin
I	'Lancifolia Aurea' **new**	EHrv
	'Last Dance' (v)	IBal
	'Laura Z'	IBal
	'Lavender Doll'	IBal
	'Lavender Lace'	IBal
	'Leading Lady'	IBal
	'Leather Sheen'	EGol EMic
	'Leatherneck'	IBal
	'Lederhosen'	EMic IBal
	'Lee Armiger' (*tokudama* hybrid)	EGol
	'Lemon Delight'	EGol EMic EPGN IBal LRHS NMyG NNor WWEG
	'Lemon Frost'	EMic IBal
	'Lemon Juice' **new**	EBee NMyG
	'Lemon Lime'	EGol EMic IBal MHom MNrw NMyG NNor NPro WPat WTin WWEG
	'Lemon Twist'	IBal
	'Lemonade'	IBal
	'Leola Fraim' (v)	EGol EMic IBal LRHS NMyG
	'Let Me Entertain You'	EMic
	'Leviathan'	EMic
	'Libby'	EMic IBal
	'Liberty'[PBR] (v)	CWGN EMic EPGN GBin IBal LRHS MBri NBro NGdn NMyG NNor SApp WFar
	'Li'l Abner' (v)	IBal
*	***lilacina***	WFar
	'Lily Blue Eyes' **new**	EMic
	'Lily Pad'	EPGN
	'Lime Fizz'	EGol EMic IBal SApp

'Lime Piecrust' EGol IBal
'Lime Shag' (*sieboldii* f. *spathulata*) EGol IBal
'Limey Lisa' EGol EMic EPGN IBal WWEG
'Linda Sue' (v) IBal
'Lionheart' (v) **new** EMic IBal
'Little Aurora' (*tokudama* hybrid) EGol EMic IBal WWEG
'Little Bit' IBal
'Little Black Scape' EGol EMic IBal LSRN MHom NEgg NGdn NHol NLar NPro
'Little Blue' (*ventricosa*) EGol EMic
'Little Bo Beep' (v) EGol IBal WWEG
'Little Boy' IBal
'Little Caesar' (v) EGol EMic EPGN IBal
'Little Devil' EMic IBal
'Little Doll' (v) EGol IBal
'Little Jay' (v) EGol EMic IBal SApp
'Little Maddie' **new** EGol EMic
'Little Miss Magic' IBal
'Little Miss Muffett' **new** EGol
'Little Razor' EGol IBal
'Little Red Joy' EGol EMic IBal
'Little Red Rooster' EMic EPGN IBal NGdn NNor WWEG
'Little Stiffy' EGol EMic SApp
'Little Sunspot' (v) EGol EMic EPGN NHar
'Little Treasure' (v) **new** EGol EMic
'Little White Lines' (v) EGol EMic EPGN GKev IBal
'Little Willie' (v) EGol
'Little Wonder' (v) EGol EMic EPGN IBal WWEG
'Lizard Lick' IBal
'Lollapalooza' (v) IBal
'London Fog' (v) IBal
'Lonesome Dove' (v) EMic
longipes EGol SApp
- B&SWJ 10806 WCru
'Lothar the Giant' IBal
'Louisa' (*sieboldii*) (v) LRHS
'Love Pat' ♀H4 CCon EGol EMic EPGN EPfP GAbr GBin IBal LRHS LSRN MAvo MRav NGdn NLar NMyG NNor SApp WCAu
'Lovely Loretta' IBal
'Loyalist'PBR (v) EMic LRHS NGdn NLar SApp SPoG WFar WWEG
'Lucy Vitols' (v) EGol EMic IBal
'Lullabye' EMic
'Lunar Eclipse' (v) CHid EMic IPot NEgg SApp WWEG
'Machete' IBal
'Mack the Knife' EMic IBal
'Maekawa' EGol EMic
'Magic Fire'PBR (v) EMic EPGN EPfP IBal MNrw
'Magic Island' **new** EMic
'Majesty' EGol EMic IBal MBri NGdn
'Malabar' (v) **new** EMic IBal
'Mama Mia' (v) CWat EGol EMic EPGN EPfP IBal LRHS MBNS MBel NBro NGdn NHol NMyG NWad SBfd
'Manhattan' EMic
'Manzo' (v) EGol
'Maraschino Cherry' EGol EMic EWTr IBal NEgg NMyG SApp
'Marble Rim' (v) EGol IBal
'Mardi Gras' (v) EMic SApp
'Marge' (*sieboldiana* hybrid) EMic
'Margin of Error' (v) EGol EPGN IBal NMyG
'Marginata Alba' misapplied see *H.* 'Albomarginata' (*fortunei*), *H. crispula*
'Marginata Alba' ambig. (v) ECha LPBA NNor
'Marilyn' EGol EMic IBal
'Marilyn Monroe' EMic IBal IPot
'Marmalade on Toast' EMic
'Marquis' (*nakaiana* hybrid) EGol
'Marrakech' EMic
'Mary Joe' EMic IBal
'Mary Marie Ann' (*fortunei*) (v) EGol EMic EPGN IBal
'Masquerade' (v) EGol EMic EPGN IBal NHar SApp SMHy WFar WHal WThu
'Maui Buttercups' EMic IBal SApp
'May' EMic IBal
'Maya' (*fortunei*) (v) EMic IBal
'Medieval Age' (v) **new** IBal
§ 'Mediopicta' (*sieboldii*) EMic IBal
'Mediovariegata' (*undulata*) see *H. undulata* var. *undulata*
'Medusa' (v) EGol EMic IBal
'Memories of Dorothy' EMic IBal
'Mentor Gold' EGol
'Mesa Fringe' (*montana*) EMic
'Mid Afternoon' IBal
'Midas Touch' NEgg NHol NLar NNor
'Middle Ridge' EMic
'Midnight Ride' IBal
'Midwest Gold' MHom SApp
'Midwest Magic' (v) EGol EMic IBal NLar SApp
'Mieke' (v) IBal
'Mighty Mite' **new** EGol
'Mighty Mouse' (v) IBal
'Mikawa-no-yuki' IBal
'Miki' IBal
'Mildred Seaver' (v) EGol EMic GAbr IBal LRHS MHom NMyG
'Millennium' EMic EPGN SApp
'Ming Jade' SApp
'Minnie Bell' (v) EGol IBal
'Minnie Klopping' EMic
minor misapplied f. ***alba*** see *H. sieboldii* var. *alba*
§ ***minor*** Maekawa EBee EGol EPGN GEdr ITim WCot WFar XLum
- B&SWJ 1209 from Korea WCru
- B&SWJ 8775 from Korea WCru
- B&SWJ 11103 from Japan WCru
- from Korea EGol IBal
- Goldbrook form EGol
'Minor' (*ventricosa*) see *H. minor* Maekawa
'Mint Candy' IBal
'Mint Julep' (v) IBal
'Minuet' (v) IBal
'Minuteman' (*fortunei*) (v) CCon EBee ECtt EMic EPGN EPfP IBal IPot LAst MBNS MMuc NGdn NLar NNor NOrc NPnk SApp SBfd WFar WGor WTin WWEG
'Miss Linda Smith' **new** EMic IBal
'Miss Ruby' EMic IBal
'Miss Saigon' (v) IBal
'Miss Tokyo' (v) EMic IBal
'Mississippi Delta' EMic
'Mister Watson' EMic IBal SApp
'Misty Waters' (*sieboldiana*) EMic
'Moerheim' (*fortunei*) (v) EBee EGol EMic EPGN IBal WHal WWEG
'Mohegan' EMic
'Moi Marleen' **new** IBal
N ***montana*** EGol EMic GBin
- B&SWJ 4796 WCru
- B&SWJ 5585 WCru
- 'Hida-no-hana' (v) IBal

- f. ***macrophylla***	EGol IBal
'Moon Glow' (v)	EGol EMic
'Moon River' (v)	EGol EMic EPGN SApp
'Moon Shadow' (v)	EGol
'Moon Split' (v) **new**	EMic NGdn
'Moon Waves'	EGol
'Moonbeam'	EShb
'Moongate Flying Saucer' **new**	EMic
'Moonlight' (*fortunei*) (v)	EGol EMic EPGN GMaP IBal LRHS NNor SApp
'Moonlight Sonata'	EGol EMic IBal
'Moonstruck'PBR (v)	ECtt EGol EMic EPGN IBal
'Moorheim'	LRHS
'Morning Light'PBR	EBee EGol EMic EPGN EPfP IBal LBMP MAvo MBNS MBri NBro NGdn NLar NPnk SApp SRkn WBor WFar
'Morning Star' **new**	EMic
'Moscow Blue'	EGol EMic
'Mount Everest'	EMic IBal
'Mount Fuji' (*montana*)	EGol IBal
'Mount Hope' (v)	EGol
'Mount Kirishima' (*sieboldii*)	see *H.* 'Kirishima'
§ 'Mount Royal' (*sieboldii*)	IBal
'Mount Tom' (v)	EGol EMic IBal
'Mountain Snow' (*montana*) (v)	CWat EGol EMic LRHS SApp
'Mountain Sunrise' (*montana*)	EGol
'Mourning Dove' (v)	EMic IBal
'Mr Big'	IBal NGdn
'Mrs Minky'	EBee EMic EPGN LRHS
'Muffie' (v)	EMic IBal
'Munchkin' (*sieboldii*)	WPat
'My Claire' (v)	IBal
'My Cup of Tea'	IBal
'My Friend Nancy' (v)	EGol
'Mystic Star'	IBal
'Naegato'	SApp
nakaiana	EBee EMic IBal
'Nakaimo'	IBal NHol
'Nameoki'	NHol
'Nana' (*ventricosa*)	see *H. minor* Maekawa
'Nancy'	EMic
§ 'Nancy Lindsay' (*fortunei*)	CTri EMic IBal NGdn NLar SApp
'Nancy Minks'	EMic IBal
'Neat and Tidy'	IBal
'Neat Splash' (v)	CWCL NBir WWEG
'Neat Splash Rim' (v)	IBal
'Neelix' **new**	IBal
'Nemesis' (v)	IBal
'Neptune'	EMic
'Niagara Falls'	CCon EGol EMic IBal NGdn
'Nicola'	EGol EMic EPGN IBal MHom
'Night before Christmas' (v)	CCon CHid EBee EGol EMic EPGN LPBA LRHS MNrw NBro NCGa NEgg NGdn NHol NMyG NNor NPnk SApp WHoo WWEG
'Night Life'	EMic IBal
nigrescens	EGol EMic EPGN IBal LRHS NMyG
- 'Cally White'	GCal IBal NCGa
'Niko' (v) **new**	IBal
'Nokogiryama'	EMic
'None Lovelier' (v)	EMic IBal
'Nor'easter' (v)	IBal
'North Hills' (*fortunei*) (v)	EAEE EBee EGol EMic IBal MHom NBir NGdn SWvt WWEG
'Northern Exposure' (*sieboldiana*) (v)	CCon EGol EMic IBal NCGa NGdn NMyG SApp
'Northern Halo' (*sieboldiana*) (v)	EMic
'Northern Sunray' (*sieboldiana*) (v)	IBal
'Norwalk Chartreuse' **new**	IBal
'Nougat' (v)	IBal
'Nouzang'	IBal
'Nutty Professor' (v)	IBal
'Oberon'	EGol
'Obscura Marginata' (*fortunei*)	see *H. fortunei* var. *aureomarginata*
'Obsession'	EGol IBal
'Ocean Isle' (v)	IBal
'October Sky' **new**	EMic
'Oder'	IBal
'Ogon-chirifu-hime'	IBal
'Ogon-hime-tokudama' **new**	IBal
'Ogon-koba'	IBal
'Oh Cindy' (v) **new**	EMic
'O'Harra'	EGol EMic IBal
'Old Faithful'	EGol EMic
'Old Glory'PBR (v)	ECtt EGol EMic IBal
'Olga's Shiny Leaf'	EGol EMic
'Olive Bailey Langdon' (*sieboldiana*) (v)	EMic IBal SApp
'Olive Branch' (v)	EGol EMic IBal
'Olympic Edger'	EMic IBal
'Olympic Glacier' (v)	EMic IBal SApp
'Olympic Gold Medal'	EMic IBal
'Olympic Silver Medal'	EMic IBal
'Olympic Sunrise' (v)	EMic IBal
'Olympic Twilight' **new**	EMic
'On Stage'	see *H.* 'Chōkō-nishiki'
'On the Border' (v)	IBal
'One Man's Treasure'	EMic EPGN IBal IPot MBel NGdn SApp
'Ooh La La' (v)	IBal
'Ophir'	EMic IBal
'Ops' (v)	EGol EMic IBal
'Orange Crush' (v)	IBal SApp
'Orange Marmalade' (v)	EBee ECtt EMic EPGN IBal LRHS NGdn SApp SBfd
'Oriana' (*fortunei*)	EGol EMic
'Orion's Belt' (v)	IBal
'Osprey' (Tardiana Group)	EGol
'Oxheart'	EMic IBal
'Oze' (v)	IBal
pachyscapa	EMic
'Pacific Blue Edger'	CCon EGol EMic MDev MMuc NGdn NNor SApp WAul WWEG
'Painted Lady' (*sieboldii*) (v) **new**	GKev
'Pamela Lee' (v)	IBal NGdn NMyG
'Pandora's Box' (v)	EGol EPGN GEdr NHar SApp WCot
'Paradigm' (v)	EBee EGol EMic EPGN IBal LRHS NGdn SApp
'Paradise Backstage' (v)	EMic IBal
'Paradise Beach'	EMic IBal
'Paradise Blue Sky' **new**	IBal
'Paradise Expectations' (*sieboldiana*) (v)	EMic IBal SApp
'Paradise Glory'	EMic IBal
'Paradise Gold Line' (*ventricosa*) (v)	IBal
'Paradise Island'PBR (*sieboldiana*) (v)	EMic EPGN IBal MDev NGdn SApp
'Paradise Joyce'PBR	EGol EMic EPGN IBal IPot LRHS NLar NNor SApp WWEG
'Paradise Ocean'	EMic
'Paradise on Fire' (v)	EMic IBal SApp

'Paradise Parade' (v)	IBal
'Paradise Passion' (v)	IBal
'Paradise Power' PBR	EMic
'Paradise Puppet' (*venusta*)	EMic EPGN GKev IBal NMyG NNor SApp WWEG
'Paradise Red Delight' (*pycnophylla*)	EMic IBal
'Paradise Sandstorm'	IBal
'Paradise Standard' (d)	EMic IBal
'Paradise Sunset'	EGol EMic IBal
'Paradise Sunshine'	EMic
'Paradise Surprise' (v)	IBal
'Parhelion'	EMic
'Parky's Prize' (v)	EGol
'Pastures Green'	EGol IBal
'Pastures New'	EGol EMic MHom NMyG SApp WWEG
'Pathfinder' (v)	EGol EMic IBal SApp
'Patricia'	EMic
'Patrician' (v)	EGol EMic EPGN IBal
'Patriot' (v)	Widely available
'Patriot's Fire' (v)	IBal
'Patriot's Green Pride'	IBal
'Paul Revere' (v)	IBal
'Paul's Glory' (v)	EGol EMic EPGN EPfP GMaP IBal IPot LPBA LRHS MBri NBir NGdn NMRc NMyG NNor SApp WFar WWEG
'Peace' (v)	EGol EMic EPGN IBal
'Peacock Strut'	IBal
'Peanut'	EGol EMic IBal
'Pearl Lake'	EBee EGol EMic EPGN IBal MHom NBir NEgg NGdn NHol NLar NMen NMyG NNor SApp SRGP WTin
'Peedee Absinth'	EMic
'Peedee Laughing River' (v)	IBal
'Pelham Blue Tump'	EGol EMic
'Peppermint Cream' (*cathayana*)	IBal
'Peppermint Ice' (v)	EGol EMic IBal
'Percy'	EMic IBal
'Peridot' (Tardiana Group)	IBal
'Permanent Wave'	EGol IBal
'Perry's True Blue'	EMic
'Peter Pan'	EGol EMic IBal
'Peter the Rock'	IBal
'Pete's Dark Satellite'	EMic IBal
'Pewterware'	EMic IBal
'Phantom'	IBal SApp
'Philadelphia'	IBal
'Phoenix'	EGol EMic IBal NLar SApp
'Photo Finish' (v)	EGol EMic
'Phyllis Campbell' (*fortunei*)	see *H.* 'Sharmon'
'Picta' (*fortunei*)	see *H. fortunei* var. *albopicta*
'Piedmont Gold'	CHid EBee EHoe EMic EPGN IBal LHop LRHS SApp WPtf
'Pilgrim' (v)	EBee EGol ELan EMic EPGN IBal LRHS NBro NMyG NRHS SApp WFar
'Pineapple Poll'	EGol EMic EPGN NMyG NNor WTin WWEG
'Pineapple Upside Down Cake' (v)	EMic EPGN IBal NBro NLar NMyG WFar
'Pinky'	IBal
'Pinwheel' (v)	IBal
'Pistache' (v)	EMic IBal
'Pixie Vamp' (v) **new**	EGol EMic
'Pizzazz' (v)	EGol EMic IBal LRHS MHom NGdn NHol NLar NMyG SApp WFar WWEG
plantaginea	EMic IBal LEdu LPla LRHS MHom NMyG SSpi WFar WKif
– var. ***grandiflora***	see *H. plantaginea* var. *japonica*
§ – var. ***japonica*** ♀H4	CAvo ECha EHrv EPGN LRHS MNrw MRav NLar SApp SMrm WCFE WFar WPGP WWEG
'Platinum Tiara' (v)	EGol EMic IBal NBir NMyG
'Plug Nickel'	EMic IBal
'Polar Moon' (v)	IBal
'Pole Cat' (v)	IBal
'Pooh Bear' (v)	EGol EMic
'Popcorn'	EMic IBal SApp
'Popo'	EGol EMic EPGN IBal SApp
'Pot of Gold' **new**	EMic
'Potomac Pride'	EGol EMic EPGN LRHS NMyG SApp
'Powder Blue' (v)	IBal
'Powderpuff'	IBal
'Prairie Glow'	IBal
'Prairie Sky'	EMic IBal MDev NGdn WFar
'Praying Hands' (v)	EGol EMic EPGN EPfP GBin IBal IPot LRHS LSou MBNS NMyG SMrm SPoG WFar WWEG
'Prestige and Promise' (v)	EMic IBal
'Pretty Flamingo'	EMic IBal
'Prima Donna'	EMic
'Primavera Primrose'	SApp
'Prince of Wales'	EMic IBal LRHS LSqu NNor SApp SPoG SRkn
'Princess Anastasia' (v)	IBal
'Proud Sentry' **new**	EMic IPot
'Puck'	EGol
'Punky' (v)	EMic IBal
'Purple Boots'	EMic IBal
'Purple Dwarf'	EGol EMic IBal NLar WCru WHal WWEG
'Purple Glory'	EMic
'Purple Haze'	EBee EMic IBal NCGa NGdn NMyG SHar WCot
'Purple Lady Finger'	IBal WWEG
'Purple Passion'	EGol EMic
'Purple Profusion'	EGol EMic
'Quarter Note' (v)	IBal
'Queen Josephine' (v)	EGol EMic EPGN EPfP IBal IPot LRHS MBNS MHom MMuc NCGa NGdn NMyG SApp SBfd SEND SRGP WFar
'Queen of the Seas'	EMic IBal SApp
'Quill'	EMic
'Quilting Bee'	EGol EMic IBal
'Radiant Edger' (v)	EGol EMic EPGN GCra IBal NHol SBfd WWEG
'Radio Waves'	EMic IBal
'Rain Dancer' **new**	EMic
'Rain Forest'	EMic IBal
'Rainbow's End' (v)	IBal IPot
'Rainforest Sunrise' (v)	ELon EMic IBal LSou NGdn SApp
'Rascal' (v)	EGol EMic
'Raspberries and Cream' (v)	IBal
'Raspberry Sorbet'	EGol EMic EPGN IBal
rectifolia	NNor
– 'Kinbuchi Tachi' (v)	IBal
– 'Ogon Tachi' (v)	EMic IBal
'Red Cadet'	EMic IBal
'Red Dog' **new**	EMic
'Red Dragon'	IBal
'Red Hot Flash' (v)	EMic IBal
'Red Hot Poker'	IBal

	Name	Suppliers
	'Red Neck Heaven' (*kikutii* var. *caput-avis*)	IBal SApp WTin
	'Red October'	ECtt EMic EPGN EPfP GAbr GBin IBal IBoy IPot LEdu LRHS LSou MBNS MBel MPie NGdn NLar NPnk SBfd SPoG WCot WFar WWEG
	'Red Salamander'	EGol EMic IBal
	'Red Sox' **new**	IBal
	'Red Stepper'	EMic
	'Red Wing' (v)	IBal
	'Regal Chameleon'	IBal
	'Regal Rhubarb'	EGol EMic IBal
	'Regal Splendor' (v)	EGol ELon EMic EPGN LRHS MHom NBro NCGa NGdn NHol NMyG NNor SApp WAul WHoo WMnd
	'Regal Supreme' (v) **new**	EMic
	'Reginald Kaye'	EMic
	'Remember Me'[PBR]	CWCL ELan ELon EMic EPGN IBal LRHS LSRN MBNS MBri MDev MPnt NGdn NHol NLar NMyG NNor NWad SApp SMrm WFar WGor WWEG
	'Reptilian'	EGol EMic
	'Resonance' (v)	NGdn NLar
	'Restless Sea'	EMic
	'Reversed' (*sieboldiana*) (v)	EBee EGol ELan EMic EPGN IBal LRHS MDKP NBro NGdn NNor WFar WHal
	'Revolution'[PBR] (v)	EBee EGol EMic EPGN GKev IBal IPot LRHS LSRN MMuc NBro NEgg NGdn NLar NMyG NRHS SApp SPoG WAul WFar WWEG
	'Rhapsody' (*fortunei*) (v)	EGol EMic
	'Rhapsody in Blue'	EGol IBal
	'Rheingold' (v)	IBal
	'Rhinestone Cowboy' (v)	IBal
	'Rhythm and Blues'	IBal
	'Rich Uncle'	IBal
	'Richland Gold' (*fortunei*)	EGol EMic EPGN NMyG
	'Rickrack'	IBal
	'Rim Rock'	EMic
	'Ringtail' **new**	EMic
	'Rippled Honey'	COlW EGol EMic EPGN IBal NMyG NPro SApp
	'Rippling Waves'	EGol EMic
	'Riptide'	EMic
	'Risa'	IBal
	'Rising Sun'	EGol
	'Risky Business'[PBR] (v)	EMic EPGN IBal SMrm
	'Robert Frost' (v)	EGol EMic WTin
	'Robin Hood'	EMic IBal SApp
	'Robin of Loxley' **new**	EMic
	'Robusta' (*fortunei*)	see *H. sieboldiana* var. *elegans*
	'Robyn's Choice' (v)	EMic IBal
	'Rock Island Line' (v)	EMic IBal
	'Rock Princess'	IBal
§	***rohdeifolia*** (v)	LRHS
	- f. ***albopicta***	ELan
	'Roller Coaster Ride'	IBal
	'Ron Damant'	EPGN IBal
	'Rootin'-Tootin'' (v)	IBal
	'Rosedale Golden Goose'	EMic IBal
	'Rosedale Knox'	IBal
	'Rosedale Lost Dutchman'	IBal SApp
	'Rosedale Melody of Summer' (v)	IBal
	'Rosedale Misty Magic' (v)	IBal
	'Rosedale Richie Valens'	IBal
	'Rosedale Spoons'	IBal
	'Rosemoor'	EGol IBal
	'Rotunda'	EGol
	'Rough Waters'	SApp
	'Roxsanne'	EMic
	'Roy Klehm' (v)	EMic IBal
	'Royal Charm'	IBal
	'Royal Flush' (v)	IBal
	'Royal Golden Jubilee'	EMic EPGN IBal NCGa
§	'Royal Standard' ♀H4	Widely available
	'Royal Super'	EPGN
	'Royal Tapestry' (v)	IBal
	'Royal Tiara' (*nakaiana*) (v)	EGol IBal
	'Royalty'	EGol
	rupifraga	EGol IBal
	'Rusty Bee'	IBal
	'Ryan's Big One'	IBal
§	'Sagae' (v) ♀H3-4	CWat EBee EGol EMic EPGN IBal IPot LRHS MBri MHom MNrw NGdn NNor NPnk SApp SDix SPoG WAul WFar WHoo WWEG
	'Saint Elmo's Fire' (v)	EGol EMic EPGN IBal LRHS SApp
	'Saint Paul'	EMic IBal MNrw
	'Saishu-jima' (*sieboldii* f. *spathulata*)	EMic WCru
	'Saishu-yahite-site' (v)	EGol
	'Salute' (Tardiana Group)	EGol EMic
	'Samual Blue'	EGol
	'Samurai' (*sieboldiana*) (v)	EGol EMic IBal IPot MRav NBir NBro NGdn NLar NNor SApp
	'Sandhill Crane' (v)	IBal
	'Sarah Kennedy' (v)	EPGN
	'Sara's Sensation' (v) **new**	IBal
	'Satisfaction' (v)	EMic
	'Savannah'	EGol IBal
	'Sazanami' (*crispula*)	see *H. crispula*
	'Scallion Pancakes' **new**	EMic
	'Schwan'	GBin
	'Scooter' (v)	EGol EMic IBal
	'Sea Beacon' (v)	EGol
	'Sea Bunny'	EGol
	'Sea Dream' (v)	EGol EMic IBal LRHS NEgg NMyG NNor
	'Sea Drift'	EGol
	'Sea Fire'	EGol
	'Sea Frolic'	EGol IBal
	'Sea Gold Star'	EGol NMyG
	'Sea Gulf Stream'	EMic
	'Sea Hero'	EGol
	'Sea Lotus Leaf'	EGol EMic LLWP NLar NNor
	'Sea Monster'	EGol IBal
	'Sea Octopus'	EGol
	'Sea Sapphire'	EGol
	'Sea Thunder' (v)	EGol EMic EPGN
	'Sea Yellow Sunrise'	EGol EMic IBal SApp
	'Second Wind' (*fortunei*) (v)	EGol EMic EPGN NMyG SApp
	'Secret Ambition'[PBR] (v)	EMic
	'Secret Love'	EMic IBal
	'Seducer' (v)	EMic IBal
	'See Saw' (*undulata*)	EGol EMic SApp
	'September Sun' (v)	EGol EMic IBal LRHS NNor
	'Serena' (Tardiana Group)	IBal SApp
	'Serendipity'	EGol EMic GAbr MHom
	'Shade Beauty' (v)	EGol
	'Shade Fanfare' (v) ♀H4	EGol EHoe ELan EMic EPfP IBal LAst LPla LRHS MBNS MRav MWhi NBir NGdn NLar NSti SApp SPer WFar WMnd WTin WWEG

	'Shade Finale' (v)	IBal
	'Shade Master'	EGol EMic IBal
	'Shade Parade' (v)	IBal
	'Shamoa'	SApp
§	'Sharmon' (*fortunei*) (v)	EGol ELon EMic EPGN IBal MBNS NEgg NLar SApp SBfd
	'Sharp Dressed Man'	EMic IBal NGdn
	'Shazaam'	EMic
	'Sheila West'	EMic IBal
	'Shelleys' (v)	EGol IBal
	'Sherborne Profusion' (Tardiana Group)	EMic IBal
	'Sherborne Songbird' (Tardiana Group)	EGol IBal
	'Sherborne Swan' (Tardiana Group)	EGol IBal
	'Sherborne Swift' (Tardiana Group)	EGol EMic LRHS
	'Shere Khan' (v)	EGol
	'Shimmy Shake' **new**	EMic
	'Shining Tot'	EGol LLHF
	'Shiny Penny' (v)	EGol EMic IBal WWEG
	'Shirley Vaughn' (v)	EGol
	'Shogun' (v)	EGol IBal
	'Showboat' (v)	EGol EMic IBal LRHS NMyG
	sieboldiana	CMac CSBt ECha EGol EHrv ELan EMic GCra GMaP LBMP LLWP LRHS LTen MRav MSwo NChi NHol SPlb SRms WFar WMoo WWEG XLum
§	- var. ***elegans*** ♈H4	Widely available
	- 'George Smith'	EMic IBal SApp
	- var. ***mira***	EMic
	- var. ***sieboldiana***	NGdn
	sieboldiana × venusta	NGdn
	sieboldii	CWat MRav
§	- var. ***alba***	EGol IBal
§	- 'Paxton's Original' (v) ♈H4	EGol WWEG
§	- var. ***sieboldii*** f. ***kabitan*** (v)	EGol EMic EPGN LRHS NHar SApp WTin WWEG
	- - f. ***shiro-kabitan*** (v)	EGol EMic EPGN LRHS
	- f. ***spathulata***	EMic
	'Silberpfeil'	EMic IBal
	'Silk Kimono' (v)	EGol
	'Silver Bay'	EMic IBal
	'Silver Bowl'	EGol
	'Silver Crown'	see *H.* 'Albomarginata'
	'Silver Heart' (v) **new**	IBal
	'Silver Lance' (v)	EGol EMic
	'Silver Lining'	IBal
	'Silver Lode' (v)	IBal
	'Silver Moon' **new**	EMic
	'Silver Shadow' (v)	CHid EMic GBin NBir NGdn NHol NNor NWad SApp
	'Silver Spray' (v)	EGol IBal
	'Silver Star' (v) **new**	IBal
	'Silver Threads and Gold Needles' (v)	IBal
	'Silverado' (v)	IBal
	'Silvery Slugproof' (Tardiana Group)	LRHS SApp WWEG
	'Singin' the Blues'	IBal
	'Singing in the Rain' (v)	IBal
	'Sitting Pretty' (v)	EGol EPGN
	'Sky Dancer'	EMic IBal
	'Sleeping Beauty'	CWGN EMic GQue IBal NGdn NMyG SApp
	'Slick Willie'	EGol EMic
	'Slim and Trim'	EGol EMic
	'Small Parts'	EGol EMic IBal
	'Small Sum'	IBal
	'Smooth Sailing' (v)	IBal
	'Snow Cap' (v)	EBee EGol EMic IBal NGdn NLar NNor NPro SApp WWEG
	'Snow Crust' (v)	EGol EMic
	'Snow Flakes' (*sieboldii*)	CMac EGol EPGN EPfP NBro NGdn NLar NPro WFar WWEG
	'Snow Mound'	IBal
	'Snow Mouse'	EGol EMic IBal
	'Snow White' (*undulata*) (v)	EGol IBal
	'Snowbound' (v)	IBal
	'Snowden'	CPrp ECha EGol EMic EPGN ETod GMaP IBal LRHS MWat NBir NGdn NHol NNor SApp SSpi WAul WCru WWEG
	'Snowy Lake' (v)	IBal
	'So Sweet' (v)	COlW EBee ECtt EGol EHoe ELan EMic EPGN EPfP LPBA LRHS MHom MSwo NBro NGdn NHol NMyG NNor SApp SBfd SPad SPoG WFar WWEG
	'Solar Flare'	EGol EMic IBal
	'Something Blue'	EMic
	'Something Different' (*fortunei*) (v)	EGol EPGN
	'Something Else' **new**	EMic
	'Sophistication' (v)	EGol
	'Southern Gold'	EMic
	'Sparkling Burgundy'	EGol EMic
	'Sparky' (v)	EGol IBal
	'Spartacus' (v)	EMic IBal
	'Spartan Glory' (v)	IBal
	'Special Gift'	EGol EMic WWEG
	'Spellbound' (v)	IBal
	'Spilt Milk' (*tokudama*) (v)	EGol EMic EPGN IBal LRHS SApp SPoG WHoo
§	'Spinners' (*fortunei*) (v)	ECha EGol EMic LRHS NNor
	'Spinning Wheel' (v)	EGol
	'Spock's Ears' **new**	IBal
	'Spring Break' (v) **new**	EMic
	'Spring Fling'	EMic IBal
	'Spritzer' (v)	EGol EMic IBal MNrw SApp
	'Squash Casserole'	EGol
	'Squiggles' (v)	EGol
	'Stained Glass'	CBcs ECtt EGol ELon EMic EPGN IBal NGdn NMyG NNor SApp WFar WRHF
	'Star Kissed'	IBal
	'Starburst' stable (v)	IBal
	'Stardust'	IBal
	'Stargate'	IBal
§	'Starker Yellow Leaf'	EMic
	'Starship' (v)	EMic IBal
	'Stenantha Variegated' (*fortunei*) (v)	NHol
	'Step Sister'	EMic IBal
	'Stepping Out' (v)	EMic IBal
	'Stetson' (v)	EMic IBal
	'Stiletto' (v)	Widely available
	'Stimulation'	IBal
	'Stirfry'	EMic
	'Stitch in Time' (v)	IBal
	'Stonewall'	IBal
	'Stormy Dance' **new**	EPGN
	'Striker' (v)	EGol IBal
	'Striptease' (*fortunei*) (v)	CMac EGol EMic EPGN IBal LRHS MBNS MBri MNrw NGdn NHol NLar NPnk SApp WFar WHoo WWEG

'Sugar and Cream' (v)	CWat EGol EMic IBal LRHS NGdn NNor
'Sugar and Spice' (v)	EMic IBal
'Sugar Daddy'	EMic
'Sultana' (v)	EMic IBal WWEG
'Sum and Substance' ♀H4	Widely available
'Sum and Subtle' (v) **new**	EMic IBal
'Sum Cup-o-Joe' (v)	EMic
'Sum it Up' (v)	EMic
'Summer Breeze' (v)	EGol EMic IBal NGdn
'Summer Fragrance'	ECtt EGol EMic LRHS NMyG
'Summer in Georgia'	IBal
'Summer Lovin'' (v)	IBal
'Summer Music' (v)	CWCL EGol EMic EPGN IBal SApp WWEG
'Summer Serenade' (v)	EGol EMic IBal SApp
'Sun Catcher'	EMic
'Sun Glow'	EGol
'Sun Power'	EGol EMic EPfP IBal LRHS MBNS NBro NGdn NLar NMyG NSti SApp SBfd SMrm
'Sun Worshipper'	EMic IBal SApp
'Sundance' (*fortunei*) (v)	EGol
'Sunlight Child'	EGol IBal
'Sunny Smiles' (v) **new**	EMic
'Sunshine Glory'	EGol EMic IBal
'Super Bowl'	EGol
'Super Nova' (v)	EGol EMic GBin IBal SApp SPoG
'Super Sagae'	EMic IBal
'Surprised by Joy' (v)	EGol EMic IBal NNor SApp WWEG
'Susy'	IBal
'Sutter's Mill'	IBal
'Suzuki Thumbnail'	EMic
'Sweet Bo Beep'	EGol LRHS
'Sweet Bouquet'	EMic
'Sweet Home Chicago' (v)	EGol EMic IBal
'Sweet Innocence' (v)	EMic IBal
'Sweet Marjorie'	EGol
'Sweet Standard'	NMyG
'Sweet Sunshine'	EGol EMic
'Sweet Susan'	EGol EMic LPla LRHS LSRN LTen MBNS SApp SPer SWvt
'Sweet Tater Pie'	EGol EMic
'Sweetheart'	EMic
'Sweetie' (v)	EMic IBal LRHS SApp WWEG
'Sweetness'	IBal
'Swirling Hearts'	EGol IBal
'Swizzle Sticks'	IBal
'T. Rex'	EMic SApp
'Tall Boy'	CSev ECha EGol IBal NBir NNor
'Tamborine' (v)	CWat EGol EPGN IBal LRHS NMyG SApp
'Tango'	EMic IBal
'Tappen Zee' (v)	EMic IBal
Tardiana Group	EGol ELan MHom NGdn NHol
'Grey Goose' (Tardiana Group) **new**	EMic
'Just June' (Tardiana Group) (v) **new**	WWlt
'Moody Blues' (Tardiana Group) **new**	EMic
'Sherborne Swallow' (Tardiana Group) **new**	IBal
tardiflora	EBee EGol EPGN IBal SApp WCot WPGP
tardiva	LRHS
'Tattoo'PBR (v)	CWGN EGol EMic EPGN LRHS LSRN MBNS MNrw NLar SApp WWEG
'Tea and Crumpets' (v)	EPGN IBal
'Tea at Betty's'	EPGN
'Teaspoon'	EMic IBal NNor SApp
'Teatime' (v)	EMic IBal
'Teeny-weeny Bikini' (v)	EMic
'Templar Gold'	IBal
'Temple Bells'	EGol
'Temptation'	EMic IBal SApp
'Tenryu'	EGol
'Tequila Sunrise'	IBal
'Terpsichore' **new**	EMic
'Terracotta'	MCri
'Terry Wogan'	EPGN NNor
'Tet-a-Poo'	IBal
'Thai Brass'	SApp
'The King' (v) **new**	IBal
'The Leading Edge' (v)	IBal
'The Queen' (v) **new**	IBal
'The Razor's Edge'	IBal
'The Right One' (v) **new**	IBal
'The Shining'	IBal
'The Twister'	EGol IBal NMyG
'Theo's Blue'	EMic IBal
'Thomas Hogg'	see ***H. undulata*** var. ***albomarginata***
'Thumb Nail'	ECha EGol EMic IBal NNor SApp SCnR
'Thumbelina'	EGol EMic IBal
'Thunderbolt'PBR (*sieboldiana*)	EGol EMic EPGN IBal MBNS NGdn NLar SApp WFar
'Tick Tock' (v)	EMic IBal
'Tickle Me Pink'	EMic IBal
'Tidewater'	IBal
'Time Tunnel' (*sieboldiana*) (v)	EMic IBal
'Tiny Tears'	EGol GAbr IFoB
'Titanic'PBR	EMic IBal
'Toasted Waffles'	WFar
tokudama	EGol EMic IBal MHom NBir NGdn NHol NNor NSti SApp WFar XLum
§ - f. ***aureo-nebulosa*** (v)	EGol EMic EPGN IBal NGdn NSti SRms WMnd
- f. ***flavocircinalis*** (v)	CPrp EGol EMic EPGN GMaP IBal NBro SApp WFar WHoo WMnd
'Toledo' **new**	IBal
'Tom Rex'	IBal
'Tom Schmid' (v)	EGol EMic EPGN IBal NMyG
'Tom Thumb'	EGol EMic IBal SApp
'Topaz'	IBal
'Topscore'	NNor
'Torchlight' (v)	EGol EMic EPGN IBal MHom
tortifrons	EMic IBal
'Tortilla Chip'	IBal
'Tot Tot'	EGol EMic IBal
'Touch of Class'PBR (v)	EMic EPGN IBal NHol NMyG NNor WFar WWEG
'Touchstone' (v)	IBal LRHS NMyG SApp SWvt WWEG
'Toy Soldier'	EMic IBal SApp
'Trail's End'	EMic
'Tranquility' (v)	EMic
'Tremors'	EMic IBal
'Trill'	IBal SApp
'Trixi' (v)	IBal
'Tropical Dancer' **new**	EMic
'True Blue'	EGol EMic IBal SApp WWEG
'Tsugaru Komachi'	EMic
'Tsugaru Komachi Kifukurin' (v)	IBal
'Turning Point'	EGol

	'Tutu'	EGol
	'Twiggie'	EMic
	'Twilight' (*fortunei*) (v)	EGol EMic EPGN IBal LRHS MBNS MBri MDev NGdn NLar SApp SWvt WWEG
	'Twilight Time'	IBal LRHS
	'Twinkle Toes'	EGol EMic IBal
	'Twist of Lime' (v)	EGol EMic GKev IBal LRHS NNor WWEG
	'Ufo' **new**	EMic
	'Ultramarine'	IBal
	'Ultraviolet Light'	EGol
	'Unchained Melody'	IBal
	undulata	GAbr NNor WFar
§	- var. ***albomarginata***	CBcs CMac CSam EBee EGol ELan EMic EPGN EPfP GMaP LRHS LSRN MRav MWat NBid NBir NGdn NLar SBod SPer SRms SWvt WFar WMnd WPtf WTin WWEG XLum
§	- var. ***erromena*** ♀H4	EMic GMaP LPBA NNor WHrl
§	- var. ***undulata*** (v) ♀H4	EBee ELan EPGN EPfP GMaP IBal LPBA LRHS MCot MRav MSwo NEgg NGdn NLar NMyG NNor SPer SPoG WFar WWEG
	- var. ***univittata*** (v) ♀H4	ECha EGol EHrv EMic LAst MHom MWhi NBir NPro WFar WMoo
	'Unforgettable'	EMic IBal SApp
	'Upper Crust' (v)	IBal
	'Urajiro-hachijo' (*longipes* var. *latifolia*)	EGol IBal
	'Urajiro' (*hypoleuca*)	EGol IBal
	'Valentine Lace'	EGol EMic IBal
	'Valley's Cathedral'	IBal
	'Valley's Chute the Chute'	EMic IBal
	'Valley's Glacier' (v)	EMic IBal MDev
	'Valley's Vanilla Sticks'	EMic IBal
	'Van Wade' (v)	EGol EMic IBal
	'Vanilla Cream' (*cathayana*)	EGol EMic
	'Variegata' (*gracillima*)	see *H.* 'Vera Verde'
	'Variegata' (*tokudama*)	see *H. tokudama* f. *aureo-nebulosa*
	'Variegata' (*undulata*)	see *H. undulata* var. *undulata*
	'Variegata' (*ventricosa*)	see *H.* 'Aureomarginata' (*ventricosa*)
	'Variegated' (*fluctuans*)	see *H.* 'Sagae'
	'Velvet Moon' (v)	EMic IBal
	ventricosa ♀H4	CBcs CMac EGol EMic GMaP LPBA MWhi NGdn SGar WFar
	- BWJ 8160 from Sichuan	WCru
	- var. ***aureomaculata***	EGol EMic LRHS NBir NNor NSti WFar
I	'Venucosa'	EGol
	'Venus' (d)	ECtt EHrv EMic IBal LRHS NGdn SApp SMrs SPer WBrk WCot
	'Venus Star'	EGol EMic EPGN IBal NMyG
	venusta ♀H4	CCon EBee ECho EDAr EGol EMic EPGN GCra GEdr IBal LRHS MHer MRav NBid NBir NMen NMyG NNor NRHS NRya NSti SApp SRot WCot WTin WWEG
	- B&SWJ 4389	WCru
	- 'Kin Botan' (v)	GEdr
	- 'Porter'	IBal
	- 'Red Tubes'	IBal
	- ***yakusimensis***	see *H. kikutii* var. *yakusimensis*
§	'Vera Verde' (v)	GCra GQui IBal LRHS NBir NMyG
	'Verdi Valentine'	IBal
	'Verkade's No 1'	IBal
	'Verna Jean' (v)	EGol EMic IBal
	'Veronica Lake' (v)	EGol EMic IBal LRHS NMyG NNor WHal
	'Victory'	EMic IBal
	'Viking Ship'	EMic
	'Vilmoriniana'	EGol EMic IBal
	'Vim and Vigor'	EMic IBal
	'Vina'	IBal
	'Viridis Marginata'	see *H. sieboldii* var. *sieboldii* f. *kabitan*
	'Vulcan' (v)	EMic IBal
	'Wagtail' (Tardiana Group)	EGol EMic IBal
	'Wahoo' (*tokudama*) (v)	EGol
	'War Paint'	EMic EPGN IBal NMyG WFar
	'Warwick Ballerina'	EGol
	'Warwick Comet' (v)	EMic IBal SApp
	'Warwick Curtsey' (v)	EGol EMic IBal
	'Warwick Delight' (v)	EGol IBal
	'Warwick Edge' (v)	EGol EMic IBal
	'Warwick Essence'	EGol EMic
	'Warwick Sheen'	IBal
	'Waukon Glass' **new**	EMic
	'Waukon Thin Ice'	EMic
	'Waukon Water' **new**	EMic
	'Waving Winds' (v)	EGol IBal LRHS
	'Waving Wuffles'	EMic IBal NMyG
	'Wayside Blue'	EMic
	'Wayside Perfection'	see *H.* 'Royal Standard'
	'Weihenstephan' (*sieboldii*)	EGol EMic
	'Well Shaked' (v) **new**	IBal
	'Weser'	EGol
	'Wheaton Blue'	EMic LRHS
	'Whirligig' (v)	EMic
	'Whirling Dervish' (v)	IBal
	'Whirlwind' (*fortunei*) (v)	EGol EMic EPGN GQue IBal IPot LRHS MAvo MBri MNrw MRav NBro NEgg NGdn NMyG NNor NOrc SApp SMrm SPad WAul WMnd WWEG
	'Whirlwind Tour' (v)	EGol IBal SApp
	'Whiskey Sour'	IBal
	'White Bikini' (v)	IBal
	'White Ceiling'	IBal
	'White Christmas' (*undulata*) (v)	EGol EMic EPGN IBal
	'White Dove' (v)	EMic IBal
	'White Edger' **new**	EMic
	'White Fairy' (*plantaginea*) (d)	EMic IBal
	'White Feather' (*undulata*)	CHid CWGN EBee ELon EPfP LRHS NBir NGdn NMyG NNor SBfd
	'White Gold'	EGol IBal
	'White Knight'	IBal
	'White On' (*montana*)	EMic
	'White Ray'	IBal
	'White Triumphator' (*rectifolia*)	EGol EMic GBin IBal
	'White Trumpets'	EMic
	'White Vision'	EGol
	'Wide Brim' (v) ♀H4	Widely available
	'Wiggle Worms' (v)	IBal
	'William Lachman' (v)	NLar
	'Wily Willy'	IBal
	'Wind River Gold'	EGol EMic
	'Windsor Gold'	see *H.* 'Nancy Lindsay'
	'Winfield Blue'	EGol EMic IBal
	'Winfield Gold'	EGol EMic IBal
	'Winfield Mist' (v)	IBal
	'Winsome' (v)	EGol IBal
	'Winter Lightning' (v)	NNor
	'Winter Snow' (v)	EMic IBal SApp
	'Winter Vision' (v) **new**	IBal
	'Winter Warrior' (v) **new**	EMic

'Wintergreen' (v) IBal
'Wogon' (*sieboldii*) EMic GEdr GKev GMaP ITim NMen NSti
'Wogon's Boy' EGol EMic EPGN LRHS WWEG
'Wolverine' (v) EBee ECGP ECtt EGol EHoe EMic EPGN GAbr IBal LRHS LSou MHom NGdn NLBP NMyG SWvt WBrk WCot WWEG
'Woolly Mammoth' (v) IBal
'Wooly Bully' SApp
'Woop Woop' (v) EMic IBal
'World Cup' IBal
'Worldly Treasure' IBal
'Wrinkles and Crinkles' EMic
'Wylde Green Cream' EGol EMic IBal
'Xanadu' (v) IBal
'X-rated' (v) IBal
'Yakushima-mizu' (*gracillima*) EMic IBal NMyG
* ***yakushimana*** NHar NMen
'Yellow Boa' EGol EMic
'Yellow Edge' (*fortunei*) see *H. fortunei* var. *aureomarginata*
'Yellow Edge' (*sieboldiana*) see *H.* 'Frances Williams'
'Yellow River' (v) EGol EMic EPGN IBal LRHS NGdn NMyG NNor SApp
'Yellow Splash' (v) ECha EMic EPGN LRHS MHom NMyG NNor
'Yellow Splash Rim' (v) EGol EMic NCGa
'Yellow Splashed Edged' (v) EMic
'Yellow Submarine' IBal
'Yesterday's Memories' (v) EMic
'Yin' (v) EMic IBal SApp
yingeri EGol SApp WPGP
- B&SWJ 546 WCru
'Zager Blue' EMic
'Zager Green' EMic
'Zager White Edge' (*fortunei*) (v) EGol EMic IBal NMyG SApp WTin
'Zebra Stripes' (v) **new** IBal
'Zitronenfalter' EGol IBal
'Zodiac' (*fortunei*) (v) IBal
'Zounds' EBee ECtt EGol EMic EPfP EShb GBin GKev IBal LRHS MRav NGdn NLar NMyG NOrc NSti SApp SBfd SRms WBor WFar WWEG

Hottonia (*Primulaceae*)

palustris CBen EHon ELan LPBA MSKA MWts NPer SWat

Houstonia (*Rubiaceae*)

caerulea L. ECho
- var. ***alba*** SPlb
- 'Millard's Variety' **new** WIce
longifolia EWes
michauxii 'Fred Mullard' EWes

Houttuynia (*Saururaceae*)

cordata GKev GPoy SBfd SDix SWat WFar WWEG XLum
§ - 'Boo-Boo' (v) CMac EPfP NBro SBfd SMrm WWEG
§ - 'Chameleon' (v) Widely available
- 'Flame' (v) CMac CWCL EBee LRHS MAsh MBri NPri NRHS SBfd SMrm WWEG
- 'Flore Pleno' (d) CBen CMac CRow CWat EHon ELan EPfP LPBA MRav MSCN NBir NPer SIde SPer SPlb SRms SWat WFar WHrl WPnP XLum
- 'Joker's Gold' CMac EBee ECtt EPPr EPfP SMrm SPoG
- 'Pied Piper' CDoC EBee SAga SBfd SPad
- 'Tequila Sunrise' CHEx
- 'Terry Clarke' see *H. cordata* 'Boo-Boo'
- 'Tricolor' see *H. cordata* 'Chameleon'
- Variegata Group (v) LPBA NBro

Hovea (*Papilionaceae*)

celsii see *H. elliptica*
§ ***elliptica*** SPlb
montana SPlb

Hovenia (*Rhamnaceae*)

dulcis CAgr CBcs CMCN EPfP LEdu NLar
- B&SWJ 11024 WCru

Howea (*Arecaceae*)

§ ***belmoreana*** ♀H1 XBlo
§ ***forsteriana*** ♀H1 CCCN NPla XBlo

Hoya (*Apocynaceae*)

§ ***australis*** MOWG
bella see *H. lanceolata* subsp. *bella*
carnosa ♀H1 CBcs EBak EOHP SEND SWal WCot WWFP
- 'Compacta Regalis' (v) NPer
- 'Krinkle 8' NPer
- 'Tricolor' (v) NPer
* ***compacta*** 'Tricolor' NPer
darwinii misapplied see *H. australis*
lacunosa CCCN
§ ***lanceolata*** subsp. ***bella*** ♀H1 CBcs SEND

Huernia (*Apocynaceae*)

barbata LToo
guttata LToo
hislopii LToo
hystrix LToo
leachii LToo
longituba LToo
nouhuysii LToo
procumbens LToo
zebrina LToo

Humata (*Davalliaceae*)

tyermannii CMen EShb ISha WCot WFib
- 'Selcka' CMen

Humea see *Calomeria*

elegans see *Calomeria amaranthoides*

Humulus ✿ (*Cannabaceae*)

lupulus CArn CBcs CRWN EPfP GPoy MNHC NLar NMir SIde WHer
- 'Aureus' ♀H4 Widely available
- 'Aureus' (f) CRHN ELon EOHP GCal GKev SPoG WBor WCot WWFP
* - ***compactus*** GPoy
- 'Fuggle' CAgr GPoy
- 'Golden Tassels' (f) CSPN EBee ELon LBuc LHop LRHS MBri MCoo MGos MHoo MNHC NLar NPri SBfd SEND SMad SPer SPoG
- (Goldings Group) 'Mathons' CAgr
- 'Prima Donna' CAgr LHop MCoo NLar SBfd SCoo SEND SIde SPer SPoG SWvt
- 'Taff's Variegated' (v) EWes MAvo WSHC

- 'Wye Challenger'	CAgr GPoy MHer
- 'Wye Northdown'	CAgr

Hunnemannia (*Papaveraceae*)

fumariifolia	CSpe XSen

Huodendron (*Styracaceae*)

biaristatum	WPGP
tibeticum	EBee WPGP

Hutchinsia see *Pritzelago*

Hyacinthella (*Asparagaceae*)

acutiloba	ECho WCot
dalmatica 'Grandiflora'	ECho
glabrescens	WCot
heldreichii	ECho WCot
hispida	WCot
lazulina	LWst
leucophaea	ECho LWst
lineata	WCot
millingenii	ECho WCot
pallens	ECho
siirtensis	WCot

Hyacinthoides (*Asparagaceae*)

aristidis	ECho WCot
§ ***hispanica***	ECho NBir SEND
- 'Alba'	ECho
- subsp. ***algeriensis***	WCot
- 'Dainty Maid'	ECho WCot
- 'Excelsior'	ECho
- 'Miss World'	ECho WCot
- 'Mount Everest'	ECho
- 'Queen of the Pinks'	ECho WCot
- 'Rosea'	ECho
- 'White City'	ECho WCot
§ ***italica*** ♀H4	CPom ECho WShi
- BS 380	WCot
lingulata **new**	LWst
mauritanica	ECho
§ ***non-scripta***	CAvo CBct CBro CHab CTca CTri ECho EPot GKev LAma LPot LRHS MBel MCot MHer MMuc MWat NBir NMen NMir NPri NRHS SDeJ SEND SPer SRms SVic WHer WShi
- 'Alba'	CAvo ECho MMuc NBir SEND
- 'Backkum's Blue'	NMin
- 'Bracteata'	CNat
- cleistogamous **new**	CNat
- 'Rosea'	ECho MMuc SEND
§ ***vincentina***	WCot

Hyacinthus ✿ (*Asparagaceae*)

amethystinus	see *Brimeura amethystina*
azureus	see *Muscari azureum*
comosus 'Plumosus'	see *Muscari comosum* 'Plumosum'
fastigiatus	see *Brimeura fastigiata*
multi-flowered blue	SDeJ
multi-flowered pink	SDeJ
multi-flowered white	SDeJ
orientalis 'Aiolos'	SPer
- 'Amethyst'	ERCP LAma
- 'Anastasia'	CAvo
- 'Anna Liza'	MBri
- 'Anna Marie' ♀H4	CBro LAma MBri SDeJ
- 'Ben Nevis' (d)	LAma
- 'Blue Giant'	LAma SDeJ
- 'Blue Jacket' ♀H4	CBro LAma MBri SDeJ
- 'Blue Magic'	SDeJ
- 'Blue Pearl' PBR	SDeJ
- 'Blue Star'	LAma SPhx
- 'Carnegie'	CAvo CBro EPfP ERCP LAma SPhx
- 'China Pink'	SDeJ SPer
- 'City of Haarlem' ♀H4	CAvo CBro EPfP LAma MBri SDeJ SPhx
- 'Crystal Palace' (d)	LAma
- 'Delft Blue' ♀H4	CAvo CBro EPfP LAma MBri SDeJ SPer SPhx
- 'Fondant'	LAma SDeJ
- 'General Köhler' (d)	LAma SDeJ
- 'Gipsy Princess'	LAma
- 'Gipsy Queen' ♀H4	EPfP LAma MBri SDeJ WCot
- 'Hollyhock' (d) ♀H4	ERCP LAma SDeJ
- 'Jan Bos' ♀H4	LAma MBri SDeJ SPer
- 'Kronos' **new**	CAvo
- 'Lady Derby'	SDeJ
- 'L'Innocence' ♀H4	CAvo CBro
- 'Miss Saigon' ♀H4	ERCP
- multi-flowered	ERCP SDeJ
- 'Odysseus'	LAma SDeJ
- 'Ostara' ♀H4	LAma MBri
- 'Paul Hermann' ♀H4	SDeJ
- 'Peter Stuyvesant'	EPfP ERCP LAma SDeJ
- 'Pink Pearl' ♀H4	EPfP LAma MBri SDeJ SPhx
- 'Pink Royal' (d)	LAma
- 'Purple Sensation' PBR	CAvo SPhx
- 'Red Magic'	LAma SDeJ
- 'Rosette' (d)	LAma SDeJ
- 'Splendid Cornelia'	CAvo ERCP SDeJ
- 'White Pearl'	LAma MBri SDeJ
- 'Woodstock'	CAvo EPfP ERCP LAma SDeJ SPer SPhx

Hydrangea ✿ (*Hydrangeaceae*)

angustipetala	see *H. scandens* subsp. *chinensis* f. *angustipetala*
anomala subsp. ***anomala*** BWJ 8052 from China	WCru
- - HWJK 2065 from Nepal	WCru
- - 'Winter Glow'	WCru WFar
- subsp. ***glabra*** B&SWJ 6804	WCru
- - 'Crûg Coral'	WCru
§ - subsp. ***petiolaris*** ♀H4	Widely available
- - B&SWJ 5457	WCru
- - B&SWJ 5996 from Yakushima	WCru
- - B&SWJ 6081	WCru
§ - - var. ***cordifolia***	NLar
- - - B&SWJ 11487	WCru
§ - - - 'Brookside Littleleaf'	GKin IDee MBri NLar WFar
- - dwarf	see *H. anomala* subsp. *petiolaris* var. *cordifolia*
- - 'Firefly' (v) **new**	WPat
* - - var. ***minor*** B&SWJ 5991	WCru
- - 'Mirranda'	CBcs CRHN EPfP NBro SGol SPoG SWvt
* - - var. ***tiliifolia***	EBee LRHS WFar WSHC
- - - B&SWJ 4400	WCru
- - - B&SWJ 8497	WCru
- - 'Yakushima'	WCru
* - subsp. ***quelpartensis*** B&SWJ 8799	WCru
- Semiola = 'Inovalaur' PBR	EBee LLHF LRHS SBfd SGol SKHP SLim WPGP
- 'Winter Surprise'	CSpe MTPN
§ ***arborescens***	CArn CPLG MRav WFar WPGP

- 'Annabelle' ♀H4 — Widely available
- 'Bounty' — MAsh WPat
§ - subsp. ***discolor*** — LEdu WKif WPat
- - 'Sterilis' — GBin GGGa SHyH WPGP WPat
- 'Grandiflora' ♀H4 — CBcs EBee ELan EPfP LSRN MSwo NBro NEgg WPGP
- 'Hayes Starburst'PBR — CMil CWGN EBee GGGa LLHF LRHS MAsh MWat SCoo SHyH SKHP SPoG SSpi WPGP WPat
- 'Hills of Snow' — IVic NLar
- Incrediball = 'Abetwo' **new** — LRHS MBlu SPoG
§ - Invincibelle Spirit = 'Ncha1' **new** — LRHS MBlu SLon SPoG
- 'Invincible Spirit' — see *H. arborescens* Invincibelle Spirit
- 'Picadilly' — NLar
- 'Pink Pincushion' — NLar
- 'Puffed Green' — NLar
- subsp. ***radiata*** — EBee LRHS MRav SPoG WCru WPGP
- - 'Samantha' — EPfP LRHS WPGP
- 'Ryan Gainey' **new** — MPkF
- 'Vasterival' — NLar
- 'Wesser Falls' — CMil
- White Dome = 'Dardom'PBR — NBro
aspera — CMac CTri EUJe SHyH SLon SSpi SSta WCru WKif WPGP
- HWJCM 452 — WCru
- from Gongshan, China — CMil CPLG SMad WPGP
- 'Anthony Bullivant' — EBee GKin IArd LRHS NLar SHyH SKHP WKif WPat
- 'Bellevue' **new** — IVic
- Kawakamii Group — CGHE CHEx CMil CPLG CSpe EBee ESwi EWTr GBin LRHS NCGa NLar SGol SKHP WCru WPGP
- - B&SWJ 3456 — WCru
- - B&SWJ 3462 — WCru
- - B&SWJ 6702 — WCru
- - B&SWJ 6714 — WCru
- - B&SWJ 6827 — WCru
- - B&SWJ 7101 — WCru
- - 'August Abundance' — WCru
- - 'Formosa' — WCru
- - 'Maurice Mason' — CPLG
- - 'September Splendour' — WCru
- Kawakamii Group × ***involucrata*** — WPGP
- 'Macrophylla' ♀H3 — CWib EBee EPfP EWTr GCal IVic MBri MGos MRav SHil SHyH SPer WCru WFar WPGP
- 'Mauvette' — CMil EPfP LRHS LTen MBlu NBro NLar SGol SPer SSpi WCru
- 'Peter Chappell' — CMil CPLG LRHS WPat
§ - subsp. ***robusta*** — CPLG SLPl WCru WPGP
- - GWJ 9430 — WCru
- - WWJ 11888 — WCru
- 'Rocklon' — CMil NLar WCru
- 'Rosthornii' — see *H. aspera* subsp. *robusta*
- 'Sam MacDonald' — CPLG LRHS NLar SKHP SSpi WPGP WPat
§ - subsp. ***sargentiana*** ♀H3 — CBcs CDul CPLG EBee ELan ELon EPfP EUJe IArd LRHS LSRN MBlu MBri MCot MGos MRav NBir NBro NEgg NLar SHil SHyH SMad SPer SSpi SSta WCru WFar WKif WPGP
- - large-leaved — WCru WPat
- subsp. ***strigosa*** — CDul CPLG EPfP LRHS SHyH SSpi WCru WPGP WPat
- - B&SWJ 8201 — WCru
- - HWJ 653 — WCru
- - HWJ 737 — WCru
- - from Gong Shan, China — CGHE EBee
- 'Taiwan Pink' — EPfP IArd NLar
- 'Velvet and Lace' — LRHS MBri NLar SHil
§ - Villosa Group ♀H3 — Widely available
cinerea — see *H. arborescens* subsp. *discolor*
'Cohhii' — ECre
'Garden House Glory' — CGHE WPGP
glabrifolia — see *H. scandens* subsp. *chinensis*
glandulosa B&SWJ 4031 — WCru
'Glyn Church' **new** — WPGP
aff. ***gracilis*** B&SWJ 3942 — WCru
§ ***heteromalla*** — CGHE CMHG GGGa SLPl WPGP
- B&SWJ 2142 from India — WCru
- B&SWJ 2602 from Sikkim — WCru
- BWJ 7657 from China — WCru
- GWJ 9337 from Sikkim — WCru
- HWJ 938 from Vietnam — WCru
- HWJCM 180 — WCru
- HWJK 2127 from Nepal — WCru
- SBEC — GGGa
- Bretschneideri Group — EBee EPfP GQui SHyH WCru WFar WPGP
- 'Fan Si Pan' — WCru
- 'Nepal Beauty' — EBee EUJe IVic SGol WPGP
- 'Snowcap' — EPfP GQui IArd LRHS NLar SHyH SKHP SLPl SSpi WPGP
- f. ***xanthoneura*** 'Wilsonii' — WKif
hirta B&SWJ 5000 — WCru
- B&SWJ 11022 — WCru
indochinensis — CPLG
- B&SWJ 8307 — WCru
- B&SWJ 11717 — WCru
* - f. ***purpurascens*** KWJ 12233B **new** — WCru
integerrima — see *H. serratifolia*
integrifolia B&SWJ 022 — WCru
- B&SWJ 6967 — NLar WCru
involucrata — EPfP LLHF LRHS MBri MMHG NRHS SBrt SHil SHyH
- B&SWJ 4790 — WCru
- dwarf — WCru
- 'Hortensis' (d) ♀H3-4 — CMil EPfP MRav NLar SMad SSpi WCru WKif WPGP WSHC
- 'Mihara-kokonoe' — WPGP
- 'Multiplex' — WCru
- 'Oshima' **new** — WPGP
- 'Plena' (d) — EBee GGGa LRHS MRav NLar SSta WCru WFar WPGP
- 'Sterilis' — CMil WCru
- 'Viridescens' — LLHF LRHS WCru WPGP
- 'Yohraku-tama' **new** — WPGP
- 'Yokudanka' (d) — GQui MAsh NLar WPGP
kawagoeana var. ***grosseserrata*** B&SWJ 11500 — WCru
kwangsiensis B&SWJ 11717 — WCru
- WWJ 11609 — WCru
lingii B&SWJ 11790 — WCru
lobbii — see *H. scandens* subsp. *chinensis*
longifolia B&SWJ 6883 — WCru
- CWJ 12413 — WCru
longipes — CMil CPLG GQui WCru WPGP
- var. ***fulvescens*** B&SWJ 8188 — WCru
luteovenosa — WCru
- B&SWJ 5647 — WCru

	- B&SWJ 5929	WCru
	- B&SWJ 6220	WCru
	- B&SWJ 6317	WCru
	macrophylla 'AB Green Shadow'PBR	MAsh MMHG SPoG
	- 'Adria' (H)	NLar SHyH
	- 'Aduarda'	see *H. macrophylla* 'Mousmée'
	- 'All Summer Beauty' (H)	ELon MAsh
	- Alpen Glow	see *H. macrophylla* 'Alpenglühen'
§	- 'Alpenglühen' (H)	CBcs CPLG CSBt ELan IVic LRHS SHyH SLim
	- 'Altona' (H) ♀H3-4	CBcs EBee EPfP GGGa IArd LRHS MAsh MGos MRav NBir NLar SHyH SPer
	- 'Amethyst' (H/d)	CGHE
	- 'Ami Pasquier' (H) ♀H3-4	CDoC CMac COlW CSBt CTri EBee ELan EPfP IVic LRHS LSRN MMuc MRav MSwo NEgg SCoo SEND SGar SHyH SLim SSpi SWvt
*	- 'Aureomarginata' (v)	SHyH WCot
	- 'Ave Maria' (H)	GGGa MAsh
§	- 'Ayesha' (H)	Widely available
	- 'Bachstelze' (Teller Series) (L)	IVic MAsh WPGP
	- 'Bavaria' (H) **new**	WFar
	- 'Beauté Vendômoise' (L)	CGHE LRHS NLar SHyH SSpi WPGP
	- 'Bela'PBR (H)	LRHS
	- 'Benelux' (H)	CBcs
	- 'Bicolor'	see *H. macrophylla* 'Harlequin'
	- 'Black Steel Zambia' (H) **new**	SLon
	- 'Black Steel Zebra' (H) **new**	SLon
§	- 'Blauer Prinz' (H)	CSam MAsh SHyH
§	- 'Bläuling' (Teller Series) (L)	CDoC EPfP GKin LAst LSRN MGos SBfd SHyH
§	- 'Blaumeise' (Teller Series) (L)	CDoC CMHG ELon EPfP GGGa LRHS LTen MAsh MBri MDKP MGos MRav NEgg SCoo SHyH SLim SLon SPoG SSpi SWvt WPGP
	- 'Blue Bonnet' (H)	CDul EPfP LRHS LSRN MRav SHyH SPer
	- Blue Butterfly	see *H. macrophylla* 'Bläuling'
	- Blue Prince	see *H. macrophylla* 'Blauer Prinz'
	- Blue Sky	see *H. macrophylla* 'Blaumeise'
	- Blue Tit	see *H. macrophylla* 'Blaumeise'
	- 'Blue Wave'	see *H. macrophylla* 'Mariesii Perfecta'
	- Bluebird	see *H. macrophylla* 'Bläuling'
	- 'Bluebird' misapplied	see *H. serrata* 'Bluebird'
§	- 'Blushing Bride'PBR	GKin LBuc MAsh NPri SLon SPoG
	- 'Bodensee' (H)	LTen MBri MMuc SEND SHyH
	- 'Bouquet Rose' (H)	CWib ECtt LBMP MMuc SEND SHyH
	- 'Brestenburg' (H)	MAsh
	- 'Bridal Bouquet' (H)	CDoC
	- 'Brügg' (H)	EBee LRHS MAsh SHyH SLim SPer WPGP
	- 'Buchfink' (Teller Series) (L)	SHyH
	- Cardinal	see *H. macrophylla* 'Kardinal' (Teller Series)
§	- 'Cardinal Red' (H)	ECre EPfP
	- 'Cendrillon' (H) **new**	CMil
	- 'Chaperon Rouge' (H)	LRHS
	- 'Colour Fantasy' (H)	MBrN
	- 'Cordata'	see *H. arborescens*
	- 'Dandenong' (L)	GQui MAsh
	- 'Dart's Romance'	SHyH
	- 'Dart's Song'	NLar
	- 'Deutschland' (H)	CTri
	- Dolce Gipsy = 'Dolgip' (L) **new**	EPfP
	- Dolce Kiss = 'Dolkis' (L) **new**	EPfP
	- 'Domotoi'	see *H. macrophylla* 'Setsuka-yae'
	- Dragonfly	see *H. macrophylla* 'Libelle'
	- 'Eldorado' (H)	SHyH
	- Endless Summer = 'Bailmer' (H)	EPfP LBuc LRHS MAsh MGos NPri SPoG
	- Endless Summer Blushing BridePBR	see *H. macrophylla* 'Blushing Bride'
	- Endless Summer Twist-n-Shout = 'Piihm-I'	EPfP LBuc LRHS
§	- 'Enziandom' (H)	CBcs CPLG CSBt MAsh SHyH WPGP
	- 'Etoile Violette'	LRHS MAsh
	- 'Europa' (H) ♀H3-4	CBcs CPLG LRHS SHyH
	- 'Fantasia'PBR	NPnk
§	- 'Fasan' (Teller Series) (L)	MAsh
	- Firelight	see *H. macrophylla* 'Leuchtfeuer'
	- Fireworks	see *H. macrophylla* 'Hanabi'
	- Fireworks Blue	see *H. macrophylla* 'Jōgasaki'
	- Fireworks Pink	see *H. macrophylla* 'Jōgasaki'
	- Fireworks White	see *H. macrophylla* 'Hanabi'
	- Forever and Ever = 'Early Sensation' (Forever and Ever Series) (H)	CMac CMil CTrC ECrN GKin LBuc LLHF
	- 'Forever Pink' (H)	GGGa MAsh MWat NLar
§	- 'Frau Fujiyo' (Lady Series) (H)	CPLG CTrC
§	- 'Frau Katsuko' (Lady Series) (H)	SPer
§	- 'Frau Mariko' (Lady Series) (H)	MRav
§	- 'Frau Nobuko' (Lady Series) (H)	CTrC
§	- 'Frau Taiko' (Lady Series) (H)	SPer
	- 'Frillibet' (H)	CAbP MRav NLar
	- 'Ganku Bo Chokens' (H) **new**	WCot
	- 'Gartenbaudirektor Kühnert' (H)	SHyH
§	- 'Générale Vicomtesse de Vibraye' (H) ♀H3-4	CDoC CDul COlW CTri EBee EPfP LRHS MAsh SHyH SLim SPer SSpi
	- Gentian Dome	see *H. macrophylla* 'Enziandom'
	- 'Geoffrey Chadbund'	see *H. macrophylla* 'Möwe'
	- 'Gerda Steiniger' (H)	SHyH
	- 'Gertrud Glahn' (H)	SHyH WFar
	- 'Gimpel' (Teller Series) (L)	MAsh
	- 'Glowing Embers' (H)	IArd
	- Goldrush = 'Nehyosh' (v)	CDul CMil EBee LRHS NEgg SBfd SLim
	- 'Goliath' (H)	EPfP
§	- 'Grant's Choice' (L)	NBro SHyH
	- Great Star = 'Blanc Bleu'	EBee EPfP LRHS LSRN MAsh SBfd SLim WFar
	- 'Hamburg' (H)	CTri EBee ECtt EPfP MGos SDix SHyH SLim WFar
§	- 'Hanabi' (L/d)	CBcs CDoC CMil ECre LRHS MBlu NLar SHyH
§	- 'Harlequin' (H)	GGGa WCot
	- 'Harry's Red' (H)	MAsh
	- 'Hatsu-shime' (L)	NLar
	- 'Heinrich Seidel' (H)	CBcs CTri SHyH WMoo
	- 'Hobella'PBR (Hovaria Series)	MGos
	- 'Hobergine'PBR (Hovaria Series) (H)	SHyH

	Name	Suppliers
	- 'Holehird Purple'	MAsh
	- 'Homigo'PBR (Hovaria Series) (H)	SHyH
	- 'Izu-no-hana' (L/d)	CBcs CMil ELon LHop MAsh MBlu NLar SHyH SUsu WBor WPGP
	- 'James Grant'	see *H. macrophylla* 'Grant's Choice'
	- 'Jofloma'	NLar
§	- 'Jōgasaki' (L/d)	CBcs CMil CPLG LRHS MAsh MBlu NLar SDys SHyH WPGP
	- 'Joseph Banks' (H)	CBcs CTri SHyH
	- 'Kardinal'	see *H. macrophylla* 'Cardinal Red' (H)
§	- 'Kardinal' (Teller Series) (L)	MAsh SGol
	- 'King George' (H)	CBar CBcs CDoC CDul CSBt EBee EPfP LRHS MGos MMuc NEgg NHol SBfd SEND SGol SHyH SLim SPer SPoG SWvt WFar WMoo
§	- 'Klaveren'	CMil GGGa MAsh NBro SHyH
	- 'Kluis Superba' (H)	CBcs CTri SHyH
	- 'La France' (H)	COlW CTri IVic LRHS SBfd SHyH SLim WFar
	- 'Lady Fujiyo'	see *H. macrophylla* 'Frau Fujiyo'
	- 'Lady in Red' (L)	CMil LRHS SPoG
	- Lady Katsuko	see *H. macrophylla* 'Frau Katsuko'
	- 'Lady Mariko'	see *H. macrophylla* 'Frau Mariko'
	- 'Lady Nobuko'	see *H. macrophylla* 'Frau Nobuko'
	- 'Lady Taiko Blue'	see *H. macrophylla* 'Frau Taiko'
	- 'Lady Taiko Pink'	see *H. macrophylla* 'Frau Taiko'
	- 'Lanarth White' (L) ♀H3-4	CBar CBcs CDoC CPLG CSBt CTri EBee ECre ELan EPfP GGGa LBMP LRHS MAsh MMuc MSwo NLar SBod SEND SHyH SLPl SLim SPer SRms SSpi SWvt WBor WKif WPGP
	- 'Lemon Wave' (L/v)	NLar
§	- 'Leuchtfeuer' (H)	ELon LRHS MGos SHyH WMoo
§	- 'Libelle' (Teller Series) (L)	CBcs CDoC CMil EPfP GGGa LRHS MGos MRav NEgg NLar SBfd SGol SHyH SLim SPer SSpi
	- 'Lilacina'	see *H. macrophylla* 'Mariesii Lilacina'
	- 'Love You Kiss'PBR (Hovaria Series) (L)	CBcs CMil LBuc LRHS NLar SCoo SHyH SPoG SRGP WCot
§	- 'Maculata' (L/v)	ELan GQui WGwG
	- 'Madame A. Riverain' (H)	NLar SHyH
	- 'Madame Emile Mouillère' (H) ♀H3-4	Widely available
	- Magical Jade = 'Hortmaja' (H) **new**	EPfP WCot
	- Magical Ocean = 'Hortmoc' (H) **new**	WCot
	- 'Maréchal Foch' (H)	CTri NLar
	- 'Mariesii' (L)	CDoy CMHG CTrC CTri ELan LRHS MSwo NLar SDix SHyH SPer
§	- 'Mariesii Grandiflora' (L) ♀H3-4	EPfP LRHS NBro SBfd SEND SHyH SPer SRms WFar WMoo
§	- 'Mariesii Lilacina' (L) ♀H3-4	EPfP MMuc SEND SHyH SLon SPer SSpi WMoo
§	- 'Mariesii Perfecta' (L) ♀H3-4	Widely available
	- 'Mariesii Variegata' (L/v)	CWib
	- 'Masja' (H)	CBar EBee ELon GKin IArd IVic LAst MAsh MGos MMuc MRav MSwo NBro NLar SEND SGol SHyH SLim WBor
	- 'Mathilde Gütges' (H)	CDoC
	- 'Max Löbner' (H)	SHyH
	- 'Merveille Sanguine' (H)	Widely available
	- 'Messalina' (L)	MAsh SHyH
	- 'Mirai'PBR (H)	CBcs ESwi SHyH WCot WPGP
	- 'Miss Belgium' (H)	CMac CTri GKin MAsh
§	- 'Mousmée' (L)	IArd SHyH SSpi
§	- 'Möwe' (L) ♀H3-4	CBcs CDoC CMil CPLG EBee ECtt ELon EPfP LHop LSRN MAsh MMuc NLar SCoo SDix SEND SGol SHyH SLim SPer SRms SSpi SSta WPat
	- 'Mrs W.J. Hepburn'	CSBt SHyH SPer
§	- 'Nachtigall' (Teller Series) (L)	IVic MAsh SHyH WPGP
	- 'Nanping'PBR (Sturdy Series) (L)	EPfP
	- 'Niedersachsen' (H)	CDoC CTri MRav SHyH
	- Nightingale	see *H. macrophylla* 'Nachtigall'
	- 'Nigra' (H) ♀H3-4	CBcs CMac CPLG CWib EBee ELan ELon EPfP IFoB LRHS MAsh MBri MGos MMuc MRav MSCN NBro NLar SDix SEND SHyH SLim SPer WFar WGrn WGwG WPGP WPat
	- 'Nikko Blue' (H)	CBcs EPfP GKin SEND SHyH
	- var. ***normalis*** (L)	CPLG
§	- 'Nymphe' (H)	SHyH
	- 'Oregon Pride' (H)	GGGa MAsh WFar WPGP
	- 'Otaksa' (H)	NLar
	- 'Papagei' (Teller Series)	SPer
	- 'Parzifal' (H) ♀H3-4	CDul GGGa SHyH
	- 'Pax'	see *H. macrophylla* 'Nymphe'
	- 'Pfau' (Teller Series) (L)	CMil ELon MAsh SHyH
	- Pheasant	see *H. macrophylla* 'Fasan'
	- 'Pia' (H)	CDoC CMil CPLG ELan GGGa LBMP LBuc LRHS MAsh MGos MRav SHyH SMad SPer SRms WBor WCru WFar WGrn
	- Pigeon	see *H. macrophylla* 'Taube'
	- 'Pirate's Gold'	CMil EBee EHoe ELon GGGa WFar WHar WMoo
	- 'Prinses Beatrix' (H)	SHyH
	- 'Quadricolor' (L/v)	CHll CMac CPLG EHoe GCal MGos MRav SDix SGar SHyH SLim SPer SPlb SRms WCot WSHC
	- 'Queen Elizabeth' (H)	GKin
	- 'R.F. Felton' (H)	SHyH
	- 'Red Baron'	see *H. macrophylla* 'Schöne Bautznerin'
	- 'Red Red' (H)	MAsh
	- Redbreast	see *H. macrophylla* 'Rotkehlchen'
	- 'Regula' (H)	SHyH
	- 'Renate Steiniger' (H)	CBar LRHS LTen MGos MMuc MRav SEND SHyH
	- 'Romance'	LBuc WCot
	- 'Rosea'	MCri
	- 'Rosita' (H)	MAsh NBir WFar
§	- 'Rotkehlchen' (Teller Series) (L)	CDoC EPfP NEgg SLim SPlb SPoG SWvt
	- 'Rotschwanz' (Teller Series) (L)	CMil EBee LLHF LRHS MAsh SHyH WPGP WPat
	- 'Sabrina'PBR (H)	CBcs CMil MBri MGos MWat SPoG
	- 'Salsa'	CMil MAsh MBri MWat
	- 'Sandra' (Dutch Ladies Series) (L)	CBcs CMil ELon
	- 'Schneeball' (H)	MAsh SHyH
§	- 'Schöne Bautznerin'	LRHS MWat NCGa SHyH SLim WMoo
	- 'Sea Foam' (L)	MGos NLar
	- 'Selina'	CBcs EPfP LAst LLHF LSRN MBri MDKP SCoo SPoG
	- 'Selma'PBR (Dutch Ladies Series) (L)	CBcs MBri

§ - 'Setsuka-yae' (L/d) CMil NLar
- 'Shakira' (H) new SPer
- 'Sheila' (Dutch Ladies Series) (L) CBcs EPfP LSRN MBri SPoG
- 'Sibilla' (H) SPlb
- 'Sindarella' MBri
- Sister Therese see *H. macrophylla* 'Soeur Thérèse'
§ - 'Soeur Thérèse' (H) CBar EBee MAsh MMuc NLar SEND SGol SWvt WGwG
- 'Soraya'PBR (Dutch Ladies Series) (L) CBcs
- 'Sumida-no-hanabi' (L/d) WPGP
§ - 'Taube' (Teller Series) (L) CBcs CDoC CMHG CPLG EPfP GQui MAsh MGos SCoo SHyH SPoG SWvt
- 'Teller Pink' see *H. macrophylla* 'Taube'
- 'Teller Red' see *H. macrophylla* 'Rotkehlchen'
N - Teller variegated see *H. macrophylla* 'Tricolor'
N - Teller Weiss see *H. macrophylla* 'Libelle'
- var. ***thunbergii*** see *H. serrata* var. *thunbergii*
- 'Tivoli' (H) new WFar
- 'Tokyo Delight' (L) ♀H3-4 CGHE CMil CPLG LRHS MAsh SDys SHyH WPGP
§ - 'Tricolor' (L/v) CBcs CDoC CDul CTri ELon LAst LRHS MGos SHyH SLon SPer WFar WMoo
- 'Variegata' see *H. macrophylla* 'Maculata'
- 'Veitchii' (L) ♀H3-4 CBcs CDoy CDul CMHG CPLG CSBt EBee ECre EPfP EWTr LPot LRHS MGos MRav MSwo SDix SGar SHyH SPer SSpi WPGP
- 'Vicomte de Vibraye' see *H. macrophylla* 'Générale Vicomtesse de Vibraye'
- 'Westfalen' (H) ♀H3-4 CMac IArd SDix
I - 'White Lace' (L) ELan GKin
- 'White Mop' (H) CWib
- 'White Wave' see *H. macrophylla* 'Mariesii Grandiflora'
- 'Zaunkoenig' (L) MAsh
- 'Zebra'PBR (H) EPfP ESwi LBuc MGos WCot
- 'Zhuni Hito' NLar
- 'Zorro'PBR CBcs CDoC CMil EBee EPfP ESwi GGGa GKin LBuc LRHS MAsh SBfd SCoo SLim SLon SPoG SSpi WCot
aff. ***mangshanensis*** BWJ 8120 GGGa WCru
'Mars' (Cityline Series) new SGar
paniculata CMCN
- B&SWJ 3556 from Taiwan WCru
- B&SWJ 5413 from Japan WCru
- B&SWJ 8894 from Japan WCru
- from Taiwan SKHP WFar
- 'Ammarin' GQui LLHF NLar WPat
- Angel's Blush see *H. paniculata* 'Ruby'
- 'Big Ben' ♀H4 EPfP GGGa GQui LRHS MBri NLar SKHP
- 'Bombshell' new LBuc SPtl
- 'Brussels Lace' CAbP CDul EPfP LRHS LSRN MBri MRav NLar NRHS SGol SHyH SLon SPoG SSta WGrn WPat
- 'Burgundy Lace' CBcs MBlu MBri NLar
- 'Chantilly Lace' CMil LRHS MBri NRHS SHil
- Dart's Little Dot = 'Darlido'PBR IVic LLHF LSRN MAsh NLar WFar WPGP WPat
- 'Dharuma' GKin LLHF LRHS SGol WPat
- 'Dolly' GQui LRHS SHyH
- Early Sensation = 'Bulk'PBR EBee EThi GKin LRHS MSwo SHyH SKHP SMDP SPoG WFar WMoo
- 'Everest' CAbP CMil EBee EPfP LRHS MAsh SHyH SPoG WPat
- 'Floribunda' CGHE EBee ELan EPfP LRHS MAsh NRHS SHyH WPGP
- 'Grandiflora' ♀H4 Widely available
- 'Great Escape' NLar
- 'Greenspire' EBee EPfP LRHS MAsh MBlu MRav SHyH WFar WPat
- 'Harry's Souvenir' NLar
- 'Kyushu' ♀H4 Widely available
- 'Last Post' GQui
- 'Limelight'PBR ♀H4 Widely available
- Magical Candle = 'Bokraflame' new EPPr EPfP WCot
- 'Mathilde' NLar
- Mega Mindy = 'Ilvomindy' new SKHP
- 'Mega Pearl' LSRN NLar
- 'Melody' NLar
- 'Mount Aso' CMil EWld GQui NBro WPGP
- 'October Bride' GQui MBri NLar WPGP
- 'Papillon' WPGP WPat
- 'Pee Wee' LLHF NLar
- 'Phantom' ♀H4 CBcs CMCN CMil EBee ELon EMil EPfP GGGa GKin LRHS LSRN LSqu MAsh MBri MDKP MRav NBro NCGa NLar SCoo SHyH SPoG WCot WFar WPGP WPat
- 'Pink Beauty'PBR (H) CTri LSRN WFar
- Pink Diamond = 'Interhydia' ♀H4 Widely available
- 'Pink Jewel' CWib LLHF WPat
- 'Pink Lady' WFar
- Pinky-Winky = 'Dvppinky'PBR ♀H4 CWGN EBee EPPr EPfP ESwi GKin GQui IArd IVic LBuc LLHF LRHS MBlu NLar SGol SHil SHyH SKHP SPoG SSta WFar
- 'Praecox' EWTr GQui MRav WKif
- 'Rosy Morn' LRHS SPoG
§ - 'Ruby' CBcs IArd LSRN
- 'Silver Dollar' ♀H4 EBee EPfP LRHS LSRN MBri SHyH
- 'Tardiva' CBcs CDoC EBee EPfP GKin GQui LRHS MGos MRav NBro SDix SHyH SPer SRms SWvt WFar WPGP WPat
- 'Tender Rose' NLar
- 'Unique' ♀H4 Widely available
- Vanille Fraise = 'Renhy'PBR CBcs CDoC CPne CWGN EBee EPfP EThi GGGa LAst LBuc LRHS LSRN MAsh MBlu MBri MRav MWat NCGa SBfd SGol SHyH SMad SWvt WFar WGrn WPGP
- 'White Goliath' GQui IArd NLar
- 'White Lace' NLar
- 'White Lady' CBcs
- 'White Moth' CAbP CBcs CDul EBee EPfP GGGa LLHF LRHS NBro NLar SHyH WPat
- 'Wim's Red' MMHG SGol
- 'Yuan-Yang' WCru
peruviana* × *seemanii GKin IArd IDee NRHS SSta
petiolaris see *H. anomala* subsp. *petiolaris*
'Preziosa' ♀H3-4 Widely available
* ***quelpartensis*** CRHN GQui
- B&SWJ 8846 WCru
quercifolia ♀H3-4 Widely available

- 'Alice' CJun EBee EPfP ESwi LRHS MAsh NRHS SGol SHyH SSpi WPGP
- 'Alison' EPfP SGol
I - 'Amethyst' Dirr SGol
- 'Applause' LRHS NLar
- 'Back Porch' NLar SGol
- 'Burgundy' CBcs CJun CMil EBee EPfP ESwi GBin IArd IDee IVic NCGa NLar SGol WPGP
- 'Flore Pleno' see *H. quercifolia* Snowflake
- 'Harmony' CJun CMil EBee ELon EPfP ESwi IArd LRHS NLar SHil SHyH SKHP SSta WPGP WPat
- 'Ice Crystal' IVic SGol WPGP
- 'Lady Anne' EBee EPfP MRav WPGP
- 'Little Honey'PBR SGol SSpi
- Little Honey = 'Brihon' CAbP EBee EPfP IVic LRHS MAsh SPoG
* - 'Pee Wee' CAbP CBcs CDoC CJun EBee ELan EPfP LRHS MAsh MPkF NLar SGol SHyH SKHP SLon SPoG SReu SSta WPGP WPat
- 'Sike's Dwarf' CJun EBee IVic LTen MPkF MRav SGol WCot WPat
- 'Snow Giant' CJun
- Snow Queen = 'Flemygea' CBcs CDoC CDul CTri EBee ELan EPfP EThi EWTr IVic LRHS MAsh MBri MGos MPkF MRav NCGa NLar SGol SHyH SKHP SLim SMad SPer SPoG SWvt WFar WGrn WPGP WPat
- 'Snowdrift' CJun CMil
§ - Snowflake = 'Brido' (d) CAbP CBcs CDoC CMil CSPN CWGN EBee ELan EPfP LRHS MAsh MGos MRav NLar SHyH SKHP SLon SPer SPoG SSpi SSta WPGP WPat
- 'Stardust' MMHG
- 'Tennessee Clone' CJun EBee ESwi NLar SKHP

sargentiana see *H. aspera* subsp. *sargentiana*

scandens NBro
- B&SWJ 5448 WCru
- B&SWJ 5481 WCru
- B&SWJ 5496 WCru
- B&SWJ 5523 WCru
- B&SWJ 5602 WCru
- B&SWJ 5893 WCru
- B&SWJ 5929 WCru
- B&SWJ 6159 WCru
- B&SWJ 6317 WCru
§ - subsp. ***chinensis*** CBcs CPLG WFar
- - B&SWJ 1488 WCru
- - B&SWJ 3214 WCru
- - B&SWJ 3420 WCru
- - B&SWJ 3869 WCru
- - B&SWJ 3410 from Taiwan WCru
- - B&SWJ 3423 WCru
- - B&SWJ 3487 WCru
- - BWJ 8000 from Sichuan WCru
§ - - f. ***angustipetala*** B&SWJ 3454 WCru
- - - B&SWJ 3553 WCru
- - - B&SWJ 3667 WCru
- - - B&SWJ 3733 WCru
- - - B&SWJ 3814 WCru
- - - B&SWJ 6038 from Yakushima WCru
- - - B&SWJ 6041 from Yakushima WCru
- - - B&SWJ 6056 from Yakushima WCru
- - - B&SWJ 6787 WCru
- - - B&SWJ 6802 WCru
- - - B&SWJ 7121 WCru
- - - B&SWJ 7128 WCru
- - f. ***formosana*** B&SWJ 1488 WCru
- - - B&SWJ 3271 WCru
- - - B&SWJ 7058 NLar WCru
- - - B&SWJ 7097 NLar WCru
- - f. ***macrosepala*** B&SWJ 3423 WCru
- - - B&SWJ 3476 WCru
- - - CWJ 12441 WCru
- - f. ***obovatifolia*** B&SWJ 3487b WCru
- - - B&SWJ 3683 WCru
- - - B&SWJ 7121 WCru
- subsp. ***liukiuensis*** WCru
- - B&SWJ 6022 WCru
- - B&SWJ 11471 WCru
- 'Splash' (v) CMil

seemannii Widely available
- 'Roger Grounds' (v) **new** WCot

serrata CPLG CTri CWib WKif
- B&SWJ 4817 WCru
- B&SWJ 6241 WCru
- 'Acuminata' see *H. serrata* 'Bluebird'
- 'Aigaku' (L) CMil CPLG
- 'Aka Beni-yama' GQui
- 'Akabe-yama' NBro NLar
- 'Akishino-temari' **new** WPGP
- Amacha Group CGHE
- - 'Amagi-amacha' (L) CMil GQui NBro NLar
- - 'Ō-amacha' CMil GQui WPGP
- 'Amagyana' (L) CGHE CPLG
- subsp. ***angustata*** WCru
- 'Ao-yama' **new** WPGP
- Avelroz = 'Dolmyf'PBR SBfd
- 'Belladonna' GQui
- 'Belle Deckle' see *H. serrata* 'Blue Deckle'
- 'Beni-gaku' (L) CMil CPLG ECre LRHS MAsh NBro NLar SHyH WPGP
- 'Beni-yama' (L) CGHE CMil GQui WPGP
- 'Blue Billow' (L) GGGa NBro NLar
§ - 'Blue Deckle' (L) CMHG CMac MAsh MGos MRav NBro SDys SHyH WPGP
§ - 'Bluebird' (L) ♀H3-4 Widely available
- 'Cap Sizun' **new** WPGP
- 'Chiba Cherry-lips' WCru
- 'Chiri-san Sue' (d) WCru
- 'Crûg Cobalt' WCru
- 'Diadem' (L) ♀H3-4 CMil CPLG EPfP GQui LRHS NBro SDix SHyH WPGP
- dwarf white-flowered (L) WCru
- 'Forget Me Not' GQui
- 'Fuji Snowstorm' (v) CMil
- 'Fuji Waterfall' see *H. serrata* 'Fuji-no-taki'
- 'Fuji-no-shirayuki' (L/d) **new** CMil
§ - 'Fuji-no-taki' (L/d) CAbP ELon LAst LLHF NCGa NEgg SMad WBor WFar WPGP
- 'Golden Showers' (L) NBro
- 'Golden Sunlight'PBR (L) CDoC SWvt
- 'Graciosa' (L) LLHF WPGP WPat
- 'Grayswood' (L) ♀H3-4 CBcs CMac CPLG CSBt EBee EPfP GQui LRHS MAsh MRav NBro SDix SGol SHyH SLim SPer SSpi WBor WKif WPGP

- 'Hakucho' (L/d) NBro WPGP
- 'Hallasan' misapplied see *H. serrata* 'Maiko', 'Spreading Beauty'
- 'Hallasan' ambig. CMil
- 'Hallasan' R. & J. de Belder (L) CMil WPGP
- 'Hime-benigaku' (L) CMil MAsh WFar
- 'Impératrice Eugénie' (L) GQui
- 'Intermedia' (L) CPLG NBro
- 'Isusai-jaku' (L) GQui
- 'Kiyosumi' (L) CDoC CGHE CLAP CMil CPLG ECre ELon GQui NBir SBrt SHyH WBor WCot WCru WPGP WPat
- 'Klaveren' see *H. macrophylla* 'Klaveren'
- 'Koreana' (L) MAsh
- 'Kurenai' (L) NBro NLar WPGP
- 'Kurohime' (L) CMil NBro WPGP
- 'Macrosepala' (L) MAsh SHyH WPGP

§ - 'Maiko' (L) IArd
- 'Midori' (L) CPLG SHyH
- 'Mikata Yae' WPGP
- 'Miranda' (L) ♀H3-4 CPLG CSam EPfP LRHS MAsh NBro NLar SDys SHyH SSpi WFar
- 'Miyama-yae-murasaki' (L/d) CGHE CLAP CMil CPLG CSpe MAsh SHyH WPGP
- 'Momo-beni-yama' CMil
- 'Odoriko-amacha' **new** WPGP
- 'Pretty Maiden' see *H. serrata* 'Shichidanka'
- 'Professeur Iida' (L) WPGP

§ - 'Prolifera' (L/d) CGHE CMil LLHF WPGP WPat
- 'Pulchella' see *H. serrata* 'Prolifera'
- 'Ramis Pictis' (L) GQui NBro NLar SHyH WPGP
- 'Rosalba' (L) ♀H3-4 CLAP CPLG ECre IVic NBro WFar WSHC
- 'Sapphirine' (L) GQui
- 'Sekka' **new** WPGP

§ - 'Shichidanka' (L/d) EBee LLHF LRHS NBro WPat
- 'Shichidanka-nishiki' (L/d/v) CDoC CGHE CPLG ECre GQui SHyH WBor
- 'Shinonome' (L/d) CMil CPLG GQui WPGP
- 'Shirofuji' (L/d) CLAP CMil EWld LLHF MAsh WPGP WPat
- 'Shiro-gaku' (L) MAsh NBro NLar
- 'Shirotae' (L/d) CMil CPLG EBee GGGa SHyH WPGP
- 'Shōjō' ELon MAsh WPGP WPat

§ - 'Spreading Beauty' (L) WPGP
- 'Suiro-maiko' **new** WPGP
- 'Suzukayama-yama' **new** WPGP

§ - var. ***thunbergii*** (L) GQui WFar

* - - 'Plena' (L/d) GQui WCru
- 'Tiara' (L) ♀H3-4 CAbb CDul CMil CPLG ELon EPfP GGGa IVic LRHS LSRN MAsh NBir NBro NLar SDix SDys SHyH SLim WPGP WPat
- 'Uzu-azisai' WPGP
- 'Woodlander' (L) WPat
- 'Yae-no-amacha' (L/d) CBcs CPLG NBro SHyH WPGP
- subsp. ***yezoensis*** CMil GQui NLar
- - 'Hime-gaku' CMil

§ ***serratifolia*** CHEx CPLG EPfP IArd IDee SSpi SSta WFar WPGP
- HCM 98056 WCru

sikokiana CLAP
- B&SWJ 5035 WCru
- B&SWJ 5855 WCru
- B&SWJ 11174 WCru
- B&SWJ 11381 WCru

'Silver Slipper' see *H. macrophylla* 'Ayesha'

tiliifolia see *H. anomala* subsp. *petiolaris*

villosa see *H. aspera* Villosa Group

xanthoneura see *H. heteromalla*

'Zambia' EPfP LBuc MGos WCot

Hydrastis (*Ranunculaceae*)

canadensis CArn GPoy LEdu

Hydrocharis (*Hydrocharitaceae*)

morsus-ranae CBen CHab CRow CWat EHon EWay LPBA MSKA MWts NPer SWat

Hydrocleys (*Alismataceae*)

nymphoides XBlo

Hydrocotyle (*Araliaceae*)

asiatica see *Centella asiatica*

vulgaris CWat

Hydrophyllum (*Boraginaceae*)

canadense EBee

'Spring Silver' SKHP

Hylomecon (*Papaveraceae*)

* ***hylomecoides*** WCru

§ ***japonica*** CLAP EBee ECho EHrv ELan EWld GBBs GCra GEdr GKev LEdu LRHS MAvo NBir NLBP NMen NRya WCru WFar

Hylotelephium see *Sedum*

Hymenanthera see *Melicytus*

Hymenocallis (*Amaryllidaceae*)

'Advance' ECho LAma

§ ***caroliniana*** ECho

× ***festalis*** ♀H1 CCCN CPne ECho EPfP LAma SDeJ SPav WFar
- 'Zwanenburg' CGrW ECho

harrisiana CCCN CTca ECho EPfP SDeJ

littoralis GHim

§ ***longipetala*** ECho

occidentalis see *H. caroliniana*

'Sulphur Queen' ♀H1 CGrW ECho SDeJ SPav

'Tropical Giant' **new** GHim

Hymenolepis (*Asteraceae*)

parviflora see *Athanasia parviflora*

Hymenosporum (*Pittosporaceae*)

flavum EShb EUJe MOWG

Hymenoxys (*Asteraceae*)

acaulis* var. *caespitosa see *Tetraneuris acaulis* var. *caespitosa*

grandiflora see *Tetraneuris grandiflora*

§ ***hoopesii*** CMac EBee ELan EPfP GMaP LHop LRHS NBir NChi NEgg NPri SPer SPoG SRms WCot WFar WMnd WPer WWEG

Hyoscyamus (*Solanaceae*)

niger CArn GPoy MNHC

reticulatus WCot

Hypericum ✿ (*Hypericaceae*)

CC 4131 CPLG

CC 4544 CPLG

	SDR 6106	GKev
	acmosepalum	MAsh WPat
	aegypticum	ECho EPot MHer NMen SBrt WAbe WFar WPer WThu
	amblycalyx	WAbe
	androsaemum	CArn CRWN ECha ELan MHer MRav MSwo NPer WHfH WMoo WOut
§	- 'Albury Purple'	ELan EShb LDai MRav NLar WHrl WMoo XLum
	- 'Autumn Blaze'	CBcs
§	- 'Dart's Golden Penny'	SPer
	- 'Excellent Flair'	NLar
§	- f. ***variegatum*** 'Mrs Gladis Brabazon' (v)	NBir NLar WCot WHrl
	athoum	WAbe WIce WThu
	balearicum	EHrv WAbe XSen
	barbatum	WFar
	bellum	EBee GCal SLon
	buckleyi	WAbe
	calycinum	CBcs CDul CMac CTrC CTri EBee ELan ELon EPfP LAst LBuc MGos MRav MWat NWea SBfd SEND SGol SPer SWvt WGwG WMoo XLum
	- 'Brigadoon'	LRHS MAsh SGol
	- 'Senior'	LAst
	cerastioides	CMea CTri CWib EDAr EDif NGdn SMrm SRms WAbe WFar WPat WPer XSen
	coris	EWes MWat NMen SRms WAbe
	cuneatum	see *H. pallens*
	× ***cyathiflorum*** 'Gold Cup'	CMac EBee LRHS SPoG
	× ***dummeri*** 'Peter Dummer'	MAsh NLar
	'Eastleigh Gold'	CMac
	'Elite Baby Green'	EPfP
	'Elite Mayor'	EPfP
	'Elite Sweet Lion'	EPfP
	elodes	CWat MSKA
	elongatum	MWat
	empetrifolium 'Prostratum'	see *H. empetrifolium* subsp. *tortuosum*
§	- subsp. ***tortuosum***	EWes
	foliosum NJM 08.031	WPGP
	forrestii 🏆H4	EBee MMuc SEND WFar
N	***fragile*** misapplied	see *H. olympicum* f. *minus*
	frondosum 'Buttercup'	NLar
	- 'Sunburst'	EBee
	'Gold Penny'	see *H. androsaemum* 'Dart's Golden Penny'
	Golden Beacon = 'Wilhyp'[PBR] **new**	CSpe EBee ESwi GAbr LAst LHop LRHS LSou NEgg NLar SBfd SPad WCot WFar WH
	grandiflorum	see *H. kouytchense*
	henryi	SLPl
	- L 753	SRms
	'Hidcote' 🏆H4	Widely available
	'Hidcote Variegated' (v)	LRHS MAsh MWat SLim SRms WFar
	hirsutum	CHab NMir
	(Hypearls Series) Hypearls Annelies **new**	SHil
	- Hypearls Ella **new**	SHil
	- Hypearls Jacqueline **new**	SHil
	× ***inodorum*** 'Albury Purple'	see *H. androsaemum* 'Albury Purple'
	- 'Autumn Surprise'[PBR]	NEgg NHol WHar
	- 'Dream'	NLar
	- 'Elstead'	EBee ECrN ECtt ELan EPfP MRav MWat NHol NLar NWea
	- Magical Cherry = 'Kolmcherrip'	EPfP
	- 'Rheingold'	MAsh
	- 'Ysella'	MRav
	japonicum	ECho EWes
	kalmianum	EWes WCot
	kamtschaticum	XLum
	kelleri	ITim
§	***kouytchense*** 🏆H4	CDul CMCN EBee ELon EPfP EWes GQui LAst LHop LRHS MAsh MMuc MRav SEND SPoG WCFE WCot WPat
	lancasteri	EBee EPfP LRHS MAsh SPoG WPat
	leschenaultii misapplied	see *H.* 'Rowallane'
	linarioides	EBee
	maclarenii	EWes
	Magical Beauty = 'Kolmbeau'[PBR]	ELon NLar NPnk SPoG
	Magical Red = 'Kolmred'[PBR]	NLar SPoG
	Magical White = 'Kolmawhi'[PBR] **new**	SPoG
	Miracle Fantasy = 'Hymirfan'	NLar
	Miracle Summer = 'Hymirsum'	EPfP NLar
	Miracle Wonder = 'Hymirwon'	NLar
	× ***moserianum*** 🏆H4	CBar CDul CMac EPfP LRHS MGos MRav NPer SHil SLon SPer SRms
	- 'Daybreak'	EBee LRHS MAsh SPoG
§	- 'Tricolor' (v)	Widely available
	- 'Variegatum'	see *H.* × *moserianum* 'Tricolor'
	'Mrs Brabazon'	see *H. androsaemum* f. *variegatum* 'Mrs Gladis Brabazon'
	nummularium	NMen WAbe
	oblongifolium	CPLG
	- CC 4546	WCot
	olympicum 🏆H4	CEnt CTri ECha ECho ELan GJos LRHS MAsh MBrN MWat NRHS SEND SPer SRms SWvt WAbe WFar WIce XLum XSen
	- 'Grandiflorum'	see *H. olympicum* f. *uniflorum*
§	- f. ***minus***	CTri ECho ECtt NGdn SPlb SRms WHrl WPer XLum
§	- - 'Sulphureum'	CPrp ECho ELon EWTr EWes GMaP LRHS MLHP NBir SPer SRms SWvt WCFE
	- - 'Variegatum' (v)	CWan EWes NBir SPoG SWvt
§	- f. ***uniflorum***	ECho NBro WPer
	- - 'Citrinum' 🏆H4	CMea CSpe EBee ECha ECtt EPfP GBuc LRHS MRav MWat NBro SEND SRot WAbe WCot WHoo WKif WRHF
	orientale	EWes
§	***pallens***	ECho NMen WAbe
	perforatum	CArn CHab CHby CWan EBee ENfk EPfP GPoy MHer MHoo MNHC NMir SEND SIde WHer WHfH WJek WMoo WSFF
	polyphyllum	see *H. olympicum* f. *minus*
	- 'Citrinum'	see *H. olympicum* f. *minus* 'Sulphureum'
	- 'Grandiflorum'	see *H. olympicum* f. *uniflorum*
	prolificum	MMHG WCFE
	quadrangulum L.	see *H. tetrapterum*
	reptans misapplied	see *H. olympicum* f. *minus*
	reptans Dyer	CMea EWes
	revolutum **new**	LEdu
§	'Rowallane' 🏆H3	CTri GCal SDix SMrm SSpi
	'Sonnenbrut'	SLPl

stellatum	WFar
subsessile	CPLG
'Sungold'	see *H. kouytchense*
'Sweet Lion' new	CMac
§ ***tetrapterum***	CArn
tomentosum	XSen
trichocaulon	ECho EWes
uralum HWJ 520	WCru
xylosteifolium	SLon

Hypocalyptus (*Papilionaceae*)

sophoroides	SPlb

Hypochaeris (*Asteraceae*)

radicata	CHab NMir

Hypocyrta see *Nematanthus*

Hypoestes (*Acanthaceae*)

aristata	CPLG EShb

Hypolepis (*Dennstaedtiaceae*)

millefolium	LRHS NRHS WCot
punctata	EFer

Hypoxis (*Hypoxidaceae*)

hemerocallidea new	WCot
- 'Bloemfontein'	ECho
hirsuta	CCCN ECho WCot
hygrometrica	ECho ECou IBal NMen WThu
krebsii	ECho
obtusa 'Harrismith'	ECho
parvula	NMen
§ - var. ***albiflora*** 'Hebron Farm Biscuit'	CBro CCCN ECho EWes GEdr SUsu WAbe WFar
rigidula 'Harrismith'	ECho
villosa	ECho

Hypoxis × *Rhodohypoxis* see × *Rhodoxis*

H. parvula × ***R. baurii***	see × *Rhodoxis hybrida*

Hypsela (*Campanulaceae*)

longiflora	see *H. reniformis*
§ ***reniformis***	ECho EDAr GAbr LBee LRHS MAsh MRav WFar

Hyssopus ✿ (*Lamiaceae*)

from Georgia new	EWes
officinalis	Widely available
- f. ***albus***	CWan ECha EGHP ELau ENfk EPfP EWhm GPoy MHer MHoo MNHC SIde SPer SPlb WHfH WJek WPer XLum XSen
- subsp. ***aristatus***	CArn EBee ELau ELon ENfk EPfP EWhm GPoy LLWP LRHS MHer MHoo MNHC SIde SPoG WJek XLum XSen
- 'Roseus'	CEnt ECha EGHP ELau ENfk EPfP EWhm GPoy LLWP MHer MHoo MNHC SEND SIde SPer SPoG WJek WPer XLum XSen

Hysterionica (*Asteraceae*)

pulchella	CPBP

Hystrix (*Poaceae*)

patula	CKno EBee EHoe EPPr EShb GCal LLWP MBel MMoz MNrw MWhi SPlb SSvw WPer WTin XLum

I

Iberis (*Brassicaceae*)

Absolutely Amethyst = 'B2401' new	CBct CMea NPri
aurosica 'Sweetheart'	EDAr GEdr WFar
candolleana	see *I. pruitii* Candolleana Group
commutata	see *I. sempervirens*
'Correvoniana'	MAsh
gibraltarica	ECho SRms WGor
- 'Betty Swainson'	EWTr EWld SBch SMrm SPhx SUsu
'Masterpiece' new	WHlf
§ ***pruitii*** Candolleana Group	ECho GEdr NMen WAbe WFar
saxatilis	ECho GKev LHop LRHS NRHS WThu
semperflorens	WCFE WWEG
§ ***sempervirens*** ♀H4	CMea CTri CWib ECho ELan EPfP IFoB LAst MAsh MWat NBro NOrc SEND SRms WCFE WFar WPer XLum
- 'Compacta'	ECho
- 'Elfenreigen'	GCal
- 'Fischbeck'	SRot
- 'Golden Candy'	CTri EHoe MAvo SPoG WFar
- 'Little Gem'	see *I. sempervirens* 'Weisser Zwerg'
- 'Pygmaea'	ECho NMen
- Schneeflocke	see *I. sempervirens* 'Snowflake'
- 'Snow Cushion'	EDAr EPfP GEdr WWEG
§ - 'Snowflake' ♀H4	CBar ECho EPfP GEdr IFoB LHop MAsh MWat NBre NPri NRya SBch SPer SPoG SWvt WFar XLum
- 'Tahoe'	EDAr LPot
§ - 'Weisser Zwerg'	CMea ECha ECho ECtt ELan GEdr MHer MRav MWat NMen NRya SBch SRms
taurica new	WAbe

Ichthyoselmis (*Papaveraceae*)

§ ***macrantha***	CDes CEnt CLAP ECha EPfP EWld GCra LAma LHop MNrw WCru WPGP WSHC

Idesia (*Salicaceae*)

polycarpa	CAbP CBcs CDul CMCN EBtc EPfP IVic LHop NLar SEND WFar

Ilex ✿ (*Aquifoliaceae*)

N × ***altaclerensis***	WFar
§ - 'Belgica Aurea' (f/v) ♀H4	CBcs CDoC CJun CTho EPfP MBri MSwo NHol WFar
- 'Camelliifolia' (f) ♀H4	CDul CTho ELan EPfP LMaj MBlu NEgg NPCo SGol WFar
- 'Camelliifolia Variegata' (f/v)	CMac
- 'Golden King' (f/v) ♀H4	Widely available
- 'Hendersonii' (f)	NPCo
- 'Hodginsii' (m) ♀H4	CTri WFar
- 'James G. Esson' (f)	LRHS
- 'Lady Valerie' (f/v)	IArd
- 'Lawsoniana' (f/v) ♀H4	CDoC CJun CMac CSBt CTri EBee EHoe ELan EPfP LRHS MAsh MMuc MWat NEgg NLar NPCo NWea SBfd SEND SGol SHil SLim SLon SPer SPoG SRms WFar WMou WPat

	- 'Purple Shaft' (f)	CMCN MRav
	- 'Ripley Gold' (f/v)	LRHS MAsh MBri NWea SEND
	- 'Silver Sentinel'	see *I.* × *altaclerensis* 'Belgica Aurea'
	- 'Wilsonii' (f)	EPfP NPCo NWea
	aquifolium ♀H4	CBar CBcs CCVT CDul CHab CJun CRWN CSBt CTho CTri CWib EBee ECrN EPfP MBri MGos MMuc MRav MSwo NLar NPri NWea SBfd SEND SEWo SGol SPer WMoo WMou
	- 'Alaska' (f)	CCVT CDoC CDul CJun CMCN LBuc LRHS MAsh MBri NLar NRHS NSti NWea SBfd SGol SHil SWvt WFar WGob
	- 'Amber' (f) ♀H4	CTri NPCo NWea
	- 'Angustifolia' (f)	EBee LRHS WCFE WFar
	- 'Angustifolia' (m or f)	EPfP MWat SPoG WFar
	- 'Angustimarginata Aurea' (m/v)	NPCo
§	- 'Argentea Marginata' (f/v) ♀H4	Widely available
§	- 'Argentea Marginata Pendula' (f/v)	CDoC CMac CTri ELan EPfP LRHS MAsh MRav NLar NWea SPer SRms WFar WPat
	- 'Argentea Pendula'	see *I. aquifolium* 'Argentea Marginata Pendula'
	- 'Argentea Variegata'	see *I. aquifolium* 'Argentea Marginata'
	- 'Atlas' (m)	CBcs CDoC LBuc
	- 'Aurea Marginata' (f/v)	CMac EPfP LBuc MGos NPCo SEWo WCFE WFar WPat
	- 'Aurea Marginata Pendula' (f/v)	CDoC WPat
	- 'Aurea Regina'	see *I. aquifolium* 'Golden Queen'
	- 'Aureovariegata Pendula'	see *I. aquifolium* 'Weeping Golden Milkmaid'
	- 'Aurifodina' (f)	CJun NPCo
	- 'Bacciflava' (f)	CBcs CDoC CDul CMac CTho CTri ELan ELon EPfP IArd LMaj LTen MBlu MGos MRav NEgg NLar NPCo NWea SLim SPer SPoG SRms SWvt WCFE WFar
	- 'Bowland' (f/v)	NHol
	- 'Chris Whittle'	NHol
	- 'Crassifolia' (f)	CWib IArd SMad
	- 'Elegantissima' (m/v)	CJun SCoo
	- 'Fastigiata Sartori'	NLar
	- 'Ferox' (m)	CJun EBee ELan EPfP LRHS SPer SPoG
	- 'Ferox Argentea' (m/v) ♀H4	Widely available
*	- 'Ferox Argentea Picta' (m/v)	WFar
	- 'Ferox Aurea' (m/v)	CDoC CJun CWib ELan ELon EPfP LRHS MAsh NEgg NPCo
§	- 'Flavescens' (f)	EPfP MBlu NPCo
	- 'Gold Flash' (f/v)	LRHS MAsh MGos NEgg NLar
I	- 'Golden Hedgehog'	LRHS SPer
	- 'Golden Milkboy' (m/v)	CMac ELan EPfP MAsh MGos SGol WPat
§	- 'Golden Queen' (m/v) ♀H4	CDoC CMac CWib IArd MGos NBir NPCo SRms WPat
	- 'Golden van Tol' (f/v)	CBcs CDoC CSBt CTri CWSG EBee ECrN ELan ELon EPfP LRHS LTen MAsh MBlu MGos MSwo NEgg NLar NPCo SCoo SGol SRms WGob WMoo
	- 'Green Minaret'	IVic
§	- 'Green Pillar' (f)	EPfP
	- 'Green Spire'	see *I. aquifolium* 'Green Pillar'
	- 'Handsworth New Silver' (f/v) ♀H4	Widely available
	- 'Harpune' (f)	IArd
§	- 'Hascombensis'	CDoC LHop NMen NWea
	- 'Hastata' (m)	CWib IArd IDee
	- 'J.C. van Tol' (f) ♀H4	Widely available
	- 'Laurifolia' (m)	IArd
	- 'Lichtenthalii' (f)	IArd IVic NPCo
	- 'Madame Briot' (f/v) ♀H4	Widely available
	- 'Marijo' **new**	LRHS
	- moonlight holly	see *I. aquifolium* 'Flavescens'
	- 'Myrtifolia' (f)	NEgg NPCo
	- 'Myrtifolia' (m)	ELan EPfP GCal MGos NEgg NLar NPCo SCoo SMad WFar WMoo
	- 'Myrtifolia Aurea' (m/v)	NEgg SWvt WFar WGob
	- 'Myrtifolia Aurea Maculata' (m/v) ♀H4	CDoC CJun CTri EBee ELan EPfP LRHS MAsh MRav NEgg NPCo NWea SMad SPoG SWvt WFar WPat
	- 'Northern Lights' (v) **new**	EBee
	- 'Pendula' (f)	MRav NWea
	- 'Pendula Mediopicta'	see *I. aquifolium* 'Weeping Golden Milkmaid'
	- 'Pyramidalis' (f) ♀H4	CDoC CDul CMac CTri EBee ELan EWTr LRHS MAsh MBri MGos NLar NPCo NWea SEND SGol SHil SRms WFar WMoo
	- 'Pyramidalis Aureomarginata' (f/v)	CDoC NLar
	- 'Pyramidalis Fructu Luteo' (f) ♀H4	MAsh MBri
	- 'Recurva' (m)	CMac
	- 'Rubricaulis Aurea' (f/v)	NLar NPCo WGob
	- 'Scotica' (f)	NWea
	- Siberia = 'Limsi'PBR (f)	IVic
	- 'Silver King'	see *I. aquifolium* 'Silver Queen'
	- 'Silver Milkboy' (f/v)	EBee ELan EPfP MBlu WFar
	- 'Silver Milkmaid' (f/v)	CDoC EBee EPfP LRHS MAsh NEgg NHol SLim SPer SWvt WGob WMoo WMou
§	- 'Silver Queen' (m/v) ♀H4	CBcs CCVT CDoC CMac CWib EBee EHoe EPfP LRHS MAsh MBri MGos MRav MSwo NBir NEgg NHol NLar NPCo NPri NRHS NWea SHil SLim SLon SPer SRGP SWvt WFar
	- 'Silver Sentinel'	see *I.* × *altaclerensis* 'Belgica Aurea'
	- 'Silver van Tol' (f/v)	CDoC CJun EBee ELan LRHS MAsh NEgg NLar NPCo NPer NWea SPer WFar
	- 'Somerset Cream' (f/v)	CJun CTri CWib
	- 'Sterntaler'	IVic
§	- 'Watereriana' (m/v)	MAsh
	- 'Waterer's Gold'	see *I. aquifolium* 'Watereriana'
§	- 'Weeping Golden Milkmaid' (f/v)	MRav WPat
	- 'White Cream' (m/v)	IVic MBri
	- 'Wichtel'	IVic
	- 'Yellow Star' (f/v)	IVic
	× ***aquipernyi*** Dragon Lady = 'Meschick' (f)	CDoC NPCo
	× ***attenuata***	WFar
	- 'Sunny Foster' (f/v)	CDoC EPfP WFar
§	***bioritsensis***	CMCN CTri NWea
	'Brilliant' (f)	NPCo
	'Clusterberry' (f)	NPCo
	colchica	CMCN IDee
	cornuta	EPfP ERom WFar
	- B&SWJ 8756	WCru
	- 'Ira S. Nelson' (f/v)	IArd IDee WCot
	crenata	CDul CMCN CTri EPfP ERom GCra MGos MRav NHol NWea STrG WFar

*	- 'Akagi'	WFar
	- 'Aureovariegata'	see *I. crenata* 'Variegata'
	- 'Convexa' (f) ♀H4	EBee EPfP MAsh MRav NEgg NPCo NWea WFar WGwG WPat
	- 'Convexed Gold' (f/v)	LRHS MBri SPoG
	- 'Dwarf Pagoda' (f)	IVic
	- 'Fastigiata' (f)	CDoC EBee EPfP LRHS MAsh MBri MGos MWat NHol NLar SLim SPer SPoG WFar
*	- 'Glory Gem' (f)	CBcs
	- 'Golden Gem' (f/v) ♀H4	CDoC CSBt CTri EBee ELan ELon EPfP IVic LRHS LTen MAsh MGos NWea SCoo SGol SPer SPoG SWvt WFar WPat
	- 'Golden Rock' PBR **new**	EBee
*	- 'Green Hedge'	LBuc
	- 'Helleri' (f)	EPfP MAsh WPat
	- 'Ivory Tower' (f)	NEgg NPCo
	- 'Luteovariegata'	see *I. crenata* 'Variegata'
	- 'Mariesii' (f)	CMac EBee MBlu
I	- 'Pyramidalis' (f)	MRav NWea
§	- 'Shiro-fukurin' (f/v)	CMCN EBee ELan EPfP LRHS SLon
	- 'Sky Pencil' (f)	CMCN
	- 'Snowflake'	see *I. crenata* 'Shiro-fukurin'
	- 'Stokes' (m)	NLar
§	- 'Variegata' (v)	CMac EPfP LRHS
	dimorphophylla	CBcs CDoC CMac
	dipyrena	CBcs IArd
	'Doctor Kassab' (f)	CMCN
	'Elegance' (f)	MBlu WFar
	'Good Taste' (f)	CDoC WFar
	hascombensis	see *I. aquifolium* 'Hascombensis'
	hookeri	CDoC
	'Indian Chief' (f)	NPCo WFar
	insignis	see *I. kingiana*
§	***kingiana***	WFar
	× ***koehneana***	CDul ELan
	- 'Chestnut Leaf' (f) ♀H4	CCVT CDoC CLnd CMCN EBtc EPfP MRav NPCo SEND SSta WFar WGrn WMou
	laevigata **new**	CMCN
	latifolia	CBcs CHEx CMCN NLar WPGP
*	'Little Diamond'	LSRN
	'Lydia Morris' (f)	CSam WFar
	maximowicziana var. ***kanehirae***	CBcs
	× ***meserveae*** Blue Angel = 'Conang' (f)	CBcs CDoC CDul CMac CWSG EBee ELan EPfP IFoB LRHS MAsh MBri MRav NEgg NLar NPCo NWea SPoG SRms WFar WMoo
	- Blue Bunny = 'Meseal' (f)	IVic
	- 'Blue Girl' (f)	CTri
	- Blue Maid = 'Mesid' (f)	EWTr NLar NPCo
	- Blue Prince = 'Conablu' (m)	CBcs CDoC CDul CMCN CMac EBee ELan LBuc LRHS MAsh MBlu NEgg NHol NLar NWea SLim SPer SPoG WFar
	- Blue Princess = 'Conapri' (f)	CBcs CMCN CMac EBee ELan EPfP LBuc LRHS MAsh MBlu MRav NLar NPCo NPri NSti NWea SCoo SLim SPer SPoG WMoo
	- Blue Stallion = 'Mesan' (m)	CDoC
	- Castle Spire = 'Hachfee' PBR	EBee IVic NLar WFar
	- Castle Wall = 'Hecken Star' PBR	EBee IVic WFar
	- 'Golden Prince' (m)	IArd
	- 'Heckenpracht' PBR	EBee IVic WFar
	myrtifolia	CMac MAsh MRav
	- (f) **new**	MAsh
	'Nellie R. Stevens' (f)	CDoC LMaj LTen NWea SCoo SEWo
	opaca	CMCN
	perado subsp. ***azorica*** **new**	WPGP
	- subsp. ***perado***	CBcs NPCo
	- subsp. ***platyphylla***	CBcs CMCN MBlu
	pernyi	CDoC CMCN CMac CTri EBee EPfP LRHS MAsh SLon SPoG WFar
	- var. ***veitchii***	see *I. bioritsensis*
	'September Gem' (f)	CMCN NPCo
	serrata	CMac CMen
	- 'Koshobai'	CMen
	- 'Leucocarpa'	CMen
	spinigera	CBcs
	suaveolens	CMCN
	verticillata	CMCN EBee LRHS NEgg WFar
	- (f)	CBcs EBtc ELon EPfP MMHG NLar NWea WFar
	- (m)	EBtc ELon EPfP MMHG NLar NWea
	- 'Christmas Cheer' (f)	WFar
	- f. ***chrysocarpa*** (f)	NLar
	- 'Maryland Beauty' (f)	CJun
	- 'Southern Gentleman' (m)	CJun MBlu
	- 'Winter Gold' (f)	CJun
	- 'Winter Red' (f)	CJun CMCN LTen MBlu
	vomitoria	CMCN EBtc
	× ***wandoensis***	CMCN
	yunnanensis	GQui IArd

Iliamna see *Sphaeralcea*

Illicium (*Schisandraceae*)

anisatum	CBcs CDoC CMac CPLG EBee EPfP IGor NLar WFar WPGP WSHC
floridanum	CBcs CPne EPfP GKin NLar SBrt SSpi WPat
- f. ***album***	EPfP
- 'Halley's Comet'	NLar
henryi	CDoC CGHE CMHG CPLG CWib EBee EPfP IVic NLar SSpi WPGP WSHC
aff. ***henryi***	CBcs
jiadifengpi **new**	NLar
majus WWJ 11919	WCru
oligandrum **new**	NLar
simonsii	CPLG IVic MBlu WPGP
- BWJ 8024	WCru
'Woodland Ruby'	NLar

Impatiens ✿ (*Balsaminaceae*)

CC 4980	CPLG
DJHC 98415	CDes WCru WPGP
apiculata	EBee GCal
arguta	CCon CDes CLAP CPLG CPom CSpe EBee EShb GCal MDKP MPie SBrt WHil WPGP
- 'Alba' **new**	CSpe
Athena Series (d) **new**	NPri
auricoma	WCot
auricoma × ***bicaudata***	WDib
bicaudata	CSpe MPie
congolensis	CCCN
Dezire Series **new**	NPri
- 'Dezire Lavender Splash' **new**	LAst
'Emei Dawn' **new**	WCru
flanaganae	CCon WPGP
forrestii	CLAP

gomphophylla	CCon
(Harmony Series) Harmony Dark Red = 'Danhardkrd'	WGor
- Harmony Orange Star	WGor
- Harmony Pink Smile = 'Danhar267'	WGor
- Harmony Raspberry Cream = 'Danharras'	WGor
- Harmony Violet = 'Danharvio'	WGor
hawkeri pink-flowered **new**	LAst
keilii	WDib
kerriae B&SWJ 7219	WCru
kilimanjari subsp. ***kilimanjari***	CDoC CSpe GCal MPie
kilimanjari × ***pseudoviola***	CDoC CSpe MPie WDib
langbianensis HWJ 1054	WCru
'Linda's White'	GCal
macrophylla B&SWJ 10157	WCru
'Masquerade' **new**	NPri
namchabarwensis	CDes CSpe MCot SBch WCot WCru WPGP
niamniamensis	CHll EBak EShb WCot WDib
- 'Congo Cockatoo'	CDTJ CDoC CHEx EOHP NPer SRms
- 'Golden Cockatoo' (v)	CDTJ CDoC CHll EBak EShb
noli-tangere	WSFF
omeiana	CCCN CCon CDes CHEx CLAP CPom CSpe EBee EPPr ESwi EWld GCal GEdr IGor LEdu LRHS MNrw MSCN NLar NMyG SBch SBig SUsu WBor WCru WFar WHil WPGP WPtf
- DJH C98492	WCru
- 'Ice Storm'	GCal WCru
- silver-leaved	CDes CHEx CLAP CSpe GEdr MDKP WCru WPGP
parasitica	WDib
platypetala B&SWJ 9722	WCru
pseudoviola	SDix
puberula	CCon
- HWJK 2063	CDes EBee SBrt WCru WPGP
repens ♀H1	WDib
rothii	CCon CSpe EShb GCal
scabrida	CSpe
sodenii	CCon CDTJ CSpe GCal SBHP WDib
stenantha	CCon CDes EBee
tinctoria	CCon CGHE CHEx CHll CPLG CPom CSpe GCal GCra MNrw WCot WPGP WWlt
- from Cherangani, Kenya **new**	GCal
- subsp. ***tinctoria***	IFro
tuberosa	WDib
ugandensis	CCon GCal
uniflora	CCon CDes EBee GCal SBrt WPGP
Velvetea = 'Secret Love'	CCCN WDib
walleriana 'Patchwork Peach Prism' **new**	NPri
- 'Patchwork Pink Shades' **new**	NPri
- 'Patchwork Salmon Surprise' **new**	NPri

Imperata (*Poaceae*)

cylindrica	CMen XLum
- 'Red Baron'	see *I. cylindrica* 'Rubra'
§ - 'Rubra'	Widely available

Incarvillea (*Bignoniaceae*)

arguta	LLHF XLum
brevipes	see *I. mairei*
compacta	EBee GHim LLHF
- BWJ 7620	WCru
delavayi	CBcs CSBt CWib EBee ECha ECho ELan ELon EPfP EPot GBuc GMaP LPot MGos MSCN MWhi NBir NLar SDeJ SPad SPer SRms SWvt WFar WWEG XLum
- 'Alba'	see *I. delavayi* 'Snowtop'
- 'Bees' Pink'	EBee EDAr EPfP EPot GBuc LRHS MSCN NLar
- 'Rose'	LRHS
§ - 'Snowtop'	EBee ELan EPfP EPot GCal GKev GMaP LRHS LTen NBir NLar SDeJ SPer SWvt WFar WPer WWEG XLum
cf. ***delavayi*** SDR 6715 **new**	GKev
forrestii	EBee
grandiflora	EBee ELan GKev
lutea	EBee GKev
- BWJ 7784	WCru
§ ***mairei***	CTsd ECho EDAr EPfP GEdr LRHS NLar NRHS WHil WPer XLum
- SDR 1812	GKev
- SDR 4336	GKev
- var. ***mairei***	GBuc
- - f. ***multifoliata***	see *I. zhongdianensis*
- pink-flowered	GCal
olgae	EPfP NLar
younghusbandii	GEdr
§ ***zhongdianensis***	CFis CPBP EBee GEdr GHim GKev LRHS SPhx
- ACE 1600	GBuc
- BWJ 7692	WCru
- BWJ 7978	EDAr WCru

Indigofera (*Papilionaceae*)

amblyantha ♀H4	CBcs CPLG EBee ELon EPfP LRHS MAsh MBlu MBri MMHG NLar SEND SKHP SPlb SSpi WSHC
australis	MOWG
balfouriana BWJ 7851	WCru
cassioides	WCru
decora f. ***alba***	EPfP
dielsiana	EBee EPfP LRHS WKif WPGP
'Dosua'	SEND
gerardiana	see *I. heterantha*
hancockii **new**	SKHP
hebepetala	EBee EPfP SKHP WPGP WSHC
§ ***heterantha*** ♀H4	Widely available
- from China	MBri
himalayensis	CMHG CPLG SKHP
- Yu 10941	WPGP
- 'Silk Road'	EBee EPfP LBuc LRHS MBlu MBri MGos SHil SKHP
howellii **new**	SKHP WPGP
kirilowii	EBee EPfP IVic MBri MOWG NLar SKHP WPGP WSHC
pendula	CMHG CPLG CWGN EBee EPfP LRHS MOWG SEND SKHP SPoG SSpi WKif WPGP WSHC
- B&SWJ 7741	WCru
potaninii	CMHG CMac CPLG EBee EPfP LRHS MOWG SBrt WHer
pseudotinctoria	CCCN CPom EPfP SEND SRms

subverticillata	WSHC
szechuensis new	SKHP
tinctoria	CArn

Indocalamus (*Poaceae*)

latifolius	EPPr ERod EUJe MMoz MWht NLar WJun
solidus	see *Bonia solida*
§ ***tessellatus*** ♀H4	CAbb CDoC CEnt CHEx EAmu ELon ENBC EPfP ERod GCal IDee MBri MMoz MWht NGdn NLar SMad WFar WJun WMoo WPGP
- f. ***hamadae***	ERod MMoz MWht WJun

Indosasa (*Poaceae*)

gigantea new	ERod

Inula (*Asteraceae*)

acaulis	WCot
barbata	GCal LRHS
cordata	LRHS
crithmoides	WHer
dysenterica	see *Pulicaria dysenterica*
ensifolia	CBcs ELan GJos MDKP MNFA NBro SLPl XLum
- 'Compacta'	ECho GCal LRHS
- 'Gold Star'	CMac EBee ECho MBNS MRav NBid NBir NEgg SPet SPoG WFar WMnd WPer
glandulosa	see *I. orientalis*
helenium	CArn CHab CHby CPrp CSev EBee ELau ENfk GAbr GPoy IBoy LEdu LPBA MHer MHoo MNHC NBid NBir NLar NMir SPoG SRms WGwG WHer WHfH WJek WMoo WPer
hirta	WPer
hookeri	CBre CMea CSam EBee ECha ELan GCal GJos GMaP IFro LEdu MBel MLHP MMuc MNFA NBid NChi NDov NPer NSti SAga SDix SEND WAbb WBrk WFar WWEG
- GWJ 9033	WCru
macrocephala misapplied	see *I. royleana*
magnifica	Widely available
- 'Sonnenstrahl' ♀H4	EBee GQue SEND SPhx
oculus-christi	EBee EWes NBre WCot
§ ***orientalis***	EBee EPfP GAbr GJos MBri MNFA NGBl NLar SMad SPad WFar WJek WMnd WPer WWEG
racemosa	CTca EPPr EWes GBin GCal IBlr MNrw NBid SMrm SPlb WBor WFar
- 'Sonnenspeer'	EBee GBin NBid NLar SLPl SMad WPer WPtf
rhizocephala	MDKP WPer
§ ***royleana***	CEnt GCal MDKP MNrw MRav
salicina	EBee

Iochroma (*Solanaceae*)

§ ***australe***	CHII CSpe EWld IRar LRHS MOWG SGar
§ - 'Andean Snow'	CHII CPLG EShb
§ - 'Bill Evans'	CPLG EShb
cyaneum	CCCN CDoC CHII MOWG WHil
- purple-flowered	CHII
gesnerioides	WCot
- 'Coccineum'	CCCN CDoC CHII WCot
§ ***grandiflorum***	CCCN CDoC CHII CSev SEND
warscewiczii	see *I. grandiflorum*

Ipheion ✿ (*Alliaceae*)

'Alberto Castillo'	Widely available
dialystemon	ECho EPot LLHF WAbe
- JCA 2420010	WPGP
hirtellum	CDes
'Jessie'	CBro CDes CMea CPom CPrp EBee ECho EPot GBuc LAma LHop LLHF LRHS MNrw NHol NMen NMin WCot WHil
'Rolf Fiedler' ♀H2-3	Widely available
sellowianum	CDes SCnR WCot
sessile	CDes ECho
§ ***uniflorum***	CBro CTri EBee ECha ECho LAma MMoz MNrw NMen SBch SEND SMrm SPer SRms WAbb WAul WBrk WCot WFar WPer WTin
- f. ***album***	CBro CPom CPrp EBee ECha ECho EPPr EPot EWes GKev LEdu LRHS MNrw NRHS SMrm WCot WHal
- 'Charlotte Bishop'	Widely available
- 'Froyle Mill' ♀H4	CBro CMea CPom CPrp EBee ECho ELon EPPr EPot ERCP EWes GKev LHop LLWP LRHS MNrw NMen NRHS SUsu WCot WFar WHil WHoo WTin
- subsp. ***tandiliense***	CDes
- 'Wisley Blue' ♀H4	Widely available

Ipomoea (*Convolvulaceae*)

acuminata	see *I. indica*
alba	CCCN
batatas 'Blackie'	EShb ESwi WFar
- 'Margarita'	EShb ESwi
- 'Pink Frost' (v)	EShb
- Suntory Black Tone = 'Kyuikukan 1'PBR	EShb
- (Sweet Caroline Series) 'Sweet Caroline Bronze'PBR	ESwi EUJe SMrm
- - 'Sweet Caroline Purple'PBR	EUJe
- - 'Sweet Caroline Sweetheart Light Green'PBR	ESwi
- - 'Sweet Caroline Sweetheart Purple'PBR	CSpe ESwi
carnea	CCCN
coccinea var. ***hederifolia***	see *I. hederifolia*
§ ***hederifolia***	CCCN
× ***imperialis*** 'Sunrise Serenade'	CCCN
§ ***indica*** ♀H1	CCCN CHEx CHII CRHN EShb MOWG MREP SPer
learii	see *I. indica*
lindheimeri new	WCot
§ ***lobata***	CSpe LSou NPri SBch
'Milky Way'	CCCN
muellerii	CCCN
× ***multifida***	CSpe
purpurea 'Grandpa Otts'	SEND
- 'Kniola's Black Night'	CSpe SBch
- 'Split Personality' new	NPri
- 'Star of Yelta' new	NPri
quamoclit	CSpe
versicolor	see *I. lobata*

Ipomopsis (*Polemoniaceae*)

§ ***aggregata***	GKev

Iresine (*Amaranthaceae*)

herbstii	EShb EUJe
– 'Aureoreticulata'	EShb
'Shiny Rose Purple'	LBuc

Iris ✿ (*Iridaceae*)

'Abbey Chant' (IB)	CIri WCAu XSen
'About Town' (TB)	WCAu
'Abracadabra' (SDB)	SMrm
'Absolute Treasure' (TB)	EWoo
'Action Front' (TB)	EAEE EBee ECGP EHrv EIri EPfP ESgI ETod EWoo LHop LRHS MAvo SBfd SDeJ SHil SMrm WAul WGwG WWEG
'Actress' (TB)	CWGN EAEE ETod LBuc LRHS LSRN SHil
acutiloba	LWSt
'Adobe Rose' (TB)	ESgI XSen
'Adventuress' (TB)	EWoo XSen
'African Wine'	WAul
'After Dark' (TB)	CKel
'Afternoon Delight' (TB)	ESgI EWoo WCAu
'Afternoon in Rio' (TB) **new**	WCAu
'Again and Again' (TB)	EWoo
'Agatha Christie' (IB)	WCAu
'Age of Innocence' (TB)	WCAu
'Aglow Again' (MTB) **new**	SDys
'Agnes James' (CH) ♀H3	CBro
'Agua Fresca' (TB) (v) **new**	WCAu
'Ahwahnee Princess' (SDB)	EWoo
'Aichi-no-kagayaki' (SpH)	WCot
'Air Up There' (TB)	CIri
'Alabaster Unicorn' (TB)	ESgI
'Albatross' (TB)	SMrm
albicans ♀H4	CMea ECho LEdu SEND
albomarginata	ECho LWSt
'Alcazar' (TB)	EWoo LSRN SWat WMnd WWEG
'Aldo Ratti' (TB)	ESgI
'Alene's New Love' (SDB)	EWoo
'Alene's Other Love' (SDB)	WCAu
'Alenette' (TB)	WCAu
'Alexia' (TB) ♀H4	CKel
'Alice Harding' (TB)	ESgI
'Alida' (Reticulata)	CBro ECho EPot ERCP GKev LAma LLHF SDeJ
'Alizes' (TB) ♀H4	CPar ESgI WCAu XSen
'All Night Long' (TB)	CIri
'Allison Elizabeth' (BB) ♀H4	WAul
'Alsterquelle' (SDB)	WTin
'Amadora' (TB)	CKel EIri
'Amas' (TB)	WCAu
'Amazing Grace' (TB)	EWoo
'Ambassadeur' (TB)	EWoo
'Amber Queen' (DB)	EBee ECtt ELan EPfP NBir SDeJ SPer
'Ambersand' (IB)	SIri
'Ambroisie' (TB) ♀H4	ESgI ETod EWoo
'Amelia Bedeila' (IB)	SIri
'American Patriot' (IB)	CKel WCAu
'Amethyst Dancer' (TB)	WCAu
'Amethyst Flame' (TB)	ECho ESgI NBre SRms WCAu
'Amherst Blue' (IB)	EIri SIri
'Amherst Bluebeard' (SDB)	ESgI SIri
'Amherst Caper' (SDB)	ESgI
'Amherst Glacier' (IB)	WCAu
'Amherst Jester' (BB)	SIri WAul
'Amherst Moon' (SDB)	SIri
'Amherst Mustard' (SDB)	SIri
'Amherst Purple Ribbon' (SDB)	SIri WCAu
'Amherst Sweetheart' (SDB)	SIri
'Amigo' (TB)	EWoo
'Amphora' (SDB)	CBro
'Ancient Echoes' (TB)	ESgI
'Andalou' (TB) ♀H4	CWCL EWoo XSen
'Angel Heart' (IB)	EWoo
'Angel's Tears'	see *I. histrioides* 'Angel's Tears'
'Angel's Touch' (TB)	ESgI
anglica	see *I. latifolia*
'Annabel Jane' (TB)	CKel COIW CWan ELon WCAu
'Anne Elizabeth' (SDB)	CBro
'Annikins' (IB) ♀H4	CKel
'Anniversary Celebration' (TB)	CKel
'Announcement' (TB)	CIri
'Antarctique' (IB)	ESgI
'Antiope' (Rc)	GKev
'Antler Road' (TB)	CIri
'Anvil of Darkness' (TB)	EWoo
'Aphrodisiac' (TB)	XSen
aphylla	GBin WThu
– 'Slick' **new**	SDys
'Apollo' (Dut)	CAvo GKev
'Appledore' (SDB)	CBro
'Appointer' (SpH)	NChi
'Apricorange' (TB) ♀H4	CKel WCot
'Apricot Blaze' (TB)	ESgI
'Apricot Drops' (MTB) ♀H4	ESgI WAul WCAu
'Apricot Frosty' (BB)	ESgI WCAu XSen
'Apricot Silk' (IB)	CCCN SBfd SEND SMrm WWEG
'Apricot Topping' (BB)	WAul WCAu
'Aqua Taj' (IB)	WAul
'Arab Chief' (TB)	CKel
'Arabi Pasha' (TB)	WCAu
* 'Arabic Night' (IB)	WCAu
'Arcobaleno' (TB) **new**	CIri
'Arctic Fancy' (IB) ♀H4	CKel
'Arctic Sunrise' (TB)	ESgI
'Argus Pheasant' (SDB)	ESgI
'Arizona Convention' (Spuria) **new**	CIri
'Armageddon' (TB)	ESgI
'Arms Wide Open' (TB) **new**	CIri
'Around Midnight' (TB)	LRHS WCAu
'Arpège' (TB)	XSen
'Art Deco' (TB)	SIri XSen
'Art School Angel' (TB)	CIri
'Arts Alive' (Spuria) **new**	EWoo
'As de Coeur' (TB)	XSen
'As You Were' (TB) **new**	CIri
'Ascension Crown' (TB)	ESgI
'Ask Alma' (IB)	ESgI XSen
'Astrid Cayeux' (TB)	ESgI
'Astro Flash' (TB)	ESgI
'Astrology' (TB) **new**	WCAu
'Atlantic Sky' (TB) **new**	ESgI
* 'Atlantique' (TB)	CKel
'Attention Please' (TB)	CKel ELan SMrm WWEG
attica	CBro CPBP ECho LLHF NRya WThu
– lemon-flowered	WThu
§ ***aucheri*** ♀H2	ECho EPot ERCP GKev LLHF LWSt NMin
– 'Blue Jay'	LWSt
– 'Blue Tit'	LWSt
– indigo-flowered	LWSt
– 'Leylek Ice'	LWSt
– 'Leylek Lilac'	LWSt

	Name	Suppliers
	- 'Olof'	LWst
	- 'Snow Princess'	ECho LWst
	- 'Snow White'	ECho LWst
	- 'Turkish Ice'	LWst
	- white-flowered	LWst
	'Aunt Josephine' (TB)	ESgI
	'Aurean' (IB)	CKel
	'Austrian Sky' (SDB)	CMac EBee ECtt EWTr LHop LRHS SDeJ WAul WCot
	'Autumn Apricot' (TB)	EWoo
	'Autumn Circus' (TB)	EWoo WAul
	'Autumn Echo' (TB)	ESgI XSen
	'Autumn Embers' (SDB)	WCAu
	'Autumn Encore' (TB)	EBee EWoo MHer SBfd
	'Autumn Riesling' (TB) **new**	WCAu
	'Autumn Tryst' (TB)	ESgI EWoo WCAu
	'Autumn Wine' (BB)	CIri
	'Avalon Sunset' (TB)	EIri
	'Avanelle' (IB)	GBin NBre
	'Awesome Blossom' (TB)	ESgI
	'Az Ap' (IB)	ELon MNHC WCAu WHil
	'Babbling Brook' (TB)	XSen
	'Baboon Bottom' (BB)	CIri
	'Baby Bengal' (BB)	XSen
	'Baby Blessed' (SDB)	CBro WCAu
	'Baby Prince' (SDB)	ESgI
	'Baccarat' (TB)	WCAu
	'Bach Toccata' (MTB)	SDys
	'Back in Black' (TB)	CKel
	'Badlands' (TB)	WCAu
	'Bal Masqué' (TB)	ESgI XSen
	'Ballyhoo' (TB)	WCAu XSen
	'Baltic Star' (TB)	EWoo
	'Banbury Beauty' (CH) ♀H3	MAvo
	'Banbury Ruffles' (SDB)	ESgI WAul
	'Bang' (TB)	CKel
	'Bangles' (MTB) ♀H4	SDys WCAu
	'Bar de Nuit' (TB)	ESgI EWoo
	'Barbara's Kiss' (Spuria)	CIri
	barbatula BWJ 7663	WCru
	barnumae	LWst
	'Baroque Prelude' (TB)	CKel
	'Batik' (BB)	XSen
	'Battle Star' (TB) **new**	CIri
	'Battlestar Atlantis' (TB) **new**	CIri
	'Bayberry Candle' (TB)	CIri
	'Be Mine' (TB)	CIri
	'Be My Baby' (BB)	WCAu
	'Beach Girl' (TB)	EWoo
	'Bedtime Story' (IB)	SWat WCot WWEG XSen
	'Beechfield'	LRHS
	'Bee's Knees' (SDB) ♀H4	SIri
	'Before the Storm' (TB)	CKel ELon ESgI WCAu XSen
	'Beguine' (TB)	ESgI
	'Being Busy' (SDB)	ESgI
	'Bel Azur' (IB)	ESgI EWoo
	'Bel Esprit' (TB)	WCAu
	'Belgian Princess' (TB) **new**	WCAu
	'Belise' (Spuria) ♀H4	WAul WCot
	'Belle de Nuit' (TB)	EWoo
	'Ben a Factor' (MTB)	ESgI
N	'Benton Arundel' (TB)	EMal
	'Benton Caramel'	EMal EWoo
	'Benton Cordelia' (TB)	EMal ESgI
	'Benton Daphne' (TB)	EMal
	'Benton Dierdre' (TB)	ELon EMal SRms
	'Benton Evora' (TB)	EMal
N	'Benton Lorna' (TB)	EMal
	'Benton Nigel' (TB)	EMal EWoo WCAu
	'Benton Primrose' (TB)	EMal EWoo
	'Benton Sheila' (TB)	ECha
	'Benton Susan' (TB)	EMal EWoo
	'Beotie' (TB)	EWoo
	'Bering Sea' (IB) **new**	WCAu
	'Berkeley Gold' (TB)	CSBt EBee ECtt ELan EShb EWes LRHS NOrc SBfd SDeJ SPer SWat WWEG
	'Berlin Tiger' (SpH) ♀H4	CRow EPPr EPfP MWts NLar SApp WCAu
	'Bermuda Triangle' (BB)	CIri SDys WAul
	'Best Bet' (TB)	ESgI EWoo WCAu
	'Bethany Claire' (TB)	ESgI WCAu
	'Betty Cooper' (Spuria)	WAul WCAu
	'Betty Simon' (TB)	CKel CWCL ETod EWoo XSen
	'Beverly Sills' (TB)	EAEE EBee EPfP EWTr EWoo GBin LSou MRav SDeJ SRGP WAul WCAu WGwG WHil XSen
	'Bewilderbeast' (TB)	XSen
	'Bianco' (TB)	WCAu WWEG
	'Bibury' (SDB) ♀H4	WCAu
	'Big Dipper' (TB)	ECtt
	'Big Melt' (TB)	CKel
	'Big Squeeze' (TB)	WCAu
	'Big Wheel' (CH)	SMrm
	biglumis	see *I. lactea*
	biliottii	CBro
	'Bishop's Robe' (TB)	ESgI
	'Black as Night' (TB)	XSen
N	'Black Beauty' (Dut)	EPfP
	'Black Beauty' (TB)	MWat SPer
	'Black Cherry Delight' (SDB) **new**	ESgI
	'Black Dragon' (TB)	CCCN CHid NLar XSen
	'Black Flag' (TB)	XSen
	'Black Gamecock' (La)	CCon CIri CWCL ECtt ELan IPot LPBA MBNS MNrw MSCN MWts NBro NLar NOrc SKHP SMrm WHil WMAq
	'Black Hills' (TB)	EBee
	'Black Hope' (TB)	CIri EWoo
	'Black Ink' (TB)	COIW
	'Black Knight' (TB)	MRav NLar WHrl WKif
	'Black Magic' (IB)	EWoo
	'Black Night' (IB)	EBee SRGP WWEG
	'Black Sergeant' (TB) ♀H4	CKel
	'Black Stallion' (MDB)	ESgI
	'Black Swan' (TB)	CMac ECha ECtt ELan EPfP ESgI EShb EWoo GCal LAst LRHS LSRN MCot NBre NGdn SBfd SMrm SPer SPoG WCAu WCot WHil XSen
	'Black Taffeta' (TB)	CKel
	'Black Tie Affair' (TB)	ESgI EWoo XSen
	'Blackbeard' (BB) ♀H4	CKel
	'Blackberry Towers' (TB) **new**	ESgI
	'Blackout' (TB)	ESgI EWoo
	'Blast' (IB)	CKel
	'Blatant' (TB)	ESgI EWoo WCAu XSen
	'Blazing Light' (TB)	XSen
	'Blenheim Royal' (TB)	ESgI WCAu XSen
	'Blowing Bubbles' (TB)	CIri
	'Blue Bossa' (CH) ♀H4	WAul
	'Blue Boy' (IB)	EWoo
	'Blue Denim' (SDB)	ECho ECtt EPfP GCal MRav NBir NPnk WBor WCot WHil WTin WWEG
	'Blue Eyed Brunette' (TB)	WCAu

	'Blue Gown' (TB)	EWoo
	'Blue Hendred' (SDB)	NBir WCAu
	'Blue Lamp' (TB)	CKel
	'Blue Line' (SDB) ♀H4	CDes NBre
	'Blue Meadow Fly' (Sino-Sib)	EBee
	'Blue Note Blues' (TB)	WCAu
	'Blue Note' (Reticulata) **new**	LLHF NMin
	'Blue Pigmy' (SDB)	CPBP CWat ECtt LRHS NGdn NLar SBfd SDeJ SPer
	'Blue Pools' (SDB)	MBri NBir WTin
	'Blue Rhythm' (TB)	CKel ELan ELon EPfP EWoo GMaP LRHS MAvo MRav NBre SBfd SCoo SDeJ SPer WCAu WMnd WWEG
	'Blue Sapphire' (TB)	ESgI WCAu
	'Blue Shimmer' (TB)	CSBt EBee ECha ELan EPfP ESgI EShb ETod EWoo LRHS LSRN MCot NCGa SBfd SDeJ SPer SWat WCAu WGwG WWEG
	'Blue Staccato' (TB)	CKel WCAu XSen
	'Blue Suede Shoes' (TB)	ESgI EWoo LSRN XSen
	'Blue Warlsind' (J)	LWst
	'Bluebird Wine' (TB)	WCAu
	'Blushing Moon' (TB)	WAul
	'Bob Nichol' (TB) ♀H4	CKel
	'Bob's Fancy' **new**	SDeJ
	'Bockingford' (MTB)	SIri
	'Bohemia Sekt' (TB)	CKel
	'Bohemian' (TB)	CWCL
	'Bold Pretender' (La)	ECtt ELan EPfP MBNS NLar SKHP WHil
	'Bold Print' (IB)	CWan EAEE EBee ELon IPot LAst LRHS LSRN NCGa SBea SBfd SHil SPoG WAul WCAu WWEG
	'Bollinger'	see *I.* 'Hornpipe'
	'Bonnie Davenport' (TB)	CIri
I	'Bonny' (MDB)	CBro
	'Bonus Bucks' (TB)	CKel
	'Bonus Lite' (TB) **new**	CIri
	'Boo' (SDB)	CKel CPBP WCAu XSen
	'Border Happy' (TB) **new**	WCAu
	'Bouzy Bouzy' (TB)	ESgI XSen
	bracteata	EBee GBuc IGor
	- NNS 04-223	GBuc
	bracteata* × *thompsonii	IGor
	'Braithwaite' (TB)	CKel CWGN EBee ELan ESgI EShb EWoo LRHS NBre SBfd SDeJ SPer SRms SWat WAul WCAu
	'Brandaris' (TB) **new**	ESgI
	'Brannigan' (SDB)	CBro NBir
	'Brasero' (TB)	CWCL ECtt EWoo
	'Brash and Bold' (AB) **new**	WCAu
	'Brasilia' (TB)	NBir NBre
	'Brassie' (SDB)	CBro MBNS NPnk WHil WWEG XSen
	'Brave New World' (TB) ♀H4	CIri
	'Breakers' (TB) ♀H4	CKel EWoo
	'Breaking Point' (TB)	CIri
	'Breezy Blue' (SDB)	WCAu
§	'Bride' (DB)	WMnd
	'Bride's Blush' (TB)	CIri
	'Bride's Halo' (TB)	LSRN XSen
	'Bright Button' (SDB)	CKel ESgI EWoo
	'Bright Fire' (TB)	EIri
	'Bright Vision' (SDB)	ESgI
	'Bright White' (MDB)	CBro CKel ECho SMrm
N	'Bright Yellow' (DB)	MRav
	'Brighteyes' (IB)	LRHS SRms
	'Brindisi' (TB)	XSen
	'Brise de Mer' (TB)	XSen
	'Bristo Magic' (TB)	XSen
	'Bristol Gem' (TB)	XSen
	'Broad Shoulders' (TB)	WCAu
	'Broadband' (TB)	WCAu
	'Broadleigh Angela' (CH)	CBro
	'Broadleigh Ann' (CH)	CBro
	'Broadleigh Carolyn' (CH) ♀H3	CBro CElw
N	'Broadleigh Clare' (CH)	CBro
	'Broadleigh Dorothy' (CH)	CBro MAvo
	'Broadleigh Eleanor' (CH)	CBro
	'Broadleigh Elizabeth' (CH)	CBro
N	'Broadleigh Emily' (CH)	CBro
	'Broadleigh Fenella' (CH)	CBro
N	'Broadleigh Jean' (CH)	CBro
	'Broadleigh Joan' (CH)	CBro
	'Broadleigh Lavinia' (CH)	CBro MRav
	'Broadleigh Mitre' (CH)	CBro CElw
	'Broadleigh Nancy' (CH)	CBro MAvo
	'Broadleigh Peacock' (CH)	CBro MAvo WSHC
	'Broadleigh Penny' (CH)	CBro
N	'Broadleigh Rose' (CH)	CBro CElw EPri EPyc LRHS MBrN MRav SApp SMrm WSHC
	'Broadway Baby' (IB)	ESgI SIri WAul
	'Bronzaire' (IB) ♀H4	CKel EIri WCAu WGwG
	'Bronze Age' (AB) **new**	LWst
	'Bronze Beauty' (Dut)	ERCP LAma
	'Bronze Beauty' (TB) **new**	SDeJ
	'Bronze Beauty' van Tubergen (*boogiana* hybrid)	EPfP NBir SDeJ
	'Bronze Perfection' (Dut)	WRHF
	'Bronzed Violet' (TB)	CKel
	'Brother Carl' (TB)	XSen
N	'Brown Chocolate' (TB)	WCAu
N	'Brummit's Mauve' (TB)	WCAu
	'Bruno' (TB)	LSRN NLar
	'Brussels' (TB)	ESgI
	bucharica misapplied	see *I. orchioides* Carrière
	bucharica ambig.	EBee ECho ELon EWTr MNrw SDeJ WBor
§	***bucharica*** Foster ♀H3-4	CBro ECho EPfP EPot GKev LAma
*	- 'Baldschuan Yellow' (J)	LWst
	- 'Princess'	EBee ECho
*	- 'Top Gold'	ECho
	bucharica* × *orchioides	ECho LWst
	bucharica* × *warleyensis	LWst
	'Buckwheat' (TB)	EWoo SIri
	'Bugleboy Blues' (TB)	CIri
	'Buisson de Roses' (TB)	XSen
	bulleyana	ECho GEdr GKev SRms
	- BWJ 7912	WCru
	- black-flowered	CPLG GKev
	- - SDR 1792	EBee
	- - SDR 4775	GKev
	'Bumblebee Deelite' (MTB) ♀H4	CJun CKel WCAu
	'Burgermeister' (TB)	XSen
	'Burgundy Party' (TB)	XSen
	'Burka' (TB)	ESgI
	'Burnt Toffee' (TB)	ESgI XSen
	'Burst' (TB)	CKel
	'Buto' (TB)	EWoo
	'Butter Pecan' (IB)	WCAu
	'Buttercup Bower' (TB)	WCAu
	'Buttermere' (TB)	SRms
	'Butterpat' (IB)	ESgI
	'Butterscotch Carpet' (SDB)	WCAu

	'Butterscotch Kiss' (TB)	CMac EBee ECGP ELan EPfP LDai LHop LRHS MBNS MRav NBir NLar SBfd SHil SPer
	'Buzzword' (SDB) new	WCAu
	'Bye Bye Blues' (TB)	ESgI XSen
	'Byzantine Purple' (TB) new	EWoo
	'Cabaret Royale' (TB)	ESgI XSen
	'Cable Car' (TB)	CKel CWCL ECtt ESgI EWoo SMrm WCAu
	'Cajun Rhythm' (TB)	XSen
	'Calgary' (TB) new	WCAu
	'Caliente' (TB)	CWGN MCot MRav MWhi WCAu XSen
	'California Dreamin'' (TB)	CIri
	'California Gold' (TB)	WWEG
	'California Style' (IB)	XSen
§	Californian hybrids	CElw CMac CPBP EPot GCra LRHS MCot NBir WCot
	'Calm Stream' (TB) ♀H4	CKel WCAu
	'Calypso Mood' (TB)	XSen
	'Camelot Rose' (TB)	WCAu XSen
	'Cameo Blush' (BB)	XSen
	'Cameo Queen' (SDB) ♀H4	CIri
	'Cameo Wine' (TB)	CJun ECtt ESgI XSen
	'Cameroun' (TB)	ESgI EWoo
	'Campbellii'	see *I. lutescens* 'Campbellii'
	canadensis	see *I. hookeri*
	'Canadian Kisses' (SDB) new	ESgI
	'Canadian Streaker' (TB/v)	ESgI WCot
	'Canary Bird' (TB)	ESgI
	'Candy Rock' (IB)	CIri EWoo WCAu
	'Candylane' (MTB)	CKel
	'Cannington Apricot' (IB)	CKel
	'Cannington Ochre' (SDB)	CBro
	'Cannington Skies' (IB)	CKel
	'Can't Touch This' (TB)	WCAu
	'Cantab' (Reticulata)	CBro ECho EPot ERCP GBin GKev LAma LRHS SDeJ
	'Caper' (SDB) new	EIri
	'Caprice' (TB)	EWoo
	'Capricious Candles' (TB)	CIri
	'Captain Gallant' (TB)	ESgI
	'Captain Indigo' (IB)	CKel ESgI WCAu
	'Captive Sun' (SDB)	EAEE EBee EPfP LRHS SIri
	'Caramel' (TB)	XSen
	'Carenza' (BB)	CKel
	'Caribbean Dream' (TB)	EWoo XSen
	'Carnaby' (TB)	ESgI LAst LRHS MBri MRav NCGa SBfd SDeJ WCAu WWEG XSen
	'Carnival Time' (TB)	CMac CWGN EBee ECtt EShb LBuc LDai LRHS NCGa SBfd SMrm SPer WAul XSen
	'Carol Lee' (TB) new	EBee
	'Carolina Gold' (TB)	XSen
	'Carolyn Rose' (MTB) ♀H4	EBee NBre SMrm
*	'Caronte' (IB)	ESgI
	'Carriwitched' (IB)	CKel
	'Casbah' (TB)	XSen
	'Cascade Rhythm' (TB)	WCAu
	'Cascade Springs' (TB)	CPar XSen
	'Cascade Sprite' (SDB)	SRms
	'Casual Joy' (TB)	CIri
	'Catalyst' (TB)	XSen
	'Cat's Eye' (SDB)	ESgI
	caucasica	CMac
	'Cayenne Capers' (TB)	ESgI
N	'Cedric Morris'	EWes
	'Cee Jay' (IB) ♀H4	EWoo
	'Cee Tee'	EWoo XSen
	'Celebration Song' (TB)	ESgI SIri WAul XSen
	'Celestial Glory' (TB)	XSen
	'Cerdagne' (TB)	XSen
	'Cerf-Volant' (TB)	SIri
	'Chalkhill' (SDB)	WCAu
	chamaeiris	see *I. lutescens* subsp. *lutescens*
	'Champagne Elegance' (TB)	ECtt EIri EPri NBir XSen
	'Champagne Encore' (IB)	ESgI EWoo
	'Champagne Frost' (TB)	XSen
	'Champagne Music' (TB)	WCAu
	'Champagne Waltz' (TB)	CWCL XSen
	'Change of Pace' (TB)	ESgI WCAu XSen
	'Chanted' (SDB)	EWoo WCAu XSen
	'Chantilly' (TB)	EBee ELan EPfP EWoo LRHS MNHC MRav NBir NGdn NLar SPer SWat
	'Chapeau' (TB)	ESgI
	'Chapel Bells' (TB)	CKel
	'Charlotte Maria' (TB)	CKel
	'Charmaine' (TB)	XSen
	'Chartreuse Ruffles' (TB)	ECtt SIri
	'Chasing Rainbows' (TB)	SDys WCAu
	'Château d'Auvers-sur-Oise' (TB)	SIri
	'Cher' (TB)	LSRN
	'Cherie' (TB) new	WCAu
N	'Cherished' (TB)	WWEG
	'Cherokee Lace' (Spuria)	WTin
	'Cherry Blossom Special' (TB)	CIri
	'Cherry Garden' (SDB)	Widely available
	'Cherry Orchard' (TB)	SGar
	'Cherrywood' (SDB)	CBro
	'Cherub's Smile' (TB)	XSen
	'Cheryl Ann O'Leary' (TB)	CIri
	'Chevalier de Malte' (TB)	ESgI
	'Chickee' (MTB) ♀H4	CKel
	'Chicken Little' (MDB)	CBro
	'Chief Moses' (TB)	WCAu
I	'Chieftain' (SDB)	MRav
	'China Dragon' (TB)	SWat XSen
	'China Nights' (TB)	ESgI
	'China Seas' (TB)	NBre
	'Chinese Coral' (TB)	XSen
	'Chinese Treasure' (TB)	XSen
	'Chinook Winds' (TB)	ESgI WCAu
	'Chivalry' (TB)	ESgI WTin
	'Chorus Girl' (TB)	CKel
	'Christmas Angel' (TB)	WCAu
	chrysographes ♀H4	CBro CHid CMac CWCL EHrv EPfP EPri EWll IKil LAst LRHS MBel MHer MLHP MMuc MRav NPnk NPri NSti SRot WCFE WFar
I	- 'Black Beauty'	CCon ECho EPfP
	- 'Black Gold'	EPri
I	- 'Black Knight'	CCse CPLG EDAr ELon EPfP GBuc GCal GCra ITim LHop NChi NLar SMad SWat WGwG WMnd
	- black-flowered	CDes COlW CPLG CSpe EBee ELan GAbr GBBs GBuc GCal GKev GKin LRHS LTen MNrw MSCN MWhi NGdn NMen NPnk SPer SPoG WCru WFar WHoo WMoo WPGP WPnP WSHC WWEG
	- dark-flowered new	GKev
	- 'Goldvein' new	CMac
N	- 'Inshriach'	LEdu
N	- 'Kew Black'	CPLG ECho LEdu NBir WHer WWEG

	– 'Mandarin Purple'	GCal MSpe SPer SWat
	– 'Rob'	ECho
§	– 'Rubella'	ECho GCra WFar
*	– 'Rubens'	GCal
	– 'Rubra'	see *I. chrysographes* 'Rubella'
	– yellow-flowered	WFar
	chrysographes* × *forrestii	GBin NBir
	chrysophylla	IGor
	'Chubby Cheeks' (SDB)	CKel WCAu
	'Church Stoke' (SDB)	WCAu
N	'Cider Haze' (TB)	CKel
	'Cimarron Rose' (SDB)	ESgI WAul
	'Cimarron Strip' (TB)	EPfP WWEG XSen
	'Cimarron Trail' (TB) new	WCAu
	'Cinnabar Red' (Spuria)	WAul
	'Cinnamon Stick' (Spuria)	CIri
	'Circus Stripes' (TB)	XSen
	'Cirrus Veil' (SDB)	WCAu
	'Citoyen' (TB)	XSen
	'Citronnade' (TB)	ESgI
	'City Lights' Harrell (TB)	WCAu
	'City of Paradise' (TB) new	ESgI
	'Clairette' (Reticulata)	ECho EPot LAma NMin SDeJ
	'Clara Ellen' (Spuria) new	WAul
	'Clara Garland' (IB) ♀H4	CKel WCAu
	'Clarence' (TB)	CKel ESgI EWoo XSen
	clarkei	CPrp EBee GBin WFar
	– B&SWJ 2122	WCru
	– CC 2751	CPLG
	– CC 6517	GKev
	– SDR 3819	GKev
	'Classic Look' (TB)	ESgI
	'Classic Navy' (BB) new	ESgI
	'Clay's Caper' (SDB)	NBre
	'Clear Choice' (TB) new	WCAu
	'Clearwater River' (TB) new	WCAu
N	'Cleo' (TB)	CKel
	'Cleo Murrell' (TB)	ESgI EWoo
	'Cliffs of Dover' (TB)	CKel EIri ESgI EWoo GCal MCot SGar SRms
	'Close Shave' (TB)	CIri
	'Cloud Ballet' (TB)	EWoo
	'Cloud Mistress' (IB)	ESgI
	'Cloud Pinnacle' (IB)	CKel
	'Cloudcap' (TB)	SRms
	'Clown Around' (TB)	CIri
	'Clownerie' (TB)	EWoo
	'Clyde Redmond' (La) ♀H4	WAul WMAq
	'Coalignition' (TB)	CIri ETod EWoo WCAu
	'Codicil' (TB)	EIri EWoo XSen
	'Colery'	LRHS
	'Colette Thurillet' (TB)	WCAu XSen
	collettii	ECho LWst
	'Color Carnival' (TB) new	ESgI
	'Color Me Blue' (TB)	WCAu
	'Color Splash' (TB)	XSen
	'Colorific' (La)	EPfP NBro NLar WHil
	'Colortart' (TB)	XSen
	'Combo' (SDB)	CKel
	'Come to Me' (TB)	CIri
	'Coming Up Roses' (TB)	XSen
	'Con Fuoco' (TB)	XSen
	'Concertina' (IB)	CIri EWoo WCAu
	'Confetti' (TB)	MBri
	confusa ♀H3	CHEx CPne CSev EWld IFro SBig SEND SGar SMad WFar XSen
N	– 'Martyn Rix'	CBct CDes CGHE CHEx CHid CPou EBee ELon EPfP GCal IGor LRHS MLHP MPie SBrt SEND WCot WFar WGwG WHer WMnd WPGP WPer
	'Congo Bongo' (BB)	WAul
	'Conjuration' (TB)	ESgI EWoo SIri
	'Constant Wattez' (IB)	CKel EBee ESgI NLar
	'Constantine Bay' (TB) new	ESgI
	'Consummation' (MTB)	WHil
	'Cookies Bright Spot' (MTB) new	WCAu
	'Copatonic' (TB)	ESgI
	'Copper Capers' (TB) new	ESgI
	'Copper Classic' (TB)	ESgI LSRN
	'Coquetterie' (TB)	EWoo
	'Coral Point' (TB)	WCAu
	'Coral Sunset' (TB)	WCAu XSen
	'Cordoba' (TB)	WCAu XSen
	'Corps de Ballet' (TB)	CIri
	'Côte d'Or' (TB)	XSen
	'Count Dracula' (TB)	CIri
	'County Town Red' (TB)	SIri
	'Coup de Soleil' (TB)	EWoo
	'Court Magician' (SDB)	SIri
	'Crackles' (TB)	CKel
	'Cracklin Burgundy' (TB)	XSen
	'Crackling Caldera' (TB)	WAul
N	'Craithie' (TB) new	EMal
	'Cranapple' (BB) ♀H4	ESgI WAul
	'Cranberry Ice' (TB)	ELon EWoo XSen
	'Cranberry Sauce' (TB)	WCAu
	'Cranbrook' (IB) ♀H4	SIri
	'Cream and Peaches' (SDB)	SIri
	'Cream Beauty' (Dut)	GKev LAma
	'Cream Pixie' (SDB)	WCAu
	'Cream Soda' (TB) ♀H4	CKel
	cretensis	see *I. unguicularis* subsp. *cretensis*
	'Crimson King' (IB)	EWoo
	'Crinoline' (TB)	CKel XSen
	'Crisis' (TB)	CIri
	'Crispette' (TB)	WCAu
	cristata ♀H4	EBee EPot GEdr LLHF NHar NLar SRms
	– 'Alba'	EBee GCal GEdr LLHF WAbe WThu
	cristata* × *lacustris	NMen
	crocea ♀H4	GBin GKev
	'Croftway Lemon' (TB)	COIW ELon
	'Cross Current' (TB)	WCAu
	'Crowned Heads' (TB)	CKel WCAu XSen
	'Crownette' (SDB)	CKel
	'Crushed Velvet' (TB)	WCAu
	'Crystal Fountain' (TB) new	CIri
	'Crystal Gazer' (TB) new	ESgI
	'Crystal Glitters' (TB)	ESgI
	'Crystal Phoenix'	CRow
	'Cumulus' (TB)	EWoo
	cuniculiformis	ECho WCot
	'Cup Race' (TB)	WCAu XSen
	'Curlew' (IB)	WCAu
	'Cutie' (IB)	ESgI EWoo WCAu
	'Cyanea' (DB)	ECho GEdr
	cycloglossa	ECho EPot GKev LLHF LWst
	'Dakota Smoke' (TB)	EWoo
	'Dale Dennis' (DB)	XSen
	'Dance Away' (TB)	ESgI
	'Dance for Joy' (TB)	XSen
	'Dance the Night Away' (TB) new	WCAu
	'Dancer's Veil' (TB)	CKel CMac ECtt ELon ESgI LRHS MRav NBre SPer

	'Dancing Bunnies' (SDB) **new**	WCAu
	'Dancing Gypsy' **new**	WCAu
	'Dancing Lilacs' (MTB)	ESgI
	danfordiae	CAvo CBro ECho EPfP EPot GKev LAma LRHS SDeJ SMrm SPer WFar WGwG
	'Dangerous Mood' (TB)	EWoo
	'Dante's Inferno' (TB)	EWoo
	'Dardanus' (Rc)	ECho EPot ERCP GKev LLHF SDeJ WCot
	'Dark Crystal' (SDB)	ESgI EWoo
	'Dark Rosaleen' (TB) ♀H4	NBre
	'Dark Spark' (SDB)	WCAu
	'Dark Vader' (SDB)	ESgI WAul WCAu
	'Darkness' (IB)	SIri
	'Darkside' (TB)	XSen
	darwasica	LWst
	'Dash Away' (SDB)	ESgI SIri
	'Dashing' (TB)	EWoo
	'Dauber's Delight'	CIri
	'Daughter of Stars' (TB)	ESgI EWoo
	'Dauntless' (TB)	ESgI
	'David Guest' (IB)	CKel
	'Dawn of Fall' (TB)	ESgI
	'Dawning' (TB) ♀H4	CIri ESgI EWoo
	'Dazzling Gold' (TB)	ESgI XSen
	'Dear Jean' (TB) **new**	CIri
	'Death by Chocolate' (SDB)	ESgI WAul
	'Deep Black' (TB)	CKel CPar CWGN EHrv ELan EPfP ESgI GBin IPot LAst LRHS LSRN MAvo MBNS MCot MRav MWat NCGa NLar NOrc SBfd SDeJ SPer SPoG SWat WAul WGwG WWEG
	'Deep Pacific' (TB)	MBri WCAu
	'Deep Space' (TB)	WCAu
	'Deft Touch' (TB)	CKel WCAu XSen
	delavayi ♀H4	ECho EWes GMaP IBlr MBel WRHF
	- SDR 50	CPLG GKev
N	- 'Didcot'	EBee LRHS NRHS
	'Delicate Lady' (IB) ♀H4	CKel
	'Delirium' (IB)	WAul WCAu
	'Delta Blues' (TB)	EWoo
	'Delta Butterfly' (La)	WMAq
	'Demelza' (TB)	CKel
	'Demi-Deuil' (TB)	EWoo
	'Demon' (SDB)	CJun CKel XSen
	'Denys Humphry' (TB)	CKel WCAu
	'Deputé Nomblot' (TB)	EWoo
	'Derwentwater' (TB)	SRms
I	'Desert Dream' (Sino-Sib)	GAbr
	'Desert Echo' (TB)	COIW MHer XSen
	'Desert Song' (TB)	CKel WCAu
	'Destination' (Spuria) ♀H4	CIri
	'Devil David' (TB)	CIri
	'Devil May Care' (IB)	CIri ESgI EWoo WAul
	'Devilry' (SDB)	EWoo
	'Devil's Spoon' (TB)	CIri
	'Devonshire Cream' (TB)	CIri
	'Diabolique' (TB) ♀H4	XSen
	'Diamond Ring' (TB)	SDys
	dichotoma	EWes
	'Diligence' (SDB) ♀H4	CKel
	'Disco Jewel' (MTB)	ESgI
	'Discovered Treasure' (TB) **new**	WCAu
	'Diversion' (TB)	ESgI
	'Divine' (TB)	CKel
	'Dixie Darling' (TB)	ESgI XSen
	'Dixie Pixie' (SDB)	WCAu WTin
	'Dogrose' (TB)	EWoo
	'Dolce' (SpH) **new**	WCAu
	'Doll' (IB)	EWoo
	'Doll Ribbons' (MTB)	EPfP
	'Dolly Madison' (TB)	ESgI
	domestica	CArn CBro CHll EBee ELan EPfP GKev GPoy SBfd SGar SPav SPlb SRms WGwG WHer WOut WPer WPtf WSHC
	- B&SWJ 8692B	WCru
	- 'Crûg Colossal'	WCru
	- 'Freckle Face'	CMac EBee LSou SPad WHil
	- 'Hello Yellow'	EBee EShb
	'Don Juan' (TB)	EWoo
	'Don't Touch' (TB)	CIri
	'Dorcas Lives Again' (TB)	WHil
	'Dotted Swiss' (TB)	XSen
	'Double Bubble' (TB)	EWoo
	'Double Byte' (SDB)	XSen
	'Double Click' (TB)	EWoo
	'Double Espoir' (TB)	XSen
	'Double Lament' (SDB)	CBro
	'Double Mini'	EWoo
	'Double Vision' (TB)	ESgI EWoo XSen
	'Double Your Fun' (IB)	WAul
	douglasiana ♀H4	ECho GCal GKev MHer WFar WOut
	- 'Cape Ferrelo'	SKHP
	'Dover Beach' (TB)	SIri
	'Draco' (TB)	ESgI XSen
	'Drake Carne' (TB)	CKel
	'Dream Indigo' (IB)	CKel EWoo WCAu XSen
	'Dreamsicle' (TB)	EWoo
	'Dresden Candleglow' (IB)	WCAu
	'Drive Me Wild' (TB) **new**	WCAu
	'Dualtone' (TB)	CKel
	'Dunlin' (MDB)	CBro ECho NBir
	'Dural White Butterfly' (La)	CHid LPBA MSCN
	'Durham Dream' (TB)	CIri
	'Dusky Challenger' (TB)	CJun CKel ESgI EWoo WCAu XSen
	'Dusky Evening' (TB)	XSen
	'Dutch Chocolate' (TB)	CPar ESgI ETod EWes EWoo XSen
	'Dwight Enys' (TB) ♀H4	CKel
	'Dynamite' (TB)	ESgI EWoo XSen
	'Eagle's Flight' (TB)	CKel XSen
	'Earl of Essex' (TB)	WCAu XSen
	'Early Frost' (IB)	CKel ESgI
	'Early Light' (TB) ♀H4	ESgI LPot WCAu
	'Easter' (SDB)	SIri
	'Eastertime' (TB)	ESgI EWoo
	'Easy' (MTB)	EIri SIri
	'Easy Grace' (TB)	EWoo
	'Ebony Echo' (TB)	EWoo
	'Echo de France' (TB)	ESgI EWoo XSen
	'Edge of Winter' (TB)	CKel SIri XSen
	'Edith Wolford' (TB)	CCCN CWCL ECtt ESgI GBin MMHG SRGP WWEG XSen
N	'Ed's Blue' (DB)	ELan
	'Edward' (Reticulata)	CBro ECho EPfP EPot GKev LAma LRHS MWat NMin SDeJ SMrm
	'Edward of Windsor' (TB)	ELan GMaP LRHS NLar SRGP WMnd
	'Eggnog' (TB)	EWoo
	'Egyptian' (TB)	CIri
	'Eileen Louise' (TB) ♀H4	WCAu

	Name	Suppliers
	'Eldorado' (TB)	EWoo
	'Eleanor Clare' (IB) ♀^{H4}	CKel
	'Eleanor Hill' (Spuria)	WAul
	'Eleanor Roosevelt' (IB)	EWoo
	'Eleanor's Pride' (TB)	CKel ESgI WCAu
	'Elegans' (TB)	MCot
	elegantissima	see *I. iberica* subsp. *elegantissima*
	'Elizabeth Arden' (TB)	CKel
	'Elizabeth of England' (TB)	GKev WWEG
	'Elizabeth Poldark' (TB)	ESgI XSen
	'Elsa Sass' (TB)	ESgI
	'Elsie Petty' (IB)	SIri
N	'Elvinhall'	CBro
	'Encre Bleue' (IB)	ESgI
	'Endless Love' (TB)	EIri
	'English Charm' (TB)	ESgI WAul WCAu XSen
	'English Cottage' (TB)	COIW ELon GBin GCal LSRN LTen MWat NLar SMrm WCAu WSHC WWEG XSen
	'Ennerdale' (TB)	SRms
	'Enriched' (MTB) ♀^{H4}	SIri
§	***ensata*** ♀^{H4}	CBcs CBro CHEx COIW CWat ELan EPfP GKev LPBA LRHS MHer MNrw NBro NLar SPlb SRms SWat WCFE WFar
N	- 'Activity'	CRow GBin SHar WFar WWEG
	- 'Agrippine'	SKHP
	- 'Alba'	ECha
	- 'Aldridge Prelude'	WAul
	- 'Aldridge Snow Maiden' ♀^{H4}	WAul
	- 'Aldridge Visitor' ♀^{H4}	WAul
	- 'Alpine Majesty' ♀^{H4}	CIri
	- 'Apollo'	CBen CRow
	- 'Asahimaru' new	GEdr
	- 'Asian Warrior'	LRHS NLar WFar
	- 'August Emperor'	CMHG IPot LAst SMrm
	- 'Azuma-kagami'	CCon ELan EPfP MNrw
	- 'Azure'	WFar
N	- 'Barnhawk Sybil'	SKHP
	- 'Barr Purple East' ♀^{H4}	CPrp CRow
I	- 'Blue King'	NHol SPet
I	- 'Blue Peter'	CBen CRow
	- 'Blue Prince'	CBen
	- 'Butterflies in Flight'	CRow
	- 'Caprician Butterfly' ♀^{H4}	EBee EPfP LRHS MBri SMrm WCAu
N	- 'Carnival Prince'	CCon WFar WMoo
	- 'Cascade Crest'	SWat
	- 'Center of Interest'	EBee NBir NCGa
*	- 'Charm'	NRHS
*	- 'Chico Geisho'	WAul
	- 'Chitose-no-tomo'	CRow
	- 'Chiyodajō'	CKel
	- 'Continuing Pleasure' ♀^{H4}	WAul
	- 'Cry of Rejoice'	EBee ECho ECtt NBro SWat WCAu WFar
	- 'Crystal Halo'	CIri LRHS WCAu
	- 'Dace'	GBin
	- 'Dancing Waves'	CRow
I	- 'Darling'	CRow EBee ECho EPfP MBri MMuc NBro NLar SEND SWat WFar WMoo WWEG
	- 'Diamant'	GBin
	- 'Dramatic Moment'	GBuc WFar WWEG
I	- 'Dresden China'	CRow
N	- 'Eden's Blush'	MLHP
N	- 'Eden's Charm'	ELan EPfP GBin LPBA
N	- 'Eden's Paintbrush'	ELan EPfP SPer
N	- 'Eden's Picasso'	CCon ELan
N	- 'Eden's Purple Glory'	CHid GBin WCot WTin
N	- 'Eden's Starship'	CCon
	- 'Electric Rays'	EBee WAul WFar
I	- 'Emotion'	CMac EBee WAul WFar
	- 'Flying Tiger' ♀^{H4}	CIri
I	- 'Fortune'	EBee GBin SMrm WAul
	- 'Freckled Geisha'	CIri ELon IPot LRHS NBir SPoG WCAu WFar
	- 'Frilled Enchantment' ♀^{H4}	EBee IPot SMrm
I	- 'Galatea'	CPLG CPrp LEdu WFar
	- 'Geisha Gown'	SWal
	- 'Gold Bound'	SKHP
N	- 'Gracieuse'	ELan EPfP GBin LRHS NLar SUsu SWat WFar WWEG
	- 'Gusto'	CMHG EBee ELon EPfP IPot LDai MNrw NBro NCGa SWat WBor WFar
	- 'Haru-no-umi'	CKel
	- 'Hatsubeni' new	GEdr
	- 'Hercule'	CHid CPLG CRow GAbr NBir
	- Higo hybrids	LRHS
	- Higo white	SPer
	- 'Hinomaru-nigo' new	GEdr
N	- 'Hokkaido'	CBen CRow
	- 'Hoshi-akari'	NCGa WBor WFar
	- 'Hue and Cry' ♀^{H4}	CIri
	- hybrids	EHon ESgI
*	- 'Innocence'	CKel CMac EHrv NBre NLar SWat WAul WFar WMoo
	- 'Iso-no-nami'	CDes EBee NBro WAul
	- 'Janome-gasa' new	GEdr
*	- 'Jitsugetsu'	CCon NLar
	- 'Jocasta'	CMHG EPfP MBri NCGa SMrm WFar
N	- 'Jodlesong'	ECtt
	- 'Kalamazoo'	WFar
	- 'Katy Mendez' ♀^{H4}	CMHG IPot WAul
*	- 'Kiyo-tsura'	CKel
*	- 'Kiyo-zuru'	EPfP MWts
N	- 'Kogesho'	EPfP GBuc LRHS MNrw NBro NLar
N	- 'Koh Dom'	SPer
	- 'Kuma-funjin'	CPLG CRow
	- 'Kumo-no-obi'	CMHG CPLG EBee GBuc MCot NPnk SWat
*	- 'Kunshikoku'	NLar
	- 'Lace Ruff'	CMHG MBri
	- 'Lady in Waiting'	CMHG ECtt EPfP MBri NLar SMrm SWal WHil
	- 'Landscape at Dawn'	CRow
N	- 'Laughing Lion'	EBee ECtt WAul WCAu WFar WMoo WWEG
	- 'Light at Dawn'	CEnt CMHG EPfP LDai MBel NBro WBor WFar WMoo
N	- 'Lilac Blotch'	SPer
I	- 'Loyalty'	CPLG EBee ECho WFar
	- 'Mancunian' ♀^{H4}	CKel
I	- 'Mandarin'	CBen CRow
	- 'Michinoku-kogane' new	GEdr
	- 'Midsummer Reverie'	CRow
N	- 'Momozomo'	LLHF NBro NLar
§	- 'Moonlight Waves'	CHid CMHG CPLG CPrp CRow EAEE EBee ELan EPfP EShb GAbr GBuc GCra GKin GMaP LRHS MCot MWts NGdn NHol SMrm SWat WAul WCAu WFar
	- 'Murasame' ♀^{H4}	CMHG WAul
	- 'Oase' new	ECtt

	- 'Ocean Mist'	CHid ECtt GBuc
	- 'Oku-banri'	CHEx CPLG CPrp EShb
	- 'Ol' Man River' ♀H4	WAul
	- 'Oriental Eyes'	NGdn NLar WAul
	- pale mauve-flowered	NBir SPer
	- 'Pastel Princess'	WAul
	- 'Pin Stripe'	MBri NLar SUsu SWat WMoo
	- 'Pink Frost'	CRow EBee ELan EPfP LBMP LHop LRHS MWts WFar WTin
	- 'Pinkerton'	CIri
	- 'Pleasant Earlybird'	WAul
	- 'Pleasant Journey'	ECtt EHrv
	- 'Prairie Frost'	NLar
	- 'Prairie Noble'	NLar
N	- 'Purple Glory'	ELan
	- purple-flowered	SPer
	- 'Queen's Tiara'	ELon
	- 'Rakka-no-utage'	NLar
	- 'Ranpo'	CRow
I	- 'Red Dawn'	CBen
I	- 'Reveille'	SWat WAul
	- 'Rivulets of Wine'	CIri
§	- 'Rose Queen' ♀H4	Widely available
	- 'Rowden'	CRow
	- 'Rowden Amir'	CRow
	- 'Rowden Autocrat'	CRow
	- 'Rowden Begum'	CRow
	- 'Rowden Caliph'	CRow
	- 'Rowden Consul'	CRow
	- 'Rowden Dauphin'	CRow
	- 'Rowden Dictator'	CRow
	- 'Rowden Emperor'	CRow
	- 'Rowden Empress' **new**	CRow
	- 'Rowden King'	CRow
	- 'Rowden Knight'	CRow
	- 'Rowden Mikado'	CRow
	- 'Rowden Naib'	CRow
	- 'Rowden Nuncio'	CRow
	- 'Rowden Pasha'	CRow
	- 'Rowden Prince'	CRow
	- 'Rowden Queen'	CRow
	- 'Rowden Shah'	CRow
	- 'Rowden Sirdar' **new**	CRow
	- 'Rowden Sultan' **new**	CRow
I	- 'Royal Banner'	ECtt WAul WFar WWEG
	- 'Royal Crown'	ECho XLum
I	- 'Ruby King'	LEdu WAul
	- 'Ruffled Dimity'	CBcs IPot LRHS MBel
	- 'Sandsation'	CIri
	- 'Sapphire Star'	CKel
	- 'Seigakujo' **new**	GEdr
	- 'Sennyo-no-hora'	CPrp
I	- 'Sensation'	CWCL EBee ECho ECtt GBin SMrm SWat WAul WWEG
	- 'Snowy Hills'	WAul XLum
	- 'Sorcerer's Triumph'	GBin LRHS WFar
	- var. ***spontanea***	SWat
	- - B&SWJ 1103	WCru
	- - B&SWJ 8699	WCru
	- 'Springtime Melody'	WAul
I	- 'Star'	CBen
	- 'Stippled Ripples'	CMHG IPot MWts
	- 'Summer Storm' ♀H4	CKel SPer
	- 'Taketori-hime' (v)	XLum
	- 'Tensyukaku' **new**	GEdr
	- 'The Great Mogul' ♀H4	CKel CRow
	- 'Umi-kaze'	NLar
	- 'Variegata' (v) ♀H4	Widely available
N	- 'Velvety Queen'	CPrp ECtt WAul WCAu
I	- 'White Ladies'	CSBt EBee SWat WWEG
I	- 'White Pearl'	CRow
	- 'Wine Ruffles'	CMHG LSRN SIri SMrm WFar
	- 'Yako-no-tama'	CRow WMoo
	- 'Yamato Hime'	NLar
N	- 'Yedo-yeman'	EBee WFar
N	- 'Yu Nagi'	SPer
	'Entertainer' (TB)	EWoo
	'Épée Violette' (TB) **new**	ESgI
	'Epicenter' (TB)	ESgI XSen
	'Eramosa Skies' (SDB)	WCAu
	'Erect' (IB)	CKel
	'Etched Apricot' (TB)	WCAu
	'Eternal Bliss' (TB)	EWoo
	'Evening Drama' (TB)	WCAu
	'Evening Gown' (TB)	XSen
	'Evening Pond' (MTB)	CKel
	'Ever After' (TB)	ECtt EWoo XSen
	'Evergreen Hideaway' (TB)	CIri
	'Everything Plus' (TB)	ESgI XSen
	'Exotic Isle' (TB)	ECtt ESgI XSen
	'Extra' (BB)	CPBP LLHF
	'Extra Innings' (TB)	EWoo
	'Eye Magic' (IB) ♀H4	CKel XSen
	'Eye of Tiger'	see *I.* 'Tigereye'
	'Eyebright' (SDB) ♀H4	CBro WCAu
	'Fabuleux' (TB)	SIri
	'Faenelia Hicks' (La)	WMAq
	'Falconeer' (TB)	CIri
	'Fall Empire' (TB)	EWoo
	'Fall Enterprise' (TB)	CIri
	'Fall Fiesta' (TB)	XSen
	'Fancy Brass' (TB)	SIri
	'Fancy Dress' (TB)	SIri
	'Fanfaron' (TB)	ESgI XSen
	'Farleigh Damson' (SDB)	SIri
	'Fashion Holiday' (IB)	SIri
	'Fashion Lady' (MDB)	CBro ECho
	'Fathom' (IB)	WCAu
	'Feminine Charm' (TB)	MRav WCAu
	'Festive Skirt' (TB)	CKel
	'Feu du Ciel' (TB) ♀H4	ESgI EWoo XSen
	'Fierce Fire' (IB) ♀H4	CKel
	'Fiesta Time' (TB)	CWCL ECtt XSen
	'Filibuster' (TB)	WCAu
	filifolia var. ***latifolia***	NMin
	'Film Festival' (TB)	ESgI
	'Finalist' (TB)	WCAu XSen
	'Firebeard' (TB)	CIri
	'Firebug' (IB)	ESgI XSen
	'Firecracker' (TB)	MRav WCAu
	'First Interstate' (TB)	CWCL ESgI XSen
	'First Movement' (TB)	ESgI
	'First Romance' (SDB)	LSRN SIri
	'First Violet' (TB)	ESgI
	'Fit the Bill' (TB)	EWoo
	'Five Star Admiral' (TB)	XSen
	'Flaming Dragon' (TB)	XSen
	'Flaming Victory' (TB)	XSen
	flavescens	ESgI EWoo SBch WCAu XSen
	'Fleur Collette Louise' (La)	CIri
	'Flight of Fantasy' (La)	CKel
	'Flight to Mars' (TB)	CIri
	'Flirting Again' (SDB) ♀H4	SIri
	'Floorshow' (TB)	XSen
§	'Florentina' (IB/TB) ♀H4	CArn CBro CHby COlW EBee ECGP ESgI EWoo GCal GPoy MNHC MRav NBid NBir SEND SIde WCAu WHer XSen

'Florentine Silk' (TB) WCAu
'Flumadiddle' (IB) CBro CKel WCFE
'Flushed Delight' (TB) CIri
'Flute Enchantée' (TB) CIri XSen
'Focus' (TB) XSen
foetidissima ♀H4 Widely available
- 'Aurea' GQue WCot
- ***chinensis*** see *I. foetidissima* var. *citrina*
§ - var. ***citrina*** CBre CCon ECGP EPfP EPri EWld GAbr GCal GCra IBlr LEdu NLar SChr SEND SLPl SWal WCot WGwG
- 'Fructu Albo' EBee GBin NSti
- var. ***lutescens*** CHid EPPr
- 'Variegata' (v) ♀H4 CElw EPfP MSCN NBir NPer
- yellow-seeded GCal
'Fogbound' (TB) WCAu
'Foggy Dew' (TB) EAEE EWTr LRHS NCGa NPnk
'Fondation Van Gogh' (TB) XSen
'Foolish Fancy' (TB) SIri
'Footloose' (TB) SIri XSen
'For Mary' (TB) CIri
'Foreign Legion' (TB) **new** WCAu
'Foreigner' (TB) **new** WCAu
'Forest Light' (SDB) CBro ESgI
'Forever Blue' (SDB) WCAu
'Forever Gold' (TB) EWoo XSen
'Forever Yours' (TB) WAul
'Forge Fire' (TB) ESgI
formosana ECho
- B&SWJ 3076 WCru
'Forrest Hills' (TB) EBee IPot LRHS
forrestii ♀H4 CCon CHid CMac CPLG EBee ECho GAbr GBin GCal GCra GKev ITim LPBA LRHS MBri MHer MMuc NBir NBro NGdn SRot WAbe
'Fort Apache' (TB) EWes EWoo
'Fortunata' (TB) XSen
'Fortunate Son' EWoo WCAu
'Fortune Teller' (TB) CKel
'Fourfold Blue' (SpH) GBin
'Foxy Lady' (TB) EWoo
'Framboise' (TB) XSen
'Frances Iva' (TB) EWoo
'Francheville' (TB) EWoo
'Frank Elder' (Reticulata) EBee ECho EPot GKev LAma LLHF LWst MRav SDeJ
'Frans Hals' (Dut) GKev MMHG MNrw
'Freedom Flight' (TB) CIri
'French Can Can' (TB) EWoo SIri
'French Horn' (TB) CIri
'French Rose' (TB) CKel
'Fresno Calypso' (TB) ESgI WCAu XSen
'Friday Blues' (BB) WAul
'Frigiya' (Spuria) WAul
'Frison-roche' (TB) CWCL
'Frisounette' (TB) ESgI
'Fritillary Flight' (IB) ♀H4 CKel SAga
'Frivolité' (TB) ESgI
'Frontier Lady' (TB) CIri
'Frontier Marshall' (TB) XSen
'Frost and Flame' (TB) ECtt ELan LBuc LRHS MCot MRav NBir NLar SBfd SDeJ SPer SPoG SWat WAul WWEG
'Frost Echo' (TB) EWoo
'Frosted Angel' (SDB) CBro
'Frosted Biscuit' (TB) ♀H4 CKel
'Frosted Fantasy' (TB) CIri
'Frosted Velvet' (MTB) WCAu
'Frosty Crown' (SDB) CDes
'Frosty Elegance' (IB) **new** ESgI
'Frosty Jewels' (TB) XSen
'Fruit Cocktail' (IB) CKel CRDP XSen
'Full Sun' (Spuria) **new** EWoo
fulva ♀H3 CDes CIri CRow EPri GCal LPot MMHG MWts NBir NBro NSti WBor WCot WHil WTin
- 'Marvell Gold' (La) CRow EBee
× ***fulvala*** ♀H4 CCon EWes GBin NBir NSti WTin
- 'Violacea' LRHS
'Funambule' (TB) EWoo
'Furnaceman' (SDB) CBro
'Futuriste' (TB) SIri
'Gai Luron' (TB) WWEG
'Gallant Moment' (TB) ECtt ESgI EWoo SIri XSen
'Galleon Gold' (SDB) CKel
'Galway' (IB) SIri XSen
'Game Plan' (TB) **new** WCAu
'Gandalf the Grey' (TB) **new** ESgI
N 'Gelbe Mantel' (Sino-Sib) CHid NBir NSti WFar
'Gemstone Walls' (TB) ESgI
'Gentius' (TB) WMnd
'Gentle' (SDB) WCAu
'George' (Reticulata) ♀H4 CAvo CBro ECho EPfP EPot ERCP GKev LAma LRHS NMin NRHS NWad WBrk WCot WHoo
'Gerald Darby' see *I.* × *robusta* 'Gerald Darby'
germanica ♀H4 MMuc SEND WCAu
- var. ***florentina*** see *I.* 'Florentina'
§ - 'Nepalensis' WCAu
- 'The King' see *I. germanica* 'Nepalensis'
'Gertrude' (TB) EWoo
'Ghost Train' (TB) CIri EWoo
'Gingerbread Man' (SDB) CBro CMea CPBP EHrv ESgI MBrN SMrm WCAu
'Gingersnap' (TB) EWoo
'Glacier' (TB) ECho
'Glacier Gold' (TB) XSen
'Glad Rags' (TB) XSen
'Gladys Austin' (TB) XSen
'Glowing Embers' (TB) **new** ESgI
'Gnu' (TB) XSen
'Gnus Flash' (TB) CIri
'Goddess of Green' (IB) EWoo
'Godfrey Owen' (TB) CKel WCAu
'Godsend' (TB) CIri CKel
'Going Home' (TB) ♀H4 SIri
'Going My Way' (TB) ESgI EWoo LSou SIri WCAu WWEG XSen
'Gold Burst' (TB) XSen
'Gold Country' (TB) XSen
'Gold for Bold' **new** WCAu
'Gold of Autumn' (TB) CKel SMrm
'Goldberry' (IB) WCAu
'Golden Alien' (TB) CIri
'Golden Alps' (TB) SRms WCAu
'Golden Beauty' GKev SDeJ
'Golden Child' (SDB) XSen
'Golden Encore' (TB) CKel WCAu
'Golden Forest' (TB) GBin
'Golden Immortal' (TB) EWoo
'Golden Panther' (TB) WCAu
'Golden Planet' (TB) CKel
'Golden Violet' (SDB) ESgI
'Goldfinger' (TB) **new** LWst
goniocarpa WAbe
- KR 3739 GEdr
'Good Life' **new** WCAu

'Good Looking' (TB)	ESgI WCAu
'Good Show' (TB)	ESgI EWoo XSen
'Good Vibrations' (TB)	SIri XSen
'Goodbye Girl' (TB) **new**	ESgI
'Goodbye Heart' (TB)	EWoo LSRN
'Gordon' (Reticulata)	CAvo ECho EPfP EPot ERCP GKev LAma SMrm
gormanii	see *I. tenax*
'Gosh' (SDB)	CKel
'Gossip' (SDB)	CBro ESgI
'Gracchus' (TB)	ESgI EWoo LRHS WCAu
gracilipes × lacustris	GEdr WAbe
graeberiana	ECho EPot GKev SDeJ
- yellow fall	ECho LWst
graminea ♀H4	CAvo CBro CHid CMac CPne CRow EBee ECha ECho EHrv ELan EPfP EPri GKev IFro LLWP LRHS NBir NMen NSti SBch SEND WAul WCAu WCot
- var. ***pseudocyperus***	GCal NMRc SDys
graminifolia	see *I. kerneriana*
'Granada Gold' (TB)	SRms XSen
'Grand Circle' (TB)	CIri EWoo
'Grand Illusion' (Spuria) **new**	EWoo
'Grand Waltz' (TB)	XSen
'Grape Cordial' (SDB)	WAul
'Grapelet' (MDB)	CPBP WCAu
'Grapeshot' (TB)	CIri
'Grapetizer' (TB) **new**	WCAu
'Great Gatsby' (TB)	CKel
'Great Lakes' (TB)	ESgI EWoo
'Grecian Skies' (TB)	ESgI
'Green Eyed Lady' (TB) **new**	ESgI
'Green Ice' (TB)	CKel LRHS MRav
'Green Prophecy' (TB)	CKel
'Green Spot' (SDB) ♀H4	CBro CKel EBee ECho ECtt EHrv ELan ESgI GBuc LAst LHop LRHS MRav NBir NLar SDeJ SPer WAul
'Green Streak' (TB)	CIri
'Gringo' (TB)	WCAu
'Grooving' (BB) **new**	ESgI
'Guatemala' (TB)	WCAu
'Guess Who I Am' (TB) **new**	WCAu
'Gwyneth Evans' (BB) ♀H4	CKel
'Gypsy Beauty' (Dut)	CAvo EPfP GKev LAma MWat SDeJ
'Gypsy Jewels' (TB)	CKel ESgI LTen XSen
'Gypsy Romance' (TB) ♀H4	EIri ESgI EWoo SIri WCAu
'Habit' (TB)	EWoo WAul WCAu
'Hafnium' (SDB)	CKel
'Hakuna Matata' (AB)	SDys
halophila	see *I. spuria* subsp. *halophila*
'Happenstance' (TB)	EWoo
'Happy Hugs' (TB) **new**	WCAu
'Happy Mood' (IB) ♀H4	NBre WCAu
'Harbor Blue' (TB)	CKel MWat SWat WCAu WWEG
'Harlow Gold' (IB)	ESgI
'Harmony' ambig.	SPer
'Harmony' (Reticulata)	CAvo CBro ECho EPfP EPot GKev LAma LRHS MBri MWat NWad SDeJ
'Harriette Halloway' (TB)	CWGN EPfP EShb ETod LRHS LSRN NLar SMrm SRGP WCot
hartwegii	ECho
- subsp. ***hartwegii***	IGor
- subsp. ***pinetorum***	IGor
'Harvest King' (TB)	ECtt ESgI XSen
'Harvest of Memories' (TB)	ESgI EWoo WWEG
'Haut les Voiles' (TB)	CWCL

	'Haute Couture' (TB)	XSen
	'Haviland' (TB)	XSen
	'Headcorn' (MTB) ♀H4	SIri WAul
	'Headline Banner' (BB)	EWoo WCAu
	'Heartbeat Away' (TB)	CIri
	'Heart's Radiance' (MTB)	SDys
	'Heather Carpet' (SDB)	WCAu
	'Heather Sky' (TB)	CIri
	'Heavenly Days' (TB)	WCAu
	'Heaven's Edge' (TB)	WCAu
	'Helen Collingwood' (TB)	ESgI EWoo
	'Helen Dawn' (TB) ♀H4	SIri
	'Helen McGregor' (TB)	CKel EWoo
	'Helen Proctor' (IB)	ESgI WCAu WCot XSen
	'Helena Terry' (TB) **new**	ESgI
	'Helene C.' (TB)	EWoo XSen
	'Helge' (IB)	COlW ECho NBre SWat
	'Hellcat' (IB)	EWoo WAul WCAu
	'Hello Darkness' (TB) ♀H4	ESgI EWoo WCAu WCot XSen
	'Hell's Fire' (TB)	ELon EWoo MBri WCAu
	'Hemstitched' (TB)	EWoo
	'Her Majesty' (TB)	EWoo
	'Her Royal Highness' (TB) **new**	ECtt
	'Hercules' (Reticulata)	ECho LAma NMin
	'Here Comes The Sun' (TB)	WCAu
	'Heure Bleue' (TB)	EWoo
	'Hi' (IB)	CIri
	'High Barbaree' (TB)	EWoo
	'High Blue Sky' (TB)	WCAu
	'High Command' (TB)	CKel
	'High Impact' (TB)	EWoo
	'High Peak'	WCAu
	'High Roller' (TB) ♀H4	CIri
	'Highline Amethyst' (Spuria)	EPri WAul
	'Highline Halo' (Spuria) **new**	EWoo
	'Hildegarde' (Dut)	SDeJ
	'His Royal Highness'	WCAu
	'Hissy-Fit' (IB)	CKel
	histrio	ECho EPot
	- subsp. ***aintabensis***	ECho GKev LAma
	histrioides	ECho
§	- 'Angel's Tears' (Reticulata)	CAvo ECho GKev NMin
	- 'Halkis' (Reticulata)	EPot ERCP GKev LAma NMin
	- 'Lady Beatrix Stanley'	CBro ECho EPot ERCP LAma LLHF NMen NMin
N	- 'Major'	CDes ECho GKev LAma NMin
N	- 'Michael Tears'	ECho
	- var. ***sophenensis***	ECho
	'Hocus Pocus' (SDB)	CWGN EAEE EBee ECho EPfP EWTr EWoo GBuc LRHS WAul
	'Holden Clough' (SpH) ♀H4	CPLG CPrp ELan EPfP GBin GCra GMaP LEdu MBel MRav NBir NEgg NGdn NSti WAul WBrk WFar WHer WSHC WWEG
	'Holden's Child'	CWat MWts
	Hollingsworth seedling **new**	WCAu
	'Hollywood Nights' (TB)	EWoo
	'Holy Night' (TB)	CKel
	'Honey Behold' (SDB)	CKel
	'Honey Glazed' (IB)	ESgI WAul WCAu
	'Honey Mocha Lotta' (Spuria) **new**	EWoo
	'Honeylove' (SDB)	SDys
	'Honeymoon Suite' (TB)	EWoo
	'Honeyplic' (IB) ♀H4	ESgI SIri
	'Honington' (SDB)	WCAu

	'Honky Tonk Blues' (TB)	CKel ESgI LSRN
	'Honky Tonk Hussy' (BB)	CKel
	'Honorabile' (MTB)	ESgI EWoo WCAu
	hoogiana ♀H3	ECho EPot GKev LRHS LWst
	- 'Purpurea'	ECho
§	***hookeri***	COIW CPBP EBee ECho ELan GBin GEdr GKev GMaP IGor MGos SMrm WCAu
	- SDR 2202	GKev
	hookeriana	LRHS
	'Hoptoit' (TB) **new**	CIri
	'Horizon Bleu' (TB)	EWoo
	'Horned Rosyred' (TB)	EWoo
§	'Hornpipe' (TB)	WCAu
	'Hortensia Rose' (TB)	SIri
	'Hot Spiced Wine' (TB)	EWoo
	'Hot to Trot' (TB)	ESgI
	'Howard Weed' (TB)	MNrw
	'Huckleberry Fudge' (TB)	WAul XSen
	'Hula Hands' (IB)	CIri
	'Hula Moon' (TB)	ESgI
	hyrcana	ECho
	'I Repeat' (TB)	ESgI XSen
	'I Seek You' (TB)	ESgI
	iberica	ECho
§	- subsp. ***elegantissima***	ECho LWst
	'Ice Dancer' (TB) ♀H4	CKel
	'Iced Tea' (TB) ♀H4	CIri
	'Ida' (Reticulata)	ECho LAma
	'Idol' (TB)	EWoo
	'Ila Crawford' (Spuria) ♀H4	XSen
	'I'll Be Back' (IB)	WAul
	illyrica	see *I. pallida*
	'I'm Back' (TB) **new**	WCAu
	imbricata	GKev
	'Immortality' (TB)	CKel CWGN ESgI WCAu WWEG XSen
	'Imperative' (IB)	EWoo SIri
	'Imperator' (Dut)	ECho
	'Imperial Bronze' (Spuria)	SMrm WAul WCAu
	'Impetuous' (BB) ♀H4	CKel
	'Imprimis' (TB)	EWoo XSen
	'In Concert' (TB)	SMrm
	'In Limbo' (IB)	CKel
	'In Love' (TB)	XSen
	'In Town' (TB)	EWoo XSen
	'Incentive' (TB)	ECtt EWoo
*	'Incoscente' (TB)	ESgI
	'Indeed' (IB)	ESgI
	'Indian Chief' (TB)	CCCN CWCL EPfP ESgI EWoo LTen MRav WCAu WWEG
	'Indian Hills' (TB)	EWoo
	'Indian Idyll' (IB)	CKel EWoo
	'Indian Jewel' (SDB)	ECho
	'Indian Pow Wow' (SDB)	CRDP CSev
N	'Indiana Sunset' (TB)	CKel
	'Indigo Flight' (IB)	CKel
	'Indigo Princess' (TB)	CKel EWoo XSen
	'Infanta' (SDB) **new**	WCAu
	'Infernal Fire' (TB)	CIri
	'Inferno' (TB)	EWoo
	'Infrared' (TB) **new**	WCAu
	'Innocent Devil' (TB)	CIri
	'Innocent Heart' (IB) ♀H4	WCAu
	'Innocent Pink' (TB)	ESgI
	innominata	CAvo EBee ECha ECho EPot GAbr GKev IBlr LHop LRHS NBir NBro NMen SRms WWEG
	- JCA 1	GEdr
	- apricot-flowered	IBlr
	- Ballyrogan hybrids	IBlr
	- bronze-flowered	MMuc
	- dwarf	NMen
	- 'Peacock'	GEdr
	- yellow-flowered	NMen NRya
	'Inscription' (SDB)	ECho
	'Instant Hit' (TB)	WCAu
	'Interpol' (TB)	ESgI EWoo XSen
	'Invicta Daybreak' (IB)	SIri
	'Invicta Garnet' (SDB)	SIri
	'Invicta Gold' (SDB)	SIri
	'Invisible' (SDB) **new**	WCAu
	'Irish Chant' (SDB)	WCAu
	'Irish Doll' (MDB)	WCAu
	'Irish Harp' (SDB) **new**	ESgI
	'Irish Tune' (TB)	ESgI
	'Iron Eagle' (TB)	CIri
	'Isabelle'	LSRN XSen
	'Island Sunset' (TB)	ESgI SIri
	'Isoline' (TB)	ESgI
	'Italian Velvet' (TB) **new**	WCAu
	'J.S. Dijt' (Reticulata)	CAvo CBro ECho EPfP EPot ERCP GKev LAma MBri MGos SDeJ SPhx
	'Jabal' (SDB)	SIri
	'Jack Attack' (La)	SMrm SPoG
	'Jacquessiana'	EWoo WCAu
	'Jade Mist' (SDB)	ECho
	'Jaguar Blue' (TB)	EWoo WCAu
	'Jane Phillips' (TB) ♀H4	Widely available
	'Jane Taylor' (SDB)	CBro
	'Janet Lane' (BB)	CKel
	'Janine Louise' (TB) ♀H4	CKel
	japonica ♀H3	CBcs CHEx CPLG ECho EPfP GHim NLar NPer WAul XLum XSen
	- B&SWJ 8921	WCru
	- 'Bourne Graceful'	CPLG
	- 'Ledger'	CAvo CDes CHll CMac CPLG CPrp ECha EHrv ELan EPfP IGor MRav SEND SMad WWFP
I	- 'Purple Heart'	CAvo
N	- 'Rudolph Spring'	GCal WWFP
I	- 'Snowflake'	CAvo
§	- 'Variegata' (v) ♀H3	CBro CDes CHEx CKel CPrp ECha ECho EHrv ELan ELon ESwi MHer NBro NPer SAga SBfd SEND SMad WHil WWFP XSen
	'Jasper Gem' (MDB)	ECho NBir
	'Jayceetee' (TB)	CIri
	'Jazz Festival' (TB)	SIri WCAu XSen
	'Jazz Solo' (TB) **new**	WCAu
	'Jazzed Up' (TB)	XSen
	'Je l'Adore' (TB)	EWoo
	'Jean Cayeux' (TB)	ESgI
	'Jean Guymer' (TB)	ESgI NBir
	'Jeanne Price' (TB)	ESgI EWoo LSRN WCAu
	'Jelly Belly' (SDB)	EWoo
	'Jennie Grace' (SDB)	SIri
	'Jeremy Brian' (SDB) ♀H4	WCAu
	'Jeremy Jets On' (TB) **new**	CIri
	'Jesse Lee' (SDB)	CKel
	'Jesse's Song' (TB)	ESgI WCAu XSen
	'Jet-Setter' (TB)	CIri
	'Jeunesse' (TB)	ESgI
	'Jewel Baby' (SDB)	CBro CKel
	'Jeweler's Art' (SDB)	ESgI EWoo
	'Jiansada' (SDB)	CBro
	'Jigsaw' (TB)	ESgI XSen

	Name	Suppliers
	'Jitterbug' (TB)	EHrv
	'Jive' (SDB) **new**	WCAu
	'Joanna' (TB)	LSRN NLar WWEG
	'John' (IB)	CKel LSRN
	'Joli Coeur' (TB)	EWoo
	'Joseph Henry' (TB)	WCAu
	'Joyce' (Reticulata)	CBro ECho EPfP EPot GKev LAma MBri NLar SDeJ SPhx
	'Joyce Terry' (TB)	CWan
	'Jubilant Spirit' (Spuria)	EWes
	'Jubilation' (TB)	EWoo
	'Jubilee Gem' (TB)	CKel
	'Jud Paynter' (TB)	CKel
	'Judy Mogil' (TB) **new**	CIri
	'Julia Vennor' (TB)	CKel
	'Juliet' (TB)	ESgI
	'Jump Start' (IB)	EWoo WCAu
	'Jumping Jupiter' (TB) **new**	CIri
	'June Prom' (IB)	EAEE LRHS MNHC SRGP
	'Jungle Fires' (TB)	WCAu
	'Jungle Shadows' (BB)	ESgI EWoo MRav NBir WCAu
	'Jungle Warrior' (SDB)	CKel
	'Jurassic Park' (TB)	ESgI EWoo WCAu XSen
	'Just Dance' (IB)	ESgI
	'Just Jennifer' (BB)	WAul WCAu
	kaempferi	see *I. ensata*
	'Karen' (TB)	LSRN
	kashmiriana	ECre
	'Katharine Hodgkin' (Reticulata) ♀H4	Widely available
	- dark-flowered	NMin
	'Katie-Koo' (IB) ♀H4	CKel
	'Katy Petts' (SDB)	ESgI WCAu
	'Kayleigh-Jayne Louise' (TB)	CKel
	'Kelway Renaissance' (TB)	CKel
	'Ken's Choice' (TB) ♀H4	CKel
	'Kent Blackguard' (IB)	SIri
	'Kent Compote' (IB)	SIri
	'Kent Pride' (TB)	CSBt CWGN EAEE EBee ECha ECtt EPfP ESgI ETod EWoo GBin IPot LRHS MCot MRav SBea SBfd SGar SPoG SWat WAul WTin WWlt
	'Kentish Icon' (SDB)	SIri
	'Kentucky Bluegrass' (SDB)	WCAu
	'Kentucky Derby' (TB)	XSen
§	***kerneriana*** ♀H4	GBuc LRHS MBel NBir
	'Kharput' (IB)	EWoo
	'Kildonan' (TB)	WCAu
	'King's Jester' (TB)	EWoo
	'Kirkstone' (TB)	WCAu
	kirkwoodii	ECho LWst
	'Kiss of Summer' (TB) ♀H4	ESgI SDys WAul
	'Kissing Circle' (TB)	ESgI EWoo SBfd
	'Kiwi Slices' (SDB)	CPBP ESgI
	'Knick Knack' (MDB)	CBro CMea CPBP ECho ELan EPfP GKev GMaP LBee MRav SDeJ SMrs SPoG WAul
	'Koi' (TB) **new**	ESgI
	korolkowii	ECho LWst
	'La Meije' (TB)	SIri
	'La Nina Rosa' (BB)	WCAu
	'La Senda' (Spuria)	WCot
	'Lace Legacy' (TB)	ECtt EWoo LSRN
	'Laced Cotton' (TB)	XSen
	'Laced Lemonade' (SDB)	MBri
§	***lactea*** ♀H4	XSen
	- CC 3768	WCot
	lacustris ♀H4	CBro NMen WAbe XSen
	'Lacy Snowflake' (TB)	LHop
	'Lad' **new**	WCAu
	'Lady Belle' (MTB) ♀H4	ESgI
	'Lady Essex' (TB)	EWoo
	'Lady Friend' (TB)	WCAu XSen
	'Lady Gale' (IB)	CKel
	'Lady Ilse' (TB)	WCAu
	'Lady in Red' (SDB)	ESgI WCAu
	'Lady Mohr' (AB)	CKel
	'Lady Phyllis' (MTB) **new**	CIri
	'Lady R' (SDB)	ECho
	laevigata ♀H4	CRow ECha ECho EHon ELan EPfP EWay ITim LPBA MMuc MRav NBro NPer SEND SGar SPer SWat WFar WMAq WMoo WShi WWEG
	- var. ***alba***	CRow ECha ECho EHon ELan EPfP EWTr LPBA SWat WFar WMoo
	- 'Atropurpurea'	CRow
	- 'Colchesterensis'	CRow EPri ITim NGdn NPer SWat WMAq
I	- 'Dorothy'	LPBA NGdn
N	- 'Dorothy Robinson'	LRHS SWat
	- 'Elegant'	see *I. laevigata* 'Weymouth Elegant'
I	- 'Elegante'	EWay
*	- 'Elgar'	WMAq
	- 'Liam Johns'	CRow
	- 'Midnight'	see *I. laevigata* 'Weymouth Midnight'
N	- 'Monstrosa'	CDes EWay
	- 'Plena' (d)	CRow
	- 'Rashomon'	CRow
	- 'Regal'	CWat
	- 'Richard Greaney'	CRow EWay
	- 'Rose Queen'	see *I. ensata* 'Rose Queen'
	- 'Rowden Starlight'	CRow CWat
	- 'Shirasagi'	CRow
I	- 'Snowdrift'	CRow CWat EWay LPBA LRHS NBir NGdn NLar NPer NRHS SPer SWat WFar WMAq
	- 'Variegata' (v) ♀H4	CBen CRow CWat EAEE ECha ECho EHoe EPfP EWay LPBA LRHS MWts NBro NGdn NPer SPer SWat WMAq WMoo WTin
	- 'Violet Garth'	EWay
	- 'Weymouth'	see *I. laevigata* 'Weymouth Blue'
§	- 'Weymouth Blue'	CBen CRow EWay
§	- 'Weymouth Elegant'	CRow
§	- 'Weymouth Midnight'	CMil CRow LPBA SWat
	- 'Weymouth Purity'	EWay
	'Lamia' (TB) **new**	CIri
N	'Langport Chapter' (IB)	CKel ESgI
N	'Langport Chief' (IB)	CKel
N	'Langport Claret' (IB)	CKel ESgI
N	'Langport Curlew' (IB)	CKel ESgI SMrm
N	'Langport Duchess' (IB)	ESgI WTin
N	'Langport Fairy' (IB)	CKel
N	'Langport Flame' (IB)	CKel ESgI WTin
N	'Langport Hope' (IB)	CKel
N	'Langport Jane' (IB)	CKel
N	'Langport Lady' (IB)	CKel
N	'Langport Lord' (IB)	ESgI
	'Langport Minstrel' (IB)	CKel ESgI
N	'Langport Pearl' (IB)	CKel
	'Langport Phoenix' (IB)	CKel
N	'Langport Pinnacle' (IB)	CKel
N	'Langport Smoke' (IB)	CKel
	'Langport Snow' (IB)	CKel
N	'Langport Song' (IB)	CKel
N	'Langport Star' (IB)	CKel ESgI

	Name	Suppliers
	'Langport Storm' (IB)	CKel EAEE ECGP EPfP MRav WAul WTin
N	'Langport Sun' (IB)	CKel ESgI
N	'Langport Swift' (IB)	CKel
	'Langport Sylvia' (IB)	CKel
N	'Langport Tartan' (IB)	CKel
N	'Langport Violet' (IB)	CKel ESgI
	'Langport Vista' (IB)	CKel
	'Langport Warrior' (IB)	CKel
	'Langport Wren' (IB) ΨH4	CBro CKel EAEE EBee EPfP EPri ESgI GBuc GCal GQue LAst LHop LRHS MBri MCot MWhi NBir NGdn SBch SBfd WAul WTin WWEG
	'Lark Rise' (TB) ΨH4	CKel
	'Larry Gaulter' (TB)	WCAu
	'Late Liftoff' (TB)	CIri
§	***latifolia*** ΨH4	ECho GKev MMuc NMin SEND WShi
	– 'Duchess of York'	EBee ECho GKev
	– 'Isabella'	ECho GKev WCot
	– 'King of the Blues'	CAvo EBee ECho GKev
	– 'Mansfield'	ECho GKev
	– 'Montblanc'	CAvo EBee ECho GKev
	– 'Queen of the Blues' (Eng)	ECho
	– wild-collected	GCal
	'Latin Lark' (TB)	ESgI
	'Laura Jean' (TB)	EWoo
	'Laura Louise' (La)	SKHP
	'Lava Moonscape' (TB)	CIri
	lazica ΨH4	CBct CBro CHll CMac CPrp CRow EBee EPPr EPfP EPot ESgI IBlr LRHS MRav NBir NCGa NSti SBch SEND SPer WCot WGwG WHil
	– 'Joy Bishop'	CJun WCot
*	– 'Richard Nutt'	CJun ELon WCot
N	– 'Turkish Blue'	CPrp IBlr
	'Lazuline'	LWst
	'Legato' (TB)	ESgI
*	'Lemon Beauty' (TB)	LHop
	'Lemon Brocade' (TB)	EWoo WCAu
	'Lemon Fever' (TB)	ESgI
	'Lemon Flare' (SDB)	EIri MRav SRms
	'Lemon Flurry' (IB)	SBch
	'Lemon Ice' (TB)	ECha EPfP GBin LBuc LRHS SBfd SDeJ SPer WCAu
	'Lemon Lyric' (TB)	ESgI
*	'Lemon Peel' (IB)	CKel
	'Lemon Pop' (IB)	WCAu
	'Lemon Puff' (MDB)	CBro WCAu
	'Lemon Tree' (TB)	WCAu
	'Lemon Whip' (IB)	EWoo
N	'Lena' (SDB)	CBro
	'Lenkoran' (Spuria)	WAul
	'Lenna M' (SDB)	CKel CPBP ECho
	'Lenora Pearl' (BB)	XSen
	'Lent A. Williamson' (TB)	GMaP WWEG
	'Leprechaun's Delight' (SDB)	CKel
	'Leprechaun's Purse' (SDB)	WCAu
	'Let's Elope' (IB)	ESgI
	'Licorice Stick' (TB)	EBee XSen
	'Light Beam' (TB)	XSen
	'Light Cavalry' (IB)	ESgI EWoo
	'Light Laughter' (IB)	WCAu
	'Light Rebuff' (TB)	EWoo
	'Lilac Times'	EWoo
	'Lilli-white' (SDB)	CKel CWat EBee EHrv ELan EPfP LRHS MBNS MRav SBfd SPhx SPoG WCAu WWEG
	'Lilting' (TB)	XSen
	'Lima Colada' (SDB)	SMrm
	'Limbo' (SpH)	CRow
	'Lime Fizz' (TB)	XSen
	'Limelight' (TB)	SRms
	'Lion King' (Dut) **new**	WFar
	'Little Black Belt' (SDB)	EWoo
	'Little Blackfoot' (SDB)	CDes ESgI WCAu WCot
	'Little Blue-eyes' (SDB)	ESgI WCAu
	'Little Bluets' (SDB)	ESgI
	'Little Dandy' (SDB)	ECho
	'Little Dogie' (SDB)	ECho
	'Little Dream' (SDB)	WCAu
	'Little Firecracker' (SDB)	WCAu
	'Little Paul' (MTB)	ESgI
	'Little Rosy Wings' (SDB)	CBro CPBP
	'Little Shadow' (IB)	MRav SRms WWEG
	'Little Showoff' (SDB)	ESgI
	'Little Snowman'	LRHS
	'Little Tilgates' (CH) ΨH3	WCot
	'Living Waters' (TB) **new**	ESgI
	'Local Color' (TB)	ESgI EWoo SIri XSen
	'Lodore' (TB)	SRms
	'Logo' (IB)	WCAu
	'Lohengrin' (TB)	EWoo
	'Lollipop' (SDB)	ESgI SIri
	longipetala	EWes NBir
	'Looking Forward' (TB) **new**	ESgI
	'Lookingglass Eyes' (Spuria)	CIri
	'Loop the Loop' (TB)	CMac EBee EWoo LAst NBre SCoo SPoG SWat
	'Loose Valley' (MTB) ΨH4	SIri
	'Lord Warden' (TB)	ECGP ECtt EPfP LDai LRHS MCot SMrm
	'Lorilee' (TB)	ESgI WCAu
	'Lothario' (TB)	WCAu
	'Lottie Lou' (TB) **new**	SIri
	'Lotus Land' (TB)	WCAu
	'Louisa's Song' (TB) **new**	WCAu
	'Louvois' (TB)	ESgI EWoo NLar
	'Love Power' (BB)	WAul
	'Love the Sun' (TB)	ESgI XSen
	'Lovely Again' (TB)	LRHS MRav WCAu
	'Lovely Dawn' (TB)	WCAu
	'Lovely Leilani' (TB)	ESgI
	'Lovely Señorita' (TB)	WCAu
	'Love's Tune' (IB)	LBuc SRGP SWat
	'Low Ho Silver' (IB)	WCAu
	'Loyalist' (TB)	CPar EWoo SIri
	'Lucky Charm' (MTB)	CMea
	'Lucky Devil' (Spuria) ΨH4	CIri
	'Lucy's Gift' (MTB) ΨH4	SRGP WAul
	'Lugano' (TB)	ESgI EWoo
	'Lula Marguerite' (TB)	EWoo
	'Luli-Ann' (SDB) ΨH4	CKel
	'Lullaby of Spring' (TB)	CKel
	'Lumarco' (TB)	EWoo
	'Lumière d'Automne' (TB)	ESgI XSen
	'Luminosity' (TB)	ESgI
	'Lunar Frost' (IB)	SIri
	'Lure of Gold' (IB)	WCAu
	lutescens ΨH4	ECho EPot GCra WCot
§	– 'Campbellii'	ECho
§	– subsp. ***lutescens***	XSen
	'Lyrique' (BB)	CKel WAul
	maackii	GEdr
	macrosiphon	EBee IGor
	'Madame Lynn' (Spuria) **new**	EWoo

	'Madeira Belle' (TB)	ESgI
	'Madeleine Frances' (SDB)	SIri
	'Magharee' (TB)	ESgI
	'Magic Kingdom' (TB)	CIri
	'Magic Man' (TB)	XSen
	'Magical Encounter' (TB)	EWoo
	magnifica ♀H3-4	ECho ELon GKev
N	- 'Agalik'	ECho
	- 'Alba'	ECho GKev LWst
*	'Mahogany Mix' (Dut)	LAma
	'Maid of Orange' (BB) **new**	WCAu
	'Maisie Lowe' (TB)	ESgI EWoo
	'Majestic Ruler' (TB)	WCAu
	'Making Eyes' (SDB)	WCAu
	'Man About Town' (TB)	WCAu
	'Mandarin Purple' (Sino-Sib)	NGdn
	mandshurica	CPBP
	'Mango Entree' (TB)	WCAu
	'Mango Smoothy' (BB) **new**	ESgI
	'Many Mahalos'	WAul
	'Mara' (IB)	CKel
	maracandica	LWst
	'Margrave' (TB)	EWoo XSen
	'Marguérite' (Reticulata/v)	ECho
	mariae	LWst
	'Mariposa Autumn' (TB)	ESgI EWoo SIri
	'Mariposa Skies' (TB)	ESgI
	'Mariposa Wizard' (IB)	WAul
	'Marmalade Skies' (BB)	WCAu
	'Maroon Caper' (IB)	SBch
	'Martyn Rix'	see *I. confusa* 'Martyn Rix'
	'Mary Constance' (IB) ♀H4	CKel
	'Mary Frances' (TB)	ESgI LSRN WCAu XSen
	'Mary McIlroy' (SDB) ♀H4	CBro CKel WTin
	'Master Touch' (TB)	ELon XSen
	'Masterwork' (TB)	CIri
	'Matinata' (TB)	CKel XSen
	'Matt McNames' (TB)	EWoo
	'Maui Moonlight' (IB) ♀H4	CKel ESgI EWoo NLar WAul WCAu
	'May Melody' (TB)	WCAu
	'Maya Mint' (MDB)	LLHF
	'Meadow Court' (SDB)	CBro CKel WCAu WWEG
	'Medallion' (Spuria) **new**	EWoo
	'Media Luz' (Spuria)	WCAu
	'Medici Prince' (TB)	EWoo
	'Medway Valley' (MTB) ♀H4	SIri WCAu
	'Meg's Mantle' (TB) ♀H4	CKel
	'Melbreak' (TB)	ESgI WCAu
	mellita	see *I. suaveolens*
	'Melon Honey' (SDB)	CKel ELon WCAu
	'Menton' (SDB)	CKel
	'Mer du Sud' (TB) ♀H4	EIri ESgI EWoo LRHS XSen
*	'Merebrook Blue Lagoon' (La)	WMAq
	'Merebrook Jemma J' (La)	WMAq
*	'Merebrook Lemon Maid' (La)	WMAq
	'Merebrook Malvern Shadow' (La)	WMAq
	'Merebrook Purpla' (La)	WMAq
	'Merebrook Rum 'n' Raisin' (La) **new**	WMAq
*	'Merebrook Rusty Red' (La)	WMAq
*	'Merebrook Snowflake' (La)	WMAq
	'Merebrook Sunnyside Up' (La)	WMAq
	'Merebrook Symphony' (La) **new**	WMAq
	'Merry Dance' (SDB)	CKel
	'Mesmerizer' (TB)	ESgI
	'Messy Jessi' (TB) **new**	CIri
	'Metaphor' (TB)	WCAu
	'Mezza Cartuccia' (IB)	ESgI
I	'Midnight Blue' (MDB)	CBro
	'Midnight Caller' (TB)	ESgI EWoo XSen
	'Midnight Majesty' (TB)	EWoo
	'Midnight Mango'	see *I.* 'Midnight Web'
	'Midnight Oil' (TB)	CIri EWoo WCAu
	'Midnight Treat' (TB) **new**	WCAu
§	'Midnight Web' (IB) ♀H4	CKel
	'Midsummer Night's Dream' (IB)	ESgI EWoo WAul
	'Mighty Mouse'	EWoo
	'Mighty Warrior' (TB) **new**	CIri
	'Miles Ahead' (TB) **new**	WCAu
	milesii ♀H4	CPLG IGor NBir WSHC
	'Millennium Falcon' (TB)	WAul
	'Millennium Sunrise' (TB)	WCAu
	'Mini Big Horn' (IB)	CIri
	'Mini-Agnes' (SDB)	CBro
	'Minisa' (TB) **new**	ESgI
	'Minnis Bay' (SDB)	SIri
	'Miss Carla' (IB)	ESgI NBre
	'Miss Nellie' (BB)	CKel
	'Missouri Streams' (Spuria) **new**	EWoo
	missouriensis ♀H4	CAvo CMac EBee IGor
	'Mister Matthew' (TB) ♀H4	CKel
	'Mister Roberts' (SDB)	ESgI
	'Mistress of Camelot' (TB) **new**	SDys
	'Mme Chéreau' (TB)	ESgI EWoo WCAu
	'Monet's Blue' (TB)	EWoo
	'Monsieur-Monsieur' (TB)	ESgI
	Monspur Group	WCot
	'Moon Journey' (TB)	SIri WAul
	'Moon Sparkle' (IB)	CKel
	'Moonbeam' (TB)	CKel
	'Moonlight Waves'	see *I. ensata* 'Moonlight Waves'
	'Moonlit Waves' (TB)	CKel
	'Moonstruck' (TB)	EWoo
	'Morning Splendor' (TB) **new**	EWoo
	'Morning's Blush' (SDB) ♀H4	CIri
	'Morwenna' (TB) ♀H4	CKel ESgI
	'Mosaic of Blessing' (TB) **new**	ESgI
	'Mote Park' (MTB)	WAul
	'Mother Earth' (TB)	ESgI EWoo WAul
	'Mountain Music'	EWoo
	'Mrs Horace Darwin' (TB)	CCon SWat WMnd
	'Mrs Nate Rudolph' (SDB)	WCAu
	'Mrs Tait' (Spuria)	NChi
	'Muggles' (SDB) **new**	SIri
	'Mukaddam' (TB)	CIri
	'Murder Mystery' (TB) **new**	WCAu
	'Muriel Neville' (TB)	WCAu
	'Must Unite' (TB)	WCAu
	'Muted Melody' (TB) **new**	CIri
	'My Honeycomb' (TB)	WCAu
	'My Kayla' (SDB)	ESgI
N	'My Seedling' (MDB)	CBro
	'Myra' (SDB)	XSen
	'Mysterieux' (TB)	SIri
	'Mystic Beauty' (Dut)	LAma
	'Mystic Dragon' (TB)	SDys

	Name	Suppliers
	'Naivasha' (TB)	CKel
	'Nancy' (TB)	SApp
	'Nancy Hardy' (MDB)	CBro
	narbutii (J)	LWst
	narcissiflora	WCot
	'Nassak' (TB)	EWoo
	'Natascha' (Reticulata)	ECho EPfP EPot LAma NMin NWad SDeJ
	'Natchez Trace' (TB)	EPri XSen
	'Navajo Code' (TB)	CIri
	'Navajo Jewel' (TB)	ESgI EWoo XSen
	'Nectar of the Gods' (TB) **new**	WCAu
	'Needlecraft' (TB)	NBre XSen
	'Needlepoint' (TB)	ESgI
	'Negro Modelo' (SDB)	WCAu
	'Neige de Mai' (TB)	ESgI
	'Neil's Choice' (TB) **new**	CIri
*	'Nel Jupe' (TB)	LRHS NLar
	'Neon' (TB) **new**	ESgI
	nertschinskia	see *I. sanguinea*
	'Neutron' (SDB) **new**	WCAu
	'Neutron Dance' (TB) **new**	WCAu
	'New Centurion' (TB)	EWoo XSen
	'New Creation' (TB) **new**	ESgI
	'New Day Dawning' (TB)	CIri
	'New Face' (TB) **new**	WCAu
	'New Flame' (TB) **new**	ESgI
	'New Idea' (MTB)	ESgI WCAu
	'New Leaf' (TB)	WCAu
	'New Snow' (TB)	WCAu
	'Next in Line'	EWoo
	'Next Millenium' (TB)	EWoo
	'Nibelungen' (TB)	CJun ELon ESgI MNrw NBre WFar WGwG XSen
	'Nice 'n' Nifty' (IB)	WTin
	'Nicola Jane' (TB) 🏆H4	CKel
	nicolai	GKev
	- RM 8276	LWst
	- VV QQ.175	LWst
	- red-flowered **new**	LWst
	- yellow-flowered **new**	LWst
	'Night Edition' (TB)	CJun ESgI EWoo XSen
	'Night Game' (TB)	EWoo XSen
	'Night Owl' (TB)	CKel ELan ELon ESgI LAst LHop MCot MHer SPoG WHrl
	'Night Ruler' (TB)	ESgI EWoo WCAu
	'Night Shift' (IB)	NBre
	'Nightfall' (TB)	EBee ESgI
	'Nightmare' (TB)	CIri
	'Nights of Gladness' (TB)	ESgI
	nigricans	LWst
	'Noble Lady' (TB)	CIri
	'Noctambule' (TB)	EWoo
	'Noon Siesta' (TB)	ESgI
	'Nora Eileen' (TB) 🏆H4	CKel
	'Nordica' (TB)	ESgI
	'Norfolk Belle' (TB) 🏆H4	WAul
*	× ***norrisii***	EBee EWes SBfd
	- 'Butterfly Magic' **new**	EBee
	- 'Dazzler'	MBel NLBP
	- 'Heart of Darkness' **new**	EBee
	'North Downs' (BB)	SIri
	'Northern Jewel' (IB)	SIri
	'Northwest Pride' (TB)	EWoo WCAu
	'Now This' (Spuria) **new**	EWoo
	'Nuee d'Orage' (TB)	EWoo
	'Oasis Angel' (TB)	CIri
	'Oasis Dragon' (TB)	CIri
	'Oasis Sydney' (TB) **new**	CIri
	'Oblivion' (IB)	WAul
	'Obsidian' (TB)	CIri WAul WCAu
	'Ocean Depths' (TB)	ESgI
	'Ocelot' (TB)	ESgI
	'Ochraurea' (Spuria)	SMrm
	'Ochre Doll' (SDB)	CBro CKel
	ochroleuca	see *I. orientalis* Mill.
	'O'Cool' (IB)	CKel
	'Octave' (AB) **new**	WCAu
	'October' (TB)	ESgI
	'October Storm' (IB)	EWoo
	odaesanensis	SBrt
	'Oh Jamaica' (TB)	XSen
	'Oh So Cool' (MTB)	ESgI
	'Oklahoma' (TB)	EWoo
	'Oktoberfest' (TB)	XSen
	'Ola Kalá' (TB)	EAEE EWll GMaP LRHS MCot MWat NBre NLar SHil SPer WCAu WWEG XSen
	'Old Black Magic' (TB)	ESgI EWoo XSen
	'Old Flame' (TB)	XSen
	'Olympiad' (TB)	ESgI XSen
	'Olympic Challenge' (TB)	ESgI MRav
	'Olympic Torch' (TB)	WCAu
	'Ominous Stranger' (TB)	ESgI WCAu
	'Once Again' (TB)	EWoo XSen
	'One Desire' (TB)	XSen
	'Open Sky' (SDB)	EWoo SIri XSen
	'Orageux' (IB)	CWCL SIri
	'Orange Caper' (SDB)	CMac ECtt EPfP ESgI GBuc MRav NLar NRHS SBfd
	'Orange Encore' (SDB)	WAul
	'Orange Harvest' (TB)	ESgI EWoo XSen
	'Orange Order' (TB)	WCAu
N	'Orange Plaza'	WHil
	'Orange Pop' (BB)	WAul
	'Orchardist' (TB)	CKel
	'Orchidarium' (TB)	CKel
	'Orchidea Selvaggia' (TB)	ESgI
	orchioides misapplied	see *I. bucharica* Foster
§	***orchioides*** Carrière	ECho
	- deep yellow-flowered	LWst
	- dwarf	LWst
N	- 'Urungachsai'	EPot
	orchioides* × *warleyensis	LWst
	'Oregon Skies' (TB)	ESgI ETod EWoo
	'Oreo' (TB)	WCAu
	'Oriental Baby' (IB)	CKel
	'Oriental Beauty' (Dut)	GKev LAma MBel SPhx WFar
	'Oriental Beauty' (TB)	SDeJ
	'Oriental Glory' (TB)	WCAu
	orientalis Thunb.	see *I. sanguinea*
	- 'Alba'	see *I. sanguinea* 'Alba'
	orientalis ambig.	EWes SLPl WCAu
§	***orientalis*** Mill. 🏆H4	GBin GCal NLar SGar WCru XSen
	'Orinoco Flow' (BB) 🏆H4	CKel ESgI WCAu
	'Orloff' (TB)	ESgI
	'Oro Antico' (TB)	CIri
	'Osage Buff' (TB)	CKel
	'Osay Canuc' (TB)	CIri
	'Ostrogoth' (TB)	CIri
	'Othello' (TB)	EWoo
	'Oulo' (TB)	ESgI XSen
	'Our House' (TB)	ESgI
	'Out Yonder' (TB)	WCAu
	'Outrage' (SDB) **new**	CIri
	'Over Easy' (SDB)	CKel
	'Overjoyed' (TB)	XSen

	'Overnight Sensation' (TB)	EWoo
	'O'What' (SDB)	ESgI
	'Ozark Maid' (MTB)	SDys
	'Ozone Alert' (TB)	CIri
	Pacific Coast hybrids	see *I.* Californian hybrids
	'Pacific Gambler' (TB)	SMrm
	'Pacific Mist' (TB)	WCAu
	'Pacific Panorama' (TB)	XSen
	'Pagan Dance' (TB)	EWoo
	'Pagan Goddess' (TB)	EWoo
	'Pagan Pink' (TB)	XSen
	'Pagan Princess' (TB)	WCAu
	'Paint It Black' (TB)	ETod EWoo XSen
	'Painter's Choice' (Spuria)	CIri
	'Pale Shades' (IB) ♀H4	CBro CKel
§	***pallida***	EBee ESgI EWoo GMaP MRav MWat SEND SRms WCAu WMnd XSen
§	- 'Argentea Variegata' (TB/v)	CSBt EBee ECha EHoe EHrv EPfP EWoo GBuc GKev GMaP LAst LRHS MAsh MBrN MCot MNFA MRav NBir NBro NSti SBfd SPer SPoG WAul WHoo WWEG XSen
	- 'Aurea'	see *I. pallida* 'Variegata' Hort.
	- 'Aurea Variegata'	see *I. pallida* 'Variegata' Hort.
	- subsp. ***cengialtii***	XSen
	- var. ***dalmatica***	see *I. pallida* subsp. *pallida*
§	- subsp. ***pallida*** ♀H4	CArn CKel CPLG CWan EAEE ECha ELan EPfP GCal LRHS SDix SPer WCFE
	- 'Variegata' misapplied	see *I. pallida* 'Argentea Variegata'
§	- 'Variegata' Hort. (v) ♀H4	CBcs CBro CMac CWat EBee ECha ELan EPfP ESgI LRHS MAsh MAvo MBri MCot MRav NSti SDix SPer SPet SPlb SRot SWvt WCFE WCot WFar WWEG XSen
	'Palm Springs' (IB)	LLHF NMin
	'Palomino' (TB)	WCAu
	'Paltec' (IB)	CPou
	'Pane e Vino' (TB)	ESgI
	'Pansy Top' (SDB)	SIri
	'Paradise' (TB)	CKel
	'Paradise Bird' (TB) ♀H4	WCAu
	paradoxa	ECho LWst
	'Paricutin' (SDB)	CBro
	'Paris Lights' (TB)	XSen
	'Parisien' (TB)	CWCL EIri
	'Parts Plus' (IB)	CIri
	'Party Dress' (TB)	CMac EBee ELan EPfP LRHS MRav MWhi NBir NGdn NLar SBfd SPer SPoG SRms SWat WGwG
	'Paso Doble' (TB) **new**	ESgI
	'Pastel Charm' (SDB)	NPnk SMrm WMnd
	'Patina' (TB)	ECtt EIri ETod EWoo WAul WCAu
	'Patterdale' (TB)	NBir NBre
	'Paul Black' (TB) ♀H4	CIri
	'Pauline' (Reticulata)	CAvo CBro ECho EPfP ERCP GKev LAma LRHS MWat SMrm SPhx
	'Peaceful Waters' (TB)	ECtt XSen
	'Peach Eyes' (SDB)	CBro CKel
	'Peach Picotee' (TB)	ESgI XSen
	'Peach Spot' (TB)	CJun
	'Peachy Face' (IB)	ESgI XSen
	'Pearls of Autumn' (TB)	WCAu
	'Pearly Dawn' (TB)	ECtt SPer SRGP SWat WWEG
*	'Pêche Melba' (TB)	XSen
	'Pegaletta' (La)	NBro
	'Peggy Chambers' (IB) ♀H4	SMrm
	'Pelion Hills' **new**	LRHS
	'Penny a Pinch' (TB)	WWEG
	'Pepita' (SDB)	EWoo
	'Perfect Interlude' (TB)	ECtt EIri XSen
	'Performer' (MTB)	EIri SIri
	'Perfume Shop' (IB)	CKel
	'Persian Berry' (TB)	WCAu XSen
	'Persuit of Happiness' (TB) **new**	WCAu
	'Petite Monet' (MTB)	ESgI
	'Phaeton' (TB)	WCAu
	'Pharaoh's Daughter' (IB)	EWoo SIri
	'Phil Keen' (TB) ♀H4	CKel
N	'Picadee'	CDes EPfP
	'Pigeon' (SDB)	XSen
	'Pilot' (SDB) **new**	WCAu
	'Pinewood Charmer' (CH)	CElw
	'Pinewood Sunshine' (CH)	MAvo
	'Pink Attraction' (TB)	ESgI XSen
	'Pink Bubbles' (BB)	XSen
	'Pink Charm' (TB)	EAEE EPfP LBuc LRHS NCGa SBfd SDeJ SPlb SPoG WAul
	'Pink Clover' (TB)	ESgI
	'Pink Confetti' (TB)	EWoo XSen
	'Pink Horizon' (TB)	XSen
	'Pink Invasion' (TB) **new**	WCAu
	'Pink Kitten' (IB)	WCAu WGwG XSen
N	'Pink Lavender' (TB)	ELon
	'Pink Parchment' (BB) ♀H4	CKel
	'Pink Pele' (IB)	ESgI WAul
	'Pink Pinafore' (TB)	EWoo
	'Pink Pussycat' (TB)	MBri
	'Pink Quartz' (TB) **new**	ESgI
	'Pink Reprise' (BB)	EWoo
	'Pink Swan' (TB)	XSen
	'Pink Taffeta' (TB)	XSen
	'Pinnacle' (TB)	CKel GCal SWat
	'Pipes of Pan' (TB)	ESgI WCAu
	'Pirate's Quest' (TB)	ESgI EWoo XSen
	'Piroska' (TB) ♀H4	ESgI XSen
*	'Piu Blue' (TB)	ESgI
	'Pixie' (DB)	GKev WRHF
	'Pixie' (Reticulata) ♀H4	ECho ELan EPot LAma LHop NLar SDeJ SMrm
	planifolia	ECho LWst
	'Platinum' (TB)	WCAu
	'Pledge Allegiance' (TB)	ECtt ESgI EWoo
	'Plickadee' (SDB)	CBro
	'Plum Lucky' (SDB)	SIri
	'Plum Wine' (SDB)	CJun CKel
	'Poem of Ecstasy' (TB)	WCAu
	'Pogo' (SDB)	CMac ECho ECtt ELan EPfP EPot ETod GBuc GMaP LRHS MRav NBir SBfd SDeJ SMrm SRms
	'Polvere di Stelle' (TB) **new**	ESgI
	'Pookanilly' (IB)	CJun
	'Poppa John' (TB)	CIri
	'Port of Call' (Spuria)	EWoo
	'Powder Blue Cadillac' (TB)	CKel
	'Power Point' (TB)	CIri
	'Prairie Sunset' (TB)	EWoo
	'Prairie Thunder' (AB) **new**	WCAu
	'Preatorian Guard' (TB) **new**	CIri
	'Precious Heather' (TB) ♀H4	CKel
	'Presence' (TB)	SIri
	'Pretender' (TB)	WCAu
	'Pretty Please' (TB)	ESgI
	'Primrose Drift' (TB)	ESgI
	'Prince Indigo' (TB)	MRav
	'Princess Beatrice' (TB)	WCAu

	Name	Suppliers
	'Princess Sabra' (TB) $\mathbb{Y}^{H4}$	CKel
	'Princesse Caroline de Monaco' (TB)	ESgI EWoo
	prismatica	GKev
	- ***alba***	IGor
	'Professor Blaauw' (Dut) $\mathbb{Y}^{H4}$	CAvo EPfP GKev
	'Progressive Attitude' (TB)	EPri
	'Protocol' (IB)	CKel
	'Proud Tradition' (TB)	ESgI SIri WCAu XSen
	'Provençal' (TB)	CJun CKel CPar CWCL ECtt ESgI ETod EWoo WAul WCAu XSen
	'Prudy' (BB) $\mathbb{Y}^{H4}$	CKel
	pseudacorus $\mathbb{Y}^{H4}$	Widely available
	- B&SWJ 5018 from Japan	WCru
	- from Korea	CRow
	- 'Alba'	CPrp GCal MRav MSKA MWts NGdn SWat
	- var. ***bastardii***	CBen CRow CWat ECha ELon EPfP ESgI LPBA MSKA NPer SLon SPer SWat WBrk WCAu WFar WMoo WPnP WTin XLum
	- 'Beuron'	CRow
	- cream-flowered	NBir SWat WAul
N	- 'Crème de la Crème'	ELon GBin GQue NLar NSti WHil
	- 'Esk'	GCal
N	- 'Flore Pleno' (d)	CBen CPrp CRow ECho ESgI GCra LPBA MSKA NLar NPer WBrk WCAu WCot WFar WPnP WWEG
N	- 'Golden Daggers'	CRow
I	- 'Golden Fleece'	SPer
	- 'Golden Queen'	CRow EWay
	- 'Ilgengold'	CRow
N	- 'Ivory'	CRow
	- 'Krill'	WHil
	- 'Mandchurica'	XBlo
*	- ***nana***	CRow
	- 'Roy Davidson' $\mathbb{Y}^{H4}$	CBro CPrp CRow GCal IBlr LPBA NLar SUsu WCot WFar WHil WTin
N	- 'Sulphur Queen'	GBin WCot WWEG
	- 'Sun Cascade'	CRow
N	- 'Tiger Brother'	CBro WBrk
	- 'Tiggah'	CRow
N	- 'Turnipseed'	WCot
	- 'Variegata' (v) $\mathbb{Y}^{H4}$	Widely available
*	***pseudocapnoides*** (J)	LWst
	'Pulse Rate' (SDB)	CBro
	pumila	CPBP LRHS MCot MWat NRHS SWal
	- f. ***atroviolacea***	CKel WMnd
N	- 'Gelber Mantel'	NBir
	- 'Violacea' (DB)	SRms
	'Pumpin' Iron' (SDB) $\mathbb{Y}^{H4}$	CJun CKel ESgI
	'Punch' (BB)	WAul
	'Punchline' (TB)	CWCL ECtt
	'Punk' (MDB)	CIri
	purdyi	IGor
	'Pure As Gold' (TB)	CWCL ESgI EWoo XSen
	'Purple Gem' (Reticulata)	ECho EPfP EPot GKev LAma
	'Purple People Eater' (TB)	CIri
	'Purple Sensation' (Dut)	ECho SDeJ
	'Purr for Mints' (TB)	CIri
	'Pussycat Pink' (SDB) **new**	ESgI WCAu
	'Quaker Lady' (TB)	ESgI EWoo SIri
	'Quantum Leap' (TB)	CIri
	'Quark' (SDB)	CBro CKel CPBP
	'Quechee' (TB)	CWCL EAEE EBee EPfP ESgI ETod EWoo GMaP IPot LBuc LDai LRHS LSRN MCot MRav MWat NCGa NLar SDeJ SMrm SPer SWat WAul WGwG
	'Queen in Calico' (TB)	ESgI
	'Queen of Angels' (TB)	WCAu
	'Queen of Hearts' (TB)	XSen
	'Queen of May' (TB)	EWoo
	'Queen's Circle' (TB) $\mathbb{Y}^{H4}$	CIri WCAu
	'Queen's Ivory' (SDB)	SMrs
	'Queen's Prize' (SDB)	SIri
	'Rabbit's Foot' (SDB)	LSRN SIri
	'Radiant Apogee' (TB)	ECtt EIri
	'Radiant Burst' (IB)	SIri
	'Rain Dance' (SDB) $\mathbb{Y}^{H4}$	ESgI
	Rainbow Grand Mixture	SDeJ
	'Rainbow Rim' (SDB)	ESgI
	'Rajah' (TB)	EBee EHrv ELan EPfP EShb EWoo GMaP LRHS LSRN MCot MLHP MRav NCGa NOrc SBfd SPer SPoG WMnd
	'Rameses' (TB)	ESgI EWoo WCAu
	'Rancho Rose' (TB)	CKel XSen
	'Rapture in Blue' (TB)	EWoo
	'Rare Edition' (IB)	CKel EWoo NBir NBre WAul XSen
	'Rare Quality' (TB)	WAul XSen
	'Rare Treat' (TB)	XSen
	'Raspberry Acres' (IB)	MRav WCAu
	'Raspberry Blush' (IB) $\mathbb{Y}^{H4}$	CKel CPar EAEE EIri EPfP GBin IPot LBMP LRHS LSou MRav NBre NCGa NGdn SBea SWat WAul WGwG WWFP XSen
	'Razoo' (SDB)	CKel
	'Real Coquette' (SDB)	SIri
	'Realm' (TB)	ESgI
	'Rebecca Perret' (TB)	WCAu
	'Rebus' (SDB)	SIri
	'Red Canyon Glow' (TB)	CIri
	'Red Dazzler' (La) **new**	CIri
	'Red Echo' (La) **new**	CIri
	'Red Flash' (TB)	ESgI
	'Red Heart' (SDB)	ELon ESgI MRav WTin WWEG XSen
	'Red Orchid' (IB)	ELan ESgI LHop NBre SRms WCAu WWEG
	'Red Revival' (TB)	MRav WCAu
N	'Red Rum' (TB)	CKel EWes
	'Red Zinger' (IB)	CJun ESgI EWoo LRHS WAul
	'Redelta' (TB)	XSen
	'Redondo' (IB)	EWoo
	'Reflets Safran' (TB)	SIri XSen
	'Regal Surprise' (SpH) $\mathbb{Y}^{H4}$	CRow EBee WAul
	'Regards' (SDB)	CBro EBee GEdr XSen
§	***reichenbachii***	EPot WAbe WThu
	'Reincarnation' (TB)	CIri EWoo
	'Remembering Vic' (Spuria) **new**	EWoo
	'Renewal' (TB)	EWoo
	'Renown' (TB)	EWoo
	'Repartee' (TB)	XSen
	'Replicator' (SDB)	EWoo
	reticulata $\mathbb{Y}^{H4}$	ECho ELan EPfP LRHS SDeJ SEND SMrm SPer
	- KPPZ 90-152	LWst
	- var. ***bakeriana***	ECho LLHF NMin
N	- 'Violet Queen'	ECho
	'Return to Bayberry' (TB)	CIri
	'Return to Sender' (TB)	EWoo
	'Réussite' (TB)	EWoo
	'Rhages' (TB)	EWoo
	'Rhapsody' (Reticulata) **new**	SDeJ

	'Rheinfels' (TB)	EWoo
	'Rheingauperle' (TB)	ESgI EWoo
	'Rime Frost' (TB)	WCAu
	'Ringdove' (TB) **new**	ESgI
	'Ringo' (TB)	CKel EWoo LSRN MRav
	'Rings of Saturn' (TB) **new**	CIri
	'Rio Rojo' (TB) **new**	WCAu
	'Rip City' (TB)	ESgI
	'Ripple Chip' (SDB)	WTin
	'Risen in Glory' (TB) **new**	ESgI
	'Rising Moon' (TB)	EWoo SIri
	'Ritz' (SDB)	WWEG
	'Rive Gauche' (TB)	ESgI
	'Riverbuds'	SIri WCAu
	'Rob Cornell' (TB) **new**	ESgI
	'Robe d'Été' (TB)	CWCL
§	× ***robusta*** 'Dark Aura' ♀H4	MAvo MWts WCot WTin
§	- 'Gerald Darby' ♀H4	Widely available
	- 'Mountain Brook'	CRow
	- 'Nutfield Blue'	WTin
	'Rock Star' (TB)	CIri
§	'Rocket' (TB)	EPfP GMaP LBuc LRHS MRav NBir NBre SDeJ SPer WAul
	'Rocket Master' (TB)	ESgI
	'Rocket Randy' (TB) **new**	CIri
	'Roman Carnival' (TB)	EWoo
	'Romance' (TB)	EWoo
	'Romano' (Dut)	LRHS
	'Romantic Evening' (TB)	EIri EWoo XSen
	'Romantic Mood' (TB)	CKel
	'Romney Marsh' (IB)	SIri
	'Rosalie Figge' (TB)	ESgI EWoo WCot
	'Rosé' (TB)	LSRN
	'Rose Queen'	see *I. ensata* 'Rose Queen'
	'Rose-Marie' (TB)	EWoo
	'Rosemary's Dream' (MTB)	NBre
	rosenbachiana	ECho LWSt
	- 'Darwas'	LWSt
N	- 'Harangon'	ECho LWSt
	- 'Tovil-Dara'	LWSt
	'Roseplic' (TB)	LRHS
	'Rosette Wine' (TB)	ESgI WCAu
	'Rosy Veil' (TB)	ESgI EWoo
	'Rosy Wings' (TB)	ECho ESgI EWoo
	'Roucoulade' (TB)	SIri
	'Rouge Gorge' (TB)	SIri
	'Roulette' (TB)	MBri
N	'Roy Elliott'	NMen
	'Royal Crusader' (TB)	CCse CJun XSen
	'Royal Elegance' (TB)	SIri
	'Royal Intrigue' (TB)	SIri
	'Royal Magician' (SDB)	WTin
	'Royal Satin' (TB)	CHid WGwG
	'Royal Snowcap' (TB) **new**	WCAu
	'Royal Tapestry' (TB)	NBre
	'Royalist' (TB)	CKel
	'Rubacuori' (TB)	ESgI EWoo
	'Rubistar' (TB)	EWoo
	'Ruby Chimes' (IB)	ESgI WCAu
	'Ruby Contrast' (TB)	WCAu
	'Ruby Eruption'	WCAu
	rudskyi	see *I. variegata*
	'Russet Crown' (TB)	CKel
	'Rustic Cedar' (TB)	ESgI WCAu
	'Rustle of Spring' (TB)	WCAu
	'Rustler' (TB)	WCAu
	'Rusty Beauty' (Dut)	LAma SDeJ
	'Rusty Magnificence' (TB)	EWoo
	'Ruth Rowlands' (TB)	ESgI EWoo
	ruthenica	ECho WCot
	- var. ***nana***	CPLG GKev
	'Ryan James' (TB)	CKel
	'Sable' (TB)	EBee EHrv ELan EPfP ESgI ETod EWoo GMaP LBuc LRHS LSRN MAsh MCot MRav MWat MWhi NLar NOrc SEND SMrm SPer WAul WCAu WWEG
	'Sable Night' (TB)	CKel ESgI
	'Sager Cedric' (TB)	WCAu
	'Saint Crispin' (TB)	EPfP GCra GMaP LRHS MRav SBfd SPer SPoG WGwG WWlt
	'Sally Jane' (TB)	WCAu
	'Salmon Sunset' (Spuria) **new**	EWoo
	'Salonique' (TB)	ESgI MMHG NLar WCAu
	'Saltwood' (SDB)	CBro ESgI NBre SIri
	'Sam Carne' (TB)	WCAu
	'Samarcande' (TB) **new**	ESgI
	× ***sambucina***	EBee XSen
	'San Diego' (TB) **new**	ESgI
	'San Francisco' (TB)	ESgI
	'San Gabriel' (TB)	EWoo
	'San Leandro' (TB)	MBri
	'San Leon' (DB)	GBin
	'Sandling Sunset' (TB) **new**	SIri
	'Sandstone Sentinel' (BB)	CIri
	'Sandy Caper' (IB)	WCAu WTin
	'Sangone' (IB)	ESgI
§	***sanguinea*** ♀H4	CMCN
§	- 'Alba'	IBlr
	- 'Nana Alba'	EWoo GBin IBlr
§	- 'Snow Queen'	CAvo CBcs EBee ELan EPfP EPri EWoo GBin GKev GMaP LPBA LPot LRHS MBri MGos MSCN NPri NSti SPer SWat WCAu WCot WHoo WMnd WMoo WWEG
	'Sapphire Beauty' (Dut)	SDeJ
	'Sapphire Gem' (SDB)	CKel ESgI EWoo LSRN WAul WCAu
	'Sapphire Hills' (TB)	WCAu XSen
	'Sarah Taylor' (SDB) ♀H4	CBro ECho EWoo WCAu
*	'Sarajaavo' (AB)	CKel
	sari	ECho LWSt
	'Sasha Borisovich' (TB) **new**	ESgI
	'Sass with Class' (SDB)	CKel WTin
	'Saturn' (TB) **new**	WCAu
	'Scottish Warrior' (TB)	CIri
	'Scribe' (MDB)	CBro NBir WCAu
	'Sea Double' (TB)	WWEG
	'Sea Fret' (SDB)	CBro
	'Sea Monster' (SDB)	CJun
	'Sea of Joy' (TB)	XSen
	'Sea Wisp' (La)	NBro SKHP
	'Seakist' (TB)	WCAu
	'Season Ticket' (IB)	XSen
	'Seastone' (SDB)	WCAu
	'Second Look' (TB)	XSen
	'Second Wind' (TB)	ECtt EWoo
	'Secret Melody' (TB)	XSen
	'Secret Rites' (TB)	CIri
	'Self Evident' (MDB)	LLHF
	'Semola' (SDB)	ESgI
	'Senlac' (TB)	EPfP NLar WMnd
	'Señor Frog' (SDB)	ESgI
	serbica	see *I. reichenbachii*
	'Serene Moment' (TB)	SIri
	'Serenity Prayer' (SDB)	WCAu

	setosa 🏆H4	CBro CMac CTri CWCL EBee ECho GCra GKev IGor LEdu LPBA LRHS MNrw NRHS SBfd WAbe
	- ***alba***	NLar
	- var. ***arctica***	GBuc LEdu WPer
I	- 'Baby Blue'	EPfP LRHS NPri
	- subsp. ***canadensis***	see *I. hookeri*
	- dark violet-flowered	EPri
	- var. ***nana***	see *I. hookeri*
	'Seven Hills' (TB) **new**	ESgI
	'Severn Side' (TB) 🏆H4	CKel
	'Shahryar'	LWst
	'Shakespeare's Sonnet' (SDB)	ESgI
	'Shameless' (IB)	NBre
	'Shampoo' (IB)	CKel SIri WCAu
	'Share the Spirit' (TB)	WCAu
	'Sheila Ann Germaney' (Reticulata)	EBee ECho EPot GKev LAma LLHF LWst NHol NMen NMin NWad WCot
	'Shelby Lynne' (TB) **new**	CIri
	'Shelford Giant' (Spuria) 🏆H4	CIri NEgg
	'Sherbet Lemon' (IB) 🏆H4	CKel WCAu
	'Shifnal' **new**	WCAu
	'Shirley Chandler' (IB) 🏆H4	SIri
	'Short Distance' (IB)	EWoo SIri
	shrevei	see *I. virginica* var. *shrevei*
	'Shurton Brook' (TB)	CKel
	'Shurton Inn' (TB)	CKel WCAu
	sibirica 🏆H4	CAvo CMHG COIW CWat EDAr EHon EHrv ESgI GAbr GBBs GKev LAma LAst LLWP MLHP MMuc NChi SEND SPlb WBrk WCot WFar WHer WMoo WShi
	- 'Ann Dasch'	WAul
	- 'Annemarie Troeger' 🏆H4	NBre SMrm
	- 'Annick'	EBee
	- 'Anniversary'	SMrm
	- 'Atlantic Crossing'	SIri WAul
	- 'Baby Sister'	CMHG EBee EWoo GAbr GBin GBuc LSRN NBre NBro NRHS SRGP SWat WAul
	- 'Banish Misfortune'	CIri WAul
	- 'Berlin Bluebird'	CGHE SMHy
	- 'Berlin Purple Wine'	EPri
	- 'Berlin Ruffles' 🏆H4	CIri EWes EWoo
	- 'Berlin Sky'	ESgI EWes
	- 'Bickley Cape'	WWEG
	- 'Blue Burgee'	ECha
I	- 'Blue Butterfly'	CPrp ELan EPfP MDev MNrw MSCN NGdn
	- 'Blue Cape' **new**	EBee
	- 'Blue Celeste' **new**	EBee
	- 'Blue King'	CHid CKel EBee ELan EPfP GBin GMaP MRav NBro NGdn SMrm SPer WMnd WMoo WWEG
	- 'Blue Mere'	MCot WAul
	- 'Blue Moon'	CPrp EBee WFar
	- 'Blue Reverie'	ESgI EWoo
N	- 'Blue Sceptre'	IBlr
	- 'Blueberry Fair'	CIri
	- 'Bournemouth Ball Gown'	SIri
	- 'Bracknell'	WBor
	- 'Bridal Jig'	EBee
	- 'Butter and Sugar' 🏆H4	Widely available
	- 'Caesar'	CRow EWoo SDys SRms
	- 'Caesar's Brother'	CBar CCon CHid CPrp EBee ELan EPfP EWoo GBin IBlr LRHS MNFA NBro SBfd SPer SPet SWal SWat WCAu WHoo WNew WPtf WWEG

	- 'Cambridge' 🏆H4	EBee EHoe EIri GBin GBuc LRHS MNFA MWat NBre NGdn SWat WAul WFar WHoo WWlt
	- 'Chandler's Choice'	EWes
	- 'Chartreuse Bounty'	EPri EWes GBin NLar NSti
	- 'Chilled Wine'	EBee ELon
	- 'Circle Round'	CSpe
	- 'Cleedownton' 🏆H4	WAul
	- 'Cleve Dodge'	EPri ESgI EWoo SIri XLum
N	- 'Colin's Pale Blue'	SMHy
	- 'Contrast in Styles'	EBee EPri GAbr LSou MSCN SPoG WBor WCAu WFar WHil
	- 'Cool Spring'	MSpe
	- 'Coquet Waters'	NBid
	- 'Coronation Anthem'	EWoo WAul
	- 'Dance Ballerina Dance'	CCon CHid CWCL EBee EPfP EPri LRHS MRav NMRc SMrm WFar
	- 'Dancing Nanou'	ECtt SBfd SWat
	- 'Dark Desire'	EWoo MRav WAul
	- 'Dawn Waltz' **new**	WCAu
	- 'Dear Delight'	LLHF LRHS MAvo WBor WFar WPtf
	- 'Dear Dianne'	CHid CKel ECha
	- 'Demure Illini' **new**	EBee
	- 'Dewful'	EBee
	- 'Dirigo Black Velvet'	CIri
	- 'Double Standards'	CIri EBee EPri WHil
	- 'Dreaming Orange'	ECtt EPri
	- 'Dreaming Spires' 🏆H4	ESgI SIri WCot
	- 'Dreaming Yellow' 🏆H4	CBre CMHG CSam EAEE EBee ECha EHon EPfP EPri EShb GBin GBuc GKin LEdu LRHS MMuc MRav NGdn NRHS SApp SBfd SEND SMrm SPer SVic WAul WCAu WMoo WNew WWlt
	- 'Dunkler Wein'	EBee EWes
	- 'Ego'	CAvo CHid CYeo ECha ELon EPfP EPri EWoo GAbr GBuc MGos NBro SWat WCAu WMoo
	- 'Ellenbank Sapphire'	GBin
	- 'Ellesmere'	EBee NGdn
	- 'Emma Ripeka'	WAul
	- 'Emperor'	CRow CWat EBee NBre NSti SWat
	- 'Eric the Red'	EWoo IBlr
	- 'Erste Sahne'	GBin
	- 'Ever Again'	EWoo
	- 'Ewen'	CHid CPou CRow EWoo GBin GKin GMaP IBlr LEdu MNrw NGdn SMrm SWat WCot WFar WWEG WWlt
	- 'Exuberant Encore' 🏆H4	WCAu
	- 'Flight of Butterflies'	Widely available
	- 'Fond Kiss' **new**	WCAu
	- 'Fourfold Lavender'	EWes MSpe NLar WAul
	- 'Fourfold White'	ESgI
N	- 'Gerbel Mantel'	GBin GKin MSpe SPet WFar
	- 'Golden Crimping' **new**	EWoo
	- 'Golden Edge'	EWoo GQue MAvo MBel MWts SMrm WWlt
*	- 'Goldkind'	WAul
	- grey-flowered	SApp
	- 'Gull's Wing'	LHop MBel NSti SMrm
	- 'Gustav' **new**	EWoo
	- 'Harpswell Hallelujah'	EWoo SBch
	- 'Harpswell Happiness' 🏆H4	CPrp EBee EPfP EPri GBin GCra MBel SBch SWat WAul WMoo
	- 'Harpswell Haze'	ECha WMoo
	- 'Helen Astor'	CRow CTri MRav SApp SWal SWat
	- 'Heliotrope Bouquet' **new**	EWoo

N - 'Himmel von Komi' GBin
- 'Hohe Warte' ♀H4 GBin
- 'Höhenflug' GBin
- 'Hubbard' CEnt EPri EShb GBin MAvo MBel MNrw NBro SBch WFar
- 'Illini Charm' CHid EBee SSvw WFar WMoo
I - 'Imperial Velvet' **new** EWoo
- 'Isabelle' LSRN
- 'Ivory Queen' **new** EWoo
- 'Jac-y-do' EWes
- 'Jennifer Hewitt' **new** EPri
- 'Jewelled Crown' WFar
- 'Kathleen Mary' ♀H4 WAul
- 'Kent Arrival' SIri
- Kenta No Se129 **new** EPri
- 'King of Kings' **new** WCAu
- 'Kita-no-seiza' **new** EBee
- 'Lady Vanessa' CPou EBee GBin MBel MRav NSti WAul
§ - 'Lake Niklas' ELon GBin NCGa
- 'Langthorns Pink' CCse ELan MRav
- 'Laurenbuhl' CPLG
- 'Lavender Bounty' CHid NBre NBro SPet
- 'Lavender Fair' CIri
- 'Limeheart' CPou LLHF
- 'Linda Mary' **new** EWoo
- 'Little Blue' WAul
N - 'Little Twinkle Star' EWTr GBin NPro WFar
- 'Mabel Coday' EPri EWoo
- 'Maranatha' EWoo
- 'Marilyn Holmes' GBin GQue WCot
§ - 'Melton Red Flare' EBee EHon ELan GBin LRHS LSou MBNS MSpe SDys SMrm WFar
- 'Memphis Memory' EBee ELan ELon GBin GCra MBel MNrw NGdn NLar SBch SPer
- 'Moon Silk' EBee ECtt ELon EPri GAbr GBin GBuc LLHF LRHS WCot WFar
- 'Mountain Lake' EShb GBin LRHS SWat WCot WFar WPtf
- 'Mrs Rowe' CPou CRow EIri GBuc LLWP MRav MWat SWat WAul WCAu WFar
- 'Mrs Saunders' WAul
- 'My Love' GBin
- 'Navy Brass' EPri
- new hybrids WOut
- 'Night Breeze' EPri SIri
- 'Niklas Sea' see *I. sibirica* 'Lake Niklas'
- 'Nora Distin' WCAu
- 'Nottingham Lace' GBin LLHF SWat
- 'Oban' ♀H4 ESgI GBuc
- 'Orville Fay' WBor WCot
- 'Other Worlds' WAul
- 'Ottawa' CPou CRow CWat EBee ELan LPot LRHS MBNS NRHS SWat WFar
- 'Outset' ELon SSvw WWEG
- 'Over in Gloryland' **new** WCAu
I - 'Pageant' WCot
- 'Pansy Purple' EBee
- 'Papillon' CBar CSev CTri EBee ECtt ELan ELon EWoo GAbr LHop LRHS MBel MWat NBir NBro NGdn NSti SApp SDeJ SMrm SPer SWal SWat WBor WCAu WFar WWEG
N - 'Pearl Queen' MCot WFar
- 'Peg Edwards' EWoo
- 'Percheron' EBee EPri ESgI EWoo SIri
- 'Perfect Vision' ♀H4 CIri
- 'Perry's Blue' CBcs CMac CSBt EBee EHon EHrv EPfP EPri GKin GMaP LRHS LTen MGos MRav MSpe NBir NBro NGdn NPer SBch SBfd SPer SRms SSvw SWat WAul WCAu WFar WMnd
I - 'Perry's Favourite' CRow
- 'Persimmon' misapplied see *I. sibirica* 'Tycoon'
- 'Persimmon' ambig. CCon CHid CYeo ECtt GCra GKin LRHS MWat SWat WMoo
- 'Peter Hewitt' ♀H4 CIri WAul
- 'Pink Haze' CRow EPfP ESgI GBin MBel NBro WWEG
- 'Pirate Prince' NPer
- 'Pleasures of May' EBee WBor
- 'Plissée' ♀H4 GBin
- 'Pounsley Purple' CPou EPri
- 'Primrose Cream' WCot
- 'Prussian Blue' ♀H4 CIri SMHy
- 'Purple Mere' WAul
- 'Reddy Maid' WCAu
- 'Redflare' see *I. sibirica* 'Melton Red Flare'
N - 'Regality' CWCL MHer MMuc NBro
- 'Regency Belle' ♀H4 EWoo SIri
- 'Regency Buck' EWoo SBch WCot
- 'Rikugi-sakura' EPri GBin LLHF WCot
- 'Riverdance' **new** EWoo
- 'Roanoke's Choice' CBro CElw ELon EWes GAbr GBin MBel NCGa WBor WFar
- 'Roaring Jelly' CIri EPri EWes LRHS NLar WCot
- 'Rosace' **new** EWoo
I - 'Royal Blue' ECha SWat
- 'Ruby Wine' CCon EPri LEdu NLar
- 'Ruffled Velvet' ♀H4 CElw CHid CKel CMHG EBee ECho ECtt ELan EPfP EPri ESgI EWoo IPot LPBA LRHS LTen MBri MCot MRav NBro SMrm SPer SPet SWat WAul WBor WCAu WFar WMoo WWEG
- 'Ruffles Plus' EPri MBel WFar
- 'Salamander Crossing' CIri
- 'Savoir Faire' ECha
- 'Scramble' **new** EBee ESwi WCot
- 'Sea Horse' WAul
- 'Sea Shadows' EPri ESgI NBir
- 'Shaker's Prayer' ♀H4 CIri CPrp EWes GAbr MBrN WAul
- 'Shall We Dance' ♀H4 CIri EWes WAul
- 'Shirley Pope' ♀H4 COIW EBee EWes EWoo GAbr GBin GBuc LRHS MBri MNFA NCGa NSti WAul WFar WMoo WNew WWEG
- 'Shirley's Choice' EPri SIri
- 'Showdown' EBee ECtt GMaP SAga SWat WFar
- 'Silver Edge' ♀H4 Widely available
- 'Sky Wings' CRow ECha EWoo GQue MArl MSpe WMoo
- 'Snow Prince' EPri WAul
- 'Snow Queen' see *I. sanguinea* 'Snow Queen'
- 'Snowcrest' CBre MRav SBfd
- 'Soft Blue' ♀H4 NBre WAul
N - 'Southcombe White' CRow WWEG
- 'Sparkle' WAul
- 'Sparkling Rosé' Widely available
- 'Stephen Wilcox' EPri WAul
- 'Steve' CPar EWes SWat
- 'Steve Varner' EBee EPri EWoo
- 'Strawberry Fair' ♀H4 CIri
- 'Sultan's Ruby' **new** EWoo
- 'Summer Revels' EPri
- 'Summer Sky' CBre GBin LEdu MSCN NCGa SWat WAul WCot WTin WWEG
- 'Sutton Valence' SIri WAul

	Name	Suppliers
	- 'Swank'	WAul
	- 'Sweet Surrender'	EPri
	- 'Taldra'	WAul
	- 'Tal-y-Bont'	WAul
	- 'Tanz Nochmal'	GBin
	- 'Teal Velvet'	EBee ECha EPfP EPri EWoo WCAu WFar
	- 'Temper Tantrum'	CEnt CKel CPrp MBNS WCAu
	- 'Tropic Night'	CCon CPrp CSam CTri CYeo EBee ECtt EHrv EIri EPri EWoo GKin LHop LPBA LRHS MRav NGdn NRya NSti SBfd SMrm SPer SWat WAul WCot WFar WWEG
§	- 'Tycoon'	EShb EWoo GBin IBlr LRHS SMrm SPer WCAu
	- 'Valda'	EBee
	- 'Vi Luihn'	CBcs EBee ECha WAul WMoo
	- 'Victoria's Secret' **new**	WCAu
	- 'Viel Schnee'	GBin
N	- 'Violet Skies'	GBin
	- 'Visual Treat'	SIri
	- 'Wall Street Blues'	EWoo WAul
	- 'Waterloo'	WAul
	- 'Wealden Butterfly' ♀H4	SIri WAul
	- 'Wealden Carousel'	SIri
	- 'Wealden Mystery'	EPri SIri WAul
	- 'Wealden Skies'	SIri WAul
	- 'Welcome Return'	CElw EWoo GQue MBNS MMuc NBro NLar SEND SWat WFar WMoo
N	- 'Welfenfürstin'	GBin
	- 'Welfenprinz' ♀H4	WAul
I	- 'White Queen'	ESgI SWat
I	- 'White Swan'	EPri
	- 'White Swirl' ♀H4	CBro CKel CPrp CTri EBee ECtt EHrv ELon EPfP EWoo LAst LPBA LRHS MCot MNFA MWat NBro NLar NSti SAga SBfd SPet SWat WBor WCot WFar WPnP WTin
	- 'White Triangles'	EWoo
	- 'Yankee Consul'	WAul
	- 'Zakopane' ♀H4	EBee EWes
	- 'Zweites Hundert'	WFar
	'Sibirica Alba'	ECha EPfP EPri GBBs LLWP SWat WBrk WCFE WFar
	'Sibirica Baxteri'	WAul
	'Sibtosa Princess' (SpH)	WCAu
	sichuanensis	CPLG
	'Side Effect' **new**	WCAu
	sieboldii	see *I. sanguinea*
	'Sierra Blue' (TB)	ESgI
	'Sierra Grande' (TB)	XSen
	'Sierra Nevada' (Spuria)	SMrm XSen
	'Sign of Leo' (TB)	XSen
	'Silkirim' (TB)	CKel
	'Silver Shower' (TB)	EWoo
	'Silverado' (TB)	CKel ECtt ESgI EWoo GBin LRHS WCAu
	'Silvery Beauty' (Dut)	LAma MBel MBri NBir SDeJ SPhx
	sindjarensis	see *I. aucheri*
	'Sindpers' (J) ♀H3	LWst
	'Sing to Me' (TB) **new**	WCAu
	'Sinister Desire' (IB)	EWoo SIri
	sintenisii ♀H4	CBro CPBP ECho LWst WTin XSen
	'Sir Michael' (TB)	ESgI EWoo
	'Siva Siva' (TB)	EBee MRav
	'Six Pack' (TB)	CIri
	'Sixteen Candles' (IB)	EWoo
	'Sixtine C' (TB)	SIri
	'Skating Party' (TB)	CKel ESgI EWoo XSen
	'Sky Beauty' (Dut) **new**	SDeJ
	'Sky Hooks' (TB)	XSen
	'Sky Tracery' (MTB)	SDys
	'Skydancer' (SDB)	WCAu
	'Skyfire' (TB)	CWCL ESgI EWoo WWEG
	'Skylark's Song' (TB)	EIri EWoo
	'Slap Bang' (SDB)	ESgI
	'Slovak Prince' (TB)	CIri
	'Small Sky' (SDB)	CBro
	'Smart Aleck' (TB)	ECtt ESgI EWoo
N	'Smart Girl' (TB)	CKel EIri
	'Smart Move' (TB)	CWCL ESgI
	'Smash' (MTB)	ESgI
	'Smiling Faces' (TB)	WCAu
	'Smitten Kitten' (IB)	LSRN WCAu
	'Smokey Dream' (TB)	CKel
	'Smokey Salmon' (TB)	CKel
	'Smooth' (SDB) **new**	SDys
	'Snow and Wind' (TB)	WAul
	'Snow Fiddler' (MTB)	EWoo
	'Snow Plum' (IB)	SIri
	'Snow Season' (SDB)	ESgI
	'Snow Tracery' (TB)	LRHS MBri NCGa NPnk
	'Snow Troll' (SDB)	WCAu
	'Snowcone' (IB)	EWoo
	'Snowdrift' (*laevigata*)	see *I. laevigata* 'Snowdrift'
	'Snowmound' (TB)	CCCN CKel ESgI EWoo WCAu
	'Snowy Owl' (TB) ♀H4	CKel SAga WCAu
	'Snugglebug' (SDB)	EWoo
	'Social Event' (TB)	ESgI XSen
	'Socialist' (TB)	WCAu
	'Soft Return'	EWoo
	'Solar Fire' (TB)	CIri
	'Solar Fusion' (Spuria) **new**	EWoo
	'Solid Mahogany' (TB)	MRav
	'Soligo' (MDB) **new**	ESgI
	'Solo Flight' (TB) **new**	SDys
	'Somerset Blue' (TB) ♀H4	CKel
	'Somerset Cider' (TB) **new**	SIri
N	'Somerset Vale' (TB)	SMrm
	'Somerton Brocade' (SDB)	CKel
	'Somerton Dance' (SDB)	CKel
	'Song of Norway' (TB)	ECtt EIri EWoo XSen
	'Sonoran Sands' (IB)	SDys
	'Sopra il Vulcano' (BB)	ESgI EWoo
	'Sostenique' (TB)	ESgI
	'Souvenir de Madame Gaudichau' (TB)	ESgI EWoo
	'Sparkling Waters' (TB) **new**	ESgI
	'Sparkplug' (SDB)	ESgI
	'Spartan' (TB)	CKel
	'Special Feature' (TB)	CIri
	'Spellbreaker' (TB)	SIri
	'Spice Lord' (TB)	WCAu
	'Spiced Custard' (TB)	CKel EIri ESgI EWoo
	'Spiced Tiger' (TB)	ESgI
	'Spicy Cajun' (La)	WHil
	'Spinning Wheel' (TB)	SIri
	'Spirit of Memphis' (TB)	XSen
	'Splashacata' (TB)	WCAu XSen
	'Splashdown' (Sino-Sib)	SWat
	'Splat' (IB)	CIri
	'Spreckles' (TB)	ESgI
	'Spring Blush' (MTB)	SIri
	'Spring Festival' (TB)	WCAu
	'Spring Kiss' (TB)	SIri
	'Spring Madness' (TB) **new**	CIri
	'Spring Time' (Reticulata)	ECho LAma NMin SDeJ

spuria CMac CPou WCot
§ - subsp. ***halophila*** EBee GBin GKev
- subsp. ***ochroleuca*** see *I. orientalis* Mill.
'Spy' (BB) **new** WCAu
'Square Dance Skirt' (TB) **new** SDys
'St Louis Blues' (TB) ESgI XSen
'Stairway to Heaven' (TB) ESgI WCAu
'Stapleford' (SDB) CBro
'Staplehurst' (MTB) ♀H4 SIri WAul
'Star Rider' (Spuria) **new** CIri
'Star Shine' (TB) CKel ESgI WCAu
'Starcrest' (TB) EWoo
'Stardate' (SDB) CKel
'Starlette Rose' (TB) EWoo
'Starring' (TB) EWoo WCAu
'Starship' (TB) XSen
'Starship Enterprise' (TB) CIri
'Starwoman' (IB) SDys WCAu
'Staten Island' (TB) ESgI SEND SRms WCAu WTin
'Stella Polaris' (TB) COIW CWan ELon
'Stellar Lights' (TB) EIri EWoo WCAu
'Stepping Out' (TB) ♀H4 CMac CPar EAEE EBee EPfP ESgI GBin LDai LRHS MCot NBre NCGa WAul WBor
'Stinger' (SDB) ♀H4 CIri
'Stingray' (TB) CIri ESgI
'Stitch in Time' (TB) EIri EWoo
'Stockholm' (SDB) CKel
stolonifera ECho LWst
- 'Zwanenburg Beauty' ECho
'Stop the Music' (TB) XSen
'Storm Center' (TB) EWoo
'Stormy Circle' (SDB) WCAu
N 'Storrington' (TB) EMal
'Strange Brew' (TB) WCAu
'Strathmore' (TB) **new** EMal
'Strawberry Love' (IB) ♀H4 CKel
'Strike it Rich' (TB) **new** ESgI
'Striking' (TB) EWoo
'Strozzapreti' (TB) ESgI
'Strut' (TB) **new** WCAu
'Study In Black' (TB) XSen
stylosa see *I. unguicularis*
§ ***suaveolens*** CPou ECho NMen NWad
* - var. ***flavescens*** LWst
* - var. ***violacea*** ECho GCal LWst
'Subtle' **new** WCAu
'Succès Fou' (TB) SIri
'Suffering Became Beauty' (TB) **new** ESgI
'Sugar' (IB) WCAu
'Sugar Magnolia' (TB) EWoo
'Sultan's Palace' (TB) CWCL EBee ECho ESgI EWoo LRHS LTen WWEG XSen
'Summer Holidays' (TB) XSen
'Summer's Smile' (TB) ESgI EWoo
'Summertime Blues' (TB) EWoo
'Sun Ada Beach' (TB) CIri
'Sun Doll' (SDB) ♀H4 CKel
'Sunblaze' (TB) WCAu
'Sunny and Warm' (TB) CKel
'Sunny Dawn' (IB) ♀H4 CKel
'Sunny Disposition' (TB) XSen
'Sunny Side Up' LWst
'Sunnyside Delight' (TB) WCAu
'Sunrise in Sonora' (Spuria) ♀H4 CIri SGar
'Sunshine Boy' (IB) CKel
'Superstition' (TB) ♀H4 EBee EIri ELan ESgI EWes EWoo GBin LRHS MRav SMrm WCAu WCot WWEG XSen
'Supreme Sultan' (TB) CWCL ESgI ETod EWoo WCAu XSen
'Susan Bliss' (TB) CKel EBee ELan EPfP ESgI NBre SMrm WCAu
'Susan Gillespie' (IB) ♀H4 CKel
'Suspect' (AB) **new** WCAu
'Suspicion' (TB) CIri
svetlanae LWst
'Swain' (TB) ESgI
'Swan Ballet' (TB) **new** ESgI
'Swazi Princess' (TB) CKel ELon ESgI
'Sweet Kate' (SDB) ♀H4 WCAu
'Sweet Lena' (TB) ESgI
'Sweet Musette' (TB) WCAu
'Sweeter than Wine' (TB) MRav
'Swingtown' (TB) EWoo WCAu
'Swiss Majesty' (TB) WCAu
'Swizzle' (IB) XSen
'Sybil' (TB) GBin GCra NHar
'Sylvan' (TB) XSen
'Sylvia Murray' (TB) WCAu
'Symphony' (Dut) ECho NBir SDeJ
'Syncopation' (TB) CKel ESgI XSen
'Tabac Blond' (TB) EWoo
'Tact' (IB) SIri
'Tahitian Pearl' (TB) CIri
'Take Me Away' (TB) SDys
'Tall Chief' (TB) WCAu
'Tamerlan' (TB) EWoo
'Tan Tingo' (IB) XSen
N 'Tanex' ECho
'Tangerine Sky' (TB) EWoo
'Tangfu' (IB) ESgI
'Tangled Web' (TB) **new** ESgI
'Tango Music' (SpH) ♀H4 GBin
'Tantara' (SDB) XSen
'Tantrum' (IB) WAul WCAu XSen
'Tanzanian Tangerine' (TB) WCAu
'Tarheel Elf' (SDB) ESgI
'Tarn Hows' (TB) ESgI SRms WCAu
'Teapot Tempest' (BB) **new** WCAu
'Teasaucer Hill' (MTB) ♀H4 SIri
tectorum CCse CHEx GHim GKev LRHS SChr SDix WAul WCot XSen
- BWJ 8191 WCru
- 'Alba' WThu XSen
- 'Cruella' **new** EBee
- 'Variegata' misapplied see *I. japonica* 'Variegata'
- 'Variegata' (v) NSti
'Tell Fibs' (SDB) CBro CKel
'Temple Gold' (TB) CKel NPer
'Temple Meads' (IB) ESgI WCAu
'Templecloud' (IB) ♀H4 CKel
'Tempting Fate' (TB) CPar EWoo
§ ***tenax*** ECho GBuc GEdr SMrm
- subsp. ***tenax*** IGor
'Tennessee Woman' (TB) CIri
'Tennison Ridge' (TB) WCAu
tenuissima subsp. ***tenuissima*** IGor NMen
'Thaïs' (TB) ESgI
'The Black Douglas' (TB) EWoo
'The Bride' see *I.* 'Bride'
'The Citadel' (TB) ELon
'The Red Douglas' (TB) ESgI
'The Rocket' see *I.* 'Rocket'

	'Theatre' (TB)	ESgI
	'Theodolinda' (TB)	EWoo
	'Third Charm' (SDB)	CBro
	'Third World' (SDB)	CBro
	'This and That' (IB)	WCAu
	thompsonii	IGor
	'Thornbird' (TB) ♀H4	ECtt EIri ESgI EWoo WCAu
	'Three Cherries' (MDB)	CBro ECho SIri
	'Thriller' (TB)	ESgI EWoo WCAu XSen
	thunbergii	see *I. sanguinea*
	'Thunder Echo' (TB)	ESgI SIri
	'Thundering Hills' (TB)	CKel
	'Tide's In' (TB)	ECtt EWoo
	'Tiffany' (TB)	EWoo WTin
	'Tiger Shark' (TB)	CIri
§	'Tigereye' (Dut)	ERCP GKev LAma
	tigridia	CPLG
	'Tilgate' **new**	WRHF
	'Time Piece' (TB)	CKel
	'Time Zone' (TB) **new**	WCAu
	'Tinkerbell' (SDB)	CPBP GMaP LRHS NBir NGdn SDeJ SWal
	'Tintinara' (TB) ♀H4	CKel
	'Tishomingo'	EWoo
	'Titan's Glory' (TB) ♀H4	ESgI EWoo LEdu MRav WCot
	'To the Point' (TB)	CIri
	'Tollong' ♀H4	IKil
	'Tom Johnson' (TB) ♀H4	EWoo
	'Tom Tit' (TB)	WCAu
	'Tomorrow's Child' (TB)	EWoo
	'Toni Lynn' (MDB)	ECho
	'Toots' (SDB)	ECho WTin
	'Top Flight' (TB)	EBee ELan SPer SRms
	'Top Gun' (TB)	CJun ESgI
N	'Topolino' (TB)	CKel SAga
	'Topsy Turvy' (MTB)	NBre
	'Torchlight' (TB)	SEND
	'Torero' (TB)	EWoo SIri
	'Total Eclipse' (TB)	SRms
	'Totally Cool' (SDB)	LSRN SIri
	'Touch of Frost' (BB) **new**	ESgI
	'Touch of Mahogany' (TB)	WCAu
	'Toy Clown' (SDB)	EWoo
	'Trade Secret' (TB)	CIri
	'Trails West' (TB)	EWoo
	'Trajectory' (SDB) **new**	WCAu
	'Trapel' (TB)	ESgI
	'Trencavel' (TB)	ESgI
	'Trenwith' (TB)	CKel ESgI
	'Triffid' (TB)	CIri
	'Trillion' (TB)	CIri
	'Triple Whammy' (TB)	ESgI XSen
	'Triplicate' (SDB)	SMrm
	tuberosa	CArn CAvo CBro CDes CHid CPrp CTri CWCL EBee ECGP ECha ECho EPfP ERCP GKev LAma MBel MCot NMin SDeJ SMrm WCot WTin
	- BS 348	WCot
	- MS 76	WCot
	- MS 729	WCot
	- MS 731	WCot
	- MS 821	WCot
	- MS 964	WCot
	- PB	ELan WCot
	'Tumultueux' (TB)	EWoo
	'Tut's Gold' (TB)	ECtt ESgI WCAu
	'Tuxedo' (TB)	XSen
	'Tyland Blue' (TB) **new**	SIri
	typhifolia	SBrt
	'Tyrian Dream' (IB)	WCAu
	'UFO' (TB)	CIri
	'Ultimate' (SDB)	CIri
	'Uncle Charlie' (TB)	WCAu
§	***unguicularis*** ♀H4	Widely available
	- from Lady Gibson	GEdr
	- 'Abington Purple'	CAvo CBro CJun EIri
	- 'Alba'	CAvo CBct CPLG ECha ESgI XSen
N	- 'Bob Thompson'	CAvo
§	- subsp. ***cretensis***	ECho EPot GKev NMen SKHP WAbe XSen
N	- 'Diana Clare'	CJun WCot
	- 'Kilbroney Marble' **new**	EPri
N	- 'Marondera'	CAvo CJun
	- 'Mary Barnard' ♀H4	CAvo CBro CJun CPou CTca ECGP ECha ECho EHrv GEdr IBlr NBir NMen SSvw WMnd
N	- 'Oxford Dwarf'	CBro ECho LLHF
N	- 'Palette'	ELan
§	- 'Walter Butt'	CAvo CBro CJun ECGP NBir WCot
	uromovii	MArl
	'Ursula Warleggan' (TB)	CKel
	'Vague à l'Ame' (TB)	ESgI EWoo
	'Val de Loire'	EWoo
	'Valerie Joyce' **new**	WCAu
	'Vamp' (IB)	CKel EWoo SIri SMrm XSen
	'Vandal Spirit' (TB)	ESgI
	'Vanilla Skies' (TB)	WCAu
	'Vanity' (TB) ♀H4	ESgI XSen
	'Vanity's Child' (TB)	XSen
§	***variegata*** ♀H4	IGor XSen
	'Vegas Heat' (BB)	CIri
	'Velvet Dusk' (TB)	EWoo
	'Velvet King' (TB) **new**	ESgI
	'Velvet Purple'	XBlo
	'Verity Blamey' (TB)	CKel
	versicolor ♀H4	CArn CBen CRow CWat EHon GBin GKev GMaP IBlr LPBA MGos MMuc MNHC MWts SEND SPlb SRms SWat WBrk WFar WMAq WMoo WPnP WShi WTin
	- 'Algonquin' **new**	CRow
	- 'Between the Lines'	CRow
	- 'China West Lake'	CRow
	- 'Claret Cup'	CPou EWoo WWEG
	- 'Dottie's Double'	CRow
*	- 'Georgia Bay'	CRow
	- 'Kermesina'	COIW CRow CWat EBee ECha EHon ELan ESgI GBuc IBlr LPBA MGos MWts NPer NSti SRms SWat WFar WMAq WMoo WPnP
	- 'Mysterious Monique'	CCse CDes CWat
	- 'Party Line'	SIri
	- purple-flowered	EWay
	- 'Rosea'	CRow EWay
	- 'Rowden Allegro'	CRow
	- 'Rowden Aria'	CRow
	- 'Rowden Cadenza'	CRow
	- 'Rowden Calypso'	CRow
	- 'Rowden Cantata'	CRow
	- 'Rowden Concerto'	CRow
	- 'Rowden Descant' **new**	CRow
	- 'Rowden Harmony'	CRow
	- 'Rowden Jingle' **new**	CRow
	- 'Rowden Lullaby'	CRow
	- 'Rowden Lyric'	CRow
	- 'Rowden Mazurka'	CRow
	- 'Rowden Melody'	CRow

	- 'Rowden Minuet' **new**	CRow
	- 'Rowden Nocturne'	CRow
	- 'Rowden Pastorale'	CRow
	- 'Rowden Refrain'	CRow
	- 'Rowden Rondo'	CRow
	- 'Rowden Sonata'	CRow
	- 'Rowden Symphony'	CRow
	- 'Rowden Waltz'	CRow
	- 'Silvington'	CRow
	- 'Whodunit'	CRow
	'Vibrant' (TB)	WCAu
	'Vibrations' (TB)	ESgI WCAu
	vicaria	ECho GKev LWst
	- RM 8269	LWst
	- 'Morgiana'	LWst
*	- 'Prominence'	LWst
I	- 'Sina'	LWst
	'Victoria Falls' (TB)	ESgI EWoo WCAu
	'Vin Nouveau' (TB)	XSen
	'Vinho Verde' (IB) ♀H4	CKel
	'Vino Rosso' (SDB)	ESgI
	'Violet Beauty' (Reticulata)	ECho ERCP GKev LAma NWad
	'Violet Classic' (TB)	WCAu
	'Violet Fusion' (Spuria) **new**	EWoo
	'Violet Harmony' (TB)	ESgI
	'Violet Icing' (TB) ♀H4	CKel
	'Violet Rings' (TB)	WCAu
	'Viper' (IB)	CIri EWoo
	virginica 'De Luxe'	see *I.* × *robusta* 'Dark Aura'
I	- 'Pink Butterfly'	MDev
	- 'Pond Crown Point'	CRow
	- 'Pond Lilac Dream'	CRow
N	- 'Purple Fan'	CRow
§	- var. ***shrevei***	CRow
	'Vision in Pink' (TB)	WCAu
	'Vitafire' (TB)	ECtt ESgI EWoo
	'Vitality' (IB)	ELon ESgI
	'Viva Mexico' (TB)	EWoo
	'Voilà' (IB)	ESgI
	'Volts' (SDB)	CKel XSen
	'Voluminous' (TB)	CIri
	'Volute' (TB)	ESgI
I	'Vonnies Wedding Iris'	ELon
	'Voyage' (SDB)	EWoo XSen
	'Wabash' (TB)	ELan LRHS WCAu WTin XSen
	'Walter Butt'	see *I. unguicularis* 'Walter Butt'
	'War Chief' (TB)	ESgI MRav
	'War Sails' (TB)	EWoo SIri WCAu
	warleyensis	ECho LWst
	'Warlsind' (J)	LWst
	'Warrior King' (TB)	EWoo
	'Waters Of Miraba' (BB)	EWoo
	wattii	CPLG GCal
	'Waxen Image' (IB)	WAul
	'Way to Go' (TB)	CIri
	'Wealden Canary' (Spuria)	WAul
	'Wealden Elegance' (Spuria)	WAul
	'Wealden Sunshine' (Spuria)	WAul
	'Wearing Rubies' (TB) **new**	ESgI WCAu
	'Webelos' (SDB)	MRav
	'Webmaster' (SDB)	SIri
	'Wedding Vow' (TB)	CKel EIri
	'Wedgwood' (Dut)	NBre
	'Welch's Reward' (MTB) ♀H4	CKel ESgI
	'Welcome Discovery' **new**	WCAu
	'Well Suited' (SDB)	EWoo
	'Wench' (TB)	EWoo
	'Westar' (SDB) ♀H4	CKel EIri
	'Westpointer' (TB)	CIri
	'Westwell' (SDB)	WCAu
	'What Again' (SDB)	XSen
	'Wheels' (SDB)	WTin
	'White City' (TB)	EAEE EPfP ESgI EWTr EWoo GMaP LRHS MCot MRav MWat MWhi NPer SBfd SDeJ SMrm SPer SRms SWat WCAu WMnd
	'White Excelsior' (Dut)	ECho
	'White Gem' (SDB)	ESgI EWoo
	'White Knight' (TB)	EBee ELan EPfP ESgI NBre WHrl WMnd WWEG
	'White Reprise' (TB)	ESgI XSen
	'White van Vliet' (Dut)	SDeJ
	'White Wine' (MTB)	WCAu
	'Whitewater River' (Spuria)	CIri
	'White-Wave'	XBlo
	'Whole Cloth' (TB)	ESgI
	'Whoopsi Daisy' (BB) **new**	CIri
	'Widow's Veil' (SDB) **new**	ESgI
N	'Wild Echo' (TB)	CKel
	'Wild Jasmine' (TB)	ECtt
	'Wild Ruby' (SDB)	CKel
	'Wild West' (TB)	CKel
	'Wild Wings' (TB)	EWoo MCot NCGa
	willmottiana	ECho LWst
	- 'Alba'	ECho
	wilsonii ♀H4	CPLG EBee GBin GKev WCot
	'Windjammer Seas' (TB)	SDys WAul
	'Winemaster' (TB)	ECtt EWoo SIri
	'Winesap' (TB)	ESgI EWoo
	'Wings of Peace' (TB)	CIri
	'Winner's Circle' (TB)	SMrm
	winogradowii ♀H4	CBro ECho GKev LAma LLHF WAbe
	'Winter Crystal' (TB) ♀H4	CKel
	'Winter Olympics' (TB)	EAEE EBee EPfP EShb LBuc LRHS MRav WGwG
	'Winter Pearl' (IB)	EWoo
	'Wise' (SDB)	WCAu
	'Wishful Thinking' (TB)	SIri
	'Wisteria Sachet' (IB)	WCAu
	'Witch's Wand' (TB)	ESgI EWoo
	'Wonders Never Cease' (TB) **new**	WCAu
	'Wondrous' (TB)	ESgI
	'Wrangler' (IB)	EWoo SIri
	'Xillia' (IB)	CKel
	xiphioides	see *I. latifolia*
	xiphium	ECho
	'Yellow and White'	GAbr
	'Yellow Flirt' (MTB)	WCAu
	'Yellow Joy' **new**	EABi
	'Yes' (TB)	CJun ESgI
	'Yosemite Nights' (TB)	EWoo
	'Yosemite Star' (TB)	EWoo
	'Youth Dew' (TB)	EWoo
	'Zantha' (TB)	XSen
	zenaidae ARJA 9715	LWst
	- 'Dessert'	LWst
	'Zero' (SDB) ♀H4	CKel

Isatis (*Brassicaceae*)

glauca	CFis
tinctoria	CArn CHab CHby CRWN CSev ENfk EOHP GAbr GJos GPoy MHer MHoo MNHC NPnk SIde SPav WHfH WJek XLum

Ismene see *Hymenocallis*

Isodon (Lamiaceae)

calycinus	SPlb
longitubus B&SWJ 11027	WCru
rubescens new	WCot

Isolepis (Cyperaceae)

§ ***cernua***	CBen CWat MBri MSKA MWts NOak SBfd SCoo SHDw WMAq

Isoloma see Kohleria

Isomeris see Cleome

Isoplexis (Scrophulariaceae)

canariensis	CAbb CBcs CCCN CDTJ CHEx CHll CRHN CSpe EBee ESwi EWll ITim SEND SGar SPlb SPoG WCFE WWlt
isabelliana	CCCN CDTJ LDai
sceptrum	CCCN CDTJ CHEx CHll CPLG SPlb WPGP

Isopogon (Proteaceae)

anemonifolius	SPlb
anethifolius	SPlb

Isopyrum (Ranunculaceae)

biternatum	NLar
dicarpon	see *Dichocarpum dicarpon*
nipponicum	CLAP GEdr WCot WCru WPGP
stoloniferum	WCru
thalictroides	EBee EPot GEdr LLHF SCnR SDys WCot

Isotoma (Campanulaceae)

sp.	SWvt
'Avant-garde Blue' new	SPoG
§ ***axillaris***	CSpe LAst NPer SCoo SPer SPet SPoG
- 'Fairy Carpet'	SRms
fluviatilis	NLar

Itea (Iteaceae)

chinensis	CPLG
ilicifolia ♀H3	Widely available
* - 'Rubrifolia'	EBee LRHS SLon SPoG
japonica 'Beppu'	SLPl SSpi
virginica	CAbP CBcs CMCN ELan EWTr MRav SLim SLon WFar
§ - 'Henry's Garnet'	CAbP CDoC CJun CMCN CMac CSBt EBee ECrN EPfP GBin IDee LAst LBMP LEdu LRHS MBri MGos NLar NPri SBfd SHil SLim SPer SPoG SRGP SSpi SWvt WCot WFar
- Little Henry = 'Sprich'PBR	CHGN CMac CSBt EBee ELan ELon IVic LRHS LSRN NLar SPtl
- 'Long Spire'	CJun NLar
- 'Merlot'	CJun EBee NLar
- 'Sarah Eve'	CJun CMCN NLar SRGP
- 'Saturnalia'	NLar
- Swarthmore form	see *I. virginica* 'Henry's Garnet'
yunnanensis	CPLG MBlu NLar SSpi WSHC

Ixeris (Asteraceae)

stolonifera	XLum

Ixia (Iridaceae)

aurea 'Saldanha'	ECho
'Blue Bird'	CCon ECho LAma SDeJ SMrm
capillaris 'Citrusdal'	ECho
'Castor'	CAvo CPrp ECho
curta	ECho
dubia	ECho
flexuosa	ECho
'Gemini'	ECho
'Giant'	CAvo CTca ECho SDeJ
'Hogarth'	CPrp ECho LAma WHil
'Holland Glory'	ECho
latifolia var. ***latifolia***	ECho
longituba 'Citrusdal'	ECho
lutea	ECho
'Mabel'	CAvo ECho WCot
maculata	ECho
marginifolia from Komsberg	ECho
'Marquette'	ECho
metelerkampiae	ECho
- 'Goudini'	ECho
mixed	SDeJ
monadelpha	ECho
orientalis	ECho
paniculata	ECho WHil
'Panorama'	ECho
polystachya	ECho
- var. ***longistylis***	ECho
- var. ***lutea***	ECho
pumilio	WCot
purpureorosea 'Saldanha'	ECho
rapunculoides	ECho
- var. ***rigida***	ECho
- var. ***subpendula***	ECho
'Rose Emperor'	ECho LAma SDeJ WHil
scillaris var. ***subundulata***	ECho
'Spotlight'	ECho WHil
thomasiae	WCot
trifolia	ECho
'Venus'	CCon CTca ECho LAma SDeJ WHil
versicolor	ECho
viridiflora	CDes ECho WCot
- var. ***minor***	ECho
'Vulcan'	CPrp ECho WHil
'Yellow Emperor'	CTca ECho SDeJ

Ixiolirion (Ixioliriaceae)

montanum	ECho
pallasii	see *I. tataricum*
§ ***tataricum***	ECho LAma MCot
- Ledebourii Group	CAvo EBee

J

Jaborosa (Solanaceae)

integrifolia	CCon CPLG EBee ELan LEdu LRHS MAvo WCot WPGP XLum

Jacaranda (Bignoniaceae)

acutifolia misapplied	see *J. mimosifolia*
§ ***mimosifolia***	CBcs CCCN EShb MREP SPlb

Jacobinia see Justicia

Jamesia (Hydrangeaceae)

americana	NLar

Jasione (Campanulaceae)

§ ***heldreichii***	LRHS NBir SRms

	jankae	see *J. heldreichii*
§	***laevis***	ECho GAbr GKev LRHS SRms
§	- 'Blaulicht'	CMHG EBee ECha EPfP LPot LRHS MBNS NEgg NLar SBfd SMrm SPlb WMoo
	- Blue Light	see *J. laevis* 'Blaulicht'
	montana	ECho EDAr MNHC WPnn
	perennis	see *J. laevis*

Jasminum ✿ (*Oleaceae*)

	CC 4728	CPLG
	adenophyllum	MOWG
	affine	see *J. officinale* f. *affine*
	angulare ♀H1	CPLG CRHN EShb MOWG SEND
	azoricum ♀H1	CCCN CDoC CRHN CTrC ELan EPfP EShb GCal MOWG
	beesianum	Widely available
	bignoniaceum	WSHC
	blinii	see *J. polyanthum*
	dispermum	CRHN
	diversifolium	see *J. subhumile*
	farreri	see *J. humile* f. *farreri*
	floridum	EWes
	fruticans	CMac EBee ELon EPfP LRHS SBrt SEND WCru XLum
	giraldii misapplied	see *J. humile* f. *farreri*
	grandiflorum misapplied	see *J. officinale* f. *affine*
	grandiflorum L.	IDee
	- 'De Grasse' ♀H1	CRHN EShb MOWG
	heterophyllum	see *J. subhumile*
	humile	CEnt CPLG MBrN SEND WFar WKif
§	- f. ***farreri***	MBri
	- var. ***glabrum***	see *J. humile* f. *wallichianum*
§	- 'Revolutum' ♀H4	CBcs CDul CMac CRHN CSBt CTrC CWSG CWib EBee ELan EPfP GCal LAst LHop LRHS MGos MRav NLar SBfd SEND SLon SPer SPoG SRms SWvt WFar WGwG WSHC WWFP
§	- f. ***wallichianum*** B&SWJ 2559	WCru
§	***laurifolium*** f. ***nitidum***	MOWG
§	***mesnyi*** ♀H2-3	CCCN CDoy CEnt CMac CPLG CRHN CTri CWib EBak EBee ELan EPfP IGor LRHS MOWG MRav MWat SBfd SEND SPer WSHC
	multiflorum	CCCN MOWG
	multipartitum	EShb
	- bushy	CSpe
	nitidum	see *J. laurifolium* f. *nitidum*
§	***nudiflorum*** ♀H4	Widely available
	- 'Argenteum'	see *J. nudiflorum* 'Mystique'
	- 'Aureum'	EBee ELan MAsh MBNS MRav NSti SPer SRms WCot
*	- 'Compactum'	MAsh
§	- 'Mystique' (v)	EBee ELan LRHS MAsh MRav SLon SPer SPoG WCot
	odoratissimum	EShb MOWG
	officinale ♀H4	Widely available
	- CC 1709	WMoo
§	- f. ***affine***	CBcs CCCN CRHN CSPN CTri CWSG CWib EBee ELan EPfP LAst LRHS MRav SCoo SDix SLim SRms WCru WFar
§	- 'Argenteovariegatum' (v) ♀H4	Widely available
	- 'Aureovariegatum'	see *J. officinale* 'Aureum'
§	- 'Aureum' (v)	CBcs CDoC CHby CMac CWSG CWib EBee ECtt ELan EPfP IBoy LBMP LRHS MAsh MBri MHer MREP NBir SBfd SCoo SLim SLon SPer SRms WPat
	- 'Clotted Cream'PBR	see *J. officinale* 'Devon Cream'
	- 'Crûg's Collection'	WCru
§	- 'Devon Cream'PBR	CBcs CCCN CDul CSBt CWGN EBee ECrN EPfP LAst LBMP LBuc LRHS LSRN MBri MGos MREP MRav NHol NLar NRHS SBfd SCoo SHil SLim SPer SPoG WCot WPat
	- Fiona Sunrise = 'Frojas'PBR	Widely available
	- 'Grandiflorum'	see *J. officinale* f. *affine*
	- 'Inverleith' ♀H4	CCCN CDoC CMac CTrC CWSG EBee ELan EPfP EShb IArd LAst LBMP LHop LRHS MAsh MBNS MBri MGos MRav SBfd SCoo SHil SLim SMad SPad SPer SPoG WFar WGrn WSHC
	- 'Variegatum'	see *J. officinale* 'Argenteovariegatum'
	parkeri	CBcs CCCN CJun CMac CMea CTri EBee ECho ELon EPfP GCal GEdr LRHS MBNS NLar NMen WPat
	- 'Bychan' **new**	WAbe
§	***polyanthum*** ♀H1-2	CArn CBcs CPLG CRHN CSBt CTrC CTri EBak EBee ELan EPfP ERom LRHS MBri MOWG NEgg SBfd SEND SLim SPer SRms
	- dark red-leaved	CPLG WPGP
	primulinum	see *J. mesnyi*
	reevesii hort.	see *J. humile* 'Revolutum'
	sambac ♀H1	CArn CCCN CDoC CHll CRHN EAmu ELan EPfP EShb MOWG
	- 'Grand Duke of Tuscany' (d)	MOWG
	sieboldianum	see *J. nudiflorum*
§	***simplicifolium*** subsp. ***suavissimum***	CRHN
	stenalobium	MOWG
	× ***stephanense***	Widely available
	suavissimum	see *J. simplicifolium* subsp. *suavissimum*
§	***subhumile***	IRar

Jatropha (*Euphorbiaceae*)

integerrima	CCCN
multifida	SPlb

Jeffersonia (*Berberidaceae*)

diphylla	CArn CBro CLAP EBee ECho EPPr EPri GAbr LAma LEdu LRHS MMoz MNrw NBir NHol NLar NMyG NRHS WAbe WCru WFar
dubia	CBro CCon CLAP EBee ECho EWes GEdr LEdu LLHF LRHS MNrw NBir NHar NMen NSla WAbe WCru

jostaberry see *Ribes* × *culverwellii*

Jovellana (*Calceolariaceae*)

punctata	CCCN CDoC CMac CPLG EBee SPlb
repens	CCon
sinclairii	CHll CPLG ECou LLHF SMrm SUsu
violacea ♀H3	CAbP CAbb CBcs CCCN CDoC CEnt CMac CPLG CTrC CTsd CWib EBee EPfP GCal IVic LRHS SGar SUsu WCru WPGP WPat WSHC WWlt

Jovibarba ✿ (*Crassulaceae*)

§	***allionii***	CMea CTri CWil EDAr EPot LBMP LRHS MAsh MHer MSCN NHol NMen NPri WAbe WHal WHoo WIvy WPer WTin
	- 'Oki'	ECho LRHS NMen
	allionii* × *hirta	CWil MSCN NMen SDys SFgr
§	***arenaria***	CWil GAbr NMen XLum
	- from Passo di Monte Croce Carnico	CWil NMen
	'Autumn Fires'	MSCN
*	***echiniformis***	XLum
	'Emerald Spring'	NMen SFgr
§	***heuffelii***	ECho LRHS NHol NMen WIvy WPer
	- 'Aga'	NHol WIvy
	- 'Aiolos'	NHol
	- 'Alemene'	NHol
	- 'Almkroon'	NHol
	- 'Angel Wings'	CWil LRHS NHol NMen WHoo
§	- 'Apache'	CWil NMen
	- 'Aquarius'	CWil NMen WIvy
	- 'Artemis'	NHol
	- 'Aurora'	NHol
	- 'Be Mine'	CWil WGor
	- 'Beacon Hill'	CWil WIvy
	- 'Belcore'	CWil WIvy
	- 'Benjamin'	CWil NHol
	- 'Bermuda'	WIvy
	- 'Bermuda Sunset'	NHol
	- 'Big Red'	NHol
	- 'Blaze'	CWil
	- 'Brandaris'	NHol SDys
	- 'Brocade'	MSCN NHol WIvy
	- 'Bronze Ingot'	CWil WCot
	- 'Bulgarien'	CWil
	- 'Cakor'	NHol
§	- 'Cherry Glow'	CWil NHol
	- 'Chocoleto'	NMen WTin
	- 'Cleopatra'	NHol
	- 'Copper King'	CWil WIvy
	- 'Dunbar Red'	NHol
	- 'Fandango'	CWil MHom NMen WIvy
	- 'Gento'	NHol
	- 'Geronimo'	NHol
	- 'Giuseppi Spiny'	MHom NHol NMen WTin
	- var. ***glabra***	LRHS WHoo
	- - from Araba Konak, Bulgaria	CWil MHom NHol NMen WTin
	- - from Anthoborio	CWil NMen WTin
	- - from Backovo, Bulgaria	NHol
	- - from Galičica, Balkans	NHol
	- - from Haila, Montenegro/ Kosovo	CWil NHol NMen SFgr WIvy
	- - from Jakupica, Macedonia	CWil NMen WIvy
	- - from Ljuboten, Balkans	CWil NHol NMen WTin
	- - from Ošljak, Albania	CWil NMen
	- - from Pasina Glava, Macedonia	CWil NMen
	- - from Rhodope, Bulgaria	CWil MHom NHol
	- - from Treska Gorge, Macedonia	CWil NMen WTin
	- - from Vitse, Greece	WIvy
§	- - 'Cameo'	NHol WIvy
	- 'Gold Rand'	NHol
	- 'Grand Slam'	CWil
	- 'Green Land'	CWil
	- 'Greenstone'	CWil MHom NHol NMen WAbe WIvy WTin
	- 'Harmony'	CWil NHol
	- 'Henry Correvon'	CWil
	- 'Hot Lips'	CWil
	- 'Hystyle'	WIvy
	- 'Ikaros'	NHol
	- 'Inferno'	MHom NHol NMen
§	- 'Inge'	NMen
	- 'Iole'	WIvy
	- 'Ithaca'	NHol
	- 'Iuno'	CWil NHol
	- 'Jade'	CWil NMen WIvy
	- 'Kapo'	WIvy
	- var. ***kopaonikensis***	CWil LRHS MHom NMen
	- 'Mary Ann'	MHom NMen WIvy
	- 'Miller's Violet'	CWil NMen WIvy WTin
	- 'Mink'	CWil
	- 'Minuta'	CWil NHol NMen WIvy WTin
	- 'Mystique'	CMea CWil LRHS NMen WIvy
	- 'Nannette'	CWil
	- 'Nobel'	NHol
	- 'Opele'	NHol
	- 'Orion'	CMea CWil NHol NMen
	- var. ***patens***	NMen
	- 'Pink Skies'	CWil NMen WIvy
	- 'Pink Star'	CWil NMen
	- 'Prisma'	CWil NMen WIvy WTin
	- 'Purple Haze'	WIvy
	- 'Red Rose'	CWil NMen
	- 'Serenade'	CWil NMen WGor
	- 'Springael's Choice'	CWil NMen
	- 'Sungold'	NHol
	- 'Suntan'	CWil NHol NMen WIvy
	- 'Sylvan Memory'	CWil WGor
	- 'Tan'	CWil NHol NMen WTin
	- 'Tancredi'	NMen
	- 'Torrid Zone'	MBrN NMen WIvy WTin
	- 'Tuxedo'	CWil NMen
	- 'Vesta'	CWil
	- 'Violet'	SDys WIvy
	- 'Xanthoheuff' **new**	NMen
§	***hirta***	CWil EDAr EUJe GAbr NHol NMen SFgr WPer XLum
	- from Wintergraben, Austria	SPlb
	- 'Belansky Tatra'	CWil NMen
§	- subsp. ***borealis***	CWil NHol
	- subsp. ***glabrescens***	EPot WHil
	- - from High Tatra	XLum
	- - from Smeryouka	CWil NMen
I	- 'Glauca'	SFgr
	- 'Hedgehog'	SFgr
	- var. ***neilreichii***	ECho LRHS MHom NMen NRHS
	- 'Purpurea'	XLum
	- 'Rax'	SFgr
	preissiana	NHol NMen SFgr WIvy WTin
§	***sobolifera***	CHEx CWil EDAr EPot GKev NHol NMen SFgr SPlb WAbe WHal WIvy WPer XLum
	- 'August Cream'	LRHS
	- 'Bronze Globe'	SFgr
	- 'Green Globe'	ECho LRHS NRHS SDys WTin
	- 'Miss Lorraine'	SFgr

Juania (*Arecaceae*)

	australis	EAmu

Jubaea (*Arecaceae*)

§	***chilensis***	CBcs CBrP CPHo EAmu IDee SBig SPlb
	spectabilis	see *J. chilensis*

Juglans ✿ (*Juglandaceae*)

§ ***ailanthifolia*** CMCN EGFP
- var. ***cordiformis*** 'Brock' (F) CAgr
- - 'Campbell Cw3' (F) CAgr
- - 'Fodermaier' seedling CAgr
- - 'Rhodes' (F) CAgr
ailanthifolia* × *cinerea see *J.* × *bixbyi*
§ × ***bixbyi*** CAgr
cinerea 'Beckwith' (F) CAgr
- 'Booth' seedlings (F) CAgr
- 'Craxezy' (F) CAgr
- 'Kenworthy' seedling CAgr
- 'Myjoy' (F) CAgr
hindsii EBtc
mandshurica (F) CBcs
- BWJ 8097 from China WCru
- RWJ 9905 from Taiwan WCru
* - subsp. ***sieboldiana*** B&SWJ 11026 WCru
microcarpa CMCN
nigra (F) ♀H4 CBcs CCVT CDul CLnd CMCN CMac CSBt CTho CWib EBee ECrN ELan EPfP GTwe LAst LRHS MAsh MBri MGos NWea SEND SGol SPer WCFE WFar WMou
- 'Bicentennial' (F) CAgr
- 'Emma Kay' (F) CAgr
- 'Laciniata' EPfP MBlu MBri WPat
- 'Purpurea' WPat
- 'Thomas' (F) CAgr
- 'Weschke' (F) CAgr
regia (F) ♀H4 Widely available
- 'Axel' (F) CAgr
- 'Broadview' (F) CAgr CSBt CTho ELan EPom GTwe IVic LAst LBuc LRHS MBlu MBri MCoo MGos NEgg NWea SCoo SEWo SKee SPer SPoG SVic WHar
- 'Buccaneer' (F) CAgr CMam CTho ECrN EPom GTwe MWat SKee WHar
- 'Chandler' (F) CAgr CMam
- 'Corne du Périgord' (F) CAgr CMam
- 'Ferjean' (F) CAgr
- 'Fernette'PBR (F) CAgr CMam WHar
- 'Fernor' (F) CAgr CMam WHar
- 'Franquette' (F) CAgr EBee GTwe MCoo WHar
- 'Hansen' (F) CAgr
- 'Hartley' (F) CAgr
- 'Jupiter' (F) CAgr
- 'Laciniata' WPat
- 'Lara' (F) CAgr GTwe
- 'Mayette' (F) CAgr
- 'Meylannaise' (F) CAgr CMam
- number 16 (F) CAgr WHar
- 'Parisienne' (F) CAgr SGol
- 'Plovdivski' (F) CAgr MBri WHar
- 'Proslavski' (F) CAgr CDul EBee MBri WHar
- 'Purpurea' CMCN MBlu MBri
- 'Rita' (F) CAgr LBuc MBri
- 'Ronde de Montignac' (F) CAgr
- 'Saturn' (F) CAgr
- 'Soleze' (F) CAgr
sieboldiana see *J. ailanthifolia*

jujube see *Ziziphus jujuba*

Juncus (*Juncaceae*)

articulatus XLum
bulbosus CNat CRWN
'Curly Gold Strike' (v) LRHS MSKA SBfd
§ ***decipiens*** 'Curly-wurly' EBee EPfP EWes LPBA LRHS NOak SWal SWat
- 'Spiralis' see *J. decipiens* 'Curly-wurly'
effusus CHEx CRWN CWat EHon LPBA MSKA NPer SBfd SWat WMAq XLum
- 'Carman's Japanese' CKno
- 'Gold Strike' (v) CWat EPPr
§ - f. ***spiralis*** CBen CRow CSpe CWat EHoe EHon ELan EPfP GKev LPBA LRHS LTen MAsh NBir NLar NOak NWsh SBfd SLim SPlb SPoG SVic WHal WMAq WPGP WPnP XLum
§ - - 'Unicorn'PBR EBee LRHS SApp SBfd SPoG
ensifolius CKno CRow CWat EHoe EWay EWes LPBA MMHG MSKA MWts NPer
filiformis 'Spiralis' EBee LPot SApp WWEG
inflexus CBen CRWN CWat EHon MMuc MSKA SEND SWat
- 'Afro' EBee ELan EPfP MMuc NBro NOak SEND SPlb SWal WHal WWEG
pallidus EPPr GCal
patens 'Carman's Gray' CKno CWCL EPPr GCal GQue LRHS MMoz MMuc NGdn NNor NOak NWad NWsh SApp SEND WMoo WPtf WWEG
- 'Elk Blue' CKno WWEG
'Unicorn'PBR see *J. effusus* f. *spiralis* 'Unicorn'
xiphioides EHoe

Junellia (*Verbenaceae*)

§ ***micrantha*** GEdr
odonnellii WAbe

Juniperus ✿ (*Cupressaceae*)

chinensis CMen SEND
- 'Aurea' ♀H4 CBcs CMac EHul LRHS MGos
§ - 'Blaauw' ♀H4 CDoC CMac CMen EHul MGos SGol WEve WFar
- 'Blue Alps' CJun EHul LRHS MGos MMuc NEgg SCoo SEND SGol SLim WEve WFar
- 'Densa Spartan' see *J. chinensis* 'Spartan'
- 'Echiniformis' CKen
- 'Expansa Aureospicata' (v) CDoC CKen EHul EPfP MGos SEND SLim SPoG
§ - 'Expansa Variegata' (v) CDoC CWib EHul EPfP MGos WFar
- 'Ferngold' CDoC
- 'Itoigawa' CMen
§ - 'Kaizuka' ♀H4 EHul LBee NLar SGol SLim SMad
- 'Kaizuka Variegata' see *J. chinensis* 'Variegated Kaizuka'
- 'Kuriwao Gold' see *J.* × *pfitzeriana* 'Kuriwao Gold'
- 'Obelisk' ♀H4 EHul
- 'Oblonga' CDoC EHul
- 'Plumosa Aurea' ♀H4 EHul WFar
- 'Plumosa Aureovariegata' (v) CKen
- 'Pyramidalis' ♀H4 CDoC EHul EPfP MAsh MWat NPri SCoo WFar
- 'Robust Green' NLar SEND
- 'San José' CMen EHul LRHS MAsh
§ - var. ***sargentii*** CMen
- 'Shimpaku' CKen CMen NLar
§ - 'Spartan' EHul
- 'Stricta' CSBt EHul LBee LRHS MGos SGol SLim

	- 'Sulphur Spray'	see *J.* × *pfitzeriana* 'Sulphur Spray'
	- 'Torulosa'	see *J. chinensis* 'Kaizuka'
§	- 'Variegated Kaizuka' (v)	EHul SCoo WFar
	communis	CArn CDul CHab CRWN EHul GPoy MNHC NWea SIde WAbe
	- (f)	SIde
	- 'Arnold'	CDul
	- 'Arnold Sentinel'	CKen
	- 'Atholl'	CKen
	- 'Barton'	NLar
	- 'Barton Gem'	NWad
	- 'Berkshire'	CKen
	- 'Brien'	CDoC CKen
	- 'Brynhyfryd Gold'	CKen
	- 'Compressa' ♀H4	CBcs CDoC CKen CMac CSBt CTri CWib EHul EPfP EPot GEdr LAst LBee LRHS MAsh MBri MGos NEgg NHol NMen NWad NWea SLim SPer SPoG WEve WFar WPat
§	- 'Constance Franklin' (v)	EHul
	- 'Corielagan'	CKen NLar
	- 'Cracovia'	CKen
	- var. ***depressa***	GPoy SGol
	- 'Depressa Aurea'	CKen CSBt EHul LBee MGos WFar
	- 'Depressed Star'	EHul SPoG WGor
	- 'Derrynane'	EHul
	- 'Effusa'	CKen
	- 'Gelb'	see *J. communis* 'Schneverdingen Goldmachangel'
	- 'Gold Cone'	CKen EHul EPfP LBee LRHS MAsh MGos SLim SPoG WFar WGor
	- 'Golden Showers'	see *J. communis* 'Schneverdingen Goldmachangel'
	- 'Goldschatz'	CKen LAst SPoG
	- 'Green Carpet' ♀H4	CDoC CKen CMen EHul EPfP GKin LBuc LRHS MAsh NEgg NHol SCoo SLim SPoG WCFE
	- 'Haverbeck'	CKen
	- 'Hibernica' ♀H4	CDul CSBt CTri EHul EPfP LAst LRHS MGos NWea SBfd SLPl SLim SPer SPoG WEve
	- 'Hibernica Aurea'	CMac
	- 'Hibernica Variegata'	see *J. communis* 'Constance Franklin'
	- 'Hornibrookii' ♀H4	EHul MGos NWea SRms
	- 'Horstmann'	GKin NLar
I	- 'Horstmann's Pendula'	CDoC
	- 'Kenwith Castle'	CKen
	- 'Meyer'	GKin
	- 'Prostrata'	WFar
	- 'Pyramidalis'	SPlb
	- 'Rakete'	IVic
	- 'Repanda' ♀H4	CBcs CDoC CMac CSBt CWib EHul EPfP EPot LAst LRHS MAsh MGos SCoo SEND SGol SLim SPer SPoG WEve WFar
§	- 'Schneverdingen Goldmachangel'	LRHS MAsh MGos NLar SLim SPoG
	- 'Sentinel'	CDoC EHul LRHS SLim WCFE WEve WMou
	- 'Sieben Steinhauser'	CKen
	- 'Silver Mist'	CKen
	- 'Spotty Spreader' (v)	LRHS SLim SPoG
	- Suecica Group	EHul NWea
	- - 'Suecica Aurea'	EHul
	- 'Zeal'	CKen
	conferta	see *J. rigida* subsp. *conferta*
	- var. ***maritima***	see *J. taxifolia*
	davurica	EHul
	- 'Expansa Albopicta'	see *J. chinensis* 'Expansa Variegata'
	- 'Expansa Variegata'	see *J. chinensis* 'Expansa Variegata'
	- 'Leningrad' **new**	LPot
	excelsa subsp. ***polycarpos***	CMen
	'Fitz Kukuri Gold'	MMuc
	foetidissima	CMen
	× ***gracilis*** 'Blaauw'	see *J. chinensis* 'Blaauw'
	'Grey Owl' ♀H4	EHul ELan EPfP LRHS NWea SCoo SEND SGol SLim WFar
	horizontalis	CDul NWea
§	- 'Andorra Compact'	NLar SCoo
	- 'Bar Harbor'	CKen CMac EHul MGos NWea
§	- 'Blue Chip'	EHul ELan EPfP LBee LRHS MGos NBir SCoo SLim SPer SPoG
	- 'Blue Horizon'	LRHS
	- 'Blue Moon'	see *J. horizontalis* 'Blue Chip'
	- 'Blue Pygmy'	CKen
	- 'Blue Rug'	see *J. horizontalis* 'Wiltonii'
	- 'Douglasii'	CKen EHul
	- 'Emerald Spreader'	CKen EHul ELan
	- 'Glacier'	CKen
	- Glauca Group	EHul MGos NWea SPoG
	- 'Glomerata'	CKen
	- 'Golden Carpet'	ELan EPfP LBuc MGos NLar SPoG
	- 'Golden Spreader'	CDoC
	- 'Grey Pearl'	CKen EHul
	- 'Hughes'	EHul LBee MRav NWea
	- Icee Blue = 'Monber'	CKen GKin MAsh NLar SLim SPoG
	- 'Jade River'	EHul
	- 'Limeglow'	CDoC CKen EPfP LAst LRHS MGos NEgg NLar SCoo SLim SPer SPoG WGor
	- 'Mother Lode'	CKen
	- 'Neumann'	CKen
	- 'Plumosa Compacta'	see *J. horizontalis* 'Andorra Compact'
	- 'Prince of Wales'	EHul MAsh MGos WEve
	- 'Turquoise Spreader'	CSBt EHul NWea SGol
	- 'Venusta'	see *J. virginiana* 'Venusta'
	- 'Villa Marie'	CKen
§	- 'Wiltonii' ♀H4	EHul
	- 'Winter Blue'	LBee LRHS SLim SPer
	- 'Youngstown'	SEND WFar
	- 'Yukon Belle'	CKen
N	× ***media***	see *J.* × *pfitzeriana*
§	× ***pfitzeriana***	CDul SGol WEve
	- 'Armstrongii'	EHul
	- 'Blaauw'	see *J. chinensis* 'Blaauw'
	- 'Blue and Gold' (v)	CKen EHul
	- 'Blue Cloud'	see *J. virginiana* 'Blue Cloud'
§	- 'Carbery Gold'	CBcs CDoC CDul CMac CSBt EHul GKin LBee LRHS MAsh MBri MGos MWat SCoo SLim SPoG WEve WFar
	- 'Daub's Frosted'	SLim
	- 'Gold Coast'	CDoC CKen CSBt EHul EPfP LBee LRHS MBri MGos SGol SLim SPer WEve
	- Gold Sovereign = 'Blound'PBR	LBee MAsh
*	- 'Golden Joy'	LRHS SLim SPoG
	- 'King of Spring'	SLim
§	- 'Kuriwao Gold'	CMac EHul GKin LRHS MGos MRav NLar NPri SCoo SEND SGol SPoG WFar
	- 'Mint Julep'	CSBt EHul LRHS LTen MGos SCoo SGol SLim WEve WFar
	- 'Mordigan Gold'	WEve
	- 'Old Gold' ♀H4	CKen EHul EPfP GKin LBee LRHS MBri MGos MWat NEgg NPri NWea

SCoo SEND SGol SLim SPlb SPoG WEve WFar
- 'Old Gold Carbery' see *J.* × *pfitzeriana* 'Carbery Gold'
- 'Pfitzeriana' see *J.* × *pfitzeriana* 'Wilhelm Pfitzer'
- 'Pfitzeriana Aurea' EHul EPfP EPot MGos NWea SGol WEve WFar
- 'Pfitzeriana Compacta' 𝕐H4 EHul SCoo
- 'Pfitzeriana Glauca' EHul LRHS SCoo
§ - 'Sulphur Spray' 𝕐H4 CDul CWib EHul MAsh MGos MMuc SEND SGol SLim WCFE WEve WFar
§ - 'Wilhelm Pfitzer' EHul EPfP NWea
§ ***pingii*** 'Glassell' CDoC MAsh NLar
- 'Hulsdonk Yellow' PBR SLim
§ - var. ***wilsonii*** CDoC CKen NLar
procera WPGP
procumbens 'Bonin Isles' LRHS SPoG
- 'Nana' 𝕐H4 CDoC CKen CMac CSBt EHul EPfP LAst LBee LPot LRHS MAsh MGos NEgg NHol SCoo SLim SPoG WCFE WEve WFar
recurva CDoC
- 'Castlewellan' CDoC NLar
- var. ***coxii*** CDoC CMac EHul MGos NHol NLar SMad WCFE
§ - 'Densa' CDoC CKen EHul
- 'Nana' see *J. recurva* 'Densa'
rigida CMen NLar
§ - subsp. ***conferta*** CMac MWat SEND SGol WEve
- - 'All Gold' SLim
* - - 'Blue Ice' CKen WFar
- - 'Blue Pacific' EHul NLar SGol WCFE WFar
- - 'Blue Tosho' CDul SPoG
- - 'Emerald Sea' EHul
- - 'Schlager' SLim
- - 'Silver Mist' CKen
sabina NWea
§ - 'Blaue Donau' EHul
- Blue Danube see *J. sabina* 'Blaue Donau'
- 'Broadmoor' EHul
- 'Buffalo' EHul
- 'Knap Hill' see *J.* × *pfitzeriana* 'Wilhelm Pfitzer'
- 'Mountaineer' see *J. scopulorum* 'Mountaineer'
- 'Rockery Gem' EHul LRHS SLim SPoG
- 'Skandia' CKen
- 'Tamariscifolia' CBcs CDul CWib EHul GKin LBee LRHS LTen MAsh MGos NWea SEND SGol SLim SPer SPoG WCFE WEve WFar
- 'Variegata' (v) EHul
sargentii see *J. chinensis* var. *sargentii*
scopulorum CKen
- 'Blue Arrow' CDoC CDul CKen CSBt CWib ELan EPfP GKin LAst LBee LRHS MAsh MBri MGos NEgg NHol NLar NPCo NWea SCoo SGol SLim SPer WBor WEve WFar
- 'Blue Banff' CKen
- 'Blue Heaven' EHul
- 'Blue Pyramid' EHul
- 'Boothman' EHul
- 'Moonglow' EHul
§ - 'Mountaineer' EHul
- 'Mrs Marriage' CKen
- 'Silver Star' (v) EHul
- 'Skyrocket' CBcs CCVT CDul CMac CSBt CTri CWib ECrN EHul EPfP EPot LAst MGos MRav MWat NPCo NWea SEND SPlb WCFE WEve WFar WMou
- 'Snow Flurries' SLim
- 'Springbank' EHul WCFE
- 'Wichita Blue' EHul EPfP IVic WEve
squamata 'Blue Carpet' 𝕐H4 CBcs CDoC CDul CKen CMac CSBt CWib EHul EPfP LAst LBuc LPot LRHS MAsh MBri MGos NEgg NHol NPri NWea SBfd SEND SGol SLim SPer SPoG WCFE WEve WFar
- 'Blue Spider' CKen LRHS SCoo SLim
- 'Blue Star' 𝕐H4 Widely available
- 'Blue Star Variegated' see *J. squamata* 'Golden Flame'
- 'Chinese Silver' EHul SLim
- 'Dream Joy' CKen LRHS NLar SLim SPoG
- 'Filborna' CKen LBee LRHS SLim
- 'Glassell' see *J. pingii* 'Glassell'
§ - 'Golden Flame' (v) CKen
- 'Holger' 𝕐H4 CDoC CDul CMac CSBt EHul EPfP GEdr LAst LBee LRHS MAsh MBri MGos NHol SCoo SGol SLim SPoG WEve
- 'Loderi' see *J. pingii* var. *wilsonii*
- 'Meyeri' EHul GKev NWea SCoo SGol WFar
- 'Wilsonii' see *J. pingii* var. *wilsonii*
§ ***taxifolia*** CSBt
§ ***virginiana*** 'Blue Cloud' EHul LRHS LTen SLim
- 'Burkii' EHul WEve
- 'Frosty Morn' CKen EHul WFar
- 'Glauca' EHul NWea
- 'Golden Spring' CKen
- 'Helle' see *J. chinensis* 'Spartan'
- 'Hetzii' EHul NLar NWea WFar
- 'Hillspire' EHul
- Silver Spreader = 'Mona' CKen EHul
- 'Sulphur Spray' see *J.* × *pfitzeriana* 'Sulphur Spray'
§ - 'Venusta' CKen

Jurinea (*Asteraceae*)

glycacantha LRHS
ledebourii LRHS
mollis SPhx

Jurinella see *Jurinea*

Jussiaea see *Ludwigia*

Justicia (*Acanthaceae*)

aconitiflora WHil
aurea EShb
§ ***brandegeeana*** 𝕐H1 CCCN EShb MOWG
- 'Lutea' see *J. brandegeeana* 'Yellow Queen'
- variegated (v) EShb
§ - 'Yellow Queen' EShb
- yellow-flowered EShb
§ ***carnea*** CHII EBak EShb GCal MOWG SMad SUsu WCot WHil
- 'Alba' CCCN EShb
- dark-leaved CHII WCot
- 'Radiant' **new** SMad
§ ***floribunda*** CBcs
guttata see *J. brandegeeana*
pauciflora see *J. floribunda*
'Penrhosiensis' EShb WHil
pohliana see *J. carnea*
rizzinii 𝕐H1 CBcs CCCN CHII SMad WHil
scheidweileri EShb
spicigera EShb WHil
suberecta see *Dicliptera sericea*

K

Kadsura (Schisandraceae)

coccinea B&SWJ 11793	WCru
japonica	CBcs
- B&SWJ 1027	WCru WPGP
- B&SWJ 4463 from Korea	WCru
- B&SWJ 11109 from Japan	WCru
- 'Fukurin' (v)	NLar
- 'Variegata' (v)	CCCN EBee EPfP LRHS SEND WSHC
- white fruit	CBcs

Kaempferia ✿ (Zingiberaceae)

parishii new	GHim
roscoeana new	GHim
rotunda	CCCN GHim LAma LEdu
- 'Himalayan Easter' new	GHim

Kageneckia (Rosaceae)

oblonga	SPlb

Kalanchoe (Crassulaceae)

beharensis ♀H1	CAbb CCCN CDTJ EShb
- 'Fang'	CDTJ
- 'Rusty'	CDTJ CSpe
§ ***delagoensis***	CCCN EShb
fedtschenkoi	EShb
laciniata	EShb
orgyalis	EShb
prolifera	EShb
pubescens	EShb
pumila ♀H1	EShb EWoo SBch SPet
rhombopilosa	EShb
sexangularis	EShb
'Tessa' ♀H1	WCot
thyrsiflora 'Bronze Sculpture'	CAbb EUJe WCot
tomentosa ♀H1	EShb WCot
tubiflora	see *K. delagoensis*

Kalimeris (Asteraceae)

§ ***incisa***	EBee MRav WBor
- 'Alba'	EBee ECha LHop NLar WFar XLum
- 'Blue Star'	EBee ECha EWll LHop LRHS NLar WCAu WFar WPtf WSHC
- 'Charlotte'	EBee EWes NBre NDov
- 'Madiva'	CSam EBee ECha LHop LPla NDov
- 'Nana Blue'	NDov
§ ***mongolica***	CDes CMac EBee ECha MMuc SEND WFar WSHC
- 'Antonia'	NDov
§ ***pinnatifida***	EBee LRHS
- 'Hortensis'	ECtt
§ ***yomena*** 'Shogun' (v)	CPrp EBee ECha EHoe ELan EMil EPfP EShb LRHS NBir NBre NLar SAga SMrm SPer WFar WPer WWEG XLum
- 'Variegata'	see *K. yomena* 'Shogun'

Kalmia ✿ (Ericaceae)

angustifolia ♀H4	GKev SRms WFar
- f. ***rubra*** ♀H4	CBcs CDoC CDul EBee ELan EPfP LRHS MAsh NLar NPri SBfd SPer SReu WFar
I - 'Rubra Nana'	CMac
cuneata	GGGa
latifolia ♀H4	CBcs ELan EPfP LRHS LSou MMuc NPri NWea SEND SPer SWvt WFar
- 'Bigboy'	GGGa
- 'Bullseye'	NLar
- 'Carousel'	CBcs CCCN GEdr NLar
- 'Clementine Churchill'	CMac
- 'Freckles' ♀H4	ELan EPfP GGGa NPCo SPoG
- 'Fresca'	NPCo
- 'Galaxy'	GGGa IVic
- 'Kaleidoscope'	GGGa IVic
- 'Minuet'	CBcs CCCN CDoC EBee EPfP GEdr GGGa IVic LRHS MLea MPkF NLar NPCo SLim SPoG SSpi SWvt
- 'Mitternacht'	GGGa
- f. ***myrtifolia***	LRHS
- - 'Elf'	EPfP GEdr IVic LRHS MAsh MGos MPkF NLar NRHS SLim
- 'Nipmuck'	CMac
- 'Olympic Fire' ♀H4	EBee GGGa IVic LRHS MPkF NLar SLim
- 'Olympic Wedding'	NLar
- 'Ostbo Red'	CBcs CDoC CDul CMac EBee EPfP GEdr IVic LRHS MLea MPkF NCGa NPCo SPoG SReu SSpi SWvt
- 'Peppermint'	GGGa IVic MPkF SLim
- 'Pink Charm' ♀H4	IVic
- 'Pink Frost'	NPCo
- 'Pinwheel'	EBee MPkF NLar SLim
- 'Quinnipiac'	MPkF
- 'Sarah'	LRHS MLea NPCo
§ ***microphylla***	WAbe
polifolia	CBcs EPfP NHar NMen SPer WThu
- var. ***compacta***	WSHC
- 'Glauca'	see *K. microphylla*
- f. ***leucantha***	NHar NMen WThu

Kalmiopsis (Ericaceae)

* ***leachiana*** 'Shooting Star'	WThu

× Kalmiothamnus (Ericaceae)

'Haytor'	ITim WAbe
ornithomma 'Cosdon'	WAbe WThu
'Sindelberg'	ITim WAbe

Kalopanax (Araliaceae)

pictus	see *K. septemlobus*
§ ***septemlobus***	CBcs CDul ELan EPfP GBin NLar SEND
- var. ***magnificus*** B&SWJ 10900	WCru
- f. ***maximowiczii***	CDoC EBee EPfP IVic MBlu WCot

Keckiella (Plantaginaceae)

§ ***antirrhinoides***	SBrt

Kelseya (Rosaceae)

uniflora	WAbe

Kennedia (Papilionaceae)

coccinea	CCCN
macrophylla	CBcs CRHN
nigricans	CCCN MOWG
prostrata	SPlb
rubicunda	CCCN CRHN

Kentia (*Arecaceae*)

belmoreana	see *Howea belmoreana*
forsteriana	see *Howea forsteriana*

Kentranthus see *Centranthus*

Kerria (*Rosaceae*)

japonica misapplied single	see *K. japonica* 'Simplex'
japonica (d)	see *K. japonica* 'Pleniflora'
- 'Albescens'	WCot WFar
- 'Golden Guinea' ♀H4	CMac CPLG EBee ECtt ELan EPfP EWTr IFro LRHS MAsh MGos MNrw MRav MSwo SBfd SCoo SHil SPer SRms SWal SWvt WFar
§ - 'Picta' (v)	CDul CWib EBee ECrN ELan LRHS MGos MRav MSwo SBfd SGol SLim SLon SPer SPoG SRms WFar WSHC
§ - 'Pleniflora' (d) ♀H4	Widely available
§ - 'Simplex'	CMac CPLG NWea
- 'Variegata'	see *K. japonica* 'Picta'

Khadia (*Aizoaceae*)

acutipetala	CCCN

Kirengeshoma (*Hydrangeaceae*)

palmata ♀H4	Widely available
- Koreana Group	CCon CLAP CPLG EBee ELan EPPr EPfP GBuc GCal IPot ITim LAst LEdu LHop LRHS MCot MRav NBid NHol NLar NPnk SPad SPer SPoG WCot WCru WFar WGwG WWEG WWlt

Kitaibela (*Malvaceae*)

vitifolia	CPLG EBee ELan GCal MBel MPie NBid SBrt SEND SGar SPav SPlb WPer WPtf

Kitchingia see *Kalanchoe*

kiwi fruit see *Actinidia deliciosa*

Kleinia (*Asteraceae*)

articulata	see *Senecio articulatus*
grantii	WCot
repens	see *Senecio serpens*

Knautia (*Caprifoliaceae*)

§ ***arvensis***	CArn CHab CHII CRWN EPfP MHer MNHC NLan NLar NMir SEND WFar WHer WMoo WOut WSFF
- 'Rachael'	CElw
dipsacifolia	SHar
'Jardin d'en Face'	EBee ELan EPfP LRHS WCot
§ ***macedonica***	Widely available
- 'Crimson Cushion'	CSpe ECtt LSou WCot WFar
- 'Mars Midget'	Widely available
- Melton pastels	COIW CPLG EBee ELan EPfP EShb GJos LRHS LSRN LSou MGos NLar NPer NRHS SPet SPoG SRot SWat SWvt WFar WWEG
- pink-flowered	CSam
- 'Red Knight'	EPfP MBNS WCot
- red-flowered	CWib
- short	ECtt SPad
- tall, pale-flowered	SPhx
- 'Thunder and Lightning' (v)	CWGN EBee ECtt LSou NPri SPer WCot
sarajevensis	SUsu

Knightia (*Proteaceae*)

excelsa	CBcs IDee

Kniphofia ✿ (*Asphodelaceae*)

sp.	SVic
'Ada'	EWTr EWes LRHS NRHS
albescens	SGar SPlb
'Alcazar'	CBcs CPrp EBee ECtt EPfP LRHS LSRN MAvo MBri MHer MSCN SBfd SPer SRkn SWvt WCAu WCot WFar WMnd
* ***alpina***	LRHS
'Amber'	NBre
'Ample Dwarf'	ECtt WCot
'Amsterdam'	MWat SHar
angustifolia	SPlb
'Apricot'	LRHS NRHS
'Apricot Souffle'	EPri WCot
'Apricots and Cream'	WCot
'Atlanta'	LRHS SBfd
'Aurora' **new**	XLum
'Barbie' **new**	WCot
'Barton Fever'	WCot
baurii	CPLG IGor SPlb
'Bees' Flame'	EBee
'Bees' Jubilee'	MNrw WHoo
'Bees' Lemon'	Widely available
'Bees' Sunset' ♀H4	CAvo CDes EBee GCra GQue LPla MNFA MNrw SMHy SMrm SUsu WCot WHil WWEG
'Bengal Fire'	LRHS
'Bicolor'	EBee ECtt NSti
'Bitter Chocolate'	WCot
'Bob's Choice'	WCot
'Border Ballet'	LBMP LRHS NBir NBre NGdn NLar SWat WFar
brachystachya	ELon GAbr GBin GCal SPlb WCot
'Bressingham Comet'	EBee ECtt LRHS MBri NBir NCGa SHil WWEG
'Bressingham Gleam'	LRHS WCot
Bressingham hybrids	IFoB
Bressingham Sunbeam = 'Bresun'	EBee ECtt LRHS NBir NRHS WWEG
'Bressingham Yellow'	EBee ECtt
'Brimstone' Bloom ♀H4	CElw EBee ECtt EHrv EPPr EPfP LAst LEdu LHop LRHS MBri MCot MSpe NBir NSti NWsh SAga SRkn SWvt WAbb WAul WCot WFar WGwG WMnd WWEG
bruceae	EPri
buchananii	CDes
'Buttercup' ♀H4	CAvo LSRN WSHC
'Candlelight'	CCse COIW EBee ECtt EPri LRHS MAvo NBre SBfd
'Candlemass'	CTca SBfd
'Carole's Crush'	WCot
caulescens ♀H3-4	Widely available
- 'Coral Breakers'	CPLG CTca EBee ECtt GAbr LRHS MNFA NEgg SBfd SDix SKHP SMad SPer SPoG WCot
- 'John May'	EBee ECtt GBin LRHS SMad
	WCot
- short	ECha
'Chichi'	WCot
'Christmas Cheer' **new**	CDes
citrina	CCon CTrC EPfP GCra LAst LRHS MAvo MBrN NBre NLar NPri WCot WHil XLum

	'Citrina' **new**	LRHS
	'C.M. Prichard' misapplied	see *K. rooperi*
	'C.M. Prichard' Prichard	WCot
	'Cobra'	EBee ECtt GBin GMaP LRHS SBfd SUsu WCot WHil
	'Comet'	ECtt
I	'Cooperi' **new**	EPri
	'Coral Sceptre'	LPla WCot
	'Dingaan'	CAbb EBee ECtt GQue MBel MNrw NBir NEgg SAga WCot
	'Dorset Sentry'	CAbb COlW EBee ECtt ELon EPfP GCal LRHS MCot MGos MNrw NBir NEgg NLar NOrc NSti SBfd SKHP WCAu WCot WFar WWEG
	'Drummore Apricot'	CMHG EAEE EBee ECha ECtt ELan GBuc GCal IBoy LRHS LSRN MAvo MBel NBir NCGa NEgg NSti SEND WCot WFar WGwG
I	'Earliest of All'	EBee
	'Early Buttercup'	CTca SBfd WCot WFar
	ensifolia	CTca ECtt NGdn WMnd XLum
	'Ernest Mitchell'	WCot
	Express hybrids	NBre NLar XLum
	'Fairyland'	NGBl SGar WBrk WTin
	'Feuerkerze'	EBee
	'Fiery Fred'	EBee ELan LRHS MRav NBre NRHS SBfd SMrm WCot
	'Firefly'	LRHS
	'First Sunrise'[PBR]	EBee ECtt NCGa
	'Flamenco'	COlW EBee EWll LRHS NBre NGdn NHol SBfd SPet WRHF WWEG
	'Florence Bedecked' **new**	WCot
	foliosa Hochst.	LEdu
	'Frances Victoria'	WCot
	galpinii misapplied	see *K. triangularis* subsp. *triangularis*
	galpinii ambig.	LAst SPer WWEG XLum
	galpinii Baker ♀H4	EBee NBre SEND
	'Gilt Bronze'	EBee WCot
	'Gladness'	ECtt MAvo NBir NBre NCGa NSti WCot WWEG
	'Gloire d'Orléans' **new**	XLum
	'Goldelse'	EBee NBir WCot
	'Goldfinch'	CCse CSam
	gracilis	LEdu
	'Green and Cream'	MNrw
	'Green Jade'	Widely available
	'Green Lemon'	NBre
	'H.E. Beale'	ECtt GCal WCot
	'Hen and Chickens'	EBee MAvo WCot
	hirsuta	CCon EBee GBin LRHS NRHS SPad WCot WSHC
	- JCA 3.461.900	SKHP
	- 'Fire Dance'	EBee LRHS
	- 'Traffic Lights'	GBin
	'Hollard's Gold'	WCot
	'Ice Queen'	CAvo CCon CPar EBee ECtt ELon EPPr EPri IPot LAst LRHS MAvo MRav NChi NLar SBfd SEND SGar SRms SWvt WCot WTin WWEG
	ichopensis	WPGP
	'Incandesce'	WCot
	'Ingénue'	WCot
	'Innocence'	LRHS NBre
	'Jane Henry'	EBee MAvo
	'Jenny Bloom'	CAvo CMac COlW EBee ECtt ELan ELon EPfP EWTr GBuc GCal GMaP ITim LAst LRHS MRav MWat NEgg NLar NPri SPer WCAu WCot WFar WMnd WWEG
	'John Benary'	EAEE EBee ECtt GMaP IKil LRHS LSou MAvo MBel MCot NBir NEgg NGdn NLar SBfd SEND SMrm SPer WCot WKif WTin WWEG
	'Jonathan'	ECtt WCot
	laxiflora	EPri WPGP
	'Lemon Ice'	EBee WCot
	'Light of the World'	see *K. triangularis* subsp. *triangularis* 'Light of the World'
	linearifolia	CPLG CTrC EBee GCra MBel MNrw SGar SPlb WCot
	'Little Elf'	XLum
	'Little Maid'	Widely available
	'Lord Roberts'	GCal MRav SBfd SMad WCot WPGP
	'Luna'	WCot
	macowanii	see *K. triangularis* subsp. *triangularis*
	'Maid of Orleans'	LRHS
	'Mermaiden'	CCon CMHG EBee ECtt LAst MNrw WCAu WCot
	'Minister Verschuur'	EBee ECtt GQue LRHS MBri WMnd
	'Modesta'	WSHC
	'Moonstone'	EBee ECtt WCot
	'Mount Etna'	WCot
	multiflora	CTca ECtt
	'Nancy's Red'	Widely available
	nelsonii Mast.	see *K. triangularis* subsp. *triangularis*
	'New England'	EBee
	'Nobilis'	see *K. uvaria* 'Nobilis'
	northiae ♀H4	CHEx CPLG CTca EAmu EBee ECtt ELan ELon EPri EUJe EWes EWll GCal GKev LEdu LRHS MAvo MNrw NLar NMRc SBfd SDix SEND SMad SPlb SWal WCot WCru WPGP XLum
	- JCA 3.462.600	WCot
	'November Glory'	CTca WCot
	'Old Court Seedling'	WCot
§	'Painted Lady'	CAvo COlW CSam CTca CTri CYeo EBee ECtt EPfP GAbr GMaP LAst MNFA MNrw NCGa NLar SMHy WCot
	pauciflora	WCot
	'Percy's Pride'	Widely available
	'Pfitzeri'	SRms
	× ***praecox***	LRHS MAvo SGar WCFE WCot
	'Primrose Upward' **new**	WCot
I	'Primulina' Bloom	LRHS
	'Prince Igor' misapplied	see *K. uvaria* 'Nobilis'
	'Prince Igor' Prichard	GAbr LRHS MLHP NBir WCot
	pumila	LLHF
	'Raging Inferno'	WCot
	'Red Rocket'	WCot
	'Rich Echoes'	WCot
	ritualis	CPLG LSou SKHP WWEG
§	***rooperi*** ♀H4	Widely available
I	- 'Torchlight'	CPne
	'Royal Castle'	CPLG GMaP LRHS NBir NGdn NOrc SEND WFar WWEG XLum
	'Royal Standard' ♀H4	CBcs CMac CPrp EBee ECtt ELan EPfP EShb LRHS LSRN MCot NCGa NLar SBfd SPer SPoG SWvt WFar WMnd WWEG
	rufa Baker	MAvo SUsu
	- CD&R 1032	SGar
	'Safranvogel'	EBee ECtt MAvo MSpe SMad WCot

'Samuel's Sensation' misapplied — see *K.* 'Painted Lady'
'Samuel's Sensation' Samuel ♀H4 — CCon EBee ELan LRHS NLar NSti SEND SRGP WCot WWEG
sarmentosa — CTrC SGar SPlb WCot
'Scorched Corn' **new** — MAvo MSpe WCot
'Sherbet Lemon' — ECtt MNrw WCot
'Shining Sceptre' — CSam CTca EBee ECha ECtt LRHS MAvo NLar SBfd SGar SMad SPoG SWvt WAul WWEG
'Springtime' — WCot
'Star of Baden-Baden' — CDes EBee NBir SEND SMad WCot WWEG
Stark's Early Perpetual-Flowering Hybrids **new** — XLum
'Strawberries and Cream' — CAvo CBcs CCon CMac COlW CWCL CYeo EBee ECha ECtt EPfP GQue LAst MAvo SBfd SPer SWvt WCot
stricta — WCot
'Sunningdale Yellow' ♀H4 — CCse CDes COlW CYeo EBee ECha ECtt EHrv EPfP GMaP LRHS MLHP SMHy SRms WHoo WWEG
'Tawny King' — Widely available
'Tetbury Torch'PBR — CWGN EAEE EBee ECGP ECtt GBin GQue LHop LRHS LSou MAvo NCGa NLar WAul WPtf WWEG
thomsonii — GCal NGdn SBod
- var. ***snowdenii*** misapplied — see *K. thomsonii* var. *thomsonii*
- var. ***snowdenii*** ambig. — CPLG CPne WPGP XLum
§ - var. ***thomsonii*** — CEnt MAvo SAga SMHy SUsu WHal
'Timothy' — Widely available
'Toffee Nosed' ♀H4 — Widely available
'Torchbearer' — NBre WCot
triangularis — EPfP EShb MBlu NCGa WFar XLum
§ - subsp. ***triangularis*** — CBro COlW EBee EPfP GBuc GCal LAst LRHS LSRN SDix SMrm SRms SWat WCot
§ - - 'Light of the World' — CAvo CBcs CTca EAEE EBee ECtt LAst LEdu LRHS MAvo MBel MBlu MHer NBir NLar SPer SUsu SWvt WCot WFar WGrn WPtf WWEG
'Tubergeniana' — WCot
'Tuckii' — SRms
typhoides — CDes EBee NBir SPlb
tysonii — SPlb
uvaria — CTrC LRHS NBir SEND SRms WCot WMnd XSen
- 'Grandiflora' — CMac MWhi SBfd WFar
§ - 'Nobilis' ♀H4 — Widely available
'Vanilla' — CCon EBee LAst LRHS LSRN MAvo NGdn SBfd SEND WAul WWEG
'Vincent Lepage' — EBee GBin LHop NLar
'Wol's Red Seedling' — CAvo CBct CBro CEnt COlW CSam CYeo EBee ECtt ELon EWTr GAbr LSou MCot MNrw NCGa NEgg NGdn NLar SBfd SPoG WCot WGrn WGwG WHoo
'Wrexham Buttercup' — COlW CSam EBee ECtt ELan EPfP GAbr GBin GMaP GQue LRHS LSRN MCot MNrw NPri NWsh SBfd SMad WCot WHal WHoo WWEG WWlt
'Yellow Cheer' — WCot
'Yellow Hammer' Slieve Donard — CSam EBee NBre SBfd SEND SGar
'Zululandii' — WCot

Knowltonia (*Ranunculaceae*)

filia — CPLG

Koeleria (*Poaceae*)

cristata misapplied — see *K. macrantha*
glauca — CWib EBee ECha EHoe EPPr EPfP EUJe GMaP LEdu LRHS LTen MBNS MWhi NBro NGdn NRHS NWsh SBfd SLim SMrm SPlb SWvt WFar WMnd WWEG XLum
§ ***macrantha*** — NLar XLum
pyramidata — SMea XLum
vallesiana — EHoe LRHS SMea
- 'Mountain Breeze' — EPPr

Koelreuteria (*Sapindaceae*)

bipinnata — CMCN
paniculata ♀H4 — Widely available
- 'Coral Sun'PBR — CGHE CMHG CPLG EBee EPfP LRHS MBlu MBri MGos NLar SChF WPGP WPat
- 'Fastigiata' — CDul EBee EPfP MBlu MBri MWat SCoo SSpi WHar
- 'Rosseels' — NLar
- 'September' — EPfP

Kohleria (*Gesneriaceae*)

'Ampallang' **new** — WDib
'Cybele' — EABi WDib
'Dark Velvet' — WDib
eriantha ♀H1 — CDoC WDib
hirsuta — WDib
'Jester' ♀H1 — EABi WDib
'Marquis de Sade' — EABi
'Red Ryder' — EABi
'Ruby Red' — WDib
'Silver Feather' **new** — WDib
§ 'Sunrise'PBR — WDib
'Sunshine'PBR — see *K.* 'Sunrise'
warscewiczii ♀H1 — EABi WDib

Kolkwitzia (*Caprifoliaceae*)

amabilis — CDoy CPLG CSBt CTri ECGP ELan EPfP MGos NWea SGol SPlb SRms WCFE WHar WMoo WRHF
- Dream Catcher = 'Maradco' — CMac CWSG EPfP MRav NLar NPro SPoG WPat
- 'Pink Cloud' ♀H4 — Widely available

Kosteletzkya (*Malvaceae*)

virginica — MAvo SPhx

kumquat see *Fortunella*

Kunzea (*Myrtaceae*)

ambigua — EBee ECou ESwi IDee MOWG SPlb
- pink-flowered — ECou
- prostrate — ECou
baxteri — ECou ESwi MOWG
ericifolia — SPlb
§ ***ericoides*** — CTsd ECou
- 'Auckland' — ECou
- 'Bemm' — ECou
parvifolia — ECou

L

Lablab (Papilionaceae)

§	***purpureus***	LSou SHDw
	- 'Ruby Moon'	CSpe

+ *Laburnocytisus* (Papilionaceae)

	'Adamii'	CDul CJun CLnd CMac EBee ECrN ELan EPfP IVic LAst LSRN MGos MPkF NLar SMad SPer

Laburnum ✿ (Papilionaceae)

	alpinum	EPfP NWea SPlb
	- 'Pendulum'	CDoC CDul CLnd ELan LSRN MAsh MBri MGos NEgg NPri SCrf SGol SLim SPer SPoG
§	***anagyroides***	CDul CWib MMuc NWea SEND SRms
	vulgare	see *L. anagyroides*
	× ***watereri*** 'Sunspire' **new**	MPkF
	- 'Vossii' ♀H4	Widely available

Lachenalia (Asparagaceae)

	alba 'Nieuwoudtville'	ECho
	algoensis	ECho
§	***aloides***	CDoC CGrW CTca ECho EPot GKev NMen
	- var. ***aurea*** ♀H1	CTca ECho EPot SBch WCot
I	- var. ***luteola***	ECho
	- 'Nelsonii'	ECho WCot
	- 'Pearsonii'	ECho GKev
	- var. ***quadricolor*** ♀H1	CGrW CPrp CTca ECho WCot
	- var. ***vanzyliae*** ♀H1	WCot
	angelica 'Agterkop'	ECho
	anguinea	ECho
	arbuthnotiae 'Somerset West'	ECho
	attenuata	ECho WCot
	barkeriana	ECho
	bolusii	ECho
§	***bulbifera*** ♀H1	CTca ECho WCot
	- 'George' ♀H1	ECho WCot
	capensis	ECho
	carnosa	ECho
	cernua 'Goudini'	ECho
	comptonii	ECho
	congesta 'Roggeveld'	ECho
	contaminata ♀H1	CGrW CPrp ECho EPfP WCot
	doleritica	ECho
	elegans	ECho
	- var. ***flava*** **new**	GKev
	- var. ***membranacea***	ECho
	- var. ***suaveolens***	ECho
	fistulosa	ECho
	- 'Klein Drakenstein'	ECho
	framesii	ECho
	'Fransie' PBR	ECho
	gillettii	ECho
	glaucophylla	ECho
	hirta	ECho
	juncifolia	ECho
	- var. ***juncifolia***	ECho
	kliprandensis 'Kliprand'	ECho
*	***komsbergensis*** **new**	WCot
	lactosa	ECho
	latimerae	ECho
	leipoldtii	ECho
	'Lemon Ripple' (v)	WCot
	liliiflora	CGrW ECho
	longibracteata	ECho
	longituba	WCot
	marginata	ECho
	mathewsii	ECho
	maximilianii 'Cederberg'	ECho
	mediana	ECho
	montana	ECho
	muirii 'Bredasdorp'	ECho
	multifolia	ECho
	mutabilis	CTca ECho WCot
	'Namakwa' (African Beauty Series)	CTca ECho
	namaquensis	ECho
	namibiensis	ECho
	nardoubergensis	ECho
	neilii	ECho
	nervosa	ECho WCot
	obscura	ECho WCot
	orchioides var. ***glaucina***	CDes ECho WCot
	orthopetala	CDes ECho GKev WCot
	pallida	ECho
	peersii 'Betty's Bay'	ECho
	pendula	see *L. bulbifera*
	polyphylla	ECho
	polypodantha 'Varsputs'	ECho
	purpureocoerulea 'Darling'	ECho
	pusilla	ECho WCot
	pustulata ♀H1	CTca ECho EPot WCot
	- blue-flowered	CGrW ECho GKev
	- 'Meerlust'	ECho
	- yellow-flowered	CTca ECho
	reflexa	ECho EPot
	'Robijn'	CPrp ECho
	'Rolina'	ECho
	'Romaud'	ECho WCot
	'Romelia' PBR	ECho WCot
	'Ronina' (African Beauty Series)	CPrp ECho GKev WCot
	'Rosabeth'	ECho WCot
	rosea	ECho EPot GKev
	rubida	CGrW ECho WCot
	'Rupert' (African Beauty Series)	CPrp ECho GKev
	salteri 'Elim'	ECho
	splendida	ECho
	stayneri	CLak
	thomasiae	ECho
	trichophylla	ECho
	tricolor	see *L. aloides*
	unicolor	ECho WCot
	unifolia	ECho
	variegata 'Mamre'	ECho
	violacea	ECho WCot
	- var. ***glauca***	ECho
	viridiflora ♀H1	CTca ECho EPot GKev SBch WCot
	xerophila	ECho
	youngii 'Humansdorp'	ECho
	zebrina	ECho
	- f. ***densiflora*** 'Tanqua'	ECho
	zeyheri	ECho

Lactuca (Asteraceae)

	alpina	see *Cicerbita alpina*
	perennis	CPom EPPr LRHS NLar WHer
	virosa	CArn

Lagarostrobos (*Podocarpaceae*)

§ ***franklinii*** CBcs CDoC IDee
- 'Fota' (f) WThu
- 'Picton Castle' (m) WThu

Lagerstroemia (*Lythraceae*)

indica ♀H1 CCCN CDul EPfP ERom EShb SEND SPlb SSpi WSHC
- 'Baton Rouge' **new** MGos MPkF
- 'Berlingot Menthe' SEND
- 'Cordon Bleu' **new** MGos MPkF
- 'Dwarf Purple' LRHS
- Dynamite = 'Whit II' LRHS SSpi
- Little Chief hybrids EShb
- 'Red Imperator' SEND
- 'Rosea' CBcs SEND
- 'World's Fair' LRHS

subcostata CWJ 12352 WCru

Lagunaria (*Malvaceae*)

patersonii CHII WPGP

Lagurus (*Poaceae*)

ovatus ♀H3 CKno NGBl SBch

Lamiastrum see *Lamium*

Lamium ✿ (*Lamiaceae*)

album CArn CHab MWat NMir
- 'Friday' (v) NBir WHer WWEG

flexuosum EBee EPPr

§ ***galeobdolon*** CArn CTri CWib EShb MHer SRms WHer
- § 'Florentinum' (v) CMac CWan EBee ECha EPfP MMuc MRav SEND WPer WWEG
- 'Hermann's Pride' EBee EHoe ELon EPfP GMaP LBMP LRHS MNFA NBir NDov NMir SMrm SPer SPoG SRms SWvt WAul WFar WHoo WMoo WWEG XLum
- 'Kirkcudbright Dwarf' EBee EWes GBin NBre XLum
- § 'Silberteppich' ECha ELan MRav XLum
- 'Silver Angel' XLum
- Silver Carpet see *L. galeobdolon* 'Silberteppich'
- 'Variegatum' see *L. galeobdolon* 'Florentinum'

garganicum WSpi
- subsp. ***garganicum*** CPom EWes LPla

luteum see *L. galeobdolon*

maculatum MMuc NChi SEND SRms WFar
- 'Album' EBee ELan EPfP LRHS SHar SPer SRms
- 'Anne Greenaway' (v) EBee EWes SPet WWEG
- § 'Aureum' EHoe ELan SMrm SPet SWvt WFar XLum
- 'Beacon Silver' CMac CWib EBee ECha EHrv ELan EPfP LRHS LTen MGos MHer MLHP MSCN MWhi NBir SPer SPet SPlb SPoG SRGP SRms SWvt WFar WWEG XLum
- 'Brightstone Pearl' EWes MAvo
- 'Cannon's Gold' ECtt ELan EWes LPot LRHS SWvt WWEG
- 'Chequers' ambig. NBre SPer
- 'Elisabeth de Haas' (v) EBee EWes NBre
- 'Forncett Lustre' EWes
- 'Forncett White Lustre' NBre
- 'Ghost' **new** EBee EPPr LBuc
- 'Gold Leaf' see *L. maculatum* 'Aureum'
- Golden Anniversary = 'Dellam'PBR (v) ELan ELon LAst LSRN NBro SWvt WRHF
- 'Golden Nuggets' see *L. maculatum* 'Aureum'
- 'Golden Wedding' SRms
- 'Ickwell Beauty' (v) WWEG
- 'James Boyd Parselle' CMea WHal
- 'Margery Fish' SRms
- 'Orchid Frost' CHid ECGP EHoe EWll LHop LRHS
- Pink Chablis = 'Checkin'PBR ELon LRHS
- 'Pink Nancy' SWvt
- 'Pink Pearls' CSBt LRHS NBre SHar SMrm SPet WFar WMoo WWEG
- 'Pink Pewter' EBee ECha ECtt EHoe ELan ELon EPfP EShb GMaP LRHS SPer SPlb SPoG SUsu WWEG XLum
- 'Purple Winter' EPPr
- 'Red Nancy' CFis EBee GCal SWvt XLum
- § 'Roseum' CWib EBee ELan EPfP LTen MCot MRav MWat NChi SGar SPer WMoo XLum
- 'Shell Pink' see *L. maculatum* 'Roseum'
- 'Silver Shield' EWes
- 'Sterling Silver' CSam EBee NBre
- 'White Nancy' ♀H4 Widely available
- 'Wootton Pink' MHer NBir NLar SSvw SWvt

'Marshmallow' **new** LBuc

orvala Widely available
- 'Album' CDes CLAP CPLG CPrp EBee EHrv ELan EPPr GBin LEdu LRHS NBir NLar SHar SMrm WHer WPGP WPtf
- pink-flowered CLAP CSpe
- 'Silva' CCVN CDes CLAP CPLG CSam EBee EPPr EPfP LEdu LRHS WCot WSHC

sandrasicum CPBP

Lampranthus (*Aizoaceae*)

sp. SBod

aberdeenensis see *Delosperma aberdeenense*

aurantiacus CBcs CHEx SPet

'Bagdad' CHEx

blandus CBcs CCCN

'Blousey Pink' CHEx

§ ***brownii*** CBcs CCCN ECho ELan LRHS SPet SPlb WPnn

coccineus SPet

deltoides see *Oscularia deltoides*

edulis see *Carpobrotus edulis*

glaucus SEND

haworthii WCot

multiradiatus SEND

oscularis see *Oscularia deltoides*

'Pink' EUJe SPlb WPnn

purple-flowered EUJe

roseus CCCN CHEx ECho IRar LRHS NRHS SPet WNew

'Salmon Pink' SPlb WPnn

'Shanklin' SPlb

spectabilis CBcs CCCN CTri SBfd SPet WNew WPnn
- orange-flowered EUJe WNew
- purple-flowered SPlb WNew
- 'Tresco Apricot' CCCN ECho
- 'Tresco Brilliant' CCCN CHEx ELon SEND SPet WPnn
- 'Tresco Fire' CCCN CDoC CPLG ELon SPlb SUsu
- 'Tresco Orange' CCCN WPnn

- 'Tresco Peach'	CCCN
- 'Tresco Purple' **new**	CWCL
- 'Tresco Red'	CCCN ELon EUJe SEND WNew WPnn
- white-flowered	SPlb WPnn
- yellow-flowered	WNew WPnn
spiniformis	SGar
'Sugar Pink'	CHEx SEND

Lamprocapnos (*Papaveraceae*)

§ ***spectabilis*** ♀H4	Widely available
- 'Alba' ♀H4	Widely available
- 'Gold Heart'PBR	CBcs EBee ECha EPfP IBoy LRHS MBri MGos MMHG MRav NLar NSti SBfd SGol SPoG WCot WFar WHil
- 'Valentine'	EBee NPnk SPoG WHil

Lamprothyrsus (*Poaceae*)

hieronymi CDPR 3096	EPPr
- RCB RA K2-2	CDes EBee WCot

Lancea (*Phrymaceae*)

tibetica	CPBP

Lantana (*Verbenaceae*)

'Calippo Tutti Frutti'	ESwi EUJe LSou
camara	CArn ELan EShb WFar
- 'Kolibri'	LAst
- (Lucky Series) Lucky Red Hot Improved = 'Balucrehot'PBR **new**	SPoG
- - Lucky White = 'Balucwite'PBR **new**	SPoG
- - Lucky Yellow Improved = 'Balucimyel'PBR **new**	SPoG
- 'Mine d'Or'	EUJe
- orange-flowered	CCCN
- pink-flowered	CCCN EShb
- red-flowered	CCCN
- 'Sonja'	LAst
- variegated (v)	EShb
- white-flowered	CCCN EShb
- yellow-flowered	EShb
'Goldsome'	SEND
§ ***montevidensis***	CSam EShb
* - ***alba***	EShb
'Radiation'	EUJe
'Red and Gold'	SEND
sellowiana	see *L. montevidensis*
'Spreading Sunset'	MOWG

Lapageria ✿ (*Philesiaceae*)

rosea ♀H3	CBcs CCCN CDoy CPLG CPne CRHN CTsd EPfP NLar SChF WPGP
- var. ***albiflora***	CRHN SChF
- 'Flesh Pink'	CPLG CRHN

Lapeirousia (*Iridaceae*)

anceps	ECho
corymbosa	ECho
cruenta	see *Freesia laxa*
divaricata	ECho
fabricii 'Grey's Pass'	ECho
fastigiata	ECho
jacquinii 'Gilberg'	ECho
laxa	see *Freesia laxa*
montana 'Danielskuil'	ECho
plicata 'Nieuwoudtville'	ECho
pyramidalis 'Worcester'	ECho

Lapiedra (*Amaryllidaceae*)

martinezii	ECho

Lapsana (*Asteraceae*)

communis 'Inky'	CNat

Larix ✿ (*Pinaceae*)

decidua ♀H4	CBcs CCVT CDoC CDul CMen CRWN ELan EMil EPfP MGos MMuc NEgg NWea SEND SPer SPlb WEve WFar WMou
- 'Corley'	CKen NLar SLim
- 'Croxby Broom'	CKen
§ - var. ***decidua***	WFar
- 'Globus'	LRHS NLar SLim
- 'Grott'	NLar
- 'Horstmann Recurved'	LRHS NLar SCoo SLim
- 'Kornik'	NLar
- 'Krejci'	NLar SLim
- 'Little Bogle'	CKen MAsh NHol NLar
- 'Oberförster Karsten'	CKen NLar
- 'Pendula'	CBcs WFar
- 'Puli'	EBee LRHS MAsh MBlu MGos NHol NLar SCoo SLim SPer SPoG WFar
- 'Schwarzenburg'	NLar
× ***eurolepis***	see *L.* × *marschlinsii*
europaea DC.	see *L. decidua* var. *decidua*
gmelinii var. ***olgensis***	NLar
- 'Tharandt'	CKen LRHS SLim
griffithii	CPne
§ ***kaempferi*** ♀H4	CCVT CDoC CDoy CDul CLnd CMen ELan EPfP LBuc LMaj LRHS MAsh MMuc NWea SCoo SEWo SLim SPer WEve WFar WMou
- 'Bambino'	CKen
- 'Bingman'	CKen
- 'Blue Ball'	CKen NLar SLim WEve
- 'Blue Dwarf'	CDoC CKen LRHS MAsh MBri MGos SLim SPoG WEve WFar
- 'Blue Haze'	CKen
- 'Blue Rabbit'	CKen LRHS
- 'Blue Rabbit Weeping'	MGos SLim
- 'Cruwys Morchard'	CKen
- 'Cupido'	LRHS SLim
- 'Diana'	CKen LRHS MAsh MBlu MGos NHol NLar SLim WFar
- 'Elizabeth Rehder'	CKen
- 'Grant Haddow'	CKen
- 'Grey Pearl'	CKen MAsh NLar WFar
- 'Hanna's Broom'	SLim
- 'Hobbit'	CKen
* - 'Jakobsen's Pyramid'	CDoC CMen LRHS MAsh SLim SPoG WEve WFar
- 'Lobby Dosser'	LRHS
- 'Nana'	CKen LRHS NLar SLim WFar
I - 'Nana Prostrata'	CKen
- 'Pendula'	CDul EPfP MGos NLar SPer SPoG
- 'Peve Tunnis'	NLar
- 'Stiff Weeping'	LRHS MPkF NLar NPCo SLim
- 'Swallow Falls'	CKen
- 'Varley'	CKen
- 'Wehlen'	CKen
- 'Wolterdingen'	CKen LRHS MBlu NLar SLim
- 'Yanus Olieslagers'	CKen
laricina 'Arethusa Bog'	CKen NLar SLim
- 'Bear Swamp'	CKen SLim WFar
- 'Bingman'	CKen

- 'Hartwig Pine'	CKen
- 'Newport Beauty'	CKen
leptolepis	see *L. kaempferi*
§ × ***marschlinsii***	CCVT MMuc NWea SEND
- 'Domino'	CKen SLim
- 'Gail'	CKen
- 'Julie'	CKen
'Varied Directions'	SLim

Larryleachia (*Asclepiadaceae*)

cactiformis	LToo

Laser (*Apiaceae*)

trilobum	SPhx

Laserpitium (*Apiaceae*)

latifolium	EPPr
§ ***siler***	CArn CSpe EBee SMHy SPhx SPlb WSHC

Lasiagrostis see *Stipa*

Lasiospermum (*Asteraceae*)

bipinnatum	SPlb

Lastreopsis (*Dryopteridaceae*)

hispida	ESwi

Lathraea (*Orobanchaceae*)

clandestina new	CAvo

Lathyrus ✿ (*Papilionaceae*)

§ ***articulatus***	CSpe
§ ***aureus***	CLAP CMac CPom CSpe EBee GBuc GCal IFro LRHS MCot MHer NBid NBir NCGa NChi NSti SKHP SMrm SUsu WAul WFar WHal WHoo WKif WPGP WViv WWEG
- 'Cally Variegated' (v)	GCal
chilensis	CCon LLHF
chloranthus	SPav
cirrhosus	CDes WPGP
clymenum articulatus	see *L. articulatus*
cyaneus misapplied	see *L. vernus*
davidii	CPom EBee EWes EWld GCal LLHF WCot WSHC
eucosmus new	LLHF
fremontii hort.	see *L. laxiflorus*
grandiflorus	CPom CSev CTri EBee ECGP NLar SDix SMrm SSvw SWat WCot
heterophyllus	EBee
incurvus	MPet
inermis	see *L. laxiflorus*
japonicus	EBee
- subsp. ***maritimus***	NLar SPhx
'Lamorna's Love'	WViv
latifolius ♀H4	CArn CRHN CRWN EBee EPfP LAst MWat MWhi NPer SPoG SRms SVic SWal WBrk WFar WHer WPer XLum
§ - 'Albus' ♀H4	CTri ELan SPav SRms WKif XLum
- 'Blushing Bride'	CSpe WCot
- deep pink-flowered	MHer NLar NSti
- pale pink-flowered	NSti
- Pink Pearl	see *L. latifolius* 'Rosa Perle'
- 'Red Pearl'	CBcs EBee ECtt ELan EPfP GAbr LBuc LRHS LSRN MBri MCot MLHP MNHC MWat NPri SEND SPav SPer SPlb SPoG SSvw WPer
§ - 'Rosa Perle' ♀H4	CBcs CTri EBee ECha ECtt LHop LRHS LSRN MBri MCot MLHP MNHC MRav NBir NLar NPer NPri SMrm SPer SSvw WMoo WWEG XLum
- Weisse Perle	see *L. latifolius* 'White Pearl'
- 'White Pearl' misapplied	see *L. latifolius* 'Albus'
§ - 'White Pearl' ♀H4	CBcs ECha EPfP GAbr GCal LRHS LSRN MBri MCot MHer MLHP MRav NBir NLar NPer NPri NSti SMrm SPer SPoG SSvw WFar WPer WSHC
§ ***laxiflorus***	CDes CPom EBee SSvw WMoo WPGP WSHC
linifolius	EBee NLar WCot WHfH WPGP
montanus	GPoy
nervosus	CHid CSpe EBee EWes GBin SMrm SRms
neurolobus	CPom EBee
nevadensis	WHil
niger	CSpe EBee LHop LRHS LSou MCot MHer MMHG NLar SSvw WKif WWEG
odoratus	SVic
- 'Anniversary' new	MCot
- 'Betty Maiden' new	MCot
- 'Blue Medley' new	MCot
- 'Burnished Bronze' new	MCot
- 'Charlie's Angel' ♀H4 new	MCot
- 'Cupani'	SPhx
- 'Dancing Queen'	MPet
- 'Dark Passion' new	MCot
- 'Dawn' new	MCot
- 'Evening Glow' ♀H4 new	MCot
- 'George Priestley' new	MCot
- 'Honey Pink' new	MCot
- 'Jilly' ♀H4 new	MCot
- 'Lord Nelson' new	SPhx
- 'Lucinda Jane'	MPet
- 'Mammoth Mixed'	MPet
- 'Marion' new	MCot
- 'Matucana'	CSpe MWat WBrk
- 'Midnight' new	SPhx
- 'Milly' new	MCot
- 'Misty Mountain' new	MCot
- 'Mollie Rilestone' new	MCot
- 'Mrs Bernard Jones' ♀H4 new	MCot
- 'Mrs Collier' new	SPhx
- 'Our Harry' new	MCot
- 'Restormel' new	MCot
- 'Richard and Judy' new	MCot
- 'Wedding Day' ♀H4 new	MCot
- 'White Frills' new	SPhx
- Winter Elegance Series	MPet
odoratus × ***belinensis*** 'Erewhon'	MPet
odoratus × ***belinensis*** 'Navy'	MPet
palustris	EBee NLar SPlb
polyphyllus	EBee MPet NSti
pratensis	CHab EBee NMir WSFF
pubescens	EBee MPet
roseus	GCal WSHC WViv
rotundifolius ♀H4	CHid EBee GLog MNrw NSti SPhx WHoo
- 'Tillyperone'	EBee SSvw
sativus	CHid CSpe ELan
- f. ***albus***	CSpe

subandinus new — SBrt SPlb WCot
sylvestris — EBee SBch SEND WBrk
tingitanus — CSpe SWal
- 'Roseus' — SBch
transsylvanicus — CPom EBee GBin SPhx
tuberosus — CArn EBee WCot WSHC
'Tubro' — EBee
venetus — CSpe EBee EWes GCal MNrw WSHC
§ **vernus** ♀H4 — Widely available
- 'Albiflorus' new — XEll
- 'Alboroseus' ♀H4 — CLAP EBee ELan ELon EPfP GBuc GCal GCra GMaP IFro LHop MAvo MHer MNrw NBir NChi NPnk SAga SMrm SPhx SPoG SWat SWvt WCot WFar WHoo WViv
- var. **albus** — CDes CLAP CMea WCot WPGP
- **aurantiacus** — see *L. aureus*
- 'Caeruleus' — CLAP ECGP MNFA WHoo WPGP
* - 'Cyaneus' — SAga SWat WCot
I - 'Filifolius' — CSpe
- 'Flaccidus' — CFis SBrt WCot WKif WTin
* - 'Gracilis' — WViv
- 'Indigo Eyes' — CDes
- 'Madelaine' — WCot
- purple-flowered — LRHS MMuc SEND
- 'Rainbow' — CLAP EPfP GAbr LRHS MMHG SMrm WFar WWEG
- 'Rosenelfe' — CMea EBee GBuc LBMP MCot MDKP NPri SMrm SPhx WCot WHal WHil WKif WPGP WSHC XLum
- f. **roseus** — CDes EBee ECha LRHS MMuc MRav NBir NCGa SEND SRms WBrk WCot
- 'Spring Beauty' — CLAP
- 'Spring Delight' — LRHS
- 'Spring Melody' — EHrv MRav
- 'Subtle Hints' — WCot

Laurelia (*Atherospermataceae*)

§ **sempervirens** — CBcs CTrC WPGP
serrata — see *L. sempervirens*

Laureliopsis (*Atherospermataceae*)

philippiana — NLar

Laurentia see *Isotoma*

Laurus (*Lauraceae*)

§ **azorica** — CBcs
canariensis — see *L. azorica*
nobilis ♀H4 — Widely available
- f. **angustifolia** — CMac CTsd EBee EOHP IDee LRHS MBlu MHer MRav NLar SEND
- 'Aurea' ♀H4 — CBcs CDul CMac EBee ELan ELon EPfP LHop LRHS MGos MHer NEgg NLar SEND SLim SLon SPer SPoG SWvt WFar WMoo
- clipped pyramid — LSRN
- 'Crispa' — MRav
- 'Sunspot' (v) — WCot
- variegated (v) — CMac

Lavandula ✿ (*Lamiaceae*)

'After Midnight' — see *L.* 'Avonview'
'Alba' — see *L. angustifolia* 'Alba', *L.* × *intermedia* 'Alba'
'Alba' ambig. — CWib EBee NYoL SIde SPer WPer
'Alexandra'PBR — MWat SBfd
§ **angustifolia** — CArn CBar CCVT CWCL CWib EBee ELau ENfk EPfP GPoy LBuc LRHS LSRN MBri MGos MHer MHoo MWat NGdn NPer NPri NYoL SBfd SDow SLim SPlb SVic WFar XLum XSen
- 'Alba' misapplied — see *L. angustifolia* 'Blue Mountain White'
§ - 'Alba' — EPfP GPoy LBuc LRHS LSRN LTen MHer MHoo MRav MSwo NMen NYoL SBch SLon SPlb WFar WJek
- 'Alba Nana' — see *L. angustifolia* 'Nana Alba'
- 'Arctic Snow' — CBcs CEnt CHab CSev EBee EPfP LRHS LSRN MBri MGos MHer MSwo MWat NGdn NPri NYoL SDow SFai SHil SPoG WLav
- Aromatico Blue = 'Lablusa'PBR new — LRHS
- 'Ashdown Forest' — CWan ENfk EWhm LRHS MHer MHoo MLHP NYoL SBch SDow SIde SPer WHoo WJek WLav
- 'Backhouse Purple' — SDow
- 'Beechwood Blue' ♀H4 — MHoo NYoL SDow WLav
- 'Belle Hélène' new — XSen
- 'Betty's Blue' — SDow
- Blue Cushion = 'Lavandula Schola'PBR — LRHS LSRN MAsh NYoL SDow SFai WFar WLav
- Blue Ice = 'Dow3'PBR — EBee EGHP ENfk LRHS MNHC MWat NLar NYoL SDow SFai SLim SPoG WLav
§ - 'Blue Mountain White' — SDow WLav
- 'Blue Rider' — LRHS NGdn NYoL SWal WLav
- 'Blue River'PBR — EBee WFar
- Blue Scent = 'Syngablusc' — LRHS
§ - 'Bowles's Early' — NYoL WFar
- 'Bowles's Grey' — see *L. angustifolia* 'Bowles's Early'
- 'Bowles's Variety' — see *L. angustifolia* 'Bowles's Early'
- 'Cedar Blue' — CWan ELau ENfk EWhm MHer MHoo NYoL SBfd SDow SHDw SIde WFar WJek WLav
- 'Coconut Ice'PBR — CWCL CWSG NYoL WLav
- 'Compacta' — SDow WLav
- 'Dwarf Blue' — EPfP LSRN NYoL WFar
- 'Elizabeth' — LRHS LSRN NYoL SDow SFai SPoG WLav
- 'Ellagance Ice' — LRHS
- 'Ellagance Purple' — LBuc LRHS SHil
- 'Ellagance Sky' — LBuc LRHS SHil
- 'Folgate' — CArn CWCL ECtt ELau ENfk EPfP LSou MHer MHoo MNHC NGdn NYoL SDow SGol SIde WFar WHoo WJek WLav WMnd XSen
- 'Fring A' — SDow
- Garden Beauty = 'Lowmar'PBR (v) — LBuc LRHS NPri SPoG
- 'Granny's Bouquet' — LSRN NYoL SBfd
§ - 'Hidcote' ♀H4 — Widely available
- 'Hidcote Pink' — CEnt CWCL CWib LSRN LSou MHer MHoo MNHC MRav NGdn NYoL SDow SWal SWat WFar WMnd WPer XSen
- 'Hidcote Superior' — LBMP LSRN NGdn
- 'Imperial Gem' ♀H4 — Widely available
- 'Jean Davis' — see *L. angustifolia* 'Rosea'
- 'Lady' — MHoo NPer SBfd SWal WPer
- 'Lady Ann' — CWCL SDow WLav
I - 'Lavender Haze' — SFai
- 'Lavenite Petite'PBR — CSev EBee LLHF LRHS LSRN NLar NYoL SDow SFai SPoG WLav

	– Little Lady = 'Batlad'	CMea CSev EBee ECtt LAst LBMP LRHS LSRN MAsh MSwo NDov NLar NYoL SAll SFai SGol SLim SWvt WLav
	– Little Lottie = 'Clarmo' ♀H4	CWCL EBee EOHP EWTr LSRN MHer MHoo NYoL SDow SIde SWvt WLav
	– 'Loddon Blue' ♀H4	CEnt CWCL EBee EPfP EWhm LBMP LRHS MBri MHoo NYoL SDow SFai SHil SIde WLav
§	– 'Loddon Pink' ♀H4	CWCL CWan EBee ELan EPfP GMaP LRHS MAsh MBri MHoo MLHP MMuc MNHC MRav NGdn NRHS NYoL SEND SFai SHil WFar WLav
	– 'Luberon'	XSen
	– 'Lullaby Blue'	SDow
	– 'Lumières des Alpes'	XSen
	– 'Maillette'	EGHP NGdn NYoL SDow SIde SPet WLav
	– 'Matheronne'	XSen
	– Melissa Lilac = 'Dow4'PBR	CBcs CSBt CSev EBee ENfk LBMP LRHS LSRN LSou MBri MGos MHer MNHC NDov NLar NYoL SDow SFai SHil SPoG SRkn WLav
	– 'Middachten'	EBee
	– 'Miss Donnington'	see *L. angustifolia* 'Bowles's Early'
	– 'Miss Katherine'PBR ♀H4	CWCL EBee ECtt ELan EPfP LRHS LSRN MAsh NLar NYoL SDow SPer WLav
	– Miss Muffet = 'Scholmis' ♀H4	CWCL EOHP LLHF NYoL SDow WLav
	– 'Mont Ventoux'	XSen
	– 'Munstead'	Widely available
§	– 'Nana Alba' ♀H4	CArn CMea CWan EBee ECha ELan ENfk EPfP GMaP GPoy LRHS MAsh MHer MHoo MNHC MWat NYoL SBch SDow SPer SWvt WHoo WJek XSen
	– 'Nana Atropurpurea'	SDow
	– 'Nikita' **new**	XSen
	– 'No 9'	SDow
	– 'Oxford Gem'	SFai
	– 'Pacific Blue'	LRHS MBri SHil
	– 'Perle de Rosée' **new**	XSen
	– 'Peter Pan'	CWCL ECtt EGHP ELau GBuc LSRN MHer MHoo NDov NGdn NYoL SBch SDow WLav
	– 'Princess Blue'	CWCL EBee ELan EWhm LRHS MAsh MHoo MWat NYoL SDow SIde WFar WLav WPer
§	– 'Rosea'	Widely available
	– 'Royal Purple'	CBcs CHab CWCL EWes LSou MWat NGdn NYoL SDow SFai SIde SWvt WLav
	– 'Royal Velvet'	SDow
	– 'Saint Jean'	SDow
	– 'Silver Blue' **new**	XSen
	– 'Silver Mist'	CMea EPfP LRHS NYoL WHer
	– 'Thumbelina Leigh'PBR	LBMP NYoL SDow SFai
	– 'Twickel Purple'	CBcs CWCL EBee EGHP ENfk EPfP LHop LRHS LSRN MHoo MNHC MRav NGdn NYoL SBfd SDow SFai SIde SPer SWat SWvt WFar WLav XSen
	– 'Walberton's Silver Edge'	see *L.* × *intermedia* Walberton's Silver Edge
	– 'Wendy Carlile' ♀H4	CSev
	aristibracteata	MHer WLav
§	'Avonview'	CWCL EWhm MHer SDow WHoo WLav
	'Ballerina'	CWCL LRHS SDow
§	'Bee Brilliant'PBR	ENfk EWhm WLav
§	'Bee Cool'PBR	ENfk EWhm MHer NYoL WLav
§	'Bee Happy'	CWCL ENfk EWhm NBir NYoL WJek WLav
§	'Bee Pretty'	ENfk EWhm
	'Blue Star'	EBee EGHP EPfP EWhm LRHS NGdn WFar WGwG
	'Bowers Beauty'	LRHS
	buchii var. ***buchii***	SDow WLav
	'Bulls Cross'	WLav
	Butterfly Garden = 'Avenue'PBR	CWSG
	canariensis	MHer SDow WLav
	× ***chaytoriae*** 'Gorgeous'	SDow
	– 'Joan Head' **new**	XSen
	– 'Richard Gray' ♀H3-4	CArn CBar EBee LSRN MHer MNHC NYoL SBfd SDow SLim SSvw WAbe WLav WMnd XSen
§	– 'Sawyers' ♀H4	Widely available
	– 'Silver Sands'	EPfP LBMP LSRN LSou NYoL SBfd SFai SPoG
	× ***christiana***	CArn LRHS NLar NPri NYoL SBfd SDow SFai SHDw WJek WLav
	'Cornard Blue'	see *L.* × *chaytoriae* 'Sawyers'
	dentata	CEnt ENfk GCal GPoy MHoo MNHC MRav SBod SEND SGar WJek
§	– var. ***candicans***	MHer MNHC NYoL SBch SBfd SDow WJek WLav
	– var. ***dentata*** **new**	NYoL
	– – 'Dusky Maiden'	SDow WLav
	– – 'Ploughman's Blue'	CWCL NYoL WLav
	– – f. ***rosea***	SDow
	– – 'Royal Crown' ♀H2-3	MHer WLav
	– – 'Silver Queen'	WLav
	– silver-leaved	see *L. dentata* var. *candicans*
	'Devonshire Compact'	CSBt CWCL EWhm LRHS SBch WJek
	'Devonshire Compact White'	CWCL EWhm
	'Fathead'	CBcs CWCL EBee ECtt EGHP ELan EPfP LRHS LSRN LSou MGos MHer MNHC MWat NBir NEgg NGdn NPri NYoL SCoo SDow SFai SGol SLim SPoG WJek WLav
	× ***ginginsii*** 'Goodwin Creek Grey'	MHer NYoL SDow SGol WGwG WLav
	'Hazel'	EPfP LRHS
	'Heavenly Blue' **new**	EPfP
	'Helmsdale'PBR	CSBt CWCL EBee ECrN EHrv ELan EPfP GAbr IKil LRHS LSRN LSou MAsh MGos MHer MRav MSwo MWat NGdn NYoL SAll SBfd SCoo SDow SFai SGol SLim SPer SPoG WJek
	heterophylla misapplied	see *L.* × *heterophylla* Viv. Gaston Allard Group
§	× ***heterophylla*** Viv. Gaston Allard Group	EGHP EOHP EShb WLav
	– – 'African Pride'	NYoL
	'Hidcote Blue'	see *L. angustifolia* 'Hidcote'
	× ***intermedia*** 'Abrialii'	SDow
§	– 'Alba' ♀H4	CMea EPfP MHer MHoo MMuc MNHC NYoL SDow SEND WKif XSen
	– 'Arabian Night'	see *L.* × *intermedia* 'Impress Purple', 'Sussex'

§	- Dutch Group	CSBt CWan CWib ENfk EPfP MAsh MRav MSwo MWat NYoL SBfd SCoo SDow SFai SLim SPer SPoG SWat WPer XSen
	- 'Edelweiss'	CBar CWan EGHP ENfk EPfP LRHS MHoo MNHC MRav NEgg NGdn NYoL SDow SGol SPoG SWal SWvt WLav XSen
	- 'Enigma' **new**	CBar
	- 'Fragrant Memories'	EPfP MHoo NYoL SDow SIde WLav
	- 'Fred Boutin' **new**	SGol
	- Goldburg = 'Burgoldeen' (v)	EWhm MWat
	- 'Grappenhall' misapplied	see *L.* × *intermedia* 'Pale Pretender'
	- 'Grey Hedge'	CWan EWhm MHoo MNHC NYoL WLav
	- 'Gros Bleu'	SDow WLav XSen
	- 'Grosso'	Widely available
	- 'Hidcote Giant' ♀H4	CArn EPfP LRHS MBri NPer NYoL SDow SHil WKif WLav XSen
§	- 'Impress Purple'	MNHC NYoL SDow WLav XSen
	- 'Jaubert'	XSen
	- 'Julien'	XSen
	- 'Lullingstone Castle'	ENfk EWhm MHoo MNHC NYoL SDow WGwG WJek WLav
	- 'Nizza' **new**	XSen
	- 'Old English' misapplied	see *L.* × *intermedia* 'Seal'
	- 'Old English'	ENfk SDow
	- Old English Group	CArn ELau MMuc MNHC NYoL SEND WHoo WJek WLav
§	- 'Pale Pretender'	CSBt CTri EGHP MHer MHoo MSwo NYoL SDow SPer SWal WFar WJek WMnd XSen
	- 'Provence' **new**	LRHS MHoo
§	- 'Seal'	CArn ELau ENfk EWhm GMaP MHoo MNHC NYoL SDow WFar WJek WMnd XSen
	- 'Sumian'	XSen
	- 'Super'	XSen
§	- 'Sussex' ♀H4	LRHS NYoL SDow WLav XSen
	- 'Twickel Purple'	CWib ECtt EWes LSRN MHoo NLar NYoL SGol SWat WJek WMnd
§	- Walberton's Silver Edge = 'Walvera' (v)	CSBt EPfP LBuc LRHS MGos MWat NEgg SBfd SCoo SDow SFai SIde SLim SPoG
	'Jamboree'	WLav
	'Jean Davis'	see *L. angustifolia* 'Rosea'
	lanata ♀H3	CArn ECha GPoy WJek WLav
§	***latifolia***	CArn XSen
I	'Lavender Lace'	CWSG LSRN SCoo
	'Loddon Pink'	see *L. angustifolia* 'Loddon Pink'
	'Madrid Blue'	see *L.* 'Bee Happy'
	'Madrid Pink'	see *L.* 'Bee Pretty'
	'Madrid Purple' PBR	see *L.* 'Bee Brilliant'
	'Madrid White' PBR	see *L.* 'Bee Cool'
	'Marshwood' PBR	CTri SCoo SDow SIde SLim
	minutolii	SDow
	multifida	CSev LDai MHer WLav
	officinalis	see *L. angustifolia*
	'Passionné'	CWSG LRHS MGos WLav
	pedunculata	XSen
§	- subsp. ***pedunculata*** ♀H3-4	Widely available
	- - 'James Compton'	CWib ECha LRHS MAsh NGdn NYoL
	- - 'Wine'	CBcs
	- subsp. ***sampaiana*** 'Purple Emperor'	LRHS MBri NYoL SHil WLav
	- - 'Roman Candles'	WLav
	pinnata	CSev ENfk EPfP LPot LRHS MHer MHoo MNHC SDow
	'Pretty Polly'	CBcs CSev EGHP EPfP LBMP LRHS NYoL SDow SFai SRkn WLav
	'Pukehou'	EPfP LRHS SCoo SDow WLav
	'Regal Splendour' PBR	CSBt CWCL EBee ECtt EGHP ELan EPfP LRHS LSRN LSou MAsh MBri MGos MHer MNHC NPri NRHS NYoL SCoo SDow SFai SHil SLim SPoG WLav
	Rocky Road = 'Fair09' PBR	EBee LBMP LRHS LSRN MGos NGdn NYoL SDow SFai SRkn WLav
	'Rosea'	see *L. angustifolia* 'Rosea'
	rotundifolia	SDow
	'Roxlea Park'	CWCL
	'Russian Anna'	LSRN
	'Saint Brelade'	CWCL EPfP LRHS SDow WLav
	'Silver Edge'	see *L.* × *intermedia* Walberton's Silver Edge
	'Somerset Mist'	EWhm WLav
N	***spica*** nom. rejic.	see *L. angustifolia*, *L. latifolia*
	- 'Hidcote Purple'	see *L. angustifolia* 'Hidcote'
	stoechas ♀H3-4	Widely available
	- from Corsica	LRHS
	- var. ***albiflora***	see *L. stoechas* subsp. *stoechas* f. *leucantha*
	- 'Anouk' PBR	EBee EPfP LRHS NGdn SPoG
	- 'Barcelona White' (Barcelona Series)	CWCL
	- 'Blueberries and Cream'	CSev LRHS LSou
	- 'Boysenberry Ruffles' PBR (Ruffles Series)	LRHS LSRN
	- 'Lace'	LSRN WLav
	- Lavender Lace = 'Colace' PBR **new**	NYoL
	- Lilac Wings = 'Prolil' PBR	CSev EPfP LLHF LRHS LSRN MBri SCoo SFai SHil WLav
	- (Little Bee Series) Little Bee Deep Purple	LBuc LRHS MBri SHil
	- - Little Bee Deep Rose	LBuc LRHS MBri SHil
	- - Little Bee Lilac = 'Florvendula Lilac'	CWSG LRHS SHil
	- - Little Bee Rose = 'Florvendula Rose'	CWSG LRHS
	- subsp. ***luisieri*** 'Tickled Pink' PBR	CWCL ECtt
	- 'Night of Passion'	LRHS SDow
	- 'Papillon'	see *L. pedunculata* subsp. *pedunculata*
	- subsp. ***pedunculata***	see *L. pedunculata* subsp. *pedunculata*
	- 'Purley'	CWan
	- 'Raspberry Ruffles' (Ruffles Series)	MWat
	- 'Rocky Red'	CSev LSRN
	- Ruffles Series **new**	ENfk
	- 'Silver Anouk' PBR	EBee EPfP LRHS
§	- subsp. ***stoechas*** f. ***leucantha***	CWCL CWan CWib ECha EPfP LRHS MBri MNHC MSwo MWat SBfd SDow SHil SPer WFar
	- - - 'Snowman'	CBcs CHab CSBt EPfP LRHS MHer MWat SBfd SCoo SFai SLim SPoG SWvt WFar
	- - 'Liberty'	CWCL
	- - 'Provençal'	LRHS MBri NRHS SCoo SHil
	- - 'Purple Wings'	EPfP LRHS LSou MAsh MGos SFai SLim SRkn
	- - f. ***rosea*** 'Kew Red'	CBcs CTri CWCL CWan ENfk LBMP LSRN MGos MHer MNHC NYoL

SDow SFai SLim SWvt WGwG WJek WLav
- 'Sugarberry Ruffles'PBR (Ruffles Series) ENfk
- 'Victory' LRHS MGos SHil SPoG
- 'With Love'PBR LRHS SDow
'Sugar Plum' WLav
Tiara = 'Fair 10'PBR CSBt EGHP ENfk EPfP LRHS LSRN MBri MGos MWat NPri NRHS NYoL SCoo SDow SFai SHil SLim SPoG WLav
'Van Gogh' SDow
vera misapplied see *L.* × *intermedia* Dutch Group
vera DC. see *L. angustifolia*
viridis CArn ELan ELau EPfP LRHS MHer MHoo NPer SDow WAbe WJek WLav
'Whero Iti' SDow
'Willow Vale' ♀H3-4 CTri CWCL EBee EPfP EWhm LBMP LBuc LRHS LSRN MAsh MHer NYoL SAga SDow SWvt WJek
'Willowbridge Calico'PBR NGdn NYoL WLav

Lavatera (*Malvaceae*)

arborea CArn SChr SEND WHer
- 'Rosea' see *L.* × *clementii* 'Rosea'
- 'Variegata' (v) ELan NPer NSti SDix SEND SGar WCot
bicolor see *L. maritima*
cachemiriana NBir NPer SPhx WPer
Chamallow = 'Inovera'PBR EPfP LBuc LRHS LSRN LSou MGos SPoG
× ***clementii*** 'Barnsley' Widely available
- 'Barnsley Baby' EBee ELon LBuc LRHS NGdn NHol NLar NPer NPri SPer SWvt WHil
- 'Blushing Bride' CDoC ELon EPfP LBMP LRHS LSRN MBri MGos NLar NRHS SBfd SEND SHil SPer
- 'Bredon Springs' ♀H3-4 CBar CDoC CDul CSBt CWSG EBee ECha EPfP LHop LRHS LSRN MAsh MSwo MWat NGdn NLar SEND SGol SLim SPer SWvt WFar WHar
- 'Burgundy Wine' ♀H3-4 CBar CBcs CMac EBee ELan EPfP EUJe LRHS MAsh MBri MGos MSwo NBir NEgg NGdn NHol NLar NPer NPri NRHS SBfd SHil SLim SLon SPer SPoG SWvt WFar
- 'Candy Floss' ♀H3-4 EBee EPfP LRHS MAsh MGos NBir NLar NPer SGol
- 'Kew Rose' CDoC LRHS MSwo NPer SEND SLim SRms
- 'Lavender Lady' LHop NPer SEND
- 'Lisanne' LRHS MSwo SGol
- 'Mary Hope' EBee EPfP LRHS MAsh
- Memories = 'Stelav' LRHS LSRN NLar SLim
- 'Pavlova' CPLG
§ - 'Rosea' ♀H3-4 CBcs CMac CWSG EBee ECrN EPfP LAst LRHS LSRN MAsh MGos MWat NBir NEgg NPri SBfd SGol SHil SLon SPer SPoG SWvt WFar
§ - 'Wembdon Variegated' (v) NPer
'Grey Beauty' LHop MAsh
§ ***maritima*** ♀H2-3 CDoC CMac CPLG CRHN EBee ECtt ELan EPfP LHop LRHS MCot SBfd SEND SPer SPoG SWvt WKif WSHC
N ***olbia*** SPlb SRms
- 'Eye Catcher' IVic LRHS MSwo NLar SPer SPoG SWal
- 'Lilac Lady' EBee ECha ECrN ELan EPfP LRHS MGos SLim SPer WFar WKif
§ - 'Pink Frills' MGos SWvt WCot
'Peppermint Ice' see *L. thuringiaca* 'Ice Cool'
'Pink Frills' see *L. olbia* 'Pink Frills'
'Rosea' see *L.* × *clementii* 'Rosea'
'Sweet Dreams'PBR NLar
N ***thuringiaca*** GCal NNor WFar
- 'First Light' EDAr EWll GCal SPhx
§ - 'Ice Cool' ECha GCal MGos SWvt WKif
- Red Rum = 'Rigrum'PBR CMac EBee EPfP LAst LBuc LLHF LRHS LSRN MAsh MGos NEgg NLar NPri SEND SHar SLim SPoG SWvt WHar
'Variegata' see *L.* × *clementii* 'Wembdon Variegated'
'White Angel'PBR NLar
'White Satin'PBR NLar

Lecanthus (*Urticaceae*)

peduncularis CHEx

Ledebouria (*Asparagaceae*)

adlamii see *L. cooperi*
concolor misapplied see *L. socialis*
§ ***cooperi*** CDes CSev CYeo ECho ELan EPri LEdu LHop LRHS SUsu WPGP WTcb
ovalifolia ECho
§ ***socialis*** CSev ECho LToo MCot SBHP SBch
violacea see *L. socialis*

× *Ledodendron* (*Ericaceae*)

§ 'Arctic Tern' ♀H4 CDoC CSBt CTri ECho GQui LMil MGos MLea SPer

Ledum (*Ericaceae*)

glandulosum SIN 1828 GLin
§ ***groenlandicum*** EBee GKin IDee MLea NLar SPer WSHC
- 'Compactum' EBee GKin NLar
- 'Helma' IVic NLar
- 'Lenie' NLar
palustre GPoy NLar WThu

Legousia (*Campanulaceae*)

pentagonica 'Midnight Stars' CSpe

Leiophyllum (*Ericaceae*)

buxifolium ♀H4 EPfP NLar SSpi WThu
- var. ***hugeri*** GBin
- 'Maryfield' WAbe

Lembotropis see *Cytisus*

Lemna (*Araceae*)

gibba NPer
minor CWat LPBA MSKA NPer SWat
trisulca CWat EHon LPBA MSKA NPer SWat

lemon see *Citrus limon*

lemon balm see *Melissa officinalis*

lemon grass see *Cymbopogon citratus*

lemon verbena see *Aloysia citrodora*

Leonotis (*Lamiaceae*)

leonitis	see *L. ocymifolia*
leonurus	CBcs CCCN CDTJ CHEx CHGN CHll ECre EPfP EShb EWes LEdu LRHS MNrw SLim SLon SMad SMrm SPlb SPoG XLum
- var. ***albiflora***	CCCN WHil
nepetifolia	CHll
- var. ***nepetifolia*** 'Staircase'	CCCN SPav
§ ***ocymifolia***	CCCN CPLG LSou WPGP
- var. ***raineriana***	CHll

Leontice (*Berberidaceae*)

albertii	see *Gymnospermium albertii*
armeniaca new	WCot

Leontochir (*Alstroemeriaceae*)

ovallei	CCCN

Leontodon (*Asteraceae*)

autumnalis	CHab NMir
hispidus	CHab NMir
§ ***rigens***	EBee LRHS MHer MLHP MMuc NBid NBir SDix SMad SMrm WFar WMoo
- 'Girandole'	see *L. rigens*

Leontopodium (*Asteraceae*)

alpinum	CTri CWib ECho EPfP GAbr GEdr GKev LRHS MAsh MWat SPlb SPoG SRms WPer XLum
- 'Everest' new	EDAr
- 'Mignon'	ECho EWes GEdr GMaP WAbe WHoo
- subsp. ***nivale***	GKev
coreanum	GKev
himalayanum	GKev
§ ***ochroleucum*** var. ***campestre***	MDKP NLar XLum
palibinianum	see *L. ochroleucum* var. *campestre*
souliei	XLum

Leonurus (*Lamiaceae*)

artemisia	see *L. japonicus*
cardiaca	CArn CWan GPoy MHer MHoo MNHC SIde WHfH
§ ***japonicus***	CArn SMad
macranthus	EFEx
- var. ***alba***	EFEx
sibiricus misapplied	see *L. japonicus*
sibiricus L.	CArn GCal MHoo

Leopoldia (*Hyacinthaceae*)

comosa	see *Muscari comosum*
spreitzenhoferi	see *Muscari spreitzenhoferi*
tenuiflora	see *Muscari tenuiflorum*

Lepechinia (*Lamiaceae*)

bella	CSpe SDys
chamaedryoides	CHll CPLG CSpe
floribunda	CSev
hastata	CCse CDoC CPom CSpe SBHP WHil WJek WWlt
salviae	EPri SUsu

Lepidium (*Brassicaceae*)

campestre	CArn CHab
latifolium	CArn ENfk LEdu

Lepidothamnus (*Podocarpaceae*)

§ ***laxifolius***	WThu

Lepidozamia (*Zamiaceae*)

peroffskyana	CBrP

Leptecophylla (*Ericaceae*)

§ ***juniperina***	IRar

Leptinella (*Asteraceae*)

§ ***atrata***	SMad
- subsp. ***luteola***	EBee EPfP GEdr
'County Park'	ECho ECou EDAr MMuc
dendyi	ECho ECou EWes GEdr MHer NMen NSla WIce
dioica	CTrC GBin
filicula	ECou
hispida	see *Cotula hispida* (DC.) Harv.
§ ***minor***	WMoo
§ ***potentillina***	CTri EBee ECha ECho EHoe GBin GEdr MBNS NLar SRms WMoo WPer WPtf XLum
§ ***pyrethrifolia***	ECho EDAr GEdr NMen
- 'Macabe'	ECou
§ ***rotundata***	ECou
§ ***serrulata***	ECho
§ ***squalida***	ECha ECho EDAr EPPr GBin MWat NLar NRya NSti WMoo
§ - 'Platt's Black'	CPBP EBee ECha ECho EDAr EHoe EPPr EShb EWes GAbr GBin GEdr GKev LEdu MSCN NDov NLar NRya NSti SBch SPet WFar WHoo WMoo WNew WPer WPtf WWFP XLum
traillii	GEdr

Leptocodon (*Campanulaceae*)

gracilis	EWld
- HWJK 2155	WCru

Leptodactylon (*Polemoniaceae*)

§ ***californicum***	CPBP
watsonii	CPBP

Leptospermum ✿ (*Myrtaceae*)

argenteum	CBcs
citratum	see *L. petersonii*
'Confetti'	ECou
'Copper Sheen'	CBcs CTrC
'County Park Blush'	ECou ELon
cunninghamii	see *L. myrtifolium*
'Electric Red' (Galaxy Series)	LRHS SLim
ericoides	see *Kunzea ericoides*
flavescens misapplied	see *L. glaucescens*
flavescens Sm.	see *L. polygalifolium*
§ ***glaucescens***	ECou SPlb
§ ***grandiflorum***	CTrC ELan EPfP SSpi WSHC
grandifolium	ECou LRHS
'Havering Hardy'	ECou
humifusum	see *L. rupestre*
juniperinum	CBcs CTrC SPlb
'Karo Pearl Star'	CBcs CTrC
'Karo Spectrobay' PBR	CBcs
laevigatum 'Yarrum'	ECou
§ ***lanigerum***	CBcs CMHG CPLG CTrC CTri CTsd EBee ECou EPfP GAbr SPlb
- 'Cunninghamii'	see *L. myrtifolium*
- 'Wellington'	ECou

liversidgei	ECou
minutifolium	ECou
morrisonii	ECou
§ ***myrtifolium***	CTrC CTri ECou EWes SPer
- 'Newnes Forest'	ECou
myrtifolium* × *scoparium	ECou
nitidum	CBcs CTrC ECou SPlb
- 'Cradle'	ECou
§ ***petersonii***	CArn ECou EShb MHer MOWG
- 'Chlorinda'	ECou
phylicoides	see *Kunzea ericoides*
'Pink Cascade' new	IVic
'Pink Surprise'	ECou MOWG
§ ***polygalifolium***	CBcs CTrC ECou SPlb
prostratum	see *L. rupestre*
pubescens	see *L. lanigerum*
'Red Cascade'	SWvt
rodwayanum	see *L. grandiflorum*
rotundifolium	CTrC ECou
§ ***rupestre*** ♀H4	CDoC CTrC CTri ECou IRar NHar SPlb WSHC
rupestre* × *scoparium	ECou
scoparium	CArn CTsd ECou ELau ERom MNHC SPlb WJek
- 'Adrianne'	ELan EPfP LRHS MRav
- 'Album'	CTrC
- 'Appleblossom'	EPfP SGol SLim
- 'Autumn Glory'	EBee SLim
- 'Blossom' (d)	CBcs CMac ECou LRHS MOWG
- 'Burgundy Queen' (d)	CBcs CMac CSBt EUJe IVic
- 'Chapmanii'	CMHG
- 'Coral Candy'	CBcs EBee LRHS MMuc SEND
- 'County Park Pink'	ECou
- 'County Park Red'	ECou
- 'Crimson Glory' (d)	CSBt
- 'Elizabeth Jane'	WFar
- 'Essex'	ECou
- 'Fred's Red'	WPat
- 'Gaiety Girl' (d)	CSBt
- var. ***incanum***	CTrC MOWG
'Keatleyi' ♀H3	
- 'Jubilee' (d)	CBcs CMac IVic SLim
- 'Kerry'	CAbP
- 'Lady Bird' new	ECou
- 'Lambethii'	EBee
- 'Leonard Wilson' (d)	CTri EBee ECou
- 'Lyndon'	ECou
- 'Martini'	CAbb CBcs CDoC CMac CSBt CTrC EBee EPfP IVic LRHS SEND
- 'McLean'	ECou
- 'Moko'	ECou
- (Nanum Group) 'Huia'	LBuc
- - 'Kea'	CBcs ECou MHer MRav SEND WFar
- - 'Kiwi' ♀H3	CAbP CAbb CBcs CCCN CDoC CSBt CTrC CWSG EBee ECou ELan EPfP EUJe EWes LRHS MAsh SLim SLon WFar
- - 'Nanum'	ECou NMen
- - 'Pipit'	EWes WAbe
- - 'Tui'	CSBt CTrC
- 'Nichollsii' ♀H3	EBee WSHC
- 'Nichollsii Nanum' ♀H2-3	WAbe WPat WThu
- 'Pink Cascade'	CAbb CBcs CMac CTrC CTri CWib EBee LRHS SEND SLim
- 'Pink Damask'	IVic SLim SWvt
- 'Pink Falls'	ECou
- 'Pink Frills'	ECou
- 'Pink Queen'	LRHS
- 'Pink Splash'	ECou
- 'Pom Pom'	LRHS
- var. ***prostratum*** hort.	see *L. rupestre*
- 'Red Damask' (d) ♀H3	CBcs CDoC CDul CMac CPLG CTrC CTri CWib EBee EHoe ELan EPfP LRHS LSRN MAsh MOWG MRav NPCo SGol SPad SPlb SPoG SWvt WFar WSHC
- 'Red Falls'	CBcs CPLG CTrC ECou
- 'Redpoll'	ECou
- 'Roseum'	MRav
* - 'Ruby Wedding'	ELan EPfP LRHS LSRN MAsh SLon SPoG
- 'Snow Flurry'	CTrC EPfP LRHS SEND SGol SLim
- 'Snow White'	LRHS
- 'Wingletye'	ECou
- 'Winter Cheer' (d)	EPfP LRHS SGol
- 'Wiri Joan' (d)	CBcs
- 'Wiri Linda'	CMac
- 'Zeehan'	ECou
sericeum	ECou MOWG
'Silver Sheen' ♀H3	EBee ECou ELan EPfP LHop LRHS MAsh NLar SPlb SPoG WPGP WPat
'Snow Column'	ECou
squarrosum	CTrC
turbinatum	ECou
- 'Thunder Cloud'	ECou
'Wellington Dwarf'	ECou

Lespedeza (*Papilionaceae*)

bicolor	CCCN CSpe EBee LRHS MHer MMuc SEND SKHP WCFE WFar WGob WSHC
buergeri	EPfP LRHS MMHG NLar WSHC
japonica	SPlb
thunbergii ♀H4	CBcs CDul CHll CSpe CWib EBee ELan EPPr EPfP EPri IVic LHop LRHS MAsh MBlu MBri MGos MOWG NRHS SBod SLon SMad SPer SPoG SSpi SSta WPGP WSHC
- 'Albiflora'	CAbP LRHS SPer WPGP
- 'Avalanche'	NLar
- 'Edo-shibori'	NLar
- 'Summer Beauty'	CBcs EBee EPPr EPfP LRHS MGos
- 'White Fountain'	EBee EPfP LRHS NRHS SKHP SPoG
tiliifolia	see *Desmodium elegans*

Leucadendron (*Proteaceae*)

argenteum	CBcs CCCN CHEx CTrC EAmu SPlb
daphnoides	SPlb
discolor	SPlb
eucalyptifolium	CTrC SPlb
'Inca Gold'	CTrC EAmu MOWG
laureolum	CCCN
'Maui Sunset'	CTrC
'Mrs Stanley'	CTrC
'Safari Sunset'	CBcs CCCN CDoC CTrC EAmu SBig
'Safari Sunshine'	CTrC
salicifolium	SPlb
salignum	CCCN
- 'Early Yellow'	CTrC
- 'Fireglow'	CDoC CTrC
strobilinum	CDoC

Leucaena (*Mimosaceae*)

leucocephala	SPlb

Leucanthemella (*Asteraceae*)

§ ***serotina*** ♀H4	Widely available
- 'Herbststern'	NLar

Leucanthemopsis (*Asteraceae*)

§	***alpina***	ECho
	hosmariensis	see *Rhodanthemum hosmariense*

Leucanthemum ✿ (*Asteraceae*)

	'Angel'	CMea NPri WGrn
	atlanticum	see *Rhodanthemum atlanticum*
	catananche	see *Rhodanthemum catananche*
	graminifolium	EPfP LRHS WPer
	hosmariense	see *Rhodanthemum hosmariense*
	mawii	see *Rhodanthemum gayanum*
	maximum misapplied	see *L.* × *superbum*
§	***maximum*** (Ramond) DC.	NBro NPer
	- ***uliginosum***	see *Leucanthemella serotina*
	nipponicum	see *Nipponanthemum nipponicum*
	'Osiris Neige'	ECtt NLar
	'Real Galaxy' **new**	LBuc
	'Sante'	CCVN
	'Sunshine Peach'	CFis GBin MBri SPad SRot WCot
§	× ***superbum***	CMac MHer MLHP MMuc SEND WFar
	- 'Aglaia' (d) ♀^{H4}	Widely available
	- 'Alaska'	CAni CPLG EBee EPfP LAst LHop LRHS NGdn SBfd SPer SWvt WFar WPer WRHF WWEG
	- 'Amelia'	NBre NLar SRGP
	- 'Andernach'	CAni
	- 'Anita Allen' (d)	CAni CElw CPrp EBee MAvo WCot WPer WWEG
	- 'Anna Camilla'	CAni
	- 'Antwerp Star'	NBre NLar WBrk
	- 'Banwell'	CAni
	- 'Barbara Bush' (v/d)	ECtt NBir SWvt
§	- 'Beauté Nivelloise'	CAni CCVN CPrp CWCL EBee ECtt EPfP GBin LRHS MAvo MDKP NBre NCGa NLar NPri SMad SPoG SRms SWat WPer WPtf WWEG
	- 'Becky'	CCse CMac CWan EBee ECha ELon EWes LLHF LRHS LSRN LSou MAvo NBre NLar NPro NRHS SRGP SSvw WCAu WWEG
	- 'Bishopstone'	CAni EBee ECtt ELan LBMP LEdu LLHF MSpe NCGa SMrm WPer WWEG
	- 'Brightside'	GQue LRHS MWat NRHS
	- Broadway Lights = 'Leumayel'^{PBR}	EBee ECtt EPfP GBin IBoy IPot LBMP LRHS MAsh MAvo MBri MRav MSCN NBir NPnk SHil SPoG SUsu WCAu WFar WGrn WHil WWEG
	- 'Christine Hagemann'	CAni CPrp EBee ECtt EWes GBin MAvo MDKP MRav NCGa NLar SHar WWEG
	- 'Cobham Gold' (d)	CAni CWCL NBre NOrc SUsu SWal
	- 'Coconut Ice'	WPer WWEG
	- 'Colwall'	CAni WWEG
	- 'Crazy Daisy'	CAni CTri CWib EBee LRHS NLar SRot SWal SWvt WHrl
	- 'Crazy Daisy Butterfly'	LAst
	- 'Devon Mist'	CAni
	- 'Dipsy Daisy'	WPer
	- 'Droitwich Beauty'	CAni CPrp ECtt LLHF MAvo WCFE WHoo WWEG
	- 'Duchess of Abercorn'	CAni
	- 'Dwarf Snow Lady'	NBre NLar
	- 'Easton Lady'	CAni
	- 'Eclipse'	CAni MAvo
	- 'Edgebrook Giant'	CAni MAvo WWEG
	- 'Edward VII'	CAni
	- 'Eisstern'	CDes EBee LEdu MAvo NCGa
	- 'Elworthy Sparkler'	CElw MAvo WWEG
	- 'Esther Read' (d)	CWCL EBee ECtt ELan EPfP GBin GMaP LHop LRHS LSRN MBel MBri MMuc NBro NEgg NPri SPoG SRGP SRms SWat SWvt WCot WFar WMnd WWEG
	- 'Etoile d'Anvers'	EBee
§	- 'Everest'	CAni SRms WWEG
	- 'Exhibition'	NBre WWEG
	- 'Fiona Coghill' (d)	CAni CElw CPrp CWGN EAEE EBee ECtt EPfP EWTr GBin IBoy LBMP LHop LRHS LSou MAvo MDKP MNrw MSpe NBir NCGa NEgg NGdn NLar WCot WFar WHoo WWEG
	- 'Firnglanz'	CAni GBin MAvo WWEG
	- 'Flore Pleno' (d)	SPlb
	- 'Goldrausch'^{PBR}	Widely available
	- 'Gruppenstolz'	CAni EBee GBin
	- 'H. Seibert'	CAni CPrp MArl MAvo WWEG
	- 'Harry'	CAni
	- 'Highland White Dream'^{PBR}	LRHS
	- 'Horace Read' (d)	CAni CElw CPrp ECtt ELan NBir SAga SBch SWvt WPer WWEG
	- 'Jennifer Read'	CAni CPrp MAvo MSpe WCot WWEG
§	- 'John Murray' (d)	CAni EWes MDKP NBir SMrm WAbb WCot WWEG
	- 'Little Miss Muffet'	CSBt CWGN EAEE EBee ECtt EHrv LAst LLHF LRHS LSou MBNS NCGa NPro NWad WWEG
	- 'Little Princess'	see *L.* × *superbum* 'Silberprinzesschen'
	- 'Majestic'	CAni
	- 'Manhattan'	CAni CCse EBee EWes GBin LRHS NBre
	- 'Margaretchen'	CAni EBee MAvo WWEG
	- 'Marion Bilsland'	CAni MDKP MSpe NCGa NChi WBrk
	- 'Marion Collyer'	CAni
	- 'Mayfield Giant'	CAni CTri WPer
	- 'Mount Everest'	see *L.* × *superbum* 'Everest'
	- 'Octopus'	CAni EBee MAvo WBrk
	- 'Old Court'	see *L.* × *superbum* 'Beauté Nivelloise'
	- 'Paladin' **new**	EBee ECtt
	- 'Phyllis Smith'	CAni COlW EBee ECtt LSRN MAvo MBri MHer MRav MSpe NCGa NGdn SAga SMad SMrm SPer SPoG SUsu WAbb WBrk WCAu WCot WFar WMoo WWEG
	- 'Polaris'	EBee LRHS MBNS NBre WMoo XLum
	- 'Rags and Tatters'	CAni ECtt EWes MAvo WWEG
	- 'Rijnsburg Glory'	WPer
	- 'Schwabengruss'	CAni
	- 'Shaggy'	see *L.* × *superbum* 'Beauté Nivelloise'
§	- 'Silberprinzesschen'	CAni CSBt EBee ELon EPfP GJos LPot LRHS NEgg NPri SBfd SPlb SRms WFar WMoo WPer WRHF WWEG XLum
	- 'Silver Spoon'	EPfP WPer
	- 'Snehurka'	CAni EBee LLHF LRHS LSou MAvo SUsu WCot WWEG

- 'Snow Lady' EBee LRHS NEgg NPer NPri SBfd SRms WFar
- 'Snowcap' CHid EBee ECha EPfP LRHS MRav NEgg NGdn SBea SPer SPoG SWvt WCAu WTin
- 'Snowdrift' CAni LRHS MAvo NBre NLar SBfd WCot WPer WWEG
- 'Snowstorm' MAvo

§ - 'Sonnenschein' Widely available
- 'Starburst' (d) SRms
- 'Stina' EBee GBin MAvo WWEG
- 'Summer Snowball' see *L.* × *superbum* 'John Murray'
- 'Sunny Killin' CAni
- 'Sunny Side Up'PBR EBee ECtt LHop LRHS MBri NCGa NLar SMrm WFar WWEG
- Sunshine see *L.* × *superbum* 'Sonnenschein'
- 'T.E. Killin' (d) ♀H4 CPrp EBee ECha ECtt EPfP EWTr GBuc LRHS MBri MRav MWat NRHS SHil SPoG WCot WFar WHoo WWEG WWlt
- 'Victorian Secret' **new** EBee
- 'White Iceberg' (d) CAni WPer
- 'Wirral Pride' CAni CCVN ELon EPfP MAvo WBrk WMnd WWEG
- 'Wirral Supreme' (d) ♀H4 Widely available

'Tizi-n-Test' see *Rhodanthemum catananche* 'Tizi-n-Test'

§ ***vulgare*** CArn CHab CMac CRWN ENfk EPfP EShb MHer MNHC NLan NMir SBch SBfd SIde WFar WHer WJek WMoo WSFF WShi XLum
- 'Filigran' EShb LRHS SIde WFar

§ - 'Maikönigin' LHop WHrl XLum
- May Queen see *L. vulgare* 'Maikönigin'
- 'Sunny' CBre EWes

'White Knight' LRHS NBre NLar

Leucochrysum (*Asteraceae*)

albicans subsp. ***alpinum*** GKev

Leucocoryne (*Alliaceae*)

alliacea ECho
'Andes' CCCN ECho
'Caravelle' ECho
hybrids CGrW ECho
ixioides ECho
* - ***alba*** ECho
purpurea ♀H1 CGrW ECho

Leucogenes (*Asteraceae*)

grandiceps EPot NRHS NSla WAbe
leontopodium EPot NSla WAbe
tarahaoa GEdr WAbe

Leucogenes × *Raoulia* see × *Leucoraoulia*

Leucojum ✿ (*Amaryllidaceae*)

aestivum CBcs CTri EBee ECGP ECho EPfP GCal ITim LAma LHop MAvo MCot NEgg NHol SEND SRms WBor WCot WFar WShi GKev LAma LHop MAvo MBel MNrw NBir NEgg NHol NMen NWad SDeJ SMrm SRms WCot WFar WHer WHoo WShi
- 'Gravetye Giant' ♀H4 Widely available

autumnale see *Acis autumnalis*
longifolium see *Acis longifolia*
roseum see *Acis rosea*
tingitanum see *Acis tingitana*
trichophyllum see *Acis trichophylla*
valentinum see *Acis valentina*
vernum ♀H4 CAvo CBro CHid CPLG CWCL ECho ELan EPfP EPot GBuc GCal
- var. ***carpathicum*** CLAP ECha ECho EHrv GEdr NMen
- var. ***vagneri*** CLAP EBee ECha EHrv GEdr IGor SDys WTin

Leucophysalis (*Solanaceae*)

sinense BWJ 8093 LHop WCru

Leucophyta (*Asteraceae*)

§ ***brownii*** WCot
- 'Challenge' **new** EDAr

Leucopogon (*Ericaceae*)

§ ***colensoi*** EBee WThu

§ ***fraseri*** ECou GEdr NHar WThu
- bronze-leaved NHar

§ ***parviflorus*** ECou

× *Leucoraoulia* (*Asteraceae*)

§ ***loganii*** WAbe

Leucosceptrum (*Lamiaceae*)

canum CPLG
- GWJ 9424 WCru
japonicum B&SWJ 10804 WCru
- B&SWJ 10981 WCru
- 'Golden Angel' WCot
stellipilum WCru
var. ***formosanum*** B&SWJ 1926
- - RWJ 9907 WCru
- var. ***tosaense*** WCru B&SWJ 8892

Leucospermum (*Proteaceae*)

glabrum **new** SPlb
'Scarlet Ribbon' CCCN

Leucothoe (*Ericaceae*)

axillaris 'Curly Red'PBR CWSG EBee ELan EPfP IVic LBuc LRHS MGos MMHG MPkF NLar SBfd SLim SLon SPoG SWvt
- 'Scarletta' see *L.* Scarletta

Carinella = 'Zebekot' EPfP LRHS NLar SBfd SPoG
davisiae NLar

§ ***fontanesiana*** ♀H4 CMCN CMac EPfP
- 'Rainbow' (v) CBcs CDul CMac CSBt CWSG CWib EBee ELan EPfP LRHS MAsh MGos NEgg NLar NPnk NPri SBfd SGol SHil SLim SPad SPer SPoG SReu SRms SSta SWvt WFar WGwG WMoo
- 'Rollissonii' ♀H4 MRav SRms
- Whitewater = 'Howw' (v) **new** LRHS MPkF

keiskei EPfP
- 'Royal Ruby' EPfP LRHS LSou MGos MPkF NEgg NLar SGol SHil SLim SPoG WFar WMoo

Lovita = 'Zebonard' EPfP LRHS MBri MGos MRav NHol NLar SBfd SCoo

Red Lips = 'Lipsbolwi'PBR CDoC EBee ELan EPfP IVic MGos NPla

§ Scarletta = 'Zeblid' Widely available
walteri see *L. fontanesiana*

Leuzea (Asteraceae)

centaureoides	see *Stemmacantha centaureoides*

Levisticum (Apiaceae)

officinale	CArn CHby CPrp CSev EGHP ELau ENfk EPfP GAbr GPoy LEdu MHer MHoo MNHC NPri SBfd SDix SEND SGar SIde SPlb SVic SWat WHer WHfH WJek WPer

Lewisia ✿ (Portulacaceae)

'Archangel'	NRya
Ashwood Carousel hybrids	CTri ECho MAsh NHar
'Ashwood Pearl'	MAsh
'Ben Chace'	MAsh
Birch strain	CBcs ECho ELan
brachycalyx ♀H2	CPBP ECho EWes LLHF MAsh WPer
- pink-flowered	MAsh
brachycalyx* × *nevadensis 'Rosea'	GKev
cantelovii	CWCL MAsh
columbiana	MAsh WPer
- 'Alba'	MAsh
- 'Rosea'	GKev NSla
- subsp. ***rupicola***	ITim LLHF MAsh
- subsp. ***wallowensis***	MAsh NMen
congdonii	MAsh
'Constant Comment'	SEND
cotyledon ♀H4	CWCL ECho GKev ITim LLHF LRHS NRHS NSla WFar
- f. ***alba***	MAsh
- - 'Snowstorm'	LLHF
- 'Ashwood Ruby'	MAsh
- Ashwood strain	ECho EPfP EWes LRHS MAsh SRms WGor
- 'Brannan Bar'	MAsh
- 'Bright Eyes'	GKev
- var. ***cotyledon***	LLHF
- double-flowered (d)	GKev
- - white (d) **new**	GKev
- 'Fransi'	NLar
- var. ***howellii***	LLHF
- hybrid	ECho EPot LHop SPoG WGor
- 'John's Special'	MAsh
- magenta-flowered	ECho MAsh
§ - 'Regenbogen'	WGor WPer
- Sunset Group ♀H4	ECho EPfP LAst MHer NLar SEND WNew WPer WRHF
'George Henley'	ECho EPfP EWes LLHF MAsh NMen NRya WAbe WGor
leeana	GKev
'Little Peach'	CPBP EDAr GKev WGor WPer
'Little Plum'	CMea CPBP ECho EDAr EPfP ITim MDKP NLar NRya WGor WHoo WPer
§ ***longipetala***	ECho
§ ***nevadensis***	ECho EDAr EPot GEdr ITim LRHS MAsh NMen NRHS NRya WHoo WPer
I - 'Alba'	GKev
- ***bernardina***	see *L. nevadensis*
- 'Rosea'	MAsh
oppositifolia 'Richeyi'	GKev
'Pinkie'	MAsh NMen
pygmaea	CPBP CWCL ECho EWes GEdr ITim LAst LRHS MAsh MHer MWat NBir NMen NRHS NRya NSla
- subsp. ***longipetala***	see *L. longipetala*
Rainbow mixture	see *L. cotyledon* 'Regenbogen'
'Rawreth'	LLHF
rediviva	CPBP EWes GEdr LLHF MAsh WAbe
- subsp. ***minor***	EPot
- white-flowered	GKev
serrata	LLHF MAsh
'Trevosia'	MAsh
tweedyi ♀H2	ECho EPfP LHop LRHS MAsh NRHS WAbe
- 'Alba'	WAbe
- 'Rosea'	ECho LHop LRHS NRHS

Leycesteria (Caprifoliaceae)

crocothyrsos	CBcs CWib EBee ELan EPfP LAst MDKP NLar
formosa ♀H4	Widely available
- brown-stemmed	IFoB
- Golden Lanterns = 'Notbruce'PBR	CBcs CDoC CMac CSBt EBee ELan EPfP LBuc LRHS LSRN LTen MAsh MBri MGos MMHG MMuc NEgg NLar SBfd SCoo SHil SLim SPoG SPtl SWvt WFar WMoo
- 'Gold Leaf'	MDKP
- 'Golden Pheasant' (v)	EHoe
- 'Lydia'	EBee
- 'Purple Rain'	EBee EWes GBin LRHS LTen NLar SBfd SHil SLim

Leymus (Poaceae)

from Falkland Islands	EPPr
§ ***arenarius***	Widely available
cinereus **new**	WCot
hispidus	see *Elymus hispidus*

Lhotzkya see Calytrix

Liatris (Asteraceae)

aspera	EBee NLBP
cylindracea	SPhx
elegans	EBee EPfP NBre NLBP NLar SPlb
ligulistylis	EBee LRHS NLBP SBea SPhx
mucronata	NLBP NLar
punctata	EBee LRHS
pycnostachya	CRWN EBee NLBP NLar SRms
scariosa 'Alba'	EBee SMrm
§ ***spicata***	Widely available
- 'Alba'	CMac CPrp CSBt CSpe EBee ECha ECtt ELan EPfP LAma LAst LEdu LSRN MNrw MSCN NGdn NLar NPri SBfd SPer SPet SPlb STes WPer XLum
- ***callilepis***	see *L. spicata*
- 'Floristan Violett'	CTri EBee EHrv EPfP GMaP LRHS MAvo MBel MHer MWat MWhi NDov NEgg NLBP NLar SCoo SPlb SPoG SWal SWvt WFar WGwG WMnd WMoo WPer WWEG WWlt XLum
- 'Floristan Weiss'	CPLG CTri EBee EHrv EPPr EPfP ERCP GMaP LRHS MAvo MBel MHer MRav MWat MWhi NCGa NDov NLar SDeJ SPoG SWal SWvt WFar WGwG WMnd WMoo WPer WWEG
- Goblin	see *L. spicata* 'Kobold'
§ - 'Kobold'	Widely available
squarrosa	LRHS SPhx

Libanotis (*Umbelliferae*)

montana	see *Seseli libanotis*

Libertia ✿ (*Iridaceae*)

HCM 98.089	WPGP
'Amazing Grace'	CDes EBee GCal SBch
'Ballyrogan Blue'	CDes
* ***breunioides***	CDes CPLG WPGP
caerulescens	CCCN CMac COIW CPLG EBee ECho EPfP EShb EWll LRHS MNrw NBir NCGa SGar SMad SMrm WHer WMoo
chilensis	see *L. formosa*
elegans	CPLG
§ ***formosa***	CBcs CBro CCVN CElw CHid CPLG CTri EBee ECho ELan GCal GCra LRHS NChi NRHS NSti SBfd SGar SPer SRms STes SWvt WHer WKif WPer XLum
- brown-stemmed	IFoB
grandiflora 🏆H4	Widely available
'Highlander'	LBuc LRHS NWad
ixioides	CBcs EBee ECha ECho ECou GKev LEdu MCot SBfd SLPl WPGP WRHF WSpi
- 'Goldfinger' (v)	Widely available
- hybrid	SDix
- 'Tricolor'	LDai LRHS MRav WMoo WPat
ixioides* × *peregrinans new	WSpi
'Nelson Dwarf'	EBee GCal
paniculata	CPLG WSHC
peregrinans	Widely available
- 'Gold Leaf'	CBcs CCCN CElw CJun CPrp CSpe CTri CTsd EBee EPfP GBuc LAst LHop LRHS NOak SHil SMad SPoG SWvt WFar WHoo
- 'Gold Stripe'	EBee EPPr LRHS WPer
* ***procera***	CDes CSpe EBee EPfP IVic LEdu LRHS SKHP WPGP WSHC
pulchella	EBee
sessiliflora	CPLG EBee NBir
- RB 94073	SMad
'Taupo Blaze'	CBcs CKno CMac CPrp EBee LHop LRHS LSRN LSou NHol SBfd SGol SKHP SLon SPoG
'Taupo Sunset' PBR	CCCN CPLG EBee ELon EPfP ETod EUJe EWes LAst LRHS LSou MBNS MBel MPkF NBir NOak NPnk SBfd SGol SKHP SWvt WSpi
tricococca HCM 98.089	EBee

Libocedrus (*Cupressaceae*)

chilensis	see *Austrocedrus chilensis*
decurrens	see *Calocedrus decurrens*

Libonia see *Justicia*

Ligularia ✿ (*Asteraceae*)

'Britt Marie Crawford' PBR	Widely available
'Cheju Charmer'	ELon LEdu WCru WFar WWEG
clivorum	see *L. dentata*
§ ***dentata***	CRow EBee ECtt NBro NLar SBea SBfd SRms SWat WFar
- 'Dark Beauty'	MMuc MWhi NBre WMnd
- dark-leaved	WWEG
- 'Desdemona' 🏆H4	Widely available
- 'Enkelrig'	EBee
- 'Midnight Lady'	EBee NHol NLar WWEG
- 'Orange Princess'	NPer WPer
- 'Osiris Fantaisie' (v)	CAbP COIW CPLG EBee ECtt EWes GBee GBin IBoy IPot LLHF MAsh MAvo MNrw MWts NLar NMyG NPnk NSti SMad SPoG SUsu WBor WCot WFar WPnP WWEG
- 'Othello'	CCon CRow EBee ECtt EHon EPfP EShb LAst LPot LRHS MSCN NBid NCGa NEgg NGdn NLar NPri SBfd SPav SPet SPoG SWat SWvt WBor WFar WWEG WWlt
- 'Sommergold'	ECha
- 'Twilight'	CBct ECtt MBNS
§ ***fischeri***	ECha LEdu NBre WPer
- B&SWJ 2570	WCru
- B&SWJ 4381	WCru
- B&SWJ 4478	WCru
- B&SWJ 5653	WCru
- B&SWJ 8802	WCru
'Franz Marc' new	GCal
'Gold Torch'	CBct ECtt NLar
'Granito'	MAsh
§ 'Gregynog Gold' 🏆H4	EBee ECha ECtt EPfP GAbr GMaP LRHS LTen MRav MWhi NBro NLar NOrc NRHS SPav SPer WFar WWEG WWlt
× ***hessei***	GMaP MMuc NLar SWat WFar
hodgsonii	CKno EPPr LEdu LRHS MRav WPer
- B&SWJ 10855	WCru
intermedia B&SWJ 606a	WCru
japonica	CLAP CRow ECha GCra LEdu LRHS MWhi NLar NRHS WFar
- B&SWJ 2883	WCru
- 'Rising Sun'	CLAP CPLG GEdr WCru
'Laternchen' PBR	EBee IBal MBri MWts
'Little Rocket' PBR	CBct CPLG EBee ECtt MBNS MBri MWts NBro NGdn NLar
macrophylla	LRHS NRHS
'Osiris Café Noir'	CAbb EBee ECtt IPot NLar
'Osiris Pistache' (v)	EBee ECtt
× ***palmatiloba***	see *L.* × *yoshizoeana* 'Palmatiloba'
§ ***przewalskii*** 🏆H4	Widely available
- 'Dragon's Breath' new	ECtt
- 'Light Fingered'	NBre
sibirica	CSam EShb GAbr LRHS NLar WMoo WPer WWEG
- B&SWJ 4383	WCru
- B&SWJ 5806	WCru
- B&SWJ 5841	WCru
- var. ***speciosa***	see *L. fischeri*
smithii	see *Senecio smithii*
speciosa	see *L. fischeri*
stenocephala	EBee LRHS MCot NBro NGdn NLar SHar SWat WFar WTcb XLum
'Sungold'	CMac CSam EBee ECtt GBin LRHS NCGa NGdn NRHS
tangutica	see *Sinacalia tangutica*
'The Rocket' 🏆H4	Widely available
tussilaginea	see *Farfugium japonicum*
- 'Aureo-maculata'	see *Farfugium japonicum* 'Aureomaculatum'
veitchiana	CCon CDoy CRow CSam EPfP GAbr GCal GKev LAst LEdu LRHS NCGa SWat WFar
vorobievii	GAbr GCal NLar
'Weihenstephan'	GCal
wilsoniana	CCon CHEx CRow ECtt LRHS MMuc MRav NBre SEND SWat WFar

§	× ***yoshizoeana*** 'Palmatiloba'	CHEx EBee ELan ELon EWes GBee GCal LEdu LRHS MRav NRHS SPhx SWat WFar WWEG
	'Zepter'	CBct CMHG EBee ECtt GBuc GCal GQue MBNS MWhi MWts NEgg NLar NWad WCot WFar WWEG

Ligusticum (*Apiaceae*)

	lucidum	CMCN EBee EPfP IVic MAvo SPhx SUsu WPGP
	porteri	CArn
§	***scoticum***	CArn EBee EShb EWTr EWes GPoy LEdu MCot MDKP MHer MHoo NPnk SUsu WHrl WJek WPtf
	striatum B&SWJ 7259	WCru

Ligustrum ✿ (*Oleaceae*)

§	***delavayanum***	EBtc EPfP ERom MGos NLar STrG WFar
	- B&L 12083	CPLG
	ibota	EBtc NLar
	ionandrum	see *L. delavayanum*
	japonicum	ECrN LRHS LTen SEND SGol SPer WFar
	- 'Coriaceum'	see *L. japonicum* 'Rotundifolium'
*	- 'Coriaceum Aureum'	LRHS
	- 'Macrophyllum'	EPfP
§	- 'Rotundifolium'	CAbP CBcs CDoC CDul CHEx CMac CPLG EBee ELan EPfP IVic LBMP LRHS MAsh MGos MRav NLar SBfd SCoo SMad SPer SPoG WCFE WFar
§	- 'Silver Star' (v)	MGos NLar SEND SGol SLon
§	- 'Texanum'	EWes NLar SEWo WCFE
	- 'Texanum Argenteum'	see *L. japonicum* 'Silver Star'
	- 'Variegatum' (v)	LMaj SGol
	lucidum ♀H4	CBar CCVT CDoC CDul CSBt CTri ELan EWTr IDee LAst LPla MGos MRav NLar NWea SBfd SEND SGol SPer SWvt WFar
	- Guiz 296	CPLG
	- 'Excelsum Superbum' (v) ♀H4	CJun CMac ECrN ELan EPfP LAst LHop MGos SGol SSpi SWal
	- 'Golden Wax'	CJun MRav SSpi
	- 'Tricolor' (v)	CJun EBee ELan EPfP LRHS MAsh NLar SBfd SPer SPoG SSpi SWvt
	obtusifolium 'Dart's Perfecta'	SLPl
	ovalifolium	Widely available
§	- 'Argenteum' (v)	CBcs CCVT CDoC CDul CMac CTri CWib EBee ECrN EHoe LBuc LRHS MMuc MRav MWat NEgg NLar SBfd SEND SGol SLim SPer SPoG SWvt WFar
	- 'Aureomarginatum'	see *L. ovalifolium* 'Aureum'
§	- 'Aureum' (v) ♀H4	Widely available
	- 'Lemon and Lime' (v)	CDoC EBee EHoe EPfP LRHS SCoo SHil SWvt
	- 'Variegatum'	see *L. ovalifolium* 'Argenteum'
	quihoui ♀H4	EBee ECre ELan EPfP GKin IDee LHop LRHS SDix SEND SKHP SLon SMad SPer SSpi WPat
	sempervirens	EPfP
	sinense	CMCN EPfP GLin MRav SBfd WFar
	- 'Multiflorum'	CWib WFar
	- 'Pendulum'	LRHS
	- 'Variegatum' (v)	CJun EWes LHop MRav SPer
	strongylophyllum	CDoC CPLG
	texanum	see *L. japonicum* 'Texanum'
	undulatum 'Lemon Lime and Clippers'	LRHS MAsh NLar NPri SDix SLim
	'Vicaryi'	CJun ELan EPfP EWTr MGos MMuc NHol NPro SEND SGol SHil WFar
	vulgare	CArn CBcs CCVT CDul CHab CMac CRWN CTri CWan ECrN EPfP LAst LBuc MMuc MSwo NWea SEND SEWo SWvt WMou WSFF
	- 'Aureovariegatum' (v)	CNat
	- 'Lodense'	EBtc

Lilium ✿ (*Liliaceae*)

	'Acapulco' (VII-/d)	LAma MCri NGdn SDeJ
	African Queen Group (VI-/a) ♀H4	ERCP LAma LRHS NLar SCoo SPer SRms
	- 'African Queen' (VIb-c/a)	CBro MCri SDeJ
	'Algarve' (VIIIa-b/c)	MBri
	'Altari' (VIIIa-b/b)	MCri SDeJ
	amabile var. ***luteum*** (IXc/d)	MCri
	'Ambergate' **new**	SDeJ
	'Anastasia' (VIIIb-c/b-d)	LAma SDeJ
	'Angela North' (Ic)	GEdr
	'Annemarie's Dream' **new**	SDeJ
	'Apeldoorn' (Ia/b)	MCri NNor
	'Apollo' (Ia-b) ♀H4	LAma NNor SDeJ
	'Arena' (VIIa/b)	EPfP LRHS MCri SCoo WFar
	'Ariadne' (Ic-d)	CDes
	'Aristo'	see *L.* 'Orange Aristo'
	Asiatic hybrids (I)	LAma NGdn
	auratum (IXb/c)	CDoy ECho EFEx EPfP GBuc GKev WGwG
	- 'Gold Band'	see *L. auratum* var. *platyphyllum*
	- 'Golden Ray'	GBuc
	- 'Perfection' (IXb/c)	LRHS
§	- var. ***platyphyllum*** (IXb/c)	MCri NNor SDeJ
	- - B&SWJ 4824	WCru
	- - B&SWJ 5041	WCru
	- var. ***virginale*** (IXb/c)	MCri SDeJ
	'Avignon' (Ia/b)	MCri
	'Bach' (VIIIa-b/b)	MBri
	Backhouse hybrids	see *L.* × *dalhansonii* Backhouse Group
	bakerianum (IXc/b)	LAma
	'Barbara North' (Ic)	GEdr
	'Barbaresco' (VIIa-b/b)	SCoo
	'Barcelona' (Ia/b-c)	NNor
	'Belgrado' PBR (VIIa/b-c) **new**	SDeJ
	'Belle Epoque' (VIIb/b-c) **new**	SDeJ
	Bellingham Group (IVc/d)	GEdr
	'Bergamo' (VIIb/b)	EPfP SCoo SDeJ WFar
	'Black Beauty' (VIIIb-c/d)	EPfP GBin GKev LAma LRHS MCri NNor SDeJ
	'Black Dragon'	see *L. leucanthum* var. *centifolium* 'Black Dragon'
	'Black Pearl'	EPfP SPer
	'Black Tie' (VIIa-b/b)	MCri
	'Boogie Woogie' (VIIIa-b/b)	SDeJ
	Brasilia = 'Zora' (VII)	SDeJ
	Bright Pixie = 'Ceb Bright' (Ia/b)	SDeJ
	'Bright Star' (VIb-c/c)	LAma MCri
	brownii (IXb-c/a)	ECho LAma MCri
	bulbiferum (IXa/b)	ECho
	'Burgundy Splash' (I)	LAma
	'Butter Pixie' PBR (Ia/b)	NNor SDeJ WGor

	Name	Suppliers
	'Buzzer' (VII) **new**	MAsh
§	***canadense*** (IXc/a)	CBro CDes CRDP GBuc LAma WCru XEll
	- var. ***coccineum*** (IXc/a)	CRDP GBuc
	- var. ***flavum***	see *L. canadense*
	candidum (IXb/a) ♀H4	CAvo CBcs CBro CTca CWCL EBee ECha ECho EHrv ELan EPfP EPot ERCP GKev LAma MCri MHer NLar SDeJ SEND SRms WCot XLum
	'Capuchino' (Ia-b/c)	LAma MCri
	carniolicum	see *L. pyrenaicum* subsp. *carniolicum*
	'Casa Blanca' (VIIb/b-c) ♀H4	CAvo CBro CSut EPfP GKev LAma MCri NBir NLar NNor SCoo SDeJ WCot WFar
	'Centerfold' (Ia-b/b)	LAma NNor
	cernuum (IXc/d)	ECho GKev LAma MCri SDeJ SPer
*	- 'Album'	EBee ECho SDeJ
	ciliatum	LWst
	Citronella Group (Ic/d)	ECGP ECho LAma MCri SDeJ WFar
	'Claude Shride' (IIc/d) **new**	SDeJ
	columbianum (IXc/d)	ECho NMen WHal
	- B&SWJ 9564	WCru
	- dwarf (IXc/d)	NMen
	'Con Amore' (VIIb/b)	SCoo WFar
	'Conca d'Or' PBR (VIIIb/b)	LAma SDeJ
	concolor (IXa/c)	LRHS
	'Connecticut King' (Ia/b)	LAma MCri
	'Corina' (Ia/b)	NNor
	'Côte d'Azur' (Ia/b-c)	LAma NNor
	'Coulance' (VII-/d)	LRHS
	'Creation' (VIa/b) **new**	SDeJ
	'Crimson Pixie' (Ia/b)	CBro SDeJ SPet
	× ***dalhansonii*** (IIc/d)	SPhx WCot
§	- Backhouse Group (IIc/d)	GEdr
§	- 'Marhan' (IIc/d)	ECho GBuc
	- 'Mrs R.O. Backhouse' (IIc/d)	ECho GEdr SDeJ
	dauricum var. ***alpinum*** (IX)	MCri
	davidii (IXc/d)	CPLG EBee ECho GBuc GEdr GKev LAma MCri MMoz SDeJ WCru
	- var. ***unicolor***	GBuc
§	- var. ***willmottiae*** (IXc/d)	MCri WCot WCru
	'Diabora' (Ia/b)	GBuc
	'Dimention' (I)	LAma
	distichum (IXb-c/d)	WCot
	- - B&SWJ 794	WCru
	- - B&SWJ 4465	WCru
	'Dizzy' (VIIa-b/b-c)	MCri NNor SDeJ
	duchartrei (IXc/d)	CDes CDoy CPLG ECho GEdr LAma LWst NSla WAbe WCru
	'Ebony' (Ic/d)	LAma
	'Eileen North' (Ic/-)	GEdr
	'Electric' (Ia/b-c)	MCri NNor
	'Elodie' PBR (1a/b)	CAvo LAma
	'Elusive' **new**	SDeJ
	'Enchantment' (Ia/b)	SDeJ
	'Eros' (Ic/d)	GEdr
	'Expression' (VII)	SDeJ
	'Eyeliner' PBR	LAma
	'Fancy Joy' (Ia/b-c)	MBri
	'Fangio' (VIIIa/b)	NNor
	'Fata Morgana' (Ia/b) ♀H4	LAma NNor SCoo SDeJ
	'Fire King' (Ib/d)	EPfP LAma MCri SCoo SDeJ SRms WFar
	'Fopapo' **new**	SDeJ
	formosanum (IXb/a)	CPne LRHS MCri
	- RWJ 10005	WCru
	- var. ***pricei*** (IXb/a)	ECho ELan EPot GBin GEdr LRHS MHer NMen NRHS NSla SHil SPoG WIce
	- - 'Snow Queen' (Vb/a)	SDeJ
	'Garden Party' (VIIb/b) ♀H4	SDeJ WFar
	'Glossy Wings' (VIIIa-b/b)	NNor
	'Golden Joy' (Ia/-)	MBri
	Golden Splendor Group (VIb-c/a) ♀H4	LAma MCri SCoo SDeJ
	'Golden Stone' (VIIIa-b/b) **new**	SDeJ
	'Graffity' (I)	LAma
	'Gran Paradiso' (Ia/b)	MCri SRms
	'Grand Cru' (Ia/b) ♀H4	LRHS MCri NNor SDeJ
	grayi (IX)	GBuc
	Green Magic Group (VI-/a)	NNor
	'Hannah North' (Ic)	GEdr
	hansonii (IXb-c/d)	ECha ECho GBuc GEdr LAma MCri SDeJ
	- B&SWJ 4756 from Aomori, Japan	WCru
	- B&SWJ 8506	WCru
	- B&SWJ 8528	WCru
	henryi (IXc/d) ♀H4	EBee ECho EPfP GKev LAma MCri NLar NNor SDeJ WCru
	'Hit Parade' (VII)	SDeJ
	× ***hollandicum*** (Ia/b)	MCri
	'Honeymoon' (VIIIa-b/b)	SDeJ
	'Hot Lips' (VIIb/b-d)	EPfP
	'Ibarra' (Ia/b)	MCri
	'Ice Pixie' (Ia/b) **new**	SDeJ
	'Italia' (Ia)	LRHS
	'Ivory Pixie' (Ia/b)	GKev SPet
	'Jacqueline'	LRHS
	japonicum (IXb/a)	EFEx
	'Jo's Choice' **new**	SDeJ
	'Josephine' **new**	SDeJ
	'Journey's End' (VIIb/c)	LAma
§	'Joy' (VIIa-b/b) ♀H4	LAma MCri NNor SDeJ
	'Karen North' (Ic)	GEdr
	'King Pete' (Ib/b-c) ♀H4	SDeJ
	'Kingdom' PBR (VIIIa/b-c) **new**	SDeJ
	'Lady Alice' (VI-/d)	SDeJ WGwG
	'Lake Tulare' (IV) **new**	GEdr
§	***lancifolium*** (IXc/d)	CArn CHid GBin WBrk WFar
	- B&SWJ 4352	WCru
*	- ***album***	GHim
	- var. ***flaviflorum*** (IXc/d)	CBro GBuc MCri SDeJ
	- 'Flore Pleno' (IXc/d)	EPPr GCal LHop LRHS MHer MMHG NBir NNor NRHS SDeJ SMrm WCot WCru WFar WHil WTin
*	- var. ***forrestii*** (IX)	MCri
	- Forrest's form (IX)	LRHS
	- var. ***fortunei*** (IXc/d)	GCal SDix
	- - B&SWJ 539	WCru
	- pink-flowered	SDeJ
	- 'Splendens' (IXc/d) ♀H4	CBro EBee ECGP ECho EPfP GKev LAma MCri NBid NNor SDeJ SPhx
	'Landini' PBR (Ia/b)	SDeJ
	lankongense (IXc/d)	CWCL EPot GBuc GEdr GGGa LAma MCri WCru
	- BWJ 7691	WCru
	'Latvia' (Ia/b)	MCri SDeJ
	'Lazy Lady' **new**	SDeJ
	'Le Rêve'	see *L.* 'Joy'
	leichtlinii (IXc/d)	CBro ECho EPot GEdr GKev LRHS MCri SDeJ

	- B&SWJ 4519	WCru
	- 'Iwashimiza' (IXc/d)	MCri
	'Lemon Pixie' (Ia/b)	LAma SPet
	leucanthum (IXb-c/a)	LAma
	- var. ***centifolium*** (IXb-c/a)	MCri WCru
	- - BWJ 8130	WCru
§	- - 'Black Dragon' (IXb-c/a)	MCri
	lijiangense (IXc/d)	GEdr MCri
	'Linda' (Ia/b) **new**	SDeJ
	'Little John' (VIIa-b/b)	MBri SDeJ SPer
	Lollypop = 'Holebibi' (Ia/b)	GBuc MBri NNor SCoo SPet
	longiflorum (IXb/a) ♀H2-3	EBee ECho LAma MCri SCoo
	- B&SWJ 11376	WCru
	- 'Memories'	MBri
	- 'Rose' **new**	SDeJ
§	- 'White American' (Vb/a)	CBro ECho LRHS SPer
	- 'White Heaven'PBR (Vb/a)	EPfP
	lophophorum (IXc/b)	LAma LWst
	'Lovely Girl' (VII-/b)	CSut SDeJ
	'Luxor' (Ib)	MCri NBir
	'Luzia' (VII) **new**	NCGa
	mackliniae (IXc/a)	CWCL EBee ECho GBuc GCal GCra GEdr GGGa GHim GMaP NBir NMen WAbe WHal
	- from Nagaland, India	GGGa
	- deep pink-flowered	GGGa
	'Mambo'PBR (VII)	LAma
	'Marco Polo' (Ia/-)	SCoo SDeJ WFar
	'Marhan'	see *L.* × *dalhansonii* 'Marhan'
	martagon (IXc/d) ♀H4	CBro CCon CTca CWCL EBee ECha ECho EHrv ELan EPot ERCP GBuc GEdr GKev GPoy LAma LRHS MCot NBir NLar NPnk SDeJ SRms WAul WCot WFar WPnP WShi WTin
	- var. ***albiflorum*** (IXc/d)	EHrv GBuc
	- var. ***album*** (IXc/d) ♀H4	CAvo CBro CWCL EBee ECho ELan EPfP EPot GEdr GKev GMaP LAma LRHS NBir NChi SDeJ WPtf WShi
	- var. ***cattaniae*** (IXc/d)	GBuc GEdr MCri WCot
	- 'Plenum' (IXc/d)	WCot
*	- var. ***rubrum***	CWCL
	medeoloides (IXc/d)	ECho EFEx GBuc LWst NMen
	'Mediterrannee' (VIIb/d)	NNor
	michiganense (IXc/d)	GBuc
	'Miss Feya' (VIII)	LAma
	'Miss France' (VIIb/b-c)	EPfP SDeJ
	'Miss Lily' **new**	SDeJ
	'Miss Lucy'PBR (VIIa-b/b-c)	CHid LAma SDeJ
	'Miss Rio' (VII)	SCoo
	'Mona Lisa' (VIIb/b-c)	EPfP GKev LAma LRHS MBri MCri NGdn NNor SDeJ WFar
	monadelphum (IXc/d)	ECho GKev LAma SDeJ
	'Mont Blanc' (Ia)	SDeJ
	'Monte Negro' (Ia/b)	CBro LRHS MCri NGdn
	'Montezuma'PBR (VIIa-b/b) **new**	SDeJ
	'Montreux' (Ia/b-c)	LAma SDeJ
	'Mount Duckling'	GKev
	'Mr Job' **new**	SDeJ
	'Muscadet'PBR (VIIa-b/b)	CSut LAma NGdn SDeJ
§	***nanum*** (IXc/b)	ECho GEdr LAma LWst NMen WAbe WCru WHal
	- AGS/ES	NMen
	- from Bhutan (IX)	NMen WCru
	- var. ***flavidum*** (IXc/b)	GEdr LWst NMen
	nepalense (IXc/a)	CBcs CBro CCon CHid CPLG CTca EBee ECho EPot ERCP GBuc GEdr GHim GKev LAma MCri SDeJ WCot WCru WFar WWFP XLum
	- B&SWJ 2985	WCru
	'Nerone' (Ia/b)	CHid NNor
	'Netty's Pride' (Ia/b-c)	CAvo CBro CHid EPfP ERCP GBuc MCri SDeJ SPer WCot
	'New Wave' (Ia/b)	SDeJ
	'Night Flyer' (Ib-c/b-c) **new**	SDeJ
	nobilissimum (IXa-b/a)	EFEx
	'Nove Cento' (Ia/b) ♀H4	MCri SDeJ
	'Odeon' (VI-/a)	MCri
	'Olivia' (Ia)	LAma MCri
	Olympic Group (VI-/a)	MCri
§	'Orange Aristo' (Ia)	WCot
	'Orange County' (Ia/b) **new**	SDeJ
	'Orange Electric' (Ia/b)	SDeJ
	'Orange Marmalade' (IIb/c-d) **new**	SDeJ
	'Orange Pixie' (Ia/b)	MCri NNor SCoo SPet WGor
	'Orange Twinkle' (Ib-c/b)	SDeJ
*	Oriental Superb Group	NGdn
§	***oxypetalum*** (IXb-c/b)	ECho LWst
	- var. ***insigne*** (IXb-c/b)	ECho GBin GBuc LWst NMen WAbe WCru WHal
	'Painted Pixie' (Ia)	MAsh
	'Pan' (Ic)	GEdr
	papilliferum (IXc/d)	LAma
	pardalinum (IXc/d) ♀H4	CBro CWCL EBee ECho ERCP GKev LWst MCot MMoz WBor WCru WHal
	- var. ***giganteum*** (IXc/d)	EPfP MCri MNrw
	- subsp. ***pardalinum*** (IX)	GBuc
	- subsp. ***shastense*** (IXc/d)	NMen
§	- subsp. ***vollmeri*** (IXc/d)	GBuc NMen WCru
§	- subsp. ***wigginsii*** (IXc/d)	MCri
	× ***parkmanii*** Imperial Silver Group (VIIb/c)	LAma
	- 'Rosy Dimple' (VIIa/b) **new**	SDeJ
	- 'Sam' (VIIb/c) ♀H4	EPfP
	parryi (IXb-c/a)	WHal
	parvum (IXa-b/a)	ECho GBuc
	'Patricia's Pride'	MCri SDeJ
	'Peach Butterflies' (Ic/d)	SDeJ
	'Peach Pixie' (Ia/b)	NBir SCoo
	'Pearl Jennifer' (Ib-a/c) **new**	SDeJ
	'Pearl Jessica' (Ib-c/b-c) **new**	SDeJ
	'Pearl Justien' (Ia-b/c) **new**	SDeJ
	'Pearl Loraine' (Ib-c/b-c) **new**	SDeJ
	'Pearl Sonja' **new**	SDeJ
	'Pearl Stacey' (Ib-c/c) **new**	SDeJ
	'Peggy North' (Ic/d)	GEdr
	philippinense (IXa-b/a)	CDes GHim LAma MCri WPGP
	'Pimento' (VIIa/b) **new**	NCGa SDeJ
	'Pink Flavour' **new**	SDeJ
	Pink Perfection Group (VIb/a) ♀H4	CBro EPfP ERCP LAma LRHS MCri NNor SCoo SDeJ SPer WFar
	'Pink Pixie'PBR (Ia/b)	NNor SDeJ SPet
	'Pink Tiger' (VIIIb/c)	CAvo MCri NNor WGor
	'Pink Twinkle'	CBro
	poilanei HWJ 681	WCru
	- WWJ 11679	WCru
	polyphyllum	GLin
	primulinum var. ***ochraceum*** (IXc/a)	LAma LWst MCri WCru
§	***pumilum*** (IXc/d) ♀H4	EBee ECho EPot ERCP GKev LAma MCri SDeJ
	'Purple Prince' (VIIIa-b/a-b)	SDeJ
	pyrenaicum (IXc/d)	ECho GBuc IBlr LWst MCri WPGP WShi
§	- subsp. ***carniolicum*** (IXc/d)	MCri

Red Band Group (VII-/b) WFar
'Red Carpet' (Ia/b) MCri NBir NNor SDeJ
'Red County' (Ia/c-b) **new** SDeJ
'Red Electric' (Ia/b) **new** SDeJ
'Red Hot' (VIIIc-d/b) SDeJ
Red Rum = 'Zanlorum' MBri
'Red Star' LRHS
'Red Twinkle' SDeJ
'Red Velvet' (Ic/d) SDeJ
regale (IXb/a) ♀H4 CAvo CBro CCon CDoy CMea CTca EBee ECha EHrv ELan EPfP ERCP GKev GMaP LAma LRHS MCot MCri NLar NNor SDeJ SPer WCot WFar
- 'Album' (IXb/a) CAvo EBee ERCP GKev LAma LRHS MCri NLar NNor SCoo SDeJ WCot WFar WGwG XLum
§ - 'Royal Gold' (IXb/a) MCri
'Reinesse' (Ia/b) MBri SDeJ
'Rina's Twinkle' LRHS
'Robert Swanson' LAma SDeJ
'Robina' (VIIIa-b/b-c) LAma WCot
'Roma' (Ia/b) NBir
'Rosefire' (Ia/b) NNor
'Rosella's Dream' (I) **new** SDeJ
'Rosemary North' (Ic/d) CDes GEdr
'Rosita' (Ia/b-c) WFar
'Rosselini' **new** SDeJ
rosthornii (IXc/d) CPLG EBee GEdr LAma WCot WCru
'Royal Fantasy' (VIII) NNor
'Royal Gold' see *L. regale* 'Royal Gold'
rubellum (IXb/a) EFEx
* 'Rubina' MCri
'Ruud' (VIIb/b-c) LAma
sachalinense (IXa/b) RBS 0235 EPPr
'Salinas' (VII a/b) **new** SDeJ
'Salmon Star' PBR **new** NCGa
'Salmon Tiger' **new** SDeJ
'Salmon Twinkle' (Ib-c/c) LRHS SDeJ WFar
'San Vincenzo' EPfP
sargentiae (IXb-c/a) EBee GEdr MCri NMen WCot WCru
'Satisfaction' (VIIIa-b/-) SDeJ
'Scarlet Delight' (VIIb-c/c-d) **new** SDeJ
'Scheherazade' (VIIIc/d) LAma MCri SDeJ
'Set Point' (VIIb/b) SDeJ
'Silly Girl' (Ia/-) NNor
'Smokey Mountain' (VIIIc/d) **new** SDeJ
§ 'Snow Crystal' (Ia/b) EPfP
'Souvenir' PBR (VIIa-b/b) NGdn
'Spark' NNor
speciosum (IXb-c/d) B&SWJ 4847 WCru
- - B&SWJ 4924 WCru
- var. ***album*** (IXb-c/d) EBee ECho EPfP GKev LEdu MCri NBir SDeJ
- var. ***gloriosoides*** (IXb-c/d) LAma
- var. ***rubrum*** (IXb-c/d) EBee ECha ECho EPfP GKev LAma MCri NBir SDeJ SPer SRms
§ - 'Uchida' (IXb-c/d) CPLG EPfP MCri SDeJ
'Sphinx' (Ia/d) CAbP NNor WCot
'Spring Pink' (Ia) ERCP SDeJ
'Staccato' (Ia/c) MCri
'Stainless Steel' (Ia/b) **new** SDeJ
'Star Gazer' (VIIa/c) CBro CSut GKev LAma LRHS MCri NNor SCoo SDeJ WFar
'Starfighter' (VIIa-b/c) GKev MCri SDeJ
'Sterling Star' (Ia/b) MCri NNor
Stones = 'Holebobo' (Ia/b) NNor
'Sulphur King' WCot
sulphureum (IXb-c/a) LAma MCri
'Sumatra' (VIIb/b) LAma
'Sun Ray' (Ia/b) MCri
superbum (IXc/d) EBee GBuc LAma WCru WPGP
'Sutter's Gold' (I) **new** MCri
'Sutton Court' (II) GBuc GEdr
'Sweet Lord' SDeJ
'Sweet Surrender' (Ib-c/c-d) EPfP MCri NNor SDeJ
'Sweet-kiss' (Ia-b/b) MBri
'Tailor Made' (Ia/b) **new** SDeJ
taliense (IXc/d) ECho GEdr LAma MCri WCru
'Tarragona' PBR (VIIIb/b) **new** SDeJ
tenuifolium see *L. pumilum*
'Tiger Woods' (VII) EPfP LAma
tigrinum see *L. lancifolium*
'Tom Pouce' (VIIa/b) EPfP MCri SDeJ
'Toscane' (Ia/b-c) **new** SDeJ
'Touch' (VIIb/-) MCri
Triumphator = 'Zanlophator' PBR (VIIIb/a-b) EPfP MCri NNor SDeJ
tsingtauense (IXa/c) EBee MCri SDeJ
- B&SWJ 4263 WCru
- B&SWJ 4698 WCru
- B&SWJ 519 WCru
'Uchida Kanoka' see *L. speciosum* 'Uchida'
'Urandi' (VIIIc/b) **new** SDeJ
'Val Di Sole' PBR (Ia/b) **new** SDeJ
'Venezuela' PBR (VIIa-b/b-c) **new** SDeJ
'Venture' (1a) NNor
'Vermeer' (Ia-b/b-c) LRHS WFar
'Victory Joy' MBri
'Visaversa' (VIIIa-b/b) **new** SDeJ
'Vivaldi' (Ia/b) SDeJ
vollmeri see *L. pardalinum* subsp. *vollmeri*
wallichianum (IXb/a) EBee ECho EPot GHim LAma SDeJ XLum
wardii (IXc/d) CPLG
'White American' see *L. longiflorum* 'White American'
'White Paradise' (V) SCoo
White Pixie see *L.* 'Snow Crystal'
'White Present' (Vb/a) **new** SDeJ
'White Twinkle' (Ia-b/b) CAvo SDeJ
wigginsii see *L. pardalinum* subsp. *wigginsii*
willmottiae see *L. davidii* var. *willmottiae*
wilsonii var. ***luteum*** MCri
'Wine Electric' (Ia/c) **new** SDeJ
xanthellum var. ***luteum*** (IXb-c/d) CDes WCru
'Yellow Electric' MCri SDeJ
'Yellow Eye' **new** SDeJ

lime see *Citrus aurantiifolia*

lime, Philippine see × *Citrofortunella microcarpa*

Limnanthes (*Limnanthaceae*)

douglasii ♀H4 CArn EPfP SIde
- subsp. ***rosea*** CSpe

Limonium (*Plumbaginaceae*)

bellidifolium CMea ECha EDAr MWat WPer
- 'Dazzling Blue' WHrl

	chilwellii	ECGP SEND
	cosyrense	CMea GEdr MHer NMen WAbe WPer
	dregeanum	WThu
	dumosum	see *Goniolimon tataricum* var. *angustifolium*
	gmelinii	SPlb WPer
*	- subsp. ***hungaricum***	NLar XLum
	gougetianum	LLHF WPer
	latifolium	see *L. platyphyllum*
	paradoxum	WAbe
	perezii	CCon WPer
§	***platyphyllum***	CKno CMea EBee EPPr EPfP GMaP LHop LRHS MBel MHer MWat NChi NMir SBfd SEND SMHy SPer SRms WAul WHoo WPer WTin WWEG
	- 'Robert Butler'	CPrp GCal GQue MRav SUsu
	- 'Violetta'	EBee ECGP ECha ELan EPfP GCal LAst LRHS MBel MBri MRav NOrc SPer SPoG WHoo
	sinuatum new	SVic
	tataricum	see *Goniolimon tataricum*
	vulgare	WHer

Linaria (*Plantaginaceae*)

	aeruginea	CPBP CSpe WPtf
	- 'Neon Lights'	CSpe EDAr LRHS NGdn SBfd
	- subsp. ***nevadensis*** 'Gemstones'	SBch
	alpina	CSpe ECtt NRHS NRya NSla SRms
	anticaria 'Antique Silver'	CPLG LSou MRav WPtf WWEG
	Blue Lace = 'Yalin'	LSou
	cymbalaria	see *Cymbalaria muralis*
§	***dalmatica***	EBee ECha ELan EPPr IFro MPie NBid NBre SBch WCot WMoo WPer WWEG
	dalmatica × ***purpurea***	WCot
	× ***dominii*** 'Carnforth'	SBch SHar WCot WWEG
	- 'Yuppie Surprise'	CHid NBir
	genistifolia	MDKP
	- subsp. ***dalmatica***	see *L. dalmatica*
	hepaticifolia	see *Cymbalaria hepaticifolia*
*	***lobata alba***	ECho SPlb
	origanifolia	see *Chaenorhinum origanifolium*
	pallida	see *Cymbalaria pallida*
	'Peachy'	CSpe
	pilosa	see *Cymbalaria pilosa*
	purpurea	CTri EBee EHoe ELan EPfP IFoB LRHS MHer MNHC NBro NPer NPri SEND SPhx SRms WCot WFar WMoo WPer WSFF
	- 'Alba'	see *L. purpurea* 'Springside White'
	- 'Brown's White Strain'	CSpe EBee IBoy MBel MPie SPad WCot WRHF
	- 'Canon Came'	CNat
	- 'Canon Went'	Widely available
	- 'Freefolk Piccolo' new	SHar
	- pink-flowered	CSpe
	- 'Radcliffe Innocence'	see *L. purpurea* 'Springside White'
§	- 'Springside White'	EBee ECha ECtt LBMP LRHS MBri NBir NGdn SBch SPer SPhx SSvw WAul WFar WPer WSHC WWEG XLum
	- 'Thurgarton Beauty'	MDKP
	repens	CPom WCot WHer
	× ***sepium***	WCot
	triornithophora	CCon ECha LRHS MHer MSpe SBfd SPlb WHrl WKif WMoo WPtf
	- 'Pink Budgies'	LLHF LSou
	- purple-flowered	WMoo
	- 'Rosea'	CSpe
	vulgaris	CArn CHab LDai MDKP MHer MHoo MNHC NMir SEND WHer WHfH WJek
	- 'Peloria'	CPBP MDKP
	'Winifrid's Delight'	NBre

Lindelofia (*Boraginaceae*)

	anchusoides misapplied	see *L. longiflora*
	anchusoides (Lindl.) Lehm.	EPPr NBid
§	***longiflora***	EBee GCal GCra GMaP LPla

Lindera (*Lauraceae*)

benzoin	CBcs EPfP LRHS MBlu NLar
erythrocarpa	EPfP
- B&SWJ 6271	WCru
- B&SWJ 8730	WCru
megaphylla	CHEx
obtusiloba ♀H4	CAbP EPfP SSpi
- B&SWJ 8723	WCru
- B&SWJ 11054	WCru
praecox	EPfP
- B&SWJ 10802	WCru
- B&SWJ 10953 from north Japan	WCru
- B&SWJ 11125 from south Japan	WCru
reflexa	NLar
sericea B&SWJ 11123	WCru
- B&SWJ 11141	WCru
- var. ***lancea*** B&SWJ 11071	WCru
- - B&SWJ 11118	WCru
strychnifolia	EPfP
triloba	SSpi
- B&SWJ 11121	WCru
- B&SWJ 11466	WCru
- B&SWJ 5570	WCru
umbellata B&SWJ 10881	WCru
- var. ***membranacea*** B&SWJ 6227	WCru
- - B&SWJ 10837	WCru

Linnaea (*Caprifoliaceae*)

borealis	CPLG EPot WAbe
- subsp. ***americana***	NHar WAbe

Linum (*Linaceae*)

	arboreum ♀H4	LLHF NBir WPat
	campanulatum	WThu
	capitatum	NSla
	flavum	EPfP GKev XSen
	- 'Compactum'	CMea EBee ECho LLHF SRms WCot
	'Gemmell's Hybrid' ♀H4	ECho EPot EWes NBir NMen WAbe WThu
	grandiflorum 'Rubrum' new	CSpe
	leonii	LRHS
	monogynum	ECou LLHF
§	- var. ***diffusum***	ECou
	- 'Nelson'	see *L. monogynum* var. *diffusum*
	narbonense	CCse EDif LDai LRHS SBch SPhx
	- 'Heavenly Blue'	NCGa
§	***perenne***	CArn CRWN EBee ECha ELan ENfk EPfP GMaP MAsh MBel MHer MNHC NLar SIde SPer SPoG WJek WPer WWEG
	- 'Album'	EBee ECha ELan EPfP NLar SPer WJek WPer

	- subsp. ***alpinum*** 'Alice Blue'	WAbe
§	- 'Blau Saphir'	EBee GQue MWat NHol NLar
	- Blue Sapphire	see *L. perenne* 'Blau Saphir'
	- 'Himmelszelt'	NLar
	- subsp. ***lewisii***	NBir
	- 'Nanum Diamond'	NLar
	- 'Nanum Sapphire'	see *L. perenne* 'Blau Saphir'
	- 'White Diamond'	SPoG
	sibiricum	see *L. perenne*
	suffruticosum	WPat WThu
	subsp. ***salsoloides*** 'Nanum'	
	uninerve	WAbe
	usitatissimum	CRWN MHer SIde
	- 'Blue Dress' new	CSpe SPhx

Lippia (*Verbenaceae*)

sp.	SWvt
alba	CArn
canescens	see *Phyla nodiflora* var. *canescens*
chamaedrifolia	see *Verbena peruviana*
citriodora	see *Aloysia citrodora*
dulcis	CArn EOHP
nodiflora	see *Phyla nodiflora*
repens	see *Phyla nodiflora*

Liquidambar ✿ (*Altingiaceae*)

	acalycina	CDul CJun CLnd EBee EBtc ELan EMil EPfP MGos MRav NLar SBir SCoo SGol SLim SPoG SSpi SSta WPGP WPat
	- 'Burgundy Flush'	CJun NLar SSta
	- 'Spinners'	LRHS SSpi
	formosana	CDul CMCN CMac EPfP IArd LAst MGos MSnd NPCo SBir SGol SSta WPGP
	- 'Afterglow'	CJun SSta
	- 'Ellen'	CJun NLar SSta
	- 'Gail'	SSta
	- Monticola Group	CJun EPfP SBir SSta
	- 'Woodleigh'	SSta
	orientalis	CDul CJun CLnd CMCN EBtc EPfP LLHF NPCo SBir SSta
	- 'M. Foster' new	NLar
	styraciflua	Widely available
	- 'Andrew Hewson'	CAbP CJun CLnd EBee EPfP IVic LRHS MAsh MBlu NLar NRHS SBir SSta WPat
	- 'Anja'	CJun MBlu SBir SSta WPat
	- 'Anneke'	CJun SBir SSta
	- 'Aurea'	see *L. styraciflua* 'Variegata' Overeynder
	- 'Aurea Variegata'	see *L. styraciflua* 'Variegata' Overeynder
	- 'Aurora'	CJun EBee SBir
	- 'Brodsman'	NLar
	- 'Burgundy'	CJun CLnd LLHF MBlu SBir SSta WPat
	- Cherokee = 'Ward' new	MGos
	- 'Elstead Mill'	CAbP
	- 'Festeri'	SBir SSta WPat
	- 'Festival'	CJun MBlu SSta
	- 'Frosty' (v)	CJun SSta
	- 'Globe'	see *L. styraciflua* 'Gum Ball'
	- 'Gold Beacon'	MPkF
	- 'Golden Treasure' (v)	CDul CJun CMCN LRHS MAsh MBri MGos NLar SPer SPoG SReu SSta WPat
	- 'Goldmember'	CJun SSta
	- 'Granary Sunset'	SBir SSta
§	- 'Gum Ball'	CJun CLnd CMCN ELon EPfP ERom EWes LLHF MGos NLar NPCo SBir SLim SMad SSta WPat
	- Happidaze = 'Hapdell'	CJun NLar SBir SSta WPat
	- 'Jennifer Carol'	CJun NLar SBir SSta
	- 'Kia'	CAbP CJun LLHF NLar SBir WPat
	- 'Kirsten'	CJun
	- 'Lane Roberts' ♀H4	CDoC CDul CLnd CMCN CMac CSBt CTho EBee ELan EPfP IArd LHop LRHS LSRN MAsh MBlu MBri MGos MWat NLar SBfd SBir SCoo SEWo SMad SPoG SReu SSta SWvt WPat
	- 'Lynn' new	SSta
	- 'Manon' (v)	CDoC CJun SLim
	- 'Midwest Sunset'	CJun MBlu WPat
	- 'Moonbeam' (v)	CJun NLar SBir SLim SSta WPat
	- 'Moraine'	CJun SBir
	- 'Naree'	CJun NLar SBir SSta
	- 'Nina' new	SSta
	- 'Oconee'	EPfP LLHF MAsh SLim SSta WPat
	- 'Paarl' (v)	CJun NLar
	- 'Palo Alto'	CJun LLHF LRHS MAsh MBlu NLar SBir SCoo SLim SSta WPGP WPat
	- 'Parasol'	CAbP CJun CLnd EBtc NLar NPCo SBir SSta
	- 'Pendula'	CJun CLnd MBlu SBir SSta
	- 'Penwood'	CJun NLar SSta
	- 'Professor Louwjan'	NLar
	- 'Red Sunset'	SSta
	- 'Rotundiloba'	CJun CLnd CMCN ECrN EPfP LLHF MAsh MBlu SSta WPat
	- 'Savill Torch' new	SSta
	- 'Schock's Gold'	CJun MAsh SSta WPat
	- 'Silver King' (v)	CJun CMCN CMac EBee ECrN MBri MGos MMHG MPkF NHol NLar NPCo SCoo SLim SPer SReu SSta WFar WPat
	- 'Simone' new	SSta
	- 'Slender Silhouette'	CAbP CDul CJun EBee EPfP GKin LLHF LRHS MAsh MBlu NLar SBir SCoo SGol SLim SPoG SReu SSpi SSta WMou WPat
	- 'Stared'	CDul CJun CLnd EBee EBtc LRHS LTen MBlu MBri MGos NLar SBir SCoo SLim SSta WPGP WPat
	- 'Thea'	CAbP CJun CLnd EMil EPfP LRHS MAsh MBlu MBri SBir SSta
	- 'Variegata' misapplied	see *L. styraciflua* 'Silver King'
§	- 'Variegata' Overeynder (v)	CBcs CDul CJun CLnd CMac EBee ELan EPfP LRHS MAsh MGos SLim SSta
	- 'White Star' (v)	CJun SSta
	- 'Woorby Rose'	SBir SSta
	- 'Worplesdon' ♀H4	Widely available

Liriodendron ✿ (*Magnoliaceae*)

'Chapel Hill'	MBlu NLar WPat
chinense	CBcs CDul CGHE CMCN EPfP MBlu SGol WPGP
chinense × ***tulipifera***	WPGP
'Doc Deforce's Delight'	MBlu NLar
tulipifera ♀H4	Widely available
- 'Ardis'	NLar
- 'Arnold'	SGol
- 'Aureomarginatum' (v) ♀H4	Widely available

- 'Fastigiatum'	CDoC CDul CMCN CTho EBee ECrN ELan EPfP GKin MAsh MBlu MBri MGos NLar SSta WPat
- 'Glen Gold'	GKin MBlu NLar
- 'Heltorf' **new**	NLar
- 'Purgatory'	MBlu

Liriope ✿ (*Asparagaceae*)

	'Big Blue'	see *L. muscari* 'Big Blue'
§	***exiliflora***	CLAP NLar WCot WWEG
	- 'Ariaka-janshige' (v)	LRHS WWEG
	- Silvery Sunproof misapplied	see *L. spicata* 'Gin-ryu', *L. muscari* 'Variegata'
§	***gigantea***	CLAP EPPr
	graminifolia misapplied	see *L. muscari*
	hyacinthifolia	see *Reineckea carnea*
	koreana	EBee EPPr GCal
	- B&SWJ 8821	WCru
	'Majestic'	CBct CLAP MHer WFar WHoo
	'Minnow'	WCot
	minor	CMac
§	***muscari*** ♀H4	Widely available
	- B&SWJ 561	WCru
	- 'Alba'	see *L. muscari* 'Monroe White'
	- Amethyst = 'Liptp'	LAst NPri
§	- 'Big Blue'	CAbb CBct CLAP CMac CPLG EBee ECtt ELan ELon EPPr EPfP EPri EShb LAst LEdu LHop LRHS LSRN MRav MSwo NLar SBfd SEND SUsu SWvt WMoo WWEG
	- 'Christmas Tree'	EPPr WHoo WMoo WWEG
	- 'Evergreen Giant'	see *L. gigantea*
	- 'Gold-banded' (v)	CBct CLAP EBee EPPr EPfP LHop LRHS NSti WCot WFar
	- 'Goldfinger'	CPLG EBee
	- 'Ingwersen'	CPLG EBee ECho EHrv ELon EPPr EPfP LRHS NMRc XLum
	- Isabella = 'Lirf' **new**	EBee
	- 'John Burch' (v)	CBct CLAP CPLG EBee ELon EShb LAst LHop NLar NOak SMad WGrn WWEG
	- 'Lilac Wonder' **new**	EPPr
	- 'Majestic' misapplied	see *L. exiliflora*
	- 'Moneymaker'	EBee ECtt EPPr LAst LRHS XEll
§	- 'Monroe White'	CBct CLAP CMac CPLG EBee ECha EHrv ELan ELon EPPr EPfP EShb LAst LEdu LRHS MBri MRav NBid NLar NOak SPer SPet WAul WCot WFar WWEG
	- 'Okina' (v)	CKno CYeo EBee ECtt ELon EWes GEdr LLHF MAvo MCot NLar NMyG NSti SMad SPer SPlb WCot WRHF
	- 'Paul Aden'	EBee EPfP WPGP
	- 'Pee Dee Ingot'	EBee ECtt EPPr EShb LRHS LSou NLar
	- 'Royal Purple'	CBct CLAP EBee ELon EPPr EPfP NGdn NLar SBfd SPer WGrn WWEG
	- 'Silver Ribbon'	CBro CLAP CWGN EBee EPfP EWhm LRHS LSRN MGos NOak WWEG
	- 'Super Blue'	EPPr
	- 'Superba'	WCot
§	- 'Variegata' (v)	CCon CDes CKno CLAP CPLG EAEE EBee ECho EHrv ELan EPPr EPfP EWes LAst LEdu LRHS MAsh NBir NOak NSti SBfd SMrm SPer SPoG SWvt WCot WFar WPGP WWEG
	- variegated, white-flowered (v)	CCon ECho
	- 'Webster Wideleaf'	EBee WCot
	platyphylla	see *L. muscari*
	'Samantha'	ECha NOak SBch
	spicata	EBee ECho WWEG XLum
	- 'Alba'	ECho MRav WTin
§	- 'Gin-ryu' (v)	CBct CLAP CMac CPLG CPrp EBee ELan ELon EPPr EShb EWes LEdu LSRN MBri MRav SLPl SMad SPer WCot WWEG XLum
	- 'Silver Dragon'	see *L. spicata* 'Gin-ryu'
	- 'Small Green'	WWEG

Listera (*Orchidaceae*)

ovata	WHer

Litchi (*Sapindaceae*)

chinensis	CCCN

Lithocarpus ✿ (*Fagaceae*)

cleistocarpa	CHEx
edulis	CGHE CHEx CPLG EBee SKHP WPGP

Lithodora (*Boraginaceae*)

§	***diffusa***	ECho MWat SGol SRot
	- 'Alba'	CTri ECho GEdr GKev MGos NCGa SPer SPoG WFar
	- 'Baby Barbara'	GKev
	- 'Cambridge Blue'	NWad
	- 'Compacta'	EWes WAbe WPat
§	- 'Grace Ward' ♀H4	EPfP LLHF MMuc WAbe WPat
§	- 'Heavenly Blue' ♀H4	Widely available
	- 'Inverleith'	ECho EWes LLHF
	- 'Pete's Favourite'	ECtt LLHF WAbe
	- 'Picos'	CMea ECho EPot NLar NMen NSla WAbe WPat WThu
	- 'Star' PBR	CMHG EPfP EPot LRHS MAvo NCGa NLar SCoo SPer SPoG SRot SWvt WIce
	fruticosa	CArn
	× ***intermedia***	see *Moltkia* × *intermedia*
§	***oleifolia*** ♀H4	ECho EPot LLHF LRHS MWat NBir NMen NRHS SBch
	rosmarinifolia	WCFE
	zahnii	ECho EPot LHop LLHF LRHS
	- 'Azureness'	CSpe WAbe

Lithophragma (*Saxifragaceae*)

parviflorum	EWes WAbe

Lithospermum (*Boraginaceae*)

diffusum	see *Lithodora diffusa*
doerfleri	see *Moltkia doerfleri*
'Grace Ward'	see *Lithodora diffusa* 'Grace Ward'
'Heavenly Blue'	see *Lithodora diffusa* 'Heavenly Blue'
officinale	CArn GPoy NMir
oleifolium	see *Lithodora oleifolia*
purpureocaeruleum	see *Buglossoides purpurocaerulea*

Litsea (*Lauraceae*)

glauca	see *Neolitsea sericea*

Littonia (*Colchicaceae*)

modesta	CPne CRHN ECho

Livistona (*Arecaceae*)

australis	EAmu
chinensis ♀H1	CPHo EAmu SBig

decora	EAmu
nitida	EAmu SChr
saribus	EAmu

Loasa (*Loasaceae*)

triphylla var. ***volcanica***	EWes WSHC

Lobelia (*Campanulaceae*)

aberdarica	CHEx
angulata	see *Pratia angulata*
bridgesii	CDTJ CPLG EBee EWes GCal NGBl WHer WHil WKif WMoo WPGP
§ ***cardinalis*** ♀H3	CArn CHEx CMac CRWN EHon ELon EPfP GMaP LPBA LRHS NGBl NLar NPer SMrm SPer SPet SPlb SRms SWat SWvt WFar WMAq
- 'Bee's Flame'	CCon CPrp CWGN GBuc LBMP LRHS MCot MRav MSpe NBre NEgg NGdn SPad
§ - 'Elmfeuer'	CMHG EBee ECtt EHoe EPfP EShb LAst LSou NLar NPri SBfd SPlb SWvt XLum
- 'Eulalia Berridge'	EBee ECtt NPnk SMrm WSHC
- subsp. ***graminea*** var. ***multiflora***	CCon
§ - 'Queen Victoria' ♀H3	Widely available
N - 'Russian Princess' misapplied	CWCL EPfP LRHS MAsh NGdn NPnk SWvt WWEG
'Cinnabar Deep Red'	see *L.* × *speciosa* 'Fan Tiefrot'
'Cinnabar Rose'	see *L.* × *speciosa* 'Fan Zinnoberrosa'
Compliment Blue	see *L.* × *speciosa* 'Kompliment Blau'
Compliment Deep Red	see *L.* × *speciosa* 'Kompliment Tiefrot'
Compliment Purple	see *L.* × *speciosa* 'Kompliment Purpur'
Compliment Scarlet	see *L.* × *speciosa* 'Kompliment Scharlach'
Elizabeth Strangman selection	NDov
erinus Big Blue = 'Weslobigblue'PBR	LAst
- Cascade Series ♀H3 **new**	SEND
- 'Crystal Palace' ♀H3 **new**	NPri SEND
- 'Kathleen Mallard' (d)	CCCN LAst SWvt
- 'Purple Star'	LBMP LSou
- 'Richardii'	see *L. richardsonii*
- 'String of Pearls' ♀H3 **new**	SEND
- 'Waterfall Light Blue With Eye' (Waterfall Series)	NPri
excelsa	MTPN
- B&SWJ 9513	WCru
Fan Deep Red	see *L.* × *speciosa* 'Fan Tiefrot'
Fan Deep Rose	see *L.* × *speciosa* 'Fan Orchidrosa'
Fan Salmon	see *L.* × *speciosa* 'Fan Lachs'
'Flamingo'	see *L.* × *speciosa* 'Pink Flamingo'
fulgens	see *L. cardinalis*
- Saint Elmo's Fire	see *L. cardinalis* 'Elmfeuer'
× ***gerardii***	see *L.* × *speciosa*
gibberoa	CDTJ CHEx
'Gladys Lindley'	NLar
'Hadspen Purple'PBR	see *L.* × *speciosa* 'Hadspen Purple'
inflata	CArn EOHP GPoy
kalmii	WPer
laxiflora	CFis CHll SHom
- B&SWJ 9064	WCru
- var. ***angustifolia***	CDTJ CHEx CPrp CSam EBee ECtt EPfP EWld GCal LRHS SMHy SMrm SPav SRms
linnaeoides	SPlb
'Lipstick'	WWEG
montana	EWld
- B&SWJ 8220	WCru
pedunculata	see *Pratia pedunculata*
'Pink Passion'	LRHS
'Queen Victoria'	see *L. cardinalis* 'Queen Victoria'
§ ***richardsonii*** ♀H1+3	LAst SWvt
sessilifolia	CPLG EBee LPBA WCot WPer
- B&SWJ 8875	WCru
siphilitica	Widely available
- 'Alba'	CEnt CSam EBee EPfP GCal LPBA LRHS SBch SBfd SPav SRms SWat SWvt WBor WFar WHrl WMnd WMoo WPer WShi XLum
- blue-flowered	CSpe NCGa NLar SWat SWvt
- 'Rosea'	MNrw
§ × ***speciosa***	CEnt IKil NBre SVic SWat WBor WFar WMoo XLum
- 'Butterfly Blue'	EBee LBMP SPad
- 'Butterfly Rose'	SRot
- 'Cherry Ripe'	CPrp GCra LLHF NHol
- 'Dark Crusader'	CPrp EBee ECtt ELan EPfP LAst LBMP LRHS MCot NDov NHol SAga SMrm SWat WMnd
- Fan Series **new**	MRav
- - 'Fan Blau'	EPfP LPot LRHS WWEG
- - 'Fan Burgundy'	CEnt CPrp EPfP LRHS MHer NGdn NLar SPet WHil
§ - - 'Fan Lachs'	EPfP LRHS SAga SPet
§ - - 'Fan Orchidrosa' ♀H3-4	CHEx EPfP LRHS NGdn NLar SPet SRot
- - 'Fan Scharlach' ♀H3-4	EBee EPfP LRHS MAvo MGos NLar SGar SPoG SRot SWvt WHil WShi
§ - - 'Fan Tiefrot' ♀H3-4	EPfP LRHS SPet SRms SWvt WPer
§ - - 'Fan Zinnoberrosa' ♀H3-4	CEnt EBee SRms SRot SWvt WMoo WPer
- 'Grape Knee-high'	EBee EPfP GCra LLHF LSRN
§ - 'Hadspen Purple'PBR	CMHG CMac CSpe CWGN EBee ELan EPfP IPot LRHS LSRN MAsh MBri MCot MRav NCGa NRHS NSti SHar SPoG SWat SWvt
- 'Kimbridge Beet'	CMac
- Kompliment Series	WWEG
§ - - 'Kompliment Blau'	CWat SPet SWvt WPer
§ - - 'Kompliment Purpur'	MNrw SPet SWvt
§ - - 'Kompliment Scharlach' ♀H3-4	CWat EBee EPfP LHop MNrw NHol NPer SPer SPet SWvt WFar WMnd WPer WWEG
§ - - 'Kompliment Tiefrot'	MNrw NLar SMrm SPet SWvt WPer
- 'Monet Moment'	EBee EWes GCal SPoG SWvt
- 'Pauline'	ECtt
- 'Pink Elephant' ♀H4	GCra MDKP NBre SHar WFar WWEG
§ - 'Pink Flamingo'	LRHS NLar SPer WFar WMoo WShi
- 'Rosenkavalier'	EBee ECtt MCot WFar
- 'Ruby Slippers'	EBee ELan EPfP LRHS LSRN NCGa WWEG
N - 'Russian Princess' purple-flowered	CCon CPrp EBee ECtt EHoe ELan LAst LBMP LHop LPBA LSou MBel MBri MCot MHer MSpe MWat NCGa NDov NHol NRHS SAga SBfd SMrm SPer WFar WMnd
- 'Sparkle deVine'	SMrm
- 'Sparkling Burgundy'	LRHS
- 'Sparkling Ruby'	EBee EPfP LBuc MCot
- 'Tania'	Widely available
§ - 'Vedrariensis'	CMac CPrp CSpe CWib EBee EHon ELan EPfP GBuc LPBA LRHS MBel MCot MHer MMuc MNrw NPnk SBfd

SEND SGar SPer SPoG SRms SWvt WFar WHil WHoo WMnd XLum
- 'Will Scarlet' LRHS
'Star Sky' LSou
'Super Star' **new** LAst LSou
'Tania's Sister' WGrn
treadwellii see *Pratia angulata* 'Treadwellii'
tupa Widely available
- JCA 12527 IBlr
- Archibald's form CPLG GCra WCot
urens CRDP WPGP
valida SWvt
- 'Delft Blue' **new** NPri
- 'True Blue' CWGN EPfP SWvt
vedrariensis see *L.* × *speciosa* 'Vedrariensis'
wollastonii SPlb

Lobularia (*Brassicaceae*)

maritima Easter Bonnet Series ♀H3 **new** NPri
- 'Snow Crystals' **new** NPri

Loeselia (*Polemoniaceae*)

mexicana CHll

loganberry see *Rubus* × *loganobaccus*

Lomandra (*Asparagaceae*)

confertifolia ECou
filiformis Savanna Blue = 'Lmf500' ESwi LSou NOak
hystrix SPlb
longifolia ECou GCal LEdu SPlb
- 'Kulnura' ECou
- Nyalla = 'Lm400'PBR LHop
- 'Orford' ECou
- Tanika = 'Lm300'PBR EBee ESwi LTen NOak

Lomaria see *Blechnum*

Lomatia (*Proteaceae*)

dentata LRHS MRav
ferruginea CBcs CDoC CPLG EPfP IDee SKHP WCru WPGP
fraseri EPfP LRHS SSpi
hirsuta SKHP
longifolia see *L. myricoides*
§ ***myricoides*** CBcs CCCN CDoC CPLG CTsd EBee ELan EPfP LRHS MAsh MBri NLar SHil SKHP SLon SPer SSpi
silaifolia LRHS
tinctoria CBcs CDoC CPLG EBee EPfP GBin IDee LRHS MAsh NLar SSpi

Lomatium (*Apiaceae*)

foeniculaceum subsp. ***fimbriatum*** NNS 06-349 WCot
grayi SPhx

Lonicera ✿ (*Caprifoliaceae*)

sp. CMen
B&SWJ 2654 from Sikkim WCru
KR 291 ELon
SDR 6044 GKev
§ ***acuminata*** CCon EBee LRHS WWau
- B&SWJ 3480 WCru
- B&SWJ 6743 WCru
- B&SWJ 6815 WCru
alberti MBNS MMuc NLar SEND WWau
alseuosmoides CDul EBee IArd LRHS NLar SEND SKHP SLon SPoG WCru WPGP WSHC WWau
× ***americana*** misapplied see *L.* × *italica*
§ × ***americana*** (Miller) K. Koch CBcs CRHN EPfP MGos MRav MSwo MWhi NLar NWea SEND SKHP SLim SRms WBor WWau
§ × ***brownii*** 'Dropmore Scarlet' Widely available
- 'Fuchsioides' misapplied see *L.* × *brownii* 'Dropmore Scarlet'
- 'Fuchsioides' K. Koch EBee WSHC
caerulea EPPr MRav
- var. ***altaica*** LEdu
- var. ***edulis*** CAgr LBuc LEdu MCoo WWau
- var. ***kamtschatica*** CAgr EPom NLar WWau
§ ***caprifolium*** ♀H4 CDoC CRHN EBee ELan EPfP LRHS NLar SPer WWau
- 'Anna Fletcher' CRHN CSPN LSRN WCFE
- 'Cornish Cream' SGol
- f. ***pauciflora*** see *L.* × *italica*
chaetocarpa MRav WSHC
chamissoi NLar
'Clavey's Dwarf' see *L.* × *xylosteoides* 'Clavey's Dwarf'
crassifolia SBrt WCot
- 'Little Honey' EPPr MMHG MRav WCot WWau
deflexicalyx EPfP NLar WWau
'Early Cream' see *L. caprifolium*
elisae CAbP CJun CMac EPfP NLar WPat WSHC
etrusca CCon MRav
- 'Donald Waterer' ♀H4 CRHN EBee EPfP LRHS LSRN NLar WFar WGor WWau
- 'Michael Rosse' EBee IArd LRHS MBNS SKHP SRms WWau
- 'Superba' ♀H4 CRHN EBee ELan EPfP LRHS NLar SEND SLim SPer SPoG WFar WSHC WWau
'Fire Cracker' EBee SLon
flexuosa see *L. japonica* var. *repens*
fragrantissima Widely available
giraldii misapplied see *L. acuminata*
giraldii Rehder EBee EPfP MRav SLim WWau
glabrata SCoo SLim WWau
- B&SWJ 2150 WCru
glaucescens **new** WPat
'Golden Trumpet' CWGN LRHS LSRN WWau
grata see *L.* × *americana* (Miller) K. Koch
× ***heckrottii*** CDoC CRHN CSBt ECtt MGos NLar
§ - 'American Beauty' EBee WWau
- 'Gold Flame' misapplied see *L.* × *heckrottii* 'American Beauty'
- 'Gold Flame' ambig. GKin LSRN LTen NLar WWau
- 'Gold Flame' hort. CDul CMac COlW EBee ELan EPfP LBuc LRHS MAsh MBri MGos MRav SBfd SLim SPer SPoG SRms WFar WMoo WSHC
§ ***henryi*** Widely available
- B&SWJ 8109 WCru
- Sich 1489 WPGP
- 'Copper Beauty'PBR CCon EBee ECrN EPPr GKin IBoy LBMP LBuc LHop LRHS LSRN LSou MAsh MGos MRav MWat NLar NPri NRHS SGol SLon SPoG WPGP WWau
- var. ***subcoriacea*** see *L. henryi*
hildebrandiana CCCN CHll CPLG CRHN EBee EUJe LRHS MOWG SKHP WPGP

	Name	Suppliers
	'Honey Baby'PBR	EBee ELon EPfP LLHF LRHS MAsh NHol NWad
	insularis	see *L. morrowii*
	involucrata	CHll CMCN CMHG CPLG CWib EPPr GQui LHop MBNS MBlu MMuc NChi SEND SPer WCFE WFar
	- var. ***ledebourii***	CEnt EBee ELan EPfP LAst LLHF LRHS MRav SDys SKHP WGob
	- 'Orange Dwarf'	SKHP
§	× ***italica*** ♀H4	CRHN CSam CTri EBee ECtt LRHS MBNS MSwo NEgg NPer SCoo SKHP SPer WFar
§	- Harlequin = 'Sherlite'PBR (v)	CMac CSPN EBee EHoe EPfP GKin LHop LRHS LSRN MGos SLim SPlb SRms SWvt
	japonica	CCVT CMen IBoy MHoo
§	- 'Aureoreticulata' (v)	CDul CMac CWib EBee ECrN EHoe ELan EPfP EShb LRHS LSRN MGos MRav MWhi NPer SGol SPer SPet SRms WFar WWau
	- 'Cream Cascade'	COlW EBee LRHS MSwo NLar SCoo SGol WWau
	- 'Dart's Acumen'	CRHN
	- 'Dart's World'	EBee MBri WFar WWau
	- 'Halliana' ♀H4	Widely available
	- 'Hall's Prolific'	CDoC CDul CSBt CWSG EBee ECrN ELan EPfP LBuc LRHS LSRN MAsh MBlu MBri MGos MHer MRav MSwo MWat NEgg SBfd SGol SLim SPad SPoG SWvt WFar
§	- 'Horwood Gem' (v)	EBee ECtt LSRN NLar SCoo SLim WFar WWau
	- 'Maskerade' (v)	LLHF NBro NLar WWau
	- 'Mint Crisp'PBR (v)	CDul CMac CSBt CSPN CWGN CWSG EBee ECrN ECtt ELan EPfP LAst LRHS LSRN LSou MBri MGos MWat NLar SBfd SGol SLim SLon SPad SPer SPoG SWvt WFar
	- 'Peter Adams'	see *L. japonica* 'Horwood Gem'
	- 'Red World'	WWau
§	- var. ***repens*** ♀H4	CDul CMac COlW CSBt CTri CWSG EBee ECrN ECtt ELan EPfP LAst LRHS MBri MRav MSwo MWat NLar SCoo SGol SLPl SLim SLon SPad SPer SRms WFar WMoo
	- 'Variegata'	see *L. japonica* 'Aureoreticulata'
	korolkowii	CJun EPPr EPfP MBNS NBir NLar SEND SPoG WCFE WSHC WWau
	- 'Blue Velvet'	MCoo NLar WWau
	- var. ***zabelii*** misapplied	see *L. tatarica* 'Zabelii'
	- var. ***zabelii*** (Rehder) Rehder	ELan
	lanceolata BWJ 7935	WCru
	maackii	CHll CJun CMCN EBee EPPr EPfP IGor MMHG MRav NLar WCFE WWau
	- f. ***podocarpa***	SPoG
*	***macgregorii***	CMCN
	macrantha B&SWJ 11687	WCru
	- WWJ 11606	WCru
	'Mandarin'	CDoC CRHN EBee ELan LRHS MBlu MGos NLar SCoo SGol SLim SWvt WPat WSHC WWau
	maximowiczii var. ***sachalinensis***	WWau
§	***morrowii***	CMCN
	nitida	CBar CBcs CCVT CDul CMac CMen CSBt CTri ECrN EPfP NWea SBfd SEND SEWo SGol SPer SWal WFar WHar WWau
	- 'Baggesen's Gold' ♀H4	Widely available
	- 'Eden Spring'	NPro
	- Edmée Gold = 'Briloni'	MAsh
	- 'Elegant'	WWau
	- 'Ernest Wilson'	WWau
	- 'Fertilis'	SPer
	- 'Lemon Beauty' (v)	Widely available
	- 'Lemon Queen'	CWib ELan MSwo SEND WWau
	- 'Lemon Spreader'	CBcs
§	- 'Maigrün'	CBar CBcs CCVT CDul EBee EPfP MSwo NPro SBfd SPer SWvt WFar WWau
	- Maygreen	see *L. nitida* 'Maigrün'
	- 'Red Tips'	EHoe EPfP GKin MGos SBfd SCoo WFar WMoo WWau
	- 'Silver Beauty' (v)	CDul CMac CWib EBee ECrN EHoe EPfP LAst LHop MGos MSwo NEgg SAga SBfd SPer SPlb SRms SWvt WFar WMoo WWau
	- 'Twiggy' (v)	CDoC CSBt EDAr EHoe ELon LBuc LHop LRHS MAsh NEgg NHol NLar SBfd WGrn WWau
	periclymenum	CArn CCVT CRWN CTri ECrN GPoy MHer MLHP MRav NLar NMir NWea SPlb WPnn WSFF
	- 'Belgica' misapplied	see *L.* × *italica*
	- 'Belgica'	Widely available
	- Caprilia Imperial = 'Inov86'	SBfd
	- 'Florida'	see *L. periclymenum* 'Serotina'
	- 'Graham Thomas' ♀H4	Widely available
	- 'Harlequin'PBR	see *L.* × *italica* Harlequin
	- 'Heaven Scent'	EBee LBuc LSRN MNHC NLar WFar WPnn WWau
	- 'Honeybush'	CDoC CJun CSPN CWGN LBMP MAsh MBri MGos NHol NWad SLim WMoo
	- 'La Gasnérie'	EBee SLim WPnn WWau
	- 'Munster'	WPnn WSHC
	- 'Red Gables'	CRHN CWan EBee ELon LSRN MBNS MGos NLar SCoo SEND SLim WCot WGor WKif WPat WPnn WWau
	- 'Scentsation'PBR	CMac CSBt CWGN EBee EPfP LAst LBMP LBuc LRHS MAsh MBri NCGa NLar SCoo SLon SPoG WWau
N	- 'Serotina' ♀H4	Widely available
	- 'Sweet Sue'	COlW CRHN CSPN CSpe EBee ECtt ELan ELon EPfP LBuc LRHS LSRN MAsh MBNS MBri MGos MLHP MSwo NEgg SCoo SPoG SWvt WFar WMoo WWau
	- yellow	NEgg
	pileata	CBcs CCVT CDoy CDul CMac CSBt CTri EBee ECrN EHoe ELan EPfP EShb EWTr LBuc LRHS MGos MRav MSwo MWhi NPer NWea SBfd SGol SPer SPoG SRms WCFE WFar WHar
	- 'Craibstone Compact' **new**	SLPl
	- 'Loughall Evergreen' **new**	SLPl
	- 'Moss Green'	CDoC EBee
	- 'Pilot'	SLPl
	- 'Silver Lining' (v)	WCFE
	- 'Stockholm'	SLPl
	pilosa Willd. F&M 207	WPGP
	- F&M 256	WPGP

	× ***purpusii***	CDoC CHll CMac COlW CRHN CTri CWSG CWib EBee ECrN EPfP LSRN MBNS MGos MLHP MWat SBfd SPer SRms WCFE WFar WSHC
	- 'Spring Romance'	CMac
	- 'Winter Beauty' ♀H4	Widely available
	ramosissima	NLar WWau
	saccata	CJun EPfP
	sempervirens ♀H4	CMac CRHN CSBt EBee MBNS MRav WFar WSHC
	- 'Cedar Lane'	CRHN EBee LRHS
	- 'Dropmore Scarlet'	see *L.* × *brownii* 'Dropmore Scarlet'
	- 'Leo'	CWGN
N	- f. ***sulphurea***	EPfP WSHC
	- - 'John Clayton'	EBee LRHS SKHP
	setifera 'Daphnis'	CJun EPfP
	similis var. ***delavayi*** ♀H4	CRHN CSPN CWGN EBee ELan EPfP LRHS MAsh MBri MNHC MRav NEgg SBfd SDix SEND SLPl SRms WCot WCru WFar WPGP WSHC
	splendida	WSHC
	'Spring Bouquet'	LRHS
	standishii	CTri WFar
	- 'Budapest'	EBee LEdu LLHF LRHS MAsh MBlu MBri MRav NLar SPoG WPat WWau
	stenantha	IGor
	subaequalis	CGHE
	- Og 93.329	SKHP WPGP WSHC
	Sweet Isabel = 'Genbel'PBR	CWGN EBee EPfP LRHS SKHP
	syringantha	CArn CRHN EBee ECrN ELan EPfP EWTr LAst LEdu MBri MGos MMuc MNrw MRav MWhi NEgg NLar NPro SEND SLPl SPer WBor WCFE WFar WPat WSHC WWau
	- 'Grandiflora'	GQui
	tatarica	CHll CMCN CWib EBee MRav WWau
	- 'Alba'	CJun EBee EPPr EWTr
	- 'Arnold Red'	CBcs EBee ELan EPPr EPfP MBlu MHer NLar SEND WBor
	- 'Hack's Red'	CWib EBee ELon EPPr EPfP LHop LRHS LSou MRav SAga SCoo SKHP SMDP SPer SPoG SWvt WFar WWau
	- 'Rosea'	EPPr
§	- 'Zabelii'	EBee EPfP EWTr
	× ***tellmanniana***	CBar CBcs CDoC CDul CMac CPLG CRHN EBee ECtt ELan EPfP LBMP LRHS LSRN MAsh MBri MSwo NEgg SAga SBfd SEND SLim SPer SPet SRms WFar WSHC
	- 'Joan Sayers'	EBee LSRN SCoo SLim WCFE
	thibetica	MBlu SPer
	tragophylla ♀H4	CDoC CDoy CSBt EBee ELan EPfP LRHS LSRN MAsh MBNS MBri MRav SCoo SEND SLim SPer SSpi SWvt WPat WSHC WWau
	- 'Maurice Foster'	ELan MBNS SMDP WSHC
	- 'Pharaoh's Trumpet'	EBee EPfP LRHS SLon WWau
	vesicaria	WWau
	webbiana	ELan WWau
§	× ***xylosteoides*** 'Clavey's Dwarf'	EBee EPPr GKin LLHF
	xylosteum	CArn EBee EBtc EPPr NLar WWau

Lophomyrtus (*Myrtaceae*)

§	***bullata***	CAbP CDTJ CTrC SPer WFar
	- 'Matai Bay'	CTrC EBee
	× ***ralphii*** 'Black Pearl'	CTrC CWGN EBee EShb LBuc LRHS MBri SBfd SCoo SHil SLim SPoG SPtl SRkn
	- 'Gloriosa' (v)	CDoC CTrC EPfP
	- 'Kathryn'	CBcs CDoC EBee ELan EPfP LRHS NLar SPoG SRGP
	- 'Little Star' (v)	CBcs CDoC CTrC LRHS SLim SPoG WPat
	- Logan's form (v)	CBcs EBee LRHS SEND
	- 'Magic Dragon' (v) **new**	SPoG
	- 'Multicolor' (v)	CBcs CTrC EBee EPfP LRHS NPri SLim
	- 'Pixie'	CBcs CDoC CTrC EBee EPfP LRHS MAsh MGos SEND SLim SPoG WPat
	- 'Purpurea' **new**	MPkF
	- 'Red Dragon'	CBcs CMac CTrC CWSG EBee IDee LEdu LRHS LSou MAsh SLim WFar WPat
	- 'Red Pixie'	CDoC
	- 'Red Wing'	LRHS
§	- 'Traversii' (v)	SPoG
	- 'Tricolor' (v)	WFar
	- 'Wild Cherry'	CTrC LRHS

Lophosoria (*Dicksoniaceae*)

	quadripinnata	CBty CCon CDTJ CKel EAmu SBig WPGP

Lophospermum (*Plantaginaceae*)

	'Cream Delight'	CCCN
§	***erubescens*** ♀H2-3	CRHN SBch SGar
§	'Magic Dragon'	LSou SEND SLim SVic
§	'Red Dragon'	CCCN EShb SBch SGar
§	***scandens***	CCCN CRHN
	- 'Mystic Rose' **new**	NPri
	'Summer Cream'	LAst
	'Wine Red'	LAst WBor

loquat see *Eriobotrya japonica*

Loropetalum (*Hamamelidaceae*)

	chinense	CWib
	- Black Pearl	see *L. chinense* 'Pearl'
	- 'China Pink'	CBcs
	- 'Ming Dynasty'	CAbP CTrC MAsh SEND SSta
§	- 'Pearl'	CWSG
	- 'Rose Blush'	ECho
	- f. ***rubrum***	CBcs CPLG CWib
	- - 'Blush'	CJun EBee SBfd SSpi
	- - 'Burgundy'	CTrC MPkF
	- - 'Daybreak's Flame'	CJun CTrC LRHS MPkF SSta WGob
	- - 'Fire Dance'	CAbP CBcs CCCN CDoC CHll CJun CPLG CTrC EBee ELon EPfP IDee LRHS MAsh MGos MPkF SBfd SEND SPad SPoG SPtl SRkn SSpi SWvt WCot WFar WGrn WHlf WPat
	- - 'Fire Glow'	LRHS SHil
	- - 'Pipa's Red'	MGos MPkF
	- 'Snowdance'	CAbP
	- 'Tang Dynasty'	CTrC ESwi LRHS SSta

Lotus (*Papilionaceae*)

	berthelotii	CCCN CDTJ CHEx ECtt ELan EOHP EUJe LPot MCot SBfd SEND SPet
	- deep red-flowered ♀H1+3	SBfd SWvt
	berthelotii × ***maculatus*** ♀H1+3	CCCN MSCN

corniculatus	CArn CHab MCoo MHer MMuc MNHC NLan NMir SEND SIde WSFF XLum
- 'Plenus' (d)	EPot NLar WPer
'Gold Flash'	LAst SBfd SEND
hirsutus ♀H3-4	Widely available
- 'Brimstone' (v)	CWSG CWib ECtt LHop LRHS MRav SBfd SPer SPoG SWvt XSen
- Little Boy Blue = 'Lisbob'PBR	CSBt EBee EPfP LBMP LRHS LSou LSqu MAsh SBfd SPoG SSpi
- 'Lois'	EPfP LHop LRHS MDKP SPoG WPGP
jacobaeus	MCot
maculatus	EOHP EUJe MOWG SMrm SPet
maritimus	CPom SRot
pedunculatus	CHab MCoo NMir WSFF
pentaphyllus	NLar XSen
tetragonolobus	CPom SPhx SVic

lovage see *Levisticum officinale*

Loxostigma (*Gesneriaceae*)

kurzii GWJ 9342	WCru

Ludwigia (*Onagraceae*)

uruguayensis	LPBA

Luetkea (*Rosaceae*)

pectinata	GEdr

Luffa (*Cucurbitaceae*)

aegyptiaca new	SVic

Luma (*Myrtaceae*)

§ ***apiculata*** ♀H3	Widely available
§ - 'Glanleam Gold' (v) ♀H3	Widely available
- 'Nana'	LEdu WJek
- 'Penlee'	WJek
- 'Saint Hilary' (v)	EPfP LRHS SBfd WJek
- 'Variegata' (v)	CMHG CTri SLim
§ ***chequen***	CBcs EBee IDee LRHS MHer NLar WFar WJek WMoo

Lunaria (*Brassicaceae*)

§ ***annua***	MNHC NPri SIde SWat WCot WJek WSFF
- var. ***albiflora*** ♀H4	MMuc NBir SEND SUsu SWat WCot
I - - 'Alba Variegata' (v)	CSpe LBMP WBrk WTin
- 'Chedglow'	CNat
- 'Corfu Blue'	CDes CSpe EDif WCot
- 'Munstead Purple'	CSpe
- 'Nettleton'	CNat
- 'Variegata' (v)	NBir SWat WCot WHer
- violet-flowered	NBir
biennis	see *L. annua*
rediviva	CSpe EBee ECGP ECha EPPr GAbr GBin GCal GCra IBlr IFro LEdu LRHS MHer MMuc NBid NPer NSti SEND SUsu WFar WHer WPGP
- 'Partway White'	WCot

Lunathyrium (*Woodsiaceae*)

pycnosorum	ISha

Lupinus ✿ (*Papilionaceae*)

'African Sunset'	CWCL
albus	CArn
'Animal'	CWCL
'Approaching Storm'	SMrm
arboreus ♀H4	Widely available
- blue and white-flowered	NChi
- 'Blue Boy'	EBee ELan LSRN
- blue-flowered	CTrC CWCL LRHS MCot SBfd SPer SPlb SPoG SWvt WCot WFar
- 'Chelsea Blue'	EPfP LRHS
- prostrate	MDKP
- 'Rhubarb and Custard'	CWCL
- 'Snow Queen'	CWCL LRHS SPoG
- 'Sulphur Yellow'	SWvt
- white-flowered	CSpe MCot SPlb
- yellow and blue-flowered	NBir SRkn
- yellow-flowered	CTrC ELan MCot MLHP WWEG
arcticus	CSpe EBee
Band of Nobles Series ♀H4	WFar
'Beefeater'	CWCL EBee LLHF
'Bishop's Tipple'	CWCL EWes
'Blossom'PBR	CWCL CWGN EBee GBin IPot LLHF LRHS LSRN MBri SPoG
'Blue Streak'	CWCL
'Brimstone'	CWCL
'Bruiser'	CWCL
'Bubblegum'	CWCL
'Camelot Blue'	EPfP
'Carmen'	CWCL
'Chameleon'	CWCL GBin LRHS
chamissonis	CHll CSpe CWCL ELan EWes LHop LRHS MCot SMrm SPer
'Chandelier' (Band of Nobles Series)	CBcs CSBt CTri EBee ECtt ELan ELon EPfP IBoy LHop LRHS MAsh MBri MCot MNHC MWat NBir NGBl NPri NRHS SBfd SHil SMrm SPer SPoG SWvt WCAu WFar WMnd XLum
'Desert Sun'	CWCL EBee
'Dwarf Lulu'	see *L.* 'Lulu'
Gallery Series	CSBt MAsh SCoo SPlb WFar
- 'Gallery Blue'	ECtt ELan EPfP LRHS LSRN NLar NPri SCoo SMrm SPer SPoG WFar
- 'Gallery Pink'	ELan EPfP LRHS NLar NPri SCoo SMrm SPer SPoG WFar
- 'Gallery Red'	ECtt ELan EPfP GAbr LRHS NLar NPri SCoo SMrm SPer SPoG WFar
- 'Gallery Rose'	LSRN SPoG
- 'Gallery White'	ELan EPfP GAbr LRHS NLar NPri SCoo SPer SPoG WFar
- 'Gallery Yellow'	ECtt ELan EPfP GAbr LRHS NLar NPri SPer SPoG
'Gladiator'	CWCL EBee EWes LLHF SPoG
'Heathcliffe Blue'	WOut
'Imperial Robe'	CWCL
'Inspiration'	CWCL
'Le Gentilhomme' (Band of Nobles Series)	MCot XLum
'Lindy Lou'	CWCL
§ 'Lulu'	EPfP LRHS MWat SBfd SPer SPoG SWvt WFar WMoo
'Manhattan Lights'PBR	CWCL CWGN EWes IPot LLHF LRHS MBri
'Masterpiece'PBR	CWCL LLHF LRHS MBri
Minarette Group	CTri LRHS SPet SRms WFar
'Morello Cherry'	CWCL
'Mrs Perkins'	SMrm
'My Castle' (Band of Nobles Series)	CBcs CSBt CTri EBee ECtt ELan EPfP LBMP LRHS LSRN MAsh MBri MGos MNHC MWat NGBl NPri NRHS SBfd SHil SMrm SPer SPoG SWal SWvt WFar WMnd WMoo XLum

'Neptune'	CWCL
'Noble Maiden' (Band of Nobles Series)	Widely available
nootkatensis	GLog LDai LRHS
'Pauly'	CWCL
'Pen and Ink'	CWCL
perennis	LRHS
'Persian Slipper' PBR	CWCL CWGN EWes GBin IPot LLHF LRHS MBri SPoG
'Pluto'	CWCL
'Polar Princess'	EWes LRHS SWat
propinquus	CEnt SPhx
'Purple Emperor' **new**	EBee
'Queen of Hearts'	EBee
'Red Arrow'	CWCL
'Red Rum' PBR	CWCL CWGN GBin LBuc LRHS MBri SPoG
'Redhead'	CWCL
'Rote Flamme'	CPrp EWes SMrm WOut XLum
Russell hybrids	CSBt EPfP LAst MHer MLHP SBfd SEND SGar SPet SPlb SRms SVic SWvt WFar
'Saffron' PBR	CWCL GBin LRHS LSRN MBri
'Salmon Star' PBR	CWCL GBin LRHS SPoG
'Sand Pink'	EWes
'Silver Fleece'	WHer
'Snowgoose'	CWCL
'Tequila Flame'	CWCL EBee GBin IPot LLHF LRHS MBri
'Terracotta'	CWCL EBee GBin SPoG
texensis	CSpe
'The Chatelaine' (Band of Nobles Series)	Widely available
'The Governor' (Band of Nobles Series)	Widely available
'The Page' (Band of N obles Series)	CBcs EBee ELan ELon EPfP LHop LRHS LSRN MAsh MBel MBri MCot MNHC MWat NPri SBfd SMrm SPer SPoG SWvt WCFE WFar WMnd WMoo XLum
'Thundercloud'	CDes SMrm
'Towering Inferno'	CWCL EBee EWes
variicolor	CHid LDai SMHy SMad
Woodfield hybrids	SMrm

Luzula (*Juncaceae*)

alpinopilosa	EPPr GBin MMHG
× ***borreri***	EPPr
- 'Botany Bay' (v)	EPPr GBin WWEG
'Engel'	EPPr EWes
luzuloides	WPtf
- 'Schneehäschen'	GBin GCal NWsh WSHC
maxima	see *L. sylvatica*
nivalis	GAbr
nivea	Widely available
- 'Lucius'	LTen
- 'Schattenkind'	EBee
pedemontana	EPPr SMea
pilosa	GCal
- 'Igel'	CKno EBee LEdu NBid SLPl SMad WWEG
purpureosplendens	LEdu NOak
rufa	ECou
§ ***sylvatica***	CHEx CRWN CRow ELan EPPr EPfP LRHS MMoz MMuc MRav NBro NMir NOrc SBfd SEND WHer WShi WWEG XLum
- from Tatra Mountains, Czechoslovakia	EPPr
- 'A. Rutherford'	see *L. sylvatica* 'Taggart's Cream'
- 'Aurea'	CHEx CKno ECha EPPr EPfP LAst LBMP LRHS MMoz MRav NBid NOak NRHS NSti NWsh SApp SEND WCot WFar WGrn WMoo WPtf
- 'Aureomarginata'	see *L. sylvatica* 'Marginata'
I - 'Auslese'	EPPr EPfP WMoo
- 'Barcode' (v)	CNat
- 'Hohe Tatra'	CElw CPrp CSpe EBee ECtt EHoe EPPr EWes GMaP LEdu MBNS MWhi NBro NGdn NLar NOak SBfd SLPl SPer SPoG WPnP WWEG XLum
§ - 'Marginata' (v)	CHEx CPrp ECha EHoe EPPr GMaP LBMP MAvo MBNS MMoz MMuc MRav MWhi NBid NBro NGdn NSti NWad SEND SLPl SPer SWal WCot WHoo WMoo WWEG XLum
* - f. ***nova***	ELon EPPr
- 'Schattenlicht'	EBee
- 'Solar Flair'	CTrC MWhi WPtf
§ - 'Taggart's Cream' (v)	EHoe MBNS NBid NHol SApp WGrn WMoo WWEG
- 'Tauernpass'	EBee EHoe EPPr GCal SLPl
- 'Wäldler'	EPPr MBNS NHol
ulophylla	ECou WThu

Luzuriaga (*Luzuriagaceae*)

polyphylla HCM 98202	WCru
radicans	CCCN ECou IBlr WCru WSHC
- RH 0602	WCru

Lychnis (*Caryophyllaceae*)

alpina	CMac EBee ECho EDAr EPfP GKev GMaP MAsh NGdn XLum
- 'Rosea'	NBir
- 'Snow Flurry'	EDAr NLar
§ × ***arkwrightii***	ECha ELan LRHS
- 'Orange Zwerg'	CWCL MBNS SMrm
- 'Vesuvius'	CBcs CMac CWGN EAEE EBee LRHS MWat NBir NPnk SMrm SPad SPer SRms STes WMnd WPer WWEG XLum
chalcedonica ♀H4	Widely available
- var. ***albiflora***	EBee EPfP MBel NBro NMRc SMrm WFar WHrl WMoo WPer
- 'Carnea'	LRHS MBNS NBre NGdn SMrm SPhx WPer WWEG
- 'Dusky Salmon'	MDKP WOut
- 'Flore Pleno' (d)	EBee ELan EShb GCal NLar WFar
- 'Morgenrot'	LRHS MBel
- 'Pinkie'	ELan NLar
- 'Rauhreif'	NBre SPhx XLum
- 'Rosea'	EBee EPfP LRHS NBir WFar WHrl WMoo WPer
* - 'Salmonea'	NBir SRms
- 'Summer Sparkle Pink'	SWal
- 'Summer Sparkle Red'	SWal
cognata	MDKP
- B&SWJ 4234	WCru
§ ***coronaria*** ♀H4	Widely available
- MESE 356	SPhx
- 'Abbotswood Rose'	see *L.* × *walkeri* 'Abbotswood Rose'
- 'Alba' ♀H4	Widely available
- 'Angel's Blush'	MDKP NBir SPav SRkn
- Atrosanguinea Group	CBre EBee GMaP IBlr LRHS MBel MRav MSpe NEgg NGdn NPri NRHS NSti NWad SMrm SPer WGwG

- 'Blood Red'	CSpe WRHF
- 'Cerise'	MArl MDKP NBir WRHF
- 'Dancing Ladies'	WMnd
- dark red-flowered **new**	MAvo
- Gardeners' World = 'Blych' (d)	CDes CElw CSpe EBee ECtt ELon EWes LRHS LSou MBNS MBel NGdn NSti SMrm SPer SUsu WBrk WCot WFar
- 'Hutchinson's Cream' (v)	NBir NPro
- Oculata Group	CElw CSpe EBee EPfP LEdu LPot SBfd SGar SMrm SPav SPet SPlb WFar WKif WMoo WWEG
§ ***coronata*** var. ***sieboldii***	SBrt
dioica	see *Silene dioica*
flos-cuculi	CArn CBen CEnt CHab CPom CRWN CWat EBee ECho EHon EHrv EPfP LEdu LPBA MHer MMuc MNHC NLan NMir NPri SEND WHer WMAq WMoo WPnP WSFF WWFP XLum
- var. ***albiflora***	CBre CElw EWld LPBA MSKA NBro NLar WHer WMnd WMoo WWFP
- Jenny = 'Lychjen'PBR (d)	CWCL EBee ELan ELon GQue LAst LBMP LRHS MBNS MBel MNrw NSti SBfd SHar SPoG SRkn SUsu WCot WGrn WHer
- 'Nana'	CBre ECho EDAr GAbr IFro MSKA NGdn NLar SBch
- 'White Robin'	CBre CEnt EHrv EPfP EWTr GQue IFro IKil LBMP LEdu LRHS MBNS MBel MWat NCGa NGdn NPnk SHar SMrm SPoG WAul WBor WFar WPnP WPtf WWEG
flos-jovis ♀H4	ECha EPfP GJos LRHS MBel NBir NLar NRHS SRms WMoo XLum
- 'Alba'	WPtf
- 'Hort's Variety'	EBee LRHS NBir
- 'Minor'	see *L. flos-jovis* 'Nana'
§ - 'Nana'	LRHS MSCN SBch
- 'Peggy'	EShb LRHS NBre NGdn NLar NRHS
fulgens	NBre
× ***haageana***	EBee NLar SRms
- 'Lumina Bronze Leaf Red'	LRHS
'Hill Grounds'	CDes CElw WCot WSHC
lagascae	see *Petrocoptis pyrenaica* subsp. *glaucifolia*
miqueliana	WMoo
'Molten Lava'	EBee EPfP NLar WPer
'Rollie's Favorite'PBR	EBee ECtt MAvo NDov NPri SHil SPoG WBor
* ***sikkimensis***	EBee NBre
'Terry's Pink'	NCGa
§ ***viscaria***	CArn ECha GCra GJos LDai SBch WFar WMoo WTin
- 'Alba'	EBee ECha NBre NBro SBch XLum
- ***alpina***	see *L. viscaria*
§ - subsp. ***atropurpurea***	CFis EBee EWes LSou NBre SBHP SRms WHrl WPtf
- 'Feuer'	EBee EWes GJos LRHS NLar WMoo
- 'Firebird'	EWes NBre
- 'Plena' (d)	NBir SRkn
- 'Schnee'	LRHS NEgg
- 'Splendens'	EPfP SPet XLum
- 'Splendens Plena' (d) ♀H4	EBee NBre NBro SUsu WFar XLum
§ × ***walkeri*** 'Abbotswood Rose' ♀H4	IBlr
§ ***yunnanensis***	EBee GKev NBid SBHP SPhx WPtf XLum
- ***alba***	see *L. yunnanensis*

Lycianthes (*Solanaceae*)

quichensis B&SWJ 10395	WCru
§ ***rantonnetii***	CBcs CCCN CHll ELan EPfP EShb EUJe IDee LRHS MOWG SEND SPer SPoG WWlt
- 'Royal Robe'	CRHN
- 'Variegatum' (v)	CHll EShb MSCN WCot

Lycium (*Solanaceae*)

barbarum	CAgr CBcs CCCN CSpe EBee EPfP EPom EWes IDee LBuc LEdu LRHS MCoo SBfd SEND SMad SPlb SPoG SVic WHar
- 'Big Life Berry' **new**	MCoo
chinense	CArn NLar

Lycopodium (*Lycopodiaceae*)

clavatum	GPoy

Lycopsis see *Anchusa*

Lycopus (*Lamiaceae*)

americanus	CArn
europaeus	CArn CHab ELau GPoy WGwG

Lycoris (*Amaryllidaceae*)

albiflora	ECho WCot
aurea	EBee ECho GHim GKev
haywardii	WCot
incarnata	ECho
radiata	CCCN EBee ECho GBin GHim
sanguinea	ECho
sprengeri	ECho
squamigera	ECho

Lygodium (*Lygodiaceae*)

japonicum	ISha WFib

Lyonia (*Ericaceae*)

ligustrina	NLar
mariana	NLar

Lyonothamnus (*Rosaceae*)

floribundus	CCCN CDoC CGHE CPLG EUJe
subsp. ***aspleniifolius***	NLar SSpi WPGP

Lysichiton (*Araceae*)

americanus ♀H4	Widely available
americanus × ***camtschatcensis***	ECha
camtschatcensis ♀H4	Widely available

Lysimachia ✿ (*Primulaceae*)

albescens	CPLG EBee GKev MCot SPad WHer
§ ***atropurpurea***	CSpe EBee EHrv ELan EPfP GJos LRHS NRHS SBfd SPer SPlb WMnd WWEG
- 'Beaujolais'	CPLG GAbr GJos LPot LRHS LSRN MBri MPie NPnk NPri SHil SMrm SPoG WHil
- 'Geronimo'	CSpe
barystachys	CPrp CSam EBee LPla LRHS MRav NPnk SHar WCot WFar WWEG
Candela = 'Innlyscand'	CSpe LHop LSou MBri SMrm SPoG WHil
candida	WCot

ciliata	CMHG CMac EBee ECha EHoe ELan GMaP MNrw NBir NGdn SWat WCot WMnd
§ - 'Firecracker' ♀H4	Widely available
- 'Purpurea'	see *L. ciliata* 'Firecracker'
clethroides ♀H4	Widely available
- 'Geisha' (v)	EBee EWes LLHF WCot
- 'Lady Jane'	CCon MNrw SRms
§ ***congestiflora***	NPer SPet
- 'Outback Sunset'PBR (v)	LAst
ephemerum	Widely available
fortunei	EBee EWld LRHS MWat SBch
hybrida	WCot
lichiangensis	CPLG GKev LRHS MSCN NBir NRHS WMoo
lyssii	see *L. congestiflora*
mauritiana	LRHS
'Midnight Sun'	LAst
minoricensis	CCon ELan SWat
nemorum subsp. ***azorica***	WCot
- 'Pale Star'	CBre EBee
nummularia	COIW CSBt CTri CWat ECtt EHon EPfP GPoy LPBA NBir SGol SWat WBrk WHfH
- 'Aurea' ♀H4	Widely available
paridiformis	WCot
- var. ***stenophylla***	CPLG
- - DJHC 704	EBee WCot
punctata misapplied	see *L. verticillaris*
punctata L.	CRow CSBt EBee ECha EHon EPfP GMaP MHer MMuc MRav MWat NBro NHol NMir NPer SBfd SEND SGar SPer SPlb SRms SWat WBrk WMAq WMoo WPer WPnP
§ - 'Alexander' (v)	Widely available
- 'Gaulthier Brousse'	EBee WCot WWEG
- Golden Alexander = 'Walgoldalex'PBR (v)	CPLG EBee ELon LRHS MBNS MBel MBri MMuc NHol NLar SBfd SPoG WOut WWEG
- 'Golden Glory' (v)	WCot
- 'Hometown Hero'	EBee
- 'Irish Butter' **new**	WCot
- 'Ivy Maclean' (v)	EBee SWvt WCot WWEG
- 'Variegata'	see *L. punctata* 'Alexander'
- ***verticillata***	see *L. verticillaris*
'Purpurea'	see *L. atropurpurea*
pyramidalis	WPtf WWEG
quadrifolia	EBee
Snow Candles = 'L9902'	CCVN COIW EBee LHop
thyrsiflora	CWat EBee EHon EWay NPer SWat WCot WMAq
§ ***verticillaris***	CTri WCot
vulgaris	CArn CHab CRWN EBee LPBA MSKA SIde WJek WMoo
- subsp. ***davurica***	WCot
- - B&SWJ 8632	WCru

Lysionotus (*Gesneriaceae*)

gamosepalus B&SWJ 7241	WCru
aff. ***kwangsiensis*** HWJ 643	WCru
'Lavender Lady'	CSpe EBee NCGa WHil
pauciflorus	CDes WAbe WSHC
- B&SWJ 189	WCru
- B&SWJ 303	WCru
- B&SWJ 335	WCru
serratus HWJK 2426	WCru

Lythrum (*Lythraceae*)

alatum	NDov
anceps	NBre NLar
salicaria	Widely available
- 'Augenweide'	XLum
- 'Blush' ♀H4	Widely available
- 'Brightness'	WHil
§ - 'Feuerkerze' ♀H4	CKno CMea CPrp EAEE EBee ECtt ELan ELon EPfP LAst LBMP LHop LRHS LSou MBel MBri MCot MNFA MRav MSpe MWts NBir NEgg NHol NSti SAga SPer WFar WHil WWEG
- Firecandle	see *L. salicaria* 'Feuerkerze'
- 'Happy'	ELon LRHS SMrm
- 'Lady Sackville'	EBee ECtt ELon EPPr GBin GMaP IPot LRHS MCot NLar SMrm WSHC WWEG
- 'Little Robert'	SBea
- 'Morden Pink'	EBee MBri MDKP MMuc NLar SEND SPhx SSvw WFar WPtf
- 'Prichard's Variety'	CKno WPGP
- 'Robert'	Widely available
- 'Robin'	EBee LLHF LRHS MAsh MCot SRot SWvt
- 'Rose'	ELan NBir SWvt
- 'Stichflamme'	SMrm
- 'Swirl'	EBee ECtt MDKP NDov NLar SHar SMrm WFar WHoo
- 'The Beacon'	EBee MDKP NLar SRms
- Ulverscroft form	WHil
- 'Zigeunerblut'	CElw CKno CMHG EBee ELon EPPr IPot LHop MDKP MRav NLar SMrm SPhx SSvw SWat
virgatum	CMHG NDov SMHy SPhx SSvw SUsu WCFE WMoo WOut WSHC
- 'Dropmore Purple'	CPrp CSam EBee ECtt ELon EPPr EPfP LAst LHop LRHS LSRN MAsh MBri MCot MDKP MRav MSpe NDov NEgg NPri SPhx WCAu WFar WSHC XLum
- 'Rose Queen'	ECha MDKP NDov SMHy WFar WPer
- 'Rosy Gem'	EBee EPfP GMaP LAst LRHS MWat MWhi NBro SRms SWvt WCFE WFar WPer WWEG
- 'The Rocket'	CSam CTri EBee EPPr EPfP GBee LAst LRHS MRav NBro NDov SPer SWvt WWlt

Lytocaryum (*Arecaceae*)

§ ***weddellianum*** ♀H1	EAmu

M

Maackia (*Papilionaceae*)

amurensis	CBcs CHGN ELan EPfP IArd IDee IVic LRHS WSHC
- var. ***buergeri***	CDul
chinensis	MBlu NLar

Macbridea (*Lamiaceae*)

caroliniana	WPGP

mace, English see *Achillea ageratum*

Macfadyena (*Bignoniaceae*)

uncata	MOWG
§ ***unguis-cati***	CCCN CRHN EShb SGar

Machaerina (*Cyperaceae*)

sinclairii ECou

Machilus see *Persea*

Mackaya (*Acanthaceae*)

§ **bella** ♀H1 CHll EShb WHil

Macleaya (*Papaveraceae*)

cordata misapplied see *M.* × *kewensis*
§ **cordata** (Willd.) R. Br. ♀H4 EBee ELan EPfP LHop LRHS MBri MSCN MWhi NBir NOrc NPri SBfd SEND SPer SPlb SRms WCot WMnd WMoo XLum
§ × **kewensis** CWan EWTr
- 'Flamingo' ♀H4 CPLG EBee ECha ECtt GBuc GQue LAst LRHS MBNS MBel MNFA NPnk SMrm SWvt WHoo WWEG
§ **microcarpa** EHoe SGar SWat WWEG
- 'Kelway's Coral Plume' ♀H4 Widely available
- 'Spetchley Ruby' CPLG GBin MRav SPhx SUsu WCot WPGP WWEG
'Plum Tassel' WCot

Maclura (*Moraceae*)

pomifera CArn CBcs EBee IVic NLar SPlb
- 'Pretty Woman' NLar
tricuspidata EGFP

Macrodiervilla see *Weigela*

Macropiper (*Piperaceae*)

§ **excelsum** CHEx ECou

Macrozamia (*Zamiaceae*)

communis CBrP EAmu
diplomera CBrP
dyeri see *M. riedlei*
glaucophylla CBrP
johnsonii CBrP
lucida CBrP
miquelii CBrP
moorei CBrP
mountperiensis CBrP
§ **riedlei** CBrP

Maddenia (*Rosaceae*)

hypocleuca NLar

Maesa (*Primulaceae*)

japonica CPLG
- CWJ 12371 WCru
montana CPLG

Magnolia ✿ (*Magnoliaceae*)

acuminata CBcs CDul CMCN EPfP LMaj NLar
- 'Blue Opal' CBcs CJun
* - 'Kinju' CJun MBri NLar
- 'Koban Dori' CBcs CJun
- large yellow-flowered NLar
- 'Moegi Dori' NLar
- 'Patriot' SKHP
- 'Patriot' × (× **brooklynensis** 'Yellow Bird') CJun
- 'Seiju' CJun
§ - var. **subcordata** CBcs NLar
- - 'Miss Honeybee' CBcs CJun
- - 'Mister Yellowjacket' CJun
acuminata × 'Elizabeth' **new** SEWo
'Advance' CBcs CJun
'Albatross' CBcs CDoC WPGP
'Alex' CJun SSta
'Alixeed' CJun
* **alternifolia** NHim
'Amber' CJun
'Ambrosia' CBcs CJun
amoena CTho
- 'Multiogeca' CBcs CWib
'Angelica' **new** CJun
'Anilou' CJun
'Ann' ♀H4 CPLG NLar
'Anna' CJun
'Anne Rosse' SKHP WPGP
'Anticipation' CJun CMHG
'Apollo' CBcs CDoC CDul CJun IVic LSRN SKHP SSta WPGP
'Archangel' CJun
ashei see *M. macrophylla* subsp. *ashei*
'Asian Artistry' CJun
'Athene' CBcs CDoC CJun CMHG IVic SSta WPGP
'Atlas' CBcs CDoC CJun CTho GGGa NHim WPGP
'Aurora' CBcs CDoC CJun
'Banana Split' CJun NHim
'Betty' ♀H4 CDoC CDul CMac EBee ECrN EPfP GEdr LRHS LSRN MGos NLar NPla SKHP SLim SSta
'Big Dude' CDoC CJun IArd LSRN MBri
biondii CBcs LSRN NLar
'Black Beauty' CBcs CJun MBri
Black Tulip = 'Jurmag1'PBR CBcs CDul ELan EPfP IVic LBuc LRHS SCoo SKHP SLon WPGP
'Blushing Belle' CJun
'Brenda' CJun
× **brooklynensis** 'Evamaria' CBcs CTho
- 'Golden Joy' CDoC CJun
- 'Hattie Carthan' CBcs CJun NLar
- 'Woodsman' CBcs NLar
- 'Yellow Bird' CBcs CDoC CJun CMHG CTho EBee EPfP GKin IArd LSRN MBlu MBri MGos NEgg NHol NLar SKHP
'Butterbowl' CBcs CJun
'Butterflies' CBcs CDoC CDul CJun CTho EBee ELan ELon EPfP GGGa LRHS LSRN MBlu MBri MGos NLar SGol SKHP SLim SSta WFar WGob
'Caerhays Belle' CBcs CJun IVic NHim NLar SKHP SSpi SSta WPGP
'Caerhays New Purple' CLnd
'Caerhays Surprise' CBcs CJun SKHP SSpi SSta WPGP
campbellii CBcs CMCN ELan EPfP IDee LRHS SKHP SSpi
- Alba Group CBcs WPGP
- - 'Ethel Hillier' CBcs
- - 'Sir Harold Hillier' CJun
- 'Ambrose Congreve' WPGP
- 'Betty Jessel' CJun CMHG WPGP
- 'Darjeeling' CBcs CDoC CJun IVic LRHS SKHP
- 'John Gallagher' SKHP
- 'Lamellan Pink' CTho
- 'Lamellan White' CTho
- subsp. **mollicomata** CHEx EPfP IArd WFar

	- - 'Lanarth'	CBcs CJun LRHS WPGP
	- - 'Peter Borlase'	GGGa
	- 'Queen Caroline'	WPGP
	- (Raffillii Group) 'Charles Raffill'	CBcs CDoC CDul ELan EPfP LRHS MGos SLim WMou WPGP
	- - 'Kew's Surprise'	CBcs CDoC CJun CMHG WPGP
	- 'Sidbury'	MBri
	campbellii* × *sprengeri	WPGP
	'Candy Cane'	CJun
	'Carlos'	CJun
	cathcartii B&SWJ 11802	WCru
	- HWJ 874	WCru
	cavaleriei var. ***platypetala***	CBcs CPLG
	'Cecil Nice'	CDoC
	Chameleon	see *M.* 'Chang Hua'
	champaca	CCCN
§	'Chang Hua'	CJun NLar
	chapensis	CBcs SKHP
	'Charles Coates'	CJun EPfP MBri NLar WPGP
	chevalieri B&SWJ 11802	WCru
	- DJHV 06037	WCru
	- HWJ 533	WCru
	- HWJ 621	WCru
	China Town = 'Jing Ning'	CJun
	'Columbus'	CJun SKHP WPGP
	'Columnar Pink'	NLar
	compressa	CCCN EPfP
	'Coral Lake'	CJun SKHP
	cordata	see *M. acuminata* var. *subcordata*
	'Crystal Chalice'	CJun SSta
	'Cup Cake'	CJun
	'Curly Locks'	CJun
	cylindrica misapplied	see *M.* 'Pegasus'
	cylindrica ambig.	CBcs CMCN
	cylindrica E.H.Wilson	EPfP
	- 'Bjuv'	CJun
	'Daphne'	CBcs CJun CMHG IVic LMil LRHS LSRN MAsh NLar SKHP SPoG WPGP
	'Darrell Dean'	CJun
	'David Clulow'	CBcs CJun EBee IArd LRHS SKHP WPGP
	dawsoniana	CBcs EPfP NLar
	- 'Barbara Cook'	CJun
	- 'Strybing' new	GGGa
	- 'Valley Splendour'	CJun
	'Daybreak'	CBcs CJun MBlu MBri MRav SGol SSpi SSta WPGP
	'Deborah'	CJun
	decidua	SKHP
	delavayi	CBcs CBrP CDoy CDul CHEx CMCN EBee EGFP EPfP EUJe IArd IDee SMad SSpi WPGP
§	***denudata*** 🏆$^{H3-4}$	CBcs CDoy CDul CMCN CTho CWib EPfP IArd LMaj LMil LRHS MBlu MGos NLar SSpi SSta
	- 'Double Diamond'	CJun
	- 'Dubbel'	CBcs NHim
	- 'Forrest's Pink'	CBcs LRHS
	- Fragrant Cloud = 'Dan Xin'	CBcs CJun CWib MBri NHim NLar
	- 'Gere'	CBcs CJun
	- 'Ghost Ship'	CJun
	- 'Rubiflora'	SSta
	- Yellow River = 'Fei Huang'	CBcs CJun CWib LRHS LSou MBri MWat NLar
	doltsopa	CBcs CCCN CGHE CHEx CPLG EBee EPfP SKHP SSta WPGP
	- 'Silver Cloud'	CBcs CDoC CPLG
	'Dr M. Oesthook'	SSta
	'Early Rose'	CJun GGGa
	'Eleanor May'	CJun
	'Elegance'	CJun
	'Elisa Odenwald'	CJun NHim
	'Elizabeth' 🏆^{H4}	CBcs CDoC CDul CJun CMCN CTho EBee ELan EPfP GGGa LAst LMil LRHS LSRN MAsh MBlu MGos NLar SKHP SPer SPoG SSpi SSta SWvt
§	***ernestii***	CPLG CWib
§	- subsp. ***ernestii*** new	NLar
	'Eskimo'	CJun SKHP SSpi
	'Felicity'	CJun
	Felix Jury = 'Jurmag2'^{PBR}	CBcs ELan EPfP LRHS SSpi WPGP
	figo	CBcs CCCN CDoC CPLG EBee EPfP LRHS SKHP SSta WPGP
	- var. ***crassipes***	CBcs
	figo* × *laevifolia	SKHP
	'Fireglow'	CJun CTho MBri
	'Flamingo'	CJun
	floribunda WWJ 11929 new	WCru
	- WWJ 12003	WCru
	aff. ***floribunda*** var. ***tonkinensis*** DJHV06 105	WCru
	fordiana	CBcs CPLG
§	***foveolata***	CBcs CWib
	- B&SWJ 11749	WCru
	- WWJ 11929	WCru
	- WWJ 11955	WCru
	'Frank Gladney'	CJun CTho
	'Frank's Masterpiece'	CJun SKHP
	fraseri	CBcs SKHP
	- var. ***pyramidata***	SKHP
	'Galaxy' 🏆^{H4}	CBcs CDoC CDul CJun CMHG CMac EBee ELon EPfP GGGa LMil LRHS MAsh MBri MGos NLar SEWo SLim SSpi SSta WGob
	'Genie'^{PBR}	CBcs CDoC
	'George Henry Kern'	CBcs CDoC CDul EBee GEdr IDee LRHS MBri MGos NEgg NLar NPCo SHil WCFE WFar WGob
	'Gladys Carlson'	CJun
	globosa	CBcs CPLG WFar WGob
	'Gold Crown'	CBcs CJun MBri
	'Gold Star'	CBcs CDoC CJun CMHG CTho EPfP LMil LRHS MGos NLar SKHP SSpi SSta
	'Golden Endeavour'	CJun
	'Golden Gala'	CJun
	'Golden Gift'	CJun EBee LRHS MAsh SPoG SSpi
	'Golden Pond'	CJun MBri
	'Golden Rain'	CJun
	'Golden Sun'	CBcs CJun
	'Goldfinch'	CJun
I	× ***gotoburgensis*** Chollipo clone	WPGP
	- clone 2	CJun
	grandiflora	CMCN CWib EPfP ESwi LEdu LRHS LSRN MGos MRav NEgg NLar SBfd SEWo WFar
	- 'Blanchard'	CBcs CJun EUJe
	- 'Bracken's Brown Beauty'	CMCN
	- 'Charles Dickens'	CJun
	- 'Edith Bogue'	CBcs CJun GKin LMil NEgg NPCo WGob
	- 'Exmouth' 🏆$^{H3-4}$	Widely available
	- 'Ferruginea'	CBcs CJun CTho EBee LRHS NLar SGol

	– 'François Treyve'	EPfP LRHS LTen SBfd
	– 'Galissonnière'	CBcs CCVT CWib EBee ECrN EPfP ERom LMaj LRHS LTen MGos MREP SBfd SGol SKHP SLim SSpi SWvt WPGP
I	– 'Galissonnière Nana'	LMaj
	– 'Goliath'	CBcs CDul CHEx EBee ELan EPfP LRHS SBfd SEWo SKHP SLdr SLim SPer SSpi WPGP
	– 'Harold Poole'	CJun
	– 'Kay Parris'	CJun EPfP LRHS SKHP SPoG SSpi
	– 'Little Gem'	CBcs CDoC CJun ELan EPfP EUJe LRHS MBri MGos NLar SGol SHil SSpi
	– 'Mainstreet'	CJun
	– 'Monlia'	CJun
	– 'Nannetensis'	CJun LRHS MBri SHil
	– 'Overton'	CJun
	– 'Russet'	CJun
	– 'Saint Mary'	CBcs CJun
	– 'Samuel Sommer'	CBcs CJun SSpi
	– 'Symmes Select'	CJun
	– 'Treyvei'	CJun
	– 'Victoria' ♀H3-4	CDoC CDul CJun CTho EBee ELan ELon EPfP LMil LRHS LSRN MAsh MBlu MGos MWat NHim NLar SGol SHil SLim SPer SPoG SReu SSpi SSta WGob WPGP
	'Green Bee'	CBcs CJun
	'Green Mist'	CJun LMil LRHS SSpi
	'Hawk'	WPGP
	'Heaven Scent' ♀H4	Widely available
	'Helen Fogg'	CJun
	heptapeta	see *M. denudata*
	'Honey Flower'	CJun NLar
§	'Hong Yur'	CJun
	'Hot Flash'	CBcs CJun MBri
	'Hot Lips'	CJun
	hypoleuca	see *M. obovata* Thunb.
	'Ian's Red'	CBcs CDoC CJun IVic MBri WPGP
§	***insignis***	CHEx CPLG SKHP WPGP
	'Iolanthe'	CBcs CDoC CGHE CJun CMCN CMHG CTho EBee ELan EPfP IVic MAsh MBri MGos SHil SSta WPGP
	'Iufer'	CJun SSta
	'J.C.Williams'	CBcs CDoC CJun CTho IVic WPGP
	'Jack Fogg'	MPkF SKHP
	'Jane' ♀H4	CDoC CJun CMac EBee ELan EPfP LMil LRHS MAsh MGos MRav SPer
	'Jersey Belle'	CJun
	'Joe McDaniel'	CBcs CJun IArd NHim NLar SKHP
	'John Bond'	SSta
	'John Congreve'	WPGP
	'Joli Pompom'	CJun
	'Judy Zuk'	SKHP SSta
	'Kate Brook'	NLar
	× ***kewensis*** 'Wada's Memory'	see *M. salicifolia* 'Wada's Memory'
	kobus	CBcs CCVT CDoy CDul CLnd CMCN CTho CTsd EPfP GKin IArd IDee LMaj MBlu MMuc NLar NWea SEWo SLdr WGob
	– 'Esveld Select'	CJun MBri SSpi
	– 'Janaki Ammal'	CJun
§	– 'Norman Gould'	CDoC CJun EPfP MBri NLar NPla SSta
	– 'Octopus'	CJun
	– pink-flowered	CBcs CJun
	– 'White Elegance'	CJun
	– 'Wisley Star'	SSta
	laevifolia ambig.	WSHC
§	***laevifolia*** (Y.W.Law R.Y.F.Wu) Noot	CBcs CHid CPLG EBee EPfP NLar SChF SKHP WPGP
	– arborescent	SKHP
	– 'Dali Velvet'	CPLG
	– 'Gail's Favourite'	EBee LRHS MAsh SKHP SPoG SSpi
	– 'Velvet and Cream'	IVic
	– 'Willow Leaf'	SKHP
	'Laura Saylor'	CJun
	'Leda'	CJun MBri SSta
	'Legacy'	CJun NLar SKHP WPGP
	'Legend'	CJun EPfP
	'Lemon Star' **new**	MBri
	'Lennarth Jonsson'	CJun
§	***liliiflora***	CBcs GKin NHim
	– 'Darkest Purple'	CJun
§	– 'Nigra' ♀H4	Widely available
	– 'Raven'	SKHP
*	'Limelight'	CJun EBee SSpi WPGP
	× ***loebneri***	NEgg
	– 'Ballerina'	CBcs CDoC NLar
	– 'Donna'	CJun EBee EPfP LMil LRHS LSRN MAsh MBri NLar SHil SKHP SSpi SSta
	– 'Encore'	CJun
	– 'Leonard Messel' ♀H4	Widely available
	– 'Lesley Jane'	CJun
	– 'Merrill' ♀H4	CBcs CDul CJun CMCN CMHG CMac CTho CWib EBee ELan EPfP LMaj LMil LRHS MAsh MBri MGos MMuc MRav NLar NPCo SEND SGol SKHP SPer SReu SSpi SSta WFar WGob
	– 'Neil McEacharn'	CJun
	– 'Pink Cloud'	CJun
	– 'Powder Puff'	CJun
	– 'Raspberry Fun'	CJun IArd
	– 'Snowdrift'	CJun NLar SSta
	– 'Star Bright'	CJun
	– 'White Stardust'	CJun
	– 'Wildcat'	CJun NLar SKHP
	– 'Willow Wood'	CJun
	'Lois'	CBcs CJun EPfP GGGa LRHS LSRN MAsh NLar SKHP SPoG SSpi WPGP
	'Lombardy Rose'	NLar
	lotungensis	NLar
	'Lotus'	CJun
	'Lucy Carlson'	CJun
	macclurei	CBcs
	macrophylla	CBcs CBrP CMac EPfP IArd IDee LRHS MBlu MBri MPkF NLar SKHP WPGP
§	– subsp. ***ashei***	CBcs CMCN SKHP WPGP
	– subsp. ***ashei*** × ***virginiana***	CJun
	macrophylla × ***macrophylla*** subsp. ***ashei***	SKHP
	macrophylla × ***sieboldii***	CJun
	'Mag's Pirouette'	MBri SKHP
	'Malin'	CJun CMHG
	'Manchu Fan'	CBcs CJun EMil EPfP IArd IVic LRHS LSRN LTen NLar SKHP SLim SSpi

§	'March Til Frost'	CJun NLar SKHP WPGP
	'Margaret Helen'	CBcs CDoC CJun CMHG
	'Marj Gossler'	CJun
	'Marjorie Congreve'	WPGP
	'Mark Jury'	CBcs SKHP WPGP
	martinii	CBcs SKHP
	'Mary Bee'	SKHP
	'Mary Nell'	CJun
	'Maryland'	CJun CWib GGGa SKHP SSpi
	maudiae	CBcs CDoC CPLG EPfP IDee NLar SKHP SSpi WPGP
	'Maxine Merrill'	CJun IDee MBri SSta
	'May to Frost'	see *M.* 'March Til Frost'
	'Milky Way' ♀H4	CBcs CDoC CGHE CJun CMHG CTho EBee EPfP GGGa MGos SKHP SSpi SSta WPGP
	'Moondance'	CJun
	'Morning Calm'	SKHP
	'Nimbus'	CJun SKHP SSpi
	nitida	CBcs CPLG
	obovata Diels	see *M. officinalis*
§	***obovata*** Thunb. ♀H4	CBcs CDul CJun CMCN CTho EPfP IDee MGos NLar NWea SSpi WMou WPGP
	obovata* × *officinalis new	CMHG
	odora	CWib
§	***officinalis***	CBcs EPfP NLar WFar
	- var. ***biloba***	CGHE NLar WPGP
	'Old Port'	CBcs
	'Olivia'	CJun MBri
	'Orchid' new	MBri
	'Paul Cook' new	MBri
	'Peachy'	CBcs CJun MBri NLar
§	'Pegasus'	CBcs CJun GGGa LRHS MBri SKHP SSpi SSta
	'Peppermint Stick'	CBcs SSta
	'Peter Smithers'	CJun MBri
	'Phelan Bright'	CJun
	'Phillip Tregunna'	CBcs CMHG CTho SKHP
	'Phil's Masterpiece'	CJun
	'Pickard's Garnet' new	CBcs
	'Pickard's Stardust'	EPfP
	'Pickard's Sundew'	see *M.* 'Sundew'
	'Piet van Veen'	CJun
	'Pink Delight'	CJun
	'Pink Goblet'	LRHS NHim
	'Pink Surprise'	CJun
	'Pinkie' ♀H4	CJun EMil LSRN MGos NEgg NLar SSta WGob
	'Pirouette'	CJun EPfP LLHF LRHS NHim SSpi SSta
	'Porcelain Dove'	CJun NHim SKHP SSpi
	'Princess Margaret'	CBcs CDoC CJun MBri
	× ***proctoriana***	CAbP CDoC CGHE EBee LMil LRHS NLar SChF SKHP WPGP
	- Gloster form	NLar
	- 'Robert's Dream'	CJun EBee LRHS MAsh SPoG SSpi SSta
	- 'Slavin's No 44'	CJun
	'Purple Globe'	CJun SKHP
	'Purple Sensation'	CBcs CJun
	quinquepeta	see *M. liliiflora*
	'Raspberry Ice'	CBcs CDoC CMHG CMac CTho EBee ELon EPfP LMil LRHS MAsh NLar SLim SPoG SRms WFar WGob
	'Raspberry Swirl'	SSta
	'Red As'	CBcs
	'Red as Red'	CDoC
	'Red Baron'	CJun
	'Red Lion'	CJun
	'Ricki'	CBcs CJun EMil EPfP LSRN MBlu MGos NLar WFar
	'Roseanne'	CJun
	rostrata	CBcs CGHE ELan SKHP WPGP
	'Rouged Alabaster'	CDoC NLar
	'Royal Crown'	CBcs CDoC EPfP IDee LRHS MRav NEgg NLar NPCo SLim
	'Ruby'	CBcs CJun
	salicifolia ♀H3-4	CBcs CMCN EPfP SSpi
	- 'Jermyns'	CJun
	- 'Louisa Fete'	CJun
*	- 'Rosea'	CBcs CJun
	- upright	WPGP
	- 'Van Veen'	CJun
§	- 'Wada's Memory' ♀H4	CDoC CHid CJun CMCN CPLG CTho EBee ELan EPfP LMil LRHS MAsh MBlu MBri MMuc NLar SEND SKHP SLdr SSpi SSta WFar
	- 'Windsor Beauty'	CJun NHim SSta
*	***sapaensis*** NJM 09.139 new	WPGP
	- NJM 09.143	WPGP
	- NJM 09.168	WPGP
	'Sara Koe' new	MBri
	sargentiana	CBcs SSta
	- 'Broadleas'	CJun
	- var. ***robusta***	CBcs CMCN ELan EPfP MGos NLar SSpi
	- - 'Blood Moon'	CJun
	- - 'Multipetal'	WPGP
	- - 'Trengwainton Glory'	NHim
	'Satisfaction'	CDul CJun NLar
	'Sayonara' ♀H4	CBcs CJun SSpi
	'Schmetterling'	see *M.* × *soulangeana* 'Pickard's Schmetterling'
	'Serene'	CBcs CJun CMHG EPfP MBri MGos SSta WPGP
	'Shirazz'	CBcs CDoC CJun SKHP WPGP
	sieboldii	CBcs CDul CGHE CJun CLnd CMCN CMac CTho ELan EPfP GKin IDee LRHS LSRN MBlu MBri MGos NLar SHil SKHP SLim SPad SSpi WFar WPGP
	- B&SWJ 4127	WCru
	- 'Colossus'	CJun IArd MBlu MBri SKHP
	- 'Genesis'	CJun
	- 'Genesis' × ***tripetala***	CJun
	- 'Genesis' × ***virginiana***	CJun
	- 'Michiko Renge'	CJun NLar
	- 'Min Pyong-gal'	CJun
	- 'Pride of Norway'	CJun
	- subsp. ***sinensis***	CDoC CJun CTho ELan EPfP MBlu NLar WPGP
I	- - 'Grandiflora'	CJun
	'Sir Harold Hillier'	CBcs WPGP
	'Sleeping Beauty' new	SKHP
	'Snow Goose'	CJun
	'Solar Flair'	CBcs CJun MBri SKHP
	× ***soulangeana***	Widely available
	- 'Alba Superba'	CBcs CDoC CTri EPfP LRHS MBlu MGos MRav SLim WFar
	- 'Alexandrina'	EPfP MBlu NLar
	- 'Amabilis'	SBfd
	- 'Brozzonii' ♀H3-4	CDoC CDul CMac EPfP GCra IArd LMil LRHS MBri MGos NEgg NLar NPCo SSta WGob
	- 'Burgundy'	CDoC NPCo WFar WGob
	- 'Fukuju'	CJun

	- 'Lennei' $\mathbb{Y}^{H3-4}$	CBcs CDoC CMCN CMac CSBt EBee EPfP GEdr IArd LAst LRHS MBri MGos MSwo NLar SLim SRms WFar WGob
	- 'Lennei Alba' $\mathbb{Y}^{H3-4}$	CBcs CDoC CMCN CMac IArd MBlu WFar WGob
	- 'Nigra'	see *M. liliiflora* 'Nigra'
	- 'Pickard's Ruby'	MBri
§	- 'Pickard's Schmetterling'	CDoC LMil LRHS MAsh MBri NHim
	- 'Pickard's Snow Queen'	CJun
	- 'Pickard's Sundew'	see *M.* 'Sundew'
	- 'Picture'	CDoC CMac CTri NLar WGob
	- Red Lucky	see *M.* 'Hong Yur'
	- 'Rosea'	LMaj
	- 'Rubra' misapplied	see *M.* × *soulangeana* 'Rustica Rubra'
§	- 'Rustica Rubra' $\mathbb{Y}^{H3-4}$	CBcs CDoC CDul CMCN CMac CTri EBee ELan EPfP LAst LMil LRHS LSRN MAsh MBri MGos NLar SGol SPer SPoG SReu SRms SSpi WFar WGob
	- 'San José'	CJun LMil LRHS MAsh NHim NLar WFar
	- 'Speciosa'	SSta
	- 'Superba'	CMac SBfd SBod
	- 'Verbanica'	CCVT LMil LRHS MAsh
	'Spectrum'	CBcs CDoC CJun EBee EMil IArd IDee LMil LRHS MBri MGos NLar SKHP SLdr SSpi SSta
	sprengeri	CWib
	- 'Copeland Court'	CJun NHim SSta
	- var. ***diva***	CBcs CPLG EPfP MBri NLar SKHP WPGP
	- - 'Burncoose'	CBcs CDoC
	- - 'Claret Cup'	GGGa
	- - 'Dark Diva'	CJun
	- - 'Diva'	NHim WPGP
	- - 'Eric Savill'	CJun IVic SKHP WPGP
	- - 'Lanhydrock'	CJun MBri SKHP SSta WPGP
	- - 'Westonbirt'	WPGP
	- var. ***elongata***	SKHP
	- 'Marwood Spring'	CMHG MBri SKHP SSta WPGP
	'Spring Rite'	CJun SKHP
	'Star Wars' $\mathbb{Y}^{H4}$	CBcs CDoC CJun CPLG CTho EBee ELan EPfP GGGa LMil LRHS LTen MBri MGos NLar SKHP SPoG SSpi SSta WPGP
	'Stellar Acclaim'	CBcs CJun
	stellata $\mathbb{Y}^{H4}$	Widely available
	- 'Centennial'	CDoC CJun CTho MBri NLar SSta
	- 'Chrysanthemumiflora'	CJun EPfP SKHP
	- 'Dawn'	CJun
	- 'Jane Platt'	CBcs CJun EBee ELan EPfP EWes LMil LRHS MBri MGos SKHP SSpi SSta WPGP
	- f. ***keiskei***	CBcs CJun EPfP MGos NHol NLar SKHP
	- 'Kikuzaki'	CJun
	- 'King Rose'	CBcs CDoC CJun CTsd EPfP LAst LMil LRHS MAsh NHim SPoG
	- 'Massey'	CJun
	- 'Norman Gould'	see *M. kobus* 'Norman Gould'
	- 'Rosea'	CBar CJun CMCN CTho ELan ELon GEdr GKev LMil MGos MRav MSwo NEgg NLar SKHP
I	- 'Rosea Massey'	CJun WFar
	- 'Royal Star'	Widely available
	- 'Scented Silver'	CJun LRHS MAsh SKHP SPoG
	- 'Shi-banchi Rosea'	CJun
	- 'Two Stones'	SKHP
	- 'Water Lily' $\mathbb{Y}^{H4}$	CBcs CJun CMCN CMac CTho EBee ELan ELon EPfP GKev LAst LMil LRHS LSRN LTen MAsh MBlu NHim NLar NPCo NRHS SHil SKHP SLim SPer SPoG SSta WFar WPGP
	- 'Wisley Stardust'	LRHS
	'Summer Solstice'	CBcs CJun MBri NHim
	'Sun Ray'	CBcs CJun
	'Sunburst'	CBcs CJun SRms
	'Sundance'	CBcs CJun MBri NLar
§	'Sundew'	CBcs CDoC EPfP NHim NLar NPCo
	'Sunsation'	CBcs CDoC CJun SSta
	'Sunspire'	CBcs CJun NLar
	'Suntown'	CJun
	'Susan' $\mathbb{Y}^{H4}$	Widely available
	'Susanna van Veen'	CBcs CDoC CJun WPGP
	'Swedish Star'	CJun
	'Sweet Merlot'	CBcs CDoC CJun
	'Sweet Valentine'	CBcs CJun
	'Sweetheart'	CJun SSpi
	'Theodora'	MBri NLar
	× ***thompsoniana***	CBcs CMCN EPfP NLar SSpi
	- 'Olmenhof'	IArd
	'Thousand Butterflies'	CBcs CJun
	'Tina Durio'	CBcs MBri SKHP
	'Todd Gresham'	CJun
	'Todd's Forty Niner'	CJun
	'Touch of Pink'	CBcs NLar
	'Tranquility'	CBcs CJun SKHP
	tripetala	CBcs CMCN CPLG CTho EBee ELan EPfP NLar SKHP SSpi SSta WPGP
	- 'Bloomfield'	CJun
	- 'Petite' **new**	SKHP
	'Ultimate Yellow'	CJun NLar
	× ***veitchii***	CBcs EPfP
	- 'Peter Veitch'	CTho
	virginiana	CBcs CJun CMCN EPfP IDee NLar SBig SKHP SSpi WPGP
	- 'Aiken County'	SKHP
	- var. ***australis*** 'Green Shadow'	SGol
	- 'Havener'	SKHP
	- 'Henry Hicks'	CJun
	- 'Moonglow'	CJun EPfP LRHS MBlu MBri
	- 'Pink Halo'	CJun
	- 'Satellite'	CJun MBri
	'Vulcan'	CBcs CDoC CJun ELan EPfP MBri SCoo
	× ***watsonii***	see *M.* × *wieseneri*
	'White Mystery'	CJun
§	× ***wieseneri***	CBcs CGHE CJun CMHG EBee ELan EPfP LRHS MBlu NLar SKHP SPer SSpi WPGP
	- 'Aashild Kalleberg'	CBcs CJun SKHP SSpi
	- 'Lupo Osti'	SKHP
	- 'William Watson'	MBri SSta
	wilsonii $\mathbb{Y}^{H4}$	Widely available
	- 'Highdownensis' **new**	MBri
	'Yaeko'	CJun
	'Yellow Fever'	CBcs CJun CTho
	'Yellow Garland'	CJun
	'Yellow Lantern'	CAbP CBcs CDoC CJun EBee EPfP EWTr GGGa LMil LRHS LSRN MAsh MBlu MWat NLar SSpi SSta
	'Yellow Sea'	CJun SKHP
	Yuchelia No. 1 **new**	CBcs

yunnanensis	CCCN CHll MBri MPkF SSpi
zenii	CBcs CMCN
- 'Pink Parchment'	CJun

× *Mahoberberis* (*Berberidaceae*)

aquisargentii	CMac EBee EPfP GCal IVic LRHS MMuc MRav SEND SKHP WFar
'Dart's Desire'	NLar
'Magic'	NLar
miethkeana	LRHS SRms
neubertii	NLar

Mahonia ✿ (*Berberidaceae*)

§	***aquifolium***	CBcs CDul EBee ECrN MGos MMuc MRav NWea SGol SPer SPlb SReu
	- 'Apollo' ♀H4	CBcs CDul CSBt CWib EBee ELan ELon EPfP LAst LHop LRHS LSRN MAsh MGos MRav MWat NEgg NLar SCoo SEND SPer SPoG
	- 'Atropurpurea'	CMac CSBt ELan EPfP LRHS NLar SPer
	- 'Cosmo Crawl'	LRHS MBri SHil
	- 'Euro'	NLar
	- 'Fascicularis'	see *M.* × *wagneri* 'Pinnacle'
	- 'Green Ripple'	CJun EPfP NLar
	- 'Orange Flame'	CJun EPfP NLar
	- 'Smaragd'	CDoC CMac ELan EPfP LRHS LSRN MBlu MGos MRav SLPl
	- 'Versicolor'	MBlu
	bealei	see *M. japonica* Bealei Group
	'Bokrafoot'PBR	EBee EPfP LRHS MAsh MBlu SLon SSta
	confusa	CDoC CGHE CHEx EBee LLHF LRHS NLar SKHP WPGP
	eurybracteata new	EBee
	eutriphylla	see *M. trifolia*
	fortunei	CBcs IDee NLar WSHC
	- 'Winter Prince'	NLar
	gracilipes	CGHE CHEx EBee EPfP GCal IArd IDee MBlu NLar SKHP SLon SSpi WPGP
	japonica ♀H4	Widely available
§	- Bealei Group	CBcs CDul CSBt EBee ELan ELon EPfP LAst LRHS MAsh MGos MRav MSwo NPer NPla NWea SBfd SCoo SGol SKHP SLim SWvt WFar
	- 'Gold Dust'	CMac NLar NWea
	- 'Hiemalis'	see *M. japonica* 'Hivernant'
§	- 'Hivernant'	EBee EPfP LTen NEgg NWea
	lanceolata	WPGP
	leschenaultii B&SWJ 9535	WCru
	× ***lindsayae***	WPGP
	- 'Cantab'	WPGP
	lomariifolia ♀H3	CHEx EBee EPfP EWes LRHS MAsh MBlu SBfd SKHP SSpi
	longibracteata	GKin
	× ***media*** 'Buckland' ♀H4	CBcs CDul CHab CMac CTrC EBee EPfP MRav MWat NEgg NLar SBfd SDix SPer SRms WPat
	- 'Charity'	Widely available
	- 'Hope'	NLar
	- 'Lionel Fortescue' ♀H4	CBcs CMac CSBt CTrC EBee ELan EPfP GKin LAst LHop LRHS MAsh MCoo MRav NEgg NRHS SBfd SDix SKHP SMad SPer SPoG SSpi WCFE
	- 'Winter Sun' ♀H4	Widely available
	moranensis T 292 new	WPGP
	nervosa	CBcs CMac EPfP MBlu NEgg NLar WCru
	- B&SWJ 9562	WCru
	nitens	CBcs
	- 'Cabaret'PBR	EBee EPfP LRHS MAsh MWat SPoG
	oiwakensis B&SWJ 371	WCru
	- B&SWJ 3660	WCru
	pallida	SKHP SSpi WPGP
	pinnata misapplied	see *M.* × *wagneri* 'Pinnacle'
	pinnata ambig.	EPfP
	pinnata (Lag.) Fedde 'Ken S. Howard'	NLar
	- 'Maurice Foster'	NLar
	repens	GCal NLar
	× ***savilliana***	WPGP
	- 'Commissioner'	CWib
	Sioux = 'Bokrasio'PBR	EBee LRHS MAsh SPoG
§	***trifolia***	GCal
	trifoliolata var. ***glauca***	CJun
	× ***wagneri*** 'Fireflame'	GCal
	- 'Hastings Elegant'	CJun IDee NLar
	- 'Moseri'	NLar WPat
§	- 'Pinnacle' ♀H4	EBee ELan EPfP IDee LRHS MAsh NLar SPer SPoG
	- 'Sunset'	CJun GKin MBlu NLar
	- 'Undulata'	EPfP LRHS MBlu NLar SPer SRms

Maianthemum (*Asparagaceae*)

	amoenum	LEdu
	- B&SWJ 10390	WCru
	atropurpureum	WCru
	bicolor	CDes LEdu SWat
	bifolium	CAvo CBct CDes CHid EBee ECho GCra LEdu MAvo MMoz MNrw NBro NMen NPnk SBch SRms WCru WPtf WWEG XLum
§	- subsp. ***kamtschaticum***	CLAP EBee ECha EHrv EPPr EPot LEdu LRHS MAvo NLar NRya WCot WTin WWEG
	- - B&SWJ 4360	WCru
	- - CD&R 2300	WCru
*	- - var. ***minimum***	EBee GCal WCru
	canadense	EBee ECho EPot GBuc GCal MNrw NBid NMen WCru WHil
	chasmanthum	see *M. bifolium* subsp. *kamtschaticum*
	comaltepecense B&SWJ 10215	WCru
	dilatatum	see *M. bifolium* subsp. *kamtschaticum*
	flexuosum	LEdu
	- B&SWJ 9069	WCru
	- B&SWJ 9079	WCru
	- B&SWJ 9150	WCru
	aff. ***flexuosum*** B&SWJ 9026	WCru
	- B&SWJ 9055	WCru
	formosanum B&SWJ 349	EPPr WCru
	fuscum	GBin GHim WCru
	- var. ***cordatum***	WCru
	gigas B&SWJ 10470	WCru
	henryi	ECho GEdr LEdu WCru
	japonicum	EHrv LEdu LWst
	- B&SWJ 1179	WCru
	- B&SWJ 4714	WCru
	oleraceum	CBct CPLG GBin GEdr GHim LEdu LWst MMoz
	- B&SWJ 2148	WCru
	- purple-flowered	GEdr
	paniculatum B&SWJ 9137	WCru
	- B&SWJ 9140	WCru

- purple-flowered B&SWJ 9139	WCru
pendent, B&SWJ 10305 from Guatemala	WCru
purpureum	GHim
- G-W&P 150	EPPr
racemosum 🏆H4	Widely available
- subsp. ***amplexicaule***	GCal
- - 'Emily Moody'	CBct CDes CPLG CPou EBee EPPr EPfP SKHP WPGP
- dwarf	ECho
- 'Wisley Spangles'	LRHS
aff. ***salvinii*** B&SWJ 9000	WCru
- B&SWJ 9088	WCru
- B&SWJ 10402	WCru
scilloideum B&SWJ 10407	WCru
* - var. ***roseum*** B&SWJ 10335	WCru
stellatum	CBct EBee ECha ECho EPPr EPfP EPot GBBs GBin GBuc GCal LEdu LHop LRHS MAvo NChi NLar NPnk SMad WCru WGwG WHil WPnP WTin XLum
szechuanicum	WCru
tatsienense	CBct CPLG LEdu WCru

Maihuenia (*Cactaceae*)

poeppigii	SPlb
- F&W 9670	WCot

Maireana (*Amaranthaceae*)

georgei	SPlb

Malacothamnus (*Malvaceae*)

fremontii	MDKP

Malus ✿ (*Rosaceae*)

§ 'Adirondack'	EPfP LRHS MAsh MBri MMuc NLar SCoo SEND SLim SLon SPoG WJas
'Admiration'	see *M.* 'Adirondack'
× ***adstringens*** 'Almey'	ECrN
- 'Hopa'	CDul
- 'Simcoe'	EBee
'Aldenhamensis'	see *M.* × *purpurea* 'Aldenhamensis'
'Amberina'	CLnd
× ***arnoldiana***	LMaj
× ***atrosanguinea*** 'Gorgeous'	CDul CLnd CMac CTho EBee GTwe LBuc LHop LRHS LSRN MAsh MBri MGos MSwo NLar NWea SCoo SEWo SLim SPer SPoG WJas WMou
baccata	CDul CLnd CMCN CTho GTwe MMuc NWea SCoo SEND SPlb
- 'Dolgo'	EPom SKee WHar
- 'Lady Northcliffe'	CDul CLnd SFam
- var. ***mandshurica***	CTho
- 'Street Parade'	LMaj
aff. ***baccata***	MAsh NWea
§ ***bhutanica***	CDul CLnd MAsh SCrf
- 'Mandarin'	MBri NLar SCoo
brevipes	CLnd LRHS SCoo
- 'Wedding Bouquet'	CWSG EBee LBuc MAsh MBri MWat NLar SEWo
'Butterball'	CDul CLnd CTho EPfP LAst LBuc LMaj LTen NLar NWea SCoo SLim SPer WHar WJas WMou
'Candymint Sargent'	CLnd
'Cave Hill'	CLnd
* 'Cheal's Weeping'	CMac LAst MMuc NEgg
Coccinella = 'Courtarou'	MMuc SGol
'Comtessa de Paris'	CLnd EPfP LTen MAsh
'Coralburst'	MAsh MBri
coronaria var. ***dasycalyx*** 'Charlottae' (d)	CDul CLnd EBee EPfP SPer
- 'Elk River'	LRHS MAsh SCoo
'Crimson Brilliant'	CLnd
'Crittenden'	MAsh MRav
* 'Directeur Moerlands'	CCVT CDoC ECrN EPfP IArd SBfd SPer
domestica 'Acklam Russet' (D)	SKee
- 'Acme' (D)	ECrN MCoo
- 'Adams's Pearmain' (D)	CCAT CTho CTri ECrN GTwe MCoo SFam SKee WHar
- 'Admiral' (D)	ECrN
§ - 'Alexander' (C)	SKee
- 'Alfriston' (C)	CAgr SKee
§ - 'Alkmene' (D) 🏆H4	CAgr ECrN SKee
- 'All Doer' (C/D/Cider)	CCAT CTho
- 'Allen's Everlasting' (D)	SKee
- 'Allington Pippin' (D)	CSBt CTho CTri ECrN IArd LRHS SFam SKee WHar
- Ambassy = 'Dalil'[PBR] (D)	IArd
- 'American Mother'	see *M. domestica* 'Mother'
- 'Ananas Reinette' (D)	ECrN
- 'Annie Elizabeth' (C)	CAgr CCAT CTho CWib ECrN EMil GTwe IArd LAst LRHS MCoo SFam SKee SVic WHar WJas
- 'Api Rose' (D)	SKee
- 'Ard Cairn Russet' (D)	ECrN IArd SKee
- 'Aromatic Russet' (D)	SKee
- 'Arthur Turner' (C) 🏆H4	CCVT CTri ECrN EPom GTwe IArd LAst LBuc MWat SCrf SFam SKee WHar WJas
- 'Ashmead's Kernel' (D) 🏆H4	CAgr CCAT CDul CSBt CTho CTri CWSG CWib ECrN EPfP EPom GTwe IArd LBuc LRHS MCoo MRav MWat NWea SCrf SFam SKee SLim SVic WHar WJas
- 'Ashton Bitter' (Cider)	CCAT CTho CTri GTwe
- 'Ashton Brown Jersey' (Cider)	CCAT
- 'Askham Pippin' (F) **new**	MCoo
- 'Autumn Pearmain' (D)	WHar
- 'Aynho Scarlet' (F)	LBuc
- 'Baker's Delicious' (D)	ECrN SKee WHar
- 'Ball's Bittersweet' (Cider)	CCAT CTho
- 'Ballyfatten' (C)	IArd
- 'Ballyvaughan Seedling' (D)	IArd
- 'Balsam'	see *M. domestica* 'Green Balsam'
- 'Banana Pippin'	CDoC
- 'Banns' (D)	ECrN
- 'Bardsey' (D)	CAgr EPom WGwG WHar
- 'Barnack Beauty' (D)	CTho CTri SKee
- 'Barnack Orange' (D)	SKee
- 'Baxter's Pearmain' (D)	ECrN SKee
- 'Beauty of Bath' (D)	CAgr CCAT CCVT CDoC CTho CTri CWib ECrN ELan EWTr GTwe LAst LBuc MRav SFam SKee SPer WHar WJas
- 'Beauty of Hants' (D)	ECrN SKee
- 'Beauty of Kent' (C)	SKee
- 'Beauty of Moray' (C)	GQui SKee
- 'Bedwyn Beauty' (C)	CTho
- 'Beeley Pippin' (D)	SKee
- 'Belfleur Kitaika' (D)	SKee
- 'Belfleur Krasnyi' (D)	SKee
- 'Bell Apple' (Cider/C)	CCAT CTho
- 'Belle de Boskoop' (C/D) 🏆H4	CAgr CCAT ECrN GTwe MCoo SKee

- 'Belvoir Seedling' (D/C) SKee
- 'Benenden Early' (D) SKee
- 'Ben's Red' (D) CAgr CCAT CDoC CTho SKee
- 'Bess Pool' (D) CCAT MCoo SFam
- 'Bewley Down Pippin' see *M. domestica* 'Crimson King' (Cider/C)
- 'Bickington Grey' (Cider) CCAT CTho
- 'Billy Down Pippin' (F) CTho
- 'Bismarck' (C) CCAT SKee
- 'Black Dabinett' (Cider) CCAT CTho
- 'Black Tom Putt' (C/D) CTho
- 'Black Vallis' (Cider) **new** CCAT
- 'Blenheim Orange' (C/D) ♀H4 Widely available
- 'Blood of the Boyne' (D) **new** IArd
- 'Bloody Ploughman' (D) ECrN GTwe SKee SLon WHar
- 'Blue Sweet' (Cider) CTho
- Bolero = 'Tuscan'PBR (D/Ball) MCoo SKee
- 'Boston Russet' see *M. domestica* 'Roxbury Russet'
- 'Bountiful' (C) CAgr CDoC CDul CMac CSBt CTri CWSG CWib ECrN EPom GTwe IArd LRHS LSRN MBri NLar SKee SPoG WHar
- 'Box Apple' (D) CDoC
- 'Braddick Nonpareil' (D) SKee
- 'Braeburn' (D) CAgr CDul CSut CTri ECrN EPom LAst LBuc LRHS MWat SBfd SCrf SEWo SFam SKee SPer WHar WJas
- 'Braeburn Hillwell' (D) **new** EPom
- 'Braintree Seedling' (D) ECrN
- 'Bramley's Seedling' (C) ♀H4 Widely available
- 'Bramley's Seedling' clone 20 CDoC LRHS MBri NLar SCoo SKee SLim SPoG WHar
- 'Bramshott Rectory' (D/C) SKee
- 'Bread Fruit' (C/D) CDoC CTho
- 'Breakwell's Seedling' (Cider) CCAT CTho
- 'Bridgwater Pippin' (C) CCAT CTho
- 'Bright Future' (D) EPom LBuc MCoo
- 'Broad-eyed Pippin' (C) SKee
- 'Broadholm Beauty' EPom WHar
- 'Brookes's' (D) WHar
- 'Brown Crofton' (D) IArd
- 'Brown Snout' (Cider) CCAT CTho
- 'Brownlees Russet' (D) CAgr CTho CTri GTwe MCoo NEgg NWea SFam SKee WHar
- 'Brown's Apple' (Cider) CAgr CCAT GTwe
- 'Broxwood Foxwhelp' (Cider) CCAT
- 'Burn's Seedling' (D) CTho
- 'Burrowhill Early' (Cider) CTho
- 'Buttery Do' CCAT CTho
- 'Byfleet Seedling' (C) SKee
- 'Cadbury' CCAT
- 'Calville Blanc d'Hiver' (D) SKee
- 'Cambusnethan Pippin' (D) GQui SKee
- 'Camelot' (Cider/C) CCAT
- 'Cap of Liberty' (Cider) CCAT
- 'Captain Broad' (D/Cider) CCAT CTho
- 'Captain Kidd' (D) EPom SKee WHar
- 'Carlisle Codlin' (C) GTwe NLar NWea
- 'Caroline' (D) ECrN
- 'Catherine' (C) ECrN SKee
- 'Catshead' (C) CAgr CCAT CTri ECrN GQui IArd SKee WHar
- 'Caudal Market' (F) LBuc
- 'Cellini' (C/D) SKee
- 'Chacewater Longstem' (F) **new** CDoC
- 'Charles Ross' (C/D) ♀H4 CAgr CCAT CCVT CDul CMac CSBt CTho CTri ECrN EPom GTwe IArd LAst LBuc LRHS LSRN MBri MCoo MRav NEgg NLar NWea SCrf SFam SKee SLim SPer WHar WJas
- 'Chaxhill Red' (Cider/D) CCAT CTho
- 'Cheddar Cross' (D) CAgr CCVT CTri ECrN
- 'Chelmsford Wonder' (C) ECrN SKee
- 'Chisel Jersey' (Cider) CAgr CCAT CTri SKee
- 'Chivers Delight' (D) CAgr CCAT CSBt ECrN GTwe LRHS MCoo SKee WHar WJas
- 'Chorister Boy' (D) CTho
- 'Christmas Pearmain' (D) CAgr CTho ECrN GTwe SFam SKee
- 'Cider Lady's Finger' (Cider) CCAT SKee
- 'Cissy' (D) WGwG
- 'Claygate Pearmain' (D) ♀H4 CAgr CCAT CDoC CTho CTri ECrN GTwe LRHS MCoo SFam SKee SVic WHar
- 'Cleeve' (D) SKee
- 'Clopton Red' (D) ECrN SKee
- 'Clydeside' GQui
- 'Coat Jersey' (Cider) CCAT
- 'Cobra' CDoC LBuc LRHS MBri MCoo WHar WJas
- 'Cockle Pippin' (D) CAgr CTho SKee
- 'Coeur de Boeuf' (C/D) SKee
- 'Coleman's Seedling' (Cider) CTho
- 'Collogett Pippin' (C/Cider) CCAT CDoC CTho
- 'Colonel Vaughan' (C/D) SKee
- 'Cornish Aromatic' (D) CAgr CCAT CDoC CTho CTri GTwe SCrf SFam SKee WHar
- 'Cornish Gilliflower' (D) CAgr CCAT CDoC CDul CTho ECrN MCoo SFam SKee WHar
- 'Cornish Honeypin' (D) CTho
- 'Cornish Longstem' (D) CAgr CDoC CTho
- 'Cornish Mother' (D) CDoC CTho
- 'Cornish Pine' (D) CDoC CTho
- 'Corse Hill' (D) CCAT CTho
- 'Costard' (C) CCAT SKee
- 'Cottenham Seedling' (C) SKee
- 'Coul Blush' (D) SKee
- 'Court of Wick' (D) CAgr CCAT CDoC CTho CTri ECrN SKee SVic WHar
- 'Court Pendu Plat' (D) CAgr CCAT CDoC CTho MWat NWea SFam SKee WHar WJas
- 'Court Royal' (Cider) CCAT
- 'Cox Cymraeg' (D) WGwG
- 'Cox's Orange Pippin' (D) CBcs CCAT CCVT CDul CMac CSBt CTri CWib ECrN ELan EPom GKin GTwe LAst LRHS LSRN MGos MMuc MWat NLar NPri SBfd SCrf SEWo SFam SKee SLim SWvt WJas
- 'Cox's Pomona' (C/D) SKee WHar
- 'Cox's Rouge de Flandres' (D) SKee
- 'Cox's Selfing' (D) CDoC CTri CWSG CWib EPfP EPom GTwe LBuc LRHS MBri MGos MNHC SCrf SKee SPer SPoG WHar WJas
- 'Crawley Beauty' (C) CAgr CCAT CDoC GTwe SFam SKee WHar

	- 'Crimson Beauty of Bath' (D)	CAgr
	- 'Crimson Bramley' (C)	CCAT IArd LAst
§	- 'Crimson King' (Cider/C)	CAgr CCAT
	- 'Crimson King' (D)	CAgr CTri
	- 'Crimson Queening' (D)	SKee WHar
	- 'Crimson Victoria' (Cider)	CTho
	- Crispin	see *M. domestica* 'Mutsu'
	- 'Croen Mochyn' (D)	WGwG
§	- 'Crowngold' (D)	EPom GTwe
	- Cybèle = 'Delrouval'	LRHS
	- 'Dabinett' (Cider)	CAgr CCAT CTho CTri GTwe LBuc SCrf SKee WHar
	- 'D'Arcy Spice' (D)	CAgr CCAT CDoC ECrN EPfP MCoo MWat SFam SKee WHar
	- 'Decio' (D)	SKee
	- Delbarestivale = 'Delcorf' (red) (D) ♀H4	LRHS
	- 'Devon Crimson Queen' (D)	CDoC CTho
	- 'Devonshire Buckland' (C)	CTho
	- 'Devonshire Quarrenden' (D)	CAgr CCAT CDoC CDul CTho SFam SKee SVic WHar WJas
	- 'Diamond' (D)	WGwG
	- 'Discovery' (D) ♀H4	Widely available
	- 'Doctor Clifford' (C) **new**	SKee
	- 'Doctor Harvey' (C)	ECrN SFam SKee
	- 'Doctor Kidd's Orange Red'	see *M. domestica* 'Kidd's Orange Red'
	- 'Domino' (C)	MCoo
	- 'Don's Delight' (C)	CTho
	- 'Dove' (Cider)	CCAT
	- 'Downton Pippin' (D)	WHar
	- 'Dredge's Fame' (D)	CTho
	- 'Duchess of Oldenburg' (C/D)	SKee
	- 'Duchess's Favourite' (D)	SKee
	- 'Dufflin' (Cider)	CCAT CTho
	- 'Duke of Cornwall' (C)	CDoC CTho
	- 'Duke of Devonshire' (D)	CCAT CSBt CTho CTri SFam SKee
N	- 'Dumeller's Seedling'	see *M. domestica* 'Dummellor's Seedling'
§	- 'Dummellor's Seedling' (C) ♀H4	CCAT CTri SKee WHar
	- 'Dunkerton Late Sweet' (Cider)	CCAT CCVT CTho LBuc
§	- 'Dutch Mignonne' (D)	SKee
	- 'Dymock Red' (Cider)	CCAT LBuc
	- 'Early Blenheim' (D/C)	CCAT CTho
	- 'Early Julyan' (C)	GQui SKee
	- 'Early Victoria'	see *M. domestica* 'Emneth Early'
	- Early Windsor	see *M. domestica* 'Alkmene'
	- 'Early Worcester'	see *M. domestica* 'Tydeman's Early Worcester'
	- 'East Lothian Pippin' (C)	GQui
	- 'Easter Orange' (D)	GTwe SKee
	- 'Ecklinville' (C)	SKee
	- 'Edelborsdorfer' (D) **new**	SKee
	- 'Eden'	LBuc
	- 'Edith Hopwood' (D)	ECrN
	- 'Edward VII' (C) ♀H4	CCAT GTwe SCrf SFam SKee WHar
	- 'Egremont Russet' (D) ♀H4	Widely available
	- 'Ellis' Bitter' (Cider)	CCAT CTho GTwe LBuc SKee SVic
	- 'Ellison's Orange' (D) ♀H4	CAgr CCAT CDul CMac CSBt CTri CWib ECrN EPfP EPom GTwe LAst LBuc MMuc MWat NWea SFam SKee SPer SVic WHar WJas
	- 'Elstar' (D) ♀H4	CCVT CDoC CWib ECrN EPom GTwe LAst SKee WHar
	- 'Elton Beauty' (D)	SKee
§	- 'Emneth Early' (C) ♀H4	CAgr ECrN GTwe SFam SKee WJas
	- 'Emperor Alexander'	see *M. domestica* 'Alexander'
	- 'Empire' (D)	LAst SKee
	- 'English Codlin' (C)	CCAT CTho CTri
	- 'Epicure'	see *M. domestica* 'Laxton's Epicure'
	- 'Eros' (D)	ECrN
	- 'Essex Pippin' (D)	ECrN
	- 'Excelsior' (C)	ECrN
	- 'Exeter Cross' (D)	CCAT CSBt ECrN SFam
	- 'Eynsham Challenger' (F)	LBuc
	- 'Fair Maid of Devon' (Cider)	CAgr CCAT CTho
	- 'Fairfield' (D)	CTho
	- 'Falstaff' PBR (D) ♀H4	CAgr CCAT CDul ECrN EPfP EPom GTwe LSRN MGos NPri SCoo SKee SPer WHar WJas
	- 'Farmer's Glory' (D)	CAgr CCAT CTho
	- 'Feltham Beauty' (D)	LBuc
	- 'Fiesta' PBR (D) ♀H4	Widely available
	- 'Fillbarrel' (Cider)	CCAT
	- 'Fillingham Pippin' (C)	SKee
	- 'Flame' (D)	ECrN
	- 'Flamenco' PBR	see *M. domestica* 'Obelisk'
§	- 'Flower of Kent' (C)	SCrf SKee
	- 'Forfar'	see *M. domestica* 'Dutch Mignonne'
	- 'Forge' (D)	CAgr SKee
	- 'Fortune'	see *M. domestica* 'Laxton's Fortune'
	- 'Four Square' (F) **new**	CCAT
	- 'Foxwhelp' (Cider)	LBuc SKee
	- 'Francis' (D)	ECrN
	- 'Frederick' (Cider)	CCAT CTho
	- 'Freyberg' (D)	SKee
	- 'Fuji' (D)	LAst SKee
	- 'Gala' (D)	CMac CSBt EPom GTwe LAst SCoo SCrf SFam SKee SLim WHar
	- 'Gala Musk' (D) **new**	LAst
	- 'Galloway Pippin' (C)	GQui GTwe SKee
	- 'Gascoyne's Scarlet' (D)	CCAT SFam SKee WHar
	- 'Gavin' (D)	CAgr SKee
	- 'Genet Moyle' (C/Cider)	CTri WHar
	- 'George Carpenter' (D)	SKee
	- 'George Cave' (D)	CDul CTho ECrN GTwe IArd MCoo SFam SKee WHar WJas
	- 'George Neal' (C) ♀H4	CAgr CDoC SFam
	- 'Gibbon's Russet' (D)	IArd
	- 'Gilliflower of Gloucester' (D)	CTho
	- 'Gin' (Cider)	CCAT
	- 'Gladstone' (D)	CAgr CCAT CTho SKee WHar
	- 'Glansevin' (D)	WGwG
§	- 'Glass Apple' (C/D)	CCAT CTho
	- 'Gloria Mundi' (C)	SKee
	- 'Gloucester Royal' (D)	CTho
	- 'Gloucester Underleaf'	CTho
	- 'Golden Ball' (Cider)	CCAT CTho
	- 'Golden Bittersweet' (D)	CAgr CTho
	- 'Golden Bromham' (F)	LBuc
	- 'Golden Delicious' (D) ♀H4	CCVT CDul CMac CSBt CWib ECrN ELan EPfP LAst LBuc MMuc SBfd SCrf SEWo SKee SVic WHar
	- 'Golden Harvey' (D)	CAgr CCAT
	- 'Golden Knob' (D)	CCAT CTho CTri SKee
	- 'Golden Noble' (C) ♀H4	CAgr CCAT CDul CTho CTri ECrN GTwe IArd MCoo SFam SKee
	- 'Golden Nugget' (D)	CAgr SKee
	- 'Golden Pippin' (C)	CAgr CCAT SKee WHar
	- 'Golden Reinette' (D)	SFam SKee
	- 'Golden Russet' (D)	CAgr ECrN SKee WHar

	– 'Golden Spire' (C)	MCoo SKee WHar		
	– 'Gooseberry' (C)	LSRN		
	– 'Gooseberry Apple' (Ronald's) (F)	LBuc		
	– 'Goring' (Cider)	CCAT CTho		
	– 'Grand Sultan' (D)	CCAT		
	– 'Grandpa Ailes' (F) **new**	CTho		
	– 'Granny Smith' (D)	CBcs CDul CWib ECrN GTwe LAst LSRN SCrf SKee SPer SVic WHar		
	– 'Gravenstein' (D)	CCAT GQui SFam SKee		
§	– 'Green Balsam' (D)	CTri		
	– 'Green Kilpandy Pippin' (C)	GQui		
	– 'Greensleeves'[PBR] (D) ♀H4	CAgr CDoC CDul CMac CSBt CTri CWib ECrN EPfP EPom GTwe LAst MGos MMuc NLar SKee SLim SPoG WHar WJas		
	– 'Grenadier' (C) ♀H4	CAgr CDoC CSBt CTri ECrN GTwe LAst MGos MMuc MWat SFam SKee SLon SVic WHar WJas		
	– 'Gwell Na Mil' (D)	WGwG		
	– 'Hagloe Crab' (Cider)	LBuc		
	– 'Halstow Natural' (Cider)	CAgr CTho		
	– 'Hambledon Deux Ans' (C)	SFam SKee		
	– 'Hangy Down' (Cider)	CCAT CTho		
	– 'Harling Hero' (D) **new**	ECrN		
	– Harmonie = 'Delorina' (F)	LRHS		
§	– 'Harry Master's Jersey' (Cider)	CAgr CCAT CTho CTri MWat SKee WHar		
	– 'Harvester' (D)	CTho		
	– 'Hawthornden' (C)	GQui GTwe SKee		
	– 'Herefordshire Redstreak' (Cider)	CDul LBuc WHar		
	– 'Herefordshire Russet'[PBR] (D)	CDoC CDul CWSG EPom LBuc LRHS MBri MCoo MWat NLar SKee SLim WHar WJas		
	– 'Herring's Pippin' (D)	CTri LBuc SKee		
	– 'Hibb's Seedling' (C)	SKee		
	– 'High View Pippin' (D)	SKee		
	– 'Hoary Morning' (C)	CCAT CTho ECrN SKee		
	– 'Hocking's Green' (C/D)	CAgr CCAT CTho		
	– 'Holland Pippin' (C)	WHar		
	– 'Hollow Core' (C)	CAgr CTho		
	– 'Holstein' (D)	CTho SKee		
	– 'Honey Pippin' (D)	ECrN SKee		
	– 'Honey String' (F)	CCAT		
	– 'Horneburger Pfannkuchen' (C)	SKee		
	– 'Horsford Prolific' (D)	ECrN		
	– 'Hounslow Wonder' (C) **new**	MWat		
	– 'Howgate Wonder' (C)	CAgr CCVT CDul CSBt CWib ECrN GTwe LAst LBuc MMuc SCrf SFam SKee SPer SVic WHar WJas		
	– 'Hubbard's Pearmain' (D)	ECrN SKee		
	– 'Hunter's Majestic' (D/C)	ECrN		
	– 'Hunt's Duke of Gloucester' (D)	CTho LBuc		
	– 'Idared' (D) ♀H4	CCAT CWib ECrN SKee SVic WHar		
	– 'Improved Dove' (Cider)	CCAT		
	– 'Improved Keswick' (C/D)	CCAT CDoC CTho		
	– 'Improved Lambrook Pippin' (Cider)	CCAT CTho CTri		
	– 'Improved Redstreak' (Cider)	CTho		
	– 'Ingall's Pippin' (D)	SKee		
	– 'Ingall's Red' (D)	SKee		
	– 'Ingrid Marie' (D)	SKee		
	– 'Irish Peach' (D)	CAgr CCAT CTri ECrN GTwe IArd MCoo SFam SKee WHar		
	– 'Isaac Newton's Tree'	see *M. domestica* 'Flower of Kent'		
	– 'Isle of Wight Pippin' (D)	LBuc		
	– 'Jackson's'	see *M. domestica* 'Crimson King' (Cider/C)		
	– 'James Grieve' (D) ♀H4	Widely available		
	– 'Jester' (D)	ECrN SKee		
	– 'Joaneting' (D)	CAgr		
	– 'John Broad' (F)	CDoC		
	– 'John Standish' (D)	CAgr CCAT CTri GTwe		
	– 'John Toucher's'	see *M. domestica* 'Crimson King' (Cider/C)		
	– 'Johnny Andrews' (Cider)	CAgr CCAT CTho		
	– 'Johnny Voun' (D)	CTho		
	– 'Jonagold' (D) ♀H4	CTri CWib ECrN ELan EPom GTwe IArd NLar SBfd SCrf SFam SKee SPer SVic		
	– 'Jonagold Crowngold'	see *M. domestica* 'Crowngold'		
§	– 'Jonagored'[PBR] (D)	WHar		
	– 'Jonared' (D)	GTwe		
	– 'Jonathan' (D)	SKee		
	– 'Joybells' (D)	SKee		
	– 'Jubilee'	see *M. domestica* 'Royal Jubilee'		
	– 'Julie's Late Golden' (F)	CTri		
	– 'Jumbo'	LRHS MBri MCoo SKee WHar WJas		
	– 'Jupiter'[PBR] (D) ♀H4	CAgr CSBt CTri CWib ECrN EWTr GTwe LAst LSRN MRav SBfd SKee SLon WHar WJas		
	– 'Kandil Sinap' (D)	SKee		
	– 'Karmijn de Sonnaville' (D)	SKee		
§	– 'Katja' (D)	CAgr CCAT CCVT CDoC CDul CMac CTri CWib ECrN EWTr GKin GTwe IArd LAst LBuc MMuc MRav NEgg NLar SBfd SCoo SEWo SKee SPer WHar WJas		
	– Katy	see *M. domestica* 'Katja'		
	– 'Kent' (D)	ECrN NLar SCrf SKee		
	– 'Kentish Fillbasket' (C)	SKee		
	– 'Kerry Pippin' (D)	IArd SKee		
	– 'Keswick Codlin' (C)	CTho ECrN GTwe MBri MCoo NEgg NLar NWea SKee WHar WJas		
§	– 'Kidd's Orange Red' (D) ♀H4	CAgr CCAT CMac CTri ECrN EPfP EPom GQui GTwe LBuc LRHS MWat SBfd SCrf SFam SKee SLon WHar		
	– 'Kilkenny Pearmain' (D)	IArd		
	– 'Kill Boy'	CTho		
	– 'Killerton Sharp' (Cider)	CTho		
	– 'Killerton Sweet' (Cider)	CTho		
	– 'King Byerd' (C/D)	CCAT CDoC CTho		
§	– 'King of the Pippins' (D) ♀H4	CCAT CTho CTri ECrN GTwe MCoo SCrf SFam SKee SVic WHar		
	– 'King of Tompkins County' (D)	SFam		
	– 'King's Acre Pippin' (D)	CCAT SFam WHar		
	– 'Kingston Bitter' (Cider)	CTho		
	– 'Kingston Black' (Cider/C)	CCAT CTho CTri ECrN GTwe LBuc SKee		
	– 'Kirton Fair' (D)	CTho		
	– 'Knobby Russet' (D)	SKee		
	– 'Korobovka' (D)	SKee		
	– 'Lady Henniker' (D)	CCAT CTho ECrN SKee WHar		
	– 'Lady of the Wemyss' (C)	GQui SKee		
	– 'Lady Sudeley' (D)	CCAT CDoC CTho SKee		
	– 'Lady's Finger' (C/D)	CDoC		

	Cultivar	Suppliers
	- 'Lady's Finger of Lancaster' (C/D)	SKee
	- 'Lady's Finger of Offaly' (D)	IArd
	- 'Lake's Kernel' (D)	CTho
	- 'Lamb's Seedling' (D)	SKee
	- 'Lane's Prince Albert' (C) ♀H4	CAgr CCAT CSBt ECrN GTwe IArd MGos MRav MWat NLar NWea SCoo SCrf SFam SKee SVic WHar WJas
§	- 'Langworthy' (Cider)	CCAT CTho
	- 'Lass o' Gowrie' (C)	GQui
§	- 'Laxton's Epicure' (D) ♀H4	CAgr CDul ECrN GTwe LAst SFam SKee WHar
§	- 'Laxton's Fortune' (D) ♀H4	CCAT CMac CSBt CTri CWib ECrN GTwe IArd LAst SCrf SFam SKee WHar WJas
	- 'Laxton's Pearmain' (D)	MCoo SFam
§	- 'Laxton's Superb' (D)	CBcs CCAT CCVT CDul CMac CSBt CTri CWib ECrN EPom EWTr GKin GTwe LAst LBuc LHop MCoo MWat NPri NWea SBfd SCrf SEWo SKee SPer SVic WHar WJas
	- 'Leathercoat Russet' (D)	CAgr CCAT CDoC CTri SKee
	- 'Lemon Pippin' (C)	CCAT ECrN WHar
	- 'Lemon Pippin of Gloucestershire' (D)	CTho
	- 'Limberland' (C)	CTho
	- 'Limelight' (D)	CDoC LRHS MBri MCoo MWat NLar SBfd SCoo SKee WHar
	- 'Linda' (D)	SKee
	- 'Lodgemore Nonpareil' (D)	LBuc SKee
	- 'London Pearmain' (D)	ECrN
	- 'London Pippin' (C)	CAgr CTho
	- 'Longkeeper' (D)	CAgr CDoC CTho
	- 'Longney Russet' (D/Cider)	CCAT LBuc
	- 'Longstem' (Cider)	CTho
	- 'Lord Derby' (C)	CAgr CCAT CDul CMac CTho CWib ECrN EPom EWTr GTwe LRHS MRav SFam SKee SVic WHar
	- 'Lord Grosvenor' (C)	SKee WHar
	- 'Lord Hindlip' (D)	SFam
	- 'Lord Lambourne' (D) ♀H4	CAgr CCAT CDoC CDul CMac CSBt CSut CTri CWib ECrN EPfP GTwe LAst LRHS LSRN MCoo MGos MWat SBfd SCrf SFam SKee SPer WHar WJas
	- 'Lord of the Isles' (F)	CAgr CCAT CDoC
	- 'Lord Stradbroke' (C)	ECrN SKee
	- 'Lord Suffield' (C)	CTri ECrN SKee
	- 'Lough Tree of Wexford' (D)	IArd
	- 'Lucombe's Pine' (D)	CAgr CCAT CTho ECrN SVic
	- 'Lucombe's Seedling' (D)	CTho
	- 'Lynn's Pippin' (D)	ECrN
	- 'Machen' (D)	WGwG
	- 'Maclean's Favourite' (D)	ECrN
	- 'Maggie Sinclair' (D)	GQui
	- 'Maid of Kent'	CCAT
	- 'Major' (Cider)	CCAT
	- 'Maldon Wonder' (D)	ECrN
	- 'Malling Kent' (D)	SFam
	- 'Maltster' (D)	MCoo
	- 'Manaccan Primrose' (C/D)	CDoC
	- 'Margil' (D)	CCAT SFam SKee WHar
	- 'Markham Pippin' (D) **new**	MCoo
	- 'Marriage-maker' (D)	SKee
	- 'Maxton' (D)	ECrN SKee
	- 'May Beauty' (D)	SKee

	Cultivar	Suppliers
	- 'May Queen' (D)	SFam
	- 'Maypole' PBR (D/Ball)	MAsh
	- 'McIntosh' (D)	SKee
	- 'Médaille d'Or' (Cider)	CCAT SKee
	- 'Melrose' (D)	ECrN SVic
	- 'Merchant Apple' (D)	CCAT CTho CTri
	- 'Mère de Ménage' (C)	SFam SKee WHar
	- 'Meridian' PBR (D)	CAgr CDoC ECrN MCoo MWat
	- 'Merton Knave' (D)	SFam
	- 'Merton Worcester' (D)	ECrN SKee
	- 'Michaelmas Red' (D)	GTwe NEgg SKee
	- 'Michelin' (Cider)	CAgr CCAT CTri GTwe SKee WHar
	- 'Miller's Seedling' (D)	SKee
	- 'Mollie's Delicious' (D)	SKee
	- 'Monarch' (C)	CAgr CCAT CTri ECrN GTwe SFam SKee
	- 'Montfort' (D)	ECrN
	- 'Morgan's Sweet' (C/Cider)	CCAT CTho CTri SKee
§	- 'Mother' (D) ♀H4	CAgr CCAT CTri ECrN GTwe SCrf SKee
§	- 'Mutsu' (D)	CCAT CTri ECrN LAst MRav SKee SPer
	- 'Nanny' (D)	SKee
	- 'Nant Gwrtheyrn' (D)	WGwG
	- 'Newton Wonder' (D/C) ♀H4	CAgr CCAT CDoC CDul CSBt CTho CTri CWib ECrN GTwe IArd LAst MCoo MGos SCrf SFam SKee WHar WJas
	- 'Nine Square' (D)	CTho
	- 'No Pip' (C)	CTho
	- 'Nolan Pippin' (D)	ECrN
	- 'Nonpareil' (D)	SKee WHar
	- 'Norfolk Beauty' (C)	ECrN SKee
	- 'Norfolk Beefing' (C)	ECrN SFam SKee
	- 'Norfolk Royal' (D)	CDoC ECrN GTwe
	- 'Norfolk Royal Russet' (D)	ECrN LRHS SKee
	- 'North Aston Nonpareil' (F)	LBuc
	- 'Northcott Superb' (D)	CTho
	- 'Northern Greening' (C)	SKee WHar
§	- 'Northwood' (Cider)	CCAT CTho
	- 'Nutmeg Pippin' (D)	CCAT ECrN SFam
	- Nuvar Freckles (D)	SKee
	- Nuvar Golden Elf (D)	SKee
	- Nuvar Golden Hills (D)	SKee
	- Nuvar Home Farm (D)	SKee
	- Nuvar Melody (D)	SKee
	- 'Oaken Pin' (D)	CCAT CTho
§	- 'Obelisk' PBR (D)	NPri SKee
	- 'Old Pearmain' (D)	WHar
	- 'Old Somerset Russet' (D)	CCAT CTho
	- 'Opalescent' (D)	SKee
	- 'Orkney Apple' (F)	SKee
	- 'Orleans Reinette' (D)	CAgr CCAT CDul CTho CTri CWib ECrN GTwe IArd LBuc LRHS MWat NEgg SCrf SFam SKee WHar WJas
	- 'Oslin' (D)	SKee
	- 'Otava' PBR (C/D)	SKee
	- 'Owen Thomas' (D)	CTri
	- 'Paignton Marigold' (Cider)	CCAT CTho
	- 'Palmer's Rosey' (D)	SKee
	- 'Pascoe's Pippin' (D/C)	CTho
	- 'Payhembury' (C/Cider)	CAgr CTho CTri
	- 'Pear Apple' (D)	CAgr CCAT CDoC CTho
	- 'Peasgood's Nonsuch' (C) ♀H4	CAgr CCAT CDoC ECrN GTwe IArd NEgg SCrf SFam SKee SLon
	- 'Pendragon' (D)	CTho
	- 'Penhallow Pippin' (D)	CDoC CTho
	- 'Pennard Bitter' (Cider)	CCAT
	- 'Pépin Shafrannyi' (D)	SKee

Cultivar	Suppliers
- 'Peter Lock' (C/D)	CAgr CCAT CTho SKee
- 'Pethyre' (Cider)	CCVT
- 'Phelp's Favourite' (D)	LBuc
- 'Pig Aderyn' (C)	WGwG
- 'Pig y Colomen' (C) **new**	WGwG
- 'Pig's Nose Pippin' (D)	SKee
- 'Pig's Nose Pippin' Type III (D)	CAgr CCAT CTho
- 'Pig's Snout' (Cider/C/D)	CCAT CTho
- 'Pine Apple Russet' (C/D)	CAgr
- 'Pine Golden Pippin' (D)	SKee
- 'Pinova'[PBR] (D)	CAgr EPom MCoo WHar
- 'Pitmaston Pine Apple' (D)	CCAT CTho CTri ECrN IArd LAst MCoo MWat SFam SKee SLon WHar
- 'Pixie' (D) 🏆[H4]	CDoC CWib EPom GTwe MWat SBfd SFam SKee SLon WHar WJas
- 'Plum Vite' (D)	CAgr CTho CTri
- 'Plymouth Cross' (D)	SKee
- 'Plympton Pippin' (C)	CTho CTri
- Polka = 'Trajan'[PBR] (D/Ball)	SKee
- 'Polly' (C/D)	CDoC
- 'Polly Prosser' (D)	SKee
- 'Polly Whitehair' (C/D)	CCAT CTho
- 'Poltimore Seedling' (D)	CTho
- 'Pomeroy of Somerset' (D)	CCAT CTho CTri
- 'Ponsford' (C)	CAgr CCAT CTho
- 'Port Allen Russet' (C/D)	GQui
- 'Port Wine'	see *M. domestica* 'Harry Master's Jersey'
- 'Porter's Perfection' (Cider)	CCAT
- 'Pott's Seedling' (C)	SKee
- 'Princesse'	ECrN
- 'Profit'	CCAT CTho
- 'Quarry Apple' (C)	CTho
- 'Queen' (C)	CAgr CTho ECrN SKee
- 'Queen Cox' (D)	CTri ECrN EPom LSRN SKee SLon
- 'Queen Cox' self-fertile	CDul CSut CWib EPom LSRN SWvt WHar
- 'Queenie' (D) **new**	CCAT
- 'Queens' (D)	CTho
- 'Quench' (D/Cider)	CTho
- 'Rajka'[PBR] (D)	CDoC SKee
- 'Red Alkmene' (D)	MBri
- 'Red Belle de Boskoop' (D)	CAgr
- 'Red Bramley' (C)	CWib ECrN
- 'Red Delicious' (D)	SCrf SKee
- 'Red Devil' (D)	CAgr CMac CTri CWSG ECrN EPom GTwe LAst LRHS MBri MRav MWat SBfd SCoo SKee SLim SLon WHar WJas
- 'Red Ellison' (D)	CTho CTri ECrN GTwe
- 'Red Elstar' (D)	IArd
- 'Red Falstaff'[PBR] (D)	CAgr CCAT CCVT CDoC CDul CMac CTri ECrN EPfP GKin LBuc LRHS LSRN MBri MCoo MWat NLar SBfd SKee SLim SLon SPer SPoG WHar
- 'Red James Grieve' (D)	LSRN
- 'Red Jersey' (Cider)	CCAT
- 'Red Joaneting' (D)	SKee WHar
- 'Red Jonagold'[PBR]	see *M. domestica* 'Jonagored'
- 'Red Miller's Seedling' (D)	ECrN SCrf SKee
- 'Red Rattler' (D)	CTho CTri
- 'Red Roller' (D)	CTho
- 'Red Ruby' (F)	CTho
- 'Red Victoria' (C)	GTwe
- 'Red Windsor' (F)	CDoC CMac EPom LBuc LRHS MWat NLar SCoo SKee SLim SPoG WHar WJas
- Redlove Era (C/D) **new**	CSut
- 'Redsleeves' (D)	CAgr ECrN GTwe IArd SKee
- 'Redstrake' (Cider)	CCAT
- Regali = 'Delkistar'[PBR] (D)	LRHS
- 'Reine des Reinettes'	see *M. domestica* 'King of the Pippins'
- 'Reinette Descardre' (D)	SVic
- 'Reinette d'Obry' (Cider)	CCAT
- 'Reinette du Canada' (D)	SKee
- 'Reverend McCormick' (F)	CTho
- 'Reverend W. Wilks' (C)	CAgr CDoC CDoy CSBt CTri ECrN LAst LRHS MBri SCrf SFam SKee SPer WHar WJas
- 'Ribston Pippin' (D) 🏆[H4]	CCAT CTho CTri CWib ECrN GTwe LBuc LRHS MCoo MRav MWat SCrf SFam SKee SLon WHar WJas
- 'Rival' (D)	CAgr
- 'Robert Blatchford' (C)	ECrN
- 'Rosemary Russet' (D) 🏆[H4]	CAgr CCAT CDoC CTho GTwe MCoo SCrf SFam SKee WHar
- 'Ross Nonpareil' (D)	CAgr IArd SKee WHar
- 'Rosy Blenheim' (D)	ECrN
- 'Roundway Magnum Bonum' (D)	CAgr CTho
§ - 'Roxbury Russet' (D)	SKee
- 'Royal Gala' (D) 🏆[H4]	CMac ECrN EPom LAst LBuc MRav SLon
§ - 'Royal Jubilee' (C)	CCAT SKee
- 'Royal Russet' (C)	ECrN
- 'Royal Snow' (D)	SKee
- 'Royal Somerset' (C/Cider)	CCAT CTho CTri
- 'Rubinette' (D)	ECrN
- 'Rubinola'[PBR] (D)	SKee
- 'Ruby' Thorrington (D) **new**	ECrN
- 'Saint Cecilia' (D)	WGwG
§ - 'Saint Edmund's Pippin' (D) 🏆[H4]	CDul CTho ECrN GTwe LRHS MCoo SCrf SFam SKee
- 'Saint Edmund's Russet'	see *M. domestica* 'Saint Edmund's Pippin'
- 'Saint Everard' (D)	SKee
- 'Sam Young' (D)	CAgr IArd SKee
- 'Sandringham' (C)	ECrN
- 'Sanspareil' (D)	CAgr LBuc SKee
- 'Santana' (D)	MBri
- 'Saturn' (D)	CAgr CCVT CDoC CTri SKee WHar
- 'Saw Pits' (F)	CAgr
- 'Scarlet Crofton' (D)	IArd
- 'Schoolmaster' (C)	SKee
- 'Scotch Bridget' (C)	NBid SCoo SKee WHar
- 'Scotch Dumpling' (C)	GKin GTwe MCoo WHar
- 'Scrumptious'[PBR] (D) 🏆[H4]	CAgr CCVT CDoC CMac CTri EPfP EPom GKin LBuc LHop LRHS LSRN MBri MWat NLar NWea SBfd SCoo SEWo SKee SLim SLon SPer SPoG WHar WJas
- 'Sercombe's Natural' (Cider)	CCAT CTho
- 'Severn Bank' (C)	CCAT CTho
- 'Sheep's Nose' (C)	CCAT CTho IArd
- 'Shenandoah' (C)	SKee
- 'Shilling' (F)	LBuc
- 'Shoesmith' (C)	SKee
- 'Sidney Strake' (C)	CAgr
- 'Sir Isaac Newton's'	see *M. domestica* 'Flower of Kent'
- 'Sisson's Worksop Newtown' (D)	MCoo
- 'Slack Ma Girdle' (Cider)	CCAT CTho
- 'Snell's Glass Apple'	see *M. domestica* 'Glass Apple'

– 'Somerset Lasting' (C)	CTri
– 'Somerset Redstreak' (Cider)	CCAT CTho CTri GTwe WHar
– 'Sops in Wine' (C/Cider)	CCAT CTho SVic
– 'Sour Bay' (Cider)	CAgr CTho
– 'Sour Natural'	see *M. domestica* 'Langworthy'
– 'Spartan' (D)	CCAT CCVT CDoC CMac CSBt CTri CWib ECrN ELan EWTr GKin GTwe LAst LRHS MCoo MGos MWat NPri SBfd SCrf SFam SKee SPer SVic WHar WJas
– 'Spencer' (D)	CTri ECrN SKee
– 'Spotted Dick' (Cider)	CTho
– 'Spout Apple' (D)	LBuc
– 'Stable Jersey' (Cider)	CCAT
– 'Stanway Seedling' (C)	ECrN
– 'Star of Devon' (D)	CCAT
– 'Starking' (D)	ECrN
– 'Stark's Earliest' (D)	SVic
– 'Stembridge Cluster' (Cider)	CCAT
– 'Stembridge Jersey' (Cider)	CCAT
– 'Stirling Castle' (C)	CAgr GQui SKee
– 'Stobo Castle' (C)	GQui SKee
– 'Stockbearer' (C)	CTho
– 'Stoke Edith Pippin' (D)	WHar
– 'Stoke Red' (Cider)	CCAT CTho SKee
– 'Strawberry Pippin' (D)	CTho
– 'Striped Beefing' (C)	ECrN
– 'Sturmer Pippin' (D)	CCAT CSBt CTri ECrN GTwe MWat SCrf SFam SKee WHar
* – 'Sugar Apple'	CTho
– 'Sugar Bush' (C/D)	CTho
– 'Sugar Loaf'	see *M. domestica* 'Sugar Apple'
– 'Summer Golden Pippin' (D)	SKee
– 'Summerred' (D)	ECrN
– 'Sunburn' (D)	ECrN
– 'Sunlight'[PBR] (F) **new**	MWat
– 'Sunrise'[PBR] (D)	SKee WHar
– 'Sunset' (D) ♀H4	Widely available
– 'Suntan' (D) ♀H4	CCAT CDoC CWib ECrN LAst MWat SKee
– 'Superb'	see *M. domestica* 'Laxton's Superb'
– 'Sweet Alford' (Cider)	CCAT CTho ECrN
– 'Sweet Bay' (Cider)	CAgr CTho
– 'Sweet Cleave' (Cider)	CTho
– 'Sweet Coppin' (Cider)	CCAT CTho CTri
– 'Sweet Society' (D)	EMil LBuc MCoo SKee WHar WJas
– 'Tale Sweet' (Cider)	CCAT CTho
– 'Tan Harvey' (Cider)	CCAT CTho
– 'Taunton Cross' (D)	CAgr
– 'Taunton Fair Maid' (Cider)	CCAT CTho
– 'Taylor's' (Cider)	CCAT
– 'Ten Commandments' (D/Cider)	CCAT SKee
– 'Tewkesbury Baron' (D)	CTho
– 'The Rattler' (F)	CDoC
– 'Thorle Pippin' (D)	SKee
– 'Tidicombe Seedling' (D)	CTho
– 'Tom Putt' (C)	CAgr CCAT CCVT CDul CTho CTri CWib ECrN GTwe LBuc SKee WHar WJas
– 'Tommy Knight' (D)	CAgr CCAT CDoC CTho
– 'Topaz'[PBR] (D)	CDoC SKee
– 'Totnes Apple' (D)	CTho
– 'Tower of Glamis' (C)	GQui GTwe SKee
– Town Farm Number 59 (Cider)	CTho
– 'Transparent Codlin' (C/D)	LBuc
– 'Tregonna King' (C/D)	CCAT CDoC CTho
– 'Tremlett's Bitter' (Cider)	CAgr CCAT CTho SKee SVic
– 'Trwyn Mochyn' (C)	WGwG
– 'Twinings Pippin' (D)	SKee
§ – 'Tydeman's Early Worcester' (D)	CAgr CDul CWib ECrN GTwe SVic
– 'Tydeman's Late Orange' (D)	CCAT CDoC CMac CTri ECrN EMil GTwe IArd LAst MCoo SFam SKee WHar
– 'Uncle John's Cooker' (C)	IArd
– 'Upton Pyne' (C/D)	CCAT CDoC CTho
– 'Vallis Apple' (Cider)	CCAT CTho
– 'Veitch's Perfection' (C/D)	CTho
– 'Veitch's Prolific' (F) **new**	CDoC
– 'Vicary's Late Keeper'	CTho
– 'Victory' (C) **new**	SKee
– 'Vileberie' (Cider)	CCAT
– 'Vista-bella' (D)	ECrN
– 'Waltham Abbey Seedling' (C)	ECrN
– 'Warner's King' (C) ♀H4	CTho CTri SCrf SKee WHar
– 'Warrior' (F)	CCAT CTho
– 'Wellington' (C)	see *M. domestica* 'Dummellor's Seedling'
– 'Wellington' (Cider)	CAgr CTho
– 'Wern' (C)	WGwG
– 'West View Seedling' (D)	ECrN
– 'Wheeler's Russet' (D)	LBuc SKee
– 'White Alphington' (Cider)	CTho
– 'White Close Pippin' (Cider)	CTho
– 'White Jersey' (Cider)	CCAT
– 'White Melrose' (C)	GTwe SKee
– 'White Transparent' (C/D)	SKee
– 'Wick White Styre' (Cider)	CTho
– 'William Crump' (D)	CCAT CTho ECrN SFam SKee WHar
– 'Willoughby' (D) **new**	MCoo
– 'Winston' (D) ♀H4	CAgr CCAT CCVT CMac CSBt CTri ECrN GTwe MCoo NWea SFam SKee SVic WHar
– 'Winter Banana' (D)	ECrN MCoo SVic WHar
– 'Winter Gem' (D)	CAgr CCVT CDul ECrN EMil EPom LAst LBuc SKee WHar WJas
– 'Winter Lawrence' (F)	CTho
– 'Winter Lemon' (C/D)	GQui SKee
– 'Winter Peach' (D/C)	CAgr CDoC CTho ECrN
– 'Winter Pearmain' (D)	WHar
– 'Winter Stubbard' (C)	CTho
– 'Wintergreen' (C) **new**	CDoC
– 'Woodbine'	see *M. domestica* 'Northwood'
– 'Woodford' (C)	ECrN
– 'Woolbrook Pippin' (D)	CAgr CTho
– 'Woolbrook Russet' (C)	CTho ECrN
– 'Worcester Pearmain' (D) ♀H4	Widely available
– 'Wormsley Pippin' (D)	ECrN
– 'Wyatt's Seedling'	see *M. domestica* 'Langworthy'
– 'Wyken Pippin' (D)	CCAT ECrN SFam SKee
– 'Yarlington Mill' (Cider)	CAgr CCAT CTho CTri SKee SVic
– 'Yellow Ingestrie' (D)	LRHS MCoo SFam WHar WJas
– 'Yellow Styre' (Cider)	CTho
– 'Yorkshire Greening' (C)	SKee WHar
'Donald Wyman'	CLnd EPfP NLar SCoo
'Echtermeyer'	see *M.* × *gloriosa* 'Oekonomierat Echtermeyer'
florentina	CLnd CTho EPfP LLHF SSpi

	- 'Rosemoor'	EBee
	- 'Skopje'	EPfP WMou
	floribunda ♀H4	Widely available
	'Gardener's Gold'	CTho
§	× ***gloriosa*** 'Oekonomierat Echtermeyer'	SGol
	'Golden Gem'	EMil EPfP MAsh SEWo SLim SPer
	'Golden Hornet'	see *M.* × *zumi* 'Golden Hornet'
	'Harry Baker'	CCVT CDul CLnd EBee ECrN EMil EPfP EPom LRHS MAsh MBlu MBri MWat NLar SCoo SLim SPoG WJas
	× ***hartwigii***	CLnd
	'Hillieri'	see *M.* × *scheideckeri* 'Hillieri'
	hupehensis ♀H4	CDoy CDul CLnd CMCN CSBt CTho EBee EPfP LHop MBlu MGos MRav NWea SCrf SFam SPer WPat
	'Hyde Hall Spire'	EBee MAsh SCoo
	'Indian Magic'	CLnd EBee LRHS MAsh MBri
	'Indian Summer' **new**	CLnd
	Jelly King = 'Mattfru'	LRHS MBri MWat NLar
	'John Downie' (C) ♀H4	Widely available
	'Kaido'	see *M.* × *micromalus*
	kansuensis	CLnd EPfP
	'Laura'	CDul EPfP EPom LRHS LSRN MAsh MBri MWat NLar SCoo SKee SLim SLon SPoG WJas
	'Louisa'	CWSG MAsh NWea SCoo SGol
	× ***magdeburgensis***	CCVT CDul CLnd CSBt
	'Mary Potter'	CLnd
§	× ***micromalus***	CLnd NLar
	× ***moerlandsii***	CLnd
	- 'Liset'	CDul CSBt CWib EBee ECrN LHop MRav NEgg SCoo SEWo SFam SPer SPoG WFar WMou
§	- 'Profusion'	CBcs CDul CMac CTri EBee ECrN ELan LAst MGos MMuc MRav MSwo MWat NPri NWea SBfd SCrf SEND SGol SPer SWvt WFar WJas
	- 'Profusion Improved'	CSBt CWSG LRHS MAsh MWat SCoo SWvt WHar
	'Mokum'	CCVT CLnd LTen
	'Molten Lava'	CLnd MAsh
	niedzwetzkyana	CLnd CTho
	Nuvar Marble	MAsh MBri SKee
	orthocarpa	CLnd
	Perpetu = 'Evereste'	Widely available
	'Pink Glow'	CLnd CSBt EPom MAsh MBlu MWat NLar SBfd SCoo SEWo SLim SPer SPoG WHar
	'Pink Mushroom'	NLar
	'Pink Perfection'	CDoC ECrN NLar NWea
	Pom'Zaï = 'Courtabri'	CDoC
	'Pond Red'	CLnd
	'Prairie Fire'	CDul CLnd LRHS MAsh MBri SCoo SLim SLon SPoG
	prattii	CLnd CTho EPfP
	- 'Pourpre Noir' **new**	CLnd
	'Princeton Cardinal'	CLnd CMac EPfP MBri SCoo SLim
	'Professor Sprenger'	see *M.* × *zumi* 'Professor Sprenger'
	'Profusion'	see *M.* × *moerlandsii* 'Profusion'
	prunifolia	MBlu
	- var. ***rinkii***	CLnd
	pumila 'Cowichan'	CLnd ECrN
	- 'Dartmouth'	CDul CLnd CSBt CTri ECrN NEgg NPCo SFam
	- 'Montreal Beauty'	CLnd WJas
	'Purple Prince'	CLnd
§	× ***purpurea*** 'Aldenhamensis'	CLnd WHar
	- 'Eleyi'	CDul LAst NWea
	- 'Lemoinei'	CDul CLnd
	- 'Neville Copeman'	CCVT CDoC CDul CLnd EBee ECrN EPom EWTr SBfd WJas WMou
	- 'Pendula'	see *M.* × *gloriosa* 'Oekonomierat Echtermeyer'
	'R.J. Fulcher'	CTho
	'Ralph Shay'	CLnd
	'Red Ace'	CDul
	'Red Barron'	CLnd
	'Red Glow'	CDul CLnd ECrN MAsh MMuc SEND WJas
	'Red Jade'	see *M.* × *scheideckeri* 'Red Jade'
	'Red Obelisk'	CWSG LRHS MAsh MBri SCoo SPoG
	'Red Peacock'	CLnd
	'Robinson'	CLnd
§	× ***robusta***	CLnd GTwe LSRN NWea SBfd SCrf SLon
	- 'Red Sentinel' ♀H4	Widely available
	- 'Red Siberian'	SPer
	- 'Yellow Siberian'	CLnd
	'Rosehip' **new**	MBri
	'Royal Beauty' ♀H4	CDoC CDul CLnd CWib EPfP LAst LRHS MAsh MBri MGos MSwo SBfd SCoo SCrf SLon SPer WHar WMou
	'Royalty'	CBcs CDul CLnd CMac CSBt EBee ECrN ELan GTwe LAst LBuc LHop MGos MRav MSwo MWat NEgg NPla SBfd SCrf SEND SEWo SGol SPer WHar WJas
	'Rudolph'	CCVT CDul CLnd EBee ECrN EWTr GKin LBuc LHop LMaj MAsh MGos SCoo SEWo SLim SPer WJas WMou
	'Ruth Ann'	CLnd
	sargentii	CDul CTho EWTr LRHS NWea SFam
	- 'Tina'	CWSG MAsh
	'Satin Cloud'	CLnd
§	× ***scheideckeri*** 'Hillieri'	CDul CLnd ECrN SFam
§	- 'Red Jade'	CDul CTri CWib EBee ECrN ELan LAst MGos MMuc MRav MSwo MWat NEgg NPri NWea SBfd SEND SPer WFar WJas
	Siberian crab	see *M.* × *robusta*
	sieboldii	see *M. toringo*
	sieversii	CDul
	'Silver Drift'	CLnd
	'Snowcloud'	CDul CLnd ECrN MAsh SLim SPer
	'Snowdrift' **new**	CLnd
	'Street Parade'	CLnd
	× ***sublobata***	CLnd
	Sugar Tyme = 'Sutyzam' **new**	CLnd
	'Sun Rival'	CCVT CDoC CDul CLnd CSBt EPfP GTwe LRHS MAsh MBri NLar SBfd SCoo SEWo SLim SPoG WHar WJas
	sylvestris	CCVT CDul CHab CLnd CRWN ECrN EPfP LBuc MMuc MRav NLar NWea SEND SEWo SPer WMou
§	***toringo***	CLnd CTho ECrN EPfP LEdu LMaj MBri WSHC
I	- var. ***arborescens***	CLnd CTho
	- 'Browers'	LMaj
	- 'Scarlett'	CLnd IArd LRHS MBri NLar NWea SCoo SLim SPoG WJas WMou

- 'Wintergold'	MMuc
toringoides	see *M. bhutanica*
transitoria ♀H4	CDoC CDul CLnd CTho EBee ECrN ELan EMil EPfP LRHS MAsh MBlu MBri MRav NLar NWea SCoo SFam SSpi WMou WPGP
- 'Thornhayes Tansy'	CDul CTho EBee LRHS MAsh SLim SPoG
trilobata	CDul CLnd CTho EBee ELan EMil EPfP LHop LMaj MBlu MGos MMuc SCoo SEND
- 'Guardsman'	EBee MBri NLar SSpi WMou
tschonoskii ♀H4	CDoC CDul CLnd CMCN CMac CSBt CTho CTri CWib EBee ELan EPfP GTwe LAst LMaj LRHS MAsh MBlu MBri MGos MMuc NPri NWea SBfd SEND SPer SWvt WJas WMou
'Van Eseltine'	CDul CLnd CSBt CWib EBee ECrN EPfP MAsh MMuc MWat SFam WHar WJas
'Veitch's Scarlet'	CDoy CDul CLnd CSBt NEgg NPCo SFam
Weeping Candied Apple = 'Weepcanzam'	CLnd
'White Star'	CCVT CDoC CDul CLnd CSBt EBee ECrN LRHS SBfd SLon
'Winter Gold'	CDul LMaj MMuc SCrf SGol
'Wisley Crab'	CLnd SFam SLon WMou
yunnanensis	EPfP
- var. ***veitchii***	CTho
× ***zumi*** var. ***calocarpa***	CLnd
§ - 'Golden Hornet' ♀H4	Widely available
§ - 'Professor Sprenger'	CLnd CSam EPfP LMaj MBri SCoo

Malva (*Malvaceae*)

alcea var. ***fastigiata***	CMac EBee ECGP NBro SRms WFar WPer XLum
bicolor	see *Lavatera maritima*
'Gibbortello'	LRHS
moschata	CArn CBcs CPrp CRWN EBee ECtt ELan ENfk EPfP GAbr GJos GPoy MHer MMuc MNHC NLar NMir SIde SPer SPlb SWat WHer WJek WMoo XLum
- f. ***alba*** ♀H4	CArn CBcs CPrp CSpe EBee ECha ELan EPfP GJos GMaP LHop LRHS MHer MMuc MNHC NBir NBro NEgg NGBl NLar SBfd SPer SPoG SWvt WBrk WCAu WKif WMnd WMoo
- 'Appleblossom'	EBee
- 'Romney Marsh'	see *Althaea officinalis* 'Romney Marsh'
- ***rosea***	EPfP GMaP LAst NEgg NPer SBfd SPoG SWvt
pusilla	CCCN
'Sweet Sixteen'	EBee
sylvestris	CArn NBro SWat WHfH WJek WMoo
- 'Blue Fountain' PBR	LSou WKif
- 'Brave Heart'	SPav SWvt
- Marina = 'Dema' PBR	ELan NLar
- var. ***mauritiana***	NPer WMoo
- - 'Bibor Fehlo'	CSpe
- - 'Mystic Merlin'	CWCL SPav
- - 'Primley Blue'	EBee ECtt ELan EPfP GMaP MRav NPer WNew
- - 'Zebrina'	EBee EPfP LDai NPer SWvt WMoo
- 'Perry's Blue'	NPer

Malvastrum (*Malvaceae*)

× ***hypomadarum***	see *Anisodontea* × *hypomadara* (Sprague) D.M. Bates

Malvaviscus (*Malvaceae*)

arboreus	CHII

mandarin see *Citrus reticulata* Mandarin Group

Mandevilla (*Apocynaceae*)

§ × ***amabilis***	CCCN
- 'Alice du Pont' ♀H1	CCCN ELan EShb LRHS MOWG
- 'Passion Pink' (Parfait Series) (d)	LRHS
× ***amoena***	see *M.* × *amabilis*
boliviensis ♀H1	CCCN CRHN LRHS MOWG
§ ***laxa*** ♀H2	CCCN CHEx CHGN CHII CRHN CSpe ECre ELan EShb IRar LRHS MOWG SAga SGar WPGP WSHC
sanderi	CCCN EShb
splendens ♀H1	CCCN CHII MOWG
suaveolens	see *M. laxa*
Sundaville Pink = 'Sunmandecripi' PBR	LSou
Sundaville Red = 'Sunmandecrim' PBR	LAst LSou
Sweet Passion (Perlavilla Series)	LRHS

Mandragora (*Solanaceae*)

autumnalis	SMad WCot
§ ***officinarum***	CArn CRDP GCal GPoy SMad WCot

Manettia (*Rubiaceae*)

inflata	see *M. luteorubra*
§ ***luteorubra***	CCCN CHII

Manfreda see *Agave*

× *Mangave* see *Agave*

Mangifera (*Anacardiaceae*)

indica (F)	CCCN EAmu
- 'Osteen' (F) **new**	NPla
- 'Tommy Atkins' (F) **new**	NPla

Manglietia see *Magnolia*

yunnanensis	see *Magnolia insignis*

mango see *Mangifera indica*

Manihot (*Euphorbiaceae*)

carthaginensis	SPlb
esculenta 'Variegata'	EAmu GHim

Mantisalca (*Asteraceae*)

salmantica **new**	WCot

Mantisia (*Zingiberaceae*)

saltatoria **new**	WCot

Maranta (*Marantaceae*)

leuconeura var. ***erythroneura*** ♀H1	XBlo
- var. ***kerchoveana*** ♀H1	XBlo

Marchantia (*Marchantiaceae*)

polymorpha	CArn

Margyricarpus (*Rosaceae*)

§ **pinnatus** GEdr WPer
setosus see *M. pinnatus*

Mariscus see *Cyperus*

marjoram, pot see *Origanum onites*

marjoram, sweet see *Origanum majorana*

marjoram, wild, or oregano see *Origanum vulgare*

Marrubium (*Lamiaceae*)

§ **bourgaei** var. **bourgaei** EBee ECha ECtt LRHS MRav NEgg
'All Hallows Green' WOut XSen
candidissimum see *M. incanum*
cylleneum EWll
* - 'Velvetissimum' XSen
§ **incanum** XSen
libanoticum WPer
supinum CArn
vulgare CArn ENfk GPoy MHer MHoo MNHC SIde WJek XLum

Marsdenia (*Asclepiadaceae*)

formosana CWJ 12354 WCru

Marshallia (*Asteraceae*)

grandiflora CDes EBee SUsu
mohrii EBee
trinerva ELon

Marsilea (*Marsileaceae*)

mutica EWay
quadrifolia EWay

Massonia (*Asparagaceae*)

depressa ECho
- 'Branvlei Dam' ECho
- 'Reitfontein Gamoep' ECho
echinata ECho WCot
aff. **echinata** ECho WCot
jasminiflora ECho
pustulata ECho EUJe WCot
pygmaea ECho
subsp. **kamiesbergensis**
- subsp. **pygmaea** ECho

Mathiasella (*Apiaceae*)

bupleuroides CDes CHid LSou
- 'Green Dream' CAbP CAvo CBcs CBre CMea CSpe EBee ECtt EWll GBin LRHS MBel MNrw MPie MPnt MWat NCGa NPnk NSti SDix SLon SMrm SPoG SUsu WCot

Matricaria (*Asteraceae*)

chamomilla see *M. recutita*
parthenium see *Tanacetum parthenium*
§ **recutita** CArn GPoy MNHC
tchihatchewii XSen
'White Star' EPfP

Matteuccia (*Onocleaceae*)

orientalis CBty CDTJ CDes CKel CLAP EFer EPfP ERod GCal GEdr GMaP LRHS NBid NLar NMyG NOrc WFar WMoo WPnP WWEG XLum
pensylvanica CLAP EBee MMoz
struthiopteris ♀H4 Widely available
* - 'Depauperata' CLAP
- 'Jumbo' CBty CCCN CLAP EBee ISha LRHS
- 'The King' WCot

Matthiola (*Brassicaceae*)

fruticulosa 'Alba' CDes LEdu WPGP
- subsp. **perennis** NSti WHal
incana EBee LRHS MArl SPad WFar WKif
- **alba** CHid CMea ECha ELan LSou NCGa SEND SMad SPav WCot WRHF
- 'Legacy' mixed **new** NPri
- 'Pillow Talk' **new** WCAu
- purple-flowered SEND
montana LLHF
white-flowered perennial CArn CSev CSpe MSCN NPer

Maurandya (*Plantaginaceae*)

§ **barclayana** CDTJ CHll MBri SGar
'Bridal Bouquet' CCCN LSou
erubescens see *Lophospermum erubescens*
lophantha see *Lophospermum scandens*
lophospermum see *Lophospermum scandens*
'Magic Dragon' see *Lophospermum* 'Magic Dragon'
'Red Dragon' see *Lophospermum* 'Red Dragon'

Maytenus (*Celastraceae*)

boaria CBcs CMCN EPfP IArd IDee LEdu MBri MGos NLar SEND WSHC
disticha (Hook.f.) Urb. LEdu

Mazus (*Phrymaceae*)

novae-zeelandiae CTrC
reptans EBee ECho EPfP EPot MSKA NLBP NLar NPer XLum
- B&SWJ CPLG GEdr
- 'Albus' EBee ECho EPfP MSKA NLar SPlb XLum

Mecardonia (*Plantaginaceae*)

'Goldflake' CCCN
'Sundona Early Yellow' LAst

Meconopsis ✿ (*Papaveraceae*)

aculeata GCra
Ballyrogan form GEdr
betonicifolia ♀H4 CBcs CGHE CSBt CTri CWCL EBee ELan EPau EPfP GAbr GBuc GCra GGGa GKev GKin IBoy ITim LRHS MBri MCot NBir NEgg NLar NPri NRHS NSum SPoG WFar WMoo WSpi
- var. **alba** EBee ELan GBin GCra GGGa GKev LRHS NGdn NLar NSum
- 'Hensol Violet' GBuc GCra GGGa NLar NSum
- violet-flowered ITim
cambrica CCCN CMac CPLG CTri EHrv ELan EPfP GJos MMuc NPri SGar WBrk WFar WHer WPtf WSpi
- 'Anne Greenaway' (d) WCot
- var. **aurantiaca** SBch WCot WFar
- double-flowered (d) WCot WFar
- - orange (d) NBir WCot
§ - 'Frances Perry' EWld GCal WCot WFar
- 'Muriel Brown' (d) GCal WCot

	- 'Rubra'	see *M. cambrica* 'Frances Perry'
	chelidoniifolia	EWld GCra IGor NBid WCru WFar
	× ***cookei***	GKev
	- 'Old Rose'	GBin GBuc GEdr GGGa
N	Fertile Blue Group	ITim
N	- 'Blue Ice'	see *M.* (Fertile Blue Group) 'Lingholm'
	- 'Cally Lingholm' new	GCal
N	- 'Lingholm'	Widely available
	- 'Mop-head'	GEdr
§	George Sherriff Group	GCal GCra GEdr NBir
	- 'Ascreavie'	GBuc GEdr GMaP
	- 'Barney's Blue'	GEdr GMaP
	- 'Branklyn' ambig.	CGHE CPLG GEdr LRHS WPGP
	- 'Dalemain'	GBuc GMaP
	- 'Huntfield'	GBin GEdr GGGa GMaP
	- 'Jimmy Bayne'	GBin GEdr GGGa GMaP
	- 'Susan's Reward' new	GMaP
	grandis misapplied	see *M.* George Sherriff Group
	grandis ambig.	GEdr GLin WFar
	grandis Prain	GKev
	- GS 600	see *M.* George Sherriff Group
	- 'Alba'	WSpi
	- Balruddery form	GGGa
	- 'Tromso'	GEdr
	horridula	CPBP GCra GGGa
	- CC 6554	GKev
	- CC 6634	GKev
	(Infertile Blue Group) 'Bobby Masterton'	GCra GEdr GMaP
	- 'Crarae'	GGGa
	- 'Crewdson Hybrid'	GBuc GEdr GMaP
	- 'Dawyck'	see *M.* (Infertile Blue Group) 'Slieve Donard'
	- 'Maggie Sharp'	GEdr
	- 'Mrs Jebb'	GBuc GCra GEdr GMaP
§	- 'Slieve Donard' ♀H4	GBuc GCal GCra GEdr GGGa GKev GKin GMaP LRHS NRHS
	integrifolia	CCCN GBin GEdr GGGa WAbe
N	***napaulensis*** misapplied	GCra GEdr GKev ITim LHop NLar WMoo
	- from Solukhumbu, Nepal	GCra
	- pink-flowered	LRHS NGdn
	- red-flowered	CBcs ITim
	nudicaulis	see *Papaver nudicaule*
	paniculata	GGGa GKev LRHS
	- from Bhutan	GCra
	- from Ghunsa, Nepal	CLAP
	- ginger foliage	CHid
	pseudointegrifolia	GGGa
	punicea	GGGa GKev WAbe
	quintuplinervia ♀H4	CLAP GCra NHar NSla
	- Farrer's form	GKev
	regia misapplied	WMoo
	- hybrids	GGGa
	× ***sheldonii*** misapplied (fertile)	see *M.* Fertile Blue Group
	× ***sheldonii*** misapplied (sterile)	see *M.* Infertile Blue Group
	× ***sheldonii*** ambig.	CBcs EBee GAbr ITim MCot NBir NLar NPer WFar
	simplicifolia	GGGa
	'Stewart Annand'	GEdr
	superba	GGGa GKev WAbe
	villosa	GCra GGGa GLin
	wallichii misapplied	see *M. wallichii* Hook.
	wallichii ambig.	GLin
§	***wallichii*** Hook.	GGGa
	'Willie Duncan'	GMaP
	wilsonii subsp. ***australis***	GGGa GLin

Medicago (*Papilionaceae*)

arborea	CArn SEND SPlb
lupulina	CHab
sativa	NLar WHer WSFF

Medinilla (*Melastomataceae*)

magnifica ♀H1	CCCN MBri

medlar see *Mespilus germanica*

Meehania (*Lamiaceae*)

cordata	CDes EBee
fargesii	CLAP
urticifolia	EPPr GCal GEdr WSHC
- B&SWJ 1210	WCru
- 'Wandering Minstrel' (v)	WCot

Megacarpaea (*Brassicaceae*)

polyandra	WCot

Melaleuca (*Myrtaceae*)

	acuminata	SPlb
	alternifolia	CArn CBcs CCCN CTsd ECou EOHP GPoy IDee MHer MHoo SPlb WHer WHfH
	armillaris	CCCN CDoC IDee SEND SPlb
	blaeriifolia	ECou
	bracteata	ECou
	cuticularis	SPlb
	decussata	CBcs ECou MOWG SPlb
§	***diosmatifolia***	CBcs CPLG
	elliptica	MOWG
	ericifolia	CTri CTsd GLin SEND SPlb
	erubescens	see *M. diosmatifolia*
	fulgens	ECou MOWG SPlb
	- apricot-flowered	MOWG
*	- 'Hot Pink'	MOWG
	- purple-flowered	MOWG
	gibbosa	CPLG CTrC EBee ECou ELan EUJe IDee IVic LRHS LSou MOWG SEND WSHC
	hypericifolia	CDoC CPLG CTrC MOWG SPlb
	incana	MOWG
	lateritia	ECou MOWG
	linariifolia	CCCN ECou SPlb
	nesophila	ECou EShb MOWG SPlb
	pentagona var. ***subulifolia***	ECou
	pulchella	ECou MOWG
	pungens	SPlb
	pustulata	ECou MOWG
	squamea	CTsd SEND SPlb
*	***squarmania***	MOWG
	squarrosa	CPLG CTrC ECou IDee LRHS MOWG SPlb
	tamariscina new	ECou
	thymifolia	ECou LRHS MOWG SPlb WAbe
	trichophylla new	SPlb
	wilsonii	ECou IDee

Melandrium see *Vaccaria*

rubrum	see *Silene dioica*

Melanoselinum (*Apiaceae*)

§	***decipiens***	CAbb CArn CHEx CSpe EBee EWes LEdu SMad WCot WJek WPGP

Melasphaerula (*Iridaceae*)

	graminea	see *M. ramosa*
§	***ramosa***	CBre ECho

Melastoma (*Melastomataceae*)

	sp.	CCCN

Melia (*Meliaceae*)

§	***azedarach***	CArn CBcs CCCN EPfP EShb GPoy LEdu SEND SPlb
	- B&SWJ 7039	WCru
	- var. ***japonica***	see *M. azedarach*

Melianthus (*Melianthaceae*)

	comosus	CDTJ EAmu EBee ELan EPri EShb ESwi EWes NLar SCoo SGar SPlb WSpi
	major ♀H3	Widely available
	minor	CCon CHid
	villosus	CCon CDes CHGN EWes SGar SPlb WOut WPGP

Melica (*Poaceae*)

	altissima 'Alba'	MLHP
	- 'Atropurpurea'	CTrC CWCL EBee ECha EHoe EPPr LEdu LHop LLWP LRHS MCot MMoz MNrw MWat MWhi NBid NLar SEND SGar SPlb WFar WMnd WMoo WPtf WWEG
	californica new	EPPr
	ciliata	EHoe EPPr EPfP MMoz MWhi WMnd WPtf WWEG XLum
	macra	EHoe EPPr SApp
	nutans	CWCL EBee EHoe EPPr EShb GQue MAsh NMRc NOak NWsh SBch SMHy SMrm WCot
	penicillaris	EPPr
	transsilvanica 'Atropurpurea'	EBee MMuc
	- 'Red Spire'	CWib MBNS MWhi SBfd SGol SHDw SMea SMrm WMoo XLum
	uniflora	MBel NOak
	- f. ***albida***	ECha EHoe GCal MAvo NDov NOak SLPl SMHy SUsu WCot WSHC
	- 'Variegata' (v)	CBre ECGP ECha EHoe ELon GCal MAvo MMoz NOak SUsu WCot WMoo WTin WWEG

Melicytus (*Violaceae*)

	alpinus	ECou
	angustifolius	ECou
	crassifolius	ECou
	obovatus	ECou NLar
	ramiflorus	CHEx ECou

Melilotus (*Papilionaceae*)

	officinalis	CArn CHab GPoy SIde WHer
	- subsp. ***albus***	CArn

Melinis (*Poaceae*)

	nerviglumis	LEdu
	- 'Savannah'	CWib

Meliosma (*Sabiaceae*)

	cuneifolia	CBcs NLar
	dilleniifolia subsp. ***tenuis***	CPLG
	myriantha	SSpi
	veitchiorum	EGFP NLar

Melissa ✿ (*Lamiaceae*)

	officinalis	CArn CHab CPbn CTri CWan ELau ENfk GJos GMaP GPoy LPot MBri MHer MHoo MNHC NBir SBfd SEND SIde SPlb SVic WHfH WJek
	- 'All Gold'	CArn CBre CPbn CSev ECha EHoe ELan ELau ENfk EOHP MHoo MNHC NBid SPer SPoG
§	- 'Aurea' (v)	CArn CPLG CPrp CSev CWan ELan ELau GCra GMaP GPoy MBri MHer MHoo MNHC MRav NBid NBir NBro NPri SBfd SIde SPer SPoG SRms WFar WJek WMnd WMoo XLum
*	- 'Compacta'	CPbn GPoy
	- 'Lime Balm'	CPbn EOHP MHoo
	- 'Quedlinburger Niederliegende'	CArn CPbn
N	- 'Variegata' misapplied	see *M. officinalis* 'Aurea'

Melittis (*Lamiaceae*)

	melissophyllum	CArn CLAP CMea CPom CRDP CSpe EBee ELon ITim LEdu LRHS LSou MNrw MRav NMen SSvw SUsu WCot WOut
	- subsp. ***albida***	EBee WCot
	- 'Apple Blossom'	CDes
	- pink-flowered	CLAP LEdu SUsu WBor WCot WPtf
	- 'Royal Velvet Distinction'PBR	CSpe EBee LBMP MAvo MBri MRav NDov SHar WCot WHil

Melliodendron (*Styracaceae*)

	xylocarpum	CPLG

Menispermum (*Menispermaceae*)

	canadense	CTri GPoy
	davuricum	GKin NLar

Menstruocalamus (*Poaceae*)

	sichuanensis	WPGP

Mentha ✿ (*Lamiaceae*)

	sp.	CHab
	SJ 2075	WCot
	from Jamaica	CArn
	angustifolia Corb.	see *M.* × *villosa*
	angustifolia Host	see *M. arvensis*
	angustifolia ambig.	CPbn SIde
	aquatica	CArn CBen CHab CPbn CRow CWat EHon EPfP GPoy LEdu LPBA MHer MHoo MNHC MWts NMir NPer NYoL SIde SPlb SVic SWat WHer WMAq WMoo WPnP WSFF XLum
§	- var. ***crispa***	CPbn NYoL SIde
	- krause minze	see *M. aquatica* var. *crispa*
	- 'Mandeliensis'	CPbn
§	***arvensis***	CArn CPbn ELau MHer NYoL SIde
	- 'Banana'	CPbn EGHP ENfk LEdu MHer MHoo MNHC NPri NYoL SIde WJek
	- var. ***piperascens***	LEdu MHer SIde WJek
§	- - 'Sayakaze'	CArn ELau
	- var. ***villosa***	CPbn
	asiatica	CPbn ELau MHer SIde
	'Berries and Cream'	ENfk LEdu WJek
	'Betty's Slovakian'	CPbn
	Bowles's mint	see *M.* × *villosa* var. *alopecuroides* Bowles's mint

*	***brevifolia***	CPbn SIde
	cervina	CArn CBen CPbn CWat EHon LEdu LPBA MHer MSKA NLar SIde SWat WJek XLum
*	**- *alba***	CPbn LPBA MHer MSKA NLar NYoL WMAq
I	'Chocolate Peppermint'	ENfk EWhm GAbr MHoo NBir NYoL
	citrata	see *M.* × *piperita* f. *citrata*
	'Clarissa's Millennium'	CPbn SIde
	cordifolia	see *M.* × *villosa*
	corsica	see *M. requienii*
	crispa L. (1753)	see *M. spicata* var. *crispa*
	crispa L. (1763)	see *M. aquatica* var. *crispa*
	crispa ambig. × (× ***piperita***)	CArn CPbn
	cucumber mint **new**	CPbn
	'Dionysus'	CPbn SIde
	× ***dumetorum***	CPbn NYoL
	- wine mint **new**	CPbn
	'Eau de Cologne'	see *M.* × *piperita* f. *citrata*
	eucalyptus mint	CPbn EGHP ELau MHer WGwG
	gattefossei	CArn
	× ***gentilis***	see *M.* × *gracilis*
§	× ***gracilis***	CArn CPbn EGHP ELau ENfk NPri NYoL SIde
	- 'Aurea'	see *M.* × *gracilis* 'Variegata'
§	- 'Variegata' (v)	CPbn CSev CWan ECha ELau GPoy LEdu MCot MHer MNHC NPri NYoL SPlb SWal WFar WHer WPer XLum
	graveolens **new**	MHoo
	haplocalyx	CArn ELau NYoL SIde
	'Herbert McHale' **new**	LEdu
*	'Hillary's Sweet Lemon'	CPbn ELau ENfk MHer NYoL SIde
	'Julia's Sweet Citrus'	CPbn MHer SIde
*	***lacerata***	NYoL SIde
	lavender mint	EGHP ELau GPoy LEdu MHer MNHC NYoL WJek
§	***longifolia***	CPbn CWan ELau ENfk LEdu MHoo MMuc NYoL SEND SIde SPlb WHer
	- Buddleia Mint Group	CArn CPbn EBee EGHP ELau ENfk LEdu MHer MHoo MRav NYoL SIde WJek XLum
	- - variegated (v)	LEdu WJek
	- dwarf	CPbn
	- subsp. ***schimperi***	LEdu NYoL SIde WJek
	- silver-leaved	CArn CPbn ELau GAbr LEdu MHer MHoo MNHC NLar NYoL SEND WJek
*	- 'Variegata' (v)	CPbn ELau GAbr NYoL
	Nile Valley mint	CArn ELau EWhm LEdu NYoL SHDw SIde
	× ***piperita***	CArn CHab CHby CPbn CSev CWan ECha EGHP EHoe ELau GJos GPoy LHop MBri MCot MHer MNHC NPri NYoL SPlb WPer
	- 'Black Mitcham'	CArn CPbn NYoL XLum
	- black peppermint	CHby CPbn EGHP ENfk EPfP EWhm GAbr LEdu MHoo MMuc MNHC NBir NLar NYoL SEND SWal WJek
§	- f. ***citrata***	CArn CHab CHby COlW CPbn CTri ECha EGHP ELau GJos GMaP GPoy LEdu MBri MHer MHoo MNHC MRav NBir NYoL SBfd SEND SHDw SIde SPlb SVic WJek WPer XLum
	- - from Portugal	CPbn
*	- - 'Basil'	CPbn CWan EGHP ELau GAbr LEdu MHer MNHC MRav NYoL SBfd SHDw SIde WGwG WJek XLum
	- - 'Bergamot'	CPbn XLum
	- - 'Chocolate'	CArn CPbn CWan EGHP ELau ENfk EOHP EPfP GJos LEdu MHer MNHC NYoL SBfd SHDw SIde SPlb WGwG WJek XLum
	- - 'Grapefruit'	CPbn CWan EGHP EWhm GAbr LSou MHer MNHC NYoL WJek
	- - 'Lemon'	CPbn CWan EGHP ELau ENfk EWhm GPoy LEdu MBri MHer MHoo MNHC NYoL SBfd SHDw SIde WJek WPer
	- - 'Lime'	CPbn CWan EGHP ENfk EWhm GAbr LBuc LEdu LSou MHer MHoo NYoL SBfd SHDw SIde SPlb WGwG WJek
	- - 'Orange'	CPbn EGHP ENfk LEdu MHer MMuc MNHC NYoL SEND WHil WJek
	- - 'Reverchonii'	CPbn SIde
	- - 'Swiss Ricola'	MHer NYoL SIde
	- 'Logee's' (v)	CPbn SIde
	- 'Milly Mitcham' **new**	CPbn
	- f. ***officinalis***	CPbn ELau SIde
	- var. ***ouweneellii*** Belgian mint	CPbn SIde
	- 'Persephone' **new**	CPbn
	- 'Reine Rouge'	CPbn SIde
	- 'Swiss'	EGHP EWhm LEdu MHoo NLar WJek
I	- Swiss mint	CArn CPbn ENfk
*	- white-flowered	CArn CPbn
	'Polynesian Mint'	CPbn
	pulegium	CArn CHby CPbn CRWN CSev CTri CWan ELau ENfk GPoy MHer MHoo MNHC MSKA NPri SIde SPlb SRms SVic WHer WHfH WJek WPer XLum
	- 'Upright'	CArn CPbn ENfk GPoy MHer MHoo SBfd SHDw SIde WJek WPer
§	***requienii***	Widely available
	rotundifolia misapplied	see *M. suaveolens*
	rotundifolia (L.) Hudson	see *M.* × *villosa*
	rubra var. ***raripila***	see *M.* × *smithiana*
	'Russian' curled leaf	CPbn
	'Russian' plain leaf	CPbn NYoL
	'Sayakaze'	see *M. arvensis* var. *piperascens* 'Sayakaze'
§	× ***smithiana***	CArn CPbn CWan EGHP ELau ENfk GPoy MHer MHoo MNHC MRav NBir NPri NYoL WJek WPer
	- 'Capel Ulo' (v)	ELau
	'South of France'	CPbn
§	***spicata***	CArn CHby COlW CPbn CPrp CSev CTri CWan EGHP ELau ENfk GJos GPoy LPot MBri MCot MHer MHoo MNHC NPri NYoL SEND SPlb SRms SWal WHer WJek WPer XLum
	- Algerian fruity	CPbn SIde
	- 'Austrian'	CPbn
*	- 'Brundall'	CPbn ELau NYoL SIde
	- 'Canaries'	CPbn
*	- var. ***crispa***	CArn CPbn CWan ECha EGHP ELau ENfk LEdu LHop LPot MHer MMuc MNHC NRya NYoL SBfd SIde SPlb WJek WPer

	- - 'Moroccan'	CArn CPbn CPrp CSev EGHP ELau ENfk EOHP GAbr GJos GPoy LEdu MHer MHoo MNHC NPri NYoL SBfd SEND SHDw SIde SUsu WJek
	- - 'Persian'	CPbn
	- 'Crispula' **new**	GAbr XLum
	- 'Guernsey'	CPbn SBfd SHDw SIde
	- 'Irish'	CPbn
	- 'Kentucky Colonel'	CPbn LEdu
	- 'Mexican'	CArn CPbn
	- 'Newbourne'	CPbn ELau SIde
	- 'Pharaoh'	CArn CPbn
	- 'Rhodos'	CPbn
	- 'Russian'	CArn EGHP MHer SIde
	- 'Small Dole' (v)	SBfd SHDw
	- 'Spanish'	LEdu
	- 'Spanish Furry'	CPbn MHer SIde
	- 'Spanish Pointed'	CPbn ELau SIde WJek
	- 'Tashkent'	CArn CHby CPbn EGHP ELau ENfk EOHP EWhm LEdu MHer MNHC NYoL SBfd SHDw SIde WGwG WJek
	- subsp. ***tomentosa***	CPbn
*	- 'Variegata' (v)	CPbn SBfd SHDw
	- 'Verte Blanche'	CPbn
§	***suaveolens***	CArn CHby CPbn CWan EGHP ELau ENfk GJos GMaP GPoy MBri MHer MHoo MLHP MNHC NYoL SBfd SEND SIde SPlb SVic SWal WJek WPer WSFF
*	- 'Grapefruit'	EGHP LEdu
	- 'Jokka'	CPbn EBee
*	- 'Mobillei'	CPbn SIde
*	- 'Pineapple'	ENfk LBuc MHoo WJek
	- subsp. ***timija***	CPbn ELau LEdu MHer SIde WJek
	- 'Variegata' (v)	CArn COIW CPbn CPrp CTri CWan ECha EHoe ELau GMaP GPoy LEdu MBri MCot MHer MNHC MRav NPri SBfd SEND SIde SPlb SRms SWal WHer WPer XLum
	'Sweet Pear'	MHer NYoL
	sylvestris L.	see *M. longifolia*
*	***verona***	CPbn NYoL
	× ***verticillata***	WJek
§	× ***villosa***	CArn CPbn SEND SIde
§	- var. ***alopecuroides*** Bowles's mint	CBre CPbn CPrp EGHP ELau GPoy LEdu MHer MNHC NBir NYoL SBfd SIde SWat WGwG WHer WJek
	- 'Jack Green' **new**	LEdu
	viridis	see *M. spicata*

Mentzelia (*Loasaceae*)

decapetala	CSpe

Menyanthes (*Menyanthaceae*)

trifoliata	CBen CRow CWat EHon EWay GPoy LPBA MSKA MWts NLar NPer WHal WMAq WSFF XLum

Menziesia (*Ericaceae*)

	alba	see *Daboecia cantabrica* f. *alba*
	ciliicalyx 'Honshu Blue'	GGGa
	- 'Judith' **new**	WAbe
	- ***lasiophylla***	see *M. ciliicalyx* var. *purpurea*
	- var. ***multiflora***	EPfP
	- 'Plum Drops'	GGGa
§	- var. ***purpurea***	GGGa
	- 'Slieve Donard'	CMac
	ferruginea	IVic
	polifolia	see *Daboecia cantabrica*
	'Spring Morning'	WAbe

Mercurialis (*Euphorbiaceae*)

perennis	GPoy WHer WHfH WSFF WShi

Merendera (*Colchicaceae*)

	attica	ECho LWst
	eichleri	see *M. trigyna*
	filifolia	ECho
§	***montana***	CPBP ECho EPot LWst WIvy
	pyrenaica	see *M. montana*
	raddeana	see *M. trigyna*
	sobolifera	WCot
§	***trigyna***	ECho
	- bright pink-flowered	LWst
	- white-flowered clone	LWst

Mertensia (*Boraginaceae*)

	ciliata	CCse SWat
§	***maritima***	CSpe CWCL EBee ECho EWld GBee GEdr GPoy LEdu NBir SMrm SPlb WHoo WWEG
	- subsp. ***asiatica***	see *M. maritima*
	primuloides	LLHF
	pterocarpa	see *M. sibirica*
	pulmonarioides	see *M. virginica*
§	***sibirica***	CLAP CSpe SPlb
§	***virginica*** ♀H4	CBro CLAP CSpe CWCL EBee ECho ECtt EHrv ELan EPfP EWTr LAma LEdu LHop LRHS MBel MMoz MNrw NBir NLar NPnk NPri SMrm SRms WFar

Merwilla (*Asparagaceae*)

§	***plumbea***	WCot

Merxmuellera see *Rytidosperma*

Mesembryanthemum (*Aizoaceae*)

'Basutoland'	see *Delosperma nubigenum*
brownii	see *Lampranthus brownii*

Mespilus ✿ (*Rosaceae*)

germanica (F)	CBcs CDul CLnd CMCN CTri EBee ECrN ELan EWTr IDee LMaj LTen NEgg NLar SLon WFar WMou
- 'Bredase Reus' (F)	NLar SKee
- 'Dutch' (F)	SFam SKee
- 'Iranian' (F)	SKee
- 'Large Russian' (F)	CAgr
- 'Macrocarpa' (F)	SKee
- 'Nottingham' (F)	Widely available
- 'Royal' (F)	CAgr CMam LRHS MBri MCoo SCoo SKee WHar
- 'Westerveld' (F)	CLnd NLar SKee

Metapanax (*Araliaceae*)

davidii	IRar SLon
delavayi	SBig

Metaplexis (*Apocynaceae*)

japonica B&SWJ 8459	WCru

Metasequoia ✿ (*Cupressaceae*)

glyptostroboides ♀H4	Widely available

- 'All Bronze' NLar
- 'Chubby' new NLar
- 'Emerald Feathers' SLim
- 'Fastigiata' see *M. glyptostroboides* 'National'
- 'Gold Rush' Widely available
- 'Golden Dawn' NLar SLim
- 'Green Mantle' EHul
- 'Hamlet's Broom' new SLim
- 'Little Creamy' NLar
- 'Little Giant' MBlu
- 'Matthaei Broom' LRHS NLar SLim
- 'McCracken's White' (v) NLar SLim
- 'Miss Grace' MAsh NLar SLim

§ - 'National' MBlu
- 'Ōgon' SGol
- 'Royal Air' new NLar WBor
- 'Schirrmann's Nordlicht' SLim
- 'Sheridan Spire' MBlu
- 'Spring Cream' NLar
- 'Waasland' MBlu
- 'White Spot' (v) MBlu NPCo SLim WEve

Metrosideros (*Myrtaceae*)

carminea CCCN CTsd
§ **excelsa** CHll CTsd EBak ECou ESwi
- 'Aurea' ECou MGos
- 'Parnell' CBcs CCCN
- 'Vibrance' CCCN

kermadecensis ECou
- 'Red and Gold' CBcs CDoC
- 'Twisty' (v) CBcs
- 'Variegata' (v) CBcs CDoC ECou MGos SMrm

lucida see *M. umbellata*
Moonlight = 'Lowmoo' CTrC CWGN EBee LRHS SLim
'Pink Lady' CTrC
robusta CCCN CHEx MREP
- **aureovariegata** CCCN EShb
§ 'Springfire' CCCN LRHS
× **subtomentosa** 'Mistral' ECou
'Thomasii' see *M.* 'Springfire'
tomentosa see *M. excelsa*
§ **umbellata** CBcs CCCN CDoC CHEx CTrC CTsd EBee ECou
- Gold Nugget = 'Lownug' LRHS MSCN SLim SPtl

Meum (*Apiaceae*)

athamanticum CArn CSpe EBee EHrv GCal GPoy LHop LPla LRHS MAvo MCot MRav SPhx WFar WPer WTin

Michauxia (*Campanulaceae*)

campanuloides CSpe
tchihatchewii CCCN CDTJ CSpe NGBl

Michelia see *Magnolia*

fulgens see *Magnolia foveolata*
sinensis see *Magnolia ernestii* subsp. *ernestii*
wilsonii see *Magnolia ernestii*
yunnanensis see *Magnolia laevifolia*

Microbiota (*Cupressaceae*)

decussata ♀H4 CBcs CDoC CKen CMac CSBt ECho EHul LAst LBee LRHS MGos MMuc MWat NHol NWea SEND SLim SPoG WEve
- 'Gold Spot' CDoC SLim
- 'Jakobsen' CDoC CKen
- 'Trompenburg' CKen

Microcachrys (*Podocarpaceae*)

tetragona CDoC ECou EHul LRHS SCoo WThu

Microcoelum see *Lytocaryum*

Microglossa (*Asteraceae*)

albescens see *Aster albescens*

Microlaena see *Ehrharta*

Microlepia (*Dennstaedtiaceae*)

speluncae EShb
strigosa CBty CCCN CLAP ISha LRHS

Micromeria (*Lamiaceae*)

corsica see *Acinos corsicus*
croatica NMen
dalmatica XLum
fruticosa WJek
graeca CArn
rupestris see *M. thymifolia*
§ **thymifolia** NMen SPlb
viminea see *Satureja viminea*

Microseris (*Asteraceae*)

ringens hort. see *Leontodon rigens*

Microsorum (*Polypodiaceae*)

diversifolium see *Phymatosorus diversifolius*
scolopendria CBty

Microtropis (*Celastraceae*)

petelotii HWJ 719 WCru

Mikania (*Asteraceae*)

araucana LSou

Milium (*Poaceae*)

effusum 'Aureum' ♀H4 Widely available
- var. **esthonicum** EPPr
- 'Yaffle' (v) CBre CKno EBee EPPr EShb LEdu MWat SGar SSvw WCot WPnP

Millettia (*Papilionaceae*)

japonica 'Hime Fuji' NLar
murasaki-natsu-fuji see *M. reticulata*
§ **reticulata** CPLG

Mimosa (*Mimosaceae*)

pudica CCCN CDTJ WTou

Mimulus (*Phrymaceae*)

sp. SVic
'Andean Nymph' see *M. naiandinus*
§ **aurantiacus** ♀H2-3 CMac CSpe CTri EBak ECtt LHop LPot LRHS MAsh NBir NPer SAga SBch SBfd SGar SPlb SUsu WPer
× **bartonianus** see *M.* × *harrisonii*
bifidus 'Trish' CSpe SUsu
- 'Verity Buff' MAsh
§ - 'Verity Purple' EDif MAsh
- 'Wine' see *M. bifidus* 'Verity Purple'

× **burnetii** ECho LPBA SRms
cardinalis ♀H3 CEnt EBee ELan EPfP EWes LPBA MNrw MSKA NBir NMRc SMrm WMoo WPer WWEG
- 'Dark Throat' SGar

- gold-flowered	WHil
- 'Red Dragon'	WHrl
cupreus 'Minor'	ECho
- 'Whitecroft Scarlet' 🏆H4	ECho ELan EPfP MAsh SRms
'Dawn' **new**	SUsu
'Eleanor'	ECtt LSou SAga SGar SHom SMrm SUsu
glutinosus	see *M. aurantiacus*
- ***atrosanguineus***	see *M. puniceus*
- ***luteus***	see *M. aurantiacus*
§ ***guttatus***	NMir NPer SRms WMoo WPnP
§ × ***harrisonii***	EPfP EWes LSou SAga
'Highland Orange'	ECho EPfP MAsh SPlb SPoG WGor
'Highland Pink'	ECho EPfP MAsh SPlb SPoG WGor
'Highland Pink Rose'	WFar
'Highland Red' 🏆H4	ECho ECtt EPfP GKev LPBA MAsh NPri SPlb SPoG SRms WFar WIce WNew
'Highland Yellow'	ECho ECtt GKev LPBA MAsh SPlb SPoG WFar WIce
hose-in-hose (d)	NPer
'Inca Sunset'	EWes
langsdorffii	see *M. guttatus*
lewisii 🏆H3	CHll EWes SRms
longiflorus	MAsh
'Lothian Fire'	CWat
luteus	CWat EHon EWay GAbr LPBA NPer SPlb WBrk WMAq XLum
§ - 'Gaby' (v)	LPBA
- 'Variegatus'	see *M. luteus* 'Gaby'
- 'Variegatus' ambig. (v)	NPer
Magic Series 🏆H4 **new**	NPri
'Malibu Orange'	EPfP
minimus	ECho
'Moonlight' **new**	SUsu
moschatus	EBee
§ ***naiandinus*** 🏆H3	CEnt EWes GKev SPlb WPer
'Orange Glow'	WHal
orange hose-in-hose (d)	NBir
§ 'Orkney Gold' (d)	ECtt
'Popacatapetl'	CSpe EDif MAsh SBHP SHom SUsu
'Prairie Buff'	EDif
'Prairie Caramel'	EDif
'Prairie Cerise'	EDif
'Prairie Citron'	EDif
'Prairie Coral'	EDif
'Prairie Dawn'	EDif
'Prairie Frost'	EDif
'Prairie Lilac Frost'	EDif
'Prairie Pink'	EDif
'Prairie Scarlet'	EDif
'Prairie Sunrise'	EDif
'Prairie Sunshine'	EDif
'Prairie Violet'	EDif
primuloides	ECho EWes MAsh SPlb
'Puck'	ECho SPoG
§ ***puniceus***	CTri EDif IRar LHop MAsh SBHP SHom SMrm SRkn
'Quetzalcoatl'	LHop SMrm
Red Emperor	see *M.* 'Roter Kaiser'
ringens	CBen CWat EHon LHop LPBA MSKA NBir NPer SPlb SRms WHil WMAq WMoo WWEG
§ 'Roter Kaiser'	EPfP
'Threave Variegated' (v)	MRav NBir
'Vortex'	LSou
'Wine Red'	see *M. bifidus* 'Verity Purple'
'Wisley Red'	ECho SRms
yellow hose-in-hose	see *M.* 'Orkney Gold'

Mina see *Ipomoea*

mint, apple see *Mentha suaveolens*

mint, Bowles's see *M.* × *villosa* var. *alopecuroides*

mint, curly see *M. spicata* var. *crispa*

mint, eau-de-Cologne see *M.* × *piperita* f. *citrata*

mint, ginger see *M.* × *gracilis*

mint, horse or long-leaved see *M. longifolia*

mint, pennyroyal see *M. pulegium*

mint (peppermint) see *M.* × *piperita*

mint, round-leaved see *M. suaveolens*

mint (spearmint) see *M. spicata*

Minuartia (*Caryophyllaceae*)

capillacea	ECho
laricifolia	NMen XSen
parnassica	see *M. stellata*
saxifraga	ITim
subsp. ***tmolea*** **new**	
§ ***stellata***	EPot NMen WPat
§ ***verna***	ECho NMen
- subsp. ***caespitosa***	CTri ECho
- - 'Aurea'	see *Sagina subulata* var. *glabrata* 'Aurea'

Mirabilis (*Nyctaginaceae*)

dichotoma	EShb
jalapa	CArn CPLG EPfP LAma LEdu SEND SRms WHil WTou
- 'Buttermilk'	CCCN
- red-flowered	SEND WTou
- white-flowered	CSpe WTou
- yellow-flowered	WTou
longiflora	WHil

Miscanthus ✿ (*Poaceae*)

sp.	MBNS
capensis	SPlb
chejuensis B&SWJ 8803	WCru
'Dronning Ingrid'	CKno EBee EPPr XLum
'Elfin'	CKno
flavidus B&SWJ 6749	WCru
floridulus misapplied	see *M.* × *giganteus*
floridulus ambig.	CCon EBee MMuc MNrw SEND SPlb WFar XLum
floridulus (Labill.) Warb. ex K. Schum. & Lauterb. HWJ 522	WCru
§ × ***giganteus***	CKno CSpe EHoe ELon EPPr EUJe GCal GQue MAsh MMoz MNrw MWat NDov NWsh SApp SDix SDys SMad SVic WCot WFar WPGP WWEG
- 'Gilt Edge' (v)	CKno EPPr NWsh SApp
- 'Gotemba' (v)	EBee ELon EPPr EWes NWsh SApp
'Gotemba Gold'	SApp
'Mount Washington'	SApp

	Name	Suppliers
	nepalensis	CElw CEnt CKno CPLG ECha ECre EHoe EPGN EWes GCal LEdu MAvo MNrw NOak NWsh SDix SMrm SUsu
	- NJM 09.141	WPGP
	- 'Shikola'	WCru
	oligostachyus	SDys
§	- 'Afrika'	CDes CKno EBee EPPr LHop MAvo MNrw WPGP XLum
I	- 'Nanus Variegatus' (v)	CKno EHoe EWes LEdu WCot WPGP WWEG
	'Pos'	SApp
§	'Purpurascens'	CKno COIW CWCL ECha EHoe EShb IBoy LBMP LPla LPot LRHS LSRN MAvo MMoz MWhi NOak SApp SGol SPer WCot WMoo WTin
	sacchariflorus misapplied	see *M.* × *giganteus*
	sacchariflorus ambig.	CBcs CHEx CKno EBee ECha EHrv ELan EPfP EShb LPBA LRHS MBrN NGdn SBfd SPer WFar WMoo XLum
	sacchariflorus (Maxim.) Hack.	MWhi WWEG
	sinensis	CEnt CHEx CTri LEdu NGBl NOak WMoo WWEG
	- from Yakushima	LAst
	- 'Abundance'	CBar CKno EPfP LSqu NRHS
	- 'Adagio'	CKno EAEE EBee EHoe EPPr GBin GQue LRHS LTen MWhi SHDw SLPl SMHy SMea WCot XLum
	- 'Afrika'	see *M. oligostachyus* 'Afrika'
	- 'Aldebaran' **new**	EBee
	- 'Andante'	CKno
	- 'Arabesque'	EPPr MMoz SApp WWEG XLum
	- 'Augustfeder'	EBee EPPr LEdu SMea WWEG XLum
	- 'Autumn Light'	CKno EPPr MMoz SMea XLum
	- 'Blütenwunder'	CKno EBee
	- 'China'	CCon CKno EAEE EBee EHoe ELon EPPr EShb EWes GBin LEdu LRHS MAvo MNrw NCGa NOrc NPnk SApp SBea SDys SHDw SRms SWat WMoo WPGP WWEG XLum
	- var. ***condensatus***	LRHS LSou SMHy
	- - 'Cabaret' (v)	CHEx CKno CWCL EAEE EBee EHoe ELon EPPr EUJe GMaP IPot LEdu LHop LRHS LSRN MAsh NCGa NOak NPnk NWsh SBfd SEND SHDw WCot WHal WMoo WPGP WWEG XLum
	- - 'Central Park'	see *M. sinensis* var. *condensatus* 'Cosmo Revert'
§	- - 'Cosmo Revert'	LEdu MMoz NWsh
	- - 'Cosmopolitan' (v) ♀H4	Widely available
	- - 'Emerald Giant'	see *M. sinensis* var. *condensatus* 'Cosmo Revert'
	- 'David'	EBee ELon EPPr LEdu MAvo MBNS
	- 'Dixieland' (v)	CKno EHoe ELan EPPr EWes IFoB LEdu LRHS NWsh SApp WWEG XLum
	- 'Dreadlocks' **new**	EBee MAvo
	- 'Emmanuel Lepage'	CKno EBee EPPr LRHS XLum
	- 'Etincelle'	CKno EWes NLar XLum
	- 'Federriese'	XLum
	- 'Ferner Osten'	Widely available
	- 'Flamingo' ♀H4	Widely available
	- 'Flammenmeer'	XLum
	- 'Gaa'	SApp
	- 'Gearmella'	EPPr LEdu LRHS NWsh XLum
	- 'Gewitterwolke' ♀H4	EPPr EWes LRHS SMHy SMad XLum

	Name	Suppliers
	- 'Ghana' ♀H4	CKno EBee ELon EPPr LHop LRHS MAvo MBri SDys SMHy SUsu XLum
	- 'Giraffe'	CDTJ CKno EBee EWes LEdu WPGP WWEG XLum
	- 'Gnome'	CKno EAEE EBee EHoe EPPr LRHS MAsh MMHG MWhi WWEG
	- 'Gold Bar' PBR (v)	Widely available
	- 'Goldfeder' (v)	XLum
	- 'Goliath'	CKno EHoe ELan ELon EPPr GBin GQue IPot LBMP LEdu LRHS MBNS MMoz NRHS NWsh WFar WWEG XLum
	- 'Gracillimus'	Widely available
	- 'Gracillimus Nanus'	CKno
	- 'Graziella'	CCon CKno COIW CSam CWCL CWib EBee EHoe EHrv EPPr EPfP LEdu LRHS LTen MBri MMoz MWhi NGdn NOak NOrc NRHS SHil SLPl SPer SRms WBor WPGP XLum
	- 'Grosse Fontäne' ♀H4	CCon CWCL EBee EHoe ELan EPPr LEdu LRHS LSRN MWhi NWsh SMHy WAul WCot WMoo WWEG XLum
	- 'Gutenberg Gold'	XLum
	- 'Haiku'	CKno EPPr LEdu LRHS XLum
	- 'Helga Reich'	EWes LRHS SApp
	- 'Hercules'	LRHS MAvo MMoz SApp XLum
	- 'Hermann Müssel'	CKno EBee EPPr EWes GBin GQue LEdu LPla LRHS NOak SMHy SMea XLum
	- 'Hinjo' (v)	CHGN EBee ECGP ECha ECtt EHoe ELon EPPr GBin GBuc GQue LBMP LRHS LSou MMoz NGdn NLar NWsh SApp WCot WFar WPGP WWEG
	- hybrids	SGol
I	- 'Jubilaris' (v)	EPPr EWes
	- 'Juli'	MMoz XLum
	- 'Kaskade' ♀H4	CKno COIW CWCL EBee EHoe EPPr IPot LEdu MMoz MMuc MWhi NDov SApp SEND SMrm SUsu WFar WMoo WWEG XLum
	- 'Kirk Alexander' (v)	SApp
	- 'Kleine Fontäne' ♀H4	Widely available
	- 'Kleine Silberspinne' ♀H4	Widely available
	- 'Krater'	CKno EHoe EPPr LPla MBrN SDys SGar SMea SWat XLum
	- 'Kupferberg'	XLum
§	- 'Little Kitten'	CKno EBee LEdu NWsh SMad SMea WMoo WPGP WWEG XLum
	- 'Little Zebra' PBR (v)	EBee EPPr EPfP EUJe LHop LSRN NOak NWsh SMad SRms
	- 'Malepartus'	Widely available
	- 'Morning Light' (v) ♀H4	Widely available
	- 'Nippon'	CBar CCon CElw CKno CPrp CWCL EAEE EBee EHoe EPPr GBin LEdu LPla LRHS MMoz MWhi NBro NDov NGdn NOrc NWsh SDys SMrm SPer WPGP WWEG XLum
	- 'Nishidake'	XLum
	- 'November Sunset'	EPPr EWes MMoz NRHS XLum
	- 'Overdam'	IFoB NGdn XLum
	- 'Pagel's Pride'	EBee GBin LRHS
	- 'Poseidon'	EPPr LRHS MAvo NChi SDys SMad XLum
	- 'Positano'	CKno MMoz WPGP XLum
	- 'Professor Richard Hansen'	CKno LRHS SMHy XLum
	- 'Pünktchen' (v)	CWCL EAEE EAmu EBee ECha EHoe EPPr GBin LEdu LRHS MAsh

	MAvo NCGa NOak SApp SBfd SHDw SMHy SMad SMrm SRms WMoo WPnP WWEG XLum
- 'Purple Fall'	EBee LRHS MAvo
- var. ***purpurascens*** misapplied	see *M.* 'Purpurascens'
- 'Red Chief'	EPPr EWes GQue
- 'Red Meister' **new**	CKno EPfP
- 'Red Star' **new**	SRms
- 'Rigoletto' (v)	EPPr LRHS SApp
- 'Roland'	CKno EBee EHoe EPPr LRHS NWsh XLum
- 'Roterpfeil'	EBee EPPr
- 'Rotfeder'	EPPr SBfd XLum
- 'Rotfuchs'	EBee LLWP LPla LRHS WFar XLum
- 'Rotsilber'	CKno CPrp CSpe CWib EBee ECha EHoe EPPr GBin GMaP IArd LEdu LRHS MAvo MWhi NOak NRHS NWsh WFar WHoo WMoo WPtf WWEG XLum
- 'Russia' **new**	NWsh
- 'Samurai'	CEnt EPPr GMaP GQue MAvo SMrm
- 'Sarabande'	EBee EHoe EHul ELan EPPr GQue IPot NWsh SApp SMHy SMrm WFar WMoo XLum
- 'Septemberrot' ♀H4	CKno CPrp CWCL EBee LEdu MMuc SEND
§ - 'Silberfeder' ♀H4	Widely available
- 'Silberpfeil' (v)	NWsh
- 'Silberspinne'	CCse GBin LEdu MWat NDov NGdn SApp SBfd SMHy SMea SPlb WAul XLum
- 'Silberturm'	EBee EPPr LPla
- Silver Feather	see *M. sinensis* 'Silberfeder'
- 'Silver Sceptre'	SMHy
- 'Silver Stripe'	EPPr MAvo
- 'Sioux'	CEnt EBee EHoe EPPr EPfP EShb GBin GQue LEdu LRHS MAvo MBNS MMoz NCGa NWsh SPer SUsu WWEG
- 'Sirene'	CCon EAEE EBee EHoe EPPr GQue LRHS MBNS MBlu MBri MSpe NRHS NWsh WFar XLum
- 'Strictus' (v) ♀H4	Widely available
- 'Tiger Cub' (v)	CWCL EWes LRHS MAvo SApp
- 'Undine' ♀H4	CCon CKno CMea EBee ECha EHoe EHrv ELan EPPr EPfP LEdu LRHS MBel MBrN MSnd NWsh SLPl WMoo XLum
- 'Variegatus' (v)	Widely available
- 'Vorläufer'	EBee EHoe EPPr NWsh XLum
- 'Westacre Wine'	EWes
- 'Wetterfahne'	LEdu XLum
§ - 'Yaku-jima'	CSam EBee ECha EPPr LHop MWhi SMea
- 'Yakushima Dwarf'	Widely available
- 'Zebrinus' (v) ♀H4	Widely available
- 'Zwergelefant'	MMoz SMHy XLum
I 'Spartina'	SApp
tinctorius 'Nanus Variegatus' misapplied	see *M. oligostachyus* 'Nanus Variegatus'
transmorrisonensis	CKno EBee EHoe ELan EPPr LPla MAvo MBel MMoz NWsh SApp SMHy SPhx SWal WCot WWEG XLum
- B&SWJ 3697	WCru
yakushimensis	see *M. sinensis* 'Yaku-jima', *M. sinensis* 'Little Kitten'

Mitchella (*Rubiaceae*)

repens	CBcs EBee GBin WCru
undulata B&SWJ 10928	WCru
* - f. ***quelpartensis*** B&SWJ 4402	WCru

Mitella (*Saxifragaceae*)

acerina B&SWJ 11029 **new**	WCru
breweri	CCon CHid CMac ECha GCal MMoz MRav SBch SRms WFar WMoo WOut WPnP WTin
caulescens	ECha NBro WMoo
diphylla	EPPr
formosana B&SWJ 125	EPPr WCru
furusei var. ***subramosa*** B&SWJ 11097 **new**	WCru
× ***inami*** B&SWJ 11122	WCru
japonica B&SWJ 4971	WCru
kiusiana	CLAP
- B&SWJ 5888	WCru
makinoi	CLAP EBee EWld
- B&SWJ 4992	CPLG WCru
ovalis	EBee EPPr
pauciflora B&SWJ 6361	WCru
stylosa B&SWJ 5669	WCru
yoshinagae B&SWJ 4893	CHid CPLG EPPr GEdr WCru WMoo

Mitraria (*Gesneriaceae*)

coccinea	CBcs CCCN CDoy CEnt CHll CMac CPLG CTsd CWib ECho ELan GAbr IBoy IDee IRos LRHS LSou MBlu SLim SLon SPer SPlb SSpi
- Clark's form	CTrC EBee EUJe LAst NLar
- 'Lake Caburgua'	CCCN CSpe EBee ELon EWld GCal IArd NLar NSti WHor
- 'Lake Puyehue'	CAbb CBcs CCCN CDoC CPLG EBee EPfP LHop LRHS MAsh MGos SPoG SWvt WCru WFar WGwG WSHC

Modiolastrum (*Malvaceae*)

lateritium	CRHN CSpe CTri EBee ELan EPfP EPri GBin LAst LHop LRHS MAvo NBir NSti SMad SMrm SPet SPhx SRms SUsu WHal WHil WHoo WPGP WPer WPtf WSHC XLum

Moehringia (*Caryophyllaceae*)

muscosa	WCot

Molinia ✿ (*Poaceae*)

altissima	see *M. caerulea* subsp. *arundinacea*
'Autumn Charm'	CKno
caerulea	CKno CRWN CWib EPPr MAsh MBlu NChi NGBl
§ - subsp. ***arundinacea***	CKno CWCL ECha EPPr NLar SApp SLPl WPtf WWEG XLum
- - 'Bergfreund'	CKno CSam EBee EHoe EPPr GBin LHop MAvo NWsh SApp SMHy WMoo
- - 'Breeze' **new**	CKno
- - 'Cordoba'	CKno EPPr GQue NDov SMHy SPhx XLum
- - 'Fontäne'	CSam EBee EHoe EPPr GCal GQue LEdu LPla MAvo NDov NWsh SApp SPhx

- - 'Karl Foerster'	Widely available
- - 'Skyracer'	CCVN CKno COlW CPrp EBee EHoe EPPr EPfP GBin GCal GQue MAsh MAvo MMoz MWhi NRHS NWsh SMHy SPhx SUsu WCot WFar WGrn WMoo WWEG
- - 'Staefa'	EHoe
- - 'Transparent'	Widely available
- - 'Windsaule'	CKno EBee EPPr SPhx
- - 'Windspiel'	Widely available
- - 'Zuneigung'	CKno CSam EPPr LPla MAvo SApp SPhx
- subsp. ***caerulea*** 'Carmarthen' (v)	EHoe EPPr SApp SUsu WHal WWEG
- - 'Claerwen' (v)	ECha EPPr SMHy SPhx WMoo
- - 'Coneyhill Gold' (v)	EPPr
- - 'Dauerstrahl'	CKno EBee EPPr GCal GQue LPla MAvo MNrw NDov
- - 'Edith Dudszus'	CKno COlW CWCL EAEE EBee ECha EHoe ELon EPPr GBin GQue IPot LHop LPla LRHS MAvo MBrN MBri NDov NGdn NOrc NWsh SApp SMHy SPer SPhx WCot WGrn WMoo WWEG
- - 'Heidebraut'	EAEE EBee EHoe EHrv EPPr GBin GQue IBoy MBri MRav NBro NDov NOrc SApp SBfd SPhx WMoo WWEG
- - 'Moorflamme'	CSam EBee EHoe EPPr MAvo NDov SPhx
- - 'Moorhexe'	CPrp CSam CWCL EBee ECha EHoe ELon EPPr EPfP GBin GMaP IKil IPot LRHS MAvo NBid NDov NGdn NOak NSti SApp SLPl SMrm SPhx SWal WCot WFar WMoo WPtf WWEG
- - 'Overdam'	MMuc MNrw NDov SEND
- - 'Poul Petersen'	CKno EBee EPPr NDov SPhx WWEG
- - 'Strahlenquelle'	CSam EBee ELan EPPr GCal GQue LPla MAvo MNFA MSpe MWat NBro NDov SPhx WWEG
- - 'Variegata' (v) ♀H4	Widely available
- 'Dark Defender'	SPhx
- 'Showers of Gold'	SPhx
- 'Winterfreude'	NDov
litoralis	see *M. caerulea* subsp. *arundinacea*

Molopospermum (*Apiaceae*)

peloponnesiacum	CArn CSpe GBin GCal LEdu SBrt SMHy SPhx WCru WPnP WPtf WSHC

Moltkia (*Boraginaceae*)

§ ***doerfleri***	GCal NBir NChi WSHC
§ × ***intermedia*** ♀H4	CMea CSpe IRar SAga SBch WPat WThu
petraea	LHop LLHF LRHS MWat NRHS

Moluccella (*Lamiaceae*)

laevis **new**	SVic
- 'Pixie Bells'	CSpe

Monarda (*Lamiaceae*)

sp.	ENfk
'Adam'	EBee GBuc GCal LRHS LSRN MPkF MSpe NBre NGdn NLar WSHC
'Amethyst'	ECtt EWes SIde
'Aquarius'	EBee EPPr GQue IKil LRHS MSpe SHar SPet WCAu XLum
austromontana	see *M. citriodora* subsp. *austromontana*
'Baby Spice'	EBee
§ 'Balance'	EBee ECtt EPfP GCal LAst LRHS MCot MRav MSpe NBro NDov NGdn NSti SMrm WFar WSHC WWEG XLum
'Beauty of Cobham' ♀H4	CPrp CWCL EBee ECha ECtt ELan EPfP GBin GMaP LEdu MBri MCot MHer MNrw MPie MSpe NDov NHol NLar NPri SBch SMad SPer SPhx SWvt WBor WCAu WHlf WWEG XLum
'Blaukranz'	NBre
§ 'Blaustrumpf'	CElw EBee ECtt ELon EPfP EWes GBBs GQue LPot LRHS MPie NLar SPer WSHC
Blue Stocking	see *M.* 'Blaustrumpf'
Bowman	see *M.* 'Sagittarius'
bradburyana	EBee NBre NLar SBrt
'Cambridge Scarlet' ♀H4	Widely available
'Capricorn'	NBre WWEG XLum
'Chippawa'	LRHS
citriodora	EBee GPoy LRHS MHoo NSti SGar SIde SRms SWat XLum
§ - subsp. ***austromontana***	NBir SBch SIde
- - 'Bee's Favourite'	SPad
'Comanche'	EBee EHrv EWes
'Croftway Pink' ♀H4	Widely available
didyma	CArn CWan ENfk EPfP LPot MHoo NBro SBfd SVic SWat WJek
- 'Coral Reef'	EWes WWEG
- 'Cranberry Lace' **new**	EBee NLar
- 'Duddiscombe'	CSam CWCL
- 'Goldmelise'	WMoo
- 'Pink Lace'PBR	ECtt LSou MBri MNrw NCGa NLar STes WFar WHil
'Earl Grey'	ECtt GAbr MSpe NDov
'Elsie's Lavender'	EBee LPla MSpe MTis NDov NLar WWEG
'Elworthy'	CElw
'Fireball'PBR	CCVN CPrp CWCL EBee ECtt ELon GAbr LEdu LHop LLHF LRHS LSou MNrw NCGa NHol NLar NPri SBfd SGar WBor WFar WHil
§ 'Fishes'	CMac CPLG EAEE EBee ECtt EHrv ELan EPPr EWes IKil LRHS LSou MCot MRav MSpe NDov NGdn NLar SMrm SPet WFar WPtf WSHC WWEG
fistulosa	CArn CHby CMac GPoy MHer MHoo MNHC WJek WMoo XLum
'Gardenview Scarlet' ♀H4	Widely available
Gemini	see *M.* 'Twins'
'Gewitterwolke'	CSam EBee MSpe MTis NDov SDys WPer
'Hartswood Wine'	ECtt EWes SMad SMrm WPer WWEG
'Heidelerche'	EPPr
'Jacob Cline'	ECtt EPPr EWes GBin IPot LRHS MSpe MTis NBre NCGa NDov NRHS SPhx STes WPtf WWEG
'Kardinal'	EBee GBin LPla LRHS NDov NLar
Libra	see *M.* 'Balance'
'Loddon Crown'	COlW CPrp EBee ECtt ELon GQue LRHS MBri MDKP MHoo NHol NLar SBfd SHar SIde WCAu WSHC WWEG

	'Mahogany'	CPrp EBee ELan GBin GKev GMaP IKil LPla LRHS MCot MNrw MRav SPer SPhx WWEG
	'Marshall's Delight' ♀H4	CPrp CSam CWCL EBee ECtt EWTr EWes EWhm GBee LRHS MRav MTis NLar SGar SMrm WFar
	'Melissa'	LSRN NBre NLar
	menthifolia	EBee GCal MCot SMrm
	'Mohawk'	CPrp EAEE EBee ECtt EHrv EPPr EPfP EWhm GQue LRHS MSpe MTis MWat NDov NGdn NOrc SDix WWEG
	'Mrs Perry'	EWes
	'Neon'	MSpe MTis NDov SPhx
	'Night Rider'	EWes
	'On Parade'	CElw CSam CWCL EAEE EBee ECtt LRHS MMHG MSpe MTis NDov NGdn NHol
	'Othello'	CSam MTis NDov
	'Ou Charm'	EBee EWes GBin LRHS MMHG MTis NDov NLar SMad SMrm WFar
	'Panorama'	MHoo NLar SPet SPlb WMoo
	'Panorama Red Shades' (Panorama Series)	CWib MNHC SPet WCFE
	'Pawnee'	LRHS MTis NDov
	Petite Delight = 'Acpetdel'	CBcs EBee ELan LHop LSou MPkF NHol NLar NPri SMad WFar WWEG
	'Petite Pink Supreme'	EBee
	'Pink Supreme'PBR	EBee ECtt ELon EPfP GAbr LSou MTis NCGa NHol NLar SBfd WFar WHil
	'Pink Tourmaline'	EWhm MTis NDov SMrm WWEG
	Pisces	see *M.* 'Fishes'
	'Poyntzfield Pink'	GPoy
	Prairie Night	see *M.* 'Prärienacht'
§	'Prärienacht'	CPrp CSBt CSam EBee ECha ELan EPfP LRHS MCot MHer MSpe NBro NGdn NHol NPri SBch SPer SPlb SRms SWvt WFar WPer WSHC WWEG
	punctata	CArn ELan MCot SPhx SWat WFar
	'Purple Ann'	EBee
	'Purpurkrone' **new**	GBin
	'Raspberry Wine'	EBee ECtt EPPr LRHS MSpe
	'Ruby Glow'	CSam CWCL EBee EHrv LRHS LSRN MBri MMHG NDov SAga SMrm
§	'Sagittarius'	EAEE EBee EWTr LRHS MMHG MSpe NGdn NSti WPer
	'Saxon Purple'	MTis NDov NLar
§	'Schneewittchen'	CWCL EBee ECha ECtt EHrv ELan EPfP GBin LRHS MGos MHer MRav NLar NPri NSti SBea SIde SPer SWvt WCAu WFar WWEG
	'Scorpion'	EBee ECtt EHrv ELan EPPr EPfP GBin LEdu LRHS MCot MRav MSpe NBir NEgg NGdn NLar NOrc SMrm SPet SPhx SWvt WCAu WGwG WSHC WWlt XLum
	'Shelley'	ECha
	'Sioux'	EBee EHrv EWes LRHS WFar
	'Snow Maiden'	see *M.* 'Schneewittchen'
	'Snow Queen'	EBee ECtt EPPr EWTr LRHS MBel MSpe MWat NPro SMrm WPer
	Snow White	see *M.* 'Schneewittchen'
	'Squaw' ♀H4	Widely available
	'Talud' ♀H4	EBee MSpe NDov
§	'Twins'	CWCL EBee EPPr LRHS LSRN NLar SWvt WSHC WWEG
	'Velvet Queen'	LSou
	'Vintage Wine'	CWCL ECtt MTis NDov WFar
	'Violacea'	NHol
	'Violet Queen' ♀H4	CWCL EAEE EBee ECtt ELan EWes GQue LRHS MBel MCot MTis NBre NPro SCoo SMrm WFar WPtf WWlt
	'Violette'	EBee MSpe
	'Westacre Purple'	EPPr EWes

Monardella (*Lamiaceae*)

	macrantha	CPBP
	odoratissima	CArn
	villosa	WCot

Monochoria (*Pontederiaceae*)

§	***hastata***	MSKA

Monstera (*Araceae*)

	deliciosa (F) ♀H1	MBri XBlo
	- 'Variegata' (v) ♀H1	MBri

Montbretia see *Crocosmia*

Montia (*Portulacaceae*)

	perfoliata	see *Claytonia perfoliata*
	sibirica	see *Claytonia sibirica*

Moraea (*Iridaceae*)

	alticola	CPne ECho GCal WHer
§	***aristata***	CDes ECho WCot
§	***bellendenii***	ECho WCot
	bifida from Roggeveld	ECho
	bipartita	WCot
	britteniae	ECho
	calcicola	ECho
	ciliata	ECho
	citrina	ECho
§	***collina***	ECho
	crispa from Roggeveld	ECho
	elegans	CDes ECho
	fergusoniae from Swellendam	ECho
	flaccida	ECho
	- from Roggeveld	ECho
	fugacissima	ECho
	gigandra	ECho WCot
	glaucopsis	see *M. aristata*
	huttonii	CCCN CCon CDes CSpe CTca CTrC ECre EPri MHer SMad WCot WHil WKif WSHC
	- from Eastern Cape	ECho
	inclinata from Howick	ECho
	incurva	ECho
	iridioides	see *Dietes iridioides*
	longiaristata from Caledon	ECho
	loubseri	WCot
	lurida	WCot
	- from Bredasdorp	ECho
	macronyx from Komsberg	ECho
	marlothii	ECho
	mediterranea	ECho
	neglecta	ECho
	ochroleuca	ECho
	papilionacea from Gordon's Bay	ECho

	pavonia var. ***lutea***	see *M. bellendenii*
	polystachya	CGrW ECho
	reflexa from Calvinia	ECho
	robusta	GCal
	serpentina	ECho
	setifolia	ECho
	sisyrinchium	EBee ECho
	spathacea	see *M. spathulata*
§	***spathulata***	CPLG CTca EBee ECho GCal LEdu WCot WKif
	speciosa from Tanqua	ECho
	tortilis from Nababeep	ECho
	tricolor	ECho
	trifida from Sentinel Peak	ECho
	tripetala from Riverlands	ECho
	tulbaghensis	EBee
	unibracteata from Sentinel Peak	ECho
	vegeta	CPBP ECho WCot
	versicolor from Paarl	ECho
	villosa	ECho WCot

Morella (*Myricaceae*)

	californica	NLar
	cerifera	CArn NLar
	pensylvanica	CArn IVic NLar
	rubra	CAgr

Moricandia (*Brassicaceae*)

	arvensis	EBee WCot

Morina (*Caprifoliaceae*)

*	***afghanica***	GAbr
	alba	GCra
	longifolia	Widely available
	persica	EWes EWld SPhx

Morinda (*Rubiaceae*)

	umbellata WWJ 11688	WCru

Morisia (*Brassicaceae*)

	hypogaea	see *M. monanthos*
§	***monanthos***	EPfP EPot MAsh SRot
	- 'Fred Hemingway'	ECho ECtt LRHS NMen NSla WAbe

Morus ✿ (*Moraceae*)

	alba	CAgr CArn CBcs CCVT CDul CLnd CMCN CTho CWib ECrN ELan EPfP GTwe LBuc LHop LMaj MGos SMrm SVic
	- 'Chaparral'	LRHS
	- 'Issai'	LRHS SHil
	- 'Laciniata'	EBee
	- 'Macrophylla'	CMCN NLar
	- 'Nana'	NLar
	- 'Pendula'	CDoC CDul CMac CTho CTri ECrN ELan GTwe LAst MAsh MBlu MBri NLar SBfd SCoo SLim
	- 'Platanifolia'	LMaj MBlu
	- var. ***tatarica***	CAgr LEdu NLar
§	***bombycis***	ERom MAsh SEND
	'Capsrum' (F)	CAgr
	'Carmen' (F)	CAgr
	'Illinois Everbearing' (F)	CAgr
	'Italian' (F)	CAgr
	'Ivory' (F)	CAgr
	kagayamae	see *M. bombycis*
	latifolia 'Spirata'	NLar SEND
	nigra (F) 𝕐H4	Widely available
§	- 'Chelsea' (F)	CDul CTho CTri EPfP EPom GTwe IVic LRHS MBri MGos MWat NWea SCoo SEWo SKee SLim SPer SPoG WHar
	- 'Jerusalem' (F)	CTho LRHS MCoo MWat WHar
	- 'King James'	see *M. nigra* 'Chelsea'
	- 'Large Black' (F)	EPom
	rubra	CAgr NLar
	- 'Nana'	NLar
	'Wellington' (F)	CAgr NPri

Mosla (*Lamiaceae*)

	dianthera	EBee EWld GCal MAvo MNrw

Muehlenbeckia (*Polygonaceae*)

	astonii	CDoC ECou LRHS WPGP
	australis	ECou
	axillaris misapplied	see *M. complexa*
§	***axillaris*** Walp.	CBcs CTri ECou SBig
	- 'Mount Cook' (f)	ECou
	- 'Ohau' (m)	ECou
§	***complexa***	CBcs CDoC CHEx CHll CMac CTrC CTri CWib EBee ECou EPfP EShb ETod EUJe GBin LRHS LTen NLBP NSti SEND SLim SLon SPer SPoG SWvt WCFE WPGP WSHC XLum
	- (f)	ECou
	- 'Nana'	see *M. axillaris* Walp.
	- small-leaved	ETod
	- 'Spotlight'[PBR] (v)	EShb
	- var. ***trilobata***	CBcs CHEx CTrC EShb ESwi EUJe GCal MPie SSta XLum
	- 'Ward' (m)	ECou
	ephedroides	CTrC ECou
	- 'Clarence Pass'	ECou
*	- var. ***muricatula***	ECou
	gunnii	ECou
	platyclados	see *Homalocladium platycladum*

Muhlenbergia (*Poaceae*)

	capillaris	CFis CTrC SBfd SHDw SMrm
	dubia	WPGP
	dumosa	CKno
	japonica 'Cream Delight' (v)	EHoe LEdu SBfd SHDw
	lindheimeri	CKno SMea WCot
	mexicana	LEdu SRms
	rigens	CKno SApp WPGP

Mukdenia (*Saxifragaceae*)

	acanthifolia	CDes CLAP WCru
	rossii	CLAP EBee EHrv ELon GCal IFro LEdu MBel MBri MNrw NBid NLar NMyG NPnk SHil SMad WCru WPGP WSHC WThu WTin XLum
	- from Japan **new**	GCal
	- 'Crimson Fans'	see *M. rossii* 'Karasuba'
	- dwarf	CDes CLAP GCal MNrw
§	- 'Karasuba'	CLAP CWGN EBee EPfP GEdr GHim LBMP LSou MAvo MMHG MPnt NLar NMyG NPnk SPoG WHil
	- 'Ōgon'	CLAP
	- 'Shishiba'	GEdr

mulberry see *Morus*

Murraya (*Rutaceae*)

*	***elliptica***	MOWG
	exotica	see *M. paniculata*

	koenigii	EOHP GPoy
§	***paniculata***	CArn GPoy

Musa ✿ (*Musaceae*)

	from Yunnan, China	see *M. itinerans* 'Yunnan'
§	***acuminata***	LRHS MBri
§	- 'Dwarf Cavendish' (AAA Group) (F) ♀H1	CDoC EAmu ELan LRHS LTen NPla SBst SPlb XBlo
	- 'Grand Nain' × ***acuminata*** 'Zebrina'	EAmu
	- 'Siam Ruby' (AA Group) (F)	EAmu EUJe
	- 'Williams' (AAA Group) (F)	EAmu XBlo
	- 'Zebrina' ♀H1+3	CDTJ EAmu LRHS XBlo
	balbisiana	EAmu
	- 'Black Thai' **new**	EAmu
	basjoo ♀H3-4	CAbb CBcs CDoC CDoy CHEx CHll CSBt CSpe CTrC EAmu EBee ELan EPfP EUJe LEdu LRHS LSRN MGos NPla SBfd SBst SChr SEND SHil SLim SPer SPlb SPoG SRkn
	- 'Little Prince'	LRHS
I	- 'Rubra'	CCCN EAmu ESwi
	'Blue Java'	see *M.* 'Ice Cream'
	'Cavendish Super Dwarf'	LRHS
	cavendishii	see *M. acuminata* 'Dwarf Cavendish'
§	***coccinea*** ♀H1	XBlo
	ensete	see *Ensete ventricosum*
	'Ghew-kera' **new**	EAmu
	'Helen'	EAmu
	hookeri	see *M. sikkimensis*
§	'Ice Cream' (ABB)	EAmu
	itinerans	WCot
§	- 'Yunnan'	EAmu
	lasiocarpa	CDTJ CDoC CHEx CHll EAmu ESwi ETod EUJe LRHS MBri NPla SBfd SBig SBst SHil SPlb
	laterita	GHim
	mannii	EAmu
	nana misapplied	see *M. acuminata* 'Dwarf Cavendish'
	nana Lour.	see *M. acuminata*
	'Orange' **new**	EAmu
	ornata ♀H1	CCCN XBlo
	× ***paradisiaca*** 'Hajaré' (ABB Group) (F)	EAmu
	- 'Malbhog' (AAB Group) (F)	EAmu
	- 'Monthan' (ABB Group) (F)	EAmu
	- 'Ney Poovan' (AB Group) (F)	CCCN EAmu GHim SBst
	- 'Orinoco' (ABB Group) (F)	EAmu
	- 'Rajapuri' (AAB Group) (F)	EAmu
§	***sikkimensis***	CDTJ EAmu ELan ESwi ETod EUJe EWes GHim SBig SBst SPlb XBlo
	- 'Red Tiger'	CCCN CDTJ EAmu SBst
	'Tropicana'	XBlo
	uranoscopus misapplied	see *M. coccinea*
	velutina ♀H1+3	CCCN CDoC EAmu GHim SBig SBst

Muscari ✿ (*Asparagaceae*)

	'Aleyna'	ECho NMin
	ambrosiacum	see *M. muscarimi*
	anatolicum	ECho
	armeniacum ♀H4	CBro CTri ECho EPfP LPot LRHS MBri MMuc SEND SPer SRms WCot WFar WShi
	- 'Argaei Album'	ECho EPot LAma
	- 'Atlantic'	ECho EPfP LRHS
	- 'Blue Pearl'	ECho GKev
	- 'Blue Spike' (d)	CBro CTca ECho EPfP GKev LAma MBri NBir NEgg SDeJ SPer WCot WFar WGwG
	- 'Bright Eyes'	GKev
	- 'Cantab'	ECho GKev SDeJ
	- 'Christmas Pearl' ♀H4	ECho GKev WCot
	- 'Côte d'Azur'	GKev
	- 'Cupido'	CGrW GKev
	- 'Dark Eyes'	ECho EPfP SMrm SPer WFar
	- 'Early Giant'	ECho SDeJ
	- 'Fantasy Creation'	ECho EPot SDeJ
	- 'Gul'	WCot
	- 'Heavenly Blue'	ECho
	- 'New Creation'	ECho
	- 'Peppermint'	CTca ECho EPfP EPot ERCP LAma NMin SPhx WCot
	- 'Saffier' ♀H4	ECho LAma WCot
	- 'Valerie Finnis'	CAvo CBre CBro CTca EBee ECho EPPr EPfP EPot ERCP GMaP LAma MBri NLar SDeJ SMrm SPer SPhx WAul WBor WBrk WCot
	aucheri ♀H4	ECho LAma NRya
*	- var. ***bicolor***	WCot
	- 'Blue Magic'	ECho EPot ERCP LAma SDeJ
	- 'Ocean Magic'	CBro ECho GKev LAma MBri NLar
§	- 'Tubergenianum'	ECho LRHS
	- 'White Magic'	CAvo CBro ECho ERCP LAma SDeJ WCot
§	***azureum*** ♀H4	CAvo CBro CTca ECho ELan EPfP ERCP EWTr GMaP LAma LPot LRHS NLar NMen SPhx WCot
	- 'Album'	ECho LAma LRHS SPhx WCot
	'Baby's Breath'	see *M.* 'Jenny Robinson'
	'Big Smile'	GKev WCot
	'Blue Dream'	ECho
	'Blue Eyes'	ECho WCot
	'Blue Star'	ECho GKev
	botryoides	CAvo ECho LAma
	- 'Album'	CAvo CBro CTca CTri ECho EPfP LAma MBri SDeJ SMrm SPer SRms WCot WShi
	caucasicum	ECho WCot
	chalusicum	see *M. pseudomuscari*
	coeleste KPPZ 90-318	LWst
	commutatum	ECho
	- HOA 0130	LWst
§	***comosum***	CArn CBro ECho EPfP ERCP MCot NEgg WCot
	- 'Monstrosum'	see *M. comosum* 'Plumosum'
§	- 'Plumosum'	ECho ELan EPfP GKev LAma LRHS MBri SDeJ WCot
	dionysicum	ECho
	- HOA 8965	ECho LWst WCot
	grandifolium	LWst
	- JCA 689.450	WCot
	inconstrictum	ECho
	'Ivor's Pink'	WCot
§	'Jenny Robinson' ♀H4	EHrv IFoB SDys SMad WCot
	latifolium ♀H4	CAvo CBro CTca ECho EPfP EPot ERCP LAma LRHS MBri MWat NEgg NLar SBch SDeJ SMrm SPhx WBor WCot WTin
*	- 'Blue Angels'	NBir
	macbeathianum **new**	WCot
§	***macrocarpum***	CBro CPom CTca EBee ECha ECho EPot LAma LRHS SCnR WAbe WCot

	– 'Golden Fragrance'PBR	CAvo CHid CPLG ECho ERCP GKev IFoB LAma MCot MNrw NMin SDeJ WCot WHil
	mirum	ECho
	moschatum	see *M. muscarimi*
	'Mount Hood'	ECho ERCP LRHS SDeJ WBor
§	***muscarimi***	CAvo CBro CTca ECho IFoB LAma MCot NLar SDeJ WCot
	– var. ***flavum***	see *M. macrocarpum*
§	***neglectum***	ECho LAma LWSt NLar SEND WCot WShi
	pallens	ECho NMin WCot
	paradoxum	see *Bellevalia paradoxa*
	parviflorum	ECho SCnR
§	***pseudomuscari*** ♀H4	WCot
	racemosum	see *M. neglectum*
	'Rosy Sunrise'	WCot
	'Sky Blue'	ECho WCot
§	***spreitzenhoferi*** HOA 0120	LWSt
	'Superstar'	ECho WCot WRHF
§	***tenuiflorum***	ECho WCot
	aff. ***tenuiflorum*** JCA 0.691.251	WCot
	tubergenianum	see *M. aucheri* 'Tubergenianum'
	weissii HOA 0003	LWSt
	'White Beauty'	ECho SPhx WBor
	'Winter Amethyst'	WCot

Muscarimia (*Asparagaceae*)

ambrosiacum	see *Muscari muscarimi*
macrocarpum	see *Muscari macrocarpum*

Musella see *Musa*

Mussaenda (*Rubiaceae*)

'Tropic Snow'	CCCN

Myoporum (*Scrophulariaceae*)

debile	see *Eremophila debilis*
laetum	CAbb CBcs CPLG CTrC

Myosotidium (*Boraginaceae*)

§	***hortensia***	CBcs CBct CGHE CPLG CSpe EBee ECre EHrv ELan EPfP EUJe EWes GCal IKil ITim LRHS MCot SChF WBor WCot WPGP
	– 'True Blue'	CHid
	nobile	see *M. hortensia*

Myosotis (*Boraginaceae*)

	alpestris 'Ruth Fischer'	NBir
	capitata	CHid
	colensoi	ECou NMen
	explanata	NMen
	My Oh My = 'Myomark'PBR	ECtt LSou NPri
	palustris	see *M. scorpioides*
	pulvinaris	WAbe
	rakiura	SBch
§	***scorpioides***	CBen CHab CWat EHon LPBA MMuc MNrw MSKA MWts NMir SCoo SPer SPlb SRms SWat WBrk WMAq WMoo WPnP XLum
	– 'Alba'	LPBA MSKA MWts
	– 'Ice Pearl'	ECha
	– Maytime = 'Blaqua' (v)	NBir
	– 'Mermaid'	CBen CRow CWat ECha EWay LPBA SBch SDix SWat WPer WPtf
	– 'Pinkie'	CWat EWay LPBA SWat
	– 'Snowflakes'	CWat EWay SWat
	– variegated (v)	CBen MSKA
	sylvatica	CRWN MMuc NMir
	'Unforgettable' (v)	NBro

Myosurus (*Ranunculaceae*)

minimus	CRDP

Myrica (*Myricaceae*)

gale	CAgr CRWN GPoy IVic MGos NLar SBfd SPoG SWat WFar WGwG WHfH

Myricaria (*Tamaricaceae*)

germanica	NLar

Myriophyllum (*Haloragaceae*)

*	'Red Stem'	LPBA
	spicatum	EHon MSKA MWts WMAq
	verticillatum	CWat SCoo

Myrrhidendron (*Apiaceae*)

glaucescens B&SWJ 10699	WCru

Myrrhis (*Apiaceae*)

odorata	CArn CBre CHby CSev CSpe CWan EBee ECha ELau ENfk GPoy IFro MHer MHoo MMuc MNHC NPri SBfd SEND SIde SPad SPer WAul WHer WJek WPer WPtf WSFF WWFP
– 'Forncett Chevron'	EBee GCal LEdu

Myrsine (*Primulaceae*)

africana	CBcs CWib EShb
aquilonia	ECou
divaricata	CTrC ECou
nummularia	WThu

Myrteola (*Myrtaceae*)

§	***nummularia***	GAbr NHar NMen WAbe WThu

Myrtus (*Myrtaceae*)

	apiculata	see *Luma apiculata*
	bullata	see *Lophomyrtus bullata*
	chequen	see *Luma chequen*
	communis ♀H3	Widely available
	– 'Flore Pleno' (d)	ELau EOHP MHer
	– 'Jenny Reitenbach'	see *M. communis* subsp. *tarentina*
	– 'Merion'	WJek
	– 'Microphylla'	see *M. communis* subsp. *tarentina*
	– 'Nana'	see *M. communis* subsp. *tarentina*
	– 'Pyewood Park'	WJek
§	– subsp. ***tarentina*** ♀H3	Widely available
	– – 'Compacta'	LRHS SLon
	– – 'Microphylla Variegata' (v)	CBcs EShb LRHS MHer MNHC SBfd SPer WJek
I	– – 'Variegata' (v)	EOHP EPfP EWhm SEND SPoG
	– 'Tricolor'	see *M. communis* 'Variegata'
§	– 'Variegata' (v)	Widely available
	'Glanleam Gold'	see *Luma apiculata* 'Glanleam Gold'
	lechleriana	see *Amomyrtus luma*
	luma	see *Luma apiculata*
	nummularia	see *Myrteola nummularia*
*	***paraguayensis***	CTrC
	'Traversii'	see *Lophomyrtus* × *ralphii* 'Traversii'
	ugni	see *Ugni molinae*

N

Nandina (*Berberidaceae*)

domestica ♀H3	Widely available
- B&SWJ 4923	WCru
- B&SWJ 11113	WCru
- 'Fire Power' ♀H3	Widely available
- 'Gulf Stream'	CBcs GBin NLar SPtl
- 'Harbour Dwarf'	CDoC EBee LRHS MAsh NLar SBfd SPoG WFar
- var. ***leucocarpa***	CMCN NLar
- 'Nana'	see *N. domestica* 'Pygmaea'
- 'Nana Purpurea'	GCal
- Plum Passion = 'Monum'	EBee LBuc LRHS MAsh
§ - 'Pygmaea'	CMen SGol
- 'Richmond'	EBee ELan EPfP LAst LRHS MAsh MGos NLar SBfd SHil SLim SPer SPoG SRkn SWvt WFar
- 'Wood's Dwarf'	CBcs NLar

Napaea (*Malvaceae*)

dioica	WCot

Narcissus ✿ (*Amaryllidaceae*)

'Abba' (4) ♀H4	CQua
'Abbey Road' (5) **new**	NMin
'Aberfoyle' (2) ♀H4	CQua
'Abstract' (11a)	CQua
'Accent' (2) ♀H4	CQua
'Achduart' (3)	CQua
'Achentoul' (4)	CQua
'Achnasheen' (3)	CQua
'Acropolis' (4)	CQua EPfP SDeJ
'Actaea' (9) ♀H4	CBro CQua CTca EPfP MBri SDeJ SEND
'Acumen' (2)	CQua
'Admiration' (8)	CQua
'Adorable Lass' (6) **new**	CQua
'Advocat' (3)	CQua
'Ahwahnee' (2)	CQua
'Ainley' (2)	CQua
'Aintree' (3)	CQua
'Aircastle' (3)	CQua
'Akala' (1) **new**	CQua
'Albatross' (3)	CQua GCro
'Albus Plenus Odoratus'	see *N. poeticus* 'Plenus' ambig.
'Alpine Glow' (1)	CQua
'Altruist' (3)	CQua ERCP
'Altun Ha' (2)	CQua
'Altun Ha Gold' (2)	CQua
'Amber Castle' (2)	CQua
'Ambergate' (2)	CQua LAma SDeJ
'Ambergris Caye' (1)	CQua
'American Goldfinch' (7)	CQua
'American Heritage' (1)	CQua
'American Robin' (6)	CQua
'American Shores' (1)	CQua
'Amstel' (4)	CQua
'Andalusia' (6)	CQua
'Andrew's Choice' (7) ♀H4	CQua
'Angel' (3)	CQua
'Angel Face' (3)	CQua
Angel's tears	see *N. triandrus* subsp. *triandrus* var. *triandrus*
'Angel's Wings' (2)	CQua
'Angkor' (4)	CQua
'An-gof' (7)	CQua
'Annequin' (3)	CQua
'Apollo Gold' (10)	CQua
'Apotheose' (4)	CQua SDeJ
'Apricot' (1)	CBro GCro
'Apricot Blush' (2)	CQua
'Apricot Whirl' (11a)	CQua
'April Love' (1)	CQua
'April Snow' (2)	CBro CQua
'April Tears' (5) ♀H4	NMin
'Ara' (6)	CQua
'Aranjuez' (2)	CQua GCro
'Aranka' (2) **new**	CQua
'Arctic Gem' (3)	CQua
'Arctic Gold' (1) ♀H4	CQua LAma
'Ard Righ' (1) **new**	GCro
'Ardress' (2)	CQua
'Areley Kings' (2)	CQua
'Argosy' (1)	CQua
'Ariel'PBR (8)	GKev
'Arish Mell' (5)	CQua
'Arkle' (1) ♀H4	CQua SDeJ
'Armoury' (4)	CQua
'Arndilly' (2)	CQua
'Arpege' (2)	CQua
'Arrowhead' (6)	NMin
'Arthurian' (1)	CQua
'Articol' (11a)	CQua
'Arwenack' (11a)	CQua
'Ashmore' (2)	CQua
'Ashton Wold' (2)	CQua
§ ***assoanus*** (13)	CBro ECho EPot GKev LAma LLHF LWst MNrw MSSP NMen NMin SPhx
'Astropink' (11a)	CQua
§ ***asturiensis*** (13) ♀H3-4	ECho NMin
- giant	see *N. asturiensis* 'Wavertree'
§ - 'Wavertree' (1)	CQua NMin
asturiensis* × *cyclamineus	NMen
'Atlas Gold'	see *N. romieuxii* 'Atlas Gold'
'Audubon' (2)	CQua SDeJ
'Aunt Betty' (1)	CQua
'Avalanche' (8) ♀H3	CQua GCro NMin SDeJ
'Avalanche of Gold' (8)	CQua
'Avalon' (2)	CQua
'Baby Boomer' (7)	LAma NMin
'Baby Moon' (7)	CQua CTca EPfP EPot ERCP GEdr GKev LAma MBri NMin SDeJ
'Baccarat' (11a)	CQua
'Back Flash' (2)	CQua
'Badanloch' (3)	CQua
'Badbury Rings' (3) ♀H4	CQua
'Bala' (4)	CQua
'Balalaika' (2)	CQua
'Baldock' (4)	CQua
'Ballygarvey' (1)	CQua
'Ballynichol' (3)	CQua
'Ballyrobert' (1)	CQua
'Balvenie' (2)	CQua
'Bandesara' (3)	CQua
'Bandit' (2)	CQua
'Banker' (2)	CQua
'Banstead Village' (2)	CQua
'Bantam' (2) ♀H4	CBro CQua NMin
'Barbary Gold' (2)	CQua
'Barlow' (6)	CQua
'Barnham' (1)	CQua
'Barnsdale Wood' (2)	CQua

'Barrett Browning' (3) SDeJ
'Barrii' (3) CQua
'Bartley' (6) CQua
'Bath's Flame' (3) CAvo CQua GCro WShi
'Bear's Gold' (4) CQua
'Beaulieu' (1) CQua
'Beautiful Dream' (3) CQua
'Beauvallon' (4) ♀H4 SDeJ
'Bebop' (7) CBro
'Bedruthan' (2) CQua
'Beersheba' (1) CQua
'Beige Beauty' (3) CQua
'Belbroughton' (2) CQua
'Belcanto' (11a) CQua SDeJ
'Belisana' (2) SDeJ
'Bell Rock' (1) CQua
'Bell Song' (7) CAvo CBro CQua EPfP GKev LSou SDeJ WShi
'Bella Estrella' (11a) ERCP
'Belzone' (2) CQua
'Ben Hee' (2) ♀H4 CQua
'Berceuse' (2) CQua
'Bere Ferrers' (4) CQua
'Bergerac' (11a) CQua
'Bernardino' (2) CQua GCro
'Beryl' (6) CBro CQua EPot NMin
'Best Friend' (3) CQua
'Best Seller' (1) SPer
'Bethal' (3) CQua
'Betsy MacDonald' (6) CQua
'Biffo' (4) CQua
* 'Big Cycla' (6) ECho
'Bilbo' (6) CBro CQua
'Billy Graham' (2) CQua
'Binkie' (2) CBro CQua SPer
'Birchwood' (3) CQua
'Birdsong' (3) CQua
'Birma' (3) LAma SDeJ
'Bishops Light' (2) CQua
'Bittern' (12) CQua SDeJ
'Blair Athol' (2) CQua
'Blarney' (3) CQua
'Blisland' (9) CQua
'Blossom' (4) CQua
'Blue Danube' (1) CQua
'Blushing Maiden' (4) CQua
'Bob Spotts' (2) CQua
'Bobbysoxer' (7) CBro CQua NMin
'Bobolink' (2) CQua
'Boconnoc' (2) CQua
'Bodelva' (2) CQua
'Bodwannick' (2) CQua
'Bold Prospect' (1) CQua
'Bonython' (1) GCro
'Bosbigal' (11a) CQua
'Boscastle' (7) CQua
'Boscoppa' (11a) CQua
'Boslowick' (11a) ♀H4 CQua
'Bosmeor' (2) CQua
'Bossa Nova' (3) CQua
'Bossiney' (11a) CQua
'Bosvale' (11a) CQua
'Bosvigo' (11a) CQua
'Boulder Bay' (2) ♀H4 CQua
'Bowles's Early Sulphur' (1) CRow
'Brandaris' (11a) CQua
'Bravoure' (1) ♀H4 CQua SDeJ
'Brentswood' (8) CQua
'Brian's Favorite' (2) **new** CQua
'Bridal Crown' (4) ♀H4 EPfP LAma LRHS
'Bright Flame' (2) CQua
'Bright Spot' (8) CQua
'Brilliancy' (3) CQua GCro
'Broadland' (2) CQua
'Broadway Star' (11b) LAma SDeJ
'Brodick' (3) CQua
'Broomhill' (2) ♀H4 CQua
'Broughshane' (1) CQua
broussonetii from Morocco WPGP
'Brunswick' (2) CQua SDeJ
'Bryanston' (2) ♀H4 CQua
'Bryher' (3) CQua
'Buckshead' (4) CQua
'Budock Bells' (5) CQua
'Budock Water' (2) CQua
'Bugle Major' (2) CQua
bulbocodium (13) ♀H3-4 CBro GKev ITim LBee LEdu LRHS SMrm SRms
- from Atlas Mountains, Morocco MSSP
§ - subsp. ***bulbocodium*** (13) CBro
§ - - var. ***citrinus*** (13) LRHS SSpi
- - - MS 577 MSSP
- - var. ***conspicuus*** (13) CBro CQua CTca ECho EPfP EPot ERCP GEdr GKev LAma MSSP NMen SDeJ WCot WIce XLum
* - - var. ***filifolius*** (13) CBro
- - var. ***nivalis*** (13) ECho EPot GKev ITim
- - var. ***pallidus*** (13) GEdr
§ - - var. ***tenuifolius*** (13) EPot NMen WCot
- var. ***filifolius*** (13) MSSP
§ - Golden Bells Group (10) CAvo CBro CHid CQua CTri CWCL ECho EPot GKev LRHS MBri NHol NMin SDeJ
- 'Ice Warrior' (10) SKHP
- var. ***mesatlanticus*** see *N. romieuxii* subsp. *romieuxii* var. *mesatlanticus*
- subsp. ***obesus*** (13) ECho MSSP WAbe WCot
§ - - 'Diamond Ring' (10) CQua EPot LAma NMin
- subsp. ***praecox*** (13) ECho LRHS WCot
- - var. ***paucinervis*** (13) ECho
- subsp. ***tananicus*** see *N. cantabricus* subsp. *tananicus*
- subsp. ***vulgaris*** see ***N. bulbocodium*** subsp. ***bulbocodium***
bulbocodium × ***romieuxii*** (13) WCot
'Bunchie' (5) CQua
'Bunclody' (2) CQua
'Bunting' (7) ♀H4 CQua
'Burravoe' (1) CQua
'Bute Park' (4) CQua
'Butter and Eggs' (4) CAvo
'Butterscotch' (2) CQua
'C.J. Backhouse' (2) GCro
'Cadgwith' (2) CQua
'Cairngorm' (2) SDeJ
'Cairntoul' (3) CQua
'Calamansack' (2) CQua
'Camden' (1) CQua
'Camelot' (2) ♀H4 CQua EPfP SDeJ SPer
'Cameo King' (2) CQua
'Cameo Marie' (3) CQua
'Camilla Duchess of Cornwall' (2) CQua
'Camoro' (10) MSSP NMen
'Campernelli' (7) CQua
'Campernelli Plenus' see *N.* × *odorus* 'Double Campernelle'

'Campion' (9)	CQua
canaliculatus Gussone	see *N. tazetta* subsp. *lacticolor*
'Canaliculatus' (8)	CBro CQua CTri ECho EPfP ERCP GKev LAma LRHS MBri SDeJ SEND SPer
'Canary' (7)	CQua
'Canarybird' (8)	CQua WShi
'Canasta' (11a)	CQua
'Candida' (4)	CQua
'Canisp' (2)	CQua
'Cantabile' (9) ♀H4	CQua
cantabricus (13)	ECho
- subsp. ***cantabricus*** (13)	NMin
- - var. ***foliosus*** (13) ♀H2	ECho EPot GKev NMen SCnR WAbe WCot
§ - subsp. ***tananicus*** (13)	ECho EPot
cantabricus × ***romieuxii*** subsp. ***albidus*** var. ***zaianicus*** f. ***lutescens*** (13) **new**	WCot
'Cantatrice' (1)	CQua
'Canterbury' (5)	CQua
'Capax Plenus'	see *N.* 'Eystettensis'
'Cape Cornwall' (2)	CQua
'Capisco' (3)	CQua
'Carbineer' (2)	CQua GCro SDeJ
'Cardiff' (2)	CQua
'Cargreen' (9)	CQua
'Carib Gipsy' (2) ♀H4	CQua
'Caribbean Snow' (2)	CQua
'Carlton' (2) ♀H4	CQua EPfP GKev LAma SDeJ
'Carnearny' (3)	CQua
'Carnkeeran' (2)	CQua
'Carnkief' (2)	CQua
'Carnyorth' (11a)	CQua
'Carole Lombard' (3)	CQua
'Carwinion' (2)	CQua
'Casiah' (2)	CQua
'Cassata' (11a)	EPfP LAma NBir SDeJ
'Casterbridge' (2)	CQua
'Castle Rings' (4) **new**	CQua
'Catistock' (2)	CQua
'Cavalli King' (4)	CQua
'Cawdron' (2)	CQua
'Caye Chapel' (3)	CQua
'Cazique' (6)	CQua
× ***cazorlanus*** (13)	MSSP NSla
'Cedar Hills' (3)	CQua
'Cedric Morris' (1)	CDes CLAP ECha EWoo GBuc WCot
'Celestial Fire' (2)	CQua
'Celtic Gold' (2)	CQua
'Centrefold' (3)	CQua
'Cha-cha' (6)	CBro CQua
'Changing Colors' (11a)	CQua EPfP SDeJ
'Chanson' (1) ♀H4	CQua
'Chanterelle' (11a)	LAma SDeJ
'Chantilly' (2)	CQua
'Charity May' (6) ♀H4	CQua
'Charleston' (2)	CQua
'Charlie Connor' (1)	CQua
'Chaste' (1)	CQua
'Chat' (7)	CQua
'Cheer Leader' (3)	CQua
'Cheerfulness' (4) ♀H4	CAvo CQua LAma MBri NPer SDeJ
'Cheesewring' (3)	CQua
'Cheetah' (1)	CQua
'Chelsea Girl' (2)	CQua
'Cheltenham' (2)	CQua
'Chérie' (7)	CQua
'Cherish' (2)	CQua
'Cherrygardens' (2)	CQua
'Chesapeake Bay' (1)	CQua
'Chesterton' (9) ♀H4	CQua
'Chickadee' (6)	CQua
'Chicken Hill' (1)	CQua
'Chickerell' (3)	CQua
'Chiloquin' (1)	CQua
'China Doll' (2)	CQua
'China Gold' (10) **new**	CQua
'Chinchilla' (2)	CQua
'Chinita' (8)	CBro CQua EPfP GCro
'Chipper' (5)	CQua NMin
'Chit Chat' (7) ♀H4	CQua EPot NMin
'Chiva' (7)	CBro GKev LLHF NMin
'Chobe River' (1)	CQua
'Churchfield Bells' (5)	CQua
'Churston Ferrers' (4)	CQua
'Chy Noweth' (2)	CQua
'Cinco de Mayo' (2)	CQua
citrinus	see *N. bulbocodium* subsp. *bulbocodium* var. *citrinus*
'Citron' (3)	CQua
'Citronita' (3)	CQua
'Clare' (7)	CBro CQua NMin
'Classic Gold' (10) ♀H4 **new**	CQua
'Claverley' (2)	CQua
'Clearbrook' (2)	CQua
'Cloud Nine' (2)	CBro
'Clouded Yellow' (2)	CQua
'Clouds Hill' (4)	CQua
'Clovelly Ayr' (9)	CQua
'Codlins and Cream'	see *N.* 'Sulphur Phoenix'
'Coker's Frome' (9)	CQua
'Coldbrook' (2)	CQua
'Colin's Joy' (2)	CQua
'Colleen Bawn' (1)	CQua NMin
'Colley Gate' (3)	CQua
'Colliford' (2)	CQua
'Colorama' (11a)	CQua
'Columbus' (2)	CQua
'Colville' (9)	CQua
'Comal' (1)	CQua
'Compressus'	see *N.* × *intermedius* 'Compressus'
'Conestoga' (2)	CQua
'Congress' (11a)	CQua
'Conly' (3)	CQua
'Conowingo' (11a)	CQua
'Conspicuus' ambig.	LAma
'Conspicuus' (3)	GCro
'Cool Autumn' (2)	CQua
'Cool Crystal' (3)	CQua
'Cool Evening' (11a)	CQua
'Cool Pink' (2)	CQua
'Cool Shades' (2)	CQua
'Coombe Creek' (6)	CQua
'Copper Rings' (3)	CQua
'Copperfield' (2)	CQua
'Cora Ann' (7)	CBro
'Coral Fair' (2)	CQua
'Corbiere' (1)	CQua
'Corbridge' (2)	CQua
'Corky's Song' (2)	CQua
'Cornet' (6)	CQua
'Cornish Chuckles' (12) ♀H4	CBro CQua
'Cornish Sun' (2)	CQua
'Cornish Vanguard' (2) ♀H4	CQua
'Corofin' (3)	CQua

Name	Suppliers
'Corozal' (3)	CQua
'Cotinga' (6)	CQua NMin SDeJ
'Countdown' (2)	CQua
'Coverack Glory' (2)	CQua
'Crackington' (4) ♀H4	CQua
'Cragford' (8)	MBri SDeJ
'Craig Stiel' (2)	CQua
'Creag Dubh' (2)	CQua
'Creed' (6)	CQua
'Crenver' (3)	CQua GCro
'Crewenna' (1)	CAvo CQua
'Crill' (7)	CQua
'Crimson Chalice' (3)	CQua
'Cristobal' (1)	CQua
'Croesus' (2)	CQua GCro
'Crofty' (6)	CQua
'Croila' (2)	CQua
'Crowndale' (4)	CQua
'Crugmeer' (11a)	CQua
'Cryptic' (1)	CQua
'Crystal Star' (2)	CQua
'Cudden Point' (2)	CQua
'Cul Beag' (3)	CQua
'Culmination' (2)	CQua
'Cultured Pearl' (2)	CQua
'Cum Laude' (11a)	ERCP SDeJ
'Curlew' (7) ♀H4	CQua GKev SDeJ
'Curly' (2)	SDeJ
'Curlylocks' (7)	NMin
cyclamineus (13) ♀H4	CBro CDes CPLG CRDP CWCL LRHS MSSP NMen SCnR SKHP SRms
'Cyclope' (1)	CQua
cypri (13)	CQua
'Cyros' (1)	CQua
'Dailmanach' (2)	CQua
'Dallas' (3)	CQua
'Dalmeny' (2)	CQua
'Damson' (2)	CQua GCro
'Dan du Plessis' (8)	CQua
'Dateline' (3)	CQua
'David Alexander' (1)	CQua
'David Mills' (2)	CQua
'Dawn Brooker' (2)	CQua
'Dawn Run' (2)	CQua
'Dawn Sky' (2)	CQua
'Daydream' (2) ♀H3	CQua
'Daymark' (8)	CQua
'Dayton Lake' (2)	CQua
'Debutante' (2)	CQua
'December Bride' (11a)	CQua
'Del Rey' (1)	CQua
'Dell Chapel' (3)	CQua
'Delnashaugh' (4)	CQua ERCP LAma NHol SDeJ
'Delos' (3)	CQua
'Demand' (2)	CQua
'Demmo' (2)	CQua
'Desdemona' (2) ♀H4	CQua SDeJ
'Desert Bells' (7)	CQua NMin
'Desert Orchid' (2)	CQua
'Diamond Ring'	see *N. bulbocodium* subsp. *obesus* 'Diamond Ring'
'Dick Wilden' (4)	CQua
'Dickcissel' (7) ♀H4	CQua ERCP GKev SPhx
'Dimity' (3)	CQua
'Dimple' (9)	CQua
'Dinkie' (3)	CBro
'Disquiet' (1)	CQua
'Doctor Hugh' (3) ♀H4	CQua
'Doctor Jazz' (2)	CQua
'Doll Baby' (7)	NMin
'Doombar' (1)	CQua
'Dorchester' (4)	CQua
'Double Campernelle'	see *N.* × *odorus* 'Double Campernelle'
'Double Itzim' (4)	NMin
double pheasant eye	see *N. poeticus* 'Plenus' ambig.
double Roman	see *N.* 'Romanus'
'Double White' (4)	CQua
'Doublet' (4)	CQua
'Doubtful' (3)	CQua
'Dover Cliffs' (2)	CQua
'Downlands' (3)	CQua
'Downpatrick' (1)	CQua
'Dragon Run' (2)	CQua
'Dreamlight' (3)	CQua
'Drumboe' (2)	CQua
dubius (13)	CBro ECho EPot
'Duchess of Westminster' (2)	GCro
'Dulcimer' (9)	CQua
'Dunkeld' (2)	CQua
'Dunkery' (4)	CQua
'Dunley Hall' (3)	CQua
'Dunmurry' (1)	CQua
'Dunskey' (3)	CQua
'Dutch Lemon Drops' (5) ♀H4	CMea CQua EPot NMin
'Dutch Master' (1) ♀H4	CQua LAma SDeJ SPer
'Early Bride' (2)	CQua
'Early Splendour' (8)	CQua
'Earthlight' (3)	CQua
'Easter Moon' (2)	CQua
'Eastern Dawn' (2)	CQua SDeJ
'Eastern Promise' (2)	CQua
'Eaton Song' (12) ♀H4	CBro CQua
'Ebony' (1)	CQua
'Eddy Canzony' (2)	CQua
'Edgbaston' (2)	CQua
'Edge Grove' (2)	CQua
'Edward Buxton' (3)	CQua GCro
'Egard' (11a)	CQua
'Egmont King' (2)	CQua
'Eland' (7)	CQua
'Elburton' (2)	CQua
'Elegans' (3)	CAvo GCro
elegans (13)	ECho EPot
'Elf' (2)	CQua
'Elfin Gold' (6)	CQua
'Elizabeth Ann' (6)	CQua
'Elka' (1)	CAvo CBro CQua LLHF MSSP NMin
'Elphin' (4)	CQua
'Elrond' (2)	CQua
'Elven Lady' (2)	CQua
'Elvira' (8)	CQua WShi
'Emcys' (6)	EPot LLHF NMin
'Emerald Pink' (3)	CQua
'Emily' (2)	NMin
'Eminent' (3)	CQua
'Emperor' (1)	CQua GCro
'Empire' (2)	GCro
'Empress of Ireland' (1) ♀H4	CQua
'English Caye' (1)	CQua
'Ensemble' (4)	CQua
'Epona' (3)	CQua
'Erin' (3)	CQua
'Erlicheer' (4)	CQua SDeJ
'Estrella' (3)	CQua
§ ***eugeniae*** (13)	WCot
'Euryalus' (1)	CQua
'Evangeline' (3)	GCro

	'Eve Robertson' (2)	CQua
	'Evelyn Roberts' (11a)	CQua
	'Evening' (2)	CQua
	'Evesham' (3)	CQua
	'Eyeglass' (3)	CQua
	'Eyelet' (3)	CQua
	'Eyrie' (3)	CQua
§	'Eystettensis' (4)	CBro CQua CRDP IBlr
	'Fair Head' (9)	CQua
	'Fair Prospect' (2)	CQua
	'Fair William' (2)	CQua
	'Fairgreen' (3)	CQua
	'Fairlawns' (3)	CQua
	'Fairmile' (3)	CQua
	'Fairy Chimes' (5)	CQua
	'Fairy Footsteps' (3)	CQua
	'Fairy Island' (3)	CQua
	'Fairy Tale' (3)	CQua
I	'Faith' (1) **new**	SDeJ
	'Falconet' (8) ♀H4	CBro CQua EPfP SPer
	'Falmouth Bay' (3)	CQua
	'Falstaff' (2)	CQua
	'Fanline' (11a)	CQua
	'Far Country' (2)	CQua
I	'Fashion' (11b)	CQua
	'Fastidious' (2)	CQua
	'February Gold' (6) ♀H4	CAvo CBro CQua CTri EPfP EPot ERCP GKev LAma LRHS MBri NBir SDeJ SEND SPer SPhx SRms WShi
	'February Silver' (1)	CBro EPot ERCP LAma SDeJ SPhx
	'Feeling Lucky' (2) ♀H4	CQua
	'Felindre' (9)	CQua EPot
	'Feock' (3)	CQua
	fernandesii (13)	ECho GEdr ITim NMin SCnR WCot WThu
	- var. ***cordubensis*** (13)	ECho EPot GEdr
	- var. ***cordubensis*** × ***jonquilla*** (13)	NMin
	'Ferndown' (3)	CQua
	'Fertile Crescent' (7)	CQua
	'Feu de Joie' (4)	GCro
	'Ffitch's Ffolly' (2)	CQua
	'Filoli' (1)	CQua
	'Finchcocks' (2)	CQua
	'Fine Gold' (1)	CQua
	'Fine Romance' (2)	CQua
	'Finland' (2)	CQua
	'Fire Tail' (3)	WShi
	'Firebrand' (3)	CQua
	'First Born' (6)	CQua NMin
	'First Formal' (3)	CQua
	'First Hope' (6)	CQua
	'Flambards Village' (4)	CQua
	'Flirt' (6)	CQua
	'Flomay' (7)	NMin
	'Flower Record' (2)	LAma
	'Flusher' (2)	CQua
	'Flycatcher' (7)	CQua
	'Flying High' (3)	CQua
	'Foff's Way' (1)	CQua
	'Foresight' (1)	CQua
	'Forge Mill' (2)	CQua
	'Fort Mitchell' (1) **new**	CQua
	'Fortissimo' (2)	SPer
	'Fortune' (2)	CQua GCro LAma MBri SDeJ
	'Fossie' (4)	CQua
	'Foundling' (6) ♀H4	CQua
	'Foxfire' (2)	CQua
	'Foxhunter' (2)	CQua
	'Fragrant Breeze' (2)	SDeJ
	'Fragrant Rose' (2)	CQua ERCP
	'Frances Delight' (11a)	CQua
	'Frank Miles' (2) **new**	GCro
	'Freedom Rings' (2)	CQua
	'Fresh Field' (2)	CQua
	'Fresh Lime' (1)	CQua
	'Frigid' (3)	CQua
	'Front Royal' (2)	CQua
	'Frostkist' (6)	CBro CQua
	'Frosty Morn' (5)	NMin
	'Frozen Jade' (1)	CQua
	'Fruit Cup' (7)	CQua SDeJ
	'Fuco' (1)	CQua NMin
	'Full House' (4)	SDeJ
	'Fulwell' (4)	CQua
	'Furbelow' (4)	CQua
	'Gabriella Rose' (4) **new**	CQua
	gaditanus (13)	CBro
	'Garden Opera' (7) ♀H4	CQua
	'Gay Cavalier' (4)	CQua
	'Gay Kybo' (4) ♀H4	CQua
	'Gay Song' (4)	CQua
	'Gay Time' (4)	SDeJ
	gayi (13)	CQua WShi
	'Geevor' (4)	CQua
	'Gellymill' (2)	CQua
	'Gemini Girl' (2)	CQua
	'George Leak' (2)	CQua
	'Geranium' (8) ♀H4	CBro CQua EPfP ERCP GCro LAma SDeJ SPer WShi
	'Gerry Smith' (2) **new**	CQua
	'Gettysburg' (2)	CQua
	'Gigantic Star' (2)	CQua
	'Gillan' (11a)	CQua
	'Gin and Lime' (1) ♀H4	CQua
	'Gipsy Moon' (2)	CQua
	'Gipsy Queen' (1)	CBro CQua ECha EPot LLHF NMin
	'Gironde' (11)	CQua
	'Glacier' (1)	CQua
	'Glasnevin' (2)	CQua
	'Glen Clova' (2)	CQua
	'Glendermott' (2)	CQua
	'Glenside' (2)	CQua
	'Glissando' (2)	CQua
	'Gloria Mundi' (2)	GCro
	'Gloriosus' (8)	CQua
	'Glover's Reef' (1)	CQua
	'Glowing Phoenix' (4)	CQua
	'Glowing Red' (4)	CQua
	'Goff's Caye' (2)	CQua
	'Golant' (2)	CQua
	'Gold Bond' (2)	CQua
	'Gold Cache' (11a)	CQua
	'Gold Charm' (2)	CQua
	'Gold Convention' (2) ♀H4	CQua
	'Gold Medallion' (1)	CQua
	'Gold Top' (2)	CQua
	'Golden Amber' (2)	CQua
	'Golden Aura' (2) ♀H4	CQua
	'Golden Bear' (4)	CQua
	'Golden Bells'	see *N. bulbocodium* Golden Bells Group
	'Golden Cheer' (2)	CQua
	'Golden Dawn' (8) ♀H3	CQua EPfP
	'Golden Ducat' (4)	CQua LAma MBri NBir SDeJ
	'Golden Halo' (2)	CQua

'Golden Harvest' (1)	CQua LAma NPer		'Helford Sunset' (2)	CQua
'Golden Incense' (7)	CQua		'Helios' (2)	CQua GCro
'Golden Jewel' (2) ♀H4	CQua		***hellenicus***	see *N. poeticus* var. *hellenicus*
'Golden Joy' (2)	CQua		***henriquesii***	see *N. jonquilla* var. *henriquesii*
'Golden Lion' (1)	CQua EPfP		'Henry Irving' (1)	CQua GCro
'Golden Marvel' (1)	CQua		'Hero' (1)	CQua
'Golden Orbit' (4)	CQua		'Heslington' (3)	CQua
'Golden Phoenix' (4)	CQua		'Hexameter' (9)	CQua
'Golden Rain' (4)	CQua		'Hexworthy' (3)	CQua
'Golden Rapture' (1) ♀H4	CQua		'Hicks Mill' (1)	CQua
'Golden Sceptre' (7)	GCro		'High Society' (2) ♀H4	CQua
'Golden Sheen' (2)	CQua		'Highfield Beauty' (8) ♀H4	CQua
'Golden Spur' (1)	CQua LAma		'Highgrove' (1)	CQua
'Golden Torch' (2)	CQua		'Highlite' (2)	CQua
'Golden Twins' (7)	CQua		'Hihitahi' (2)	CQua
'Golden Vale' (1) ♀H4	CQua		'Hilda's Pink' (2)	CQua
'Goldfinger' (1) ♀H4	CQua		'Hillstar' (7) ♀H4	CQua NMin SDeJ
'Goldhanger' (2)	CQua		***hispanicus*** (13)	ECho
'Golitha Falls' (2)	CQua		'Holland's Glory' (4)	GCro
'Good Fella' (2)	CQua		'Holme Fen' (2)	CQua
'Good Measure' (2)	CQua		'Home Fires' (2)	CQua
'Goonbell' (2)	CQua		'Honey Pink' (2)	CQua
'Goose Green' (3)	GKev		'Honeybird' (1)	CQua
'Gorran' (3)	CQua		'Hoopoe' (8) ♀H4	CQua GKev
'Gossmoor' (4)	CQua		'Horace' (9)	CQua
'Grace Note' (3)	CQua		'Horn of Plenty' (5)	CQua
'Grand Monarque'	see *N. tazetta* subsp. *lacticolor* 'Grand Monarque'		'Hors d'Oeuvre' (8)	CBro
			'Horsfieldii' (1)	GCro
'Grand Primo Citronière' (8)	CQua		'Hospodar' (2)	CQua GCro
			'Hot Gossip' (2)	CQua
'Grand Prospect' (2)	CQua		'Hotspur' (2)	CQua
'Grand Soleil d'Or' (8)	CQua LAma SDeJ		Howick Beauty (2) **new**	GCro
'Great Expectations' (2)	CQua		'Hugh Town' (8)	CAvo CQua SEND
'Great Warley' (2) **new**	GCro		'Hugus' (7)	CQua
'Greatwood' (1)	CQua		'Hummingbird' (6)	EPot
'Green Chartreuse' (2)	CQua		'Hunting Caye' (2)	CQua
'Green Island' (2)	SDeJ		'Huntley Down' (1)	CQua
'Green Lawns' (9)	CQua		'Ice Chimes' (5)	CQua
'Green Pearl' (3)	NMin		'Ice Dancer' (2)	CQua
'Greenodd' (3)	CQua		'Ice Diamond' (4)	CQua
'Grenoble' (2)	CQua		'Ice Follies' (2) ♀H4	CQua EPfP GKev LAma MBri NBir SDeJ SPer
'Gresham' (4)	CQua			
'Gribben Head' (4)	CQua		'Ice King' (4)	NBir SDeJ
'Guiding Spirit' (4)	CQua		'Ice Wings' (5) ♀H4	CAvo CBro CQua EPot NMin SDeJ WShi
'Gull' (2) **new**	CQua			
'Gulliver' (3)	CQua GCro		'Idless' (1)	CQua
'Gunwalloe' (11a)	CQua	I	'Idol' (7)	CQua EPot NMin
'Guy Wilson' (2)	CQua		'Immaculate' (2)	CQua
'Gwennap' (1)	CQua		'Inara' (4)	CQua
'Gwinear' (2)	CQua		'Inca' (6)	CQua
'Hacienda' (1)	CQua		'Inchbonnie' (2)	CQua
'Half Moon Caye' (2)	CQua		× ***incomparabilis*** (13)	SEND
'Halley's Comet' (3)	CQua		'Independence Day' (4)	CQua
'Halloon' (3)	CQua		'Indian Maid' (7) ♀H4	CQua
'Halzephron' (2)	CQua		'Indora' (4)	CQua
'Hambledon' (2) ♀H4	CQua		'Innisidgen' (8)	CQua
'Hampton Court' (2)	CQua		'Innovator' (4)	CQua
'Happy Fellow' (2)	CQua		'Interim' (2)	CQua SDeJ
'Harmony Bells' (5)	CBro CQua NMin		× ***intermedius*** (13)	CBro CQua NMin WAbe WCot
'Harpers Ferry' (1)	CQua	§	– 'Compressus' (8)	CBro CQua
'Hartlebury' (3)	CQua		'Intrigue' (7) ♀H4	CQua
'Havelock' (2)	GCro		'Invercassley' (3)	CQua
'Hawera' (5) ♀H4	CAvo CBro CHid CMea CQua CTca CTri EPfP EPot ERCP GKev LAma LSou MBri SDeJ SPer WShi		'Inverpolly' (2)	CQua
			'Irene Copeland' (4)	CQua
			'Irish Fire' (2)	CQua
'Heamoor' (4) ♀H4	CQua		'Irish Light' (2)	CQua
hedraeanthus (13)	ECho EPot		'Irish Luck' (1)	CQua
– SG 15	WCot		'Irish Minstrel' (2) ♀H4	CQua
'Helford Dawn' (2)	CQua		'Irish Mist' (2)	CQua

Plant	Suppliers
'Irish Rum' (2)	CQua
'Irish Wedding' (2)	CQua
'Isambard' (4)	CQua
'Island Pride' (8)	CQua
'Islander' (4)	CQua
'Itzim' (6) 🏆^{H4}	CBro CQua SDeJ
jacetanus (13)	MSSP NMin
'Jack Snipe' (6) 🏆^{H4}	CAvo CBro CHid CQua ECho EPfP EPot GKev LAma MBri NHol SDeJ SEND WShi
'Jack Wood' (11a)	CQua
'Jackadee' (2)	CQua
'Jacob Maurer' (6)	CQua
'Jamage' (8)	CQua
'Jamaica Inn' (4)	CQua
'Jamboree' (2)	CQua
'Janelle' (2)	CQua
'Jantje' (11a)	CQua
'Javelin' (2)	CQua
'Jeanine' (2)	CQua
'Jenny' (6) 🏆^{H4}	CBro CMea CQua ERCP GKev LAma MBri MCot NBir SDeJ SPhx WShi
'Jersey Lace' (2)	CQua
'Jersey Roundabout' (4)	CQua
'Jersey Star' (4)	CQua
'Jersey Torch' (4)	CQua
'Jetfire' (6) 🏆^{H4}	CMea CQua ECho EPfP EPot ERCP GKev LAma LPot LRHS LSou MBri NHol SDeJ SPer WShi
'Jimmy Noone' (1)	CQua
'Johanna' (5)	CBro
'John Daniel' (4)	CQua
'John Dickens' (2) **new**	CQua
'John Evelyn' (2)	GCro
'John Lanyon' (3)	CQua
'John Philip Sousa' (2)	CQua
'Johnny Dodds' (1)	CQua
'John's Delight' (3)	CQua
jonquilla (13) 🏆^{H4}	CBro CQua EPot GKev LAma NMin WShi
§ - var. ***henriquesii*** (13)	CQua ECho GKev NMin SCnR
'Joppa' (7)	CQua
'Joy Bishop'	see *N. romieuxii* 'Joy Bishop'
'Joybell' (6)	CQua
'Juanita' (2)	NPer SDeJ
'Jules Verne' (2)	CQua
'Julia Jane'	see *N. romieuxii* 'Julia Jane'
'Juliet Firstbrook' (2)	CQua
'Jumblie' (12) 🏆^{H4}	CBro EPfP EPot GKev LAma LRHS MBri SDeJ
'Jumbo Gold' (1)	CTri
juncifolius Req. ex Lag.	see *N. assoanus*
'June Lake' (2)	CQua
'Junior Miss' (12)	NMin
'Kabani' (9)	CQua
'Kalimna' (1)	CQua
'Kamms' (1)	CQua
'Kamura' (2)	CQua
'Kate Davies' (2)	CQua
'Katherine Jenkins' (7)	CQua
'Kathy's Clown' (6)	CQua
'Katie Heath' (5)	EPfP ERCP MBri SDeJ SPer
'Katrina Rea' (6)	CQua
'Kaydee' (6) 🏆^{H4}	CQua SDeJ
'Kea' (6)	CQua
'Keats' (4)	CQua NMin
'Kebaya' (2)	CQua
'Kedron' (7)	ERCP
'Kelly Bray' (1)	CQua
'Kenellis' (10)	EPot GEdr
'Kernow' (2)	CQua
'Kidling' (7)	CQua EPot NMin
'Killara' (8)	CQua
'Killearnan' (9)	CQua
'Killigrew' (2)	CQua GCro
'Killivose' (3)	CQua
'Kilmood' (2)	CQua
'Kilworth' (2)	CQua
'Kimmeridge' (3)	CQua
'King Alfred' (1)	CQua EPfP SDeJ SEND SPer
'King Size' (11a)	CQua
'Kinglet' (7)	CQua
'King's Grove' (1) 🏆^{H4}	CQua
'Kings Pipe' (2)	CQua
'Kingscourt' (1) 🏆^{H4}	CQua
'Kingsmill Lake' (2)	CQua
'Kirklington' (2)	CQua
'Kit Hill' (7)	CQua
'Kitten' (6)	CQua
'Kiwi Magic' (4)	CQua
'Kiwi Sunset' (4)	CQua
'Knightsbridge' (1)	CQua
'Kokopelli' (7) 🏆^{H4}	CBro CQua NMin
'Koomooloo' (2)	CQua
'La Belle' (7) **new**	LLHF
'La Vella' (2)	CQua
'Lady Alice' (7)	CQua
'Lady Be Good' (2)	CQua
'Lady Diana' (2)	CQua
'Lady Emily' (2)	CQua
'Lady Godiva' (3)	GCro
'Lady Hilaria' (2)	CQua
'Lady Margaret Boscawen' (2)	CQua GCro
'Lady Moore' (3) **new**	GCro
'Lady Serena' (9)	CQua
'Lalique' (3)	CQua
'Lamanva' (2)	CQua
'Lanarth' (7)	GCro
'Lancaster' (3)	CQua
'Landewednack Lady' (4)	CQua
'Langarth' (11a)	CQua
'Larkelly' (6)	CQua
'Larkhill' (2)	CQua
'Larkwhistle' (6) 🏆^{H4}	LAma SDeJ
'Las Vegas' (1)	EPfP SDeJ
'Latchley' (2)	CQua
'Latchley Meadows' (2)	CQua
'Laurens Koster' (8)	CQua
'Lavender Lass' (6)	CQua
'Lavender Mist' (2)	CQua
'Lazy River' (1)	CQua
'Lee Moor' (1)	CQua
'Lemon Beauty' (11b)	CQua SDeJ
'Lemon Drizzle' (2)	CQua
'Lemon Drops' (5)	ECho ERCP SDeJ SPhx
'Lemon Haze' (2)	CQua
'Lemon Silk' (6)	CBro CQua ECho NMin
'Lemonade' (3)	CQua
'Lennymore' (2)	CQua
'Lewis George' (1)	CQua
'Liberty Bells' (5)	CQua ECho LAma MBri
'Liebeslied' (3)	CQua
'Life' (7)	CQua
'Lighthouse' (3)	CQua
'Lighthouse Reef' (1)	CQua
'Lilac Charm' (6)	CQua

'Lilac Hue' (6)	CBro
'Lilac Mist' (2)	CQua
'Lilliput' ambig.	CQua
'Lily-May Bostock' (6)	CQua
'Limbo' (2)	CQua
'Limehurst' (2)	CQua
'Limequilla' (7)	CQua
'Lindsay Joy' (2)	CQua
'Lintie' (7)	CQua
'Little Beauty' (1) ♀H4	CBro CQua LAma NMin
'Little Dancer' (1)	CBro CQua
'Little Flik' (12)	NMin
'Little Jewel' (3)	CQua
'Little Meg' (7)	CQua
'Little Rusky' (7)	CBro CQua NMin
'Little Sentry' (7)	CBro CQua NMin
'Little Soldier' (10)	CQua NMin
'Little Tyke' (2)	CQua
'Little Witch' (6)	CBro CQua EPfP GCro GKev LAma MWat SDeJ SPhx WShi
'Littlefield' (7)	CQua
'Livelands' (1)	CQua
'Liverpool Festival' (2)	CQua
'Lobularis'	see *N. lobularis* (Haw.) Schult. & Schult. f.
lobularis misapplied	see *N. nanus*
§ ***lobularis*** (Haw.) Schult. & Schult. f.	CAvo CBro CQua CTca CTri ECho EPot GKev LRHS MBri SDeJ SEND SPer SPhx
'Loch Alsh' (3)	CQua
'Loch Assynt' (3)	CQua
'Loch Brora' (2)	CQua
'Loch Coire' (3)	CQua
'Loch Fada' (2)	CQua
'Loch Hope' (2)	CQua
'Loch Leven' (2)	CQua
'Loch Loyal' (2)	CQua
'Loch Lundie' (2)	CQua
'Loch Maberry' (2)	CQua
'Loch Naver' (2)	CQua
'Loch Owskeich' (2) ♀H4	CQua
'Loch Stac' (2)	CQua
'Logan Rock' (7)	CQua
'Lorikeet' (1)	CQua
'Lothario' (2)	LAma MBri
'Louise de Coligny' (2)	ERCP
'Love Call' (11a)	CQua
'Loveny' (2)	CQua
'Lubaantun' (1)	CQua
'Lucifer' (2)	CAvo CQua GCro WShi
'Lulworth' (2)	GCro
'Lundy Light' (2)	CQua
'Lynher' (2)	CQua
'Lyrebird' (3)	CQua
'Lyric' (9)	CQua
'Lysander' (2)	CQua
'Madam Speaker' (4)	CQua
'Madame Plemp' (1)	GCro
'Madison' (4)	CQua
'Maelor' (1)	SEND
'Magic Moment' (3)	CQua
'Magician' (2)	CQua
'Magna Carta' (2)	CQua
'Magnet' (1)	LAma NPer
'Magnificence' (1)	CQua
'Majestic Star' (1)	CQua
'Maker's Mark' (1) **new**	CQua
'Malpas' (3)	CQua
'Malvern City' (1)	CQua
'Manaccan' (1)	CQua
'Mangaweka' (6)	CQua
'Manly' (4) ♀H4	CQua ERCP
'Mantle' (2)	CQua
'Marabou' (4)	CQua
'Margaret Herbert' (7)	CQua
'Marie Curie Diamond' (7) ♀H4	CQua
'Marieke' (1)	LAma SDeJ
'Marilyn Anne' (2)	CQua
'Marjorie Hine' (2)	CQua
'Marjorie Treveal' (4)	CQua
'Marlborough' (2)	CQua
'Marlborough Freya' (2)	CQua
'Marshfire' (2)	CQua
'Martha Washington' (8)	CBro CQua
'Martinette' (8)	CQua CTca SDeJ
'Martinsville' (8)	CQua
'Mary Copeland' (4)	CQua
'Mary Kate' (2)	CQua
'Mary Plumstead' (5)	NMin
'Mary Rosina' (4)	CQua
'Mary Veronica' (3)	CQua
'Marzo' (7)	NMin
'Matador' (8)	CQua
'Mawla' (1)	CQua
'Max' (11a)	CQua
'Maximus Superbus' (1)	CQua
'Maya Dynasty' (2)	CQua
'Mayor's Choice' (11a)	CQua
'Maywood' (11a)	CQua
'Mazzard' (4)	CQua
× ***medioluteus*** (13)	CBro CQua NMin
'Medusa' (8)	CBro GCro
'Melancholy' (1)	CQua
'Melbury' (2)	CQua
'Meldrum' (1)	CQua
'Memento' (1)	CQua
'Menabilly' (4)	CQua
'Mên-an-Tol' (2)	CQua
'Menehay' (11a) ♀H4	CQua
'Mereworth' (2)	CQua
'Merlin' (3) ♀H4	CQua LAma SDeJ
'Merry Bells' (5)	CQua
'Merrymeet' (4)	CQua
'Mersing' (3)	CQua
'Merthan' (9)	CQua
'Michaels Gold' (2)	CQua
'Midas Touch' (1)	CQua
'Midget'	see *N. nanus* 'Midget'
Midtown Aerolite (2) **new**	GCro
Midtown Alfie (1) **new**	GCro
Midtown Autocrat (2) **new**	GCro
Midtown Brigadier (2) **new**	GCro
Midtown Elegance (2) **new**	GCro
Midtown Noble (1) **new**	GCro
Midtown Torch (2) **new**	GCro
'Mike Pollock' (8)	CQua
'Milan' (9)	CQua
'Millennium Sunrise' (2)	CQua
'Millennium Sunset' (2)	CQua
'Milly's Magic' (2)	CQua
Minicycla Group (6)	ECho MSSP WAbe
minimus misapplied	see *N. asturiensis*
'Minnow' (8) ♀H3	CAvo CBro CMea CQua ECho EPfP EPot ERCP GKev LAma LPot LRHS MBri NBir SDeJ SPer SPhx
minor (13) ♀H4	CBro CQua ECha ECho EPot GEdr GKev LAma NMin WCot WShi

Name	Suppliers
- 'Little Gem' (1) ΨH4	CBro CQua CTri EPfP ITim LAma SPhx
- var. ***pumilus*** 'Plenus'	see *N.* 'Rip van Winkle'
- Ulster form (13)	IBlr MSSP
'Mint Julep' (3) ΨH4	SDeJ SPhx
'Minute Waltz' (6)	CQua
'Mirar' (2)	CQua
'Misquote' (1)	CQua
'Miss Klein' (7)	LLHF NMin
'Miss Muffit' (1)	CQua
'Mission Bells' (5) ΨH4	CQua NMin SPhx
'Mission Impossible' (11a)	CQua
'Mist of Avalon' (4)	CQua
'Misty Glen' (2) ΨH4	CQua
'Mite' (6) ΨH4	CAvo CBro CQua EPot GEdr LAma LLHF NMin
'Mithrel' (11a)	CQua
'Mitylene' (2)	GCro
'Mitzy' (6)	LLHF NMin
'Modern Art' (2)	CQua
'Modulation' (2)	EPfP
'Mondragon' (11a)	CQua
'Mongleath' (2)	CQua
'Monks Wood' (1)	CQua
'Monksilver' (3)	CQua
'Montclair' (2)	CQua
'Montego' (3)	CQua
'Moon Dream' (1)	CQua
'Moon Ranger' (3)	CQua
'Moon Shadow' (3)	CQua
'Moonstruck' (1)	CQua
'Morab' (1)	CQua
'Morval' (2)	CQua
moschatus (13) ΨH4	CBro CQua ECho EPot LAma NMin SPhx WShi
'Mount Fuji' (2)	CQua
'Mount Hood' (1) ΨH4	EPfP GKev LAma NBir SDeJ SEND SPer
'Mowser' (7)	CQua
'Mr Julian' (6)	CQua
'Mrs Langtry' (2)	GCro WShi
'Mrs R.O. Backhouse' (2)	CQua WShi
'Mulatto' (1)	GCro
'Mullion' (3)	CQua
'Mulroy Bay' (1)	CQua
'Murlough' (9)	CQua
'Muscadet' (2)	CQua
'My Sunshine' (2)	CQua
'My Sweetheart' (3)	CQua
'Mystic' (3)	CQua
'Namraj' (2)	CQua
'Nancegollan' (7)	CBro CQua
'Nangiles' (4)	CQua
'Nanpee' (7)	CQua
'Nansidwell' (2)	CQua
'Nanstallon' (1)	CQua
§ ***nanus*** (13)	CWCL GBuc
§ - 'Midget' (1)	CBro CQua ECho ERCP GKev LAma SKHP
'Neon Light' (2)	CQua
'Nessa' (7)	CQua
'Nether Barr' (2)	CQua
nevadensis (13)	SKHP
'New Hope' (3)	CQua
'New Life' (3)	CQua
'New Paris' (2)	CQua
'New Penny' (3)	CQua
'New World' (2)	CQua
'New-Baby' (7)	CQua EPfP NMin SDeJ
'Newcastle' (1)	CQua
'Newcomer' (3)	CQua
'Nicole' (2) **new**	EPfP
'Night Music' (4)	CQua
'Nightcap' (1)	CQua
'Nirvana' (7)	CBro
'Niveth' (5)	CQua
§ ***nobilis*** (13)	CQua EPot
- var. ***nobilis*** (13)	NMin
'Nonchalant' (3)	CQua
'Norma Jean' (2)	CQua
'North Liberty' (2)	CQua
'North Rim' (2)	CQua
'Noss Mayo' (6)	CQua
'Notre Dame' (2) ΨH4	CQua
Nylon Group (10)	CBro ECho EPot EPri GEdr MSSP WCot
- yellow-flowered (10)	ECho
'Oak Wood Sprite' (1)	NMin
'Obdam' (4)	SDeJ
'Obsession' (2)	CQua
obvallaris (13) ΨH4	CAvo CBro CQua CTca ECho EPfP EPot ERCP GKev LRHS MBri NMin SDeJ SPer SPhx WHer WShi
'Ocarino' (4)	CQua
'Odd Job' (12)	CQua
× ***odorus*** (13)	WShi
§ - 'Double Campernelle' (4)	CQua ECho ERCP MBri SDeJ WShi
'Oecumene' (11a)	CQua
'Ohau Lights' (1)	CQua
old pheasant's eye	see *N. poeticus* var. *recurvus*
'Ombersley' (1)	CQua
'Orange Phoenix' (4) **new**	GCro
'Orange Tint' (2)	CQua
'Orange Walk' (3)	CQua
'Orangery' (11a)	LAma SDeJ
'Orchard Place' (3)	CQua
'Oregon Bells' (7)	CQua
'Orkney' (2)	CQua
'Ormeau' (2) ΨH4	CQua
'Ornatus Maximus' (9)	NMin
'Oryx' (7) ΨH4	CQua
'Osceola' (2)	CQua
'Osmington' (2)	CQua
'Ouma' (1)	CQua
'Ouzel' (6)	CQua
'Owyhee' (2)	CQua
'Oxford Gold' (10) **new**	CQua
'Oykel' (3)	CQua
'Oz' (12)	LLHF
pachybolbus (13)	NMin
'Pacific Coast' (8) ΨH4	CQua EPfP LAma LLHF NMin
'Pacific Mist' (11a)	CQua
'Pacific Rim' (2)	CQua
'Painted Desert' (3)	CQua
'Pale Sunlight' (2)	CQua
pallidiflorus (13)	ECha
'Palmares' (11a)	CQua SDeJ
'Pamela Hubble' (2)	CQua
'Pamela Joan' (2)	CQua
'Pampaluna' (11a)	CQua
'Panache' (1)	CQua
panizzianus (13)	CQua WPGP
'Paper White'	see *N. papyraceus*
'Paper White Grandiflorus' (8)	CQua EPfP MBri SDeJ SPer
'Papillon Blanc' (11b)	ERCP
'Papua' (4) ΨH4	CQua
§ ***papyraceus*** (13)	CAvo CQua CTca GKev LAma NMin

	Name	Suppliers
	'Parcpat' (7)	CBro
	'Parisienne' (11a)	SDeJ
	'Park Springs' (3)	CQua
	'Parkdene' (2)	CQua
	'Passionale' (2) 𝕐H4	CQua EPfP LAma NBir
	'Pastiche' (2)	CQua
	'Pat Brown' (2)	CQua
	'Patabundy' (2)	CQua
	'Patrick Hacket' (1) 𝕐H4	CQua
	'Paula Cottell' (3)	NMin
	'Pay Day' (1)	CQua
	'Peach Prince' (4)	CQua
	'Pearl Wedding' (3)	CQua
	'Pearlshell' (11a)	CQua
	'Peeping Tom' (6) 𝕐H4	CBro ECho ERCP LAma SDeJ SRms
	'Pelynt' (3)	CQua
	'Pemboa' (1)	CQua
	'Pencrebar' (4)	CAvo CQua EPot LAma LRHS NMin SDeJ WShi
	'Pend Oreille' (3)	CQua
	'Pengarth' (2)	CQua
	'Penjerrick' (9)	CQua
	'Penkivel' (2) 𝕐H4	CQua
	'Pennance Mill' (2)	CQua
	'Pennine Way' (1)	CQua
	'Penny Perowne' (7)	CQua
	'Pennyfield' (2)	CQua
	'Penpol' (7)	CBro CQua
	'Penril' (6)	CQua
	'Penstraze' (7)	CQua
	'Pentewan' (2)	CQua GCro
	'Pentille' (1)	CQua
	'Pentire' (11a)	CQua
	'Penvale' (7)	CQua
	'Peppercorn' (6)	CQua
	'Percuil' (6)	CQua
	'Perdredda' (3)	CQua
	perez-chiscanoi (13)	SKHP WPGP
	'Perimeter' (3)	CQua
	'Peripheral Pink' (2)	CQua
	'Perky' 1964 (6)	NMin
	'Perlax' (11a)	CQua
	'Perpetuation' (7)	CQua
	'Personable' (2)	CQua
	'Petit Four' (4)	LAma SDeJ
	'Petrel' (5)	CBro CQua EPot ERCP GKev NMin SDeJ SPhx
	'Phantom' (11a)	CQua
	'Phil's Gift' (1)	CQua
	'Phoenician' (2)	CQua
	'Picoblanco' (2)	CBro CQua NMin
	'Pigeon' (2)	CQua
	'Pineapple Prince' (2) 𝕐H4	CQua
	'Pink Angel' (7)	CQua
	'Pink Champagne' (4)	CQua
	'Pink Charm' (2)	CQua
	'Pink China' (2)	CQua
	'Pink Clover' (2)	CQua
	'Pink Evening' (2)	CQua
	'Pink Formal' (11a)	CQua
	'Pink Glacier' (11a)	CQua
	'Pink Holly' (11a)	CQua
	'Pink Ice' (2)	CQua
	'Pink Pageant' (4)	CQua
	'Pink Paradise' (4)	CQua
	'Pink Parasol' (1)	SDeJ
	'Pink Silk' (1)	CQua
	'Pink Surprise' (2)	CQua
	'Pink Tango' (11a)	CQua
	'Pinza' (2) 𝕐H4	CQua SDeJ
	'Pipe Major' (2)	CQua EPfP
	'Pipers Barn' (7)	CQua
	'Piper's End' (3)	CQua
	'Piper's Gold' (1)	CQua
	'Pipestone' (2)	CQua
	'Pipit' (7) 𝕐H4	CAvo CBro CQua ECho EPfP EPot ERCP GKev LAma LPot MBri NBir NMin SDeJ WShi
	'Pismo Beach' (2)	CQua
	'Pitchroy' (2)	CQua
	'Pixie's Sister' (7) 𝕐H4	CQua LLHF NMin
	'Pledge' (1)	NMin
	poeticus (13)	WHer
§	- var. ***hellenicus*** (13)	CBro CQua
	- old pheasant's eye	see *N. poeticus* var. ***recurvus***
	- var. ***physaloides*** (13)	CQua
	- 'Plenus' misapplied	see *N.* 'Tamar Double White'
§	- 'Plenus' ambig. (4)	CBro CQua EPot ERCP GQui SDeJ WShi
§	- var. ***recurvus*** (13) 𝕐H4	CAvo CBro CQua CTca ECho EPfP ERCP GKev LAma MCot NBir SDeJ SEND SPhx WShi
	- white-flowered (13) **new**	SDeJ
	'Poet's Way' (9)	CQua
	'Pol Crocan' (2)	CQua
	'Pol Dornie' (2)	CQua
	'Pol Voulin' (2)	CQua
	'Polar Ice' (3)	CQua LAma SDeJ SPhx
	'Polar Morn' (3)	CQua
	'Polglase' (8)	CBro
	'Polgooth' (2)	CQua
	'Polly's Pearl' (8)	CQua
	'Polnesk' (7)	GCro
	'Polonaise' (2)	CQua
	'Polwheveral' (2)	CQua
	'Pomona' (3)	GCro
	'Popeye' (4) **new**	EPfP
	'Poppy's Choice' (4)	CQua
	'Pops Legacy' (1)	CQua
	'Porthchapel' (7)	CQua
	'Portloe Bay' (3)	CQua
	'Portrait' (2)	CQua
	'Portrush' (3)	CQua
	'Potential' (1)	CQua
	'Praecox' (9)	CBro
	'Prairie Fire' (3)	CQua
	'Preamble' (1)	CQua
I	'Precocious' (2) 𝕐H4	CQua SDeJ
	'Premiere' (2)	CQua
	'Presidential Pink' (2)	CQua
	'Pretty Baby' (3)	CQua
	'Pride of Cornwall' (8)	CBro CQua
	'Primrose Beauty' (4)	CQua
	'Princeps' (1)	CAvo CQua GCro
	'Princess Zaide' (3)	CQua
	'Princeton' (3)	CQua
	'Printal' (11a)	SDeJ
	'Prism' (2)	CQua
	'Probus' (1)	CQua
	'Professor Einstein' (2)	EPfP SDeJ
	'Prologue' (1)	CQua
	'Prussia Cove' (2)	CQua
	pseudonarcissus (13) 𝕐H4	CHab CQua CRow LAma LPot MMuc SEND SPhx WHer WShi
	- subsp. ***eugeniae***	see *N. eugeniae*
	- subsp. ***nobilis***	see *N. nobilis*
	- 'Plenus' (4) **new**	GCro

- subsp. ***pseudonarcissus*** double-flowered (4) **new** CQua
'Ptolemy' (1) GCro
'Pueblo' (7) CQua SDeJ
'Pukenui' (4) CQua
pumilus ambig. (13) CQua ECho LLHF NMin SDeJ WShi
'Punchline' (7) ♀H4 CQua
'Puppet' (5) CQua
'Purbeck' (3) ♀H4 CQua
'Quail' (7) ♀H4 CQua CTca EPfP GKev LAma LSou MBri
'Quasar' (2) ♀H4 CQua
Queen Anne's double daffodil see *N.* 'Eystettensis'
'Queen Juliana' (1) CQua
'Queen Mum' (1) CQua
'Queen of Spain' (10) CQua NMin
'Queen of the North' (3) GCro
'Quick Step' (7) CQua
'Quiet Day' (2) CQua
'Radiant Gem' (8) CQua
radiiflorus (13) EPot
- var. ***poetarum*** (13) CBro CQua GCro
- var. ***radiiflorus*** (13) **new** GCro
'Radjel' (4) CQua
'Rainbow' (2) ♀H4 CQua SPer
'Rame Head' (1) CQua
'Rameses' (2) CQua
'Raoul Wallenberg' (2) EPfP
'Rapture' (6) ♀H4 CBro CQua ERCP MBri NMin
'Rashee' (1) CQua
'Raspberry Ring' (2) CQua
'Rathowen Gold' (1) CQua
'Ravenhill' (3) CQua
'Rebekah' (4) CQua
'Recital' (2) CQua
'Red Devon' (2) ♀H4 SDeJ
'Red Era' (3) CQua
'Red Legend' (2) CQua
'Red Lips' (2) CQua
'Red Socks' (6) CQua
'Red Spartan' (2) CQua
'Refrain' (2) CQua
'Regal Bliss' (2) CQua
'Reggae' (6) ♀H4 CBro CQua EPfP SDeJ WShi
'Rembrandt' (1) CQua
'Rendezvous Caye' (2) CQua
'Replete' (4) CQua
requienii see *N. assoanus*
'Resolute' (2) GCro
'Reverse Image' (11a) CQua
rifanus see *N. romieuxii* subsp. *romieuxii* var. *rifanus*
'Right Stuff' (6) **new** NMin
'Rijnveld's Early Sensation' (1) ♀H4 CAvo CBro CMea CQua ECha ERCP SEND WCot
'Rikki' (7) CBro CQua NMin
'Rima' (1) CQua
'Rimmon' (3) CQua
'Ringing Bells' (5) CQua
'Ringleader' (2) CQua
'Ringmaster' (2) CQua
'Ringmer' (3) CQua
§ 'Rip van Winkle' (4) CBro CQua CTca EPfP EPot ERCP IFro LAma MBri NHol SDeJ WShi
'Rippling Waters' (5) ♀H4 CQua LAma
'Ristin' (1) CQua
'Rival' (6) CQua
'River Queen' (2) CQua
'Rockall' (3) CQua
'Rockery White' (1) NMin
'Roger' (6) CQua
'Rogue' (2) CBro
'Romance' (2) ♀H4 LAma
§ 'Romanus' (4) CAvo CQua
romieuxii (13) ♀H2-3 CBro CDes CPBP EPri ITim LRHS MSSP SCnR WCot
- JCA 805 EPot LWst
- SF 370 WCot
- subsp. ***albidus*** (13) ECho EPot WCot
§ - - var. ***zaianicus*** (13) ECho
- - - SB&L 82 MSSP WCot
I - - - f. ***lutescens*** (13) GEdr
§ - 'Atlas Gold' (10) EPot GEdr SCnR
§ - 'Joy Bishop' (10) GEdr NMen SCnR
§ - 'Julia Jane' (10) ECho EPot GKev NMin SCnR WCot
* - subsp. ***pallidus*** SB&L 237 **new** WCot
- subsp. ***romieuxii*** (13) GKev
§ - - var. ***mesatlanticus*** (13) WCot
§ - - var. ***rifanus*** (13) ECho GKev
- - - B 8927 WCot
- - - B 8929 WCot
§ - 'Treble Chance' (10) EPot
'Rory's Glen' (2) CQua
'Rosannor Gold' (11a) CQua
'Roscarrick' (6) CQua
'Rose of May' (4) CQua WShi
'Rose of Tralee' (2) CQua
'Rose Royale' (2) CQua
'Rose Sheen' (2) CQua
'Rose Villa' (2) CQua
'Rosemerryn' (2) CQua
'Rosemoor Gold' ♀H4 CBro CQua
'Rosemullion' (4) CQua
'Rosevine' (3) CQua
'Rosy Wonder' (2) CQua
'Round Oak' (1) CQua
'Royal Connection' (8) CQua
'Royal Marine' (2) CQua
'Royal Princess' (3) CQua ERCP
'Royal Regiment' (2) CQua
'Ruby Red' (2) CQua
'Rubythroat' (2) CQua
'Rugulosus' (7) ♀H4 CBro CQua ECho
* 'Rugulosus Flore Pleno' (d) ECho
rupicola (13) CBro CQua CWCL ECho EPot GKev LLHF MSSP NMen NMin SPhx
§ - subsp. ***watieri*** (13) CQua ECho EPot GKev ITim LLHF MSSP NMin SPhx
'Rustom Pasha' (2) CQua GCro
'Rytha' (2) CQua
'Saberwing' (5) CQua
'Sabine Hay' (3) CQua ERCP
'Sabrosa' (7) ♀H4 CBro CQua LLHF NMin
'Sagana' (9) CQua
'Sailboat' (7) ♀H4 CGrW CQua EPfP MBri SPer
'Saint Agnes' (8) CQua
'Saint Budock' (1) CQua
'Saint Day' (5) CQua
'Saint Dilpe' (2) CQua
'Saint Keverne' (2) ♀H4 CQua EPfP SDeJ SEND
'Saint Keyne' (8) CQua
'Saint Olaf' (3) GCro
'Saint Patrick's Day' (2) CQua LAma SDeJ
'Saint Peter' (4) CQua

'Saint Petroc' (9)	CQua
'Saint Piran' (7)	CQua
'Salakee' (2)	CQua
'Salcey Forest' (1)	CQua
'Salmon Trout' (2)	CQua
'Salome' (2) ♀H4	CQua LAma NBir NPer SDeJ SEND
'Salute' (2)	CQua
'Samantha' (4)	CQua
'Sandycove' (2)	CQua
'Sandymount' (2)	CQua
'Sarah Dear' (2)	CQua
'Sarah Markillie' (11a)	CQua
'Sarchedon' (9) **new**	GCro
'Sargeant's Caye' (1)	CQua
'Satchmo' (1)	CQua
'Saturn' (3)	CQua
scaberulus (13)	EPot
'Scarlet Chord' (2)	CQua
'Scarlet Elegance' (2)	CQua
'Scarlet Gem' (8)	SDeJ
'Scarlett O'Hara' (2)	CQua
'Scilly Spring' (8)	CAvo
'Scilly White' (8)	CQua
'Scorrier' (2)	CQua
'Scrumpy' (2)	CQua
'Sea Dream' (3)	CQua
'Sea Gift' (7)	CBro
'Sea Green' (9)	CQua
'Sea Legend' (2)	CQua
'Sea Princess' (3)	CQua
'Seagull' (3)	CAvo CQua GCro LAma WShi
'Sealing Wax' (2)	CQua
'Segovia' (3) ♀H4	CBro CQua EPot LAma NMin SCnR SPhx
'Sempre Avanti' (2)	LAma SDeJ
'Seraglio' (3)	CQua
'Serena Lodge' (4) ♀H4	CQua
serotinus (13)	ECho EPot GKev
'Sextant' (6)	CQua
'Sheelagh Rowan' (2)	CQua
'Sheer Joy' (6)	CQua
'Shepherd's Hey' (7)	CQua EPfP SDeJ
'Sherborne' (4) ♀H4	CQua
'Sherpa' (1)	CQua
'Shining Light' (2)	CQua
'Shockwave' (2)	CQua
'Shortcake' (2)	CQua
'Sidley' (3)	CQua
'Silent Valley' (1) ♀H4	CQua
'Silk Cut' (2)	CQua
'Silkwood' (3)	CQua
'Silver Bells' (5)	CQua
'Silver Chimes' (8)	CAvo CBro CQua CTca ECho EPfP LAma NBir SDeJ SPhx
'Silver Convention' (1)	CQua
'Silver Crystal' (3)	CQua
'Silver Kiwi' (2)	CQua
'Silver Minx' (1)	CQua
'Silver Plate' (11a)	CQua
'Silver Smiles' (7)	SPhx
'Silver Surf' (2)	CQua
'Silversmith' (2)	CQua
'Silverthorne' (3)	CQua
'Silverwood' (3)	CQua
'Sinopel' (3)	LAma SDeJ
'Sir Samuel' (2)	CQua
'Sir Watkin' (2)	CAvo CQua GCro
'Sir Winston Churchill' (4) ♀H4	CQua EPfP LAma SDeJ SPer
'Sirius' (2) **new**	GCro
'Sissy' (6)	CQua
'Skerry' (2)	CQua
'Skilliwidden' (2) ♀H4	CQua
'Skookum' (3)	CQua
'Slieveboy' (1)	CQua
'Small Fry' (1)	CQua
'Small Talk' (1) ♀H4	CQua LLHF NMin
'Smokey Bear' (4)	CQua
'Smooth Sails' (3)	CQua
'Snipe' (6)	CQua NMin WShi
'Snoopie' (6)	CQua
'Snow Bunting' (7)	CBro
'Snowcrest' (3)	CQua
'Snowshill' (2)	CQua
'Solar Tan' (3)	CQua
'Soleil d'Or' (8)	CQua
'Solferique' (2)	CQua
'Solveig's Song' (12)	WAbe
'Sonata' (9)	CQua
'Songket' (2)	CQua
'Sophie Girl' (2)	CQua
'Sophie's Choice' (4) **new**	CAvo
'Soprano' (2)	CQua
'Sorcerer' (3)	CQua
'South Street' (2)	CQua
'Southease' (2)	CQua
'Spaniards Inn' (4)	CQua
'Sparkling Tarts' (8)	CQua
'Sparnon' (11a)	CQua
'Sparrow' (6)	CQua
'Special Envoy' (2) ♀H4	CQua
'Spellbinder' (1) ♀H4	CQua SDeJ
'Spencer Tracy' (2)	CQua
'Spirit of Rame' (3)	CQua
'Sportsman' (2)	CQua
'Spring Dawn' (2)	EPfP SPer
'Spring Glory' (1)	GCro
'Spring Morn' (2)	CQua
'Spun Honey' (4)	CQua
'Stadium' (2)	LAma
'Stainless' (2)	SPhx
'Stann Creek' (1)	CQua
'Stanway' (3)	CQua
'Star Glow' (2)	CQua
'Starfire' (7)	CQua
'State Express' (2)	CQua
'Stella' (2)	GCro WShi
'Stenalees' (6)	CQua
'Step Child' (6)	CQua
'Step Forward' (7)	CQua
'Steve's Favorite' (2) **new**	CQua
'Stilton' (9)	CQua GCro
'Stinger' (2)	CQua
'Stint' (5) ♀H4	CBro CQua SDeJ SPhx
'Stocken' (7)	CBro CQua EPri NMin WAbe
'Stoke Charity' (2)	CQua
'Stoke Doyle' (2)	CQua
'Stormy Weather' (1)	CQua
'Stratosphere' (7) ♀H4	CQua NMin SDeJ
'Strines' (2) ♀H4	CQua
'Suave' (3)	CQua
'Sugar and Spice' (3)	CQua
'Sugar Cups' (8)	CQua
'Sugar Loaf' (4)	CQua
'Sugarbush' (7)	WShi
'Suisgill' (4)	CQua
'Sukey' (6)	CQua
§ 'Sulphur Phoenix' (4)	CQua GCro WShi

	Sulphur Star (2) **new**	GCro
	'Sumo Jewel' (6)	CQua
	'Sun Disc' (7) ♀^{H4}	CBro CQua CTri ECho GKev LAma LSou MBri NMin SDeJ WShi
	'Sunday Chimes' (5)	CQua
	'Sundial' (7)	CBro GKev LAma NMin
	'Sunrise' (3)	CQua GCro
	'Suntory' (3)	CQua
	'Surfside' (6) ♀^{H4}	CQua NMin
	'Surrey' (2)	CQua
	'Suzy' (7) ♀^{H4}	CBro SDeJ
	'Swaledale' (2)	CQua
	'Swallow' (6)	CQua LAma SDeJ
	'Swanpool' (3)	CQua
	'Sweet Blanche' (7)	CQua
	'Sweet Lorraine' (2)	CQua
	'Sweet Memory' (2)	CQua
	'Sweet Pepper' (7)	CBro
	'Sweet Sue' (3)	CQua
	'Sweetness' (7) ♀^{H4}	CAvo CBro CQua GCro LAma WShi
	'Swift Arrow' (6) ♀^{H4}	CQua
	'Swing Wing' (6)	CQua
	'Taffeta' (10)	CBro EPri
	'Tahiti' (4) ♀^{H4}	CQua EPfP LAma SDeJ
	× ***taitii*** (13)	NMin WShi
	'Talgarth' (2)	CQua
§	'Tamar Double White' (4)	CBro
	'Tamar Fire' (4) ♀^{H4}	CQua
	'Tamar Lad' (2)	CQua
	'Tamar Lass' (3)	CQua
	'Tamar Snow' (2)	CQua
	'Tamara' (2)	CQua EPfP
	'Tangent' (2)	CQua
	'Tarlatan' (10)	CBro
	'Tarnished Gold' (2)	CQua
	'Tasgem' (4)	CQua
	'Taslass' (4)	CQua
	tazetta (13)	ECho
	- subsp. ***italicus*** from France (13)	SEND
§	- subsp. ***lacticolor*** (13)	CQua ERCP LAma SDeJ
§	- - 'Grand Monarque' (8)	CBro CQua
	- subsp. ***ochroleucus*** (13)	CQua
*	- var. ***odoratus***	CQua NMin
	'Teal' (1)	CQua
	'Tehidy' (3)	CQua
§	'Telamonius Plenus' (4)	CBro CQua IGor SEND WCot WShi
	'Tenedos' (2) **new**	GCro
	tenuifolius	see *N. bulbocodium* subsp. *bulbocodium* var. *tenuifolius*
	× ***tenuior*** (13)	NMin
	'Terracotta' (2)	CQua
	'Tête-à-tête' (12) ♀^{H4}	CAvo CBro CQua CTca CWCL EPfP EPot ERCP GAbr GKev LAma LPot LRHS LSou MBri MNHC SDeJ SEND SPer
	'Texas' (4)	CQua
	'Thalia' (5)	CAvo CBro CQua CTca EPfP ERCP GKev LAma LPot MBri MCot NBir NHol SDeJ SEND SPer SPhx WShi
	'The Alliance' (6) ♀^{H4}	CBro CQua
	'The Caley' (2)	CQua
	'The Grange' (1)	CQua
	'The Knave' (6)	CQua
	'The Little Gentleman' (6)	NMin
	'Thomas Kinkade' (2) **new**	CQua
	'Thoresby' (3)	CQua
	'Thoughtful' (5)	CBro CQua
	'Three Oaks' (1) **new**	CQua
	'Tibet' (2)	CQua
	'Tideford' (2)	CQua
	'Tiercel' (1)	CQua
	'Tiffany Jade' (3)	CQua
	'Tiger Moth' (6)	CQua
	'Timolin' (3)	CQua
	'Tinhay' (7)	CQua
	'Tiny Bubbles' (12)	NMin
	'Tiritomba' (11a)	CQua
	'Titania' (6)	CQua
	'Tittle-tattle' (7)	CQua
	'Toby' (2)	SDeJ
	'Toby the First' (6)	CAvo CQua
	'Tommora Gold' (2)	CQua
	'Tommy White' (2)	CQua
	'Top Hit' (11a)	CQua
	'Topolino' (1) ♀^{H4}	CAvo CBro CQua EPot LAma LRHS
	'Torianne' (2) ♀^{H4}	CQua
	'Torridon' (2)	CQua
	'Toto' (12) ♀^{H4}	CBro CMea CQua ERCP MBri SDeJ SPhx
	'Tracey' (6) ♀^{H4}	CQua LAma
	'Trebah' (2) ♀^{H4}	CQua
	'Treble Chance'	see *N. romieuxii* 'Treble Chance'
	'Treble Two' (7)	CQua
	'Trecara' (3)	CQua
	'Trefusis' (1)	CQua
	'Trehane' (6)	CQua
	'Trelawney Gold' (2)	CQua
	'Trelissick' (7)	CQua
	'Tremough Dale' (11a)	CQua
	'Trena' (6) ♀^{H4}	CQua ERCP NMin
	'Trenwith' (1)	CQua
	'Trepolo' (11b)	ERCP
	'Tresamble' (5)	CBro CQua GCro LAma MBri SDeJ
	'Trevaunance' (6)	CQua
	'Treverva' (6)	CQua
	'Treviddo' (2)	CQua
	'Trevithian' (7) ♀^{H4}	CBro CQua LAma SDeJ WShi
	'Trewarvas' (2)	CQua
	'Trewirgie' (6)	CQua
	'Trewoon' (4)	CQua
	triandrus var. ***albus***	see *N. triandrus* subsp. *triandrus* var. *triandrus*
	- subsp. ***pallidulus*** (13) SG 13 **new**	WCot
	- subsp. ***triandrus*** (13)	MSSP
§	- - var. ***triandrus*** (13)	CQua
	'Tricollet' (11a)	SDeJ
	'Trident' (3)	CQua
	'Trigonometry' (11a) ♀^{H4}	CQua
	'Tripartite' (11a) ♀^{H4}	CQua GKev NMin SDeJ
	'Triple Crown' (3) ♀^{H4}	CQua
	'Tristram' (2)	CQua
	'Tropic Isle' (4)	CQua
	'Trousseau' (1)	CQua
	'Troutbeck' (3)	CQua
	'Tru' (3)	CQua
	'Truculent' (3)	CQua
	'Trumpet Warrior' (1) ♀^{H4}	CQua
	'Tryst' (2)	CQua
	'Tudor Minstrel' (2)	CQua
	'Tuesday's Child' (5) ♀^{H4}	CQua
	'Tullyroyal' (2)	CQua
	'Tunis' (2)	GCro
	'Turncoat' (6)	CQua
	'Tutankhamun' (2)	CQua

'Tweety Bird' (6) **new**	EPfP
'Twink' (4)	CQua
'Tyee' (2)	CQua
Tyndrum Conspicuus **new**	GCro
'Tyrian Rose' (2)	CQua
'Tyrone Gold' (1) ♀H4	CQua
'Tywara' (1)	CQua
'Ulster Bank' (3)	CQua
'Ulster Bride' (4)	CQua
'Ultimus' (2)	CQua
'Uncle Bill' (1)	CQua
'Uncle Duncan' (1)	CQua
'Unique' (4) ♀H4	LAma SDeJ
'Unsurpassable' (1)	CQua GCro LAma
'Upalong' (12)	CQua
'Upshot' (3)	CQua
'Utiku' (6)	CQua
'Val d'Incles' (3)	CQua
'Valdrome' (11a)	CQua
'Valinor' (2)	CQua
'Valley Dew' (2)	CQua
'Van Sion'	see *N.* 'Telamonius Plenus'
'Vaticaan' (1)	SDeJ
'Velvet Spring' (2)	CQua
'Verdin' (7)	CQua NHol
'Verger' (3)	LAma MBri SDeJ
'Vernal Prince' (3) ♀H4	CQua
'Verona' (3) ♀H4	CQua
'Vers Libre' (9)	CQua
'Vice-President' (2) ♀H4	CQua
'Victoria' (1)	CQua
'Vigil' (1) ♀H4	CQua
'Viking' (1) ♀H4	CQua
'Violetta' (2)	CQua
'Virginia Waters' (3)	CQua
viridiflorus (13)	WCot
'Volare' (2)	CQua
'Vulcan' (2) ♀H4	CQua
'W.P. Milner' (1)	CAvo CBro CQua EPfP EPot ERCP LAma MBri NMin SDeJ SEND SMrm SPhx WShi
'Waldon Pond' (3)	CQua
'Waldorf Astoria' (4)	CQua
'Walton' (7)	CQua
'Warbler' (6) ♀H4	CQua LAma NMin
'Warmington' (3)	CQua
'Waterperry' (7)	CBro LAma SEND
'Watership Down' (2)	CQua
'Watersmeet' (4)	CQua
watieri	see *N. rupicola* subsp. *watieri*
'Wave' (4)	CQua
'Wavertree'	see *N. asturiensis* 'Wavertree'
'Waxwing' (5)	CQua
'Wee Bee' (1)	CQua
'Weena' (2)	CQua
'Welcome' (2)	CQua
'Welsh Rugby Union' (1)	CQua
'Westward' (4)	CQua
'Whang-hi' (6)	CQua
'Wheal Bush' (4)	CQua
'Wheal Coates' (7) ♀H4	CQua
'Wheal Honey' (1)	CQua
'Wheal Jane' (2)	CQua
'Wheal Kitty' (7)	CQua
'Wheal Rose' (4)	CQua
'Wheatear' (6)	CQua NMin
'Whetstone' (1)	CQua
'Whisky Galore' (2)	CQua
'Whisky Mac' (2)	CQua
'White Emperor' (1)	CQua GCro
'White Empress' (1)	CQua
'White Giant' (1)	GKev
'White Lady' (3)	CAvo CQua GCro LAma WShi
'White Lion' (4) ♀H4	CQua LAma SDeJ
'White Marvel' (4)	CQua
'White Nile' (2)	CQua GCro
'White Tea' (2)	CQua
'White Tie' (3)	CQua
'Wicklow Hills' (3)	CQua
'Wild Honey' (2)	CQua
'Will Scarlett' (2)	CQua
willkommii (13)	CBro CQua NMin
'Wimbledon County Girl' (2) ♀H4	CQua
'Wind Song' (2)	CQua
'Winged Victory' (6)	CQua
'Winholm Jenni' (3)	CQua
'Winter Waltz' (6)	CQua
'Wisley' (6) ♀H4	ERCP
'Woodcock' (6)	CQua
Woodcroft Beauty (2) **new**	GCro
'Woodland Prince' (3)	CQua
'Woodland Star' (3)	CQua
'Woodley Vale' (2)	CQua
'Woolsthorpe' (2)	CQua
'World Class' (5)	CQua
'Xit' (3)	CAvo CBro CQua NMin SPhx
'Xunantunich' (2)	CQua
'Yellow Cheerfulness' (4) ♀H4	CQua EPfP LAma MBri SDeJ
'Yellow River' (1) ♀H4	LAma
'Yellow Xit' (3)	CQua NMin
'Yoley's Pond' (2)	CQua
'York Minster' (1)	CQua
'Young American' (1)	CQua
'Young Blood' (2)	CQua
'Your Grace' (2)	CQua
zaianicus	see *N. romieuxii* subsp. *albidus* var. *zaianicus*
'Zekiah' (1)	CQua
'Zion Canyon' (2)	CQua
'Ziva' (8)	CAvo CGrW SDeJ

Nardostachys (*Caprifoliaceae*)

grandiflora	GPoy

Nardus (*Poaceae*)

stricta	CRWN

Nassauvia (*Asteraceae*)

gaudichaudii	WAbe

Nassella (*Poaceae*)

cernua	WPGP
poeppigiana	see *Stipa poeppigiana*
pulchra	WPGP
tenuissima	see *Stipa tenuissima*
trichotoma	CKno EHoe EPPr LDai SLim WHal WPGP

Nasturtium (*Brassicaceae*)

'Banana Split'	CCCN
officinale	MHoo MSKA SVic SWat

Natal plum see *Carissa macrocarpa*

Nauplius (*Asteraceae*)

sericeus	CSpe

nectarine see *Prunus persica* var. *nectarina*

Nectaroscordum (*Alliaceae*)

§ ***siculum*** CAvo CBre CBro CMea CTri ECho ELan ERCP GCra GKev LLWP LRHS MBel MCot NBir NChi NDov NLar NRHS NSti SDeJ SMrm SPer WBor WFar WHoo
§ - subsp. ***bulgaricum*** CBro CTca ECha EHrv EPfP EPot IBlr ITim LRHS MMoz MNrw NLar SPhx WAbb WCot WTin XLum
tripedale CAvo CBro CMea ECho

Neillia (*Rosaceae*)

affinis CDul CPLG EBee EPfP EWTr LLHF LRHS NBid NLar SWvt WCot WPat
longiracemosa see *N. thibetica*
sinensis NLar
§ ***thibetica*** Widely available
thyrsiflora WCru
var. ***tunkinensis*** HWJ 505

Nelumbo (*Nelumbonaceae*)

'Mrs Perry D. Slocum' EWay
nucifera XBlo

Nematanthus (*Gesneriaceae*)

'Apres' WDib
'Black Magic' WDib
'Christmas Holly' WDib
'Freckles' WDib
§ ***gregarius*** ♀H1 EBak SEND WDib
§ - 'Golden West' (v) WDib
- 'Variegatus' see *N. gregarius* 'Golden West'
'Lemon and Lime' WDib
radicans see *N. gregarius*
'Tropicana' ♀H1 WDib

Nemesia (*Scrophulariaceae*)

Amelie = 'Fleurame'PBR EPfP LBuc SPoG
(Aromatica Series) Aromatica Deep Blue = 'Balardeblu' NPri
- Aromatica Rose Pink = 'Balarropi'PBR NPri
Berries and Cream = 'Fleurbac'PBR ECtt EPfP LAst LBuc LSou MSCN SPoG
'Blueberry Ripple' **new** LSou
Bluebird = 'Hubbird'PBR CHll
§ ***caerulea*** WPer
§ ***denticulata*** ♀H3-4 CBar CPrp EPfP GBee LHop LRHS NEgg SAga SCoo WFar WHlf
- 'Confetti' see *N. denticulata*
- 'Maggie' LBuc LRHS
'Fleurie Blue' EPfP SPoG
foetens see *N. caerulea*
'Fragrant Cloud' ELan LSou
Fragrant Gem = 'Pengem'PBR LSRN
'Framboise' **new** SPoG
fruticans misapplied see *N. caerulea*
Golden Eye = 'Yateye'PBR EPfP LAst LSRN LSou MPnt SLon
'Honey Light Pink' **new** LBuc
Ice Pink = 'Fleuripi' EPfP
'Innocence' ♀H3 CPrp SCoo
(Karoo Series) Karoo Blue = 'Innkablue'PBR SCoo
- Karoo Dark Blue = 'Innemkadab'PBR LSou
- Karoo Pink = 'Innkapink'PBR SBfd
- Karoo Soft Blue = 'Innkarsofb'PBR CWGN
- Karoo Violet Ice = 'Innemkavic'PBR ESwi NPri
- Karoo White = 'Innkarwhi'PBR LSou SMrm
Lagoon White see *N.* Pure Lagoon
(Maritana Series) Blue Lagoon = 'Pengoon'PBR LAst LSRN SBfd SCoo
- Candy Girl = 'Pencand' SCoo
- Honey Girl = 'Penhon' LSRN SCoo
- Maritana Sky Lagoon = 'Pensky' SCoo
- Sugar Girl = 'Pensug' EPfP LSRN
Melanie = 'Fleuron' ♀H3 EPfP
'Mirabelle' **new** SPoG
(Nuvo Series) 'Nuvo Blue Bicolour' LSou
- 'Nuvo Blue' LSou WGor
- 'Nuvo Carmine' LSou WGor
- 'Nuvo Rose' LSou
'Orchard Blue' EPfP
'Provençal Dusky Blue' EPfP
'Provençal Dusky Pink' EPfP
§ Pure Lagoon = 'Penpur'PBR LAst LHop SBfd
Raspberries and Cream = 'Fleurrac' EPfP LBuc SPoG
'Rose Wings' EPfP
Sugar Frosted = 'Lowgreg' **new** SPoG
'Sugar Plum'PBR EPfP LRHS SLon
(Sunsatia Series) Sunsatia Blackberry = 'Inuppink'PBR SBfd SCoo
- Sunsatia Cranberry = 'Intraired'PBR SCoo
- Sunsatia Lemon = 'Intraigold'PBR SCoo
- Sunsatia Mango = 'Inupyel' ESwi
- Sunsatia Peach = 'Inupcream' CWGN SCoo
'Sweet Lady' **new** LAst LSou
sylvatica CSpe
'Vanilla Lady' ECtt LAst
Vanilla Mist = 'Grega'PBR EPfP LRHS LSou SLon SPoG
'White Wings' EPfP
'Wisley Vanilla' EPfP SPoG

Nemophila (*Boraginaceae*)

menziesii 'Penny Black' CSpe

Neodypsis (*Arecaceae*)

decaryi see *Dypsis decaryi*

Neolepisorus (*Polypodiaceae*)

lancifolius CPLG

Neolitsea (*Lauraceae*)

glauca see *N. sericea*
polycarpa KWJ 12309 WCru
§ ***sericea*** CBcs SSpi WSHC

Neomarica ✿ (*Iridaceae*)

caerulea EBee WCot

Neopanax (*Araliaceae*)

§ **arboreus** CDoC CHEx CTrC CTsd ECou LEdu SBig
colensoi CTrC
§ **laetus** CDoC CHEx CTrC IDee LEdu SBig

Neoregelia (*Bromeliaceae*)

carolinae (Meyendorffii Group) 'Meyendorffii' XBlo
'Hojo Rojo' XBlo
'Marconfos' XBlo

Neoshirakia (*Euphorbiaceae*)

japonica EPfP MBlu WPGP WPat
- B&SWJ 8744 WCru

Neottia (*Orchidaceae*)

ovata NLAp

Neottianthe (*Orchidaceae*)

cucullata EFEx

Nepenthes ✿ (*Nepenthaceae*)

alata CSWC NChu

Nepeta ✿ (*Lamiaceae*)

sp. LAst
from China EWes
amethystina XSen
'Blue Beauty' see *N. sibirica* 'Souvenir d'André Chaudron'
'Blue Dragon' **new** NCGa NDov
bucharica GBuc
* **buddlejifolium** MSCN NLar
camphorata SIde
cataria CArn CPrp CTri CWan EGHP ELau ENfk GJos GPoy LAst MHer MHoo MNHC NBro SBfd SIde SVic WHfH WJek WMoo
§ - 'Citriodora' CArn EGHP ELan ENfk GPoy MHer MHoo SIde SPhx WJek XLum
citriodora Dum. see *N. cataria* 'Citriodora'
clarkei EBee EPPr GMaP IFro MDKP MMuc MTis NDov SBfd SEND SIde SMHy SWat WFar WHrl WMoo
'Dropmore' LRHS
§ × **faassenii** ♀H4 Widely available
- 'Alba' COIW EBee ECtt EGHP EPfP EWhm LAst NBre NLar SBfd SEND WJek WWEG XSen
- 'Blue Wonder' EBee
- 'Kit Cat' CSpe ECGP GBuc GCal LHop LRHS LSRN MTis NCGa NDov WAul WGwG WHoo
- 'Select' WPtf
glechoma 'Variegata' see *Glechoma hederacea* 'Variegata'
govaniana Widely available
granatensis XSen
grandiflora NBre SIde WHrl WPtf
- 'Blue Danube' EBee GBin NDov SIde
- 'Bramdean' CElw CMea CPrp EBee ECtt EPfP EWes GBin LBMP LRHS MCot MTis SAga SBch SPhx WCAu WPer WWEG XLum
- 'Dawn to Dusk' Widely available
- 'Pool Bank' EBee ECtt EWes GCal LPla MAvo MTis NBre SGar SIde SMrm WHil XLum
- 'Wild Cat' EBee EPfP MAvo MBri MTis WFar
hederacea 'Variegata' see *Glechoma hederacea* 'Variegata'
italica SIde
kubanica LPla SMHy SUsu
'Lamendi' NDov
lanceolata see *N. nepetella*
latifolia SIde
- 'Super Cat' EBee
§ 'Leeds Castle' EBee EPfP LHop LRHS MHer NCGa NGdn NSti SMrm SWat WCAu WHal WMnd WPer
'Lilac Cloud' NBir
longipes hort. see *N.* 'Leeds Castle'
macrantha see *N. sibirica*
'Maurice' NDov
melissifolia SBch WPer
mussinii misapplied see *N.* × *faassenii*
mussinii Spreng. see *N. racemosa*
§ **nepetella** NBir WFar
nervosa CSpe EBee ECha ELan EPfP LAst MCot MNHC NBro NLar NPri NSti SBfd SPer WFar WJek WMnd WSHC WWEG
- 'Blue Carpet' CSpe NEgg
- 'Blue Moon' EBee EPfP EWes LRHS LSou NBid SGar SHil SMrm SPoG SRms WFar
- 'Forncett Select' CSam MRav NBre SMrm
- 'Pink Cat' EPfP LRHS LSou MDKP MNHC NLar SHil SRkn WWEG
§ **nuda** EBee ECha EWes MDKP SHar SIde SMHy WFar WHil WHrl
- 'Accent' GBin
- subsp. **albiflora** ECha
* - 'Anne's Choice' EBee SIde
* - 'Grandiflora' NBre NLar WMoo
- 'Purple Cat' EBee EPfP LLHF LSou SIde WFar
- 'Snow Cat' EBee SIde SPhx
pannonica see *N. nuda*
parnassica ECtt GQue MBel MTis NLar SEND SIde SMrm SPav SWal WHil WHrl WMnd WMoo WPer WPtf
phyllochlamys CPBP SRms XSen
Pink Candy EWll SRms WHil
'Porzellan' EBee LPla SMrm
§ **prattii** CSpe EBee MWat NLar NPro SIde SMrm WWEG
§ **racemosa** ♀H4 CArn CHby CMac CPbn CSev CWan ELau EPfP GBBs GJos LPot LRHS MCot MHoo MLHP MNHC MSCN SGar SIde WMoo XLum
- RCB AM 3 WCot
- **alba** MHoo SBfd XLum
- 'Amelia' MSpe
- 'Blue Ice' SIde
- 'Grog' SIde
- 'Little Titch' EBee ECtt EPfP GCra IPot LRHS LSRN MAsh MCot NDov NLar SIde SMrm SPoG SWat WWEG
- 'Senior' XSen
- 'Snowflake' CBcs CMea CPrp EBee ELan ELon EPfP EShb GMaP LRHS

	MBel MCot MHer MTis NBir NCGa SAga SIde SMrm SPer SPoG SWvt WFar
- 'Superba'	NBre WCot WFar
- 'Toria'	NDov
- 'Walker's Low'	Widely available
* 'Rae Crug'	ECtt EWes
reichenbachiana	see *N. racemosa*
§ ***sibirica***	COlW EBee ECha ELan EPfP MHer MSCN NBid NBro NLar NPri SBch SBfd SRkn WCAu WCot WFar WHal WJek WPer WPtf XLum
§ - 'Souvenir d'André Chaudron'	CMHG CSam CWCL EBee ECtt EHrv ELan EPfP GBuc GMaP LAst LHop LRHS MBri MCot MRav MTis SBch SPer SPoG WCAu WFar WHil WWEG
'Six Hills Giant'	Widely available
stewartiana	LDai LLHF MRav WMoo WWEG
- BWJ 7999	WCru
subsessilis	CCVN CMHG CSpe EBee ECtt EHrv ELan EPfP EShb EWTr GMaP LAst LRHS MCot MRav MSpe NBid NBir NGdn NSti NWad SBfd SPhx SRms WCru WFar WMnd WPer WWEG
- 'Blue Dreams'	ELon NLar SGar SHar WHil XLum
- 'Candy Cat'	EBee EHrv EPfP IBoy LPot MDKP NBre SBHP SPoG
- 'Cool Cat'	EBee EPfP LSRN MDKP NBre NLar NPro SIde SPoG
- Nimbus = 'Yanim'	EBee MPnt
- 'Pink Dreams'	EBee EPfP GBee GJos LBMP LRHS MHer WHil XLum
- pink-flowered	ECha SMrm SPhx WWEG
- 'Sweet Dreams'	EAEE EBee ECtt EPfP EWTr LHop LRHS MCot MDKP MRav MSpe MTis NCGa NLar NPro NSti WFar WMnd
- 'Washfield'	IPot LHop
transcaucasica 'Blue Infinity'	MSCN NLar WMnd WMoo WWEG
troodii	SIde
tuberosa	CSpe EBee LRHS MHer MPie SBch SIde SPav WCot WMnd WMoo WTcb XSen
'Veluws Blauwtje'	EBee
yunnanensis	EBee EPPr LPla SMrm WHil WOut WPGP WPer

Nephrophyllidium (*Menyanthaceae*)

crista-galli	IBlr

Nerine ✿ (*Amaryllidaceae*)

'Afterglow'	EBee ECho LAma LRHS WCot
'Alexandra'	WCot
'Ancilla' **new**	WCot
angustifolia	WCot
'Anna Fletcher' **new**	WCot
'Aries'	WCot
'Aurora'	ECho WCot
'Baghdad'	ECho WCot
'Belladonna'	WCot
'Bennett-Poë'	WCot
'Berlioz'	WCot
'Bettina' **new**	WCot
'Blanchefleur'	WCot
bowdenii ♀H3-4	Widely available
- 'Alba' ambig.	CCon CPrp CTca EBee ECho ELan EPot ERCP SCoo SMHy WCot
- 'Alba'	CBro LRHS MBel SDeJ
- 'Albivetta'	CBgR EBee ECho
- 'Blanca Perla'	CBgR WCot
- 'Chris Sanders'	WCot
- 'Codora'	see *N.* 'Codora'
- 'E.B.Anderson'	EBee WCot
- 'Ella K'	EBee EPot SPer
- Irish clone	WCot
- 'Isabel'	CBgR CBro CPrp EPot EPri ERCP EWes GAbr LRHS
- 'Linda Vista'	WCot
- 'Manina'	CCse
- 'Marjorie'	EMal
- 'Mark Fenwick'	CBro CDes ECha WOld
- 'Marnie Rogerson'	CBro CPne SMHy WCot
§ - 'Mollie Cowie' (v)	CCse CPrp GCal IBlr NCGa WCot WCru WSHC
- 'Nikita'	CBgR ECho EPot EPri ERCP LRHS SDeJ
- 'Ostara'	CBgR CPrp EBee EPot ERCP LRHS WCot
- 'Patricia'	CBgR EPot LRHS
- 'Pink Frostwork'	WCot
- 'Pink Surprise'	CAvo CDes WCot
- 'Porlock'	EBee
§ - 'Quinton Wells'	CPrp CTca SCnR SPhx WCot WHil
- 'Rowie'	CBgR CPrp EPot EPri ERCP LRHS
- 'Stefanie' **new**	SDeJ
- 'Variegata'	see *N. bowdenii* 'Mollie Cowie'
- Washfield form	SMHy
- 'Wellsii'	see *N. bowdenii* 'Quinton Wells'
'Canasta'	WCot
'Cardinal'	WCot
'Carnival'	WCot
'Carolside'	WCot
'Caryatid'	WCot
'Catherine'	WCot
'Catkin'	WCot
'Chorister' **new**	WCot
'Christmas'	WCot
'Clarabel'	WCot
'Clent Charm'	WCot
§ 'Codora'	CBgR CCCN EBee ECho LHop SPer WCot
'Corlette'	WCot
corusca 'Major'	see *N. sarniensis* var. *corusca*
'Cranfield'	WCot
'Cynthia Chance'	WCot
'Dame Alice Godman'	WCot
'Daphne' **new**	WCot
'Diana Oliver'	WCot
'Doris Vos'	WCot
'Druid'	WCot
'Elspeth'	WCot
'Enchantress'	WCot
'Eve'	WCot
'Evelyn Emmett'	WCot
'Exbury Red'	WCot
filamentosa misapplied	see *N. filifolia*
filamentosa ambig.	CBro ECho
§ ***filifolia***	CPBP CPen ECho WAbe
flexuosa	see *N. undulata* Flexuosa Group
'Fuchsine' **new**	WCot
'Fucine'	CDes EBee
gaberonensis **new**	WAbe WCot

	'Gaiety'	WCot
	'George' new	WCot
	gracilis	ECho WCot
	'Grilse'	WCot
	'Hamlet'	WCot
	'Harlequin'	WCot
	'Hera'	CBro SPhx
	'Hertha Berg'	WCot
*	***hirsuta***	ECho WAbe
	humilis	ECho WCot
	- Breachiae Group	SBch
	huttoniae	ECho
	'Iman'	WCot
	'Innominata'	WCot
	'Isobel' new	XEll
	'Janet'	WCot
	'Jenny Wren'	CDes WCot WHil
I	'Judith'	WCot
	'Kashmir'	CDes WCot
	'Kenilworth' new	WCot
	'Killarney'	WCot
	'King Leopold'	WCot
	'King of the Belgians'	ECho LAma WCot
	'Kinn McIntosh'	CDes WCot
	krigei	CPen ECho
	'Kyoto'	WCot
	'Lady Cynthia Colville'	WCot
	'Lady Downe' new	WCot
	'Lady Eleanor Keane'	WCot
	'Lady Havelock-Allen'	CDes WCot
	'Lady Llewellyn'	WCot
	'Lady St Aldwyn'	WCot
	laticoma	ECho WCot
	'Lawlord'	CDes WCot
	'Leila Hughes'	WCot
	'Lucinda'	WCot
	'Lyndhurst Salmon'	WCot
	'Maria'	CBgR WCot
	'Mars'	WCot
	masoniorum	CBro CPen ECho NMen SBch WCot
	'Miss E. Cator'	WCot
	'Miss Florence Brown'	WCot
	'Miss Frances Clarke'	WCot
	'Mrs Berkeley' new	WCot
	'Mrs Cooper'	WCot
	'Mrs Dent Brocklehurst'	WCot
	'Nena'	WCot
	'November Cheer'	ECho
	peersii	WCot
	'Pink Fairy' new	WCot
	'Pink Parfait' new	WCot
	'Pink Triumph'	CAbP CBcs CBgR EBee ECho ERCP EShb GQui IBlr LAma LHop LRHS SDeJ WCot WHoo
	'Plymouth'	SChr WCot
	pudica	SBch
	- pink-flowered	WCot
	pusilla	CLak
	'Quivotina'	WCot
	'Red Pimpernel'	ECho LAma
	'Regina'	WCot
	'Rushmere Star'	EBee SChr WCot
	'Ruth'	WCot
	sarniensis ♀H2-3	CBro CPne ECha ECho EPot EPri GKev LRHS SKHP WCot
*	- 'Borde Hill White'	WCot
§	- var. ***corusca***	LAma
	- - 'Major'	ECho SChr WCot
	- var. ***curvifolia*** f. ***fothergillii***	ECho WCot
	- 'Harry Dalton'	WCot
	- late, dull red-flowered	CDes
	'Shardlow Beauty'	WCot
	'Smokey Special'	WCot
	'Snowflake'	WCot
	'Stephanie'	CBgR CBro CCCN CTca EBee ECho ERCP EShb LAma LHop LRHS MAvo MNrw WCot WHoo
	'Susan Norris' new	WCot
	'Timoshenko'	WCot
	undulata	CBgR CBro CCCN CPne CTca ECha ECho EHrv EPri GCal LAma LSou SDeJ SPer
*	- 'Alba'	ECho
§	- Flexuosa Group	CPne ECho MRav
	- - 'Alba'	CBgR CBro EBee ECha ECho EPri MRav WAbe WCot
	× ***versicolor*** 'Mansellii'	CBro GKev SKHP
	'Vicky'	WCot
	'Virgo'	ECho LAma
	'White Swan'	ECho
	'Wolsey'	ECho WCot
	'Wombe' new	WCot
	'Zeal Giant' ♀H3-4	CAvo CBro CPne CPrp ECho GCal WCot
	'Zeal Grilse'	CDes CPne

Nerium ✿ (*Apocynaceae*)

	oleander L.	CAbb CArn CBcs CHll CTri EBak ELan EShb LRHS NLar SChr SEND SPer SPlb SPoG SRms
	- 'Album'	CTri
	- 'Album Plenum' (d)	XSen
*	- 'Atlas'	XSen
	- 'Cavalaire' (d)	XSen
*	- 'Claudia'	SEND
	- 'Commandant Barthélemy' (d)	XSen
	- 'Flavescens Plenum' (d)	EShb XSen
	- 'Madame Allen' (d)	EShb
	- 'Magaly'	SEND
	- 'Pink Beauty'	SEND
	- 'Professeur Granel' (d)	EShb
	- 'Provence' (d)	XSen
	- 'Red Beauty'	XSen
	- 'Rosario' (d)	EShb
	- 'Roseum Plenum' (d)	CRHN SEND
	- salmon-flowered	SEND
	- 'Splendens Giganteum' (d)	EShb
	- 'Variegatum' (v) ♀H1+3	CHll EShb LRHS SHil
	- 'Variegatum Plenum' (d/v)	WCot
	- 'Villa Romaine'	XSen
	- white-flowered	SEND

Neviusia (*Rosaceae*)

	alabamensis	NLar

Nicandra (*Solanaceae*)

	physalodes	CArn CHby ENfk EOHP GBee NBir SMrm WSFF
	- 'Splash of Cream' (v)	CCCN
	- 'Violacea'	CSpe SRms SWvt

Nicotiana (*Solanaceae*)

	alata	CSpe EPfP WSFF

glauca	CCCN CDTJ CHGN CHll CSpe EShb EUJe LDai NGBo SPav SPlb
'Hopleys'	CSpe
knightiana	CDTJ CSpe
langsdorffii ♀H3	CSpe SPav SPhx
- 'Hot Chocolate'	CSpe
'Lime Green' ♀H3	CSpe
mutabilis	CHll CSpe LDai SBch SDys SPhx
'Perfume Deep Purple' (Perfume Series) **new**	CSpe
suaveolens	CBre SPhx
sylvestris ♀H3	CDTJ CSpe CWSG EBee ELan EPfP SBfd SDys SEND SPav SPoG SWvt WTou
tabacum	CArn
- var. ***macrophylla***	CDTJ
'Tinkerbell'	CSpe

Nidularium (*Bromeliaceae*)

innocentii	XBlo

Nierembergia (*Solanaceae*)

§ ***repens***	CDoy ECho EDAr NLar
rivularis	see *N. repens*

Nigella (*Ranunculaceae*)

papillosa 'African Bride'	CSpe
- 'Midnight'	CSpe
sativa	MHoo

Nigritella see *Gymnadenia*

× *Niphimenes* (*Gesneriaceae*)

'Lemonade'	GHim

Nipponanthemum (*Asteraceae*)

§ ***nipponicum***	CWan EBee ECho GBin GCal IVic LAst NSti SRms WHil XLum

Noccaea see *Thlaspi*

Nolina (*Asparagaceae*)

bigelovii	XSen
durangensis	EGri
- F&M 333	WPGP
longifolia	EAmu EGri
microcarpa	WCot XSen
nelsonii	EAmu EGri SPlb
- F&M 307	EBee WPGP
parviflora	EGri
- NJM 05.010	EBee WPGP
texana	CTrC WCot XSen

Nomocharis (*Liliaceae*)

sp. **new**	EHrv
aperta	CPLG GBin GBuc GCra GEdr GGGa GHim GLin LAma WCru
- ACE 2271	EHrv LWst
- CLD 229	EHrv LWst
- CLD 524	LWst
× ***finlayorum***	LWst
mairei	see *N. pardanthina*
meleagrina	LAma LWst WAbe
nana	see *Lilium nanum*
oxypetala	see *Lilium oxypetalum*
§ ***pardanthina***	GBuc WAbe
- CLD 1490	GBuc LWst
- f. ***punctulata***	GBuc GGGa LWst WCru
saluenensis	GGGa LWst WAbe

Nonea (*Boraginaceae*)

lutea	LSou NOrc NSti WHal

Nothochelone see *Penstemon*

Nothofagus ✿ (*Nothofagaceae*)

§ × ***alpina***	CBcs CMCN GBin
antarctica	CBcs CCVT CDul CMCN CTho EBee ECrN ELan EPfP GBin GKin IVic LTen MBlu MBri MGos NWea WSHC
- 'Benmore'	NLar
betuloides	CBcs GBin IArd IDee SPlb
cunninghamii	CTrC IArd IDee SPlb
dombeyi	CBcs CDoC CDul EBee EPfP GBin IArd IVic MBlu NWea WPGP
fusca	CDoC IArd
glauca	CBcs GBin IArd IVic
menziesii	CTrC
nitida	CBcs GBin IDee
obliqua	CBcs CDul CMCN GAbr GBin IVic SPlb
procera misapplied	see *N.* × *alpina*
pumilio	GBin

Notholaena see *Cheilanthes*

Notholirion (*Liliaceae*)

bulbuliferum	EBee ECho GCra
- Cox 5074	LWst
- SDR 2865	GKev
campanulatum	EBee ECho GKev LWst
macrophyllum	EBee ECho GKev LWst
thomsonianum	ECho LWst

Nothoscordum (*Alliaceae*)

sp.	GCal
gracile	CCon
montevidense	LWst
neriniflorum	see *Caloscordum neriniflorum*
ostenii	SCnR
strictum	EBee ECho

Nuphar (*Nymphaeaceae*)

advenum	LPBA
japonica var. ***variegata*** (v)	CRow NLar
lutea	CBen CHab CRow EHon LPBA MSKA SCoo SWat

Nylandtia (*Polygalaceae*)

spinosa	SPlb

Nymphaea ✿ (*Nymphaeaceae*)

alba (H)	CBen CHab CRWN CRow CWat EHon GQue LPBA MSKA NBir SCoo SVic SWat WHil WMAq
'Albatros' misapplied	see *N.* 'Hermine'
§ 'Albatros' Latour-Marliac (H)	CWat LPBA MSKA NPer SWat
'Albatross'	see *N.* 'Albatros' Latour-Marliac, *N.* 'Hermine'
* 'Albida'	WMAq XBlo
'Almost Black' (H)	CBen MSKA
'Amabilis' (H)	CBen CRow EWay LPBA MSKA SWat WMAq
'American Star' (H)	CBen SWat WMAq
'Andreana' (H)	EWay LPBA MSKA
'Arc-en-ciel' (H)	CBen LPBA SCoo SWat WMAq
'Arethusa' (H)	LPBA

	'Atropurpurea' (H)	CBen LPBA MSKA NPer SWat WMAq
	'Attraction' (H)	CBen CRow EHon LPBA MSKA NPer SCoo SVic SWat WMAq XBlo
	'Aurora' (H)	CBen GQue LPBA MWts SVic SWat WMAq
	'Barbara Davies' (H)	MSKA
	'Barbara Dobbins' (H)	CBen EWay LPBA MSKA
	'Bateau' (H)	CBen
	'Berit Strawn' (H)	EWay
	'Bernice Ikins' (H)	MSKA
	'Black Princess' (H)	CRow EWay
	'Brakeleyi Rosea' (H)	LPBA MSKA WMAq
	'Burgundy Princess' (H)	CWat EWay MSKA NPer
	candida (H)	CBen EHon MSKA MWts NPer WMAq
	'Candidissima' (H)	SWat
§	***capensis*** (T/D)	XBlo
	'Caroliniana Nivea' (H)	CBen EHon
	'Caroliniana Perfecta' (H)	CBen LPBA MSKA SWat
	'Celebration' (H)	MSKA
	'Charlene Strawn' (H)	CWat EWay LPBA WMAq
	'Charles' Choice' (H)	EWay
	'Charles de Meurville' (H)	CBen CRow LPBA MSKA NPer SVic WMAq
	'Clyde Ikins' (H)	EWay MSKA
	'Colonel A.J. Welch' (H)	CBen EHon LPBA MSKA NPer SCoo SWat WMAq
	'Colorado' (H)	CBen EWay MSKA NPer
	colorata	see *N. capensis*
	'Colossea' (H)	CBen CWat LPBA MSKA NPer
	'Comanche' (H)	CBen MSKA NPer WMAq
	'Conqueror' (H)	CBen IArd LPBA MSKA NPer SCoo SVic SWat
§	'Darwin' (H)	CBen CWat LPBA MSKA NPer SLon SWat WMAq
	× ***daubenyana*** (T/D)	ECho
	'David' (H)	CBen EWay
	'Denver' (H)	EWay MSKA
	'Deva' (H)	CBen
	'Ellisiana' (H)	CBen LPBA MSKA NPer SWat
	'Escarboucle' (H) 🏆H4	CBen CRow CWat EWay LPBA MSKA NLar NPer SCoo SVic SWat WMAq XBlo
§	'Fabiola' (H)	CBen CRow EHon LPBA MSKA NPer SCoo WMAq
	'Fiesta'	CBen MSKA
	'Fire Crest' (H)	CBen GQue LPBA MSKA NPer SCoo SVic SWat WMAq
	'Fireball' (H)	MSKA
	'Fritz Junge' (H)	CBen
	'Froebelii' (H)	CBen CRow CWat EHon EWay LPBA MSKA NPer SWat WMAq
	'Galatée' (H)	CBen MSKA
	'Geisha Girl'	MSKA
	'Georgia Peach' (H)	EWay MSKA
	'Gladstoniana' (H) 🏆H4	CBen CRow EHon LPBA MSKA NPer SCoo SWat WMAq
	'Gloire du Temple-sur-Lot' (H)	CBen EHon NPer SWat WMAq
	'Gloriosa' (H)	CBen LPBA NPer SCoo SWat
	'Gold Medal' (H)	CBen EWay MSKA
	'Gonnère' (H) 🏆H4	CBen CRow CWat EHon EWay LPBA MSKA MWts NPer SLon SWat WMAq
	'Graziella' (H)	CBen LPBA MSKA WMAq
	'Gypsy' (H)	EWay
	'Helen Fowler' (H)	WMAq
	× ***helvola***	see *N.* 'Pygmaea Helvola'
§	'Hermine' (H)	CBen MSKA NPer SWat WMAq
	'Hollandia' misapplied	see *N.* 'Darwin'
	'Hollandia' Koster (H)	CBen SWat
	'Indiana' (H)	CBen LPBA MSKA NPer WMAq
	'Inner Light'	EWay MSKA
	'J.C.N. Forestier' (H)	CBen
	'James Brydon' (H) 🏆H4	CBen CRow CWat EHon EWay LPBA MSKA NLar NPer SCoo SLon SVic SWat WMAq
	'Jean de Lamarsalle' (H)	MSKA
	'Jerusalem Dawn'	MSKA
	'Joey Tomocik' (H)	CBen CWat EWay LPBA MSKA SCoo WMAq
	'Lactea' (H)	CBen
	'Laydekeri Fulgens' (H)	CBen EWay LPBA MSKA SWat WMAq
	'Laydekeri Lilacea' (H)	CBen CRow LPBA SWat WMAq
	'Laydekeri Purpurata' (H)	EWay LPBA SWat
	'Laydekeri Rosea' misapplied	see *N.* 'Laydekeri Rosea Prolifera'
§	'Laydekeri Rosea Prolifera' (H)	CBen EWay LPBA
	'Lemon Chiffon' (H)	CBen CRow MSKA
	'Lemon Mist'	MSKA
	'Lily Pons' (H)	CBen MSKA
	'Liou' (H)	CBen MSKA
	'Little Sue' (H)	EWay MSKA
	'Lucida' (H)	CBen LPBA MSKA SWat WMAq
	'Madame Wilfon Gonnère' (H)	CBen CWat EHon LPBA MSKA MWts NPer SVic SWat WMAq
	'Marliacea Albida' (H)	CBen CWat EHon EWay LPBA MSKA NPer SWat WMAq XBlo
	'Marliacea Carnea' (H)	CBen CRow EHon LPBA MSKA NPer SCoo SWat WMAq
§	'Marliacea Chromatella' (H) 🏆H4	CBen CRow CWat EHon EWay GQue LPBA MSKA MWts NLar SCoo SVic SWat WMAq XBlo
	'Marliacea Flammea' (H)	CBen
	'Marliacea Rosea' (H)	CBen MSKA SWat WMAq XBlo
	'Marliacea Rubra Punctata' (H)	LPBA
	'Martha' (H)	EWay
	'Masaniello' (H)	CBen CRow EHon LPBA MSKA SWat WMAq
	'Maurice Laydeker' (H)	CBen
	'Maxima'	see *N.* 'Odorata Maxima'
	'Mayla'	CBen LPBA MSKA NPer
§	'Météor' (H)	CBen EWay MSKA WMAq
	mexicana	MSKA
	'Millennium Pink'	MSKA
	'Moorei' (H)	CBen LPBA MSKA SWat WMAq
	'Mrs Richmond' misapplied	see *N.* 'Fabiola'
	'Mrs Richmond' Latour-Marliac (H)	CBen SWat XBlo
	'Newchapel Beauty'	WMAq
	'Newton' (H)	CBen EWay MSKA SWat WMAq
	'Nigel' (H)	MSKA SWat
	'Norma Gedye' (H)	CBen CWat LPBA MSKA SWat WMAq
§	***odorata*** (H)	CBen CRow EHon LPBA MSKA SCoo WMAq
§	- var. ***minor*** (H)	CBen CRow LPBA MSKA SWat WMAq
	- 'Pumila'	see *N. odorata* var. ***minor***
	- subsp. ***tuberosa*** (H)	CBen LPBA
	'Odorata Alba'	see *N. odorata*
§	'Odorata Maxima' (H)	WMAq
	'Odorata Sulphurea' (H)	SWat
§	'Odorata Sulphurea Grandiflora' (H)	CBen CRow LPBA MSKA SCoo SWat XBlo

§	'Odorata Turicensis' (H)	LPBA MSKA
	'Odorata William B. Shaw'	see *N.* 'W.B. Shaw'
	'Pam Bennett' (H)	CBen
	'Panama Pacific' (T/D)	XBlo
	'Patio Joe'	MSKA
	'Paul Hariot' (H)	CWat LPBA MSKA NPer SWat WMAq
	'Peace Lily'	MSKA
	'Peach Glow'	EWay MSKA
	'Peaches and Cream' (H)	MSKA
	Pearl of the Pool (H)	SWat
	'Perry's Baby Red' (H)	CBen CWat EWay MSKA MWts NPer SCoo WMAq
	'Perry's Crinkled Pink' (H)	CBen
	'Perry's Double White' (H)	MSKA NPer
	'Perry's Double Yellow'	MSKA
	'Perry's Dwarf Red' (H)	CBen MSKA
	'Perry's Fire Opal' (H)	MSKA NPer
	'Perry's Orange Sunset'	MSKA
	'Perry's Pink' (H)	SWat WMAq
	'Perry's Red Glow' (H)	MSKA
	'Perry's Red Star' (H)	EWay MSKA
	'Perry's Red Wonder' (H)	CBen
	'Perry's Viviparous Pink' (H)	CBen
	'Peter Slocum' (H)	CBen EWay SWat
	'Phoebus' (H)	CBen SWat
	'Pink Domino'	MSKA
	'Pink Grapefruit' (H)	XBlo
	'Pink Opal' (H)	CBen CWat LPBA
	'Pink Peony' (H)	MSKA
	'Pink Pumpkin' (H)	MSKA
	'Pink Sensation' (H)	CBen EWay MSKA NPer SLon SWat WMAq
	'Pink Sunrise' (H)	MSKA
	'Pöstlingberg' (H)	LPBA MSKA
	'Princess Elizabeth' (H)	CBen EHon LPBA
	'Pygmaea Alba'	see *N. tetragona*
§	'Pygmaea Helvola' (H) ♀H4	CBen CRow CWat EWay GQue LPBA MSKA MWts NLar NPer SCoo SLon SVic SWat WMAq
	'Pygmaea Rubis' (H)	CRow LPBA SWat WMAq
	'Pygmaea Rubra' (H)	CBen CRow CWat EWay MSKA MWts NLar NPer SCoo SVic WMAq
	'Ray Davies' (H)	CBen
	'Red Paradise' (H)	MSKA
	'Red Spider' (H)	LPBA MSKA NPer SVic
	'Rembrandt' misapplied	see *N.* 'Météor'
	'Rembrandt' Koster (H)	CBen LPBA
	'René Gérard' (H)	CBen CWat EHon GQue LPBA MSKA NPer SWat WMAq
	'Rosanna Supreme' (H)	SWat
	'Rose Arey' (H)	CBen EWay LPBA MSKA NPer SCoo SVic SWat WMAq
	'Rose Magnolia' (H)	CWat SWat
	'Rosea' (H)	LPBA
	'Rosennymphe' (H)	CBen LPBA MSKA NPer SWat WMAq
	'Rosy Morn' (H)	CBen MSKA
	'Shady Lady'	MSKA MWts
	'Sioux' (H)	CBen LPBA MSKA NPer SVic WMAq XBlo
	'Sirius' (H)	CBen LPBA MSKA SWat
	'Snow Princess'	EWay LPBA
	'Solfatare' (H)	EWay
	'Splendida' (H)	WMAq
	'Starbright'	EWay
	'Starburst' (H)	MSKA
	'Sultan' (H)	MSKA
	'Sunny Pink'	MSKA
	'Sunrise'	see *N.* 'Odorata Sulphurea Grandiflora'
§	***tetragona*** (H)	CRow CWat EWay LPBA NPer WMAq
	- 'Alba'	see *N. tetragona*
	'Texas Dawn' (H)	CBen CWat EWay MSKA SLon WMAq
	'Tuberosa Flavescens'	see *N.* 'Marliacea Chromatella'
	'Tuberosa Richardsonii' (H)	CBen EHon MSKA NPer
	'Turicensis'	see *N.* 'Odorata Turicensis'
	'Venusta' (H)	EWay
	'Vésuve' (H)	MSKA SWat
	'Virginalis' (H)	CBen LPBA MSKA NPer SWat WMAq
§	'W.B. Shaw' (H)	CBen EHon LPBA MSKA NPer SWat WMAq
	'Walter Pagels' (H)	EWay MWts WMAq
	'Weymouth Red' (H)	CBen
	'White Sultan' (H)	CWat MSKA
	'William Doogue' (H)	MSKA
	'William Falconer' (H)	CBen CWat LPBA MSKA NPer SWat
	'Wow' (H)	MSKA
	'Yellow Queen' (H)	MSKA
	'Yul Ling' (H)	EWay MSKA
	'Zeus'	MSKA

Nymphoides (*Menyanthaceae*)

	indica	XBlo
	peltata	CBen CHab CWat EHon EWay MSKA NLar NPer SCoo SVic WMAq
§	- 'Bennettii'	LPBA

Nyssa ✿ (*Nyssaceae*)

	aquatica	CBcs
	leptophylla	IArd NLar SBir SSta
	ogeche	SSta
	sinensis ♀H4	CAbP CBcs CDoC CDoy CDul CMCN CMac CTho EBee ELan EPfP LRHS MAsh MBlu MPkF MWat SBir SPer SSpi SSta WPat
	- 'Jim Russell'	SBir SSta
	- Nymans form	SBir
	sylvatica ♀H4	Widely available
	- 'Autumn Cascades'	EBee EPfP LRHS MBlu NLar SBir SSpi SSta WPGP
	- Bulk's form **new**	SSta
	- 'Dirr'	SSpi
	- 'Haymen's Red'	see *N. sylvatica* Red Rage
	- 'Isabel Grace'	EBee LRHS MAsh MBri SBir SSpi SSta
	- 'Jermyns Flame'	CAbP EBee EPfP LRHS MAsh NLar NRHS SBir SSpi
	- Jolly = 'Yiping' (v)	MPkF NLar
	- 'Lakeside Weeper' **new**	SSta
	- 'Miss Scarlet' (f)	NLar SBir SSta
	- 'Pendula'	SSta
§	- Red Rage = 'Haymanred'	MPkF
	- 'Red Red Wine'	CGHE EBee EPfP IVic NLar SBir SSta WPGP
	- 'Sheffield Park'	CAbP EBee LRHS MAsh SBir SLim SSta
	- 'Valley Scorcher' **new**	SSta
	- 'Wildfire'	LRHS MPkF SBir SGol SSpi SSta
	- 'Windsor'	EBee EPfP LRHS MAsh NLar SBir
	- 'Wisley Bonfire' (m)	CAbP CGHE EBee EPfP LRHS MAsh MWat NLar NRHS SBir SMad SPoG SSpi SSta WPGP
	ursina	CBcs SSta

Oakesiella see *Uvularia*

Ochagavia (*Bromeliaceae*)

	carnea RCB RA S-2	EBee LSou
§	***litoralis***	CMac SMad
*	***rosea***	CHEx SPlb

Ochna (*Ochnaceae*)

	serrulata	CCCN

Ocimum (*Lamiaceae*)

	'African Blue'	CArn CSpe EGHP ELau ENfk EOHP GPoy LSou MHer NPri SPoG WCot
§	***americanum***	EGHP WJek
	- 'Meng Luk'	see *O. americanum*
	basilicum	CArn ELau GPoy MHoo NPri SBfd SIde SWat WJek
	- 'Anise'	see *O. basilicum* 'Horapha'
	- 'Ararat'	EGHP ELau ENfk
	- ***camphorata***	see *O. kilimandscharicum*
	- 'Cinnamon'	EGHP ELau ENfk MNHC SBfd SHDw WJek
	- 'Gecofure'	ELau
	- 'Genovese'	EGHP ELau MHer MNHC
	- 'Genovese Special Select'	ELau
	- 'Glycyrrhiza'	see *O. basilicum* 'Horapha'
	- 'Green Globe'	EGHP
	- 'Green Ruffles'	ELau EPfP WJek
	- 'Holy'	see *O. tenuiflorum*
§	- 'Horapha'	CArn EGHP ELau ENfk MHer MNHC SIde WJek
*	- 'Horapha Nanum'	EGHP ENfk WJek
	- 'Magic Michael'	ELau
	- 'Magic Mountain'	SPoG
	- 'Magic White'	EGHP SPoG
	- 'Mexican'	ELau
	- 'Mrs Burns'	EGHP WJek
	- 'Napolitano'	EGHP ELau ENfk SIde SWat WJek
	- 'New Guinea'	ELau
	- 'Osmin'PBR	ELau
	- 'Pistou'	ELau
	- 'Purple Delight'	ELau
	- var. ***purpurascens***	SIde
	- - 'Dark Opal'	EGHP ENfk MNHC SBfd SHDw
	- - 'Purple Ruffles'	ENfk EPfP MNHC SIde SWat WJek
	- - 'Red Rubin'	MHer MNHC WJek
	- var. ***purpurascens*** × ***kilimandscharicum***	CSpe GPoy
	- 'Queenette'	ELau
	- 'Sweet Genovase'	SVic
	- 'Thai'	see *O. basilicum* 'Horapha'
	canum	see *O. americanum*
	× ***citriodorum***	EGHP ENfk MNHC SBfd SHDw SIde WJek
	- 'Lime'	EGHP ENfk MNHC
	- 'Pesto Perpetuo'	EGHP ENfk
	- 'Siam Queen'	EGHP ELau MHer WJek
	gratissimum	CArn ELau
§	***kilimandscharicum***	ELau GPoy
	minimum	EGHP ELau ENfk MHer MNHC SBfd SIde WJek
	sanctum	see *O. tenuiflorum*
	'Spice'	EGHP ELau ENfk
	'Spicy Globe'	ELau
§	***tenuiflorum***	CArn EGHP ELau GPoy MNHC SBfd SHDw SIde WJek

Odontonema (*Acanthaceae*)

	schomburgkianum	CCCN
	tubaeforme	CCCN MOWG

Oemleria (*Rosaceae*)

	cerasiformis	CBcs CHGN CJun CTri EBee EBtc EPfP LRHS NLar SSpi WCot WSHC

Oenanthe (*Apiaceae*)

	fistulosa	MSKA
	javanica 'Flamingo' (v)	CWat ELan EPfP EWay GCal LEdu LPBA MSKA MWts NBro WFar WMAq WSHC XLum
	lachenalii	SDix
	pimpinelloides	CHab

Oenothera ✿ (*Onagraceae*)

§	***acaulis***	CMea CPBP CSpe MDKP MNrw SBch WCFE WCot WPGP
§	- 'Aurea'	GKev XLum
	- 'Lutea'	see *O. acaulis* 'Aurea'
	'Apricot Delight'	EHoe GJos IPot LRHS MBel WMnd WMoo
§	***biennis***	CArn CSev CWan EGHP ELan ENfk GAbr GPoy MHer MHoo NBro SBfd SIde SPhx WBrk WHer WJek WSFF
	- SDR 6501	GKev
	'Blood Orange'	MDKP SMrm
*	***campylocalyx***	LDai
	childsii	see *O. speciosa*
	cinaeus	see *O. fruticosa* subsp. *glauca*
	'Cold Crick'	EBee
	'Colin Porter'	MDKP WMoo
	'Copper Canyon'	SPad
	'Crown Imperial'	CMac EBee LEdu LSou MArl NHol SHar SLon SPer
	Crown of Gold = 'Lishal'	ELan LLHF
§	***elata*** subsp. ***hookeri***	EWes NBre
	erythrosepala	see *O. glazioviana*
	'Finlay's Fancy'	WCru
	flava	EWld
§	***fruticosa***	NLar SEND SPlb XSen
	- 'African Sun'PBR	EBee EWes SRot
	- 'Camel' (v)	LDai MDKP NPro WHrl WWEG XLum
	- Fireworks	see *O. fruticosa* 'Fyrverkeri'
§	- 'Fyrverkeri' ♀H4	CBcs CMea CPrp EBee ECtt ELan GMaP LEdu LHop LRHS MRav NGdn SPer SWvt WAul WMnd WWEG XLum
§	- subsp. ***glauca*** ♀H4	CElw CEnt EPfP MDKP SBfd SMrm SRms WJek WPer
	- - 'Erica Robin' (v)	CMea CPrp ECtt EHoe GBin LRHS LSou MNrw MRav NEgg NGdn SAga SMad SMrm SRot SWvt WCot WHoo WWEG
	- - 'Longest Day'	MBrN
	- - Solstice	see *O. fruticosa* subsp. *glauca* 'Sonnenwende'
§	- - 'Sonnenwende'	CBre CElw CEnt EBee LRHS MAvo NLar NPro WMoo WWEG XLum
	- 'Lady Brookeborough'	MRav
	- 'Michelle Ploeger'	NBre SUsu
	- 'Yellow River'	CElw EBee
	- 'Youngii'	CWan EPfP LEdu WJek WPer WWEG

'Give-me-Sunshine' **new** SLon
glabra Miller see *O. biennis*
glabra misapplied ECha NSti
§ ***glazioviana*** MNHC NBir
hookeri see *O. elata* subsp. *hookeri*
kunthiana CEnt ECha ECho MDKP WMnd WMoo
- 'Glowing Magenta' SPoG
lamarckiana see *O. glazioviana*
Lemon Drop = 'Innoeno131'[PBR] **new** MBri MPkF SHil
'Lemon Sunset' CCVN LSou SWal WHil WMoo
linearis see *O. fruticosa*
§ ***macrocarpa*** ♀H4 Widely available
- subsp. ***fremontii*** XSen
- - 'Silver Wings' EBee SMrm SPhx
- subsp. ***incana*** CMea CSpe SPhx WHoo
- 'Yellow Queen' GJos
* ***minima*** MDKP
missouriensis see *O. macrocarpa*
oakesiana SPhx
odorata misapplied see *O. stricta*
odorata Hook. & Arn. see *O. biennis*
organensis CDes EBee MNrw
§ ***perennis*** CEnt NPro SRms WPer WThu XLum
pumila see *O. perennis*
rosea CMea
'Silky Orchid' ELon
§ ***speciosa*** EBee NBre SEND SPhx WFar WJek XLum
* - 'Alba' EBee EWes
- var. ***childsii*** see *O. speciosa*
- 'Pink Petticoats' ECha NPer
- 'Rosea' ECho LAst LEdu SPlb
- 'Siskiyou' CSpe EAEE EBee ECtt EPfP EShb EWld LEdu LRHS LSou MNrw NBro NPri SCoo SGar SMad SMrm SPer SPoG SUsu WGwG XLum
- Twilight = 'Turner01'[PBR] (v) EBee LHop
- 'Woodside White' ELon SMrm
§ ***stricta*** CMea GCal MNrw WBrk
- 'Sulphurea' CMHG CMea CSpe EBee ECGP ELan EWld GCal GMaP IFro MNFA NPer SBch SGar SMrm SPhx WAbb WAbe WCot
'Summer Sun' EAEE EBee LRHS SPer SPoG
taraxacifolia see *O. acaulis*
tetragona see *O. fruticosa* subsp. *glauca*
- var. ***fraseri*** see *O. fruticosa* subsp. *glauca*
versicolor CSev WCFE
- 'Sunset Boulevard' CSpe GCal LDai MBNS SBfd SGar SPad SPer WMoo XLum

Olea (Oleaceae)

europaea (F) Widely available
- subsp. ***africana*** CTrC WPGP
- 'Aglandau' (F) CAgr
- 'Arbequina' (F) CDoy ETod SBig
- 'Bouteillan' (F) CAgr
- 'Cailletier' (F) CAgr
- 'Chelsea Physic Garden' (F) CDoC CDoy
§ - 'Cipressino' (F) ESwi MGos SBfd SBig
- 'Cornicabra' (F) ETod
- 'El Greco' (F) CBcs
- subsp. ***europaea*** var. ***sylvestris*** SEND
- 'Fastigiata' EBee SBfd
- 'Frantoio' (F) CAgr CDoy SBfd SBig
- 'Hojiblanca' (F) CDoy EBee SBig
- 'Leccino' (F) CDoy SBig
- 'Manzanillo' (F) ETod
- 'Maurino' (F) SBig
- 'Peace' CDoy
- 'Pendolino' (F) SBig
- 'Picual' (F) CDoy ETod SBig
- 'Pyramidalis' see *O. europaea* 'Cipressino'
- 'Serrana' ETod
- 'Villalonga' ETod

Olearia ✿ (*Asteraceae*)

albida var. ***angulata*** CTrC
arborescens EWld
argophylla CPLG ECou
avicenniifolia CBcs CMac CTrC ECou IVic SEND
bullata ECou
× ***capillaris*** CDoC ECou
chathamica IVic
§ ***cheesemanii*** CBcs CDoC CPLG CTrC LRHS NLar
coriacea ECou
'County Park' ECou
erubescens CDoC
floribunda CTrC
furfuracea ECou GLin SEND
glandulosa ECou
gunniana see *O. phlogopappa*
× ***haastii*** Widely available
- 'McKenzie' ECou ELon
'Havering Blush' ECou
hectorii ECou
§ 'Henry Travers' CBcs CCCN CPLG EPfP GCal GQui IVic
ilicifolia CDoC EBee EPfP IDee IVic LRHS NLar
insignis see *Pachystegia insignis*
lacunosa WHor
lepidophylla ECou
- 'Silver Knight' NLar
- silver-leaved ECou
lirata ECou
macrodonta ♀H3 Widely available
- 'Major' CCCN LTen NLar
- 'Minor' CBcs CCCN CDoC CMac CTrC ELan EPfP GCal GQui IVic SPlb
× ***mollis*** (Kirk) Cockayne CMac EBee GQui LRHS SPer
- 'Zennorensis' ♀H3 CBcs CCCN CDoC EBee EPfP IArd IDee IVic NLar
nummularifolia CBcs CCCN CDoC CHll CTrC CTri EBee ECou ELan EPfP GKin IVic LRHS NLar SBod SEND SPer SPoG SWvt
- var. ***cymbifolia*** ECou
- hybrids ECou
- 'Little Lou' ECou
odorata ECou NLar WFar
oleifolia see *O.* 'Waikariensis'
paniculata CDoC CMHG CTrC CTri CTsd EBee EPfP IVic LRHS SEND
§ ***phlogopappa*** CTri ECou EWld GLin
- 'Comber's Blue' CBcs CCCN EBee ELan EPfP GKin IVic LRHS LSRN MAsh SCoo SLim SPer
§ - 'Comber's Pink' CBcs CCCN CDoC CHid CPLG EBee ELan ELon EPfP GKin LRHS LSRN MNHC NPer NSti SCoo SLim SPer SPoG WGrn WKif WSHC

	Name	Suppliers
	- 'Rosea'	see *O. phlogopappa* 'Comber's Pink'
I	- var. ***subrepanda*** (DC.) J.H. Willis	CTrC
	ramulosa	CCCN CDoC CPLG
	- 'Blue Stars'	CMac ECou SLon SRms WGrn
	rani misapplied	see *O. cheesemanii*
	rani Druce	CTrC
*	***rossii***	CTrC
	× ***scilloniensis*** misapplied	see *O. stellulata* DC.
	× ***scilloniensis*** ambig.	CBcs EWld LAst SAga SGar SPoG
	× ***scilloniensis*** Dorrien-Smith 🏆H3	CCCN CTsd LRHS MRav
	- 'Compacta'	CBcs
	- 'Master Michael'	CCCN CDoC CTri EBee ELon EPfP GBin IVic LRHS MAsh MOWG NLar SBfd SPer SPoG WCFE WGrn WPGP WSHC
	semidentata misapplied	see *O.* 'Henry Travers'
	solandri	CCCN CDoC CMac CTrC CTsd ECou EHoe IDee LRHS SDix SEND SPer
	- 'Aurea'	CBcs GQui
	'Stardust'	CTrC LRHS SPlb
	stellulata misapplied	see *O. phlogopappa*
§	***stellulata*** DC.	CMac CPLG CSBt CWSG CWib EBee ECou EPfP LRHS SCoo SDix SLim SPer
	- 'Michael's Pride'	CPLG
	- var. ***rugosa***	ECou
	traversii	CBcs CCCN CDoC CMHG CSBt CTrC CTsd EBee EPfP EWld LRHS SBfd SEND WHer
	- 'Tweedledee' (v)	SEND
	- 'Tweedledum' (v)	CCCN CDoC CWib ECou EHoe SBfd
	- 'Variegata' (v)	CBcs CTrC CTsd EBee
	virgata	CCCN CHEx ECou GBin GQui IDee MCot
	- var. ***laxiflora***	CTrC WHer
	- var. ***lineata***	CDoC ECou NLar SEND WHer WSHC
	- - 'Dartonii'	CDoC EBee ECou EPfP GBin LRHS SLPl SPlb SPoG
§	'Waikariensis'	CMHG CMac CPLG CTrC EBee ECou GKin IDee IVic LRHS MAsh MSCN SEND SLon SPoG WCFE

Oligoneuron see *Solidago*

Oligostachyum (*Poaceae*)

	Name	Suppliers
	lubricum	see *Semiarundinaria lubrica*
	oedogonatum	WPGP

olive see *Olea europaea*

Olsynium (*Iridaceae*)

	Name	Suppliers
§	***douglasii*** 🏆H4	CBro CMea EBee GKev LLHF NMen NRHS NRya NSla
	- 'Album'	CDes CWCL ELon EPot GAbr GBin GEdr LLHF NHar NMen NRHS NRya NSla WHal
	- dwarf	GEdr
	- var. ***inflatum***	EWes
§	***filifolium***	GAbr
§	***junceum***	CSpe LLHF MDKP WPGP
	trinerve B&SWJ 10459	WCru

Omphalodes ✿ (*Boraginaceae*)

	Name	Suppliers
	cappadocica 🏆H4	CElw EBee EPfP EPot EShb IFoB LEdu LRHS MMuc NBro NDov NPer NSla SRms SWat WBrk WFar
	- 'Alba'	CMac
	- 'Anthea Bloom'	NEgg
	- 'Cherry Ingram' 🏆H4	Widely available
	- 'Lilac Mist'	CLAP EBee GBuc LLWP MRav SRms SSvw SWvt WWEG
	- 'Parisian Skies'	CDes CLAP
	- 'Starry Eyes'	Widely available
§	***linifolia*** 🏆H4	CSpe MCot NMen SBch SPhx
	- ***alba***	see *O. linifolia*
	luciliae	CLAP
	nitida	CSpe LRHS MMuc MNrw NLBP NRya WWEG
	verna	Widely available
	- 'Alba'	Widely available
	- 'Elfenauge'	CDes EBee NBir NLar NRya SMrm SSvw WCot WWEG
	- ***grandiflora***	WCot

Omphalogramma (*Primulaceae*)

	Name	Suppliers
	delavayi	GKev
	- SDR 5167	GKev
	minus **new**	GKev

Oncostema see *Scilla*

onion see *Allium cepa*

Onixotis (*Colchicaceae*)

	Name	Suppliers
	stricta	CDes CLak WCot

Onoclea (*Onocleaceae*)

	Name	Suppliers
	sensibilis 🏆H4	Widely available
	- copper-leaved	CHEx CJun CRow WPGP

Ononis (*Papilionaceae*)

	Name	Suppliers
	repens	CArn NMir
	rotundifolia	CPom
	spinosa	MHer SMrm SPhx WPer WSpi XLum

Onopordum (*Asteraceae*)

	Name	Suppliers
	acanthium	CArn EBee ECha ELan ENfk EPfP GAbr GMaP LRHS MHer MWat NBid NEgg SBfd SIde SPhx WCot WFar WHer WMnd
	arabicum	see *O. nervosum*
§	***nervosum*** 🏆H4	CSpe EBee SEND

Onosma (*Boraginaceae*)

	Name	Suppliers
	alborosea	CCse ECha GCal GCra SEND WKif WPat
	echioides	WIce
	helvetica	GEdr
	nana	WAbe

Onychium (*Pteridaceae*)

	Name	Suppliers
	contiguum	WCot
	japonicum	CBty CPLG EFer GQui ISha

Ophiopogon ✿ (*Asparagaceae*)

	Name	Suppliers
	BWJ 8244 from Vietnam	WCru
	ACE 2362	NMen
	from India	GCal
	'Black Dragon'	see *O. planiscapus* 'Nigrescens'

bodinieri CBct ECho EShb EWes LEdu
- B&L 12505 CLAP EBee EPPr
caulescens B&SWJ 8230 WCru
- B&SWJ 11813 WCru
aff. ***caulescens*** HWJ 590 WCru WPGP
chingii EBee EPPr EWes GCal LEdu SCnR
clarkei GHim MMoz
clavatus KWJ 12267 new WCru
formosanus CPrp GBin
- B&SWJ 3659 WCru
'Gin-ryu' see *Liriope spicata* 'Gin-ryu'
graminifolius see *Liriope muscari*
intermedius CBct CJun CPBP CSpe EPPr EShb GHim NLar WAbe WCot
- GWJ 9387 WCru
§ - 'Argenteomarginatus' (v) ECho EWes
- 'Variegatus' see *O. intermedius* 'Argenteomarginatus'
§ ***jaburan*** CMac ECho EWTr LEdu NPnk WMoo
- 'Variegatus' see *O. jaburan* 'Vittatus'
§ - 'Vittatus' (v) ECho EHoe ELan EPfP EWes LEdu MGos WCot WFar
japonicus CMac ECho EPPr EPfP EShb GPoy LEdu XLum
- B&SWJ 1871 WCru
- 'Albus' CLAP ECho EPri MWat
- 'Compactus' CDoC EBee WPGP
- 'Gyoku-Ryu' GCal
- 'Kigimafukiduma' CMac CPLG EBee LRHS MRav
- 'Kyoto' EBee EPPr ESwi NOak
- 'Minor' CBct CKno ELon EPPr EPfP LBMP NLar WPGP WWEG XLum
- 'Nanus Variegatus' (v) EBee
- 'Nippon' CPrp EBee ECho EHoe EPPr NGdn
- 'Silver Dragon' (v) new EPPr WCFE
- 'Tama-ryu' WAbe
* - 'Tama-ryu Number Two' ECho EPPr
* - 'Variegatus' (v) CDTJ CMac CPrp ECho LEdu SLPl SPer
parviflorus GWJ 9387 WCru
- HWJK 2093 WCru
planiscapus CKno CMHG CPLG CSev EBee ECho EPPr NBro SBfd SPad WMoo WWEG
* - 'Albovariegatus' (v) WMoo
- 'Black Beard' CKno CTrC GBin LHop MAsh WCot
- ***leucanthus*** EPPr SLPl WCot
- 'Little Tabby' (v) CDes CLAP EBee ECho MDKP MMoz MWhi NPro WAbe WCot WGrn WHal WTin WWEG
* - ***minimus*** ECho
§ - 'Nigrescens' ♀H4 Widely available
- 'Silver Ribbon' ECho
scaber B&SWJ 1842 WCru
- B&SWJ 3655 WCru
'Spring Gold' EShb

Ophrys (*Orchidaceae*)

apifera CCon NLAp WHer
- subsp. ***trollii*** NLAp
apifera × ***holoserica*** NLAp
apifera × ***scolopax*** NLAp
arachnitiformis new NLAp
bombyliflora NLAp
ferrum-equinum new NLAp
fuciflora NLAp
fusca new NLAp
heldreichii NLAp
insectifera NLAp
lutea new NLAp
- subsp. ***galilaea*** new NLAp
reinholdii NLAp
scolopax NLAp
subsp. ***cornuta*** new
speculum NLAp
sphegodes NLAp
- subsp. ***helenae*** new NLAp
- subsp. ***mammosa*** new NLAp
strausii NLAp
tenthredinifera new NLAp

Oplopanax (*Araliaceae*)

horridus CArn
- B&SWJ 9551 WCru
japonicus new WCru

Opopanax (*Apiaceae*)

chironium CArn LEdu SPhx

Opuntia (*Cactaceae*)

compressa see *O. humifusa*
erinacea var. ***utahensis*** WCot
× ***polycantha*** NNS 99-263
fragilis SChr SKHP XSen
§ ***humifusa*** CDTJ EAmu EGri ETod SChr SMad WCot XLum XSen
§ ***polyacantha*** EGri SChr SPlb XSen
rhodantha see *O. polyacantha*

orange, sour or Seville see *Citrus aurantium*

orange, sweet see *Citrus sinensis*

Orbea (*Apocynaceae*)

cooperi LToo
lugardii LToo
paradoxa LToo
pulchella LToo
semota LToo
speciosa LToo
§ ***variegata*** ♀H1 LToo

Orbexilum (*Papilionaceae*)

pedunculatum SBrt SPhx
var. ***psoralioides*** new

Orchis (*Orchidaceae*)

anthropophora EFEx NLAp
elata see *Dactylorhiza elata*
foliosa see *Dactylorhiza foliosa*
fuchsii see *Dactylorhiza fuchsii*
italica NLAp
laxiflora see *Anacamptis laxiflora*
maculata see *Dactylorhiza maculata*
maderensis see *Dactylorhiza foliosa*
majalis see *Dactylorhiza majalis*
§ ***mascula*** ECho NLAp WHer
militaris NLAp
morio see *Anacamptis morio*
pallens new NLAp
purpurea NLAp
simia NLAp

oregano see *Origanum vulgare*

Oreocharis (*Gesneriaceae*)

aurea new	WCot

Oreomyrrhis (*Apiaceae*)

argentea	GKev NMen SPhx

Oreorchis (*Orchidaceae*)

patens	LWst

Origanum ✿ (*Lamiaceae*)

from Kalamata	SEND
acutidens	XSen
amanum ♀H2-3	CPBP ECho EPot EWes NBir NMen NRHS NSla SBch WAbe WPat
- var. ***album***	ECho NSla WAbe
× ***applii***	ELau
'Barbara Tingey'	CRDP ECho ELan EWes MNrw WCFE
'Bristol Cross'	EPot MHer XSen
'Buckland'	CPrp CRDP ECho ECtt EPot MHer NMen WAbe WSHC
caespitosum	see *O. vulgare* 'Nanum'
§ ***calcaratum***	ECho LLHF WAbe
'Carol's Delight'	MHer
creticum	see *O. vulgare* subsp. *hirtum*
dictamnus	CMea ECho GPoy LLHF MHer SBfd SHDw WJek XSen
'Dingle Fairy'	CWCL EBee ECho ELon EPot EWes MHer MNrw NBir SBch SIde SRot WGwG WMoo XSen
ehrenbergii	XSen
'Emma Stanley'	WAbe
'Frank Tingey'	ECho LLHF
'Gold Splash'	CPbn EPfP SIde WMoo
heracleoticum L.	see *O. vulgare* subsp. *hirtum*
'Hot and Spicy'	CPbn ENfk LBuc MHer WJek XSen
'Jekka's Beauty' new	WJek
'Kent Beauty'	CKno CMea CSpe CWCL EBee ECho ECtt ELan EPfP EShb GCal LAst LRHS LSou MHer MRav MSCN NBir NMen SBfd SPhx SUsu SWvt WAbe WJek WKif WSHC XSen
'Kent Beauty Variegated' (v)	ECho
laevigatum ♀H3	CMHG ECho ELan EPfP EPot GBee MHer NBro NMir NPer SIde SUsu WKif WMoo WPer WSHC XSen
- 'Herrenhausen' ♀H4	Widely available
- 'Hopleys'	CMea CPbn CPrp CSev CTri EBee ECha EHrv ELan EPfP GCal LAst LHop LRHS MBri MHer MRav MWat NBir NCGa NDov SBfd SEND SPer WGwG WHoo WPer WSHC XSen
- 'Purple Charm'	EDAr MNHC SIde
'Lynda Windsor'	CRDP
majorana	CArn CHab CPbn CSev ELan ELau ENfk GPoy MHer MHoo MNHC SIde SWat WJek WPer
I - 'Aureum'	GKev
- Pagoda Bells = 'Lizbell'PBR	LPot SIde SMrm SRot WHoo
'Marchants Seedling'	SMHy
microphyllum	CArn CPbn EDAr NMen
minutiflorum	ECho LLHF
'Norton Gold'	CBre EBee ECha ECtt LRHS MHer NBre NPer SIde
'Nymphenburg'	LSou SIde
onites	CHby CPbn CWan ELau ENfk MHer MHoo MNHC SBfd SIde SPlb WJek WPer
Overseas Farm hybrid	MHer
'Rosenkuppel'	CMea CPbn EBee ECha ECtt EHoe ELan EPot LHop LRHS MAvo MHer MLHP SBch SPer SPhx SPlb WJek WMoo WPer WPnn WTin WWEG
'Rotkugel'	CMHG CPrp ELon WCFE WCru WWEG
rotundifolium ♀H4	CMea EBee ECho ELan LLHF MDKP MHer NBir SBch XSen
- hybrid	MDKP
scabrum	SBch
subsp. ***pulchrum*** 'Newleaze'	
syriacum	CArn
tournefortii	see *O. calcaratum*
virens	CArn
vulgare	CArn CHab CPbn CRWN CSev CWan GJos GMaP GPoy MHer MHoo MMuc MNHC NBro NLan NMir NPri SBfd SEND SGar SIde SPlb SVic WHer WJek WPer WSFF
- from Israel	ELau
- 'Acorn Bank'	CArn CPbn CPrp EBee ELau ENfk EWes MNHC NLar SIde SPoG WGwG WHer WJek
- var. ***album***	ELau
- 'Aureum' ♀H4	Widely available
- 'Aureum Crispum'	CPbn CPrp CWan ECha ELau ENfk GPoy NBid SBch SBfd SIde SWat WJek
- 'Compactum'	CArn CMea CPbn CPrp CSev EBee ECha ELau ENfk GCal GPoy LEdu MHer MNHC NBir NSla SIde SPlb SWat WJek WPer WTin XLum XSen
- 'Country Cream' (v)	CElw CPbn CPrp EBee ECtt ELau ELon ENfk EPfP EShb EWes GMaP LPot LRHS MAsh MHer MHoo MLHP MNHC NBir NGdn SBfd SHDw SPer SPlb SPoG SRot SWat WCFE WWEG
- var. ***formosanum*** B&SWJ 3180	WCru
§ - 'Gold Tip' (v)	CEnt CMea CPbn CSev EBee ELau ENfk MCot MHer MHoo MNHC NWad SBfd SIde SPlb SWat WFar WHer WJek WWEG
- 'Golden Shine'	EHoe EWes MHoo SIde
§ - subsp. ***hirtum***	CArn CHby CPbn GPoy SPlb WJek WPer
- - 'Greek'	CEnt CPrp CWan EGHP ELau ENfk LEdu MHer MNHC SBfd SEND WGwG
§ - 'Nanum'	LHop LRHS WJek
- 'Nyamba'	GPoy
- 'Pink Mist'	MNrw
- 'Polyphant' (v)	CPbn CSev LSou NBir WJek XLum XSen
- 'Thumble's Variety'	CElw CMea CPrp EAEE EBee ECha EHoe EPfP GCal LHop LRHS MAsh MBri MHer MRav NRHS NWad SAga SIde SSvw SWat WCFE WHer WMnd WMoo WWEG XLum XSen
- 'Tomintoul'	GPoy
- 'Variegatum'	see *O. vulgare* 'Gold Tip'
- 'White Charm'	CPbn MHoo NWad SIde
'Z'Attar'	MHer SIde WJek

Orixa (*Rutaceae*)

japonica	CPLG EBee MBri NLar WPGP
- 'Variegata' (v)	LLHF LRHS NLar

Orlaya (*Apiaceae*)

grandiflora	CBre CCon CSam CSpe EBee LBMP SBch SPhx SUsu WCot WHal

Ornithogalum (*Asparagaceae*)

algeriense	ECho
arabicum	CBro CCCN CCon CHid ECho GKev LAma MBri SDeJ WCot
arcuatum	WCot
arianum	ECho
balansae	see *O. oligophyllum*
caudatum	see *O. longibracteatum*
chionophilum	EBee ECho
dubium ♀H1	CBro ECho LRHS WBor WHlf
- hybrids **new**	CGrW
fimbriatum	ECho WCot
- HOA 0152	LWst
lanceolatum	ECho GKev WCot
§ ***longibracteatum***	CHEx EBee ECho SChr WGwG
maculatum	ECho
magnum	CAvo CBro EBee ECho EPot ERCP GBuc GKev MCot MNrw SDeJ SPad SPhx WCot
multifolium 'Loeriesfontein'	ECho
'Namib Gold' **new**	SDeJ
nanum	see *O. sigmoideum*
narbonense	EBee ECho GKev SPhx WCot
nutans ♀H4	CAvo CBro CHid CPrp EBee ECho EPfP EPot GBin GBuc GCal GHim GKev LAma LHop LRHS MCot MNrw NBir NMRc NMen SDeJ SEND SPhx WCot
§ ***oligophyllum***	EBee ECho EPfP EPot MNrw NMen
§ ***orthophyllum***	ECho
ponticum	ECho
pyramidale	CPom EBee ECho EPot MNrw SCnR SPhx WCot
- short	SMHy
pyrenaicum	CAvo ECha WShi
reverchonii	EBee ECho EPot SPhx
saundersiae	EBee ECho
sibthorpii	see *O. sigmoideum*
§ ***sigmoideum***	EBee GKev
sintenisii	EBee ECho
suaveolens 'Saldanha'	ECho
tenuifolium	see *O. orthophyllum*
- subsp. ***aridum***	ECho
thyrsoides ♀H1	CCCN ECho EPfP GBin GHim LAma LRHS SDeJ
ulophyllum	ECho
umbellatum	CAvo CBro CTri ECho EPfP GKev GPoy LAma LHop MBri MCot MNrw NMen SDeJ SEND SMrm SPer SRms WHil WPer WShi

Ornithoglossum (*Colchicaceae*)

viride	CLak

Orontium (*Araceae*)

aquaticum	CWat EHon EWay LPBA MSKA MWts NLar NPer SWat WMAq

Orostachys (*Crassulaceae*)

§ ***spinosa***	EWes GKev NMen SPlb WCot

Orthrosanthus (*Iridaceae*)

chimboracensis	CCon EWld MDKP NLar WPer
- JCA 13743	CPou
laxus	CCon ECou EWTr LLHF MAvo MCot NBir SEND SHom SMad WMoo WWEG
multiflorus	CBro CSpe EPri
polystachyus	CCVN CSpe CTsd CYeo LPla SMrm WSHC

Orychophragmus (*Brassicaceae*)

violaceus	CCCN

Oryzopsis (*Poaceae*)

hymenoides	LDai
- 'Rimrock'	SPhx
lessoniana	see *Anemanthele lessoniana*
miliacea	CKno CSpe EBee ECha EHoe EPPr LDai MMoz NDov NWsh SEND SMHy SUsu WCot WPGP WWEG

Oscularia (*Aizoaceae*)

§ ***deltoides*** ♀H1-2	CCCN CHEx WCot

Osmanthus (*Oleaceae*)

armatus	CAbP CBcs CMac EBee EPfP NLar SGol
§ × ***burkwoodii*** ♀H4	Widely available
§ ***decorus***	CBcs CMac CTri EBee ELan EPfP MGos MRav NLar NWea SBrt SEND SGol SPer WFar
- 'Angustifolius'	NLar
delavayi ♀H4	Widely available
- 'George Gardner'	CMac
- 'Latifolius'	CJun CPLG EBee EPfP LRHS MAsh SLon SPoG
forrestii	see *O. yunnanensis*
× ***fortunei***	CPLG EBee EPfP LLHF LRHS SEND
fragrans	CBcs CDoC CMCN GBin MBri SLon
§ ***heterophyllus***	CBcs CDul CMac ECrN EPfP MGos MRav NLar SGol SPer SRms SSta WFar
§ - all gold	CDoC
- 'Argenteomarginatus'	see *O. heterophyllus* 'Variegatus'
§ - 'Aureomarginatus' (v)	CBcs CDoC CMHG CTsd EHoe ELon GKin NWea SLon SPer WCFE
- 'Aureus' misapplied	see *O. heterophyllus* all gold
- 'Aureus' Rehder	see *O. heterophyllus* 'Aureomarginatus'
§ - 'Goshiki' (v)	Widely available
N - 'Gulftide' ♀H4	CDul EBee EPfP LRHS MAsh MGos NLar SCoo WFar
- 'Kembu' (v)	NLar
- 'Myrtifolius'	CMac NLar
- 'Ōgon'	EPfP
- 'Purple Shaft'	CAbP EBee ELan EPfP LRHS MAsh
- 'Purpureus'	CBar CBcs CDoC CDul CMHG CMac CWib ELon GBin MBri MGos MRav MSwo NHol NLar SCoo SEND SGol SLim SLon SPer SPoG SSpi WCFE
- 'Rotundifolius'	CBcs CMac NLar
- Tricolor	see *O. heterophyllus* 'Goshiki'
§ - 'Variegatus' (v) ♀H4	Widely available
ilicifolius	see *O. heterophyllus*
rigidus	NLar
serrulatus	NLar
suavis	NLar

§ ***yunnanensis***	CMHG EPfP MBlu MBri MRav NLar WFar WPGP WPat

× *Osmarea* see *Osmanthus*

Osmaronia see *Oemleria*

Osmorhiza (*Apiaceae*)

aristata B&SWJ 1607	WCru

Osmunda ✿ (*Osmundaceae*)

sp.	CCCN
asiatica **new**	WCru
cinnamomea ♀H4	CBty CCCN CKel CLAP CWCL EBee EWes GBin GCal ISha LRHS LTen NLar NMyG
claytoniana ♀H4	CLAP EFer GBin GLin ISha LRHS NLar NMyG WCru WPnP XLum
japonica	CHid CLAP GBin ISha NCGa
regalis ♀H4	Widely available
- from southern USA	CLAP
- 'Cristata' ♀H4	CBty CFwr CLAP EBee ELan EPfP GBin LRHS MMoz MRav NBid NLar SWvt WFib
- 'Purpurascens'	CHid CLAP CPrp CWCL EBee ELan ELon EPfP ERod GEdr GQui LRHS MAvo MGos MRav NBid NBir NHol NLar SBfd SGol SHil SWat WFar WFib WMoo WPGP WPnP WWEG XLum
- var. ***spectabilis***	CCCN CLAP ISha LRHS
- 'Undulata'	WFib

Osteospermum (*Asteraceae*)

'African Queen'	see *O.* 'Nairobi Purple'
'Almach' (Springstar Series)	LSou
'Arusha'PBR (Cape Daisy Series)	LSou
'Astra Outback Purple' (Astra Series)	LAst
Banana Symphony = 'Sekiin47' (Symphony Series)	CCCN
barberae misapplied	see *O. jucundum* (Phillips) Norlindh
- 'Compactum' **new**	CBar
'Blue Streak'	CCCN CMac
'Brickell's Hybrid'	see *O.* 'Chris Brickell'
'Buttermilk' ♀H1+3	CCCN ELan WWlt
'Cannington John'	CCCN LSRN
'Cannington Roy'	CBar CBcs CCCN CWCL EBee ECtt ELan EPfP GAbr GBee LSRN SPoG
caulescens misapplied	see *O.* 'White Pim'
§ 'Chris Brickell'	GCal
compact white-flowered	CHEx
ecklonis	CBcs CCCN CDTJ CHll CTri EBee EPfP GMaP NBro NGdn WPer
- var. ***prostratum***	see *O.* 'White Pim'
'Giles Gilbey' (v)	CCCN MBNS
'Gold Sparkler' (v)	SEND
'Gweek Variegated' (v)	CCCN
'Helen Dimond'	LBuc LRHS
'Hopleys' ♀H3-4	MHer SEND
'Iced Gem'	LBuc LRHS
'Irish'	EPot IGor LBMP LSou SMrm
§ ***jucundum*** ♀H3-4	CEnt CTri CWCL ECha EPfP LRHS LSRN MLHP MRav NBir NPer SEND SMrm SPlb SRms WBrk WIce
- 'Blackthorn Seedling' ♀H3-4	CCCN CMea CWGN EBee IVic NGdn SAga
- var. ***compactum***	CHEx CMac EBee ELan ELon EPfP GCal GMaP LBMP LRHS LSRN MBri NPer NPri SMrm SPer SPoG SWvt WAbe WHil WHoo WNew WPat
- 'Killerton Pink'	WPer
- 'Langtrees' ♀H3-4	SMrm
- 'Nanum'	EDAr
'Keia' (Springstar Series)	CCCN
§ 'Lady Leitrim' ♀H3-4	CBar CCCN CWCL CWGN EBee ECha ELan ELon EPfP GCra LBMP LHop LSRN MGos MSpe NPer SAga SPer SPoG SWvt WAbe WFar WHlf WPtf
'Lemon Symphony'PBR (Symphony Series)	CBcs
'Mango Symphony' (Symphony Series)	CWCL LAst
Milk Symphony = 'Seiremi' (Symphony Series)	CCCN CWCL LAst
'Mirach' (Springstar Series)	CWCL
§ 'Nairobi Purple'	CBcs CCCN CHEx CWCL EBee ELan EPfP ESwi MBNS MBri NDov NPri SEND SMrm SWvt WBor WCot WHil WNew
Nasinga Cream = 'Aknam'PBR (Cape Daisy Series)	CCCN
Nasinga Purple = 'Aksullo' (Cape Daisy Series)	EPfP
oppositifolium	CCCN
Orange Symphony = 'Seimora'PBR (Symphony Series)	CBcs CCCN CWCL LAst MBNS
'Pale Face'	see *O.* 'Lady Leitrim'
'Peggyi'	see *O.* 'Nairobi Purple'
'Pink Whirls' ♀H1+3	CCCN
'Port Wine'	see *O.* 'Nairobi Purple'
'Seaside' (Side Series)	EPfP
(Serenity Series) Serenity Lemonade = 'Balserlem' **new**	CWGN
- Serenity Sunset = 'Balserset' **new**	CWGN
'Silver Sparkler' (v) ♀H1+3	CCCN CDTJ ELan MHer
'Snow Pixie'	CSpe CWGN EDAr LHop NPri SWvt WHil
Sonja = 'Sunny Sonja'PBR	EPfP
'Sparkler'	CCCN CHEx
Springstar Series	CBcs
'Stardust'PBR	EPfP LBuc LRHS NPer SCoo SPoG
'Sunny Amanda'PBR	LSou SPoG
'Sunny Bianca'PBR **new**	SPoG
'Sunny Dark Florence'	LSou
'Sunny Dark Martha'	EPfP
'Sunny Davina'	LSou
'Sunny Elena'PBR **new**	LSou WGor
'Sunny Felix'PBR **new**	SPoG
'Sunny Mary'PBR	SPoG WGor
'Sunny Nathalie'	CSpe
'Sunny Sheila'	WGor
'Sunny Victoria'PBR **new**	LSou
* 'Superbum'	CHEx CWCL
I 'Superbum' × 'Lady Leitrim'	CHEx
'Tauranga'	see *O.* 'Whirlygig'
'Tresco Peggy'	see *O.* 'Nairobi Purple'
'Tresco Pink'	CCCN
'Tresco Purple'	see *O.* 'Nairobi Purple'

Voltage Yellow = 'Balvoyelo' new	LSqH
'Weetwood' ♀H3-4	CCCN CWGN EBee ECtt ELan GCal LHop LRHS MHer MLHP SAga SPer SPoG SWvt WAbe WFar
§ 'Whirlygig' ♀H1+3	CCCN
§ 'White Pim' ♀H3-4	CDTJ CHll ELan ELon NPer SDix SEND SMrm SUsu
'Wine Purple'	see *O.* 'Nairobi Purple'
'Wisley Pink'	NEgg
'Zaurak' (Springstar Series)	CCCN CWCL
'Zulu' (Cape Daisy Series)	CCCN

Ostrowskia (*Campanulaceae*)

magnifica	LWst

Ostrya (*Betulaceae*)

carpinifolia	CBcs CCVT CDul CLnd CMCN CTho CWib EBee EMil EPfP EWTr MBlu MMuc NLar NWea SEND SGol SWvt
japonica	CDul CMCN NLar
virginiana	EPfP

Otatea (*Poaceae*)

aztecorum	ERod

Othonna (*Asteraceae*)

sp.	XLum
cheirifolia	CCCN CMea CSpe EHoe ELan EWes NBir SAga SEND WBrk WPer WSHC XLum XSen

Othonnopsis see *Othonna*

Ourisia (*Plantaginaceae*)

× ***bitternensis*** 'Cliftonville Canary'	WAbe
- 'Cliftonville Crimson'	WAbe
- 'Cliftonville Damask'	WAbe
- 'Cliftonville Ling'	WAbe
- 'Cliftonville Old Rose'	WAbe
- 'Cliftonville Pink'	WAbe
- 'Cliftonville Roset'	CPBP WAbe
caespitosa var. ***gracilis***	EPot
coccinea	EBee GAbr GCra GEdr GKev NBir NMen
crosbyi	GEdr
'Loch Ewe'	CPLG GAbr
macrophylla	LLHF
microphylla	WAbe
- f. ***alba***	WAbe
- 'Hollowcliffe'	WAbe
modesta	GBin
polyantha 'Cliftonville Scarlet'	WAbe
'Snowflake' ♀H4	GAbr GEdr NLBP NMen WAbe

Oxalis (*Oxalidaceae*)

sp.	NMen
from Mount Stewart	WMoo
acetosella	CRWN MHer NLBP NMir WHer WShi
- var. ***subpurpurascens***	IFro WCot
adenophylla ♀H4	CElw CPLG CTri ECho EPfP EPot GAbr GKev GMaP LAma LHop LRHS MAsh NEgg NHol NLar NMen SDeJ SPoG SRms WHoo WPer
adenophylla × ***enneaphylla***	CPBP
'Anne Christie'	CPBP
anomala	ECho WCot
arenaria F&W 10584	WCot
§ ***articulata***	LRHS NPer SEND WCot XLum
- 'Alba'	WCot XLum
§ - subsp. ***rubra***	SDeJ
'Black Velvet' (Xalis Series)	SPoG
bowiei	ECho EPot WPtf
- 'Amarantha'	ECho
brasiliensis	ECho EPot
'Dark Eye'	EPot
deppei	see *O. tetraphylla*
§ ***depressa***	CTri ECho EPot EWes GEdr LLHF NBir NMen NRHS NRya NSla SDeJ SRms
ecklóniana	ECho
- var. ***sonderi***	EBee ECho WCot
enneaphylla ♀H4	CElw ECho ELon EPot GAbr LHop LLHF LRHS NMen NRHS NRya SBch
- 'Alba'	ECho GEdr GHim NMen NRHS NSla
- subsp. ***ibari***	ECho EPot GEdr GHim NMen NSla
- 'Minutifolia'	LLHF NMen NRya NSla
- 'Rosea'	ECho EPot GKev LLHF NLar NRya NSla SBch WIce
- 'Sheffield Swan'	ECho GEdr LLHF NMen NRHS NSla WPtf
falcatula	WCot
'Fanny'	EBee ECho
flava	CGrW ECho WCot
floribunda misapplied	see *O. articulata*
fourcadei	ECho WCot
glabra	CPBP
griffithii double-flowered (d)	LWst
- 'Pink Charm' new	GEdr
- 'Snowflake' new	GEdr
'Gwen McBride'	CPBP NMen
hedysaroides misapplied	see *O. spiralis subsp. vulcanicola*
hedysaroides Kunth	CCCN GCal
'Hemswell Knight'	CPBP NMen SBch
hirta	CPBP EPot SBch
- 'Gothenburg'	CPBP EBee ECho NMen SBch
imbricata	CPBP ECho LLHF
inops	see *O. depressa*
'Ione Hecker' ♀H4	CMea ECho ELon EPot GEdr GKev ITim NHar NLar NMRc NMen NRya WCot WIce
'Irish Mist' (v)	EBee ECho WHil
* ***karroica***	ECho NMen WCot
§ ***laciniata***	ECho NHar NMen
- hybrid	NHar
lactea double-flowered	see *O. magellanica* 'Nelson'
lasiandra	CCCN ECho
loricata	ECho NMen
magellanica	CRow CSpe CTri ECho EDAr LBee LRHS NChi SPlb WFar WMoo
- 'Flore Pleno'	see *O. magellanica* 'Nelson'
§ - 'Nelson' (d)	CSpe EBee ECho EWes GCal LBee MMuc NBir NPer WMoo WPtf
mallobolba 'Citrino'	WAbe
massoniana	CSpe ECho EPot NMen WAbe WCot WHil
'Matthew Forrest'	NMen
§ ***megalorrhiza***	CHEx SChr
§ ***melanosticta***	ECho EPot LLHF SDeJ WCot WIce
monophylla	ECho
namaquana	ECho
obtriangulata	ECho

obtusa	ECho NMen SCnR WIce
- apricot-flowered	WCot
oregana	CHid CMac CRow EBee ECho ELon SPhx WCot WCru WPGP WSHC
- 'Klamath Ruby'	WSHC
- f. ***smalliana***	EWes GEdr LHop WCru
palmifrons	ECho EPot LLHF
perdicaria	ECho EPot EWes LHop LRHS NRHS SBch WAbe WIce
pes-caprae	CGrW
polyphylla	EBee ECho
- var. ***pentaphylla***	CPBP EPot
§ ***purpurea***	ECho WAbe
- 'Ken Aslet'	see *O. melanosticta*
regnellii	see *O. triangularis* subsp. *papilionacea*
'Ridgeway Jewel' **new**	CPBP
rosea misapplied	see *O. articulata* subsp. *rubra*
semiloba	ECho GCal NCGa
Slack Top hybrids	NSla
speciosa	see *O. purpurea*
§ ***spiralis***	CCCN LSou SDix
subsp. ***vulcanicola***	
- - 'Burgundy'	NPri
squamata	LLHF
squamoso-radicosa	see *O. laciniata*
stipularis	ECho LLHF
succulenta Barnéoud	see *O. megalorrhiza*
succulenta ambig.	CHll
'Sunny'	ECho
'Sunset Velvet'	EBee WCot
§ ***tetraphylla***	CPLG EBee ECho LAma NPer
* - ***alba***	ECho
- 'Iron Cross'	CCVN CHEx CHid EBee ECho EPot GAbr LAma NBir NPnk SDeJ
triangularis	CCCN CHEx CPLG ECho EOHP EPot LAma MAvo NBir NPer
- 'Birgit'	EBee ECho SDeJ
- Burgundy Wine = 'JR Oxburwi' (Xalis Series)	CWGN EUJe NPer
- 'Cupido'	EBee ECho WPer
- 'Mijke'	EBee ECho NMRc
§ - subsp. ***papilionacea*** ♀H1	EBee ECho LAma
- - 'Atropurpurea'	CSpe EBee LHop SDeJ
* - - ***rosea***	WCot
- subsp. ***triangularis***	CHid EBee ECho EUJe LDai
tuberosa	GPoy LEdu
'Ute'	GEdr NMen NSla
valdiviensis	MDKP
versicolor ♀H1	ECho EPot NBir NMen SCnR SDeJ WAbe WCot WHil
I 'Waverley Hybrid'	NMen

Oxycoccus see *Vaccinium*

Oxydendrum ✿ (*Ericaceae*)

arboreum	CAbP CBcs CDoC CMCN EBee EPfP IDee IVic LRHS MMuc NLar SCoo SPer SSpi SSta WPGP
- 'Chameleon'	SSta

Oxypetalum (*Apocynaceae*)

caeruleum	see *Tweedia caerulea*

Oxytropis (*Papilionaceae*)

campestris	EBee
coerulea **new**	CPBP
hailarensis var. ***chankaensis***	CPBP
lagopus **new**	CPBP
purpurea	LLHF

Oziroë (*Hyacinthaceae*)

§ ***biflora***	LLHF

Ozothamnus (*Asteraceae*)

antennaria	WSHC
§ ***coralloides*** ♀H2-3	ECou IRar WAbe
§ 'County Park Silver'	EWes GEdr GKev ITim MDKP WPat
diosmifolius **new**	EBee
§ ***hookeri***	CBcs CDoC LRHS MBrN MRav WJek WPat
§ ***ledifolius*** ♀H4	CBcs CDoC EBee ELan EPfP MBri NBir SLon SPer WAbe WPat
§ ***rosmarinifolius***	CBcs CDoC CTsd EBee ELan EPfP LRHS MAsh MSwo NChi SBfd SPer WPnn
- 'Kiandra'	ECou
- 'Silver Jubilee' ♀H3	CBcs CDoC CEnt CSBt EBee ECrN ELan EPfP GCal LRHS MGos MNHC MRav MSwo NSti SLim SLon SPer SPlb SRkn
scutellifolius	ECou
§ ***selago***	ECou WCot WPat WThu
§ - var. ***tumidus***	ITim WPat WThu
'Sussex Silver'	CDoC WPnn
'Threave Seedling'	CDoC EBee ELan IVic MAsh SPer WGrn

P

Pachyphragma (*Brassicaceae*)

§ ***macrophyllum***	CPom CSev EBee ECGP ECha EHrv ELan ELon EWTr GCal IBlr MNFA NLar NMRc NSti WCot WCru WPGP WPtf WSHC

Pachyphytum (*Crassulaceae*)

bracteosum	EUJe
glutinicaule RE 477 **new**	CDoC
werdermannii **new**	CDoC

Pachypodium (*Apocynaceae*)

geayi ♀H1	EAmu
lamerei ♀H1	EAmu
succulentum	LToo

Pachysandra (*Buxaceae*)

axillaris	CLAP EBee EPPr GCal SKHP WCot
- BWJ 8032	WCru
- 'Crûg's Cover'	EWld WCru
procumbens	CLAP EBee EHrv LHop NLar SKHP WCot WCru
- 'Angola' (v)	WCot
stylosa	CHEx MRav NLar SMad
terminalis	Widely available
- 'Green Carpet' ♀H4	Widely available
- 'Green Sheen'	ECha EPPr EPfP ESwi LRHS SMad WFar
- 'Variegata' (v) ♀H4	Widely available

Pachystachys (*Acanthaceae*)

lutea ♀H1	CCCN

Pachystegia (*Asteraceae*)

§ ***insignis***	CPne LRHS
- Daizea = 'Hardec'	EBee

Pachystima see *Paxistima*

× *Pachyveria* (*Crassulaceae*)

'Mrs Coombes' **new**	CDoC

Paederota (*Plantaginaceae*)

§ ***bonarota***	WAbe
lutea	WAbe

Paeonia ✿ (*Paeoniaceae*)

'Age of Gold' (S)	GBin WCAu
'Age of Victoria'	GBin
albiflora	see *P. lactiflora*
'America'	GBin WCAu
'Angelet'	WCAu
'Anna Marie' (S)	GBin
anomala	CCon GEdr GKev LWst MPhe NLar WCot
- var. ***intermedia***	GCal
'Argosy'	WCAu
arietina	see *P. mascula* subsp. *arietina*
'Athena'	GBin WCAu
'Avant Garde'	WCAu
banatica	see *P. officinalis* subsp. *banatica*
'Banquet' (S)	GBin
§ 'Bartzella' (d)	CKel ELan GBin NLar WCAu WCot
beresowskii	EBee LWst
'Black Monarch'	WCAu
'Black Pirate' (S)	CKel
'Blaze'	GMaP LRHS NCGa NSti WCAu
'Border Charm'	GBin
'Boreas' (S)	GBin
'Bravura'	GBin
'Bridal Icing'	GBin WCAu
'Bride's Dream'	GBin
'Brocaded Gown' (S)	GBin
broteroi	SKHP WCot
brownii	EPot
'Buckeye Belle' (d)	CKel EBee ELan EPfP EWTr GBin IBoy LRHS LSRN MBri MHom NCGa SHar SMrm SPer SPoG SWat WCAu WCot WWEG
'Burma Joy' **new**	WCAu
'Burma Midnight'	GBin
'Burma Ruby'	GBin WCAu
californica	CCon
'Callie's Memory'	CKel GBin WCAu WHlf
cambessedesii ♀H2-3	CBro CSpe EBee EPot GEdr GKev LRHS NBir NMen NRHS SSpi SUsu WAbe WCot WKif
- dwarf	EPot
'Canary Brilliant' PBR	GBin WCAu
'Carina'	GBin
'Carol'	WCAu
caucasica	see *P. mascula* subsp. *mascula*
'Chalice'	GBin
× ***chamaeleon***	SKHP
'Cheddar Royal'	GBin
'Cherry Ruffles'	GBin
'Chinese Dragon' (S)	CKel
'Claire de Lune'	CKel EBee GBin SHar WCAu
'Command Performance'	GBin
'Copper Kettle'	CKel GBin WCAu
'Cora Louise'	CKel GBin WCAu
'Coral Charm'	CKel GBin MMHG NCGa SDeJ SKHP WCAu WCot
'Coral Fay'	GBin WCAu
'Coral 'n' Gold'	WCAu
'Coral Sunset'	CKel GBin SDeJ SMrm WCAu
'Coral Supreme'	GBin
corallina	see *P. mascula* subsp. *mascula*
coriacea	EBee
- var. ***atlantica***	CBro
Crimson Red	see *P. suffruticosa* 'Hu Hong'
'Cytherea'	MHom
'Dancing Butterflies'	see *P. lactiflora* 'Zi Yu Nu'
'Daredevil' (S)	GBin
daurica	see *P. mascula* subsp. *triternata*
- subsp. ***coriifolia*** RCB UA 12 **new**	WCot
decomposita	MPhe
decora	see *P. peregrina*
delavayi (S) ♀H4	CKel ELan EPfP GAbr GBin GCal GKev GMaP IFro LHop LRHS MAsh MGos NBir NEgg NLar SDix SEND SKHP SLPl SPer SPoG SRms SSpi WCAu WCot WFar
- BWJ 7775	WCru
- SDR 4327	GKev
- from China (S)	MPhe
- var. ***angustiloba*** f. ***alba*** (S)	CPLG
§ - - f. ***angustiloba*** (S)	GBin GKev SSpi WCot
- - - 'Coffee Cream' (S)	CKel
§ - - f. ***trollioides*** (S)	CPLG
§ - var. ***delavayi*** f. ***lutea*** (S)	CCVT CDul CSpe EBee EPfP IBoy IFro LEdu LRHS MAsh MGos NBir NEgg SGar SLon SPhx SPoG SRms SUsu WFar WHar WHoo WTin
- var. ***lutea***	see *P. delavayi* var. *delavayi* f. *lutea*
- 'Mrs Colville' (S)	GBin GCal
- 'Mrs Sarson' (S)	CHid ELan EWes NCGa SWat
- Potaninii Group	see *P. delavayi* var. *angustiloba* f. *angustiloba*
- 'Tapestry'	CSpe
- Trollioides Group	see *P. delavayi* var. *angustiloba* f. *trollioides*
delavayi × ***suffruticosa***	LSRN
'Diana Parks'	GBin
Drizzling Rain Cloud	see *P. suffruticosa* 'Shiguregumo'
'Early Bird'	GBin LRHS
'Early Glow'	GBin WCAu
'Early Scout'	GBin MHom WCAu WCot
'Echt Klasse'	GBin
'Eden's Perfume'	EBee GBin LRHS MBri NLar SPoG
'Elizabeth Foster'	GBin WCAu
'Ellen Cowley'	GBin WCAu
emodi	CKel GKev SHar
'Ezra Pound' (S)	GBin WCAu
'F. Koppius'	CKel
'Fairy Princess'	MBri WAul WCAu
'Firelight'	GBin WCAu
'First Arrival'	CKel GBin WCAu
'First Dutch Yellow'	see *P.* 'Garden Treasure'
'Flame'	CKel EBee EPfP EWTr MNrw NLar NSti SDeJ WAul WCAu
Fragrant Jade	see *P.* 'Xiang Yu'
'Friendship' **new**	WCAu
§ Gansu Group (S)	CKel MPhe
- 'Bai Bi Fen Xia' (S)	MPhe
- 'Bai Bi Lan Xia' (S)	MPhe
- 'Bing Shan Xue Lian' (S)	MPhe
- 'Bing Xin Zi' (S) **new**	MPhe

– 'Cheng Xin' (S)	MPhe
– 'Fen He' (S)	MPhe
– 'Fen Jin Yu Zhu' (S)	MPhe
– 'Fen Mian Tao Sai' (S) **new**	MPhe
– 'Feng Xian' (S)	MPhe
– 'Gu Cheng Xiang Hui' (S) **new**	MPhe
– 'He Hua Deng' (S)	MPhe
– 'He Ping Lian' (S)	MPhe
– 'Hei Feng Die' (S)	MPhe
– 'Hei Tian E' (S)	MPhe
– 'Hei Xuan Feng' (S)	MPhe
– 'Hei Yuan Shuai' (S) **new**	MPhe
– 'Hong Lian' (S)	MPhe
– 'Hong Xia Ying Xue' (S)	MPhe
– 'Huang He' (S)	MPhe
– 'Hui He' (S)	MPhe
– 'Jiao Rong' (S)	MPhe
– 'Jin Cheng Ming Yue' (S)	MPhe
– 'Ju Hua Fen' (S)	MPhe
– 'Lan Hai Yiu Bo' (S)	MPhe
– 'Lan He' (S)	MPhe
– 'Lan Tian Meng' (S)	MPhe
– 'Lan Yu San Cai' (S) **new**	MPhe
– 'Li Xiang' (S)	MPhe
– 'Lian Chun' (S)	MPhe
– 'Long Yuan Hong' (S)	MPhe
– 'Mo Hai Yin Bo' (S)	MPhe
– 'Mo Hai Yin Zhou' (S)	MPhe
– 'Ri Yue Tong Hui' (S) **new**	MPhe
– 'Shu Sheng Peng Mo' (S)	MPhe
– 'Tao Hua Nu' (S)	MPhe
– 'Tie Mian Wu Si' (S)	MPhe
– 'Xiang Lu Zi Yan' (S)	MPhe
– 'Xiong Mao' (S)	MPhe
– 'Xue Hai Bing Xin' (S)	MPhe
– 'Xue Lian' (S)	MPhe
– 'Xue Yuan Yu Hui' (S) **new**	MPhe
– 'Ye Guang Bei' (S)	MPhe
– 'Yu Ban Xiu Qiu' (S)	MPhe
– 'Yu Guan Lan Dai' (S)	MPhe
– 'Yu Lu Lian Dan' (S)	MPhe
– 'Yu Rong Dan Xin' (S)	MPhe
– 'Yuan Yang Pu' (S) **new**	MPhe
– 'Zi Die Ying Feng' (S)	MPhe
– 'Zi Hai Yin Bo' (S)	MPhe
– 'Zong Ban Bai' (S)	MPhe
Gansu Mudan Group	see *P.* Gansu Group
§ 'Garden Treasure'	GBin SDeJ WCAu
'Gauguin' (S)	WCAu
'Gold Standard'	GBin WAul
'Golden Bowl'	CKel GBin
'Golden Dream'	see *P.* 'Bartzella'
'Golden Isles'	CKel
'Golden Thunder'	CKel
'Golden Wings'	GBin
'Grace Root'	GBin
'Hephestos' (S)	GBin
'Heritage'	GBin
'Hillary'	CKel GBin WCAu
'Ho-gioku'	GBin
'Honor'	WCAu
'Horizon'	GBin WCAu
humilis	see *P. officinalis* subsp. *microcarpa*
'Illini Belle'	GBin
'Illini Warrior'	WAul WCAu
'In the Mood'	GBin
intermedia	WCot
'Isani Gidui'	see *P. lactiflora* 'Isami-jishi'
japonica misapplied	see *P. lactiflora*
japonica ambig.	GEdr
japonica (Makino) Miyabe & Takeda B&SWJ 10985	WCru
'Jay Cee'	GBin
jishanensis	MPhe
'Joseph Rock'	see *P. rockii*
'Joyce Ellen'	GBin
'Jubilation'	GBin
'Julia Rose'	CKel GBin WCAu
'Kathryn Ann'	GBin
kavachensis	EBee GCal LWst
'Kinkaku'	see *P.* × *lemoinei* 'Souvenir de Maxime Cornu'
'Kinko'	see *P.* × *lemoinei* 'Alice Harding'
'Kinshi'	see *P.* × *lemoinei* 'Chromatella'
'Kintei'	see *P.* × *lemoinei* 'L'Espérance'
'Koikagura'	CKel
'Kokamon'	CKel
§ ***lactiflora***	CArn GCal GKev LWst MBel MPhe MRav WCAu WCot
– 'Abalone Pearl'	GBin
– 'Adolphe Rousseau'	CBcs CKel EBee NLar WCAu
* – 'Afterglow'	CKel
– 'Agida'	GBin LRHS MRav
– 'Agnes Mary Kelway'	CKel
– ***alba***	MBel WBor
– 'Albâtre'	CKel
– 'Albert Crousse'	CBcs CKel GBin MRav NBir SWat WCAu
– 'Alexander Fleming'	EBee MAvo MBNS NBir SMrm SWat WCAu
– 'Algae Adamson'	CKel
– 'Alice Harding'	CKel GBin WCAu
– 'Amibilis'	WCAu
– 'Angel Cheeks'	CKel EBee GBin MBri WCAu
– 'Anna Pavlova'	CKel
– 'Antwerpen'	LRHS
– 'Arabian Prince'	CKel
– 'Arcadia' **new**	WCAu
– 'Argentine'	CKel EBee
– 'Armistice' (d) **new**	WCAu
– 'Asa Gray'	CKel
– 'Auguste Dessert'	CKel GBin WCAu WCFE WCot
§ – 'Augustin d'Hour'	CKel WCAu
– 'Aureole'	CKel MRav
– 'Avalanche'	CKel EPfP GBin NLar SHar SMrm
– 'Ballerina'	CKel MRav
– 'Barbara'	CKel NCGa WCAu
– 'Baroness Schröder'	EBee ELan GBin
– 'Barrington Belle'	EBee EPfP GBin WCAu
– 'Barrymore'	CKel
– 'Beacon'	CKel
– 'Beatrice Kelway'	CKel
– 'Belle Center'	GBin WCAu
– 'Best Man'	EBee MBri NGdn WCAu
– 'Bethcar'	CKel
– 'Better Times'	WCAu
– 'Bev'	GBin
– 'Big Ben'	GBin NLar SHar STes
– 'Blaze of Beauty'	CKel
– 'Bluebird'	CKel
– 'Blush Queen'	CKel WCAu
– 'Border Gem'	LRHS MRav
– 'Bouchela'	EBee NLar
– 'Boule de Neige'	EWll GBin LHop NLar
– 'Bouquet Perfect' **new**	WCAu
– 'Bower of Roses'	CKel
– 'Bowl of Beauty' $\heartsuit^{H4}$	Widely available

– 'Bowl of Cream'	CKel EBee GBin SWat SWvt WCAu
– 'Break o' Day'	WCAu
– 'Bridal Gown'	WCAu
– 'Bridal Veil'	CKel
– 'Bridesmaid'	CKel
– 'Bright Knight'	WCAu
– 'British Beauty'	CKel
– 'Bunker Hill'	CKel LRHS SBfd SWvt WCAu
– 'Bu-te'	GBin
– 'Butter Bowl'	GBin WCAu
– 'Canarie'	CKel MBri
– 'Candeur'	CKel
– 'Cang Long'	CKel
– 'Captivation'	CKel
– 'Carnival'	CKel
– 'Caroline Allain'	CKel
– 'Carrara'	GBin
– 'Cascade'	CKel
– 'Catherine Fontijn'	CKel GBin WCAu
– 'Charles Burgess'	MSCN SPoG WCAu
– 'Charles' White'	CKel GBin LRHS NLar SDeJ WCAu
– 'Charm'	GBin
– 'Cheddar Charm'	GBin WAul WCAu
– 'Cheddar Cheese'	WCot
– 'Cheddar Supreme'	GBin
– 'Cherry Hill'	WCAu
– 'Chestine Gowdy'	CKel
– 'Chief Wapello'	GBin
– 'Chippewa'	EBee GBin
– 'Chun Xiao'	CKel
– 'Circus Circus'	GBin
– 'Claire Dubois'	CKel GBin WCAu
– 'Cora Stubbs'	GBin MBri
– 'Cornelia Shaylor'	CKel WCAu
– 'Corsair' **new**	WCAu
– 'Couronne d'Or'	GBin
– 'Cream Puff' **new**	WCAu
– 'Crimson Glory'	CKel
– 'Crinkles Linens'	GBin
– 'Dawn Crest'	CKel
– 'Dayspring'	CKel
– 'Daystar'	MRav
– 'Dayton' **new**	WCAu
– 'Decorative'	CKel
– 'Dei Xian Jin' **new**	WCAu
– 'Delachei'	CKel
– 'Dinner Plate'	GBin MAsh MBri SPer WCAu
– 'Do Tell'	EBee GBin MBri NCGa NGdn NLar SPer WCAu
– 'Docteur H. Barnsby'	CKel
– 'Doctor Alexander Fleming'	CKel GBin LRHS MDev SDeJ SHar SRot STes SWat SWvt WHoo
– 'Dominion'	CKel
– 'Don Juan'	CKel
– 'Doreen'	CKel GBin NCGa SHar WCAu
– 'Doris Cooper'	WCAu
– 'Dorothy Welsh'	CKel
– 'Dragon'	CKel
– 'Dresden'	WCAu
– 'Duchesse de Nemours' ♀H4	Widely available
– 'Eden's Temptation'	SPer
– 'Edouard Doriat'	WCAu
– 'Edulis Superba'	CKel EBee ELan EWTr GBin LRHS LSRN MBNS MRav NLar NPer
– 'Elaine'	MRav
– 'Eliza Lundy' (d) **new**	WCAu
– 'Elizabeth Stone'	CKel
– 'Ella Christine Kelway'	CKel
– 'Elsa Sass'	EBee GBin SHar SMrm WCAu
– 'Emma Klehm'	WCAu
– 'Emperor of India'	CKel
– 'Enchantment'	CKel
– 'English Princess'	CKel
– 'Ethereal'	CKel
– 'Evening Glow'	CKel
– 'Evening World'	CKel
– 'Fairy's Petticoat'	GBin WCAu
– 'Fashion Show'	CKel
– 'Félix Crousse' ♀H4	CBcs CKel CMac CTri ELan GBin GMaP IBoy LHop LRHS LSRN MBNS MDev MRav NBir NRHS SDeJ SPer SWat WCAu WFar
– 'Felix Supreme'	GBin
– 'Festiva Maxima' ♀H4	CKel CSBt CTri EBee ELan EPfP GBin LRHS MBri NBir NEgg NLar NRHS SBfd SMrm SPer SRkn SRot SWat SWvt WCAu WFar WHoo WWEG
– 'Festiva Supreme'	GBin
– 'Fiesta Posey' **new**	WCAu
– 'Fiona' (d) **new**	WCAu
– 'Firebelle' **new**	WCAu
– 'Florence Ellis'	WCAu
– 'Florence Nicholls'	CKel GBin
– 'Foxtrot' **new**	WCAu
– 'France'	CKel
– 'Fuji-no-mine'	GBin
– 'Garden Lace'	WCAu
– 'Gardenia'	CKel EBee EPfP GBin NLar SDeJ WCAu
– 'Gay Paree'	CKel EWTr GBin NCGa NLar SHar SPer WCAu
– 'Gayborder June'	CKel
– 'Général Joffre'	MRav
– 'Général MacMahon'	see *P. lactiflora* 'Augustin d'Hour'
– 'General Wolfe'	CKel
– 'Germaine Bigot'	CKel GBin MRav WCAu
– 'Gilbert Barthelot'	CKel WCAu
– 'Gladys McArthur'	GBin
– 'Gleam of Light'	CKel MBri
– 'Globe of Light'	GBin
– 'Glory Hallelujah'	WCAu
– 'Glowing Candles'	WCAu
– 'Go-Daigo'	GBin
– 'Golden Fleece'	WCAu
– 'Great Sport'	MRav
– 'Green Lotus'	WAul
– 'Guidon'	WCAu
– 'Gypsy Girl'	CKel
– 'Hakodate'	CKel
– 'Happy Days' **new**	WCAu
– 'Heartbeat'	CKel
– 'Helen Hayes'	WCAu
– 'Henri Potin'	GBin
– 'Henry Bockstoce'	CKel GBin
– 'Her Grace'	CKel
– 'Herbert Oliver'	CKel
– 'Hermione'	CKel GBin WCAu
– 'Highlight' **new**	WCAu
– 'Hit Parade'	WCAu
– 'Honey Gold'	CKel ELan GBin WAul WCAu
– 'Hyperion'	CKel
– 'Immaculée'	CKel EBee EPfP GBin LRHS LSRN MBri NCGa SPoG
– 'Inspecteur Lavergne'	CKel EBee GBin IBoy LRHS MBri MSCN NGdn SPer WAul WCAu WCot WWEG

Cultivar	Suppliers
– 'Instituteur Doriat'	CKel GBin WCAu
§ – 'Isami-jishi'	GBin
– 'Jacorma'	CCon GBin
– 'Jacques Doriat'	CKel
– 'James Kelway'	CKel GBin
– 'Jan van Leeuwen'	CKel EBee EPfP GBin GMaP MBri SPer WCAu WCot
– 'Jappensha-ikhu'	GBin
– 'Jeanne d'Arc'	CKel
– 'Jin Chi Yu'	CKel
– 'John Howard Wigell'	WCAu
– 'Joy of Life'	CKel
– 'Judith Eileen'	GBin
– 'June Morning'	CKel
– 'June Rose'	WCAu
– 'Kakoden'	GBin
– 'Kansas'	CKel EBee ELan EPfP GBin IBoy LRHS MBri NBir NGdn NLar SPoG WCAu WFar
– 'Karen Gray'	GBin WCAu
– 'Karl Rosenfield'	CKel CSBt EBee EPfP GBBs GBin IBoy LAst LRHS LSRN MNrw MRav MSCN NEgg NLar SBfd SHar SPer SPoG SRms SRot SWvt WCAu WFar WHil WHoo WWEG XSen
– 'Kathleen Mavoureen'	CKel
– 'Kelway's Betty'	CKel
– 'Kelway's Brilliant'	CKel
– 'Kelway's Circe'	CKel
– 'Kelway's Daystar'	CKel
– 'Kelway's Exquisite'	CKel
– 'Kelway's Glorious'	CKel EBee EPfP GBin MBNS MRav NLar WCAu WGwG
– 'Kelway's Lovely'	CKel GBin
– 'Kelway's Lovely Lady'	CKel
– 'Kelway's Majestic'	CKel MRav
– 'Kelway's Scented Rose'	CKel
– 'Kelway's Supreme'	CKel SWat
– 'King of England'	GBin
– 'Knighthood'	CKel
– 'Königswinter'	GBin
§ – 'Koningin Wilhelmina'	EBee GBin MNrw
– 'Krekler's Red' **new**	WCAu
– 'Krinkled White'	CKel EBee EPfP EWTr GBBs GBin GMaP LRHS MHom MRav NCGa NLar NSti SBfd SDeJ SHar SKHP SUsu WAul WCAu WCot WWEG
– 'La Belle Hélène'	CKel
– 'La Lorraine'	CKel
– 'Lady Alexandra Duff' $\mathbb{Y}^{H4}$	CKel EPfP GBin LRHS MRav NBir NGdn SMrm SWvt WCAu WWEG
– 'Lady Ley'	CKel
– 'Lady Mayoress'	CKel
– 'Lady Orchid'	EPfP NGdn WCAu
– 'Lancaster Imp'	GBin WAul WCAu
– 'Langport Triumph'	CKel
– 'Largo'	WCAu
– 'Laura Dessert' $\mathbb{Y}^{H4}$	CKel EBee GBin NCGa WCAu
– 'Laura Shaylor' **new**	WCAu
– 'Lavender Whisper' **new**	WCAu
– 'Le Jour'	WCAu
– 'L'Éclatante'	CKel GBin LRHS WGwG
– 'Legion of Honor'	CKel
– 'Lemon Ice'	CKel
– 'Lemon Queen'	GBin
– 'L'Étincelante'	GBin
– 'Lian Dai' **new**	WCAu
– 'Liebchen' **new**	WCAu
– 'Lights Out'	GBin
– 'Lillian Wild'	GBin
– 'Little Medicineman'	EBee GBin
– 'Lois Kelsey'	GBin WCAu
– 'Lollipop' (d) **new**	WCAu
– 'Longfellow'	CKel GBin
– 'Lord Kitchener'	CKel GBin LRHS
– 'Lorna Doone'	CKel
– 'Lotus Queen'	GBin NLar WCAu
– 'Louis van Houtte'	CKel NEgg SBfd
– 'Love's Touch' (d) **new**	WCAu
– 'Lyric'	CKel WCAu
– 'Madame Calot'	WCAu
– 'Madame de Verneville'	WCAu
– 'Madame Ducel'	CKel WCAu
– 'Madame Emile Debatène'	CKel EBee MAsh MBNS NOrc WCAu WFar
– 'Madame Gaudichau'	WCot
– 'Madame Jules Dessert'	EBee WCAu
– 'Madelon'	CKel WCAu
– 'Maestro'	GBin
– 'Magenta Moon'	WCAu
– 'Magic Orb'	CKel
– 'Mandarin's Coat'	GBin
– 'Margaret Clark' **new**	WCAu
– 'Margaret Truman'	CKel WCAu
– 'Marguérite Gerard'	WCAu
– 'Marie Crousse'	WCAu
– 'Marie Lemoine'	CKel GBin LRHS WCAu WCot
– 'Marietta Sisson'	WCAu
– 'Mary Brand'	WCAu
– 'Masterpiece'	CKel
– 'May Treat'	WCAu
– 'Merry Mayshine'	GBin WCAu
– 'Midnight Sun'	MBri WCAu
– 'Minnie Shaylor'	WCAu
– 'Mischief'	MRav WCAu
– 'Miss America'	EBee EPfP GBin MBri WCAu WCot
– 'Miss Eckhart'	CKel EBee GBin WCAu
– 'Miss Mary'	EBee EWTr
– 'Missie's Blush'	GBin
– 'Mister Ed'	GBin WCAu
– 'Mistral'	CKel
– 'Monsieur Jules Elie' $\mathbb{Y}^{H4}$	CKel EBee EPfP GBin IBoy LRHS MBri MHom NGdn NLar SBfd SPer WAul WCAu WHoo WWEG
– 'Monsieur Martin Cahuzac'	CKel GBin LRHS WCAu
– 'Moon River'	EPfP GBin MSCN SMrm WCAu WHoo
– 'Moonstone' **new**	CKel EBee
– 'Mother's Choice'	CKel GBin LSRN NGdn NLar WCAu WCot
– 'Mr G.F. Hemerik'	CKel GBin WCAu WCot
– 'Mr Thim'	WCAu
– 'Mrs Edward Harding'	CKel WCAu
– 'Mrs Franklin D. Roosevelt'	GBin WCAu
– 'Mrs J.V. Edlund'	GBin WCAu
– 'Murillo' **new**	EBee
– 'My Pal Rudy'	GBin WCAu
– 'My Petite Cherie' **new**	WCAu
– 'Myrtle Gentry'	CKel GBin WCAu
– 'Nancy Nicholls'	WCAu
– 'Nancy Nora'	MBri NGdn SPer WCAu
– 'Neomy Demay'	CKel GBin
– 'Neon'	NCGa
– 'Nice Gal'	GBin WCAu
– 'Nick Shaylor'	CKel GBin WCAu
– 'Nippon Beauty'	EBee GBin LRHS MMHG NCGa NLar SBfd SHar SKHP WCot WFar
– 'Nippon Gold' **new**	WCAu

	- 'Noemie Demay'	LRHS
	- 'Norma Volz'	GBin WCAu
	- 'Nymphe'	CKel MRav NLar WAul WCAu
	- 'Orlando Roberts'	GBin
	- 'Ornament'	CKel
	- 'Orpen'	CKel
	- 'Paola'	CKel
	- 'Paul Bunyan'	GBin
	- 'Paul M. Wild'	CKel WCAu
*	- 'Pecher'	CKel LRHS NLar NPer
	- 'Peter Brand'	CKel EBee GBin NLar
	- 'Petite Porcelain' **new**	WCAu
	- 'Philippe Rivoire'	CKel WCAu
	- 'Philomèle'	WCAu
	- 'Pico'	WCAu
	- 'Picotee' **new**	WCAu
	- 'Pillow Talk'	CKel EBee GBin MBri SPer WCAu
	- 'Pink Cameo'	NLar WCAu WCot
	- 'Pink Dawn'	EPfP MBri SPer WCAu
	- 'Pink Delight'	WCAu
	- 'Pink Giant'	WCAu
	- 'Pink Parfait'	GBin LRHS SPer WCAu
	- 'Pink Princess'	GBin WCAu
	- 'Plainsman'	GBin
	- 'Polar King'	WCAu
	- 'President Franklin D. Roosevelt'	LRHS SWat
	- 'President Lincoln' **new**	WCAu
	- 'Président Poincaré'	CKel MRav SWat WCAu
	- 'President Taft'	see *P. lactiflora* 'Reine Hortense'
	- 'Primevère'	CKel EBee EPfP GBin LAst NBir NLar SHar SPer SPoG WCAu WWEG
	- 'Princess Margaret'	WCAu
	- 'Queen of Sheba'	WCAu
	- 'Queen Victoria'	GBin
	- 'Queen Wilhelmina'	see *P. lactiflora* 'Koningin Wilhelmina'
	- 'Raoul Dessert'	WCAu
	- 'Raspberry Sundae'	CKel ELan GBin MRav NLar SPer STes WCAu WCot
	- 'Ray Payton'	GBin
	- 'Red Dwarf'	CKel
	- 'Red Emperor'	WCAu
	- 'Red Sarah Bernhardt'	ELan SMrm WWEG
§	- 'Reine Hortense'	CKel GBin LRHS MRav SHar
	- 'Renato'	EBee GBin STes WCAu
	- 'Richard Carvel'	WCAu
	- 'Ruth Cobb'	WCAu
	- 'Sante Fe'	CKel EPfP WCAu
	- 'Sarah Bernhardt' ♀H4	Widely available
	- 'Scarlet O'Hara'	CMac GBin NGdn SPer SPoG WCAu
	- 'Schaffe'	GBin
	- 'Sea Shell'	EBee EPfP GBin GMaP LRHS WCAu
	- 'Serene Pastel' **new**	WCAu
	- 'Shawnee Chief'	GBin
	- 'Shen Tao Hua'	CKel
	- 'Shimmering Velvet'	CKel
	- 'Shirley Temple' (d)	CKel EBee ELan EPfP GBin LRHS LTen MBNS MBel MBri MRav NBir NGdn NRHS SBfd SDeJ SPoG WCAu WWEG
	- 'Silver Flare'	CKel
	- 'Sir Ernest Shackleton' (d) **new**	MRav
	- 'Soft Salmon Joy'	GBin
	- 'Solange'	CKel GBin LRHS NLar WCAu
	- 'Sorbet'	CKel EBee EPfP LHop NBir NCGa NLar NPer SBfd STes WBor WWEG
	- 'Starlight'	CKel EBee GBin LRHS SHar WCAu WCot
	- 'Strephon'	CKel
	- 'Super Gal' **new**	WCAu
	- 'Sweet Melody'	GBin WCAu
	- 'Sweet Sixteen'	WCAu
	- 'Sword Dance'	CKel EWll GBBs GBin SDeJ
	- 'Tamate-boko'	WCAu
	- 'The Mighty Mo'	GBin
	- 'The Nymph'	LRHS NBir WWEG
	- 'Thérèse'	WCAu
	- 'Tom Eckhardt'	CKel GBin SPer WCAu
	- 'Top Brass'	CKel GBin MBri MRav NLar WCAu WWEG
	- 'Topeka Garnet'	GBin
	- 'Toro-no-maki'	WCAu
	- 'Translucient'	CKel
	- 'Victoire de la Marne'	CKel
	- 'Violet Dawson'	GBin
	- 'Vogue'	CKel GBin MRav NCGa SWvt WCAu
	- 'W.F. Turner'	CKel
	- 'Walter Faxon'	GBin
	- 'West Elkton'	GBin
	- 'Westerner'	GBin
	- 'White Grace'	WCAu
	- 'White Rose of Sharon'	CKel
	- 'White Sands'	GBin
	- 'White Wings'	CBcs CKel CMac CTri EBee ELan EPfP GBin LRHS MAvo NLar STes SWat SWvt WAul WCAu WCot WWEG
	- 'Whitleyi Major' ♀H4	MPhe WCot
	- 'Wilbur Wright'	GBin
	- 'Wladyslawa'	GBin LRHS NLar SHar
§	- 'Zi Yu Nu'	EBee LSRN
	- 'Zuzu'	GBin WAul WCAu
	'Lafayette Escadrille' (S)	WCAu
	'Late Windflower'	CKel GCra MHom
	'Leda' (S)	GBin
	'Legion of Honour'	GBin WCAu
	× ***lemoinei*** (S)	WHal
§	- 'Alice Harding' (S)	CKel
§	- 'Chromatella' (S)	CKel LAma
	- 'High Noon' (S)	CKel MPhe SKHP SWat WCAu
§	- 'L'Espérance' (S)	LAma
	- 'Marchioness' (S)	CKel GBin WCAu
§	- 'Souvenir de Maxime Cornu' (S)	CKel EPfP LAma MWat SKHP SPer
	'Lemon Dream' PBR	CKel
	'Lilith' (S)	GBin
	lithophila	see *P. tenuifolia* subsp. *lithophila*
	'Little Joe'	WCAu
	'Little Red Gem'	GBin
	lobata 'Fire King'	see *P. peregrina*
	'Lovebirds'	GBin WCAu
	ludlowii (S) ♀H4	Widely available
	lutea	see *P. delavayi* var. *delavayi* f. *lutea*
	macrophylla	MPhe
	'Magenta Gem'	WAul
	'Mai Fleuri'	WCAu
	mairei	CCon CPLG GGGa MPhe
	'Many Happy Returns'	GBin
	mascula	CBro EPfP GKev LLHF NBir SHar WWEG
	- from Sicily	MPhe
§	- subsp. ***arietina***	EBee GKev MWat
	- - 'Northern Glory'	LRHS
	- subsp. ***hellenica*** from Sicily	MPhe

§	- subsp. ***mascula***	GKev
	- - from Georgia	MPhe
§	- subsp. ***russoi***	LWst WCot WThu
	- - from Sardinia	MPhe
	- - 'Picotee'	GBin
§	- subsp. ***triternata***	CKel LRHS LWst NLar WCot
	'Mikuhino-akebono'	CKel
	mlokosewitschii ♀H4	CBcs CBro CKel CPLG ECha ECho EPPr GEdr GKev GMaP LHop LRHS MCot MHom MNrw MPhe MWat NBir NMen NRHS SDix SUsu SWvt WAbe WCAu WCot WHoo WKif WSHC WTin
	- hybrids	GKev
	mollis	see *P. officinalis* subsp. *villosa*
	'Moonrise'	WCAu
	'Morning Lilac'	WCAu
	'Murad of Hershey Bar' (S)	GBin WCAu
	'Normie' (d) **new**	WCAu
	'Nosegay' **new**	WCAu
	'Nova'	GBin
	obovata ♀H4	CCon CPne LRHS MPhe
	- var. ***alba*** ♀H4	CPLG EBee GBin GEdr GKev LLHF WAbe WCot WThu
	- 'Grandiflora'	LRHS
	- var. ***willmottiae***	CPLG MPhe
	officinalis	CArn GCra GKev
	- WM 9821 from Slovenia	MPhe
	- 'Alba Plena'	CKel CPou LRHS MRav NEgg SWvt WCAu WWEG
	- 'Anemoniflora Rosea' ♀H4	LRHS MHom SWvt
§	- subsp. ***banatica***	LWst MHom MPhe WCAu WCot
	- 'China Rose'	GBin
	- subsp. ***humilis***	see *P. officinalis* subsp. *microcarpa*
	- 'Lize van Veen'	GBin
§	- subsp. ***microcarpa***	WCAu
	- 'Mutabilis Plena'	IBlr WCAu
	- 'Rosea Plena' ♀H4	CKel CMac EBee ECtt EPfP GMaP LAst LRHS NEgg SPer SWat SWvt WCAu WFar WWEG
	- 'Rubra Plena' ♀H4	CKel CPou CTri EBee ECtt EPfP GAbr GBin GCra GMaP LAst LHop LRHS MBri MHom MRav NEgg NGdn NLar SEND SPer SRms STes SWat SWvt WCAu WCot WFar
§	- subsp. ***villosa***	CKel ELan GKev LRHS WFar
	'Old Rose Dandy'	GBin
	'Oriental Gold'	CKel
	ostii (S)	CKel CPLG EPfP MPhe SKHP
§	- 'Feng Dan Bai' (S)	CKel GBin MPhe
	'Pageant'	GBin
	'Paladin'	GBin
	papaveracea	see *P. suffruticosa*
	paradoxa	see *P. officinalis* subsp. *microcarpa*
	'Pastel Splendor'	CKel GBin WCAu
	'Paula Fay'	CKel EBee EPfP GBin MBri MRav SDeJ STes WCAu WCot
§	***peregrina***	CBro CKel ECho GEdr MHom MPhe SKHP SSpi WAbe WCAu
	- 'Fire King'	CKel GBin NLar
§	- 'Otto Froebel' ♀H4	CKel GBin GCra NLar
	- 'Sunshine'	see *P. peregrina* 'Otto Froebel'
	'Pink Hawaiian Coral'	CKel GBin NLar
	'Postilion'	GBin
	potaninii	see *P. delavayi* var. *angustiloba* f. *angustiloba*
	'Prairie Charm'	GBin WCAu
	'Prairie Moon'	EBee GBin NLar WCAu
	'Prince Charming' **new**	WCAu
	qiui	MPhe
	'Raspberry Charm' **new**	WCAu
	'Red Charm'	CKel GBin IBoy MBri NCGa WCAu
	'Red Magic'	SMrm WFar
	'Red Red Rose'	GBin WCAu
	'Renown' (S)	CKel
	'Requiem'	GBin WCAu
§	***rockii*** (S)	CBcs CKel EPfP GBin MPhe
	- from Tianshui, Gansu	MPhe
	- from Wenshian, Gansu	MPhe
	- hybrid	see *P.* Gansu Group
	- subsp. ***linyanshanii*** (S)	MPhe
	'Roman Gold'	CKel GBin
	romanica	see *P. peregrina*
	'Rose Flame' (S) **new**	WCAu
	'Rosedale' **new**	WCAu
	'Roselette'	GBin
	'Roselette's Child'	GBin
	'Roy Pehrson's Best Yellow'	GBin
	ruprechtiana	GKev
	russoi	see *P. mascula* subsp. *russoi*
	'Scarlet Heaven'	CKel GBin WCAu
	'Serenade' **new**	WCAu
	'Shimano-fuji'	CKel
	'Shining Light'	GBin NLar
	'Show Girl'	GBin WCAu
	'Showanohokori'	CKel
	'Silver Dawn'	GBin
	sinensis	see *P. lactiflora*
	'Soshi'	GBin
	'Spring Carnival' (S)	GBin
	'Squirt'	GBin
	steveniana	EBee MHom MPhe WCot
§	***suffruticosa*** (S)	CWib ELan GKev MGos SSpi
	- 'Akashigata' (S)	CKel
	- 'Alice Palmer' (S)	CKel
I	- 'Better than Snow Tower' (S)	LRHS
	- Bird of Rimpo	see *P. suffruticosa* 'Rimpo'
	- Black Dragon Brocade	see *P. suffruticosa* 'Kokuryū-nishiki'
	- Brocade of the Naniwa	see *P. suffruticosa* 'Naniwa-nishiki'
	- 'Burgundy Wine' (S)	GBin
	- 'Cardinal Vaughan' (S)	CKel
	- Charming Age	see *P. suffruticosa* 'Howki'
	- 'Da Hu Hong' (S)	LBuc SPoG
	- 'Dou Lu' (S)	CKel
	- Double Cherry	see *P. suffruticosa* 'Yae-zakura'
	- 'Duchess of Kent' (S)	CKel
	- 'Duchess of Marlborough' (S)	CKel
	- Eternal Camellias	see *P. suffruticosa* 'Yachiyo-tsubaki'
	- Flight of Cranes	see *P. suffruticosa* 'Renkaku'
	- Floral Rivalry	see *P. suffruticosa* 'Hana-kisoi'
	- 'Frost on Peach Blossom' (S)	LRHS
*	- 'Glory of Huish' (S)	CKel
	- 'Godaishu' (S)	CKel GBin LAma SKHP SPer
	- 'Guardian of the Monastry' (S)	GBin
	- 'Hai Huang' (S)	WKif
§	- 'Hakuo-jisi' (S/d)	CKel EPfP WCAu
§	- 'Hana-daijin' (S)	LAma
§	- 'Hana-kisoi' (S)	CKel GBin LAma WCAu
	- 'Haru-no-akebono' (S)	CKel
§	- 'Higurashi' (S)	EPfP
§	- 'Howki' (S)	WCAu
§	- 'Hu Hong' (S)	LTen
	- 'Hu's Family Red' (S)	LRHS
	- Jewel in the Lotus	see *P. suffruticosa* 'Tama-fuyo'

	- Jewelled Screen	see *P. suffruticosa* 'Tama-sudare'
	- 'Jing Ge' (S)	WKif
	- 'Jitsugetsu-nishiki' (S)	CKel
	- 'Joseph Rock'	see *P. rockii*
	- Kamada Brocade	see *P. suffruticosa* 'Kamada-nishiki'
§	- 'Kamada-nishiki' (S)	CKel
§	- 'Kaow' (S)	CKel
	- King of Flowers	see *P. suffruticosa* 'Kaow'
	- King of White Lions	see *P. suffruticosa* 'Hakuo-jisi'
	- 'Kinkaku'	see *P.* × *lemoinei* 'Souvenir de Maxime Cornu'
	- 'Kinshi'	see *P.* × *lemoinei* 'Alice Harding'
	- 'Kokucho' (S)	CKel
§	- 'Kokuryū-nishiki' (S)	CKel LAma LRHS SKHP SPer
	- 'Koshi-no-yuki' (S)	CKel
	- 'Lan Bao Shi' (S)	WKif
	- Magnificent Flower	see *P. suffruticosa* 'Hana-daijin'
	- 'Montrose' (S)	CKel
*	- 'Mrs Shirley Fry' (S)	CKel
	- 'Mrs William Kelway' (S)	CKel
§	- 'Naniwa-nishiki' (S)	CKel
	- 'Nigata Akashigata' (S)	CKel
	- Pride of Taisho	see *P. suffruticosa* 'Taisho-no-hokori'
	- 'Princess Chiffon' (S)	GBin
	- 'Reine Elisabeth' (S)	CKel
§	- 'Renkaku' (S)	CKel SKHP SPer
§	- 'Rimpo' (S)	CKel EPfP GBin LAma MWat SKHP SPer
	- subsp. ***rockii***	see *P. rockii*
	- 'Rou Fu Rong' (S)	LTen
§	- 'Shiguregumo' (S)	CKel
	- 'Shimadaigin' (S)	CKel
	- 'Shimane-chōjuraku' (S)	CKel GBin
	- 'Shimane-hakugan' (S)	CKel
	- 'Shimane-seidai' (S)	CKel
	- 'Shimanishiki' (S)	CKel MWat SKHP SPer
	- 'Shin Shima Kagayaki' (S)	CKel
	- 'Shintoyen' (S)	CKel
	- 'Sumi-no-ichi' (S)	CKel
	- 'Superb' (S)	CKel
§	- 'Taisho-no-hokori' (S)	CKel
§	- 'Taiyo' (S)	CKel EPfP LAma SKHP SPer
§	- 'Tama-fuyo' (S)	CKel
§	- 'Tama-sudare' (S)	CKel GBin
	- 'Tao Hua Fei Xue' (S) new	LBuc
	- The Sun	see *P. suffruticosa* 'Taiyo'
	- Twilight	see *P. suffruticosa* 'Higurashi'
	- 'Wu Long Peng Sheng' (S)	CKel LBuc SPoG
	- 'Xue Ta' (S)	CKel LBuc LRHS SPoG
§	- 'Yachiyo-tsubaki' (S)	CKel LAma SKHP
§	- 'Yae-zakura' (S)	LAma WCAu
	- 'Yin Hong Qiao Dui' (S)	CKel
	- 'Ying Ri Hong'	WKif
	- 'Yoshinogawa' (S)	CKel EPfP
	- 'Yu Ban Bai' (S)	WKif
	- 'Zhao Fen' (S)	LBuc LRHS NPer SPoG
	'Sugar 'n' Spice' new	WCAu
	'Sunshine'	see *P. peregrina* 'Otto Froebel'
*	***szowitsianum***	EPot
	'Taiheko'	CKel
	'Tango' new	WCAu
	'Ten' i'	CKel
	tenuifolia	EWll GBin GCal GKev LRHS MHom NLar NMen NSla SKHP SMad WCAu WCot
	- RCB UA 11	WCot
§	- subsp. ***lithophila***	MHom MPhe
	- 'Plena'	EPot GEdr
	tomentosa	MPhe
	'Tria' (S)	GBin
	'Vanilla Twist'	WAul
	veitchii	CKel EPfP GCal GEdr GKev GMaP MHom NLar NMen SSpi WCAu WCot
	- from China	MPhe
	- pale-flowered	GCal
	- var. ***woodwardii***	CCon ECho EPot GBin GCra GKev SSpi WCAu WCot WThu
	'Vesuvian'	CKel
	'Viking Full Moon'	GBin WCAu
	'White Emperor'	WCAu
	White Phoenix	see *P. ostii* 'Feng Dan Bai'
	wittmanniana	CKel GBin GCal WCot
§	'Xiang Yu' (S)	LBuc LRHS
	'Yellow Crown'	CKel GBin SHar WCAu
	'Yellow Dream'	GBin

Paesia (*Dennstaedtiaceae*)

	scaberula	CLAP NBir SSpi WFib

Paliurus (*Rhamnaceae*)

	spina-christi	CArn CBcs NLar SLon

Pallenis (*Asteraceae*)

§	***maritima***	CCCN

Panax (*Araliaceae*)

	ginseng	EBee GPoy
	japonicus	WCru
	- BWJ 7932	WCru

Pancratium (*Amaryllidaceae*)

	maritimum	CArn CSpe ECho GKev SDeJ

Pandanus (*Pandanaceae*)

	utilis	EAmu

Pandorea (*Bignoniaceae*)

	jasminoides	CCCN CDoC CHll CRHN CTri CTsd EBak ECou EShb MOWG
§	- 'Charisma' (v)	CBcs CCCN CHll EBee EPfP EShb LSou MOWG SEND SLim SPer SPoG
	- 'Lady Di'	CCCN MOWG
	- 'Rosea'	CCCN
	- 'Rosea Superba' ♀H1	CBcs CHEx CRHN LHop SEND SLim
	- 'Variegata'	see *P. jasminoides* 'Charisma'
	lindleyana	see *Clytostoma calystegioides*
	pandorana	CHll CRHN EBee SLim SMrm
	- 'Golden Showers'	CBcs CCCN CDoC CRHN MOWG MRav SEND SLim

Panicum (*Poaceae*)

	amarum 'Dewey Blue'	CKno EPPr MAvo SMHy SUsu
	bulbosum	CKno EHoe EPPr
	clandestinum	CSpe EBee EHoe EPPr EWes MWhi SMea WWEG XLum
§	'Fibre Optics'	CSpe
	miliaceum	EBee NRHS
	- 'Purple Majesty'	CWib SPhx
	- 'Violaceum'	SPhx
	virgatum	CRWN CTri MAsh SMrm WMnd WPer WWEG XLum
	- 'Blue Tower'	CKno ELon MAvo SApp SMea
	- 'Cardinal' new	EBee
	- 'Cloud Nine'	CKno EBee EPPr MAvo MSnd NOak SApp SMHy SUsu WHal

- 'Dallas Blues' CKno CPrp EBee ECha EHoe EPPr EWes LAst LEdu LHop LRHS MAvo MRav MWhi NOak NWsh SApp SHDw SMHy SMrm SPer WFar WMoo WPGP XLum

- 'Farbende Auslese' MAvo WWEG

- 'Hänse Herms' CKno EBee EHoe EPPr MAvo MWhi SApp SMea WFar WTin WWEG

- 'Heavy Metal' Widely available

- 'Heiliger Hain' CKno CSpe EBee EPPr LHop MAvo SUsu WCot

I - 'Kupferhirse' CKno EBee EPPr

- 'Northwind' CKno EBee EPPr LRHS MAvo SApp SHDw SMHy SMad SPhx WFar

- 'Pathfinder' SApp

- 'Prairie Sky' CKno CPrp CWCL EAEE EBee EHoe ELon EPPr LEdu LRHS MAsh MAvo MBri MNFA NBro NLar NRHS SDix SMHy SMea SUsu WAul WFar WMoo WPGP WTin

- 'Purple Haze' EBee EPPr

- 'Red Cloud' CKno SMHy

- 'Rehbraun' EBee EHoe EPPr EPfP LEdu LHop LRHS LTen NMRc NOak NRHS NWsh SApp SGol WCAu WFar WTin WWEG

- 'Rotstrahlbusch' CKno CPrp CWib EBee EHoe EPPr GMaP MAvo MWhi NOak NOrc NWsh SPer SWal WCot WMnd WMoo WPGP WWEG

- 'Rubrum' ECha EHoe ELan EPPr MAvo MWat SApp SDix WMoo

- 'Shenandoah' Widely available

- 'Squaw' CKno CMac CPrp CWCL CWib EAEE EBee EHoe EPPr EPfP IPot LRHS MMuc MNFA NOak NOrc NRHS NWsh SApp SBea SEND SMad SWal WCot WFar WMoo WTin WWEG XLum

- 'Strictum' EBee EHoe EPPr EWes GQue LEdu LPla LRHS SApp SMHy SPhx SUsu WMoo

- 'Warrior' CKno CPrp CWCL EAEE EBee EHoe EHrv EPPr LHop LRHS MAvo MBri MCot MRav MWhi NBid NCGa NRHS NWsh SApp SUsu SWal WAul WFar WPGP WTin WWEG XLum

- 'Wood's Variegated' (v) WCot

Papaver ✿ (*Papaveraceae*)

aculeatum CTca

alboroseum LLHF LRHS

'Alpha Centauri' (SPS) LLHF SWat

alpinum CSpe GJos GKev LRHS MAsh NGdn NRHS NSla SPet SWat WFar

- 'Flore Pleno' (d) NBir

amurense SWat

anomalum album CSpe

atlanticum LDai NBro NGdn SPlb

- 'Flore Pleno' (d) CSpe IFro NBro NGdn WCot WFar

'Aurora' (SPS) SWat

'Beyond Red' (SPS) SWat

bracteatum see *P. orientale* var. *bracteatum*

'Bright Star' (SPS) SWat

burseri SRot

'Cathay' (SPS) SWat

commutatum Υ^{H4} CSpe ELan SPhx SWat

- 'Ladybird' Υ^{H4} **new** NPri SUsu

corona-sancti-stephani SWat

'Danish Flag' NNor

degenii CPBP

'Eccentric Silk' (SPS) SWat

fauriei GKev WAbe

§ 'Fire Ball' (d) ECha GCal LHop NBid NBro SWat WMnd WWEG

'Harlequin' (SPS) ELon

'Heartbeat'[PBR] (SPS) EBee IPot LRHS MAvo MBel SMrm SWat WFar

heldreichii see *P. pilosum* subsp. *spicatum*

hybridum 'Flore Pleno' (d) NSti SWat

'Jacinth' (SPS) CDes EBee LLHF SWat

kerneri **new** WAbe

lateritium CHid CPou SRms

- 'Nanum Flore Pleno' see *P.* 'Fire Ball'

'Lauffeuer' ELon SWat

'Matador'[PBR] Υ^{H4} CWCL EBee NNor WCot WFar

'Medallion' (SPS) CDes EBee EPri LLHF LRHS SWat WHoo

microcarpum LLHF

§ ***miyabeanum*** CSpe ECho ELan LRHS MAsh MMuc SRot WFar

- ***tatewakii*** see *P. miyabeanum*

'Moondance' **new** NPri

nanum 'Flore Pleno' see *P.* 'Fire Ball'

§ ***nudicaule*** LPot

- 'Aurora Borealis' CSpe

- Champagne Bubbles Group NNor SPet SWat WFar

- - 'Champagne Bubbles Orange' NPri

- - 'Champagne Bubbles Pink' NPri

- - 'Champagne Bubbles White' NPri

- - 'Champagne Bubbles Yellow' NPri

- var. ***croceum*** 'Flamenco' NNor

- Garden Gnome Group see *P. nudicaule* Gartenzwerg Group

§ - Gartenzwerg Group Υ^{H4} CSpe EPfP LRHS MBri NGdn SBfd SPet SPlb SPoG SRot WFar WGor WWEG

- 'Pacino' CMea EWll LRHS NLar SPet WFar

- 'Solar Fire Orange' Υ^{H4} MBel

- 'Summer Breeze' SPet

- 'Summer Breeze Orange' Υ^{H4} NPri

- 'Summer Breeze Yellow' NPri

- Wonderland Series NNor SPet

- - 'Wonderland Orange' NPri

- - 'Wonderland Pink Shades' NPri

- - 'Wonderland White' NPri

orientale CBcs EPfP SRms SWat WFar

- 'Abu Hassan' SWat

- 'Aglaja' Υ^{H4} CElw CKno CWCL EBee ECtt ELon LRHS NEgg NGdn NSti SMad SUsu SWat WCot WHoo

- 'Aladin' SWat

- 'Ali Baba' GCra SWat

- 'Alison' SWat

- 'Allegro' CSBt EBee ELon EPfP GMaP LAst LRHS MBNS MBri MRav NGdn NRHS SBfd SPer SPlb SVic SWat SWvt WWEG XLum

- 'Allegro Vivace' LRHS

	- 'Arwide'	SWat
	- 'Aslahan'	ECha ELon MRav SWat
	- 'Atrosanguineum'	SWat
	- 'Avebury Crimson'	MWat SWat
	- 'Baby Kiss'PBR	EBee ECtt NLar SWat WFar
	- 'Ballkleid'	ECha ELon SWat
	- 'Beauty Queen'	EBee ECha LRHS MRav NGdn SDix SWat
	- 'Bergermeister Rot'	SWat
	- 'Big Jim'	SWat
	- 'Black and White' ♀H4	CMac EBee ECha ELan EPfP GMaP LRHS MNrw MRav NEgg NPri SApp SPer SWat WCot
	- 'Blackberry Queen'	ECtt SWat
	- 'Blickfang'	SWat
	- 'Bolero'	ECtt NLar
	- 'Bonfire'	LRHS LSou MBri
	- 'Bonfire Red'	EBee LRHS SWat
§	- var. ***bracteatum*** ♀H4	NBir SWat
	- 'Brilliant'	EBee GJos LRHS LTen MWat NBre NGdn SWat WFar WMoo XLum
	- 'Brooklyn' (New York Series)	ECtt LRHS LSRN MAvo SWat
	- 'Burning Heart'	CPar ECtt LRHS MSCN NLar SBfd SPer SPoG SWat
	- 'Carmen'PBR	ECtt ELon GAbr MAsh MNrw MSCN WCot
*	- 'Carneum'	LRHS NBre NLar WWEG
	- 'Carnival'	EBee NBre SWat
	- 'Casino'	MAsh
	- 'Castagnette'	EBee
	- 'Catherina'	NBre SWat
	- 'Cedar Hill'	EBee ECtt ELon EWes GCal MRav MWat NBre NGdn SMrm SWat
	- 'Cedric Morris' ♀H4	ECha ELan GMaP MRav SWat WCot WHoo WMnd
	- 'Central Park' (New York Series)	SWat WFar
I	- 'Charming' pink-flowered	CMac EBee ECtt MWat NCGa NGdn SPhx SWat
	- 'Charming' red-flowered	LRHS
	- 'China Boy'	SWat WHrl
	- 'Clochard'	CElw ECtt ELon SUsu SWat WCot
	- 'Coral Reef'	ECtt ELon MHer MLHP SWat WMoo
	- 'Corrina'	SWat
	- 'Curlilocks'	CPar EBee ECtt ELan ELon EPfP IBoy LRHS MRav MWat NGdn SBfd SPer SRms SWat SWvt WCot WWEG
	- 'Derwisch'	ELon SWat
*	- 'Diana'	SWat
	- 'Double Pleasure'	EBee ECtt MSCN NBre SWat WHrl
	- double red shades (d)	NGdn
	- 'Doubloon' (d)	EBee NBre NGdn SWat
	- 'Dwarf Allegro'	WMnd
	- 'Dwarf Allegro Vivace'	LRHS
	- 'Earl Grey'	SWat
	- 'Effendi' ♀H4	CWCL ECtt SUsu SWat WCot
	- 'Elam Pink'	SWat WCot
	- 'Erste Zuneigung'	ECha ELon MAvo SWat
	- 'Eskimo Pie'	SWat
	- 'Eyecatcher'	EBee ELon
	- 'Fancy Feathers'PBR	EBee ECtt NGdn NLar SWat WHil
	- 'Fatima'	SWat
	- 'Feuerriese'	SWat
	- 'Feuerzwerg'	SWat
	- 'Fiesta'	ELon NBre SWat
	- 'Firefly'PBR	SWat
	- 'Flamenco'	CBcs ELon SWat
	- 'Flamingo'	ELon MBri MSCN SWat
*	- 'Flore Pleno' (d)	NGdn
	- 'Forncett Summer'	CPar ECtt ELon MRav NBre NGdn NLar SMrs SPer SWat WCAu WCot WHoo WHrl WTin WWEG
	- 'Frosty' (v)	SHar
	- 'Fruit Punch'	GJos SWal
	- 'Garden Glory'	EBee ECtt ELon GCra LRHS LSRN MArl NBre SWat WCAu
	- 'Glowing Embers'	ECtt SWat
	- 'Glowing Rose'	ELon MDKP NBre SWat
	- Goliath Group	ECha ELan ELon LHop LRHS MRav NBro SDix SRms SWat WFar WMnd WWEG
	- - 'Beauty of Livermere'	Widely available
§	- - 'Beauty of Livermere' clonal	ECtt WCot
	- 'Graue Witwe'	ELon SApp SWat WHrl
	- 'Guardsman'	see *P. orientale* (Goliath Group) 'Beauty of Livermere' clonal
	- 'Halima'	SWat
	- 'Harlem' (New York Series)	CElw CSpe EBee IPot MSCN NLar NPnk SMrm SWat
	- 'Harvest Moon' (d)	EBee ECtt LRHS NPer NPri SWat WHal WWEG
	- 'Heidi'	SWat
	- 'Hewitt's Old Rose'	NBre
	- 'Hula Hula'	ECha ELon SWat
	- 'Indian Chief'	EBee IPot MBel MDev NLar NPer NPri SRot WFar WWEG
	- 'Inferno'PBR	ECtt
	- 'John III' ♀H4	SPhx SWat
	- 'John Metcalf'	EBee ECtt LHop LRHS NBre NSti SWat
	- 'Juliane'	ECha ECtt ELon NSti SWat WTin
	- 'Karine' ♀H4	CElw CSam EBee ECha ELan EPPr EPfP GMaP LHop LRHS MNrw NLar SPoG SWat WCAu WHoo WTin
	- 'Khedive' (d) ♀H4	CWCL EBee SWat
	- 'King George'	SWat
	- 'King Kong'	CPar ECtt NLar SWat WCot
	- 'Kleine Tänzerin'	CSam ECtt EWTr LRHS LSou MAsh MBel MHer MMuc MRav MSCN NBre NSti SEND SWat WCAu WCot
	- 'Kollebloem'	EBee SWat
	- 'Lady Frederick Moore'	LHop LRHS NBre SWat WWEG
	- 'Lady Roscoe'	NBre SWat
	- 'Ladybird'	EPfP LRHS NBre
	- 'Laffeuer'	SUsu
	- 'Lambada'	SWat
	- 'Lauren's Lilac'	EAEE EBee ECtt ELon LSRN NBre NCGa SMrs SWat
	- 'Leuchtfeuer' ♀H4	CDes ECha LRHS NBre SWat
	- 'Lighthouse' ♀H4	SWat
	- 'Lilac Girl'	EBee ECha ECtt ELon GMaP MAvo MBel NLar SApp SWat WHrl
	- 'Little Candyfloss'PBR	MAsh SWat
	- 'Louvre' (Parisienne Series)	EBee ECtt ELon SEND SPoG SWat WCot WFar
	- 'Maiden's Blush'	ECtt NBre NSti SWat
	- 'Mandarin'PBR	LRHS MAsh WCot
	- 'Manhattan' (New York Series)	CElw CSam CSpe EBee ECtt ELon EPfP EWes MNrw NEgg NGdn NPnk NSti SPer SPoG SWat WFar WHoo
	- 'Marcus Perry'	EBee ECtt EWes GMaP LRHS NEgg NGdn SBfd SPoG SWat WFar
	- 'Marlene'	IPot MBri MSCN SWat
	- 'Mary Finnan'	CTca SWat
	- 'Master Richard'	SWat

	– 'May Queen' (d)	ECtt EWes IBlr MRav NBre NBro NLar NSti SWat WCot WHrl WPnn
	– 'May Sadler'	NBre NLar SWat
	– 'Midnight'	ELon NBre SWat
	– 'Miss Piggy'PBR	EBee ECtt IKil LLHF MBri SMrm SWat WCot WFar
	– 'Mrs H.G. Stobart'	SWat
	– 'Mrs Marrow's Plum'	see *P. orientale* 'Patty's Plum'
	– 'Mrs Perry'	CMac CMea CSBt EBee ECtt ELan GMaP IFro LRHS MBel MWat NGdn NPer SPer SRms SWat WBrk WCAu WFar WMnd WTin
	– 'Nanum Flore Pleno'	see *P.* 'Fire Ball'
	– 'Noema'	SWat
	– 'Orange Glow'	EBee MBel SWat WMoo
	– 'Orangeade Maison'	SWat
	– 'Oriana'	SWat
	– 'Oriental'	SWat
	– 'Pagode'	NCGa
	– 'Pale Face'	SWat
	– 'Papillon'PBR	EBee WFar
	– 'Paradiso'	MBri MSCN NCGa
§	– 'Patty's Plum'	Widely available
	– 'Perry's White'	CBcs CSBt EBee ECtt ELan ELon EPfP GMaP LAst LHop LRHS MCot MMuc MRav SBfd SMrm SPer SPoG SWat SWvt WCAu WFar WMnd WTin WWEG
	– 'Peter Pan'	ELon NBre SWat
	– 'Petticoat'	ECtt ELan NBre SWat
	– 'Picotée'	EBee ECtt ELan EShb LRHS LSou MBri MRav NEgg NLar NRHS SPer SPoG SRot SWat SWvt WFar WHil WMoo WWEG
	– 'Pink Lassie'	NBre SWat
	– 'Pink Panda'	SWat
	– 'Pink Pearl'PBR	NCGa SWat
	– 'Pink Ruffles'PBR	CBcs EBee ECtt SPoG SWat WCot WFar
	– 'Pinnacle'	EBee ELon SWat WFar
	– 'Pizzicato'	CEnt CWib LBMP LRHS NNor NPer SBfd SGar SPet SWal SWat WFar WMoo WWEG
	– 'Place Pigalle' (Parisienne Series)	EBee ECtt ELon EPfP LHop LSou MAsh MBel NEgg NPri SMad SPer SPoG SWat WCot
	– 'Polka'	SWat
	– 'Prince of Orange'	SWat WWEG
	– Princess Victoria Louise	see *P. orientale* 'Prinzessin Victoria Louise'
	– 'Prinz Eugen'	ELon GMaP LRHS NBre SWat
§	– 'Prinzessin Victoria Louise'	EBee EPfP GMaP LAst LRHS NGdn NLar NNor NRHS SGar SMrm SWat WBrk WFar WWEG XLum
	– 'Prospero'	NBre SWat
	– 'Queen Alexandra'	LBMP NGdn NLar WWEG XLum
	– 'Raspberry Queen'	CCon CDes CMac CMea EBee ECtt ELan ELon EWTr GMaP IBoy MArl MBel MRav MWat NLar NSti SApp SBfd SMrm SWat WCot WFar WHal WHoo WMnd WTin WWEG
	– 'Raspberry Ruffles'	NBre SWat
	– 'Rembrandt'	MDKP NBre SWat WCot
	– 'Rose Queen'	NBre WCot
	– 'Rosenpokal'	SWat
	– 'Roter Zwerg'	ECha ELon SWat
	– 'Royal Chocolate Distinction'	CElw CSpe CWCL EBee ECtt ELon EPPr EPfP EWTr LRHS LSRN MAvo MBel NLar SBfd SPoG SWat WFar
	– 'Royal Wedding'	Widely available
	– 'Ruffled Patty'PBR	EBee ECtt EPfP MAsh NCGa NSti SWat WHrl
	– 'Ruffled Princess of Orange'PBR **new**	SWat
*	– 'Saffron'	SWat
	– 'Salmon Glow' (d)	SWat WFar WWEG
	– 'Salome'	SWat
	– 'Scarlet King'	CMac LRHS SWat
	– 'Scarlett O'Hara'PBR (d)	CPar EBee ECtt EPfP LLHF LRHS MAsh MBri NPri SWat WBor WFar
	– 'Showgirl'	ELon MBel NBre SWat
*	– 'Silberosa'	SWat
	– 'Sindbad'	ELon NEgg SWat
	– 'Snow Goose'	CMea EBee ECtt ELon ESwi IBoy IPot LHop LRHS MAvo MBel MCot SMad SWat WCot WHoo
	– 'Snow Queen'	GAbr MAsh
	– 'Spätzünder'	NBre SWat
	– 'Springtime'	ELon EWes LAst MRav SWat WTin
	– 'Staten Island' (New York Series)	ECtt MAvo MNrw
	– Stormtorch	see *P. orientale* 'Sturmfackel'
§	– 'Sturmfackel'	NBre SWat
	– 'Suleika'	SWat
	– 'Sultana'	EBee ECha ELon MArl SWat WCAu
	– 'Sunset'PBR	SWat
	– 'The Promise'	NBre SWat
	– 'Tiffany'	CMac ECtt ELon GAbr LSRN MAvo MCot NEgg NGdn SPer SWat WWEG
	– 'Trinity'	SWat
	– 'Türkenlouis'	EBee ECGP ECtt ELon EPfP GAbr GCra GMaP LAst LRHS LSRN MSCN MWat NGdn NLar SMrm SUsu SWat WCAu WCot WFar WHil WHoo WTin WWEG
	– 'Turkish Delight'	EBee ECtt EHrv ELon GCra GMaP LRHS LSRN MAvo MBel MMuc MRav NBir NLar NPri NRHS SBfd SEND SMrm SWat SWvt WCAu WFar WMnd WWEG
	– 'Tutu'	SWat
	– 'Victoria Dreyfuss'	SWat
	– 'Viola'	SWat
	– 'Violetta'	SWat
	– 'Walking Fire'	MNrw
	– 'Water Babies'	SWat
	– 'Watermelon'	ECtt IPot LRHS NLar SMrm SPer SWat WFar
	– 'White Ruffles' PBR	EBee ECtt EWTr IKil MAvo NCGa SWat
	– 'Wild Salmon'	NBre
	– 'Wisley Beacon'	ELon SWat
	– 'Wunderkind'	EBee ECtt LRHS SWat
	'Party Fun'	CSpe SWal
	paucifoliatum	WHrl
	pilosum	SWat WTin
§	– subsp. ***spicatum***	CCon CMea CSev CSpe ECha ELon GBin LHop LPla NBir WCot WHer WMoo
	'Rhapsody in Red' (SPS)	SWat
	rhoeas	CArn CHab GJos GPoy MNHC NNor WJek
	– Angels' Choir Group (d)	NNor SWat
	– Mother of Pearl Group	CSpe MCot SPhx SWat
	– Shirley Group	NNor
	rupifragum	CEnt ECha GAbr LEdu SGar WFar WPer WPnn

	- 'Double Tangerine Gem'	see *P. rupifragum* 'Flore Pleno'
§	- 'Flore Pleno' (d)	CSpe LRHS MHer NCGa SVic WBrk WFar WMoo
	- 'Tangerine Dream'	SPet WPer
	'Serena' (SPS)	SWat
	'Shasta' (SPS)	CDes EBee LLHF MAvo MBel SWat WCot WFar
	'Snow White' (SPS)	SWat
	somniferum	CArn ELau ENfk GPoy SVic SWat
	- var. ***album*** new	CArn
	- 'Blackcurrant Fizz' (d)	SPhx
	- 'Boudoir Babe' (d) new	CSpe
	- (Laciniatum Group) 'Crimson Feathers'	NNor
	- - 'Swansdown' (d)	CSpe
	- 'Lauren's Grape'	CSpe
	- Paeoniiflorum Group (d)	SWat
	- - 'Black Beauty' (d)	CSpe SDeJ SVic SWat
	- 'Pink Chiffon'	SWat
	- 'Ragged Red' (d) new	CSpe
	- subsp. ***setigerum***	NNor
	- single white-flowered	CSpe
	- 'White Cloud' (d)	SWat
	'Tequila Sunrise' (SPS)	CDes EBee MAvo SWat
	'The Cardinal'	NBre
	'The Falklands' (SPS)	SWat
	triniifolium	CSpe LRHS SPhx WCot
	'Vesuvius' (SPS)	SWat
	'Viva' (SPS)	SWat
*	'Witchery'	MAvo

papaya (paw paw) see *Carica papaya*

Parabenzoin see *Lindera*

Parachampionella see *Strobilanthes*

Paradisea (*Asparagaceae*)

	liliastrum ♀H4	CBro CHid CPrp EBee ECho EPri GCal IGor NBid NChi
	- 'Major'	EBee ECho SPhx
	lusitanica	CAvo CBro CDes CHid CMHG CPom CSam CSpe CTca EBee ECho EPri GBin GCal GKev IBlr IBoy LEdu MCot SPhx WPGP

Parahebe (*Plantaginaceae*)

	'Angela'	MSCN
	× ***bidwillii***	GJos MHer SRms SRot
	- 'Kea'	MDKP SRot WPer
	canescens	ECou
§	***catarractae***	CPLG CTri CWib ECho ECou EPfP GAbr GCra MLHP MRav MSCN MWat NBir NBro SRms WFar WKif WMnd WPer
	- from Chatham Island	EWes
	- blue-flowered	CDoC SPer
	- 'County Park'	ECou
	- 'Cuckoo'	ECou
§	- 'Delight' ♀H3	CPLG ECou EWes GCal GMaP GQue LHop LRHS MHer NPer SDix SRot WFar
	- subsp. ***diffusa***	NPer
	- 'Miss Willmott'	SPer SPlb WPer
	- 'Porlock'	CBar GKev WHoo
	- 'Porlock Purple'	see *P. catarractae* 'Delight'
	- 'Rosea'	ECho SRms WFar
	- white-flowered	CSpe IRar MLHP SRms WPer
	densifolia	see *Chionohebe densifolia*
§	***formosa***	SPlb
	'Gillian'	WPer
	'Greencourt'	see *P. catarractae* 'Delight'
	'Joy'	EWes
	linifolia	CTri
§	***lyallii***	ECho EPfP GJos GMaP LAst MCot MHer MMuc MRav MSwo MWat NLBP SEND SPlb SRms WKif
	- 'Julie-Anne' ♀H3	GCal LRHS
	- 'Rosea'	CTri WPer
	- 'Summer Snow'	ECou
	'Mervyn'	CTri MDKP WPer
§	***perfoliata*** ♀H3-4	CMac CMea CPLG CSpe EBee ECha ELan EPfP EPri GCal GCra GMaP LEdu LHop MAsh MCot MNrw MRav NChi SDix SEND SPer SRms SUsu WCFE WPat WPer WWFP XLum
	- dark blue-flowered	XLum
	'Snow Clouds'	CMea EPfP GKev LHop LRHS SBch SDix SRot SUsu SWal WFar
	'Snowcap'	CDoC LAst LRHS MRav NRHS SPlb SRms

Parajubaea (*Arecaceae*)

	torallyi var. ***torallyi***	EAmu

Parakmeria see *Magnolia*

Paranomus (*Proteaceae*)

	reflexus	SPlb

Paraquilegia (*Ranunculaceae*)

§	***anemonoides***	CPLG GKev WAbe
	grandiflora	see *P. anemonoides*

Parasenecio (*Asteraceae*)

	delphiniifolius	GEdr
	- B&SWJ 5789	WCru
	- B&SWJ 10885	WCru
	- B&SWJ 11189	WCru
	- B&SWJ 11415	WCru
	farfarifolius var. ***acerinus*** B&SWJ 11549	WCru
	- - B&SWJ 11554	WCru
	- var. ***bulbifer***	WCru
	hastatus var. ***farfarifolius***	see *P. maximowiczianus*
	kiusianus B&SWJ 11460	WCru
§	***maximowiczianus*** B&SWJ 11468	WCru
	mortonii GWJ 9419	WCru
	- HWJK 2214	WCru
	tebakoensis B&SWJ 11167	WCru
	- B&SWJ 11536	WCru
	aff. ***yatabei*** B&SWJ 11117	WCru

Paraserianthes (*Mimosaceae*)

	distachya	see *P. lophantha*
§	***lophantha*** ♀H1	CHEx CPLG EBak ELan EShb SEND SPlb

Parasyringa see *Ligustrum*

Parathelypteris (*Thelypteridaceae*)

§	***novae-boracensis***	ISha

Parietaria (*Urticaceae*)

	judaica	CArn GPoy WHer WSFF

Paris ✿ (*Melanthiaceae*)

chinensis	WCru
- B&SWJ 265 from Taiwan	WCru
cronquistii	CLAP
delavayi	WCru
fargesii	LAma LWst WCru
- var. ***brevipetalata***	WCru
- var. ***petiolata***	WCru
forrestii	WCru
incompleta	CLAP GCal WCru
- VVTR.1755	LWst
japonica	LAma LWst WCru
lancifolia B&SWJ 3044 from Taiwan	WCru
mairei	WCru
polyphylla ♀H4	CArn CBct CBro CCon CLAP EBee ECho GEdr GHim LAma LRHS LWst MNrw SKHP SPhx WCru WFar WPnP WSHC WShi
- B&SWJ 2125	WCru
- Forrest 5945	GCal
- HWJCM 475	WCru
- var. ***alba***	CCon
- var. ***stenophylla***	CCon EBee LAma LWst WCru
* - var. ***yunnanensis alba***	GCal
quadrifolia	CLAP CSpe ECho EPfP EWld GCal GPoy MAvo NHar NLar NMen NMyG SKHP SPhx SSpi WBor WCru WHer WPGP WPnP WShi WTin
- SDR 2828	GKev
tetraphylla	GEdr WCru
thibetica	CCon GHim LWst SKHP WCru
- var. ***apetala***	WCru
verticillata	CLAP GEdr LAma WCru
- 'Ryokutei' (d)	WCru

Parnassia (*Celastraceae*)

SDR 5128	GKev
palustris	GEdr
var. ***izuinsularis*** **new**	

Parochetus (*Papilionaceae*)

§ ***africanus*** ♀H2	CHid ECre
* - 'Blue Gem'	CCCN CSpe
communis misapplied	see *P. africanus*
communis ambig.	CCon CPLG MSCN NPer XLum
communis Buch.-Ham. ex D. Don from Himalaya	GCra

Paronychia (*Caryophyllaceae*)

argentea	WPat
§ ***capitata***	CTri SRms WHoo
kapela	SPlb XSen
- 'Binsted Gold' (v)	WPer XLum XSen
§ - subsp. ***serpyllifolia***	GBin NRya XLum
nivea	see *P. capitata*
serpyllifolia	see *P. kapela* subsp. *serpyllifolia*

Parrotia (*Hamamelidaceae*)

persica ♀H4	Widely available
- 'Biltmore'	CJun NLar SSta
- 'Burgundy'	CJun NLar
- 'Felicie'	CJun EPfP NLar
- 'Globosa'	NLar
- 'Het Plantsoen' **new**	NLar
- 'Jodrell Bank'	CJun MBlu NLar
§ - 'Lamplighter' (v)	CJun
- 'Pendula'	CJun CMCN EPfP SSta
- 'Persian Carpet' **new**	NLar
- 'Summer Bronze'	EBee LRHS MAsh SBir SSpi SSta
- 'Vanessa'	CBcs CDoC CDul CJun CLnd CMCN CMac EBee EPfP EWes GBin GKin IArd LRHS LTen MAsh MBlu MGos NLar SBir SGol SLPl SPoG SSta WMou
- 'Variegata'	see *P. persica* 'Lamplighter'
subaequalis **new**	NLar

Parrotiopsis (*Hamamelidaceae*)

jacquemontiana	CBcs CJun IVic MBlu NLar SSpi

Parrya (*Brassicaceae*)

menziesii	see *Phoenicaulis cheiranthoides*

parsley see *Petroselinum crispum*

Parsonsia (*Apocynaceae*)

capsularis	ECou
heterophylla	ECou

Parthenium (*Asteraceae*)

integrifolium	CArn EBee GPoy LRHS SPhx

Parthenocissus (*Vitaceae*)

§ ***henryana*** ♀H4	Widely available
himalayana	CBcs
- 'Purpurea'	see *P. himalayana* var. *rubrifolia*
§ - var. ***rubrifolia***	CBcs CRHN CWCL EBee ELan LRHS LTen MAsh MRav NLar SBfd SLim SLon SPoG WCru WFar WGrn
inserta misapplied	see *P. quinquefolia*
inserta ambig.	CMac CTsd NLar
laetevirens	NLar
§ ***quinquefolia*** ♀H4	Widely available
- var. ***engelmannii***	CBcs EBee LAst LBuc SBfd SPer WCFE
- 'Guy's Garnet'	WCru
- Star Showers = 'Monham' (v)	EBee EPfP NLar
semicordata B&SWJ 6551	WCru
striata	see *Cissus striata*
thomsonii	see *Cayratia thomsonii*
§ ***tricuspidata*** ♀H4	CCVT EBee EHoe EPfP MAsh MGos SGol SPer WFar
- 'Beverley Brook'	CRHN EBee LBuc LRHS LSRN MBri NLar SBod SPer SRms WFar
- 'Crûg Compact'	WCru
- 'Fenway Park'	EBee MRav NLar
- 'Green Spring'	CBcs EBee IArd MGos NLar SPer
- 'Lowii'	CMac EBee EPfP LBuc LRHS MBlu MGos MRav NLar SLon SPer
- 'Minutifolia'	EBee
- 'Robusta'	CHEx EBee SBfd
§ - 'Veitchii'	Widely available

Pasithea (*Hemerocallidaceae*)

caerulea	CAvo EBee ESwi SPer WCot

Paspalum (*Poaceae*)

glaucifolium	MNrw
quadrifarium	CKno EPPr LDai
- RCB RA S-5	WCot

Passiflora ✿ (*Passifloraceae*)

actinia	CCCN CRHN
'Adularia'	CCCN
alata (F) ♀H1	CCCN

	× ***alatocaerulea***	see *P.* × *belotii*
	'Allardii'	CCCN
	ambigua	CCCN
§	'Amethyst' ♀H1	CCCN CRHN CSBt CSPN EAmu EShb LHop LRHS LSRN MRav SPoG WFar WPGP
	amethystina misapplied	see *P.* 'Amethyst'
§	***amethystina*** Mikan	CBcs ECre
	'Anastasia'	CCCN
	'Andy'	CCCN
	'Angelo Blu'	CCCN
	'Annika' new	CCCN
	antioquiensis misapplied	see *P.* × *exoniensis*
	antioquiensis ambig.	CBcs CDoC CSPN MOWG SEND
	antioquiensis ambig. ×(× ***exoniensis*** 'Hill House')	CHll
	antioquiensis Karst ♀H2	CHll CRHN
	'Ariane'	CCCN
	× ***atropurpurea***	CCCN
§	***aurantia***	CCCN LRHS
	banksii	see *P. aurantia*
§	× ***belotii***	CCCN CRHN LRHS SLim
	- 'Impératrice Eugénie'	see *P.* × *belotii*
	'Betty Myles Young'	CRHN
	'Blue Bird'	CCCN
	'Blue Crown' new	CCCN
	'Blue Moon'	CCCN
	'Blue Stripper' new	CCCN
	'Blue Velvet' new	CCCN
	'Byron Beauty'	CCCN
	'Byte' new	CCCN
§	***caerulea*** ♀H3	Widely available
	- 'Clear Sky' PBR	CCCN CSPN EPfP LHop LRHS
	- 'Constance Eliott'	CBcs CCCN CDoC CMac CRHN CSBt CSPN CWSG CWib EAmu EBee ELan EPfP LBMP LHop LRHS MAsh MBri MOWG MREP MRav MWat NLar SBfd SEND SGol SPer SWvt WFar
	- ***rubra***	CSBt WFar
	× ***caeruleoracemosa***	see *P.* × *violacea*
	× ***caponii***	CCCN
	- 'John Innes' new	CCCN
	chinensis	see *P. caerulea*
	citrifolia	CCCN
	citrina	CCCN LRHS MOWG SLim
	× ***colvillii***	CHll
	'Coordination'	CCCN
§	***coriacea***	CCCN
	'Crimson Tears'	CCCN
	'Crimson Trees'	CCCN
	'Daylight' new	CCCN
	'Debby'	CCCN CSPN LSRN
	× ***decaisneana*** (F)	CCCN
	Eden = 'Hil Pas Eden'	CCCN CSBt CSPN EAmu LRHS MBri SCoo SLim SRkn
	edulis (F)	CAgr CBcs CCCN ELau SVic
	- 'Parati' new	CCCN
	'Elizabeth' (F)	CCCN
	'Empress Eugenie'	see *P.* × *belotii*
*	'Evatoria'	CCCN
§	× ***exoniensis*** ♀H1	CCCN CHll CRHN CSBt ECre
	'Fairylights'	CCCN
	'Fantasma' new	CCCN
	'Fata Confetto' new	CCCN
	'Fledermouse'	CCCN
	'Flying V'	CCCN
	'Grand Duchess'	CCCN
	gritensis	CCCN
	'Heidi' new	CCCN
	incarnata (F)	CAgr CArn SPlb
	'Incense' (F) ♀H1	CCCN SPlb WFar
	'Inspiration'	CCCN
	'Jelly Joker'	CCCN
	'Justine Lyons'	CRHN
	karwinskii	CCCN
	× ***kewensis***	CCCN
	'Lady Margaret'	LRHS
	'Lambiekins'	CRHN
§	***ligularis*** (F)	CCCN
	'Lilac Lady'	see *P.* × *violacea* 'Tresederi'
	'Livie' new	CCCN
	lowei	see *P. ligularis*
	lutea	CCCN
	'Luzmarina' new	CCCN
	maliformis (F)	CHll
	'Maria'	CCCN
	'Mary Jane'	CCCN
I	***matthewsii*** 'Alba'	CRHN
	'Mavis Mastics'	see *P.* × *violacea* 'Tresederi'
	mayana	see *P. caerulea*
	membranacea (F)	CCCN
	'Michael' new	CCCN
	'Minai' new	CCCN
	'Mini Lamb'	CRHN
	mixta (F)	CCCN SEND
	mollissima misapplied	see *P. tarminiana*
	mollissima ambig. (F)	CBcs CCCN CHll MOWG SPlb
	mollissima (Kunth) L.H.Bailey (F) ♀H1	CRHN
	mucronata	CCCN
	murucuja	CCCN
	'New Incense'	CCCN
	'Nightshift' new	CCCN
	obtusifolia	see *P. coriacea*
	onychina	see *P. amethystina* Mikan
	'Panda' new	CCCN
	'Peter Lawerence'	CCCN
	'Pink Festival'	CCCN
	'Pinky' new	CCCN
	× ***piresiae***	CCCN
	'Precioso'	CCCN
	'Purple Haze'	CCCN CSPN CWib EBee LRHS NEgg NLar
	'Purple Rain'	CCCN
	quadrangularis (F) ♀H1	CCCN CHll CWSG
	quinquangularis	CBcs CCCN
	racemosa ♀H2	CCCN EBee LAst MNHC
	- 'Buzios'	CCCN
	'Red Inca'	CCCN
	reitzii new	CCCN
	riparia new	CCCN
	rubra	CCCN EBee SLim
	sexocellata	see *P. coriacea*
	'Simply Red'	CCCN
	'Star of Bristol' ♀H2	CSPN EBee SLim
	'Star of Kingston'	CCCN
	'Star of Surbiton'	CRHN
	'Sunburst'	CCCN CHEx
§	***tarminiana*** (F)	CCCN CRHN CSBt
	tetrandra	CPLG ECou
	× ***tresederi***	see *P.* × *violacea* 'Tresederi'
	trifasciata	CCCN
	tulae	CCCN LRHS
§	***variolata*** from French Guiana	CCCN
§	× ***violacea*** ♀H1	CBcs CCCN CRHN WFar

- 'Eynsford Gem' CCCN EAmu
- 'Lilac Lady' see *P.* × *violacea* 'Tresederi'
- 'Sabin' CCCN LHop
§ - 'Tresederi' CCCN SEND WFar
- 'Twin Star' **new** CCCN
- 'Victoria' CCCN CSBt CSPN EBee NLar SLim
vitifolia (F) CCCN
'White Lightning' CSPN LBuc LRHS LSqu NPri SBfd SLim SPoG SWvt
'White Wedding' CCCN
'Wilgen Heintje' **new** CCCN
'Winterland' **new** CCCN
wurdackii see *P. variolata* from French Guiana

passion fruit see *Passiflora*

passion fruit, banana see *Passiflora mollissima* (Kunth) L.H. Bailey

Pastinaca (*Apiaceae*)

sativa CHab SVic

Patersonia (*Iridaceae*)

occidentalis LRHS SPlb

Patrinia ✿ (*Caprifoliaceae*)

gibbosa CSam CSpe EBee EDAr GEdr GKev LRHS MLHP MMHG MPie NLar SPhx WMoo WPnP
- B&SWJ 874 WCru
scabiosifolia CHll CKno CSpe EBee ECha ECtt GAbr GCal LRHS MNFA NBir NLar SPhx SUsu WAul WFar WHoo WMoo WPGP WTcb
- B&SWJ 8740 WCru
- 'Nagoya' MNrw
triloba CRDP CSpe ECho GCal GEdr LRHS LSou MMHG SUsu WFar WMoo
* - 'Minor' ECho
- var. ***palmata*** GKev WMoo
villosa CPLG EBee GCal LRHS MMHG NGdn SPhx SSvw

Paulownia (*Paulowniaceae*)

catalpifolia LLHF MBri NLar
elongata NLar
fortunei CDul IVic MBlu NLar SPlb
- Fast Blue = 'Minfast' CHGN CPLG EBee EPfP ESwi LLHF LSRN SBfd SEND SGol SLim WHar WMou
kawakamii WPGP
- RWJ 9909 WCru
tomentosa ♀H3 Widely available
- 'Coreana' CHll
- - B&SWJ 8503 WCru

Pavonia (*Malvaceae*)

missionum CSpe
multiflora ambig. CCCN
praemorsa CSpe
strictiflora CCCN
* ***volubilis*** CCCN

paw paw (false banana) see *Asimina triloba*

paw paw (papaya) see *Carica papaya*

Paxistima (*Celastraceae*)

canbyi WPat WThu

peach see *Prunus persica*

pear see *Pyrus communis*

pear, Asian see *Pyrus pyrifolia*

pecan see *Carya illinoinensis*

Peganum (*Nitrariaceae*)

harmala CArn

Pelargonium (*Geraniaceae*)

'A.M. Mayne' (Z/d) WFib
'Abb and Mab' (Sc) MBPg
'Abba' (Z/d) WFib
abrotanifolium (Sc) ENfk EWoo MBPg MHer SSea WFib WGwG
'Abundance' (Sc) CSev LDea
acetosum CSev EWoo GCal MHer SMrm WCot
'Ada Green' (R) WFib
'Ada Sutterby' (Dw/d) SKen
'Adam's Quilt' (Z/C) SKen
'Ade's Elf' (Z/St) NFir SSea
'Ailsa' (Min/d) SKen
'Ainsdale Beauty' (Z) SSea WFib
'Ainsdale Duke' (Z) NFir
'Ainsdale Eyeful' (Z) WFib
'Alan West' (Z/St) SSea
Alba = 'Fisalb' (Z/d) SKen
alchemilloides CRHN
'Alcyone' (Dw/d) SKen
'Alde' (Min) NFir SKen SSea
'Aldwyck' (R) CWCL WFib
'Alex Kitson' (Z) WFib
'Algenon' (Min/d) WFib
I 'Alice' (Min) WFib
'Alice Greenfield' (Z) NFir
alpinum MHer
'Amari' (R) WFib
'Ambrose' (Min/d) WFib
Amelit = 'Pacameli'PBR (I/d) LAst NPri SSea
'American Prince of Orange' (Sc) MBPg
Ameta = 'Pacmeta'PBR (Z) **new** LAst
'Amethyst' (R) SCoo SPet WFib
§ Amethyst = 'Fisdel'PBR (I/d) ♀H1+3 SKen
'Androcles' (A) LDea
'Angela Woodberry' (Z) WFib
(Angeleyes Series) Angeleyes Bicolor = 'Pacbicolor'PBR (A) LAst NPri
- Angeleyes Burgundy = 'Pacburg'PBR (A) LAst SSea
- Angeleyes Josie (A) SKen
- Angeleyes Orange = 'Paccrio'PBR (A) EWoo LAst LSou
- Angeleyes Randy (A) SSea
'Angelique' (Dw/d) WFib
'Ann Hoystead' (R) ♀H1+3 NFir WFib
'Anna Lisa Pope' (R) MGbk
'Annsbrook Aquarius' (St) NFir
'Annsbrook Beauty' (A/C) NFir WFib
'Annsbrook Fruit Sundae' (A) LDea
'Annsbrook Jupitor' (Z/St) NFir

Name	Suppliers
'Annsbrook Mulberry Blotch' (Z/v)	MGbk
Anthony = 'Pacan'[PBR] (Z/d)	LAst
Antik Scarlet = 'Tikscarl'[PBR] (Antik Series) (Z) **new**	LAst
'Antoine Crozy' (Z × I/d)	WFib
'Apache' (Z/d) 𝕐[H1+3]	WFib
appendiculatum	CLak MHer WCot
'Apple Betty' (Sc)	EWoo MBPg WFib
'Apple Blossom Rosebud' (Z/d) 𝕐[H1+3]	EShb MBri MHer NEgg SKen SMrm SSea WBrk WFib
'Appleblossom' (Angeleyes Series)	LAst SWal
'Apricot' (Dw/v) **new**	SKen
'Apricot' (Z/St)	LAst
'April Hamilton' (I)	CWCL WFib
'April Showers' (A)	LDea WFib
'Archie Pope' (R)	MGbk
'Arctic Frost'	WFib
§ 'Arctic Star' (Z/St)	CSpe NFir SKen SSea WBrk WFib
'Ardens'	CHll CSev CSpe EBee EWoo LSou MCot MHer NFir SMrm SSea SUsu SWvt WCot WFib WWFP
'Ardwick Cinnamon' (Sc)	ENfk EWoo MBPg MHer NFir WFib
aridum	WCot
(Aristo Series) Aristo Beauty = 'Regbeauty'[PBR] (R)	LAst
- Aristo Clara Schumann (R)	LAst
'Arizona' (Min/d)	SKen
'Arnside Fringed Aztec' (R)	MHer WFib
'Aroma' (Sc)	EWoo MBPg
'Ashby' (U/Sc)	CWCL ENfk EWoo MBPg MHer NFir SBch SSea
'Ashfield Jubilee' (Z/C)	NFir SKen
'Ashfield Monarch' (Z/d) 𝕐[H1+3]	NFir
'Ashfield Serenade' (Z) 𝕐[H1+3]	WFib
'Askham Fringed Aztec' (R) 𝕐[H1+3]	CWCL WFib
asperum Ehr. ex Willd.	see *P.* 'Graveolens'
'Atlantic Burgundy'	CWCL MCot
§ 'Atomic Snowflake' (Sc/v)	ENfk LDea MBPg MNHC SIde SKen SPet WFib
'Atrium' (U)	MHer WFib
'Attar of Roses' (Sc) 𝕐[H1+3]	CArn CHby CRHN ENfk LDea MBPg MCot MHer NFir NPri SBch SGar SIde SSea WBrk WFib WGwG
'Auntie Billie' (A)	LDea
'Aurelia' (A)	LDea
'Aurora' (Z/d)	SKen WGor
australe	CRHN CSpe EWoo MCot SBch WFib
'Australian Mystery' (R/Dec)	CSpe NFir WFib
'Aztec' (R) 𝕐[H1+3]	NFir WFib
'Baby Bird's Egg' (Min)	WFib
'Baby Harry' (Dw/v)	WFib
'Baby Snooks' (A)	LDea
Balcon Imperial	see *P.* 'Roi des Balcons Impérial'
'Balcon Rose'	see *P.* 'Hederinum'
'Balcon Rouge'	see *P.* 'Roi des Balcons Impérial'
'Balcon Royale'	see *P.* 'Roi des Balcons Impérial'
'Ballerina' (R)	see *P.* 'Carisbrooke'
I 'Ballerina' (Min)	WFib
'Barbara Lambert' (Z/St)	MGbk
§ 'Barbe Bleu' (I/d)	NFir SKen SSea WFib
'Barking' (Min/Z)	NFir
'Barnston Dale' (Dw/d)	NFir

Name	Suppliers
'Bath Beauty' (Dw)	CSpe SKen
'Beatrice Cottington' (I/d)	SKen WFib
Beau Jangles Tom (I)	NPri
'Beauty of Eastbourne' misapplied	see *P.* 'Lachskönigin', *P.* 'Eastbourne Beauty'
'Beauty of El Segundo' (Z/d)	SKen
'Belinda Adams' (Min/d) 𝕐[H1+3]	NFir SSea
Belladonna = 'Fisopa' (I/d)	SCoo
'Bembridge' (Z/St/d)	NFir SSea WFib
'Ben Franklin' (Z/d/v) 𝕐[H1+3]	NFir SSea
'Ben Matt' (R)	WFib
'Berkswell Beacon' (A)	LDea
'Berkswell Blush' (A)	LDea
'Berkswell Bonanza' (A)	LDea
'Berkswell Bounty' (A) **new**	MGbk
'Berkswell Calypso' (A)	LDea
'Berkswell Carnival' (A)	LDea
'Berkswell Champagne' (A)	LDea
'Berkswell Charm' (A)	LDea
'Berkswell Dainty' (A)	LDea
'Berkswell Debonair' (A)	LDea
'Berkswell Fondant' (A)	LDea
'Berkswell Gaiety' (A)	LDea
'Berkswell Gala' (A) **new**	MGbk
'Berkswell Gipsy' (A)	LDea
'Berkswell Jester' (A)	LDea
'Berkswell Lace' (A)	LDea MHer
'Berkswell Nocturne' (A)	LDea MGbk
'Berkswell Petticote' (A)	LDea
'Berkswell Pixie' (A)	LDea
'Berkswell Rosette' (A)	LDea
'Berkswell Sparkler' (A)	LDea
'Berkswell Trinket' (A)	LDea
'Berkswell Windmill' (A)	LDea
'Berliner Balkon' (I)	SKen
'Bernice Ladroot'	LDea
'Beromünster' (Dec)	EWoo MHer NFir WFib
'Bert Pearce' (R)	WFib
'Beryl Reid' (R)	CWCL WFib
'Bette Shellard' (Z/d/v)	NFir
'Betty Catchpole' (Z)	EWoo
betulinum	EWoo WFib
'Betwixt' (Z/v)	SKen SSea
'Big Apple' (Sc)	MBPg
'Bird Dancer' (Dw/St) 𝕐[H1+3]	CSpe MHer MNHC NFir SBch SKen SSea SWal WBrk
(Birdbush Series) 'Birdbush Anchor' (Sc) **new**	MBPg
- 'Birdbush Andy Pandy' (Sc)	MBPg
- 'Birdbush Beautiful' (Sc)	MBPg
- 'Birdbush Belinda' (Sc)	MBPg
- 'Birdbush Bella' (Sc)	MBPg
- 'Birdbush Betty' (Sc)	MBPg
- 'Birdbush Big Ears' (Sc) **new**	MBPg
- 'Birdbush Billy' (Sc)	MBPg
- 'Birdbush Blanco' (Sc)	MBPg
- 'Birdbush Blush' (Sc)	MBPg
- 'Birdbush Bobby' (Sc)	MBPg
- 'Birdbush Bold and Beautiful' (Sc)	MBPg
- 'Birdbush Bolero' (Sc)	MBPg
- 'Birdbush Bonny' (Sc)	MBPg
- 'Birdbush Bountiful' (Sc)	MBPg
- 'Birdbush Bramley' (Sc)	MBPg
- 'Birdbush Brandy' (Sc)	MBPg
- 'Birdbush Brilliant' (Sc)	MBPg
- 'Birdbush Champion' (Sc)	MBPg

- 'Birdbush Chloe' (St)	MBPg
- 'Birdbush Claire Louise' (Sc)	MBPg
- 'Birdbush Dawndew' (Sc)	MBPg
- 'Birdbush Eleanor' (Z)	MBPg WFib
- 'Birdbush Julie Anne' (Sc)	MBPg
- 'Birdbush Kay Lye' (Sc)	MBPg
- 'Birdbush Lemonside' (Sc)	MBPg
- 'Birdbush Limey' (Sc)	MBPg
- 'Birdbush Linda Creasey' (Sc)	MBPg
- 'Birdbush Marion Louise' (Sc)	MBPg
- 'Birdbush Matty'	MBPg
- 'Birdbush Miriam' (Sc)	MBPg
- 'Birdbush Nutty' (Sc)	MBPg
- 'Birdbush Pink and Perky' (U)	MBPg
- 'Birdbush Pinky' (Sc)	MBPg
- 'Birdbush Sensation' (Sc) **new**	MBPg
- 'Birdbush Suzy' (Sc)	MBPg
- 'Birdbush Sweetness' (Sc)	MBPg
- 'Birdbush Too Too O' (Sc)	MBPg
- 'Birdbush Velvet' (Sc)	MBPg
- 'Birdbush Victoria' (Sc)	MBPg
'Birthday Girl' (R)	CWCL WFib
'Bitter Lemon' (Sc)	EWoo MBPg
'Black Butterfly'	see *P.* 'Brown's Butterfly'
'Black Knight' (A)	NFir
'Black Knight' (R)	CSpe EWoo MHer
'Black Knight' Lea (Dw/d/C)	NFir
'Black Prince' (R/Dec)	CSpe EWoo NFir WFib
'Black Velvet' (R)	EWoo MCot
'Black Vesuvius'	see *P.* 'Red Black Vesuvius'
'Blackcurrant Yhu' (Dec)	NFir
'Blackdown Delight' (Z)	NFir
'Blackdown Sensation' (Dw/Z)	NFir
Blanca = 'Penwei'PBR (Dark Line Series) (Z/d)	LAst LBMP
Blanche Roche = 'Guitoblanc' (I/d)	LAst LBMP LSou NPri SCoo
§ 'Blandfordianum' (Sc)	EWoo LDea MHer
'Blandfordianum Roseum' (Sc)	EWoo LDea
'Blaze Away'	SSea
'Blazonry' (Z/v)	SKen SSea WFib
'Blue Beard'	see *P.* 'Barbe Bleu'
'Blue Peter' (I/d)	SKen
Blue Sybil = 'Pacblusy'PBR (I/d)	LAst LSou NPri
Blue Wonder = 'Pacbla'PBR (Z/d)	LAst WGor
Blue-Blizzard = 'Fisrain'PBR (I)	SCoo
'Blushing Bride' (I/d)	SKen
'Blushing Sophie'	LAst
'Bob Newing' (Min/St)	WFib
'Bobberstone' (Z/St)	WFib
'Bold Appleblossom' (Z)	WFib
'Bold Carmine' (Z/d)	NFir
'Bold Carousel' (Z/d)	WFib
'Bold Cherub' (Z/d)	MGbk
'Bold Elf' (Z/Min/d) **new**	MGbk
'Bold Flame' (Z/d)	WFib
'Bold Gem' (Z/d)	MGbk
'Bold Limelight' (Z/d)	WFib
'Bold Minstrel' (Z/d) **new**	MGbk WFib
'Bold Pixie' (Dw/d)	WFib
'Bold Princess' (Z/d)	MGbk
'Bold Sunrise' (Z/d)	NFir
'Bold Sunset' (Z/d)	NFir WFib
'Bold White' (Z)	NFir
'Bolero' (U) ♀H1+3	NFir WFib
'Bon Bon' (Min/St)	WFib
'Bontrosai'PBR (Sc) **new**	MCot
'Bosham' (R)	WFib
'Both's Snowflake' (Sc/v)	MBPg
bowkeri	WFib
'Brackenwood' (Dw/d) ♀H1+3	NFir
Bravo = 'Fisbravo'PBR (Z/d)	WFib
'Brenda' (Min/d)	WFib
'Brenda Hyatt' (Dw/d)	WFib
'Brian West' (Min/St/C)	WFib
'Brian West Butterfly' (Z/St)	MGbk WFib
'Briarlyn Beauty' (A)	LDea MBPg
'Briarlyn Moonglow' (A)	LDea
'Bridesmaid' (Dw/d)	NFir SKen
'Brightstone' (Z/d)	WFib
'Brilliant' (Dec)	ENfk WFib
'Brilliantine' (Sc)	CSev ENfk EWoo MBPg MHer WFib WGwG
'Bristol' (Z/v)	SSea
'Brixworth Pearl' (Z)	WFib
'Bronze Corinne' (Z/C/d)	SKen SPet
'Brook's Purple'	see *P.* 'Royal Purple'
'Brookside Fiesta' (Min/d)	MGbk
'Brookside Flamenco' (Dw/d)	WFib
'Brookside Primrose' (Min/C/d)	SKen WFib
'Brookside Serenade' (Dw)	WFib
§ 'Brown's Butterfly' (R)	ECtt NFir WFib
'Brunswick' (Sc)	EWoo LDea MHer WFib
'Burgundy' (R)	LBMP
'Burns Country' (Dw)	NFir
'Bushfire' (R) ♀H1+3	EWoo WFib
Butterfly = 'Fisam'PBR (I)	NFir SCoo
'Cal'	see *P.* 'Salmon Irene'
Calais = 'Paclai'PBR	LAst
'California Brilliant' (U)	MHer
'Calignon' (Z/St)	WFib
'Camphor Rose' (Sc)	MBPg NFir SSea
'Can-can' (I/d)	WFib
canescens	see *P.* 'Blandfordianum'
'Cape Beauty'	EWoo
'Cape Town' (Dw/z/v) **new**	WFib
capitatum	ENfk MBPg MHer MNHC WFib
'Capri' (Sc)	MBPg WFib
'Captain Starlight' (A)	EWoo LDea MHer NFir SKen SSea WFib
'Caravan' (A)	LDea
'Cardinal'	see *P.* 'Kardinal'
'Carefree' (U)	NFir WFib
§ 'Carisbrooke' (R) ♀H1+3	WFib
'Carl Gaffney'	LDea
'Carmel' (Z)	WFib
carnosum	MHer
'Carol Gibbons' (Z/d)	NFir
'Caroline Schmidt' (Z/d/v)	MCot NFir SKen SSea WBrk WFib
'Carolyn Dean' (St)	NFir
'Carolyn Hardy' (Z/d)	WFib
Cascade Pink	see *P.* 'Hederinum'
'Catford Belle' (A) ♀H1+3	LDea
'Cathay' (Z/St)	NFir

'Cathy' (R) NFir
caucalifolium MHer
subsp. ***caucalifolium***
- subsp. ***convolvulifolium*** WFib
'Cayucas' (I/d) SKen
'Cézanne' (R) MCot
'Charity' (Sc) ♀H1+3 ENfk LDea MBPg MCot MHer NFir SKen WFib
'Charlotte Bronte' (Dw/v) WFib
'Charmay Alf' (A) LDea
'Charmay Aria' (A) LDea
'Charmay Bagatelle' (A) LDea
'Charmay Cocky' (Z/d) **new** MGbk
'Charmay Electra' (A) LDea
'Charmay Marjorie' (A) LDea
'Charmay Snowflake' (Sc/v) MBPg
'Chelsea Gem' (Z/d/v) ♀H1+3 SKen SSea WFib
'Chelsea Morning' (Z/d) WFib
'Chelsea Star' (Z/d/v) MGbk
'Cherie Maid' (Z/v) SSea
'Cherry' (Min) WFib
'Cherry Baby' (Dec) MHer NFir
'Cherry Orchard' (R) WFib
'Chew Magna' (R) WFib
'Chieko' (Min/d) WFib
'Chinz' (R) NFir
§ 'Chocolate Peppermint' (Sc) CRHN CSev ENfk EWoo LDea MBPg MHer MNHC NFir SIde SSea WBrk WFib
'Chocolate Tomentosum' see *P.* 'Chocolate Peppermint'
'Chocolate Twist' (St/C) LAst
'Chrissie' (R) WFib
'Cindy' (Dw/d) WFib
'Citriodorum' (Sc) ♀H1+3 LDea MBPg MCot MHer WFib
'Citronella' (Sc) CRHN LDea MBPg WFib WGwG
citronellum (Sc) MBPg
'City of Bath' CWCL
'Claret Rock Unique' (U) EWoo SKen SSea WFib
'Clatterbridge' (Dw/d) NFir
'Clorinda' (U/Sc) CRHN ENfk EShb EWoo MBPg MCot MHer MNHC SBch SIde SKen SSea SWal WFib WGwG
Coco-Rico (I) SKen
'Coddenham' (Dw/d) WFib
'Cola Bottles' NPer NPri
§ 'Colonel Baden-Powell' (I/d) WFib
'Colwell' (Min/d) MGbk WFib
'Concolor Lace' see *P.* 'Shottesham Pet'
'Contrast' (Z/C/v) CWCL MBri NEgg SCoo SKen SPoG SSea WFib
'Cook's Peachblossom' WFib
'Copthorne' (U/Sc) ♀H1+3 CRHN EWoo LDea MBPg MCot MHer SSea WFib
cordifolium CRHN EWoo WFib
- var. ***rubrocinctum*** NFir
I - 'Valentine' **new** CSpe
coriandrifolium see *P. myrrhifolium* var. *coriandrifolium*
'Cornell' (I/d) WFib
cortusifolium MHer
'Cottenham Beauty' (A) LDea NFir
'Cottenham Charm' (A) LDea
'Cottenham Delight' (A) LDea NFir
'Cottenham Glamour' (A) MHer NFir
'Cottenham Harmony' (A) LDea
'Cottenham Jubilee' (A) LDea MHer
'Cottenham Special' (A) MGbk
'Cottenham Surprise' (A) LDea NFir
'Cottenham Treasure' (A) LDea
'Cottenham Wonder' (A) NFir
'Cottontail' (Min) WFib
cotyledonis CSpe WFib
'Countess Mariza' see *P.* 'Gräfin Mariza'
'Countess of Scarborough' see *P.* 'Lady Scarborough'
'Country Girl' (R) SPet
'Cover Girl' (Z/d) WFib
'Covina' (R) WFib
'Cramdon Red' (Dw) SKen WFib
'Cransley Star' (A) LDea
'Cream 'n' Green' (R/v) NFir
'Creamery' (d) WFib
'Creamy Nutmeg' (Sc/v) ENfk EShb EWoo LDea MHer NFir SSea WBrk
'Crimson Fire' (Z/d) MBri
'Crimson Unique' (U) ♀H1+3 CSpe ENfk EWoo MCot MHer SKen SSea WFib
§ ***crispum*** (Sc) ENfk GPoy MBPg NEgg SBch
§ - 'Golden Well Sweep' (Sc/v) MBPg WFib
- 'Major' (Sc) MCot WFib
- 'Peach Cream' (Sc/v) ENfk MBPg WFib
- 'Prince Rupert' (Sc) MBPg
- 'Variegatum' (Sc/v) ♀H1+3 CRHN ENfk GPoy LDea MBPg MHer NFir SBch SIde SPet SSea WCot WFib
crithmifolium MHer
'Crocketta' (I/d/v) NFir SKen
'Crocodile' (I/C/d) ECtt EShb MHer NFir SKen SSea WBrk WFib
'Crystal Palace Gem' (Z/v) SKen SSea WFib
cucullatum WFib
- 'Flore Pleno' (d) MHer WFib
- subsp. ***strigifolium*** EWoo
'Cupid' (Min/Dw/d) WFib
§ 'Czar' (Z/C) SCoo
'Dainty Maid' (Sc) CSpe ENfk NFir
'Dale Queen' (Z) WFib
'Damilola' (Z/St/Min/C) **new** MGbk
'Danielle Marie' (A) LDea
'Dark Gigette' (Min) **new** NFir
'Dark Red Irene' (Z/d) SKen WFib
'Dark Secret' (R) CSpe SMrm WFib
'Dark Venus' (R) EWoo WFib
Dark-Red-Blizzard = 'Fisblizdark' (I) CWCL EWoo
'Darmsden' (A) ♀H1+3 LDea NFir
'Davina' (Min/d) WFib
'Dawn Star' (Z/St) NFir
'Deacon Arlon' (Dw/d) SKen
'Deacon Avalon' (Dw/d) WFib
'Deacon Barbecue' (Z/d) SKen WFib
'Deacon Birthday' (Z/d) WFib
'Deacon Bonanza' (Z/d) SKen WFib
'Deacon Clarion' (Z/d) SKen WFib
'Deacon Coral Reef' (Z/d) WFib
'Deacon Fireball' (Z/d) WFib
'Deacon Gala' (Z/d) WFib
'Deacon Golden Bonanza' (Z/C/d) WFib
'Deacon Golden Gala' (Z/C/d) SKen
'Deacon Golden Lilac Mist' (Z/C/d) WFib
'Deacon Jubilant' (Z/d) SKen
'Deacon Lilac Mist' (Z/d) WFib
'Deacon Mandarin' (Z/d) SKen WFib
'Deacon Minuet' (Z/d) NFir WFib
'Deacon Peacock' (Z/C/d) WFib
'Deacon Picotee' (Z/d) SKen WFib

§ 'Deacon Summertime' (Z/d) WFib
'Dean's Delight' (Sc) LDea MBPg
'Debbie' (A) LDea
'Deborah Miliken' (Z/d) NFir WFib
'Decora Lavender' see *P.* 'Decora Lilas'
§ 'Decora Lilas' (I) ECtt LAst SKen SPet
'Decora Mauve' see *P.* 'Decora Lilas'
'Decora Pink' see *P.* 'Decora Rouge'
'Decora Red' see *P.* 'Decora Rouge'
§ 'Decora Rose' (I) ECtt SPet
§ 'Decora Rouge' (I) ECtt LAst SPet
'Decora Scarlet' (I) SKen
'Deerwood Darling' (Min/v/d) WFib
'Deerwood Lavender Lad' (Sc) CSev ENfk EWoo LDea MBPg MHer SSea WFib
'Deerwood Lavender Lass' LDea MBPg MCot MHer
'Deerwood Pink Puff' (St/d) WFib
'Delightful' (R) WFib
'Delli' (R) CWCL MHer NFir NPer SMrm WFib
'Dennis Hunt' (Z/C) NFir
denticulatum MHer SKen SSea
§ - 'Filicifolium' (Sc) CRHN ENfk EShb LDea MBPg MCot MHer SSea WFib
'Diane Louise' (d) SSea
'Dibbinsdale' (Z) NFir
dichondrifolium (Sc) CSev CSpe MBPg MHer NFir SSea WFib
dichondrifolium* × *reniforme (Sc) NFir
'Didi' (Min) SKen
'Display' ambig. (Dw/v) WFib
'Distinction' (Z) NFir SKen SPoG SSea WFib
'Dollar Princess' (Z/C) SKen
'Dolly Varden' (Z/v) ♀H1+3 NFir SKen SSea WFib
'Don's Helen Bainbridge' (Z/C) NFir
'Don's Mona Noble' (Z/C) NFir
'Don's Richard A. Costain' (Z/C) NFir
'Don's Silva Perle' (Dw/v) SKen
'Don's Southport' (Z/v) NFir
'Dorcus Bingham' (Sc) MBPg
'Doreen' (Z/d) MGbk
'Doris Hancock' (R) WFib
'Dorothy May' (A) LDea
'Double Bird's Egg' (Z/d) SKen
'Double Orange' (Z/d) SKen
'Double Pink' (R/d) WFib
'Dovedale' (Dw/C) WFib
'Dovepoint' (Dw/2) NFir
'Downlands' (Z/d) WFib
'Dresden White' (Dw) WFib
Dresdner Apricot = 'Pacbriap'PBR (I/d) NPri
'Dubai Star' (Z) MGbk
'Duchess of Devonshire' (U) WFib
'Duke of Edinburgh' see *P.* 'Hederinum Variegatum'
'Dunkery Beacon' (R) WFib
'E. Dabner' (Z/d) SKen WFib
'Earliana' (Dec) LDea SUsu
§ 'Eastbourne Beauty' (I/d) SKen
echinatum EWoo MHer
- 'Album' SSea WFib
'Eclipse' (Dw/d) SKen
'Eclipse' (I/d) SKen
'Eden Gem' (Min/d) WFib
'Edmond Lachenal' (Z/d) WFib
'Edward Humphris' (Z) SKen
'Edwards Michael' (A) LDea
'Eileen Nancy' (Z) NFir
'Eileen Postle' (R) ♀H1+3 WFib
Elbe Silver = 'Pensil' (I) NFir SCoo
'Elizabeth Angus' (Z) SKen
'Elmsett' (Dw/C/d) NFir SSea WFib
'Els' (Dw/St) SKen WBrk
'Elsi' (I × Z/d/v) WFib
'Elsie Gillam' (St) WFib
'Elsie Portas' (Z/C/d) SKen
'Embassy' (Min) WFib
'Emerald' (I) SKen
Emilia = 'Pactina'PBR LAst
'Emma Hössle' see *P.* 'Frau Emma Hössle'
'Emma Jane Read' (Dw/d) WFib
'Emma Louise' (Z) SKen
'Enchantress' (I) SKen
'Encore' (Z/d/v) SSea
endlicherianum SPhx WCot
'Endsleigh' (Sc) MBPg
'Erwarton' (Min/d) NFir
'Eskay Gold' (A) WFib
'Eskay Jewel' (A) WFib
'Eskay Ruby' (A) MHer
'Eskay Sugar Candy' (A) WFib
'Eskay Verglo' (A) WFib
'Evka'PBR (I/v) CWCL LAst SCoo SSea
exhibens WCot
exstipulatum EShb EWoo SSea
'Fair Ellen' (Sc) LDea MBPg MHer WFib
'Fairlee' (DwI) WFib
'Fairy Lights' (Dw/St) NFir
'Fairy Orchid' (A) LDea WFib
'Fairy Queen' LDea
'Fandango' (Z/St) NFir SMrm WFib
'Fanny Eden' (R) EWoo WFib
'Fantasia' white-flowered (Dw/d) ♀H1+3 WFib
'Fareham' (R) ♀H1+3 WFib
'Fenton Farm' (Dw/C) NFir
'Feuerriese' (Z) SKen
'Fiat' (Z/d) SKen
'Fiat Queen' (Z/d) SKen WFib
'Fiat Supreme' (Z/d) SKen
'Fieldings Unique' (U) **new** NFir
'Fifth Avenue' (R) WFib
'Filicifolium' see *P. denticulatum* 'Filicifolium'
'Fir Trees Audrey B' (St) NFir
'Fir Trees Betty' (U) NFir
'Fir Trees Echoes of Pink' (A) EWoo
'Fir Trees Eileen' (St) NFir SMrm
'Fir Trees Ele' (A/v) NFir
'Fir Trees Fantail' (Min) NFir
'Fir Trees Fiesta' (R) **new** NFir
'Fir Trees Flamingo' (Dw) NFir
'Fir Trees Jack' (Z/Dw) NFir
'Fir Trees Janet' (Dw) NFir
'Fir Trees Jennifer' (R/Dec) NFir
'Fir Trees John Grainger' (Z/v) NFir
'Fir Trees Mark' (R/Dec/v) NFir
'Fir Trees Nan' (R/Dec) NFir
'Fir Trees Pink Pom-Pom' (Dw/St/C/d) NFir
'Fir Trees Ruby Wedding' (C) NFir
'Fir Trees Silver Wedding' (Z/C/d) NFir
'Fir Trees Sparkler' (Min/C) NFir
'Fir Trees Val' (Z) NFir

(Fireworks Series) Fireworks Cherry = 'Fiwocherry'PBR (Z) SBfd
- Fireworks Cherry-white = 'Fiwocher'PBR (Z) SSea
- Fireworks Light Pink = 'Fiwopink'PBR (Z/St) SBfd SWal
- Fireworks Red-white = 'Fiworewhi'PBR (Z) SBfd
- Fireworks White = 'Fiwowit'PBR (Z) SBfd
'First Blush' (R) WFib
'First Love' (Z) NFir
'Flaming Katy' (Min) NFir
'Fleur-de-lys' (A) LDea
'Fleurette' (Min/d) SKen
'Fleurisse' (Z) WFib
'Floral Cascade' (Fr/d) SSea
'Florence Hunt' (R) NFir
'Floria Moore' (Dec) EWoo NFir SSea
'Flower Basket' (R/d) EWoo
(Flower Fairy Series) Flower Fairy Rose = 'Swero'PBR (Z) LSou
- Flower Fairy White Splash = 'Swewhi'PBR (Z) LAst LSou
'Flower of Spring' (Z/v) ♀H1+3 SSea
Foxy = 'Pacfox'PBR (Z) LSou
fragrans ENfk SWal
Fragrans Group (Sc) CRHN CSev EWoo GPoy MBPg MCot MHer SKen SPet SSea WFib WGwG
§ - 'Fragrans Variegatum' (Sc/v) CSev MBPg NFir SKen SWal WBrk WFib
- 'Snowy Nutmeg' see *P.* (Fragrans Group) 'Fragrans Variegatum'
'Fraiche Beauté' (Z/d) WFib
'Francis Gibbon' (Z/d) WFib
'Francis Parrett' (Min/d) ♀H1+3 SKen WFib
'Frank Hazel' (Dw/Z) NFir
'Frank Headley' (Z/v) ♀H1+3 MCot NPer SCoo SIde SKen SMrm SSea WFib WOld
§ 'Frau Emma Hössle' (Dw/d) WFib
'Freak of Nature' (Z/v) MHer NFir SKen SSea WFib
'Frensham' (Sc) ENfk LDea MBPg MHer WFib
'Freshfields Suki' (Dw) NFir
'Freshwater' (St/C) WFib
'Friary Wood' (Z/C/d) NFir WFib
'Friesdorf' (Dw/Fr) MCot MHer NFir SKen WBrk WFib
'Fringed Apple' (Sc) LDea MBPg
'Fringed Aztec' (R) ♀H1+3 CWCL NFir SPet WFib
'Fringed Jer'Ray' (A) LDea SSea
'Frosty' misapplied see *P.* 'Variegated Kleine Liebling'
'Frosty Petit Pierre' see *P.* 'Variegated Kleine Liebling'
'Fruity' (Sc) MBPg
frutetorum MHer
fruticosum EWoo WFib
'Fuji' (R) NFir
fulgidum EWoo MCot WFib
'Gabriel' (A) EWoo LDea
'Galilee' (I/d) ♀H1+3 SKen
'Galway Star' (Sc/v) ♀H1+3 MBPg MHer WFib
'Gareth Mark Pratt' (Z/C) **new** MGbk
'Garnet Rosebud' (Min/d) NFir WFib
'Gartendirektor Herman' (Dec) EWoo NFir WFib
'Gaudy' (Z) WFib
'Gemini' (Z/St/d) CWCL NFir WFib
'Gemma' (R) NFir
'Gemstone' (Sc) ♀H1+3 CSev ENfk LDea MBPg MHer
'Genie' (Z/d) WFib
'Gentle Georgia' (R) WFib
'Georgia' (R) WFib
'Georgia Peach' (R) WFib
'Georgina Blythe' (R) ♀H1+3 WFib
'Gerainbow Neon' (Gerainbow Series) (I) LAst
'Giant Oak' (Sc) MBPg
gibbosum EWoo MHer SSea WFib WGwG WHer
'Ginger Frost' (Sc/v) WFib WGwG
'Ginger Rogers' (Z) NFir
'Glacier Crimson' (Z) SKen
'Glacis'PBR (Quality Series) (Z/d) LAst LSou SSea
'Gladys Evelyn' (Z/d) WFib
'Gladys Weller' (Z/d) WFib
glaucum see *P. lanceolatum*
§ ***glutinosum*** WFib
Golden Angel see *P.* 'Sarah Don'
'Golden Brilliantissimum' (Z/v) SSea WFib
'Golden Chalice' (Min/v) WFib
'Golden Clorinda' (U/Sc/C) CRHN LDea MBPg NFir SSea
'Golden Ears' (Dw/St/C) NFir NPer WFib
'Golden Edinburgh' (I/v) WFib
'Golden Gates' (Z/C) SKen
'Golden Harry Hieover' (Z/C) ♀H1+3 MBri SSea
'Golden Lilac Gem' (I/d) WFib
'Golden Lilac Mist' SKen
'Golden Petit Pierre' (Min/C) SSea
'Golden Princess' (Min/C) WFib
'Golden Square' (Dw/St) WFib
'Golden Staphs' (Z/St/C) MHer NFir
'Golden Wedding' (Z/d/v) NFir
'Golden Well Sweep' see *P. crispum* 'Golden Well Sweep'
'Goldstone Copper' (Min/d) MGbk
'Gooseberry Leaf' see *P. grossularioides*
'Gordano Midnight' (R) EWoo
'Gordon Quale' (Z/d) WFib
'Gosbeck' (A) SSea
'Gosbrook Berry Zest' (A/Sc) **new** MGbk
'Gosbrook Clifford Taylor' (Min/d) MGbk
'Gosbrook Gillian Martin' (Min/d) MGbk
'Gosbrook Jacky Tickner' (Z/Dw/d) **new** MGbk
'Gosbrook Robyn Louise' (Z/St/d) MGbk
'Gosbrook Ryan David' (Z/Dw/d) **new** MGbk
'Gosbrook Snowcap' (Z/St/d) MGbk
'Grace' (A) LDea
'Grace Thomas' (Sc) ♀H1+3 CSev LDea MBPg MHer WFib
'Grace Wells' (Min) WFib
§ 'Gräfin Mariza' (Z/d) SKen
'Grand Slam' (R) CWCL NFir WFib
'Grandad Mac' (Dw/St) NFir SSea
grandiflorum EWoo MCot MHer WFib
graveolens L'Hér. see *P.* 'Graveolens'

	Name	Suppliers
	graveolens *sensu* J.J.A. van der Walt	LDea SBch WFib
§	'Graveolens' (Sc)	ENfk GPoy MBPg MHer SWal WBrk WFib
	'Graveolens Minor' (Sc)	EWoo
	'Great Glemham Lemon' (Sc)	EWoo
	'Green Eyes' (I/d)	MHer SKen
	'Green Goddess' (I/d)	SKen
§	'Greengold Kleine Liebling' (Min/C/v)	SKen
	'Greengold Petit Pierre'	see *P.* 'Greengold Kleine Liebling'
	'Greetings' (Min/v)	MBri WFib
	'Grey Lady Plymouth' (Sc/v)	LDea MBPg MCot MHer WFib
	'Grey Sprite' (Min/v)	WFib
§	***grossularioides***	EOHP MBPg MHer
	- 'Coconut'	MBPg
	'Guernsey Flair' (Z)	LSou
	'Gustav Emich' (Z/d)	SKen
	'Gwen' (Min/v)	NFir
	'H. Rigler' (Z)	SKen
§	'Hannaford Star' (Z/St)	WFib
	'Hannah West' (Z/C)	SSea
	'Hansen's Pinkie' (R)	EWoo
	'Hansen's Wild Spice' (Sc)	MBPg
	'Happy Anniversary' (Dw/C)	NFir
	'Happy Appleblossom' (Z/v/d)	NFir
	(Happy Face Series) Happy Face Mex = 'Pacvet'PBR (I)	NPri
	- Happy Face Velvet Red = 'Pachafvel'PBR (I)	NPri
	'Happy Thought' (Z/v) ♀H1+3	MBri MCot NFir SCoo SKen SSea WFib
	'Harbour Lights' (R)	WFib
	'Harewood Slam' (R)	WFib
	'Harlequin Mahogany' (I/d)	SKen
	'Harlequin Pretty Girl' (I × Z/d)	WFib
	'Harlequin Rosie O'Day' (I)	SKen WFib
	'Harvard' (I/d)	WFib
	havlasae	ECou
	'Hazel' (R)	WFib
	'Hazel Cherry' (R)	CWCL WFib
	'Hazel Choice' (R)	NFir
	'Hazel Perfection' (R)	NFir
	'Hazel Star' (R)	WFib
	'Hazel Stardust' (R)	NFir
§	'Hederinum' (I)	LSou
§	'Hederinum Variegatum' (I/v)	MCot NFir SPet WFib
	'Helen Christine' (Z/St)	NFir WFib
	'Hemingstone' (A)	LDea
	'Hemley' (Sc)	LDea
	'Henry Weller' (A)	NFir WFib
	'Hermione' (Z/d)	WFib
	'Highfields Appleblossom' (Z)	SKen
	'Highfields Attracta' (Z/d)	SKen WFib
	'Highfields Candy Floss' (Z/d)	NFir
	'Highfields Choice' (Z)	SKen
	'Highfields Comet' (Z)	SKen
	'Highfields Contessa' (Z/d)	SKen
	'Highfields Delight' (Z)	WFib
	'Highfields Fancy' (Z/d)	NFir SKen
	'Highfields Festival' (Z/d)	NFir SKen WFib
	'Highfields Melody' (Z/d)	WFib
	'Highfields Pride' (Z)	SKen WFib
	'Highfields Prima Donna' (Z/d)	SKen
	'Highfields Symphony' (Z)	WFib
	'Hilbre Island' (Z/C/d)	NFir
	'Hills of Snow' (Z/v)	MBri MHer SKen SSea WFib
	'Hillscheider Amethyst'PBR	see *P.* Amethyst = 'Fisdel'
	'Hindoo' (R × U)	CSpe EWoo NFir SBch SSea WFib
	hispidum	MHer
	'Hitcham' (Min/d)	WFib
	'Holbrook' (Dw/C/d)	NFir WFib
	'Holt Beauty'	EWoo
	'Honeywood Suzanne' (Min/Fr)	SKen
	'Honne Frühling' (Z)	SKen
	'Honnestolz' (Dw)	SKen
	'Hope Valley' (Dw/C/d) ♀H1+3	NFir SKen
	'House and Garden' (R)	NFir
	'Hula' (R × U)	EWoo
	'Hunter's Moon' (Z/C)	NFir
	'Icing Sugar' (I/d)	WFib
	'Immaculatum' (Z)	WFib
	'Imperial Butterfly' (A/Sc)	CRHN ENfk LDea NFir SSea WFib
	ionidiflorum	CSpe EShb MCot MHer MNHC SPhx
	'Irene' (Z/d) ♀H1+3	SKen WFib
	'Irene Picardy' (Z/d)	SKen
	'Irene Toyon' (Z) ♀H1+3	SKen WFib
	'Isidel' (I/d) ♀H1+3	SKen
	'Islington Peppermint' (Sc)	NFir SBch WFib
	'Isobel Eden' (Sc)	LDea MBPg
	'Italian Gem' (I)	SKen
	'Ivalo' (Z/d)	SKen WFib
	'Ivory Snow' (Z/d/v)	NFir WFib
	'Jacey' (Z/d)	SKen
	'Jack of Hearts' (I × Z/d)	WFib
	'Jack Wood' (Z/d)	NFir
§	'Jackie' (I/d)	MBri WFib
	'Jackie Davies' (R)	EWoo
	'Jackie Gall'	see *P.* 'Jackie'
	'Jackie Totlis' (Z/St)	WFib
	'Jackpot Wild Rose' (Z/d)	WFib
	'Jacqueline' (Z/d)	SKen
	'Jane Biggin' (Dw/C/d)	SKen
	'Janet Hofman' (Z/d)	WFib
	'Janet Kerrigan' (Min/d)	WFib
	'Jayne Eyre' (Min/d)	SKen WFib
	'Jean Bart' (I)	SSea
	'Jean Caws' (Z/St)	WFib
	'Jean Oberle' (Z/d)	SKen
	'Jeanie Hunt' (Z/C/d)	NFir
§	'Jeanne d'Arc' (I/d)	SKen WFib
	'Jer'Rey' (A)	EWoo LDea NFir SSea WFib
	'Jessel's Unique' (U)	SPet
	'Jill Brown' (Min/St/C)	MGbk
	'Jip's Bunjy' **new**	NFir
	'Jip's Desert Dawn' (Z/Min) **new**	WFib
	'Jip's Desert Poppy' (Z/Min) **new**	WFib
	'Jip's Freda Burgess' (Z/C/d)	NFir
	'Jip's John Morbey' (Z/C/d) **new**	MGbk
	'Jip's Pip' (Z/C/d)	MGbk NFir
	'Jip's Rosy Glow' (Min/d)	NFir
	'Jip's Timmy' (Z/C/Dw/d) **new**	MGbk
	'Joan Fontaine' (Z)	WFib
	'Joan Morf' (R)	EWoo NFir WFib

	Name	Suppliers
	'Joan of Arc'	see *P.* 'Jeanne d'Arc'
	'John's Pride' (Dw)	MBri NFir
	'Joseph Wheeler' (A)	LDea
	'Joy' (I)	SPet
	'Joy' (R) ♀H1+3	CSpe NFir WFib
I	'Joy' (Z/d)	SKen
	'Joy Lucille' (Sc)	LDea MBPg
	'Juliana' (R)	LAst
	'Julie Smith' (R)	WFib
	'Juniper' (Sc)	MBPg
	'Just Bella' (d)	NFir
	'Just Beth' (Z/C/d)	NFir
	'Just Joss' (Dw/d)	NFir
	'Just Rita' (A)	SSea
	'Just William' (Min/C/d)	WFib
	'Kamahl' (R)	WFib
§	'Kardinal' (Z/d)	SPet
	'Karen' (Dw/C)	LSou
	'Karl Hagele' (Z/d)	WFib
	'Karmin Ball'	WFib
	'Karrooense'	see *P. quercifolium*
	'Katie' (R)	EWoo
	'Katrine'	CWCL LAst NPri
	'Kayleigh Aitken' (R)	CWCL
	'Kayleigh West' (Min)	SSea
	'Keepsake' (Min/d)	WFib
	'Keith Vernon' (Z)	NFir
	'Ken Lea Butterfly' (Z/d)	MGbk
	'Kenny's Double' (Z/d)	WFib
	'Kensington' (A)	LDea
	'Kerensa' (Min/d)	WFib
	'Kesgrave' (Min/d)	WFib
	'Kettlebaston' (A) ♀H1+3	LDea
	'Kewense' (Z)	EShb
	'Kimono' (R)	NFir
	'Kinder Gaisha' (R)	NFir
	'King Edmund' (R)	NFir
	'King of Balcon'	see *P.* 'Hederinum'
	'King of Denmark' (Z/d)	WFib
	'King Solomon' (R)	WFib
§	'Kleine Liebling' (Min)	WFib
	'Kyoto' (R)	NFir
	'La France' (I/d) ♀H1+3	MCot SKen WFib
	'La Paloma' (R)	WFib
	Laced Red Mini Cascade = 'Achspen' (I)	NFir
§	'Lachskönigin' (I/d)	SKen SPet WFib
	'Lady Ilchester' (Z/d)	SKen WFib
	'Lady Love Song' (R)	NFir WFib
	'Lady Mary' (Sc)	EWoo MBPg MHer
	'Lady Mavis Pilkington' (Z/d)	WFib
	'Lady Plymouth' (Sc/v) ♀H1+3	CRHN CSpe ENfk EPfP EShb EWoo LDea MBPg MCot MHer MNHC MSCN NEgg NFir SBfd SKen SPet SSea SWal WFib WGwG
§	'Lady Scarborough' (Sc)	ENfk EWoo MBPg MHer WFib
	'Lady Woods' (Z)	SSea
	laevigatum	MHer
	'Lakeland' (I)	SKen SSea
	'Lancastrian' (Z/d)	WFib
§	***lanceolatum***	MHer
	'Lara Aladin' (A)	LDea
	'Lara Ballerina'	NFir SBch
	'Lara Candy Dancer' (Sc) ♀H1+3	CRHN LDea MBPg SBch WFib
	'Lara Jester' (Sc)	ENfk EWoo WFib
	'Lara Nomad' (Sc)	LDea MBPg
	'Lara Rajah' (R)	EWoo

	Name	Suppliers
	'Lara Starshine' (Sc) ♀H1+3	ENfk EWoo MHer NFir WFib
	'Lara Waltz' (R/d)	WFib
	'Larkfield' (Z/v)	SSea
N	'Lass o' Gowrie' (Z/v)	NFir SKen
	'Lateripes' (I)	SKen
	Laura = 'Penlau' (Z) **new**	WMoo
	'Laura Wheeler' (A)	LDea
	'Laurel Hayward' (R)	WFib
	'Lauren Alexandra' (Z/d)	WFib
	'Lavender Grand Slam' (R) ♀H1+3	NFir
	'Lavender Mini Cascade'PBR	see *P.* Lilac Mini Cascade
	'Lavender Sensation' (R)	WFib
	'Lawrenceanum'	WFib
	'L'Élégante' (I/v) ♀H1+3	EWoo MCot MHer SKen SSea WFib
	'Lemon Air' (Sc)	MBPg
	'Lemon Crisp'	see *P. crispum*
	'Lemon Fancy' (Sc)	LDea MBPg MCot MHer NFir WFib
	'Lemon Fizz' **new**	ENfk
	'Lemon Kiss' (Sc)	CSpe EWoo MBPg
	'Lemon Meringue' (Sc)	MBPg
	'Lemon Toby' (Sc)	MBPg
	'Leslie William Burrows'	EWoo
	'Letitia' (A)	ENfk
	Lila Compakt-Cascade	see *P.* 'Decora Lilas'
	'Lilac Gem' (Min/I/d)	ENfk MCot SKen
§	Lilac Mini Cascade = 'Lilamica'PBR (I)	NFir
	'Lili Marlene' (I)	SKen SPet
	'Lilian' (I/d) **new**	SKen
	'Lilian Pottinger' (Sc)	CRHN CSev ENfk EWoo LDea MBPg MHer NFir SKen SSea
	'Lilian Woodberry' (Z)	WFib
	Lilly = 'Paclill'PBR	NPri
	'Limoneum' (Sc)	CSev ENfk MBPg MHer
	'Lindy Portas' (I/d)	SKen
	'Lipstick' (St)	WFib
	'Lisa Jo' (St/v/Dw/d)	WFib
	'Little Alice' (Dw/d) ♀H1+3	NFir WFib
	'Little Blakenham' (A)	LDea
	'Little Gem' (Sc)	ENfk MBPg MHer SSea WFib
	'Little Jim' (Min/d)	NFir
	'Little Jip' (Z/d/v)	NFir WFib
	'Little Spikey' (St/Min/d)	WFib
	'Lord Baden-Powell'	see *P.* 'Colonel Baden-Powell'
	'Lord Bute' (R) ♀H1+3	CSpe ECtt EWoo MCot MHer MSCN NFir NPer SBch SGar SIde SKen SMrm SPet SSea SUsu WFib WGwG
	'Lord de Ramsey'	see *P.* 'Tip Top Duet'
	'Lord Roberts' (Z)	WFib
	Lorena = 'Pacdala'PBR (Dark Line Series) (Z/d)	LAst
	'Lorna' (Dw/d)	LAst
	'Lotusland' (Dw/St/C)	NFir WFib
I	'Louise' (R)	NFir
	'Love Song' (R/v)	NFir WFib
	'Lucy Gunnett' (Z/d/v)	NFir
	luridum	WCot
	'Lyewood Bonanza' (R)	CWCL WFib
	'Lyric' (Min/d)	SKen
	'Mabel Grey' (Sc) ♀H1+3	CRHN CSev CSpe ENfk EWoo MBPg MCot MHer MNHC NFir NPer SBch SIde SSea WFib
§	'Madame Auguste Nonin' (U/Sc)	ENfk MHer NFir SBch WFib
	'Madame Butterfly' (Z/d/v)	NFir SKen
	'Madame Crousse' (I/d) ♀H1+3	EWoo WFib
	'Madame Hibbault' (Z)	SKen

	'Madame Layal' (A)	EWoo MHer NFir SBch WFib
	'Madame Margot'	see *P.* 'Hederinum Variegatum'
	'Madame Salleron' (Min/v) 🏆$^{H1+3}$	LDea LSou WBrk
	'Madge Taylor' (R)	NFir
	'Magaluf' (I/C/d)	SSea
	'Magic Lantern' (Z/C)	NFir
	'Magnum' (R)	WFib
	'Mairi' (A)	LDea
	'Majesta' (Z/d)	SKen
	'Mamie' (Z/d)	SKen
	'Mangles' Variegated' (Z/v)	WFib
	'Manx Maid' (A)	LDea NFir
	'Maple Leaf' (Sc)	EWoo MBPg
	'Marble Sunset'	see *P.* 'Wood's Surprise'
	'Marchioness of Bute' (R/Dec)	MHer NFir WFib
	'Maréchal MacMahon' (Z/C)	ENfk SKen SSea
	'Margaret Soley' (R) 🏆$^{H1+3}$	WFib
	'Margaret Waite' (R)	WFib
	'Margery Stimpson' (Min/d)	WFib
	'Marie Thomas' (Sc)	LDea MBPg SBch
	Marimba = 'Fisrimba'^{PBR}	SCoo
	'Mariquita' (R)	WFib
	'Mark' (Dw/d)	WFib
	'Marquis of Bute' (R/v)	NFir
	'Martin Parrett' (Min/d)	WFib
	'Mary Harrison' (Z/d)	WFib
	'Masquerade' (R)	SPet
	'Masterpiece' (Z/C/d)	SKen
I	'Maureen' Hoddinott (Z/d) **new**	MHer
	'Mauve Beauty' (I/d)	SKen WFib
	'Maxime Kovalevski' (Z)	WFib
	'Maxine' (Z/C)	NFir
	'May Day' (R)	WFib
	'May Magic' (R)	NFir WFib
	'Meadowside Dark and Dainty' (St)	NFir SKen WFib
	'Meadowside Harvest' (Z/St/C)	NFir
	'Meadowside Julie Colley' (Dw)	NFir
	'Meadowside Midnight' (St/C)	WFib
	'Medallion' (Z/C)	SSea
	'Medley' (Min/d)	WFib
	'Megan Hannah' (Dw/c/d)	MGbk NFir
	'Melanie Day' (St)	NFir
	'Memento' (Min/d)	WFib
	'Mendip' (R)	WFib
	'Mendip Anne' (R)	NFir
	'Mendip Barbie' (R)	NFir
	'Mendip Blanche' (R)	NFir
	'Mendip Lorraine' (R)	NFir
	'Mendip Louise' (R)	NFir
	'Mendip Sarah' (R)	NFir
	'Meon Maid' (R)	WFib
	'Mere Casino' (Z)	WFib
	'Merry-go-round' (Z/C/v)	MGbk
	'Mexican Beauty' (I)	SKen WFib
	'Mexicana'	see *P.* 'Rouletta'
	'Mexicanerin'	see *P.* 'Rouletta'
	'Michael' (A)	LDea MHer NFir
	'Michelle' (Min/C)	LDea
	'Michelle West' (Min)	WFib
	'Milden' (Dw/Z/C)	NFir
	'Millfield Gem' (I/d)	WFib
	'Millfield Rose' (I/d)	EWoo
	'Mini-Czech' (Min/St)	WBrk
	'Minnie' (Z/d/St)	WBrk
	'Minstrel Boy' (R)	EWoo WFib
	'Minx' (Min/d)	WFib
	'Miss Burdett Coutts' (Z/v)	MHer SKen SSea WFib
	'Miss McKinsey' (Z/St/d)	NFir
	'Miss Muffett' (Min/d)	WFib
§	'Miss Stapleton'	EWoo MHer WFib
	'Misterioso' (R)	EWoo WFib
	'Misty Morning' (R)	EWoo WFib
	'Modesty' (Z/d)	WFib
	'Mohawk' (R)	NFir WFib
	'Mole'	see *P.* 'The Mole'
	mollicomum	WCot
	'Monica Bennett' (Dw)	SKen
	'Monkwood Rose' (A)	LDea NFir
	'Monsal Dale' (Dw/C/d)	SKen
	'Monsieur Ninon' misapplied	see *P.* 'Madame Auguste Nonin'
§	'Monsieur Ninon' (U)	CRHN WFib
	'Mont Blanc' (Z/v)	WFib
	'Montague Garabaldi Smith' (R)	CWCL WFib
	'Moon Maiden' (A)	EWoo LDea WFib
	Morning Sun = 'Pacmorsu' (Green Leaf Series) (Z) **new**	LAst
	'Morse' (Z)	SKen
	'Morval' (Dw/C/d) 🏆$^{H1+3}$	WFib
	'Morwenna' (R)	MHer NFir SMrm WCot WFib
	'Mosaic Gay Baby' (I/v/d)	WFib
	'Mr Henry Cox' (Z/v) 🏆$^{H1+3}$	MHer NFir SKen WFib
	'Mr Wren' (Z)	SKen WFib
	'Mrs A.M. Mayne' (Z)	SKen
	'Mrs Cannell' (Z)	WFib
	'Mrs Dumbrill' (A)	LDea
	'Mrs Eve Scott' (Z/d)	MGbk
	'Mrs Farren' (Z/v)	MCot SKen
	'Mrs G.H. Smith' (A)	LDea MBPg NFir WFib
	'Mrs J.C. Mappin' (Z/v) 🏆$^{H1+3}$	SKen
	'Mrs Kingsbury' (U)	SKen WFib
	'Mrs Martin' (I/d)	WFib
	'Mrs May Last' (Z/St/v)	MGbk
	'Mrs McKenzie' (Z/St)	WFib
	'Mrs Parker' (Z/d/v)	NFir SKen WFib
	'Mrs Pat' (Dw/St/C)	NFir
	'Mrs Pollock' (Z/v)	EUJe LAst MCot NEgg SCoo SKen SSea WBrk WFib
	'Mrs Quilter' (Z/C) 🏆$^{H1+3}$	MBri SKen SMrm SSea WBrk WFib
	'Mrs Strang' (Z/d/v)	SKen SSea
	'Mrs Taylor' (Sc)	MBPg
	'Mrs W.A.R. Clifton' (I/d)	LDea SKen WFib
	mutans	WFib
§	'Mutzel' (I/v)	NFir
	'My Chance' (Dec)	NFir WFib
§	***myrrhifolium*** var. ***coriandrifolium***	CSpe MHer NFir WCot WFib
	'Mystery' (U) 🏆$^{H1+3}$	CWCL NFir SSea WFib
	'Nancy Grey' (Min)	NFir
	'Narina' (I)	SCoo
	Nealit 2 = 'Pennea'^{PBR} (I/d)	NPri
	'Needham Market' (A)	LDea
	'Neil Jameson' (Z/v)	SKen
	'Nellie Nuttall' (Z)	WFib
	'Nervosum' (Sc)	MBPg
	'Nervous Mabel' (Sc) 🏆$^{H1+3}$	LDea MHer WBrk WFib
	'New Day' (A)	LDea

	Name	Suppliers
	'New Gypsy' (R) **new**	CWCL
	'New Life' (Z)	NFir
	'Nicola Buck' (R)	NFir
	'Nicor Star' (Min)	WFib
	'Nikki' (A)	LDea
	'Noche' (R)	SMrm
	'Noele Gordon' (Z/d)	WFib
	'Notting Hill Beauty' (Z)	SKen
	oblongatum	NFir
	'Occold Profusion' (Dw/d)	NFir
	'Occold Shield' (Dw/C/d)	NEgg NFir SMrm SSea WBrk WFib
	'Occold Tangerine' (Z)	WFib
	'Occold Volcano' (Dw/C/d)	WFib
	'Octavia Hill' (Z) **new**	LAst
	odoratissimum (Sc)	ENfk EWoo GPoy LDea MBPg MHer NFir SKen SSea WFib WGwG
	'Odyssey' (Min)	WFib
	'Old Orchard' (A)	LDea
	'Old Rose' (Z/d)	WFib
	'Old Spice' (Sc/v)	ENfk EWoo LDea MBPg MCot NFir SWal WFib WGwG
	'Oldbury Duet' (A/v)	LDea MHer NFir SSea
	'Olga Shipstone' (Sc)	MBPg
	'Olivia' (R)	WFib
	'Onalee' (Dw)	WFib
	'Opera House' (R)	WFib
	'Orange Fizz' (Sc)	EWoo MHer NFir
	'Orange Fizz' (Z/d)	LDea
	'Orange King' (Z/s) **new**	SKen
	'Orange Parfait' (R)	WFib
I	'Orange Princeanum' (Sc)	MBPg
	'Orange Splash' (Z)	SKen
	'Orangeade' (Dw/d)	WFib
	'Orchid Clorinda' (Sc)	MBPg WFib
	'Orchid Paloma' (Dw/d)	SKen
	'Orion' (Min/d)	SKen SSea WFib
	'Orsett' (Sc) ♀H1+3	LDea
	'Osna' (Z)	SKen
	'Otto's Red' (R)	NFir
	'Our Amy' (Z/d)	SSea
	'Our Flynn' (Z/St) **new**	WFib
	'Our Gynette' (Dec)	EWoo
	'Overchurch' (Dw)	NFir
	PAC cultivars	see under selling name
	'Pagoda' (Z/St/d)	MHer SKen WFib
	'Paisley Red' (Z/d)	NFir WFib
	'Pam Tutcher' (St) **new**	NFir
	'Pamela Vaughan' (Z/St)	WFib
	'Pampered Lady' (A)	LDea NFir
	panduriforme	WFib
	papilionaceum	CHEx CRHN EWoo MCot MHer SSea WFib
	'Parisienne' (R)	CWCL EWoo WFib
	'Party Dress' (Z/d)	WFib
	'Pascal' (Z)	SKen
	'Pat Hannam' (St)	WFib
	'Paton's Unique' (U/Sc) ♀H1+3	CRHN ENfk EWoo MCot MHer NFir SPet SSea WCot WFib
	'Patricia Andrea' (T)	NFir NPer WFib
	'Patsy 'Q'' (Z/C)	SKen
	'Paul Crampel' (Z)	MCot MHer SSea WFib
	'Paul Gotz' (Z)	SKen
	'Paul West' (Min/d)	SBch
	'Peace' (Min/C)	WFib
	'Peach Princess' (R)	NFir
	'Peaches and Cream' (R)	MBPg
	'Peacock'	LDea
	Pearl Necklace	see *P.* 'Perlenkette'
	PELFI cultivars	see under selling name
	peltatum	WFib
	'Penny' (Z/d)	WFib
	'Penny Dixon' (R)	NFir
	'Penny Lane' (Z)	WFib
	'Penny Serenade' (Dw/C)	SKen
	'Pensby' (Dw)	NFir
	'Peppermint Lace' (Sc)	CSev EWoo MBPg
	'Peppermint Scented Rose' (Sc)	MBPg MSCN
	'Percy Hunt' (R)	NFir
	'Perfect' (Z)	WFib
§	'Perlenkette' (Z/d)	MHer
	'Pershore Princess'	WBrk
	'Petals' (Z/v)	SKen
	'Peter Godwin' (R)	WFib
	'Peter's Choice' (R)	WFib
	'Peter's Luck' (Sc) ♀H1+3	MBPg
	'Petit Pierre'	see *P.* 'Kleine Liebling'
	'Philomel' (I/d)	SPet
	'Phyllis' (U/v)	ENfk EWoo MBPg MHer NFir SSea
	'Phyllis Variegated' (v)	MCot MSCN WCot
	'Picotee'	MHer
	'Pink Aurore' (U)	WFib
	'Pink Bonanza' (R)	NFir WFib
	'Pink Capitatum'	see *P.* 'Pink Capricorn'
§	'Pink Capricorn' (Sc)	CRHN ENfk EWoo MBPg WFib
	'Pink Cascade'	see *P.* 'Hederinum'
	'Pink Champagne' (Sc)	CRHN MCot MHer
	'Pink Countess Mariza' (Z)	SKen
	'Pink Dolly Varden' (Z/v)	WFib
	'Pink Fondant' (Min/d)	WFib
	'Pink Gay Baby'	see *P.* 'Sugar Baby'
	'Pink Happy Thought' (Z/v)	SWal WFib
	'Pink Hindoo' (Dec)	EWoo
	'Pink Ice' (Min/d)	NFir
	'Pink Mini Cascade'	see *P.* 'Rosa Mini-cascade'
	'Pink Needles' (Min/St)	WFib
	'Pink Pet' (U) **new**	NFir
	'Pink Rambler' (Z/d)	SKen WFib
	'Pink Rosebud' (Z/d)	WFib
	Pink Sybil = 'Pacpisyb' (I/d) **new**	NPri
	'Pippa' (Min/Dw)	NFir
	'Playmate' (Min/St)	WFib
	'Plum Rambler' (Z/d)	EShb WBrk WFib
	'Poetesse' (A)	LDea
	'Polka' (U)	EWoo NFir WFib
	'Pompeii' (R)	NFir WFib
	'Poquita' (Sc)	MBPg
	'Porchfield' (Min/St)	WBrk
	'Potpourri' (Min)	SKen
	'Preston Park' (Z/C)	SKen WFib
	'Pretty Girl' (I)	MCot
	'Pretty Polly' (Sc)	LDea WFib
	'Prim' (Dw/St/d)	WFib
	'Prince of Orange' (Sc)	CSev ENfk EWoo GPoy LDea MBPg MCot MHer NFir SBch SIde SPet SSea SWal WFib WGwG
	'Princeanum' (Sc) ♀H1+3	MBPg WFib
	'Princess Abigail' (Dw/d)	NFir
	'Princess Alexandra' (Z/d/v)	SKen
	'Princess Anne' (Z)	CSpe
	'Princess Josephine' (R)	WFib
	'Princess of Wales' (R)	WFib
	'Princess Virginia' (R/v)	WFib
	'Priory Coral' (Z/St/v)	MGbk
	'Priory Salmon' (St/d)	EShb
	'Priory Star' (St/Min/d)	WFib
	'Prosperity' (Sc)	LDea MBPg

	pseudoglutinosum	WFib
	'Purple Heart' (Dw/St/C)	NFir
	'Purple Rogue' (R)	WFib
	'Purple Unique' (U/Sc)	ENfk EWoo MCot MHer NFir SKen WFib
	'Pygmalion' (Z/d/v)	SSea WFib
	'Quantock' (R)	WFib
	'Quantock Angelique' (A)	NFir
	'Quantock Beauty' (A)	LDea
	'Quantock Blonde' (A)	LDea
	'Quantock Candy' (A)	EWoo NFir
	'Quantock Clare' (A)	NFir
	'Quantock Classic' (A)	EWoo NFir
	'Quantock Darren' (A)	NFir
	'Quantock Double Dymond' (A)	NFir
	'Quantock Kendy' (A)	CWCL LDea NFir
	'Quantock Kirsty' (A)	EWoo LDea NFir
	'Quantock Louise' (A)	NFir
	'Quantock Marjorie' (A)	LDea NFir SSea
	'Quantock Matty' (A)	LDea NFir
	'Quantock May' (A)	LDea NFir
	'Quantock Medoc' (A)	LDea
	'Quantock Millennium' (A)	CWCL LDea
	'Quantock Mr Nunn' (A)	NFir
	'Quantock Perfection' (A)	NFir
	'Quantock Rory' (A)	LDea
	'Quantock Rose' (A)	LDea
	'Quantock Sally' (A/d)	NFir
	'Quantock Sapphire' (A)	LDea
	'Quantock Shirley' (A)	LDea
	'Quantock Star' (A)	CWCL LDea NFir
	'Quantock Ultimate' (A)	NFir
	'Queen of Denmark' (Z/d)	SKen WFib
	'Queen of Hearts' (I × Z/d)	WFib
	'Queen of the Lemons'	EWoo
N	***quercifolium*** (Sc)	CRHN CSev GPoy MBPg MNHC SKen WFib
	- variegated (v)	MBPg SKen
	quinquelobatum	CSpe
	radens (Sc)	ENfk WFib
	'Rads Star' (Z/St)	NFir
	'Radula' (Sc) ϒH1+3	CSev ENfk LDea MBPg MHer MNHC SBch SSea SWal WFib
	'Radula Roseum' (Sc)	EWoo SSea WFib
	'Raphael' (A)	LDea
	'Raspberry Ripple' (A)	LDea NFir
	'Raspberry Surprise' (R)	SSea
	'Ray Bidwell' (Min)	NFir WFib
	'Red Admiral' (Min/d/v)	SKen
§	'Red Black Vesuvius' (Min/C)	SKen SSea WFib
	'Red Cactus' (St)	NFir
	'Red Capri' (Sc)	MBPg
	'Red Cascade' (I) ϒH1+3	WFib
	'Red Ice' (Min/d)	NFir
	'Red Magic Lantern' (Z/C)	SKen
	'Red Pandora' (Z)	NFir WFib
	'Red Rambler' (Z/d)	SKen WBrk WFib
	'Red Robin' (R)	WCot
	'Red Silver Cascade'	see *P.* 'Mutzel'
	'Red Spider' (Dw/Ca)	WFib
	'Red Startel' (Z/St/d)	SKen WFib
	'Red Susan Pearce' (R)	WFib
	Red Sybil = 'Pensyb'PBR (I/d)	NPri
	'Red Velvet' (R)	LBMP
	'Red Witch' (Dw/St/d)	MHer WBrk WFib
	Red-Blizzard = 'Fizzard' (I)	MCot SCoo
§	Red-Mini-Cascade = 'Rotemica' (I)	SKen
	'Reflections' (Z/d)	WFib
	'Reg 'Q'' (Z/C)	NFir
	'Regina' (Z/d)	SKen WFib
	'Rembrandt' (R)	WFib
	'Renate Parsley'	MCot MHer NFir SSea WFib
	reniforme	GPoy MBPg MHer SSea SUsu WFib
	'Retah's Crystal' (Z/v)	MGbk
	'Reverend David Harley' (Z)	NFir
	'Rhian Harris' (A)	LDea
	'Rhineland' (I)	SKen
	'Richard Gibbs' (Sc)	ENfk LDea MBPg MHer
	'Richard Key' (Z/d/C)	WFib
	'Richard Upward' (Z/d)	MGbk
	'Ricky Black Velvet' (A)	LDea
	'Ricky Cheerful' (A)	LDea
	'Ricky Promise' (A)	LDea
	'Ricky Ruby' (A)	LDea
	'Rietje van der Lee' (A)	ENfk WFib
	'Rigel' (Min/d)	NFir SKen
	'Rigi' (I/d)	MBri SKen
	'Rimey' (St)	NFir
	'Rimfire' (R)	CWCL EWoo MHer NFir WFib
	'Rio Grande' (I/d)	MHer NFir SKen SPet SWal WFib
	'Rising Sun'	NFir
	'Rita Scheen' (A/v)	SSea
	'Rober's Lemon Rose' (Sc)	CRHN ENfk MBPg MCot MHer SIde SSea WBrk
	'Robert Fish' (Z/C)	SCoo
	'Robert McElwain' (Z/d)	WFib
	'Robin' (Sc)	MBPg
	'Robin's Unique' (U)	EWoo WFib
	'Robyn Hannah' (St/d)	NFir
	rodneyanum	CDes
	'Rogue' (R)	WFib
	'Roi des Balcons'	see *P.* 'Hederinum'
	'Roi des Balcons Des Rameaux' (I)	SKen
§	'Roi des Balcons Impérial' (I) ϒH1+3	SKen
	'Roi des Balcons Mauve' (I)	SKen
	'Roi des Balcons Rose'	see *P.* 'Hederinum'
	'Roller's Echo' (A)	LDea WFib
	'Roller's Pioneer' (I/v)	ENfk EWoo SKen
	'Roller's Satinique' (U) ϒH1+3	MHer
	'Roller's Shadow' (A)	LDea
	'Rollison's Unique' (U)	MHer WFib
	'Romeo' (R)	EWoo
	'Rookley' (St/d)	NFir
§	'Rosa Mini-cascade' (I)	NFir
	'Rose Bengal' (A)	ENfk LDea
	'Rose of Amsterdam' (Min/d)	WFib
	'Rose Paton's Unique' (U/Sc)	SMrm
	'Rose Pope' (R)	MGbk
	'Rose Silver Cascade' (I)	MCot MHer
	'Rose Startel' (Z/St)	SKen
	'Rosebud Supreme' (Z/d)	WFib
	'Rosette' (Dw/d)	SKen
	'Rosmaroy' (R)	WFib
	'Rospen' (Z/d)	SKen
	'Rosy Dawn' (Min/d)	WFib
	'Rote Mini-cascade'	see *P.* Red-Mini-Cascade
§	'Rouletta' (I/d)	LAst SKen WFib
	'Royal Ascot' (R)	NFir SPet SSea
	'Royal Norfolk' (Min/d)	NFir SKen

	Cultivar	Suppliers
	'Royal Oak' (Sc) 🏆H1+3	CRHN CSev ENfk LDea MBPg MCot MHer MNHC SBch SPet SSea SWal WFib
§	'Royal Purple' (Z/d)	SKen WFib
	'Royal Sovereign' (Z/C/d)	LDea
	'Royal Surprise' (R)	EWoo NFir
	'Ruben' (d)	LSou
	'Ruby' (Min/d)	WFib
	'Ruby Orchid' (A)	LDea
	'Ruffled Velvet' (R)	EWoo
	'Rushmere' (Dw/d)	WFib
	'Rushmoor Golden Rosebud' (Z)	MGbk WFib
	'Rushmoor Golden Ruffles' (Z/St/Min/C/d) **new**	MGbk
	'Rushmoor Jazz' (Z/St/v)	MGbk
	'Rushmoor Mrs Eve Scott' (Z/d) **new**	WFib
	'Rushmoor Rhapsody' (St)	MGbk
	'Rushmoor Wind Chimes' (St)	MGbk
	'Saint Elmo's Fire' (St/Min/d)	MHer WFib
	Saint Malo = 'Guisaint' (I)	NFir
	'Salmon Beauty' (Dw/d)	WFib
§	'Salmon Irene' (Z/d)	WFib
	Salmon Princess = 'Pacsalpri' PBR	LAst LSou
	'Salmon Queen'	see *P.* 'Lachskönigin'
	'Samantha' (R)	WFib
	'Samantha Stamp' (Dw/d/C)	WFib
	Samelia = 'Pensam' PBR (Dark Line Series) (Z/d)	LAst LBMP SWal WGor
	'Sancho Panza' (Dec) 🏆H1+3	CSpe LDea SKen SSea WFib
	'Sandra Lorraine' (I/d)	WFib
	'Sanguineum'	CSev CSpe
	'Sanibel' (Min/d)	MGbk
	'Santa Maria' (Z/d)	SKen
	'Santa Paula' (I/d)	SKen
§	'Sarah Don' (A/v)	WFib
	'Sarah Hunt' (Min/d)	NFir
	'Sarah Jane' (Sc)	MBPg
	'Sassa' PBR (Quality Series) (Z/d)	LAst
	'Satsuki' (R)	NFir
	'Scarborough Fair' (A)	NFir
	'Scarlet Gem' (Z/St)	WBrk WFib
	'Scarlet Pet' (U)	MBPg NFir SMrm
	'Scarlet Rambler' (Z/d)	EShb SMrm WFib
	'Scarlet Unique' (U)	CRHN EWoo MCot SKen SSea WFib
	schizopetalum	WFib
§	'Schneekönigin' (I/d)	SKen
	'Schottii'	MHer NFir WFib
	'Scottow Star' (Z/C)	WFib
	'Seale Star' (Dw/St/C)	SSea
	'Seaview Lilac' (Z/Min/C) **new**	MGbk
	'Seaview Silver' (Min/St)	WFib
	'Seaview Sparkler' (Z/St)	WFib
	'Secret Love' (Sc)	LDea MBPg
	'Seeley's Pansy' (A)	EWoo LDea MHer
	'Sefton' (R) 🏆H1+3	WFib
	'Selena' (Min)	LDea
	'Semer' (Min)	SKen
	'Shan Hoy' (Dw)	NFir
	'Shanks' (Z)	NFir
	'Shannon'	EWoo SBch WFib
	'Shelley' (Dw)	SKen
	'Shirley Ash' (A)	LDea
	Shocking Orange = 'Pacshorg' (Quality Series)	LAst
	Shocking Pink = 'Pensho' PBR (Quality Series) (Z/d)	LAst
	Shocking Violet = 'Pacshovi' PBR (Quality Series) (Z/d)	LAst
	'Shogan' (R)	NFir
§	'Shottesham Pet' (Sc)	ENfk EWoo MHer MNHC
	'Shrubland Pet' (U/Sc)	SKen
	sidoides	CDes CEnt CSpe EWoo GPoy LAst MBPg MCot MHer NFir SBch SMHy SMrm SPhx SSea WFib WGwG WHer
	- black-flowered	CTca SBrt
	- 'Sloe Gin Fizz'	CSpe
	Sidonia = 'Pensid' PBR (Dark Line Series) (Z/d)	LAst WGor
	'Sienna' (R)	NFir
	'Sil Falko' PBR (I)	LSou WGor
	'Sil Hero' PBR (Z)	WGor
	'Sil Linus' PBR (Z)	LSou
	'Sil Malaika' PBR (I)	LSou
	'Sil Pia' PBR (I)	LSou
	'Sil Tomke' PBR (I)	LSou
	'Sil Wittje' PBR (I)	LAst
	'Silver Anne' (R/v)	NFir
	'Silver Blazon' (Z/Dw/C/v) **new**	MGbk WFib
	'Silver Delight' (v/d)	WFib
	'Silver Kewense' (Dw/v)	WFib
	'Silver Lady' (Z/d/v)	MGbk
	'Silver Leaf Rose' (Sc)	MBPg
	'Silver Shadow' (Z/Dw/C/d/v) **new**	MGbk
	'Silver Snow' (Min/St/d)	WFib
	'Silver Splash' (Z/v)	MGbk
	'Silver Wings' (Z/v)	NFir
	'Simon Portas' (I/d)	SKen
	'Sir Colin' (Z)	SSea
	'Skelly's Pride' (Z)	SKen WFib
	'Skies of Italy' (Z/C/d)	MBri SKen SSea WFib
	'Small Fortune' (Min/d)	SKen
	'Sneezy' (Min)	NFir
	'Snow Cap' (MinI)	NFir
	'Snow Flurry' (Sc)	WBrk
	Snow Queen	see *P.* 'Schneekönigin'
	'Snowbaby' (Min/d)	WFib
	'Snowbright' (St/d)	MGbk
	'Snowdrift' (I/d)	WFib
	'Snowflake' (Min)	see *P.* 'Atomic Snowflake'
	'Snowstorm' (Z)	SKen WFib
	'Sofie'	see *P.* 'Decora Rose'
	'Solferino' (A)	ENfk LDea
	Solidor (I/d) 🏆H1+3	NFir
	'Something Special' (Z/d)	NFir WFib
	'Sophia' (Z)	LAst
	Sophie Casade	see *P.* 'Decora Rose'
	'Sophie Dumaresque' (Z/v)	MBri NFir SKen SSea WFib
	'Sophie Emma' (Z)	NFir
	'Sophie Marion' (Dw/Z)	MGbk
	'Sorcery' (Dw/C)	SKen
	'Sound Appeal' (A)	LDea
	'South African Sun' (Z/d)	MGbk
	'South American Bronze' (R) 🏆H1+3	SMrm WFib
	'Southern Belle' (A)	LDea

'Southern Cherub' (A)	LDea
'Souvenir de Prue'	EWoo
'Spanish Angel' (A) ♀H1+3	CWCL LDea MHer NFir SSea WFib
'Spellbound' (R)	WFib
'Spital Dam' (Dw/d)	NFir
'Spitfire' (Z/Ca/d/v)	WFib
§ 'Splendide'	CSpe EPfP MBPg MHer NFir SSea SWvt WFib
'Spot-on-bonanza' (R)	NFir WFib
'Spring Park' (A)	SSea
'Springfield Black' (R)	MCot
'Springfield Glory' (Z)	MGbk
'Springtime' (Z/d)	WFib
'Stadt Bern' (Z/C)	MBri NFir SKen
× ***stapletoniae***	see *P.* 'Miss Stapleton'
'Star Flecks' (St)	NFir
'Starlight Magic' (A) ♀H1+3	LDea
'Startel Salmon' (Z/St)	MHer
'Stella Ballerina'	SMrm
'Stellar Arctic Star'	see *P.* 'Arctic Star'
'Stellar Hannaford Star'	see *P.* 'Hannaford Star'
'Strawberries and Cream' (Z/St)	NFir
'Strawberry Fayre' (Dw/St)	WFib
'Stringer's Souvenir' (Dw/d/v)	SSea
§ 'Sugar Baby' (DwI)	ECtt MBri MHer SKen WFib
'Summer Cloud' (Z/d)	WFib
'Summertime' (Z/d)	see *P.* 'Deacon Summertime'
'Sun Rocket' (Dw/d)	WFib
'Sundridge Moonlight' (Z/C)	WFib
'Sundridge Surprise' (Z)	WFib
'Sunny Jim' (Z)	SSea
'Sunraysia' (Z/St)	WFib
'Sunridge Moonlight' (Dw)	NFir
'Sunset Snow' (R)	WFib
'Sunspot' (Min/C)	NFir
'Sunspot Kleine Liebling' (Min)	SSea
'Sunspot Petit Pierre' (Min/v)	WFib
'Sunstar' (Min/d)	WFib
'Super Rose' (I)	SKen SPet
'Supernova' (Z/St/d)	SKen WFib
'Surcouf' (I)	CWCL WFib
'Susan Payne' (Dw/d)	MHer
'Susie 'Q'' (Z/C)	SKen SSea
'Sussex Delight' (Min)	SPet
'Sussex Gem' (Min/d)	SKen WFib
'Sussex Lace'	see *P.* 'White Mesh'
'Swanland Lace' (I/d/v)	WFib
'Swedish Angel' (A)	LDea NFir WFib
'Sweet Lady Mary' (Sc)	ENfk MBPg
'Sweet Mimosa' (Sc) ♀H1+3	CRHN ENfk EWoo LAst LPot MCot MHer NEgg NFir SBch SSea SWal WBrk WFib WGwG
'Sweet Miriam' (Sc)	LDea MBPg
'Sweet Sixteen' (R)	WFib
'Swilland' (A)	LDea
'Sybil Holmes' (I/d)	MBri SKen SPet WFib
'Sylvia Marie' (d)	SKen
'Tamie' (Dw/d)	NFir
'Telstar' (Min/d)	SKen
tetragonum	CRHN EWoo MBPg MHer SSea WFib
'The Alde'	EWoo
'The Axe' (A)	LDea
'The Barle' (A) ♀H1+3	LDea WFib
'The Boar' (Fr) ♀H1+3	EWoo MCot WFib
'The Bray' (A)	LDea
'The Creedy' (A)	LDea
'The Culm' (A)	EWoo LDea SSea WFib
'The Czar'	see *P.* 'Czar'
'The Dart' (A)	LDea
'The Heddon' (A)	LDea
'The Joker' (I/d)	WFib
'The Kenn-Lad' (A)	EWoo LDea
'The Lowman' (A)	LDea
'The Lyn' (A)	LDea
§ 'The Mole' (A)	LDea WFib
'The Okement' (A)	LDea
'The Otter' (A)	LDea
'The Speaker' (Z/d)	SKen
'The Tamar' (A)	EWoo LDea MHer
'The Tone' (A) ♀H1+3	LDea
'The Yar' (Z/St)	WFib
'Thomas' (Sc)	MBPg
'Thomas Earle' (Z)	WFib
'Thomas Gerald' (Dw/C)	SKen
'Tilly' (Min)	NFir
'Tinker West' (Z/St/Dw) **new**	WFib
'Tinkerbell' (A)	LDea
'Tiny Tinker' (Z/St/Min/C/d/v) **new**	MGbk
§ 'Tip Top Duet' (A) ♀H1+3	EWoo LDea MHer NFir SKen SMrm SSea WFib
'Tirley Garth' (A)	WFib
'Tomcat'[PBR] (I/d)	SSea
tomentosum (Sc) ♀H1+3	CHEx CSev CSpe ENfk EShb EWoo GPoy LDea MBPg MCot MHer MNHC NFir SKen SSea WFib WGwG
- 'Chocolate'	see *P.* 'Chocolate Peppermint'
'Tomgirl' (A)	NPri
Tomgirl = 'Pactomgi'[PBR] (I × Z/d)	LAst
Tommy = 'Pactommy' (I) **new**	LAst NPri
'Topscore' (Z/d)	WFib
'Tornado' (R)	CWCL NFir WFib
'Torrento' (Sc)	LDea MBPg MHer WFib
'Tortoiseshell' (R)	WFib
'Toscana Okka' (Toscana Series) (I)	LSou SPet
'Tracy' (Min/d)	NFir
transvaalense	NFir
tricolor misapplied	see *P.* 'Splendide'
tricolor Curt.	NFir
tricuspidatum	EWoo WCot
trifidum	EWoo MBPg SSea WFib
'Triomphe de Nancy' (Z/d)	WFib
triste	EWoo MCot MHer SSea WCot WFib
'Trudie' (Dw/Fr)	MHer SKen WBrk WFib
'Trulls Hatch' (Z/d)	SKen
'Tuesday's Child' (Dw/C)	SKen
'Turkish Coffee' (R)	NFir WFib
'Turkish Delight' (Dw/C)	NFir WFib
'Turtle's Surprise' (Z/d/v)	SKen WBrk
'Tweenaway' (Dw)	MGbk NFir
'Tyabb Princess' (R)	EWoo
'Unique Aurore' (U)	MHer SKen
'Unique Mons Ninon'	see *P.* 'Monsieur Ninon'
'Urban White' (Dec)	WFib
'Urchin' (Min/St)	NFir WFib
'Ursula Key' (Z/c)	SKen WFib
'Ursula's Choice' (A)	WFib

'Val Merrick' (Dw/St) WFib
'Valentine' (Z/C) WFib
'Valley Court' (I) LAst
'Vancouver Centennial' (Dw/St/C) ♀H1+3 CSpe MBri MCot MHer NEgg NFir SCoo SKen SSea WBrk WFib
'Vandersea' EWoo
'Variegated Clorinda' (Sc/v) WFib
'Variegated Fragrans' see *P.* (Fragrans Group) 'Fragrans Variegatum'
'Variegated Joy Lucille' (Sc/v) MBPg
§ 'Variegated Kleine Liebling' (Min/v) SSea WFib
'Variegated Petit Pierre' (Min/v) MHer WFib
'Variegated Wootton's Unique' (v) EWoo
'Vectis Blaze' (I) EWoo
'Vectis Cascade' EWoo
'Vectis Dazzler' (Z/St/d) MGbk
'Vectis Embers' (Z/d/v) MGbk
'Vectis Finery' (St/d) NFir
'Vectis Glitter' (Z/St) NFir SSea WBrk WFib
'Vectis Pink' (Dw/St) WFib
'Vectis Purple' (Z/d) WFib
'Vectis Sparkler' (Dw/St) NFir
'Vectis Starbright' (Dw/St) WFib
'Vectis Volcano' (Z/St) WFib
'Velvet Duet' (A) ♀H1+3 LDea NFir
'Vera Dillon' (Z) SKen
'Verdale' (A) LDea
'Verona' (Z/C) MBri SKen SSea
'Verona Contreras' (A) CWCL LDea NFir
'Veronica' (Z/d) SKen
'Vic Claws' (Dw/St) NFir
'Vicki' (R) EWoo
'Vicki Town' (R) WFib
'Vicky Claire' (R) EWoo NFir SMrm WFib
Vicky = 'Pacvicky'PBR (I) LAst NPri
Victor = 'Pacvi'PBR (Quality Series) (Z/d) LBMP LSou
'Victoria' (Z/d) SKen
'Viking' (Min/d) SKen
'Village Hill Oak' (Sc) LDea MBPg
Ville de Dresden = 'Pendresd'PBR (I) EWoo
'Ville de Paris' see *P.* 'Hederinum'
'Vina' (Dw/C/d) SKen WFib
'Vincent Gerris' (A) LDea
Vinco = 'Guivin'PBR (I/d) WGor
violareum misapplied see *P.* 'Splendide'
'Virginia' (R) SPet
'Viscossisimum' (Sc) MHer
viscosum see *P. glutinosum*
'Vivat Regina' (Z/d) WFib
'Voodoo' (U) ♀H1+3 CSpe CWCL EWoo LAst MCot MHer NFir SMrm SPet SSea SUsu WCot WFib
'Wantirna' (Z/v) ECtt NFir
'Warrenorth Coral' (Z/C/d) NFir WFib
'Warrenorth Pearl' (Z/d) MGbk
'Warrenorth Platinum' (Z/v/d) MGbk
'Warrenorth Rubellite' (Z/v) MGbk
'Warrenorth Thulite' MGbk
'Washbrook' (Min/d) NFir
'Wayward Angel' (A) ♀H1+3 LDea
'Wedding Royale' (Dw/d) WFib
'Welling' (Sc) LDea MBPg MHer NFir
'Wendy Anne' SKen
'Wendy Jane' (Dw/d) WFib
'Wendy Read' (Dw/d) WFib
'Westdale Appleblossom' (Z/d/C) WBrk WFib
'Westside' (Z/d) WFib
'Westwood' (Z/St) WFib
'Whisper' (R) EWoo WFib
'White Bird's Egg' (Z) WFib
'White Boar' (Fr) CSpe EShb EWoo WFib
'White Bonanza' (R) WFib
'White Cascade' (I) SKen
'White Duet' (A) LDea
'White Eggshell' (Min) WFib
'White Feather' (Z/St) MHer
'White Glory' (R) ♀H1+3 NFir
§ 'White Mesh' (I/v) MBri NFir SKen
'White Prince of Orange' (Sc) MBPg
'White Unique' (U) SBch SPet WFib
White-Blizzard = 'Fisbliz'PBR SCoo
Wico = 'Guimongol'PBR (I/d) CWCL WGor
'Wild Spice' (Sc) LDea
'Wilhelm Kolle' (Z) WFib
'Wilhelm Langath' SCoo WBrk
'Willa' (Dec) WFib
'Winner' LAst
'Wolverton' (Z) WFib
§ 'Wood's Surprise' (Min/I/d/v) SKen SPet SWal
'Wootton's Unique' CSev CSpe EWoo
'Wychwood' (A/Sc) EWoo LDea
'Wyck Beacon' (I/d) SKen
'Yale' (I/d) ♀H1+3 MBri SKen WFib
'Yhu' (R) NFir SMrm WFib
'York Minster' (Dw/v) SKen
'Yvonne' (Z) WFib
'Zama' (R) NFir
'Zinc' (Z/d) WFib
'Zoe' (A) LDea
'Zofia Pope' (R) MGbk
zonale WFib
'Zulu King' (R) WFib
'Zulu Warrior' (R) WFib

Peliosanthes (*Asparagaceae*)

arisanensis B&SWJ 3639 WCru
caesia B&SWJ 5183 WCru
teta subsp. ***humilis*** RWJ 10044 **new** WCru

Pellaea (*Pteridaceae*)

atropurpurea CLAP
falcata CLAP
rotundifolia ♀H2 CBty CLAP GBin ISha LRHS
viridis WPGP

Pellionia see *Elatostema*

Peltandra (*Araceae*)

alba see *P. sagittifolia*
§ ***sagittifolia*** CRow EWay
undulata see *P. virginica* (L.) Schott
§ ***virginica*** (L.) Schott CRow LPBA NLar NPer SWat
- 'Snow Splash' (v) CRow

Peltaria (*Brassicaceae*)

alliacea CSpe GBin LEdu WCot

Peltiphyllum see *Darmera*

Peltoboykinia (*Saxifragaceae*)

§	***tellimoides***	CLAP GCal GEdr GKev NBir WFar WMoo WPnP
	watanabei	CDes CLAP CSpe EBee GEdr LEdu LRHS NLar WCot WCru WMoo WPGP

Pennantia (*Pennantiaceae*)

	baylisiana	ECou
	corymbosa	ECou
	- 'Akoroa'	ECou
	- 'Woodside'	ECou

Pennellianthus see *Penstemon*

Pennisetum ✿ (*Poaceae*)

	× ***advena*** 'Eaton Canyon'	see *P. setaceum* 'Eaton Canyon'
§	***alopecuroides***	CWCL EBee EHoe EPfP LRHS MBrN MWat NGdn SApp SLim SPer SPlb SWat SWvt WFar WWEG XLum
	- B&SWJ 11434	WCru
	- Autumn Wizard	see *P. alopecuroides* 'Herbstzauber'
	- 'Black Beauty'	CSpe SMHy
	- 'Cassian's Choice'	CKno CSam EBee EHoe ELon EWes SMrm
	- 'Caudatum'	CKno EBee SApp
	- f. ***erythrochaetum***	EBee
	- - 'Ferris'	WCru
	- 'Foxtrot'	IPot MAvo
	- 'Gelbstiel'	EPPr
	- 'Goldstrich' **new**	EBee
	- 'Hameln'	Widely available
§	- 'Herbstzauber'	CCon CKno CSam EBee EHoe EPfP LHop LRHS MAvo NRHS NWsh WGwG
	- 'Little Bunny'	CKno CWib EBee EHoe ELan EPPr EPfP GCal IVic LRHS LSRN LTen NGdn NLar SApp SMea SMrm SWvt WFar WWEG
	- 'Little Honey' (v)	CKno EBee LPot MBNS MBri NLar XLum
	- 'Magic'	ELon EPPr MAvo MDKP WWEG
	- 'Moudry'	CKno CPLG CSam EBee EHoe ELon EPPr EPfP LRHS MAvo MBri SBfd SHDw XLum
	- 'National Arboretum'	CKno EHoe EPPr LEdu SApp WCot
	- var. ***purpurascens***	CWCL
	- 'Reborn'	EBee MAvo
	- 'Red Head'	CKno CMea CSpe ELon EUJe EWes IPot LRHS LSou MAvo MBNS NRHS
	- f. ***viridescens***	CKno ECha EHoe ELan EPPr EPfP EShb LEdu LRHS MRav MWhi NRHS NWsh SApp SDix SMrm WPer WPnP WPtf WWEG XLum
	- 'Weserbergland'	CKno CSam EBee EHoe EPPr LRHS SApp WWEG
	- 'Woodside'	CKno CWCL EBee EHoe EPPr LEdu MBNS SApp SMad
	compressum	see *P. alopecuroides*
	'Fairy Tails'	CKno EPfP LSqu NRHS SMHy SUsu
	flaccidum	EBee EHul EPPr
	glaucum 'Purple Baron'	EPfP SBfd
	- 'Purple Majesty'	CSpe MNrw NGBl SBfd SMrm
	incomptum	EHoe XLum
	- purple-flowered	CCon MMoz
	longistylum misapplied	see *P. villosum*
	macrourum	Widely available
	- 'Short Stuff'	CKno
	massaicum 'Red Bunny Tails'	ELon LRHS
	- 'Red Buttons'	see *P. thunbergii* 'Red Buttons'
	orientale ♀H3	CKno COlW CPrp CSpe CWCL EBee ECha EHoe EPfP LHop LRHS MNrw MRav NBir NWsh SApp SEND SGar SPer SUsu WCot WHoo WKif WWEG XLum
	- 'Karley Rose' [PBR]	CKno CPar EBee EHoe EHrv EWes IPot LHop LRHS MAvo MWhi NDov NOak NPnk NWsh SBfd SSvw SUsu WWEG
I	- 'Robustum'	EPPr MAvo SApp WPGP
	- 'Shenandoah'	SApp
	- 'Shogun'	CKno CSam EBee EPPr MAvo NRHS WCot
	- 'Tall Tails'	CKno EBee ECGP EHoe EPPr EWes LBMP LEdu LRHS MWhi NPnk NSti SMea WWEG XLum
	'Paul's Giant'	CKno SApp
	rueppellii	see *P. setaceum*
§	***setaceum*** ♀H3	CKno CWib EPfP NWsh SBfd SHDw SIde
§	- 'Eaton Canyon'	LRHS
	- 'Emelia Mae'	SBfd SHDw
	- 'Fireworks' (v)	EBee LRHS MAsh NSti SBfd SLon SPad SPoG WCot
	- 'Rubrum' ♀H4	CAbb CBcs CKno CPLG CSam CWCL EShb LAst LSRN MAsh MGos NSti NWsh SBfd SCoo SHDw SMad SPoG SRot SUsu SWvt WCot
	thunbergii	EBee LRHS NRHS
§	- 'Red Buttons'	CKno ECha EHoe ELon EPPr EPfP LEdu LSqu MAvo MDKP NOak NRHS SBfd SHDw SMHy SMea SSvw SUsu WGrn WHoo
§	***villosum*** ♀H3	Widely available
	- 'Cream Falls'	LRHS

pennyroyal see *Mentha pulegium*

Penstemon ✿ (*Plantaginaceae*)

	sp.	SVic
	NJM 09.028	WPGP
	'Abberley'	MBNS WPer
	'Abbey Dore'	SLon
	'Abbotsmerry'	ECtt EPfP LLHF MBNS MCot SAga SGar SLon
	'Agnes Laing'	LPen MBNS SPlb
	albertinus	see *P. humilis*
§	'Alice Hindley' ♀H3	Widely available
§	'Andenken an Friedrich Hahn' ♀H4	Widely available
	antirrhinoides	see *Keckiella antirrhinoides*
	'Apple Blossom' misapplied	see *P.* 'Thorn'
	'Apple Blossom' ♀H3-4	Widely available
	arizonicus	see *P. whippleanus*
	'Ashton'	LPen MBNS SAga
	'Audrey Cooper'	CMac MBNS
	'Axe Valley Pixie'	MBel SAga
	azureus	CCon
	- subsp. ***azureus***	CCon
	- - NNS 05-527	GKev
	'Baby Lips'	LLHF
	'Barbara Barker'	see *P.* 'Beech Park'
§	***barbatus***	ELan SRms WFar
	- 'Cambridge Mixed'	LAst

	Name	Suppliers
	- subsp. ***coccineus***	CCon GBin LPen MBNS NLar SPhx
	- 'Iron Maiden'	LRHS
	- 'Jingle Bells'	EPfP LPen MDKP SPav
	- orange-flowered	SPlb
	- 'Peter Catt'	MDKP SMrm
	- Pinacolada Series	LRHS
	- var. ***praecox***	EPfP MBNS SRot WPer
	- - f. ***nanus*** 'Rondo'	LPen LRHS NLar
	barrettiae	LLHF
	'Beckford'	EPfP LLHF MBNS
§	'Beech Park' ♀H3	EPfP EWes LPen MBNS NBir WCot
	'Bisham Seedling'	see *P.* 'White Bedder'
	'Blackbird'	Widely available
	'Blue Spring' misapplied	see *P. heterophyllus* 'Blue Spring'
	'Blueberry Fudge' (Ice Cream Series)	MBri MTis
	'Blueberry Taffy' new	WHlf
	'Bodnant'	LAst LLHF LSou MBNS SAga WHoo WPer WWEG
	bradburii	see *P. grandiflorus*
	'Bredon'	MBNS SAga
	bridgesii	see *P. rostriflorus*
	'Burford Purple'	see *P.* 'Burgundy'
	'Burford Seedling'	see *P.* 'Burgundy'
	'Burford White'	see *P.* 'White Bedder'
§	'Burgundy'	CCon CMac CPrp CSam CWCL EBee ECtt ELon GMaP LLWP LPen LRHS MCot NBir NPer NPri SAga SMrm SPer SPoG SRms WFar WPer XLum
	caespitosus	GKev
	- subsp. ***suffruticosus***	see *P. tusharensis*
	californicus	WAbe WFar XSen
§	***campanulatus***	EPfP EPot EWes GEdr NMen SAga SRms WFar WPer
	- PC&H 148	SDys SGar
	- ***pulchellus***	see *P. campanulatus*
	- 'Roseus' misapplied	see *P. kunthii*
	'Candy Pink'	see *P.* 'Old Candy Pink'
	cardwellii	EWes
	cardwellii × ***davidsonii***	WAbe
	'Castle Forbes'	GMaP LPen MBNS SAga SRms WPer
	'Cathedral Rose'	EPfP
	'Catherine de la Mare'	see *P. heterophyllus* 'Catherine de la Mare'
	'Centra'	LPen MBNS XLum
	'Charles Rudd'	CWCL EBee ECtt ELon EPfP LPen LSRN MBNS SAga SRGP SRms SWvt WCot
§	'Cherry' ♀H3	GBee LPen MBNS SGar SHar SMrm SPlb WPer WWEG
	'Cherry Ripe' misapplied	see *P.* 'Cherry'
§	'Chester Scarlet' ♀H3	ECtt LPen MBNS MRav SDix SGar SLon WCFE WKif WPer XLum
	'Choirboy'	EWes
	cinicola	LLHF
	'Claret'	SAga
	cobaea	LPen WPer
	'Comberton'	MBNS SAga
	confertus	CTri ECho EPot LPen MBNS NChi NMen SBrt WPer
	- RCB/MO A-7	WCot
	'Connie's Pink' ♀H3	ECtt LPen MBNS SGar SLon SRms WWEG
	'Cottage Garden Red'	see *P.* 'Windsor Red'
§	'Countess of Dalkeith'	CBcs COlW ECtt ELan EWes LLWP LPen MBel MCot MRav SAga SPer SPlb SRms SUsu SWvt WCot WFar
	cristatus	see *P. eriantherus*
	cyananthus new	LPen
*	- var. ***utahensis***	WCot
	cyaneus	GKev
	davidsonii	ECho EWes NMen WAbe WFar WPat WThu
	- var. ***davidsonii***	CPBP WAbe
	- var. ***menziesii*** ♀H4	GEdr LRHS
	- - 'Microphyllus'	EPot GEdr LLHF NHar WAbe
	- var. ***praeteritus***	GEdr MDKP
	'Dazzler'	LPen MBNS SAga SWvt WPer
§	***deaveri***	EBee
	'Devonshire Cream'	CWCL ECtt LPen MBNS SAga
	diffusus	see *P. serrulatus*
	digitalis	CRWN EBee GCal LPen LRHS MBNS WFar WPer
§	- 'Husker Red'	Widely available
	- 'Huskers Lilac'	WSpi
	- 'Joke'	IPot
	- 'Mystica'	EDif EWll LBuc LHop
	- 'Purpureus'	see *P. digitalis* 'Husker Red'
	- 'Ruby Tuesday'	CDes EWes SUsu WPGP
	discolor pale lavender-flowered	NBir
§	'Drinkstone Red'	ECtt EHrv EPfP LPen MBNS SDix SDys WPer
	'Drinkwater Red'	see *P.* 'Drinkstone Red'
	(Elgar Series) 'Elgar Crown of India'	EBee
	- 'Elgar Enigma' new	LLHF
	- 'Elgar Firefly'	EBee
	- 'Elgar Nimrod'	EBee
	'Ellenbank Amethyst'	SDys
	'Ellwood Red Phoenix'	MBNS
	'Elmley'	EPfP MBNS WCot
§	***eriantherus***	LLHF
	- var. ***redactus*** new	CPBP
	Etna = 'Yatna'	ECtt EPfP GKev LHop LPen LRHS MBNS NEgg SAll SBfd SMrm SRms WHlf
	euglaucus	EBee GKev LLHF
	- NNS 07-397	GKev
§	'Evelyn' ♀H4	Widely available
	'Evelyn' × 'Papal Purple'	LPen
	'Firebird'	see *P.* 'Schoenholzeri'
	'Flame'	LPen MBNS SAga SLon WPer WWEG
	'Flamingo'	CWCL EBee ECtt EPfP EWes LAst LPen LRHS LSRN MBNS NBir NLar SAga SBfd SMrm SPet SPoG SRms SWvt WFar WHoo WWEG
	fruticosus	WAbe
§	- var. ***scouleri*** ♀H4	MAsh
	- - f. ***albus*** ♀H4	CSpe WAbe
	- - 'Amethyst'	GEdr SRms WAbe
	- var. ***serratus*** 'Holly'	NMen
	Fujiyama = 'Yayama'PBR	CSam CWGN ECtt EPfP LHop LPen LPot LRHS SAll SBfd SLon SMrm SRms SWvt WFar WHlf
	'Garden Red'	see *P.* 'Windsor Red'
	'Garnet'	see *P.* 'Andenken an Friedrich Hahn'
	gentianoides B&SWJ 10271	WCru
	'Geoff Hamilton'	EBee ECtt EPfP LPen LSRN MBNS SAga SLon SPoG
	'George Elrick'	LLHF LPen WHoo
§	'George Home' ♀H3	ECtt ELon EWes LPen MBNS SMrm SRms
	'George Moon'	ECtt EPfP LRHS SPad
	'Gilchrist'	ECtt SLon

	Name	Suppliers
	glaber	CMHG CMea GBee LHop LLWP LPen LSRN SPlb WKif WPer
	- 'Roundway Snowflake'	SHar SPhx
	- white-flowered	SGar
	'Gloire des Quatre Rues'	MBNS XLum
	gormanii	SGar
	gracilis	WPer
§	***grandiflorus***	CCon EBee LPen SBfd SBrt SPhx
	- 'War Axe' **new**	LPen WHil
	'Great Witley'	WPer
	hallii	EPot EWes SBrt WPat
	harbourii	CPBP
	hartwegii ♀H3-4	LPen WPer
	- 'Albus'	LPen SBch SGar SHar SRms
I	- 'Giganteus' **new**	LPen
	- 'Picotee Red'	CWCL LPen LRHS SHil
	- 'Tubular Bells Rose'	NGBl SPet
	'Helenetti'	SDys
§	***heterophyllus***	LPen LRHS MNrw MSCN NBir NGBl SPet SRkn SRms WPer
	- 'Blue Eye'	MBrN
	- 'Blue Gem'	CTri NMen WHil
§	- 'Blue Spring'	CSpe EBee ECtt EPfP LHop LPen LRHS MRav NLar SPhx SPoG WAbe WWEG
§	- 'Catherine de la Mare' ♀H4	ELan LHop LPen LRHS LSRN MHer MWat NBir SAga SBch SMrm SPer SRGP SWvt WFar WHrl WKif
	- 'Electric Blue'	CWCL LRHS
	- 'Heavenly Blue'	CPrp CSBt CWCL EBee ECtt EPfP GMaP LAst LPen LRHS MBNS MLHP MWat NEgg SAll SBfd SGar SMrm SPer SPet SPoG SUsu SWat SWvt WFar WHil WMnd WWEG
	- 'Les Holmes'	LPen
	- 'Misty Blue Shades'	LRHS
	- subsp. ***purdyi***	EPyc
	- 'Roundway White'	WCot
	- 'True Blue'	see *P. heterophyllus*
	- 'Züriblau'	CCon EPfP GAbr LPen SPhx SPlb
§	'Hewell Pink Bedder' ♀H3	COlW EBee EPfP GBuc LPen LPot LRHS MBNS MRav NCGa NLar NPri SGar SMrm SRms SWvt WFar WMnd WPer
	'Hewitt's Pink'	CBcs SLon
	hidalgensis	CDes
	'Hidcote Pink' ♀H3-4	Widely available
	'Hidcote Purple'	SHar WHoo XLum
*	'Hidcote White'	LPot MHer SAga SWvt WWEG
	'Hillview Pink'	SLon
	'Hillview Red'	MBNS
§	***hirsutus***	EBee LRHS WPer
	- f. ***albiflorus***	WAbe WPtf
	- var. ***pygmaeus***	CMea CPBP EBee ECho EShb EWTr GEdr GKev LBMP LPen MHer NMen SGar SPlb WAbe WHoo WIce
*	- - f. ***albus***	EBee GEdr WHoo
	'Hopleys Variegated' (v)	LRHS MBNS SWvt
§	***humilis***	SBrt
	idahoensis	EDAr
	isophyllus ♀H3-4	LPen LPot SAga WPer
	'James Bowden'	MBNS
	Jean Grace = 'Penbow'	CSpe LHop NDov WHlf
	'Jessica'	CWGN SAga
	'Jingle Bells'	NLar
	'John Booth'	MBNS
	'John Nash' misapplied	see *P.* 'Alice Hindley'
	'John Nash'	MHer SAga SRms
	'John Spedan Lewis'	SLon
	'Joy'	ECtt LPen MBNS WPer
	'Juicy Grape' (Ice Cream Series)	MBri SAll WHil
	'June'	see *P.* 'Pennington Gem'
	'Kate Gilchrist'	SLon
	Kilimanjaro = 'Yajaro'	EPfP LRHS SLon SRms
	'King George V'	Widely available
	'Knight's Purple'	ECtt MBNS
	'Knightwick'	LPen MBNS WPer
§	***kunthii***	EBee GEdr LLWP LPen MDKP WPer
	- upright	SGar
§	***laetus*** subsp. ***roezlii***	ECho EPot LRHS MAsh NRHS
§	'Le Phare'	LPen MBNS WPer XLum
	'Lilac and Burgundy'	LPen MBNS MBel SMrm SRms SWvt WFar WWEG
	'Lilac Frost'	ECtt LLHF MWhi WPer
	'Lilliput'	CMea ELon GKev LHop SBfd SLon SPet WHil WHoo
	linarioides 'Marilyn Ross'	ECtt MBNS
	'Little Witley'	WPer
	'Lord Home'	see *P.* 'George Home'
	'Louise Wilson'	WHlf
	'Lucinda Gilchrist'	SLon
	lyallii	CCon ELan GKev LPen SRms WCot WHil WPer
	'Lynette'	LPen MBNS SBch SPlb WPer
	'Macpenny's Pink'	CMac ECtt LPen MBNS SAga
	'Madame Golding'	LPen MBNS SGar SPlb WPer
	'Malvern Springs'	MBNS
	'Margery Fish' ♀H3	CElw CFis CWCL ECtt EPyc EWes LPen WPer WWEG
	'Martley'	WPer
	'Marylin'	WHlf
	'Maurice Gibbs' ♀H3	CBcs CWCL ECtt EPfP EWes LHop LPen LSRN LSqH MBNS SAga SRGP SRms WMnd WWEG
	Mexicali hybrids	LPen MBel
	× ***mexicanus*** 'Sunburst Amethyst'	LPen LRHS SBfd SPad SPhx SRms WPer
	- 'Sunburst Ruby'	LPen LRHS SBfd SLon SPhx
	'Midnight'	CSam ECtt ELan EPfP EWTr GBBs LPen LPot MBNS MRav SAga SEND SGar SWvt WCFE WMnd WPer WWEG
	'Minibird Purple' (Minibird Series)	LPen
	'Mint Pink'	SAga
	'Modesty'	EPfP LPen MBNS SAga SRms WPer
	'Mother of Pearl'	CBcs CCon CWCL EBee EHrv EPfP EShb GMaP LHop LPen LRHS LSRN MBNS MBel MCot MSwo MWat SPlb SRms SWvt WFar WMoo WPer WWEG WWlt
	'Mrs Miller'	LPen MBNS
	'Mrs Morse'	see *P.* 'Chester Scarlet'
	'Mrs Oliver'	EWes
	multiflorus	LPen
§	'Myddelton Gem'	LPen MWat SRms WCot
	'Myddelton Red'	see *P.* 'Myddelton Gem'
	newberryi ♀H4	WIce
	- f. ***humilior***	EPot
§	- subsp. ***sonomensis***	GEdr SRms WAbe
*	'Newbury Gem'	LPen LSRN MBNS SRGP SWvt
	'Oaklea Red'	SEND
§	'Old Candy Pink'	LPen MBNS SWvt WPer
	'Osprey' ♀H3	CMac CWCL EBee ECtt ELan EPfP EShb EWes LAst LRHS MAsh MBNS NBir NGdn SBfd SMrm SRms SWvt WHoo WMnd WPer WWEG

	ovatus	CCon CMac EBee ELan LPen NBre NLar SGar SPhx SRms
	'Overbury'	ECtt LPen MBNS SRms
	'Papal Purple'	LLWP LPen MAsh MBNS MHer NBir NCGa SAga SLon SPhx SRms XLum
	'Patio Bells Pink'	LPen MLHP SBfd
	Patio Bells Red = 'Yapbred'	LPen SBfd
	'Patio Bells Shell'	CSpe LHop SLon SMrm
	'Peace'	GBin LPen MBNS SLon WHoo
§	'Pennington Gem' ♀H3	CPrp ELan GQue LPen LRHS MHer MSCN NBir SRms SWvt WPer
	'Pensax'	WPer
	'Pensham Amelia Jane'	CWGN EBee ECtt ELon EPfP LHop LPen LRHS LSRN LSou MAsh MAvo MBNS MBri MSCN MTis NCGa NRHS SAga SAll SHil SLon SMrm SPer SRkn SRms SWvt WBor WHil
	'Pensham Arctic Fox'	ECtt LHop LRHS SAga SBch SLon
	'Pensham Arctic Sunset'	SLon WHrl
	'Pensham Avonbelle'	MBNS SRms
	'Pensham Bilberry Ice'	EPyc MBNS SWvt WMnd
	'Pensham Blackberry Ice'	ECtt EPfP EPyc LPen LSou MBNS SAll SLon SRms WMnd
	'Pensham Blueberry Ice'	ECtt EPyc LPen LSou MBNS SWvt WFar WMnd
	'Pensham Bow Bells'	SAga
	'Pensham Capricorn Moon'	ECtt NLar SLon SRGP
	'Pensham Charlotte Louise'	ECtt ELon LRHS MAsh MBri NLar SAll SRms SWal
	'Pensham Czar'	EBee ECtt EPfP LHop LRHS LSou LSqH MAsh MBNS MBri MCot MTis NCGa NRHS SAga SAll SHil SLon SMrm SPer SRkn SRms SWvt WHrl
	'Pensham Dorothy Wilson'	EBee EPyc SMrm
	'Pensham Edith Biggs'	ECtt EPfP WMoo
	'Pensham Eleanor Young'	EBee ECtt LRHS LSou MBNS NCGa SAll SLon SWvt
	'Pensham Freshwater Pearl'	CElw SAga SRms WHlf WHoo
	'Pensham Great Expectations'	EBee ECtt
	'Pensham Jessica Mai'	ECtt ELon LRHS LSou MAsh MAvo NRHS SPer SRkn SRms SWvt WHil
	'Pensham Just Jayne'	EBee ECtt ELon EPfP EPyc LRHS LSRN MBNS SAll SLon SRGP SRkn SRms SWvt WHoo WMnd WMoo
	'Pensham Kay Burton'	EPfP EPyc SRGP WMnd
	'Pensham Laura'	CSam CWGN EBee ECtt EPfP LHop LPen LRHS LSRN LSqH MAsh MAvo MBNS MBel MBri MTis NRHS SAga SAll SHil SLon SMrm SPer SRGP SRkn SWvt WBor WHlf WPer
	'Pensham Loganberry Ice'	EBee LSou MBNS MBri NCGa SAga SLon
	'Pensham Marjorie Lewis'	WMnd
	'Pensham Miss Wilson'	SAga SRms
	'Pensham Petticoat'	EBee
	'Pensham Plum Jerkum'	CWGN EBee ECtt ELon EPfP EPyc LHop LRHS LSou MBNS MBri MCot NLar SAga SAll SHil SLon SPer SRkn SUsu SWvt WHil WMnd WMoo
	'Pensham Raspberry Ice'	MBNS MBri SLon WMnd
	'Pensham Saint James's'	WHlf
	'Pensham Son of Raven'	SAga
	'Pensham Tayberry Ice'	ECtt EPyc MBNS SLon WMnd
	'Pensham Tiger Belle Coral'	NChi SAga
	'Pensham Victoria Plum'	CElw MHer SHar WHoo
	'Pensham Wedding Bells'	SRms WPer
	'Pensham Wedding Day'	CWCL EBee EPfP LHop LPen LRHS LSRN LSou MBNS MBri NLar SAga SAll SLon SPer SPoG SRGP WHlf WHoo
	'Persham Skies'	WHlf
	'Pershore Carnival'	SRms WHrl
	'Pershore Fanfare'	SAga WHrl
	'Pershore Pink Necklace'	CWCL ECtt LPen LRHS SAga SRms SWvt WCot WHlf WWEG
	petiolatus	CPBP
	'Phare'	see *P.* 'Le Phare'
	'Phoenix Red' (Phoenix Series)	LRHS WCFE
	'Phyllis'	see *P.* 'Evelyn'
	pinifolius ♀H4	CCon CMea CTri ECho EDAr EPot GKev LHop LRHS MAsh MBel NHar NRHS SGar SPhx SPoG WFar WPat XLum XSen
	- 'Compactum'	GKev
	- dwarf	XSen
	- 'Mersea Yellow'	CCon CMea ECho EDAr EPfP EPot GEdr GKev LHop LRHS MAsh NHar NRHS SAga SLon SPhx SPlb SPoG WFar WPat WPer XLum XSen
	- 'Wisley Flame' ♀H4	ECho EPfP EPot EWes GEdr MBNS MHer MSCN MWat NRya XSen
	'Pink Bedder'	see *P.* 'Hewell Pink Bedder', 'Sutton's Pink Bedder'
	'Pink Endurance'	LPen MBNS SRkn WHal WPer
	'Pink Ice'	LPen
	'Polaris Red' **new**	EPfP
	'Port Wine' ♀H3	CMea CSam CTri CWCL ELon EPfP GMaP LPen LPot LRHS LSRN MCot MWat NBir SMrm SPoG SWvt WKif WMnd WPer WWEG
	'Powis Castle'	ECtt EWes WPer
	'Priory Purple'	MBNS WHrl WPer
	procerus	WPer
	- var. ***brachyanthus***	GKev
§	- var. ***formosus***	GEdr GKev NMen WAbe
§	- 'Roy Davidson' ♀H4	CMea CYeo EPot LRHS NHar NMen WAbe WFar WPat
	- var. ***tolmiei***	EPot GCal GEdr GKev NMen
	pubescens	see *P. hirsutus*
	pulchellus Greene	see *P. procerus* var. *formosus*
	pulchellus Lindl.	see *P. campanulatus*
	'Purple and White'	see *P.* 'Countess of Dalkeith'
	'Purple Bedder'	CMac COlW EBee EPfP LPen LRHS LSRN MLHP MWat NBir SBfd SMrm SPoG SRkn SRms SWvt WCFE WFar WGor
	'Purple Passion'	CElw EBee EHrv EPfP EWes LRHS WWEG
	'Purple Pixie'	LPen
	'Purple Sea'	SGar
	'Purpureus Albus'	see *P.* 'Countess of Dalkeith'
	'Raspberry Ripple'	MBri MTis
	'Raven' ♀H3	CBar CMac CSam CWCL EBee ECtt EShb GCra LAst LBMP LHop LLWP LPen LRHS MCot MHer SAll SEND SPer SRms SWvt WCAu WFar WHal WHil WPer WWEG
	'Razzle Dazzle'	LPen MBNS SPlb WCot WPer
	'Red Emperor'	LPen SPlb WPer WWEG
	'Red Knight'	GCra LPen MBNS
	'Red Riding Hood'[PBR]	EPfP
	'Red Rocks'	LRHS WCot
	'Red Sea'	SGar
	'Rich Purple'	EPyc MBNS SPlb
	'Rich Ruby'	COlW CWCL CWGN EBee ECtt EHrv ELan EPfP EWes LLWP LPen

		LRHS MCot NBir SAga SPlb SRGP SWvt WCot WPer WWEG
	richardsonii	LPen WPer
	'Ridgeway Red'	MBNS
	roezlii Regel	see *P. laetus* subsp. *roezlii*
	'Ron Sidwell'	SGar SLon WCFE
§	***rostriflorus***	LLHF
	'Rosy Blush'	MBNS SAga SPlb
	'Roy Davidson'	see *P. procerus* 'Roy Davidson'
	'Royal White'	see *P.* 'White Bedder'
	'Rubicundus' 🏆H3	CWCL EBee ELan EPfP GBin LPen LRHS LSRN MAsh MBNS SAga SBfd SMrm SWvt WCot WFar WMnd
	'Ruby' misapplied	see *P.* 'Schoenholzeri'
	'Ruby Field'	EPyc MSCN WCFE
	'Ruby Gem'	LPen
	rupicola 🏆H4	GEdr LHop LRHS NRHS
	- 'Albus'	GKev
	- 'Conwy Lilac'	SRms WAbe
	- 'Conwy Rose'	WAbe
	- 'Puyallup Pink' **new**	GKev
	'Russian River'	CPrp EBee ECtt EPfP EWes LHop LPen LRHS LSRN MBNS SPlb SWvt WPer
	rydbergii	CFis EBee
	'Samsong'	WCFE
*	Saskatoon hybrids	LHop
	Saskatoon hybrids rose-flowered	SLon
	Scarlet Queen	see *P.* 'Scharlachkönigin'
§	'Scharlachkönigin'	ECtt LPen
§	'Schoenholzeri' 🏆H4	Widely available
	scouleri	see *P. fruticosus* var. *scouleri*
§	***serrulatus***	EPot EWes
	- 'Albus'	EBee LPen SPhx
	'Shell Pink'	LPen WPer
	'Sherbourne Blue'	LPen LPot SAga WCot WPer
*	'Shrawley'	WPer
	'Sissinghurst Pink'	see *P.* 'Evelyn'
	'Six Hills'	WAbe
	'Skyline'	EPfP
	smallii	CDes CEnt EBee EDAr EPPr EPfP EWes LPen LRHS LSRN MHer SPhx SRkn WPGP WPer
	'Snow Storm'	see *P.* 'White Bedder'
	'Snowflake'	see *P.* 'White Bedder'
	sonomensis	see *P. newberryi* subsp. *sonomensis*
	'Sour Grapes' misapplied	see *P.* 'Stapleford Gem'
	'Sour Grapes' ambig.	LPot MBel MCot MGos NGdn SAll SMrm WWEG
§	'Sour Grapes' M. Fish 🏆H3-4	Widely available
	'Southcombe Pink'	LPen
	'Southgate Gem'	GBee GKev LPen MBNS MWat SRms SWvt
	'Souvenir d'Adrian Regnier'	MBNS SGar
	'Souvenir d'André Torres' misapplied	see *P.* 'Chester Scarlet'
	speciosus subsp. ***kennedyi***	CPBP
	spectabilis	SBrt
§	'Stapleford Gem' 🏆H3	CWCL ECtt EHrv ELan EUJe GBuc LPen LRHS MBel MCot MLHP MRav MWhi NChi NPri SAga SMrm SPet SPlb SRms SWvt WCot WFar WHoo WMnd WMoo WWEG
	'Strawberries and Cream' (Ice Cream Series)	MBri MTis NLar SRkn WHil
	'Strawberry and Blackberry Fancy'	EBee
	strictus	CCon EBee EPPr LPen LRHS MBNS MNFA WPer
	Stromboli = 'Yaboli'	LRHS
	superbus	SBrt
§	'Sutton's Pink Bedder'	MBNS SPlb
	'Sweet Cherry' (Ice Cream Series)	ECtt MBri
	'Sweet Joanne' **new**	EBee
	tall pink-flowered	see *P.* 'Welsh Dawn'
N	'Taoensis'	EWes MBNS
	'Ted's Purple'	WHlf
	teucrioides	EPot
	- JCA 1717050	CPBP
	'The Juggler'	ECtt EPfP LPen MBNS MBel SMrm SWvt WFar WMnd
§	'Thorn'	ECtt ELan EShb LPen LRHS MWat NBir SEND SPhx SRms SWvt WWEG
	'Threave Pink'	EBee ECtt LLWP LRHS MBNS MRav SEND SHar SMrm SPer SWvt WWEG
	'Thundercloud'	ECtt LPen
	'Torquay Gem'	LLHF LPen MBNS SDys WPer
	'True Sour Grapes'	see *P.* 'Sour Grapes' M. Fish
	'Tubular Bells Red'	NGBl
§	***tusharensis***	GKev
	utahensis	GBee LRHS SAga
	'Vanilla Plum' (Ice Cream Series)	MBri
	Vesuvius = 'Yasius'	EBee ECtt EPfP LPen LRHS NEgg SBfd SGar SLon SMrm SRms WCAu WFar WHlf
	virens	CPBP EBee WPer
	virgatus	see *P. deaveri*
	subsp. ***arizonicus***	
	- 'Blue Buckle'	EBee EWTr IPot SPlb
	'Wallington Pink'	LRHS
	watsonii	SBrt
§	'Welsh Dawn'	CEnt LPen MBNS
§	***whippleanus***	EBee GEdr LPen LRHS SPhx WAbb
§	'White Bedder' 🏆H3	Widely available
	'Whitethroat' Sidwell	LPen MBNS
I	'Whitethroat' purple-flowered	SMrm WCot WPer
	'Willy's Purple'	ECtt MBNS
§	'Windsor Red'	CTri EBee ECtt EPfP LPen LRHS MBNS SBfd SLon SRms SWvt WCot
	'Woodpecker'	ECtt LPen MAvo MBNS SAga SGar SRms SUsu

Pentachondra (*Ericaceae*)

	pumila	IBlr

Pentaglottis (*Boraginaceae*)

§	***sempervirens***	CArn EPfP MHer WSFF

Pentapanax see *Aralia*

Pentapterygium see *Agapetes*

Pentas (*Rubiaceae*)

	lanceolata	CCCN ELan EShb

pepino see *Solanum muricatum*

peppermint see *Mentha × piperita*

Pericallis (*Asteraceae*)

	aurita	CRHN

× ***hybrida*** Senetti Series — MGos NPer NPri SPoG
- - Senetti Blue Bicolor = 'Sunseneribuba'PBR — LAst MGos SPoG
- - Senetti Blue = 'Sunsenebu'PBR **new** — SPoG
- - Senetti Magenta Bicolor = 'Sunsenereba'PBR — LAst MGos SPoG
- - Senetti Magenta = 'Sunsenere'PBR **new** — SPoG

lanata ambig. — CRHN IRar
§ ***lanata*** (L'Hér.) B. Nord. — CHll EShb
- Kew form — CSpe

Perilla (*Lamiaceae*)

§ ***frutescens*** var. ***crispa*** ♀H2 — CSpe SHDw
- green-leaved — ELau
- var. ***japonica*** — GPoy
- var. ***nankinensis*** — see *P. frutescens* var. *crispa*
- var. ***purpurascens*** — CArn ELau WJek

Periploca (*Apocynaceae*)

graeca — CBcs CMac CRHN EBee SLon
purpurea B&SWJ 7235 — WCru
sepium — CPLG

Pernettya see *Gaultheria*

N ***mucronata*** — see *Gaultheria mucronata*

Perovskia (*Lamiaceae*)

abrotanoides — LRHS XLum
atriplicifolia — CArn CBcs CMea ELan MHer MNHC NSti WKif WMnd WPer XSen
- 'Blue Shadow' — EBee LRHS
- Lacey Blue = 'Lisslitt'PBR — CSpe LBuc
- 'Little Spire'PBR — CBar CMac CSBt CSpe EBee EHoe EPfP EWes GBin GMaP GQue LRHS LSRN MAsh NBid NLar NRHS SBfd SGol SPer SPoG WHil

'Blue Haze' — GCal LRHS SMHy
'Blue Spire' ♀H4 — Widely available
'Filigran' — EBee ELan EUJe GBin GBuc LRHS LSou MWhi SBfd SEND SMad SPoG WFar WPat XSen
'Hybrida' — LRHS SBfd
'Longin' — EBee LHop NDov

Persea (*Lauraceae*)

americana — CCCN
indica — CCCN
japonica B&SWJ 8410 — WCru
lingue — CBcs IDee
thunbergii — CBcs CHEx

Persicaria (*Polygonaceae*)

B&SWJ 11268 from Sumatra — WCru
§ ***affinis*** — CBcs CBen CSBt EBee EHrv GAbr MWhi NBro NSti SWat WBrk WFar WMoo
- 'Darjeeling Red' ♀H4 — Widely available
- 'Dimity' — see *P. affinis* 'Superba'
- 'Donald Lowndes' ♀H4 — CEnt CMac CTri CYeo EBee ELan EPfP GKev GMaP IVic LAst LHop LPBA LPot LRHS LSRN MHer MNrw MRav MWat NPri SPer SRms SWat SWvt WFar WMoo WPer WWEG
- 'Kabouter' — EBee GBin IPot NLar WBor
- 'Ron McBeath' — LRHS
§ - 'Superba' ♀H4 — Widely available

alata — see *P. nepalensis*
alpina — CDes CSpe ECha EHrv ELan EPPr EWTr GBin GMaP LRHS MAvo MCot NDov SBch SDix SMad WCot WFar WMoo WWEG
amphibia — MSKA SWat XLum
§ ***amplexicaulis*** — CBre CKno CPrp CRow CSpe ELan EWes GMaP MBel MCot MHer NOrc WBor WFar WGwG WMoo WRHF WTin XLum
- 'Alba' — Widely available
- 'Anouk' **new** — EBee
- 'Arun Gem' — see *P. amplexicaulis* var. *pendula*
- 'Atrosanguinea' — CKno CMac CRow CTri EBee ECha ELan LRHS MMuc MNFA MRav MSpe MWat NBir NLar SEND SPer SRms SWat SWvt WFar WOld WWEG
- 'Baron' — CRow
- 'Betty Brandt' — GBin
- 'Blackfield'PBR — CBct EBee ECtt ELon EPPr EWes GBin GQue LRHS LSou MBNS NDov NLar WCot WHil
- 'Blush Clent' — WHoo WTin
- 'Clent Charm' — NChi WWEG
- 'Cottesbrooke Gold' — CRow ECtt
- 'Dikke Floskes' — CRow MSpe WCot
- 'Eastfield' (v) — WCot
- 'Fascination' — WCot
- 'Fat Domino'PBR — EBee GBin IPot NDov NLar
- 'Firedance' — CKno EBee EHoe ELon EPPr GQue IPot MSpe NDov SMHy SMrm SPhx SWat WCot
- 'Firetail' ♀H4 — Widely available
- 'Golden Arrow' (v) **new** — LBuc
- 'High Society' — EBee GBin
- 'Inverleith' — CBct CBre CDes CKno CRow EBee ECGP ECha ECtt EPPr GBin GBuc GMaP GQue LBMP LRHS MAvo MBel MMuc MNFA MSpe SEND SPhx WCot WMoo WOut WPGP WPnP

I - 'Jo and Guido's Form' — EBee ELon MSpe NLar SUsu WCAu WFar
- 'JS Caliente'PBR — CKno CMea CYeo EBee ECtt ELon GBin GQue LRHS MBel NCGa WCot
- Orange Field = 'Orangofield'PBR — CKno EBee EPPr GBin GQue LHop LRHS NCGa NDov

* - var. ***pendula*** — EBee EPPr GQue NBir WFar WMoo
- - HWJK 2255 — WCru
- 'Pink Elephant' — CSam EBee EPPr GBee GBin GQue MSCN MSpe NDov NLar WHil WWEG
- 'Pink Lady' — CRow NLar
- 'Rosea' — Widely available
- 'Rowden Gem' — CRow WMoo
- 'Rowden Jewel' — CRow
- 'Rowden Rose Quartz' — CRow
- 'September Spires' — NDov
- 'Summer Dance' — EBee ECtt EPPr GQue LPla NLar
- Taurus = 'Blotau' — CElw CKno CSam EBee ECha EPPr GBin LRHS MBri NCGa NLar NSti SMHy WCAu WFar WPGP WPnP WTin WWEG

§ ***bistorta*** — CArn CRow ELau GPoy MHer MMuc MNHC MWhi NBir NLar SEND SRms SWat WOut

	- subsp. ***carnea***	EBee ECha EHoe ELon EPPr GBin LPla LRHS MBNS MDKP MMuc MSpe NBir NBro NDov SEND WCot WMoo
	- 'Hohe Tatra'	CDes EBee EPPr LRHS NDov WFar
	- 'Superba' ♀H4	Widely available
	campanulata	CElw CRow EBee ECha ECtt EHoe GAbr GMaP IFro LPot MMuc MRav MSpe MWhi NBro NEgg SEND SPer SUsu WFar WMoo WOld WOut
	- Alba Group	CElw CFis EBee GBin NBro WMoo
	- var. ***lichiangense***	GBin
	- 'Madame Jigard'	CRow GBin
	- 'Rosenrot'	CBre CRow GBin LRHS NBir NHol SWat WFar WOld WWEG
	- 'Southcombe White'	CRow GBin LRHS WPer WWEG
§	***capitata***	XLum
	- 'Pink Bubbles'	EHoe SPet SWvt
	chinensis B&SWJ 11268	WCru
	conspicua	EBee
	dshawachischwilii	SUsu
*	***elata***	LRHS
	emodi	CRow
	hydropiper 'Fastigiata'	CArn
*	***kahil***	GBin WCot
*	***macrophylla***	LDai LRHS WFar
I	- 'Cally Strain'	GCal
	microcephala	CRow EWes
	- 'Red Dragon'PBR	Widely available
	milletii	EBee GBuc NLar WCru
§	***mollis***	LRHS WPGP
	nakaii	EBee
	neofiliformis	EShb MWhi
§	***nepalensis***	CPLG CRow EBee EPPr EShb MAvo MSpe MTPN
	'October Pink'	CSam
§	***odorata***	CArn EGHP ELau ENfk EOHP GPoy MHer MHoo MNHC SBfd SHDw SIde WJek
	orientalis	SMrm SUsu
	polystachya	see *P. wallichii*
	'Red Baron'	EPPr
§	***runcinata***	CRow EBee NBir WMoo
	- Needham's form	CRow CSpe
	scoparia	see *Polygonum scoparium*
	sphaerostachya Meisn.	see *P. macrophylla*
	tenuicaulis	CBre CEnt CRow CSpe EBee EHrv GBin MNFA NLar SBch WCru WFar WMoo
§	***tinctoria***	EOHP WSFF
§	***vacciniifolia*** ♀H4	Widely available
	- 'Ron McBeath'	CRow
§	***virginiana***	CRow EPPr GCal LRHS NRHS WMoo
	- var. ***filiformis***	CHEx CSpe EBee ECtt LBMP LPla MMoz MPie SBfd SWvt WCot WHil WTcb WWEG
	- - 'Ballet'	WCot
	- - 'Batwings'	ESwi LRHS
	- - Compton's form	CBct CHEx CRow ECha EPPr EPfP EShb GCal LDai LHop LPla LRHS MMoz SUsu WAul WCot
	- - 'Lance Corporal'	CMac CRow EHoe EPPr EShb GBin NLar SMrm SUsu WMnd
	- - 'Moorland Moss'	WMoo
	- Variegated Group (v)	CRow ECha EShb MBNS WCot WMoo WOld
	- - 'Painter's Palette' (v)	Widely available
	- white-flowered	CKno EPPr
	vivipara	MMHG NLar
§	***wallichii***	MMuc NLar SDix SEND SWat WCot WMoo WPtf WWEG XLum
§	***weyrichii***	EPPr GCal NBir NBro NLar WMoo XLum

persimmon see *Diospyros virginiana*

persimmon, Japanese see *Diospyros kaki*

Petalostemon see *Dalea*

Petamenes see *Gladiolus*

Petasites (*Asteraceae*)

	albus	GPoy MHer NLar
	fragrans	EBee ELan MHer SWat WFar XLum
§	***frigidus*** var. ***palmatus***	EBee LEdu NLar
	- - JLS 86317CLOR	SMad
	- - 'Golden Palms'	EHrv EUJe NMRc
	hybridus	EBee LEdu MSKA SWat
*	- 'Variegatus' (v)	XLum
	japonicus	CBcs GPoy
	- var. ***giganteus***	CArn CHEx CMac CRow EBee ECha ELan EPfP EUJe LEdu MBel SWat WCru
§	- - 'Nishiki-buki' (v)	CHEx CMac CRow EBee EPPr EUJe EWld GQue MBel MHer MSKA NBir NEgg NSti SMad WBor WFar WPtf WWEG
	- - 'Variegatus'	see *P. japonicus* var. *giganteus* 'Nishiki-buki'
	- f. ***purpureus***	EPPr EWes
	palmatus	see *P. frigidus* var. *palmatus*
	paradoxus	CDes CLAP EPPr EWes EWld LEdu MBel WCot

× *Petchoa* (*Solanaceae*)

(Supercal Series) Supercal Cherry	LAst NPri
- SuperCal Neon Rose ='Kakegawa S89'PBR	LSou
- SuperCal Terracotta ='Kakegawa S91'PBR	LSou NPri
- SuperCal Vanilla Blush ='Sakpxc005'	NPri

Petrea (*Verbenaceae*)

volubilis	CCCN

Petrocallis (*Brassicaceae*)

	lagascae	see *P. pyrenaica*
§	***pyrenaica***	WAbe
	- ***alba***	WAbe

Petrocoptis (*Caryophyllaceae*)

	pyrenaica	SRms
§	- subsp. ***glaucifolia***	ITim

Petrocosmea (*Gesneriaceae*)

begoniifolia	WAbe
formosa 'Crûg's Capricious'	WCru
forrestii	WAbe
grandiflora	WAbe
- 'Crème de Crûg'	WCru
iodioides	WAbe
kerrii	WCot
aff. ***martini***	WAbe
minor	CPBP WAbe

rosettifolia	WAbe WThu
sericea	WAbe

Petrophytum (*Rosaceae*)

caespitosum	EPot WAbe
cinerascens	WAbe
§ ***hendersonii***	WAbe

Petrorhagia (*Caryophyllaceae*)

'Pink Starlets'	EPfP LHop
saxifraga ♀H4	CSpe ECho EDAr LBMP SRms SWal WMoo WPnn

Petroselinum (*Apiaceae*)

§ ***crispum***	CArn EGHP ENfk GPoy LPot MHoo MNHC SBfd SIde SPoG SWal WJek WPer
- 'Bravour' ♀H4	ELau MHer MHoo
- 'Champion Moss Curled'	SVic
- 'Darki'	EGHP ELau MHoo NPri
- French	CArn ELau ENfk MHer MHoo MNHC NPri SPoG WJek
- 'Italian'	see *P. crispum* var. *neapolitanum* plain-leaved
- 'Moss Curled' ♀H4	MHoo
§ - var. ***neapolitanum***	ELau ENfk MHoo SBfd SIde SPoG
plain-leaved	SVic
- 'Super Moss Curled'	SWal
§ - var. ***tuberosum***	MHer MNHC SIde SVic
hortense	see *P. crispum*
tuberosum	see *P. crispum* var. *tuberosum*

Petteria (*Papilionaceae*)

ramentacea	EBtc

Petunia (*Solanaceae*)

Black Velvet = 'Balpevac' **new**	LAst NPri
Candyfloss = 'Kercan'PBR (Tumbelina Series) (d)	LSou NPri
(Cascadias Series) Cascadias Bicolor Pastel = 'Dancasbipas'PBR	NPri
- Cascadias Rim Violet	LAst NPri
Cherry Ripple = 'Kerripcherry'PBR (Tumbelina Series) (d)	LSou NPri
Clara = 'Kerclara'PBR (Tumbelina Series) (d)	LSou
Conchita Blossom White = 'Conbloss'PBR (Conchita Series)	NPri
(Corona Series) 'Corona Amethyst'	NPri
- 'Corona Rose Rim' **new**	NPri
'Empaurea'	NPri
(Fanfare Series) 'Fanfare Crème de Cassis' **new**	NPri
- 'Fanfare Hot Rose' **new**	NPri
- 'Fanfare Yellow' **new**	NPri
(Frenzy Series) 'Frenzy Blue Star' **new**	NPri
- 'Frenzy Plum Bicolour' **new**	NPri
- 'Frenzy Rose Star' **new**	NPri
- 'Frenzy Rose Vein' **new**	NPri
- 'Frenzy Yellow' **new**	NPri
Inga (Tumbelina Series) (d) **new**	LSou
Joanna (Tumbelina Series)	LAst LSou
Katrina = 'Kerkat'PBR (Tumbelina Series) (d)	LAst
(Littletunia Series) Littletunia Bicolour Illusion	LSou NPri
- Littletunia Blue Vein **new**	LAst NPri
- Littletunia Breezy Pink = 'Dantun2'	LSou
- Littletunia Sweet Pink = 'Dantun3'	LSou
- Littletunia Ultra Purple	LSou
Melissa = 'Kermelis'PBR (Tumbelina Series) (d)	LAst LSou
'Mini Me Pink Star' (Mini Me Series)	LAst
patagonica	WAbe
'Potunia Papaya' (Potunia Series) **new**	LAst
Priscilla = 'Kerpril'PBR (Tumbelina Series) (d)	LAst LSou NPri
(Supertunia Series) Supertunia Pretty Much Picasso = 'Bhtun31501' **new**	NPri
- Supertunia Raspberry Blast = 'Temari'	ESwi NPri
- Supertunia Royal Velvet = 'Kakegawa S28'PBR	ESwi
- Supertunia Vista Bubblegum = 'Ustuni6001'	ESwi
- Supertunia White = 'Kakegawa S30'PBR	ESwi
(Surfinia Series) Surfinia Baby Pink Morn = 'Sunbapimo'PBR	LSou
- Surfinia Blue Picotee	LSou
- Surfinia Blue = 'Sunblu'	LAst LSou NPri WGor
- Surfinia Blue Vein = 'Sunsolos'PBR	LAst WGor
- Surfinia Burgundy = 'Keiburtel'PBR	LAst NPri WGor
- Surfinia Crazy Pink = 'Sunrovein'PBR	LAst NPri
- Surfinia Double Blue Star = 'Sunsurfelevi' (d)	LAst NPri
- Surfinia Hot Pink = 'Marrose'PBR	LSou WGor
- Surfinia Hot Red = 'Sunhore'PBR	NPri
- Surfinia Lime = 'Keiyeul'PBR	LAst NPri WGor
- Surfinia Pastel 2000 = 'Sunpapi'PBR	WGor
- Surfinia Pink Ice = 'Hakice'PBR (v)	LAst NPri WGor
- Surfinia Purple = 'Shihi Brilliant' ♀H3	LAst LSou NPri WGor
- Surfinia Red = 'Keirekul'PBR	LAst NPri WGor
- Surfinia Rose Vein = 'Sunrove'PBR	LAst WGor
- Surfinia Sky Blue = 'Keilavbu'PBR ♀H3	LAst NPri WGor
- Surfinia Sweet Pink = 'Sunsurfmomo'PBR	LSou
- Surfinia Vanilla = 'Sunvanilla'PBR	LSou
- Surfinia Victorian Yellow = 'Sunpatiki'PBR	LAst NPri

- Surfinia White = 'Kesupite'	LAst
Susanna (Tumbelina Series)	LAst
Veranda Yellow = 'Kerveryello'[PBR] (Veranda Series) new	NPri
Victoria = 'Kervic'[PBR] (Tumbelina Series)	LAst LSou

Peucedanum (*Apiaceae*)

caffrum new	SPlb
japonicum B&SWJ 8816B	WCru
officinale	CSpe EBee LRHS NLar SPlb
ostruthium	GPoy LEdu MSCN NCGa WPtf
- 'Daphnis' (v)	CDes CElw CSpe EBee LEdu LPla MAvo MMoz NChi NLar NMRc NPro SUsu WCFE WCot WHrl WWFP XLum
verticillare	CArn CSpe EBee LRHS MBel MCot MNFA SDix SKHP SPhx WSHC WWEG

Peumus (*Monimiaceae*)

boldus	CBcs IArd IDee

Phacelia (*Boraginaceae*)

bolanderi	LDai
sericea	GKev
- subsp. ***sericea*** NNS 08-352	GKev
tanacetifolia	SPhx

Phaedranassa (*Amaryllidaceae*)

BKBlount 2623	WCot
carmiolii	WCot
cinerea	ECho WCot
dubia	ECho WCot
* ***montana***	ECho
tunguraguae	ECho
viridiflora	ECho WCot

Phaenocoma (*Asteraceae*)

prolifera	SPlb

Phaenosperma (*Poaceae*)

globosa	CSam CSpe EBee EHoe EPPr EWes LEdu NWsh WCot WPGP XLum

Phagnalon (*Asteraceae*)

saxatile (L.) Cass. RCB RL -21	WCot

Phaiophleps see *Olsynium*

nigricans	see *Sisyrinchium striatum*

Phalaris (*Poaceae*)

arundinacea	LPot MBNS MSKA SPlb SVic SWat WTin
- cream-flowered	WWEG
- 'Elegantissima'	see *P. arundinacea* var. *picta* 'Picta'
- var. ***picta***	CDul CHEx CTri CWCL CWib MSKA NBid NBir NPer SApp SPoG WFar XLum
- - 'Arctic Sun' (v)	CKno ELon EPPr SBfd SDix SPoG
- - 'Aureovariegata' (v)	CBcs MRav NGdn NPer SWat WMoo XLum
- - 'Feesey' (v)	Widely available
- - 'Luteopicta' (v)	EBee EHoe EPPr MMuc SEND WTin XLum
§ - - 'Picta' (v) ♀H4	COIW EBee ELan EPfP LBMP LPBA LRHS MMuc SBfd SEND SPer SWal SWat WMoo
- - 'Streamlined' (v)	EPPr NWsh SLPl WFar
- - 'Tricolor' (v)	EHoe

Phanerophlebia (*Dryopteridaceae*)

caryotidea	see *Cyrtomium caryotideum*
falcata	see *Cyrtomium falcatum*
fortunei	see *Cyrtomium fortunei*

Pharbitis see *Ipomoea*

Phaseolus (*Papilionaceae*)

caracalla	see *Vigna caracalla*
vulgaris 'Yin Yang'	LSou

Phedimus see *Sedum*

Phegopteris (*Thelypteridaceae*)

§ ***connectilis***	EFer WAbe
decursive-pinnata	CDes CLAP LRHS NLar NMyG WFib WPnP

Phellodendron (*Rutaceae*)

amurense	CBcs CCCN CDul CMCN EBee ELan EPfP GBin IDee IVic LEdu NLar WBor WPGP
- B&SWJ 11000	WCru
- var. ***sachalinense***	LEdu
japonicum B&SWJ 11175	WCru

Phenakospermum (*Strelitziaceae*)

guianense	XBlo

Pherosphaera (*Podocarpaceae*)

fitzgeraldii	CKen WThu

Philadelphus ✿ (*Hydrangeaceae*)

SDR 2823	CPLG
SDR 4862	GKev
SDR 4945	GKev
SDR 4946	CPLG GKev
SDR 5111	GKev
'Avalanche'	CMHG CPLG NLar NPro SEND SPer SRms
'Beauclerk' ♀H4	CDoC CDul CTri EBee ECrN EPfP GQui IVic LRHS MBri MGos MRav NBro NEgg NRHS NWea SHil SKHP SLim SPer SPoG SRms SWvt WPat
'Belle Etoile' ♀H4	Widely available
'Bicolore'	NLar
'Bouquet Blanc'	MRav NLar SRms WPat
brachybotrys	MRav
'Buckley's Quill' (d)	ECrN EPfP EWes LRHS MRav SGol SWvt WGrn
'Burfordensis'	CWSG EPfP LAst MRav SEND
§ ***calvescens*** new	MRav
aff. ***calvescens***	MRav
- BWJ 8005	WCru
coronarius	CBcs CDul EBee EPfP LBuc MLHP MRav MWhi NWea SEND SPer
- 'Aureus' ♀H4	Widely available
- 'Bowles's Variety'	see *P. coronarius* 'Variegatus'
§ - 'Variegatus' (v) ♀H4	CDul CJun CMHG CWib EBee ELan EPfP EWTr LAst LHop LPot LRHS MAsh MGos MMuc MRav MSwo NBir SLim SMad SPer SPoG SRms WCFE WCot WFar WKif WMoo WPat WSHC
coulteri	WPGP

'Coupe d'Argent' MRav
'Dainty Lady' LRHS SLon
'Dame Blanche' (d) EPfP EWTr MRav
delavayi CGHE EBee EPfP GBin SKHP WPGP
- var. ***calvescens*** see *P. calvescens*
- var. ***melanocalyx*** EBee EPfP GCra MRav SChF WPGP
- - B&L 12168 WPGP
- 'Nymans' CPLG EPfP SKHP WKif
'Enchantement' (d) MRav SDix
'Erectus' CSBt CWib EBee ELon EPfP LRHS MGos MNHC MRav SKHP SLim SPer SPoG WPat
'Etoile Rose' WMoo
'Falconeri' new MRav
'Frosty Morn' (d) CBcs EBee EPfP LRHS MMuc MRav NBro SEND SPer
incanus B&SWJ 8616 WCru
§ 'Innocence' (v) CMac CPLG EBee ECrN EHoe ELan EPfP LAst LRHS MBri MGos MMuc MRav MSwo NLar NPro SAga SBfd SEND SKHP SLim SPad SPer SPoG SRms WFar WPat
'Innocence Variegatus' see *P.* 'Innocence'
§ ***insignis*** MRav
'Kelmarsh' SLPl
× ***lemoinei*** CBcs CDul CTri EBee EWTr LBMP MGos MWat NLar WFar
I - 'Lemoinei' NWea
lewisii CPLG
- L 1896 CPLG
'Limestone' MRav
maculatus WPat
- 'Mexican Jewel' CGHE CPLG EBee ELon SKHP WKif WPGP WPat
- 'Scented Storm' CMHG CSam
- 'Sweet Clare' new LRHS
madrensis CGHE LHop MRav
- F&M 326 WPGP
'Manteau d'Hermine' (d) ♀H4 Widely available
'Marjorie' NLar
mexicanus GCal WSHC
- B&SWJ 10253 WCru
- 'Rose Syringa' CGHE CPLG EBee SKHP WPGP
- × ***palmeri*** new WPGP
microphyllus CDul CMCN CTri EBee ELan ELon EPfP LAst MAsh MGos MRav MWhi SKHP SLon SPer SPhx SPoG SSpi WKif WPGP WPat WSHC
'Miniature Snowflake' (d) CSpe MAsh SEND WPat
'Minnesota Snowflake' (d) CBcs EWes LRHS LSRN MMuc MRav NEgg NLar NPro SBfd SGol
'Mont Blanc' CBcs EBee GKin MRav
'Mrs E.L. Robinson' (d) CMac EBee ELon LAst LLHF LRHS MAsh MGos NEgg NLar SHil WBor WCFE WPat
myrtoides B&SWJ 10436 WCru
'Natchez' (d) CMac EBee ELon LLHF NLar WPat
'Oeil de Pourpre' MRav
palmeri CGHE WPGP WPat
pekinensis CPLG
'Perryhill' MRav
'Polar Star' EBee ELon GBin WKif
purpurascens CPLG EBee EPfP EWes GQui LLHF MRav SChF SKHP WPGP WPat
- BWJ 7540 WCru
× ***purpureomaculatus*** ELon LLHF MAsh MRav WPat
satsumi SLPl
- B&SWJ 10811 WCru
- B&SWJ 11004 WCru
schrenkii NLar
- B&SWJ 8465 WCru
§ 'Silberregen' CDul CMac CSam EBee ELon EPfP EWTr LBMP LRHS MAsh MGos MMuc MRav NLar NPro SRms SWvt WPat
Silver Showers see *P.* 'Silberregen'
'Snow Velvet' EBee EPfP LLHF LRHS
'Snowbelle' (d) EBee LBMP LRHS MAsh MBri MWat NBro NHol NLar SKHP SWvt
'Snowflake' EBee WMoo
'Souvenir de Billiard' see *P. insignis*
'Starbright' new LRHS
subcanus CPLG
- L 524 CPLG WPGP
'Sybille' ♀H4 CDul CMHG EPfP LHop LRHS MAsh MRav MSwo SDix SKHP SPer SRms SSpi WPat WSHC
tenuifolius NLar SLPl
tomentosus CPLG
- B&SWJ 2707 WCru
- GWJ 9215 WCru
'Virginal' (d) Widely available
'Voie Lactée' MRav
White Icicle = 'Bialy Sopel' CCCN
White Rock = 'Pekphil' CDoC CMac EBee EPfP IVic LLHF LRHS LSRN MRav SKHP SLim SPer
'Yellow Cab' CWSG NEgg NLar SLim
'Yellow Hill' CMac EPfP LRHS NEgg NLar SBfd SKHP SLim
zeyheri SLPl

Philesia (*Philesiaceae*)

buxifolia see *P. magellanica*
§ ***magellanica*** CPLG GGGa IBlr SSpi WAbe WCru WSHC
- 'Rosea' CWib EPfP IBlr SSpi

Phillyrea (*Oleaceae*)

angustifolia CDul CGHE CMCN EBee ELan EPfP ERom EUJe EWTr IVic LRHS MBri MGos MRav NLar SBfd SBig SEND SHil SPer SSpi WFar WPGP WSHC XSen
- f. ***rosmarinifolia*** CCCN CPLG EBee ELan EPfP LAst NLar SLPl
- - 'French Fries' WPGP
decora see *Osmanthus decorus*
§ ***latifolia*** CDul EBee EGFP ELan EPfP LRHS NLar SBfd SEND SSpi WPGP
I - 'Rodrigueziensis' WCFE
media see *P. latifolia*

Philodendron (*Araceae*)

bipinnatifidum ♀H1 EAmu SEND XBlo
* ***rubrum*** XBlo
scandens 'Mica' XBlo
xanadu XBlo

Phlebodium (*Polypodiaceae*)

§ ***aureum*** ♀H1 CSpe
pseudoaureum ISha WCot

Phleum (*Poaceae*)

bertolonii CRWN
phleoides EBee LRHS
pratense EHoe MAvo NMir WSFF

Phlox ✿ (*Polemoniaceae*)

	adsurgens ♀H4	MAsh WAbe
	- 'Alba'	WAbe
	- 'Mary Ellen'	ITim
	- 'Red Buttes'	ECho
	- 'Wagon Wheel'	CMea CWCL ECho ECtt EWes GBuc LHop LRHS NHar SMrm SPlb SRms SRot WAbe WFar WIce
	amplifolia	EBee NBre WFar
	- 'Winnetou' **new**	EBee
	× ***arendsii*** 'Andrew'	WCot
	- 'Aureole' **new**	LSou MAsh MSCN
	- 'Autumn's Pink Explosion' **new**	WCot
	- 'Babyface'	LSou MAsh MSCN NGdn WFar
	- 'Casablanca'	NDov
	- 'Dougal'	WCot
	- 'Dylan'	WCot
	- 'Early Star'	EBee LSou
	- 'Eyecatcher'	NBro
	- 'Gary'	WCot
	- 'Hesperis'	EBee ECha ELon GBin GQue IPot MCot NDov NLar SMrm SPhx WFar
	- 'Lilac Girl'	NBre
	- 'Luc's Lilac'	CPrp ECtt GBin LLHF LRHS MCot MSpe NBro NCGa NDov NEgg NGdn NSti SMrm SPhx SPoG WAul WFar WWlt
	- 'Miss Jessica' (Spring Pearl Series)	LAst NRHS
§	- 'Miss Jill' (Spring Pearl Series)	EPfP SPet WCot WTin
§	- 'Miss Karen' (Spring Pearl Series)	NBro
§	- 'Miss Margie' (Spring Pearl Series)	LEdu
§	- 'Miss Mary' (Spring Pearl Series)	ECtt EPfP GMaP MDKP MSpe
§	- 'Miss Wilma' (Spring Pearl Series)	EPfP
	- 'Neon Flare Blue' (Neon Series) **new**	LSou
	- 'Paul'	WCot
	- 'Ping Pong'	LDai
	- 'Pink Attraction'	MNrw NBro NCGa
	- 'Purple Star'	EBee
	- 'Roger'	WCot
	- 'Rosa Star'	NBre
	- 'Sweet William'	MSpe NEgg
	- 'Utopia'	CDes CSam ELon LPla MCot NLar SMrm SPhx SUsu WCot
	austromontana	EPot GKev ITim NWad
	bifida	ECho
	- 'Alba'	ECho LLHF MWat
	- blue-flowered	ECho SUsu
	- 'Colvin's White'	ECho XLum
	- 'Frohnleiten'	NHar WPer
	- 'Minima Colvin'	ECho ECtt EPot GKev
	- 'Ralph Haywood'	CMea CPBP CWCL ECtt EPot ITim
	- 'Thefi'	EWes MNrw WIce
	borealis	see *P. sibirica* subsp. *borealis*
*	- ***arctica***	EPot
	bryoides	see *P. hoodii* subsp. *muscoides*
	caespitosa	CMea ECho EWes
	- subsp. ***pulvinata***	see *P. pulvinata*
	- 'Zigeunerblut'	CPBP NHar
	canadensis	see *P. divaricata*
	carolina subsp. ***angusta***	SUsu
	- 'Bill Baker' ♀H4	Widely available
	- 'Magnificence'	EBee EWes MDKP NLar SMad SPhx WCot WSHC
	- 'Miss Lingard' ♀H4	CSam CWCL EBee ECtt ELon LRHS LSou MCot MSpe MWat NBir NGdn NLar NSti SMrm WAul WCot WFar WRHF WWEG
	'Charles Ricardo'	EWes LRHS WHoo
	'Chattahoochee'	see *P. divaricata* subsp. *laphamii* 'Chattahoochee'
§	***condensata***	WAbe
	Coral Flame (Flame Series)	CMac LRHS LSou SRkn
	covillei	see *P. condensata*
	'Daniel's Cushion'	see *P. subulata* 'McDaniel's Cushion'
	diffusa	EPot
§	***divaricata*** ♀H4	EWTr SPlb XLum
	- 'Blue Dreams'	CCon ECtt LRHS MNrw SUsu WFar WHal WWlt
	- 'Blue Perfume'	CPrp EBee ECtt LSou NBro NGdn NLar WFar
	- 'Clouds of Perfume'	CWCL EAEE ECtt EPfP EWTr GBuc GMaP LRHS LSRN LSou MSCN MSpe NDov NEgg NLar NPnk SGar SMrm SPoG STes SWvt WFar WGwG WWEG
	- 'Dirigo Ice'	ECho LHop LRHS NRHS WSHC
	- 'Eco Texas Purple'	CPrp ECtt MSCN NCGa WFar WSHC WWlt
	- 'Fuller's White'	CWCL LRHS
	- subsp. ***laphamii***	EHrv EWes
§	- - 'Chattahoochee' ♀H4	CBcs CPrp CSpe CWCL ECho ECtt ELan ELon EPfP EWes GBin GBuc LHop LPot LRHS MCot MNrw MWat NLar NRHS SMrm SPoG SRot SWvt WCFE WFar WHil WHoo
§	- 'Louisiana Purple'	WSHC
	- 'May Breeze'	EBee ECho EHrv GCra GMaP LHop LRHS MNrw MSCN NCGa NPnk NRHS SUsu WSHC WWEG WWlt
	- 'Plum Perfect'	ECtt LLHF
*	- 'White Perfume'	CPrp CWCL EBee EWes LRHS LSou MDKP NBro NCGa NLar SMrm SPet WWEG
	douglasii	SEND SRms
	- 'Alba'	GJos
	- 'Apollo'	CTri ECho ECtt LLHF NHar NMen
	- 'Boothman's Variety' ♀H4	CPBP ECha ECho ECtt EDAr ELan EPfP ITim MLHP MWat NMen SRms
	- 'Crackerjack' ♀H4	CMea CTri ECho ECtt EDAr ELan ELon EPfP EPot GAbr GJos GMaP ITim LRHS MAsh MHer MLHP MWat NBir NEgg NMen NSla SPoG WFar WIce
	- 'Eva'	ECho ECtt EDAr EPot GMaP ITim LHop LRHS LSRN MAsh MSCN NBir NLar NMen NPri NSla NWad WFar WNew
	- 'Georg Arends'	ECtt EPot GJos
	- 'Ice Mountain'	CMea CYeo ECho ECtt ELan EPot GMaP NEgg NWad SPoG SRot WFar WNew
	- 'Iceberg' ♀H4	GJos NMen
	- 'J.A. Hibberson'	EPot
	- 'Lilac Cloud'	CYeo ECho ECtt EDAr GJos NPro
	- Lilac Queen	see *P. douglasii* 'Lilakönigin'
	- 'Lilac Wonder'	CPBP
§	- 'Lilakönigin'	CTri

	- 'Napoleon'	ECho ECtt EPot ITim LLHF NMen NWad
	- 'Ochsenblut'	ECho LLHF LRHS MHer MLHP MSCN NHar NLar WAbe
	- 'Red Admiral' Υ^{H4}	CYeo ECho ECtt EPfP EWes GMaP MAsh MWat NLar WCFE WFar
	- 'Rose Cushion'	ECho EDAr EWes MHer
	- 'Rose Queen'	ECho
	- 'Rosea'	CMea ECho EDAr ELan LRHS MAsh NMen WFar WNew
	- 'Silver Rose'	ECho MWat
	- 'Sprite'	SRms
	- 'Tycoon'	see *P. subulata* 'Tamaongalei'
	- 'Violet Queen'	ECho EWes WFar WPat
	- 'Waterloo'	CMea ECho ECtt EPot ITim LRHS MAsh NMen
I	- 'White Admiral'	CTri CYeo ECho ECtt LHop LSRN WPer
	- 'Zeigeurnerblut'	CMea WAbe
	drummondii 'Classic Cassis'	LSou SPoG
	'Fancy Feelings' (Feelings Series)	NBro NLar
	glaberrima 'Morris Berd'	CDes EBee WSHC
	hendersonii	WAbe
§	***hoodii*** subsp. ***muscoides***	WAbe
	idahoensis	SPhx
	'Jeff's Pink' **new**	WHlf
	'Kelly's Eye' Υ^{H4}	ECho ECtt GEdr LRHS NBir NHar SPoG WFar
	kelseyi	WAbe
	- 'Lemhi Purple'	CPBP WAbe
	- 'Rosette'	ECho MDKP WFar WPer
	Light Pink Flame = 'Bareleven'^{PBR}	ECtt EPfP LRHS NPri SPoG
	Lilac Flame = 'Barten'^{PBR}	EPfP SPoG WHil
	longifolia subsp. ***brevifolia***	CPBP WAbe
	'Louisiana'	see *P. divaricata* 'Louisiana Purple'
	maculata	NOrc WPer
	- 'Alba'	WCAu
	- 'Alpha' Υ^{H4}	CPrp CSam CWCL EBee ECha ECtt EPfP GBuc GCal GCra GMaP LRHS MMuc MSpe NDov NLar NOrc SKHP SPer SWvt WAul WFar WSHC WWlt
	- Avalanche	see *P. maculata* 'Schneelawine'
	- 'Delta'	EBee EPPr GBuc LRHS MMuc NLar SBfd SPer SRkn SWvt WFar
	- 'Natascha'	Widely available
	- 'Omega' Υ^{H4}	CMac CPLG CPrp EAEE EBee ECtt EWTr GAbr GBuc LAst LHop LRHS MCot MMuc MNrw MSpe NGdn NLar NPnk SBfd SKHP SMad SPer SPoG SWvt WAul WCAu WFar WWEG
	- 'Princess Sturdza' Υ^{H4}	SDix WCot
	- 'Reine du Jour'	CSam ELon IVic LPla MDKP NDov SMrm SPhx WSHC
	- 'Rosalinde'	CPrp EBee ECtt ELon GBuc LRHS MMuc NLar SBfd SWvt WCAu WFar WSHC WWEG
§	- 'Schneelawine'	SPlb
	'Matineus'	SPhx
	'Millstream'	see *P.* × *procumbens* 'Millstream'
	'Millstream Blue'	EPfP
	'Millstream Jupiter'	ECho
	'Minnie Pearl'	EWes SKHP
	muscoides	see *P. hoodii* subsp. *muscoides*

	nana 'Arroya' **new**	WAbe
	- 'Mary Maslin'	WAbe
	nivalis	MWat
	- 'Nivea'	EPot GJos
	paniculata	CPne ECha GCra NBid NDov SDix SWal WCot
	- var. ***alba***	SDix WCot WTin
	- 'Alba Grandiflora' Υ^{H4}	GMaP MAvo MNrw WCot WHoo
	- 'Alexandra'^{PBR}	EBee MSCN
	- 'All in One'	ECtt LSou
	- 'Amethyst' misapplied	see *P. paniculata* 'Lilac Time'
	- 'Amethyst' Foerster	CCon CSam GQue LRHS NBir NLar NOrc SPet SWat WCAu WFar
	- 'Anne' **new**	CSam
I	- 'Aureovariegata Undulata' (v)	WCot
	- 'Auslese D. Bach' **new**	CSam
	- 'Balmoral'	CMac EBee ECtt GCra LRHS MLHP NEgg NSti SBfd SMrs SWat SWvt WWEG
	- 'Barnwell'	SWat
	- 'Becky Towe'^{PBR} (v)	EBee ECtt LLHF LRHS LSou MNrw NEgg NLar
	- 'Betty Margarite'	NDov
	- 'Blauer Morgen'	IPot
	- 'Blue Boy'	COlW EBee ECtt EPfP GKev GMaP LAst LRHS MDKP MTis NBir NBro NEgg NLar SKHP SMrm SRms SWvt WFar WMnd
	- 'Blue Ice' Υ^{H4}	EBee ELan NBro
	- 'Blue Paradise'	Widely available
	- 'Blushing Bride'	SRms
	- 'Blushing Shortwood' **new**	EBee
	- 'Border Gem'	CBcs CMac EBee ECtt LAst LRHS MAvo MCot MRav MSpe MWat NChi NDov NHol NLar SDix SWat SWvt WBrk WHrl WSHC WWEG WWlt
	- 'Branklyn'	GCra LRHS
	- 'Brigadier' Υ^{H4}	CPrp CTri EBee ECtt ELan GMaP LRHS MCot MDKP MSpe MWat NEgg NGdn SBfd SMrm SPer SRms WFar
	- 'Bright Eyes' Υ^{H4}	Widely available
	- 'Burgi'	SDix
	- 'Candy Floss'	ELon LLHF
	- 'Cardinal'	MAvo NDov
	- 'Caroline van den Berg'	SRms
	- 'Cecil Hanbury'	NLar
	- 'Chintz'	MRav SRms
	- 'Cinderella'	ECtt MTis
	- 'Cool Best'	NDov
§	- 'Cool of the Evening'	WKif
	- 'Coral Queen'	MSpe
	- 'Cosmopolitan'^{PBR}	LSou MNrw NCGa WFar
	- Count Zeppelin	see *P. paniculata* 'Graf Zeppelin'
	- 'Crème de Menthe' (v)	CWGN EBee
	- 'Danielle'	CSBt LSou MSCN SPet WHil
	- 'Darwin's Choice'	see *P. paniculata* 'Norah Leigh'
	- 'David'	Widely available
	- 'David's Lavender'	CElw EBee
	- 'Delilah'^{PBR}	MAsh
	- 'Discovery'	EBee EHrv EWes MCot MRav MSpe NEgg SBfd SWat
	- 'Doghouse Pink'	SDix
	- 'Dresden China'	MAvo MTis SWat
§	- 'Düsterlohe'	CSBt CSam ECtt GBin GBuc GQue MTis NBir NLar SMrm SPer SWat WCot WHoo XLum

- 'Early Light Pink' **new**	IPot
- 'Early Velvet' **new**	IPot
- 'Eclaireur' misapplied	see *P. paniculata* 'Düsterlohe'
- 'Eclaireur' Lemoine	SWat
- 'Eden's Crush'	NBre
- 'Eden's Flash'	CElw ECtt LRHS MSpe NBre
- 'Eden's Smile'	ECtt
- 'Elisabeth' (v)	ECtt EPfP LSRN MSpe WHil
- 'Elizabeth Arden'	ECtt MSpe NLar SWat
- 'Elizabeth Campbell'	GCal
- 'Empty Feelings' (Feelings Series)	NBro
- 'Ending Blue'	MTis
- 'Etoile de Paris'	see *P. paniculata* 'Toits de Paris' Symons-Jeune
- 'Europa'	EBee ECtt ELan MCot NBir NGdn NLar SPer WCAu WFar
- 'Eva Cullum'	CSam EBee ECtt EHrv ELon EPfP GBin GCra GMaP LHop LRHS MArl MCot MSpe NHol NLar SBfd SPer SPet SWat WCAu WCot WWEG WWlt
- 'Eva Foerster'	GBin NRHS
- 'Eventide' ♀H4	CMac CSam CWCL EBee ECGP ECtt EPfP LHop LPot LRHS MArl MCot MNrw MRav MSpe MWat SBfd SPer SPet SWat WFar WPtf
- 'Excelsior'	MRav
- 'Ferris Wheel'	LSou NCGa
- 'Flamingo'	EBee ECtt LRHS NLar SWvt
- 'Fondant Fancy' PBR	LSou SPoG WFar
- 'Franz Schubert'	CSam EBee ECtt EPfP GBin GCra LPot LRHS MBel MCot MLHP MSpe MWat MWhi NBir NGdn NLar NSti SBfd SGar SPer SWat SWvt WCot WFar WKif WWEG WWlt
§ - 'Frau Alfred von Mauthner'	ECtt GBin SMrm
- 'Frosted Elegance' (v)	WWEG
- 'Fujiyama'	see *P. paniculata* 'Mount Fuji'
- 'Goldmine' PBR (v)	LSou MNrw
§ - 'Graf Zeppelin'	ECtt ELan LRHS SRms SRot XLum
- 'Grenadine Dream' PBR	EBee LAst LSou MBri SPoG WFar
- 'Harlequin' (v)	CBcs CWGN EBee ECha ECtt ELon GMaP LRHS NBro NEgg NLar NSti SPer SPoG WCot WFar WWEG WWlt
- 'Hochgesang' **new**	EBee
- 'Irene Mast' **new**	CSam
- 'Iris'	SMrm SRms WCot
- 'Jade'	CWGN EBee ECGP ECtt ELon MAvo MBel MNrw NDov NLar NSti WCot WHlf
- 'Judy'	LSRN NBro NCGa
- 'Jules Sandeau'	LRHS
§ - 'Juliglut'	SWat WCot
- July Glow	see *P. paniculata* 'Juliglut'
- 'Junior Bouquet'	ECtt NLar
- 'Junior Dance'	ECtt NLar SRot
- 'Junior Dream'	ECtt NLar SRot
- 'Junior Fountain'	ECtt NLar
- 'Katarina'	CElw ECtt NLar
- 'Katherine'	NLar NRHS
- 'Kirchenfürst'	CElw IPot LPla LRHS MSpe NBir SBfd SMrm
- 'Kirmesländler'	ECtt GBin NLar SWat
- 'Lads Pink'	SDix
- 'Lady Clare'	SRms
- 'Landhochzeit'	GBin
- 'Laura'	EBee ECtt ELon EPfP GBin IPot LHop LRHS MTis NBro NCGa NPri SMrm SPet SRkn SRms STes SWvt WBor WFar WHoo WMnd WSHC WTin
§ - 'Lavendelwolke'	CSam GCal NBir NLar SWat
- Lavender Cloud	see *P. paniculata* 'Lavendelwolke'
- 'Le Mahdi' ♀H4	ELan MTis SRms SWat
- 'Lichtspel'	LPla NDov SAga SPhx
- 'Lila Miniatur'	NDov
§ - 'Lilac Time'	CElw EBee ECtt ELon EPfP LSRN MDKP NLar SHil SWat SWvt WWEG
- 'Little Boy'	CElw ECtt ELon MDKP MNrw NLar WFar
- 'Little Laura'	CElw CWGN EBee ECtt EWTr LRHS LSRN MSpe NDov NHol NLar NOrc NPri SPoG WCot WFar WWlt
- 'Little Princess'	ELon LLHF LRHS NLar SMrm WMnd
- 'Little Sara'	NDov
- 'Lizzy' PBR	NLar
- 'Logan Black'	GCal
- 'Magic Blue'	LSou
- 'Manoir d'Hézèques'	WCot
- 'Mary Christine' (v)	CDes NBid
- 'Maude Stella Dagley'	MSpe
- 'Mia Ruys'	MArl MLHP
- 'Midnight Feelings' (Feelings Series)	NBro NLar
- 'Milly van Hoboken'	WKif
- 'Miss Elie'	LAst NBre WFar
- 'Miss Holland'	LAst NGdn SPet WWEG
- 'Miss Jill'	see *P.* × *arendsii* 'Miss Jill'
- 'Miss Karen'	see *P.* × *arendsii* 'Miss Karen'
- 'Miss Kelly'	EHrv LRHS LSou MSpe WHoo WWlt
- 'Miss Margie'	see *P.* × *arendsii* 'Miss Margie'
- 'Miss Mary'	see *P.* × *arendsii* 'Miss Mary'
- 'Miss Pepper'	CWCL ECtt ELon LSou MMuc NGdn NLar SEND SMrm SRkn WBor WFar
- 'Miss Universe'	NBre WHil WWEG
- 'Miss Wilma'	see *P.* × *arendsii* 'Miss Wilma'
- 'Monica Lynden-Bell'	Widely available
- 'Monte Cristallo' **new**	EBee
- 'Mother of Pearl' ♀H4	EBee ECtt ELan GQue IPot LRHS MAvo MSpe MWat NEgg SPer WFar WWEG
§ - 'Mount Fuji' ♀H4	Widely available
- 'Mount Fujiyama'	see *P. paniculata* 'Mount Fuji'
- 'Mrs A.E. Jeans'	SRms
- 'Mystique Black' **new**	LSou
- 'Nadia' **new**	EBee
- 'Natural Feelings' PBR (Feelings Series)	NBro NLar WWlt
- 'Newbird'	ECtt SHil SRms WWEG
- 'Nicky'	see *P. paniculata* 'Düsterlohe'
- 'Nirvana' **new**	CSam
§ - 'Norah Leigh' (v)	Widely available
- 'Orange Perfection'	see *P. paniculata* 'Prince of Orange'
- 'Othello'	CSam EBee ECGP ECtt EWTr LRHS MSpe NSti SBfd SMrs WFar WMnd WWlt
- 'Otley Choice'	EBee ECtt LRHS MRav MWat NLar SWat
- 'Otley Purple'	MHer
- 'P.D. Williams'	WCot
- 'Pastorale'	WCot
- 'Peppermint Twist'	CWCL CWGN EBee ELon GKev LRHS LSou MAsh MBri MNrw NEgg

	NLar NPri SMad SPad SPoG SWvt WCot WFar WWlt
– 'Picasso'	ECtt LSou
– 'Pina Colada'PBR	CWGN LSou MAsh NLar SPoG WFar WHil
– Pink Eye Flame = 'Barthirtyfive'PBR	EPfP LBMP LSou MTis NPri SKHP SPoG
– 'Pink Posie' (v)	WCot
– Pink Red Eye Flame	EPfP LRHS LSou NPri SPoG
– 'Pinky Hill'	CElw CSBt LSou MTis
– 'Pleasant Feelings'PBR (Feelings Series)	NBro
– 'Popeye'	ECtt LPla NLar
– 'Prime Minister'	ELon
§ – 'Prince of Orange' ♀H4	Widely available
– 'Prospero' ♀H4	CSam CSpe EBee LRHS MCot MRav NBid SRkn SWat
– Purple Eye Flame = 'Barthirtythree'PBR	LLHF LSou MTis NPri SBfd SHar SKHP WFar WHil
– 'Purple Kiss'PBR	CWGN LSou MBri MHer WFar
– 'Rainbow'	ELon
– 'Rectory Pink'	MSpe
– 'Red Caribbean'	LSou MBri
– 'Red Feelings' (Feelings Series)	NBro
– 'Red Flame'	CBct CWGN EBee ECtt EPfP LRHS LSou MTis SBfd SHil SKHP SPoG WCot WFar
– 'Red Riding Hood'	ECtt LAst LSou MAsh MBri SPet SRkn
I – 'Reddish Hesperis'	MAvo NDov
– 'Rembrandt'	CPLG LRHS MTis
– 'Rijnstroom'	CBcs EBee ECha ECtt ELon LRHS MArl NLar SMrm SRot WBrk WFar
– 'Robert Poore'	ELon
– 'Rosa Goliath' **new**	CSam
– 'Rosa Pastell'	CSpe ECGP ECtt EHrv ELon GQue IPot LHop LPla LSou MAvo MBel MTis NDov SAga SMrm SPer SPoG WCot WWlt
– 'Rosanne' **new**	MAvo
– 'Rowie'	NBid
– 'Rubymine' (v)	LLHF WFar
– 'Sandringham'	EBee EHrv LRHS MArl MLHP MRav MSpe NBir NDov NHol SBfd SPer SPoG SWvt
§ – 'Schneerausch'	LPla SPhx
– 'Septemberglut'	NLar SHil
– 'Skylight'	EBee EHrv LSRN NBre NBro SBfd SDix
– 'Snow White'	NBre
– Snowdrift	see *P. paniculata* 'Schneerausch'
– 'Speed Limit 45'	WCot
– 'Spitfire'	see *P. paniculata* 'Frau Alfred von Mauthner'
– 'Starburst'	EBee NBro
– 'Starfire' ♀H4	Widely available
– 'Starlight'	NHar
– 'Steeple Bumpstead'	LSou WCot
– 'Sternhimmel'	LPla
– 'Strawberry Daiquiri'	LSou MAsh NCGa SPoG WFar
– 'Swizzle'	LSou MAsh MBri MHer NCGa SMrm SPoG WBor WFar
– 'Tenor'	CCon CMac CTri EBee ECtt ELon EPfP GBuc LAst LRHS MCot MDKP MWat NHol NLar NPri SBfd SPet SPoG SWvt WFar WGwG WWEG
– 'Tequila Sunrise'	MBri
– 'The King'	EBee ECtt LRHS MDKP NBro NLar SWat WHlf WSHC
– 'Tiara' (d)	CWGN EBee ECtt ELon LSou MBel MTis NCGa SPer SWvt WCot
– 'Toits de Paris' misapplied	see *P. paniculata* 'Cool of the Evening'
§ – 'Toits de Paris' Symons-Jeune	WSHC
– 'Twister' **new**	LSou MAsh MAvo
– 'Uspekh'	COlW CSam EBee ECtt EPPr EWes LRHS MCot MDKP MRav MSpe MTis NBro NOrc NSti SAga SBfd SMrs SPer SUsu WCAu WFar WGwG WHrl WWEG
– 'Van Gogh'	CCse EHrv
– 'Velvet Flame'	CAbP EPfP LBMP LSou MBel NPri SHar SKHP WCot
– 'Vintage Wine'	MNrw
– 'Violetta Gloriosa'	ELon LPla SMrm
– 'Watermelon Punch'	LSou MBri MHer WFar
– 'Wendy House'	LEdu LLHF MNrw
– 'Wenn Schon Denn Schon'	GBin
– 'White Admiral' ♀H4	CBcs CElw CWCL EBee ECtt EHrv ELan ELon EPfP GAbr GCra GMaP LHop LRHS MCot MHer MSpe MWat NEgg SBfd SPer SPhx SPoG SRms SWat SWvt WMnd WSHC WWEG
– White Flame = 'Bartwentynine'PBR	CBct ECtt EPPr EPfP LBMP LRHS LSou MTis SBfd SHil SKHP WCot WHil
– 'Wilhelm Kesselring'	EBee ECtt ELon NBre WBor
– 'Windsor' ♀H4	EBee ECtt ELon EPfP GCal LRHS MSpe NDov NEgg NHol NLar SBfd SPoG SRms SWvt WCAu WFar WWEG
'Petticoat'	CMea CPBP ECtt EPot MDKP MWat NHar SBch WFar WIce
pilosa	EDAr NPro
Pink Flame = 'Bartwelve'PBR	CBct EPfP LLHF LRHS LSou SBfd SHil SPoG
'Pride of Rochester'	ECtt GJos LHop LRHS NRHS
§ × ***procumbens*** 'Millstream' ♀H4	ECtt
– 'Variegata' (v)	ECha ECho ECtt MDKP SPlb SRot WRHF
§ ***pulvinata***	WAbe
– blue-flowered **new**	GKev
Purple Flame = 'Barfourteen'PBR	CBct EPfP LBMP LSou SBfd SHar SHil SPoG WFar
× ***rugelii***	EPot
'Sherbet Cocktail'PBR	CWGN NLar WCot WPtf
§ ***sibirica*** subsp. ***borealis***	EDAr
'Sileniflora'	EPot
stolonifera	IFro MNrw
I – 'Alba'	EBee EPfP
– 'Ariane'	ECha EWld LSou MCot SBch
– 'Blue Ridge' ♀H4	CPLG ECha ECtt EPfP LRHS LSRN SRms
– 'Fran's Purple'	EWld MNrw NBro SBch WCFE
– 'Home Fires'	EBee ECho ECtt EPfP LEdu LRHS NBro SMrm SPlb WRHF XLum
– 'Mary Belle Frey'	CEnt
– 'Montrose Tricolor' (v)	NBro
– 'Pink Ridge'	SBch
– 'Purpurea'	CWCL EBee EPfP LEdu LSou
– 'Violet Vere'	LRHS
subulata 'Alexander's Surprise'	ECho ECtt EDAr EPfP LBee LRHS MAsh NBir NLar SPlb

	– 'Amazing Grace'	CTri CWCL CYeo ECho EDAr EPfP EPot EWes IPot LAst LHop LRHS MAsh SEND SPoG WAbe WIce WPer
	– 'Apple Blossom'	EDAr NHol SPet SPoG SRms WFar WHoo
	– 'Atropurpurea'	EDAr EPfP LRHS MAsh SPoG XLum
	– 'Bavaria'	LLHF
	– Beauty of Ronsdorf	see *P. subulata* 'Ronsdorfer Schöne'
	– 'Blue Eyes'	see *P. subulata* 'Oakington Blue Eyes'
	– 'Bonita'	CPBP ECho ECtt EPot GJos LRHS MAsh NLar WHoo WIce XLum
	– 'Bressingham Blue Eyes'	see *P. subulata* 'Oakington Blue Eyes'
	– 'Candy Stripe'	see *P. subulata* 'Tamaongalei'
	– 'Cavaldes White'	NPri SPoG
	– 'Drumm'	see *P. subulata* 'Tamaongalei'
	– 'Emerald Cushion'	CMea CTri CWCL ECho ECtt EDAr ELon LRHS MDKP MWat NHol NLar WCFE WHil WNew WRHF
	– 'Emerald Cushion Blue'	CPLG CTri CYeo ECho EPfP GJos LAst LRHS MAsh NBir NMen NPnk NPri NPro SBch SPlb SPoG WAbe WFar WPer
	– 'Fairy'	WPer
	– 'Fort Hill'	NHar
	– 'G.F. Wilson'	see *P. subulata* 'Lilacina'
*	– 'Holly'	ECtt EPot ITim LLHF NHol NWad
	– 'Jupiter'	ECho
	– 'Kimono'	see *P. subulata* 'Tamaongalei'
§	– 'Lilacina'	CMea ECho MWat WIce
§	– 'Maischnee'	CPBP CTri ECho ECtt MWat SPlb WFar
	– 'Marjorie'	CYeo ECho ECtt GJos LBee MAsh MHer NBir SPoG WFar WHoo WNew
	– May Snow	see *P. subulata* 'Maischnee'
§	– 'McDaniel's Cushion' ♀H4	Widely available
	– 'Mikado'	see *P. subulata* 'Tamaongalei'
	– 'Millstream Daphne'	ECho
	– 'Moonlight'	ECtt EDAr GJos
	– 'Nettleton Variation' (v)	CYeo ECho ECtt EDAr EPfP EPot EWes GKev LBMP LHop LRHS MAsh MDKP NLar SPlb SPoG SWal
§	– 'Oakington Blue Eyes'	CTri LRHS MAsh SRms
	– 'Pink Pearl'	EWes
	– 'Purple Beauty'	CMea CWCL ECho EPot GJos LLHF LRHS NHar NMRc NRHS NWad SPoG STes WCFE WFar WPer WSHC
	– 'Red Wings' ♀H4	CMea ECho ECtt EPfP EPot MAsh SRms
§	– 'Ronsdorfer Schöne'	EPot LBee LLHF MSCN NBir
	– 'Samson'	EDAr LSRN MAsh
	– 'Sarah'	LLHF
	– 'Scarlet Flame'	CBar CMea ECho ECtt EDAr EPfP EPot MAsh NHol WFar WHoo
	– 'Snow Queen'	see *P. subulata* 'Maischnee'
	– 'Snowflake'	MSCN
	– 'Starglow'	MAsh
§	– 'Tamaongalei'	CMea CTri CWCL CYeo ECtt EDAr ELon EPfP EPot EWes GEdr GJos GKev GMaP LRHS MMuc MSCN NRHS SEND SPet STes WCFE WHil WHoo WIce WNew WPer XLum
	– 'Temiskaming'	CTri ECho ECtt EDAr EWes LHop LRHS MLHP NMen SRms WAbe WSHC
	– 'Tschernobyl'	EPot
	– 'White Delight'	CBar CMea ECho ECtt EDAr EPfP GJos LAst LBee LRHS MAsh NMen SPet SPoG STes WFar WHil WPer
	– 'Winifred'	NEgg
	'Swirly Burly'	GQue NLar
	'Tiny Bugles'	CPBP
	Violet Flame = 'Barsixtyone'	LRHS MAvo WCot
	White Eye Flame = 'Barsixty'	EPfP LRHS
	'White Kimono'	ECho LHop LRHS NRHS
	'Zwergenteppich'	LLHF WPer

Phlomis (*Lamiaceae*)

*	***anatolica***	LRHS NLar
I	– 'Lloyd's Variety'	CAbP CSam EBee ELan LRHS MAsh SEND SPer
	angustifolia	EBee LRHS XSen
	anisodonta white-flowered	XSen
	armeniaca	XSen
	atropurpurea BWJ 7922	WCru
	bourgaei	XSen
	bovei subsp. ***maroccana***	SEND WHal WOut XLum XSen
	capitata	XSen
	cashmeriana	CCon CSam ECha EHoe EPfP LAst LDai LSou MMuc NLar SBea SBfd SKHP SMad SPhx WCFE WWEG
	chrysophylla ♀H3	CAbP CTrC EBee ECha ELan EPfP LRHS MAsh MRav NLar SDix SEND SPer WCFE XSen
	cretica	XSen
	crinita	EBee XSen
	cypria	XSen
	'Edward Bowles'	EBee ECha LRHS LSRN MRav NLar SKHP SLPl SWvt XSen
*	'Elliot's Variety'	CPLG
	fruticosa ♀H4	Widely available
	– white-flowered	ECrN
	grandiflora	SEND XSen
	herba-venti	XSen
	italica	Widely available
	– 'Pink Glory'	CMac
	lanata ♀H3-4	CAbP EBee ELan EPfP LAst LRHS NLar SBrt SPer WCFE WKif XSen
	– 'Pygmy'	CHVG NPro XSen
	'Le Sud'	XSen
	leucophracta	XSen
	longifolia	EBee EPfP LHop LRHS LSou MNrw NLar SEND SKHP SPer SSvw WGrn WPGP XSen
	– var. ***bailanica***	CSam EPfP LRHS
	lunariifolia	XSen
	lychnitis	XSen
	lycia	XSen
	macrophylla	SPhx
	monocephala	XSen
	nissolei	XSen
	platystegia	XSen
	purpurea	CAbP CArn CPLG EBee ELan EPfP IDee LRHS MAsh MNrw NBir SBfd SEND WCot WGrn XSen
	– ***alba***	EBee EPfP LRHS SKHP XSen
	– subsp. ***almeriensis***	CCse CPom XSen
	– subsp. ***caballeroi***	XSen
§	***russeliana*** ♀H4	Widely available
	– 'Dappled Shade' (v) new	WCot
	– 'Mosaic' (v)	MAvo XSen
	samia Boiss.	see *P. russeliana*

samia L. CKno CSpe EBee LBMP LDai LHop LRHS NBir NChi NGdn NLar SKHP SMrm WOut WPtf XSen
- 'Green Glory' WTin
taurica EPfP LRHS NRHS SGar SPhx
tuberosa CArn CBcs CCon CKno CMac CPou EBee EPfP EWTr LEdu LRHS LSRN NGdn NLar SBfd SPet WGwG WHoo WMnd WPtf XSen
- 'Amazone' CSev EBee ECha EHrv EPfP GBin LHop MBel MRav NBid NCGa NDov NOrc NPnk NSti SMad SWal WCot WFar WMnd XSen
- 'Bronze Flamingo' CKno EBee ECGP EPfP ETod GBin GMaP LAst LBMP LRHS LSou MNrw MPnt MRav NBid NOrc SKHP SMrm SPoG WMnd WPer
viscosa misapplied see *P. russeliana*

Phoenix (*Arecaceae*)

canariensis 🏆[H1+3] CBcs CPLG CTrC CWSG CWib EAmu EGri EPfP EUJe IVic LRHS MBri MREP NPri SBfd SBst SEND SLim SPlb SPoG STrG
dactylifera (F) EAmu SBig
reclinata EAmu XBlo
roebelenii 🏆[H1+3] CDTJ CDoC LRHS MBri SBig
- 'Multistem' XBlo
rupicola EAmu
sylvestris EAmu
theophrasti CPHo EAmu

Phoenicaulis (*Brassicaceae*)

§ ***cheiranthoides*** LLHF

Phormium ✿ (*Hemerocallidaceae*)

§ 'Alison Blackman'[PBR] CBcs CDoC CKno COlW CTrC EBee EPfP ESwi GBin IVic LHop LRHS LSRN MAsh MBri MGos MRav NPla SBfd SCoo SEND SHil SPoG SRkn SWvt
'Amazing Red' CTrC ESwi SBfd
'Apricot Queen' (v) CAbb CBcs CCCN CDoC CSBt CTrC CWib EBee EPfP ESwi LRHS LSRN LTen MAsh MBri MGos MWat NEgg NLar SBfd SBod SEND SEWo SHil SPer SPoG SRkn WPat
'Back in Black' LBuc NPri SBfd WFar
'Black Edge' MRav
'Black Rage' CBcs LHop LRHS
Black Velvet = 'Seivel' IBoy NPla SBfd SEND
'Bronze Baby' Widely available
'Buckland Ruby' CDoC
'Carousel' CTrC ESwi
'Chocolate Fingers' CBcs
'Chocomint' CBcs CTrC
colensoi see *P. cookianum*
§ ***cookianum*** CHEx CTrC EPfP
- 'Black Adder'[PBR] CBcs ELon ESwi EUJe IBoy LBuc LRHS LSRN MAsh MDev MGos SBfd SPoG
- dwarf SLPl
- 'Flamingo' (v) CBcs CCCN CDTJ CSBt CTrC EBee ELan ELon EPfP ESwi LRHS LSou MAsh MBri MGos NLar SBfd SEWo SLim SPer SPoG SRkn WPat
- subsp. ***hookeri*** 'Cream Delight' (v) 🏆[H3-4] CAbb CBcs CCCN CDoC COlW CSBt CWib EBee EHoe EPfP EUJe LRHS LSRN MGos MRav MSwo NPri NRHS SBfd SCoo SGol SHil SPer SWvt WGrn
- - 'Tricolor' (v) 🏆[H3-4] Widely available
'Crimson Devil' CBcs CTrC NPri SBfd SLim
Dark Avocado = 'Westado'[PBR] EBee MAsh SLim
'Dark Delight' CBcs CDoC
'Dazzler' (v) CBcs CDoC LSRN
'Duet' (v) 🏆[H3] CCCN CDoC CTrC CWib EBee EHoe ELon EPfP ESwi LHop LRHS NLar SEND SEWo SWvt
'Dusky Chief' CSBt CTrC EPfP ESwi LRHS
'Dusky Princess' ESwi LRHS
'Emerald Isle' CDoC
'Evening Glow' (v) CBcs CCCN CSBt CTrC EBee ELan ELon EPfP ESwi ETod EUJe LRHS LSRN MAsh MBri MGos MWat SBfd SEND SEWo SHil SPoG SRkn SWvt WGrn WPat
'Firebird' ESwi EUJe LSRN SWvt
'Glowing Embers' CBcs COlW CTrC EAmu ELon IVic
'Gold Ray' CBcs CTrC EBee ELon ESwi LRHS MBri NLar NPri SBfd SCoo SHil SWvt WCot WGrn
'Gold Sword' (v) CCCN CDoC CMHG CSBt CTrC EBee EPfP ESwi LRHS MDev MPie MWat NEgg SBfd
'Golden Alison'[PBR] see *P.* 'Alison Blackman'
'Golden Ray' (v) EUJe LAst LRHS
'Green Sword' CBcs CCCN
'Jack Spratt' (v) CBcs ECou EHoe SWvt
'Jester' (v) Widely available
'Limelight' SBfd SWvt
§ 'Maori Chief' CSBt EPfP LRHS SWvt WGrn WPat
§ 'Maori Maiden' (v) CBcs CCCN CDoC CDul CTrC CTri EBee EHoe EPfP ESwi LRHS MGos MRav SRkn SWvt
§ 'Maori Queen' (v) CBcs CCCN CDTJ CDoC COlW CSBt CTrC EBee ELan EPfP ESwi LRHS MBri MGos MSwo MWat NPri SBfd SCoo SEND SHil SLPl SPer SPoG SRkn SWvt
§ 'Maori Sunrise' (v) CBcs CCCN CDoC CTrC EBee ELon EPfP IArd LRHS LSRN MBrN MGos MRav NPla SBfd SCoo SLim SPer SWvt
'Margaret Jones'[PBR] CCCN CKno CTrC LSRN SLim
'Merlot'[PBR] NPri
'Moonraker' CBcs CTrC
'Peach Melba' CTrC
'Pink Panther' (v) CAbb CBcs CCCN CDoC CTrC CWib EBee ECtt ELan ELon EPfP LAst LHop LRHS LSRN LTen MAsh MBri MGos MRav MSwo MWat NGdn NPla NPri SCoo SHil SPer SPoG WPat
'Pink Stripe' (v) CBcs CDoC CMHG CSBt EAmu EBee ESwi LRHS MBri MGos NPri NRHS SBfd SHil SPoG SWvt WCot
'Platt's Black' Widely available
'Rainbow Chief' see *P.* 'Maori Chief'
'Rainbow Maiden' see *P.* 'Maori Maiden'
'Rainbow Queen' see *P.* 'Maori Queen'
'Rainbow Sunrise' see *P.* 'Maori Sunrise'
'Red Fingers' CBcs
'Red Sensation' ELon EPfP LRHS SEWo
I 'Rubrum' CTrC EUJe LRHS
'Sundowner' (v) 🏆[H3] CBcs CCCN CDoC CDul CSBt CTrC EBee EHoe ELan EPfP LHop

LRHS MAsh MBri MGos MRav NBir NEgg SBfd SBod SCoo SEND SHil SLim SPer SPlb SPoG SWvt WGrn WPat
'Sunset' (v) CBcs CCCN CSBt EUJe SWvt WCot
'Surfer' (v) CBcs LHop MBel MBri WGrn
'Surfer Boy' LTen
'Surfer Bronze' CBcs CCCN CSBt ETod LSou SBfd
'Surfer Green' CCCN ESwi SBfd
'Sussex Velvet' EBee SCoo SLim
'Taya' **new** CBcs CTrC
tenax ♀H4 Widely available
- 'All Black'PBR LBuc LRHS MBri MGos NRHS SCoo SHil
- 'Bronze' SWal SWvt
- 'Chocolate Dream' EPfP
- 'Co-ordination' CBcs CCCN EBee EPfP SBfd
- 'Darkside' WCot
- 'Deep Purple' CHEx
- dwarf SLPl
I - 'Giganteum' CHEx
- 'Joker' CBcs CTrC
* - ***lineatum*** SEND
- Purpureum Group ♀H3-4 Widely available
- Sweet Mist = 'Phos2' NOak
- 'Variegatum' (v) ♀H3-4 CDTJ CDoy CTrC EBee ELon EPfP ETod EUJe LRHS MGos MWat SBfd SEND SEWo SPer SRms
- 'Veitchianum' (v) CDoy EUJe SPer
'Thumbelina' CBcs CCCN ESwi MAsh WPat
'Tom Thumb' CBcs
'Wings of Gold' ESwi ETod
'Yellow Wave' (v) ♀H3 Widely available

Photinia ✿ (*Rosaceae*)

arbutifolia see *Heteromeles salicifolia*
beauverdiana IRar WWau
- var. ***notabilis*** EPfP
Corallina = 'Bourfrits'PBR **new** EUJe NLar
davidiana CDul CMac CTri ELan EPfP MRav NLar SRms WFar WWau
- 'Palette' (v) CBcs CDul CMac CWib EBee EHoe ELan ELon EPfP LAst LHop LRHS MAsh MGos MMuc MSwo NEgg NLar NPri SBfd SLim SPer SPoG SRms SWvt WFar WHar WMoo
- var. ***undulata*** 'Fructu Luteo' CAbP MRav NLar SEND WWau
- - 'Prostrata' CMac CTri ELan MRav NLar WFar WWau
×***fraseri*** WWau
- 'Allyn Sprite'PBR NEgg SBfd
I - 'Atropurpurea Nana' EPfP LBMP MGos
- 'Birmingham' CMac EWes
- 'Canivily' CTrC EBee EMil EWes IVic LRHS MBri NLar SBfd SGol SHil SLim
- Cracklin' Red = 'Parred' **new** NLar
- Dynamo Red = 'Parsur' **new** NLar
- Fireball Red = 'Parbri' **new** NLar
* - 'Ilexifolium' ESwi
- 'Little Red Robin' CBar CSBt EBee EHoe ELan ELon EPfP EShb IVic LAst LBuc LRHS LSRN MAsh MRav MWat NHol NLar NRHS SBfd SGol SHil SLim SLon SPad SPer SPoG SWvt
- Pink Marble = 'Cassini' (v) CBcs EBee ELan EPfP EWTr LBuc LRHS MBri MPkF NHol SBfd SHil SLim SLon SPoG SRms
- 'Red Robin' ♀H4 Widely available
- 'Red Select' NPri WPat
- 'Robusta' CMac CTrC EBee EPfP LRHS SWvt
I - 'Robusta Compacta' WFar
glabra WWau
§ - 'Parfait' (v) CAbP EBee LRHS MAsh SLon WWau
- 'Pink Lady' see *P. glabra* 'Parfait'
- 'Rubens' EBee EPfP LRHS MAsh MRav WWau
- 'Variegata' see *P. glabra* 'Parfait'
integrifolia HWJ 946 WCru
lasiogyna CMCN
lucida WCru
microphylla B&SWJ 11837 WCru
- HWJ 564 WCru
niitakayamensis IGor
parvifolia EPfP
'Redstart' CAbP CMac EBee EPfP LRHS LSou MGos NEgg NLar NPro SEND SLim SLon SPer SWvt WMoo
§ ***serratifolia*** CAbP CBcs CDul CHEx EBee EPfP NLar SBfd SEND SPer WFar WWau
I - 'Compacta' WFar
- 'Jenny' CDul CTrC LRHS LSou NEgg NLar
serrulata see *P. serratifolia*
- Curly Fantasy = 'Kolcurl'PBR EBee EMil IVic LBuc LRHS MGos MRav NLar SBfd SPoG WWau
'Super Hedge'PBR see *P.* Super Hedge
§ Super Hedge = 'Branpara'PBR CTrC EBee EShb LRHS LSou WHar WWau
'Super Red' CSBt EBee EUJe MNHC MWat NLar SLim
villosa ♀H4 CAbP CGHE CTho SPoG WWau
- B&SWJ 8665 WCru
- var. ***coreana*** B&SWJ 8789 WCru
- var. ***laevis*** CPLG EPfP MBri WWau
- - B&SWJ 8877 WCru
- f. ***maximowicziana*** EPfP MBri
* - var. ***zollingeri*** B&SWJ 8903 WCru

Phragmites (*Poaceae*)

sp. **new** CHab
from Sichuan, China EPPr
§ ***australis*** CBen CHab CRWN CWat LPBA MSKA NLar NMir SVic SWat WMAq WPnP XLum
- subsp. ***australis*** var. ***striatopictus*** EPPr
- - 'Variegatus' (v) CBen CKno CWCL CWat EBee EPPr EShb LPBA LRHS MMuc MWhi NBir NLar NWsh SEND SMad SWal WWEG XLum
- subsp. ***humilis*** **new** CHab
- subsp. ***pseudodonax*** EPPr MMoz
communis see *P. australis*
karka EPPr
- 'Candy Stripe' (v) CBen EPPr MSKA

Phrynium (*Marantaceae*)

pubinerve GHim

Phuopsis (*Rubiaceae*)

§ ***stylosa*** CHVG CSev CTri EBee ECha ELan ELon EPfP GAbr GMaP IFoB LBMP LRHS LSou MHer MLHP NBid NBir

NBro NChi SEND SPoG SRms WFar WMoo WPer WPtf XLum

- 'Purpurea' CElw GBin MNrw MRav NChi NDov

Phygelius ✿ (*Scrophulariaceae*)

aequalis CTca MRav WMoo
- ***albus*** see *P. aequalis* 'Yellow Trumpet'
- 'Aureus' see *P. aequalis* 'Yellow Trumpet'
- Cedric Morris form SHom
- 'Cream Trumpet' see *P. aequalis* 'Yellow Trumpet'
- 'Indian Chief' see *P.* × *rectus* 'African Queen'
- 'Pink Trumpet' SCoo SMrm SPet
- 'Sani Pass' CPrp ELon EPfP GMaP LSRN MHer MSCN SCoo SEND SHom SPet SPlb SWvt WCot
- 'Trewidden Pink' ♀H4 CWib EBee ELan ELon EPfP GBin LAst LHop MSCN SBfd SHom SLim SWvt WMnd WMoo WWEG XLum

§ - 'Yellow Trumpet' ♀H3-4 CBcs CSBt CTca CWib EBee ELan ELon EPfP GMaP IBoy LBMP LPot LSRN MAsh MLHP SBfd SEND SHom SLim SPad SPet SWal SWvt WHoo WMnd WMoo WWEG XLum

(Candy Drops Series) Candy Drops Cream = 'Kerphycrem'PBR LRHS SVic
- Candy Drops Peach = 'Kerphypeach'PBR **new** SVic
- Candy Drops Purple = 'Kerphypur'PBR SGar SVic
- Candy Drops Salmon Orange = 'Kerphysalm'PBR LRHS
- Candy Drops Tangerine = 'Kerphytan'PBR LRHS SVic

§ ***capensis*** ♀H3-4 CDoy CDul CHll CWib ELan GCra MHer NLar SHom SPet SRms WMnd
- ***coccineus*** see *P. capensis*
- orange-flowered LHop SHom

'Golden Gate' see *P. aequalis* 'Yellow Trumpet'

'Midas Touch' ELon NLar

New Sensation = 'Blaphy'PBR ECtt EPfP LRHS MNrw MRav SWvt

'Passionate'PBR NLar

§ × ***rectus*** 'African Queen' ♀H3-4 EBee ELan EPfP LPot MLHP MRav MSwo NBir NGdn SEND SMad SPlb SWvt WKif WMnd WMoo WWEG
- 'Aylesham's Pride' SHom
- 'Cherry Swirl' **new** SHom
- 'Devil's Tears' ♀H4 CBcs EBee ELan EPfP LAst LPot LRHS NEgg NLar SBfd SEND SLim SPad SWvt WHil WMnd WMoo
- 'Fantasia' SHom
- 'Ivory Twist' ELon LHop LRHS SEND SHom
- 'Jodie Southon' LSou SDys SHom SUsu WCot

* - 'Logan's Pink' LSRN
- 'Moonraker' CHll CTri EBee ELan EPfP GBin LAst LHop LRHS MBri MHer MRav NEgg NGdn NLar SBfd SEND SHom SMrm SPer SPlb SRms SWal WKif WMoo XLum
- 'Raspberry Swirl' LRHS SHom
- 'Red Alert' **new** SHom
- 'Salmon Leap' ♀H4 CTri EBee ELan EPfP GBin GBuc LAst LRHS LSRN MBNS MGos MRav NEgg NLar SBfd SBod SEND SHom SLim SMrm SPlb SWal SWvt WMnd WMoo
- Somerford Funfair Apricot = 'Yapapr' SWvt
- Somerford Funfair Coral = 'Yapcor'PBR CDoC EBee EPfP GKev LPot LRHS MBri NEgg NLar SLim SRkn SWvt WFar
- Somerford Funfair Cream = 'Yapcre'PBR CDoC EBee EPfP LBMP LRHS NEgg NLar NPri SGar SLim SMrm SWvt WFar WPtf
- Somerford Funfair Orange = 'Yapor'PBR EBee LBMP LRHS MBri NLar NPri SHil SLim SPoG SWvt WFar
- Somerford Funfair Wine = 'Yapwin' EBee ELan EPfP EShb LPot LRHS LSou MBNS MBri NEgg NLar NPri SBfd SHil SLim SMrm SPoG SWvt WFar WPtf
- Somerford Funfair Yellow = 'Yapyel'PBR EBee LRHS SHil SLim SPoG SWvt
- 'Sunshine' EBee ELan MDKP SHom SMrm WCot
- 'Sweet Dreams' LRHS SHom

§ - 'Winchester Fanfare' CSBt ELan EPfP GBin GMaP LBMP LRHS MGos MRav SBod SEND SLim SMrm SPer SWvt WKif WMoo WWEG
- 'Winton Fanfare' see *P.* × *rectus* 'Winchester Fanfare'

'Rory'PBR SRms

Phyla (*Verbenaceae*)

§ ***nodiflora*** ECha WJek WPer
- 'Alba' SEND

§ - var. ***canescens*** WHal XLum

Phyllanthus (*Euphorbiaceae*)

emblica **new** CArn

× *Phylliopsis* (*Ericaceae*)

'Coppelia' ♀H4 GEdr GKev NHar WAbe WPat

hillieri 'Askival' WThu
- 'Pinocchio' NHar WPat WThu

'Hobgoblin' WAbe

'Mermaid' ITim NHar WAbe WThu

'Sprite' EBee WPat

'Sugar Plum' CCCN CWSG LRHS NHar NLar SWvt WThu

'Swanhilde' WAbe

Phyllitis see *Asplenium*

scolopendrium see *Asplenium scolopendrium*

Phyllocladus (*Podocarpaceae*)

alpinus CDoC CDul ECou NLar NWad

Phyllodoce (*Ericaceae*)

aleutica ECho NHar SRms WThu

caerulea ♀H4 ECho
- ***japonica*** see *P. nipponica*
- 'Murray Lyon' NHar WAbe WThu
- 'W.M. Buchanan's Peach Seedling' NHar

empetriformis ECho SRms WThu

§ ***nipponica*** ♀H4 NHar NMen WThu

'Peach' **new** WThu

Phyllostachys ✿ (*Poaceae*)

angusta ERod MWht SBig

arcana WJun
- 'Luteosulcata' CEnt ERod GBin MMoz MMuc MWht NLar WJun

§ ***atrovaginata*** ERod SGol WJun

aurea ♀H4	Widely available
- 'Albovariegata' (v)	CDTJ ENBC EPfP ERod LRHS MWht WJun
- 'Flavescens Inversa'	ERod MWht SEND WJun
- 'Holochrysa'	CDTJ ERod MWht WJun
- 'Koi'	CDTJ CEnt ERod MMoz MWht SBig SGol WJun WPGP
aureocaulis	see *P. aureosulcata* f. *aureocaulis*, *P. vivax* f. *aureocaulis*
aureosulcata	CWib ENBC ERod LEdu MMoz MWht WJun WMoo
- f. ***alata***	see *P. aureosulcata* f. *pekinensis*
§ - f. ***aureocaulis*** ♀H4	Widely available
- 'Harbin'	ERod
- 'Harbin Inversa'	CDTJ ERod
- 'Lama Tempel'	CDTJ WPGP
§ - f. ***pekinensis***	MMoz SBig
- f. ***spectabilis*** ♀H4	Widely available
bambusoides	CDTJ ERod SBig SDix WJun
- 'Albovariegata' (v)	ETod
- 'Allgold'	see *P. bambusoides* 'Holochrysa'
- 'Castilloni Inversa'	EAmu ERod ETod EWes LEdu MMoz MWht WJun
- 'Castillonii'	CBcs CEnt EAmu ENBC ERod EUJe EWes LEdu MMoz MWht NLar SBig SDix SEND WJun WPGP
- 'Castillonis Inversa Variegata' (v)	WJun
- 'Castillonis Variegata' (v) **new**	ERod
§ - 'Holochrysa'	CDTJ CDoC CEnt ERod MMoz MWht SEND WJun WPGP
- 'Kawadana' (v)	ERod WJun
- f. ***lacrima-deae***	CAgr CDTJ CTrC EPfP EUJe GBin
- 'Marliacea'	ERod SBig WJun
- 'Sulphurea'	see *P. bambusoides* 'Holochrysa'
- 'Tanakae'	CDTJ ENBC MMoz SBig
- 'Violascens'	SBig
bissetii	Widely available
congesta misapplied	see *P. atrovaginata*
decora	ERod MMoz MMuc MWht NLar SEND WJun
dulcis	CEnt EPfP ERod MWht SBig WJun
§ ***edulis***	CAgr CDTJ CTrC ELon ERod MMoz MWht SBig SBst WJun
- 'Bicolor'	WJun
§ - 'Heterocycla'	XBlo
- f. ***pubescens***	see *P. edulis*
fimbriligula	WJun
flexuosa	CBcs CEnt LRHS MWht SGol SHil WJun
glauca	CDTJ EPfP ERod ETod MMoz MWht NLar SBig
- f. ***yunzhu***	ERod MWht WJun
'Green Groove'	NHim
heteroclada	CAgr CDTJ CEnt WJun
- 'Solid Stem' misapplied	see *P. purpurata* 'Straight Stem'
heterocycla	see *P. edulis* 'Heterocycla'
- f. ***pubescens***	see *P. edulis*
humilis	CEnt ENBC ERod EUJe MGos MMoz MMuc MWhi MWht NLar SBig SEND WJun
incarnata	WJun
iridescens	ERod ETod NLar SBig WJun
lithophila	ERod
makinoi	ERod
mannii	ERod MWht
nidularia	ERod MMoz SBig WJun
nigra ♀H4	Widely available
- 'Boryana'	CCVT CDoC CEnt EAmu EPfP ERod EUJe MGos MMoz MMuc MWht SBig SEND SWvt WFar WJun WMoo
- 'Hale'	MWht
- f. ***henonis*** ♀H4	EAmu ENBC ERod MMoz MMuc MREP MWht NLar SBig SEND SGol WJun WPGP
- 'Megurochiku'	ENBC ERod MWht WJun
- f. ***punctata***	CDoC ENBC ERod MAvo MMuc MWht NGdn SEND WJun WMoo
- 'Tosaensis'	ERod
nuda	EAmu ERod MMoz MMuc MWht NLar SEND WJun
- f. ***localis***	ERod MWht
parvifolia	CEnt ERod MWht WJun
platyglossa	ERod
praecox	ETod WJun
- f. ***viridisulcata***	EAmu ERod WJun
prominens	ERod
propinqua	CDoC EAmu ERod GBin MMoz MWht WJun
* ***pubescens*** 'Mazel'	SPlb
§ ***purpurata*** 'Straight Stem'	MWht
rubicunda	WJun
rubromarginata	CDTJ CEnt ERod MMuc MWht NLar WJun
'Shanghai 3'	EAmu ERod ETod
stimulosa	ERod MWht WJun
sulphurea	CDTJ
- 'Houzeau'	ERod MMuc SEND
§ - f. ***sulphurea***	ERod WJun
- 'Sulphurea'	see *P. sulphurea* f. *sulphurea*
§ - f. ***viridis***	ERod SBig
violascens	CEnt ERod EUJe MMoz MWht SBig WJun
viridiglaucescens	CDTJ ERod ETod MBrN MMoz MWht NLar SBig SEND WJun
viridis	see *P. sulphurea* f. *viridis*
vivax	EPfP ERod EUJe GQui LEdu MMoz MWht NLar SBig SEND WJun
§ - f. ***aureocaulis*** ♀H4	Widely available
- - 'Huanwenzii'	CDTJ CTrC EAmu ENBC ERod ETod EUJe MGos MMoz MWht NPla WJun
- 'Katrin'	LEdu
* - 'Sulphurea'	XBlo

× *Phyllothamnus* (*Ericaceae*)

erectus	WAbe WPat

Phymatosorus (*Polypodiaceae*)

§ ***diversifolius***	WCot WPGP

Phymosia (*Malvaceae*)

§ ***umbellata***	MOWG WPGP

Phyodina see *Callisia*

Physalis (*Solanaceae*)

alkekengi ♀H4	CTri NBir NLar SWvt XLum
- var. ***franchetii***	CArn CDoy CMac CSBt EBee ECha ELan EPfP LAst LRHS MHer MWat NBir NBro NEgg NGdn NPri SBfd SMad SPer SPoG SRms WFar WMnd WOld WPer
- - dwarf	LRHS NLar
- - 'Gigantea'	ECGP MNHC NGBl NLar SPlb
- - 'Gnome'	see *P. alkekengi* var. *franchetii* 'Zwerg'

- - 'Variegata' (v)	EWes LEdu NPro SEND WOld
§ - - 'Zwerg'	EWll LRHS
- 'Halloween King' new	EBee LRHS SPoG
- 'Halloween Queen' new	EBee LRHS SPoG SPtl
angulata B&SWJ 7016	LLHF
campanula B&SWJ 10409	WCru
edulis	see *P. peruviana*
§ ***peruviana*** (F)	CCCN MHoo SBfd SHDw SPlb SVic

Physaria (*Brassicaceae*)

alpina	GKev

Physocarpus (*Rosaceae*)

'Burning Embers'	LBuc SRms
§ 'Donna May'	LBuc
Little Devil	see *P.* 'Donna May'
malvaceus	EWes
monogynus	NLar
opulifolius	CDul
- 'Angel Gold'	EBee ELan EMil EPfP MAsh SBfd
- Coppertina[PBR]	see *P. opulifolius* Diable D'Or
- 'Dart's Gold' ♀H4	Widely available
§ - Diable D'Or = 'Mindia'[PBR]	CDoC EMil EPfP LBuc LRHS MAsh MBlu MBri MPkF NEgg NPla NRHS SBfd SGol SHil WMoo
- 'Diabolo'[PBR] ♀H4	Widely available
- Lady in Red = 'Tuilad'[PBR]	CMac CSBt EBee ELon EPPr EPfP EShb EWes LAst LHop LRHS LSqu MAsh MGos MPkF MWat NHol NLBP NLar SHar SKHP SLim SLon SPoG SPtl SRkn WFar WGrn WMoo WPat
§ - 'Luteus'	CDoC CWib MRav WFar WMoo
- 'Nugget'	LBuc LRHS SHil
- Summer Wine = 'Seward'[PBR]	EBee EPfP EWTr EWes LHop
- 'Tilden Park'	EBee SGol
ribesifolius 'Aureus'	see *P. opulifolius* 'Luteus'

Physochlaina (*Solanaceae*)

orientalis	GEdr GHim SPhx

Physoplexis (*Campanulaceae*)

§ ***comosa*** ♀H2-3	EPot NMen NSla WAbe

Physostegia (*Lamiaceae*)

angustifolia	GQui NBre
§ ***virginiana***	CSBt CTri GMaP LHop LRHS MBel SBfd SGar SPoG SRms SWat WBrk WCFE XLum
- 'Alba'	CSBt CTri EBee EHrv ELon GAbr GJos GMaP LBMP LEdu LRHS MBel NChi SMrm SPet SPlb WHrl XLum
§ - 'Crown of Snow'	CCon EBee ECtt EPfP MHer MRav MWat NPri SBea SBfd SHar SPoG SWvt WFar WHil WMoo WPer WWEG
- 'Galadriel'	EBee
- 'Grandiflora'	CCon
- 'Miss Manners'	CMac EAEE EBee ECGP ECtt LRHS MBri MCot NBre NCGa NGdn NLar SRGP SUsu WHil
- 'Red Beauty'	EBee
- 'Rose Crown'	SPer
- 'Rose Queen'	CTri MWat NBre NChi NPri SBfd
- 'Rosea'	EBee EPfP GJos IFoB MMuc NBre NGdn SHar SPoG SWal SWvt WFar WHrl WPer WWEG
- Schneekrone	see *P. virginiana* 'Crown of Snow'
- 'Snow Queen'	see *P. virginiana* 'Summer Snow'
§ - var. ***speciosa*** 'Bouquet Rose'	CPrp EBee ECGP ECha EHrv EPfP LEdu LRHS MCot MNFA MRav NBir NLar NRHS SPer SWvt WCAu WGwG WMoo WRHF WWEG XLum
- - Rose Bouquet	see *P. virginiana* var. *speciosa* 'Bouquet Rose'
- - 'Variegata' (v)	CMac CSBt EBee ECtt EHoe EHrv ELan ELon EPfP LHop MRav NBir NGdn NPnk SBea SPer SRms SWat WBrk WCAu WCot WFar WHoo WMnd WWEG XLum
§ - 'Summer Snow' ♀H4	CBcs CPrp EBee ECha ELan EPfP LHop LRHS NLar SPer SRms SWat WBrk WCAu WCot WFar WMnd
- 'Summer Spire'	EHrv ELan LRHS
- 'Vivid' ♀H4	Widely available
- 'Wassenhove'	SMrm

Phyteuma (*Campanulaceae*)

balbisii	see *P. cordatum*
comosum	see *Physoplexis comosa*
§ ***cordatum***	EDif GJos
hemisphaericum	ECho
humile	EDAr LRHS WThu
nigrum	ECho LLHF NBid WBor WPGP
orbiculare	GEdr
scheuchzeri	CSpe EBee ECho EPfP EWld GBin GEdr NSla SGar SMad SRms SRot WIce WPGP XLum
spicatum	CDes NBro

Phytolacca (*Phytolaccaceae*)

acinosa	GKev GPoy SWat
- HWJ 647	WCru
§ ***americana***	CArn CSev ELan EPfP ESwi EUJe GPoy MBNS MHer MNHC MPie NLar SIde SRms SWat WAbb WFar WJek WMnd WMoo XLum
- B&SWJ 1000	WCru
- B&SWJ 8817A	WCru
- 'Silberstein' (v)	CBct EBee ECtt ESwi LDai MBNS NLar WCot WHer
- 'Variegata' (v)	MMHG NBir
clavigera	see *P. polyandra*
decandra	see *P. americana*
dioica	CHEx CPLG
esculenta	LEdu SEND
icosandra B&SWJ 8988	WCru
- B&SWJ 9033	WCru
- Purpurascens Group B&SWJ 11251	SRms WCru
japonica B&SWJ 3005	NBid WCru
- B&SWJ 3522	WCru
'Laka Boom'	LHop
octandra B&SWJ 9514	WCru
- B&SWJ 10151	WCru
§ ***polyandra***	NBid NBro SRms
rivinoides B&SWJ 10264	WCru
rugosa B&SWJ 10263	WCru

Picea (*Pinaceae*)

§ ***abies***	CCVT CDul CLnd CMac CSBt CTri CWib EHul EPfP LAst LBuc MBri MGos MMuc NEgg NWea SCoo SEND SLim SPer SPoG WEve WMou
- 'Acrocona'	EHul MBri MGos NLar WEve
- 'Archer'	CKen
- 'Argenteospica' (v)	NPCo

	- 'Aurea'	NPCo WEve
	- 'Capitata'	CKen NLar
	- 'Clanbrassiliana'	CKen MGos NLar NWad WEve WFar WGor
	- Compacta Group	LBee NPCo
I	- 'Congesta'	CKen
	- 'Crippsii'	CKen
I	- 'Cruenta'	CKen SLim
	- 'Cupressina'	CKen
	- 'Decumbens' **new**	NLar
	- 'Diffusa'	CKen NLar
	- 'Dumpy'	CKen NHol NLar NWad WGor
	- 'Ellwangeriana'	NLar WEve
	- 'Excelsa'	see *P. abies*
	- 'Fahndrich'	CKen CMen
	- 'Finedonensis'	NLar WEve
	- 'Formanek'	CDoC CKen CMen
	- 'Four Winds'	CKen NLar
	- 'Frohburg'	CKen MGos NLar NPri
	- 'Gold Drift'	NLar
	- 'Gregoryana'	CKen CMac
	- 'Heartland Gem'	CKen
	- 'Himfa'	NLar
	- 'Horace Wilson'	CKen CMen
	- 'Humilis'	CKen
	- 'Hystrix'	CMen NLar NWad
	- 'Inversa'	CDul CKen MBlu MGos NLar SLim WEve
	- 'J.W. Daisy's White'	see *P. glauca* 'J.W. Daisy's White'
	- 'Jana'	CKen
	- 'Kral'	CKen
	- 'Little Gem' ♀H4	CDoC CKen CMen EHul GEdr LBee LRHS MAsh NHol NLar NWad NWea SCoo SLim SPer SPoG WEve WFar
	- 'Marcel'	CKen
	- 'Maxwellii'	EHul
	- 'Mikulasovice'	NLar
	- 'Nana Compacta'	CKen CMen EHul LAst MAsh WFar WGor
	- 'Nidiformis' ♀H4	CDoC CKen CMac CMen CSBt CTri EHul LAst LPot LRHS MWat NHol NLar NPCo NWea SCoo SGol SLim SPer SPoG SRms WEve WFar
	- 'Norrkoping'	CKen
	- 'Ohlendorffii'	CKen EHul MGos NLar
	- 'Pachyphylla'	CKen
	- 'Pseudomaxwellii'	NLar
	- 'Pumila Nigra'	EHul LRHS MGos SLim WGor
	- 'Pusch'	CKen CMen NLar SLim
	- 'Pygmaea'	CKen NLar WGor
	- 'Reflexa'	MAsh NPCo WEve
	- 'Remontii'	NWea
	- 'Rydal'	CBcs CDoC CDul CKen MAsh MBri NHol NLar NWea SLim WEve
	- 'Saint James'	CKen
	- 'Silberkugel'	NLar
	- 'Sonnenberg'	NLar
	- 'Starý Smolivec'	NLar
	- 'Tompa'	LRHS MBri NLar SLim
	- 'Vermont Gold'	CKen NLar
	- Will's Dwarf	see *P. abies* 'Wills Zwerg'
§	- 'Wills Zwerg'	SGol
§	***alcoquiana*** var. ***alcoquiana***	NWea SLim
	- var. ***reflexa***	MPkF
	asperata	NWea
	bicolor	see *P. alcoquiana* var. *alcoquiana*
	breweriana ♀H4	CCVT CDoC CDul CMac EHul EPfP GKin IDee LEdu LRHS MBlu MGos MMuc NEgg NPCo NPri NWea SEND SLim SSta WCFE WEve WFar WMou
	- 'Kohout's Dwarf'	CKen
	chihuahuana	SLim
	engelmannii	CDul NWea
	- 'Compact'	SLim
	- subsp. ***engelmannii***	CKen NPCo
	- 'Jasper'	NLar
	- 'Lace'	NLar
	glauca	CDul NWea WEve
	- Alberta Blue = 'Haal'[PBR]	CKen LRHS MAsh WEve WFar
	- var. ***albertiana*** 'Alberta Globe'	CDoC CSBt EHul EPot GKin LBee LRHS MAsh MBri MGos NEgg NWad SCoo SLim SPoG WEve WFar
	- - 'Conica'	CBcs CDoC CDul CMac CMea CSBt EHul EPfP EUJe LBee MAsh MBri MGos NEgg NHol NWad NWea SBod SEND SGol SLim SPer SPoG SRms WCFE WEve WFar
	- - 'Gnome'	CKen WEve
	- - 'Laurin'	CKen MGos NPCo NWad WEve WGor
	- - 'Tiny'	CKen NWad WEve WGor
	- 'Arneson's Blue Variegated' (v)	CDoC CKen LRHS MAsh MBri SLim WFar
	- 'Biesenthaler Frühling'	CKen SLim
	- 'Blue Planet'	CKen IVic NLar
	- 'Coerulea'	NPCo
	- 'Cy's Wonder'	CKen
	- 'Echiniformis' ♀H4	CKen GKin LBee MBri
	- var. ***glauca***	WEve
	- 'Goldilocks'	CKen MBri
§	- 'J.W. Daisy's White'	CBcs CDoC CKen EHul EPfP GKin LRHS MAsh MGos NEgg NHol NLar NWad NWea SBod SCoo SLim SPer SPoG WEve WFar WGor
	- 'Jean Dilly'	NLar
I	- 'Julian Potts Monstrosa'	NLar
	- 'Lilliput'	CKen EHul MBri MGos NLar NWad NWea WGor
§	- 'Nana'	CKen
	- 'Piccolo'	CBcs CKen LRHS MGos NHol NLar SLim WEve
	- 'Pixie'	CKen WEve
	- 'Rainbow's End' (v)	CKen LRHS NLar SLim WFar
	- 'Sander's Blue'	CKen EHul EPfP GKin LBee LRHS MBri MGos SLim SPoG WEve WFar WGor
	- 'Spring Surprise' **new**	CKen
	- 'Zuckerhut'	GKin LRHS MBri
	glehnii 'Sasanosei'	CKen
	- 'Shimezusei'	CKen
	jezoensis	CKen CMen MGos NWea
	- 'Aurea'	SLim
	- subsp. ***hondoensis***	CMen
	- 'Marianbad'	CKen
	- 'Yatsabusa'	CKen CMen
	koraiensis	CDul NLar NWea
	kosteri 'Glauca'	see *P. pungens* 'Koster'
	koyamae 'Bedgebury Cascade'	SLim
	likiangensis	CDul CMCN EPfP NLar NWea
	- var. ***balfouriana***	see *P. likiangensis* var. *rubescens*
§	- var. ***rubescens***	LRHS MGos SLim
	mariana	EPfP NWea
	- 'Aureovariegata' (v)	WFar

	- 'Austria Broom'	CKen
	- 'Bill Archer'	NWad
	- 'Fastigiata'	CKen
	- 'Nana' 𝕐H4	CDoC CKen CMac CMen EHul EPfP EPot GEdr LRHS MAsh MMuc NHol NWad NWea SCoo SEND SLim SPoG WEve WFar
I	- 'Pygmaea'	CKen NWad
	× ***mariorika*** 'Machala'	MBri
	morrisonicola	CKen
	omorika 𝕐H4	CBcs CCVT CDul CJun CMCN CTho EPfP EWTr MGos MMuc NWea SEND SEWo WCFE WEve WFar
	- 'de Ruyter'	IVic
	- 'Frohnleiten'	CKen
	- 'Frondenberg'	CKen
	- 'Karel'	CKen MBri NLar
	- 'Minimax'	CKen
	- 'Nana' 𝕐H4	EHul LRHS MGos NPCo SCoo SLim SPoG WCFE WEve WFar
	- 'Pendula' 𝕐H4	CDoC LRHS MBlu NLar SLim SSta WEve
	- 'Pendula Bruns'	LRHS NLar SLim
	- 'Peve Tijn'	LRHS NLar SPoG
	- 'Pimoko'	CKen LRHS MBri MGos NLar NPCo SLim
	- 'Pimpf'	IVic
	- 'Pygmy'	CKen
	- 'Schneverdingen'	CKen
	- 'Tijn'	CKen SLim
	- 'Treblitsch'	CKen NLar
	- 'Tremonia' **new**	NLar
	orientalis 𝕐H4	CDul NWea WThu
	- 'Aurea' (v) 𝕐H4	CMac EHul ELan MBri MGos NLar NPri SCoo SLim SMad
	- 'Aureospicata'	CDoC CTho MAsh MBlu NLar NPCo SCoo WEve
	- 'Bergman's Gem'	CKen
	- 'Early Gold' (v)	MBri WFar
	- 'Golden Start'	LRHS MBri NLar SLim
	- 'Juwel'	CKen NLar
	- 'Kenwith'	CKen
	- 'Kosteri'	MAsh
	- 'Mount Vernon'	CKen
	- Nana Group	GKin
	- 'Professor Langner'	CKen MAsh SLim
	- 'Skylands'	CKen ELan LRHS MAsh MBri MGos NHol NLar SLim SPoG WEve
	- 'Tom Thumb'	CKen MAsh NLar SLim
	- 'Wittboldt'	CKen MBri
	pungens	WEve
	- 'Baby Blueeyes'	WFar
	- 'Blaukissen'	CKen SLim
	- 'Blue Pearl'	NLar
	- 'Blue Trinket'	WGor
	- 'Edith'	CKen LRHS NLar NPCo SLim SPer WFar WGor
	- 'Erich Frahm'	LTen MAsh MBri MGos WFar
	- 'Fat Albert'	LRHS MGos NEgg NLar NPCo NWea SLim WFar
	- 'Frieda'	LRHS SBod SLim
	- Glauca Group	CDul CLnd CMac MMuc NWea SCoo SEND SPoG WEve WFar WMou
	- - 'Glauca Procumbens'	CMen NLar NWea
§	- - 'Glauca Prostrata'	EHul SLim WEve
	- 'Glauca Globosa'	see *P. pungens* 'Globosa'
	- 'Globe'	CKen CMen
I	- 'Globosa' 𝕐H4	CBcs CKen CSBt EHul LAst LRHS MAsh MBri MGos NHol NPCo NPri NWea SCoo SLim SPer SPoG WEve WFar
	- 'Gloria'	CKen SLim
	- 'Hoopsii' 𝕐H4	CDoC CDul CSBt EHul EPfP GKin IVic LAst LRHS MAsh MBri MGos MWat NEgg NLar NPCo NPri NWea SEWo SLim SPoG SWvt WEve WFar
	- 'Hoto'	EHul MGos
	- 'Hunnewelliana'	EPfP
	- 'Iseli Fastigiate'	GKin MAsh MBri NPCo SCoo SLim SPer SPoG WEve
	- 'Iseli Foxtail'	LAst NLar
§	- 'Koster' 𝕐H4	CSBt EHul EPfP LAst LRHS MGos NEgg NPri NWea SLim SPoG WEve WFar WMou
	- 'Koster Fastigiata'	NEgg
	- 'Lucky Strike'	CKen MBri MGos NLar
	- 'Maigold' (v)	CKen IVic NLar SLim
	- 'Moerheimii'	EHul NLar WEve
	- 'Montgomery'	CKen NLar WEve
	- 'Mrs Cesarini'	CKen NLar SLim
	- 'Niemitz' **new**	SLim CKen
	- 'Oldenburg'	NEgg NLar NPCo NWea SLim
	- 'Procumbens'	CKen
	- 'Prostrata'	see *P. pungens* 'Glauca Prostrata'
	- 'Prostrate Blue Mist'	WEve
	- 'Rovelli's Monument'	NLar
	- 'Saint Mary's Broom'	CKen NLar NPCo
	- 'Schovenhorst'	EHul WFar
	- 'Snowkiss'	NPCo WFar
	- 'Thomsen'	EHul
	- 'Thuem'	EHul EPfP MGos NLar NPCo WFar
	- 'Waldbrunn'	CKen MBri WEve
	- 'Wendy'	CKen
	- 'Yvette' **new**	NLar
	purpurea	WEve
	retroflexa	NWea
	rubens	NLar WEve
	schrenkiana	CMCN
	sitchensis	CDul MAsh NWea
	- 'Papoose'	see *P. sitchensis* 'Tenas'
	- 'Pévé Wiesje'	NLar
	- 'Silberzwerg'	CKen LRHS NLar SLim SPoG
	- 'Strypemonde'	CKen
§	- 'Tenas'	CKen LRHS NLar SLim SPoG
	smithiana	CDul EPfP GBin NLar NWea WEve
	- 'Sunray'	LRHS SLim
	wilsonii	CKen NLar

Picrasma (*Simaroubaceae*)

	ailanthoides	see *P. quassioides*
§	***quassioides***	CMCN EBee EPfP MBri WPGP

Picris (*Asteraceae*)

echioides	CArn WHer

Picrorhiza (*Plantaginaceae*)

kurrooa	GPoy

Pieris (*Ericaceae*)

'Balls of Fire'	CMac
'Bert Chandler'	CMac GKin
'Firecrest' 𝕐H4	CMHG MMuc NLar SSpi
'Flaming Silver' (v) 𝕐H4	Widely available
'Forest Flame' 𝕐H4	Widely available
formosa B&SWJ 2257	WCru
- var. ***forrestii***	CDoC CWib GLin

	- - 'Charles Michael'	CPLG
	- - 'Jermyns'	CMac MRav
	- - 'Wakehurst' 𝕐H3	CAbP CDul CMac CPLG CTri ELon EPfP GKin LRHS MAsh MGos MRav MSnd SPer SPoG SSpi WFar
	Havila = 'Mouwsvila' (v)	CMac MAsh MGos NWad
	japonica	CMac MGos SReu
	- 'Astrid'	IVic
	- 'Blush' 𝕐H4	MAsh
	- 'Bonfire'	CCCN ELan IVic LRHS MBri MGos MMuc NEgg NLar SBfd SEND SHil SLim SPoG
	- 'Carnaval' (v)	CCCN CDoC CMac CSBt CWCL CWib ELan ELon IVic LBuc LRHS LSRN MAsh MBri MGos MRav NLar NPCo SBfd SCoo SHil SLim SPer SPoG SWvt WFar
	- 'Cavatine' 𝕐H4	CMHG IVic
§	- 'Christmas Cheer'	CMac LSRN WMoo
	- 'Cupido'	CDoC IVic MAsh MGos NLar SBfd SLim SPoG WFar
	- 'Debutante' 𝕐H4	CBcs CWib ELan GBin GKin IVic LRHS MAsh MBri MGos NLar NPCo NPri NRHS SBfd SCoo SHil SSpi SWvt WFar
	- 'Don'	see *P. japonica* 'Pygmaea'
	- 'Dorothy Wyckoff'	MAsh SSta
	- 'Flaming Star'	SWvt
	- 'Flamingo'	CMac GEdr
I	- 'Katsura' PBR	Widely available
	- 'Little Heath' (v) 𝕐H4	Widely available
	- 'Little Heath Green' 𝕐H4	CDoC CMac ELon GKin MAsh MGos MMuc NEgg NPCo SBfd SPer SPoG SWvt WFar WMoo
	- 'Minor'	GKev NWad WThu
	- 'Mountain Fire' 𝕐H4	Widely available
	- 'Passion' PBR	GBin IVic MPkF SBfd
	- 'Pink Delight' 𝕐H4	CAbP CDoC LRHS LSRN MRav NEgg SBfd SRms
	- 'Prelude' 𝕐H4	CSBt CWCL LRHS MAsh NLar NMen NRHS WAbe
	- 'Purity' 𝕐H4	CBcs CDoC CMHG CMac LRHS MGos NEgg SBfd SLim SPer SReu SWvt WFar WGwG WHar
§	- 'Pygmaea'	CMac GKev NWad SSta WThu
	- 'Ralto' PBR **new**	MBri MRav
	- 'Red Mill'	IVic MAsh SLim SPer SSpi
	- 'Rondo'	IVic
	- 'Rosalinda'	LTen MAsh MGos NLar WFar
	- 'Sarabande' 𝕐H4	GKin IVic MAsh MGos MMuc MPkF NHol NLar
	- 'Scarlett O'Hara'	CSBt
	- Taiwanensis Group	GKin LRHS MMuc NLar SBfd SEND SRms WFar
	- 'Temple Bells'	CSBt LTen SBfd
	- 'Valley Rose'	CGHE CSBt ELan GKin IVic LLHF MGos NLar SPoG SSpi WFar
	- 'Valley Valentine' 𝕐H4	CBcs CDoC CDul CMac CSBt CWib EPfP GEdr IVic LRHS LSRN MAsh MBri MGos MMuc MPkF NPCo NRHS SBfd SCoo SEND SHil SLim SPer SPoG SReu SWvt WFar
	- 'Variegata' misapplied	see *P. japonica* 'White Rim'
	- 'Variegata' ambig.	NLar
	- 'Variegata' (Carrière) Bean (v)	CMHG EPfP LRHS MGos MRav NHol SBfd WFar WHar
	- 'Wada's Pink'	see *P. japonica* 'Christmas Cheer'
	- 'White Pearl'	CAbP CMac EPfP IVic MAsh
§	- 'White Rim' (v) 𝕐H4	CDul CMac MAsh SPlb
	- 'William Buchanan'	WThu
	- var. ***yakushimensis***	NLar
	nana	WThu
	'Tilford'	CMac

Pilea (*Urticaceae*)

§	***microphylla***	EBak EShb
	muscosa	see *P. microphylla*
	peperomioides 𝕐H1	CSev

Pileostegia (*Hydrangeaceae*)

viburnoides 𝕐H4	Widely available
- B&SWJ 3565	WCru
- B&SWJ 3570 from Taiwan	WCru
- B&SWJ 7132	WCru

Pilosella (*Asteraceae*)

§	***aurantiaca***	CArn CRWN EBee ELan IRos LEdu MHer MNHC NBid NOrc SEND SGar SIde WCot WHer WMoo WOut WSFF
§	- subsp. ***carpathicola***	MMuc
§	***officinarum***	NRya
	tardans **new**	CFis

Pilularia (*Marsileaceae*)

globulifera	MSKA

Pimelea (*Thymelaeaceae*)

	coarctata	see *P. prostrata*
	drupacea	IDee
	ferruginea	ECou WAbe
	- 'Magenta Mist'	MOWG
	filiformis	ECou
	oreophila	WThu
§	***prostrata***	CTrC CTri ECho ECou WPer WThu
	- 'Misty Blue'	CTrC
	- f. ***parvifolia***	ECou
	sericeovillosa	WThu
	tomentosa	ECou LRHS

Pimpinella (*Apiaceae*)

anisum	CArn SIde SVic
bicknellii	WPGP
major 'Rosea'	CDes CHid CMea CPLG CPom CSam CSpe EBee ECtt GCal LDai LHop LRHS LSou MBel MHer NCGa NChi NDov NGdn NOrc SMrm SPer SPhx SUsu WCot WFar WHal WHil WPGP
saxifraga	CHab

pineapple see *Ananas comosus*

pineapple guava see *Acca sellowiana*

Pinellia (*Araceae*)

	cordata	CPom EBee LEdu LWst MDKP NMen SChF WCru
	pedatisecta	CDes EBee GEdr MDKP SChF WCot
	pinnatisecta	see *P. tripartita*
	ternata	EBee GEdr NLar NMen WCot WPnP
	- B&SWJ 3532	WCru
§	***tripartita***	CPLG EBee ECho EPPr MDKP WCot
	- B&SWJ 1102	WCru
	- 'Dragon Tails' (v)	SKHP
	- 'Purple Face'	WCru

Pinguicula (*Lentibulariaceae*)

	ehlersiae	EFEx
	esseriana	EFEx
	grandiflora	CSWC EECP EFEx NMen NRya
	longifolia subsp. ***longifolia***	EFEx
	moranensis var. ***caudata***	EFEx
	- ***moreana***	EFEx
	- ***superba***	EFEx
	vulgaris	EFEx WHer
	'Weser'	CSWC NChu

pinkcurrant see *Ribes rubrum* (P)

Pinus ✿ (*Pinaceae*)

	albicaulis 'Flinck'	CKen
	- 'Nana'	see *P. albicaulis* 'Noble's Dwarf'
	- 'No. 3'	CKen
§	- 'Noble's Dwarf'	CKen
	aristata	CDul CLnd CMen EHul MGos WEve
	- 'Cecilia'	CKen
	- 'Kohout's Mini'	CKen
	- 'Sherwood Compact'	CKen MAsh MBri NLar SLim
	- 'So Tight'	CKen
	armandii	CAgr CDoC CDul CMCN CTrC WPGP
	- 'Gold Tip'	CKen
	austriaca	see *P. nigra* subsp. *nigra*
N	***ayacahuite***	CKen CPne
	- var. ***veitchii***	WPGP
	balfouriana dwarf	CKen
	banksiana	CDul
	- 'Arctis'	NLar
	- 'Chippewa'	CKen
I	- 'Compacta'	CKen
	- 'H.J. Welch'	CKen
	- 'Manomet'	CKen
	- 'Neponset'	CKen
	- 'Schneverdingen'	CKen
	- 'Schoodic'	LRHS NLar SLim
	- 'Wisconsin'	CKen
	bhutanica	WPGP
	brutia	IGor
	bungeana	CDoC CDul CLnd EPfP MBlu SLPl WEve
	- 'Diamant'	CKen
	- 'June's Broom'	CKen
	cembra	CAgr CDul CLnd NLar NWea SEND WEve
	- 'Aurea'	see *P. cembra* 'Aureovariegata'
§	- 'Aureovariegata' (v)	LRHS NPCo WEve
	- 'Barnhourie'	CKen
	- 'Blue Mound'	CKen
	- 'Chalet'	CKen
	- 'Compacta Glauca'	MBri
	- Glauca Group	WEve
	- 'Inverleith'	CKen
	- 'Jermyns'	CKen
	- 'King's Dwarf'	CKen
	- 'Ortler'	CKen NLar
	- 'Roughills'	CKen
	- 'Stricta'	CDoC CKen
	- witches' broom	CKen
	cembroides NJM 09.022A	WPGP
	contorta	CBcs CDoC CDul MGos NWea SPlb WWau
	- 'Asher'	CKen
	- 'Chief Joseph'	CKen MAsh NLar SLim
	- 'Frisian Gold'	CKen SLim
	- var. ***latifolia***	CDul CLnd
	- 'Spaan's Dwarf'	CKen LRHS MGos NLar SCoo SLim SPoG WEve
	- 'Taylor's Sunburst'	CKen MAsh NLar
	coulteri ♀H4	CDul SBig SKHP WPGP WWau
	densiflora	CDul CMCN EUJe IGor
	- 'Alice Verkade'	CDoC CMen EHul LRHS MAsh MBri NLar SCoo SLim WEve WFar
	- 'Aurea'	LRHS NLar
	- 'Golden Ghost'	MAsh NLar SLim
	- 'Jane Kluis'	CMen EHul LRHS LTen NLar SCoo SLim WEve WFar
	- 'Jim Cross'	CKen
	- 'Low Glow'	CKen LRHS NLar NPCo SLim
	- 'Oculus-draconis' (v)	LRHS MGos NEgg NLar SLim WEve WFar
	- 'Pendula'	CKen LRHS NEgg NLar SCoo SLim WEve WFar
	- 'Umbraculifera'	CMen GKin MAsh MGos NLar NPCo SSta WEve WFar
§	***devoniana***	LRHS SLim
	'Edsal Wood'	NLar
	edulis	CAgr
	- 'Juno'	CKen
	elliottii	SBig
	- var. ***densa***	CKen
	engelmanii 'Glauca'	WFar
	fenzeliana	CKen
	flexilis	CDul IGor
	- 'Blackfoot'	NLar
	- 'Cesarini Blue'	NLar
	- 'Firmament'	LRHS NLar SLim
	- 'Glenmore Dwarf'	CKen
	- 'Nana'	CKen
	- 'Piute'	NLar
	- 'Tara Mae'	NLar
	- 'Tarryall'	CKen
	- 'Tinby Temple'	NLar
	- 'Vanderwolf's Pyramid'	CDoC MAsh MBri NLar
	- WB No 1	CKen
	- WB No 2	CKen
	funebris	IGor
	greggii	CDul
	- NJM 09.014	WPGP
	griffithii	see *P. wallichiana*
	halepensis	CDul SEND
§	***hartwegii*** NJM 09.029	WPGP
§	***heldreichii*** ♀H4	CDoC CDul GKin MGos NWea WFar
	- 'Aureospicata'	NLar WEve
	- 'Compact Gem'	CDoC CKen LRHS MBri MGos NLar SLim WEve
	- 'Dolce Dorme'	CKen NLar
	- 'Groen'	CKen
	- 'Kalous'	NLar
	- var. ***leucodermis***	see *P. heldreichii*
	- - 'Irish Bell'	NLar
	- - 'Pirin 7'	NLar
	- 'Malink'	CKen IVic LRHS SLim
	- 'Ottocek'	CKen
	- 'Pygmy'	CKen
	- 'Pyramid'	NLar
	- 'Satellit'	CKen EHul LRHS MAsh MGos NLar NPCo SLim WEve
	- 'Schmidtii'	see *P. heldreichii* 'Smidtii'
§	- 'Smidtii' ♀H4	CDoC CKen CMen LRHS MAsh MBri MGos NLar SLim WEve WGor
	- 'Zwerg Schneverdingen'	CKen NLar NPCo

	× ***holfordiana***	CDoC WPGP
	jeffreyi ♀H4	CDul CMCN CTho NWea
	- 'Joppi'	CKen NLar SLim
	koraiensis	GKin LRHS
	- 'Bergman'	CKen
	- 'Dragon Eye'	CKen SLim
	- 'Jack Corbit'	CKen
	- 'Shibamichi' (v)	CKen
	- 'Silver Lining'	NPCo
	- 'Silveray'	NLar
	- 'Silvergrey'	CKen
	- 'Spring Grove'	NLar
	- 'Winton'	CKen NLar
	leucodermis	see *P. heldreichii*
	magnifica	see *P. devoniana*
	massoniana	NLar
	monophylla 'Tioga Pass'	NLar
	montezumae misapplied	see *P. hartwegii*
	montezumae Lamb.	WPGP
	NJM 09.016	
	- 'Sheffield Park'	SLim
	monticola 'Pendula'	CKen
	- 'Pygmy'	see *P. monticola* 'Raraflora'
§	- 'Raraflora'	CKen
	- 'Skyline'	NLar WEve
	- 'Windsor Dwarf'	CKen
	mugo	CArn CBcs CDul CMac EHul MGos NWea SEND WBor WEve WFar
	- 'Allgau'	CKen
	- 'Amber Glow'	NLar
	- 'Benjamin'	CKen MGos NLar
	- 'Bisley Green'	NLar
	- 'Brownie'	CKen
	- 'Carsten'	CKen MGos SCoo SLim WEve WGor
	- 'Carsten's Wintergold'	CDoC EMil LRHS MAsh MBri NLar SPoG WEve
	- 'Chameleon'	NLar
	- 'Columbo'	NLar
	- 'Corley's Mat'	CKen LAst MWat NLar SLim WEve
	- 'Devon Gem'	NPCo
	- 'Dezember Gold'	IVic LRHS NLar SLim
	- 'Flanders Belle'	LRHS SLim
	- 'Gnom'	CDul EHul GKin MAsh MBri MGos MWat NEgg NLar NPCo SCoo WEve WFar
	- 'Gold Star'	CMen SLim
	- 'Golden Glow'	CKen LRHS MBri NLar SCoo SLim
	- 'Heinis Triumph'	MBri
	- 'Hesse'	SCoo
	- 'Hoersholm'	CKen
	- 'Hulk'	CKen
	- 'Humpy'	CKen CMen LRHS MAsh MBri MGos NPCo SCoo SLim WCFE WEve WFar
	- 'Ironsides'	CKen
	- 'Jacobsen'	CKen NLar
	- 'Janovsky'	CKen
	- 'Kamila'	NLar
	- 'Kissen'	CKen MBri MGos NLar SLim WEve
	- 'Klosterkotter'	NLar WFar
	- 'Kobold'	NEgg WFar
	- 'Krauskopf'	CKen
	- 'Laarheide'	WEve
	- 'Laurin'	CKen
	- 'Little Lady'	NLar
	- 'Marand'	NLar
	- 'March'	CKen
	- 'Mini Mops'	CKen NLar WEve
	- 'Minikin'	CKen MBri
	- 'Mops' ♀H4	CDul CMac CMen EHul EPfP LRHS LTen MAsh MBlu MBri MGos NHol NPCo NWea SBfd SBod SCoo SLim SPer SPoG SSta WEve WFar
	- 'Mops Midget'	CMen MAsh MBri NPCo WEve
	- 'Mops Snezna'	NLar
	- var. ***mughus***	see *P. mugo* subsp. *mugo*
§	- subsp. ***mugo***	NWea SGol WFar
	- 'Mumpitz'	CKen
	- 'Northern Lights'	CKen
	- 'Ophir'	CBcs CDul CKen CMen EHul EPfP LAst LRHS MAsh MBri MGos NLar SCoo SLim SPer SSta WEve WFar
	- 'Pal Maleter' (v)	LRHS NLar NPCo SCoo SLim SPoG
	- 'Paradekissen'	NPCo
	- 'Paul's Dwarf'	CKen
	- 'Picobello'	LRHS MAsh NLar SLim
	- 'Piggelmee'	CKen IVic NLar
	- Pumilio Group ♀H4	CDoC CDul CLnd EHul MGos NWea SBfd WFar WMoo
	- var. ***rostrata***	see *P. mugo* subsp. *uncinata*
	- 'Rushmore'	CKen
	- 'Spaan'	CKen
	- 'Sunshine' (v)	CKen NLar
	- 'Suzi'	CKen
	- 'Trompenburg'	NPCo
	- 'Tuffet'	NLar
	- 'Uelzen'	CKen NLar
§	- subsp. ***uncinata***	LMaj NWea SLim WFar
	- - 'Grüne Welle'	CKen NLar SLim
	- - 'Paradekissen'	CKen NLar
	- 'Varella'	CKen LRHS NLar SCoo SLim
	- 'White Tip'	CKen
	- 'Winter Gold'	CKen EHul EPfP LAst MGos MWat NLar NPCo NWea SSta WEve WFar WGor
	- 'Winter Sun'	MAsh NLar
	- 'Winzig'	CKen
	- 'Zundert'	CKen MGos NLar SPoG WEve
	- 'Zwergkugel'	CKen
	muricata ♀H4	CDoC CDul CLnd MGos NWea
	nigra ♀H4	CBcs CDul CLnd CMac CTri LMaj LRHS MGos SBfd SGol WEve WMou
	- var. ***austriaca***	see *P. nigra* subsp. *nigra*
	- 'Bambino'	CKen
	- 'Black Prince'	CKen LRHS MGos NLar NPCo SLim WEve WFar
	- var. ***calabrica***	see *P. nigra* subsp. *laricio*
	- var. ***caramanica***	see *P. nigra* subsp. *pallasiana*
N	- 'Cebennensis Nana'	CKen
	- var. ***corsicana***	see *P. nigra* subsp. *laricio*
*	- 'Fastigiata'	NPCo
	- 'Frank'	CKen LRHS NLar SLim
	- 'Green Tower'	NLar
	- 'Hornibrookiana'	CKen NLar
	- 'Komet'	IVic NLar SCoo SLim
§	- subsp. ***laricio*** ♀H4	CCVT CDoC CDul CMac IVic LRHS MGos MMuc NWea SEND WWau
	- - 'Aurea'	MBlu
	- - 'Bobby McGregor'	CKen
	- - 'Globosa Viridis'	NEgg NPCo
	- - 'Goldfingers'	CKen NLar
	- - 'Moseri'	CKen
	- - 'Pygmaea'	CKen WFar
	- - 'Spingarn'	CKen
	- - 'Talland Bay'	CKen
	- - 'Wurstle'	CKen
	- subsp. ***maritima***	see *P. nigra* subsp. *laricio*
	- 'Nana'	MBri NLar

§	- subsp. ***nigra***	CCVT CDoC CJun CLnd CTho LBuc MGos MMuc NLar NWea SBfd SEND SEWo SGol WFar WWau
	- - 'Birte'	CKen
	- - 'Bright Eyes'	NLar SPoG WEve
	- - 'Helga'	CKen NLar
	- - 'Schovenhorst'	CKen
	- - 'Skyborn'	CKen
	- - 'Strypemonde'	CKen NPCo
	- - 'Yaffle Hill'	CKen NLar
	- 'Obelisk'	CKen NLar
§	- subsp. ***pallasiana***	CDul
	- - 'Pyramidalis'	CDoC NLar
	- 'Pierrick Bregeon'PBR	LRHS
	- 'Richard'	CKen LRHS NLar
	- 'Rondello'	NLar
	- 'Spielberg'	NLar
	palustris	CDoC CLnd IVic SBig SKHP
	parviflora	CDul SPlb
	- 'Aaba-jo'	CKen
	- 'Adcock's Dwarf' ♀H4	CDoC CKen LRHS MBri MGos NLar NPCo SLim SPoG WEve
	- 'Al Fordham'	CKen
	- 'Aoi'	CKen CMen
	- 'Ara-kawa'	CKen CMen
	- 'Atco-goyo'	CKen
	- Azuma-goyo Group	CKen CMen
I	- 'Baasch's Form'	CKen MGos NLar
	- 'Bergman'	CDoC MAsh NLar
	- 'Blauer Engel'	CDoC MBlu MGos NLar
	- 'Blue Giant'	IArd LTen MBri NLar
	- 'Blue Lou'	NLar
	- 'Bonnie Bergman'	CDoC CKen NHol NLar WEve
	- 'Brevifolia'	NLar
	- 'Chikusa Goten'	IArd NLar
	- 'Dai-ho'	CKen
	- 'Daisetsusan'	CKen
	- 'Doctor Landis Gold'	CKen SLim
	- 'Dougal'	CKen
	- 'Fukai' (v)	CKen MGos NLar WBor
	- 'Fukiju'	CKen
	- Fukushima-goyo Group	CKen CMen
	- 'Fuku-zu-mi'	CKen IVic NLar WEve
	- 'Fu-shiro'	CKen
	- 'Gimborn's Ideal'	IVic NLar
	- 'Gin-sho-chuba'	CKen
	- Glauca Group	EHul MAsh MBlu MBri MGos NPCo SGol SKHP WEve WFar
I	- 'Glauca Nana'	CKen
	- 'Goldilocks'	CKen MAsh NLar
	- 'Green Wave'	CKen
	- 'Gyok-ke-sen'	CKen
	- 'Gyo-ko-haku'	CKen
	- 'Gyokuei'	CKen
	- 'Gyokusen Sämling'	CKen NLar
	- 'Gyo-ku-sui'	CKen CMen
	- 'H2'	CKen
	- 'Hagaromo Seedling'	CKen CMen NLar
	- 'Hakko'	CKen
	- 'Hatchichi'	CKen
	- 'Hatsumari'	NLar
	- 'Ibo-can'	CKen CMen
	- 'Ichi-no-se'	CKen
	- 'Iri-fune'	CKen
	- Ishizuchi-goyo Group	CKen
	- 'Ka-ho'	CKen
	- 'Kanrico'	CKen
	- 'Kanzan'	CKen
	- 'Kin-po'	NLar
	- 'Kiyomatsu'	CKen NLar
	- 'Kobe'	CKen NLar WEve
	- 'Kokonoe'	CKen CMen
	- 'Kokuho'	CKen NLar
	- 'Koraku'	CKen
	- 'Kusu-dama'	CKen
	- 'Meiko'	CKen CMen
	- 'Michinoku'	CKen
	- 'Momo-yama'	CKen
	- 'Myo-jo'	CKen
	- Nasu-goyo Group	CKen
	- 'Negishi'	CDoC CKen CMen LRHS MAsh MBri NLar SCoo SLim WEve
	- 'Ogon-janome'	CKen MAsh SLim
	- 'Ossorio Dwarf'	CKen
	- var. ***pentaphylla***	IVic
	- 'Regenhold'	CKen
	- 'Richard Lee'	CKen
	- 'Ryo-ku-ho'	CKen
	- 'Ryu-ju'	CKen NLar
	- 'Sa-dai-jin'	CKen
	- 'San-bo'	CKen
§	- 'Saphir'	CKen
	- 'Schoon's Bonsai'	CDoC NLar
	- 'Setsugekka'	CKen NLar
	- 'Shika-shima'	CKen
	- 'Shimada'	CKen
	- Shiobara-goyo Group	CKen
	- 'Shirobana'	NLar
	- 'Shizukagoten'	CKen MBri
	- 'Shu-re'	CKen
	- 'Sieryoden'	CKen
	- 'Smout'	CKen
	- 'Tani-mano-uki'	CKen
	- 'Tempelhof'	LMaj NLar NPCo
	- 'Tenysu-kazu'	CKen
	- 'Tokyo Dwarf'	CKen
	- 'Tribune'	NLar
	- 'Walker's Dwarf'	CKen
	- 'Watnong'	CKen
	- 'Zelkova'	CMen
	- 'Zui-sho'	CKen
	patula ♀H2-3	CBcs CCCN CDoC CDul CHll CLnd CMCN EPfP EUJe IDee IVic LAst LRHS SBfd SBig SCoo SLim SMad SPlb WEve WPGP
	peuce	GLin IGor NLar NWea
	- 'Arnold Dwarf'	CKen
	- 'Cesarini'	CKen
	- 'Thessaloniki Broom'	CKen
	pinaster ♀H4	CBcs CDoC CDul CLnd IVic MMuc SEND
	- subsp. ***escarena***	WWau
	pinea ♀H4	CAgr CArn CCVT CDoC CDul CLnd CTho ELau EPfP EUJe IVic LHop LMaj LRHS MGos MMuc SBfd SCoo SEND SEWo SGol SLim SPlb WEve
	- 'Queensway'	CKen
	ponderosa ♀H4	CDul CLnd NWea WEve
	- var. ***scopulorum***	NWea
	pseudostrobus	WPGP
	- NJM 09.009A	WPGP
	pumila	CDul
	- 'Buchanan'	CKen
	- 'Draijer's Dwarf'	LRHS SCoo SLim WEve
	- 'Dwarf Blue'	NLar
	- 'Glauca' ♀H4	CDoC CKen MAsh NLar
	- 'Globe'	MAsh NLar SLim
	- 'Jeddeloh'	CKen

	– 'Knightshayes'	CKen
	– 'Pinocchio'	CKen
	– 'Säntis'	CKen
	– 'Saphir'	see *P. parviflora* 'Saphir'
	radiata ♀H3-4	CBcs CCVT CDoC CDul CLnd CMac CTrC CTri ECrN ELan EPfP EUJe LRHS MMuc NWea SBfd SCoo SEND SMad WEve WFar WWau
	– Aurea Group	CDoC CDul CKen LRHS MAsh MGos NEgg NPCo SCoo SLim SPoG WEve WFar
	– 'Bodnant'	CKen
	– 'Isca'	CKen
	– 'Marshwood' (v)	CKen SLim
	resinosa 'Don Smith'	CKen
	– 'Joel's Broom'	CKen
	– 'Nana'	NLar
	– 'Quinobequin'	CKen
	× ***schwerinii***	CDoC CKen MBri
	– 'Wiethorst'	CKen IArd IDee LRHS NLar SLim
	sibirica 'Blue Smoke'	CKen
	– 'Mariko'	CKen
	strobiformis 'Coronado'	CKen
	– 'Loma Linda'	CKen SLim
	strobus	CBcs CCVT CDul CLnd CMen EPfP MGos MMuc NWea SEND SLim WEve WFar
§	– 'Alba'	SLim
	– 'Amelia's Dwarf'	CKen
	– 'Anna Fiele'	CKen
	– 'Bergman's Mini'	CKen NLar
	– 'Bergman's Pendula Broom'	CKen
I	– 'Bergman's Sport of Prostrata'	CKen
	– 'Beth'	CKen
	– 'Bloomer's Dark Globe'	CKen
	– 'Blue Shag'	LRHS MGos NLar SCoo SLim SPer SPoG
	– 'Brevifolia'	CKen
	– 'Cesarini'	CKen
	– 'Compacta'	NPCo
	– 'Contorta'	CDoC
	– 'Densa'	CKen
	– 'Dove's Dwarf'	CKen
	– 'Ed's Broom'	CKen
	– 'Elkins Dwarf'	CKen NHol NLar
	– 'Fastigiata'	CKen
	– 'Golden Showers'	NLar
	– 'Green Curls'	CKen
	– 'Green Twist'	NLar SLim
	– 'Greg'	CKen
	– 'Hershey'	CKen
	– 'Hillside Gem'	CKen
	– 'Himmelblau'	IDee MBlu NLar SLim
	– 'Horsford'	CDoC CKen LRHS SLim
	– 'Horsford Sister' **new**	CKen
	– 'Jericho'	CKen
	– 'Julian Pott'	CKen
	– 'Julian's Dwarf'	CKen
	– 'Krügers Lilliput'	LRHS NLar SLim
	– 'Louie'	CKen LRHS NLar
	– 'Macopin'	NLar
	– 'Mary Butler'	CKen NLar
	– 'Merrimack'	CKen NLar
	– 'Minima'	CDoC CDul CKen LRHS MBlu MBri MGos NLar NPCo NWea SLim SPoG WGor
	– 'Minuta'	CKen
§	– Nana Group	NPri SEWo WEve
	– 'Nana'	see *P. strobus* Nana Group
	– 'Nana Compacta'	LRHS
	– 'Nivea'	see *P. strobus* 'Alba'
	– 'Northway Broom'	CKen LRHS SLim
	– 'Pendula'	CKen
I	– 'Pendula Broom'	CKen
	– 'Radiata'	CTri EHul NLar
I	– 'Radiata Aurea'	LRHS
	– 'Reinshaus'	CKen
	– 'Sayville'	CKen
	– 'Sea Urchin'	CKen LRHS SLim SPoG
	– 'Secrest'	NLar
	– 'Stowe Pillar'	NLar SLim
	– 'Tiny Kurls'	CKen MAsh NLar SLim
I	– 'Tortuosa'	NLar
	– 'Torulosa'	MBlu SMad
	– 'Uncatena'	CKen
	– 'Verkade's Broom'	CKen
	– 'Wendy'	NLar
	sylvestris ♀H4	CBcs CCVT CDoC CDul CHab CMac CRWN CTho CTri ECrN EHul ELan EPfP LAst LBuc LRHS MGos MMuc NEgg NLar NWea SBfd SEND SEWo SGol SPer SPoG WEve WMou
	– 'Abergeldie'	CKen
	– 'Alderly Edge'	CMen WEve WFar
	– 'Andorra'	CKen
§	– 'Argentea'	CMen SLim
§	– Aurea Group ♀H4	CDul CKen CMac CMen EHul EMil LRHS MAsh MBlu MBri NEgg NLar NPCo NPri NWea SCoo SLim SPer SPoG SSta WEve WFar
	– 'Aurea'	see *P. sylvestris* Aurea Group
	– 'Avondene'	CKen
	– 'Bergfield'	CMen NLar
	– 'Beuvronensis' ♀H4	CMen MGos NEgg NLar NPCo SLim WEve
	– 'Blue Sky'	NLar
	– 'Bonna'	LRHS SLim
	– 'Buchanan's Gold'	CKen
	– 'Burghfield'	CKen CMen WFar
	– 'Chantry Blue'	CMen EHul LRHS MAsh MBri MGos NEgg NLar NPCo SCoo SLim WEve WFar
	– 'Clumber Blue'	CKen
	– 'Compressa'	SLim
	– 'Dereham'	CKen
	– 'Doone Valley'	CKen MGos NEgg NPCo WEve WFar
	– 'Edwin Hillier'	see *P. sylvestris* 'Argentea'
	– Fastigiata Group	CDoC CDul CKen CMac CMen IDee LRHS MGos NPCo SCoo SLim SPoG WCFE WEve WFar
	– 'Frensham'	CKen MAsh MBri MGos NLar NPCo WEve WFar
	– 'Globosa'	NPCo
	– 'Gold Coin'	CDoC CDul CKen CMen EPfP LRHS MAsh MGos NEgg NHol NLar NPCo SCoo SLim SPoG WEve WFar
	– 'Gold Medal'	CKen SLim WEve WFar
	– 'Grand Rapids'	CKen
	– 'Gwydyr Castle'	CKen
	– 'Hesley Dwarf'	NLar
	– 'Hillside Creeper'	CKen LRHS NLar SLim SPoG WEve
	– 'Humble Pie'	CKen
	– 'Inverleith' (v)	EHul MGos SCoo SLim SPoG WEve WFar
	– 'Jeremy'	CKen NEgg NPCo SLim SPoG WEve

	- 'John Boy'	CMen NLar
	- 'Kelpie'	LRHS
	- 'Kenwith'	CKen
	- 'Kosice'	NLar
	- 'Lakeside Dwarf'	CMen
	- 'Lodge Hill'	CMen LRHS MAsh NPCo SCoo SLim WEve
	- 'Longmoor'	CKen NLar
	- 'Martham'	CKen CMen WEve
	- 'Mitsch Weeping'	CKen
*	- 'Moseri'	MAsh NPCo
	- 'Mount Vernon Blue'	NLar
	- 'Munches Blue'	CKen
	- 'Nana' misapplied	see *P. sylvestris* 'Watereri'
	- 'Nana Compacta'	CMen
§	- 'Nisbet's Gem'	CKen CMen
	- 'Padworth'	CMen NLar
	- 'Peve Heiheks'	NLar
	- 'Peve Miba'	NLar
I	- 'Pine Glen'	CKen
	- 'Piskowitz'	CKen
	- 'Pixie'	CKen NLar
I	- 'Prostrata'	NPCo
	- 'Pygmaea'	SLim
	- 'Repens'	CKen
	- 'Saint George'	CKen
	- 'Saxatilis'	CKen CMen WEve
	- subsp. ***scotica***	GQue NWea
	- 'Scott's Dwarf'	see *P. sylvestris* 'Nisbet's Gem'
	- 'Scrubby'	NLar
	- 'Sentinel'	CKen NLar SLim
	- 'Skjak I'	CKen NLar
	- 'Skjak II'	CKen LRHS
	- 'Skogbygdi'	NLar
	- 'Slimkin'	CKen
	- 'Spaan's Slow Column'	CKen LRHS SCoo SLim
	- 'Tage'	CKen
	- 'Tanya'	CKen
	- 'Tilhead'	CKen
	- 'Treasure'	CKen MBri
	- 'Trefrew Quarry'	CKen
	- 'Troll Guld'	NLar SLim
	- 'Vargguld'	CKen
§	- 'Watereri'	EHul LAst LRHS LTen MBri MGos NLar NPri SCoo SLim WFar
	- 'Westonbirt'	CKen CMen EHul MAsh NLar WEve
	- 'Xawrey 1'	NLar
	tabuliformis	CDul CMCN
	taeda	CDul EPfP WPGP
	taiwanensis	CDoC CDul
	thunbergii	CDul CLnd CMCN CMen ELan MGos MMuc SEND
	- 'Akame'	CKen CMen
	- 'Akame Yatsabusa'	CMen
	- 'Aocha-matsu' (v)	CKen CMen NLar
	- 'Arakawa-sho'	CKen CMen
	- 'Banshosho'	CKen CMen LRHS MGos NLar SLim WEve
	- 'Beni-kujaku'	CKen CMen
	- 'Compacta'	CKen CMen
	- var. ***corticosa*** 'Fuji'	CMen
	- - 'Iihara'	CMen
	- 'Dainagon'	CKen CMen
	- 'Eechee-nee'	CKen
	- 'Hayabusa'	CMen
	- 'Iwai'	CMen
	- 'Janome'	CMen
	- 'Katsuga'	CMen
	- 'Kotobuki'	CKen CMen NLar NPCo WEve WFar
	- 'Koyosho'	CMen
	- 'Kujaku'	CKen CMen
	- 'Kyokko'	CKen CMen
	- 'Kyushu'	CKen CMen
	- 'Maijima'	NLar
	- 'Mikawa'	CMen MBlu
	- 'Miyajuna'	CKen CMen
	- 'Nishiki-ne'	CKen CMen
	- 'Nishiki-tsusaka'	CMen
	- 'Oculus-draconis' (v)	CMen NPCo
	- 'Ōgon'	CKen CMen LRHS NLar SLim
	- 'Porky'	CKen CMen
§	- 'Sayonara'	CMen LRHS MAsh MBri NLar SLim
	- 'Senryu'	CKen CMen
	- 'Shinsho'	CKen CMen
	- 'Shio-guro'	CKen CMen
	- 'Suchiro'	NEgg NPCo
	- 'Suchiro Yatabusa'	CKen CMen
	- 'Sunsho'	CKen CMen
	- 'Taihei'	CKen CMen
I	- 'Thunderhead'	CDoC CKen CMen LRHS NLar SLim
	- 'W.B.'	CKen
	- 'Yatsubusa'	see *P. thunbergii* 'Sayonara'
	- 'Ye-i-kan'	CKen
	- 'Yoshimura'	CMen
	- 'Yumaki'	CKen CMen MGos
	uncinata	see *P. mugo* subsp. *uncinata*
	- 'Etschtal'	CKen
	- 'Grünne Welle' **new**	SLim
	- 'Jezek'	CKen NLar
	- 'Leuco-like'	CKen
	- 'Litomysl'	NLar
	- 'Offenpass'	CKen
	- 'Susse Perle'	CKen
	virginiana 'Wate's Golden'	CKen NLar SLim
§	***wallichiana*** ♀H4	Widely available
	- 'Densa'	NLar SLim
	- 'Densa Hill'	LRHS
	- 'Frosty'	CKen
	- 'Nana'	CKen LRHS NLar SCoo SLim SPoG WEve
	- 'Umbraculifera'	MBri
	- var. ***wallichiana*** **new**	EUJe
	- 'Winter Light'	NLar
	- 'Zebrina' (v)	MBlu NLar
	yunnanensis	CDoC WBor

Piper (*Piperaceae*)

	auritum	GPoy
	excelsum	see *Macropiper excelsum*

Piptanthus (*Papilionaceae*)

	forrestii	see *P. nepalensis*
	laburnifolius	see *P. nepalensis*
§	***nepalensis***	CBcs CSpe EBee EGri ELan EPau EPfP IDee LAst LHop LRHS MGos MPie MSCN NBid NLar SEND SGar SHil SMad SPer SPoG SRms
	- SDR 6729	GKev
	tomentosus	EBee MMHG

Pistacia (*Anacardiaceae*)

	chinensis	EBtc EPfP WPGP
	lentiscus	CArn CBcs EBee ERom EUJe SEND WCot XSen
	terebinthus	XSen

Pistia (*Araceae*)

	stratiotes	CBen LPBA MSKA NPer SCoo

Pitcairnia (*Bromeliaceae*)

bergii	CHll
heterophylla	WCot

Pittosporum ✿ (*Pittosporaceae*)

anomalum	CTrC ECou MOWG
- (f)	ECou
- (m)	ECou
- 'Falcon'	ECou
- 'Raven' (f)	ECou
- 'Starling' (m)	ECou
* ***argyrophyllum***	LTen
'Arundel Green'	CDoC EBee EPfP EUJe LRHS LSRN MAsh NRHS SBfd SHil SLim SWvt
bicolor	CTrC CTsd GQui WPGP
buchananii	SGar
colensoi	ECou
- 'Cobb' (f)	ECou
- 'Wanaka' (m)	ECou
'Collaig Silver'	LRHS MAsh SBfd SLim
crassifolium	CBcs CCCN CHEx CHGN CTrC CTsd ECou EWld IDee LRHS
- 'Havering Dwarf' (f)	ECou
- 'Napier' (f)	ECou
- 'Variegatum' (v)	CCCN WPat
'Crinkles' (f)	ECou
daphniphylloides	CHEx EBee ELan WPGP
- B&SWJ 6789	WCru
- RWJ 9913	WCru
'Dark Delight' (m)	ECou
'Essex' (f/v)	ECou
eugenioides	CHEx CSam ESwi SEND
- 'Mini Green'	SBfd
- 'Platinum' (v)	CBcs CCCN LRHS
- 'Variegatum' (v) ♀H3	CBcs CCCN CDoC CDul CHEx CMac CTrC EBee EHoe EPfP EUJe GQui IArd IDee LAst LHop LRHS MBri MGos NLar NPri SBfd SEND SHil SKHP SLim SPoG WSHC
'Garnettii' (v) ♀H3	Widely available
glabratum B&SWJ 11685 <u>**new**</u>	WCru
heterophyllum	ECou ECrN ELan EWes SEND
- variegated (v)	EBee EBtc ECou LRHS MAsh SEND SPoG
'Holbrook' (v)	CSam
'Humpty Dumpty'	ECou
illicioides	WCru
var. ***angustifolium*** B&SWJ 6771	
- - RWJ 9846	WCru
- var. ***illicioides*** B&SWJ 6712	WCru
× ***intermedium***	CWib ECou SWvt
- 'Craxten' (f)	CCCN ECou LRHS
michiei	ECou
- (f)	ECou
- (m)	ECou
- 'Jack' (m)	ECou
- 'Jill' (f)	ECou
'Nanum Variegatum'	see *P. tobira* 'Variegatum'
obcordatum	ECou
- var. ***kaitaiaense***	ECou
oblongilimbum DJHV 06137	WCru
'Oliver Twist'	CTrC LRHS LSRN SBfd SCoo SPtl
omeiense	ECou EWes SKHP
pimeleoides	ECou
var. ***reflexum*** (m)	
ralphii	CCCN CTsd ECou
- 'Green Globe'	SKHP
- 'Variegatum' (v)	CCCN CGHE LRHS SKHP SSpi WPGP
ralphii × ***tenuifolium***	ECou
'Saundersii' (v)	SCoo
'Tadina Gold'	SEND
tenuifolium ♀H3	Widely available
- 'Abbotsbury Gold' (f/v)	CAbb CBcs CCCN CDoC CMac CTri EBee ECou EHoe ELan EPfP EUJe EWes LAst LRHS MGos MREP MSwo MWat SBfd SEND SGol SLim SPer SWvt WSHC
- 'Atropurpureum'	ELan
- 'Brockhill Compact'	EBee LRHS
- 'County Park'	CCCN EUJe LRHS WFar
- 'County Park Dwarf'	ECou MAsh
- 'County Park Green'	ELon
- 'Deborah' (v)	ECou
- 'Dixie'	ECou
§ - 'Eila Keightley' (v)	CMHG
- 'Elizabeth' (m/v)	CAbP CBcs CDoC CMac CTrC EBee ECou EHoe EPfP EUJe IArd LAst LRHS LSRN MAsh MBri MGos MREP MRav NLar NRHS SBfd SEND SHil SLim SPoG
- 'French Lace'	CBcs CCCN ECou ELan LRHS NLar SBfd SEND WFar
- 'Gold Star'	CDoC CWSG EBee ECou EHoe ELan ELon EPfP EWTr LAst LBMP LRHS MAsh MGos SBfd SCoo SLim SPer SPoG SWvt WFar WMoo
- 'Golden Cut'	NLar
- 'Golden King'	CCCN CDoC CMHG CMac CSBt EBee EPfP LRHS MAsh MGos NEgg NPla NRHS SBfd SHil SLim SPoG SRms
- 'Golden Princess' (f)	ECou
- 'Golf Ball' PBR	CBcs CDoC CTrC EBee EUJe LRHS
- 'Green Elf'	ECou
- 'Green Thumb'	CMac ELan
- 'Irene Paterson' (m/v) ♀H3	Widely available
- 'James Stirling'	CCCN ECou EPfP
- 'John Flanagan'	see *P. tenuifolium* 'Margaret Turnbull'
- 'Limelight' (v)	CBcs CSBt EBtc EPfP LHop LRHS LSRN MGos MREP SLim SPoG
- 'Loxhill Gold'	CCCN CWSG IArd LRHS MGos NPla SEND SGol
§ - 'Margaret Turnbull' (v)	CBcs CTrC ECou ELan EWes GKin LHop LRHS LSRN MGos SGol
- 'Marjory Channon' (v)	EBee ELan EPfP EWTr LRHS LSRN SPtl
- 'Mellow Yellow'	CAbP
- 'Moonlight' (v)	CBcs CTrC EBee EHoe LRHS MRav
- 'Mountain Green'	CMac SBfd
- 'Nutty's Leprechaun'	CCCN LAst
- 'Pompom'	CCCN EBee IVic LRHS
- 'Purpureum' (m)	CCCN CMac CSBt CSam CTri EBee EHoe EPfP EUJe LAst LRHS LSRN MBri MREP MWat NEgg NLar SBfd SCoo SEND SHil SLim SPer SPoG SRms
- 'Silver Magic' (v)	CBcs EPfP LRHS MGos NLar SBfd
- 'Silver Princess' (f)	ECou
- 'Silver Queen' (f/v) ♀H3	Widely available

- 'Silver Sheen' (m) CBcs CJun ECou LRHS SBfd
- 'Stevens Island' CBcs CJun CTrC LRHS MGos
- 'Stirling Gold' (f/v) ECou EPfP EWes
- 'Sunburst' see *P. tenuifolium* 'Eila Keightley'
- 'Tandara Gold' (v) CBcs CCCN CDoC CDul CSBt CTrC EBee ECou EHoe ELan ELon EPfP EUJe LBMP LRHS LSRN MAsh MGos SBfd SCoo SLim SPoG WFar WGob
- 'Tiki' (m) CBcs CCCN CTrC ECou LRHS
- 'Tom Thumb' ♀H3 Widely available
- 'Tresederi' (f/m) CCCN CTrC CTsd ECou
- 'Variegatum' (m/v) CBar CBcs CDoC CSBt EBee ECou LRHS LSRN MGos MSwo SHil SLim SPer SPoG SWvt WGob
- 'Victoria' (v) CBcs CCCN CDoC CTrC EBee LRHS LSRN MGos SLim SPoG WFar
- 'Warnham Gold' (m) ♀H3 CBcs CDoC CMac CWib EBee ECou ELan EPfP GKin IVic LHop LRHS MAsh MGos SBfd SLim SPer SPoG SSpi
- 'Wendle Channon' (m/v) CCCN CMHG CMac CSBt EBee ECou EHoe EPfP LRHS MAsh SGol SLim SPer WSHC
- 'Wrinkled Blue' CBcs CTrC EBee EPfP LRHS MAsh MRav SBfd SPoG

tobira ♀H3 CBcs CDoC CDul CMac CTri EBee ELan EPfP EUJe IDee IVic LAst LRHS LSRN MBri MGos MRav NBir SBfd SBod SEND SPer SPoG SRkn SSpi SSta WCot WKif WPat WSHC
- B&SWJ 4362 LAst
* - 'Cuneatum' CCCN CDoC CPLG EBee ELan EPfP LHop LRHS LSRN SKHP
* - 'Nanum' CBcs CCCN CDoC CMac EBee ELan EPfP ERom ETod EUJe LRHS LTen MGos MOWG SBfd SLim SPer SPoG
§ - 'Variegatum' (v) ♀H2-3 CBcs CCCN CHll CMac EBee ELan EPfP EUJe IVic LHop LRHS LSRN MGos NLar SAga SBfd SEND SKHP SLim SLon SPer SPoG SSta WSHC

'Trim's Hedger' CTho
truncatum EWes
undulatum CHEx
viridiflorum EShb

Plagianthus (*Malvaceae*)

betulinus see *P. regius*
divaricatus CBcs CTrC
lyallii see *Hoberia lyallii*
§ ***regius*** CBcs SBig

Plagiorhegma see *Jeffersonia*

Plantago (*Plantaginaceae*)

asiatica 'Variegata' (v) NBro
coronopus ELau
holosteum GKev
lanceolata CArn CHab NMir WHfH WSFF
- 'Golden Spears' CBre EBee
- 'Streaker' (v) WCot

major WSFF
- 'Atropurpurea' see *P. major* 'Rubrifolia'
- 'Bowles's Variety' see *P. major* 'Rosularis'
§ - 'Rosularis' CArn CRow CSpe EBee LEdu MHer NBro NChi NPri SPav WHer
§ - 'Rubrifolia' CArn CHid CRow CSpe EShb LDai MBNS MHer NBid NBro NChi NDov NLBP WHer WMoo WSFF

maritima WHer
media CHab MHer
nivalis GEdr
psyllium L. CArn
rosea see *P. major* 'Rosularis'
subulata **new** GEdr MHer

Platanthera (*Orchidaceae*)

bifolia NLAp
chlorantha NLAp
hologlottis EFEx
metabifolia EFEx LWSt NLAp

Platanus ✿ (*Platanaceae*)

× ***acerifolia*** see *P.* × *hispanica*
§ × ***hispanica*** ♀H4 CBcs CCVT CDul CLnd CMCN EBee ECrN EPfP LAst LBuc LMaj MGos MMuc NWea SEND SEWo SGol SPer WFar WMou
- 'Alphen's Globe' SEWo
- 'Bloodgood' CTho
- 'Suttneri' (v) WMou

orientalis ♀H4 CCVT CDul CMCN CTho EPfP LEdu NLar SLPl
- PAB 346 LEdu
- 'Cuneata' ECrN
§ - f. ***digitata*** ♀H4 CCVT CDoC CDul CLnd CMCN CTho EBee EPfP ERod MBlu
- var. ***insularis*** WPGP
- 'Laciniata' see *P. orientalis* f. *digitata*
- 'Minaret' CDul
- 'Mirkovec' CDoC IArd MBri SPer

racemosa EGFP

Platycarya (*Juglandaceae*)

strobilacea CBcs CMCN NLar

Platycerium (*Polypodiaceae*)

alcicorne misapplied see *P. bifurcatum*
§ ***bifurcatum*** ♀H1 CCCN XBlo

Platycladus (*Cupressaceae*)

§ ***orientalis*** 'Aurea Nana' ♀H4 CDoC CKen CMac CSBt CWib EHul EPfP EPot LBee LRHS MGos MWat NWea SGol SLim SPoG WEve WFar
- 'Autumn Glow' CKen SCoo WGor
- 'Beverleyensis' NLar WEve
- 'Collen's Gold' EHul
- 'Conspicua' CKen CSBt CWib EHul SPoG
- 'Elegantissima' ♀H4 EHul LRHS
- 'Franky Boy' CDoC LAst LRHS MGos NHol NLar SLim SPoG
- 'Golden Pygmy' CKen
- 'Juniperoides' EHul
- 'Kenwith' CKen
- 'Lemon 'n' Lime' WEve
- 'Magnifica' EHul
- 'Meldensis' CDoC CTri EHul
- 'Minima' EHul WGor
- 'Minima Glauca' CKen
- 'Morgan' NLar WEve
- 'Purple King' SCoo
I - 'Pyramidalis Aurea' LBee SCoo WEve
- 'Raffles' WBor
- 'Rosedalis' CKen CSBt EHul EPfP LBee LRHS SCoo
- 'Sanderi' WCFE
- 'Sieboldii' EHul
- 'Southport' LBee
- 'Summer Cream' CKen EHul

– 'Westmont' (v)	CKen NLar

Platycodon ✿ (*Campanulaceae*)

	grandiflorus ♀H4	CArn CTri EBee ECha ELau EPfP GKev LHop LRHS MHer SRms WHoo
	– 'Albus'	CBro CMac EBee EPfP LRHS SPer SWvt WHoo WPer
	– Apoyama Group ♀H4	NMen WHoo WPer WThu
	– – 'Fairy Snow'	EBee ELan EShb EWTr NBre WHoo
	– (Astra Series) 'Astra Blue'	ELon EPfP LHop SPoG SRot
	– – 'Astra Pink'	SPoG
	– – 'Astra White'	SPoG
	– 'Blue Pearl'	WHoo
	– 'Blue Star'PBR	LRHS
	– 'Fuji Blue'	EBee ELon MAvo NLar WHoo WWEG XLum
	– 'Fuji Pink'	CPrp EAEE ELan ELon EPfP LAst LHop LRHS MAvo MRav NLar SWvt WHoo WWEG XLum
	– 'Fuji White'	ELan ELon GKev NLar WWEG XLum
	– 'Hakone'	MRav WHoo
	– 'Hakone Blue'	EPfP LAst NBre NLar
*	– 'Hakone Double Blue' (d)	EAEE ELan MBNS SRms
	– 'Hakone White'	CPrp EBee EPfP MRav NLar NMen WHoo
	– 'Mariesii' ♀H4	CBro CDoy CMea CSBt EAEE EBee EPfP LAst LRHS MNHC MRav MWat NBir NEgg NMen SEND SPer SPlb SRms SWvt WHoo WPer WSHC WWlt
	– Mother of Pearl	see *P. grandiflorus* 'Perlmutterschale'
§	– 'Perlmutterschale'	CPrp EAEE EBee EPfP LBMP MRav WAul WHoo
	– 'Pink Star'	EBee LRHS
	– ***pumilus***	GKev WHoo
	– 'Sentimental Blue'	CMac CWib NLar SPet XLum
	– 'Shell Pink'	see *P. grandiflorus* 'Perlmutterschale'
	– small **new**	GKev
	– 'Willy'	XLum
	– 'Zwerg'	EShb LBMP NBre

Platycrater (*Hydrangeaceae*)

arguta	WCru
– B&SWJ 6266	WCru

Plecostachys (*Asteraceae*)

§	***serpyllifolia***	LAst

Plectocephalus (*Asteraceae*)

varians	GCal

Plectranthus (*Lamiaceae*)

	sp.	LAst
	from Puerto Rico	CArn
	ambiguus	EOHP
	– 'Manguzuku'	EOHP
	– 'Nico'	EOHP SBch
	– 'Umigoye'	EOHP
	amboinicus	CArn EOHP WJek
*	– 'Variegatus' (v)	EOHP
	– 'Well Sweep Wedgewood' (v)	EOHP
	argentatus ♀H2	CDoC CPom CSpe EOHP EShb EUJe IDee MCot SDix SEND SGar SRkn WKif WWlt
	– 'Hill House' (v)	CHll EOHP
	australis misapplied	see *P. verticillatus*
	barbatus **new**	EOHP
	– 'Vicki'	CPne
	behrii	see *P. fruticosus*
	Blue Angel = 'Edelblau' (Cape Angels Series)	EOHP
	caninus	SPoG
	ciliatus	CPne EOHP EShb SGar SRkn WWlt
	– 'Easy Gold' (v)	CPne EOHP
	– 'Sasha' (v)	CCCN CDoC CHll ECtt EShb SPet
	'Cloud Nine'	EOHP
	coleoides 'Marginatus'	see *P. forsteri* 'Marginatus'
	– 'Variegatus'	see *P. madagascariensis* 'Variegated Mintleaf'
	Cuban oregano	EOHP
	ecklonii	EOHP
	– 'Medley Wood'	EOHP
	ernstii	EOHP
	excisus	CDes EBee WPGP
§	***forsteri*** 'Marginatus'	EOHP
	'Frills'	CPne EOHP
§	***fruticosus***	CPne EOHP
	– 'Behr's Pride'	EOHP
	– 'James'	EOHP
	hadiensis	EOHP
	var. ***tomentosus*** 'Carnegie'	
	– – green-leaved	EOHP
	– – 'Penge' (v)	EOHP
	– var. ***woodii***	EOHP
	hereroensis **new**	CSpe
	madagascariensis	EOHP
	– gold-leaved	EOHP
	– 'Lothlorien' (v)	EOHP
§	– 'Variegated Mintleaf' (v) ♀H1	EOHP MNHC SPet SRms WJek
	'Marble Ruffles'	EOHP
	menthol-scented, large-leaved	EOHP
	menthol-scented, small-leaved	EOHP
	mutabilis	EOHP
	neochilus	CSpe
§	***oertendahlii*** ♀H1	EBak EOHP
	– silver-leaved	EOHP
	ornatus	EOHP NPla
	– 'Pee Off'	EOHP
	– variegated (v)	EOHP
	prostratus	EOHP
	purpuratus large-leaved	EOHP
	– small-leaved	EOHP
	rehmannii	EOHP
	saccatus	EOHP
	subsp. ***longitubus***	
	– subsp. ***pondoensis***	EOHP
	sinensis	LRHS
	spicatus	EOHP
	– 'Nelspruit'	EOHP
	strigosus	EOHP
	Swedish ivy	see *P. verticillatus*, *P. oertendahlii*
§	***thyrsoideus***	ECre EOHP
§	***verticillatus***	EOHP
	– 'Barberton'	EOHP
	– 'Pink Surprise'	EOHP
	Vick's plant	EOHP
	zatarhendii	EOHP
	zuluensis	CArn CDoC CPne EOHP EShb SBch SDix SRkn WBor
	– dark-leaved	EOHP
	– 'Sky'	EOHP

Pleioblastus (Poaceae)

	akebono	see *P. argenteostriatus* 'Akebono'
§	***argenteostriatus*** 'Akebono'	ERod
§	- f. ***pumilus***	CDoC EHoe ERod MBlu MWht SPlb WFar
	auricomus	see *P. viridistriatus*
	- 'Vagans'	see *Sasaella ramosa*
	chino f. ***angustifolius***	see *P. chino* 'Murakamianus'
	- f. ***aureostriatus*** (v)	MMoz
	- f. ***elegantissimus***	CCon CDoC CEnt EPfP ERod MGos MMoz MMuc NLar SBig SEND WJun WMoo
	- var. ***hisauchii***	ERod MWht WJun
	- 'Kimmei'	MMuc
§	- 'Murakamianus'	GBin
	fortunei	see *P. variegatus* 'Fortunei'
*	***funghomii***	MMuc
	'Gauntlettii'	see *P. argenteostriatus* f. *pumilus*
	glaber 'Albostriatus'	see *Sasaella masamuneana* 'Albostriata'
	gramineus	IArd
§	***hindsii***	ERod MMoz SEND
§	***humilis***	ENBC MMuc MWhi SEND
	- var. ***pumilus***	see *P. argenteostriatus* f. *pumilus*
	linearis	CAbb EAmu ERod LRHS MMoz MWht NLar SBig WJun WMoo
§	***pygmaeus***	CBcs CDoC CDul CTri EHoe EHul ELan ENBC GBin LEdu MBrN MGos MWhi NBro NGdn NLar SGol SRms WFar WMoo
§	- 'Distichus'	CEnt EHul ENBC EPPr MGos MMuc MWht NGdn NLar SEND WMoo
§	- 'Mirrezuzume'	CPLG GBin
*	- var. ***pygmaeus*** 'Mini'	MMuc SEND
§	***simonii***	LRHS MMuc MWht NLar SEND XBlo
	- 'Variegatus' (v)	LRHS NGdn SPer
§	***variegatus*** (v) ♀H4	CBcs CDoC CDul CEnt EHoe EHul ELan ELon ENBC EPfP LEdu LPot LRHS MBrN MGos MMuc MWht NGdn SBfd SDix SLim SPlb SWal SWvt WFar WJun WMoo XBlo
§	- 'Fortunei' (v)	SEND SGol
	- 'Tsuboii' (v)	CAbb CDTJ CDoC EPPr ERod GQui MBrN MBri MMoz MWhi MWht NLar SGol WFar WJun WMoo
§	***viridistriatus*** ♀H4	Widely available
	- f. ***variegatus*** (v)	SAga SWvt WMoo

Pleione ✿ (Orchidaceae)

	sp.	NDav
	Adams gx	LYaf
	albiflora	CFwr
	Alishan gx 'Merlin'	LYaf
	- 'Mother's Day'	LYaf
	- 'Mount Fuji'	LYaf
	Asama gx 'Red Grouse'	GEdr LYaf
	Askia gx	GEdr
	aurita	CFwr EPot GEdr LYaf
	Bandai-san gx 'Sand Grouse'	LYaf
	× ***barbarae***	EPot IFoB LYaf
	Barcena gx	EPot LYaf
	Berapi gx 'Purple Sandpiper'	EPot LYaf
	Betty Arnold gx	LYaf
	Brigadoon gx	EPot GEdr
	- 'Stonechat'	EPot LYaf
	Britannia gx 'Doreen'	EPot LYaf
§	***bulbocodioides***	EPot GEdr LYaf
	- 'New Forest'	GEdr
§	- 'Yunnan'	EPot GEdr IFoB
	Burnsall gx	GEdr
	Captain Hook gx	LYaf
	Caroli gx 'Cape Robin' **new**	LYaf
	chunii	EFEx GEdr LAma LYaf
	Danan gx	LYaf
	Deriba gx	EPot LYaf
	Eastfield gx 'Purple Emperor'	LYaf
	Eiger gx	LYaf
	El Pico gx 'Goldcrest'	EPot
	- 'Kestrel'	EPot
	- 'Pheasant'	EPot LYaf
	Erebus gx 'Brambling'	EPot
	- 'Redpoll'	GEdr LYaf
	Etna gx 'Bullfinch'	EPot
	formosana ♀H2	CCon CPne ECho EFEx EPot GEdr LAma LEdu WFar WPGP
	- Alba Group	CFwr ECho WFar
	- - 'Claire'	GEdr IFoB LEdu LYaf
	- - 'Snow Bunting'	LEdu LYaf
	- 'Blush of Dawn'	GLin LYaf
	- 'Cairngorm'	IFoB
	- 'Greenhill'	LYaf
	- Hyb 8001 **new**	IFoB
	- 'Iris'	IFoB
	- 'Pitlochry'	LYaf
	- (Pricei Group) 'Oriental Grace'	IFoB LYaf
	- - 'Oriental Splendour'	GEdr LYaf
	- 'Snow Cap'	GEdr
	- 'Snow White'	LEdu LYaf WPGP
	forrestii	CFwr ECho EFEx EPot LAma
	Fuego gx	IFoB
	Ganymede gx	LYaf
	Gerry Mundey gx	GEdr
	- 'Tinney's Firs'	LYaf
§	***grandiflora***	CFwr GEdr LYaf
	Harlequin gx 'Norman'	LYaf
	Hekla gx	IFoB
	- 'Locking Stumps'	GEdr
	- 'Partridge'	LYaf
	- 'Partridge' × **Zeus Weinstein gx**	GEdr
	hookeriana	LWSt
	humilis	LWSt LYaf
	Irazu gx	IFoB
	- 'Cheryl'	EPot
	Jorullo gx 'Long-tailed Tit'	GEdr LYaf
	Keith Rattray gx 'Kelty'	LYaf
	Kenya gx	LYaf
	- 'Bald Eagle'	LYaf
	Kohala gx	LYaf
	Krakatoa gx 'Wheatear'	LYaf
	Lascar gx 'Dipper'	LYaf
	- 'Purple Finch' **new**	LYaf
	Leda gx	LYaf
	Lhasa gx 'Blushes'	LYaf
	limprichtii ♀H2	CFwr ECho EFEx EPot IFoB LEdu LWSt LYaf
	Lyn Butterfield gx	LYaf
	maculata	EFEx LWSt
	Marion Johnson gx	LYaf
	Mauna Loa gx	LYaf
	- 'Glossy Starling'	LYaf

Mawenzi gx	LYaf
Novarupta gx 'Goshawk'	LYaf
- 'Raven'	LYaf
Orinoco gx 'Gemini'	GEdr
Orizaba gx	LYaf
- 'Fish Eagle'	LYaf
Paricutin gx	LYaf
pinkepankii	see *P. grandiflora*
Piton gx	EPot LYaf
§ ***pleionoides***	EPot LYaf
pogonioides misapplied	see *P. pleionoides*
pogonioides (Rolfe) Rolfe	see *P. bulbocodioides*
praecox	LWst
Quizapu gx 'Peregrine'	LYaf
Rakata gx	EPot GEdr IFoB
- 'Locking Stumps'	EPot GEdr
- 'Redwing'	LYaf
- 'Shot Silk'	LYaf
- 'Skylark'	GEdr LYaf
San Salvador gx	LYaf
Sangay gx	LYaf
Santorini gx	LYaf
- 'Yellow Wagtail'	LYaf
saxicola	CFwr LYaf
scopulorum	EFEx LYaf
Shantung gx	CCon EPot LAma
- 'Ducat'	EPot GEdr LYaf
- 'Gerry Mundey'	LYaf
- 'Ridgeway'	GEdr LYaf
- 'Silver Anniversary'	LYaf
Sharon Ann Winter gx	LYaf
Sorea gx	GEdr
Soufrière gx	LYaf
speciosa Ames & Schltr.	see *P. pleionoides*
St Helens gx	LYaf
Stromboli gx 'Fireball'	EPot
Surtsey gx	EPot
- 'Stephanie Rose'	EPot
Taal gx 'Red-tailed Hawk'	LYaf
× ***taliensis***	LYaf
Tarawera gx	LYaf
Tibesti gx new	LYaf
Toff gx	LYaf
Tolima gx 'Moorhen'	LEdu LYaf
Tongariro gx	CPBP EPot GEdr
Ueli Wackernagel gx	GEdr
Versailles gx	EPot
- 'Bucklebury' ♕H2	EPot LYaf
Vesuvius gx	EPot
- 'Grey Wagtail'	LYaf
- 'Leopard'	LYaf
- 'Phoenix'	EPot LYaf
- 'Tawny Owl'	GEdr LYaf
Volcanello gx 'Honey Buzzard'	GEdr LYaf
- 'Song Thrush'	EPot LYaf
Whakari gx	LYaf
'Wharfedale Pine Warbler'	LYaf
yunnanensis misapplied	see *P. bulbocodioides* 'Yunnan'
yunnanensis ambig.	GEdr LAma
yunnanensis (Rolfe) Rolfe	LYaf
Zeus Weinstein gx	GEdr IFoB LYaf
- 'Desert Sands'	GEdr

Pleomele see *Dracaena*

Pleurospermum (*Apiaceae*)

from Nepal	WCot
aff. ***album*** KWJ 12281	WCru
aff. ***amabile*** BWJ 7886	WCru
benthamii B&SWJ 2988	WCru
brunonis	EBee
calcareum B&SWJ 8008	WCru
yunnanense BWJ 7952A	WCru

plum see *Prunus domestica*

Plumbago (*Plumbaginaceae*)

§ ***auriculata*** ♕H1-2	CBcs CCCN CDoC CHEx CRHN CSBt CTri CWCL EBak EBee ELan EPfP EPri EShb EUJe LRHS MOWG MRav SEND SMrm SPer SPoG SRms SVic
- f. ***alba*** ♕H1-2	CBcs CHEx CRHN CSev CWCL EPfP EShb MOWG SEND
- 'Crystal Waters'	CCCN EShb
- dark blue-flowered	CSpe
capensis	see *P. auriculata*
§ ***indica*** ♕H1	CCCN
- ***rosea***	see *P. indica*
larpentiae	see *Ceratostigma plumbaginoides*

Plumeria (*Apocynaceae*)

sp.	WSFF
rubra ♕H1	LRHS XBlo
- 'Golden Glow'	XBlo
- 'Velvet Red'	XBlo

Poa (*Poaceae*)

alpina	NLar SMea XLum
- var. ***nodosa***	SWal
chaixii	EHoe EPPr NLar XLum
colensoi	CKno EBee EHoe GAbr MAvo
× ***jemtlandica***	EHoe EPPr
labillardierei	CKno CWCL EBee ECha EHoe EPPr MAvo NRHS NWsh SEND SPer SUsu WMoo XLum
pratensis	CHab
trivialis	CRWN
I 'Variegata' (v)	SApp

Podalyria (*Papilionaceae*)

calyptrata	SPlb
sericea	SPlb

Podocarpus ✿ (*Podocarpaceae*)

acutifolius	CBcs CDoC ECou IGor
- (f)	ECou
- (m)	ECou
alpinus R. Br. ex Hook. f.	CDul
andinus	see *Prumnopitys andina*
'Autumn Shades' (m)	ECou
'Blaze' (f)	CBcs CDoC ECou LEdu LRHS MBrN NHol NLar SCoo SLim SPoG WFar
chilinus	see *P. salignus*
'Chocolate Box' (f)	ECou MAsh NLar NWad SLim
'County Park Fire' PBR (f)	CBcs CDoC ECou EHul EPfP ESwi LAst LRHS MGos MWat NEgg NHol NLar NWad SCoo SLim SPoG SWvt WEve WFar WGor
'County Park Treasure'	ECou
cunninghamii	ECou
- 'Kiwi' (f)	ECou
- 'Roro' (m)	CBcs CDoC ECou
cunninghamii × ***nivalis*** (f)	ECou
dacrydioides	see *Dacrycarpus dacrydioides*
elongatus	CTrC

– 'Blue Chip'	CBcs
ferrugineus	see *Prumnopitys ferruginea*
'Flame'	CDoC ECou EHul MAsh NLar NPCo
'Guardsman' new	ECou
'Havering' (f)	CDoC ECou
henkelii	CTrC
'Jill' (f)	ECou
latifolius	ECou
lawrencei	EHul WThu
– (f)	ECou
– 'Alpine Lass' (f)	ECou
– 'Blue Gem' (f)	CDoC ECou LRHS MAsh MGos MMuc SCoo SEND SLim WFar
– 'Kiandra'	ECou
– 'Kosciuszko'	ECou
– 'Pine Lake'	ECou
– 'Red Tip'	CDoC LRHS SCoo SLim
'Lucky Lad'	ECou
'Macho' (m)	ECou
macrophyllus	CDoC CHEx ERom SMad WFar
– (m)	ECou WFar
– 'Aureus'	CBcs
'Maori Prince' (m)	CDoC ECou
nivalis	CBcs CDul CMac CTrC ECou GCal SRms WThu
– 'Arthur' (m)	ECou
– 'Bronze'	CDoC ECou GCal
– 'Christmas Lights' (f)	CKen ECou
– 'Clarence' (m)	ECou
– 'Cover Girl'	LRHS SPoG
– 'Green Queen' (f)	ECou
– 'Hikurangi'	CDoC
– 'Jack's Pass' (m)	ECou WFar
– 'Kaweka' (m)	ECou
– 'Kilworth Cream' (v)	CBcs CDoC CMen ECou ESwi LRHS MGos NHol NLar SLim SPoG SWvt WGor
– 'Little Lady' (f)	ECou
– 'Livingstone' (f)	ECou
– 'Lodestone' (m)	ECou
– 'Moffat' (f)	CBcs CDoC ECou
– 'Otari' (m)	CDoC ECou MAsh NLar
– 'Park Cover'	ECou
– 'Princess' (f)	ECou MBrN
– 'Ruapehu' (m)	CDoC ECou
– 'Trompenburg'	NLar
nubigenus	CBcs
'Orangeade' (f)	CBcs CDoC MGos NHol NLar
'Red Embers' (f)	CDoC ECou ESwi NEgg SCoo WFar WGor
* 'Redtip'	CMen
§ ***salignus*** ♀H3	CBcs CDoC CDul CHEx CPLG EPfP EUJe IDee LRHS SLim WFar WSHC WThu
– (f)	ECou WFar
– (m)	ECou
'Soldier Boy'	ECou
spicatus	see *Prumnopitys taxifolia*
'Spring Sunshine' (f)	CBcs CDoC ECou MGos NLar
totara	CBcs CBrP CTrC ECou LEdu WFar
– 'Albany Gold'	CTrC
– 'Aureus'	CBcs CDoC ECou WFar
– 'Pendulus'	CDoC ECou
'Young Rusty' (f)	CBcs CDoC ECou MAsh MGos NHol NLar WEve WFar

Podophyllum (*Berberidaceae*)

sp.	WBor
aurantiocaule	CPLG GGGa
§ ***delavayi***	CBct CCon CDes CLAP CPLG GEdr NLar SKHP WAbe WCot WCru
difforme	CBct CLAP GEdr SKHP WCru
emodi	see *Sinopodophyllum hexandrum* var. *emodi*
– var. ***chinense***	see *Sinopodophyllum hexandrum* var. *chinense*
hexandrum	see *Sinopodophyllum hexandrum*
– var. ***chinense***	see *Sinopodophyllum hexandrum* var. *chinense*
× ***inexpectatum*** new	MNrw
'Kaleidoscope' (v)	CBct CLAP EBee ESwi EUJe GEdr NCGa NPnk WCot
peltatum	CArn CBct CBro CDes CHid CLAP CWCL EBee ECho EHrv EWTr EWld GAbr GBBs GBin GEdr GPoy LAma LEdu NLar NMyG NSti SPhx WBor WCot WCru WFar WPGP WPnP
– var. ***peltatum*** f. ***deamii***	EBee
pleianthum	CBct CDes CLAP GEdr LRHS WCru
– B&SWJ 282 from Taiwan	WCru
– short	WCru WFar
veitchii	see *P. delavayi*
versipelle	CLAP LEdu LWSt SKHP WCru
– 'Spotty Dotty'PBR (v)	CBct CLAP CPLG EBee ESwi EUJe GEdr LRHS MAvo MMHG MMoz MNrw NLar NPnk NSti SHeu SKHP SMad WCot WFar

Podranea (*Bignoniaceae*)

§ ***ricasoliana***	CRHN EBee LRHS MOWG SPoG WBor

Pogonatherum (*Poaceae*)

* ***distichum***	XBlo

Pogonia (*Orchidaceae*)

sp.	NDav

Pogostemon (*Lamiaceae*)

from An Veleniki Herb Farm, Pennsylvania	CArn
§ ***cablin***	EOHP GPoy
patchouly	see *P. cablin*

Polemonium ✿ (*Polemoniaceae*)

ambervicsii	see *P. pauciflorum* subsp. *hinckleyi*
'Apricot Beauty'	see *P. carneum* 'Apricot Delight'
N ***archibaldiae*** ♀H4	NBir SRms
'Blue Pearl'	CMea ELan EPfP GJos LRHS MBri MNrw NBro NGdn NLar SBfd SPer WFar WPtf
§ ***boreale***	EBee LRHS SWvt WMoo
– 'Heavenly Habit'	EBee GJos LRHS MBNS NGdn WJek XLum
brandegeei misapplied	see *P. pauciflorum*
§ ***brandegeei*** Greene	CCVN GKev
– subsp. ***mellitum***	see *P. brandegeei* Greene
§ ***caeruleum***	Widely available
– 'Bambino Blue'	EBee LRHS SWvt
– 'Blue Bell'	LRHS
– Brise d'Anjou = 'Blanjou'PBR (v)	CMac CMea EBee ECtt ELan EPfP EShb EWes LRHS MAsh MBri NBir NGdn SBfd SMad SPer SWvt WFar WWEG
– subsp. ***caeruleum*** f. ***albiflorum***	CBre CSBt CWCL ECha EHrv ELan EPfP EWTr GAbr MBNS MHer MRav

NBro SBfd SEND SPer SPoG SRms STes WMoo XLum
- 'Filigree Clouds' LRHS NGdn NLar SMrm
- 'Filigree Skies' LRHS NGdn NLar
- var. ***grandiflorum*** see *P. caeruleum* subsp. *himalayanum*
§ - subsp. ***himalayanum*** CSpe GAbr WJek WMoo
- 'Humile' see *P.* 'Northern Lights'
- 'Snow and Sapphires' (v) EBee LSou MBri MPnt NPer SWvt
- white-flowered GJos MMuc
carneum CTri CWan EBee ECha GMaP LRHS MNrw NLar NRHS WMoo
§ - 'Apricot Delight' EBee GJos MNrw NBir NGdn NLar SBfd SGar SIde SPer SPoG STes WFar WHer WJek WPer WPtf WWEG
cashmerianum see *P. caeruleum* subsp. *himalayanum*
chartaceum LLHF
'Churchills' CBre EBee WPGP WSHC
'Eastbury Purple' CElw CWCL MAvo
'Elworthy Amethyst' CElw WPGP
eximium ECho LLHF
foliosissimum misapplied see *P. archibaldiae*
- 'Cottage Cream' CDes WCot WPGP
- var. ***foliosissimum*** EWes
'Glebe Cottage Lilac' GCra NBir SBch WPGP
'Hannah Billcliffe' CDes CElw EBee ECtt EWes MBrN MTis NCot WPGP
'Heaven Scent' EBee NDov NLar
§ 'Hopleys' GCal LHop
× ***jacobaea*** EBee EWes NCot WCot WPGP
'Katie Daley' see *P.* 'Hopleys'
'Lambrook Mauve' ♀H4 Widely available
mellitum see *P. brandegeei* Greene
'North Tyne' NChi
§ 'Northern Lights' CDes CMea CSev CWCL EBee ECGP ECtt ELon EWes IBoy MBel MCot MNFA MNrw MPie MTis NCot NDov NLar SBch STes SUsu WCot WFar WMoo WPGP WWFP
'Norwell Mauve' MAvo MNrw
'Onslow Blue' **new** SUsu
§ ***pauciflorum*** CEnt EBee ECtt EPfP IFro LRHS NBir WJek WMoo WTou
§ - subsp. ***hinckleyi*** GKev LRHS NLBP SBch
§ - subsp. ***pauciflorum*** SPav
- silver-leaved see *P. pauciflorum* subsp. *pauciflorum*
- 'Sulphur Trumpets' SPad SWvt
- subsp. ***typicum*** see *P. pauciflorum* subsp. *pauciflorum*
'Pink Beauty' EBee ELan EPfP GBuc NBre NGdn WWEG
pulchellum Salisb. see *P. reptans*
pulchellum Turcz. see *P. caeruleum*
pulchellum Willd. EDAr
pulcherrimum misapplied see *P. boreale*
- 'Tricolor' see *P. boreale*
pulcherrimum Hook. ECho GKev NBro WPer
- subsp. ***pulcherrimum*** LLHF
'Rainbow Magic' **new** NLar
§ ***reptans*** CArn GPoy MHer NBro WAul WMoo WPtf XLum
- 'Album' see *P. reptans* 'Virginia White'
- 'Firmament' EBee MAvo WPGP
* - 'Sky Blue' NBro
- 'Stairway to Heaven'PBR (v) Widely available
- 'Touch of Class'PBR (v) EBee LSou NLar
§ - 'Virginia White' CBre CDes CElw CMea CSev EBee EWes MAvo MTis NChi SUsu WFar WPGP
- 'White Pearl' MBel NPri
× ***richardsonii*** misapplied see *P.* 'Northern Lights'
× ***richardsonii*** Graham see *P. boreale*
'Sapphire' CBre LRHS
'Sonia's Bluebell' CDes CElw EBee ECGP ECtt EPPr EWes MAvo MDKP MNrw MTis NDov NLar NSti SBch STes SUsu WPGP
'Theddingworth' WFar
viscosum LLHF
yezoense CBre NBre
- var. ***hidakanum*** EBee ECtt ELan EWes GBin LHop
Bressingham Purple = 'Polbress' LRHS MAsh MBNS MBri MWat NCGa NDov NHol NLar NOrc NPri NSti NWad SBfd SMrm SPer SPoG SPtl
- - 'Purple Rain' Widely available

Polianthes (*Agavaceae*)

elongata WCot
§ ***geminiflora*** WCot
tuberosa ♀H1-2 CBcs CCCN EPfP GHim WCot XLum
- 'The Pearl' (d) LAma SDeJ WCot WPGP XLum

Poliomintha (*Lamiaceae*)

bustamanta NBir SPhx WSHC

Poliothyrsis (*Salicaceae*)

sinensis ♀H4 CBcs EPfP IArd IDee MBri NLar SSpi WPGP

Pollia (*Commelinaceae*)

japonica EShb ESwi EWes SBrt

Polygala (*Polygalaceae*)

calcarea WPat
- Bulley's form EPot
- 'Lillet' ♀H4 CPBP ECho EPot EWes GEdr LHop LLHF LRHS NMen NRHS WAbe WPat WThu
chamaebuxus ♀H4 CBcs GKev MAsh MDKP MGos MMuc NLar NSla SPoG SRms WThu
I - ***alba*** LBee LRHS NLar SChF WAbe
§ - var. ***grandiflora*** ♀H4 CBcs CCon ECho EPfP EPot GAbr GEdr GKev IVic LBee LHop LRHS MAsh MGos MWat NMen NSla SChF SPoG WAbe WIce WPat
- 'Kamniski' EPot
- 'Loibl' EPot
- 'Purpurea' see *P. chamaebuxus* var. *grandiflora*
- 'Rhodoptera' see *P. chamaebuxus* var. *grandiflora*
§ × ***dalmaisiana*** ♀H1 CAbb CCCN CHEx CHll CRHN CSpe CWGN EBee EPfP EPri SEND SGar SPlb WAbe WCFE
fruticosa 'Southern Shores' **new** CSpe
myrtifolia CCCN CTrC MGos SMrm SPlb SPoG
- Bibi Pink = 'Polylap' LBuc LHop LRHS MBri SHil SPoG
- 'Grandiflora' see *P.* × *dalmaisiana*
'Purple Passion' **new** WHlf
virgata CCCN

Polygonatum ✿ (*Asparagaceae*)

	CC 5729	EWld
	Og 94047	CDes
	altelobatum B&SWJ 286	WCru
	- B&SWJ 1886	WCru
	arisanense B&SWJ 271	WCru
	- B&SWJ 3839	WCru
§	***biflorum***	Widely available
	canaliculatum	see *P. biflorum*
	cathcartii B&SWJ 2429	WCru
	cirrhifolium	CCon CCse CDes CLAP CPom EBee ELan EPot GBin GEdr GHim MMoz MNrw SKHP WCru WPGP
	- red-flowered	EBee NLar WCot
	commutatum	see *P. biflorum*
	'Corsley'	CPou
	cryptanthum	WCru
	curvistylum	CAvo CBct CCon CLAP CPom ECha EHrv EPPr GEdr IFoB IGor MNFA NLar NRya SPhx WCru WFar WHil WSHC
	- CLD 761	GEdr
	- pink-flowered **new**	SBch
	cyrtonema misapplied	see *Disporopsis pernyi*
	cyrtonema Hua	WCru
*	***desoulavyi*** var. ***yezoense*** B&SWJ 764	WCru
	falcatum misapplied	see *P. humile*
	falcatum A. Gray	EBee NRya
	- B&SWJ 1077	WCru
	- silver-striped	CLAP GEdr SMHy
	- - B&SWJ 5101	NMyG WCru
	- 'Variegatum'	see *P. odoratum* var. *pluriflorum* 'Variegatum'
	'Falcon'	see *P. humile*
	filipes	EPPr WCru
	fuscum	WCru
	geminiflorum	CBct CLAP CPom IGor LRHS WCru WFar
	- McB 2448	CLAP GEdr
	giganteum	see *P. biflorum*
	glaberrimum	CBct WCot WFar
§	***graminifolium***	CBct CLAP CPBP CPom EBee ECho EPPr GEdr LRHS SCnR WCot WCru WThu
	- G-W&P 803	ECho EPot IPot NMen
§	***hirtum***	CBct CLAP CPom CPrp ECho EPPr IFoB LEdu MAvo MMoz NMyG WCru WFar WTin
	- BM 7012	EBee ECho
	- 'Robustum' **new**	LWst
	hookeri	CBct CBro CMac CPLG EBee ECho EDAr EHrv EPPr EPot GBin GEdr GHim IBal ITim LEdu LWst NBid NCGa NHol NLar NMen NMyG NRya NSla SPhx WCru WFar WHil WWEG
	- McB 1413	GEdr
§	***humile***	CBct CLAP EBee ECho EHrv EPPr EPfP GCal GHim IBal LHop LWst MAvo MHer NGdn NLar NMen NMyG NPnk SMad WAul WCru WFar WHil XLum
I	- 'Variegatum' (v)	CMac
§	× ***hybridum*** ♀H4	Widely available
	- 'Betberg'	CBct CCon CLAP CRow ECha EHrv EPPr MAvo NBir WCot
	- 'Flore Pleno' (d)	CBct ELon WHer
	- 'Nanum'	CBct CHid WCot
	- 'Purple Katie'	MAvo NMyG
§	- 'Striatum' (v)	Widely available
	- 'Variegatum'	see *P.* × *hybridum* 'Striatum'
	- 'Wakehurst'	EHrv
	- 'Weihenstephan'	EBee GCal IPot
	- 'Welsh Gold' (v)	CAvo
	inflatum	EBee ECho WCru
	- B&SWJ 922	WCru
	involucratum	ECho WCru
	- B&SWJ 4285	WCru
	japonicum	see *P. odoratum*
	kingianum yellow-flowered	CDes
	- - B&SWJ 6545	WCru
	- - B&SWJ 6562	WCru
	'Langthorn's Variegated' (v)	ELan
	lasianthum	CPom LWst SMHy WCru
	- B&SWJ 671	NMyG WCru
	latifolium	see *P. hirtum*
	leptophyllum KEKE 844	GEdr
	maximowiczii	CPom EBee EPPr GCal WCru
	'Multifide'	EBee
	multiflorum misapplied	see *P.* × *hybridum*
	multiflorum L.	CBcs CElw CMac CPrp CRow CSBt CWCL EBee ECha ECho EHrv EPot GAbr GCal MRav NGdn NLar NMyG NPnk SKHP SMrm SPlb SRms WBor WCAu WFar WHer WMoo WWEG XLum
	- ***giganteum*** hort.	see *P. biflorum*
*	- 'Ramosissima'	SMHy
*	***nanum*** 'Variegatum' (v)	CBcs ECho
	nodosum	WCru
§	***odoratum*** ♀H4	CAvo CBct CBro CDes CPom CRow EBee ECho EHrv GMaP MAvo NBid NLar NMyG NPnk NRya SWal WCru WFar WHil WWEG
§	- dwarf	ECho LEdu
	- 'Flore Pleno' (d) ♀H4	CAvo CDes CLAP CPom CRDP ECha ECho EHrv LEdu MMoz NMyG SCnR WCot WFar WHoo WTin
	- 'Grace Barker'	see *P.* × *hybridum* 'Striatum'
	- Kew form	EPot
	- var. ***pluriflorum***	EBee EHrv
§	- - 'Variegatum' (v) ♀H4	Widely available
	- 'Red Stem'	ECho MAvo WCru
	- 'Silver Wings' (v)	CBct CLAP ECha EHrv NBir NLar
	- var. ***thunbergii***	WCru
	- 'Ussuriland'	EPPr GCal
	- 'Ussuriland Roundleaf'	GCal
	officinale	see *P. odoratum*
	oppositifolium	GHim
	- B&SWJ 2537	WCru
§	***orientale***	CBct CLAP ECho ELau
	pluriflorum	see *P. graminifolium*
	polyanthemum	see *P. orientale*
	prattii	ECho LWst WCru
	- CLD 325	GEdr
	pubescens	CBct EBee ECho LEdu WCru WThu
	pumilum	see *P. odoratum* dwarf
	punctatum	CRDP GHim LEdu WFar
	- B&SWJ 2395	CBct WCru
	roseum	CLAP CPom EBee EPPr GEdr GKev LLHF MAvo MMoz WCot WCru
	sewerzowii	EPPr
	sibiricum	CAvo CBct CPom CRDP GEdr IGor WCru WFar

- DJHC 600 CDes EBee WCot WPGP
stenanthum CPom LWst
- B&SWJ 5727 WCru
stenophyllum CAvo WCru
stewartianum CLAP EPPr NRya
aff. ***tessellatum*** B&SWJ 9752 WCru
tonkinense LEdu
- B&SWJ 8246 WCru
- HWJ 551 WCru WFar
- HWJ 567 WCru
- white-flowered HWJ 861 WCru
verticillatum CBct CBro CGHE CHid CRow ECha EPfP EPot GHim IFoB LEdu MNFA MNrw MRav SKHP SMad WCot WCru WFar WPGP
- CLD 1308 EPPr
- 'Giant One' IPot
- 'Himalayan Giant' CHid ECho IPot LWst WPnP
* - 'Roseum' CAvo
- 'Rubrum' CArn CBct CLAP CRow EBee EHrv EPPr GEdr IGor LEdu LHop LRHS MAvo NBid NChi NLar WCot WCru WHil
- 'Serbian Dwarf' CBct CHid EBee ECho EPot IPot
aff. ***verticillatum*** CSpe
wardii WCot
aff. ***wardii*** WCot
- B&SWJ 6599 WCru
zanlanscianense CBct EBee EHrv IGor WCru WFar

Polygonum (*Polygonaceae*)

affine see *Persicaria affinis*
amplexicaule see *Persicaria amplexicaulis*
aubertii see *Fallopia baldschuanica*
aviculare CArn
baldschuanicum see *Fallopia baldschuanica*
bistorta see *Persicaria bistorta*
capitatum see *Persicaria capitata*
compactum see *Fallopia japonica* var. *compacta*
equisetiforme misapplied see *P. scoparium*
filiforme see *Persicaria virginiana*
molle see *Persicaria mollis*
multiflorum see *Fallopia multiflora*
odoratum see *Persicaria odorata*
polystachyum see *Persicaria wallichii*
runciforme see *Persicaria runcinata*
§ ***scoparium*** EHoe ESwi SDys WFar WOld XLum
tinctorium see *Persicaria tinctoria*
vacciniifolium see *Persicaria vacciniifolia*
weyrichii see *Persicaria weyrichii*

Polylepis (*Rosaceae*)

australis CSpe ESwi LEdu MBri SEND SMad WCot
- tall WPGP

Polymnia (*Asteraceae*)

sonchifolia LEdu

Polypodium ✿ (*Polypodiaceae*)

aureum see *Phlebodium aureum*
- 'Glaucum' CSpe
australe see *P. cambricum*
§ ***cambricum*** EBee EFer WCot WFib WTin
- 'Barrowii' CLAP WAbe WFib
I - 'Cambricum' ♀H4 CLAP GCal WAbe
- 'Conwy' WFib
- 'Cristatum' CLAP WFib
- (Cristatum Group) 'Grandiceps Forster' CLAP
- - 'Grandiceps Fox' ♀H4 MRav WFib
- 'Hornet' WFib
- 'Macrostachyon' CLAP GBin NBid NMyG WFib
- 'Oakleyae' MMoz SMHy WCot
- 'Omnilacerum Oxford' CLAP
- 'Prestonii' CDes WCot WFib
- Pulcherrimum Group CLAP SDys WAbe
- - 'Pulcherrimum Addison' CDes WCot WFib WPGP
- - 'Pulchritudine' CLAP WCot
- 'Richard Kayse' CDes CLAP EBee MMoz WAbe WCot WFib WPGP
- Semilacerum Group EFer
- - 'Carew Lane' WFib
- - 'Falcatum O'Kelly' CDes
- - 'Robustum' WFib
- 'Whilharris' ♀H4 CLAP CRDP SMHy
I × ***coughlinii*** bifid WFib
glycyrrhiza CLAP GPoy WFib
- bifid see *P.* × *coughlinii* bifid
- 'Longicaudatum' ♀H4 CLAP MWhi NMyG WCot WFib
- 'Malahatense' CLAP
- 'Malahatense' (sterile) CDes WAbe WPGP
interjectum CLAP EFer LRHS MMoz MRav
- 'Cornubiense' ♀H4 CHVG CLAP GBin GEdr MMoz NBid NBir SMHy WAbe WTin
- 'Glomeratum Mullins' WFib
× ***mantoniae*** WFib WIvy
- 'Bifidograndiceps' NBid WFib
scouleri CBty CLAP EFer ISha NBro WPGP
vulgare Widely available
- 'Bifidocristatum' see *P. vulgare* 'Bifidomultifidum'
- 'Bifidomulticeps' WCot
§ - 'Bifidomultifidum' CBty CLAP CWCL ELon EWTr GCal GEdr ISha LLWP LRHS MGos MRav NLar WCot WRHF WWEG
* - 'Congestum Cristatum' SRms
- 'Cornubiense Grandiceps' GCal SRms WIvy
* - 'Cornubiense Multifidum' EBee WCot
- 'Elegantissimum' NBid WFib
- 'Parsley' WCot
- 'Trichomanoides Backhouse' CLAP GCal WAbe WFib
'Whitley Giant' WCot

Polypompholyx see *Utricularia*

Polyspora (*Theaceae*)

§ ***axillaris*** CCCN CHll EBee
- CWJ 12363 WCru
longicarpa DJHV 06041 WCru
- WWJ 11604 WCru
speciosa B&SWJ 11750 WCru
- WWJ 11934 WCru

Polystichum ✿ (*Dryopteridaceae*)

acrostichoides CBty CDTJ CDes CKel CLAP EBee ERod LRHS MBri NCGa NLar NMyG SBfd WPGP XLum
aculeatum ♀H4 Widely available
I - Densum Group EFer
- Grandiceps Group EFer
- 'Portia' WFib
andersonii CLAP
bissectum CPLG
braunii CBcs CMac CWCL EBee GBin GMaP IKil LRHS MMoz MMuc NBid NLar SBfd WFib WPnP WWEG XLum

	caryotideum	see *Cyrtomium caryotideum*
	× ***dycei***	CBty GBin ISha LRHS
	falcatum	see *Cyrtomium falcatum*
	falcinellum	GLin
	fortunei	see *Cyrtomium fortunei*
	imbricans	CLAP
	interjectum	MRav
	makinoi	CBty CCCN CLAP EBee EPPr ETod GBin ISha LRHS NBid WFib
	munitum ♀H4	Widely available
	neolobatum	WFib
	- BWJ 8182	WCru
	polyblepharum ♀H4	Widely available
	- 'Jade'	CMac LRHS LTen
	proliferum misapplied	see *P. setiferum* Acutilobum Group
	proliferum ambig.	CBty EAmu WPtf
	proliferum (R. Br.) C. Presl	CLAP GCal SBig WFib WPGP
*	- ***plumosum***	LAst SPad SWvt
	richardii	SBig
	rigens	CBty CLAP CPrp EBee EFer ISha LAst LRHS LSou NLar NMyG SBfd SRms SRot WCru WFib WWEG
	setiferum ♀H4	Widely available
§	- Acutilobum Group	CLAP CPrp EBee ECha EHrv GMaP LRHS NHol SDix SGol SPer SRms WBor WMoo WPGP
	- Congestum Group	EHrv GBin MMoz NCGa NEgg NHol NLar SBfd SPer SRms WFib WPat
	- - 'Congestum'	CBty CLAP CWCL EBee ELan EPPr EPfP ERod IKil ISha LBMP LRHS LTen MRav MWhi NBir NGdn NHol NMyG SPoG WGor WMoo XLum
	- - 'Congestum Cristatum'	LAst
	- 'Cristatopinnulum'	CGHE CLAP NHar WPGP
	- Cristatum Group	CLAP EHrv SRms
	- Cruciatum Group	CLAP
	- Divisilobum Group	CBcs CLAP EFer ELan LPBA MCot MGos MLHP MMoz MWat MWhi SRms WAul WFar WFib WHoo WIvy WKif WPGP WTin
	- - 'Caernarfon'	CLAP
	- - 'Dahlem'	CBty CDoC CEnt CLAP EBee ECha EFer ELan ELon EPfP GBin GMaP LRHS LSRN MCot MMoz MWhi SPer SPoG WFib WKif WMoo WPnP WPtf WWEG
	- - 'Divisilobum Densum' ♀H4	CLAP EHrv EPfP MRav NBir NOrc
	- - 'Divisilobum Iveryanum' ♀H4	CLAP EFer SRms WFib
	- - 'Divisilobum Laxum'	CLAP
	- - 'Divisilobum Wollaston'	CDTJ CKel CLAP CWCL ETod LRHS MRav NBid NLar
	- - 'Herrenhausen'	Widely available
	- - 'Madame Patti'	MMoz
	- - 'Mrs Goffey'	WFib
	- Foliosum Group	CLAP EFer
	- 'Gracile'	LTen MRav NBir
	- 'Grandiceps'	CGHE CLAP EFer ELan
	- 'Hamlet'	WFib
	- 'Helena'	WFib
	- 'Hirondelle'	SRms
	- Lineare Group	WFib
	- Multilobum Group	CLAP SRms WFib
	- 'Othello'	WFib
	- Perserratum Group	GBin NBid WFib
	- 'Plumo-Densum'	see *P. setiferum* 'Plumosomultilobum'
	- 'Plumosodensum'	see *P. setiferum* 'Plumosomultilobum'
	- Plumosodivisilobum Group	CLAP ECha GBin LSou NBid SMHy WFib
	- - 'Baldwinii'	CLAP WFib
	- - 'Bland'	WFib
	- Plumosomultilobum Group **new**	NCGa
I	- - 'Plumosomultilobum'	CBty CGHE CLAP CWCL EBee EPfP GBin ISha MCot MGos MMoz NBir NLar SBfd WCot WFib WGwG WHoo WMoo WPat
I	- - 'Plumosomultilobum Densum'	CMea LRHS MBel SEND WCot WWEG
	- Plumosum Group	CGHE CLAP CMac CSpe EFer ELon LTen NOrc SRot
	- - dwarf	CSBt MMuc
*	- ***plumosum grande*** 'Moly'	SRms
	- Proliferum Group	see *P. setiferum* Acutilobum Group
*	- 'Proliferum Wollaston'	CBty CPrp EBee ELon ETod ISha MMoz MMuc WWEG
	- 'Pulcherrimum Bevis' ♀H4	CBty CHVG CHid CLAP CMea CSpe EBee ECGP ELon ESwi GBin MAvo MMuc MRav NGdn NMyG SDix SEND SUsu SWvt WCot WFib WKif WPGP WPat WPnP WSpi
	- Rotundatum Group	CBty CLAP
	- - 'Cristatum'	CLAP ISha
	- - 'Rotundatum Ramosum'	CLAP
	- 'Smith's Cruciate'	CLAP LLHF MRav WFib
	- 'Wakeleyanum'	EFer SRms
	tsussimense ♀H4	Widely available
	vestitum	CLAP CTrC MMoz SBig

Polyxena (*Hyacinthaceae*)

*	***brevifolia***	ECho
	corymbosa	ECho NMen
§	***ensifolia***	ECho LLHF WCot
	longituba	CPBP ECho WCot
	odorata	ECho NRya
	paucifolia	ECho
	pygmaea	see *P. ensifolia*

Pomaderris (*Rhamnaceae*)

apetala	CPLG
elliptica	CPLG ECou
kumeraho	CCCN

pomegranate see *Punica granatum*

Poncirus (*Rutaceae*)

§	***trifoliata***	CAgr CArn CBcs CCCN CDoC EBee ELan EPfP GBin IDee LEdu LRHS MBlu MRav NEgg SMad SPer SPlb SPoG SVic WFar WSHC
	- 'Flying Dragon'	IVic SMad

Ponerorchis (*Orchidaceae*)

graminifolia	LAma LWst

Pontederia (*Pontederiaceae*)

cordata ♀H4	CBen CHEx CRow CWat EHon ELan EPfP EWay LPBA MSKA MWts NPer SCoo SPlb SWat WFar WMAq XLum
- f. ***albiflora***	CRow CWat EPfP EWay LPBA MWts NLar WMAq XLum
- 'Blue Spires'	MSKA

§ – var. ***lancifolia*** CBen CRow EWay LPBA MNrw MSKA MWts NPer SWat WTin
– 'Pink Pons' CRow LPBA NLar
dilatata see *Monochoria hastata*
lanceolata see *P. cordata* var. *lancifolia*

Populus ✿ (*Salicaceae*)

× ***acuminata*** WMou
alba CBcs CCVT CDoC CDul CLnd CMac CSBt CTho CTri CWib ECrN LBuc NWea SBfd SEWo SGol SPer WMou
– 'Bolleana' see *P. alba* f. *pyramidalis*
– 'Nivea' MMuc SEND
§ – f. ***pyramidalis*** SRms WMou
§ – 'Raket' CCVT CLnd CTho ECrN ELan SPer
– 'Richardii' EBtc EGFP MAsh WCot WMou
– Rocket see *P. alba* 'Raket'
§ 'Balsam Spire' (f) ♀H4 CDoC CDul CLnd CTho WMou
§ ***balsamifera*** CCVT CLnd CSBt CTri MGos SBfd SPer WCot
– 'Vita Sackville West' MBlu
× ***canadensis*** CMam ECrN
§ – 'Aurea' ♀H4 CDul CLnd CTho CWib MGos MRav NEgg SPer WFar WMou
– 'Columbia' WMou
– 'Eugenei' (m) WMou
– 'Robusta' (m) CCVT CDoC CDul CLnd CTri LBuc NWea WMou
– 'Serotina' (m) CDoC CDul WMou
× ***canescens*** CDoC CLnd NWea
deltoides 'Fuego' SGol
– 'Purple Tower' new SMad
× ***generosa*** 'Beaupré' WMou
× ***jackii*** 'Aurora' (f/v) CBcs CCVT CDul CLnd CMac CSBt ELan LBuc LPot MGos MMuc NPri NWea SBfd SGol SPer WFar WHar WMou
lasiocarpa ♀H4 CGHE CMCN CPLG CTho EBee ELan EPfP IArd IDee MBlu SGol SLPl WMou WPGP
nigra CDul CHab CLnd CMac CTho EBee EPfP MMuc NWea SEND WSFF
– (f) ECrN SLPl
– (m) SLPl
– subsp. ***betulifolia*** CCVT CDul CHab CLnd CWan NWea WMou
– – (f) EBtc WMou
– – (m) EBtc WMou
§ – 'Italica' (m) ♀H4 CCVT CDoC CDul CLnd CMac CSBt CTho CTri CWib ECrN ELan LBuc MGos NWea SBfd SEWo SPer WMou
– 'Pyramidalis' see *P. nigra* 'Italica'
'Serotina Aurea' see *P.* × *canadensis* 'Aurea'
simonii 'Fastigiata' WMou
szechuanica WMou
§ – var. ***tibetica*** WMou
tacamahaca see *P. balsamifera*
'Tacatricho 32' see *P.* 'Balsam Spire'
tremula ♀H4 CCVT CDoC CDul CHab CLnd CMac CRWN CSBt CTho CTri CWib EBee ECrN ELan GAbr LBuc MMuc NWea SBfd SEND SEWo SPer WHar WMou WSFF
§ – 'Erecta' CDul CLnd CTho EBee MBlu SMad WMou
– 'Fastigiata' see *P. tremula* 'Erecta'
– 'Pendula' (m) CTho ECrN IDee WMou
trichocarpa SPer
– 'Fritzi Pauley' (f) CDul CTho WMou
– 'Trichobel' new CMam
violascens see *P. szechuanica* var. *tibetica*
wilsonii WPGP
yunnanensis WMou

Porophyllum (*Asteraceae*)

ruderale CArn ELau

Portulaca (*Portulacaceae*)

oleracea CArn ENfk MHer MNHC SIde SVic WJek
– var. ***aurea*** MNHC WJek

Potamogeton (*Potamogetonaceae*)

crispus CBen CWat EHon MSKA MWts WMAq WSFF
natans MSKA

Potentilla ✿ (*Rosaceae*)

CC 5226 GKev
CC 5356 GKev
CC 5780 GKev
alba CTri EBee ECha ECho ELan GCal MAsh MLHP MRav MWat NChi NWad WAul
alchemilloides CMac LRHS WPer
alpicola WPer
ambigua see *P. cuneata*
anglica CArn
anserina CArn MHer NMir WHer XLum
– 'Golden Treasure' (v) EBee WHer
anserinoides WMoo WPer
arbuscula misapplied see *P. fruticosa* 'Elizabeth'
– 'Beesii' see *P. fruticosa* 'Beesii'
'Arc-en-ciel' Widely available
argentea CRWN LRHS MBNS SPlb WFar XLum
arguta EBee
argyrophylla see *P. atrosanguinea* var. *argyrophylla*
– 'Alfred Salter' LRHS
atrosanguinea Widely available
§ – var. ***argyrophylla*** CCon COlW CSam CWCL EBee ECha ELan EPfP GCal LRHS MMuc MWat NBir NBro SEND SRms WAul WFar WMoo XLum
– – 'Golden Starlit' LRHS
§ – – 'Scarlet Starlit' EBee LRHS NCGa
– 'Fireball' (d) EPfP GJos WPer
– var. ***leucochroa*** see *P. atrosanguinea* var. *argyrophylla*
* – 'Sundermannii' LLHF
aurea ECho ECtt EPfP GBin WNew WPat
– 'Aurantiaca' EWes NLar NPro
§ – subsp. ***chrysocraspeda*** NMen
§ – 'Goldklumpen' ECtt MRav NPro
'Blazeaway' EBee ECtt LRHS LSou MArl MBNS NGdn NPro WFar
calabra EBee ECha EWes WHer
§ ***cinerea*** CTri ECho LBee LLHF LRHS
collina LLHF
§ ***crantzii*** CMea SRms
– 'Nana' see *P. crantzii* 'Pygmaea'
§ – 'Pygmaea' ECho ECtt EPfP NBir NMen
§ ***cuneata*** ♀H4 ECho GAbr GKev MMuc SEND WPer
davurica 'Abbotswood' see *P. fruticosa* 'Abbotswood'

	delavayi	LRHS MNrw
	detommasii	LLHF
	- MESE 400	EBee
	dickinsii	NMen
	'Emilie' (d)	CSpe CWCL EBee ECtt GAbr GBuc GCal LRHS MAvo MBNS MBel MCot MNrw NLar NMRc NPro SWvt WBor WCot WFar WHil WWlt
§	***erecta***	CRWN CWan GPoy MNHC WHfH WNew
	eriocarpa	EBee ECho EPau GEdr NMen NRHS NSla WAbe WIce WPat
	- CC 6352	GKev
	- var. ***tsarongensis***	WAbe
	'Esta Ann'	CMac EBee ECtt GBuc LHop MArl MAvo MBNS MCot NCGa NPro SRGP
	'Etna'	CEnt EBee ECtt ELan GBuc LRHS MAvo MLHP MNFA MNrw NBir NLar NPnk SPad SWal WHrl WMoo WPer WPtf
	'Everest'	see *P. fruticosa* 'Mount Everest'
	'Fireflame'	ECha NLar WMoo
	fissa	MNrw NBir SPhx
	'Flambeau' (d)	CWCL EBee ECtt EShb GBuc GKin IPot LDai LHop LPla LRHS MArl MNFA MRav NGdn NLar NPro WCAu WMoo
	'Flamenco'	CSam CTri ECtt MArl MAvo MBNS MBri MLHP MNrw MRav NBir NCGa SUsu WAbb WFar WMoo
	fragariiformis	see *P. megalantha*
	fruticosa	LBuc NWea
§	- 'Abbotswood' ♀H4	Widely available
	- 'Abbotswood Silver' (v)	MSwo WMoo
	- 'Annette'	CMac MBrN NPro
	- 'Apple Blossom'	CWib
	- var. ***arbuscula*** hort.	see *P. fruticosa* 'Elizabeth'
	- 'Argentea Nana'	see *P. fruticosa* 'Beesii'
	- 'Baby Bethan'PBR (d)	LLHF NHol
§	- 'Beesii'	EBee ELan EPfP
	- 'Chelsea Star' ♀H4	CDoC CMac EBee LBuc LRHS LSRN MAsh MGos SBfd SHil
	- 'Chilo' (v)	NEgg WMoo
	- var. ***dahurica*** 'Hersii'	see *P. fruticosa* 'Snowflake'
	- 'Dart's Golddigger'	CTri NWad
	- 'Daydawn'	CBcs CDul CMac CTri CWSG EBee ECtt ELan EPfP LBMP LHop LRHS MAsh MLHP MRav MSwo NBir NEgg NHol NLar NWad SGol SLim SPer SWvt WFar WMoo
§	- 'Elizabeth'	CBar CBcs CDul CWib EBee ELan EPfP LAst LRHS LSRN MGos MNHC MSwo NHol NWea SBfd SGol SLim SPer SRms SWvt WCFE WFar WMoo
	- 'Farreri'	see *P. fruticosa* 'Gold Drop'
	- 'Floppy Disc'	ELan EPfP
	- 'Glenroy Pinkie'	EBee MRav NLar
§	- 'Gold Drop'	CMac
	- 'Golden Spreader'	LRHS
	- 'Goldfinger'	CMac CSBt CWSG EBee ELan EPfP GBin LHop LRHS MAsh MGos MMuc MRav MSwo MWat NEgg NHol SCoo SEND SLim SPer SPlb SPoG WFar
	- Goldkugel	see *P. fruticosa* 'Gold Drop'
	- 'Goldstar'	CBar CDul CWSG EBee IArd LRHS MGos NPri SBfd SCoo SEND SLim SLon SRms WFar
	- 'Goldteppich'	LBuc
	- 'Grace Darling'	ELan EPfP EWes GBin NBir NEgg NHol NLar SRGP SWvt WMoo
	- 'Groneland' ♀H4	EPfP LRHS MAsh SCoo SPoG
	- 'Haytor's Orange'	CWib
	- 'Hopleys Orange' ♀H4	CDoC CSBt CWSG EBee ELon EPfP EWes LHop LRHS MWat NHol NPri NRHS SCoo SEND SGol SHil SRms WGor WMoo
	- 'Hurstbourne'	NPro
	- 'Jackman's Variety' ♀H4	CWib EPfP LRHS MAsh SRms
	- 'Katherine Dykes'	CDul CTri CWib EBee EPfP GKin LAst LBMP LRHS LSRN MAsh MGos MNHC MWat NEgg NWea SCoo SLim SPer SPoG SRms WFar WHar WMoo
*	- 'King Cup' ♀H4	EPfP LRHS MAsh
§	- 'Klondike'	CBcs CSBt NEgg NWea
	- 'Kobold'	CDul
*	- 'Lemon and Lime'	LRHS NBir NPro
	- 'Limelight' ♀H4	CDoC CSBt EBee ELan EPfP GBin GKin LHop LRHS MAsh MBri MRav MSwo SHil SRms WFar
	- 'Longacre Variety'	CMac CTri IArd MSwo NWea
	- 'Lovely Pink'PBR	see *P. fruticosa* 'Pink Beauty'
§	- 'Maanelys'	CSBt EBee ELan MWat NHol NWea SPer WMoo
	- 'Macpenny's Cream'	CMac
§	- 'Manchu'	CMac EBee MRav MWat SPer WPat
	- Mango Tango = 'Uman'PBR	CSBt EBee LRHS LSRN MWat
§	- Marian Red Robin = 'Marrob'PBR ♀H4	CDoC CSBt CWib EBee ELan EPfP GKin LAst LRHS MBri MRav MSwo MWat NEgg NHol NPri NWea SCoo SLim SLon SPer SPoG SWvt
	- 'McKay's White'	NLar
	- 'Medicine Wheel Mountain' ♀H4	ELan EWes IArd LRHS MAsh MGos MRav NHol NLar NPro NRHS NWad SCoo SHil SLim SPer SPoG
	- Moonlight	see *P. fruticosa* 'Maanelys'
§	- 'Mount Everest'	CTri EBee MMuc NWea SEND SLon
	- 'Nana Argentea'	see *P. fruticosa* 'Beesii'
	- 'New Dawn'	GKin LBuc SHil WFar
	- 'Orangeade'	EBee EPfP LRHS MAsh NLar SCoo SPoG
*	- 'Peachy Proud'	NPro
§	- 'Pink Beauty'PBR ♀H4	CBar CDoC CSBt CWSG EBee ELan ELon EPfP GKin LRHS LSRN MAsh MBrN MBri MRav MWat NCGa NEgg NHol NPri SBfd SCoo SEND SLim SPer SPoG SRms SWvt WHar WMoo
	- 'Pink Pearl'	WMoo
	- 'Pink Queen'	NLar
	- 'Pink Whisper'	NPro
	- 'Pretty Polly'	ELan LAst LRHS MGos MSwo NHol NLar WFar WMoo
	- 'Primrose Beauty' ♀H4	CDoC CDul CMac EBee ELan ELon EPfP LAst LPot LRHS LSRN MAsh MMuc MRav MSwo MWat NEgg NHol SCoo SEND SLPl SLim SPer SPlb SPoG WFar WMoo
§	- Princess = 'Blink'	CBcs CDul CWSG EBee ELan EPfP LBMP LRHS MAsh MRav NEgg SCoo SGol SLim SRms WFar WMoo
	- var. ***pumila***	GKev
	- 'Red Ace'	Widely available
	- Red RobinPBR	see *P. fruticosa* Marian Red Robin
	- 'Red Surprise' **new**	WFar

- 'Setting Sun' LBuc
- 'Snowbird' EBee EPfP MGos NPro SLim WFar
§ - 'Snowflake' CBcs WMoo
- 'Sommerflor' ♀H4 CDoC EBee EPfP LRHS MAsh NCGa
- 'Sophie's Blush' MRav NWea WSHC
- 'Summer Dawn' LBuc
- 'Summer Sorbet' LRHS
- 'Sunset' CBcs CMac CWib ECrN ELan GKin LSRN MGos NBir NEgg NWea SCoo SLim SRms WFar WMoo
- 'Tangerine' Widely available
- 'Tilford Cream' CSBt CTri EBee ELan EPfP EWTr GBin GKin LAst LRHS LSRN MRav MSwo MWat NBir NEgg NHol SGol SLim SPer SPoG SRms WFar WMoo
- 'Tom Conway' CMac NLar
- var. ***veitchii*** CDoy CSBt
- 'Vilmoriniana' CTri EBee ELan EPfP GCal LRHS MAsh MLHP MRav NWea SPer SPoG SSpi SWvt WSHC
- 'Whirligig' CMac
- 'Wickwar Beauty' CWib
- 'Yellow Bird' ♀H4 LRHS MAsh
'Gibson's Scarlet' ♀H4 Widely available
§ ***glandulosa*** CTri ECho EWld GEdr MAsh SRms
subsp. ***nevadensis*** new
'Gloire de Nancy' (d) CWCL EBee LBMP MRav NBir NChi NLar WCot
'Gold Clogs' see *P. aurea* 'Goldklumpen'
gracilis EBee
'Helen Jane' EPfP GBee GBuc GJos LRHS MAsh MBNS MHer NBir NLar STes WFar WMnd WPtf WWFP
'Herzblut' NLar
× ***hopwoodiana*** CMea CSpe CWCL EBee ECha ECtt ELan EPPr EPfP GCal GJos LAst LHop MCot MNrw MRav NBir NCGa NChi NDov NLar NPnk SPer SUsu WAbb WCAu WMoo WPtf WWEG
× ***hybrida*** 'Jean Jabber' EBee MRav NLar NPro SRGP
hyparctica MDKP
- 'Nana' ITim
'Jack Elliot' NPro
kurdica XLum
leuconota LRHS
'Light My Fire' EBee ECtt LLHF MAvo MBNS MBri NCGa WWlt
§ 'Majland' NDov
'Mandshurica' see *P. fruticosa* 'Manchu'
'Maynard's' see *P.* 'Majland'
§ ***megalantha*** ♀H4 Widely available
- 'Gold Sovereign' EAEE EPfP LRHS LSou NPro SPoG
'Melton' EBee MNrw
* 'Melton Fire' CEnt CWan ECtt EPfP GBee GJos GKin GQue MNHC NBir SGar SUsu WFar WMnd WMoo WPnP
'Monarch's Velvet' see *P. thurberi* 'Monarch's Velvet'
'Monsieur Rouillard' (d) CMac CSam CWCL EBee ECtt GCra IPot LRHS MArl MCot MNrw MRav MWat NGdn WHoo WMnd
'Mont d'Or' MRav
montana WPer
morefieldii CPBP
nepalensis CEnt EHoe GKev MLHP NBro NChi NPro WHrl XLum
- 'Helen Jane' new SBea
- 'Master Floris' WHal
§ - 'Miss Willmott' ♀H4 Widely available
- 'Ron McBeath' CCon COlW CWCL EBee ECtt ELan EPfP GBin GCal GCra ITim LAst LHop MCot MRav MSCN NGdn NHol NLar NMRc NSti SBfd SPer SPoG SRGP SWvt WHoo WMoo WPtf WWEG
- 'Roxana' CCon EBee ELan MRav NBro NLar SRGP WAbb WFar WMoo WPer
- 'Shogran' COlW EBee GJos GQue LAst LBMP MAvo MBNS NHol NLar WHrl WPtf
§ ***neumanniana*** MAsh NBir NPri
- 'Goldrausch' LEdu MRav
§ - 'Nana' ECho ECtt EPot LBee MHer MWat NMen NRya NWad SPlb SRms WIce WMoo WPat XLum
- white-flowered LAst
nevadensis see *P. glandulosa subsp. nevadensis*
nitida GEdr GKev MAsh NMen SRms WAbe
- 'Alba' ECho EPot NMen
- 'Rubra' CMea ECho EDAr MWat NBir NSla SRms WAbe
nivalis ECho
ovina var. ***ovina*** LLHF
- - NNS 08-374 GKev
palustris CWat EBee NLar NMir WMoo XLum
parvifolia 'Klondike' see *P. fruticosa* 'Klondike'
pedata LLWP NChi XLum
pensylvanica LLHF
'Pink Panther' see *P. fruticosa* Princess
aff. ***polyphylla*** CHP&W 314 GKev
recta COlW MArl NPri WTou XLum
- 'Alba' CEnt GMaP LAst LDai NBre NEgg WPtf
- 'Citrina' see *P. recta* var. *sulphurea*
- 'Macrantha' see *P. recta* 'Warrenii'
§ - var. ***sulphurea*** CEnt CMea GKev LAst MCot MHer MLHP MNFA MNrw NBir NBre NLar NSti SBch SPhx WBrk WFar WHal WHoo WHrl WMnd WMoo WPer WPtf WTin XLum
§ - 'Warrenii' CSBt EBee EPfP GMaP LAst LRHS MRav NBir NEgg SPer SRms WFar WHal WHrl WMoo WPer XLum
reptans CArn CRWN
'Roxanne' (d) LRHS MHer
rupestris CMea ECha MHer NLar NSti SGar WCAu WFar WHal WMoo WOut WPer WPtf
'Scarlet Starlet' see *P. atrosanguinea* var. *argyrophylla* 'Scarlet Starlit'
simplex EBee
speciosa EWes WMoo
sterilis CHid WHer WSFF
* ***sundermanii*** WHrl
tabernaemontani see *P. neumanniana*
ternata see *P. aurea* subsp. *chrysocraspeda*
thurberi LRHS MCot MNFA MNrw NLar SPhx WMoo XLum
§ - 'Monarch's Velvet' Widely available
tommasiniana see *P. cinerea*
× ***tonguei*** ♀H4 CCon CMea COlW CPrp EBee ECha ECho ECtt EPfP GMaP LAst LHop MHer MMuc MNrw MRav NBir NChi NDov SEND SPad SPer SPoG SRkn SRms WFar WIce WMnd WMoo WPtf
tormentilla see *P. erecta*
'Twinkling Star' EBee WPtf

verna misapplied	see *P. neumanniana*
- 'Pygmaea'	see *P. neumanniana* 'Nana'
'Versicolor Plena' (d)	NLar
villosa	see *P. crantzii*
'Volcan'	CWCL EBee ECtt ETod EWes GBuc GQue MAvo NPro SMHy SUsu WAbb WCAu WFar WHal
'White Queen'	MNrw MRav NBre SHar
'William Rollisson' ♀H4	Widely available
willmottiae	see *P. nepalensis* 'Miss Willmott'
'Yellow Queen'	CBcs CMac CTri GKin GMaP LHop LPot MNrw MRav NLar SBod WCAu WFar

Poterium see *Sanguisorba*

sanguisorba	see *Sanguisorba minor*

Pratia (*Campanulaceae*)

§ ***angulata***	CDoy
- 'Jack's Pass'	NEgg
§ - 'Treadwellii'	ECha ECho EPfP GEdr LRHS SPlb WHal
§ ***pedunculata***	CBar CTri ECha ECho ECou ECtt EDAr ELan EPfP LBee LRHS MAsh NChi NRya SPet SPlb SRms SRot WFar WMoo WPer WPtf
I - 'Alba'	CYeo EWes
- 'County Park'	CBar CEnt CMea CPLG CSpe CTri ECha ECho ECou ECtt EDAr ELan GAbr ITim LBMP LRHS MAsh MMuc SEND SPlb SPoG SRms SRot WHil WMoo WPer XLum
- 'Tom Stone'	ECtt
- 'White Stars'	ECho EDAr

Premna (*Verbenaceae*)

* ***vanrensburgii***	CCCN

Preslia see *Mentha*

Primula ✿ (*Primulaceae*)

sp.	SVic
* ***abyssinica*** new	LEdu
acaulis	see *P. vulgaris*
'Adrian Jones' (Au)	IPen WAbe
advena var. ***euprepes***	see *P. euprepes*
agleniana (Cy)	IPen
'Alan Robb' (Pr/Prim/d)	ECtt EPfP NGdn NMRc SPer WFar
albenensis (Au)	EPot IPen
'Alexina' (*allionii* hybrid) (Au)	MFie NHar
algida (Al)	ECho GKev
- 'Sibirica'	GKev
§ ***allionii*** (Au) ♀H2	IPen NSum WAbe
- HNG 12	ITim
- 'Agnes' (Au)	MFie NMen WAbe
- 'Aire Waves'	see *P.* × *loiseleurii* 'Aire Waves'
- 'Alan Burrow' (Au) new	IPen
- var. ***alba*** (Au)	IPen
- 'Allen Moonbeam' (Au)	ITim
- 'Allen Queen' (Au)	IPen WAbe
- 'Andrew' (Au)	IPen WAbe
- 'Anna Griffith' (Au)	CPBP IPen MFie WAbe
- 'Anne' (Au)	IPen
- 'Aphrodite' (Au)	NHar
- 'Apple Blossom' (Au)	GKev
- 'Archer' (Au)	IPen ITim NWad
- 'Ares' (Au)	NHar
- 'Aries Violet' (Au)	NHar
- 'Austen' (Au)	MFie WAbe
- 'Avalanche' (Au)	IPen WAbe
- 'Beryl' (Au)	IPen
- 'Biddy' (Au)	IPen
- 'Bill Martin' (Au)	IPen ITim NWad
- 'Blood Flake' (Au)	IPen ITim
- Burnley form (Au)	NWad
- 'Cherry' (Au)	WAbe
- 'Chivalry' (Au)	MFie
- 'Circe's Flute' (Au)	NHar
- 'Cissie' (Au)	IPen ITim
- 'Claude Flight' (Au)	MFie
- 'Crowsley Variety' (Au)	NMen
- 'Crystal' (Au)	MFie WAbe
- 'Daniel Burrow' (Au) new	IPen
- 'David Burrow' (Au) new	IPen
§ - 'Edinburgh' (Au)	GKev IPen NWad
- 'Edrom' (Au)	IPen ITim
- 'Elizabeth Baker' (Au)	IPen ITim MFie WAbe
- 'Elizabeth Burrow' (Au)	WAbe
- 'Elizabeth Earle' (Au)	ITim WAbe
- 'Elliott's Large'	see *P. allionii* 'Edinburgh'
- 'Elliott's Variety'	see *P. allionii* 'Edinburgh'
- 'Emily Jane' (Au)	IPen
- 'Eureka' (Au)	CPBP
- 'Eveline Burrow' (Au)	WAbe
- 'Fanfare' (Au)	IPen NHar
- 'Flute' (Au)	IPen
- 'Frank Barker' (Au)	IPen
- 'Gabriele' (Au) new	MFie
- 'Gavin Brown' (Au)	IPen
- 'Gilderdale Glow' (Au)	CPBP GKev
- 'Giuseppi's Form'	see *P. allionii* 'Mrs Dyas'
- 'Grace Burrow' (Au) new	IPen
- 'Grandiflora' (Au)	ITim
- 'Hartside' (Au)	NWad
- 'Hartside 12' (Au)	IPen
- 'Hartside 6' (Au)	IPen ITim NHar
- 'Hazey' (Au)	ITim
- 'Hocker Edge' (Au)	GKev ITim MFie NWad
- 'Horwood' (Au)	ITim
- 'Huntsman' (Au)	MFie
- 'Imp' (Au)	IPen
- 'Io 2' (Au)	NHar
- 'Ion's Amethyst' (Au)	NHar
- 'Isobel' (Au)	IPen
- 'James' (Au)	IPen
- 'Jan' (Au)	IPen
- 'Joe Elliott' (Au)	IPen ITim
- 'Julia' (Au)	IPen
- K R W	see *P. allionii* 'Ken's Seedling'
§ - 'Kath Dryden' (Au)	IPen LLHF
§ - 'Ken's Seedling' (Au)	IPen MFie
- 'Lindisfarne' (Au)	IPen
- 'Lismore 81/19/2' (Au) new	MFie
- 'Lismore 87/3/2' (Au) new	MFie
- 'Little O' (Au)	WAbe
- 'Louise' (Au)	IPen
- 'Lucy' (Au)	IPen NHar
- 'Malcolm' (Au)	IPen ITim WAbe
- 'Margaret Earle' (Au)	IPen WAbe
- 'Marion' (Au)	ITim
- 'Marjorie Wooster' (Au)	IPen ITim MFie
- 'Martin' (Au)	IPen ITim
- 'Mary Anne' (Au)	WAbe
- 'Mary Berry' (Au)	IPen MFie NWad
- 'Maurice Dryden' (Au)	IPen WAbe
- 'Megan' (Au) new	ITim
- 'Molly' (Au)	IPen

§ – 'Mrs Dyas' (Au)	IPen MFie NWad WAbe
– 'Neon' (Au)	IPen
– 'Neptunes Wave' (Au)	NHar
– 'New Dawn' (Au)	ITim NHar
– 'Pale Venus' (Au)	IPen NHar
– 'Peace' (Au)	MFie
– 'Peggy Wilson' (Au)	EWld GKev NWad WThu
– 'Pennine Pink' (Au)	IPen
– 'Perkie' (Au)	IPen
– 'Phoebe's Moon' (Au)	IPen NHar
– 'Pink Ice' (Au)	EBee ITim MFie
– 'Pinkie' (Au)	IPen WAbe
– 'Praecox' (Au)	IPen
– 'Quip' (Au)	IPen
– RAH form (Au) new	MFie
– 'Raymond Wooster' (Au)	GKev IPen NWad
– 'Scimitar' (Au)	IPen MFie
– 'Serendipity' (Au)	IPen
– 'Snowflake' (Au)	CPBP GKev IPen WAbe
– 'Stanton House' (Au)	MFie
– white-flowered, thrum-eyed (Au)	IPen
– 'Tranquillity' (Au)	ITim NHar WAbe
– 'Travellers' (Au)	IPen
– 'Viscountess Byng' (Au)	WAbe
– 'William Earle' (Au)	CPBP GKev IPen ITim WAbe
allionii* × *auricula	ECho NWad
misapplied 'Old Red Dusty Miller' (Au)	
allionii* × *auricula 'Blairside Yellow' (Au)	ECho IPen NSum WFar
allionii* × *clusiana (Au)	ECho WAbe
allionii* × *hirsuta (Au)	NWad
allionii* × *pedemontana	see *P.* × *sendtneri*
allionii* × *pubescens (Au)	ECho
allionii* × *pubescens 'Harlow Car' (Au)	GAgs
allionii × 'Lismore Treasure' (Au)	CPBP MFie
allionii × 'Snow Ruffles' (Au)	IPen ITim MFie
allionii × 'White Linda Pope' (Au)	IPen MFie NHar
alpicola (Si) ♀H4	CLAP GAbr GEdr GKev IPen LPBA LRHS NBid NBro NCGa NGdn NSum SBfd WAbe
– var. ***alba*** (Si)	GBuc GEdr GKev IPen LRHS MNrw NBid SEND
§ – var. ***alpicola*** (Si)	CLAP GBin GBuc GCra GEdr GKev IPen MNrw WAbe
– hybrids (Si)	WMoo
– 'La Luna' (Si)	MMuc SEND
– var. ***luna***	see *P. alpicola* var. *alpicola*
– var. ***violacea*** (Si)	CCVN CCon CLAP GAbr GBin GCra GKev IPen LRHS MMuc MNrw NBid SEND WAbe WFar WHil WPer
'Altaica'	see *P. elatior* subsp. *meyeri*
altaica grandiflora	see *P. elatior* subsp. *meyeri*
amethystina (Am)	WAbe
amoena	see *P. elatior* subsp. *meyeri*
'Amy Smith'	GAbr
anisodora	see *P. wilsonii* var. *anisodora*
'Annemijne'	GEdr WCot
'April Rose' (Pr/Prim/d)	NBid
× ***arctotis***	see *P.* × *pubescens*
aurantiaca (Pf)	CCon GEdr GKev IPen
– SDR 6713	GKev
aureata (Pe)	WAbe
auricula ambig. (Au)	CTsd
auricula L. (Au) ♀H4	EDAr IPen MFie NBro SPer SPet SPlb SPoG WAbe
auricula misapplied '2nd Vic' (Au/S)	SPop WFar
– A74 (Au)	SEND SWal
– K85 (Au/S)	ITim SPop
– 'Abdor' (Au/St)	SPop
– 'Abrigde' (Au/d)	WAln
– 'Abundance' (Au/A)	NDro SPop
– 'Achates' (Au/A)	IPen WAln
– 'Admiral' (Au/A)	EWoo WAln WCre
– 'Adrian' (Au/A)	GAbr GAgs IPen MFie NBro NDro SPop WBla WCre WHil
– 'Adrienne' (Au/A) new	SPop
– 'Adrienne Ruan' (Au/A)	WAln
– 'Aga Khan' (Au/A)	WAln
– 'Agamemnon' (Au/A)	EWoo MFie WAln WCre
– 'Alamo' (Au/A)	MFie NDro WCre
– 'Alan Ball' (Au)	WAln WCre
– 'Alan Ravenscroft' (Au/A)	MFie SPop WFar
– 'Albert Bailey' (Au/d)	EWoo GAbr GAgs IPen MFie NDro NEgg SPop WCre WHil
– 'Albury' (Au/d)	IPen
– 'Alchemist' (Au/S)	IPen WCre
– 'Alexandra Georgina' (Au/A)	MFie NDro WAln
– 'Alf' (Au/A)	IPen MFie NDro SPop WHil
– 'Alfred Charles' (Au/A)	WAln
– 'Alfred Niblett' (Au/S)	IPen
– 'Alice' (Au/d)	IPen
– 'Alice Haysom' (Au/S)	CWCL ELan EWoo GAbr GAgs IPen ITim MAsh NDro SPop WCre WFar WHil
– 'Alicia' (Au/A)	EWoo GAbr MFie NDro SPop WCre
– 'Alison Jane' (Au/A)	CPBP GAgs IPen MFie NDro WAln WCre WHil
– 'Alison Telford' (Au/A)	WHil
– 'Allard' (Au/A) new	WAln
– 'Allegro' (Au/A) new	WAln
– 'Allensford' (Au/A)	WCre
– 'Alloway' (Au/d)	WAln
– 'Almand' (Au/d)	WAln
– 'Almondbury' (Au/S)	NDro
– alpine mixed (Au/A)	EPfP SRms
– 'Amber Light' (Au/S)	SPop WAln
– 'Amber Waves' (Au)	GAbr
– 'Amethyst' (Au/S) new	WAln
– 'Amicable' (Au/A)	EWoo GAgs IPen MFie NDro SPop WCre WHil
– 'Ancient Order' (Au/A)	IPen WAln
– 'Ancient Society' (Au/A)	EWoo GAbr IPen MFie NDro SPop WFar WHil
– 'Andrea Julie' (Au/A)	GAgs IPen MFie NDro SPop WCre WHil
– 'Andrew Hunter' (Au/A)	IPen MFie NDro SPop
– 'Andy Cole' (Au/A)	EWoo IPen NDro SPop WAln
– 'Angel Eyes' (Au/St)	IPen SPop
– 'Angel Islington' (Au/S)	NDro
– 'Angela Gould' (Au)	GAbr MFie
– 'Angela Short' (Au/St)	IPen NDro SPop WAln
– 'Angostura' (Au/d)	IPen SPop
– 'Ann Taylor' (Au/A)	IPen WAln
– 'Anne Hyatt' (Au/d)	GAbr NDro
– 'Anne Swithinbank' (Au/d)	IPen WAln
– 'Annie Tustin' (Au/S)	SPop
– 'Antoc' (Au/S)	EWoo SPop

- 'Anwar Sadat' (Au/A) EWoo GAbr MFie NDro WCre WFar WHil
- 'Apple Blossom' (Au/B) NDro
- 'Applecross' (Au/A) IPen NDro SPop WCre WFar WHil
- 'April Moon' (Au/S) MAsh MFie NDro SPop
- 'April Tiger' (Au/St) EWoo WAln
- 'Aquarius' (Au/d) **new** SPop
- 'Arab Prince' (Au/A) **new** WAln
- 'Arab Queen' (Au/A) **new** WAln
- 'Arabian Night' (Au/A) WAln
- 'Arapaho' (Au/A) WAln
- 'Arctic Fox' (Au) MFie WAln
- 'Argus' (Au/A) EWoo GAbr GAgs IPen MAsh MFie NDro SPop WCre WHil
- 'Arlene' (Au/A) WAln
- 'Arthur Delbridge' (Au/A) MFie NDro WFar WHil
- 'Arundel Cross' (Au) IPen NEgg
- 'Arundell' (Au/S/St) CPBP CWCL GAbr GAgs IPen MAsh MFie NDro SPop WCre WFar WHil
- 'Arwen' (Au/A) MFie SPop
- 'Ascot Gavotte' (Au/S) **new** WAln
- 'Ashcliffe Gem' (Au/A) IPen NDro WAln
- 'Astolat' (Au/S) EBee GAbr GAgs GKev IPen ITim NDro SPop WCre WHil
- 'Athene' (Au/S) IPen NDro SPop WAln
- 'Atlantic' (Au/S) NDro NEgg
- 'Aubergine' (Au/B) NDro
- 'Audacity' (Au/d) IPen WAln
- 'Audrey' (Au/S) **new** SPop
- 'Aurora' (Au/A) EDAr MFie NDro WAln WCre
- 'Austin' (Au/A) IPen NDro SPop WAln
- 'Autumn Fire' (Au/A) EWoo GAgs SPop
- 'Autumn Glow' (Au/d) **new** SPop
- 'Aviemore' (Au/A) WCre
- 'Avon Carrier' (Au/d) SPop
- 'Avon Citronella' (Au) SPop
- 'Avon Twist' (Au/d) SPop
- 'Avril' (Au/A) IPen NDro SPop WAln WCre
- 'Avril Hunter' (Au/A) GAgs IPen MFie NDro SPop WCre WHil
- 'Aztec' (Au/d) WAln
- 'Bacchante' (Au/d) SPop WAln
- 'Bacchus' (Au/A) MFie NDro SPop
- 'Baggage' (Au) GAbr IPen
- 'Balbithan' (Au/B) GAbr
- 'Baltic Amber' (Au) GAgs MFie SPop WHil
- 'Bank Error' (Au/S) IPen NDro
- 'Barbara Mason' WAln
- 'Barbarella' (Au/S) IPen MFie NDro SPop WCre
- 'Barbarian' (Au) WFar
- Barnhaven doubles (Au/d) CWCL GAbr NSum
- 'Barnhaven Gold' (Au) IPen
- 'Barr Beacon' (Au/A) NDro
- 'Basilio' (Au/S) NDro WAln
- 'Basuto' (Au/A) IPen ITim MFie NDro SPop WCre WHil
- 'Beatrice' (Au/A) CTri EWoo GAbr IPen MFie NDro SPop WCre WFar WHil
- 'Beauty of Bath' (Au/S) WAln
- 'Beckminster' (Au/A) WAln
- 'Bedford Lad' (Au/A) NDro WCre
- 'Beechen Green' (Au/S) EWoo GAbr IPen ITim MAsh NDro SPop WCre
- 'Behold' (Au) WCre
- 'Belgravia Gold' (Au/B) NDro
- 'Bellamy Pride' (Au/B) GAbr IPen NDro SPop WCre
- 'Belle Zana' (Au/S) EWoo GAgs IPen MFie NDro SPop
- 'Ben Lawers' (Au/S) SPop WBla
- 'Ben Wyves' (Au/S) SPop WBla WCre
- 'Bendigo' (Au/S) EWoo MFie SPop WAln
- 'Bengal Rose' (Au/S) SPop
- 'Benno' (Au/St) NDro
- 'Benny Green' (Au/S) IPen SPop WCre
- 'Beppi' (Au) WHil
- 'Bethan McSparron' (Au/B) NDro
- 'Betty Stewart' (Au/A) **new** WAln
- 'Bewitched' (Au/A) MFie NDro WAln
- 'Bilbao' (Au/A) WAln
- 'Bilbo Baggins' (Au/A) NDro SPop WAln
- 'Bill Bailey' (Au/d) EWoo GAbr NDro SPop WCre
- 'Bilton' (Au/S) SPop WCre
- 'Bingley Folk' (Au/B) SPop
- 'Bizarre' (Au) GAgs WCre
- 'Black Diamond' (Au/d) **new** WHil
- 'Black Ice' (Au/S) NDro WAln
- 'Black Jack'PBR (Au/d) GKin NDov NPri SMrm
- 'Blackfield' (Au/S) SPop
- 'Blackhill' (Au/S) ITim MFie SPop
- 'Blackpool Rock' (Au/St) CWCL WAln WBla
- 'Blairside Yellow' (Au/B) ECho EWes LLHF NDro WAbe
- 'Blakeney' (Au/d) MFie NDro
- 'Blossom' (Au/A) GAbr MFie WBla WFar
- 'Blue Bonnet' (Au/A/d) EWoo GAbr GAgs NDro WAln WCre
- 'Blue Boy' (Au/S) NDro SBea WAln WBla WHil
- 'Blue Chip' (Au/S) GAgs MFie NDro SPop WCre
- 'Blue Cliff' (Au/S) IPen SPop WAln
- 'Blue Fire' (Au/S) SPop
- 'Blue Frills' (Au) WAln
- 'Blue Heaven' (Au/A) IPen NDro SPop WCre
- 'Blue Jean' (Au/S) GAbr IPen MFie NDro SPop
- 'Blue Lace' (Au) WAln
- 'Blue Night' (Au/B) **new** ITim
- 'Blue Nile' (Au/S) SPop WCre
- 'Blue Ridge' (Au/A) WAln
- 'Blue Skies' (Au/St) SPop
- 'Blue Velvet' (Au/B) GAbr GAgs IPen LLHF MFie NBro NDro WCre WHil
- 'Blue Wave' (Au/d) MSCN SPop
- 'Blue Yodeler' (Au/A) GAgs MFie NDro SPop WBla WCre WHil
- 'Blush Baby' (Au/St) EWoo GAbr GAgs NDro SPop WBla
- 'Blyth Spirit' (Au/A) **new** WAln
- 'Bob Dingley' (Au/A) IPen WCre
- 'Bob Lancashire' (Au/S) CWCL GAbr GAgs IPen ITim MFie NDro SPop WCre
- 'Bokay' (Au/d) WAln
- 'Bold Tartan' (Au/St) IPen NDro WAln
- 'Bolero' (Au/A) WAln
- 'Bollin Tiger' (Au/St) WAln
- 'Bonafide' (Au/d) WAln
- 'Bonanza' (Au/S) SPop WAln
- 'Bookham Firefly' (Au/A) GAbr GAgs IPen MFie SPop WBla WCre WFar WHil
- 'Bookham Star' (Au/S) SPop
- 'Border Bandit' (Au/B) SPop WAln
- 'Border Beauty' (Au/St) NDro
- 'Border Blue' (Au/B) **new** WAln
- 'Border Patrol' (Au/B) **new** WAln
- 'Border Tawny' (Au/B) NDro
- 'Boromir' (Au/A) EWoo NDro WAln
- 'Bournebrook' (Au/A) **new** WAln
- 'Bradford City' (Au/A) CWCL NDro SPop WHil
- 'Bradmore Bluebell' (Au) GAbr NDro
- 'Bramley Rose' (Au/B) SPop
- 'Bran' (Au/B) NDro
- 'Brandaris' (Au/A) **new** WAln

- 'Branno' (Au/S) WAln
- 'Brass Dog' (Au/S) new WAln
- 'Brasso' (Au) MFie NDro SPop WAln
- 'Brazen Hussy' (Au/d) WAln
- 'Brazil' (Au/S) EBee GAbr IPen MFie NDro SPop WCre WHil
- 'Brazos River' (Au/A) EWoo MFie WAln WHil
- 'Breckland Joy' (Au/A) NDro WAln
- 'Brenda's Choice' (Au/A) EWoo IPen MFie NDro SPop WBla WCre WFar
- 'Brentford Bees' (Au/St) WAln
- 'Bright Eyes' (Au/A) IPen MFie WCre
- 'Bright Ginger' (Au/S) EWoo
- 'Brimstone and Treacle' (Au/d) SPop WAln
- 'Broad Gold' (Au/A) MFie SPop WBla WCre
- 'Broadwell Gold' (Au/B) GAbr NDro SPop WCre
- 'Brookfield' (Au/S) GAgs IPen ITim MAsh MFie NDro SPop WBla WCre
- 'Broughton' (Au/S) MFie SPop
- 'Brown Ben' (Au) EWoo MFie WFar WHil
- 'Brown Bess' (Au/A) GAbr GAgs IPen MAsh MFie NDro WBla WCot WCre WFar WHil
- 'Brownie' (Au/B) CWCL NBir NDro SPop WHil
- 'Bucks Green' (Au/S) GAbr NDro SPop
- 'Bunty' (Au/A) MFie
- 'Buoyance' (Au/A) new WAln
- 'Bush Baby' (Au/B) NDro
- 'Butternut' (Au/S) new WAln
- 'Butterwick' (Au/A) EWoo GAbr GAgs GMaP IPen MFie NDro NEgg SPop WBla WCre
- 'C.G. Haysom' (Au/S) GAbr MFie NDro SPop WCre
- 'C.W. Needham' (Au/A) IPen MFie NDro SPop WCre
- 'Cadiz Bay' (Au/d) WAln
- 'Calypso' (Au/d) SPop WAln
- 'Cambodunum' (Au/A) IPen MFie NDro SPop WCre WFar WHil
- 'Camelot' (Au/d) EBee ELan EWoo GAgs MFie NBro NDro SPop WCre WFar WHil
- 'Cameo' (Au/A) WCre
- 'Cameo Beauty' (Au/d) SPop
- 'Camilla' (Au/A) WAln
- 'Candida' (Au/d) EWoo IPen MFie NDro SPop WBla WCre
- 'Candy Stripe' (Au/St) SPop WBla
- 'Cappela' (Au/d) WAln
- 'Caramel' (Au/A) IPen WAln
- 'Cardinal Red' (Au/d) NDro SPop
- 'Cardington' (Au/A) new WAln
- 'Carioca' (Au/A) WAln
- 'Carl Andrew' (Au/S) new WAln
- 'Carmel' (Au/d) SPop WAln
- 'Carnival' (Au/A) new WAln
- 'Carole' (Au/A) MFie SPop WBla WCre WFar
- 'Carreras' (Au) MFie NDro
- 'Carzon' (Au/A) NDro
- 'Catherine Wheel' (Au/St) WAln
- 'Celtic One' (Au/St) new SPop
- 'Ceri Nicolle' (Au/B) NDro
- 'Chadwick End' (Au/S) new WAln
- 'Chaffinch' (Au/S) EWoo GAbr GAgs IPen NDro SPop WBla
- 'Chamois' (Au/B) GAbr IPen MFie NDro WHil
- 'Chanel' (Au/S) SPop WAln WCre
- 'Chantilly Cream' (Au/d) WAln
- 'Charles Bronson' (Au/d) GAbr MFie NDro WAln
- 'Charles Rennie' (Au/B) MFie NDro SPop WAln WHil
- 'Charlie's Aunt' (Au/A) WAln
- 'Checkmate' (Au) EWoo MFie SPop WAln
- 'Chelsea Bridge' (Au/A) EWoo IPen MFie NDro SPop WBla WCre WHil
- 'Cheops' (Au/A) IPen MFie NDro NEgg
- 'Cherry' (Au/S) GAbr GAgs IPen NDro WCre
- 'Cherry Picker' (Au/A) MFie NDro SPop WCre WFar
- 'Cheyenne' (Au/S) EWoo GAbr GAgs MFie NDro WCre WFar
- 'Chiffon' (Au/S) CPBP EWoo IPen MAsh NDro SPop
- 'Chiquita' (Au/d) SPop
- 'Chirichua' (Au/S) WAln
- 'Chloë' (Au/S) IPen NDro SPop
- 'Chloris' (Au/S) SPop
- 'Choir Boy' (Au/A) new WAln
- 'Chorister' (Au/S) CPBP EBee GAbr GAgs IPen ITim MFie NDro WCre WHil
- 'Chyne' (Au) EWoo
- 'Cicero' (Au/A) MFie SPop WAln
- 'Cindy' (Au/A) NDro
- 'Cinnamon' (Au/d) EWoo GAgs ITim MAsh MFie NDro SPop WBla WCre
- 'Cinnamon' (Au/S) GAbr WHil
- 'Ciribiribin' (Au/A) WAln
- 'Citron-Ella' (Au/d) SPop
- 'Clara' (Au/d) new SPop
- 'Clare' (Au/S) IPen MFie NDro SPop WCre
- 'Clarish' (Au) new ITim
- 'Classic' (Au/A) new WAln
- 'Clatter-Ha' (Au/d) MAsh WHil
- 'Claudia Taylor' (Au) EWoo SPop
- 'Cleft Stick' (Au) new IPen
- 'Clipper' (Au/S) new WAln
- 'Clotted Cream' (Au/B) new NDro
- 'Cloud Nine' (Au/S) WCre
- 'Clouded Yellow' (Au/S) SPop WBla WHil
- 'Cloudy Bay' (Au) NDro WCot WFar
- 'Cloverdale' (Au/d) WAln
- 'Clunie' (Au/S) IPen NDro WCre
- 'Clunie II' (Au/S) GAgs IPen WFar
- 'Cobden Meadows' (Au/A) WAln WCre
- 'Cockle' (Au/S) new SPop
- 'Coffee' (Au/S) IPen MFie NDro SPop WCre WFar
- 'Colbury' (Au/S) NDro SPop
- 'Colonel Champney' (Au/S) EWoo NDro SPop WCre
- 'Comet' (Au/S) IPen NDro
- 'Confederate' (Au/S) WAln
- 'Connaught Court' (Au/A) EWoo IPen NDro WCre
- 'Conquistador' (Au/A) NDro WAln
- 'Conservative' (Au/S) EWoo GAbr IPen NDro WFar
- 'Consett' (Au/S) EWoo IPen MFie SPop WHil
- 'Cooper's Gold' (Au/B) NDro
- 'Copper King' (Au/B) new WAln
- 'Coppi' (Au/A) EWoo IPen NDro SPop
- 'Coral' (Au/S) EWoo GAgs NDro
- 'Cornish Cream' (Au/B) IPen NDro
- 'Cornmeal' (Au/S) GAgs ITim MFie NDro SPop WAln WCre WHil
- 'Corntime' (Au/S) SPop WAln WCre
- 'Corona' (Au/S) WAln
- 'Corporal Jones' (Au/S) SPop WCre
- 'Corporal Kate' (Au/St) WAln WCre
- 'Corrie Files' (Au/d) MFie WAln
- 'Cortez Silver' (Au/S) WAln
- 'Cortina' (Au/S) CPBP ECho EWoo GAbr GAgs IPen MFie NDro SPop WBla WCre WFar WHil
- 'Country Maid' (Au/A) new WAln
- 'County Park Red' (Au/B) NDro
- 'Coventry Street' (Au/S) MAsh MFie NDro SPop

- 'Crackley Tagetes' (Au/d) ECho
- 'Craig Nordie' (Au/B) new NDro
- 'Craig Vaughan' (Au/A) MFie SPop
- 'Cranborne' (Au/A) SPop WAln
- 'Crecy' (Au/A) MFie SPop WAln
- 'Cressida' (Au/d) new SPop
- 'Crimple' (Au/S) NDro SPop WAln
- 'Crimson Glow' (Au/d) EWoo GAbr GAgs MFie NDro SPop WBla
- 'Crinoline' (Au/S) NDro SPop
- 'Cuckoo Fair' (Au/S) EWoo GAbr IPen NDro SPop WCre
- 'Cuddles' (Au/A) EWoo MFie NDro WAln
- 'Curly Wurlie' (Au) new GAbr
- 'Curry Blend' (Au/B) GAbr NDro
- 'Cutie Pie' (Au/St) IPen WCre
- 'Cuttlefish' (Au/St) SPop
- 'Daftie Green' (Au/S) EWoo GAbr GAgs IPen NDro WCre
- 'Dakota' (Au/S) EWoo MFie
- 'Dales Red' (Au/B) EWoo GAbr GAgs IGor IPen MFie NDro SPop WCre WHil
- 'Dan Tiger' (Au/St) EWoo MFie NDro SPop WAln WHil
- 'Daniel' (Au/A) EWoo NDro WAln
- 'Daphnis' (Au/S) GAbr SPop WAln
- 'Dark Eyes' (Au/d) EWoo GAbr GAgs MFie NDro SPop
- 'Dark Lady' (Au/A) WAln
- 'Dark Red' (Au/S) IPen
- 'David Beckham' (Au/d) SPop WAln
- 'Decaff' (Au/St) WAln
- 'Deckchair' (Au/St) MFie NDro SPop
- 'Dedham' (Au/d) WAln
- 'Del Boy' (Au/A) new WAln
- 'Delilah' (Au/d) GAbr GAgs MFie NDro SPop WHil
- 'Denise' (Au/S) WAln
- 'Denna Snuffer' (Au/d) EWoo GAbr NDro
- 'Devon Cream' (Au/d) ECho MFie SPop WFar
- 'Diamond' (Au/d) WAln
- 'Diane' (Au/A) MFie
- 'Dick Rogers' (Au/B) NDro
- 'Digby' (Au/d) EWoo NDro WAln
- 'Digit' (Au/d) NDro WAln
- 'Dilemma' (Au/A) SPop
- * - 'Dill' (Au/A) IPen NDro SPop WAln WHil
- 'Dilly Dilly' (Au/A) NDro SPop
- 'Divint Dunch' (Au/A) GAgs IPen MFie NDro SPop WCre WFar WHil
- 'Doctor Duthie' (Au/S) SPop WAln
- 'Doctor Lennon's White' (Au/B) GAbr IPen MFie NDro SPop WCre WHil
- 'Dolly Viney' (Au/d) GAbr WAln
- 'Donhead' (Au/A) MFie NDro SPop WCre WFar WHil
- 'Donna Clancy' (Au/S) EWoo SPop
- 'Dorado' (Au/d) WAln
- 'Doreen Stephens' (Au/A) MFie WFar
- 'Doris Jean' (Au/A) MFie WFar
- 'Dorothy' (Au/S) WAln
- 'Doublet' (Au/d) ECho GAbr GAgs IPen MFie NDro SPop WCre WFar WHil
- 'Doubloon' (Au/d) ECho
- 'Doublure' (Au/d) EWoo GAbr GAgs NDro SPop WCre WHil
- 'Douglas Bader' (Au/A) EWoo GAbr MFie NDro SPop WCre WHil
- 'Douglas Black' (Au/S) EWoo GAbr IPen MFie NDro SPop WCre WHil
- 'Douglas Green' (Au/S) EWoo IPen NDro
- 'Douglas White' (Au/S) MFie SPop
- 'Dovedale' (Au/S) NDro SPop WAln
- 'Dowager' (Au/A) MFie
- Downtown Doubles (Au/d) SPop
- 'Doyen' (Au/d) EWoo IPen ITim MAsh MFie WAln WFar WHil
- 'Drax' (Au/A) WAln
- 'Dream' (Au/St) SPop
- 'Dubarii' (Au/A) MFie WAln
- 'Duchess of Malfi' (Au/S) SPop WAln
- 'Duchess of York' (Au) LLHF
- 'Duke of Edinburgh' (Au/B) NDro WAln
- * - 'Dusky' (Au) WFar
- 'Dusky Girl' (Au/A) NDro WAln
- 'Dusky Maiden' (Au/A) EWoo GAbr GAgs MFie NDro SPop WBla WCre WHil
- 'Dusky Yellow' (Au/B) ECho NDro
- 'Dusty Miller' (Au/B) ECho NBir
- 'Eastern Promise' (Au/A) GAgs MFie NDro SPop WBla WFar WHil
- 'Ed Spivey' (Au/A) NDro WBla WCre
- 'Eddy Gordon' (Au/A) WAln
- 'Eden Alexander' (Au/B) MFie NDro
- 'Eden Blue Star' (Au/B) EWoo SPop
- 'Eden Carmine' (Au/B) MFie SPop
- 'Eden Cynthia' (Au/B) new MFie
- 'Eden David' (Au/B) MFie SPop WHil
- 'Eden Goldfinch' (Au/B) SPop WBla
- 'Eden Greenfinch' (Au/B) EWoo GAgs NDro SPop
- 'Eden Moonlight' (Au/B) WAln WHil
- 'Eden Sunrise' (Au/B) new NDro
- 'Edinburgh' (Au/A) new WAln
- 'Edith Allen' (Au/A) WAln
- 'Edith Major' (Au/d) CPBP MFie SPop
- 'Edith Mather' (Au/S) new WAln
- 'Edward Sweeney' (Au/S) WAln
- 'Eglinton' (Au) WCre
- 'Eileen K' (Au/S) NDro
- 'Elf Star' (Au/A) SPop WAln
- 'Eli Jenkins' (Au) WAln
- 'Elizabeth Ann' (Au/A) GAbr NDro SPop
- 'Ellen Thompson' (Au/A) EWoo GAbr GAgs IPen MFie NDro SPop WCre WFar WHil
- 'Elsie' (Au/A) WCre
- 'Elsie May' (Au/A) EWoo ITim MAsh MFie NDro SPop WCre WHil
- 'Elsinore' (Au/S) IPen WCre
- 'Emberglow' (Au/d) WAln
- 'Embley' (Au/S) NDro SPop WCre
- 'Emery Down' (Au/S) NDro SPop WBla
- 'Emily' (Au/d) IPen
- 'Emma Louise' (Au) IPen
- 'Emmett Smith' (Au/A) NBro NDro WAln
- 'Emorydown' (Au/S) WCre
- 'Enigma' (Au/S) SPop WAln
- 'Enlightened' (Au/A) MFie NDro
- 'Envy' (Au/S) MFie
- 'Erica' (Au/A) IPen MFie NDro SPop WCre WHil
- 'Erjon' (Au/S) MFie NDro SPop
- 'Error' (Au/S) MFie WAln
- 'Eschman Starflower' (Au/S) new WHil
- 'Esso' (Au/S) NDro WAln
- 'Ethel' (Au) NDro WCre
- 'Ethel Wild' (Au/d) SPop
- 'Ethel Wilkes' (Au/d) new WAln
- 'Etna' (Au/S) WAln
- 'Ettrick' (Au/S) WAln
- 'Europa' (Au/d) new SPop
- 'Eve Guest' (Au/A) EWoo NDro SPop WAln

- 'Eventide' (Au/S) SPop
- 'Everest Blue' (Au/S) GAbr SPop WCre
- 'Excalibur' (Au/d) EWoo GAbr GAgs NDro SPop WFar
- 'Eyeopener' (Au/A) IPen MFie NDro SPop WCre WHil
- 'Fabuloso' (Au/St) EWoo SPop WBla
- 'Fairy' (Au/A) NDro WAln
- 'Fairy Light' (Au/S) new WAln
- 'Fairy Moon' (Au/S) IPen WAln
- 'Fairy Queen' (Au/S) WAln
- 'Falcon' (Au/S) SPop
- 'Faliraki Fanciful' (Au) EWoo
- 'Falstaff' (Au/d) WAln
- 'Fanciful' (Au/S) EWoo MFie NDro WHil
- 'Fancy Free' (Au) SPop
- 'Fandancer' (Au/A) WAln
- 'Fanfare' (Au/S) EWoo MAsh MFie NDro SPop WBla
- 'Fanny Meerbeck' (Au/S) GAbr IPen MFie NDro SPop WBla WFar WHil
- 'Fantasia' (Au/d) new WAln
- 'Faro' (Au/S) MAsh NDro SPop WBla WCre
- 'Favourite' (Au/S) EWoo GAbr GAgs IPen ITim MAsh MFie NDro SPop WBla WCre WFar WHil
- 'Fearless' (Au/S) new WAln
- 'Fen Tiger' (Au/St) SPop WAln
- 'Fennay' (Au/S) EWoo WAln
- 'Ferrybridge' (Au/A) IPen WAln
- 'Fiddler's Green' (Au/d) CPBP EWoo GAbr GAgs NDro SPop
- 'Figaro' (Au/S) MFie NDro SPop WCre
- 'Figurine' (Au/d) new WAln
- 'Finchfield' (Au/A) GAbr IPen MFie NDro WAln
- 'Firecracker' (Au) IPen WAln
- 'Firenze' (Au/A) MFie SPop
- 'Firsby' (Au/d) NDro SPop WAln WBla WCre WHil
- 'First Lady' (Au/A) SPop WAln WBla
- 'First Light' (Au/B) NDro
- 'Fishtoft' (Au/d) MFie
- 'Fitzroy' (Au/d) SPop
- 'Fleet Street' (Au/S) MFie NDro
- 'Fleminghouse' (Au/S) GAbr MFie NDro SPop WCre
- 'Florence Brown' (Au/S) IPen
- 'For You' (Au/St) new SPop
- 'Forest Burgundy' (Au/d) SPop
- 'Forest Cappuccino' (Au/d) EWoo SPop
- 'Forest Duet' (Au/d) EWoo SPop
- 'Forest Fire' (Au/d) EWoo SPop
- 'Forest Lemon' (Au/d) SPop
- 'Forest Pines' (Au/S) WAln
- 'Forest Sunlight' (Au/d) SPop
- 'Forest Twilight' (Au/d) new SPop
- 'Foxfire' (Au/A) new WAln
- 'Fradley' (Au/A) IPen MFie WAln WHil
- 'Frank Bailey' (Au/d) MAsh SPop WAln
- 'Frank Crosland' (Au/A) MFie NDro WCre WFar WHil
- 'Frank Faulkner' (Au/A) WAln
- 'Frank Jenning' (Au/A) NDro WAln
- 'Frank Taylor' (Au/S) EWoo
- 'Fred Booley' (Au/d) EWoo GAbr IPen MAsh MFie NDro SPop WCre WFar WHil
- 'Fred Livesley' (Au/A) NDro WAln
- 'Fresco' (Au/A) SPop WAln
- 'Freya' (Au/S) new SPop
- 'Friskney' (Au/d) EWoo WAln
- 'Frittenden Yellow' (Au/B) GAbr SPop WFar
- 'Frosty' (Au/S) NDro WBla WCre
- 'Fuller's Red' (Au/S) ITim NDro SPop WCre WFar WHil
- 'Funny Valentine' (Au/d) EWoo IPen MFie SPop
- 'Fuzzy' (Au/St) WAln
- 'G.L.Taylor' (Au/A) IPen NDro
- 'Gaia' (Au/d) MFie SPop
- 'Gail Atkinson' (Au/A) SPop WAln WBla
- 'Galatea' (Au/S) WAln
- 'Galator' (Au/A) new WAln
- 'Galen' (Au/A) WCre WFar
- 'Ganymede' (Au/d) SPop WAln
- 'Gary Pallister' (Au/A) WAln WBla
- 'Gavin Ward' (Au/S) WAln
- 'Gay Crusader' (Au/A) GAbr IPen MFie NDro SPop WCre WFar WHil
- 'Gazza' (Au/A) WAln
- 'Gee Cross' (Au/A) GAbr IPen
- 'Geldersome Green' (Au/S) NDro SPop WCre WFar
- 'Gemini' (Au/S) NDro
- 'General Champney' (Au) WCre
- 'Generosity' (Au/A) MFie NDro WCre WHil
- 'Geordie' (Au/A) WAln
- 'George Edge' (Au/B) NDro
- 'George Harrison' (Au/B) GAbr NDro SPop
- 'George Jennings' (Au/A) MFie NDro
- 'George Swinford's Leathercoat' (Au/B) GAbr NDro
- 'Geronimo' (Au/S) GAbr IPen MAsh MFie NDro SPop WBla WCre
- 'Ghost Grey' (Au) WBla WCre
- 'Gimli' (Au/A) WAln
- 'Girl Guide' (Au/S) WHil
- 'Gizabroon' (Au/S) CFis CPBP CWCL EBee EWoo GAbr GAgs MFie NDro NEgg SPop WBla WCre WFar WHil
- 'Glasnost' (Au/S) WAln
- 'Gleam' (Au/S) CWCL EBee ECho EDAr LLHF MFie NDro SPop WBla WCre WFar WHil
- 'Glencoe' (Au/S) EWoo
- 'Gleneagles' (Au/S) EWoo IPen NDro SPop WAln WBla WCre
- 'Glenelg' (Au/S) EWoo GAbr ITim MFie NDro SPop WBla WCre WHil
- 'Glenluce' (Au/S) EWoo SPop
- 'Gnome' (Au/B) GAbr IPen NDro
- 'Goeblii' (Au/B) new NDro WHil
- 'Gold Blaze' (Au/S) NDro
- 'Gold Seal' (Au/d) SPop
- 'Gold Seam' (Au/A) EWoo MFie WAln
- 'Golden Boy' (Au/A) MFie NDro SPop WAln
- 'Golden Chartreuse' (Au/d) EWoo SPop
- 'Golden Fleece' (Au/S) EWoo GAbr MFie NDro SPop
- 'Golden Girl' (Au/A) WAln
- 'Golden Glory' (Au/A) WAln
- 'Golden Harvest' (Au/A) SPop
- 'Golden Hill' (Au/S) EWoo MAsh SPop
- 'Golden Hind' (Au/d) EWoo MFie NBro NDro SPop WBla WCre
- 'Golden Splendour' (Au/d) EWoo GAgs IPen ITim MAsh MFie NDro SPop WBla WCre WFar WHil
- 'Golden Wedding' (Au/A) IPen MFie SPop WAln WBla WHil
- 'Goldie' (Au/S) NDro
- 'Goldthorn' (Au/A) WCre
- 'Goldwin' (Au/A) NDro
- 'Gollum' (Au/A) MFie NDro SPop WAln WBla
- 'Good Report' (Au/A) GAgs MAsh MFie NDro SPop WBla WFar WHil
- 'Goody Goody' (Au/St) SPop
- 'Googie' (Au/d) new SPop
- 'Gorey' (Au/A) MFie NDro WCre WHil
- 'Gorgeous George' (Au/St) SPop

- 'Grabley' (Au/S)	SPop
- 'Grace' (Au/S)	WAln
- 'Grace Ellen' (Au/S)	WAln
- 'Grandad's Favourite' (Au/B)	NDro SPop
- 'Green Abundance' (Au/B)	EWoo
- 'Green Finger' (Au/S)	MFie SPop WHil
- 'Green Frill' (Au)	GAgs NDro
- 'Green Goddess' (Au/St)	WAln
- 'Green Heart' (Au/S)	SPop
- 'Green Isle' (Au/S)	EWoo GAbr IPen MFie NDro SPop WCre WFar
- 'Green Jacket' (Au/S)	IPen SPop WCre
- 'Green Meadows' (Au/S)	SPop WAln
- 'Green Parrot' (Au/S)	GAbr NDro SPop WCre WHil
- 'Green Shank' (Au/S)	EWoo GAgs IPen NDro SPop WFar WHil
- 'Greenfield's Fancy' (Au)	EBee
- 'Greenfinch' (Au/S)	EWoo
- 'Greenfinger' (Au/S)	WAln
- 'Greenheart' (Au/S)	EWoo SPop
- 'Greenpeace' (Au/S)	GAbr NDro SPop WAln WBla
- 'Greswolde' (Au/d)	SPop
- 'Greta' (Au/S)	CWCL ECho EWoo GAbr IPen ITim MFie NDro SPop WFar WHil
- 'Gretna Green' (Au/S)	SPop
- 'Grey Bonnet' (Au/S)	SPop WAln
- 'Grey Dawn' (Au/S)	WAln
- 'Grey Edge' (Au)	ECho
- 'Grey Friar' (Au/S)	WAln
- 'Grey Hawk' (Au/S)	IPen SPop WAln
- 'Grey Lady' (Au/S)	WAln
- 'Grey Lag' (Au/S)	SPop WHil
- 'Grey Monarch' (Au/S)	GAbr MAsh MFie NDro SPop WAln WCre WHil
- 'Grey Owl' (Au/S)	WAln
- 'Grey Ridge' (Au/S) **new**	WAln
- 'Grey Shrike' (Au/S)	WAln
- 'Grizedale' (Au/S)	SPop
- 'Groupie' (Au/St) **new**	SPop
- 'Grüner Veltliner' (Au/S)	NDro SPop WCre
- 'Guinea' (Au/S)	EWoo GAbr IPen ITim MFie NDro SPop
- 'Gwai Loh' (Au) **new**	NDro
- 'Gwen' (Au/A)	NDro SPop WAln WCre
- 'Gwen Baker' (Au/d)	GAbr MFie NDro WAln WCre
- 'Gwenda' (Au/A)	SPop WAln WHil
- 'Gypsy Rose Lee' (Au/A)	MFie
- 'Habanera' (Au/A)	MFie NDro SPop WCre WFar
- 'Hadrian's Shooting Star' (Au/d)	WAln
- 'Haffner' (Au/S)	NDro SPop
- 'Hallmark' (Au/A)	MFie NDro WAln
- 'Handsome Lass' (Au/St)	EWoo IPen SPop
- 'Hannah' (Au/A) **new**	WAln
- 'Harlequin' (Au/B)	NDro
- 'Harmony' (Au/B)	EWoo MFie NBro
- 'Harry Hotspur' (Au/A)	EWoo IPen MFie NDro SPop WFar WHil
- 'Harry 'O'' (Au/S)	MFie NDro SPop WCre
- 'Harthorpeburn' (Au/B)	NDro
- 'Harvest Glow' (Au/S)	IPen NDro SPop WHil
- 'Havanna' (Au/d) **new**	WAln
- 'Hawkwood' (Au/S)	CPBP CWCL GAbr GAgs IPen MAsh MFie NDro NEgg SPop WBla WFar WHil
* - 'Hazel' (Au/A)	IPen MFie NDro SPop WCre WHil
- 'Headdress' (Au/S)	EWoo GAbr MFie SPop WCre
- 'Heady' (Au/A)	EWoo MFie NDro WHil
- 'Heart of Gold' (Au/A)	MAsh MFie SPop WAln
- 'Hebers' (Au)	NDro SPop WAln
- 'Helen' (Au/S)	GAbr IPen MFie NDro SPop WCre WHil
- 'Helen Barter' (Au/S)	NDro SPop WHil
- 'Helen Ruane' (Au/d)	EBee EWoo GAgs GKev SPop WCre WFar
- 'Helena' (Au/S)	IPen MAsh MFie NDro SPop WAln WFar WHil
- 'Helena Brown' (Au/S)	WAln
- 'Helena Dean' (Au/d)	SPop WAln
- 'Her Nibs' (Au/St)	MAsh
- 'Hermia' (Au/A)	MFie SPop
- 'Hetty Woolf' (Au/S)	GAbr NDro SPop WCre
- 'Hew Dalrymple' (Au/S)	NDro SPop
- 'High Hopes' (Au)	NDro WAln
- 'Highland Park' (Au/A)	NDro SPop
- 'Hillhook' (Au/A) **new**	WAln
- 'Hillview Hermes' (Au/S) **new**	WHil
- 'Hinton Admiral' (Au/S)	EWoo IPen NDro SPop
- 'Hinton Fields' (Au/S)	CPBP CSev EBee EShb GAbr GAgs IPen MAsh MFie NDro NEgg SPop WBla WCre WFar WHil
- 'Hobby Horse' (Au)	EWoo ITim NDro
- 'Holyrood' (Au/S)	EWoo GAbr IPen NDro SPop
- 'Honey' (Au/d)	GAbr NBro NDro NEgg SPop
- 'Hopleys Coffee' (Au/d)	EWoo GAbr NDro SPop WAln WCre
- 'Hopton Gem' (Au/B) **new**	NDro
- 'Howard Telford' (Au/A)	MFie NDro SPop
- 'Hughie' (Au/A) **new**	WAln
- 'Hurstwood Midnight' (Au)	MFie WAln
- 'Iago' (Au/S)	NDro SPop WAln
- 'Ian Greville' (Au/A)	IPen MFie NDro SPop WBla WCre
- 'Ibis' (Au/S)	WAln WCre
- 'Ice Maiden' (Au/A)	EWoo GAbr IPen MFie NDro SPop WBla WHil
- 'Icon' (Au/St) **new**	SPop
- 'Ida' (Au/A) **new**	IPen
- 'Idmiston' (Au/S)	CWCL EWoo GAbr IPen MAsh NDro SPop WCre WFar WHil
- 'Ilona' (Au/d)	SPop
- 'Imari Stripe' (Au/St)	MAsh WBla
- 'Immaculate' (Au/A)	MFie SPop WBla WCre WHil
- 'Impassioned' (Au/A)	MFie SPop WBla WCre WFar
- 'Impeccable' (Au/A)	IPen MFie
- 'Imperturbable' (Au/A)	IPen MFie NDro SPop
- 'Indian Love Call' (Au/A)	GAbr GAgs IPen ITim MFie NDro SPop WBla WCre WFar WHil
- 'Innsworth' (Au/A) **new**	WAln
- 'Iris Scott' (Au/A)	NDro
- 'Isabella' (Au/A)	NDro WAln
- 'Jack Dean' (Au/A)	EWoo MFie SPop WCre WFar WHil
- 'Jack Horner' (Au) **new**	WAln
- 'Jack Redfern' (Au/A)	NDro
- 'Jaffa' (Au/A) **new**	EWoo WAln
- 'James Arnot' (Au/S)	GAbr IPen MFie NDro SPop WAln WFar
- 'James Watham' (Au/S) **new**	WAln
- 'Jane' (Au/S)	WAln
- 'Jane Myers' (Au/d)	WAln WHil
- 'Janet' (Au)	ECho GEdr
- 'Janet Watts' (Au)	GAgs
- 'Janie Hill' (Au/A)	GAbr MFie SPop WBla WCre
- 'Jean Fielder' (Au/A)	SPop WAln
- 'Jean Jacques' (Au/A)	WAln
- 'Jeanne' (Au/A)	EWoo MFie
- 'Jeannie Telford' (Au/A)	MFie NDro SPop WCre WHil
- 'Jeff Scruton' (Au/A) **new**	SPop WAln

– 'Jenny' (Au/A)	EWoo GEdr IPen MFie NDro SPop WCre WFar
– 'Jersey Bounce' (Au/A)	EWoo GAbr NDro WAln
– 'Jesmond' (Au/S)	WAln
– 'Jessie' (Au/d)	EWoo
– 'Jilting Jessie' (Au/St)	IPen NDro SPop
– 'Joan Curtis' (Au/d)	SPop
– 'Joan Elliott' (Au/A)	GAbr
– 'Joanne' (Au/A)	EWoo GAbr MFie SPop WCre
– 'Joe Perks' (Au/A)	EWoo IPen MFie NBro NDro SPop WBla WFar WHil
– 'Joel' (Au/S)	EWoo GAgs IPen ITim MFie NDro SPop WBla WCre WHil
– 'Johann Bach' (Au/B)	SPop
– 'John Stewart' (Au/A)	MFie SPop
– 'John Wayne' (Au/A)	EWoo GAbr MAsh MFie NDro WBla WCre WFar
– 'John Woolf' (Au/S)	NDro
– 'Jolly Green Giant' (Au/S) **new**	WAln
– 'Jonathon' (Au/A)	EWoo NDro WAln
– 'Jorvic' (Au/S)	NDro
– 'Joy' (Au/A)	IPen LLHF MAsh MFie NDro SPop WCre WFar WHil
– 'Joyce' (Au/A)	EWoo GAbr GAgs IPen MFie NDro SPop WCre WFar WHil
– 'Judith' (Au/B)	NDro
– 'Judith Borman' (Au/d)	GAgs NDro
– 'Julia' (Au/S)	NDro WAln
– 'Julie Nuttall' (Au/B)	NDro
– 'June' (Au/A)	NDro SPop
– 'Jungfrau' (Au/d)	NDro SPop WAln
– 'Jupiter' (Au/S)	NDro SPop WAln
– 'Jupp' (Au) **new**	EBee
– 'Jura' (Au/A)	WAln
– 'Just Steven' (Au/A)	SPop WAln
– 'K S' (Au/S)	NDro
– 'Karen Cordrey' (Au/S)	EBee ECho EWoo GAbr GAgs GKev IPen ITim MFie NDro SPop WBla WCre WFar WHil
– 'Karen McDonald' (Au/A)	MFie NDro SPop
– 'Kate Haywood' (Au/B)	NDro WHil
– 'Kath Dryden'	see *P. allionii* 'Kath Dryden'
– 'Kelso' (Au/A)	MFie
– 'Ken Chilton' (Au/A)	EWoo MFie NDro SPop WFar WHil
– 'Kentucky Blues' (Au/d)	SPop
– 'Kercup' (Au/A)	MFie NDro SPop WCre
– 'Kerry'	GKev WAln
– 'Kevin' (Au/A) **new**	WAln
– 'Kevin Keegan' (Au/A)	MFie NDro SPop WHil
– 'Key West' (Au/A)	SPop WAln
– 'Khachaturian' (Au/A)	MFie NDro WAln
– 'Kilby' (Au/A)	SPop WBla
– 'Kim' (Au/A)	GAbr IPen MFie NDro WCre
– 'Kincraig' (Au/S)	WAln WBla
– 'King Kong' (Au) **new**	WAln
– 'Kingcup' (Au/A)	GAbr MFie NDro SPop WCre
– 'Kingfisher' (Au/A)	EWoo GAbr ITim MFie NDro SPop WHil
– 'Kingpin' (Au/St)	NDro
– 'Kintail' (Au/A)	MFie
– 'Kiowa' (Au/S)	SPop
– 'Kirklands' (Au/d)	EWoo ITim MFie NDro SPop
– 'Kohinoor' (Au)	MFie WHil
– 'Königin der Nacht' (Au/St)	MFie NDro SPop WCre
– 'Lady Daresbury' (Au/A)	MFie NDro SPop WFar
– 'Lady Day' (Au/d)	SPop WAln
– 'Lady Diana' (Au/S)	EWoo NDro
– 'Lady Emma Monson' (Au/S)	EWoo NDro SPop
– 'Lady Joyful' (Au/S)	WCre
– 'Lady of the Vale' (Au/A)	NDro WAln
– 'Lady Penelope' (Au/S)	WAln
– 'Lady Zoë' (Au/S)	EWoo MAsh MFie NDro SPop WCre
– 'Lambert's Gold' (Au)	GAbr SPop
– 'Lamplugh' (Au/d)	IPen WHil
– 'Lancelot' (Au/d)	EWoo SPop
– 'Landy' (Au/A)	MFie NDro SPop WCre
– 'Langley Park' (Au/A)	GAgs IPen MAsh MFie NDro SPop WCre WHil
– 'Laptop' (Au/St)	SPop WBla
– 'Lara' (Au/A)	MFie NDro
– 'Laredo' (Au/A)	EWoo WAln
– 'Larry' (Au/A)	EWoo GAgs MFie NDro SPop WCre WFar
– 'Late Romantic' (Au) **new**	ECtt NDov NPnk SMrm
– 'Lavender Lady' (Au/B)	IPen NDro NEgg
– 'Lavender Ridge' (Au/B) **new**	WAln
– 'Lavenham' (Au/S)	WAln
– 'Laverock' (Au/S)	MFie NBir NBro NEgg WBla WCre WHil
– 'Laverock Fancy' (Au/S)	GAbr IPen ITim NDro
– 'Lazy River' (Au/A)	EWoo NDro WAln WCre
– 'Leather Jacket' (Au)	GAbr WHil
– 'Leathercoat' (Au)	EWoo
– 'Lechistan' (Au/S)	GAbr GAgs IPen ITim MAsh MFie NDro SPop WCre WHil
– 'Lee' (Au/A)	IPen NDro WAln WCre
– 'Lee Clark' (Au/A)	MFie WAln
– 'Lee Paul' (Au/A)	EWoo GAbr GAgs IPen MAsh MFie NDro SPop WAln WBla WCre WHil
– 'Lee Sharpe' (Au/A)	EWoo IPen MFie NDro SPop WAln
– 'Legolas' (Au/A) **new**	SPop WAln
– 'Lemmy Getatem' (Au/d)	NDro WHil
– 'Lemon Drizzle' (Au/S) **new**	WAln
– 'Lemon Drop' (Au/S)	EWoo ITim MAsh MFie NBro NDro SPop
– 'Lemon Ice' (Au/S) **new**	WAln
– 'Lemon Sherbet' (Au/B)	GAbr GAgs NDro SPop WHil
– 'Lemonade' (Au)	GAgs
– 'Lepton Jubilee' (Au/S)	EWoo GAbr NDro WAln
– 'Leroy Brown' (Au/A)	WAln
– 'Lester' (Au/d)	SPop WAln
– 'Leverton' (Au/d)	EWoo SPop
– 'Lewis Telford' (Au/A)	SPop
– 'Lich' (Au/S)	EWoo NDro
– 'Lichfield' (Au/A/d)	EWoo IPen SPop WCre
– 'Light Hearted' (Au/A)	CWCL MFie NDro WFar
– 'Light Music' (Au/d)	WAln
– 'Likely Lad' (Au/St)	SPop
– 'Lila' (Au/S)	EWoo NDro SPop WAln
– 'Lilac Domino' (Au/S)	EWoo GAbr GAgs IPen MFie NDro NEgg SPop WFar WHil
– 'Lilac Ladywood' (Au/d)	SPop
– 'Lillian Hill' (Au/A)	EWoo MFie WAln WBla
– 'Lillibet' (Au/A) **new**	NDro
– 'Lima' (Au/d)	MFie WAln
– 'Lime 'n' Lemon' (Au)	ITim
– 'Lime Ridge' (Au) **new**	WAln
– 'Limelight' (Au/A)	EWoo NDro SPop
– 'Limelight' (Au/S)	IPen
– 'Lincoln Bullion' (Au/d)	EWoo SPop
– 'Lincoln Charm' (Au/d)	GAbr SPop
– 'Lincoln Chestnut' (Au/d)	SPop

- 'Lincoln Glow' (Au/d) SPop
- 'Linda' (Au/A) **new** WAln
- 'Lindley' (Au/S) ITim MAsh NDro SPop
- 'Lindsey Moreno' (Au/S) WAln
- 'Ling' (Au/A) MFie NDro SPop WCre
- 'Linnet' (Au/B) NDro
- 'Lintz' (Au/B) MAsh MFie NDro SPop
- 'Linze 2' (Au/S) MFie NDro
- 'Lisa' (Au/A) EWoo IPen MFie NDro SPop WCre WFar WHil
- 'Lisa Clara' (Au/S) EWoo GAbr GAgs IPen ITim MAsh MFie NDro SPop WCre WFar
- 'Lisa's Smile' (Au/S) EWoo MFie NDro SPop WHil
- 'Little Bo Peep' (Au) **new** WAln
- 'Little Rosetta' (Au/d) GAbr MFie NDro WHil
- 'Lizzie Files' (Au/A) **new** SPop WAln
- 'Lockyer's Gem' (Au/B/St) NDro NEgg
- 'Lockyer's Green' (Au) EWoo
- 'Lofty' (Au/St) NDro
- 'Lolita' (Au/St) EWoo SPop WHil
- 'Lord Saye and Sele' (Au/St) CWCL EWoo GAbr IPen ITim MAsh MFie NCGa NDro NEgg SPop WCre WHil
- 'Lothlorien' (Au/A) WAln
- 'Louisa Woolhead' (Au/d) EWoo SPop
- 'Lovebird' (Au/S) CPBP GAbr MAsh NDro SPop WHil
- 'Lucky Strike' (Au) WAln
- 'Lucy Locket' (Au/B) EBee EWoo GAbr IPen ITim NDro NEgg NLar WCre WHil
- 'Ludlow' (Au/S) GAbr
- 'Lune Tiger' (Au/St) MFie
- 'Lupy Minstrel' (Au/S) NDro SPop WAln
- 'Lusty Lad' (Au/St) SPop
- 'Lynn' (Au/A) WAln
- 'Lynn Cooper' (Au) SPop WBla WFar
- 'MacWatt's Blue' (Au/B) GAbr IGor IPen NDro SPop WCre WHil
- 'Madelaine Palmer' (Au/d) SPop
- 'Maggie' (Au/S) GAbr NDro SPop WCre
- 'Magnolia' (Au/B) WCre
- 'Mandarin' (Au/A) CWCL GAbr GAgs MFie NDro SPop WBla WCre WFar WHil
- 'Mardi Gras' (Au/d) WAln
- 'Margaret' (Au/S) GAbr
- 'Margaret Faulkner' (Au/A) GAbr MFie NDro WBla WCre
- 'Margaret Irene' (Au/A) IPen SPop WCre
- 'Margaret Martin' (Au/S) IPen MFie NDro SPop WCre
- 'Margaret Merril' (Au) **new** GAbr
- 'Margot Fonteyn' (Au/A) GAbr MFie SPop WAln WBla WHil
- 'Marie Crousse' (Au/d) CMea CPBP EWoo GMaP MFie NDro SPop WCre WFar
- 'Marigold' (Au/d) WFar
- 'Marion Howard Spring' (Au/A) MFie WCre
- 'Marion Tiger' (Au/St) NDro WAln
- 'Mark' (Au/A) CFis IPen MAsh MFie NBro NDro SPop WCre WFar
- 'Marmion' (Au/S) EWoo GAbr IPen MFie NDro SPop WBla WCre WFar WHil
- 'Martha Livesley' (Au/A) WAln
- 'Martha's Choice' (Au/A) WAln
- 'Martin Fish' (Au) WCre
- 'Martin Luther King' (Au/S) EWoo NDro WHil
- 'Mary' (Au/d) GAbr NDro SPop WAln
- 'Mary Taylor' (Au/S) WAln
- 'Mary Zach' (Au/S) EWoo MFie NDro SPop WAln WHil
- 'Matthew Yates' (Au/d) CMea EBee GAbr IPen MAsh MFie NDro SPop WCot WCre WHil
- 'Maureen Millward' (Au/A) IPen MFie NDro SPop WCre
- 'May' (Au/A) NDro WCre
- 'Mazetta Stripe' (Au/S/St) GAbr MFie NBro NDro NLar SPop WBla WHil
- 'Meadow Sweet' (Au/S) **new** WAln
- 'Meadowlark' (Au/A) EWoo MFie NDro SPop WCre WFar WHil
- 'Mease Tiger' (Au/St) GAbr
- 'Megan' (Au/d) WAln
- 'Mehta' (Au/A) MFie NDro WAln
- 'Mellifluous' (Au) MFie WBla WCre WFar WHil
- 'Melody' (Au/S) IPen SPop
- 'Mere Green' (Au/S) WAln
- 'Mere Peppermint' (Au) EWoo WAln
- 'Merlin' (Au/A) EBee IPen
- 'Merlin' (Au/S) MFie
- 'Merlin Stripe' (Au/St) CWCL IPen NDro SPop WBla WCre WHil
- 'Mermaid' (Au/d) NDro
- 'Merridale' (Au/A) MFie WCre WHil
- 'Mersey Tiger' (Au/S) EWoo ITim MAsh MFie NDro SPop WCre WHil
- 'Metis' (Au/d) SPop
- 'Mexicano' (Au/A) WAln
- 'Michael' (Au/S) MFie SPop WAln
- 'Michael Wattam' (Au/S) SPop WAln
- 'Mick' (Au/A) MFie WCre WHil
- 'Midland Marvel' (Au/St) SPop WBla
- 'Midnight' (Au/A) WAln
- 'Mikado' (Au/S) IPen MAsh MFie SPop WBla WCre WHil
- 'Milkmaid' (Au/A) MFie WMAq
- 'Millicent' (Au/A) MFie WFar WHil
- 'Mink' (Au/A) MFie NDro WFar
- 'Minley' (Au/S) CPBP GAbr MFie NBir NBro NDro NEgg SPop WCre
- 'Minstead' (Au/S) SPop
- 'Minstrel' (Au/S) MFie NDro WCre
- 'Mipsie Miranda' (Au/d) SPop
- 'Mirabella Bay' (Au/A) WAln
- 'Mirandinha' (Au/A) MFie
- 'Miriam' (Au/A) EWoo SPop WAln
- 'Mish Mish' (Au/d) GAbr NDro WHil
- 'Miss Bluey' (Au/d) EWoo NDro SPop WAln
- 'Miss Muffet' (Au/S) **new** WAln
- 'Miss Newman' (Au/A) SPop
- 'Miss Pinky' (Au) EWoo NDro SPop
- 'Mojave' (Au/S) EWoo GAbr GAgs IPen MFie NDro NEgg SPop WCre WHil
- 'Mollie Langford' (Au/A) MFie NDro SPop WHil
- 'Monet' (Au/S) WAln
- 'Moneymoon' (Au/S) EWoo GAgs IPen NDro SPop WCre WHil
- 'Monica' (Au/A) MFie
- 'Monk' (Au/S) MFie NDro WBla WHil
- 'Monmouth Star' (Au/St) NDro
- 'Moody Cow' (Au/St) MAsh
- 'Moon Fairy' (Au/S) NDro SPop WAln
- 'Moonglow' (Au/S) EWoo NDro
- 'Moonlight' (Au/S) WAln
- 'Moonrise' (Au/S) EWoo MFie NDro
- 'Moonriver' (Au/A) EWoo SPop WCre WFar WHil
- 'Moonshadow' (Au/d) WAln
- 'Moscow' (Au/S) SPop
- 'Moselle' (Au/S) MAsh NDro WAln
- 'Mr A' (Au/S) EWoo NDro SPop WHil
- 'Mr Bojangles' (Au/d) SPop WAln
- 'Mr Greenfingers' (Au) WCre

- 'Mrs Cairn's Blue' (Au/B) NDro
- 'Mrs Dargan' (Au/d) NDro
- 'Mrs J.H. Watson' (Au) WCre
- 'Mrs L. Hearn' (Au/A) EWoo GAbr IPen ITim NDro SPop WHil
- 'Mrs R. Bolton' (Au/A) WCre WFar
- 'Mrs Robinson' (Au/St) NDro
- 'Mrs Wilson' (Au) GAbr
- 'Murray Lakes' (Au/A) NDro
- 'Murray Lanes' (Au/A) EWoo WAln
- 'Mustard Sauce' (Au/B) NDro
- 'My Buddy' (Au/St) SPop
- 'My Fair Lady' (Au/A) MFie
- 'My Friend' (Au/B) NDro
- 'Myrtle Park' (Au/A) WAln
- 'Mystery' (Au) GAbr
- 'Nancy Dalgetty' (Au/B) NDro
- 'Naniconan' (Au/A) NDro
- 'Nankenan' (Au/S) MFie NDro WBla
- 'Neat and Tidy' (Au/S) EWoo GAbr GAgs MFie NDro SPop WBla WCre WFar
- 'Nefertiti' (Au/A) EWoo IPen MFie NDro SPop WCre WHil
- 'Nessun Dorma' (Au/A) EWoo NDro SPop WAln
- 'Neville Telford' (Au/S) GAbr IPen MAsh MFie NDro SPop WFar WHil
- 'Newbottle' (Au/S) **new** WAln
- 'Newton Harcourt' (Au/A) **new** SPop
- 'Nick Drake' (Au/d) SPop
- 'Nickity' (Au/A) GAbr GAgs IPen ITim MAsh MFie NDro SPop WAln WCre WFar WHil
- 'Nicola Jane' (Au/A) EWoo SPop WAln
- 'Nigel' (Au/d) EWoo GAbr MFie NDro
- 'Night and Day' (Au/St) NDro SPop
- 'Nightwink' (Au/S) MFie WAln
- 'Nil Amber' (Au) SPop
- 'Nina' (Au/A) NDro WAln
- 'Nita' (Au/d) SPop WAln
- 'No 21' (Au/S) NDro SPop
- 'Nocturne' (Au/S) EWoo IPen NBro NDro SPop WBla WCre
- 'Noelle' (Au/S) EWoo IPen
- 'Nona' (Au/d) EWoo NDro SPop
- 'Nonchalance' (Au/A) MFie NDro SPop WHil
- 'Norma' (Au/A) MFie NDro
- 'Nymph' (Au/d) EWoo GAbr MFie NDro SPop WBla WHil
- 'Oakes Blue' (Au/S) NDro
- 'Oakie' (Au/S) WAln
- 'Oban' (Au/S) MFie NDro SPop WBla
- 'Odette' (Au) **new** IPen
- 'Oikos' (Au/B) SPop
- 'Ol' Blue Eyes' (Au/St) SPop WAln
- 'Old Black Isle Dusty Miller' (Au/B) NDro
- 'Old Clove Red' (Au/B) EWoo GAbr GAgs MFie NDro WCre WHil
- 'Old Cottage Blue' (Au/B) GAbr NDro WFar
- 'Old Dublin Blue' (Au/B) NDro
- 'Old England' (Au/S) EWoo MFie NDro SPop WBla
- 'Old Gold' (Au/S) GAbr IPen NDro WAln WBla WFar
- 'Old Gold Dusty Miller' (Au/B) NDro
- 'Old Irish Blue' (Au/B) ITim NDro NEgg WCre
- 'Old Irish Green' (Au/B) GAbr NDro
- 'Old Irish Scented' (Au/B) EWoo IPen MFie NBro NDro WHil
- 'Old Irish Yellow' (Au/B) NDro NEgg
- 'Old Mustard' (Au/B) NDov NDro SMHy
- 'Old Pink Dusty Miller' (Au/B) GAbr IPen

§ - 'Old Purple Dusty Miller' (Au/B) GAbr
- 'Old Red Dusty Miller' (Au/B) GAbr LLHF NDro SPop WHil
- 'Old Red Elvet' (Au/S) GAbr NDro SPop
- 'Old Smokey' (Au/A) EWoo NDro SPop WBla WHil
- 'Old Suffolk Bronze' (Au/B) GAgs NDro
- 'Old Timer' (Au/S) SPop
- 'Old Yellow Dusty Miller' (Au/B) EWes EWoo GAbr IGor IPen NBro NDro NLar NRya WCre WHil
- 'Old-Fashioned' (Au/B) **new** NDro
- 'Olivia' (Au/d) SPop
- 'Olton' (Au/A) IPen MFie
- 'Optimist' (Au/St) EWoo IPen SPop WCre
- 'Opus One' (Au/A) EWoo WAln
- 'Orb' (Au/S) IPen MAsh MFie NDro SPop WBla WCre WHil
- 'Ordvic' (Au/S) WAln
- 'Orlando' (Au/S) MFie NDro SPop WAln
- 'Orwell Tiger' (Au/St) EWoo GAgs IPen SPop WCre
- 'Osbaston Bullseye' (Au/St) SPop
- 'Osborne Green' (Au/B) GAbr GAgs GBin IGor MFie NDov NDro SPop WCre WHil
- 'Ossett Saphire' (Au/A) NDro SPop
- 'Otto Dix' (Au/A) WAln
- 'Overdale' (Au/A) NDro WAln
- 'Paddlin' Madeleine' (Au/A) EWoo NDro WAln
- 'Paleface' (Au/A) EWoo IPen MFie NDro WBla WCre
- 'Pam Tiger' (Au/St) WAln WCre
- 'Panache' (Au/S) WAln
- 'Papageno' (Au/St) WAln
- 'Paphos' (Au/d) IPen SPop
- 'Paradise Yellow' (Au/B) EWoo GAbr GEdr MFie NDro NEgg SPop
- 'Paragon' (Au/A) IPen ITim MFie WHil
- 'Parakeet' (Au/S) **new** WAln
- 'Paris' (Au/S) WAln
- 'Party Time' (Au/S) IPen WBla
- 'Pass Me By' (Au) **new** IPen
- 'Passing Cloud' (Au/d) **new** WAln
- 'Pastiche' (Au/A) MFie NDro WCre
- 'Pastures New' (Au) **new** WAln
- 'Pat' (Au/S) SPop
- 'Pat Barnard' (Au) IPen
- 'Patience' (Au/S) ITim NDro SPop WHil
- 'Patricia Barras' (Au/S) EWoo WAln
- 'Pauline' (Au/A) EWoo MFie
- 'Pavarotti' (Au/A) NDro SPop
- 'Peewit' (Au/S) **new** WAln
- 'Pegasus' (Au/d) EWoo NDro SPop
- 'Peggy' (Au/A) GAbr WHil
- 'Pequod' (Au/A) MFie NDro WBla
- 'Perdito' (Au/S) **new** WAln
- 'Perseus' (Au/S) **new** WAln
- 'Phantom' (Au/d) SPop WAln
- 'Pharaoh' (Au/A) CWCL EWoo GAbr GAgs MFie NDro SPop WBla WFar
- 'Phoenix' (Au/A) **new** WAln
- 'Phyllis Douglas' (Au/A) EWoo IPen MFie NDro NEgg SPop WCre WHil
- 'Piccadilly' (Au/S) MFie
- 'Pierot' (Au/A) IPen MFie NDro SPop WCre WHil

- 'Piers Telford' (Au/A) CPBP CWCL EWoo GAbr GAgs IPen MFie NDro NEgg NLar SBch SPop WCre WHil
- 'Piglet' (Au/d) EWoo GAbr GAgs NDro SPop
- 'Pimroagh' (Au/A) EWoo NDro
- 'Pink Fondant' (Au/d) GAbr NDro
- 'Pink Hint' (Au/B) NDro
- 'Pink Lady' (Au/A) GAbr MFie NBro SPop WHil
- 'Pink Lilac' (Au/A/S) NDro
- 'Pinkerton' (Au/d) SPop WAln
- 'Pinkie' (Au/A) WHil
- 'Pinkie Dawn' (Au/B) IPen NDro WCre
- 'Pinstripe' (Au) EWoo GAbr GAgs IPen NDro SPop WCre WHil
- 'Pioneer Stripe' (Au/S) GAbr GAgs IPen SPop WCre
- 'Pippin' (Au/A) CPBP CWCL GAbr GAgs IPen MFie NBro NDro SPop WCre WFar WHil
- 'Pixie' (Au/A) EWoo IPen MFie SPop
- 'Plain Jane' (Au) MAsh
- 'Playboy' (Au/A) NDro SPop WAln
- 'Plum Pudding' (Au/d) **new** SPop WAln
- 'Polestar' (Au/A) MFie NDro SPop WBla WCre WFar WHil
- 'Polly' (Au/B) EBee GAgs GKev NDro
- 'Pop's Blue' (Au/S/d) NEgg SPop
- 'Portree' (Au/S) GAbr SPop
- 'Pot o' Gold' (Au/S) CPBP EBee ECho EWoo GAgs IPen MAsh MFie NDro NEgg SPop WBla WCre WFar WHil
- 'Powder and Paint' (Au/A) **new** WAln
- 'Powder Puff' (Au/B) **new** SPop
- 'Prague' (Au/S) IPen MAsh MFie NBir NDro SPop WCre
- 'Pretender' (Au/A) MFie SPop
- 'Pride of Poland' (Au/S) SPop
- 'Prince Bishops' (Au/S) NDro SPop WAln
- 'Prince Charming' (Au/S) GAgs IPen ITim MFie NDro SPop
- 'Prince John' (Au/A) MFie NBro NDro SPop WBla WCre WFar WHil
- 'Proctor's Yellow' (Au/B) NDro
- 'Prometheus' (Au/d) EWoo MAsh MFie NDro SPop WCre WHil
- 'Prosperine' (Au/S) SPop WAln WCre
- 'Psyche' (Au/S) **new** SPop WAln
- 'Ptarmigan' (Au) **new** WAln
- 'Pumpkin' (Au) **new** GAbr
- 'Purple Dusty Miller' see *P. auricula* 'Old Purple Dusty Miller'
- 'Purple Emperor' (Au/A) MFie
- 'Purple Frills' (Au) MFie
- 'Purple Glow' (Au/d) WAln
- 'Purple Haze' (Au) SPop
- 'Purple Lovely' (Au) MFie SPop
- 'Purple Orient' (Au/d) **new** SPop
- 'Purple Patch' (Au/d) **new** SPop
- 'Purple Promise' (Au) GAbr ITim
- 'Purple Prose' (Au/St) MFie SPop
- 'Purple Royale' (Au/B) NDro
- 'Purple Sage' (Au/S) EWoo ITim MFie NDro WHil
- 'Purple Star' (Au/d) **new** SPop
- 'Purple Velvet' (Au/S) CWCL IPen NDro SPop
- 'Quatro' (Au/d) EWoo SPop
- 'Queen Alexandra' (Au/B) EWoo GAbr NDro WHil
- 'Queen Bee' (Au/S) GAbr MFie NDro SPop WBla WCre WFar
- 'Queen's Bower' (Au/S) SPop WCre
- 'Queenswood' (Au/S) WCre
- 'Quintessence' (Au/A) MFie WCre WHil
- 'R.L. Bowes' (Au/A) NDro
- 'Rab C. Nesbitt' (Au/A) WAln
- 'Rabley Heath' (Au/A) GAbr MFie NDro SPop WCre WHil
- 'Rachel' (Au/A) EWoo WAln WCre
- 'Rachel de Thame' (Au/S) **new** WAln
- 'Rachel Labouchere' (Au/S) **new** WAln
- 'Radiant' (Au/A) IPen
- 'Rag Doll' (Au/S) NDro
- 'Ragnald the Magnificent' (Au/S) **new** WAln
- 'Rainy Days' (Au/B) **new** NDro
- 'Rajah' (Au/S) EBee ECho EWoo GAbr GAgs IPen ITim MFie NDro NEgg NLar SPop WBla WCre WFar WHil
- 'Raleigh Stripe' (Au/St) EWoo GAbr GAgs IPen ITim WAln WBla WCre
- 'Ralph's Tan' (Au/B) NDro
- 'Rameses' (Au/A) IPen MFie NDro WCre
- 'Rebecca Baker' (Au/d) SPop
- 'Red Admiral' (Au) NDro SPop WAln
- 'Red and White Stripe' (Au/S/St) WFar
- 'Red Arrows' (Au) SPop WAln
- 'Red Baron' (Au/S) WAln
- 'Red Beret' (Au/S) SPop
- 'Red Bordeaux' (Au/S) NDro
- 'Red Carpet' (Au/S) SPop
- 'Red Diamond' (Au/d) **new** WAln
- 'Red Embers' (Au/S) SPop WAln
- 'Red Ensign' (Au/B) NDro
- 'Red Gauntlet' (Au/S) EWoo GAbr GKev IPen MFie NDro SPop WCre WFar
- 'Red Mark' (Au/A) MFie SPop WHil
- 'Red Rum' (Au/S) MFie WAln
- 'Red Sonata' (Au/S) SPop
- 'Red Vulcan' (Au) WCre
- 'Red Wire' (Au/St) MAsh NDro SPop
- 'Redcar' (Au/A) MFie NDro WCre
- 'Reddown Bat' (Au/d) SPop
- 'Redstart' (Au/B) GKev ITim
- 'Redstart' (Au/S) GAgs IPen ITim WHil
- 'Regency' (Au/A) NDro WAln
- 'Regency Dandy' (Au/St) SPop
- 'Regency Denja' (Au) **new** IPen
- 'Regency Emperor' (Au/St) IPen SPop
- 'Regency Saint Clements' (Au/St) SPop WAln
- 'Remus' (Au/S) CPBP ECho ELan EWoo GAbr IPen ITim LLHF MAsh MFie NDro NEgg SPop WCre WFar WHil
- 'Renata' (Au/S) NDro
- 'Rene' (Au/A) EWoo GAbr IPen MFie NDro WCre
- 'Renown' (Au/A) IPen NDro WAln WCre
- 'Requiem' (Au/d) **new** WAln
- 'Resi' WHil
- 'Respectable' (Au/A) WAln
- 'Reverie' (Au/d) WAln
- 'Reynardyne' (Au/d) SPop
- 'Riatty' (Au/d) GAbr NDro SPop
- 'Richard Shaw' (Au/A) IPen SPop
- 'Ring of Bells' (Au/S) SPop WAln
- 'Risdene' (Au) IPen WAln WCre
- 'Rivendell' (Au/A) **new** WAln
- 'Robbo' (Au/B) EWoo NDro
- 'Robert Green' (Au/S) EWoo SPop WAln

- 'Robert Lee' (Au/A) WAln
- 'Roberto' (Au/S) MAsh WAln
- 'Robin Hood Stripe' (Au/St) EWoo NDro SPop WBla
- 'Robinette' (Au/d) GAbr SPop
- 'Rock Sand' (Au/S) EWoo GAbr MFie NDro WBla WFar WHil
- 'Rodeo' (Au/A) EWoo GAbr IPen SPop
- 'Rolts' (Au/S) ECho EWoo GAbr GAgs GKev IPen MAsh MFie NBro NDro SPop WBla WCre WFar WHil
- 'Rondy' (Au/S) ITim MFie SPop WAln WHil
- 'Ronnie Johnson' (Au) WAln
- 'Ronny Simpson' (Au) WCre
- 'Rosalie' (Au) SPop
- 'Rosalie Edwards' (Au/S) EWoo MFie SPop WCre
- 'Rose Conjou' (Au/d) EWoo GAbr IPen MFie NDro SPop WFar WHil
- 'Rose Kaye' (Au/A) GAbr IPen WCre
- 'Rosebud' (Au/S) EWoo GAbr NDro SPop
- 'Rosemarket Rackler' (Au/B) NDro
- 'Rosemary' (Au/S) EWoo ITim MAsh MFie NDro SPop WCre WHil
- 'Rosewood' (Au) SPop WCre
- 'Rosie' (Au/S) NDro
- 'Rostock' (Au/B) **new** NDro
- 'Rothesay Robin' (Au/A) WAln
- 'Rowena' (Au/A) IPen MFie NBro NDro SPop WCre WHil
- 'Roxborough' (Au/A) EWoo GAgs IPen
- 'Roxburgh' (Au/A) MFie NDro SPop WCre
- 'Roy Keane' (Au/A) IPen MFie SPop WAln WBla
- 'Royal Mail' (Au/S) MFie NDro SPop WAln WBla WCre
- 'Royal Marine' (Au/S) MFie SPop WAln
- 'Royal Scot' (Au/S) WCre
- 'Royal Velvet' (Au/S) GAbr GAgs IPen NDro WHil
- 'Ruby Hyde' (Au/B) EWoo GAbr NDro
- 'Ruby Sutton' (Au/d) EWoo
- 'Ruddy Duck' (Au/S) SPop WBla WCre
- 'Rumbled' (Au/St) MAsh
- 'Rusty Dusty' (Au) GAbr
- 'Rusty Red' (Au/B) NDro
- 'Ryecroft' (Au/A) WAln
- 'Sabrina' (Au/A) WAln
- 'Saginaw' (Au/A) EWoo WAln
- 'Sailor Boy' (Au/S) MFie NDro SPop WAln WHil
- 'Saint Boswells' (Au/S) GAbr NDro SPop
- 'Saint Elmo' (Au/A) MFie SPop
- 'Saint Quentin' (Au/S) WAln
- 'Salad' (Au/S) GAbr
- 'Sale Green' (Au/S) MFie SPop
- 'Sally' (Au/A) MFie
- 'Sam Brown' (Au/S) WBla
- 'Sam Gamgee' (Au/A) NDro WAln
- 'Sam Hunter' (Au/A) NDro SPop
- 'Samantha' (Au/A) EWoo WAln WCre
- 'Samantha' (Au/d) SPop
- 'Sandhills' (Au/A) MAsh MFie WBla WCre WHil
- 'Sandmartin' (Au/S) MFie
- 'Sandra' (Au/A) ELan GAbr GAgs IPen MAsh MFie NDro SPop WBla WCre WHil
- 'Sandra's Lass' (Au/A) EWoo SPop
- 'Sandwood Bay' (Au/A) EWoo GAbr GAgs MFie NBro NDro NEgg SPop WCre WHil
- 'Sappho' (Au/S) **new** WAln
- 'Sarah Gisby' (Au/d) MFie SPop WBla
- 'Sarah Lodge' (Au/d) EWoo GAbr IPen MAsh NDro SPop WCre WHil
- 'Saruman' (Au/A) **new** WAln
- 'Sasha Files' (Au/A) **new** WAln
- 'Satin Doll' (Au/d) MFie SPop
- 'Scaraben' (Au) **new** GAbr
- 'Scipio' (Au/S) NDro SPop WAln
- 'Scorcher' (Au/S) IPen MFie NDro SPop
- 'Sea Lavender' (Au/d) **new** WAln
- 'Sea Mist' (Au/d) WAln
- 'Searchlight' (Au) WCre
- 'Second Victory' (Au) CPBP NDro WCre WHil
- 'Serenity' (Au/S) MFie NDro SPop WBla WCre WHil
- 'Sergeant Wilson' (Au) SPop WAln
- 'Shalford' (Au/d) EWoo GAbr MFie NDro SPop WCre WFar WHil
- 'Sharmans Cross' (Au/S) MFie WAln
- 'Sharon Louise' (Au/S) IPen NDro SPop WCre
- 'Shaun' (Au/d) **new** ECtt GAbr NDov NPri
- 'Sheila' (Au/S) GAbr MAsh NDro SPop WBla WCre WFar WHil
- 'Shere' (Au/S) EWoo MFie NDro SPop WCre
- 'Shergold' (Au/A) MFie WCre
- 'Sherwood' (Au/S) CWCL EWoo IPen MAsh MFie NDro SPop WHil
- 'Shirley' (Au/S) SPop WAln
- 'Shotley' (Au/A) MFie SPop
- 'Show Bandit' (Au/St) SPop
- 'Showtime' (Au/S) NDro
- 'Sibsey' (Au/d) CWCL MAsh NDro SPop WHil
- 'Sidney' (Au/A) WAln
- 'Silmaril' (Au) SPop WAln
- 'Silver City' (Au/S) **new** WAln
- 'Silver Rose' (Au) WCre
- 'Silverway' (Au/S) EWoo ITim MAsh SPop WAln WCre WHil
- 'Simply Red' (Au) IPen MAsh MFie NDro SPop WAln WBla
- 'Sir John' (Au/A) MAsh MFie WBla WFar WHil
- 'Sir John Hall' (Au) MFie
- 'Sir Robert' (Au/d) WAln
- 'Sirbol' (Au/A) EWoo IPen MFie NDro SPop WBla WCre WFar WHil
- 'Sirius' (Au/A) CWCL EWoo GAbr IPen MFie NDro SPop WBla WCre WFar
- 'Skylark' (Au/A) EWoo GAbr GAgs IPen NDro SPop WBla WCre WHil
- 'Skyliner' (Au/A) NDro
- 'Slack Top Red' (Au) NSla
- 'Slim Whitman' (Au/A) NDro SPop WAln WBla
- 'Slioch' (Au/S) EWoo GAbr GAgs IPen MAsh MFie NDro SPop WCre WHil
- 'Slip Anchor' (Au/A) WAln
- 'Smart Tar' (Au/S) WAln WCre
- 'Smoothy' (Au/St) SPop
- 'Snooty Fox' (Au/A) GAbr IPen MFie SPop WCre
- 'Snooty Fox II' (Au/A) MFie NDro WBla
- 'Snow Maiden' (Au/d) **new** WAln
- 'Snowy Owl' (Au/S) GAbr MFie NDro SPop WCre
- 'Soliloquy' (Au) MAsh
- 'Soncy Face' (Au/A) MFie SPop WBla WCre WHil
- 'Sonia Nicolle' (Au/B) NDro
- 'Sonny Boy' (Au/A) NDro SPop WAln WBla
- 'Sooty' (Au/d) **new** IPen
- 'Sophie' (Au/d) SPop WAln
- 'South Barrow' (Au/d) GAbr SPop WCre WHil
- 'Southease Jane' (Au) WAln
- 'Southport' (Au) GAbr NDro
- 'Sparky' (Au/A) MFie NDro WAln
- 'Spartan' (Au) WAln
- 'Spitfire' (Au/S) MFie

- 'Spokey' (Au) IPen
- 'Spring Meadows' (Au/S) EWoo GAbr MAsh MFie NDro NEgg SPop WHil
- 'Springtime' (Au/A) SPop
- 'Standish' (Au/d) GAbr
- 'Stant's Blue' (Au/S) IPen MFie NBro NDro WCre WFar
- 'Star Spangle' (Au/St) NDro
- 'Star Wars' (Au/S) GAbr MAsh MFie NDro SPop WAln WCre WHil
- 'Star Wars II' (Au) GAgs
- 'Stardust' (Au/S) WCre
- 'Starling' (Au/B) EWoo GAbr IPen NDro SPop
- 'Starry' (Au/S) NDro
- 'Starsand' (Au/S) WCre
- 'Stella' (Au/S) NDro SPop
- 'Stella Coop' (Au/d) NDro WAln
- 'Stella South' (Au/A) **new** SPop
- 'Stetson' (Au/A) WAln
- 'Stoke Poges' (Au/A) WAln
- 'Stoney Cross' (Au/S) SPop WAln
- 'Stonnal' (Au/A) MFie NDro SPop WHil
- 'Stormin' Norman' (Au/A) EWoo MFie NDro SPop WHil
- 'Stormy Weather' (Au/St) SPop
- 'Stripe Tease' (Au/St) **new** SPop
- 'Striped Ace' (Au/St) NDro SPop WCre WHil
- 'Stripey' (Au/d) IPen WCre
- 'Stromboli' (Au/d) NDro SPop WBla
- 'Stuart West' (Au/A) WCre
- 'Stubb's Tartan' (Au/S) MFie
- 'Sue' (Au/A) MFie SPop WCre WFar
- 'Sue Ritchie' (Au/d) SPop
- 'Suede Shoes' (Au/S) SPop
- 'Sugar Plum Fairy' (Au/S) EWoo GAbr NDro SPop WHil
- 'Sultan' (Au/A) WAln
- 'Summer Sky' (Au/A) NDro SPop WCre
- 'Summer Wine' (Au/A) EWoo MFie NDro SPop
- 'Sumo' (Au/A) EWoo GAbr GAgs MFie NDro SPop WBla WCre WFar WHil
- 'Sunflower' (Au/A/S) EWoo GAbr ITim MAsh MFie NDro SPop WCre
- 'Sunlight' (Au/A) **new** WAln
- 'Sunlit Tiger' (Au/S) EWoo
- 'Sunsplash' (Au) WBla WCre
- 'Sunspot' (Au/A) **new** EWoo WAln
- 'Sunstar' (Au/S) NDro
- 'Super Para' (Au/S) EWoo GAbr IPen MFie NDro SPop WBla WHil
- 'Superb' (Au/S) MFie WAln WBla
- 'Surething' (Au/A) **new** WAln
- 'Susan' (Au/A) MFie NDro WCre
- 'Susannah' (Au/d) EWoo GAbr GAgs GMaP IPen MFie NDro SPop WCre WFar WHil
- 'Sweet Georgia Brown' (Au/A) MFie SPop WAln
- 'Sweet Pastures' (Au/S) CPBP GAbr IPen MFie NDro SPop WCre
- 'Swiss Royal Velvet' (Au/B) NDro
- 'Sword' (Au/d) CPBP CWCL EWoo GAbr GAgs IPen ITim MAsh MFie NDro SPop WCre WFar WHil
- 'Symphony' (Au/A) EWoo ITim MFie NDro SPop WBla WCre WFar WHil
- 'T.A. Hadfield' (Au/A) EWoo GAgs MFie NDro SPop WBla WFar WHil
- 'Taffeta' (Au/S) EWoo GAbr LHop NDro SPop WCre WHil
- 'Tall Purple Dusty Miller' (Au/B) SPop
- 'Tally-ho' (Au/A) NDro WAln
- 'Tamar Gold' (Au/d) **new** WAln
- 'Tamar Mist' (Au) WAln
- 'Tamino' (Au/S) IPen NDro SPop WAln
- 'Tango' (Au/d) **new** WAln
- 'Tarantella' (Au/A) GAbr MFie NDro SPop
- 'Tawny Owl' (Au/B) GAbr NBro
- 'Tay Tiger' (Au/St) GAbr MAsh MFie SPop WHil
- 'Teawell Pride' (Au/d) EWoo SPop WHil
- 'Ted Gibbs' (Au/A) MFie NDro SPop WBla WCre WHil
- 'Ted Roberts' (Au/A) MFie NDro SPop WBla WCre WFar WHil
- 'Teem' (Au/S) GAbr IPen MAsh NDro SPop WCre
- 'Telesto' (Au/d) **new** SPop
- 'Telford's Surprise' (Au/A) **new** WAln
- 'Temeraire' (Au/A) MFie
- 'Tenby Grey' (Au/S) SPop WCre
- 'Tender Trap' (Au/A) WAln
- 'Terpo' (Au/A) MFie NDro WAln WBla
- 'The Argylls' (Au/St) SPop
- 'The Baron' (Au/S) EBee GAbr GAgs GKev IPen MFie NDro SPop WBla WCre WFar WHil
- 'The Bishop' (Au/S) GAbr IPen SPop WHil
- 'The Bride' (Au/S) MFie NDro SPop WCre
- 'The Cardinal' (Au/d) EWoo WAln
- 'The Czar' (Au/A) MFie NDro SPop
- 'The Egyptian' (Au/A) IPen MFie NDro SPop WBla WHil
- 'The Few' (Au/St) **new** SPop
- 'The Hobbit' (Au/A) WAln WBla
- 'The Lady Galadriel' (Au/A) NDro
- 'The Maverick' (Au/S) MFie SPop
- 'The President' (Au/d) **new** WAln
- 'The Raven' (Au/S) EBee GAbr GAgs GKev ITim MAsh MFie NDro SPop WBla WCre
- 'The Sneep' (Au/A) EWoo IPen MFie NDro SPop WBla WCre WFar
- 'The Snods' (Au/S) EWoo IPen MFie NDro SPop WBla
- 'The Wrekin' (Au/S) SPop
- 'Thetis' (Au/A) EWoo MFie SPop WCre WFar
- 'Thisbe' (Au/A) NDro
- 'Three Way Stripe' (St) EWoo GAbr GAgs WBla WCre WHil
- 'Thunderstorm' (Au) MAsh
- 'Thutmoses' (Au/A) NDro WAln
- 'Tiger Tim' (Au/St) EWoo WAln
- 'Tim' (Au) GAbr IPen SPop
- 'Tim's Fancy' (Au/S) NDro
- 'Tinkerbell' (Au/S) IPen MFie SPop WCre WFar
- 'Tiptoe' (Au/St) **new** SPop
- 'Titania' (Au) SPop
- 'Toddington Green' (Au/S) WAln
- 'Toffee Crisp' (Au/A) EWoo IPen NDro SPop WBla
- 'Tom Farmer' (Au) WBla WCre
- 'Tomboy' (Au/S) IPen MAsh NDro SPop WBla
- 'Toolyn' (Au/S) EWoo GAgs NDro WAln
- 'Top Style' (Au/d) **new** WAln
- 'Tosca' (Au/S) CWCL GAbr IPen MAsh NDro SPop WBla WCre WFar WHil
- 'Trafalgar Square' (Au/S) GAbr GAgs MFie NDro SPop WBla
- 'Trident' (Au/d) **new** WAln
- 'Trish' (Au) GAbr
- 'Trojan' (Au/S) EBee GKev WCre
- 'Trouble' (Au/d) EWoo GAbr GMaP IPen MAsh MFie NDro SPop WCre WHil
- 'Troy Aykman' (Au/A) MFie SPop WAln WBla
- 'Trudy' (Au/S) EWoo GAbr IPen ITim MAsh MFie NDro SPop WCre WHil
- 'True Briton' (Au/S) IPen MFie NDro SPop WBla WCre
- 'Trumpet Blue' (Au/S) MFie SPop WFar WHil

- 'Tudor Rose' (Au/S)	NDov NDro
- 'Tumbledown' (Au/A)	EWoo MFie SPop
- 'Tummel' (Au/A)	EWoo MFie NDro SPop WBla WHil
- 'Tupelo Honey' (Au/d) new	WAln
- 'Turnberry' (Au/S)	SPop
- 'Twiggy' (Au/S)	NDro SPop
- 'Typhoon' (Au/A)	EWoo IPen MFie SPop WCre WHil
- 'Uncle Arthur' (Au/A)	MFie WAln WHil
- 'Unforgettable' (Au/A)	MFie
- 'Upper Crust' (Au/St)	SPop WBla
- 'Upton Belle' (Au/S)	IPen MAsh MFie NDro SPop WAln WCre WFar
- 'Ursula' (Au/d) new	WAln
- 'Ushba' (Au/d)	SPop
- 'V2 Green' (Au/S)	WCre
- 'Valerie' (Au/A)	IPen MFie SPop WCre
- 'Valerie Clare' (Au)	MFie WAln WHil
- 'Vee Too' (Au/A)	GAbr MFie NDro SPop WBla WCre WFar WHil
- 'Vega' (Au/A)	SPop
- 'Velvet Moon' (Au/A)	MFie WAln WFar
- 'Venetian' (Au/A)	MFie NDro SPop WAln WBla WFar WHil
- 'Venus' (Au/A)	WAln
- 'Vera' (Au/A)	NDro SPop WAln
- 'Vera Eden' (Au)	WAln
- 'Vera Hill' (Au/A)	WAln
- 'Verdi' (Au/A)	SPop WAln
- 'Vesuvius' (Au/d)	IPen NDro SPop
- 'Victoria' (Au/S)	SPop WAln
- 'Victoria de Wemyss' (Au/A)	IPen MFie WBla WCre WHil
- 'Victoria Jane' (Au/A) new	WAln
- 'Victoria Park' (Au/A)	WAln
- 'Violet Surprise' (Au/St)	NDro
- 'Vulcan' (Au/A)	MAsh MFie NBro
- 'W. Muller' (Au)	NBro
- 'Walhampton' (Au/S)	SPop
- 'Walter Lomas' (Au/S)	WAln
- 'Walton' (Au/A)	CPBP GAbr MAsh MFie NDro SPop WCre WFar
- 'Walton Heath' (Au/d)	GAbr GAgs IPen MAsh MFie NDro SPop WBla WCre WFar
- 'Waltz Time' (Au/A)	MFie
- 'Wanda's Moonlight' (Au/d)	WAln
- 'Warpaint' (Au/St)	NDro
- 'Warwick' (Au/S)	MFie SPop
- 'Wayward' (Au/S)	WAln WCre
- 'Wedding Day' (Au/S)	EWoo ITim MFie NDro WBla
- 'Wentworth' (Au/A)	IPen WAln
- 'Werner Müller' (Au/B) new	NDro
- 'Whistlejacket' (Au/S)	MFie NDro SPop WBla
- 'White Ensign' (Au/S)	EWoo GAbr IPen NDro SPop WCre WFar WHil
- 'White Satin' (Au/S)	SPop WAln WCre
- 'White Water' (Au/A)	EWoo MFie NDro SPop WCre WHil
- 'White Wings' (Au/S)	EWoo GAgs IPen ITim MFie NDro SPop WCre
- 'Whitecap' (Au/S)	WAln
- 'Whoopee' (Au/A)	WAln
- 'Wichita Falls' (Au/A)	NDro WAln
- 'Wide Awake' (Au/A)	NDro SPop
- 'Wild and Grey' (Au/S)	NDro
- 'Wilf Booth' (Au/A)	MFie SPop WBla WFar
- 'William Gunn' (Au/d)	MFie SPop
- 'Willow Tree' (Au/S) new	WAln
- 'Wincha' (Au/S)	ITim MFie NDro NEgg SPop WBla WCre WFar
- 'Windways Mystery' (Au/B)	GAbr NDro
- 'Windways Pisces' (Au/d)	WAln
- 'Winifrid' (Au/A)	GAbr GAgs NDro SPop WCre WFar WHil
- 'Witchcraft' (Au)	SPop WCre
- 'Woodlands Lilac' (Au/B)	NDro
- 'Woodmill' (Au/A)	EWoo IPen MFie NDro SPop WBla WHil
- 'Wookey Hole' (Au/A)	MFie NDro SPop
- 'Wor Jackie' (Au/S)	SPop
- 'Wycliffe Harmony' (Au/B)	NDro
- 'Wycliffe Midnight' (Au/B)	EWoo GAbr NDro WAln
- 'Wye Hen' (Au/St)	SPop WAln
- 'Wye Lemon' (Au/S)	SPop
- 'X2' (Au)	WBla WHil
- 'Xavier' (Au) new	EBee
- 'Yellow Hammer' (Au/S)	WAln
- 'Yellow Isle' (Au/S)	WAln
- 'Yellow Muff' (Au/S) new	WAln
- 'Yitzhak Rabin' (Au/A)	WHil
- 'Yorkshire Grey' (Au/S)	GAbr IPen MFie NBro SPop
- 'Zambia' (Au/d)	GAbr MFie NDro WCre
- 'Zimmer' (Au/St)	SPop
- 'Zircon' (Au/S)	SPop WAln
- 'Zodiac' (Au/S)	WAln
- 'Zoe' (Au/A)	WAln
- 'Zoe Ann' (Au/S)	WAln
- 'Zorro' (Au/St)	WAln
auriculata (Or)	GKev
- subsp. ***olgae*** (Or)	EBee GKev
'Barbara Barker' (Au)	GEdr NMen
'Barbara Midwinter' (Pr)	CDes CJun EBee GAbr GEdr LLHF NHar SHar WAbe WCot
Barnhaven Blues Group (Pr/Prim) ♀H4	GAbr NCGa NSum WHil
Barnhaven doubles (Pr/Prim/d)	CWCL
Barnhaven Gold-laced Group	see *P.* Gold-laced Group Barnhaven
Barnhaven hybrids	NSum
'Beatrice Wooster' (Au)	GAbr GAgs GKev IPen MFie WFar
'Beeches' Pink'	GAbr NHar NSum
beesiana (Pf)	Widely available
(Belarina Series) 'Belarina Butter Yellow' (Pr/Prim/d)	CMea CPLG CWCL EPfP EWll GAbr LLHF MBNS MFie NDov NLar NPnk SMrm SRot
- 'Belarina Cobalt Blue' (Pr/Prim/d)	CMea CPLG CWCL EWll LLHF MBNS MFie NPnk SMrm SRot
- Belarina Cream = 'Kerbelcrem'PBR (Pr/Prim/d)	CPLG CWCL ELon EPot EWll LLHF MFie NPnk SMrm SRot WBor WCot WHil
- 'Belarina Pink Ice' (Pr/Prim/d)	CWCL ELon EWll LHop MBNS MFie NLar NPnk WBor
- 'Belarina Rosette Nectarine' (Pr/Prim/d)	CPLG CWCL ECtt ELon EPot EWll LHop MBNS MFie NLar NPnk SMrm WHil WPtf
bellidifolia (Mu)	GKev IPen NGdn
§ - subsp. ***hyacinthina*** (Mu)	WAbe
beluensis	see *P.* × *pubescens* 'Freedom'
§ × ***berninae*** 'Windrush' (Au)	WAbe
'Bewerley White'	see *P.* × *pubescens* 'Bewerley White'
bhutanica	see *P. whitei* 'Sherriff's Variety'
bileckii	see *P.* × *forsteri* 'Bileckii'
'Blue Julianas' (Pr)	NCGa NSum
'Blue Riband' (Pr/Prim)	CDes EBee LLHF WFar

'Blue Ribbon' IGor
'Blue Sapphire' (Pr/Prim/d) CDes GAbr GBin MFie NCGa NDov WHil
'Blutenkissen' (Pr/Prim) GAbr GEdr
'Bon Accord Cerise' (Pr/Poly/d) GAbr
'Bon Accord Purple' (Pr/Poly/d) WFar WRHF
boothii (Pe) NSum
- 'Alba' (Pe) LLHF NHar
- subsp. ***repens*** (Pe) CEnt MNrw
'Boothman's Ruby' see *P.* × *pubescens* 'Boothman's Variety'
boreiocalliantha new GKev
bracteata (Bu) GKev WAbe
§ ***bracteosa*** (Pe) GKev
Bressingham (Pf) WFar
brevicula (Cy) SDR 4452 GKev
- SDR 6844 GKev
'Broadwell Milkmaid' IPen WAbe
'Broadwell Oliver' (Au) IPen
'Broadwell Pink' (Au) IPen
'Broadwell Ruby' (Au) WAbe
'Broadwell Violet' IPen
'Broxbourne' MFie
'Buckland Wine' (Pr/Prim) CElw GAbr
× ***bulleesiana*** (Pf) CWCL EBee EPfP GBuc GKev LBMP LRHS MBri MCot MFie MSCN NBro NChi NEgg NGdn NHol NLar NRHS NSum SPet SWat WFar WMnd WMoo WPer WPnP WWEG XLum
- Moerheim hybrids (Pf) WFar
bulleyana (Pf) ♀H4 Widely available
- ACE 2484 SWat
burmanica (Pf) EBee GBuc GEdr GKev IPen MMuc SWat WFar WMoo
- SDR 5801 GKev
'Butter's Bronze' (Pr/Prim) GAbr
'Butterscotch' (Pr/Prim) NCGa NSum WHil
'Caerulea Plena' (Pr/Prim) NBid
calderiana subsp. ***calderiana*** (Pe) GKev
- subsp. ***strumosa*** (Pe) GKev
Candelabra hybrids (Pf) CBre CBro CHVG GAbr IPen ITim LSou NBir NGdn SMrm SPet SWat WFar WOut
Candelabra hybrids orange-flowered (Pf) SMrm
Candy Pinks Group (Pr/Prim) NCGa NSum WHil
capitata (Ca) CMac EBee ECho EPfP EWld GCal GKev IPen SPer WFar
- CC 3843 GKev
- subsp. ***mooreana*** (Ca) CCon CFis CHid CLAP CPLG CPrp CTsd CYeo EPfP GKev IPen LRHS NGdn NSum SMrm SPet SPlb SRot WAbe XLum
- 'Norverna Blue' (Ca) SGar
'Captain Blood' (Pr/Prim/d) EPfP GAbr IPot WFar
'Carmen' (Pr/Prim/d) EPfP
carniolica (Au) EPot GKev WCot
cernua (Mu) GKev IPen NSum
'Charlotte' (Pr/Prim) new IPen
§ ***chionantha*** (Cy) ♀H4 CLAP CWCL EPfP GBin GBuc GCra GKev MFie MMuc NBir NCGa NGdn NSum SBfd SPer WAbe WFar
- SDR 4426 GKev
- SDR 4610 SEND
- SDR 4847 GKev
- subsp. ***chionantha*** (Cy) GBuc GKev IPen
- cream-flowered MMuc
§ - subsp. ***sinoplantaginea*** (Cy) SDR 2747 GKev
- - SDR 4563 GKev
- - SDR 4773 GKev
§ - subsp. ***sinopurpurea*** (Cy) CLAP CWCL EBee EPfP GBin GBuc GKev IPen MMuc NBir NCGa NLar NSum WAbe WHil
- - SDR 4418 GKev
chungensis (Pf) CLAP CWCL EBee EPfP GBin GCra GEdr GKev IPen MFie MMuc NGdn NSum SBfd SWvt WAbe WMoo
§ ***chungensis*** × ***pulverulenta*** (Pf) CHid CLAP GEdr GKev NLar WMnd WWEG
× ***chunglenta*** see *P. chungensis* × *P. pulverulenta*
'Cisca' WCot
'Clarence Elliott' (Au) CDes CPBP IPen ITim MFie NHar NMen NWad WAbe WFar WThu
clarkei (Or) GEdr WAbe
clusiana 'Murray-Lyon' (Au) NMen
cockburniana (Pf) ♀H4 GEdr GKev GQui IPen LRHS NCGa NGdn SWat WAbe WFar
- SDR 1967 EBee
- SDR 5939 GKev
- 'Edrom Primrose' (Pf) GEdr
- hybrids (Pf) SWat
- 'Kevock Sunshine' (Pf) GKev IPen
concholoba (Mu) GKev
'Corporal Baxter' (Pr/Prim/d) EPfP LLHF SPer
cortusoides (Co) CLAP EBee EPfP GCra GKev IPen
Cowichan strain (Pr/Poly) CElw
Cowichan Amethyst Group (Pr/Poly) CDes CWCL EBee GAbr NCGa
Cowichan Blue Group (Pr/Poly) GAbr NCGa NSum
Cowichan Garnet Group (Pr/Poly) CDes CWCL EWoo GAbr NCGa NSum
Cowichan Red Group (Pr/Poly) WFar
Cowichan Venetian Group (Pr/Poly) CDes CWCL GAbr NCGa NSum WFar
Cowichan Yellow Group (Pr/Poly) CDes NCGa NSum
'Coy' (Au) WAbe
'Craven Gem' (Pr/Poly) GBuc
Crescendo Series (Pr/Poly) GAbr
- 'Crescendo Blue Shades' (Pr/Poly) ♀H4 new LSou SEND
- 'Crescendo Bright Red' (Pr/Poly) ♀H4 new LSou SEND
- 'Crescendo Golden' (Pr/Poly) ♀H4 new SEND
- 'Crescendo Lemon Yellow' (Pr/Poly) new LSou
- 'Crescendo Pink and Rose Shades' (Pr/Poly) ♀H4 new SEND
- 'Crescendo White' (Pr/Poly) new LSou
'Crimson Velvet' (Au) GAbr IPen WThu
crispa see *P. glomerata*
cuneifolia subsp. ***heterodonta*** (Cu) GEdr
- - white-flowered new GEdr
daonensis (Au) GAgs
darialica (Al) GKev LLHF
'Dark Rosaleen' (Pr/Poly) CPLG CWGN EBee ECtt EWTr GAbr GBuc GEdr IGor ITim LLHF

	Name	Suppliers
		MBNS MFie MNrw MPie NCGa NDov SSvw SUsu WCot
	'David Valentine' (Pr)	GAbr GBuc GEdr WAbe WCot
	'Dawn Ansell' (Pr/Prim/d)	CDes CRow CWCL ECtt EPfP GAbr GBuc IGor MBNS MFie MNrw MRav NBir NCGa NDov NLar NPnk SUsu WHer WHil
	Daybreak Group (Pr/Poly)	CWCL NCGa
	deflexa (Mu)	IPen WAbe
	denticulata (De) ♀[H4]	Widely available
	- CC 4629	GKev
	- var. ***alba*** (De)	CBcs CBen CTri EBee ECha ECho EPfP GAbr GBin GCra GMaP MBel MFie MWat NGdn NHol NLar NPri SMrm SPer SPoG WMoo WPer WWEG
	- blue-flowered (De)	CWCL ECho GAbr NLar NPri SMrm WFar
	- 'Bressingham Beauty' (De)	LRHS
	- 'Glenroy Crimson' (De)	CLAP EBee LLHF
	- 'Karryann' (De/v)	WCot WHil
	- lilac-flowered (De)	ECho EHon MWat NPri SMrm WWEG
	- purple-flowered (De)	ECho WMoo
	- red-flowered (De)	ECho MFie NBir WMoo
	- 'Robinson's Red' (De)	GBuc
	- 'Ronsdorf' (De)	ELon NLar
	- 'Rubin' (De)	CWCL CWat ECho EHon GAbr GBin GMaP MBrN MLHP NChi NLar SMrm SPer SPoG SRms WPer WWEG XLum
	- 'Rubinball' (De)	WCot
	'Desert Sunset' (Pr/Poly)	CWCL NCGa WHil
	dickieana (Am) **new**	GKev
	'Don Keefe'[PBR]	CMHG EBee ECtt GAbr GBin GEdr LLHF LSou MBNS MFie MNrw NGdn NLar NPnk SPoG SUsu WCot WWlt
	'Dorothy' (Pr/Poly)	MRav
	'Double Lilac'	see *P. vulgaris* 'Lilacina Plena'
	'Duchess of York' (Pr/Poly)	GAbr LLWP WCot
	'Duckyls Red' (Pr/Prim)	WHal
	'Dusky Lady'	CLAP MBri
	'Early Bird' (*allionii* hybrid) (Au)	IPen ITim MFie
	'Easter Bonnet' (Pr/Prim)	NBid
	edgeworthii	see *P. nana*
§	***elatior*** (Pr) ♀[H4]	CArn CMac CRWN CRow CSev EBee ECho GKev MHer MNHC MNrw NChi NEgg NLar NMen NPnk NPri SBch SBfd SPer SPoG SUsu SWvt WBrk WCot WFar
	- SDR 6327	GKev
	- hose-in-hose (Pr/d)	NBid
	- hybrids (Pr)	EPfP MWat SPlb
§	- subsp. ***meyeri*** (Pr)	GKev LLHF
	- subsp. ***pallasii*** (Pr)	GKev
	- subsp. ***pseudoelatior*** (Pr) **new**	WAbe
	'Elizabeth Browning'	GAbr WCot
	'Elizabeth Killelay'[PBR] (Pr/Poly/d)	CBct CCVN CPLG CWCL CWGN EBee ECtt ELan GBin GBuc GEdr GMaP LDai LSou MAvo MBel MFie MNrw NBir NEgg NGdn NLar NPnk NSti SPer SPoG SSvw SUsu WCot WFar
	'Ellen Page' (Au)	MFie
	'Ethel Barker' (Au)	IPen MFie NWad
	'Eugénie' (Pr/Prim/d)	ECtt LLHF MRav NCGa
§	***euprepes***	GKev
	'Fairy Rose' (Au)	IPen NWad
	farinosa (Al)	GKev IPen NGdn WFar
	fasciculata (Ar)	GKev
	- CLD 345	WAbe
	- SDR 3092	GKev
	'Favorit de Fred' **new**	WCot
	'Fire Opal'	LRHS
	Firefly Group (Pr/Poly)	NCGa WCot
§	***firmipes*** (Si)	EWes GKev IPen LPot
§	***flaccida*** (Mu)	GEdr GKev IPen NSum SBfd WAbe
	Flamingo Group (Pr/Poly)	NCGa WHil
	florida (Y)	GKev LLHF
	florindae (Si) ♀[H4]	Widely available
	- SDR 4626	GKev
	- bronze-flowered (Si)	GQui NBir
	- hybrids (Si)	CMac EHrv GAbr GEdr GMaP NCGa NSti SMrm
	- Keillour hybrids (Si)	CLAP NGdn NHol NLar
	- magenta-flowered (Si)	MDKP
	- 'Muadh' (Si)	MMuc SEND
	- orange-flowered (Si)	CSam GCal IPen MDKP MNrw WFar WMoo
	- peach-flowered (Si)	CSpe MDKP
	- 'Ray's Ruby' (Si)	CLAP GEdr MDKP MNrw NBir NGdn WCot
	- red-flowered (Si)	GBin GKev IPen MFie MMuc NBid NLar NSum WFar
	- terracotta-flowered (Si)	NGdn SUsu
	Footlight Parade Group (Pr/Prim)	NCGa
	forbesii (Mo) CC 4084	CPLG
	forrestii (Bu)	GKev IPen WAbe
	- SDR 4304	CPLG GKev
§	× ***forsteri*** 'Bileckii' (Au)	GMaP LLHF NBir
	- 'Dianne' (Au)	EDAr GAbr GKev LLHF NBro NRya WAbe
	'Francisca' (Pr/Poly)	Widely available
	frondosa (Al) ♀[H4]	ECho GCra GKev IPen MLHP NMen SBch WAbe
	Fuchsia Victorians Group (Pr/Poly)	CWCL
	'Garnet' (*allionii* hybrid) (Au)	MFie
	'Garryarde Crimson'	LLHF
	'Garryarde Guinevere'	see *P.* 'Guinevere'
	gemmifera (Ar)	GKev
	- SSSE 242	GKev
	- var. ***monantha*** (Ar)	GKev
	geraniifolia (Co)	CLAP GCra GEdr GKev
§	'Gigha' (Pr/Prim)	CDes CLAP CWCL EBee GCal
	'Gilded Ginger'	CWCL NCGa
	'Ginger Spice' (Au)	NDro
	glaucescens (Au)	EPot
§	***glomerata*** (Ca)	GKev IPen
	- CC 6748	GKev
	- SDR 3924	GKev
	'Glowing Embers' (Pf)	GKev LLHF NBir
	glutinosa All.	see *P. allionii*
	Gold-laced Group (Pr/Poly)	Widely available
§	- Barnhaven (Pr/Poly)	GAbr GBuc NBir
	- Beeches strain (Pr/Poly) ♀[H4]	CWCL
	- red-flowered (Pr/Poly)	LBMP XEll
	gracilipes (Pe)	CLAP LLHF WAbe
	- GOS 146	GEdr
	- L&S 1166	CLAP
	- early-flowering (Pe)	GCra WAbe
	- late-flowering (Pe)	CLAP GCra

Mark	Plant	Suppliers
	– 'Major'	see *P. bracteosa*
	– 'Minor'	see *P. petiolaris* Wall.
	graminifolia	see *P. chionantha*
	Grand Canyon Group (Pr/Poly)	CWCL NCGa
	grandis (Sr)	GKev IPen
	'Groenekan's Glorie' (Pr/Prim)	GAbr GBuc GEdr NBir NSum WFar
§	'Guinevere' (Pr/Poly) ♀H4	CPLG CSam CSpe EBee ECtt EHoe EWTr GAbr GBuc GEdr GMaP IGor LSou MBri MFie MNrw NBid NBir NBro NDov NSla NSum SPlb SPoG WAbe WCot WFar WHil
	'Hall Barn Blue' (Pr/Prim)	CSam GAbr GEdr GMaP MFie NHar NMyG WCot WHil
§	***halleri*** (Al)	GKev IPen WAbe
	– 'Longiflora'	see *P. halleri*
	handeliana	GKev
	HEHEHE 077 **new**	
	aff. ***handeliana***	GKev
	Harbinger Group (Pr/Prim)	CWCL WHil
	Harbour Lights mixture (Pr/Poly)	CWCL GAbr NCGa
	Harlow Carr hybrids (Pf)	EPfP GQui NCGa NRHS NSla WHil WMoo
	Harvest Yellows Group (Pr/Poly)	CWCL NCGa WCot
	'Hazel's White'	GAbr GKev
	'Helmswell Abbey' (Au)	GAgs GKev
	helodoxa	see *P. prolifera*
	'Hemswell Blush' (Au)	CSpe GKev ITim LLHF NLar WCre
	'Hemswell Ember' (Au)	CPBP ECtt GAgs NRya NWad
	heucherifolia (Co)	IPen
	– SDR 3224	GKev
	hidakana (R)	GEdr
	'High Point' (Au)	NMen WAbe
	hirsuta (Au)	GAgs GKev IPen SEND WAbe
	– 'Lismore Snow' (Au)	NHar NWad
	– red-flowered (Au)	EBee GAgs GKev MMuc
	– subsp. ***valcuvianensis*** (Au)	EPot
	hoffmanniana **new**	GEdr
	hose-in-hose (Pr/Poly/d)	MNrw
	'Hyacinthia' (Au)	GAgs IPen MFie NLar
	hyacinthina	see *P. bellidifolia* subsp. *hyacinthina*
	ianthina	see *P. prolifera*
	'Ilana' **new**	IPen
	incana (Al)	GKev
	Indian Reds Group (Pr/Poly)	CWCL WHil
	'Ingram's Blue' (Pr/Poly)	CDes EBee GAbr MBel WCot
	Inshriach hybrids (Pf)	CMHG LRHS WFar
	integrifolia (Au)	GEdr
§	'Inverewe' (Pf) ♀H4	CRow GBin GBuc GCra GKev GQui NBir NBre SUsu
	involucrata	see *P. munroi*
	ioessa (Si)	EWes GCra GQui NGdn
	– hybrids (Si)	WAbe
	'Iris Mainwaring' (Pr/Prim)	ECtt GAbr GCra GEdr LLHF MCot
	'Jackie Richards' (Au)	MFie NWad
	Jack-in-the-Green Group (Pr/Poly)	CLAP CWCL MNrw NSla WBor WFar WMoo
	– white-flowered (Pr/Poly)	IFro
	– red-flowered (Pr/Poly)	WHil
	japonica (Pf)	CMHG CSam ECha GQui IPen LPBA LRHS MSCN NBro NGdn SPer SWat WAbe WFar WMoo

Mark	Plant	Suppliers
	– 'Alba' (Pf)	CPrp CTri EBee EHrv EPfP GBuc GCal GEdr IPen MFie NGdn NWad SPer WAbe WFar WHil WWEG
	– 'Apple Blossom' (Pf)	Widely available
*	– 'Carminea' (Pf)	CHid EBee GEdr GKev IPen MFie MSCN NBro NGdn NLar NWad WFar WHil WPnP
	– 'Fuji' (Pf)	NBro
	– 'Fuji' hybrids (Pf)	NLar
	– hybrids (Pf)	CMac GCra MRav
	– 'Jim Saunders' (Pf)	SLon
	– 'Merve's Red' (Pf)	EBee
	– 'Miller's Crimson' (Pf) ♀H4	Widely available
	– 'Oriental Sunrise' (Pf)	CCVN CMil EHrv GBuc GKev LLHF
	– pale pink-flowered (Pf)	ITim NSum
	– 'Peninsula Pink' (Pf)	IPen
	– 'Pink Pagoda' (Pf)	EBee GKev ITim
	– 'Pinkie' (Pf)	IPen
	– 'Postford White' (Pf) ♀H4	Widely available
	– Redfield strain (Pf)	IPen
	– red-flowered (Pf)	IPen WAbe
	– 'Splendens' (Pf)	IFro IPen
	– 'Valley Red' (Pf)	IPen ITim LRHS MFie
	jesoana (Co)	LLHF
	– B&SWJ 618	WCru
	– var. ***pubescens*** (Co)	EBee
	'Joan Hughes' (*allionii* hybrid) (Au)	WAbe
	'Joanna'	ECou GBuc
	'Johanna' (Pu)	GAbr GEdr GKev LLHF NGdn NHar NPnk NSum WAbe
	'John Fielding' (Sr × Pr)	CBro CElw EBee GAbr GEdr MCot WCot
	'Jo-Jo' (Au)	MFie WAbe
	juliae (Pr)	ECho EDAr GEdr LRHS NBid NHar NPnk NRHS NSum SPlb WAbe
I	– 'Millicent' (Pr)	WCot
	– white-flowered (Pr)	NSum
	'Juliana's Fireflies' (Pr/Poly)	CWCL
	'Ken Dearman' (Pr/Prim/d)	ECtt EPfP MRav NBir SPer
	kialensis (Y)	WAbe
	'Kinlough Beauty' (Pr/Poly)	ECtt GAbr GBuc GEdr GMaP LLHF LRHS NPnk
§	***kisoana*** (Co)	CLAP CPLG GKev IPen LLHF LRHS WCru
	– var. ***alba*** (Co)	CLAP
	– var. ***shikokiana***	see *P. kisoana*
	– 'Velvet' (Co)	CLAP GEdr
	'Kusum Krishna'	GEdr NHar NMen WCot
	'Lady Greer' (Pr/Poly) ♀H4	CMac CSam EBee EDAr EPfP GAbr GBuc GEdr GKev GMaP IGor LHop LLWP MCot MHer NChi NGdn NHar NLar NSum SUsu WHer
	'Lambrook Mauve' (Pr/Poly)	GAbr
§	***latifolia*** (Au)	GKev
	latisecta (Co)	GEdr IPen WCot
§	***laurentiana*** (Al)	GKev NMen WAbe
	'Lea Gardens' (*allionii* hybrid) (Au)	IPen MFie NWad
	'Lee Myers' (*allionii* hybrid) (Au)	IPen MFie
	'Lemon and Lime' **new**	CMea
	leucophylla	see *P. elatior*
	'Lilac Domino' (Au)	IPen WCre
	lilacina	GKev IPen
	– SDR 3088	GKev
	'Lilian Harvey' (Pr/Prim/d)	SPer
	limbata	GKev

'Lindum Buttermilk' **new**	IPen
'Lindum Crepes Suzette' **new**	IPen MFie
'Lindum First Kiss' **new**	IPen
'Lindum Frosty Moon' **new**	IPen
'Lindum Lace' **new**	IPen
'Lindum Malcolm's Mate'	CPBP
'Lindum Moonlight'	IPen MFie
'Lindum Serenade' (Au)	IPen
'Lindum Smoke' **new**	IPen
'Lindum Wedgwood' (Au)	IPen
'Lingwood Beauty' (Pr/Prim)	CFis CSam GAbr WAbe
'Lismore' (Au)	GAgs
'Lismore 79/7'	NWad
'Lismore Bay' (Au)	GKev
'Lismore Jewel' (Au)	NMen
'Lismore Sunshine'	NHar WThu
'Lismore Treasure' (Au)	NMen
'Lismore Yellow' (Au)	CPBP NHar WAbe
Lissadel hybrids (Pf)	NCGa
'Little Egypt' (Pr/Poly)	CWCL GAbr NCGa
littoniana	see *P. vialii*
× ***loiseleurii*** 'Aire Mist' (Au)	GKev IPen NHar NMen NRya NSum NWad WAbe WThu
§ - 'Aire Waves' (Au)	CWCL ITim NHar NMen NWad
- 'White Waves' (Au)	IPen
longiflora	see *P. halleri*
luteola (Or)	ECho GKev LLHF NGdn NSum WFar WPer
macrocalyx	see *P. veris*
'MacWatt's Claret' (Pr/Poly)	GAbr GBuc LLWP
'MacWatt's Cream' (Pr/Poly)	CFis EBee GAbr GCra GEdr LLHF LRHS SSvw WCot WHil
magellanica (Al)	WAbe
'Maisie Michael'	LLHF WAbe
marginata (Au) ♀H4	CPne ECho EWoo IPen LHop LRHS MFie MMuc NRHS NSla NSum SBch SEND WAbe WFar
- from the Dolomites (Au)	NWad
- 'Adrian Evans' (Au)	ITim SBch
- 'Adrian Jones' (Au)	ITim
- 'Alba' (Au)	MFie NBro NRHS NRya NWad WFar WThu
- 'Ardfearn' (Au)	GAgs
- 'Baldock's Purple' (Au)	IPen
- 'Barbara Clough' (Au)	GEdr IPen MFie NWad WFar
- 'Beamish' (Au) ♀H4	NBro NRya NSla NWad
- 'Beatrice Lascaris' (Au)	MFie NRya WThu
- 'Caerulea' (Au)	MFie NWad
- 'Clear's Variety' (Au)	GKev IPen ITim
- dark (Au)	EPot
- 'Doctor Jenkins' (Au)	IPen NLar NRya NWad
- 'Drake's Form' (Au)	GKev IPen NLar NRya
- dwarf (Au)	ECho GEdr LRHS MFie
- 'Earl L. Bolton'	see *P. marginata* 'El Bolton'
§ - 'El Bolton' (Au)	IPen NWad WAbe
- 'Elizabeth Fry' (Au)	IPen MFie
- 'F.W. Millard' (Au)	CWCL
- 'Grandiflora' (Au)	IPen NWad
- 'Highland Twilight' (Au)	IPen NSla WAbe
- 'Holden Variety' (Au)	GKev IPen ITim MFie NRya NWad WAbe
- 'Holly Leaf' (Au) **new**	GEdr
- 'Ivy Agee' (Au)	IPen NRya
- 'Janet' (Au)	GEdr WCre
- 'Jenkins Variety' (Au)	ECho
- 'Kesselring's Variety' (Au)	ECho GEdr IPen MFie NWad WAbe WFar WTin
- 'Laciniata' (Au)	ECho IPen LRHS NRHS
- 'Lemon Sorbet' (Au) **new**	IPen
- lilac-flowered (Au)	IPen
- 'Linda Pope' (Au) ♀H4	GAgs GKev IPen NBir NHar NSla NSum WAbe
- maritime form (Au)	IPen
- 'Millard's Variety' (Au)	IPen ITim NWad
- 'Miss Fell' (Au)	IPen
- 'Mrs Carter Walmsley' (Au)	NRya
- 'Nancy Lucy' (Au)	WAbe
- 'Napoleon' (Au)	GEdr IPen MFie MSCN
- 'Prichard's Variety' (Au) ♀H4	ECho GEdr IPen ITim MFie MSCN NRya WAbe WFar
- 'Rosea' (Au)	IPen
- 'Sheila Denby' (Au)	IPen
- 'The President' (Au)	GAgs
- violet-flowered (Au)	ECho
- 'Waithman's Variety' (Au)	IPen NRya
- wild-collected (Au)	MFie NWad
'Maria Talbot' (*allionii* hybrid) (Au)	IPen
'Marianne Davey' (Pr/Prim/d)	WKif
'Marie Crousse' (Pr/Prim/d)	CWCL EPfP WHal
Marine Blues Group (Pr/Poly)	CWCL NCGa NSum
'Maris Tabbard' (Au)	IPen MFie NLar WAbe
'Mark Viette' **new**	EBee
'Mars' (*allionii* hybrid) (Au)	IPen MFie NRya NWad
'Marven' (Au)	GEdr IPen
'Mary Anne'	GAbr
maximowiczii (Cy)	EWTr GBuc IPen LLHF MMHG NGdn NSum SPad WHil
- Red-flowered Group **new**	GBuc GEdr GKev IPen
megaseifolia (Pr)	EBee GBuc GKev IPen
× ***meridiana*** (Au)	NWad
§ - 'Miniera' (Au)	IPen MFie WAbe
'Mexico'	LLHF
Midnight Group	CWCL NCGa
'Mike Smith' **new**	IPen
'Miniera'	see *P. × meridiana* 'Miniera'
minima (Au)	NBro NLar WAbe
- SDR 5517	GKev
- var. ***alba*** (Au)	NLar NRya
minor (Cy)	GKev
'Miss Indigo' (Pr/Prim/d)	ECtt EPfP EWll GMaP MBNS MFie MRav NLar SGar WFar WHil
mistassinica (Al)	WAbe
- var. ***macropoda***	see *P. laurentiana*
miyabeana (Pf)	GKev IPen
modesta var. ***faurieae*** (Al)	IPen
- - f. ***leucantha*** (Al)	GKev
monticola **new**	GKev
'Moorland Apricot'	WMoo
moupinensis	CLAP CPLG GEdr LLHF
- subsp. ***barkamensis*** **new**	GKev
* 'Mrs Eagland'	GAbr
'Mrs Frank Neave' (Pr/Prim)	GEdr IPen
'Mrs Marjorie Banks' (Pr) **new**	GKev
'Mrs McGillivray' (Pr/Prim)	GAbr
§ ***munroi*** (Ar)	CDes GEdr GKev IPen NHar WAbe
- CC 5311	GKev
- white-flowered (Al)	WAbe
§ - subsp. ***yargongensis*** (Al)	GKev IPen
- - SDR 3096	GKev
- - SDR 6121	GKev
muscarioides (Mu)	GKev IPen WAbe

	Muted Victorians Group (Pr/Poly)	NCGa NSum WHil
§	***nana*** (Pe)	IPen
	'Netta Dennis' (Pe)	LLHF NHar
	neurocalyx new	GKev
	New Pinks Group (Pr/Poly)	CWCL NCGa NSum
	nipponica (Su)	GEdr
	nivalis ambig.	NSum
	nivalis Pallas	see *P. chionantha*
	'No Eye Cow'	WPGP
	nutans Delavay ex Franch.	see *P. flaccida*
	obconica (Ob) SDR 6706	GKev
	'Oberau' new	IPen
	obtusifolia (Cy)	GKev
	'Old Port' (Pr/Poly)	CElw CSam GKev LLWP NMen NSum SBch
	Old Rose Victorians Group (Pr/Poly)	NSum
	orbicularis (Cy)	GEdr GKev LLHF
	'Oriental Sunset'	GAbr MDKP
	Osiered Amber Group (Pr/Prim)	NSum
*	'Page'	IPen MFie
	palinuri (Au)	IPen
	palmata (Co)	EBee GEdr GKev
	'Paris '90' (Pr/Poly)	CWCL NCGa NSum WHil
	parryi (Pa)	EPfP GKev SBfd
	- NNS 04-423	WCot
	pedemontana 'Alba' (Au)	LLHF MFie WThu
	'Perle von Bottrop' (Pr/Prim)	GAbr GEdr WCot
	'Peter Klein' (Or)	GBuc GKev LLHF WAbe WTin
	petiolaris misapplied	see *P.* 'Redpoll'
§	***petiolaris*** Wall. (Pe)	GCra GEdr GKev NHar NSum
	- Sherriff's form	see *P.* 'Redpoll'
	'Petticoat'	EPfP SPer
	'Pink Aire' (Au)	MFie NMen NRya
	'Pink Fairy' (Au)	IPen
	'Pink Ice' (*allionii* hybrid) (Au)	CPBP GKev MFie NRya NWad
	poissonii (Pf)	CBen CTri EBee ELan EPfP GAbr GBin GCra GEdr GKev GQui IBal IPen LPBA LRHS NGdn NSum SBfd WAbe WAul WShi
	- ACE 2030	EPot
	- SDR 5126	GKev
	- SDR 5959	GKev
	polyanthus (Pr/Poly)	WFar
	polyneura (Co)	GKev IPen MSnd NGdn WHil
	- SDR 4728	GKev
	'Port Wine' (Pr)	GAbr GCra
	'Powdery Pink'	LRHS
	prenantha (Pf)	GKev WAbe
	- SDR 3909	GKev
	Primlet Series (Pr/Prim) new	SPoG
§	***prolifera*** (Pf) ♀H4	CMHG CWCL EBee EPfP GBuc GCra GEdr GKev GQui IPen LHop LPBA LRHS NCGa NGdn SPer SWat WAbe WMoo
§	× ***pubescens*** (Au) ♀H4	GEdr IPen MHer NDro NGdn WPer
	- 'Apple Blossom' (Au)	GAgs IPen MFie
§	- 'Bewerley White' (Au)	EBee ECho EPfP GAgs IPen NDro WCre WFar
	- 'Blue Wave' (Au)	IPen MFie SPop
§	- 'Boothman's Variety' (Au)	CTri ECho EPfP EWoo GKev ITim MFie NSla WFar WHoo WTin
	- 'Carmen'	see *P.* × *pubescens* 'Boothman's Variety'
	- 'Chamois' (Au)	MFie
	- 'Christine' (Au)	CDes CMea EBee GAgs GKev IPen NBir NSum WCot
	- 'Cream Viscosa' (Au)	EWoo
	- 'Deep Mrs Wilson' (Au)	MFie
	- 'Faldonside' (Au)	IPen MFie NPnk NSum WCre WThu
§	- 'Freedom' (Au)	CTri ECho EWoo GAgs GKev IPen MFie NBir NLar NSla
	- 'George Harrison' (Au)	MFie
	- 'Harlow Car' (Au)	CMea GQui IPen MFie NSum WFar WTin
	- 'Hazel's White' (Au)	GAgs
	- 'Joan Danger' (Au)	IPen
	- 'Joan Gibbs' (Au)	IPen ITim MFie WCre
	- 'Kath Dryden' (Au)	ITim
	- 'Lilac Fairy' (Au)	IPen ITim NPnk NWad WThu
	- 'Moonlight' (Au) new	NDro
	- 'Mrs J.H. Wilson' (Au)	GEdr MFie NRya
	- 'Pat Barwick' (Au)	IPen MFie NDro NRya WTin
	- 'Peggy Fell' (Au)	WHil
	- 'Rufus' (Au)	EWes GAbr GAgs NDro WThu
	- 'Sid Skelton' (Au)	IPen
	- 'Snowcap' (Au)	IPen ITim
	- 'Sonya' (Au)	IPen
	- 'The General' (Au)	CTri IPen MFie
§	- 'Wedgwood' (Au)	GAbr IPen MFie WHil
	- 'Winnifred' (Au)	NDro
	- yellow-flowered (Au)	IPen
	pulverulenta (Pf) ♀H4	Widely available
	- 'Bartley'	WHil
	- Bartley hybrids (Pf) ♀H4	ITim LRHS LSou NSum
	- 'Bartley Pink' (Pf)	GBuc
	purdomii	GKev
	'Quaker's Bonnet'	see *P. vulgaris* 'Lilacina Plena'
	'Rachel Kinnen' (Au)	GAbr IPen MFie WFar
	'Ramona' (Pr/Poly)	CWCL NCGa
	'Ravenglass Vermilion'	see *P.* 'Inverewe'
	'Red Ruffles' (Pr/Poly/d)	EWll GAbr WHil
§	'Redpoll' (Pe)	CLAP GBuc LLHF NHar
	reidii (So)	GEdr GKev
	- var. ***williamsii*** (So)	IPen
	reticulata (Si)	GKev
	'Reverie' (Pr/Poly)	CWCL NCGa
	'Rheniana' (Au)	IPen MFie NLar NRya
	'Rick Lupp' new	IPen
	'Romeo' (Pr/Prim)	CLAP LLHF WCot
	rosea (Or) ♀H4	CElw CWCL EBee ECho EPfP GEdr GKev IPen MAsh MFie MMuc NBid NBir NRya
	- CC 5260	GKev
	- 'Delight'	see *P. rosea* 'Micia Visser-de Geer'
	- 'Gigas' (Or)	GAbr LRHS NRya WBor WFar
	- 'Grandiflora' (Or)	CMac CPrp ECho EPfP GKev LHop LPBA LRHS NCGa SBfd SPoG SRms SWal SWat WFar WHil WPer XLum
§	- 'Micia Visser-de Geer' (Or)	WTin
	'Rosemary Cottage' new	GAbr
§	***rotundifolia*** (Cf) CC 6537	GKev
	'Rowallane Rose' (Pf)	IPen
I	'Rowena'	GAbr GCra LLHF WCot
	roxburghii	see *P. rotundifolia*
	'Roy Cope' (Pr/Prim/d)	EPfP NBir
	rubra	see *P. firmipes*
	rusbyi (Pa)	GKev
	- subsp. ***ellisiae*** (Pa)	IPen
	'Saracen'	IPen MFie
	saxatilis ambig. (Co)	MFie
	scandinavica (Al)	GKev
§	'Schneekissen' (Pr/Prim)	CSam CWCL EBee GAbr GBuc GCra GEdr LLHF LRHS MHer NBro NChi NPro WHil
	scotica (Al)	GKev GPoy NRHS NSla WAbe

	secundiflora (Pf)	CLAP CWCL EBee ELan GBuc GCra GKev LPBA NBir NSum SBfd SBrt SPer SPlb SWat WAbe WFar WHoo WMoo
	- SDR 4401	GKev
	- SDR 4435	GKev
§	× ***sendtneri*** (Au)	MFie
	serratifolia (Pf) SDR 5165	GKev
	'Shizuko Hara'	IPen
	sibthorpii	see *P. vulgaris* subsp. *sibthorpii*
	sieboldii (Co) ♀H4	CEnt GKev IPen MCot MLHP MNrw NMen NSla SBch SRms SUsu WAbe WFar
	- 'Aimayama' (Co)	NHar
	- 'Akinoysool' (Co)	WFar
	- 'Ankoan' (Co)	WFar
	- 'Asahi' (Co)	WFar
	- 'Asahigata' (Co)	NHar
	- 'Ayanami' (Co)	WFar
	- 'Bide-a-Wee Blue' (Co)	NBid
	- 'Bijyonomai' (Co)	WFar
I	- 'Blue Lagoon' (Co)	EBee LLHF NLar
	- 'Blue Shades' (Co)	IPen NMen
	- blue-flowered (Co)	CLAP CWCL NMen
	- 'Blush' (Co)	CLAP WWEG
	- 'Boykavitch' (Co)	NHar
	- 'Bureikou' (Co)	NHar WFar
	- 'Carefree' (Co)	CLAP IPen LLHF NBro NLar NMen
	- 'Cherubim' (Co)	CLAP EBee GCra LLHF
	- 'Daiminnisiki' (Co)	NHar
	- 'Dancing Ladies' (Co)	CLAP IPen NBro NHar WFar
	- 'Dart Rapids' (Co)	CDes
	- 'Duane's Choice' (Co)	CDes CLAP EBee MNrw NHar SBch
	- 'Edasango' (Co)	WFar
	- 'Edomurasaki' (Co)	WFar
	- 'Frilly Blue' (Co)	EBee
	- 'Galaxy' (Co)	NBro
	- 'Geisha Girl' (Co)	CCon CLAP CSpe EBee MRav NLar WAbe WFar WWEG
	- 'Ginhukurin' (Co)	NHar WFar
	- 'Godaisyo' (Co)	WFar
	- 'Hantack Botanic Garden' (Co)	NHar
	- 'Hatagarasi' (Co)	WFar
	- 'Hatusugato' (Co)	NHar
	- 'Higurasi' (Co)	NHar WFar
	- 'Hinokoromo' (Co)	WFar
	- 'Hujikosi' (Co)	WFar
	- 'Hukiageakura' (Co)	NHar
	- 'Hutaezuru' (Co)	WFar
	- 'Inikina White' (Co)	WFar
	- 'Inokima Minoura' (Co)	WFar
	- 'Izuto' (Co)	WFar
	- 'Jyuuyuunoutage' (Co)	NHar WFar
	- 'Kaedegari' (Co)	WFar
	- 'Kansenden' (Co)	WFar
	- 'Karagoromo' (Co)	WFar
	- 'Koba-no-fue' (Co)	NHar
	- 'Kokoroiki' (Co)	WFar
	- 'Kosijimoyuki' (Co)	WFar
	- 'Kotonosirabe' (Co)	WFar
	- 'Kourohou' (Co)	WFar
	- 'Kurama' (Co)	WFar
	- 'Lacewing' (Co)	SBch
	- f. ***lactiflora*** (Co)	CLAP IPen NBro NMen SMHy SRot WFar WTin
	- 'Lilac Sunbonnet' (Co)	CLAP EPfP LLHF NHar WFar
	- 'Lisujyanome' (Co)	WFar
	- 'Maiougi' (Co)	WFar
	- 'Makazebeni' (Co)	WFar
	- 'Managuruma' (Co)	WFar
	- 'Manakoora' (Co)	CLAP EBee EHrv IPen NBro NSum WFar
	- 'Mangetu' (Co)	WFar
	- 'Masasino' (Co)	WFar
	- 'Matso-no-yuki' (Co)	NHar
	- 'Matunoyuki' (Co)	WFar
	- 'Mihonokoji' (Co)	WFar
	- 'Mikado' (Co)	CLAP EBee IPen WFar WWEG
	- 'Mikininonomare' (Co)	WFar
	- 'Mitanohikari' (Co)	WFar
	- 'Miyakowakare' (Co)	WFar
	- 'Miyuki' (Co)	WFar
	- 'Momotidori' (Co)	NHar
	- 'Musasi' (Co)	WFar
	- 'Myoutiriki' (Co)	WFar
	- 'Nankinkozakura' (Co)	NHar
	- 'Noboruko' (Co)	NHar
	- 'Nuretubame' (Co)	NHar
	- 'Okinanotomo' (Co)	NHar
	- 'Okinatomo' (Co)	WFar
	- 'Oshibori' (Co)	NHar
	- 'Pago-Pago' (Co)	CDes CLAP EBee EHrv IPen MNrw NBro WFar
	- 'Pink Laced' (Co)	WFar
	- pink-flowered (Co)	CWCL NBir
	- 'Rasyoumon' (Co)	WFar
	- 'Rock Candy' (Co)	NHar WFar
	- 'Saiun' (Co)	NHar
	- 'Sakuragana' (Co)	WFar
	- 'Sasanari' (Co)	WFar
	- 'Sekidaiko' (Co)	NHar
	- 'Senyuu' (Co)	WFar
	- 'Seraphim' (Co)	CLAP EBee MMHG NLar SBch WWEG
	- 'Seto-no-ume' (Co)	NHar
	- 'Shiokemuri' (Co)	NHar
	- 'Shirousagi' (Co)	NHar WFar
	- 'Sikoubai' (Co)	WFar
	- 'Sinipukurn' (Co)	WFar
	- 'Sinnkirou' (Co)	WFar
	- 'Sinseiu' (Co)	WFar
	- 'Siritonbo' (Co)	WFar
	- 'Sitikenjin' (Co)	WFar
	- 'Snowdrop' (Co)	LHop LSou NCGa NMyG WCot WMoo
	- 'Snowflake' (Co)	CDes CLAP EBee NLar NMen NSla SBch WAbe WFar
	- 'Sotodorihime' (Co)	WFar
	- 'Sousiarai' (Co)	NHar WFar
	- 'Sumidanohatu' (Co)	WFar
	- 'Sumisonegawa' (Co)	WFar
	- 'Sumizomegenji' (Co)	NHar
	- 'Sweetie' (Co)	WFar
	- 'Syunkou' (Co)	WFar
	- 'Syutyuka' (Co)	WFar
	- 'Tagonoura' (Co)	NHar WFar
	- 'Tah-ni' (Co)	NBro NSum
	- 'Taoyami' (Co)	NHar
	- 'Tatutanoy' (Co)	WFar
	- 'Tidoriasobi' (Co)	WFar
	- 'Tokinohina' (Co)	WFar
	- 'Toyonoharu' (Co)	NHar WFar
	- 'Tukinomiyaka' (Co)	WFar
	- 'Turunokegoromo' (Co)	NHar
	- 'Winter Dreams' (Co)	CLAP CWCL EHrv NBid NBro NHar NSum WFar
	- 'Yukiguruma' (Co)	WFar

- 'Yuuhibeni' (Co) NHar
sikkimensis (Si) ♀H4 CEnt EBee ECho GEdr GKev IPen LRHS MSnd NGdn NSum SBfd SPoG WFar
- CC 5730 GKev
- CC 5986 GKev
- CC 6397 GKev
- CC&McK 1022 GQui
- from Bhutan LEdu
- var. ***pseudosikkimensis*** (Si) GKev IPen
- - SDR 4528 GKev
- var. ***pudibunda*** (Si) GEdr GKev
- - SDR 3099 GKev
- - SDR 4919 GKev
- 'Ruby Shades' (Si) GEdr
- 'Tilman Number 2' (Si) GBuc
aff. ***sikkimensis*** (Si) IPen NCGa NGdn
'Silver Lace Charlotte' **new** WIce
Silver-laced Group (Pr/Poly) EPfP LBMP NLar SPoG SWvt WFar WIce
- black-flowered (Pr/Poly) **new** XEll
'Silverwells' (Pf) GEdr
simensis (Sp) GKev
sinoplantaginea see *P. chionantha* subsp. *sinoplantaginea*
sinopurpurea see *P. chionantha* subsp. *sinopurpurea*
'Siobhan' WCot
'Sir Bedivere' (Pr/Prim) CDes GAbr GBuc GKev NHar WCot
smithiana see *P. prolifera*
'Snow Carpet' see *P.* 'Schneekissen'
'Snow White' (Pr/Poly) GEdr MRav
Snowcushion see *P.* 'Schneekissen'
'Snowruffles' ITim
sonchifolia (Pe) CCon CLAP GKev
- subsp. ***emeiensis*** **new** GKev
- subsp. ***sonchifolia*** **new** GKev
sorachiana see *P. yuparensis*
'Sorbet' CWCL
'Sparkling Eyes' WCot
spectabilis (Au) GEdr GKev
Spice Shades Group (Pr/Poly) NCGa
'Stonewash' LRHS
'Stradbrook Charm' (Au) CPBP CWCL EPot MFie WFar WThu
'Stradbrook Dainty' (Au) MFie NWad WFar
'Stradbrook Dream' (Au) ITim MFie WFar
'Stradbrook Lilac Lustre' (Au) MFie
'Stradbrook Lucy' (Au) IPen ITim NWad WFar
'Stradbrook Mauve Magic' (Au) MFie
stricta (Al) GKev
Striped Victorians Group (Pr/Poly) NCGa NSum WHil
'Strong Beer' (d) **new** EBee LSou
'Sue Jervis' (Pr/Prim/d) CWCL EPfP MRav NBir NLar SPer WHal
suffrutescens (Su) WAbe
'Sunshine Susie' (Pr/Prim/d) EPfP GMaP SPer WHil
szechuanica (Cy) GKev IPen
takedana (Bu) LLHF
'Tango' (Pr/Prim) NCGa
tangutica (Cy) IPen
tanneri (Pe) GKev
'Tantallon' (Pe) CLAP LLHF NHar
Tartan Reds Group (Pr/Prim) CWCL
'Tawny Port' (Pr/Poly) CLAP NBro
'Theodora' (Pr) **new** GAbr
'Tie Dye' (Pr/Prim) LLHF MNrw NGBo NLar WCot
'Tinney's Moonlight' (Pe) NHar
'Tipperary Purple' (Pr/Prim) GAbr GEdr
'Tomato Red' (Pr/Prim) CDes EBee GAbr LLHF WCot
'Tony' (Au) CPBP IPen MFie WAbe
'Top Affair' (Au/d) IPen
'Torchlight' (Pr/Prim/d) IGor
'Tortoiseshell' (Pr/d) **new** GEdr
tschuktschorum (Cy) GKev
* ***urumiensis*** GKev
'Val Horncastle' (Pr/Prim/d) ECtt EPfP GAbr GMaP MFie NLar SPer WCot
Valentine Victorians Group (Pr/Poly) NCGa
× ***venusta*** GKev
'Vera Maud' (Pr) NCGa NSum
§ ***veris*** (Pr) ♀H4 Widely available
- subsp. ***columnae*** (Pr) EBee
I - 'Coronation Cowslips' (Pr) GBuc
- hybrids (Pr) LBMP MBel NHol SGar
- 'Katy McSparron' (Pr/d) CMea CPLG ECtt GAbr GCra LSou MFie MNrw SPer SPoG SUsu WBor WCot
- subsp. ***macrocalyx*** (Pr) GKev MHoo WCot
- orange-flowered (Pr) MHer WMoo
- red-flowered (Pr) NBid NGdn SWal WMoo
- 'Sunset Shades' (Pr) CSpe ECGP GBuc LBMP MHoo NGdn NLar SBch WFar XEll
vernalis see *P. vulgaris*
verticillata (Sp) IPen
§ ***vialii*** (So) ♀H4 Widely available
'Vicky' **new** IPen
Violet Victorians Group (Pr/Poly) NCGa
viscosa see *P. latifolia*
§ ***vulgaris*** (Pr/Prim) ♀H4 Widely available
- var. ***alba*** (Pr/Prim) CRow NSla WBrk
- - 'Alba Plena' (Pr/Prim/d) CRow GAbr GCal MBri NSum
- green-flowered see *P. vulgaris* 'Viridis'
- hybrids (Pr/Prim) **new** EPot
§ - 'Lilacina Plena' (Pr/Prim/d) CDes CWCL EBee EPfP GCal IFro IGor LLHF MRav NCGa NDov NSum WFar
§ - subsp. ***sibthorpii*** (Pr/Prim) ♀H4 CMHG CSam EBee ECho ELon EPfP GBuc GEdr IPen ITim LLWP LRHS MCot MFie MHer MLHP MNrw MRav NBro NChi NDov NMyG SKHP SRms WHil
- - pale-flowered (Pr/Prim) **new** GBuc
- 'Taigetos' (Pr/Prim) CBro CPLG
§ - 'Viridis' (Pr/Prim/d) CCon EOHP MNrw
waltonii (Si) CCVN CLAP CWCL EBee EDAr EPfP GBin GEdr GKev IPen MDKP MNrw NCGa NSum SBfd SPoG WHil
- hybrids (Si) ELon MCot
Wanda Group (Pr/Prim) ECho LBMP SVic
- 'Wanda' (Pr/Prim) ♀H4 CBcs CPne CTri ECho GAbr GCra LBMP LLWP MBel MCot MFie MHer MMuc NBid NDov NPnk SEND SRms WBrk WCFE WCot WFar WHil WTin
- 'Wanda Grace' NPnk

	- 'Wanda Hose-in-hose' (Pr/Prim/d)	GCra LLWP MMHG NBir SSvw WHer WHil
	- 'Wanda Jack-in-the-Green' (Pr/Prim)	CLAP WCot WFar
	wardii	see *P. munroi*
	warshenewskiana (Or)	CLAP ECtt EWes GBuc GEdr GKev NHar NMen NRya WAbe
	watsonii (Mu)	EWes GKev NHar SWat
	- ACE 1402	IPen
	- SDR 1626	GKev
	- SDR 1673	GKev
	'Wedgwood'	see *P.* × *pubescens* 'Wedgwood'
	'Welsh Blue'	CSpe
	'Wharfedale Bluebell' (Au)	IPen NBir WAbe WThu
	'Wharfedale Buttercup' (Au)	IPen NHar NWad
	'Wharfedale Butterfly' (Au)	NWad
	'Wharfedale Crusader' (Au)	IPen
	'Wharfedale Gem' (*allionii* hybrid) (Au)	MFie NWad
	'Wharfedale Ling' (*allionii* hybrid) (Au)	CPBP GKev MFie NLar NWad
	'Wharfedale Sunshine' (Au)	GKev IPen NWad
	'Wharfedale Village' (Au)	IPen WAbe WThu
	'White Linda Pope' (Au)	GAgs NMen NWad
	'White Wanda' (Pr/Prim)	GAbr
	'White Waves' (*allionii* hybrid) (Au)	ITim
§	***whitei*** 'Sherriff's Variety' (Pe)	CLAP
	'William Genders' (Pr/Poly)	GAbr GEdr LLHF
	wilsonii (Pf)	CTri CTsd CWCL LDai MCot NGdn SWat
§	- var. ***anisodora*** (Pf)	CLAP EWld GKev GQui IPen MFie NGdn
	- var. ***wilsonii*** (Pf) new	GKev
	'Windrush'	see *P.* × *berninae* 'Windrush'
	'Winter White'	see *P.* 'Gigha'
	'Wisley Crimson'	see *P.* 'Wisley Red'
§	'Wisley Red' (Pr/Prim)	CElw LRHS
	wollastonii (So) CC 6210	GKev
	- CC 6551	GKev
	'Woodland Walk' (Pr/Prim) new	EPfP
	woodwardii new	GKev
	wulfeniana (Au)	EPot GEdr GKev
	yargongensis	see *P. munroi* subsp. *yargongensis*
	yunnanensis (Y)	NLar
§	***yuparensis*** (Al)	GBuc GKev IPen WHil
	- white-flowered (Al)	GKev
	zambalensis (Ar)	GKev IPen
	- SDR 1716	GKev
	'Zenobia'	WCre

Prinsepia (*Rosaceae*)

sinensis	CArn CBcs MBlu NLar SLon WSHC
utilis	CTrC

Pritchardia (*Arecaceae*)

affinis	XBlo
pacifica	XBlo

Pritzelago (*Brassicaceae*)

alpina	GEdr NRHS NSla

Prostanthera (*Lamiaceae*)

	'Alpine Gold' new	MAsh
	aspalathoides	CCCN CTsd EWes MOWG
	'Badja Peak'	CTrC CTsd EBee EWes LRHS MAsh MOWG SLim
	baxteri	CTrC ECou MOWG
	- 'Silver Ghost' new	SLim
	cuneata ♀H4	Widely available
	- 'Alpine Gold'	CMHG CWSG LRHS
	- Kew form	WPGP
*	***digitiformis***	CTsd ECou
	incisa	CTsd SGar
	- 'Rosea'	EOHP
	'La Provence' PBR	LRHS
	lasianthos	CBcs CCCN CDoC CEnt CHVG CHll CTsd EWes LRHS MOWG SHDw SLim SPlb WCFE WJek
	- 'Kallista Pink'	CTsd MOWG
	- var. ***subcoriacea***	CPLG
	latifolia	CTsd
	melissifolia	CArn CTsd ECre
§	- var. ***parvifolia***	CCCN EBee
	'Mint Delight'	SLim
	'Mint Royale'	EBee LBuc LRHS SLim
	'Mint-Ice'	SLim
	nivea	ECou
	ovalifolia ♀H2	CCCN EBee ECou IRar MOWG WJek
I	- 'Variegata' (v)	CBcs CCCN CHGN CMac CPLG CTrC CTsd ECou LRHS MOWG SEND SPoG WCFE WGrn WWFP
	phylicifolia	CAbb
	'Poorinda Ballerina'	CDoC CTsd EBee ECou EOHP LRHS MAsh MGos SLim SPer SPoG SRkn WWFP
	'Poorinda Petite'	CCCN CDoC CTsd EBee LRHS
	rotundifolia ♀H2	CAbb CCCN CHEx CSev CSpe CTri CTsd CWSG EBee ECho EOHP ESwi MHoo MNHC MOWG MSCN SBod SPer WCFE WGrn
	- 'Chelsea Girl'	see *P. rotundifolia* 'Rosea'
§	- 'Rosea' ♀H2	CCCN CDoC CTrC CTsd EBee ECou EPfP LHop LRHS MOWG SEND WGrn
	scutellarioides 'Lavender Lady'	ECou
	sericea	LRHS
	sieberi misapplied	see *P. melissifolia* var. *parvifolia*
	sieberi Benth.	CTrC CTsd MOWG
	walteri	CCCN LRHS MOWG

Protea (*Proteaceae*)

aurea	SPlb
burchellii	SPlb
coronata	SPlb
cynaroides	CBcs CCCN CHEx CTrC EAmu LTen SBig SPlb
effusa	SPlb
eximia	CBcs CCCN EAmu SPlb
grandiceps	CCCN SPlb
lacticolor	SPlb
laurifolia	SPlb
nana	SPlb
neriifolia	CCCN SPlb
obtusifolia	SPlb
'Pink Ice'	CTrC
repens	SPlb
scolymocephala	SPlb
subvestita	CTrC SPlb
susannae	SPlb
venusta	CTrC

Prumnopitys (*Podocarpaceae*)

§	***andina***	CBcs CDoC IArd IDee LRHS SLim

elegans	see *P. andina*
§ ***ferruginea***	IGor
§ ***taxifolia***	CDoC CTrC ECou

Prunella (*Lamiaceae*)

§ ***grandiflora***	CHby CPrp ECha SBfd SPer SWat WFar WWEG
- 'Alba'	CBre EBee ECha EPfP GMaP LRHS MSCN NLar SPer WFar
- 'Blue Loveliness'	GBee SWvt
- 'Carminea'	EBee SPer
- light blue-flowered	NLar WFar WOut
- 'Loveliness' ♀H4	CDoC CMac EBee ECha GMaP MBel MRav NBro NGdn NSti SPer SPlb SRGP WCAu WFar
- 'Pagoda'	CEnt CSpe NLar
- 'Pink Loveliness'	CPrp EBee SRms
- 'Rosea'	EBee
- 'Rubra'	GAbr NLar WPer
- violet-flowered	EPfP LRHS
- 'White Loveliness'	CMac CPrp WWEG
hyssopifolia	XSen
incisa	see *P. vulgaris*
Summer Daze = 'Binsumdaz'[PBR]	EBee LSou NSti SPoG
§ ***vulgaris***	CArn CHab CRWN ENfk GPoy MHer MHoo MNHC NLan NMir WHer WHfH WJek WMoo
- f. ***leucantha***	WHer
- 'Rose Pearl'	LRHS
× ***webbiana***	see *P. grandiflora*
- 'Gruss aus Isernhagen'	EBee

Prunus ✿ (*Rosaceae*)

'Accolade' ♀H4	Widely available
§ 'Amanogawa' ♀H4	Widely available
americana	EUJe
amygdalus	see *P. dulcis*
armeniaca 'Alfred' (F)	CDul GTwe SFam SKee WHar
- 'Bredase' (F)	CWib
- 'De Nancy'	see *P. armeniaca* 'Gros Pêche'
- 'Early Moorpark' (F)	CAgr CWib EPfP GTwe LAst MBri SEND SLon WHar
- Flavorcot = 'Bayoto'[PBR] (F)	CAgr CMam CSut EPfP EPom MCoo SKee SPer
- 'Garden Aprigold' (F)	SPoG
- 'Goldcot' (F)	CAgr CTho LRHS MBri MCoo SKee WHar
- 'Golden Glow' (F)	CAgr CTho EPom LRHS MBri MCoo MWat SKee WHar
- 'Goldrich' (F)	CAgr
§ - 'Gros Pêche' (F)	SVic
- 'Hargrand' (F)	CAgr SVic
- 'Harogem' (F)	CAgr
- 'Hemskirke' (F)	SKee
- 'Isabella' (F)	CAgr
- 'Moorpark' (F) ♀H3	CHab CSBt CTri CWib GTwe LAst MGos MRav SBfd SKee SPer
- 'New Large Early' (F)	SEND SKee
- 'Tomcot' (F)	CAgr CDul CTho CTri EPom LBuc LRHS LSRN MBri MCoo SFam SKee SLim SPoG WHar
- 'Tross Orange' (F)	CWib LBuc
avium ♀H4	Widely available
- 'Amber Heart' (F)	SKee
- 'Archduke' (F) **new**	SKee
- 'Bigarreau Gaucher' (F)	SKee WHar
§ - 'Bigarreau Napoléon' (F)	GTwe LSRN SCrf SKee SVic
- 'Birchenhayes'	see *P. avium* 'Early Birchenhayes'
- 'Black Eagle' (F)	SKee
- 'Black Elton' (F)	SKee
- 'Black Heart' (F)	CWib MMuc SEND
- 'Black Tartarian' (F)	SKee
- 'Bottlers'	see *P. avium* 'Preserving'
- 'Bradbourne Black' (F)	SCrf SKee WHar
- 'Bullion' (F)	CTho
- 'Burcombe' (F)	CTho
- Celeste = 'Sumpaca'[PBR] (D)	CAgr CMac CTri EMil GTwe LRHS MBri MCoo NLar SFam SKee SLim SPoG WHar
- 'Cherokee'	see *P. avium* 'Lapins'
- 'Colney' (F) ♀H4	CDul GTwe IArd NLar SFam SKee WJas
- 'Coroon' (F) **new**	SKee
- 'Dun' (F)	CTho
§ - 'Early Birchenhayes' (F)	CTho
- 'Early Rivers' (F)	CSBt CWib GTwe IArd LAst LSRN NLar SKee SVic WHar
- 'Elton Heart' (F)	SKee
- 'Emperor Francis' (F)	SKee
- 'Fastigiata'	WHar
- 'Fice' (F)	CTho
- 'Florence' (F)	SKee
- 'Governor Wood' (F)	GTwe SKee
- 'Grandiflora'	see *P. avium* 'Plena'
- 'Greenstem Black' (F)	CTho
- 'Hannaford' (D/C)	CTho
- 'Hertford' (F) ♀H4	SFam SKee WHar
- 'Inga' (F)	SFam SKee
- 'Ironsides' (F)	SKee
- 'Kentish Red' (F)	SKee
- 'Kordia' (D)	EPom GTwe SFam SKee WHar
§ - 'Lapins' (F)	CAgr CDul CTho CTri ECrN EPfP EPom GTwe LAst MBri MRav NLar SFam SKee SPoG WHar WJas
- 'May Duke'	see *P.* × *gondouinii* 'May Duke'
- 'Merchant' (F) ♀H4	SKee
- 'Mermat' (F)	SKee
- 'Merpet' (F)	SKee
- 'Merton Bigarreau' (F)	WHar
- 'Merton Crane' (F)	SKee
- 'Merton Favourite' (F)	SKee
- 'Merton Glory' (F)	CAgr CDul CSBt EPfP GTwe IArd MGos SCrf SEND SFam SKee SLim WHar
- 'Merton Late' (F)	SKee
- 'Merton Marvel' (F)	SKee
- 'Merton Premier' (F)	EWTr SKee SVic
- 'Nabella' (F)	IArd WJas
- 'Napoléon'	see *P. avium* 'Bigarreau Napoléon'
- 'Noble' (F)	SKee
- 'Noir de Guben' (F)	IArd SKee WHar
- 'Noir de Meched' (D)	SKee
- 'Old Black Heart' (F)	SKee
- 'Penny'[PBR] (F)	CAgr EPom SKee WHar
§ - 'Plena' (d) ♀H4	Widely available
§ - 'Preserving' (F)	CTho
- 'Regina' (F)	CSut NLar SFam
- 'Ronald's Heart' (F)	SKee
- 'Roundel Heart' (F)	SKee WHar
- 'Small Black' (F)	CTho
- 'Stella' (F) ♀H4	Widely available
- 'Stella Compact' (F)	CWib EWTr LAst LSRN WHar
- 'Summer Sun' (D) ♀H4	CAgr CSut CTho CTri EPfP EPom GTwe LBuc LRHS MBri MCoo NLar SBfd SCoo SFam SKee SLim SPoG WHar
- 'Summit' (F)	SKee

	Name	Suppliers
	- 'Sunburst' (D)	CAgr CCVT CDul CMac CMam CTho CTri CWib ECrN GTwe IArd LBuc LRHS LSRN MBri SBfd SCoo SEWo SFam SKee SLim SPer SPoG SVic SWvt WHar WJas
	- 'Sweetheart' (F)	CAgr CDul EPom GTwe LRHS LSRN MBri SKee SLim SPoG WHar
	- 'Sylvia' (F)	CAgr SFam
	- 'Turkish Black' (F)	SKee
	- 'Van' (F)	CSBt GTwe IArd SFam SKee WHar
	- 'Vega' (F)	CAgr GTwe IArd SKee WHar WJas
	- 'Waterloo' (F)	SKee
	- 'White Heart' (F)	CWib ECrN SKee
	'Beni-yutaka'	CCVT LAst MAsh MBri MRav SCoo SLim SPoG
	besseyi	CAgr
	'Blaze'	see *P. cerasifera* 'Nigra'
	× ***blireana*** (d) ♀H4	CDul CLnd CTri EPfP LAst MAsh MBri MGos MRav MSwo MWat NLar NWea SBfd SCoo SPer SPoG WFar WHar
	'Blushing Bride'	see *P.* 'Shōgetsu'
	campanulata 'Felix Jury'	LRHS
	'Candy Floss'	see *P.* 'Matsumae-beni-murasaki'
	cerasifera	CDul CHab CRWN CTri ECrN EPfP GAbr LBuc NWea SPer SVic
	- 'Cherry Plum' (F)	CTri ECrN MMuc SKee
	- 'Crimson Dwarf'	MBri SCoo SWvt
	- 'First' (F)	CAgr
	- 'Golden Sphere' (F)	CAgr CTho CTri EPom LRHS SLim WHar
	- 'Gypsy' (F)	CAgr CTho LRHS SLim WHar
	- 'Hessei' (v)	MAsh MBri MRav NLar SBfd
	- 'Kentish Red' (F)	SEND
§	- Myrobalan Group (F)	ECrN MRav SVic
	- - 'Magda Jensen' (C)	CAgr
§	- 'Nigra' ♀H4	Widely available
	- 'Pendula'	ECrN SWvt WFar
§	- 'Pissardii'	CDul CWib ECrN EPfP LMaj LSRN MMuc NWea SCoo SFam SLim SLon SWvt WFar WJas WMou
	- 'Rosea'	NLar
	- 'Ruby'	CAgr EPom MBri
	- 'Spring Glow'	CCVT CDul EBee EPfP MSwo SBfd SCoo SLim SLon
	cerasus 'Maynard'	LSRN
	- 'Montmorency' (F)	SKee
	- 'Morello' (C) ♀H4	Widely available
	- 'Nabella' (F)	SKee
	- 'Rhexii' (d)	CDul ECrN MAsh MBri NEgg NPCo
	'Cheal's Weeping'	see *P.* 'Kiku-shidare-zakura'
	Chocolate Ice	see *P.* 'Matsumae-fuki'
§	× ***cistena*** ♀H4	CDul CSBt EBee ELan EPfP LAst LRHS MAsh MBri MGos MSwo NRHS SBfd SCoo SGol SHil SPoG SWvt
	- 'Crimson Dwarf'	see *P.* × *cistena*
	'Collingwood Ingram'	EBee LRHS MBlu MBri MGos MWat SLim SPoG
	conradinae	see *P. hirtipes*
	'Daikoku'	EBee
	davidiana	SPlb
	domestica 'Angelina Burdett' (D)	GTwe SKee
	- 'Anna Späth' (C/D)	SKee
	- 'Ariel' (C/D)	SKee
	- 'Autumn Compote' (C)	SKee
	- 'Avalon' (D)	CAgr CCAT CCVT GTwe IArd LBuc SFam SKee WHar
	- 'Beauty' (D)	CSut
	- 'Belgian Purple' (C)	SKee
	- 'Belle de Louvain' (C)	CTho CTri GTwe SKee WHar
	- 'Blaisdon Red' (C)	CTho GTwe WHar
	- 'Blue Rock' (C/D) ♀H4	SKee
	- 'Blue Tit' (C/D) ♀H4	CAgr CTho EPom GTwe SEND SKee WHar
	- 'Bonne de Bry' (D)	SKee
	- 'Brandy Gage' (C/D)	SKee
	- 'Bryanston Gage' (D)	CTho SKee
	- 'Burbank's Giant'	see *P. domestica* 'Giant Prune'
	- 'Cambridge Gage' (D) ♀H4	CAgr CCVT CDoC CDul CMac CMam CTri CWib ECrN EPfP EPom EWTr GTwe IArd LAst LRHS MBri MMuc MWat SBfd SCoo SEND SEWo SFam SKee SLim SPer SPoG WHar WJas
	- 'Chrislin' (F)	CAgr CTho
	- 'Coe's Golden Drop' (D)	CCAT ECrN GTwe IArd LAst MBri MGos MRav SFam SKee SPer WHar
	- 'Count Althann's Gage' (D)	GTwe NEgg SFam SKee
	- 'Cox's Emperor' (C)	SKee
	- 'Crimson Drop' (D)	SKee
	- 'Cropper'	see *P. domestica* 'Laxton's Cropper'
	- 'Curlew' (C)	SKee
	- 'Czar' (C) ♀H4	Widely available
	- 'Denbigh Plum' (D)	WGwG
	- 'Denniston's Superb'	see *P. domestica* 'Imperial Gage'
	- 'Des Bejonnieres' (D)	SKee
	- 'Diamond' (C)	SKee
	- 'Dittisham Black' (C)	CAgr CTho
	- 'Dittisham Ploughman' (C)	CTho SKee
	- 'Dunster Plum' (F)	CAgr CTho CTri CWib
	- 'Early Green Gage' (D)	NEgg
	- 'Early Laxton' (C/D) ♀H4	GTwe LAst SEND SFam SKee
	- 'Early Prolific'	see *P. domestica* 'Early Rivers'
§	- 'Early Rivers' (C)	CAgr CCAT CDul CSBt CTho CTri GTwe LRHS LSRN NWea SCoo SFam SKee WHar
	- 'Early Transparent Gage' (C/D)	CCAT CMac CSBt CTho CTri GTwe IArd LAst LBuc LRHS MBri MCoo SCoo SFam SKee WHar
	- 'Edda' (D)	WHar
	- 'Edwards' (C/D) ♀H4	CTri CWib EMil GTwe NEgg SKee
	- 'Excalibur' (D)	CAgr GTwe IArd LBuc SFam SKee WHar
§	- German Prune Group (C)	MCoo SKee
§	- 'Giant Prune' (C)	CDul GTwe MMuc SEND SFam SKee
	- 'Golden Transparent' (D)	GTwe LAst MCoo SFam SKee
	- 'Goldfinch' (D)	GTwe MCoo SKee
	- 'Gordon Castle'	NLar SKee WHar
	- Green Gage Group	see *P. domestica* Reine-Claude Group
	- 'Grey Plum' (F)	CAgr CTho
	- 'Guinevere' (F)	CAgr LRHS MBri MCoo WHar
	- 'Guthrie's Late Green' (D)	SKee
	- 'Haganta'PBR (F)	CAgr
	- 'Herman' (C/D)	CAgr GTwe LAst LRHS MBri MCoo SFam SKee SPoG WHar
	- 'Heron' (F)	GTwe SKee WHar
	- 'Impérial Epineuse' (D)	SKee
§	- 'Imperial Gage' (C/D) ♀H4	CAgr CCAT CSBt CTho CTri EMil EPom EWTr GTwe NLar SEND SFam SKee WHar
	- 'Italian Prune' (F)	MCoo
	- 'Jefferson' (D) ♀H4	CAgr ECrN GTwe IArd NLar SFam SKee SVic WHar

	Name	Suppliers
*	– 'Jubilaeum' (D)	CAgr CSut EPom GTwe LRHS SCoo SEWo SFam SKee
	– 'Kea' (C)	CAgr CTho SKee
	– 'Kirke's' (D)	CCAT CTho GTwe SFam SKee WHar
	– 'Landkey Yellow' (F)	CAgr CTho
	– 'Langley Gage' (F)	CAgr
	– 'Late Muscatelle' (D)	SKee
	– 'Late Transparent Gage' (D)	SKee
	– 'Lawson's Golden' (D) **new**	SKee
§	– 'Laxton's Cropper' (C)	CTri GTwe LAst SKee WHar
	– 'Laxton's Delight' (D) $\mathbb{Y}^{H4}$	GTwe
	– 'Laxton's Gage' (D)	SKee
	– 'Laxton's Jubilee' (C/D) **new**	CSBt
	– 'Mallard' (D) $\mathbb{Y}^{H4}$	SKee WHar
	– 'Manaccan' (C)	CAgr CTho
	– 'Marjorie's Seedling' (C) $\mathbb{Y}^{H4}$	Widely available
	– 'McLaughlin' (D)	SKee
	– 'Merton Gage' (D)	SKee
	– 'Merton Gem' (C/D)	SKee
	– 'Monarch' (C)	SKee
	– 'Monsieur Jaune' (C/D)	SKee
	– Old English gage	CMac ECrN EPom SBfd
	– 'Olympia' (C/D)	SKee
	– 'Ontario' (C/D)	SKee
	– 'Opal' (D) $\mathbb{Y}^{H4}$	CAgr CCAT CCVT CDoC CDul CMac CWSG CWib EPom GTwe LBuc LRHS MBri MGos MMuc MWat NLar NWea SCoo SCrf SEND SFam SKee SLim SPoG WHar
	– 'Orleans' (C)	SKee
	– 'Oullins Gage' (C/D) $\mathbb{Y}^{H4}$	CAgr CCAT CCVT CDoC CDul CMac CSBt CTri CWib EPfP GTwe IArd LAst LBuc LRHS MBri MMuc MRav NPri SBfd SEND SEWo SFam SKee SPer SVic SWvt WHar WJas
	– 'Pershore' (C) $\mathbb{Y}^{H4}$	CAgr CWib GTwe LRHS MBri NEgg SFam SKee WHar
	– 'Pond's Seedling' (C)	CSBt SKee
	– 'President' (C/D)	SEND SKee
	– 'Purple Pershore' (C)	CAgr CTri CWib GTwe IArd NEgg SFam SKee WHar
	– 'Quetsche d'Alsace'	see *P. domestica* German Prune Group
	– 'Reeves' (C) $\mathbb{Y}^{H4}$	GTwe IArd SFam SKee WHar
	– 'Reine-Claude Dorée'	see *P. domestica* Reine-Claude Group
§	– Reine-Claude Group (C/D)	CSBt GTwe SFam SKee SLim SPer
	– – 'Old Green Gage'	see *P. domestica* (Reine-Claude Group) 'Reine-Claude Vraie'
	– – 'Reine-Claude de Bavais' (D)	CCAT CTho CTri GTwe SFam SKee WHar
	– – 'Reine-Claude de Vars' (D)	SVic
	– – 'Reine-Claude Violette' (D)	SKee
§	– – 'Reine-Claude Vraie' (C/D)	CAgr CCVT CDul CMac CSBt CWib EPfP LBuc LRHS LSRN NPri SPoG WJas
§	– – 'Willingham Gage' (C/D)	GTwe LAst LRHS SKee WHar
	– 'Royale de Vilvoorde' (D)	SKee
	– 'Sanctus Hubertus' (D) $\mathbb{Y}^{H4}$	CTri GTwe IArd SKee WHar
	– 'Seneca' (D)	EPom WHar
	– 'Severn Cross' (D)	GTwe SKee
	– 'Stanley' (C/D)	SVic
	– 'Stella'	CCVT LAst LSRN NEgg NPri SLim WHar
	– 'Stella's Star'	LBuc LRHS MCoo
	– 'Swan' (C)	GTwe IArd SKee WHar
	– 'Syston White'	MGos
	– 'Thames Cross' (D)	CSut SKee
	– 'Transparent Gage' (D)	SKee
	– 'Utility' (D)	SKee
	– 'Valor' (C/D) $\mathbb{Y}^{H4}$	WHar
	– 'Verity' (C/D)	SKee
	– 'Victoria' (C/D) $\mathbb{Y}^{H4}$	Widely available
	– 'Violetta'^{PBR} (C/D)	CAgr GTwe SFam WHar
	– 'Wangenheimer Frühzwetsche' (F)	SKee
	– 'Warwickshire Drooper' (C)	CAgr CTho CWib GTwe IArd NEgg NLar SBfd SFam SKee SLon WHar
	– 'Washington' (D)	SKee
	– 'Willingham'	see *P. domestica* (Reine-Claude Group) 'Willingham Gage'
	– 'Zimmers Frühzwetsche' (F)	SKee
§	***dulcis***	CDul CHab CLnd CTri CWib ECrN EPfP EPom LAst LRHS MGos MREP MWat NWea SBfd SCoo SCrf SEND SFam SWvt
	– 'Ai' (F)	CAgr
	– 'Ardechoise' (F)	CAgr
	– 'Ferraduel' (F)	CAgr
	– 'Ferragnes' (F)	CAgr
	– 'Lauranne' (F)	CAgr
	– 'Mandaline' (F)	CAgr
*	– 'Phoebe' (F)	CAgr
	– 'Supernova' (F)	CCCN
	– 'Tuono' (F)	CCCN
	Easter Bonnet = 'Comet'^{PBR}	CTri EPfP LRHS MWat
	Fragrant Cloud	see *P.* 'Shizuka'
	'Fugenzō'	CDoy CSBt EBee
	glandulosa 'Alba Plena' (d)	CMac CSBt LBMP MAsh SGol SPlb SPoG SRms SWvt WCFE
	– 'Rosea Plena'	see *P. glandulosa* 'Sinensis'
§	– 'Sinensis' (d)	CPLG CSBt SPoG SRms
§	× ***gondouinii*** 'May Duke' (F)	SKee SVic WHar
	'Hally Jolivette'	ELan GKin MAsh SPoG
	'Hillieri Spire'	see *P.* 'Spire'
	'Hilling's Weeping'	SLon
§	***hirtipes***	CLnd
	'Hokusai'	CDul EPfP LRHS SGol
	Hollywood	see *P.* 'Trailblazer'
	'Horinji'	EBee MBri SCoo
	'Ichiyo' (d) $\mathbb{Y}^{H4}$	CDul CLnd ECrN EPfP LAst MBri SCoo SCrf
	incisa	CTri NEgg NWea
	– 'Ariane'	LMaj
	– 'Beniomi'	MRav
	– 'February Pink'	CJun SGol
	– 'Fujima'	EBee LAst SBfd
	– 'Kojo-no-mai'	Widely available
	– 'Mikinori'	CMac CSBt EPfP LBMP MAsh MBlu NLar SCoo WFar
	– 'Oshidori' (d)	CMac CSBt ELon EPfP LRHS MBri MRav NEgg NLar SLim SRms
	– 'Pendula'	SCoo
	– 'Praecox' $\mathbb{Y}^{H4}$	CHGN CSBt CTho EPfP LRHS MWat SCoo
§	– f. ***yamadae***	CJun LBMP NLar
	insititia (F)	CRWN

	– 'Blue Violet Damson' (F)	CAgr GTwe MCoo WHar
§	– 'Bradley's King Damson' (C)	MCoo SKee WHar
	– bullace (C)	LEdu NWea
	– 'Countess' (C)	CTri
	– 'Dittisham Damson' (C)	CTho
	– 'Farleigh Damson' (C) ♀H4	CAgr CWib GTwe IArd LAst LBuc MMuc NWea SBfd SFam SKee SPer SVic WHar WJas
	– 'Golden Bullace'	see *P. insititia* 'White Bullace'
	– 'King of Damsons'	see *P. insititia* 'Bradley's King Damson'
	– 'Langley Bullace' (C)	CAgr GTwe NLar SKee WHar
	– 'Lisna' (C)	CTri
	– 'Merryweather Damson' (C)	Widely available
	– 'Mirabelle de Nancy' (C)	CAgr CDul CTho GTwe LAst LMaj SFam SKee SLim WHar
	– 'Mirabelle Ruby' (F)	LRHS
§	– 'Prune Damson' (C) ♀H4	CAgr CDoC CDul CTho CTri EPom GTwe IArd LBuc LRHS MBri MMuc MWat NLar SBfd SEND SFam SKee SPer WHar WJas
	– 'Shepherd's Bullace' (C)	CAgr CTho SKee
	– 'Shropshire Damson'	see *P. insititia* 'Prune Damson'
	– 'Small Bullace' (C)	CAgr SKee
§	– 'White Bullace' (C)	CAgr
	– 'Yellow Apricot' (C)	SKee
§	***jamasakura***	CDul
	'Jō-nioi'	CDul CLnd CTho MBri
§	'Kanzan' ♀H4	Widely available
§	'Kiku-shidare-zakura' ♀H4	Widely available
	Korean hill cherry	see *P. verecunda*
	'Kuboko-zakura' **new**	EBee
	'Kulilensis Ruby'	LSRN SLPl
	'Kursar' ♀H4	CDul CLnd CSBt CTho CTri EPfP GKin LRHS LSRN MAsh MBri NLar NWea SBfd SCoo SCrf SLim SLon SPer SPoG SWvt WMou
	laurocerasus ♀H4	CBcs CCVT CDul CMac CWSG EBee ECrN ELan EPfP EShb GKin LAst MGos MMuc MRav NPri NWea SCob SEND SGol SPer SPoG SReu WFar WMoo WMou WWau
	– 'Aureovariegata'	see *P. laurocerasus* 'Taff's Golden Gleam'
	– 'Camelliifolia'	CMac CTri MBlu WCFE WWau
N	– 'Castlewellan' (v)	CDoC CDul CTri EPfP LAst LHop LRHS MGos MRav MSwo NLar NPro NWad SBfd SDix SLim SPer SPoG SSta WFar WGrn WHar WMoo WWau
	– 'Caucasica'	LTen NLar SBfd SEND SGol WWau
	– 'Cherry Brandy'	MRav SGol SLPl WWau
	– Dart's Lowgreen	see *P. laurocerasus* Low 'n' Green
	– Etna = 'Anbri'PBR	CMac EBee EPfP LBuc LRHS LSou MAsh MBri MWat NPri SWvt WMou WWau
	– 'Gajo'PBR	NPro SPer WWau
	– Genolia = 'Mariblon'PBR	SGol
	– 'Green Marble' (v)	CTri EBee EHoe WWau
	– 'Herbergii'	MAsh
§	– 'Latifolia'	CHEx EUJe SLPl WWau
§	– Low 'n' Green = 'Interlo'	MRav
	– 'Magnoliifolia'	see *P. laurocerasus* 'Latifolia'
	– 'Marbled White'	see *P. laurocerasus* 'Castlewellan'
	– 'Miky'	CJun
	– 'Mischeana'	SLPl
	– 'Mount Vernon'	CTri LBuc MBlu WWau
	– 'Novita'	CWSG EPfP
	– 'Otto Luyken' ♀H4	CBcs CCVT CDul CMac CTri EBee EHoe ELan EPfP LAst LBMP LBuc LHop LPot LRHS LSRN LTen MAsh MGos MRav MSwo MWhi NBir NEgg NWea SBfd SGol SPer SPlb WFar
	– 'Prostrata'	NWad
	– 'Reynvaanii'	CJun MBri SLPl
	– 'Rotundifolia'	CBar CDoC CMac CSBt CTri CWib EBee ECrN ELan EPfP LBuc LRHS LSRN MBri MGos MSwo MWat NEgg NLar NWea SBfd SEWo SGol SHil SLim SPoG SRms SWvt WHar WMoo
	– 'Schipkaensis'	SLPl
	– 'Schipkaensis Macrophylla' **new**	SEND
§	– 'Taff's Golden Gleam' (v)	CJun WWau
	– 'Van Nes'	CJun EBee MAsh WWau
	– 'Variegata' misapplied	see *P. laurocerasus* 'Castlewellan'
	– 'Variegata' ambig. (v)	CWib SRms
	– 'Whitespot'	SEND
	– 'Zabeliana'	CDul CMac CTri EBee EPfP MSwo NEgg NWad NWea SPer SRms WFar WWau
	litigiosa	EBee SCoo
	'Little Pink Perfection'	CDul MBri SCoo SPoG
	lusitanica ♀H4	Widely available
	– subsp. ***azorica***	CDoC CPLG LRHS MRav WFar WPGP
	– 'Myrtifolia'	CBar CTri EBee EPfP LRHS MBri MRav SBfd SGol SHil SLon SWvt WCFE WMoo
	– 'Variegata' (v)	CBar CDul CMac CTri CWib EBee ELan ELon LAst LHop MGos MLHP MRav MSwo SBfd SDix SEND SGol SLim SPer SPoG SSta SWvt WFar WMoo
	maackii	MMuc SEND
	– 'Amber Beauty'	CBcs CDoC CDul EPfP GBin GKin LMaj LSRN MRav SBfd SGol SHil SLon WFar
	'Mahogany Lustre'	see *P. serrula* 'Mahogany Lustre'
§	'Matsumae-beni-murasaki'	NLar SCoo
§	'Matsumae-fuki'	CWSG LRHS LSRN MBri MWat NLar NWea SBfd SLim
§	'Matsumae-hanagasa'	LRHS MBri NLar WMou
	maximowiczii	IPen
	– B&SWJ 10967	WCru
	'Mount Fuji'	see *P.* 'Shirotae'
	mume	CMCN CMen
	– 'Beni-chidori'	CMac CWib EBee EPfP IVic LRHS MBlu MBri NLar SCoo SLim SPoG WCot WJas
§	– 'Omoi-no-mama' (d)	CMen
	– 'Omoi-no-wac'	see *P. mume* 'Omoi-no-mama'
	myrobalana	see *P. cerasifera* Myrobalan Group
	nipponica var. ***kurilensis*** 'Brilliant'	CBcs CSBt GBin LRHS MBri NLar SBfd SPoG
	– – 'Ruby'	CBcs GBin LSRN MBri NEgg WFar
	'Okamé' ♀H4	Widely available
	'Okumiyako' misapplied	see *P.* 'Shōgetsu'
	padus	CCVT CDul CHab CLnd CMac CRWN CSBt CTri ECrN EWTr LBuc MGos MMuc MSwo NWea SEND SEWo WMou
	– 'Albertii'	CCVT MBri SCoo
	– 'Colorata' ♀H4	CBcs CDoC CDul CMac CTho EBee ECrN ELan EWTr LHop LMaj MAsh

	Name	Suppliers
		MGos MRav NLar SCoo SGol SPer SWvt WFar
	- 'Grandiflora'	see *P. padus* 'Watereri'
	- 'Purple Queen'	ECrN SGol
§	- 'Watereri' ♀H4	CCVT CDoC CDul CLnd CMCN CMac CTho CWib ECrN ELan EPfP GBin LAst LHop LMaj NWea SCoo SEWo SGol SLim SPer SPoG WMou
	'Pandora' ♀H4	CCVT CDul CLnd EBee ECrN EPfP LAst LHop LRHS MAsh MBri MGos MMuc MRav MSwo NPCo NWea SBfd SCoo SEND SEWo SHil SPer SPoG WFar
	pendula	SCrf
§	- 'Pendula Rosea' ♀H4	CDoC CDul CTri CWib EPfP MAsh SCrf WFar WJas
§	- 'Pendula Rubra' ♀H4	CCVT CDoC CLnd CMac CSBt CWib EBee EPfP EWTr LHop LRHS MBri MSwo SBfd SCoo SLim SPer SPoG WFar WMou
§	- 'Stellata'	MAsh MBri
	pensylvanica	LMaj
	persica 'Amsden June' (F)	CLnd CWib EBtc GTwe MCoo MWat NLar SFam SKee WHar
	- 'Avalon Pride' (F)	CAgr CSut EPfP EPom LBuc MCoo SKee
	- 'Bellegarde' (F)	SFam
	- 'Bonanza' (F)	EPom LSRN
	- 'Champion' (F) **new**	CLnd
	- 'Darling' (F)	SVic
	- 'Dixi Red' (F)	CAgr
	- 'Duke of York' (F) ♀H3	CTri GTwe SFam
	- 'Foliis Rubris' (F)	CDul LRHS
	- 'Francis' (F)	SKee
	- 'Garden Lady' (F)	CMam GTwe SLim WHar
	- 'Hale's Early' (F)	GTwe MRav MWat SFam SKee SLim SPer WHar
	- 'Mesembrine' PBR (F)	EPom
	- var. ***nectarina*** 'Early Rivers' (F) ♀H3	GTwe LAst LSRN
	- - 'Fantasia' (F)	EPfP
	- - 'Flavortop' (F)	EPfP SPer
	- - 'Garden Beauty' (F/d)	SPoG
	- - 'Gulfcrimson' (F) **new**	LAst
	- - 'Humboldt' (F)	CAgr GTwe LAst SFam SKee WHar
	- - 'John Rivers' (F)	GTwe SPer
	- - 'Lord Napier' (F) ♀H3	CAgr CDoC CDul CSBt CTri CWSG CWib EPfP EPom LAst LBuc LRHS MGos MWat SEND SFam SKee SLim SPer SVic WHar
	- - 'Nectared' (F)	CWib
	- - 'Nectarella' (F)	CMam EPom LSRN SLim WHar
	- - 'Pineapple' (F)	CAgr CTri GTwe SFam SKee WHar
	- - 'Terrace Ruby' (F)	SPoG
	- 'Peregrine' (F) ♀H3	CAgr CDul CLnd CSBt CTri CWSG CWib EPfP EPom EWTr GTwe LAst LBuc LRHS LSRN MBri MGos MWat NLar SEND SFam SKee SLim SPer SPoG WHar WJas
	- 'Pink Peachy' (F)	NLar
	- 'Purpurea'	GKin
	- 'Red Haven' (F)	CAgr CWib GTwe SKee SVic WHar
	- 'Red Top' (F)	EPfP
	- 'Redwing' (F)	CAgr
	- 'Robin Redbreast' (F)	CAgr
	- 'Rochester' (F) ♀H3	CAgr CMam CSBt CTri CWSG CWib EPom GTwe LAst LSRN MBri NLar SEND SFam SKee SLim SPer SPoG WHar
	- 'Royal George' (F)	GTwe SFam SPer
	- 'Sagami-shidare'	LAst
	- 'Saturne' (F)	EPom SKee WHar
	- 'Terrace Amber' (F)	SPoG
	- 'Terrace Diamond' (F)	SPoG
	- 'Terrace Pearl'	LSRN
	- 'White Peachy' (F)	NLar
	× ***persicoides*** 'Ingrid' (F)	CAgr CMam EBtc LBuc LRHS MBri MCoo SCoo WHar
	- 'Pollardii' (F)	NWea WJas
	- 'Robijn' (F)	CAgr EPom LBuc MCoo SVic
	- 'Spring Glow' (F)	CDoC LAst MBri NWea SEND WJas
	'Pink Parasol'	see *P.* 'Matsumae-hanagasa'
	'Pink Perfection' ♀H4	CBcs CDul CLnd CSBt CWib ECrN EPfP LAst LRHS MBri MGos MWat NLar SBfd SPer WFar WHar WJas
	'Pink Shell' ♀H4	CAbP EPfP MAsh MBri
	pissardii	see *P. cerasifera* 'Pissardii'
	'Pissardii Nigra'	see *P. cerasifera* 'Nigra'
*	***prostrata*** var. ***discolor***	NLar
	- 'Nana' **new**	ECho
	pumila var. ***depressa***	MRav NLar NPro
	'Royal Burgundy' (d)	CCVT CDul CLnd CMac CWGN EBee EMil EPfP LAst LRHS LSRN MAsh MBri MGos MWat SBfd SCoo SEWo SGol SLim SPer SPoG WFar WHar
	rufa	CDul CJun CLnd CTho EBee EBtc GKin SKHP SLon WPat
	salicina 'Lizzie' **new**	EPom
	- 'Methley' (D)	ECrN SPoG WHar
	sargentii ♀H4	Widely available
	- 'Charles Sargent'	EBee MAsh
	- 'Columnaris'	EBee LRHS MBri
	- 'Rancho'	CLnd SCoo SLim SPer WFar
	× ***schmittii***	CCVT ECrN MMuc SCoo SEND SPer WJas
	'Sekiyama'	see *P.* 'Kanzan'
	serotina	CDul NLar
§	***serrula*** ♀H4	Widely available
	- Branklyn form	MGos
	- Dorothy Clive form	EBee LSRN
§	- 'Mahogany Lustre'	WFar
	- 'Princesse Sturdza' **new**	MBlu
	- var. ***tibetica***	see *P. serrula*
	serrula × ***serrulata***	CBcs CTho
	serrulata 'Erecta'	see *P.* 'Amanogawa'
	- 'Grandiflora'	see *P.* 'Ukon'
	- 'Longipes'	see *P.* 'Shōgetsu'
	- 'Miyako' misapplied	see *P.* 'Shōgetsu'
N	- var. ***pubescens***	see *P. verecunda*
	- 'Rosea'	see *P.* 'Kiku-shidare-zakura'
	- var. ***spontanea***	see *P. jamasakura*
	'Shidare-zakura'	see *P.* 'Kiku-shidare-zakura'
	'Shimizu-zakura'	see *P.* 'Shōgetsu'
	'Shirofugen' ♀H4	CBcs CDoC CDul CLnd CMCN CMac CSBt CTho CWSG CWib EBee ECrN EPfP EWTr GKin LBuc LRHS LSRN MAsh MBri MMuc MRav MWat SBfd SEND SGol SPer WFar WHar WJas
§	'Shirotae' ♀H4	Widely available
§	'Shizuka'	CWSG CWib EBee LRHS MBri NLar SBfd SCoo SPer SPoG
§	'Shōgetsu' ♀H4	CBcs CDul CLnd CSBt CTho EBee ECrN ELan EPfP EWTr LAst LMaj LRHS MAsh MBri MRav NEgg NLar SBfd SEWo SFam SLim SPer SPoG

'Shosar'	CWib MAsh NLar SCoo SPer
× ***sieboldii*** 'Caespitosa'	MBri SCoo
'Snow Goose'	CDoC EBee LAst LHop LMaj LRHS NEgg SCoo SGol WFar
'Snow Showers'	CCVT CMac EBee LRHS LSRN MAsh MBri MGos MWat NWea SBfd SEND SEWo SPer SPoG
spinosa	CCVT CDoC CDul CHab CMac CRWN CTri ECrN EPfP EPom EShb GAbr LAst LBuc LSRN MAsh MBlu NLar NWea SBfd SEWo SPer SPoG SVic WFar WMou WSFF
- 'Plena' (d)	CTho MBlu
- 'Purpurea'	CDul CTho EGFP MAsh MBlu MBri NLar WFar WMou
§ 'Spire' ♀H4	Widely available
× ***subhirtella*** 'Autumnalis' ♀H4	Widely available
- 'Autumnalis Rosea' ♀H4	Widely available
- 'Falling Stars'	SLon
- 'Fukubana'	CLnd CMac EBee EPfP MAsh MBri NLar
- 'Pendula' misapplied	see *P. pendula* 'Pendula Rosea'
- 'Pendula Plena Rosea' (d)	LAst
- 'Pendula Rosea'	see *P. pendula* 'Pendula Rosea'
- 'Pendula Rubra'	see *P. pendula* 'Pendula Rubra'
N - 'Rosea'	CLnd MRav
- 'Stellata'	see *P. pendula* 'Stellata'
'Sunset Boulevard'	LRHS MBri
'Taihaku' ♀H4	Widely available
'Taoyame'	CLnd
tenella	CAgr ECha ELan SEND
- 'Fire Hill'	CBcs CJun CWib ECho ELan EPfP LRHS LSRN MGos MRav SKHP SPer WCFE WCot WJas
'The Bride'	CDul LRHS MAsh MBri SCoo
tibetica	see *P. serrula*
'Tiltstone Hellfire'	EBee LRHS MBri NLar
tomentosa	CAgr GBin LLHF MAsh SEND
§ 'Trailblazer' (C/D)	CLnd CMac CSBt ECrN IVic LAst MRav MSwo SLon SPer WMou
triloba	CBcs CWib ECha ECrN LAst MBlu NWea
- 'Multiplex' (d)	SPoG SRms WJas
§ 'Ukon' ♀H4	CBcs CDoC CDul CLnd CMCN CMac CTho CTri EBee ECrN EPfP EWTr LRHS MAsh MBri MGos MMuc MRav MWat NEgg NLar NWea SBfd SCrf SEND SGol SPer WFar WHar
'Umineko'	CCVT CDoC CLnd CWib ECrN MGos MMuc SEND SEWo SLPl SPer WHar
§ ***verecunda***	NWea WJas
virginiana 'Schubert'	CDul EBee ECrN SCoo WFar WMou
'White Cloud'	CDul
yamadae	see *P. incisa* f. *yamadae*
× ***yedoensis***	CCVT CDul LMaj MAsh MBri MRav SBfd SLon SPer WMou
- 'Ivensii'	CBcs CDul CSBt CWib LHop LMaj MMuc NEgg NWea SCoo SEND SPer
- 'Pendula'	see *P.* × *yedoensis* 'Shidare-yoshino'
- 'Perpendens'	see *P.* × *yedoensis* 'Shidare-yoshino'
§ - 'Shidare-Yoshino'	CCVT CDul CLnd CSBt ECrN LRHS MAsh MBri MGos MRav MSwo MWat NWea SBfd SLim SLon SPoG
§ - 'Somei-Yoshino' ♀H4	CCVT CLnd CTho CTri EPfP LAst MBri NWea SLim SPer WHar WJas
'Yoshino'	see *P.* × *yedoensis* 'Somei-Yoshino'
'Yoshino Pendula'	see *P.* × *yedoensis* 'Shidare-yoshino'

Psacalium (*Asteraceae*)

pinetorum B&SWJ 10269	WCru

Pseuderanthemum (*Acanthaceae*)

carruthersii var. ***atropurpureum*** 'Rubrum'	LSou
laxiflorum	CCCN
reticulatum orange-flowered	CCCN

Pseudocydonia (*Rosaceae*)

§ ***sinensis***	CAgr CBcs CMen NLar

Pseudofumaria see *Corydalis*

alba	see *Corydalis ochroleuca*
lutea	see *Corydalis lutea*

Pseudogynoxys (*Asteraceae*)

§ ***chenopodioides***	CCCN CSpe

Pseudolarix (*Pinaceae*)

§ ***amabilis*** ♀H4	CBcs CDoC CMCN CTho EHul EPfP GBin LRHS MBlu MBri MPkF NHol NPCo NPnk NWea SBfd SCoo SKHP SLim SPoG WFar
kaempferi	see *P. amabilis*

Pseudomuscari see *Muscari*

azureum	see *Muscari azureum*

Pseudopanax (*Araliaceae*)

(Adiantifolius Group) 'Adiantifolius'	CDoC CHEx CTrC ESwi
- 'Cyril Watson' ♀H1	CBcs CDoC CHEx ELan IDee LRHS LTen SBig SLim WCot
arboreus	see *Neopanax arboreus*
chathamicus	CDoC CHEx
crassifolius	CAbb CBcs CBrP CCCN CDTJ CHEx CTrC EAmu EBee ELon ESwi EUJe GBin IDee LRHS SBig SPoG WCot
- var. ***trifoliolatus***	CHEx
discolor	ECou IDee LEdu
ferox	CAbb CBcs CBrP CDTJ CTsd EAmu ESwi EUJe GBin SBig SLim SMad
'Forest Gem'	CDoC
laetus	see *Neopanax laetus*
lessonii	CBcs CBrP CHEx ECou ELan
- 'Black Ruby'	ECou
- 'Gold Splash' (v) ♀H1	CBcs CDoC CHEx CTrC ELan IDee IVic LRHS SBig SEND SLim
- 'Goldfinger'	CBcs
- 'Nigra'	CTrC
- 'Rangitira'	CBcs CDoC CTrC EUJe IDee LRHS SBig SLim
'Linearifolius'	CHEx CTrC IDee LEdu
'Purpureus' ♀H1	CDoC CTrC ESwi SEND
'Sabre'	CBcs CDoC CHEx CTrC EUJe LRHS SLim
'Trident'	CDoC CHEx CTrC ECou IDee LRHS SBig SLim

Pseudophoenix (*Arecaceae*)

* ***nativo***	MBri

Pseudosasa (Poaceae)

	amabilis misapplied	see *Arundinaria gigantea*
§	***amabilis*** (McClure) Keng f.	CEnt WFar
§	***japonica*** ♀H4	CAbb CBcs CDoC CEnt CHEx CTrC CWib ENBC EPfP LEdu LRHS MMoz MMuc MWhi MWht NGdn NLar SBfd SEND SEWo SHil SPoG WCFE WFar WJun WMoo
§	- 'Akebonosuji' (v)	CEnt MWht WJun WPGP
I	- var. ***pleioblastoides***	MWht
	- 'Tsutsumiana'	CHEx ELon ERod EUJe MMoz MWht NLar SBig WJun
	- 'Variegata'	see *P. japonica* 'Akebonosuji'
	usawai	WJun
	viridula	ERod MWht

Pseudotsuga (Pinaceae)

§	***menziesii*** ♀H4	CBcs CDul CLnd EPfP MBlu MMuc NWea SEND WFar
	- 'Bhiela Lhota'	CKen
	- 'Blue Wonder'	CKen
	- 'Densa'	CKen
	- 'Fastigiata'	CKen
	- 'Fletcheri'	CKen SLim
	- 'Geijsteren'	NLar
	- var. ***glauca***	CDul
	- 'Glauca Pendula'	CKen
I	- 'Gotelli's Pendula'	CKen
	- 'Graceful Grace'	CKen
	- 'Idaho Gem'	CKen
	- 'Julie'	CKen
	- 'Little Jamie'	CKen
	- 'Lohbrunner'	CKen
	- 'McKenzie'	CKen
	- 'Nana'	CKen
	- 'Oudemansii'	NLar
	- Pendula Group	NPCo
	- 'Stairii'	CKen
	- 'Uwes Golden'	NLar
	taxifolia	see *P. menziesii*

Pseudowintera (Winteraceae)

§	***colorata***	CBcs CDoC CMac CPLG CTrC CWib GAbr GKin IVic MPkF MRav NLar NPnk WFar
	- 'Marjorie Congreve'	IVic LRHS
	- 'Moulin Rouge'	CBcs LBuc LRHS SPoG
	- 'Mount Congreve'	CBcs GKin IArd MBri NLar
	- 'Red Leopard'	LBuc LRHS NLar NPnk

Psidium (Myrtaceae)

	cattleyanum	see *P. littorale* var. *longipes*
	guajava (F)	CCCN SPlb XBlo
§	***littorale*** var. ***longipes*** (F)	CCCN EDif XBlo

Psilotum (Psilotaceae)

	nudum	ECou

Psoralea (Papilionaceae)

*	***fleta***	SPlb
	glabra	SPlb
	glandulosa	CArn SBrt SPlb WSHC
	oligophylla	SPlb
	onobrychis new	SPhx
	pinnata	CPLG CTrC IRar

Psychotria (Rubiaceae)

	capensis	CPLG

Ptelea (Rutaceae)

	trifoliata	CArn CBcs CDul CLnd CMac CWib ELan EPfP MBlu MBri SPer SRms WPGP
	- 'Aurea' ♀H4	CAbP CBcs CJun CLnd CMac CPLG EBee ELan EPfP EWTr GBin LHop LRHS MAsh MBlu MBri NLar SPer SPoG SSpi WPGP
	- 'Fastigiata'	EPfP

Pteracanthus see Strobilanthes

Pteridophyllum (Papaveraceae)

	racemosum	EFEx GEdr LWSt WCru

Pteris (Pteridaceae)

	from Yunnan	CLAP
§	***actiniopteroides***	WCot
	angustipinna B&SWJ 6738	WCru
	cretica ♀H1+3	CHEx
	- var. ***albolineata*** ♀H1	CBty LRHS SRms XBlo
	- 'Mayi' (v)	CBty
	- 'Rowei'	CBty LRHS XBlo
	- 'Wimsettii'	CBty LRHS
	ensiformis 'Evergemiensis' (v)	CBty
	gallinopes	CLAP
	henryi	see *P. actiniopteroides*
*	***staminea***	XBlo
	tremula	SRms
	tricolor	CBty
	wallichiana	CBty CGHE CHEx EBee WPGP

Pterocactus (Cactaceae)

	hickenii F&W 10240 new	WCot

Pterocarya ✿ (Juglandaceae)

	fraxinifolia ♀H4	CBcs CCVT CDul CMCN CTho ECrN EGFP EPfP GQui IArd IDee LMaj LRHS MBlu MMuc MRav SEND
	macroptera var. ***insignis***	WPGP
	× ***rehderiana***	CTho MBlu WMou
	stenoptera	CBcs CDTJ CMCN CTho EGFP NLar
	- 'Fern Leaf'	EPfP MBlu MBri WMou WPGP
	tonkinensis new	EGFP

Pterocephalus (Caprifoliaceae)

	parnassi	see *P. perennis*
§	***perennis***	CMea ECho MHer NBir NMen NRya SRms WAbe WHoo XSen
	- subsp. ***perennis***	WHrl
	pinardii	WAbe XSen

Pterostylis (Orchidaceae)

	coccina	ECho
	curta	ECho LLHF

Pterostyrax (Styracaceae)

	corymbosa	CBcs CJun CMCN IArd MBri NLar SSpi
	hispida ♀H4	CAbP CBcs CDoC CDul CHGN CJun CMCN CWib EBee EPfP GBin IArd IDee IVic LRHS MBlu MBri MGos MRav NLar SChF SHil SPoG SSpi WFar
	psilophyllus	WPGP

Ptilostemon (*Asteraceae*)

	afer	CCse
§	***diacantha***	ELan EPfP IFoB LRHS WCot
	echinocephalus	MDKP

Ptilotrichum see *Alyssum*

Ptilotus (*Amaranthaceae*)

exaltatus	SPlb

Pueraria (*Papilionaceae*)

montana var. ***lobata***	CArn

Pulicaria (*Asteraceae*)

§	***dysenterica***	CArn CHab NMir SIde WSFF
	odora **new**	WCot

Pulmonaria (*Boraginaceae*)

	angustifolia ♀H4	CMac EBee EPfP GKev GMaP MNrw NOrc SEND SRms WTin
*	- ***alba***	IFoB
	- 'Azurea'	CBro CElw CHVG CTca EBee ELan EPPr EPfP GAbr GMaP IGor LRHS MCot MMuc MRav NBro NLar SBfd SPer SRms WFar WMnd
	- 'Blaues Meer'	ECtt EPfP GAbr WCru
	- 'Munstead Blue'	CElw CLAP CMac GBuc MCot MRav NRya SRms
	'Apple Frost'	EBee LRHS NLar SGol WWEG
	'Baby Blue'	COIW
	'Barfield Regalia'	IGor LLHF NSti WCru
	'Benediction'	CDes LLHF MAvo MNrw NSti WCot
	'Beth's Pink'	GAbr WFar
	'Blauer Hügel'	LLHF NSti
	'Blauhimmel'	GCra
	'Blue Buttons'	CCon ECtt WWEG
	'Blue Crown'	CElw CSev EBee EWes
	'Blue Ensign'	Widely available
	'Blue Moon'	see *P. officinalis* 'Blue Mist'
	'Bonnie'	CMea
	'Botanic Hybrid'	WCru
	'Bubble Gum'PBR	EBee SPtl
	Cally hybrid	CLAP GCal SMrm WCru
	'Cedric Morris'	CElw
	'Chintz'	CLAP MAvo SMrm
	'Coral Springs'	EBee GBuc LLHF NLar
	'Corsage'	ECtt
	'Cotton Cool'	Widely available
	'Crawshay Chance'	CElw SMHy
	'De Vroomen's Pride' (v)	WMnd
	'Diana Clare'	Widely available
	'Elworthy Rubies'	CElw EPPr
	'Emerald Isles'	SWvt
	'Excalibur'	EBee ECtt EHrv NLar
	'Fiona'	WWEG
	'Glacier'	CBro CTca EBee EPfP MNrw NSti SAga WWEG
	'Hazel Kaye's Red'	LLWP
	'Highdown'	see *P.* 'Lewis Palmer'
	'Ice Ballet' (Classic Series)	CLAP EBee MAvo SPtl
§	'Lewis Palmer' ♀H4	CBro CSam CTca EBee ELan GCal GMaP LPot LRHS MBri MNrw NBir NLar SRGP SRms WBrk WCot WHoo WTin WWEG
	'Little Star'	ECtt GBuc LRHS MAvo NSti SRGP SUsu WCru WFar
	longifolia	CPrp EAEE EBee ECha EHoe ELan EPfP GAbr GBin GKev LRHS NBir NLar NOrc NSti WBrk
§	- 'Ankum'	CElw CLAP EPfP NBir NSti WSHC WWEG
	- 'Ballyrogan Blue'	IBlr
	- 'Bertram Anderson'	CPrp CTca EBee ECtt GMaP LRHS NBir NLar SBfd SPer SPoG SRGP SRms SWvt WBrk WCru WFar WMnd WWEG
	- subsp. ***cevennensis***	CLAP EBee LRHS MBel NCGa NLar NSti WPtf WWEG
	- 'Coen Jansen'	see *P. longifolia* 'Ankum'
	- 'Dordogne'	CLAP NBir NLar
	- 'Howard Eggins'	EBee
	'Majesté'	CLAP CWib EBee ECha EHoe EHrv ELan EPfP EWes GMaP IFro LAst LHop LRHS MRav NBir NEgg NOrc NSti SApp SBfd SPer SPoG WBor WBrk WCot WFar WMnd WWEG
	'Margery Fish' ♀H4	CBro CLAP CSam EBee EPfP LRHS MWhi SPer WMnd
	'Mary Mottram'	CElw ECtt ELan NBir NSti WMnd
	'Matese Blue'	CLAP
	'Mawson's Blue'	CLAP EWes MRav MSpe NBir NChi SWvt WBrk WMoo WSHC
	'May Bouquet'PBR	LLHF
	'Melancholia'	IBlr
	'Merlin'	CLAP SKHP
§	'Milchstrasse'	EBee
	Milky Way	see *P.* 'Milchstrasse'
	mollis	EBee ECGP GCal MNrw NSti WCru
	- 'Royal Blue'	MRav
	- 'Samobor'	CLAP
	'Moonstone'	CElw
	'Mountain Magic'PBR	ECtt LRHS SIde
	'Mrs Kittle'	CCon EBee IFoB LRHS MRav NBir NSti WAul WBrk WFar WMnd WWEG
	'Netta Statham'	LLHF NSti
	'Nürnberg'	WWEG
	officinalis	CArn CBro CHby IFoB MHoo MLHP MNHC NChi SIde WBrk WFar
	- 'Alba'	WBrk
§	- 'Blue Mist'	CBro CLAP EBee ELan GMaP MBel NBir WBrk WCot WHoo WMnd WMoo WTin
	- 'Bowles's Blue'	see *P. officinalis* 'Blue Mist'
	- Cambridge Blue Group	EBee LRHS MRav MWat NBir WCot WPtf
	- 'Marjorie Lawley'	LRHS
	- 'Stillingfleet Gran'	LLHF
	- 'White Wings'	CLAP EBee NLar SIde
	- 'Wuppertal'	EBee
	'Oliver Wyatt's White'	CLAP EBee SRGP
	Opal = 'Ocupol'	Widely available
	'Open Skies' (v) **new**	CDes
	'Pink Haze'PBR	CYeo ECtt LPla MBel MBri NSti SBfd SPoG SWvt WBrk WCot WRHF
	'Polar Splash'	EBee LRHS SIde
	'Raspberry Ice'	EBee
	'Raspberry Splash'PBR	CLAP COIW ECtt GBin GKev LRHS MTis NLar SGol SIde SMrm SPoG
*	'Rowlatt Choules'	MAvo
	'Roy Davidson'	CLAP CSam CTca EBee ECGP ECtt EHrv EPfP IGor LHop LRHS MBel NBir NCGa NSti SRms SWvt WFar WPtf WWEG

	rubra ♀H4	CBcs CElw CHab CPom ECha ELan EShb GAbr LBMP LLWP MLHP MMuc MNrw NBid NOrc NSti SEND SRms WCAu WFar WTin
	- var. ***alba***	see *P. rubra* var. *albocorollata*
§	- var. ***albocorollata***	CBre EBtc EHrv GAbr GBin MBel NBid WBrk WFar WWEG
	- 'Ann'	CLAP
	- 'Barfield Pink'	CBro ELan GCal IFro MBel NBir NLar NMRc WCru
	- 'Bowles's Red'	CMac EBee ECtt EHrv EPfP IFoB LRHS MNrw MRav MWat NBir NCGa NGdn NPnk SIde SPer WFar WGwG WMnd
	- 'David Ward' (v)	CBro CCon CMac ECha ECtt EHrv ELan EPfP GCra GEdr GMaP LHop LRHS MRav NBir NLar NPnk SMrm SPer WBrk WCFE WHil WMnd WPtf WWEG
	- 'Rachel Vernie' (v)	CLAP CPou MAvo WBrk
	- 'Redstart'	CBro CMac CSBt CSam CTca EBee ECtt EPfP IGor LEdu LHop LLWP LRHS MBel MNrw MRav NBir NEgg NGdn NLar SRms SWvt WBrk WFar WMnd WMoo WWEG
§	***saccharata***	ECha ELan GMaP IFro MMuc NEgg NPnk SEND SIde SRms WFar
	- 'Alba'	CBro CElw ECha IFro MMuc SRms
	- Argentea Group ♀H4	CBro CSev CTri EBee ELan EPfP GMaP LRHS MBel MRav NGdn WBrk WWEG
	- 'Dora Bielefeld'	CHVG CLAP EBee ECha ECtt EHrv EPPr EPfP EWTr GBuc GMaP LLWP LRHS MNrw MRav NBir NCGa NGdn NHol SBfd SMrm SPer SRGP SWvt WAul WFar WHil WHoo WMnd WWlt
	- 'Frühlingshimmel'	CBro CElw EBee ECtt EPfP LRHS MNrw MRav NSti WFar WPtf
	- 'Glebe Cottage Blue'	ECGP
	- 'Leopard'	CEnt CLAP CMac CMea CSam CTca CWCL EBee ECha ECtt GBin GBuc GMaP LRHS MBel MNrw NBir NLar SApp WBrk WCot WFar WHoo WWEG WWlt
	- 'Mrs Moon'	CTri CWib EBee ECtt ELon EPfP GMaP LRHS LTen MWat NLar NOrc SBfd SPer SWvt WHil WMnd WWEG
	- 'Old Rectory Silver'	NBir
	- 'Picta'	see *P. saccharata*
	- 'Pink Dawn'	CMHG EBee WMnd
	- 'Reginald Kaye'	EBee ECha EWes MAvo MNrw
	- 'Silverado'PBR	EBee ECtt LRHS MBel NLar NOrc
	- 'Stanhoe'	EWes
	'Saint Ann's'	EBee LLHF NSti WCru
	'Samurai'	GBin NSti
	'Silver Bouquet'PBR **new**	LSou
	'Silver Sabre'	IBlr
	'Silver Surprise'	WCot
	'Sissinghurst White' ♀H4	Widely available
	'Smoky Blue'	CLAP EBee ECtt EPfP LHop MRav SWat WMnd WWEG
	'Spilled Milk'	NLar
	'Spotted Bob'	WCAu
	'Stillingfleet Meg'	CLAP EAEE EBee ECtt LAst LHop LRHS MBel MNrw NSti NWad SRGP WPtf
	'Trevi Fountain'	CLAP COIW CWCL EBee ECtt EShb GBin GJos LRHS MTis NPri SIde SMrm SPoG WCot WPtf
	'Vera May' ♀H4	EBee
	'Victorian Brooch'PBR	CLAP COIW CSam CWCL EBee ECtt GBin GKev LSou MNrw MTis NEgg NLar NPri SIde SMrm SPoG WFar WPtf WWEG
	'Weetwood Blue'	CBre CLAP CTca EBee EPfP MNrw

Pulsatilla (Ranunculaceae)

	alba	CBro
	albana	CBro ECho LHop LLHF LRHS NRHS
	- 'Lutea'	GKev LLHF
	alpina	NGdn SRms
§	- subsp. ***apiifolia*** ♀H4	EPot IFro
	- subsp. ***sulphurea*** misapplied	see *P. alpina* subsp. *apiifolia*
	ambigua	GKev LLHF
	campanella	LLHF
	caucasica	CBro ECho LRHS NRHS
	cernua	LHop LRHS
	georgica	EDAr GEdr WIce
	halleri ♀H4	EBee GKev
	- subsp. ***rhodopaea*** **new**	EPot
	- subsp. ***slavica*** ♀H4	GEdr LLHF
	- subsp. ***taurica***	LRHS
	lutea	see *P. alpina* subsp. *apiifolia*
	montana	LLHF NMen SPlb
§	***patens***	EDAr LLHF NGdn WIce
	- subsp. ***flavescens***	EDAr
	pratensis	GPoy SRms
	- subsp. ***nigricans***	LHop LRHS
I	- 'Semiplena'	MMoz
	rubra	GKev NGdn SPad SRot
*	***serotina***	EBee GKev
	subslavica **new**	GKev
	turczaninovii	GKev LLHF LPla LRHS
§	***vernalis*** ♀H2	NLar NSla WAbe
	violacea	CBcs
§	***vulgaris*** ♀H4	Widely available
	- 'Alba' ♀H4	Widely available
	- 'Barton's Pink'	CBro ECho EWes LHop LLHF LRHS NRHS SRot
	- 'Blaue Glocke'	EPot GEdr LRHS MCot MWat NPri SHar SMrm SWvt WFar WHil XSen
	- 'Eva Constance'	CBro ECho LHop LLHF LRHS NRHS WAbe
	- 'Gotlandica'	LLHF
	- subsp. ***grandis***	LRHS NMen NSla
	- - 'Budapest'	CRDP
	- - 'Papageno'	CSpe EAEE EBee ECho ELon EPot GAbr GEdr GMaP LBMP LRHS MAvo NCGa NDov NLar NSla SMrm WFar WHil WIce WPer
	- Heiler hybrids	CPrp EAEE LLHF MRav NCGa NDov NEgg NGdn NSla SEND
	- 'Perlen Glocke'	EDAr EWTr MHer
	- pink-flowered	CMea LLHF NSla
	- Red Clock	see *P. vulgaris* 'Röde Klokke'
§	- 'Röde Klokke'	EBee ECtt EPot GEdr GKev LRHS MCot MNrw MWat MWhi NPri NWad SHar SMrm SWvt WHil WPer XLum XSen
	- ***rosea***	GAbr
	- Rote Glocke	see *P. vulgaris* 'Röde Klokke'
	- var. ***rubra***	CMea EBee ECho ELan EPPr EPfP GMaP LRHS MBri MHer MNHC MRav NBir NLar NRHS NSla SBfd

	SGar SPer SPet SPoG SRms SRot WFar WHoo WIce
§ - 'Weisse Schwan'	EPfP GMaP NMen SRot
- 'White Bells'	EPot GEdr NHol
- White Swan	see *P. vulgaris* 'Weisse Schwan'

Pultenaea (*Papilionaceae*)

juniperina	SPlb

pummelo see *Citrus maxima*

Punica (*Lythraceae*)

granatum	CArn CBcs CHEx CMen EAmu EPfP ERom IDee LRHS MGos MOWG MREP SLim SVic WSHC
- 'André le Roi' (F)	SLPl
- 'Chico'	CBcs SEND
- 'Fina Tendral'	CCCN
- 'Flore Pleno'	see *P. granatum* f. *plena* 'Rubrum Flore Pleno'
- 'Legrelleae' (F/d)	SEND SLPl
- 'Maxima Rubra'	EShb XSen
- var. ***nana*** ♀H3	CAgr CArn CCCN CMen EBee EBtc ELau EOHP EPfP EShb LEdu LRHS MREP SMrm WPat
- f. ***plena*** (d)	CBcs LRHS MRav WCFE WPat
- - 'Flore Pleno Luteo' (d)	LRHS
§ - - 'Rubrum Flore Pleno' (d) ♀H3	SEND
- 'Provence'	XSen
* - 'Striata'	MOWG

Purshia (*Rosaceae*)

plicata NJM 09.015 **new**	WPGP

Puschkinia (*Asparagaceae*)

scilloides	ECho NBir
- 'Aragat's Gem'	ECho LWst
- large-flowered clone	LWst
§ - var. ***libanotica***	ECho EPfP EPot GKev LAma LEdu LRHS SDeJ SMrm SPer WRHF WShi
- - 'Alba'	ECho EPot GKev LAma SPer WCot
- 'Snowdrift'	LWst

Puya (*Bromeliaceae*)

alpestris	CCCN CTrC EAmu EBee EShb ETod SBig SPlb WPGP
berteroana	CAbb CBcs CCCN CDTJ CDoC CHEx EGri EShb ETod SPlb
chilensis	CAbb CBcs CCCN CDTJ CDoC CHEx CPne EAmu LRHS SPlb
coerulea	CCCN CCon CDTJ EAmu ELon EWld SGar SPlb
ferruginea	SPlb
laxa	EGri SChr
mirabilis	CDTJ EBee EGri ESwi
- RCB/Arg L-3	WCot
raimondii	WPGP
spathacea RCB/Arg S-2	WCot
venusta	CArn CCCN CDTJ EGri ETod SPlb

Pycnanthemum (*Lamiaceae*)

montanum	GBin
muticum	CArn MSCN
pilosum	CArn EBee ELau MHer NLar SIde SWal XLum
tenuifolium	NLar
virginianum	GCal SPhx

Pycnostachys (*Lamiaceae*)

reticulata	EOHP
urticifolia	EOHP EWes

Pygmea see *Chionohebe*

Pyracantha (*Rosaceae*)

Alexander Pendula = 'Renolex'	LHop MRav MSwo SRms WFar
angustifolia	WCFE
§ ***atalantioides***	SPlb WCFE
'Brilliant'	EPfP SCoo
§ ***coccinea*** 'Lalandei'	CMac
- 'Red Column'	Widely available
- 'Red Cushion'	MRav SRms
Dart's Red = 'Interrada'	CSBt SBfd SLim WHar
'Fiery Cascade'	LRHS SPoG
gibbsii	see *P. atalantioides*
'Golden Charmer' ♀H4	CDul CMac EBee EPfP IBoy LRHS MAsh MGos MSwo NEgg NLar NPri NWea SBfd SCoo SGol SLPl SPer SPoG SRms SWvt WFar WGwG WRHF
'Golden Glow'	SLim
'Golden Sun'	see *P.* 'Soleil d'Or'
'Harlequin' (v)	SGol WFar
'Knap Hill Lemon'	MBlu
'Mohave'	CMac CTri EBee ECrN ELan ELon IBoy LRHS MAsh MWat NPri SCoo SGol SLim SRms SWvt
'Mohave Silver' (v)	CMac CWSG ELan EShb LAst LBMP LRHS MAsh SBfd
'Molten Lava'	MBri
'Monrovia'	see *P. coccinea* 'Lalandei'
'Navaho'	SEWo
'Orange Charmer'	CBar CMac CTri ELan LHop LRHS MAsh MGos MWat NLar NWea SPer SPlb WFar
'Orange Glow' ♀H4	CSBt CTri CWib EBee ECrN EPfP IBoy LAst LBuc LPot LRHS MAsh MBri MGos MMuc MSwo NPri NWea SEND SEWo SGol SHil SLim SPer SPoG SRms SWvt WFar WGwG WHar
'Renault d'Or'	SLPl
rogersiana ♀H4	CDul ECrN EPfP MRav WFar
- 'Flava' ♀H4	CDul CSBt EBee EPfP LRHS NEgg SBfd SPoG SWvt
'Rosedale'	LRHS WHar
Saphyr Jaune = 'Cadaune'PBR	CBar CBcs CCVT CDoC CSBt CWSG EBee ECrN EMil EPfP LRHS LTen MAsh MGos MRav MWat NCGa NLar NPri SCoo SGol SPer
Saphyr Orange = 'Cadange'PBR ♀H4	CBar CBcs CCVT CDoC CMac CSBt CWSG EBee EMil EPfP LRHS LTen MAsh MBri MGos MRav NEgg NLar NPri SCoo SGol SPer
Saphyr Panache = 'Cadvar'PBR (v)	EBee MWat
Saphyr Rouge = 'Cadrou'PBR ♀H4	CBar CBcs CCVT CDoC CDul CMac CSBt CWSG EBee ELan EMil EPfP LRHS LTen MBri MGos MMuc MRav MWat NLar NPri SCoo SEND SGol SPer SWvt WFar
'Shawnee'	CMac CWib MSwo MWat
§ 'Soleil d'Or'	CBar CDul CTri CWib EBee ECrN ELan EPfP IBoy LAst LBuc LRHS MAsh MBri MMuc MRav NLar

SEND SEWo SGol SHil SLPl SLim SLon SPer SPlb SWvt WFar WHar
'Sparkler' (v) CMac EHoe
'Teton' 🏆H4 CMac CWSG EBee ELan EPfP LAst LRHS MAsh MSwo NEgg NWea SGol SPoG SRms
'Ventoux Red' SCoo
'Watereri' NWea SLPl WFar
'Yellow Sun' see *P.* 'Soleil d'Or'

Pyrethropsis see *Rhodanthemum*

Pyrethrum see *Tanacetum*

Pyrola (*Ericaceae*)

minor NMen
rotundifolia LEdu WHer

Pyrostegia (*Bignoniaceae*)

venusta CCCN MOWG

Pyrrocoma (*Asteraceae*)

clementis EBee

Pyrrosia (*Polypodiaceae*)

hastata CMen
lingua CMen WPGP
polydactyla CMen
sheareri **new** ISha

Pyrus ✿ (*Rosaceae*)

amygdaliformis CLnd SCoo
var. ***cuneifolia***
betulifolia CMCN
calleryana 'Bradford' CLnd
- 'Chanticleer' 🏆H4 Widely available
- 'Chanticleer' variegated (v) CDul MAsh
communis (F) CCVT CDul CTri LBuc NWea SPer SPlb WMou
- 'Abbé Fétel' (D) SKee
- 'Bambinella' (D) **new** SKee
- 'Baronne de Mello' (D) CTho SFam SKee
- 'Beech Hill' (F) CDul EBee ECrN SGol SPer
- 'Belle Guérandaise' (D) SKee
- 'Belle Julie' (D) SKee
- 'Bellissime d'Hiver' (C) SKee
- 'Bergamotte Esperen' (D) SKee
- 'Beth' (D) 🏆H4 CAgr CDoC CMac CSBt CTri CWib ECrN EPfP GTwe IArd LAst LBuc LRHS MBri MGos NLar NPri SFam SKee SLim SPer WHar
- 'Beurré Alexandre Lucas' (D) SKee
- 'Beurré Bedford' (D) SKee
- 'Beurré Clairgeau' (C/D) SKee
- 'Beurré d'Amanlis' (D) SKee
- 'Beurré d'Avalon' (D) SKee
- 'Beurré de Beugny' (D) SKee
- 'Beurré Diel' (D) SKee
- 'Beurré Dumont' (D) CAgr SFam
- 'Beurré Giffard' (D) CAgr
- 'Beurré Hardy' (D) 🏆H4 CAgr CCVT CDoC CDul CMac CSBt CTho CTri CWib ELan EPfP EPom EWTr GTwe IArd LAst LRHS MBri MCoo MMuc MWat NEgg NLar SBfd SEND SFam SKee WHar
- 'Beurré Mortillet' (D) SKee
- 'Beurré Superfin' (D) 🏆H4 ECrN GTwe MCoo SFam SKee WHar
- 'Bianchettone' (D) SKee
- 'Bishop's Thumb' (D) SKee
- 'Black Worcester' (C) GTwe SFam SKee WHar WJas
- 'Blakeney Red' (Perry) SKee WHar
- 'Blickling' (D) SKee
- 'Bon Chrétien d'Hiver' (D) **new** SKee
- 'Brandy' (Perry) CAgr IArd SKee WHar
- 'Bristol Cross' (D) CAgr GTwe SKee
- 'Calebasse Bosc' (D) SKee
- 'Catillac' (C/D) 🏆H4 CAgr GTwe SFam SKee WHar
- 'Charneaux' (F) SVic
- 'Chaumontel' (D) SKee
- 'Clapp's Favourite' (D) CTho ECrN ELan SKee SVic
- 'Concorde'[PBR] (D) 🏆H4 Widely available
- 'Conference' (D) 🏆H4 Widely available
- Delbardélice = 'Delété' LRHS
- 'Docteur Jules Guyot' (D) CAgr SKee
- 'Doyenné Blanc' (F) SKee
- 'Doyenné Boussoch' (D) SKee
- 'Doyenné d'Été' (D) MCoo SFam SKee
- 'Doyenné du Comice' (D) 🏆H4 Widely available
- 'Duchesse d'Angoulême' (D) SKee
- 'Durondeau' (D) GTwe SFam SKee
- 'Easter Beurré' (D) SKee
- 'Emile d'Heyst' (D) GTwe MCoo WHar
- 'Fertility Improved' see *P. communis* 'Improved Fertility'
- 'Fondante d'Automne' (D) CAgr CTho SKee WHar
- 'Forelle' (D) SKee
- 'Glou Morceau' (D) CAgr ECrN GTwe MCoo MWat SFam SKee WHar
- 'Glow Red Williams' (D) SFam
- 'Gorham' (D) 🏆H4 CAgr CTho ECrN GTwe MCoo SFam SKee WHar
- 'Green Horse' (Perry) CCAT
- 'Hacon's Imcomparable' (D) SKee
- 'Harley Gum' (F) WHar
- 'Harvest Queen' (D/C) CAgr
- 'Hellen's Early' (Perry) CCAT IArd SKee WHar
- 'Hendre Huffcap' (Perry) CCAT SKee WHar
- 'Hessle' (D) CAgr GTwe MCoo NWea SFam SKee
- Humbug = 'Pysanka' (F) **new** EPom LBuc MBri MCoo
§ - 'Improved Fertility' (D) CAgr CDoC
- Invincible = 'Delwinor' (D/C) CAgr CDul CSut CTho EPom LBuc LRHS MBri MCoo SLim WHar
- 'Jargonelle' (D) CAgr CTho ECrN GTwe SFam SKee WHar
- 'Jeanne d'Arc' (D) SVic
- 'Joséphine de Malines' (D) 🏆H4 CAgr GTwe IArd MWat SFam SKee WHar
- 'Judge Amphlett' (Perry) WHar
- 'Kieffer' (C) CAgr
- 'Laxton's Foremost' (D) CAgr SKee
- 'Laxton's Satisfaction' (D) SFam
- 'Légipont' (F) CAgr
- 'Louise Bonne of Jersey' (D) 🏆H4 CAgr CDoC CMac CTri ECrN GTwe IArd LAst MGos SFam SKee WHar
- 'Marguérite Marillat' (D) SKee
- 'Marie-Louise' (D) SKee WHar
- 'Marquise' (D) **new** SKee
- 'Merton Pride' (D) CAgr CTho GTwe IArd MCoo MWat SFam SKee WHar
- 'Merton Star' (D) SKee

- 'Moonglow' CAgr
- 'Moorcroft' (Perry) SKee
- 'Mrs Seden' (D) new SKee
- 'Nouveau Poiteau' (C/D) CAgr ECrN GTwe SKee
- 'Nuvar Celebration' (F) SKee
- 'Nye Russet Bartlett' (F) CAgr
- 'Olivier de Serres' (D) SKee
- 'Onward' (D) ♀H4 CAgr CDul CTho CTri CWib ECrN EPom GTwe IArd LRHS MBri NEgg NLar NWea SFam SKee WHar
- 'Ovid' (D) CAgr
§ - 'Packham's Triumph' (D) CAgr CDoC CTri CWib ECrN GTwe LAst SKee SVic WHar
- 'Passe Crassane' (D) SKee
- 'Penrhyn' (D) new WGwG
- 'Pero Nobile' (D) SKee
- 'Pitmaston Duchess' (C/D) ♀H4 ECrN GTwe MCoo SFam SKee WHar
- 'Précoce de Trévoux' (D) WHar
- 'Red Comice' (D/C) GTwe SKee
- 'Red Sensation Bartlett' (D/C) GTwe LBuc LRHS SKee
- 'Robin' (C/D) IArd SKee
- 'Santa Claus' (D) SFam SKee
- 'Seckel' (D) SFam SKee
- 'Sierra' (D) CAgr
- 'Snowdon Queen' (D) WGwG
- 'Souvenir du Congrès' (D) CAgr
- 'Swan's Egg' (D) SKee
- 'Terrace Pearl' (D) SPoG
- 'Thompson's' (D) SFam SKee
- 'Thorn' (Perry) CAgr SKee WHar
- 'Triomphe de Vienne' (D) SFam
- 'Triumph' see *P. communis* 'Packham's Triumph'
- 'Uvedale's St Germain' (C) SFam SKee
- 'Verbelu' SKee
- 'Vicar of Winkfield' (C/D) GTwe SKee
- 'Williams' Bon Chrétien' (D/C) ♀H4 Widely available
- 'Williams Red' (D/C) GTwe LHop SKee
- 'Winnal's Longdon' (Perry) WHar
- 'Winter Nelis' (D) CAgr CTri CWib ECrN GTwe LRHS SFam SKee WHar
- 'Winter Orange' (D) new SKee
- 'Zéphirin Grégoire' (D) SKee

cordata CDul CTho
elaeagnifolia CDul SLim
var. ***kotschyana***
- 'Silver Sails' CLnd EMil LAst MBlu MBri NLar SCoo SSpi

fauriei CTho
nivalis CDul CLnd CTho EBee ECrN EPfP LMaj LRHS MBri MRav SCoo SPer
- 'Catalia' MAsh MBri SCoo

pashia NLar
pyraster CDul CHab WCot
pyrifolia '20th Century' see *P. pyrifolia* 'Nijisseiki'
- 'Hosui' (F) CAgr SVic
- 'Kosui' (F) SVic
- 'Kumoi' (F) LRHS MCoo WHar
§ - 'Nijisseiki' (F) SVic
- 'Shinko' (F) CAgr
- 'Shinseiki' (F) CAgr MWat SKee WHar
- 'Shinsui' (F) SKee

* ***salicifolia*** var. ***orientalis*** CTho
- 'Pendula' ♀H4 Widely available

ussuriensis CTho

Q

Qiongzhuea see *Chimonobambusa*

Quercus ✿ (*Fagaceae*)

NJM 09.121 WPGP
NJM 09.181 WPGP
acerifolia EPfP
acherdophylla SBir WPGP
§ ***acuta*** CBcs
acutifolia SBir
acutifolia* × *mexicana SBir
acutissima CBcs CDul CMCN EPfP SBir
aegilops see *Q. ithaburensis* subsp. *macrolepis*
affinis EPfP MBri SBir
agrifolia CBcs CDul CMCN EBtc EGFP
ajudaghiensis see *Q. hartwissiana*
alba CMCN SBir
aliena CDul CMCN SBir
alnifolia CDul
arkansana CMCN SBir
× ***atlantica*** SBir
austrina CMCN SBir
× ***beadlei*** see *Q.* × *saulii*
× ***benderi*** SBir
berberidifolia CMCN SBir
bicolor CMCN EPfP SBir
× ***bimundorum*** SBir
§ - 'Crimschmidt' EPfP MBlu MBri

borealis see *Q. rubra*
breweri see *Q. garryana* var. *breweri*
buckleyi CDul CMCN SBir
× ***bushii*** CMCN EPfP MBlu MBri SBir
- 'Seattle Trident' EPfP MBlu

canariensis ♀H4 CBcs CLnd CMCN CTho EPfP WMou WPGP
candicans new SBir
castanea new WPGP
castaneifolia CDul CMCN
- 'Green Spire' ♀H4 CDul CMCN EPfP IArd MBlu SBir SEND

cerris CBcs CCVT CDoC CDul CLnd CMCN ECrN ELan EPfP LAst LMaj MGos NWea SEND SPer WFar
- 'Afyon Lace' MBlu SBir
§ - 'Argenteovariegata' (v) CBcs CDul CMCN EBee ELan EPfP IArd MAsh MBlu MBri MPkF SBir SMad WCot WPat
- 'Athena' new MBlu
- 'Marmor Star' SEND
- 'Variegata' see *Q. cerris* 'Argenteovariegata'
- 'Wodan' MBlu

chenii CDul CMCN SBir
chrysolepis CMCN EPfP SBir
coccifera CGHE CMCN SSpi WPGP
- subsp. ***calliprinos*** SBir

coccinea CBcs CDul CMCN CTho CTri EBee ECrN EPfP MBlu MWht NEgg NWea SBir SEWo SLim SPer SPoG WPat
- 'Splendens' ♀H4 CDoC CDul CHll CJun CMCN CTri EBee ELan EPfP IArd MAsh MBlu MBri NLar SMad SPer WPat

conspersa SBir
crassifolia WPGP

	Name	Suppliers
	Crimson Spire	see *Q.* × ***bimundorum*** 'Crimschmidt'
	crispipilis	SBir
	dalechampii	CMCN SBir
	dentata	CDul CMCN
	- 'Carl Ferris Miller'	CBcs CMCN EPfP LLHF MBlu MBri SBir SEND WCot WMou WPGP WPat
	- 'Pinnatifida'	CMCN EPfP IDee MBlu MPkF SMad WCot WPat
	- 'Sir Harold Hillier'	MBlu MBri
	- subsp. ***yunnanensis***	CDul SBir
	dolicholepis	CMCN SBir
	'Doring's Zweizack'	SBir
	douglasii	CMCN SSpi
	- G 261	WPGP
	dumosa	CMCN
	- G 315	WPGP
	- G 316	WPGP
	durifolia new	SBir
	× ***dysophylla*** new	WPGP
	elliottii	SBir
	ellipsoidalis	CDul CMCN SBir
	- 'Hemelrijk'	EPfP IDee MBlu MBri SBir
	× ***exacta***	SBir
	fabrei	CMCN EGFP SBir
	faginea	CDul EGFP
	falcata	CMCN EBtc SBir
	- var. ***pagodifolia***	see *Q. pagoda*
	× ***fernaldii***	CMCN EPfP MBlu
	frainetto	CDoC CDul CMCN CTho EBee ECrN ELan EPfP LMaj NWea SEND SPer WMou
	- 'Hungarian Crown' ♀H4	CMCN EPfP MBlu SBir
	- 'Tortworth'	MBri SMad WMou
	- 'Trump'	CMCN MPkF
	franchetii	SBir
	gambelii	CMCN EGFP MPkF
	garryana	CMCN WPGP
§	- var. ***breweri***	EGFP
	- var. ***fruticosa***	see *Q. garryana* var. *breweri*
	georgiana	CMCN EPfP SBir
	gilva	CMCN SBir
	glabrescens	WPGP
	glandulifera	see *Q. serrata* Thunb.
§	***glauca***	CBcs CDul CMCN EPfP IArd NLar SBir WPGP
	graciliformis	SBir
	gravesii	CMCN EPfP SBir
	greggii	SBir WPGP
§	***hartwissiana***	SBir
	× ***hastingsii***	CMCN SBir
	havardii	CMCN
	× ***hawkinsiae***	SBir
	× ***haynaldiana***	SBir
	hemisphaerica	EPfP SBir
	× ***heterophylla***	CMCN EPfP SBir
	× ***hickelii***	CMCN EPfP SBir
	- 'Giesselhorst'	CDul
	hirtifolia new	WPGP
§	× ***hispanica***	CLnd
	- 'Ambrozyana'	CDul CMCN
	- 'Bloemendaal'	MBlu MBri
	- 'Diversifolia'	CMCN EPfP MBlu
	- 'Fulhamensis'	CMCN MBlu MBri SBir SEND WMou
§	- 'Lucombeana' ♀H4	CBcs CDul CHGN CMCN CSBt CTho EBee ELan EPfP IArd IDee MBlu SBir SEND SPer
§	- 'Pseudoturneri'	CBcs CDul EBee ELan MBlu SEND
	- 'Suberosa'	CTho
	- 'Waasland Select'	IArd MBri NLar SBir
	- 'Wageningen'	CDul CMCN MBri SBir
	hypoleucoides	CDul CMCN EPfP
	ilex ♀H4	Widely available
	- 'Fordii'	SBir
	ilicifolia	CMCN EPfP SBir WPGP
	imbricaria	CDul CLnd CMCN EPfP SBir
	incana Roxb.	see *Q. leucotrichophora*
	× ***introgressa***	SBir
§	***ithaburensis*** subsp. ***macrolepis***	CMCN LEdu SBir
	- - 'Hemelrijk Silver'	MBlu SBir WPat
	× ***jackiana***	EPfP
	john-tuckeri G 271	WPGP
	kelloggii	CBcs CLnd CMCN EPfP MBri SBir WPGP
	× ***kewensis***	CMCN LMaj SBir
	laevigata	see *Q. acuta*
	laevis	CDul CMCN EPfP SBir
	'Langtry'	SBir
§	***laurifolia***	CDul CLnd CMCN EGFP EPfP SBir
	laurina	SBir WPGP
§	***leucotrichophora***	CDul CMCN SBir
	liaotungensis	see *Q. wutaishanica*
	× ***libanerris***	SBir
	- 'Rotterdam'	CMCN SBir
	libani	CMCN EPfP
	lobata	CMCN EGFP LEdu
	× ***lucombeana***	see *Q.* × *hispanica*
	- 'William Lucombe'	see *Q.* × *hispanica* 'Lucombeana'
	× ***ludoviciana***	CDul CMCN EPfP SBir
	lyrata	CDul CMCN SGol
	macranthera	CMCN EPfP MBri SBir
	macrocarpa	CDul CMCN EPfP
	macrolepis	see *Q. ithaburensis* subsp. *macrolepis*
	marilandica	CDul CMCN EPfP IDee MBlu SBir
	'Mauri'	IArd MBlu MBri
	mexicana	IArd SBir WPGP
§	***michauxii***	CDul CMCN EPfP MBlu SBir
	mongolica	CDul MBlu SBir
	- subsp. ***crispula*** var. ***grosseserrata***	CMCN
	monimotricha new	SBir
	muhlenbergii	CMCN MBlu MPkF SBir
	× ***mutabilis***	SBir
	myrsinifolia	see *Q. glauca*
	myrtifolia	SBir
	nigra	CDul CMCN MBri NLar SBir
	- 'Beethoven'	MBlu MBri SBir
I	- 'Nyewoodii'	SBir
	nuttallii	see *Q. texana*
	obtusa	see *Q. laurifolia*
	oglethorpensis	SBir
	oxyodon new	SBir
	pacifica G 301	WPGP
	- G 305	WPGP
	- G 313	WPGP
§	***pagoda***	CMCN IGor SBir
	palustris ♀H4	CCVT CDoC CDul CLnd CMCN CTho EBee ECrN ELan EPfP EWTr IArd LMaj MAsh MBlu NEgg NLar NWea SBir SEWo SGol SPer
	- 'Green Dwarf'	CMCN MBlu SEWo
	- 'Isabel' new	EPfP
	- 'Pendula'	CMCN
	- 'Silhouette'	CJun SBir

	– 'Swamp Pygmy'	CMCN EPfP MBlu
	– 'Windischleuba'	MBlu
	pannosa	SBir
	parvula var. ***parvula***	SBir
§	× ***pauciloba***	CMCN
	pedunculata	see *Q. robur*
	pedunculiflora	see *Q. robur* subsp. *pedunculiflora*
§	***petraea*** 🏆H4	CDoC CDul CHab CLnd CTri ECrN EPfP GAbr MBlu NLar NWea SGol SPer WFar WMou
	– 'Acutiloba'	SBir
§	– 'Insecata'	CDul CMCN EPfP MBlu
	– 'Laciniata'	see *Q. petraea* 'Insecata'
	– Mespilifolia Group	CDul
§	– 'Purpurea'	CMCN MBlu NLar
	– 'Rubicunda'	see *Q. petraea* 'Purpurea'
§	***phellos***	CDul CLnd CMCN EBee EBtc EPfP EWTr MBlu MBri SBir SLPl
	phillyreoides	CBcs CDul CMCN EPfP SBir SLPl
	polymorpha	CDul CMCN MBri MPkF
	Pondaim Group	CMCN WMou
	pontica	CDul CMCN EPfP IArd LLHF MBlu MPkF WPat
	prinus misapplied	see *Q. michauxii*
§	***prinus*** L.	CMCN EPfP MBri
	pubescens	CMCN SEND
	pumila Michx.	see *Q. prinus* L.
	pumila Walt.	see *Q. phellos*
	pungens	CMCN
	pyrenaica	CDul CLnd CMCN CTho EBtc MBri SEND
	– 'Pendula'	CMCN EPfP
	Regal Prince	see *Q.* × *warei* 'Long'
	rhysophylla	CBcs CDul CMCN EPfP IDee MBlu SBir WPGP
	– 'Maya'	CDul EBee ELan EPfP IArd MBri MPkF NLar SBir
	× ***riparia***	SBir
§	***robur*** 🏆H4	Widely available
	– 'Argenteomarginata' (v)	CDul CMCN MBlu WPat
	– 'Atropurpurea'	MPkF NWea
	– 'Compacta'	MBlu
	– 'Concordia'	CBcs CLnd CMCN EBee EBtc ELan EPfP MBlu MPkF NLar NWea SKHP
	– 'Dissecta'	CMCN
	– 'Facrist'	SBir
	– f. ***fastigiata***	CDoC CDul CLnd CTho EBee ECrN EPfP IArd IVic LHop MGos NWea SBir SGol SLPl SLim SPer WFar
	– – 'Koster' 🏆H4	CDul CMCN CMac CTri EPfP LMaj MBlu SBir
	– 'Fennessyi'	IArd
	– 'Filicifolia' misapplied	see *Q. robur* 'Pectinata'
	– 'Filicifolia'	WPat
	– var. ***haas***	CDul
	– – 'Cankiri'	SBir
	– 'Irtha'	EPfP
	– 'Menhir'	LLHF MBlu WCot WPat
§	– 'Pectinata'	EPfP MBlu
§	– subsp. ***pedunculiflora***	CMCN
	– 'Pendula'	CMCN MBlu
	– 'Purpurascens'	CMCN
	– 'Purpurea'	MBlu
	– 'Raba'	CMCN
	– 'Rita's Gold'	MBri
§	– 'Salfast'	MBlu
	– 'Salicifolia Fastigiata'	see *Q. robur* 'Salfast'
	– 'Strypemonde'	CMCN
	– 'Timuki'	IArd MBlu
	– f. ***variegata*** (v)	CJun
	– – 'Fürst Schwarzenburg' (v)	MBlu
	– 'Zeeland'	SBir
	robur × ***macrocarpa***	SBir
	× ***virginiana***	
	rotundifolia	CAgr CMCN EPfP WPGP
§	***rubra*** 🏆H4	Widely available
	– 'Aurea'	CJun CMCN EBee EPfP MBlu
	– 'Boltes Gold'	CJun MBlu MBri
	– 'Cyrille'	SBir
	– 'Magic Fire'	CDul CMCN EPfP MBlu NLar SBir
	– 'Red Queen'	MBlu
*	– 'Sunshine'	CMCN MBlu WPat
	rugosa	CMCN SBir
	× ***runcinata***	SBir
	salicina	WPGP
	× ***sargentii*** 'Thomas' **new**	EPfP MBri
	sartorii	SBir WPGP
§	× ***saulii***	CMCN SBir
	× ***schochiana***	EPfP MBlu MBri
	× ***schuettei***	SBir
	semecarpifolia	MBlu
§	***serrata*** Thunb.	CDul CMCN EGFP EPfP LEdu MBri SBir
	sessiliflora	see *Q. petraea*
	shumardii	CDul CMCN EPfP MBlu MBri NLar SBir SGol
	sinuata subsp. ***breviloba***	SBir
	stellata	CDul CMCN EPfP SBir
	suber	CAgr CBcs CCVT CDoC CDul CMCN CTho EBee ELan EPfP IArd LEdu LMaj MGos MREP SEND WPGP
	– 'Sopron'	EPfP MBlu
§	***texana***	CMCN EPfP SBir
	– New Madrid Group	CDul EBee EPfP MBlu MBri SBir
	tomentella	SBir
	trojana	CDul CMCN SBir
	tuberculata **new**	WPGP
	turbinella	CMCN
	× ***turneri***	CDoC CLnd CMCN CTho EPfP MBri WMou
	– 'Pseudoturneri'	see *Q.* × *hispanica* 'Pseudoturneri'
	undulata Torr.	see *Q.* × *pauciloba*
	variabilis	CDul CMCN EPfP MPkF SGol
	velutina	CBcs CDul CJun CLnd CMCN CTho EPfP IVic NLar SBir
	– 'Albertsii'	CJun IArd MBlu
	– 'Oakridge Walker'	MBlu
	– 'Rubrifolia'	CJun CMCN EPfP
	'Vilmoriana'	CMCN IDee
	virginiana	CBcs CMCN SBir
	× ***warburgii***	EPfP
	× ***warei***	SBir
	– 'Chimney Fire' **new**	EPfP
§	– 'Long'	EPfP MBlu MPkF
	– 'Windcandle'	MBlu SBir
	wislizeni	CDul CMCN NLar SBir
	– G 265	CBcs WPGP
§	***wutaishanica***	CMCN

Quillaja (*Quillajaceae*)

saponaria	CArn CBcs CCCN IArd IDee

quince see *Cydonia oblonga*

Quisqualis (*Combretaceae*)

indica	CCCN MOWG

R

Rabiea (*Aizoaceae*)

	difformis **new**	CPBP

Racosperma see *Acacia*

× *Ramberlea* (*Gesneriaceae*)

	'Inchgarth' **new**	GKev

Ramonda (*Gesneriaceae*)

§	***myconi*** ♀H4	CLAP CPBP ECho EWes GEdr LLHF NMen NSla SChF SRms WAbe
	- var. ***alba***	CLAP ECho GEdr GKev WThu
	- 'Jim's Shadow'	WAbe
	- 'Rosea'	CLAP LLHF
	nathaliae ♀H4	CLAP ECho WAbe WThu
	- 'Alba'	CLAP NSla WAbe
	pyrenaica	see *R. myconi*
	serbica	NSla WThu

Randia (*Rubiaceae*)

	formosa	CCCN

Ranunculus (*Ranunculaceae*)

	abnormis	WAbe
	aconitifolius	EBee ECha ECho GCra GKev GMaP NLar SHar SWat WHal WMnd WMoo
	- 'Flore Pleno' (d) ♀H4	Widely available
	acris	CHab NBir NLan NMir NPer WSFF
	- subsp. ***acris*** 'Stevenii'	EBee EPPr IGor LPla SDix WHal
	- 'Citrinus'	CElw GBin LRHS NCGa WHal WMoo
	- 'Flore Pleno' (d) ♀H4	CDes CElw CWCL EBee ECha ECho EHrv ELan EPfP GBin GQue LEdu LPot LRHS MCot MRav NBid NBro NGdn NRya NWad SPoG SRms SUsu WFar WHil WMoo XLum
	- 'Hedgehog'	ECho EPPr MMHG
	- 'Sulphureus'	CBre WFar WHal
	alpestris	ECho GEdr NMen NRya
	amplexicaulis	EBee ELon EPot GKev GMaP NHar NMen
	aquatilis	CWat EHon MSKA MWts SWat WMAq WSFF
	× ***arendsii*** 'Moonlight'	CElw CRDP LRHS
	asiaticus	ERCP
	baurii	ECho SBrt
	bilobus	NMen
§	***bulbosus*** 'F.M. Burton'	GBuc NRya WCot
	- ***farreri***	see *R. bulbosus* 'F.M. Burton'
	- 'Speciosus Plenus'	see *R. constantinopolitanus* 'Plenus'
	calandrinioides ♀H2-3	EBee ECho EWes IFoB NBir WAbe WCot
	- SF 137	WCot
§	***constantinopolitanus*** 'Plenus' (d)	EWld GCal MRav NBid NBro SUsu WCot WFar WMoo
	cortusifolius	SWat
	crenatus	ECho GEdr NMen NRya
	creticus	ECho
	extorris 'Flore Pleno' (d)	EBee
	ficaria	CArn CTri ESwi MHer SEND WHer WSFF WShi
	- 'Aglow in the Dark'	CHid
	- var. ***albus***	CHid CSam ELon LEdu NRya WOut
	- anemone-centred	see *R. ficaria* 'Collarette'
	- 'Art Nouveau'	CDes EBee
	- 'Ashen Primrose'	EBee
§	- var. ***aurantiacus***	ECha ECho MHer NLar NRya SPhx SRms WFar
	- 'Bowles's Double'	see *R. ficaria* 'Double Bronze', 'Picton's Double'
	- 'Brambling'	CBre CHid CLAP ECho LEdu NLar SBch
	- 'Brazen Child'	MDKP SHar
	- 'Brazen Daughter'	ECho
	- 'Brazen Hussy'	Widely available
	- 'Broadleas Black'	ECho
	- subsp. ***bulbilifer*** 'Chedglow'	MDKP WCot
	- 'Chocolate Cream'	ECho
§	- subsp. ***chrysocephalus***	CDes ECha ELon IFro SBch WCot WFar
	- 'Coffee Cream'	EBee
§	- 'Collarette' (d)	CHid EBee ECho ELon EPot GBuc IGor LEdu MHer NBir NLar NMen NRya WFar WOut
	- 'Coppernob'	CHid ECho ELon MDKP SBch WCot WFar
	- 'Cupreus'	see *R. ficaria* var. *aurantiacus*
	- 'Damerham' (d)	CHid
	- 'Deborah Jope'	SUsu
	- double, cream-flowered	see *R. ficaria* 'Double Mud'
	- - yellow-flowered	see *R. ficaria* Flore Pleno Group
	- - green-eyed (d)	CHid LEdu
§	- 'Double Bronze' (d)	CHid EBee ECho GBuc LEdu MDKP MHer NBir NLar NRya SHar
§	- 'Double Mud' (d)	CHid CLAP ECho GAbr GBuc IFro LEdu NLar NRya SHar WFar WHal
	- 'Dusky Maiden'	ECho NLar SBch WFar
	- 'E.A. Bowles'	see *R. ficaria* 'Collarette'
	- 'Elan' (d)	CDes EBee MMoz
§	- Flore Pleno Group (d)	CHid CTri ECha ECho ELan ELon EPPr GAbr NRya NSti SBch SRms WCot WFar
	- 'Fried Egg'	ECho
	- 'Granby Cream'	ECho
	- 'Green Mantle'	ECho
	- 'Green Petal'	CHid EBee ECho EPPr GBuc LEdu MCot MDKP MHer NBir NLar NRya SSvw WHal WHer
	- 'Holly'	see *R. ficaria* 'Holly Green'
§	- 'Holly Green'	ECho
	- 'Hyde Hall'	ECho NLar SBch WFar
	- 'Jake Perry'	MNrw
	- 'Jane's Dress'	CHid
	- 'Ken Aslet Double' (d)	CDes EBee LEdu MHer NLar WHal
	- 'Lambrook Black'	WHer
	- 'Lambrook Variegated' (v)	CFis EPPr
	- 'Lemon Queen'	CHid
	- 'Leo'	MDKP MNrw
	- subsp. ***major***	see *R. ficaria* subsp. *chrysocephalus*
	- 'Melanie Jope'	EBee
	- 'Mobled Jade'	CHid
	- 'Monksilver'	IFro
	- 'Mud'	MDKP
	- 'Newton Abbot'	CBre
I	- 'Nigrifolia'	MDKP
	- 'Old Master'	NCGa WCot
	- 'Orange Sorbet'	LEdu MNrw NLar
§	- 'Picton's Double' (d)	MNrw
	- 'Primrose'	CHid NLar NRya
	- 'Primrose Elf'	EBee
	- 'Ragamuffin' (d)	CDes EBee LEdu

- 'Randall's White'	CFis EBee EPfP MCot NCGa SHar WFar
- 'Richard and Val'	WCot
- 'Salad Bowl' (d)	ECho
- 'Salmon's White'	CBre EBee ECho ELan ELon EPPr NBir NLar NRya SHar WFar WHal WPtf
- 'Sheldon Silver'	CHid
- 'Silver Collar'	LEdu
- 'Single Cream'	MNrw
- 'Torquay Elf'	EBee
- 'Tortoiseshell'	CHid EBee MDKP WFar
- 'Wisley Double'	see *R. ficaria* 'Double Bronze'
- 'Wisley White'	NSti
- 'Witchampton'	CDes EBee
- 'Yaffle'	CFis CHid EBee ECho MDKP
flammula	CBen CHab CRow CWat EHon EWay LPBA MSKA SWat WPnP
- subsp. ***minimus***	CRow
gouanii	NRya
gramineus ♀H4	CCon CSpe CWCL EBee ECho EDAr GBin GEdr GMaP LBee LRHS MNrw MWat NMen NRya SMrm SRms SUsu WCAu WFar WPer
- 'Pardal'	SCnR WCot WFar
* ***guttatus***	NMen
illyricus	EBee ECha EDAr EPPr LRHS NRya WAbe WHal
kochii	EBee ECho EPot WCot
lanuginosus	EPPr
lingua	SPlb
- 'Grandiflorus'	CBen CRow EHon LPBA MSKA NPer SWat WHal WMAq WPnP
lyallii	EBee
macauleyi	GEdr NRya
millefoliatus	CPBP ECho GBuc NMen WAbe
montanus double-flowered (d)	CPBP SHar WCot
- 'Molten Gold' ♀H4	ECho ECtt GEdr GMaP MMHG MRav
nivicola	WCot
parnassiifolius	GEdr NMen WAbe
platanifolius	LPla NRHS SMHy
'Purple Heart' (d) **new**	EPfP
pyrenaeus	NMen
repens 'Buttered Popcorn' (v)	CRow NLar WMoo
- 'Cat's Eyes' (v)	EBee
- 'Gloria Spale'	CBre CRow
- var. ***pleniflorus*** (d)	CBre CRow SRot WFar
- 'Snowdrift' (v)	CDes EBee LEdu
- 'Timothy Clark' (d)	CBre
seguieri	ECho LHop LLHF LRHS NRHS WAbe
serbicus	EBee
speciosus 'Flore Pleno'	see *R. constantinopolitanus* 'Plenus'

Ranzania (*Berberidaceae*)

japonica	CDes WCru

Raoulia (*Asteraceae*)

australis misapplied	see *R. hookeri*
australis ambig.	SMad
australis Hook.f. ex Raoul	CEnt CYeo EDAr EPot GEdr GKev ITim MAsh MWat
§ - Lutescens Group	ECha ECho
glabra	EPot
haastii	ECou
§ ***hookeri***	CMea ECha ECho EPot ITim MAsh SPlb SRms WAbe WPat WThu
- var. ***laxa***	EWes
× ***loganii***	see × *Leucoraoulia loganii*
lutescens	see *R. australis* Lutescens Group
monroi	EPot
petriensis	WAbe
× ***petrimia*** 'Margaret Pringle'	WAbe
subsericea	EWes NMen
tenuicaulis	ECha SPlb

raspberry see *Rubus idaeus*

Ratibida (*Asteraceae*)

columnifera	CRWN EBee EPfP SPet SPhx
- f. ***pulcherrima***	CSpe EPfP LRHS NRHS SMad SPet SPhx XLum
- - 'Red Midget'	CSpe EBee LRHS NRHS SBfd SPet SPhx
- - 'Red Midnight'	EBee
pinnata	CEnt CRWN CSam EBee EPfP LSRN NBir SMad SPet SPhx SPlb WCot WMnd WSHC XLum

Ravenala (*Strelitziaceae*)

madagascariensis	EAmu SPlb XBlo

Ravenea (*Arecaceae*)

rivularis	CCCN EAmu XBlo

Rechsteineria see *Sinningia*

redcurrant see *Ribes rubrum* (R)

Rehderodendron (*Styracaceae*)

macrocarpum	WPGP

Rehmannia (*Plantaginaceae*)

angulata misapplied	see *R. elata*
§ ***elata*** ♀H2	CCon CSam CSpe ELan EPfP LAst LBMP LHop LLWP LRHS MHer MNHC NOrc SDys SGar SMrm WFar WHil WTcb WWEG WWlt XLum
glutinosa ♀H3	CSpe EWTr
piasezkii	WPGP

Reineckea (*Asparagaceae*)

§ ***carnea***	CCon CHid CHll CPLG EBee ECha ELan EPPr EWTr GBin GCal GEdr GKev LEdu LRHS MPie NSti SDys SEND SPlb SUsu WCot WCru WPGP WPtf XLum
- B&SWJ 4808	ELon WCru
- SDR 330	EBee EPPr GKev
- 'Baoxing Booty'	WCru
- 'Crûg's Broadleaf'	WCru
- RBGE form	GEdr
- 'Variegata' (v)	EShb WCot
aff. ***carnea*** from Sichuan	WCot

Reinwardtia (*Linaceae*)

§ ***indica***	CCCN CHll CPLG EShb SMrm
trigyna	see *R. indica*

Remusatia (*Araceae*)

hookeriana	EBee GBin GHim
- B&SWJ 2529	WCru

pumila	EBee GBin GHim
vivipara	EBee GBin GHim

Reseda (*Resedaceae*)

alba	MHer
lutea	SIde
luteola	CHab CHby GPoy MHer WHer WHfH WSFF

Restio (*Restionaceae*)

festuciformis	CPrp EHoe GBin
paniculatus	CCCN CDTJ CHEx
subverticillatus	CAbb CHEx
tetraphyllus	CAbb CCon CHid CTrC CTsd EHoe GBin SPlb SPoG

Reynoutria see *Fallopia*

Rhamnus (*Rhamnaceae*)

alaternus	WFar
var. ***angustifolia***	
§ - 'Argenteovariegata' (v) ♀H4	Widely available
- 'Variegata'	see *R. alaternus* 'Argenteovariegata'
cathartica	CCVT CDul CHab CLnd CTri ECrN EPfP EShb LBuc NLar NWea SEWo WMou WSFF
frangula	see *Frangula alnus*
imeretina	EBee WPGP WPat
pallasii	NLar
pumila	NLar
taquetii	NLar

× *Rhaphiobotrya* (*Rosaceae*)

§ 'Coppertone'	EPfP SEND

Rhaphiolepis (*Rosaceae*)

× ***delacourii***	CWib EBee ECrN ELan EPfP LAst SEND SRms
- 'Coates' Crimson'	CDoC CTsd EBee ELan EPfP IVic LAst LHop LRHS SLim WPat WSHC
- Enchantress = 'Moness'	CTsd EBee ELan EPfP LRHS MAsh MRav SLon
- 'Pink Cloud'	CBcs EPfP LRHS
- 'Spring Song'	SLon
indica	ERom SEND
- B&SWJ 8405	WCru
- 'Coppertone'	see × *Rhaphiobotrya* 'Coppertone'
- Springtime = 'Monme'	CBcs EBee IVic LRHS SLim
umbellata ♀H2-3	CBcs CHEx CTri CWib EBee ELan EPfP LAst LHop LRHS SBrt SEND SHil SLon WFar WPGP WPat WSHC
- f. ***ovata***	WCot
- - B&SWJ 4706	WCru

Rhaphithamnus (*Verbenaceae*)

cyanocarpus	see *R. spinosus*
§ ***spinosus***	CBcs CMCN EBee EPfP GAbr GBin LEdu LRHS

Rhapidophyllum (*Arecaceae*)

hystrix	CBrP

Rhapis ✿ (*Arecaceae*)

§ ***excelsa*** ♀H1	CCCN EAmu XBlo
- 'Variegata' (v) **new**	EAmu

Rhazya (*Apocynaceae*)

orientalis	see *Amsonia orientalis*

Rheum ✿ (*Polygonaceae*)

CC 5243	EWld
GWJ 9329 from Sikkim	WCru
SDR 5004	GKev
SDR 5919	GKev
§ 'Ace of Hearts'	Widely available
'Ace of Spades'	see *R.* 'Ace of Hearts'
acuminatum	EBee
- HWJCM 252	WCru
- HWJK 2354	WCru
- PAB 2487	LEdu
alexandrae	EWTr EWes GCal LEdu MMHG NLar WFar
- SDR 2924	EBee
- SDR 4602	GKev
- SDR 4757	GKev
- SDR 6031	GKev
altaicum	LEdu
'Andrew's Red'	GTwe
§ ***australe***	CAgr CArn CCon CSpe EBee GCal LEdu LPBA NBro NLar WCot WFar WHoo WMnd XLum
'Cally Dwarf'	GCal
'Cally Giant'	GBin GCal
delavayi	GCal NLar
emodi	see *R. australe*
N × ***hybridum*** from Burston Hall	LRHS
- from Gledhill	LRHS
- from Hartley	LRHS
- from Holt	LRHS
- from Isle of Ely Horticultural Institute	LRHS
- from Maldon, Essex	LRHS
- from Ramsden	LRHS
- from Sherburn Park	LRHS
- 'Amerikanske Kaempe'	LRHS
- 'Amstel Seedling'	LRHS
- 'Appleton's Forcing'	LRHS
- 'Baker's All Season'	GTwe LRHS
- 'Bedford Scarlet'	LRHS
- 'Brandy Carr Scarlet'	ECrN EGHP MRav
- 'Brown's Crimson'	LRHS
- 'Brown's Red'	LRHS
- 'Canada Red'	GTwe LRHS
- 'Carter's Forcing'	LRHS
- 'Cawood Advance'	LRHS
- 'Cawood Castle'	LRHS
- 'Cawood Delight'	GTwe LRHS SMHy
- 'Cawood Ensign'	LRHS
- 'Cawood Oak'	LRHS
- 'Champagne'	CAgr ECrN EGHP EPfP EPom GTwe LBuc LRHS NRHS SPer SWal
* - 'Champagne Rood'	LRHS
- 'Collis's Ruby'	LRHS
- 'Coutt's Red Stick'	LRHS
- 'Crimson Queen'	LRHS
- 'Crimson Wine'	LRHS
- 'Cutbush's Seedling'	LRHS
- 'Dawe's Challenge'	LRHS
- 'Daw's Champion'	GTwe LRHS
- 'Donkere Bloedrede Zoet'	LRHS
- 'Drust's Red'	LRHS
- 'Early Champagne'	LRHS
- 'Early Cherry'	LRHS
- 'Early Devon'	LRHS
- 'Early Mitchell'	LRHS
- 'Early Superb'	LRHS

	- 'Early Victoria'	LRHS
	- 'Exhibition Red'	LRHS
	- 'Fenton's Special'	CTri EGHP GTwe LRHS MCoo MRav
*	- 'Frambozenrood Limburg'	LRHS
	- 'Fulton's Strawberry Surprise' ♀H4	GTwe LRHS
	- 'German Wine'	LRHS
	- 'Giant Grooveless Crimson'	LRHS
	- 'Glaskin's Perpetual'	CAgr CWib EMil EPfP LAst LBuc LRHS MHoo NPri NRHS SWal
	- 'Goliath'	LRHS MCoo
	- 'Grandad's Favorite' ♀H4	LRHS NRHS
	- 'Green Jam'	LRHS
	- 'Greengage'	GTwe LRHS
	- 'Guardsman'	LRHS
	- 'Hadspen Crimson'	CBct WCot
	- 'Hammond's Early'	GTwe LRHS
	- 'Harbinger'	GTwe LRHS
	- 'Hawke's Champagne' ♀H4	GTwe LRHS WCot
	- 'Holsteiner Blut'	EPfP LRHS SPoG
	- 'Irish Apple'	LRHS
	- 'Kentville'	LRHS
	- 'Larne'	LRHS
	- 'Laxton's No 1'	LRHS NRHS
	- 'Linnaeus'	LRHS
	- 'Livingstone'PBR	LRHS
	- 'Mac Red' ♀H4	GTwe
	- 'Marshall's Early'	LRHS
	- 'McDonald'	LRHS
	- 'Merton's Banner'	LRHS
	- 'Merton's Broadleaf'	LRHS
	- 'Merton's Foremost'	LRHS
	- 'Merton's Yardstick'	LRHS
	- 'Mikoot'	LRHS
	- 'Mira'	LRHS
	- 'Mitchell's Early Albert'	LRHS
	- 'Mitchell's Royal Albert'	LRHS
	- 'Mrs McKenzie'	LRHS
	- 'Perpetual'	LRHS
	- 'Pink Champagne'	EPfP SPoG
	- 'Prince Albert'	EGHP GTwe LRHS NEgg
*	- 'Ras Versteeg'	LRHS
	- 'Raspberry Red'	EPfP EPom LBuc LRHS NRHS
	- 'Red Champagne'	EGHP EPfP LBuc LRHS SPoG
	- 'Red Prolific'	GTwe
	- 'Red Victoria'	LRHS
	- 'Reed's Champagne'	LRHS
	- 'Reed's Early Superb' ♀H4	GTwe LRHS
	- 'Reed's Red'	LRHS
	- 'Riverside Giant'	LRHS
	- 'Rosenhagen'	LRHS
	- 'Ruby'	LRHS
	- 'Saint Kevin'	LRHS
	- 'Seedling Le Grice'	LRHS
	- 'Seedling Piggot'	LRHS
	- 'Stein's Champagne' ♀H4	GTwe LRHS
	- 'Stockbridge'	LRHS
	- 'Stockbridge Arrow'	CMac CSut CTri ECrN EGHP EMil GTwe LRHS NEgg
	- 'Stockbridge Bingo'	GTwe LRHS
	- 'Stockbridge Cropper'	LRHS
	- 'Stockbridge Emerald'	GTwe LRHS
	- 'Stockbridge Guardsman'	GTwe
	- 'Stockbridge Harbinger'	LRHS
	- 'Stockbridge Smith'	LRHS
	- 'Stott's Monarch'	LRHS
	- 'Strawberry'	GTwe LRHS NBir NRHS
	- 'Strawberry Red'	LRHS
	- 'Strawberry Taylor'	LRHS
	- 'Sutton's Cherry Red'	GTwe LRHS
	- 'The Appleton'	LRHS
	- 'The Sutton'	CWib GTwe LRHS
	- 'Timperley Early' ♀H4	CDoC CMac CSBt CTri CWib EGHP EMil EPfP EPom GTwe LAst LRHS LSRN MGos MMuc MRav NEgg NPri NRHS SBfd SCoo SEND SKee SLim SPer SPoG SWal WGwG WHar
	- 'Tingley Cherry'	GTwe
	- 'Valentine'	LRHS
	- 'Victoria'	CAgr CDoC CMac CSBt CTri CWib EGHP ELau EMil EPfP EPom GTwe LBuc LRHS LSRN MCoo MGos MHer MHoo MNHC NRHS SLim SPoG SVic SWal WGwG WHar
	- 'Victoria 2' **new**	LAst
	- 'Vinrabarber Svenborg'	LRHS
	- 'Vroege Engelse'	LRHS
	- 'Zwolle Seedling'	GTwe
	kialense	CBct CDes EBee LEdu NBid NSti WPGP WWEG
	officinale	CArn CBct CHEx EBee GCal LRHS MBri SIde SWat
	palmatum	CArn CBcs EBee ECha ELan EPfP GCra LPBA LRHS MGos MNHC MRav NGdn SWat WFar
	- 'Atropurpureum'	see *R. palmatum* 'Atrosanguineum'
§	- 'Atrosanguineum' ♀H4	CBct CCon CMac EBee ECha ELan EPfP EShb GCal IFro LBMP LPBA LRHS MBri MGos MMuc MRav NBid NBro NEgg NRHS NWad SEND SHil SPlb SWat WCru WMnd
	- 'Bowles's Crimson'	CBct LRHS MBri MRav NBid SHil WCot
	- 'Red Herald'	CBct LRHS SHil WCot WWEG
	- 'Rubrum'	CBct EBee LRHS NBir NHol WFar
	- 'Savill'	LRHS MBri MRav SHil WWEG
	- var. ***tanguticum***	Widely available
	rhaponticum	NLar
	ribes	WCot WCru
	tataricum	LEdu

Rhinanthus (*Orobanchaceae*)

	minor	CHab GJos

Rhodanthe (*Asteraceae*)

§	***anthemoides***	IRar

Rhodanthemum (*Asteraceae*)

	'African Eyes'	ECho EPfP LRHS MBrN MBri MGos NPri SPoG SRot SUsu WNew
	Agadir **new**	LBuc
§	***atlanticum***	ECho EWes
§	***catananche***	CCCN ECho EPot EWes MBNS SRot WAbe
§	- 'Tizi-n-Test'	ECho
	- 'Tizi-n-Tichka'	CPBP ECho EWes LHop LRHS NRHS
§	***gayanum***	CCCN ECho EWes IRar
	- 'Flamingo'	see *R. gayanum*
§	***hosmariense*** ♀H4	CCCN CMea ECha ECho EDAr ELan ELon EPfP EPot GMaP LHop LRHS MAsh MCot MWat NRHS NSla SCoo SEND SPer SPoG SRms SRot WAbe WHoo WPat
	Marrakech	see *R.* Moondance

§	Moondance = 'Usrhod0701' **new**	LBuc WHlf
	Tangier **new**	LBuc WHlf

Rhodiola (*Crassulaceae*)

	CC 5344	GKev
	SDR 5015	GKev
	crassipes	see *R. wallichiana*
	cretinii HWJK 2283	WCru
§	***fastigiata***	EBee GCal GKev NMen WCot
	- BWJ 7544	SKHP WCru
§	***heterodonta***	ECha ELan LRHS MRav WCot
	himalensis misapplied	see *R.* 'Keston'
	himalensis (D. Don) Fu	CTri
	integrifolia subsp. ***integrifolia***	EDAr
§	***ishidae***	CTri
§	'Keston'	CTri XLum
§	***pachyclados***	ECho ECtt EDAr EUJe GJos GMaP LBee LRHS MHer MMuc NBir NRHS NRya NWad SEND SGar SPlb SRot SWal SWvt WAbe WFar WPer XLum
	aff. ***purpureoviridis***	WFar
	- BWJ 7544	WCru
	rhodantha	NSla
§	***rosea***	Widely available
	semenovii	NLar
	sinuata HWJK 2318	WCru
	- HWJK 2326	WCru
§	***trollii***	ECho LHop LRHS NRHS SPlb WAbe
§	***wallichiana***	MLHP NBid
	- GWJ 9263	WCru
	- HWJK 2352	WCru

Rhodochiton (*Plantaginaceae*)

§	***atrosanguineus*** ♀H1-2	CCCN CHll CSpe ELan EPfP GBee IDee LRHS MAsh MPie NPri SGar SLon SPer SPoG
	volubilis	see *R. atrosanguineus*

Rhodocoma (*Restionaceae*)

arida	CCCN GBin
capensis	CAbb CCCN CCon CPrp CTrC CTsd GBin GCal LRHS
gigantea	CCCN CCon CTrC EAmu ETod GBin SPlb

Rhododendron ✿ (*Ericaceae*)

	sp.	GKin SEWo
	'A.J. Ivens'	see *R.* 'Arthur J. Ivens'
	'Abegail'	SLdr
	aberconwayi	LMil
	- 'His Lordship'	GGGa LMil MSnd
	acrophilum (V)	GGGa
	'Addy Wery' (EA) ♀H3-4	CDoC ECho GKin MGos SPer
	adenogynum	GGGa LMil MSnd
§	- Adenophorum Group F 20444	SLdr
	adenophorum	see *R. adenogynum* Adenophorum Group
	adenopodum	GGGa MSnd
	adenosum	GGGa
	'Admiral Piet Hein'	SReu
	'Adonis' (EA/d)	CBcs CMac LMil NLar SLdr
	'Adriaan Koster' (hybrid)	SHea
	'Advance' (EA)	MSnd
	aeruginosum	see *R. campanulatum* subsp. *aeruginosum*
	aganniphum	MSnd
	- var. ***flavorufum***	MSnd
	- 'Rusty'	MSnd
	'Aida' (R/d)	CSBt SReu
	'Aksel Olsen'	CTri GEdr LRHS
	'Aladdin' (*auriculatum* hybrid)	GGGa
	'Aladdin' (EA)	CMac ECho NEgg
	Aladdin Group	SReu
	Albatross Group	SReu
	'Albatross Townhill Pink'	LMil
	'Albert Schweitzer' ♀H4	CDoC CWri LMil NLar SLdr SLim WFar
	albertsenianum	GGGa MSnd
	albrechtii (A)	GGGa IVic LMil
	- Whitney form (A)	LMil
	'Alena'	GGGa
	'Alexander' (EA) ♀H4	IVic LMil LSRN MAsh MGos
	'Alfred'	GGGa
	'Alice' (EA)	SLdr
	'Alice' (hybrid) ♀H4	CMac LMil SHea SLdr
	'Alison Johnstone'	GGGa SHea WThu
	Alison Johnstone Group	CBcs LMil MSnd SLdr SReu
	'Alpine Gem'	IVic
	Alpine Gem Group	GQui
	'Altaclerense' **new**	LMil
	'Altair' (K)	SHea
§	***alutaceum*** var. ***alutaceum*** Globigerum Group	GGGa
§	- var. ***iodes***	MSnd
§	- var. ***russotinctum***	MSnd NHim
	- - R 158	SLdr
§	- - Triplonaevium Group	GGGa
	amagianum (A)	LMil NHim
	Amalfi Group	LMil
	'Amber Rain' (A)	SHea
	ambiguum	LMil MSnd
I	- 'Crosswater'	LMil
	- 'Golden Summit'	GGGa
	- 'Jane Banks'	LMil
	'Ambrosia' (EA)	CSBt
	'Ambush'	SHea
	'America'	SHea
	'Amity'	CWri ECho LMil MAsh MMuc MSnd NPCo SEND SLdr WGwG
	'Amoenum Coccineum' (EA/d)	MAsh MSnd SLdr SReu
	Amor Group	SHea
	'Amoretto'	IVic
	'Anah Kruschke'	GGGa MAsh SPoG
	'Analin'	see *R.* 'Anuschka'
	'Anatta Gold' (V)	GGGa
	'Anchorite' (EA)	SLdr
	'Androcles'	LMil
	'Angelo'	LMil
	Angelo Group	CWri LMil SReu
	Anita Group	SHea
	'Anna Baldsiefen'	ELon GKin MGos NHim NPCo SEND SLim SPoG
	'Anna Kauser'	MSnd
	'Anna Rose Whitney'	CBcs CTri CWri LRHS LTen MAsh MGos NEgg SLim
	'Annabella' (K) ♀H4	NLar SReu SSta
	annae	GGGa LMil NHim
	'Anne Frank' (EA)	MGos
	'Anne Teese'	GGGa LMil
	'Annegret Hansmann'	GGGa
	'Anneke' (A)	EPfP LMil NLar SPoG SReu SSta
	anthopogon	LMil
	- 'Betty Graham'	GGGa

	- subsp. ***hypenanthum*** 'Annapurna'	GGGa ITim WAbe
§	***anthosphaerum***	GGGa
	'Antilope' (Vs)	CBcs CWri ECho LMil MAsh MBri MGos MLea MMuc NEgg NLar SHea SLdr SPer SReu SSta
	'Antonio'	LMil
§	'Anuschka'	MAsh MMuc
	anwheiense	GGGa SHea
	aperantum	GGGa
	apodectum	see *R. dichroanthum* subsp. *apodectum*
	'Apple Blossom' ambig.	CMac GKin
	'Apple Blossom' Wezelenburg (M)	SLdr
N	'Appleblossom' (EA)	see *R.* 'Ho-o'
	'Apricot Blaze' (A)	SReu SSta
	'Apricot Fantasy'	LMil
	'Apricot Surprise'	CTri LRHS MAsh
	'April Chimes'	WThu
	'April Showers' (A)	LMil
	'Aquamarin'	IVic NLar
	'Arabesk' (EA)	GKin LMil MAsh MBri MGos SLdr
	'Arabesque'	SHil
	araiophyllum	LMil
	- KR 7483	LMil
	arborescens (A)	GGGa LMil
	- pink-flowered (A)	LMil
	arboreum	CDoC CHEx GGGa IDee LMil LRHS MSnd NHim NLar SReu
	- B&SWJ 2244	WCru
	- subsp. ***arboreum***	MSnd
	- subsp. ***cinnamomeum***	CDoC GGGa LMil MSnd SLdr SReu
	- - var. ***album***	GGGa MSnd SReu
	- - 'Everest Reunion' new	LMil
	- - var. ***roseum***	GGGa
	- - - 'Tony Schilling'	GKin LMil NLar SReu
	- subsp. ***delavayi***	GGGa LMil MSnd
	- - KR 3909	LMil
	- - var. ***delavayi***	GLin
	- - var. ***peramoenum*** AC 5577	GLin
	- 'Heligan'	SReu
§	- subsp. ***nilagiricum***	GLin
	- var. ***roseum***	NHim SHea
§	- subsp. ***zeylanicum***	GGGa
	'Arctic Fox' (EA)	GGGa
	'Arctic Regent' (K)	GQui
	'Arctic Tern'	see × *Ledodendron* 'Arctic Tern'
§	***argipeplum***	GGGa MSnd
	'Argosy' ♀H4	LMil SReu
	argyrophyllum	MSnd SLdr
	- subsp. ***argyrophyllum***	GGGa SLdr
§	- subsp. ***hypoglaucum***	GGGa MSnd
	- subsp. ***nankingense***	GGGa
	- - 'Chinese Silver' ♀H4	CDoC GGGa LMil MSnd SLdr SReu
	arizelum	GGGa LMil MAsh MSnd
	- subsp. ***arizelum*** Rubicosum Group	GGGa LMil
	'Arkona'	IVic
	armitii (V)	GGGa
	'Arneson Gem' (M)	CDoC GGGa LMil MAsh MMuc NLar SEND SLdr
	'Arneson Ruby' (K)	GGGa
	'Arpege' (Vs)	LMil MBri SReu
	'Arthur Bedford'	CBcs CSBt SLdr SReu
§	'Arthur J. Ivens'	SLdr
	'Arthur Osborn'	SLdr SSpi
	'Arthur Stevens'	MSnd SLdr
	'Asa-gasumi' (Kurume) (EA)	NHim SLdr
	asterochnoum	GGGa MSnd
	'Astrid'	IVic LMil LSRN
	'Astronaut' (K)	SHea
	atlanticum (A)	GGGa LMil SReu SSta
	- 'Seaboard' (A)	LMil
	augustinii	CWri GGGa LMil MLea MSnd NLar SLdr SSpi SSta
§	- subsp. ***chasmanthum***	GGGa
	- compact EGM 293	LMil
§	- 'Electra' ♀H3-4	GGGa
	- Electra Group	CDoC LMil MLea SLdr
	- Exbury form	GGGa LMil SReu
§	- subsp. ***hardyi***	GGGa
*	- 'Trewithen'	GGGa LMil
I	- 'Werrington'	CPLG SLdr SReu
§	***aureum***	GGGa WThu
	auriculatum	GGGa LMil MSnd NHim SLdr SReu SSta
	- Reuthe's form	SReu
	auriculatum × ***hemsleyanum***	GGGa
	auritum	SLdr
	'Aurora' (K)	SLdr
	austrinum (A)	LMil NLar
	- yellow-flowered (A)	LMil
	'Avalanche' ♀H4	LMil SReu
	Avocet Group	LMil
	'Award'	LMil
	'Ayah'	LMil
	Azor Group	SHea
	Azrie Group	SLdr
§	'Azuma-kagami' (Kurume) (EA)	LMil LSRN
	'Azurika'	IVic
	'Azurro'	GGGa LMil NLar
	B.B.C. Group	LMil
	'Babette'	see *R.* (Volker Group) 'Babette'
	'Babuschka'	LMil
	'Baden-Baden'	CMac CTri ECho GEdr GKin MAsh MGos MSnd NEgg NLar SLdr SPoG WFar
	'Bagshot Ruby'	SHea
	baileyi	MSnd NHim
	'Bakkarat' (K)	SHea
	balangense	GGGa
	balfourianum	GGGa
	'Ballerina' (K)	SHea
	'Balzac' (K)	CDoC ECho GKin MAsh MGos NEgg SHea SPer
	'Banana Boat'	IVic
	'Bandoola'	SReu
	'Barbara Coats' (EA)	SLdr
	'Barbarella'	GGGa IVic
	barbatum	CDoC CHEx GGGa LMil MSnd
	- B&SWJ 2160	WCru
	- B&SWJ 2237	WCru
	- B&SWJ 2624	WCru
	'Barbecue' (K)	LMil LRHS
	'Barmstedt'	CWri MAsh WMoo
	'Barnaby Sunset'	GGGa LMil LRHS
	'Bartholo Lazzari' (G)	SReu SSta
	'Bashful' ♀H4	CBcs CSBt ECho EPfP MGos SLdr
§	***basilicum***	CDoC GGGa IDee LMil NHim SLdr
	- AC 616	MSnd
	- KR 7532	LMil
	- KR 7540	LMil

× ***bathyphyllum***	GGGa
bauhiniiflorum	see *R. triflorum* var. *bauhiniiflorum*
beanianum	GGGa NHim
- APA 60	GGGa
- KC 0122	GGGa
- compact	see *R. piercei*
'Beatrice Keir'	LMil MSnd SReu
'Beau Brummell'	LMil
'Beaulieu' (K)	SHea
'Beaulieu Manor'	GQui
'Beauty of Littleworth'	SReu
'Beaver' (EA)	MMuc
'Beefeater' × ***yakushimanum***	SLdr
beesianum	GGGa MSnd
'Beethoven' (EA) ♀H3-4	MSnd SLdr
'Belami'	IVic
'Belkanto'	CDoC GKin
'Belle Heller'	SLdr
'Ben Cruachan' (K) **new**	GGGa
'Ben Lawers' (K) **new**	GGGa
'Ben Lomond' (K) **new**	GGGa
'Ben Vorlich' (K) **new**	GGGa
'Ben Vrackie' (K) **new**	GGGa
'Bengal'	ECho GEdr LRHS LSRN SLdr SLim
'Bengal Fire' (EA)	CMac SLdr
'Beni-giri' (EA)	CMac
'Bergensiana'	SReu SSta
'Bergie Larson'	CBcs ECho IVic LMil MAsh MLea MMuc NPCo SEND SLdr
'Berg's 10'	MLea
'Berg's Yellow'	CWri ECho LMil MGos MLea MMuc MSnd SEND SLdr
'Bernstein'	LMil LRHS MAsh NLar
'Berryrose' (K) ♀H4	CBcs CMac CSBt CTri CWri ECho EPfP GKin LMil MAsh MGos MMuc MSnd NLar SEND SLdr SPer SReu
'Beryl Taylor'	GGGa
'Betty Anne Voss' (EA)	ECho LRHS LSRN MAsh MBri MGos SCoo SLdr
'Betty Wormald'	CDul CMac CWri ECho MBri MGos MLea MMuc SEND SHea SLdr SPer
bhutanense	GGGa
- KR 8233	LMil
Bibiani Group	LMil SHea
'Bijou de Ledeberg' (EA)	CMac
'Billy Budd'	SLdr
'Birthday Girl'	CBcs ECho ELon LMil LSRN MAsh MLea NHim SBod SLdr
'Biskra'	GGGa LMil
'Blaauw's Pink' (EA) ♀H3-4	CDoC CMac CSBt ECho ELon EPfP GKin GQui LMil MBri MGos MMuc MSnd NPCo SEND SLdr SPer SPlb SPoG SReu WFar
'Black Knight' (EA)	SLdr
'Black Magic'	CDoC CWri GKin LMil
'Black Sport'	MLea
Blaue Donau	see *R.* 'Blue Danube'
'Blazecheck'	SCoo
'Blewbury' ♀H4	LMil SLdr SReu SSta
'Blue Bell'	SHea
'Blue Boy'	CDoC LMil
'Blue Chip'	SLdr
§ 'Blue Danube' (EA) ♀H3-4	CDoC CMac CSBt CTri ECho ELon EPfP GGGa GKin IVic LMil LRHS MAsh MBri MGos MMuc MSnd NPCo NPri SEND SHil SLdr SLim SPer SPoG SReu SSta WFar

'Blue Diamond'	CMac CSBt ECho ELon LRHS LSRN MGos NPCo SLdr SPer WGwG
Blue Diamond Group	CBcs ECho EPfP MGos MSnd SReu
'Blue Monday' (EA)	SLdr
'Blue Moon' (EA)	ELon LMil SLdr
'Blue Peter' ♀H4	CBcs CSBt CWri ECho ELon EPfP LMil LRHS MAsh MGos MLea NLar SLdr SPer SReu SSta
'Blue Pool'	LMil
'Blue Star'	GEdr NMen
'Blue Steel'	see *R. fastigiatum* 'Blue Steel'
Blue Tit Group	CBcs CDoC EPfP GGGa LRHS MSnd SLim SReu SSta
Bluebird Group	CMac CSBt MGos
'Blurettia'	CDoC CWri MMuc SEND
'Blutopia'	LMil
Bobolink Group **new**	LMil
'Boddaertianum'	SHea SLdr SReu
'Bodnant Yellow'	LMil
Bohlken's Laura **new**	GGGa
'Bonfire'	SHea SReu
boothii	GGGa
- HECC 10077	GGGa
'Bo-peep'	GQui LMil SLdr
Bo-peep Group	CBcs
'Boskoop Ostara'	CBcs LMil MGos
'Bouquet de Flore' (G) ♀H4	CDoC EPfP LMil MLea NLar SReu
'Bow Bells' ♀H4	ECho EPfP GEdr LMil LRHS MAsh MBri MSnd NHim NLar NPri SHea SLdr WFar
Bow Bells Group	MGos MLea
'Bow Street'	SHea
'Bowjingles' **new**	GGGa
brachyanthum subsp. ***hypolepidotum***	GGGa
brachyanthum × ***viridescens*** **new**	GGGa
brachycarpum	GKev GLin
- 'Roseum Dwarf'	GGGa
'Brambling'	GGGa
'Brazier' (EA)	SLdr
'Brazil' (K)	CSBt SHea
'Bremen'	LMil
brevinerve	MSnd
'Briane' (EA)	GGGa
'Bric-à-brac'	SLdr WThu
Bric-à-brac Group	CBcs
'Bright Forecast' (K)	CWri IVic MLea SLdr
'Brigitte'	CWri IVic LMil LRHS LSRN MAsh SLdr
'Brilliant' (EA)	SHil
'Brilliant' (hybrid)	MGos WFar
'Brilliant Blue' (EA)	MAsh
'Britannia'	CSBt CWri EPfP LMil SReu WFar
'Brocade'	MSnd SHea SLdr
'Bronze Fire' (A)	SLdr SReu SSta
'Brown Eyes'	ECho GKin MMuc SEND SLdr
'Bruce Brechtbill' ♀H4	CDoC CWri ECho GGGa GKin LMil MAsh MBri MGos MMuc NPCo SEND SLdr SReu SSta
'Bruce Hancock' (Ad)	ECho ELon MMuc SLdr
§ 'Bruns Gloria'	LMil
'Bruns Schneewitchen'	SPoG SReu
'Buccaneer' (EA)	SLdr
bullatum	see *R. edgeworthii*
'Bungo-nishiki' (EA/d)	CMac WThu
bureavii ♀H4	GGGa GLin LMil MGos MSnd NHim NLar SReu SSta
- 'Berg' **new**	GGGa

	bureavii* × *yakushimanum	SReu
	bureavioides	LMil MSnd
	'Burletta'	IVic LMil
	burmanicum	GGGa SLdr
	'Busuki'	GGGa LMil
	'Butter Brickle'	LMil MLea SLdr
	'Butter Yellow'	ECho GEdr
	'Butterfly'	LMil SHea
	'Buttermint'	ECho MGos MLea
	'Buzzard' (K)	LMil
	calendulaceum (A)	GGGa LMil
	- red-flowered (A)	LMil
	- yellow-flowered (A)	LMil
	'Calfort' new	GGGa
	Calfort Group	SLdr
	callimorphum	GGGa LMil
	- var. ***myiagrum***	MSnd
	calophytum ♀H4	GGGa IDee LMil LRHS MSnd NHim NLar SLdr
	calostrotum	IDee WAbe
	- subsp. ***calostrotum***	GKev
	- 'Gigha' ♀H4	GGGa LMil MAsh MGos SLdr WAbe
§	- subsp. ***keleticum*** ♀H4	CDoC GEdr GGGa GKev MGos
	- - R 58	GGGa LMil
§	- - Radicans Group	GEdr GGGa IVic MLea WAbe WThu
	- - - USDAPI 59182/R11188	MLea
	- subsp. ***riparium***	GLin
	- - Calciphilum Group	GGGa WThu
§	- - Nitens Group	CDoC GGGa MAsh NMen WAbe
	caloxanthum	see *R. campylocarpum* subsp. *caloxanthum*
	'Calsap'	GGGa
	Calstocker Group	LMil
	camelliiflorum	GGGa
	campanulatum	GGGa IDee LMil LRHS MSnd SReu WAbe
	- CC 5124	GKev
§	- subsp. ***aeruginosum***	GGGa LMil MSnd SLdr SReu
	- 'Knaphill'	MSnd
	campylocarpum	GGGa LMil MSnd SReu
	- KR 8212	LMil
§	- subsp. ***caloxanthum***	GGGa LMil
§	- - Telopeum Group	MSnd
	campylogynum ♀H4	CBcs GGGa LMil MLea NMen NPCo SSpi WAbe
	- SBEC 0519	GGGa
	- 'Album'	see *R.* 'Leucanthum'
	- black-flowered	IVic
	- Charopoeum Group	WThu
	- - 'Patricia'	ECho EPot GEdr LLHF LMil NLar SLdr
	- (Cremastum Group) 'Bodnant Red'	GGGa WThu
	- Myrtilloides Group	CDoC ECho GGGa GKev GQui LMil MAsh MGos MSnd NMen SReu WAbe WThu
	- plum-flowered	WAbe
	- salmon pink-flowered	ECho GEdr WAbe
	camtschaticum	GGGa LMil WThu
	- var. ***albiflorum***	GGGa NMen
	- red-flowered	GGGa
	canadense (A)	GGGa
	- f. ***albiflorum*** (A)	GGGa LMil
	- dark-flowered (A)	LMil
	'Candy Striped Pink'	IVic
	canescens (A)	LMil
	'Cannon's Double' (K/d) ♀H4	CBcs CWri GKin LMil MAsh MBri MGos MLea NLar SLdr SPer
	'Canzonetta' (EA) ♀H4	ECho ELon GGGa LMil LRHS MAsh MBri MGos MMuc
	'Captain Jack'	GGGa
	'Carat' (A)	NLar SReu
	cardiobasis	see *R. orbiculare* subsp. *cardiobasis*
	Carita Group	SHea
	'Carita Charm'	LMil
	'Carita Golden Dream'	LMil
	'Carita Inchmery'	SHea
	'Carmen'	CWri ECho GEdr GGGa GKev GKin LMil MAsh MGos MLea NPCo SLdr SReu
	'Carmine'	MSnd
	carneum	GGGa
	'Caroline Allbrook' ♀H4	CWri ECho GGGa IDee MAsh MGos MLea NEgg NLar SEND SLdr
	'Caruso'	IVic
	'Cary Ann'	CBcs CTri LMil LRHS MAsh SLdr SReu WFar
	'Casablanca' (EA)	LBuc SLdr
	'Cassata'	LMil
	'Cassley' (Vs)	LMil
	catacosmum	GGGa
	catawbiense	GKev GLin SLdr
	'Catawbiense Album'	CTri MAsh
	'Catawbiense Boursault'	SLdr
	'Catawbiense Grandiflorum'	CWri MAsh
	'Catharine van Tol'	LMil
	caucasicum	GGGa
	'Caucasicum Pictum'	LMil MSnd SLdr
	'Cayenne' (EA)	SLdr
	'Cecile' (K) ♀H4	CBcs CDoC CMac CWri ECho GBin GKin LMil LSRN MAsh MBri MGos MMuc SEND SLdr SPer SReu
	'Celestial' (EA)	CMac
	'Centennial'	see *R.* 'Washington State Centennial'
	cephalanthum	GGGa LMil
	- subsp. ***cephalanthum*** SBEC 0751	WThu
	- - Crebreflorum Group	GGGa LMil WAbe WThu
	- - - Week's form	ITim
	- - Nmaiense Group	GGGa
	- subsp. ***platyphyllum***	GGGa
	cerasinum	LMil MSnd
	- 'Cherry Brandy'	GGGa MSnd
	- 'Coals of Fire'	GGGa MSnd
	'Cetewayo' ♀H4	CWri LMil SReu
	chaetomallum	see *R. haematodes* subsp. *chaetomallum*
	chamaethomsonii	GGGa
	- var. ***chamaethomsonii***	MSnd
	- - Rock form	GGGa
§	'Champagne' ♀H3-4	CSBt EPfP LMil LRHS MAsh SHea SReu
	championae new	GGGa
	'Chanel' (Vs)	SReu SSta
	changii	GGGa
	'Chanticleer' (EA)	SLdr
	chapaense	see *R. maddenii* subsp. *crassum*
	'Chariots of Fire' (EA)	LMil
	charitopes	LMil
	- F 25570	GGGa LMil
§	- subsp. ***tsangpoense***	GGGa GQui
	'Charlotte Megan' (A) new	LMil
	'Charme La'	GGGa
	chasmanthum	see *R. augustinii* subsp. *chasmanthum*

'Cheer'	CWri MAsh MMuc NEgg SEND SLdr SLim WFar
'Chelsea Reach' (K/d)	SHea SLdr
'Chelsea Seventy'	MAsh MSnd SLdr
'Chenille' (K/d)	SHea SLdr
'Cherie' (EA)	MAsh
'Cherokee' (EA)	MSnd NHim SLdr
'Cherries and Cream'	LMil
'Cherry Drops' (EA)	LRHS MAsh
'Chetco' (K)	LMil NLar
'Chevalier Félix de Sauvage' ♀H4	LMil SHea SReu
'Chikor'	CBcs ECho GBin GGGa GKin MAsh MBri MGos MSnd WFar WThu
'Chinchilla' (EA)	GQui
'Chink'	CBcs MSnd SLdr
'Chionoides'	CMac SLdr
'Chipmunk' (EA/d)	GGGa LRHS MAsh MBri
'Chippewa' (EA)	CTri IVic LMil
'Chocolate Ice' (K/d)	SHea
'Choremia' ♀H3	LMil MLea SHea SReu
christi (V)	GGGa
'Christina' (EA/d)	LMil MMuc
'Christmas Cheer' (EA/d)	see *R.* 'Ima-shojo'
'Christmas Cheer' (hybrid)	CBcs CDoC CMac CSBt CWri GBin GGGa GKin LMil MAsh MGos MLea MSnd NLar SEND SLdr SReu
chrysanthum	see *R. aureum*
chrysodoron	LMil
ciliatum	CBcs GGGa LMil SLdr
'Cilpinense' ♀H3-4	CMac CSBt CWri ECho EPfP GKev LMil LRHS MMuc NLar NPri SEND SHea SLdr SPoG SReu WGwG
Cilpinense Group	CBcs GGGa MSnd SPer WFar
cinnabarinum	CBcs LMil MSnd SLdr
- subsp. ***cinnabarinum*** BL&M 234	LMil
- - Blandfordiiflorum Group	GGGa LMil MSnd
§ - - 'Conroy'	CTsd LMil
- - 'Nepal'	LMil
- - Roylei Group	GGGa LMil NHim
- - - 'Vin Rosé'	LMil
§ - subsp. ***tamaense***	LMil NHim
§ - subsp. ***xanthocodon***	CBcs GGGa LMil MSnd NHim
§ - - Concatenans Group	GGGa LMil MSnd NHim SLdr
- - - KW 5874	LMil
- - - 'Amber'	LMil
- - Purpurellum Group	GGGa MSnd
Cinzan Group	LMil
circinnatum new	GGGa
citriniflorum	LMil
- R 108	LMil
- Brodick form	LMil
- var. ***citriniflorum***	LMil MSnd
- var. ***horaeum***	GGGa MSnd
'Clarice' (K)	SHea
'Claudine'	IVic
clementinae	GGGa MSnd
- F 25705	LMil
- SDR 3230	GKev
'Cliff Garland'	GQui LMil LRHS
'Coccineum Speciosum' (G) ♀H4	CDoC CMac CSBt GKin LMil SLdr SReu SSta
coeloneuron	GGGa LMil
- EGM 334	LMil
collettianum	GGGa
'Colonel Coen'	CWri ELon GKin LMil LRHS MBri MGos MLea MMuc NLar SEND SLdr
Colonel Rogers Group	SLdr SReu
'Colyer' (EA)	SLdr
comisteum C 6541 new	GGGa
concatenans	see *R. cinnabarinum* subsp. *xanthocodon* Concatenans Group
concinnum	CWri GGGa SLdr
- Pseudoyanthinum Group	GGGa GQui SLdr
'Conroy'	see *R. cinnabarinum* subsp. *cinnabarinum* 'Conroy'
'Contina'	LMil
'Conversation Piece' (EA)	SLdr
'Conyan Apricot'	SLdr
cookeanum	see *R. sikangense* var. *sikangense* Cookeanum Group
'Cool Haven'	LMil
'Coral Mist'	GGGa
'Coral Reef'	SLdr
'Coral Sea' (EA)	SReu
'Coral Seas' (V)	GGGa
coriaceum	GGGa LMil MSnd SLdr
'Corinna'	GGGa
'Corneille' (G/d) ♀H4	CSBt LMil SReu SSta
'Corona'	SHea
'Coronation Day'	LMil SReu
'Coronation Lady' (K)	SHea
coryanum 'Chelsea Chimes'	MSnd
'Cosmopolitan'	CWri LMil MGos MMuc SBfd SEND SPoG WMoo
Cote Group (A)	SLdr
'Countess of Derby'	SHea SLdr SReu
'Countess of Haddington' ♀H2	CBcs LMil SLdr
cowanianum	GGGa
'Cowslip'	LRHS NLar
Cowslip Group	CTri LMil MAsh MGos MLea MSnd
coxianum	GGGa
'Craig Faragher' (V)	GGGa
'Crane' ♀H4	EPfP GGGa GQui IVic LLHF LMil LRHS MAsh SLdr
crassum	see *R. maddenii* subsp. *crassum*
'Cream Crest'	GKin GQui LMil NLar SLdr SLim
'Creamy Chiffon'	CWri ECho MGos MLea NHim NLar WGwG
§ 'Creeping Jenny'	ECho GEdr GGGa MSnd SLdr
crenulatum new	GGGa
'Crest' ♀H3-4	CWri GGGa LMil MGos
'Crete' ♀H4	LMil
'Crimson Pippin'	LMil
crinigerum	GGGa IDee LMil
- var. ***crinigerum***	MSnd
- var. ***euadenium***	MSnd
'Crinoline' (EA)	SLdr
Crossbill Group	CBcs SLdr
'Crossroads'	MSnd
'Crosswater Belle'	LMil
'Crosswater Red' (K)	LMil
'Csárdás'	GGGa IVic
cubittii	see *R. veitchianum* Cubittii Group
cucullatum	see *R. roxieanum* var. *cucullatum*
cumberlandense (A)	GGGa IDee LMil
- 'Sunlight' (A)	LMil
'Cunningham's White'	CBcs CTri CWri ELan EPfP GGGa LMil LRHS LTen MAsh MGos MMuc MSnd NPri SBfd SEND SLdr SLim SPoG SReu WFar
'Cupcake' new	GGGa
'Curlew' ♀H4	CBcs CMac GEdr GKev GKin LMil MAsh MBri MGos MSnd NLar SLdr SReu SSpi

	Name	Suppliers
	cyanocarpum	GGGa MSnd
	'Cynthia' 🏆H4	CBcs CMac CWri ECho EPfP GGGa LMil LSRN MGos MSnd NEgg SEND SLdr SPer SReu SSta
	'Dagmar'	IVic
	dalhousieae new	GGGa
§	- var. ***rhabdotum***	GGGa
	'Damozel'	SHea SLdr
	'Danger' (K)	SHea SLdr
	'Danuta'	IVic
	'Daphne Daffarn'	SHea
	'Daphne Millais'	SHea
	'Dartmoor Pixie'	WThu
	dasycladum	see *R. selense* subsp. *dasycladum*
	dauricum 'Album'	see *R. dauricum* 'Hokkaido'
§	- 'Hokkaido'	GGGa
	- 'Mid-winter' 🏆H4	GGGa LMil
	'David' 🏆H4	SHea
	davidii	GGGa LMil
	davidsonianum 🏆H3-4	GGGa LMil MSnd NHim SLdr
	- Bodnant form	LMil
	- 'Caerhays Blotched'	GGGa SLdr
	- 'Caerhays Pink'	SLdr
	- 'Ruth Lyons'	LMil
	'Daviesii' (G) 🏆H4	CBcs CDoC CSBt CTri CWri ECho ELan EPfP GGGa GKin GQui LMil LRHS MAsh MBri MLea MMuc MSnd NPCo NPri SLdr SPer SPoG SReu SSpi
	'Day Dream'	SHea SLdr
N	'Daybreak'	see *R.* 'Kirin'
	'Daybreak' (K)	GQui SHea
	'Dear Barbara'	LMil LSRN
	'Dear Grandad' (EA)	CTri LMil LSRN SCoo
	'Dear Grandma'	LMil LSRN
	'Dearest' (EA)	LRHS MAsh NPri
	'Debutante'	NHol SHea
	decorum 🏆H4	CDoC GGGa IDee LLHF LMil MSnd SLdr SReu SSpi
	- KR 2496	LMil
	- SDR 4208	GKev
	- SDR 5026	GKev
	- SDR 5805	GKev
	- subsp. ***cordatum*** C&H 7132 new	GGGa
	- 'Cox's Uranium Green'	SReu
§	- subsp. ***diaprepes***	MSnd
	- - 'Gargantua'	SReu
	- late-flowering	LMil
	- pink-flowered	GGGa
	decorum* × *yakushimanum	SLdr SReu
	degronianum	NHim
§	- subsp. ***degronianum***	GGGa LMil MSnd
	- subsp. ***heptamerum*** 'Ho Emma'	IDee LMil
	- - 'Oki Island'	LMil
	- 'Rae's Delight'	IDee LMil
	dekatanum	GGGa
	deleiense	see *R. tephropeplum*
	'Delicatissimum' (O)	CBcs CDoC CWri ECho GGGa GKin GQui MBri MGos MLea MMuc MSnd NEgg NPCo SEND SHea SLdr SPer WGwG
	'Delta'	NLar SLim
	dendrocharis	LMil NHim
	- Cox 5016	GGGa WAbe
	- Glendoick Gem = 'Gle002'	GGGa
	'Denise'	IVic
*	'Denny's Rose' (A)	LMil SReu
	'Denny's Scarlet'	SReu SSta
	'Denny's White' (A)	LMil NHol SReu SSta
	denudatum	GLin LMil MSnd
	- EGM 294	LMil
	desquamatum	see *R. rubiginosum* Desquamatum Group
	'Diabolo' (K)	SHea
	Diamant Group lilac-flowered (EA)	ECho LMil MLea
	- pink-flowered (EA)	ECho MGos MLea
§	- purple-flowered (EA)	ECho MGos MLea SLdr
§	- red-flowered (EA)	ECho MLea SLdr
	- rosy red-flowered (EA)	ECho
	- white-flowered (EA)	ECho MLea
	'Diamant Purpur'	see *R.* Diamant Group purple-flowered
	'Diamant Rot'	see *R.* Diamant Group red-flowered
	'Diane'	CMac
	diaprepes	see *R. decorum* subsp. *diaprepes*
	dichroanthum	GGGa LMil
§	- subsp. ***apodectum***	GGGa LMil MSnd
	- subsp. ***dichroanthum***	MSnd
§	- subsp. ***scyphocalyx***	GGGa LMil LTen MSnd NLar SBfd
	- subsp. ***septentrionale*** new	GGGa
	dictyotum	see *R. traillianum* var. *dictyotum*
	didymum	see *R. sanguineum* subsp. *didymum*
	'Diorama' (Vs)	GKin LMil SReu SSta
	discolor	see *R. fortunei* subsp. *discolor*
	diversipilosum 'Milky Way' new	GGGa
	'Doc'	CMac EPfP MAsh MGos SLdr SReu WFar
	'Doctor A. Blok'	SLdr
	'Doctor M. Oosthoek' (M) 🏆H4	CSBt GKin SReu
	'Doctor Reiger' new	NLar
	'Doctor Stocker'	LMil MSnd
	'Doctor V.H. Rutgers'	WFar
	'Doncaster'	WFar
	'Dopey' 🏆H4	CBcs CDul CSBt CWri ECho ELon EPfP GGGa LMil LRHS MAsh MBri MGos MLea MSnd NEgg NHol SLdr SLim SPoG SReu
	'Dora Amateis' 🏆H4	CDoC ECho GGGa IVic LMil LRHS MAsh MBri MGos SLdr SLim SReu WThu
	Dormouse Group	CBcs ECho LMil MAsh MMuc NLar SEND SLdr SReu
	'Dorothy Corston' (K)	SHea
	'Dörte Reich'	GGGa
	'Dotella' new	GGGa
	'Double Beauty' (EA/d)	SReu SSta
	'Double Damask' (K/d) 🏆H4	SLdr
	'Double Date' (d)	SLdr
	'Double Dots' (d) new	LMil
	double yellow-flowered (A/d)	SLdr
	'Douglas McEwan'	SLdr
	'Dracula' (K)	GGGa
	Dragonfly Group	SReu
	'Dreamland' 🏆H4	CBcs CDoC CSBt CWri ECho LMil LRHS MAsh MGos MLea MSnd NLar SLim SPoG SReu
	'Drury Lane' (K)	GQui LMil
	dryophyllum misapplied	see *R. phaeochrysum* var. *levistratum*

	Name	Suppliers
	'Dufthecke'[PBR]	see *R.* White Dufthecke
	'Dusky Dawn'	SLdr
	'Dusky Orange'	SReu
	'Düsselfeuer'	IVic
	'Dusty Miller'	LRHS MAsh MBri MGos MSnd NLar SLdr
	eastmanii (A)	GGGa
	'Ebony Pearl'	CBcs ECho ELon MGos MMuc SEND SLdr WGwG
	eclecteum	GGGa LMil MSnd
§	***edgeworthii*** 🏆H2-3	CBcs GGGa WAbe
	'Edith Bosley'	NLar
	'Edna Bee' (EA)	LMil
	'Egret' 🏆H4	ECho EPot GEdr GGGa LMil MBri MGos MLea MSnd SLdr WThu
	'Eider'	GGGa MAsh SLdr
	'Eileen'	LMil
N	'Eisenhower' (K)	SHea
	'El Camino'	ECho LMil MBri MMuc MSnd SEND SLdr
	'El Greco'	SLdr
	Eldorado Group	GQui
	'Eleanore'	SLdr
	'Electra'	see *R. augustinii* 'Electra'
	elegantulum	LMil MSnd
	'Elisabeth Hobbie' 🏆H4	ECho LMil NLar
	'Eliska'	IVic
	'Elizabeth'	CTri CTsd CWri ECho LRHS LSRN MGos MSnd SBod SHea
N	'Elizabeth' (EA)	CMac CSBt EPfP MGos SLdr
	Elizabeth Group	CBcs LMil MAsh SLdr SPer SReu WFar
	'Elizabeth Jenny'	see *R.* 'Creeping Jenny'
	'Elizabeth Lockhart'	ECho GEdr GQui MGos
	'Elizabeth Red Foliage'	CTri GGGa LMil LRHS MAsh MBri SPer SReu
	'Else Frye'	GGGa
	'Elsie Lee' (EA/d) 🏆H3-4	CSBt CTrh ECho LMil MAsh MGos MMuc
	'Elsie Pratt' (A)	NHol SHea
	'Emasculum'	LMil SLdr
	'Emma Williams'	CBcs
	'Endsleigh Pink'	CBcs CWri LMil MMuc SEND
	eriogynum	see *R. facetum*
	eritimum	see *R. anthosphaerum*
	'Ernest Inman'	LMil SLdr
	erosum	MSnd
	'Eruption'	IVic
	'Esmeralda'	CMac
	'Etna' (EA)	SLdr
	'Etta Burrows'	CWri GGGa
	'Euan Cox'	GGGa
	euchroum	MSnd
	eudoxum	MSnd NHim
	'Europa'	SReu
	eurysiphon	GGGa MSnd
	'Eva Goude' (K)	SHea
	'Evelyn Hyde' (EA)	SLdr
	'Evening Fragrance' (A)	LMil
	'Everbloom' (EA)	SLdr
	'Everest' (EA)	SPoG
	'Everestianum'	SHea
	Everred = '851C'[PBR]	GGGa
	exasperatum	GGGa
	Exburiense Group	MMuc
	'Exbury Calstocker'	LMil
	'Exbury Naomi'	LMil
	'Exbury White' (K)	GQui
	excellens	GGGa IDee LMil
	eximium	see *R. falconeri* subsp. *eximium*
	'Exquisitum' (O) 🏆H4	CBcs CDoC CWri ECho EPfP GGGa GKin LMil MBri MMuc SLdr SPer
	exquisitum	see *R. oreotrephes* Exquisitum Group
	'Extraordinaire'	GGGa SReu SSta
	faberi	GGGa LMil
	'Fabia' 🏆H3	CBcs CMac GGGa GKin LMil MSnd SHea SLdr
	Fabia Group	CWri
§	'Fabia Tangerine'	CMac MLea
	'Fabia Waterer'	LMil
§	***facetum***	GGGa IDee LMil
	- KR 7593	LMil
	'Faggetter's Favourite' 🏆H4	LMil SHea SReu SSta
	Fairy Light Group	LMil
	falconeri 🏆H3-4	CDoC CHEx CHll GGGa LMil MGos MSnd NHim NPCo SLdr
§	- subsp. ***eximium***	CDoC GGGa IDee LMil MSnd NLar
	'Falling Snow'	IVic
	'Fanal' (K)	MBri
	'Fanny'	see *R.* 'Pucella'
	'Fantastica' 🏆H4	CDoC CWri ELan ELon EPfP GGGa GKev IDee LMil LRHS MAsh MBri MGos MLea NLar NPCo NPri SLdr SLim SPoG
	fargesii	see *R. oreodoxa* var. *fargesii*
	farinosum	NHim
	farrerae	NHim
	'Fashion' (EA)	SLdr
	fastigiatum	GEdr LMil MSnd SLdr
	- SBEC 804/4869	GGGa WThu
§	- 'Blue Steel' 🏆H4	CBcs CTri ECho ELon GKin IVic LMil LRHS MAsh MGos NPCo SLdr SPlb WPat
	- 'Indigo Steel' **new**	GGGa
	'Fastuosum Flore Pleno' (d) 🏆H4	CBcs CDul CMac CSBt CWri EPfP GGGa LMil MGos MLea MSnd NLar SHea SLdr SPer SReu SSta WFar
	'Fatima'	LMil
	faucium	GGGa
	'Favor Major' (K)	SHea
	'Favorite' ambig. (EA)	SLdr
	'Fawley' (K)	SHea SLdr
	'Feenkissen' (EA) **new**	IVic
	'Fénelon' (G)	SReu SSta
	ferrugineum	GGGa LMil MGos
	'Feuerwerk' (K)	GGGa IVic SHea
	fictolacteum	see *R. rex* subsp. *fictolacteum*
	Fire Bird Group	SHea SLdr
	'Fireball' (K) 🏆H4	CBcs CDoC CTri CWri EPfP GGGa GKev GKin LMil MAsh MBri MGos MLea MMuc NLar SEND SLdr SPer SPoG
	'Fireglow' (EA)	CSBt GKin LMil LRHS
	'Firelight' (hybrid)	GKin LMil NLar
	'Firetail'	SHea
	'Flaming Bronze'	SReu
	'Flaming Gold'	EPfP LRHS MAsh NPri
§	***flammeum*** (A)	LMil
	'Flanagan's Daughter'	LMil MAsh
	'Flautando'	IVic LMil
	Flava Group	see *R.* Volker Group
	flavidum	GGGa
	- 'Album'	WThu
	fletcherianum 'Yellow Bunting'	GGGa
	aff. ***flinckii*** AC 5441	GLin
	floccigerum	LMil MSnd

- bicolored	GGGa
'Floradora' (M)	SReu
'Floriade' × ***yakushimanum***	SLdr
floribundum	GGGa LMil SLdr
'Florida' (EA/d) ♀H3-4	CMac LMil SLdr SReu
'Flower Arranger' (EA)	LMil LRHS MAsh MBri SCoo
formosanum	GGGa
formosum	CBcs GGGa GQui SLdr
§ - var. ***formosum*** Iteaphyllum Group	GGGa
- - 'Khasia'	GGGa
- var. ***inaequale***	GGGa
forrestii KR 6113	LMil
- subsp. ***forrestii***	LMil
- - Repens Group	LMil
- - - 'Seinghku'	GGGa WThu
- Tumescens Group	GGGa WThu
Fortune Group	SLdr
fortunei	GGGa LMil SLdr
§ - subsp. ***discolor*** ♀H4	LMil MSnd SLdr
- - (Houlstonii Group) 'John R. Elcock'	LMil
- - 'Hummeltanz' **new**	IVic
- - var. ***kwangfuense*** AC 5208	LMil
- 'Mrs Butler'	see *R. fortunei* 'Sir Charles Butler'
§ - 'Sir Charles Butler'	LMil
'Fox Hunter'	SLdr
fragariiflorum	GGGa
'Fragrant Star' (A)	GGGa
'Fragrantissimum' ♀H2-3	CBcs CMac CSBt CTsd CWri ECre GGGa IDee LMil MRav NLar SKHP SLdr
'Francesca'	GGGa
Francis Hanger Group	SReu
'Frank Galsworthy' ♀H4	LMil SReu
'Fred Peste'	CDoC ECho GKin LMil MAsh MBri MGos MLea MMuc MSnd NLar SEND SLim
'Fred Wynniatt'	LMil MSnd SLdr
'Fred Wynniatt Stanway'	see *R.* 'Stanway'
'Freda' (EA)	SLdr
'Freya' (R/d)	LMil LSRN
'Fridoline' (EA)	IVic
'Frigate' (EA)	SLdr
'Frills' (K/d)	SHea
'Frome' (K)	SHea
'Frosted Orange' (EA)	LMil MAsh
'Frosthexe'	WAbe
'Frühlingsbeginn'	IVic
'Frühlingsglühen' **new**	IVic
'Fulbrook'	LMil
fulgens	GGGa GLin LMil MSnd
- KR 8204	LMil
fulvum ♀H4	CDoC GGGa GKin LMil MSnd SReu SSta
- KR 7614	LMil
- subsp. ***fulvoides***	GGGa LMil MSnd
§ 'Fumiko' (EA)	CBcs CSBt ELon LRHS MAsh MGos MLea MMuc NPCo SHil
'Furnivall's Daughter' ♀H4	CMac CSBt CWri ECho EPfP GGGa LMil LRHS MGos MMuc MSnd NLar SEND SHea SLdr SPer SReu SSta WFar
'Fusilier'	SHea SReu
'Gabrielle Hill' (EA)	MAsh SLdr
'Gaiety' (EA)	LMil SLdr SReu
galactinum	GGGa IDee LMil NHim
'Galathea' (EA)	MMuc
'Gallipoli' (K)	SHea
'Gandy Dancer'	CWri MLea SLdr
'Garden State Glow' (EA/d)	SLdr
'Garibaldi'	SHea
'Garnet'	SHea
'Gartendirektor Glocker'	CWri ECho GGGa IVic MAsh MSnd SLim
'Gartendirektor Rieger' ♀H4	CWri GGGa IVic LMil SHea SReu
'Gauche' (A)	GQui SLdr
'Gaugin'	GQui
'Geisha Lilac'	see *R.* 'Hanako'
'Geisha Orange'	see *R.* 'Satschiko'
'Geisha Pink'	see *R.* 'Momoko'
'Geisha Purple'	see *R.* 'Fumiko'
'Geisha Red'	see *R.* 'Kazuko'
'Gena Mae' (A/d)	GGGa SLdr
'General Eisenhower'	SHea SReu
'General Eric Harrison'	SLdr
'General Practitioner'	MSnd SLdr
'General Wavell' (EA)	CMac SLdr
'Gene's Favourite'	SReu
genestierianum	GGGa
'Geoffrey Millais'	LMil
'Georg Arends' (Ad)	EPfP LRHS MAsh SLdr
'George Hyde' (EA)	LRHS LSRN MAsh SCoo
'George Johnstone'	SLdr
'George's Delight'	MSnd
§ × ***geraldii***	SLdr
'Germania'	LMil LRHS MAsh NHim NPri SPoG SReu
Gertrud Schäle Group	CDoC CTri GEdr NLar SHea
Gibraltar Group	LMil
'Gibraltar' (K) ♀H4	CBcs CDoC CMac CSBt CTri CWri EPfP GGGa GKin LMil LRHS MAsh MBri MGos NLar SLdr SLim SPoG SReu SSta WFar
'Gilbert Mullie' (EA)	LMil SLim
'Gill's Crimson'	SHea SReu
'Ginger' (K)	CSBt CWri GKin LMil
'Ginny Gee' ♀H4	CBcs CDoC CSBt CWri ECho EPfP EPot GEdr GGGa GKev GKin IVic LMil LRHS MAsh MBri MGos MLea MMuc MSnd NEgg NLar SEND SReu SSta WFar WPat
§ 'Girard's Hot Shot' (EA)	ECho GQui MAsh MGos SReu
'Girard's Hot Shot' variegated (EA/v)	ECho GGGa LMil LRHS MAsh MMuc
glanduliferum	GGGa
- EGM 347	LMil
glaucophyllum	GGGa LMil MSnd NHim
- B&SWJ 2638	WCru
- Borde Hill form	LMil
- var. ***glaucophyllum***	MSnd
§ - subsp. ***tubiforme***	GGGa
Glendoick Butterscotch = 'Gle003'	GGGa
Glendoick Crimson = 'Gle004' (EA)	GGGa
Glendoick Dream = 'Gle005' (EA)	GGGa
Glendoick Ermine = 'Gle006' (EA)	GGGa
Glendoick Frolic = 'Gle007'	GGGa
Glendoick Garnet = 'Gle008' (EA)	GGGa
Glendoick Glacier = 'Gle009' (EA)	GGGa

Glendoick Goblin = 'Gle010' (EA)	GGGa
Glendoick Gold = 'Gle011'	GGGa
Glendoick Ice Cream = 'Gle013'	GGGa
Glendoick Mystique = 'Gle014'	GGGa
Glendoick Petticoats = 'Gle015'	GGGa
Glendoick Rosebud = 'Gle022' (EA)	GGGa
Glendoick Ruby = 'Gle016'	GGGa
'Glendoick Silver'	GGGa
Glendoick Snowflakes = 'Gle001' (EA)	GGGa
Glendoick Vanilla = 'Gle017'	GGGa
Glendoick Velvet = 'Gle018'	GGGa
'Glenna' **new**	GGGa
'Gletschernacht'	IVic
glischrum	GGGa NHim
- subsp. ***glischroides***	GGGa LMil
§ - subsp. ***rude***	GGGa
globigerum	see *R. alutaceum* var. *alutaceum* Globigerum Group
'Glockenspiel' (K/d)	SHea SLdr
'Gloria'	see *R.* 'Bruns Gloria'
'Gloria Mundi' (G)	SHea
'Glory of Littleworth' (Ad)	LMil
'Glowing Embers' (K)	CBcs CDoC CMac CTri CWri ECho GKin MAsh MBri MLea NHol SHea SLdr SLim SPer SReu SSta
'Goblin'	MSnd SLdr
'Gog' (K)	CSBt SHea
§ 'Goldbukett'	GGGa
'Goldcrest' (A)	SHea
'Golden Belle'	MAsh
Golden Bouquet	see *R.* 'Goldbukett'
'Golden Coach'	CWri ECho MGos MLea MSnd SBod SLdr
'Golden Eagle' (K)	CBcs CDoC ECho GKin LMil MAsh MGos MSnd NLar SHea SReu SSta WMoo
'Golden Flare' (A)	CBcs CDoC CSBt CWri ECho GBin GKin LRHS MAsh MBri MGos MLea MMuc NEgg NPCo SLdr
'Golden Gate'	CDoC CSBt ECho MBri MLea MMuc NLar SEND SLdr WFar
'Golden Hind' (A)	SHea
'Golden Horn'	SLdr
'Golden Horn' (K)	GQui SHea
'Golden Lights' (A)	CWri ECho GKin LMil MBri MGos MLea NEgg NPCo WGwG
(Golden Oriole Group) 'Talavera'	LMil SSpi
'Golden Princess'	LMil
'Golden Ruby'	CBcs ECho MLea NHim SLdr SPer
'Golden Splendour'	LMil
'Golden Sunset' (K)	CMac ECho LMil MAsh MBri MGos MLea NHol NLar SHea SLdr
'Golden Torch' ♀H4	CBcs CDoC CDul CWri ECho EPfP LMil LRHS MAsh MBri MGos MLea MSnd NLar SLdr SLim SPoG SReu SSta WFar
'Golden Wedding'	CBcs CDul CSBt CWri ECho ELon LMil LSRN MAsh MGos MMuc MSnd SBod SEND SLdr SPer
'Golden Wit'	MAsh MMHG MMuc NEgg SEND
'Goldfinch' (K)	SHea
'Goldflimmer' (v)	CDoC EPfP GGGa GKin LMil LRHS MAsh MBri MGos MMuc NLar NPri SBfd SEND SLim SPoG
'Goldfort'	SReu
'Goldika'	LMil
'Goldkollier'	IVic
'Goldkrone' ♀H4	CWri ELon EPfP GBin GGGa LMil MAsh MBri MGos MLea SPer SPoG SReu
'Goldpracht' (K)	IVic
Goldschatz = 'Goldprinz'	IVic LMil
'Goldsworth Orange'	CWri ECho LMil MGos MSnd SBod SLdr
'Goldsworth Orange' × ***insigne***	MAsh
'Goldsworth Yellow'	CSBt
'Goldtopas' (K)	GGGa GKin LMil LRHS
'Golfer'	LMil
'Gomer Waterer' ♀H4	CDoC CDul CMac CSBt CWri ECho EPfP GGGa LMil LRHS LTen MAsh MBri MGos MMuc MSnd NLar SEND SLdr SPoG SReu SSta WFar
gongashanense	NHim
'Gorbella'	SReu
Gowenianum Group (Ad)	LMil
'Grace Seabrook'	CDul CSBt CTri CWri ECho GGGa MBri MGos MMuc MSnd NPCo SBod SEND SLdr SPer SReu
'Graciosum' (O)	SReu
'Graf Lennart'	GGGa
'Graffito'	GGGa IVic LMil
'Graham Thomas'	LMil SReu
'Grand Slam'	ECho MLea MSnd
grande	GGGa LMil MSnd SLdr
- pink-flowered	MSnd
gratum	see *R. basilicum*
'Graziella'	GGGa LMil
'Greensleeves'	LMil
'Greenway' (EA)	CBcs SLdr
'Grenadier'	LMil SHea
griersonianum	CBcs GGGa LMil
griersonianum × ***yakushimanum***	SLdr
griffithianum	MSnd NHim SLdr
'Gristede' ♀H4	ECho LMil LRHS MGos NHim SReu
groenlandicum	see *Ledum groenlandicum*
'Grosclaude'	CMac SHea
'Grouse' × ***keiskei*** var. ***ozawae*** 'Yaku Fairy'	ECho
'Grumpy'	CBcs CSBt CWri ECho GBin LMil LRHS MAsh MBri MGos NHim SLdr SReu
'Gumpo' (EA)	CMac SLdr
'Gumpo Pink' (EA)	SLdr
'Gumpo White' (EA)	LRHS MAsh MGos
'Gundula'	LMil
'Gunter Dinger'	IVic
'Gwenda' (EA)	CTri SLdr
'Gwendoline' (A)	SReu SSta
'Gwillt-king'	CBcs
habrotrichum	GGGa LMil
'Hachmann's Anastasia'	LMil
'Hachmann's Charmant'	GGGa LMil SPoG
'Hachmann's Constanze'	LMil
'Hachmann's Diadem'	LMil
'Hachmann's Eskimo'	LMil
'Hachmann's Junifeuer'	SReu SSta

	'Hachmann's Kabarett'	LMil LRHS NLar
	'Hachmann's Marianne'	LMil
	'Hachmann's Marlis' ♀H4	LMil SReu
	'Hachmann's Picobello' new	GGGa
§	'Hachmann's Polaris' ♀H4	CDoC LMil MBri NLar SLdr
	'Hachmann's Porzellan' ♀H4	LMil
§	'Hachmann's Rokoko' (EA)	LMil
	haematodes	GGGa IDee LMil LRHS SLdr
§	- subsp. ***chaetomallum***	GGGa LMil MSnd
	- subsp. ***haematodes***	LMil
	'Halfdan Lem'	CBcs CDoC ECho GGGa GKin LMil LTen MAsh MBri MGos MLea MMuc MSnd NLar SEND SLdr SLim SPer SReu SSta
	'Hallelujah'	IVic MAsh
	'Halopeanum'	SHea SLdr
	'Hamlet' (M)	LMil
	'Hammondii'	LMil
	'Hampshire Belle'	LMil
	'Hana-asobi' (EA)	MSnd
§	'Hanako' (EA)	MGos MLea
	hanceanum 'Canton Consul'	GGGa
	- Nanum Group	CBcs GGGa
	'Hanger's Flame' (A)	LMil
	'Hansel'	CDoC CWri ECho GQui LMil MAsh MMuc SEND SLdr
	Happy Group	ECho
	'Hardijzer Beauty' (Ad)	MSnd SLdr
	'Hardy Gardenia' (EA/d)	SReu SSta
	hardyi	see *R. augustinii* subsp. *hardyi*
	'Harkwood Moonlight'	LMil
	'Harkwood Red' (EA)	SLdr
	Harry White's hybrid (A)	SReu SSta
	'Harvest Moon' (K)	NLar SCoo SHea SLdr SSta
	'Harvest Moon' (hybrid)	MMuc SEND
	'Hatsu-giri' (EA)	CMac LMil MSnd SLdr SReu
	'Heather Macleod' (EA)	SLdr
	heatheriae	GGGa LMil NHim
	- KR 6176	LMil
	- KR 6187	LMil
	'Heidi'PBR (EA)	SLdr
	'Helen Close' (EA)	SLdr
	'Helena Evelyn' (A) new	LMil
	'Helene Schiffner' ♀H4	LMil SReu
	heliolepis	GGGa LMil
	- var. ***fumidum***	see *R. heliolepis* var. *heliolepis*
§	- var. ***heliolepis***	GGGa
	hemidartum	see *R. pocophorum* var. *hemidartum*
	hemsleyanum	LMil MSnd NHim
	'Herbert' (EA)	CMac SLim
	'Herbstzauber'	LMil
	'Heureuse Surprise' (G)	SLdr
	'High Summer'	LMil
	'Hilda Margaret'	SReu
	'Hille'	LMil
	'Himmelberg' new	GGGa
	'Hinamayo'	see *R.* (Obtusum Group) 'Hinomayo'
	'Hino-crimson' (EA) ♀H3-4	CBcs CDoC CMac CSBt CTri ELon GKin LMil LRHS MAsh MBri MGos MMuc NHim NHol SEND SLdr SPer SPoG SReu SSta WFar
	'Hinodegiri' (EA)	CMac CSBt SLdr SReu
	'Hino-scarlet' (EA)	CBcs
	hippophaeoides	GKev LMil MSnd SLdr WAbe WFar
	- 'Bei-ma-shan'	see *R. hippophaeoides* 'Haba Shan'
	- 'Blue Silver'	GGGa IVic LMil MAsh
	- Glendoick Iceberg = 'Gle019'	GGGa
§	- 'Haba Shan' ♀H4	GGGa LMil WThu
	hirsutum	LMil
	- 'Flore Pleno' (d)	ECho EPot GEdr GKev
	hirtipes	GGGa MSnd NHim
	hodgsonii	LMil MSnd SLdr
	'Homebush' (K/d) ♀H4	CBcs CDoC CMac CTri CWri EPfP LMil MAsh MBri MGos NPCo SLdr SPer SPoG SReu SSta
	'Honey Butter'	LMil SLim
	'Honeysuckle' (K)	SHea SReu SSta
§	'Ho-o' (EA)	CBcs SLdr
	hookeri	LMil
	- Tigh-na-Rudha form	GGGa
	'Hoppy'	CBcs CWri LMil MAsh MGos MLea MMuc MSnd NLar SEND SLdr SLim SPer SPoG
	'Horizon Monarch' ♀H3-4	CDoC CWri GGGa GKin IVic LMil LRHS MBri MLea NLar SBfd SLdr SLim SReu SSta
	horlickianum	GGGa
	'Hortulanus H. Witte' (M)	CSBt SReu
	'Hot Shot'	see *R.* 'Girard's Hot Shot'
	'Hot Shot Variegated' (EA/v)	CDoC GGGa NEgg SHil SLdr
	'Hotei' ♀H4	CDoC CSBt CWri ECho EPfP GKin LMil LRHS MAsh MGos NEgg NPCo SLdr SPer SReu
	'Hotspur' (K)	CSBt CWri ECho GBin MGos NLar SLdr
	'Hotspur Red' (K) ♀H4	CDoC GKev GKin LMil MAsh NEgg NPCo SHea WMoo
	huanum	GGGa LMil
	- EGM 316	LMil
	'Hugh Koster'	CSBt SLdr
	aff. ***huidongense***	LMil
	- KR 7315	LMil
	'Hullaballoo'	LMil
	Humming Bird Group	CMHG GEdr LMil SLdr
	hunnewellianum	MSnd
	'Hussar'	CWri LMil
	'Hyde and Seek'	GQui
	'Hydie' (EA/d)	SPoG
	'Hydon Dawn' ♀H4	CBcs CDoC CWri LMil LRHS MAsh MGos MLea MSnd SHea SLdr SPer SReu SSta
	'Hydon Hunter' ♀H4	MSnd SHea SLdr SReu SSta
	'Hydon Pink'	SHea
	'Hydon Velvet'	LMil SReu
	hylaeum	MSnd
	Hyperion Group	SReu SSta
	hyperythrum	GGGa LMil MSnd
	hypoglaucum	see *R. argyrophyllum* subsp. *hypoglaucum*
	'Ice Cube'	ECho MLea MMuc NHim NLar SEND SLdr SPer
	'Iceberg'	see *R.* 'Lodauric Iceberg'
	'Idealist'	LMil
	'Ightham Gold'	SReu
	'Ightham Peach'	SReu
	'Ightham Purple'	SReu
	'Ightham Yellow'	SHea SReu
	'Ilam Carmen' (K)	SHea
§	'Ilam Melford Lemon' (A)	LMil
§	'Ilam Ming' (A)	LMil
	'Ilam Violet'	LMil
	'Imago' (K/d)	LMil SLdr
§	'Ima-shojo' (EA/d)	CMac LRHS LSRN MGos SBfd

	Name	Suppliers
	impeditum	CBcs CSBt CWib ECho GEdr GKev GQui MAsh MGos MLea MMuc MSnd SEND SLdr SPer SReu SSta WFar
	- 'Blue Steel'	see *R. fastigiatum* 'Blue Steel'
	- 'Indigo'	GKin LLHF MAsh MGos NPCo SLdr WAbe
	- 'Pygmaeum'	GEdr NHar WAbe WThu
	- Reuthe's form	SReu
	imperator	see *R. uniflorum* var. *imperator*
§	***indicum*** 'Macranthum' (EA)	SLdr
	'Ingrid Mehlquist' **new**	GGGa
	Inkarho Lilac Dufthecke = 'Rhodunter 149'PBR	LMil
	insigne ♀H4	GGGa GLin LMil MSnd
	- Reuthe's form	SReu
	insigne × ***yakushimanum***	SReu
	Intrifast Group	GGGa
	iodes	see *R. alutaceum* var. *iodes*
	'Irene Koster' (O) ♀H4	CDoC CSBt CWri EPfP GGGa GKin LMil MAsh MBri MLea NEgg NLar SLdr SLim SPer SSpi
	'Irohayama' (EA) ♀H3-4	CMac ELon EPfP GQui LMil LRHS MAsh MMuc NPri SEND SLdr
	irroratum	LMil
	- subsp. ***irroratum***	MSnd
*	- subsp. ***kontumense*** var. ***ningyuenense***	GGGa GLin
	- 'Polka Dot'	GGGa LMil
	- subsp. ***yiliangense*** EGM 339	LMil
	'Isabel'	NPri
	'Isabel' (EA)	LRHS MAsh
	'Isola Bella'	GGGa
	iteaphyllum	see *R. formosum* var. *formosum* Iteaphyllum Group
	'Ivette' (EA)	CMac
	'Izabelle' (EA)	MBri
	'J.C. Williams'	CBcs
	'J.G. Millais'	SLdr
	'J.M. de Montague'	see *R.* 'The Hon. Jean Marie de Montague'
	'Jalisco Eclipse'	LMil
	'Jalisco Elect'	CWri SLdr
	'Jalisco Janet'	LMil SHea
	'James Burchett' ♀H4	LMil SLdr SReu
	'James Gable' (EA)	MAsh SLdr
	'Janet Blair'	CWri
	'Janet Rhea' (EA)	SLdr
	'Janet Ward'	SReu
	japonicum (A. Gray) Valcken	see *R. molle* subsp. *japonicum*
	- var. ***pentamerum***	see *R. degronianum* subsp. *degronianum*
	jasminiflorum (V)	GGGa
	javanicum (V)	GGGa
	'Jean Marie Montague'	see *R.* 'The Hon. Jean Marie de Montague'
	'Jeff Hill' (EA)	ECho MMuc SEND SLdr
	'Jenny'	see *R.* 'Creeping Jenny'
	'Jeremy Davies'	SReu
	'Jessica Rose' (A) **new**	LMil
	'Jim Russell' (*ciliicalyx* hybrid) **new**	GGGa
	'Jingle Bells'	GGGa
	'Joan Paton' (A)	SLdr
	'Joanna'	MMuc
	'Jocelyne'	LMil
	'Jock'	SLdr
	Jock Group	CBcs CMHG
	'Jock Brydon' (O)	GGGa LMil SHea
	'Johanna' (EA) ♀H4	CDoC CTri EPfP IVic LMil LRHS MAsh NHol NLar NPri SLdr SPer SReu
	'John Cairns' (EA)	CMac MSnd SLdr
	'John Walter'	SHea
	'John Waterer'	SHea WFar
	'Johnny Bender'	SLdr
	johnstoneanum	CBcs GGGa LMil NHim SLdr
	- KW 7732	SLdr
	- 'Double Diamond' (d)	LMil
	'Jolie Madame' (Vs)	CWri ECho GKin LMil LRHS MAsh MBri MLea MMuc NLar NPri SLdr SReu SSta
	'Joseph Baumann' (G)	SLdr
	'Joseph Hill' (EA)	ECho ELon MGos MMuc SLdr
	'Jubilant'	LMil SHea
	'Jubilee'	SLdr
	'Juliette' (EA) **new**	IVic
	'June Fire' (A)	GGGa SReu
	kaempferi (EA)	LMil SLdr
	- 'Damio'	see *R. kaempferi* 'Mikado'
§	- 'Mikado' (EA)	LMil SReu
	- orange-flowered (EA)	CMac
	'Kalinka'	LMil MAsh NLar SLdr
	'Karen Triplett'	LMil
	'Karin'	SLdr
	'Kasane-kagaribi' (EA)	SLdr
	'Kate Waterer' ♀H4	CWri MGos SReu WFar
N	'Kathleen' de Rothschild (K)	SHea
	'Kathleen' van Nes (EA)	SLdr
	'Katisha' (EA)	SLdr
	'Katy Watson'	SReu SSta
§	'Kazuko' (EA)	MGos SHil
	'Keija' (EA)	SLdr
	keiskei	LLHF
	- var. ***ozawae*** 'Yaku Fairy' ♀H4	LMil WAbe WThu
	keleticum	see *R. calostrotum* subsp. ***keleticum***
	'Kelsay's Double'	MLea
	'Ken Janeck' ♀H4	GGGa
§	***kendrickii***	GGGa
	'Kentucky Colonel'	SLdr
	'Kermesinum' (EA)	CTri MAsh MGos NWad SHil SLdr SLim SReu
I	'Kermesinum Rosé' (EA)	CSBt ECho ELon LMil MGos MLea SLdr SLim SReu
	kesangiae	GGGa LMil
	- AC 5343	LMil
	- var. ***album***	GGGa
	keysii	GGGa
	- EGM 064	LMil
	'Kilian' (A)	MAsh
	'Kilimanjaro'	LMil SReu
	'Kimbeth'	GGGa
	'King George' Loder	see *R.* 'Loderi King George'
	kingianum	see *R. arboreum* subsp. *zeylanicum*
§	'Kirin' (Kurume) (EA/d)	CBcs CMac LMil SLdr
	'Kirsten Begeer'	IVic
	kiusianum (EA) ♀H4	LMil MSnd SReu
I	- 'Album' (EA)	LMil SReu
	- 'Hillier's Pink' (EA)	LMil
	'Kiwi Majic'	LMil
	'Klondyke' (K) ♀H4	CBcs CSBt CTri EPfP GGGa GKin LMil LRHS MAsh MGos NLar NPri SHea SLdr SReu
	'Kluis Sensation' ♀H4	CMac CSBt MSnd SLdr SReu

'Kluis Triumph'	SReu
'Knap Hill Apricot' (K)	LMil SHea
'Knap Hill Red' (K)	CDoC LMil SHea
'Knap Hill Yellow' (K)	SHea
'Kobold' (EA)	SLdr
'Koichiro Wada'	see *R. yakushimanum* 'Koichiro Wada'
'Kokardia'	LMil NHim
'Kokette'	IVic
kongboense	GGGa WAbe
'Königstein' (EA)	IVic LMil SHil
§ 'Koningin Emma' (M)	GKin LMil NLar
'Konsonanz'	IVic
'Koromo-shikibu' (EA)	GGGa
'Koromo-shikibu White' (EA)	GGGa
'Koster's Brilliant Red' (M)	CSBt EPfP MGos SReu SSta
§ 'Kure-no-yuki' (EA/d)	LMil MAsh MMuc
kyawii	GGGa
'Lackblatt'	see *R.* (Volker Group) 'Lackblatt'
lacteum	GGGa LMil
'Lady Alice Fitzwilliam' ♀H2-3	CBcs CMHG CMac ECre GGGa GKin IDee LMil
'Lady Chamberlain Salmon Trout'	see *R.* 'Salmon Trout'
'Lady Clare' (K)	SHea
'Lady Clementine Mitford' ♀H4	CSBt CWri ECho EPfP GQui LMil MAsh MBri MGos MLea MMuc SEND SHea SLdr SReu
'Lady Eleanor Cathcart'	SHea SLdr
'Lady Louise' (EA)	SLdr
'Lady Montagu' **new**	LMil
'Lady Robin' (EA)	SLdr
'Lady Romsey' ♀H4	LMil MSnd SLdr
laetum (V)	GGGa
'Lamplighter'	LMil SReu
lanatoides	GGGa LMil
§ ***lanatum***	ECho GGGa LMil
- Flinckii Group	see *R. lanatum*
'Langworth'	CWri ECho GQui LMil MGos MLea MMuc MSnd SEND SLdr SReu
lanigerum	LMil SReu
'Lanzette'	IVic
lapponicum Parviflorum Group	GGGa
'Lapwing' (K)	SLdr
'Laramie'	GGGa
'Late Love' (EA)	CDoC
* ***laterifolium***	GGGa
§ ***latoucheae*** (EA)	LMil
Laura Aberconway Group	SHea SLdr
'Lavender Brilliant' (EA)	SLdr
'Lavender Girl' ♀H4	CMac LMil MSnd SLdr SReu SSta
'Lea Rainbow'	MLea
'Ledifolium'	see *R. × mucronatum*
'Ledifolium Album'	see *R. × mucronatum*
'Lee's Dark Purple'	CWri LMil WFar
'Lee's Scarlet'	LMil
'Lemon Dream'	LMil LRHS MAsh NLar NPri SLdr SLim
* 'Lemon Drop' (A)	GGGa
'Lemon Lights' (A)	LMil
'Lemon Meringue'	LMil
'Lemonora' (M)	CBcs GKin
'Lem's 45'	CBcs CWri ECho MBri SLdr SPer
'Lem's Cameo' ♀H3	GGGa LMil SReu SSta
'Lem's Monarch' ♀H4	CBcs CDoC CWri ELon GGGa LMil MBri MGos MLea MMuc NHim SEND SLdr SReu SSta
'Lem's Tangerine'	CDoC LMil
'Lemur' (EA)	ECho GEdr GGGa LMil MLea WThu
'Leni'	LRHS MAsh
'Leo' (EA)	GQui MSnd SLdr
'Leonardslee Giles'	SLdr
'Leonardslee Primrose'	SLdr
'Leonore' **new**	LMil
lepidostylum	CBcs CMac CWri GGGa LMil SReu
lepidotum	GGGa
- var. ***album***	GGGa
- yellow-flowered McB 110	WThu
§ ***leptocarpum***	GGGa
leptopeplum	NHim
§ 'Leucanthum'	GGGa WThu
leucaspis	SLdr
'Leuchtpolster'	IVic
'Lewis Monarch'	GQui
'Lila Pedigo'	CWri ECho MAsh MGos NHim SPer
'Lilactina'	SLdr
'Lilliput' (EA)	MAsh
'Lily Marleen' (EA)	CTri SCoo
'Limetta' (K) **new**	GGGa
'Linda' ♀H4	CBcs CTri CWri ECho EPfP GGGa LMil LSRN MAsh MBri MGos MMuc SEND SLdr
'Linda Stuart' (EA) **new**	GGGa
lindleyi	CBcs GGGa GQui NHim
- 'Dame Edith Sitwell'	LMil
- 'Geordie Sherriff' **new**	GGGa
'Linearifolium'	see *R. stenopetalum* 'Linearifolium'
'Linnet' (K/d)	SHea SLdr
'Lionel's First'	LMil
Lionel's Triumph Group	LMil
'Little Beauty' (EA)	SLdr
'Little Ben'	ECho GEdr
'Loch Arkaig' **new**	GGGa
'Loch Awe'	GGGa
'Loch Earn'	GGGa
'Loch Laggan'	GGGa
'Loch Leven'	GGGa
'Loch Linnhe'	GGGa
'Loch Lomond'	GGGa
'Loch Morar'	GGGa
'Loch o' the Lowes'	MGos
'Loch Tummel'	GGGa
lochiae (V)	GGGa
'Lochinch Spinbur'	GQui
Lodauric Group	SReu
§ 'Lodauric Iceberg' ♀H3-4	LMil MSnd SReu
'Lodbrit'	SReu
Loderi Group	SLdr
'Loderi Fairy Queen'	SLdr
'Loderi Game Chick' ♀H3-4	SLdr
'Loderi Georgette'	SLdr
'Loderi Helen'	SLdr
§ 'Loderi King George' ♀H3-4	CBcs CDoC CDul CHll CWri ECho GGGa GKin IVic LMil MGos MLea MSnd NLar SLdr SPer SReu SSta WGwG
'Loderi Patience'	SLdr
'Loderi Pink Coral'	LMil SLdr
'Loderi Pink Diamond' ♀H3-4	CDoC CWri LMil SLdr
'Loderi Pink Topaz' ♀H3-4	SLdr
'Loderi Pretty Polly'	CWri SLdr
'Loderi Princess Marina'	SLdr
'Loderi Sir Edmund'	MSnd SLdr
'Loderi Sir Joseph Hooker'	MSnd SLdr
'Loderi Titan'	SLdr SReu
'Loderi Venus' ♀H3-4	MSnd SLdr SReu SSta

	'Loderi White Diamond'	SLdr
	'Loder's White' ♀H3-4	LMil MLea SHea SLdr SReu SSta
	longesquamatum	GGGa MSnd
	longipes	GGGa LMil MSnd SLdr
	- EGM 336	LMil
	- var. ***chienianum***	LMil MSnd
	lopsangianum	GGGa NHim
	'Lord Roberts' ♀H4	CBcs CDoC CDul CMac CSBt CTri CWri ECho EPfP GGGa LMil LRHS MAsh MGos MLea MMuc MSnd NEgg NLar SEND SHea SLdr SLim SPer SReu WFar WMoo
	'Lori Eichelser'	GEdr
	'Louis Pasteur'	SReu
	'Louisa' (EA)	MAsh
	'Louise Dowdle' (EA)	SLdr
	'Lovely William'	CMac LMil MSnd SLdr
	'Lucy Lou'	GGGa
	ludlowii	GGGa
	'Luisella'	IVic
	'Lullaby' (EA)	SLdr
	'Lunar Queen'	SLdr
	luteiflorum	GGGa MSnd
	lutescens	CBcs LMil MSnd SLdr SReu SSta WAbe WThu
	- 'Bagshot Sands' ♀H3-4	GGGa IDee LMil LRHS NLar SLdr
	- 'Exbury'	CPLG
	luteum (A) ♀H4	Widely available
	- 'Golden Comet' (A)	GGGa
	lyi	GGGa
*	'Mac Ovata'	CMac
	macabeanum ♀H3-4	CBcs CDoC CWri GGGa GKev GKin IDee LMil LRHS MLea MMuc MSnd NPCo SEND SLdr SPer SReu SSpi SSta WFar
	- NAPE 052	GGGa
	- Reuthe's form	SReu
	macabeanum × ***wardii***	GGGa
	'Macarena'	IVic
	macgregoriae (V)	GGGa
	macranthum	see *R. indicum* 'Macranthum'
	macrosmithii	see *R. argipeplum*
	maculiferum	GGGa NHim
	'Madame Ad. van Hecke' (EA)	CTri GKin IVic LMil MAsh MBri MMuc SHil SLdr SLim WFar
	'Madame Masson'	CDoC CDul CTri CWri ECho LMil LRHS MAsh MBri MGos MLea MMuc MSnd NLar NPri SBfd SBod SEND SPer SReu SSta WFar
	maddenii	CDoC LMil
§	- subsp. ***crassum***	CBcs CPLG GGGa GLin IVic MSnd SKHP SLdr
§	- subsp. ***maddenii*** Polyandrum Group	CBcs GGGa GQui
	'Madeleine' (K)	SHea
	'Maggie'	IVic
	'Maggie Brown' (A) **new**	GGGa
	'Magic Flute' (EA)	LRHS MAsh MBri MGos
I	'Magic Flute' (V)	LMil SCoo
	'Magnificum' (O)	SHea SLdr
	magnificum	GGGa SReu
	magniflorum **new**	GGGa
	'Maharani'	GGGa
	'Mai-ogi' (EA)	IVic
	'Maischnee' (EA)	GGGa
	'Maja' (G)	SReu SSta
§	***makinoi*** ♀H4	GGGa LLHF LMil LRHS NHim SReu SSpi SSta WAbe
	- 'Fuju-kaku-no-matsu'	MGos
	'Makiyak'	LMil
	'Malahat'	MSnd
	malayanum **new**	GGGa
	mallotum	GGGa IDee LMil LRHS MSnd NHim SReu
	'Manda Sue'	MMuc SEND
	Mandalay Group	SHea
	'Mandarin Lights' (A)	LMil MBri
	'Manderley'	LMil
	maoerense	GGGa
	'Maraschino' (EA)	GGGa IVic
	'Marcel Ménard'	CDoC CDul GGGa LMil LRHS MAsh NLar NPri SBfd SReu SSta WFar
	'Marchioness of Lansdowne'	CWri SHea
	'Mardi Gras'	CDoC NEgg NLar SLdr
	Margaret Dunn Group	CWri
	'Margaret Falmouth'	SReu
	'Marie Curie'	LMil
	'Marie Hoffman'	LMil
	'Marilee' (EA)	CDoC ECho ELon IVic LRHS MAsh MGos SLdr
	Mariloo Group	LMil MSnd
	'Marina' (K)	SHea
	'Marion Merriman' (K)	SHea
	'Marion Street' ♀H4	LMil SReu
	'Markeeta's Prize' ♀H4	CDoC CWri ECho EPfP GGGa LMil LRHS MAsh MBri MGos MLea MMuc NLar NPri SEND SHea SLdr SLim SReu
	'Marley Hedges'	LMil
	'Marlies' (A)	MBri
	'Marmot' (EA)	ECho MLea
	'Mars'	SLdr
	'Marsalla'	LMil
	'Martha Isaacson' (Ad) ♀H4	CWri LMil MGos SLdr SReu
	'Martha Wright' **new**	GGGa NPri
	martinianum	GGGa SLdr
	'Maruschka' (EA)	GGGa IVic LMil LRHS MAsh SPoG
	'Mary Claire' (K)	SHea
	'Mary Forte'	SBfd
	'Mary Helen' (EA)	LRHS MAsh MBri SCoo SLim
	'Mary Poppins' (K)	GKin LMil LSRN MAsh NLar SCoo SLdr SLim WMoo
	'Master of Elphinstone' (EA)	SLdr
	'Matador'	GGGa LMil MSnd SHea SLdr
	Matador Group	SReu
	maximum	GGGa
§	'Maxwellii' (EA)	CMac SLdr
	'May Day' ♀H3-4	CMac MAsh NEgg NLar SHea SLdr
	May Day Group	CBcs CWri MGos MSnd
	'Mayor Johnstone'	CTri MAsh NPri
	'Mazurka' (K)	IVic SHea SLdr
	Medea Group	SLdr
	Medusa Group	SHea
	megacalyx	GGGa
	'Megan' (EA)	ECho ELon LMil LSRN MAsh MGos MMuc NLar SLdr WGwG
	megaphyllum	see *R. basilicum*
	megeratum	GGGa NHim SLdr
	- 'Bodnant'	GGGa ITim WAbe WThu
	mekongense var. ***mekongense*** Rubroluteum Group	see *R. viridescens* Rubroluteum Group
	- - Viridescens Group	see *R. viridescens*
	'Melford Lemon'	see *R.* 'Ilam Melford Lemon'
	'Melidioso'	LMil
	'Melina' (EA/d)	LMil
	'Melville' **new**	SReu SSta

'Mendosina'	IVic
mengtszense	MSnd
'Mephistopheles' (K)	SHea
'Merganser' ♀H4	GEdr GGGa LMil MLea
'Merlin' (EA)	LMil SLdr
metternichii var. ***pentamerum***	see *R. degronianum* subsp. *degronianum*
'Mi Amor'	GGGa LMil
'Miami' (A)	SLdr
'Michael Hill' (EA)	MAsh
'Michael Waterer'	MSnd SLdr
'Michael's Pride'	CBcs GQui LMil
'Michiko' (EA) **new**	IVic
microgynum	GGGa MSnd
- Gymnocarpum Group	MSnd
microleucum	see *R. orthocladum* var. *microleucum*
micromeres	see *R. leptocarpum*
'Midnight Mystique'	SReu SSta
'Midnight Ruby'	GGGa
'Midsummer'	IVic SHea
'Midsummer Mermaid' (A)	LMil
'Mikado' (EA)	see *R. kaempferi* 'Mikado'
'Milton' (R)	LMil
mimetes	GKev
'Mimi' (EA)	CMac
'Mindy's Love'	LMil NHim
'Ming'	see *R.* 'Ilam Ming'
miniatum	GGGa
- CER 9927	GGGa
'Minikin' (K)	SHea
minus	GQui
- var. ***minus*** (Carolinianum Group) 'Epoch'	LMil
'Miss Muffet' (EA)	SLdr
'Moerheim' ♀H4	CBcs CWri ECho LRHS MGos MMuc NPCo NPri SEND SLdr SLim SReu
§ 'Moerheim's Pink'	LMil MSnd SLdr
'Moidart' (Vs)	LMil
'Moira Salmon' (EA)	SLdr
§ ***molle*** subsp. ***japonicum*** (A)	LMil
- subsp. ***molle*** (A)	LMil
mollicomum	NHim
Mollis orange-flowered (M)	GKin SRms
Mollis pink-flowered (M)	GKin SRms
Mollis red-flowered (M)	GKin
Mollis salmon-flowered (M)	GQui
Mollis yellow-flowered (M)	GKin GQui SRms
'Molly Ann'	ECho LSRN MBri MGos MSnd NLar
'Molten Gold' (v)	GGGa LMil LRHS MAsh
§ 'Momoko' (EA)	MAsh
monanthum	GGGa
monosematum	see *R. pachytrichum* var. *monosematum*
montroseanum	CDoC GGGa LMil MSnd NHim SLdr
'Moon Maiden' (EA)	ECho ELon GQui MMuc NLar
Moonstone Group	MLea
'Moonstone Pink'	MSnd SLdr
'Moonstone Yellow'	MSnd SLdr
'Moonwax'	SLdr
§ 'Morgenrot'	MGos NLar WFar
morii	GGGa
morii × ***pachysanthum*** **new**	GGGa
'Morning Cloud' ♀H4	ECho EPfP LRHS MAsh NHol SLdr SLim SReu
Morning Red	see *R.* 'Morgenrot'

'Moser's Maroon'	CBcs CWri ECho GGGa MGos MLea SEND SLdr SPoG
'Motet' (K/d)	SHea
'Mother's Day' (EA) ♀H4	CDoC CMac CSBt CTri ECho EPfP GKin GQui LMil LRHS LSRN MAsh MBri MGos MMuc NEgg NHol NPCo NPri SEND SLdr SLim SPer SPoG SReu SSta WFar
'Mount Everest'	LMil SReu SSta
'Mount Rainier' (K)	SLdr
'Mount Saint Helens' (A)	LMil NLar SLdr SLim
'Mount Seven Star'	see *R. nakaharae* 'Mount Seven Star'
moupinense	GGGa GLin MSnd SLdr
- 'Fulmar' **new**	GGGa
'Mrs A.C. Kenrick'	SHea SLdr
'Mrs A.T. de la Mare' ♀H4	CWri LMil SHea SReu SSta
'Mrs Betty Robertson'	CMac ECho GBin MGos MMuc SEND SLdr
'Mrs Charles E. Pearson' ♀H4	CDul CSBt LMil MSnd SHea SLdr
'Mrs Davies Evans' ♀H4	SReu SSta
'Mrs Emil Hager' (EA)	SLdr
'Mrs Furnivall' ♀H4	CBcs CDoC CWri ECho GGGa LMil MGos MLea MMuc SEND SLdr SReu
'Mrs G.W. Leak'	CDul CSBt CWri GGGa LMil MLea SHea SReu
'Mrs J.C. Williams' ♀H4	LMil
'Mrs J.G. Millais'	LMil SHea
'Mrs James Horlick'	CWri
'Mrs Kingsmill'	SLdr
'Mrs Lionel de Rothschild' ♀H4	CWri SReu
'Mrs P.D. Williams'	SReu
'Mrs Peter Koster' (M)	SLdr WFar
'Mrs R.S. Holford' ♀H4	MSnd SHea SLdr
'Mrs T.H. Lowinsky' ♀H4	CDoC CDul CMac ECho GGGa GKin LMil MAsh MGos MLea MMuc MSnd NHim NLar SEND SHea SLdr SLim SPer SReu SSta
§ × ***mucronatum*** (EA)	CBcs MSnd
'Mucronatum'	see *R.* × *mucronatum*
mucronulatum	CBcs MSnd
- B&SWJ 786	WCru
- var. ***chejuense***	see *R. mucronulatum* var. *taquetii*
- 'Cornell Pink' ♀H4	GGGa WFar
§ - var. ***taquetii***	GGGa
- - B&SWJ 4486	WCru
'Mulroy Cream' **new**	LMil
'Muneira' (EA) **new**	IVic
'Nabucco' (A)	EPfP GGGa MMuc SEND WMoo
nakaharae (EA)	MSnd NHim SLdr SReu WAbe
- 'Mariko' (EA)	WAbe WThu
§ - 'Mount Seven Star' (EA) ♀H4	ECho GGGa LMil MGos NWad SLdr WAbe
§ - orange-flowered (EA)	ECho LMil LRHS MAsh MGos MMuc SLdr SReu
- pink-flowered (EA)	ECho MGos MMuc NLar SLdr SPer SReu SSta
- red-flowered (EA)	ECho MGos
'Nakahari Orange'	see *R. nakaharae* orange-flowered
nakotiltum	MSnd
'Nancor'	CBcs
'Nancy' (EA)	MAsh
'Nancy Buchanan' (K)	SLdr
'Nancy Evans' ♀H3-4	CDoC CSBt ECho EPfP GGGa GKin LMil LSRN MAsh MLea NLar NPCo NPri SLdr SLim SReu SSpi SSta WFar
'Nancy of Robinhill' (EA)	SReu

	Name	Suppliers
	'Nancy Waterer' (G) ♀H4	EPfP LMil NLar SReu
	'Nanki Poo' (EA)	SLdr
	'Naomi' (EA)	GQui MSnd SLdr
	Naomi Group	CWri MSnd
	'Naomi Hope'	LMil
	'Naomi Nautilus'	LMil
	'Naomi Pink Beauty'	LMil
	'Naomi Stella Maris'	LMil
	'Narcissiflorum' (G/d) ♀H4	CSBt EPfP GKin LMil NLar SReu SSta
	'Naselle'	GGGa SReu
	'Nassau' (EA/d)	LMil
	'Ne Plus Ultra' (V)	GGGa
	neriiflorum	GGGa LMil MSnd
§	- subsp. ***neriiflorum*** Phoenicodum Group	GGGa
§	- subsp. ***phaedropum***	GGGa LMil
	'Newcomb's Sweetheart'	LMil
	'Niagara' (EA) ♀H3-4	CMac LMil MGos SLdr SPoG
	'Nichola' (EA)	LSRN
	'Nico' (EA)	CMac LRHS MAsh
	'Nicoletta'	LMil
	'Night Sky'	CDoC ECho GGGa LMil LRHS MAsh MGos MMuc MSnd NLar NPCo SLdr
	'Nightingale'	SReu
	nigroglandulosum	GGGa
	nilagiricum	see *R. arboreum* subsp. *nilagiricum*
	'Ninotschka' new	IVic
	nipponicum	GGGa
	'Nishiki' (EA)	CMac
	nitens	see *R. calostrotum* subsp. *riparium* Nitens Group
	nitidulum var. ***omeiense***	GGGa MSnd
	nivale subsp. ***boreale*** Ramosissimum Group	GGGa
§	- subsp. ***nivale***	GKev ITim
	niveum ♀H4	GGGa LMil MSnd NHim SReu
	- B&SWJ 2611	WCru
	- B&SWJ 2659	WCru
	- B&SWJ 2675	WCru
	nobleanum	see *R.* Nobleanum Group
§	Nobleanum Group	GGGa LMil MLea MSnd SLdr SSta
	'Nobleanum Album'	GGGa LMil SReu SSta
	'Nobleanum Coccineum'	SReu
	'Nobleanum Venustum'	CWri LMil SReu SSta
	'Nordlicht' (EA)	SLdr
	'Norfolk Candy'	LMil LRHS
	'Noriko' (EA)	SLdr
N	'Norma' (R/d) ♀H4	SReu
	'Northern Hi-Lights' (A)	GKin LMil NLar SLdr SLim
	'Nova Zembla'	CBcs CDoC CTri ECho EPfP GGGa LMil LRHS MAsh MGos MMuc NEgg SEND SLim SPer SPoG SReu SSta
	nudiflorum	see *R. periclymenoides*
	nudipes	LMil
	nuttallii	GGGa LMil
	'Oban'	EPot GEdr WAbe WThu
	Obtusum Group (EA)	MSnd SLdr
	- 'Amoenum' (EA/d)	CBcs CDoC CMac CSBt ECho LMil MGos MSnd SBfd SLdr SPer WFar
§	- 'Hinomayo' (EA) ♀H3-4	CMac CTri EPfP GKin GQui LMil MSnd NHim SLdr SPer SReu
	occidentale (A) ♀H4	CDul GKin LMil SHea
	- SIN 1830	GGGa GLin
	- 'Crescent City Double'	GGGa
	- 'Exquisitum' new	GGGa
	ochraceum	GGGa LMil
	'Odee Wright'	CTri CWri LRHS MAsh SLdr
	'Odoratum' (Ad)	MLea
	'Oh! Kitty'	CWri ECho MLea NPCo SLdr
	'Old Copper'	CWri
	'Old Gold' (K)	ECho SHea SLdr
	'Old Port' ♀H4	CWri LMil
	'Olga' ♀H4	CBcs LMil SHea SReu SSta
	'Olga Niblett' (EA)	SReu SSta
	oligocarpum	GGGa LMil
	'Olive'	LMil SLdr
	'Olympic Flame' (EA)	LMil
	'Olympic Sunrise'	LMil
§	'One Thousand Butterflies'	MSnd SLdr
	'Ophelia' (EA)	SLdr
	'Opossum' (EA)	GGGa
	'Orange Beauty' (EA) ♀H3-4	CBcs CDoC CMac CSBt ECho GGGa MAsh MGos MSnd SLdr SReu WFar
	'Orange King' (EA)	LMil MGos SPoG
	'Orangeade' (K)	SHea
	orbiculare ♀H3-4	GGGa LMil MSnd
§	- subsp. ***cardiobasis***	GGGa NHim
	'Orchid Lights'	MAsh
	'Oregon' (EA)	SLdr
	Oregonia Group	LMil
	oreodoxa	LMil
§	- var. ***fargesii*** ♀H4	GGGa LMil MSnd
	- var. ***oreodoxa***	GGGa LMil
	oreotrephes	GKev IDee IVic LMil MSnd NLar SHea SLdr
	- 'Bluecalyptus'	GGGa
§	- Exquisitum Group	SLdr
	- 'Pentland'	GGGa LMil
	'Orient' (K)	SHea
§	***orthocladum*** var. ***microleucum***	GGGa GKev WThu
	'Oryx' (O)	SHea SLdr
	'Osaraku Seedling' (EA)	EPfP LRHS
	'Osmar' ♀H4	GGGa MGos MSnd
	'Ostara'	MGos
	'Osterschnee'	IVic
	'Oudijk's Favorite'	SLdr
	'Oudijk's Sensation'	CBcs CWri ECho GQui MAsh MGos MMuc NHim NPCo SEND SHea SLdr
	'Oxydol' (K)	IVic MMuc SHea SLdr
§	***pachypodum***	GGGa
	pachysanthum ♀H4	CDoC GGGa GKin IDee LMil LRHS MSnd NLar SLdr SReu SSpi
	- 'Crosswater'	LMil
	pachysanthum × ***yakushimanum***	SReu
	pachytrichum	GGGa NHim SLdr
§	- var. ***monosematum***	MSnd
	'Palestrina' (EA) ♀H3-4	CBcs CMac CSBt ECho EPfP GBin GKin MAsh MGos MMuc NLar NPCo SEND SLdr SPer SReu SSta WFar
	'Pallas' (G)	GKin SReu
	paludosum	see *R. nivale* subsp. *nivale*
	'Pancake'	CMac
	'Panda' (EA) ♀H4	CSBt CTri ECho EPfP GGGa LMil LRHS MAsh MLea NPri SReu
	'Papaya Punch'	LMil
	'Paprika Spiced'	CWri ECho LMil MAsh MGos MLea NHim NLar NPCo SLdr
	'Parfait' (EA) new	LMil
	'Parkfeuer' (A)	GGGa IVic LMil
	parmulatum	GGGa LMil

	- KW 5876	GGGa LMil
	- 'Ocelot'	GGGa
	parryae AM (*roseatum*)	GGGa
	'Patty Bee' ♀H4	CBcs CSBt CTri CWri ECho EPfP EPot GEdr GGGa GKev IDee ITim LMil LRHS MAsh MBri MGos MLea NLar NPri SLdr SLim SReu SSpi SSta WFar
	patulum	see *R. pemakoense* Patulum Group
	'Pavane' (K)	SHea
	'Peep-bo' (EA)	SLdr
	'Peeping Tom'	SReu
	pemakoense	GGGa MSnd SLdr SReu WThu
§	- Patulum Group	GEdr SLdr
	'Pemakofairy'	WThu
	pendulum	GGGa
	Penelope Group	SReu
	'Penheale Blue' ♀H4	GKin LMil
	'Penjerrick' **new**	GGGa
	'Penny Tomlin'	SReu SSta
	pentaphyllum (A)	GGGa
	'Peppina'	GGGa
	'Percy Wiseman' ♀H4	CBcs CDoC CDul CSBt CWri ECho EPfP GGGa GKin LMil LRHS MAsh MBri MGos MLea MMuc MSnd NEgg SBfd SEND SLdr SLim SPer SPoG SReu SSta WFar
	'Perfect Lady'	LMil
§	***periclymenoides*** (A)	GGGa GKev LMil
	'Persil' (K) ♀H4	CBcs CMac CSBt CTri CWri ECho EPfP GBin GGGa GKin LMil LRHS MAsh MBri MGos MLea MMuc NLar SCoo SEND SLdr SReu SSta WMoo
	'Peter Chapell' **new**	GGGa
	'Peter Gable' (EA)	SLdr
	'Peter Koster' (M)	SHea
	'Peter Koster' (hybrid)	GKin SLdr
	petrocharis	GGGa
	'Petrouchka' (K)	SHea
	'Pfauenauge'	GGGa
	phaedropum	see *R. neriiflorum* subsp. *phaedropum*
	phaeochrysum	MSnd SLdr
	- var. ***agglutianum***	GKev NHim
§	- var. ***levistratum***	MSnd SLdr
	- var. ***phaeochrysum***	GKev
	'Phalarope'	GEdr SLdr SReu
	phoenicodum	see *R. neriiflorum* subsp. *neriiflorum* Phoenicodum Group
	'Phyllis Korn'	CWri IVic LMil LTen SLdr
	'Picotee' (K)	LMil
§	***piercei***	GGGa LMil MSnd
	'Pilgrim' **new**	LMil
	'Pine Marten' (EA) **new**	GGGa
	pingianum	GGGa SLdr
	'Pink Bride'	SLdr
	'Pink Cameo'	CWri
	'Pink Cherub' ♀H4	ECho ELon LMil MAsh SLdr SReu
	'Pink Delight' ambig.	GQui MAsh
I	'Pink Delight' (K)	GKin MBri MGos SHea SLdr
	'Pink Delight' (V)	MMuc
	'Pink Drift'	CSBt ECho GEdr LMil MGos MMuc NPCo SEND SLdr SPer WThu
	'Pink Gin'	LMil LRHS NHim
	'Pink Mimosa' (Vs)	SLdr
	'Pink Pancake' (EA) ♀H4	ECho ELon EPfP GKin LMil LRHS MAsh MGos MMuc NPri SLdr
	'Pink Pearl' (EA)	see *R.* 'Azuma-kagami'
	'Pink Pearl' (hybrid)	CBcs CMac CSBt CTri CWri ECho EPfP GGGa LMil MAsh MBri MGos MMuc MSnd NLar NPri SHea SLdr SPer SPoG SReu SSta WFar
	'Pink Pebble' ♀H3-4	CBcs CPLG ELon MLea SLdr
	'Pink Perfection'	CMac MGos MSnd SHea SLdr WFar
	'Pink Polar Bear'	GKin LMil
	'Pink Ruffles' (K)	SHea SLdr
	'Pinkerton'	LMil
	'Pintail'	GGGa LMil LRHS MAsh
	'Pipit'	GGGa
	'Pippa' (EA)	CMac
	'PJM Elite'	NLar
	'PJM Regal'	IVic
	'Plover'	GGGa
	pocophorum	MSnd NHim
§	- var. ***hemidartum***	MSnd
	- var. ***pocophorum***	GGGa
	'Point Defiance'	CWri ECho MSnd
	'Polar Bear' ♀H3-4	CBcs CHll CSBt GGGa GKin IVic LMil MGos NHim SLdr SReu
	Polar Bear Group	CWri ECho LMil MLea
	'Polaris'	see *R.* 'Hachmann's Polaris'
	'Polarnacht'	CDoC GGGa GKin IVic LMil LRHS MAsh
	poluninii	GGGa
	- KR 8231	LMil
	polyandrum	see *R. maddenii* subsp. *maddenii* Polyandrum Group
§	***polycladum*** Scintillans Group	GGGa SLdr
	polylepis	MSnd
	'Polyroy' **new**	GGGa
	'Pomegranate Splash' **new**	GGGa
	ponticum	CBcs CDul CMac CTri CWri MGos SBfd WFar
	- 'Filigran' **new**	IVic
§	- 'Variegatum' (v)	CBcs CMac CSBt EPfP LRHS MAsh MGos MLea MSnd NPri SBfd SLdr SPoG SRms SSta WFar
	'Popocatapetl'	SReu
	populare **new**	GGGa
	'Praecox' ♀H4	CBcs CSBt ECho ELon EPfP GGGa GKev GKin LMil LRHS MAsh MGos MMuc NLar NPri SEND SLdr SLim SPer SPoG SReu SSta WFar
	praestans	GGGa GKin IDee LMil LRHS MSnd SLdr
	prattii	GGGa NHim
	- 'Perry Wood'	LMil
	preptum	GGGa SLdr
	'President Roosevelt' (v)	CSBt EPfP GKin MAsh MGos NPri SBfd SPoG SReu
	'Pridenjoy'	LMil
	primuliflorum	MSnd WAbe
	- 'Doker-La'	GGGa LMil
	'Prince Camille de Rohan'	LMil SHea
	'Princess Alice'	CBcs WAbe
	'Princess Anne' ♀H4	CBcs CMHG ECho EPot GEdr LMil LRHS MAsh MGos MLea SHea SLdr SLim SPer SPoG SReu SSta
	'Princess Galadriel'	SLdr
	'Princess Juliana'	ECho MGos
	'Princess Margaret of Windsor' (K)	GQui LMil
	principis	GGGa LMil SLdr
	- 'Lost Horizon'	CDoC LMil MSnd SLdr
§	- Vellereum Group	SLdr
§	***prinophyllum*** (A)	GGGa GKin LMil

'Prins Bernhard' (EA)	SLdr
'Prinses Juliana' (EA)	MMuc SLdr SReu
'Professor Hugo de Vries' ♀H4	SHea SLdr
pronum	GGGa
- R.B. Cooke form	GGGa
- Towercourt form	GGGa
prostratum	see *R. saluenense* subsp. *chameunum* Prostratum Group
proteoides	GGGa
proteoides* × *tsariense	GGGa
protistum	GGGa
pruniflorum	GGGa
prunifolium (A)	GGGa LMil
przewalskii	GGGa MSnd
pseudochrysanthum ♀H4	GGGa IDee LMil MSnd SReu
- dwarf	GGGa
pseudociliipes	GGGa
'Ptarmigan' ♀H3-4	ECho GEdr GGGa LMil MAsh MGos MMuc MSnd NPri SEND SLdr SReu WFar WPat WThu
pubescens	GGGa
pubicostatum	GLin MSnd
§ 'Pucella' (G) ♀H4	CWri
pudorosum	GGGa
'Pulchrum Maxwellii'	see *R.* 'Maxwellii'
pumilum	GGGa WAbe WThu
'Pumuckl' **new**	IVic
'Puncta'	SLdr
'Purple Cushion' (EA)	LRHS MAsh NPri
'Purple Diamond'	see *R.* Diamant Group purple-flowered
purple Glenn Dale (EA)	SLdr
'Purple Passion'PBR	NLar
'Purple Queen' (EA/d)	MAsh
'Purple Splendor' (EA)	CMac MMuc SEND SLdr
'Purple Splendour' ♀H4	CBcs CSBt CWri ECho ELon EPfP LMil MGos MLea MMuc NEgg NPCo SEND SPer SPoG SReu SSta WFar WMoo
'Purple Triumph' (EA) ♀H3	LMil SLdr SSta
'Purpurtraum' (EA) ♀H4	LMil
qiaojiaense NN 0903 **new**	GGGa
'Quail'	GGGa LMil SLdr
'Queen Alice'	LMil
Queen Emma	see *R.* 'Koningin Emma'
'Queen Louise' (K)	SHea
'Queen Mary'	SReu SSta
'Queen of Hearts'	LMil SHea SLdr
'Queen Souriya'	SReu
'Quentin Metsys' (R)	SLdr SReu SSta
quinquefolium (A)	GGGa LMil MSnd
'Rabatz'	GGGa IVic LMil
'Raby' (A)	LMil
racemosum ♀H4	CBcs GKev LMil MSnd SLdr
- 'Rock Rose' ♀H3-4	IDee LMil
'Racine' (G)	SLdr SReu SSta
'Racoon' (EA) ♀H4	GGGa
radicans	see *R. calostrotum* subsp. *keleticum* Radicans Group
'Raimunde' (K)	IVic
'Ramapo' ♀H4	CDoC ECho EPfP GGGa LMil LRHS MAsh MBri MGos MSnd SLdr SLim SReu
'Raoul Millais'	LMil
'Raphael de Smet' (G/d)	SReu
'Razorbill' ♀H4	CDoC ECho GGGa GKin LMil LRHS MGos SLim
recurvoides	GGGa IDee LMil MSnd SLdr SReu
- Keillour form	GGGa
recurvum	see *R. roxieanum* var. *roxieanum*
'Red and Gold'	GGGa
'Red Dawn'	LRHS
'Red Delicious'	CWri LMil SLdr
'Red Diamond'	see *R.* Diamant Group red-flowered
'Red Fountain' (EA)	ECho MMuc
'Red Jack'	CWri LMil SReu SSta
'Red Panda' (EA)	GGGa
'Red Pimpernel' (EA)	SLdr
'Red Sunset' (A)	SLdr
'Red Velour'	MSnd SLdr
'Red Wood'	GGGa
'Redwing' (EA)	CDoC MAsh SLdr
'Rennie' (A)	ECho GKin MGos MLea MMuc SHea
'Renoir' ♀H4	CSBt LMil SLdr SReu
reticulatum (A)	CBcs LMil MSnd SReu
'Reuthe's Purple'	SReu WAbe WThu
'Rêve d'Amour' (Vs)	SReu SSta
'Rex' (EA)	MAsh SLdr
rex	CDoC GGGa GKin LMil SLdr
- EGM 295	LMil
§ - subsp. ***fictolacteum*** ♀H3-4	CDoC GGGa GKin IDee LMil MSnd NHim SLdr SReu
- subsp. ***gratum***	LMil
- subsp. ***rex*** ♀H3-4	MSnd
rex* × *yakushimanum	SReu
rhabdotum	see *R. dalhousieae* var. *rhabdotum*
'Ria Hardijzer'	LMil
rigidum	GGGa GLin
* - ***album***	LMil
'Ring of Fire'	CWri ECho IVic LMil MGos MLea MSnd NHim SLdr
'Ripe Corn'	MSnd
'Ripples' (EA)	CTrh
ririei	GGGa LMil SLdr SReu
- AC 2036	LMil
'Robert Croux'	MSnd SLdr
'Robert Seleger'	GGGa GKin LMil LRHS MAsh MMuc SEND SReu
'Robin Hill Frosty' (EA)	SLdr
'Robin Hill Gillie' (EA)	SLdr
'Robinette'	CBcs CWri ECho MAsh
'Rocket'	CDoC CTri ECho LMil MAsh MGos MLea MMuc SEND SHea SLdr SLim SPoG
'Roehr's Peggy Ann' (EA)	LMil
'Rokoko'	see *R.* 'Hachmann's Rokoko'
(Romany Chai Group) 'Romany Chai'	SHea
'Romany Chal'	SHea
'Rosa' (EA)	LMil
'Rosa Mundi'	CSBt
Rosalind Group	CMac
'Rosalinda' (EA)	SLdr
'Rosata' (Vs) ♀H4	GGGa GKin SReu SSta
'Rose Bud'	CSBt CTri
'Rose Elf'	WThu
'Rose Glow' (A)	SReu
'Rose Gown'	SReu
'Rose Greeley' (EA)	CDoC ECho GQui SLdr SLim SPer SReu WFar WGwG
'Rose Haze' (Vs)	SLdr SReu
'Rose Torch' (A)	SReu
'Rosebud' (EA/d) ♀H3-4	CBcs CMac MGos NHol SLdr SReu
roseum	see *R. prinophyllum*
'Roseum Elegans'	CDoC MAsh SLim WFar

'Rosevallon'	MSnd
Rosinetta = 'Hachrosi' (EA) **new**	GGGa
'Rosy Dream'	CWri ECho MAsh MBri MMuc MSnd SEND
'Rosy Fire' (A)	LMil SReu
'Rosy Lea'	MLea
'Rosy Lights' (A)	CTri LMil NLar SLdr
'Rotglocke'	IVic
'Rothenburg'	SLdr
rothschildii	CDoC GGGa IDee LMil MSnd NHim SLdr
'Rotkäppchen'	IVic
'Rouge'	SHea
rousei (V)	GGGa
roxieanum	GGGa LMil MSnd SLdr
§ - var. ***cucullatum***	GGGa
- var. ***oreonastes*** ♀H4	GGGa IVic LMil MSnd SSta
- - Nymans form	SReu
- var. ***parvum***	GGGa
§ - var. ***roxieanum***	NHim
'Royal Command' (K)	CTri CWri GKin LMil SHea
'Royal Lodge' (K)	SHea
'Royal Mail'	SHea
'Royal Ruby' (K)	CWri ECho MAsh MGos MMuc SHea SLdr
'Roza Stevenson'	LMil
'Rubicon'	CWri ECho GGGa GQui MAsh MMuc SEND SLdr
rubiginosum	CBcs GGGa LMil MSnd NHim
- SDR 5142	GKev
§ - Desquamatum Group	CBcs SLdr
- pink-flowered	LMil
'Rubinetta' (EA)	WFar
rubroluteum	see *R. viridescens* Rubroluteum Group
'Ruby F. Bowman'	SReu
'Ruby Hart'	GGGa LSRN MMuc
'Ruddy Duck' (K)	SHea
rude	see *R. glischrum* subsp. *rude*
rufum	GGGa
rugosum Sinclair 240 (V)	GGGa
'Rumba' (K)	SHea
rushforthii **new**	GGGa
russatum ♀H4	EPfP GGGa LMil MSnd SLdr SSpi WAbe
- blue-black-flowered	GKin LMil
* - 'Collingwood Ingram' **new**	GGGa
- 'Purple Pillow'	CSBt
Russautinii Group	MSnd SLdr
russotinctum	see *R. alutaceum* var. *russotinctum*
'Ryde Heron' (EA)	SLdr
'Sabina' (EA)	SLdr
'Sacko'	CWri GGGa LLHF LMil MAsh NLar SLim
'Saffron Queen'	CBcs MMuc SEND SLdr
'Sahara' (K)	LMil SHea
'Saint Breward'	GQui MSnd SLdr
'Saint Merryn' ♀H4	CBcs CWri ECho MBri MMuc SEND SLdr
'Saint Minver'	SLdr
'Saint Tudy'	SLdr
'Saint Valentine' (V)	GGGa
'Salmon Sander' (EA)	SLdr
§ 'Salmon Trout'	LMil LSRN
'Salmon's Leap' (EA/v)	CMac CSBt ELan LMil LRHS MAsh MBri SLdr SReu WFar
saluenense	LMil MSnd SLdr WThu

§ - subsp. ***chameunum*** Prostratum Group	GGGa
'Sammetglut'	CWri
'Samuel Taylor Coleridge' (M)	GKin NLar
sanguineum	LMil MSnd SLdr
§ - subsp. ***didymum***	GGGa MSnd SLdr
- subsp. ***sanguineum*** var. ***haemaleum***	GGGa LMil MSnd
- - var. ***sanguineum*** F 25521	LMil
'Santa Maria' (EA)	ECho ELon LMil LSRN MBri MGos SReu SSta
santapaui (V)	GGGa
'Sapphire'	MAsh WThu
'Sappho'	CBcs CMac CSBt CWri ECho EPfP GBin GGGa GKin LMil MGos MLea NEgg NPCo SEND SLdr SReu SSta WFar WGwG
'Sapporo'	LMil
sargentianum	GGGa NHar WAbe WThu
- 'Whitebait'	GGGa
'Sarled' ♀H4	GGGa ITim LMil NHar SHea WPat WThu
Sarled Group	WAbe
'Saroi' (EA)	SLdr
'Saskia' (K)	IVic
'Satan' (K) ♀H4	CSBt SHea SReu
§ 'Satschiko' (EA) ♀H4	CSBt GGGa LRHS MAsh MGos NHim NPri SHil SLdr
'Satsop Surprise'	SLdr
Satsuki type (EA)	ECho SLdr
'Saturnus' (M)	GKin
§ ***scabrifolium*** var. ***spiciferum***	SLdr WAbe
'Scandinavia'	SHea
'Scarlet Pimpernel' (K)	SHea
'Scarlet Wonder' ♀H4	CBcs CDoC CMHG CSBt CWri ECho EPfP GGGa GKev GKin LMil LRHS MAsh MBri MGos NPri SEND SHea SLdr SPer SReu WFar
'Sceptre' (K)	SHea
schistocalyx F 17637	MSnd
schlippenbachii (A)	GGGa GKev LMil MSnd
- 'Sid's Royal Pink' (A)	LMil
'Schneekrone' ♀H4	GGGa MBri
'Schneeperle' (EA)	IVic LMil SHil
'Schneespiegel'	GGGa
scintillans	see *R. polycladum* Scintillans Group
'Scintillation'	CBcs CWri GGGa LMil LTen MAsh MBri MGos MLea MMuc MSnd NLar SEND SLdr
scopulorum	GGGa MMuc SEND SLdr
'Scotian Bells'	GGGa
scottianum	see *R. pachypodum*
'Scout' (EA)	MAsh SLdr
scyphocalyx	see *R. dichroanthum* subsp. *scyphocalyx*
'Seaview Sunset'	GGGa
'Seb'	SLdr
'Second Honeymoon'	CBcs CWri ECho MLea MSnd NHim SEND SLdr
'Seikai' (EA)	SLdr
seinghkuense	GGGa LMil
- CCH&H 8106	GGGa LMil
§ ***selense*** subsp. ***dasycladum***	MSnd
- subsp. ***jucundum***	GGGa

semibarbatum	GLin
semnoides	GGGa LMil SLdr
'Sennocke'	LMil
'September Song'	CBcs CMac CWri ECho GGGa LMil MAsh MGos MLea MMuc NHol NLar NPCo SEND SLdr SPer
serotinum	GGGa GLin LMil
serpyllifolium (A)	CBcs SLdr
'Sesterianum'	CMHG SLdr
'Seta'	CAbP CBcs SHea SLdr WThu
Seta Group	SReu
'Seville'	SHea
'Shamrock'	CDoC EPfP GEdr LRHS MAsh MBri MGos MLea NEgg SBfd SEND SLdr SLim SPoG WFar
'Shanty' (K/d)	SHea
'Sheila' (EA)	CSBt LRHS MAsh NPri
'Shelley' (EA)	LMil LSRN
shepherdii	see *R. kendrickii*
sherriffii	GGGa MSnd
'Shiko' (EA)	MAsh
'Shiko Lavender' (A)	SPoG
Shilsonii Group	LMil
'Shi-no-noe' (EA)	SLdr
'Shrimp Girl'	GKin MAsh MSnd
sichotense	GGGa
sidereum	GGGa
siderophyllum	GGGa GLin MSnd
sikangense	GGGa MSnd SLdr
- var. ***exquisitum***	GGGa GLin
§ - var. ***sikangense*** Cookeanum Group	SLdr
'Silbervelours'	IVic
§ 'Silberwolke' ♀H4	IVic LMil MAsh
'Silkeborg Silence' **new**	GGGa
Silver Cloud	see *R.* 'Silberwolke'
'Silver Edge'	see *R. ponticum* 'Variegatum'
'Silver Glow' (EA)	CMac
'Silver Jubilee' ♀H4	LMil
'Silver Moon' (EA)	SLdr
'Silver Queen' (EA)	ECho ELon MGos NEgg SLdr SPer
'Silver Sixpence'	CBcs ECho EPfP LRHS LSRN MAsh MBri MGos MMuc MSnd NPCo SEND SLdr
'Silver Skies'	LMil
'Silver Slipper' (K) ♀H4	CBcs GKin LMil MAsh MLea NHol NLar SHea SLdr SReu SSta WFar
'Silver Sword' (EA/v) **new**	EPfP
'Silver Thimbles' (V)	GGGa
'Silverwood' (K)	LMil
'Silvester' (EA)	CTri LMil LRHS MAsh MBri MGos SLdr SReu
'Simona'	LMil SReu
simsii (EA)	CMac LMil SLdr
sinofalconeri	GGGa LMil
- KR 7342	LMil
- SEH 229	LMil
sinogrande ♀H3	CAbb CBcs CDoC CHEx CHll CWri ELon GBin GGGa GKin IDee LMil MMuc NPCo SEND SLdr
- KR 4027	LMil
'Sir Charles Lemon' ♀H3-4	CDoC CWri ECho GGGa LMil MAsh MBri MGos MLea MSnd NLar NPCo SHea SLdr SPer
'Sir Robert' (EA)	LRHS MAsh
'Sleeping Beauty'	WAbe
'Sleepy'	CBcs CSBt ECho MAsh MGos MSnd SLdr
smirnowii	GGGa IDee LMil MSnd
smithii	see *R. argipeplum*
'Sneezy'	CBcs CSBt CWri ECho EPfP GGGa LMil LRHS MAsh MGos MSnd SLdr SLim
'Snipe'	CBcs CTri ECho GEdr LMil LRHS MAsh MBri MGos NLar SLdr SLim SReu
'Snow' (EA)	SLdr
'Snow Crown' (*lindleyi* hybrid)	MAsh MLea
'Snow Hill' (EA)	GBin GQui LMil MGos SLdr
'Snow Lady'	CBcs ECho EPfP EPot GEdr GKin GQui MAsh MGos MMuc SEND SLdr SReu
'Snow Pearl'	LRHS MAsh
'Snow Queen'	LMil
Snow Queen Group	SReu
'Snowbird' (A)	LMil SLdr
'Snowflake' (EA/d)	see *R.* 'Kure-no-yuki'
'Snowstorm'	MMuc SEND
'Snowwhite' (EA)	LMil
'Soft Lips' (K)	SHea
'Soho' (EA)	GQui
'Soir de Paris' (Vs)	CSBt GGGa GKin IVic LMil MBri MLea MMuc NLar SEND SLdr SReu SSta WGwG
'Soldier Sam'	SReu
'Solidarity'	ECho MAsh MBri MGos SLdr WBor
'Solway' (Vs)	LMil
'Sommerduft' (A)	IVic
'Son de Paris' (A)	GQui
'Sonata'	CWri GGGa SReu
'Songbird'	LMil MAsh MSnd SLdr
'Sophie Hedges' (K/d)	SLdr
sororium (V)	GGGa LMil
- KR 3085	LMil
souliei	LMil SSpi
- deep pink-flowered	GGGa
'Southern Cross'	SLdr
'Souvenir de D.A. Koster'	SLdr
'Souvenir de Doctor S. Endtz' ♀H4	SHea SLdr
'Souvenir of Anthony Waterer' ♀H4	SHea SReu
'Souvenir of W.C. Slocock'	SReu
'Spätlese'	IVic
speciosum	see *R. flammeum*
'Spek's Orange' (M) ♀H4	GGGa GKin
sperabile	GGGa LMil NHim
- var. ***weihsiense***	LMil MSnd SLdr
sphaeranthum	see *R. trichostomum*
sphaeroblastum	GGGa MSnd
- var. ***wumengense***	GGGa GLin
- - KR 1481	MSnd
spiciferum	see *R. scabrifolium* var. *spiciferum*
'Spicy Lights' (A)	LMil
spilotum	LMil NHim
'Spinner's Glory'	MAsh
spinuliferum	GGGa
'Spitfire'	NHol
'Spring Beauty' (EA)	CMac MSnd SLdr SReu
'Spring Magic'	MSnd SLdr
'Spring Pearl'	see *R.* 'Moerheim's Pink'
'Spring Rose'	SLdr
'Spring Sunshine'	LMil
'Springday'	CMac
'Squirrel' (EA) ♀H4	CDoC ECho GEdr GGGa GKin LMil MAsh MGos MLea SLdr SLim SReu
'Staccato'	IVic

Stadt Essen Group	LMil SLdr
'Stadt Westerstede'	LMil
stamineum	GGGa NHim
§ 'Stanway'	LMil
'Starbright Champagne'	GGGa LMil
'Statuette'	IVic
§ ***stenopetalum*** 'Linearifolium' (EA)	CMac LMil SLdr WAbe
stenophyllum	see *R. makinoi*
stewartianum	GGGa LMil SLdr
'Stewartstonian' (EA)	CMac ELon SReu
'Stoat' (EA)	GQui
'Stopham Girl' (A)	LMil
'Stopham Lad' (A)	LMil
'Stour' (K)	SHea
'Strategist'	SHea SLdr
'Strawberry Cream'	GGGa LRHS MAsh
'Strawberry Ice' (K) ♀H4	CBcs CDoC CSBt CWri ECho ELan EPfP GBin GGGa GKin LMil LRHS MAsh MBri MGos MMHG MMuc NEgg SEND SLdr SPer SReu WMoo
'Strawberry Sundae'	MLea MMuc NEgg SEND SLdr
strigillosum	GGGa GLin MSnd
- Reuthe's form	SReu
subansiriense	GGGa
suberosum	see *R. yunnanense* Suberosum Group
succothii	GGGa SLdr
'Suga-no-ito' (EA)	SLdr
sulfureum	GGGa
'Summer Blaze' (A)	SLdr SReu
'Summer Dawn'	LMil
'Summer Flame'	SReu
'Summer Fragrance' (O) ♀H4	LMil SReu SSta
'Summer Snow'	IVic
'Summer Sorbet' new	LMil
'Sun Chariot' (K)	CBcs LMil MAsh MMHG
'Sun Fire' new	LMil
'Sun of Austerlitz'	SHea SLdr
Sunkist Group	SLdr
(Sunrise Group) 'Sunrise'	MSnd SLdr
'Sunset Pink' (K)	ELan SLdr
'Sunte Nectarine' (K) ♀H4	ECho GKin GQui IDee LMil MLea MMuc NLar SHea SLdr
'Surprise' ambig. (EA)	CDoC CTri SLdr
'Surrey Heath'	CBcs CDoC CDul CWri ECho EPfP LMil MAsh MGos MMuc MSnd NLar SEND SLdr SLim
'Susan' (EA)	MSnd
'Susan' J.C. Williams ♀H4	LMil SReu
'Susannah Hill' (EA)	CDoC MGos SLdr
sutchuenense	GGGa LMil MSnd NHim
- var. ***geraldii***	see *R.* × *geraldii*
'Swamp Beauty'	CWri ECho MAsh MGos MLea MMuc MSnd SEND SLdr WGwG
'Swansong' (EA)	CMac SLdr
'Sweet Simplicity'	CWri SHea SLdr
'Sweet Sue'	MSnd SLdr
'Swift'	ECho GGGa GQui LLHF LMil LRHS MAsh MBri MMuc NPCo SEND SLdr
'Sylphides' (K)	CMac
'T.S. Black' (EA)	SLdr
taggianum	GGGa
'Taka-no-tsukasa' (EA)	SLdr
taliense	GGGa LMil
- SBEC 0350	GGGa
- SDR 1804	NHim
Tally Ho Group	SHea
tamaense	see *R. cinnabarinum* subsp. *tamaense*
'Tama-no-utena' (EA)	SLdr
'Tanager' (EA/k)	SLdr
'Tangerine'	see *R.* 'Fabia Tangerine'
'Tangiers' (K)	SHea SLdr
tapetiforme	GGGa
'Tarantella'	NEgg
'Taurus' ♀H4	CDoC CWri ECho ELon GKin IVic LMil LRHS MAsh MGos MMuc MSnd NPCo SEND SLdr SReu
taxifolium (v)	GGGa
'Tay' (K)	SLdr
'Teal'	ECho GEdr MGos MLea
'Ted Millais'	LMil
'Teddy Bear'	CWri LMil MLea
telopeum	see *R. campylocarpum* subsp. *caloxanthum* Telopeum Group
temenium var. ***gilvum*** 'Cruachan'	GGGa
'Temple Belle'	ECho SLdr
'Tender Heart' (K)	SLdr
'Teniers' (R)	SReu SSta
§ ***tephropeplum***	GGGa MSnd NHim WAbe
- Deleiense Group	see *R. tephropeplum*
'Tequila Sunrise'	LMil
'Terra-cotta'	LMil
'Terra-cotta Beauty' (EA)	NWad WPat WThu
'Tessa'	CBcs ECho ELon MMuc SEND SLdr
Tessa Group	LMil
'Tessa Roza' (EA) ♀H4	GKev GQui
thayerianum	GGGa MSnd
§ 'The Hon. Jean Marie de Montague' ♀H4	CWri ELon EPfP GGGa GKin LMil MAsh MBri MGos MLea MMuc MSnd NLar SEND SLdr SPer SReu
'Thomas David' (A) new	LMil
thomsonii	CDoC GGGa GKin IDee LMil MSnd SLdr SReu
- AC 113	MSnd
'Thor'	GGGa SReu
'Thousand Butterflies'	see *R.* 'One Thousand Butterflies'
'Thunderstorm'	SReu
thymifolium	NHim
'Tibet' ♀H3-4	GQui LMil
'Tidbit' ♀H4	CMac GGGa LMil MGos MLea MSnd SLdr
'Tinkerbird'	GGGa LRHS NPri
'Tinsmith' (K)	SLdr
titapuriense	GGGa
'Titian Beauty'	CBcs CDoC CSBt CWri ECho EPfP GGGa LMil LRHS MAsh MGos MMuc MSnd NEgg NPCo NPri SEND SLdr SLim SPer WBor WFar WMoo
'Titness Delight'	SLdr
'Tit-Willow' (EA)	LRHS MAsh SCoo
'Tolkien'	SReu
'Tom Hyde' (EA)	LSRN
'Top Banana'	SLdr
'Torchlight' (EA)	LMil LRHS
'Toreador' (EA)	MSnd SLdr
'Tornado'	MAsh
'Torridon' (Vs)	LMil
'Tortoiseshell Champagne'	see *R.* 'Champagne'
'Tortoiseshell Orange' ♀H3-4	CBcs CSBt CWri LMil MBri NLar SHea SLim SReu SSta
'Tortoiseshell Salome'	SHea
'Tortoiseshell Wonder' ♀H3-4	EPfP LMil LRHS MAsh NPri SHea

	Name	Suppliers
	'Toucan' (K)	CSBt SHea SLdr
	'Tower Beauty' (A)	SHea SLdr
	'Tower Dainty' (A)	SHea
	'Tower Daring' (A)	SHea
	'Tower Dragon' (A)	LMil SHea SLdr
	traillianum	LMil MSnd
§	- var. ***dictyotum***	NHim
	'Treecreeper'	GGGa GKin LMil SLdr
	'Tregedna Red'	SReu
	'Trewithen Orange'	SLdr
	'Trewithen Purple'	GGGa
	trichanthum	GGGa
	- 'Honey Wood'	LMil
§	***trichostomum***	GGGa SSpi WAbe
	- Ledoides Group	LMil
	triflorum	GGGa LMil NHim
§	- var. ***bauhiniiflorum***	CBcs GGGa SLdr
	- var. ***triflorum*** Mahogani Group	GGGa MSnd
	trilectorum	GGGa
	'Trill' (EA)	SLdr
	triplonaevium	see *R. alutaceum* var. *russotinctum* Triplonaevium Group
	'Tromba'	LMil
	'Troupial' (K)	SHea
	tsangpoense	see *R. charitopes* subsp. *tsangpoense*
	tsariense	GGGa IDee LMil MSnd
	- var. ***trimoense***	GGGa LMil
	- - KW 8288	LMil
	- 'Yum Yum'	GGGa
	tubiforme	see *R. glaucophyllum* subsp. *tubiforme*
	'Tuffet' (EA)	SLdr SReu
	'Tunis' (K)	LRHS MAsh NPri
	'Turaço'	GGGa LMil MGos SLdr
	'Turnstone'	GGGa
	'Twilight Pink'	SLdr
	'Umpqua Queen' (K)	SLdr
	ungernii	GGGa MSnd SLdr
§	***uniflorum*** var. ***imperator***	GGGa
	'Unique' (G)	ECho EPfP GGGa MGos MMuc SEND SPer
	'Unique' (*campylocarpum* hybrid) ♀H4	CBcs MAsh MBri MSnd SHea SLdr SReu
	'Unique Marmalade'	ECho LMil MAsh MMuc NLar SEND SLdr
	'Ursine' **new**	IVic
	uvariifolium var. ***griseum***	LMil MSnd NHim
	- 'Reginald Childs'	LMil
	'Valencia' **new**	IVic
	valentinianum	CBcs GGGa MSnd SLdr WAbe
	- F 24347	MSnd
	- var. ***oblongilobatum***	GGGa
	'Van'	LMil NLar SLim
	'Van Houttei Flore Pleno' (G)	SLdr SReu SSta
	'Van Nes Sensation'	LMil
	Vanessa Group	LMil
	'Vanessa Pastel' ♀H3-4	CMac GGGa LMil SReu
	vaseyi (A) ♀H3-4	GGGa GLin LMil
	- SDR 2209	GKev
	- 'White Find'	GGGa
	- white-flowered (A)	LMil
	'Vayo' (A)	SLdr
	veitchianum	GGGa NHim
§	- Cubittii Group	GGGa
	- KNE Cox 9001	GGGa
	vellereum	see *R. principis* Vellereum Group

	Name	Suppliers
	'Velvet Gown' (EA)	SPoG
	venator	GGGa MSnd
	aff. ***venator*** KC 0104 **new**	GGGa
	'Venetian Chimes'	CSBt ECho MGos MSnd SLdr SPoG
	vernicosum	CWri GGGa MSnd NHim
	'Vespers' (EA)	CTrh
	'Victoria Hallett'	SLdr
	'Vida Brown' (EA/d)	CMac SLdr SReu WThu
	'Vinecourt Dream' (M)	GKin MBri MLea MMuc NLar SEND SLdr
	'Vinecourt Duke' (R/d)	CWri ECho GKin MAsh MMuc NEgg NLar NPCo
	'Vinecourt Troubador' (K/d)	LMil MAsh NPCo
	'Vineland Dream' (K/d)	CWri ECho GKin
	'Vineland Fragrance'	SLdr
	'Vintage Rosé' ♀H4	GBin LMil MLea SLdr
	'Violetta' (EA)	SLdr
	'Violette Funken'	LMil
	'Virginia Richards'	LRHS SLdr
	Virginia Richards Group	CWri MAsh MBri MGos
§	***viridescens***	MSnd NHim WThu
	- 'Doshong La'	GGGa LMil
§	- Rubroluteum Group	SLdr
	viscidifolium	GGGa
	'Viscosepalum' (G)	SHea SLdr
	viscosum (A) ♀H4	GGGa GQui LMil MLea MMHG MMuc SHea SPer SReu WGwG
	- 'Grey Leaf' (Vs)	LMil
	- var. ***montanum*** (A)	IBlr
	- f. ***rhodanthum*** (A)	LMil
	- 'Roseum' (Vs)	LMil SHea
	'Viscount Powerscourt'	SLdr
	'Viscy' ♀H4	CDul CWri ECho EPfP GKin GQui LMil LRHS MAsh MGos MMuc MSnd NLar SLdr
§	Volker Group	CWri LMil LRHS MAsh MBri SSta
§	- 'Babette'	LMil
§	- 'Lackblatt'	MBri MGos MSnd
	'Vollblut' **new**	SReu SSta
	'Vulcan' ♀H4	GGGa LMil MLea
	'Vuyk's Rosyred' (EA) ♀H4	CBcs CDoC CMac CTri GKin GQui LMil MAsh MGos NHol NWad SLdr SPer SPoG SReu WFar
	'Vuyk's Scarlet' (EA) ♀H4	CBcs CDoC CMac CSBt CTri EPfP GKin GQui LRHS MAsh MGos MMuc MSnd NHol NPri NWad SEND SLdr SPer SPlb SReu SSta WFar
	'W.E. Gumbleton' (M)	SReu
	'W.F.H.' ♀H4	CWri IDee LMil MSnd SLdr SSpi
	'Wagtail'	GGGa
	'Walküre'	LMil
	wallichii	GGGa LMil MSnd SLdr
	- KR 8227	LMil
	- Heftii Group	GGGa GLin
	'Wallowa Red' (K)	ECho GBin LMil MBri MLea MMHG MMuc SEND SLdr
	'Wally Miller'	ECho MAsh MBri SReu
	walongense	GGGa
	wardii	GGGa LMil LRHS MSnd NLar SHea
	- L&S 5679	GGGa MSnd
	- var. ***puralbum***	GGGa
	- var. ***wardii*** Litiense Group	NHim
	'Ward's Ruby' (EA)	CTrh
§	'Washington State Centennial' (A)	GGGa
	wasonii	LMil MSnd
	- SIN 1852	GLin

- f. ***rhododactylum***	MSnd
- var. ***wenchuanense***	GGGa
- yellow-flowered	GGGa
'Water Baby' (A)	LMil
'Water Girl' (A)	GGGa LMil
'Waterfall'	SLdr
watsonii	MSnd
'Waxwing'	SHea
'Wee Bee' ♀H4	CDoC ECho EPfP EPot GEdr GKin LLHF LMil LRHS MAsh MLea NLar NPCo SLdr SLim SReu
'Wendy'	MAsh
'Westminster' (O)	LMil
'Weston's Pink Diamond' (d)	LMil
'What a Dane'	GGGa
'Whidbey Island'	LMil
'Whisperingrose'	LMil
'White Brocade'	SSta
§ White Dufthecke = 'Rhodunter 48'PBR	LMil
'White Frills' (EA)	ECho NLar SLdr
'White Glory'	SLdr
'White Gold'	GGGa
'White Grandeur' (EA)	CTrh
'White Jade' (EA)	SLdr
'White Lady' (EA)	SLdr
'White Lights' (A) ♀H4	EPfP LMil NLar
'White Pearl' (EA)	LSRN
'White Perfume' (A)	SReu SSta
'White Rosebud' (EA)	SReu
'White Swan' (K)	GKin MGos MMuc SHea SLdr
'White Swan' (hybrid)	CBcs SReu
'White Wings'	GQui
'Whitethroat' (K/d) ♀H4	CWri ECho EPfP GQui LMil LRHS MAsh MBri MMHG MMuc NEgg SEND SLdr SPer SReu SSta
'Whitney's Dwarf Red'	SLdr
'Wigeon'	LMil
wightii	GGGa GLin MSnd
'Wilgen's Ruby'	CDoC CSBt LMil MGos MSnd SLdr SLim WFar
'Willbrit'	CBcs CWri ECho MAsh MBri MGos SLdr
'William III' (G)	SLdr
williamsianum ♀H4	CBcs CMac ECho GGGa LMil MAsh MLea MSnd NLar SReu SSpi WFar
- 'Andrea'	IVic
- Caerhays form	CPLG
- white-flowered	GGGa
'Willy' (EA)	LMil SLdr
wilsoniae	see *R. latoucheae*
wiltonii ♀H4	GGGa IDee LMil NLar SLdr
'Windlesham Scarlet'	SLdr
'Windsor Hawk'	CWri
'Windsor Lad'	SReu
'Windsor Sunbeam' (K)	CWri
'Wine and Roses'PBR	GGGa
'Winsome' (hybrid) ♀H3	CBcs GKin NLar NPri SHea SLdr
Winsome Group	CMac CWri GGGa MAsh MSnd
'Winston Churchill' (M)	SReu SSta
'Winter Spice' **new**	GGGa
'Wintergreen' (EA)	MMuc SEND
'Winterpurpur'	IVic
'Wishmoor'	SReu
'Wisley Blush'	LMil
'Witchery'	GGGa
'Wombat' (EA) ♀H4	CTri EPfP GGGa LMil LRHS MAsh MGos NHim NLar NPri SLdr SReu
wongii	GGGa GQui MSnd SLdr
'Woodcock'	SHea SLdr
'Wren'	ECho EPot GEdr GGGa GKev IVic LMil LRHS MAsh MGos MLea MMuc SEND SLdr SReu WThu
'Wryneck' (K)	SHea SLdr
'Wye' (K)	SLdr
xanthocodon	see *R. cinnabarinum* subsp. *xanthocodon*
xanthostephanum	GGGa
'XXL' **new**	SReu SSta
'Yaku Angel'	IVic
'Yaku Incense'	ECho LMil MAsh MLea MMuc MSnd NLar SEND SLdr
'Yaku Prince'	ECho MAsh MGos MMuc NHim SEND SLdr
'Yaku Princess'	CBcs
yakushimanum	CBcs CMHG CWri ECho GKin LMil MBri MGos MLea MMuc MSnd NHol NLar SLdr SPer SReu SSta WFar
- 'Edelweiss' ♀H4	LMil LRHS
- Exbury form	CMac SReu
- FCC form	see *R. yakushimanum* 'Koichiro Wada'
§ - 'Koichiro Wada' ♀H4	CMac CPLG EPfP GGGa IDee IVic LMil LRHS MGos SLdr SPoG SReu
yaoshanense **new**	GGGa
'Yaye' (EA)	SLdr
'Yellow Cloud' (A)	ECho MBri MLea NPCo
'Yellow Hammer' ♀H4	CBcs CMac ECho GGGa GKin LMil MBri NLar SLdr WFar
Yellow Hammer Group	CWri MGos MSnd SPer SReu SSta
'Yoga' (K)	SHea
'Yol'	SLdr
yuefengense	GGGa
yunnanense	CBcs GGGa GKev LMil MSnd SLdr SSpi
- SDR 4217	GKev
- SDR 4957	GKev
- SDR 4960	GKev
- 'Openwood' ♀H3-4	IDee LMil
- pink-flowered	GGGa
- 'Red Throat'	SLdr
- red-blotched	LMil
§ - Suberosum Group	SLdr
- white-flowered	GGGa
aff. ***yunnanense***	IDee
zaleucum	GGGa LMil
- Flaviflorum Group	GGGa
- var. ***zaleucum***	MSnd
zeylanicum	see *R. arboreum* subsp. *zeylanicum*
ziyuanense AC 4211 **new**	MSnd

Rhodohypoxis ✿ (*Hypoxidaceae*)

'1000 Cranes' **new**	IBal
'Andromeda'	EWes
baurii ♀H4	CAvo CCCN CPBP ECho GEdr IBal ITim LRHS MAsh MBel NBir NMen NSla SEND SPoG WAbe WFar WIce XLum
- 'Abigail'	EWes
- 'Alba'	CRDP ECho IBal NMen
- 'Albrighton'	CRDP CTri ECho EWes GEdr IBal ITim LAma NBir NHol NMen NWad WAbe WPat
- 'Apple Blossom'	CTca CYeo ECho ELon EPot EWes IBal ITim LBee LRHS NHol NMen NWad SCnR WAbe WFar
- 'Badger'	NWad WAbe

– var. ***baurii***	CYeo ECho EWes LBee
– var. ***baurii*** × ***baurii*** var. ***platypetala*** new	ECho NMen
– 'Bridal Bouquet' (d)	EWes IBal NHol NMen WAbe WFar
– 'Coconut Ice'	EPot EWes IBal
– var. ***confecta***	ECho EWes NHol
– 'Daphne Mary'	EWes
– 'David Scott'	EWes
– 'Dawn'	CYeo ECho EPot EWes GEdr IBal LAma LRHS NMen WAbe WFar
– 'Douglas'	CYeo ECho EPfP EPot EWes GEdr IBal LAma NBir NHol NMen WAbe WFar
– 'Dulcie'	ECho EPot EWes GEdr SCnR WAbe WFar
– 'Emily Peel'	ECho EPot EWes IBal LLHF WAbe
– 'Eva-Kate'	ECho EWes IBal LAma WAbe WFar WPat
– 'Fred Broome'	CTca CYeo ECho EPot EWes GEdr IBal LAma NHol NMen NWad WAbe WFar WPat
– 'Goliath'	EWes
– 'Harlequin'	ECho EWes GEdr IBal LAma NHol NMen NWad WAbe WFar
§ – 'Helen'	ECho EPot EWes GEdr IBal NHol WAbe WFar
– 'Jacqueline Potterton'	EPot
– 'Kitty'	EWes
– 'Lily Jean' (d)	CEnt CRDP CTri CYeo ECho ELon EPfP EWes GEdr IBal ITim LRHS NMen SMrm WCot WFar
– 'Luna'	EWes
– 'Margaret Rose'	CTca ECho EWes IBal ITim LLHF NHol NMen WAbe WFar
– 'Mars'	EWes NBir NHol
– 'Monique'	EWes
– 'Pearl'	ECho
– 'Perle'	CYeo ECho EWes GEdr IBal NHol NSla NWad SCnR
– 'Pictus' (v)	CRDP ECho EPot EWes GEdr IBal LAma LBee LRHS NHol NMen NWad WAbe WFar WPat
– 'Pink Pearl'	EWes IBal NHol WAbe
– pink-flowered	ECho SEND
– var. ***baurii***	CRDP CYeo ECho EPfP EPot EWes GEdr IBal NHol NMen NWad WAbe WFar XLum
– – Burtt 6981	EWes
– var. ***baurii*** × ***milloides***	IBal LLHF NHol WAbe
– 'Rebecca'	ECho EWes
– 'Red King'	EWes IBal
– red-flowered	ECho NRHS SPlb
– 'Ruth'	CEnt ECho EPfP EPot EWes IBal LAma NHol NMen SDeJ WAbe WFar
– 'Susan Garnett-Botfield'	ECho EWes GEdr IBal NMen WAbe WFar
– 'Tetra Red'	CEnt CYeo ECho EPot EWes IBal LRHS NHol NMen SDeJ WAbe WFar
– 'The Bride'	EWes
– white-flowered	CTca ECho EPot NMen
'Betsy Carmine'	CCCN ELon GEdr IBal NWad WAbe WFar
'Blush'	CYeo ECho IBal
'Bright Eyes' (d)	CRDP EWes
'Candy Stripe'	ECho EPot EWes GEdr LRHS
'Carina'	ECho EWes NMen
'Cayasan'	ECho WAbe
'Confusion'	EWes NHol WAbe WFar
'Dainty Dee' (d)	EWes
deflexa	CPBP CRDP CWCL CYeo ECho EPot EWes GEdr IBal ITim LRHS NHol NMen NRHS NSla NWad SCnR SMrm WAbe WFar
'Donald Mann'	ECho EWes ITim LLHF NHol NMen WAbe
'Dusky'	ECho EWes GEdr NMen
'E.A. Bowles'	ECho EWes IBal NMen NRHS NSla WAbe WFar
'Ellicks'	IBal
'Garnett'	ECho EPot EWes IBal NMen WAbe
'Goya' (d)	ECho EPot IBal NMen WPat
'Great Scot'	ECho EPot EWes GEdr IBal LRHS NMen WAbe WFar
'Hebron Farm Biscuit'	see *Hypoxis parvula* var. *albiflora* 'Hebron Farm Biscuit'
'Hebron Farm Cerise'	see × *Rhodoxis* 'Hebron Farm Cerise'
'Hebron Farm Pink'	see × *Rhodoxis hybrida* 'Hebron Farm Pink'
'Hinky Pinky'	GEdr
'Holden Rose' (d)	ECho NHol NWad
hybrids	CWCL ELan MWat
'Jupiter'	GEdr NMen
'Kiwi Joy' (d)	CRDP CWCL CYeo EPot EWes GEdr IBal LLHF NHol NMen NWad SDeJ WAbe WFar
'Knockdolian Red'	NHol
'Lily Fan'	WFar
'Midori'	ECho EWes GEdr SUsu
milloides	CEnt CRDP CTca CYeo ECho EPfP EPot EWes GEdr IBal ITim LBee LRHS NHol NMen NRHS NWad SGar WAbe WFar
– 'Claret'	CEnt CRDP CSam CYeo ECho EPot EWes ITim LLHF LRHS NHol SUsu WAbe WFar WPat
– 'Damask'	CRDP ECho EPot EWes NMen
– 'Drakensberg Snow'	EWes
– giant	ECho WFar
– pink-flowered new	NMen
I – 'Super Milloides'	LRHS
'Monty'	ECho EWes GEdr WAbe
'Mystery'	EWes NHol WAbe
'Naomi'	ECho EWes
'New Look'	CYeo ECho EWes GEdr IBal LLHF NMen NWad SMrm WAbe WFar WGor
'Ori Zuru'	ECho GEdr
'Origami' new	IBal
'Pearl White'	ECho
'Pink Ice'	GEdr IBal NBir
'Pink Star'	WFar
'Pinkeen'	ECho EPot EWes GEdr IBal LLHF NMen WAbe WFar
'Pinkie'	EPot IBal
'Pintado'	ECho EWes GEdr NWad WAbe
'Raspberry Ice'	ECho NHol NWad
'Rosie Lee'	EWes WAbe
'Shell Pink'	EWes IBal ITim NHol NWad WAbe
'Snow'	EWes
'Snow White'	EWes NHol NMen
'Starlett'	CYeo EWes IBal NHol
'Starry Eyes' (d)	CRDP ECho EWes
'Stella'	CCCN ECho EPot EWes GEdr IBal NHol NMen NRHS NWad WAbe
'Telios' new	IBal
'Tetra Pink'	ECho EWes IBal NHol NWad WAbe
'Tetra Rose'	GEdr WFar

'Tetra White' see *R. baurii* 'Helen'
thodiana CRDP ECho EPot EWes GEdr IBal NHol NMen SCnR WAbe WFar
'Twinkle Star Mixed' ECho LRHS SPoG
'Two Tone' EWes
'Venetia' CMea ECho IBal NHol NMen NWad SBch WAbe
'Westacre Picotee' EWes
'Wild Cherry Blossom' ECho EWes IBal

Rhodohypoxis × *Hypoxis* ✿ (*Hypoxidaceae*)

R. baurii* × *H. parvula see × *Rhodoxis hybrida*

Rhodoleia (*Hamamelidaceae*)

aff. ***henryi*** B&SWJ 11782 **new** WCru

Rhodophiala (*Amaryllidaceae*)

§ ***advena*** EPot
§ ***bifida*** SCnR WCot
chilensis F&W 9700 WCot
'Harry Hay' WCot
rosea GHim LAma

Rhodora see *Rhododendron*

Rhodothamnus (*Ericaceae*)

sessilifolius WThu

Rhodotypos (*Rosaceae*)

kerrioides see *R. scandens*
§ ***scandens*** CDul CPLG CTri CWib EBee ELan EPfP EShb EWTr GKin IGor LHop LRHS MBri MMHG MNrw NHol NLar SEND SLon SPoG SSpi WCru WSHC

× *Rhodoxis* ✿ (*Hypoxidaceae*)

'Anne Crock' CYeo IBal
'Aurora' EWes
'Bloodstone' EWes NHol NWad
'Hebron Farm Biscuit' see *Hypoxis parvula* var. *albiflora* 'Hebron Farm Biscuit'
§ 'Hebron Farm Cerise' CCCN CYeo ECho ELon EPot EWes GEdr NMen WFar
'Hebron Farm Rose' LLHF
§ ***hybrida*** ECho EWes IBal ITim NMen SUsu WAbe XLum
- 'Aya San' CYeo EWes IBal
§ - 'Hebron Farm Pink' CBro CYeo ECho EWes GEdr IBal NHol NMen SCnR WAbe WFar
- 'Hebron Farm Red Eye' CCCN CYeo ELon EWes GEdr IBal SCnR WAbe WFar
- 'Pink Stars' CYeo IBal
- (*R. baurii* var. *baurii* × *H. parvula*) **new** ECho IBal
'Little Pink Pet' EWes

Rhoeo see *Tradescantia*

Rhopalostylis (*Arecaceae*)

baueri CBrP
sapida CBrP CTrC
- 'East Cape' SBig

rhubarb see *Rheum* × *hybridum*

Rhus (*Anacardiaceae*)

ambigua B&SWJ 3656 WCru
- large-leaved B&SWJ 10884 WCru
§ ***aromatica*** CArn EBtc ELan LRHS NLar
chinensis CMCN NLar
- var. ***roxburghii*** SSpi
copallinum EBtc ELan
coriaria CArn EPfP NLar
cotinus see *Cotinus coggygria*
glabra CArn CBcs CDoC EBtc EPfP MGos SPer
- 'Laciniata' misapplied see *R.* × *pulvinata* Autumn Lace Group
- 'Laciniata' Carrière NLar
glauca EShb
N ***hirta*** see *R. typhina*
incisa SPlb
krebsiana WHil
magalismontana EShb
potaninii EBee EPfP LRHS MAsh SBfd
§ × ***pulvinata*** Autumn Lace Group EPfP MGos WFar
- - 'Red Autumn Lace' ♀H4 LBuc LRHS MBlu MBri MRav SBfd SHil SPer SPoG
punjabensis EGFP
§ ***radicans*** CArn GPoy WHer
succedanea CDTJ
- NJM 09.216 WPGP
toxicodendron see *R. radicans*
trilobata see *R. aromatica*
N ***typhina*** ♀H4 CBcs CDoC CDul CHEx CLnd CMac CTri EBee ELan EPfP GKin LBMP LRHS MAsh MGos MMuc MRav NEgg NLar NWea SBfd SEND SGol SPer SPoG SSta WFar
§ - 'Dissecta' ♀H4 CBcs CDoC CDul CLnd CMac EBee ELan EPfP LAst LRHS MAsh MBri MGos MRav MWat NEgg NLar NPri SBfd SEND SGol SPer WFar
- 'Laciniata' hort. see *R. typhina* 'Dissecta'
- Radiance = 'Sinrus' EBee LRHS MAsh MBlu SPoG
- Tiger Eyes = 'Bailtiger'PBR EBee ELan EMil EPfP GKin LBuc LRHS MAsh MBri MGos NLar NPri NRHS SCoo SHil SPoG SPtl SWvt
§ ***verniciflua*** EGFP NLar SSpi

Rhynchelytrum see *Melinis*

Rhynchospora (*Cyperaceae*)

colorata NPer SHom
latifolia CKno SDix SHDw

Ribes ✿ (*Grossulariaceae*)

alpinum CPLG EPfP MRav MWht NWea SPer SRms WOut
- 'Aureum' CAbP EHoe NEgg
americanum SBfd
- 'Variegatum' (v) EHoe ELan NLar WPat
aureum misapplied see *R. odoratum*
'Ben Hope'PBR (B) CAgr EPom MCoo SCoo SWvt WHar WWFS
'Black Velvet' (D) CAgr MCoo
§ × ***culverwellii*** (F) CAgr CCCN CWib EMil EPom GTwe LBuc LEdu LSRN NLar SPoG SVic WHar WWFS
divaricatum CAgr GPri LEdu
gayanum NLar
glaciale NLar
× ***gordonianum*** Widely available
griffithii LEdu

Name	Suppliers
- GWJ 9331	WCru
jostaberry	see *R.* × *culverwellii*
'Kathleen'	EPfP
laurifolium	CBcs CDoC CDul CHGN CMHG CPLG CTri ELan EWTr LAst MRav NLar SBrt SPer WFar WKif WSHC
- (f)	CMac EPfP SBrt SRms
- (m)	EPfP SBrt
- 'Mrs Amy Doncaster'	CMac WCot WPat
- Rosemoor form	CDoC CSam EBee SKHP WPGP
longeracemosum	GGGa
menziesii	CHll EWes GBin NLBP WCot
nigrum	LTen
- 'Baldwin' (B)	CDoC CTri EPfP LRHS NLar SKee SLim SPer SPoG WHar
- 'Barchatnaja' (B)	CAgr
- 'Ben Alder'[PBR] (B)	CAgr CWib LRHS SCoo WWFS
- 'Ben Connan'[PBR] (B) ♀H4	CAgr CMac CSBt CWib EPfP EPom GPri GTwe LBuc LHop LRHS LSRN MBri MGos MMuc NLar NWea SCoo SKee SLim SPer SPoG SWvt WHar WWFS
- 'Ben Gairn'[PBR] (B)	CAgr CSBt MCoo WHar WWFS
- 'Ben Lomond'[PBR] (B) ♀H4	CAgr CMac CSBt CTri CWib ECrN EPfP GPri GTwe LBuc LRHS LSRN MGos MRav NEgg NPri NWea SEND SKee SPer SVic WHar
- 'Ben More' (B)	CAgr CWib MBri
- 'Ben Nevis' (B)	CAgr CTri CWib SKee SPer
- 'Ben Sarek' (B) ♀H4	CAgr CDoC CMac CSBt CSut CTri CWib ECrN EMil EPfP GTwe LAst LBuc LHop LRHS LSRN MGos MRav NLar NWea SBfd SKee SLim SPer SPoG SWvt WHar WWFS
- 'Ben Tirran'[PBR] (B)	CAgr CDoC CSBt CWib LBuc LRHS LSRN MBri MGos NLar SBfd SCoo SPoG SWvt WHar WWFS
- 'Big Ben' (B)	CSut EPom LSRN NPri
- 'Black Reward' (B)	CAgr MCoo
- 'Boskoop Giant' (B)	CAgr GTwe NEgg SLim WHar
* - 'Byelorussian Sweet' (B)	CAgr
- 'Consort' (B)	CAgr
- 'Ebony' (B)	CMac EMil SLon SVic
* - 'Hystawneznaya' (B)	CAgr
- 'Jet' (B)	CAgr GTwe NEgg
* - 'Kosmicheskaya' (B)	CAgr
- 'Loch Ness' (B)	WHar
- 'Pilot Alexander Mamkin' (B)	CAgr
- 'Seabrook's' (B)	CAgr
- 'Titania' (B)	LRHS SPoG
- 'Tsema' (B)	MCoo
- 'Wellington XXX' (B)	CAgr GTwe LBuc NWea SPer
§ ***odoratum***	Widely available
- 'Crandall'	CAgr LEdu
'Pink Perfection'	CMCN
praecox	CBcs MMuc SEND
rubrum 'Blanka' (W)	CAgr CMac CSut GPri SBfd
- 'Cascade' (R)	CAgr
- 'Cherry' (R)	CAgr MCoo
- 'Hollande Rose' (P)	GTwe
- 'Jonkheer van Tets' (R) ♀H4	CAgr CSBt CWib EMil EPfP EPom GPri GTwe IArd LRHS LSRN MCoo MMuc NLar NWea SEND SKee SLim SPer WHar WWFS
- 'Junifer' (R)	CAgr GTwe LRHS SKee
- 'Laxton's Number One' (R)	CAgr CTri GPri GTwe LRHS LSRN MNHC NLar NWea SLim SPer SPoG WGwG WHar
- 'Laxton's Perfection' (R)	MCoo
- 'Red Lake' (R) ♀H4	CAgr CTri CWib EPfP GPri GTwe LBuc LRHS MGos NEgg NLar NPri SKee SPer SPoG
- 'Redstart' (R)	CAgr CSBt CTri CWib GTwe LBuc LRHS NLar SKee SPoG WHar WWFS
- 'Rondom' (R)	CAgr SVic
- 'Rosetta' (R)	MCoo
- 'Rovada' (R)	CAgr CMac CSBt CSut CWib EPom GPri GTwe LRHS LSRN SBfd SKee SVic WHar WWFS
- 'Roxby Red' (R)	MCoo
- 'Stanza' (R) ♀H4	CAgr GTwe MCoo MMuc SEND
- 'Transparent' (W)	GTwe
§ - 'Versailles Blanche' (W/C)	CAgr CSBt CTri CWib EPfP EPom GPri GTwe LBuc LRHS LSRN MBri MGos MMuc NPri SEND SKee SLim SPer SPoG WHar WWFS
- 'White Dutch' (W)	MCoo
- 'White Grape' (W) ♀H4	GTwe
- 'White Pearl' (W)	MCoo SVic
- White Versailles	see *R. rubrum* 'Versailles Blanche'
- 'Wilson's Long Bunch' (R)	GTwe
sanguineum	CDul CWCL NEgg WFar WMoo
- 'Brianjou' **new**	EBee
- 'Brocklebankii'	CMac CPLG EBee ELan MGos MRav MWat NLar SAga SLim SPer SRms WBor WCFE WSHC
- 'Carneum' **new**	LRHS
- double-flowered	see *R. sanguineum* 'Plenum'
- 'Elkington's White'	EPfP LBuc LRHS MBri NRHS SHil SLon
- 'Flore Pleno'	see *R. sanguineum* 'Plenum'
- 'King Edward VII'	Widely available
- 'Koja'	EBee GBin LBuc LPot LRHS LSRN MGos MWat NPri NRHS SHil SPoG WCot WPat
- 'Lombartsii'	EPfP MRav
§ - 'Plenum' (d)	EPfP
- 'Poky's Pink'	CMac LLHF LRHS MRav SPoG
- 'Pulborough Scarlet' ♀H4	Widely available
- 'Red Bross'	SWvt
- 'Red Pimpernel'	EBee EPfP LRHS LSRN MAsh MBNS SCoo SPoG SWvt
- 'Tydeman's White'	CPLG CSBt ELan EPfP MGos NLar NPri NWea WSHC
- var. ***variegata***	CMac
- White Icicle = 'Ubric' ♀H4	CBcs CDoC CTri CWib EBee EPfP EWTr GBin LAst LBMP LPot LRHS MAsh MBlu MHer MRav MWat NBir NLar NPri SLim SPer SPoG SRms SWvt WFar WPat
speciosum ♀H3	Widely available
uva-crispa 'Achilles' (D)	GTwe
- 'Admiral Beattie' (F)	GTwe NEgg
- 'Annelii' (F)	CAgr
- 'Bedford Red' (C/D)	GTwe
- 'Bedford Yellow' (C/D)	GTwe
- 'Beech Tree Nestling' (D)	GTwe
- 'Blucher' (D)	GTwe
- 'Bright Venus' (D)	GTwe
- 'Broom Girl' (D)	GTwe
- 'Captivator' (C)	CSBt GTwe LBuc NEgg
- 'Careless' (C/D) ♀H4	CMac CSBt EMil GTwe LRHS LSRN MGos NLar SKee SPer WGwG WHar
- 'Cook's Eagle' (C)	GTwe
- 'Cousen's Seedling' (D)	GTwe
- 'Criterion' (D)	GTwe

- 'Crown Bob' (C/D)	GTwe
- 'Dan's Mistake' (D)	GTwe
- 'Drill' (D)	GTwe
- 'Early Sulphur' (D)	GTwe
- 'Espera' (D) **new**	CSut
- 'Firbob' (D)	GTwe NEgg
- 'Forester' (D)	GTwe
- 'Freedom' (C)	GTwe
- 'Gipsy Queen' (D)	GTwe
- 'Glenton Green' (D)	GTwe
- 'Golden Drop' (D)	GTwe
- 'Green Gem' (C/D)	GTwe
- 'Green Ocean' (D)	GTwe
- 'Greenfinch' (C) ♀H4	CAgr GTwe WWFS
- 'Guido' (F)	GTwe
- 'Gunner' (C/D)	GTwe NEgg
- 'Heart of Oak' (F)	GTwe
- 'Hedgehog' (D)	GTwe
- 'Hero of the Nile' (D)	GTwe
- 'High Sheriff' (D)	GTwe
- 'Hinnonmäki' (F)	CAgr LBuc SPer
- 'Hinnonmäki Grön' (F)	CSBt EMil EPfP LRHS LSRN MNHC MRav WHar
- 'Hinnonmäki Gul' (D)	CAgr CSBt CSut CTri EMil EPfP EPom GTwe LBuc LRHS MGos MNHC NLar SBfd SKee SPer SPoG SVic WHar
- 'Hinnonmäki Röd' (C/D)	CAgr CMac CTri EMil EPfP EPom GTwe LBuc LRHS LSRN MBri MCoo MRav NLar SBfd SPer SPoG SVic WHar
- 'Howard's Lancer' (C/D)	GTwe
- 'Invicta' (C/D) ♀H4	Widely available
- 'Ironmonger' (D)	GTwe
- 'Jubilee' (C/D)	LBuc
- 'Keen's Seedling' (D)	GTwe
- 'Keepsake' (C/D)	GTwe
- 'King of Trumps' (F)	GTwe
- 'Lady Sun' (F) **new**	CSut
- 'Lancashire Lad' (C/D)	GTwe
- 'Langley Gage' (D)	GTwe MCoo NEgg
- 'Laxton's Amber' (D)	GTwe
- 'Leveller' (D) ♀H4	CTri GTwe LAst LBuc MCoo MGos SPer WHar
- 'London' (C/D)	GTwe
- 'Lord Derby' (C/D)	GTwe
- 'Martlet' (F)	CAgr GTwe LRHS MCoo SLim WWFS
- 'Pax' PBR (D)	CAgr CDoC EPfP GTwe LBuc LRHS NLar SKee SLim SPoG WWFS
- 'Peru' (D)	GTwe
- 'Pitmaston Green Gage' (D)	GTwe
- 'Plunder' (C)	GTwe
- 'Queen of Trumps' (D)	GTwe
- var. ***reclinatum*** 'Aston Red'	see *R. uva-crispa* 'Warrington'
- 'Red Champagne' (D)	GTwe
- 'Rifleman' (D)	GTwe
- 'Rokula' PBR (C/D)	CDoC GTwe LRHS MBri SLim
- 'Rosebery' (D)	GTwe
- 'Scotch Red Rough' (D)	GTwe
- 'Scottish Chieftan' (D)	GTwe
- 'Snow' (F)	EPfP SCoo
- 'Snowdrop' (D)	GTwe
- 'Spinefree' (C)	GTwe
- 'Surprise' (D)	GTwe
- 'Telegraph' (F)	GTwe
- 'Victoria' (C/D)	GTwe
§ - 'Warrington' (F)	GTwe
- 'Whinham's Industry' (C/D) ♀H4	CSBt CTri GPri GTwe LAst LBuc LHop LRHS LSRN MGos MMuc NEgg NPri SEND SPer WGwG WHar
- 'White Lion' (C/D)	GTwe
- 'White Transparent' (C)	GTwe
- 'Whitesmith' (C/D)	CTri GTwe LSRN MCoo
- 'Woodpecker' (D)	GTwe NEgg
- 'Xenia' (D)	EPom
- 'Yellow Champagne' (D)	GTwe
valdivianum	WCot
viburnifolium	NLar
'Worcesterberry' (C)	SPer

Ricinocarpos (*Euphorbiaceae*)

pinifolius	ECou

Ricinus (*Euphorbiaceae*)

communis	CDTJ MBel SBfd SPlb
- 'Carmencita' ♀H3	SDys SGar
- 'Carmencita Bright Red' **new**	NPri
- 'Carmencita Pink'	CDTJ
- 'Carmencita Red'	CDTJ NPri SBfd
- 'Dominican Republic'	CDTJ
- 'Gibsonii'	CDTJ SBst SMrm
- 'Impala'	CDTJ SBst SGar SMrm
- 'New Zealand Black'	CDTJ CSpe
- 'Zanzibariensis'	CDTJ SGar

Rigidella see *Tigridia*

Riocreuxia (*Apocynaceae*)

torulosa	CCCN SPlb

Robinia (*Papilionaceae*)

× ***ambigua***	SKHP SSpi
§ ***boyntonii***	LSRN
§ ***hispida***	CDul CWib ECrN ELan EPfP EWTr MBlu NLar SPer
- 'Macrophylla'	NLar
- 'Rosea' misapplied	see *R. boyntonii*, *R. hispida*
- 'Rosea' ambig.	CBcs EBee
kelseyi	CDul EBee EWes SPer
× ***margaretta*** Casque Rouge	see *R.* × *margaretta* 'Pink Cascade'
§ - 'Pink Cascade'	CCVT CDoC CDul CLnd CMac CTrC CTri EPfP LAst MAsh MBlu MGos SBfd SCoo SCrf SEND SEWo SGol SLim SPer
pseudoacacia	CCVT CDul CHab CLnd ELan LBuc MCoo NEgg SEND SGol SPlb WFar
- 'Bessoniana'	CDul EBee LAst LMaj
- 'Frisia' ♀H4	Widely available
- 'Inermis' hort.	see *R. pseudoacacia* 'Umbraculifera'
§ - 'Lace Lady' PBR	CSBt CWSG ELan EPfP LRHS MAsh MBri MGos NLar SCoo SLim SPoG
- 'Rozynskiana'	CDul
- 'Tortuosa'	EBee EBtc ELan LAst MBlu SBfd SPer
- 'Twisty Baby' PBR	see *R. pseudoacacia* 'Lace Lady'
§ - 'Umbraculifera'	CDul LMaj LTen MBri MGos SCoo
- 'Unifoliola'	LMaj
× ***slavinii*** 'Hillieri' ♀H4	CDoC CDul EBee ECrN ELan EPfP EUJe LSRN MAsh MBlu MBri MWat NLar SBfd SCrf SEND SLon SPer SPoG

Rochea see *Crassula*

Rodgersia (Saxifragaceae)

ACE 2303 SDix
CLD 1432 CPLG
aesculifolia ♀H4 Widely available
- green bud IBlr
- var. **henrici** CLAP CRow GBin GCal MRav NBro NMyG SWat WHoo WMoo
- - hybrid CHid EBee EWTr IVic NLar WAul WWEG XLum
- pink-flowered SSpi
- 'Red Dawn' IBlr
- 'Red Leaf' GCal IFoB
'Badenweiter' ECha
'Blickfang' IBlr
'Bloody Mary' CBcs CElw EBee ECtt EPPr SKHP
'Borodin' EBee
Cally strain GCal
'Dark Pokers' NLar
'Die Anmutige' CLAP CRow
'Die Schöne' CLAP EBee NLar
'Die Stolze' EBee GBin LEdu MBrN
'Elfenbeinturm' IBlr
'Fascination' IBlr
'Herkules' EBee ECha ECtt EHoe ELon GBin GCal GMaP IFoB LHop LSou MBNS NEgg NLBP NLar SKHP SSpi WCot WFar WPnP WWEG WWFP
'Irish Bronze' ♀H4 CLAP CPrp EAEE EBee ECtt ELan GBin GQue IVic LBMP LEdu LRHS LSRN MAvo NPnk WAul WMoo WPnP WWEG
'Koriata' IBlr
'Kupfermond' CRow IBlr NBir
'La Blanche' CMil EBee ECtt ELon LEdu LRHS NCGa NEgg NGdn SPer WCot WPnP WWEG
'Maigrün' IBlr
nepalensis CLAP LRHS
- EMAK 713 CLAP IBlr WPGP
- HWJK 2140 WCru
'Parasol' CBro CLAP CMac IBlr NBir NHol SKHP SSpi WPGP
pinnata Widely available
- B&SWJ 7741A CBcs WCru WFar
- L 1670 CLAP CPLG ELan IBlr SSpi WPGP
- SDR 3301 GKev
- 'Alba' GCal IBlr NHol
- 'Buckland Beauty' CDes EBee IBlr NRHS SSpi WMoo WPGP
- 'Cally Coffee' GCal
- 'Cally Coral' **new** GCal
- 'Cally Salmon' EWes GCal IBlr
- 'Chocolate Wing' Widely available
- 'Crûg Cardinal' GCal WCru
- 'Elegans' CCon EBee EHoe ELan EPfP GKev GMaP IBlr LAst LBMP LEdu LRHS MRav NEgg NHol NOrc SPer SWvt WGwG
- 'Fireworks'PBR CCon CHid CLAP EBee ECtt ELan GBin IPot LEdu LSou MBri NLar SMrm SPer WFar WHil
- 'Jade Dragon Mountain' CDes GCal IBlr SKHP
- 'Maurice Mason' CLAP CPLG ECtt GKev IBlr LTen NLar SMHy WWEG
- 'Mont Blanc' IBlr
- Mount Stewart form IBlr
- 'Panache' IBlr
- 'Perthshire Bronze' IBlr
- pink-flowered WCru
- 'Rosea' IBlr
- 'Superba' ♀H4 Widely available
- white-flowered GAbr SWat WCru
pinnata × sambucifolia IBlr
podophylla ♀H4 Widely available
- B&SWJ 10818 WCru
- B&SWJ 10823 WCru
- 'Braunlaub' CLAP EBee GQue NBro SMad WFar WMoo WPnP WWEG
- 'Bronceblad' IBlr
- Donard selection IBlr MBri
- 'Rotlaub' CDes CLAP CRow EBee GBin IBlr IPot IVic WBor WMoo
- 'Smaragd' CDes CLAP CRow EBee GBin GCal IBlr MRav NBir NLar NRHS
purdomii hort. CLAP GCal WCot WPGP
'Reinecke Fuchs' IBlr
'Rosenlicht' CRow
'Rosenzipfel' IBlr
sambucifolia CBcs CLAP CMac CRow EBee EWTr GBBs GBee GBin GCal LEdu LRHS MLHP MMuc NBir NEgg NLar NSti SEND SWat WFar WMoo WPnP WWEG XLum
- B&SWJ 7899 WCru
- dwarf pink-flowered IBlr
- dwarf white-flowered IBlr
- large red-stemmed NBir
- 'Mountain Select' EBee GCal WFar
tabularis see *Astilboides tabularis*

Roemeria (Papaveraceae)

hybrida CSpe

Rohdea (Asparagaceae)

japonica CHEx LRHS WCot WPGP
- B&SWJ 4853 WCru
- B&SWJ 5091 WCru
- 'Godaishu' (v) WCot
- 'Gunjaku' (v) WCot
- 'Lance Leaf' LEdu
- long-leaved WCot WFar
- 'Miyakonojo' (v) WCot
- 'Talbot Manor' (v) CDes WCot
- 'Tama-jishi' (v) WCot
- 'Tuneshige Rokujo' (v) WCot
tonkinensis HWJ 562 WCru
watanabei B&SWJ 1911 WCru

Romanzoffia (Boraginaceae)

§ **sitchensis** CTri
suksdorfii Greene see *R. sitchensis*
tracyi CDes CLAP GEdr NRya
unalaschcensis CLAP SRms

Romneya (Papaveraceae)

coulteri ♀H4 Widely available
§ - var. **trichocalyx** CCon CGHE
§ - 'White Cloud' ♀H4 CBct CPLG EBee ELan SChF WPGP WSpi
× **hybrida** see *R. coulteri* 'White Cloud'
trichocalyx see *R. coulteri* var. *trichocalyx*

Romulea (Iridaceae)

B&F MA 14 WCot
amoena 'Nieuwoudtville' ECho
austinii 'Komsberg' ECho
§ **autumnalis** ECho

barkerae 'Paternoster' ECho
biflora 'Vanrhynsdorp' ECho
bulbocodium CBro ECho WAbe
- var. ***clusiana*** ECho
- var. ***crocea*** ECho
* - 'Knightshayes' SCnR
- var. ***leichtliniana*** CDes
citrina from Tweerivier ECho
- 'Kamiesberg' ECho
columnae ECho
- subsp. ***columnae*** ECho
congoensis GCal
cruciata var. ***cruciata*** 'Riverlands' ECho
- var. ***intermedia*** 'Somerset West' ECho
dichotoma ECho
discifera 'Grasberg' ECho
diversiformis 'Komsberg' ECho
eximia ECho
flava var. ***minor*** 'Dassenberg' ECho
- 'Rawsonville' ECho
hirsuta var. ***cuprea*** 'Rawsonville' ECho
- var. ***hirsuta*** 'Klipheuwel' ECho
- var. ***zeyheri*** 'Malmesbury' ECho
hirta ECho
kamisensis ECho
leipoldtii ECho
linaresii ECho
longipes 'Coega' ECho
longituba see *R. macowanii*
* ***luteoflora*** var. ***sanguinea*** ECho
§ ***macowanii*** ECho
montana ECho
namaquensis ECho
nivalis ECho
obscura var. ***blanda*** ECho
- var. ***obscura*** ECho
- var. ***subtestacea*** ECho
pratensis ECho
ramiflora CPLG ECho LWst
rosea ECho
- var. ***rosea*** 'Caledon' ECho
- var. ***speciosa*** see *R. autumnalis*
sanguinalis from Tweerivier ECho
setifolia var. ***aggregata*** 'Rawsonville' ECho
sladenii 'Gifberg' ECho
stellata 'Nardouwsberg' ECho
subfistulosa from Roggeveld ECho
tabularis ECho
tempskyana ECho
tetragona var. ***flavandra*** 'Matjiesfontein' ECho
tortuosa subsp. ***aurea*** 'Komsberg' ECho
- var. ***tortuosa*** 'Botuin' ECho
toximontana 'Gifberg' ECho
triflora 'Riverlands' ECho
* ***zahnii*** GKev

Rondeletia (*Rubiaceae*)

amoena MOWG

Rorippa (*Brassicaceae*)

amphibia MSKA
nasturtium-aquaticum WMAq

Rosa ✿ (*Rosaceae*)

A Shropshire Lad = 'Ausled'PBR (S) LRHS LStr MAsh MAus MBri NEgg SMrm SSea SWCr
A Whiter Shade of Pale = 'Peafanfare'PBR (HT) ECnt ELon ESty GCoc LStr MAus MRav SWCr
Abbeyfield Gold = 'Korquelda'PBR (F) SWCr
Abbeyfield Rose = 'Cocbrose' (HT) ♀H4 GCoc MRav SMrm SPer
Abigaile = 'Tanelaigib' (F) LSRN
Abracadabra = 'Korhocsel' (HT) new ESty
Abraham Darby = 'Auscot' (S) CTri EBee EPfP GCoc IBoy LRHS LSRN LStr MAus MBri MRav MWat NEgg NLar SEND SLon SMrm SPer SPoG SWCr
Absent Friends = 'Dicemblem'PBR (F) ESty IBoy IDic SRGP
Absolutely Fabulous = 'Wekvossutono'PBR (F) CGro CSBt CWSG EBee ECnt EPfP ESty GCoc LBuc LRHS LSRN LShp LStr MAsh MBri MRav MWat NPri SCoo SMrm SPer SPoG SWCr
abyssinica new LEdu
Accademia = 'Baracc'PBR (S) EBee ECnt
'Adam' (ClT) LSRN
'Adam Messerich' (Bb) SLon
Adam's Rose = 'Wekromico' (F) LSRN
'Adélaïde d'Orléans' (Ra) ♀H4 CRHN EBee LRHS MAus MBri MRav SEND SFam SPer SWCr
'Aglaia' (Ra) CPou MAus SMrm
'Agnes' (Ru) ♀H4 CGro ELon EPfP EWTr GCoc IArd MAus MRav MWat NLar SPer SRGP
'Aimée Vibert' (N) CSam MAus MRav NLar SEND SPer SRGP
'Alain Blanchard' (G) CPou EBee MAus
Alan Titchmarsh = 'Ausjive'PBR (S) CSBt CWSG ESty LRHS LSRN MAus MBri SCoo SPer
§ × ***alba*** 'Alba Maxima' (A) CArn EWTr GCoc LRHS MAus MRav NLar SEND SPer SWCr WHer
§ - 'Alba Semiplena' (A) ♀H4 GCoc LRHS MAsh MAus SPer SWCr WHer
- Celestial see *R.* 'Céleste'
- 'Maxima' see *R.* × ***alba*** 'Alba Maxima'
'Albéric Barbier' (Ra) ♀H4 CRHN CSBt CSam CTri EBee ECnt ELan EPfP EWTr LRHS LStr MAus MBri MRav MWat NPri NWea SEND SMad SMrm SPer SPoG SSea SWCr WHer
'Albertine' (Ra) ♀H4 CBcs CGro CSBt CSam CWSG EBee ECnt ELan ELon EPfP ESty GCoc IBoy LAst LRHS LStr MAus MBri MGos MRav MWat NEgg NPri SEND SMad SMrm SPer SPoG SSea SWCr
'Alchymist' (S/Cl) CPou EPfP ESty LRHS LTen MAus MBri MRav NLar SEND SPer
Alec's Red = 'Cored' (HT) CBcs CTri CWSG GCoc IBoy LBuc LRHS LSRN LStr MAsh MAus MRav MWat SMrm SPer SPoG SRGP SWCr
Alexander = 'Harlex' (HT) ♀H4 CGro GCoc IBoy LSRN LStr MAus MRav SPer SSea SWCr
'Alexander von Humboldt' (Cl) NLar
Alexander's Issie = 'Dicland'PBR (F) IDic

	Name	Suppliers
	'Alexandre Girault' (Ra)	CRHN LRHS MAus MBri NLar SPer SWCr WHer
	'Alfred de Dalmas' misapplied	see *R.* 'Mousseline'
	Alfred Sisley = 'Delstrijor'[PBR] (S) **new**	MRav
	'Alfresco'[PBR] (ClHT)	MBri SSea
	Alibaba = 'Chewalibaba' (Cl)	EBee ECnt ESty SWCr
	'Alida Lovett' (Ra)	LRHS MAus
	Alison = 'Coclibee'[PBR] (F)	GCoc LSRN SWCr
	Alissar, Princess of Phoenicia = 'Harsidon' **new**	ESty
§	'Alister Stella Gray' (N)	EBee EPfP EWTr LRHS MAus MBri MCot MMuc NEgg NLar SEND SLon SPer SSea SWCr
	All American Magic = 'Meiroylear' (HT) **new**	ESty
	'Allen Chandler' (ClHT)	MAus
§	Alnwick Castle = 'Ausgrab'[PBR] (S)	EPfP IBoy LRHS LStr MAus MBri SCoo SMrm SPer SSea
	'Aloha' (ClHT) 𝕐H4	CBcs CGro CTri EBee ELon EPfP ESty EWTr LAst LRHS LStr MAus MCot MRav NLar SEND SMrm SPer SPoG SSea SWCr
	alpina	see *R. pendulina*
	'Alpine Sunset' (HT)	CTri ELon ESty MAsh MBri MRav SPer SPoG SWCr
	altaica Willd.	see *R. spinosissima*
	Altissimo = 'Delmur' (Cl)	CGro EBee LRHS MAus SEND SPer SSea SWCr
	'Amadis' (Bs)	MAus
	Amanda = 'Beesian' (F)	ESty LSRN
	Amber Abundance = 'Harfizz'[PBR] (Abundance Series) (S)	ESty
	Amber Cover = 'Poulbambe'[PBR] (Towne & Country Series) (GC)	MAsh
	Amber Nectar = 'Mehamber'[PBR] (F)	MAsh
	Amber Queen = 'Harroony' (F) 𝕐H4	CGro CSBt CTri EPfP GCoc IArd IBoy LBuc LStr MAsh MAus MRav SPer SWCr
	amblyotis RBS 0262	GBin NLar
	Ambridge Rose = 'Auswonder' (S)	LRHS MAus
	'Amélia'	see *R.* 'Celsiana'
	Amelia = 'Poulen011'[PBR] (Renaissance Series) (S)	ECnt SWCr
	'American Pillar' (Ra)	CGro CSBt CTri CWSG EBee ECnt ELan EPfP IBoy LRHS LStr MAus MMuc MRav NLar SEND SPer SPoG SSea SWCr WBor WKif
	'Amy Robsart' (RH)	MAus
	Anabell = 'Korbell' (F)	LSRN
	'Anaïs Ségalas' (G)	MAus
	'Andersonii' (*canina* hybrid)	MAus
§	'Anemone' (Cl)	MAus
	anemoniflora	see *R.* × *beanii*
	anemonoides	see *R.* 'Anemone'
	Angela = 'Grifgela'	LSRN
	Angela Rippon = 'Ocaru' (Min)	CSBt MBri SPer
	'Angela's Choice' (F)	LSRN
	Anisley Dickson = 'Dickimono' (F) 𝕐H4	SPer
	Ann = 'Ausfete'[PBR] (S)	LSRN MAus
	Ann Henderson = 'Fryhoncho' (F)	LSRN
	Anna Ford = 'Harpiccolo' (Min/Patio) 𝕐H4	LStr SPer
	Anna Livia = 'Kormetter'[PBR] (F) 𝕐H4	ECnt
	Anne Boleyn = 'Ausecret'[PBR] (S)	IBoy LRHS MAus MBri NEgg SCoo
	'Anne Dakin' (ClHT)	MAus
	Anne Harkness = 'Harkaramel' (F)	MAus SPer
	Antique = 'Antike' (F)	CPou
	Aperitif = 'Macwaira'[PBR] (HT)	ESty
	Aphrodite = 'Tan00847'[PBR] (S) **new**	ESty MRav SWCr
	apothecary's rose	see *R. gallica* var. *officinalis*
	'Apple Blossom' (Ra)	SMrm
	'Apricot Nectar' (F)	GCoc MAus SPer
	'Apricot Silk' (HT)	CTri MBri SPer
	Apricot Sunblaze = 'Savamark' (Min)	CSBt
	'Archiduc Joseph' misapplied	see *R.* 'Général Schablikine'
	'Arethusa' (Ch)	EBee
	Art Nouveau = 'Pejamark' (F)	ESty SWCr
	'Arthur Bell' (F) 𝕐H4	CSBt CTri ELon EPfP ESty IArd IBoy LAst LRHS LStr MAsh MAus MBri MRav MWat NEgg NPri SMrm SPer SPoG SRGP SSea SWCr WBor
	'Arthur de Sansal' (DPo)	MAus MBri WBor
	Artistic Licence = 'Guesmarble' (HT)	SWCr
	arvensis	CCVT CHab CRWN LBuc MAus NWea
	'Assemblage des Beautés' (G)	MAus
	'Auguste Gervais' (Ra)	MAus
	Austrian copper rose	see *R. foetida* 'Bicolor'
	Austrian yellow	see *R. foetida*
	'Autumn' (HT)	LSRN
	Autumn Fire	see *R.* 'Herbstfeuer'
	'Autumnalis'	see *R.* 'Princesse de Nassau'
	'Avignon' (F)	EBee
	Avon = 'Poulmulti'[PBR] (GC) 𝕐H4	ELan EPfP GCoc MRav SPer SWCr
	Awakening = 'Probuzení' (ClHT)	EWTr NLar SWCr
	'Ayrshire Splendens'	see *R.* 'Splendens'
	'Baby Bio' (F/Patio)	ESty SWCr
	'Baby Faurax' (Poly)	MAus
	Baby Love = 'Scrivluv'[PBR] (Min/Patio) 𝕐H4	MAus
	Baby Masquerade = 'Tanba' (Min)	GCoc MRav MWat SPer SWCr
	Babyface = 'Rawril'[PBR] (Min)	ESty
	'Ballerina' (HM/Poly) 𝕐H4	Widely available
	Ballindalloch Castle = 'Cocneel'[PBR] (F)	GCoc
	'Baltimore Belle' (Ra)	CRHN MAus
	banksiae (Ra)	CPou SRms
	– ***alba***	see *R. banksiae* var. *banksiae*
§	– var. ***banksiae*** (Ra/d)	CHll CPou CRHN CSBt CSPN CTri EBee ELan EPfP ERom GQui LRHS LStr MAus SLon SPer WCot XSen

	Name	Suppliers
	– 'Lutea' (Ra/d) ♀H3	Widely available
	– 'Lutescens' (Ra)	CHll
	– var. ***normalis*** (Ra)	CSBt CSam MAus SKHP SLon WCot WHer WPGP
I	– 'Rosea'	MWat NLar
	banksiae × ***gigantea*** **new**	WPGP
	'Bantry Bay' (ClHT)	CSBt ELan LSRN LStr SEND SLon SPer SSea SWCr
	Barbara Austin = 'Austop'PBR (S)	MAus
	Barbara Windsor = 'Ganleon'PBR (F)	GCoc SWCr
	Barkarole = 'Tanelorak'PBR (HT)	CSBt ESty LStr SWCr
	'Baron Girod de l'Ain' (HP)	ELon ESty LAst LRHS MAsh MAus MBri MMuc MRav NEgg NLar SEND SMrm SPer SWCr WBor
	'Baroness Rothschild' ambig.	see *R.* 'Baronne Adolph de Rothschild' (HP), *R.* Climbing Baronne Edmond de Rothschild (ClHT)
§	'Baronne Adolph de Rothschild' (HP)	MBri
	'Baronne Prévost' (HP)	MAus SFam
	Baroque Floorshow = 'Harbaroque'PBR (S)	MRav
	Barry Stephens = 'Horcabellero' (HT)	LSRN
§	× ***beanii*** (Ra)	IFro
	'Beau Narcisse' (G)	MAus
	Beautiful Britain = 'Dicfire' (F)	LStr MRav SWCr
	Beautiful Sunrise = 'Bostimebide'PBR (ClPatio)	SWCr
	'Belinda' (HM) **new**	LSRN
§	Bella = 'Pouljill'PBR (Renaissance Series) (S)	CPou
	'Belle Amour' (A × D)	CPou MAus
	Belle Blonde = 'Menap' (HT)	SPer
	'Belle de Crécy' (G) ♀H4	CPou CSam CTri IBoy LRHS LStr MAsh MAus MBri NPri SEND SFam SKHP SPer SWCr
	'Belle des Jardins' misapplied	see *R.* × *centifolia* 'Unique Panachée'
	Belle Epoque = 'Fryyaboo'PBR (HT)	GCoc LStr SMad SMrm SWCr
	'Belle Isis' (G)	MAus SPer
	'Belle Portugaise' (ClT)	MAus
	Belmonte = 'Harpearl'PBR (F)	GCoc
§	'Belvedere' (Ra)	CPou IBoy MAus SPer WBor
	Benita = 'Dicquarrel' (HT)	IDic
	Benjamin Britten = 'Ausencart'PBR (S)	CSBt EPfP IBoy LRHS MAus MBri NEgg
	Berkshire = 'Korpinka'PBR (GC) ♀H4	LStr NLar SWCr
	Beryl Joyce = 'Tan96145'PBR (HT)	ESty MRav SWCr
	Best of Friends = 'Pouldunk'PBR (HT)	LSRN SWCr
	Best Wishes = 'Chessnut'PBR (ClHT/v)	LAst LBuc LSRN SRGP
	'Betty Prior' (F)	GCoc
	'Betty's Smile' (HT) **new**	LSRN
	'Bewitched' (HT) **new**	LSRN
§	Bewitched = 'Poulbella'PBR (Castle Series) (F)	EPfP MAsh SWCr
	Bianco = 'Cocblanco' (Patio/Min)	GCoc MAus MRav MWat
	Big Purple = 'Stebigpu'PBR (HT)	ECnt ESty
	Birthday Boy = 'Tan97607'PBR (HT)	CGro ESty LSRN LStr MRav SWCr
	Birthday Girl = 'Meilasso'PBR (F)	CSBt ESty LBuc LSRN LStr MAsh MRav MWat NPri SCoo SMrm SRGP SSea SVic SWCr
	Birthday Wishes = 'Guesdelay' (HT)	CTri LRHS LSRN SSea
	Birthday Wishes (Patio)	see *R.* Shrimp Hit
	Bishop Elphinstone = 'Cocjolly' (F)	GCoc
	Black Baccara = 'Meidebenne'PBR (HT)	CGro ESty SMrm SWCr
	Black Beauty = 'Korfleur' (HT)	MAus
	'Black Ice' (F)	SPer SWCr
	'Black Jack' (Ce)	see *R.* 'Tour de Malakoff'
	'Blairii Number Two' (ClBb) ♀H4	CSam EBee EPfP MAus MRav NEgg NLar SEND SPer
	'Blanche Double de Coubert' (Ru) ♀H4	CDul CSBt CSam CTri EBee ECnt ELan EPfP GBin GCoc LBuc LSRN LStr MAus MCot NEgg NLar SEND SMrm SPer SSea SWCr
	'Blanche Moreau' (CeMo)	MAus NLar SKHP SLon SPer
	'Blanchefleur' (Ce × G)	CPou EBee MAus
	'Blesma Soul' (HT)	CSBt
	'Blessings' (HT) ♀H4	CBcs CGro CSBt CTri GCoc LBuc LSRN LStr MAsh MAus MBri MGos MRav SPer SWCr
	'Bleu Magenta' (Ra) ♀H4	EBee EWTr IArd MAus MCot MRav NLar SEND SMrm SWCr WKif
	'Bloomfield Abundance' (Poly)	CPou EPfP MAus SPer SWCr WHer
	'Blossomtime' (Cl)	SMad SPer
	Blue for You = 'Pejamblu'PBR (F)	CGro ECnt ELon ESty GCoc LBuc LRHS LStr MAsh MAus SCoo SMad SPoG SWCr
	Blue Moon = 'Tannacht' (HT)	CTri ELan GCoc IBoy MBri MGos MRav SPer SPoG SRGP
	Blue Peter = 'Ruiblun' (Min)	ESty IBoy
	'Blush Excelsior' **new**	SMrm
	'Blush Hip' (A)	MAus
	'Blush Noisette'	see *R.* 'Noisette Carnée'
	'Blush Rambler' (Ra)	CSBt EBee EPfP MAus MMuc SEND SPer
	'Blushing Lucy' (Ra)	MTPN SMrm
	Blythe Spirit = 'Auschool'PBR (S)	LRHS MAus MBri NEgg
	'Bobbie James' (Ra) ♀H4	CTri EBee EPfP EWTr GCoc LBuc LRHS LStr MAus MBri MRav NEgg NLar SPer SPoG SSea SWCr
	'Bobby Charlton' (HT)	LSRN
	Bonica = 'Meidomonac' (GC) ♀H4	CSam CTri EBee ECnt ELan EPfP ESty EWTr GCoc IBoy LRHS LShp LStr MAsh MAus MBri MRav MWat NEgg NLar NPri SEND SMad SMrm SPer SPoG SSea SWCr WBor WKif
§	Bonita = 'Poulen009'PBR (Renaissance Series) (S)	ECnt
	Boogie-Woogie = 'Poulyc006'PBR (Courtyard Series) (ClHT)	ECnt SWCr
	Born Again	see *R.* Renaissance
	'Botzaris' (D)	SFam

'Boule de Neige' (Bb)	CBcs CTri EBee ECnt ELan ELon EPfP GCoc IBoy LRHS LSRN LStr MAsh MAus MBri MRav MWat NLar SFam SMrm SPer SWCr
'Bouquet d'Or' (N)	MAus NLar
'Bouquet Tout Fait' misapplied	see *R.* 'Nastarana'
'Bouquet Tout Fait' (N)	EBee
Bow Bells = 'Ausbells' (S)	MAus
Bowled Over = 'Tandolgnil'PBR (F)	ESty SWCr
§ ***bracteata***	CHll CRHN EWes GQui MAus
Brass Ring	see *R.* Peek-a-boo
Brave Heart = 'Horbondsmile' (F)	MAus MRav SPoG
Breath of Life = 'Harquanne'PBR (ClHT)	ELan LStr MAus MRav SPer SWCr
Breathtaking = 'Hargalore'PBR (HT)	ESty SWCr
Bredon = 'Ausbred' (S)	MAus
§ 'Brenda Colvin' (Ra)	MAus
'Brian's Star' (F)	LSRN
Bride and Groom = 'Smi10-98' (HT)	ESty
Bride = 'Fryyearn'PBR (HT)	GCoc LSRN LStr MRav SWCr
Bridge of Sighs = 'Harglowing'PBR (Cl)	ECnt ESty LShp LStr SPoG SSea SWCr
Bright Fire = 'Peaxi'PBR (ClHT)	MBri SPer SSea SWCr
Bright Future = 'Kirora'PBR (Cl)	ECnt ESty
Bright Smile = 'Dicdance' (F/Patio)	MAus
Brilliant Pink Iceberg = 'Probril' (F)	LStr SWCr
Britannia = 'Frycalm'PBR (HT)	ECnt MAsh
Broadlands = 'Tanmirsch'PBR (GC)	GCoc NLar SLon SWCr
Brother Cadfael = 'Ausglobe'PBR (S)	ELon LAst LRHS LStr MAus MBri NEgg NLar SCoo SLon SMrm SPer SSea SWCr
Brown Velvet = 'Maccultra' (F)	ESty SWCr
§ ***brunonii*** (Ra)	CPLG EWes MAus
- CC 4515	WCot
- CC 5147	GKev
§ - 'La Mortola' (Ra)	MAus MRav NLar
Brush-strokes = 'Guescolour' (F)	ESty SWCr
'Buff Beauty' (HM) ♀H4	CSBt CSam CTri CWSG EBee ECnt ELan EPfP GCoc IBoy LRHS LSRN LStr MAsh MAus MCot MRav MWat NEgg NLar NPri SFam SMad SPer SSea SWCr WCFE
'Bullata'	see *R.* × *centifolia* 'Bullata'
Burgundy Ice = 'Prose'PBR (F)	CGro CSBt EBee ECnt ELon ESty GCoc LBuc LShp LStr MRav SCoo SMad SMrm SPoG SSea SWCr
'Burgundy Iceberg'PBR	see *R.* Burgundy Ice
'Burma Star' (F)	GCoc
burnet, double pink	see *R. spinosissima* double pink-flowered
burnet, double white	see *R. spinosissima* double white-flowered
Buttercup = 'Ausband'PBR (S)	LRHS MAus
Buxom Beauty = 'Korbilant'PBR (HT)	ECnt ESty GCoc LRHS MAsh MBri MGos MWat SCoo SPoG SWCr
'C.F. Meyer'	see *R.* 'Conrad Ferdinand Meyer'
californica (S)	MAus
- 'Plena'	see *R. nutkana* 'Plena'
'Callisto' (HM)	CSam MAus
§ Calypso = 'Poulclimb'PBR (ClHT)	ECnt SWCr
'Camayeux' (G)	CPou ECnt MAus NLar SPer
Cambridgeshire = 'Korhaugen'PBR (GC)	CTri LStr MAus SPer SSea SWCr
'Canary Bird'	see *R.* × *xanthina* 'Canary Bird'
canina (S)	CArn CCVT CDul CHab CLnd CRWN CTri ECrN EPfP LBuc MAus MRav NWea SBfd SEWo SPer SPoG WMou
'Cantabrigiensis' (S) ♀H4	CSam EPfP MAus NLar SLon SPer SSea
'Capitaine Basroger' (CeMo)	MAus
'Capitaine John Ingram' (CeMo) ♀H4	MAus SEND SLon
'Captain Christy'	see *R.* 'Climbing Captain Christy'
'Captain Scarlet' (ClMin)	ESty
'Cardinal de Richelieu' (G) ♀H4	Widely available
Cardinal Hume = 'Harregale' (S)	EBee ESty
Carefree Days = 'Meirivouri' (Patio)	EPfP IBoy LRHS NPri SMrm SPoG
Cariad = 'Auspanier' (HM) **new**	LRHS MAsh MAus
Caring for You ambig.	LSRN
Caring for You = 'Coclust'PBR (HT)	GCoc
'Carol' (Gn)	see *R.* 'Carol Amling'
§ 'Carol Amling' (F)	LSRN
carolina	SLPl
'Caroline Testout'	see *R.* 'Madame Caroline Testout'
Caroline Victoria = 'Harprior'PBR (HT)	LSRN SWCr
Carris = 'Harmanna'PBR (HT)	ESty
Cascade = 'Poulskab'PBR (ClMin)	ECnt
§ Casino = 'Macca' (ClHT)	CTri EBee ELon IBoy LBuc MBri MRav SPer
'Castle Apricot'PBR	see *R.* Lazy Days
'Castle Cream'	see *R.* Perfect Day
'Castle Fuchsia Pink'PBR	see *R.* Bewitched (F)
Castle of Mey = 'Coclucid' (F)	GCoc
'Castle Peach'PBR	see *R.* Imagination
'Castle Shrimp Pink'PBR	see *R.* Fascination (F)
'Castle Yellow'PBR	see *R.* Summer Gold
'Catherine Mermet' (T)	MAus
§ 'Cécile Brünner' (Poly) ♀H4	CSam CTri EBee ELan EWTr GCoc LRHS LSRN LStr MAus MCot NLar SMad SMrm SPer SSea SWCr
Celebration 2000 = 'Horcoffitup'PBR (S)	MAus
§ 'Céleste' (A) ♀H4	EBee EPfP GCoc LStr MAus MRav NLar SEND SFam SPer SSea
'Célina' (CeMo)	LSRN
'Céline Forestier' (N) ♀H3	CPou EBee EWTr MAus MRav NLar SEND SMrm SPer SPoG
§ 'Celsiana' (D)	CPou CSam EWTr LSRN MAus SFam SPer
Centenary = 'Koreledas'PBR (F) ♀H4	SPer
§ × ***centifolia*** (Ce)	CArn LRHS MAus MRav SMad SPer

§	– 'Bullata' (Ce)	MAus
§	– 'Cristata' (Ce) ♀H4	ECnt ELon IBoy LRHS LStr MAsh MAus MRav NLar SEND SFam SPer SWCr WBor
§	– 'De Meaux' (Ce)	MAus NLar SPer
§	– 'Muscosa' (CeMo)	GCoc LRHS LStr MRav MWat SEND SFam
§	– 'Shailer's White Moss' (CeMo)	MAus SFam
	– 'Spong' (Ce)	MAus
§	– 'Unique' (Ce)	MAus NLar
§	– 'Unique Panachée' (Ce)	CPou MAus
	'Centifolia Variegata'	see *R.* × *centifolia* 'Unique Panachée'
	Centre Stage = 'Chewcreepy'PBR (S/GC)	MAsh MAus
	'Cerise Bouquet' (S) ♀H4	MAus MRav SPer
	César = 'Meisardan'PBR (ClHT) **new**	SSea
	'Champagne Dream' (Patio)	SWCr
§	Champagne Moments = 'Korvanaber'PBR (F)	CBcs CSBt EBee ECnt ELan EPfP ESty GCoc IBoy LRHS LSRN LStr MAsh MAus MGos MRav MWat NPri SPer SPoG SRGP SSea SWCr
	'Champneys Pink Cluster' (China hybrid)	LRHS MAus
	Chandos Beauty = 'Harmisty'PBR (HT)	ECnt ESty GCoc LRHS LStr MAsh MRav SSea SWCr
	'Chanelle' (F)	SDix SPer
	Chantal Merieux = 'Masmaric' (Generosa Series) (S)	MRav
	Chapeau de Napoléon	see *R.* × *centifolia* 'Cristata'
	Charles Austin = 'Ausles' (S)	MAus MRav SMrm
	Charles Darwin = 'Auspeet'PBR (S)	CWSG EPfP LRHS MAus MBri NEgg SCoo SMrm SPer SWCr
	Charles de Gaulle	see *R.* Katherine Mansfield
	'Charles de Mills' (G) ♀H4	CSam CTri EBee ECnt ELan EPfP GCra LRHS LShp LStr MAus MBri MRav MWat NLar SFam SKHP SPer SWCr WHer
	Charles Rennie Mackintosh = 'Ausren'PBR (S)	CSBt LRHS MAus MBri NEgg SWCr
	Charlie's Rose = 'Tanellepa' (HT)	ESty LSRN SWCr
	Charlotte = 'Auspoly'PBR (S) ♀H4	EPfP ESty IBoy LRHS LSRN MAus MBri NEgg SCoo SEND SPer SSea SWCr
	Charmant = 'Korpeligo'PBR (Min)	LRHS
	Charmian = 'Ausmian' (S)	MAus
	Chartreuse de Parme = 'Delviola' (S)	ESty MRav SLon
	'Château de Clos-Vougeot' (HT)	IArd
	Chatsworth = 'Tanotax'PBR (Patio/F)	MRav SPer SSea
	Chaucer = 'Auscer' (S)	MAus
§	Cheek to Cheek = 'Poulslas'PBR (Courtyard Series) (ClMin)	SWCr
	Cheerful Charlie = 'Cocquimmer'PBR (F)	LSRN MRav
	CheriePBR	see *R.* Songs of Praise
	Cherry Brandy '85 = 'Tanryrandy'PBR (HT)	CSBt
	Cheshire = 'Fryelise'PBR (HT)	GCoc
	Cheshire = 'Korkonopi'PBR (County Rose Series) (S)	MAus SWCr
	'Cheshire Life' (HT)	MAus
	Chianti = 'Auswine' (S)	EBee MAus NLar
	Chicago Peace = 'Johnago' (HT)	SWCr
	Child of AchievementPBR	see *R.* Bella
	Childhood Memories = 'Ferho' (ClHM)	SWCr
	Chilterns = 'Kortemma'PBR (GC)	SWCr
	'Chinatown' (F/S) ♀H4	CGro CTri IBoy LStr MAsh MAus MBri MRav SMrm SPer SPoG SSea SWCr
	chinensis misapplied	see *R.* × *odorata*
	– 'Minima' *sensu stricto* hort.	see *R.* 'Pompon de Paris'
	– 'Mutabilis'	see *R.* × *odorata* 'Mutabilis'
	– 'Old Blush'	see *R.* × *odorata* 'Pallida'
	– var. ***spontanea*** **new**	WPGP
	Chloe = 'Poulen003'PBR (Renaissance Series) (S)	CPou EBee ECnt LSRN SLon SMrm SWCr
	Chris Beardshaw = 'Wekmeredoc'PBR (HT)	SWCr
	Chris = 'Kirsan'PBR (ClHT)	ECnt ESty GCoc LSRN MAus SWCr WGor
	Christopher = 'Cocopher' (HT)	GCoc SWCr
	Christopher Columbus = 'Meinronsse' (HT)	IArd
	Christopher Marlowe = 'Ausjump'PBR (S)	LRHS MAus MBri SCoo
§	'Chromatella' (N)	MAus
	Cider Cup = 'Dicladida'PBR (Min/Patio) ♀H4	ESty IBoy IDic LStr MAus SWCr
	'Cinderella' (Ra) **new**	WBor
	'Cinderella' (Min)	CSBt
	Cinderella = 'Korfobalt' (ClS)	CPou SWCr
	City Lights = 'Poulgan'PBR (Patio)	CSBt
	City of CarlsbadPBR	see *R.* Hanky Panky
	'City of Leeds' (F)	MAsh SPer
	City of London = 'Harukfore'PBR (F)	CSBt SPer SWCr
	City of York = 'Direktör Benschop' (Cl/HT)	MCot
	Clair Matin = 'Meimont' (ClS)	CPou MAus
	Claire Austin = 'Ausprior'PBR (S)	CWSG EPfP ESty LRHS MAus MBNS MBri SSea SWCr
	'Claire Jacquier' (N)	CSam EBee EPfP MAus SPer SWCr
	Claire Rose = 'Auslight'PBR (S)	LSRN MAus MRav SMrm SPer
	Claret = 'Frykristal'PBR (HT)	EBee ECnt ESty GCoc LStr MRav SSea SWCr
	Clarinda = 'Cocsummery'PBR (F)	GCoc
	Claude Monet = 'Jacdesa' (HT)	MRav
	'Clementina Carbonieri' (T)	NLar
	Cleo = 'Beebop' (HT)	LSRN
	'Cliff Richard' (F)	ESty LBuc LSRN SWCr
	'Climbing Alec's Red' (ClHT)	ELon MBri
	'Climbing Allgold' (ClF)	SLon
	'Climbing Arthur Bell' (ClF) ♀H4	CSBt CTri ESty IBoy LAst LBuc SPer SPoG SSea SWCr

	'Climbing Ballerina' (Ra)	CSBt SWCr
§	Climbing Baronne Edmond de Rothschild = 'Meigrisosar' (ClHT)	CSBt
	'Climbing Blue Moon' (ClHT)	GCoc LBuc SWCr
§	'Climbing Captain Christy' (ClHT)	MAus
	'Climbing Cécile Brünner' (ClPoly) ♡H4	CSBt CTri EBee ECnt EPfP LSRN LStr MAus MBri MCot MRav NLar SEND SPer SSea SWCr
	'Climbing Château de Clos-Vougeot' (ClHT)	MAus
	'Climbing Christine' (ClHT)	MAus
§	'Climbing Columbia' (ClHT)	EShb SPer
	'Climbing Crimson Glory' (ClHT)	CPou GCoc MAus MBri
§	'Climbing Devoniensis' (ClT)	CPou
	'Climbing Ena Harkness' (ClHT)	CTri GCoc MAus MRav SEND SPer SPoG SSea SWCr
	'Climbing Etoile de Hollande' (ClHT) ♡H4	CSBt CSam CTri CWSG EPfP GCoc IBoy LStr MAus MBri MRav NPri SEND SFam SMad SPer SPoG SSea SWCr
	Climbing Fragrant Cloud = 'Colfragrasar' (ClHT)	CBcs ELan
	'Climbing Home Sweet Home' (ClHT)	LSRN
	'Climbing Iceberg' (ClF) ♡H4	CGro CSBt CTri EBee ELan EPfP ESty GCoc IArd LSRN LStr MAus MBri MMuc MRav MWat NEgg NLar SMrm SPer SPoG SSea SWCr
	'Climbing Jazz'PBR	see *R.* That's Jazz
	'Climbing la France' (ClHT)	MRav
§	'Climbing Lady Hillingdon' (ClT) ♡H3	EBee EPfP LRHS MAus MBri MRav NEgg NLar SEND SPer SWCr
	'Climbing Lady Sylvia' (ClHT)	CSBt EBee LRHS MAus SPer
	'Climbing Little White Pet'	see *R.* 'Félicité Perpétue'
	'Climbing Madame Abel Chatenay' (ClHT)	MAus
	'Climbing Madame Butterfly' (ClHT)	MAus NLar SPer
	'Climbing Madame Caroline Testout' (ClHT)	CPou CTri MAus MRav SEND SPer
§	'Climbing Madame Edouard Herriot' (ClHT)	MAus
	'Climbing Masquerade' (ClF)	CTri LBuc MAus MRav NEgg SEND SPer SSea SWCr
	'Climbing Mrs Herbert Stevens' (ClHT)	EPfP LRHS MAus MRav SEND SMrm SPer SWCr
	'Climbing Mrs Sam McGredy' (ClHT) ♡H4	CSBt MAus
	'Climbing Niphetos' (ClT)	MAus
	'Climbing Ophelia' (ClHT)	MAus SEND SPer
	Climbing Orange Sunblaze = 'Meiji Katarsar'PBR (ClMin)	SPer
§	'Climbing Paul Lédé' (ClT)	LRHS MAus SEND SWCr
	'Climbing Peace' (ClHT)	SPer
§	'Climbing Pompon de Paris' (ClMinCh)	CTri MAus SEND SLPl SMrm SPer
	'Climbing Ruby Wedding' (ClHT)	LSRN
	'Climbing Shot Silk' (ClHT) ♡H4	SPer SWCr
§	'Climbing Souvenir de la Malmaison' (ClBb)	CPou MAus SPer
	'Climbing White Cloud'PBR	see *R.* White Cloud
	'Cloth of Gold'	see *R.* 'Chromatella'
	Cloud Nine = 'Fryextra'PBR (HT)	ECnt GCoc
	Colchester Beauty = 'Cansend' (F)	ECnt
§	'Colonel Fabvier' (Ch)	MAus
	colonial white	see *R.* 'Sombreuil'
	'Columbia' (HT)	CPou
	'Columbian'	see *R.* 'Climbing Columbia'
	'Commandant Beaurepaire' (Bb)	CPou EWTr MAus
	common moss	see *R.* × *centifolia* 'Muscosa'
	Commonwealth Glory = 'Harclue'PBR (HT)	SWCr
	'Compassion' (ClHT) ♡H4	Widely available
*	'Compassionate' (F)	MRav
	'Complicata' (G) ♡H4	CPou CTri EPfP LRHS LStr MAus MBri MRav NLar SEND SKHP SPer SSea SWCr
	'Comte de Chambord' misapplied	see *R.* 'Madame Knorr'
	Comte de Champagne = 'Ausufo'PBR (S)	ESty LRHS MAsh MAus MBri SCoo
	'Comtesse Cécile de Chabrillant' (HP)	CPou EBee MAus
	'Comtesse de Lacépède' misapplied	see *R.* 'Du Maître d'Ecole'
§	'Comtesse de Murinais' (DMo)	MAus SFam
§	'Comtesse du Caÿla' (Ch)	MAus
	ConcertPBR	see *R.* Calypso
	'Conditorum' (G)	SFam
	Congratulations = 'Korlift' (HT)	CSBt ECnt IArd IBoy LBuc LSRN LStr MAus MGos MRav NPri SMrm SPer SSea SVic SWCr
	Connie = 'Boselftay'PBR (F)	ESty GCoc LSRN SWCr
§	'Conrad Ferdinand Meyer' (Ru)	EBee SPer
	Conservation = 'Cocdimple' (Min/Patio)	GCoc MBri SMrm SWCr
	Constance Finn = 'Hareden'PBR (F)	SWCr
	'Constance Spry' (ClS) ♡H4	CTri EPfP LRHS LStr MAus MBri MCot MMuc MRav MWat NEgg NLar NPri SEND SMrm SPer SWCr
§	'Cooperi' (Ra)	CAbP CSam CWib EWTr SSea SWCr WPGP
	Cooper's Burmese	see *R.* 'Cooperi'
	'Coral Cluster' (Poly)	MAus
	Coral PalacePBR	see *R.* Imagination
	Cordelia = 'Ausbottle'PBR (S)	LRHS MAus MBri
	'Cornelia' (HM) ♡H4	CBcs CSam CTri EBee EPfP EWTr GCoc IArd IBoy LRHS LSRN LStr MAsh MAus MBri MRav MWat NLar SEND SFam SMad SPer SRGP SWCr
	Coronation Street = 'Wekswetrup' (F)	LSRN
	Corvedale = 'Ausnetting'PBR (S)	LRHS MAus
	cottage maid	see *R.* × *centifolia* 'Unique Panachée'
	Cottage Maid = 'Poulspan' (S) **new**	MAus
	Cottage Rose = 'Ausglisten'PBR (S)	CGro LRHS LSRN MAus MBri MRav SMrm SWCr
	Countess CelestePBR	see *R.* Imagination
	'Coupe d'Hébé' (Bb)	MAus

	Name	Suppliers
	Courage = 'Poulduf'[PBR] (HT)	ECnt
	Courvoisier = 'Macsee' (F)	CSBt
	'Cramoisi Picotée' (G)	MAus
	'Cramoisi Supérieur' (Ch)	EWTr MAus
	Crathes Castle = 'Cocathes' (F)	GCoc
	Crazy for You = 'Wekroalt'[PBR] (F)	ECnt ESty LSRN MAsh SSea SWCr
	Cream Abundance = 'Harflax'[PBR] (Abundance Series) (F)	EBee ESty LStr SSea SWCr
	Crème Anglaise = 'Ganang'[PBR] (ClHT)	GCoc
	Crème Brûlée = 'Ganbru'[PBR] (Cl)	GCoc
	Crème de la Crème = 'Gancre'[PBR] (ClHT)	CSBt EBee ECnt ELon ESty GCoc MAus MRav SPer SPoG SRGP SSea SWCr WBor
	'Crépuscule' (N)	MAus NLar SWCr
	Cressida = 'Auscress' (S)	MAus
	crested moss	see *R.* × *centifolia* 'Cristata'
	Cricri = 'Meicri' (Min)	MAus
	Crimson Cascade = 'Fryclimbdown'[PBR] (ClHT)	ESty LRHS MBri MRav SPer SPoG SSea SWCr
	crimson damask	see *R. gallica* var. *officinalis*
	'Crimson Descant' (ClHT)	EBee ECnt SWCr
	'Crimson Glory' (HT)	GCoc
	'Crimson Shower' (Ra) ♀H4	CSam CTri EBee EWTr LRHS MAus MBNS MBri MMuc MRav NEgg SEND SMrm SPer WHer
	'Cristata'	see *R.* × *centifolia* 'Cristata'
	Crocus Rose = 'Ausquest'[PBR] (S)	EBee EPfP LRHS LStr MAus MBri MRav MWat NEgg SMrm SPer SWCr
	Crown Princess Margareta = 'Auswinter'[PBR] (S)	ECnt EPfP ESty LAst LRHS MAsh MAus MBri NEgg SCoo SMad SMrm SPer SSea SWCr
	cuisse de nymphe	see *R.* 'Great Maiden's Blush'
	'Cupid' (ClHT)	EBee EWTr MAus SPer
I	'Cutie' (Patio)	ESty SWCr
	Cymbeline = 'Auslean' (S)	SPer
	Dacapo = 'Poulcy012'[PBR] (Courtyard Series) (ClPatio)	ECnt
	'D'Aguesseau' (G)	EBee MAus
	'Daily Mail'	see *R.* 'Climbing Madame Edouard Herriot'
	'Dainty Bess' (HT)	MAus SSea SWCr
	'Dale Farm' (F/Patio)	ESty
	× ***damascena*** var. ***bifera***	see *R.* × *damascena* var. *semperflorens*
§	- var. ***semperflorens*** (D)	MAus MCot MRav NLar SSea SWCr
	- 'Trigintipetala' misapplied	see *R.* 'Professeur Emile Perrot'
§	- 'Versicolor' (D)	MAus SPer SSea SWCr
	Dame Wendy = 'Canson' (F)	MAus
	'Danaë' (HM)	CSam MAus
	Dancing Queen = 'Fryfeston' (ClHT)	ECnt ESty GCoc LRHS MBri MRav SWCr
	Danny Boy = 'Dicxcon'[PBR] (Patio)	IDic LSRN WGor
	'Danse du Feu' (ClF)	CBcs CSBt CTri ELan EPfP IBoy LAst LRHS LStr MAus MRav NPri SPer SPoG SWCr
	Dapple Dawn = 'Ausapple' (S)	MAus
	Darcey Bussell = 'Ausdecorum'[PBR] (S)	CSBt EPfP ESty IBoy LRHS MAus MBri SSea SWCr

	Name	Suppliers
	'Darling Jenny' (HT) **new**	LSRN
	'Dart's Defender' (Ru)	SLPl
	David Whitfield = 'Gana'[PBR] (F)	GCoc LSRN
	davidii	MAus
	Dawn Chorus = 'Dicquasar'[PBR] (HT) ♀H4	CGro CSBt CWSG EPfP ESty IBoy IDic LStr MAsh MBri MRav MWat SPer SPoG SSea SWCr
	'Daybreak' (HM)	CTri EBee MAus
	'De Meaux'	see *R.* × *centifolia* 'De Meaux'
	'De Meaux, White'	see *R.* 'White de Meaux'
§	'De Resht' (DPo) ♀H4	CPou CTri EBee ECnt EPfP GCoc LRHS MAsh MRav MWat NLar SBfd SMrm SPer SWCr
	'Dear Daughter' (F)	ESty
	'Dearest' (F)	CBcs SPer SWCr
	'Debbie Thomas' (HT)	LSRN
	Deb's Delight = 'Legsweet'[PBR] (F)	LSRN
	'Debutante' (Ra)	CSam EWTr LRHS MAus
	'Deep Secret' (HT) ♀H4	CBcs CSBt CTri CWSG ECnt ELon EPfP ESty GCoc LBuc LRHS LStr MAsh MBri MRav NPri SPer SRGP SSea SWCr
	'Deidre Hall' (HT) **new**	LSRN
	'Delambre' (DPo)	MAus
	Della Balfour = 'Harblend'[PBR] (ClHT)	SWCr
	Dentelle de Malines = 'Lenfro' (S)	MAus
	Desert Island = 'Dicfizz'[PBR] (F)	ELon GCoc IDic
	'Designer Sunset' (Patio)	SWCr
§	'Desprez à Fleur Jaune' (N)	IArd LRHS MAus MGos MRav NEgg NLar SEND SFam SPer SWCr
	'Devon Maid' (ClHT)	SWCr
	'Devoniensis' (ClT)	see *R.* 'Climbing Devoniensis'
	Diamond Anniversary = 'Morsixty' (Min)	LSRN
	'Diamond Celebration' (HT)	LSRN SWCr
	Diamond Days Forever = 'Fryjess'[PBR] (F)	ESty LSRN
	'Diamond Jubilee' (HT)	CSBt SWCr
	Diamond = 'Korgazell'[PBR] (Patio)	EPfP ESty LSRN LStr
	'Diamond Wishes'[PBR]	see *R.* Misty Hit
	Diamonds Forever = 'Mattdiafor' (HT) **new**	CWSG
	Diana = 'Tananaid'[PBR] (HT) **new**	LSRN
	Dick's Delight = 'Dicwhistle' (GC)	LSRN SWCr
	Dizzy Heights = 'Fryblissful'[PBR] (ClHT)	GCoc MAus MRav SPer SWCr
	'Docteur Grill' (T)	MAus
	Doctor Goldberg = 'Gandol' (HT)	GCoc
	Doctor Jackson = 'Ausdoctor' (S)	MAus
	Doctor Jo = 'Fryatlanta'[PBR] (F)	SWCr
	'Doctor W. Van Fleet' (Ra/Cl)	MAus
	'Don Charlton' (HT)	NEgg
	'Don Juan' (ClHT)	SWCr
	'Doncasteri'	MAus
	'Doreen' (HT)	LSRN
	'Doris Tysterman' (HT)	CGro CTri LBuc LStr MAus SPer

Dorothy = 'Cocrocket'PBR (F) — GCoc LSRN MRav
'Dorothy Perkins' (Ra) — CGro CTri LRHS MAus MRav MWat NLar NPer NWea SPer SRGP WHer
'Dortmund' (S) ♀H4 — EPfP EWTr GCoc MAus NLar SPer SWCr
Double Delight = 'Andeli' (HT) — ESty GCoc IBoy LSRN SPer SWCr
Douglas = 'Cocfresco' (F) — GCoc
Dream Lover = 'Peayetti'PBR (Patio) — ESty SWCr
'Dreaming Spires' (Cl) — SPer SWCr
§ 'Du Maître d'Ecole' (G) — ELon LRHS MAus WHer
Dublin Bay = 'Macdub' (ClF) ♀H4 — CSBt CSam CTri ECnt ELan ELon EPfP GCoc IArd IBoy LAst LRHS LStr MCot MRav MWat NLar SEND SMrm SPer SPoG SSea SWCr WBor
'Duc de Guiche' (G) ♀H4 — CSam MAus SEND SFam SLon SPer WHer
Duchess of Cornwall = 'Tan97157' (HT) — CSBt MRav SWCr
'Duchess of Portland' — see *R.* 'Portlandica'
Duchess of YorkPBR — see *R.* Sunseeker
'Duchesse d'Angoulême' (Ce × G) — MAus SFam
'Duchesse de Buccleugh' (G) — MAus MRav
§ 'Duchesse de Montebello' (G) ♀H4 — CPou CSam EWTr LRHS MAus NLar SFam SLon SPer
'Duchesse de Verneuil' (CeMo) — MAus SFam
'Duke of Edinburgh' (HP) — MAus
Duke of EdinburghPBR (Patio) — see *R.* The Gold Award Rose
'Duke of Wellington' (HP) — CPou
'Duke of Windsor' (HT) — SPer
'Dundee Rambler' (Ra) — MAus
'Dupontii' (S) — EWTr GCoc MAus SFam SKHP SPer
Durrell = 'Tan02876' (F) — SWCr
'Dusky Maiden' (F) — EBee MAus MCot SWCr
Dusty Springfield = 'Horluvdust' (F) — LBuc
'Dutch Gold' (HT) — GCoc MAus MBri SPer
'E.H. Morse' — see *R.* 'Ernest H. Morse'
'Easlea's Golden Rambler' (Ra) ♀H4 — EPfP LRHS MAus MRav NEgg NLar SLon SMrm
'Easter Morning' (Min) — SPer
Easy Does It = 'Harpageant' (F) **new** — ECnt ESty
Easy Going = 'Harflow'PBR (F) — IArd MAsh MRav SWCr
ecae — MAus
'Eddie's Jewel' (*moyesii* hybrid) — LSRN MAus
'Eden Rose' (HT) — GCoc
Eden Rose '88 = 'Meiviolin'PBR (ClHT) — CPou EBee MCot SPer SWCr
Edward's Rose = 'Smi73/7/97' (F) — ESty
eglanteria — see *R. rubiginosa*
Eglantyne = 'Ausmak'PBR (S) ♀H4 — CSBt ELan ELon EPfP ESty GCoc LRHS MAus MBri MRav SMrm SPer SPoG SSea SWCr
'Eleanor' (Patio) — LSRN
Eleanor Masson = 'Cocdesire' (F) — GCoc
Eleanor = 'Poulberin'PBR (S) — ECnt SLon SWCr
§ ***elegantula*** 'Persetosa' (S) — MAus NLar SKHP
§ Elina = 'Dicjana' (HT) ♀H4 — EBee ECnt ELon GCoc IBoy LStr MAus MRav SPer SPoG SWCr
Elizabeth = 'Coctail'PBR (F) — GCoc
'Elizabeth Harkness' (HT) — MAus
Elizabeth of Glamis = 'Macel' (F) — CTri GCoc SPer SWCr
Elizabeth Stuart = 'Maselstu' (Generosa Series) (S) — LSRN MRav
Elle = 'Meibderos'PBR (HT) — ESty LSRN SWCr
Ellen = 'Auscup' (S) — LSRN MAus
'Ellen Willmott' (HT) — EBee MAus SPer
'Elmshorn' (S) — CBcs
Eloise = 'Kirsandra'PBR (HT) — ESty
Elspeth Marshall = 'Coczefma' (HT) — GCoc
Emilien Guillot = 'Masemgui' (Generosa Series) (S) — MRav
Emily = 'Ausburton' (S) — LSRN
'Emily Gray' (Ra) — ECnt EPfP EWTr LSRN LStr MAus MRav SPer
Emily Victoria = 'Boshipeacon' (F) — LSRN
'Emma Wright' (HT) — MAus
'Emmerdale' (F) — LBuc
'Empereur du Maroc' (HP) — EBee IBoy MAus MRav
'Empress Josephine' — see *R.* 'Impératrice Joséphine'
Empress Michiko = 'Dicnifty'PBR (HT) — ESty IDic
'Ena Harkness' (HT) — CTri ELan GCoc LRHS SRGP SWCr
England's Rose = 'Auslounge' (S) **new** — ESty MAus
§ England's Rose = 'Ausrace' (S) — LRHS MAsh
English Elegance = 'Ausleaf' (S) — MAus
English Garden = 'Ausbuff' (S) — CGro CTri EPfP LSRN MAus MRav SMrm SPer
'English Miss' (F) ♀H4 — EBee ECnt ELon EPfP ESty IBoy LBuc LRHS LStr MAsh MAus MBri MRav SMrm SPer SPoG SWCr
English SonnetPBR — see *R.* Samaritan
'Eos' (*moyesii* hybrid) — MAus
'Erfurt' (HM) — EBee EWTr MAus SPer
§ 'Ernest H. Morse' (HT) — CSBt CTri GCoc IBoy MRav SPer SPoG SWCr
Escapade = 'Harpade' (F) ♀H4 — MAus
Especially for You = 'Fryworthy'PBR (HT) — CSBt ELon ESty GCoc LSRN LStr SCoo SSea SWCr
Essex = 'Poulnoz'PBR (GC) — MRav SPer SPoG SWCr
'Etain' (Ra) — ECnt
§ 'Étendard' (ClHT) — MRav SPer SPoG SWCr
Eternal Flame = 'Korassenet'PBR (F) — MAsh
Eternally Yours = 'Macspeego'PBR (HT) — EBee ESty
'Ethel' (Ra) — CPou EBee LSRN
'Étoile de Hollande' (HT) — ELan GBin LRHS MBNS MCot NEgg NLar SLon
'Eugénie Guinoisseau' (Mo) — CPou
Euphoria = 'Intereup'PBR (GC/S) — IDic LBuc SWCr
'Europeana' (F) — GCoc
'Evangeline' (Ra) — MAus

Name	Suppliers
Evelyn = 'Aussaucer'PBR (S) ♀H4	CSBt EPfP ESty EWTr GCoc LRHS LSRN MAus MBri MRav MWat NEgg NLar SLon SMrm SPer SWCr
§ Evelyn Fison = 'Macev' (F)	CSBt CTri ELan GCoc IBoy LSRN MAus MWat SPer
'Excelsa' (Ra)	CSBt CTri EPfP IArd IBoy LAst MRav NWea SPoG
Eye Paint = 'Maceye' (F)	MAus SMrm
'Eyecatcher' (F)	EBee
Eyes for You = 'Pejbigeye' (F)	ESty LStr
'F.E. Lester'	see *R.* 'Francis E. Lester'
§ 'F.J. Grootendorst' (Ru)	IBoy NEgg SPer
'Fabvier'	see *R.* 'Colonel Fabvier'
Fair Bianca = 'Ausca' (S)	MAus
Fairy Prince = 'Harnougette' (GC)	ESty
Fairy Queen = 'Sperien' (Poly/GC)	IDic LBuc
'Fairy Rose'	see *R.* 'The Fairy'
Fairy Snow = 'Holfairy' (S)	SWCr
Faithful Friend = 'Beachallenge' (S)	LSRN
Falstaff = 'Ausverse'PBR (S)	CGro CSBt ELon EPfP LRHS LSRN LStr MAsh MAus MBNS MBri MGos MRav NEgg SMrm SPer SPoG SSea SWCr
'Fantin-Latour' (*centifolia* hybrid) ♀H4	CTri ECnt ELan EPfP GCoc GCra IBoy LAst LRHS LStr MAus MBri MRav MWat NEgg NLar SEND SFam SMad SPer SSea SWCr WKif
farreri var. ***persetosa***	see *R. elegantula* 'Persetosa'
Fascination = 'Jacoyel' (Castle Series) (HT)	LStr SCoo
§ Fascination = 'Poulmax'PBR (F) ♀H4	EBee ECnt EPfP IBoy MAsh MBri MRav SPer SWCr
Father's Favourite = 'Gandoug'PBR (F)	GCoc LSRN SWCr
fedtschenkoana misapplied	MAus
fedtschenkoana Regel	SLPl
Fée des Neiges	see *R.* Iceberg
'Felicia' (HM) ♀H4	CSBt CSam CTri EBee ECnt ELan EPfP EWTr GCoc LRHS LStr MAsh MAus MRav MWat NLar SEND SFam SKHP SMrm SPer SWCr WKif
'Félicité Parmentier' (A × D) ♀H4	LRHS MAus MBri MRav MWat NLar SFam SPer SWCr
§ 'Félicité Perpétue' (Ra) ♀H4	CBcs ELan EPfP EWTr GCoc IBoy LRHS LShp LStr MAus MBri MRav NEgg NLar SEND SFam SPer SPoG SSea SWCr
'Fellemberg' (ClCh)	MAus
Fellowship = 'Harwelcome'PBR (F) ♀H4	ESty GCoc LStr MAus MRav SCoo SSea SWCr
'Ferdinand Pichard' (Bb) ♀H4	CPou CSBt CTri EBee ECnt ELon EPfP ESty EWTr GCoc LAst LRHS MAus MBri MCot MRav NEgg NLar SEND SKHP SPer SPoG SSea SWCr WKif
Ferdy = 'Keitoli'PBR (GC)	SPer
Fergie = 'Ganfer'PBR (F/Patio)	SWCr
ferruginea	see *R. glauca* Pourr.
Festival = 'Kordialo'PBR (Patio)	ESty IBoy LStr MBri MRav SPer SPoG SWCr
Fetzer Syrah Rosé = 'Harextra'PBR (S)	ESty
Fiery Hit = 'Poulfiry'PBR (PatioHit Series) (Min/Patio)	LRHS
§ ***filipes*** 'Kiftsgate' (Ra) ♀H4	Widely available
§ 'Fimbriata' (Ru)	CPou ELon EWTr MAus NLar SPer WBor
Financial Times Centenary = 'Ausfin' (S)	MAus
Fiona = 'Meibeluxen' (S/GC)	LSRN
First Great Western = 'Oracharpam'PBR (HT)	ESty LStr SMrm SWCr
'Fisher and Holmes' (HP)	MAus
Fisherman's Friend = 'Auschild'PBR (S)	MAus
Flashdance = 'Poulyc004'PBR (ClMin)	ECnt SWCr
'Flora' (HT)	MAus
'Flore' (Ra)	CRHN
'Florence Mary Morse' (S)	SDix
Florence Nightingale = 'Ganflor'PBR (F)	GCoc SPer
'Flower Carpet Amber' (GC)	IBoy LRHS SCoo SPoG SWCr
'Flower Carpet Coral'PBR (GC)	CGro GCoc IBal LRHS MBri SCoo SWCr
Flower Carpet Gold = 'Noalesa'PBR (GC)	CGro ECnt GCoc IBoy LRHS MBri NPri SPoG SWCr
Flower Carpet PinkPBR	see *R.* Pink Flower Carpet
Flower Carpet Red Velvet = 'Noare'PBR (GC/S)	CGro ECnt ELan EPfP GCoc IBal IBoy LRHS LStr MBri NPri SCoo SPer SPoG SWCr
Flower Carpet Ruby (GC)	LBuc LRHS SCoo SPoG
Flower Carpet Scarlet = 'Noa83100b'PBR (GC)	LBuc LRHS
§ Flower Carpet Sunshine = 'Noason'PBR (GC)	ELan EPfP LRHS LStr SCoo SPer
Flower Carpet White = 'Noaschnee'PBR (GC) ♀H4	CGro CTri ECnt ELan EPfP GCoc IBoy LRHS LStr MAus MBri NPri SCoo SPer SPoG SWCr
Flower Power = 'Frycassia'PBR (Patio)	CSBt ECnt ELon ESty GCoc IBoy LStr MAus MRav MWat SPoG SWCr
Flower Power Gold = 'Fryneon' (Patio)	ECnt ESty LStr
§ ***foetida*** (S)	EBee MAus
§ - 'Bicolor' (S)	MAus
§ - 'Persiana' (S)	MAus SPer
foliolosa	SLPl
Fond Memories = 'Kirfelix'PBR (Patio)	ESty LSRN LStr SWCr
For You With Love = 'Fryjangle' (Patio)	GCoc LBuc LSRN
Forever Royal = 'Franmite' (F)	ESty
Forget Me Not = 'Coccharm'PBR (HT)	GCoc
forrestiana	LRHS MAus
Fortune's double yellow	see *R.* × *odorata* 'Pseudindica'
'Fountain' (HT)	MAus SPer SWCr
Fragrant Cloud = 'Tanellis' (HT)	CTri CWSG ELon EPfP ESty GCoc IBoy LRHS LStr MAsh MAus MBri MGos MRav NPri SMrm SPer SPoG SSea SWCr
'Fragrant Delight' (F) ♀H4	CSBt ELan GCoc LStr MAus MBri MRav MWat SPer SPoG SSea
Fragrant Dream = 'Dicodour'PBR (HT)	CGro ESty IBoy IDic LStr MRav SMrm SSea SWCr
Fragrant Memories = 'Korpastato'PBR (HT)	CSBt MGos SCoo SKHP

	Name	Suppliers
	'Francesca' (HM)	EWTr LRHS LSRN MAus SFam SPer
	Francine Austin = 'Ausram'PBR (S/GC)	LRHS MAus MBri NEgg SPer
§	'Francis E. Lester' (HM/Ra) ♀H4	CRHN CSam ELan EPfP LRHS MAus MBri MMuc NLar SEND SMrm SPer SRGP SSea SWCr WBor
	× ***francofurtana*** misapplied	see *R.* 'Impératrice Joséphine'
	'François Juranville' (Ra) ♀H4	CPou CRHN EBee EPfP IBoy LRHS LShp LStr LTen MAus MBri MMuc MRav NLar SEND SLon SPer SWCr WHer
§	'Frau Karl Druschki' (HP)	EBee MAus
	'Fred Loads' (F) ♀H4	MAus
	Freddie Mercury = 'Batmercury' (HT)	LSRN NEgg
	Free Spirit = 'Fryjeru'PBR (F)	ECnt GCoc
	Freedom = 'Dicjem' (HT) ♀H4	CTri EBee ECnt GCoc LStr MAus MRav SPer SVic
	'Frensham' (F)	GCoc SSea SWCr
	Friend for Life = 'Cocnanne'PBR (F) ♀H4	GCoc LSRN MRav
	Friends Forever = 'Korapriber' (F)	EPfP GCoc MAsh
	'Fritz Nobis' (S) ♀H4	CPou GCoc LStr MAus NLar SPer WKif
	Frothy = 'Macfrothy'PBR (Patio)	ECnt ESty
	'Fru Dagmar Hastrup' (Ru) ♀H4	CDul CSBt CTri EBee ECnt ELan EMil EPfP GCoc IBoy LBuc LRHS LStr MAus NEgg NLar NWea SEND SPer SWCr WBor
	'Frühlingsduft' (SpH)	EWTr
	'Frühlingsgold' (SpH) ♀H4	CBcs ELan GCoc LRHS LStr MAus NLar NWea SPer
	'Frühlingsmorgen' (SpH)	EWTr GCoc LStr MAus SLon SMad SPer
	Fulton Mackay = 'Cocdana'PBR (HT)	GCoc
	Fyvie Castle = 'Cocbamber' (HT)	GCoc
§	***gallica*** var. ***officinalis*** (G) ♀H4	CArn CPrp CSam CTri EPfP GCoc GPoy LRHS MAsh MAus MBri MRav NLar SFam SKHP SPer SSea SWCr
§	- 'Versicolor' (G) ♀H4	CArn CSBt CSam CTri ECnt ELan EPfP EWTr GCoc GCra GPoy IBoy LRHS LShp LStr MAsh MAus MBri MNHC MRav NPri NSti SMad SMrm SPer SPoG SSea SWCr WBor WKif
	Galway Bay = 'Macba' (ClHT)	IBoy LRHS MRav SPer SPoG SWCr
§	Garden News = 'Poulrim'PBR (HT)	EBee
	Garden of Roses	see *R.* Joie de Vivre
	'Gardeners Glory'PBR (ClHT)	ECnt ESty LRHS SMad
	'Gardenia' (Ra)	EWTr LRHS MAus NLar SPer
	'Garnette Carol'	see *R.* 'Carol Amling'
	'Garnette Pink'	see *R.* 'Carol Amling'
	'Gaujard'	see *R.* Rose Gaujard
	'Gelbe Dagmar Hastrup'PBR	see *R.* Yellow Dagmar Hastrup
	'Général Jacqueminot' (HP)	MAus
	'Général Kléber' (CeMo)	MAus SFam
§	'Général Schablikine' (T)	MAus NLar
	Genesis = 'Fryjuicy'PBR (Patio)	CGro ECnt ESty LBuc MRav SWCr
N	***gentiliana*** misapplied	see *R.* 'Polyantha Grandiflora'
N	***gentiliana*** H. Lév. & Variot	see *R. multiflora* var. *cathayensis*
	Gentle Hermione = 'Ausrumba'PBR (S)	ELan EPfP IBoy LRHS MAus MBri SWCr
	Gentle Touch = 'Diclulu' (Min/Patio)	CSBt LBuc MRav SMad SPer SPoG
	Geoff Hamilton = 'Ausham'PBR (S)	EPfP ESty IBoy LRHS LSRN LStr MAsh MAus MBNS MBri NEgg SCoo SMrm SPer SSea SWCr
	'Geoffrey Smith' (Cl) **new**	LSRN
	'Georg Arends' (HP)	MAus
	George Best = 'Dichimanher'PBR (Patio)	ESty IDic LBuc LSRN SWCr
	'George Dickson' (HT)	MAus
	'Georges Vibert' (G)	MAus
	'Geranium' (*moyesii* hybrid) ♀H4	CBcs CDul CSam CTri EBee ELan EPfP GCoc IArd IBoy LRHS LStr MAsh MAus MBri MCot MRav MWat NLar SEND SPer SSea SWCr WBor
	Gerbe d'Or	see *R.* Casino
	'Gerbe Rose' (Ra)	MAus
	Gertrude Jekyll = 'Ausbord'PBR (S) ♀H4	Widely available
	'Ghislaine de Féligonde' (Ra/S)	CPou CSam EPfP EWTr GCoc LStr MAus NLar SEND SMrm SPer SWCr
	GhitaPBR	see *R.* Millie
	Giardina = 'Tan97286' (Cl) **new**	ESty SWCr
	gigantea × ***longicuspis*** **new**	WPGP
	Ginger Syllabub = 'Harjolina'PBR (ClHT)	CWSG ECnt ELon ESty GCoc MBri MRav SPoG SRGP SWCr
	Gingernut = 'Coccrazy'PBR (Patio)	SWCr
	Gipsy Boy	see *R.* 'Zigeunerknabe'
	Glad Tidings = 'Tantide'PBR (F)	IBoy MRav SPer SWCr
	Glamis Castle = 'Auslevel'PBR (S)	CBcs CTri EPfP IBoy LRHS LStr MAsh MAus MBri NEgg SCoo SMrm SPer SWCr
	glauca ambig.	GCra MHer NLar SBfd
§	***glauca*** Pourr. (S) ♀H4	CMea CPom CSBt CTri EBee ECnt EPfP EWTr GCoc IBoy LBuc LHop LRHS LStr MAus MLHP MMuc MRav NEgg NSti NWea SEND SGol SKHP SPer SSea SWCr WMoo
	'Glenfiddich' (F)	CSBt CTri CWSG GCoc LStr MAus MBri MRav SPer
	Glenshane = 'Dicvood' (GC/S)	MRav
	Global Beauty = 'Tan 94448' (HT)	MRav SWCr
	'Gloire de Dijon' (ClT)	CGro CSBt CTri CWSG EBee ECnt ELan EPfP IBoy LAst LRHS LSRN LStr MAus MBri MCot MRav NEgg NLar NPri SPer SPoG SRGP SSea SWCr
	'Gloire de Ducher' (HP)	MAus
	'Gloire de France' (G)	MAus MRav WHer
	'Gloire de Guilan' (D)	MAus
	'Gloire des Mousseuses' (CeMo)	LRHS MAus SFam
	'Gloire du Midi' (Poly)	MAus
	'Gloire Lyonnaise' (HP)	SLon
	'Gloria Mundi' (Poly)	NEgg
	Gloriana = 'Chewpope'PBR (ClMin)	CGro ECnt ESty LRHS MAus MBri MRav MWat SCoo SKHP SMrm SPer SPoG SSea SWCr

Glorious = 'Interictira'[PBR] (HT) — ESty IDic SWCr
'Glory of Seale' (S) — SSea
Glowing Amber = 'Manglow' (Min) — ESty
Gold Rush = 'Jacrebin'[PBR] (F) — ESty GCoc
Gold Symphonie = 'Macfraba' (Min) — LBuc
'Golden Anniversary' (Patio) — IBoy LStr MBri SPer SWCr
'Golden Autumn' (HT) — LSRN
Golden Beauty = 'Korberbeni'[PBR] (F) — CPou ESty MAsh MBri
Golden Celebration = 'Ausgold'[PBR] (S) ♀H4 — CSBt CTri CWSG EBee ECnt EPfP ESty GCoc IBoy LAst LRHS LSRN LStr MAsh MAus MBri MRav NLar SLon SMad SMrm SPer SPoG SSea SWCr
'Golden Chersonese' (S) — MAus
Golden Future = 'Horanymoll'[PBR] (ClHT) — MAus SWCr
'Golden Gate' ambig. — EBee
Golden Gate = 'Korgolgat'[PBR] (ClHT) — ECnt ESty LStr MAus SWCr
Golden Jewel = 'Tanledolg'[PBR] (F/Patio) — ESty
Golden Jubilee = 'Cocagold' (HT) — GCoc MRav SWCr
Golden Kiss = 'Dicalways'[PBR] (HT) — IDic
Golden Memories = 'Korholesea'[PBR] (F) — CBcs CGro CSBt ESty GCoc LStr MAsh MBri MGos MRav SCoo SPer SWCr
Golden Moment = 'Smi-99-2-04' (HT) **new** — ESty
'Golden Rambler' — see *R.* 'Alister Stella Gray'
'Golden Showers' (Cl) ♀H4 — CGro CSBt CTri CWSG EBee ELan EPfP GCoc IBoy LAst LRHS LSRN LStr LTen MAus MBri MRav MWat NEgg NLar NPri SMrm SPer SPoG SSea SWCr
Golden Smiles = 'Frykeyno'[PBR] (F) — ECnt ESty GCoc
Golden Symphonie = 'Meitoleil' (Min/Patio) — ELon
Golden Trust = 'Hardish'[PBR] (Patio) — LStr MWat
Golden Wedding Anniversary (F) — LSRN
Golden Wedding = 'Arokris'[PBR] (F) — CGro CSBt CTri CWSG EBee ECnt ELan EPfP ESty GCoc IArd IBoy LRHS LSRN LStr MAsh MAus MGos MRav MWat NEgg NPri SMrm SPer SPoG SSea SVic SWCr
'Golden Wedding Celebration' (F) — ESty LSRN SWCr
'Golden Wings' (S) ♀H4 — CPou CTri ELan EPfP GCoc IBoy LRHS LStr MAus MRav NLar SKHP SPer SSea SWCr
Golden Years = 'Harween'[PBR] (F) — ESty
'Goldfinch' (Ra) — ELan EPfP LRHS LStr MAus MBri MRav NEgg NLar SEND SPer SPoG SWCr WBor
Goldstar = 'Candide' (HT) — ECnt
Good as Gold = 'Chewsunbeam'[PBR] (ClMin) — CSBt ECnt ESty LStr SPer SSea SWCr
Good Life = 'Cococircus'[PBR] (HT) — GCoc SCoo
Gordon Snell = 'Dicwriter' (F) — IDic
Gordon's College = 'Cocjabby'[PBR] (F) ♀H4 — GCoc
'Grace Abounding' (F) — LSRN
Grace = 'Auskeppy'[PBR] (S) — CSBt EBee EPfP ESty LRHS LSRN LStr MAsh MAus MBri NEgg SMrm SPer SSea SWCr
Gracious Queen = 'Bedqueen' (HT) — GCoc SWCr
Graham Thomas = 'Ausmas' (S) ♀H4 — Widely available
Grande Amore = 'Korcoluma'[PBR] (HT) — CSBt LRHS LSRN
'Grandma' (F) — LSRN
'Grandpa Dickson' (HT) — CBcs GCoc IBoy LBuc MAsh MAus MBri MRav SPer
Granny's Favourite (Patio/F) — LSRN
Great Expectations = 'Jacdal' (F) — SPoG
Great Expectations = 'Lanican' (HT) — CBcs
Great Expectations = 'Mackalves'[PBR] (F) — EPfP ESty GCoc IArd LBuc LStr MAsh MRav SCoo SPer SWCr
§ 'Great Maiden's Blush' (A) — GCoc MRav NLar SFam
'Great News' (F) — MAus
Greenall's Glory = 'Kirmac'[PBR] (F/Patio) — MAus MRav
Greetings = 'Jacdreco'[PBR] (F) — ELon IDic LBuc MAsh MRav
Grenadine = 'Poulgrena'[PBR] (HT) — ECnt
'Grootendorst' — see *R.* 'F.J. Grootendorst'
'Grootendorst Supreme' (Ru) — SPer
Grouse 2000 = 'Korteilhab'[PBR] (GC) — CTri MAus
Grouse = 'Korimro' (S/GC) ♀H4 — EPfP MAus NLar SEND SLon SPer
'Gruss an Aachen' (Poly) — EPfP EWTr LStr MAus NLar SPer SWCr
'Gruss an Teplitz' (China hybrid) — MAus SPer
'Guinée' (ClHT) — CSBt ELan ELon EPfP LAst LRHS LStr MAus MCot MRav NPri SMrm SPer SRGP SSea WCot
'Gustav Grünerwald' (HT) — MAus
Guy Savoy = 'Delstrimen'[PBR] (F) — ESty EWTr MRav SLon
Guy's Gold = 'Harmatch'[PBR] (HT) — ESty
Gwen Mayor = 'Cocover'[PBR] (HT) — GCoc
Gwent = 'Poulurt'[PBR] (GC) — CSBt ELan LSRN LStr SEND SPer SSea
§ ***gymnocarpa*** var. ***willmottiae*** — SPer SSea
Gypsy Boy — see *R.* 'Zigeunerknabe'
'Hakuun' (F/Patio) ♀H4 — MAus
'Hamburger Phönix' (Ra) — SPer
Hampshire = 'Korhamp'[PBR] (GC) — MAus
Hand in Hand = 'Haraztec'[PBR] (Patio/Min) — MWat SPoG

Name	Suppliers
Händel = 'Macha' (ClHT) ♀H4	CSBt CTri CWSG ELan EPfP IBoy LAst LBuc LRHS LStr MRav MWat NEgg NLar SBfd SPer SPlb SPoG SSea SWCr
§ Hanky Panky = 'Wektorcent' PBR (F)	CGro ESty GCoc MAsh MRav SCoo SWCr
Hannah Gordon = 'Korweiso' (F)	SPer SWCr
'Hansa' (Ru)	EBee EMil GCoc LBuc MAus SPer SWCr
Happy Anniversary = 'Bedfranc' PBR (F)	LSRN SWCr
Happy Anniversary = 'Delpre' (F)	CGro CTri LRHS LStr MAsh MRav SPoG
'Happy Birthday' (Min/Patio)	CGro CWSG ESty IBoy LBuc LSRN LStr SPoG SWCr
Happy Child = 'Auscomp' PBR (S)	LRHS MAus
Happy Retirement = 'Tantoras' PBR (F)	CGro ESty GCoc LBuc LSRN LStr MAsh MRav SCoo SPoG SSea SWCr
§ × ***harisonii*** 'Harison's Yellow' (SpH)	MAus
§ - 'Lutea Maxima' (SpH)	MAus
§ - 'Williams Double Yellow' (SpH)	EWTr GCoc MAus
Harlow Carr = 'Aushouse' PBR (S)	EPfP IBoy MAus MRav SCoo SMrm SPer
Harlow Carr = 'Kirlyl' (F)	MBri
'Harry Edland' (F)	SSea SWCr
'Harry Wheatcroft' (HT)	IBoy MAus SPer
Harvest Fayre = 'Dicnorth' PBR (F)	IDic MBri SPer
'Headleyensis' (S)	MAus SLon
Heart of Gold = 'Coctarlotte' PBR (HT)	EBee ECnt ESty GCoc MRav
Heather Austin = 'Auscook' PBR (S)	LRHS MAus
Heavenly Rosalind = 'Ausmash' PBR (S)	LRHS MAus
§ 'Hebe's Lip' (D ×RH)	MAus
'Helen Knight' (*ecae* hybrid) (S)	MAsh MAus SSea
helenae	CTri MAus NLar SPer
hemisphaerica (S)	MAus
§ 'Henri Martin' (CeMo)	IBoy LEdu LRHS MAus NEgg NLar SKHP SLon SPer
Henri Matisse = 'Delstrobla' (HT)	ESty MRav SPoG
'Henry Nevard' (HP)	MAus
Her Majesty = 'Dicxotic' PBR (F)	IDic
§ 'Herbstfeuer' (RH)	CPou EBee SPer
Heritage = 'Ausblush' (S)	CGro CTri EBee ELan ELon EPfP LStr MAus MBri MRav MWat NEgg NLar SEND SLon SMrm SPer SPoG SSea
'Hermosa' (Ch)	EWTr LRHS MAus MRav
Hero = 'Aushero' (S)	MAus
Hertfordshire = 'Kortenay' PBR (GC) ♀H4	ELan MAus MRav SEND SPer SWCr
× ***hibernica***	MAus
'Hidcote Gold' (S)	MAus
§ 'Hidcote Yellow' (Cl)	LRHS SPer
Hide and Seek = 'Diczodiac' PBR (F)	IDic
High Flier = 'Fryfandango' PBR (ClHT)	MWat SWCr
High Hopes = 'Haryup' PBR (ClHT) ♀H4	EPfP GCoc IBoy LStr MAus SPer SPoG SSea SWCr
'Highdownensis' (*moyesii* hybrid) (S)	ELan SPer
Highfield = 'Harcomp' (ClHT)	MAus SPer
Hilda Murrell = 'Ausmurr' (S)	MAus
'Hillieri' (*moyesii* hybrid)	MAus
'Hippolyte' (G)	MAus
Hole-in-one = 'Horeagle' (F)	LSRN
holy rose	see *R.* × *richardii*
'Homère' (T)	MAus
Hommage à Barbara = 'Delchifrou' PBR (HT) **new**	MRav SMrm
Honey Bunch = 'Cocglen' PBR (F)	MRav SPer SRGP
Honey Dijon = 'Weksproulses' PBR (F)	CSBt EBee ECnt ESty SWCr
Honeybun = 'Tan98264' PBR (Patio)	ESty SWCr
'Honorine de Brabant' (Bb)	CPou LRHS MAus MCot NLar SPer SWCr
Hospitality = 'Horcoff' PBR (F)	ESty
Hot Chocolate = 'Wekpaltez' (F)	CGro CSBt EBee ECnt ELan ELon EPfP ESty GCoc IBoy LBuc LRHS LStr MAsh MBri MRav NPri SCoo SMad SMrm SPer SPoG SRGP SSea SWCr WBor
Hot Stuff = 'Maclarayspo' (Min)	SWCr
House Beautiful = 'Harbingo' (Patio)	MRav
'Hugh Dickson' (HP)	CPou LSRN MAus NLar
hugonis	see *R. xanthina* f. *hugonis*
- 'Plenissima'	see *R. xanthina* f. *hugonis*
Humanity = 'Harcross' PBR (F)	MRav SMrm
Hyde Hall = 'Ausbosky' PBR (S)	MAus SCoo
I Love You = 'Geelove' (HT)	LBuc
Ice Cream = 'Korzuri' PBR (HT) ♀H4	CGro CSBt CWSG EBee ECnt ESty GCoc IBoy LStr MAus MRav MWat SPoG SWCr
§ Iceberg = 'Korbin' (F) ♀H4	CBcs CGro CSBt CTri CWSG EBee ECnt EPfP ESty GCoc IBoy LAst LRHS LStr MAsh MAus MGos MRav MWat NPri NWea SMrm SPer SPoG SSea SWCr
'Illusion' (ClF)	SWCr
§ Imagination = 'Pouldron' PBR (F)	MAsh
§ 'Impératrice Joséphine' (Ga) ♀H4	CSam IBoy LRHS MAsh MAus MRav NLar SFam
In Memory Of	LSRN
Indian Summer = 'Peaperfume' PBR (HT) ♀H4	CSBt CWSG ELon GCoc MAsh MRav MWat SMrm SPoG SWCr
'Indigo' (DPo)	CPou ELon MAus
Ingrid Bergman = 'Poulman' PBR (HT) ♀H4	CTri ECnt ELon EPfP GCoc IBoy LBuc LRHS LSRN LStr MAsh MBri MGos MRav SMrm SPer SPoG SWCr
Innocence = 'Cocoray' PBR (Patio)	CGro GCoc
Intrigue = 'Korlech' (F)	LStr
Invincible = 'Runatru' (F)	LBuc
'Ipsilanté' (G)	MAus

	Name	Suppliers
	'Irène Watts' (Ch)	CPou ECre EPfP LSRN NLar SKHP SWCr
	'Irene's Delight' (HT)	LSRN
	Iris = 'Coczero' (HT)	GCoc LSRN
	Iris = 'Ferecha' (HT)	LSRN SWCr
	Irish Eyes = 'Dicwitness'PBR (F)	CBcs CGro CWSG EPfP ESty IArd IBoy IDic LBuc LStr MAsh MBri MRav MWat SCoo SPer SWCr
	Irish Hope = 'Harexclaim'PBR (F)	SWCr
	Irish Wonder	see *R.* Evelyn Fison
	Isabella = 'Poulisab'PBR (Renaissance Series) (S)	CPou CTri ECnt SLon SWCr
	IsisPBR (HT)	see *R.* Silver Anniversary = 'Poulari'
	Isn't She Lovely = 'Diciluvit'PBR (HT)	ECnt ESty GCoc IDic LBuc LSRN MAsh SWCr
	'Ispahan' (D) ♀H4	EPfP LRHS MAus MBri MCot NEgg NLar SFam SLPl SLon SPer
	Ivory Castle = 'Guesoverlay' (HT)	SWCr
	Jack's Wish = 'Kirsil' (HT)	LSRN
§	× *jacksonii* 'Max Graf' (GC/Ru)	LRHS MAus NLar
	- Red Max Graf	see *R.* Rote Max Graf
	Jacobite rose	see *R.* × *alba* 'Alba Maxima'
	Jacqueline du Pré = 'Harwanna'PBR (S) ♀H4	EBee ECnt EPfP ESty GCoc LSRN MAus MCot MRav MWat NLar SLon SPer SSea SWCr WBor
	Jacquenetta = 'Ausjac' (S)	MAus
N	'Jacques Cartier' misapplied	see *R.* 'Marchesa Boccella'
	James Galway = 'Auscrystal'PBR (S)	CSBt IBoy LRHS LStr MAus MBri NEgg SCoo SSea
	'James Mason' (G)	MAus
	'James Mitchell' (CeMo)	MAus
	'James Veitch' (DPoMo)	MAus
	Janet = 'Auspishus'PBR (S)	LRHS LSRN MAus MBri SSea SWCr
§	'Japonica' (CeMo)	MAus
§	Jardins de Bagatelle = 'Meimafris' (HT)	LSRN MRav
	Jasmina = 'Korcentex'PBR (ClHT)	CPou EPfP ESty MGos SWCr
	'Jaune Desprez'	see *R.* 'Desprez à Fleur Jaune'
	Jayne Austin = 'Ausbreak'PBR (S)	CSBt LRHS MAus SPer
	JazzPBR	see *R.* That's Jazz
	'Jazz' (F)	LSRN
	Jean = 'Cocupland'PBR (Patio)	GCoc LSRN
	'Jean Mermoz' (Poly)	MAus
	'Jeanne de Montfort' (CeMo)	MAus
	'Jenny Duval' misapplied	see *R.* 'Président de Sèze'
	Jenny's Rose = 'Cansit' (F)	EBee ECnt GCoc LSRN SWCr
	Jill's Rose = 'Ganjil'PBR (F)	GCoc LSRN SWCr
	John Clare = 'Auscent'PBR (S)	LRHS MAus
	'John Hopper' (HP)	EWTr MAus SWCr
§	Joie de Vivre = 'Korfloci 01'PBR (Patio/S)	CSBt CWSG ECnt ESty GCoc IBoy LBuc LShp LStr MAsh MBri MRav MWat NPri SCoo SMad SMrm SPoG SWCr
	'Josephine Bruce' (HT)	CBcs LSRN
	'Joseph's Coat' (ClS)	IArd LBuc LStr SWCr
	'Jubilee Celebration' (F)	EPfP
	Jubilee Celebration = 'Aushunter'PBR (S)	CSBt EPfP ESty LRHS MAus MBri SMrm SSea
	Jude the Obscure = 'Ausjo'PBR (S)	CSBt ESty LRHS MAus MBri NEgg SWCr
	'Julia's Rose' (HT)	LSRN LStr MAus SPer SWCr
	Julio Iglesias = 'Meistemon'PBR (F)	ESty LSRN
	'Juno' (Ch)	CPou MAus
	Just for You = 'Moryou' (Min)	LSRN
	'Just Jenny' (Min)	LSRN
	'Just Joey' (HT) ♀H4	CBcs CGro CSBt CWSG ECnt ELan EPfP GCoc IArd IBoy LStr MAus MRav MWat NEgg NPri SMrm SPer SPoG SRGP SSea SWCr
	'Katharina Zeimet' (Poly)	CTri MAus NLar
§	Katherine Mansfield = 'Meilanein' (HT)	CSBt
	'Kathleen' (HM)	LSRN
	'Kathleen Harrop' (Bb)	EBee ELon EWTr LRHS LStr MAus MMuc NLar SEND SFam SPer SRGP SSea SWCr
	Kathleen Jane = 'Horcoed' (S/F)	LSRN
	Kathleen's Rose = 'Kirkitt' (F)	LSRN
	Kathryn McGredy = 'Macauclad' (HT)	ESty
	Kathryn Morley = 'Ausclub'PBR (F)	MAus
	'Katie' (ClF)	LSRN SWCr
N	'Kazanlik' misapplied	see *R.* 'Professeur Emile Perrot'
	Keep Smiling = 'Fryflorida' (HT)	GCoc LBuc LStr MAsh MRav MWat SWCr
§	Kent = 'Poulcov'PBR (Towne & Country Series) (S/GC) ♀H4	CSBt ECnt ELan EPfP ESty GCoc IBoy LBuc LSRN LStr MRav MWat NLar SEND SMrm SPer SSea SWCr
	Kew Gardens = 'Ausfence' (S)	LRHS MAus
	'Kew Rambler' (Ra)	CRHN CSam EBee MAus NLar SFam SLon SPer
	'Kiftsgate'	see *R. filipes* 'Kiftsgate'
	'Kim' (Patio)	LSRN
	Kind Regards = 'Peatiger' (F)	LSRN
	King's Macc = 'Frydisco'PBR (HT)	CGro LRHS MAsh MAus MWat SPoG SWCr
	'King's Ransom' (HT)	CSBt MRav SPer SPoG SWCr
	Knirps = 'Korverlandus'PBR (GC)	SWCr
	Knock Out = 'Dadler' (F)	MAsh SWCr
§	'Königin von Dänemark' (A) ♀H4	ECnt ELon EPfP GCoc IBoy LRHS MAus MBri MRav MWat NEgg NLar SKHP SPer SSea SWCr
	Korona = 'Kornita' (F)	SPer
	'Korresia' (F)	CSBt CTri ECnt ELon EPfP ESty GCoc IBoy LBuc LStr MAsh MAus MBri MRav MWat SPer SPoG SWCr
	'Kronprinzessin Viktoria von Preussen' (Bb)	MAus
	L.D. Braithwaite = 'Auscrim'PBR (S) ♀H4	CBcs ELan EPfP GCoc IBoy LRHS LStr MAus MBNS MBri MRav NLar SLon SMad SPer SWCr
	'La Belle Distinguée' (RH)	EBee
	'La Belle Sultane'	see *R.* 'Violacea'
	'La France' (HT)	MAus
	'La Mortola'	see *R. brunonii* 'La Mortola'
	'La Perle' (Ra)	CRHN
	'La Reine Victoria'	see *R.* 'Reine Victoria'
	La Rose de Molinard = 'Delgrarose' (S) **new**	ESty
	La Rose de Petit Prince = 'Delgramau' (F) **new**	MRav

'La Rubanée'	see *R.* × *centifolia* 'Unique Panachée'
La Sévillana = 'Meigekanu' (F/GC)	SPer WCot
'La Ville de Bruxelles' (D) ♀H4	CSam LRHS MAus SLon SPer
Lady Emma Hamilton = 'Ausbrother'PBR (S)	EPfP ESty IBoy LRHS MAus MBri SCoo SPer SSea SWCr
'Lady Gay' (Ra)	WBor
'Lady Godiva' (Ra)	MAus
'Lady Hillingdon' (ClT)	see *R.* 'Climbing Lady Hillingdon'
'Lady Hillingdon' (T)	MAus
'Lady Iliffe' (HT)	GCoc SWCr
Lady MacRobert = 'Coclent' (F)	GCoc
Lady Mitchell = 'Haryearn' (HT)	ECnt
Lady of Megginch = 'Ausvolume'PBR (S)	CWSG ESty LRHS MAus MBri SSea
Lady of Shalott = 'Ausnyson' (S)	LRHS MAus MBri SSea
Lady Penelope = 'Chewdor'PBR (ClHT)	CSBt
§ 'Lady Penzance' (RH) ♀H4	CBcs CHab MAus SPer
Lady Rachel = 'Candoodle' (F)	EBee ECnt
Lady Rose = 'Korlady' (HT)	MAsh
'Lady Sylvia' (HT)	CTri LSRN MAus NEgg SPer
Lady Taylor = 'Smitling' (F/Patio)	ESty
'Lady Waterlow' (ClHT)	MAus NLar
laevigata (Ra)	MAus MMuc NLar
- 'Anemonoides'	see *R.* 'Anemone'
L'Aimant = 'Harzola'PBR (F) ♀H4	CSBt ELon ESty GCoc LStr MAus MRav SWCr
'Lamarque' (N)	CPou MAus
Lancashire = 'Korstesgli'PBR (GC) ♀H4	ECnt ESty GCoc LSRN LStr MAus MRav SMrm SWCr
Laura Ford = 'Chewarvel'PBR (ClMin) ♀H4	CGro CTri IBoy LRHS LStr MAus MGos MRav MWat SBfd SPer SPoG SSea
'Laura Louisa' (Cl)	EBee
'Laure Davoust' (Ra)	CPou MMuc
Lavender Ice = 'Tan04249' (F)	ECnt ESty LStr SWCr
'Lavender Jewel' (Min)	MAus
'Lavender Lassie' (HM) ♀H4	CPou CSam EBee MAus NLar SPer SSea SWCr
Lavender Parfum de Provence = 'Meibriacus'PBR (HT)	ESty
Lavender Symphonie = 'Meiptima' (Patio)	ESty SMrm
Lavinia	see *R.* Lawinia
§ Lawinia = 'Tanklewi' (ClHT) ♀H4	CSBt EPfP LStr MRav SPer SWCr
'Lawrence Johnston'	see *R.* 'Hidcote Yellow'
§ Lazy Days = 'Poulkalm'PBR (F)	EBee ECnt MAsh
'Le Rêve' (Cl)	EWTr
'Le Vésuve' (Ch)	CPou MAus
Lea = 'Poulren019' (ClS)	ECnt
Leander = 'Auslea' (S)	MAus
Leaping Salmon = 'Peamight'PBR (ClHT)	CGro CSBt ELan ELon ESty GCoc LAst LSRN LStr MAus MRav SPer SRGP SWCr
'Leda' (D)	ELon MAus NLar SFam SPer
'Lemon Pillar'	see *R.* 'Paul's Lemon Pillar'
Léonardo de Vinci = 'Meideauri'PBR (F)	CSBt
'Léontine Gervais' (Ra)	CRHN LRHS MAus MBri NLar
'Leo's Eye'	CPou EPfP
Leslie's Dream = 'Dicjoon' (HT)	IDic
'Leverkusen' (ClF) ♀H4	EWTr LRHS MAus MRav NLar SEND SMrm SPer SWCr
Lichfield Angel = 'Ausrelate'PBR (S)	IBoy LRHS MAus MBri SCoo
Lichtkönigin Lucia = 'Korlillub' (S)	SSea
Life Begins at 40! = 'Horhohoho' (F)	LSRN SWCr
Light Fantastic = 'Dicgottago' (F)	ESty GCoc IDic MAsh
'Lilac Dream' (F)	SWCr
Lilac Rose = 'Auslilac' (S)	MAus
Lilian Austin = 'Ausli' (S)	MAus
Liliana = 'Poulsyng'PBR (S)	CPou ECnt SLon SMrm SWCr
Lilli Marlene = 'Korlima' (F)	CSBt GCoc IBoy SPer
Lincoln Cathedral = 'Glanlin'PBR (HT)	SPer
Lincolnshire Poacher = 'Glareabit' (HT)	NEgg
'Lincolnshire Yellow Belly' (F)	ESty
Lion's Fairy TalePBR	see *R.* Champagne Moments
Lisa = 'Kirdisco' (F)	LSRN
Little Amy = 'Battamy' (Min)	LSRN
'Little Buckaroo' (Min)	MBri SPer
Little Cherub = 'Tan00814'PBR (Patio)	SWCr
'Little Flirt' (Min)	MAus
'Little Gem' (DPMo)	MAus
Little Jackie = 'Savor' (Min)	LSRN
Little Miss Sunshine = 'Dicgungho' (F) **new**	IDic
Little Rambler = 'Chewramb'PBR (MinRa) ♀H4	CSBt ECnt ESty LStr MAus MGos MMuc MRav MWat SCoo SMrm SPer SSea SWCr
'Little White Pet'	see *R.* 'White Pet'
Lochinvar = 'Ausbilda'PBR (S)	LRHS
'Lolabelle'	CPou
'Long John Silver' (Cl)	MAus SSea
longicuspis misapplied	see *R. mulliganii*
longicuspis Bertol. (Ra)	EBee EWTr
§ - var. ***sinowilsonii*** (Ra)	GCal MAus
aff. ***longicuspis***	EWTr SWCr
Lord Byron = 'Meitosier' (ClHT)	LStr SSea SWCr
'Lord Penzance' (RH)	SPer
Lorna = 'Cocringer' (F)	GCoc LSRN
'L'Ouche' misapplied	see *R.* 'Louise Odier'
'Louis Gimard' (CeMo)	MAus SFam
'Louis XIV' (Ch)	EWTr MCot
§ 'Louise Odier' (Bb)	CTri ECnt ELon EPfP GCoc IArd LRHS LStr MAus MBri MRav MWat NLar SFam SPer SRGP SSea SWCr
Love & Peace = 'Baipeace'PBR (HT)	ELan ESty SPoG SWCr
Love Knot = 'Chewglorious'PBR (ClMin)	CSBt ECnt ELon ESty LRHS MRav MWat SBfd SCoo SMrm SSea SWCr WGor
§ Lovely Bride = 'Meiratcan'PBR (Patio)	EPfP LRHS MBri SPoG SWCr
Lovely Fairy = 'Spevu'PBR (Poly/GC)	ELon IDic

Lovely Lady = 'Dicjubell'PBR (HT) ♀H4	CSBt ECnt ESty GCoc IDic LBuc LSRN LStr MAus MRav MWat SSea SWCr
Lovely MeidilandPBR	see *R.* Lovely Bride
'Lovers' Meeting' (HT)	GCoc IBoy MRav SPer SWCr
Loving Memory = 'Korgund' (HT)	CGro CSBt CWSG ECnt ESty GCoc IArd LSRN LStr MAsh MGos MRav NPri SPer SPoG SSea SVic SWCr
Lucetta = 'Ausemi' (S)	MAus
luciae var. ***onoei***	EPot
'Lucky' (F)	CGro CWSG EBee EPfP ESty LRHS LShp LStr NPri SMrm SPer
Lucky! = 'Frylucy' (F)	CSBt ECnt ELon GCoc LBuc LSRN MAsh MBri MRav SCoo SMad SPoG SSea SWCr
Lucy = 'Kirlis' (F)	LSRN
Ludlow Castle	see *R.* England's Rose
Luscious Lucy = 'Tucklucy' (Patio) **new**	LSRN
'Lutea Maxima'	see *R.* × *harisonii* 'Lutea Maxima'
'Lykkefund' (Ra)	MAus
'Mabel Morrison' (HP)	MAus
Macartney rose	see *R. bracteata*, *R.* The McCartney Rose
Macmillan Nurse = 'Beamac' (S)	ESty MCot
'Macrantha' (Gallica hybrid)	MAus
macrophylla	MAus
- B&SWJ 2603	WCru
- CC 6259	GKev
§ - 'Master Hugh' ♀H4	MAus
'Madame Abel Chatenay' (HT)	MAus
'Madame Alfred Carrière' (N) ♀H4	Widely available
'Madame Alice Garnier' (Ra)	CPou MMuc SPer
'Madame Bravy' (T)	MAus
'Madame Butterfly' (HT)	LRHS MAus SPer
§ 'Madame Caroline Testout' (HT)	CTri LRHS SEND SPoG SRGP
'Madame de la Roche-Lambert' (DPMo)	CPou MAus
'Madame de Sancy de Parabère' (Bs)	EWTr IArd MAus SWCr
'Madame Driout' (ClT)	CPou
'Madame Ernest Calvat' (Bb)	CPou
'Madame Eugène Résal' misapplied	see *R.* 'Comtesse du Caÿla'
Madame Figaro = 'Delrona' (S)	MRav
§ 'Madame Grégoire Staechelin' (ClHT) ♀H4	CTri ECnt ELan EPfP IBoy LAst LRHS LSRN LStr MAus MBri MRav NEgg SMrm SPer SPlb SPoG SWCr
'Madame Hardy' (ClD) ♀H4	CPou CSBt ECnt EPfP EWTr GCoc LRHS LStr MAus MBri MCot MRav NChi NEgg NLar SFam SMrm SPer SSea SWCr
'Madame Isaac Pereire' (ClBb) ♀H4	CSBt CTri EBee ECnt EPfP GCoc IBoy LRHS LStr MAsh MAus MBri MCot MRav MWat NLar NPri SFam SMad SMrm SPer SPoG SSea SWCr
'Madame Jules Gravereaux' (ClT)	MAus
§ 'Madame Knorr' (DPo) ♀H4	CPou ECnt ELon EPfP LRHS MAsh MAus MCot MRav NLar SPer SSea SWCr WBor
'Madame Laurette Messimy' (Ch)	CPou MAus
'Madame Lauriol de Barny' (Bb)	MAus MRav NLar SFam SLon
'Madame Legras de Saint Germain' (A × N)	CPou EBee EWTr LRHS MAus NLar SFam SPer
'Madame Louis Lévêque' (DPMo)	CPou NLar
'Madame Pierre Oger' (Bb)	CTri EBee ECnt LRHS LStr MAus MCot MRav SKHP SPer SWCr
'Madame Plantier' (A × N)	CPou LRHS MAus MRav NLar SEND SPer
'Madame Scipion Cochet' (HP) **new**	CPou
'Madame Zöetmans' (D)	MAus
'Madge' (HM)	SDix
Magic Carpet = 'Jaclover'PBR (S/GC) ♀H4	CWSG ELan GCoc IBoy IDic LBuc MAus MGos MRav MWat SMrm SPer SSea SWCr
'Magnifica' (RH)	LRHS MAus
Maid Marion = 'Austobias' (HM) **new**	LRHS MAsh MAus
Maid of Honour = 'Jacwhink' (F) **new**	IDic
'Maid of Kent'PBR (Cl)	MAus SCoo SPer SWCr
'Maiden's Blush' (A) ♀H4	CArn CTri ELan LRHS MAsh MAus SFam SPer SSea SWCr WHer
'Maiden's Blush, Great'	see *R.* 'Great Maiden's Blush'
'Maigold' (ClPiH) ♀H4	CBcs CGro CTri EBee ECnt ELan ELon EPfP GCoc LRHS LStr MAus MRav MWat NLar SEND SMad SPer SWCr
Make a Wish = 'Mehpat'PBR (Min/Patio)	ESty
Maltese rose	see *R.* 'Cécile Brünner'
Malvern Hills = 'Auscanary'PBR (Ra)	CSBt EPfP LRHS MAus MBri SPer SSea SWCr
Mamma Mia! = 'Fryjolly'PBR (HT)	ECnt ESty GCoc LBuc MAsh MBri MRav NPri SPoG SWCr
'Mandarin' (F) **new**	SSea
Mandarin = 'Korcelin'PBR (Min)	ESty IBoy LStr MRav
Many Happy Returns = 'Harwanted'PBR (F) ♀H4	CBcs CGro CSBt CWSG ECnt ELan EPfP GCoc IBoy LRHS LSRN LStr MAsh MGos MRav MWat NPri SPer SPoG SSea SVic SWCr
'Marbrée' (DPo)	MAus
'Märchenland' (F)	MAus
§ 'Marchesa Boccella' (DPo) ♀H4	CPou CSam CTri EBee EPfP GCoc LRHS MAsh MBri NLar NPri SPer SPoG SSea SWCr WBor WHer
'Maréchal Davoust' (CeMo)	MAus SFam
'Maréchal Niel' (N)	EShb MAus SPer
'Margaret' (HT)	GCoc LSRN
Margaret Merril = 'Harkuly' (F) ♀H4	CBcs CGro CSBt CTri CWSG EBee ECnt ELan EPfP ESty GCoc IArd IBoy LRHS LSRN LStr MAsh MAus MRav MWat NPri SPer SPoG SRGP SSea SWCr
'Marguerite Hilling' (S) ♀H4	CTri EPfP MAus MCot MRav NLar SPer
'Mariae-Graebnerae'	SLPl
'Marie Louise' (D)	EBee MAus SFam
'Marie Pavič' (Poly)	CPou MAus
'Marie van Houtte' (T)	MAus
'Marie-Jeanne' (Poly)	MAus
Marinette = 'Auscam'PBR (S)	MAus
Marjorie Fair = 'Harhero' (Poly/S) ♀H4	EPfP ESty GCoc MAsh MAus MRav SWCr
'Marlena' (F/Patio)	GCoc MAus

	Name	Suppliers
	Marry Me = 'Dicwonder'PBR (Patio) 🏆H4	ESty IDic LBuc
	'Martha' (Bb)	LSRN
	'Martian Glow' (F)	NLar
	'Martin Frobisher' (Ru)	MAus
I	'Mary' (Poly)	LStr
	Mary Magdalene = 'Ausjolly'PBR (S)	MAus
	'Mary Manners' (Ru)	NLar
	Mary Rose = 'Ausmary' (S) 🏆H4	CSBt CTri CWSG EBee ELan EPfP GCoc IBoy LRHS LSRN LStr MAsh MAus MBri MRav MWat NLar NPri SLon SMrm SPer SPoG SSea SWCr WKif
	'Mary Wallace' (Cl)	MAus
	Mary Webb = 'Auswebb' (S)	MAus
	'Masquerade' (F)	CTri CWSG ELan GCoc MRav SMrm SPer SSea SWCr
	'Master Hugh'	see *R. macrophylla* 'Master Hugh'
	Matawhero MagicPBR	see *R.* Simply the Best
	'Max Graf'	see *R.* × *jacksonii* 'Max Graf'
	'Maxima'	see *R.* × *alba* 'Alba Maxima'
	'May Queen' (Ra)	CPou LRHS MAus MBri MRav NLar SEND SFam SPer SWCr
	Mayor of Casterbridge = 'Ausbrid'PBR (S)	LRHS MAus
	'McCartney Rose'PBR	see *R.* The McCartney Rose
	'Meg' (ClHT)	EWTr LRHS LSRN MAus MCot SPer SRGP
	'Meg Merrilies' (RH)	NLar
	Melody Maker = 'Dicqueen'PBR (F)	IBoy IDic
	'Memories Are Made of This' (F)	GCoc
	Memory Lane = 'Peavoodoo'PBR (F)	LSRN MBri SWCr
	'Mermaid' (Cl) 🏆H3-4	CBcs CSBt EBee ECnt ELon EPfP LHop LRHS LStr MAus MBri NLar SEND SMrm SPer SPoG SSea SWCr
§	Message = 'Meban' (HT)	MBri
§	'Mevrouw Nathalie Nypels' (Poly) 🏆H4	CTri LRHS LStr MAus MMuc MRav NLar SPer SWCr WKif
	'Michèle Meilland' (HT)	MAus
	× ***micrugosa***	MAus
	- 'Alba'	MAus
	Middlesborough Football Club = 'Horflame' (HT)	LSRN
§	Millie = 'Poulren013'PBR (Renaissance Series) (S)	EBee ECnt EPfP LRHS LSRN MAsh MBri NPri SPoG SWCr
	Millie Rose = 'Wekblunez'PBR (HT)	CWSG
	Millionaire = 'Peazara' (F)	LSRN
	'Minnehaha' (Ra)	MAus
	mirifica stellata	see *R. stellata* var. *mirifica*
	Mischief = 'Macmi' (HT)	LSRN SPer
	Miss Alice = 'Ausjake'PBR (S)	LRHS LSRN MAus MBri SWCr
	'Miss Edith Cavell' (Poly)	MAus
§	'Mister Lincoln' (HT)	MBri SPer
	Mistress Quickly = 'Ausky'PBR (S)	MAus
§	Misty Hit = 'Poulhi011'PBR (PatioHit Series) (Patio)	ECnt LRHS LSRN LStr SWCr
	Molineux = 'Ausmol'PBR (S) 🏆H4	EBee EPfP IBoy LRHS MAsh MAus MBri SWCr
	Moment in Time = 'Korcastrav' **new**	ECnt LStr
	Monsieur Pélisson	see *R.* 'Pélisson'
	Moody Blue = 'Fryniche' (HT)	EBee ECnt ELon ESty GCoc IBoy MRav SMrm
	Moonbeam = 'Ausbeam' (S)	MAus
	'Moonlight' (HM)	CSam CTri EBee ELan EWTr LRHS MAus MRav SMrm SPer SPoG SWCr
	Moonshine = 'Tan97123'PBR (HT)	ESty
	'Morgengruss' (Cl)	SPer SWCr
	'Morletii' (Bs)	MMuc MRav
	'Morning Jewel' (ClF) 🏆H4	GCoc SPer SWCr
	Morning Mist = 'Ausfire' (S)	LRHS MAus SSea WCot
§	'Morsdag' (Poly/F)	LSRN LStr SVic
	Mortimer Sackler = 'Ausorts'PBR (S)	CWSG LAst LRHS MAsh MAus MBri SCoo
	moschata (Ra)	MAus MRav NLar SSea
	- 'Autumnalis'	see *R.* 'Princesse de Nassau'
	- var. ***nepalensis***	see *R. brunonii*
	Mother's Day	see *R.* 'Morsdag'
I	'Mother's Day'	SRGP
	Mother's Joy = 'Horsiltrop' (F)	LSRN
	Mountain Snow = 'Aussnow' (Ra)	LRHS MAus MBri
	Mountbatten = 'Harmantelle' (F) 🏆H4	ELan EPfP LBuc LStr MAsh MAus MBri MRav NPri SPer SPoG SSea SWCr
§	'Mousseline' (DPoMo)	CPou EWTr MAus MCot NLar SFam SPer
	'Mousseuse du Japon'	see *R.* 'Japonica'
	moyesii (S)	CDoy CTri ELan EWTr GCra MAus NEgg NWea SKHP SPer
	'Mr Bluebird' (MinCh)	MAus
	'Mr Lincoln'	see *R.* 'Mister Lincoln'
	'Mrs Anthony Waterer' (Ru)	EBee MAus SPer
	Mrs Doreen Pike = 'Ausdor'PBR (Ru)	LRHS MAus
	'Mrs Honey Dyson' (Ra)	CPou EBee EWTr
	'Mrs John Laing' (HP)	EPfP LRHS MAus NLar SFam SLon SPer SWCr
	'Mrs Oakley Fisher' (HT)	EBee EWTr MAus MCot SDix SMad SMrm SPer SWCr
	'Mrs Paul' (Bb)	MAus
	'Mrs Sam McGredy' (HT)	CPou LRHS NEgg SSea
	'Mullard Jubilee' (HT)	SWCr
§	***mulliganii*** (Ra) 🏆H4	EPfP GKin MAus SPer SWCr
	multibracteata (S)	MAus
	multiflora (Ra)	LBuc MAus
§	- var. ***cathayensis*** (Ra)	WBor
§	- 'Grevillei' (Ra)	SPer
	- 'Platyphylla'	see *R. multiflora* 'Grevillei'
	- wild-collected	GCal
	Mum in a MillionPBR	see *R.* Millie
	MummyPBR	see *R.* Newly Wed
	Mum's Blessing = 'Guesimage' (F)	SWCr
	mundi	see *R. gallica* 'Versicolor'
	Munstead Wood = 'Ausbernard'PBR (S)	ESty LRHS LSRN MAsh MAus SSea
	'Muscosa Alba'	see *R.* × *centifolia* 'Shailer's White Moss'
	'Mutabilis'	see *R.* × *odorata* 'Mutabilis'
	My Everything = 'Coccastle'PBR (F)	ESty GCoc
	My Girl = 'Tan00798'PBR (HT) **new**	ESty
	'My Joy' (HT)	LSRN
	My Mum = 'Webmorrow'PBR (F)	ESty GCoc LBuc LSRN SWCr
	My Valentine = 'Mormyval' (Min)	LSRN MAsh SPoG SWCr
	Myriam = 'Cocgrand' (HT)	GCoc LSRN

	Mystery Girl = 'Dicdothis'[PBR] (HT)	EBee ECnt ELon ESty GCoc IDic LBuc
	Nahéma = 'Deléri' (ClHT)	SWCr
	Nancy = 'Poulninga'[PBR] (Renaissance Series) (S)	CPou EBee LSRN
	'Narrow Water' (Ra)	CPou NLar SWCr
§	'Nastarana' (N)	EWTr NLar
	'Nathalie Nypels'	see *R.* 'Mevrouw Nathalie Nypels'
	'National Trust' (HT)	CBcs CTri IArd IBoy MAsh SPer
	'Nestor' (G)	EBee MAus
	'Nevada' (S) ♀H4	CSBt CTri ECnt ELan EPfP EWTr GCoc IArd IBoy LRHS LStr MAus MRav NLar SPer SSea SWCr WKif
	Never Forgotten = 'Gregart' (HT)	LSRN
	New Arrival	see *R.* 'Red Patio'
	New Beginnings = 'Korprofko'[PBR] (F)	GCoc
§	'New Dawn' (Cl) ♀H4	Widely available
	'New Home'	LSRN
	New Life = 'Cocwarble'[PBR] (F)	GCoc
	New Zealand = 'Macgenev'[PBR] (HT)	SWCr
§	Newly Wed = 'Dicwhynot'[PBR] (Patio)	IDic LBuc LStr
	News = 'Legnews' (F)	MAus SWCr
	Nice Day = 'Chewsea'[PBR] (ClMin) ♀H4	CGro ELon EPfP ESty IBoy LRHS LStr MRav MWat SBfd SPer SPoG SWCr
	'Nicola' (F)	LSRN
	Night Light = 'Poullight'[PBR] (Courtyard Series) (Cl)	ECnt MRav
	Night Sky = 'Dicetch'[PBR] (F)	IDic
	Nina = 'Mehnina'[PBR] (S)	LSRN SWCr WBor
	Nina = 'Poulren018'[PBR] (Renaissance Series) (S)	ECnt
	nitida	LRHS MAus NWea SEND SLPl SPer WHer
	Noble Antony = 'Ausway'[PBR] (S)	CWSG LRHS LStr MAus MBri SSea
§	'Noisette Carnée' (N)	CSam EBee EPfP EWTr GCra LRHS LStr MBNS MBri MCot MRav NLar SLPl SPer SSea SWCr
	Norfolk = 'Poulfolk'[PBR] (GC)	CTri ESty NLar SMrm SPer
	'Northern Lights' (HT)	GCoc
	'Norwich Pink' (S)	MAus
	Nostalgia = 'Savarita' (Min)	MAsh MAus
	Nostalgie = 'Taneiglat'[PBR] (HT)	CSBt ECnt ELon ESty GCoc LStr MBri MRav SPoG SSea SWCr
	'Nozomi' (ClMin/GC) ♀H4	CGro CTri ELan EPfP ESty GCoc MAus MRav NLar SMrm SPer
	'Nuits de Young' (CeMo) ♀H4	GCoc LRHS MAus MBri SEND SFam SKHP WHer
	'Nur Mahal' (HM)	MAus
	Nurse Tracey Davies = 'Frykookie'[PBR] (F)	ESty
	nutkana (S)	MAus
§	- 'Plena' (S/D) ♀H4	EPfP EWTr GCoc NLar SKHP WHer
	'Nymphenburg' (HM)	EBee SPer
	'Nyveldt's White' (Ru)	MAus
	Octavia Hill = 'Harzeal'[PBR] (F)	CWSG EBee EWTr MRav NLar SPer SWCr
§	× ***odorata***	SVic
	- 'Fortune's Double Yellow'	see *R.* × *odorata* 'Pseudindica'
§	- 'Mutabilis' (Ch) ♀H3-4	CPou CRHN EBee ECre EPfP EWTr GBin GCoc LRHS MAus MCot MRav SEND SKHP SMrm SPer SPoG SSea SWCr WCFE WCot WKif XSen
§	- 'Pallida' (Ch)	EPfP LRHS MCot MRav SPer SSea SWCr WBor
§	- 'Pseudindica' (ClCh)	MAus
§	- Sanguinea Group (Ch)	XSen
	- - 'Bengal Crimson' (Ch)	EPfP EWTr LPla LRHS LSRN SKHP SLon SPoG WCot WKif
	- - 'Bob's Beauty' (Ch)	WCot
§	- 'Viridiflora' (Ch)	CPou EBee LRHS MAus SLon SMad SPer SSea WCot WHer
	Odyssey = 'Franski'[PBR] (F)	ESty SWCr
	'Oeillet Flamand'	see *R.* 'Oeillet Parfait'
§	'Oeillet Parfait' (G)	MAus
	officinalis	see *R. gallica* var. *officinalis*
	old blush China	see *R.* × *odorata* 'Pallida'
	old cabbage	see *R.* × *centifolia*
	Old John = 'Dicwillynilly' (F)	IDic
	old pink moss rose	see *R.* × *centifolia* 'Muscosa'
	Old Port = 'Mackati'[PBR] (F)	ESty IArd
	old red moss	see *R.* 'Henri Martin'
	old velvet moss	see *R.* 'William Lobb'
	'Old Velvet Rose'	see *R.* 'Tuscany'
	old yellow Scotch (SpH)	see *R.* × *harisonii* 'Williams Double Yellow'
	Olivia = 'Wekquahofa' (HT)	LSRN
	Olympic Spirit = 'Peaprince' (F)	LRHS MAsh
	'Omar Khayyám' (D)	MAus MRav
	omeiensis	see *R. sericea* subsp. *omeiensis*
	Open Arms = 'Chewpixcel'[PBR] (ClMin) ♀H4	ESty MAus SMad SMrm SPer SSea SWCr
	'Ophelia' (HT)	LRHS MAus
	'Orange Sensation' (F)	CTri MAus
§	Orange Sunblaze = 'Meijikatar'[PBR] (Min)	CSBt SPer
	Oranges and Lemons = 'Macoranlem'[PBR] (S/F)	CGro CSBt ELan ESty IBoy LBuc LStr MAsh MAus SPoG SSea SWCr
	Othello = 'Auslo'[PBR] (S)	MAus SPer
	'Our Beth' (S)	LSRN
	Our George = 'Kirrush' (Patio)	LSRN
	Our Jubilee = 'Coccages' (HT)	ESty LBuc SVic
	Our Molly = 'Dicreason' (GC/S)	IDic LSRN SWCr
	Oxfordshire = 'Korfullwind'[PBR] (GC) ♀H4	LStr MRav MWat
	Paddy Stephens = 'Macclack'[PBR] (HT)	SWCr
	Painted Moon = 'Dicpaint' (HT)	ESty
	Panache = 'Poultop'[PBR] (Patio/Min)	ECnt IBoy LStr SWCr
	'Papa Gontier' (T)	MAus
	Papa Meilland = 'Meisar' (HT)	CSBt GCoc MAus SPer
	Paper Anniversary (Patio)	LSRN
	Papi Delbard = 'Delaby' (ClHT)	ESty MRav
§	'Para Ti' (Min)	MAus SPer
I	'Parade' (Cl) ♀H4	MAus MRav SMad SWCr
	'Parkdirektor Riggers' (F)	CSam LStr MAus MBri NLar SPer SWCr
	Parson's pink China	see *R.* × *odorata* 'Pallida'
	Partridge = 'Korweirim' (GC)	MAus
	Pascali = 'Lenip' (HT)	CTri GCoc IBoy LBuc MAus MBri SPer

	Pat Austin = 'Ausmum'PBR (S) ♀H4	CSBt CTri EBee ELon EPfP IBoy LRHS LSRN LStr LTen MAus MBNS MBri MRav MWat NEgg NLar SEND SPer SPoG SWCr
	Patricia = 'Korpatri' (F)	SWCr
	'Paul Lédé' (ClT)	see *R.* 'Climbing Paul Lédé'
	Paul McCartneyPBR (HT)	see *R.* The McCartney Rose
	'Paul Neyron' (HP)	EWTr MAus MCot SPer
	'Paul Noël' (Ra)	MAus
	'Paul Ricault' (Ce × HP)	MAus
	Paul Shirville = 'Harqueterwife'PBR (HT) ♀H4	ELan ELon MAus SPer SWCr
	'Paul Transon' (Ra) ♀H4	CPou CRHN EBee EPfP LRHS MBri MMuc NEgg NLar SEND SPer SRGP SWCr WHer
	'Paulii Rosea' (Ru/GC)	MAus
	'Paul's Himalayan Musk' (Ra) ♀H3-4	CPLG CRHN CSBt CSam CTri ECnt EPfP EWTr GKin IArd IBoy LRHS LStr MAus MBri MCot MRav NEgg NLar SEND SFam SMad SMrm SPer SPoG SRGP SSea SWCr WKif
§	'Paul's Lemon Pillar' (ClHT)	LAst LRHS MAus NLar SMrm SSea
	'Paul's Scarlet Climber' (Cl/Ra)	CGro ELan IBoy LAst LStr MAus MRav NPri SEND SPer SRGP
	'Pax' (HM)	CPou MAus WKif
	Peace = 'Madame A. Meilland' (HT) ♀H4	CSBt CTri ECnt ELan EPfP ESty GCoc IBoy LRHS LSRN LStr MAsh MAus MRav MWat NEgg NPri SMrm SPer SPoG SRGP SSea SWCr
	Peacekeeper = 'Harbella'PBR (F)	CSBt
	Peach Blossom = 'Ausblossom' (S)	MAus
	'Peach Grootendorst' (Ru)	CPou
§	Pearl Abundance = 'Harfrisky'PBR (F)	ESty SWCr
	Pearl Anniversary = 'Whitston'PBR (Min/Patio)	CSBt ESty LSRN LStr MRav SPoG SWCr
	Pearl Drift = 'Leggab' (S)	EBee MAus MCot MWat SMrm SPer SWCr
	Pearl = 'Korterschi'PBR (F)	MAsh MRav SWCr
	Pearl = 'Wekpearl' (HT) **new**	MAsh
	Peaudouce	see *R.* Elina
§	Peek-a-boo = 'Dicgrow' (Min/Patio)	SPer
	Peer Gynt = 'Korol' (HT)	SWCr
	Pegasus = 'Ausmoon'PBR (S)	MAus
§	'Pélisson' (CeMo)	SFam
§	***pendulina***	LBuc MAus
	'Penelope' (HM) ♀H4	CSBt CSam CTri EBee ECnt ELan EPfP EWTr GCoc IBoy LRHS LSRN LStr MAsh MAus MBri MCot MRav MWat NLar NPri SEND SFam SMad SPer SRGP SSea SWCr WKif
	Penny Lane = 'Hardwell'PBR (ClHT) ♀H4	CSBt ECnt ELon EPfP ESty GCoc IBoy LAst LRHS LStr MAus MBri MRav MWat NLar SCoo SPer SPoG SSea SWCr
	× ***penzanceana***	see *R.* 'Lady Penzance'
	Peppermint SplashPBR	see *R.* Rachel Louise Moran
	Perception = 'Harzippee'PBR (HT)	SWCr
	Perdita = 'Ausperd' (S)	ESty LRHS MAus
	Perennial Blue = 'Mehr9601' (Ra)	ESty MRav SSea SWCr
	Perennial Blush = 'Mehbarbie'PBR (Ra)	ESty MRav SWCr
§	Perfect Day = 'Poulrem' (F)	EBee ECnt
	'Perle des Jardins' (T)	MAus
§	'Perle d'Or' (Poly) ♀H4	EBee LRHS MAus MMuc NLar SDix SLon SMad SPer
	Perpetually Yours = 'Harfable'PBR (Cl)	CGro LStr MRav MWat SCoo
	Persian yellow	see *R. foetida* 'Persiana'
	Peter Pan = 'Chewpan'PBR (Min)	MAus MWat SWCr
	Peter Pan = 'Sunpete' (Patio)	EPfP NPri SPoG
	'Petite de Hollande' (Ce)	MAus NLar SPer
	'Petite Lisette' (Ce × D)	MAus NLar
	'Petito' (F)	SMrm
	Phab Gold = 'Frybountiful'PBR (F)	ESty GCoc MAsh
	Pheasant = 'Kordapt'PBR (GC)	MAus SPer SWCr
	Phillipa = 'Poulheart'PBR (S)	LSRN
	Phoebe (Ru)	see *R.* 'Fimbriata'
	'Phyllis Bide' (Ra) ♀H4	EBee EPfP EWTr IArd LPot LRHS LStr MAus MBri MCot NLar SEND SPer SRGP SSea SWCr
	Piccadilly = 'Macar' (HT)	CGro CSBt CTri GCoc IBoy MBri MRav SPer SWCr
	Piccolo = 'Tanolokip' (F/Patio)	CGro ESty LStr SWCr
	'Picture' (HT)	MAus SPer
	Pigalle '84 = 'Meicloux' (F)	SWCr
	'Pilgrim'PBR	see *R.* The Pilgrim
	pimpinellifolia	see *R. spinosissima*
	- double yellow-flowered	see *R.* × *harisonii* 'Williams Double Yellow'
	- 'Harisonii'	see *R.* × *harisonii* 'Harison's Yellow'
	- 'Lutea'	see *R.* × *harisonii* 'Lutea Maxima'
	Pink Abundance = 'Harfrothy'PBR (Abundance Series) (F)	ESty LStr MAus
	'Pink Bouquet' (Ra)	CRHN
	'Pink Favorite' (HT)	SPer
	Pink Fizz = 'Poulycool' (ClPatio)	ECnt
§	Pink Flower Carpet = 'Noatraum'PBR (GC) ♀H4	CGro CSBt CTri ECnt ELan GCoc IBoy LRHS LStr MBri NPri SCoo SEND SPer SPoG SWCr
	'Pink Garnette'	see *R.* 'Carol Amling'
	'Pink Grootendorst' (Ru) ♀H4	EPfP LRHS MAus NEgg NLar SPer SWCr
§	Pink Hit = 'Poultipe'PBR (Min/Patio)	ECnt IBoy LRHS LSRN LStr SWCr
	Pink Knock Out = 'Radcon' (S)	MAsh
	'Pink Leda' (D)	EBee
	'Pink Medley' (F)	MBri
	pink moss	see *R.* × *centifolia* 'Muscosa'
	'Pink Parfait' (F)	SPer
	Pink Peace = 'Meibil' (HT)	IBoy SWCr
	Pink Perfection = 'Korpauvio'PBR (HT)	ESty
	'Pink Perpétué' (Cl)	CBcs CGro CSBt CTri ECnt ELan ELon EPfP GCoc IBoy LBuc LRHS LStr MAus MBri MRav SBfd SMrm SPer SPoG SSea SWCr
	'Pink Prosperity' (HM)	MAus
	Pirouette = 'Poulyc003'PBR (ClS)	ECnt SWCr
	'Plaisanterie' (HM)	MAus

	Name	Suppliers
	'Playboy' (F)	GCoc
	Playtime = 'Morplati' (F)	MAus
	Pleine de Grâce = 'Lengra' (S)	MAus
	Polar Star = 'Tanlarpost' (HT)	CSBt ECnt LBuc LStr MBri MRav MWat SPer SWCr
	× ***polliniana***	SLPl
	'Polly' (HT)	GCoc LSRN
§	'Polyantha Grandiflora' (Ra)	MAus
	'Pompon Blanc Parfait' (A)	MAus
	'Pompon de Paris' (ClMinCh)	see *R.* 'Climbing Pompon de Paris'
§	'Pompon de Paris' (MinCh)	SMrm WAbe
	'Pompon Panaché' (G)	MAus
	Pomponella = 'Korpompan'[PBR] (F) **new**	ESty
	Port Sunlight = 'Auslofty'[PBR] (HM)	IBoy LRHS MAus SSea
	Portland rose	see *R.* 'Portlandica'
§	'Portlandica' (Po)	CTri LRHS MAus SPer
	Portmeirion = 'Ausguard'[PBR] (S)	MAus SCoo
	Pot o' Gold = 'Dicdivine' (HT)	SPer SWCr
	Pour Toi	see *R.* 'Para Ti'
	prairie rose	see *R. setigera*
	'Precious Memories' (Min)	LSRN
	Precious Memories = 'Dichello'[PBR] (F)	ESty GCoc IDic
	'Precious Platinum' (HT)	MBri SPer
§	'Président de Sèze' (G) 𝕐H4	CPou CSam MAus NLar SFam SPer
	Pretty in Pink = 'Dicumpteen'[PBR] (GC)	ECnt IDic LBuc SWCr
	Pretty Jessica = 'Ausjess' (S)	CGro LRHS LSRN MAus MRav SMrm SPer
	Pretty Lady = 'Scrivo'[PBR] (F) 𝕐H4	MAus
	Pretty Polly = 'Meitonje'[PBR] (Min) 𝕐H4	CGro EPfP ESty IBoy LRHS LStr MBri MRav MWat SMrm SPer SPoG SWCr
	Pretty Sunrise = 'Meipelmel'[PBR] (S)	MAsh
	Pride of England = 'Harencore'[PBR] (HT)	GCoc
	Pride of Scotland = 'Macwhitba' (HT)	GCoc
	'Prima Ballerina' (HT)	CTri GCoc LStr MAsh SPer SPoG SSea
	primula (S) 𝕐H3-4	EShb GCoc MAus NLar SPer WBor
	'Prince Camille de Rohan' (HP)	EBee MAus
	'Prince Charles' (Bb)	MAus NLar WKif
	Prince Jardinier = 'Meitroni'[PBR] (HT) **new**	ESty
	Prince Regent = 'Genpen' (S)	SSea
	Princess Alexandra of Kent = 'Ausmerchant'[PBR] (S)	EPfP ESty LRHS MAus MBri SSea
	Princess Alexandra = 'Pouldra'[PBR] (Renaissance Series) (S)	CTri ECnt EPfP SMrm SWCr
	Princess Anne = 'Auskitchen' (S) **new**	LRHS MAsh MAus
	Princess = 'Korspobux'[PBR] (HT)	ECnt
	Princess Nobuko = 'Coclistine'[PBR] (HT)	GCoc
	'Princess of Wales' (HP)	EPfP
	Princess of Wales = 'Hardinkum'[PBR] (F) 𝕐H4	EPfP GCoc LStr MAsh MRav SCoo SPer SWCr
	Princess Royal = 'Dicroyal'[PBR] (HT)	IDic
§	'Princesse de Nassau' (Ra)	MAus SEND SKHP
	'Princesse Louise' (Ra)	CRHN MAus SFam
	'Princesse Marie' misapplied	see *R.* 'Belvedere'
	'Pristine' (HT)	MAus
§	'Professeur Emile Perrot' (D)	SMad
	'Prolifera de Redouté' misapplied	see *R.* 'Duchesse de Montebello'
	Proper Job = 'Tan02733' (HT)	CWSG SWCr
	'Prosperity' (HM) 𝕐H4	CSam CTri EBee EPfP GCoc LRHS MAus MCot MRav NLar SLon SMrm SPer SWCr
	Prospero = 'Auspero' (S)	MAus NLar SEND
	Pure Bliss = 'Dictator'[PBR] (HT)	ELon IDic SWCr
	Pure Gold = 'Harhappen'[PBR] (F)	CSBt
	'Purezza' (Ra)	NLar
	Purple Skyliner = 'Franwekpurp'[PBR] (ClS)	ESty
	Purple Tiger = 'Jacpurr'[PBR] (F)	ESty IDic LStr SMrm SSea SWCr
	Quaker Star = 'Dicperhaps' (F)	IDic
	quatre saisons	see *R.* × *damascena* var. *semperflorens*
	Queen Elizabeth	see *R.* 'The Queen Elizabeth'
	Queen Mother = 'Korquemu'[PBR] (Patio) 𝕐H4	CSBt ELan GCoc LStr MAus MRav SPer SPoG SWCr
	'Queen of Bourbons' (Bb)	MAus NLar
	Queen of Denmark	see *R.* 'Königin von Dänemark'
	Queen of Sweden = 'Austiger'[PBR] (S)	EBee ECnt LRHS MAus MBri SMrm SPer SWCr
	'Rachel' (HT)	LSRN
§	Rachel Louise Moran = 'Jacdrama'[PBR] (HT)	ESty
	Rachel = 'Tangust'[PBR] (HT)	CSBt ESty LStr MRav SPoG SWCr
	Racy Lady = 'Dicwaffle'[PBR] (HT)	IDic
	Radio Times = 'Aussal'[PBR] (S)	MAus
	Rainbow Magic = 'Dicxplosion'[PBR] (Patio)	IDic
	'Rambling Rector' (Ra) 𝕐H4	Widely available
	Rambling Rosie = 'Horjasper'[PBR] (Ra)	CGro EBee ECnt EPfP ESty GCoc LSRN MAus SWCr WBor
	'Ramona' (Ra)	SWCr
	'Raspberry Royale' (F/Patio)	LRHS
	'Raubritter' ('Macrantha' hybrid)	EPfP LRHS MAsh MAus MMuc SPer SWCr
	Ray of Hope = 'Cocnilly'[PBR] (F)	GCoc
	Ray of Sunshine = 'Cocclare'[PBR] (Patio)	GCoc
	Raymond Blanc = 'Delnado' (HT)	MRav SLon
	'Raymond Carver' (S)	MCot
	'Raymond Chenault' (S)	CGro SWCr
	Rebecca (Patio)	ESty LSRN
	'Rebecca Claire' (HT)	LSRN

Rebecca Mary = 'Dicjury'PBR (F) IDic
Reconciliation = 'Hartillery'PBR (HT) MBri SWCr
Red AbundancePBR see R. Songs of Praise
Red Blanket = 'Intercell' (S/GC) LAst MAus SPer
Red Coat = 'Auscoat' (F) MAus
Red Devil = 'Dicam' (HT) ESty GCoc IBoy MAsh MBri SCoo SPoG
Red Eden Rose = 'Meidrason'PBR (Cl) ESty SSea SWCr
Red Finesse = 'Korvillade'PBR (F) ECnt MAsh
'Red Grootendorst' see R. 'F.J. Grootendorst'
'Red Max Graf' see R. Rote Max Graf
Red Medley = 'Noapu'PBR (Min) MBri
red moss see R. 'Henri Martin'
Red New Dawn see R. 'Étendard'
§ 'Red Patio' (F/Patio) LSRN
Red Rascal = 'Jacbed'PBR (S/Patio) CSBt ELon IDic
red rose of Lancaster see R. gallica var. officinalis
Redouté = 'Auspale'PBR (S) LRHS MAus
Reflections = 'Simref' (F) SWCr
Regensberg = 'Macyoumis'PBR (F/Patio) IBoy MAus SPer SWCr
'Reine des Centfeuilles' (Ce) SFam
'Reine des Violettes' (HP) CPou CWSG ELon EPfP IArd LRHS LStr MAsh MAus MBri MRav MWat NLar SPer SRGP SWCr
§ 'Reine Victoria' (Bb) EBee EPfP IBoy LRHS LStr MAus MBri MRav SPer SWCr
Remember Me = 'Cocdestin' (HT) ♀H4 CGro CSBt CWSG ECnt ESty GCoc IArd IBoy LSRN LStr MAus MBri MGos MRav NEgg NPri SPer SPoG SWCr
§ Remember = 'Poulht001'PBR (HT) ECnt EPfP LRHS MAsh SWCr
Remembrance = 'Harxampton'PBR (F) ♀H4 CTri CWSG ESty GCoc LBuc LSRN LStr MAsh MRav NPri SPer SPoG SSea SWCr
§ Renaissance = 'Harzart'PBR (HT) CSBt ELon GCoc LStr MRav SWCr
'René André' (Ra) CPou CRHN EBee MAus NLar
'René d'Anjou' (CeMo) LRHS MAus
'Rescht' see R. 'De Resht'
'Rêve d'Or' (N) MAus MCot SLon SPer
'Réveil Dijonnais' (ClHT) MAus
Rhapsody in Blue = 'Frantasia'PBR (S) CGro CSBt CWSG EBee ECnt ELan ELon EPfP ESty GCoc IBoy LAst LRHS LStr MAsh MAus MBri MGos MRav MWat NPri SCoo SMad SMrm SPer SPoG SSea SWCr
§ × *richardii* GCoc MAus
Rick Stein = 'Tan96205'PBR (HT) LSRN LStr SWCr
'Rival de Paestum' (T) MAus
'River Gardens' NPer
Rob Roy = 'Cocrob' (F) GCoc SPer
Robbie Burns = 'Ausburn' (SpH) MAus
'Robert le Diable' (Ce × G) MAus NLar
Rock & Roll = 'Wekgobnez' (HT) new ESty
Rockabye Baby = 'Dicdwarf' (Patio) ESty IDic SWCr

'Roger Lambelin' (HP) MAus
Romance = 'Tanezamor'PBR (S) IBoy LSRN MRav
'Rosa Mundi' see R. gallica 'Versicolor'
Rosabell = 'Cocceleste'PBR (F/Patio) ESty GCoc
'Rose à Parfum de l'Haÿ' (Ru) CTri
'Rose de Meaux' see R. × centifolia 'De Meaux'
'Rose de Meaux White' see R. 'White de Meaux'
'Rose de Rescht' see R. 'De Resht'
Rose des Cisterciens = 'Delarle' (HT) ESty
'Rose des Maures' misapplied see R. 'Sissinghurst Castle'
'Rose du Maître d'Ecole' see R. 'Du Maître d'Ecole'
'Rose du Roi' (HP/DPo) ELon EWTr LRHS MAus
§ Rose Gaujard = 'Gaumo' (HT) LAst
Rose of Picardy = 'Ausfudge' (S) LRHS MAus MBri SSea
'Rose-Marie Viaud' (Ra) CPou CSam MAus MMuc
Rosemary Harkness = 'Harrowbond' (HT) ESty LStr MBri MRav SMrm SPer SRGP
'Rosemary Rose' (F) SPer
Rosemoor = 'Austough'PBR (S) CSBt LRHS MAsh MAus MBri SSea
'Roseraie de l'Haÿ' (Ru) ♀H4 Widely available
Roses des Cistercians = 'Deltisse' MRav
Rosie = 'Benros' (Min) LSRN
Rosy Cushion = 'Interall' (S/GC) ♀H4 EWTr GCoc MAsh MAus MCot SBfd SLon SPer
Rosy Future = 'Harwaderox' (F/Patio) SWCr
'Rosy Mantle' (ClHT) CSBt SPer SWCr
§ Rotary Sunrise = 'Fryglitzy' (HT) CSBt
§ Rote Max Graf = 'Kormax' (GC/Ru) CDul EPfP NLar
Rouge Royale = 'Meikarouz' (HT) ESty
roxburghii (S) CBcs EPfP LEdu MAus SKHP
- 'Plena' see R. roxburghii f. roxburghii
§ - f. ***roxburghii*** (d/S) MAus
'Royal Air Force' (HT) new SMrm
'Royal Albert Hall' (HT) GCoc
Royal CopenhagenPBR see R. Remember
'Royal Occasion' (F) SPer
Royal William = 'Korzaun'PBR (HT) ♀H4 CSBt ELan ELon EPfP ESty GCoc LSRN LStr MAsh MAus MBri MGos MRav SPer SSea SWCr
§ ***rubiginosa*** CArn CCVT CDul CRWN EPfP GPoy IFro LBuc MAus MRav NWea SFam SPer WMou
rubrifolia see R. glauca Pourr.
'Rubrotincta' see R. 'Hebe's Lip'
rubus (Ra) MAus
Ruby Anniversary = 'Harbonny'PBR (Patio) CSBt CWSG ESty LBuc LRHS LSRN LStr MRav MWat SCoo SPoG SSea SVic SWCr
Ruby Celebration = 'Peawinner'PBR (F) ESty MRav SWCr
Ruby Rambler = 'Chewrubyramb' (Ra) LBuc
Ruby Ruby see R. Ruby Slippers
§ Ruby Slippers = 'Weksactrumi' (Min) LRHS SPoG

'Ruby Wedding' (HT) CBcs CGro CSBt CTri CWSG ECnt ELan EPfP GCoc IArd IBoy LRHS LSRN LStr MAsh MAus MBri MGos MRav NPri SMrm SPer SPoG SSea SVic SWCr
'Ruby Wedding Anniversary' (F) LSRN
rugosa (Ru) CBar CDul CLnd CTri ECrN EPfP EPom LBuc LRHS MAus MBri MHer MRav NWea SBfd SGol SPlb SVic SWCr WMou
- 'Alba' (Ru) ♀H4 CBcs CCVT CDul CHab CTri EBee ECnt ELan EPfP GBin GCoc LAst LBuc LRHS LStr MAus MRav NWea SBfd SGol SMrm SPer SSea SVic SWCr WBor
- 'Rubra' (Ru) ♀H4 CBcs CCVT CHab CTri CWib EPfP GCoc LAst LBuc LStr SBfd SEWo SMrm SPer SPoG SSea SVic
'Rugosa Atropurpurea' (Ru) SBfd
Rushing Stream = 'Austream' (GC) MAus
'Russelliana' (Ra) MAus MMuc SFam WKif
Safe Haven = 'Jacreraz'[PBR] (F) IDic LBuc
Saint Alban = 'Auschesnut'[PBR] (S) MAus
Saint Boniface = 'Kormatt' (F/Patio) CSBt
Saint Cecilia = 'Ausmit'[PBR] (S) MAus
Saint Edmunds Rose[PBR] see *R.* Bonita
Saint John's rose see *R.* × *richardii*
'Saint Nicholas' (D) MAus
Saint Swithun = 'Auswith'[PBR] (S) EPfP LRHS MAsh MAus MBri SSea
'Salet' (DPMo) CPou MAus WHer
'Sally Holmes' (S) ♀H4 EBee ECnt EPfP EWTr GCoc LRHS MAus MRav MWat SEND SLon SMad SPer SSea SWCr
Sally Kane = 'Frygroovy'[PBR] (HT) CGro EBee ECnt MRav
Sally's Rose = 'Canrem' (HT) EBee ECnt GCoc LSRN
Salsa[PBR] see *R.* Cheek to Cheek
Salvation = 'Harlark'[PBR] (F) EBee ESty SWCr
§ Samaritan = 'Harverag'[PBR] (HT) CSBt ESty MRav SPoG SWCr
sambucina <u>**new**</u> WPGP
sancta see *R.* × *richardii*
'Sander's White Rambler' (Ra) ♀H4 CRHN CSam CTri EBee EPfP LRHS MAus MBri MRav NLar SPer SWCr
Sandra = 'Carsandra' EPfP SLon
Sandra = 'Koreinek'[PBR] (HT) <u>**new**</u> LSRN
Sandra = 'Poulen055'[PBR] (Renaissance Series) (S) LSRN
'Sanguinea' see *R.* × *odorata* Sanguinea Group
Sarah (HT) see *R.* Jardins de Bagatelle
'Sarah van Fleet' (Ru) CTri EBee EPfP GCoc IArd IBoy LRHS LStr MAus MBri MRav MWat NEgg NLar SPer
Sarah, Duchess of York[PBR] see *R.* Sunseeker
Savoy Hotel = 'Harvintage'[PBR] (HT) ♀H4 ECnt GCoc LStr MAus MBri MRav SMrm SPer SPoG SWCr
'Scabrosa' (Ru) ♀H4 ECnt EPfP GCoc LRHS MAsh MAus NLar SLon SPer SPoG
Scarborough Fair = 'Ausoran' (S) MAus
Scarlet Fire see *R.* 'Scharlachglut'
Scarlet Glow see *R.* 'Scharlachglut'
Scarlet Hit = 'Poulmo'[PBR] (PatioHit Series) (Min/Patio) ECnt IBoy LRHS LSRN LStr SWCr
Scarlet Patio = 'Kortingle'[PBR] (Patio) ESty MWat SSea
Scarlet Queen Elizabeth = 'Dicel' (F) CBcs LBuc MRav
'Scented Air' (F) SPer
Scented Carpet = 'Chewground'[PBR] (GC) ECnt MAus SWCr
Scented Memory = 'Poulht002'[PBR] (HT) ECnt
Scentimental = 'Wekplapep'[PBR] (F) ESty LRHS LStr MAsh MRav SCoo SSea SWCr
Scent-sation = 'Fryromeo'[PBR] (HT) CWSG ELon GCoc LRHS LStr MAsh MRav SCoo SPoG SWCr
Scepter'd Isle = 'Ausland'[PBR] (S) ♀H4 CSBt LRHS MAus MBri SCoo SPer SSea SWCr
§ 'Scharlachglut' (ClS) ♀H4 CPou EPfP SPer
Schneewittchen see *R.* Iceberg
§ 'Schneezwerg' (Ru) ♀H4 GCoc MAus MRav NLar SPer SSea SWCr
'Schoolgirl' (ClHT) CBcs CTri CWSG ELan ELon EPfP GCoc IBoy LAst LBuc LRHS LStr MRav MWat NEgg SPer SPoG SSea SWCr
'Scintillation' (S/GC) MAus
Scotch rose see *R.* ***spinosissima***
Scotch yellow (SpH) see *R.* × *harisonii* 'Williams Double Yellow'
'Seagull' (Ra) ♀H4 CGro CTri CWSG EBee ECnt EPfP ESty IBoy LAst LRHS LSRN LStr MAus MRav MWat NLar NWea SLon SMad SMrm SPer SPoG SWCr WHer
'Seale Pink Diamond' (S) SSea
'Sealing Wax' (*moyesii* hybrid) NLar
'Semiplena' see *R.* × *alba* 'Alba Semiplena'
sericea (S) MAus
- var. ***morrisonensis*** B&SWJ 7139 WCru
§ - subsp. ***omeiensis*** BWJ 7550 WCru
- - f. ***pteracantha*** (S) CBcs CDul CSBt ELan EPfP EWTr GCoc LRHS LTen MAus MRav NLar NSti NWea SPer SSea
- - - 'Atrosanguinea' (S) CArn
§ ***setigera*** MAus
setipoda (S) MAus
seven sisters rose see *R. multiflora* 'Grevillei'
Seventh Heaven = 'Fryfantasy'[PBR] (HT) GCoc SWCr
Sexy Rexy = 'Macrexy' (F) ♀H4 CGro EPfP ESty GCoc IBoy LSRN LStr MAsh MAus MBri MRav SMrm SPer SPoG SRGP SWCr
'Shailer's White Moss' see *R.* × *centifolia* 'Shailer's White Moss'
Sharifa Asma = 'Ausreef'[PBR] (S) CSBt ELan ELon EWTr LRHS LStr MAus MBri MRav NEgg NLar SLon SMrm SPer SWCr
Sheila's Perfume = 'Harsherry' (F) CGro ECnt ESty GCoc IBoy LRHS LSRN LStr MAsh MRav SPer SPoG SWCr
Shine On = 'Dictalent'[PBR] (Patio) ♀H4 CSBt ECnt ESty IBoy IDic LBuc LStr MBri MWat SPoG SWCr

	Name	Suppliers
	Shining Light = 'Cocshimmer'PBR (Patio)	GCoc MRav SCoo
	Shocking Blue = 'Korblue' (F)	SPer
	Shona = 'Dicdrum' (F)	IDic
	Showmee Sunshine = 'Kenveron' (GC) **new**	ESty
	Showtime = 'Baitime' (ClS)	MAsh
§	Shrimp Hit = 'Poulshrimp'PBR (Patio)	ECnt LStr
	'Shropshire Lass' (S)	MAus
	Silver Anniversary ambig.	LSRN SBfd
	Silver Anniversary = 'Jaclav' (HT) **new**	MBri
§	Silver Anniversary = 'Poulari'PBR (HT) ♀H4	CGro CSBt CTri CWSG ECnt ELan GCoc LRHS LSRN LStr MAsh MAus MGos MRav MWat NPri SCoo SMrm SPer SPoG SSea SVic SWCr
	Silver Ghost = 'Kormifari'PBR (S)	MAsh
	'Silver Jubilee' (HT) ♀H4	CGro EPfP GCoc IArd IBoy LBuc LRHS LStr MAsh MAus MBri MRav SPer SPoG SVic SWCr
	'Silver Lining' (HT)	ELon MBri SRGP
	'Silver Wedding' (HT)	ELan GCoc IArd MAus MRav NEgg SMrm SPer SVic SWCr WBor
	'Silver Wedding Celebration' (F)	CTri ESty
	Silver WishesPBR	see *R.* Pink Hit
	Simba = 'Korbelma' (HT)	LSRN
	'Simplex Multiflora'	CWib
	Simply Heaven = 'Diczombie'PBR (HT)	ESty GCoc IDic MBri
§	Simply the Best = 'Macamster'PBR (HT)	CGro CSBt CWSG ECnt ELan ELon ESty GCoc LSRN LStr MAsh MAus MBri MGos MRav MWat NPri SCoo SMrm SPer SPoG SWCr
	sinowilsonii	see *R. longicuspis* var. *sinowilsonii*
	'Sir Cedric Morris' (Ra)	NLar SSea
	Sir Clough = 'Ausclough' (S)	MAus
	Sir Edward Elgar = 'Ausprima'PBR (S)	MAus
I	'Sir Galahad' white-flowered (F)	MRav
	Sir John Betjeman = 'Ausvivid'PBR (S)	CWSG EPfP IBoy LRHS MAus
	'Sir Joseph Paxton' (Bb)	CPou MAus
	Sir Walter Raleigh = 'Ausspry' (S)	MAus MRav MWat SMrm
§	'Sissinghurst Castle' (G)	MAus
	Sister Elizabeth = 'Auspalette'PBR (S)	LSRN MAus MBri SCoo
	Skylark = 'Ausimple'PBR (S)	LRHS MAus MBri
	'Skyrocket'	see *R.* 'Wilhelm'
	Smarty = 'Intersmart' (S/GC)	MAus SPer
	Snow Carpet = 'Maccarpe' (Min/GC)	MAus
	'Snow Dwarf'	see *R.* 'Schneezwerg'
	Snow Goose = 'Auspom'PBR (ClS)	CSBt EPfP LRHS MAus MBri SSea
	Snow Hit = 'Poulsnows'PBR (Min/Patio)	ECnt SWCr
	'Snow Queen'	see *R.* 'Frau Karl Druschki'
	Snow Sunblaze = 'Meigovin' (Min)	CSBt
	Snowball = 'Macangeli' (Min/GC)	LSRN
	Snowcap = 'Harfleet'PBR (Patio)	ESty SMrm
	'Snowdon' (Ru)	LRHS MAus
	Soeur Emmanuelle = 'Delamo'PBR (S) **new**	MRav SLon SMrm
	'Soldier Boy' (Cl)	CPou SWCr
§	Solo Mio = 'Poulen002'PBR (Renaissance Series) (S)	CTri ECnt
§	'Sombreuil' (ClT)	EBee EPfP IArd LRHS MAus MBri MRav NEgg NLar SEND SPer SWCr
	Something Special = 'Macwyo'PBR (HT)	ESty SWCr
	Song and Dance = 'Frydishy'PBR (HT)	ESty GCoc SWCr
§	Songs of Praise = 'Harkimono'PBR (Abundance Series) (F)	ESty MAsh SWCr
	Sonia	see *R.* Sweet Promise
	'Sophia'PBR	see *R.* Solo Mio
	'Sophie's Perpetual' (ClCh)	CPou EWTr GCoc LRHS MAus SLon SPer SWCr WBor
	Sophy's Rose = 'Auslot'PBR (S)	LRHS LSRN MAus MBNS MBri NEgg NPri SMrm SPer SSea SWCr
	Sorbet Fruité = 'Meihestries'PBR (Cl) **new**	SSea
	soulieana (Ra/S) ♀H3-4	MAus
	'Soupert et Notting' (DPoMo)	CPou LRHS MAus MRav SPer
	'Southampton' (F) ♀H4	LSRN LStr MAsh MAus SPer SSea SWCr
	'Souvenir de Claudius Denoyel' (ClHT)	CPou SPer
	'Souvenir de Jeanne Balandreau' (HP)	CPou EBee
	'Souvenir de la Malmaison' (ClBb)	see *R.* 'Climbing Souvenir de la Malmaison'
	'Souvenir de la Malmaison' (Bb)	EPfP GCoc LRHS MAus MRav MWat NLar SPer
	'Souvenir de Madame Léonie Viennot' (ClT)	MAus MRav
	'Souvenir de Saint Anne's' (Bb)	MAus
	'Souvenir di Castagneto' (HP)	MRav
	'Souvenir du Docteur Jamain' (ClHP)	CPou CSBt EBee ELan ELon EPfP ESty EWTr GCoc LRHS LStr MAus MCot MRav NLar SFam SMrm SPer SPoG SSea SWCr WKif
	'Spanish Beauty'	see *R.* 'Madame Grégoire Staechelin'
	Sparkle = 'Frymerlin' (HT) **new**	ECnt ESty GCoc
	SparklerPBR	see *R.* Kent
	Sparkling Scarlet = 'Meihati' (ClF)	ELan
	Special Anniversary = 'Whastiluc'PBR (HT)	CGro CSBt EPfP ESty GCoc LRHS LSRN MAsh MRav MWat NPri SCoo SMrm SPoG SWCr
	Special Child = 'Taniripsa'PBR (F/Patio)	ECnt LStr MRav SSea SWCr
	Special Event = 'Meibrelon' (HT)	ESty
	Special Friend = 'Kirspec'PBR (Patio)	CWSG ESty GCoc LSRN LStr MWat SWCr
	Special Occasion = 'Fryyoung'PBR (HT)	ESty GCoc MRav SMrm SWCr
	Special Son (F)	ESty
	'Spectabilis' (Ra)	CPou EWTr SKHP
	SpellboundPBR	see *R.* Garden News

Name	Suppliers
Spice of Life = 'Diccheeky'PBR (F/Patio)	IDic
§ ***spinosissima***	CDul ECrN LBuc MAus NWea SGol SPer SSea WCot
- 'Andrewsii' ♀H4	MAus MRav
§ - double pink-flowered	SKHP WBor
§ - double white-flowered	ECha GCoc IGor MAus SSea
- 'Dunwich Rose'	CSam EPfP GCoc MAus NLar SKHP SPer WCot
- 'Falkland'	ECha GCra MAus
- 'Glory of Edzell'	MAus
- 'Marbled Pink'	MAus
- 'Mary, Queen of Scots'	MAus SRms
- 'Mrs Colville'	MAus
- 'Ormiston Roy'	MAus
- 'Single Cherry'	MAus SSea
- 'William III'	EWes GCra MAus SLPl
Spirit of Freedom = 'Ausbite'PBR (S)	ESty LRHS MAus MBri NEgg SSea
§ 'Splendens' (Ra)	SLPl
St Helena = 'Canlish' (F)	ECnt
'Stanwell Perpetual' (SpH)	CSam EPfP GCoc IBoy LStr MAus MRav MWat NLar SEND SFam SPer SSea SWCr WBor
Star Dust = 'Morstar' (Min) **new**	ELon
'Star Performer'PBR (ClPatio)	CSBt ECnt EPfP ESty SBfd SPoG SSea SWCr
Stardust = 'Peavandyke'PBR (Patio/F)	CPou ESty
Starlight Express = 'Trobstar'PBR (Cl)	IBoy LRHS MBri MRav SBfd SCoo SMrm SPer SPoG
Starry Eyed = 'Horcoexist' (Patio)	SWCr
'Stars 'n' Stripes' (Min)	MAus
Stella (HT)	GCoc LSRN
stellata	MAus
§ - var. ***mirifica***	MAus
Strawberries and Cream = 'Geestraw' (Min/Patio)	ELan ESty LBuc
Strawberry Fayre = 'Arowillip'PBR (Min/Patio)	ESty MRav SPoG
Strawberry Hill = 'Ausrimini'PBR (S)	CSBt EBee ECnt ESty LRHS MAus MBri SCoo SSea
Strike It Rich = 'Wekbepmey' (HT) **new**	GCoc
§ Sue Hipkin = 'Harzazz'PBR (HT)	ESty MRav SWCr
Suffolk = 'Kormixal'PBR (S/GC)	CGro CSBt ELan GCoc LStr MAus MRav SEND SPer SSea
Sugar and Spice = 'Peaallure'PBR (Patio)	SPoG
Sugar Baby = 'Tanabagus'PBR (Patio)	ESty SWCr
Sugar 'n' Spice = 'Tinspice' (Min)	MRav
Suma = 'Harsuma' (GC)	ESty SMrm
Summer Beauty = 'Kororbe'PBR (F)	ECnt ESty
Summer Fever = 'Tan99106' (Patio)	SWCr
Summer Fragrance = 'Tanfudermos'PBR (Castle Series) (HT)	ELon MBri
§ Summer Gold = 'Poulreb'PBR (F)	EBee ECnt ESty MAsh SWCr
Summer Love = 'Franluv' (F)	CBcs
Summer Song = 'Austango'PBR (S)	EPfP ESty IBoy LRHS MAus MBri SWCr
Summer Wine = 'Korizont'PBR (Cl) ♀H4	CSBt EBee ECnt EPfP LRHS MGos SCoo SPer SPoG SWCr
Summertime = 'Chewlarmoll'PBR (ClPatio)	CGro CSBt EBee ECnt ELan EPfP GCoc IBoy LRHS LStr MAus MRav MWat NPri SBfd SCoo SMrm SPer SPoG SSea
Sun Hit = 'Poulsun'PBR (PatioHit Series) (Min/Patio)	CSBt ECnt LRHS LStr MRav SWCr
'Sunblaze'PBR	see *R.* Orange Sunblaze
Sunblest = 'Landora' (HT)	MAsh MRav
Sunfire = 'Jacko' (F)	ECnt
Sunrise = 'Kormarter'PBR (S)	CGro EPfP ESty LBuc MWat SWCr
§ Sunseeker = 'Dicracer'PBR (F/Patio)	EPfP IDic MRav SPoG SWCr
Sunset Boulevard = 'Harbabble'PBR (F) ♀H4	ECnt GCoc LStr MAsh MAus MBri MRav SCoo SPer SWCr
Sunset CelebrationPBR	see *R.* Warm Wishes
Sunshine Abundance	SWCr
Super Dorothy = 'Heldoro' (Ra)	LSRN MAus SSea SWCr
Super Elfin = 'Helkleger'PBR (Ra) ♀H4	EBee LBuc LStr MAus MRav SMrm SPer SSea SWCr
Super Excelsa = 'Helexa' (Ra)	ESty IBoy LStr MAus SSea SWCr
Super Fairy = 'Helsufair'PBR (Ra)	EBee ECnt LStr MAus MRav SMad SPer SSea SWCr
Super Sparkle = 'Helfels'PBR (Ra)	LStr SSea
§ Super Star = 'Tanorstar' (HT)	GCoc LStr MAus MRav MWat SWCr
Super Trouper = 'Fryleyeca' (F)	CSBt ECnt ESty GCoc IBoy LStr MAsh MRav SCoo SWCr
'Surpasse Tout' (G)	MAus
Surprise = 'Presur'PBR (HT)	SWCr
Surrey = 'Korlanum'PBR (GC) ♀H4	CSBt CTri EBee ELan EPfP ESty GCoc LSRN LStr MAus MRav MWat NLar SPer SSea SWCr
Susan = 'Poulsue' (S)	ECnt LSRN SLon SWCr
Susan Williams-Ellis = 'Ausquirk' (S) **new**	LRHS MAsh MAus
Sussex = 'Poulave'PBR (GC)	CSBt GCoc LStr MRav SMrm SPer SSea SWCr
Swan = 'Auswhite' (S)	MAus
Swan Lake = 'Macmed' (Cl)	CPou EBee ECnt ELan EPfP IBoy LBuc LStr MRav NLar NPri SMrm SPer SWCr
Swany = 'Meiburenac' (Min/GC) ♀H4	ESty LSRN MAus SPer SWCr
'Sweet Ballymaloe' **new**	IBoy
Sweet Caroline = 'Micaroline' (Min)	LSRN
Sweet Child of Mine (HT) **new**	CWSG
Sweet Dream = 'Fryminicot'PBR (Patio) ♀H4	CGro CSBt CTri ECnt ELan EPfP ESty GCoc IBoy LAst LSRN LStr MAus MBri MRav MWat NPri SMad SMrm SPer SPoG SRGP SSea SWCr
'Sweet Fairy' (Min)	CSBt NMen
Sweet Haze = 'Tan97274'PBR (F)	CSBt EPfP ESty GCoc IBoy LRHS LStr MAsh MRav SCoo SPer SWCr
Sweet Juliet = 'Ausleap'PBR (S)	CSBt ECnt ESty IBoy LRHS MAus SMrm SPer SWCr

	Name	Suppliers
*	'Sweet Lemon Dream' (Patio)	CTri
	Sweet Magic = 'Dicmagic'PBR (Min/Patio) ♀H4	CGro CTri ELon EPfP IBoy IDic LBuc LRHS LStr MRav NPri SPoG
	Sweet Memories = 'Whamemo' (Patio)	CTri ECnt ELon EPfP ESty IBoy LRHS LStr MRav SCoo SMrm SPer SPoG SWCr
	Sweet Parfum de Provence = 'Meiclusif'PBR (HT)	ESty
	Sweet PrettyPBR	see *R.* The Charlatan
§	Sweet Promise = 'Meihelvet' (GC)	SPer
	Sweet Remembrance = 'Kirr' (HT)	LStr SCoo
	'Sweet Revelation'PBR	see *R.* Sue Hipkin
	Sweet Symphonie = 'Meibarke'PBR (Patio)	LAst
	'Sweet Wonder' (Patio)	EPfP MBri SPoG
N	Sweetheart = 'Cocapeer' (HT)	GCoc
	'Sweetie' (Patio)	ESty SWCr
	sweginzowii	MAus
	'Sydonie' (HP)	CPou EBee
	'Sylvia Dot' (F)	LSRN
	'Sympathie' (ClHT)	MGos SPer SSea SWCr
	Tall Story = 'Dickooky' (F) ♀H4	EBee MRav SWCr
	Tam O'Shanter = 'Auscerise' (S)	LRHS MAus
	Tamora = 'Austamora' (S)	MAus
	Tango Showground = 'Chewpattens'PBR (GC)	SSea
	Tatoo = 'Poulyc002'PBR (ClPatio)	EBee
	Tatton = 'Fryentice'PBR (F)	ESty MAus MRav SMrm SWCr
	Tawny Tiger = 'Frygolly'PBR (F)	CGro GCoc SWCr
	Tea Clipper = 'Ausrover'PBR (S)	CSBt ESty LRHS MAsh MAus MBri SCoo SSea
	Tear Drop = 'Dicomo'PBR (Min/Patio)	IBoy IDic LBuc LStr SMrm SPer SWCr
	Teasing Georgia = 'Ausbaker'PBR (S)	EBee ECnt EPfP ESty IBoy LRHS LSRN MAus MBri SCoo SSea SWCr
	Temptress = 'Korramal' (ClS)	EPfP SBfd
	Tenacious = 'Macblackpo'PBR (F)	ESty LStr SWCr
	Tequila Sunrise = 'Dicobey'PBR (HT) ♀H4	CGro CTri ELan EPfP ESty IBoy IDic LStr MAsh MAus MBri MRav SMrm SPer SSea SWCr
§	Terracotta = 'Meicobuis' (HT)	ESty SWCr
	Tess of the d'Urbervilles = 'Ausmove'PBR (S)	ESty IBoy LRHS LStr MAus MBri NEgg SCoo SPer SWCr
	'Tessa' (F)	LSRN
	Thank You = 'Chesdeep'PBR (Patio)	ESty LBuc LStr SMrm SWCr
§	That's Jazz = 'Poulnorm'PBR (Courtyard Series) (ClF)	ECnt MWat SWCr
	The Alexandra Rose = 'Ausday'PBR (S)	LRHS MAus SEND SSea
	The Alnwick RosePBR	see *R.* Alnwick Castle
I	'The Anniversary Rose' **new**	MAsh
	The Attenborough Rose = 'Dicelope'PBR (F)	IDic
	'The Bishop' (Ce × G)	MAus
	'The Bishop of Bradford' (ClPiH)	EBee ECnt
§	The Charlatan = 'Meiguimov'PBR (S)	MAsh
	The Compass Rose = 'Korwisco'PBR (S)	EPfP
	The Countryman = 'Ausman'PBR (S)	LRHS LStr MAus SSea
	The Dark Lady = 'Ausbloom'PBR (S)	LAst MAus MBri NEgg SPer
	'The Ednaston Rose' (Cl)	WHil
§	'The Fairy' (Poly) ♀H4	CSBt CTri EBee ECnt ELan EPfP EWTr GCoc IBoy LRHS LStr MAus MRav MWat NLar SBfd SEND SMad SMrm SPer SPoG SSea SWCr WCFE
	'The Garland' (Ra) ♀H4	CRHN EBee EPfP LRHS MAus MBri MMuc NLar SFam SPer SWCr
	The Generous Gardener = 'Ausdrawn'PBR (S)	CWSG EPfP LRHS MAus MBri SCoo SPer SSea SWCr
§	The Gold Award Rose = 'Poulac008' (Palace Series) (Patio)	ECnt
	The Herbalist = 'Aussemi' (S)	LRHS MAus SSea
	The Hilda Ogden Rose = 'Korchason' (Patio) **new**	LBuc
	The Ingenious Mr Fairchild = 'Austijus'PBR (S)	LRHS MAus MBri SCoo
	The Jack Duckworth Rose = 'Korlutmag'PBR (Patio) **new**	LBuc
	The Jubilee Rose = 'Poulbrido'PBR (F)	ECnt SCoo
	The Lady's Blush = 'Ausoscar' (S) **new**	LRHS MAus
	The Maidstone Rose = 'Kordauerpa' (S)	SCoo
	'The Margaret Coppola Rose'PBR	see *R.* White Gold
	The Mayflower = 'Austilly'PBR (S)	CSBt IBoy LRHS LStr MAus MBri SMrm
§	The McCartney Rose = 'Meizeli'PBR (HT)	CWSG SPer SWCr
	'The New Dawn'	see *R.* 'New Dawn'
	The Nun = 'Ausnun' (S)	MAus
	The Painter = 'Mactemaik'PBR (F)	LSRN LStr
§	The Pilgrim = 'Auswalker'PBR (S)	CSBt EPfP ESty LRHS LStr MAus MBri SEND SPer SSea SWCr
	The Prince = 'Ausvelvet'PBR (S)	LRHS MAus NLar SPer
	The Prince's Trust = 'Harholding'PBR (Cl)	LStr MAus SPoG
	'The Prioress' (S)	MAus
§	'The Queen Elizabeth' (F)	CBcs CGro CSBt CTri GCoc IBoy LSRN LStr MAsh MAus MBri MRav MWat NPri SPer SRGP SWCr WBor
	The Reeve = 'Ausreeve' (S)	MAus
	The Rita Sullivan Rose = 'Korzweenu' (Patio) **new**	LBuc
	The Rotarian	see *R.* Rotary Sunrise
I	'The Rugby Rose' (HT)	LSRN
	The Shepherdess = 'Austwist'PBR (S)	IBoy LRHS MAsh MAus MBri SMrm SSea
	The Soham RosePBR	see *R.* Pearl Abundance
	The Squire = 'Ausquire' (S)	MAus
	The Times Rose = 'Korpeahn' (F) ♀H4	ECnt LStr MAus MRav SPer SWCr
	The Wedgwood Rose = 'Ausjosiah' (ClS)	LRHS MAus

Name	Suppliers
The Wren = 'Kormamtiza'PBR (F/Patio)	EPfP
'Thelma' (Ra)	MAus
'Thérèse Bugnet' (Ru)	MAus
Thinking of You = 'Frydandy'PBR (HT)	ESty GCoc IBoy LStr MAsh MAus NPri SRGP SVic SWCr
'Thisbe' (HM)	CPou EBee MAus SPer
Thomas Barton = 'Meihirvin' (HT)	LStr
'Threave' (Bb)	CPou
Three Cheers = 'Dicdomino'PBR (F)	IDic
threepenny bit rose	see *R. elegantula* 'Persetosa'
Tickled Pink = 'Fryhunky'PBR (F)	CSBt EPfP ESty GCoc LRHS LSRN LShp MAsh MBri MRav MWat SCoo SPer SPoG SWCr
Times Past = 'Harhilt'PBR (ClHT)	ELon ESty GCoc LStr MBri MRav SPoG SRGP SWCr
'Tina Turner' (HT)	LSRN
Tintinara = 'Dicuptight'PBR (HT)	ECnt IDic
Tip Top = 'Tanope' (F/Patio)	SPer
'Tipo Ideale'	see *R.* × *odorata* 'Mutabilis'
Together Forever = 'Dicecho'PBR (F)	GCoc IDic MAsh
'Tom Marshall'	EBee LSRN
Top Marks = 'Fryministar'PBR (Min/Patio)	CGro CSBt GCoc LStr MRav MWat SCoo SPer SWCr
Topaz JewelPBR	see *R.* Yellow Dagmar Hastrup
Toprose = 'Cocgold'PBR (F)	GCoc MAsh
'Topsi' (F/Patio)	SPer
§ 'Tour de Malakoff' (Ce)	CPou IBoy LRHS MAus MRav NLar SFam SPer
Tradescant = 'Ausdir'PBR (S)	MAus
'Treasure Trove' (Ra)	CRHN LRHS MAus NLar SMrm SWCr
Trevor Griffiths = 'Ausold'PBR (S)	MAus
'Tricolore de Flandre' (G)	MAus
'Trier' (Ra)	CPou EBee MAus
'Trigintipetala' misapplied	see *R.* 'Professeur Emile Perrot'
'Triomphe de l'Exposition' (HP)	MAus
'Triomphe du Luxembourg' (T)	MAus
triphylla	see *R.* × *beanii*
Troika = 'Poumidor' (HT) ♀H4	CSBt ELan EPfP GCoc IBoy LRHS LStr MAus MRav SMrm SPer SPoG SWCr
Troilus = 'Ausoil' (S)	MAus
'Tropicana'	see *R.* Super Star
Trumpeter = 'Mactru' (F) ♀H4	CTri EBee ECnt GCoc IArd IBoy LBuc LStr MAsh MAus MRav MWat SPer SPoG SSea SWCr WCot
§ 'Tuscany' (G)	GCoc MAus SPer
'Tuscany Superb' (G) ♀H4	CPou CSBt CSam CTri EBee EPfP EWTr LAst LRHS MAsh MAus MBri MRav NChi NLar SEND SFam SKHP SMrm SPer SSea SWCr WBor WHer WKif
Twenty-one Again! = 'Meinimo'PBR (HT)	LSRN SWCr
Twice in a Blue Moon = 'Tan96138'PBR (HT)	CGro CSBt EBee ECnt ESty GCoc IBoy LBuc MRav MWat SCoo SMrm SPoG SSea SWCr
Twist = 'Poulstri'PBR (Courtyard Series) (ClPatio)	CGro EBee ECnt ESty MWat
Tynwald = 'Mattwyt' (HT)	LStr SPer
'Ulrich Brünner'	see *R.* 'Ulrich Brünner Fils'
§ 'Ulrich Brünner Fils' (HP)	MAus
'Unique Blanche'	see *R.* × *centifolia* 'Unique'
Valencia = 'Koreklia'PBR (HT) ♀H4	MAus
Valentine Heart = 'Dicogle'PBR (F) ♀H4	CSBt CWSG ESty IArd IDic LSRN MAsh MAus MRav SPoG SWCr
Vanilla Twist = 'Dicghost' (F)	IDic
'Vanity' (HM)	MAus
Varenna Allen = 'Harmode'PBR (F)	EBee ECnt
'Variegata di Bologna' (Bb)	EPfP EWTr LRHS MAus MMuc MRav SLon SMrm SSea SWCr
'Vatertag' (Min)	LSRN
'Veilchenblau' (Ra) ♀H4	CRHN CSBt CSam CTri ECnt ELan EPfP LRHS LStr MAus MCot MRav NEgg NLar SEND SMrm SPer SPoG SSea SWCr WBor WKif
Velvet Fragrance = 'Fryperdee'PBR (HT)	CGro CSBt ECnt ELon ESty GCoc LStr MAus MRav MWat SMrm SPoG SSea SWCr
'Venusta Pendula' (Ra)	MAus
'Verschuren' (HT/v)	ESty
versicolor	see *R. gallica* 'Versicolor'
'Vick's Caprice' (HP)	MAus NLar
'Vicomtesse Pierre du Fou' (ClHT)	MAus
Victoria Joy = 'Diciwill' (F)	IDic
Viking PrincessPBR	see *R.* Imagination
'Village Maid'	see *R.* × *centifolia* 'Unique Panachée'
§ 'Violacea' (G)	EBee MAus
'Violette' (Ra)	CPou CRHN LRHS LTen MAus SPer WHer
virginiana ♀H4	GCal MAus NWea
'Viridiflora'	see *R.* × *odorata* 'Viridiflora'
Waltz = 'Poulkrid'PBR (Courtyard Series) (ClPatio)	ECnt
wardii* var. *culta	MAus
Warm Welcome = 'Chewizz'PBR (ClMin) ♀H4	CGro CWSG ECnt EPfP ESty GCoc IBoy LRHS LSRN LStr MAus MBri MGos MRav SBfd SMad SMrm SPer SPoG SSea SWCr
§ Warm Wishes = 'Fryxotic'PBR (HT) ♀H4	CSBt ECnt ESty GCoc IBoy LBuc LRHS LSRN LStr MAsh MAus MBri MGos MRav MWat SPoG SSea SWCr
'Warrior' (F)	GCoc
Warwick Castle = 'Auslian' (S)	MAus
webbiana	MAus SKHP
Wedding Celebration = 'Poulht006'PBR (HT)	ECnt SWCr
'Wedding Day' (Ra)	CRHN CSBt CSam CTri CWSG ECnt ELan EPfP ESty IBoy LEdu LRHS LSRN LStr MAus MBri MGos MRav MWat NEgg NLar NPri SEND SMrm SPer SSea SWCr
Wee Cracker = 'Cocmarris'PBR (Patio)	ESty GCoc
Wee Jock = 'Cocabest' (F/Patio)	GCoc IBoy SMrm
'Weetwood' (Ra)	CRHN
Weisse WolckePBR	see *R.* White Cloud

Well-Being = 'Harjangle'PBR (S) — CSBt ELon ESty SWCr
'Wendy Cussons' (HT) — CTri GCoc MRav SPer SWCr
Wenlock = 'Auswen' (S) — MAus SPer
Westerland = 'Korwest' (S) ♀H4 — GCoc MRav SWCr WCot
Where the Heart Is = 'Cocoplan'PBR (HT) — ESty
Whisky Mac = 'Tanky' (HT) — CBcs CSBt CTri ELan GCoc LBuc MBri MRav NPri SMrm SPer SRGP
'White Bath' — see *R.* × *centifolia* 'Shailer's White Moss'
'White Christmas' (HT) — GCoc
§ White Cloud = 'Korstacha'PBR (S/ClHT) ♀H4 — EPfP ESty LRHS MWat SKHP SPoG SWCr
'White Cockade' (Cl) — CPou ESwi GCoc SMrm SPer SWCr
White CoverPBR — see *R.* Kent
§ 'White de Meaux' (Ce) — MAus
White Diamond = 'Interamon'PBR (S) — EBee ECnt IDic LBuc
§ White Gold = 'Cocquiriam'PBR (F) — CSBt GCoc
'White Grootendorst' (Ru) — LRHS
White Knight (HT) — see *R.* Message
White Meidiland = 'Meicoublan'PBR (S/GC) — MAsh
white moss — see *R.* 'Comtesse de Murinais', *R.* × *centifolia* 'Shailer's White Moss'
White Parfum de Provence = 'Meidiaphaz' (HT) — CSBt ESty
'White Patio' (Min/Patio) — LRHS
§ 'White Pet' (Poly) ♀H4 — CSBt CTri EBee ECnt EPfP EWTr GCoc LRHS LStr MBri MCot MRav SEND SMrm SPer SWCr
white Provence — see *R.* × *centifolia* 'Unique'
white rose of York — see *R.* × *alba* 'Alba Semiplena'
White Star = 'Harquill' (ClHT) — EBee ECnt ESty
'White Wings' (HT) — IBoy SPer WKif
N ***wichurana*** (Ra) — CBcs EWTr GCal GLin MAus SKHP
- 'Variegata' (Ra/v) — EPot
* - 'Variegata Nana' (Ra/v) — MRav
'Wickwar' (Ra) — EWTr GCal
Wife of Bath = 'Ausbath' (S) — MAus
Wild Edric = 'Aushedge'PBR (Ru) — LRHS MAus SCoo
Wild Rover = 'Dichirap'PBR (F) — ESty IDic LRHS LStr MAsh MBri
Wild Thing = 'Jactoose'PBR (S) — IDic LBuc MAsh
Wildeve = 'Ausbonny'PBR (S) — LRHS MAus MBri SMrm
Wildfire = 'Fryessex' (Patio) — ECnt ELon ESty IBoy LRHS MAus MWat SMrm SPoG SWCr
§ 'Wilhelm' (HM) — CPou MAus SPer
'Will Scarlet' (HM) — MAus
'William Allen Richardson' (N) — MAus
'William Cobbett' (F) — SSea
§ 'William Lobb' (CeMo) ♀H4 — CDoy CGro CPou CRHN EPfP IBoy LRHS LStr MAus MBri MRav NEgg NLar SPer SWCr WBor WHer WKif
William Morris = 'Auswill'PBR (S) — CSBt LRHS MAus MBri NEgg SSea SWCr
William Shakespeare 2000 = 'Ausromeo'PBR (S) — CSBt EBee ECnt EPfP ESty LRHS LStr MAsh MAus MBNS MBri NEgg SCoo SSea SWCr
William Shakespeare = 'Ausroyal'PBR (S) — CGro CWSG IBoy MCot SMrm SPer
'William Tyndale' (Ra) — CPou CSam EBee
'Williams' Double Yellow' — see *R.* × *harisonii* 'Williams Double Yellow'
willmottiae — see *R. gymnocarpa* var. *willmottiae*
Wilton = 'Eurosa' — SWCr
Wiltshire = 'Kormuse'PBR (S/GC) ♀H4 — CSBt CTri ECnt ESty IBoy LSRN LStr MRav SEND SLon SSea SWCr
Winchester Cathedral = 'Auscat'PBR (S) — CGro CSBt CTri ECnt ELon EPfP ESty IBoy LAst LRHS LSRN LStr MAsh MAus MBri MRav MWat NEgg NLar SLon SMad SMrm SPer SSea SWCr
Windflower = 'Auscross' (S) — MAus
Windrush = 'Ausrush' (S) — MAus SPer
Wise Portia = 'Ausport' (S) — MAus
Wisley 2008 = 'Ausbreeze' (S) — CSBt ECnt EPfP IBoy LRHS MAsh MAus SSea
Wisley = 'Ausintense'PBR (S) — EBee SCoo
With All My Love = 'Coczodiac'PBR (HT) — CSBt ESty GCoc LStr
With Love = 'Andwit' (HT) — SWCr
With Thanks = 'Fransmoov'PBR (HT) — ESty MBri SWCr
Wizard (HT) **new** — ESty
Wonderful News = 'Jonone'PBR (Patio) — CGro ESty MWat
Wonderful = 'Poulpmt005'PBR (HT) — ECnt SWCr
§ ***woodsii*** — MAus
- var. ***fendleri*** — see *R. woodsii*
Worcestershire = 'Korlalon'PBR (GC) — GCoc MAus MRav SPer SSea SWCr
§ ***xanthina*** 'Canary Bird' (S) ♀H4 — Widely available
§ - f. ***hugonis*** ♀H4 — CTri ELan MAus SKHP SPer
'Yellow Cécile Brünner' — see *R.* 'Perle d'Or'
Yellow Charles Austin = 'Ausyel' (S) — MAus
§ Yellow Dagmar Hastrup = 'Moryelrug'PBR (Ru) — CPou SPer
Yellow Floorshow = 'Harfully'PBR (GC) — MRav
Yellow Flower CarpetPBR — see *R.* Flower Carpet Sunshine
'Yellow Patio' (Min/Patio) — LRHS LStr NPri SSea SWCr
yellow Scotch — see *R.* × *harisonii* 'Williams Double Yellow'
Yellow Sunblaze = 'Meitrisical' (Min) — CSBt
'Yesterday' (Poly/F/S) ♀H4 — MAsh MAus NLar
York and Lancaster — see *R.* × *damascena* 'Versicolor'
Yorkshire = 'Korbarkeit'PBR (GC) — GCoc LStr MRav SSea
'Yorkshire Lady' (HT) — NEgg
You Are My Sunshine = 'Frykwango'PBR (HT) — ECnt ESty GCoc LBuc MAsh MBri
Young Lycidas = 'Ausvibrant'PBR (S) — CSBt IBoy LRHS MAus SSea SWCr
Young Princess = 'Tan02670' (F) — SWCr
'Yvonne Rabier' (Poly) ♀H4 — MAus MRav NLar SLon SPer
'Zéphirine Drouhin' (Bb) — Widely available
§ 'Zigeunerknabe' (S) — EBee ECnt GCoc MAus MCot MRav NLar SKHP SPer

Roscoea ✿ (*Zingiberaceae*)

ACE 2539 — GEdr
CC 6142 — EWld

Name	Suppliers
from Sikkim **new**	WHil
alpina	CBro CLAP CPLG CPrp EBee ECho EHrv GBuc GEdr GHim GKev LWst NGdn WCru
– CC 1820	IBlr
– CC 3667	EPPr GEdr
– 'Leaping Salmon'	CCon
– pink-flowered	IBlr
– purple-flowered	IBlr
– short	WCru
§ ***auriculata***	Widely available
– B&SWJ 2594	WCru
– brown-stemmed × ***purpurea***	IBlr
– early-flowering	IBlr WCru
– 'Floriade'	CDes CLAP EBee GBuc IBlr LRHS LWst
– green-stemmed × ***purpurea***	IBlr
– late-flowering	WCru
– 'Special'	CLAP
– 'White Cap'	EBee LWst
auriculata × australis	IBlr
auriculata × capitata	IBlr
australis	CCon CSam ELon GBuc GEdr MNrw WCru
– pink-flowered KW 22124	IBlr
– purple-flowered KW 22124	IBlr
australis × humeana	IBlr
'Ballyrogan Lavender'	IBlr
× ***beesiana*** 'Ballyrogan Purple'	IBlr
– Cream Group	CBct CDes CFwr CLAP EBee EHrv ELon EPfP EWld GBuc GEdr IBlr LEdu MMHG NBir NPnk SKHP WCru WPGP
– Dark Group	ELon IBlr
– Gestreept Group	CAvo CBro CCon CFwr CHEx CLAP CMea EBee ECtt EPot GBuc GEdr IBlr LAma LWst MCot NHar SKHP SPlb SPoG WCru WHar WWEG
– 'Lemon and Lavender' **new**	IBlr
– 'Monique'	CDes CLAP EBee IBlr LEdu LWst NHar WPGP
– 'Moonlight' **new**	IBlr
– 'Petite Purple'	IBlr
Blackthorn strain	IBlr
brandisii misapplied	see *R. tumjensis*
capitata	CLAP IBlr
cautleyoides ♀H4	Widely available
– CLD 772	IBlr
– var. ***cautleyoides*** f. ***atropurpurea***	IBlr
– – – 'Giraffe'	IBlr
– – white-flowered	CRDP
– cream-flowered × ***humeana*** **new**	LWst
– 'Crûg's Late Lemon'	WCru
– 'Doge Purple'	IBlr
– dwarf, from Kew	LRHS
– 'Early Purple'	CDes CLAP ECho GBuc WPGP
– 'Early Yellow'	EBee LWst
– 'Himalaya'	CLAP EBee LWst
– 'Jeffrey Thomas'	CBct CFwr CLAP CSam EBee ECho ELan ELon EPPr EPot GBuc GCal GEdr GHim IBlr LWst MLHP SRGP WCot WHil
– 'Kew Beauty' ♀H4	CCon CDes CLAP CMea CPLG CRDP EBee EPfP GBuc GCal GEdr LRHS LSou MMoz NGdn SKHP SMHy WCot WHil WPGP WWlt
– late, lavender-flowered	IBlr
– late, yellow-flowered	IBlr NCot
– 'Lemon Giraffe'	IBlr
– 'Pennine Purple'	IBlr NHar
– plum-flowered	IBlr
– var. ***pubescens***	IBlr
– – CLD 687	GEdr
– 'Purple Giant'	CLAP GHim LWst SKHP
– purple-flowered	IBlr NHar
– red-mauve-flowered **new**	WHil
– 'Reinier'	CLAP EBee GCal IBlr LWst SKHP
– f. ***sinopurpurea***	IBlr
– 'Vanilla'	EBee LEdu LWst SKHP WHil
– 'Washfield Purple'	IBlr
– 'Yeti'	CLAP EBee LWst SKHP
cautleyoides × humeana	CLAP IBlr LWst NCot WHar
cautleyoides × purpurea f. ***rubra*** 'Red Gurkha' **new**	IFoB
cautleyoides × scillifolia f. ***atropurpurea***	IBlr
debilis var. ***debilis***	IBlr
forrestii f. ***forrestii***	IBlr
– f. ***purpurea***	IBlr
– f. ***purpurea × humeana***	IBlr
humeana ♀H4	CBct CBro CLAP ECho GBuc GEdr LAma LRHS LWst MBri NRHS WThu
– ACE 2539	IBlr
– f. ***alba***	IBlr
– Forrest's form	IBlr
– lavender-flowered	IBlr
– 'Long Acre Sunrise'	CLAP WPGP
– f. ***lutea***	CLAP GEdr IBlr
– pink-flowered	IBlr
– 'Purple Streaker'	CDes CLAP EBee WPGP
– 'Rosemoor Plum'	CDes CLAP GEdr WPGP
– 'Snowy Owl'	CLAP
– 'Two Tone' **new**	IBlr
– f. ***tyria***	EBee IBlr
– – 'Inkling'	GBuc
'Ice Maiden'	IBlr
praecox	IBlr
– BWJ 7848	WCru
procera misapplied	see *R. auriculata*
procera Wall.	see *R. purpurea*
'Purple King'	EBee LWst
§ ***purpurea***	CAvo CBro CHEx EBee ECha ELan ELon EPPr EPfP EPot GCal GEdr IBlr IFoB LAma LEdu LRHS LSou MCot NBir NGdn WCru WHer WHil WKif WWEG
– CC 1757	IBlr
– CC 3628	CPLG IBlr
– HWJK 2020	WCru
– HWJK 2169	WCru
– HWJK 2175	WCru
– HWJK 2400	WCru
– HWJK 2407	WCru
– KW 13755	IBlr
– MECC 2	IBlr
– MECC 10	IBlr
– f. ***alba***	GEdr
– 'Brown Peach'	LRHS
– 'Brown Peacock'	CDes CLAP GBuc IBlr LWst SKHP WCru WPGP
– 'Dalai Lama'	LWst SPlb
– var. ***gigantea*** CC 1757	IBlr MNrw

- 'Himalayan Delight'	IBlr
- 'Nico'	EBee ELan IBlr LRHS LWst SKHP WCot
- 'Niedrig'	EBee IBlr SKHP
- 'Peacock'	CLAP EBee IBlr LWst SKHP WHil
- 'Peacock Eye'	IBlr LRHS LWst SKHP
- var. ***procera***	see *R. purpurea*
- Rosemoor form	CLAP LWst
- f. ***rubra*** 'Red Gurkha'	CDes CLAP IBlr LEdu
- short	CLAP IBlr
- tall	CLAP WCru WPGP
- 'Twin Towers' **new**	EBee
- 'Typico'	IBlr
- 'Vannin'	LEdu WCru
- 'Vincent'	EBee LWst
- 'Wisley Amethyst'	CLAP GEdr IBlr LLHF LRHS LWst MBri NCot SKHP SPoG SPtl WHil
schneideriana	IBlr WHil WThu
- robust form	IBlr
scillifolia	CBro CCon CPBP ECho GBuc GKev LAma LHop LRHS NBir NRHS SDeJ WHar
- f. ***atropurpurea***	CDes CPom EHrv GBuc GEdr IBlr WAul WCru WPGP WThu WWEG
- f. ***scillifolia***	CDes CYeo EBee EHrv GEdr IBlr IFoB WCru WHar WHil WThu
aff. ***scillifolia*** purple-flowered	IBlr
tibetica	CCon CLAP EBee GEdr GKev IBlr WCru WThu
- ACE 2538	IBlr WCru
- BWJ 7878	WCru
- f. ***atropurpurea*** BWJ 7640	WCru
aff. ***tibetica***	IBlr
aff. ***tibetica*** f. ***albo-purpurea***	IBlr
§ ***tumjensis***	CLAP EBee EWes IBlr WPGP
wardii	CPLG IBlr

rosemary see *Rosmarinus officinalis*

Rosenia (*Asteraceae*)

humilis	CPBP

Rosmarinus ✿ (*Lamiaceae*)

sp.	CHab
* 'Compactus Albus'	MWat
corsicus 'Prostratus'	see *R. officinalis* Prostratus Group
lavandulaceus misapplied	see *R. officinalis* Prostratus Group
× ***noeanus***	XSen
officinalis	Widely available
- var. ***albiflorus***	CArn CSev EBee ELau ENfk EOHP EPfP EWhm GPoy LRHS MHer MHoo MNHC SBfd SDow SEND SHDw SLim SPlb WGwG WJek XSen
- - 'Lady in White'	CSBt EBee ELan EPfP LRHS MHer SDow SLim SPer SPoG WGwG WJek
- 'Alderney'	MHer SDow
§ - var. ***angustissimus*** 'Benenden Blue' ♀H4	CSBt CWan CWib EBee EPfP GPoy MHoo SBfd SDix SPer SPlb SPoG SUsu WGwG WJek WPnn WRHF
- - 'Corsican Blue'	CArn EBee ELan EPfP GPoy MHer MNHC MRav SBfd SGol SHDw SIde SPer WPer
- - 'Corsicus Prostratus'	SHil
- 'Aureovariegatus'	see *R. officinalis* 'Aureus'
§ - 'Aureus' (v)	EOHP WJek
- 'Baby P.J.'	EOHP
- 'Baie d'Audierne'	XSen
- 'Barbecue' PBR	EGHP ELau SIde
- 'Blue Lagoon'	EGHP ELau ENfk EWhm LRHS MHer MHoo MNHC SIde SPtl WGwG WHer WJek WPnn
- 'Blue Rain'	EBee EGHP EPfP MHer SIde WHfH WPnn
- 'Boule'	CArn ELau MHer SDow WGwG WJek XSen
- 'Capercaillie'	SDow
- 'Collingwood Ingram'	see *R. officinalis* var. *angustissimus* 'Benenden Blue'
- 'Cottage White'	SUsu WGwG WHer
- dwarf, blue-flowered	ELau
- 'Farinole'	CArn ELau MNHC
- 'Fastigiatus'	see *R. officinalis* 'Miss Jessopp's Upright'
- 'Fota Blue'	CArn CSpe CTsd CWib ELau IArd IGor LRHS MHer MHoo MNHC SAga SBfd SDow SGol SHDw SIde SPoG SWvt WGwG WJek WPnn
- 'Foxtail'	LBuc LRHS SPtl WJek
- 'Frimley Blue'	see *R. officinalis* 'Primley Blue'
- 'Genges Gold' (v)	MHer SBfd
- 'Golden Rain'	see *R. officinalis* 'Joyce DeBaggio'
- 'Gorizia'	CArn CBcs EHoe SDow SLim WGwG WPnn
- 'Green Ginger'	CArn CPrp EBee EGHP ELan ELau EOHP EPfP GBin LHop LRHS MAsh MHer MHoo MNHC MRav MSCN NPer SDow SPer SPoG WGwG WJek WMnd WPnn
- 'Guilded'	see *R. officinalis* 'Aureus'
- 'Haifa'	EBtc ECtt ELau ENfk EWhm LRHS MHoo NLBP SIde WJek WPnn
- 'Henfield Blue'	SBfd SHDw
- 'Huntington Carpet' **new**	LAst
- 'Iden Blue'	SIde
- 'Iden Blue Boy'	CSpe SIde
- 'Iden Pillar'	SIde
§ - 'Joyce DeBaggio' (v)	MHer SDow WGwG WHer
- 'Knightshayes Blue'	LRHS
- 'Lady in Blue'	WGwG
- ***lavandulaceus***	see *R. officinalis* Prostratus Group
- 'Lilies Blue'	GPoy
- 'Lockwood Variety'	see *R. officinalis* (Prostratus Group) 'Lockwood de Forest'
- 'Majorca Pink'	CBcs CHab CSBt CSpe CWan EBee ELau ENfk LRHS MHer MNHC MSCN NPri SDow SIde SPer WGwG WJek XLum
- 'Marenca'	ELau MNHC
- 'McConnell's Blue' ♀H4	CArn CDoC CPrp EBee ELan ELau ENfk IGor LHop LRHS MAsh MGos MNHC SBfd SDow SHDw WFar WGwG WHer WHoo WJek WPGP
§ - 'Miss Jessopp's Upright' ♀H4	Widely available
- 'Pat Vlasto'	SUsu
- 'Pointe du Raz'	CAbP CArn EBee ELan EPfP LRHS MAsh SChF SLim
§ - 'Primley Blue'	CBcs CMea CSev CTsd EBee ECtt ELau ENfk MHoo MNHC MRav SGol SIde WFar WJek WPer
§ - Prostratus Group	Widely available
- - 'Capri'	CAbP CSBt ECtt ELau EPfP LRHS MBrN MHer SPoG WJek
- - 'Gethsemane'	CArn SIde WGwG

– – 'Jackman's Prostrate'	CBcs CHab ECtt
§ – – 'Lockwood de Forest'	WGwG WHer
– – 'Sheila Dore'	SPlb
– f. ***pyramidalis***	see *R. officinalis* 'Miss Jessopp's Upright'
– ***repens***	see *R. officinalis* Prostratus Group
– 'Rex'	ELau
– 'Roman Beauty'PBR	CBcs CSev EBee LAst LRHS LSRN SLim SPtl SWvt WHer
– 'Roseus'	CArn CEnt CPrp CWib EBee ELan ELau ENfk EPfP GPoy LHop LRHS MAsh MHer MHoo MNHC MWat NEgg SBfd SDow SEND SLim SPoG WGwG WHer WJek WMnd WPer WPnn
– 'Salem'	MHer
– 'Sea Level'	ELau MHer WGwG
– 'Severn Sea' ♀H4	CArn CBcs CPrp CSBt CTri CWSG CWan EBee ECtt ELan ELau ENfk EPfP GPoy LRHS MAsh MGos MHer MNHC MRav MSwo SDow SIde SLon SPer WCFE WGwG WHoo WJek WPer
– 'Shimmering Stars'	SDow
– 'Silver Sparkler'	WPat
– Silver Spires = 'Wolros'	MNHC
– 'Sissinghurst Blue' ♀H4	CArn CWan EBee ECha ECrN ELan ELau ENfk EPfP LRHS MAsh MHer MLHP MNHC MRav SBfd SDow SGol SIde SLim SPer SPlb SRms SWvt WGwG WJek
– 'Sissinghurst White'	WGwG
– 'Sorcerer's Apprentice'	WGwG
– 'South Downs Blue'	SBfd SHDw
– 'Spanish Snow'	WGwG
– 'Sudbury Blue'	ELau ENfk EPfP MHoo MNHC SBfd SDow SHDw SPad WJek WPnn XSen
– 'Sunkissed' **new**	LBuc LRHS
– 'Trusty'	CWan
– 'Tuscan Blue'	Widely available
– 'Variegatus'	see *R. officinalis* 'Aureus'
– 'Vicomte de Noailles'	XSen
– 'Wilma's Gold'	EBee
repens	see *R. officinalis* Prostratus Group
Salcombe form	CHll
'Sappho'	CHll

Rostrinucula (*Lamiaceae*)

dependens	ECre EPfP EWes MTPN NLar WCFE
sinensis	CPLG

Rosularia ✿ (*Crassulaceae*)

sp.	MWat
from Sandras Dag, Turkey	CWil LBee LRHS
§ ***aizoon***	ECho LRHS NRHS
alba	see *R. sedoides* var. *alba*
alpestris from Rhotang Pass, Himalaya	WThu
§ ***chrysantha***	ECho EDAr LRHS NMen NRHS SPlb
crassipes	see *Rhodiola wallichiana*
libanotica RCB RL 20	WCot
pallida A. Berger	see *R. chrysantha*
pallida Stapf	see *R. aizoon*
pallida ambig.	EPot SFgr
sedoides	CWil MMuc
§ – var. ***alba***	ECho EDAr EPot WNew
sempervivum	CWil ECho EWes NMen
§ – subsp. ***glaucophylla***	CWil WAbe WThu
spatulata hort.	see *R. sempervivum* subsp. *glaucophylla*

Rubia (*Rubiaceae*)

peregrina	CArn GPoy
tinctorum	CArn CHab CHby EOHP GPoy SWat WHfH WSFF

Rubus ✿ (*Rosaceae*)

RCB/Eq C-1	WCot
SDR 4635	GKev
alceifolius Poir.	SDys
arcticus	EBee ECtt EPPr GEdr NHar NLar SRms SRot SSvw WCru WPat WThu XLum
– subsp. ***stellatus***	NHar
× ***barkeri***	ECou
'Benenden' ♀H4	Widely available
'Betty Ashburner'	CAgr CBcs CDoC CDul EBee EPPr EWTr GQui LAst MGos MRav MWhi SLPl SPer WMoo XLum
biflorus ♀H4	EWes MBlu MMuc NLar SEND WPGP
'Black Butte'	EPom GPri LRHS SLon SVic
'Boysenberry' (F)	LRHS
boysenberry, thornless (F)	CMac EMil GPri GTwe LBuc LSRN NPri SPer
buergeri B&SWJ 5555	WCru
caesius **new**	WCot
calophyllus	CDul WPGP
calycinoides Hayata	see *R. rolfei*
calycinoides Kuntze	EBtc GKev SGol
chamaemorus	GPoy
§ ***chingii*** var. ***chingii*** **new**	SEND
cockburnianus (F)	CArn CBcs CTri CWib EBee ELan EPfP EWTr GCra GKin IFoB LBuc MRav MSwo NLar NSti NWea SPer SPlb SRms WFar
– 'Goldenvale' ♀H4	CDoC CDul EBee EHoe EPfP EWTr GQui IFro LHop LRHS MAsh MBlu MGos MMuc MRav MSwo MWhi NBir NEgg NLar NSti SEND SLon SPer SPoG WFar WTin
crataegifolius	LEdu MRav WPat
'Emerald Spreader'	WMoo
fockeanus misapplied	see *R. rolfei*
formosensis B&SWJ 1798	ESwi WCru
N ***fruticosus*** agg.	NWea WSFF
– 'Adrienne' (F)	CAgr CSBt LRHS MBri SEND WHar
– 'Ashton Cross' (F)	CDoC GTwe LBuc
– 'Bedford Giant' (F)	CSBt GTwe LRHS LSRN MGos MMuc SEND SKee SLim SPoG WHar
– 'Black Satin' (F)	CAgr LRHS NLar NPri SVic
– 'Chester' (F)	LRHS SBfd SKee
– 'Helen' (F)	CAgr CSut GPri MCoo
– 'Himalayan Giant' (F)	GTwe MRav NEgg NLar
– 'John Innes' (F)	GPri MCoo
– 'Kotata' (F)	MRav
– 'Loch Maree' (F/d)	CMac EPom LRHS SLon
– 'Loch Ness'PBR (F) ♀H4	CAgr CWib EPom GPri GTwe IArd LBuc LRHS LSRN SCoo SKee SVic WHar
– 'Loch Tay'PBR (F)	CMac EPom GPri LRHS SBfd SPer
– 'Merton Thornless' (F)	CSBt CWib GTwe LAst LSRN MGos SPlb WHar
– 'Natchez' (F) **new**	SPer
– 'Navaho Big and Early' (F) **new**	CSut

- 'Oregon Thornless' (F)	CAgr CCVT CDoC CSBt CWib ECrN EPfP GTwe LRHS LSRN MBri MRav NEgg NLar SCoo SKee SLim SPoG SRms WHar
* - 'Sylvan' (F)	MCoo MMuc
- 'Thornfree' (F)	CAgr CDoC CTri LRHS NLar SKee SLim
- 'Variegatus' (v)	CMac CRDP MBlu WCot
- 'Waldo' (F)	CAgr CSBt CWib ECrN LBuc LSRN MBri MGos NPri SEND WHar
aff. ***gachetensis*** B&SWJ 10603	WCru
'Glencoe'	GPri MCoo
'Golden Showers'	CWib
henryi	EBee ESwi IGor LRHS MRav NSti WCot
- var. ***bambusarum***	ESwi MRav WCru
'Hildaberry' (F)	GPri
ichangensis	CBcs ESwi LEdu
idaeus	GPoy
- 'All Gold' (F) ♀H4	CAgr CSut EMil GPri LRHS MCoo MNHC SBfd SCoo SPer SVic WHar
- 'Aureus' (F)	ECha ELan EWes LEdu MRav NBid WCot WFar
- 'Autumn Bliss' (F) ♀H4	Widely available
- 'Autumn Treasure' (F)	CSut LRHS NPri SLon WWFS
- 'Cascade Delight' (F)	CSut EPom
- 'Erika' (F) **new**	NPri
- 'Fallgold' (F)	CWib EPfP MMuc SEND SKee SPoG
- 'Glen Ample'[PBR] (F) ♀H4	CAgr CMac CSBt CTri CWSG CWib EMil EPfP EPom GPri GTwe LBuc LRHS LSRN MBri MCoo MNHC NWea SBfd SCoo SEND SKee SLim SPer SPoG SVic WHar WWFS
- 'Glen Clova' (F)	CAgr CSBt CTri CWib GTwe LRHS LSRN MGos MRav NLar SBfd SKee SLim SPer SPoG SVic WHar
- 'Glen Doll'[PBR] (F)	CAgr GTwe LBuc LRHS MCoo SCoo WWFS
- 'Glen Fyne'[PBR] (F) **new**	GTwe
- 'Glen Lyon'[PBR] (F)	CWib GKin LAst LBuc MBri SCoo WHar
- 'Glen Magna'[PBR] (F) ♀H4	CAgr CMac CSBt CWSG CWib GKin LRHS MBri NLar SCoo SKee SLim SPoG WWFS
- 'Glen Moy'[PBR] (F) ♀H4	CAgr CSBt CTri CWib ECrN EPfP GPri GTwe LAst LRHS LSRN MGos NEgg NWea SCoo SKee SLim WHar WWFS
- 'Glen Prosen'[PBR] (F) ♀H4	CAgr CSBt CWib EPfP GKin GTwe LRHS LSRN MBri MGos MRav NEgg NPri SCoo SKee SLim SPer SPlb WHar
- 'Heritage' (F)	CWib SCoo
- Himbo Top = 'Rafzaqu'[PBR] (F)	GPri
- 'Joan J'[PBR] (F) ♀H4	CMac CSut EMil EPom GPri GTwe LRHS
- 'Julia' (F)	MCoo
- 'Leo'[PBR] (F) ♀H4	CSBt CTri CWib GTwe SCoo SKee SPer WHar
- 'Malling Admiral' (F) ♀H4	CSBt CTri CWib EPom GTwe LAst LSRN NWea SCoo SKee SPer
- 'Malling Delight' (F)	CSBt CWib SCoo SPlb
- 'Malling Jewel' (F) ♀H4	CSBt CWib EPom GTwe LAst LBuc LSRN SKee SPer WHar WWFS
- 'Malling Promise' (F)	CWib
- 'Octavia'[PBR] (F)	CAgr CSBt EMil EPom LBuc LRHS MCoo NLar NWea SLim SPoG WHar WWFS
- 'Polka'[PBR] (F) ♀H4	EPom GPri LBuc LRHS LSRN MCoo MRav SCoo SKee SLim SVic WHar
- 'Summer Gold' (F)	GTwe
- 'Tulameen' (F) ♀H4	CAgr CSBt CWib ECrN EMil EPom GPri LRHS LSRN MBri MNHC NLar SBfd SCoo SKee SLim SPer SPoG SVic WWFS
- 'Valentina' (F)	GPri SVic
- 'Zeva Herbsternte' (F)	CWib
illecebrosus (F)	XLum
irenaeus	LEdu LRHS SEND SSpi
Japanese wineberry	see *R. phoenicolasius*
'Karaka Black'[PBR]	GPri LBuc LRHS SVic
'Kenneth Ashburner'	CDoC NLar WTin
lineatus	CDTJ CDoC CSpe CWib EBee EPfP EWTr EWes GBin LHop LRHS MCot MMuc NSti SKHP WCru WPGP
- B&SWJ 11261 from Sumatra	WCru
- HWJ 892 from Vietnam	ESwi WCru
- HWJK 2045 from Nepal	GQui WCru
- from Nepal	GCra
× ***loganobaccus*** (F) **new**	LRHS
- 'Brandywine' (F)	GPri
- 'Ly 59' (F) ♀H4	ECrN EPfP GTwe MMuc MRav SEND SKee SRms
- 'Ly 654' (F) ♀H4	CSBt EPom GTwe LBuc MBri NEgg NPri SPer WHar
- thornless (F)	CAgr CTri CWSG CWib EPom GPri GTwe SBfd SPoG SVic
'Malling Minerva' (F)	CMac CSut WWFS
'Margaret Gordon'	MRav
microphyllus 'Variegatus' (v)	MRav
§ ***nepalensis***	CAgr CDoC GKev LEdu
- from Nepal	GCra
nutans	see *R. nepalensis*
occidentalis 'Ebony'	LRHS
- 'Haut'	GPri
- 'Jewel'	GPri
odoratus	CPLG EBee ELan EPPr EPfP EWTr LEdu MBlu MRav NBid SPer WFar WTin
'Ouachita' (F)	SPer
palmatus	see *R. chingii* var. *chingii*
- var. ***coptophyllus***	MMuc
parviflorus	CArn
- double-flowered (d)	EPPr
- 'Sunshine Spreader'	EHoe LEdu WPat
parvus	LEdu
pectinellus var. ***trilobus***	EWld WCot
- - B&SWJ 1669B	NLar WCru
peltatus	CGHE EBee NLar WPGP
pentalobus	see *R. rolfei*
§ ***phoenicolasius***	CAgr CCCN CDul CHGN CMac EBee EMil EPPr EPfP EWTr GTwe LEdu LHop LRHS MBlu MCoo MRav NLar SGol SPer SPoG SVic WAbb WPGP
§ ***rolfei***	CTri GEdr
- B&SWJ 3546 from Taiwan	WCru
- B&SWJ 3878 from the Philippines	WCru
- 'Emerald Carpet'	CAgr EBee NLar
rosifolius 'Coronarius' (d)	ELan LSou NLar NPro WCot
sanctus	CNat
setchuenensis	CMCN EWes NLar

'Silvan' (F) ♀H4 — GPri GTwe SEND
spectabilis — CBcs CWib ELan EPPr LEdu MMuc MRav SEND WFar WSHC
- 'Flore Pleno' — see *R. spectabilis* 'Olympic Double'
§ - 'Olympic Double' (d) — Widely available
splendidissimus B&SWJ 2361 — ESwi WCru
squarrosus — ECou SMad
'Sunberry' (F) — CCCN GTwe
swinhoei B&SWJ 1735 — WCru
taiwanicola B&SWJ 317 — EDAr ESwi GEdr LHop WCru
- CWJ 12400 — WCru
Tayberry Group (F) ♀H4 — CSBt CTri GTwe LAst LRHS LSRN MGos NLar NPri SPer SRms SVic WHar
- 'Buckingham' (F) — CSut EMil EPom GPri GTwe LBuc LRHS SBfd SVic
- 'Medana Tayberry' (F) — CAgr EPfP GPri LRHS MBri SKee SPoG
§ ***thibetanus*** ♀H4 — Widely available
- 'Silver Fern' — see *R. thibetanus*
treutleri B&SWJ 2139 — WCru
tricolor — CAgr CBcs CDul CSBt CTri CWib EBee ECrN EPfP GKev GKin MBlu MCoo MMuc MRav MSwo NEgg NLar SBfd SDix SEND SGol SPer WMoo
trilobus B&SWJ 9096 — WCru
'Tummelberry' (F) — EMil GPri GTwe LRHS MCoo SBfd SVic
ulmifolius 'Bellidiflorus' (d) — GCal MBlu MRav MSwo WAbb WHrl
ursinus — SBfd
'Veitchberry' (F) — CDoy GPri
xanthocarpus — NLar XLum
'Youngberry' thornless (F) — GPri

Rudbeckia ✿ (*Asteraceae*)

Autumn Sun — see *R. laciniata* 'Herbstsonne'
'Berlin' — EBee LRHS SPoG WCot WGrn
deamii — see *R. fulgida* var. *deamii*
'Dublin' — EBee LRHS SPoG SPtl WCot
fulgida — SWvt
- 'City Garden' — ECtt GBin NCGa NDov NLar SRms
§ - var. ***deamii*** ♀H4 — Widely available
- 'Early Bird Gold' — EBee GBin NDov NLar SBfd WCot
- var. ***fulgida*** — CMea EBee EPfP SBfd SPoG
§ - var. ***speciosa*** ♀H4 — CKno CPrp EBee ECha ECtt EHrv ELan EPfP GAbr MMuc MSpe SBch SEND SPhx SPlb SRms SWal SWvt WFar WMoo WOut WPer WPtf WTin WWEG XLum
- var. ***sullivantii*** 'Goldsturm' ♀H4 — Widely available
- - 'Pot of Gold' — LSou WHil
- Viette's Little Suzy = 'Blovi' — EBee SRms
gloriosa — see *R. hirta*
'Golden Jubilee' — LRHS
grandiflora 'Sundance' — CSam EBee LRHS SBfd SPhx WPtf
§ ***hirta*** — LRHS MNHC NBir NRHS SVic
- 'Autumn Colours' (mixed) — CMea SPhx WCAu
- 'Cappuccino' — MSCN
- 'Cherokee Sunset' (d) — CSpe
- 'Cherry Brandy' — LRHS LSou NOrc NPri SPhx
- 'Chim Chiminee' — NGBl
- 'Goldilocks' — SVic
- 'Indian Summer' ♀H3 — EPfP SPav SPhx
- 'Irish Eyes' — SPav SVic
- 'Marmalade' — EPfP LRHS NGBl SVic
- 'Prairie Sun' — ELon EPfP LRHS MBel NGBl SPhx
- 'Sonora' — NGBl
- 'Tiger Eye' — LRHS SPoG
- 'Toto' ♀H3 — SPav SWvt
July Gold — see *R. laciniata* 'Juligold'
laciniata — CElw CHVG CKno CMac CSpe EBee ELan GCal GQue LEdu MDKP MSpe NCGa NDov NGBl NLar NOrc SBfd SGar SMHy SPhx WCot WMoo WOld WWEG XLum
- 'Golden Glow' — see *R. laciniata* 'Hortensia'
- 'Goldkugel' (d) ♀H4 — MSpe
- 'Goldquelle' (d) ♀H4 — CWCL EBee ECha ECtt ELan EPfP GMaP IVic LHop LRHS MSpe NGdn NOrc NPnk NPri SBea SMrm SPer SPoG SRms SRot SWvt WBor WCot WFar WMnd WWEG XLum
§ - 'Herbstsonne' ♀H4 — Widely available
§ - 'Hortensia' (d) — EBee GQue MAvo MBel MRav WBrk WCot WOld WWEG
§ - 'Juligold' — CPrp EBee LBMP LRHS MBNS MCot NBre NDov NEgg NGdn SMrm SPoG WFar WWEG WWFP
- 'Starcadia Razzle Dazzle' — WCot WWEG
'Little Gold Star' **new** — WCot
maxima — CKno CSpe EBee ECha GBin IFoB LEdu LHop LRHS MBel MBri MSpe NCGa NLar NSti SBfd SKHP SMad SMrm SPhx SPlb SUsu WCot WFar WWEG XLum
missouriensis — EBee LRHS SBfd
mollis — EBee NBre
newmannii — see *R. fulgida* var. *speciosa*
nitida — EBee
occidentalis — GKev LRHS NBre NLar
- 'Black Beauty' PBR — EBee EPfP WMnd
- 'Green Wizard' — CMac CWib EBee ECtt EHrv ELan EPfP GBin IBoy LRHS MCot MLHP NDov NLar NRHS NSti SBfd SGar SMad SPav SPer SRms WTin WWEG
* ***paniculata*** — EBee LLHF NBre WCot
'Peking' — EBee LRHS SPoG WCot WGrn
purpurea — see *Echinacea purpurea*
speciosa — see *R. fulgida* var. *speciosa*
subtomentosa — CSam EBee EWes GCal LPla MDKP MSpe MTis NBre NDov NPnk NSti SMHy SUsu WOld XLum
- 'Henry Eilers' — CKno ECtt ELan EPfP GBin GQue IKil IPot LBMP LRHS LSou MBri MMHG MTis NPnk SBfd SKHP SPoG SRms SWvt WCot WHil
'Takao' — EBee LSou MDKP
triloba ♀H4 — CDes CMea CSam EBee ECha ELon EPfP EShb LEdu LRHS MNrw MSpe NGdn NPnk NRHS SMad SMrm SPhx SUsu WCAu WFar WMoo WPGP WTcb
- 'Prairie Glow' — EBee EDAr NPnk SPhx
'Vitamin C' — EBee

rue see *Ruta graveolens*

Ruellia (*Acanthaceae*)

amoena — see *R. brevifolia*
§ ***brevifolia*** — ECre EShb
humilis — EBee EPPr EShb SPhx WHil
macrantha — CCCN EShb
makoyana ♀H1 — CSev EShb MBri
tweediana — EShb

Rulingia (*Sterculiaceae*)

hermanniifolia	ECou MOWG

Rumex (*Polygonaceae*)

acetosa	CArn CHab CHby CSev CWan EGHP ELau ENfk GPoy MCoo MHer MHoo MMuc MNHC NBir SBfd SEND SIde WHer WJek WSFF
- 'Abundance'	ELau LEdu
- subsp. ***acetosa*** 'Saucy' (v)	LEdu WCot
- 'De Belleville'	CPrp
- 'Profusion'	GPoy MHer
- subsp. ***vinealis***	EBee
acetosella	CArn CHab NMir WSFF
alpinus	EBee LEdu SPhx WCot
crispus	ELau
flexuosus	CSpe EBee EPPr GCal MDKP NLar WJek
hydrolapathum	CArn CHab LPBA MMuc MSKA SEND SPlb WSFF
patientia	CArn CHab ELau
sanguineus	CTri ENfk EShb LPBA MSKA NLBP NLar SBfd WFar
- var. ***sanguineus***	CArn CElw CRow CSev EBee ELan IFoB MHer MNHC NBro NPri WHer
'Schavel'	LEdu
scutatus	CArn CHby CSev ELau ENfk GPoy MHoo MNHC SBfd SIde SPlb WHer WHfH WJek
- subsp. ***induratus*** new	SEND
- 'Silver Shield'	CRow ELau LEdu MHer SIde WJek

Rumohra (*Dryopteridaceae*)

adiantiformis ♀H1	CCCN ISha LRHS SEND WFib WPGP
- RCB/Arg D-2	WCot

Ruscus ✿ (*Asparagaceae*)

aculeatus	CArn CBcs CDul CMac CRWN ELan EPfP ERom GPoy IDee LEdu LTen MGos MRav NLar NWea SBfd SLim SPlb SRms WBor WPGP WRHF
- hermaphrodite	EPfP EWes GCal MBri SEND SMad WPGP WPat WThu
- var. ***aculeatus*** 'Lanceolatus' (f)	GCal
- var. ***angustifolius*** PAB 254	LEdu
- 'Christmas Berry'	EPfP
- 'John Redmond' PBR	CSBt EBee ELan ELon EPfP EShb EWes LAst LHop LLHF LRHS LSqu MAsh MREP NHol NLar SBfd SCoo SEND SKHP SLon SPer SPoG SSpi WBor WCot WPGP
* - 'Wheeler's Variety' (f/m)	CJun MRav WPGP
hypoglossum	SEND WCot WPGP
racemosus	see *Danae racemosa*

Ruspolia (*Acanthaceae*)

hypocrateriformis	CCCN
seticalyx	EShb

Russelia (*Plantaginaceae*)

§ ***equisetiformis*** ♀H1	CAbb CPne EShb MOWG
- 'Lemon Falls'	EShb MOWG
juncea	see *R. equisetiformis*

Ruta (*Rutaceae*)

chalepensis	CArn XLum XSen
corsica	CArn XLum
graveolens	CArn CHab CWan ENfk EPfP GPoy MHoo SBfd SIde SWal WJek WSpi XLum
- 'Jackman's Blue'	CBcs CSev CTri EHoe ELan EOHP EPfP GMaP GPoy MGos MHer MNHC MRav MSwo NLar SBfd SLim WMnd WSpi XLum
- 'Variegata' (v)	CWan ELan MNHC NPer

Ruttya (*Acanthaceae*)

fruticosa	CCCN
- 'Scholesii'	EShb

× *Ruttyruspolia* (*Acanthaceae*)

lutea	CCCN

Rytidosperma (*Poaceae*)

* ***arundinaceum***	EShb

S

Sabal (*Arecaceae*)

§ ***bermudana***	EAmu
causiarum	EAmu
§ ***mexicana***	EAmu
minor	CHEx CPHo EAmu MREP SBig SPlb
palmetto	CDoC EAmu
princeps	see *S. bermudana*
texana	see *S. mexicana*

Saccharum (*Poaceae*)

arundinaceum	CKno
ravennae	EPPr SApp SMad SMrm SPlb WCot

sage see *Salvia officinalis*

sage, annual clary see *Salvia viridis*

sage, biennial clary see *Salvia sclarea*

sage, pineapple see *Salvia elegans*

Sageretia (*Rhamnaceae*)

§ ***thea***	CMen
theezans	see *S. thea*

Sagina (*Caryophyllaceae*)

subulata	ECho EHoe LRHS SVic XLum
§ - var. ***glabrata*** 'Aurea'	CMea CTri ECha ECho ECtt EDAr GMaP SPoG WPer

Sagittaria (*Alismataceae*)

'Bloomin' Babe'	CRow
graminea 'Crushed Ice' (v)	CRow MWts
japonica	see *S. sagittifolia*
latifolia	LPBA MWts NPer
* ***leucopetala*** 'Flore Pleno' (d)	NLar NPer
§ ***sagittifolia***	CBen CRow CWat EHon LPBA MSKA WMAq
- 'Flore Pleno' (d)	CWat EWay LPBA WMAq
- var. ***leucopetala***	WMAq

Saintpaulia (*Gesneriaceae*)

'Aca's Pink Delight' WDib
'Aca's Red Ember' (v) WDib
'Allegro Appalachian Trail' WDib
'Always Pink' WDib
'Aly's Rosy Baby' WDib
'Anouk' **new** WDib
'Arctic Frost' (d) WDib
'Baby Brian' **new** WDib
'Baby's Breath' WDib
'Beacon Trail' WDib
'Beatrice Trail' WDib
'Betty Stoehr' WDib
'Blackie Bryant' WDib
'Blue Dragon' (d) WDib
'Blue Tail Fly' WDib
'Blushing Trail' WDib
'Bob Serbin' (d) WDib
'Buffalo Hunt' (d) WDib
'Candy Swirls' WDib
'Cathedral' WDib
'Chantaspring' WDib
'Cherries 'n' Cream' WDib
'Chiffon Fiesta' WDib
'Chiffon Moonmoth' WDib
'Chiffon Vesper' WDib
'Coral Sparkle Trail' WDib
'Crimson Ice' WDib
'Cupid's Jewel' **new** WDib
'Deer Trail' WDib
'Delft' (d) WDib
'Desir' WDib
'Dibley's Beate' **new** WDib
'Dibley's Lis' **new** WDib
'Electric Dreams' WDib
'Emerald Love' WDib
'Falling Raindrops' WDib
'Favorite Child' WDib
'Fire Mountain' **new** WDib
'Flashy Angel' (v) WDib
'Flower Drum' **new** WDib
'Fun Trail' WDib
'Genetic Blush' WDib
'Gillian' (d) WDib
'Golden Eye' WDib
'Golden Glow' (d) WDib
'Grandmother's Halo' WDib
'Green Ice' WDib
'Green Lace' (d) WDib
'Halo's Aglitter' WDib
'Happy Cricket' WDib
'Indigo Ruffles' WDib
'Irish Flirt' (d) WDib
'Jolly Cutie Pie' **new** WDib
'King's Trail' (d) WDib
'Kostina Fantaziya' WDib
'Lemon Drop' (d) WDib
'Lemon Whip' (d) WDib
'Little Axel' WDib
'Lollipop' WDib
'Looking Glass' WDib
'Louisiana Lagniappe' WDib
'Louisiana Lullaby' (d) WDib
'Love Spots' WDib
'Lucky Lee Ann' (d) WDib
'Luminescence' WDib
'Lyon's Paprika' WDib
'Lyon's Plum Pudding' WDib
'Mac's Black Jack' WDib
'Mac's Carnival Clown' WDib
'Mac's Cheery Cherry' **new** WDib
'Mac's Circus Clown' WDib
'Mac's Coral Cutie' WDib
'Mac's Exquisite Extravaganza' WDib
'Mac's Just Jeff' (d/v) WDib
'Mac's Nocturne' (d) WDib
'Mac's Strawberry Sundae' **new** WDib
'Mair' WDib
'Ma's Corsage' WDib
'Ma's Easter Parade' **new** WDib
'Ma's Lily Pad' WDib
'Midget Lilian' (v) WDib
'Midnight Flame' (d) WDib
'Midnight Magic' WDib
'Midnight Rascal' (d) WDib
'Midnight Waltz' (d) WDib
'Milky Way Trail' WDib
'Minnie Mine' WDib
'Minstrel's Mary Ruth' WDib
'Motley Crew' WDib
'Ness' Antique Red' WDib
'Ness' Bangle Blue' WDib
'Ness' Cherry Smoke' WDib
'Ness' Crinkle Blue' (d) WDib
'Ness' Dynomite' WDib
'Ness' Midnight Fantasy' WDib
'Ness' Satin Rose' WDib
'Ness' Sheer Peach' **new** WDib
'Ness' Sno Fun' WDib
'Ness' Viking Maiden' WDib
'Newtown Ohio' WDib
nitida **new** WDib
'Ode to Beauty' WDib
'Okie Easter Bunny' WDib
'Oksana' WDib
'Optimara Little Seneca' WDib
'Otoe' (d) WDib
'Pink Duchess' (d) WDib
'Pink Wink' WDib
'Pirate's Treasure' **new** WDib
'Pixie Blue' WDib
'Pixie Pink' WDib
'Pixie Show-off' WDib
'Powder Keg' (d) WDib
'Powwow' (d/v) WDib
'Purple Passion' **new** WDib
'Rain Man' WDib
'Rainbow's Limelight' (d) WDib
'Rainbow's Quiet Riot' WDib
'Ramblin' Amethyst' WDib
'Ramblin' Angel' (d) WDib
'Ramblin' Dots' WDib
'Ramblin' Lassie' WDib
'Ramblin' Magic' (d) WDib
'Ramblin' Sunshine' WDib
'Rapid Transit' (d) WDib
'Rare Tapestry' WDib
'Raspberry Crisp' WDib
'Red Lantern' (d) WDib
'Red Summit' WDib
'Rhapsodie Clementine' WDib
'Rhapsodie Rosalie' WDib
'Robert Mayer' WDib
'Rob's Bamboozle' (d) WDib
'Rob's Blue Cat' WDib

	Plant	Suppliers
	'Rob's Blue Socks'	WDib
	'Rob's Boo Hoo'	WDib
	'Rob's Chilly Willy' (d/v)	WDib
	'Rob's Cloudy Skies' (d)	WDib
	'Rob's Dandy Lion' (d/v)	WDib
	'Rob's Denim Demon' (d/v)	WDib
	'Rob's Dust Storm' (d)	WDib
	'Rob's Gundaroo' (d)	WDib
	'Rob's Hallucination'	WDib
	'Rob's Heebie Jeebie'	WDib
	'Rob's Hopscotch' (d)	WDib
	'Rob's Hot Tamale'	WDib
	'Rob's Ice Ripples' (d)	WDib
	'Rob's Jitterbug'	WDib
	'Rob's June Bug' (d/v)	WDib
	'Rob's Love Bite' (d)	WDib
	'Rob's Peedletuck'	WDib
	'Rob's Pink Buttercups' (v)	WDib
	'Rob's Rinky Dink' (d)	WDib
	'Rob's Ruff Stuff'	WDib
	'Rob's Sarsparilla' (d)	WDib
	'Rob's Scarecrow'	WDib
	'Rob's Scrumptious'	WDib
	'Rob's Seduction' (d/v)	WDib
	'Rob's Shadow Magic' (d/v)	WDib
	'Rob's Smarty Pants' (d)	WDib
	'Rob's Sticky Wicket' (d)	WDib
	'Rob's Toorooka' (d)	WDib
	'Rob's Twinkle Blue' (d)	WDib
	'Rob's Vanilla Trail' (d)	WDib
	'Rob's Wooloomooloo' (d)	WDib
	'Roll Along Blue' (d)	WDib
	'Santa Anita'	WDib
	shumensis	WDib
	'Silly Girl' **new**	WDib
	'Sky Bells' (v)	WDib
	'Snow Leopard' **new**	WDib
	'Sweet Amy Sue' (d)	WDib
	'Taffeta Blue' (d)	WDib
	'Taffeta Petticoats'	WDib
	'Teen Thunder'	WDib
	'The Madam'	WDib
	'Tula' **new**	WDib
	'Twist 'n' Shout'	WDib
	'Warm Sunshine'	WDib
	'Whirligig Star'	WDib
	'Wisteria' (d)	WDib
	'Witch Doctor' (d)	WDib
	'Yesterday's Child'	WDib

Salix ✿ (*Salicaceae*)

	Plant	Suppliers
	acutifolia	ELan
	- 'Blue Streak' (m) ♀H4	CWiW CWon EPfP EWes MBlu NBir NLar SMHy SWat WFar WMou
	- 'Pendulifolia' (m)	SGol
	'Aegma Brno' (f)	CWon WMou
	aegyptiaca	CDoC CWon EBtc MBlu NWea WMou
	alba	CCVT CDul CHab CLnd CWiW LBuc LMaj NWea SEWo SGol WJPR WMou
	- f. ***argentea***	see *S. alba* var. *sericea*
	- 'Aurea'	CTho CWon WIvy WMou
	- 'Belders' (m)	CWon
	- var. ***caerulea***	CDul CLnd CWon NWea WMou
	- - 'Wantage Hall' (f)	CWiW CWon
	- 'Cardinalis' (f)	CWiW CWon SWat
	- 'Chermesina' hort.	see *S. alba* var. *vitellina* 'Britzensis'
	- 'Dart's Snake'	CWon ELan EPfP MAsh MBrN MRav NLar WCot
	- 'Flame'	CWon
	- 'Golden Ness'	EBee LRHS MAsh MBlu SPoG WFar
	- 'Hutchinson's Yellow'	CDoC CTho CWon MGos NLar SLim
	- 'Liempde' (m)	NWea
	- 'Raesfeld' (m)	CWiW CWon
§	- var. ***sericea*** ♀H4	CBcs CDul CLnd CTho CWon EPfP MBlu MRav MWat NLar NWea SPer WIvy WMou
	- 'Splendens'	see *S. alba* var. *sericea*
	- 'Tristis' misapplied	see *S.* × *sepulcralis* var. *chrysocoma*
§	- 'Tristis' ambig.	CCVT CLnd CTri CWon ELan LAst MBri MGos MRav MSwo NLar NWea SEND SEWo SLim SWat WFar WHar
	- var. ***vitellina*** ♀H4	CDul CTri CWon EPfP GQue LBuc MBNS MBrN NLar NWea SGol SLon SWat WIvy
§	- - 'Britzensis' (m) ♀H4	Widely available
	- - 'Nova'	SWat
§	- - 'Yelverton'	CWon EBee MAsh SPoG SWat WFar
	- 'Vitellina Pendula'	see *S. alba* 'Tristis' ambig.
	- 'Vitellina Tristis'	see *S. alba* 'Tristis' ambig.
	alba × ***amygdaloides*** × ***nigra***	CWon
§	***alpina***	ECho NHar
	'Americana'	CWiW CWon
	amplexicaulis	CWon
	- 'Pescara' (m)	CWiW
	amygdaloides	CWiW CWon
	'Aokautere'	see *S.* × *sepulcralis* 'Aokautere'
	apennina 'Cisa Pass'	CWon
	apoda	CWon
	- (m)	WPer
	appendiculata	CWon
§	***arbuscula***	CWon ECho NLar
	arenaria	see *S. repens* var. *argentea*
	aurita	NLar NWea
	babylonica	CDul CWon WMou
	- 'Annularis'	see *S. babylonica* 'Crispa'
	- 'Bijdorp'	MBri NLar
§	- 'Crispa'	CWon ELan LHop LRHS MBri MTPN MWts SMad SPoG WFar
	- 'Pan Chih-kang'	CWiW NLar
	- var. ***pekinensis***	CWon
	- - 'Pendula'	NLar
	- - 'Snake'	CWon
§	- - 'Tortuosa' ♀H4	Widely available
*	- 'Tortuosa Aurea'	SGol SWvt
	× ***balfourii***	CWon
	bebbiana	CWon
	bicolor	CWon NWea
	'Blackskin' (f)	CWiW
	bockii	EBee EBtc ELan LLHF LRHS MMuc SKHP
§	'Bowles's Hybrid'	CMam WMou
	'Boydii' (f) ♀H4	CWon ECho EPfP EPot GAbr GBin GEdr GKev ITim LEdu LRHS MGos NBir NMen NRya NSla WAbe WFar WPat WWFP
§	'Boyd's Pendulous' (m)	CWib
	burjatica	CWon
	- 'Germany'	CMam CWon
	- 'Korso'	CWon
	caesia	WIvy
	× ***calodendron*** (f)	CWon
	candida	CMam CWon

	cantabrica	CWon
	caprea	CBcs CCVT CDul CHab CLnd CTri CWon EPfP LBuc LMaj NWea SEWo SPer WMou WSFF
	- 'Black Stem'	CDul
§	- 'Kilmarnock' (m)	Widely available
	- var. ***pendula*** (m)	see *S. caprea* 'Kilmarnock' (m)
	caprea × lanata	CWon
	× ***capreola***	CWon
	cashmiriana	CWon GEdr
	caspica	CWon
*	- ***rubra nana***	SWat
	chaenomeloides	CWon
	'Chrysocoma'	see *S.* × *sepulcralis* var. *chrysocoma*
	cinerea	CBcs CDoC CTri CWon LBuc NWea SEWo WJPR WMou
	- 'Bude'	CWon
	- subsp. ***oleifolia*** × ***phylicifolia***	CWon
	- 'Tricolor' (v)	NPro
	cordata	CWon SLPl
	- 'Purpurescens'	CWon
	daphnoides	CCVT CDoC CDul CLnd CMac CWon EBee EPPr EPfP LRHS MGos MMuc MSwo NRHS NWea SEND SGol SPer SRms SWat WFar WMou WSFF
	- 'Aglaia' (m)	CBcs CDul CWon GQue WIvy
	- 'Continental Purple'	CWon
	- 'Lady Aldenham'	CWon
	- 'Meikle' (f)	CWiW SWat
	- 'Netta Statham' (m)	CWiW CWon
	- 'Ovaro Udine' (m)	CWiW
	- 'Oxford Violet' (m)	CWon NWea WIvy
	- 'Pendulifolia'	CWon
	- 'Purple Heart'	CWon
	- 'Sinker'	WIvy
	- 'Stewartstown'	CWiW
	- 'Wynter Bloom'	CWon
	× ***dasyclados***	CWon
	- 'Grandis'	NWea
	discolor	CWon
	discolor × elaeagnos	CWon
§	× ***doniana*** 'Kumeti'	CWiW CWon
	'E.A. Bowles'	see *S.* 'Bowles's Hybrid'
	× ***ehrhartiana***	CNat CWon
§	***elaeagnos***	CCVT CDoC CLnd CTho CTri ECrN EPfP MBrN MMuc NWea SEND SLon SPer SWat WFar WMou
§	- subsp. ***angustifolia*** ♀H4	CBcs CDul CWon ELan EPfP MRav MSwo NLar NPCo NWea SEND SRms WIvy
	'Elegantissima'	see *S.* × *pendulina* var. *elegantissima*
	× ***erdingeri***	CWon
	eriocephala 'American Mackay' (m)	CWiW
	- 'Green USA'	CWon
	- 'Kerksii' (m)	CWiW CWon
	- 'Mawdesley' (m)	CWiW CWon
	- 'Russelliana' (f)	CWiW CWon
§	'Erythroflexuosa'	CBcs CDoC CDul CWon EBee ELan EPPr EPfP LAst LBMP LHop MAsh MGos MMuc MRav NWea SBfd SEND SGol SLim SPer SPoG SWat WCFE WFar WHer
	exigua	Widely available
	fargesii	Widely available
§	× ***finnmarchica***	GEdr WAbe
	× ***forbyana***	CWon
	formosa	see *S. arbuscula*
	fragilis	CCVT CDul CHab CLnd MRav NWea WMou
	- var. ***decipiens***	CWon
§	- var. ***furcata***	CTri CWon GKev
	- 'Legomey'	WIvy
	× ***fruticosa*** 'McElroy' (f)	CWiW CWon
	fruticulosa	see *S. fragilis* var. *furcata*
	'Fuiri-koriyanagi'	see *S. integra* 'Hakuro-nishiki'
	furcata	see *S. fragilis* var. *furcata*
	gilgiana	CWon
	glabra	CWon
	glauca	CNat
	glaucophylloides	CWon
	'Golden Curls'	see *S.* 'Erythroflexuosa'
	gracilistyla	CTho CWon NWea SCoo SLPl WMou
§	- 'Melanostachys' (m)	Widely available
	× ***greyi***	NPro
	hastata (f)	SWat
	- 'Wehrhahnii' (m) ♀H4	CBcs CDul CWon ECho ELan EPfP GCra GKev IVic LEdu MBlu MMuc MRav MSwo NBir NWea SEND SPer SWat
	helvetica ♀H4	CBcs CDul CMac CWon EBee ECho ELan EPfP GAbr IVic MBlu MMuc MRav NBir NEgg NLar NWea SEND SPer WFar
	herbacea	ECho GEdr NMen WAbe
	hibernica	see *S. phylicifolia*
I	***himalayas***	CWon
	× ***hirtei*** 'Delamere'	CWon
	- 'Rosewarne'	CWon
	hookeriana	CDul CWon ELan MBlu MBrN MBri NLar SLPl SSpi WCFE WIvy WMou
	humilis var. ***microphylla***	CWon
	incana	see *S. elaeagnos*
	integra	CWon
	- 'Albomaculata'	see *S. integra* 'Hakuro-nishiki'
	- 'Flamingo'[PBR]	SPoG
§	- 'Hakuro-nishiki' (v)	Widely available
	- 'Pendula' (f)	MAsh MBri
	irrorata	CDul CLnd CWon EBee EPfP LRHS MBlu MSwo NLar SWat
	'Jacquinii'	see *S. alpina*
	kinuyanagi (m)	CWon ELan LHop WIvy
§	***koriyanagi***	CWiW CWon
	'Kumeti'	see *S.* × *doniana* 'Kumeti'
	'Kuro-me'	see *S. gracilistyla* 'Melanostachys'
	laggeri	CWon
	lanata ♀H4	CBcs CMac CMea CWon EBee ECho ELan ELon EPfP GAbr GKev MAsh MGos MRav NBir NEgg NHol NLar NMen NWea SBrt SPer SWat WFar
	- 'Drake's Hybrid'	NMen
	- 'Mrs Mac' (m)	CWon
	lapponum	GEdr NLar NWea SRms WAbe
	- compact **new**	GKev
	lasiandra	CWon
	× ***laurina*** (f)	CWon
§	***lindleyana***	CWon
	lucida	CWon
	mackenzieana	CWon
	magnifica ♀H4	CDul CGHE CLnd CTho CWon EBee ELan EPfP EWTr IArd LEdu LRHS MSnd NWea SKHP SMad SSpi SWat WFar WMou WPGP

	'Mark Postill' (f)	CDoC CWon EBee ELon GBin LRHS MBNS MMuc NLar SEND
	matsudana 'Tortuosa'	see *S. babylonica* var. *pekinensis* 'Tortuosa'
	- 'Tortuosa Aureopendula'	see *S.* 'Erythroflexuosa'
	'Melanostachys'	see *S. gracilistyla* 'Melanostachys'
	× ***meyeriana***	CWon WIvy
	- 'Daza'	CWon
	- 'Lumley' (f)	CWiW
	mielichhoferi	CWon
	miyabeana	CMam CWon
I	- 'Purpurascens'	CWon
	miyabeana × ***schwerinii***	CWon
	× ***mollissima***	CWiW
	var. ***hippophaifolia*** 'Jefferies' (m)	
	- - 'Notts Spaniard' (m)	CWiW
	- - 'Stinchcombe'	WIvy
	- - 'Trustworthy' (m)	CWiW CWon
	- 'Pheasant Brown'	CWon
	- 'Q83'	CMam CWon
	- var. ***undulata*** 'Kottenheider Weide' (f)	CWiW CWon
	moupinensis	CWon EPfP GKev MBri WAbe
	- EDHCH 97.319	WPGP
	aff. ***moupinensis*** from Vietnam	WPGP
§	***myrsinifolia***	EBee MBlu MMuc NLar SEND WGrn
	- subsp. ***alpicola***	CWon
	- 'Cotinifolia'	CWon
	- 'Faucille'	CWon
	myrsinites var. ***jacquiniana***	see *S. alpina*
	myrtilloides 'Pink Tassels' (m)	ECho GEdr NHar SBrt
	myrtilloides × ***repens***	see *S.* × *finnmarchica*
	nakamurana var. ***yezoalpina***	CWon EBee ELan EWes GAbr GEdr GKev GQui IVic LRHS MBlu MMuc MRav NHar NLar WAbe WFar WPat
	nepalensis	see *S. lindleyana*
	nigra	CWon
	nigricans	see *S. myrsinifolia*
	nivalis	see *S. reticulata* subsp. *nivalis*
	× ***ovata***	NMen
	× ***pendulina***	CWon
§	- var. ***elegantissima***	CWon SWat
	pentandra	CDul NWea WFar WJPR WMou
	- 'Dark French'	CWon
	- 'Patent Lumley'	CWiW CWon
	petiolaris	CWon
§	***phylicifolia***	NWea WJPR WMou
	- 'Malham' (m)	CWiW CWon
§	***purpurea***	CCVT CDul NWea WGwG WJPR WMou
	- 'Brittany Green' (f)	CWiW
	- 'Continental Reeks'	CWiW CWon WIvy
	- 'Dark Dicks' (f)	CWiW CWon NLar WIvy WSFF
	- 'Dicky Meadows' (m)	CWiW CWon WIvy
*	- 'Elegantissima'	CWon
	- 'Goldstones'	CWiW NLar WIvy
	- f. ***gracilis***	see *S. purpurea* 'Nana'
	- 'Green Dicks'	CWiW CWon WIvy
	- 'Helix'	see *S. purpurea*
	- 'Howki' (m)	CWon WMou
	- 'Irette' (m)	CWiW CWon
	- 'Jagiellonka' (f)	CWiW CWon WIvy
	- var. ***japonica***	see *S. koriyanagi*
	- subsp. ***lambertiana***	CWiW CWon WIvy
	- 'Lancashire Dicks' (m)	CWiW
	- 'Leicestershire Dicks' (m)	CWiW
	- 'Light Dicks'	CWiW CWon
	- 'Lincolnshire Dutch' (f)	CWiW
§	- 'Nana'	EPfP MMuc NLar NWea SEND SLPl SLon WFar WMoo
	- 'Nancy Saunders' (f)	CTho CWiW CWon EHoe GCal MBNS MBlu MBrN MRav NBir NLar NPro NSti SMHy SUsu WCot WIvy
I	- 'Nicholsonii Purpurascens'	CWon
	- 'Pendula' ♀H4	CCVT CWon EBee ECrN MAsh MBri MGos MSwo NPri NWea SBfd SPoG
	- 'Procumbens'	CWon
	- 'Read' (f)	CWiW
	- 'Reeks' (f)	CWiW CWon
	- 'Richartii' (f)	CWiW CWon
	- 'Uralensis' (f)	CWiW CWon
	pyrenaica	EWes WAbe
	pyrenaica × ***retusa***	ECho
	pyrifolia	CWon NWea
	rehderiana	CWon
	reinii	CWon
	repens	NLar NWea SRms SWat WGwG WKif
§	- var. ***argentea***	CDul CWon ELan EPfP EWes LRHS MMuc MRav NWea SPer WFar
	- 'Armando'PBR	NLar
	- 'Iona' (m)	NLar
	- ***pendula***	see *S.* 'Boyd's Pendulous' (m)
	- 'Voorthuizen' (f)	ECho
	reticulata ♀H4	ECho EPot GKev NBir NMen NSla WAbe
§	- subsp. ***nivalis***	EPot
	retusa	CTri NBir
	'Robin Redbreast'	CWon
	rosmarinifolia misapplied	see *S. elaeagnos* subsp. *angustifolia*
	× ***rubens*** 'Basfordiana' (m)	CDoC CDul CLnd CTho CWiW CWon EWes MBNS SWat WMou
	- 'Bouton Aigu'	CWiW CWon
	- 'Farndon'	CWiW
	- 'Farndon Red'	CWon
	- 'Flanders Red' (f)	CWiW CWon
	- 'Fransgeel Rood' (m)	CWiW CWon
	- 'Glaucescens' (m)	CWiW CWon
	- 'Golden Willow'	CWiW CWon
	- 'Hutchinson's Brown'	CWon
	- 'Jaune de Falaise'	CWiW CWon
	- 'Jaune Hâtive'	CWiW
	- 'Laurina'	CWiW
	- 'Natural Red' (f)	CWiW CWon
	- 'Parsons'	CWiW CWon
	- 'Rouge Ardennais'	CWiW CWon
	- 'Rouge Folle'	CWiW
	- 'Russet' (f)	CWiW
	× ***rubra***	CWiW
	- 'Abbey's Harrison' (f)	CWiW
	- 'Continental Osier' (f)	CWiW CWon
	- 'Eugenei' (m)	CDul CWon GQui MBlu SWat WIvy
	- 'Fidkin' (f)	CWiW CWon
	- 'Harrison's' (f)	CWiW CWon
	- 'Harrison's Seedling A' (f)	CWiW
	- 'Mawdesley'	CWiW CWon
	- 'Mawdesley Seedling A' (f)	CWiW
	- 'Pyramidalis'	CWiW CWon
	sachalinensis 'Kioryo'	CWon
	salviifolia	CWon

× ***savensis***	CWon
Scarlet Curls = 'Scarcuzam'	CWon WPat
schwerinii	CWon
- 'Hilliers'	CWon
schwerinii* × *viminalis new	CMam
scouleriana	CWon
× ***sepulcralis***	NWea
§ - 'Aokautere'	CWiW CWon
- 'Caradoc'	CWiW CWon
§ - var. ***chrysocoma***	Widely available
× ***sericans***	CWon
× ***seringeana***	CWon
serissaefolia	CWon
serpyllifolia	CTri NHar NMen WPat WThu
- 'Chamonix'	NSla
serpyllum	see *S. fragilis* var. *furcata*
'Setsuka'	see *S. udensis* 'Sekka'
silesiaca	CWon
× ***simulatrix***	EBee
sitchensis	NWea
× ***smithiana***	CLnd CWon NWea
× ***stipularis*** (f)	NWea
'Stuartii'	NMen
subopposita	EBee EBtc ELan EWes MMuc SEND WAbe WGwG
triandra	CDul CWon WMou
- 'Black German' (m)	CWiW
- 'Black Hollander' (m)	CWiW CWon NLar WIvy
- 'Black Maul'	CWiW
- 'Brilliant'	CWon
- 'Champion B'	CWon
- 'Grisette de Falaise'	CWiW CWon
- 'Grisette Droda' (f)	CWiW CWon
- var. ***hoffmanniana***	CWon
- 'Houghton's Black'	CWon
- 'Light French'	CWon
- 'Long Bud'	CWiW
- 'Noir de Challans'	CWiW CWon
- 'Noir de Touraine'	CWiW CWon
- 'Noir de Villaines' (m)	CWiW CWon WIvy
- 'Oliveacea'	CWon
- 'Rouge d'Orléans'	CWon EBtc
- 'Sarda d'Anjou'	CWiW
- 'Semperflorens' (m)	CWon NLar
- 'Whissander'	CWiW CWon WIvy
- 'Zwarre Driebast'	CWon
× ***tsugaluensis*** 'Ginme' (f)	CWon SLPl
udensis	NWea
§ - 'Sekka' (m)	CWon ELan EPfP LTen MBlu MMuc NBir NWea SEND SWat WFar WIvy WMou
uva-ursi	WAbe
viminalis	CCVT CLnd CMac CMam CWon EPfP LBuc NWea SEWo SVic WJPR WMou WSFF
- 'Black Satin'	CWon
- 'Brown Merrin'	WIvy
- 'Gigantea' (m)	CMam CWon
- 'Green Gotz'	CWiW WIvy
- 'Reader's Red' (m)	WIvy
- 'Riefenweide'	WIvy
- 'Romanin'	CWon
- 'Yellow Osier'	WIvy
vitellina 'Pendula'	see *S. alba* 'Tristis' ambig.
waldsteiniana	CWon EBee
'Yelverton'	see *S. alba* var. *vitellina* 'Yelverton'

Salicornia (*Amaranthaceae*)

europaea	SVic

Salsola (*Amaranthaceae*)

soda	CArn ELau

Salvia ✿ (*Lamiaceae*)

sp.	CHab
ACE 2172	SPin
CC 6306	GKev
CD&R 1162	EPyc SPhx
CD&R 1458	SPin
CD&R 1495	SPin
CD&R 3071	SPin
PC&H 226	SPin
from Catamarca, Argentina new	SDys
acetabulosa	see *S. multicaulis*
adenophora	EPyc SPin XSen
aerea	CPom
aethiopis	EWes SDix SPav SPin XSen
§ ***africana***	CSpe SPin WHil XSen
africana-caerulea	see *S. africana*
africana-lutea	see *S. aurea*
agnes	EPyc SPin
algeriensis	EPyc SBch
'Allen Chickering'	XSen
amarissima	EPyc SPin XSen
'Amber'	LHop SBrt SPin SUsu XSen
ambigens	see *S. guaranitica* 'Blue Enigma'
'Amistad' new	WHlf
ampelophylla B&SWJ 10751	SPin WCru
§ ***amplexicaulis***	EPyc NLar SMrm SPin SRms WHrl WPer XSen
amplifrons	SPin
angustifolia Cav.	see *S. reptans*
angustifolia Mich.	see *S. azurea*
'Anna' new	SDys
'Anthony Parker'	SAga WOut XSen
'Anthony Waterer' new	EWld
apiana	CArn EOHP EPyc MHer SGar SPin WHfH XSen
arenaria	SPin
argentea ♀H3	CBcs CSpe EBee ECha ECtt ELan EPfP GKev GMaP LHop LRHS MSpe NRHS SBfd SGar SMad SMrm SPav SPer SPin SWat WCAu WFar WJek WKif WMnd WWEG XLum XSen
- 'Artemis' new	EBee
arizonica	CCon EPyc EWld GCal LHop LPla MAsh SDys SPin SUsu XSen
aspera	SPin XSen
atrocyanea	CSpe ECre EPyc EWes EWld MAsh MSpe SDys SGar SPin WHal WKif WWlt XSen
§ ***aurea***	CHll CSev CSpe SBch SGar SPin SPlb SWal XLum XSen
- 'Kirstenbosch'	CDes CSev EBee ECtt EPyc EWld MRav SDys SGar SPin WKif WPGP WPer XSen
aurita	SPin
- var. ***galpinii***	SPin XSen
austriaca	SPin XSen
§ ***azurea***	CRWN EPyc LRHS SMrm SPhx SPin XSen
- var. ***grandiflora***	SPin WCot
bacheriana	see *S. buchananii*
§ ***barrelieri***	ESwi SPin XSen
'Bee's Bliss'	XSen
'Belhaven'	EWld GCal SPin

bertolonii	see *S. pratensis* Bertolonii Group
bicolor	see *S. barrelieri*
'Black Knight'	CWGN EPyc SDys SPin WPGP
blancoana	see *S. lavandulifolia* subsp. *blancoana*
blepharophylla	CPrp ECtt EGHP EPyc LHop MHer MSCN SPin SRkn XSen
- 'Diablo'	ECtt SAga SPin
- 'Painted Lady'	CWGN MAsh SDys SPin WWlt
'Blue Chiquita'	SPin
'Blue Sky'	EWld
bracteata	XSen
brandegeei	SPin
broussonetii	SPin XSen
§ ***buchananii*** ♀H1+3	CHll CSam EBee ECtt EGHP EPyc LHop MAsh MHer MRav SAga SDys SPin SRkn SWal XSen
bulleyana misapplied	see *S. flava* var. *megalantha*
bulleyana Diels	CPLG EBee EWes EWld MDKP MHoo MMHG SGar WCru WPer XSen
- 'Blue Lips' **new**	WHlf
bullulata **new**	SPin
cacaliifolia ♀H1+3	CPLG CRHN ECtt EGHP EPyc EWld GCal MAsh MHer MSCN SDys SGar SPer SPin SRkn SUsu WSHC WWlt XSen
cadmica	SPin WHil
caerulea misapplied	see *S. guaranitica* 'Black and Blue'
caerulea L.	see *S. africana*
caespitosa	NMen SPin XSen
campanulata	CPom CPou EWld SPin
- B&SWJ 9232	WCru
- DJHC C394	SPin
- GWJ 9294	SPin WCru
- var. ***hirtella*** GWJ 9397	WCru
canariensis	IDee SPin WOut XSen
- f. ***albiflora***	XSen
- f. ***candidissima***	SPin XSen
candelabrum ♀H3-4	CAbP CSev CSpe EWes GCal MHer SAga SBch SPav SPhx SPin WCot WKif WPnn WWlt XSen
candidissima	SPin XSen
canescens	XSen
cardinalis	see *S. fulgens*
cardiophylla **new**	SPin
carnea	EWld MHom SPin
- from Valle de Bravo, Mexico	EPyc SDys
castanea	LRHS SPin
caudata	SPin XSen
§ ***chamaedryoides***	CSev EGHP EPyc MHom SBrt SGar SPet SPhx SPin SUsu WPGP XLum XSen
- var. ***isochroma***	EPyc IRar MAsh SGar SPin SUsu WPGP XSen
- 'Marine Blue'	MAsh MCot
- silver-leaved	CSpe SPin WHil XLum
aff. ***chamaedryoides*** B&SWJ 9032 from Guatemala	SPin WCru
chamelaeagnea	EPyc SPin SUsu XSen
chapalensis	SPin WWlt
chiapensis	MAsh SPin SUsu WWlt XSen
chinensis	see *S. japonica*
chionophylla	SPin
'Christine Yeo'	CSev EBee ECtt EGHP ELon EPfP EPri EPyc MAsh MSpe SAga SBch SDys SEND SGar SPin SUsu WHil WHoo WMnd WPGP XSen

cinnabarina	SPin
cleistogama misapplied	see *S. glutinosa*
clevelandii	EWes MHer SPav SPin WJek XSen
- 'Winnifred Gilman'	SDys
clinopodioides	CDes EBee SPin
'Clotted Cream' **new**	EWld
coahuilensis misapplied	see *S. greggii* × *serpyllifolia*
coahuilensis ambig.	EPyc LSou MAsh SGar SKHP SLon SMrm SPin SRkn WSHC XLum
coahuilensis Fernald	LHop
coccinea	SPin
- 'Brenthurst'	SPin
- 'Coral Nymph' (Nymph Series)	ECtt EPyc LDai SPav SPin
- 'Forest Fire'	EPyc
- 'Lady in Red' (Nymph Series) ♀H3	ECtt SPav
* - 'Snow Nymph' (Nymph Series)	ECtt EPyc
concolor misapplied	see *S. guaranitica*
concolor Lamb. ex Benth.	EPyc EWld GCal MHom SDys SPin WPGP WSHC XSen
confertiflora	CCon CHEx CPLG CSam CSpe CWCL ECre ECtt EGHP ELan EPyc EShb GCal MAsh MHer MHom MSCN SAga SDys SGar SPin SPlb SRkn SUsu SWal WKif WPGP WWlt XSen
corrugata	CCon CPne EBee ECtt EPyc EWld GCal LRHS MAsh MHer SAga SDys SPhx SPin SRkn SWal WPGP WWlt XSen
'Crème Caramel'	CWGN ECtt EPyc MAsh MHom
cruickshanksii	SPin
cryptantha	XSen
aff. ***curtiflora*** B&SWJ 10356	WCru
curviflora	CSpe EPyc SBch SDys SPin XSen
cyanescens	CMea CPBP EBee EPot EPyc SBch SPin XSen
cyanicalyx	EPyc SDys SPin XSen
cyclostegia	CPLG
daghestanica	GKev SPin XSen
'Dale Blue'	EWld
I ***dangitalis*** SDR 4332	CPLG EBee
darcyi misapplied	see *S. roemeriana*
darcyi J. Compton	CHll CPLG CSpe EPyc EWes EWld MCot SDys SPin WSHC WWlt XSen
davidsonii	SPin
decumbens	SPin
dentata	SPin
desoleana	SPin WHil XSen
'Didi'	NDov
digitaloides	XSen
- BWJ 7777	SPin WCru
'Dinah'	SUsu
discolor ♀H1	CSev CSpe ECtt ELan EPyc EWld GCal LDai MAsh MBel MCot MHer SAga SDys SEND SGar SPet SPin WWlt XSen
* - ***nigra***	CArn CCse
disermas	SPin SPlb XSen
- pink-flowered	SPin
disjuncta	SPin XSen
divinorum	CArn EOHP GPoy LEdu WHfH XSen
dolichantha	CCVN CCon EBee EPyc LRHS MCot MDKP NBir NLar SEND SPin WHer WMoo WPtf XSen
dolomitica	SPav SPin

	Name	Suppliers
	dombeyi	CPne EPyc SDys SPin
	dominica	CArn SPin XSen
	dorisiana	MAsh SDys SPin WHer XSen
	'Dorset Wonder'	NDov
	durifolia new	SPin
	'Dyson's Crimson'	SDys
	eigii	SPin XSen
	eizi-matudae	EPyc SPin
	elegans	ELau EWes GCal GCra MHom MHoo XSen
	- 'Golden Delicious'	ECtt ENfk EWes LHop MHer MHoo MNHC SBfd SPin WFar WHer WHil WOut
	- 'Honey Melon'	EGHP ENfk EPyc MAsh MHoo SDys
§	- 'Scarlet Pineapple'	Widely available
	- 'Sonoran Red'	SDys
	- 'Tangerine'	CArn CPrp CWan EGHP ELau ENfk EOHP EPyc LAst LSou MHer MHoo MNHC NLBP SBfd SPin SWal WJek
	eremostachya	XSen
	euphratica new	XSen
	evansiana	SPin XSen
	'Eveline'	CSev CWGN ECtt EPfP LRHS NLar
	excelsa	SPin XSen
	fallax	SPin XSen
	farinacea	EPfP SPin
	- 'Victoria' ♀H3	LRHS SGar WHrl
§	***flava*** var. ***megalantha***	ELan LSRN SPin XSen
	- - BWJ 7974	WCru
	florida	SPin XSen
	forreri	EBee EPyc MAsh NDov SBHP SEND SPin WPGP XSen
	- 'Karen Dyson'	SDys
§	***forsskaolii***	Widely available
	- white-flowered	SPin XSen
§	***fruticosa***	CArn ELau EPyc LRHS SIde SLon SPin XSen
§	***fulgens*** ♀H3	EPyc EWld GCal MAsh MHoo SAga SBHP SDys SGar SPin SRkn WFar WWlt XSen
	- from Mt Popacatapetl, Mexico new	SDys
	gesneriiflora	CSpe ECtt EPyc EWld SDys SGar SPin WPGP XSen
	- mountain form new	WPGP
	- 'Tequila'	SPin WOut WWlt
	gilliesii	SPin
	glabrescens	SPin
	- B&SWJ 11152	WCru
*	- var. ***robusta*** B&SWJ 11147	WCru
	glechomifolia	SPin XSen
§	***glutinosa***	CArn CMac CSpe EBee EPyc EWld GCal LDai LRHS MCot MNrw NBro NLar SPav SPin WCAu WCot WPer WTcb XSen
	graciliramulosa	SPin XSen
	gracilis	SPin
	grahamii	see *S. microphylla* var. *microphylla*
	gravida	SPin
	'Great Comp'	SDys
	greggii	ECtt EGHP EPyc EWes LRHS MHer WPer WTcb XLum XSen
	- CD&R 1148	MCot SDys
	- 'Alba'	EGHP EPyc SAga SPin XLum XSen
	- 'Blush Pink'	see *S. microphylla* 'Pink Blush'
	- 'Caramba' (v)	EBee EGHP LHop LRHS SAga SPet WHil
	- 'Devon Cream'	see *S. greggii* 'Sungold'
	- 'Icing Sugar' PBR	CCVN CWGN ECtt EPPr EPyc LHop LPot LRHS MAsh MCot NDov NPri SDys SPet SPoG SRkn WBor WHil WPer WSHC
	- 'Keter's Red'	WHil
	- 'Lara' new	WHlf
	- 'Lipstick'	CPLG EBee ECtt MAsh
	- 'Magenta'	WHil
	- 'Magnet'	SPin
	- (Navajo Series) 'Navajo Bright Red'	EPyc
*	- - 'Navajo Cream'	EPyc
*	- - 'Navajo Dark Purple'	EPyc SAga
*	- - 'Navajo Purple'	EPyc MCot
	- - Navajo Salmon Red = 'Rfds016'	EPyc
*	- - 'Navajo White'	EPyc
	- 'Peach' misapplied	see *S.* × *jamensis* 'Pat Vlasto'
	- 'Peach'	CSpe CWGN EGHP ELau EPfP EPyc MAsh MHer MHoo SAga SGar SPet SPoG SUsu WMnd WPGP WWlt XLum XSen
	- 'Pink Preference'	MAsh SUsu
	- 'Raspberry Red'	MCot XLum
	- salmon-flowered	MHoo
	- 'Sierra San Antonio'	see *S.* × *jamensis* 'Sierra San Antonio'
	- 'Sparkler' (v)	EPfP LRHS MAsh SLon SPoG
	- 'Stormy Pink'	CDes CHll CSam CSpe EPyc LRHS MAsh MCot NDov SAga SUsu WHil WIvy WPGP WPer WSHC WWlt XSen
§	- 'Sungold'	CWGN ECtt EGHP EPfP EPyc LRHS MAsh MHoo NDov SDys SHom SPin SUsu WHil WMnd WWlt XSen
	- variegated (v)	EHoe XSen
	- yellow-flowered	XLum
	greggii* × *lycioides	see *S. greggii* × *serpyllifolia*
§	***greggii* × *serpyllifolia***	CAbP CSpe EPyc MCot MHoo NDov NPri SDys SGar SPin WSHC
	grewiifolia	SPin
	guadalujarensis new	SPin
§	***guaranitica***	CBcs CEnt CHEx ECtt EShb EWld LRHS MHer SAga SPin SWal WKif WPGP WWlt XLum XSen
	- 'Argentina Skies'	CHGN CSpe EPPr EPyc SAga SMrm SPin WWlt XSen
§	- 'Black and Blue'	CCon CPLG CRHN CSpe CWCL CWGN EBee ECre ECtt EGHP EPfP EPyc GCal LHop LRHS LSRN NPri SAga SBod SDys SGar SMrm SPin SUsu WPGP WSHC WTcb XSen
§	- 'Blue Enigma' ♀H3-4	CArn CPLG CSev CSpe CWGN EBee ECha ECtt EGHP EHrv EPfP EShb GCal LHop LRHS MAsh MCot MGos MRav MSpe SDix SDys SEND SMrm SPin WMnd WWlt XLum XSen
	- 'Brazil'	LRHS
	- 'Costa Rica Blue' new	SDys
	- 'Indigo Blue'	ECtt EPfP MAsh SPin WWlt
	- 'Purple Splendor'	EShb MHer
	- purple-flowered	CSam
	haematodes	see *S. pratensis* Haematodes Group
	haenkei	SPin XSen
	- 'Prawn Chorus'	CSpe CWGN LRHS MAsh WWlt
	heerii	SPin
	heldreichiana	SPin XSen
	henryi	SPin

hians	CPom EBee EWld GCal GCra MDKP NLar SBfd SGar SRms WPer XLum
- CC 1787	CPLG
hierosolymitana	CHid LRHS XSen
hirtella	SPin
hispanica misapplied	see *S. lavandulifolia*
hispanica L.	CSam SPin
holwayi	EPyc SPin XSen
- B&SWJ 8995	WCru
horminum	see *S. viridis* var. *comata*
huberi	XSen
'Huntsman's Red'	IRar
hydrangea **new**	SPin
hypargeia	XSen
'Ice Blue' **new**	MHom
inconspicua	SPin
indica	XSen
'Indigo Spires'	CHll CMHG CPLG CSpe CWGN ECre ECtt EPyc EShb EWld MAsh MCot NDov SAga SDys SMrm SPhx SPin SUsu WSHC WWlt XLum XSen
interrupta	MCot MHer SAga SPin XSen
involucrata ♀H3	CCon CPom CSev CSpe EPyc EWld GCra MCot MHom NBro SDys SPin SUsu WHrl WSHC XSen
- 'Bethellii' ♀H3-4	CArn CMHG EBee ECtt ELan EPfP EPyc LRHS MAsh MHer SAga SBch SDix SDys SGar SKHP SMrm SPin SRkn WGrn WKif WWlt XLum XSen
- 'Boutin' ♀H3	EPyc MAsh MHom SDys WWlt
§ - 'Hadspen'	CCon CDes CHll CRHN CSam CSpe EWes GCal SBch SPin XLum XSen
- 'Joan'	CWGN EPyc MAsh SDys SPin SUsu WWlt
- 'Mrs Pope'	see *S. involucrata* 'Hadspen'
- 'Pink Icicles' **new**	SDys
* - var. ***puberula***	MHom SPin XSen
iodantha	SDys SPin
- 'Louis Saso'	SPin
iodochroa	EBee
- B&SWJ 10252	SPin WCru
× ***jamensis***	EBee ELau EWes NPri SPin
- 'California Sunset'	EWld MAsh SDys SUsu
- 'Cherry Queen'	CWGN EBee EPyc MAsh SAga SPin WWlt XSen
- 'Dark Dancer'	CSpe MAsh SPhx WHil WWlt XSen
- 'Desert Blaze' (v)	CDes CWGN ECtt EGHP EPyc LBuc MCot MHer NCGa SDys SMrm SPin WGrn WPGP WTcb WWlt XLum
- 'Devantville'	NDov XLum
- 'Dysons' Orangy Pink'	CDes CSpe NDov SAga
- 'El Durazno'	MHoo WTcb
§ - 'Hot Lips'	Widely available
- 'James Compton'	EPyc SMrm
- 'Kentish Pink'	SDys
- 'La Luna'	CDes CEnt CSam CSpe ECtt EPyc LHop MAsh MCot MHer MHom MRav MSCN NDov SGar SPin SUsu WHil WIvy WMnd WPGP WPer WSHC WTcb XLum XSen
- 'La Siesta'	EBee EGHP EPyc MHoo SAga WTcb XSen
- 'La Tarde'	CEnt CTri EGHP EPyc MAsh MHom SBch WTcb WWlt XSen
- 'Los Lirios' ♀H3-4	CPom CSpe CTri EPyc SAga SMrm SPin SUsu WHil WIvy WWlt
- 'Maraschino'	EBee EPfP EPyc LHop LRHS MAsh SDys SPin SRms WMnd WWlt XLum XSen
* - 'Mauve'	EPyc NDov
- 'Moonlight Over Ashwood' (v)	EPyc MAsh SBHP SPin WSHC WWlt
- 'Moonlight Serenade'	EPyc MAsh SAga SDys SUsu
§ - 'Pat Vlasto'	EPyc SPin SUsu
- 'Peter Vidgeon'	CSpe CWGN EPyc MCot SDys SPin SUsu WWlt
- 'Pleasant Pink'	EPyc MAsh SUsu XSen
- 'Plum Wine'	WWlt
- 'Raspberry Royale' ♀H3-4	CDes CPom EBee ECtt EGHP EPfP EPyc LHop LRHS MAsh MCot MHer MHoo SBch SGar SMrm SPin WIvy WMnd WSHC WTcb XSen
- 'Red Velvet'	ECtt EGHP ELon EPyc EWld MAsh MHom SDys SUsu WHrl WSHC WWlt XSen
- 'Señorita Leah'	CWGN EPyc MAsh SDys SUsu WWlt
§ - 'Sierra San Antonio'	CDes CWGN EPfP EPyc LRHS MAsh MHom NDov SAga SBHP SDys SMrm SUsu WPGP WTcb XLum XSen
- 'Stormy Sunrise'	SDys
§ - 'Trebah'	CPom CSpe ECre EPyc EShb LRHS MAsh MCot MHom SDys SGar SPin SPoG SRot WHil WIvy WSHC WWlt XSen
- 'Trenance'	CSpe ECre ELon EPyc LHop LRHS MHom SAga SBch SGar SPin SRot WHil WIvy WWlt XSen
§ ***japonica***	SPin XSen
- 'Alba'	SPin
'Jean's Purple Passion'	EPyc SDys SPin
judaica	CMac SPin WGrn XSen
jurisicii	CWib EBee EPyc LRHS MAsh SEND SGar SPav SPin WJek WSHC XLum XSen
- 'Alba'	XSen
- pink-flowered	CSpe SPin XSen
karwinskyi	SPin XSen
- B&SWJ 9081	WCru
keerlii	SPin XSen
koyamae	LRHS SPin
- B&SWJ 10919	WCru
kronenburgii **new**	XSen
'Lady Strybing'	SPin
'Lalarsha' **new**	SDys
lanceolata	CSpe EPyc LHop SPin WWlt XSen
lanigera	SPin
'Lararsha'	MCot SUsu
lasiantha	SPin XSen
§ ***lavandulifolia***	Widely available
§ - subsp. ***blancoana***	CMea ECha ELau EPyc MHer SPin XSen
- subsp. ***pyrenaeorum*** **new**	XSen
- subsp. ***vellerea*** **new**	XSen
lavanduloides	SPin
- B&SWJ 9053	CDes WCru
lemmonii	see *S. microphylla* var. *wislizeni*
'Lemon Pie' **new**	WHlf
leptophylla	see *S. reptans*
leucantha ♀H1	CArn CSev CSpe ELan EPyc MAsh MCot MHer MRav MSCN SAga SEND SGar SPin SPlb SRkn SWal WTcb XSen
- 'Danielle's Dream' **new**	EBee

- 'Eder' (v) — MAsh SDys SPin
- 'Midnight' — CSam
- 'Purple Velvet' — ECtt EGHP EPyc MAsh MHer MHom SDix SDys SPin SUsu WWlt XSen
- 'San Marcos Lavender' — CSev SPin
- 'Santa Barbara' — CHll LRHS MAsh SDys XSen
- 'White Mischief' new — EBee

leucocephala — CSev EPyc SGar SPin XSen
leucophylla — XSen
- NNS 01-375 — SPin WCot

limbata new — XSen
littae — SPin XSen
longispicata — SPin
longistyla — SPin WPGP XSen
* ***luzentzii*** F&W 11499 — IFoB
lycioides misapplied — see *S. greggii* × *serpyllifolia*
lycioides A. Gray — CAbP CHll LRHS SEND SPhx SPin
lyrata — EOHP SGar XSen
- 'Burgundy Bliss' — see *S. lyrata* 'Purple Knockout'
§ - 'Purple Knockout' — EBee EGHP EPfP EPyc LAst NLBP SBfd SGar SMrm SPin WHer WPtf XSen
- 'Purple Vulcano' — see *S. lyrata* 'Purple Knockout'

macellaria misapplied — see *S. microphylla*
macellaria Epling — CSam
macrophylla — GCal SDys SPin WPGP XSen
- Cally selection — SPin
- 'Wendy's Surprise' — SUsu WWlt

macrophylla* × *sagittata new — SDys
macrosiphon — SPin
'Madeline' — CWGN EBee EPfP LRHS LSou MAvo
madrensis — EPyc SPin XSen
- 'Dunham' — GCal WWlt

'Magic Potion' — CWGN
melissodora — SPin
mellifera — CArn SPin XSen
merjamie 'Mint-sauce' — LRHS
mexicana — SPin
- B&SWJ 10288 — WCru
- 'Lollie Jackson' — WWlt
- var. ***mexicana*** — XSen
- var. ***minor*** — EPyc SDys SPin
- 'Snowflake' — XSen

meyeri — CPom EPyc EWld MHom SPin WWlt
§ ***microphylla*** — CArn CMHG CMac CPom CPrp CTri CWan ELau EOHP EWes LAst LHop MHer MHoo MSCN NSti SPet WCFE WPer XLum
- CD&R 1141 — SPin
- F&M 157 — WPGP
- 'Belize' — CPrp EGHP MAsh NDov SBri SUsu WHil WWlt
- 'Cerro Potosi' — CCse CPom CPrp CSev CSpe EGHP ELon EPfP EPyc LRHS MAsh SAga SDys SGar SMrm SPin SUsu WCFE WIvy WWlt XLum
- 'Hot Lips' — see *S.* × *jamensis* 'Hot Lips'
- 'Huntington' — EOHP EPyc SPin XSen
- 'Kew Red' ♀H3-4 — CCon EGHP EWld MHoo MNrw SPin WHil WHoo WPGP
- 'La Trinidad' — XSen
I - 'Lutea' — MAsh SUsu
- 'Maroon' — CWGN EPyc SDys SUsu
§ - var. ***microphylla*** — CRHN CSev CSpe CTri CWib EBee ECtt EGHP ELan ENfk EOHP EPfP EPyc LSRN MCot MHer MHoo MNHC MRav NPri SEND SPin SRkn WHfH WJek WPer WSHC XSen
- - 'La Foux' — EPyc MCot SBch SMrm XLum XSen
- - 'Newby Hall' ♀H3-4 — CDes CPom ECtt EGHP EPyc EShb EWes MHoo SPhx WPGP XSen
N - var. ***neurepia*** — see *S. microphylla* var. *microphylla*
- 'Orange Door' — EPyc SDys XSen
- orange-red-flowered new — MRav
- 'Oregon Peach' — EPfP LRHS
- 'Oxford' — EGHP SPin
§ - 'Pink Blush' ♀H3-4 — EABi EBee ECtt EGHP ELan EPfP EPyc LRHS MAsh MCot MHer MHom MHoo SEND SMrm SPin SPoG SRkn WHil WHoo WIvy WKif WPGP WPer WSHC WTcb WWlt XSen
- 'Pleasant View' ♀H3-4 — EPyc SUsu WHil WWlt XSen
- 'Robin's Pride' — EPyc SDys SUsu
- 'Rodbaston Current Purple' — MSpe
- 'Rodbaston Red' — WWlt
- 'Rosy Cheeks' — WOut
§ - 'Ruth Stungo' (v) — ECre IRar
- 'San Carlos Festival' — CPom EGHP EPyc MAsh NCGa SBch SDys SPhx SPin SUsu WPGP WWlt XSen
- 'Trelawny Rose Pink' — see *S.* 'Trelawney'
- 'Trelissick Creamy Yellow' — see *S.* 'Trelissick'
- 'Trewithen Cerise' — see *S.* 'Trewithen'
- 'Variegata' splashed — see *S. microphylla* 'Ruth Stungo'
- 'Violette' — EPfP EPyc
- 'Wild Watermelon' — CPrp CWGN EPfP EPyc MAsh MCot SAga SDys WWFP WWlt XSen
§ - var. ***wislizeni*** — CPom EPyc SPin
- 'Zaragoza' — SPin

microstegia — XSen
miltiorhiza — CArn CSpe MHoo SPhx SPin XSen
miniata — CSpe EPyc SBHP SPin XSen
misella — SPin
mohavensis — SPin XSen
moorcroftiana — EPyc WHil
moschata — SPin
'Mrs Beard' — XSen
muelleri misapplied — see *S. greggii* × *serpyllifolia*
muelleri Epling — EBee EPyc
muirii — SPin
'Mulberry Jam' — CCse CHGN CHll CSev CSpe EBee ECtt EPfP EPyc EWes LHop MAsh MCot MHom NDov SAga SBch SDys SPin SRkn SUsu WKif WPGP WSHC WTcb WWFP WWlt XSen
§ ***multicaulis*** ♀H4 — EPyc MAsh SPin XSen
munzii — CCon SDys SPin XSen
* ***murrayi*** — CAbP SPin
Mystic Spires Blue = 'Balsalmisp'PBR — CSpe CWGN EPyc
'Nachtvlinder' new — SDys
namaensis — CSev SGar SPin XSen
nana B&SWJ 10272 — SPin WCru WHil
napifolia — EBee LPot LRHS NLar SAga SPav SPin XSen
- 'Baby Blue' — EBee LRHS

'Nazareth' — MAsh SPin XSen
'Nel' — LHop
nemorosa — EPyc LRHS SPin SRms XLum XSen
- 'Amethyst' ♀H4 — EBee ELon EPfP GQue IKil LPot LRHS MBel MRav MSpe NDov

		NRHS SDys SMHy SMrm SPhx SPin SRms WCAu WCot WKif WWEG WWlt XSen
	- 'Blaureiter'	LRHS
	- Blue Mound	see *S.* × *sylvestris* 'Blauhügel'
	- 'Caradonna'	Widely available
	- East Friesland	see *S. nemorosa* 'Ostfriesland'
	- 'Indigo Friesland'	LRHS
	- 'Kleine Amethyst'	NDov
	- 'Lubecca' ♀H4	EBee ECtt EHrv ETod LHop LRHS MBel MCot MSpe NDov NEgg NGdn NLar SPer WFar WMnd WWEG XSen
	- Marcus = 'Haeumanarc'PBR	CWGN EBee ECtt ELan EPfP LAst LBMP LRHS LSRN LSou MBNS MBri MRav NDov NLar SBfd SDys SPoG WFar WSHC
	- 'Midsummer'	EWld
	- 'New Dimension Blue' **new**	EBee
	- 'New Dimension Rose' **new**	EBee
§	- 'Ostfriesland' ♀H4	Widely available
	- 'Phoenix Pink'	SPhx
	- 'Pink Beauty'	MWat
	- 'Pink Friesland'PBR	EBee ECtt ELon EPPr EWTr GQue LRHS LSou MGos MSpe NDov SMrm
	- 'Plumosa'	see *S. nemorosa* 'Pusztaflamme'
	- 'Porzellan' ♀H4	ECtt
§	- 'Pusztaflamme' ♀H4	EBee ECha ECtt ELon EPPr EPfP GQue LRHS LSou MRav MSpe NOrc SMrm SUsu WWEG XSen
	- 'Rose Queen'	ECtt ELon LAst MWat NBir SWat WCot WFar XLum XSen
	- 'Rosenwein'	EBee LDai LRHS MDKP NGdn SMrm SPhx XSen
	- 'Royal Distinction'	EBee ECtt
	- 'Schneekönig'	LSou
	- 'Schwellenburg'	CMea CSpe EBee ECtt ELon GBin GQue LHop LRHS LSou MBel NLar SPad SUsu WCot XSen
I	- (Sensation Series) 'Sensation Blue Improved'	LRHS
	- - 'Sensation Blue'	IPot
	- - 'Sensation Deep Blue' **new**	ELon
I	- - 'Sensation Deep Rose Improved'	LRHS
	- - 'Sensation Rose'	CCVN EBee LBMP LLHF LRHS LSou MAsh MBri NDov SHil WCot
	- - 'Sensation Sky Blue'	LRHS
	- - 'Sensation White'	CSev CWGN
§	- subsp. ***tesquicola***	ECha EPyc LSRN MWhi NGdn NLar SMrm SPhx WFar
	- 'Wesuwe'	EBee ELon EPPr ETod NDov XSen
	neurepia	see *S. microphylla* var. *microphylla*
*	***nevadensis***	SPin
	'Newe Ya'ar'	EPfP
	nilotica	LRHS SPin XSen
	nipponica B&SWJ 5829	SPin WCru
	- var. ***trisecta***	SPin
	nubicola	CPLG GPoy SPin WOut XSen
	- BWJ 7639	WCru
	- CC 4607	EBee
	- CC 4762	NLar
	'Nuchi' **new**	SPin
	nutans	SPin XSen
	oblongifolia B&SWJ 10315	WCru
	officinalis	Widely available
	- 'Albiflora'	CArn CSev ECtt EOHP MHoo SPin WJek XSen
N	- 'Aurea' ambig.	CWib GPoy MHoo
	- 'Berggarten'	CArn CPrp ECha ELau EPfP GCal LEdu LHop MCot MHer MRav SDix SPhx SPin SUsu WHer WJek WMnd XLum XSen
§	- broad-leaved	ELau EWhm MHer SWat WJek
	- 'Crispa'	EOHP SPin XSen
	- 'Extrakta'	EWhm SPhx
	- 'Grete Stolze'	SEND XSen
	- 'Growers Friend'	LAst LBMP
§	- 'Icterina' (v) ♀H4	Widely available
	- 'Kew Gold'	MRav
	- ***latifolia***	see *S. officinalis* broad-leaved
	- narrow-leaved	see *S. lavandulifolia*
	- 'Nazareth'PBR	ELau WJek XSen
	- ***prostrata***	see *S. lavandulifolia*
	- 'Purpurascens' ♀H4	Widely available
	- 'Robin Hill'	ECtt EWhm GQue LSou NDov
	- 'Rosea'	CArn EOHP WJek XSen
	- 'Tricolor' (v)	CTri EBee ECho ELan ELau ENfk EPfP EShb LAst LBMP MAsh MBri MHer MHoo MLHP MNHC MRav NGdn SBfd SGol SPer SPin SPlb SPoG SWal WFar WJek WMnd XSen
	- 'Variegata'	see *S. officinalis* 'Icterina'
	- variegated (v)	ECho MHer
	- 'Würzburg'	XSen
	ombrophila	SPin
	omeiana BWJ 8062	SPin WCru
	- 'Crûg Thundercloud'	WCru
	oppositiflora misapplied	see *S. tubiflora*
	oppositiflora ambig.	EPyc SDys SPin XSen
	orbignaei	SPin XSen
	orthostachys **new**	SPin
	oxyphora	EPyc SDys SPin XSen
	pachyphylla	SPin XSen
	palaestina	XSen
	pallida **new**	SDys SPin
§	***patens*** ♀H3	Widely available
	- 'Alba' misapplied	see *S. patens* 'White Trophy'
	- 'Blue Angel'	EBee EPfP EWes IFoB SPad SPet WIvy WWEG
	- 'Cambridge Blue' ♀H3	CPLG CPrp CSpe EBee ECtt EHrv ELan EPfP LAst LHop LRHS MAsh MBel MCot MHer MHoo MRav MSpe NLar NPer NPri SBfd SDys SMrm SPer SPhx SPin WFar WWlt XSen
	- 'Chilcombe'	EPyc MCot MHer MSpe SDys SPin WIvy WOut WWlt XSen
	- 'Dot's Delight'	CPLG CSpe ECtt EPyc EWes GBin LHop LRHS MAsh MSpe NCGa SAga SBch SDys SMrm SPin SRkn SUsu
	- 'Guanajuato'	CBcs CPLG CSam CSpe EBee ECtt EPyc EWes IFoB MAsh MBel MHer NLar SBfd SDys SMad SMrm SPin SRkn SRot WBor WHil WSHC
	- large	CSpe
	- lavender-flowered	MBel
	- light blue-flowered	EPfP
	- 'Oxford Blue'	see *S. patens*
	- (Patio Series) 'Patio Deep Blue' **new**	NPri
	- - 'Patio Sky Blue' **new**	NPri

	- 'Peggy's Pink' new	MSpe
	- 'Pink Ice'	CPom EPyc WHil WOut
	- pink-flowered	SPin
	- 'Royal Blue'	see *S. patens*
§	- 'White Trophy'	CBcs CPLG CPrp ECtt ELan EPyc EWld LRHS SDys SGar SMrm SPer SPin WIvy WOut
	pauciserrata	SPin
	pennellii new	SPin
	'Penny's Smile'	EPyc LBuc SDys SPin SUsu WHoo WWlt
	'Peru Blue'	CSpe EPyc SDys
	'Phyllis' Fancy'	CSam CSpe CWGN EPyc MAsh SDys SGar SPlb SUsu WSHC XSen
	pinguifolia	SPin XSen
	'Pink Icing' new	SPin
	pinnata new	SPin
	pisidica	SPin XSen
	plectranthoides	SPin XSen
	pogonochila	SPin XSen
	polystachya	SPin XSen
	- B&SWJ 8985	WCru
	pomifera	SPin XSen
*	'Powis Castle'	MHom
	pratensis	CArn CWib EBee EGHP ELan EPfP EPyc GJos MHer MNHC NChi SPin WCot XSen
	- 'Albiflora'	CDes
§	- Bertolonii Group	EPyc SPin XSen
	- 'Dear Anja'	see *S.* × *sylvestris* 'Dear Anja'
§	- Haematodes Group ♀[H4]	ELan EPyc LDai MNrw NLar SPav SPin SRms
	- 'Indigo' ♀[H4]	CDes CPrp EBee ECtt ELon EPfP EWTr GMaP LRHS LSou MCot MRav NCGa NDov NEgg NLar SPhx SPin SPoG SUsu WCot WMnd WPGP
	- 'Lapis Lazuli'	CDes EPyc EWes SPhx SUsu
	- 'Pink Delight'[PBR]	EBee ECGP ECtt EPfP LRHS NCGa NDov NLar SPoG
	- 'Rose Rhapsody' (Ballet Series)	EBee EPPr EPfP EPyc LBMP LDai LRHS MHer SPhx WFar XSen
	- 'Rosea'	ECha SPhx SPin
	- 'Swan Lake' (Ballet Series)	EBee EPPr EPfP EPyc LRHS NChi NLar SPhx SPin SPlb SSvw XSen
	- 'Sweet Esmeralda' (Ballet Series)	EBee EPyc LRHS NGdn NLar SPhx XSen
	- 'Tenorei'	LRHS
	- 'Twilight Serenade' (Ballet Series)	EBee ECtt EPyc LRHS NCGa SBfd WHil XSen
	pratensis* × *transylvanica	GJos
	procurrens	EPyc SPin XSen
	prostrata	EOHP
	prunelloides	SPin XSen
	przewalskii	CPLG EPyc EWld LRHS NMRc SPhx SPin WPer WTcb XSen
	- ACE 1157	WCru
	- BWJ 7920	SPin WCru
	- var. ***mandarinorum***	LRHS
	pubescens	SPin
	pulchella	SPin
	'Purple Majesty'	CHll CSam EPyc EShb LHop SAga SDys SMrm SPhx SPin SRkn WKif WWlt
	'Purple Queen'	EPyc LRHS LSou SDys WWlt
	purpurea	LBMP LSRN SPin
	radula	EPyc SPin XSen
	ranzaniana	SPin XSen
	raymondii subsp. ***mairanae***	SPin XSen
	recognita	SPin WSHC XSen
	recurva	SPin
	red-flowered, B&SWJ 10375 from Guatemala	WCru
	reflexa	SPin
	regeliana misapplied	see *S. virgata* Jacq.
	regeliana Trautv.	LRHS NBir XSen
	regla	LRHS MAsh SPin WPGP XSen
	- 'Jame'	SPin
	- 'Mount Emory'	SPin
	- 'Royal'	SPin
	repens	EBee EPyc SPhx SPin XSen
	- var. ***repens***	SGar XSen
§	***reptans***	SPin XSen
	- from Western Texas	CWGN SDys SUsu WCot
	retinervia	SPin
	rhinosima new	EPyc
	'Ribbon Belle' new	MAsh
	ringens	SPin XSen
	riparia misapplied	see *S. rypara*
	roborowskii	SPin
§	***roemeriana*** ♀[H3]	CPBP CSpe EBee EPyc IFoB SBch SPin WPGP
	- 'Bordeaux Steel Blue'	LRHS SRms
	- 'Red Dwarf'	LRHS
	'Rolando' new	SDys SPin
	roscida	SPin
	rosifolia new	XSen
	'Royal Bumble'	CSpe EBee EPfP EPyc IPot LHop LRHS MAsh NDov SUsu WPGP XLum XSen
	'Royal Crimson Distinction'[PBR]	EPPr
	rubescens	SPin XSen
	rubiginosa	SPin XSen
	runcinata	EPyc SPin
	rutilans	see *S. elegans* 'Scarlet Pineapple'
§	***rypara***	CPom SPin XSen
	sagittata	EPyc GCal SPin WWlt XSen
	(Savannah Series) 'Savannah Purple'	LRHS SRot
	- 'Savannah Red'	EPfP LRHS
	- 'Savannah Salmon Rose'	IFoB LRHS SRot
	scabra	CSpe EPyc SPin WOut XSen
	schlechteri	SPin
	sclarea	CArn CHab CHby ECtt ENfk GPoy LRHS MHer MHoo MNHC NGdn SIde SPin WHfH WJek XLum XSen
	- var. ***sclarea***	ECtt
	- var. ***turkestanica*** hort.	CPom CSev CSpe EBee ECtt EHrv ELan EPfP LRHS LSRN MCot MHoo MRav NEgg NGdn NRHS SBfd SEND SGar SMad SMrm SPav SPer SPhx SWat WKif WMnd XLum XSen
	- var. ***turkestaniana*** Mottet	MSpe WWEG
§	- 'Vatican White'	CSpe EBee EPfP LDai LRHS MHoo MSpe SBch SMad SMrm SPad WJek WMnd WWEG XLum XSen
	- white-bracted	CWib NLar SPin SWal SWvt
*	***scordifolia***	SPin
	scutellarioides	SPin XSen
	semiatrata misapplied	see *S. chamaedryoides*
	semiatrata ambig.	EPyc IFoB
	semiatrata Zucc.	CDes CSpe EWld SAga SPin XSen
	'Serenade'	EBee LRHS MTis NDov SPhx
	serpyllifolia	SPin XSen
	- white-flowered	SPin

sessei	SPin XSen
setulosa	SPin XSen
'Shame'	NDov
'Silas Dyson'	CDes CSpe ECre ECtt EPyc EWld IPot LRHS MHom NDov SBch SDys SPhx SPin SPoG SUsu WOut WPGP WWlt
'Silke's Dream'	CDes CPom CWGN EBee ECtt EPyc EWld LRHS MAsh NDov SBHP SBch SDys SPin SUsu WHoo WPGP WWlt XSen
sinaloensis	MAsh SPin XSen
smithii	SPin
somalensis	SPin XSen
sonomensis	XSen
'Southern Belle' **new**	SPin
spathacea ♀H3-4	SPhx SPin
- 'Avis Keedy'	SPin
spinosa	XSen
splendens	SPin
- 'Dancing Flame' (v)	EPyc
- 'Helen Dillon'	EPyc SPin WWlt
- 'Jimi's Good Red'	CSpe SDys
- 'Peach'	SPin
- 'Vanguard' ♀H3	LAst NPri
§ - 'Van-Houttei' ♀H3	CSam CSev ECre EPyc EShb EWld SDys SPin WWlt
- 'Vista Purple' **new**	LAst
sprucei	SPin XSen
squalens	SPin
stachydifolia	SPin WPGP XSen
§ ***staminea***	LRHS SDys
stenophylla	WHil XSen
'Stephanie'	EPyc SDys SPin
stolonifera	CSpe SDys XSen
stoteonifera	SPin
striata	EPyc SPin XSen
- red-flowered	SPin
styphelus	SDys SPin
subpalmatinervis	SPin
subrotunda	EPyc EWld SDys SPin
summa	XSen
× ***superba*** ♀H4	CPrp CSBt EBee ECtt ELan EPfP EPyc LRHS LSRN MBel MBri MWat SBfd SDix SRms WCAu WGwG WHoo
- 'Adora Blue'	LRHS MBri SHil
- 'Adrian'	EBee ECtt EPfP LRHS LSRN LSou MSpe SPoG
- 'Merleau'	EBee LRHS
- 'Merleau Rose'	EBee LPot MRav SRms WGor
* - 'Rosea'	EBee
- 'Rubin' ♀H4	ECtt MBNS NBre SMrm SPhx
I - 'Superba'	CSev ECha ECtt MRav SPhx SRkn
× ***sylvestris***	LSRN SGar SPin
§ - 'Blauhügel' ♀H4	EBee ECha ECtt ELan EPfP EShb LSou MArl MCot MRav MSpe NDov NPri SHil SMrm SPhx WHoo WPer WPtf WWEG XSen
§ - 'Blaukönigin'	EBee ELon EPfP EWTr GKev GMaP LAst LRHS MWat NGBl NLar NRHS SBfd SPer SPet SPlb SPoG SRms SWvt WPer WWEG XSen
- Blue Queen	see *S.* × *sylvestris* 'Blaukönigin'
§ - 'Dear Anja'	EBee IPot LHop LPla MTis NCGa NDov SPhx WHlf
- 'Lye End'	MRav MWat WCot
§ - 'Mainacht' ♀H4	Widely available
- May Night	see *S.* × *sylvestris* 'Mainacht'
- 'Negrito'	EBee ELon EWll MTis NGdn NLar SMrm XSen
- 'Rhapsody in Blue' PBR	CAbP EBee LRHS MAvo MBNS MTis NDov NLar WCot
- 'Rose Queen'	EBee ECha ECtt ELan ELon EPfP LHop LRHS MRav NGBl NOrc SBfd SCoo SPet SPhx SPoG SWvt WPer WWEG XSen
- 'Rügen'	EBee ELon MTis XSen
- 'Schneehügel'	CMac CSBt EBee ECha EHoe ELan ELon EPPr EPfP GMaP LAst LRHS MBNS MRav MSpe NBre NEgg NPri NPro SHil SMrm SPer WCAu WHil WMnd WWEG XSen
- 'Superba' **new**	GBuc
- 'Tänzerin' ♀H4	EBee ELon EPPr LPla LRHS MTis NDov SUsu WHlf XSen
- 'Viola Klose'	CPrp EAEE EBee ECha ECtt GBuc LRHS LSRN MBri MCot MSpe MTis NCGa NDov NGdn NLar NRHS SRms XSen
tachiei hort.	see *S. forsskaolii*
taraxacifolia	SPin WHil XSen
tarayensis	SPin
tesquicola	see *S. nemorosa* subsp. *tesquicola*
thymoides **new**	WHil
tianschanica	SPin
tiliifolia	SPav SPin SRms
tingitana	SPin XSen
tomentosa	SPin XSen
tortuosa **new**	SPin
transcaucasica	see *S. staminea*
transsylvanica	LDai SGar SMrm SPav SPhx SPin WPer WTcb XSen
- 'Baumgartenii'	LRHS
- 'Blue Spire'	CMea EBee MCot MWhi SPav
'Trebah Lilac White'	see *S.* × *jamensis* 'Trebah'
§ 'Trelawney'	EPPr EPyc LRHS MHom SRot WBor WWlt XSen
§ 'Trelissick'	ECre EPPr EPyc LHop LRHS MAsh MHom SEND SPet SPin SRkn SRot WBor WWlt
§ 'Trewithen'	CPLG CPom ECre EPyc LRHS MHom SPin SPoG SRot WHil XSen
trijuga	EPyc SPin
triloba	see *S. fruticosa*
tubifera	SPin
§ ***tubiflora*** ♀H1+3	CSpe EPyc EWld MAsh SPin XSen
uliginosa ♀H3-4	Widely available
- 'African Skies'	EBee IPot SPin WHlf
- 'Ballon Azul'	CSpe NDov SDys WSHC
univerticillata **new**	SPin
urica	SPin XSen
- short	SDys
uruapana	SPin
'Valerie'	EPyc SDys
'Van-Houttei'	see *S. splendens* 'Van-Houttei'
variana	SPin
vaseyi **new**	XSen
'Vatican City'	see *S. sclarea* 'Vatican White'
verbenaca	CArn EPyc LRHS MHer SPin XSen
- pink-flowered	SPhx
verticillata	EBee EPfP EPyc LEdu NLar SPin WFar XSen
§ - 'Alba'	CAbP EBee ECtt EPfP GJos GQue LRHS MCot MRav NGdn NLar SPer SPin WCAu XSen
- 'Endless Love'	EBee LSou NDov
- 'Hannay's Blue'	EBee EPPr MAvo NDov SMrm

	- 'Hannay's Purple'	EPPr
	- 'Purple Rain'	Widely available
	- 'Smouldering Torches'	LHop LPla MTis NDov SPhx
	- 'White Rain'	see *S. verticillata* 'Alba'
	villicaulis	see *S. amplexicaulis*
	villosa	WHil
§	***virgata*** Jacq.	EBee SGar SPin WOut XSen
	viridis	CHby MNHC SPin
§	- var. ***comata***	MCot SIde WJek
	- 'Marble Arch Blue' (Marble Arch Series) new	CSpe
	- var. ***viridis***	WHrl
	viscosa ambig.	EPyc SGar
	viscosa Jacq.	SPin WOut XSen
	vitifolia	CSpe EPyc SDys
	- B&SWJ 10236	SPin WCru
	wagneriana	SPin
	'Waverly'	CSam EBee EPyc EWld MAsh MCot MHer SAga SDys WWlt XSen
	'Wendy's Wish' new	CSam CWGN NPri SPin
	× ***westerae***	SPin XSen
	xalapensis	SPin
	yunnanensis	SPin
	- BWJ 7874	WCru
	aff. ***yunnanensis***	SPin

Salvinia (*Salviniaceae*)

sp.	LPBA
natans	MSKA

Sambucus ✿ (*Adoxaceae*)

	adnata	SDix WFar
	caerulea	see *S. nigra* subsp. *caerulea*
	callicarpa	NLar WCot
	chinensis	WCot
	coraensis	see *S. williamsii* subsp. *coreana*
	ebulus	LEdu NLar SMad WCot WSFF
	formosana	WCot
	gaudichaudiana new	ECou
*	***himalayensis***	WCot
	mexicana B&SWJ 10349	WCot WCru
	miquelii	WCot
	nigra	CArn CBcs CCVT CDul CHab ECrN EPom GPoy LBuc NWea SBfd SEWo SIde SPer WFar WMou WSFF
	- 'Albomarginata'	see *S. nigra* 'Marginata'
	- 'Albovariegata' (v)	CMac SEND WCot WMoo
*	- 'Ardwall'	CAgr GCal WCot
N	- 'Aurea' ♀H4	CBcs CDul CMac CSBt CWan ELan EPfP EWTr MRav NWea SPer WCot WFar WMoo
	- 'Aureomarginata' (v)	ECrN ELan EPPr EPfP LPot MRav NLar SBfd WCFE WCot WFar
	- 'Bradet'	CAgr NLar WCot
	- 'Cae Rhos Lligwy'	CAgr WCot
§	- subsp. ***caerulea***	EPfP
	- subsp. ***canadensis*** 'Adams' (F)	WCot
	- - 'Aurea'	CWib WCot WHar
	- - 'John's'	CAgr WCot
	- - 'Maxima'	EWes SMad WCot
	- - 'Rubra'	WCot
	- - 'York' (F)	CAgr WCot
	- 'Castledean'	WCot
	- 'Dolomite' (v)	WCot
	- 'Donau'	CAgr WCot
	- 'Frances' (v)	EPPr WCot
	- 'Franzi'	CAgr WCot
	- 'Fructu Luteo'	NLar WCot
	- 'Godshill' (F)	CAgr WCot
	- 'Haschberg'	CAgr WCot
	- 'Heterophylla'	see *S. nigra* 'Linearis'
	- 'Hillier's Dwarf'	WCot
	- 'Ina'	CAgr WCot
	- 'Körsör' (F)	NLar WCot
	- f. ***laciniata*** ♀H4	CDul ELan EPPr EPfP GCal LPot LRHS MBlu MMuc MRav NLar NWea SDix SLon SPer SPoG WCFE WCot WFar WPGP
§	- 'Linearis'	ELan NLar WCot WFar
	- 'Long Tooth'	CDul WCot
	- 'Lutea Punctata'	WCot
	- 'Madonna' (v)	CMac LEdu LTen MBlu MGos MRav NLBP NLar SBfd SMad SPer WCot
§	- 'Marginata' (v)	CDul CWan CWib EHoe MHer MRav SDix SPer SPoG WCot WFar
	- 'Marion Bull' (v)	CDul NLar WCot
I	- 'Marmorata'	NLar WCot
	- 'Mint Julep'	WCot
I	- 'Monstrosa'	NLar WCot
	- 'Nana'	WCot
	- 'Naomi'	WCot
	- 'Norfolk Speckled' (v)	WCot
	- 'Pingo Trail' new	WCot
	- 'Plena' (d)	WCot
	- f. ***porphyrophylla*** 'Black Beauty'PBR	see *S. nigra* f. *porphyrophylla* 'Gerda'
	- - 'Black Lace'PBR	see *S. nigra* f. *porphyrophylla* 'Eva'
	- - 'Black Tower' new	EAmu MPkF
	- - 'Dart's Greenlace'	WCot
§	- - 'Eva'PBR	Widely available
§	- - 'Gerda'PBR ♀H4	Widely available
§	- - 'Guincho Purple'	CBcs CDul CMac CTri EBee ELan EPPr EPfP MHer MRav NLar NWea SGol SPlb WCot WFar WMoo
	- - 'Purple Pete'	CDul WCot
	- - 'Thundercloud'	CDul CMHG ELon EPPr EWes MAsh MBri MNrw NChi NLar NPro WCot WFar WMoo
	- 'Pulverulenta' (v)	CWib EPPr GCal LHop MRav NLBP NLar SPer WCot WFar
	- 'Purpurea'	see *S. nigra* f. *porphyrophylla* 'Guincho Purple'
	- 'Pyramidalis'	MRav NLar WCot
	- 'Riese aus Vossloch'	WCot
	- 'Robert Piggin' (v)	WCot
	- var. ***rotundifolia***	WCot
	- 'Sambu' (F)	CAgr WCot
	- 'Samdal' (F)	CAgr WCot
	- 'Samidan' (F)	CAgr WCot
	- 'Samnor' (F)	CAgr WCot
	- 'Sampo' (F)	CAgr WCot
	- 'Samyl' (F)	CAgr WCot
	- 'Urban Lace'	CAgr WCot
	- 'Variegata'	see *S. nigra* 'Marginata'
	- f. ***viridis***	CAgr WCot
	palmensis	WCot
	racemosa	EPfP NWea WCot
	- 'Aurea'	EHoe
	- 'Crûg Lace'	WCru
	- 'Goldenlocks'	EWes MSwo NLar WCot
	- subsp. ***kamtschatica***	WCot
	- 'Plumosa Aurea'	CBcs CSBt CWib EBee ELan EPfP GCra LRHS MBri MRav MSwo NLar NWea SLim WFar
	- var. ***pubens***	WCot
§	- var. ***sieboldiana***	WCot
	- 'Sutherland Gold' ♀H4	Widely available

- 'Tenuifolia' EPfP WCot
- 'Welsh Gold' **new** SPoG

sieboldiana see *S. racemosa* var. *sieboldiana*

tigranii NLar WCot

§ ***williamsii*** subsp. ***coreana*** WCot

Samolus (*Primulaceae*)

repens ECou LLHF

Sandersonia (*Colchicaceae*)

aurantiaca ECho EPot ERCP LAma SDeJ

Sanguinaria (*Papaveraceae*)

canadensis CArn CAvo CBct CBro CCon EBee ECho EPfP EPot EWTr GEdr GKev GPoy LAma LEdu LRHS MBel MHoo NHol NLar NMen NRHS NRya SDeJ SMHy SWat WAbe WCru WPGP WShi

- f. ***multiplex*** (d) CLAP ECho GEdr IFro NBir WSHC
- - 'Plena' (d) ♀H4 Widely available
- 'Paint Creek Double' (d) **new** GHim
- 'Peter Harrison' EBee

Sanguisorba ✿ (*Rosaceae*)

§ ***albiflora*** CCVN CDes CKno EBee ELan EShb GBuc LBMP LPla MAvo MRav NGdn NLar NPro SEND SMrm SPhx SWat WFar WHil WHlf WMoo WOut WPGP

'All Time High' MAvo NDov

applanata MAvo WCot

armena CElw EBee EWes MAvo MBel MNrw SSvw WTin

'Autumn Bliss' **new** MAvo

benthamiana CHEx

'Blackthorn' EBee ECtt MAvo MTis NDov SMHy WCot

'Burr Blanc' MAvo SMHy SPhx

canadensis CDes CKno CMac CRow EBee ECha ECtt EPPr EPfP GCal GMaP GPoy LPla MAvo MNrw MRav NBir NLar NSti SPhx SWat WAul WCot WFar WMoo WOld WOut WTin WWEG XEll

- hybrid **new** MAvo

'Cangshan Cranberry' CDes MAvo NLar SMHy SUsu WCot

* ***caucasica*** EBee EPPr EWes GBee GBin LEdu LPla MAvo NBre SPhx

'Chocolate Tip' EBee ECtt IPot NBro

dodecandra CDes MAvo

hakusanensis CDes CKno EBee GBBs GCal IFro IPot LEdu MAvo MNFA MNrw NBir NBre NBro NChi NLar NPro SUsu WCot WFar WPGP WSHC WTin WWEG

- B&SWJ 8709 WCru
- 'Lilac Squirrel' **new** EBee

'John Coke' NLar

magnifica CDes EWes GCal LEdu SUsu WCot WPGP

- ***alba*** see *S. albiflora*

menziesii Widely available

- 'Dali Marble' (v) CCVN EBee ECtt NLar SPoG WMoo
- 'Wake Up' NDov

§ ***minor*** CArn CHby CPrp EBee EGHP ELau GPoy MHer MHoo MNHC NBro NMir SIde SPhx SPlb WGwG WHer WJek WMoo

- subsp. ***minor*** CHab

obtusa Widely available

- 'Chatto' EBee ECha
- silver-leaved MNrw
- white-flowered CDes MAvo MMuc WPGP

officinalis CArn CHab CKno COIW CPom CWan EBee EHoe GBin GQue MHer MHoo MNFA NMir NPro SPer SPhx SWat WCAu WFar WMoo WWEG

- CDC 262 EPPr SSvw
- CDC 282 CSpe SPhx
- CDC 292 GQue WCot
- from Mongolia LEdu MAvo
- 'Arnhem' CCse CKno EBee ECtt EPPr LEdu LPla LRHS MAvo MTis NDov SMHy SMrm SPhx SUsu WCot WPGP WTin
- 'Crimson Queen' **new** EBee GQue MTis
- dark-flowered **new** MAvo
- early-flowering **new** CDes
- 'False Tanna' CWib WFar
- 'Lemon Splash' (v) EBee LEdu MAvo WCot WFar
- 'Martin's Mulberry' CDes EWes GCal MAvo NDov SUsu
- 'Morning Select' **new** ECtt
- 'Pink Tanna' CDes CElw CKno CPrp EBee EPPr GBBs GBin GBuc LEdu LHop MAvo MCot MDKP MGos MMuc MNFA MTis NBid NBro NSti SEND SMHy SPhx SUsu WCAu WCot WMoo WWEG
- 'Red Thunder' CDes CKno CSpe EBee ECtt EPPr GBin IPot LPla LRHS MAvo NCGa NDov NLar NOrc WCAu WWEG
- 'Shiro-fukurin' (v) EBee EWes MAvo NLar WCot WHer WSHC

parviflora see *S. tenuifolia* var. *parviflora*

pimpinella see *S. minor*

'Pink Brushes' EBee IPot LPla MAvo NCGa NDov NLar WCAu

'Raspberry Mivvi' **new** SPhx

'Rock and Roll' ECtt EPPr GQue IPot MAvo MTis NLar SBea

sitchensis see *S. stipulata*

§ ***stipulata*** EBee GCal LPla MAvo MNrw WCAu

- var. ***riishirensis*** EBee MAvo

'Tanna' Widely available

'Tanna' seedling EPPr EShb

tenuifolia CEnt EHrv GCal IFro MCot MHer NChi NLar SBHP SMrm SPhx

- var. ***alba*** CKno CPrp CWCL EBee EPPr EPfP EWTr EWes EWll GQue MAvo MCot NDov NPro SMrm SPhx WCot WFar WHoo WMoo WOld WPer WWEG
- - CDC GCal MRav
- - 'Korean Snow' MAvo MNFA NDov SMHy SPhx SUsu
- 'Big Pink' GCal MAvo MNrw

§ - var. ***parviflora*** CDes EBee LEdu MAvo MNrw NLar WPGP WTin

- 'Pink Elephant' CKno EBee ECtt EPPr EWTr GBin GQue LDai LEdu LHop MAvo NCGa NDov NLar SMad WMoo WPGP WTin WWFP
- 'Pink Tickler' MAvo
- var. ***purpurea*** CDes WCAu
- 'Purpurea' CKno EBee EPPr LEdu MAvo NLar SPhx WCot WFar WPGP

- 'Stand Up Comedian'	EBee LEdu MAvo NLar WWEG
- 'Sturdy Guard'	EBee MAvo
- 'White Tanna'	EPPr MAvo

Sanicula (*Apiaceae*)

europaea	CArn GPoy WTin

Santolina (*Asteraceae*)

benthamiana	XSen
§ ***chamaecyparissus*** ♀H4	Widely available
- var. ***corsica***	see *S. chamaecyparissus* 'Nana'
- 'Double Lemon' (d)	EPfP
- subsp. ***insularis***	XSen
- 'Lambrook Silver'	CDoC EBee ECtt ENfk EOHP EPfP EWTr LRHS MAsh NLar SBfd SCoo SLim SPoG WJek
- 'Lemon Queen'	CDoC EBee ENfk EPfP LRHS MAsh MGos MNHC MSwo MWat NBir NLar SBfd SIde SWat WGwG WJek XSen
- subsp. ***magonica***	WAbe
§ - 'Nana' ♀H4	CBar CMHG CPrp EPfP LRHS MAsh MHer MNHC MRav MSwo SPoG SRms SWat WGrn WPer XSen
- 'Pretty Carroll'	EBee ECtt ELan EPfP LRHS LSRN LTen MAsh MBri NLar SIde WJek
- 'Small-Ness'	CMea EBee ECho ELan EPfP EWes GEdr LRHS MAsh MHer NRHS NSla SWvt WHer WJek WPer
- 'Weston'	ECho
incana	see *S. chamaecyparissus*
* ***lindavica***	XSen
pectinata	see *S. rosmarinifolia* subsp. *canescens*
pinnata	CArn MHer MLHP WPer
§ - subsp. ***neapolitana*** ♀H4	CArn CSBt CSev CWib EBee ECha ELan ENfk EPfP MBri MNHC MRav SBod SDix SEND SIde WMnd WWEG
- - cream-flowered	see *S. pinnata* subsp. *neapolitana* 'Edward Bowles'
§ - - 'Edward Bowles'	Widely available
- - 'Sulphurea'	CArn CMea EBee EPfP LRHS MAsh SBfd SPer SPhx WKif WPer XSen
rosmarinifolia	CArn CDoC CDul CWan GPoy LRHS MRav MSCN SBod SEND SLon SPlb SPoG SRms
§ - subsp. ***canescens***	EPfP WPer
- 'Lemon Fizz'	EBee EHoe ELan EMil ENfk EPPr EPfP LBMP LRHS LSou MAsh NBir NPri SBfd SCoo SHil SPer SPoG SPtl SWvt WHer WPnn
§ - subsp. ***rosmarinifolia***	CSev ECha ECrN ELan ENfk EPfP MHer MHoo MRav SBfd SDix SIde SPer SWvt WFar WGwG WHoo WJek XSen
- - 'Primrose Gem' ♀H4	CBcs CDoC CPrp CSBt CSam CTri EBee ECha EPfP LHop LRHS MAsh MAvo MRav MSwo MWat NLar NPri SBfd SEND SPer SPoG SWvt WHoo WJek
- - white-flowered	SSvw WHer XSen
Shades of Jade = 'Sant101'	EBee WRHF
tomentosa	see *S. pinnata* subsp. *neapolitana*
virens	see *S. rosmarinifolia* subsp. *rosmarinifolia*
viridis	see *S. rosmarinifolia* subsp. *rosmarinifolia*

Sanvitalia (*Asteraceae*)

Aztekengold = 'Starbini'PBR	LAst WGor
'Little Sun'	SPet
procumbens 'Irish Eyes'	CSpe
'Sunbini'PBR	CCCN CSpe LSou NPri

Saponaria (*Caryophyllaceae*)

× ***boissieri***	EPot
'Bressingham' ♀H4	ECho ECtt EDAr EPfP EPot LBee NMen WAbe WIce WPat
Bressingham hybrid	GKev LRHS MAsh
caespitosa	EDAr EWes
× ***lempergii*** 'Max Frei'	CSam EBee ELon EPPr LSou MCot MRav SAga SPhx WCot XLum
ocymoides ♀H4	CMea EBee ECha ECho ECtt EDAr EHon EPfP LAst LRHS MAsh MLHP MNHC NMen NPri SEND SPlb SPoG SRms SRot SWal WBor WCFE WFar WPer XLum
- 'Alba'	ECha XLum
- 'Snow Tip'	ECho EDAr NGdn NLar SBch XLum
officinalis	CArn CBre CPbn CWan ENfk GPoy MHer MHoo MLHP MNHC SIde SPlb SWal WFar WHer WJek WMoo WPer WPtf
- 'Alba Plena' (d)	CBre EBee LRHS MMuc NLar SEND WFar WPer WPtf WTin XLum
- 'Betty Arnold' (d)	ECtt EWes MHer WCot WTin
§ - 'Dazzler' (v)	WWEG
- 'Flore Pleno' (d) **new**	GAbr
- 'Rosea Plena' (d)	Widely available
- 'Rubra Plena' (d)	CPrp ELan EWes MMuc MSCN MWhi NBre SEND SHar WHer WTin
- 'Variegata'	see *S. officinalis* 'Dazzler'
× ***olivana*** ♀H4	CPBP ECho ECtt GKev MAsh NLar NMen XLum
pumila	EDAr
'Rosenteppich'	ECtt
zawadskii	see *Silene zawadskii*

Saposhnikovia (*Apiaceae*)

divaricata	CArn SPhx

Sarcocapnos (*Papaveraceae*)

enneaphylla	LSRN

Sarcococca ✿ (*Buxaceae*)

confusa ♀H4	Widely available
hookeriana ♀H4	ELon EPfP GKin IFoB LBMP LSRN LTen MBlu MSwo NLar NPri SBfd WFar WPGP
- B&SWJ 2585	WCru
- HWJK 2393	WCru
- HWJK 2428	WCru
- Sch 1160	CPLG
- Sch 2396	CPLG
- var. ***digyna*** ♀H4	Widely available
- - 'Purple Stem'	CJun CPLG CTri EBee EPfP GBin GKin LAst LRHS MGos MNrw MRav NLar NPnk SBfd SCoo SPoG SWvt WCru
* - - 'Schillingii'	CJun WCru
- var. ***hookeriana***	CJun LSRN
- - GWJ 9369	WCru
- - HWJK 2102	WCru
- var. ***humilis***	Widely available
orientalis	CAbP CJun CMCN CPLG EBee ELan ELon EPfP IArd LRHS MAsh MGos

	NLar NRHS SPoG SSpi WFar WPGP WPat
'Roy Lancaster'	see *S. ruscifolia* var. *chinensis* 'Dragon Gate'
ruscifolia	Widely available
– var. ***chinensis*** ♀H4	CJun CSam EPfP SLon WCru WFar WPGP
§ – – 'Dragon Gate'	CDoC CGHE CJun CPLG EBee ELan EPfP LHop LLHF LRHS LSRN MAsh NLar SChF SLim SLon SPoG SReu SWvt WCru WPGP WPat
saligna	CBcs CJun EBee EBtc EPfP LRHS MRav NLar SLon SPoG WCru
– MF P2056	WCru
trinervia B&SWJ 9500	WCru
vagans B&SWJ 7285	WCru
wallichii	CGHE CPLG ELon MBlu SEND SPoG WPGP WPat
– B&SWJ 2291	CJun WCru
– GWJ 9427	WCru
zeylanica var. ***brevifolia*** GWJ 9480	WCru

Sarmienta (*Gesneriaceae*)

repens ♀H2	CGHE CPLG CPne WAbe WPGP

Sarothamnus see *Cytisus*

Sarracenia ✿ (*Sarraceniaceae*)

× ***ahlesii***	CHew
alata	CHew CSWC EECP NChu WSSs
– 'Black Tube'	WSSs
– heavily veined	WSSs
– pubescent	EECP NChu WSSs
– 'Red Lid'	EECP NChu WSSs
– 'Red Lid' × ***flava*** red pitcher	EECP
– wavy lid	WSSs
– white-flowered	WSSs
alata × ***flava*** var. ***maxima***	CSWC NChu WSSs
× ***areolata***	CHew CSWC NChu WSSs
× ***catesbyi*** ♀H1	CHew CSWC NChu WSSs
× ***courtii***	CSWC NChu
'Dixie Lace'	CSWC
× ***excellens*** ♀H1	CSWC NChu WSSs
× ***exornata***	CSWC NChu SPlb
× ***farnhamii***	CSWC EECP NChu
flava ♀H1	CSWC MREP NChu WSSs
– all green giant	see *S. flava* var. *maxima*
– var. ***atropurpurea***	EECP WSSs
– 'Burgundy'	WSSs
– 'Claret' **new**	WSSs
– var. ***cuprea***	CSWC NChu WSSs
– var. ***flava***	CHew EECP WSSs
§ – var. ***maxima***	CHew CSWC EECP NChu WSSs
– var. ***ornata***	CHew CSWC EECP NChu WSSs
– var. ***rubricorpora***	CHew EECP NChu WSSs
– var. ***rugelii***	CHew EECP WSSs
– veinless	CSWC
× ***harperi***	CSWC NChu
'Juthatip Soper'	WSSs
'Ladies in Waiting'	CSWC
leucophylla ♀H1	CHew CSWC NChu SPlb WSSs
– green	WSSs
– green and white	WSSs
– pubescent	WSSs
– 'Schnell's Ghost'	WSSs
– 'Tarnok'	WSSs
leucophylla × ***oreophila***	CSWC EECP NChu
leucophylla × (× ***popei***)	EECP
'Lynda Butt'	CSWC WSSs
'Mardi Gras'	CSWC
× ***miniata***	EECP WSSs
minor	CSWC EECP NChu WSSs
– var. ***minor***	CHew
§ – 'Okee Giant'	CSWC NChu WSSs
– 'Okefenokee Giant'	see *S. minor* 'Okee Giant'
– var. ***okefenokeensis***	CHew WSSs
minor × ***oreophila***	CSWC
× ***mitchelliana*** ♀H1	WSSs
× ***moorei***	CHew WSSs
– 'Brook's Hybrid'	CHew CSWC EECP NChu WSSs
oreophila	CHew CSWC NChu WSSs
oreophila × ***purpurea*** subsp. ***venosa***	CSWC NChu
× ***popei***	CSWC NChu WSSs
psittacina	CHew CSWC EECP NChu WSSs
* – f. ***heterophylla***	CSWC
purpurea	MREP SPlb
– subsp. ***purpurea***	CHew CSWC NChu WSSs
– – f. ***heterophylla***	CSWC WSSs
– subsp. ***venosa***	CHew CSWC WSSs
– – var. ***burkii***	CSWC NChu WSSs
× ***readii***	WSSs
rubra	CSWC EECP NChu WSSs
– subsp. ***alabamensis***	CHew CSWC NChu WSSs
– subsp. ***gulfensis***	CHew CSWC NChu WSSs
* – – f. ***heterophylla***	CSWC WSSs
– subsp. ***jonesii***	CSWC EECP NChu WSSs
* – – f. ***heterophylla***	CSWC WSSs
– subsp. ***rubra***	CHew CSWC WSSs
– subsp. ***wherryi***	CHew CSWC EECP NChu WSSs
– – giant	WSSs
– – yellow-flowered	WSSs
× ***wrigleyana*** ♀H1	MREP

Saruma (*Aristolochiaceae*)

henryi	CLAP CPom ESwi EWTr EWld GEdr LEdu SUsu WCot WCru WPGP WSHC

Sasa (*Poaceae*)

disticha 'Mirrezuzume'	see *Pleioblastus pygmaeus* 'Mirrezuzume'
glabra f. ***albostriata***	see *Sasaella masamuneana* 'Albostriata'
kagamiana	NLar
kurilensis	MWhi MWht WFar WJun
§ – 'Shima-shimofuri' (v)	EPPr EPfP ERod MMoz MWht WJun
– 'Shimofuri'	see *S. kurilensis* 'Shima-shimofuri'
nana	see *S. veitchii* f. *minor*
§ ***palmata***	CDul CWib EHoe MMuc MWhi SBfd SEND SLim WFar WHer
– f. ***nebulosa***	CBcs CCon CDoC CHEx ENBC EPfP EWes MBrN MMoz MWht NLar WFar WJun WMoo
quelpaertensis	MWht
tessellata	see *Indocalamus tessellatus*
tsuboiana	CBcs CDoC ENBC GQui LRHS MMoz MWht NGdn NLar SBig SGol WFar WMoo WPnP
§ ***veitchii***	CBcs CDoy CTrC ECha EHoe ENBC MMoz MMuc MRav MWht NLar SEND SGol SPer WFar WJun WMoo
§ – f. ***minor***	WMoo

Sasaella (Poaceae)

	glabra	see *S. masamuneana*
§	***masamuneana***	ENBC
§	- 'Albostriata' (v)	CDoC CEnt ENBC EPPr ERod LEdu LRHS MMoz MMuc MWht SBig SEND WFar WJun WMoo WPGP
	- f. ***aureostriata*** (v)	MMoz
§	***ramosa***	CHEx MWht

Sassafras (Lauraceae)

albidum	CArn CBcs CCCN CMCN EBee EPfP LRHS MAsh NLar SBfd SKHP SLon SPoG SSpi WPGP
tzumu	WPGP

satsuma see *Citrus unshiu*

Satureja ✿ (Lamiaceae)

	coerulea ♀H4	CWan EWes NBir XSen
	douglasii	EOHP SBfd SHDw WJek
	- 'Indian Mint'PBR	CArn ENfk MHer
	hortensis	ELau ENfk GPoy MHer MHoo MNHC SBfd SIde WJek
	- 'Selektion'	LLWP
	intricata	XSen
	macedonica	LLWP
	montana	CArn CHby CWan EGHP ELau ENfk GKev GPoy LLWP MBri MHer MHoo MNHC NMen SBfd SDix SIde SRms SVic WHfH WJek WPer XSen
*	- ***citriodora***	GPoy LLWP MHer MHoo XSen
§	- subsp. ***illyrica***	CPBP MHoo SPhx WJek WPer XLum XSen
	- 'Purple Mountain'	GPoy LLWP MHer
	- ***subspicata***	see *S. montana* subsp. *illyrica*
	obovata	XSen
	parnassica	LLWP WPer
	repanda	see *S. spicigera*
	seleriana	SDys
§	***spicigera***	CArn CPrp ELau ENfk EPot LEdu LLWP MHer MHoo NBir NMen SIde SPhx WJek WPer XLum
*	- 'Prostrata' new	WAbe
	spinosa	XSen
	thymbra	CArn SBfd SHDw XSen
§	***viminea***	EOHP

Saurauia (Actinidiaceae)

subspinosa	CHEx

Sauromatum (Araceae)

	guttatum	see *S. venosum*
§	***venosum***	CArn CPLG EAmu EBee ECho EShb GCal GHim LAma LEdu LRHS MMoz NLar SBig SBst WCru WPGP

Saururus (Saururaceae)

cernuus	CArn CBen CHEx CRow CWat EHon ELan LPBA MSKA MWts SRms SWat WMAq
chinensis	CRow GEdr

Saussurea (Asteraceae)

costus	GPoy
nepalensis	GEdr

savory, summer see *Satureja hortensis*

savory, winter see *Satureja montana*

Saxegothaea (Podocarpaceae)

conspicua	CBcs CDoC GBin IArd NLar

Saxifraga ✿ (Saxifragaceae)

	McB 1377	NMen
	McB 1377/1 (7)	NWad
	McB 1377/2 (7)	NWad
	SEP 45	NMen
	'Ada' (× *petraschii*) (7)	NMen
	'Aemula' (× *borisii*) (7)	NMen
	'Affinis' (× *petraschii*) (7)	NMen
§	'Afrodite' (*sempervivum*) (7)	EPot NMen
	aizoides (9)	ECho
	- SDR 5497	GKev
	- var. ***atrorubens*** (9)	ECho GKev
	'Aladdin' (× *borisii*) (7)	NMen
	'Alan Hayhurst' (8)	CPBP GEdr WAbe WFar
	'Alan Martin' (× *boydilacina*) (7)	ECho EPot NLar NMen
	'Alba' ambig.	LRHS
	'Alba' (× *apiculata*) (7)	ECho EDAr MAsh MHer NMen NRHS NRya SPlb WFar WIce WPat
	'Alba' (× *arco-valleyi*)	see *S.* 'Ophelia'
	'Alba' (*oppositifolia*) (7)	ECho ELan EWes ITim NWad WAbe
	'Alba' (*sempervivum*)	see *S.* 'Zita'
	'Albert Einstein' (× *apiculata*) (7)	NMen
	'Albertii' (*callosa*)	see *S.* 'Albida'
§	'Albida' (*callosa*) (8)	ECho WAbe
	'Albrecht Dürer' (Lasciva Group) (7)	EPot WAbe
	'Aldebaran' (× *borisii*) (7)	NMen
	'Aldo Bacci' (Milford Group) (7)	NMen
	'Alfons Mucha' (7)	EPot NMen WPat
	'Alice' (Milford Group) (*marginata* 'Milica' × *aretioides*) (7) new	NMen
	'Allendale Acclaim' (× *lismorensis*) (7)	NMen
	'Allendale Accord' (*diapensioides* × *lilacina*) (7)	NMen
	'Allendale Allure' (*aretiodes* × *stolitzkae*) (7)	NMen
	'Allendale Amber' (7)	NMen
	'Allendale Andante' (× *arco-valleyi*) (7)	NMen
	'Allendale Angel' (× *kepleri*) (7)	NMen WAbe
	'Allendale Argonaut' (7)	NMen WAbe
	'Allendale Ballad' (7)	NMen WAbe
	'Allendale Ballet' (7)	NMen
	'Allendale Bamby' (× *lismorensis*) (7)	EPot NMen
	'Allendale Banshee' (7)	NMen
	'Allendale Baron' (*aretioides* × *andersonii*) (7) new	NMen
	'Allendale Bauble' (*media* × *lilacina*) (7) new	NMen
	'Allendale Beau' (× *lismorensis*) (7)	CPBP NMen
	'Allendale Beauty' (*aretiodes* × *cinerea*) (7)	CPBP NMen
	'Allendale Betty' (× *lismorensis*) (7)	NMen

'Allendale Billows' (7)	NMen
'Allendale Blossom' (× *limorensis*) (7)	NMen
'Allendale Blush' (*lilacina* × *rosinae*) (7) **new**	NMen
'Allendale Bonny' (7)	EPot NMen WAbe
'Allendale Boon' (× *izari*) (7)	NMen
'Allendale Bounty' (7)	NMen
'Allendale Bravo' (× *lismorensis*) (7)	NMen WAbe
'Allendale Cabal' (7)	CPBP ITim NMen
'Allendale Carol' (7)	NMen
'Allendale Celt' (× *novacastelensis*) (7)	NMen
'Allendale Charm' (Swing Group) (7)	ITim NMen WAbe
'Allendale Chick' (7)	NHar NMen
'Allendale Citation' (*cinerea* × *diapensioides*) (7) **new**	NMen
'Allendale Comet' (7)	NMen
'Allendale Czech' (*aretiodes* × *georgei*) (7) **new**	NMen
'Allendale Dance' (7)	CBct NMen
'Allendale Delight' (*lowndesii* hybrid) (7) **new**	NMen
'Allendale Desire' (7)	NMen WAbe
'Allendale Divine' (7)	NMen WAbe
'Allendale Dream' (7)	EPot NMen
'Allendale Duo' (*aretiodes* × *georgei*) (7)	NMen WAbe
'Allendale Elegance' (7)	NMen
'Allendale Elf' (7)	EPot NMen WAbe
'Allendale Elite' (7)	NMen
'Allendale Enchantment' (7)	NMen
'Allendale Envoy' (7)	ITim NMen WAbe
'Allendale Epic' (*ferdinandi-coburgi* × *wendelboi*) (7)	NHar WAbe
'Allendale Fairy' (7)	ITim NHar NMen
'Allendale Fame' (7)	NMen
'Allendale Fancy' (7)	WAbe
'Allendale Frost' (7)	NMen
'Allendale Ghost' (7)	NMen WAbe
'Allendale Goblin' (7)	NMen WAbe
'Allendale Grace' (7)	NMen WAbe
'Allendale Gremlin' (7)	NMen
'Allendale Harvest' (7)	NMen
'Allendale Hobbit' (*matta-florida* × *poluminiana*) (7)	EPot NHar WAbe
'Allendale Host' (*andersonii* × *poluminiana*) (7)	WAbe
'Allendale Ice' (*diapensioides* × *vandellii*) (7) **new**	NMen
'Allendale Icon' (× *polulacina*) (7)	NMen WAbe
'Allendale Imp' (7)	WAbe
'Allendale Ina' (7)	NHar NMen WAbe
'Allendale Jinn' **new**	NMen WAbe
'Allendale Jo' **new**	NMen WAbe
'Allendale Joy' (× *wendelacina*) (7)	NMen
'Allendale King'	NMen
'Allendale Magic'	NMen
'Allendale Noon' **new**	NMen
'Allendale Pearl' (× *novacastelensis*) (7)	NMen
'Allendale Ruby' (7)	NMen WAbe
'Allendale Snow' (× *rayei*) (7)	NMen
'Alpenglow' (7)	NMen
alpigena (7)	WAbe
'Amberine' (× *anglica*) (7) **new**	NMen
'Amitie' (× *gloriana*) (7)	NMen
andersonii (7)	NMen NRya
'Andrea Cesalpino' (Renaissance Group) (7)	NMen
angustifolia Haw.	see *S. hypnoides*
'Anne Beddall' (× *goringiana*) (7)	NMen WAbe
'Antonio Vivaldi' (7)	WAbe
'Aphrodite' (*sempervivum*)	see *S.* 'Afrodite'
× ***apiculata*** (7) **new**	GKev
× ***apiculata*** *sensu stricto* hort.	see *S.* 'Gregor Mendel'
'Apple Blossom' (15)	ECtt EPfP GKev NPro NRya WGor WHoo
'Arabella' (× *edithae*) (7)	ECho
'Aramis' (7) **new**	NMen
§ 'Arco' (× *arco-valleyi*) (7)	NMen
× ***arco-valleyi*** *sensu stricto* hort.	see *S.* 'Arco'
× ***arendsii*** purple-flowered (15)	SGar SPlb
§ 'Aretiastrum' (× *boydii*) (7)	NMen
aretioides (7)	NMen
'Argia Romani' (7)	NMen
'Ariel' (× *hornibrookii*) (7)	NMen
'Arthur' (× *anglica*) (7)	NMen
'Asahi' (*fortunei*) (5)	IVic
'Assimilis' (× *petraschii*) (7)	EPot NMen
'Aufheiter von Eri' (*fortunei*) (5)	IVic
'August Hayek' (× *leyboldii*) (7)	NMen
'Auguste Renoir' (Decora Group) (7) **new**	NMen
'Aurea Maculata' (*cuneifolia*)	see *S.* 'Aureopunctata'
'Aurea' (*umbrosa*)	see *S.* 'Aureopunctata'
§ 'Aureopunctata' (× *urbium*) (11/v)	CMac CTri ECha ECho ELan GKev GMaP LPot LRHS MHer MLHP MRav NDov SBfd SPer SPlb SPoG SRms WMoo WPtf XLum
'Autumn Tribute' (*fortunei*) (5)	CBct CLAP WAbe WFar
'Ayako' (*fortunei*) (5)	NHar
'Ayer's Rock' (7)	WAbe
'Balcana' (*paniculata*) (8)	EPot WAbe
'Baldensis'	see *S. paniculata* var. *minutifolia*
'Beatles' (7)	EPot NMen
§ 'Beatrix Stanley' (7)	ECho LRHS MHer NMen NRHS NRya NWad WGor
'Becky Foster' (× *borisii*) (7)	NMen
'Bellisant' (× *hornibrookii*) (7)	NMen
'Beni-komachi' (*fortunei*)	NHar
'Berenika' (× *bertolonii*) (7)	EPot
'Beryl' (× *anglica*) (7)	NMen
× ***biasolettoi*** *sensu stricto* hort.	see *S.* 'Phoenix'
× ***bilekii*** (7)	ECho NMen
'Birch Yellow'	see *S.* 'Pseudoborisii'
'Black Beauty' (15)	ECtt LPot MHer
'Black Ruby' (*fortunei*) (5)	Widely available
'Blackberry and Apple Pie' (*fortunei*) (5)	CBct CElw CLAP CPLG EBee ECtt EPfP GAbr GEdr IBal LRHS MBrN

	MLHP MNrw NHar NMyG SBch SBfd SPet SWvt WAul WCot WFar WMoo WWEG
'Blaník' (× *borisii*) (7)	NMen
'Blanka' (× *borisii*) (7)	NMen
'Bob Hawkins' (15/v)	EDAr LRHS NHol NWad
§ 'Bodensee' (× *hofmannii*) (7)	WPat
'Bohdalec' (× *megaseiflora*) (7)	NMen
'Bohemia' (7)	ECho EPot NLar NMen
× ***borisii*** *sensu stricto* hort.	see *S.* 'Sofia'
'Bornmuelleri' (7)	NMen
'Boston Spa' (× *elisabethae*) (7)	ECho ECtt LRHS MAsh MHer NLar NMen NRHS SPlb WPat
'Brailes' (× *poluanglica*) (7)	NMen
'Brian Arundel' (Magnus Group) (7)	NMen
'Bridget' (× *edithae*) (7)	ECho LRHS NMen NRHS
'Brimstone' (7)	NMen WAbe
'Brno' (× *elisabethae*) (7)	EPot NMen
'Brookside' (*burseriana*) (7)	EPot NMen
brunoniana	see *S. brunonis*
§ ***brunonis*** (1) CC 5315	GKev
'Bryn Llwyd'	WAbe
bryoides (10)	ECho
'Buchholzii' (× *fleischeri*) (7)	NMen
* 'Buckland' (*fortunei*) (5)	WCot
'Bürgel' (× *poluanglica*) (7) **new**	GKev
× ***burnatii*** (8)	LRHS NMen NPro NRHS NSla WGor
burseriana (7)	ECho WAbe WGor
'Buttercup' (× *kayei*) (7)	WHoo
× ***byam-groundsii*** (7)	WFar
× ***caesia*** misapplied (× *fritschiana*)	see *S.* 'Krain'
caesia L. (8)	SRms WAbe
§ ***callosa*** (8) ♀H4	ECho EDAr GEdr MDKP MHer MLHP MMuc NMen SEND WAbe WFar WPat
- subsp. ***callosa*** (8)	ECho
§ - - var. ***australis*** (8)	GJos NBro NMen
- var. ***lantoscana***	see *S. callosa* subsp. *callosa* var. *australis*
- ***lingulata***	see *S. callosa*
'Cambridge Seedling' (7)	NMen
'Camyra' (7)	WAbe
× ***canis-dalmatica***	see *S.* 'Canis-dalmatica'
§ 'Canis-dalmatica' (× *gaudinii*) (8) ♀H4	ECho ECtt EPot GEdr GJos LRHS NHar NRHS NWad WGor WPer
§ 'Carmen' (× *elisabethae*) (7)	WAbe
§ 'Carniolica' (*paniculata*) (8)	NBro NHol NMen
'Carniolica' (× *pectinata*) (8)	WAbe
carolinica	see *S.* 'Carniolica' (*paniculata*)
cartilaginea	see *S. paniculata* subsp. *cartilaginea*
'Castor' (× *bilekii*) (7)	NMen
'Caterhamensis' (*cotyledon*) (8)	NHar
'Cathy Reed' (× *polulacina*) (7)	NMen
caucasica (7)	ECho WAbe
cebennensis (15) ♀H2	NMen NRya
- dwarf (15)	WAbe
'Cecil Davies' (8)	NHar
'Celebration' **new**	WAbe
cespitosa (15)	NMen WAbe
'Chambers' Pink Pride'	see *S.* 'Miss Chambers'
'Charles Chaplin' (7)	ECho EPot NHar NMen
'Charles Darwin' (7)	CPBP EPot
'Cheap Confections' (*fortunei*) (4)	CBct CLAP EBee ECtt IFoB LLHF SBch SBfd WBor WFar WMoo WOld WPGP WWEG
§ ***cherlerioides*** (10)	NRya WFar
'Cherry Pie' (*fortunei*) (5)	CBct CLAP EBee GEdr LLHF LRHS NBir NHar NMyG
'Cherrytrees' (× *boydii*) (7)	NMen
* 'Chetwynd' (*marginata*) (7)	NMen
'Chez Nous' (× *gloriana*) (7/v)	NMen
'Chodov' (7)	EPot NMen
'Christian Huygens' (7) **new**	NMen
'Christine' (× *anglica*) (7)	ECho NMen
cinerea (7)	NMen WAbe
- McB 1376	NWad
'Cio-Cio-San' (*poluniniana* × *lowndesii*) (Vanessa Group) (7)	CPBP NMen WAbe
'Citronella' (7)	ECho NMen WAbe
'Claire Felstead' (*cinerea* × *poluniniana*) (7)	NMen
'Clare' (× *anglica*) (7)	ECtt NHol NMen
§ 'Clarence Elliott' (*umbrosa*) (11) ♀H4	CMea CTri ECho EWes GAbr GBin GCal GKev GMaP MDKP MHer NDov NHol NLar NMen NRya SEND SMad WFar WIce WPat WWEG
'Claude Monet' (Impressio Group) (7)	NMen
'Claudia' (× *borisii*) (7)	NMen
'Cleo' (× *boydii*) (7)	NMen
'Cloth of Gold' (*exarata* subsp. *moschata*) (15)	CElw ECha ECho ECtt EDAr ELan GKev GMaP LRHS MAsh MHer NHol NMen NRHS NRya NSla NWad SPlb SPoG SRms WAbe WFar WIce
cochlearis (8)	CTri GEdr LRHS MAsh NBro NMen NRHS NSla SBch SEND WAbe WPer
'Cockscomb' (*paniculata*) (8)	ECho GEdr NHar NMen NRya NWad WAbe
columnaris (7)	NMen WAbe
'Combrook' (× *poluanglica*) (7)	NMen
'Coningsby Queen' (× *hornibrookii*) (7)	NMen
'Conwy Snow' (*fortunei*) (5)	CDes CLAP NHar WAbe WFar
'Conwy Star' (*fortunei*) (5)	CLAP NHar WAbe WFar
'Coolock Gem' (7)	NMen WAbe
'Coolock Jean' (7)	NMen
'Coolock Kate' (7)	NMen WAbe
'Cordata' (*burseriana*) (7)	NMen
'Corona' (× *boydii*) (7)	NMen
'Corrennie Claret' (15)	EWes
'Correvoniana' misapplied	see *S.* 'Lagraveana'
'Correvoniana' Farrer (*paniculata*) (8)	EDAr EPot MHer MSCN SEND WFar
cortusifolia (5)	CLAP ECho
- B&SWJ 5879	WCru
- var. ***stolonifera*** (5)	CBct ECho GCal
- - B&SWJ 6205	WCru
§ ***corymbosa*** (7)	EPot
'Cotton Crochet' (*fortunei*) (5/d)	CAbP CBct CYeo EBee ECtt ESwi GEdr LRHS NHar NMyG SBfd SEND SHeu WBor WCot WFar WMoo WOld
cotyledon (8)	ECho SEND WAbe WCFE WPer
§ 'Cranbourne' (× *anglica*) (7) ♀H4	ECho EPot LRHS MAsh NMen WPat

	'Cream' (*paniculata*) (8)	ECho
	'Cream Seedling' (× *elisabethae*) (7)	ECho MAsh NMen
	'Crenata' (*burseriana*) (7)	EPot NMen
	'Crimscote-love' (*poluanglica*) (7)	NMen
	'Crimson Diall' (× *irvingii*) (7)	NMen
	'Crimson Rose' (*paniculata*)	see *S.* 'Rosea' (*paniculata*)
§	***crustata*** (8)	CPBP ECho MDKP NHar NMen WAbe WThu
	- var. ***vochinensis***	see *S. crustata*
	'Crystal Pink' (*fortunei*) (5/v)	CBct CPLG ECtt GAbr GEdr IFoB LRHS MNrw NHar NLar NMen NMyG NPnk WCot WFar WGrn WOld
	'Crystalie' (× *biasolettoi*) (7)	LRHS NMen WPat
	'Cultrata' (*paniculata*) (8)	NBro
	'Cumulus' (*iranica* hybrid) (7) ♀H4	EDAr EPot GKev NMen WAbe
	cuneata (15)	NHol
§	***cuneifolia*** (11)	ECho LBee MHer MLHP MWat NWad SEND WFar WMoo WPer
	- var. ***capillipes***	see *S. cuneifolia* subsp. *cuneifolia*
§	- subsp. ***cuneifolia*** (11)	ECtt GJos
*	- var. ***subintegra*** (11)	ECho
	'Cuscutiformis' (*stolonifera*) (5)	CElw CHid CPLG EBee EWld GBuc GEdr LRHS MBel MRav MSCN SBch SMrm SRms WBor WCru WPGP XLum
	dahurica	see *S. cuneifolia*
	'Dainty Dame' (× *arco-valleyi*) (7)	NMen WAbe
	'Dana' (× *megaseiflora*) (7)	NMen
	'Dartington Double' (15/d)	EWes WFar
	'Dartington Double White' (15/d)	NHol
	'David' (7)	NMen
	'Dawn Frost' (7)	NMen WIce
	'Delia' (× *hornibrookii*) (7)	EPot ITim NMen
	'Demeter' (× *petraschii*) (7) **new**	NMen
§	'Denisa' (× *pseudokotschyi*) (7)	NMen
	densa	see *S. cherlerioides*
	'Dentata' (× *geum*)	see *S.* 'Dentata' (× *polita*)
§	'Dentata' (× *polita*) (11)	CSpe ECha ECho GCal MAvo WMoo WWEG
	'Dentata' (× *urbium*)	see *S.* 'Dentata' (× *polita*)
	desoulavyi (7)	NMen
	'Diana' ambig.	NLar
	diapensioides (7)	NMen WAbe
	dinnikii (7)	NMen WAbe
	× ***dinninaris*** (7)	NMen
	'Discovery' (7) **new**	NMen
	'Dobruška' (× *irvingii*) (7)	NMen
	'Doctor Clay' (*paniculata*) (8)	GEdr GKev LRHS NHar NHol NMen NRHS NRya SPlb WAbe
	'Doctor Ramsey' (8)	ECho EWes GEdr LRHS NBro NHol NMen NRHS NWad WAbe WGor WPnn
	'Don Giovanni' (7)	NMen WAbe
	'Donald Mann' (15)	EWes
	'Donnington Chalice'	NMen
	'Donnington Gold'	NMen
	'Donnington Veil'	NMen
	'Dora Ross' (× *baccii*) (7) **new**	NMen
	'Dorothy Milne' (7)	NMen
	'Drakula' (*ferdinandi-coburgi*) (7)	ECho LRHS NMen NRHS
	'Dubarry' (15)	EWes
	'Dulcimer' (× *petraschii*) (7)	NMen
	aff. ***duthiei*** **new**	CPBP
	'Dwight Ripley' (7)	NMen
	'Edgar Irmscher' (7)	NMen
	'Edith' (× *edithae*) (7)	ECho LRHS NRHS
	'Edouard Manet' (Impressio Group) (7) **new**	NMen
	'Edward Elgar' (× *megaseiflora*) (7)	NMen
	'Egmont' (7)	NMen
	'Elf' (7)	see *S.* 'Beatrix Stanley'
	'Eliot Hodgkin' (× *millstreamiana*) (7)	NMen
	× ***elisabethae*** *sensu stricto* hort.	see *S.* 'Carmen'
	× ***elisabethae*** Sünd. (7)	EDAr
	'Elizabeth Sinclair' (× *elisabethae*) (7)	EPot GKev NMen
	'Ellie Brinckerhoff' (× *hornibrookii*) (7)	NMen
	'Elliott's Variety'	see *S.* 'Clarence Elliott' (*umbrosa*)
	epiphylla (5) BWJ 8177	WCru
§	'Ernst Heinrich' (× *heinrichii*) (7)	NMen
	'Esther' (× *burnatii*) (8)	CMea ECho GEdr GKev LRHS MAsh NMen SRGP WAbe WPnn
§	'Eulenspiegel' (× *geuderi*) (7)	EPot NMen NWad
	'Eva Hanzliková' (× *izari*) (7)	NMen WAbe
	exarata (15)	NMen WAbe
	- subsp. ***moschata*** 'Elf' (15)	ECtt NMen SRms WGor
	'Excellent' (Exclusive Group) (7)	EPot
	fair maids of France	see *S.* 'Flore Pleno'
	'Fairy' (*exarata* subsp. *moschata*) (15)	CMea ECtt NBir
	'Faldonside' (× *boydii*) (7) ♀H4	MAsh NMen NRya WPat
	'Falstaff' (*burseriana*) (7)	NRya WAbe
	× ***farreri*** hort.	see *S.* (Silver Farreri Group) 'Reginald Farrer'
§	'Faust' (× *borisii*) (7)	NMen
	'Favorit' (× *bilekii*) (7)	NMen
§	***federici-augusti*** subsp. ***grisebachii*** (7) ♀H2-3	ECho EPot GKev LRHS NRHS NSla WAbe WFar
	'Felicity' (× *anglica*) (7) **new**	NMen
	'Ferdinand' (× *hofmannii*) (7)	NMen
	ferdinandi-coburgi (7) ♀H4	ECtt NMen SBch WAbe
§	- subsp. ***chrysosplenifolia*** var. ***rhodopea*** (7)	ECho EPot LRHS NMen
	- var. ***pravislavii***	see *S. ferdinandi-coburgi* subsp. *chrysosplenifolia* var. *rhodopea*
	- var. ***radoslavoffii***	see *S. ferdinandi-coburgi* subsp. *chrysosplenifolia* var. *rhodopea*
	'Findling' (15)	EPfP MAsh NMen NWad SPoG WAbe
	'Firebrand' (× *kochii*) (7)	NMen WAbe
	'Five Color' (*fortunei*)	see *S.* 'Go-nishiki'
§	***flagellaris*** (1)	NMen WAbe
	'Flamenco' (× *anglica*) (7) **new**	NMen

'Flavescens' misapplied see *S.* 'Lutea' (*paniculata*)

× ***fleischeri*** (7) NMen

§ 'Flore Pleno' (*granulata*) (15/d) CRDP EWes NBir SUsu WAbe WFar

'Flowers of Sulphur' see *S.* 'Schwefelblüte'

'Flush' (× *petraschii*) (7) NMen

fortunei (5) ♀^{H4} CHEx CLAP CMac ECho GMaP NBir NPnk SRms WAbe

- B&SWJ 6346 WCru

- f. ***alpina*** (5) CLAP

- - from Hokkaido (5) CLAP WCru

- var. ***koraiensis*** (5) B&SWJ 8688 WCru

- 'Musgrove Pink' CLAP

- var. ***obtusocuneata*** (5) CLAP ECho LLHF NMen WAbe

- f. ***partita*** (5) CLAP GEdr WCot WCru

- var. ***pilosissima*** (5) B&SWJ 8557 WCru

- pink-flowered (5) CLAP WAbe WFar

- var. ***suwoensis*** (5) CLAP

'Foster's Gold' (× *elisabethae*) (7) NMen

'Four Winds' (15) EPfP EWes MBrN SPoG

'Francesco Redi' (Renaissance Group) NMen

'Francis Cade' (8) GAbr WAbe

'Frank Sinatra' (× *poluanglica*) (7) NMen

'Franz Liszt' (7) WAbe

'Franzii' (× *paulinae*) (7) NMen

'Freckles' CYeo GKev

'Frederik Chopin' (7) EPot NMen WAbe

'Friar Tuck' (× *boydii*) (7) NMen NWad

'Friesei' (× *salmonica*) (7) EPot NMen

× ***fritschiana*** (8) NMen

'Fumiko' (*fortunei*) (5) CLAP WAbe WCru

'Funkii' (× *petraschii*) (7) NMen

'G.W. Gould No. 1' **new** NMen

'Gaertneri' (× *mariae-theresiae*) (7) NMen

'Gaiety' (15) ECho LRHS NRHS SPoG WFar

'Galahad' (× *elizabethae*) (7) NMen

'Galaxie' (× *megaseiflora*) (7) NMen

'Ganymede' (*burseriana*) (7) NMen WAbe

'Gelber Findling' (7) EPot NMen WAbe

'Gelbes Monster' (*fortunei*) (5) IVic

'Gem' (× *irvingii*) (7) EPot NMen WIce

'General Joffre' (15) see *S.* 'Maréchal Joffre'

'Geoff Wilson' (× *biasolettoi*) NMen

'George Gershwin' (Blues Group) (7) NMen

georgei (7) EPot NMen WAbe

- F&W 83 (7) **new** NMen

'Gerard Philipe' (7) **new** EPot NMen

'Gertie Pritchard' (× *megaseiflora*) see *S.* 'Mrs Gertie Prichard'

× ***geuderi*** sensu stricto hort. see *S.* 'Eulenspiegel'

§ × ***geum*** (11) CHid MRav WFar WMoo

- Dixter form (11) ECha SMHy WFar WWEG

'Gina Lollobrigida' (Blues Group) (7) **new** NMen

'Gleborg' (15) EWes SPoG

'Gloria' (*burseriana*) (7) ♀^{H4} ECho LRHS MAsh NMen NRHS WIce WPat

'Gloriana' see *S.* 'Godiva'

× ***gloriana*** sensu stricto hort. (7) see *S.* 'Godiva'

'Gloriosa' (× *gloriana*) (7) see *S.* 'Godiva'

'Glückliches Mädchen' (*fortunei*) (5) IVic

§ 'Godiva' (× *gloriana*) (7) NMen WAbe

'Gold Dust' (× *eudoxiana*) (7) ECho MAsh NMen NRya

'Gold Mound' WNew

'Golden Falls' (15/v) EWes LRHS SPlb SPoG

Golden Prague (× *pragensis*) see *S.* 'Zlatá Praha'

'Golem' (× *megaseiflora*) (7) **new** WAbe

§ 'Go-nishiki' (*fortunei*) (5) CBct GEdr LLHF NHar NMyG

'Gorges du Verdon' (8) GKev

'Goring White' (7) NMen

'Gothenburg' (7) NMen WAbe WPat

'Grace Farwell' (× *anglica*) (7) ECho NLar NMen NRya WHoo

'Grace' (× *arendsii*) (15/v) see *S.* 'Seaspray'

'Grandiflora' (*burseriana*) (7) NMen

granulata (15) CRWN ECho EDAr GJos MHer NMir NRHS NSla WAbe WFar

'Gratoides' (× *grata*) (7) NMen

§ 'Gregor Mendel' (× *apiculata*) (7) ♀^{H4} CSam CYeo ECho ECtt EPot LRHS NLar NMen NRHS SRms WAbe WFar WHoo

'Gregor' (× *poluanglica*) (7) **new** NMen

grisebachii see *S. federici-augusti* subsp. *grisebachii*

'Haagii' (× *eudoxiana*) (7) CTri ECho GKev MAsh NLar NMen

'Harbinger' (7) NMen WAbe

'Hare Knoll Beauty' (8) CPBP ECho EPot GKev LRHS NHar NHol NMen NRHS NRya NSla WAbe

'Harley' (7) NMen

'Harlow Car' (7) EPot NMen NSla

'Harold Bevington' (*paniculata*) (8) GEdr

'Harold Lloyd' (7) NMen

'Harry Marshall' (× *irvingii*) (7) NMen NWad

'Hartswood White' (15) MWat

'Harvest Moon' (*stolonifera*) (5) CHEx WBor WHer

'Heda' (*marginata*) (7) **new** NMen

'Hedwig' (× *malbyana*) (7) NMen WAbe

× ***heinreichii*** sensu stricto hort. see *S.* 'Ernst Heinrich'

'Heisel Kurenai' (*fortunei*) (5) IVic

'Hi-Ace' (15/v) ECtt EDAr MHer SPlb

'Hime' (*stolonifera*) (5) WCru

'Hindhead Seedling' (× *boydii*) (7) LRHS NMen WAbe

hirsuta (11) EBee EHrv EWTr EWld LRHS MMuc NRHS WCru

- subsp. ***hirsuta*** (11) **new** SEND

'Hirsuta' (× *geum*) see *S.* × *geum*

'Hirtella' Ingwersen (*paniculata*) (8) EPot

'Hirtifolia' (*paniculata*) (8) GJos

'His Majesty' (× *irvingii*) (7) NMen WFar

'Hiten' (*fortunei*) GKev

'Hitomebore' (*fortunei*) (5) NHar

'Hocker Edge' (× *arco-valleyi*) (7) ITim NMen WAbe

'Holden Seedling' (15) ECtt EWes

'Honington' (× *poluanglica*) (7) NMen

	hostii (8)	ECho EDAr GKev NWad WTin
	- subsp. ***hostii*** (8)	GEdr XLum
	- subsp. ***rhaetica*** (8)	NBro NMen
	'Hradčany' (× *megaseiflora*) (7)	NMen
	'Hsitou Silver' (*stolonifera*) (5)	EPPr MDKP SPhx
	'Hunscote' (× *poluanglica*) (7)	NMen
	hybrid JB 11	NMen
§	***hypnoides*** (15)	NMir SPoG WAbe
	hypostoma (7)	WAbe
	'Iceland' (*oppositifolia*) (7)	EWes WAbe
	'Icicle' (× *elisabethae*) (7)	NMen
	'Idlecote'	NMen
	'Ignaz Dörfler' (× *doerfleri*) (7)	NMen WAbe
	imparilis (5)	CLAP EHrv GEdr WCru
	'Ingeborg' (15)	CElw ECha
	iranica (7)	NMen
	'Irena' (7) **new**	NMen
	'Irene Bacci' (× *baccii*) (7)	NMen
	'Iris Prichard' (× *hardingii*) (7)	NMen
	× ***irvingii*** (7)	ECho EPot
	× ***irvingii*** *sensu stricto* hort.	see *S.* 'Walter Irving'
	'Ivana' (× *caroliquarti*) (7)	NMen WAbe
	'James' (7)	NMen
	'Jan Amos Kómensky' (× *anglica*) (7) **new**	NMen
	'Jan Neruda' (× *megaseiflora*) (7)	CPBP NMen
	'Jan Palach' (× *krausii*) (7)	NMen
	'Jaromir' (8) **new**	NHar NMen
	'Jason' (× *elisabethae*) (7)	NMen
	'Jenkinsiae' (× *irvingii*) (7) ♀H4	CYeo ECho EDAr EPot LRHS MAsh MMuc NMen NRya NWad SEND WAbe WIce WPat
	'Joachim Barrande' (× *siluris*) (7)	NMen
§	'Johann Kellerer' (× *kellereri*) (7)	EPot WAbe
	'Johann Wolfgang Goethe' (7) **new**	WAbe
	'John Byam-Grounds' (Honor Group) (7)	WAbe
	'John Tomlinson' (*burseriana*) (7)	NMen
	'Jorg' (× *biasolettoi*) (7)	EPot
	'Josef Čapek' (× *megaseiflora*) (7)	NMen
	'Josef Mánes' (× *borisii*) (7)	NMen
	'Joy'	see *S.* 'Kaspar Maria Sternberg'
	'Joy Bishop' (7)	NMen WAbe
	'Joyce Carruthers' (7) **new**	NMen
	'Judith Shackleton' (× *abingdonensis*) (7)	NMen WAbe
	'Juliet'	see *S.* 'Riverslea'
§	***juniperifolia*** (7)	CYeo ECho EDAr GAbr MAsh SRms
	'Jupiter' (× *megaseiflora*) (7)	NMen
	'Kampa' (7)	NMen
	'Kanna' (*fortunei*) (5)	IVic
	karadzicensis (7)	NMen
	'Karasin' (7)	NMen
	'Karel Čapek' (× *megaseiflora*) (7)	ECho LRHS NMen NRHS NWad WAbe
	'Karel Hynek Mácha' (7) **new**	NMen
	'Karel Stivín' (× *edithae*) (7)	NMen
	'Karlštejn' (× *borisii*) (7)	EPot
§	'Kaspar Maria Sternberg' (× *petraschii*) (7)	LRHS NMen WPat
	'Kath Dryden' (7)	ECho ECtt GEdr GKev ITim NMen NWad
	'Kathleen Pinsent' (8) ♀H4	ECho
	'Kathleen' (× *polulacina*) (7)	EPot NMen WFar
	× ***kellereri*** *sensu stricto* hort.	see *S.* 'Johann Kellerer'
	'Ken McGregor' (7)	NMen WAbe
	'Kestoniensis' (× *salmonica*) (7)	NMen
	'Kew Gem' (× *petraschii*) (7)	ECho NMen
	'Kewensis' (× *kellereri*) (7)	NMen WAbe
	'Kineton' (× *poluanglica*) (7)	ITim NMen
	'King Lear' (× *bursiculata*) (7)	ECho LRHS NMen
	'Kinki Purple' (*stolonifera*) (5)	EHrv ELon EShb EWld WCru WPGP
	'Knapton Pink' (15)	ECtt EDAr EPfP MAsh NPro NRya SPoG WAbe WFar WIce
	'Knebworth' (8)	ECho
*	'Koigokora' (*fortunei*) (5)	NHar
	'Kokaku' (*fortunei*)	LLHF
§	'Kolbiana' (× *paulinae*) (7)	NMen
	'Kon Tiki' (7)	WAbe
*	'Kosumosu' (*fortunei*) (5)	NHar WOld
	kotschyi × ***wendelboi***	EPot
	'Koukan' (*fortunei*) (5)	IVic
§	'Krain' (× *fritschiana*) (8)	ECho GEdr
	'Krákatit' (× *megaseiflora*) (7)	NMen
	'Krasava' (× *megaseiflora*) (7)	ITim NMen
	'Kyrilli' (× *borisii*) (7)	NMen
	'Labe' (× *arco-valleyi*) (7)	NMen WAbe
	'Ladislav Čelakovský' (7)	NMen WAbe
	'Lady Beatrix Stanley'	see *S.* 'Beatrix Stanley'
§	'Lagraveana' (*paniculata*) (8) ♀H4	ECho EDAr GKev LRHS NRHS NRya WGor
	'Laka' (7)	EPot NMen WAbe
	× ***landaueri*** *sensu stricto* hort.	see *S.* 'Leonore'
	'Lemon Hybrid' (× *boydii*) (7)	NMen
	'Lemon Spires' (7)	NMen WAbe
	'Lenka' (× *byam-groundsii*) (7)	NMen WAbe
	'Leo Gordon Godseff' (× *elisabethae*) (7)	ECho LRHS NMen NRHS
	'Leonardo da Vinci' (7) **new**	NMen WAbe
§	'Leonore' (× *landaueri*) (7)	ECho LRHS NRHS WAbe WFar
	'Letchworth Gem' (× *urbium*) (11)	ECho GCal
	× ***lhommei*** (8) **new**	WAbe
	'Licht des Cerise' (*fortunei*) (5)	IVic
	'Lidice' (7)	EPot NMen WAbe WHoo
	'Lilac Time' (× *youngiana*) (7)	NMen WAbe
	lilacina (7)	NMen WAbe WPat WThu
	'Limelight' (*callosa* subsp. *callosa* var. *australis*) (8)	NWad WAbe
	'Lincoln Foster' (8) **new**	NHar
	'Lindau' (7)	NMen
	lingulata	see *S. callosa*
	'Lismore Carmine' (× *lismorensis*) (7)	EPot NMen
	'Lismore Gem' (× *lismorensis*) (7)	ECho NMen

'Lismore Mist' (× *lismorensis*) (7)	CPBP NMen
'Lismore Pink' (× *lismorensis*) (7)	NMen
'Lissadell' (*callosa*) (8)	GKev IFoB ITim
* 'Little Piggy' (*epiphylla*) (5)	CDes GEdr WCru
'Lizzy' (7)	EPot
llonakhensis **new**	WAbe
'Lohengrin' (× *boerhammeri*) (7)	EPot NMen
'Lohmuelleri' (× *biasolettoi*) (7)	GKev
lolaensis (7) **new**	WAbe
'Long Acre Pink' (*fortunei*) (5)	CLAP
longifolia (8)	ECho NSla
- hybrids	WAbe
'Louis Armstrong' (Blues Group) (7)	EPot NMen WAbe
Love Me	see *S.* 'Miluj Mne'
lowndesii (7)	WAbe
'Loxley' (*poluanglica*) (7)	GEdr NMen
'Ludmila Šubrová' (× *bertolonii*) (7)	NMen
'Lutea' ambig.	GJos
'Lutea' (*aizoon*)	see *S.* 'Lutea' (*paniculata*)
'Lutea' (*diapensioides*)	see *S.* 'Wilhelm Tell', 'Primulina'
'Lutea' (*marginata*)	see *S.* 'Faust'
§ 'Lutea' (*paniculata*) (8) ♀H4	ECho EDAr EHoe GEdr GMaP NBro NHol NWad WFar
§ 'Luteola' (× *boydii*) (7) ♀H4	WAbe
luteoviridis	see *S. corymbosa*
'Lužníce' (× *poluluteopurpurea*) (7)	NMen
macedonica	see *S. juniperifolia*
'Magdalena' (× *thomasiana*) (7)	NMen
'Magna' (*burseriana*) (7)	NMen
'Maigrün' (*fortunei*) (5)	NHar
'Maiko' (*fortunei*) (5)	NHar
'Major' (*cochlearis*) (8) ♀H4	MMuc WGor
'Major Lutea'	see *S.* 'Luteola'
'Maly Trpaslík' (*vandellii* × *sempervivum*) (7)	WAbe
'Mangart' (*burseriana*) (7) **new**	ITim NMen
'Marc Chagall' (Decora Group) (7)	NMen WAbe
§ 'Maréchal Joffre' (15)	NEgg
'Margarete' (× *borisii*) (7)	NMen
marginata (7)	WAbe
- var. ***balcanica***	see *S. marginata* subsp. *marginata* var. *rocheliana*
- subsp. ***marginata*** var. ***boryi*** (7)	EPot NMen WAbe
- - var. ***coriophylla*** (7)	EPot NMen WAbe
§ - - var. ***rocheliana*** (7)	ITim NMen
'Maria Callas' (× *poluanglica*) (7)	WAbe WGor
'Maria Luisa' (× *salmonica*) (7)	CPBP NMen WAbe WPat
'Marianna' (× *borisii*) (7)	EPot NMen
'Marie Stivínová' (× *borisii*) (7)	EPot
'Marilyn Monroe' (Vanessa Group) (7) **new**	NMen
'Maroon Beauty' (*stolonifera*) (5)	CCVN EBee ECtt EPPr LPot MDKP NBid NBre NGBo WCot WWEG
'Marpha Moonlight' **new**	WAbe
'Mars' (× *elisabethae*) (7)	NMen
'Marshal Joffre' (15)	see *S.* 'Maréchal Joffre' (15)
'Marsilio Ficino' (Milford Group) (7)	NMen
§ 'Martha' (× *semmleri*) (7)	NMen
'Mary Golds' (Swing Group) (7)	GKev ITim NLar WGor
matta-florida (7)	NMen
'May Queen' (7)	NMen
'Meg' (7) **new**	NMen
× ***megaseiflora*** *sensu stricto* hort.	see *S.* 'Robin Hood'
'Melrose' (× *salmonica*) (7)	NMen
mertensiana (6)	GEdr NBir WCru WSHC
'Meteor' (7)	NHol NRya NSla
micranthidifolia (4)	CLAP
'Mikuláš Koperník' (× *zenittensis*) (7)	NMen WAbe
'Millstream Cream' (× *elisabethae*) (7)	ECho NMen
§ 'Miluj Mne' (× *poluanglica*) (7)	ECho ITim NMen WHoo
'Minnehaha' (× *elisabethae*) (7)	WAbe
'Minor' (*cochlearis*) (8) ♀H4	ECho EPot GKev LRHS NHar NMen NRHS NWad WGor WPat
'Mirko Webr' (Harmonia Group) (*aretioides* × *cinerea*) (7)	NMen WAbe
§ 'Miss Chambers' (× *urbium*) (11)	SMHy WCot WMoo WSHC
'Momo Sekisui' (*fortunei*) (5)	IVic
'Momo Tarou' (*fortunei*) (5)	NHar
'Mona Lisa' (× *borisii*) (7)	NMen NWad WAbe
'Monarch' (8) ♀H4	GAbr GKev NWad WAbe
§ 'Mondscheinsonate' (× *boydii*) (7)	WAbe
'Monika' (*webrii*) (7) **new**	NMen
'Moonlight Sonata' (× *boydii*)	see *S.* 'Mondscheinsonate'
'Moonlight' (× *boydii*)	see *S.* 'Sulphurea'
'Morava' (7)	NMen
Mossy Group (15)	LRHS
* 'Mossy Pink'	SPoG
'Mossy Red'	SPoG WNew
'Mossy Triumph'	see *S.* 'Triumph'
'Mossy White'	GAbr WNew
'Mother of Pearl' (× *irvingii*) (7)	ECho NMen WIce
'Mother Queen' (× *irvingii*) (7)	NMen WPat
'Mount Nachi' (*fortunei*) (5)	CBct CDes CElw CWCL EBee EPfP EWes GAbr GEdr GMaP IBal LRHS MCot MLHP NBro NMen NMyG SPlb SUsu WAbe WCot WFar WMoo WPGP WPer WWEG
§ 'Mrs Gertie Prichard' (× *megaseiflora*) (7)	NMen
'Mrs Helen Terry' (× *salmonica*) (7)	EPot NMen WIce
'Mrs Leng' (× *elisabethae*) (7)	MDKP NMen
mutata (9)	GKev
'Myra Cambria' (× *anglica*) (7)	NMen NWad
'Myra' (× *anglica*) (7)	ECho NMen WHoo WPat
'Myriad' (7)	NMen
'Naarden' (7) **new**	NMen

‘Nancye’ (× *goringiana*) (7) EPot ITim NMen WAbe
‘Neptun’ (7) NMen
‘Nicholas’ (8) **new** GKev
‘Nimbus’ (*iranica*) (7) NMen
‘Niobe’ (× *pulvilacina*) (7) NMen
‘Nisi’ (*fortunei*) (5) IVic
‘Norvegica’ (*cotyledon*) (8) WAbe WThu
‘Nottingham Gold’ (× *boydii*) (7) EPot NMen NWad
‘Obristii’ (× *salmonica*) (7) NMen
§ ***obtusa*** (7) EPot MHer NMen WAbe
‘Ochroleuca’ (× *elisabethae*) (7) NMen
‘Odysseus’ (*sancta*) (7) NMen
‘Olymp’ (*scardica*) (7) NMen
‘Omar Khayyám’ EPot NMen WAbe
‘Opalescent’ (7) NMen
§ ‘Ophelia’ (× *arco-valleyi*) (7) NMen
oppositifolia (7) MWat NHol NSla SPlb SRms WAbe WFar
I - ‘Holden Variety’ (7) NRya NWad
- ‘Le Bourg d’Oisans’ (7) WAbe
- subsp. ***oppositifolia*** var. ***latina*** (7) ECho
‘Orava’ (7) **new** NMen
‘Oriole’ (× *boydii*) (7) NMen
‘Orion’ (× *kepleri*) (7) **new** NMen
‘Orjen’ (*paniculata* var. *orientalis*) (8) GEdr
‘Ottawa’ **new** NMen
‘Ottone Rosai’ (Toscana Group) (7) NMen
‘Oxhill’ (7) NMen
‘Pablo Picasso’ (Conspecta Group) (7) **new** NMen WAbe
paniculata (8) ECho EDAr EHoe GKev GMaP MAsh MDKP MHer MWat NSla SPlb SRms WAbe WFar WHoo WNew
§ - subsp. ***cartilaginea*** (8) GKev WAbe
- - ‘Atropurpurea’ (8) NHar NHol WIce
- - hybrid **new** EPot
- subsp. ***kolenatiana*** see *S. paniculata* subsp. *cartilaginea*
§ - var. ***minutifolia*** (8) CPBP CTri CYeo ECho LRHS MAsh MSCN MWat NBro NHar NMen NRya NSla SPlb WAbe
‘Pankrác’ (7) **new** GKev NMen
paradoxa (15) ECho EPot GEdr LRHS NHol NRHS NWad WGor
‘Parcevalis’ (× *finnisiae*) (7 × 9) NMen WAbe
‘Parsee’ (× *margoxiana*) (7) NMen
‘Paul Gauguin’ **new** WAbe
‘Paula’ (× *paulinae*) (7) NMen
‘Peach Blossom’ (7) NMen
‘Peach Melba’ (7) CPBP EPot NLar NMen WAbe WFar
* ‘Peachy Head’ NMen WAbe
‘Pearl Rose’ (× *anglica*) (7) EPot NMen
‘Pearly Gates’ (× *irvingii*) (7) NMen
‘Pearly Gold’ (15) NRya WFar
‘Pearly King’ (15) ECtt GMaP MAsh WAbe WFar WRHF
× ***pectinata*** Schott, Nyman & Kotschy see *S.* ‘Krain’
pedemontana from Mount Kazbek, Georgia (15) WAbe
‘Penelope’ (× *boydilacina*) (7) ECho LRHS NLar NMen NRHS WAbe WHoo WPat
pensylvanica (4) GCal GCra WCot

‘Perikles’ (7) NMen
‘Peter Burrow’ (× *poluanglica*) (7) ♀H4 ECho ITim NMen WIce
‘Peter Pan’ (15) EDAr EPfP GJos GMaP LRHS MAsh MHer NHol NMen NRya NWad SPoG WFar WNew WPat
‘Petra’ (7) EPot NMen WFar
§ ‘Phoenix’ (× *biasolettoi*) (7) ECho LRHS
‘Pierantonio Micheli’ (Renaissance Group) **new** NMen
‘Pilatus’ (× *boydii*) (7) NMen
‘Pink Cloud’ (*fortunei*) (5) CLAP NHar WAbe WFar
‘Pink Haze’ (*fortunei*) (5) CLAP NHar WAbe
‘Pink Mist’ (*fortunei*) (5) CLAP NHar WAbe WFar
‘Pink Pagoda’ (*nipponica*) (5) CDes CLAP EBee GEdr WCot WCru WPGP
‘Pink Pearl’ (7) NMen SBch
‘Pink Ray’ (*fortunei*) (5) **new** LLHF
‘Pink Star’ (× *boydilacina*) (7) NLar
‘Pixie’ (15) CTri ECtt LRHS MAsh NHol NMen NRya NWad SPoG SRms
‘Pixie Alba’ see *S.* ‘White Pixie’
‘Plena’ (*granulata*) see *S.* ‘Flore Pleno’
‘Polar Drift’ NHar NSla WAbe
‘Pollux’ (× *boydii*) (7) NMen
poluniniana (7) WAbe
poluniniana × ‘Winifred’ (× *poluanglica*) (7) ECho EPot
‘Pompadour’ (15) NPro
‘Popelka’ (subsp. *marginata* var. *rocheliana*) (7) LRHS NMen NRHS
porophylla (7) NMen
- var. ***thessalica*** see *S. sempervivum* f. *stenophylla*
‘Precious Piggy’ (*epiphylla*) (5) WCru
‘Primrose Bee’ (× *apiculata*) (7) ITim NMen
‘Primrose Dame’ (× *elisabethae*) (7) ECho MDKP NMen WAbe WIce
‘Primulaize’ (9 × 11) MWat NMen
‘Primulaize Salmon’ (9 × 11) NHar WHoo WPer
§ ‘Primulina’ (× *malbyana*) (7) NMen
‘Primuloides’ (*umbrosa*) (11) ♀H4 ECho EDAr MMuc NMen SRms SWvt WFar
‘Prince Hal’ (*burseriana*) (7) ECho EPot LRHS NMen
‘Princess’ (*burseriana*) (7) ECho LRHS NMen
‘Probynii’ (*cochlearis*) (8) EPot MWat NMen NWad WAbe
‘Prospero’ (× *petraschii*) (7) NMen
× ***prossenii*** *sensu stricto* hort. see *S.* ‘Regina’
× ***proximae*** ‘Květy Coventry’ (7) EPot
§ ‘Pseudoborisii’ (× *borisii*) (7) NMen
× ***pseudokotschyi*** *sensu stricto* hort. see *S.* ‘Denisa’
‘Pseudoscardica’ (× *wehrhahnii*) (7) NMen
‘Pseudo-valdensis’ (*cochlearis*) (8) WAbe
‘Psycho’ (7) **new** WAbe
pubescens (15) WAbe
- subsp. ***iratiana*** (15) CPBP
‘Punctatissima’ (*paniculata*) (8) NHar
* ***punctissima*** NWad
‘Pungens’ (× *apiculata*) (7) NMen
‘Purple Piggy’ (*epiphylla*) (5) CLAP WCru

	Name	Suppliers
	'Purpurea' (*fortunei*)	see *S.* 'Rubrifolia'
§	'Pygmalion' (× *webrii*) (7)	WGor
	'Pyramidalis' (*cotyledon*) (8)	EPfP EWTr SRms
	'Pyrenaica' (*oppositifolia*) (7)	ECho NMen
	quadrifaria (7)	WAbe
	'Quarry Wood' (× *anglica*) (7)	NMen
	'Radvan Horný' (× *cullinanii*) (7)	WAbe
	'Rainsley Seedling' (8)	GKev NBro NMen
	ramulosa (7)	NMen
	'Red Poll' (× *poluanglica*) (7)	NMen NRya
*	'Regent'	WAbe
§	'Regina' (× *prossenii*) (7)	MHer NMen
§	'Reginald Farrer' (Silver Farreri Group) (8) 🏆H4	GEdr
	'Rembrandt van Rijn' (7) **new**	NMen WAbe
	retusa (7)	NMen WAbe
	'Rex' (*paniculata*) (8)	NWad
	rhodopetala (7)	ECho
§	'Riverslea' (× *hornibrookii*) (7)	NMen WAbe
§	'Robin Hood' (× *megaseiflora*) (7)	EPot NMen WHoo WPat
	'Rokoko' (*megaseiflora*) (7) **new**	NMen
	'Rokujō' (*fortunei*) (5)	CLAP EBee IVic NLar NPnk NPro SHeu WFar
	'Romeo' (× *hornibrookii*) (7)	NMen
	'Rosa Tubbs'	GKev
	rosacea (15)	EDAr
	'Rosalind' (7) **new**	NMen
	'Rosea' (*cortusifolia*) (5)	CLAP NHar NPri
§	'Rosea' (*paniculata*) (8) 🏆H4	GMaP LBMP NBro NMen NSla SEND SRms WFar
I	'Rosea Spendens' (*paniculata*) **new**	SEND
	'Rosea' (× *stuartii*) (7)	NMen
	'Rosemarie' (7)	ECho EPot NMen
	'Rosenzwerg' (15)	WFar
	'Rosina Sündermann' (× *rosinae*) (7)	ECho LRHS NMen
	'Rote Stadt' (*fortunei*) (5)	IVic
	rotundifolia (12)	EBee ECha EWTr GMaP MDKP SBfd
	'Roy Clutterbuck' (7)	NMen
	'Rubella' (× *irvingii*) (7)	EPot
	'Rubra' (*aizoon*)	see *S.* 'Rosea' (*paniculata*)
§	'Rubrifolia' (*fortunei*) (5)	CLAP CMac CSpe EBee ECha ECtt EHoe GAbr GEdr IBal LAst LRHS MBri MCot NMen NMyG NPnk SMad SPet SWvt WBor WCot WCru WFar WMoo WWEG
*	'Ruby Red'	NPro
*	'Ruby Wedding' (*cortusifolia*) (5)	CLAP WCru WFar
	rufescens (5) BWJ 7510	EHrv GEdr WCru
	- BWJ 7684	GEdr WCru
	'Rufina' (7) **new**	NMen
	'Rusalka' (× *borisii*) (7)	NMen
	'Russell V. Prichard' (× *irvingii*) (7)	NMen NWad
	'Ruth Draper' (*oppositifolia*) (7)	WAbe WFar
	'Ruth McConnell' (15)	CMea SBch
	'Sabrina' (× *fallsvillagensis*) (7)	NMen
	'Saint John's' (8)	ECho GEdr GKev
	'Saint Kilda' (*oppositifolia*) (7)	ITim
	× ***salmonica*** *sensu stricto* hort.	see *S.* 'Salomonii'
§	'Salomonii' (× *salmonica*) (7)	EPot NMen SRms
	'Samo' (× *bertolonii*) (7)	NMen
	sancta (7)	ECho EPot LRHS NMen NRHS SRms
	- subsp. ***pseudosancta***	see *S. juniperifolia*
	- - var. ***macedonica***	see *S. juniperifolia*
	'Sandpiper' (7)	NMen
	'Šárka' (7)	NMen
	sarmentosa	see *S. stolonifera*
	'Sartorii'	see *S.* 'Pygmalion'
	'Satchmo' (Blues Group) (7)	EPot NMen
	'Saturn' (× *megaseiflora*) (7)	NMen WFar
	'Sázava' (× *poluluteopurpurea*) (7)	NMen
	scardica (7)	EPot NBro NMen WAbe
	- var. ***dalmatica***	see *S. obtusa*
§	'Schelleri' (× *petraschii*) (7)	EPfP NMen
	'Schöne Mädchen' (*fortunei*) (5)	IVic
§	'Schwefelblüte' (15)	ECho GMaP LRHS WPat
	scleropoda (7)	NMen
§	'Seaspray' (× *arendsii*) (15/v)	EWes
	'Seissera' (*burseriana*) (7)	NMen
	'Semafor' (Holenka's Miracle Group) (× *megaseiflora*) (7)	NMen
	× ***semmleri*** *sensu stricto* hort.	see *S.* 'Martha'
	sempervivum (7)	NGdn NMen WAbe
§	- f. ***stenophylla*** (7)	ECho MHer
	sendaica (5)	WCru
	- B&SWJ 7448	GEdr
	'Sergio Bacci' (7)	NMen
	'Sherlock Holmes' (7)	NMen WAbe
	'Shimmy' **new**	WAbe
	'Shinkunomai' (*fortunei*) (5)	IVic
	'Shiragiku' (*fortunei*) (5)	NHar WCot
	'Silver Beads' (*paniculata*) (8)	NHar
§	'Silver Cushion' (15/v)	CMea CTri ECho ELan LRHS MAsh MBrN NEgg NRHS SBch SPlb SPoG WAbe WFar WNew
	'Silver Edge' (× *arco-valleyi*) (7)	NMen WAbe
	'Silver Maid' (× *engleri*) (8)	GEdr NMen NSla WAbe
	'Silver Mound'	see *S.* 'Silver Cushion'
	'Silver Velvet' (*fortunei*) (5)	CAbP CBct CLAP CSpe ECtt ESwi GEdr IFoB LRHS NMyG SHeu WBor WCot
	'Sir Douglas Haig' (15)	NWad
	'Sissi' (7)	CPBP NMen WAbe
	'Slack's Ruby Southside' (Southside Seedling Group) 🏆H4	MDKP NMen NSla NWad WFar WIce
	'Slack's Sensation'	NSla
	'Slack's Supreme'	NHar NSla
	'Slzy Coventry' (× *proximae*) (7)	WAbe
	'Snowcap' (*pubescens*) (15)	NMen WAbe
	'Snowdon' (*burseriana*) (7)	NMen
	'Snowflake' (Silver Farreri Group) (8) 🏆H4	WAbe
§	'Sofia' (× *borisii*) (7)	EPot NMen WFar
	'Sorrento' (*marginata*) (7)	NMen
	Southside Seedling Group (8) 🏆H4	Widely available
	- 'Southside Star' 🏆H4	WAbe WFar
	'Soyokaze' (*fortunei*) (5)	NHar

	spathularis (11)	CEnt WCot
	'Splendens' (*oppositifolia*) (7) ♀H4	CYeo ECho EPfP MMuc NHar SRms WAbe WPat
	'Spotted Dog'	see *S.* 'Canis-dalmatica'
	'Sprite' (15)	SPoG
	spruneri (7)	ECho LRHS NMen NRHS WAbe
	- var. ***deorum*** (7)	NMen
	'Stansfieldii' (*rosacea*) (15)	MAsh NMen SPlb SPoG WFar
	'Star Dust' (7)	EPot
	stellaris (4)	WAbe
	stenophylla subsp. ***stenophylla***	see *S. flagellaris*
	stolitzkae (7)	NMen WAbe
§	***stolonifera*** (5) ♀H2	CArn CCVN CEnt CHEx CSpe ECho EShb EWTr LDai NBro NPnk SDix SWvt WCot WFar WMoo WPnn
	- large-flowered (5)	WCot WGrn
	stribrnyi (7)	NMen WAbe
	'Sturmiana' (*paniculata*) (8)	NMen SRms
	'Sue Drew' (*fortunei*) (5)	LLHF
	'Sue Tubbs'	GKev
	'Suendermannii Major' (× *kellereri*) (7)	ECho LRHS NRya
	'Suendermannii' (× *kellereri*) (7)	ECho LRHS NRHS
	'Sugar Plum Fairy' (*fortunei*) (5)	ECtt EShb ESwi IVic LRHS SMad SPer WCot
§	'Sulphurea' (× *boydii*) (7)	ECho LRHS MAsh NMen NWad WPat
	'Swan' (× *fallsvillagensis*) (7)	NMen
	'Sylva' (× *elisabethae*) (7)	NMen
	'Symons-Jeunei' (8)	GEdr NWad WAbe
	'Tábor' (× *schottii*) (7)	NMen
	'Teide' (Swirly Group) (7)	NMen
	'Tenerife' (Swirly Group) (7)	CPBP NMen WAbe
	'Thalia' (7) **new**	NMen
	'Theoden' (*oppositifolia*) (7) ♀H4	CMea CPBP ECho EWes NHar WAbe
	'Theresa Cooper' (7)	EPot WAbe
	'Theresia' (× *mariae-theresiae*) (7)	NMen
	'Thorpei' (× *gusmusii*) (7)	NMen
	'Timmy Foster' (× *irvingii*) (7)	NMen
	tolmiei (3)	WAbe
	tombeanensis (7)	NMen
	'Tricolor' (*stolonifera*) (5) ♀H2	CHEx EBak
§	'Triumph' (× *arendsii*) (15)	ECtt EPfP GMaP MAsh NEgg SPoG
	'Tully' (× *elisabethae*) (7)	WGor WPat
	'Tumbling Waters' (8) ♀H4	ECho EPot GAbr LHop LRHS MRav NHol NMen NRHS NSla WAbe WFar WGor WPat
§	'Tvoje Píseň' (× *poluanglica*) (7)	GKev NMen WHoo WThu
§	'Tvůňj Den' (× *polulacina*) (7)	NMen
§	'Tvůj Polibek' (× *poluanglica*) (7)	MDKP NMen
§	'Tvůj Přítel' (× *poluanglica*) (7)	NMen
	'Tvůěj Sen' (× *poluanglica*) (7) **new**	NMen
§	'Tvůj Úsměv' (× *poluanglica*) (7)	NLar NMen
§	'Tvůj Úspěch' (× *poluanglica*) (7)	EPot NMen WAbe
	'Tycho Brahe' (× *doerfleri*) (7)	NMen WAbe
	'Tysoe' (7)	NMen
	umbrosa (11)	CMac CTri EBee ECho EDAr LAst LEdu LRHS MMuc MRav SBfd SEND SPlb SPoG SRms STes SWvt WFar WMoo XLum
*	- ***subinteger***	SEND
	'Unique'	see *S.* 'Bodensee'
	× ***urbium*** (11) ♀H4	CHEx CTri EBee ECho ELan EPfP EWTr GMaP LEdu MBel NPri SBfd SPer SRms WBrk WCAu WFar WPer WWEG
	'Vaccariana' (*oppositifolia*) (7)	ECho EPot
	'Václav Hollar' (× *gusmusii*) (7)	NMen
	'Vahlii' (× *smithii*) (7)	NMen
	'Valborg'	see *S.* 'Cranbourne'
	'Valentine'	see *S.* 'Cranbourne'
	'Valerie Finnis'	see *S.* 'Aretiastrum'
	'Valerie Keevil' (× *anglica*) (7)	NMen
I	'Variegata' (*cuneifolia*) (11/v)	ECho ECtt EPfP LRHS NHol NWad SPet SPlb SPoG WFar WMoo WPer
I	'Variegata' (*exarata* subsp. *moschata*) (15/v) **new**	GMaP
	'Variegata' (*umbrosa*)	see *S.* 'Aureopunctata'
I	'Variegata' (× *urbium*) (11/v)	EBee ECho EPfP LAst LRHS MBel MSpe NLar SRms WFar WNew WWEG
	'Večerní Hvězda'	WAbe
	veitchiana (5)	GEdr NBro
	'Verona' (× *caroli-langii*) (7)	WAbe
	'Vesna' (× *borisii*) (7)	NMen
	'Vincent van Gogh' (× *borisii*) (7)	EPot NMen
	'Vladana' (× *megaseiflora*) (7)	CPBP ECho EPot LRHS NMen NRHS WAbe
	'Vlasta' (7)	NMen
	'Vlasta Burian' (7)	WAbe
	'Vltava' (7)	EPot NMen
	'Volgeri' (× *hofmannii*) (7)	NMen
	'Vreny' (8)	GKev
	'Vysoké Mýto' (7)	EPot NMen WAbe
	'Wada' (*fortunei*) (5)	CAbP CDes CLAP EAEE EBee ECtt ELon EWTr GAbr GBuc GEdr LAst LRHS MCot MNrw MSpe NBir NMyG NPri SPer WBor WCot WFar WOld WPGP WSHC WWEG
	'Waithman's Variety' (8)	GEdr
	'Wallacei' (15)	NMen
	'Walpole's Variety' (8)	WAbe WPer
	'Walter Ingwersen' (*umbrosa*) (11)	SRms
§	'Walter Irving' (× *irvingii*) (7)	NMen WAbe
	'Warmes Herz' (*fortunei*) (5)	IVic
	'Wartosque' (*callosa*) (8)	EPot
	'Weisser Zwerg' (15)	NMen
	'Welsh Dragon' (15)	WAbe
	'Welsh Red' (15)	WAbe WFar
	'Welsh Rose' (15)	WAbe
	wendelboi (7)	NMen WAbe
	'Wendrush' (× *wendelacina*) (7)	NMen
	'Wendy' (× *wendelacina*) (7)	NMen WAbe
	'Wheatley Gem' (7)	NMen
	'Wheatley Lion' (× *borisii*) (7)	NMen
	'Wheatley Rose' (7)	ECho LRHS NRHS

	'White Cap' (× *boydii*) (7)	NMen
	'White Imp' (7)	NMen
§	'White Pixie' (15)	ECtt EDAr EPfP MAsh MHer NHol NPri NPro NRya NWad SPlb SPoG SRms WFar WIce WNew
	'White Star' (× *petraschii*)	see *S.* 'Schelleri'
	'Whitehill' (8) ♀H4	CMea CPBP ECho ELan GEdr GJos GMaP LRHS MAsh MDKP NBro NHol NMen NRHS NRya NSla NWad SBch SPet WFar WHoo WNew WPat WTin
§	'Wilhelm Tell' (× *malbyana*) (7)	NMen
	'William Boyd' (× *boydii*) (7)	WAbe
	'William Shakespeare' (Blues Group) (7)	WAbe
	'Winifred Bevington' (8 × 11) ♀H4	CPBP ECho EDAr GEdr LHop LRHS MMuc NBro NLar NMen NRHS NRya NWad WAbe WFar WHoo WPer WPnn
	'Winifred' (× *anglica*) (7)	ECho EPot NMen WAbe
	'Winston Churchill' (15)	CElw CTri ECho ECtt LRHS MAsh NHol NRHS NWad
I	'Winston Churchill Variegata' (15/v)	ECtt NHol NWad
	'Winton' (× *paulinae*) (7)	NMen
	'Wisley' (*federici-augusti* subsp. *grisebachii*) (7) ♀H2-3	GKev NMen WPat
	'Wisley Primrose'	see *S.* 'Kolbiana'
	'Woodside Ross' (15)	ECtt
	'Yellow Rock' (7)	MWat NMen NRya
	'Youkuy' (*fortunei*) (5)	IVic
	Your Day	see *S.* 'Tvůj Den'
	Your Friend	see *S.* 'Tvůj Přítel'
	Your Good Fortune	see *S.* 'Tvůj Úspěch'
	Your Kiss	see *S.* 'Tvůj Polibek'
	Your Smile	see *S.* 'Tvůj Úsměv'
	Your Song	see *S.* 'Tvoje Píseň'
	Your Success	see *S.* 'Tvůj Úspěch'
	'Yunagi' (*fortunei*) (5)	IVic NHar WOld
	× ***zimmeteri*** (8 × 11)	ECho NMen
§	'Zita' (*sempervivum*) (7)	NMen
§	'Zlatá Praha' (× *pragensis*) (7)	NMen WAbe
	'Zlín' (× *leyboldii*) (7)	NMen

Scabiosa (*Caprifoliaceae*)

	africana	EBee EWes SHar
	- 'Jocelyn'	SHar
	alpina L.	see *Cephalaria alpina*
	argentea	EBee EWes LEdu
	atropurpurea	SPav
	- 'Ace of Spades'	CWCL ELan MCot SMad SPav SPhx
	- 'Beaujolais Bonnets'	EPfP EWTr LRHS SHil SPer WHrl
§	- 'Chile Black'	CBcs CHab EBee ECtt EHoe EHrv ELan EPfP EUJe EWes GCal LAst LHop LRHS LSRN LSou MWat NPri SMrm SPav SPer SPet SRkn SWvt WMnd WWEG WWlt XLum
§	- 'Chilli Pepper'	CWCL EHrv EPfP LHop LRHS MBri
§	- 'Chilli Sauce'	CWCL EHrv EPfP LHop LRHS
	- 'Derry's Black'	CSpe
	- 'Nona'	LLHF
	- 'Oxford Blue' **new**	SPhx
	- 'Peter Ray'	WWlt
	banatica	see *S. columbaria*
	'Barocca'	CSpe LRHS WHil
	'Blue Diamonds'	EBee LRHS MHer
	Burgundy Bonnets = 'Scabon'PBR	EPfP LRHS
§	'Butterfly Blue'	CBar CMHG EBee ECtt ELon EPPr EPfP GAbr LRHS LSRN LSou MBri NHol NLar SCoo SHil SMrm SPer SPoG SWvt WAul WBrk WCAu WCot WFar WWEG
	caucasica	CMac EPfP GKev LAst LEdu NRHS WFar WHoo
	- var. ***alba***	CBcs CKno EPfP NGBl WFar WHoo
	- 'Blauer Atlas'	EBee
	- 'Blausiegel'	CMac CSam EBee ECtt EHrv MCot MRav NBre NDov SMrm SPet WFar
	- 'Clive Greaves' ♀H4	EBee ECha ECtt ELan EPfP GBuc IBoy MBri MPkF NPri SPad SRms SWvt WFar
	- 'Deep Waters'	CSpe EBee LRHS WPtf
	- 'Fama'	CSpe CWib EBee NBir NGBl NLar SMrm SPlb SRms WFar WWEG XLum
	- 'Goldingensis'	MHer NGdn NPri WPer
	- House's hybrids	CSBt NGdn SRms
	- 'Isaac House'	ELon NLar SPhx XLum
	- 'Kompliment'	NBre NLar SMrm WWEG
	- 'Lavender Blue'	WFar
	- 'Miss Willmott' ♀H4	CMac CSam EBee ECha ECtt EHoe EHrv ELan EPfP IPot LHop LRHS MBri MCot MHer MLHP MRav NCGa NPri SWvt WCAu WFar WGwG WHrl WMnd WWFP
	- 'Moerheim Blue'	EBee
	- Perfecta Series	CWib EBee LRHS MMHG NGdn NLar SBfd SPoG SWat
	- - 'Perfecta Alba'	COIW CWib EBee ECtt GMaP LAst LRHS MSpe MWat NChi NLar NOrc NPri SBfd SMrm SPad SPer SPoG SWat WPtf WWEG XLum
	- - 'Perfecta Blue'	MSpe XLum
	- - 'Perfecta Lilac Blue'	CWib EPfP GMaP SBfd SPer WWEG
	- 'Stäfa'	EBee ECha GBee LRHS MBri MCot MRav MSpe NCGa NEgg NLar SUsu WMnd
	- 'Thorp's Variegated' (v)	WCot
	'Chile Black'	see *S. atropurpurea* 'Chile Black'
	'Chile Pepper'	see *S. atropurpurea* 'Chilli Pepper'
	'Chile Sauce'	see *S. atropurpurea* 'Chilli Sauce'
	'Chile Spice'	MBri
	cinerea	SPhx
§	***columbaria***	CHab EBee LRHS MPet NBre NEgg NLan NMir SMrm WHer WJek WSFF WWEG
*	- ***alpina***	WAbe
	- 'Misty Butterflies'	CCVN ECtt EDAr EPfP LBMP LHop LSou NEgg NGdn NLar SBfd SMrm WFar WWEG
	- 'Nana'	CCse CMea EBee LRHS NBir NGdn NLar NMen SBch SBea WCFE WFar WHrl WWFP XLum
§	- subsp. ***ochroleuca***	CKno CSpe ECha EHrv GCal GLin LRHS MCot MSpe NBir NLar SPhx SPoG SRms WFar WPGP
	- - MESE 344	EBee
	- - 'Moon Dance'	CCon CMea EBee EDAr GCal LLHF LRHS MSpe NCGa NPri NRHS SBfd SMad WHoo
	- 'Pincushion Blue'	EDAr
	- 'Pincushion Pink'	EDAr NGdn SBea WFar WWEG
	- pink-flowered	LRHS
	cretica	EBee XSen

drakensbergensis	EBee EWes GAbr LRHS MTPN SLon WCot WHrl WPtf
farinosa	ECtt MMuc SEND SGar WAbe WFar
gigantea	see *Cephalaria gigantea*
graminifolia	ECho GKev NBir NMen SBch SRms WWEG XLum
- JM 990	EBee
- ***rosea***	EWes
'Helen Dillon'	EBee ECtt EWes LSou WWEG
'Irish Perpetual Flowering'	see *S.* 'Butterfly Blue'
japonica var. ***acutiloba***	SPhx
- var. ***alpina***	CEnt CPrp EBee EPfP GAbr GKev MMuc MWat NGdn SBfd SEND SPet SPhx WHoo WNew WTin WWFP XLum
- - 'Blue Star'	NBre NCGa
- 'Ritz Blue'	EPfP SPad
lachnophylla	EBee GCal SPhx
- 'Blue Horizon'	EBee WHil
'Little Emily'	ELon LSou SAga SUsu
lucida	EAEE EBee ECho ECtt EPfP LRHS MRav WHrl WPGP WPer XLum
'Midnight'	CMea
'Midnight Moon' **new**	WHlf
'Miss Havisham'	ECtt EWes
montana Mill.	see *Knautia arvensis*
ochroleuca	see *S. columbaria* subsp. *ochroleuca*
parnassi	see *Pterocephalus perennis*
'Perpetual Flowering'	see *S.* 'Butterfly Blue'
Pink Buttons = 'Walminipink'	CCon EBee LRHS LSou
'Pink Diamonds'	CMac EBee EPfP MBri
'Pink Mist'[PBR]	CBar EBee ECtt EPfP IBoy LRHS MBri MPkF NBir NLar SCoo SMrm SPer SPoG SRms WCAu
pterocephala	see *Pterocephalus perennis*
rhodopensis	EBee
'Rosie's Pink'	ECtt
rumelica	see *Knautia macedonica*
'Sapphire Moon' **new**	WHlf
'Satchmo'	see *S. atropurpurea* 'Chile Black'
'Silvery Moon' **new**	WHlf
succisa	see *Succisa pratensis*
tatarica	see *Cephalaria gigantea*
tenuis	SPhx
triandra	EBee LHop
'Vivid Violet'	CAbP ECtt LSou MNrw NDov NLar SHar SHil SMrm SUsu WBor WCot

Scadoxus ✿ (*Amaryllidaceae*)

multiflorus	CCCN CPrp ECho GHim LAma SDeJ
§ - subsp. ***katherinae*** ♀H1	CPne ECho WCot
§ - subsp. ***multiflorus*** ♀H1	WCot
natalensis	see *S. puniceus*
§ ***puniceus***	CLak GHim WCot

Scaevola (*Goodeniaceae*)

aemula 'Blue Fan'[PBR]	see *S. aemula* 'Blue Wonder'
§ - 'Blue Wonder'[PBR]	NPer SWvt
- 'Purple Fan'	LAst
- White Wonder = 'Scax0226' **new**	LHop
- 'Zig Zag'[PBR]	CCCN NPri
Blauer Facher = 'Saphira'[PBR]	CCCN LHop
'Brillant'[PBR]	LSou
crassifolia	SPlb
'Mini Blue'	CCCN
'Topaz Pink'	LHop LSou

Sceletium (*Aizoaceae*)

tortuosum	SPlb

Schefflera (*Araliaceae*)

sp.	WPGP
alpina	IVic
- B&SWJ 8247	WCru
- B&SWJ 11827	WCru
- HWJ 936	WCru
arboricola ♀H1	CHEx SEND XBlo
- 'Gold Capella' ♀H1	SEND XBlo
- 'Kalahari'	XBlo
brevipedicellata HWJ 870	WCru
- KWJ 12224	WCru
§ ***chapana*** B&SWJ 11848	WCru
- HWJ 983	WCru
delavayi	CHEx WPGP
elegantissima ♀H1	EShb
enneaphylla B&SWJ 11727	WCru
- HWJ 1018	WCru
fantsipanensis B&SWJ 11666	WCru
- B&SWJ 11671	WCru
fengii	GLin
gracilis HWJ 622	WCru
- HWJ 878	WCru
hoi B&SWJ 11747	WCru
kornasii B&SWJ 11830	WCru
- HWJ 918	WCru
lenticellata B&SWJ 9762	WCru
macrophylla	LEdu
- B&SWJ 8210	WCru
- B&SWJ 9788	WCru
microphylla B&SWJ 3872	WCru
multinervia B&SWJ 11727 **new**	WCru
aff. ***myriocarpa*** B&SWJ 11828	WCru
rhododendrifolia	CHEx WPGP
- GWJ 9375	WCru
taiwaniana	CHEx IVic
- B&SWJ 3575	WCru
- B&SWJ 7096	WCru
- RWJ 10000	WCru
- RWJ 10016	WCru
vietnamensis	see *S. chapana*

Schima (*Theaceae*)

wallichii	CPLG EBee
- subsp. ***noronhae*** var. ***superba***	CCCN CPLG EPfP
- subsp. ***wallichii*** var. ***khasiana***	CBcs

Schinus (*Anacardiaceae*)

latifolius	CBcs
lentiscifolius	SPlb
molle	SPlb
polygamus	CBcs SPlb

Schisandra (*Schisandraceae*)

sp.	LAst
arisanensis B&SWJ 3050	WCru
aff. ***bicolor*** BWJ 8151	WCru
chinensis	CAgr CArn CBcs GPoy LEdu MSwo NLar
- B&SWJ 4204	WCru

grandiflora	CBcs CDoC EBee ELan EPfP LRHS MBlu NLar SKHP SMDP SPer WGwG
- B&SWJ 2245	WCru
- var. ***cathayensis***	see *S. sphaerandra*
- 'Jamu' (m)	WCru
- 'Lahlu' (f/F)	WCru
grandiflora × rubriflora	WCru
henryi subsp. ***yunnanensis*** B&SWJ 6546	WCru
incarnata × ***rubriflora*** new	WCru
nigra	see *S. repanda*
aff. ***plena*** HWJ 664	WCru
propinqua subsp. ***sinensis***	CMac LEdu MBlu NLar WSHC
- BWJ 8148	WCru
§ ***repanda*** B&SWJ 5897	WCru
- B&SWJ 11455	WCru
rubriflora	CBcs CHEx CTri CWSG EBee EPfP IDee LRHS MBlu MGos SKHP SLon SMDP SPoG SSpi
- (f)	ELan WSHC
- (m)	NHol
- BWJ 7557	WCru
§ ***sphaerandra*** BWJ 7739	WCru
sphenanthera	ELan LRHS NLar WSHC

Schivereckia (Brassicaceae)

doerfleri	MWat

Schizachyrium (Poaceae)

§ ***scoparium***	CKno EBee EHoe EPPr LBMP LRHS MWhi SPhx SUsu WCot XLum
- 'Blaze'	EPPr
- 'Blue Heaven' new	EBee
- 'Cairo'	EBee
- 'Explosion' new	EBee
- 'Prairie Blues'	CKno EBee EShb LRHS SMea SMrm SPhx WCot
- 'The Blues'	EBee
- 'Wildwest' new	EBee

Schizocarphus (Hyacinthaceae)

nervosus	ECho WCot

Schizocodon see Shortia

Schizopetalon (Brassicaceae)

walkeri	CSpe

Schizophragma (Hydrangeaceae)

corylifolium	NLar
- BWJ 8150	WCru WPGP
aff. ***elliptifolium*** WWJ 11905	WCru
hydrangeoides	CBcs CDoC CDul EBee ELan EPfP EWTr GKin LAst LRHS MBlu MGos SGol SLim SLon SPer SPoG SWvt
- B&SWJ 5489	WCru
- B&SWJ 5732	WCru
- B&SWJ 5954	WCru
- B&SWJ 6119 from Yakushima, Japan	WCru
- B&SWJ 8505 from Ulleungdo, Korea	WCru
- B&SWJ 8522 from Ulleungdo, Korea	WCru
- 'Brookside Littleleaf'	see *Hydrangea anomala* subsp. *petiolaris* var. *cordifolia* 'Brookside Littleleaf'
- 'Cheju's Early'	WCru
- 'Iwa Garami'	NLar
- 'Moonlight'	Widely available
* - f. ***quelpartensis*** B&SWJ 8771	WCru
- 'Roseum' ♀H4	CBcs CDoC CMac CMil CSPN EBee ELan EPfP EWes GKin IArd LRHS MBlu MBri MGos NCGa NLar NPri NRHS SGol SKHP SLim SPer SPoG SSpi SWvt WCru WFar WPGP
integrifolium ♀H4	CBcs CMac EBee ELan EPfP EWTr LRHS NLar SKHP SSpi WKif WPGP WSHC
- var. ***fauriei***	NLar WSHC
- - B&SWJ 1701	WCru
- - B&SWJ 7052	WCru
- - CWJ 12433	WCru

Schizostachyum (Poaceae)

§ ***funghomii***	SEND

Schizostylis see Hesperantha

coccinea 'Gigantea'	see *Hesperantha coccinea* 'Major'
- 'Grandiflora'	see *Hesperantha coccinea* 'Major'
- 'Sunset'	see *Hesperantha coccinea* 'Sunrise'
'Pink Princess'	see *Hesperantha coccinea* 'Wilfred H. Bryant'

Schoenoplectus (Cyperaceae)

§ ***lacustris***	CWat MMuc MSKA SEND
- subsp. ***tabernaemontani*** 'Albescens' (v)	CBen CWat LPBA MNrw MSKA MWts SWat WHal
- - 'Zebrinus' (v)	CBen CWat ELan EPfP EUJe LPBA MNrw MSKA MWts NPla SPlb SWat WFar WHal WMAq WPnP

Schoenus (Cyperaceae)

pauciflorus	CWCL EHoe EWes NOak SUsu WMoo

Sciadopitys (Sciadopityaceae)

verticillata ♀H4	CBcs CDoC CDoy CDul CKen CSBt CTho EHul EPfP ERom GKin IDee LRHS MBlu MBri MGos NHol NWea SBfd SCoo SEND SLim SPoG SSpi SWvt WEve WFar WHar
I - 'Compacta'	LRHS
- 'Firework'	CKen
- 'Globe'	CKen
- 'Gold Star'	CKen
- 'Goldammer'	NLar
- 'Golden Rush'	CKen NLar WEve
- 'Goldmahne'	CKen
- 'Grüne Kugel'	CKen NLar
- 'Jeddeloh Compact'	CKen
- 'Kugelblitz'	WEve
- 'Kupferschirm'	CKen
- 'Mecki'	CKen MDev WEve
- 'Megaschirm'	CKen
- 'Ossorio Gold'	CKen WEve
- 'Picola'	CKen NLar
- 'Pygmy'	CKen
- 'Richie's Cream' new	CKen
- 'Richie's Cushion'	CKen WEve
- 'Shorty'	CKen
- 'Speerspitze'	CKen

- 'Star Wars' CKen
- 'Starburst' CKen
- 'Sternschnuppe' CKen MDev NLar WEve
- 'Wintergreen' CKen

Scilla (*Asparagaceae*)

adlamii see *Ledebouria cooperi*
× ***allenii*** see × *Chionoscilla allenii*
amethystina see *S. litardierei*
amoena ECho WCot
aristidis from Algeria ECho
autumnalis CAvo CDes CPom ECho EPot GKev LAma LLHF WShi WThu
bifolia ♀H4 CAvo CBro CPom CTca ECho EPot GKev LAma LLWP SBch SDeJ SPhx WShi
- RS 156/83 ECho LWst
- 'Alba' ECho EPot SPhx
- 'Rosea' ECho EPot GKev LAma LLWP MWat SDeJ
bithynica ♀H4 WShi
campanulata see *Hyacinthoides hispanica*
caucasica LWst
chinensis see *S. scilloides*
cilicica ECho SPhx
greilhuberi ECho EPPr EPot LLHF WAbe WCot
hohenackeri LLHF SPhx WThu
- BSBE 559 LWst
- BSBE 811 CDes WCot
§ ***hughii*** CDes ECho
hyacinthoides CDes ECho WCot
ingridiae ECho LWst
- var. ***taurica*** ECho
italica see *Hyacinthoides italica*
japonica see *S. scilloides*
latifolia from Morocco ECho
libanotica see *Puschkinia scilloides* var. *libanotica*
liliohyacinthus CAvo CBro CRow ECho GHim IBlr LWst MMHG WSHC WShi
- 'Alba' CAvo
lingulata ECho LLHF NMen WCot
- S&F 253 CDes
- var. ***ciliolata*** CBro CPBP ECho EPot SBch
- var. ***lingulata*** ECho
§ ***litardierei*** ♀H4 CTca ECho EPPr EPot IFro LAma NMen SBch SDeJ SEND SPhx WShi
lutea hort. see *Ledebouria socialis*
madeirensis CLak WCot
melaina EPot WCot
- VVTA.118 LWst
mesopotamica LWst
messeniaca CPom
- HOA 0168 LWst
- MS 38 from Greece WCot
mischtschenkoana ♀H4 CAvo CBro CHid ECho EPot IFro LAma MBri NRHS SDeJ WShi
§ - 'Tubergeniana' ♀H4 CMea ECho GKev SPhx WCot
- 'Zwanenburg' ECho
monophyllos ECho LWst
morrisii LWst
natalensis see *Merwilla plumbea*
non-scripta see *Hyacinthoides non-scripta*
nutans see *Hyacinthoides non-scripta*
obtusifolia ECho
persica ♀H4 CDes ECho SPhx WCot
peruviana Widely available
- S&L 285 WCot
- SB&L 20/1 WCot
- 'Alba' CBro CDes CFwr CPrp CTca ECho WCot XLum
* - var. ***ciliata*** WCot
- var. ***elegans*** CDes WCot
- 'Hughii' see *S. hughii*
- 'Paul Voelcker' **new** CDes
- var. ***venusta*** CDes
- - S&L 311/2 WCot
pratensis see *S. litardierei*
puschkinioides ECho
reverchonii ECho
- from Spain WCot
rosenii ECho
§ ***scilloides*** ECho GKev SCnR
- B&SWJ 8812 WCru
* - 'Alba' **new** SDeJ
siberica ♀H4 CAvo CBro CTca ECho EPfP GAbr GKev LAma LRHS MMuc MWat SBch SEND SMrm SPer SPhx WRHF WShi
- 'Alba' CTca ECho EPfP EPot GKev LAma SBch SDeJ SMrm WShi
- 'Boreas' LWst
- 'Enem' **new** LWst
- 'Spring Beauty' CCse CMea ECGP ECho EPot GKev LAma MBri SDeJ SPhx SRms
'Tubergeniana' see *S. mischtschenkoana* 'Tubergeniana'
verna CDes ECho WCot WShi WThu
vicentina see *Hyacinthoides vincentina*
violacea see *Ledebouria socialis*
vvedenskyi RM 8257 **new** LWst

Scirpoides (*Cyperaceae*)

§ ***holoschoenus*** CRWN

Scirpus (*Cyperaceae*)

cernuus see *Isolepis cernua*
holoschoenus see *Scirpoides holoschoenus*
lacustris see *Schoenoplectus lacustris*
- 'Spiralis' see *Juncus effusus* f. *spiralis*
maritimus see *Bolboschoenus maritimus*

Scleranthus (*Caryophyllaceae*)

biflorus CTrC ECho EDAr EUJe EWes LEdu MAsh NSla SPlb WPer XLum
singuliflorus WPat
uniflorus CTrC ECho EShb LEdu SMad SPlb XLum

Sclerochiton (*Acanthaceae*)

harveyanus EShb

Scoliopus (*Liliaceae*)

bigelowii LWst SCnR WHal
hallii EBee GEdr LEdu LWst NMen WCru

Scolopendrium see *Asplenium*

Scopolia (*Solanaceae*)

anomala EBee
carniolica CArn CCon EBee ELan EWld GKev GPoy LEdu MPhe NChi NLar NSti SPlb WAul WCru WFar WPGP WSHC XLum
- from Poland LEdu
- from Slovenia WCot
§ - var. ***brevifolia*** EHrv EPPr EWld LEdu SPhx WTin
- - WM 9811 MPhe
- subsp. ***hladnikiana*** see *S. carniolica* var. *brevifolia*

- 'Zwanenburg'	EHrv EPPr EWes LEdu NLar SPhx XLum
lurida	see *Anisodus luridus*

Scorzonera (*Asteraceae*)

hispanica	SVic

Scrophularia (*Scrophulariaceae*)

aquatica	see *S. auriculata*
§ ***auriculata***	CHab LPBA MHer NMir NPer WHer
§ - 'Variegata' (v)	CBcs EBee ECha EHoe ELan EPfP EShb GCal LPBA LRHS MHer NBid NEgg SBfd SPer SPoG WCot WSHC
buergeriana 'Lemon and Lime' misapplied	see *Teucrium viscidum* 'Lemon and Lime'
- 'Lemon and Lime' (v)	NEgg
callianthа	MDKP
canina	GKev
grandiflora	CPom
nodosa	CArn CRWN EBee GPoy NMir WHer WHfH
- ***variegata***	see *S. auriculata* 'Variegata'
scopolii	EBee

Scutellaria ✿ (*Lamiaceae*)

albida	WOut
§ ***alpina***	ECho GJos SPlb SRms SRot WGor WPer
- 'Arcobaleno'	GEdr LLHF SMrm
- 'Moonbeam'	GEdr LRHS
altissima	CFis ECha ELan ELon LRHS MMuc NBro SBfd SEND SGar SPlb WOut WPtf XSen
'Amazing Grace'	EWes
baicalensis	CArn CDes EBee GJos GPoy MHoo SMrm WPtf
barbata	CArn
canescens	see *S. incana*
galericulata	CHab CWan ENfk GPoy MHer
hastata	see *S. hastifolia*
§ ***hastifolia***	CTri ECtt
§ ***incana***	EBee ECGP ELan ELon EPPr GMaP LHop LPla SUsu WCot WHlf
indica	EWld LSou WCot
- var. ***japonica***	see *S. indica* var. *parvifolia*
§ - var. ***parvifolia***	EBee ECho EWes GEdr GJos LRHS SRot
- - 'Alba'	CPBP ECho LLHF
integrifolia	CFis
lateriflora	CArn GPoy LRHS SMrm WJek
maekawae	EBee WPGP
- B&SWJ 557a	WCru
'Mood Indigo'	EPPr LRHS
novae-zelandiae	ECou
orientalis	EBee ECtt GCal WAbe
- subsp. ***bicolor***	ECtt
- subsp. ***pinnatifida***	XSen
pontica	CPBP EBee EDAr GEdr SBch SMrm
scordiifolia	CMea CSam EBee ECha ECho EDAr LRHS MAsh MAvo NRya NWad SBHP SBch SRms WFar WHal WHoo WTin
- 'Seoul Sapphire'	CSpe EWes GAbr LEdu LRHS LSou NMen WPtf
sevanensis	EBee LHop WCot WIce
'Sherbert Lemon'	CMea ELon SBfd SRot
suffrutescens 'Texas Rose'	CMea CSpe EBee EDAr IPot LHop LLHF LRHS MAsh SBch SBfd SRot WNew
supina	see *S. alpina*
tournefortii	ECtt LLWP
* ***zhongdianensis***	WPtf

seakale see *Crambe maritima*

Sebaea (*Gentianaceae*)

rehmanii	SPlb
thomasii	GEdr WAbe
- 'Bychan' **new**	WAbe

Securigera (*Papilionaceae*)

§ ***varia***	CArn ELon EPfP LHop MMuc NPri SEND SRms XLum

Sedastrum see *Sedum*

× *Sedeveria* (*Crassulaceae*)

'Darley Dale' **new**	CDoC
'Letizia' **new**	EUJe

Sedum ✿ (*Crassulaceae*)

'Abbey Dore'	EBee ELan EPfP GCal LPla LRHS LSou MTis NCGa NRHS SBfd SPhx WAbb WAul WCAu WPGP
acre	CTri ECho EPfP GPoy LEdu LRHS MAsh MHer MNHC NMir NRHS SEND SPlb XLum
- 'Aureum'	ECho EDAr EHoe EPfP LAst MAsh NLar NPri NRya SPer SPoG WFar WPat XLum
- 'Elegans'	ECtt
- 'Golden Queen'	ECho LRHS MSCN NRHS SPlb SPoG
- 'Helvetica'	WCot
- 'Minus'	ECho EDAr
§ - subsp. ***neglectum*** var. ***majus***	EPfP NLar
- 'Oktoberfest'	EDAr
adolphi	EPfP
aizoon	ECho GCal LAst NBre SIde SPlb WFar XLum
- 'Aurantiacum'	see *S. aizoon* 'Euphorbioides'
§ - 'Euphorbioides'	ECha ECtt ELan LDai MHer MRav NLar SEND SGar SHar SPer SPlb WFar WTin
albescens	see *S. forsterianum* f. *purpureum*
alboroseum	see *S. erythrostictum*
§ ***album***	ECho LRHS NBro NMir NRHS SEND XLum
- 'Coral Carpet'	ECho ECtt EDAr EPPr EPfP EPot GAbr GJos GKev MAsh MRav MWat NRya SFgr SPoG WFar XLum
- subsp. ***gypsicola***	see *S. gypsicola*
- subsp. ***teretifolium*** var. ***micranthum*** 'Chloroticum'	XLum
§ - - var. ***murale***	CTri XLum
alpestre	XLum
altissimum	see *S. sediforme*
* ***altum***	NBre WFar
anacampseros	MHer SEND SUsu XLum
athoum	see *S. album*
atlanticum	see *S. dasyphyllum* subsp. *dasyphyllum* var. *mesatlanticum*
'Autumn Charm'	see *S.* (Herbstfreude Group) 'Lajos'
Autumn Joy	see *S.* (Herbstfreude Group) 'Herbstfreude'
beauverdii HWJ 824	WCru
'Bertram Anderson' ♀H4	Widely available

	Name	Suppliers
	beyrichianum misapplied	see *S. glaucophyllum*
	bithynicum 'Aureum'	see *S. hispanicum* var. *minus* 'Aureum'
	Black Beauty = 'Florseblab'	LBuc LRHS SHil
	'Blade Runner'	EBee LRHS LSou
§	***brevifolium*** var. ***quinquefarium***	WIce
	burrito	EShb
	'Carl'	Widely available
	caucasicum	WAbb
	cauticola ΨH4	CSpe ECho EDAr GBuc GCal GEdr MAvo MBrN MHer MRav NBre SRms SRot WAbe WIce XLum
	- from Lida	ECho
	- 'Coca-Cola'	CCVN CMac CWGN EAEE EBee ECtt EHoe GJos LAst LBMP LRHS MAsh MCot NDov NMen NPri SBfd SPhx SPoG SWvt WBor WFar WHoo WNew
	- 'Lidakense' ΨH4	CMea CSpe CWCL ECha ECho ECtt GBuc LRHS MAsh MBri MLHP MSCN NHol NRHS NSla SBch SPlb SRot WCot WFar WHil XLum
	- 'Purpurine'	ECho GCal
	- 'Robustum'	see *S.* 'Ruby Glow'
	'Chocolate Drop' **new**	NLar
	chrysicaulum	EPot
	'Class Act' PBR ΨH4 **new**	ECtt GBin
	'Cloud Walker' PBR	CAbP EBee ECtt NCGa WCot
	compressum	see *S. palmeri* subsp. *palmeri* tetraploid
	confusum Hemsl.	SEND WFar WHoo WPer
	crassipes	see *Rhodiola wallichiana*
	crassularia	see *Crassula setulosa* 'Milfordiae'
	'Crazy Ruffles'	EBee ECtt EWTr WCot
	cryptomerioides B&SWJ 054	WCru
	'Crystal Pink' **new**	EBee NLar
	'Dark Jack'	EBee MAvo NCGa NGdn SMrm WFar
	dasyphyllum	ECho EDAr MWat NRya SPlb SRms
§	- subsp. ***dasyphyllum*** var. ***mesatlanticum***	GKev NBir
	- ***mucronatis***	see *S. dasyphyllum* subsp. *dasyphyllum* var. *mesatlanticum*
	'Diamond Edge' (v)	EBee ECtt WWEG
	divergens	XLum
	douglasii	see *S. stenopetalum* 'Douglasii'
	drymarioides	LRHS NBre WHil
	'Dudley Field'	MHer
	'Eleanor Fisher'	see *S. telephium* subsp. *ruprechtii*
	ellacombeanum	see *S. kamtschaticum* var. *ellacombeanum*
	'Elworthy Rose'	CElw
§	***erythrostictum***	CWan LRHS WAbb XLum
	- 'Frosty Morn' (v)	Widely available
§	- 'Mediovariegatum' (v)	EAEE EBee ELan LRHS MHer MNrw MRav NLar NPnk NRHS SBfd SWvt WFar WMnd WMoo WWEG XLum
	ewersii	ECho ECtt EDAr MAsh MMuc NBro NLar NSla SPhx SPlb XLum
	- CC 5288	EWld
	- var. ***homophyllum*** 'Rosenteppich'	EPPr LRHS MBrN NRHS SWvt WMoo
	fabaria	see *S. telephium* subsp. *fabaria*
	fastigiatum	see *Rhodiola fastigiata*
	forsterianum subsp. ***elegans***	SPlb XLum
§	- f. ***purpureum***	NRya
	'Frosted Fire'	EBee LSou MAsh
	furfuraceum	NMen WAbe
	Garnet Brocade = 'Garbro' PBR	CCVN ECtt WMoo
§	***glaucophyllum***	WFar XLum
	'Gold Mound'	EPfP LAst LRHS MAsh NLar SSvw
	'Goldie' **new**	CDoC
	'Green Expectations'	ECtt GBin MNFA MRav MWat NBre
§	***gypsicola***	EBee
	hakonense 'Chocolate Ball' **new**	LAst
	Herbstfreude Group **new**	EHrv NWsh
	- 'Autumn Fire'	EBee MAsh
	- 'Beka' (v)	LSou
	- 'Elsie's Gold' (v)	EBee ECtt LRHS MAsh NLar SPoG
§	- 'Herbstfreude' ΨH4	Widely available
	- 'Jaws' PBR	CKno EBee ECtt IKil SMrm WCot
§	- 'Lajos' (v)	EBee LSou MAsh NPro
	- 'Mini Joy'	LRHS MBri WRHF
	heterodontum	see *Rhodiola heterodonta*
	hidakanum	ECtt EHoe EPot GMaP NBro NHol NMen NWad WHoo WTin
	himalense misapplied	see *Rhodiola* 'Keston'
	hispanicum	ECho EDAr NBre SPlb
	- ***glaucum***	see *S. hispanicum* var. *minus*
§	- var. ***minus***	ECho ECtt MMuc SEND SPlb
§	- - 'Aureum'	ECho
	humifusum	WThu
§	***hybridum***	XLum
	- 'Czar's Gold'	NGdn
	'Indian Chief'	see *S.* (Herbstfreude Group) 'Herbstfreude'
	ishidae	see *Rhodiola ishidae*
	'James Windsor'	CRDP
	'José Aubergine' PBR	CPrp EBee ECtt GBin IPot LRHS MAvo MBri MCot MTis NCGa NDov NLar SBfd SPoG SUsu WPGP WWEG
	'Joyce Henderson'	EBee ECtt EPfP GQue LHop MCot MRav MTis NLar NRHS SMrm SPer SRGP SUsu WBrk WCot WMoo WTin WWEG
	kamtschaticum ΨH4	ECho GJos WFar
	- B&SWJ 10870	WCru
§	- var. ***ellacombeanum*** ΨH4	MMuc NMen SEND WCot XLum
	- - B&SWJ 8853	WCru
§	- var. ***floriferum*** 'Weihenstephaner Gold'	CEnt CTri ECho ECtt EDAr EPfP GAbr GEdr GMaP LPot MAsh MHer MMuc MRav MWat NBir NMen SEND SPlb SPoG SRms WAbe WFar XLum
	- var. ***kamtschaticum*** 'Variegatum' (v) ΨH4	CMea ECho ECtt EDAr EHoe EPfP LAst LBMP LRHS MAsh MHer MMuc MWat NPri NRHS SEND SPoG SRms SRot SWvt XLum
	lanceolatum	NBre
	lineare 'Variegatum' (v)	LAst XLum
	'Little Gem'	see × *Cremnosedum* 'Little Gem'
§	***lydium***	CTri ECho MAsh MHer SFgr SPlb
	- 'Aureum'	see *S. hispanicum* var. *minus* 'Aureum'
	- 'Bronze Queen'	see *S. lydium*
	makinoi 'Ōgon'	EBee
I	'Marchants Best Red' ΨH4	SMHy SPhx SUsu WCot
	'Matrona' ΨH4	Widely available
	maweanum	see *S. acre* subsp. *neglectum* var. *majus*

	middendorffianum	ECho MAsh MBrN MHer MWat NMen SEND SRms SRot WFar XLum
	'Moonglow'	ECtt NMen
	'Moonlight Serenade' **new**	MAsh MTis
	moranense	SEND XLum
	morganianum ♀H1	EBak EShb
	morrisonense B&SWJ 7078	WCru
	'Mr Goodbud' PBR ♀H4	CPrp EBee ECtt GBin LRHS MNrw NDov SBfd WCot WWEG
	'Munstead Red'	CMea COIW CPrp CWCL EBee ECha ECtt EHrv EPfP GAbr GBin LAst LDai LRHS MAsh MRav MTis MWat NLar SBfd SGar SMrm SPer SPhx SPoG WFar WKif WMnd WMoo
	murale	see *S. album* subsp. *teretifolium* var. *murale*
	nevii misapplied	see *S. glaucophyllum*
	nevii ambig.	SPlb
	nicaeense	see *S. sediforme*
	niveum	NMen
	obcordatum	NMen
	obtusatum misapplied	see *S. oreganum*
§	***obtusatum*** A. Gray	NBro NSla WFar WPnn
	obtusifolium	MAsh
	- var. ***listoniae***	EDAr
	ochroleucum	MMuc NBre SEND
	oppositifolium	see *S. spurium* 'Album'
§	***oreganum***	ECha ECho EDAr GAbr GKev GMaP MHer MSCN MWat NMen SPlb SRms SRot XLum
	- 'Procumbens'	see *S. oreganum* subsp. *tenue*
§	- subsp. ***tenue***	LEdu NHol NRya NWad WAbe WPat
§	***oregonense***	ECho LRHS NMen NRHS
	pachyclados	see *Rhodiola pachyclados*
	pachyphyllum	EPfP WNew
	palmeri	CHEx LSou MRav NBir SChr XLum
§	- subsp. ***palmeri*** tetraploid	SEND
	'Parish Plum'	SBch
	'Pewter'	ECho
	pilosum	NMen
	'Pink Dove'	SBch
	'Pinky'	EBee MAsh WFar
§	***pluricaule***	ECho LRHS NRHS NSla SPlb SRms
	populifolium	ECha GCal GJos MHer MMuc NLar SPhx WPer XLum
	praealtum	SChr SEND
	quinquefarium	see *S. brevifolium* var. *quinquefarium*
	'Red Cauli' ♀H4	Widely available
	'Red Rum'	LPla SPhx
	'Red Setter' **new**	WPGP
	reflexum L.	see *S. rupestre* L.
	reptans	ECho
	rhodiola	see *Rhodiola rosea*
	'Ripe Rhubarb'	SMHy
	rosea	see *Rhodiola rosea*
	rubroglaucum misapplied	see *S. oregonense*
	rubroglaucum Praeger	see *S. obtusatum* A. Gray
	× ***rubrotinctum***	CHEx SEND
	- 'Aurora'	SChr
§	'Ruby Glow' ♀H4	Widely available
	'Ruby Glow' variegated (v)	WPer
	'Ruby Port'	CSpe
§	***rupestre*** L.	ECho GJos MBNS MMuc MWat SEND SPlb WFar XLum
	- 'Angelina'	CKno EBee EPPr EWes LRHS MAsh MAvo MGos MHer NBir NDov NHol NPri NPro NWad SPoG SRGP WCot WGrn XLum
	- 'Monstrosum Cristatum'	NBir SMad XLum
	ruprechtii	see *S. telephium* subsp. *ruprechtii*
	sarcocaule hort.	see *Crassula sarcocaulis*
	sarmentosum	ECho XLum
§	***sediforme***	EDAr EPot GAbr LRHS
	- B&F MA 25	WCot
	- ***nicaeense***	see *S. sediforme*
	selskianum	GJos NBre SBch WFar XLum
	- 'Goldilocks'	GJos
	sempervivoides	ECho
	sexangulare	ECho EDAr EPot MAsh MHer NRya SEND SFgr SPlb SRms WFar WPer XLum
	sibiricum	see *S. hybridum*
	sieboldii	CFis ECho
	- 'Dragon'	LRHS
	- 'Mediovariegatum' (v) ♀H2-3	CFis CHEx COIW ECho LPot MHer NPri NWsh SPlb WFar XLum
	'Silvermoon'	NWad
	spathulifolium	CTri ECha ECho MDKP
	- 'Aureum'	ECho ECtt MWat WAbe
	- 'Cape Blanco' ♀H4	Widely available
	- 'Purpureum' ♀H4	Widely available
	- subsp. ***yosemitense*** 'Red Raver'	CPBP
	spectabile ♀H4	CArn CHEx CHab CPrp CTri EBee ELan EPfP GJos GMaP LRHS MCot MHer MRav NGdn SBfd SGar SPer SPlb SRms WBor WBrk WCAu WFar WSFF WTin WWEG
	- 'Album'	CHEx
	- Brilliant Group	CBar CHab LBMP LRHS WCAu
	- - 'Brilliant' ♀H4	CBcs CKno CSBt CTri EBee ECha ECtt ELan EPfP LAst LPot LRHS MAsh MBri MGos MRav NGdn NOrc NRHS SBfd SPer SPoG SWvt WFar WMoo WWEG
	- - 'Carmen'	EBee LRHS XLum
	- - 'Hot Stuff'	ELon NPri WCot
	- - 'Lisa'	GBin MTPN NDov NLar
	- - 'Meteor'	CPrp EBee LPla MWat NLar SMrm SPhx WPer WWEG
	- - 'Neon'	EBee LRHS MAsh NCGa NDov
	- - 'Rosenteller'	CKno EBee NBre SMrm WFar
§	- - 'Septemberglut'	EBee NBre WCot XLum
	- - 'Steven Ward'	CKno EBee EWes SRGP WCot
	- 'Humile'	XLum
	- 'Iceberg'	Widely available
*	- 'Mini'	ELan MRav
	- 'Pink Chablis' PBR (v)	EBee NLar WCot
	- September Glow	see *S. spectabile* (Brilliant Group) 'Septemberglut'
	- 'Stardust'	CKno CPrp CTri EBee EPfP GKev GMaP LAst LRHS LSou MRav MTis NCGa NLar SMrm SPer SPet WFar WGor WWEG XLum
	- 'Variegatum'	see *S. erythrostictum* 'Mediovariegatum'
	spinosum	see *Orostachys spinosa*
	spurium	CHEx ECho GAbr GJos MMuc NPro SEND SRms XSen
§	- 'Album'	NRya XLum
	- 'Atropurpureum'	ECha ECho WMoo XLum
	- 'Coccineum'	ECho GJos MNHC SEND
	- Dragon's Blood	see *S. spurium* 'Schorbuser Blut'

- 'Erdblut' NMen
- 'Fuldaglut' CTri ECho EHoe EPfP GMaP GQue IPot LRHS MAsh MNrw NMen NRHS NRya SMrm WFar WMoo WNew WPer WPnn
- 'Green Mantle' EBee ECha ECho EPfP NRHS
- 'John Creech' **new** EBee
- Purple Carpet see *S. spurium* 'Purpurteppich'
- 'Purpureum' SRms

§ - 'Purpurteppich' EBee ECho ECtt GJos MRav NBro NLar NWad SRms
- 'Roseum' SRms
- 'Ruby Mantle' EWll GKev MSCN NBro NPro SBch SPoG SWvt WMoo XLum

§ - 'Schorbuser Blut' ℽH4 CMea EBee ECho ECtt EPau EPfP GJos GKev MCot MLHP MWat NBir NRya NSla SPlb SRGP SRms WFar WHoo WIce XLum

I - 'Splendens Roseum' XLum
- 'Summer Glory' NLar

§ - 'Tricolor' (v) CTri EBee ECha ECho EHoe GEdr GJos GKev MAsh MHer MLHP MRav MSCN NRya SPlb SPoG WFar WMoo XLum
- 'Variegatum' see *S. spurium* 'Tricolor'
- 'Voodoo' CEnt ECtt EPfP EWes GEdr LBMP LPot MAsh MHer MSCN NBro NGdn SGar WFar XLum

stefco XLum

stenopetalum SPlb

§ - 'Douglasii' MHer SRms

'Stewed Rhubarb Mountain' CKno CPrp EAEE EBee ECha ECtt EPfP LDai LHop LRHS MBNS MCot MNFA MRav NBro NCGa NLar NOrc SBfd WCAu WFar WMoo WWEG

stoloniferum ECho

stribrnyi see *S. urvillei* Stribrnyi Group

'Sunset Cloud' CHEx CMHG EBee ECtt EWes GCal IPot LPla LPot MRav NBre

takesimense XLum
- B&SWJ 8518 WCru

telephium CArn NBir SRms XLum

§ - Atropurpureum Group ℽH4 COIW EBee ELan EPfP MRav SWvt WWEG
- - 'African Pearl' WCFE WCot WWEG
- - 'Arthur Branch' CPrp GBin LRHS WWEG

I - - 'Atropurpureum Nanum' WWEG
- - 'Bon Bon' CPrp EBee LRHS MBNS MBel NLar SGar SPoG
- - 'Bressingham Purple' EPPr
- - 'Chocolate' EBee ECtt EPPr LRHS MAvo NLar
- - 'Dark Knight' LRHS
- - 'El Cid' EBee EWes
- - 'Hester' EBee WWEG
- - 'Karfunkelstein' ℽH4 CKno EBee ECha ECtt EPPr GBin MAvo MTis NDov SPhx SUsu WCot
- - 'Leonore Zuuntz' EBee NBre
- - 'Lynda et Rodney' EWes
- - 'Lynda Windsor' EBee ECtt EPfP GAbr NLar NPnk NPro SWvt WFar
- - 'Möhrchen' EBee EHrv GBin GMaP LRHS MRav MTis NGdn NLar NPnk NWsh SBfd SPhx SPoG WFar WMnd WMoo
- - 'Picolette' EBee ECtt LRHS LSou MNrw NCGa NRHS SPoG WCot
- - 'Postman's Pride' PBR CKno CWGN EBee ECtt EPfP LPla LRHS LSou MWat NGdn NLBP SPad SUsu WCot

§ - - 'Purple Emperor' ℽH4 Widely available
- - 'Ringmore Ruby' MHer WCot WPGP WWEG
- - 'Xenox' PBR ℽH4 CWGN EBee ECtt EPPr EPfP ETod EWll GBin IPot LRHS MAsh MAvo MBNS MCot MNrw MTis NLar SBfd SHar SMrm WFar WHil WPGP
- 'Bronco' PBR ECtt
- 'Dentate' **new** SUsu
- Emperor's Waves Group NGdn

§ - subsp. ***fabaria*** ECtt MRav NWsh SMrm WAbb WCot WFar WWEG
- - var. ***borderei*** CElw LBMP LPla SBch SPhx SUsu
- 'Jennifer' EBee ECtt WCot
- subsp. ***maximum*** 'Atropurpureum' see *S. telephium* Atropurpureum Group
- - 'Gooseberry Fool' COIW CPrp EBee ECGP ECtt EPfP GMaP SBch SPhx WFar WWEG
- 'Rainbow Xenox' **new** LSou MAsh
- 'Roseum' WWEG

§ - subsp. ***ruprechtii*** CPrp EAEE ECha ECtt EPPr EPfP GMaP LRHS LSou MCot MRav NSti SPer SPet SPhx WFar WGwG WMoo WPer
- - 'Citrus Twist' EBee ECtt LRHS MRav MTis NPnk
- - 'Hab Gray' CSpe EBee ECtt ETod EWes GBin GQue LAst LRHS MTis NLar SAga SMrm SUsu WCot
- - 'Pink Dome' ECha
- 'Strawberries and Cream' Widely available
- 'Sunkissed' PBR **new** ECtt NCGa
- subsp. ***telephium*** GCra
- 'Variegatum' (v) MDKP
- 'Yellow Xenox' **new** LSou

ternatum MHer WFar

tetractinum LRHS
- 'Coral Reef' WFar

trollii see *Rhodiola trollii*

'Twinkling Star' **new** EBee MAsh

urvillei Sartorianum Group MHer XLum

§ - Stribrnyi Group XLum

ussuriense EBee EPfP GCal NBir SBfd SUsu
- 'Chuwangsan' EWld WCru

'Veluwse Wakel' GBin

'Vera Jameson' ℽH4 Widely available

viviparum B&SWJ 8662 WCru

'Washfield Purple' see *S. telephium* 'Purple Emperor'

'Weihenstephaner Gold' see *S. kamtschaticum* var. *floriferum* 'Weihenstephaner Gold'

weinbergii see *Graptopetalum paraguayense*

'Winky' LSou MAsh MBel

yezoense see *S. pluricaule*

'Zebra' LRHS

Seemannia see *Gloxinia*

Selaginella (Selaginellaceae)

braunii CLAP WCot

erythropus var. ***sanguinea*** CBty LRHS

kraussiana ℽH1 CLAP EDAr EShb
- 'Aurea' CBty CCCN ISha LRHS SMad
- 'Brownii' ℽH1 CBty CCCN ISha LRHS
- 'Gold Tips' CBty CCCN ISha LRHS

lepidophylla SVic

moellendorfii CBty ISha LRHS

tamariscina WAbe

uncinata ℽH1 CBty CLAP ISha

Selago (Scrophulariaceae)

thunbergii LHop

Selinum (Apiaceae)

sp. new WHil
carvifolium EBee EShb LDai LRHS WWEG
tenuifolium see *S. wallichianum*
§ ***wallichianum*** COlW CPom CSam CSpe ELan EPri EShb EWTr GBuc GCal GCra LBMP LRHS MAvo MWat NCGa NDov NLar SMHy SMrm SPhx SUsu WFar WHil WSHC WWEG
- EMAK 886 EBee GPoy SDix
- HWJK 2224 WCru
- HWJK 2347 WCru
- PAB 3579 LEdu

Selliera (Goodeniaceae)

radicans ECou EDAr GAbr GBin GEdr

Semele (Asparagaceae)

androgyna CHEx CRHN

Semiaquilegia (Ranunculaceae)

'Early Dwarf' EDif
§ ***ecalcarata*** CDes CPom EBee ECho EHrv GCal GJos GKev LDai MNrw NGdn SBea SRms SSvw WCru WFar WHal WPGP WTou
- Australian CDes
* - f. ***bicolor*** WCru
- 'Flore Pleno' (d) WTou
- 'Snowbell' WCru
simulatrix see *S. ecalcarata*
'Sugar Plum Fairy' EPfP LRHS SPoG

Semiarundinaria (Poaceae)

§ ***fastuosa*** ♀H4 CBcs CDoC CEnt CHEx CJun EAmu ENBC EPfP ERod EUJe MMoz MMuc MWht SEND SPlb WJun
- var. ***viridis*** CEnt ERod MWht SBig WCru WJun
kagamiana CDoC ENBC EPfP MMoz MMuc MWhi MWht SBig SEND WJun
§ ***lubrica*** MWht
makinoi EAmu MWht SLPl WJun
nitida see *Fargesia nitida*
§ ***okuboi*** CEnt ENBC ERod MMoz MWht
villosa see *S. okuboi*
yamadorii ERod MMoz MWht WJun
yashadake CEnt ERod WJun
- f. ***kimmei*** CDoC CEnt ERod LRHS MGos MMoz MMuc MWht NLar SBig SEND WFar WJun WMoo WPGP
I - - 'Inversa' CEnt

Semnanthe see *Erepsia*

Sempervivella see *Rosularia*

Sempervivum ✿ (Crassulaceae)

sp. SVic
from Andorra ESem
from Sierra Nova ESem
'Aaroundina' CWil
'Abba' EDAr NMen WHal WPer
'Adelaar' CWil NMen
'Adelmoed' CWil NMen SFgr
'Ageet' CWil NMen
'Aglow' MHom NMen
'Aladdin' CWil ESem GEdr MSCN NMen SRms
'Alaric' NMen
'Albernelli' SFgr
'Alchimist' NMen XLum
'Aldo Moro' CWil ECha EDAr ESem GAbr LBee LRHS MHom NMen SFgr WIce WIvy XLum
'Alice' ESem MSCN
'Alidae' ESem
allionii see *Jovibarba allionii*
'Alluring' ESem GAbr NMen
'Alpha' ESem LBee LRHS NMen SFgr SRms WHal WPer WTin XLum
altum CWil ESem LRHS MHom NMen NRHS SPlb XLum
'Amanda' CWil ECha EDAr ESem MBrN NMen SRms WHoo WPer WTin
'Ambergreen' NMen
andreanum see *S. tectorum* var. *alpinum*
'Apache' Payne see *Jovibarba heuffelii* 'Apache'
'Apache' Haberer NMen
'Apollo' SFgr XLum
'Apple Blossom' CMea ECha ESem NMen
arachnoideum ♀H4 Widely available
- 'Ararat' SDys
- 'Boria' ESem
- var. ***bryoides*** CWil ESem LLHF LRHS NMen NRHS WIvy WPer
- 'Cebennense' ESem
- 'Clärchen' EPot ESem MSCN NMen NSla SFgr WAbe
- cristate CWil
* - ***densum*** EDAr MTis NMen WAbe WFar
- subsp. ***doellianum*** see *S. arachnoideum* subsp. *tomentosum* var. *glabrescens*
- form No 1 ECho
- 'Laggeri' see *S. arachnoideum* subsp. *tomentosum* (C.B. Lehm. & Schnittsp.) Schinz & Thell.
- 'Opitz' NMen WPer
- red NMen
- 'Red Papaver' NMen
- 'Red Wings' ECha NMen XLum
- 'Rubrum' CHEx ECho EUJe GMaP LRHS NRHS SPlb XLum
- 'Sultan' ESem
- subsp. ***tomentosum*** misapplied see *S.* × *barbulatum* 'Hookeri'
§ - subsp. ***tomentosum*** (C.B. Lehm. & Schnittsp.) Schinz & Thell. ♀H4 CHEx CWil ECho LRHS MSCN NMen NPer NRHS SFgr SPlb SRms WAbe WGor WPer
- - GDJ 92.04 CWil
§ - - var. ***glabrescens*** NMen SDys WPat
- - 'Minus' NMen
§ - - 'Stansfieldii' ECho GAbr LRHS NMen NRHS WHal
§ - 'White Christmas' CWil MHer NMen
arachnoideum* × *calcareum CWil NMen WIvy WTin
arachnoideum* × *montanum see *S.* × *barbulatum*
arachnoideum* × *nevadense CWil SDys
arachnoideum* × *pittonii CWil MTis NMen WAbe
arenarium see *Jovibarba arenaria*
'Arlet' EDAr

armenum	ESem NMen
– var. ***insigne***	ESem
'Arondina'	CWil NMen
'Aross'	CMea ESem GAbr NMen
'Arrowheads Red'	NMen
'Artist'	CWil ESem NMen SFgr
'Ashes of Roses'	EPot ESem MHom NHol NMen WAbe WGor WPer XLum
'Asteroid'	CWil ESem NMen
'Astrid'	CWil
atlanticum	ESem MHom NMen NSla SRot
– from Atlas Mountains, Morocco	CWil ESem
– from Oukaïmeden, Morocco	CWil ESem GAbr NMen SRms WTin
– 'Edward Balls'	CWil ESem NMen SDys SFgr
'Atlantis' ambig.	ESem
'Atropurpureum' ambig.	CHEx CWil EDAr GAbr GEdr MBrN NMen WGor WPer
'Aureum'	see *Greenovia aurea*
'Averil'	CWil NMen
'Aymon Correvon'	ESem NMen
'Baby Skrocki'	CWil NMen
balcanicum	CWil EDAr ESem NMen WIvy XLum
ballsii	ECho LLHF LRHS NMen NRHS
– from Kambeecho, Greece	MHom
– from Smólikas, Greece	CWil MHom NMen
– from Tschumba Petzi, Greece	CWil MHom SDys XLum
'Banderi'	NMen
'Banjo'	NMen
'Banyan'	ECho LRHS NMen NRHS
'Barbarosa'	CWil ESem
§ × ***barbulatum***	ESem GAbr LBee LRHS NMen SDys SFgr WHoo WPer
§ – 'Hookeri'	CTri CWil EPot ESem NLar NMen SFgr WAbe WPer
'Bascour Zilver'	CMea CWil ECha ESem GAbr LBee LRHS MSCN NMen SRms WHal
'Beaute'	ESem NMen
'Bedazzled'	ESem NMen
'Bedivere'	CWil LBee LRHS NMen SRms
'Bedivere Crested'	NMen
* 'Bedley Hi'	MHom NMen
'Bella Donna'	ESem MHom NMen WPer
'Bella Meade'	CWil EDAr NMen SFgr SRms WPer
'Bellotts Pourpre'	CWil NMen
'Benny Hill'	CWil
'Bernstein'	CWil EDAr EPot ESem MHer NMen NWad SFgr WHal XLum
'Beta'	ESem MHom NMen WAbe WPer WTin XLum
'Bethany'	CMea CWil ESem NMen NWad WHal
'Bicolor' ambig.	EPfP
'Big Mal'	NMen
'Big Red'	NMen
'Big Slipper'	ESem NMen
'Binstead'	ESem
'Birchmaier'	NMen SFgr
'Black Beauty'	EPot NMen
'Black Cap'	NMen
'Black Claret'	NMen
'Black Knight'	ECho LRHS MHer NMen NRHS SPlb SRms WHal
'Black Mini'	CWil EPot GAbr GKev MDKP NBir NMen SRms
'Black Mountain'	CHEx CWil ESem GKev LBee LRHS NMen
'Black Prince'	ECha ESem NMen
'Black Velvet'	ESem NMen WIvy WPer
'Bladon'	WPer
'Blood of Winter'	WGor
'Blood Sucker'	WGor
'Blood Tip'	CHEx CMea CWil ECha ECho ESem GAbr GCra GKev LAst LRHS MAsh MHer MMuc MSCN NHol NMen NRHS NRya NWad SBch SEND SPlb SPoG SRms WFar WGor WHal WHoo WPer
'Bloodgood' **new**	ECho
'Bloody Goose' **new**	NMen
'Blue Boy'	CWil ECha ECho EPPr EPot GAbr LBee LRHS MSCN NMen NRHS SFgr SRms WPer
'Blue Moon'	ESem NMen
'Blue Time'	EPot GEdr SFgr WHoo WTin XLum
'Blush'	EDAr ESem
'Boissieri'	see *S. tectorum* subsp. *tectorum* 'Boissieri'
'Bold Chick'	ESem NMen
'Bombardier'	EDAr
'Booth's Red'	CHEx NMen WGor
'Boreale'	see *Jovibarba hirta* subsp. *borealis*
borisii	see *S. ciliosum* var. *borisii*
borissovae	EPot ESem MHom NMen SDys
'Boromir'	CWil EDAr ESem NMen XLum
'Boule de Neige'	GEdr NMen NRya
'Bowles's Variety'	NMen WPer
'Braune Maus'	ESem SFgr
'Britta'	ESem SDys
'Brock'	ECha ECho ESem LRHS MHer MHom NMen NRHS WPer
'Bronco' ♀H4	CDes CHEx CWil ECho ESem GAbr LBee LRHS MHom MMuc NHol NMen NRya NWad SRms WCot WFar WHfH WPGP XLum
'Bronze Beauty'	EDAr
'Bronze Pastel'	CWil ECha EDAr ESem MHom MMuc MSCN NMen NSla SEND SFgr SRms SRot WGor WTin
'Brown Owl'	CWil ECho ESem NMen SRms WFar
'Brownii'	ESem GAbr NMen WPer WTin
'Brunette'	ECho GAbr
bungeanum hort. **new**	NMen
'Burgundy'	ECha ESem NMen
'Burgundy Velvet'	ESem NMen
'Burnatii'	see *S. montanum* subsp. *burnatii*
'Burning Desire'	WGor
'Burnished Bronze'	ESem NMen
'Butterbur'	ESem
'Butterfly'	ESem NMen
'Café'	CWil MSCN NHol NMen NWad SFgr SRms WIvy WPer
* ***calabricum*** **new**	NHol
× ***calcaratum***	EDAr
calcareum	CMea CWil ECho EPfP EUJe EWll GKev LRHS MAsh MMuc NBro NEgg NHol NMen SEND SPlb SPoG SRms SRot WFar WHoo WPer XLum
– from Alps, France	CWil ESem NMen
– from Calde la Vanoise, France	CWil NMen
– from Ceüze, France	CWil ESem WIvy
– from Cleizé, France	see *S. calcareum* 'Limelight'
– from Col Bayard, France	CWil ESem GAbr NMen
– from Colle St Michel, France	CWil ESem NMen SFgr SRms

	– from Gorges supérieures du Cians, France	CWil ESem NMen
	– from Mont Ventoux, France	CWil ESem
	– from Petite Ceüse, France	ESem SRot
	– – GDJ 92.15	CWil
	– – GDJ 92.16	CWil SRms
	– from Queyras, France	CWil ESem NMen
	– from Route d'Annôt, France	CWil ESem NMen
	– from Triora, Italy	CWil ESem NMen
	– 'Benz'	ESem SDys
	– 'Extra' ♀H4	CHEx CWil ESem GAbr GEdr MSCN NMen SFgr SRot
	– 'Greenii'	CWil ECho ESem GKev LRHS MMuc NMen NRHS SEND SPlb
§	– 'Grigg's Surprise'	CWil ESem NMen SPlb WFar
	– 'Guillaumes' ♀H4	CWil ESem NMen SFgr SRot WHoo
§	– 'Limelight'	CMea CWil EDAr LRHS NMen WHal WIvy WPer WTin
	– 'Monstrosum'	see *S. calcareum* 'Grigg's Surprise'
	– 'Mrs Giuseppi'	CWil ECho ESem ETod GAbr LBee LRHS NMen SFgr SRms WAbe WFar WIce WPer XLum
	– 'Pink Pearl'	CWil MSCN NMen SDys SFgr WIvy WTin XLum
	– 'Sir William Lawrence' ♀H4	CMea CWil ECho EDAr ESem NMen SFgr SRms WAbe WHal WHoo WIvy WPer WThu WTin XLum
	'Caliph's Hat'	NMen
*	***calopticum* × *nevadense***	WTin
	'Cameo'	see *Jovibarba heuffelii* var. *glabra* 'Cameo'
	'Canada Kate'	CWil ESem NMen WPer
	'Cancer'	XLum
	'Candy Floss'	CWil NMen WGor
	cantabricum	CWil ESem MMuc NMen SEND WThu XLum
	– from Cue Vas de Sol	ESem
	– from Cuengas Piedras	ESem
	– from Cuevas del Sil, Spain	CWil
	– from Navafria, Spain	CWil NMen WTin
	– from Peña Prieta, Spain	NMen
	– from Piedrafita, Spain	ESem
	– from Riaño, Spain	CWil ESem GAbr
	– from San Glorio, Spain	CWil ESem GAbr NMen
	– from Ticeros	ESem NMen XLum
	– from Tizneros, Spain	CWil
	– from Valvanera, Spain	ESem NMen
	– subsp. ***cantabricum*** from Leitariegos, Spain	CWil GAbr MHom NMen
	– – from Peña de Llesba, Spain GDJ 93.13	CWil
	– – from Pico del Lobo, Spain	CWil
	– subsp. ***guadarramense***	see *S. vicentei* subsp. *paui*
	– – from Pico del Lobo, Spain, No 1	SRms SRot
	– – from Pico del Lobo, Spain, No 2	ESem
	– – from Valvanera, Spain, No 1	CWil NMen
	– subsp. ***urbionense***	CWil GEdr SRms
	– – from El Gatón, Spain	CWil
	– – from Picos de Urbión, Spain	CWil ESem NMen
	cantabricum* × *montanum subsp. ***stiriacum***	WTin
	cantabricum* × *montanum subsp. ***stiriacum*** 'Lloyd Praeger'	CWil
	'Caramel'	ESem NMen
*	× ***carlsii***	ESem
	'Carluke'	NMen
	'Carmen'	ESem GAbr NMen SFgr
	'Carneum'	ESem NMen
	'Carnival'	ESem NMen WPer
	caucasicum	CWil ESem MHom NMen NRHS XLum
	'Cavo Doro'	CWil NMen SFgr
	'Celon'	ESem NMen
	'Centennial'	ESem NMen
	'Cerluke'	ESem
	charadzeae	CWil ESem LBee LRHS NMen XLum
	'Charolensis'	ESem
	'Chartbury'	EDAr
	'Cherry Frost'	ECho NHol NMen NRya SFgr XLum
	'Cherry Glow'	see *Jovibarba heuffelii* 'Cherry Glow'
	'Chilli Pepper'	CYeo
	'Chivalry'	ESem NMen
	'Chocolate'	NMen WAbe WPer
§	× ***christii***	ESem NMen
	'Christmas Time'	NMen SFgr
	chrysanthum	ESem
	ciliosum ♀H4	CMea CPBP CWil ECho ESem NMen NRya
	– from Alí Butús, Bulgaria	SDys
	– from Ochrid	NMen
	– from Pestani	ESem
§	– var. ***borisii***	EPfP ESem GCal GKev NMen NRya WAbe WHal
	– var. ***ciliosum*** × ***ciliosum*** var. ***borisii***	CTri NMen
	– var. ***galicicum*** 'Mali Hat'	CPBP NMen WPer
	ciliosum* × *grandiflorum	CWil ESem NMen
	ciliosum* × *marmoreum	ESem NMen
	ciliosum* × *tectorum	WTin
	'Cindy'	ESem SRms
	'Circlet'	CWil ESem NMen
	'Clara Noyes'	ESem NMen WFar WPer
	'Clare'	ESem MHer NMen
	'Claudine'	ESem
	'Clemanum'	ESem
	'Cleveland Morgan'	ECha ESem MHom NBro NMen XLum
	'Climax' ambig.	ECho EPfP ESem MHom NMen WFar
	'Clisette'	ESem
	'Cobweb Capers'	ESem MHom MTis NMen
	'Cobweb Centres'	NMen
	'Cochise'	ESem
	'Collage'	ESem WPer
	'Collecteur Anchisi'	ESem SDys SFgr
	'Commander Hay' ♀H4	CHEx EDAr EPfP ETod EWes GAbr GCra GKev MHom MSCN NDov NMen NPer SRGP SRms WHal WIvy WJek WPer XLum
	'Comte de Congae'	ESem MTis NMen
	'Concorde'	LRHS
	'Congo'	ESem NMen SFgr XLum
	'Conran'	NMen
	'Corio'	ESem NMen
	'Cornstone'	ECha ESem
	'Corona'	CWil ESem NMen SFgr WPer
	'Coronet'	ESem

'Corsair'	CWil ECha EPPr ESem GEdr MBrN NMen SEND SFgr WGor WIvy WPer WTin
'Cotopaxi'	CWil NMen
'Cranberry'	ESem NMen
'Cresta'	ESem
'Crimson King'	SFgr
'Crimson Velvet'	CHEx CMea ESem LBee LRHS NMen SFgr WPer XLum
'Crimson Webb'	ESem
§ 'Crispyn' ♀H4	CWil EPot ESem LBee LRHS MHer MHom MMuc MSCN NMen SFgr WPer
'Croky'	ESem
'Croton'	ESem NMen WPer
'Crucify' **new**	NMen
'Cupream'	CWil ESem NMen SRms WPer
'Dakota'	CWil EDAr ESem NMen SFgr
'Dallas'	CWil NMen SRms
'Damask'	CWil LBee LRHS NMen SFgr WPer
'Dame Arsac'	ESem
'Dancer'	ESem
'Dancer's Veil'	ESem
'Darjeeling'	CWil NMen
'Dark Beauty'	CMea CWil ECha ECho ESem LRHS MSCN NHol NMen NRHS SFgr WAbe WCot WGor WHal WPer
'Dark Cloud'	CWil ESem GAbr LBee LRHS NMen WHoo WIvy WPer XLum
'Dark Point'	CWil ESem MHom NMen SFgr
'Dark Velvet'	CMea NMen
'Darkie'	CWil ESem SFgr WPer
davisii	ECha NMen
'De Kardijk'	NMen
'Deep Fire'	CWil ESem NMen SRms WIvy WTin
× ***degenianum***	ESem GAbr NMen SFgr WPer
'Delta' ♀H4	MHom NMen WHoo WTin
densum	see *S. tectorum*
'Devon Glow'	MSCN
'Devon Jewel'	WGor
'Diamant'	ESem
'Diane'	CWil ESem SFgr
'Director Jacobs'	CWil EDAr ESem NMen SEND SFgr WPer WTin
'Direktor General'	GEdr
'Disco Dancer'	ESem
dolomiticum	ESem NMen XLum
dolomiticum* × *montanum	ESem NBro NMen SFgr WTin
'Donarrose'	ESem SFgr
'Downland Queen'	CWil ESem NMen
'Dragoness'	ESem NMen
'Dream Catcher' **new**	NMen
'Duke of Windsor'	NMen SFgr
'Dunscar Hybrid'	ESem
'Dusky'	ESem
'Dyke'	CTri CWil EDAr ESem GAbr NMen SFgr WHal
dzhavachischvilii	ESem NMen XLum
'Edge of Night'	CWil NMen
'Eefje'	CWil ESem NMen
'El Greco'	ESem NMen
'El Toro'	ECha ESem MHom NMen
'Elgar'	NMen WPer
'Elizabeth'	WPer
'Elvis'	CWil GAbr MHom NMen SFgr
'Emerald Giant'	CWil ESem SFgr WPer WTin
'Emerson's Giant'	CWil ESem NMen
'Eminent'	ESem

'Emma Jane'	ESem
'Emmchen'	CWil NMen SFgr
'Engle's'	CMea CTri ECha ECho ESem GKev LRHS MHer MMuc MSCN MTis NMen SEND SRms WHal WPer
'Engle's 13-2'	ESem NBro NMen
'Engle's Rubrum'	CPBP EPot LBee NMen
erythraeum	CMea ECho ESem LLHF LRHS MHom NMen NRHS SPlb WAbe WHal
- from Pirin, Bulgaria	NMen
- from Rila, Bulgaria	NMen
- 'Red Velvet'	NMen
'Excalibur'	ESem NMen WIvy
'Exhibita'	CWil EPPr ESem NMen SDys
'Exorna'	CWil ECha EDAr ESem MHom NMen SFgr WIvy WPer
'Fair Lady'	CWil ESem MHom MTis NMen
'Fairy'	EPot
'Fame'	ESem WGor
'Fat Jack'	CWil NMen
× ***fauconnetii***	CWil EDAr ESem NMen SFgr
- 'Rubellum'	ESem NMen
- 'Thompsonii'	CWil ESem NMen
'Feldmaier'	ESem NMen
'Fernwood'	ESem
'Festival'	EDAr ESem NMen
'Fiery Furness'	ESem NMen
'Fiesta' ambig.	WHal
fimbriatum	see *S.* × ***barbulatum***
'Finerpointe'	ESem NMen
'Fire Glint'	CWil ESem GEdr NMen SRms WIvy
'Firebird'	NMen SFgr
'Firefly'	ESem
'Firgrove Silver'	SFgr
'First Try'	ESem
flagelliforme	ESem XLum
'Flaming Heart'	CWil EDAr ESem MAsh MBrN NMen WGor WPer
'Flamingo'	ECha ESem NMen
'Flanders Passion'	ECha LBee LRHS MMuc NMen SRms WPer
'Flasher'	NMen WPer
'Fluweel'	MSCN NMen
'Forden'	CHEx NMen SFgr WGor
'Ford's Amiability'	ESem SDys
'Ford's Giant'	XLum
'Ford's Shadows'	SDys
'Ford's Spring'	CWil ESem NMen WIvy WPer
'Freckles'	NMen
'Freeland'	WPer
'Frigidum'	ESem
'Frolic'	ESem
'Fronika'	CWil NMen
'Frosty'	CWil ESem NMen SFgr SRms
'Fuego' ♀H4	CWil ESem MHom NMen SFgr
'Fuji'	ESem NMen
× ***funckii***	CHEx CWil EDAr ESem MAsh MBrN NMen SDys SFgr WPer WTin XLum
'Furryness'	ESem NMen
'Fusilier'	NMen
'Fuzzy Wuzzy'	EDAr ESem MTis NMen
'Galahad'	NMen
'Gallivarda' ♀H4	CWil ESem MSCN NMen
'Gambol'	ESem NWad
'Gamma'	CHEx CWil ESem LBee LRHS NMen WTin

Name	Suppliers
'Garnet'	ECho ESem WGor WIvy WPer
'Gay Jester'	CTri CWil ESem NMen SFgr WHoo WTin
'Gazelle'	ESem NMen WIvy WPer XLum
'Genevione'	CWil ESem NMen
'Georgette'	CWil ECha ESem NMen WPer XLum
'Gilosum'	EDAr
'Ginger'	ESem
'Ginnie's Delight'	CWil NMen
'Gipsy'	NMen
giuseppii ♀H4	ECho GKev LBee MHer MMuc NMen NRHS WPer
- from Coriscao, Spain	LRHS
- - GDJ 93.17	CWil
- from Cumbre de Cebolleda GDJ 93.04	CWil
- from Peña Espigüete, Spain	CWil ESem NMen SDys
- from Peña Prieta, Spain	CWil NMen
× ***guiseppii***	ESem SEND
'Gizmo'	CWil ESem NMen SFgr
'Gleam'	ESem
'Gloriosum' ambig.	EDAr ESem MSCN SFgr WPer
'Glowing Embers'	CWil ESem MHom NMen WHal WPer XLum
'Godaert'	MMuc SEND XLum
'Goldie'	ESem NMen SFgr
'Gollum'	NMen
'Goya'	ESem
'Graceum'	ESem
'Grammens'	ESem
'Granada'	EDAr ESem NMen
'Granat'	ESem LRHS MHer NMen SRms WPer XLum
'Granby'	CWil ECho LBee LRHS MMuc NMen SDys
grandiflorum	CWil ESem NMen WPer WThu XLum
- from Valpine	ESem NMen
- 'Fasciatum'	ESem NMen
- 'Keston'	ESem
grandiflorum* × *montanum	see *S.* × *christii*
'Grannie's Favourite'	NMen
'Grape Idol'	CWil ESem NMen
'Grapetone'	ESem MHom NMen SDys WHal
'Graupurpur'	CWil XLum
'Green Apple'	CWil GAbr MHom NMen SDys
'Green Disk'	SRms
'Green Dragon'	ECho ESem LRHS MSCN NMen NRHS SRms WOut
'Green Gables'	EDAr ESem WPer
'Green Giant'	ESem
'Green Ice'	CWil NMen
'Greenwich Time'	EDAr ESem NMen
* ***greigii***	EPot
'Grenadier'	ESem
'Grey Dawn'	ECho ESem LRHS MHom MTis NMen NRHS XLum
'Grey Ghost'	ESem NMen WIvy WPer
'Grey Green'	CWil
'Grey Lady'	CMea CWil ESem NMen
'Grey Owl'	ECho LRHS NMen SRms
'Grey Velvet'	CWil NMen
'Greyfriars'	CMea ECho EDAr EPot ESem LBee LRHS MTis NMen SFgr WGor WPer
'Greyolla'	CWil ESem WPer
'Grünrand'	ESem

Name	Suppliers
'Grünschnabel'	XLum
'Gulle Dame'	CWil ESem MHom NMen SFgr
'Hades'	ESem
'Halemaumau'	CWil ESem NMen
I 'Hall's Hybrid'	CWil ESem GAbr MSCN NBro NMen
'Hall's Seedling'	NMen
'Happy'	CWil ESem NMen SFgr SRms WGor WIvy WPer WThu
'Hart'	CWil NMen WTin
'Haullauer's Seedling'	NMen
'Havana'	ESem NMen
'Hayling'	ECho ESem LRHS NMen NRHS SRms WPer XLum
'Heigham Red'	CWil ECho EPPr ESem GKev LBee LRHS NMen NRHS WIce WPer
'Heike'	CWil NMen
'Helen'	EDAr
'Heliotroop'	ESem NMen SDys SRot
helveticum	see *S. montanum*
'Hester'	CHEx CWil ECho ESem MAsh MBrN NBro NMen WFar
'Hey-hey'	ECho EPot LBee LRHS MAsh MBrN NDov NMen NRHS SPlb WPer XLum
'Hidde'	CWil ESem NMen SFgr WPer
'Hidde's Roosje'	ESem NMen
'Hirsutum'	see *Jovibarba allionii*
hirtum	see *Jovibarba hirta*
'Hispidulum'	ESem
'Hookeri'	see *S.* × *barbulatum* 'Hookeri'
'Hopi'	CWil NMen
'Hortulanus Smit'	NMen XLum
'Hot Peppermint'	ESem
'Huggable Helen' **new**	GKev
'Hullabaloo'	EDAr ESem NMen SFgr
'Hurricane'	CWil ESem MSCN MTis NMen WIvy WPer
'Icicle'	CHEx CMea ECho ESem LRHS MSCN NBro NHol NMen NRHS SRms WAbe WGor WOut
imbricatum	see *S.* × *barbulatum*
'Imperial'	CWil MHom
'Inge'	see *Jovibarba heuffelii* 'Inge'
ingwersenii	ESem MHom NMen XLum
ingwersenii* × *pumilum	CWil ESem NMen
- - from Spain	NMen
'Iophon'	LBee LRHS
iranicum	NMen
'Irazu'	CWil ESem GAbr LRHS MSCN NMen NRHS SDys SFgr SRms WPer
'Irene'	ESem SFgr
'Isaac Dyson'	SDys SRot
'Isabelle'	CWil NMen
italicum	ESem MHom NMen XLum
'Itchen'	ESem NMen
'Ivonne'	CWil NMen
'Iwo'	CHEx NMen SFgr
'Jack Frost'	CWil NBro NMen SFgr XLum
'Jacquette'	CWil ESem NMen
'Jadestern'	CWil NMen
'Jamie's Pride'	WGor
'Jane'	ESem
'Jasper'	ESem
'Jaspis'	ESem
'Jelly Bean'	CWil NMen SFgr
'Jet Stream' ♀H4	CWil ECho ESem LRHS MHom NMen NRHS SDys SPlb SRms WGor
'Jewel Case'	CWil ECho ESem LRHS NMen

I	'John Hobbs seedling No. 2'	ESem NMen
	'John T.'	ESem NMen
	'Jolly Green Giant'	ESem MHom NMen
	'Jubilee'	CMea CWil ECho EDAr ELan EPot ESem GEdr MAsh MHer NMen WGor WPer XLum
	'Jubilee Tricolor'	ESem GEdr NHol NMen SFgr WAbe
*	'Julia'	ESem
	'Jungle Fires'	CMea CWil EPot ESem NMen SDys SRms WHoo
	'Jungle Shadows'	EDAr ESem NMen XLum
	'Jupiter'	GKev XLum
	'Justine's Choice'	CWil NMen SRms
	'Kalinda'	ESem MHom NMen
	'Kappa'	CTri CWil ESem NBro NMen SDys SRot WPer
	'Katmai'	CWil ESem NMen
	'Kaya'	CWil
	'Kelly Jo'	CWil ESem NBro NMen SFgr WFar WTin
	'Kelut'	ESem NMen
	'Kermit'	ESem MHom NMen
	'Kia'	CWil NMen
	'Kiara'	CWil NMen
	'Kibo'	ESem NMen WIvy
	'Kimba' **new**	NMen
	'Kimble'	ESem NMen WPer
	'Kimono'	ESem NWad
	kindingeri	CWil ESem MHom NMen XLum
	'King George'	CTri CWil ECha ESem GKev LBee LRHS MMuc NMen SFgr SRms WGor WHal WHoo WPer WTin XLum
	'King Lear'	ESem NMen
	'Kip'	CMea ECha NMen WIvy WPer
	'Koko Flanel'	CWil ESem NMen SFgr
	'Korspel Glory'	NMen
	'Korspelsegietje'	CWil GAbr NMen SRms
	kosaninii	ESem NMen SFgr WPer WTin
	- from Koprivnik, Slovenia	MSCN NMen SDys WAbe XLum
*	- from Visitor	CWil
	'Krakeling'	NMen
	'Kramer's Purpur'	NMen
	'Kramer's Spinrad'	CHEx CMea CPBP CWil ECha EPPr EPot ESem GAbr LBee LRHS NMen SDys SFgr SPlb SRms WHoo WIvy WTin
	'Krater'	CWil ESem NMen
	'Kubi'	ESem
	'Lady Kelly'	ESem NMen WIvy
	'L'Arte'	ESem
	'Launcelot'	ECha ESem NMen WPer
	'Laura Lee'	ESem MMuc NMen SEND
	'Lavender and Old Lace'	CHEx CWil ECho ESem GAbr LRHS MSCN NMen NRHS SFgr SPlb SRms WIce WNew WPer
	'Laysan'	CWil
	Le Clair's hybrid No 4	NMen
	'Lemon and Lime'	ESem
	'Lennik's Glory'	see *S.* 'Crispyn'
	'Lennik's Glory No. 2'	ESem
	'Lennik's Time'	ESem
	'Lentezon'	ESem
	'Leocadia's Nephew'	ESem NMen
	'Leon Smits'	CWil ESem
	'Les Yielding'	ESem
	leucanthum	XLum
	'Lilac Time' ♀H4	CMea CWil ECho EPPr ESem GAbr LRHS MBrN MHer MSCN NMen NRHS SFgr SPlb SRms WHal WIvy WOut WPer XLum
	'Lime Frost'	ESem
	'Lion King'	CWil ESem MSCN NMen
	'Lipari'	ECha ESem NMen WCot XLum
	'Lipstick'	ESem NMen
	'Little Bo Bo'	ESem
	'Little Flirt'	MSCN
	'Lively Bug'	CWil ECho EDAr ESem LBee LRHS MMuc MSCN NMen NRHS SDys SEND SRms WGor WPer
	'Lloyd Praeger'	see *S. montanum* subsp. *stiriacum* 'Lloyd Praeger'
	'Long Shanks'	MSCN
	'Lonzo'	CWil SRms
	'Lord Alan' **new**	GKev
	'Lynn's Choice'	CWil GAbr NMen SFgr WHal WIvy WPer
	macedonicum	ESem NMen WTin XLum
	- from Ljuboten, Macedonia/Kosovo	CWil ESem NMen
	'Madeleine'	CWil ESem NMen
	'Magic Spell'	CWil ESem NMen
	'Magical'	CWil NMen
	'Magnificum'	CWil ESem NMen WGor
	'Mahogany'	CHEx CTri CWil ECho EDAr ESem GKev LBee LRHS MAsh MHer NHol NMen SFgr SRms WGor WHal WIvy WNew XLum
	'Maigret'	CWil NMen WPer
	'Majestic'	CWil ESem LBee LRHS NMen
	'Major White'	CHEx
	'Malby's Hybrid'	see *S.* 'Reginald Malby'
	'Marella'	ESem WPer
	'Maria Laach'	CWil ESem MMuc NMen
	'Marijntje'	CWil ESem NMen WPer
	'Marjorie Newton'	CWil ESem NMen WPer
	'Marmalade'	ESem
§	***marmoreum***	ECho EPot LBee LRHS MAsh NMen SRms WFar WHal WPer
	- from Kanzan Gorge, Bulgaria	ESem NMen
	- from Monte Tirone, Italy	LRHS SDys
	- from Okol, Albania	ESem NMen
	- 'Brunneifolium'	CWil ESem GAbr GCal LBee LRHS NMen WIvy WPer XLum
	- subsp. ***marmoreum*** var. ***dinaricum***	ESem MHer NMen
	- - - from Karawanken	ESem
§	- - 'Rubrifolium'	XLum
	'Marshall'	NMen
	'Martin'	ESem
	'Mate'	ESem NMen
	'Matthew's Day Dream' **new**	GKev
	'Maubi'	CHEx
	'Mauna Kea'	NMen WPer
	'Mauvine'	NMen XLum
	'Mayfair'	EDAr
	'Mayfair Imp'	NMen
	'Maytime'	ESem
	'Medallion'	ESem SFgr
	'Meisse'	ECho NMen
	'Melanie'	CWil ESem MBrN NMen WIvy
	'Memorial Merit'	ESem
	'Mercury'	CWil ECho ESem GAbr LRHS NBro NMen NRHS SRms
	'Merlin'	ESem MSCN
	'Metallicum'	ESem

	mettenianum **new**	NMen
	'Midas'	CWil ECha ECho ESem LRHS NMen NRHS SFgr
	'Milá'	CWil
	'Mini Frost'	CWil NMen WPer
	'Minuet'	NMen
	'Missouri Rose'	NMen
	'Mixed Spice'	CWil
	'Moerkerk's Merit'	CWil ESem GAbr MTis NMen XLum
	'Mohair'	NMen
	'Mondstein'	CWil ESem WIvy WPer
	'Monique'	WPer
	'Monseigneur Desmet'	ESem
	'Montage'	CWil
§	***montanum***	ESem NMen WPer
	- from Arbizion, France	CWil
	- from Gavarnie, France	ESem
	- from Monte Tirone, Italy	LBee
	- from Monte Tonale, Italy	CWil
	- from Windachtal, Germany	CWil NMen
§	- subsp. ***burnatii***	CWil ESem MHom NMen WIvy
	- 'Caesar'	MSCN
	- subsp. ***carpaticum***	CWil XLum
	- - 'Cmiral's Yellow'	ESem MSCN SFgr WAbe WIvy
*	- Fragell form	SFgr
	- subsp. ***montanum***	CWil
	- 'Rubrum'	see *S.* 'Red Mountain'
	- subsp. ***stiriacum***	CWil ESem NMen SFgr
	- - from Mauterndorf, Austria	ESem NMen
	- - from Puerto de San Francisco, USA	ESem
§	- - 'Lloyd Praeger'	CWil ESem LBee LRHS NMen SDys SFgr WIvy WPer
	montanum × tectorum var. ***boutignyanum*** GDJ 94.15	CWil
	'Moondrops'	CWil
	'More Honey'	CWil NMen SFgr
	'Morning Glow'	NMen WGor WHal WPer
	'Mount Hood'	ECho ESem ETod LRHS NMen NRHS WHal
	'Mount Usher'	NMen
	'Mrs Elliott'	NMen
	'Mulberry Wine'	CWil ESem LBee LRHS NMen SRms WGor WHoo
	'Mystic'	CWil ESem MBrN NMen WPer
	'Neon'	CWil NMen
	nevadense	CWil EPot NMen SFgr SRms
	- from Calar de Santa Barbara, Spain GDJ 96A-07	CWil
	- from Puerto de San Francisco	CWil ESem
	- 'Hirtellum'	CWil NMen
	'Nico'	CWil NMen NWad SRms
	'Night Raven'	CMea MTis NMen WIvy WPer
	'Nigrum'	see *S. tectorum* 'Nigrum'
	'Niobe'	ESem SFgr WHal
	'Noellie'	CWil NMen
	'Noir'	CWil EDAr ESem MSCN NBro NMen WAbe WGor
	'Norbert'	CWil EDAr SRms WIvy WPer XLum
	'Norne'	ESem
	'Nouveau Pastel'	CFis CMea CWil ESem NMen WHal WPer XLum
	'Octet'	CWil NMen
	octopodes	NBir SIde XLum
	- var. ***apetalum***	CWil ESem GAbr MSCN NMen SRms WIvy
	'Oddity'	ECha ESem ETod MBrN MHer NMen WHal WPer
	'Ohio'	NMen
	'Ohio Burgundy'	ECha ECho ESem LRHS NMen NRHS SRms WAbe WPer WTin
	'Old Copper'	ESem
	'Old Rose'	NMen
	'Olivette'	ECha ESem NMen WPer WTin XLum
	'Omega'	NMen WPer
	'Ornatum'	EPot ESem MHer MHom MWat NMen WAbe WHal WIvy WPer
	ossetiense	CWil EDAr ESem GAbr NMen XLum
	'Othello' ♀H4	CDes CTri EPfP GCra MMuc NBir NMen WPGP WPer WTin XLum
	'Ottelein'	CWil NMen
	'Pacific Feather Power'	NMen
	'Pacific Opal'	CWil NMen
	'Pacific Purple Shadows'	CWil NMen
	'Pacific Spring Frost' **new**	SFgr
	'Packardian'	CWil NMen NWad SFgr WIvy
	'Painted Lady'	CWil ESem NMen
	'Palissander'	EDAr GAbr NMen SFgr WPer XLum
	'Pam Wain'	MHom NMen
	'Panola Fire'	WFar
	'Passionata'	CWil ESem NMen SFgr
	'Pastel'	CWil ESem MHer NMen
	patens	see *Jovibarba heuffelii*
	'Patrician'	CWil ESem LBee LRHS SRms
	'Peggy'	CWil ESem NMen WGor
	'Pekinese'	CWil ECho EDAr EPot ESem GEdr LRHS MBrN NBro NMen NRHS SFgr SRms WGor WPer XLum
	'Peterson's Ornatum'	SDys
	'Petsy'	ESem NMen SRms
	'Phoebe' **new**	NMen
	'Pilatus'	ECha EWes SRms WFar WPer
	× ***piliferum*** 'Hausmannii'	NMen
	'Pine Cone'	WGor
	'Pink Astrid'	CWil ESem
	'Pink Button'	CWil
	'Pink Cloud'	CWil LRHS NMen
	'Pink Dawn'	ESem
	'Pink Delight'	ESem MSCN
	'Pink Flamingoes'	NMen
	'Pink Lemonade'	CWil ESem MHom NMen
	'Pink Mist'	NMen SRms WPer
	'Pink Puff'	CWil ESem MHom NMen SFgr
	'Pippin'	CWil ESem NMen SRms WPer
	'Piran'	CWil
	pittonii ♀H4	CMea CWil EPot ESem NMen WHal XLum
	'Pixie'	CPBP CWil ESem NMen SFgr WIvy WPer
	'Plum Frosting'	MSCN WGor
	'Plum Mist'	NWad
	'Plumb Rose'	CWil ESem NMen WIvy WPer
	'Pluto'	CWil ESem LBee LRHS NMen XLum
	'Poke Eat'	ESem NMen
	'Polaris'	CWil ESem MHom NMen
	'Poldark'	ESem NMen
	'Pompeon'	ESem
	'Ponderosa'	CWil NMen
	'Pottsii'	CWil ESem
I	'Powellii'	ESem
	'Precious'	ESem
	'President Arsac'	NMen XLum

	Name	Suppliers
	'Probus' **new**	NMen
	'Procton'	ESem NMen
	'Proud Zelda'	CWil EDAr ESem GAbr MTis NMen
	'Průhonice'	CWil NMen WFar
	'Pseudo-ornatum'	LBee LRHS SRms
	'Pumaros'	NMen SDys
	pumilum	CWil ECho GKev LRHS NMen NRHS
	- from Adyl-Su, Chechnya, No 1	CWil
	- from Armkhi, Ingushetia	ESem SDys
	- from El'brus, Russia, No 1	CWil ESem
	- from Techensis	CWil NMen
	- 'Sopa'	CWil ESem NMen
	'Purdy'	MHom MSCN NMen WAbe
	'Purdy's 50-6'	CWil ESem NMen
	'Purdy's 70-40'	ESem
	'Purple Beauty'	EPot ESem GKev NMen
	'Purple King'	CMea MHom MTis NMen SDys
	'Purple Passion'	ESem NMen
	'Purple Queen'	CWil EDAr ESem LRHS NMen NRHS
	'Pygmalion'	CWil ESem NMen
	'Queen Amalia'	see *S. reginae-amaliae*
	'Quintessence'	CWil NMen SFgr SRms
	'Racey'	ESem NMen
	'Ragtime'	ESem
	'Ramses'	ESem SDys
	'Raspberry Ice'	CFis CMea LBee LRHS MSCN NBro NMen WPer
	'Rauer Kulm'	CWil ESem NMen
*	'Rauheit'	WFar
	'Rauhreif'	ESem WFar XLum
	'Red Ace'	CWil ECha GEdr MBel NBro NDov NMen SFgr WFar WPer
	'Red Beam'	CWil ESem MSCN NMen
	'Red Chips'	EDAr MHom
	'Red Delta'	CDes CWil NBir NMen SFgr WCot WPGP
	'Red Devil'	CMea CWil ECha ECho ESem LRHS NMen NRHS SFgr SPlb WHoo WPer WTin
	'Red Giant'	ESem NMen
	'Red Lion'	CWil GEdr NMen SFgr
	'Red Lynn'	CWil ESem
§	'Red Mountain'	CWil ESem LBee LRHS NMen SRms
	'Red Pink'	CWil
	'Red Robin'	EDAr ESem NMen
	'Red Rum'	WPer
	'Red Shadows'	LBee LRHS NMen WPer WTin
	'Red Spider'	CWil EPot ESem MHom NBro NMen
	'Red Summer'	ESem
	'Red West' **new**	NMen
	'Regal'	ESem NMen
	'Regina'	NMen
	reginae	see *S. reginae-amaliae*
§	***reginae-amaliae***	CWil EPot ESem GKev NMen XLum
	- from Kambeecho, Greece, No 2	NMen SDys
	- from Mavri Petri, Greece	CWil ESem SDys
	- from Sarpun, Turkey	CWil ESem NMen SDys WTin
	- from Vardusa, Serbia	CWil ESem SDys
§	'Reginald Malby'	CTri ECho ESem GMaP LRHS NMen NRHS SFgr SRms WIvy
	'Reinhard' ♀H4	CMea CWil CYeo ECha ECho EDAr EPot ESem GEdr LRHS MAsh MBrN MHer MSCN NMen NRya SPlb SRms WFar WHal WHoo WIvy WPer
	'Remus'	CWil ECha ELan ESem NMen SDys SFgr WGor
	'Rex'	NMen
	'Rhône'	CWil ESem LBee LRHS NMen
	'Rich 'n' Fruity'	MSCN
	'Risque'	CWil ESem LBee LRHS NMen WPer
	'Rita Jane'	CWil ECha ESem MHom NMen SFgr WTin
	'Robin'	LBee LRHS NBro NHol NMen WTin
	'Ronny'	CWil ESem NMen
	'Roosemaryn'	EDAr ESem NMen
	'Rose Queen'	ESem
	× ***roseum***	ESem NMen
	'Rosie'	CMea CPBP CWil ECho EPot GAbr GEdr GMaP LBee LRHS MAsh MSCN NHol NMen NRHS SEND SRms WHal WHoo WIce WPer WTin
	'Rotkopf' ♀H4	CWil ESem MSCN NMen SFgr XLum
	'Rotmantel'	NMen SDys WTin
	'Rotund'	CWil ESem GEdr MSCN
	'Rouge'	ESem NMen
	'Royal Mail'	ESem
	'Royal Opera'	CWil EDAr ESem NMen
	'Royal Ruby'	ECha ESem LBee NMen WIvy
	'Royale'	SFgr
	'Rubellum Mahogany'	SFgr
	'Rubikon Improved'	ESem NMen
	'Rubin'	CMea CTri ECha EPfP GKev MAsh MSCN NBir NEgg NMen NPri SPoG SRms WAbe WHoo WIce WNew WPer XLum
I	'Rubra Ash'	CWil ESem NMen WAbe WTin
I	'Rubra Ray'	CWil EDAr ESem NMen
	'Rubrifolium'	see *S. marmoreum* subsp. *marmoreum* 'Rubrifolium'
*	'Ruby Glow'	EDAr
	'Ruby Heart'	EDAr
	'Russian River'	CMea NMen WHoo WTin
	'Rusty'	CWil ESem SFgr
	ruthenicum	ECho ESem LLHF LRHS MHom NRHS NRya
	- 'Regis-Fernandii'	ECho XLum
	'Safara'	CWil ESem
	'Saffron'	NMen
	'Saga'	ESem MHom
	'Sanford's Hybrid'	NMen
	'Santis'	ESem
	'Sarah'	EDAr ESem NMen
	'Sarotte'	CWil NMen
	'Sassy Frass'	ESem NMen
	'Saturn'	ESem NMen SRms
	schlehanii	see *S. marmoreum*
	schnittspahnii	ESem XLum
	'Seminole'	CWil ESem NMen
	'Serendipity'	EDAr
	'Shadri'	ESem
	'Sha-Na'	CWil NMen
	'Sharon's Pencil'	CWil NMen
	'Sheila'	GAbr
	'Shirley Moore'	CWil EDAr ESem NMen SFgr WTin
	'Shirley's Joy'	ESem NMen WTin XLum
	'Sideshow'	CWil ESem NMen
	'Sigi'	ESem
	'Sigma'	ESem NMen
	'Silberkarneol' misapplied	see *S.* 'Silver Jubilee'
	'Silberspitz'	CWil ECho LRHS MHer MHom NBro NMen NRHS SPlb WPer

	'Silver Cup'	CWil ESem NMen SFgr WIvy
§	'Silver Jubilee'	CMea CWil ECha ECho EDAr ESem GAbr LRHS NBro NMen NRHS NRya SPlb SRms WGor XLum
	'Silver Queen'	CWil ESem SFgr
	'Silver Shadow'	MSCN WGor
	'Silver Spring'	ESem NMen
	'Silver Thaw'	CWil ECha EDAr NMen SFgr
	'Silverine'	CWil EDAr NMen
	'Silvertone'	CWil ESem NMen
	'Simonkaianum'	see *Jovibarba hirta*
	'Sioux'	CWil ESem LBee LRHS MBrN NHol NMen WFar WHal WIvy WPer WTin
	'Skrocki's Bronze'	ESem GAbr LRHS NMen WPer
	'Slabber's Seedling'	CWil NMen
	'Smaragd'	CWil ECha ESem LBee LRHS NMen WFar XLum
	'Smokey Jet'	ESem NMen SFgr
	'Smokey Quartz'	WGor
	'Snowberger'	CWil EPot ESem MSCN NMen SFgr SRms WGor WHal WPer
	'Soarte'	ESem
	soboliferum	see *Jovibarba sobolifera*
	'Soothsayer'	CWil NMen
	sosnowskyi	CWil NMen
	'Spanish Dancer'	NMen
	'Speciosum'	ESem
	'Spherette'	CWil EDAr MBrN MSCN NMen WAbe WPer
	'Spider's Lair' ♀H4	EDAr MHom
	'Spinellii'	NMen WThu WTin
	'Spiver's Velvet'	NMen
	'Springmist'	CWil ECho EPot ESem GAbr LRHS MAsh MTis NMen NRHS SFgr SRms WGor WPer WTin
	'Sprite'	CWil GEdr MBel MTis NMen SDys WOut WTin
	'Squib'	CWil ESem MSCN
	stansfieldii	see *S. arachnoideum* subsp. *tomentosum* 'Stansfieldii'
	'Starburst'	CWil NMen
	'Starion'	CWil
	'Starshine'	NMen SFgr
	'State Fair'	CWil EDAr NMen WIvy WPer
*	***stoloniferum***	GAbr
	'Strawberry Fields'	ESem
	'Strawberry Sundae'	ESem NMen
	'Strider'	CWil GAbr WTin
	'Stuffed Olive'	CWil SDys SRms SRot
I	'Subanum'	ESem
	'Sugary'	ESem
	'Sun Waves'	CWil ESem NMen SDys SFgr
	'Sunkist'	NMen
	'Sunray Desire'	WGor
	'Sunray Magic'	WGor
	'Sunrise'	ESem
	'Super Dome'	CWil NMen
	'Superama'	ESem
	'Supernova'	ESem
	'Syston Flame'	CWil NMen
	'Tamberlane'	EDAr
	'Tarita'	CWil NMen
	'Teck'	NMen
§	***tectorum*** ♀H4	CArn CHby CTri ECho EDAr ELan EPfP GPoy LBee LPot LRHS MHer MHoo MMuc MNHC NMen SBfd SIde SPlb WFar WJek XLum
	- from Eporn	CWil NMen
§	- var. ***alpinum***	CWil ECho ESem LRHS MHom NBro NMen NRHS SRms
	- var. ***andreanum***	CWil XLum
	- 'Atropurpureum'	ECho ELan NMen WTin
	- 'Atroviolaceum'	EDAr ESem NLar NMen SPlb WFar WIvy WTin XLum
*	- 'Aureum'	SFgr
	- var. ***boutignyanum***	ESem
	from Route de Tuixén, Spain	
	- - - GDJ 94.04	CWil SRms
	- - from Sant Joan de Caselles, Andorra GDJ 94.02	CWil
	- - - GDJ 94.03	CWil
	- var. ***calcareum***	ECho
§	- 'Nigrum'	ESem LBee LRHS MHer NBro NMen SDys WGor WTin
	- 'Red Flush'	CWil EDAr EPPr MBrN NMen SDys SFgr WFar WPer
	- 'Royanum' ♀H4	ESem GAbr MSCN
*	- subsp. ***sanguineum***	EDAr
	- 'Sunset'	CMea EDAr ESem GAbr NMen SDys SFgr WHal
	- subsp. ***tectorum***	ESem GEdr NMen
§	- - 'Boissieri'	CWil NMen WIvy
	- - 'Triste'	CHEx CWil LBee LRHS NMen WFar XLum
	- 'Tokajense'	ESem
	- 'Violaceum'	MHom SRms WAbe WGor
	tectorum* × *zeleborii	WTin
	'Tederheid'	ESem
	'Telfan'	NMen
	'Terlamen'	NMen
	'Terracotta Baby'	CWil ESem NMen SFgr
	'Thayne'	NMen
	'The Platters'	CWil NMen
	'The Rocket'	CWil NMen
	× ***thompsonianum***	CWil NMen SFgr
	'Thunder'	CWil NMen
	'Tiffany'	WPer
	'Tiger Bay'	NMen
	'Tina'	WPer
	'Tip Top'	CWil ESem GEdr NMen SFgr
	'Titania'	CWil NBro NMen WHal WTin
	'Tombago'	ESem
	'Topaz'	CWil ECha ESem LBee LRHS NMen SFgr SRms XLum
	'Tordeur's Memory'	CWil ESem GEdr LBee LRHS MMuc MSCN NMen SEND
	'Tracy Sue'	EDAr XLum
	'Trail Walker'	CWil LBee LRHS NMen SRms
	transcaucasicum	CWil XLum
	'Tree Beard'	CWil NMen
	'Trine'	CWil
	'Tristesse' ♀H4	CWil EDAr GAbr MBrN NMen SFgr WGor
	'Truva'	CWil ESem NMen SFgr
	'Twilight Blues'	CWil ECho ESem LRHS NMen NRHS SFgr SRms
	'Twizzler' **new**	MSCN
	'Undine'	CWil ESem NMen SFgr
	'Unicorn'	ESem
	'Utopian'	ESem
	× ***vaccarii***	CWil NMen XLum
	'Van der Steen'	GAbr NMen
	'Vanbaelen'	CWil GAbr NMen SDys
	'Vanessa'	CWil
	'Veuchelen'	CWil ESem

	vicentei	ESem MHom NMen WFar WTin
	– from Gaton	ESem LBee LRHS NMen
§	– subsp. ***paui***	NHol NMen NSla
	'Victorian'	ESem
	'Video'	CWil ESem MHom NMen SFgr
	'Vignola'	CWil NMen
	'Viking'	NMen
	'Violet Queen'	ESem NMen
	'Virgil'	CWil EDAr ESem GAbr MBrN MSCN MTis NMen NWad SDys WAbe WCot WGor WIce WPer WTin
I	'Virginius'	CWil GAbr
	'Vulcano'	ESem NMen
	'Waldalina'	CWil NMen
	'Warners Pink'	MDKP
	'Warrior'	EDAr
	'Wasti' **new**	NMen
	'Watermelon Rind'	ESem MTis NMen
	webbianum	see *S. arachnoideum* subsp. *tomentosum* (C.B. Lehm. & Schnittsp.) Schinz & Thell.
	'Webby Flame'	CWil NMen
	'Webby Ola'	NMen
	'Webbyola'	ESem NMen
	'Wega'	NMen
	'Weirdo'	CWil ESem NMen
	'Wendy'	ESem NMen
	'Westerlin'	CWil ECha ESem NMen
	'White Bouquet' **new**	NMen
	'White Christmas'	see *S. arachnoideum* 'White Christmas'
	'White Eyes'	NMen
	'White Ladies'	ESem NMen
	'Whitening'	EDAr GAbr NMen
	× ***widderi***	NMen
	'Wilhelm Tell' **new**	NMen
I	'Woolcott's Variety'	CWil ECho ESem MDKP MSCN NBir NMen WFar WPer WTin
	wulfenii	CWil NMen
*	– ***roseum***	EDAr
	'Xaviera'	CWil ESem NMen
	'Yanisha'	CWil NMen
	'Yarnton'	ESem NMen
	'Yvette'	CWil NMen
	'Zackenkrone'	NMen
	'Zaza'	CWil ESem NMen
	zeleborii	ESem SDys WHal
	'Zenith'	CWil EDAr ESem GAbr NMen SFgr SRms
	'Zenobia'	ESem MHom
	'Zenocrate'	NHol NMen WHal
	'Zepherin'	CWil ESem MSCN NMen
	'Zeppelin No 3'	NMen
	'Zilver Moon'	CWil ESem NMen
	'Zilver Snowflake'	CWil NMen
	'Zilver Suzanna'	CWil NMen
	'Zilverprinsesje'	CWil
	'Zircon'	EDAr ESem NMen
	'Zone'	CHEx ESem MTis NMen
	'Zorba'	NMen
	'Zulu'	ECha NMen SFgr

Senecio (*Asteraceae*)

§	***articulatus***	EShb
	bidwillii	see *Brachyglottis bidwillii*
	buchananii	see *Brachyglottis buchananii*
	candicans misapplied	see *S. cineraria*
	chrysanthemoides	see *Euryops chrysanthemoides*
§	***cineraria***	LPot SEND
	– 'Silver Dust' ♀H3	EPfP
	– 'White Diamond'	ECha
*	***coccinilifera***	SBch
	compactus	see *Brachyglottis compacta*
	confusus	see *Pseudogynoxys chenopodioides*
	crassissimus	EShb
	cristobalensis **new**	WCot
	doria	EShb LRHS WFar WHil WHrl
	ficoides	EShb
	formosoides B&SWJ 10736	WCru
	formosus B&SWJ 10700	WCru
	– B&SWJ 10746	WCru
	gerberifolius B&SWJ 10357	WCru
	– B&SWJ 10361	WCru
	glastifolius	LRHS
	grandifolius	see *Telanthophora grandifolia*
	'Gregynog Gold'	see *Ligularia* 'Gregynog Gold'
	greyi misapplied	see *Brachyglottis* (Dunedin Group) 'Sunshine'
	greyi Hook.	see *Brachyglottis greyi* (Hook. f.) B. Nord.
	heritieri DC.	see *Pericallis lanata* (L'Hér.) B. Nord.
	hoffmannii	EShb
	integrifolius subsp. ***capitatus***	SPlb
	kleiniiformis	EShb
	laxifolius hort.	see *Brachyglottis* (Dunedin Group) 'Sunshine'
	leucostachys	see *S. viravira*
	macroglossus	CHll CRHN EShb WFar
	– 'Variegatus' (v) ♀H1	EShb
	maritimus	see *S. cineraria*
	monroi	see *Brachyglottis monroi*
	petasitis	CBcs CHEx CTrC SDix WCot
	polyodon	CCCN CDes CSpe EDAr EPPr EShb EWll GAbr GBin MNrw MPie MSpe NDov NGdn NLar SPhx WMoo WPGP WSHC WWEG
	– S&SH 29	EBee NCGa
	– subsp. ***subglaber***	EWes
	przewalskii	see *Ligularia przewalskii*
	pulcher	CDTJ CDes CGHE EBee LEdu MNrw NCGa SBch SHar SMrm SUsu WAbb WPGP
	reinholdii	see *Brachyglottis rotundifolia*
	rowleyanus	EBak
	scandens	CBre CCCN CPLG EShb MNrw WPGP
	seminiveus	EBee
§	***serpens***	CDoC EShb EUJe SEND
§	***smithii***	ELan GBee NBid SEND WCot WCru WFar WWEG
	squalidus	WHer
	subulatus	GKev
	var. ***subulatus*** CC 6515 **new**	
	– – CC 6516	EWld
	'Sunshine'	see *Brachyglottis* (Dunedin Group) 'Sunshine'
	talinoides	EShb
	subsp. ***cylindricus*** 'Himalaya'	
	tanguticus	see *Sinacalia tangutica*
§	***viravira*** ♀H3-4	CMea EPfP EUJe MCot SDix SMad SMrm SPer WSHC

Senna (*Caesalpiniaceae*)

alata B&SWJ 9772	WCru
alexandrina	CCCN EShb LRHS WPGP
§ ***corymbosa***	CBcs CCCN CHEx CRHN CTri EAmu SEND SGar SMrm
× ***floribunda***	EBee LRHS
hebecarpa	LRHS SBrt SPhx
§ ***marilandica***	CArn EBee ELan EWes LRHS
multiglandulosa	CBcs WPGP
retusa	CHEx
septemtrionalis	CCCN EBee LRHS

Sequoia (*Cupressaceae*)

sempervirens ♀H4	CBcs CDoC CDul CLnd CMCN CMac CMen ECrN EHul EPfP ERom EWTr GKin LMaj LRHS MBlu MMuc NWea SEND SGol SLim SPoG WEve WMou
- 'Adpressa'	CDoC CDul CTho EHul LRHS MAsh MBri MGos NWea SCoo SLim WFar
- 'Cantab'	CDoC SLim WMou
- 'Henderson Blue'	SLim
- 'Prostrata'	CDoC LRHS SEND SLim WFar
- 'Simpson's Silver'	SLim

Sequoiadendron (*Cupressaceae*)

giganteum ♀H4	CBcs CCVT CDoC CDoy CDul CMCN CMac CTho CTri EHul ELan EPfP EWTr LMaj LRHS MAsh MBlu MBri MGos MMuc NEgg NWea SEND SEWo SGol SPer SPlb WEve WFar WMou
- 'Bajojeka'	NLar
- 'Barabits Requiem'	IArd LRHS MBlu NLar SLim SMad
- 'Blauer Eichzwerg'	NLar SLim
- 'Blue Iceberg'	CKen
- 'Bultinck Yellow'	MBlu NLar SMad
- 'Cannibal'	NLar
- 'Curly Green'	NLar
- 'French Beauty'	NLar
- 'Glaucum'	CDoC CDul CTho LRHS MBlu MBri NLar SLim SPoG WMou
* - 'Glaucum Compactum'	MBlu
- 'Greenpeace'	MBlu NLar
- 'Hazel Smith'	SEND
- 'Little Stan'	CKen NLar
- 'Pendulum'	CCVT CDoC CKen ERod MBlu MGos NLar SLim SMad WEve
- 'Philip Curtis'	NLar
- 'Pierie'	NLar
- 'Pirat'	NLar
- 'Powdered Blue'	LRHS NLar SLim
- 'Von Martin'	NLar

Serapias (*Orchidaceae*)

lingua	SChF

Serenoa (*Arecaceae*)

repens	EAmu EGri

Seriphidium (*Asteraceae*)

caerulescens var. ***gallicum***	CEls
§ ***canum***	CEls MHer
§ ***ferganense***	CEls
§ ***fragrans***	CEls
§ ***maritimum***	CArn MHer
- 'Coca-Cola' **new**	EBee
- var. ***maritimum***	CEls
§ ***nutans***	CEls MCot MRav
§ ***tridentatum***	CArn WHer
§ ***vallesiacum*** ♀H4	CEls

Serratula (*Asteraceae*)

coronata	EBee LRHS
- subsp. ***insularis*** B&SWJ 8698 **new**	WCru
- - f. ***alba***	GAbr
§ ***seoanei***	CKno CMea CPom EBee ECha EDAr LHop LPla LRHS MHer MLHP MNrw MPie MRav MWat NBid SBch SDix SPhx SRms SUsu WCot WFar WPGP WPat WTin
shawii	see *S. seoanei*
tinctoria	CArn NLar NMir SPhx
- subsp. ***macrocephala***	EBee
wolffii	EBee

Serruria (*Proteaceae*)

florida	SPlb
phylicoides	SPlb

Sesamum (*Pedaliaceae*)

indicum	CArn

Sesbania (*Papilionaceae*)

punicea	CCCN

Seseli (*Apiaceae*)

gummiferum	CArn CHid CSam CSpe LDai SKHP SPhx WHil WPtf
- fine-leaved **new**	CSpe
hippomarathrum	EBee SPhx WCot WHrl WPGP
§ ***libanotis***	CSam CSpe LEdu LPla NDov NLar SAga SDix SPhx WPtf
montanum	CSpe LHop WPGP
petraeum RCB UA 13 **new**	WCot

Sesleria (*Poaceae*)

§ ***albicans***	EPPr
§ ***argentea***	EBee EHoe
autumnalis	CKno EBee LEdu LPla SPhx
caerulea	CKno CSam EBee EHoe ELan EPfP GQue LEdu LTen MBrN MWhi SPoG WPtf
- subsp. ***calcarea***	see *S. albicans*
- 'Malvern Mop'	EBee WHrl WPGP WWEG
* ***candida***	EPPr
cylindrica	see *S. argentea*
glauca	EHoe NLar NOak SBfd
'Greenlee'	CKno
heufleriana	CWCL EBee EHoe EPPr MBel NLar SMea SPhx SPlb WCot WWEG
insularis	EBee EPPr EShb
'Morning Dew'	EBee GCal
nitida	CKno EBee EHoe LEdu MBrN MMoz SApp SPhx WCot WPGP
rigida	EHoe
sadleriana	EBee EPPr EWes

Setaria (*Poaceae*)

macrostachya ♀H3	CKno LLWP NDov SBch SPhx
palmifolia	CHEx CHll CKno EUJe SPlb WCot
- BWJ 8132	WCru
viridis	CSpe WCot WTin

Setcreasea see *Tradescantia*

Sharon fruit see *Diospyros kaki*

Shepherdia (*Elaeagnaceae*)

argentea	CBcs NLar

Shibataea (*Poaceae*)

chinensis	CBcs
kumasaca	CAbb CBcs CDoC CEnt CHEx ENBC EPfP ERod GCal IBal LEdu LRHS MBrN MMoz MWht SBig SGol SLPl WJun WPGP
lancifolia	WJun

Shortia (*Diapensiaceae*)

galacifolia	GKev IBlr
soldanelloides	GKev IBlr
- var. ***ilicifolia***	IBlr
- var. ***magna***	IBlr
uniflora	IBlr NHar
- var. ***kantoensis***	GKev
- var. ***orbicularis*** 'Grandiflora'	IBlr

Sibbaldia (*Rosaceae*)

procumbens	GKev

Sibbaldiopsis (*Rosaceae*)

tridentata 'Lemon Mac'	CYeo NHar
- 'Nuuk'	CCon EPPr GJos

Sibthorpia (*Plantaginaceae*)

europaea	CGHE CHEx CPLG

Sida (*Malvaceae*)

hermaphrodita	EBee

Sidalcea (*Malvaceae*)

'Brilliant'	CBcs EBee EHrv EPfP LAst LRHS MDKP MDev MNrw MSCN NBir NPri NRHS SHar SPer WCAu WMoo WWEG
campestris from Oregon, USA	EPPr
candida	CPrp CSam EBee ECtt ELan EPfP GCra GMaP LAst LHop LRHS MBNS MBel MCot MMuc MRav MTis NEgg NGdn NLar NSti SEND SMHy SMrm SPer WCAu WCot WPtf
- 'Bianca'	CHVG EBee EHrv EPfP MSCN NGBl NLar WFar WHal WMoo WPer WWEG
'Candy Girl'	EBee MDev
'Croftway Red'	CCon EBee ELan EPfP GCra LRHS MBel MCot NBro NGdn NWad SAga SMrm SPer SPet SWvt WFar
cusickii	WOut
'Elsie Heugh' ♀H4	Widely available
hendersonii	EBee
hickmanii subsp. ***anomala***	EBee
hirtipes	EBee
'Interlaken'	LRHS
'Little Princess'PBR	CCon CElw EBee EPfP EWes LBuc LRHS LSou MAsh NDov NGdn NLar SPoG WFar
'Loveliness'	EBee ECtt ELan EShb LHop LSou MRav NBro NCGa NGdn NLar NWad SAga
malviflora	SRms
- 'Alba'	WFar
'Monarch'	MDKP
'Moorland Rose Coronet'	WMoo
'Mr Lindbergh'	EBee EPfP MAvo SAga WFar
'Mrs Borrodaile'	CMac CPrp EBee MRav NBro NGdn NPro SMrm WFar WMoo WWEG
'Mrs Galloway'	WFar
'Mrs T. Alderson'	EBee WFar
'My Love'	NDov SMrm
'Oberon'	EBee MRav NRHS WFar
oregana (Nutt. ex Torr. & A. Gray) A. Gray	NBid NGdn WOut
- subsp. ***spicata***	WMoo
'Party Girl'	Widely available
'Präriebrand'	SMrm
'Purpetta'	EBee NGBl NGdn NLar NPro SBfd SPad WPer
reptans	CDes EBee WWFP
'Reverend Page Roberts'	MAvo MRav WCot WFar WWEG
'Rosaly'	EBee ELon IFoB LRHS NGdn NLar WFar WGor WHal
'Rosanna'	EBee GMaP LRHS NGdn NLar NRHS SBfd WHal WPer WPtf
'Rose Bud'	CElw CPrp EBee MAvo
'Rose Queen'	EBee ECha LHop MCot MRav NBro NHol SPer SRms WFar
'Rosy Gem'	ECtt NBre WFar
Stark's hybrids	LRHS SRms
'Sussex Beauty'	CPrp CSam EBee MArl MBel MCot MLHP MRav NCGa NDov NEgg NGdn NHol SMrm WAul WFar WMoo WOut WWlt
'Sweet Joy'	SMrm
'William Smith' ♀H4	CPrp CSam EBee ECha ECtt EPfP EWes GBuc LRHS LSRN MBel MMuc MRav MWat NBir NCGa NChi NGdn NLar NOrc SBea SEND SPer WFar WMoo WWEG
'Wine Red'	CCon CMHG CPrp EBee EShb LAst LRHS LSou MCot MDKP MTis NEgg NGdn NHol SMrm SPoG SWvt WFar WWEG WWFP

Sideritis (*Lamiaceae*)

clandestina	XSen
cypria	XSen
hyssopifolia	EBee
perfoliata	XSen
phlomoides	XSen
phrygia	XSen
scardica	XSen
syriaca	CArn NBre XSen
taurica	XSen

Sieversia (*Rosaceae*)

§ ***pentapetala***	GEdr WAbe
reptans	see *Geum reptans*

Silaum (*Apiaceae*)

silaus	NMir

Silene (*Caryophyllaceae*)

RBS	EPPr
SDR 6174	GKev
from Uzbekistan	GCal
acaulis	ECho EDAr GJos MAsh NLar NMen SRms WAbe
§ - subsp. ***acaulis***	ECho SPlb SRms

	- 'Alba'	ECho EDAr EWes NLan NLar NMen WAbe WThu
	- 'Blush'	NMen NRHS NSla WAbe
§	- subsp. ***bryoides***	NLar
	- 'Correvoniana'	NLar
	- subsp. ***elongata***	see *S. acaulis* subsp. *acaulis*
	- subsp. ***exscapa***	see *S. acaulis* subsp. *bryoides*
	- 'Frances'	CYeo GMaP ITim NHar NMen NRHS NRya NSla WAbe
	- 'Francis Copeland'	ECho NMen
	- 'Helen's Double' (d)	ECho EDAr EPot GJos
	- 'Mount Snowdon'	ECho ECtt EDAr ELan EPfP EPot EWes GMaP MAsh NLar NMen NRya SPlb SPoG SRms SRot WHoo WPat
	- 'Pedunculata'	see *S. acaulis* subsp. *acaulis*
	alba	see *S. latifolia* subsp. *alba*
§	***alpestris***	NLar SBch SRms SRot WMoo WThu
	- 'Flore Pleno' (d) ♀H4	CMea CPBP EWes LBee LRHS NSla SBch WAbe WIce
	araratica	ITim WAbe
	argaea	WAbe
	× ***arkwrightii***	see *Lychnis* × *arkwrightii*
	armeria	SDys WHer
	- 'Aphrodite' new	CSpe
	- 'Electra'	CSpe WWFP
	asterias	GCal GCra MNrw NSti SBrt WWFP
	- MESE 429	GBin
	atropurpurea	see *Lychnis viscaria* subsp. *atropurpurea*
	bolanthoides new	LLHF SBrt
§	***compacta***	NLar
	'Confetti'	EDif WTou
	'Country Comet'	NChi
§	***davidii***	GKev WAbe
	delavayi	LRHS
	dinarica	WAbe
§	***dioica***	CArn CHab CMac CRWN EWTr LEdu MHer MNHC NLan NLar NMir SGar SPoG SWat WMoo WOut WSFF WShi
	- 'Clifford Moor' (v)	EBee ECtt MSCN NSti SCoo
	- 'Compacta'	see *S. dioica* 'Minikin'
	- 'Firefly'PBR (d)	CMac CWCL ECtt GBee LBMP LSou NSti SHar SPoG SRkn WWlt
§	- 'Flore Pleno' (d)	GCra MRav NBid NBro NChi NGdn SMrm SSvw WFar WHoo WTin
	- 'Inane'	CDes EBee WBor WPGP WRHF WWFP
	- 'Innocence'	NChi
	- f. ***lactea***	MHer
§	- 'Minikin'	ECha MSCN MTis NGdn WTin
	- 'Purple Prince'	EBee NChi WMoo WOut WTou
I	- 'Ray's Golden Campion' new	WOut WTou
	- 'Richmond' (d)	EBee
	- 'Rubra Plena'	see *S. dioica* 'Flore Pleno'
	- 'Thelma Kay' (d/v)	ECtt EWes NBre NGdn WMoo WWFP
	- 'Underdine'	EBee EWes
	- 'Valley High' (v)	EBee ECtt EWes SPoG WHer WHil
	elisabethae	EWTr EWld LSou SBrt WCot
§	***fimbriata***	CCon CSpe EBee EHrv ELan EPPr EPyc EShb LPla MCot MMHG MNFA MRav NLar NSti SBri SGar SMrm WAbb WBor WCot WMoo WPGP WPtf WRHF WTin
	gigantea	EBee
	hookeri	CPBP GKev
	- Ingramii Group	GKev WAbe
	kantzeensis	see *S. davidii*
	keiskei var. ***minor***	CPBP ECho EWes LRHS NRHS WAbe
	laciniata 'Jack Flash'	GJos
	latifolia	CArn CHab MMuc NMir SEND WPtf
§	- subsp. ***alba***	MNHC SEND
	maritima	see *S. uniflora*
	maroccana	CRWN
	multifida	see *S. fimbriata*
	noctiflora	CHab WSFF
	nutans	CArn EBee SRms WSFF
	orientalis	see *S. compacta*
	pharnaceifolia new	CPBP
	pusilla	CPBP ITim NLar NMen
	quadridentata	see *S. alpestris*
	regia	EBee SPhx
	rubra	see *S. dioica*
	saxifraga	NLar
	schafta ♀H4	CTri ECha ECho ECtt EPfP EWTr MAsh MMuc MRav NBid NHol SRms WFar WHoo WNew WPer XLum
	- 'Abbotswood'	see *Lychnis* × *walkeri* 'Abbotswood Rose'
	- 'Persian Carpet'	SBch
	- 'Robusta'	LRHS NDov
	- 'Shell Pink'	CPBP ECha EWes GJos LBee LRHS NBid NDov WHoo
	sieboldii	see *Lychnis coronata* var. *sieboldii*
§	***uniflora***	CHab ECho ECtt EPfP MMuc MSCN MWat NBro SBch SEND SPlb SRms SRot SWal WMoo XLum
	- 'Alba Plena'	see *S. uniflora* 'Robin Whitebreast'
I	- 'Compacta'	ECho WMoo
§	- 'Druett's Variegated' (v)	CMea CTri ECha ECho ECtt EDAr ELon EPfP EPot EWes GJos LHop LRHS MAsh MHer NBid NMen NPri NRHS SPet SPlb SPoG SRms WFar WIce WPat XLum
	- 'Flore Pleno'	see *S. uniflora* 'Robin Whitebreast'
§	- 'Robin Whitebreast' (d)	CMea ECha ECho ECtt EPfP GCal NBid NBro SRms SRot SUsu WMoo WRHF WSHC
	- 'Rosea'	EBee ECho EPfP MMuc SEND SPlb SRot SUsu WPer
	- 'Variegata'	see *S. uniflora* 'Druett's Variegated'
	- Weisskehlchen	see *S. uniflora* 'Robin Whitebreast'
	- 'White Bells'	CTri MAsh WKif WSHC
	virginica	GKev
§	***vulgaris***	CArn CHab CRWN ELau LEdu MHer MNHC NLan NMir WOut
	- subsp. ***maritima***	see *S. uniflora*
	wallichiana	see *S. vulgaris*
	'Wisley Pink'	ECtt
	yunnanensis	SPhx WSHC
§	***zawadskii***	LRHS MDKP NWad SBrt SWal

Siler (*Umbelliferae*)

montanum	see *Laserpitium siler*

Silphium (*Asteraceae*)

integrifolium	NBre SAga SMad SPhx WCot WOld XLum
laciniatum	CArn CWCL EBee NBre SMad SMrm SPhx WCot XLum
perfoliatum ♀H4	CArn CFis EBee ELon GPoy NBre NDov NLar SMrm SPhx SUsu WCot WOld WWEG XLum

- var. ***connatum***	SPhx
radula	EBee
terebinthinaceum	EBee SPhx WCot XLum
trifoliatum	WCot

Silybum (*Asteraceae*)

marianum	CArn EGHP ELan EPfP GAbr GPoy LRHS MHoo MNHC SIde SPav WFar WHer WHfH WOut WTou
- 'Adriana'	SPav

Simmondsia (*Simmondsiaceae*)

chinensis	CArn

Sinacalia (*Asteraceae*)

§ ***tangutica***	CSam ECha LHop MBel NBid NBro NLar SDix WAbb WCot

Sinarundinaria (*Poaceae*)

anceps	see *Yushania anceps*
jaunsarensis	see *Yushania anceps*
maling	see *Yushania maling*
murielae	see *Fargesia murielae*
nitida	see *Fargesia nitida*

Sinningia (*Gesneriaceae*)

sp.	EABi
* ***caerulea***	WDib
calcaria new	WDib
canescens ♀H1	WDib
§ ***cardinalis***	CSpe EBak WDib
- 'Innocent'	WDib
conspicua	WDib
nivalis	WDib
speciosa 'Blanche de Méru'	SDeJ
- 'Hollywood'	SDeJ
- 'Kaiser Friedrich'	SDeJ
- 'Kaiser Wilhelm'	SDeJ
- 'Mont Blanc'	SDeJ
tuberosa	MCot
tubiflora	CSpe SUsu WCot WKif XLum

Sinobambusa (*Poaceae*)

tootsik	WJun

× *Sinocalycalycanthus* (*Calycanthaceae*)

raulstonii 'Hartlage Wine'	CJun EPfP GKin IArd IDee LRHS MBlu MBri MWat NLar SHil SPoG SSpi
'Venus'	EBee EPfP LRHS MBlu SPoG SSpi

Sinocalycanthus (*Calycanthaceae*)

chinensis	CArn CBcs CHll CJun CMCN CMac EBee ELan EPfP EUJe GKin LRHS MBlu MPkF NLar SHil SMad WSHC

Sinofranchetia (*Lardizabalaceae*)

chinensis	CBcs WPGP

Sinojackia (*Styracaceae*)

xylocarpa	CBcs NLar

Sinopodophyllum (*Berberidaceae*)

§ ***hexandrum***	CArn CBct CBro CRow EBee ECho GAbr GBuc GCra GPoy LAma LRHS MBri MCot MNrw MRav NBid NBir NChi NMen SKHP SPhx SPlb WCot WFar WPnP
§ - var. ***chinense***	CLAP CRow EBee ECho EWld GCal GEdr IBlr LEdu LRHS LWst WCru
- - BWJ 7908	WCru
- - SDR 4409	CPLG
- 'Chinese White'	CPLG WCot
§ - var. ***emodi*** new	GBuc
- - 'Majus'	CCon CLAP EBee GBin WHal

Sinowilsonia (*Hamamelidaceae*)

henryi	NLar

Siphocampylus (*Campanulaceae*)

foliosus RCB RA S4	WCot

Siphocranion (*Lamiaceae*)

§ ***macranthum***	CDes EWes WPGP

Sison (*Apiaceae*)

amomum	CBre

Sisymbrium (*Brassicaceae*)

§ ***luteum***	WHil

Sisyrinchium ✿ (*Iridaceae*)

× ***anceps***	see *S. angustifolium*
§ ***angustifolium***	CMHG ECha EDAr LPBA MCot NBir NChi NLar SChF SPlb SRms WBrk WPer WPtf
- f. ***album***	EDAr MCot NChi NLar
- 'Holly' (v) new	WCot
§ ***arenarium***	MAvo SPet
atlanticum	EDAr NBro
bellum hort.	see *S. idahoense* var. *bellum*
bermudiana	see *S. angustifolium*
- 'Album'	see *S. graminoides* 'Album'
'Biscutella'	CEnt CKno CPrp CTri EBee ECho ECtt EPfP GMaP LEdu LHop NMen NRya SAga SPad SPlb SWal WFar WHal WHoo WKif WNew
'Blue Ice'	CMea CWCL EDAr GEdr LRHS MAvo MCot MWat WAbe WMoo WPer
'Blue Skies' new	EDAr
boreale	see *S. californicum*
brachypus	see *S. californicum* Brachypus Group
'Californian Skies'	CBro CElw CKno CPLG CTri CYeo EBee ECha ECho ECtt GMaP LHop LRHS MAsh MAvo MNrw NBir NDov NMen NRHS NSla SMrm SWvt WFar WKif WMoo
§ ***californicum***	CBen ECho EDAr EHon LPBA LRHS NBro WFar WMAq WNew WPer XLum
§ - Brachypus Group	ECho EDAr EPfP EPot GAbr LPot MAsh MWat NBir NLar SGar SPlb SWal SWvt WMoo
* ***capsicum***	CPLG
coeruleum	see *Gelasine coerulea*
convolutum	NDov
- B&SWJ 9117	WCru
cuspidatum	see *S. arenarium*
'Deep Seas'	MAvo SUsu
depauperatum	MNrw WPer
'Devon Skies'	CElw CHid CTca CWCL CYeo ECho LRHS MDKP MNrw NMen NRHS SBch SWvt WAbe WFar WIce
'Doctor Bailey' new	GKev
douglasii	see *Olsynium douglasii*

	'Dragon's Eye'	CElw CKno CMea CYeo ECtt EDAr EWes MAvo MBrN MHer NRya SMrm SSvw WIce WPer
	'E.K. Balls'	Widely available
	filifolium	see *Olsynium filifolium*
	graminoides	IFoB NBro
§	- 'Album'	NBro
	grandiflorum	see *Olsynium douglasii*
	'Hemswell Sky'	EHoe GAbr NRya
	'Iceberg'	CElw EDAr MWat SMrm
	idahoense	CYeo ECha ECtt EDAr GAbr GEdr GKev LSou MHer NRya SPlb SRms
§	- var. ***bellum***	CKno ECho EDAr EPfP IFro SPet SRms SWal WMoo WNew XLum
	- - pale-flowered	CKno SMHy SSvw
	- - 'Rocky Point'	CElw CSpe EBee EPfP EWes GJos LRHS MAvo SPoG
	- var. ***macounii***	EBee GEdr NRHS NSla SPlb WFar
§	- - 'Album' ♀H4	CElw CMea ECho EPot GAbr GEdr GKev LPot MAvo MWat SPet SPlb WAbe
	iridifolium	see *S. micranthum*
	junceum	see *Olsynium junceum*
	littorale	CPLG NLar
	macrocarpon misapplied	see *S. macrocarpum*
	macrocarpon E.P. Bicknell ♀H2-3	MNrw NMen
§	***macrocarpum***	ECho EDAr MDKP WPer
	'Marion'	CElw CMea CPBP CSpe EDAr MAvo MBrN NDov NLar SMrm SPet WPer
	'May Snow'	see *S. idahoense* var. *macounii* 'Album'
§	***micranthum***	ECho
	montanum* × *nudicaule	ECho GAbr MNrw NRHS NRya NSla SRot
	'Mrs Spivey'	ECtt MHer NBir
	'North Star'	see *S.* 'Pole Star'
	palmifolium	CDes CSpe CTrC LEdu MAvo MDKP MHer MNHC MNrw SBch SGar SMad SPoG WCot WHer WPer WSHC XLum
	patagonicum	CPLG EDAr WPer
§	'Pole Star'	WPer
	'Quaint and Queer'	COIW CPLG CWCL ECha ECtt EHoe LPot MBrN MLHP MNrw NBir NBro NChi WMnd WPer WSHC
	'Raspberry'	CFis CMea EBee
	'Sapphire'	CFis CPrp CYeo ECtt GEdr GJos LRHS NPri SPoG WFar WGrn WMoo
	'Sisland Blue'	EWes
§	***striatum***	Widely available
§	- 'Aunt May' (v)	Widely available
	- 'Variegatum'	see *S. striatum* 'Aunt May'
	aff. ***unispathaceum*** B&SWJ 10683	WCru

Sium (*Apiaceae*)

sisarum	ELau GPoy MHer

Skimmia ✿ (*Rutaceae*)

	anquetilia	CMac
	- (f)	IVic WCru
	- (m)	WCru
	arborescens B&SWJ 11799	WCru
	- subsp. ***nitida*** B&SWJ 8239	WCru
	arisanensis B&SWJ 7114	WCru
	- CWJ 12417	WCru
	black-fruited, B&SWJ 8259 from northern Vietnam (f/m)	WCru
	× ***confusa*** 'Kew Green' (m) ♀H4	Widely available
	japonica	CDul CMHG CMac CWib GQui MGos NPla SSta WFar
	- (f)	CDoy CMac CTri ELan EPfP SRms
	- B&SWJ 5053 (f) and (m)	WCru
	- 'Alba'	see *S. japonica* 'Wakehurst White'
	- 'Bowles's Dwarf Female' (f)	CDoC CMHG ELan EPfP MBri MGos MRav MWht NHol SLim SLon
	- 'Bowles's Dwarf Male' (m)	CMHG ELan NHol NWad SLim
	- 'Bronze Knight' (m)	CMac IVic MBri MRav NWad WFar
	- 'Carberry' **new**	IVic
	- 'Cecilia Brown' (f)	WFar
	- 'Chameleon'	CDul MBri NHol NLar
	- 'Dad's Red Dragon'	MBri NHol
	- 'Emerald King' (m)	MAsh MBri WFar
	- 'Finchy'PBR **new**	MBri
N	- 'Foremanii'	see *S. japonica* 'Veitchii'
§	- 'Fragrans' (m) ♀H4	CDoC CMac CSBt CTri CWSG CWib EBee EPfP LRHS LSRN MAsh MBri MGos MRav MWat NHol NLar NPri NWea SBfd SHil SLim SPer SPoG SWvt WFar WGob WGwG
	- 'Fragrant Cloud'	see *S. japonica* 'Fragrans'
	- 'Fructu Albo'	see *S. japonica* 'Wakehurst White'
	- 'Godrie's Dwarf' (m)	EPfP LRHS NLar NRHS SHil WFar
	- var. ***intermedia*** f. ***repens***	WFar
	- - B&SWJ 5560	WCru
	- - B&SWJ 11165	WCru
	- 'Kew White' (f)	CAbP CDoC CWib EBee ELan EPfP IArd LRHS MAsh MBri MGos NHol NLar NWad SLim SLon SPer SSta SWvt WCFE WCot WFar
	- Luwian = 'Wanto'	WCFE WFar
	- 'Magic Marlot'PBR (v)	EBee EPfP LRHS MAsh MGos MRav MWat NLar SPoG
	- 'Marlot' (m)	EPfP LRHS MAsh MWat NLar SPoG
	- 'Nymans' (f) ♀H4	CDoC CSam EBee ELan EPfP LPot LRHS MAsh MBri MGos MRav SBfd SLim SPer SPoG SReu SRms SSpi WFar WGob
	- Obsession = 'Obsbolwi'PBR	LBuc MAsh NPri
	- 'Pigmy' (f)	CPLG
	- 'Red Dragon' (f)	CMac
	- 'Red Princess' (f)	MAsh WFar
*	- 'Red Riding Hood'	ELon LRHS MAsh NHol SHil SLon SPer
	- 'Redruth' (f)	CBcs CDoC CMac CSBt CSam ELon LRHS MAsh MGos MWat NLar SEND WFar
§	- subsp. ***reevesiana***	CBcs CDoC CDul CMHG CMac CSBt CTri CWSG CWib EBee EPfP GQui IVic LRHS MBri MGos MRav MSwo NLar NRHS SBfd SHil SPoG SSpi SWvt WFar
	- - B&SWJ 3763	MAsh WCru
	- - var. ***reevesiana***	SPer
	- - - B&SWJ 3544	WCru
§	- Rogersii Group	CMac CTri
	- - 'George Gardner'	LRHS
	- - 'Nana Mascula' (m)	CTri
	- 'Rubella' (m) ♀H4	Widely available
	- 'Rubinetta' (m)	EBee EPfP IArd LSRN MAsh MGos SLim WFar

- 'Ruby Dome' (m) MBri WFar
- 'Ruby King' (m) CDoC CSBt IArd LSRN NHol NLar
- 'Scarlet Dwarf' (f) MBri NHol
- 'Snow White'PBR MWat
- 'Tansley Gem' (f) EBee LRHS MAsh MBri MWht SPoG WFar
- 'Temptation'PBR **new** ELan EPfP LRHS MWat
- 'Thelma King' WFar
- 'Thereza'PBR (m) EBee EPfP LBuc MAsh NLar

§ - 'Veitchii' (f) CBar CBcs CDoy CDul CMac CSBt CTri EBee ELan EPfP IArd LRHS LSRN LTen MAsh MBri MGos MRav MWat NHol NLar SEND SLim SPoG SSta SWvt

§ - 'Wakehurst White' (f) CBcs CMHG CMac CSBt CTri ELan EPPr EPfP IVic LRHS MBri MRav NLar SLim SLon SPoG SReu WFar

- 'Winifred Crook' (f) LHop LRHS MBri WFar
- 'Wisley Female' (f) CTri NHol

laureola CDoC CPLG CSam MRav SGar SRms WFar WSHC
- GWJ 9364 WCru
- subsp. ***laureola*** HWJK 2095 WCru
- subsp. ***multinervia*** GWJ 9374 WCru

'Olympic Fire' CWSG
'Olympic Flame' IArd LRHS MAsh MBlu MGos SPoG WFar
reevesiana see *S. japonica* subsp. *reevesiana*
rogersii see *S. japonica* Rogersii Group

Smilax (*Smilacaceae*)

sp. WBor
B&SWJ 6628 from Thailand WCru
aspera CArn CMac EShb EWld LEdu WCru WPGP
china B&SWJ 4427 WCru
discotis CBcs SEND
glaucophylla B&SWJ 2971 WCru
nipponica B&SWJ 4331 WCru
rotundifolia LEdu
sieboldii LEdu MRav
- B&SWJ 744 WCru

Smilacina see *Maianthemum*

Smithiantha (*Gesneriaceae*)

'Extra Sassy' EABi
'Little One' WDib
'Multiflora' EABi
'Santa Clara' EABi

I 'Temple Bells' EABi

Smyrnium (*Apiaceae*)

olusatrum CArn CHab CSev CSpe MHer MNHC SIde SWat WHer WSFF
perfoliatum CHid CSpe EBee EHrv ELan ELon EWes NBir SBrt SDix SMrm WCot WHal WSHC
rotundifolium WCot

Solandra (*Solanaceae*)

grandiflora misapplied see *S. maxima*
hartwegii see *S. maxima*

§ ***maxima*** CCCN CHll

Solanum (*Solanaceae*)

atropurpureum CDTJ CSpe SPlb
aviculare G.Forst. LRHS
betaceum (F) CCCN EShb SVic
capsicastrum SPlb
conchifolium hort. see *S. linearifolium*
crispum NBir SGar
- 'Autumnale' see *S. crispum* 'Glasnevin'
- 'Elizabeth Jane Dunn' (v) WCot WSHC

§ - 'Glasnevin' ♀H3 Widely available

dulcamara CArn GPoy WHfH
- var. ***album*** EHoe LSRN
- 'Variegatum' (v) CMac CWan EHoe MAsh WFar
hispidum CHEx
incanum **new** LEdu
jasminoides see *S. laxum*
laciniatum CCCN CDTJ CHEx CPLG CSev CSpe EShb EWes MCot SBfd SBig SBst SEND SGar SPav SPlb WWlt

§ ***laxum*** EBee EShb LRHS SPer SRms SWvt WSHC

- 'Album' ♀H3 Widely available
- 'Album Variegatum' (v) CWib LRHS WSHC

* - 'Aureovariegatum' (v) CMac EBee EShb LBMP MGos NEgg SLim SPlb

- 'Coldham' EShb GCal SMad
- 'Creche ar Pape' ECha

§ ***linearifolium*** CSpe EBee LBMP SKHP WCot WPGP

muricatum (F) CCCN CHll EShb SPlb
pseudocapsicum 'Thurino' EPfP
- variegated (v) WCot
pyracanthum CDTJ SMad
quitoense (F) CDTJ CSpe SBig
rantonnetii see *Lycianthes rantonnetii*
seaforthianum MOWG
sisymbriifolium SBst WWlt
aff. ***stenophyllum*** B&SWJ 10744 WCru
wendlandii CHll

Solaria (*Alliaceae*)

sp. GCal

Soldanella (*Primulaceae*)

alpicola GJos
alpina CPBP EBee ECho GCra GKev LLHF MAsh NMen SRms WAbe
- SDR 6332 GKev

I - 'Alba' ECho GEdr NSla WAbe

carpatica ECho GKev LLHF NSla WAbe
- 'Alba' MDKP NHar NSla WAbe
- hybrid NMen
carpatica* × *pusilla CPBP ECho ITim NHar NMen NRya NWad WAbe
carpatica* × *villosa ECho LEdu MDKP
cyanaster EBee ECho GEdr GJos GKev LLHF NLBP NMen NRya WAbe
dimoniei EBee ECho GEdr GKev ITim NMen WAbe
hungarica ECho WAbe
minima ECho GJos NMen
montana ECho GEdr GJos LLHF NLar NMen SBch
pindicola ECho EWes NMen WAbe WFar
pusilla NWad
'Spring Symphony' GEdr LLHF
'Sudden Spring' GEdr WAbe
villosa EBee ECho GAbr GEdr GKev LEdu NMen NRya NWad SBch WFar WMoo WPtf WSHC WThu

Soleirolia (*Urticaceae*)

	soleirolii	CHEx CTri EPot EUJe LPBA MWhi SMad SPer SVic SWvt WHer XLum
	– 'Argentea'	see *S. soleirolii* 'Variegata'
§	– 'Aurea'	CTca CTri SVic SWvt
	– 'Golden Queen'	see *S. soleirolii* 'Aurea'
	– 'Silver Queen'	see *S. soleirolii* 'Variegata'
§	– 'Variegata' (v)	LPBA SVic WHer

Solenopsis (*Campanulaceae*)

axillaris	see *Isotoma axillaris*

Solenostemon ✿ (*Lamiaceae*)

'Autumn Rainbow'	WDib
'Beauty' (v)	WDib
'Beauty of Lyons'	WDib
'Black Heart'	WDib
'Black Prince'	WDib
'Brilliant' (v)	WDib
'Bronze Pagoda'	WDib
'Buttercup'	WDib
'Chamaeleon' (v)	WDib
'City of Sunderland'	WDib
'Combat' (v)	ECtt WDib
'Crimson Ruffles' (v) ♀H1	WDib
'Dazzler' (v)	WDib
'Display'	WDib
'Durham Gala'	WDib
'Firelight'	WDib
'Freckles' (v)	WDib
'Gay's Delight' **new**	NPri
'Gingernut' **new**	EUJe NPri
'Illumination'	WDib
'Inky Fingers' (v)	WDib
'Juliet Quartermain'	EUJe WDib
'Jupiter'	WDib
'Kentish Fire' (v)	WDib
'Kiwi Fern' (v)	WDib
'Lemon Chiffon'	WDib
'Lord Falmouth' ♀H1	WDib
'Midnight'	EUJe
'Mrs Pilkington' (v)	WDib
'Muriel Pedley' (v)	WDib
'Paisley Shawl' (v) ♀H1	WDib
'Palisandra'	CSpe
'Peter Wonder' (v)	WDib
'Picturatus' (v) ♀H1	WDib
'Pineapple Beauty' (v) ♀H1	WDib
'Pineapplette' ♀H1	WDib
'Pink Chaos'	WDib
'Red Angel'	WDib
'Red Velvet'	WDib
'Rose Blush' (v)	WDib
'Roy Pedley'	WDib
'Royal Scot' (v) ♀H1	WDib
'Salmon Plumes' (v)	WDib
'Saturn'	WDib
scutellarioides Henna = 'Balcenna'PBR	ECtt NPri
'The Flume'	WDib
thyrsoideus	see *Plectranthus thyrsoideus*
'Timotei'	WDib
Trusty Rusty = 'Uf06419' **new**	NPri SMrm
'Walter Turner' (v) ♀H1	ECtt WDib
'Winsome' (v)	WDib
'Winter Sun' (v)	WDib
'Wisley Flame'	WDib
'Wisley Tapestry' (v) ♀H1	WDib

Solidago (*Asteraceae*)

	Babygold	see *S.* 'Goldkind'
	brachystachys	see *S. cutleri*
	caesia	EWes NBir SMHy WOld
	canadensis	CTri EBee ELan MBel MMuc SEND SPlb WFar WHer XLum
	– var. ***salebrosa***	LRHS
	– var. ***scabra***	WOld WTin
	'Citronella'	ECtt EWll GQue
	'Cloth of Gold'	CMac EBee ECtt EPfP LRHS NPro SPoG SWvt WGwG WMnd
§	'Crown of Rays'	CPrp ECtt ELon EPfP LRHS MRav WFar WMnd WWEG
§	***cutleri***	EBee ECho ELan GEdr MWat NLar SPlb SRms WFar
	– 'Goldrush' **new**	EBee
I	– ***nana***	ECho EWes
	'Ducky'	EBee
	'Early Bird'	NLar WFar
	'Featherbush'	LRHS
§	***flexicaulis***	GMaP XLum
	– 'Variegata' (v)	CWan EBee ECtt ELan GMaP NLar WFar WHer WPer WWEG XLum
	'Gardone' ♀H4	WFar
	gigantea	WFar WPer
	glomerata	EBee NLar SMrm WPer
	Golden Baby	see *S.* 'Goldkind'
§	'Golden Dwarf'	CWCL WPtf WWEG XLum
	'Golden Falls'	LRHS
	'Golden Fleece'	see *S. sphacelata* 'Golden Fleece'
	Golden Gate = 'Dansolgold'	LRHS
	'Golden Rays'	see *S.* 'Goldstrahl'
	'Golden Thumb'	see *S.* 'Queenie'
	'Golden Wings'	CBre MWat
	'Goldenmosa' ♀H4	CMac CSBt EBee EPfP EWes GMaP LRHS SPer SSvw WCot WFar
	'Goldilocks'	NPri SRms
§	'Goldkind'	CSBt CTri EBee ECtt EPfP GAbr IBoy LPot LRHS MCot MMuc MWhi NEgg NOrc SBfd SEND SWvt WBrk WFar WWEG
§	'Goldstrahl'	LRHS NRHS
	'Goldwedel'	EBee
	Goldzwerg	see *S.* 'Golden Dwarf'
	'Harvest Gold'	CElw
	hybrida	see *S.* × *luteus*
	latifolia	see *S. flexicaulis*
	'Laurin'	EBee LRHS NLar XLum
	'Ledsham'	EBee ECtt EWll LEdu LRHS MCot NBre SPoG WMnd
	'Lena' **new**	NRHS SRms
	'Leraft'	EBee
	'Linner Gold'	NBre
§	× ***luteus***	EBee SRms WFar WHil XLum
	– 'Lemore' ♀H4	CPrp EBee ELan EPfP GBuc GMaP GQue LAst LDai LHop LRHS LSou MWat NCGa NSti SMrm SPer SPhx SRms WCot WFar WWEG XLum
	ohioensis	XLum
§	***ptarmicoides***	EBee WPer XEll XLum
	– 'Mago'	EBee
§	'Queenie'	ECha MHer MLHP NBre WWEG
	riddellii	EBee
	rigida	LRHS SMrm WCot
	rugosa	ECha MBNS MMuc SEND SPhx WCot

- 'Fireworks'	CBre CHVG CMHG COlW CPrp CSam EBee ECtt ELon GCal GQue LHop MAvo MNFA NLar NRHS SDys SPhx SUsu WBrk WCot WFar WHoo WOld WTin WWEG WWlt XLum
sempervirens	WCot WFar WOld
- 'Goldene Wellen'	EBee
'Septembergold'	CSam
shortii	EBee
'Sonnenschein'	NBre
speciosa	LRHS SPhx
spectabilis var. ***confinis***	EBee
§ ***sphacelata*** 'Golden Fleece'	CBcs EBee NBre SRms WMnd WWEG
Strahlenkrone	see *S.* 'Crown of Rays'
'Summer Sunshine'	WWEG
'Super'	CPrp WCot
Sweety = 'Barseven' PBR	SPtl
'Tom Thumb'	CMac MRav NBir SRms
uliginosa	EShb XLum
ulmifolia	EBee
virgaurea	CArn EBee GPoy MHer MNHC NLar WHer
- var. ***cambrica***	see *S. virgaurea* subsp. *minuta*
§ - subsp. ***minuta***	GBin
§ - 'Variegata' (v)	CBre EHoe NPro
vulgaris 'Variegata'	see *S. virgaurea* 'Variegata'
'Yellow Springs'	GJos

× *Solidaster* see *Solidago*

hybridus	see *Solidago* × *luteus*

Sollya (*Pittosporaceae*)

fusiformis	see *S. heterophylla*
§ ***heterophylla*** 🏆H1	Widely available
- 'Alba'	CBcs CCCN CSPN EBee ELan EPfP LRHS MCot SLim SLon SWvt WSHC
- mauve-flowered	ECou
- 'Pink Charmer'	CBcs EBee ELan LRHS SLon
- pink-flowered	CCCN CHGN CHll CSPN LBMP LRHS SEND SLim SWvt

Sonchus (*Asteraceae*)

fruticosus	CHEx IDee
giganteus	CHll
pinnatus	SPlb

Sophora (*Papilionaceae*)

cassioides NJM 08.008 **new**	WPGP
§ ***davidii***	CBcs CGHE CPLG CWGN CWib EBee EPfP LRHS MBlu MGos MOWG SBrt SEND SPoG SSpi WPGP WSHC
flavescens	SBrt
fulvida	ECou WPGP
howinsula	ECou IRar
japonica	see *Styphnolobium japonicum*
§ 'Little Baby'	CAbP CWib EBee ELan EPfP EUJe IVic LAst LBuc LRHS LSRN MGos SPoG SPtl SWvt WGrn
longicarinata	ECou
macrocarpa	CBcs
microphylla	CHEx CTri ECou EPfP EUJe LHop LRHS SEND WPGP
molloyi	ECou
- 'Dragon's Gold'	CBcs EBee ECou ELan EPfP LRHS MAsh SCoo SPoG SSpi SSta WPGP
- 'Early Gold'	WPGP
prostrata misapplied	see *S.* 'Little Baby'
prostrata ambig.	CBcs CGHE LRHS SEND
prostrata Buch.	CMac ECou
Sun King = 'Hilsop' PBR 🏆H4	CBcs CWGN EBee ELan EPfP EWes IVic LRHS LSRN MBlu MGos NLar SBfd SCoo SHil SLim SLon SPoG SPtl SWvt
tetraptera 🏆H3	CAbP CBcs CMac CTsd EBee ECou EPfP LRHS NGBo SEND SPer WBor WPGP
viciifolia	see *S. davidii*

Sorbaria (*Rosaceae*)

aitchisonii	see *S. tomentosa* var. *angustifolia*
arborea	see *S. kirilowii*
aff. ***assurgens*** BWJ 8185	WCru
§ ***kirilowii***	CMac CPLG MRav NLar SMad WOut
- AC 3433	MSnd
sorbifolia	CAbP CBcs CCVT CMCN EBee MLHP MMuc NLar NPro SBrt SEND SPer SPlb SPoG WFar
- 'Sem' PBR	Widely available
- var. ***stellipila***	SLPl
- - B&SWJ 776	WCru
§ ***tomentosa*** var. ***angustifolia*** 🏆H4	CBcs CDul CTri CWan EBee ELan EPfP IDee LRHS MMuc MRav NBid NPro SEND SLon SPer WHer

× *Sorbopyrus* (*Rosaceae*)

auricularis	MCoo
- 'Shipova' (F)	CAgr

Sorbus ✿ (*Rosaceae*)

sp.	CMen
MF 96072	GKev
adamii	CMCN
alnifolia	CJun CLnd CMCN EPfP MBlu SLPl
- B&SWJ 8461	WCru
- B&SWJ 10948	WCru
- 'Red Bird'	EPfP MBlu MBri
americana	CLnd NWea
anglica	CDul CNat
'Apricot Lady'	GBin
'Apricot Queen'	CDul CLnd EBee ECrN LAst MMuc NEgg SGol WFar
aria	CCVT CDul CHab CLnd CSBt CTri ECrN LBuc MGos MMuc NWea SEND SEWo SGol WMou
- 'Aurea'	CLnd SPer WFar
- 'Chrysophylla'	CDul CSBt EBee ECrN NWea SPoG
- 'Decaisneana'	see *S. aria* 'Majestica'
- 'Lutescens' 🏆H4	Widely available
- 'Magnifica'	CDoC ECrN ELan LMaj NEgg SCoo SEWo WJas
§ - 'Majestica' 🏆H4	CCVT CDoC CDul CLnd CMac EBee ECrN LHop MAsh MRav NWea SCoo SPer WHar WJas
- 'Mitchellii'	see *S. thibetica* 'John Mitchell'
arnoldiana 'Golden Wonder'	see *S.* 'Lombarts Golden Wonder'
aronioides misapplied	see *S. caloneura*
arranensis	WPat
§ ***aucuparia***	Widely available
- 'Aspleniifolia'	CBcs CCVT CDul CLnd CMCN CMac CSBt CWSG EBee ECrN GBin LAst LRHS MGos MRav MWat NPCo NWea SBfd SLim SPer WFar WJas

§	- 'Beissneri'	CAgr CDul GBin MGos MRav NLar NWea SCoo SLon WHCr
	- Cardinal Royal = 'Michred'	CCVT CDoC ECrN MMuc NEgg SBfd SCoo SEND SEWo SHil SLon WJas
	- 'Dirkenii'	GBin MAsh SGol WJas
§	- var. ***edulis*** (F)	CBcs CDul CLnd CTho EBee ECrN LBuc LMaj MCoo MGos SCoo SPer
	- - 'Rossica' misapplied	see *S. aucuparia* var. *edulis* 'Rossica Major'
§	- - 'Rossica Major'	CDul ECrN GQui SCoo SEWo WFar
§	- 'Fastigiata'	CTri EPfP GKin LAst LMaj MAsh MBlu MGos NPCo WFar
	- 'Hilling's Spire'	CTho
	- ***pluripinnata***	see *S. scalaris* Koehne
	- var. ***rossica*** Koehne	see *S. aucuparia* var. *edulis*
	- 'Sheerwater Seedling' ♀^{H4}	CBcs CCVT CDoC CDul CMCN CSBt EBee ECrN ELan EPfP GKin LAst LHop LMaj MGos MMuc MRav MSwo NPri SBfd SEND SEWo SGol SLim SPer WFar
	- var. ***xanthocarpa*** ♀^{H4}	ECrN EPfP LMaj
	Autumn Spire = 'Flanrock'	CDoC CLnd LRHS MAsh MBri MGos NLar SBfd SCoo SLim SLon SPoG SWvt WHCr WHar
	bakonyensis	IGor
	'Bellona'	WPat
	bissetii	WPat
	brevipetiolata B&SWJ 11771	WCru
§	***caloneura***	EPfP MBlu WPGP WPat
	- Guiz 80	WCru
	carmesina B&L 12545	WCru
	cashmiriana Hedl. ♀^{H4}	Widely available
	aff. ***cashmiriana*** B751 **new**	WCru
	'Chamois Glow'	MAsh WJas
	'Chinese Lace'	Widely available
§	***commixta***	CBcs CDul CLnd CMCN CSto CTho EBee ECrN LAst MBlu MGos MMuc MSwo NLar SEND SGol SLim SPer WJas
	- B&SWJ 10839	WCru
	- B&SWJ 11043	WCru
	- 'Embley' ♀^{H4}	CBcs CCVT CDul CMCN CSBt CTho CTri ECrN ELan EPfP LHop MBlu MGos MMuc MRav NEgg NLar NPCo NWea SEND SGol SPer SPoG WFar
	- Olympic Flame = 'Dodong'	EPfP IArd IDee LRHS MAsh MBlu MBri MWat NLar SCoo SEWo SLim WHar
	- 'Ravensbill'	EBee EPfP NLar SCoo WHCr WHar WMou
	- var. ***rufoferruginea***	GQui
	- - B&SWJ 11486	WCru
	- var. ***sachalinensis*** B&SWJ 8496	WCru
	- - B&SWJ 8515	WCru
	conradinae misapplied	see *S. pohuashanensis* (Hance) Hedlund
	conradinae Koehne	see *S. esserteauana*
	'Copper Kettle'	EBee EPfP MAsh MBri MWat NLar SCoo WHCr WHar
	'Coral Beauty'	CLnd
	corymbifera WWJ 11860	WCru
	croceocarpa	CDul
	'Croft Coral'	MAsh
	cuspidata	see *S. vestita*
*	***decora*** 'Grootendorst'	CDul
	- var. ***nana***	see *S. aucuparia* 'Fastigiata'
	devoniensis	CDoC CDul CNat CTho
	- 'Devon Beauty'	CAgr
	discolor misapplied	see *S. commixta*
	discolor (Maxim.) Maxim.	CLnd EBee EGFP LAst MBlu MMuc NWea SEND WJas
	- MF 96172	MAsh
	domestica	CDul EPfP MMuc NWea SEND SLPl
	- 'Maliformis'	see *S. domestica* f. *pomifera*
§	- f. ***pomifera***	CLnd
	- 'Rosie'	CAgr
	'Eastern Promise'	EBee ECrN EPfP GBin MAsh MBlu MBri MMuc MWat NLar NWea SCoo SLim WHCr WJas WMou
§	***eburnea*** Harry Smith 12799	GQui
	eminens	CDul CNat
	epidendron WWJ 11930	WCru
§	***esserteauana***	CTho EPfP WPat
	'Fastigiata'	see *S. aucuparia* 'Fastigiata', *S.* × *thuringiaca* 'Fastigiata'
	aff. ***filipes*** KR 6453 **new**	WCru
	folgneri	CJun
	- 'Emiel'	EPfP MBlu MBri
	- 'Lemon Drop'	CDul CJun CLnd CWSG EPfP MAsh NLar SCoo SMad
§	***foliolosa***	NWea
	forrestii	CBcs CMCN EPfP GKev LRHS SEND SLPl
*	***fortunei***	CLnd
§	***frutescens***	EPfP NWea WPGP
	fruticosa Crantz	CSto GKev NSla
	- 'Koehneana'	see *S. koehneana* C.K. Schneid.
	'Ghose'	CLnd EBee MBri SCoo
	glabrescens	CSto
	glabriuscula	GKev
	'Glendoick Gleam'	GGGa
	'Glendoick Glory'	GGGa
	'Glendoick Ivory'	GGGa
	'Glendoick Pearl'	GGGa
	'Glendoick Ruby'	GGGa
	'Glendoick Spire'	GGGa
	'Glendoick White Baby'	GGGa
	glomerulata	LLHF
	'Golden Wonder'	see *S.* 'Lombarts Golden Wonder'
	gonggashanica	EPfP GKev
*	***gorrodini***	CLnd
§	***graeca***	WPat
	granulosa HWJ 1041	WCru
	harrowiana	WPGP WPat
	hazslinszkyana	IGor
	hedlundii	CPLG EBee EBtc EPfP GBin NLar NWea SKHP WPGP
	- KR 1687	WPGP
	- KR 1810	WPGP
	hemsleyi	CDul CLnd CPLG EPfP WPGP WPat
	- 'John Bond'	EBee LRHS MAsh NLar SPoG
	hugh-mcallisteri CLD 310	GKev
	hupehensis C.K. Schneid. ♀^{H4}	CBcs CDul CLnd CMCN CMac CTho CTri EBee EPfP LHop MMuc MRav NWea SBfd SEND SGol SLPl SPer WFar WHar WJas WMou
	- MF 96170	EPfP
	- 'November Pink'	see *S. hupehensis* 'Pink Pagoda'
§	- var. ***obtusa*** ♀^{H4}	CCVT CDoC CDul CLnd EPfP NEgg NPCo
§	- 'Pink Pagoda'	CDoC CDul CLnd EBee EPfP IArd LRHS LSRN MAsh MBlu MGos MMuc MRav MWat NLar NPri

		NWea SBfd SCoo SEND SEWo SLim SLon SPer SPoG WBor WFar WHCr WMou
	- 'Rosea'	see *S. hupehensis* var. *obtusa*
	hybrida L.	ECrN
	- 'Gibbsii' 🏆H4	CDoC CLnd EBee ELan EPfP EWTr SPoG WHar
	insignis	EPfP WPGP WPat
	intermedia	CBcs CCVT CDul CLnd CSBt CTho CTri CWib ECrN MGos NWea SEND SGol WHar WMou
	- 'Brouwers'	ELan LMaj SEND WMou
	japonica B&SWJ 10813	WCru
	- B&SWJ 11048	WCru
	'Joseph Rock'	Widely available
§	× ***kewensis***	CDul CLnd NWea SPlb
	'Kirsten Pink'	CLnd CWib EBee ECrN SPer WFar
	koehneana misapplied	see *S. frutescens*
§	***koehneana*** C.K.Schneid. 🏆H4	CBcs GKev GQui IDee NMen NWea WTin
	aff. ***koehneana*** C.K.Schneid.	see *S. eburnea*
	lanata misapplied	see *S. vestita*
	lancastriensis	CNat
	latifolia	NWea
	- 'Henk Vink'	CCVT LMaj
	'Leonard Messel'	EBee MAsh MBri SCoo WHCr
	'Leonard Springer'	ECrN EPfP
	'Likjornaja'	EPfP
§	'Lombarts Golden Wonder'	CBcs CDul CLnd MMuc NWea SEND SGol WJas
	maderensis **new**	WPat
	'Maidenblush'	SGol
	matsumurana misapplied	see *S. commixta*
	megalocarpa	CDoC CDul CJun EPfP SKHP SSpi WPGP
	meliosmifolia B&SWJ 11709	WCru
	microphylla	CMCN
	- GWJ 9252	WCru
	minima	WPat
	monbeigii (Card.) Yü	CLnd
	moravica 'Laciniata'	see *S. aucuparia* 'Beissneri'
§	***munda***	GBin
	aff. ***ovalis*** H 1948	EBee
	'Pearly King'	CTho MAsh WJas
§	'Pink Pearl'	CDul
	'Pink Veil'	NLar
	'Pink-Ness'	MBlu MWat NLar SCoo
	pohuashanensis misapplied	see *S.* × *kewensis*
§	***pohuashanensis*** (Hance) Hedlund	WPat
	porrigentiformis	CDul
	poteriifolia	NHar WPat
	prattii misapplied	see *S. munda*
	prattii Koehne	EBee GKev MBri MMuc SEND
	- var. ***subarachnoidea***	see *S. munda*
	pseudohupehensis	MSnd
	pseudovilmorinii	CDul CPom EBee GBin LRHS MBri
	- CLD 1437	GKev
	- MF 93044	SSpi
	randaiensis	CSto GKev GQui SPlb
	- B&SWJ 3202	EPfP SSpi WCru
	'Red Tip'	CDul MWat
	reducta 🏆H4	CBcs GAbr GBin GEdr GKev GQui MBlu MMuc NHar NHol NSla SEND SPer WFar WPat
	reflexipetala misapplied	see *S. commixta*
	rehderiana misapplied	see *S. aucuparia*
	rehderiana Koehne	CDul CLnd
	rosea	GKev
	- SEP 492	WCru
	- 'Rosiness'	CLnd EBee EPfP MBri SCoo SLim
	sambucifolia	SKHP
	sargentiana 🏆H4	CCVT CDul CLnd CMCN CTho CTri EBee ECrN EGFP ELan EPfP GQui MBlu MBri MGos MRav MSwo NLar NWea SLim SPer SPoG WHCr WMou
	scalaris ambig.	CMCN IDee MAsh MGos MSwo NWea WMou
§	***scalaris*** Koehne	CBcs CCVT CDul CLnd CTho CTri EBee EPfP IDee LHop MBlu MGos SBfd SCoo SPer SPoG WJas
	'Schouten'	ECrN
	scopulina misapplied	see *S. aucuparia* 'Fastigiata'
	simonkaiana	IGor
	subulata HWJ 925	WCru
	- KWJ 12272	WCru
	sudetica **new**	GKev
	'Sunshine'	CCVT CDoC CDul CLnd LTen MAsh MBri MGos MMuc NLar SEND WJas
	thibetica AGS/ES 347	WPGP
§	- 'John Mitchell' 🏆H4	CAgr CDul CLnd CMCN CWib EBee ECrN EPfP MAsh MBlu MBri MGos MRav NWea SLim SPer SPoG WFar WMou
	aff. ***thibetica*** BWJ 7757a	WCru
	thomsonii GWJ 9363	WCru
	- HWJ 984	WCru
	- WWJ 12004	WCru
§	× ***thuringiaca*** 'Fastigiata'	CBcs CCVT CDul CLnd CSBt EPfP MAsh MMuc NEgg SCoo WJas
	torminalis	CBcs CCVT CDul CHab CLnd CMCN CMac CTho CTri EBee ECrN ELan EPfP MBri MGos MMuc MRav MSnd NLar NWea SCoo SEND SEWo SLPl SPer SPoG WFar WHar WMou
	umbellata var. ***cretica***	see *S. graeca*
	ursina	see *S. foliolosa*
	× ***vagensis***	WMou
§	***vestita***	CLnd CTho EPfP WCru
	vexans	CDul GBin
	vilmorinii 🏆H4	Widely available
	- 'Robusta'	see *S.* 'Pink Pearl'
	aff. ***vilmorinii***	GKin
	wardii	CBcs CDul CLnd CTho EPfP MBlu MBri
	'White Swan'	ECrN NLar
	'White Wax'	CDul EPfP LAst MGos SGol SPer SPoG
	'Wilfrid Fox'	CLnd EBee SLPl
	wilmottiana	CDul WPat
	wilsoniana	CLnd GGGa GQui
	'Wisley Gold'	CWSG EBee LRHS MAsh NLar SCoo SLim SPoG WHCr WMou

Sorghastrum (*Poaceae*)

	avenaceum	see *S. nutans*
§	***nutans***	CKno CRWN CWCL SMad SPhx
	- 'Indian Steel'	CMHG EBee GQue SDix WWEG XLum

sorrel, common see *Rumex acetosa*

sorrel, French see *Rumex scutatus*

Souliea see *Actaea*

Sparaxis (*Iridaceae*)

auriculata 'Vanrhynsdorp'	ECho
bulbifera	ECho
fragrans 'Napier'	ECho
grandiflora	ECho
subsp. ***acutiloba***	
- subsp. ***fimbriata***	ECho
- subsp. ***grandiflora***	CGrW ECho WCot
- subsp. ***violacea*** 'Botriver'	ECho
hybrids	LAma
meterlekampiae	ECho
'Piekenierskloof'	
- 'Rawsonville'	ECho
mixed **new**	SDeJ
parviflora	ECho
'Red Reflex'	ECho
tricolor	CGrW ECho SDeJ
variegata (v)	ECho
villosa	ECho GKev

Sparganium (*Sparganiaceae*)

§ ***erectum***	CRow CWat EHon LPBA NMir NPer SWat WMAq WSFF
ramosum	see *S. erectum*

Sparrmannia (*Malvaceae*)

africana ♀H1	CBcs CHEx CHll EAmu EShb LRHS MBri SEND
- 'Flore Pleno' (d)	CBcs

Spartina (*Poaceae*)

'Dafken'	EBee
patens	EPPr
pectinata	SGol XLum
- 'Aureomarginata' (v)	CHEx CPrp CWCL EBee EHoe ELan EPPr EPfP GMaP LBMP LRHS LTen MBri MLHP MMoz MMuc MWhi NLar NOak NWsh SApp SBfd SEND SGar SMrm SPer WFar WMoo WWEG

Spartium (*Papilionaceae*)

junceum ♀H4	CArn CBcs CDoC CDul CTri ECrN ELan ELon EPfP GCal LAst MGos MSCN MWat SBfd SDix SEND SPer SPoG SRms WBor XSen
- 'Brockhill Compact'	CDoC EBee EPfP IVic LRHS

Spartocytisus see *Cytisus*

Spathantheum (*Araceae*)

orbignyanum	WCot

Spathipappus see *Tanacetum*

Spathodea (*Bignoniaceae*)

campanulata	SPlb

spearmint see *Mentha spicata*

Speirantha (*Asparagaceae*)

§ ***convallarioides***	CDes CGHE CLAP CPom EBee ECho EHrv ELon EPPr EPfP LEdu MNrw WCot WCru WHil WPGP
gardenii	see *S. convallarioides*

Sphacele see *Lepechinia*

Sphaeralcea (*Malvaceae*)

ambigua	SPlb
'Childerley'	CSpe EBee ECtt LHop MCot SAga SMrm SPoG WCot
coccinea	SPlb WCot
fendleri	CHll
- subsp. ***venusta***	LHop
'Hopleys Lavender'	EBee LAst LHop LSou SAga SWvt
'Hyde Hall'	ELan
incana	CSpe LHop LSou SAga
- 'Sourup' **new**	CSpe EBee WCot
malviflora	CDTJ
miniata	CCCN CHll SAga SMrm
munroana	CDTJ CPom CSev ELan SAga SRkn WSHC
- pale pink-flowered	CSam ECtt
* - 'Shell Pink'	CSpe
'Newleaze Coral'	CWGN EBee ECtt EWld LAst LBMP LHop LSou MAsh SAga SPad SPoG SRkn SUsu SWvt WCot WWFP
'Newleaze Pink'	LHop SAga SRkn
obtusiloba	SAga
remota	CPLG EBee SPhx SPlb
rivularis	EBee LPla
umbellata	see *Phymosia umbellata*

Sphaeromeria (*Asteraceae*)

§ ***capitata***	CPBP

Sphenomeris (*Dennstaedtiaceae*)

chinensis B&SWJ 6108	WCru

Spigelia (*Loganiaceae*)

marilandica	CDes EBee SKHP
- 'Red Feather'	NLar
- 'Wisley Jester'	SKHP

Spilanthes (*Asteraceae*)

acmella misapplied	see *Acmella oleracea*
oleracea	see *Acmella oleracea*

Spiloxene (*Hypoxidaceae*)

canaliculata 'Kamiesberg'	ECho
capensis 'Somerset West'	ECho
minuta 'Nay'	ECho
serrata 'Saldanha'	ECho

Spiraea (*Rosaceae*)

SDR 6047	GKev
'Abigail'	CDoC
albiflora	see *S. japonica* var. *albiflora*
arborea	see *Sorbaria kirilowii*
§ 'Arguta' ♀H4	Widely available
aff. 'Arguta' **new**	SHil
× ***arguta*** 'Bridal Wreath'	see *S.* 'Arguta'
bella	SLon WTin
betulifolia	EBee GKin MRav
- var. ***aemiliana***	ECtt MAsh MMuc SLPl WFar
- 'Tor'	EPPr
× ***billardii*** misapplied	see *S.* × *pseudosalicifolia*
× ***bumalda*** 'Wulfenii'	see *S. japonica* 'Walluf'
callosa 'Alba'	see *S. japonica* var. *albiflora*
canescens	CPLG GKin
- AC 1354	MSnd

§	***cantoniensis*** 'Flore Pleno' (d)	SLon
	- 'Lanceata'	see *S. cantoniensis* 'Flore Pleno'
	× ***cinerea*** 'Grefsheim' ΨH4	CDoC CSBt EBee MBri MGos SEND SGol SLim SPer SPlb
	crispifolia	see *S. japonica* 'Bullata'
	decumbens	EBee
	douglasii	CMac
	formosana B&SWJ 1597	CPLG WCru
§	× ***foxii***	SLPl
	fritschiana	CMac SLPl SLon
	hayatana	SLon
	- RWJ 10014	WCru
	hendersonii	see *Petrophytum hendersonii*
	japonica	WFar
§	- var. ***albiflora***	CBcs CMac CSBt CTri CWib ECrN ELan ELon EPfP LRHS MGos MMuc MRav MSwo MWat NEgg NPri NWad SBfd SEND SGol SLim SPad SPer SRms SWvt WFar WMoo
	- 'Alpina'	see *S. japonica* 'Nana'
	- 'Alpine Gold'	GBin NPro
	- 'Anthony Waterer' (v)	Widely available
	- 'Barkby Gold'	MGos
	- 'Blenheim'	SRms
§	- 'Bullata'	CMac GEdr NLar NMen SRms WAbe WPat
	- 'Candlelight' ΨH4	CSBt EBee EPfP GKin LAst LRHS MAsh MBri MGos NEgg NLar SCoo SGol SLim SPer SPoG SWvt WMoo
	- 'Crispa'	EPfP NPro WFar WGrn WMoo
	- 'Dart's Red' ΨH4	CDul GKin IVic MWat WFar
	- 'Firelight'	Widely available
§	- 'Genpei'	CMac SGol SPer SPoG
	- 'Gold Mound'	CBar CMac CPLG CWSG CWib EBee EHoe ELan EPfP LRHS MAsh MGos MMuc MRav MSwo NLar SCoo SEND SLim SPlb SRms WFar WHar
	- Golden Princess = 'Lisp' ΨH4	CMac CTri EPfP LBuc LRHS MAsh MGos NEgg NPri SCoo SGol SHil SRms SSta WFar WMoo
	- 'Goldflame'	Widely available
	- 'Little Princess'	CBar CBcs CDul CMac CWSG CWib EBee ECrN EShb LRHS MAsh MRav MSwo MWat NRHS NWea SBfd SCoo SGol SHil SLim SPer SRGP SRms SSta SWvt WFar WHar WMoo
§	- 'Macrophylla'	WGrn WPat
	- Magic Carpet = 'Walbuma' PBR (v) ΨH4	EPfP GBin LBuc LRHS MAsh MMuc NLar SCoo SEND SPoG
	- 'Magnifica'	see *S. japonica* 'Macrophylla'
§	- 'Nana' ΨH4	CMac CSBt ECho GEdr MAsh MRav SRms
	- 'Nyewoods'	see *S. japonica* 'Nana'
	- 'Shiburi'	see *S. japonica* var. *albiflora*
N	- 'Shirobana' misapplied	see *S. japonica* 'Genpei'
N	- 'Shirobana'	see *S. japonica* var. *albiflora*
	- 'Snow Cap'	CWib
§	- 'Walluf'	CMac CTri CWib
	- 'White Gold' PBR	CSBt EBee ECrN ELan EPfP LAst LRHS LSqu MAsh MBri NHol NPro NWad SCoo SLim SPer SPoG SWvt WHar WMoo
	latifolia	MMuc SEND
	'Margaritae'	SPer SWvt
	micrantha	CPLG
	nipponica	CBcs
	- 'Halward's Silver'	MRav NPro SLPl
§	- 'Snowmound' ΨH4	Widely available
	- var. ***tosaensis*** misapplied	see *S. nipponica* 'Snowmound'
	- var. ***tosaensis*** (Yatabe) Makino	LHop
	palmata 'Elegans'	see *Filipendula purpurea* 'Elegans'
	prunifolia (d)	CMac ELan LRHS MBlu MRav SHil SPer WCFE WGrn WPat
§	× ***pseudosalicifolia***	EBee
	- 'Triumphans'	MMuc SEND
	salicifolia	MMuc SEND WFar
	'Sparkling Champagne' **new**	LBuc LRHS SLon
	'Summersnow'	SLPl
	'Superba'	see *S.* × *foxii*
	thunbergii ΨH4	CDul CTri CWib EBee EPfP MMuc MRav NWea SBfd SCoo SEND SGol SLim SRms
	- 'Golden Times'	LRHS SPoG
	- 'Mellow Yellow'	see *S. thunbergii* 'Ōgon'
	- 'Mount Fuji'	CMac CWib EHoe MMuc MRav NPro SEND WFar
§	- 'Ōgon'	WFar
	ulmaria	see *Filipendula ulmaria*
	× ***vanhouttei***	CBcs CDul CTri EBee EPfP MMuc MRav MSwo SEND SLim SPer SRms WFar
	- 'Gold Fountain'	CWSG EBee EPfP EShb GBin NHol SCoo SPoG WFar
	- 'Pink Ice' (v)	CDoC CWib EBee EHoe EPfP LAst LBMP LHop LRHS MGos MMuc MRav SBfd SPer SPlb SPoG SWvt WFar
	veitchii	MRav
	venusta 'Magnifica'	see *Filipendula rubra* 'Venusta'

Spiranthes (*Orchidaceae*)

	aestivalis	NLAp
	cernua	NGdn
	- var. ***odorata***	EHrv LSou
	- - 'Chadd's Ford'	CBcs CBro CDes CPLG EBee ECha ECho ECtt EHrv EWTr IKil LHop LRHS MBel MCot MNrw NBir NCGa NLar NMen NPnk NSti SPad SUsu WCot WFar WPnP WWEG
	spiralis	NLAp WHer

Spodiopogon (*Poaceae*)

	sibiricus	CKno EBee EHoe EPPr LDai SMad
	- 'West Lake'	EBee

Sporobolus (*Poaceae*)

	airoides	CKno EBee EHoe EPPr EShb GCal LPla SMHy SMad WCot WHrl
	heterolepis	CKno EBee EHoe EShb GCal NDov SMHy SMad SMea SPhx SUsu
	- 'Cloud'	EBee GBin
	- 'Weinheim' **new**	EBee
I	- 'Wisconsin Strain'	EPPr LPla
	wrightii	EBee EPPr MWhi SMad SPhx

Sprekelia (*Amaryllidaceae*)

	formosissima	CCon CSpe ECho GHim LAma LEdu SDeJ SPav

Stachys ✿ (*Lamiaceae*)

	RCB UA 2 **new**	WCot
	aethiopica 'Danielle'	see *S. thunbergii* 'Danielle'
§	***affinis***	CArn CCon GPoy LEdu SPlb SVic
	albens	IFro XSen
	albotomentosa	CFis CMea MDKP WCot WWlt

	alpina	EBee
	balcanica	CDes GKev
	- MESE	EBee WPGP
	betonica	see *S. officinalis*
§	***byzantina***	Widely available
§	- 'Big Ears'	Widely available
§	- 'Cotton Boll'	COlW EBee ECha GCal SBch WFar WWEG XLum
	- 'Countess Helen von Stein'	see *S. byzantina* 'Big Ears'
	- gold-leaved	see *S. byzantina* 'Primrose Heron'
	- large-leaved	see *S. byzantina* 'Big Ears'
	- 'Limelight'	WCot XLum
§	- 'Primrose Heron'	EBee ECha GBee GKev LRHS MRav NBid NLar NOrc NSti SMrm SPer SPoG SWvt WFar XLum
	- 'Sheila McQueen'	see *S. byzantina* 'Cotton Boll'
	- 'Silky Fleece'	EBee ECha EPfP EShb EWTr LRHS NBre SBfd SRms WWEG XSen
	- 'Silver Carpet'	CBcs COlW EBee ECha EHoe EHrv ELon EPfP EWTr GMaP LAst LRHS LSRN MBel MCot MRav NOrc NSti SCob SPer SRms SWat SWvt WCAu WCot WFar WHoo WMnd WWEG XLum
	chamissonis var. ***cooleyae***	EBee
	citrina	CMea GCal WAbe XSen
	coccinea	ECtt MCot SBch WMoo
	cretica	XSen
	- subsp. ***salviifolia***	XSen
	densiflora	see *S. monieri* (Gouan) P.W. Ball
§	***discolor***	CFis CMea EBee IKil MDKP NLar
	germanica	EBee NBre
	- subsp. ***bithynica***	SMrm
	- subsp. ***cordigera*** new	SEND
	glutinosa	MDKP XSen
	grandidentata new	WPGP
	grandiflora	see *S. macrantha*
	heraclea	LRHS
	'Hidalgo'	CSpe
	lanata	see *S. byzantina*
	lavandulifolia	WAbe XSen
§	***macrantha***	CKno CMac CTri EBee ECha LEdu LRHS LSRN MCot MLHP MWat NBir NOrc NSti SGar SPhx SRms SWat WCFE WCot WFar WTin WWEG
*	- 'Alba'	EBee ECha
	- 'Hummelo'	see *S. officinalis* 'Hummelo'
	- 'Morning Blush'	WPer
	- 'Motley' (v) new	LEdu
*	- 'Nivea'	CSam ELan NBir
	- 'Robusta' $\mathbb{Y}^{H4}$	ELan GCal LEdu LRHS MMuc NBro NGdn SMrm WCot WRHF WWEG
	- 'Rosea'	CElw CMHG EBee ELan GBee GMaP LLWP LRHS MArl MLHP SPlb SWat WPer
	- 'Superba'	CPrp CSpe EBee ECtt EPfP GCra GKev GMaP LAst LEdu MAvo MRav MWhi NEgg SPer SWvt WBor WCot WFar WMnd WMoo XLum
	- 'Violacea'	EBee GKev LRHS MBrN NChi WCot
	mexicana misapplied	see *S. thunbergii*
	monieri misapplied	see *S. officinalis*
	monieri ambig.	EBee EShb LBMP NLar NSti WOut
	- white-flowered	CSpe GKev
§	***monieri*** (Gouan) P.W. Ball	CEnt GBin LEdu LRHS
*	- 'Rosea'	EBee LEdu NBre NDov NLar
	nivea	see *S. discolor*
	obliqua	NBre WOut
§	***officinalis***	CArn CCVN CEnt CHab CPrp CRWN CSev CWan EBee GPoy LEdu MCot MHer MHoo MMuc MNHC MWhi NLan NMir WCot WHer WHfH WJek
	- SDR 3554	GKev
	- 'Alba'	CArn CPrp EBee LEdu MMuc NBro WFar WTin
	- dwarf	LRHS
	- dwarf, white-flowered	GCal
§	- 'Hummelo'	CPrp CSam EBee ECtt ELon EPPr EPfP GAbr GQue IKil IPot LDai LHop LPla LRHS LSou MBel MDKP MRav NDov NLar SMrm SPhx SUsu WFar WHoo WPtf WWEG XLum
	- 'Marchant's Pink' new	SMHy
	- mauve-flowered	WTin
	- 'Powder Puff'	EBee
	- 'Rosea'	CCVN GCal GQue NBro WFar WSHC WTin WWEG
	- 'Rosea Superba'	EBee ECha MDKP NBre WCAu WCot WFar
	- 'Saharan Pink'	CMHG EBee EPfP LSou MMuc WOut WWEG
	- 'Spitzenberg'	SUsu
	- 'Wisley White'	EBee GQue LRHS NPri SRms WCot
	olympica	see *S. byzantina*
	ossetica	CDes EBee
	palustris	CArn CHab LPBA MMuc NLan NLar NMir SEND
	- from Islay, Hebrides	MMuc SEND
	- pale-flowered new	WOut
	recta	CEnt NLar
	scardica MESE 362	MDKP
	setifera	NBre
	spicata	see *S. macrantha*
	stricta	LRHS
	- 'Alba'	LRHS
	swainsonii	XSen
	sylvatica	CArn CHab NLan NMir WHer WSFF
	thirkei	XSen
§	***thunbergii***	CDes LEdu MBrN MDKP MWhi SBch SUsu WCot WPGP
§	- 'Danielle'	CMac CSpe EBee LAst LHop LRHS LSRN MHer SDys SRkn SRms
	tuberifera	see *S. affinis*

Stachyurus (*Stachyuraceae*)

chinensis	CBcs CJun CMCN CTri CWib IArd MGos NLar SMad SPoG
- 'Celina'	CJun GKin LRHS MBlu NLar SHil
- 'Goldbeater'	NLar
- 'Joy Forever' (v)	CBcs CDoC CMac EBee EMil EPfP IArd IVic LLHF LRHS LSRN MBri MGos NLar NRHS SHil SKHP SLim SPer SPoG SSpi SSta SWvt
- 'Senna'	LRHS NLar
- 'Wonderful Image' new	NLar
himalaicus	NLar
- HWJCM 009	WCru
- HWJK 2035	WCru
- 'Dolly' new	NLar
aff. ***himalaicus*** HWJK 2052	WCru
'Magpie' (v)	CJun EPfP MBri NLar
praecox $\mathbb{Y}^{H4}$	Widely available
- B&SWJ 8898	WCru
- B&SWJ 10899	EWTr LHop WCru
- var. ***leucotrichus***	CJun NLar
- var. ***matsuzakii***	CJun NLar

- - B&SWJ 2817	WCru
- - B&SWJ 11229	WCru
- - 'Issai'	LRHS NRHS SHil SSta
- 'Oriental Sun'	MBri
- 'Petra'	CJun
retusus	CPLG NLar
'Rubriflorus'	CJun ELan EPfP LRHS MAsh MBri NLar SChF WPGP
salicifolius	CBcs CGHE CJun CPLG EBee EPfP IDee MBri NLar SKHP WPGP WPat
sigeyosii	CBcs NLar
- B&SWJ 6915	WCru
- CWJ 12420	WCru
- RWJ 10094	WCru
aff. ***szechuanensis***	CPLG
- BWJ 8153	WCru
yunnanensis	CBcs CJun IArd NLar WSHC

Stanleya (*Brassicaceae*)

pinnata	SBrt

Stapelia (*Apocynaceae*)

divaricata	LToo
gettliffei	LToo
marmoratum	see *Orbea variegata*
variegata	see *Orbea variegata*

Staphylea ✿ (*Staphyleaceae*)

bolanderi	CBcs
bumalda	CJun NLar
- B&SWJ 11053	WCru
colchica	CBcs CDul CHll CJun CMCN EBee ELan EPfP EWTr EWes LRHS MGos MMHG MRav SPer WKif WPat WSHC
holocarpa	CJun EPfP
- 'Innocence'	CDul NLar
N - var. ***rosea***	CJun EPfP SMad
N - 'Rosea'	CBcs CJun MBlu NLar SSpi
pinnata	CAgr CJun EBtc EPfP IVic NLar SEND
trifolia	CBcs CJun NEgg

Statice see *Limonium*

Stauntonia (*Lardizabalaceae*)

B&SWJ 8223	WCru
NJM 09.081	WPGP
aff. ***chinensis*** DJHV 06175	WCru
hexaphylla	CBcs CDoC CHEx CHll CRHN CTri CWGN EBee EPfP ESwi LRHS MAsh NLar SKHP SPer SPoG SSpi SSta WSHC
- B&SWJ 4858	WCru
leucantha KWJ 12218	WCru
obovatifoliola B&SWJ 3685	WCru
- CWJ 12353	WCru
purpurea	NLar
- B&SWJ 3690	WCru
yaoshanensis B&SWJ 8223	WCru
- HWJ 1024	NLar WCru

Stegnogramma (*Thelypteridaceae*)

pozoi	EFer

Stellaria (*Caryophyllaceae*)

graminea	CHab
holostea	CHab CRWN NBir NMir WPtf WShi

Stemmacantha (*Asteraceae*)

carthamoides	CArn
§ ***centaureoides***	ECGP ECha EPPr GAbr GCal GQue LPla NBid SUsu WCAu WCot

Stenanthium (*Melanthiaceae*)

gramineum	EWes
robustum	WPGP

Stenomesson (*Amaryllidaceae*)

§ ***miniatum***	WCot
pearcei	ECho WCot
variegatum	WCot
- yellow-flowered	WCot

Stenotaphrum (*Poaceae*)

secundatum	EShb
- 'Variegatum' (v) ♀H1	EShb LSou

Stephanandra (*Rosaceae*)

chinensis	SLon
incisa	CBcs CPLG
§ - 'Crispa'	CDoC CDul CMac CTri EBee ELan EPfP EWTr GKin LAst LHop LTen MBlu MRav NEgg NHol NLar SPer WCFE WMoo
- 'Dart's Horizon'	SLPl
- 'Prostrata'	see *S. incisa* 'Crispa'
tanakae	CBcs CDoC CDul CMac CPLG CTri EBee ELan EPfP EWTr LAst MBlu MRav NEgg SLPl SLon SPer

Stephania (*Menispermaceae*)

longa KWJ 12163	WCru
rotunda B&SWJ 2396	WCru
sinica BWJ 8094	WCru
aff. ***tetrandra*** WWJ 11896	WCru

Stephanotis (*Asclepiadaceae*)

floribunda ♀H1	CBcs CCCN CSpe EBak MBri

Sternbergia (*Amaryllidaceae*)

'Autumn Gold'	ECho LAma
candida	CBro
fischeriana	CBro
greuteriana	ECho EPot LWst SCnR
lutea	CAvo CBro ECha ECho EPot ERCP EWes LAma LHop LRHS NRHS SChF SDeJ SDix WTin
- Angustifolia Group	CAvo CBro CDes CMea ECho WCot
sicula	CBro ECho EPot GKev NRya
- from Dodona, Greece	LWst
- 'Arcadian Sun'	ECho GKev LWst
- var. ***graeca***	ECho
- - from Crete	ECho
- 'John Marr'	WThu

Stevia (*Asteraceae*)

rebaudiana	CArn ENfk EOHP EUJe GPoy MHoo WCot WJek

Stewartia ✿ (*Theaceae*)

gemmata	see *S. sinensis*
'Korean Splendor'	see *S. pseudocamellia* Koreana Group
koreana	see *S. pseudocamellia* Koreana Group

	malacodendron ♀H4	EPfP LRHS SSpi
	monadelpha	CBcs CMen LLHF MPkF NLar SSpi
	ovata	LRHS SSpi
	pseudocamellia ♀H4	Widely available
	- B&SWJ 11044 from North Japan	WCru
§	- Koreana Group ♀H4	CDul CMCN EPfP LRHS MBri NLar SHil SSpi
	pteropetiolata	CMHG IVic
	- B&SWJ 11726	WCru
	- WWJ 11939	WCru
	rostrata	CBcs CJun ELan EPfP IArd IDee MBlu MPkF NLar SSpi WCru
	serrata	CJun CMen MPkF NLar
§	***sinensis*** ♀H4	CBcs CDul CJun EPfP MBlu MMuc MPkF NLar SEND SSpi

Stigmaphyllon (*Malpighiaceae*)

ciliatum	CCCN
littorale	CCCN

Stipa (*Poaceae*)

	F&M 248	CDes WPGP
	arundinacea	see *Anemanthele lessoniana*
	barbata	CKno CSpe ECha ELon EPPr EWes SApp SUsu WKif
	brachytricha	see *Calamagrostis brachytricha*
§	***calamagrostis***	Widely available
	- 'Algau'	WCot
	- 'Lemperg'	NDov
	capillata	EBee EPPr GCal MWhi
	- 'Brautschleier'	CWib SWal WNew WPtf
*	- 'Lace Veil'	MBel
	comata	EBee MSnd
	elegantissima	CKno EHoe SHDw
	extremiorientalis	CKno ECha EPPr SMad
*	***gerardi***	SApp
	gigantea ♀H4	Widely available
	- 'Gold Fontaene'	CCon CDes CElw CKno EBee EPPr EWes LRHS MAvo MMoz MNrw NDov SMad SUsu WCot WMoo WPGP WWEG
	- 'Pixie'	NWsh SApp WWEG
	grandis	CKno ECha EPPr GBin WMoo WPer
	ichu	CKno MAvo SDix SMHy
	- F&M 32	WPGP
	joannis	GCal
	lasiagrostis	see *S. calamagrostis*
	leptostachya new	WCot
	lessingiana	CPLG EBee EHoe EHul EPPr LRHS SBfd SEND WMoo
	offneri	EBee EPPr EWes LRHS SSvw
	pennata	CKno CSpe EBee EPPr LRHS SBfd
§	***poeppigiana***	GCal
	pseudoichu	CSpe MAvo WCot WWEG
	- RCB/Arg Y-1	EBee ECGP ELon NCGa SUsu
	pulcherrima	EBee EPPr GCal LRHS
	- 'Windfeder'	CCon
	ramosissima	CKno
	robusta	EBee EPPr SPhx
	splendens misapplied	see *S. calamagrostis*
	stenophylla	see *S. tirsa*
	tenacissima	EBee EHul LSRN MAsh SUsu
	tenuifolia misapplied	see *S. tenuissima*
	tenuifolia Steud.	CMea EBee EHul EPfP LRHS MBri MRav NBir NBro NOak NSti WHal WMoo XLum XSen
§	***tenuissima***	Widely available
	- 'Wind Whispers'	CSpe MBel SBfd
§	***tirsa***	EPPr SPhx
	turkestanica	EBee SBfd SUsu SWal SWat
	ucrainica	EPPr

Stokesia ✿ (*Asteraceae*)

	cyanea	see *S. laevis*
§	***laevis***	CPrp EBee ECGP ECha EPfP EWTr LRHS MMuc NLar SBea SEND SMrm SPet SPlb WFar WMoo WPGP WPer WWEG XLum
	- 'Alba'	CCVN COIW EBee ECha EHrv ELan EPfP EPri LEdu LRHS MRav NPnk SPer SPhx
	- 'Blue Star'	CBcs COIW CSam CWGN EBee ELan ELon EPfP GBin LAst LBMP LEdu LRHS MBel MBri MRav NHol NPnk NPri SBfd SMrm SPad SPer SPhx SRot SWvt WHoo WMnd WMoo WSHC
	- 'Klaus Jelitto'	CFwr EBee IPot LEdu LRHS NMRc SHar SPoG
	- 'Mary Gregory'	Widely available
	- mixed	CPou
	- 'Omega Skyrocket'	CPou EBee GBin NHol NLar SBea SMrm WPer WWEG
	- 'Peach Melba'	EBee ECtt NCGa WMoo
	- 'Purple Parasols'	CCVN COIW CWGN EAEE EBee ECtt EPfP EShb GBin IKil LHop LRHS LSou MBel MWat NCGa NPnk NRHS SMrm SPoG STes SUsu SWvt WAul WGwG WMoo WWEG
	- 'Silver Moon'	CAbP EAEE EBee ECtt EPfP LAst LRHS MBel MTPN NBir NHol SMrm WAul WWEG
§	- 'Träumerei'	CWGN EAEE EBee EPfP LAst LRHS NLar NPnk SBfd SMrm SPet WMnd WMoo WPer WWEG
	- 'White Star'	see *S. laevis* 'Träumerei'

Stranvaesia see *Photinia*

× *Stranvinia* see *Photinia*

Stratiotes (*Hydrocharitaceae*)

aloides	CBen CWat EHon EWay LPBA MWts NPer SVic SWat WMAq WPnP

strawberry see *Fragaria*

Strelitzia (*Strelitziaceae*)

alba	CCCN EAmu NPla
juncea	XBlo
nicolai	CAbb CDTJ EAmu EGri NPer SPlb XBlo
reginae ♀H1	CAbb CBcs ELan EShb EUJe LRHS MREP NPer NPla SBig SChr SEND SPlb XBlo
- 'Kirstenbosch Gold'	XBlo

Streptocarpella see *Streptocarpus*

Streptocarpus ✿ (*Gesneriaceae*)

'Albatross' ♀H1	WDib
'Alissa'PBR	WDib
'Amanda' Dibley ♀H1	WDib
'Amanda'PBR Fleischle (Marleen Series)	WDib
'Anne'	CSpe WDib

'Athena'	WDib
'Awena'	WDib
baudertii	WDib
'Bethan' ♀H1	WDib
'Bianca'	WDib
'Black Gardenia'	WDib
'Black Panther'	WDib
'Blue Bird'	SBrm
'Blue Gem'	WDib
'Blue Moon'	WDib
'Blue Nymph'	WDib
'Blushing Bride' (d)	WDib
* 'Boysenberry Delight'	WDib
'Branwen'	WDib
'Brimstone'	SBrm
'Bristol's Black Bird'	WDib
'Bristol's Very Best'	WDib
'Buttons'	SBrm
caeruleus	WDib
'Caitlin'	WDib
candidus	WDib
'Carol'	WDib
'Carolyn Ann'	SBrm
'Carys' ♀H1	WDib
caulescens	WDib
- var. ***pallescens***	WDib
'Charlotte'	SBrm WDib
'Cherub' **new**	CSpe
'Chloe'	WDib
'Chorus Line' ♀H1	WDib
'Christine'	SBrm
'Clouds'	CSpe
'Concord Blue'	WDib
'Constant Nymph'	WDib
'Copper Knob'	SBrm
'Crystal Beauty'	WDib
'Crystal Blush'	WDib
'Crystal Charm'	WDib
'Crystal Dawn'	WDib
'Crystal Ice'PBR ♀H1	WDib
'Crystal Snow'	WDib
'Crystal Wonder'	WDib
cyaneus	WDib
- subsp. ***polackii***	WDib
'Cynthia' ♀H1	WDib
'Dainty Lady'	SBrm
'Daphne' ♀H1	WDib
'Dark Eyes Mary'	SBrm
'Denim'	WDib
denticulatus	WDib
'Diana'	WDib
'Dinas'	WDib
'Dreamtime'	SBrm
dunnii	WDib
'Elegance'	SBrm
'Elizabeth'	SBrm
'Ella'	SBrm
'Ella Mae'	SBrm
'Ellie'	WDib
'Elsi'	WDib
'Emily'	WDib
'Emma'	WDib
'Eve' **new**	WDib
'Falling Stars' ♀H1	CSpe WDib
'Festival Wales'	WDib
'Fiona'	WDib
floribundus hort.	WDib
'Frances'	SBrm
'Franken Alison'	SBrm
'Franken Jenny'	SBrm
'Franken Kelly'	SBrm
'Franken Misty Blue'	SBrm
'Franken Texas Sunset'	SBrm
'Frosty Diamond'	WDib
gardenii	WDib
'Gillian'	SBrm
glandulosissimus ♀H1	WDib
'Gloria' ♀H1	CSpe WDib
'Gwen'	WDib
'Hannah'	WDib
'Hannah Ellis'	SBrm
'Happy Snappy' ♀H1	WDib
'Harlequin Blue'	WDib
'Harriet'	WDib
'Heidi' ♀H1	WDib
'Helen' ♀H1	WDib
'Hope'	WDib
'Ida'	SBrm
'Inky Fingers'	SBrm
'Iona'	WDib
'Isabella' **new**	WDib
'Izzy'	SBrm
'Jacquie'	WDib
'Jane Elizabeth'	SBrm
'Jennifer' ♀H1	WDib
'Jessica'	WDib
'Joanna'	WDib
johannis	WDib
'Josie'	SBrm
'Judith'	SBrm
'Karen'	WDib
'Katie'PBR	WDib
kentaniensis	WDib
'Kerry's Gold'	SBrm
'Kim' ♀H1	CSpe WDib
kirkii	WDib
'Kisie'	SBrm
'Lady Lavender'	SBrm
'Largesse'	SBrm
'Laura' ♀H1	WDib
'Leyla'PBR	WDib
'Louise'	WDib
'Lucy'	WDib
'Lynne'	WDib
'Maassen's White' ♀H1	WDib
'Magpie'	SBrm
'Margaret' Gavin Brown	WDib
'Marie'	WDib
'Mary'	SBrm
'Megan'	WDib
'Melanie' Dibley ♀H1	WDib
meyeri	WDib
'Midnight Flame'	WDib
'Mini Nymph'	WDib
'Misty Pink'	SBrm
'Modbury Lady'	SBrm
modestus	WDib
'Molly'	SBrm
'Monica's Magic'	SBrm
'Moonlight'	WDib
'Myfanwy'	WDib
'Neptune'	WDib
'Nerys'	WDib
'Nia'	WDib
'Nicola'	WDib
'Olga'	WDib
'Olwen'	WDib
'Padarn'	WDib

'Pale Rider' SBrm
'Party Doll' WDib
'Patricia' SBrm
'Paula' ♀H1 WDib
pentherianus WDib
'Pink Leyla'PBR WDib
'Pink Souffle' WDib
polyanthus WDib
subsp. ***dracomontanus***
primulifolius WDib
- subsp. ***formosus*** WDib
'Princesse' (Marleen Series) WDib
prolixus WDib
'Raspberry Dream' SBrm
rexii WDib
'Rhiannon' WDib
'Rose Halo' **new** WDib
'Rosebud' WDib
'Rosemary' (d) WDib
(Roulette Series) 'Roulette Azur' WDib
- 'Roulette Cherry' WDib
'Rubina'PBR WDib
'Ruby' ♀H1 WDib
'Ruby Anniversary' SBrm
'Ruffles' SBrm
'Sally' WDib
'Sandra' WDib
'Sarah' WDib
saxorum ♀H1 CCCN EOHP LSou WDib
- compact CCCN EOHP WDib
'Scarlett' WDib
'Seren'PBR WDib
'Shannon' SBrm
'Sian' WDib
silvaticus WDib
'Sioned' **new** WDib
'Snow White' ♀H1 CSpe WDib
'Sophie' WDib
'Southshore' WDib
'Spirit'PBR WDib
'Stacey' SBrm
'Stella'PBR ♀H1 WDib
'Stephanie' WDib
stomandrus WDib
'Strawberry Fondant' SBrm
'Susan' ♀H1 WDib
'Swaybelle' SBrm
'Targa' (Marleen Series) WDib
'Tatan Blue' SBrm
'Teleri' **new** WDib
'Terracotta' SBrm
'Texas Hot Chili' WDib
'Texas Sunrise' SBrm
thompsonii WDib
'Tina' ♀H1 WDib
'Tracey' WDib
vandeleurii WDib
'Vanessa' SBrm
variabilis WDib
'Velvet Underground' SBrm
'Vera' SBrm
'Watermelon Wine' WDib
wendlandii WDib
'Wendy' WDib
'White Butterfly' **new** WDib
'White Wings' SBrm
'Wiesmoor Red' WDib
'Winifred' WDib

Streptopus (*Liliaceae*)

amplexifolius EBee ECho MNrw WCru
- var. ***papillatus*** **new** GEdr
roseus EBee ECho
streptopoides EBee EPPr LRHS MMHG

Streptosolen (*Solanaceae*)

jamesonii ♀H1 CHll EBak ELan EShb IDee SAga SWvt

Strobilanthes (*Acanthaceae*)

sp. WBor
CC 4071 CPLG
CC 4573 CPLG
anisophylla EShb SDys WCot
atropurpurea misapplied see *S. attenuata*
atropurpurea Nees see *S. wallichii*
§ ***attenuata*** CCon EBee ECGP ECha ECtt ELan EPfP GCal GCra IVic LHop LRHS MBel MCot MRav NCGa NChi NDov NSti SGar WCru WFar WMoo WPer WWlt XLum
- 'Blue Carpet' NDov
- subsp. ***nepalensis*** CHll CLAP MWhi
- 'Out of the Ocean' WOut
dyeriana ♀H1 CAbP EAmu EBak ELan EShb WCot
flexicaulis EBee WPGP
- B&SWJ 354 WCru
aff. ***inflata*** B&SWJ 7754 WCru
nutans CDes CPou EBee NSti SBrt
pendula WBor
aff. ***pentstemonoides*** HWJK 2019 WCru
rankanensis CCon EBee EPPr NMRc SBch SDys SMHy SUsu XLum
- B&SWJ 1771 WCru
violacea CPrp EShb EWTr LHop WPer
§ ***wallichii*** CMac CSam EBee EWes EWld LLWP NSti SUsu WCot WCru WFar WMoo WOld WSHC WWEG
'Wollerton' WWlt

Stromanthe (*Marantaceae*)

sanguinea 'Triostar'PBR (v) XBlo

Strongylodon (*Papilionaceae*)

macrobotrys MOWG

Strophanthus (*Apocynaceae*)

speciosus CCCN CHll EShb

Strumaria (*Amaryllidaceae*)

aestivalis ECho
chaplinii ECho
discifera WCot
subsp. ***bulbifera*** **new**
karooica 'Komsberg' ECho
leipoldtii 'Vanrhynsdorp' ECho
massoniella 'Reitfontein' ECho
salteri 'Nardouwsberg' ECho
truncata ECho
- 'Garies' ECho

Struthiopteris (*Blechnaceae*)

niponica see *Blechnum niponicum*

Stuartia see *Stewartia*

Stylidium (*Stylidiaceae*)

adnatum	ECou MOWG
graminifolium	SPlb
- Little Saphire = 'St116'	NOak SRot
- 'Tiny Trina'	LRHS NOak

Stylophorum (*Papaveraceae*)

diphyllum	CPou EBee EWld GEdr MRav WCru WFar WPnP
lasiocarpum	CPLG CPom CSpe EWes EWld IGor NBid SGar WCru

Styphelia (*Epacridaceae*)

colensoi	see *Leucopogon colensoi*

Styphnolobium (*Leguminosae*)

§ ***japonicum*** ♀H4	CAbP CHab CTho CWib EPfP EWTr LMaj MGos MMuc SPer SPlb
- 'Pendulum'	ELan LMaj MBlu

Styrax (*Styracaceae*)

americanus	NLar
formosanus	CGHE
- var. ***formosanus***	CJun CPLG EPfP WPGP WPat
- - B&SWJ 3803	WCru
- - B&SWJ 6786	WCru
- var. ***hayatiana*** B&SWJ 6823	WCru
hemsleyanus ♀H4	CAbP CBcs CPLG CTho EPfP GBin IArd IDee MBlu MMuc NLar SEND SPer SSpi
hookeri	CPLG
japonicus ♀H4	CBcs CDoC CDul CMCN CPLG CTho CTri CWib EBee ELan EPfP GKin IDee LRHS MAsh MBlu MGos MMuc MRav SChF SEND SPer SPoG SReu SSpi SSta WFar WPGP WPat
- B&SWJ 4405	WCru
- B&SWJ 8770	WCru
- Guiz 216	WPGP
- (Benibana Group) 'Pink Chimes'	CBcs CJun CMac CPLG ELan EPfP GKin MBlu MPkF NLar SCoo SPer SSpi WPat
- 'Carillon'	CJun
- 'Fargesii'	CBcs CDoC CDul CJun CPLG CTho EPfP GBin IVic SCoo SKHP SSpi
- 'Fragrant Fountain' **new**	MBlu
- 'Hyme' **new**	NLar
- 'Issai' **new**	NLar
- 'Pendulus'	CBcs NLar
- 'Purple Dress'	CJun MBlu MBri NLar
- 'Snowfall'	CJun NLar
- 'Sohuksan'	CJun MBlu NLar SSpi
obassia ♀H4	CBcs CDul CMCN CTho EPfP GBin IDee IVic LRHS MBlu MBri NLar SPoG SSpi
- B&SWJ 6023	WCru
- B&SWJ 10890	WCru
odoratissimus	CPLG
officinalis	CBcs
suberifolius WWJ 11868	WCru
* ***taiwanensis***	SKHP
* ***triloba***	CPLG
wilsonii	CPLG
wuyuanensis	CBcs NLar

Succisa (*Caprifoliaceae*)

§ ***pratensis***	CArn CHab CMac CRDP EBee EPri LEdu LRHS MHer MNHC MPie NLan NLar NMen SBch SMHy SPhx SUsu WCAu WHer WHoo WPtf WSFF WTin WWFP XLum
- 'Alba'	EWes
- 'Buttermilk'	CRDP
- 'Cassop'	GEdr NRya
- 'Derby Purple'	CSpe
- 'Peddar's Pink'	EWes LEdu SPhx

Succisella (*Caprifoliaceae*)

inflexa	MSpe SPhx
- 'Frosted Pearls'	CMHG EBee EDif LLWP MWat WHil WWFP

Sullivantia (*Saxifragaceae*)

sullivantii dwarf	WThu

sunberry see *Rubus* 'Sunberry'

Sutera (*Scrophulariaceae*)

(Abunda Series) Abunda Blue Improved = 'Balabimblu'	LAst
- Abunda Colossal Sky Blue = 'Balabolav'	NPri
- Abunda Colossal White = 'Balabowite'PBR	NPri
Cabana Trailing White = 'Sutcatrwhi'PBR (Cabana Series)	WGor
(Copia Series) Copia Dark Pink = 'Dancop19'PBR	LAst NPri
- Copia Double White (d)	LAst
- Copia Gulliver Lavender = 'Dangul16'	LSou
- Copia Gulliver White = 'Dangul14'PBR	LAst LSou
cordata 'Blizzard'	LSou
- 'Olympic Gold' (v)	SCoo
- 'Pink Domino'	SPet
- Scopia Double Pink Pearl (Scopia Series) **new**	LAst
§ - 'Snowflake'	LAst NPer SCoo SPet SPoG
Great Purple = 'Dancop21'PBR (Scopia Series)	LSou
Gulliver Lilac = 'Dancop24'PBR (Scopia Series)	LSou
'Lime Delight' **new**	LAst
neglecta	SPlb WPGP
Scopia Golden Leaves = 'Dancopgoleav' (Scopia Series)	NPri
'Secrets Blue Delight'	LSou
'Secrets Central Pink'	LSou
'Secrets Silver Sky'	LSou

Sutherlandia ✿ (*Papilionaceae*)

frutescens	CArn CSpe SPlb WJek
montana	CSpe

Swainsona (*Papilionaceae*)

galegifolia	CHll
- 'Albiflora'	MOWG WWlt

sweet cicely see *Myrrhis odorata*

Syagrus (*Arecaceae*)

botryophora XBlo
§ **romanzoffiana** EAmu XBlo
- 'Santa Caterina' EAmu
weddelliana see *Lytocaryum weddellianum*

× *Sycoparrotia* (*Hamamelidaceae*)

semidecidua CJun MBlu NLar SLPl
- 'Purple Haze' CJun NLar

Sycopsis (*Hamamelidaceae*)

sinensis CAbP CBcs CPLG CWib EBee EMil EPfP LHop LRHS NLar SKHP SPoG SSpi WFar WHor WPGP WSHC

Symphoricarpos (*Caprifoliaceae*)

albus CDul CMac MSwo NWea SHil
- 'Constance Spry' SRms
§ - var. **laevigatus** EPfP LBuc
§ - 'Taff's White' (v) WMoo
- 'Variegatus' see *S. albus* 'Taff's White'
× **chenaultii** 'Brain de Soleil'PBR **new** EBee
- 'Hancock' CBar CDul CMac EBee ECrN ELan EPfP MGos MMuc MRav MSwo NPro SEND SGol SLim SPer WCFE
× **doorenbosii** 'Magic Berry' MRav NWea SGol
- 'Mother of Pearl' EBee ELan EPfP MMuc MRav NWea SEND SPer
- 'White Hedge' CSBt EBee ELan LBuc MMuc NWea SEND SPer SPlb
guatemalensis B&SWJ 1016 WCru
Magical Candy = 'Kolmcan'PBR EBee EPfP
Magical Galaxy = 'Kolmgala'PBR EBee EPfP MBri
Magical Sweet = 'Kolmaswet'PBR **new** MBri
orbiculatus EBee SLon
- 'Albovariegatus' see *S. orbiculatus* 'Taff's Silver Edge'
- 'Argenteovariegatus' see *S. orbiculatus* 'Taff's Silver Edge'
- 'Bowles's Golden Variegated' see *S. orbiculatus* 'Foliis Variegatis'
§ - 'Foliis Variegatis' (v) CMac CTri EHoe ELan EPfP MGos MRav SGol SPer WSHC
- 'George Gardiner' **new** CMac
§ - 'Taff's Silver Edge' (v) EHoe SGol
- 'Variegatus' see *S. orbiculatus* 'Foliis Variegatis'
rivularis see *S. albus* var. *laevigatus*

Symphyandra see *Campanula*

asiatica see *Hanabusaya asiatica*

Symphyotrichum see *Aster*

Symphytum (*Boraginaceae*)

asperum CSev ECha ELan MRav NLar WMoo
* **azureum** EBee ELan LTen NLar WMnd
'Belsay' GBuc
'Belsay Gold' NBir SDix
caucasicum ♀H4 CElw CMHG EBee ECha GPoy GQue IFro LEdu SBch SEND SIde SSvw WHer WHil WMoo WOut XLum
- 'Norwich Sky' CKno CPLG EWld
cordatum EBee EPPr LEdu MNrw SKHP
'Denford Variegated' (v) NBid
§ 'Goldsmith' (v) CMea CSam EBee ECha EHrv ELan EPfP LAst LBMP LRHS LSou MBri MCot MSCN NBid NBir NEgg NGdn NLar NOrc NPer NPri SBfd SPer WBrk WFar WHoo WJek WMnd WWEG
grandiflorum CArn CMac CTri CWan EBee GPoy LEdu
I - 'Miraculum' **new** EBee
* - 'Sky-blue-pink' EBee IFro
'Grandiflorum' variegated (v) LRHS
'Hidcote Blue' CBar CBre CPrp CTri EBee ECha ECtt EPfP LBMP LRHS MHoo MMuc NBro NEgg NOrc SBfd SEND SLPl SPer SPoG WCru WGwG WMnd WMoo WOut WPtf WWEG
§ 'Hidcote Pink' CWCL EBee ECha ECtt LBMP LPot LRHS MMuc NBir NEgg SBch SEND SLPl SPer SPoG WFar WGwG WMnd WMoo WPnP WWEG
'Hidcote Variegated' (v) CMac
ibericum CArn CSam EBee ECha EHrv EPfP GKev GMaP GPoy LHop LRHS MHoo MLHP MMuc NSti SEND SGar SRms WGwG WJek WMoo WOut
- 'All Gold' ECha ECtt MHer MNrw WMoo
- 'Blaueglocken' CSev EBee ECha LPla WMoo
- dwarf IFro WMoo
- 'Gold in Spring' NLar WFar
- 'Jubilee' see *S.* 'Goldsmith'
- 'Lilacinum' CFis LRHS WHer
- 'Variegatum' see *S.* 'Goldsmith'
- 'Wisley Blue' CBcs CHab CPrp EBee EPfP WFar WMnd WMoo WWEG
'Lambrook Gold' **new** LHop
'Lambrook Sunrise' CMac LEdu MBri NBro WCot WMoo WWEG
'Langthorns Pink' CPom EBee ELan GCal
'Mereworth' see *S.* × *uplandicum* 'Mereworth'
officinale CArn CHab CSev CWan EBee EGHP ENfk GJos GPoy MHer MHoo MNHC MNrw NPer NPri SBfd SIde SPoG SRms WHer WHfH WJek
* - blue SEND
- 'Bohemicum' ECho
- var. **ochroleucum** WHer
orientale CPom GCal MBel SEND
peregrinum see *S.* × *uplandicum*
'Roseum' see *S.* 'Hidcote Pink'
'Rubrum' CDes CEnt EAEE EBee EHrv ELan EPfP EWes GBin GCra LBMP LEdu LRHS NBro NOrc SPer WFar WGwG WPGP XLum
'Sera Howys' WOut
'Snape Cottage' CMea
tuberosum CArn CBre CElw CEnt CPom CSam EPPr GPoy LEdu MHer MMuc SEND WBor WCot WFar WHer
§ × **uplandicum** CSev CTri EBee ELan GCra GPoy SIde SVic WJek
- 'Axminster Gold' (v) CEnt CMea EWes WCot

- 'Bocking 14'	CAgr CEnt CHby CPbn CPrp EOHP EWhm GAbr MNHC SIde WSFF XLum
- 'Droitwich' (v)	WCot
§ - 'Mereworth' (v)	CBct LRHS MMuc NRHS SEND
- 'Moorland Heather'	MHer WMoo
- purple-flowered	MMuc SEND
- 'Variegatum' (v) ♀H4	ECha ECtt ELan EPfP EWes GBuc MBri NBir NGdn NSti SDix SPoG WFar WMoo WWlt

Symplocarpus (*Araceae*)

foetidus	WCot
renifolius	WCru

Symplocos (*Symplocaceae*)

paniculata	see *S. sawafutagi*
§ ***sawafutagi***	CBcs EPfP NLar WPGP WPat

Syneilesis (*Asteraceae*)

aconitifolia	CLAP GEdr WCot
- B&SWJ 879	CDes WCru
palmata	CLAP GEdr LEdu WCot
- B&SWJ 1003	WCru
- B&SWJ 11226	WCru
subglabrata B&SWJ 298	LEdu WCru
aff. ***tagawae*** B&SWJ 11191	WCru

Syngonium (*Araceae*)

podophyllum ♀H1	XBlo

Synnotia see *Sparaxis*

Synthyris (*Plantaginaceae*)

laciniata	EBee
missurica	CLAP
- subsp. ***missurica*** **new**	GBuc
- var. ***stellata***	CLAP EAEE EBee ECre EPfP EWes GBuc GCal LRHS MMHG NCGa NSti SPoG WAul WFar WGwG WHal WMoo WPGP
reniformis	CLAP GBuc WPGP WWEG

Syringa ✿ (*Oleaceae*)

afghanica misapplied	see *S. protolaciniata*
afghanica C.K. Schneid.	IDee IVic
'Alexander's Pink'	WGob
× ***chinensis*** 'Alba'	see *S.* 'Correlata'
- 'Persian Lilac'	WGob
- 'Saugeana'	EWTr NLar SLPl SPer
§ 'Correlata' (graft-chimaera)	EBee
emodi 'Aurea'	NLar
- 'Aureovariegata'	see *S. emodi* 'Elegantissima'
§ - 'Elegantissima' (v)	CBcs CDoC CMac EBee EBtc EPfP GQui LLHF LRHS MAsh NEgg SKHP SPoG SSpi
- 'Variegata' (v)	LRHS WPat
'Hagny'	WGob
× ***hyacinthiflora*** 'Clarke's Giant'	NLar
- 'Esther Staley' ♀H4	CLnd EPfP MRav SKHP
- 'Pocahontas'	EBee GBin NLar
Josée = 'Morjos 060f'	CDoC ELon EPfP LBMP MAsh NLar SPoG SWvt WGob WPat
× ***josiflexa***	CPLG
- 'Agnes Smith'	EBee LAst MMuc NLar WGob WSHC
- 'Anna Amhoff'	GBin NLar
- 'Bellicent' ♀H4	CMac EBee ELan EPfP LAst LRHS MAsh MMuc MRav NLar NSti SKHP SPer SPlb SPoG SRms SWvt WCFE WGob WPat
- 'James MacFarlane'	NLar WGob
- 'Lynette'	NPro
- 'Redwine'	NLar SKHP
§ - 'Royalty'	LRHS LTen NLar SKHP WGob
josikaea	CMCN CSBt EBee NLar SPer WGob
'Kim'	MRav
komarowii	GGGa
§ - subsp. ***reflexa***	CDul EPfP EWTr IDee LLHF MGos SLon WGob
§ × ***laciniata*** Mill.	CJun EBee ELan EPfP EWTr LRHS MGos MRav NLar SPer SPoG SSpi WCFE WGor WPGP
§ ***meyeri*** 'Palibin' ♀H4	Widely available
'Minuet'	CBcs EBee NLar SKHP WGob
'Miss Canada'	NLar WGob
oblata	CMCN
palibiniana	see *S. meyeri* 'Palibin'
patula misapplied	see *S. meyeri* 'Palibin'
patula (Palibin) Nakai	see *S. pubescens* subsp. *patula*
pekinensis	see *S. reticulata* subsp. *pekinensis*
× ***persica*** ♀H4	CJun CPLG CTri EPfP EWTr IDee MGos MRav NLar SLon SPer WFar
- 'Alba' ♀H4	CJun LTen MAsh MRav WFar WPat WSHC
- var. ***laciniata***	see *S.* × *laciniata* Mill.
pinnatifolia	CBcs IArd NLar
× ***prestoniae*** 'Desdemona'	EBtc LRHS MMuc SKHP SSta
- 'Donald Wyman'	WGob
- 'Elinor' ♀H4	CMHG EPfP MRav NSti SKHP
- 'Helen'	MAsh
- 'Nocturne'	WGob
- 'Royalty'	see *S.* × *josiflexa* 'Royalty'
§ ***protolaciniata***	LBMP MAsh NLar SKHP WFar
- 'Kabul'	EPfP NLar
pubescens subsp. ***julianae*** 'George Eastman'	MRav WGob
- subsp. ***microphylla*** 'Superba' ♀H4	Widely available
§ - subsp. ***patula***	CMac ECho LRHS MMuc MRav NWea SEND
- - 'Miss Kim' ♀H4	CDoC CMac CSBt EBee ELan ELon IArd LAst LRHS LSRN MAsh MBri MGos MRav MSwo NEgg NHol NLar SCoo SKHP SLim SPoG SSta WFar WGob WPat
'Red Pixie'	CHll CMac EBee ELon LBuc LRHS MAsh MBri MGos MMHG NLar SCoo SHil SKHP WGob
reflexa	see *S. komarowii* subsp. *reflexa*
reticulata	MBlu
- 'Ivory Silk'	EPfP LLHF NLar SKHP
§ - subsp. ***pekinensis***	CMCN GBin
- - China Snow = 'Morton'	SKHP
- - 'Yellow Fragrance'	NLar
× ***swegiflexa***	CDul CPLG NLar
sweginzowii	GKin SPer
tomentella	NWea SRms
velutina	see *S. pubescens* subsp. *patula*
villosa	SPlb WGob
vulgaris	CDul EPfP LBuc NWea
- 'Albert F. Holden'	WGob
§ - 'Andenken an Ludwig Späth' ♀H4	Widely available
- 'Aurea'	LBuc MGos MRav NPro WFar
- Beauty of Moscow	see *S. vulgaris* 'Krasavitsa Moskvy'

- 'Belle de Nancy' (d) CCCN CDul CLnd CMac CWib EBee ELan ELon LAst MAsh MMuc MRav NEgg SEND SGol SWvt WGob
- 'Charles Joly' (d) ♀H4 Widely available
- 'Congo' LSRN MRav WGob
- 'Decaisne' SPer
- 'Edith Cavell' (d) **new** WGob
- 'Edward J. Gardner' (d) ELon SEND
- 'Firmament' ♀H4 ELan EPfP MRav NEgg SEND SPer WGob
- 'Hope' see *S. vulgaris* 'Nadezhda'
- 'Katherine Havemeyer' (d) ♀H4 Widely available
§ - 'Krasavitsa Moskvy' (d) EPfP EWes IArd LRHS MBri MGos MRav NLar SHil
- 'Lee Jewett Walker' SSta
- 'Lila Wonder' PBR **new** EBee EPfP
- 'Madame Florent Stepman' CMac NLar WGob
- 'Madame Lemoine' (d) ♀H4 Widely available
- 'Masséna' MRav SPer
- 'Maud Notcutt' EWes
- 'Michel Buchner' (d) CBcs CDul CWib EBee ELan LAst MBlu MGos MRav NLar SBfd SCoo SLim SPer WGob
- 'Miss Ellen Willmott' (d) IArd MRav NLar
- 'Mrs Edward Harding' (d) ♀H4 EBee EPfP LAst LBuc MRav NLar NWea SCoo SPer WGob
§ - 'Nadezhda' (d) MBri
- 'Olivier de Serres' (d) NLar
- 'Pat Pesata' WGob
- 'Paul Deschanel' (d) NLar
- 'Paul Thirion' (d) WGob
- 'Président Grévy' (d) CBar CDoC CMac EBee EMil EPfP LRHS MAsh SLim
- 'Primrose' CBcs CCCN CDul CMac CWib EBee ELan ELon EPfP GBin IArd LRHS MAsh MBri MGos MMuc MSnd NEgg NLar SCoo SEND SHil SKHP SPer WFar WGob
- 'Prince Wolkonsky' (d) EBee EMil EPfP LSRN LTen SPer WGob
- 'Princesse Sturdza' EMil MAsh
- 'Professor Hoser' **new** WGob
- 'Ruhm von Horstenstein' MBri
- 'Sensation' CBcs CDoC CMac CSBt CWSG EBee ELon EPfP IArd LAst LRHS LSRN LSou MAsh MBri MGos MMuc MRav MSwo NEgg NLar NWea SCoo SEND SHil SKHP SLim SPer SPoG WGob
- 'Souvenir de Louis Spaeth' see *S. vulgaris* 'Andenken an Ludwig Späth'
- 'Ukraina' WGob
- variegated (v) EWes
- 'Vestale' ♀H4 EWes MRav
- 'Victor Lemoine' (d) **new** MBri WGob
- 'Viviand-Morel' (d) CMac GAbr LLHF NEgg SKHP WGob
- 'William Robinson' (d) SPer

wolfii CArn EBtc
yunnanensis CPLG GGGa LLHF
- 'Prophecy' WGob

Syringodea (*Iridaceae*)

longituba 'Perdekraal' ECho

Syzygium (*Myrtaceae*)

australe ERom EShb
paniculatum CPLG EShb IDee

T

Tabernaemontana (*Apocynaceae*)

coronaria see *T. divaricata*
§ ***divaricata*** CCCN

Tacca (*Taccaceae*)

chantrieri CCCN EAmu
- 'Green Isle' **new** GHim
- f. ***macrantha*** **new** GHim
integrifolia EAmu GHim

Tacitus see *Graptopetalum*

Tagetes (*Asteraceae*)

'Cinnabar' SDix
lemmonii SBfd SDix SHDw WJek
'Lemon Gem' WJek
lucida CArn ENfk EOHP LEdu MHoo WJek
patula Durango Series **new** NPri
- - 'Durango Bee' **new** NPri
- - 'Durango Flame' **new** NPri
- - 'Durango Orange' **new** NPri
- - 'Durango Yellow' **new** NPri
- - 'Durango Yellow Fire' **new** NPri

Talbotia (*Velloziaceae*)

§ ***elegans*** CSpe WCot

Talinum (*Portulacaceae*)

'Zoe' CPBP

Tamarix (*Tamaricaceae*)

chinensis CSBt
gallica CMen CSBt MGos NWea SEND WSHC
hampeana SEND
§ ***parviflora*** CMac EPfP IVic LRHS MGos SPoG
pentandra see *T. ramosissima*
§ ***ramosissima*** CCCN CMac CTri ECrN ELan EPfP MAsh MWhi SEWo SLim SLon SRms WSHC
- 'Hulsdonk White' **new** EBee
- 'Pink Cascade' CBcs CCCN CDul CSBt EBee ELon EPfP LRHS MBlu MBri MGos MREP MRav NEgg SBfd SBod SEND SGol SPer SPoG SWvt
- 'Rosea' CBcs
§ - 'Rubra' ♀H4 CDoC CWSG EBee EPfP IVic MGos NLar SLon SPer
- 'Summer Glow' see *T. ramosissima* 'Rubra'
tetrandra ♀H4 CBcs CCVT CDul CMac CSBt CWib EBee ELan EPfP LRHS MAsh MBlu MBri MRav MSwo MWat NLar NPer SBfd SEND SGol SHil SPer SPlb SRms SWvt WHar
- 'Africance' EBee ERom
- var. ***purpurea*** see *T. parviflora*

tamarillo see *Solanum betaceum*

tamarind see *Tamarindus indica*

Tamarindus (*Caesalpiniaceae*)

indica (F) SPlb

Tamus (*Dioscoreaceae*)

communis	CArn

Tanacetum ✿ (*Asteraceae*)

CC 6343	GKev
§ ***argenteum***	ECho MRav SIde
– subsp. ***canum***	ECho EWes LRHS MAsh SLon
§ ***balsamita***	CArn CHby CPrp EBee ELan ELau ENfk GPoy LEdu MHer MHoo MNHC WHfH WJek WTin XLum XSen
§ – subsp. ***balsamita***	GPoy SIde
§ – subsp. ***balsamitoides***	CHby CPrp MHer WJek
– var. ***tanacetoides***	see *T. balsamita* subsp. *balsamita*
– ***tomentosum***	see *T. balsamita* subsp. *balsamitoides*
capitatum	see *Sphaeromeria capitata*
§ ***cinerariifolium***	CArn CPrp CWan GPoy MNHC WJek
coccineum 'Aphrodite' (d)	NEgg
– 'Beauty of Stapleford'	NEgg
– 'Bees' Pink Delight'	NEgg
– 'Brenda'	EPfP
– 'Duro'	EBee LRHS
– 'Eileen May Robinson' ♀H4	EBee EPfP LRHS LSRN NGdn
– 'Evenglow'	EPfP
– 'James Kelway' ♀H4	EPfP MRav NBir
– 'King Size'	SGar WFar
– Robinson's giant-flowered	SRms
– Robinson's pink-flowered	CCse EBee ELan EPfP EWll GMaP SBfd WPer WWEG XLum
– Robinson's red-flowered	CSBt EBee EPfP GMaP MLHP SBfd SPlb SWvt WPer WWEG XLum
– Robinson's rose-flowered	SBfd
– Robinson's, mixed	SBfd
– 'Scarlet Glow'	EWll
– 'Snow Cloud'	ECtt ELan EPfP WWEG
– 'Vanessa'	LRHS MNrw
§ ***corymbosum***	GCal
– 'Festtafel'	LPla
densum	ECho EDAr WCFE
– subsp. ***amani***	EBee ECha ECho GMaP LRHS MAsh MWat XSen
– subsp. ***sivasicum***	XSen
§ ***haradjanii***	ECho ECtt SBch WKif
huronense	EBee
macrophyllum misapplied	see *Achillea grandifolia* Friv.
§ ***macrophyllum*** (Waldst. & Kit.) Sch.Bip.	CPrp ECtt EPPr LPla SPhx
– 'Cream Klenza'	WCot
niveum	ECha WCot
– 'Jackpot'	CWib EBee EPfP EWes SSvw SWvt
§ ***parthenium***	CArn CHab CHby CPbn CWan ELau ENfk GPoy MHer MHoo MNHC NPer SBfd SIde SRms SVic WHer WJek XLum
– 'Aureum'	CHid CPbn CPrp CRow CWan ECha EGHP ELan ELau ENfk EWes GPoy LPot MBri MHer MLHP MNHC MRav SBfd SPer SPlb SRms SWvt WFar WHer WJek WMoo XLum
– 'Cartwheels'	MAvo SUsu
– double white-flowered (d)	MHoo NPer SRms
– 'Golden Ball'	EPfP
– 'Golden Moss'	XLum
– 'Plenum' (d)	EHrv SBch
§ – 'Rowallane' (d)	MMuc SEND WCot
– 'Sissinghurst White'	see *T. parthenium* 'Rowallane'
– 'Snowball' (d)	EPfP
poteriifolium	EBee LRHS MAvo
§ ***ptarmiciflorum*** ♀H3-4	WCot
– 'Silver Feather'	WJek
* ***tommansii***	LRHS
vulgare	CArn CHab CHby CMac CSev ECha ECtt ELau ENfk GPoy MHer MHoo MNHC SBfd SIde SVic WJek WMoo WSFF XSen
– 'All Gold'	CSev SMad
– var. ***crispum***	CPrp CWan EBee ELau ENfk MHer MNHC MRav SBfd SIde SMad WFar WJek
– 'Golden Fleece'	ECtt EWes LEdu LRHS LSou NSti SPer SUsu WCot WGrn WRHF
– 'Isla Gold' (v)	EBee ECtt EWes GMaP LDai LEdu LHop LPla MHer MMuc MRav SEND SMrm WAbb WCot WFar WJek WMoo
– 'Silver Lace' (v)	CBre EBee EGHP EWes NBid SEND WFar WHer WJek WMoo

Tanakaea (*Saxifragaceae*)

radicans	WCru

tangelo see *Citrus × tangelo*

tangerine see *Citrus reticulata*

Taraxacum (*Asteraceae*)

albidum	GLin
faeroense	EPPr WCot
officinale agg.	CArn CHab
– 'Nettleton'	CNat
rubrifolium	CBre CSpe EPPr

tarragon see *Artemisia dracunculus*

Tasmannia see *Drimys*

Taxodium (*Cupressaceae*)

ascendens 'Nutans'	see *T. distichum* var. *imbricarium* 'Nutans'
distichum ♀H4	Widely available
– 'Cascade Falls'PBR	IArd LRHS MBlu MBri MGos NLar NPri SLim
– 'Cave Hill'	SLim
– 'Falling Waters'	CBcs SGol SKHP WMou
– 'Gee Whiz' new	SLim
– 'Hursley Park'	NLar SLim
– var. ***imbricarium***	CMCN EPfP LRHS
§ – – 'Nutans' ♀H4	CBcs EPfP IArd LRHS MBlu NLar SCoo SGol SLim SMad
– 'Little Leaf'	NLar SLim
– 'Minaret'	IArd MBlu
* – 'Pendulum'	IArd IDee
– 'Peve Minaret'	CDoC CMen LRHS MBri MGos NLar SEWo SGol SKHP SLim SPoG
– 'Peve Yellow'	MBlu NLar
– 'Schloss Herten'	LRHS NLar SLim
– 'Secrest'	CBcs MBlu NLar SLim
– Shawnee Brave = 'Mickelson'	MBlu
mucronatum	CDoC CPLG
– NJM 09.037	WPGP

Taxus ✿ (*Taxaceae*)

baccata ♀H4	Widely available

	– 'Adpressa Aurea' (v)	CKen GKin
	– 'Adpressa Variegata' (m/v) ♀H4	CDoC
	– 'Aldenham Gold'	CKen
	– 'Amersfoort'	CDoC GKin LRHS NLar SCoo
	– Aurea Group	CDul EOHP SRms
I	– 'Aureomarginata' (v)	CBcs MAsh NEgg SWvt WGor
	– 'Autumn Shades'	CBcs NLar
	– 'Bridget's Gold'	CKen
	– 'Corleys Coppertip'	CKen EBtc LRHS MBri MRav NHol NLar SCoo SEND SLim WEve WFar
	– 'Cristata'	CKen MAsh NLar
	– 'David'	IArd MBri NLar SPoG WEve
	– 'Dovastoniana' (f) ♀H4	CMac NLar NWea WMou
	– 'Dovastonii Aurea' (m/v) ♀H4	CBcs EPfP GKin MBlu MBri NEgg NLar NPCo NWea SGol SLim WCFE WFar
	– 'Elegantissima' (f/v)	CTho ECrN EHul EPfP LRHS NPCo NWea SCoo WFar WGor
	– 'Erecta' (f)	EHul
§	– 'Fastigiata' (f) ♀H4	CBcs CDul CMac CSBt CTho CTri CWib ECrN EHul ELan EPfP LAst MGos MRav MSwo MWat NEgg NPCo NWea SBfd SEWo SGol SLim SPer SPoG SRms SWvt WFar WHar
	– Fastigiata Aurea Group	CLnd CMac CWib EPfP GKev IArd LBuc LMaj MAsh MGos MWat NHol SGol SRms WFar WHar
	– 'Fastigiata Aureomarginata' (m/v) ♀H4	CDoC CDul CMac CSBt CTri EHul EPfP LBee LRHS MBri MGos NWea SAga SBfd SCoo SLim SLon SPer SPoG SWvt WEve
	– 'Fastigiata Robusta' (f)	CDoC CSBt EBtc EPfP LRHS MBri NHol NLar NPCo SCoo SLim SPoG WEve WFar
	– 'Goud Elsje'	CKen NLar
	– 'Grayswood Hill'	NLar
	– 'Green Column'	CKen
	– 'Green Diamond'	CKen NLar
	– 'Green Rocket'	CDul NLar
	– 'Hibernica'	see *T. baccata* 'Fastigiata'
	– 'Icicle'	CBcs LRHS MAsh MGos NHol NLar NWad SLim WEve
	– 'Itsy Bitsy'	CKen
	– 'Ivory Tower'	CBcs CDoC CKen ELan MGos NEgg NHol NLar NPCo NWad SLim WEve WFar WGor
	– 'Klitzeklein'	CKen
	– 'Litfass'	NLar
	– 'Lutea' (f)	SLim
	– 'Nutans'	CDoC CKen
	– 'Pendula'	MRav
	– 'Prostrata'	CMac WFar
	– 'Pygmaea'	CKen WEve
	– 'Repandens' (f) ♀H4	EHul IArd NWea WCFE WFar
I	– 'Repens Aurea' (v) ♀H4	CDoC CDul CKen CMac EHul MBri MGos NEgg SCoo WEve WFar
	– 'Rushmore'	MBri
	– 'Semperaurea' (m) ♀H4	CBcs CDoC CMac EHul LBuc LTen MAsh MBri MGos NWea SCoo SGol SLim SPoG WFar
	– 'Silver Spire' (v)	CKen MDKP
	– 'Standishii' (f) ♀H4	Widely available
	– 'Stove Pipe'	CKen
	– 'Summergold' (v)	EHul ELan EPfP LRHS MAsh MGos MRav MWat NBir NEgg NHol NLar SCoo SLim WEve WFar
	– 'White Icicle'	MGos WGor
	brevifolia	NHol NLar
	cuspidata	CMen
	– 'Aurescens' (v)	CKen
	– 'Minuet'	CKen
	– 'Robusta'	EHul
	– 'Silver Queen'	SLim
	– 'Straight Hedge'	LRHS SBod SLim
	× ***media*** 'Brownii'	LBuc
	– 'Hicksii' (f) ♀H4	CDul LBuc LMaj LRHS MGos NLar NWea SCoo SGol SLim WFar
	– 'Hillii'	LBMP LBuc LTen
	– 'Lodi'	LBee
	– 'Nixe'	SLim

Tayberry see *Rubus* Tayberry Group

Tecoma (*Bignoniaceae*)

	capensis ♀H1	CHII CRHN MOWG
	– 'Aurea'	MOWG
	cochabambensis RCB RA L-8	WCot
	'Orange Glow'	MOWG
	ricasoliana	see *Podranea ricasoliana*
	stans	EUJe

Tecomanthe (*Bignoniaceae*)

	speciosa	ECou

Tecomaria see *Tecoma*

Tecophilaea (*Tecophilaeaceae*)

	cyanocrocus ♀H2	ECho LAma LLHF LRHS NMin NRHS
	– 'Leichtlinii' ♀H2	ECho EPot LAma LLHF LRHS NMin NRHS SCnR SDeJ
	– 'Purpurea'	see *T. cyanocrocus* 'Violacea'
	– Storm Cloud Group	ECho LLHF
§	– 'Violacea'	ECho EPot LLHF LRHS NMin NRHS
	violiflora	ECho LAma

Telanthophora (*Asteraceae*)

§	***grandifolia***	CHEx

Telekia (*Asteraceae*)

§	***speciosa***	CCon CMac COIW CSam CSpe EBee ELan EPPr EPfP GAbr LRHS MBel MMuc MRav NBro NChi NLar SDix SEND SLPl SPlb WBrk WCFE WFar WHer WMoo WWEG

Telesonix see *Boykinia*

Teline see *Genista*

Tellima (*Saxifragaceae*)

	grandiflora	Widely available
	– 'Bob's Choice'	WCot
	– 'Delphine' (v)	EBee EPPr XLum
	– 'Forest Frost'	CBct CFis CMac EBee ECGP LAst LHop LRHS NBre NDov NLar NOrc SBch WCot WGwG WHoo WMoo WOut WWEG
	– Odorata Group	CBre ECha EHrv MRav WCot WMoo
	– 'Purpurea'	see *T. grandiflora* Rubra Group
	– 'Purpurteppich'	EBee ECha EHoe EHrv EPPr LHop LRHS MRav NDov NRHS WCot WMnd WMoo WPtf WWEG
§	– Rubra Group	Widely available
	– 'Silver Select'	EPPr

Telopea (*Proteaceae*)

'Dawn Fire' CTrC
oreades SPlb
speciosissima CCCN SPlb
- 'Red Embers' CTrC
truncata CCCN SPlb WCru

Templetonia (*Papilionaceae*)

retusa ECou

Temu see *Blepharocalyx*

Tetracentron (*Trochodendraceae*)

sinense CBcs EPfP IArd NLar

Tetradenia (*Lamiaceae*)

riparia EOHP

Tetradium (*Rutaceae*)

austrosinense WPGP
NJM 09.215 **new**
§ ***daniellii*** CBcs CCVT CMCN EPfP IArd IDee LEdu LRHS SSpi WPGP
* ***- henryi*** NLar
§ - Hupehense Group CMCN CTho GBin MBri MSnd NLar
glabrifolium B&SWJ 6882 WCru
- CWJ 12364 WCru
ruticarpum LEdu WPGP
- B&SWJ 3541 WCru
* ***velutinum*** NLar

Tetragonia (*Aizoaceae*)

tetragonoides CArn

Tetragonolobus see *Lotus*

Tetraneuris (*Asteraceae*)

§ ***acaulis*** var. ***caespitosa*** CPBP
§ ***grandiflora*** WIce
- NNS 08-210 GKev
scaposa EPot

Tetrapanax (*Araliaceae*)

§ ***papyrifer*** ♀H2-3 CBrP CDTJ CHEx CHGN ESwi MBri NLar SBig SBst XBlo
- B&SWJ 7135 CBcs EUJe SEND WCru
- 'Di-Sue-Shan' WCru
- 'Empress' WCru
- 'Rex' Widely available
- 'Steroidal Giant' CDTJ SBig SKHP

Tetrapathaea see *Passiflora*

Tetrastigma (*Vitaceae*)

obtectum CCCN CTsd EBee ECre EWes WCFE

Tetratheca (*Elaeocarpaceae*)

'Bicentennial Belle' LRHS
ciliata var. ***alba*** MOWG
thymifolia pink-flowered MOWG

Teucridium (*Lamiaceae*)

parvifolium ECou MPie

Teucrium (*Lamiaceae*)

* ***ackermannii*** CMea ECho LBee NMen SBch WAbe WHoo WTin XSen
arduinoi SEND XSen
aroanium ECho EPot GEdr MWat XSen
asiaticum XSen
botrys MHer
canadense XSen
chamaedrys misapplied see *T.* × ***lucidrys***
chamaedrys L. CBar CPom CPrp CWan CWib ELon ENfk GMaP GPoy LAst LRHS LSRN MHoo MNHC MSwo NWad SBfd SEND SLim SMad SPlb SRms WBrk WHfH WJek WWEG XSen
- 'Nanum' ECho
divaricatum XSen
dunense XSen
flavum CArn EDAr EPPr NBre WJek XSen
fruticans Widely available
- 'Azureum' ♀H3 CBcs COlW CWSG EBee ELan EPfP LAst LRHS LSRN MGos MRav SBfd SEND SMad SPer SPoG SPtl WCFE WKif XSen
- 'Compactum' CDoC EBee ELan ELon EWTr LAst LRHS LSRN MGos SLim SLon SPer SPoG WCFE WPGP WPnn
- 'Drysdale' CDoC CSBt EBee LRHS SLim
gnaphalodes XSen
hircanicum CArn CSam CSev EBee ECtt ELan EPfP IFro LLWP LRHS LSRN MMuc MNrw MWhi NBir NLar SBfd SEND SGar SMrm SPhx SRkn WCFE WCot WJek WMoo WPtf WTin XSen
- 'Flowtime' EBee
- 'Paradise Delight' EBee ECtt NLar NPnk WBor
- 'Purple Tails' COlW CPrp CWib EPfP LSou MDev MNHC NBir SMad SPad SWal WPer WWEG
§ × ***lucidrys*** CArn CMea CSev CWan EBee ECha ECrN ELan ENfk EPfP LRHS MGos MHer MMuc MNHC MRav SGar SIde SPer SPoG WCFE WCot WHoo WJek WPnn XSen
lucidum GCal MWat
marum CArn CMea CTri NMen WJek XSen
massiliense misapplied see *T.* × ***lucidrys***
massiliense L. EBee XSen
montanum EDAr WJek XSen
musimonum EPot
nivale EBee
orientale XSen
polium MWat WJek WThu XSen
- subsp. ***aureum*** XSen
pseudochamaepitys **new** XSen
pyrenaicum CMea CPBP CPom EPot EWes GEdr SBch XSen
- subsp. ***guarense*** XSen
scordium CNat
scorodonia CArn CHab CRWN GPoy MCot MHer MNHC NLar NMir WHer WJek XSen
- 'Binsted Gold' EBee LDai MMoz NSti
- 'Crispum' EHrv LEdu LRHS MHer MMuc NBro NLar SBch SEND SPer SRms WGrn WGwG WJek WKif WMnd WMoo WPer
- 'Crispum Marginatum' (v) CFis COlW EBee ECGP ECha EHoe EPPr EPfP LEdu LSou MNrw MRav NSti WTin WWEG
- 'Spring Morn' EBee
- 'Winterdown' (v) EBee NPro SBch
subspinosum ECho GEdr LBee LLHF LRHS MWat NMen NWad WHoo WThu XSen

§ ***viscidum*** 'Lemon and Lime' (v) — EBee LSou
webbianum — ECho XSen

Thalia (*Marantaceae*)

dealbata — CBen CHEx EAmu EUJe EWay LPBA MSKA MWts NLar SBig SDix SLon WMAq
geniculata* f. *rheumoides new — EAmu

Thalictrum (*Ranunculaceae*)

CC 4576 — CPLG
from Afghanistan — see *T. isopyroides*
actaeifolium — CLAP CWib MDKP
- B&SWJ 4664 — WCru
- B&SWJ 6310 — WCru
- var. ***brevistylum*** B&SWJ 8819 — CDes WCru
- - 'Twinkling Star' — EBee ECtt
- 'Perfume Star' — NLar WCot
adiantifolium — see *T. minus* 'Adiantifolium'
alpinum — EDAr EPPr XLum
angustifolium — see *T. lucidum*
'Anne' PBR — EBee ECtt IPot NLar WCot
aquilegiifolium — Widely available
- var. ***album*** — CSpe EBee ECha ELan EPfP GCra IPot LAst LHop LRHS MMuc NBid SEND SKHP SPhx SWvt WMnd WPer WPtf WTcb WWEG
- 'Gold Lace' — ECtt
* - 'Hybridum' — WFar WMoo WPer
- var. ***intermedium*** B&SWJ 10965 new — WCru
- 'Purpureum' — CPom CSev LRHS NLar WHoo
- var. ***sibiricum*** B&SWJ 11007 — WCru
- 'Small Thundercloud' — GCal LAst
- 'Thundercloud' ♀H4 — CBct CCVN CCon CPLG EBee ECtt ELon EPfP LHop LRHS MBri MCot NEgg NLar NSti SKHP SMrm SPer WBor WCot
baicalense — CPom
'Black Stockings' — CKno CMac CPLG EBee ECtt EShb GBin IPot LRHS LSou NCGa NDov NLar NPnk NSti SKHP SPoG SRkn WHil WWlt
chelidonii — GMaP LRHS
- HWJK 2216 — WCru
clavatum — CLAP WPGP
coreanum — see *T. ichangense*
cultratum — CDes EBee WPGP
- HWJCM 367 — NLar
dasycarpum — EBee MDKP NBre NLar WCot WFar WPnP
§ ***delavayi*** ♀H4 — Widely available
- BWJ 7903 — WCru
- var. ***acuminatum*** BWJ 7535 — WCru
- - BWJ 7971 — WCru
- 'Album' — Widely available
- 'Ankum' — EBee
- var. ***decorum*** — CElw CLAP CPom CWCL EPPr GEdr MCot NCGa NPnk WCot WCru WPGP WSHC
- - BWJ 7770 — WCru
- aff. var. ***decorum*** — CPLG
- 'Gold Laced' — NLar
- 'Hewitt's Double' (d) ♀H4 — Widely available
- 'Hinkley' new — NLar
- var. ***mucronatum*** — WCru
- - DJHC 473 — WCru
- purple-stemmed BWJ 7748 — WCru
diffusiflorum — CLAP WCru WSHC
dipterocarpum misapplied — see *T. delavayi*
dipterocarpum Franch. — CMac EBee LRHS WMnd XLum
- ACE 4.878.280 — CMil
'Elin' — Widely available
fendleri — GBin
- NNS 06-547 — WCot
- var. ***polycarpum*** — EBee WOut
filamentosum — EBee EPPr
- B&SWJ 777 — WCru
- B&SWJ 4145 — WCru
- var. ***yakusimense*** B&SWJ 6094 — WCru
finetii — CLAP
aff. ***finetii*** DJHC 473 — CLAP
flavum — CHab CMac CWan ECtt EHon LRHS NBro NMir NRHS SMHy SMrm SPhx SWat WShi WTou WWEG
- 'Chollerton' — see *T. isopyroides*
§ - subsp. ***glaucum*** ♀H4 — Widely available
- - dwarf — CDes WPGP
- - 'True Blue' — NDov
- 'Illuminator' — CDes CTri EBee ECtt ELon EPfP LRHS MArl MRav SBfd SMad SMrm SPoG WCot WFar
flexuosum — see *T. minus* subsp. *minus*
foetidum — NBre
grandiflorum — WCot
honanense — EBee SKHP
- BWJ 7962 — WCru
- 'Marble Leaf' — SKHP
§ ***ichangense*** — CSpe GEdr LRHS MBel WCot WSHC
- B&SWJ 8203 — WCru
- Evening Star strain (v) new — ECtt
- var. ***minus*** 'Chinese Chintz' — WCru
- 'Purple Marble' — CWGN GEdr MCot MTis NCGa SHar SUsu WCot
§ ***isopyroides*** — CCon CPom EAEE EBee GBin GCal GKev LAst MCot MMuc MNFA MRav NChi NLar NMen NPnk NRHS SEND SMrm WCot WKif
javanicum — LEdu
- B&SWJ 9506 — WCru
- var. ***puberulum*** B&SWJ 6770 — WCru
johnstonii B&SWJ 9127 — WCru
kiusianum — EBee ECha ECho ECtt EHoe EWes GAbr GCra GEdr GMaP ITim LRHS MBel MCot MMuc MPie NBir NEgg NMen NPnk NRHS NSla SEND SKHP SWvt WAbe WCot WFar WWEG XEll
- Kew form — WSHC
koreanum — see *T. ichangense*
§ ***lucidum*** — CElw CPLG EBee ECtt ELan EShb GBin GCal LRHS MMuc NBre NLar NSti SEND SKHP SPhx WCot WTcb
minus — CArn EBee ECGP ELan LRHS MBel MMuc NBre SEND
§ - 'Adiantifolium' — CMac EBee GBin IPot MBel MRav NBre NGdn NLar SHar SRms WFar WPer XLum
- var. ***hypoleucum*** B&SWJ 8634 — WCru

	- subsp. ***kemense***	EBee
§	- subsp. ***minus***	NBre
	- subsp. ***saxatile***	WPer
	- var. ***sipellatum*** B&SWJ 5051	WCru
	morisonii	LRHS NBid
	'Nishiki' new	GEdr
	omeiense BWJ 8049	WCru
	- DJHC 762	CDes
	orientale	EWes
	osmundifolium	WCru
	petaloideum	ECha EPPr GCal MDKP NLar WCot WTcb
	platycarpum B&SWJ 2261	WCru
	polygamum	see *T. pubescens* Pursh
	przewalskii	WCru
§	***pubescens*** Pursh	EBee ECha ECtt GMaP LRHS NBre NDov SUsu WCot
	punctatum	CLAP
	- B&SWJ 1272	WCru
	ramosum BWJ 8126	WCru
	reniforme	CCon IGor WCot
	- B&SWJ 2610	WCru
	- GWJ 9311	WCru
	- HWJK 2403	WCru
	rochebrunianum	Widely available
	rubescens B&SWJ 10006	WCru
*	***rugosum***	LRHS
	sachalinense	CCon WOut WPGP WTcb
	- RBS 0279	EBee EPPr
	shensiense	CPLG GEdr
	simplex var. ***brevipes*** B&SWJ 4794	WCru
	speciosissimum	see *T. flavum* subsp. *glaucum*
*	***sphaerostachyum***	CElw ECtt MNrw MWhi NBre SMrm WHal
	'Splendide'	CPLG CSpe ECtt ELon EPfP IPot MAvo MBel MNrw MTis NCGa NDov NLar SEND SUsu WCot WHil
	squarrosum	EBee LRHS WPGP WTcb
	tenuisubulatum BWJ 7929	WCru
	tuberosum	CDes CElw CMea CRDP CSpe LLHF SHar SUsu
	tubiferum B&SWJ 10999	WCru
	'Tukker Princess' new	EBee WCot
	uchiyamae	CDes EBee GBin GKev LRHS WCot WPGP WTcb
	urbainii	GEdr
	'Yubari' new	GEdr
	yunnanense	WCru

Thamnocalamus (*Poaceae*)

	aristatus	EPfP
	crassinodus	SBig
	- 'Gosainkund'	CEnt ERod MMoz MWht
	- 'Kew Beauty'	CAbb CDTJ CDoC CEnt EPfP ERod EUJe MBrN MMoz MWht SBig WJun WPGP
	- 'Lang Tang'	CEnt ERod MMoz MWht WJun WPGP
	- 'Merlyn'	CDoC CEnt EPfP ERod MMoz MWht WJun WPGP
	falconeri	see *Himalayacalamus falconeri*
	funghomii	see *Schizostachyum funghomii*
	khasianus	see *Drepanostachyum khasianum*
	maling	see *Yushania maling*
	spathaceus misapplied	see *Fargesia murielae*
§	***spathiflorus***	CEnt WJun
	- subsp. ***nepalensis***	ERod MMuc MWht SBig SEND WPGP
§	***tessellatus***	ERod MMuc MWht SEND WJun

Thamnochortus (*Restionaceae*)

cinereus	CTrC
insignis	CSpe SPlb
lucens	SPlb
rigidus	CCCN

Thapsia (*Apiaceae*)

decipiens	see *Melanoselinum decipiens*
villosa	CArn

Thea see *Camellia*

Theilera (*Campanulaceae*)

robusta new	EUJe

Thelypteris (*Thelypteridaceae*)

kunthii	ISha
noveboracensis	see *Parathelypteris novae-boracensis*
ovata var. ***lindheimeri***	ISha
palustris	CKel CRWN EBee LPBA MMoz NLar SRms WFib WPnP WShi XLum
phegopteris	see *Phegopteris connectilis*

Themeda (*Poaceae*)

triandra	SMad

Thermopsis (*Papilionaceae*)

	caroliniana	see *T. villosa*
	chinensis	EBee NRHS SBea WHil
	fabacea	see *T. lupinoides*
	lanceolata	CMea CTri EBee EPfP EWTr GBin LRHS NRHS NSti SAga SHar SMrm WAul WFar WHil WHrl WKif WPer
§	***lupinoides***	ECha EHrv LRHS MHer
	mollis	CPLG NBid
	montana	see *T. rhombifolia* var. *montana*
§	***rhombifolia*** var. ***montana***	CMHG CWCL EAEE EBee EHrv ELan ELon EPfP GAbr GCra GMaP LHop LRHS NBir NCGa NLar NOrc NSti NWad SEND SPer SPoG WAbb WBor WHil WPer WWEG
§	***villosa***	CAbP CPom CWCL EBee ELon EPPr LRHS MRav NDov NGdn NLar SGar SMHy WCot WHil WHoo

Therorhodion see *Rhododendron*

Thevetia (*Apocynaceae*)

neriifolia	CCCN

Thladiantha (*Cucurbitaceae*)

dubia	SDix WCot

Thlaspi (*Brassicaceae*)

sp.	NGdn
biebersteinii	see *Pachyphragma macrophyllum*
stylosum	GEdr

Thryptomene (*Myrtaceae*)

baeckeacea	CCCN
saxicola	ECou

Thuja ✿ (*Cupressaceae*)

'Extra Gold'	see *T. plicata* 'Irish Gold'
'Green Giant'	SLim

§	***koraiensis***	CDoC IDee SCoo
	occidentalis	NWea SEND
	- 'Amber Glow'	CDoC CKen CSBt LRHS MGos NHol NLar NWad SCoo SLim SPoG WBor WEve
	- 'Aureospicata'	EHul
	- 'Bateman Broom'	CKen
	- 'Beaufort' (v)	CKen EHul
	- 'Brabant'	CDul LMaj LRHS NLar SCoo SLim WMou
	- 'Brobecks Tower'	CDoC CKen LRHS NLar SLim
	- 'Caespitosa'	CKen WEve WGor
	- 'Cristata Aurea'	CKen
	- 'Danica' ♀H4	CMac EHul GKin LPot MBri MMuc NWea SCoo SEND SLim SRms WBor WCFE WEve WFar
	- 'Degroot's Spire'	CKen LRHS NLar SLim
	- 'Dicksonii'	EHul
	- 'Douglasii Aurea' (v)	CKen
	- Emerald	see *T. occidentalis* 'Smaragd'
	- 'Ericoides'	CDoC EHul MGos SRms
	- 'Europa Gold'	CDoC EHul MGos NLar SGol SLim
	- 'Filiformis'	CKen
I	- 'Globosa Variegata' (v)	CKen
	- 'Gold Drop'	CKen
	- 'Golden Globe'	CDoC EHul LRHS MGos SCoo SLim
	- 'Golden Minaret'	EHul
	- 'Golden Tuffet'	CDoC EHul GKin LRHS MBri MGos MPkF SCoo SLim SPer WGor
	- 'Hetz Midget'	CKen EHul GKin LAst LRHS NLar NWad SCoo SLim SPlb WFar
	- 'Holmstrup' ♀H4	CDoC CMac CTri CWib EHul SCoo SGol SLim SPoG SRms WEve WFar
	- 'Holmstrup's Yellow'	EHul LRHS SLim SPoG
	- 'Hoveyi'	CTri EHul MWat
	- 'Linesville'	CKen
	- 'Little Champion'	EHul NLar
	- 'Little Gem'	EHul MGos NHol NLar SRms
	- 'Lutea Nana' ♀H4	EHul WCFE
	- 'Malonyana'	NLar
	- 'Malonyana Holub'	SLim
	- 'Marrisen's Sulphur'	CDoC EHul
	- 'Meineke's Zwerg' (v)	CKen NLar
	- 'Miky'	CKen
	- 'Mr Bowling Ball'	CDoC LRHS NLar SLim SPoG
	- 'Ohlendorffii'	CDoC CKen EHul
I	- 'Pumila Sudworth'	NLar
I	- 'Pygmaea'	CKen
	- 'Pyramidalis Aurea'	WEve
	- 'Pyramidalis Compacta'	EHul WEve WGor
	- 'Recurva Nana'	EHul NWad
	- 'Rheingold' ♀H4	Widely available
§	- 'Smaragd' ♀H4	CDoC CDul CSBt CWib EHul EPfP LAst LBuc LRHS MAsh MGos MWat NLar NWea SBfd SCoo SGol SLim SPer SPoG SWvt WCFE WEve WFar WMou
*	- 'Smaragd Variegated' (v)	CKen
	- 'Smokey'	CKen
	- 'Southport'	CKen WEve
	- 'Spaethii'	EHul
	- 'Spiralis'	EHul NLar WCFE
§	- 'Stolwijk' (v)	EHul MGos
	- 'Sunkist'	CKen CMac CTri CWib EHul LAst MBri MGos NEgg SCoo SGol SLim WFar
	- 'Teddy'	CDoC EHul LBee LRHS MBri MWat NHol NWad SCoo SLim SPoG WFar WGor
	- 'Tiny Tim'	CDoC CMac CWib EHul MGos SGol WEve WFar WGor
	- 'Trompenburg'	CDoC EHul NLar
	- 'Wansdyke Silver' (v)	CMac EHul SCoo SLim
	- 'Wareana'	CMac
	- 'Wareana Aurea'	see *T. occidentalis* 'Wareana Lutescens'
§	- 'Wareana Lutescens'	CWib EHul MGos
	- 'Waterfield'	MAsh NWad
	- 'Yellow Ribbon'	CKen CSBt EHul LRHS NLar SCoo SGol SLim SPoG WBor WEve WFar WHar
	orientalis	see *Platycladus orientalis*
	- 'Lemon 'n' Lime' (v)	LRHS
	- 'Miller's Gold'	see *Platycladus orientalis* 'Aurea Nana'
	plicata	CCVT CDoy CDul CMac CTho EHul EPfP MGos NWea SLim SPer WMou
	- 'Atrovirens' ♀H4	CDul CTri LBee LBuc LMaj LTen MAsh MBri MGos MMuc SBfd SCoo SEND SEWo SGol SLim SRms WEve WHar WMou
*	- 'Atrovirens Aurea'	WEve
	- 'Aurea' ♀H4	EHul LRHS MAsh SLim SPoG SRms
	- 'Brooks Gold'	CKen
	- 'Can-can' (v)	MAsh NLar SCoo
I	- 'Cole's Variety'	CDul CWib MGos
	- 'Collyer's Gold'	CDul EHul NLar SRms WEve
	- 'Copper Kettle'	CKen EHul GKin LRHS NLar SCoo SLim WEve WGor
	- 'Cuprea'	CKen EHul
	- 'Doone Valley'	CKen EHul WFar
	- 'Emerald'PBR	EUJe
	- 'Excelsa'	CDul LMaj
	- 'Fastigiata' ♀H4	CDul
	- 'Gelderland'	EHul LRHS LTen NEgg NLar SCoo SLim WFar
	- Goldy = '4ever'PBR	CDoC MBri SPoG
	- 'Gracilis Aurea'	EHul
	- 'Hillieri'	CDoC CDul
§	- 'Irish Gold' (v) ♀H4	CDul CMac LRHS
	- 'Martin'	CJun
	- 'Rogersii'	CDoC CKen CMac EHul MAsh MGos NHol SCoo SPoG SRms WFar
	- 'Semperaurescens' (v)	CMac
	- 'Stolwijk's Gold'	see *T. occidentalis* 'Stolwijk'
	- 'Stoneham Gold' ♀H4	CDoC CMac EHul GKin LRHS MAsh MGos MMuc NPCo SPer SRms WEve
	- 'Sunshine'	CKen
	- Verigold = 'Courtapli'	CCVT MMuc SEND
	- 'Whipcord'	CBcs CKen EHul EPfP LRHS MPkF NLar SCoo SLim SPer SPoG WEve
*	- 'Windsor Gold'	EHul
	- 'Winter Pink' (v)	CKen
	- 'Zebrina' (v)	CBcs CDoC CDul CMac CTri CWib EHul ELan EPfP LRHS MAsh MGos MMuc NEgg NLar NPri NWea SCoo SEND SLim SMad SPer SPoG SWvt WEve WFar WHar
	plicata* × *standishii	CDul

Thujopsis (*Cupressaceae*)

dolabrata ♀H4	CBcs CDul EHul GKin MMuc NEgg NLar NWea SEND WEve WFar
- 'Aurea' (v)	CDoC CKen EHul LRHS MGos NLar SCoo SLim WEve
- 'Laetevirens'	see *T. dolabrata* 'Nana'

- 'Melbourne Gold'	NLar WEve
§ - 'Nana'	CDoC CKen CMac EHul LRHS MGos NLar SCoo SLim SRms WEve WFar
- 'Variegata' (v)	CMac EHul GKin LRHS MGos NLar SCoo SLim SPoG WEve WFar
koraiensis (Nakai) hort.	see *Thuja koraiensis*

Thunbergia (*Acanthaceae*)

alata	EPfP SPoG WTou
- 'African Sunset'	CSpe
- 'Lemon'	LSou
- 'Lemon Queen'	CHII
- 'Orange Beauty'	LSou NPri WBor
* ***arborea***	CCCN
battiscombeii	CCCN EShb MOWG
coccinea	CCCN
erecta	CCCN MOWG
fragrans GWJ 9441	WCru
grandiflora ♀H1	CCCN CHII MOWG
- 'Alba'	CCCN CHII
gregorii ♀H1+3	CCCN CHII EShb MOWG
- 'Mango'	SPoG
laurifolia B&SWJ 7166	WCru
'Moonglow'	CCCN
mysorensis ♀H1	MOWG
natalensis	CCCN EShb
'Orange Wonder'	CCCN

thyme, caraway see *Thymus herba-barona*

thyme, garden see *Thymus vulgaris*

thyme, lemon see *Thymus citriodorus*

thyme, wild see *Thymus serpyllum*

Thymus ✿ (*Lamiaceae*)

from Albania	CArn
from Turkey	EWes LLWP SBfd SHDw
§ 'Alan Bloom'	LLWP
'Albus' new	ENfk
'Anderson's Gold'	see *T. pulegioides* 'Bertram Anderson'
azoricus	see *T. caespititius*
'Bressingham'	CArn CMea CPrp CTri CWan ECtt EDAr EGHP ELau GMaP LBee LLWP LRHS MHer MHoo MMuc MNHC NPri NYoL SBfd SEND SPlb SRms SWal WFar WIce WJek WPat WPer WWEG
'Caborn Fragrant Cloud'	LLWP
'Caborn Grey Lady'	LLWP
'Caborn Lilac Gem'	LLWP SBfd SHDw
'Caborn Pink Beauty'	LLWP
'Caborn Pink Carpet'	LLWP
'Caborn Rosanne'	LLWP
'Caborn Wine and Roses'	ENfk LLWP
§ ***caespititius***	CArn EDAr ELau GMaP GPoy MHer NMen NRya NYoL SBfd SPlb SRot WAbe WHer WPer WWEG
caespitosus	CTri
camphoratus	CArn EGHP ELau ENfk ESwi EWes MHer MHoo MNHC NMen NSla SBfd WJek WWEG
- 'A Touch of Frost'	SBfd SHDw
- 'Derry'	CSpe
capitatus	CArn
§ ***carnosus***	MHer NYoL WPer XSen
'Carol Ann' (v)	ELau ENfk EWes MNHC NYoL WWEG
'Caroline'	SBfd
ciliatus	LLWP WPer XSen
cilicicus misapplied	see *T. caespititius*
cilicicus ambig.	MNHC NMen WJek WWEG
cilicicus Boiss. & Bail.	EWes WAbe
- Göteborg	ITim
citriodorus misapplied	see *T.* 'Culinary Lemon'
citriodorus ambig.	EPot SWal WCFE XLum
citriodorus (Pers.) Schreb. new	NYoL
- 'Archer's Gold'	see *T. pulegioides* 'Archer's Gold'
- 'Aureus'	see *T. pulegioides* 'Aureus'
- 'Bertram Anderson'	see *T. pulegioides* 'Bertram Anderson'
- 'Silver Posie'	see *T.* 'Silver Posie'
'Coccineus'	see *T.* Coccineus Group
§ Coccineus Group ♀H4	Widely available
- 'Atropurpureus' Schleipfer	see *T.* 'Purple Beauty'
- 'Bethany'	SGar
§ - 'Purple Beauty'	EPot LLWP MHer SBfd SHDw WWEG
§ - 'Red Elf'	ENfk GAbr MHer NMen NYoL SBfd WJek WWEG
'Coccineus Major'	CMea CWan EDAr LRHS MHer MNHC NRHS SIde WJek
comosus misapplied	NYoL SBfd SHDw WJek WPer
'Cow Green'	SBfd
'Creeping Lemon' misapplied	see *T. pulegioides* 'Kurt'
§ 'Culinary Lemon'	CArn CHby CWan EDAr EGHP ELau ENfk GPoy LLWP MBrN MHer MNHC MWat NPri NYoL SBfd WJek WPer XSen
'Dark Eyes'	SBfd SHDw
'Dartmoor'	LLWP SBfd SHDw WJek WWEG
'Desboro'	see *T. serpyllum* 'Desborough'
'Dillington' new	ENfk
doerfleri	ECha LLWP NYoL XSen
'Doone Valley' (v)	Widely available
drucei	see *T. polytrichus* subsp. *britannicus*
'E.B.Anderson'	see *T. pulegioides* 'Bertram Anderson'
'Eastgrove Pink'	LLWP SBfd SHDw
'Emma's Pink'	LLWP
erectus	see *T. vulgaris* 'Erectus'
'Fragrantissimus'	CArn CEnt CMea CWan EGHP ELau ENfk EWhm GPoy LLWP MHer MHoo MNHC MWat NPri SIde SPlb SWal WJek WOut WPer XSen
'Golden King' (v)	CWan ECha EDAr EGHP ELan ENfk LHop LLWP LRHS LSRN MAsh MBri MHer WWEG
'Golden Lemon' misapplied	see *T. pulegioides* 'Aureus'
'Golden Lemon' (v)	LLWP WJek
'Golden Queen' (v)	EDAr EGHP MWat NPri NYoL SBfd SPet SRms WFar
'Gratian'	SBfd SHDw
§ 'Hartington Silver' (v)	ECha ECho ECtt ENfk EPot EWes GKev LBMP LHop LRHS MHer MHoo NRHS NRya NSla NYoL SPlb SPoG WHoo WJek WPer WWEG
herba-barona	CArn CMea CPrp CTri CWan ECha EDAr ELau ENfk GPoy LEdu LLWP MHer MHoo MNHC MWat NYoL SEND SIde SRms WJek WPer WWEG

	- ***citrata***	see *T. herba-barona* 'Lemon-scented'
§	- 'Lemon-scented'	ECha GPoy LLWP MHer NYoL SBfd SHDw SIde WJek
	'Highdown'	ECtt SBfd SHDw
	'Highdown Adur'	SBfd SHDw
	'Highdown Lemon'	SBfd SHDw
	'Highdown Red'	SBfd SHDw
	'Highdown Stretham'	SBfd SHDw
	'Highland Cream'	see *T.* 'Hartington Silver'
	hirsutus	SWal
	hyemalis	GPoy
§	'Iden'	WJek WWEG
	'Jekka'	WJek WWEG
	'Jürgens Rosenteppich'	LLWP SBfd
	'Kurt'	see *T. pulegioides* 'Kurt'
	'Lavender Sea'	EWes LLWP
	'Lemon Beauty'	LLWP
	'Lemon Caraway'	see *T. herba-barona* 'Lemon-scented'
	'Lemon Curd'	CPrp ELau ENfk LLWP MHoo MNHC NHol NYoL SBfd SHDw SIde SPlb SPoG WFar WJek WWEG
	'Lemon Sorbet'	SBfd SHDw
	'Lemon Supreme'	LLWP
*	'Lemon Variegated' (v)	EDAr ELau ENfk EPfP EWhm MNHC NYoL SPer SPoG WWEG
	leucotrichus	XSen
	'Lilac Time'	ECtt EGHP ENfk EWes LLWP MHer SBfd SHDw SIde SPlb WJek WPer WWEG
	'Lime'	LEdu
	'Lindisfarne'	LLWP
	linearis **new**	XSen
	longicaulis	CArn ECha ELau LLWP MHer WJek
	'Magic Carpet' **new**	SPhx
	'Marjorie'	LLWP
	marschallianus	see *T. pannonicus*
§	'Massa'	LLWP SBfd SHDw
	mastichina	CArn MHoo WPer XSen
	- 'Didi'	MHer
	membranaceus	WAbe
	micans	see *T. caespititius*
	minus	see *Calamintha nepeta*
	'Mountain Select'	LLWP SBfd SHDw
	neiceffii	CMea ECha ELau LLWP SBch WWEG XSen
§	'Nettleton Pink Carpet'	LLWP WPer
	'New Hall'	SBfd
	'Orange' **new**	LEdu
§	Orange Spice = 'Tm95'	LLWP SBfd SHDw XSen
	pallasianus	ELau SBfd SHDw
§	***pannonicus***	LLWP MHer NYoL WPer
	'Peter Davis'	EGHP ENfk LHop LRHS LSRN MAsh MHer MHoo NBir NSla NYoL SBfd SIde SPoG XSen
§	'Pinewood'	LLWP MHer SIde XSen
	'Pink Ripple'	CMea ECtt ELau ENfk EPot EWes LLWP MHer MNHC SBch SBfd SHDw SIde WHal WHoo WJek WPer WWEG
	polytrichus misapplied	see *T. praecox*
§	***polytrichus*** A. Kern. ex Borbás subsp. ***britannicus***	CArn CHab CTri CWan ECha EDAr EPot GJos GMaP GPoy MBNS MBri MHer MLHP MNHC NBir NYoL SBfd SEND SHDw SPlb SRms WHoo WJek WPer WWEG
	- - 'Minor'	see *T.* 'Nettleton Pink Carpet'
	'Porlock'	CMea CPrp CTri CWan EGHP ELau EPfP GPoy LLWP MAsh MHer NYoL SIde SRms WHoo WJek WPer WWEG
§	***praecox***	GJos MHer NLan NMir
	- 'Albiflorus'	EPot
	- subsp. ***arcticus***	see *T. polytrichus* subsp. *britannicus*
	- - 'Albus'	see *T.* 'Thomas's White'
	pulegioides	CArn CHby ELau ENfk GPoy LLWP MBri MHer MNHC NYoL SBch SBfd SHDw SIde WJek WPer
§	- 'Archer's Gold'	Widely available
§	- 'Aureus' ♀H4	ENfk EPot GKev GMaP LLWP MAsh MBri MHer NPri SBfd SPer SPlb WFar WHoo WJek
§	- 'Bertram Anderson' ♀H4	CMea CSam ECha ECtt EGHP ELau ENfk EPfP GMaP LAst LLWP MAsh MHer MHoo NBir NPri NRya NYoL SBfd SIde SPer SPoG SRms WAbe WFar WHoo WIce WJek WWEG
	- 'Foxley' (v)	CWan EGHP EHoe ELau ENfk EPfP EWhm LLWP MHer MHoo MNHC NPri NYoL SBfd SHDw SIde SPlb SPoG WHer WJek WWEG
	- 'Hans'	LLWP
§	- 'Kurt'	ELau ENfk LEdu LLWP MHer SBfd SHDw WJek WNew WWEG
	- 'Sir John Lawes'	LLWP MHer SBfd
	- 'Tabor'	EGHP ENfk EWhm GMaP MNHC NYoL SBfd SHDw
	'Rainbow Falls' (v)	EPfP LLWP MHoo MNHC NYoL SBfd SHDw SIde WWEG
	'Rasta' (v)	LLWP MHer
§	'Red Glow'	LLWP
	'Redstart'	ECha ELau ENfk EPot LBee LLWP MHer NYoL SBch SBfd SHDw SIde WJek WWEG
	richardii subsp. ***nitidus*** 'Compactus Albus'	see *T. vulgaris* 'Snow White'
	'Rosa Ceeping'	LLWP SBfd SHDw
	'Rosalicht'	see *T.* 'Rosedrift'
	'Rosalind'	SBfd
§	'Rosedrift'	LLWP SBfd SHDw
	rotundifolius misapplied	see *T. vulgaris* 'Elsbeth'
	'Ruby Glow'	CEnt ECtt ELau EPot EWes MHer SBfd SHDw WWEG
	serpyllum ambig.	SIde SPet SVic XLum
	serpyllum L.	CArn GJos LLWP MBri MMuc SPlb SRms WJek WPer
	- var. ***albus***	CPrp ECha ELau GMaP GPoy LAst LLWP LRHS MNHC NPri SIde SPer SRms WAbe WHoo WJek WWEG
	- 'Albus Variegatus'	see *T.* 'Hartington Silver'
	- 'Annie Hall'	CPrp CWan EDAr ELau EPfP EPot LHop LLWP LRHS MAsh MHer NPri NRHS SBfd SIde WCFE WJek WPer
	- 'Atropurpureus'	see *T.* (Coccineus Group) 'Atropurpureus' misapplied
	- ***coccineus*** 'Minor' misapplied	see *T.* Coccineus Group
	- - 'Minor' Bloom	see *T.* 'Alan Bloom'
	- 'Conwy Rose'	CPBP WAbe
§	- 'Desborough'	LLWP MHer WWEG
	- 'East Lodge'	LLWP MNHC
	- 'Elfin'	ECho EPot EWes LBee MBri SBfd SPlb WAbe WWEG
	- 'Fulney Red'	EWes

	- 'Goldstream' (v)	CMea CPrp EGHP ELau ENfk EPfP LHop LLWP LRHS MBri MHer NRHS NYoL SPlb SRms WJek WPer
	- 'Iden'	see *T.* 'Iden'
	- 'Minimalist'	see *T. serpyllum* 'Minor'
	- 'Minimus'	see *T. serpyllum* 'Minor'
§	- 'Minor'	Widely available
	- 'Minus'	see *T. serpyllum* 'Minor'
	- 'Petite'	EWes LLWP
	- 'Pink Chintz' ♀H4	CArn CMea ECha ECtt EDAr ELau ENfk EPfP EPot GMaP GPoy LLWP LRHS MAsh MBri MHer MHoo MNHC NYoL SBfd SPer SPlb SPoG WHoo WJek WPer WWEG
	- 'Posh Pinky'	EPot LLWP NMen
	- 'Purple Beauty'	see *T.* (Coccineus Group) 'Purple Beauty'
	- 'Pygmaeus'	LLWP
	- 'Red Carpet'	ECtt NYoL
	- 'Red Elf'	see *T.* (Coccineus Group) 'Red Elf'
	- 'Red Glow'	see *T.* 'Red Glow'
	- 'Roseus'	SIde
	- 'Russetings'	CPrp CYeo ECtt ELau ENfk EPfP EPot LLWP MAsh MHer MHoo MNHC NYoL SBch SBfd SIde SPoG SRms WJek WNew WWEG
	- 'September'	LLWP MHer
	- 'Snowdrift'	CArn CMea CWan ECtt ELau ENfk EPfP EPot GKev LLWP MHer MNHC MWat NMen NWad SBch SIde SPlb WCFE WFar WJek WPat WPer WWEG
	- 'Variegatus'	see *T.* 'Hartington Silver'
	- 'Vey'	CPBP EPot EWes GMaP LHop LLWP LRHS MHer NRHS SBfd SHDw WJek WWEG
	sibthorpii	CArn
	'Silver King' (v)	ENfk
§	'Silver Posie'	Widely available
	'Silver Queen' (v) ♀H4	CBcs CSam CWan ECha EDAr EGHP ELan ENfk EPfP GKev GMaP LAst LLWP MHer MHoo MNHC NYoL SBfd SPlb SWal WFar WJek WNew WWEG
	'Snowdonia Idris'	LLWP
	'Snowdonia Ifor'	LLWP
	'Snowdonia Iorwerth'	LLWP
	'Snowdonia Isolde'	LLWP
	'Snowdonia Lass'	LLWP SBfd
	'Snowdonia Pedr'	LLWP
	'Snowdonia Pink Gem'	LLWP
	'Snowdonia Pryderi'	LLWP
	'Snowdonia Pwyll'	LLWP
	'Snowdonia Rhiannon'	LLWP
	'Snowdonia Rowena'	LLWP
	'Snowman'	SBfd
	'Spicy Orange'	see *T.* Orange Spice
§	'Thomas's White' ♀H4	CTri NYoL
	valesiacus	see *T.* 'Massa'
§	***vulgaris***	Widely available
	- 'Aranjuez'	LLWP
	- 'Château Queribus'	LLWP
*	- 'Compactus'	CSam ENfk GPoy LLWP MHer MNHC MRav WJek
	- 'Deutsche Auslese'	see *T. vulgaris*
	- 'Diamantis'	LLWP
	- 'Dorcas White'	LLWP MHer WPer
§	- 'Elsbeth'	ELau LLWP MHer SBfd SHDw
	- 'English Winter'	ENfk SIde
	- 'Erectus'	see *T. carnosus*
	- French	see *T. vulgaris*
	- French, summer	NYoL SIde
	- 'Golden Pins'	MHer
	- 'Lemon Queen'	ELau
	- 'Lucy'	LLWP MHer MNHC
	- 'Pinewood'	see *T.* 'Pinewood'
§	- 'Snow White'	ELau EWes LLWP SBfd SHDw WJek
	'Widecombe' (v)	LLWP SBfd SHDw
	zygis	CArn MHoo

Tiarella (*Saxifragaceae*)

	'Appalachian Trail'	LSou MPnt NPnk SHeu SUsu
	'Black Snowflake' PBR	EBee MPnt
	'Black Velvet'	EBee MBel MPnt SHeu
	'Braveheart'	EBee LHop MPnt SHeu WWEG
	'Butter and Sugar' **new**	MPnt
	'Butterfly Wings'	MPnt
	'Candy Striper' **new**	MPnt SHeu
	'Cascade Creeper'	LSou MPnt NPnk
	collina	see *T. wherryi*
	cordifolia ♀H4	Widely available
	- 'Glossy'	CBct CCon MPnt
	- 'Milk Chocolate'	MMoz MPnt
	- 'Oakleaf'	CCon EBee MBel MPnt NBro
	- 'Rosalie'	see × *Heucherella alba* 'Rosalie'
	- 'Running Tapestry'	EBee MPnt
	- 'Slick Rock'	EPPr
	'Crow Feather' PBR	EBee LSou MPnt SHeu
	'Cygnet'	CBct CLAP COIW EBee ECtt LHop MPnt NPnk SHeu SPer SRot WFar
	'Dunvegan'	EBee MPnt
	'Elizabeth Oliver'	CLAP MPnt
	'Freckles'	LRHS MRav
	'Happy Trails'	MPnt NPnk SHeu
	'Hidden Carpet'	CHid
	'Inkblot'	EBee ELan LRHS MPnt NBro SHeu WFar WMoo
	'Iron Butterfly' PBR (v)	CBct CLAP CMac CSpe CWCL EBee ECha ECtt EPfP GBin GMaP LBMP LHop LRHS LSRN MNrw MPnt MRav NBro NPnk SMrm SPer SPoG SRot STes WFar WPGP
	'Iron Cross' **new**	SPlb
	'Jeepers Creepers' PBR	EBee MPnt NCGa NPnk NWad SHar SHeu
*	'Laciniate Runner'	CLAP
	'Martha Oliver'	CLAP EBee MPnt SBch WPGP
	'Mint Chocolate' PBR	CLAP CYeo EAEE EBee ECha ECtt EHoe EHrv ELan EPfP GMaP LPot MBel MNrw MPnt MRav MWhi NBir NGdn NLar NPnk SPer SWvt WFar WPGP
	Morning Star = 'Tntia042' PBR	CHid CWCL EWll LBMP LRHS MBri MPnt NPnk SHeu SMrm SRkn SRot WFar
	'Mystic Mist' PBR (v)	EBee ECtt LSou MPnt NLar NPnk NWad SHeu SPoG
	'Neon Lights' PBR	CSpe EBee ECGP EWes MAsh MPnt NBir NCGa NPnk SHeu SWvt
§	'Ninja' PBR	CHid EBee ECha ECtt EHrv ELan EUJe GMaP LAst LRHS MPnt MRav NBir NLar NSti SPer SWvt WCot WFar
	'Oregon Trail' **new**	MPnt NPnk
	'Pacific Crest' **new**	MPnt SHeu
	'Pink Bouquet'	CAbP CLAP CMac CSpe CWGN EAEE EBee ECtt EHrv GJos LRHS

Name	Suppliers
	MBel MBri MNFA MPie MPnt NBro NPnk NRHS SBch WFar WMoo WPnP
'Pink Brushes'PBR	CLAP MPnt WPnP
'Pink Skyrocket'PBR	CAbP CLAP CWGN CYeo EBee ECtt ELan LLHF LRHS LSRN MAvo MBel MPnt NBir NGdn NHol NPnk NWad SHar SHeu SPer WCot
'Pinwheel'	EBee LRHS MPnt MRav NRHS
'Pirate's Patch'PBR	LLHF MPnt SHeu
polyphylla	EBee ELan MPnt NLar SBch SWal WCru WFar
- 'Baoxing Pink'	CLAP LAst MPnt WCru
- 'Filigran'	EBee EPfP MPnt NLar NWad WPtf
- 'Moorgrün'	GCal LRHS
- pink-flowered	CLAP EHrv GBin
'Running Tiger'	MPnt
'Sea Foam'	MPnt NPnk SHeu
'Simsalabim'	EBee MPnt
'Skeleton Key'	EBee MPnt
'Skid's Variegated' (v)	EBee ECtt LRHS MNrw MPie MPnt NSti SHeu SWvt WCot
'Skyrocket'	ECtt
'Spanish Cross'	MPnt SHeu
'Spring Symphony'PBR	CLAP CWCL EBee ECtt EShb GBin GBuc LBMP LRHS LSou MBel MBri MPnt MWat NCGa NLar NPer NPnk SBfd SHil WFar WHoo
Starburst = 'Tntia041'PBR	MPnt NPnk SHeu
'Sugar and Spice'PBR	EBee MBrN MPnt NCGa NHol NPnk NWad SHeu
'Sunset Ridge' **new**	MPnt SHeu
'Tiger Stripe'	EBee EPfP MPnt MRav NBro NPnk SHeu WFar
'Timbuktu'	MPnt SHeu
trifoliata	MPnt MRav WFar
- var. ***unifoliata***	MPnt WWEG
'Viking Ship'PBR	see × *Heucherella* 'Viking Ship'
§ ***wherryi*** ♀H4	CBcs CWCL EBee ELan ELon EPfP EWTr GMaP LAst LPot LRHS MPnt NBir NBro NOrc NPri SBch SPer SPlb SRot SWvt WFar WPer WPnP WWEG XLum
- 'Bronze Beauty'	CLAP GBuc IGor MPnt MRav SBch WFar WPGP
- 'Green Velvet'	ECha MPnt
- 'Heronswood Mist' (v)	CAbP CBct CCon EBee ECtt MMoz MNrw MPnt SHeu SPer SWvt WCot
- 'Montrose'	WPGP

Tibouchina (*Melastomataceae*)

Name	Suppliers
grandifolia	CCCN
granulosa	MOWG
heteromalla	CCCN CRHN
'Jules'	MOWG
organensis	CCCN CHll MOWG SHeu WPGP
paratropica	CRHN
- RCB/Arg X-4	WCot
semidecandra hort.	see *T. urvilleana*
§ ***urvilleana*** ♀H1	CBcs CCCN CDoC CHEx CRHN CSBt CTri CTsd EBak ELan EPfP EUJe LRHS MCot MOWG NCGa SEND SPer SPoG SRkn WCot
- 'Compacta'	CCCN LRHS
- 'Edwardsii'	LSou SMrm SUsu WCot
- 'Nana'	CDoC
- 'Rich Blue Sun'	CSpe LRHS
- variegated (v)	CCCN LSou SUsu WCot

Tigridia ✿ (*Iridaceae*)

Name	Suppliers
catarinensis **new**	SDeJ
§ ***immaculata*** B&SWJ 10393 **new**	WCru
lutea	ECho
orthantha 'Red-Hot Tiger'	WCru
pavonia	CBro CPLG ECho EWll LAma MBri SDeJ
- 'Alba Immaculata'	CSpe
- 'Aurea'	MDev
- 'Canariensis'	CTca
- 'Lilacea'	ECho MDev SDeJ
- 'Speciosa'	CTca SDeJ

Tilia ✿ (*Malvaceae*)

Name	Suppliers
HRS 2808 **new**	WPGP
americana	CMCN
- 'Dentata'	CDul
- 'Nova'	CDoC
amurensis	CMCN
argentea	see *T. tomentosa*
begoniifolia	see *T. dasystyla*
chenmoui	CMCN EPfP MBlu WPGP
chinensis	CMCN EBee NPCo WPGP
- F 30558	WPGP
chingiana	CDul CMCN SBir SLon
cordata ♀H4	CBcs CCVT CDul CHab CLnd CMac CSBt CTho CTri EBee ECrN ELan EPfP LBuc LMaj LPot MAsh MMuc MSwo NWea SBfd SCoo SEND SEWo SPer WMou
§ - 'Böhlje'	CDul ECrN SLPl
- 'Dainty Leaf'	CDul
- 'Erecta'	see *T. cordata* 'Böhlje'
- 'Greenspire' ♀H4	CCVT CDoC CDul CLnd CWib ECrN LMaj LTen MRav SBfd SEWo
- 'Len Parvin'	WPGP
- 'Lico'	LMaj
- 'Roelvo'	CDul
- 'Swedish Upright'	CDul CTho
- 'Winter Orange'	CDul EBee EPfP MBlu MBri MWat NPCo SBfd SBir SCoo SEWo
§ ***dasystyla***	CMCN EBee
- subsp. ***caucasica***	WPGP
endochrysea **new**	WPGP
× ***euchlora*** ♀H4	CBcs CCVT CDul CLnd CMCN EBee ECrN EPfP LMaj NWea SBfd SEWo SPer WFar
§ × ***europaea***	CDul CLnd CRWN ELan EWTr MMuc NWea SEND
- 'Koningslinde'	CDul
- 'Pallida'	CDul CLnd LMaj LTen MBlu NWea
- 'Wratislaviensis' ♀H4	CDoC CDul CLnd EBee EPfP MAsh MBlu NLar NWea
§ 'Harold Hillier'	MBlu
henryana	CBcs CDoC CDul CLnd CMCN CTho CWib EBee ELan EMil EPfP ERod IArd IDee LRHS MBlu MBri MMuc MREP NWea SBir SCoo WPGP
- 'Arnold Select'	MBri WMou
§ ***heterophylla***	CMCN EPfP MBlu MBri WPGP
'Hillieri'	see *T.* 'Harold Hillier'
insularis misapplied	see *T. japonica* 'Ernest Wilson'
intonsa	CMCN
japonica	CDul CMCN EBee WPGP
§ - 'Ernest Wilson'	CMCN MBlu

kiusiana	CDul CMCN EBee MBlu WMou WPGP
mandshurica	CDul CMCN EBee WPGP
maximowicziana	WPGP
mexicana	WPGP
- CD&R 1318	WPGP
miqueliana	CMCN
'Moltkei'	CMCN EBee MBri WPGP
mongolica	CBcs CDoC CDul CMCN EBee EPfP MBlu MMuc SCoo WMou WPGP
monticola	see *T. heterophylla*
nobilis KR 226 **new**	WPGP
oliveri	CDul CMCN EBee MBlu NWea SBir WMou WPGP
paucicostata	WPGP
'Petiolaris' ♀H4	CBcs CCVT CDoC CDul CLnd CMCN EBee ECrN ELan EPfP MBlu MSwo NWea SEND SPer WMou
platyphyllos	CCVT CDul CHab CLnd CMCN CSBt CTho CTri EBee ECrN EMil EPfP EWTr LAst LBuc MMuc NWea SBfd SCoo SEND SPer WMou
- 'Aurea'	CDul CTho ECrN MBlu
- 'Corallina'	see *T. platyphyllos* 'Rubra'
- 'Erecta'	see *T. platyphyllos* 'Fastigiata'
§ - 'Fastigiata'	CDul SLPl
- 'Laciniata'	CDul CMCN CTho LMaj MBlu
§ - 'Rubra' ♀H4	CCVT CDoC CDul CLnd CTho EPfP LBuc MGos NWea SEWo WFar
- 'Tortuosa'	MBlu WMou
§ ***tomentosa***	CDul CLnd CMCN ELan EMil LMaj MMuc NWea SCoo WMou
- 'Brabant' ♀H4	CDoC CDul EPfP LMaj WFar
tuan	CMCN WPGP
× ***vulgaris***	see *T.* × *europaea*

Tilingia (*Apiaceae*)

ajanensis B&SWJ 11202	WCru

Tillaea see *Crassula*

Tillandsia (*Bromeliaceae*)

sp.	XBlo
aeranthos	SChr

Tinantia (*Commelinaceae*)

pringlei	LEdu SBrt SDys SUsu WHil WPGP
- AIM 77	EBee WCot
- variegated (v)	WCot

Titanopsis (*Aizoaceae*)

calcarea ♀H1	CCCN EPfP

Tithonia (*Asteraceae*)

rotundifolia	CSpe
- 'Torch'	CSpe SMrm

Tofieldia (*Tofieldiaceae*)

coccinea	GCal GEdr WCru

Tolmiea (*Saxifragaceae*)

menziesii	CMac EWld MCot SWal XLum
- 'Goldsplash'	see *T. menziesii* 'Taff's Gold'
- 'Maculata'	see *T. menziesii* 'Taff's Gold'
§ - 'Taff's Gold' (v) ♀H4	CWan EHoe EHrv EOHP EShb GMaP NBid SPlb WHoo XLum
- 'Variegata'	see *T. menziesii* 'Taff's Gold'

Tolpis (*Asteraceae*)

barbata	CSpe

Tonestus (*Asteraceae*)

§ ***lyallii***	WPer

Toona (*Meliaceae*)

§ ***sinensis***	CArn CBcs CDul CGHE CTho CWib EBee ELan EPfP LEdu MMuc SEND WPGP
- 'Flamingo' (v)	CBcs EBee EPfP ESwi GKin IVic LEdu LRHS MAsh MGos NLar SHil SPoG WCot

Torenia (*Linderniaceae*)

Purple Moon = 'Dantopur'PBR (Moon Series)	LSou
Summer Wave Series	CCCN SCoo

Torilis (*Apiaceae*)

japonica	CBre CHab

Townsendia (*Asteraceae*)

alpigena	GKev
§ - var. ***alpigena***	CPBP GKev
condensata	CPBP
formosa	ECho
hookeri	CPBP NMen
incana	WAbe
leptotes	CPBP
mensana	GKev
montana	see *T. alpigena* var. *alpigena*
§ ***rothrockii***	NMen
spathulata	CPBP
wilcoxiana misapplied	see *T. rothrockii*

Toxicodendron (*Anacardiaceae*)

vernicifluum	see *Rhus verniciflua*

Trachelium (*Campanulaceae*)

§ ***asperuloides***	WAbe
caeruleum ♀H1	SGar
- 'Black Knight'	CSpe

Trachelospermum ✿ (*Apocynaceae*)

from Nanking, China	EShb
§ ***asiaticum*** ♀H2-3	Widely available
- B&SWJ 4814	WCru
- 'Golden Memories'	CPLG CSPN CWGN EBee ELan ELon EPfP LRHS LSRN LSqu MGos SKHP SLon SPoG SSpi SSta SWvt WCot WPat
- 'Goshiki' (v)	EShb WPat
- var. ***intermedium***	WPGP
* - 'Kiejiu Chirimen'	SKHP
- 'Kulu Chirimen'	WCot
- 'Nagaba' (v)	SKHP
- 'Ōgon-nishiki' (v)	LRHS SKHP SPoG
- 'Pink Showers'	SKHP
- 'Shirofu Chirimen' (v)	SKHP
- 'Summer Sunset' **new**	EPfP MPkF
- 'Theta'	SKHP WCot WPGP WPat
'Chameleon'	SKHP
jasminoides ♀H3-4	Widely available
- B&SWJ 5117	WCru
- 'Big White Star'	EPfP
§ - 'Japonicum'	CRHN CSPN LRHS NPri SLon SPer SPoG WSHC
- 'Major'	CSPN EBee ELan SEND SSpi
* - 'Oblanceolatum'	GCal

- 'Star of Toscana'	EPfP LRHS
- 'Tricolor' (v)	CBcs CTrC EBee LRHS SGol SLim SWvt WCot
- 'Variegatum' (v) ♀H3-4	Widely available
- 'Waterwheel'	EBee ELan LRHS SKHP SSpi WPGP WSHC
- 'Wilsonii'	CMac CPLG CSPN CTrC EBee ELan EPfP GCal LRHS LSRN NLar SEND SKHP SLim SPer SPoG SWvt WCot WCru WHar WPGP WPat
majus misapplied	see *T. jasminoides* 'Japonicum'
majus Nakai	see *T. asiaticum*

Trachycarpus (*Arecaceae*)

sp.	EAmu
from Manipur	EAmu SChr
§ ***fortunei*** ♀H3-4	Widely available
fortunei* × *wagnerianus	EBee WPGP
latisectus	EAmu SBig
martianus	CDTJ CTrC EAmu SBig SChr
nanus	CDTJ
'Nova'	EAmu
princeps	CBrP
takil Becc.	CBrP CDTJ EAmu
wagnerianus	CBrP CDTJ CGHE CHid CPHo CPLG CTrC EAmu EBee ETod NPla SBig SChr SMad WPGP

Trachymene (*Apiaceae*)

coerulea	CSpe

Trachyspermum (*Apiaceae*)

ammi	CArn

Trachystemon (*Boraginaceae*)

orientalis	CBre CHEx CMac CPLG CSev EBee ECha EHrv ELan EPfP IKil LEdu LHop MCot MRav NBid NLar SBch SBig SEND SKHP WBrk WCot WCru WFar WHer WMoo

Tradescantia ✿ (*Commelinaceae*)

albiflora	see *T. fluminensis*
× ***andersoniana*** W. Ludwig & Rohw. nom. inval.	see *T.* Andersoniana Group
§ Andersoniana Group	CWib SPet SWal WHil WPer
- 'Baby Doll'	XLum
- 'Bilberry Ice'	CMac CPrp CWCL EBee ECtt EPfP GJos GMaP LBMP LHop LRHS MBel MWat MWhi NBir NBro NCGa NGdn NLar NPnk SApp SBfd SMrm SPoG WCAu WHoo WMnd WWEG XLum
- 'Blanca'	WWEG
- 'Blue and Gold'	CBcs EBee ECtt ELon EPPr EPfP LAst LHop LRHS MRav NHol NLar NSti WCot WWEG
- 'Blue Stone'	CCse CMea CSBt EBee ECha ECtt MAvo MRav SPad SRms WHoo WTin XLum
- 'Bridal Veil'	CHll
- 'Caerulea Plena'	see *T. virginiana* 'Caerulea Plena'
- Carmine Glow	see *T.* (Andersoniana Group) 'Karminglut'
- 'Charlotte'	CTca EBee ECha ECtt LRHS LSRN MAvo MCot NBre NBro NGdn NLar NRHS SBfd SMrm WCAu WMnd WWEG
- 'Chedglow'	WWEG
- 'Concord Grape'	Widely available
- 'Danielle'	EPfP
- 'Domaine de Courson'	EBee ECtt XLum
- 'In the Navy'	LDai NBre NLar
- 'Innocence'	CMHG CSBt CTri EBee ECha ECtt ELan EPfP GCra GJos GMaP LAst LHop LRHS MBel MMuc NBir NCGa NGdn NPnk NSti SBfd SEND SPer WMnd XLum
- 'Iris Prichard'	CPrp CTca EBee ELan EPfP GCra GLog GMaP LAst NBre NCGa NLar
- 'Isis' ♀H4	CPrp CTri EBee ECtt ELan EPfP GCra LBMP LRHS MMuc MRav NBir NCGa NGdn NOrc SBfd SEND SPer WKif WMnd WNew WTin
- 'J.C. Weguelin' ♀H4	EBee EPfP LPot NBir NMRc NPnk SRms WCAu WMnd WWEG XLum
§ - 'Karminglut'	EBee ECtt ELan EPfP GLog GMaP NBir NGdn NPnk WCAu WHoo WWEG XLum
- 'Leonora'	EBee EPfP LRHS MMuc NLar SEND XLum
- 'Little Doll'	CTca CWCL ECtt EPfP GLog LAst LRHS MDKP MGos MNFA NBro NLar WWEG XLum
- 'Little White Doll'	CPrp CWCL EBee ECtt LAst MDKP MNFA NBre NLar WWEG
- 'Mariella'	EBee
- 'Mrs Loewer'	MAvo
- 'Osprey' ♀H4	CBcs CTri EBee ECha ECtt ELan EPfP GCal LRHS MAvo MLHP MRav MWhi NBro NCGa NGdn NLar NPri NRHS NSti SPer SPoG SRms WCAu WHoo WKif WWEG XLum
- 'Pauline'	EBee ECtt ELon LAst MRav NBir NLar NMRc WHoo WTin WWEG XLum
- 'Perinne's Pink'	CWCL EBee ECtt EPfP LRHS MDev NLar NPnk NSti SPoG SUsu
- 'Pink Chablis'	CWCL ECtt MNFA NBro NLar SUsu
- 'Purewell Giant'	CMac CTri EBee GLog LHop LRHS NBro NLar NRHS SPer WGor WKif WMnd
- 'Purple Dome'	EBee ECtt GMaP LAst LRHS MAvo MCot MMuc MRav MWat NBir NBro NCGa NGdn SBfd SEND SPoG WMnd WTin
- 'Red Grape'	CTca EBee ECtt EWll LPot LRHS MBel MWhi NPro NRHS NSti WWEG
- 'Rosi'	EBee
- 'Rubra'	CPrp EBee NOrc SRms XLum
- 'Satin Doll'[PBR]	CBcs EBee ECtt EPfP
- 'Snowbank'	EBee
- 'Sunshine Charm'	NLar
- 'Sweet Kate'	CBct CMac CWCL EBee ECtt LBMP LRHS LSRN MBNS NBro SHil SPoG SRGP XLum
- 'Sylvana'	EBee SApp
- 'Temptation'	ECtt
- 'Valour'	CSBt EBee
- 'Zwanenburg Blue'	EBee ECha ECtt EHrv ELan GLog LAst LRHS MLHP NCGa NPnk SPlb WMnd WWEG XLum
'Angel Eyes'	ECtt MDKP
'Blushing Bride' (v)	MPkF
canaliculata	see *T. ohiensis*
crassifolia F&M 258 new	WPGP

	crassula new	EOHP
§	***fluminensis***	SChr
	- 'Albovittata'	EShb
§	- 'Aurea' ♀H1	EShb
	- 'Maiden's Blush' (v)	CSpe EShb SGar SPlb SRms
	- 'Quicksilver' (v) ♀H1	EShb
	- 'Variegata'	see *T. fluminensis* 'Aurea'
	'Gold Mound'	WRHF
	'Lucky Charm' new	NLar
§	***ohiensis***	LPBA MAvo
	pallida 'Kartuz Giant'	CSpe EShb WCot
§	- 'Purpurea' ♀H2-3	EOHP EShb
	pendula	see *T. zebrina*
	'Purple Sabre'	CBcs LAst MWhi SMrm
	purpurea	see *T. pallida* 'Purpurea'
	sillamontana ♀H1	EShb
	spathacea	EShb
	- 'Vittata' ♀H1	WCot
	tricolor	see *T. zebrina*
	virginiana	LPot MWhi SGar
	- 'Alba'	CMac GCal WPer
*	- 'Brevicaulis'	ECha ECtt NBre NBro WWEG
§	- 'Caerulea Plena' (d)	EBee ELan EPfP MRav SPer SRms WTin WWEG
	- 'Rubra'	SPlb
§	***zebrina*** ♀H1	EShb
	- ***pendula***	see *T. zebrina*
	- 'Purpusii' ♀H1	SRms

Tragopogon (*Asteraceae*)

crocifolius	CCVN CSpe SPhx
porrifolius	GCal MCot SVic WCot
pratensis	CArn NMir

Trapa (*Lythraceae*)

natans	CBen

Trautvetteria (*Ranunculaceae*)

carolinensis	CLAP GEdr WCru
var. ***japonica***	
- - B&SWJ 10861	WCru
- var. ***occidentalis***	EBee GEdr WCru

Triadica (*Euphorbiaceae*)

sebifera	LEdu

Trichodiadema (*Aizoaceae*)

bulbosum new	SPlb

Trichopetalum (*Asparagaceae*)

§	***plumosum***	CBro

Trichostema (*Lamiaceae*)

dichotomum RCB RL 15	WCot

Tricuspidaria see *Crinodendron*

Tricyrtis (*Liliaceae*)

	B&SWJ 3229 from Taiwan	WCru WFar
	from Taiwan	WFar
	'Adbane'	CBct CLAP EBee ELan EPPr EWes GBuc GKev IKil LRHS MMoz NGdn SMrm WFar WGwG WWEG
	affinis B&SWJ 2804	CLAP WCru
	- B&SWJ 5645	WCru
	- B&SWJ 6182	WCru
	- B&SWJ 11169	WCru
	- B&SWJ 11442	WCru
	- 'Early Bird'	WCru WFar
	- 'Lunar Landing' new	EThi
	- 'Sansyoku'	GEdr
	'Amanagowa'	CLAP
	bakeri	see *T. latifolia*
	'Blackberry Mousse' new	EBee
	'Blue Wonder'	LRHS LSou MSCN NLar NPro SPer SPet
	dilatata	see *T. macropoda*
	'Empress'	CBct CPLG EBee ECha ELon EPfP EThi EWes GBuc IBal LAst LEdu LSou MTis NEgg NPnk SMrm SPet SPoG SRkn WFar WWEG
	flava	EBee LRHS WCru WFar
	formosana ♀H4	Widely available
	- B&SWJ 306	CLAP MNrw WFar
	- B&SWJ 355	WCru WFar
	- B&SWJ 3073	WCru WFar
	- B&SWJ 3616	CPLG WCru WFar
	- B&SWJ 3635	CLAP
	- B&SWJ 3712	WCru WFar
	- B&SWJ 6705	CLAP
	- B&SWJ 6741	WCru WFar
	- B&SWJ 6970	WCru WFar
	- B&SWJ 7071	WFar
	- RWJ 10109	WCru
	- 'Dark Beauty'	CDes CLAP CPLG CWCL EBee ECtt EHrv EWTr GBuc MAvo MBel MBri MNrw MTis MWat NPri SMrm SPad SUsu WFar WPGP
	- dark-flowered	GAbr NCGa WFar
	- 'Emperor' (v)	EBee ESwi
	- 'Gilt Edge' (v)	CBct CPLG CWCL EBee ECtt ELon EPfP EPri EThi EWTr GBuc IBal LRHS LSou MBNS MBel MDKP MTis NBid NBro NEgg NGdn NHol NLar NPnk NSti SPoG SUsu WFar WWEG
	- f. ***glandosa*** B&SWJ 7084	WCru WFar
	- aff. f. ***glandosa*** 'Blu-Shing Toad'	WCru WFar
	- var. ***grandiflora*** 'W-Ho-ping Toad'	WCru WFar
	- 'Kestrel' (v)	WCot
	- pale-flowered	CBct EThi WFar WWEG
	- 'Purple Beauty'	EBee LSou MDKP MNrw MPkF MTis NPnk
	- 'Samurai' (v)	CLAP CWCL EPPr EWes NPnk WFar
	- 'Seiryu'	EBee
	- 'Shelley's'	CBct CLAP NBro WFar WWEG
	- 'Small Wonder'	WCru WFar
	- 'Spotted Toad'	LEdu WCru
§	- Stolonifera Group	CAvo CBcs CBro CMac EBee EHrv ELan EPfP LEdu LRHS MCot MWat NHol SDix WFar WMnd
	- - B&SWJ 7046	WCru WFar
	- 'Taiwan Toad'	CPLG WFar
	- 'Taroko Toad'	WCru
	- 'Tiny Toad'	WCru WFar
	- 'Variegata' (v)	CBct LEdu NBir WCru WFar
	- 'Velvet Toad'	WCru WFar
	'Golden Leopard'	EPfP LSou NCGa SPer
	'Harlequin'	LEdu WFar WWEG
§	***hirta***	CBcs CDes CHid CMac CPrp CTri CWCL EBee ECho EHrv EPfP GAbr ITim LRHS MCot MMuc NBro NHol SEND SGar SPet SPlb SWal SWvt WFar WWEG
	- B&SWJ 5971	WCru
	- B&SWJ 11182	WCru
	- B&SWJ 11227	WCru

- 'Alba' CMac EHrv WFar
- 'Albomarginata' (v) CMac CPrp EAEE EBee EHrv EPPr EPfP GCra LRHS MAvo NEgg NLar NSti SWvt WFar WPGP
- 'Golden Gleam' LRHS WCot WFar
- 'Makinoi Gold' WFar
- var. ***masamunei*** WCru
- 'Matsukaze' CLAP CPLG CPom EWes MAvo SUsu WFar
- 'Miyazaki' CCon CLAP CMac ECtt EPfP GBuc IFoB LBMP LRHS MCot MHer MNrw MPkF MTis NCGa NLar WFar WWEG
- 'Taiwan Atrianne' CFis EBee ECtt LDai LRHS MDKP MNrw NBro NCGa NEgg NHol WFar
- 'Variegata' (v) CBct CTri EBee ELon EWes GCra GKev NRHS WCot WFar WWEG

N Hototogisu CBct CBro CLAP CPLG CPom EAEE EBee ECtt ELan ELon LHop LRHS MCot MWat NBir NEgg NHol NLar NPnk WFar WMnd WWEG

'Imperial Banner' (v) EBee MAvo

ishiiana CLAP EHrv MMoz SUsu WCot WCru WFar WPGP WSHC
- var. ***surugensis*** LEdu WCru WFar

'Ivory Queen' WFar

japonica see *T. hirta*

'Kohaku' CBct CLAP ELan EThi EWes GEdr GKev NPro WFar WPGP WWEG

lasiocarpa CLAP EBee EHrv LEdu MAvo MTis
- B&SWJ 3635 CLAP CPLG WCru WFar
- B&SWJ 6861 WCru WFar
- B&SWJ 7013 CBct WCru WFar
- B&SWJ 7103 WCru
- 'Royal Toad' WCru

§ ***latifolia*** ELan EThi GAbr GLog GMaP LEdu LRHS NLar WCru WFar WWEG
- B&SWJ 10996 from Japan WCru
- from Japan WFar
- 'Yellow Sunrise' CBcs EBee ECtt EPPr MCot NSti SPoG WFar

'Lemon Lime' (v) NPro WFar WWEG

'Lightning Strike' (v) CBct EBee ECtt EWes LEdu NHol NPnk SPoG WCot WFar

'Lilac Towers' CBct ELan MAvo WCru WFar WWEG

macrantha EBee GAbr GKev GLog WCru WSHC

§ - subsp. ***macranthopsis*** CBct CLAP CPLG GBuc GEdr LHop MDKP WCot WCru WFar
- - 'Juro' (d) WCru

macranthopsis see *T. macrantha* subsp. *macranthopsis*

N ***macropoda*** CBct EBee ELan EPfP GLog LEdu LHop LRHS MAvo NGdn SMad WFar WMnd WWEG
- B&SWJ 1271 WCru WFar
- B&SWJ 5013 WCru WFar
- B&SWJ 5556 WCru
- B&SWJ 5847 from Japan WCru WFar
- B&SWJ 6209 WCru WFar
- B&SWJ 8700 WCru WFar
- B&SWJ 8829 from Korea WCru WFar
- from Yungi Temple, China CLAP EPPr NCGa WFar
- 'Tricolor' CDes WCot

maculata HWJCM 470 WCru
- HWJK 2010 WCru WFar
- HWJK 2411 WCru WFar

'Moonlight Treasure'PBR CLAP CPLG EBee NHol WCot

nana WCru
- B&SWJ 11399 WCru
- 'Karasuba' GEdr
- 'Raven's Back' WCru

ohsumiensis CBct CLAP CPom ECha EHrv GBuc GEdr LRHS MDKP SUsu WCru WFar WPGP
- 'Nakatsugawa' (v) GEdr

perfoliata CLAP LEdu WCru WFar
- 'Spring Shine' (v) WCru WFar

pilosa EBee GKev

Pink Freckles CBct ELon ESwi EThi LRHS LSou
= 'Innotripf'PBR MPnt SPoG

'Raspberry Mousse' CLAP CWCL EBee EHrv EPfP EWTr IFoB IPot LHop LSou MAvo MBNS NSti SMrm WPGP

ravenii B&SWJ 3229 **new** WCru

setouchiensis WCru WFar

'Shimone' CHid CLAP CPLG CPom ECha ELan NCGa WFar

'Sinonome' EBee MAvo MPkF

stolonifera see *T. formosana* Stolonifera Group

suzukii RWJ 10111 WCru WFar

'Taipei Silk'PBR EBee ESwi IFoB LSou NCGa NLar NPri SBfd

'Tojen' Widely available

'Tresahor White' WFar

'Variegata' (*affinis* hybrid) (v) WFar WWEG

'Washfields' WFar WPGP

'White Towers' CBro CHid CLAP CPLG CWCL EAEE EBee ECha EHrv EPPr EPfP GBuc IFoB LRHS MAvo MBel MRav NCGa NEgg NLar NPnk NSti SBfd SPer SRms WAul WFar WGwG

Trientalis (*Primulaceae*)

europaea f. ***rosea*** WHil

Trifolium (*Papilionaceae*)

angustifolium CArn

incarnatum CSpe MHer

nanum LLHF

ochroleucon CHab EBee EHrv EPPr GMaP LEdu LRHS MAvo MCot MMuc MNFA MPie MSCN NSti SBch SEND SMHy SMad SSvw SWal WAul WFar WMoo WPer WWEG

pannonicum CCVN CMea EHrv GCal MNrw SUsu WOut WTin
- 'White Tiara' **new** EBee

pratense CHab MHer NMir WSFF
- 'Dolly North' see *T. pratense* 'Susan Smith'
- 'Ice Cool' see *T. repens* 'Green Ice'

§ - 'Susan Smith' (v) CBre CCCN EBee EPfP EWes MNrw WFar WHer

repens SVic WSFF
- 'Douglas Dawson' LDai
- 'Dragon's Blood' CDes CMea LEdu MPie NPro SMrm SPoG WFar WPGP
- 'Gold Net' see *T. pratense* 'Susan Smith'

§ - 'Green Ice' CBre EAEE EBee ECGP LRHS NDov NSti WFar WHal
- 'Harlequin' (v) EBee MHer WCot WFar WMoo WOut WPer
- 'Hullavington' CNat
- 'Purpurascens' CArn CBre CEnt EAEE EPfP LRHS MAsh MBNS MHer MPie NEgg NSti SPoG WNew

§ - 'Purpurascens Quadrifolium' CMea CWan EBee ECha EHoe EPau EWes GAbr MCot NEgg NMir NPer NPri SPer SPlb WFar WHer
- 'Tetraphyllum Purpureum' see *T. repens* 'Purpurascens Quadrifolium'
- 'Wheatfen' CNat CRow EBee NDov NPer
- 'William' CBre ECGP LEdu NDov WCot WFar WOut
rubens CArn CCVN CMea CWCL EBee EHrv EPPr EShb GCal LEdu LRHS MAvo MCot MMHG MMuc MNFA MNHC MNrw SPer SPhx SPlb SSvw SUsu WAul WCAu WFar WMoo WSHC WTin
- 'Drama' MNrw SUsu
- 'Peach Pink' CSpe EBee ELon EPPr LHop MBel MMHG SBch SPhx SSvw SUsu WCot
- 'Red Feathers' ELon EPPr LRHS SMad SMrm WPer WWEG
trichocephalum EPPr

Triglochin (*Juncaginaceae*)

maritimum CRWN
palustre CRWN

Trigonella (*Papilionaceae*)

foenum-graecum CArn SIde

Trillidium see *Trillium*

Trillium ✿ (*Melanthiaceae*)

albidum CWCL ECho GBuc GMaP LLHF LRHS LWst MNrw NMen SKHP SSpi WHal
albidum* × *kurabayashii new LWst
angustipetalum GEdr LWst
apetalon GEdr LWst
camschatcense CPLG GEdr LAma NMen
- from Japan LWst
§ ***catesbyi*** CLAP CPLG CWCL EBee ECho EPot GEdr GKev LAma LLHF LWst MBel MNrw NHol NMen
cernuum CLAP CWCL ECho GCra LRHS WCru WSHC
chloropetalum GBBs GBuc SChF SSpi WPGP
- var. ***chloropetalum*** new GBuc
- var. ***chloropetalum* × *parviflorum*** SKHP
§ - var. ***giganteum*** 🏆H4 CLAP CPLG GBuc GEdr LWst NMen NSla SPhx SSpi WCru
- pink-flowered new GEdr
- var. ***rubrum*** see *T. chloropetalum* var. *giganteum*
- white-flowered ECha
cuneatum Widely available
- 'Ghost' SKHP
- 'Moonshine' SKHP
decipiens GEdr LWst
decumbens GEdr LWst SKHP
discolor GEdr LWst
erectum 🏆H4 Widely available
- f. ***albiflorum*** CCon CLAP CWCL EBee ECho GBuc GEdr LAma LWst MBel MMoz MNrw NHol NMen NMyG SKHP SSpi WCru
- 'Beige' GKev
- f. ***luteum*** LWst SKHP
- red-flowered GKev
erectum* × *flexipes CLAP EBee ECho GBuc GEdr LWst MNrw NBir NMen SKHP SSpi
flexipes CLAP CWCL EBee ECho EHrv GEdr GKev LAma LWst MNrw NMen NMyG SKHP SSpi
- erect EHrv LWst NMen
I - 'Harvington Selection' LRHS LWst MBri SKHP
foetidissimum LWst SKHP
govanianum EBee GHim LWst
gracile LWst
grandiflorum 🏆H4 Widely available
- 'Kath's Dwarf' GEdr
- f. ***polymerum*** 'Flore Pleno' (d) CLAP ECho LLHF LWst SCnR SKHP
- - 'Snowbunting' (d) EBee EWes LWst MMHG NHar WThu
- 'Quicksilver' SKHP
- f. ***roseum*** LWst
kurabayashii CBct CCon CDes CPLG ECho EHrv GBuc LRHS LWst MNrw NMen SChF SKHP SSpi WCru WHal WPGP
lancifolium GEdr LWst
ludovicianum GEdr LWst
luteum 🏆H4 Widely available
maculatum LWst
nivale EBee NHar
ovatum CLAP SSpi
- f. ***hibbersonii*** GBuc GCra
- 'Roy Elliott' CPLG MNrw NMen
parviflorum ECho GEdr LWst SKHP
pusillum CLAP CPLG CWCL EBee ECho ELan EPot GBBs GEdr GKev LLHF LWst MNrw NHol NMen
* - var. ***alabamicum*** SKHP
I - var. ***georgianum*** new SKHP
- var. ***pusillum*** NSla
- var. ***virginianum*** CLAP LAma
recurvatum CBcs CWCL ECho EHrv EPot GBBs GEdr GKev LAma LWst NHol NMen NPnk SKHP WCru WFar WPnP
reliquum LWst
rivale 🏆H3 CLAP CPLG ECho GBBs GBuc LLHF NMen WFar WThu
- pink-flowered GEdr NMen
- 'Purple Heart' CLAP GEdr
rugelii CLAP EBee ECho EHrv EWes GAbr LWst MNrw NMen SKHP SSpi
- Askival hybrids EBee ECho GBuc LWst MNrw SKHP SSpi
- 'Orchard Pink' LWst MNrw
rugelii* × *vaseyi EHrv EWes LWst MNrw NMen SKHP SSpi
sessile CPLG CWCL EBee ECho GBBs GBuc GKev LAma LRHS LWst MAvo NBir NMen NPnk SDeJ SKHP SMrm WCot WFar WKif WSHC WShi
- 'Rubrum' see *T. chloropetalum* var. *giganteum*
simile CLAP ECho LLHF LRHS MNrw SKHP SSpi
smallii WCru
stamineum ECho GEdr
stylosum see *T. catesbyi*
sulcatum CLAP CPLG CWCL EBee ECho EHrv GAbr GBuc GEdr GGGa GMaP LRHS LWst MBri MNrw NMen SKHP SSpi WCot WFar
- cream-flowered LWst
taiwanense B&SWJ 3411 WCru
texanum SKHP

tschonoskii	ECho GEdr LAma
underwoodii	GEdr LWst
undulatum	EBee ECho GEdr LAma LWst MNrw NHol
vaseyi	CLAP CWCL ECho EHrv EWes GBBs GEdr GKev LAma LRHS LWst MNrw NMen SKHP SSpi
- horizontal inflorescence	MNrw
viride	GBBs WFar
viridescens	EBee ECho GEdr LAma LWst WFar

Triosteum (*Caprifoliaceae*)

erythrocarpum	EBee
himalayanum	EBee GCal GEdr GKev WSHC
- BWJ 7907	CLAP WCru
pinnatifidum	CLAP CPom EBee GCal

Tripterospermum (*Gentianaceae*)

* aff. ***chevalieri*** B&SWJ 8359	WCru
cordifolium B&SWJ 081	WCru
distylum B&SWJ 11491	WCru
fasciculatum B&SWJ 7197	WCru
- B&SWJ 11297	WCru
hirticalyx B&SWJ 11725	WCru
- B&SWJ 11786	WCru
japonicum	GEdr LLHF WCot
- B&SWJ 8920	WCru
- B&SWJ 10876	WCru
lanceolatum B&SWJ 085	WCru
- RWJ 9918	WCru
volubile B&SWJ 11774	WCru

Tripterygium (*Celastraceae*)

doianum B&SWJ 11467 **new**	WCru
regelii B&SWJ 5453	WCru
- B&SWJ 10921	WCru
wilfordii BWJ 7852 from China **new**	WCru
- WWJ 12009	WCru

Tristagma (*Alliaceae*)

nivale f. ***nivale*** F&W 10284	WCot

Triteleia (*Asparagaceae*)

'4U'	CAvo CBro EBee ECho WCot
bridgesii	ECho
- NNS 00-731	WCot
californica	see *Brodiaea californica*
§ 'Corrina'	CAvo CBro EBee ECho EPot
dudleyi NNS 01-401	WCot
grandiflora	ECho WCot
hyacinthina	EBee ECho GKev WCot
ixioides	ECho
- subsp. ***anilina*** NNS 95-537	WCot
- 'Splendens'	EBee ECho
- 'Starlight'	CAvo CBro CTri EBee ECho EPot ERCP GKev SDeJ SMrm SPer
§ ***laxa***	ECho
- NNS 00-742	WCot
- NNS 00-743	WCot
- 'Allure'	EBee ECho GKev
- 'Dexter' **new**	EBee WCot
§ - 'Koningin Fabiola'	CBro CMea CSpe CTri EBee ECho EPot GKev IPot LAma MLHP MNrw NBir SDeJ SEND SPer WCot WRHF
- Queen Fabiola	see *T. laxa* 'Koningin Fabiola'
lilacina	ECho
'Ocean Queen' **new**	CMea EBee
§ ***peduncularis***	EBee ECho WCot
'Royal Blue'	EPot ERCP WCot
'Rudy'	CAvo CBro CHid CMea EBee ECho ERCP SDeJ WCot
× ***tubergenii***	ECho
uniflora	see *Ipheion uniflorum*

Trithrinax (*Arecaceae*)

brasiliensis	EAmu SBig
campestris	CBrP EAmu SBig

Tritoma see *Kniphofia*

Tritonia (*Iridaceae*)

crocata ♀H2-3	CPou ECho WCot
- 'Baby Doll'	CPrp EBee LEdu WHil
- 'Pink Sensation'	CDes CSpe EBee ECho
- 'Plymouth Pastel'	CDes
- 'Prince of Orange'	CDes CPou
- 'Princess Beatrix'	CDes
- 'Riversdale'	ECho
- 'Serendipity'	CDes CPrp EBee EPri
- 'Tangerine'	CDes CPBP
deusta	CDes EPri
§ ***disticha***	Widely available
subsp. ***rubrolucens***	
- - short, red-pink-flowered	CDes
- - tall, clear pink-flowered	CDes CTca
flabellifolia	ECho
florentiae 'Tanqua Karoo'	ECho
hyalina	CPou
karooica 'Middlepos'	ECho
laxifolia	CDes CPrp CTca EBee ECho EPot LEdu
lineata	CDes CPou CTca EBee ECho EPri WHil WPGP
- 'Parvifolia'	EBee
pallida	ECho SPlb
rosea	see *T. disticha* subsp. ***rubrolucens***
securigera	CDes ECho LEdu
squalida	ECho EPri

Trochocarpa (*Ericaceae*)

clarkei	WThu
gunnii	WThu
thymifolia	WAbe WThu
- white-flowered	WThu

Trochodendron (*Trochodendraceae*)

aralioides	CBcs CDoC CHEx CMac CSam CTho CTsd CWib EBee EPfP GKin IVic MBlu MBri MGos MMuc NLar SDix SEND SKHP SLPl SLon SPer SReu SSpi SSta WCot WPGP
- B&SWJ 1651 from Taiwan	WCru
- CWJ 12357 from Taiwan	WCru
- RWJ 9845 from Taiwan	WCru

Trollius (*Ranunculaceae*)

ACE 1187	CPLG GEdr
SDR 4816	GKev
acaulis	ECho EWes NMen WFar WPat
asiaticus	EBee GKev
§ ***chinensis***	ECha GCal GKev SWat
- 'Golden Queen' ♀H4	Widely available
× ***cultorum*** 'Alabaster'	Widely available
- 'Baudirektor Linne'	ECtt MRav NGdn WFar
- 'Byrne's Giant'	EBee ECtt GBin

– 'Canary Bird'	ELan EPfP GCal NGdn SRms
– 'Cheddar'	CWCL EBee ECtt ELon EPPr EPfP EWTr GCal GMaP LHop LSou MBNS MBel MBri MMHG MRav MWts NBro NEgg NLar NOrc NPnk NPro SKHP SPoG SPtl SWvt WBor WFar WWEG
– 'Commander-in-Chief'	EBee SMad
– 'Earliest of All'	CSam CWCL EBee MBri NGdn SPer WFar WWEG
– 'Empire Day'	MBri
– 'Etna'	EBee SHar WWEG
§ – 'Feuertroll'	CMea EBee ECha ECtt LRHS MBri MCot MRav NEgg NGdn NPro
– Fireglobe	see *T.* × *cultorum* 'Feuertroll'
– 'Golden Cup'	NBir NGdn
– 'Goldquelle' ♀H4	GBuc
– 'Goliath'	EWes
– 'Helios'	CSam GBuc LLHF LRHS
– 'Lemon Queen'	CMac CWCL CWat EBee ECtt EHrv EPfP GBin GKev GMaP LPBA LRHS MBri MNFA MRav NLar NPnk SPer SWat WFar WHil
– 'Maigold'	MAvo
– 'Orange Crest'	EBee ECtt GCal LSou SPoG WFar WHal WWEG
– 'Orange Globe'	EBee SMrm WFar
– 'Orange Glow'	EBee SMad
– 'Orange Princess' ♀H4	CWCL CWat EBee EPfP GMaP NBro NLar SPer SRms
– 'Orange Queen'	SWvt
– 'Prichard's Giant'	CMHG EBee ECtt ELan NBro NEgg NGdn NLBP WCFE WFar WWEG
§ – 'Superbus' ♀H4	CDes CWCL EBee ELan EPfP GMaP NGdn SPer WFar
– 'T. Smith'	NBro WWEG
– 'Taleggio'	LEdu
europaeus	CRWN CWCL EBee ECha GCal LAst LEdu LHop MLHP MMuc MRav NGdn NHol NMir SBfd SBrt SPet SPhx SRot SWat WAbe WAul WCFE WFar WHoo WWEG
– SDR 5441	GKev
– SDR 5473	GKev SEND
– SDR 6306	GKev
– 'Superbus'	see *T.* × *cultorum* 'Superbus'
hondoensis	EBee GCal GKev LLHF NLar NPro
ircuticus	EBee
laxus	EWes
– 'Albiflorus'	CPLG
ledebourii misapplied	see *T. chinensis*
pumilus	ECha ECho ELan EPfP GCal GKev LRHS NLar NSla SBfd SPer WAbe WFar WPer
– ACE 1818	CPLG EBee GCal MHer NHol NRHS
– 'Wargrave'	ECho
ranunculinus	GKev
ranunculoides	GKev
riederianus	LRHS
stenopetalus	CDes CWCL EWes MBri MNrw MRav NPnk
vaginatus	EBee GKev
yunnanensis	EBee GKev NRHS WFar
– orange-flowered	CPLG GKev

Tropaeolum ✿ (*Tropaeolaceae*)

azureum	CCCN EPot WPGP
beuthii	ECho WCot
brachyceras	CCCN ECho EPot WCot
ciliatum ♀H1	CCCN CCon CGHE ECho ELan GCal NBid NLar WCot WCru WFar WPGP
hookerianum subsp. ***austropurpureum***	CDes CGHE
incisum	CCCN CWCL WCot
majus	ENfk MHoo SVic
– Alaska Series (v) ♀H3	CPrp ENfk MNHC NPri SEND SIde WJek
– 'Apricot Twist'	GBee
– 'Banana Split'	NPri
– 'Crimson Beauty'	CSpe
§ – 'Darjeeling Double' (d) ♀H4	GBee WCot
– 'Darjeeling Gold'	see *T. majus* 'Darjeeling Double'
– 'Empress of India'	CPrp MNHC WJek
– 'Hermine Grashoff' (d) ♀H2-3	CSpe GBee GCal NPer
– Jewel Series **new**	ENfk
– 'Margaret Long' (d)	CSpe GCal WCot
* – 'Peaches and Cream'	WJek
– 'Red Wonder'	CCCN CSpe EPfP NPri
– 'Sunset Pink'	CPrp
– Tom Thumb mixed	MNHC WJek
pentaphyllum	CSpe EBee ECho ELan EWes GCal LLHF WCot WPGP
peregrinum	ECho SBfd
polyphyllum	CCCN CWCL EBee ECho EPfP EPot GBuc GGGa NBir SCnR SMHy WAbe WCot WPGP
sessilifolium	EBee ECho
speciosum ♀H4	Widely available
tricolor ♀H1	CAvo CCCN EBee ECho ELan GCal
tuberosum	ECho GPoy SDeJ WHer
– var. ***lineamaculatum*** 'Ken Aslet' ♀H3	CBcs CBro CCCN CSpe CWCL EBee ECha ECho ELan EOHP EPfP EPot IFro LAma LHop LRHS SPer SPoG

Tsuga ✿ (*Pinaceae*)

canadensis	CDul EPfP NWea WEve
– 'Abbott's Dwarf'	CDoC CKen MGos NHol WGor
§ – 'Abbott's Pygmy'	CKen
– 'Albospica' (v)	WFar
– 'Arnold Gold Weeper'	CKen
– 'Aurea' (v)	NLar WEve
– 'Bacon Cristate'	CKen
– 'Betty Rose' (v)	CKen
– 'Birkett's White'	CKen
– 'Brandley'	CKen
§ – 'Branklyn'	CKen
– 'Cappy's Choice'	CKen
– 'Cinnamonea'	CKen
– 'Coffin'	CKen
– 'Cole's Prostrate'	CKen MAsh NLar SLim
– 'Creamey' (v)	CKen
– 'Curley'	CKen
– 'Curtis Ideal'	CKen
– 'Dr Hornbeck'	see *T. canadensis* 'Hornbeck'
– 'Eisburg' **new**	SLim
– 'Essex'	NWad
* – 'Everitt's Dense Leaf'	CKen
– 'Everitt's Golden'	CKen
– 'Fantana'	LRHS MAsh NHol NLar SCoo SLim WEve
– 'Gentsch White' (v)	NLar
– 'Gracilis'	WThu
– 'Hedgehog'	CDoC NLar
§ – 'Hornbeck'	CKen

	– 'Horsford'	CKen NLar NWad
	– 'Horstmann' No 1	CKen
	– 'Hussii'	CKen NHol NLar
	– 'Jacqueline Verkade'	CKen MAsh NLar
	– 'Jeddeloh' ♀H4	CDoC CMac EPot LRHS MAsh MGos NEgg NHol SCoo SGol SLim SPoG WEve
	– 'Jervis'	CKen NHol NLar NWad
	– 'Julianne'	CKen
	– 'Kingsville Spreader'	CKen
	– 'Little Joe'	CKen
	– 'Little Snow'	CKen
I	– 'Lutea'	CKen
	– 'Many Cones'	CKen
	– 'Minima'	CKen
	– 'Minuta'	CDoC CKen MGos NHol NLar NWad WGor
	– 'Moon Frost'	MAsh NLar
	– 'Palomino'	CKen NLar
	– 'Pendula' ♀H4	CKen EPfP LRHS MAsh MBri SLim WEve WFar
	– 'Pincushion'	CKen
	– 'Prostrata'	see *T. canadensis* 'Branklyn'
	– 'Pygmaea'	see *T. canadensis* 'Abbott's Pygmy'
	– 'Rugg's Washington Dwarf'	CKen
	– 'Snowflake'	CKen
	– 'Stewart's Gem'	CKen
	– 'Verkade Petite'	CKen
	– 'Verkade Recurved'	CKen NLar
	– 'Vermeulen's Wintergold'	NLar
	– 'Von Helms' Dwarf'	CKen
	– 'Warnham'	CKen MAsh
	caroliniana 'La Bar Weeping'	CKen NLar
	chinensis	CKen
	diversifolia 'Gotelli'	CKen
	dumosa	CKen
	heterophylla ♀H4	CBcs CCVT CDul EPfP LBuc MMuc NWea SEND SEWo SGol SMad WEve
	– 'Iron Springs'	CKen
	– 'Laursen's Column'	CKen
	– 'Thorsens Weeping'	CKen
	menziesii	see *Pseudotsuga menziesii*
	mertensiana 'Blue Star'	CKen MAsh
	– 'Elizabeth'	CKen
	– 'Glauca'	CKen
I	– 'Glauca Nana'	CKen
I	– 'Horstmann'	CKen
	– 'Quartz Mountain'	CKen
	sieboldii 'Baldwin'	CKen
	– 'Green Ball'	CKen
	– 'Honeywell Estate'	CKen
	– 'Nana'	CKen

Tuberaria (*Cistaceae*)

	lignosa	WAbe WCot

Tulbaghia ✿ (*Alliaceae*)

	acutiloba	CAvo CTca LEdu MHom NHoy WTul
	'African Moon'	NHoy
	alliacea	CAvo ECho EShb MHom NHoy SCnR WCot
	alliacea* × *violacea	ECho
*	***allioides***	CBro
	'Bob Brown'	CDes WTul
	'Bright Eyes'	NHoy
	capensis	CDes CPou NBir NHoy WCot WTul
	capensis* × *violacea CGV 1970	WTul
	'Cariad'	WTul
	cernua CD&R 199	CDes WTul
	– hybrid	EPri NHoy WTul
	cernua* × *violacea	WTul
§	***coddii***	CPne EBee MHom NHoy WCot WTul
	coddii* × *violacea	NHoy WTul
	cominsii	CPLG EPri SBch WTul
	– 'Harry Hay's Pink'	NHoy
	cominsii* × *violacea	CAvo CPLG CTca EBee MHom NHoy WTul
	– – soft pink-flowered	WTul
	'Cosmic'	CDes CPou EPri LEdu NHoy WTul
	'Crystal'	NHoy
	'Dreaming Spires'	NHoy
	dregeana	NHoy WCot
	'Elaine Ann'	NHoy
	'Enigma'	NHoy
	'Fairy Snow'	WTul
	'Fairy Star'	CDes CTca EBee EShb LEdu NHoy WCot WPGP WTul
	fragrans	see *T. simmleri*
	– 'Alba'	ELan EPot EWTr SDeJ
	galpinii	NHoy WTul
	'Grey Dawn'	NHoy
	'Hazel'	CDes CPou CYeo MHer NHoy WTul
	'Janet'	NHoy
	'John May's Special'	CDes CKno EBee EShb LEdu MHom NHoy SMrm SUsu WPGP WTul
	leucantha	CDes CTca EBee MHom NHoy WPGP WTul
	– H&B 11996	CDes WTul
	– from Sentinel Peak, South Africa	WTul
	'Lilian'	WTul
	ludwigiana	CPne
	maritima	see *T. violacea* var. *maritima*
	Marwood seedling	EBee MHer MHom MTPN NHoy
	montana	EBee MHer NHoy WCot WTul
	natalensis	CBro CPou CPrp ECho LEdu NHoy WHoo
	– B&V 421	EBee SUsu
	– – clone 1 white	NHoy WTul
	– – clone 2 pink	NHoy WTul
	– CD&R 84	NHoy WTul
	– pink-flowered	CTca ECho MHom NHoy WTul
	– white-flowered	CTca
	natalensis* × *verdoorniae	WTul
	– – VOS 1966	WTul
	natalensis* × *violacea	NHoy WTul
	poetica	see *T. coddii*
	'Premier'	NHoy
	'Purple Eye'	CPne WTul
	'Rainbow'	NHoy
§	***simmleri***	CPou EBee ECho EHrv EPot EPri EShb EWes GKev LAma LEdu NHoy SDeJ WTul
	– 'Cheryl Renshaw'	WCot WTul
	– pink-flowered	CTca
	– 'Snow Queen'	CPrp
	– white-flowered	CPou CPrp CTca NHoy WTul
	'Snowball'	NHoy
	'Suzanne'	NHoy
	verdoorniae	NHoy WHil
	violacea	Widely available

	– from RBGE	MHom NHoy
*	– 'Alba'	EBee EHrv EPPr EPri GCal MCot MHer NHoy NMRc SMrm SWat WFar WTin
	– 'Dissect White'	NHoy WTul
I	– 'Fine Form'	CKno NHoy WKif
*	– ***grandiflora***	CAvo
	– 'John Rider'	NHoy WTul
	– 'Lowan'	WTul
*	– var. ***maritima***	CPne CYeo EShb LEdu MHom NHoy SMrm WCot WTul
	– var. ***obtusa***	NHoy WTul
	– 'Pallida'	CBro CCse CDes CPou CTca ECho LEdu NHoy WPGP WTul
	– 'Pearl'	CPou NHoy WTul
	– 'Peppermint Garlic'	CDes CTca WPGP WTul
	– var. ***robustior***	CPou CTca EWes NHoy WTul
	– 'Seren'	WTul
§	– 'Silver Lace' (v)	Widely available
	– 'Variegata'	see *T. violacea* 'Silver Lace'
	– var. ***violacea***	NHoy WTul
	– 'White Goddess'	CPou WTul
	– 'White Star'	EBee
	violacea × ***violacea*** var. ***maritima***	WTul
	white-flowered	WHil

Tulipa ✿ (*Liliaceae*)

	'Abba' (2)	SDeJ
	'Absalon' (9)	GKev LAma
	'Abu Hassan' (3)	CAvo CMea ERCP LAma MBri SDeJ
	acuminata (15)	CAvo CBro CTca ECho ERCP LAma NMin SDeJ SPhx
	'Ad Rem' (4)	MBri
	'Addis' (14) ♀H4	LAma
	affinis new	LWst
	'African Queen' (3)	LAma
	aitchisonii	see *T. clusiana*
	'Aladdin' (6)	LAma SDeJ
	'Aladdin's Record' (6)	CAvo CBro SDeJ
	'Albert Heijn' (13) new	SDeJ
	albertii (15)	ECho LAma NMin
	'Aleppo' (7)	SDeJ
	'Alfred Cortot' (12) ♀H4	LAma SDeJ
	'Allegretto' (11)	MBri
	altaica (15) ♀H4	ECho EPot LAma
	amabilis	see *T. hoogiana*
	'American Eagle' (7)	SDeJ
	'Analita' (13)	LAma
	'Ancilla' (12) ♀H4	CBro LAma
	'Angélique' (11) ♀H4	CAvo CTca EPfP ERCP GKev LAma MBri NBir SDeJ SPer
	'Annie Schilder' (3)	ERCP
	'Antoinette'PBR (5)	LAma
	'Apeldoorn' (4)	GKev LAma MBri SDeJ SPer
	'Apeldoorn's Elite' (4) ♀H4	LAma MBri SDeJ
	'Apricot Beauty' (1) ♀H4	CHid CTca ERCP LAma MBri MMHG NBir SDeJ
	'Apricot Emperor' (13)	MCot
	'Apricot Impression'PBR (4)	LAma
	'Apricot Jewel'	see *T. linifolia* (Batalinii Group) 'Apricot Jewel'
	'Apricot Parrot' (10) ♀H4	CAvo LAma MBri MCot SDeJ
	'Arabian Mystery' (3)	CAvo ERCP LAma NHol SDeJ
	'Aria Card' (7) new	ERCP
	'Artist' (8) ♀H4	EPfP ERCP LAma SDeJ
	'Atlantis' (5) new	MBri
	'Attila' (3)	CAvo LAma
	aucheriana (15) ♀H4	CBro ECho EPot LAma LLHF NMin
	australis (15)	ECho
	aximensis (15)	ECho LAma NMin
	'Bacchus' (7)	LAma
	bakeri	see *T. saxatilis* Bakeri Group
	'Ballade' (6) ♀H4	CAvo ERCP LAma MCot SDeJ
	Ballade Dream = 'Sonnet' (6)	SDeJ
	'Ballerina' (6) ♀H4	CAvo CBro CMea CTca ECho EPfP ERCP LAma MBri MCot SDeJ SPer SPhx
	'Banja Luka' (4)	SDeJ
	'Barbados' (7)	LAma
	'Barcelona' (3) ♀H4	ERCP
	'Baronesse' (5) new	SDeJ
	'Bastogne Parrot'PBR (10)	LAma
	batalinii	see *T. linifolia* Batalinii Group
	'Beau Monde' (3) ♀H4	SDeJ
	'Beauty of Apeldoorn' (4)	LAma MBri
	'Beauty Queen' (1)	SDeJ
	'Belicia' (2)	LAma
	'Bellflower' (7)	LAma
	'Bellona' (3)	SDeJ
	'Berlioz' (12)	SDeJ
	'Bestseller' (1)	SDeJ
	biebersteiniana (15)	ECho NMin
§	***biflora*** (15)	CAvo CTca ECho EPot GKev IFro LAma LWst SBch SDeJ SPhx WShi
	bifloriformis (15)	ECho LLHF
I	– 'Maxima' (15)	ECho NMin SPhx
	– 'Starlight' (15) ♀H4	ECho LWst NMin SPhx
	'Big Chief' (4) ♀H4	LAma
	'Black Hero' (11)	CAvo EPfP ERCP LAma MCot SDeJ
	'Black Jewel' (7)	ERCP LAma SDeJ
	'Black Parrot' (10) ♀H4	CAvo CBro CHid EPfP ERCP LAma MBri SDeJ SPer
	'Black Stallion' (11)	LAma
	'Black Swan' (5)	SDeJ
	'Bleu Aimable' (5)	CAvo ERCP SDeJ
	'Blue Diamond' (11)	CAvo ERCP SDeJ
	'Blue Heron' (7) ♀H4	CAvo ERCP LAma MCot SDeJ
	'Blue Parrot' (10)	CAvo EPfP ERCP LAma SDeJ
	'Blue Ribbon' (3)	CAvo
	Blueberry Ripple	see *T.* 'Zurel'
	'Blushing Beauty' (5)	SDeJ
	'Blushing Bride' (5)	SDeJ
	'Blushing Lady' (5)	MCot
	'Boutade' (14)	NPer
	'Bridesmaid' (5)	LAma
	'Burgundy' (6)	CTca ERCP LAma SDeJ
	'Burgundy Lace' (7)	LAma SDeJ
	'Burning Heart' (4) ♀H4	SDeJ
	'Buttercup' (14) ♀H4 new	SDeJ
	'Café Noir' (5)	ERCP LAma
	'Cairo'	ERCP
	'Calgary' (3) ♀H4	EPfP LAma
	'Calypso' (14) ♀H4	LRHS
	'Canasta' (7)	SDeJ
	'Candela' (13) ♀H4	LAma SDeJ
	'Candy Club' (5)	LAma
	'Candy Prince'PBR (1)	EPfP
	'Canova' (7)	SDeJ
	'Cantata' (13)	LAma
	'Cape Cod' (14)	LAma
	'Cardinal Mindszenty' (2)	ERCP SDeJ
	carinata (15)	ECho LWst NMin
	'Carlton' (2)	MCot
	'Carnaval de Nice' (11/v) ♀H4	CBro CTca ERCP LAma MBri SDeJ SPer
	'Carrousel' (7)	SDeJ

	Name	Suppliers
	'Cassini' (3)	LAma SDeJ
§	***celsiana*** (15)	ECho LAma
	'China Lady' (14) ♀H4	ECho SDeJ
	'China Pink' (6) ♀H4	CAvo CBro CMea CTca EPfP ERCP LAma MBri MCot SDeJ
	'China Town' (8) ♀H4	ERCP LAma MBri SDeJ
	'Christmas Dream' (1)	SDeJ
	'Christmas Marvel' (1)	LAma
	chrysantha Boiss. ex Baker	see *T. montana*
	'Cistula' (6) **new**	SDeJ
	'City of Vancouver' (5)	EPfP
	'Claudia' (6)	SPer
	'Cloud Nine' (5)	ECho
§	***clusiana*** (15)	CBro ECho ERCP LAma LWSt MBri NMin SPhx WHer
	- var. ***chrysantha*** (15) ♀H4	CAvo CPLG ECho LAma SPhx WHoo WShi
	- - 'Tubergen's Gem' (15)	ECho EPot GKev LAma MBri NMin SPhx
	- 'Cynthia' (15) ♀H4	CTca ECho EPot ERCP GKev LAma MBri NMin SDeJ SPhx
	- 'Sheila' (15)	ECho IFro NMin SPhx
§	- var. ***stellata*** (15)	ECho
	'Columbine' (5)	ECho LAma
	'Concerto' (13)	CBro MBri NPer SDeJ
	'Coquette' (1) **new**	SDeJ
	'Corona' (12)	ECho SDeJ
	'Corsage' (14) ♀H4	SDeJ
	'Cortina' (9)	SDeJ
	'Couleur Cardinal' (3)	CBro ERCP LAma SDeJ
	'Creme Upstar' (11)	MBri SDeJ
	cretica (15)	ECho EPot LAma LWSt NMin
	'Crispion Dark' (7)	ERCP
	'Cum Laude' (5)	LAma
	'Cummins' (7)	CAvo ERCP
	'Curly Sue' (7)	CAvo ERCP LAma MCot
	'Czaar Peter' (14) ♀H4	CAvo EPfP MBri NPer
	'Dance' (13)	SDeJ
	'Dancing Queen' **new**	MBri
	'Dancing Show' (8)	LAma
	dasystemon (15)	ECho EPot LAma SPhx
	dasystemonoides (15)	ECho
	'Davenport' (7)	ERCP
	'David Teniers' (2)	ERCP
	'Daydream' (4) ♀H4	SPer
	'Daytona' (7)	CAvo
	didieri misapplied	see *T. passeriniana*
	'Doll's Minuet' (8)	ERCP LAma
	'Don Quichotte' (3) ♀H4	MBri SDeJ
	'Donald Duck' (14) ♀H4 **new**	MBri
	'Donauperle' (14) **new**	SDeJ
	'Donna Bella' (14) ♀H4	EPfP SDeJ
	'Dordogne' (5) ♀H4	SDeJ
	'Double Price' (2)	ERCP
	'Double Red Riding Hood' (14v) **new**	SDeJ
	'Dreamboat' (14)	MBri
	'Dreaming Maid' (3)	LAma MBri
	'Dreamland' (5) ♀H4	MBri SDeJ
	'Duc van Tol Max Cramoisie' (1)	LAma
	'Duc van Tol Primrose' (1)	LAma
	'Duc van Tol Red and Yellow' (I)	GKev WHer
	'Duc van Tol Rose' (1)	LAma
	'Duc van Tol Salmon' (1)	LAma
	'Duc van Tol Violet' (1)	LAma
	'Duc van Tol White' (1)	LAma
	'Dutch Gold' (3)	MBri
	'Dynasty' (3)	SPer
	'Early Harvest' (12) ♀H4	CAvo SDeJ
	'Easter Surprise' (14) ♀H4	MBri NHol SDeJ
	eichleri	see *T. undulatifolia*
	'Electra' (5)	LAma MBri
	'Elegans Alba' (6)	LAma
	'Elegant Lady' (6)	CAvo CBro LAma MCot SDeJ
	'Esperanto' (8/v) ♀H4	LAma SDeJ
	'Estella Rijnveld' (10)	ERCP LAma SDeJ
	'Eternal Flame' (2)	ERCP LAma
	'Exotic Emperor'	LAma
	'Fancy Frills' (7) ♀H4	ERCP LAma SDeJ
	'Fantasy' (10) ♀H4	LAma
	ferganica (15)	ECho LAma LWSt NMin
	'Fidelio' (3) ♀H4	SDeJ
*	'Finola' (11)	MCot
	'Fire Queen' (3) ♀H4	LAma
	'Flair' (1)	LAma SDeJ
	'Flaming Parrot' (10)	CAvo ERCP GKev LAma MBri
I	'Flaming Purissima' (13)	CAvo MBri SDeJ
	'Flaming Springgreen' (8)	CAvo ERCP LAma SDeJ
	'Flig Flag' **new**	ERCP
	'Florosa' (8)	ERCP SDeJ
	'Foxtrot' PBR (2)	EPfP ERCP
	'Françoise' (3)	SDeJ
	'Franz Léhar' (12)	SDeJ
	'Fringed Family' (7)	SDeJ
	'Fritz Kreisler' (12)	LAma SDeJ
	'Fulgens' (6)	ECho LAma
	'Für Elise' (14)	SDeJ
	'Gaiety' (12)	SDeJ
	'Garden Party' (3) ♀H4	LAma SDeJ
	'Gavota' (3) ♀H4	CAvo CBro EPfP LAma MCot SDeJ SPer
	'Gemma' (10)	LAma
	'Generaal de Wet' (1)	LAma SDeJ SPhx
	'Georgette' (5)	LAma MBri
	'Gerbrand Kieft' (11) ♀H4	ERCP
	'Giuseppe Verdi' (12)	LAma MBri
	'Glück' (12) ♀H4	ECho LRHS
	'Golden Apeldoorn' (4)	LAma MBri SDeJ
	'Golden Artist' (8)	EPfP LAma MBri SDeJ
	'Golden Emperor' (13)	LAma SDeJ SPer
	'Golden Melody' (3)	SDeJ
	'Golden Oxford' (4)	LAma
	'Golden Parade' (4)	LAma
	'Gordon Cooper' (4)	SDeJ
	'Goudstuk' (12)	LAma
	'Grand Perfection' PBR (3) ♀H4 **new**	EPfP
	'Green Eyes' (8)	SDeJ
	'Green River' (8)	SDeJ
	'Green Wave' (10)	ERCP LAma SDeJ
	grengiolensis (15)	ECho LAma NMin
	'Groenland' (8)	CAvo CBro LAma MBri MCot
	'Gudoshnik' (4)	LAma
	hageri (15)	ECho LAma MBri
	- 'Red Cup' (13)	NMin
	- 'Splendens' (15)	ECho EPot LAma SPhx
	'Hamilton' (7) ♀H4	LAma SDeJ
	'Happy Family' (3)	LAma
	'Happy Generation' (3)	LAma MBri
	'Happy Hour' (7) ♀H4	ERCP
	'Havran' (3)	CAvo ERCP LAma
	'Heart's Delight' (12)	CBro ECho LAma MBri SDeJ
	'Hemisphere' (3)	EPfP ERCP LAma SDeJ
	'Hermitage' (3)	ERCP LAma
	heweri (15)	ECho LAma NMin

	Name	Suppliers
	hissarica (15)	ECho
	'Hocus Pocus' (5)	SDeJ
	'Holland Baby' (2) **new**	SDeJ
	'Holland Bouquet' (3)	LAma
	'Holland Chic' (6)	LAma MCot SDeJ
	'Hollandia' (3)	MBri
	'Hollands Glorie' (4) 🏆H4	SDeJ
	'Hollywood' (8)	LAma
	'Honeymoon' (7)	LAma
	'Honky Tonk' (15) 🏆H4	CAvo ECho GKev MBri NMin
§	***hoogiana*** (15)	ECho
	'Hotpants' (3)	LAma
§	***humilis*** (15)	CBro ECho GKev LAma MBri WShi
	- 'China Carol' (15)	ECGP ECho IFro SDeJ
	- 'Eastern Spice' (15)	ECho LAma NMin
	- 'Eastern Star' (15)	ECho GKev LAma MBri NMin SPhx
	- 'Helene' (15)	ECho
§	- 'Lilliput' (15)	CBro CMea ECho EPot GKev LAma LRHS NMin SPhx
	- 'Magenta Queen' (15)	ECho
	- 'Odalisque' (15)	ECho EPot ERCP GKev LAma NMin
	- 'Pallida' (15)	ECho
	- 'Pegasus' (15)	NMin
	- 'Persian Pearl' (15)	CAvo CMea ECho EPfP EPot ERCP GKev LAma MBri NMin SDeJ SMrm
*	- 'Pink Charm' (15)	ECho
§	- var. ***pulchella***	ECho SPhx
	- - Albocaerulea Oculata Group (15)	CPou CTca ECho EPot ERCP GKev LAma LLHF LWst MCot NMin SPhx
§	- Violacea Group (15)	CAvo CMea ECho LAma MBri
	- - black base (15)	CBro ECho EPot ERCP GKev MBri NMin SBch
	- - yellow base (15)	ECho EPot GKev LAma
	- 'Zephyr' (15)	NMin
	'Humming Bird' (8)	LAma
	hungarica **new**	ECho
	'Ile de France' (5)	ERCP LAma SDeJ SPer
	iliensis (15)	CMea ECho EPot LLHF LWst NMin
	'India' (3)	ERCP
	'Indian Summer' (3)	MCot
	ingens (15)	ECho LAma NMin SPhx
	'Insulinde' (9)	LAma
	'Inzell' (3)	EPfP LAma
	'Ivory Floradale' (4) 🏆H4	LAma SDeJ
	'Jan Reus' (3)	CAvo ERCP
	'Jazz' (6)	ERCP
	'Jewel of Spring' (4) 🏆H4	LAma
	'Joffre' (1)	MBri
	'Johann Strauss' (12)	ECho LAma MBri
	'Juan' (13) 🏆H4	MBri
	julia (15)	ECho NMin
	karabaghensis (15)	ECho
	'Karel Doorman' (10)	LAma
	kaufmanniana (12)	ECho EPot
§	'Kees Nelis' (3)	MBri
	'Keizerskroon' (1) 🏆H4	LAma SDeJ
	'Kingsblood' (5) 🏆H4	SDeJ
	kolpakowskiana (15) 🏆H4	ECho EPfP EPot ERCP LAma MBri NMin WShi
	kurdica (15)	ECho LAma SPhx
	- purple-flowered (15)	ECho LWst
	- red-flowered (15)	LWst
	'Lac van Rijn' (1)	GKev LAma
*	'Lady Diana' (14)	MBri
	'Lady Jane' (15) 🏆H4	CAvo CBro ECho EPfP ERCP NMin SPer SPhx WShi
	lanata (15)	ECho NMin
	'Latvian Gold' (15)	ECho NMin
	'Leen van der Mark' (3)	LAma MBri
	'Libretto Parrot' (10)	LAma SDeJ
	'Lighting Sun' (4)	LAma
	'Lilac Perfection' (11)	CTca ERCP MBri SDeJ
	'Lilac Wonder'	see *T. saxatilis* (Bakeri Group) 'Lilac Wonder'
	'Lilliput'	see *T. humilis* 'Lilliput'
	'Lilyfire' (6) **new**	ECGP SDeJ
	linifolia (15) 🏆H4	CAvo CBro ECho EPfP EPot ERCP GKev LAma MBri NMin SDeJ SPhx WShi
§	- Batalinii Group (15) 🏆H4	ECho LAma LWst MBri SPhx
§	- - 'Apricot Jewel' (15)	CBro ECho EPot ERCP GKev
	- - 'Bright Gem' (15) 🏆H4	CBro ECho EPot GKev LAma MBri NPer SPhx WHoo
	- - 'Bronze Charm' (15)	CAvo CMea ECGP ECho EPot LAma MBri NMin SDeJ SPhx
	- - 'Red Gem' (15)	ECho GKev LAma SPhx
	- - 'Red Hunter' (15) 🏆H4	ECho ERCP GKev MBri SPer
	- - 'Red Jewel' (15)	ECho
	- - 'Salmon Gem' (15) **new**	ECho
	- - 'Yellow Jewel' (15)	ECho GKev LAma LWst SPhx
§	- Maximowiczii Group (15)	ECho EPot LAma
	'Lion King' (7) **new**	ERCP
	'Lipgloss' (3)	LAma
	'Little Beauty' (15) 🏆H4	CAvo CBro CMea ECho EPfP GKev LAma MBri SBch SDeJ SMrm SPhx WHoo
	'Little Princess' (15) 🏆H4	CAvo CBro CMea CTca ECho ERCP GKev LAma SPhx
	'Little Star' (15) **new**	NMin
	'Lovely Surprise' (14)	SDeJ
	'Lucky Strike' (3)	MBri
§	'Lustige Witwe' (3)	SDeJ
	'Mabel' (9)	LAma
§	'Madame Lefeber' (13)	MBri SDeJ
	'Madonna' (10)	EPfP
	'Magier' (5)	MBri
	'Maja' (7)	MBri MCot
	'March of Time' (14)	MBri
	'Marie José' (14) **new**	SDeJ
	'Mariette' (6)	CBro LAma MBri SDeJ SPer
	'Marilyn' (6)	ERCP LAma SDeJ
	marjolletii (15)	CBro ECho LAma NMin
	'Maroon'	ERCP
	'Mary Ann' (14)	LAma
	'Matchpoint' (7/d)	ERCP SDeJ
	'Maureen' (5) 🏆H4	ERCP LAma SDeJ
	mauritiana (15)	ECho
	- 'Cindy' (15)	ECho NMin SPhx
	maximowiczii	see *T. linifolia* Maximowiczii Group
	'Maytime' (6)	ERCP LAma MBri MCot SDeJ
	'Maywonder' (11) 🏆H4	MBri
	'Menton' (5) 🏆H4	ERCP LAma SDeJ
	'Menton Exotic' **new**	ERCP
	Merry Widow	see *T.* 'Lustige Witwe'
	'Mickey Mouse' (1)	MBri
	'Miskodeed' (14)	SDeJ
	'Miss Holland' (3)	MBri
	'Mona Lisa' (6)	LAma SDeJ
	'Moneymaker' (6) **new**	ERCP
§	***montana*** (15)	CTca ECho EPot LAma LWst NMin SPhx
	- yellow-flowered	ECho GKev LAma NMin SPhx
	'Monte Carlo' (2) 🏆H4	LAma MBri
	'Montreux' (2)	ECho LAma
	'Mount Tacoma' (11)	CAvo CBro EPfP ERCP LAma MBri MCot NHol SDeJ SPer
	'Mr Van der Hoef' (2)	LAma MBri SDeJ

'Mrs John T. Scheepers' (5) ♀H4	SDeJ
'Muriel' (10)	ERCP
'Negrita' (3)	ERCP LAma MBri MCot SDeJ
neustruevae (15)	ECho EPot NMin SPhx
'New Design' (3/v)	LAma MBri
'Nightrider' (8)	CAvo ERCP MCot
'Ollioules' (4) ♀H4	SDeJ
'Olympic Flame' (4) ♀H4	SDeJ
'Orange Bouquet' (3) ♀H4	LAma MBri
'Orange Elite' (14)	MBri
'Orange Emperor' (13) ♀H4	CAvo LAma MBri MCot SDeJ
'Orange Favourite' (10)	ERCP LAma
'Orange Princess' (11) ♀H4	CTca ERCP SDeJ
'Orange Sun'	see *T.* 'Oranjezon'
'Orange Triumph' (11)	MBri
'Oranje Nassau' (2) ♀H4	LAma MBri
§ 'Oranjezon' (4) ♀H4	ERCP
'Oratorio' (14) ♀H4	MBri SDeJ
'Oriental Beauty' (14) ♀H4	EPfP
orithyioides	ECho NMin
orphanidea (15)	ECho LAma NMin SCnR
- 'Flava' (15)	ECho EPot LAma SPhx
§ - Whittallii Group (15) ♀H4	CAvo ECho EPot ERCP GKev LAma NMin SPhx
ostrowskiana (15)	ECho LAma LWst NMin
'Oxford' (4) ♀H4	LAma
'Oxford's Elite' (4)	LAma
'Page Polka' (3)	MBri SDeJ
'Palestrina' (3)	EPfP
'Pandour' (14)	MBri
'Papillon' (9)	LAma
'Parade' (4) ♀H4	MBri
§ ***passeriniana*** (15)	ECho
'Passionale' (3) ♀H4	EPfP SDeJ SPer
patens	ECho
'Paul Scherer' (3) ♀H4	ERCP
'Peach Blossom' (2)	ERCP LAma MBri SDeJ SPer
'Peppermintstick' (15) ♀H4	CAvo CTca ECho NMin SDeJ
'Perestroyka' (5)	MBri SDeJ
'Perfecta' (10)	GKev
persica	see *T. celsiana*
'Philippe de Comines' (5)	LAma
'Piccolo' (15)	LAma
'Picture' (5) ♀H4	ERCP LAma SDeJ
'Pieter de Leur' (6)	EPfP LAma MBri SPer
'Pimpernel' (8/v)	LAma SDeJ
'Pink Diamond' (5)	EPfP ERCP SDeJ
'Pink Dwarf' (12)	SDeJ
'Pink Impression' (4) ♀H4	LAma MBri SDeJ
'Pink Sensation' (14) ♀H4 **new**	SDeJ
'Pinocchio' (14)	LRHS MBri SDeJ
'Plaisir' (14) ♀H4	LAma MBri
planifolia (15)	ECho
platystigma (15)	ECho LAma NMin
'Poco Loco' (13) **new**	SDeJ
polychroma	see *T. biflora*
praestans (15)	ECho LAma SPer WShi
- 'Bloemenlust' (15) **new**	ECho
- 'Fusilier' (15) ♀H4	CBro CPLG ECGP ECho EPfP EPot LAma MBri NBir SDeJ
- 'Moondance' (15) **new**	ECho
- 'Red Sun' (15) **new**	ECho
- 'Shogun' (15) **new**	ECho ERCP
- 'Unicum' (15/v)	ECho ERCP LAma MBri NMin SDeJ
- 'Van Tubergen's Variety' (15)	ECho LAma NPer
- 'Yari' (15) **new**	ECho
- 'Zwanenburg Variety' (15)	ECho
'Princeps' (13)	LAma MBri SDeJ
'Princess Unique'PBR (11)	LAma
'Princesse Charmante' (14) ♀H4	MBri
'Prinses Irene' (3) ♀H4	CAvo CBro CMea CTca EPfP ERCP LAma LRHS MBri MCot NBir SDeJ
'Prinses Margriet' (3)	ERCP
'Professor Röntgen' (10)	ERCP LAma SDeJ
pulchella	see *T. humilis* var. *pulchella*
- humilis	see *T. humilis*
§ 'Purissima' (13) ♀H4	CAvo CBro EPfP LAma MBri MCot SDeJ SPer SPhx
'Purple Bouquet' (3)	LAma
'Purple Prince' (5)	LAma LRHS SDeJ
'Quebec' (14)	SDeJ
'Queen of Marvel' (2)	SDeJ
'Queen of Night' (5)	CAvo CBro CMea CTca EPfP ERCP GKev LAma MBri MCot NHol SPer SPhx WPtf
'Queen of Sheba' (6) ♀H4	LAma
'Quest' (3)	LAma
'Recreado' (5)	CAvo ERCP SDeJ
'Red Emperor'	see *T.* 'Madame Lefeber'
'Red Georgette' (5) ♀H4	LAma MBri NBir
'Red Princess' (11) ♀H4	ERCP
'Red Riding Hood' (14) ♀H4	CAvo CBro EPfP GKev LAma LRHS MBri NBir SDeJ SPer
'Red Shine' (6) ♀H4	CAvo CBro LAma MBri SDeJ
'Red Springgreen' (8)	LAma SDeJ
'Red Wing' (7) ♀H4	SDeJ
regelii (15) **new**	ECho
Rembrandt mix (9)	MBri
'Renown' (5)	SDeJ
'Renown Unique' (11)	LAma
rhodopea	see *T. urumoffii*
'Ringo'	see *T.* 'Kees Nelis'
'Rococo' (10)	CBro ERCP MBri SDeJ
'Ronaldo' (3)	EPfP ERCP LAma
* 'Rose Emperor' (13)	MBri
'Rosy Dream' (13)	SDeJ
'Salmon Impression'PBR (4)	MBri
'Salut' (13)	MCot
'Sapporro' (6)	ERCP LAma
saracenica	ECho LWst
saxatilis (15)	CBro CMea ECho EPfP GKev LAma MBri SDeJ WShi
§ - Bakeri Group (15)	CPou ECho
§ - - 'Lilac Wonder' (15) ♀H4	CAvo CBro CPLG ECho EPot ERCP GKev LAma MBri NPer SEND SPhx
'Scarlet Baby' (12)	EPfP MBri
schmidtii **new**	ECho
'Schoonoord' (2)	LAma MBri
schrenkii (15)	ECho ERCP LAma NMin
'Scotch Lassie' (5)	ECho
'Sensual Touch' (7) ♀H4 **new**	SDeJ
'Shakespeare' (12)	CBro ECho LAma SDeJ
'Shirley' (3)	CAvo EPfP ERCP LAma MBri MCot SDeJ SPer
'Shirley Dream' (3)	SDeJ
'Showtime' (14) **new**	SDeJ
'Showwinner' (12) ♀H4	CAvo CBro LAma MBri NHol
'Silverstream' (4)	LAma
'Snow Parrot' (10)	ERCP
sogdiana (15)	ECho LAma LLHF LWst NMin
'Sorbet' (5) ♀H4	LAma SDeJ
sosnowskyi (15)	ECho

sprengeri (15) 𝕐H4	CAvo CBro CDes CLAP CPLG CRDP CTca ECGP ECha ECho EPot ERCP LAma LLHF SCnR WHal WIvy WShi
- Trotter's form (15)	WCot
'Spring Green' (8) 𝕐H4	CAvo CBro EPfP ERCP GKev LAma MBri MMHG SDeJ SPer SPhx
'Spryng' (3) 𝕐H4	SDeJ
'Starfighter' (7)	SDeJ
stellata	see *T. clusiana* var. *stellata*
'Stockholm' (2) 𝕐H4	LAma
'Stresa' (12) 𝕐H4	CBro LAma LRHS SDeJ
subpraestans (15)	ECho LAma
'Super Parrot' (10)	LAma
'Swan Wings' (7)	ERCP LAma SDeJ SPer
'Sweet Harmony' (5) 𝕐H4	MBri
'Sweetheart' (13)	MBri SDeJ
sylvestris (15)	CAvo CBro CTca ECho EPfP EPot ERCP LAma MBri NBir NMin SDeJ SPhx WCot WHer WShi
systola (15)	ECho NMin
'Taco' (15) **new**	ECho MBri
tarda (15) 𝕐H4	CAvo CBro CPLG ECho EPfP ERCP GKev LAma LPot LRHS MBri NSla SDeJ SPhx
- 'Kazakhstan' (15)	ECho
'Temple of Beauty' (5) 𝕐H4	SPhx
'Temple's Favourite' (5) **new**	MBri
'Tequila Sun' (3)	LAma
tetraphylla (15)	ECho LAma LWst NMin
'Texas Flame' (10)	MBri SDeJ
'Texas Gold' (10)	LAma SDeJ
'The First' (12)	CAvo
'The Lizard' (9)	LAma
'Theeroos' (2)	LAma
'Tinka' (15) 𝕐H4	ECho EPfP LSou NMin SPhx
'Toplips' (11)	SDeJ
'Topparrot' (10) **new**	SDeJ
'Toronto' (14) 𝕐H4	CTca LAma MBri SDeJ
'Toronto Double' (2) **new**	SDeJ
'Toulon' (13) 𝕐H4	MBri
'Très Chic' (6)	CTca EPfP MBri SPer
'Trinket' (14) 𝕐H4	LAma
tschimganica (15)	ECho LAma LWst
tubergeniana (15)	ECho
- 'Keukenhof' (15)	ECho
turkestanica (15) 𝕐H4	CBro CPLG CTca ECho EPfP EPot ERCP GKev LAma LPot MBri NPer SDeJ SPhx WHoo
'Turkish Delight' (14)	NPer
'Typhoon' (3)	LAma
'Uncle Tom' (11)	ERCP LAma MBri SDeJ
§ ***undulatifolia*** (15)	ECho LAma
- 'Clare Benedict' (15)	ECho NMin
- 'Excelsa' (15)	ECho NMin
'Union Jack' (5) 𝕐H4	LAma
'United States' (14)	NPer
urumiensis (15) 𝕐H4	CBro ECho EPot GKev LAma LPot MBri NMin SBch SDeJ SPhx
§ ***urumoffii*** (15)	ECho LAma
'Valentine' (3) 𝕐H4	SDeJ
'Valery Gergiev' (7)	ERCP
'Van der Neer' (1)	SDeJ
'Velvet Lily' (6)	NMin
'Verona' (2)	SDeJ
'Véronique Sanson' (3)	SDeJ
violacea	see *T. humilis* Violacea Group
'Violet Bird' (8)	ERCP SDeJ
'Virichic' (8)	ERCP MCot
vvedenskyi (15)	ECho EPot GKev SPhx
- 'Girlfriend' **new**	ECho
- 'Tangerine Beauty' (15) 𝕐H4	ECho GKev MBri
'Warbler' (7)	SDeJ
* 'Water Lily'	ECho
'Weber's Parrot' (10)	ERCP MBri
'Weisse Berliner' (3)	CBro LAma
'West Point' (6) 𝕐H4	CAvo CBro CTca ERCP LAma MBri SDeJ
'White Dream' (3)	CAvo EPfP LAma MBri SDeJ
'White Emperor'	see *T.* 'Purissima'
'White Parrot' (10)	CAvo ERCP LAma SDeJ
'White Triumphator' (6) 𝕐H4	CAvo CBro CMea ERCP GKev LAma MBri MCot NBir SDeJ SPhx
whittallii	see *T. orphanidea* Whittallii Group
'Wildhof' (3) 𝕐H4	ERCP
'Willemsoord' (2)	LAma MBri SDeJ
'William of Orange'	SDeJ
wilsoniana	see *T. montana*
'Wisley' (5) **new**	MBri
'World Expression' (5) 𝕐H4	SDeJ
'Yellow Crown' (3)	LAma
'Yellow Emperor' (5)	MBri
'Yellow Flight' (3)	LAma SDeJ
'Yellow Pompenette'PBR (11) 𝕐H4	SDeJ
I 'Yellow Purissima' (13) 𝕐H4	EPfP
'Yellow Springgreen' (8)	ERCP
'Yokohama' (3)	LAma SDeJ
'Zampa' (14) 𝕐H4	MBri
zenaidae (15)	ECho
'Zombie' (13)	LAma
'Zomerschoon' (5)	LAma
§ 'Zurel' (3)	EPfP ERCP LAma MCot

tummelberry see *Rubus* 'Tummelberry'

Tunica see *Petrorhagia*

Tupistra (*Asparagaceae*)

aurantiaca	GEdr
- B&SWJ 2267	WCot WCru
- B&SWJ 2401	WCru
chinensis 'Eco China Ruffles'	WCot
fimbriata	WCot
grandistigma	WCot
nutans	EBee GHim
urotepala HWJ 562	WCru
wattii B&SWJ 8297	WCru

Tussilago (*Asteraceae*)

farfara	CArn GPoy MHer NMir WHer WHfH WSFF

Tweedia (*Asclepiadaceae*)

§ ***caerulea*** 𝕐H2	CBcs CCCN CDTJ CHII CSPN CSpe EShb EUJe SGar SPad SWal

Typha (*Typhaceae*)

angustifolia	CBen CKno CRow CWat EHon LPBA MMuc MSKA NLar NPer SEND SLPl SPlb SWat WPnP
latifolia	CBen CRow CWat EHon LPBA MSKA NBir NLar NPer SEND SVic SWat WHer WMAq WPnP
- 'Variegata' (v)	CRow ELan LPBA MSKA MWts NLar NPla WCot WMAq

§	***laxmannii***	CBen CRow EHon LPBA MSKA NLar WPnP
	lugdunensis	MWts
	minima	CBen CCon CRow CWat EHoe EHon ELan EPfP LPBA MSKA MWts NLar NPer SCoo SWat WMAq WPnP
	shuttleworthii	CRow
	stenophylla	see *T. laxmannii*

Typhonium (*Araceae*)

	alpinum	EBee WCot
	giganteum	SKHP WCot
	roxburghii	GHim
	venosum	EUJe

Typhonodorum (*Araceae*)

	lindleyanum	XBlo

U

Uapaca (*Euphorbiaceae*)

	kirkiana (F)	XBlo

Ugni (*Myrtaceae*)

§	***molinae***	CAgr CBcs CCon CDoy CDul CHll CPLG CPrp EBee ELan ELon EShb IDee IVic LEdu LRHS MCoo MHer MOWG SBfd SLPl SWvt WFar WGwG WJek WMoo
	- 'Butterball' **new**	EShb
	- 'Flambeau'	CAgr CBcs CMac CPLG EBee ELan EPfP EShb IVic LBMP LEdu LHop LRHS MAsh MGos NLar SBfd SHil SLon SPoG SPtl SWvt WGrn
	- orange-leaved **new**	WJek
	- 'Variegata' (v)	LEdu WJek

Ulex (*Papilionaceae*)

	europaeus	CArn CBcs CCVT CDoC CDul CHab CMac CRWN CTri ECrN ELan EPfP LBuc MCoo MGos MMuc NEgg NWea SEND SEWo SPer WHar
§	- 'Flore Pleno' (d) ♀[H4]	CBcs CDoC CDul CMac CSBt CTri ELan ELon EPfP GAbr GCal IArd MBlu MGos MMuc NLar NWea SEND SPer WFar WHer
	- 'Plenus'	see *U. europaeus* 'Flore Pleno'
	gallii	NLar
	- 'Mizen Head'	CTrC ELan GCal MWhi SLon

Ulmus ✿ (*Ulmaceae*)

	alata	EGFP
	americana **new**	EGFP
	- 'Princeton'	CKno SGol
	- 'Valley Forge' **new**	SGol
	crassifolia	EGFP
	'Dodoens'	IArd SCoo
	'Frontiez'	SGol
§	***glabra***	CDul CRWN EPfP NWea SCoo
	- 'Camperdownii'	CMac EBee ECrN ELan LAst WMou
	- 'Exoniensis'	CTho IVic
	- 'Gittisham'	CTho
	- 'Horizontalis'	see *U. glabra* 'Pendula'
	- 'Lutescens'	CTho CTri NLar NPri NWea SCoo SEWo
§	- 'Pendula'	CMac
§	× ***hollandica*** 'Dampieri Aurea'	CDul CTho EBee ELan EPfP LBuc MAsh MBlu MRav MWat NLar NWea SPer SPoG
	- 'Jacqueline Hillier'	CMac CSpe ECho ELan LAst LBuc LMaj MMuc MRav NLar SEND SGol WCFE WFar WPat
	- 'Wredei'	see *U.* × *hollandica* 'Dampieri Aurea'
	laevis	CDul ECrN EGFP
	'Lobel'	CCVT
	Lutèce = 'Nanguen'	CDoC CDul SGol
	minor	CDul
	- subsp. ***angustifolia***	EGFP
	- 'Dampieri Aurea'	see *U.* × *hollandica* 'Dampieri Aurea'
	montana	see *U. glabra*
	'Morton Glossy'	CDul
	parvifolia	CMCN CMen WPGP
	- Everclear = 'Bsnupf'	SGol
	- 'Frosty' (v)	ECho
	- 'Geisha' (v)	ECho ELan MAsh MGos MRav WPat
§	- 'Hokkaido'	CMen EWes GEdr LLHF WAbe WPat WThu
	- 'Pygmaea'	see *U. parvifolia* 'Hokkaido'
	- 'Yatsubusa'	ECho EWes MRav NLar
	procera	CDul LBuc MCoo MGos SLon WSFF
	pumila 'Beijing Gold'	NLar
	rubra	CArn
	'Sapporo Autumn Gold'	CCVT EBee LBuc LMaj MRav SGol WCFE
	serotina	EGFP
	Vada = 'Wanoux'[PBR]	SGol

Umbellularia (*Lauraceae*)

	californica	CArn CMCN EPfP IDee SSpi

Umbilicus (*Crassulaceae*)

	rupestris	CArn CRWN SChr WHer WShi

Uncinia (*Cyperaceae*)

*	***cyparissias*** from Chile	NBir
	divaricata	ECou
	egmontiana	CTrC EBee ECou EPfP LRHS SHil SPad WGrn WMnd WMoo
N	***rubra***	Widely available
	- 'Everflame'	CKno CWGN EBee IBoy LRHS NSti SPoG WCot
	uncinata	CBcs ECha NHol SDix
*	- ***rubra***	CCon CKno CTri CWCL ELon IFro LAst LBMP LRHS SBfd SLim SMrm SRms SUsu SWvt

Uniola (*Poaceae*)

	latifolia	see *Chasmanthium latifolium*
	paniculata	SApp

Urceolina (*Amaryllidaceae*)

	miniata	see *Stenomesson miniatum*
	peruviana	see *Stenomesson miniatum*

Urginea (*Hyacinthaceae*)

	capitata 'Sentinel Peak'	ECho
	fugax	EBee
	macrocentra	ECho
	maritima	CArn ECho LAma WCot
	ollivieri	ECho

undulata	ECho

Urospermum (*Asteraceae*)

dalechampii	CSam ECha LRHS MMHG SGar SUsu

Ursinia (*Asteraceae*)

alpina	CPBP
anthemoides **new**	WHil

Urtica (*Urticaceae*)

dioica 'Chedglow 2' (v)	CNat
- 'Dog Trap Lane'	CNat
- 'Judith' **new**	CNat
- OGG mutant	CNat
- 'Winter Yellow'	CNat

Utricularia (*Lentibulariaceae*)

sp.	EECP
alpina	CSWC
australis	EFEx
biloba	CHew
bisquamata	CSWC
- 'Betty's Bay'	CHew
dichotoma	CHew EFEx
exoleta R. Brown	see *U. gibba*
§ ***gibba***	EFEx
heterosepala	CHew
intermedia	EFEx
lateriflora	CHew EFEx
livida	CHew CSWC EECP EFEx
longifolia	CSWC
menziesii	EFEx
microcalyx	CHew
monanthos	CHew EFEx
nephrophylla	CHew
novae-zelandiae	CHew
ochroleuca	EFEx
paulineae	CHew
praelonga	CHew CSWC
prehensilis	CHew
pubescens	CSWC
reniformis	EFEx
- ***nana***	EFEx
sandersonii	CHew CSWC EECP
- blue-flowered	EECP
simplex	CHew
subulata	EFEx
tricolor	CHew
uniflora	CHew
vulgaris	EFEx
warburgii	CHew
welwitschii	CHew

Uvularia (*Colchicaceae*)

§ ***caroliniana***	ECho
disporum	ECho
grandiflora ♀^{H4}	Widely available
- dwarf	ECho
- gold-leaved	MAvo
- 'Lynda Windsor'	CRDP SKHP
- orange-flowered	SKHP
- var. ***pallida***	CAvo CBct CLAP CPom EBee ECha ECho EHrv EPPr EPfP EPot GCal GEdr IBlr LEdu LRHS MNFA MRav NCGa NHar NPnk SMHy SUsu WAbe WCru WFar WPnP
- 'Susie Lewis'	WCru
grandiflora × ***perfoliata***	ECho NBir WWEG
perfoliata	CBct CLAP CPLG EBee ECha ECho EPPr EPfP EPot EWTr GBuc IBlr LEdu MRav NBir NPnk WAbe WCru
- tall	EPPr
pudica	see *U. caroliniana*
sessilifolia	CBct CLAP CPLG CRDP EBee ECho EPot GEdr IBlr LEdu LRHS MMHG SSvw WCru
- 'Cobblewood Gold' (v)	WCru

Vaccinium ✿ (*Ericaceae*)

sp.	LSRN
angustifolium var. ***laevifolium***	GLin
arctostaphylos	NLar SWvt
'Berkeley' (F)	CAgr CCCN CTrh CWib GKin LBuc LSRN MAsh MBlu NPla SPoG WHar
'Bluecrop' (F)	Widely available
'Bluejay' (F)	CWib LAst LRHS SCoo SLon WHar
'Blueray' (F)	CWib GKin GPri
'Brigitta' (F)	CTrh EMil GTwe LRHS NPla SPoG
chaetothrix	WAbe WThu
'Chandler' (F)	CAgr CMac CTrh EMil EPom GKin GPri LRHS LSRN MCoo NPla SBfd SKee SPoG
consanguineum B&SWJ 10486	WCru
corymbosum (F) ♀^{H4}	CBcs MGos MNHC SBfd SCoo SReu SSta
- 'Blauweiss-Goldtraube' (F)	CSBt CWSG CWib EPfP GKin LSRN MAsh MGos NLar SPoG SVic WFar WGwG WHar
- 'Blue Duke' (F)	LSRN
- 'Bluegold' (F)	CTrh EMil LRHS SPer
- 'Bluetta' (F)	CAgr CTrh CTri CWib GPri GTwe MGos SCoo SPoG WFar
- 'Coville' (F)	CWib NLar
- 'Darrow' (F)	CAgr CTrh GTwe LBuc LRHS MAsh
- 'Dixie' (F)	CSBt MSCN NPla WGwG
- 'Duke' (F) ♀^{H4}	CTrh CWib ELan EPfP EPom GPri LRHS MAsh MGos NPla NWea SPoG
- 'Elizabeth' (F)	GPri
- 'Elliott' (F)	LSRN SBfd SPer
- 'Grover' (F)	NLar
- 'Hannah's Choice' (F)	GPri
- 'Hardyblue' (F)	CAgr
- 'Ivanhoe' (F)	GKin
- 'Jersey' (F)	CAgr CWib EPfP LAst LRHS MAsh MCoo MGos MMuc NLar SCoo SEND SPer SPoG SVic
- 'Legacy' (F)	CTrh
- 'Nelson' (F)	GPri LRHS NPla SCoo
- 'Nui' (F)	EPom LSRN SPer
- 'Patriot' (F)	CAgr CSBt CTrh CWib GKin GPri GTwe LBuc LRHS MBri MGos MPkF MRav NPla SBfd SCoo SHil SPoG WGwG
- 'Reka' (F)	CAgr
- 'Sierra' (F)	GPri
- 'Spartan' (F) ♀^{H4}	CTrh CWib EPom GTwe LRHS LSRN MAsh MGos NPla SBfd SKee SPer SPoG

- 'Stanley' (F)	ELan LRHS MAsh
- 'Toro' (F)	GPri GTwe LBuc LRHS MAsh MGos
crassifolium subsp. ***sempervirens*** 'Well's Delight' (F)	EBee LRHS MAsh SPoG
cylindraceum ♀H4	CBcs EPfP MAsh NLar WFar WPat
delavayi	EBee LRHS MAsh NHar NMen WAbe WFar WPat WThu
dunalianum	WCru
var. ***caudatifolium*** B&SWJ 1716	
- var. ***megaphyllum*** HWJ 515	WCru
'Earliblue' (F)	CAgr CSBt GKin MBri MGos WFar
floribundum	CBcs CDoC CMHG EBee LRHS MAsh NLar SSpi
glaucoalbum ♀H3-4	CAbP CDoC CMac EBee EPfP LRHS MAsh MRav SPer SPoG SSpi WPGP WPat
'Goldtraube 71'	LRHS MAsh NPla
* ***grandiflorum***	ECho
griffithianum	SSta
'Groover'	LSRN
'Herbert' (F)	CAgr CMac EPom LBuc MGos
macrocarpon (F)	CArn ECho ELan GTwe LRHS MAsh NHar SPoG SRms
- 'Centennial' (F)	NHar
- 'CN' (F)	CAgr NLar
- 'Early Black' (F)	EPom GKin SVic
- 'Franklin' (F)	CAgr
- 'Hamilton'	GEdr LLHF NMen WThu
- 'Howes' (F)	NHar
- 'Langlois' (F)	NLar
- 'Olson's Honkers' (F)	CAgr NLar
- 'Pilgrim' (F)	CAgr CMac CTrh GKin LEdu LRHS NHar WHar
- 'Red Star' (F)	CTrh
- 'Stevens' (F) new	CTrh
'Misty' (F)	CAgr
moupinense	CDoC EBee IDee LRHS MAsh NMen WAbe WThu
- 'Variegatum' (v)	LLHF
myrtillus	CAgr EPom GPoy NLar SVic
'Northblue' (F)	CTrh
'Northland' (F)	CSBt CWib EPfP GTwe LRHS MBri NLar NPla SCoo SPoG
nummularia	ECho GEdr LRHS NHar NMen SSpi WAbe WThu
ovatum	CBcs CMHG CMac CTsd GKev IDee WThu
- 'Thundercloud'	CAbP EBee LRHS MAsh
§ ***oxycoccos*** (F)	CAgr CArn GPoy MCoo MGos NHar WThu
'Ozarkblue' (F)	CTrh EPom GTwe LSRN SPer
padifolium	WPGP
pallidum	IBlr
palustre	see *V. oxycoccos*
'Poppins' new	CTrh
retusum	IRar
'Sunrise' (F)	GTwe
'Sunshine Blue' (F)	CAgr CTrh EMil EPom LBuc LRHS SPoG
'Tophat' (F)	CCCN MPkF
vitis-idaea	CArn EPfP EWes GPoy MGos NWea SVic WFar
- 'Autumn Beauty'	NLar
- 'Compactum'	EWes LLHF
- 'Ida'	LBuc
- Koralle Group ♀H4	CAgr EPfP GKin MBri MCoo NLar NWad SPoG
- subsp. ***minus***	GEdr GPri NLar NMen WAbe WThu
- 'Red Candy' new	ELan EPfP
- 'Red Pearl'	CSBt EPfP EPom LRHS MAsh MGos NLar
* - 'Variegatum' (v)	EWes

Vagaria (*Amaryllidaceae*)

ollivieri	ECho

Valeriana (*Caprifoliaceae*)

'Alba'	see *Centranthus ruber* 'Albus'
alliariifolia	EBee GCal NBro WCot
- 'Sirene'	EBee
'Coccinea'	see *Centranthus ruber*
dioica	CHab
jatamansi	CArn GPoy
montana	NBro NRya SRms SWat
officinalis	Widely available
- subsp. ***officinalis*** new	MSpe
- subsp. ***sambucifolia***	EPPr GCal MNrw MSpe SHar WHil
phu 'Aurea'	CArn CHby CMac EBee ECha EHoe EHrv ELan EPfP GKin LHop LRHS MBri MCot MLHP MRav NBid NBir NBro NEgg NSti NWad SMrm SPer SRms WMoo
pyrenaica	ECha EHrv EPPr GCal LPla LRHS MMHG MMuc MNrw SEND SPhx WCot WMoo
saxatilis	NLar NRya
supina	CPBP
wallrothii	EBee WCot

Valerianella (*Caprifoliaceae*)

§ ***locusta***	GPoy SVic
olitoria	see *V. locusta*

Vallea (*Elaeocarpaceae*)

stipularis	CHll CTsd IGor

Vallota see *Cyrtanthus*

Vancouveria (*Berberidaceae*)

chrysantha	CCon CLAP CMil CPLG CPom EPPr GEdr LEdu MRav NLar NRya SBch SKHP SMad WMoo WPGP WPtf
hexandra	CBct CCon CGHE CLAP CMac CPLG ECha EHrv EPPr EPfP GAbr GEdr GKev LEdu NRya NSti SKHP SPhx WCru WMoo WPGP WWEG
- NNS 08-423	GKev
planipetala	CLAP WCru

Vania see *Thlaspi*

veitchberry see *Rubus* 'Veitchberry'

Vellozia (*Velloziaceae*)

elegans	see *Talbotia elegans*

Veltheimia ✿ (*Asparagaceae*)

§ ***bracteata*** ♀H1	CCse CHll CLak EBak ECho IBlr LToo WCot
viridifolia Jacq.	see *V. bracteata*

× *Venidioarctotis* see *Arctotis*

Venidium see *Arctotis*

Veratrum ✿ (*Melanthiaceae*)

album ♀H4	CBct CCon CPne EBee ECha ECho GCal GPoy LEdu LWst MNrw MRav NBid WCot WCru
- var. ***flavum***	GCal LPla MNrw SPhx WCru
- subsp. ***lobelianum***	EBee GCal
- 'Lorna's Green'	GCal
- var. ***oxysepalum***	WCru
californicum	CHGN EBee ECha GCal MNrw NBid
dolichopetalum B&SWJ 4195	WCru
formosanum	CDes EWld MNrw
- B&SWJ 1575	EHrv GEdr WCru
- RWJ 9806	WCru
grandiflorum B&SWJ 4416	WCru
longebracteatum	WCru
maackii	GEdr
- var. ***japonicum***	WCru
- var. ***maackii*** B&SWJ 5831	WCru
- var. ***parviflorum***	GCal
nigrum ♀H4	CBct EBee GCal GMaP IKil LPla LWst MAvo MLHP MNrw MRav NBid NBir NCGa NLar SMad SPhx SPlb WBor WCot WCru WFar WPnP WSpi
- B&SWJ 4450 from South Korea	WCru
schindleri B&SWJ 4068	WCru
stamineum	WCru
viride	CBct EBee ECha EWes GCal MNrw NBid

Verbascum (*Scrophulariaceae*)

acaule	EPot
'Annie May'	EBee LSRN NOrc SUsu
'Apricot Sunset'	EBee SPhx
'Arctic Summer'	see *V. bombyciferum* 'Polarsommer'
'Aurora'	SPhx
'Aztec Gold'	EBee
'Bill Bishop'	ECho
blattaria	EHrv GKev NBir SPav SWat WFar WHer WWEG
- f. ***albiflorum***	CSpe EBee EWTr IFro LLWP NDov SGar SPlb SWal WHer WMoo WTin
- yellow-flowered	SPav SWat
'Blushing Bride'PBR	LLHF
boerhavii	WHil
§ ***bombyciferum***	CBre CSev ECha GMaP NGBl
* - 'Arctic Snow'	SPav SPoG
§ - 'Polarsommer'	CSpe EBee EPfP MBri NBir SMad SPer SPet SWat WWEG
- 'Silver Lining'	NLar NPer
'Broussa'	see *V. bombyciferum*
'Buttercup'	EBee ECtt LRHS
'Butterscotch'	SUsu
'Caribbean Crush'	CBcs CHab EBee ECtt ELan ELon EPfP EWll IBoy LRHS NLar SBfd SPer
chaixii	CSam ECha MBel MMHG NBir WFar WMoo XLum
- 'Album' ♀H4	Widely available
- 'Blackberry Crush'	MDKP
- 'Sixteen Candles'	GJos LRHS MBNS NChi NLar WHil WPtf
- 'Wedding Candles'	EBee NGdn NLar SBea WHil
chaixii × 'Wendy's Choice'	MDKP
'Cherokee'	SUsu
'Cherry Helen'PBR	EBee ECtt LRHS LSRN MBri NEgg NGdn NLar NPnk SBfd SPer
'Christo's Yellow Lightning' ♀H4 **new**	SUsu WCot
'Clementine'	EBee LBuc LPla SPhx SUsu WHlf
'Coneyhill Yellow'	EPPr
(Cotswold Group) 'Cotswold Beauty' ♀H4	CSam EAEE EBee ECtt EPfP LRHS MBel MRav MWat NGdn SPer WHoo WMnd
- 'Cotswold Gem'	ECtt
- 'Cotswold Queen'	CBcs CHab EAEE EBee ECtt ELan EPPr EPfP LRHS MDKP MRav MWat NGdn SBea SPer SWvt WCAu WMnd
- 'Gainsborough' ♀H4	CSBt EAEE EBee ECha ECtt EHrv ELan EPfP GMaP LAst LHop LPot LRHS LSRN MBel MBri MGos MRav NGdn NLar NPri NSti SBfd SPer SWat SWvt WCAu WFar WHil WMnd
- 'Mont Blanc'	EAEE EBee EHrv LRHS SWat
- 'Pink Domino' ♀H4	CBcs CSam EBee ECtt EHrv ELan EPPr EPfP GMaP LRHS MAvo MLHP MRav MWat NGdn SBea SPer SWvt WFar WMnd WWFP WWlt
- 'Royal Highland'	EBee ECtt EHrv ELan EPfP NGdn NLar SWvt
- 'White Domino'	EBee ECtt
'Cotswold King'	see *V. creticum*
§ ***creticum***	CSpe EBee IKil SPav WCot
'Dark Eyes'PBR	EBee ECtt MTis
§ ***densiflorum***	CArn EBee WWEG
- BSSS 232	WCru
'Dijon'	EWes
dumulosum ♀H2-3	WAbe
epixanthinum ♀	CSpe LRHS
'Flower of Scotland'	ECtt
'Golden Wings' ♀H2-3	ECtt NMen WAbe
'Helen Johnson'	CBcs CHab CWCL EAEE EBee ECtt EPfP GMaP LHop LRHS LSRN MGos MRav NLar NPnk NPri SBfd SCoo SPer SRkn SWvt WCAu WFar WWEG
'Hiawatha'	SPhx
× ***hybridum*** 'Banana Custard'	EBee MNHC NGBl
- 'Copper Rose'	EPfP MBri
- 'Snow Maiden'	CTri EPfP MHer
- 'Wega'	NLar
'Hyde Hall Sunrise'	EPfP
'Innocence'	MDKP
'Jackie'	CBcs EBee ECtt EHrv ELan LRHS LSRN MBri MSCN NGdn NRHS SCoo SPer SPoG WFar WHil WWEG
'Jackie in Pink'	EWes LRHS MDev NGdn NRHS SHil WFar
'Jackie in Yellow'PBR	EBee LLHF MDev NGdn
'Jester'	EBee ECtt LBuc SPoG WHlf
'Jolly Eyes'	EBee ECtt MBri
'June Johnson'	EAEE EBee ECtt LRHS SHar
'Kalypso'	SPhx
'Lavender Lass'	ECtt
'Letitia' ♀H3	CBcs CMea EBee ECho ECtt ELan EWes GCal IPot ITim LRHS NMen NRHS SRot SWvt WAbe
'Linda' **new**	EBee
longifolium var. ***pannosum***	see *V. olympicum*
lychnitis	CArn SPhx

'Megan's Mauve' EAEE EBee LRHS
'Merlin'PBR EAEE ECtt LRHS LSRN LSou MBNS MBel MBri SMrm SPoG
'Monster' EBee
'Moonlight' ECtt
'Moonshadow' SPhx
'Mystery Blonde' SPhx
nigrum CArn CHab EBee LHop NGdn NLar WMnd WMoo
- var. ***album*** NChi NGdn NLar WMoo
'Norfolk Dawn' EBee ECtt SPhx
§ ***olympicum*** EBee ELan EPfP GJos LPot LRHS MBNS MWat NGBl SDix SEND SMrm WCAu WCot WWEG
'Pandora' LRHS
'Patricia' EBee SPhx
'Petra' LPla SPhx
phoeniceum ELan EPfP GJos GKev LRHS NBid NBro SBfd SGar SPlb SPoG SWal WMoo XLum
* - 'Album' XLum
- 'Antique Rose' WHrl
- 'Flush of White' ECtt EPPr EPfP GQue IFro NGBl NGdn NLar NPnk SBea SPav SSvw WCFE WMoo WWEG XLum
- hybrids CTri GMaP NEgg NGdn SRms SWat WFar WPer WWEG
- 'Rosetta' CMea EPfP NGBl NGdn WHil
- 'Violetta' CCVN CMea CSpe ECtt EPPr EPfP EWll LAst LBMP MLHP MWat NEgg NGBl NGdn NSti SBea SPav SPer WCFE WCot WFar WHrl WMoo WPtf XLum
'Phoenix' CTsd EBee
'Pink Ice' MDKP
'Pink Kisses' CWCL EBee LLHF LRHS LSRN
'Pink Petticoats' LRHS SBfd SPoG
(Pixie Series) 'Pixie Apricot' ECtt
- 'Pixie Blue' EBee ECtt LSou
- 'Pixie Pink' LSou
- 'Pixie White' ECtt
'Plum Smokey'PBR EBee ECtt IBoy LLHF LRHS SBfd
'Primrose Cottage' MBri
'Primrose Path' EBee ECtt ELon EPfP LRHS NPri SBfd SRot
'Purple Prince' ECtt
pyramidatum SPhx
'Raspberry Ripple' EBee ECtt ELan LLHF SPer
'Rosie' EBee SPoG
'Sierra Sunset' ECtt EPfP MTis
'Southern Charm' EBee ECtt EPfP EWll GJos GMaP MBri MHer NLBP NPnk SPoG WFar WHil WPtf
'Spica' NLar
'Sugar Plum'PBR EBee ECtt ELon EWll LLHF MTis SPoG
'Summer Sorbet' EBee ECtt ELan EPfP LRHS SPoG
Sunset shades GJos
thapsiforme see *V. densiflorum*
thapsus CHab ENfk GPoy MHer MHoo MNHC NBir NMir SEND
'Twilight' LRHS

Verbena (*Verbenaceae*)

(Aztec Series) Aztec Blue Velvet = 'Balazvelu' (G) **new** NPri
- Aztec Cherry Red = 'Balazcherd'PBR (G) NPri
- Aztec Coral = 'Balazcoral'PBR (G) NPri
- Aztec Dark Pink Magic = 'Balazdapima' (G) NPri
- Aztec Pearl = 'Balazpearl'PBR (G) SCoo
- Aztec Plum Magic = 'Balazplum'PBR (G) NPri
- Aztec Red = 'Balazred' (G) SCoo
- Aztec Silver Magic = 'Balazsilma'PBR (G) ♀H3 LSou NPri SCoo
'Betty Lee' (G) ECtt
'Blue Prince' (G) CSpe MAsh SUsu
§ ***bonariensis*** ♀H3-4 Widely available
- 'Lollipop' **new** EBee
'Boughton House' (G) EBee
brasiliensis misapplied see *V. bonariensis*
canadensis 'Perfecta' (G) CSpe
'Candy Carousel' (G) SPet
chamaedrifolia see *V. peruviana*
§ 'Claret' (G) ♀H3 CCVN CMac CSev CSpe EBee ECtt ELan ELon EPfP LAst LRHS LSRN LSou MAsh MCot MGos MTis SAga SBfd SCoo SHil SMrm SPet SUsu WWEG
corymbosa CEnt CHid CHll CWCL EBee ECGP ECha EPPr LRHS MMuc MSpe NLar SAga SBfd WMoo WPer
- 'Gravetye' CPrp EBee LPot WFar
'Diamond Merci' (G) WHoo
(Donalena Series) Donalena Twinkle Purple (G) **new** NPri
- Donalena Twinkle Pink (G) NPri
'Edith Eddleman' (G) CMac CWGN EBee EPfP LRHS LSqH MAsh SHil
'Empress Peach Flair' **new** LAst
'Fiesta' (G) LRHS
'Hammerstein Pink' EBee EPfP
hastata CSpe EBee ECtt EPfP LAst LEdu LRHS MNrw NDov NSti SMrm SPhx SPlb SWat SWvt WBor WFar WMnd WMoo WPer WSHC
* - 'Alba' EBee EPfP GCal LDai MDKP MNrw NLar WMoo WWFP
- 'Blue Spires' EPfP IPot WWEG
- f. ***rosea*** CElw CMea CSpe EBee EHoe ELan EPfP GKev LRHS MDKP MLHP MNrw MRav NBid NDov SBfd SPhx SPoG SUsu SWat WMoo WSHC WWEG WWFP
- - 'Pink Spires' ECtt EPfP LHop WWEG
- 'White Spires' CMea EPfP WWEG
'Homestead Purple' (G) CBar CMac COlW CPrp CSev EBee ECtt EPfP EShb LDai LRHS LSRN MAsh MCot MGos MNrw NDov SAga SBfd SMrm SPer SPet SUsu SWvt WHoo WWEG
'Jenny's Wine' see *V.* 'Claret'
'La France' (G) CHGN EBee ECha ECtt EPfP LRHS LSou SAga SDix SMHy SMrm SPhx SUsu WMnd WSHC
'Lavender Spires' SPhx
'Lois' Ruby' see *V.* 'Claret'
macdougalii LHop MDKP SPhx
officinalis CArn CRWN CWan ENfk GPoy MHer MNHC SIde WHer WJek WPer

patagonica see *V. bonariensis*
§ ***peruviana*** (G) EBee ECho ELan EPfP LBMP LHop LRHS MAsh NRHS SChF SRms XLum
'Pink Bouquet' see *V.* 'Silver Anne'
'Pink Parfait' (G) EPfP SBfd
pink-flowered **new** SEND
purple-flowered **new** SEND
Quartz Series ♀H3 **new** NPri
- 'Quartz Red Polka Dot' SBfd
'Red Cascade' SPet
§ ***rigida*** ♀H3 Widely available
- f. ***lilacina*** LSRN NLar
- - 'Lilac Haze' CMac EPfP LBMP LRHS NSti SPoG SRkn
- - 'Polaris' CPrp EBee ELon EPfP LHop LRHS MAvo MNrw MRav NWad SHar SMHy SMrm SPer SPet SPhx SUsu WSHC
Seabrook's Lavender = 'Sealav'PBR CBar CSev EPfP ESwi LHop LRHS LSRN LSqH MAsh MNrw MTis SBfd SHar SPer SWvt WSHC
serpyllifolia see *Junellia micrantha*
§ 'Silver Anne' (G) ♀H3 LDai MCot SAga SMrm SUsu
§ 'Sissinghurst' (G) ♀H2-3 ECtt MAsh SAga SBfd SMrm SRms
'Sissinghurst Pink' SPer
'Strawberry Kiss' LAst MTis SHil
stricta LRHS MDKP NLar SPhx
Superbena Ruby Red = 'Usbena5122'PBR (Superbena Series) (G) ♀H3 SBfd
(Tapien Series) Tapien Compact Velvet = 'Suntapikovel' (G) **new** LSou
- Tapien Pink Parfait = 'Suntapipipa'PBR (G) LSou
- Tapien Pink = 'Sunver'PBR (G) LAst
- Tapien Red (G) LAst LSou
- Tapien Salmon = 'Suntapiro'PBR (G) ♀H3 LAst LSou WGor
- Tapien Sky Blue = 'Suntapilabu'PBR (G) ♀H3 LAst LSou
- Tapien Violet = 'Sunvop'PBR (G) LAst LHop LSou WGor
- Tapien White = 'Suntapipurew'PBR (G) LAst LSou
(Temari Series) Temari Blue = 'Sunmariribu'PBR (G) LAst LSou
- Temari Burgundy = 'Sunmariwaba'PBR (G) LSou
- Temari Coral Pink = 'Sunmariripi'PBR (G) LAst LSou
- Temari Neon Red = 'Sunmarineopi'PBR (G) ♀H3 LAst
- Temari Patio Red = 'Sunmaribisu'PBR (G) **new** LAst
- Temari Vanilla = 'Sunmarivani'PBR (G) LAst LSou
'Tenerife' see *V.* 'Sissinghurst'
tenuisecta (G) WPer
'Vegas Appleblossom' (Vegas Series) (G) WGor
venosa see *V. rigida*
'Voodoo Star' (G) **new** LSou
'White Cascade' SPet

Verbesina (*Asteraceae*)

alternifolia CArn
- 'Goldstrahl' EPPr WPer

Vernicia (*Euphorbiaceae*)

fordii SPlb

Vernonia (*Asteraceae*)

angustifolia × ***missurica*** **new** WCot
§ ***arkansana*** CHGN ECha EPPr EWes EWhm LRHS MMuc NLar SDix SEND SMad SPhx WWEG XLum
- 'Alba' **new** EBee
- 'Betty Blindeman' EBee
- 'Mammuth' CDes EBee ECtt EWes GQue LEdu LHop SPhx WFar WPGP
crinita see *V. arkansana*
fasciculata CSpe EBee EShb EWes LPla MRav NLar SMHy SMrm SPhx WCot
gigantea EBee EWes MMuc MNrw NLar SBHP SEND SMad SPhx WHrl
glauca **new** WCot
lindheimeri **new** SPhx WCot
missurica EBee
noveboracensis EBee EWhm NLar SGar SMad SMrm SPhx WPer XLum
- 'Albiflora' EPPr EWes

Veronica (*Plantaginaceae*)

amethystina see *V. spuria* L.
'Anna'PBR NDov
armena ECho EDAr EWTr EWes MDKP MHer MWat NMen SBch SRot WIce WPat XSen
'Atomic Blue' LSou MAsh
'Atomic Lilac' LSou
'Atomic Pink' LSou MAsh MBri
'Atomic Sky Ray' **new** LSou
'Atomic Violet' MBri
'Atomic Violet Ray' **new** LSou
§ ***austriaca*** NBre NChi WFar WMoo XLum
- dark blue-flowered **new** NChi
- var. ***dubia*** see *V. prostrata*
- 'Ionian Skies' CElw CTri EBee ECha ECho ECtt EPPr EWes LRHS MMuc NEgg NWad SEND SMrm SPer WFar WIce WKif WPat WPer WSHC WWEG
§ - subsp. ***teucrium*** CArn CSam CTri EBee ECho SRms WFar WKif WPer
- - 'Crater Lake Blue' ♀H4 EBee ECtt ELan EPfP EShb LEdu LHop LRHS MAvo MCot MNFA MRav NBre NGdn SMrm SPlb SRms WCot WFar WMnd WPer WSHC
- - 'Kapitän' ECha ECho GBuc LHop LRHS MMuc MNrw NGdn NPro SEND WFar WPer
- - 'Knallblau' SMrm SSvw WFar
- - 'Royal Blue' ♀H4 CCVN EBee EPfP EShb GMaP LRHS MWhi NCGa NSti SBch SBfd SPer SRms WFar WKif WMnd XLum XSen
'Baby Blue'PBR **new** WHil
'Baby Doll'PBR LRHS LSou MBNS MBri NCGa NLar
bachofenii WTin

beccabunga	CArn CBen CHab CWat EHon EWay GPoy LPBA MMuc MSKA MWts NMir NPer SEND SWat WHer WMAq WSFF XLum
'Bergen's Blue'	CMac NLar SHar
Blue Bouquet	see *V. longifolia* 'Blaubündel'
'Blue Indigo'	ELan MNrw MTis NBre NGdn
'Blue Spire'	SWat WPer
bombycina	ECho WAbe
bonarota	see *Paederota bonarota*
caespitosa	CPBP
- subsp. ***caespitosa***	NMen WAbe
candida	see *V. spicata* subsp. *incana*
× ***cantiana*** 'Kentish Pink'	WCFE WFar WMoo WPer WWEG
caucasica	MWat XSen
chamaedrys	ECho NMir XLum
- 'Pam' (v)	ECtt
'Christy'	EPfP LRHS
cinerea ♀H4	GMaP MLHP SBch SBrt WHoo WSHC XSen
dabneyi	CDes EBee WPGP
'Darwin's Blue'PBR	NGdn NLar NOrc WHrl
'Ellen Mae'	CElw ECtt EWes WCAu WMnd
'Eveline'PBR	EBee ECtt EPfP MBri NDov NLar WCot
exaltata (d)	LRHS NChi SMHy SMrm WCot WPer
'Fairytale'PBR	CCVN EPfP LRHS LSou MBNS MBel MBri MDev NCGa NGdn NSti SMrm WGrn WHil
'Fantasy'	MTis NDov
filiformis	XLum
- 'Fairyland' (v)	EWes
'First Love'	LSou MAsh MBri NGdn
formosa	see *Parahebe formosa*
§ ***fruticans***	ECho GJos NMen
fruticulosa	LLHF
gentianoides ♀H4	Widely available
- 'Alba'	CMea GCal LEdu LRHS NBre NChi NSti
- 'Barbara Sherwood'	GBin LRHS NBre NGdn NRHS WWEG
- 'Blue Streak'	LRHS WRHF
- 'Lilacina'	EBee ECho LRHS
- 'Nana'	EBee
- 'Pallida'	EBee EPfP GAbr GKev MBrN MMuc MRav SEND SPlb WBor WFar WWEG
- 'Robusta'	EBee ECtt LRHS NCGa NEgg NGdn SBea WHoo WMnd
- 'Tissington White'	Widely available
- 'Variegata' (v)	EBee ECha ECtt EHrv ELan EPfP GCra GMaP LAst MHer MRav MSCN NBir NEgg NPnk NWad SBfd SPer SWat WFar WMnd WWEG
'Giles van Hees'	EBee WCot
grandis	EBee GAbr IFro LEdu MDKP MMuc MWhi NChi NLar SBfd SEND SMad WFar WHrl WMoo WPtf
× ***guthrieana***	SRms
hendersonii	see *V. subsessilis hendersonii*
incana	see *V. spicata* subsp. *incana*
* - 'Candidissima'	GCal
'Ink'	MAvo SPhx
'Inspiration'	CCse NBre NDov SMrm
'Inspire Blue'	EBee EPfP LBMP LSou MPnt
'Inspire Pink'	EBee LBMP LSou MPnt
kellereri	see *V. spicata*
kiusiana	CMHG IFro LPla LRHS NLar NRHS SPhx WHrl
* - var. ***maxima***	WPtf
kotschyana	XSen
'Lavender Plume' **new**	WHil
liwanensis	ECho NMen
- Mac&W 5936	MDKP
longifolia	CMac CMea CSBt ECha ELan GCra LRHS MLHP NSti WFar WMoo WOut XLum
- 'Alba'	EBee ELan MMuc MWat NLar SEND WMoo
- 'Antarctica' **new**	MTis
- 'Blaubart'	XLum
§ - 'Blaubündel'	CCse EBee NGdn
- 'Blauer Sommer'	EAEE EHrv EPfP LBMP MCot NDov NEgg NGdn SPoG
§ - 'Blauriesin'	CCVN CTri EBee ECtt EPfP GMaP LRHS NBre NPnk NSti SPer SSvw
- Blue Giantess	see *V. longifolia* 'Blauriesin'
- 'Blue John'	EBee EPfP NBre NSti WCot
- blue-flowered	MWat
- 'Charming Pink'	EBee LRHS MAsh SMrm
- 'Fascination'	ECtt LAst NGdn NPro
- 'Foerster's Blue'	see *V. longifolia* 'Blauriesin'
- 'Joseph's Coat' (v)	MBel NBre
- 'Lila Karina'	EBee WPer
- 'Lilac Fantasy'	MBri MRav NSti WWlt
- 'Oxford Blue'	CBar LRHS WHoo
- 'Pacific Ocean'PBR	ECtt
- 'Pink Eveline'PBR	EBee NDov
- pink-flowered	EShb
- 'Rose Tone'	GJos NLar WMoo
- 'Rosea'	SBfd WPer
- 'Schneeriesin'	CPrp EAEE EBee ECha EHrv EPfP GMaP LEdu MRav NBir NLar NPnk SPer SPoG
lyallii	see *Parahebe lyallii*
macrostachya	SKHP
'Martje'	SMrm XLum
'Mini Spires Blue'	EPfP LRHS MGos
montana 'Corinne Tremaine' (v)	NBir NLar SRms WHer
officinalis	CArn XLum XSen
oltensis	CPBP ECho EWes GJos ITim LLHF MHer NMen WAbe WPat
orchidea	GEdr LRHS SRms
orientalis subsp. ***orientalis***	NMen
ornata	WOld WPer
pectinata 'Rosea'	ECho ECtt EWes XSen
peduncularis 'Oxford Blue'	see *V. umbrosa* 'Georgia Blue'
perfoliata	see *Parahebe perfoliata*
petraea 'Madame Mercier'	SMrm XLum
'Pink Damask'	CSpe CWCL EBee ECtt ELan ELon EPfP GMaP MCot MRav MTis MWat NEgg NGdn NLar NSti SDys SMrm SPhx WFar WHoo WMnd WTin WWEG
pinnata 'Blue Feathers'	EDAr
porphyriana	EBee EDAr MMuc
prenja	see *V. austriaca*
§ ***prostrata*** ♀H4	CMea CSpe CTri ECho ECtt EDAr EPfP GJos GKev LAst LBee LRHS MLHP MMuc NEgg NHar NPri SEND SRms WBor WFar WHoo WIce WMoo WNew XLum

	– 'Alba'	MLHP MWat WFar
	– 'Aztec Gold'PBR	CMac MSCN NLar NPro
§	– 'Blauspiegel'	CPBP
	– 'Blue Ice'	SMrm
	– Blue Mirror	see *V. prostrata* 'Blauspiegel'
	– 'Blue Sheen'	ECho ECtt GEdr LRHS NBir NRHS WAbe WFar WPer
	– 'Goldwell'	ECtt EPPr
	– 'Lilac Time'	ECho ECtt GEdr GKev GMaP LHop LRHS NBir NHol NLar NRHS SRms WRHF
	– 'Loddon Blue'	ECho SRms
	– 'Miss Willmott'	see *V. prostrata* 'Warley Blue'
	– 'Mrs Holt'	ECho ECtt GEdr LHop LRHS MMuc NBir NMen NRHS NWad SEND SRms WAbe WBrk WFar WHoo WPat
	– 'Nana'	ECho ECtt EWes MMuc MWat NMen WAbe
	– 'Nestor'	CTri ECtt NGdn WPtf
	– 'Rosea'	ECho MWat WPer
	– 'Spode Blue' ♀H4	CBar CMac CMea ECho ECtt GMaP LHop LRHS NRHS SPoG SRms WFar
	– 'Trehane'	EBee ECho ECtt EDAr EPfP LEdu LHop LRHS MHer MWat NEgg NRHS NRya SPlb SPoG SRms WFar WHil WIce WNew
§	– 'Warley Blue'	ECho
	'Purpleicious'	EBee EPfP LRHS LSou MBri NPri SMrm
	repens	ECho EPfP GJos NPro SPlb
	– 'Sunshine'	LRHS
	'Rosalinde'	NGdn WPer
	'Royal Pink'	CPrp LAst MRav NLar NSti
	rupestris	see *V. prostrata*
	saturejoides	CPBP SRms
	saxatilis	see *V. fruticans*
	schmidtiana 'Nana'	GKev
	– 'Nana Rosea'	GKev
	selleri	see *V. wormskjoldii*
	'Shirley Blue' ♀H4	CPrp CWib EBee ELan EPfP LPot LSRN MCot MHer MMuc MWat SEND SPhx SRms WCFE WPer WWEG
§	***spicata***	CSam EBee ELan EPfP GJos LEdu LRHS MMuc NBid NPnk SRms WBrk WFar WMoo WOut WPer
	– 'Alba'	EBee GJos LPot LRHS MRav MWat NLar WPer WTin WWEG
	– 'Barcarolle'	EBee ELan EPfP MAvo
§	– 'Blaufuchs'	CSam
	– 'Blue Bouquet'	LRHS NLar NPri
	– Blue Fox	see *V. spicata* 'Blaufuchs'
§	– 'Erika'	CPrp CSam EBee ECha ECtt EPfP LSou MBri MNrw MWat NBid NBir NBre NGdn
§	– 'Glory'PBR	CPrp EBee ECtt EPfP LRHS LSou MDev MGos NBre NEgg NPri SPad SPer SPoG WWEG
	– 'Heidekind'	CCVN CWCL EBee ECho ECtt EDAr ELan EPfP EPot GKev LAst LHop MWat NBir NGdn SBfd SRms SRot SWat WFar WGrn WHil WHoo WPer WTin XLum
	– subsp. ***hybrida***	WCot WHer
	– – 'Elaine's Form' **new**	WCot
§	– 'Icicle'	EBee MAvo SSvw WCAu
§	– subsp. ***incana***	CMea CWan EBee ECho EHoe ELan EPfP GJos MMuc SBfd SEND SPlb SRms SWat WCFE WFar WMoo WPer WTin WWEG XSen
	– – 'Nana'	ECha MLHP NBir SRms
	– – 'Silbersee'	MLHP
	– – 'Silver Carpet'	CPrp EBee ECtt LAst LHop MRav SPer WGwG WMnd
	– – 'Wendy'	EWes GCal LPla SPhx WSHC
	– 'Minuet'	LRHS
	– 'Nana Blauteppich'	CPBP EPfP LRHS NBre NLar
	– 'Pink Goblin'	EBee ECtt EDAr EPfP GQue NBre WPer
	– 'Pink Panther'PBR	EBee LSou MDev
	– Red Fox	see *V. spicata* 'Rotfuchs'
	– 'Romiley Purple'	EBee NBre SPer
	– 'Rosalind'	NLar
	– ***rosea***	see *V. spicata* 'Erika'
	– 'Rosenrot'	ECho
§	– 'Rotfuchs'	CPrp EBee ECtt EHoe ELan ELon EPfP IBoy LAst LSou MBel MCot MMuc MRav NBid NBir NGdn NOrc SBfd SEND SMrm SPer SPoG SRms WCFE WFar WPer WSHC WWEG
	– 'Royal Candles'PBR	see *V. spicata* 'Glory'
	– 'Sightseeing'	CWib GJos NBir NBre SRms WFar WRHF
	– subsp. ***spicata*** 'Nana'	XSen
	– 'Total Eclipse'PBR	LSou NCGa NSti
	– 'Twilight'PBR	EBee EPfP MBri NCGa
	– 'Ulster Blue Dwarf'	EPfP LSou MAsh MAvo MBel MBri MCot NGdn SMrm WFar
§	***spuria*** L.	MMuc SEND WPer
	stelleri	see *V. wormskjoldii*
	subsessilis	WPer
	– 'Blaue Pyramide'	NBre WPtf
*	– ***hendersonii***	NBre
	'Sunny Border Blue'	EBee EPfP NBre NLar SPoG WFar
	tauricola	XSen
	telephiifolia	EWes MDKP
	teucrium	see *V. austriaca* subsp. *teucrium*
§	***umbrosa*** 'Georgia Blue'	Widely available
	virginica	see *Veronicastrum virginicum*
	'Waterperry Blue'	WPer
	wherryi	WPer
	'White Icicle'	see *V. spicata* 'Icicle'
	'White Jolanda'	MTis NSti
	whitleyi	MMuc SEND
§	***wormskjoldii***	EBee ECho ECtt EDAr MAvo MBrN MMuc NLar NWad SBch SEND SRms
	– 'Alba'	MLHP WPer

Veronicastrum (*Plantaginaceae*)

'Adoration'	LPla NCGa NDov SMHy SPhx
brunonianum	GCal WSHC
japonicum var. ***australe*** B&SWJ 11009	WCru
latifolium	CDes GCal WCot
– BWJ 8158	WCru
sibiricum	EBee ECha EShb GCal GQue LRHS MMuc NBid NBre SEND WAul WMoo WSpi XLum
– BWJ 6352	LEdu NLar WCru
– 'Kobaltkaars' **new**	SMHy SUsu
– 'Red Arrows'	EBee ECtt NDov NLar SPhx
– var. ***yezoense*** RBS 0290	NPro
villosulum	CDes CPom EBee EWes NBid NBro WCru WSHC

§ ***virginicum***	CArn CEnt CKno EBee ECtt EHrv GCra GPoy LRHS MBrN MHoo MLHP NBir SRms WMoo WPer WWEG XLum
- 'Alboroseum'	WTin
- 'Album'	Widely available
- 'Apollo'	CBct CBre EBee ECtt EHrv EPPr EPfP EWll GAbr GEdr GMaP IBoy LPla LRHS LSou MBri NBro NDov NLar NOrc NSti SMrm SPhx WAul WHrl WSpi WWEG
- 'Diane'	EBee GEdr LPla NBre NDov SPhx SUsu WCAu WSpi
- 'Erica'	CCVN EBee ECtt EPPr EPfP GBin GEdr GQue IKil IPot LPla LRHS LSou MBel MBri MNrw MTis NCGa NDov NPnk NSti SMHy SMrm SPhx SUsu WAul WBor WCot WWEG WWlt
- 'Fascination'	Widely available
- var. ***incarnatum***	see *V. virginicum* f. *roseum*
- 'Lavendelturm'	CDes CSam EBee ECha ECtt ELon EPPr EWll GMaP IPot LHop LRHS MAvo MCot MTis NCGa NDov NLar NMRc NSti SMHy SMrm SPer SPhx WAul WCot WWEG
- light blue-flowered	MMuc SEND
- 'Pointed Finger'	GCal GMaP LEdu NBre NLar SMHy SMrm SPhx
§ - f. ***roseum***	EBee ECha ELan GMaP LPla LRHS MAvo MRav NBro NDov SPer SPhx SUsu WBor WCot WFar WKif WMoo WSpi XLum
- - 'Pink Glow'	Widely available
- 'Spring Dew'	CBre EBee EPfP LPla NBid NBro NPro SPhx WMnd
- 'Temptation'	EBee EWll GBin GMaP IPot LPla MRav NBre NBro NCGa NPro SPhx SUsu WCAu WTin

Verschaffeltia (*Arecaceae*)

splendida	XBlo

Vestia (*Solanaceae*)

§ ***foetida*** ♀H1	CBcs CCCN CPLG CTsd CWib EBee ELan ELon EMil EPfP IDee LRHS MNrw NLar SBig SBrt SEND SGar WHil WSHC
lycioides	see *V. foetida*

Viburnum ✿ (*Adoxaceae*)

acerifolium	LLHF NWad WFar WPat
alnifolium	see *V. lantanoides*
annamensis B&SWJ 8281	WCru
- B&SWJ 8302	WCru
atrocyaneum	CGHE CJun CPLG EBee MBlu NLar NWad SKHP WFar WPat
- B&SWJ 7272	EPfP MRav WCru
- HIRD 113	WPGP
§ ***awabuki***	CHEx CPLG ELon EPfP LRHS MAsh MBlu MGos NLar SEND SLim SMad SSpi WPGP WPat
- B&SWJ 8404	WCru
- B&SWJ 11374 from Wabuka, Japan	WCru
- 'Emerald Lustre'	CHEx WPGP
awabuki × (× ***hillieri***) **new**	MWat
betulifolium	CAbP CBcs CJun CPLG EPfP GGGa GKin NLar SMad
- f. ***aurantiacum*** **new**	CJun
- 'Hohuanshan'	WCru
bitchiuense	CJun MRav NLar
× ***bodnantense***	CMac CTri EBee LMaj WHar
- 'Charles Lamont' ♀H4	Widely available
- 'Dawn' ♀H4	Widely available
- 'Deben' ♀H4	EPfP MMHG NLar SPer WPat
brachyandrum B&SWJ 5784 **new**	WCru
bracteatum	NLar
buddlejifolium	CMac EBee EBtc EPfP EWes MMuc SKHP WCru WPGP
× ***burkwoodii***	Widely available
- 'Anika'	NLar
- 'Anne Russell' ♀H4	Widely available
- 'Chenaultii'	MRav
- 'Compact Beauty'	CJun CSpe WCFE WPat
- 'Conoy'	CJun ELon MAsh MWat WPat
- 'Fulbrook' ♀H4	CAbP EBee EPfP LEdu LRHS MAsh MGos NLar WPat
- 'Mohawk'	CAbP CDoC CJun EBee ELan ELon EPfP LRHS MAsh MBri NLar SCoo SHil SKHP SWvt WPat
- 'Park Farm Hybrid' ♀H4	CAbP CDoC CJun CMac CPLG CSam CTri CWib EBee ECrN ELan ELon EPfP LAst LBMP LEdu LRHS MAsh MBri MRav MSwo NLar NSti SLPl SPer SPoG SRms WPat
calvum	CPLG
aff. ***calvum*** WWJ 12012 **new**	WCru
× ***carlcephalum*** ♀H4	Widely available
- 'Cayuga'	ELon LEdu MAsh NLar WPat
* - 'Variegatum' (v)	CJun
carlesii	CBcs CDul CMac CTri CWib GKin LSRN MBlu MGos MRav MSwo SCoo SEWo SGol SLim SPer
- B&SWJ 8838	WCru
- 'Aurora' ♀H4	Widely available
- 'Charis'	CJun CSBt LRHS NLar WKif
- 'Compactum'	CJun MAsh
- 'Diana'	CDoC CJun CMHG CMac EBee EPfP LHop LRHS LSRN MAsh MBlu MRav NLar SPer SPoG SPtl SSta WPat
- 'Marlou'	CJun NLar WPat
cassinoides	CJun GBin
- 'Bullatum'	EPfP
'Chesapeake'	CDul CJun EWes MMuc SEND
chingii	CGHE CJun SLon WCru WPGP WPat
'Chippewa'	CJun
cinnamomifolium ♀H3	CAbP CDoy CHEx CPLG EBee ECre EPfP LRHS MAsh NLar SEND SLPl SLon SPer SPoG SSpi WFar WHor WPGP WSHC
cotinifolium	CPLG
- CC 4541	CPLG NLar
cylindricum	CGHE EBee EPfP LHop LRHS NLar SKHP WCru WPGP WPat
- B&SWJ 6479 from Thailand	WCru
- B&SWJ 7239	WCru WPGP
- B&SWJ 9719 from Vietnam	WCru
- HWJCM 434 from Nepal	WCru
- NJM 09.127 from Vietnam	WPGP
dasyanthum	NLar
davidii ♀H4	Widely available

Name	Suppliers
- (f)	CBcs CDoC CMac CSBt ELan EPfP EWTr LAst MAsh MGos SPer SPoG SRms WPat
- (m)	CBcs CDoC CMac CSBt ELan EPfP MGos MRav SPer SPoG SRms WPat
- 'Angustifolium'	CJun EBee LTen WPGP
dentatum	EBtc MAsh WPat
- Autumn Jazz	see *V. dentatum* 'Ralph Senior'
- Blue Muffin = 'Christom'	WPat
- Chicago Lustre	see *V. dentatum* 'Synnestvedt'
- 'Morton'	IArd
§ - 'Ralph Senior'	NLar
§ - 'Synnestvedt'	NLar
- 'White and Blue'	CJun NLar
dilatatum B&SWJ 4456	WCru
- B&SWJ 5844	WCru
- B&SWJ 8734	WCru
- B&SWJ 10894	WCru
- 'Inneke'	NLar
- 'Iroquois'	EPfP
- 'Michael Dodge'	EPfP MBri NLar
- 'Sealing Wax'	NLar
'Emerald Triumph' **new**	CJun
erosum B&SWJ 3585	WCru
- B&SWJ 8735	WCru
- B&SWJ 8893	WCru
- B&SWJ 10880	WCru
erubescens	CAbP CJun IArd NLar SBrt
- HWJK 2163	WCru
- 'Foster'	NLar
- var. ***gracilipes***	CJun EPfP IArd LLHF MAsh WPat
- 'Ward van Teylingen'	EPfP NLar
'Eskimo'	CAbP CBcs CJun CMac CSBt CWSG EBee EPfP LRHS LSRN MAsh MBNS MGos MRav SCoo SKHP SLim SPoG SSta SWvt WFar
§ ***farreri*** ♀H4	CBcs CDoC CDoy CDul CSBt CTri CWib EBee ELan EPfP LBuc LPot LRHS LSRN MGos MRav MSwo NLar NRHS SBod SGol SHil SPer SPoG SWvt WFar WHar
- 'Album'	see *V. farreri* 'Candidissimum'
§ - 'Candidissimum'	CDul CMac CPLG EBee ELan EPfP EWTr IArd LHop LRHS MAsh MRav NLar SGol SPer
- 'December Dwarf'	CJun NLar
- 'Farrer's Pink'	CAbP CJun CPLG NLar
- 'Fioretta'	NLar
- 'Nanum'	CJun CMac EBee EBtc ELan ELon EPfP LRHS MAsh MBrN MRav MWat NLar SKHP WFar WPat
foetens	see *V. grandiflorum* f. *foetens*
foetidum var. ***ceanothoides***	NLar
- var. ***rectangulatum*** B&SWJ 1888	WCru
- - B&SWJ 3451	WCru
fragrans Bunge	see *V. farreri*
'Fragrant Cloud'	ECrN
furcatum ♀H4	EPfP GKin MAsh NLar SKHP WPat
- B&SWJ 5939	WCru
× ***globosum*** 'Jermyns Globe'	CAbP CCVT CDoC CJun CMHG CMac EBee EPfP LAst MRav NLar SEND SLon SPoG WFar
grandiflorum	CJun CMac EPfP NLar
- 'De Oirsprong'	NLar
§ - f. ***foetens***	CJun EBee EPfP LRHS NLar
- - GWJ 9227	WCru
- 'Snow White'	CJun
aff. ***griffithianum*** GWJ 9388 **new**	WCru
harryanum	CAbP CDoy EBtc EPfP MBNS MOWG NLar WCru WSHC
henryi	CAbP CJun EPfP IArd NLar SBrt WPat
× ***hillieri***	CHGN MWhi
- 'Winton' ♀H4	CAbP CDoC CJun CMac CWib EBee EPfP IDee LHop LRHS LSRN LTen MBri MOWG NLar SHil SKHP SLon SPoG SSpi WFar WPGP WPat
'Huron'	EPfP
ichangense	CJun NLar
japonicum	CPLG EBee EPfP LAst LRHS NLar SLon WFar WPGP
- B&SWJ 5968	WCru
× ***juddii*** ♀H4	Widely available
kansuense	CPLG
- BWJ 7737	WCru
koreanum B&SWJ 4231	WCru
lantana	CBcs CCVT CDul CHab CLnd CRWN CTri CWib ECrN EShb LAst LBuc NLar NWea SEND SEWo SPer SVic WFar WMou
- 'Aureum'	CMHG EHoe EPfP MAsh MBlu NLar
- var. ***discolor***	NLar
- 'Mohican'	NLar
- 'Variefolium' (v)	CJun
§ ***lantanoides***	EPfP NLar SSpi
latifolium 'Chino-Crûg'	WCru
aff. ***lautum*** B&SWJ 10290 **new**	WCru
'Le Bois Marquis'PBR	EBee EMil EPfP SBfd
lentago	CAbP CMac NLar
lobophyllum	EPfP NLar
luzonicum B&SWJ 3930	WCru
- var. ***formosanum*** B&SWJ 3585 **new**	WCru
- var. ***oblongum*** B&SWJ 3549	WCru
- var. ***sinuatum*** B&SWJ 4009 **new**	WCru
macrocephalum	CJun SLon
- 'Sterile' **new**	LHop
mariesii	see *V. plicatum* f. *tomentosum* 'Mariesii'
nervosum B&SWJ 2251a	WCru
nudum	ECrN EPfP IArd IDee IVic NLar
- 'Pink Beauty'	CGHE CJun EBee EPfP LRHS LSRN MBri MMHG NLar SHil WFar WPGP WPat
- 'Winterthur'	CJun NLar
odoratissimum misapplied	see *V. awabuki*
odoratissimum Ker Gawl.	EBee LEdu
- RWJ 10046	WCru
aff. ***odoratissimum*** B&SWJ 3913 from the Philippines	WCru
- 'Arboricolum'	WCru
'Oneida'	CJun NLar
opulus	Widely available
- var. ***americanum*** 'Bailey's Compact'	MAsh WPat
- - 'Hans'	NLar
- - 'Phillips'	CAgr
- - 'Spring Red'	NLar
- - 'Wentworth'	CAgr
- 'Apricot'	NLar

- 'Aureum' CMac CSam CWib EBee EHoe ELan EPfP LAst LBMP MAsh MGos MMuc MRav NEgg NLar NMyG SPer WFar WMoo
- var. ***calvescens*** B&SWJ 10544 WCru
- 'Compactum' ♀H4 Widely available
N - 'Fructu Luteo' SGol
* - 'Harvest Gold' SCoo SLim SPoG
- 'Nanum' CAbP CBcs CMea EBee ECrN ELan ELon EPfP EShb LAst MRav NHol NLar NMen WFar WPat
- 'Notcutt's Variety' ♀H4 EPfP MAsh WPat
- 'Park Harvest' CDul EBee EBtc EPfP LRHS MAsh NLar SKHP SLPl WPat
§ - 'Roseum' ♀H4 Widely available
- 'Sterile' see *V. opulus* 'Roseum'
* - 'Sterile Compactum' LAst SWvt
N - 'Xanthocarpum' ♀H4 Widely available
parvifolium NLar
- B&SWJ 6768 WCru
phlebotrichum B&SWJ 11058 **new** WCru
pichinchense B&SWJ 10660 WCru
N ***plicatum*** CTri CWib LPot NLar
- 'Janny' WPat
- 'Mary Milton' CJun NLar
- 'Nanum' see *V. plicatum* f. *tomentosum* 'Nanum Semperflorens'
- 'Pink Sensation' CJun GBin NCGa
§ - f. ***plicatum*** EWTr
- - 'Chyverton' **new** MAsh
- - 'Grandiflorum' CAbP CDoC EPfP LRHS NLar SPer WMoo
- 'Popcorn' CAbP CJun CMac CPLG ELon EPfP LEdu LRHS LSRN MAsh MRav SLim SPoG SSta WPat
- 'Rosace' EPfP LRHS MBlu NLar SSpi WPat
- 'Shoshoni' GBin MBri NLar
N - 'Sterile' see *V. plicatum* f. *plicatum*
- f. ***tomentosum*** EPfP EWTr
- - 'Cascade' EBee EWTr LRHS NEgg NLar SSpi
- - 'Dart's Red Robin' ECtt LLHF MAsh NLar WPat
- - 'Elizabeth Bullivant' LLHF LRHS MAsh
- - 'Igloo' NLar
- - 'Lanarth' CBar CBcs CDoC CDul CMac CPLG CSBt CTri CWSG CWib EBee EPfP EWTr LHop LRHS LSRN MAsh MBlu MGos NLar NSti SCoo SGol SKHP SLim SPer SWal SWvt WFar
§ - - 'Mariesii' ♀H4 Widely available
- - 'Molly Schroeder' CJun NLar
§ - - 'Nanum Semperflorens' CDoC CMac ECtt GBin IArd MGos NLar SBfd SLPl SPoG WFar WPat WSHC
- - Newport = 'Newzam' CDoC NLar
- - 'Pink Beauty' ♀H4 Widely available
- - 'Rotundifolium' LRHS MAsh MBri MRav NLar SHil WPat
- - 'Rowallane' EPfP MBri WPat
- - 'Saint Keverne' GKin
- - 'Shasta' CDoC CMCN EPfP EWTr MBri NLar SKHP WFar
- - 'Summer Snowflake' CDoC CWGN EBee ECrN EPfP LRHS MAsh MSwo NLar SKHP SLim SPer SPoG WFar
- - 'White Beauty' **new** EPfP MAsh
- Triumph = 'Trizam' NLar
- 'Watanabe' see *V. plicatum* f. *tomentosum* 'Nanum Semperflorens'
'Pragense' ♀H4 CAbP CBcs CDul CMCN EBee EPfP LRHS MGos NHol NLar SEND SLon SPer WFar WPat
propinquum CAbP NLar
- CWJ 12426 WCru
prunifolium EBtc NLar SGol WCru
- 'Mrs Henry's Large' CJun
* 'Regenteum' CWib
× ***rhytidophylloides*** WFar
- 'Alleghany' NLar
- Dart's Duke = 'Interduke' SLPl WPat
- 'Willowwood' EBee LRHS MAsh NLar WPat
rhytidophyllum CBcs CDoy CDul CHEx CMac CTri EBee ECrN EPfP LAst LHop LRHS LTen MGos MMuc MSwo NEgg NWea SEND SGol SPer SRms WCFE WFar WMoo WSFF
- 'Aldenham' GCal LSRN
- 'Roseum' CPLG SLPl SWvt
- 'Variegatum' (v) CJun NLar WPat
- 'Wisley Pink' EBee LRHS MAsh SSpi
'Royal Guard' CJun LLHF NLar
sambucinum HWJ 838 WCru
- var. ***tomentosum*** HWJ 733 **new** WCru
sargentii B&SWJ 8695 WCru
- f. ***flavum*** NLar
- 'Onondaga' ♀H4 Widely available
- 'Susquehanna' EPfP NLar
semperflorens see *V. plicatum* f. *tomentosum* 'Nanum Semperflorens'
§ ***setigerum*** EPfP IArd NLar SLPl WPat
- 'Aurantiacum' NLar
sieboldii B&SWJ 2837 WCru
- 'Seneca' EPfP NLar
subalpinum NLar
taiwanianum B&SWJ 3009 WCru
ternatum EPfP
theiferum see *V. setigerum*
tinoides B&SWJ 10612 WCru
tinus Widely available
- 'Bewley's Variegated' (v) MRav SPer
I - 'Compactum' SWvt
- 'Eve Price' ♀H4 Widely available
- 'French White' ♀H4 CDoC CDul CMac EBee ELan ELon EPfP LRHS MGos MRav NRHS SBfd SCoo SHil SLim SPoG SWvt WFar
- 'Gwenllian' ♀H4 Widely available
- 'Israel' EBee MBNS NLar SPer
- 'Little Bognor' EBee NLar
- 'Lucidum' CBcs CJun CSam NLar WCFE
- 'Lucidum Variegatum' (v) CJun CMac SLim
* - 'Macrophyllum' EPfP LRHS NLar SPoG SWvt
- 'Purpureum' CBar CJun CSBt EBee ECrN EHoe ELon EPfP LRHS MAsh MGos MSwo MWat NEgg SBfd SCoo SGol SHil SLPl SLim SPer SPoG WFar WMoo WPat
- Spirit = 'Anvi'PBR CAbP CSBt EBee LRHS LSou MAsh NLar SBfd SCoo SPoG
- 'Spring Bouquet' MAsh NLar
- 'Variegatum' (v) CDul CMac CTri CWib EBee EHoe ELan ELon EPfP LAst LRHS MAsh MGos NEgg NLar SBfd SGol SLim SPlb SPoG SRms SWvt WFar WPat
tomentosum see *V. plicatum*
triphyllum B&SWJ 5784 WCru

urceolatum B&SWJ 6988 WCru
utile WPat WThu
aff. ***venustum*** B&SWJ 10477 WCru
wrightii MRav NLar
- B&SWJ 5871 WCru
- 'Hessei' WPat
- var. ***stipellatum*** B&SWJ 5856 WCru
- - B&SWJ 8780A WCru

Vicia (*Papilionaceae*)

americana EBee
cracca CHab NLan NMir WSFF
oroboides LRHS
sativa CHab
sylvatica EWes

Vigna (*Papilionaceae*)

§ ***caracalla*** CCCN

Viguiera (*Asteraceae*)

multiflora EBee

Villarsia (*Menyanthaceae*)

bennettii see *Nymphoides peltata* 'Bennettii'

Vinca (*Apocynaceae*)

balcanica XLum
difformis ♀H3-4 COIW CPom CTri CWan ECha LLWP LRHS MGos SBri SDix WHer XLum
* - 'Alba' CPom SBch
- Greystone form CPLG EPPr EPfP LHop NLar SEND WGwG WRHF
- 'Jenny Pym' COIW CPLG CPom EBee ECtt EPPr EWTr EWes LHop MBNS SEND SPoG WBor WFar WRHF
- 'Ruby Baker' LRHS NChi WHrl
- 'Snowmound' COIW CWan EBee LRHS MRav SPoG SWvt
herbacea RCB UA 21 WCot
'Hidcote Purple' see *V. major* var. *oxyloba*
major CBcs CDul CMac CSBt CWib ELan EPfP EShb GKev GPoy LBuc LRHS MGos MSwo NPri NWea SBfd SGol SHil SLim SPer SRms WFar WGwG WMoo XLum
- 'Alba' CMac CWib
- 'Elegantissima' see *V. major* 'Variegata'
- 'Expoflora' (v) NLar
- var. ***hirsuta*** hort. see *V. major* var. *oxyloba*
§ - subsp. ***hirsuta*** (Boiss.) Stearn CMac LPla WCot XLum
§ - 'Maculata' (v) CDoC COIW CSBt EBee EHoe EShb LRHS LSou MRav MSwo NPri SBfd SEND SLim SPer SPoG SWvt WFar WMoo
§ - var. ***oxyloba*** CFis CMac COIW CPLG CTri EBee ECha ELan EPri LHop LRHS MBel MRav MWat SPoG SRms WBor WFar WHer
- var. ***pubescens*** see *V. major* subsp. *hirsuta* (Boiss.) Stearn
- 'Surrey Marble' see *V. major* 'Maculata'
§ - 'Variegata' (v) ♀H4 Widely available
- 'Wojo's Jem' (v) CDoC CMac EBee ELan EPfP EWes LBuc LRHS LSRN MBri MGos NPri SCoo SHil SLim SPoG SWvt WCot
minor CArn CBar CBcs CDoC CDul CMac CSBt ELan EPfP GAbr GKin GPoy LAst LRHS MAsh MGos NPri NWea SBfd SCob SLim SVic WFar XLum
- f. ***alba*** ♀H4 CBcs CDoC CMac COIW EBee ECha EPPr EPfP LRHS LSRN MAsh NEgg NLar NPri SBfd SPer SWal WCot WFar WPtf XLum
§ - - 'Alba Variegata' (v) CPLG EHoe LSRN NPro SPer SRms WCot WFar WHoo
- - 'Gertrude Jekyll' ♀H4 CDoC CPLG CSBt CYeo EBee ELan EPfP EWTr GAbr IKil LHop LPot LRHS LSRN LTen MBri MGos MRav MWat NPri NRHS SBod SCoo SEND SHil SLim SPer SPoG WMoo
- 'Alba Aureovariegata' see *V. minor* f. *alba* 'Alba Variegata'
§ - 'Argenteovariegata' (v) ♀H4 Widely available
§ - 'Atropurpurea' ♀H4 Widely available
- 'Aurea' WFar
§ - 'Aureovariegata' (v) CBcs CMac ELan EPfP GAbr LRHS MGos MRav NRHS SBfd SGol SHil SLim SPer SPlb WFar
- 'Azurea' CHid MGos
§ - 'Azurea Flore Pleno' (d) ♀H4 Widely available
* - 'Blue and Gold' EAEE ECGP ELon NBre NHol
- 'Blue Drift' EWes MSwo
- 'Bowles's Blue' see *V. minor* 'La Grave'
- 'Bowles's Purple' WBor
- 'Bowles's Variety' see *V. minor* 'La Grave'
- 'Burgundy' SRms
- 'Caerulea Plena' see *V. minor* 'Azurea Flore Pleno'
- 'Dartington Star' see *V. major* var. *oxyloba*
- 'Double Burgundy' see *V. minor* 'Multiplex'
- Green Carpet see *V. minor* 'Grüner Teppich'
§ - 'Grüner Teppich' WFar
- 'Hawaii' ELon
- 'Illumination' (v) Widely available
§ - 'La Grave' ♀H4 Widely available
- 'Marie' EPPr
- 'Mrs Betty James' (d) **new** WCot
§ - 'Multiplex' (d) CYeo ECtt EPPr LBuc NChi SLim SRms WHrl WPtf
- 'Purpurea' see *V. minor* 'Atropurpurea'
- 'Ralph Shugert' CPLG CYeo EBee ELon EPPr EPfP EWes LHop LRHS LSRN LSqu MAsh NLar SBfd SCoo SGol SPoG
- 'Rubra' see *V. minor* 'Atropurpurea'
- 'Sabinka' CHid EPPr
- 'Silver Service' (d/v) CHid CWan MRav WCot
- 'Variegata' see *V. minor* 'Argenteovariegata'
- 'Variegata Aurea' see *V. minor* 'Aureovariegata'
- 'White Gold' NPro
sardoa COIW EBee EPPr EWes LRHS

Vincetoxicum (*Apocynaceae*)

cretaceum **new** LEdu
- PAB 3432 LEdu
forrestii CPLG
§ ***hirundinaria*** EBee EPPr GPoy LEdu
- CC 6289 EWld
nigrum CArn EBee GCal NChi NMyG SBrt WCot WTou
- I am a Tiny Star = 'Zotista' MGos
officinale see *V. hirundinaria*
scandens CRHN SBrt

Viola ✿ (Violaceae)

	Name	Suppliers
	'Admiration' (Va)	WBou
	adunca* var. *minor	see *V. labradorica* ambig.
§	***alba***	EWes NMen
	'Alethia' (Va)	SDys WBou
	'Alice' (Vt)	CGro CLAP
	'Alice Kate'	WBou
	'Alice Witter' (Vt)	CGro LLHF NNth WPtf
*	'Alison' (Va)	WBou
	'Amelia' (Va)	WBou
I	'Amethyst' (Vt)	CGro
	'Annette Ross' (Va)	WBou
I	'Annie' (Vt)	CGro CLAP LLHF
	'Ardross Gem' (Va)	ECho ECtt NNth WBou WKif
	arenaria	see *V. rupestris*
	'Arkwright's Ruby' (Va)	SRms
	arvensis	CHab
	'Ashvale Blue' (PVt)	CGro
	'Aspasia' (Va) ♀H4	EWoo WBou
	'Avril Lawson' (Va)	SHar WBou
	'Baby Lucia' (Va)	SRms
	'Barbara' (Va)	WBou
	'Baroness de Rothschild' misapplied	see *V.* 'Baronne Alice de Rothschild'
	'Baroness de Rothschild' ambig. (Vt)	CGro CLAP
§	'Baronne Alice de Rothschild' (Vt)	GMaP NLar WCot
	'Beatrice' (Vtta)	WBou
	'Becky Groves' (Vt)	CGro CLAP
§	'Belmont Blue' (C)	CEnt CSam CSpe CTri EBee ELon EWes EWoo GCal GMaP IFro LHop LRHS MCot MHer MMuc MRav MSCN NBir NCGa NDov NNth SBch SMrm SPer SRms WBou WCot WFar
§	***bertolonii***	WBou
	'Beshlie' (Va) ♀H4	ECtt NNth WBou
	biflora	CMHG MNrw
	'Blue Butterfly' (C)	EWoo
	'Blue Horns' (C)	ELon
	'Blue Moon' (C)	WBou
	'Blue Moonlight' (C)	CElw MMuc
	'Blue Tit' (Va)	ECtt
	'Boughton Blue'	see *V.* 'Belmont Blue'
	'Bournemouth Gem' (Vt)	CGro
§	'Bowles's Black' (T)	CSpe EPfP GCal LBMP LEdu MAsh NBro SRms WJek
	'Boy Blue' (Vtta)	ECtt
	brevistipulata* var. *hidakana new	GEdr
	'Bruneau' (dVt)	CBre ECtt EWll IBoy MAvo MBel NLar SMrm WCot
*	'Bryony' (Vtta)	WBou
	'Bullion' (Va)	NNth WBou
	'Burncoose Yellow'	WBou
	'Buttercup' (Vtta)	COIW ECtt LSRN NEgg NNth NSla SDys SPoG WBou
	'Buxton Blue' (Va)	WBou
	'Candy' (Vt)	CGro
	canina	NBro NMir
	'Carol' (Vt)	CGro
	'Carol Loxton' (Vt)	CGro
	'Catalina'	CLAP
	'Charles William Groves' (Vt) new	CGro CLAP ELon
	'Charles Winston Groves' (Vt) new	CGro
	'Charlotte'	EDAr WBou WJek
	'Chloe' (Vtta)	CGro
	'Christie's Wedding' (Vt)	CGro
	'Christmas' (Vt)	CGro
	'Clementina' (Va) ♀H4	MRav WBou
	'Cleo' (Va)	NNth WBou
	'Clive Farrell' (Vt)	CGro
	'Clive Groves' (Vt)	CGro CLAP ELon
	'Coeur d'Alsace' (Vt)	CGro CLAP CPBP ECtt GMaP NLar WHal XLum
	'Colette' (Va)	WBou
	'Colombine' (Vt)	CGro MAsh
	'Columbine' (Va)	EBee ECtt EPfP GMaP LRHS MHer NBir NDov NEgg NNth NRHS SPer SPoG WBou WCot WFar WJek
	'Comte de Chambord' (dVt)	WFar
	'Connigar'	CSam
§	'Conte di Brazza' (dPVt)	EHrv NLar SHar WFar
	'Cordelia' (Va)	WFar
	'Cordelia' (Vt)	CLAP ECtt
	cornuta ♀H4	CElw CMea ECho EPot GKev MLHP MNrw MWat NBir NBro SBch SRms WBou WFar WHoo WTou
	– Alba Group ♀H4	Widely available
	– 'Alba Minor'	CEnt ECho EPfP EWes EWoo GCal IGor NBro NRHS NSla WFar
	– blue-flowered	ECho MHer MLHP WFar WMoo
	– 'Cleopatra' (C)	GAbr
	– 'Clouded Yellow'	EWoo
	– 'Gypsy Moth' (C)	EWoo
	– 'Icy But Spicy'	EBee EWTr MCot MRav NDov NNth SMrm WBou WCot
	– Lilacina Group (C)	ECha MRav SWat WFar WMnd WPtf
	– 'Maiden's Blush'	NNth
	– 'Minor' ♀H4	CSam EWoo NBro NRHS NSla WBou
	– 'Netta Statham'	EWoo MPie NDov WBou
	– Purpurea Group	CMea ECha GCal SBch WMnd
	– 'Rosea'	ECha
	– 'Spider'	MPie SDys
	– 'Ulla'	SBfd
	– 'Victoria's Blush' (C)	CElw CSpe ECtt ELon EWTr GMaP MCot MMuc MPie NBir NDov SUsu WBou
	– 'Violacea'	EWoo
	– 'Yellow King'	EHrv
	corsica	CMea CSpe EWTr NChi SBch
§	***cucullata*** ♀H4	ECho SRms WFar
§	– 'Alba' (Vt)	CBro ECho LLWP NBir SRms
	– ***rosea***	EWes
*	– 'Striata Alba'	NBro
	'Czar'	see *V.* 'The Czar'
	'Daisy Smith' (Va)	WBou
	'Dancing Geisha' (Vt)	EPfP
	'Danielle Molly'	WBou
	'Dawn' (Vtta)	CMea EBee ECtt EPfP GMaP MAsh NEgg NNth NSla SPoG WBou
	'Delicia' (Vtta)	NDov NNth WBou
	'Desdemona' (Va)	EWoo NNth WBou
	'Devon Cream' (Va)	WBou
	'Diana Groves' (Vt)	CGro
	'Dick o' the Hills' (Vt)	CGro
	dissecta	WCot
	'Donau' (Vt)	CGro EBee WCot
	'Doreen' (Vt)	CGro
	'Duchesse de Parme' (dPVt)	CGro IFro SRms
	'D'Udine' (dPVt)	CBre EBee ECtt MTis WCot
	'Dusk'	WBou
	'E.A. Bowles'	see *V.* 'Bowles's Black'

'Eastgrove Blue Scented' (C) EWoo SDys WBou WOut WPtf
'Eastgrove Ice Blue' (C) MCot WBou WOut
'Elaine Quin' EBee ECtt MCot NDov NEgg NNth NPri SPoG WBou WKif
§ ***elatior*** EBee EPPr EWTr MNrw WHil WPer WPtf
'Elizabeth' (Va) ECtt WBou
'Elizabeth Lee' WCot
'Elliot Adam' (Va) WBou
'Elsie Coombs' (Vt) CGro
'Emperor Blue Vein' EBee EPfP NNth
erecta see *V. elatior*
'Eris' (Va) WBou
'Etain' (Va) COIW EBee ECho ECtt ELan EPfP EWes EWoo GBuc GMaP LRHS MAsh MTis NDov NEgg NNth NPri SMrm SPoG WBou WIce
'Fabiola' (Vtta) EWoo NBir
'Famecheck Apricot' CPom
* 'Fantasy' WBou
'Ferndale' (Vt) CGro
'Fiona' (Va) EWoo MCot NChi WBou
'Fiona Lawrenson' (Va) WBou
'Florence' (Va) WBou
'Foxbrook Cream' (C) WBou
'Francesca' (Va) WBou
'Freckles' see *V. sororia* 'Freckles'
(Friolina Series) Friolina Blue Yellow Cascadiz = 'Sunviopoki' **new** NPri
- Friolina Creamy Pink **new** LAst
- Friolina Orange Cascadiz = 'Sunviobare'[PBR] NPri
- Friolina Yellow Cascadiz = 'Sanvioki' **new** NPri
'George Lee' (Vt) CGro
glabella SBch
'Gladys Findlay' (Va) WBou
* 'Glenda' WBou
'Glenholme' EWoo
'Gloire de Verdun' (PVt) CGro
'Governor Herrick' (Vt) CGro CLAP ECtt LLHF NLar NNth WFar WHer
§ ***gracilis*** NBir WFar
- 'Lutea' CSam
- 'Major' WBou
'Green Goddess'[PBR] CMea NNth SMrm WFar
'Grey Owl' (Va) WBou
'Grovemount Blue' (C) CElw CMea CSpe
§ ***grypoceras*** var. ***exilis*** EBee
'Gustav Wermig' (C) WBou
'Haslemere' see *V.* 'Nellie Britton'
* 'Heaselands' SMHy SMrm
§ ***hederacea*** CPLG EBee ECou EWoo GQui IFoB SRms WFar
'Helena' (Va) WBou
'Hespera' (Va) WBou
heterophylla subsp. ***epirota*** see *V. bertolonii*
* 'Hetty Gatenby' WBou
'Hudsons Blue' CElw
'Huntercombe Purple' (Va) ♀H4 ECho LHop LRHS MCot NBir NRHS SRms WBou WHal WKif
'Iden Gem' (Va) WBou
'Inverurie Beauty' (Va) ♀H4 EWoo GMaP NDov NNth SDys WBou WKif
'Irish Elegance' see *V.* 'Sulfurea'
'Irish Molly' (Va) CSpe EBee ECho ECtt ELan EPfP EWoo GBuc LRHS MAsh MHer MTis NDov NEgg NNth NPri NRHS NSla SPer SPoG SRms WBou WFar WIce
'Isabel' NDov WBou
'Isabella' (Vt) CGro CLAP
'Ivory Queen' (Va) EWoo MRav NNth WBou
'Jack Sampson' (Vt) CGro
'Jackanapes' (Va) ♀H4 CMea EBee ECho ECtt ELan EPfP LRHS MAsh NEgg NNth SPer SPoG SRms WBou WFar WIce
'Jane Mott' (Va) EWoo
'Janet' (Va) EBee ECtt LSRN NNth NPri SDys SPoG
'Jeannie Bellew' (Va) SRms WBou WFar
'Jennifer Andrews' (Va) WBou
'Jersey Gem' (Va) NNth
'Joanna' (Va) WBou
'John Raddenbury' (Vt) GMaP
jooi CPBP EBee EPfP GKev NBir NMen SPhx SRms WAbe WPtf
'Josephine' (Vt) CGro
'Josie' (Va) WBou
'Joyce Gray' (Va) WBou
'Judy Goring' (Va) EWoo
'Julia' (Va) WBou
'Julian' (Va) EWoo NNth SRms WBou
'Juno' (Va) EWoo
'Katerina' (Va) WBou
'Kerry Girl' (Vt) CGro
'Kim' CGro CLAP
'Kitten' EWoo SDys WBou
'Kitty White' (Va) EWoo SDys
§ 'Königin Charlotte' (Vt) CGro COIW EPfP GMaP LRHS MCot MHer NEgg SBfd WCot WFar WMoo
koreana see *V. grypoceras* var. *exilis*
N ***labradorica*** misapplied see *V. riviniana* Purpurea Group
N - ***purpurea*** see *V. riviniana* Purpurea Group
§ ***labradorica*** ambig. EHrv EWTr GQui LRHS MAsh MCot NPri SMrm WFar
'Lady Hume Campbell' (PVt) CGro
'Lady Jane' (Vt) CGro
'Lady Saville' see *V.* 'Sissinghurst'
'Laura Cawthorne' NNth
'Lavender Lady' (Vt) CGro
'Lees Peachy Pink' (Vt) CGro CLAP
'Letitia' (Va) EBee MCot NNth SDys SRms WBou WFar
'Lianne' (Vt) CGro CLAP LLHF WCot
'Lindsay' WBou
'Lisa Tanner' (Va) WBou
'Little David' (Vtta) ♀H4 CSam CTri ECtt MCot NDov NNth SRms WBou
'Lizzy Wootten' (Va) **new** EWoo
'Lord Plunket' (Va) WBou
'Lorna Cawthorne' (C) SDys WBou
'Louisa' (Va) EWoo WBou WOut
§ ***lutea*** WBou
- subsp. ***elegans*** see *V. lutea*
'Luxonne' (Vt) CGro
'Lydia Groves' (Vt) CGro CLAP EBee ELon LLHF LSou WCot
'Lydia's Legacy' (Vt) CGro
'Madame Armandine Pagès' (Vt) CGro
'Maggie Mott' (Va) ♀H4 ECho ECtt EWoo LHop MCot WBou WFar WWFP
'Magic' WBou

	mandshurica 'Fuji Dawn' (v)	EBee SPad
	- f. ***hasegawae***	EPPr
	'Margaret' (Va)	WBou
	'Marie-Louise' (dPVt)	CGro ECtt NLar SHar
	'Mars' (Va)	EBee ECtt NNth SMrm
I	'Mars'	CAbP ECtt LSRN LSou MSCN WFar
	'Martin' (Va) ♀H4	COIW EBee ECha EPfP EWoo GMaP LHop LSRN MAsh MAvo MBrN MHer NDov NNth SPer SPoG WBou WFar
	'Mary Mouse'	NDov WBou
	'Mauve Haze' (Va)	WBou
	'Mauve Radiance' (Va)	ECtt EWoo WBou
	'May Mott' (Va)	WBou
	'Melinda' (Vtta)	WBou
	'Melting Moments' (Va)	NEgg
	'Mercury' (Va)	MCot WBou
	'Midnight' (Va) **new**	EWoo
	'Milkmaid' (Va)	EBee ELon NBir NNth
	'Miss Brookes' (Va)	WBou
	'Misty Guy' (Vtta)	WBou
	'Molly Sanderson' (Va) ♀H4	CSpe EBee ECha ECho ECtt ELan EPfP EPot EWoo GMaP LAst LHop LRHS MAsh MHer NEgg NNth NPri NRHS SPer SPlb SPoG WBou WFar WIce WNew
	'Moonlight' (Va) ♀H4	ECho ELan LHop LRHS MHer NRHS WBou
	'Moonraker'	NBir NNth
	'Morwenna' (Va)	ECtt MCot WBou WKif
	'Mrs Lancaster' (Va)	CMea EBee ECtt EWoo GMaP LHop LSRN NBir NNth NPri NSla SDys SPoG SRms WBou
	'Mrs Pinehurst' (Vt)	CGro GMaP
	'Mrs R. Barton' (Vt)	CGro CLAP EBee SHar
	'Mulberry' (Vt)	CGro
	'Myfawnny' (Va)	ECho ECtt ELan EWes LRHS MCot NDov NNth NRHS SDys SRms WBou WFar
	'Neapolitan'	see *V.* 'Pallida Plena'
§	'Nellie Britton' (Va) ♀H4	ECho ECtt SRms
	'Netta Statham'	see *V.* 'Belmont Blue'
	'Nora'	NDov NNth WBou
	'Norah Church' (Vt)	CGro CLAP
	'Norah Leigh' (Va)	EOHP WBou
	obliqua	see *V. cucullata*
	odorata (Vt)	CArn CBcs CGro CHab CRWN EBee EPfP GPoy MHoo MRav NMir NPri SIde SMrm SPer SRms SVic WJek
	- 'Alba' (Vt)	CGro CPom CWan EBee ECho ELan EPfP LEdu MHer NPri SEND SRms WMoo
	- 'Alba Plena' (dVt)	EHrv LSou
	- 'Albiflora' (Vt)	CEnt CLAP CPBP EPfP
	- apricot-flowered (Vt)	see *V.* 'Sulfurea'
	- 'Bethan Davies' (dVt) **new**	WCot
	- 'Dawnie' (Vt)	CGro
	- deep violet-flowered (Vt) **new**	SEND
	- var. ***dumetorum***	see *V. alba*
	- 'Ellie' (Vt) **new**	CGro
	- 'Elsmeer' (Vt)	EBee LSou WCot
	- 'Hungarian Beauty' (Vt) **new**	EBee
	- 'Katy' (Vt)	CLAP CPom ELon SBch
	- 'King of Violets' (dVt)	CBre EBee ECtt EWll LRHS LSou MAvo NEgg SHar SPer WCot WFar
	- 'Melanie' (Vt)	WCot
	- (Miracle Series) 'Miracle Bride White' (Vt) **new**	SHar
	- - 'Miracle Classy Pink' (Vt) **new**	SHar
	- - 'Miracle Intense Blue' (Vt) **new**	SHar
	- - 'Miracle Vanilla White' (Vt) **new**	SHar
	- - 'Miracle Ice White' (Vt) **new**	SHar
	- 'Perky' (Vt)	CGro
	- pink-flowered	see *V. odorata* Rosea Group
	- 'Port Breedy' (Vt)	CGro
	- 'Red Devil' (Vt)	WFar
	- ***rosea***	see *V. odorata* Rosea Group
§	- Rosea Group (Vt)	CPom EBee EWll IBoy IFoB LRHS LSou MBel MPie MRav MTis NEgg SEND SIde SMrm SPer WCot
	- 'Souvenir de Jules Josse' (Vt)	CGro
*	- subsp. ***subcarnea*** (Vt)	SEND
	- 'Sulphurea'	see *V.* 'Sulfurea'
	- 'Vin d'André Thorp' (Vt)	ECtt LEdu WCot
I	- 'Violett Charm' (Vt)	WCot
	- 'Weimar' (Vt)	GBin
	- 'Wismar' (Vt)	WCot
	'Olive Edwards' **new**	WBou
	'Opéra' (Vt)	CGro CLAP LLHF
	'Orchid Pink' (Vt)	CGro CLAP EBee GMaP
§	'Pallida Plena' (dPVt)	CGro
	palustris	CRWN WHer WSFF WShi
	'Pamela Zambra' (Vt)	CGro CLAP GMaP WSHC
	'Papilio'	NNth
	papilionacea	see *V. sororia*
	'Parchment' (Vt)	CGro
	'Parme de Toulouse' (dPVt)	CGro XLum
	'Pasha' (Va)	EWoo NNth SDys
	'Pat Creasy' (Va)	NDov NNth WBou
	'Pat Kavanagh' (C)	GAbr NDov NNth WBou
	'Patience'	WBou
	'Pearl Rose'	ELon
	pedata	CBro EBee WAbe
	- 'Bicolor'	WAbe
	pedatifida	IFoB MHer
	pensylvanica	see *V. pubescens* var. *eriocarpa*
	'Perle Rose' (Vt)	CGro CLAP
	'Petra' (Vtta)	EWoo NNth WBou
	'Phyl Dove' (Vt)	CLAP WCot
	'Pickering Blue' (Va)	WBou
	'Primrose Dame' (Va)	MHer WBou WCot
	'Primrose Pixie' (Va)	WBou
	'Prince Henry' (T)	MNHC
	'Prince John' (T)	MNHC
	'Princess Mab' (Vtta)	WBou
	'Princess of Prussia' (Vt)	CGro WCot
	'Princess of Wales'	see *V.* 'Princesse de Galles'
§	'Princesse de Galles' (Vt)	CTri
	'Pritchard's Russian' (Vt)	CGro
	'Prolific' (Vt)	CGro
§	***pubescens*** var. ***eriocarpa***	SRms
	'Purple Emperor'	SBfd
	'Purple Wings' (Va)	WBou
	'Putty'	ECou
	Queen Charlotte	see *V.* 'Königin Charlotte'
	'Queen Victoria'	see *V.* 'Victoria Regina'
	'Raven'	NNth WBou
	'Rebecca' (Vtta)	CSam EBee ECho ECtt ELan EPfP GBuc GMaP LRHS LSRN MAsh

		MCot MHer MTis NBir NDov NEgg NNth NPri SDys SMrm SPer SPoG SRms WBou WFar WIce
	'Red Charm' (Vt)	CGro EAEE EBee MWat
	'Red Giant' (Vt)	CGro EAEE MWat NEgg
	'Red Lion' (Vt)	CGro
	'Red Queen' (Vt)	CGro CLAP
	reichei	CRWN
	reichenbachiana	EBee
	'Reine des Blanches' (dVt)	CBre EBee ECtt ELon LEdu LLWP LPla LRHS MAvo MBel MTis NEgg NGdn NLar SEND SMrm SPer WCot
	reniforme	see *V. hederacea*
	riviniana	CArn CRWN MHer MMuc SEND WHer WOut WSFF WShi
	- dark pink-flowered	MMuc
	- 'Ed's Variegated' (v)	EPPr WCot
§	- Purpurea Group	Widely available
	- 'Rosea' **new**	SEND
	- white-flowered	EBee EWes MMuc SEND
	'Roscastle Black'	CMea EBee EPfP EWoo MTis NDov NNth SBfd SMrm WBou WKif
	'Rosine' (Vt)	CGro
	'Royal Elk' (Vt)	CGro
	'Rubin' (C)	LRHS
	'Rubra' (Vt)	EPfP
§	***rupestris***	CTri CWan
*	- ***rosea***	CPom EBee IFro LLWP MHer WHer WOut WPtf
	'Saint Helena' (Vt)	WCot
	schariensis	EWes
	selkirkii Pursh ex Goldie	WThu
	seoulensis **new**	LLHF
	septentrionalis	see *V. sororia*
	'Serena' (Va)	WBou
	'Sherbet Dip'	WBou
	'Sidborough Poppet'	CRDP EWes
	'Silver Samurai'	MPnt
§	'Sissinghurst' (Va)	MHer NBir
	'Sisters' (Vt)	CGro
	'Smugglers' Moon'	WBou
	somchetica **new**	WCot
	'Sophie' (Vtta)	WBou
	Sorbet Series **new**	NPri
	- 'Sorbet Sunny Royale' **new**	NPri
§	***sororia***	CPne EAEE EBee ECho EPPr EWoo MLHP MNrw NBir NBro SPhx WPtf
*	- 'Albiflora' ♀H4	CHid EBee ECho EPPr EPfP EWTr EWll EWoo LEdu MRav SPhx WCFE WFar WHil WJek XLum
	- 'Dark Freckles'	EBee ECho LHop SPhx XLum
§	- 'Freckles'	Widely available
	- 'Priceana'	EAEE EBee ECha EPri EPyc LEdu NBir SMrm WCot WPtf
	- 'Sweet Emma'	SPhx
*	'Spencer's Cottage'	WBou
	'Steyning' (Va)	WBou
	stojanowii	CSpe ECho LLHF MAsh
§	'Sulfurea' (Vt)	CLAP CPBP EBee EHrv LLWP MMHG NRya WCot WFar WPer
	'Sulfurea' lemon-flowered (Vt)	CGro
	'Sultan' (Vt)	CGro
	'Susan Chilcott' (Vt)	CGro
	'Susanne Lucas' (Vt)	CGro
	'Susie' (Va)	WBou
	'Swanley White'	see *V.* 'Conte di Brazza'
	'Sybil' (SP)	WBou
	sylvatica	CRDP
§	'The Czar' (Vt)	CBre CGro CLAP ELon SBch WCot
	'Tiger Eyes' (Va)	MAsh NNth SPoG
	'Tom Tit' (Va)	ECtt WBou
	'Tony Venison' (C/v)	ELon EPfP LEdu NEgg NNth SPoG WBou WFar WHer
	tricolor	CArn CHab CPrp ECho EGHP ENfk EPfP GPoy MHer MNHC SIde WJek
	- 'Sawyer's Black' **new**	ENfk
	'Vanessa' (Va)	NNth
	velutina	see *V. gracilis*
	verecunda	WSHC
	- B&SWJ 604a	CLAP WCru
§	- var. ***yakusimana***	CRDP WThu
	'Victoria Cawthorne' (C)	EWoo GBuc MCot MHer NDov NNth WBou
§	'Victoria Regina' (Vt)	EPfP
	'Violacea' (C)	EWoo
	'Virginia' (Va)	WBou
	'Vita' (Va)	EWoo SRms WBou
	'White Ladies'	see *V. cucullata* 'Alba'
	'White Pearl' (Va)	NNth SPhx WBou
	'William' (Va)	NDov
	'Winifred Jones' (Va)	WBou
	'Winona Cawthorne' (C)	EWoo NDov NNth
	'Wisley White'	EBee EWes LPla NNth WFar
	× ***wittrockiana*** (Fizzy Series) 'Fizzy Grape' **new**	NPri
	- - 'Fizzy Lemonberry' **new**	NPri
	- - 'Fizzy Passionfruit' **new**	NPri
	- 'Frizzle Sizzle Mix' (Frizzle Sizzle Series) **new**	NPri
	- Matrix Series **new**	NPri
	'Woodlands Cream' (Va)	MHer WBou
	'Woodlands Lilac' (Va)	WBou
	yakusimana	see *V. verecunda* var. *yakusimana*
	'Zara' (Va)	WBou
	'Zoe' (Vtta)	ECtt EPfP NEgg NNth NPri SMrm SPoG WBou WFar

Viscaria (*Caryophyllaceae*)

	vulgaris	see *Lychnis viscaria*

Viscum (*Santalaceae*)

	cruciatum B&F MA 24	WCot

Vitaliana (*Primulaceae*)

§	***primuliflora***	ECho GKev NMen NRya NSla
	- subsp. ***assoana***	EPot
	- subsp. ***chionantha***	WAbe
	- subsp. ***cinerea***	GKev
	- subsp. ***praetutiana***	CPBP NMen WAbe WPat WThu
	- subsp. ***tridentata***	NMen

Vitex (*Lamiaceae*)

	agnus-castus	CArn CBcs CHll CWSG EOHP EPri EShb GPoy LEdu LRHS MHoo MRav SBfd SEND SLon SPer WFar WSHC XSen
	- 'Alba'	CDul CWib EPfP LTen
	- var. ***latifolia***	CWib ELan EPfP LRHS LSRN MGos MHer SBfd SPoG WPGP XSen
I	- 'Rosea'	NLar XSen
	- 'Silver Spire'	CDul EBee ELan LRHS SPoG WPGP WSHC
	chinensis	see *V. negundo* var. *heterophylla*
	incisa	see *V. negundo* var. *heterophylla*
	negundo	CArn EOHP
§	- var. ***heterophylla***	EWes XSen

Vitis ✿ (*Vitaceae*)

	'Abundante' (F)	WSuV
	'Alden' (O/B)	WSuV
	'Amandin' (G/W)	WSuV
	amurensis	EPfP NLar
	- B&SWJ 4138	WCru
	- B&SWJ 4299	WCru
	'Atlantis' (O/W)	WSuV
§	'Aurore' (W)	CAgr WSuV
	'Baco Noir' (O/B)	CAgr GTwe WSuV
	betulifolia	EPfP
	'Bianca' (O/W)	WSuV
	'Birstaller Muscat' (W)	WSuV
	Black Hamburgh	see *V. vinifera* 'Schiava Grossa'
*	'Black Strawberry' (B)	CAgr WSuV
§	'Boskoop Glory' (O/B) 🏆H4	CMac EUJe LBuc MCoo NLar SCoo WSuV
	'Brant' (O/B) 🏆H4	Widely available
	'Brilliant' (B)	WSuV
	'Buffalo' (B)	WSuV
	californica (F)	NLar
	'Canadice' (O/R/S)	WSuV
	'Cascade'	see *V.* Seibel 13053
	Castel 19637 (B)	WSuV
	'Chambourcin' (B)	WSuV
	coignetiae 🏆H4	Widely available
	- B&SWJ 4550 from Korea	WCru
	- B&SWJ 4744	WCru
	- B&SWJ 8553 from Korea	WCru
	- B&SWJ 10882 from Japan	WCru
	- B&SWJ 10908 from Japan	WCru
	- Claret Cloak = 'Frovit' PBR	EBee ELan EPfP LRHS LSRN MAsh NLar SCoo SPer SSpi WPGP WPat
	- cut-leaved	CMac
	- var. ***glabrescens*** B&SWJ 8537	WCru
	- Sunningdale form	WGrn
	'Dalkauer' (W)	WSuV
I	'Diamond' (B)	WSuV
	'Dutch Black' (O/B)	WSuV
	'Edwards No 1' (O/W)	WSuV
	'Eger Csillaga' (O/W)	WSuV
	'Einset' (B/S)	WSuV
	ficifolia	see *V. thunbergii*
	flexuosa B&SWJ 5568	WCru
	- var. ***choii*** B&SWJ 4101	WCru
N	'Fragola' (O/R)	CAgr CMac CTri ECha EPfP GTwe LRHS MRav NLar SLim SPer SPoG SRms WSuV
	'Gagarin Blue' (O/B)	CAgr EPom GTwe WSuV
	'Glenora' (F/B/S)	CAgr WSuV
	'Hecker' (O/W)	WSuV
	henryana	see *Parthenocissus henryana*
	'Himrod' (O/W/S)	CCCN EMil GTwe MGos WSuV
	'Horizon' (O/W)	WSuV
	inconstans	see *Parthenocissus tricuspidata*
	'Interlaken' (O/W/S)	CAgr WSuV
	'Johanniter' (W)	WSuV
	'Kempsey Black' (O/B)	CAgr WSuV
	'Kozmapalme Muscatoly' (O/W)	WSuV
	'Kuibishevski' (O/R)	WSuV
	Landot 244 (O/B)	WSuV
	Landot 3217 (O/B)	WSuV
	'L'Arcadie Blanche' (W)	WSuV
	'Léon Millot' (O/G/B)	CAgr CSBt LSRN WSuV
	'Lucy Kuhlman' (B)	WSuV
	'Maréchal Foch' (O/B)	WSuV
	'Maréchal Joffre' (O/R)	CAgr GTwe WSuV
	'Mars' (O/B/S)	WSuV
	'Merzling' (O/W)	WSuV
	'Munson R.W.' (O/R)	WSuV
	'Muscat Bleu' (O/B)	CCCN CMam EPom LRHS NLar SLim SPoG WSuV
	'Nero' PBR	CAgr
	'New York Muscat' (O/B) 🏆H4	ECrN WSuV
	'New York Seedless' (O/W/S)	WSuV
	'Niagara' (O/W)	WSuV
	'Niederother Monschrebe' (O/R)	WSuV
	Oberlin 595 (O/B)	WSuV
	'Orion' (O/W)	LRHS WSuV
	'Paletina' (O/W)	WSuV
	parsley-leaved	see *V. vinifera* 'Ciotat'
	parvifolia	WPat
	- B&SWJ 1946	WCru
	'Perdin' (O/W)	WSuV
	'Phönix' (O/W)	CAgr CCCN EPom GTwe LRHS LSRN MBri MGos NLar NPla SKee SLim SPoG SVic WSuV
	piasezkii	WCru
*	'Pink Strawberry' (O)	WSuV
	'Pirovano 14' (O/B)	GTwe WSuV
§	'Plantet' (O/B)	WSuV
	'Poloske Muscat' (W)	CCCN CMam EPom GTwe WSuV
	purpurea 'Spetchley Park' (O/B)	CAgr WSuV
	quinquefolia	see *Parthenocissus quinquefolia*
	'Ramdas' (O/W)	WSuV
	Ravat 51 (O/W)	WSuV
	'Rayon d'Or' (O/W)	WSuV
	'Regent' PBR (O/B)	CAgr CCCN CWSG EPom GTwe LRHS MBri MCoo MGos NLar SKee SLim SPoG WSuV
	'Reliance' (O/R/S)	CAgr WSuV
	'Rembrant' (R)	CAgr WSuV
	riparia	CArn NLar
	'Romulus' (O/G/W/S)	WSuV
	'Rondo' (O/B)	CAgr SVic WSuV
	'Saturn' (O/R/S)	CAgr WSuV
	'Schuyler' (O/B)	CAgr WSuV
	Seibel (F)	GTwe
	Seibel 5279	see *V.* 'Aurore'
	Seibel 5409 (W)	WSuV
	Seibel 5455	see *V.* 'Plantet'
	Seibel 7053	WSuV
	Seibel 9549	WSuV
§	Seibel 13053 (O/B)	CMac LRHS SEND WSuV
	Seibel 138315 (R)	WSuV
	'Seneca' (W)	WSuV
	'Serena' (O/W)	WSuV
§	'Seyval Blanc' (O/W)	CAgr GTwe SEND SVic WSuV
	Seyve Villard ambig.	LRHS NPer
	Seyve Villard 12.375	see *V.* 'Villard Blanc'
	Seyve Villard 20.473 (F)	NPer
	Seyve Villard 5276	see *V.* 'Seyval Blanc'
	'Sirius' (B)	WSuV
	'Solaris' (O/W)	WSuV
	'Stauffer' (O/W)	WSuV
	'Suffolk Seedless' (B/S)	WSuV
	'Tereshkova' (O/B)	CAgr WSuV
	'Thornton' (O/S)	WSuV
§	***thunbergii*** B&SWJ 4702	WCru
	'Triomphe d'Alsace' (O/B)	CAgr CSBt NPer WSuV
	'Trollinger'	see *V. vinifera* 'Schiava Grossa'

Plant	Suppliers
'Vanessa' (O/R/S)	WSuV
§ 'Villard Blanc' (O/W)	WSuV
vinifera	EAmu EUJe LTen MGos MREP
- EM 323158B	WSuV
- 'Abouriou' (O/B)	WSuV
- 'Acolon' (O/B)	WSuV
- 'Adelheidtraube' (O/W)	WSuV
- 'Albalonga' (W)	WSuV
§ - 'Alicante' (G/B)	CBcs CMac GTwe WSuV
- 'Apiifolia'	see *V. vinifera* 'Ciotat'
- 'Augusta Louise' (O/W)	WSuV
- 'Auxerrois' (O/W)	WSuV
- 'Bacchus' (O/W)	CAgr CMam LRHS MBri NLar SLim SVic WSuV
- 'Baresana' (G/W)	NPla WSuV
- 'Beauty'	CAgr
- 'Black Alicante'	see *V. vinifera* 'Alicante'
- 'Black Frontignan' (G/O/B)	WSuV
- Black Hamburgh	see *V. vinifera* 'Schiava Grossa'
- 'Black Monukka' (G/B/S)	WSuV
- 'Black Prince' (G/B)	CAgr WSuV
- 'Blue Portuguese'	see *V. vinifera* 'Portugieser'
§ - 'Bouvier' (W)	WSuV
- 'Bouviertraube'	see *V. vinifera* 'Bouvier'
- 'Buckland Sweetwater' (G/W)	GTwe LRHS SLim WSuV
- 'Cabernet Sauvignon' (O/B)	EPfP LRHS MGos NPer SVic WSuV
- 'Cardinal' (O/R)	LRHS SHil WSuV
- 'Carla' (O/R)	WSuV
- 'Centennial' (O/N/S)	WSuV
- 'Chardonnay' (O/W)	CAgr CCCN LRHS LSRN NPer SPer SVic WSuV
§ - 'Chasselas' (G/O/W)	LRHS WSuV
- 'Chasselas Blanc' (O/W)	SVic
- 'Chasselas de Fontainebleau' (F)	CCCN LRHS SVic
- 'Chasselas de Tramontaner' (F)	LRHS
- 'Chasselas d'Or'	see *V. vinifera* 'Chasselas'
- 'Chasselas Rosé' (G/R)	CAgr SVic WSuV
- 'Chasselas Rosé Royal' (O/R)	CCCN SVic
- 'Chasselas Vibert' (G/W)	WSuV
- 'Chenin Blanc' (O/W)	SVic WSuV
§ - 'Ciotat' (F)	EShb IDee MRav WSuV
- 'Cot Précoce de Tours' (O/B)	WSuV
- 'Crimson Seedless' (R/S)	WSuV
- 'Csabyongye' (O/W)	WSuV
- 'Dattier de Beyrouth' (G/W)	WSuV
- 'Dattier Saint Vallier' (O/W)	SVic WSuV
- 'Dolcetto' (O/B)	WSuV
- 'Dornfelder' (O/R)	CCCN CSut NLar SLim SPoG WSuV
- 'Dunkelfelder' (O/R)	WSuV
- 'Early Van der Laan' (F)	CMac
- 'Ehrenfelser' (O/W)	WSuV
- 'Elbling' (O/W)	WSuV
- 'Exalta' (G/W/S)	CCCN WSuV
- 'Excelsior' (W)	WSuV
- 'Faber' (O/W)	WSuV
- 'Fiesta' (W/S)	WSuV
- 'Findling' (W)	WSuV
- 'Flame'	CAgr
- 'Flame Red' (O/D)	CCCN EPom
- 'Flame Seedless' (G/O/R/S)	CMac EPom SPoG WSuV
- 'Forta' (O/W)	WSuV
- 'Foster's Seedling' (G/W)	GTwe SVic WSuV
- 'Freisamer' (O/W)	WSuV
- 'Frühburgunder' (O/B)	WSuV
- 'Gamay Hâtif des Vosges'	WSuV
- 'Gamay Noir' (O/B)	SVic WSuV
- Gamay Teinturier Group (O/B)	WSuV
- 'Gewürztraminer' (O/R)	LRHS SVic WSuV
- 'Glory of Boskoop'	see *V.* 'Boskoop Glory'
- 'Golden Chasselas'	see *V. vinifera* 'Chasselas'
- 'Goldriesling' (O/W)	WSuV
- 'Gros Colmar' (G/B)	WSuV
- 'Grüner Veltliner' (O/W)	WSuV
- 'Gutenborner' (O/W)	WSuV
- 'Helfensteiner' (O/R)	WSuV
- 'Huxelrebe' (O/W)	WSuV
- 'Incana' (O/B)	ELon GCal MRav WCFE WCot WSHC
- 'Italia' (O/W)	LRHS NPla SHil
- 'Juliaumsrebe' (O/W)	WSuV
- 'Kanzler' (O/W)	WSuV
- 'Kerner' (O/W)	WSuV
- 'Kernling' (F)	WSuV
- 'King's Ruby' (F/S)	WSuV
- 'Lakemont' (O/W/S)	CAgr CCCN CMac CMam EPfP GTwe LRHS MBri MGos NLar NPla SKee SLim SPoG WSuV
- 'Lival' (O/B)	WSuV
- 'Madeleine Angevine' (O/W)	CAgr EPfP GTwe LRHS LSRN NPer SPoG SVic WSuV
- 'Madeleine Celine' (B)	WSuV
- 'Madeleine Royale' (G/W)	WSuV
- 'Madeleine Silvaner' (O/W)	CSBt GTwe LRHS NPer SPer SPoG WSuV
- 'Madresfield Court' (G/B)	GTwe SLim WSuV
- 'Merlot' (G/B)	LRHS SVic WSuV
§ - 'Meunier' (B)	SVic WSuV
- 'Mireille' (F)	GTwe WSuV
- 'Morio Muscat' (O/W)	WSuV
§ - 'Müller-Thurgau' (O/W)	GTwe LRHS LSRN MGos NPri SPer SVic WSuV
- 'Muscat Blanc à Petits Grains' (O/W)	SWvt WSuV
- 'Muscat de Lierval' (O/B)	WSuV
- 'Muscat de Saumur' (O/W)	WSuV
- 'Muscat Hamburg' (G/B)	LHop LRHS LSRN MGos SWvt WSuV
- 'Muscat of Alexandria' (G/W)	CBcs CCCN CMac CRHN LRHS MRav SLim SVic
- 'Muscat Ottonel' (O/W)	WSuV
- 'Muscat Saint Laurent' (W)	WSuV
- 'Nebbiolo' (O/B)	WSuV
- 'No 69' (W)	WSuV
- 'Noblessa' (W)	WSuV
- 'Noir Hâtif de Marseille' (O/B)	WSuV
- 'Olive Blanche' (O/W)	WSuV
- 'Oliver Irsay' (O/W)	WSuV
- 'Optima' (O/W)	WSuV
- 'Ora' (O/W/S)	WSuV
- 'Ortega' (O/W)	CCCN WSuV
- 'Perle' (O/W)	WSuV
- 'Perle de Czaba' (G/O/W)	WSuV
- 'Perlette' (O/W/S)	CCCN CSut EPom NPri WSuV
- 'Petit Rouge' (R)	WSuV

	- 'Pinot Blanc' (O/W)	CCCN LRHS SVic WSuV
	- 'Pinot Gris' (O/B)	SVic WSuV
	- 'Pinot Noir' (O/B)	CCCN SVic WSuV
§	- 'Portugieser' (O/B)	WSuV
	- 'Précoce de Bousquet' (O/W)	WSuV
	- 'Précoce de Malingre' (O/W)	CAgr
	- 'Prima' (O/B)	WSuV
	- 'Primavis Frontignan' (G/W)	WSuV
	- 'Purpurea' (O/B) ♀H4	Widely available
	- 'Queen of Esther' (B)	GTwe MBri NLar SKee SLim WSuV
	- 'Regner' (O/W)	WSuV
	- 'Reichensteiner' (O/G/W)	CAgr WSuV
	- 'Riesling' (O/W)	CCCN LRHS SVic WSuV
	- Riesling-Silvaner	see *V. vinifera* 'Müller-Thurgau'
	- 'Rotberger' (O/G/B)	WSuV
	- 'Royal Muscadine' (G/O/W)	SPoG WSuV
	- 'Saint Laurent' (G/O/W)	SVic WSuV
	- 'Sauvignon Blanc' (O/W)	CCCN LRHS SVic WSuV
	- 'Scheurebe' (O/W)	WSuV
§	- 'Schiava Grossa' (G/B/D)	CCCN CMac CRHN CTri ELan EPfP EPom GTwe LRHS LSRN MBri NPer NPla NPri SBfd SLim SPer SPoG SVic SWvt WFar WMoo WSuV
	- 'Schönburger' (O/W)	SVic WSuV
	- 'Schwarzriesling'	see *V. vinifera* 'Meunier'
	- 'Sémillon'	LRHS LSRN SVic
	- 'Senator' (O/W)	WSuV
	- 'Septimer' (O/W)	WSuV
	- 'Shiraz' (B)	WSuV
	- 'Siegerrebe' (O/W/D)	CAgr GTwe LRHS NPer SVic WSuV
	- 'Silvaner' (O/W)	WSuV
	- 'Spetchley Red' (O/B)	CRHN WCot WCru WPGP WPat
	- strawberry grape	see *V.* 'Fragola'
§	- 'Sultana' (W/S)	CAgr CCCN GTwe NPla WSuV
	- 'Theresa' (O/W)	MBri NLar SLim WSuV
	- 'Thompson Seedless'	see *V. vinifera* 'Sultana'
*	- 'Triomphe' (O/B)	SVic
	- 'Triomphrebe' (W)	WSuV
	- 'Vroege van der Laan' (O/W)	CCVT EUJe NLar
	- 'Wrotham Pinot' (O/B)	WSuV
	- 'Würzer' (O/W)	WSuV
	- 'Zweigeltrebe' (O/B)	WSuV
*	'White Strawberry' (O/W)	WSuV
	'Zalagyöngye' (W)	CAgr WSuV

Vriesea (*Bromeliaceae*)

	imperialis	EAmu
	splendens ♀H1	XBlo

Wachendorfia (*Haemodoraceae*)

	thyrsiflora	CAbb CCon CDes CHEx CPLG CPne EShb IGor LEdu WPGP WSHC

Wahlenbergia (*Campanulaceae*)

	albomarginata	ECho EWTr
	- 'Blue Mist'	ECho
	congesta	ECho
	gloriosa	ECou MOWG WAbe WFar
	pumilio	see *Edraianthus pumilio*
	rivularis 'Snow-cap'	SBfd
	serpyllifolia	see *Edraianthus serpyllifolius*
	undulata 'Melton Bluebird'	GJos

Waldsteinia (*Rosaceae*)

	geoides	EBee EPPr EPfP LAst LRHS MMuc NPro SPer WMoo WWEG XLum
	ternata	Widely available
§	- 'Mozaick' (v)	EBee EWes NBir NPro
	- 'Variegata'	see *W. ternata* 'Mozaick'

walnut, black see *Juglans nigra*

walnut, common see *Juglans regia*

Wasabia (*Brassicaceae*)

	wasabi	CArn GPoy LEdu

Washingtonia (*Arecaceae*)

	'Filibusta'	EAmu
	filifera ♀H1	CAbb CCCN CDoC CPHo EAmu ETod LRHS SBig SEND SPlb
	robusta	CBcs EAmu EGri LRHS SHil SPlb

Watsonia (*Iridaceae*)

	aletroides	CDes CTca EBee ECho GCal
	amatolae	IBlr
	angusta	CDes CGHE CPLG CPne CPrp EBee IBlr ITim WPGP
	ardernei	see *W. borbonica* subsp. *ardernei* (Sander) Goldblatt 'Arderne's White'
	beatricis	see *W. pillansii*
I	'Best Red'	WCot
§	***borbonica***	CDes CPne CPou CPrp
	- subsp. ***ardernei*** misapplied	see *W. borbonica* subsp. *ardernei* (Sander) Goldblatt 'Arderne's White'
§	- subsp. ***ardernei*** (Sander) Goldblatt 'Arderne's White'	CBre CCon CGHE CPLG CPrp CTca EBee ECho GCal IBlr LRHS WPGP
	- subsp. ***borbonica***	EBee IBlr WPGP
	- 'Paarl'	ECho
	brevifolia	see *W. laccata*
	brick red-flowered	CDes WPGP
	coccinea Baker	see *W. spectabilis*
	- 'Somerset West'	ECho
	densiflora	CPou IBlr
	distans	EBee
	fulgens	LEdu
	galpinii	CCon
	- lavender-flowered	IBlr
	- pink-flowered	EBee IBlr
	galpinii × ***knysnana***	IBlr
§	***humilis***	CDes CPou EBee GCal SKHP
	knysnana	CDes EBee IBlr WPGP
§	***laccata***	CCon CPne CPrp EBee
	- orange-flowered **new**	CDes
	- pink-flowered **new**	CDes
	latifolia	IBlr
	lepida	EBee ECho IBlr
	marginata	CPou CPrp EBee ECho
	- ***alba***	SKHP
	meriania	ERCP IBlr WCot
	- var. ***bulbillifera***	CGHE CPne CPrp CTca EBee ECho GCra IBlr SMrm WSHC
*	'Mount Congreve'	CTca
	'Peachy Pink Orphan'	CDes EBee WPGP
§	***pillansii***	CAbb CGHE CHEx CPLG CPne CPou CPrp CTca CYeo EBee EPri

	IBal IBlr LRHS NCGa SPoG WCot WFar WMnd
- 'Cathcart'	ECho
- hybrid	SAga
- peach-flowered	CPLG
- pink-flowered	CPLG CPrp IVic
- red-flowered	CPLG IVic
- soft pink-flowered	EPri
pink-flowered	CDes EBee
pulchra	EBee
pyramidata	see *W. borbonica*
roseoalba	see *W. humilis*
schlechteri	EBee
§ ***spectabilis***	CPne
'Stanford Scarlet'	CCon CDes CPLG CPne CPou CPrp ELon IBlr SChF SChr SUsu WPGP WSHC
stenosiphon	EBee IBlr
strubeniae	IBlr
transvaalensis	EBee
'Tresco Dwarf Pink'	CCon CDes CPLG CPrp CTca EBee IBlr LEdu WPGP
Tresco hybrids	CAbb CBcs CHll CPLG EPri LTen SAga SRkn
vanderspuyae	CPLG CPne CPrp IBlr
'White Dazzler'	SApp
wilmaniae	CPLG CPrp EBee IBlr WPGP
- JCA 3.955200	SKHP
- 'Ice Angel'	SKHP
zeyheri	EBee

Wattakaka see *Dregea*

Weigela ✿ (*Caprifoliaceae*)

CC 1231	CPLG
'Abel Carrière'	CMac CTri ECtt EPfP EWes GKin MGos NWea WCFE WFar
'Avalanche' misapplied	see *W.* 'Candida'
'Avalanche' Lemoine	see *W. praecox* 'Avalanche'
'Avant Garde'	MAsh WCot WPat
Black and White = 'Courtacad1'	CWGN EBee SBfd
'Boskoop Glory'	GQui SPer
'Bouquet Rose' **new**	LPot
§ Briant Rubidor = 'Olympiade' (v)	CDoC CMac EBee EHoe EPfP LAst LRHS MAsh MGos MMuc MRav NEgg NLar SEND SGol SHil SLim SPer SPlb SPoG WFar
'Bristol Ruby'	CBar CDul CMac CTri CWib EBee ELan EPfP GKin LRHS LTen MGos MHer MMuc MSwo NBir NPri NWea SBfd SEND SGar SHil SLon SPer SPlb SRms SWal WFar WMoo
§ 'Candida'	CTri ELan EWes MRav NLar SPer
Cappuccino = 'Verweig 2'PBR	LBuc MBlu NBro NEgg NLar SPoG
Carnaval = 'Courtalor'PBR	CBcs CWib LRHS NLar SEND
'Conquête'	SLon
coraeensis	CHll MAsh MBlu MMHG SBrt SPer WCot WPat
- 'Alba'	CHll
decora	GQui
- B&SWJ 10834	WCru
'Eva Rathke'	GKin NBir NLar NWea
'Evita'	GKin WFar
floribunda B&SWJ 10831	WCru
florida	CDul CMac EPfP MGos
- B&SWJ 8439	WCru
- f. ***alba***	CBcs WFar
* - 'Albovariegata' (v)	CPLG
- 'Bicolor'	CMac ELan
- 'Bristol Snowflake'	CDul CMac EPPr EPfP EWTr MBlu MHer MSwo NBir NLar SLon
- 'Foliis Purpureis' ♀H4	Widely available
- Magical Rainbow = 'Kolmagira'PBR **new**	LBuc
- 'Milk and Honey'	EBee GKin LRHS MBri
- Minor Black = 'Verweig 3'PBR	CWSG EBee EPfP LRHS MBri MPkF MWat NBro NHol NLar STes WMoo
- Monet = 'Verweig'PBR (v)	Widely available
- Moulin Rouge = 'Brigela'PBR	CBcs CDoC CSBt EBee ELon EPfP LBuc LRHS MBri MGos SLim
- 'Pink Princess'	EBee LRHS MSwo
- Rubigold	see *W.* Briant Rubidor
- 'Samabor'	WFar
§ - Sunny Fantasy = 'Kolsunn' **new**	EBee
- 'Suzanne' (v)	NPro
- 'Tango'	CJun LRHS MAsh NPro
'Florida Variegata' (v) ♀H4	Widely available
florida 'Versicolor'	CMHG CMac CPLG CWib GQui SLon SMrm WFar WGor
- Wine and Roses = 'Alexandra'PBR	Widely available
'Gold Rush'	NLar
'Golden Candy'	NPro
'Gustave Malet'	CMCN GQui
hortensis	CPLG
'Hulsdonk'	CWSG
japonica 'Dart's Colourdream'	EHoe ELon EWes LAst MMuc SEND SLim
'Jean's Gold'	ELan MBlu MGos MRav
'Kosteriana Variegata' (v)	CSBt EBee EPfP EWTr LRHS MAsh MMuc NEgg SBfd SEND SHil SLon WFar
'Little Red Robin' **new**	ELon
'Looymansii Aurea'	CMHG CPLG CTri EBee ELan EPfP LAst NLar SGol SPer WFar WHar
Lucifer = 'Courtared'PBR	CDoC
maximowiczii	CPLG GQui
§ ***middendorffiana***	Widely available
'Minuet'	EPfP LRHS MGos MRav MSwo NPro SLPl
'Mont Blanc'	MAsh MMHG
Nain Rouge = 'Courtanin'PBR	CBcs CTri LRHS MBri
'Nana Variegata' (v)	CPLG ECrN ELon EPfP LRHS MBri SBfd SLPl
Naomi Campbell = 'Bokrashine'PBR	EShb GBin GKin MMHG NEgg NHol NLar WFar WHar WMoo
'Newport Red'	GKin MBNS MWat NWea WFar WRHF
Pink Poppet = 'Plangen'PBR	CAbP CSBt EBee EMil EPfP GKin LAst LBMP LRHS LSRN MAsh MPkF NLar SBfd SCoo SLim SPoG SWvt
praecox	ECrN
- B&SWJ 8705	WCru
§ - 'Avalanche'	EPfP SGar
'Praecox Variegata' (v) ♀H4	CMac CTri ELan EPfP LAst LRHS MAsh MRav NBir SBfd SDix SPer SPoG SRms WCFE WCru WFar WPat
'Red Prince' ♀H4	EBee ECrN ELan EPPr EPfP LBuc LRHS MGos MSwo NEgg NLar NRHS SGol SHil SLim
Rubidor	see *W.* Briant Rubidor
Rubigold	see *W.* Briant Rubidor
'Ruby Anniversary'	LBuc SLon
'Ruby Queen'PBR	CMac EPfP

	Ruby Wedding	LSRN
	'Rumba'	CMac EWTr MRav NPro
	sessilifolia	see *Diervilla sessilifolia*
	'Snowflake'	ECrN LPot NPro SRms WFar
	'Stelzneri'	MMuc SEND
	subsessilis B&SWJ 1056	WCru
	- B&SWJ 4206	WCru
	'Victoria'	CDul CMac CWib ECrN EHoe ELan EPPr EPfP LBMP LRHS MGos MSwo NBir NWad SBfd SGol SPer WFar WGor WHar WMoo

Weinmannia (*Cunoniaceae*)

	racemosa	IVic
	- 'Kamahi'	CTrC
	trichosperma	CBcs EUJe IDee SSpi

Weldenia (*Commelinaceae*)

	candida	ECho IBlr LLHF NHar NMen WAbe

Westringia (*Lamiaceae*)

	angustifolia	MOWG
	brevifolia	ECou
	- var. ***raleighii***	ECou
§	***fruticosa*** ♀H1	CBcs CCCN CTsd EShb WJek
	- 'Smokie' (v)	CCCN CTsd MOWG
	- 'Variegata' (v)	WJek
	longifolia	CCCN ECou
	rosmariniformis	see *W. fruticosa*
	'Wynyabbie Gem'	CAbb EBee LRHS MNHC SEND

whitecurrant see *Ribes rubrum* (W)

Whiteheadia (*Hyacinthaceae*)

	bifolia 'Nardouwsberg'	ECho

Widdringtonia (*Cupressaceae*)

	schwarzii	CDoC

Wigandia (*Boraginaceae*)

	caracasana	CHII

Wikstroemia (*Thymelaeaceae*)

	gemmata	LRHS SSta

wineberry see *Rubus phoenicolasius*

Wisteria ✿ (*Papilionaceae*)

§	***brachybotrys***	CCVT SLau
§	- Murasaki-kapitan	CTri CWGN EBtc EPfP LRHS SEND SKHP
	- 'Okayama'	EPfP SKHP
	- 'Pink Chiffon'	EPfP LRHS SKHP
	- 'Shiro-beni'	CTri MGos SEND
§	- 'Shiro-kapitan'	CBcs CSPN CTri CWGN EBee EPfP IArd LRHS LSRN MBri MGos MRav NHol SEND SHil SKHP SLau SLim SPer WPGP WPat WSHC
*	- 'White Silk'	CBcs EPfP LRHS LSRN MAsh MGos NPla SLon
§	'Burford'	CSPN CWGN EPfP GBin LRHS LSRN MAsh MBri MWat NHol SCoo SEND SKHP SLau SLim WHar WPGP
	'Caroline'	CBcs CCCN CDoC CHab CSPN CWGN EBee EBtc EPfP EWTr LRHS LSRN MAsh MGos MRav NEgg NPCo SHil SLau SPer SPoG SRms SSpi WPGP WSHC
	floribunda	CBcs CCVT CRHN CWib ELan EPfP IBoy NPCo SEWo SGol WFar
§	- 'Alba' ♀H4	Widely available
	- 'Black Dragon'	see *W. floribunda* 'Yae-kokuryū'
	- 'Burford'	see *W.* 'Burford'
*	- 'Cascade'	CBcs LRHS MBri NEgg SHil
§	- 'Domino'	CBcs CCVT CMac CTri CWGN EBee ELon EPfP IArd LHop LRHS LSRN MAsh MGos MRav MWat NPla SBfd SCoo SEND SKHP SLau SLim SPer SPoG SSta WFar
	- 'Fragrantissima'	see *W. sinensis* 'Jako'
	- 'Geisha'	CBcs EBee SEND SKHP
	- 'Harlequin'	CBcs CSPN EBee ELon GCal LRHS MAsh NPCo NPla SBfd SEND SKHP WFar
	- 'Hocker Edge'	SLau
	- 'Hon-beni'	see *W. floribunda* 'Rosea'
	- 'Honey Bee Pink'	see *W. floribunda* 'Rosea'
	- 'Honko'	see *W. floribunda* 'Rosea'
	- 'Issai'	LSRN MSwo SEND SGol
	- 'Issai Perfect'	LRHS LSRN NLar SCoo SLon
	- 'Jakohn-fuji'	see *W. sinensis* 'Jako'
§	- 'Kuchi-beni'	CBcs CCVT CSPN EBee ELan GBin LRHS LSRN MAsh MBri MGos MRav NEgg NHol NLar NPCo SEND SHil SKHP SLau SPer SPoG SRms
	- 'Lawrence'	CBcs CCVT CSPN CWGN EBtc LRHS NLar SEND SKHP SLau SLim
	- 'Lipstick'	see *W. floribunda* 'Kuchi-beni'
	- 'Longissima'	see *W. floribunda* 'Multijuga'
	- 'Longissima Alba'	see *W. floribunda* 'Alba'
	- 'Macrobotrys'	see *W. floribunda* 'Multijuga'
	- 'Magenta'	LRHS NPla
§	- 'Multijuga' ♀H4	Widely available
	- Murasaki-naga	see *W. floribunda* 'Purple Patches'
	- 'Nana Richin's Purple'	SLau
	- 'Peaches and Cream'	see *W. floribunda* 'Kuchi-beni'
	- 'Pink Ice'	see *W. floribunda* 'Rosea'
§	- 'Purple Patches'	EBee
	- Reindeer	see *W. sinensis* 'Jako'
§	- 'Rosea' ♀H4	Widely available
	- 'Royal Purple'	EPfP IArd LRHS MBri SPoG WFar WGor
	- 'Russelliana'	CBcs EBee GBin LTen NLar
	- 'Shiro-naga'	see *W. floribunda* 'Alba'
	- 'Shiro-nagi'	see *W. floribunda* 'Alba'
	- 'Shiro-noda'	see *W. floribunda* 'Alba'
	- 'Snow Showers'	see *W. floribunda* 'Alba'
	- 'Variegata' (v)	CWGN
N	- 'Violacea Plena' (d)	CBcs CDoC CMac EBee EPfP LTen NLar SKHP SPer SWvt WFar
N	- 'Yae-kokuryū' (d)	Widely available
	florida Magical Fantasy = 'Kolsunn'	see *Weigela florida* Sunny Fantasy
	× ***formosa***	SLau SLim
	- 'Black Dragon'	see *W. floribunda* 'Yae-kokuryū'
	- 'Domino'	see *W. floribunda* 'Domino'
	- 'Issai' Wada *pro parte*	see *W. floribunda* 'Domino'
	- 'Kokuryū'	see *W. floribunda* 'Yae-kokuryū'
	- 'Yae-kokuryū'	see *W. floribunda* 'Yae-kokuryū'
	frutescens	EBee SLim WFar
	- 'Amethyst Falls'PBR	CWGN IArd LRHS LSRN MGos NHol NPri SCoo SLon SPoG WMoo
	- 'Longwood Purple' **new**	LRHS
	Kapitan-fuji	see *W. brachybotrys*
	'Lavender Lace'	EBee EPfP LRHS LSRN MAsh NEgg NLar SLau WFar
	macrostachya 'Blue Moon'	MGos WHar
	- 'Clara Mack'	IArd

***multijuga*'Alba'** see *W. floribunda* 'Alba'
'Showa-beni' CSPN CWGN EPfP LHop MGos SCoo SEND SKHP SLau SLim WPGP
sinensis ♀H4 Widely available
- 'Alba' ♀H4 CBcs CDoC CDul CMen CWib ELan EPfP IBoy LAst LRHS LSRN MAsh MGos MNHC MWat NEgg NPla SEND SLau SLim SPoG WFar
- 'Amethyst' CBcs CHab CSPN CWCL EPfP EShb LRHS LSRN LTen MAsh MBri MGos MRav MWat NPla NRHS NSti SHil SKHP SLau SLim SPer SPoG WPat
- 'Blue Sapphire' CBcs CHab CSPN CWGN EBee EBtc LSRN NEgg NPCo NSti SLau SRms
- 'Consequa' see *W. sinensis* 'Prolific'
- 'Cooke's Special' CWGN
§ - 'Jako' NHol
- 'Oosthoek's Variety' see *W. sinensis* 'Prolific'
I - 'Pink Ice' EWTr NEgg NPCo
- 'Prematura' see *W. floribunda* 'Domino'
- 'Prematura Alba' see *W. brachybotrys* 'Shiro-kapitan'
§ - 'Prolific' Widely available
- 'Rosea' LSRN SWvt
- 'Shiro-capital' see *W. brachybotrys* 'Shiro-kapitan'
'Tiverton' CBcs EBee EUJe NPla
venusta see *W. brachybotrys* 'Shiro-kapitan'
- 'Alba' see *W. brachybotrys* 'Shiro-kapitan'
- var. ***violacea*** misapplied see *W. brachybotrys* Murasaki-kapitan

Withania (*Solanaceae*)

somnifera CArn GPoy

Wittsteinia (*Alseuosmiaceae*)

vacciniacea WCru

Wodyetia (*Arecaceae*)

bifurcata EAmu XBlo

Wollemia (*Araucariaceae*)

nobilis CDTJ CDoC CTho EAmu EPfP ESwi EUJe GBin MGos WBor WEve WMou

Woodsia (*Woodsiaceae*)

obtusa CBty CDTJ CKel CLAP CWCL EBee EFer ISha LRHS NBro NLar NMyG SBfd SGol SPoG SRot WWEG
polystichoides ♀H4 SRms

Woodwardia (*Blechnaceae*)

from Emei Shan, China CLAP
areolata SKHP
fimbriata Widely available
orientalis CBty ESwi LRHS WFib
- var. ***formosana*** B&SWJ 6865 ESwi WCru
radicans ♀H3 CBcs CHEx CHid CLAP EWes EWld WCot WFib
unigemmata CHEx CLAP EFer EWes EWld SKHP WAbe WFib WHal
virginica CBty CLAP EBee ISha

Worcesterberry see *Ribes* 'Worcesterberry'

Wulfenia (*Plantaginaceae*)

baldaccii GKev
carinthiaca EBee ECho GAbr GEdr GKev NBir NLar NWad SBHP WPer XLum
- 'Alba' **new** EBee GKev
× ***schwarzii*** CDes EBee LEdu WPGP

Wurmbea (*Colchicaceae*)

pusilla 'Sentinel Peak' ECho
recurva ECho
spicata 'Rawsonville' ECho
stricta **new** WCot

X

Xanthium (*Asteraceae*)

sibiricum CArn

Xanthoceras (*Sapindaceae*)

sorbifolium ♀H3-4 CAgr CBcs CMCN CWib ELan EPfP MBlu NLar SSpi WBor

Xanthocyparis (*Cupressaceae*)

nootkatensis 'Aureovariegata' (v) EHul
- 'Compacta' CTri
- 'Glauca' NWea
- 'Green Arrow' CKen LRHS NLar SCoo SLim WHar
- 'Jubilee' LRHS NPCo SCoo SLim WCFE WHar
- 'Kanada' NLar
- 'Lutea' CTri NWea
- 'Nordkroken' NLar
- 'Pendula' ♀H4 CCVT CDoC CDul CKen ELan EPfP GKin LMaj LRHS MAsh MBlu MBri MGos MMuc NEgg NPCo NWea WCFE WEve
- 'Strict Weeper' CKen NLar SLim

Xanthorhiza (*Ranunculaceae*)

simplicissima CArn CBcs CGHE CRow EBee EPfP GCal IVic LEdu MBri NLar SDys SSpi WPGP

Xanthorrhoea (*Xanthorrhoeaceae*)

australis SPlb
fulva SPlb
glauca CCCN CDTJ EAmu
johnsonii SPlb
preisii CDTJ SPlb

Xanthosoma (*Araceae*)

sagittifolium CDTJ GHim
violaceum CDTJ EAmu GHim

Xerochrysum (*Asteraceae*)

§ ***bracteatum*** 'Coco' CMHG CSpe WWlt
§ - 'Dargan Hill Monarch' CHll CSpe SRms WWlt
§ - 'Skynet' WWlt
- 'Wollerton' WWlt
subundulatum **new** WAbe

Xeronema (*Xeronemataceae*)

callistemon CBrP

Xerophyllum (*Melanthiaceae*)

tenax GCal NMen

Xylotheca (*Flacourtiaceae*)

kraussiana SPlb

Ypsilandra (*Melanthiaceae*)

cavaleriei	CPLG EBee GEdr WCot
thibetica	CCon CDes CGHE CLAP CPLG CPrp CSpe EBee EPfP GEdr LAma LEdu LLHF LRHS NLar SChF SMad WCot WCru WPGP

Yucca ✿ (*Asparagaceae*)

SDR 3701	GKev
aloifolia	CCCN CDoC CHEx EAmu EGri ETod MGos MREP SBfd SBig SChr SEND SPlb
§ - f. ***marginata*** (v)	EAmu EGri MREP SBig
- 'Purpurea'	SPlb
- 'Tricolor' (v)	EGri MREP
- 'Variegata'	see *Y. aloifolia* f. *marginata*
angustifolia	see *Y. glauca*
baccata	CCCN CTrC EAmu EGri ETod SPlb
- NNS 99-510	WCot
brevifolia	EGri
campestris	EGri
carnerosana	CTrC EAmu EGri WCot
constricta new	EGri
decipiens new	EGri
§ ***elata***	CCCN CTrC EAmu EGri WPGP
§ ***elephantipes*** ♀H1	CDTJ EAmu SBfd SEND
- 'Jewel' (v)	EAmu SEND
- 'Puck' (v)	SEND
- variegated (v)	SEND
faxoniana	EAmu EGri SPlb
filamentosa ♀H4	Widely available
- 'Antwerp'	GCal
- 'Bright Edge' (v) ♀H3	Widely available
- 'Color Guard' (v)	CTrC LAst LRHS MBri NLar SChr WCot WFar
- 'Garland's Gold' (v)	CCCN CDoC MAsh MGos SBig WFar
- 'Variegata' (v) ♀H3	CBcs MGos SRms WFar
filifera	EAmu EGri ETod EUJe SPlb
flaccida	SDix
- 'Golden Sword' (v) ♀H3	CBcs CDoC CMac CTrC EBee ELan EPfP GMaP LAst LHop LRHS LSRN MAsh MGos MSCN MSwo MWat NLar SBfd SGol SLim SPer SPoG SWvt WCot
- 'Ivory' ♀H3-4	CDoC ELan ELon EPfP GCal GMaP LRHS LSRN MBlu MBri MGos MRav NLar SBfd SLPl SPer SRms
§ ***glauca***	EGri EPfP LEdu LRHS MBri WCot
gloriosa ♀H4	CBcs CDoC CHEx CMac CTri EAmu EUJe LRHS MGos MREP NPla SBfd SEND SPer SPlb SPoG SWvt WBrk
- 'Aureovariegata'	see *Y. gloriosa* 'Variegata'
- 'Bright Star'	LRHS WCot
§ - 'Variegata' (v) ♀H4	Widely available
guatemalensis	see *Y. elephantipes*
jaliscensis new	EGri
'Laddie'PBR new	IBoy
linearifolia	EAmu
linearis	see *Y. thompsoniana*
madrensis new	EGri
'Nobilis'	CHEx SDix
pallida	EGri WPGP
radiosa	see *Y. elata*
recurvifolia ♀H4	CHEx EAmu EPfP GCal MGos SBfd
- Banana Split = 'Monvil' (v)	CTrC LBuc LRHS SPoG SPtl
- 'Gold Stream' (v)	WCot
reverchonii new	EGri
rigida	CDTJ EAmu WCot WPGP
rostrata	CCCN CDTJ EAmu EGri ETod EUJe SChr SPlb WCot
- 'Sapphire Skies'	MAvo WCot
rupicola new	EGri WCot
schidigera	EAmu EGri
- NNS 03-597	WCot
schottii	CTrC
§ ***thompsoniana***	CDTJ CTrC EAmu EGri
- blue-leaved	EAmu
torreyi	CTrC EAmu
treculeana	EAmu EGri
'Vittorio Emanuele II'	SMad
whipplei	CBcs CCCN CDoC EBee EGri ELan IGor LRHS SBig SEND SPoG WPGP
- subsp. ***caespitosa***	WPGP
- subsp. ***whipplei*** NNS 05-701	WCot

Yushania (*Poaceae*)

KR 7698	ERod MWht
§ ***anceps***	CBcs CDoC CEnt CHEx CPLG ENBC EPfP MGos MMoz MMuc MWht SBig SEND WMoo
- 'Pitt White'	CEnt CPLG MWht WJun
- 'Pitt White Rejuvenated'	ERod WPGP
brevipaniculata	ERod WJun
chungii	CEnt CPLG ERod MWht WJun WPGP
* ***equatus***	WJun
maculata	CEnt CPLG ERod MMoz MWht SBig WJun
§ ***maling***	CPLG EPfP ERod MMoz WJun
Yunnan 5	CPLG

Z

Zaluzianskya (*Scrophulariaceae*)

JCA 15665	NMen WAbe
elongata new	SPlb
'Katherine'	SRot
microsiphon	SPlb
'Orange Eye'	ELon NMen NRHS NSla WAbe WIce
ovata	CPBP EBee EDAr EPfP EPot EWld GKev MSCN NRHS NSla SPet SPlb SPoG WAbe WHlf WIce
- 'Star Balsam'	EBee
pulvinata	SPlb
'Semonkong'	GCal SUsu SWvt

Zamia (*Zamiaceae*)

furfuracea	CBrP
pumila	SPlb

Zamioculcas (*Araceae*)

zamiifolia	CCCN

Zantedeschia (*Araceae*)

§ ***aethiopica*** ♀H3	Widely available
- 'Apple Court Babe'	CElw CRow ELon MNrw SMrm

- 'Childsiana'	SApp
- 'Crowborough' ♀H3	Widely available
- 'Gigantea'	CHEx
- 'Glow'	CBct CMac CPLG ECtt LRHS MRav WCot WGwG
- 'Green Goddess' ♀H3	Widely available
- 'Little Gem'	SMad
- 'Luzon Lovely'	WCru
- 'Marshmallow'	CBct ECtt ELan EPfP SPet WFar
- 'Mr Martin'	CBct CCCN CHid CMac CTrC EBee ECtt ELon LRHS MNrw SBfd SBig SMad SWvt WCot
- 'Pershore Fantasia' (v)	CBct CPLG EBee MSKA WCot WWEG
- pink-flowered	CHEx
- 'Snow White'PBR	LRHS
- 'White Gnome'	WCot WFar
- 'White Mischief'	EBee
- 'White Sail'	CBct EBee ECtt LRHS MRav NGdn SWat WFar WGwG
albomaculata	CTca LAma SPlb
'Anneke'	CCCN EPfP
'Apricot Glow'	CHll
'Ascari'PBR	CCCN
'Auckland'PBR **new**	SDeJ
'Black Eyed Beauty'	LAma
'Black Magic'	CCCN CMac EPfP
'Black Pearl'	LAma
'Black Star'	see *Z.* 'Edge of Night'
'Cameo'	CCCN LAma SDeJ
(Captain Series) 'Captain Chelsea'PBR	LAma
- 'Captain Palermo'PBR	LAma
- 'Captain Samos'	LAma
- 'Captain Tendens'PBR	LAma SDeJ
'Crystal Blush'	LAma SDeJ
§ 'Edge of Night'	CCCN ERCP EUJe LBMP SDeJ WCot
elliottiana ♀H1	CBcs CCon CHEx CSpe CTri GHim LAma
'Flame'	CCCN LBMP SPad WGwG
'Garnet Glow' **new**	WCot
'Harvest Moon'	LAma
'Helen O'Connor'	CPLG
'Kiwi Blush'	CBro CCCN CCon CHEx CPLG CSpe EAEE EBee ECtt ELan ELon EPfP EWll LHop LPBA NGdn SApp SBfd SKHP SPad SPer SPet SRkn SWat WFar WGwG
'Lime Lady'	CBct ECha EWay
'Mango'	EPri LAma WCot
'Mozart'	CCCN
'Picasso'PBR	CCCN ERCP SDeJ SPad WCot
'Pink Mist'	CBct LAma SWal
'Pink Persuasion'	LAma
'Purple Sensation'	EPfP
'Red Sox'PBR	CCCN SDeJ
rehmannii ♀H1	LAma NLar SDeJ SRms
'Silver Lining'	LAma
'Sunshine'	WCot
'White Giant'	WPGP
'White Pixie'	EPfP

Zanthorhiza see *Xanthorhiza*

Zanthoxylum (*Rutaceae*)

acanthopodium GWJ 9287	WCru
ailanthoides B&SWJ 11115 from Japan	WCru
- B&SWJ 11394 from Japan	WCru
- f. ***inermis*** RWJ 10048	WCru
americanum	ELan LEdu
armatum	CAgr
- HWJK 2178	WCru
bungeanum HWJK 2131	WCru
fauriei B&SWJ 11080	WCru
aff. ***fauriei*** B&SWJ 11371	WCru
- B&SWJ 11523	WCru
laetum WWJ 11678	WCru
- WWJ 11914	WCru
myriacanthum B&SWJ 11844	WCru
oxyphyllum HWJK 2199	WCru
piperitum	CAgr CBcs GPoy SEND
- B&SWJ 8543	WCru
- B&SWJ 11377	WCru
- B&SWJ 11433	WCru
- purple-leaved	WPGP
schinifolium	CAgr LEdu
- B&SWJ 8593	WCru
- B&SWJ 11080	WCru
- B&SWJ 11391	WCru
simulans	CAgr CArn CBcs CPLG GBin IGor IVic LEdu MBlu NLar

Zauschneria (*Onagraceae*)

§ ***californica***	CHll CSam CTri EBee ECho EDAr MBrN SLon SWat SWvt WHrl WPnn XLum
§ - subsp. ***cana***	ECha SWat
- - 'Sir Cedric Morris'	EBee EPfP LRHS
§ - 'Dublin' ♀H3	CBcs EBee ECha ECho ECtt EPfP EPot LAst LBMP LHop LRHS MAsh MHer MSCN MWat NRHS NSla SAga SEND SPer SPlb SPoG SRkn SUsu SWvt WAbe WHoo WKif WSHC XLum
- 'Ed Carman'	EBee ECtt ELon LRHS LSou MNHC SEND XLum
§ - subsp. ***garrettii***	ECho SDys SWat
- 'Glasnevin'	see *Z. californica* 'Dublin'
- subsp. ***latifolia*** 'Sally Walker'	EWes
§ - subsp. ***mexicana***	MHer SRms
- 'Olbrich Silver'	EBee ECha ECtt EShb EWes LRHS SUsu WAbe WKif XLum
- 'Solidarity Pink'	LHop WAbe
- 'Western Hills' ♀H4	CCon CSpe CTri ECha ECho EPfP LHop LRHS LSou MMuc MRav SEND SPhx SWvt WAbe WHoo XLum
cana villosa	see *Z. californica* subsp. *mexicana*
I 'Pumilio'	EPot NMen NRHS NSla
§ ***septentrionalis***	WAbe

Zea (*Poaceae*)

mays 'Quadricolor' (v)	SBfd

Zebrina see *Tradescantia*

Zelkova ✿ (*Ulmaceae*)

carpinifolia	CDul CLnd CMCN SPlb
'Kiwi Sunset'	CDul EBee LRHS MAsh NWea
schneideriana	CMCN EGFP
serrata ♀H4	CBcs CCVT CDul CLnd CMCN CMen CTho EBee ECrN ELan EPfP LMaj MGos MMuc NWea SBir SCoo SEND SGol SPer WFar WMou

- B&SWJ 8491 from Korea WCru
- 'Allgold' **new** SMad
- 'Goblin' CJun NLar WPat
- 'Green Vase' LMaj MBlu
- 'Kiwi Sunset'PBR **new** LRHS
- 'Musashino' SGol
- 'Ogon' SGol
- 'Variegata' (v) CJun CMac MBlu NLar SGol SMad

sinica CMCN CMen

× ***verschaffeltii*** EPfP MBlu

Zenobia (*Ericaceae*)

pulverulenta CAbP CBcs CDoC CMac CSBt EBee ELan EPfP IVic LRHS MAsh MBlu MGos NLar SHil SLon SSpi SSta WAbe WFar WPat WSHC

- 'Blue Sky' CAbP CBcs CMCN EBee EPfP GKin IDee LRHS MAsh MBlu MBri MGos NLar SPer SPoG SSpi SSta
- f. ***nitida*** CMac NLar
- 'Raspberry Ripple' CBcs GKin MBri NLar SSta
- 'Viridis' NLar

Zephyranthes ✿ (*Amaryllidaceae*)

atamasca SKHP

'Big Dude' **new** SKHP

candida CBro CYeo EBee ECho EPot EShb GHim ITim LAma LPot LRHS NRHS SDeJ SMrm WHil

citrina CDoy CPLG EBee ECho EPot GHim LAma SDeJ WCot

drummondii ECho WCot

flavissima CDes CPBP ECho

grandiflora ♀H2-3 GHim

'Grandjax' WCot

La Buffa Rose Group CPLG WCot

mexicana EBee

minima ECho LLHF

'Pink Beauty' **new** GHim

primulina GHim

robusta see *Habranthus robustus*

rosea EBee EPot GHim SDeJ

'Snow White' **new** GHim

Zigadenus (*Melanthiaceae*)

elegans ECGP ECha EPri EWll GCal MAvo MHer NRHS SMad SUsu WCot WSHC WTin

fremontii WCot

nuttallii CRDP EBee ECho MDKP WCot

venenosus NNS 03-605 WCot

volcanicus B&SWJ 9110 WCru

Zingiber ✿ (*Zingiberaceae*)

chrysanthum GHim

malaysianum EAmu

mioga CMac EBee GPoy LEdu SChr SPlb SWal WPGP

- 'Crûg's Zing' LEdu WCru
- 'Dancing Crane' (v) CMac EUJe IFro

officinale CTsd GHim

zerumbet GHim SBst

- 'Darceyi' (v) EBee

Zinnia (*Asteraceae*)

elegans **new** SVic

grandiflora EBee

'Red Spider' CSpe

Zizia (*Apiaceae*)

aptera LRHS SPhx

aurea SDix SPhx WSHC WTin

Ziziphus (*Rhamnaceae*)

§ ***jujuba*** (F) CAgr CBcs

- 'Lang' (F) CAgr
- 'Li' (F) CAgr
- var. ***spinosa*** CArn

sativa see *Z. jujuba*

BIBLIOGRAPHY

This is by no means exhaustive but lists some of the more useful works used in the preparation of the *RHS Plant Finder*. The websites of raisers of new plants (not listed here) are also an invaluable source of information.

GENERAL

Allan, H.H., et al. 2000. *Flora of New Zealand.* Wellington. (5 vols). http://floraseries.landcareresearch.co.nz/pages/Book.aspx?fileName=Flora%201.xml

Ball Colegrave. 2007. Plant Catalogue 2008. West Adderbury, Oxon: Ball Colegrave.

Ball Colegrave. 2007. Seed Catalogue 2008. West Adderbury, Oxon: Ball Colegrave.

Bean, W.J. 1988. *Trees and Shrubs Hardy in the British Isles.* (8th ed. edited by Sir George Taylor & D.L. Clarke & Supp. ed. D.L. Clarke). London: John Murray.

Beckett, K. (ed.). 1994. *Alpine Garden Society Encyclopaedia of Alpines.* Pershore, Worcs.: Alpine Garden Society.

Boufford, D.E., et al. (eds). 2003. *Flora of Taiwan Checklist.* A checklist of the vascular plants of Taiwan. Taipei, Taiwan: NTU. http://tai2.ntu.edu.tw

Bramwell, D. & Bramwell, Z.I. 2001. *Wild Flowers of the Canary Islands.* (2nd ed.). Madrid: Editorial Rueda, S.L.

Brickell, C. (ed.). 2008. *The Royal Horticultural Society A-Z Encyclopedia of Garden Plants.* (3rd ed.) London: Dorling Kindersley.

Brickell, C.D. et al (eds.). 2009. *International Code of Nomenclature for Cultivated Plants* (8th ed.). ISHS.

Brummitt, R.K. (comp.). 1992. *Vascular Plant Families and Genera.* Kew: Royal Botanic Gardens. http://data.kew.org

Castroviejo, S. et al. (eds). *Flora Iberica.* 1987-2007. (Vols 1-8,, 10, 14, 15, 21). Madrid: Real Jardín Botánico, C.S.I.C.

Cave, Y. & Paddison, V. 1999. *The Gardener's Encyclopaedia of New Zealand Native Plants.* Auckland: Godwit.

Cooke, I. 1998. *The Plantfinder's Guide to Tender Perennials.* Newton Abbot, Devon: David & Charles.

Cronquist, A., Holmgren, A.H., Holmgren, N.H., Reveal, J.L. & Holmgren, P.H. et al. (eds). *Intermountain Flora: Vascular Plants of the Intermountain West, USA.* (1986-97). (Vols 1, 3-6). New York: New York Botanical Garden.

Davis, P.H., Mill, R.R. & Tan, K. (eds). 1965-88. *Flora of Turkey and the East Aegean Island.* (Vols 1-10). Edinburgh University Press.

Goldblatt, P. & Manning, J. 2000. *Cape Plants. A Conspectus of the Cape Flora of South Africa.* South Africa/USA: National Botanical Institute of South Africa/Missouri Botanical Garden.

Greuter, W., Brummitt, R.K., Farr, E., Kilian, N., Kirk, P.M. & Silva, P.C. (comps). 1993. *NCU-3.*

Grierson, A.J.C., Long, D.G. & Noltie, H.J. et al. (eds). 2001. *Flora of Bhutan.* Edinburgh: Royal Botanic Garden.

Grimshaw, J. & Bayton, R. 2009. *New Trees. Recent Introductions to Cultivation.* RBG Kew: Kew Publishing.

Güner, A., Özhatay, N., Ekîm, T., Baser, K.H.C. & Hedge, I.C. 2000. *Flora of Turkey and the East Aegean Islands.* Supp. 2. Vol. 11. Edinburgh: Edinburgh University Press.

Hickman, J.C. (ed.). 1993. *The Jepson Manual. Higher Plants of California.* Berkeley & Los Angeles: University of California Press. Jan 2010. http://ucjeps.berkeley.edu/interchange.html

Hillier, J. & Coombes, A. (eds). 2002. *The Hillier Manual of Trees & Shrubs.* (7th ed.). Newton Abbot, Devon: David & Charles.

Hirose, Y. & Yokoi, M. 1998. *Variegated Plants in Colour.* Iwakuni, Japan: Varie Nine.

Hirose, Y. & Yokoi, M. 2001. *Variegated Plants in Colour.* Vol. 2. Iwakuni, Japan: Varie Nine.

Hoffman, M. (ed.). 2005. *List of Woody Plants. International Standard ENA 2005-2010.* Netherlands: Applied Plant Research.

Huxley, A., Griffiths, M. & Levy, M. (eds). 1992. *The New RHS Dictionary of Gardening.* London: Macmillan.

Iwatsuki, K., et al. 1995. *Flora of Japan.* Vols I-IIIb. Tokyo, Japan: Kodansha Ltd.

Jelitto, L. & Schacht, W.R., Simon, H. 2002. *Die Freiland-Schmuchstauden.* Germany: Verlag Eugen Ulmer.

Krüssmann, G. & Epp, M.E. (trans.). 1986. *Manual of Cultivated Broad-leaved Trees and Shrubs.* London: Batsford (3 vols).

Leslie, A.C. (trans.). *New Cultivars of Herbaceous Perennial Plants 1985-1990.* Hardy Plant Society.

Mabberley, D.J. 2008. *Mabberley's Plant Book. A Portable Dictionary of Plants, their Classification and Uses.* (3rd ed.). Cambridge: Cambridge University Press.

McNeill, J. et al. (eds). 2006. *International Code of Botanical Nomenclature (Vienna Code).* Ruggell, Liechtenstein: A.R.G. Gantner Verlag. Jan 2010. http://ibot.sav.sk.

Metcalf, L.J. 1987. *The Cultivation of New Zealand Trees and Shrubs.* Auckland: Reed Methuen.

Nelson, E.C. 2000. *A Heritage of Beauty: The Garden Plants of Ireland: An Illustrated Encyclopaedia.* Dublin: Irish Garden Plant Society.

Ohwi, J. 1965. *Flora of Japan.* Washington DC: Smithsonian Institution.
Phillips, R. & Rix, M. 1997. *Conservatory and Indoor Plants.* London: Macmillan. (2 vols).
Platt, K. (comp.). 2002. *The Seed Search.* (5th ed.). Sheffield: Karen Platt.
Press, J.R. & Short, M.J. (eds). 1994. *Flora of Madeira.* London: Natural History Museum/ HMSO.
Rehder, A. 1940. *Manual of Cultivated Trees and Shrubs Hardy in North America.* (2nd ed.). New York: Macmillan.
Rice, G. (ed.), 2006. *Encyclopedia of Perennials.* London: Dorling Kindersley.
Stace, C. 1997. *New Flora of the British Isles.* (2nd ed.). Cambridge: Cambridge University Press.
Stearn, W.T. 1992. *Botanical Latin.* (4th ed.). Newton Abbot, Devon: David & Charles.
Stearn, W.T. 1996. *Stearn's Dictionary of Plant Names for Gardeners.* London: Cassell.
Thomas, G.S. 1990. *Perennial Garden Plants. A Modern Florilegium.* (3rd ed.). London: Dent.
Trehane, P. (comp.). 1989. *Index Hortensis. Vol. 1: Perennials.* Wimborne: Quarterjack
Tutin, T.G., et al. (ed.). 1993. *Flora Europaea. Vol. 1. Psilotaceae to Platanaceae.* (2nd ed.). Cambridge University Press.
Tutin, T.G., et al. 1964. *Flora Europaea.* Cambridge University Press. Vols 1-5. http://rbg-web2.rbge.org.uk
Walter, K.S. & Gillett, H.J. (eds). 1998. *1997 IUCN Red List of Threatened Plants.* Gland, Switzerland and Cambridge, UK: IUCN.
Walters, S.M. & Cullen, J. et al. (eds). 2000. *The European Garden Flora.* Cambridge: Cambridge University Press. (6 vols).

General Periodicals

Dendroflora
New, Rare and Unusual Plants.
The Hardy Plant Society. *The Hardy Plant.*
The Hardy Plant Society. *The Sport.*
Internationale Stauden-Union. *ISU Yearbook.*
Royal Horticultural Society. *Hanburyana.*
Royal Horticultural Society. *The Garden.*
Royal Horticultural Society. *The Plantsman.*
Royal Horticultural Society. *The New Plantsman.*
Royal Horticultural Society. *The Plantsman* (new series).

General Websites

Annotated Checklist of the Flowering Plants of Nepal. Jan 2010 www.efloras.org/flora_page-aspx?_id=110
Australian Cultivar Registration Authority. Jan 2010. www.anbg.gov.au/acra
Australian Plant Breeders Rights – Database Search. Jan 2010. http://pbr.ipaustralia.optus.com.au
Australian Plant Names Index. Australian National Botanic Gardens (comp.). Jan 2010. www.anbg.gov.au/apni/index.html
Bolivia Checklist. Jan 2010. www.efloras.org/flora_page.aspx?flora_id=40
Botanical Expedition in Myanmar Checklist. Jan 2010. http://botany.si-edu/myanmar/checklistNames.cfm
Brand, H. UConn Plant Database of Trees Shrubs and Vines. Jan 2010. www.hort.uconn.edu
Canadian Ornamental Plant Foundation. Jan 2010. www.copf.org
Canadian Plant Breeders Rights Office: Canadian Food Inspection Agency. Jan 2010. www.inspection.gc.ca
Catálogo de las Plantas Vasculares de las República Argentina. Jan 2010. www.darwin.edu.ar/Publicaciones/catalogoVaseII/CatalogoVaseII.asp
Catalogue of the Vascular Plants of Madagascar. Jan 2010. www.efforas.org/flora_page.aspx?flora_id+12
Darwin Checklist of Moroccan Vascular Plants. Jan 2010. www.herbarium.rdg.ac.uk/
DEFRA Plant Varieties and Seeds Gazette. Jan 2010. www.defra.gov.uk
Flora Himalaya Database. Jan 2010. www.leca.univ-savoie.fr
Flora Mesoamericana Internet Version (W3FM). Jan 2010. Missouri Botanical Garden. www.mobot.org/MOBOT/FM/intro.html
Flora of Australia Online. Jan 2010. Australian Biological Resources Study. www.environment.gov.au/biodiversity/abrs/online-resources/flora/index.html
Flora of Chile. Jan 2010. www.efloras.org/flora_page.aspx?flora_id=60
Flora of China Checklist. Jan 2010. http://flora.huh.harvard.edu/china
Flora of Pakistan. Jan 2010. www.efloras.org/flora_page.aspd?flora_id=5
Flora of North America Website. Jan 2010. Morin, N.R., et al. www.efloras.org-page.aspx/flora_id=1
GRIN (Germplasm Resources Information Network) Taxonomy. Jan 2010. www.ars-grin.gov
Hatch, D. New Ornamentals Society Database. Jan 2010. http://members.tripod.com/~Hatch_L/nos.html
International Plant Names Index. Jan 2010. www.ipni.org
International Plant Names Index: Author Query. Jan 2010. www.ipni.org/ipni
IOPI Provisional Global Plant Checklist. Jan 2010. www.bgbm.fu-berlin.de/iopi/gpl/query.asp
Manaaki Whenua: Landcare Research in New Zealand Plants Database Jan 2010. http://nzflora.landcareresearch.co.nz
Manual de plantas de Costa Rica. Jan 2010. www.mobot.org/manual.plantas
Plant List, The. A working list of all plant species www.theplantlist.org.
Plants Database. USDA, NRCS. Jan 2010. http://plants.usda.gov

Plants of Southern Africa: an Online Checklist. Jan 2010. http://posa.sanbi.org

New Zealand Plant Variety Rights Office www.iponz.govt.nz/cms/pvr

SKUD Database for Cultivated and Utilized Plants. Jan 2010. http://skud.ngb.se

Synonymized Checklist of the Vascular Flora of the United States, Puerto Rico and the Virgin Isles. BIOTA of North America Program. Jan 2010. www.bonap.org

Tropicos. Jan 2010. www.tropicos.org

US Patent Full-Text Database. US Patent and Trademark Office, (comp.). Jan 2010. www.uspto.gov/patft

World Checklist of Selected Families. Jan 2010. apps.kew.org/wcsp

Genera and other Plant Groupings

Acer

Gregory, P. & Angus, H. 2008. *World Checklist of Maple Cultivar Names*. Forestry Commission National Arboreta.

Harris, J.G.S. 2000. *The Gardener's Guide to Growing Maples*. Newton Abbot, Devon: David & Charles.

Van Gelderen, C.J. & Van Gelderen, D.M. 1999. *Maples for Gardens*. A Color Encyclopedia. Portland, Oregon: Timber Press.

Vertrees, J.D. 2001. *Japanese Maples*. Momiji and Kaede. (3rd ed.). Portland, Oregon: Timber Press.

Actaea

Compton, J.A., Culham, A. & Jury, S.L. 1998. Reclassification of *Actaea* to Include *Cimicifuga* and *Souliea* (*Ranunculaceae*). *Taxon* 47:593-634.

Adiantum

Goudey, C.J. 1985. *Maidenhair Ferns in Cultivation*. Melbourne: Lothian.

Agapanthus

Snoeijer, W. 2004. *Agapanthus. A Revision of the Genus*. Portland, Oregon: Timber Press.

Agavaceae

Irish, M. & Irish, G. 2000. *Agaves, Yuccas and Related Plants*. A Gardener's Guide. Portland, Oregon: Timber Press.

Aizoaceae

Burgoyne, P. et al. 1998. *Mesembs of the World. Illustrated Guide to a Remarkable Succulent Group*. South Africa: Briza Publications.

Allium

Davies, D. 1992. *Alliums. The Ornamental Onions*. London: Batsford

Gregory, M., et al. 1998. *Nomenclator Alliorum*. Kew: Royal Botanic Gardens.

Mathew, B. 1996. *A Review of Allium Section Allium*. Kew: Royal Botanic Gardens.

Androsace

Smith, G. & Lowe, D. 1997. *The Genus Androsace*. Pershore, Worcs.: Alpine Garden Society.

Anemone, Japanese

McKendrick, M. 1990. Autumn Flowering Anemones. *The Plantsman* 12(3):140-151.

McKendrick, M. 1998. Japanese Anemones. *The Garden* (RHS) 123(9):628-633.

Anthemis

Leslie, A. 1997. Focus on Plants: *Anthemis tinctoria*. *The Garden* (RHS) 122(8):552-555.

Apiaceae

Pimenov, M.G. & Leonov, M.V. 1993. *The Genera of the Umbelliferae*. Kew: Royal Botanic Gardens.

Aquilegia

Munz, P.A. 1946. *Aquilegia:* the Cultivated and Wild Columbines. *Gentes Herb.* 7(1):1-150.

Araceae

Govaerts, R. & Frodin, D.G. 2002. *World Checklist and Bibliography of Araceae (and Acoraceae)*. Kew:Royal Botanic Gardens

Araliaceae

Govaerts, R. & Frodin, D.G. 2002. *World Checklist and Bibliography of Araliaceae*. Kew: Royal Botanic Gardens

Arecaceae (***Palmae,*** palms)

Craft, P. & Riffle, R.L. 2003. *Encyclopedia of Cultivated Palms*. Portland, Oregon: Timber Press.

Uhl, N.W. & Dransfield, J. 1987. *Genera Palmarum*. A Classification of Palms Based on the Work of Harold E. Moore Jr. Lawrence, Kansas: Allen Press.

Argyranthemum

Humphries, C.J. 1976. A Revision of the Macaronesian Genus *Argyranthemum*. *Bull. Brit. Mus. (Nat. Hist.) Bot.* 5(4):145-240.

Arisaema

Gusman, G. & Gusman, L. 2002. *The Genus Arisaema: A Monograph for Botanists and Nature Lovers*. Ruggell, Leichtenstein: A.R. Gantner Verlag Kommanditgesellschaft.

Pradhan, U.C. 1997. *Himalayan Cobra Lilies* (Arisaema). Their Botany and Culture. (2nd ed.). Kalimpong, West Bengal, India: Primulaceae Books.

Arum

Bown, D. 2000. *Plants of the Arum Family*. (2nd ed.). Portland, Oregon: Timber Press.

Boyce, P. 1993. *The Genus Arum*. London: HMSO.

Asclepiadaceae

Eggli, U. (ed.). 2002. *Illustrated Handbook of Succulent Plants: Asclepiadaceae*. Heidelberg, Germany: Springer-Verlag.

Aster

Picton, P. 1999. *The Gardener's Guide to Growing Asters*. Newton Abbot: David & Charles.

Asteraceae

Bremer, K. et al. 1994. *Asteraceae: Cladistics and Classification*. Portland, Oregon: Timber Press.

Cubey, J. & Grant, M. 2004. *Perennial Yellow Daisies: RHS Bulletin No 6*. Wisley, Surrey: RHS. www.rhs.org.uk/Plants/RHS-Publications/Plant-bulletins

Astilbe
Noblett, H. 2001. *Astilbe.* A Guide to the Identification of Cultivars and Common Species. Cumbria: Henry Noblett.
Aubrieta
1975. *International Registration Authority Checklist.* Weihenstephan, Germany: (Unpublished).
Bamboos
Ohrnberger, D. 1999. *The Bamboos of the World.* Amsterdam: Elsevier.
Begonia
American Begonia Society Astro Branch Begonia Data Base. Jan 2010. http://absastro.tripod.com
American Begonia Society Registered Begonias. Jan 2010. http://www.begonias.org
Ingles, J. 1990. *American Begonia Society Listing of Begonia Cultivars.* Revised Edition Buxton Checklist. American Begonia Society.
Tebbitt, M.C. 2005. *Begonias: Cultivation, Identification and Natural History.* Portland, Oregon: Timber Press.
Thompson, M.L. & Thompson, E.J. 1981. *Begonias.* The Complete Reference Guide. New York: Times Books.
Berberidaceae
Stearn, W.T. & Shaw, J.M.H. 2002. *The Genus Epimedium and Other Herbaceous Berberidaceae including the Genus Podophyllum.* Kew: Royal Botanic Gardens.
Betula
Ashburner, K. & Schilling. T. 1985. *Betula utilis* and its Varieties. *The Plantsman* 7(2):116-125.
Ashburner, K.B. 1980. *Betula* – a Survey. *The Plantsman* 2(1):31-53.
Hunt, D. (ed.). 1993. *Betula: Proceedings of the IDS Betula Symposium 1992.* Richmond, Surrey: International Dendrology Society.
Boraginaceae
Bennett, M. 2003. *Pulmonarias and the Borage Family.* London: Batsford.
Bougainvillea
Gillis, W.T. 1976. Bougainvilleas of Cultivation (*Nyctaginaceae*). *Baileya* 20(1):34-41.
Iredell, J. 1990. *The Bougainvillea Grower's Handbook.* Brookvale, Australia: Simon & Schuster.
Iredell, J. 1994. *Growing Bougainvilleas.* London: Cassell.
MacDaniels, L.H. 1981. A Study of Cultivars in *Bougainvillea* (*Nyctaginaceae*). *Baileya* 21(2):77-100.
Singh, B., Panwar, R.S., Voleti, S.R., Sharma, V.K. & Thakur, S. 1999. *The New International Bougainvillea Check List.* (2nd ed.). New Delhi: Indian Agricultural Research Institute.
Bromeliaceae
Beadle, D.A. 1991. *A Preliminary Listing of all the Known Cultivar and Grex Names for the Bromeliaceae.* Corpus Christi, Texas: Bromeliad Society.
Bromeliad Cultivar Registry Online Databases. Bromeliad Society International. Jan 2010. www.bsi.org
Brugmansia
Wreggitt, L. et al. (comp.). Jan 2010.. *Register of Brugmansia Cultivars and Checklist of Names in Use.* American Brugmansia and Datura Society. www.abads.org
Buddleja
Stuart, D.D. 2006. *Buddlejas: Royal Horticultural Society Collector Guide.* Portland, Oregon: Timber Press.
Bulbs
Leeds, R. 2000. *The Plantfinder's Guide to Early Bulbs.* Newton Abbot, Devon: David & Charles.
KAVB Online registration pages. Jan 2010. http://kavb.back2p.soft-orange.com
Buxus
Batdorf, L.R. 1995. *Boxwood Handbook. A Practical Guide to Knowing and Growing Boxwood.* Boyce, VA, USA: The American Boxwood Society. Jan 2010. www.boxwoodsociety.org
Cactaceae
Hunt, D. et al. 2006. *New Cactus Lexicon.* (2 vols.) Sherborne, Dorset: DH Books.
Camellia
Trujillo, D. J. (ed.). 2002. *Camellia Nomenclature.* (24th revd ed.). Southern California Camellia Society.
Savige, T.J. (comp.). 1993. *The International Camellia Register.* The International Camellia Society. (2 vols).
Savige, T.J. (comp.). 1997. *The International Camellia Register.* Supp. to vols 1 and 2. The International Camellia Society.
Campanula
Lewis, P. & Lynch, M. 1998. *Campanulas.* A Gardeners Guide. (2nd ed.). London: Batsford.
Lewis, P 2002. *Campanulas in the Garden.* Pershore, Worcs.: Hardy Plant Society.
Campanulaceae
Lammers, T.G. 2007. *World Checklist and Bibliography of Campanulaceae.* Kew Publishing.
Canna
Cooke, I. 2001. *The Gardener's Guide to Growing Cannas.* Newton Abbot, Devon: David & Charles.
Gray, J. & Grant, M. 2003. Canna: RHS Bulletin No 3. Wisley, Surrey: RHS. www.rhs.org.uk/Plants/RHS-Publications/Plant_bulletins
Hayward, K. Jan 2010. www.hartcanna.com
Carnivorous Plants
Schlauer, J. (comp.). Jan 2010. Carnivorous Plant Database. www.omnisterra.com
Ceanothus
Fross, D. & D. Wilken. 2006. *Ceanothus.* Portland, Oregon: Timber Press.
Cercidiphyllum
Dosmann, M.S. 1999. Katsura: a Review of *Cercidiphyllum* in Cultivation and in the Wild. *The New Plantsman* 6(1):52-62.

Dosmann, M., Andrews, S., Del Tredici, P. & Li, J. 2003. Classification and Nomenclature of Weeping Katsuras. *The Plantsman* 2(1):21-27.

Chaenomeles

Weber, C. 1963. Cultivars in the Genus *Chaenomeles. Arnoldia (Jamaica Plain)* 23(3):17-75.

Chrysanthemum

Brummitt, D. 1997. *Chrysanthemum* Once Again. *The Garden* (RHS) 122(9):662-663.

Gosling, S.G. (ed.). 1964. *British National Register of Chrysanthemums.* Whetstone, London: National Chrysanthemum Society.

National Chrysanthemum Society. 2000. *British National Register of Names of Chrysanthemums Amalgamated Edition 1964-1999.* Tamworth, Staffordshire: The National Chrysanthemum Society.

National Chrysanthemum Society UK Cultivar Database. Jan 2010. www.nationalchrysanthemumsociety.org.uk

Cistus

Demoly, J.-P. 2005. The identity of *Cistus* 'Grayswood Pink' and related plants. *The Plantsman* 4(2):76-80.

Page, R.G. Feb 2007. Cistus and Halimium Website. www.cistuspage.org.uk

Citrus

Davies, F.S. & Albrigo, L.G. 1994. *Citrus.* Wallingford, Oxon: Cab International.

Page, M. 2008. *Growing Citrus.* London: Timber Press

Saunt, J. 1990. *Citrus Varieties of the World.* An Illustrated Guide. Norwich: Sinclair

Clematis

Clematis on the Web. Jan 2008. www.clematis.hull.ac.uk

Grey-Wilson, C. 2000. *Clematis: the Genus.* London: Batsford

HelpMeFind Clematis. Nov 2006. www.helpmefind.com/clematis

Johnson, M. 2001. *The Genus Clematis.* Södertälje, Sweden: Magnus Johnsons Plantskola AB & Bengt Sundström.

Matthews, V. (comp.). 2002. *The International Clematis Register and Checklist 2002.* London: RHS.

Supps 1 (2004), 2 (2006) & 3 (2009). www.rhs.org.uk/Plants/RHS-Publications/Plant-registers

Toomey, M. & Leeds, E. 2001. *An Illustrated Encyclopedia of Clematis.* Portland, Oregon: Timber Press.

Conifers

den Ouden, P. & Boom, B.K. 1965. *Manual of Cultivated Conifers.* The Hague: Martinus Nijhof.

Eckenwalder, J.E. 2009. *Conifers of the World.* China:Timber Press

Farjon, A. 1998. *World Checklist and Bibliography of Conifers.* Kew: Royal Botanic Gardens.

Krüssmann, G. & Epp, M.E. (trans.). 1985. *Manual of Cultivated Conifers.* London: Batsford.

Lewis, J. & Leslie, A.C. 1987. *The International Conifer Register. Pt 1. Abies* to *Austrotaxus.* London: RHS.

Lewis, J. & Leslie, A.C. 1989. *The International Conifer Register. Pt 2. Belis* to *Pherosphaera,* excluding the Cypresses. London: RHS.

Lewis, J. & Leslie, A.C. 1992. *The International Conifer Register. Pt 3. The Cypresses.* London: RHS.

Lewis, J. & Leslie, A.C. 1998. *The International Conifer Register. Pt 4. Juniperus.* London: RHS.

Welch, H.J. 1979. *Manual of Dwarf Conifers.* New York: Theophrastus.

Welch, H.J. 1991. *The Conifer Manual.* Vol. 1. Dordrecht, Netherlands: Kluwer Academic Publishers.

Welch, H.J. 1993. *The World Checklist of Conifers.* Bromyard, Herefordshire: Landsman's Bookshops Ltd.

Cornus

Cappiello, P. & Shadow, D. 2005. *Dogwoods.* Portland, Oregon: Timber Press.

Howard, R.A. 1961. Registration Lists of Cultivar Names in *Cornus L. Arnoldia (Jamaica Plain)* 21(2):9-18.

Corydalis

Lidén, M. & Zetterlund, H. 1997. *Corydalis. A Gardener's Guide and a Monograph of the Tuberous Species.* Pershore, Worcs.: Alpine Garden Society Publications Ltd.

Corylus

Crawford, M. 1995. *Hazelnuts: Production and Culture.* Dartington, Devon: Agroforestry Research Trust.

Cotoneaster

Fryer, J. & Hylmö, B. 1998. Seven New Species of *Cotoneaster* in Cultivation. *The New Plantsman* 5(3):132-144.

Fryer, J. & Hylmö, B. 2001. Captivating Cotoneasters. *The New Plantsman* 8(4):227-238.

Fryer, J. & Hylmö, B. 2009. *Cotoneasters. A Comprehensive Guide to Shrubs for Flowers, Fruit and Foliage.* Portland, Oregon: Timber Press.

Crassulaceae

Rowley, G. 2003. *Crassula: A Grower's Guide.* Venegono superiore, Italy: Cactus & Co.

Eggli, U. (ed.) 2003. *Illustrated Handbook of Succulent Plants.* Springer.

Crocosmia

Goldblatt, P., Manning, J.C. & Dunlop, G. 2004. *Crocosmia and Chasmanthe.* Portland, Oregon: Timber Press.

Crocus

Jacobsen, N., van Scheepen, J. & Ørgaard, M. 1997. The *Crocus chrysanthus – biflorus* Cultivars. *The New Plantsman* 4(1):6-38.

Mathew, B. 1982. *The Crocus. A Review of the Genus Crocus (Iridaceae).* London: Batsford.

Mathew, B. 2002. *Crocus* Up-date. *The Plantsman* 1(1):44-56.

Cyclamen

Clennett, C. Jan 2010. Register of Cultivar Names. www.cyclamen.org

Grey-Wilson, C. 2003. *Cyclamen. A Guide for Gardeners, Horticulturists & Botanists.* London: Batsford.

Grey-Wilson, C. 2002 Sprenger's Alpine Cyclamen. *The Plantsman* 1(3):173-177.

Cypripedium

Cribb, P. 1997. *The Genus Cypripedium.* Portland, Oregon: Timber Press.

Dahlia

American Dahlia Society website. Jan 2010. www.dahlia.org

Bates, D. Dahlia Plant Finder 2007. Jan 2010. www.dahliaworld.co.uk

National Dahlia Society. 2005. *Classified Directory and Judging Rules.* (28th ed.) Aldershot, Hants: National Dahlia Society.

RHS & Hedge, R. (comps). 1969. *Tentative Classified List and International Register of Dahlia Names 1969.* (& Supps 1-13). London: RHS. Supps 13-20. 2002-09. http://www.rhs.org.uk/learning

Winchester Growers Ltd English National Dahlia Collection website. Jan 2010. www.national-dahlia-collection.co.uk

Daphne

Brickell, C.D. & Mathew, B. 1976. *Daphne. The Genus in the Wild and in Cultivation.* Woking, Surrey: Alpine Garden Society.

Grey-Wilson, C. (ed.). 2001. *The Smaller Daphnes. The Proceedings of 'Daphne 2000', a Conference held at the Royal Horticultural Society.* Pershore, Worcs.: Alpine Garden Society.

White, R. 2006. *Daphnes: A Practical Guide for Gardeners.* Portland, Oregon: Timber Press.

Delphinium

1949. *A Tentative Check-list of Delphinium Names.* London: RHS.

1970. *A Tentative Check-list of Delphinium Names.* Addendum to the 1949 tentative check-list of *Delphinium* names. London: RHS.

Bassett, D. & Wesley, W. 2004. *Delphinium: RHS Bulletin No 5.* Wisley, Surrey: RHS. www.rhs.org.uk/plants/documents/delph04.pdf

Leslie, A.C. 1996. *The International Delphinium Register Cumulative Supp. 1970-1995.* London: RHS.

Leslie, A.C. 1996-2005. The International Delphinium Register Supp. 1994-99. *The Delphinium Society Year Book 1996-2005.* London: RHS.

Dianthus

Galbally, J. & Galbally, E. 1997. *Carnations and Pinks for Garden and Greenhouse.* Portland, Oregon: Timber Press.

Leslie, A.C. *The International Dianthus Register.* 1983-2002. (2nd ed. & Supps 1-19). London: RHS.

Supps 19-25. 2002-08. http://www.rhs.org.uk/Plants/RHS-Publications/Plant-registers

Dierama

Hilliard, O.M. & Burtt, B.L. 1991. *Dierama. The Harebells of Africa.* Johannesburg; London: Acorn Books.

Dionysia

Grey-Wilson, C. 1989. *The Genus Dionysia.* Woking, Surrey: Alpine Garden Society.

Douglasia

Mitchell, B. 1999. Celebrating the Bicentenary of David Douglas: a Review of *Douglasia* in Cultivation. *The New Plantsman* 6(2):101-108.

Dracaena

Bos, J.J., Graven, P., Hetterscheid, W.L.A. & van de Wege, J.J. 1992. Wild and cultivated *Dracaena fragrans. Edinburgh J. Bot.* 49(3):311-331.

Echeveria

Schulz, L. & Kapitany, A. *Echeveria Cultivars.* Teesdale, Australia: Schulz Publishing.

Episcia

Dates, J.D. 1993. *The Gesneriad Register 1993.* Check List of Names with Descriptions of Cultivated Plants in the Genera *Episcia* & *Alsobia.* Galesburg, Illinois: American Gloxinia & Gesneriad Society, Inc.

Erica (see also Heathers)

Baker, H.A. & Oliver, E.G.H. 1967. *Heathers in Southern Africa.* Cape Town: Purnell.

Schumann, D., Kirsten, G. & Oliver, E.G.H. 1992. *Ericas of South Africa.* Vlaeberg, South Africa: Fernwood Press.

Erodium

Clifton, R. 1994. *Geranium Family Species Checklist. Pt 1 Erodium.* (4th ed.). The Geraniaceae Group.

Leslie, A.C. 1980. The Hybrid of *Erodium corsicum* with *Erodium reichardii. The Plantsman* 2:117-126.

Toomey, N., Cubey, J. & Culham, A. 2002. *Erodium × variabile. The Plantsman* 1(3): 166-172

Victor, D.X. (comp.). 2000. *Erodium: Register of Cultivar Names.* The Geraniaceae Group.

Erythronium

Mathew, B. 1992. A Taxonomic and Horticultural Review of *Erythronium* L. (*Liliaceae*). *J. Linn. Soc., Bot.* 109:453-471.

Mathew, B. 1998. The Genus *Erythronium. Bull. Alpine Gard. Soc. Gr. Brit.* 66(3):308-321.

Eupatorium sensu lato

Hind, D.J.N. 2006. Splitting *Eupatorium. The Plantsman* (n.s.) 5(2):185-189.

Euonymus

Brown, N. 1996. Notes on Cultivated Species of *Euonymus. The New Plantsman* 3(4):238-243.

Lancaster, C.R. 1981. An Account of *Euonymus* in Cultivation and its Availability in Commerce. *The Plantsman* 3(3):133-166.

Lancaster, C.R. 1982. *Euonymus* in Cultivation – Addendum. *The Plantsman* 4:61-64, 253-254.

Euphorbia

Govaerts, R., Frodin, D.G. & Radcliffe-Smith, A. 2000. *World Checklist and Bibliography of Euphorbiaceae.* Kew: Royal Botanic Gardens.

Turner, R. 1995. *Euphorbias. A Gardeners Guide.* London: Batsford.

Witton, D. 2000. *Euphorbias.* Pershore, Worcs.: Hardy Plant Society.

Fagales

Gocaerts, R. & Frodin, D.G. 1998. *World Checklist and Bibliography of Fagales.* RBG Kew.

Fagus

Dönig, G. 1994. *Die Park-und Gartenformen der Rotbuche Fagus sylvatica L.* Erlangen, Germany: Verlag Gartenbild Heinz Hansmann.

Wyman, D. 1964. Registration List of Cultivar Names of *Fagus* L. *J. Arnold Arbor.* 24(1):1-8.

Fascicularia

Nelson, E.C. & Zizka, G. 1997. *Fascicularia* (*Bromeliaceae*): Which Species are Cultivated and Naturalized in Northwestern Europe. *The New Plantsman* 4(4):232-239.

Nelson, E.C., Zizka, G., Horres, R. & Weising, K. 1999. Revision of the Genus *Fascicularia* Mez (*Bromeliaceae*). *Botanical Journal of the Linnean Society* 129(4):315-332.

Ferns

Checklist of World Ferns. Jan 2010. http://homepages.caverock.net.nz/nbj/fern

Johns, R.J. 1996. *Index Filicum.* Supplementum Sextum pro annis 1976-1990. Kew:Royal Botanic Gardens.

Johns, R.J. 1997. *Index Filicum.* Supplementum Septimum pro annis 1991-1995. Kew:Royal Botanic Gardens.

Jones, D.L. 1987. *Encyclopaedia of Ferns.* Melbourne, Australia: Lothian.

Kaye, R. 1968. *Hardy Ferns.* London: Faber & Faber

Rickard, M.H. 2000. *The Plantfinder's Guide to Garden Ferns.* Newton Abbot, Devon: David & Charles.

Rush, R. 1984. *A Guide to Hardy Ferns.* London: British Pteridological Society.

Forsythia

INRA Forsythia website. Jan 2010. www.angers.inra.fr/forsy

Fritillaria

Clark, T. & Grey-Wilson, C. 2003. Crown Imperials. *The Plantsman* 2(1):33-47.

Mathew, B., et al. 2000. *Fritillaria* Issue. *Bot. Mag.* 17(3):145-185.

Pratt, K. & Jefferson-Brown, M. 1997. *The Gardener's Guide to Growing Fritillaries.* Newton Abbot: David & Charles.

Turrill, W.B. & Sealy, J.R. 1980. *Studies in the Genus Fritillaria (Liliaceae).* Hooker's Icones Plantarum Vol. 39 (1 & 2). Kew: Royal Botanic Gardens.

Fruit

Brogdale Horticultural Trust National Fruit Collection. Jan 2010. www.nationalfruitcollection.org.uk

Bowling, B.L. 2000. *The Berry Grower's Companion.* Portland, Oregon: Timber Press.

Hogg, R. 1884. *The Fruit Manual.* (5th ed.). London: Journal of Horticulture Office.

Fuchsia

American Fuchsia Society Registration Database. Jan 2010. www.americanfuchsiasociety.org

Bartlett, G. 1996. *Fuchsias – A Colour Guide.* Marlborough, Wilts: Crowood Press.

Boullemier, Leo.B. (comp.). 1991. *The Checklist of Species, Hybrids and Cultivars of the Genus Fuchsia.* London, New York, Sydney: Blandford Press.

Boullemier, Leo.B. (comp.). 1995. *Addendum No 1 to the 1991 Checklist of Species, Hybrids and Cultivars of the Genus Fuchsia.* Dyfed, Wales: The British Fuchsia Society.

Goulding, E. 1995. *Fuchsias: The Complete Guide.* London: Batsford.

Johns, E.A. 1997. *Fuchsias of the 19th and Early 20th Century.* An Historical Checklist of Fuchsia Species & Cultivars, pre-1939. Kidderminster, Worcs.: British Fuchsia Society

Jones, L. & Miller, D.M. 2005. *Hardy Fuchsias: RHS Bulletin No 12.* Wisley, Surrey: RHS. www.rhs.org.uk/Plants/RHS-Publications/Plant_bulletins

Stevens, R. Jan 2010. Find That Fuchsia. www.findthatfuchsia.info

Galanthus

Bishop, M., Davis, A. & Grimshaw, J. 2001. *Snowdrops. A monograph of cultivated Galanthus.* Maidenhead: Griffin Press.

Davis, A.P., Mathew, B. (ed.) & King, C. (ill.). 1999. *The Genus Galanthus. A Botanical Magazine Monograph.* Oregon: Timber Press.

Gentiana

Bartlett, M. 1975. *Gentians.* Dorset: Blandford Press.

Halda, J.J. 1996. *The Genus Gentiana.* Dobré, Czech Republic: Sen.

Ho T.N. & Liu S. 2001. *Worldwide Monograph of Gentiana.* Beijing: Science Press.

Geranium

Armitage, J. 2005. *Hardy Geraniums – Stage 1: RHS Bulletin No 10.* Wisley, Surrey: RHS. www.rhs.org.uk/Plants/RHS-Publications/Plant_bulletins

Armitage, J. 2006. *Hardy Geraniums – Stage 2: RHS Bulletin No 14.* Wisley, Surrey: RHS. www.rhs.org.uk/Plants/RHS-Publications/Plant_bulletins

Armitage, J. 2007. *Hardy Geraniums – Stage 3: RHS Bulletin No 18.* Wisley, Surrey: RHS. www.rhs.org.uk/Plants/RHS-Publications/Plant_bulletins

Bath, T. & Jones, J. 1994. *The Gardener's Guide to Growing Hardy Geraniums.* Newton Abbot, Devon: David & Charles.

Bendtsen, B.H. 2005. *Gardening with Hardy Geraniums.* Portland, Oregon: Timber Press.

Clifton, R.T.F. 1995. *Geranium Family Species Check List Pt 2.* Geranium. (4th ed. issue 2). Dover: The Geraniaceae Group.

Jones, J., et al. 2001. *Hardy Geraniums for the Garden.* (3rd ed.). Pershore, Worcs.: Hardy Plant Society.

Victor, D.X. 2004. *Register of Geranium Cultivar Names.* (2nd ed.). The Geraniaceae Group.

Yeo, P.F. 2002. *Hardy Geraniums.* (3rd ed.). Kent: Croom Helm.

Gesneriaceae

The Gesneriad Society. Listing of registered gesneriads. Jan 2010. www.aggs.gesneriadsociety.org

Dates, J.D. 1986-1990. *The Gesneriad Register 1986-1987 & 1990.* Galesburg, Illinois: American Gloxinia & Gesneriad Society, Inc.

Gladiolus

British Gladiolus Society List of Cultivars Classified for Show Purposes 1994. Mayfield, Derbyshire: British Gladiolus Society.

1997-1998. British Gladiolus Society List of European, New Zealand & North American Cultivars Classified for Exhibition Purposes 1997 & 1998. Mayfield, Derbyshire: British Gladiolus Society.

Goldblatt, P. & Manning, J. 1998. *Gladiolus in Southern Africa.* Vlaeberg, South Africa: Fernwood Press.

Goldblatt, P. 1996. *Gladiolus in Tropical Africa.* Systematics Biology and Evolution. Oregon: Timber Press.

Lewis, G.J., Obermeyer, A.A. & Barnard, T.T. 1972. A Revision of the South African Species of *Gladiolus. J. S. African Bot.* (Supp. Vol. 10)

Gleditsia

Santamour, F.S. & McArdle, A.J. 1983. Checklist of Cultivars of Honeylocust (*Gleditsia triacanthos* L.). *J. Arboric.* 9:271-276.

Grevillea

Olde, P. & Marriott, N. 1995. *The Grevillea Book.* (3). Kenthurst, NSW: Kangaroo Press.

Haemanthus

Snijman, D. 1984. A Revision of the Genus *Haemanthus. J. S. African Bot.* (Supp. Vol. 12).

Hamamelis

Lane, C. 2005. *Witch Hazels.* Portland, Oregon: Timber Press.

Heathers

Nelson, E.C. Aug 2007. International Cultivar Registration Authority for Heathers. www.heathersociety.org.uk

Hebe

Chalk, D. 1988. *Hebes and Parahebes.* Bromley, Kent: Christopher Helm (Publishers) Ltd.

Hutchins, G. 1997. *Hebes: Here and There.* A Monograph on the Genus *Hebe.* Caversham, Berks: Hutchins & Davies.

Metcalf, L.J. 2001. *International Register of Hebe Cultivars.* Canterbury, New Zealand: Royal New Zealand Institute of Horticulture (Inc.).

Metcalf, L.J. 2006. *Hebes: A Guide to Species, Hybrids and Allied Genera.* Portland, Oregon: Timber Press.

Hedera

Jury, S. et al. 2006. *Hedera algeriensis,* a Fine Species of Ivy. *Sibbaldia* 4: 93-108.

McAllister, H. 1988. Canary and Algerian Ivies. *The Plantsman* 10(1):27-29.

McAllister, H.A. & Rutherford, A. 1990. *Hedera helix and H. hibernica* in the British Isles. *Watsonia* 18:7-15.

Rose, P.Q. 1996. *The Gardener's Guide to Growing Ivies.* Newton Abbot, Devon: David & Charles.

Rutherford, A., McAllister, H. & Mill, R.R. 1993. New Ivies from the Mediterranean Area and Macaronesia. *The Plantsman* 15(2):115-128.

Heliconia

Berry, F. & Kress, W.J. 1991. *Heliconia.* An Identification Guide. Washington: Smithsonian Institution Press.

Helleborus

Burrell, C.C. & Tyler, J.K. 2006. *Hellebores: A Comprehensive Guide.* Portland, Oregon: Timber Press.

Mathew, B. 1989. *Hellebores.* Woking: Alpine Garden Society.

Rice, G. & Strangman, E. 1993. *The Gardener's Guide to Growing Hellebores.* Newton Abbot, Devon: David & Charles.

Hemerocallis

Baxter, G.J. (comp.). American Daylily Society Registry of Daylily Cultivars. Jan 2010. www.daylilies.org

Herbs

Phillips, R. & Foy, N. 1990. *Herbs.* London: Pan Books Ltd.

Heuchera and × Heucherella

Heims, D. & Ware, G. 2005. *Heucheras and Heucherellas: Coral Bells and Foamy Bells.* Portland, Oregon: Timber Press.

Hibiscus

Noble, C. Apr 2007. Australian Hibiscus Society Database Register. www.australianhibiscus.com/

Hosta

Hosta Library. Aug 2006. www.hostalibrary.org

Grenfell, D. & Shadrack, M. 2004. *The Color Encyclopedia of Hostas.* Portland, Oregon: Timber Press.

Schmid, W.G. 1991. *The Genus Hosta.* London: Batsford.

Hyacinthaceae

Dashwood, M. & Mathew, B. 2006. *Hyacinthaceae – little blue bulbs: RHS Bulletin No 11.* Wisley, Surrey: RHS. www.rhs.org.uk/Plants/RHS-Publications/Plant_bulletins

Mathew, B. 2005. *Hardy Hyacinthaceae* Pt 1: *Muscari. The Plantsman* 4(1):40-53.

Mathew, B. 2005. *Hardy Hyacinthaceae* Pt 2: *Scilla, Chionodoxa* and × *Chinoscilla. The Plantsman* 4(2):110-121.

Hydrangea

Dirr, M.A. 2004. *Hydrangeas for American Gardens.* Portland, Oregon: Timber Press.

Haworth-Booth, M. 1975. *The Hydrangeas.* London: Garden Book Club.

Van Gelderen, C.J. & Van Gelderen, D.M. 2004. *Encyclopedia of Hydrangeas.* Portland, Oregon: Timber Press.

Hypericum

Lancaster, R. & Robson, N. 1997. Focus on Plants: Bowls of Beauty. *The Garden* (RHS) 122(8):566-571.

Ilex

Bailes, C. 2006. *Hollies for Gardeners.* Portland, Oregon: Timber Press.

Dudley, T.R. & Eisenbeiss, G.K. 1973 & 1992. *International Checklist of Cultivated Ilex.* Pt 1 *Ilex opaca* (1973), Pt 2 *Ilex crenata* (1992). Washington DC: United States Dept of Agriculture.

Galle, F.C. 1997. *Hollies: the Genus Ilex.* Portland, Oregon: Timber Press.

Impatiens

Morgan, R.J. 2007. *Impatiens: The Vibrant World of Busy Lizzies, Balsams and Touch-me-nots.* Portland, Oregon: Timber Press.

Iris

Austin, C. 2005. *Irises: A Gardener's Encyclopedia.* Oregon:Timber Press.

Hoog, M.H. 1980. Bulbous Irises . *The Plantsman* 2(3):141-64.

Keppel, K. (ed.) 2001. *Iris Check List of Registered Cultivar Names 1990-1999.* Hannibal, New York: the American Iris Society.

Mathew, B. 1981. *The Iris.* London: Batsford.

Mathew, B. 1993. The Spuria Irises. *The Plantsman* 15(1):14-25.

Service, N. 1990. *Iris unguicularis. The Plantsman* 12(1):1-9.

Stebbings, G. 1997. *The Gardener's Guide to Growing Iris.* Newton Abbot: David & Charles.

The Species Group of the British Iris Society, (ed.). 1997. *A Guide to Species Irises.* Their Identification and Cultivation. Cambridge: Cambridge University Press.

Jovibarba see under ***Sempervivum***

Kalmia

Jaynes, R.A. 1997. *Kalmia. Mountain Laurel and Related Species.* Portland, Oregon: Timber Press.

Kniphofia

Grant-Downton, R. 1997. Notes on *Kniphofia thomsonii* in Cultivation and in the Wild. *The New Plantsman* 4(3):148-156.

Taylor, J. 1985. *Kniphofia* – a Survey. *The Plantsman* 7(3):129-160.

Kohleria

Dates, J.D. (ed.) & Batcheller, F.N. (comp.). 1985. *The Gesneriad Register 1985. Check List of Names with Descriptions of Cultivated Plants in the Genus Kohleria.* Lincoln Acres, California: American Gloxinia and Gesneriad Society, Inc.

Lachenalia

Duncan, G.D. 1988. *The Lachenalia Hand Book.* Kirstenbosch, South Africa: National Botanic Gardens.

Lantana

Howard, R.A. 1969. A Check List of Names Used in the Genus *Lantana. Arnoldia.* 29(11):73-109.

Lathyrus

Norton, S. 1996. *Lathyrus. Cousins of Sweet Pea.* Surrey: NCCPG.

Lavandula

Upson, T. & Andrews, S. 2004. *The Genus Lavandula.* Kew: Royal Botanic Garden.

Legumes

ILDIS. International Legume Database and Information Service. Jan 2010. Version 10.01. www.ildis.org/LegumeWeb

Leptospermum

Check List of *Leptospermum* Cultivars. 1963. *J. Roy. New Zealand Inst. Hort.* 5(5):224-30.

Dawson, M. 1997. A History of *Leptospermum scoparium* in Cultivation – Discoveries from the Wild. *The New Plantsman* 4(1):51-59.

Dawson, M. 1997. A History of *Leptospermum scoparium* in Cultivation – Garden Selections. *The New Plantsman* 4(2):67-78.

Lewisia

Davidson, B.L.R. 2000. *Lewisias.* Portland, Oregon: Timber Press.

Elliott, R. 1978. *Lewisias.* Woking: Alpine Garden Society.

Mathew, B. 1989. *The Genus Lewisia.* Bromley, Kent: Christopher Helm.

Liliaceae sensu lato

Mathew, B. 1989. Splitting the *Liliaceae. The Plantsman* 11(2):89-105.

Lilium

Leslie, A.C. *The International Lily Register 1982-2002.* (4th ed. & 1st supp.). London: RHS.

1st supp. 2008. www.rhs.org.uk/Plants/RHS-Publications/Plant_bulletins

Online Lily Register. Jan 2010. www.lilyregister.com

Lonicera

Blahník, Z. 2006. *Lonicera* Cultivar Names: The First World List. *Acta Pruhoniciana* 81:59-64.

Magnolia

Callaway, D.J. Sep 2001. Magnolia Cultivar Checklist. www.magnoliasociety.org

Frodin, D.G. & Govaerts, R. 1996. *World Checklist and Bibliography of Magnoliaceae.* Kew: Royal Botanic Garden.

Maianthemum

Cubey, J.J. 2005 *The Incorporation of Smilacina within Maianthemum. The Plantsman* N.S.4(4).

Malus

Crawford, M. 1994. *Directory of Apple Cultivars.* Devon: Agroforestry Research Trust.

Fiala, J.L. 1994. *Flowering Crabapples.* The genus *Malus.* Portland, Oregon: Timber Press.

Rouèche, A. Oct 2007. Les Crets Fruits et Pomologie. www.pomologie.com

Smith, M.W.G. 1971. *National Apple Register of the United Kingdom*. London: MAFF

Spiers, V. 1996. *Burcombes, Queenies and Colloggetts.* St Dominic, Cornwall: West Brendon.

Meconopsis

Grey-Wilson, C. 1992. A Survey of the Genus *Meconopsis* in Cultivation. *The Plantsman* 14(1): 1-33.

Grey-Wilson, C. 2002. The True Identity of *Meconopsis napaulensis. Bot. Mag.* 23(2):176-209.

Meconopsis Group website. Jan 2010. www.meconopsis.org

Stevens, E. & Brickell, C. 2001. Problems with the Big Perennial Poppies. *The New Plantsman* 8(1):48-61.

Stevens, E. 2001. Further Observations on the Big Perennial Blue Poppies. *The New Plantsman* 8(2):105-111.

Miscanthus

Jones, L. 2004. Miscanthus: RHS Bulletin No 7. Wisley, Surrey: RHS. www.rhs.org.uk/Plants/RHS-Publications/Plant_bulletins

Moraea

Goldblatt, P. 1986. *The Moraeas of Southern Africa.* Kirstenbosch, South Africa: National Botanic Gardens.

Musa

Banana and Plantain Section of Biodiversity International 2001. http://bananas.bioversityinternational.org

INIBAP *Musa* Germplasm Information System. Jan 2010. www.crop-diversity.org/banana

Narcissus

Blanchard, J.W. 1990. *Narcissus – A Guide to Wild Daffodils.* Woking, Surrey: Alpine Garden Society.

Kington, S. (comp.). 2008. The International Daffodil Register and Classified List 2008 (4th ed. & Supps 1-2, 2007-2009). London: RHS. http://apps.rhs.org.uk/horticulturaldatabase/daffodilregister.asp

Nematanthus

Arnold, P. 1978. *The Gesneriad Register 1978.* Check List of *Nematanthus.* American Gloxinia and Gesneriad Society, Inc.

Nerium

Pagen, F.J.J. 1987. *Oleanders. Nerium L. and the Oleander Cultivars.* Wageningen, The Netherlands: Agricultural University Wageningen.

Nymphaea

Knotts, K. & Knotts, B. Victoria Adventure Website. Checklist of Waterlily Cultivars. Jan 2010. www.victoria-adventure.org

Orchidaceae

Shaw, J.M.H. Jan 2010. The International Orchid Register. http://apps.rhs.org.uk/horticulturaldatabase/orchidregister.asp

Origanum

Paton, A. 1994. Three Membranous-bracted Species of *Origanum. Kew Mag.* 11(3):109-117.

White, S. 1998. *Origanum. The Herb Marjoram and its Relatives.* Surrey: NCCPG.

Paeonia

HelpMeFind Peonies. Jan 2010. www.helpmefind.com/peony/index.php

Jakubowski, R. American Peony Society Peony Checklist. www.americanpeonysociety.org

Jakubowski, R. 2008. *Peonies 1997-2007. Registered Peony Cultivars, with a Checklist of Peony Names, References and Originators.* Missouri: American Peony Society.

Osti, G.L. 1999. *The Book of Tree Peonies.* Turin: Umberto Allemandi.

Wang, L., et al. 1998. *Chinese Tree Peony.* Beijing: China Forestry Publishing House.

Papaver

Grey-Wilson, C. 1998. Oriental Glories. *The Garden* (RHS) 123(5):320-325.

Papaveraceae

Grey-Wilson, C. 2000. *Poppies. The Poppy Family in the Wild and in Cultivation.* London: Batsford.

Tebbitt, M. Liden, M. Zetterlund, H. 2008. *Bleeding Hearts, Corydalis and their Relatives.* Portland, Oregon: Timber Press

Passiflora

King, L.A. Jan 2008. Passiflora online passion flower cultivar register. www.passionflow.co.uk

Pelargonium

Abbott, P.G. 1994. *A Guide to Scented Geraniaceae.* Angmering, West Sussex: Hill Publicity Services.

Anon. 1978. *A Checklist and Register of Pelargonium Cultivar Names.* Pt 1 A-B. Australian Pelargonium Society.

Anon. 1985. *A Checklist and Register of Pelargonium Cultivar Names.* Pt 2: C-F. Australian Pelargonium Society.

Bagust, H. 1988. *Miniature and Dwarf Geraniums.* London: Christopher Helm.

Clifford, D. 1958. *Pelargoniums.* London: Blandford Press.

Clifton, R. 1999. *Geranium Family Species Checklist, Pt 4: Pelargonium.* The Geraniaceae Group.

Complete Copy of the Spalding Pelargonium Checklist. (Unpublished). USA.

Key, H. 2000. *1001 Pelargoniums.* London: Batsford.

Miller, D. 1996. *Pelargonium.* A Gardener's Guide to the Species and Cultivars and Hybrids. London: Batsford.

Pelargonium Palette: The Geranium and Pelargonium Society of Sydney Incorporated. Varieties – Alphabetical List. Jan 2010. www.elj.com/geranium

Van der Walt, J.J.A., et al. 1977. *Pelargoniums of South Africa.* (1-3). Kirstenbosch, South Africa: National Botanic Gardens.

Penstemon
Lindgren, D.T. & Davenport, B. 1992. List and description of named cultivars in the genus *Penstemon* (1992). University of Nebraska.
Nold, R. 1999. *Penstemons.* Portland, Oregon: Timber Press.
Way, D. & James, P. 1998. *The Gardener's Guide to Growing Penstemons.* Newton Abbott, Devon: David & Charles.
Way, D. 2006. *Penstemons.* Pershore, Worcs.: Hardy Plant Society.
Phlomis
Mann Taylor, J. 1998. *Phlomis: The Neglected Genus.* Wisley: NCCPG.
Phlox
Harmer, J. & Elliott, J. 2001. *Phlox.* Pershore, Worcs.: Hardy Plant Society.
Stebbings, G. 1999. Simply Charming. *The Garden* (RHS) 124(7):518-521.
Wherry, E.T. 1955. *The Genus Phlox.* Philadelphia, Pennsylvania: Morris Arboretum.
Phormium
Heenan, P.B. 1991. *Checklist of Phormium Cultivars.* Royal New Zealand Institute of Horticulture.
McBride-Whitehead, V. 1998. Phormiums of the Future. *The Garden* (RHS) 123(1):42-45.
Pieris
Bond, J. 1982. *Pieris* – a Survey. *The Plantsman* 4(2):65-75.
Wagenknecht, B.L. 1961. Registration Lists of Cultivar Names in the Genus *Pieris* D. Don. *Arnoldia (Jamaica Plain)* 21(8):47-50.
Pittosporum
Miller, D.M. 2006. RHS Plant Assessments: *Pittosporum tenuifolium* hybrids & cultivars. www.rhs.org.uk/Plants/RHS-Publications/Plant-bulletins
Plectranthus
Addink, Wouter. Jan 2010. Coleus Finder. http://coleusfinder.org
Miller, D. & Morgan, N. 2000. Focus on Plants: A New Leaf. *The Garden* (RHS) 125(11):842-845.
Shaw, J.M.H. 1999. Notes on the Identity of Swedish Ivy and Other Cultivated *Plectranthus. The New Plantsman* 6(2):71-74.
Van Jaarsveld, E.J. 2006. *South African Plectranthus.* Vlaeberg, South Africa: Fernwood Press.
Pleione
Cribb, P. & Butterfield, I. 1999. *The Genus Pleione.* (2nd ed.). Kew: Royal Botanic Gardens.
Shaw, J.M.H. (comp.). Oct 2002. Provisional List of *Pleione* Cultivars. RHS.
***Poaceae* (*Gramineae*, grasses)**
Clayton, W.D., Harman, K.T. & Williamson, H. Jan 2010. GrassBase – The Online World Grass Flora. www.kew.org/data/grasses-syn
Clayton, W.D. & Renvoize, S.A. 1986. *Genera Graminum.* Grasses of the World. London: HMSO.
Darke, R. 2007. *Encyclopedia of Grasses for Livable Landscapes.* Portland, Oregon: Timber Press.
Govaerts, R. & Simpson, D.A. 2007 *World Checklist of Cyperaceae: Sedges.* Richmond, Surrey: RBG Kew
Grounds, R. 1998. *The Plantfinder's Guide to Ornamental Grasses.* Newton Abott, Devon: David & Charles.
Wood, T. 2002. *Garden Grasses, Rushes and Sedges.* (3rd ed.). Abingdon, Oxon: John Wood.
Polemonium
Nichol-Brown, D. 2000. *Polemonium.* Wisley: NCCPG.
Potentilla
Davidson, C.G., Enns, R.J. & Gobin, S. 1994. *A Checklist of Potentilla fruticosa: the Shrubby Potentillas.* Morden, Manitoba: Agriculture & Agri-Food Canada Research Centre. Data also on Plant Finder Reference Library professional version CD-ROM 1999/2000.
Miller, D.M. 2002. *Shrubby Potentilla: RHS Bulletin No 1.* Wisley, Surrey: RHS. www.rhs.org.uk/Plants/RHS-Publications/Plant-bulletins
Primula
Richards, J. 2002 (2nd ed.). *Primula.* London: Batsford.
Primula allionii
Archdale, B. & Richards, D. 1997. *Primula allionii Forms and Hybrids.* National Auricula & Primula Society, Midland & West Section.
Primula auricula hort.
Baker, G. *Double Auriculas.* National Auricula & Primula Society, Midland & West Section.
Baker, G. & Ward, P. 1995. *Auriculas.* London: Batsford.
Guest, A. 2009. *The Auricula History, Cultivation and Varieties.* Woodbridge, Suffolk: Garden Art Press
Hawkes, A. 1995. Striped Auriculas. National Auricula & Primula Society, Midland & West Section.
Nicholle, G. 1996. *Border Auriculas.* National Auricula & Primula Society, Midland & West Section.
Robinson, M.A. 2000. *Auriculas for Everyone.* How to Grow and Show Perfect Plants. Lewes, Sussex: Guild of Master Craftsmen Publications.
Telford, D. 1993. *Alpine Auriculas.* National Auricula & Primula Society, Midland & West Section.
Ward, P. 1991. *Show Auriculas.* National Auricula & Primula Society, Midland & West Section.
Proteaceae
International *Proteaceae* Register. July 2002. (7th ed.).
Rebelo, T. 1995. *Proteas.* A Field Guide to the Proteas of Southern Africa. Vlaeberg: Fernwood Press/National Botanical Institute.
Prunus
Crawford, M. 1996. *Plums.* Dartington, Devon: Agroforestry Research Trust.
Crawford, M. 1997. *Cherries: Production and Culture.* Dartington, Devon: Agroforestry Research Trust.

Jacobsen, A.L. 1992. *Purpleleaf Plums.* Portland, Oregon: Timber Press.

Jefferson, R.M. & Wain, K.K. 1984. *The Nomenclature of Cultivated Flowering Cherries (Prunus).* The Sato-Zakura Group. Washington DC: USDA.

Kuitert, W. 1999. *Japanese Flowering Cherries.* Portland, Oregon: Timber Press.

Pulmonaria

Bennett, M. 2003. *Pulmonarias and the borage family.* London: B.T. Batsford.

Hewitt, J. 1994. *Pulmonarias.* Pershore, Worcs.: Hardy Plant Society.

Hewitt, J. 1999. Well Spotted. *The Garden* (RHS) 124(2):98-103.

Pyracantha

Egolf, D.R. & Andrick, A.O. 1995. *A Checklist of Pyracantha Cultivars.* Washington DC: Agricultural Research Service.

Pyrus

Crawford, M. 1996. *Directory of Pear Cultivars.* Totnes, Devon: Agroforestry Research Institute.

Smith, M.W.G. 1976. *Catalogue of the British Pear.* Faversham, Kent: MAFF.

Quercus

Miller, H.A. & Lamb, S.H. 1985. *Oaks of North America.* Happy Camp, California: Naturegraph Publishers.

Mitchell, A. 1994. The Lucombe Oaks. *The Plantsman* 15(4):216-224.

Rhododendron

Argent, G., Fairweather, C. & Walter, K. 1996. *Accepted Names in Rhododendron section Vireya.* Edinburgh: Royal Botanic Garden.

Argent, G., Bond, J., Chamberlain, D., Cox, P. & Hardy, A. 1997. *The Rhododendron Handbook 1998.* Rhododendron Species in Cultivation. London: RHS.

Chamberlain, D.F. & Rae, S.J. 1990. A Revision of *Rhododendron* IV. Subgenus *Tsutsusi. Edinburgh J. Bot.* 47(2).

Chamberlain, D.F. 1982. A Revision of *Rhododendron* II. Subgenus *Hymenanthes. Notes Roy. Bot. Gard. Edinburgh* 39(2).

Chamberlain, D., Hyam, R., Argent, G., Fairweather, G. & Walter, K.S. 1996. *The Genus Rhododendron.* Edinburgh:Royal Botanic Garden.

Cullen, J. 1980. A Revision of *Rhododendron* I. Subgenus *Rhododendron* sections *Rhododendron* and *Pogonanthum. Notes Roy. Bot. Gard. Edinburgh* 39(1).

Davidian, H.H. 1982-1992 *The Rhododendron Species* (Vols 1-4). London: Batsford.

Galle, F.C. 1985. *Azaleas.* Portland, Oregon: Timber Press.

Leslie, A. C. (comp.). 1980. *The Rhododendron Handbook 1980.* London: RHS.

Leslie, A.C. (comp.) 2004. *The International Rhododendron Register and Checklist* (2nd ed. & supps. 1-5). London: RHS Supp. 1-5, 2006-2008. www.rhs.org.uk/Plants/RHS-Publications/Plant-registers

Tamura, T. (ed.). 1989. *Azaleas in Kurume.* Kurume, Japan: International Azalea Festival '89.

Ribes

Crawford, M. 1997. *Currants and Gooseberries: Production and Culture.* Dartington, Devon: Agroforestry Research Trust.

Rosa

Beales, P., Cairns, T., et al. 1998. *Botanica's Rose: The Encyclopedia of Roses.* Hoo, Kent: Grange Books.

Cairns, T. (ed.). 2000. *Modern Roses XI. The World Encyclopedia of Roses.* London: Academic Press.

Dickerson, B.C. 1999. *The Old Rose Advisor.* Portland, Oregon: Timber Press.

Haw, S.G. 1996. Notes on Some Chinese and Himalayan Rose Species of Section *Pimpinellifoliae. The New Plantsman* 3(3):143-146.

HelpMeFind Roses. Jan 2010. www.helpmefind.com

McCann, S. 1985. *Miniature Roses.* Newton Abbot, Devon: David & Charles.

Quest-Ritson, C. 2003. *Climbing Roses of the World.* Portland, Oregon: Timber Press.

Quest-Ritson, C. & Quest-Ritson, B. 2003. *The Royal Horticultural Society Encyclopedia of Roses: The Definitive A-Z Guide.* London: Dorling Kindersley.

Thomas, G.S. 1995. *The Graham Stuart Thomas Rose Book.* London: John Murray.

Verrier, S. 1996. *Rosa Gallica.* Balmain, Australia: Florilegium.

Roscoea

Cowley, J. 2007. *The Genus Roscoea.* Kew Publishing.

Rosularia

Eggli, U. 1988. A Monographic Study of the Genus *Rosularia. Bradleya* (Supp.) 6:1-118.

Saintpaulia

Goodship, G. 1987. *Saintpaulia Variety List* (Supp.). Slough, Bucks: Saintpaulia & Houseplant Society.

Moore, H.E. 1957. *African Violets, Gloxinias and Their Relatives.* A Guide to the Cultivated Gesneriads. New York: Macmillan.

Salix

Newsholme, C. 1992. *Willows.* The Genus *Salix.* London: Batsford.

Stott, K.G. 1971 *Willows for Amenity, Windbreaks and Other Uses.* Checklist of the Long Ashton Collection of Willows, with Notes on their Suitability for Various Purposes. Long Ashton Research Station: University of Bristol.

Salvia

Clebsch, B. 2003. *A Book of Salvias.* (2nd ed.). Portland, Oregon: Timber Press.

Compton, J. 1994. Mexican Salvias in Cultivation. *The Plantsman* 15(4):193-215.

Middleton, R. *Robin's Salvias.* Jan 2010. www.robinssalvias.com

Saxifraga

Bland, B. 2000. *Silver Saxifrages.* Pershore, Worcs.: Alpine Garden Society.

Dashwood, M. & Bland, B. 2005. Silver Saxifrages: RHS Bulletin No 9. Wisley, Surrey: RHS. www.rhs.org.uk/Plants/RHS-Publications/Plant-bulletins

McGregor, M. Jan 2010. Saxbase. Saxifrage Society. www.saxifraga.org

McGregor, M. 1995. *Saxifrages: The Complete Cultivars & Hybrids: International Register of Saxifrages.* (2nd ed.). Driffield, E. Yorks: Saxifrage Society.

Webb, D.A. & Gornall, R.J. 1989. *Saxifrages of Europe.* Bromley, Kent: Christopher Helm.

Sedum

Evans, R.L. 1983. *Handbook of Cultivated Sedums.* Motcombe, Dorset: Ivory Head Press.

Lord, T. 2006. *Sedum* up for assessment. *The Plantsman* 5(4):244-252.

Stephenson, R. 1994. *Sedum.* The Cultivated Stonecrops. Portland, Oregon: Timber Press.

Sempervivum

Diehm, H. Jan 2010. www.semperhorst.de

Miklánek, M. 2002. *The List of Cultivars: Sempervivum and Jovibarba v. 7.01.* Pieštany, Slovakia: M. Miklánek (private distribution).

Miklánek, M. 2000. *List of Cultivars: Sempervivum and Jovibarba* v. 15.1. http://miklanek.tripod.com

Sinningia

Dates, J.D. 1988. *The Gesneriad Register 1988. Check List of Names with Descriptions of Cultivated Plants in the Genus Sinningia.* Galesburg, Illinois: American Gloxinia and Gesneriad Society, Inc.

Solenostemon

Pedley, W.K. & Pedley, R. 1974. *Coleus – A Guide to Cultivation and Identification.* Edinburgh: Bartholemew.

Sorbus

McAllister, H. 2005. *The Genus Sorbus: Mountain Ash and Other Rowans.* Kew: Royal Botanical Gardens.

Snyers d'Attenhoven, C. 1999. *Sorbus* Lombarts hybrids *Belgische Dendrologie*: 76-81. Belgium.

Wright, D. 1981. Sorbus – a Gardener's Evaluation. *The Plantsman* 3(2):65-98.

Spiraea

Miller, D.M. 2003. *Spiraea japonica with coloured leaves: RHS Bulletin No 4.* Wisley, Surrey: Royal Horticultural Society. www.rhs.org.uk/Plants/RHS-Publications/Plant-bulletins

Streptocarpus

Arnold, P. 1979. *The Gesneriad Register 1979: Check List of Streptocarpus.* Binghamton, New York: American Gloxinia & Gesneriad.

Dibleys Nurseries Online Catalogue. Jan 2010. www.dibleys.com.

Succulents

Eggli, U. (ed.) 2002. *Illustrated Handbook of Succulent Plants.* Heidelberg, Germany: Springer-Verlag.

Eggli, U. & Taylor, N. 1994. *List of Names of Succulent Plants other than Cacti Published 1950-92.* Kew: Royal Botanic Gardens.

Grantham, K. & Klaassen, P. 1999. *The Plantfinder's Guide to Cacti and Other Succulents.* Newton Abbot, Devon: David & Charles.

Jacobsen, H. 1973. *Lexicon of Succulent Plants.* London: Blandford.

Syringa

Vrugtman, F. 2000. *International Register of Cultivar Names in the Genus Syringa L. (Oleaceae).* (Contribution No 91). Hamilton, Canada: Royal Botanic Gardens.

Thymus

Easter, M. 2009. *International Thymus Register and Checklist.* UK: Owl Prints.

Tiliaceae

Wild, H. 1984. *Flora of Southern Africa 21 (1: Tiliaceae).* Pretoria: Botanical Research Institute, Dept of Agriculture.

Tillandsia

Kiff, L.F. 1991. *A Distributional Checklist of the Genus Tillandsia.* Encino, California: Botanical Diversions.

Trillium

Case, F.W.J. & Case, R.B. 1997. *Trilliums.* Portland, Oregon: Timber Press.

Jacobs, D.L. & Jacobs, R.L. 1997. *American Treasures.* Trilliums in Woodland Garden. Decatur, Georgia: Eco-Gardens.

Tulipa

KAVB Online registration pages. http://kavb.back2p.soft-orange.com

Ulmus

Green, P.S. 1964. Registratration of Cultivar Names in *Ulmus. Arnoldia (Jamaica Plain)* 24:41-80.

Vaccinium

Trehane, J. 2004. *Blueberries, Cranberries and Other Vacciniums.* Portland, Oregon: Timber Press.

Vegetables

Official Journal of the European Communities. Oct 2007. Common catalogue of varieties of agricultural plant species: consolidated version. http://ec.europa.eu/food

Viburnum

Dirr, M.A. 2007. *Viburnums: Flowering Shrubs for Every Season.* Portland, Oregon: Timber Press.

Viola

Coombes, R.E. 2003. *Violets.* (2nd ed.). London: Batsford.

Fuller, R. 1990. *Pansies, Violas & Violettas.* The Complete Guide. Marlborough: The Crowood Press.

Perfect, E.J. 1996. *Armand Millet and his Violets.* High Wycombe: Park Farm Press.

Robinson, P.M. & Snocken, J. 2003. Checklist of the Cultivated Forms of the Genus Viola including the Register of Cultivars. American Violet Society. http://americanvioletsociety.org

Zambra, G.L. 1950. *Violets for Garden and Market.* (2nd ed.). London: Collingridge.

Vitis
Pearkes, G. 1989. *Vine Growing in Britain.* London: Dent.
Robinson, J. 1989. *Vines, Grapes and Wines.* London: Mitchell Beazley.
Watsonia
Goldblatt, P. 1989. *The Genus Watsonia.* A Systematic Monograph. South Africa: National Botanic Gardens.
Weigela
Howard, R.A. 1965. A Checklist of Cultivar Names in *Weigela. Arnoldia (Jamaica Plain)* 25:49-69.
Wisteria
Valder, P. 1995. *Wisterias.* A Comprehensive Guide. Balmain, Australia: Florilegium.
Yucca
Smith, C. 2004. *Yuccas: Giants among the Lilies.* NCCPG.
Zauschneria
Raven, P.H. 1977. Generic and Sectional Delimitation in *Onagraceae,* Tribe *Epilobieae. Ann. Missouri Bot. Gard.* 63(2):326-340.
Robinson, A. 2000. Focus on Plants: Piping Hot (*Zauschneria* Cultivars). *The Garden* (RHS) 125(9):698-699.
Zingiberaceae
Branney, T.M.E. 2005. *Hardy Gingers. Including Hedychium, Roscoea and Zingiber.* Cambridge: Timber Press.

INTERNATIONAL PLANT FINDERS

NEW ZEALAND

Gaddum, Meg (Comp.) *New Zealand Plant Finder* (2011). Lists over 50,200 plants and seeds and where to buy them. NZs largest list of plant names taken from New Zealand nursery catalogues, with data from over 180 New Zealand nurseries. Available online only at www.plantfinder.co.nz.

UNITED KINGDOM

Pawsey. Angela (ed.) *Find That Rose!* 2011-2012 (29th ed.) (2011). Lists over 3,600 varieties available in the U.K together with basic type, colour and fragrance, including all forms of standard roses. New varieties are highlighted and cross-referenced where applicable to alternative selling names. Full details of around 50 growers/outlets, many offering mail order for both bare-root and containerised plants. Also includes useful information on how to find a rose with a particular Christian name or to celebrate a special event. Includes information on charity roses and on where to see roses in bloom. To order a copy send payment of £3.85 made out to *Find That Rose!* to: 303 Mile End Road, Colchester, Essex CO4 5EA. For further information, which will include price of a CDROM version, please send sae. Visit the website on www.findthatrose.net

Pawsey. Angela, *What's in a Name* (2008). Gives the origin of the names of over 500 rose varieties. This is a companion booklet to *Find That Rose!* The simple 40 page booklet includes many roses linked with charities. Gives the background to how and why many roses got their names. In addition to the original booklet you receive updates printed in the 27th, 28th & 29th ed. of *Find That Rose!* To order send payment of £2.00 made out to *Find That Rose!* to: Angela Pawsey, 303 Mile End Road, Colchester CO4 5EA

Nurseries

The following nurseries between them stock an unrivalled choice of plants. Before making a visit, please remember to check with the nursery that the plant you seek is currently available.

Nursery Codes and Symbols

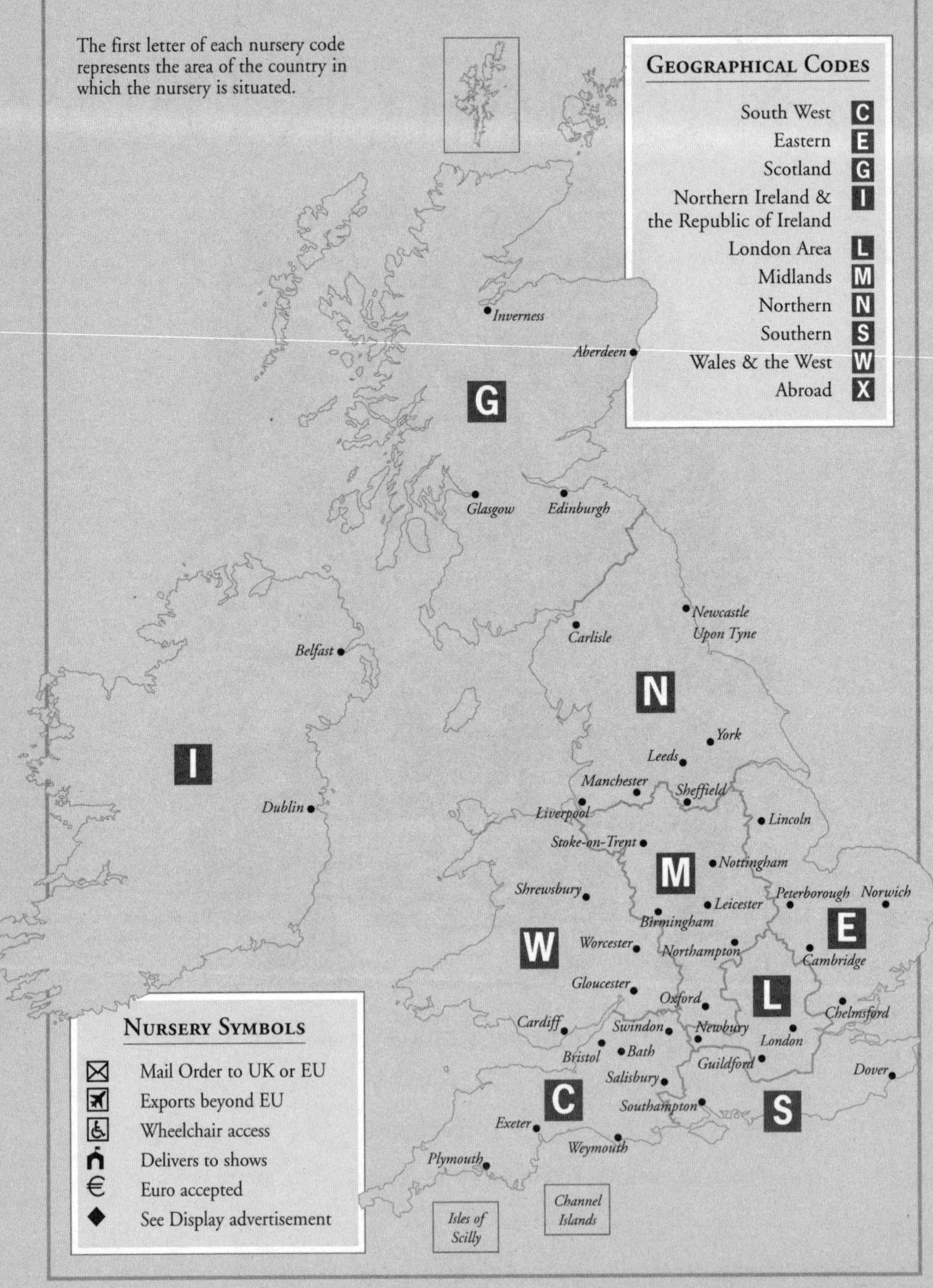

USING THE THREE NURSERY LISTINGS

Your main reference from the Plant Directory is the Nursery Details by Code listing, which includes all relevant information for each nursery in order of nursery code. The Nursery Index by Name is an alphabetical list for those who know a nursery's name but not its code and wish to check its details in the main list. The Specialist Nurseries index is to aid those searching for a particular plant group.

1 NURSERY DETAILS BY CODE

Once you have found your plant in the Plant Directory, turn to this list to find out the name, address, opening times and other details of the nurseries whose codes accompany the plant.

KEY
⊠ Mail order to UK or EU
Exports beyond EU
Wheelchair access
Delivers to shows
€ Euro accepted
◆ See Display advertisement

WHil **HILLVIEW HARDY PLANTS** ⊠ € — *Refer to the box at the base of each right-hand page for a key to the symbols*

A geographical code is followed by three letters reflecting the nursery's name

(off B4176), Worfield, Nr Bridgnorth,
Shropshire WV15 5NT
Ⓣ (01746) 716454
Ⓜ 07974 391608
Ⓕ (01746) 716454
Ⓔ hillview@themutual.net
Ⓦ www.hillviewhardyplants.com
Contact: Ingrid, John & Sarah Millington
Opening Times: 0900-1700 Mon-Sat Mar-mid Oct. At other times, please phone first.
Min Mail Order UK: £10.00 + p&p
Min Mail Order EU: £10.00 + p&p
Cat. Cost: 4 × 2nd class.
Credit Cards: All major credit/debit cards
Specialities: Choice herbaceous perennials incl. *Acanthus* & *Acanthaceae*, *Albuca*, *Aquilegia*, auricula, *Primula*, *Canna*, *Crocosmia*, *Eucomis*, *Ixia*, South African bulbs. Nat. Collections of *Acanthus* & *Albuca*. — *A brief summary of the plants available*
Notes: Also sells wholesale. — *Other information about the nursery*
Map Ref: W, B4 **OS Grid Ref:** SO772969

The map letter is followed by the map square in which the nursery is located

The Ordnance Survey national grid reference for use with OS maps

2 NURSERY INDEX BY NAME

If you seek a particular nursery, look it up in this alphabetical index. Note its code and turn to the Nursery Details by Code list for full information.

Highdown Nursery	SHDw
Hill House Nursery & Gardens	CHll
Hillier Garden Centres	SHil
Hillview Hardy Plants	WHil
Himalayan Garden Co., The	NHim
Himalayan Gardens Ltd.	GHim
Hoecroft Plants	EHoe
Holden Clough Nursery Ltd.	NHol

3 SPECIALIST NURSERIES

A list of 32 categories under which nurseries have classified themselves if they exclusively, or predominantly, supply this range of plants.

DROUGHT-TOLERANT PLANTS

ECGP, ECHA, EGRI, EHOE, ETOD, LLWP, MBPG, MPNT, NFIR, NHOY, NMRC, SALL, SDOW, SEND, SPHX, SPLB, SUSU, WFIB, WHIL, WPNN, XLUM, XSEN

How to Use the Nursery Listings

The details given for each nursery have been compiled from information supplied to us in answer to a questionnaire. In some cases, because of constraints of space, the entries have been slightly abbreviated.

Nurseries are not charged for their entries and inclusion in no way implies a value judgement.

Nursery Details by Code (*page 842*)

Each nursery is allocated a code, for example GPoy. The first letter of each code indicates the main area of the country in which the nursery is situated. In this example, G=Scotland. The remaining three letters reflect the nursery's name, in this case Poyntzfield Herb Nursery.

In this main listing the nurseries are given in alphabetical order of codes for quick reference from the Plant Directory. All of the nurseries' details, such as address, opening times, mail order service etc., will be found here.

Opening Times

Although opening times have been published as submitted and where applicable, **it is always advisable, especially if travelling a long distance, to check with the nursery first**. The initials NGS indicate that the nursery is open under the National Gardens Scheme.

Mail Order ⊠

Many nurseries provide a mail order service. **This is, however, often restricted to certain times of the year or to particular genera**. Please check the **Notes** section of each nursery's entry for any restrictions or special conditions.

In some cases, the mail order service extends to all members of the European Union. Where this is offered, the minimum charge to the EU will be noted in the Nursery entry.

Where '**No minimum charge**' (**Nmc**) is shown, please note that to send even one plant may involve the nursery in substantial postage and packing costs. Some nurseries may not be prepared to send tender or bulky plants.

Where a nursery offers a **mail order only** service, this will be noted under **Opening Times** in the nursery entry. Many nurseries also offer an online mail order facility.

Export ✈

Export refers to mail order beyond the European Union. Nurseries that are prepared to consider exporting are indicated. However, there is usually a substantial minimum charge and, in addition, all the costs of Phytosanitary Certificates and Customs have to be met by the purchaser.

Catalogue Cost

Some nurseries offer their catalogue free, or for a few stamps, but a large (at least A5) stamped addressed envelope is always appreciated as well. Overseas customers should use an equivalent number of International Reply Coupons (IRCs) in place of stamps.

Increasingly, nurseries are finding it more cost effective to produce catalogues on the Internet rather than printing them.

Wheelchair Access ♿

Nurseries are asked to indicate if their premises are suitable for wheelchair users. Where only partial access is indicated, this is noted in the **Notes** field and the nursery is not marked with the symbol.

The assessment of ease-of-access is entirely the responsibility of the individual nursery.

Specialities

Nurseries list here the plants or genera that they supply and any National Collections of plants they may hold. Please note that some nurseries may charge an entry fee to visit a National Collection. Always enquire before visiting.

Nurseries will also note here if they only have small quantities of individual plants available for sale or if they will propagate to order.

Notes

In this section, you will find notes on any restrictions to mail order or export; on limited wheelchair access; or the nursery site address, if this differs from the office address; together with any other non-horticultural information.

Delivery to Shows ⌂

Many nurseries will deliver pre-ordered plants to flower shows for collection by customers. These are indicated by a marquee symbol. Contact the nursery for details of shows they attend.

Payment in Euros €

A number of UK nurseries have indicated that they will accept payment in Euros. You should, however, check with the nursery concerned before making such a payment, as some will only accept cash and some only cheques, whilst others will expect the purchaser to pay bank charges.

Maps

If you wish to visit any of the nurseries you can find its approximate location on the relevant map (following p.945), unless the nursery has requested this is not shown. Nurseries are also encouraged to provide their Ordnance Survey national grid reference for use with OS publications such as the Land Ranger series.

Nursery Index by Name

For convenience, an alphabetical index of nurseries is included (*page 936*). This gives the names of all nurseries listed in the book in alphabetical order of nursery name together with their code.

Specialist Nurseries (*page 942*)

This list of nurseries is intended to help those with an interest in finding specialist categories of plant. Nurseries have been asked to classify themselves under one or more headings where this represents the type of plant they *predominantly* or *exclusively* have in stock. For example, if you wish to find a nursery specialising in ornamental grasses, look up 'Grasses' in the listing where you will find a list of nursery codes. Then turn to the Nursery Details by Code, for details of the nurseries.

Please note that not all nurseries shown here will have plants listed in the Plant Directory. This may be their choice or because the *RHS Plant Finder* does not list seeds or annuals and only terrestrial orchids and hardy cacti. For space reasons, it is rare to find a nursery's full catalogue listed in the Plant Directory.

In all cases, please ensure you ring to confirm the range available before embarking on a journey to the nursery.

The specialist plant groups listed in this edition are:

Acid-loving	Grasses
Alpines/rock	Hedging
Aquatics	Herbs
Bamboos	Marginal/bog
British wild flowers	Orchids
Bulbous plants	Organic
Cacti & succulents	Ornamental trees
Carnivorous	Palms
Chalk-loving	Peat-free
Climbers	Period plants
Coastal	Propagate to order
Conifers	Roses
Conservatory	Seed
Drought-tolerant	Specimen-sized
Ferns	Topiary
Fruit	Tropical

Perennials and shrubs have been omitted as these are considered to be too general and serviced by a great proportion of the nurseries.

Deleted Nurseries

Every year some nurseries ask to be removed from the book. This may be a temporary measure because they are moving, or it may be permanent due to closure, sale, retirement, or a change in the way in which they trade. Occasionally, nurseries are unable to meet the closing date and will re-enter the book in the following edition. Some nurseries simply do not reply and, as we have no current information on them, they are deleted.

Please, never use an old edition

NURSERY DETAILS BY CODE

Please note that all these nurseries are listed in alphabetical order by their code. All nurseries are listed in alphabetical order by their name in the **Nursery Index by Name** on page 936.

SOUTH WEST

CAbb ABBOTSBURY SUB-TROPICAL GARDENS ⊠ ♿
Abbotsbury, Nr Weymouth, Dorset DT3 4LA
Ⓣ (01305) 871344
Ⓕ (01305) 871344
Ⓔ info@abbotsburygardens.co.uk
Ⓦ www.abbotsburyplantsales.co.uk
Contact: David Sutton
Opening Times: 1000-1800 daily, mid Mar-1st Nov. 1000-1500, Nov-mid Mar.
Min Mail Order UK: Nmc
Cat. Cost: £2.00 + A4 sae.
Credit Cards: Access, Visa, MasterCard, Switch
Specialities: Less common & tender shrubs incl. palms, tree ferns, bamboos & plants from Australia, New Zealand & S. Africa.

CAbP ABBEY PLANTS ⊠ ♿
Chaffeymoor, Bourton, Gillingham, Dorset SP8 5BY
Ⓣ (01747) 840841
Contact: K Potts
Opening Times: 1000-1300 & 1400-1700 Wed-Sat Mar-Nov. Dec-Feb by appt.
Min Mail Order UK: Nmc
Cat. Cost: 2 × 2nd class.
Credit Cards: None
Specialities: Flowering trees & shrubs.
Map Ref: C, B4 **OS Grid Ref:** ST762304

CAby THE ABBEY NURSERY ♿
Forde Abbey, Chard, Somerset TA20 4LU
Ⓣ (01460) 220088
Ⓕ (01460) 220088
Ⓔ TheAbbeyNursery@btconnect.com
Contact: Peter Sims
Opening Times: 1000-1700 7 days, 1st Mar-31st Oct. Please phone first to check opening times in Mar.
Cat. Cost: None issued.
Credit Cards: All major credit/debit cards
Specialities: Hardy herbaceous perennials.
Map Ref: C, C4 **OS Grid Ref:** ST359052

CAgr AGROFORESTRY RESEARCH TRUST ⊠
46 Hunters Moon, Dartington, Totnes, Devon TQ9 6JT
Ⓕ (01803) 840776
Ⓔ mail@agroforestry.co.uk
Ⓦ www.agroforestry.co.uk
Contact: Martin Crawford
Opening Times: Not open. Mail order only.
Min Mail Order UK: Nmc
Min Mail Order EU: Nmc
Cat. Cost: 4 × 1st class.
Credit Cards: All major credit/debit cards
Specialities: Top & soft fruit, nut trees including *Castanea, Corylus, Juglans, Pinus*. Also seeds. Some plants in small quantities only.

CAni ANITA ALLEN ⊠
Shapcott Barton Estate, East Knowstone, South Molton, Devon EX36 4EE
Ⓣ (01398) 341664
Ⓕ (01398) 341664
Contact: Anita Allen
Opening Times: By appt. only. Garden open under NGS.
Min Mail Order UK: Nmc
Cat. Cost: 5 × 1st class & state which catalogue: Shasta daisies or *Buddleja*.
Credit Cards: None
Specialities: Nat. Collections of *Leucanthemum × superbum* & *Buddleja davidii* & hybrids, 70+ cvs. 80+ accurately named Shasta daisies, a few in very short supply. Also many hardy perennials.
Map Ref: C, B3 **OS Grid Ref:** SS846235

CArn ARNE HERBS ⊠ € ♿
Limeburn Nurseries, Limeburn Hill, Chew Magna, Bristol BS40 8QW
Ⓣ (01275) 333399

Ⓔ anthony@arneherbs.co.uk
Ⓦ www.arneherbs.co.uk
Contact: A Lyman-Dixon & Jenny Thomas
Opening Times: 1000-1600 most weekdays, prior telephone call advisable.
Min Mail Order UK: Nmc
Min Mail Order EU: Nmc
Cat. Cost: Detailed illustrated catalogue online or A4 sae for free non-descriptive plantlist. Separate Classical-early Renaissance (c.1520) list available.
Credit Cards: None
Specialities: Herbs, some very rare. North American, Mediterranean & UK wild flowers. Also plants for research, conservation projects & historical recreations.
Notes: Also sells wholesale.
Map Ref: C, A5 **OS Grid Ref:** ST563638

CAvo AVON BULBS ⊠ ⛺

Burnt House Farm, Mid-Lambrook, South Petherton, Somerset TA13 5HE
Ⓣ (01460) 242177 or 249060
Ⓕ (01460) 249025
Ⓔ info@avonbulbs.co.uk
Ⓦ www.avonbulbs.co.uk
Contact: C Ireland-Jones
Opening Times: Mail order only. Open Thu, Fri, Sat, mid-Sep to end Oct & mid-Feb to end Mar, for collection of pre-booked orders.
Min Mail Order UK: £10.00 + p&p
Min Mail Order EU: £20.00 + p&p
Cat. Cost: 4 × 2nd class.
Credit Cards: All major credit/debit cards
Specialities: Some special snowdrops are only available in small quantities.

CBar BARTERS PLANT CENTRE & NURSERY ♿

Chapmanslade, Westbury, Wiltshire BA13 4AL
Ⓣ (01373) 832694
Ⓕ (01373) 832677
Ⓔ plantcentre@barters.co.uk
Ⓦ www.barters.co.uk
Contact: Giles Hall
Opening Times: 0900-1700 Mon-Thu, 0900-1730 Fri & Sat, summer. 0900-1630 Mon-Thu, 0900-1700 Fri & Sat, winter. 1030-1630 Sun.
Cat. Cost: None issued.
Credit Cards: All, except American Express
Specialities: Wide range of shrubs. Ground cover, container trees, ferns, half-hardy perennials, grasses, herbaceous & climbers. Hedging, fruit trees, old fashioned roses & bare-root stock.
Notes: Also sells wholesale.

CBcs BURNCOOSE NURSERIES ⊠ ⛺ ♿

Gwennap, Redruth, Cornwall TR16 6BJ
Ⓣ (01209) 860316
Ⓕ (01209) 860011
Ⓔ burncoose@eclipse.co.uk
Ⓦ www.burncoose.co.uk
Contact: C H Williams
Opening Times: 0830-1700 Mon-Sat & 1100-1700 Sun.
Min Mail Order UK: Nmc
Min Mail Order EU: Individual quotations for EU sales.
Cat. Cost: Free.
Credit Cards: Visa, Switch, MasterCard, Maestro
Specialities: Extensive range of over 3500 ornamental trees & shrubs and herbaceous. Rare & unusual *Magnolia*, *Rhododendron*. Conservatory plants. 30 acre garden.
Notes: Also sells wholesale.
Map Ref: C, D1 **OS Grid Ref:** SW742395

CBct BARRACOTT PLANTS ⊠ ⛺ € ♿ ◆

Old Orchard, Calstock Road, Gunnislake, Cornwall PL18 9AA
Ⓣ (01822) 832234
Ⓜ 07811 207186
Ⓔ geoffandthelma@barracott.eclipse.co.uk
Ⓦ www.barracottplants.co.uk
Contact: Geoff & Thelma Turner
Opening Times: 0900-1700 Thu & Fri, Mar-end Sep. Other times by appt.
Min Mail Order UK: Nmc
Cat. Cost: Large 1st class.
Credit Cards: None
Specialities: Herbaceous plants: shade-loving, foliage & form. *Acanthus*, *Aspidistra*, *Astrantia*, *Bergenia*, *Convallaria*, *Disporum*, *Liriope*, *Maianthemum*, *Polygonatum*, *Roscoea*, *Trillium*, *Tricyrtis* & *Uvularia*.
Notes: Also sells wholesale.
Map Ref: C, C3 **OS Grid Ref:** SX436702

CBen BENNETTS WATER GARDENS ⊠ ♿

B3157 Chickerell Link Road, Weymouth, Dorset DT3 4AF
Ⓣ (01305) 785150
Ⓔ info@waterlily.co.uk
Ⓦ www.waterlily.co.uk
Contact: James Bennett
Opening Times: 1000-1700 Apr-Sep. Closed Sat.
Min Mail Order UK: Nmc

KEY
⊠ Mail order to UK or EU ⛺ Delivers to shows
✈ Exports beyond EU € Euro accepted
♿ Accessible by wheelchair ◆ See Display advertisement

C

Min Mail Order EU: Nmc
Cat. Cost: Sae for price list.
Credit Cards: Visa, Access, MasterCard, Switch
Specialities: Aquatic plants. Nat. Collection of *Nymphaea*.
Notes: Loose plants only by mail order. Potted plants available at nursery.
Map Ref: C, C5 **OS Grid Ref:** SY651797

CBgR **BEGGAR'S ROOST PLANTS** ⊠ €
Lilstock, Bridgwater, Somerset TA5 1SU
Ⓣ (01278) 741519
Ⓔ ro@lilstock.eclipse.co.uk
Ⓦ www.beggarsroostplants.co.uk
Contact: Rosemary FitzGerald
Opening Times: Not open. Mail order only.
Min Mail Order UK: £10.00
Min Mail Order EU: Nmc
Cat. Cost: 3 × large 2nd class.
Credit Cards: None
Specialities: *Hemerocallis* (incl. heritage) grown in British conditions. *Galanthus* (incl. West Country variants).
Notes: Mail order for specialities: *Crocosmia*, *Hemerocallis*, *Galanthus*, *Dahlia* (tubers), hardy *Nerine* (bulbs). Ask for lists.
Map Ref: C, B4 **OS Grid Ref:** ST168450

CBot **THE BOTANIC NURSERY** ⊠ ṅ €
Atworth, Nr Melksham, Wiltshire SN12 8NU
Ⓜ 07850 328756
Ⓕ (01225) 700953
Ⓔ botanicnursery@botanicguru.co.uk
Ⓦ www.botanicguru.co.uk
Contact: T. Baker
Opening Times: 1000-1700 Tue-Sat, Mar-Oct. Please avoid lunch time if possible.
Min Mail Order UK: £11.00 for 24hr carriage service. At cost for Royal Mail.
Cat. Cost: Online only.
Credit Cards: All major credit/debit cards
Specialities: Nursery propagates from large range of lime-tolerant plants in varying quantities, all peat free. Nat. Collection of *Digitalis*.
Notes: If travelling, please phone first to confirm specific plant availability. Ltd wheelchair access.
Map Ref: C, A5

CBre **BREGOVER PLANTS** ⊠ ṅ
Middlewood, North Hill, Nr Launceston, Cornwall PL15 7NN
Ⓣ (01566) 782661
Ⓔ bregoverplants@gmail.com
Contact: Jennifer Bousfield
Opening Times: 1100-1700 Wed, Mar-mid Oct and by appt.
Min Mail Order UK: Nmc
Min Mail Order EU: Nmc
Cat. Cost: 3 × 1st class. Plant list available as PDF download.
Credit Cards: None
Specialities: Unusual hardy perennials grown in small garden nursery. Available in small quantities only.
Notes: Mail order Oct-Mar only.
Map Ref: C, C2 **OS Grid Ref:** SX273752

CBro **BROADLEIGH GARDENS** ⊠ ṅ € ♿
Bishops Hull, Taunton, Somerset TA4 1AE
Ⓣ (01823) 286231
Ⓕ (01823) 323646
Ⓔ info@broadleighbulbs.co.uk
Ⓦ www.broadleighbulbs.co.uk
Contact: Lady Skelmersdale
Opening Times: 0900-1600 Mon-Fri for viewing only (charity donation). Orders collected if notice given.
Min Mail Order UK: Nmc
Min Mail Order EU: Nmc
Cat. Cost: 2 × 1st class.
Credit Cards: All major credit/debit cards
Specialities: Jan catalogue: bulbs in growth (*Galanthus*, *Cyclamen* etc.) & herbaceous woodland plants (trilliums, hellebores etc). Extensive list of *Agapanthus*. June catalogue: dwarf & unusual bulbs, *Iris* (DB & PC). Nat. Collection of Alec Grey hybrid daffodils.
Notes: Euro payment accepted as cash only.
Map Ref: C, B4 **OS Grid Ref:** ST195251

CBrP **BROOKLANDS PLANTS** ⊠ €
25 Treves Road, Dorchester, Dorset DT1 2HE
Ⓣ (01305) 265846
Ⓔ cycads@btinternet.com
Contact: Ian Watt
Opening Times: By appt. only for collection of plants.
Min Mail Order UK: £25.00 + p&p
Min Mail Order EU: £25.00 + p&p
Cat. Cost: 2 × 2nd class.
Credit Cards: None
Specialities: Cycad nursery specialising in the more cold-tolerant species of *Encephalartos*, *Dioon*, *Macrozamia* & *Cycas*. Also specialist in cold-tolerant palms as well as plants from New Zealand. Some species available in small quantities only.
Map Ref: C, C5 **OS Grid Ref:** SY682897

CBty **BENTLEY PLANTS** ⊠ ṅ € ♿
1 Bentley Wood Cottages, West Tytherley, Salisbury, Wiltshire SP5 1QB
Ⓣ (01794) 340775

Ⓕ (01794) 340775
Ⓔ john@bentleyplants.fsnet.co.uk
Ⓦ www.bentleyplants.co.uk
Contact: John Wilson
Opening Times: By appt. only.
Min Mail Order UK: Nmc
Cat. Cost: Online only.
Credit Cards: All major credit/debit cards
Specialities: Tree ferns, ground ferns & Japanese maples.
Notes: Mail order Oct-Mar.
Map Ref: C, B6 **OS Grid Ref:** SU258306

CBur **Burnham Nurseries** ⊠ ✈ ⛫ € ♿
Forches Cross, Newton Abbot, Devon
TQ12 6PZ
Ⓣ (01626) 352233
Ⓕ (01626) 362167
Ⓔ mail@orchids.uk.com
Ⓦ www.orchids.uk.com
Contact: Any member of staff
Opening Times: 1000-1600 Mon-Sun.
Min Mail Order UK: Nmc
Min Mail Order EU: £100.00 + p&p
Cat. Cost: A4 sae + 51p stamp.
Credit Cards: Visa, American Express, MasterCard, Maestro
Specialities: All types of orchid except British native types.
Notes: Please ask for details on export beyond EU.
Map Ref: C, C4 **OS Grid Ref:** SX841732

CCAT **Cider Apple Trees** ⊠ € ♿
Kerian, Corkscrew Lane, Woolston, Nr North Cadbury, Somerset BA22 7BP
Ⓣ (01963) 441101
Ⓦ www.ciderappletrees.co.uk
Contact: Mr J Dennis
Opening Times: By appt. only.
Min Mail Order UK: £9.50
Min Mail Order EU: £9.50
Cat. Cost: Free.
Credit Cards: None
Specialities: *Malus* (speciality standard trees).
Notes: Also sells wholesale.
Map Ref: C, B5

CCCN **Cross Common Nursery** ⊠ ◆
The Lizard, Helston, Cornwall TR12 7PD
Ⓣ (01326) 290722 or 290668
Ⓔ info@crosscommonnursery.co.uk
Ⓦ www.crosscommonnursery.co.uk
Contact: Kevin Bosustow
Opening Times: 1000-1700 7 days, Apr, May & Jun. Reduced hours Jul-Sep, please phone for opening times.
Min Mail Order UK: Nmc
Cat. Cost: Online only.
Credit Cards: All major credit/debit cards
Specialities: Tropical/sub-tropical, coastal plants & conservatory plants. Wide range of grapevines and citrus trees. Some plants available in small quantities only.
Map Ref: C, D1 **OS Grid Ref:** SW704116

CCha **Chapel Farm House Nursery** € ♿
Halwill Junction, Beaworthy, Devon
EX21 5UF
Ⓣ (01409) 221594
Ⓕ (01409) 221594
Contact: Robin or Toshie Hull
Opening Times: 1000-1600 Tue-Sat, 1000-1600 Sun & B/hol Mons.
Cat. Cost: None issued.
Credit Cards: None
Specialities: Plants from Japan. Also herbaceous. Japanese garden design service offered.
Notes: Newly designed & built Japanese garden.
Map Ref: C, C3

CCon **Constantine Garden Nursery (formerly Fir Tree Farm)** ⊠ ⛫ € ♿
Tresahor, Constantine, Falmouth, Cornwall
TR11 5PL
Ⓣ (01326) 340593
Ⓔ plants@cornwallgardens.com
Ⓦ www.cornwallgardens.com
Contact: Sorcha Hitchcox
Opening Times: 1000-1700 Tue-Sun (closed Mon) Feb-Jul, 1000-1700 Fri-Sun, Aug-Oct. By appt. Nov-Jan.
Min Mail Order UK: £25.00 + p&p
Min Mail Order EU: £40.00 + p&p
Cat. Cost: 6 × 1st class.
Credit Cards: Visa, Access, Delta, Switch
Specialities: Over 4000 varieties of cottage garden & rare perennials with many specialities. Also 80 varieties of *Clematis*. Some rare varieties available in small quantities only.
Notes: Free planting plans.
Map Ref: C, D1

CCse **Chase Plants (formerly Meadows Nursery)** ⊠ ⛫
Hookswood Cottage, Farnham, Blandford Forum, Dorset DT11 8DQ
Ⓣ (01725) 516394

KEY
⊠ Mail order to UK or EU ⛫ Delivers to shows
✈ Exports beyond EU € Euro accepted
♿ Accessible by wheelchair ◆ See Display advertisement

Ⓔ sales@chaseplants.co.uk
Contact: Sue Lees & Eddie Wheatley
Opening Times: By appt. only.
Min Mail Order UK: £10.00
Credit Cards: None
Specialities: Hardy perennials, shrubs & some conservatory plants.

CCVN **Culm View Nursery** ⊠ ☒ ⌂
Waterloo Farm, Clayhidon, Devon
EX15 3TN
Ⓣ (01823) 680698
Ⓔ plants@culmviewnursery.co.uk
Ⓦ www.culmviewnursery.co.uk
Contact: Brian & Alison Jacobs
Opening Times: By appt. only for collection.
Min Mail Order UK: Nmc
Min Mail Order EU: Nmc
Credit Cards: Paypal
Specialities: Hebaceous perennials grown in peat-free compost.
Notes: Mail order seed only.

CCVT **Chew Valley Trees** ⊠ ♿
Winford Road, Chew Magna, Bristol
BS40 8HJ
Ⓣ (01275) 333752
Ⓕ (01275) 333746
Ⓔ info@chewvalleytrees.co.uk
Ⓦ www.chewvalleytrees.co.uk
Contact: S Scarth
Opening Times: 0800-1700 Mon-Fri all year. 0900-1600 Sat. Closed Sat, Sun & B/hols Jul & Aug.
Min Mail Order UK: Nmc
Cat. Cost: Free.
Credit Cards: All major credit/debit cards
Specialities: Native British & ornamental trees, shrubs, fruit trees & hedging.
Notes: Also sells wholesale.
Map Ref: C, A5 **OS Grid Ref:** ST558635

CDes **Desirable Plants** ⊠ ⌂
(Office) Pentamar, Crosspark,
Totnes, Devon
TQ9 5BQ
Ⓣ (01803) 864489 evenings
Ⓔ sutton.totnes@lineone.net
Ⓦ www.desirableplants.com
Contact: Dr J J & Mrs S A Sutton
Opening Times: Not open. Mail order only.
Min Mail Order UK: £15.00
Cat. Cost: 6 × 2nd class.
Credit Cards: None
Specialities: Eclectic range of choice & interesting herbaceous perennials & bulbs by mail order.
Notes: Nursery not at this address.

CDob **Dobies of Devon** ⊠
Long Road, Paignton, Devon TQ4 7SX
Ⓣ 0844 701 7623
Ⓕ 0844 701 7624
Ⓦ www.dobies.co.uk
Contact: Customer Services
Opening Times: Not open. Mail order only. Phone line open 0830-1700 Mon-Fri (office). Also answerphone.
Min Mail Order UK: Nmc
Cat. Cost: Free.
Credit Cards: Visa, MasterCard, Switch, Delta
Specialities: Wide selection of popular flower & vegetable seeds. Also includes young plants, summer-flowering bulbs & garden sundries.
Notes: Mail order to UK & Rep. of Ireland only.

CDoC **Duchy of Cornwall** ⊠ ◆
Cott Road, Lostwithiel, Cornwall
PL22 0HW
Ⓣ (01208) 872668
Ⓕ (01208) 872835
Ⓔ sales@duchyofcornwallnursery.co.uk
Ⓦ www.duchyofcornwallnursery.co.uk
Contact: Jim Stephens
Opening Times: 0900-1700 Mon-Sat, 1000-1700 Sun & B/hols.
Min Mail Order UK: £10.00
Cat. Cost: None issued.
Credit Cards: All major credit/debit cards
Specialities: *Camellia*, *Fuchsia*, conifers & *Magnolia*. Also a huge range of garden plants incl. trees, shrubs, roses, perennials, fruit & conservatory plants.
Notes: Nursery partially accessible to wheelchair users.
Map Ref: C, C2 **OS Grid Ref:** SX112614

CDoy **Caradoc Doy** ⊠ €
PO Box 28, Exeter, Devon EX3 0WY
Ⓣ (01392) 877225
Ⓕ (01392) 877225
Ⓔ info@caradocdoy.co.uk
Ⓦ www.caradocdoy.co.uk
Contact: Caradoc Doy
Opening Times: 0900-1800 (summer), 0900-1700 (winter) 6 days, 1030-1630 Sun.
Min Mail Order UK: Nmc
Cat. Cost: Online.
Credit Cards: All major credit/debit cards
Specialities: Olive trees. Plants introduced by the Veitch Nurseries. Some varieties only available in small quantities.
Notes: Nursery located at Busy Lizzie's Craft & Plant Shop, Newton Poppleford, EX10 0DE
Map Ref: C, C4 **OS Grid Ref:** SY065895

CDTJ **Desert to Jungle** ⊠ ♠ ♿
Henlade Garden Nursery, Lower Henlade, Taunton, Somerset TA3 5NB
Ⓣ (01823) 443701
Ⓕ (01458) 250521
Ⓔ plants@deserttojungle.com
Ⓦ www.deserttojungle.com
Contact: Rob Gudge, Dave Root
Opening Times: 1000-1700 Mon-Sun, 1st Mar-31st Oct. Thu, Fri & Sat only Nov-Feb, or phone first.
Min Mail Order UK: Nmc
Credit Cards: All major credit/debit cards
Specialities: Exotic-looking plants giving a desert or jungle effect in the garden. Incl. *Canna*, aroids, succulents, tree ferns & bamboos.
Notes: Nursery shares drive with Mount Somerset Hotel. Also sells wholesale.
Map Ref: C, B4 **OS Grid Ref:** ST273232

CDul **Dulford Nurseries** ⊠ ♿
Cullompton, Devon EX15 2DG
Ⓣ (01884) 266361
Ⓕ (01884) 266663
Ⓔ dulford.nurseries@virgin.net
Ⓦ www.dulford-nurseries.co.uk
Contact: Paul Rawlings
Opening Times: 0730-1630 Mon-Fri.
Min Mail Order UK: Nmc
Min Mail Order EU: Nmc
Cat. Cost: Free.
Credit Cards: All major credit/debit cards
Specialities: Native, ornamental & unusual trees & shrubs incl. oaks, maples, beech, birch, chestnut, ash, lime, *Sorbus* & pines.
Notes: Also sells wholesale.
Map Ref: C, C4 **OS Grid Ref:** SY062062

CEls **Elsworth Herbs** ⊠
Farthingwood, Broadway, Sidmouth, Devon EX10 8HS
Ⓣ (01395) 578689
Ⓔ john.twibell@btinternet.com
Contact: Drs J D & J M Twibell
Opening Times: By appt. only.
Min Mail Order UK: £10.00
Cat. Cost: 3 × 1st class or email.
Credit Cards: None
Specialities: Nat. Collections of *Artemisia* (incl. *Seriphidium*) & *Nerium oleander*. Wide range of *Artemisia* & *Seriphidium*, *Nerium oleander*. Stock available in small quantities only. Orders may require propagation from Collection material, for which we are the primary reference source.
Notes: Partially accessible for wheelchairs.
Map Ref: C, C4 **OS Grid Ref:** SY119881

CElw **Elworthy Cottage Plants** ♠ ♿
Elworthy Cottage, Elworthy, Nr Lydeard St Lawrence, Taunton, Somerset TA4 3PX
Ⓣ (01984) 656427
Ⓔ mike@elworthy-cottage.co.uk
Ⓦ www.elworthy-cottage.co.uk
Contact: Mrs J M Spiller
Opening Times: 1000-1600 Thu, late Mar-end Aug. Also by appt. Feb-Nov.
Cat. Cost: 3 × 2nd class.
Credit Cards: None
Specialities: Unusual herbaceous plants esp. hardy *Geranium*, *Geum*, *Crocosmia*, *Monarda*, *Phlox*, *Pulmonaria*, *Astrantia*, *Viola* & *Galanthus*. Some varieties only available in small quantities.
Notes: Nursery on B3188, 5 miles north of Wiveliscombe, in centre of Elworthy village.
Map Ref: C, B4 **OS Grid Ref:** ST084349

CEnt **Entwood Farm Plants**
Harcombe, Lyme Regis, Dorset DT7 3RN
Ⓣ (01297) 444034
Ⓔ jennyhlyme@hotmail.co.uk
Contact: Jenny & Ivan Harding
Opening Times: Please phone for details.
Credit Cards: None
Specialities: Bamboo specialists, plus interesting selection of grasses, shrubs & perennials. Some stock in small quantities.
Map Ref: C, C4 **OS Grid Ref:** SY335953

CFis **Margery Fish Plant Nursery** ♿
East Lambrook Manor Gardens, East Lambrook, South Petherton, Somerset TA13 5HH
Ⓣ (01460) 240328
Ⓔ enquiries@eastlambrook.com
Ⓦ www.eastlambrook.com
Contact: Tom Wild
Opening Times: 1000-1700 Feb & May-Jul 7 days. 1000-1700 Tue-Sat & B/hol Mons Mar-Apr & Aug-Oct. Nov-Jan by appt.
Cat. Cost: None issued.
Credit Cards: All major credit/debit cards
Specialities: Hardy geraniums & cottage garden herbaceous plants. Stock available in small quantities only. Major collection of hardy geraniums on site.
Map Ref: C, B5 **OS Grid Ref:** ST431188

KEY
⊠ Mail order to UK or EU ♠ Delivers to shows
✈ Exports beyond EU € Euro accepted
♿ Accessible by wheelchair ◆ See Display advertisement

C

CFst **Forest Edge Nurseries** €
Woodlands, Wimborne, Dorset BH21 8LJ
Ⓣ (01202) 824387
Ⓕ (01202) 829564
Ⓔ davidedge@tinyworld.co.uk
Ⓦ www.forestedgenurseries.co.uk
Contact: David Edge
Opening Times: Open Mons for collection of pre-ordered plants. Other times by arrangement. Closed B/hols.
Cat. Cost: £1.00
Specialities: Heathers.
Notes: Also sells wholesale.

CFwr **The Flower Bower** ⊠
Woodlands, Shurton, Stogursey, Nr Bridgwater, Somerset TA5 1QE
Ⓣ (01278) 732134
Ⓔ theflowerbower@yahoo.co.uk
Ⓦ www.theflowerbower.co.uk
Contact: Sheila Tucker
Opening Times: By appt. only.
Min Mail Order UK: Nmc
Min Mail Order EU: Nmc
Cat. Cost: 2 × 1st class.
Credit Cards: None
Specialities: *Hemerocallis*, esp. newer varieties & spiders. *Epiphyllum* 500+ varieties
Notes: Daylilies can also be pre-ordered for Autumn delivery. Newer & rarer varieties mostly available in small quantities.
Map Ref: C, B4 **OS Grid Ref:** ST203442

CGHE **Garden House Enterprises** ⊠ ♿
The Garden House, Buckland Monachorum, Yelverton, Devon PL20 7LQ
Ⓣ (01822) 854769
Ⓕ (01822) 855358
Ⓔ office@thegardenhouse.org.uk
Ⓦ www.thegardenhouse.org.uk
Contact: Jo Selman
Opening Times: 1030-1700 7 days 1st Mar-31st Oct.
Min Mail Order UK: Nmc
Min Mail Order EU: Nmc
Cat. Cost: None issued.
Credit Cards: All major credit/debit cards
Specialities: Choice woodland plants & dieramas.
Map Ref: C, C3 **OS Grid Ref:** SX496683

CGro **C W Groves & Son Ltd** ⊠ ♿
West Bay Road, Bridport, Dorset DT6 4BA
Ⓣ (01308) 422654
Ⓕ (01308) 420888
Ⓔ garden@grovesnurseries.co.uk
Ⓦ www.grovesnurseries.co.uk
Contact: Becky Groves
Opening Times: 0830-1700 Mon-Sat, 1030-1630 Sun.
Min Mail Order UK: Nmc
Min Mail Order EU: £15.00 + p&p
Cat. Cost: 2 × 1st class.
Credit Cards: Visa, Switch, MasterCard
Specialities: Nursery & garden centre specialising in Parma & hardy *Viola*. Nat. Collection of *Viola odorata* cvs & Parma Violets. Also roses.
Notes: Mainly violets by mail order. Main display at nursery in Feb, Mar & Apr. Roses when dormant (Nov-Mar).
Map Ref: C, C5 **OS Grid Ref:** SY466918

CGrW **The Great Western Gladiolus Nursery** ⊠ €
17 Valley View, Clutton, Bristol BS39 5SN
Ⓣ (01761) 452036
Ⓕ (01761) 452036
Ⓔ clutton.glads@btinternet.com
Ⓦ www.greatwesterngladiolus.co.uk
Contact: G F Hazell
Opening Times: Mail order only. Open by appt. only.
Min Mail Order UK: Nmc
Min Mail Order EU: Nmc
Cat. Cost: 4 × 1st class (2 catalogues).
Credit Cards: None
Specialities: *Gladiolus* species & hybrids, corms & seeds. Other South African bulbous plants.
Notes: Also sells wholesale.

CHab **Habitat Aid Ltd** ⊠
The Old Rectory, Lamyatt, Somerset BA4 6NH
Ⓣ (01749) 812775
Ⓜ 07973 776613
Ⓕ (01749) 812971
Ⓔ info@habitataid.co.uk
Ⓦ www.habitataid.co.uk
Contact: Nick Mann
Opening Times: Not open. Mail order only.
Min Mail Order UK: £50.00, incl. p&p.
Cat. Cost: None issued.
Credit Cards: All major credit/debit cards
Specialities: British trees, plants and seeds. Local provenance seed mixes in small quantities only. Cottage garden perennials. Non-native trees for bees. Historic herbs.
Notes: Also sells wholesale.

CHby **The Herbary** ⊠ €
161 Chapel Street, Horningsham, Warminster, Wiltshire BA12 7LU
Ⓣ (01985) 844442
Ⓔ info@beansandherbs.co.uk

Ⓦ www.beansandherbs.co.uk
Contact: Pippa Rosen
Opening Times: May-Sep strictly by appt. only.
Min Mail Order UK: Nmc
Min Mail Order EU: Nmc
Cat. Cost: 4 × 1st class or online.
Credit Cards: None
Specialities: Culinary, medicinal & aromatic herbs organically grown in small quantities.
Notes: Mail order is for seed only and is all year for organic vegetable seed & large variety of organic bean & herb seed. Also sells wholesale.
Map Ref: C, B5 **OS Grid Ref:** ST812414

CHew **Hewitt-Cooper Carnivorous Plants** ⊠ ♠ €
The Homestead, Glastonbury Road,
West Pennard, Somerset BA6 8NN
Ⓣ (01458) 832844
Ⓕ (01458) 832712
Ⓔ sales@hccarnivorousplants.co.uk
Ⓦ www.hccarnivorousplants.co.uk
Contact: Nigel Hewitt-Cooper
Opening Times: By appt.
Min Mail Order UK: £10.00 + p&p
Min Mail Order EU: £30.00
Cat. Cost: 1 × 1st class/1× IRC.
Credit Cards: All major credit/debit cards
Specialities: Carnivorous plants.
Notes: Mail order May-Nov.

CHEx **Hardy Exotics** ⊠ ♿
Gilly Lane, Whitecross, Penzance, Cornwall
TR20 8BZ
Ⓣ (01736) 740660
Ⓕ (01736) 741101
Ⓔ contact@hardyexotics.co.uk
Ⓦ www.hardyexotics.co.uk
Contact: C Shilton/J Smith
Opening Times: 1000-1700 7 days Apr-Oct, 1000-1700 Mon-Sat Nov-Feb. Please phone first in winter months if travelling a long way.
Min Mail Order UK: £25 carriage.
Cat. Cost: 4 × 1st class (no cheques).
Credit Cards: All major credit/debit cards
Specialities: Largest selection in the UK of trees, shrubs & herbaceous plants for tropical & desert effects. Hardy & half-hardy plants for gardens, patios & conservatories. Mature plants & plantings to inspire.
Map Ref: C, D1 **OS Grid Ref:** SW524345

CHGN **High Garden Nurseries** ♿
Chiverstone Lane, Kenton, Exeter, Devon
EX6 8NJ
Ⓣ (01626) 899106
Ⓔ highgarden@highgarden.co.uk
Ⓦ www.highgarden.co.uk
Contact: Chris Britton
Opening Times: 0900-1700 Tue-Fri
Cat. Cost: None issued.
Credit Cards: None
Specialities: Quality shrubs, trees & perennials, some unusual & different.
Map Ref: C, C4 **OS Grid Ref:** SX957836

CHid **Hidden Valley Nursery** ♠ €
Umberleigh, Devon EX37 9BU
Ⓣ (01769) 560567
Ⓜ 07899 788789
Ⓔ plalindley@itsosbroadband.co.uk
Contact: Linda & Peter Lindley
Opening Times: Daylight hours, but please phone first.
Cat. Cost: None issued.
Credit Cards: None
Specialities: Hardy perennials esp. shade lovers & Chatham Islands forget-me-nots (*Myosotidium hortensia.*)
Map Ref: C, B3 **OS Grid Ref:** SS567205

CHII **Hill House Nursery & Gardens** ⊠ € ♿
Landscove, Nr Ashburton, Devon
TQ13 7LY
Ⓣ (01803) 762273
Ⓕ (01803) 158218
Ⓔ bluebird@hillhousenursery.com
Ⓦ www.hillhousenursery.com
Contact: Raymond, Sacha & Matthew Hubbard
Opening Times: 1100-1700 7 days, all year. Open all B/hols incl. Easter Sun. Closed 24th Dec-7th Jan. Tearoom open 1st Mar-30th Sep.
Min Mail Order UK: Nmc
Cat. Cost: None issued.
Credit Cards: Delta, MasterCard, Switch, Visa, Paypal
Specialities: 3000+ varieties of plants, most propagated on premises, many rare or unusual. The garden, open to the public, was laid out by Edward Hyams. Pioneers of glasshouse pest control by beneficial insects.
Map Ref: C, C3 **OS Grid Ref:** SX774664

CHVG **Hidden Valley Gardens** € ♿
Treesmill, Nr Par, Cornwall PL24 2TU
Ⓣ (01208) 873225
Ⓔ hiddenvalleygardens@yahoo.co.uk

KEY
⊠ Mail order to UK or EU ♠ Delivers to shows
✈ Exports beyond EU € Euro accepted
♿ Accessible by wheelchair ◆ See Display advertisement

Ⓦ www.hiddenvalleygardens.co.uk
Contact: Mrs P Howard
Opening Times: 1000-1800 Thu-Mon (closed Tue & Wed), 20th Mar-15th Oct. Please phone for directions. Garden open as nursery.
Cat. Cost: None issued.
Credit Cards: All major credit/debit cards
Specialities: Cottage garden plants, *Crocosmia* & many perennials which can be seen growing in the garden. Some stock available in small quantities. Display garden.
Map Ref: C, D2 **OS Grid Ref:** SX094567

CIri **THE IRIS GARDEN** ⊠ €
Yard House, Pilsdon, Bridport, Dorset DT6 5PA
Ⓣ (01308) 868797
Ⓔ the_iris_garden@yahoo.com
Ⓦ www.theirisgarden.co.uk
Contact: Clive Russell
Opening Times: Show garden open by appt. only. Please email or phone for details.
Min Mail Order UK: £15.00 + p&p
Min Mail Order EU: £25.00 + p&p
Cat. Cost: 6 × 1st class.
Credit Cards: All major credit/debit cards
Specialities: Modern bearded & beardless *Iris* from breeders in UK, USA, France, Italy & Australia. Nat. Collection of Space Age *Iris*.
Notes: Orders for bearded iris & sibiricas must be received by end Jun & by end Aug for spurias & ensatas.
Map Ref: C, C5 **OS Grid Ref:** SY421988

CJas **JASMINE COTTAGE GARDENS**
26 Channel Road, Walton St Mary, Clevedon, Somerset BS21 7BY
Ⓣ (01275) 871850
Ⓔ margaret@bologrew.net
Ⓦ http://jasminecottage.bologrew.net/
Contact: Mr & Mrs M Redgrave
Opening Times: May to Aug, daily by appt. Garden open at the same times.
Cat. Cost: None issued.
Credit Cards: None
Specialities: *Rhodochiton, Lophospermum, Maurandya, Dicentra macrocapnos, Salvia, Isotoma*, half-hardy geraniums.
Map Ref: C, A4 **OS Grid Ref:** ST405725

CJun **JUNKER'S NURSERY LTD (FORMERLY P M A PLANT SPECIALITIES)** ⊠ €
Higher Cobhay, Milverton, Somerset TA4 1NJ
Ⓣ (01823) 480774
Ⓔ karan@junker.co.uk
Ⓦ www.junker.co.uk
Contact: Karan or Nick Junker
Opening Times: Strictly by appt. only.
Min Mail Order UK: Nmc
Min Mail Order EU: Nmc
Cat. Cost: 6 × 1st class.
Credit Cards: None
Specialities: Choice & unusual shrubs & trees incl. grafted *Acer palmatum, Cornus, Daphne, Magnolia*. Many available in larger, more mature sizes. Small quantities only of some hard to propagate plants, esp. daphnes.
Notes: Reserve orders accepted. Extensive planted areas showing how the plants look growing in "real world" conditions. We propagate & grow all our own plants with an increasing number grown naturally in open ground as well as in pots. Ltd wheelchair access.
Map Ref: C, B4

CKel **KELWAYS** ⊠ ✈ ⌂ € ♿
Langport, Somerset TA10 9EZ
Ⓣ (01458) 250521
Ⓕ (01458) 253351
Ⓔ sales@kelways.co.uk
Ⓦ www.kelways.co.uk
Contact: Dave Root, Andy Martin
Opening Times: 0900-1700 Mon-Fri, 0900-1700 Sat, 1000-1600 Sun.
Min Mail Order UK: £4.00 + p&p
Min Mail Order EU: £8.00 + p&p
Cat. Cost: Online only.
Credit Cards: All major credit/debit cards
Specialities: *Paeonia, Iris, Hemerocallis* & herbaceous perennials. Nat. Collection of *Paeonia lactiflora*. Wide range of trees, shrubs & herbaceous. Hardy ferns & tree ferns.
Notes: Also sells wholesale.
Map Ref: C, B5 **OS Grid Ref:** ST434273

CKen **KENWITH NURSERY (GORDON HADDOW)** ⊠ ♿
Blinsham, Nr Torrington, Beaford, Winkleigh, Devon EX19 8NT
Ⓣ (01805) 603274
Ⓕ (01805) 603663
Ⓔ conifers@kenwith63.freeserve.co.uk
Ⓦ www.kenwithnursery.co.uk
Contact: Gordon Haddow
Opening Times: 1000-1630 Tue-Sat all year. Closed all B/hols. If travelling a long distance, please phone previous day to ensure nursery will be open.
Min Mail Order UK: £20 + p&p
Min Mail Order EU: £50 + p&p
Cat. Cost: 3 × 1st class.
Credit Cards: Visa, MasterCard
Specialities: All conifer genera. Grafting a speciality. Many new introductions to UK.

Nat. Collection of Dwarf Conifers.
Map Ref: C, B3 **OS Grid Ref:** SS518160

CKno **KNOLL GARDENS** ⊠ ♠ ♿
Hampreston, Nr Wimborne, Dorset
BH21 7ND
Ⓣ (01202) 873931
Ⓕ (01202) 870842
Ⓔ enquiries@knollgardens.co.uk
Ⓦ www.knollgardens.co.uk
Contact: N R Lucas
Opening Times: 1000-1700 Tue-Sat Apr-Oct, 1000-1600 Nov-Mar. Closed 18th Dec 2011 reopens 1st Feb 2012. Open B/hol Mons.
Min Mail Order UK: Nmc
Min Mail Order EU: Nmc
Cat. Cost: £2.00 + 50p postage.
Credit Cards: Visa, MasterCard
Specialities: Grasses (main specialism). Select perennials. Nat. Collection of *Pennisetum.*
Notes: Also sells wholesale.
Map Ref: C, C6

CLak **LAKKA BULBS** ⊠
(Office) 127 Mill Street, Torrington, North Devon EX38 8AW
Ⓣ (01805) 625071
Ⓔ lakkabulbs@talktalk.net
Contact: Jonathan Hutchinson
Opening Times: Not open. Mail order only.
Min Mail Order UK: Nmc
Min Mail Order EU: Nmc
Cat. Cost: None issued.
Credit Cards: None
Specialities: Nat. Collections of *Urginea, Veltheimia* & *Scadoxus.* Other South African bulbs of families *Amaryllidaceae* & *Hyacinthaceae.* All available in small quantities only.

CLAP **LONG ACRE PLANTS** ⊠ ♠ ♿
South Marsh, Charlton Musgrove,
Nr Wincanton, Somerset BA9 8EX
Ⓣ (01963) 32802
Ⓕ (01963) 32802
Ⓔ info@plantsforshade.co.uk
Ⓦ www.plantsforshade.co.uk
Contact: Nigel & Michelle Rowland
Opening Times: 0900-1300 & 1350-1600 Thu & Fri only, Feb-Oct.
Min Mail Order UK: £20.00 + p&p
Min Mail Order EU: Nmc
Cat. Cost: 3 × 1st class.
Credit Cards: MasterCard, Visa, Maestro, American Express, JCB
Specialities: Ferns, woodland bulbs & perennials. Marginal/bog plants.
Notes: Some plants available in small numbers only and only seasonally available. Ship to EU in autumn and winter only.
Map Ref: C, B5

CLnd **LANDFORD TREES** €
Landford Lodge, Landford, Salisbury, Wiltshire SP5 2EH
Ⓣ (01794) 390808
Ⓕ (01794) 390037
Ⓔ trees@landfordtrees.co.uk
Ⓦ www.landfordtrees.co.uk
Contact: C D Pilkington
Opening Times: 0800-1700 Mon-Fri.
Cat. Cost: Free.
Credit Cards: All, except American Express
Specialities: Deciduous ornamental trees.
Notes: Also sells wholesale.
Map Ref: C, B6 **OS Grid Ref:** SU247201

CLng **LONGCOMBE NURSERY AND GARDEN CENTRE** ⊠ ♠ ♿
Longcombe, Totnes, Devon TQ9 6PL
Ⓣ 0844 335 6915
Ⓔ info@simplyclematis.co.uk
Ⓦ www.simplyclematis.co.uk
Contact: Linda Clarke
Opening Times: 0900-1700 Mon-Sat, 1000-1600 Sun.
Min Mail Order UK: Nmc
Cat. Cost: Online only.
Credit Cards: All major credit/debit cards
Specialities: *Clematis.*
Notes: Also sells wholesale.
Map Ref: C, C3 **OS Grid Ref:** SX834601

CLoc **C S LOCKYER (FUCHSIAS)** ⊠ ✈ ♠ € ◆
Lansbury, 70 Henfield Road, Coalpit Heath, Bristol BS36 2UZ
Ⓣ (01454) 772219
Ⓕ (01454) 772219
Ⓔ sales@lockyerfuchsias.co.uk
Ⓦ www.lockyerfuchsias.co.uk
Contact: C S Lockyer
Opening Times: 1000-1300, 1430-1700 most days, please ring.
Min Mail Order UK: 6 plants + p&p
Min Mail Order EU: £12.00 + p&p
Cat. Cost: 4 × 1st class.
Credit Cards: All major credit/debit cards
Specialities: *Fuchsia.*
Notes: Many open days & coach parties. Partial wheelchair access. Also sells wholesale.
Map Ref: C, A5

KEY
⊠ Mail order to UK or EU ♠ Delivers to shows
✈ Exports beyond EU € Euro accepted
♿ Accessible by wheelchair ◆ See Display advertisement

C

CMac **MAC PENNYS NURSERIES** ⊠
154 Burley Road, Bransgore, Christchurch, Dorset BH23 8DB
Ⓣ (01425) 672348
Ⓕ (01425) 673917
Ⓔ office@macpennys.co.uk
Ⓦ www.macpennys.co.uk
Contact: T & V Lowndes & S Lowndes
Opening Times: 0900-1700 Mon-Sat, 1000-1700 Sun & B/hols, except closed Xmas-New Year.
Min Mail Order UK: Nmc
Cat. Cost: A4 sae with 4 × 1st class.
Credit Cards: All major credit/debit cards
Specialities: General. Plants available in small quantities only.
Notes: Mail order available Sep-Mar, UK only. Nursery partially accessible for wheelchairs. Also sells wholesale.
Map Ref: C, C6

CMam **MAMMOTH TREES** ⊠ ⌂ €
(Office) 6 Heath Way, Totnes, Devon TQ9 5GP
Ⓣ (01803) 864866
Ⓜ 07847 329314
Ⓔ giles@mammothtrees.co.uk
Ⓦ www.MammothTrees.co.uk
Contact: Giles Nicholson
Opening Times: Not open. Mail order only. Office open 0930-1700 for phone & email enquiries.
Min Mail Order UK: Nmc
Min Mail Order EU: Nmc
Cat. Cost: 80p.
Credit Cards: All major credit/debit cards
Specialities: *Salix* & *Populus*. Fruit & nut trees.
Notes: Credit cards accepted online only. Trees may be collected from Mammoth Trees, Wrangaton Road, South Brent, TQ10 9JE.
Map Ref: C, C3 **OS Grid Ref:** SX688587

CMCN **MALLET COURT NURSERY** ⊠ ✈ ⌂ € ♿
Curry Mallet, Taunton, Somerset TA3 6SY
Ⓣ (01823) 481493
Ⓕ (01823) 481493
Ⓔ malletcourtnursery@btinternet.com
Ⓦ www.malletcourt.co.uk
Contact: J G S & P M E Harris F.L.S.
Opening Times: 0930-1700 Mon-Fri summer, 0930-1600 winter. Sat & Sun by appt.
Min Mail Order UK: Nmc
Min Mail Order EU: Nmc
Cat. Cost: £1.50
Credit Cards: All major credit/debit cards
Specialities: Maples, oaks, *Magnolia*, hollies & other rare and unusual plants including those from China & South Korea.
Notes: Mail order Oct-Mar only. Also sells wholesale.
Map Ref: C, B4

CMea **THE MEAD NURSERY** ♿
Brokerswood, Nr Westbury, Wiltshire BA13 4EG
Ⓣ (01373) 859990
Ⓦ www.themeadnursery.co.uk
Contact: Steve & Emma Lewis-Dale
Opening Times: 0900-1700 Wed-Sat & B/hols, 1200-1700 Sun, 1st Feb-10th Oct. Closed Easter Sun.
Cat. Cost: 5 × 1st class.
Credit Cards: All major credit/debit cards
Specialities: Perennials, alpines, pot-grown bulbs and grasses.
Map Ref: C, B5 **OS Grid Ref:** ST833517

CMen **MENDIP BONSAI STUDIO** ⊠ ⌂
Byways, Back Lane, Downside, Shepton Mallet, Somerset BA4 4JR
Ⓣ (01749) 344274
Ⓜ 07711 205806
Ⓔ john@mendipbonsai.co.uk
Ⓦ www.mendipbonsai.co.uk
Contact: John Trott
Opening Times: Private nursery. Visits by appt. only.
Min Mail Order UK: £15.00
Cat. Cost: Large sae for plant & workshop lists.
Credit Cards: All major credit/debit cards
Specialities: Bonsai, Potensai, accent plants & garden stock. Acers, conifers, incl. many *Pinus thunbergii* species. Many plants available in small numbers only. Young trees for garden or bonsai culture.
Notes: Education classes, lectures, demonstrations & club talks on bonsai. Stockist of most bonsai sundries. Mail orders will be normally despatched late Mar/early Apr-late Sep/Oct. Ltd wheelchair access.
Map Ref: C, B5

CMHG **MARWOOD HILL GARDENS** ♿
Marwood, Barnstaple, Devon EX31 4EB
Ⓣ (01271) 342528
Ⓕ (01271) 342528
Ⓔ info@marwoodhillgarden.co.uk
Ⓦ www.marwoodhillgarden.co.uk
Contact: Malcolm Pharoah
Opening Times: 1100-1630, 7 days. Closed Nov-Feb.

Cat. Cost: 3 × 1st class.
Credit Cards: Visa, Delta, MasterCard, Switch, Solo
Specialities: Large range of unusual trees & shrubs. *Eucalyptus*, alpines, *Camellia*, *Astilbe*, bog plants & perennials. Nat. Collections of *Astilbe*, *Tulbaghia* & *Iris ensata*.
Map Ref: C, B3 **OS Grid Ref:** SS545375

CMil **MILL COTTAGE PLANTS** ⊠ € ♿
Henley Mill, Henley Lane, Wookey, Somerset BA5 1AW
Ⓣ (01749) 676966
Ⓜ 07851 698759
Ⓔ millcottageplants@googlemail.com
Ⓦ www.millcottageplants.co.uk
Contact: Sally Gregson
Opening Times: By appt. only. Phone for directions.
Min Mail Order UK: Nmc
Min Mail Order EU: £25.00 + p&p
Cat. Cost: 4 × 1st class.
Credit Cards: All major credit/debit cards
Specialities: Rare *Hydrangea serrata* cvs, *H. aspera* cvs, *Epimedium* & damp-loving plants.
Map Ref: C, B5

CMus **MUSGROVE WILLOWS** ⊠ ✈ ♿
Willowfields, Lakewall, Westonzoyland, Bridgwater, Somerset TA7 0LP
Ⓣ (01278) 691105
Ⓕ (01278) 699107
Ⓔ info@musgrovewillows.co.uk
Ⓦ www.musgrovewillows.co.uk
Contact: Ellen Musgrove
Opening Times: 0900-1700 Mon-Fri.
Min Mail Order UK: £12
Min Mail Order EU: Nmc
Credit Cards: All major credit/debit cards
Specialities: *Salix*. A family nursery for over 65 years.
Map Ref: C, B4

CNat **NATURAL SELECTION** ⊠ €
1 Station Cottages, Hullavington, Chippenham, Wiltshire SN14 6ET
Ⓣ (01666) 837369
Ⓜ 07800 583999
Ⓔ martin@worldmutation.demon.co.uk
Ⓦ www.worldmutation.demon.co.uk
Contact: Martin Barber
Opening Times: Please phone first.
Min Mail Order UK: £9.00 + p&p
Cat. Cost: 2 × 2nd class.
Credit Cards: None
Specialities: Unusual British natives & others. Also seed. Only available in small quantities.

CNMi **NEWPORT MILLS NURSERY** ⊠
Wrantage, Taunton, Somerset TA3 6DJ
Ⓣ (01823) 490231
Ⓜ 07940 872800
Ⓕ (01823) 490231
Ⓔ newportmillsnursery@live.co.uk
Ⓦ www.newportmillsnursery.farming.officelive.com
Contact: John Barrington
Opening Times: By appt. only.
Min Mail Order UK: Nmc, free p&p
Min Mail Order EU: Nmc, EU postal rate per order.
Cat. Cost: Free.
Credit Cards: All major credit/debit cards
Specialities: *Delphinium elatum* hybrids. English scented perpetual flowering carnations. Pinks, Exhibition, Modern & Old World.
Notes: Mail order Apr-Sep for young delphiniums in 7cm pots. Dormant plants can be sent out in autumn/winter if requested.
Map Ref: C, B4

COlW **THE OLD WITHY GARDEN NURSERY** ⊠
Grange Fruit Farm, Gweek, Helston, Cornwall TR12 6BE
Ⓣ (01326) 221171
Ⓔ sales@theoldwithygardennursery.co.uk
Ⓦ www.theoldwithygardennursery.co.uk
Contact: Sheila Chandler or Nick Chandler
Opening Times: 0930-1700 7 days, Feb-end Oct. 1000-1600 Tue-Fri, Nov.
Min Mail Order UK: £15.00
Cat. Cost: Online.
Credit Cards: Maestro, MasterCard, Visa, Delta
Specialities: Cottage garden plants, perennials, some biennials & grasses. Some varieties in small quantities only.
Notes: Partially accessible for wheelchairs (gravel paths). Also sells wholesale.
Map Ref: C, D1 **OS Grid Ref:** SW688255

CPar **PARKS PERENNIALS** ⛫
242 Wallisdown Road, Wallisdown, Bournemouth, Dorset BH10 4HZ
Ⓣ (01202) 524464
Ⓔ parks.perennials@ntlworld.com
Contact: S. Parks
Opening Times: Apr-Oct most days, please phone first.
Cat. Cost: None issued.
Credit Cards: None

KEY
⊠ Mail order to UK or EU ⛫ Delivers to shows
✈ Exports beyond EU € Euro accepted
♿ Accessible by wheelchair ◆ See Display advertisement

C

Specialities: Hardy herbaceous perennials.
Map Ref: C, C6

CPbn **PENBORN GOAT FARM** ⊠ ♿
Penborn, Bounds Cross, Holsworthy, Devon
EX22 6LH
Ⓣ (01288) 381569
Ⓔ penborngoats@btinternet.com
Ⓦ www.penborngoats.com
Contact: P R Oldfield
Opening Times: By appt. only.
Min Mail Order UK: £10.00
Min Mail Order EU: £10.00
Cat. Cost: Online.
Credit Cards: None
Specialities: *Mentha*, *Melissa*. Available in small quantities only.
Map Ref: C, C2 **OS Grid Ref:** SS290021

CPBP **PARHAM BUNGALOW PLANTS** ⊠ €
Parham Lane, Market Lavington, Devizes,
Wiltshire SN10 4QA
Ⓣ (01380) 812605
Ⓔ jjs@pbplants.freeserve.co.uk
Contact: Mrs D E Sample
Opening Times: Please ring first.
Min Mail Order UK: Nmc
Min Mail Order EU: Nmc
Cat. Cost: Sae.
Credit Cards: None
Specialities: Alpines.
Map Ref: C, B6

CPen **PENNARD PLANTS** ⊠ €
3 The Gardens, East Pennard, Shepton Mallet,
Somerset BA4 6TU
Ⓣ (01749) 860039
Ⓕ 07043 017270
Ⓔ sales@pennardplants.com
Ⓦ www.pennardplants.com
Contact: Chris Smith
Opening Times: By appt. only.
Min Mail Order UK: Nmc
Min Mail Order EU: Nmc
Cat. Cost: 3 × 1st class.
Credit Cards: All major credit/debit cards
Specialities: *Agapanthus*, *Dierama* & *Gladioli* species. Nerines (*bowdenii* hybrids).
Notes: Nursery at The Walled Garden at East Pennard.
Map Ref: C, B5

CPhi **ALAN PHIPPS CACTI** ⊠ €
62 Samuel White Road, Hanham, Bristol
BS15 3LX
Ⓣ (0117) 9607591
Ⓦ www.cactus-mall.com/alan-phipps/index.html
Contact: A Phipps
Opening Times: 1000-1700 but prior phone call essential to ensure a greeting.
Min Mail Order UK: £5.00 + p&p
Min Mail Order EU: £20.00 + p&p
Cat. Cost: Sae or 2 × IRC (EC only).
Credit Cards: None
Specialities: *Mammillaria*, *Astrophytum* & *Ariocarpus*. Species & varieties will change with times. Ample quantities exist in spring. Limited range of *Agave*.
Notes: Euro accepted as cash only. Specimen-size plants not available by mail order.
Map Ref: C, A5 **OS Grid Ref:** ST644717

CPHo **THE PALM HOUSE** ⊠
8 North Street, Ottery St Mary, Devon
EX11 1DR
Ⓣ (01404) 815450
Ⓜ 07815 673397
Ⓔ george@thepalmhouse.co.uk
Ⓦ www.thepalmhouse.co.uk
Contact: George Gregory
Opening Times: Mail order only. Open by appt. only.
Min Mail Order UK: £15.00
Min Mail Order EU: £10.00
Cat. Cost: 2 × 1st class.
Credit Cards: All major credit/debit cards
Specialities: Palms.
Notes: Also sells wholesale.
Map Ref: C, C4 **OS Grid Ref:** SY098955

CPLG **EXCLUSIVE PLANTS (INCORPORATING PINE LODGE GARDENS & NURSERY)** ⊠ ♿
Pine Lodge Gardens, Holmbush, St Austell,
Cornwall PL25 3RQ
Ⓣ (01726) 77960
Ⓜ 07775 811385
Ⓕ (01726) 77960
Ⓔ exclusiveplants@hotmail.co.uk
Ⓦ www.exclusiveplants.co.uk
Contact: Paul Bonavia
Opening Times: 1000-1700 7 days all year, except 24th/25th/26th Dec.
Min Mail Order UK: Nmc
Cat. Cost: 3 × 2nd class.
Credit Cards: All major credit/debit cards
Specialities: Rare & unusual shrubs & herbaceous, some from seed collected on plant expeditions each year. Nat. Collection of *Grevillea*.
Map Ref: C, D2 **OS Grid Ref:** SX045527

CPne **PINE COTTAGE PLANTS** ⊠ €
Pine Cottage, Fourways, Eggesford,
Chulmleigh, Devon EX18 7QZ
Ⓣ (01769) 580076
Ⓜ 07718 505053
Ⓔ sales@pcplants.co.uk

Ⓦ www.pcplants.co.uk
Contact: Dick Fulcher
Opening Times: Special open weeks for *Agapanthus*, 1000-1500 daily 25th-30th Jul & 15th-20th Aug. Other times by appt. only.
Min Mail Order UK: £20.00 + p&p
Min Mail Order EU: £50.00 + p&p
Cat. Cost: 4 × 1st class.
Credit Cards: Maestro, MasterCard, Visa
Specialities: Nat. Collection of *Agapanthus*. 200+ cvs available.
Notes: Mail order *Agapanthus* from Sep-Jun. Also sells wholesale.
Map Ref: C, B3 **OS Grid Ref:** SS683099

CPom **POMEROY PLANTS**
Tower House, Pomeroy Lane, Wingfield, Trowbridge, Wiltshire BA14 9LJ
Ⓣ (01225) 769551
Ⓜ 07895 096564
Ⓔ drsimonyoung@yahoo.co.uk
Contact: Simon Young
Opening Times: Mar-Nov. Please phone first.
Cat. Cost: 2 × 1st class.
Credit Cards: None
Specialities: Hardy, mainly species, herbaceous perennials. Many unusual and often small.
Map Ref: C, B5 **OS Grid Ref:** ST817569

CPou **POUNSLEY PLANTS** ⊠ ⌂ € ♿
Pounsley Combe, Spriddlestone, Brixton, Plymouth, Devon PL9 0DW
Ⓣ (01752) 402873
Ⓜ 07770 758501
Ⓕ (01752) 406682
Ⓔ pou599@aol.com
Ⓦ www.pounsleyplants.com
Contact: Mrs Jane Hollow
Opening Times: Normally 1000-1600 Mon-Sat but please phone first.
Min Mail Order UK: £10.00 + p&p
Min Mail Order EU: €20.00 + p&p
Cat. Cost: 2 × 1st class.
Credit Cards: None
Specialities: Unusual herbaceous perennials, cottage plants & *Clematis*. Comprehensive range of Old Roses. Large selection of South African monocots.
Notes: Mail order Nov-Feb only. Mail order roses bare root only. Also sells wholesale.
Map Ref: C, D3 **OS Grid Ref:** SX521538

CPrp **PROPERPLANTS.COM** ⊠ ✈ ⌂
Penknight, Edgcumbe Road, Lostwithiel, Cornwall PL22 0JD
Ⓣ (01208) 872291
Ⓔ info@ProperPlants.com
Ⓦ www.ProperPlants.com
Contact: Sarah Wilks
Opening Times: 1000-1800 or dusk if earlier, Tue & B/hols mid-Mar to end-Sep & by appt.
Min Mail Order UK: Nmc
Min Mail Order EU: Nmc
Cat. Cost: 4 × 1st class.
Credit Cards: All major credit/debit cards
Specialities: Wide range of unusual & easy herbaceous perennials, esp. of South African origin. Ferns & grasses. Less common herbs.
Notes: Partially accessible for wheelchair users.
Map Ref: C, C2 **OS Grid Ref:** SX093596

CQua **QUALITY DAFFODILS** ⊠ ✈ € ◆
14 Roscarrack Close, Falmouth, Cornwall TR11 4PJ
Ⓣ (01326) 317959
Ⓜ 07989 243450
Ⓕ (01326) 317959
Ⓔ rascamp@daffodils.uk.com
Ⓦ www.qualitydaffodils.com
Contact: R A Scamp
Opening Times: Not open. Mail order only. Viewing by appt. only.
Min Mail Order UK: Nmc
Min Mail Order EU: Nmc
Cat. Cost: 3 × 1st class.
Credit Cards: All major credit/debit cards
Specialities: *Narcissus* hybrids & species. Some stocks are less than 100 bulbs.
Notes: Also sells wholesale.
Map Ref: C, D1

CRDP **R D PLANTS** ♿
Homelea Farm, Chard Road, Tytherleigh, Axminster, East Devon EX13 7BG
Ⓣ (01460) 220206
Ⓕ (01460) 220206
Contact: Rodney Davey & Lynda Windsor
Opening Times: 1000-1600 most days, 1st Mar-30th Jun. Open 1st Feb for hellebores.
Cat. Cost: None issued.
Credit Cards: None
Specialities: Double & anemone-centred hellebores. Choice plants for moist shade. Established garden-worthy plants in flower for most situations.
Map Ref: C, C4 **OS Grid Ref:** ST3203

CRea **REALLY WILD FLOWERS** ⊠
H V Horticulture Ltd, Spring Mead, Bedchester, Shaftesbury, Dorset SP7 0JU
Ⓣ (01747) 811778

KEY
⊠ Mail order to UK or EU ⌂ Delivers to shows
✈ Exports beyond EU € Euro accepted
♿ Accessible by wheelchair ◆ See Display advertisement

C

Ⓕ 0844 443 2503
Ⓔ info@reallywildflowers.co.uk
Ⓦ www.reallywildflowers.co.uk
Contact: Grahame Dixie
Opening Times: Not open. Mail order only.
Min Mail Order UK: £40.00 + p&p
Cat. Cost: 3 × 1st class.
Credit Cards: All major credit/debit cards
Specialities: Native wild flowers for grasslands, woodlands & wetlands. Seeds & bulbs. Hedge plants & trees. Advisory & soil analysis services.
Notes: Credit card payment accepted for online orders only. Also sells wholesale.

CRHN **Roseland House Nursery** ⊠

Chacewater, Truro, Cornwall TR4 8QB
Ⓣ (01872) 560451
Ⓔ clematis@roselandhouse.co.uk
Ⓦ www.roselandhouse.co.uk
Contact: C R Pridham
Opening Times: 1300-1700 Tue & Wed, Apr-Sep. Other times by appt.
Min Mail Order UK: Nmc
Min Mail Order EU: Nmc
Cat. Cost: Online only.
Credit Cards: All major credit/debit cards
Specialities: Climbing & conservatory plants. Nat. Collections of *Clematis viticella* & *Lapageria rosea*. Named *Lapageria* in short supply but occasionally available.
Notes: Garden open to the public. Credit cards accepted from mail order customers only.
Map Ref: C, D1 **OS Grid Ref:** SW752445

CRow **Rowden Gardens** ⊠ ✈ ♿

Brentor, Nr Tavistock, Devon PL19 0NG
Ⓣ (01822) 810275
Ⓔ rowdengardens1@btinternet.com
Ⓦ www.rowdengardens.com
Contact: John R L Carter
Opening Times: By appt only.
Min Mail Order UK: Nmc
Min Mail Order EU: Nmc
Cat. Cost: 6 × 1st class.
Credit Cards: None
Specialities: Aquatics, damp loving & associated plants incl. rare & unusual varieties. Nat. Collections of *Caltha* & Water Iris. Some stock available in small quantities only.
Notes: Also sells wholesale.
Map Ref: C, C3

CRWN **The Really Wild Nursery** ⊠ ✈ €

19 Hoopers Way, Torrington, Devon EX38 7NS
Ⓣ (01805) 624739
Ⓕ (01805) 624739
Ⓔ thereallywildnursery@yahoo.co.uk
Ⓦ www.thereallywildnursery.co.uk
Contact: Kathryn Moore
Opening Times: Not open. Mail order only.
Min Mail Order UK: £10.00 + p&p
Min Mail Order EU: £20.00 + p&p
Cat. Cost: 3 × 1st class.
Credit Cards: Paypal
Specialities: Wildflowers, bulbs & seeds.
Notes: Mail order all year round, grown to order (plants in pots or plugs). Credit card payment accepted via Paypal online only. Also sells wholesale.

CSam **Sampford Shrubs** ⊠ € ♿

Sampford Peverell, Tiverton, Devon EX16 7EN
Ⓣ (01884) 821164
Ⓔ via website
Ⓦ www.samshrub.co.uk
Contact: M Hughes-Jones & S Proud
Opening Times: 1000-1700 Wed-Fri, 1st Apr-16th Sep incl.
Min Mail Order UK: Nmc
Cat. Cost: A5 sae.
Credit Cards: All major credit/debit cards
Specialities: Plants particularly suitable for naturalistic gardening.
Notes: Mail order only via dedicated ecommerce website. Despatched Oct-Mar.
Map Ref: C, B4 **OS Grid Ref:** ST043153

CSBt **St Bridget Nurseries Ltd** ⊠ ♿

Old Rydon Lane, Exeter, Devon EX2 7JY
Ⓣ (01392) 873672
Ⓕ (01392) 876710
Ⓔ sales@stbridgetnurseries.co.uk
Ⓦ www.stbridgetnurseries.co.uk
Contact: Garden Centre Plant Advice
Opening Times: 0900-1700 Mon-Sat, 1030-1630 Sun. Closed Xmas Day, Boxing Day, New Year's Day & Easter Sunday.
Min Mail Order UK: Nmc
Cat. Cost: Free.
Credit Cards: All major credit/debit cards
Specialities: Large general nursery, with two garden centres.
Notes: Mail order available, please contact for prices & carriage charges. Also sells wholesale.
Map Ref: C, C4 **OS Grid Ref:** SX955905

CSev **Lower Severalls Nursery** ⊠ ♿

Crewkerne, Somerset TA18 7NX
Ⓣ (01460) 73234
Ⓜ 07769 273829
Ⓔ mary@lowerseveralls.co.uk
Ⓦ www.lowerseveralls.co.uk
Contact: Mary R Pring

Opening Times: 1000-1700 Tue, Wed, Fri, Sat, Mar-end Sep. Closed Aug.
Min Mail Order UK: £20.00
Cat. Cost: 4 × 1st class.
Credit Cards: Visa, MasterCard
Specialities: Herbs, herbaceous.
Notes: Mail order perennials only.
Map Ref: C, B5 **OS Grid Ref:** ST457111

CSil **Silver Dale Nurseries** €
Shute Lane, Combe Martin, Devon EX34 0HT
Ⓣ (01271) 882539
Ⓔ silverdale.nurseries@virgin.net
Contact: Roger Gilbert
Opening Times: 1000-1700 7 days. Closed Nov-Jan.
Cat. Cost: 4 × 1st class.
Credit Cards: Visa, MasterCard, EuroCard
Specialities: Nat. Collection of *Fuchsia*. Hardy fuchsias (cultivars and species).
Map Ref: C, B3

CSna **Snape Cottage** ⊠
Chaffeymoor, Bourton, Dorset SP8 5BZ
Ⓣ (01747) 840330 (evenings only).
Ⓔ ianandangela@snapecottagegarden.co.uk
Ⓦ www.snapestakes.com
Contact: Mrs Angela Whinfield
Opening Times: 1400-1700 last w/end (Sat & Sun) in months Feb-Aug incl.
Min Mail Order UK: Nmc
Cat. Cost: Sae.
Credit Cards: None
Specialities: 'Old' forms of many popular garden plants. Plantsman's garden open same time as nursery. Stock available in small quantities. Snape Stakes plant supports.
Notes: Mail order *Galanthus* only. List issued in Feb. Group visits welcome.
Map Ref: C, B5 **OS Grid Ref:** ST762303

CSpe **Special Plants** ⊠ ⌂ €
Hill Farm Barn, Greenways Lane, Cold Ashton, Chippenham, Wiltshire SN14 8LA
Ⓣ (01225) 891686
Ⓔ derry@specialplants.net
Ⓦ www.specialplants.net
Contact: Derry Watkins
Opening Times: 1000-1700 7 days Mar-Oct. Other times please ring first to check.
Min Mail Order UK: £10.00 + p&p
Cat. Cost: 2 × 1st class for seed list.
Credit Cards: All major credit/debit cards
Specialities: Tender perennials, *Pelargonium*, *Salvia*, *Streptocarpus*, hardy geraniums, *Anemone*, *Erysimum*, *Papaver*, *Viola* & grasses. Many varieties prop. in small numbers only.
Notes: Mail order Sep-Mar only.
Map Ref: C, A5 **OS Grid Ref:** ST749726

CSPN **Sherston Parva Nursery** ⊠ ☒ ⌂ € ♿
Malmesbury Road, Sherston, Wiltshire SN16 0NX
Ⓣ (01666) 840348
Ⓜ 07887 814843
Ⓔ sherstonparva@aol.com
Ⓦ www.sherstonparva.com
Contact: Martin Rea
Opening Times: 1000-1700 7 days 1st Feb-31th Dec. Closed Jan.
Min Mail Order UK: Nmc
Min Mail Order EU: Nmc
Cat. Cost: Free.
Credit Cards: MasterCard, Delta, Visa, Switch
Specialities: *Clematis*, wall shrubs & climbers.
Map Ref: C, A5

CSto **Stone Lane Gardens** ⊠
Stone Farm, Chagford, Devon TQ13 8JU
Ⓣ (01647) 231311
Ⓔ orders@mythicgarden.eclipse.co.uk
Ⓦ www.stonelanegardens.com
Contact: Paul Bartlett
Opening Times: 0900-1700 Mon-Fri. Collection at w/ends possible. Please phone first if travelling a long distance.
Min Mail Order UK: Nmc
Min Mail Order EU: Nmc
Cat. Cost: 6 × 1st class for colour catalogue with photos.
Credit Cards: All major credit/debit cards
Specialities: Comprehensive selection of wild origin *Betula* & *Alnus*, both bare-root & in pots. Choice selection of specially grafted cvs. Nat. Collection of Birch & Alder.
Notes: Arboretum open all year with summer sculpture exhibition (charges apply). Planting service available in West Country, details on request. Credit cards accepted online only. Also sells wholesale.
Map Ref: C, C3 **OS Grid Ref:** SX708908

CSut **Suttons Seeds** ⊠
Woodview Road, Paignton, Devon TQ4 7NG
Ⓣ 0844 922 2899
Ⓕ 0844 922 2265
Ⓦ www.suttons.co.uk
Contact: Customer Services

KEY
⊠ Mail order to UK or EU ⌂ Delivers to shows
☒ Exports beyond EU € Euro accepted
♿ Accessible by wheelchair ◆ See Display advertisement

C

Opening Times: (Office) 0830-1700 Mon-Fri. Also answerphone.
Min Mail Order UK: Nmc
Min Mail Order EU: £5.00
Cat. Cost: Free.
Credit Cards: Visa, MasterCard, Switch, Delta
Specialities: Over 1,000 varieties of flower & vegetable seed, bulbs, plants & sundries.

CSWC **SOUTH WEST CARNIVOROUS PLANTS** ⊠ ☒
Blackwater Nursery, Blackwater Road, Culmstock, Cullompton, Devon EX15 3HG
Ⓣ (01823) 681669
Ⓕ 0870 705 3083
Ⓔ flytraps@littleshopofhorrors.co.uk
Ⓦ www.littleshopofhorrors.co.uk
Contact: Jenny Pearce & Alistair Pearce
Opening Times: By appt.
Min Mail Order UK: Nmc
Min Mail Order EU: Nmc
Cat. Cost: 2 × 2nd class.
Credit Cards: All major credit/debit cards
Specialities: *Cephalotus*, *Nepenthes*, *Dionea*, *Drosera*, *Darlingtonia*, *Sarracenia*, *Pinguicula* & *Utricularia*. Specialists in hardy carnivorous plants & *Dionea muscipula* cvs.
Map Ref: C, B4

CTca **TRECANNA NURSERY** ⊠ ☒ ⌂
Rose Farm, Latchley, Nr Gunnislake, Cornwall PL18 9AX
Ⓣ (01822) 834680
Ⓜ 07785 242148
Ⓔ mark@trecanna.com
Ⓦ www.trecanna.com
Contact: Mark Wash
Opening Times: 1000-1700 Fri only, Mar-Nov incl. or by prior appt. Nursery will be relocating during 2011.
Min Mail Order UK: £20
Min Mail Order EU: £40
Cat. Cost: £1.00
Credit Cards: All major credit/debit cards
Specialities: Hardy South African plants. Good collections of *Crocosmia*, *Eucomis*, *Kniphofia*, *Watsonia*, *Crinum*, *Albuca*, nerines, *Zantedeschia*, *Lachenalia* & *Moraea*. Wide range of dry bulbs from around the globe.
Notes: Talks to garden societies. Tours of the nursery. Partial wheelchair access.
Map Ref: C, C3 **OS Grid Ref:** SX247733

CTho **THORNHAYES NURSERY** ⊠ €
St Andrews Wood, Dulford, Cullompton, Devon EX15 2DF
Ⓣ (01884) 266746
Ⓕ (01884) 266739
Ⓔ trees@thornhayes-nursery.co.uk
Ⓦ www.thornhayes-nursery.co.uk
Contact: K D Croucher
Opening Times: 0800-1600 Mon-Fri. 0930-1400 Sat (Sep-Apr).
Min Mail Order UK: £100
Min Mail Order EU: £100
Credit Cards: All major credit/debit cards
Specialities: A broad range of forms of ornamental, amenity & fruit trees incl. West Country apple varieties.
Notes: Limited wheelchair access. Also sells wholesale.
Map Ref: C, C4

CTrC **TREVENA CROSS NURSERIES** ⊠ € ♿
Breage, Helston, Cornwall TR13 9PY
Ⓣ (01736) 763880
Ⓕ (01736) 762828
Ⓔ sales@trevenacross.co.uk
Ⓦ www.trevenacross.co.uk
Contact: John Eddy, Nick Hann
Opening Times: 0900-1700 Mon-Sat, 1030-1630 Sun.
Min Mail Order UK: Nmc
Cat. Cost: Online only.
Credit Cards: Access, Visa, Switch
Specialities: South African, Australian & New Zealand plants, incl. *Aloe*, *Protea*, tree ferns, palms, *Restio*, hardy succulents & wide range of other exotics.
Map Ref: C, D1 **OS Grid Ref:** SW614284

CTrh **TREHANE NURSERY** ⊠ ⌂ ♿
Stapehill Road, Hampreston, Wimborne, Dorset BH21 7ND
Ⓣ (01202) 873490
Ⓕ (01202) 873490
Ⓔ camellias@trehanenursery.co.uk
Ⓦ www.trehanenursery.co.uk
Contact: Lorraine
Opening Times: 0830-1630 Mon-Fri all year (excl. Xmas & New Year). 1000-1600 Sat-Sun in spring & by special appt.
Min Mail Order UK: Nmc
Cat. Cost: £1.50 cat./book.
Credit Cards: All major credit/debit cards
Specialities: Extensive range of *Camellia* species, cultivars & hybrids. Many new introductions. Evergreen azaleas, *Pieris* & blueberries.
Notes: Also sells wholesale.
Map Ref: C, C6 **OS Grid Ref:** SU059000

CTri **TRISCOMBE NURSERIES** ⊠ ♿ ◆
West Bagborough, Nr Taunton, Somerset TA4 3HG
Ⓣ (01984) 618267
Ⓔ triscombe.nurseries2000@virgin.net

Ⓦ www.triscombenurseries.co.uk
Contact: S Parkman
Opening Times: 0900-1730 Mon-Sat. 1400-1730 Sun & B/hols.
Min Mail Order UK: Nmc
Cat. Cost: 1 × 1st class.
Credit Cards: None
Specialities: Trees, shrubs, roses, fruit, *Clematis*, herbaceous & rock plants.
Map Ref: C, B4

CTsd **TRESEDERS** ⊠ ♿
Wallcottage Nursery, Lockengate, St. Austell, Cornwall PL26 8RU
Ⓣ (01208) 832234
Ⓔ Treseders@btconnect.com
Ⓦ www.treseders.co.uk
Contact: James Treseder
Opening Times: 0900-1700 Mon-Sat, 1000-1600 Sun.
Min Mail Order UK: Nmc
Cat. Cost: Plant list available on request.
Credit Cards: All major credit/debit cards
Specialities: A wide range of choice & unusual plants grown in peat-free compost. Establishing the Nat. Collection of *Prostanthera*.
Notes: Also sells wholesale.
Map Ref: C, C2 **OS Grid Ref:** SX034620

CTuc **EDWIN TUCKER & SONS** ⊠
Brewery Meadow, Stonepark, Ashburton, Newton Abbot, Devon TQ13 7DG
Ⓣ (01364) 652233
Ⓕ (01364) 654211
Ⓔ seeds@edwintucker.com
Ⓦ www.edwintucker.com
Contact: Geoff Penton
Opening Times: 0800-1700 Mon-Fri, 0800-1600 Sat.
Min Mail Order UK: Nmc
Min Mail Order EU: Nmc
Cat. Cost: Free.
Credit Cards: All major credit/debit cards
Specialities: Nearly 120 varieties of seed potatoes, incl. 50 organic varieties. Wide range of vegetables, flowers, green manures & sprouting seeds in packets. None treated. Nearly 200 varieties of organically produced seeds.
Notes: Also sells wholesale.

CWan **WANBOROUGH HERB NURSERY** ⛺
Callas Hill, Wanborough, Swindon, Wiltshire SN4 0DQ
Ⓣ (01793) 790327 (answering machine)
Ⓔ wanboroughnursery@btinternet.com
Ⓦ www.wanboroughherbnursery.moonfruit.com
Contact: Peter Biggs
Opening Times: 1000-1700 Fri-Mon, Mar-Oct. Other times by appt. only.
Cat. Cost: £1.00
Credit Cards: None
Specialities: Herbs, herbaceous, esp. culinary. Available in small quantities only.
Notes: Nursery located on Callas Hill between Wanborough & Fox Hill.
Map Ref: C, A6 **OS Grid Ref:** SU217828

CWat **THE WATER GARDEN** ⊠ ♿
Hinton Parva, Swindon, Wiltshire SN4 0DH
Ⓣ (01793) 790558
Ⓕ (01793) 791298
Ⓔ mike@thewatergarden.co.uk
Ⓦ www.thewatergarden.co.uk
Contact: Mike & Anne Newman
Opening Times: 1000-1700 Wed-Sun.
Min Mail Order UK: £10.00 + p&p
Cat. Cost: 4 × 1st class.
Credit Cards: Visa, Access, Switch
Specialities: Water lilies, marginal & moisture plants, oxygenators & alpines.
Notes: Also sells wholesale.
Map Ref: C, A6

CWCL **WESTCOUNTRY NURSERIES** ⊠ ⛺ ♿
Donkey Meadow, Woolsery, Devon EX39 5QH
Ⓣ (01237) 431111
Ⓔ info@westcountry-nurseries.co.uk
Ⓦ www.westcountry-nurseries.co.uk
Contact: Sarah Conibear
Opening Times: 1000-1600 Mar-Jul. Closed for lunch 1300-1330.
Min Mail Order UK: £10.00
Cat. Cost: 2 × 1st class + A5 sae for full colour cat.
Credit Cards: All major credit/debit cards
Specialities: *Lupinus*, *Lewisia*, *Hellebore*, *Clematis*, cyclamen, acers, lavender, select perennials, grasses, ferns & climbers. Nat. Collection of Lupins.
Map Ref: C, B2 **OS Grid Ref:** SS351219

CWGN **WALLED GARDEN NURSERY** ⊠ ♿ ◆
Brinkworth House, Brinkworth, Nr Malmesbury, Wiltshire SN15 5DF
Ⓣ (01666) 826637
Ⓔ f.wescott@btinternet.com
Ⓦ www.clematis-nursery.co.uk
Contact: Fraser Wescott

KEY
⊠ Mail order to UK or EU ⛺ Delivers to shows
✈ Exports beyond EU € Euro accepted
♿ Accessible by wheelchair ◆ See Display advertisement

C

Opening Times: 1000-1700, 7 days Mar-Oct. 1000-dusk, Mon-Fri Nov & Feb. Closed Dec & Jan.
Min Mail Order UK: Nmc
Credit Cards: All major credit/debit cards
Specialities: *Clematis* & climbers, with a selection of unusual perennials & shrubs.
Map Ref: C, A6 **OS Grid Ref:** SU002849

CWGr **Winchester Growers Ltd** ⊠ ☒ ♿
Varfell Farm, Long Rock, Penzance, Cornwall TR20 8AQ
Ⓣ (01736) 335851
Ⓕ (01736) 851033
Ⓔ info@national-dahlia-collection.co.uk
Ⓦ www.national-dahlia-collection.co.uk
Contact: Michael Mann
Opening Times: 1300-1630 mid-Jul to end Aug.
Min Mail Order UK: Nmc
Min Mail Order EU: Nmc
Cat. Cost: Free.
Credit Cards: Visa, Delta, MasterCard, Switch
Specialities: Nat. Collection of *Dahlia*. Due to large number of varieties, some stock available in small quantities only.
Notes: Also sells wholesale.

CWib **Wibble Farm Nurseries** ⊠ ♿
Wibble Farm, West Quantoxhead, Nr Taunton, Somerset TA4 4DD
Ⓣ (01984) 632303
Ⓕ (01984) 633168
Ⓔ sales@wibblefarmnurseries.co.uk
Ⓦ www.wibblefarmnurseries.co.uk
Contact: Mrs M L Francis
Opening Times: 0800-1700 Mon-Fri, 1000-1600 Sat. 1400-1600 Sun (open Sun Mar-Sep only). All year incl. some B/hols.
Min Mail Order UK: Nmc
Min Mail Order EU: Nmc
Cat. Cost: 3 × 1st class.
Credit Cards: All major credit/debit cards
Specialities: Growers of a wide range of hardy plants, many rare & unusual. Display gardens.
Notes: Also sells wholesale.
Map Ref: C, B4

CWil **Fernwood Nursery** ⊠ ☒ €
Peters Marland, Torrington, Devon EX38 8QG
Ⓣ (01805) 601446
Ⓔ hw@fernwood-nursery.co.uk
Ⓦ www.fernwood-nursery.co.uk
Contact: Howard Wills & Sally Wills
Opening Times: Any time by appt. Please phone or email first.
Min Mail Order UK: Nmc
Min Mail Order EU: Nmc
Cat. Cost: Sae for list.
Credit Cards: Paypal
Specialities: Nat. Collection of *Sempervivum, Jovibarba, Rosularia* & *Phormium.*
Notes: Mail order for *Sempervivum, Jovibarba* & *Rosularia* only. 5 miles from RHS Rosemoor.
Map Ref: C, C3 **OS Grid Ref:** SS479133

CWiW **Windrush Willow** ⊠ ☒ €
Higher Barn, Sidmouth Road, Aylesbeare, Exeter, Devon EX5 2JJ
Ⓣ (01395) 233669
Ⓕ (01395) 233669
Ⓔ windrushw@aol.com
Ⓦ www.windrushwillow.com
Contact: Richard Kerwood
Opening Times: Mail order only. Open by appt.
Min Mail Order UK: Nmc
Min Mail Order EU: Nmc
Cat. Cost: 2 × 1st class.
Credit Cards: None
Specialities: *Salix.* Unrooted cuttings available Dec-Mar.
Notes: Also sells wholesale.

CWon **The Wonder Tree** ⊠ ⌂
35 Beaconsfield Road, Knowle, Bristol BS4 2JE
Ⓣ 0117 908 9057
Ⓜ 07989 333507
Ⓔ Kevin@wondertree.co.uk
Ⓦ www.wondertree.co.uk
Contact: Kevin Lindegaard
Opening Times: Not open. Mail order only.
Min Mail Order UK: Nmc
Cat. Cost: Online only.
Credit Cards: All major credit/debit cards
Specialities: *Salix.*
Notes: Also sells wholesale.
Map Ref: C, A5

CWri **Nigel Wright Rhododendrons** ♿
The Old Glebe, Eggesford, Chulmleigh, Devon EX18 7QU
Ⓣ (01769) 580632
Ⓔ wrightrhodos@aol.com
Ⓦ www.wrightrhodos.com
Contact: Nigel Wright
Opening Times: By appt. only. 7 days.
Cat. Cost: 2 × 1st class.
Credit Cards: None
Specialities: *Rhododendron* & deciduous azaleas. 200 varieties field grown, root-balled, some potted. For collection only. Specialist

grower. Free advice & planting plans.
Notes: Also sells wholesale.
Map Ref: C, B3 **OS Grid Ref:** SS684106

CWSG **West Somerset Garden Centre** ⊠ ♿
Mart Road, Minehead, Somerset TA24 5BJ
Ⓣ (01643) 703812
Ⓕ (01643) 706476
Ⓔ wsgc@btconnect.com
Ⓦ www.westsomersetgardencentre.co.uk
Contact: Ms J K Webber
Opening Times: 0800-1700 Mon-Sat, 1000-1600 Sun.
Min Mail Order UK: Nmc
Cat. Cost: None issued.
Credit Cards: Visa, Solo, Maestro, MasterCard
Specialities: Wide general range. *Ceanothus.*
Map Ref: C, B4

CWVF **White Veil Fuchsias** ⊠ ♿
Verwood Road, Three Legged Cross, Wimborne, Dorset BH21 6RP
Ⓣ (01202) 813998
Contact: A. C. Holloway
Opening Times: 0900-1300 & 1400-1700 Mon-Sat, 1000-1300 & 1400-1600 Sun, Jan-Aug. Closed Sat & Sun, Sep-Dec.
Min Mail Order UK: 8 plants of your choice.
Cat. Cost: 4 × 1st class.
Credit Cards: None
Specialities: Fuchsias. Small plants grown from Jan-Apr. Available in small quantities only.

CYeo **South Yeo Nursery** ⊠ ⌂
Poughill, Crediton, Devon EX17 4LF
Ⓣ (01363) 866740
Ⓜ 07971 412132
Ⓕ (01363) 866740
Ⓔ davidross@eclecticplants.co.uk
Ⓦ www.eclecticplants.co.uk
Contact: David & Penny Ross
Opening Times: Open most days but please phone in advance to check & get directions.
Min Mail Order UK: Nmc
Min Mail Order EU: Nmc
Cat. Cost: 6 × 1st class.
Credit Cards: Paypal
Specialities: Small, family-run nursery specialising in South African & other plants. *Schizostylis, Agapanthus, Dierama, Crocosmia* & *Rhodohypoxis*. Also unusual alpines & other perennials.
Notes: Nursery located in Grade II* listed traditional Devon courtyard. Nat. Collection of *Hesperantha coccinea* cvs.
Map Ref: C, C3 **OS Grid Ref:** SS865085

Eastern

EABi **Alison Bilverstone** ⊠ €
22 Kings Street, Swaffham, Norfolk PE37 7BU
Ⓣ (01760) 725026
Ⓔ a.bilverstone@tiscali.co.uk
Contact: Alison Bilverstone
Opening Times: Not open. Mail order only.
Min Mail Order UK: Nmc
Min Mail Order EU: Nmc
Cat. Cost: A4 sae.
Credit Cards: None
Specialities: *Achemene, Kohleria* & *Smithiantha* rhizomes, available Dec to mid-Apr. Stocked in small quantities.

EACa **Alpine Campanulas (Bellflower Nursery)** ⊠ ⌂
Langham Hall Walled Garden, Langham, Nr Bury St Edmunds, Suffolk IP31 3EE
Ⓜ 07879 644958
Ⓔ campanulas@btinternet.com
Ⓦ www.alpinecampanulas.co.uk
Contact: Sue Wooster
Opening Times: 1000-1700 Thu & Fri, 1000-1300 Sat. Other times by appt.
Min Mail Order UK: £10.00
Cat. Cost: 1 × 1st class sae.
Specialities: *Campanula.* Nat. Collection of Alpine Campanulas. Most stock in small numbers only.
Notes: Hardy plant nursery at the Walled Garden, Langham Hall, Nr Bury St Edmunds, Suffolk. Groups welcome by appt.
Map Ref: E, C3 **OS Grid Ref:** TL978691

EAEE **AEE: A Lover of Plants** ⊠
38 Church Close, Roydon, Diss, Norfolk IP22 5RQ
Ⓣ (01379) 651230
Ⓕ (01379) 651230
Ⓔ aeesales@fsmail.net
Ⓦ www.aeesupplyingplantlovers.com
Contact: Anne Etheridge
Opening Times: Apr-Sep at Garden Shows & Plant Fairs. Otherwise plants available by mail order, website & at talks.
Min Mail Order UK: Nmc
Min Mail Order EU: Nmc
Cat. Cost: 3 × 1st class.
Credit Cards: Paypal
Specialities: Perennials & grasses plus a few

KEY
⊠ Mail order to UK or EU ⌂ Delivers to shows
✈ Exports beyond EU € Euro accepted
♿ Accessible by wheelchair ◆ See Display advertisement

enticing alpines & shrubs. Alpines & shrubs available in small quantities only.
Notes: Talks available. Plants may be reserved for collection with a £5.00 deposit. Plants delivered free within 10 miles of Roydon.

EAmu **AMULREE EXOTICS** ⊠ ♿
The Turnpike, Norwich Road (B1113), Fundenhall, Norwich, Norfolk NR16 1EL
Ⓣ (01508) 488101
Ⓔ SDG@exotica.fsbusiness.co.uk
Ⓦ www.turn-it-tropical.co.uk
Contact: S Gridley
Opening Times: 0930-1730 7 days spring-autumn, 1000-1630 7 days autumn-spring.
Min Mail Order UK: Nmc
Min Mail Order EU: Nmc
Cat. Cost: 2 × 1st class.
Credit Cards: Visa, MasterCard, Electron, Solo, Switch
Specialities: Hardy & half-hardy plants for home, garden & conservatory. Palms, bamboos, bananas, tree ferns, cannas, gingers, cacti, succulents & much more.
Notes: Also sells wholesale.
Map Ref: E, B3 **OS Grid Ref:** DX123740

EBak **B & H M BAKER** ♿
Bourne Brook Nurseries, Greenstead Green, Halstead, Essex CO9 1RB
Ⓣ (01787) 476369
Contact: Clive Baker
Opening Times: 0800-1600 Mon-Fri, 0900-1200 & 1400-1600 Sat & Sun, Mar-30th Jun.
Cat. Cost: 2 × 1st class + 33p.
Credit Cards: All major credit/debit cards
Specialities: *Fuchsia* & conservatory plants.
Notes: Also sells wholesale.
Map Ref: E, C2

EBee **BEECHES NURSERY** ⊠ ♿
Village Centre, Ashdon, Saffron Walden, Essex CB10 2HB
Ⓣ (01799) 584362
Ⓕ (01799) 584421
Ⓔ sales@beechesnursery.co.uk
Ⓦ www.beechesnursery.co.uk
Contact: Alan Bidwell/Kevin Marsh
Opening Times: 0830-1700 Mon-Sat, 1000-1700 Sun & B/hols.
Min Mail Order UK: £12.00
Min Mail Order EU: £20.00
Cat. Cost: 6 × 2nd class for herbaceous list.
Credit Cards: All major credit/debit cards
Specialities: Herbaceous specialists & extensive range of other garden plants. Rarieties available in ltd. numbers only.
Notes: Plants dispatched Oct-Feb only. Orders accepted throughout the year. No trees by mail order.
Map Ref: E, C2 **OS Grid Ref:** TL586420

EBla **BLACKSMITHS COTTAGE NURSERY** ⊠ ♿
Langmere Road, Langmere, Dickleburgh, Nr Diss, Norfolk IP21 4QA
Ⓣ (01379) 741136
Ⓔ Blackcottnursery@aol.com
Ⓦ www.blackcottnursery.co.uk
Contact: Ben, Sarah or Jill Potterton
Opening Times: 1000-1700 Thu-Sun & B/hol Mon, Mar-Oct.
Min Mail Order UK: Nmc
Cat. Cost: Online only.
Credit Cards: All major credit/debit cards
Specialities: Over 2000 species grown. Large selection of shade plants esp. *Anemone nemorosa* & *Poygonatum*, also large collection of *Geranium*, *Astrantia* & *Sanguisorba*.
Notes: Coffee Shop & toilets. Barn garden & bird collection. Group visits by appt.
Map Ref: E, C3 **OS Grid Ref:** TM192821

EBtc **BOTANICA** ⊠
Chantry Farm, Campsea Ashe, Wickham Market, Suffolk IP13 0PZ
Ⓣ (01728) 747113
Ⓕ (01728) 747725
Ⓔ sales@botanica.org.uk
Ⓦ www.botanica.org.uk
Contact: Daniel Everett
Opening Times: 1000-1700 6 days summer, 1000-1700 5 days August, 1000-1600 7 days winter.
Min Mail Order UK: £15 + p&p
Cat. Cost: Online only.
Credit Cards: All, except American Express
Specialities: Range of rare & unusual hardy plants.
Notes: Also sells wholesale.
Map Ref: E, C3 **OS Grid Ref:** 632824/255500

ECGP **CAMBRIDGE GARDEN PLANTS** € ♿
The Lodge, Clayhithe Road, Horningsea, Cambridgeshire CB25 9JD
Ⓣ (01223) 861370
Ⓔ kit@cambridgegardenplants.co.uk
Contact: Kit Buchdahl
Opening Times: 1100-1730 Thu-Sun mid Mar-31st Oct. Other times by appt.
Cat. Cost: 4 × 1st class.
Credit Cards: None
Specialities: Hardy perennials incl. wide range of *Geranium*, *Allium*, *Euphorbia*, *Cyclamen*, *Digitalis*.
Map Ref: E, C2 **OS Grid Ref:** TL497637

E

ECha **THE BETH CHATTO GARDENS LTD** ⊠ ♿
Elmstead Market, Colchester, Essex
CO7 7DB
Ⓣ (01206) 822007
Ⓕ (01206) 825933
Ⓔ info@bethchatto.fsnet.co.uk
Ⓦ www.bethchatto.co.uk
Contact: Beth Chatto
Opening Times: 0900-1700 Mon-Sat, 1000-1700 Sun, 1st Mar-31st Oct. 0900-1600 Mon-Sat, 1000-1600 Sun, 1st Nov to end Feb.
Min Mail Order UK: £20.00
Min Mail Order EU: Ask for details
Cat. Cost: Free plant list.
Credit Cards: Visa, MasterCard, Maestro
Specialities: Predominantly herbaceous. Many unusual for special situations.
Map Ref: E, D3 **OS Grid Ref:** TM069238

ECho **CHOICE LANDSCAPES** ⊠ ✈ ♿
Priory Farm, 101 Salts Road, West Walton, Wisbech, Cambridgeshire PE14 7EF
Ⓣ (01945) 585051
Contact: Michael Agg & Jillian Agg
Opening Times: By appt.
Min Mail Order UK: £12.00
Min Mail Order EU: £15.00 + p&p
Cat. Cost: 6 × 1st class or 6 IRC
Credit Cards: Maestro, Visa, MasterCard, Solo
Specialities: Alpines, rhododendrons, bulbs, lilies & South African bulbs & seed.
Map Ref: E, B1

ECnt **CANTS OF COLCHESTER LTD** ⊠ ✈
Nayland Road, Mile End, Colchester, Essex
CO4 5HA
Ⓣ (01206) 844008
Ⓕ (01206) 855371
Ⓔ finder@cantsroses.co.uk
Ⓦ www.cantsroses.co.uk
Contact: Angela Pawsey
Opening Times: 0900-1300, 1400-1630 Mon-Fri. Sat varied, please phone first. Sun closed.
Min Mail Order UK: Nmc
Min Mail Order EU: Nmc
Cat. Cost: Free.
Credit Cards: Visa, MasterCard, Delta, Solo, Switch
Specialities: Roses. Unstaffed rose field can be viewed dawn-dusk every day from end Jun-end Sep.
Notes: Bare-root mail order end Oct-end Mar, containers Apr-Aug. Partial wheelchair access.
Map Ref: E, C3

ECou **COUNTY PARK NURSERY**
Essex Gardens, Hornchurch, Essex
RM11 3BU
Ⓣ (01708) 445205
Ⓦ www.countyparknursery.co.uk
Contact: G Hutchins
Opening Times: 1000-1700 Mon-Sat excl. Wed, 1000-1700 Sun Mar-Oct. Nov-Feb by appt. only.
Cat. Cost: Online only.
Credit Cards: None
Specialities: Alpines & rare and unusual plants from New Zealand, Tasmania & the Falklands. Many plants in small quantities only.
Map Ref: E, D2

ECrc **THE CROCOSMIA GARDENS** ⊠ ✈ €
9 North Street, Caistor, Lincolnshire
LN7 6QU
Ⓣ (01472) 859269
Ⓜ 07506 441205
Ⓔ mark@thecrocosmiagardens.net
Ⓦ www.thecrocosmiagardens.net
Contact: Mark Fox
Opening Times: 1000-1700 Mon-Sun.
Min Mail Order UK: £5.00
Min Mail Order EU: Nmc
Credit Cards: None
Specialities: Nat. Collection of *Crocosmia*.
Map Ref: E, A1

ECre **CREAKE PLANT CENTRE** ♿
Leicester Road, South Creake, Fakenham, Norfolk NR21 9PW
Ⓣ (01328) 823018
Ⓜ 07760 762499
Ⓔ trevor-harrison@btconnect.com
Contact: Mr T Harrison
Opening Times: 1000-1300 & 1400-1730 7 days excl. Xmas.
Cat. Cost: None issued.
Credit Cards: All major credit/debit cards
Specialities: Unusual shrubs, herbaceous, conservatory plants, old roses. Hellebores.
Map Ref: E, B1 **OS Grid Ref:** TF864353

ECrN **CROWN NURSERY** ⊠ ♿
High Street, Ufford, Suffolk IP13 6EL
Ⓣ (01394) 460755
Ⓕ (01394) 460142
Ⓔ enquiries@crown-nursery.co.uk
Ⓦ www.crown-nursery.co.uk
Contact: Jill Proctor

KEY
⊠ Mail order to UK or EU — Delivers to shows
✈ Exports beyond EU — € Euro accepted
♿ Accessible by wheelchair — ◆ See Display advertisement

E

Opening Times: 0900-1700 (1600 in winter) Mon-Sat.
Min Mail Order UK: Nmc
Cat. Cost: 2 × 1st class.
Credit Cards: All major credit/debit cards
Specialities: Mature & semi-mature native, ornamental & fruit trees. Heritage fruit varieties.
Notes: Mail order for small/young stock only. Also sells wholesale.
Map Ref: E, C3 **OS Grid Ref:** TM292528

ECtt Cottage Nurseries ⊠ ♿
Thoresthorpe, Alford, Lincolnshire
LN13 0HX
Ⓣ (01507) 466968
Ⓕ (01507) 463409
Ⓔ bill@cottagenurseries.net
Ⓦ www.cottagenurseries.net
Contact: W H Denbigh
Opening Times: 0900-1700 7 days 1st Mar-31st Oct. 1000-1500 w/ends only Nov-Feb.
Min Mail Order UK: £15.00
Cat. Cost: 3 × 1st class.
Credit Cards: Visa, MasterCard, Maestro
Specialities: Hardy perennials. Wide general range.
Map Ref: E, A2 **OS Grid Ref:** TF423716

EDAr D'Arcy & Everest ⊠ ⌂ € ♿
(Office) PO Box 78, St Ives, Huntingdon, Cambridgeshire PE27 6ZA
Ⓣ (01480) 497672 answerphone
Ⓜ 07715 374440
Ⓕ (01480) 466042
Ⓔ angela@darcyeverest.co.uk
Ⓦ www.darcyeverest.co.uk
Contact: Angela Whiting, Richard Oliver
Opening Times: Wed-Fri, Mar-Sep, except show dates. Winter by appt. Coach parties welcome by appt.
Min Mail Order UK: £15.00 + p&p
Min Mail Order EU: £30.00 + p&p
Cat. Cost: 6 × 1st class.
Credit Cards: None
Specialities: Alpines & sempervivums.
Notes: Nursery is at Pidley Sheep Lane (B1040), Pidley, Huntingdon, Cambs PE28 3FL.
Map Ref: E, C2 **OS Grid Ref:** TL338762

EDif Different Plants ⌂ ♿
The Mellis Stud, Gate Farm, Cranley Green, Eye, Suffolk IP23 7NX
Ⓣ (01379) 870291
Ⓔ rickwtrs@talktalk.net
Contact: Fleur Waters
Opening Times: Sat-Thu by appt. only.
Cat. Cost: 4 × 1st class.
Credit Cards: None
Specialities: *Mimulus aurantiacus* & hybrids.
Map Ref: E, C3

EECP Essex Carnivorous Plants ⊠ ⌂
12 Strangman Avenue, Thundersley, Essex
SS7 1RB
Ⓣ (01702) 551467
Ⓔ Mark@essexcarnivorousplants.com
Ⓦ www.essexcarnivorousplants.com
Contact: Mark Haslett
Opening Times: By appt. only.
Min Mail Order UK: Nmc
Min Mail Order EU: Nmc
Cat. Cost: 2 × 1st class or online.
Credit Cards: None
Specialities: Good range of carnivorous plants. *Sarracenia, Drosera*. Nat. Collection of *Dionaea* forms & cvs. Some stock available in small quantities only. Nat. Collection of *Sarracenia* (hybrids & ssp.).
Notes: Also sells wholesale.
Map Ref: E, D2 **OS Grid Ref:** TQ797875

EExo The Exotic Garden Company ♿
Saxmundham Road, Aldeburgh, Suffolk
IP15 5JD
Ⓣ (01728) 454456
Ⓦ www.theexoticgardencompany.com
Contact: Matthew Couchy
Opening Times: 1000-1700 Mon-Sat, 1000-1600 Sun, Mar-Oct. 1000-dusk Nov-Dec. Closed Jan-Feb.
Cat. Cost: None issued.
Credit Cards: All major credit/debit cards
Specialities: General range of choice & some unusual perennials, shrubs, ferns, tree ferns, olives, palms, bamboos, herbs.
Map Ref: E, C3

EFer The Fern Nursery ⊠ ♿
Grimsby Road, Binbrook, Lincolnshire
LN8 6DH
Ⓣ (01472) 398092
Ⓔ richard@timm984.fsnet.co.uk
Ⓦ www.fernnursery.co.uk
Contact: R N Timm
Opening Times: 0900-1700 Fri, Sat & Sun Apr-Oct or by appt.
Min Mail Order UK: Nmc
Min Mail Order EU: Nmc
Cat. Cost: 2 × 1st class.
Credit Cards: None
Specialities: Ferns. Display garden.
Notes: Only plants listed in the mail order part of the catalogue will be sent mail order. Also sells wholesale.
Map Ref: E, A1 **OS Grid Ref:** TF212942

EFEx **FLORA EXOTICA** ⊠ ✈ €
Pasadena, South-Green, Fingringhoe, Colchester, Essex CO5 7DR
Ⓣ (01206) 729414
Ⓜ 07972 068679
Contact: J Beddoes
Opening Times: Not open. Mail order only.
Min Mail Order UK: Nmc
Min Mail Order EU: Nmc
Cat. Cost: 4 × 1st class.
Credit Cards: None
Specialities: Exotica flora incl. orchids.

EFly **THE FLY TRAP PLANTS** ⊠ ⌂ €
Cooke Road, Berghapton, Norwich, Norfolk NR15 1BA
Ⓣ (01508) 480348
Ⓜ 07769 2556
Ⓔ sales@tftplants.co.uk
Ⓦ tftplants.co.uk
Contact: Pauline Steward
Opening Times: By appt. only.
Min Mail Order UK: Nmc
Cat. Cost: 1 × 1st class sae.
Credit Cards: None
Specialities: All kinds of carnivorous plants, such as *Sarracenia*, *Drosera*, *Pinquicula*, to the *Utricularia* aquatic plants.

EGFP **GRANGE FARM PLANTS** ⊠ ♿
Grange Farm, 38 Fishergate Road, Sutton St James, Spalding, Lincolnshire PE12 0EZ
Ⓣ (01945) 440240
Ⓜ 07742 138760
Ⓕ (01945) 440355
Ⓔ ellis.family@tinyonline.co.uk
Contact: M C Ellis
Opening Times: Mail order only. Open by appt. only.
Min Mail Order UK: Nmc
Min Mail Order EU: Nmc
Cat. Cost: 1 × 1st class.
Credit Cards: None
Specialities: Rare trees & shrubs, esp. *Juglans*, *Fraxinus*. Some species available in small quantities only.
Map Ref: E, B2 **OS Grid Ref:** TF382186

EGHP **GREEN GARDEN HERBS** ⊠ ⌂ ♿
Beech House, 82 Leiston Road, Aldeburgh, Suffolk IP15 5PS
Ⓣ (01728) 452597
Ⓜ 07949 906290
Ⓔ info@greengardenherbs.co.uk
Ⓦ www.greengardenherbs.co.uk
Contact: Sarah Clark
Opening Times: Special open w/end 20th, 21st, 22nd May 2011. Other times by appt. only.
Min Mail Order UK: £15
Min Mail Order EU: £15
Cat. Cost: Online only. Plant list free with sae.
Credit Cards: None
Specialities: Herbs, aromatic, culinary, medicinal & ornamental, incl. *Salvia*, *Mentha*, *Thymus*. Plants & seed available.
Notes: Many plants available in small quantities. Some rarities not listed as only available in very small quantities. Also sells wholesale.
Map Ref: E, C3

EGol **GOLDBROOK PLANTS** ⊠ ✈
Hoxne, Eye, Suffolk IP21 5AN
Ⓣ (01379) 668770
Ⓕ (01379) 668770
Contact: Sandra Bond
Opening Times: 1000-1700, Thu-Sun Apr-Sep, or by appt. Other times by appt.
Min Mail Order UK: £15.00 + p&p
Min Mail Order EU: £100.00 + p&p
Cat. Cost: 3 × 1st class.
Credit Cards: None
Specialities: Very large range of *Hosta*, esp. miniature & small varieties. Some small hostas available in ltd quantities. Larger hostas being phased out.
Notes: Also sells wholesale.
Map Ref: E, C3

EGri **D GRIFFIN**
Alafin, Langford Road, Maldon, Essex CM9 4SU
Ⓣ (01621) 858384
Ⓜ 07725 876187
Contact: D Griffin
Opening Times: Open by appt. only (not Wed.). Please phone mobile number for appt.
Credit Cards: None
Specialities: *Yucca*, *Agave*. All plants available in small numbers.
Map Ref: E, D2

EHoe **HOECROFT PLANTS** ⊠ € ♿
Severals Grange, Holt Road, Wood Norton, Dereham, Norfolk NR20 5BL
Ⓣ (01362) 684206
Ⓔ hoecroft@hotmail.co.uk

KEY
⊠ Mail order to UK or EU ⌂ Delivers to shows
✈ Exports beyond EU € Euro accepted
♿ Accessible by wheelchair ◆ See Display advertisement

Ⓦ www.hoecroft.co.uk
Contact: Jane Lister
Opening Times: 1000-1600 Thu-Sun, 1st Apr-31st Oct or by appt.
Min Mail Order UK: Nmc
Min Mail Order EU: Nmc
Cat. Cost: 5 × 2nd class.
Credit Cards: None
Specialities: An extensive range of coloured & variegated-leaved shrubs & herbaceous perennials. 260 ornamental grasses. Free entry to display gardens.
Notes: Nursery 2 miles north of Guist on B1110.
Map Ref: E, B3 **OS Grid Ref:** TG008289

EHon **Honeysome Aquatic Nursery** ⊠
The Row, Sutton, Nr Ely, Cambridgeshire CB6 2PB
Ⓣ (01353) 778889
Ⓕ (01353) 777291
Ⓔ info@honeysomeaquaticnursery.co.uk
Ⓦ www.honeysomeaquaticnursery.co.uk
Contact: Mrs L S Bond
Opening Times: At all times by appt. only.
Min Mail Order UK: Nmc
Cat. Cost: 2 × 1st class.
Credit Cards: Paypal
Specialities: Hardy aquatic, bog & marginal.
Notes: Also sells wholesale.
Map Ref: E, C2

EHrv **Harveys Garden Plants** ⊠ ☒ ♠ € ♿
Great Green, Thurston,
Bury St Edmunds, Suffolk
IP31 3SJ
Ⓣ (01359) 233363
Ⓕ (01359) 233363 & answerphone
Ⓔ admin@harveysgardenplants.co.uk
Ⓦ www.harveysgardenplants.co.uk
Contact: Roger Harvey
Opening Times: 0930-1630 Tue-Sun.
Min Mail Order UK: £25 of plants + p&p
Min Mail Order EU: Please enquire.
Cat. Cost: £2.50
Credit Cards: All, except American Express
Specialities: *Helleborus*, *Anemone*, *Epimedium*, *Euphorbia*, *Eryngium*, *Galanthus*, *Astrantia*, *Pulmonaria* & other herbaceous perennials. Woodland plants.
Map Ref: E, C2 **OS Grid Ref:** 660939

EHul **Hull Farm** ⊠
Spring Valley Lane, Ardleigh, Colchester, Essex CO7 7SA
Ⓣ (01206) 230045
Ⓜ 07900 298366
Ⓔ conifers.hullfarm@tiscali.co.uk
Ⓦ www.fryersfarmshop.co.uk
Contact: Jack Fryer
Opening Times: By appt. only. Please phone for appt.
Min Mail Order UK: £50.00 + p&p
Cat. Cost: 5 × 2nd class.
Credit Cards: MasterCard, Visa
Specialities: Conifers, grasses.
Notes: Also sells wholesale.
Map Ref: E, C3 **OS Grid Ref:** GR043274

EIri **Irisesonline** ⊠
Slade Cottage, Petts Lane, Little Walden, Essex CB10 1XH
Ⓣ (01799) 526294
Ⓔ sales@irisesonline.co.uk
Ⓦ www.irisesonline.co.uk
Contact: Clare Kneen
Opening Times: By appt. only.
Min Mail Order UK: Nmc
Cat. Cost: 3 × 1st class or online.
Credit Cards: None
Specialities: *Iris*. Small family-run nursery. Some varieties available in small quantities only.
Map Ref: E, C2 **OS Grid Ref:** TL546416

EJWh **Jill White** ⊠ ♠ ♿
78 Hurst Green, Brightlingsea, Essex CO7 OEH
Ⓣ (01206) 303547
Contact: Jill White
Opening Times: By appt. only.
Min Mail Order UK: Nmc
Min Mail Order EU: Nmc
Cat. Cost: Sae.
Credit Cards: None
Specialities: *Cyclamen* species esp. *Cyclamen parviflorum*. *Cyclamen elegans*. Also seed.
Map Ref: E, D3 **OS Grid Ref:** TM088171

ELan **Langthorns Plantery** ⊠ ♿
High Cross Lane West, Little Canfield, Dunmow, Essex CM6 1TD
Ⓣ (01371) 872611
Ⓕ 0871 661 4093
Ⓔ info@langthorns.com
Ⓦ www.langthorns.com
Contact: E Cannon
Opening Times: 1000-1700 or dusk (if earlier) 7 days excl. Xmas fortnight.
Min Mail Order UK: £15.00
Cat. Cost: £1.50
Credit Cards: Visa, Access, Switch, MasterCard, Delta
Specialities: Wide general range with many unusual plants.
Notes: Mail order anything under 4ft tall.

Mail order not available during spring & summer months.
Map Ref: E, D2 **OS Grid Ref:** TL592204

ELar **Larkspur Nursery** ⊠
Fourways, Dog Drove South, Holbeach Drove, Spalding, Lincolnshire PE12 0SD
Ⓣ (01406) 330830
Ⓔ info@larkspur-nursery.co.uk
Ⓦ www.larkspur-nursery.co.uk
Contact: Ashley Ramsbottom
Opening Times: Mail order only. Open by prior arrangement. See website for details of nursery Open Days in Jun.
Min Mail Order UK: Nmc
Min Mail Order EU: Nmc
Cat. Cost: 2 × 1st class.
Credit Cards: None
Specialities: Delphiniums & *Abutilon*. Some varieties in small quantities. Order early to avoid disappointment. Also seed for sale.
Notes: Plants despatched from June in 7 or 8cm pots. See website for details.

ELau **Laurel Farm Herbs** ⊠ ♠ ♿
Main Road (A12), Kelsale, Saxmundham, Suffolk IP17 2RG
Ⓣ (01728) 668223
Ⓔ laurelfarmherbs@aol.com
Ⓦ www.laurelfarmherbs.co.uk
Contact: Chris Seagon
Opening Times: Please phone or check website for opening hours as times can vary.
Min Mail Order UK: 1 plant + p&p
Min Mail Order EU: 1 plant + p&p
Cat. Cost: Online only.
Credit Cards: Visa, MasterCard, Switch, Delta
Specialities: Herbs esp. rosemary, thyme, mint & sage.
Notes: Mail orders accepted by email, phone or post. Also sells wholesale.
Map Ref: E, C3

ELon **Long House Plants** ♿
The Long House, Church Road, Noak Hill, Romford, Essex RM4 1LD
Ⓣ (01708) 371719
Ⓕ (01708) 346649
Ⓔ tim@longhouse-plants.co.uk
Ⓦ www.longhouse-plants.co.uk
Contact: Tim Carter
Opening Times: 1000-1700 Fri, Sat & B/hols, 1000-1600 Sun, beginning Mar-end Sep, or by appt.
Cat. Cost: None issued.
Credit Cards: All major credit/debit cards
Specialities: Interesting range of choice shrubs, grasses & herbaceous perennials. Many unusual varieties.
Map Ref: E, D2 **OS Grid Ref:** TQ554194

EMal **Marshall's Malmaisons** ⊠ ♿
Hullwood Barn, Shelley, Ipswich, Suffolk IP7 5RE
Ⓣ (01473) 822400
Ⓜ 07768 454875
Ⓔ jim@malmaisons.plus.com
Ⓦ www.malmaisonsandiris.co.uk
Contact: J M Marshall/Sarah Cook
Opening Times: By appt. only.
Min Mail Order UK: £30.00 incl. p&p
Min Mail Order EU: £35.00 incl. p&p
Cat. Cost: 1st class sae.
Credit Cards: None
Specialities: Nat. Collections of Malmaison Carnations & Cedric Morris Irises. *Iris* stock only available in small quantities.
Notes: Also sells wholesale.
Map Ref: E, C3 **OS Grid Ref:** TM006394

EMic **Mickfield Hostas** ⊠ ♠ € ♿
The Poplars, Mickfield, Stowmarket, Suffolk IP14 5LH
Ⓣ (01449) 711576
Ⓕ (01449) 711576
Ⓔ mickfieldhostas@btconnect.com
Ⓦ www.mickfieldhostas.co.uk
Contact: Mr & Mrs R L C Milton
Opening Times: For specified dates see catalogue or website.
Min Mail Order UK: Nmc
Min Mail Order EU: Nmc
Cat. Cost: 4 × 1st class.
Credit Cards: All, except American Express
Specialities: Holders of Nat. Collection of *Hosta* containing over 2000 varieties. See website for details of cvs held & latest availability. Will split parent plants for customers if practical. Also operates a waiting list for rarities.
Map Ref: E, C3 **OS Grid Ref:** TM136619

EMil **Mill Race Garden Centre** ⊠ ♿
New Road, Aldham, Colchester, Essex CO6 3QT
Ⓣ (01206) 242521
Ⓕ (01206) 242073
Ⓔ plantdesk@millracegardencentre.co.uk
Ⓦ www.millracegardencentre.co.uk
Contact: Annette Bayliss
Opening Times: 0900-1730 Mon-Sat, 1000-1630 Sun.

KEY
⊠ Mail order to UK or EU ♠ Delivers to shows
✈ Exports beyond EU € Euro accepted
♿ Accessible by wheelchair ◆ See Display advertisement

E

Min Mail Order UK: £9.00
Credit Cards: All major credit/debit cards
Specialities: Stock available in small quantities only.
Notes: Trees & large shrubs not sent by mail order.
Map Ref: E, C2 **OS Grid Ref:** TL918268

ENBC **NORFOLK BAMBOO COMPANY** ⊠
Vine Cottage, The Drift, Ingoldisthorpe, King's Lynn, Norfolk PE31 6NW
Ⓣ (01485) 543935
Ⓜ 07970 310880
Ⓕ (01485) 543314
Ⓔ Lewdyer@hotmail.com
Ⓦ www.norfolkbamboo.co.uk
Contact: Lewis Dyer
Opening Times: 1000-1700 Fri, Apr-Sep, or by appt.
Min Mail Order UK: £10.00 + p&p
Cat. Cost: 1 × 1st class sae for price list.
Credit Cards: None
Specialities: Bamboos.
Map Ref: E, B2 **OS Grid Ref:** TF684334

ENfk **NORFOLK HERBS** ⊠ ♠ ♿ ◆
Blackberry Farm, Dillington, Dereham, Norfolk NR19 2QD
Ⓣ (01362) 860812
Ⓕ (01362) 860812
Ⓔ info@norfolkherbs.co.uk
Ⓦ www.norfolkherbs.co.uk
Contact: Rosemary or Oliver Clifton-Sprigg
Opening Times: 0900-1700 Mon-Sat, 1000-1600 Sun, Apr-Aug. 1000-1600 Fri & Sat, Feb, Oct & Nov. 1000-1600 Wed-Sat, Mar, Sept & Dec. Closed from Xmas to end Jan. To visit at other times, please contact nursery.
Min Mail Order UK: £5.90
Cat. Cost: 3 × 1st class.
Credit Cards: All major credit/debit cards
Specialities: Naturally raised culinary, medicinal & aromatic herb plants. Bay trees & scented pelagoniums.
Notes: Established 1986. A founding member of Norfolk Nursery Network. Also sells wholesale.
Map Ref: E, B2 **OS Grid Ref:** TF967152

EOHP **OLD HALL PLANTS** ⊠
1 The Old Hall, Barsham, Beccles, Suffolk NR34 8HB
Ⓣ (01502) 717475
Ⓔ info@oldhallplants.co.uk
Ⓦ www.oldhallplants.co.uk
Contact: Janet Elliott
Opening Times: By appt. only. Please phone first.
Min Mail Order UK: Nmc
Min Mail Order EU: Nmc
Cat. Cost: 4 × 1st class.
Credit Cards: Paypal
Specialities: A variety of rare herbs, house plants, *Plectranthus*. Some plants available in small quantities.
Notes: Partial wheelchair access. Paypal accepted for overseas orders only.
Map Ref: E, C3 **OS Grid Ref:** TM396904

EPau **PAUGERS PLANTS** ⊠ ♿
Bury Road, Depden, Bury St Edmunds, Suffolk IP29 4BU
Ⓣ (01284) 850527
Ⓜ 07906 618603
Ⓔ geraldine.arnold@btinternet.com
Contact: Geraldine Arnold
Opening Times: 0900-1730 Wed-Sat, 1000-1700 Sun & B/hols, 1st Mar-30th Nov.
Min Mail Order UK: Nmc
Cat. Cost: None issued.
Credit Cards: None
Specialities: Hardy shrubs & perennials in large or small quantities.
Notes: Also sells wholesale.
Map Ref: E, C2 **OS Grid Ref:** TL783568

EPfP **THE PLACE FOR PLANTS** ⊠ ♠ € ♿
East Bergholt Place, East Bergholt, Suffolk CO7 6UP
Ⓣ (01206) 299224
Ⓕ (01206) 299229
Ⓔ sales@placeforplants.co.uk
Ⓦ www.placeforplants.co.uk
Contact: Rupert & Sara Eley
Opening Times: 1000-1700 (or dusk if earlier) 7 days. Closed Easter Sun. Garden open Mar-Oct.
Min Mail Order UK: Nmc
Cat. Cost: 2 × 1st class.
Credit Cards: All major credit/debit cards
Specialities: Wide range of specialist & popular plants. Nat. Collection of Deciduous *Euonymus*. 20 acre mature garden with free access to RHS members during season.
Notes: Mail order from Sep-Feb only.
Map Ref: E, C3

EPGN **PARK GREEN NURSERIES** ⊠ ☒ ♠
Wetheringsett, Stowmarket, Suffolk IP14 5QH
Ⓣ (01728) 860139
Ⓜ 07909 531143
Ⓕ (01728) 861277
Ⓔ nurseries@parkgreen.co.uk
Ⓦ www.parkgreen.co.uk
Contact: Richard & Mary Ford

Opening Times: 1000-1600 Mon-Sat, 1st Mar-30th Sep.
Min Mail Order UK: £3.00
Min Mail Order EU: £5.00
Cat. Cost: 4 × 1st class.
Credit Cards: Visa, MasterCard, Delta, Maestro
Specialities: *Hosta*, ornamental grasses, ferns & other herbaceous.
Notes: Mail order *Hosta* only.
Map Ref: E, C3 **OS Grid Ref:** TM136644

EPom **POMONA FRUITS LTD** ⊠
Pomona House, 12 Third Avenue, Walton-on-the-Naze, Essex CO14 8JU
Ⓣ 0845 676 0607
Ⓕ 0845 676 0608
Ⓔ Info@PomonaFruits.co.uk
Ⓦ www.PomonaFruits.co.uk
Contact: Ming Yang/Claire Higgins
Opening Times: Not open. Mail order only.
Min Mail Order UK: Nmc
Cat. Cost: Free.
Credit Cards: All major credit/debit cards
Specialities: Fruit stock.

EPot **POTTERTONS NURSERY** ⊠ ✈ ♠ € ♿
Moortown Road, Nettleton, Caistor, Lincolnshire LN7 6HX
Ⓣ (01472) 851714
Ⓕ (01472) 852580
Ⓔ sales@pottertons.co.uk
Ⓦ www.pottertons.co.uk
Contact: Robert Potterton
Opening Times: 1000-1600 Tue-Sun. Closed Mon except B/hols. By appt. only Nov-Feb.
Min Mail Order UK: Nmc
Min Mail Order EU: Nmc
Cat. Cost: £2.00 in stamps.
Credit Cards: Maestro, MasterCard, Visa
Specialities: Alpines, dwarf bulbs & woodland plants. Hardy orchids & *Pleione*.
Notes: External talks nationally & internationally to garden clubs & societies. Group nursery tours by arrangement.
Map Ref: E, A1 **OS Grid Ref:** TA091001

EPPr **THE PLANTSMAN'S PREFERENCE** ⊠ ♠ ♿
Church Road, South Lopham, Diss, Norfolk IP22 2LW
Ⓣ Office (evenings): (01953) 681439
Ⓜ Nursery (day): 07799 855559
Ⓕ (01953) 688194
Ⓔ tim@plantpref.co.uk
Ⓦ www.plantpref.co.uk
Contact: Tim Fuller
Opening Times: 0930-1700 Fri, Sat & Sun Mar-Oct. Other times by appt.
Min Mail Order UK: £15.00
Min Mail Order EU: £30.00
Cat. Cost: Online only.
Credit Cards: All major credit/debit cards
Specialities: Hardy geraniums & ornamental grasses. Unusual & interesting perennials incl. shade/woodland. Some choice shrubs esp. *Caprifoliaceae*. Nat. Collection of *Molinia*.
Map Ref: E, C3 **OS Grid Ref:** TM041819

EPri **PRIORY PLANTS** ⊠ ♠ ♿
1 Covey Cottages, Hintlesham, Nr Ipswich, Suffolk IP8 3NY
Ⓣ (01473) 652656
Ⓕ (01473) 652656
Ⓔ sue.mann3@btinternet.com
Ⓦ www.prioryplants.co.uk
Contact: Sue Mann
Opening Times: By appt. only. Please ring first to avoid disappointment.
Min Mail Order UK: £15.00 + p&p
Min Mail Order EU: £25.00
Cat. Cost: Online only.
Credit Cards: None
Specialities: Cottage garden perennials, as well as increasing range of South African plants. *Agapanthus*, *Astrantia*, *Dierama*, *Geum*, Siberian *Iris*, *Kniphofia*, *Tritonia*, *Tulbaghia* & *Watsonia*.
Notes: Sells at plant fairs & agricultural shows.
Map Ref: E, C3 **OS Grid Ref:** TM070448

EPts **POTASH NURSERY** ⊠ ♠ ♿
Cow Green, Bacton, Stowmarket, Suffolk IP14 4HJ
Ⓣ (01449) 781671
Ⓔ enquiries@potashnursery.co.uk
Ⓦ www.potashnursery.co.uk
Contact: M W Clare
Opening Times: Pre-ordered plants can be collected by appt. only.
Min Mail Order UK: £12.90
Cat. Cost: 4 × 1st class.
Credit Cards: Visa, Delta, MasterCard
Specialities: *Fuchsia*.
Map Ref: E, C3 **OS Grid Ref:** TM0565NE

EPyc **PENNYCROSS PLANTS** ⊠
Earith Road, Colne, Huntingdon, Cambridgeshire PE28 3NL
Ⓣ (01487) 841520
Ⓔ salvias@pennycrossplants.co.uk

KEY
⊠ Mail order to UK or EU ♠ Delivers to shows
✈ Exports beyond EU € Euro accepted
♿ Accessible by wheelchair ◆ See Display advertisement

E

Ⓦ www.pennycrossplants.co.uk
Contact: Janet M Buist
Opening Times: 1000-1600 Mon-Fri, 1st Mar-31st Oct by appt.
Min Mail Order UK: Nmc
Cat. Cost: 1 × 2nd class for *Salvia* list only.
Credit Cards: None
Specialities: Hardy perennials. Salvias. Some plants available in ltd. quantities only. Will propagate salvias to order.
Notes: Mail order for young *Salvia* plants only.
Map Ref: E, C2 **OS Grid Ref:** TL378759

ERCP ROSE COTTAGE PLANTS ⊠ ♿
Bay Tree Farm, Epping Green, Essex
CM16 6PU
Ⓣ (01992) 573775
Ⓕ (01992) 561198
Ⓔ anne@rosecottageplants.co.uk
Ⓦ www.rosecottageplants.co.uk
Contact: Anne & Jack Barnard
Opening Times: By appt. & for special events (see website for details).
Min Mail Order UK: Nmc
Min Mail Order EU: £20.00
Cat. Cost: Online only.
Credit Cards: All major credit/debit cards
Specialities: Bulbs.
Notes: Mail order, bulbs only.
Map Ref: E, B1 **OS Grid Ref:** TL435053

ERhR RHODES & ROCKLIFFE ⊠ ☒ €
2 Nursery Road, Nazeing, Essex
EN9 2JE
Ⓣ (01992) 451598 (office hours)
Ⓕ (01992) 440673
Ⓔ RRBegonias@aol.com
Contact: David Rhodes or John Rockliffe
Opening Times: By appt. only.
Min Mail Order UK: £3.00 + p&p
Min Mail Order EU: £5.00 + p&p
Cat. Cost: 2 × 1st class.
Credit Cards: None
Specialities: *Begonia* species & hybrids. Nat. Collection of *Begonia*. Plants propagated to order.
Notes: Mail order Apr-Sep only.
Map Ref: E, D2

ERod THE RODINGS PLANTERY ⊠ ♿ € ⓑ
Anchor Lane, Abbess Roding, Essex
CM5 0JW
Ⓣ (01279) 876421
Ⓜ 07790 020940
Ⓔ janeandandy@therodingsplantery.co.uk
Ⓦ www.therodingsplantery.co.uk
Contact: Jane & Andy Mogridge
Opening Times: By appt. only. Occasional open days, please phone for details.
Min Mail Order UK: Nmc
Min Mail Order EU: £500.00 + p&p
Cat. Cost: 3 × 1st class.
Credit Cards: None
Specialities: Bamboos. Rare & unusual trees.
Map Ref: E, D2

ERom THE ROMANTIC GARDEN ⊠ ☒ € ⓑ ◆
Swannington, Norwich, Norfolk
NR9 5NW
Ⓣ (01603) 261488
Ⓜ 07802 722072
Ⓕ (01603) 864231
Ⓔ enquiries@romantic-garden-nursery.co.uk
Ⓦ www.romantic-garden-nursery.co.uk
Contact: John Powles/John Carrick
Opening Times: 1000-1700 Wed, Fri & Sat all year, plus B/hol Mons.
Min Mail Order UK: £5.00 + p&p
Min Mail Order EU: £30.00 + p&p
Cat. Cost: 6 × 1st class.
Credit Cards: All major credit/debit cards
Specialities: Conservatory. *Buxus* topiary, ornamental standards, large specimens. Hedging. Topiary
Notes: Also sells wholesale.
Map Ref: E, B3

ESem SEMPS BY POST ⊠
28 Mill Road, Newbourne, Woodbridge, Suffolk IP12 4NP
Ⓣ (01473) 736440
Ⓔ Tricia@sempsbypost.co.uk
Ⓦ www.sempsbypost.co.uk
Contact: Tricia Newell
Opening Times: Not open.
Min Mail Order UK: Nmc
Min Mail Order EU: Nmc
Cat. Cost: Online only.
Credit Cards: Paypal
Specialities: *Sempervivum*. Some stock available in small quantities.

ESgI SEAGATE IRISES ⊠ ☒ € ⓑ
A17 Long Sutton By-Pass, Long Sutton, Lincolnshire PE12 9RX
Ⓣ (01406) 365138
Ⓜ 07887 856389
Ⓔ sales@irises.co.uk
Ⓦ www.irises.co.uk
Contact: Julian Browse or Wendy Browse
Opening Times: 1000-1700 daily Apr-mid Jul. Please phone for appt. mid-Jul to Mar.
Min Mail Order UK: Nmc
Min Mail Order EU: Nmc. Carriage at cost.
Cat. Cost: £3.50 or €8.00
Credit Cards: Maestro, Visa, MasterCard

Specialities: Different types of *Iris*, bearded, beardless & species hybrids with about 1000 varieties in all, both historic & modern. Nat. Collection of Historic Tall Bearded Irises (pre-1965). Some only available in small quantities. Many container-grown available to callers.
Map Ref: E, B1 **OS Grid Ref:** TF437218

EShb **Shrubland Park Nurseries** ⊠ ⛺
Coddenham, Ipswich, Suffolk IP6 9QJ
Ⓣ (01473) 833187
Ⓜ 07890 527744
Ⓔ gill@shrublandparknurseries.co.uk
Ⓦ www.shrublandparknurseries.co.uk
Contact: Gill & Catherine Stitt
Opening Times: Opening times for 2011 will vary. Please ring before visiting or check website for details.
Min Mail Order UK: Nmc
Min Mail Order EU: £30.00
Cat. Cost: 6 × 1st class or free by email.
Credit Cards: All major credit/debit cards, Nochex, Paypal
Specialities: Conservatory plants, succulents, hardy perennials, climbers, shrubs, ferns & grasses.
Map Ref: E, C3 **OS Grid Ref:** TM128524

ESty **Style Roses** ⊠ ✈ ⛺ ♿
10 Meridian Walk, Holbeach, Spalding, Lincolnshire PE12 7NR
Ⓣ (01406) 424089
Ⓜ 07932 044093 or 07780 860415
Ⓕ (01406) 424089
Ⓔ info@styleroses.co.uk
Ⓦ www.styleroses.co.uk
Contact: Chris Styles, Margaret Styles
Opening Times: Vary. Nursery address is different from office, so please make an appt. before visiting.
Min Mail Order UK: Nmc
Min Mail Order EU: Nmc
Cat. Cost: Free in UK.
Credit Cards: MasterCard, Visa, Maestro, Solo
Specialities: Standard & bush roses.
Notes: Export to EU during bare-root season Nov-Mar. Other countries subject to plant health requirements. Carriage & export certificates where required charged at cost. Also sells wholesale.
Map Ref: E, B1

ESwi **Swines Meadow Farm Nursery** ⊠ ⛺ € ♿ ◆
47 Towngate East, Market Deeping, Peterborough PE6 8LQ
Ⓣ 01778 343340
Ⓜ 07811 847933
Ⓔ ceveandsons@btconnect.com
Ⓦ www.swinesmeadowfarmnursery.co.uk
Contact: Colin Ward
Opening Times: 0900-1700 Mon-Sat, 1000-1600 Sun (summer); 0900-1600 Mon-Sat, 1000-1600 Sun (winter).
Min Mail Order UK: £10.00
Min Mail Order EU: £10.00
Credit Cards: All, except American Express
Specialities: Hardy exotics, tree ferns, bamboos & phormiums. Wollemi pine stockist. Many specialities available in small quantities only.
Map Ref: E, B1 **OS Grid Ref:** TF150113

EThi **Thistlefield Plants and Design** ⊠ ⛺
65 Westgate Street, Shouldham, Kings Lynn, Norfolk PE33 0BL
Ⓣ (01366) 347365
Ⓜ 07899 994071
Ⓕ (01366) 347365
Ⓔ paul@thistlefieldplants.co.uk
Ⓦ www.thistlefieldplants.co.uk
Contact: Paul Welford
Opening Times: Not open. Sells at Plant Fairs & Shows only.
Min Mail Order UK: Nmc
Cat. Cost: Online only.
Credit Cards: None
Specialities: Perennials. *Tricyrtis* available in small quantities only.

ETho **Thorncroft Clematis** ⊠ ✈ ⛺ ♿
The Lings, Reymerston, Norwich, Norfolk NR9 4QG
Ⓣ (01953) 850407
Ⓕ (01953) 851788
Ⓔ sales@thorncroftclematis.co.uk
Ⓦ www.thorncroftclematis.co.uk
Contact: Ruth P Gooch
Opening Times: 1000-1600 Tue-Sat, Oct-Feb (closed Sun & Mon). 0900-1700 Tue-Sun, Mar-Sep, closed most Mondays but open B/hol Mon.
Min Mail Order UK: Nmc
Min Mail Order EU: Nmc
Cat. Cost: 6 × 2nd class.
Credit Cards: All major credit/debit cards
Specialities: *Clematis*.
Notes: Does not export to USA, Canada or Australia.
Map Ref: E, B3 **OS Grid Ref:** TG039062

KEY
⊠ Mail order to UK or EU ⛺ Delivers to shows
✈ Exports beyond EU € Euro accepted
♿ Accessible by wheelchair ◆ See Display advertisement

E

ETod **Todd's Botanics** ⊠ ⌂ €
West Street, Coggeshall, Colchester, Essex
CO6 1NT
Ⓣ (01376) 561212
Ⓜ 07970 643711
Ⓕ (01376) 561212
Ⓔ info@toddsbotanics.co.uk
Ⓦ www.toddsbotanics.co.uk
Contact: Mark Macdonald
Opening Times: 0900-1700 (or dusk) Thu-Sun. 1100-1600 Sun & B/hols. Open by appt. Mon-Wed. Open by appt. only in Jan.
Min Mail Order UK: Nmc
Min Mail Order EU: Nmc
Cat. Cost: Online only.
Credit Cards: All major credit/debit cards
Specialities: Hardy exotics, herbaceous. Bamboos, palms, ferns, grasses, *Canna* & *Hedychium*. Olives, incl. named varieties.
Notes: Also sells wholesale. Not all plants available mail order, contact nursery for details. Nursery partially accessible for wheelchairs.
Map Ref: E, D2 **OS Grid Ref:** TL843224

EUJe **Urban Jungle** ⊠ ⌂
The Nurseries, Ringland Lane, Old Costessey, Norwich, Norfolk NR8 5BG
Ⓣ (01603) 744997
Ⓕ (0709) 2366869
Ⓔ lizzy@urbanjungle.uk.com
Ⓦ www.urbanjungle.uk.com
Contact: Elizabeth Browne
Opening Times: 1000-1700 1st Feb-31st Oct 7 days incl B/hols. 1000-1600 Nov-Dec Thu, Fri, Sat, Sun. Closed Jan.
Min Mail Order UK: £20.00
Min Mail Order EU: £20.00
Cat. Cost: 2 × 1st class.
Credit Cards: All major credit/debit cards
Specialities: Wide range of choice plants from exotic bedding to hardy evergreens.
Notes: Display gardens & living walls. Limited wheelchair access.
Map Ref: E, B3 **OS Grid Ref:** TG1593612782

EWay **Wayside Aquatics** ⊠
Blackmore Road, Doddinghurst, Brentwood, Essex CM15 0HU
Ⓣ (01277) 823603
Ⓔ sales@waysideaquatics.co.uk
Ⓦ www.waysideaquatics.co.uk
Contact: Anna Robinson
Opening Times: 1000-1700 Wed-Sun.
Min Mail Order UK: Nmc
Min Mail Order EU: Nmc
Cat. Cost: Online only.
Credit Cards: All major credit/debit cards
Specialities: Range of water garden plants: waterlilies; floating plants; oxygenating plants; marginals; marsh plants. Some stock in small quantities.
Map Ref: E, D2 **OS Grid Ref:** TQ585995

EWes **West Acre Gardens** ⌂ ♿
West Acre, King's Lynn, Norfolk PE32 1UJ
Ⓣ (01760) 755562
Contact: J J Tuite
Opening Times: 1000-1700 7 days 1st Feb-30th Nov. Other times by appt.
Cat. Cost: None issued.
Credit Cards: Visa, MasterCard, Delta, Switch
Specialities: Very wide selection of herbaceous & other garden plants incl. *Rhodohypoxis* & *Primula auricula*.
Map Ref: E, B1 **OS Grid Ref:** TF792182

EWhm **Waltham Herbs** ⌂
Willow Vale Nursery, North Kelsey Road, Caistor, Lincolnshire LN7 6SF
Ⓣ (01472) 859481
Ⓜ 07949 883091
Ⓕ (01472) 859481
Ⓔ angelasach2@aol.com
Ⓦ www.waltham-herbs.co.uk
Contact: Angela Sach and Steve Penney
Opening Times: By appt. only.
Specialities: Herbs, lavenders and perennials, also some shrubs. Peat-free and pesticide-free.
Notes: Also sells wholesale.
Map Ref: E, A1

EWld **Woodlands**
Peppin Lane, Fotherby, Louth, Lincolnshire LN11 0UW
Ⓣ (01507) 603586
Ⓜ 07866 161864
Ⓔ annbobarmstrong@uwclub.net
Ⓦ www.woodlandsplants.co.uk
Contact: Ann Armstrong
Opening Times: Flexible but please phone or email to avoid disappointment.
Cat. Cost: None issued.
Credit Cards: None
Specialities: Small but interesting range of unusual plants, esp. woodland and *Salvia*, all grown on the nursery in limited quantity.
Notes: Mature garden, art gallery & refreshments.
Map Ref: E, A2 **OS Grid Ref:** TF322918

EWll **The Walled Garden** ♿ ◆
Park Road, Benhall, Saxmundham, Suffolk IP17 1JB
Ⓣ (01728) 602510

Ⓕ (01728) 602510
Ⓔ jim@thewalledgarden.co.uk
Ⓦ www.thewalledgarden.co.uk
Contact: Jim Mountain
Opening Times: 0930-1700 Tue-Sun Mar-Nov, 0930-dusk Tue-Sat mid Nov-mid Feb.
Cat. Cost: 2 × 1st class.
Credit Cards: All major credit/debit cards
Specialities: Tender & hardy perennials. For current information see website.
Map Ref: E, C3 **OS Grid Ref:** TM371613

EWoo **Woottens Plants** ⊠ ♿
Wenhaston, Blackheath, Halesworth, Suffolk IP19 9HD
Ⓣ (01502) 478258
Ⓕ (01502) 478888
Ⓔ sales@woottensplants.co.uk
Ⓦ www.woottensplants.co.uk
Contact: M Loftus
Opening Times: 0930-1700 7 days.
Min Mail Order UK: Nmc
Min Mail Order EU: Nmc
Cat. Cost: Online only.
Credit Cards: All, except American Express
Specialities: *Pelargonium, Hemerocallis, Primula auricula, Iris, Chrysanthemum* & *Clivia.*
Notes: Also sells wholesale.
Map Ref: E, C3 **OS Grid Ref:** TM42714375

EWTr **Walnut Tree Garden Nursery** ⊠
Flymoor Lane, Rocklands, Attleborough, Norfolk, NR17 1BP
Ⓣ (01953) 488163
Ⓔ info@wtgn.co.uk
Ⓦ www.wtgn.co.uk
Contact: Jim Paine & Clare Billington
Opening Times: 0900-1800 Tue-Sun Feb-Nov & B/hols.
Min Mail Order UK: Nmc
Cat. Cost: 4 × 1st class.
Credit Cards: All major credit/debit cards
Map Ref: E, B1 **OS Grid Ref:** TL978973

Scotland

GAbr **Abriachan Nurseries** ⊠ ♿
Loch Ness Side, Inverness, Inverness-shire IV3 8LA
Ⓣ (01463) 861232
Ⓔ info@lochnessgarden.com
Ⓦ www.lochnessgarden.com
Contact: Mr & Mrs D Davidson
Opening Times: 0900-1900 daily (dusk if earlier) Feb-Nov.
Min Mail Order UK: Nmc
Cat. Cost: 4 × 1st class.
Credit Cards: All major credit/debit cards
Specialities: Herbaceous perennials, old-fashioned *Primula, Helianthemum,* hardy geraniums, *Sempervivum* & *Primula auricula.*
Notes: Wheelchair access to nursery only.
Map Ref: G, B2 **OS Grid Ref:** NH571347

GAgs **Angusplants** ⊠ ♿
3 Balfour Cottages, Menmuir, By Brechin, Angus DD9 7RN
Ⓣ (01356) 660280
Ⓜ 07972 026109
Ⓔ alison@angusplants.co.uk
Ⓦ www.angusplants.co.uk
Contact: Dr Alison S. Goldie & Mark A. Hutson
Opening Times: By appt. only. Please phone first. Light refreshments provided.
Min Mail Order UK: Nmc
Min Mail Order EU: Nmc
Cat. Cost: A5 sae.
Credit Cards: None
Specialities: Predominantly *Primula auricula,* although other *Primula* species are offered. A few available in small quantities only.
Notes: Mail order available all year.
Map Ref: G, B3 **OS Grid Ref:** NO528643

GBBs **Border Belles** ⊠ ♿
Old Branxton Cottages, Innerwick, Nr Dunbar, East Lothian EH42 1QT
Ⓣ (01368) 840325
Ⓔ mail@borderbelles.com
Ⓦ www.borderbelles.com
Contact: Gillian Moynihan
Opening Times: Open by appt. only.
Min Mail Order UK: Nmc
Min Mail Order EU: On request
Cat. Cost: Online only.
Credit Cards: All major credit/debit cards
Specialities: Hardy perennials & woodland plants.
Notes: Also sells wholesale.

GBee **Beeches Cottage Nursery** ♿
High Boreland, Lesmahagow, South Lanarkshire ML11 9PY
Ⓣ (01555) 893369
Ⓜ 07930 343131
Ⓔ thebeeches.nursery@talktalk.net
Ⓦ www.beechescottage.co.uk
Contact: Margaret Harrison, Steven Harrison

KEY
⊠ Mail order to UK or EU — Delivers to shows
Exports beyond EU — € Euro accepted
♿ Accessible by wheelchair — ◆ See Display advertisement

Opening Times: 1000-1630 7 days incl. B/hols, mid-Apr to end Jun. Wed-Sat, Jul to end Sep. Other times by appt.
Cat. Cost: None issued.
Credit Cards: None
Specialities: Traditional & unusual hardy cottage garden perennials which can be seen growing in display gardens at 850ft. Some plants available in small quantities only. Hanging basket specialists.
Notes: Wheelchair access to nursery only. Also sells wholesale.
Map Ref: G, C2 **OS Grid Ref:** NS837403

G

GBin **Binny Plants** ⊠ € ♿
West Lodge, Binny Estate, Ecclesmachan Road, Nr Broxbourn, West Lothian EH52 6NL
Ⓣ (01506) 858931
Ⓜ 07753 626117
Ⓔ contact@binnyplants.com
Ⓦ www.binnyplants.com
Contact: Billy Carruthers
Opening Times: 1000-1700 7 days. Closed mid-Dec to mid-Jan.
Min Mail Order UK: £25.00
Min Mail Order EU: £25.00
Cat. Cost: £2.50 refundable on ordering.
Credit Cards: Visa, MasterCard, EuroCard, Maestro
Specialities: Perennials incl. *Astilbe, Geranium, Hosta, Paeonia* & *Iris*. Plus large selection of grasses & ferns.
Notes: Mail order Sep-Apr only. Also sells wholesale.
Map Ref: G, C3 **OS Grid Ref:** NT050732

GBuc **Buckland Plants** ⊠ € ♿
Whinnieliggate, Kirkcudbright, Kirkcudbrightshire DG6 4XP
Ⓣ (01557) 331323
Ⓕ (01557) 331323
Ⓔ via website
Ⓦ www.bucklandplants.co.uk
Contact: Rob or Dina Asbridge
Opening Times: 1000-1700 Thu-Sun 1st Mar-1st Nov & B/hols.
Min Mail Order UK: £20.00 + p&p
Min Mail Order EU: £50.00 + p&p
Cat. Cost: 3 × 1st class.
Credit Cards: All major credit/debit cards
Specialities: A very wide range of scarce herbaceous, woodland plants & larger alpines incl. *Anemone, Cardamine, Erythronium, Helleborus, Lilium, Meconopsis, Nomocharis, Primula, Tricyrtis* & *Trillium*.
Notes: Assisted wheelchair access.
Map Ref: G, D2 **OS Grid Ref:** NX719524

GCai **Cairnsmore Nursery** ⊠ ⌂ ♿
Chapmanton Road, Castle Douglas, Kirkcudbrightshire DG7 2NU
Ⓣ (01556) 504819
Ⓜ 07980 176458
Ⓔ cairnsmorenursery@hotmail.com
Ⓦ www.cairnsmorenursery.co.uk
Contact: Valerie Smith
Opening Times: By appt. only.
Min Mail Order UK: Nmc
Cat. Cost: 4 × 1st class.
Credit Cards: None
Specialities: *Heuchera*.
Map Ref: G, D2 **OS Grid Ref:** NX756637

GCal **Cally Gardens** ⊠ ♿
Gatehouse of Fleet, Castle Douglas, Kirkcudbrightshire DG7 2DJ
Ⓣ (01557) 815029 recorded information only.
Ⓔ info@callygardens.co.uk
Ⓦ www.callygardens.co.uk
Contact: Michael Wickenden
Opening Times: 1000-1730 Sat-Sun, 1400-1730 Tue-Fri. Easter Sat-last Sun in Sept.
Min Mail Order UK: £15.00 + p&p
Cat. Cost: 3 × 1st class.
Credit Cards: None
Specialities: Unusual perennials & grasses. Some rare shrubs, climbers & conservatory plants. 3500 varieties growing in an 2.7 acre walled garden built in the 1760s.
Notes: Also sells wholesale.
Map Ref: G, D2 **OS Grid Ref:** NX604549

GCoc **James Cocker & Sons** ⊠ ♿
Whitemyres, Lang Stracht, Aberdeen, Aberdeenshire AB15 6XH
Ⓣ (01224) 313261
Ⓕ (01224) 312531
Ⓔ sales@roses.uk.com
Ⓦ www.roses.uk.com
Contact: Alec Cocker
Opening Times: 0900-1700 Mon-Fri.
Min Mail Order UK: Nmc
Min Mail Order EU: £6.25 + p&p
Cat. Cost: Free.
Credit Cards: Visa, MasterCard, Delta, Maestro
Specialities: Roses.
Notes: Also sells wholesale.
Map Ref: G, B3

GCra **Craigieburn Garden** ♿
Craigieburn House, By Moffat, Dumfriesshire DG10 9LF
Ⓣ (01683) 221250
Ⓕ (01683) 221250
Ⓔ ajmw1@aol.com
Ⓦ www.craigieburngarden.com

Contact: Janet & Andrew Wheatcroft
Opening Times: 1030-1800 daily, Easter-31st Oct. Other times by appt.
Specialities: *Meconopsis* plants for damp gardens, herbaceous perennials.
Map Ref: G, D3

GCro **Croft 16 Daffodils** ⊠
16 Midtown of Inverasdale, Poolewe, Achnasheen, Ross-shire IV22 2LW
Ⓣ (01445) 781717
Ⓔ sales@croft16daffodils.co.uk
Ⓦ www.croft16daffodils.co.uk
Contact: Kate & Duncan Donald
Opening Times: By appt. only. Please phone or email first.
Min Mail Order UK: Nmc
Min Mail Order EU: Nmc
Cat. Cost: Online only.
Credit Cards: Paypal
Specialities: Daffodils bred pre-1930. Awarded full Nat. Collection status (2010).
Map Ref: G, A1 **OS Grid Ref:** NG822851

GEdr **Edrom Nurseries** ⊠
Coldingham, Eyemouth, Berwickshire TD14 5TZ
Ⓣ (01890) 771386
Ⓕ (01890) 771387
Ⓔ info@edrom-nurseries.co.uk
Ⓦ www.edrom-nurseries.co.uk
Contact: Mr Terry Hunt
Opening Times: 0900-1700 Thu-Mon (closed Tue-Wed), 1st Mar-30th Sep. Other times by appt.
Min Mail Order UK: Nmc
Min Mail Order EU: £20.00
Cat. Cost: Free. More plants listed online than in printed catalogue.
Credit Cards: All major credit/debit cards
Specialities: *Trillium, Arisaema, Primula, Gentiana, Meconopsis, Cypripedium, Fritillaria*, hardy orchids.
Map Ref: G, C3 **OS Grid Ref:** NT873663

GGGa **Glendoick Gardens Ltd** ⊠
Glendoick, Perth, Perthshire PH2 7NS
Ⓣ (01738) 860205
Ⓕ (01738) 860630
Ⓔ orders@glendoick.com
Ⓦ www.glendoick.com
Contact: Kenneth Cox
Opening Times: Nursery not open to the public. Garden centre open 0900-1730 (summer), 0900-1700 (winter) 7 days. Gardens open Apr & May, details on website.
Min Mail Order UK: £40.00
Min Mail Order EU: £100.00
Cat. Cost: £1.00
Credit Cards: All, except American Express
Specialities: Rhododendrons, azaleas and ericaceous, *Primula* & *Meconopsis*. Plants from wild seed. Many catalogue plants available at garden centre. 3 Nat. Collections.
Notes: Wheelchair access to Garden Centre.
Map Ref: G, C3

GHeS **Plant Ordering Service** ⊠ €
Drumterlie Farmhouse, Newton Stewart, Wigtownshire DG8 6QG
Ⓣ (01671) 401666
Ⓜ 07905 825818
Ⓔ allisonfitzearle@yahoo.co.uk
Ⓦ www.plant-orderingservice.co.uk
Contact: Allison Fitz-Earle
Opening Times: Not open. Mail order only.
Min Mail Order UK: Nmc
Min Mail Order EU: Nmc
Cat. Cost: Free.
Credit Cards: None
Specialities: Heathers.
Notes: Mail order plants available year round. Also sells wholesale.

GHim **Himalayan Gardens Ltd** ⊠ €
Inshewan Estate, Forfar, Angus DD8 3TU
Ⓣ 0141 416 3536
Ⓕ (01575) 574529
Ⓔ himalayangardens@gmail.com
Ⓦ www.himalayangardens.com
Contact: Chris Jobart
Opening Times: Not open. Mail order only.
Min Mail Order UK: Nmc
Min Mail Order EU: Nmc
Specialities: *Arisaema, Achimenes*, ginger, *Lilium*, aroids, bananas.
Notes: Also sells wholesale.

GJos **Jo's Garden Enterprise**
Easter Balmungle Farm, Eathie Road, By Rosemarkie, Ross-shire IV10 8SL
Ⓣ (01381) 621006
Ⓔ anne.chance@ukonline.co.uk
Contact: Joanna Chance
Opening Times: 1000 to dusk, 7 days.
Cat. Cost: None.
Credit Cards: None
Specialities: Alpines & herbaceous perennials. Selection of native wild flowers.
Map Ref: G, B2 **OS Grid Ref:** NH600742

KEY
⊠ Mail order to UK or EU — Delivers to shows
Exports beyond EU — € Euro accepted
Accessible by wheelchair — ◆ See Display advertisement

GKev **Kevock Garden Plants** ⊠ ⌂ €
16 Kevock Road, Lasswade, Midlothian
EH18 1HT
Ⓣ 0131 454 0660
Ⓜ 07811 321585
Ⓕ 0131 454 0660
Ⓔ info@kevockgarden.co.uk
Ⓦ www.kevockgarden.co.uk
Contact: Stella Rankin
Opening Times: Not open. Mail order & plant stalls only.
Min Mail Order UK: £20.00
Min Mail Order EU: £20.00
Cat. Cost: 4 × 1st class.
Credit Cards: Visa, MasterCard, Switch
Specialities: Chinese & Himalayan plants. *Androsace*, *Daphne*, *Paeonia*, *Primula*, *Meconopsis*, *Iris*, woodland plants, alpines, rock, marginal, bog & bulbs.
Notes: Also sells wholesale.

GKin **Kinlochlaich Garden Plant Centre**
Appin, Argyll PA38 4BB
Ⓣ (01631) 730342
Ⓜ 07881 525754
Ⓕ (01631) 730482
Ⓔ fiona@kinlochlaich.plus.com
Ⓦ www.kinlochlaichgardencentre.co.uk
Contact: Fiona Hutchison
Opening Times: 0900-1730, 7 days, Mar-Oct. (Winter) 0900-until dusk, Mon-Sat.
Cat. Cost: None issued.
Credit Cards: All major credit/debit cards
Specialities: Hardy shrubs, trees, azaleas, perennials. Also Gulf Stream plants such as *Tropaeolum*, *Embothrium*, *Eucryphia*, *Drymis* & more. Good selection of hardy seaside plants.
Notes: Do not offer mail order but will post where possible.

GLin **Linn Botanic Gardens** €
Cove, Helensburgh, Dunbartonshire
G84 0NR
Ⓣ (01436) 842084
Ⓔ jamie@linnbotanicgardens.org.uk
Ⓦ www.linnbotanicgardens.org.uk
Contact: Jamie Taggart
Opening Times: 1100-1700, 7 days.
Cat. Cost: 4 × 1st class or by email.
Credit Cards: None
Specialities: Small plant sales area offering diverse range of plants. Botanic Gardens open (charges apply).
Notes: Wheelchair access to plant sales area but not gardens.
Map Ref: G, C2 **OS Grid Ref:** NS223827

GLog **Logie Steading Plants** ♿
Forres, Moray IV36 2QN
Ⓣ (01309) 611222 or 611278
Ⓕ (01309) 611300
Ⓔ panny@logie.co.uk
Ⓦ www.logie.co.uk
Contact: Mrs Panny Laing
Opening Times: 1030-1700 hours, 7 days, April-end Oct.
Credit Cards: All major credit/debit cards
Specialities: Unusual hardy plants, grown in Scotland for Scottish gardens. Large range of hardy geraniums, bold herbaceous plants, grasses & marginal plants.
Notes: Logie House Garden open every day. Café, farm shop, gallery, secondhand books, antiques, river walk, heritage centre.
Map Ref: G, B2 **OS Grid Ref:** NJ006504

GMaP **Macplants** ⊠ ⌂ ♿
Berrybank Nursery, 5 Boggs Holdings, Pencaitland, East Lothian
EH34 5BA
Ⓣ (01875) 341179
Ⓕ (01875) 340842
Ⓔ sales@macplants.co.uk
Ⓦ www.macplants.co.uk
Contact: Gavin McNaughton
Opening Times: 1030-1700, 7 days, Mar-end Sep.
Min Mail Order UK: Nmc
Min Mail Order EU: Nmc
Cat. Cost: 4 × 2nd class.
Credit Cards: MasterCard, Switch, Visa
Specialities: Herbaceous perennials, alpines, hardy ferns, violas & grasses.
Notes: Also sells wholesale.
Map Ref: G, C3 **OS Grid Ref:** NT447703

GPoy **Poyntzfield Herb Nursery** ⊠ ☒ ♿
Nr Balblair, Black Isle, Dingwall, Ross-shire
IV7 8LX
Ⓣ (01381) 610352
Ⓕ (01381) 610352
Ⓔ info@poyntzfieldherbs.co.uk
Ⓦ www.poyntzfieldherbs.co.uk
Contact: Duncan Ross
Opening Times: 1300-1700 Mon-Sat 1st Mar-30th Sep, 1300-1700 Sun May-Aug.
Min Mail Order UK: £10.00 + p&p
Min Mail Order EU: £10.00 + p&p
Cat. Cost: 4 × 1st class.
Credit Cards: All major credit/debit cards
Specialities: Over 400 popular, unusual & rare herbs esp. medicinal. Also seeds.
Notes: Phone between 1200-1300 & 1800-1900 Mon-Sat only.
Map Ref: G, B2 **OS Grid Ref:** NH711642

GPPs **POGS PENSTEMONS** ⊠ €
Drumterlie Farmhouse, Newton Stewart, Wigtownshire DG8 6QG
Ⓣ (01671) 401666
Ⓜ 07905 825818
Ⓔ pogspenstemons@yahoo.co.uk
Ⓦ www.pogspenstemons.co.uk
Contact: Allison Fitz-Earle
Opening Times: Not open. Mail order only.
Min Mail Order UK: Nmc
Min Mail Order EU: Nmc
Cat. Cost: Free.
Credit Cards: None
Specialities: Penstemons.
Notes: Mail order plants available all year. Also sells wholesale.

GPri **PRIVICK MILL NURSERY** ⊠ ♿
Privick Mill Road, Annbank, Ayr KA6 5JA
Ⓣ (01292) 521003
Ⓔ jackie.jess@yahoo.com
Ⓦ www.privickmillnursery.co.uk
Contact: Jackie Jess
Opening Times: By appt. only for collection of plants.
Min Mail Order UK: Nmc
Cat. Cost: Free.
Credit Cards: None
Specialities: Soft fruit bushes. Blueberries. Black raspberries. *Rubus* hybrids. Available in small quantities only. All plants organically grown but not certified by Soil Assoc.
Map Ref: G, D2 **OS Grid Ref:** NS405224

GQue **QUERCUS GARDEN PLANTS** ♿
Rankeilour Gardens, Rankeilour Estate, Springfield, Fife KY15 5RE
Ⓣ (01337) 810444
Ⓕ (01337) 810444
Ⓔ colin@quercus.uk.net
Ⓦ www.quercus.uk.net
Contact: Colin McBeath
Opening Times: 1000-1700 Thu-Sun, 1st w/end Apr-mid Oct. By appt. only, Nov-Feb. 1000-1400 Sat only, Mar.
Cat. Cost: 4 × 1st class.
Credit Cards: All major credit/debit cards
Specialities: Easy & unusual plants for contemporary Scottish gardens.
Notes: Delivery service available on large orders at nursery's discretion. Also sells wholesale.
Map Ref: G, C3 **OS Grid Ref:** NO330118

GQui **QUINISH GARDEN NURSERY** ⊠
Dervaig, Isle of Mull, Argyll PA75 6QL
Ⓣ (01688) 400344
Ⓕ (01688) 400344
Ⓔ quinishplants@aol.com
Ⓦ www.Q-gardens.org
Contact: Nicholas Reed
Opening Times: By appt. only.
Min Mail Order UK: Nmc
Min Mail Order EU: Nmc
Cat. Cost: 2 × 1st class.
Credit Cards: None
Specialities: Choice garden shrubs & conservatory plants.
Map Ref: G, C1

GSPN **SPRING PARK NURSERY** ⊠ €
Drumterlie Farmhouse, Newton Stewart, Wigtownshire DG8 6QG
Ⓣ (01671) 401666
Ⓜ 07905 825818
Ⓔ julianfitzearle@aol.com
Ⓦ www.springparknursery.co.uk
Contact: Julian Fitz-Earle
Opening Times: Not open. Mail order only.
Min Mail Order UK: Nmc
Min Mail Order EU: Nmc
Cat. Cost: Free.
Credit Cards: None
Specialities: Heathers.
Notes: Mail order plants available all year.

GTwe **J TWEEDIE FRUIT TREES** ⊠
Maryfield Road Nursery, Nr Terregles, Dumfriesshire DG2 9TH
Ⓣ (01387) 720880
Contact: John Tweedie
Opening Times: Please ring for times. Collections by appt.
Min Mail Order UK: Nmc
Cat. Cost: Sae.
Credit Cards: None
Specialities: Fruit trees & bushes. A wide range of old & new varieties.
Map Ref: G, D2

N. IRELAND & REPUBLIC

IArd **ARDCARNE GARDEN CENTRE** € ♿
Ardcarne, Boyle, Co. Roscommon, Ireland
Ⓣ (353) 7196 67091
Ⓕ (353) 7196 67341
Ⓔ ardcarne@indigo.ie
Ⓦ www.ardcarnegc.com
Contact: James Wickham, Mary Frances Dwyer, Kirsty Ainge

Opening Times: 0900-1800 Mon-Sat, 1300-1800 Sun & B/hols.
Credit Cards: Access, Visa, American Express
Specialities: Native & unusual trees, fruit trees, perennials, roses, plants for coastal areas, specimen plants & semi-mature trees. Wide general range.
Map Ref: I, B1

I

IBal **BALI-HAI MAIL ORDER NURSERY** ⊠ ✈ €
42 Largy Road, Carnlough, Ballymena, Co. Antrim, N. Ireland BT44 0EZ
Ⓣ 028 2888 5289
Ⓜ 07708 257164
Ⓕ 028 2888 5289
Ⓔ balihainursery@btinternet.com
Ⓦ www.mailorderplants4me.com
Contact: Mrs M E Scroggy
Opening Times: Mon-Sat by appt. only.
Min Mail Order UK: Nmc
Min Mail Order EU: Nmc
Cat. Cost: Online only.
Credit Cards: All major credit/debit cards
Specialities: Nat. Collection of *Hosta*, part planted in 1.5 acres, open to the public by appt. *Agapanthus*, *Crocosmia*, *Rhodohypoxis*, tree ferns & other perennials.
Notes: Exports beyond EU restricted to bare root perennials, no grasses. *Hostas* grown to order. Also sells wholesale.
Map Ref: I, A3 **OS Grid Ref:** D287184

IBlr **BALLYROGAN NURSERIES** ⊠ € ♿
The Grange, Ballyrogan, Newtownards, Co. Down, N. Ireland BT23 4SD
Ⓣ 028 9181 0451 (evenings)
Ⓔ gary.dunlop@btinternet.com
Contact: Gary Dunlop
Opening Times: Only open by appt.
Min Mail Order UK: £10.00 + p&p
Min Mail Order EU: £20.00 + p&p
Cat. Cost: 2 × 1st class.
Credit Cards: None
Specialities: Choice herbaceous. *Agapanthus*, *Celmisia*, *Crocosmia*, *Rodgersia*, *Iris*, *Dierama*, *Erythronium* & *Roscoea*.
Notes: Also sells wholesale.

IBoy **BOYNE GARDEN CENTRE** €
Ardcalf, Slane, Co. Meath, Ireland
Ⓣ 00353 (0)419 824350
Ⓕ 00353 (0)419 824350
Ⓔ boynegardencentre@eircom.net
Ⓦ boynegardencentre.com
Contact: Aileen Muldoon Byrne
Opening Times: 0930-1800 Mon-Sat, 1400-1800 Sun, Mar-Sep. 0930-1800 B/hols. W/ends only Oct-Feb.
Credit Cards: All major credit/debit cards
Specialities: Hardy herbaceous perennials. David Austin roses. Unusual trees, shrubs, grasses, bamboos & ferns.
Notes: Pre-ordered plants delivered to shows.
Map Ref: I, B3

IDee **DEELISH GARDEN CENTRE** ⊠ €
Skibbereen, Co. Cork, Ireland
Ⓣ 00 (353) 28 21374
Ⓕ 00 (353) 28 21374
Ⓔ deel@eircom.net
Ⓦ www.deelish.ie
Contact: Bill & Rain Chase
Opening Times: 1000-1800 Mon-Sat, 1400-1800 Sun.
Min Mail Order EU: €50 (Ireland only).
Cat. Cost: Sae.
Credit Cards: Visa, Access
Specialities: Unusual plants for the mild coastal climate of Ireland. Conservatory plants. Sole Irish agents for Chase Organic Seeds.
Notes: No mail order outside Ireland.
Map Ref: I, D1

IDic **DICKSON NURSERIES LTD** ⊠ ✈
Milecross Road, Newtownards, Co. Down, N. Ireland BT23 4SS
Ⓣ 028 9181 2206
Ⓜ 07522 222161
Ⓕ 028 9181 3366
Ⓔ mail@dickson-roses.co.uk
Ⓦ www.dickson-roses.co.uk
Contact: Colin Dickson
Opening Times: 0800-1230 & 1300-1545 Mon-Thu. 0800-1230 Fri.
Min Mail Order UK: Nmc
Min Mail Order EU: £25.00 + p&p
Cat. Cost: Free.
Credit Cards: None
Specialities: Roses esp. modern Dickson varieties. Most varieties are available in small quantities only.
Notes: Also sells wholesale. Does not export to USA or Canada.
Map Ref: I, B3

IFoB **FIELD OF BLOOMS** ⊠ € ♿
Ballymackey, Lisnamoe, Nenagh, Co. Tipperary, Ireland
Ⓣ (353) 67 29974
Ⓜ (353) 8764 06044
Ⓔ guy2002@eircom.net
Ⓦ www.fieldofblooms.com
Contact: Guy de Schrijver
Opening Times: Strictly by appt.

Min Mail Order UK: Nmc
Min Mail Order EU: Nmc
Cat. Cost: Online only.
Credit Cards: None
Specialities: Hellebores, herbaceous, hardy perennials, ornamental grasses & woodland plants.
Map Ref: I, C2

IFro **FROGSWELL NURSERY** €
Clooncolan, Straide, Foxford, Co. Mayo, Ireland
Ⓣ (353) 94 903 1420
Ⓜ (353) 8621 06166
Ⓔ frogswell@gmail.com
Ⓦ www.frogswell.net
Contact: Celia Graebner
Opening Times: Feb-Oct by appt. Please phone first. Also Garden Open Days & occasional workshops; see website for details.
Cat. Cost: Online only.
Credit Cards: None
Specialities: A small nursery specialising in shade & woodland plants incl. hybrid hellebores & hardy geraniums, plus unusual perennials for the Irish climate, all raised on site & without chemical inputs. Some in very small quantities.
Notes: Garden visits by arrangement. See website for location map.
Map Ref: I, B1 **OS Grid Ref:** M2497

IGor **GORTKELLY CASTLE NURSERY & ARBORETUM** ⊠ ⌂ €
Upperchurch, Thurles, Co. Tipperary, Ireland
Ⓣ (353) 504 54441
Ⓔ clarevbeumer@ireland.com
Contact: Clare Beumer
Opening Times: Mail order only. Not open to the public.
Min Mail Order UK: Nmc
Min Mail Order EU: Nmc
Cat. Cost: 5 × 1st class (UK), 5 × 55c (Rep. of Ireland).
Credit Cards: None
Specialities: Choice perennials. Cultivars of Irish origin. Rare trees & shrubs in small sizes.
Map Ref: I, C2

IKil **KILMURRY NURSERY** ⊠ ⌂ € ♿
Gorey, Co. Wexford, Ireland
Ⓣ (353) 53 948 0223
Ⓜ (353) 8681 80623
Ⓕ (353) 53 948 0223
Ⓔ info@kilmurrynursery.com
Ⓦ www.kilmurrynursery.com
Contact: Paul & Orla Woods
Opening Times: 0900-1700 Mon-Fri, Mar-Sep. Wintertime by appt.
Min Mail Order UK: Nmc
Min Mail Order EU: Nmc
Cat. Cost: Online only.
Credit Cards: None
Specialities: Herbaceous perennials and grasses.
Notes: Also sells wholesale.
Map Ref: I, C3 **OS Grid Ref:** 3C

IMou **MOUNT VENUS NURSERY** ⊠ ⌂ € ♿
The Walled Garden, Mutton Lane, Dublin 16, Ireland
Ⓣ 00353 (0)1 493 3813
Ⓜ 08632 18789
Ⓔ schurmann@ireland.com
Ⓦ www.mountvenusnursery.com
Contact: Oliver & Liat Schurmann
Opening Times: 1000-1800 Mon-Sat, Feb-Nov.
Min Mail Order UK: €20
Min Mail Order EU: €35
Credit Cards: All major credit/debit cards
Specialities: Specialist perennials. Grasses & bamboos. Unusual woodland plants.
Notes: Also sells wholesale.
Map Ref: I, C3

IPen **PENINSULA PRIMULAS** ⊠ ⌂ €
72 Ballyeasborough Road,
Kircubbin, Co. Down, N. Ireland
BT22 1AD
Ⓣ 028 4277 2193
Ⓜ 07513 900762
Ⓔ Peninsula.primulas@btinternet.com
Ⓦ www.primulasandauriculas.com
Contact: Philip Bankhead
Opening Times: Mail order only. Not open.
Min Mail Order UK: Nmc
Min Mail Order EU: Nmc
Cat. Cost: Free.
Credit Cards: Paypal
Specialities: Extensive selection of *Primula* species, plus auriculas.
Notes: Also sells wholesale.

IPot **THE POTTING SHED** ⊠ ⌂ € ♿
Bolinaspick, Camolin, Enniscorthy, Co. Wexford, Ireland
Ⓣ (353) 5393 83629
Ⓕ (353) 5393 83629
Ⓔ sricher@iol.ie
Ⓦ www.camolinpottingshed.com

KEY
⊠ Mail order to UK or EU ⌂ Delivers to shows
✈ Exports beyond EU € Euro accepted
♿ Accessible by wheelchair ◆ See Display advertisement

Contact: Susan Carrick
Opening Times: 1300-1800, Thu-Sat (incl.), Mar-Sep 2011. Other times by appt.
Min Mail Order UK: Nmc
Min Mail Order EU: Nmc
Cat. Cost: 3 × 1st class.
Credit Cards: MasterCard, Visa
Specialities: We grow a wide range of unusual, hard to find and new introductions of herbaceous perennials, ornamental grasses and *Clematis*, many of which are shown to great effect in our on site Display Gardens.
Map Ref: I, C3

IPPN **Perennial Plants Nursery** ⊠ €
Nr Ballymaloe, Barnabrow, Midleton, Co. Cork, Ireland
Ⓣ (353) 21 465 2122
Ⓔ perennialplants@eircom.net
Ⓦ www.perennialplants.biz
Contact: Sandy McCarthy
Opening Times: Please ring for times.
Min Mail Order UK: Nmc
Min Mail Order EU: Nmc
Cat. Cost: None issued.
Credit Cards: None
Specialities: Many unusual herbaceous, ornamental grasses, tender perennials. Some available in small quantities only.
Notes: Will accept payment in sterling.
Map Ref: I, D2 **OS Grid Ref:** W9568

IRar **Rare Plants** ⊠ €
Kinsealy Cottage, Kinsealy Lane, Malahide, Co. Dublin, Ireland
Ⓔ info@rareplants.ie
Ⓦ www.rareplants.ie
Contact: Brian Murphy, Christopher Heavey
Opening Times: Not open to the public.
Min Mail Order UK: Nmc
Min Mail Order EU: Nmc
Cat. Cost: Online only.
Credit Cards: All major credit/debit cards
Specialities: Propagates & raises a range of rare & unusual plants incl. trees, shrubs, herbaceous & alpine. Specialises in difficult to obtain & slightly tender plants. All propagated from superior clones. Only available in small quantities.
Notes: P&p costs on request. Also sells wholesale.
Map Ref: I, C3 **OS Grid Ref:** 0 220 462

IRos **Ros Ban Wildlife Garden** €
Common, Raphoe, Co. Donegal, Ireland
Ⓣ (74) 914 5336
Ⓜ (353) 8608 05214 & 0851 191016
Ⓔ Rosbangarden@gmail.com
Contact: Ann Kavanagh
Opening Times: Garden open all year, morning to evening.
Credit Cards: None
Notes: Plants available in season from the garden. Please check plant availability with nursery before travelling.
Map Ref: I, A2 **OS Grid Ref:** C254037

ISha **Shady Plants** ⊠ €
Coolbooa, Clashmore, Youghal, Co. Cork, Ireland
Ⓣ (353) 024 96735
Ⓜ 08605 42171
Ⓔ mike@shadyplants.ie
Ⓦ www.shadyplants.net
Contact: Mike Keep
Opening Times: By appt. only Mar-May, Jul-Oct.
Min Mail Order UK: Nmc
Min Mail Order EU: Nmc
Cat. Cost: €3.00
Credit Cards: Paypal
Specialities: Specialist fern nursery based near the south coast of Ireland.
Map Ref: I, D2 **OS Grid Ref:** 613,585

ISsi **Seaside Nursery** ⊠ €
Claddaghduff, Co. Galway, Ireland
Ⓣ (353) 95 44687
Ⓜ (353) 86 3391555
Ⓔ Tom@seasidenursery.biz
Ⓦ www.seasidenursery.biz
Contact: Tom Dyck
Opening Times: 1000-1300 & 1400-1800 Mon-Sat, 1400-1800 Sun. Closed Sun 1 Oct-31 Mar.
Min Mail Order UK: Nmc
Min Mail Order EU: Nmc
Cat. Cost: €3.50
Credit Cards: Visa, MasterCard
Specialities: Plants & hedging suitable for seaside locations. Rare plants originating from Australia & New Zealand esp. *Phormium*, *Astelia*.
Notes: Also sells wholesale.
Map Ref: I, B1

ITim **Timpany Nurseries & Gardens** ⊠
77 Magheratimpany Road, Ballynahinch, Co. Down, N. Ireland BT24 8PA
Ⓣ 028 9756 2812
Ⓕ 028 9756 2812
Ⓔ s.tindall@btconnect.com
Ⓦ www.timpanynurseries.com
Contact: Susan Tindall
Opening Times: 1000-1730 Tue-Sat, Sun by appt.

Min Mail Order UK: Nmc
Min Mail Order EU: £30.00 + p&p
Cat. Cost: £2.00
Credit Cards: Visa, MasterCard
Specialities: *Celmisia, Androsace, Primula, Saxifraga, Dianthus, Meconopsis, Cassiope, Rhodohypoxis, Cyclamen* & *Primula auricula.*
Notes: Also sells wholesale.
Map Ref: I, B3

IVic **VICTORIA'S NURSERY & GARDEN** €
Upper Kells, Kells, Cahirceveen, Co. Kerry, Ireland
Ⓣ (353) 66 947 7605
Ⓜ (353) 879 111465
Ⓔ kellshouse@eircom.net
Contact: Victoria Vogel
Opening Times: 1000-1700 Wed-Sun all year except Xmas. Closed Mon & Tue, except B/hols & by arrangement.
Cat. Cost: None issued.
Credit Cards: None
Specialities: *Rhododendron*, azaleas, *Acer*, tree ferns, seaside & woodland plants, *Saxifraga fortunei* forms.
Notes: Drive along Ring of Kerry, at Kells follow signs to Kells Bay Garden towards Kells Beach, nursery to left after little bridge.
Map Ref: I, D1

LONDON AREA

LAma **JACQUES AMAND INTERNATIONAL** ⊠ ✈ ⌂ € ♿
The Nurseries, 145 Clamp Hill, Stanmore, Middlesex HA7 3JS
Ⓣ (020) 8420 7110
Ⓕ (020) 8954 6784
Ⓔ bulbs@jacquesamand.co.uk
Ⓦ www.jacquesamand.com
Contact: John Amand & Stuart Chapman
Opening Times: 0900-1700 Mon-Fri, 1000-1400 Sat.
Min Mail Order UK: Nmc
Min Mail Order EU: Nmc
Cat. Cost: 1 × 1st class.
Credit Cards: All major credit/debit cards
Specialities: Rare and unusual species bulbs esp. *Arisaema, Trillium, Fritillaria*, tulips.
Notes: Also sells wholesale.
Map Ref: L, B3

LAst **ASTERBY & CHALKCROFT NURSERY** ⊠ ♿
The Ridgeway, Blunham, Bedfordshire MK44 3PH
Ⓣ (01767) 640148
Ⓔ sales@asterbyplants.co.uk
Ⓦ www.asterbyplants.co.uk
Contact: Simon & Eva Aldridge
Opening Times: 1000-1700 7 days. Closed Xmas & Jan.
Min Mail Order UK: Nmc
Credit Cards: All major credit/debit cards
Specialities: Hardy shrubs, herbaceous & trees.
Notes: Please ring for mail order information.
Map Ref: L, A3 **OS Grid Ref:** TL151497

LAyl **AYLETT NURSERIES LTD** ♿ ◆
North Orbital Road, St Albans, Hertfordshire AL2 1DH
Ⓣ (01727) 822255
Ⓕ (01727) 823024
Ⓔ info@aylettnurseries.co.uk
Ⓦ www.aylettnurseries.co.uk
Contact: Julie Aylett
Opening Times: 0830-1730 Mon-Fri, 0830-1700 Sat, 1030-1630 Sun.
Cat. Cost: Free.
Credit Cards: All major credit/debit cards
Specialities: *Dahlia.* 2-acre trial ground adjacent to garden centre.
Map Ref: L, B3 **OS Grid Ref:** TL169049

LBee **BEECHCROFT NURSERY** ♿
127 Reigate Road, Ewell, Surrey KT17 3DE
Ⓣ (020) 8393 4265
Ⓕ (020) 8393 4265
Contact: C Kimber
Opening Times: 1000-1600 Mon-Sat, 1000-1400 Sun and B/hols. Closed Xmas-New Year week.
Cat. Cost: None issued.
Credit Cards: All major credit/debit cards
Specialities: Conifers & alpines.
Notes: Also sells wholesale.
Map Ref: L, C3

LBMP **BLOOMING MARVELLOUS PLANTS** ⌂
Korketts Farm, Aylesbury Road, Winslow, Buckinghamshire MK18 3JL
Ⓣ (01296) 714714
Ⓜ 07963 747305
Ⓔ alex@bmplants.co.uk
Ⓦ www.bmplants.co.uk
Contact: Alexia Ballance
Opening Times: 0900-1700 Tue-Sat & 1000-1600 Sun, 5th Feb-30th Oct 2011. Closed Mons. By appt. only Nov-Jan.
Credit Cards: All major credit/debit cards
Specialities: A mixture of unusual and

KEY
⊠ Mail order to UK or EU ⌂ Delivers to shows
✈ Exports beyond EU € Euro accepted
♿ Accessible by wheelchair ◆ See Display advertisement

L

familiar perennials, shrubs, grasses, ferns & bedding plants, most in more generous sizes than usually found in nurseries.
Notes: Located on the A413 just outside Winslow (heading in the Aylesbury direction). Partial wheelchair access.
Map Ref: L, A2 **OS Grid Ref:** SP777271

LBuc **BUCKINGHAM NURSERIES** ⊠ € ♿ ◆
14 Tingewick Road, Buckingham MK18 4AE
Ⓣ (01280) 822133
Ⓕ (01280) 815491
Ⓔ enquiries@buckingham-nurseries.co.uk
Ⓦ www.buckingham-nurseries.co.uk
Contact: R J & P L Brown
Opening Times: 0830-1730 (1800 in summer) Mon-Sat, 1030-1630 Sun.
Min Mail Order UK: Nmc
Min Mail Order EU: Nmc
Cat. Cost: Free.
Credit Cards: Visa, MasterCard, Switch
Specialities: Bare rooted and container grown hedging. Fruit trees, soft fruit, trees, shrubs, herbaceous perennials, alpines, grasses & ferns.
Map Ref: L, A2 **OS Grid Ref:** SP675333

L

LCla **CLAY LANE NURSERY** ⊠ ⌂
3 Clay Lane, South Nutfield, Nr Redhill, Surrey RH1 4EG
Ⓣ (01737) 823307
Ⓔ claylane.nursery@btinternet.com
Ⓦ www.claylane-fuchsias.co.uk
Contact: K W Belton
Opening Times: Variable opening times. Please phone before travelling.
Min Mail Order UK: £8.00
Cat. Cost: 3 × 2nd class.
Credit Cards: None
Specialities: *Fuchsia*. Many varieties in small quantities only.
Notes: Mail order by telephone pre-arrangement only.
Map Ref: L, C4

LCtg **COTTAGE GARDEN NURSERY** ◆
127 Barnet Road, Arkley, Barnet, Hertfordshire EN5 3JX
Ⓣ (020) 8441 8829
Ⓕ (020) 8531 3178
Ⓔ nurseryinfo@cottagegardennursery-barnet.co.uk
Ⓦ www.cottagegardennursery-barnet.co.uk
Contact: David and Wendy Spicer
Opening Times: 0930-1700 Tue-Sat Mar-Oct, 0930-1600 Tue-Sat Nov-Feb, 1000-1600 Sun & B/hol Mon all year.
Cat. Cost: None issued.
Credit Cards: All major credit/debit cards
Specialities: General range of hardy shrubs, trees, fruit trees & bushes, perennials. Architectural & exotics, *Fuchsia*, seasonal bedding, patio plants.
Map Ref: L, B3 **OS Grid Ref:** TQ226958

LDai **DAISY ROOTS** ⊠ ⌂
(Office) 8 Gosselin Road, Bengeo, Hertford, Hertfordshire SG14 3LG
Ⓣ (01992) 582401
Ⓜ 07958 563355
Ⓕ (01992) 582401
Ⓔ anne@daisyroots.com
Ⓦ www.daisyroots.com
Contact: Anne Godfrey
Opening Times: 1000-1600 Fri & Sat Mar-Oct, or by appt.
Min Mail Order UK: Nmc
Cat. Cost: Online only.
Credit Cards: All major credit/debit cards
Specialities: Ever-increasing range of choice & unusual perennials, particularly *Agastache, Anthemis, Centaurea, Digitalis, Erysimum, Salvia* & *Sedum*.
Notes: Nursery is at Jenningsbury, London Road, Hertford Heath. Also sells wholesale.
Map Ref: L, B4

LDea **DEREK LLOYD DEAN** ⌂
8 Lynwood Close, South Harrow, Middlesex HA2 9PR
Ⓣ (020) 8864 0899
Ⓔ derek@dereklloyddean.com
Ⓦ www.dereklloyddean.com
Contact: Derek Lloyd Dean
Opening Times: Not open.
Credit Cards: None
Specialities: Angel & scented leaf *Pelargonium*. Nat. Collection of Angel *Pelargonium*.

LEdu **EDULIS** ⊠ ⌂ € ♿
(Office) 1 Flowers Piece, Ashampstead, Reading, Berkshire RG8 8SG
Ⓣ (01635) 578113
Ⓜ 07802 812781
Ⓔ edulisnursery@gmail.com
Ⓦ www.edulis.co.uk
Contact: Paul Barney
Opening Times: By appt. only.
Min Mail Order UK: £10.00 + p&p
Min Mail Order EU: £50.00 + p&p
Cat. Cost: 4 × 1st class.
Credit Cards: None
Specialities: Unusual edibles, architectural plants, permaculture plants.
Notes: Nursery is at Bere Court Farm, Tidmarsh Lane, Pangbourne, RG8 8HT.

Also sells wholesale.
Map Ref: L, B2 **OS Grid Ref:** SU615747

LHel **Herts Hellebores** ⊠ €
Green Lane Farm, Levens Green, Nr Ware, Hertfordshire SG11 1HD
Ⓣ (01920) 438458
Ⓔ lorna@herts-hellebore.co.uk
Ⓦ www.herts-hellebore.co.uk
Contact: Lorna Jones
Opening Times: 1000-1600 Wed & Sat only, 2nd Feb-30th Mar 2011. Other times Jan-Apr by appt. only. Check with nursery for 2012 opening times.
Min Mail Order UK: £18
Min Mail Order EU: £18
Cat. Cost: Free.
Credit Cards: All major credit/debit cards
Specialities: Hellebore hybrids. Specialising in developments of double & anemone centred hybrids. Seed-raised plants offered by colour. Some available in small quantities only.
Map Ref: L, A4 **OS Grid Ref:** TL357224

LHop **Hopleys Plants Ltd** ⊠ ⛫ ♿
High Street, Much Hadham, Hertfordshire SG10 6BU
Ⓣ (01279) 842509
Ⓕ (01279) 843784
Ⓔ plants@hopleys.co.uk
Ⓦ www.hopleys.co.uk
Contact: Mr Aubrey Barker
Opening Times: 0900-1700 Mon & Wed-Sat, 1400-1700 Sun. Closed Nov, Jan, Feb except by appt.
Min Mail Order UK: Nmc
Cat. Cost: 5 × 1st class.
Credit Cards: Visa, Access, Switch
Specialities: Wide range of hardy & half-hardy shrubs & perennials.
Notes: Also sells wholesale.
Map Ref: L, A4 **OS Grid Ref:** TL428196

LLHF **Little Heath Farm (UK)** ⛫
Little Heath Lane, Potten End, Berkhamsted, Hertfordshire HP4 2RY
Ⓣ (01442) 864951
Ⓔ lhfnursery@gmail.com
Ⓦ www.littleheathfarmnursery.co.uk
Contact: John Spokes
Opening Times: 1000-1700 or dusk if earlier, 7 days.
Cat. Cost: Online only.
Credit Cards: Visa, MasterCard
Specialities: Large range of alpines, herbaceous, shrubs, many available in small quantities only.
Map Ref: L, B3

LLWP **L W Plants** ⊠ ⛫
23 Wroxham Way, Harpenden, Hertfordshire AL5 4PP
Ⓣ (01582) 768467
Ⓔ lwplants@waitrose.com
Ⓦ www.thymus.co.uk
Contact: Mrs Margaret Easter
Opening Times: 1000-1700 most days, but please phone first.
Min Mail Order UK: Nmc
Cat. Cost: Online only.
Credit Cards: None
Specialities: Plants from a plantsman's garden, esp. *Geranium*, grasses & *Thymus*. Some available in small quantities only. Nat. Collections of *Thymus* (Scientific), *Hyssopus* & *Satureja*. *Thymus* ICRA (provisional). *Thymus* propagated to order.
Notes: Mail order *Thymus* only.
Map Ref: L, B3 **OS Grid Ref:** TL141153

LMaj **Majestic Trees** ⛫ €
Chequers Meadow, Chequers Hill, Flamstead, St Albans, Hertfordshire AL3 8ET
Ⓣ (01582) 843881
Ⓕ (01582) 843882
Ⓔ info@majesticgroup.co.uk
Ⓦ www.majestictrees.co.uk
Contact: Andrew Austin
Opening Times: 0830-1700 Mon-Fri. 1000-1600 Sat, Nov-Feb, 1000-1700 Sat, Mar-Oct. Closed Sun, B/hols, Xmas/New Year.
Credit Cards: MasterCard, Visa, Switch, Maestro
Specialities: Semi-mature & mature containerised trees grown in airpots from 50 to 5000 ltrs.
Notes: Also sells wholesale. Disabled access by golf buggy can be arranged by appt.
Map Ref: L, B3 **OS Grid Ref:** TL08140815

LMil **Millais Nurseries** ⊠ ♿
Crosswater Farm, Crosswater Lane, Churt, Farnham, Surrey GU10 2JN
Ⓣ (01252) 792698
Ⓕ (01252) 792526
Ⓔ sales@rhododendrons.co.uk
Ⓦ www.rhododendrons.co.uk
Contact: David Millais
Opening Times: 1000-1700 Mon-Fri all year. Daily in spring.
Min Mail Order UK: Nmc
Min Mail Order EU: Nmc

KEY
⊠ Mail order to UK or EU ⛫ Delivers to shows
✈ Exports beyond EU € Euro accepted
♿ Accessible by wheelchair ◆ See Display advertisement

Cat. Cost: Free list on request. Full catalogue Online.
Credit Cards: All major credit/debit cards
Specialities: Rhododendrons, azaleas, magnolias, camellias & acers. Garden open in spring.
Notes: Mail order all year. Also sells wholesale.
Map Ref: L, C3 **OS Grid Ref:** SU856397

LPBA **Paul Bromfield – Aquatics** ⊠ ✈ € ♿
Maydencroft Lane, Gosmore, Hitchin, Hertfordshire SG4 7QD
Ⓣ (01462) 457399
Ⓜ 07969 358857
Ⓕ (01462) 422652
Ⓔ info@bromfieldaquatics.co.uk
Ⓦ www.bromfieldaquatics.co.uk
Contact: Debbie Edwards
Opening Times: Mail order only. Order online at website. Office open 1000-1700 Mon-Sat, Feb-Oct. Visitors please ring for appt.
Min Mail Order UK: Nmc
Min Mail Order EU: £100.00 incl.
Cat. Cost: Online only.
Credit Cards: Visa, MasterCard, Delta, JCB, Switch
Specialities: Water lilies, marginals & bog.
Notes: Also sells wholesale.

LPen **Penstemons by Colour** ⊠
Peterley Manor, Peterley, Prestwood, Great Missenden, Buckinghamshire HP16 0HH
Ⓣ (01494) 866420
Ⓕ (01494) 866420
Ⓔ debra@peterleymanor.co.uk
Contact: Debra Hughes
Opening Times: Any time by appt.
Min Mail Order UK: £10.00
Cat. Cost: Free.
Credit Cards: None
Specialities: *Penstemon.*
Map Ref: L, B3 **OS Grid Ref:** SU880994

LPla **The Plant Specialist**
7 Whitefield Lane, Great Missenden, Buckinghamshire HP16 0BH
Ⓣ (01494) 866650
Ⓕ (01494) 866650
Ⓔ enquire@theplantspecialist.co.uk
Ⓦ www.theplantspecialist.co.uk
Contact: Sean Walter
Opening Times: 1000-1700 Wed-Sat, 1000-1600 Sun, Apr-Oct.
Cat. Cost: None issued.
Credit Cards: All major credit/debit cards
Specialities: Herbaceous perennials, grasses, half-hardy perennials, bulbs.
Notes: Limited wheelchair access.

LPot **Potash Plants** ⌂ ♿
Potash Nursery, Drayton Parslow, Buckinghamshire
MK17 0JE
Ⓣ (01296) 720578
Ⓔ info@potashplants.co.uk
Ⓦ www.potashplants.co.uk
Contact: Gill Gallon
Opening Times: 0900-1730 Mon-Sat. 1030-1630 Sun.
Cat. Cost: Online.
Credit Cards: All, except American Express
Specialities: Wide range of traditional and unusual hardy perennials, grasses, trees & shrubs. Some available in small quantities only.
Notes: Nursery on B4032 mid-way between Aylesbury and Milton Keynes. Also sells wholesale.
Map Ref: L, A3 **OS Grid Ref:** SP834279

LRHS **Wisley Plant Centre (RHS)** ♿ ◆
RHS Garden, Wisley, Woking, Surrey
GU23 6QB
Ⓣ (01483) 211113 or 0845 060 9800
Ⓕ (01483) 212372
Ⓔ wisleyplantcentre@rhs.org.uk
Ⓦ www.rhs.org.uk/wisleyplantcentre
Opening Times: 0930-1700 Mon-Sat, Oct-Feb. 0930-1800 Mon-Sat, Mar-Sep. 1100-1700 Sun all year, browsing from 1030.
Cat. Cost: Online only.
Credit Cards: All major credit/debit cards
Specialities: Over 9,000 plants, many rare or unusual, reflecting the range of the RHS flagship garden at Wisley. Plants subject to seasonal availability. For plants not in stock, we operate a reservation service by phone & in person.
Notes: Programme of free plant events throughout the year. Please ring or check website for details.
Map Ref: L, C3

LShp **Squire's Garden Centre, Shepperton** ♿
Halliford Road, Upper Halliford, Shepperton, Middlesex
TW17 8SG
Ⓣ (01932) 784121
Ⓕ (01932) 780569
Ⓔ shepp.plants@squiresgardencentres.co.uk
Ⓦ www.squiresgardencentres.co.uk
Contact: Plant Area Manager

Opening Times: 0900-1800 Mon-Sat, 1030-1630 Sun.
Cat. Cost: None issued.
Credit Cards: All major credit/debit cards
Specialities: Roses.
Notes: Other garden centres in Middlesex & Surrey.

LSou **Southon Plants** ⊠ ♿
Mutton Hill, Dormansland, Lingfield, Surrey RH7 6NP
Ⓣ (01342) 870150
Ⓔ info@southonplants.com
Ⓦ www.southonplants.com
Contact: Mr Southon
Opening Times: 0900-1730 Feb-Oct. For Nov, Dec & Jan please phone first.
Min Mail Order UK: Nmc
Cat. Cost: Online only.
Credit Cards: All major credit/debit cards
Specialities: New & unusual hardy & tender perennials, specialising in *Agapanthus* (over 30 varieties), *Coreopsis*, *Euphorbia* & *Heuchera* (over 40 varieties).
Notes: Mail order. Please phone/email for details.
Map Ref: L, C4

LSqH **Squire's Garden Centre, West Horsley** ♿
Epsom Road, West Horsley, Leatherhead, Surrey KT24 6AR
Ⓣ (01483) 282911
Ⓕ (01483) 281380
Ⓔ hors.plants@squiresgardencentres.co.uk
Ⓦ www.squiresgardencentres.co.uk
Contact: Plant Area Manager
Opening Times: 0900-1800 Mon-Sat, 1030-1630 Sun.
Cat. Cost: None issued.
Credit Cards: All major credit/debit cards
Specialities: Herbaceous.
Notes: Other garden centres in Middlesex & Surrey.

LSqu **Squire's Garden Centre, Twickenham** ♿
Sixth Cross Road, Twickenham, Middlesex TW2 5PA
Ⓣ (020) 8977 9241
Ⓕ (020) 8943 4024
Ⓔ twic.plants@squiresgardencentres.co.uk
Ⓦ www.squiresgardencentres.co.uk
Contact: Plant Area Manager
Opening Times: 0900-1800 Mon-Sat, 1030-1630 Sun.
Credit Cards: All major credit/debit cards
Specialities: *Clematis*.
Notes: Other garden centres in Middlesex & Surrey.

LSRN **Spring Reach Nursery** ⊠ ♿
Long Reach, Ockham, Guildford, Surrey GU23 6PG
Ⓣ (01483) 284769
Ⓜ 07884 432666
Ⓕ (01483) 284769
Ⓔ info@springreachnursery.co.uk
Ⓦ www.springreachnursery.co.uk
Contact: Nick & Lissa Hourhan
Opening Times: 7 days. 1000-1700 Mon-Sat, 1030-1630 Sun. Open B/hols.
Min Mail Order UK: Nmc
Min Mail Order EU: Nmc
Credit Cards: All major credit/debit cards
Specialities: Shrubs, evergreen climbers, *Clematis*, perennials, roses, grasses, ferns, bamboos, trees, hedging, soft fruit & top fruit. Plants for chalk & clay. Deer & rabbit proof plants. Specimen & acid-loving plants.
Notes: Also sells wholesale. Please ring for mail order details.
Map Ref: L, C3

LStr **Henry Street Nursery** ⊠ ♿
Swallowfield Road, Arborfield, Reading, Berkshire, RG2 9JY
Ⓣ (0118) 9761223
Ⓕ (0118) 9761417
Ⓔ info@henrystreet.co.uk
Ⓦ www.henrystreet.co.uk
Contact: Mr M C Goold
Opening Times: 0900-1730 Mon-Sat, 1030-1630 Sun.
Min Mail Order UK: Nmc
Min Mail Order EU: Nmc
Cat. Cost: Free.
Credit Cards: All major credit/debit cards
Specialities: Roses.
Notes: Also sells wholesale.
Map Ref: L, C3

LTen **Tendercare Nurseries Ltd**
Southlands Road, Denham, Middlesex, UB9 4HD
Ⓣ (01895) 835544
Ⓕ (01895) 835036
Ⓔ sales@tendercare.co.uk
Ⓦ www.tendercare.co.uk
Contact: Saija Haivala-Kendrick
Opening Times: 0900-1700 Mon-Sat.

KEY
⊠ Mail order to UK or EU — Delivers to shows
Exports beyond EU — € Euro accepted
♿ Accessible by wheelchair — ◆ See Display advertisement

Credit Cards: All major credit/debit cards
Specialities: Mature trees, shrubs, hedging, climbers & herbaceous plants.
Notes: Also sells wholesale.

L

LToo **TOOBEES EXOTICS** ⊠ ✈ €
20 Inglewood, St Johns, Woking, Surrey, GU21 3HX
Ⓣ (01483) 722600
Ⓜ 07836 334011
Ⓕ (01483) 751995
Ⓔ bbpotter@woking.plus.com
Ⓦ www.toobees-exotics.com
Contact: Bob Potter
Opening Times: Not open. Mail order & online shop only. Visits by appt. only.
Min Mail Order UK: Nmc
Min Mail Order EU: Nmc
Cat. Cost: Sae.
Credit Cards: All major credit/debit cards
Specialities: South African & Madagascan succulents, many rare & unusual species, *Euphorbia* & *Pachypodium.* Stock varies constantly.
Notes: Credit cards accepted online only.

LTop **TOPIARY ARTS** ⊠ ♠
(Office) 224 Hospital Bridge Road, Whitton, Twickenham, Middlesex, TW2 6LF
Ⓜ 07775 602704
Ⓔ jcb@topiaryarts.com
Ⓦ www.topiaryarts.com
Contact: James Crebbin-Bailey
Opening Times: By appt. only.
Min Mail Order UK: £30
Cat. Cost: Online only.
Credit Cards: None
Specialities: Topiary with herbaceous underplanting.
Notes: Also sells wholesale. Nursery is at Copped Hall Walled Garden, Upshire, Epping, Essex CM16 5HS.

LWst **WESTONBIRT PLANTS** ⊠ ✈ ♠ €
17 Stanley Road, Carshalton, Surrey, SM5 4LE
Ⓜ 07788 676079
Ⓔ office@westonbirtplants.co.uk
Ⓦ www.westonbirtplants.co.uk
Contact: Tony Dickerson
Opening Times: Not open. Mail order & shows only.
Min Mail Order UK: Nmc
Min Mail Order EU: Nmc
Cat. Cost: 4 × 2nd class.
Credit Cards: All major credit/debit cards
Specialities: Bulbs & woodland plants incl. *Anemone nemorosa, Anemonella, Arisaema, Arum, Colchicum, Corydalis, Crocus, Erythronium, Fritillaria, Galanthus, Helleborus, Iris* (Juno & Oncocyclus), *Lilium, Nemocharis, Paeonia, Roscoea, Trillium* & hardy orchids (*Calanthe, Cypripedium* & *Epipactis*). Many rare plants in ltd. numbers.

LYaf **YAFFLES** ⊠ ♠ ♿
Harvest Hill, Bourne End, Buckinghamshire, SL8 5JJ
Ⓣ (01628) 525455
Contact: I Butterfield
Opening Times: 0900-1300 & 1400-1700. Please phone beforehand in case we are attending shows.
Min Mail Order UK: Nmc
Min Mail Order EU: £30.00 + p&p
Cat. Cost: 2 × 2nd class.
Credit Cards: None
Specialities: Nat. Collection of *Pleione. Dahlia* for collection only.
Notes: Only *Pleione* by mail order.

MIDLANDS

MArl **ARLEY HALL NURSERY** ♿
Arley Hall Nursery, Northwich, Cheshire, CW9 6NA
Ⓣ (01565) 777479 or 777231
Ⓕ (01565) 777465
Ⓦ www.arleyhallandgardens.com
Contact: Jane Foster, Rosie Jackson
Opening Times: 1100-1730 Tue-Sun 22nd Mar-end Sep. Also B/hol Mons.
Cat. Cost: 4 × 1st class.
Credit Cards: All major credit/debit cards
Specialities: Wide range of herbaceous incl. many unusual varieties, some in small quantities. Wide range of unusual pelargoniums.
Notes: Nursery is beside car park at Arley Hall Gardens.
Map Ref: M, A1 **OS Grid Ref:** SJ673808

MAsh **ASHWOOD NURSERIES LTD** ⊠ ♿ ◆
Ashwood Lower Lane, Ashwood, Kingswinford, West Midlands, DY6 0AE
Ⓣ (01384) 401996
Ⓕ (01384) 401108
Ⓔ mailorder@ashwoodnurseries.com
Ⓦ www.ashwoodnurseries.com
Contact: Karrina Gilbert & Rachel Kendall
Opening Times: 0900-1700 Mon-Sat & 0930-1700 Sun excl. Xmas & Boxing Day.
Min Mail Order UK: Nmc
Min Mail Order EU: Nmc
Cat. Cost: 6 × 1st class.
Credit Cards: All major credit/debit cards

Specialities: Large range of hardy plants, shrubs & dwarf conifers. Roses, alpines & herbaceous plants. Also specialises in *Auricula, Cyclamen, Galanthus*, hellebores, *Hepatica, Hydrangea* & *Salvia*. Nat. Collection of *Lewisia*.
Notes: Tea room overlooking display garden. Ample parking. Regular events. Groups by appt. to visit private garden.
Map Ref: M, C2 **OS Grid Ref:** SO865879

MAus **DAVID AUSTIN ROSES LTD** ⊠ ✈ € ♿ ◆
Bowling Green Lane, Albrighton, Wolverhampton, West Midlands, WV7 3HB
Ⓣ (01902) 376300
Ⓕ (01902) 375177
Ⓔ retail@davidaustinroses.co.uk
Ⓦ www.davidaustinroses.com
Contact: Customer Services Dept
Opening Times: 0900-1700, 7 days.
Min Mail Order UK: Nmc
Min Mail Order EU: Nmc
Cat. Cost: Free.
Credit Cards: Switch, Visa, MasterCard, Maestro, Access
Specialities: Roses. Nat. Collection of English Roses.
Notes: Also sells wholesale.
Map Ref: M, B2 **OS Grid Ref:** SJ798042

MAvo **AVONDALE NURSERY** ⌂ ♿
(Office) 3 Avondale Road, Earlsdon, Coventry, Warwickshire, CV5 6DZ
Ⓣ (024) 766 73662
Ⓜ 07979 093096
Ⓕ (024) 766 73662
Ⓔ enquiries@avondalenursery.co.uk
Ⓦ www.avondalenursery.co.uk
Contact: Brian Ellis
Opening Times: 1000-1230, 1400-1700 Mon-Sat, 1030-1630 Sun, Mar-Sep. Other times by appt.
Cat. Cost: 4 × 1st class.
Credit Cards: All major credit/debit cards
Specialities: Rare & unusual perennials esp. *Aster, Eryngium, Leucanthemum, Geum, Crocosmia, Sanguisorba* & grasses. Nat. Collections of *Aster novae-angliae* & *Sanguisorba*. Display garden open. Groups welcome.
Notes: Nursery is at Russell's Nursery, Mill Hill, Baginton, Nr Coventry, CV8 3AG.
Map Ref: M, C2 **OS Grid Ref:** SP339751

MBel **BLUEBELL COTTAGE NURSERY (FORMERLY LODGE LANE NURSERY)** ⊠ ♿
Lodge Lane, Dutton, Nr Warrington, Cheshire, WA4 4HP
Ⓣ (01928) 713718
Ⓕ (01928) 713718
Ⓔ info@bluebellcottage.co.uk
Ⓦ www.bluebellcottage.co.uk
Contact: Sue Beesley
Opening Times: 1000-1700 Wed-Sun & B/hols, mid Mar-mid Sep. By appt. outside these dates.
Min Mail Order UK: £10.00
Cat. Cost: Online, or by email.
Credit Cards: All major credit/debit cards
Specialities: Unusual perennials & shrubs incl. *Achillea, Astrantia, Campanula, Digitalis, Penstemon, Geranium, Heuchera, Kniphofia, Nepeta, Papaver, Salvia* & ornamental grasses.
Notes: Mail order Mar/Apr & Sep/Oct only, subject to plant size.
Map Ref: M, A1 **OS Grid Ref:** SJ586779

MBlu **BLUEBELL ARBORETUM & NURSERY** ⊠ ⌂ ♿
Annwell Lane, Smisby, Nr Ashby de la Zouch, Derbyshire LE65 2TA
Ⓣ (01530) 413700
Ⓕ (01530) 417600
Ⓔ sales@bluebellnursery.com
Ⓦ www.bluebellnursery.com
Contact: Robert & Suzette Vernon
Opening Times: 0900-1700 Mon-Sat & 1030-1630 Sun Mar-Oct, 0900-1600 Mon-Sat (not Sun) Nov-Feb. Closed 24th Dec-1st Jan incl. & Easter Sun.
Min Mail Order UK: £9.50
Min Mail Order EU: Nmc
Cat. Cost: £1.50 + 3 × 1st class.
Credit Cards: Visa, Access, Switch, MasterCard
Specialities: Uncommon trees & shrubs. Woody climbers. Display garden & arboretum.
Map Ref: M, B1 **OS Grid Ref:** SK344187

MBNS **BARNSDALE GARDENS** ⊠ ⌂ ♿
Exton Avenue, Exton, Oakham, Rutland LE15 8AH
Ⓣ (01572) 813200
Ⓕ (01572) 813346
Ⓔ info@barnsdalegardens.co.uk
Ⓦ www.barnsdalegardens.co.uk
Contact: Nick Hamilton
Opening Times: 0900-1700 Mar-May & Sep-Oct, 0900-1900 Jun-Aug, 1000-1600 Nov-Feb, 7 days. Closed 24th & 25th Dec.

KEY
⊠ Mail order to UK or EU ⌂ Delivers to shows
✈ Exports beyond EU € Euro accepted
♿ Accessible by wheelchair ◆ See Display advertisement

M

Min Mail Order UK: Nmc
Min Mail Order EU: Nmc
Cat. Cost: Online only.
Credit Cards: All major credit/debit cards
Specialities: Wide range of choice & unusual garden plants. Over 160 varieties of *Penstemon*, over 250 varieties of *Hemerocallis*.
Notes: Mail order from website or by telephone ordering only.
Map Ref: M, B3 **OS Grid Ref:** SK912108

MBPg **Barnfield Pelargoniums** ⊠
Barnfield, Off Wilnecote Lane, Belgrave, Tamworth, Staffordshire B77 2LF
Ⓣ (01827) 250123
Ⓕ (01827) 250123
Ⓔ brianandjenniewhite@hotmail.com
Contact: Brian White
Opening Times: Open by appt. only.
Min Mail Order UK: £6.00
Min Mail Order EU: £10.00
Cat. Cost: 4 × 2nd class.
Credit Cards: None
Specialities: Over 200 varieties of scented leaf pelargoniums.

MBrN **Bridge Nursery** € ♿
Tomlow Road, Napton-on-the-Hill, Nr Rugby, Warwickshire CV47 8HX
Ⓣ (01926) 812737
Ⓔ pemartino@tiscali.co.uk
Ⓦ www.Bridge-Nursery.co.uk
Contact: Christine Dakin & Philip Martino
Opening Times: 1000-1600 Mon-Sun 1st Feb-mid Dec. Other times by appt.
Cat. Cost: Online only.
Credit Cards: All major credit/debit cards
Specialities: Ornamental grasses, sedges & bamboos. Also range of shrubs & perennials. Display garden.
Notes: Also sells wholesale.
Map Ref: M, C2 **OS Grid Ref:** SP463625

MBri **Bridgemere Nurseries** € ♿
Bridgemere, Nr Nantwich, Cheshire CW5 7QB
Ⓣ (01270) 521100
Ⓕ (01270) 520215
Ⓔ customer.service@bridgemere.co.uk
Ⓦ www.bridgemere.co.uk
Contact: Keith Atkey, Roger Pierce
Opening Times: 0900-1800 7 days. Closed 25th & 26th Dec.
Cat. Cost: None issued.
Credit Cards: Visa, Access, MasterCard, Switch
Specialities: Huge range of outdoor & indoor plants, many rare & unusual. Specimen shrubs.
Map Ref: M, B1 **OS Grid Ref:** SJ727435

MCms **Chrysanthemums Direct** ⊠ ♘
Holmes Chapel Road, Over Peover, Knutsford, Cheshire WA16 9RA
Ⓣ 0800 046 7443
Ⓜ 07977 312 593
Ⓔ sales@chrysanthemumsdirect.co.uk
Ⓦ www.chrysanthemumsdirect.co.uk
Contact: Martyn Flint
Opening Times: Not open. Mail order only.
Min Mail Order UK: Nmc
Min Mail Order EU: Nmc
Cat. Cost: 4 × 1st class.
Credit Cards: All major credit/debit cards
Specialities: Chrysanthemums. Young plants grown to order. Delivery within 14 days.

MCoo **Cool Temperate** ⊠ ☒
(Office) 45 Stamford Street, Awsworth, Nottinghamshire NG16 2QL
Ⓣ (0115) 916 2673
Ⓕ (0115) 916 2673
Ⓔ phil.corbett@cooltemperate.co.uk
Ⓦ www.cooltemperate.co.uk
Contact: Phil Corbett
Opening Times: 0900-1700, 7 days. Please ring/write first.
Min Mail Order UK: Nmc
Min Mail Order EU: Nmc
Cat. Cost: 3 × 1st class.
Credit Cards: None
Specialities: Tree fruit, soft fruit, nitrogen-fixers, hedging, own-root fruit trees. Many species available in small quantities only.
Notes: Nursery at Trinity Farm, Awsworth Lane, Cossall, Notts. Also sells wholesale.
Map Ref: M, B2 **OS Grid Ref:** SK482435

MCot **Coton Manor Garden**
Guilsborough, Northampton, Northamptonshire NN6 8RQ
Ⓣ (01604) 740219
Ⓔ nursery@cotonmanor.co.uk
Ⓦ www.cotonmanor.co.uk
Contact: Caroline Tait
Opening Times: 1200-1730 Tue-Sat, 1st April (or Easter if earlier) to 30th Sep. Also Sun Apr, May & B/hol w/ends. Other times in working hours by appt.
Cat. Cost: None issued.
Credit Cards: All major credit/debit cards
Specialities: Wide-range of herbaceous perennials (3000+ varieties), some available in small quantities only. Also many tender perennials & selected shrubs.

Notes: Garden open. Tea rooms. Garden School. Partial wheelchair access.
Map Ref: M, C3 **OS Grid Ref:** SP675715

MCri **CRIN GARDENS** ⊠ €
79 Partons Road, Kings Heath, Birmingham B14 6TD
Ⓣ 0121 443 3815
Ⓜ 07805 591475
Ⓕ 0121 443 3815
Ⓔ cringardens@tiscali.co.uk
Ⓦ www.cringardens.co.uk
Contact: M Milinkovic
Opening Times: Not open. Mail order only.
Min Mail Order UK: Nmc
Min Mail Order EU: Nmc
Cat. Cost: 2 × 1st class + 1 × 2nd.
Credit Cards: None
Specialities: Lilies. Limited stock available on first come, first served basis.

MDev **DEVON CROFT NURSERY** ⊠ ♿
81 Farndon Road, Newark, Nottinghamshire NG24 4SQ
Ⓣ (01636) 704013
Ⓜ 07930 318813
Ⓔ susan@devoncroftnursery.co.uk
Ⓦ www.devoncroftnursery.co.uk
Contact: Susan Richardson
Opening Times: Wed-Sun mid-Feb to late Dec. 7 days Easter-end Jun. W/ends only Aug.
Min Mail Order UK: Nmc
Cat. Cost: Online only.
Credit Cards: All major credit/debit cards
Specialities: Wide range of *Bamboo* & hostas, many specimen-sized plants. Hardy herbaceous perennials. Some plants in small quantities.
Map Ref: M, B3 **OS Grid Ref:** SK786528

MDKP **D K PLANTS** ⛺
(Office) 19 Harbourne Road, Cheadle, Stoke on Trent, Staffordshire ST10 1JU
Ⓣ Office: (01538) 754460
Ⓜ Nursery: 07779 545015
Ⓔ davidknoxc@aol.com
Contact: Dave Knox
Opening Times: 0900-2000 (or dusk if earlier) Mon-Tue & Thu-Fri. Other times by appt.
Cat. Cost: 4 × 1st class A4 sae plus 44p 1st or 37p 2nd class.
Credit Cards: None
Specialities: Unusual hardy alpines & perennials. All grown on the nursery.
Notes: Nursery is at new roundabout across from Queen's Arms pub, Freehay Crossroads, Freehay, Cheadle, ST10 1TR.
Map Ref: M, B1

MFie **FIELD HOUSE NURSERY** ⊠ ⛺ € ♿
Leake Road, Gotham, Nottinghamshire NG11 0JN
Ⓣ (01159) 830278
Ⓜ 07504 125209
Ⓔ auricula@btinternet.com
Contact: Valerie A Woolley & Bob Taylor
Opening Times: 0900-1600 Fri-Wed or by appt.
Min Mail Order UK: 4 plants.
Min Mail Order EU: £30.00
Cat. Cost: 4 × 1st class or 4 × IRC (auriculas/primulas). 2 × 1st class (astrantias).
Credit Cards: Visa, MasterCard, Electron, Maestro, Solo
Specialities: *Primula auricula* & seed, Astrantia, herbaceous perennials. Nat. Collections of *Primula auricula* (Shows & Alpines) & *Astrantia*.
Notes: Mail order for *Astrantia*, *Auricula*, small *Primula*, & seeds.

MGbk **GOSBROOK PELARGONIUMS** ⊠
30 Damson Trees, Shrivenham, Oxfordshire SN6 8BB
Ⓣ (01793) 783329
Ⓜ 07921 089908
Ⓔ enquiries@gosbrookpelargoniums.com
Ⓦ www.gosbrookpelargoniums.com
Contact: David Taylor
Opening Times: Please ring for appt.
Min Mail Order UK: £20.00
Min Mail Order EU: £20.00
Cat. Cost: 3 × 1st class.
Specialities: *Pelargonium*.
Notes: Credit cards accepted online only.
Map Ref: M, D2 **OS Grid Ref:** SU233889

MGos **GOSCOTE NURSERIES LTD** ♿ ◆
Syston Road, Cossington, Leicestershire LE7 4UZ
Ⓣ (01509) 812121
Ⓕ (01509) 814231
Ⓔ sales@goscote.co.uk
Ⓦ www.goscote.co.uk
Contact: James Toone
Opening Times: 7 days, year round, apart from between Xmas & New Year.
Cat. Cost: Online only.
Credit Cards: Visa, Access, MasterCard, Delta, Switch
Specialities: Japanese maples, rhododendrons & azaleas, *Magnolia*, *Camellia*, *Pieris* & other

KEY
⊠ Mail order to UK or EU ⛺ Delivers to shows
✈ Exports beyond EU € Euro accepted
♿ Accessible by wheelchair ◆ See Display advertisement

M

Ericaceae. Ornamental trees & shrubs, conifers, fruit, heathers, alpines, roses, *Clematis* & unusual climbers. Show Garden to visit.
Notes: Design & landscaping service available. Also sells wholesale.
Map Ref: M, B3 **OS Grid Ref:** SK602130

MGrl **Grasslands Nursery** ⊠ ♿
Free Green Lane, Lower Peover Lane, Knutsford, Cheshire WA16 9QY
Ⓣ (01565) 722766
Ⓕ (01565) 723954
Ⓔ paul@shrubsdirect.com
Ⓦ www.shrubsdirect.com
Contact: Claire Watmore
Opening Times: 0900-1630 summer, 7 days. 1000-1600 winter, 5 days.
Min Mail Order UK: Nmc
Cat. Cost: Online only.
Credit Cards: All major credit/debit cards
Specialities: Wide general range from large specimen plants to perennials.
Map Ref: M, A1

MHer **The Herb Nursery** ♿
Thistleton, Oakham, Rutland LE15 7RE
Ⓣ (01572) 767658
Ⓔ herbnursery@southwitham.net
Ⓦ www.herbnursery.co.uk
Contact: Peter Bench
Opening Times: 0900-1800 (or dusk) 7 days excl. Xmas-New Year.
Cat. Cost: A5 sae.
Credit Cards: None
Specialities: Herbs, wild flowers, cottage garden plants, scented-leaf pelargoniums. Esp. *Thymus, Mentha, Lavandula.*
Map Ref: M, B3

MHom **Homestead Plants** ⊠
The Homestead, Normanton, Bottesford, Nottingham NG13 0EP
Ⓣ (01949) 842745
Ⓦ www.homesteadplants.co.uk
Contact: Mrs S Palmer
Opening Times: By appt.
Min Mail Order UK: Nmc
Cat. Cost: 2 × 2nd class.
Credit Cards: None
Specialities: Unusual hardy & half-hardy perennials, esp. *Paeonia* species. *Hosta, Jovibarba, Salvia, Sempervivum* & Heliotrope. Drought-tolerant asters. Most available only in small quantities. Nat. Collection of *Heliotropium* cultivars.
Notes: Mail order not offered year round. Please check with nursery for details.
Map Ref: M, B3 **OS Grid Ref:** SK812407

MHoo **Hooksgreen Herbs Ltd** ⊠ €
Hooksgreen Farm, Oulton Heath, Stone, Staffordshire ST15 8TN
Ⓣ (01782) 373770
Ⓜ 07977 886810
Ⓔ sales@hooksgreenherbs.com
Ⓦ www.hooksgreenherbs.com
Contact: Malcolm Dickson
Min Mail Order UK: £10.00
Min Mail Order EU: £10.00
Credit Cards: All major credit/debit cards
Specialities: Culinary, medicinal & scented herbs.

MJac **Jackson's Nurseries**
Clifton Campville, Nr Tamworth, Staffordshire B79 0AP
Ⓣ (01827) 373307
Contact: N Jackson
Opening Times: 0900-1800 Mon & Wed-Sat, 1000-1700 Sun.
Cat. Cost: 2 × 1st class.
Credit Cards: None
Specialities: *Fuchsia.*
Notes: Also sells wholesale.
Map Ref: M, B1

MLea **Lea Rhododendron Gardens Ltd** ⊠ ✈ ♿
Lea, Matlock, Derbyshire DE4 5GH
Ⓣ (01629) 534380/534260
Ⓕ (01629) 534260
Ⓦ www.leagarden.co.uk
Contact: Peter Tye
Opening Times: 1000-1730 7 days 20 Mar-30 Jun. Out of season by appt.
Min Mail Order UK: £15.00 + p&p
Min Mail Order EU: £15.00 + p&p
Cat. Cost: 30p + sae.
Credit Cards: All major credit/debit cards
Specialities: Rhododendrons & azaleas.
Map Ref: M, B1 **OS Grid Ref:** SK324571

MLHP **Longstone Hardy Plant Nursery** ♿
(Office) Stancil House, Barn Furlong, Great Longstone, Nr Bakewell, Derbyshire DE45 1TR
Ⓣ (01629) 640136
Ⓜ 07762 083674
Ⓔ lucyinlongstone@hotmail.com
Ⓦ www.longstonehardyplants.co.uk
Contact: Lucy Wright
Opening Times: 1300-1700 Tue-Sat & B/hols, 1st Apr-30th Sep. 1300-1700 Sat, Mar & Oct. Other times by appt.
Credit Cards: None
Specialities: Specialist peat-free nursery displaying all our own hardy perennials,

ornamental grasses, herbs & shrubs, incl. many unusual varieties. Some stock available in small quantities only. Can propagate to order.
Notes: Nursery at Station Road 150 yds on right after turning onto it at the village green. Postcode DE45 1TS.
Map Ref: M, A2 **OS Grid Ref:** SK198717

MMHG **Morton Nurseries Ltd** ⊠ ♠ ♿
Morton Hall, Ranby, Retford, Nottinghamshire DN22 8HW
Ⓣ (01777) 702530
Ⓜ 07940 434398
Ⓔ enquiries@morton-nurseries.com
Ⓦ www.morton-nurseries.co.uk
Contact: Gill McMaster
Opening Times: By appt.only
Min Mail Order UK: £5.00 + p&p
Cat. Cost: 3 × 1st class.
Credit Cards: None
Specialities: Shrubs & perennials.
Map Ref: M, A3

MMoz **Mozart House Nursery Garden** ♠
84 Central Avenue, Wigston, Leicestershire LE18 2AA
Ⓣ (0116) 288 9548
Contact: Des Martin
Opening Times: 1000-1300 last Sat of the month, Mar to Sep 2011. Other times by appt.
Cat. Cost: Phone for list.
Credit Cards: None
Specialities: Bamboos, ornamental grasses, rushes & sedges, ferns. Expanding range of shade & woodland plants. Some stock available in small quantities.
Map Ref: M, C3

MMuc **Mucklestone Nurseries** ⊠ ♿ ◆
Rock Lane, Mucklestone, Nr Market Drayton, Shropshire TF9 4DN
Ⓣ (01630) 673163
Ⓜ 07985 425829 or 07944 103987
Ⓔ info@botanyplants.co.uk
Ⓦ www.botanyplants.co.uk
Contact: Brian Watkins
Opening Times: 0900-1700 Thu-Sun, Mar-Oct but please phone first. Other times by appt.
Min Mail Order UK: Nmc
Cat. Cost: Online.
Specialities: Trees, shrubs, grasses & perennials for acid & damp soils of the north & west UK.
Notes: For mail order contact William or Louise Friend 07714 241667/8 or at email above. All plants from nurseries coded SEND & MMuc available for collection. Also sells wholesale.
Map Ref: M, B2 **OS Grid Ref:** SJ728373

MNFA **The Nursery Further Afield** ⊠ ♿
Evenley Road, Mixbury, Nr Brackley, Northamptonshire NN13 5YR
Ⓣ (01280) 848808
Ⓔ sinclair@nurseryfurtherafield.co.uk
Contact: Gerald & Mary Sinclair
Opening Times: 1000-1700 Wed-Sat, Apr-mid Sep. Other times by appt.
Min Mail Order UK: £15.00
Cat. Cost: 3 × 1st class.
Credit Cards: None
Specialities: Worthwhile hardy perennials, many unusual. Large selection of *Geranium* & *Hemerocallis*. Nat. Collection of *Hemerocallis* on display 1400-1700 16th & 17th Jul 2011.
Notes: Mail order for *Hemerocallis* only.
Map Ref: M, C3 **OS Grid Ref:** SP608344

MNHC **The National Herb Centre** ⊠ ♿
Banbury Road, Warmington, Nr Banbury, Oxfordshire OX17 1DF
Ⓣ (01295) 690999
Ⓕ (01295) 690034
Ⓦ www.herbcentre.co.uk
Contact: Plant Centre Staff
Opening Times: 0900-1730 Mon-Sat, 1030-1700 Sun.
Min Mail Order UK: Nmc
Credit Cards: All major credit/debit cards
Specialities: Herbs, culinary & medicinal. Extensive selection of rosemary, thyme & lavender, in particular.
Notes: Carriage charge of £9.00 up to 15kg, higher for heavier parcels. Next day delivery. UK mainland only. Signature required.
Map Ref: M, C2 **OS Grid Ref:** SP413471

MNrw **Norwell Nurseries** ⊠ ♠ ♿ ◆
Woodhouse Road, Norwell, Newark, Nottinghamshire NG23 6JX
Ⓣ (01636) 636337
Ⓔ wardha@aol.com
Ⓦ www.norwellnurseries.co.uk
Contact: Dr Andrew Ward
Opening Times: 1000-1700 Mon, Wed-Fri & Sun (Wed-Mon May & Jun). By appt. Aug & 20th Oct-1st Mar.
Min Mail Order UK: £15.00 + p&p
Min Mail Order EU: £40.00

KEY
⊠ Mail order to UK or EU ♠ Delivers to shows
✈ Exports beyond EU € Euro accepted
♿ Accessible by wheelchair ◆ See Display advertisement

Cat. Cost: 3 × 1st class or online.
Credit Cards: None
Specialities: A large collection of unusual & choice herbaceous perennials esp., hardy geraniums, *Geum*, pond & bog plants, cottage garden plants, *Hemerocallis*, grasses, hardy chrysanthemums & woodland plants. One acre garden open.
Notes: Also sells wholesale.
Map Ref: M, B3 **OS Grid Ref:** SK767616

MOld **Old Hall Nursery** ♿
Winkhill, Leek, Staffordshire ST13 7PN
Ⓣ (01538) 308257
Ⓜ 07866 175881
Ⓔ oldhallnursery@hotmail.co.uk
Contact: Sandra Henshall
Opening Times: 1000-1600, 7 days.
Cat. Cost: Not available.
Credit Cards: None
Specialities: Large selection of herbaceous, herbs & alpines. Also shrubs, climbers & fruit trees. All hardy.
Map Ref: M, B2 **OS Grid Ref:** SK051521

MOWG **The Old Walled Garden** ⊠ ♿
Honeybourne Road, Pebworth, Stratford-upon-Avon, Warwickshire CV37 8XP
Ⓣ (01789) 720788
Ⓕ (01789) 721162
Ⓔ Heather@oldwalledgarden.com
Ⓦ www.oldwalledgarden.com
Contact: Heather Godard-Key
Opening Times: 0900-1700 Mon-Sat, 1st Mar-31st Aug. 0900-1600 Mon-Fri, 1st Sep-28th Feb. 1030-1600 Sat & Sun, 2nd Apr-31st Jul. Closed last 2 weeks of Dec-1st week Jan, Easter Sun & Aug B/hol Mon.
Min Mail Order UK: Nmc
Min Mail Order EU: £30
Cat. Cost: 3 × 1st class.
Credit Cards: Switch, MasterCard, Visa, Maestro
Specialities: Many rare & unusual shrubs. Wide range of conservatory plants esp. Australian. *Callistemon* & *Hibiscus*.
Map Ref: M, C2 **OS Grid Ref:** SP133458

MPet **Peter Grayson (Sweet Pea Seedsman)** ⊠ €
34 Glenthorne Close, Brampton, Chesterfield, Derbyshire S40 3AR
Ⓣ (01246) 278503
Ⓕ (01246) 278503
Contact: Peter Grayson
Opening Times: Not open. Mail order only.
Min Mail Order UK: Nmc
Min Mail Order EU: Nmc
Cat. Cost: C5 sae, 1 × 2nd class.
Credit Cards: None
Specialities: *Lathyrus* species & cvs. Large collection of old-fashioned sweet peas & over 100 Spencer sweet peas incl. own cultivars and collection of old-fashioned cottage garden annuals & perennials.
Notes: Also sells wholesale. Mail order for seeds only.

MPhe **Phedar Nursery** ⊠ €
42 Bunkers Hill, Romiley, Stockport, Cheshire SK6 3DS
Ⓣ (0161) 430 3772
Ⓕ (0161) 430 3772
Ⓔ mclewin@phedar.com
Ⓦ www.phedar.com
Contact: Will McLewin
Opening Times: Frequent but irregular. Please phone to arrange appt.
Min Mail Order UK: Nmc
Min Mail Order EU: Nmc
Cat. Cost: 2 × A5 envelopes or address labels + 4 × 1st class.
Credit Cards: All major credit/debit cards
Specialities: *Helleborus*, *Paeonia*. Limited stock of some rare items.
Notes: Non-EU exports subject to destination & on an ad hoc basis only. Please contact nursery for details. Credit cards accepted for online orders only. Also sells wholesale.
Map Ref: M, A2 **OS Grid Ref:** SJ936897

MPie **Piecemeal Plants** ♿
Whatton House Gardens, Loughborough, Leicestershire LE12 5BG
Ⓜ 07950 757444
Ⓔ nursery@piecemealplants.co.uk
Ⓦ www.piecemealplants.co.uk
Contact: Mary Thomas
Opening Times: 1300-1700 4th Mar-16th Oct, most Fri & some Sun. For up to date details, please ring or see website. Also by arrangement.
Cat. Cost: Online only.
Credit Cards: None
Specialities: Interesting range of herbaceous perennials, some half-hardy or tender. Many in small quantities.
Notes: Nursery located at entrance to Whatton Gardens, off A6. Car parking in front of Whatton House at top of drive.
Map Ref: M, B3 **OS Grid Ref:** SK494242

MPkF **Packhorse Farm Nursery** ♿
Sandyford House, Lant Lane, Tansley, Matlock, Derbyshire DE4 5FW
Ⓣ (01629) 57206

Ⓜ 07974 095752
Ⓕ (01629) 57206
Contact: Hilton W Haynes
Opening Times: 1000-1700 Tues & Wed, 1st Mar-31st Oct. Any other time by appt. only.
Cat. Cost: 2 × 1st class for plant list.
Credit Cards: None
Specialities: *Acer*, rare stock is limited in supply. Other more unusual hardy shrubs, trees & conifers.
Map Ref: M, B2 **OS Grid Ref:** SK322617

MPnt PLANTAGOGO.COM ⊠ ♠ ♿
Jubilee Cottage Nursery, Snape Lane, Englesea Brook, Crewe, Cheshire CW2 5QN
Ⓣ (01270) 820335
Ⓜ 07713 518271
Ⓔ info@plantagogo.com
Ⓦ www.plantagogo.com
Contact: Vicky & Richard Fox
Opening Times: By appt. only. Also Open Days 15th & 16th Oct 2011 & 24th & 25th Mar 2012.
Min Mail Order UK: £7.95 single payment.
Min Mail Order EU: Price on application or see website.
Cat. Cost: 4 × 1st class.
Credit Cards: All major credit/debit cards
Specialities: *Heuchera*, *Heucherella*, *Tiarella*, also large selection of perennials. Nat. Collections of *Heuchera* & *Heucherella*. Nat. Collection of *Tiarella* applied for. Plants listed in ***RHS Plant Finder*** are available in good quantities. Others, not listed here, are available from our collections.
Notes: Also sells wholesale.
Map Ref: M, B1 **OS Grid Ref:** SJ750516

MRav RAVENSTHORPE NURSERY ⊠ ♿
6 East Haddon Road, Ravensthorpe, Northamptonshire NN6 8ES
Ⓣ (01604) 770548
Ⓕ (01604) 770548
Ⓔ ravensthorpenursery@hotmail.com
Contact: Jean & Richard Wiseman
Opening Times: 1000-1800 (or dusk if earlier) Tue-Sat. B/hol w/ends in May. Easter Mon.
Min Mail Order UK: Nmc
Min Mail Order EU: Nmc
Cat. Cost: None issued.
Credit Cards: Visa, MasterCard, Delta
Specialities: Over 3000 different trees, shrubs & perennials with many unusual varieties.
Notes: Search & delivery service for large orders, winter months only.
Map Ref: M, C3 **OS Grid Ref:** SP665699

MREP RARE AND EXOTIC PLANTS AT WOODSHOOT NURSERIES ⊠ ♿
King's Bromley, Burton-upon-Trent, Staffordshire DE13 7HN
Ⓣ (01543) 472233
Ⓜ 07802 737676
Ⓕ (01543) 472115
Ⓔ sales@rareandexoticplants.com
Ⓦ www.rareandexoticplants.com
Contact: Richard Flint
Opening Times: 0900-1700, 7 days.
Min Mail Order UK: £20.00 + p&p
Cat. Cost: 1 × 1st class.
Credit Cards: All major credit/debit cards
Specialities: *Acacia*, *Agave*, *Arbutus*, *Bamboo*, *Citrus*, *Cordyline*, *Dicksonia*, *Pittosporum*, palms, olives, *Yucca*, topiary & specimens.
Notes: Also sells wholesale.
Map Ref: M, B2 **OS Grid Ref:** SK127164

MSCN STONYFORD COTTAGE NURSERY ⊠ ♿
Stonyford Lane, Cuddington, Northwich, Cheshire CW8 2TF
Ⓣ (01606) 888970 or 888128 (answerphone)
Ⓜ 07714 205177
Ⓔ stonyfordcottage@yahoo.co.uk
Ⓦ www.stonyfordcottagenursery.co.uk
Contact: Andrew Overland
Opening Times: 1000-1700 Tue-Sun & B/hol Mons 1st Feb-31st Oct.
Min Mail Order UK: Nmc
Min Mail Order EU: Nmc
Cat. Cost: Not available this year.
Credit Cards: All major credit/debit cards
Specialities: Wide range of herbaceous perennials, *Iris*, hardy *Geranium*, moisture-loving & bog plants. *Sempervivum*, *Paeonia*, Candelabra *Primula*.
Notes: Also sells wholesale.
Map Ref: M, A1 **OS Grid Ref:** SJ580710

MSKA SWEET KNOWLE AQUATICS ⊠ ♿
Wimpstone-Ilmington Road, Stratford-upon-Avon, Warwickshire CV37 8NR
Ⓣ (01789) 450036
Ⓕ (01789) 450036
Ⓔ sweetknowleaquatics@hotmail.com
Ⓦ www.sweetknowleaquatics.co.uk
Contact: Zoe Harding
Opening Times: 0930-1700 Sun-Fri, closed Sat. Open B/hols.
Min Mail Order UK: Nmc
Min Mail Order EU: Nmc

KEY
⊠ Mail order to UK or EU ♠ Delivers to shows
✈ Exports beyond EU € Euro accepted
♿ Accessible by wheelchair ◆ See Display advertisement

M

Cat. Cost: By email only.
Credit Cards: All major credit/debit cards
Specialities: Aquatics. Hardy & tropical water lilies, marginals & oxygenators. 2-acre display garden open to the public (no charge).
Map Ref: M, C2 **OS Grid Ref:** SP207480

MSnd **Sound Garden Rhododendrons** ⊠ ⌂
(Office) 7 Lumber Lane, Burtonwood, Warrington, Cheshire WA5 4AS
Ⓣ (01925) 229100
Ⓜ 07931 340836
Ⓔ tim@sound-garden-design.com
Ⓦ www.sound-garden-designs.co.uk
Contact: Tim Atkinson
Opening Times: By appt. only.
Min Mail Order UK: £50.00
Min Mail Order EU: £100.00
Cat. Cost: 2 × 1st class.
Credit Cards: None
Specialities: Species *Rhododendron* & hardy hybrids. Species *Sorbus.*
Notes: Nursery at Middledale Farm, Dale Road, Marple, Cheshire SK6 6NL.
Map Ref: N, B1 **OS Grid Ref:** SJ948901

MSpe **SpecialPerennials.com** ⊠ ⌂
Yew Tree House, Hall Lane, Hankelow, Crewe, Cheshire CW3 0JB
Ⓣ (01270) 811443
Ⓜ 07716 990695
Ⓔ plants@specialperennials.com
Ⓦ www.specialperennials.com
Contact: Janet & Martin Blow
Opening Times: Nursery only open when garden open for NGS & Nat. Collection of *Helenium* Open Days, 20th/21st Aug 2011.
Min Mail Order UK: Nmc
Cat. Cost: 2 × 1st class or online.
Credit Cards: Paypal
Specialities: Herbaceous perennials. Nat. Collection of *Helenium* cvs (100+ varieties for sale). Nat. Collection of *Centaurea* applied for (50+ varieties). Also *Geum*, border *Phlox*, *Hemerocallis*, *Monada* & *Persciaria.* Some plants, esp. *Hemerocallis*, available in small quantities only.
Notes: All plants grown in garden nursery. Garden open for NGS. Talks given. Group visits to garden & nursery welcomed. Special study events. See website or send sae for details.
Map Ref: M, B1 **OS Grid Ref:** SJ699452

MSSP **S & S Perennials** ⊠
24 Main Street, Normanton Le Heath, Leicestershire LE67 2TB
Ⓣ (01530) 262250
Contact: Shirley Pierce
Opening Times: Afternoons only, otherwise please phone.
Min Mail Order UK: Nmc
Cat. Cost: 2 × 1st class.
Credit Cards: None
Specialities: *Erythronium*, *Fritillaria*, dwarf *Narcissus* & *Anemone.* Stock available in small quantities only.
Map Ref: M, B1

MSwo **Swallows Nursery** ⊠ ♿
Mixbury, Brackley, Northamptonshire NN13 5RR
Ⓣ (01280) 847721
Ⓕ (01280) 848611
Ⓔ enq@swallowsnursery.co.uk
Ⓦ www.swallowsnursery.co.uk
Contact: Chris Swallow
Opening Times: 0900-1300 & 1400-1700 (earlier in winter) Mon-Fri, 0900-1300 Sat.
Min Mail Order UK: £15.00
Cat. Cost: 3 × 1st class (plus phone number).
Credit Cards: All major credit/debit cards
Specialities: Growing a wide range, particularly shrubs, climbers, trees & roses.
Notes: Trees not for mail order unless part of larger order. Nursery transport used where possible, esp. for trees. Also sells wholesale.
Map Ref: M, C3 **OS Grid Ref:** SP607336

MTis **Tissington Nursery** ⊠ ⌂ ♿
The Old Kitchen Gardens, Tissington, Ashbourne, Derbyshire DE6 1RA
Ⓣ (01335) 390650
Ⓜ 07929 720284
Ⓔ info@tissington-nursery.co.uk
Ⓦ www.tissington-nursery.co.uk
Contact: Mairi Longdon
Opening Times: 1000-1700 daily, 3rd Mar-end Oct.
Min Mail Order UK: Nmc
Cat. Cost: 4 × 1st class.
Credit Cards: All major credit/debit cards
Specialities: Choice & unusual perennials esp. *Achillea*, *Geranium*, *Geum*, *Helenium*, *Heuchera*, *Penstemon*, *Sempervivum* & grasses.
Map Ref: M, B1 **OS Grid Ref:** SK176521

MTPN **Smart Plants** ⊠ ⌂
Sandy Hill Lane, Off Overstone Road, Moulton, Northampton NN3 7JB
Ⓣ (01604) 454106
Ⓜ 07519 339508
Ⓔ smartplants@hotmail.co.uk
Contact: Stuart Smart
Opening Times: 1000-1500 Thu & Fri, 1000-1700 Sat. Other times by appt.

Min Mail Order UK: Nmc
Cat. Cost: 3 × 1st class.
Credit Cards: None
Specialities: Wide range of herbaceous, alpines, shrubs, grasses, hardy *Geranium*. Some plants available in small quantities only.
Notes: Limited wheelchair access.

MWat WATERPERRY GARDENS LTD ⊠ ♿
Waterperry, Nr Wheatley, Oxfordshire OX33 1JZ
Ⓣ (01844) 339226/254
Ⓕ (01844) 339883
Ⓔ management@waterperrygardens.co.uk
Ⓦ www.waterperrygardens.co.uk
Contact: Mr R Jacobs
Opening Times: 1000-1730 summer. 1000-1700 winter.
Min Mail Order UK: £30.00
Cat. Cost: Online only.
Credit Cards: All major credit/debit cards
Specialities: General, large range of herbaceous esp. *Aster*, also Nat. Collection of *Saxifraga* (subsect. *Kabschia* & *Engleria*).
Map Ref: M, D3 **OS Grid Ref:** SP630064

MWhi WHITEHILL FARM NURSERY ⊠ € ♿
Whitehill Farm, Burford, Oxfordshire OX18 4DT
Ⓣ (01993) 823218
Ⓕ (01993) 822894
Ⓔ a.youngson@virgin.net
Ⓦ www.whitehillfarmnursery.co.uk
Contact: P J M Youngson
Opening Times: 0900-1800 (or dusk if earlier) 7 days, Feb-Nov.
Min Mail Order UK: £15 + p&p
Min Mail Order EU: £25 + p&p
Cat. Cost: 4 × 1st class.
Credit Cards: All major credit/debit cards
Specialities: Grasses & bamboos, less common shrubs & perennials. Some available in small quantities only.
Notes: £1.00 of catalogue cost refunded on 1st order.
Map Ref: M, D2 **OS Grid Ref:** SP268113

MWht WHITELEA NURSERY ⊠ ♿
Whitelea Lane, Tansley, Matlock, Derbyshire DE4 5FL
Ⓣ (01629) 55010
Ⓔ sales@uk-bamboos.co.uk
Ⓦ www.uk-bamboos.co.uk
Contact: David Wilson
Opening Times: By appt.
Min Mail Order UK: Nmc
Cat. Cost: Online only. Price list available 2 × 1st class.
Credit Cards: None
Specialities: Bamboos. Substantial quantities of 45 cvs & species of bamboo, remainder stocked in small numbers only. Ltd stocks of grasses, trees & shrubs.
Notes: Also sells wholesale. Mail order limited by carrier restrictions, please contact nursery or see website for details.
Map Ref: M, B1 **OS Grid Ref:** SK325603

MWts WATERSIDE NURSERY ⊠ ⌂
Sharnford, Leicestershire, LE10 3QD
Ⓣ (01455) 273730
Ⓜ 07931 557082
Ⓔ watersidenursery@yahoo.co.uk
Ⓦ www.watersidenursery.co.uk
Contact: Linda Smith
Opening Times: By appt. only.
Min Mail Order UK: Nmc
Cat. Cost: Online only.
Credit Cards: All major credit/debit cards
Specialities: Aquatics, marginal pond plants, miniature water lilies, waterlilies, bog garden plants & moisture-loving plants.

NORTHERN

NAbi ABI AND TOM'S GARDEN PLANTS ♿
Halecat Nurseries, Witherslack, Grange Over Sands, Cumbria LA11 6RT
Ⓣ (01539) 552946
Ⓜ 07904 522665
Ⓔ info@halecatplants.co.uk
Ⓦ www.halecatplants.co.uk
Contact: Tom & Abi Attwood
Opening Times: 0900-1700 Mon-Sat, 1000-1600 Sun.
Cat. Cost: Online only.
Credit Cards: All major credit/debit cards
Specialities: Hardy herbaceous perennials.
Map Ref: N, C1 **OS Grid Ref:** SD433838

NBid BIDE-A-WEE COTTAGE GARDENS ⊠ ♿
Stanton, Netherwitton, Morpeth, Northumberland NE65 8PR
Ⓣ (01670) 772238
Ⓕ (01670) 772238
Ⓔ info@bideawee.co.uk
Ⓦ www.bideawee.co.uk
Contact: Mark Robson
Opening Times: 1330-1700 Sat & Wed, 23rd Apr-31st Aug 2011. Group visits at other times, except Sun.

KEY
⊠ Mail order to UK or EU ⌂ Delivers to shows
✈ Exports beyond EU € Euro accepted
♿ Accessible by wheelchair ◆ See Display advertisement

N

Min Mail Order UK: £20.00
Cat. Cost: Online only.
Credit Cards: All major credit/debit cards
Specialities: Unusual herbaceous perennials, *Agapanthus*, *Primula*, ferns, grasses. Nat. Collection of *Centaurea*.
Map Ref: N, B2 **OS Grid Ref:** NZ132900

NBir **Birkheads Secret Gardens & Nursery** ♿
Nr Hedley Hall Woods, Sunniside, Gateshead, Tyne & Wear NE16 5EL
Ⓣ (01207) 232262
Ⓜ 07778 447920
Ⓕ (01207) 232262
Ⓔ birkheadsnursery@googlemail.com
Ⓦ www.birkheadssecretgardens.co.uk
Contact: Mrs Christine Liddle
Opening Times: 1000-1700 Wed-Sun (closed Mon & Tues) Mar-Oct. Open B/hol Mons. Coach groups by appt.
Cat. Cost: None issued.
Credit Cards: All major credit/debit cards
Specialities: Hardy herbaceous perennials, grasses, bulbs & herbs. *Allium*, *Digitalis*, *Euphorbia*, *Galanthus* & *Geranium*. Max. 30 of any plant propagated each year.
Map Ref: N, B2 **OS Grid Ref:** NZ220569

NBre **Breezy Knees Nurseries** ♿
Common Lane, Warthill, York YO19 5XS
Ⓣ (01904) 488800
Ⓦ www.breezyknees.co.uk
Contact: Any member of staff
Opening Times: 1000-1700 7 days (open 1100 Sun), 1st Apr-30th Sep.
Credit Cards: All major credit/debit cards
Specialities: Very wide range of perennials. All can be viewed in 14-acre gardens (open 22nd May-30th Sep).
Map Ref: N, C3 **OS Grid Ref:** SE675565

NBro **Brownthwaite Hardy Plants** ⊠ ⌂ ♿
Fell Yeat, Casterton, Kirkby Lonsdale, Lancashire LA6 2JW
Ⓣ (01524) 271340 (after 1800 hours).
Ⓦ www.hardyplantsofcumbria.co.uk
Contact: Chris Benson
Opening Times: 1000-1700, 1st Apr-30th Sep.
Min Mail Order UK: Nmc
Cat. Cost: 3 × 1st class for *Hydrangea* catalogue. Sae for auricula list.
Credit Cards: None
Specialities: Herbaceous perennials incl. *Geranium*, *Hosta*, also *Tiarella*, *Heucherella* & *Primula auricula*. Mail order for *Hydrangea*. Nat. Collection of *Ligularia*.
Notes: Follow brown signs from A65 between Kirkby Lonsdale & Cowan Bridge.
Map Ref: N, C1 **OS Grid Ref:** SD632794

NCGa **Caths Garden Plants** ⊠ ⌂ ♿ ◆
The Walled Garden, Heaves Hotel, Heaves, Levens, Cumbria LA8 8EF
Ⓣ (01539) 561126
Ⓕ (01539) 561126
Ⓔ cath@cathsgardenplants.co.uk
Ⓦ www.cathsgardenplants.co.uk
Contact: Bob Sanderson
Opening Times: 1030-1700 7 days, Mar-Oct. 1030-1600 Mon-Fri, Nov-Feb. Closed Xmas & New Year weeks.
Min Mail Order UK: £15.00 + p&p
Min Mail Order EU: £25.00
Cat. Cost: Online only.
Credit Cards: All major credit/debit cards
Specialities: Wide variety of perennials, incl. uncommon varieties & selections of grasses, ferns, shrubs & climbing plants.
Notes: On A590 follow signs for Heaves (not in Levens village).
Map Ref: N, C1 **OS Grid Ref:** SD497867

NChi **Chipchase Castle Nursery** ⊠ ⌂ ♿
Chipchase Castle, Wark, Hexham, Northumberland NE48 3NT
Ⓣ (01434) 230083
Ⓜ 07881 630398
Ⓔ info@chipchaseplants.co.uk
Ⓦ www.chipchaseplants.co.uk
Contact: Joyce Hunt & Alison Jones
Opening Times: 1000-1700 Thu-Sun & B/hol Mons Easter (or 1st Apr)-end Aug.
Min Mail Order UK: Nmc
Min Mail Order EU: Nmc
Cat. Cost: A5 sae for list.
Credit Cards: All major credit/debit cards
Specialities: Unusual herbaceous esp. *Eryngium*, *Geum*, *Geranium*, & *Penstemon*. Some plants only available in small quantities.
Notes: Suitable for accompanied wheelchair users.
Map Ref: N, B2 **OS Grid Ref:** NY880758

NChl **Chiltern Seeds** ⊠ ✈ €
Bortree Stile, Ulverston, Cumbria LA12 7PB
Ⓣ (01229) 581137 (24 hrs)
Ⓕ (01229) 584549
Ⓔ info@chilternseeds.co.uk
Ⓦ www.chilternseeds.co.uk
Opening Times: Mail order only. Normal office hours, Mon-Fri.
Min Mail Order UK: Nmc
Min Mail Order EU: Nmc
Cat. Cost: 3 × 2nd class.

Credit Cards: All major credit/debit cards
Specialities: Over 4,500 items of all kinds – wild flowers, trees, shrubs, cacti, annuals, houseplants, vegetables & herbs.

NChu **CHURCHTOWN CARNIVORES** ⊠ ⌂ € ♿
8 Sandheys Drive, Churchtown, Southport, Merseyside PR9 9PQ
Ⓣ (01704) 228175
Ⓜ 07928 567431
Ⓔ churchtowncarnivores@yahoo.co.uk
Ⓦ www.churchtowncarnivores.co.uk
Contact: Alan Leyland
Opening Times: By appt. only.
Min Mail Order UK: £10.00
Min Mail Order EU: £10.00
Cat. Cost: Online only.
Credit Cards: None
Specialities: Carnivorous plants. *Sarracenia, Dionaea muscipula* & forms, *Darlingtonia, Drosera.*
Map Ref: N, D1 **OS Grid Ref:** SD355183

NCot **COTTAGE GARDEN PLANTS** ⊠ ⌂ €
1 Sycamore Close, Whitehaven, Cumbria CA28 6LE
Ⓣ (01946) 695831
Ⓔ expressplants@aol.com
Ⓦ www.cottagegardenplants.com
Contact: Mrs J Purkiss
Opening Times: Open by appt. only for collecting orders & viewing garden. Consult local press & radio for charity openings.
Min Mail Order UK: Nmc
Min Mail Order EU: Nmc
Cat. Cost: 4 × 1st class sae.
Credit Cards: Paypal
Specialities: Hardy perennials incl. *Crocosmia, Galanthus, Geranium, Primula, Schizostylis* & bog plants. Small quantities only. Nat. Collection of *Geranium phaeum* Group. Viewing by appt. & on specified Open Days (check local press & radio).
Map Ref: N, C1

NCro **CROSTON CACTUS** ⊠ € ♿
43 Southport Road, Eccleston, Chorley, Lancashire PR7 6ET
Ⓣ (01257) 452555
Ⓕ (01257) 452555
Ⓔ sales@croston-cactus.co.uk
Ⓦ www.croston-cactus.co.uk
Contact: John Henshaw
Opening Times: 0930-1700 by appt. only.
Min Mail Order UK: £5.00 + p&p
Min Mail Order EU: £10.00 + p&p
Cat. Cost: 2 × 1st class or 2 × IRCs.
Credit Cards: All major credit/debit cards
Specialities: Mexican cacti, *Echeveria* hybrids & some bromeliads & *Tillandsia*. Some items held in small quantities only. See catalogue.
Notes: Credit card payment accepted for online orders only.
Map Ref: N, D1 **OS Grid Ref:** SD522186

NDav **DAVE PARKINSON PLANTS** ⊠ ⌂
4 West Bank, Carlton, Goole, East Yorkshire DN14 9PZ
Ⓣ (01405) 860693
Ⓜ 07773 564945
Ⓕ (01405) 860693
Ⓦ www.daveparkinsonplants.co.uk
Contact: Mary Parkinson
Opening Times: Not open. Mail order only.
Min Mail Order UK: £12 + p&p
Credit Cards: None
Specialities: Hardy orchids. Terrestrial South African *Disa* orchids, species & hybrids.

NDov **DOVE COTTAGE NURSERY & GARDEN** ⊠ ♿
Shibden Hall Road, Halifax, West Yorkshire HX3 9XA
Ⓣ (01422) 203553
Ⓔ info@dovecottagenursery.co.uk
Ⓦ www.dovecottagenursery.co.uk
Contact: Stephen & Kim Rogers
Opening Times: 1000-1700 Wed-Sat, 1100-1600 Sun & B/hols Mar-Dec, or by appt. at other times.
Min Mail Order UK: £20.00
Cat. Cost: 6 × 2nd class.
Credit Cards: All major credit/debit cards
Specialities: Herbaceous perennials & selected grasses, many displayed in adjoining naturalistic garden.
Map Ref: N, D2 **OS Grid Ref:** SE115256

NDro **DROINTON NURSERIES** ⊠ ✈ ⌂
Plaster Pitts, Norton Conyers, Ripon, North Yorkshire HG4 5EF
Ⓣ (01765) 641849
Ⓜ 07909 971529
Ⓕ (01765) 640888
Ⓔ info@auricula-plants.co.uk
Ⓦ www.auricula-plants.co.uk
Contact: Robin & Annabel Graham
Opening Times: Open days in spring, otherwise by appt. only.
Min Mail Order UK: Nmc
Min Mail Order EU: Nmc

KEY
⊠ Mail order to UK or EU ⌂ Delivers to shows
✈ Exports beyond EU € Euro accepted
♿ Accessible by wheelchair ◆ See Display advertisement

N

Cat. Cost: 4 × 1st class.
Credit Cards: All major credit/debit cards
Specialities: *Primula auricula*. More than 800 cvs of show, alpine, double & border auriculas. Ltd stocks of any one cultivar. Nat. Collection of *Primula auricula* (borders).
Map Ref: N, C2 **OS Grid Ref:** SE315753

NEgg **EGGLESTON HALL GARDENS** € ♿
Eggleston, Barnard Castle, Co. Durham
DL12 0AG
Ⓣ (01833) 650230
Ⓕ (01833) 650971
Ⓔ mbhock@btinternet.com
Contact: Malcolm Hockham
Opening Times: 1000-1700 7 days. Closed 24th Dec to 6th Jan each year.
Cat. Cost: Online only.
Credit Cards: All major credit/debit cards
Notes: Collection from nursery only.

N

NEqu **EQUATORIAL PLANT CO.** ✉ ✈ ⌂ €
7 Gray Lane, Barnard Castle, Co. Durham
DL12 8PD
Ⓣ (01833) 690519
Ⓕ (01833) 690519
Ⓔ equatorialplants@teesdaleonline.co.uk
Ⓦ www.equatorialplants.com
Contact: Dr Richard Warren
Opening Times: Mail order only. Open by appt. only.
Min Mail Order UK: Nmc
Min Mail Order EU: Nmc
Cat. Cost: Free.
Credit Cards: Visa, Access, Paypal
Specialities: Laboratory-raised orchids only.
Notes: Also sells wholesale.

NFir **FIR TREES PELARGONIUM NURSERY** ✉ ⌂ ♿
Stokesley, Middlesbrough, Cleveland
TS9 5LD
Ⓣ (01642) 713066
Ⓕ (01642) 713066
Ⓔ mark@firtreespelargoniums.co.uk
Ⓦ www.firtreespelargoniums.co.uk
Contact: Helen Bainbridge
Opening Times: 1000-1600 7 days 1st Apr-31st Aug, 1000-1600 Mon-Fri 1st Sep-31st Mar.
Min Mail Order UK: £4.00 + p&p
Cat. Cost: 4 × 1st class or £1.00 coin.
Credit Cards: All major credit/debit cards
Specialities: All types of *Pelargonium* – fancy leaf, regal, decorative regal, oriental regal, angel, miniature, zonal, ivy leaf, stellar, scented, dwarf, unique, golden stellar & species. Also dieramas.
Map Ref: N, C2

NGBl **GARDEN BLOOMS** ✉ ⌂ ♿
Fieldgate, Mill Field Road,
Fishlake, Doncaster, Yorkshire
DN7 5GH
Ⓣ 0845 5440964
Ⓔ info@gardenblooms.co.uk
Ⓦ www.gardenblooms.co.uk
Contact: Liz Webster
Opening Times: Thu-Sun, Mar-Sep. Please check website for exact dates.
Min Mail Order UK: Nmc
Cat. Cost: A5 sae or online.
Credit Cards: None
Specialities: Hardy & tender perennials & ornamental grasses. Available in small quantities only.
Notes: Credit cards accepted online only.
Map Ref: N, D2 **OS Grid Ref:** SE659148

NGBo **GARDENERS BOUTIQUE (FORMERLY PLANTS OF SPECIAL INTEREST)** ✉ ♿
4 High Street, Braithwell,
Nr Rotherham, South Yorkshire
S66 7AL
Ⓣ (01709) 790642
Ⓕ (01709) 790342
Ⓔ info@gardenersboutique.co.uk
Ⓦ www.gardenersboutique.co.uk
Contact: Leisha Dunstan
Opening Times: 1000-1700 Tue-Sun, Jan-Dec. Closed Mons.
Min Mail Order UK: Nmc
Cat. Cost: None issued.
Credit Cards: Switch, Visa, MasterCard, Maestro
Specialities: Wide range of herbaceous perennials, trees & shrubs.
Notes: Gift shop. Restaurant on site. RHS garden design Gold Medal.
Map Ref: N, D2

NGdn **GARDEN HOUSE NURSERY** ♿
The Square, Dalston,
Carlisle, Cumbria
CA5 7LL
Ⓣ (01228) 710297
Ⓜ 07595 219082
Ⓔ stephickso@hotmail.co.uk
Ⓦ www.gardenhousenursery.co.uk
Contact: Stephen Hickson
Opening Times: 0900-1700 7 days Mar-Oct.
Cat. Cost: Plant list online only.
Credit Cards: None
Specialities: *Geranium*, *Hosta*, *Hemerocallis*, *Iris*, grasses & bamboos.
Notes: Also sells wholesale.
Map Ref: N, B1 **OS Grid Ref:** NY369503

NHal **Halls of Heddon** ⊠ ✈
West Heddon Nurseries, Heddon-on-the-Wall, Northumberland NE15 0JS
Ⓣ (01661) 852445
Ⓕ (01661) 852398
Ⓔ enquiry@hallsofheddon.co.uk
Ⓦ www.hallsofheddon.co.uk
Contact: David Hall
Opening Times: 0900-1700 Mon-Sat 1000-1700 Sun.
Min Mail Order UK: £10.00
Min Mail Order EU: £25.00
Cat. Cost: 3 × 2nd class.
Credit Cards: MasterCard, Visa, Switch, Delta
Specialities: *Chrysanthemum* & *Dahlia*.
Notes: Also sells wholesale.
Map Ref: N, B2 **OS Grid Ref:** NZ122679

NHar **Hartside Nursery Garden** ⊠ ⌂
Nr Alston, Cumbria CA9 3BL
Ⓣ (01434) 381372
Ⓕ (01434) 381372
Ⓔ enquiries@plantswithaltitude.co.uk
Ⓦ www.plantswithaltitude.co.uk
Contact: S L & N Huntley
Opening Times: 1130-1630 Mon-Fri, 1230-1600 Sat, Sun & B/hols, mid Mar-31st Oct. All other times & winter by appt. Times may vary during show season, so please phone before travelling.
Min Mail Order UK: Nmc
Min Mail Order EU: £50.00 + p&p
Cat. Cost: 4 × 1st class or 3 × IRC
Credit Cards: All major credit/debit cards
Specialities: Alpines grown at altitude of 1100 feet in Pennines. *Primula*, ferns, *Gentian* & *Meconopsis*.
Map Ref: N, B1 **OS Grid Ref:** NY708447

NHaw **The Hawthornes Nursery** ⊠ ♿
Marsh Road, Hesketh Bank, Nr Preston, Lancashire PR4 6XT
Ⓣ (01772) 812379
Ⓔ richardhaw@talktalk.net
Ⓦ www.hawthornes-nursery.co.uk
Contact: Irene & Richard Hodson
Opening Times: 0900-1800 7 days 1st Mar-30th Jun, Thu-Sun July-Oct. Gardens open for NGS.
Min Mail Order UK: £10.00
Min Mail Order EU: Nmc
Cat. Cost: None issued.
Credit Cards: None
Specialities: *Clematis*, honeysuckle, choice selection of shrub & climbing roses, extensive range of perennials, mostly on display in the garden. Nat. Collection of *Clematis viticella*.

NHer **Herterton House Garden Nursery**
Hartington, Cambo, Morpeth, Northumberland NE61 4BN
Ⓣ (01670) 774278
Contact: Mrs M Lawley & Mr Frank Lawley
Opening Times: 1330-1730 Mon, Wed, Fri-Sun 1st Apr-end Sep. (Earlier or later in the year weather permitting.)
Cat. Cost: None issued.
Credit Cards: None
Specialities: Country garden flowers.
Map Ref: N, B2 **OS Grid Ref:** NZ022880

NHim **The Himalayan Garden Co.** ⊠ ⌂ €
The Hutts, Grewelthorpe, Ripon, Yorkshire HG4 3DA
Ⓣ (01765) 658009
Ⓕ (01765) 658912
Ⓔ info@himalayangarden.com
Ⓦ www.himalayangarden.com
Contact: Peter Roberts
Opening Times: 1000-1600, Tues-Sun & B/hol Mon, mid Apr-mid Jun. During the rest of the year by appt. only.
Min Mail Order UK: £10.00 to £15.00
Cat. Cost: Free.
Credit Cards: All major credit/debit cards
Specialities: Rare and unusual species & hybrid rhododendrons, azaleas, magnolias & *Cornus*, as well as other Himalayan plants.
Notes: Very limited wheelchair access. Also sells wholesale.
Map Ref: N, C2 **OS Grid Ref:** SE218769

NHol **Holden Clough Nursery Ltd** ⊠ ✈ ⌂ ♿
Holden, Bolton-by-Bowland, Clitheroe, Lancashire BB7 4PF
Ⓣ (01200) 447615
Ⓔ info@holdencloughnursery.co.uk
Ⓦ www.holdencloughnursery.co.uk
Contact: John Foley
Opening Times: 0900-1630 Mon-Fri Mar-Oct & B/hol Mons, 0900-1630 Sat all year. Nov-Feb by appt. only.
Min Mail Order UK: Nmc
Min Mail Order EU: Nmc
Cat. Cost: Free.
Credit Cards: All major credit/debit cards
Specialities: Large general list incl. perennials, esp. *Crocosmia*, *Astilbe* & *Hosta*, shrubs, dwarf conifers, alpines, heathers, grasses & ferns.

KEY
⊠ Mail order to UK or EU ⌂ Delivers to shows
✈ Exports beyond EU € Euro accepted
♿ Accessible by wheelchair ◆ See Display advertisement

N

Notes: Seasonal mail order on some items. Also sells wholesale on some items.
Map Ref: N, C2 **OS Grid Ref:** SD773496

NHoy **Hoyland Plant Centre** ⊠ ☒ ♠ € ♿
54 Greenside Lane, Hoyland, Barnsley, Yorkshire S74 9PZ
Ⓣ (01226) 744466
Ⓜ 07717 182169
Ⓕ (01226) 744466
Ⓔ stevenhickman@btconnect.com
Ⓦ www.somethingforthegarden.co.uk
Contact: Steven Hickman
Opening Times: All year round by appt. only.
Min Mail Order UK: Nmc
Min Mail Order EU: Nmc
Cat. Cost: 4 × 1st class.
Credit Cards: All major credit/debit cards
Specialities: *Agapanthus* (400+ cvs) & *Tulbaghia* (80+ cvs). Some available in small quantities only. Nat. Collections of *Agapanthus* & *Tulbaghia*.
Notes: Also sells wholesale. Daily practical workshops available, ring for details.
Map Ref: N, D2 **OS Grid Ref:** SE372010

NHpl **Harperley Hall Farm Nurseries** ⊠ ♠ €
Harperley, Stanley, Co. Durham DH9 9UB
Ⓣ (01207) 233318
Ⓜ 07944 644126
Ⓔ enquiries@harperleyhallfarmnurseries.co.uk
Ⓦ www.harperleyhallfarmnurseries.co.uk
Contact: Gary McDermott
Opening Times: Nursery is only open on set days as advertised on website.
Min Mail Order UK: Nmc
Min Mail Order EU: Nmc
Cat. Cost: Free.
Credit Cards: All major credit/debit cards
Specialities: Alpine rock garden plants.
Notes: Also sells wholesale.

NLan **Landlife Wildflowers Ltd** ⊠ ♿
National Wildflower Centre, Court Hey Park, Liverpool L16 3NA
Ⓣ (0151) 737 1819
Ⓕ (0151) 737 1820
Ⓔ gill@landlife.org.uk
Ⓦ www.wildflower.org.uk
Contact: Gillian Watson
Opening Times: 1000-1700, 7 days, 1st Mar-31st Aug.
Min Mail Order UK: £30.00 plants, no min. for seeds.
Cat. Cost: Free.
Credit Cards: Visa, Delta, Access, Switch, Solo
Specialities: Wild herbaceous plants & seeds.
Notes: Cafe & shop. Visitor centre, admission charge. Also sells wholesale.
Map Ref: N, D1

NLAp **Laneside Hardy Orchid Nursery** ⊠ ♠ € ♿
74 Croston Road, Garstang, Preston, Lancashire PR3 1HR
Ⓣ (01995) 605537
Ⓜ 07946 659661
Ⓔ jcrhutch@aol.com
Ⓦ www.lanesidehardyorchids.com
Contact: Jeff Hutchings
Opening Times: By telephone appt. only. Details of Open Days on website.
Min Mail Order UK: £35.00
Min Mail Order EU: £50.00
Cat. Cost: Sae or lists updated every month online.
Credit Cards: All major credit/debit cards
Specialities: 100+ species of hardy terrestrial orchids plus composts & cultivation notes. Species suitable for garden, cold or frost-free greenhouse.
Notes: Mail order for orchids during appropriate dormancy period as plants only sent bare-rooted. Also hardy orchid composts & pumice from the nursery or from Shows if ordered. See website for shows & talks.
Map Ref: N, D1

NLar **Larch Cottage Nurseries** ⊠ € ♿ ◆
Melkinthorpe, Penrith, Cumbria CA10 2DR
Ⓣ (01931) 712404
Ⓕ (01931) 712727
Ⓔ plants@larchcottage.co.uk
Ⓦ www.larchcottage.co.uk
Contact: Peter Stott & Joanne McCullock
Opening Times: Daily from 1000-1730 (or dusk in winter), all year round.
Min Mail Order UK: Nmc
Min Mail Order EU: Nmc
Cat. Cost: £7.00
Credit Cards: All major credit/debit cards
Specialities: Comprehensive plant collection in unique garden setting. Rare & unusual plants; particularly shrubs, trees, perennials, dwarf conifers & Japanese maples. *Acer*, *Hamamelis*, *Magnolia* & *Cornus kousa* cvs. Old-fashioned roses, bamboo & alpines.
Notes: Terraced restaurant & art gallery.
Map Ref: N, C1 **OS Grid Ref:** NY315602

NLBP **L.B. Plants** ⊠ ♠ ♿
Whitworth Hall Country Park, Spennymoor, Co. Durham DH16 7QX
Ⓜ 079321 59204 or 077478 95096
Ⓔ enquiries@lbplants.co.uk
Ⓦ www.lbplants.co.uk

N

Contact: Howard Leslie & Sharon Bartle
Opening Times: 1000-1800 (or sunset in winter), 7 days.
Min Mail Order UK: Nmc
Cat. Cost: 3 × 1st class.
Credit Cards: None
Specialities: Hardy herbaceous & shrubby perennials, incl. lesser known and harder to find plants.
Notes: Also sells wholesale.
Map Ref: N, B2

NMen **Mendle Nursery** ⊠ ♠ ♿
Holme, Scunthorpe, North Lincolnshire DN16 3RF
Ⓣ (01724) 850864
Ⓔ annearnshaw@lineone.net
Ⓦ www.mendlenursery.com
Contact: Mrs A Earnshaw
Opening Times: 1000-1600 Tue-Sun.
Min Mail Order UK: Nmc
Min Mail Order EU: Nmc
Cat. Cost: 3 × 1st class.
Credit Cards: All major credit/debit cards
Specialities: Many unusual alpines esp. *Saxifraga* & *Sempervivum*.
Map Ref: N, D3 **OS Grid Ref:** SE925070

NMil **Millthorpe Nursery**
(Office) 74 Meadowhead, Sheffield, Yorkshire S8 7UE
Ⓣ 0114 258 4007
Ⓜ 07899 963939
Ⓔ mail@dawson18.plus.com
Ⓦ www.millthorpenursery.co.uk
Contact: John & Anne Dawson
Opening Times: 0900-1630 Tue-Sat, 1000-1630 Sun. Closed Mon, except B/hols. Open by appt. only in Jan & Feb.
Credit Cards: None
Specialities: Good range of shrubs, herbaceous, ferns, grasses & edibles.
Notes: Nursery at Millthorpe Lane, Millthorpe, near Holmesfield, Derbyshire S18 7SA.
Map Ref: N, D2 **OS Grid Ref:** SK321767

NMin **Miniature Bulbs & Wildflower Bulbs** ⊠ ♠ €
The Warren Estate, 9 Greengate Drive, Knaresborough, North Yorkshire HG5 9EN
Ⓣ (01423) 542819
Ⓕ (01423) 542819
Ⓦ www.miniaturebulbs.co.uk
Contact: Ivor Fox
Opening Times: Not open. Mail order only.
Min Mail Order UK: £10.00
Min Mail Order EU: £15.00
Cat. Cost: 1 × 1st class.
Credit Cards: All major credit/debit cards
Specialities: Rare & unusual miniature & wildflower bulbs, incl. *Narcissus*, *Tulipa*, *Iris*, *Crocus*, *Fritillaria* & others. Spring bulb list sent out in April. Some stock in small quantities.

NMir **Mires Beck Nursery** ⊠ ♿
Low Mill Lane, North Cave, Brough, East Riding, Yorkshire HU15 2NR
Ⓣ (01430) 421543
Ⓕ (01430) 421543
Ⓔ admin@miresbeck.co.uk
Ⓦ www.miresbeck.co.uk
Contact: Judy Burrow & Martin Rowland
Opening Times: 1000-1600 Mon-Sat 1st Mar-30th Sep. 1000-1500 Mon-Fri 1st Oct-30th Nov & by appt.
Min Mail Order UK: Nmc
Cat. Cost: 3 × 1st class.
Credit Cards: None
Specialities: Wildflower plants of Yorkshire provenance.
Notes: Mail order for wildflower plants, plugs & seeds only. Also sells wholesale.
Map Ref: N, D3 **OS Grid Ref:** SE889316

NMRc **Millrace Nursery** ♿
84 Selby Road, Garforth, Leeds, LS25 1LP
Ⓣ (0113) 286 9233
Ⓕ (0113) 286 9908
Ⓔ carol@millrace-plants.co.uk
Ⓦ www.millrace-plants.co.uk
Contact: C Carthy
Opening Times: 1000-1700 Tue, Thu & Sat & by appt.
Cat. Cost: Online.
Credit Cards: None
Specialities: Unusual perennials, especially drought-resistant, incl. hardy geraniums, alliums, campanulas, penstemnons, potentillas & veronicas. Some plants in small quantities only.

NMyG **Mary Green** ⊠ ♠ ♿
The Walled Garden, Hornby, Lancaster, Lancashire LA2 8LD
Ⓣ (01524) 221989
Ⓜ 07778 910348
Ⓕ (01524) 221989
Ⓔ Marygreenplants@aol.com

KEY
⊠ Mail order to UK or EU ♠ Delivers to shows
✈ Exports beyond EU € Euro accepted
♿ Accessible by wheelchair ◆ See Display advertisement

N

Contact: Mary Green
Opening Times: By appt. only.
Min Mail Order UK: £10.00
Cat. Cost: 4 × 1st class.
Credit Cards: None
Specialities: Hostas, ferns & other shade-loving perennials.
Map Ref: N, C1 **OS Grid Ref:** SD588688

NNor **Norcroft Nurseries** ✉ € ♿
Roadends, Intack, Southwaite, Carlisle, Cumbria CA4 0LH
Ⓣ (01697) 473933
Ⓔ stellagbell@btinternet.com
Contact: Keith Bell
Opening Times: Every afternoon excl. Mon (open B/hol), Mar-Sep, or ring for appt.
Min Mail Order UK: Nmc
Cat. Cost: 2 × 2nd class.
Credit Cards: None
Specialities: Hardy herbaceous, *Dianthus*, *Aquilegia*, hostas, *Lilium*, *Papaver*.
Map Ref: N, B1 **OS Grid Ref:** NY474433

NNth **Northumberland Nurseries** ✉ ♿
Berwick Road, Wooler, Northumberland, NE71 6SL
Ⓣ (01668) 281348
Ⓜ 07723 254794
Ⓔ orders@northumberlandnurseries.co.uk
Ⓦ www.northumberlandnurseries.com
Contact: Robert O'Rourke
Opening Times: 0900-1700 Mon-Sat, 1000-1600 Sun.
Min Mail Order UK: Nmc
Cat. Cost: Free.
Credit Cards: All major credit/debit cards
Specialities: *Viola*.
Notes: Also sells wholesale.
Map Ref: N, A2 **OS Grid Ref:** NT9935828566

NOaD **Oak Dene Nurseries** ✉
10 Back Lane West, Royston, Barnsley, South Yorkshire S71 4SB
Ⓣ (01226) 722253
Contact: J Foster or G Foster
Opening Times: 0900-1230 & 1330-1800 1st Apr-30th Sep, 1000-1230 & 1330-1600 1st Oct-31st Mar. (Closed all day Wed.)
Min Mail Order UK: Phone for details.
Min Mail Order EU: Phone for details.
Cat. Cost: 1 × 2nd class for *Lithops* list.
Credit Cards: None
Specialities: Cacti, succulents (*Lithops*) & South African bulbs.
Notes: Also sells wholesale.
Map Ref: N, D2

NOak **Oak Tree Nursery** ✉ 🏠 ♿
Mill Lane, Barlow, Selby, North Yorkshire YO8 8EY
Ⓣ (01757) 618409
Ⓜ 07706 505688
Ⓔ gill@oaktreenursery.plus.com
Ⓦ www.oaktreenursery.com
Contact: Gill Plowes
Opening Times: By appt. only.
Min Mail Order UK: £10.00 + p&p
Min Mail Order EU: Nmc
Cat. Cost: 4 × 1st class.
Credit Cards: All major credit/debit cards
Specialities: Ornamental grasses & grass-like plants.
Notes: Will export seeds only beyond the EU. Also sells wholesale.

NOrc **Orchard House Nursery**
Orchard House, Wormald Green, Nr Harrogate, North Yorkshire, HG3 3NQ
Ⓣ (01765) 677541
Ⓕ (01765) 677541
Contact: Mr B M Corner
Opening Times: 0800-1630 Mon-Fri. Closed B/hols.
Cat. Cost: 4 × 1st class.
Credit Cards: None
Specialities: Herbaceous perennials, ferns, grasses, bog plants & unusual cottage garden plants.
Notes: Also sells wholesale.
Map Ref: N, C2

NPCo **Plantsman's Corner**
Sunniside, Barningham, Richmond, Yorkshire, DL11 7DW
Ⓜ 07707 694310
Ⓔ plantsmanscorner@btinternet.com
Ⓦ www.plantsmanscorner.co.uk
Contact: Malcolm Hockham
Opening Times: Not yet fully open. Visits by appt. only. Plant orders can be collected by prior arrangement or from Eggleston Hall Gardens (see nursery NEgg for opening hours). Please contact nursery for details.
Credit Cards: All major credit/debit cards
Specialities: *Cornus*, *Ilex*, & Japanese maples. Variable stock levels.

NPer **Perry's Plants** € ♿
The River Garden, Sleights, Whitby, North Yorkshire YO21 1RR
Ⓣ (01947) 810329
Ⓜ 07879 498623
Ⓔ sharon.perry@virgin.net
Ⓦ www.perrysplants.co.uk
Contact: Pat & Richard Perry
Opening Times: 1000-1700 mid-March to Oct.

Cat. Cost: None published.
Credit Cards: None
Specialities: *Lavatera, Malva, Erysimum, Euphorbia, Anthemis, Osteospermum* & *Hebe*. Uncommon hardy & container plants & aquatic plants.
Map Ref: N, C3 **OS Grid Ref:** NZ869082

NPla **The Plant Directory (formerly Scawsby Hall Nurseries)** ⊠
Barnsley Road, Scawsby, Doncaster, South Yorkshire DN5 7UB
Ⓣ (01302) 783434
Ⓔ mail@the-plant-directory.com
Ⓦ www.the-plant-directory.co.uk
Contact: David Lawson
Opening Times: Not open. Mail order only.
Min Mail Order UK: Nmc
Cat. Cost: None issued.
Credit Cards: Maestro, Visa, MasterCard, Paypal
Specialities: A wide range of herbaceous perennials, hardy trees, shrubs & indoor plants. Some indoor & aquatic plants in small quantities only.

NPnk **Primrose Bank** ⊠ ♿
Redroofs, Dauby Lane, Kexby, Yorkshire, YO41 5LH
Ⓣ (01759) 380220
Ⓜ 07774 944447
Ⓔ suegoodwill@yahoo.co.uk
Ⓦ www.primrosebank.co.uk
Contact: Sue Goodwill
Opening Times: 1000-1700, Thu-Sun, 1st Apr-30th Jun. Every day in Dec. By appt. only at other times.
Min Mail Order UK: Nmc
Cat. Cost: 4 × 1st class.
Credit Cards: All major credit/debit cards
Specialities: Unusual hardy perennials, woodland garden & shade-tolerant plants. *Astrantia, Echinacea* & *Heuchera*.
Map Ref: N, C3 **OS Grid Ref:** SE695508

NPri **Primrose Cottage Nursery** ♿
Ringway Road, Moss Nook, Wythenshawe, Manchester, M22 5WF
Ⓣ (0161) 437 1557
Ⓜ 07798 754457
Ⓔ info@primrosecottagenursery.co.uk
Ⓦ www.primrosecottagenursery.co.uk
Contact: Caroline Dumville
Opening Times: 0830-1730 Mon-Sat, 0930-1730 Sun (summer). 0830-1700 Mon-Sat, 0930-1700 Sun (winter).
Cat. Cost: Plant lists can be sent by email.
Credit Cards: All major credit/debit cards
Specialities: Hardy herbaceous perennials, alpines, herbs, roses, patio & hanging basket plants. Shrubs, ornamental trees, fruit trees, soft fruit bushes & vegetable plants.
Notes: Coffee shop open daily.
Map Ref: N, D2

NPro **ProudPlants** ⊠ ♿
East of Eden Nurseries, Ainstable, Carlisle, Cumbria CA4 9QN
Ⓣ (01768) 896604
Ⓜ 07788 142969
Ⓔ rogereastofeden@hotmail.com
Contact: Roger Proud
Opening Times: By appt. only, Mar-Oct.
Min Mail Order UK: £10.00
Cat. Cost: None issued.
Credit Cards: None
Specialities: Interesting & unusual shrubs, perennials & alpines, esp. astilbes and geums.
Notes: Mail order available Sep-Mar on geums & astilbes only.
Map Ref: N, B1 **OS Grid Ref:** NY467504

NRHS **Harlow Carr Plant Centre (RHS)** ◆
RHS Garden, Crag Lane, Harlow Carr, Harrogate, North Yorkshire HG3 1QB
Ⓣ (01423) 724667
Ⓕ (01423) 569521
Ⓔ chrisgarbutt@rhs.org.uk
Ⓦ www.rhs.org.uk
Contact: Plant Centre Staff
Specialities: Wide general range, particularly alpines.
Notes: Programme of free plant events throughout the year. Please ring or check website for details.
Map Ref: N, C2

NRib **Ribblesdale Nurseries** ♿
Newsham Hall Lane, Woodplumpton, Preston, Lancashire PR4 0AS
Ⓣ (01772) 863081
Ⓕ (01772) 861884
Ⓔ philsd@btinternet.com
Ⓦ www.ribblesdalenurseries.co.uk
Contact: Mr & Mrs Dunnett
Opening Times: 0900-1800 Mon-Sat Apr-Sep, 0900-1700 Mon-Sat Oct-Mar. 1030-1630 Sun.
Credit Cards: Visa, MasterCard, Delta, Switch

KEY
⊠ Mail order to UK or EU — Delivers to shows
Exports beyond EU — € Euro accepted
♿ Accessible by wheelchair — ◆ See Display advertisement

N

Specialities: Trees, shrubs & perennials. Conifers, hedging, alpines, fruit, climbers, herbs, aquatics, ferns & wildflowers.

NRob **W ROBINSON & SONS LTD** ⊠ ✈ € ♿
Sunny Bank, Forton, Nr Preston, Lancashire, PR3 0BN
Ⓣ (01524) 791210
Ⓕ (01524) 791933
Ⓔ info@mammothonion.co.uk
Ⓦ www.mammothonion.co.uk
Contact: Miss Robinson
Opening Times: 0900-1600 7 days Mar-Jun, 0800-1700 Mon-Fri Jul-Feb.
Min Mail Order UK: Nmc
Min Mail Order EU: Nmc
Cat. Cost: Free.
Credit Cards: Visa, Access, American Express, Switch
Specialities: Mammoth vegetable seed. Onions, leeks, tomatoes & beans. Range of vegetable plants in the spring.
Notes: Also sells wholesale.

NRya **RYAL NURSERY** ⌂ ♿
East Farm Cottage, Ryal, Northumberland NE20 0SA
Ⓣ (01661) 886562
Ⓔ alpines@ryal.freeserve.co.uk
Contact: R F Hadden
Opening Times: Mar-Jul by appt., please phone.
Cat. Cost: Sae.
Credit Cards: None
Specialities: Alpine & woodland plants. Mainly available in small quantities only. Nat. Collection of *Primula marginata*.
Notes: Also sells wholesale.
Map Ref: N, B2 **OS Grid Ref:** NZ015744

NSla **SLACK TOP NURSERIES** ⊠ ⌂ €
1 Waterloo House, 24 Slack Top, Hebden Bridge, West Yorkshire HX7 7HA
Ⓣ (01422) 845348
Ⓜ 07984 722640
Ⓔ enquiries@slacktopnurseries.co.uk
Ⓦ www.slacktopnurseries.co.uk
Contact: Michael & Allison Mitchell
Opening Times: 1000-1700 Fri-Sun 1st Mar-31st Aug & B/hols. Other times by appt.
Min Mail Order UK: £30.00
Min Mail Order EU: £50.00
Cat. Cost: 2 × 1st class A5 sae or online.
Credit Cards: None
Specialities: Alpine, rockery & woodland plants.
Notes: Some areas of garden inaccessible for wheelchairs. Talks given to gardening clubs & other groups by appt.
Map Ref: N, D2 **OS Grid Ref:** SD977286

NSti **STILLINGFLEET LODGE NURSERIES** ♿
Stewart Lane, Stillingfleet, North Yorkshire YO19 6HP
Ⓣ (01904) 728506
Ⓕ (01904) 728506
Ⓔ vanessa.cook@stillingfleetlodgenurseries.co.uk
Ⓦ www.stillingfleetlodgenurseries.co.uk
Contact: Vanessa Cook
Opening Times: 1300-1700 Wed & Fri 2nd Apr-30th Sep. 1300-1700, 1st & 3rd Sat & Sun in each month.
Cat. Cost: Online only.
Credit Cards: None
Specialities: Foliage & unusual perennials. Hardy geraniums, *Pulmonaria*, variegated plants & grasses, interesting climbers.

NSum **SUMMERDALE GARDEN NURSERY** ⌂
Summerdale House, Cow Brow, Lupton, Carnforth, Lancashire, LA6 1PE
Ⓣ (01539) 567210
Ⓔ sheals@btinternet.com
Ⓦ www.summerdalegardenplants.co.uk
Contact: Gail Sheals
Opening Times: 0930-1630 Thu, Fri & Sat, 3rd Mar-10th Sep. Other times by appt. only.
Cat. Cost: Online only.
Credit Cards: None
Specialities: Wide variety of perennials, large collection of *Primula*. Many moist and shade-loving plants incl. *Meconopsis* & hellebores.
Map Ref: N, C1 **OS Grid Ref:** SD545819

NTay **TAYLORS CLEMATIS NURSERY** ⊠ ⌂ ♿
Sutton Road, Sutton, Nr Askern, Doncaster, South Yorkshire DN6 9JZ
Ⓣ (01302) 700716
Ⓕ (01302) 708415
Ⓔ info@taylorsclematis.co.uk
Ⓦ www.taylorsclematis.co.uk
Contact: Chris & Suzy Cocks
Opening Times: Open by appt. only. Please ring for details.
Min Mail Order UK: Nmc
Min Mail Order EU: Nmc
Cat. Cost: 4 × 2nd class.
Credit Cards: All major credit/debit cards
Specialities: *Clematis* (over 350+ varieties).
Map Ref: N, D2 **OS Grid Ref:** SE552121

NWad **WADDOW LODGE GARDEN** ⊠ ♿
Clitheroe Road, Waddington, Clitheroe, Lancashire BB7 3HQ
Ⓣ (01200) 429145
Ⓔ peterfoleyhcn@hotmail.co.uk

Ⓦ www.gardentalks.co.uk
Contact: Peter Foley
Opening Times: By appt. only all year.
Min Mail Order UK: Nmc
Min Mail Order EU: Nmc
Cat. Cost: Online only.
Credit Cards: Visa, MasterCard, Delta
Specialities: A developing plantsman's garden with a wide ranging interesting plant collection.
Notes: Open for group visits by appt., incl. evenings. Also open under NGS 29th May & 31st Jul 2011. Open for other charities on 22nd May & 10th Jul 2011.
Map Ref: N, C1 **OS Grid Ref:** SD732434

NWea **WEASDALE NURSERIES LTD** ⊠
Newbiggin-on-Lune, Kirkby Stephen, Cumbria CA17 4LX
Ⓣ (01539) 623246
Ⓕ (01539) 623277
Ⓔ sales@weasdale.com
Ⓦ www.weasdale.com
Contact: Andrew Forsyth
Opening Times: 0830-1730 Mon-Fri. Closed w/ends, B/hols, Xmas through to the New Year.
Min Mail Order UK: Nmc
Min Mail Order EU: Nmc
Cat. Cost: Free of charge in UK or £2.00 to EU.
Credit Cards: All major credit/debit cards
Specialities: Hardy forest trees, hedging, broadleaved & conifers. Specimen trees & shrubs grown at 850 feet (260 metre) elevation.
Notes: Mail order a speciality. Mail order Nov-Apr only. Also sells wholesale to VAT registered customers.
Map Ref: N, C1 **OS Grid Ref:** NY690039

NWit **D S WITTON** ⊠
26 Casson Drive, Harthill, Sheffield, Yorkshire S26 7WA
Ⓣ (01909) 771366
Ⓔ donshardyeuphorbias@btopenworld.com
Ⓦ www.euphorbias.co.uk
Contact: Don Witton
Opening Times: By appt. only. Open Day, 1300-1600, Sun 8th May 2011.
Min Mail Order UK: Nmc
Cat. Cost: 1 × 1st class + sae.
Credit Cards: None
Specialities: Nat. Collection of Hardy *Euphorbia*. Over 130 varieties.
Notes: Mail order plants, Oct-Feb. Mail order seed Oct-June.
Map Ref: N, D2 **OS Grid Ref:** SK494812

NWsh **WESTSHORES NURSERIES** ⊠
82 West Street, Winterton, Lincolnshire DN15 9QF
Ⓣ (01724) 733940
Ⓔ westshnur@aol.com
Ⓦ www.westshores.co.uk
Contact: Gail & John Summerfield
Opening Times: 1st Mar-31st Oct by appt. only.
Min Mail Order UK: £15.00
Credit Cards: All major credit/debit cards
Specialities: Ornamental grasses.
Map Ref: N, D3 **OS Grid Ref:** SE927187

NYoL **YORKSHIRE LAVENDER** ⊠ ♿
Terrington, York, North Yorkshire YO60 6PB
Ⓣ (01653) 648008
Ⓕ (01653) 648008
Ⓦ www.yorkshirelavender.com
Contact: Julia Snowball
Opening Times: 1000-1700 7 days, 2nd Apr-30th Oct 2011.
Min Mail Order UK: £15.00
Cat. Cost: None issued.
Credit Cards: All major credit/debit cards
Specialities: *Lavandula*, *Mentha*, *Thymus*. Herbs.
Map Ref: N, C3 **OS Grid Ref:** SE655710

SOUTHERN

SAga **AGAR'S NURSERY** € ♿
Agars Lane, Hordle, Lymington, Hampshire SO41 0FL
Ⓜ 07508 848010
Contact: Diana Tombs
Opening Times: 1000-1700 (closed Thu), Mar-Sep. Open most days but please phone first.
Specialities: *Penstemon* & *Salvia*. Also wide range of hardy plants incl. hardy & tender shrubs, climbers & herbaceous. Many plants not listed may be available in small numbers.
Map Ref: S, D2 **OS Grid Ref:** SZ275960

SAll **ALLWOODS** ⊠ ♿
London Road, Hassocks, West Sussex BN6 9NB
Ⓣ (01273) 844229
Ⓔ info@allwoods.net
Ⓦ www.allwoods.net
Contact: David & Emma James

KEY
⊠ Mail order to UK or EU | Delivers to shows
Exports beyond EU | € Euro accepted
♿ Accessible by wheelchair | ◆ See Display advertisement

S

Opening Times: Office: 0900-1630 Mon-Fri. Answer machine all other times. Nursery: open to visitors 7 days. Check website for detailed opening times.
Min Mail Order UK: Nmc
Min Mail Order EU: Nmc
Cat. Cost: 2 × 1st class.
Credit Cards: Access, Visa, MasterCard, Switch, Maestro
Specialities: *Dianthus* incl. hardy border carnations, pinks, perpetual flowering & spray carnations, Malmaisons & *D. allwoodii*, some available as seed. Certain lavender varieties. Penstemons.
Notes: All listed varieties available as plugs but choice varies depending on time of year. Please phone before travelling to avoid disappointment and/or to ensure order is ready for collection.
Map Ref: S, D4 **OS Grid Ref:** TQ303170

S

SApp **Apple Court** ⊠ € ♿
Hordle Lane, Hordle, Lymington, Hampshire S041 0HU
Ⓣ (01590) 642130
Ⓜ 07919 280990
Ⓕ (01590) 644220
Ⓔ applecourt@btinternet.com
Ⓦ www.applecourt.com
Contact: Angela & Charles Meads
Opening Times: 1000-1700 Fri, Sat, Sun & B/hol 1st Mar-31st Oct. Closed Nov-Feb.
Min Mail Order UK: Nmc
Min Mail Order EU: Nmc
Cat. Cost: 4 × 1st class.
Credit Cards: All major credit/debit cards
Specialities: *Hemerocallis*, *Hosta*, grasses & ferns.
Notes: Groups/coach parties by prior arrangement.
Map Ref: S, D2 **OS Grid Ref:** SZ270941

SBch **Birchwood Plants** ⊠ ⌂ ♿
(Office) 10 Westering, Romsey, Hampshire SO51 7LY
Ⓣ (01794) 502192 or (02380) 814345
Ⓔ info@birchwoodplants.co.uk
Ⓦ www.birchwoodplants.co.uk
Contact: Lesley Baker
Opening Times: Open on 1st & 3rd Fri & Sat in Mar, Apr & May 2011. Plants can be collected by arrangement from nursery or from Plant Heritage sale at Longstock, Hants on 2nd May, or HPS sale at Chandlers Ford on 11th Jun. Other events will be posted on website.
Min Mail Order UK: £15 + p&p
Cat. Cost: Online only.
Credit Cards: None
Specialities: Wide range of plants, mainly herbaceous, many unusual. Good selection of hardy geraniums & *Dianthus*. Scented plants & those to attract bees & butterflies. Drought-tolerant plants & an increasing collection of alpines. Good range of Mottisfont Abbey perennials. Some stock available in small quantities only.
Notes: Nursery at Silverwood House, Gardener's Lane, Nr Romsey, SO51 6AD. Mostly accessible for wheelchairs. Mail order considered for small plants.
Map Ref: S, D2 **OS Grid Ref:** SU333190

SBea **Bean Place Nursery** ⌂
Watersfield, Bletchenden Road, Headcorn, Kent TN27 9JB
Ⓜ 07841 484822
Ⓔ beanplacenursery@googlemail.com
Contact: Anita or Tim Waters
Opening Times: By appt. only.
Credit Cards: None
Specialities: Ornamental grasses, herbaceous perennials & cottage garden plants.
Notes: Only sells at shows. Contact nursery for details of shows attended. Also sells wholesale.
Map Ref: S, C5

SBfd **Jack Dunckley's Birchfield Nursery** ⊠ ♿
Kidders Lane, Henfield, West Sussex BN5 9AB
Ⓣ (01273) 494058 or 491392
Ⓜ 07717 581584
Ⓕ (01273) 493696
Ⓔ sales@birchfieldnursery.com
Ⓦ www.birchfieldnursery.com
Contact: Jack Dunckley
Opening Times: 0830-1700 Mon-Fri, 0930-1630 Sat & Sun, all year except Xmas/New Year period. For winter hours please phone first. Please phone before visiting to ensure plant availability & to check opening hours.
Min Mail Order UK: Nmc
Cat. Cost: Online only.
Credit Cards: All, except American Express
Specialities: Very wide general range of plants incl. many unusual & new varieties, plus fruit, young veg. plants & seasonal bedding.
Notes: Also sells wholesale.
Map Ref: S, D3 **OS Grid Ref:** TQ213178

SBHP **Bleak Hill Plants** ♿
Braemoor, Bleak Hill, Harbridge, Ringwood, Hampshire, BH24 3PX
Ⓣ (01425) 652983
Ⓔ tracy@bleakhillplants.co.uk

Contact: Tracy Netherway
Opening Times: 0900-1800, Mon, Tue, Fri, Sat & 1000-1600 Sun, Mar-Oct. Closed Wed & Thu.
Cat. Cost: 2 × 1st class.
Credit Cards: None
Specialities: Hardy & half-hardy herbaceous perennials. Stock available in small quantities.
Map Ref: S, D1 **OS Grid Ref:** SU132111

SBig **Big Plant Nursery** ⊠ ♦
Hole Street, Ashington, West Sussex RH20 3DE
Ⓣ (01903) 891466
Ⓜ 07957 262845
Ⓕ (01903) 892829
Ⓔ info@bigplantnursery.co.uk
Ⓦ www.bigplantnursery.co.uk
Contact: Bruce Jordan
Opening Times: 0900-1700 Mon-Sat, 1000-1600 Sun & B/hols.
Min Mail Order UK: Please phone for further info.
Cat. Cost: A5 sae with 2 × 1st class.
Credit Cards: All major credit/debit cards
Specialities: Bamboos, hardy exotics & palms, *Ginkgo*, *Betula*.
Notes: Programme of events & propagation tuition, see nursery website for details. Also sells wholesale.
Map Ref: S, D3 **OS Grid Ref:** TQ132153

SBir **Birchfleet Nurseries** ♦
Greenfields Close, Nyewood, Petersfield, Hampshire GU31 5JQ
Ⓣ (01730) 821636
Ⓕ (01730) 821636
Ⓔ gammoak@aol.com
Ⓦ www.birchfleetnurseries.co.uk
Contact: John & Daphne Gammon
Opening Times: By appt. only. Please phone.
Cat. Cost: 2 × 1st class.
Credit Cards: None
Specialities: Oaks. Beech. *Carpinus*. Nat. Collection of *Liquidambar*.
Notes: Nursery accessible for wheelchairs in dry weather. Also sells wholesale.
Map Ref: S, C3

SBod **Bodiam Nursery**
Bodiam, Robertsbridge, East Sussex TN32 5RA
Ⓣ (01580) 830811
Ⓜ 07971 419302
Ⓔ enquiries@bodiamnursery.co.uk
Ⓦ www.bodiamnursery.co.uk
Contact: Jill Kaye
Opening Times: 1000-1700 summer, 1000-1600 winter, Tue-Sun (closed Mon). Closed Jan.
Cat. Cost: None issued.
Credit Cards: All major credit/debit cards
Specialities: *Acer*. Coastal plants.

SBri **Brickwall Cottage Nursery** ⊠
1 Brickwall Cottages, Frittenden, Cranbrook, Kent TN17 2DH
Ⓣ (01580) 852425
Ⓜ 07714 529946
Ⓔ sue.martin@talktalk.net
Ⓦ www.geumcollection.co.uk
Contact: Sue Martin
Opening Times: By appt. only.
Min Mail Order UK: Nmc
Min Mail Order EU: Nmc
Credit Cards: None
Specialities: Hardy perennials. Stock available in small quantities only. Nat. Collection of *Geum*.
Map Ref: S, C5 **OS Grid Ref:** TQ815410

SBrk **Brookfield Plants** ⊠ €
Bigelle, Sandyhurst Lane, Ashford, Kent TN25 4NX
Ⓣ (01233) 624934
Ⓜ 07944 213891
Ⓔ paulharris34@btinternet.com
Ⓦ www.brookfieldplants.com
Contact: Paul Harris
Opening Times: Visitors by appt. only.
Min Mail Order UK: Nmc
Min Mail Order EU: Nmc
Cat. Cost: £1.00
Credit Cards: All major credit/debit cards
Specialities: *Hemerocallis* & *Hosta*. Nat. Collection of *Hemerocallis* applied for.
Notes: Sells at shows.

SBrm **Brambly Hedge** ⊠
Mill Lane, Sway, Hampshire SO41 8LN
Ⓣ (01590) 683570
Contact: Kim Williams
Opening Times: By appt. only in Jul & Aug.
Min Mail Order UK: Nmc
Cat. Cost: Sae for descriptive list.
Credit Cards: None
Specialities: Nat. Collections of *Streptocarpus* & *Begonia* rex cvs. Plants available in small quantities only.
Notes: Mail order Mar-Aug, small quantities only.

KEY
⊠ Mail order to UK or EU — Delivers to shows
Exports beyond EU — € Euro accepted
Accessible by wheelchair — ♦ See Display advertisement

SBrt **BRIGHTON PLANTS** ⊠ ✈ € ♿
3 Badger Copse, Henfield, Sussex
BN5 9HE
Ⓣ (01273) 491583
Ⓔ peganum1@yahoo.co.uk
Ⓦ www.brightonplants.blogspot.com/
Contact: Steve Law
Opening Times: By appt. only.
Min Mail Order UK: Nmc
Cat. Cost: 2 × 1st class.
Credit Cards: None
Specialities: Hardy herbaceous and woody plants. Available in small quantities only.
Map Ref: S, D3 **OS Grid Ref:** TQ213167

SBst **BEAST PLANTS**
24 Arundel Road, Boyatt Wood, Eastleigh, Hampshire SO50 4PQ
Ⓜ 07887 997263 or 07887 997433
Ⓔ beastplants@tiscali.co.uk
Contact: Toni & Steve Newell
Opening Times: By appt. only.
Cat. Cost: Free.
Credit Cards: None
Specialities: Exotic, sub-tropical & unusual plants.

SCac **CACTI & SUCCULENTS** ⊠
Hammerfield, Crockham Hill, Edenbridge, Kent TN8 6RR
Ⓣ (01732) 866295
Contact: Geoff Southon
Opening Times: Flexible. Please phone first.
Min Mail Order UK: Nmc
Cat. Cost: None issued.
Credit Cards: None
Specialities: *Echeveria* & related genera & hybrids. Haworthias & gasterias. A large range of aeoniums, both species & hybrids. A large range of plants available in small quantities.

SCam **CAMELLIA GROVE NURSERY** ⊠ ✈ ⌂ € ♿
Market Garden, Lower Beeding, West Sussex RH13 6PP
Ⓣ (01403) 891412
Ⓔ sales@camellia-grove.com
Ⓦ www.camellia-grove.com
Contact: Chris Loder
Opening Times: 1000-1600 Mon-Sat, please phone first so we can give try to give you our undivided attention.
Min Mail Order UK: Nmc
Min Mail Order EU: Nmc
Cat. Cost: 2 × 1st class.
Credit Cards: All, except American Express
Specialities: Camellias & azaleas. Also rhododendrons & hydrangeas. Some in very ltd. quantities only.
Notes: Also sells wholesale.
Map Ref: S, C3 **OS Grid Ref:** TQ221255

SCan **CANNA MAN** ⊠
(Office) 4 Newland Road, Upper Beeding, Steyning, West Sussex BN44 3JJ
Ⓣ (01903) 813780
Ⓔ clivethecannaman@gmail.com
Ⓦ www.cannaman.co.uk
Contact: Colin Paker
Opening Times: Not open. Mail order only.
Min Mail Order UK: Nmc
Min Mail Order EU: Nmc
Cat. Cost: Online only.
Credit Cards: Paypal
Specialities: A wide range of disease-free *Canna*, many only available in very small numbers. All plants grown in own peat-free compost without the use of chemical pesticides.
Notes: Plants only available from May-Oct.

SChF **CHARLESHURST FARM NURSERY** ⊠ ⌂ €
Loxwood Road, Plaistow, Billingshurst, West Sussex RH14 0NY
Ⓣ (01403) 752273
Ⓜ 07736 522788
Ⓔ Charleshurstfarm@aol.com
Ⓦ www.charleshurstplants.co.uk
Contact: Clive Mellor
Opening Times: Normally 0900-1730 Fri, Sat, Sun, Feb-Oct, but please ring first before travelling.
Min Mail Order UK: Nmc
Min Mail Order EU: Nmc
Cat. Cost: 2 × 1st class.
Credit Cards: All major credit/debit cards
Specialities: Shrubs including some more unusual species. Good range of daphnes & Japanese maples.
Map Ref: S, C3 **OS Grid Ref:** TQ015308

SChr **JOHN CHURCHER** ⊠ ✈
47 Grove Avenue, Portchester, Fareham, Hampshire PO16 9EZ
Ⓣ (023) 9232 6740
Ⓜ 07917 350928
Ⓔ johnchurcher47@btinternet.com
Contact: John Churcher
Opening Times: By appt. only. Please phone or email.
Min Mail Order UK: Nmc
Min Mail Order EU: Nmc
Cat. Cost: None issued.
Credit Cards: None
Specialities: Hardy exotics for the Mediterranean-style garden, incl. palms, tree

ferns, *Musa*, hedychiums, cycads, *Agave*, *Aloe*, *Opuntia* & echiums. Stock available in small quantities only.
Map Ref: S, D2 **OS Grid Ref:** SU614047

SCmr **Cromar Nursery** ⊠ ♿
39 Livesey Street, North Pole, Wateringbury, Maidstone, Kent ME18 5BQ
Ⓣ (01622) 812380
Ⓔ CromarNursery@aol.com
Ⓦ www.cromarnursery.co.uk
Contact: Debra & Martin Cronk
Opening Times: 0930-1700 daily except Wed. Winter opening 0930-1630 Thu, Fri, Sat, Sun. Please check website or phone if travelling far.
Min Mail Order UK: Nmc
Min Mail Order EU: Nmc
Cat. Cost: 2 × 1st class.
Credit Cards: All major credit/debit cards
Specialities: Ornamental & fruit trees.
Map Ref: S, C4 **OS Grid Ref:** TQ697547

SCnR **Colin Roberts** ⊠
Tragumna, Morgay Wood Lane, Three Oaks, Guestling, East Sussex TN35 4NF
Ⓜ 07933 060905
Contact: Colin Roberts
Opening Times: Not open. Mail order only.
Min Mail Order UK: £20.00
Cat. Cost: 2 × 1st class.
Credit Cards: None
Specialities: Dwarf bulbs & woodland plants incl. many rare & unusual, in small numbers.

SCob **Coblands Nursery** ⊠
Trench Road, Tonbridge, Kent RH10 7RX
Ⓣ (01732) 770999
Ⓕ (01732) 770271
Ⓔ info@coblands.co.uk
Ⓦ www.coblands.co.uk
Contact: Sales Team
Opening Times: 0830-1700 Mon-Fri.
Min Mail Order UK: Nmc
Credit Cards: Visa, MasterCard, Maestro, American Express
Specialities: Herbaceous perennials & shrubs.
Notes: Also sells wholesale.

SCog **Coghurst Camellias** ⊠ ⛺ € ♿
Ivy House Lane, Near Three Oaks, Hastings, East Sussex TN35 4NP
Ⓣ (01424) 756228
Ⓔ rotherview@btinternet.com
Ⓦ www.rotherview.com
Contact: R Bates & W Bates
Opening Times: 0930-1600 7 days.
Min Mail Order UK: Nmc
Min Mail Order EU: Nmc
Cat. Cost: 6 × 1st class.
Credit Cards: All major credit/debit cards
Specialities: *Camellia.*
Notes: Nursery is on the same site as Rotherview Nursery. Also sells wholesale.
Map Ref: S, D5

SCoo **Cooling's Nurseries Ltd** ♿
Rushmore Hill, Knockholt, Sevenoaks, Kent TN14 7NN
Ⓣ (01959) 532269
Ⓕ (01959) 534092
Ⓔ Plantfinder@coolings.co.uk
Ⓦ www.coolings.co.uk
Contact: Mark Reeve or Toby Davies
Opening Times: 0900-1700 Mon-Sat & 1000-1630 Sun.
Cat. Cost: None issued.
Credit Cards: All, except American Express
Specialities: Large range of perennials, conifers & bedding plants. Many unusual shrubs & trees. Third generation family business.
Notes: Display garden. Coffee shop.
Map Ref: S, C4 **OS Grid Ref:** TK477610

SCrf **Crofters Nurseries** € ♿
Church Hill, Charing Heath, Near Ashford, Kent TN27 0BU
Ⓣ (01233) 712798
Ⓔ croftersnursery@yahoo.co.uk
Contact: John & Sue Webb
Opening Times: 1000-1700. Closed Sun-Tue. Please check first.
Cat. Cost: 3 × 1st class.
Credit Cards: None
Specialities: Fruit, ornamental trees. Old apple varieties. Small number of *Prunus serrula* with grafted ornamental heads.
Map Ref: S, C5 **OS Grid Ref:** TQ923493

SDay **A La Carte Daylilies** ⊠ €
Little Hermitage, St Catherine's Down, Nr Ventnor, Isle of Wight PO38 2PD
Ⓣ (01983) 730512
Ⓔ andy@alacartedaylilies.co.uk
Ⓦ www.alacartedaylilies.co.uk
Contact: Jan & Andy Wyers
Opening Times: Mail order only. Open by appt. only. Difficult to find on an unmade private road.
Min Mail Order UK: Nmc

KEY
⊠ Mail order to UK or EU ⛺ Delivers to shows
✈ Exports beyond EU € Euro accepted
♿ Accessible by wheelchair ◆ See Display advertisement

S

Min Mail Order EU: Nmc
Cat. Cost: 3 × 1st class.
Credit Cards: None
Specialities: *Hemerocallis*. Nat. Collections of Miniature & Small Flowered *Hemerocallis* & Large Flowered *Hemerocallis* (post-1960 award-winning cultivars).
Map Ref: S, D2 **OS Grid Ref:** SZ499787

SDeJ **P. de Jager & Sons Ltd** ⊠ ☒ € ♿ ◆
Church Farm, Ulcombe, Maidstone, Kent ME17 1DN
Ⓣ (01622) 840229
Ⓕ (01622) 844073
Ⓔ flowerbulbs@dejager.co.uk
Ⓦ www.dejager.co.uk
Contact: George Clowes
Opening Times: Mail order only. Orders taken from 0900-1700 Mon-Fri
Min Mail Order UK: Nmc
Min Mail Order EU: Nmc
Cat. Cost: Free.
Credit Cards: All major credit/debit cards
Specialities: Complete range of all flower bulbs.
Notes: Also sells wholesale.

SDix **Great Dixter Nurseries** ⊠
Northiam, Rye, East Sussex TN31 6PH
Ⓣ (01797) 254044
Ⓕ (01797) 252879
Ⓔ nursery@greatdixter.co.uk
Ⓦ www.greatdixter.co.uk
Contact: M. Morphy
Opening Times: 0900-1700 Mon-Fri, 0900-1230 Sat all year. Also 1400-1700 Sat, Sun & B/hols Apr-Oct.
Min Mail Order UK: Nmc
Min Mail Order EU: Nmc
Cat. Cost: 5 × 1st class.
Credit Cards: All major credit/debit cards
Specialities: *Clematis*, shrubs and plants. Gardens open.
Notes: Plants dispatched Sep-Mar only. Partially accessible for wheelchairs.

SDow **Downderry Nursery** ⊠ ☒ € ♿
Pillar Box Lane, Hadlow, Nr Tonbridge, Kent TN11 9SW
Ⓣ (01732) 810081
Ⓕ (01732) 811398
Ⓔ info@downderry-nursery.co.uk
Ⓦ www.downderry-nursery.co.uk
Contact: Dr Simon Charlesworth
Opening Times: 1000-1700 Tue-Sun 1st May-31st Oct & B/hols. Other times by appt.
Min Mail Order UK: Nmc
Min Mail Order EU: Nmc
Cat. Cost: 3 × 1st class.
Credit Cards: Delta, MasterCard, Maestro, Visa
Specialities: Nat. Collections of *Lavandula* and *Rosmarinus*.
Map Ref: S, C4 **OS Grid Ref:** TQ625521

SDys **Dysons Nurseries** ⊠ ⌂ ♿
Great Comp Garden, Platt, Sevenoaks, Kent, TN15 8QS
Ⓣ (01732) 885094
Ⓜ 07887 997663
Ⓔ dysonsorders@greatcompgarden.co.uk
Ⓦ www.greatcompgarden.co.uk
Contact: William T Dyson
Opening Times: 1100-1700 7 days 1st Apr-31st Oct. Other times by appt.
Min Mail Order UK: £24.00
Cat. Cost: Online only.
Credit Cards: All major credit/debit cards
Specialities: Salvias & an eclectic range of choice and uncommon plants.
Map Ref: S, C4

SEND **East Northdown Farm Nursery** ⊠ € ♿ ◆
Margate, Kent CT9 3TS
Ⓣ (01843) 862060
Ⓜ 07714 241668 or 241667
Ⓔ friend.northdown@btinternet.com
Ⓦ www.botanyplants.co.uk
Contact: Louise & William Friend
Opening Times: 0900-1700 Mon-Sat, 1000-1700 Sun all year. Closed Sun in Oct, Nov & Jan. Closed Xmas for 2 weeks.
Min Mail Order UK: Nmc
Cat. Cost: Online only.
Credit Cards: Visa, Switch, MasterCard
Specialities: Chalk & coast-loving plants.
Notes: Also sells wholesale.
Map Ref: S, B6 **OS Grid Ref:** TR383702

SEWo **English Woodlands** ⊠ ♿
Burrow Nursery, Herrings Lane, Cross-in-Hand, Heathfield, East Sussex TN21 0UG
Ⓣ (01435) 862992
Ⓕ (01435) 867742
Ⓔ sales@englishwoodlands.com
Ⓦ www.englishwoodlands.com
Contact: Joanne Carter
Opening Times: 0800-1700 Mon-Fri. 0800-1630 Sat. Closed Sun & B/hols.
Min Mail Order UK: £25.00
Cat. Cost: Free.
Credit Cards: All, except American Express
Specialities: Trees, shrubs, hedging.
Notes: Also sells wholesale.
Map Ref: S, C4 **OS Grid Ref:** TQ567222

SFai **Fairweather's Garden Centre** € ♿
High Street, Beaulieu, Hampshire SO42 7YB
Ⓣ (01590) 612307
Ⓕ (01590) 612519
Ⓔ info@fairweathers.co.uk
Ⓦ www.fairweathers.co.uk
Contact: Sue Greaves
Opening Times: 0900-1700 7 days.
Cat. Cost: None issued.
Credit Cards: Visa, MasterCard
Specialities: *Agapanthus*, *Heuchera* & *Lavandula*.
Notes: Also sells wholesale.
Map Ref: S, D2

SFam **Family Trees** ⊠ ♿
Sandy Lane, Shedfield, Hampshire, SO32 2HQ
Ⓣ (01329) 834812
Ⓦ www.familytreesnursery.co.uk
Contact: Philip House
Opening Times: 0930-1230 Tue, Wed, Fri & Sat mid-Oct-end Apr (closed 20th Dec-10th Jan).
Min Mail Order UK: £10.00
Cat. Cost: Free.
Credit Cards: None
Specialities: Fruit & ornamental trees. Trained fruit tree specialists: standards, espaliers, cordons. Other trees, old-fashioned & climbing roses, evergreens. Trees, except evergreens, sold bare-rooted.

SFgr **Firgrove Plants** ⊠
24 Wykeham Field, Wickham, Fareham, Hampshire PO17 5AB
Ⓣ (01329) 835206 after 1900 hours.
Ⓔ jenny@firgroveplants.demon.co.uk
Ⓦ www.firgroveplants.demon.co.uk
Contact: Jenny MacKinnon
Opening Times: Not open. Mail order only.
Min Mail Order UK: £7.00
Cat. Cost: Sae.
Credit Cards: None
Specialities: Wide range of houseleeks & smaller range of other alpines in small quantities.
Notes: Houseleeks by mail order Apr-mid Oct.

SGar **Garden Plants** ⊠ ⛺
Windy Ridge, Victory Road, St Margarets-at-Cliffe, Dover, Kent CT15 6HF
Ⓣ (01304) 853225
Ⓔ GardenPlants@GardenPlants-nursery.co.uk
Ⓦ www.GardenPlants-nursery.co.uk
Contact: Teresa Ryder & David Ryder
Opening Times: 1000-1730 summer, 1000-1700 winter. Closed Tues.
Min Mail Order UK: Nmc
Cat. Cost: 2 × 1st class + A5 sae.
Credit Cards: Visa, MasterCard
Specialities: Unusual perennials, *Penstemon* & *Salvia*.
Notes: Plantsman's garden open to view. Map essential for first visit. Access via unmade roads.
Map Ref: S, C6 **OS Grid Ref:** TR358464

SGol **Golden Hill Nurseries** ⊠ € ♿
Lordsfield, Goudhurst Road, Marden, Kent TN12 9LT
Ⓣ (01622) 833218
Ⓜ 07826 523655
Ⓕ (01622) 832528
Ⓔ enquiries@goldenhillplants.com
Ⓦ www.goldenhillplants.com
Contact: Roger Butler
Opening Times: 0900-1700 Mon-Sat, 1st Mar-31st Oct. 0900-1600 Mon-Sat, 1st Nov-28th Feb. 1100-1600 Sun from 3rd Sun in Feb until Xmas.
Min Mail Order UK: Nmc
Cat. Cost: Online only.
Credit Cards: All major credit/debit cards
Specialities: Specimen plants, shrubs, grasses, bamboos, Japanese maples, conifers & trees.
Notes: Also sells wholesale.

SHaC **Hart Canna** ⊠ ⛺ € ♿
25-27 Guildford Road West, Farnborough, Hampshire GU14 6PS
Ⓣ (01252) 514421
Ⓜ 07762 950000
Ⓔ sales@hartcanna.com
Ⓦ www.hartcanna.co.uk
Contact: Keith Hayward
Opening Times: By arrangement.
Min Mail Order UK: Nmc
Min Mail Order EU: Nmc
Cat. Cost: Sae.
Credit Cards: All major credit/debit cards
Specialities: *Canna*. Nat. Collection of *Canna*.
Notes: Also sells wholesale.
Map Ref: S, C3

SHar **Hardy's Cottage Garden Plants** ⊠ ⛺ ♿
Priory Lane Nursery, Freefolk Priors, Whitchurch, Hampshire RG28 7NJ
Ⓣ (01256) 896533
Ⓔ info@hardys-plants.co.uk
Ⓦ www.hardys-plants.co.uk
Contact: Rosemary Hardy
Opening Times: 1000-1700 7 days, 1st Mar-

KEY
⊠ Mail order to UK or EU ⛺ Delivers to shows
✈ Exports beyond EU € Euro accepted
♿ Accessible by wheelchair ◆ See Display advertisement

S

30th Sep. 1000-1600 Mon-Fri, 1st Oct-31st Oct, 1000-1500 Mon-Fri, 1st Nov-28th Feb. Closed 23rd Dec-4th Jan 2011.
Min Mail Order UK: Nmc
Cat. Cost: 10 × 1st class.
Credit Cards: Visa, Access, Electron, Switch, Solo
Specialities: Wide range of herbaceous perennials incl. *Achillea*, *Alstroemeria*, *Geranium*, *Hemerocallis*, *Heuchera*, *Paeonia*, *Penstemon* & *Salvia*.
Notes: Accepts HTA Gift Tokens. Offers trade discount.
Map Ref: S, C2

SHDw **HIGHDOWN NURSERY** ⊠ ♠ €
New Hall Lane, Small Dole, Nr Henfield, West Sussex BN5 9YH
Ⓣ (01273) 492976
Ⓜ 07900 956456
Ⓕ (01273) 492976
Ⓔ highdown.herbs@btopenworld.com
Ⓦ www.highdownnursery.com
Contact: A G & J H Shearing
Opening Times: 0900-1700 7 days.
Min Mail Order UK: £10.00 + p&p
Min Mail Order EU: £10.00 + p&p
Cat. Cost: 3 × 1st class.
Credit Cards: None
Specialities: Herbs. Grasses.
Notes: Partial wheelchair access. Also sells wholesale.
Map Ref: S, D3 **OS Grid Ref:** TV214134

SHea **HEASELANDS GARDEN NURSERY** ⊠ €
The Old Lodge, Isaacs Lane, Haywards Heath, West Sussex RH16 4SA
Ⓣ (01444) 458084
Ⓜ 07743 939490
Ⓕ (01444) 458084
Ⓔ headgardener@heaselandsnursery.co.uk
Ⓦ www.heaselandsnursery.co.uk
Contact: Stephen Harding
Opening Times: 0800-1700, Mon-Fri by appt. only so please phone first.
Min Mail Order UK: Nmc
Min Mail Order EU: Nmc
Cat. Cost: Online only. Monthly availability lists.
Credit Cards: None
Specialities: *Rhododendron* hybrids and deciduous azaleas, home-produced from cuttings. Some varieties in small quantities. Nat. Collection of Mollis Azaleas & Knaphill/Exbury Azaleas. Also *Hydragea*, *Hebe* & *Camellia*.
Notes: Also sells wholesale.
Map Ref: S, C4 **OS Grid Ref:** TQ314230

SHeu **HEUCHERAHOLICS** ⊠ ♠ ♿
(Office) The Paddock, Pilley Street, Pilley, Lymington, Hampshire SO41 5QP
Ⓣ (01590) 670581
Ⓜ 07973 291062
Ⓔ jooles.heucheraholics@googlemail.com
Ⓦ www.heucheraholics.co.uk
Contact: Julie Burton/Sean Atkinson
Opening Times: By appt. only. Please phone first.
Min Mail Order UK: Nmc
Credit Cards: All major credit/debit cards
Specialities: Heucheras, heucherellas & tiarellas. Other foliage plants. Some varieties only available in small quantities.
Notes: Nursery is located at Boldre Nurseries, Southampton Road, Boldre, Lymington, Hants.
Map Ref: S, D2 **OS Grid Ref:** SZ310934

SHil **HILLIER GARDEN CENTRES** ⊠
Ampfield House, Ampfield, Romsey, Hampshire SO51 9PA
Ⓣ (01794) 368944
Ⓕ (01794) 367830
Ⓔ info@hillier.co.uk
Ⓦ www.hillieronline.co.uk
Contact: Mark Pitman
Opening Times: Office 0830-1700 Mon-Fri. Garden Centres: 0900-1730 Mon-Sat, 1000-1630 Sun.
Min Mail Order UK: Nmc
Min Mail Order EU: £250
Cat. Cost: None issued.
Notes: Other nursery branches in the south of England.

SHom **HOME PLANTS**
52 Dorman Ave North, Aylesham, Canterbury, Kent CT3 3BW
Ⓣ (01304) 841746
Ⓔ homeplants@tiscali.co.uk
Contact: Stuart & Sue Roycroft
Opening Times: By appt. only, please phone first.
Cat. Cost: Sae for list.
Credit Cards: None
Specialities: *Phygelius* & unusual South African hardy plants. Limited stock, please phone first.

SHyH **HYDRANGEA HAVEN** ⊠ ⊠ ♠ € ♿
Market Garden, Lower Beeding, West Sussex RH13 6PP
Ⓣ (01403) 891412
Ⓔ sales@hydrangea-haven.com
Ⓦ www.hydrangea-haven.com
Contact: Chris Loder
Opening Times: 1000-1600 Mon-Sat, please

phone first, so we can give you our undivided attention.
Min Mail Order UK: Nmc
Min Mail Order EU: Nmc
Cat. Cost: 2 × 1st class.
Credit Cards: All, except American Express
Specialities: *Hydrangea*. Some available in very ltd. quantities only.
Notes: Also sells wholesale.
Map Ref: S, C3 **OS Grid Ref:** TQ221255

SIde **IDEN CROFT HERBS** ⊠ N ♿
Frittenden Road, Staplehurst, Kent TN12 0DH
Ⓣ (01580) 891432
Ⓕ (01580) 892416
Ⓔ idencroftherbs@yahoo.co.uk
Ⓦ www.uk-herbs.com
Contact: Tracey Connors-Parry
Opening Times: 0900-1700 Mon-Sat & 1100-1700 Sun & B/hols, Mar-Sep. Closed Oct-Feb.
Min Mail Order UK: £10.00
Min Mail Order EU: £25.00
Cat. Cost: 4 × 1st class.
Credit Cards: All major credit/debit cards
Specialities: Herbs, aromatic & wildflower plants & plants for bees & butterflies. Nat. Collections of *Mentha*, *Nepeta* & *Origanum*.
Notes: Wheelchairs available at nursery.
Map Ref: S, C5

SIri **IRIS OF SISSINGHURST** ⊠ € ◆
Roughlands Farm, Goudhurst Road, Marden, Kent TN12 9NH
Ⓣ (01622) 831511
Ⓔ orders@irisofsissinghurst.com
Ⓦ www.irisofsissinghurst.com
Contact: Sue Marshall
Opening Times: Contact nursery or see website for opening times.
Min Mail Order UK: Nmc
Min Mail Order EU: Nmc
Cat. Cost: 2 × 1st class.
Credit Cards: None
Specialities: *Iris*, short, intermediate & tall bearded, *ensata*, *sibirica* & many species.
Map Ref: S, C4 **OS Grid Ref:** TQ735437

SKee **KEEPERS NURSERY** ⊠
Gallants Court, Gallants Lane, East Farleigh, Maidstone, Kent ME15 0LE
Ⓣ (01622) 726465
Ⓕ 0870 705 2145
Ⓔ info@keepers-nursery.co.uk
Ⓦ www.keepers-nursery.co.uk
Contact: Hamid Habibi
Opening Times: Only on a limited number of Open Days & for collection of trees & plants by arrangement.
Min Mail Order UK: Nmc
Cat. Cost: Online only.
Credit Cards: Visa, MasterCard, Switch, Maestro
Specialities: A very large range of fruit trees incl. old & rare as well as modern varieties. Soft fruit plants & nut trees.
Map Ref: S, C4

SKen **KENT STREET NURSERIES** ⊠
Kent Street (A21), Sedlescombe, Battle, East Sussex TN33 0SF
Ⓣ (01424) 751134
Ⓔ peter@1066-countryplants.co.uk
Ⓦ www.1066-countryplants.co.uk
Contact: P Stapley
Opening Times: 0900-1700 Mon-Sat, 1030-1600 Sun.
Min Mail Order UK: £12.00
Cat. Cost: 2 × 1st class.
Credit Cards: All major credit/debit cards
Specialities: *Pelargonium*, bedding & perennials.
Notes: Mail order *Pelargonium* list only. Credit cards not accepted for mail order. Nursery partially accessible for wheelchair users.

SKHP **KEVIN HUGHES PLANTS** ⊠ ✈ € ♿
(Office) 89 Ladysmith, East Gomeldon, Salisbury, Wiltshire SP4 6LE
Ⓣ (01722) 782504
Ⓜ 07720 718671
Ⓕ (01772) 782504
Ⓔ info@kevinsplants.co.uk
Ⓦ www.kevinsplants.co.uk
Contact: Kevin Hughes
Opening Times: 1000-1700 Wed-Sun, 1st Feb-31st Oct. Other times by appt. only.
Min Mail Order UK: £10.00
Min Mail Order EU: £20.00
Cat. Cost: 3 × 1st class.
Credit Cards: All, except American Express
Specialities: Less common & new hardy garden plants with a particular emphasis on *Magnolia*, *Trillium*, climbers, *Philadelphus*, *Viburnum* & *Syringa*. We try to select plants that are garden-worthy & attract wildlife. Many plants are slow to propagate & will always be in short supply. None are from wild-dug sources.

KEY
⊠ Mail order to UK or EU
Delivers to shows
✈ Exports beyond EU
€ Euro accepted
♿ Accessible by wheelchair
◆ See Display advertisement

S

Notes: Nursery at Heale Garden, Middle Woodford, Salisbury, SP4 5NT.
Map Ref: S, C1 **OS Grid Ref:** SU125363

SLau **The Laurels Nursery** ⊠ €
Benenden, Cranbrook, Kent
TN17 4JU
Ⓣ (01580) 240463
Ⓕ (01580) 240463
Ⓦ www.thelaurelsnursery.co.uk
Contact: Peter or Sylvia Kellett
Opening Times: 0800-1600 Mon-Fri, 0900-1200 Sat, Sun by appt. only.
Min Mail Order UK: £28.00
Cat. Cost: Free.
Credit Cards: None
Specialities: Open ground & container ornamental trees, shrubs & climbers especially birch, beech & *Wisteria*.
Notes: Mail order of small Wisteria only. Also sells wholesale.
Map Ref: S, C5 **OS Grid Ref:** TQ815313

S

SLay **Layham Garden Centre & Nursery** ⊠ € ♿
Lower Road, Staple, Nr Canterbury, Kent
CT3 1LH
Ⓣ (01304) 813267
Ⓕ (01304) 814007
Ⓔ info@layhamgardencentre.co.uk
Ⓦ www.layhamgardencentre.co.uk
Contact: Ellen Wessel
Opening Times: 0900-1700 7 days.
Min Mail Order UK: Nmc
Min Mail Order EU: £25.00 + p&p
Cat. Cost: Free.
Credit Cards: Visa, MasterCard, Maestro
Specialities: Roses, herbaceous, shrubs, trees & hedging plants.
Notes: Mail order roses only. Also sells wholesale.
Map Ref: S, C6 **OS Grid Ref:** TR276567

SLBF **Little Brook Fuchsias** ♿
Ash Green Lane West, Ash Green,
Nr Aldershot, Hampshire GU12 6HL
Ⓣ (01252) 329731
Ⓔ carol.gubler@ntlbusiness.com
Ⓦ www.littlebrookfuchsias.co.uk
Contact: Carol Gubler
Opening Times: 1000-1700 Wed-Sun 1st Jan-3rd Jul.
Cat. Cost: 50p + sae.
Credit Cards: All major credit/debit cards
Specialities: Fuchsias, old & new.
Notes: Nursery located off White Lane in Ash Green.
Map Ref: S, C3 **OS Grid Ref:** SU901496

SLdr **Loder Plants** ⊠ ⊠ ⌂ € ♿
Market Garden, Lower Beeding, West Sussex
RH13 6PP
Ⓣ (01403) 891412
Ⓔ sales@rhododendrons.com
Ⓦ www.rhododendrons.com
Contact: Chris Loder
Opening Times: 1000-1600 Mon-Sat, please ring first so we can try to give you our undivided attention.
Min Mail Order UK: Nmc
Min Mail Order EU: Nmc
Cat. Cost: 2 × 1st class.
Credit Cards: All, except American Express
Specialities: Rhododendrons & azaleas in all sizes. Some in very ltd. quantities only.
Notes: Also sells wholesale.
Map Ref: S, C3 **OS Grid Ref:** TQ221255

SLim **Lime Cross Nursery** ⊠ ♿ ◆
Herstmonceux, Hailsham, East Sussex,
BN27 4RS
Ⓣ (01323) 833229
Ⓕ (01323) 833944
Ⓔ info@limecross.co.uk
Ⓦ www.limecross.co.uk
Contact: Jonathan Tate, Anita Green
Opening Times: 0830-1700 Mon-Sat & 1000-1600 Sun.
Min Mail Order UK: Nmc
Min Mail Order EU: £50.00
Cat. Cost: Free of charge.
Credit Cards: All major credit/debit cards
Specialities: Conifers, trees & shrubs, climbers.
Notes: Also sells wholesale.
Map Ref: S, D4 **OS Grid Ref:** TQ642125

SLon **Longstock Park Nursery** ⊠ ♿
Longstock, Stockbridge, Hampshire
SO20 6EH
Ⓣ (01264) 810894
Ⓕ (01264) 810924
Ⓔ longstocknursery@leckfordestate.co.uk
Ⓦ www.longstocknursery.co.uk
Contact: David Roberts
Opening Times: 0830-1630 Mon-Sat all year excl. Xmas & New Year, & 1100-1700 Sun Mar-Oct, 1000-1600 Sun, Nov-Feb.
Min Mail Order UK: Nmc
Cat. Cost: 2 × 1st class or email for lists of *Buddleja*, *Penstemon*, roses & fruit.
Credit Cards: All major credit/debit cards
Specialities: A wide range, over 2000 varieties, of trees, shrubs, perennials, climbers, aquatics & ferns. Nat. Collections of *Buddleja* & *Clematis viticella*.
Notes: Mail order for *Buddleja* only.
Map Ref: S, C2 **OS Grid Ref:** SO365389

SLPl **LANDSCAPE PLANTS** ⊠ ✈ ♿
Stocks Studio, Grafty Green, Maidstone, Kent ME17 2AP
Ⓣ (01622) 850245
Ⓕ (01622) 858063
Ⓔ landscapeplants@aol.com
Contact: Tom La Dell
Opening Times: 0800-1600 Mon-Fri, by appt. only.
Min Mail Order UK: £100.00 + p&p
Min Mail Order EU: £200.00 + p&p
Cat. Cost: 2 × 1st class.
Credit Cards: None
Specialities: Garden & landscape shrubs & perennials.
Notes: Also sells wholesale.
Map Ref: S, C5 **OS Grid Ref:** TQ772468

SMad **MADRONA NURSERY** ⊠ ⌂ € ♿
Pluckley Road, Bethersden, Kent TN26 3DD
Ⓣ (01233) 820100
Ⓕ (01233) 820091
Ⓔ madrona@hotmail.co.uk
Ⓦ www.madrona.co.uk
Contact: Liam MacKenzie
Opening Times: 1000-1700 Sat-Tue 19th Mar-31st Oct. Other times by appt.
Min Mail Order UK: Nmc
Cat. Cost: Free.
Credit Cards: All major credit/debit cards
Specialities: Unusual shrubs, conifers & perennials. Eryngiums, *Pseudopanax*.
Notes: Some plants too large to send.
Map Ref: S, C5 **OS Grid Ref:** TQ918419

SMDP **MARCUS DANCER PLANTS** ⊠ ⌂
Kilcreggan, Alderholt Road, Sandleheath, Fordingbridge, Hampshire SP6 1PT
Ⓣ (01425) 652747
Ⓜ 07709 922730
Ⓔ marcus.dancer@btopenworld.com
Ⓦ clematisplants.co.uk
Contact: Marcus Dancer
Opening Times: By appointment only.
Min Mail Order UK: Nmc
Cat. Cost: 4 × 1st class.
Credit Cards: None
Specialities: Wide range of *Clematis*, smaller range of *Daphne*. Some varieties available in small quantities only.
Map Ref: S, D1

SMea **MEADOWGATE NURSERY** ⊠ ⌂
Street End Lane, Sidlesham, Chichester, West Sussex PO20 7RG
Ⓣ (01243) 641997
Ⓜ 07736 523262
Ⓔ meadowgatenursery@tiscali.co.uk
Ⓦ www.meadowgatenursery.co.uk
Contact: David Allen
Opening Times: 1000-1700 Sat-Wed.
Min Mail Order UK: Nmc
Credit Cards: All major credit/debit cards
Specialities: Ornamental grasses and complimentary perennials.

SMHy **MARCHANTS HARDY PLANTS** € ♿
2 Marchants Cottages, Mill Lane, Laughton, East Sussex BN8 6AJ
Ⓣ (01323) 811737
Ⓕ (01323) 811737
Contact: Graham Gough
Opening Times: 0930-1730 Wed-Sat, 16th Mar-22nd Oct 2011.
Cat. Cost: 6 × 2nd class.
Credit Cards: Visa, MasterCard
Specialities: Uncommon herbaceous perennials. *Agapanthus*, *Erodium*, *Sedum*, choice grasses, *Miscanthus*, *Molinia*.
Map Ref: S, D4 **OS Grid Ref:** TQ506119

SMor **MOREHAVENS** ⊠ € ♿
Stocks Lane, Meonstoke, Hampshire SO32 3NQ
Ⓣ (01489) 878501
Ⓔ morehavens@hotmail.co.uk
Ⓦ www.camomilelawns.co.uk
Contact: E. Clements
Opening Times: Mail order only. Open only for collection.
Min Mail Order UK: £15.00
Min Mail Order EU: £15.00 + p&p
Cat. Cost: Free.
Credit Cards: Paypal
Specialities: *Camomile nobile* 'Treneague' and *C. nobile* dwarf.
Notes: Accepts payment in euros by Paypal only. Also sells wholesale.

SMrm **MERRIMENTS GARDENS** ♿
Hawkhurst Road, Hurst Green, East Sussex TN19 7RA
Ⓣ (01580) 860666
Ⓕ (01580) 860324
Ⓔ shop@merriments.co.uk
Ⓦ www.merriments.co.uk
Contact: Taryn Murrells
Opening Times: 0900-1730 Mon-Sat, 1030-1730 Sun (or dusk in winter).
Cat. Cost: Online only.
Credit Cards: Visa, Access, American Express

KEY
⊠ Mail order to UK or EU ⌂ Delivers to shows
✈ Exports beyond EU € Euro accepted
♿ Accessible by wheelchair ◆ See Display advertisement

S

Specialities: Extensive range of unusual perennials, tender perennials, grasses & annuals. Also large selection of roses & seasonal shrubs. 4-acre show garden.
Map Ref: S, C4

SMrs **MRS MITCHELL'S KITCHEN & GARDEN** ⌂ €
2 Warren Farm Cottages, The Warren, West Tytherley, Salisbury, Wiltshire SP5 1LU
Ⓣ (01980) 863101
Ⓔ julianm05@aol.com
Ⓦ www.mrsmitchellskitchenandgarden.co.uk
Contact: Louise Mitchell
Opening Times: 1400-1700 Fri & Sat, Aug & Sep. All other times by appt. only.
Cat. Cost: Online only.
Credit Cards: None
Specialities: Family-run nursery stocking less usual cottage garden plants, esp. hardy geraniums, oriental poppies, *Phlox*, Michaelmas daisies & *Chrysanthemum*. Some items in small quantities. Most plants grown in peat-free compost.
Notes: Despite postal designation, nursery is in Hampshire. Accessible, but difficult, for wheelchairs because of deep gravel. Sells mostly at plant shows & farmers' markets. See website for details of shows & markets attended.
Map Ref: S, C2 **OS Grid Ref:** SU261333

SPad **PADDOCK PLANTS** ⊠ ⌂
The Paddock, Upper Toothill Road, Rownhams, Southampton, Hampshire SO16 8AL
Ⓣ (023) 8073 9912
Ⓜ 07763 386717
Ⓔ rob@paddockplants.co.uk
Ⓦ www.paddockplants.co.uk
Contact: Robert Courtney
Opening Times: By appt. only. Please telephone in advance.
Min Mail Order UK: Nmc
Cat. Cost: Online only.
Credit Cards: All major credit/debit cards
Specialities: Family-run nursery offering interesting range of perennials, grasses, ferns & shrubs, incl. some more unusual varieties. Some varieties grown in small quantities.
Notes: Credit cards only accepted for online orders. Local delivery by our own transport.
Map Ref: S, D2 **OS Grid Ref:** SU383177

SPav **PAVILION PLANTS** ⊠
18 Pavilion Road, Worthing, West Sussex BN14 7EF
Ⓣ (01903) 821338
Ⓔ rewrew18@hotmail.com
Contact: Andrew Muggeridge
Opening Times: Mail order only. Please phone for details.
Min Mail Order UK: Nmc
Cat. Cost: 4 × 1st class.
Credit Cards: None
Specialities: Perennials and bulbs. *Digitalis*.
Map Ref: S, D3

SPer **PERRYHILL NURSERIES LTD** ⊠ ♿
Edenbridge Road, Hartfield, East Sussex TN7 4JP
Ⓣ (01892) 770377
Ⓕ (01892) 770929
Ⓔ sales@perryhillnurseries.co.uk
Ⓦ www.perryhillnurseries.co.uk
Contact: P J Chapman
Opening Times: 0900-1700 7 days 1st Mar-31st Oct. 0900-1630 1st Nov-28th Feb.
Min Mail Order UK: Nmc
Cat. Cost: Online only.
Credit Cards: Maestro, Visa, Access, MasterCard
Specialities: Wide range of trees, shrubs, perennials, roses, fruit trees, soft fruit. Unusual & rare plants may be available in small quantities.
Notes: Mail order despatch depends on size & weight of plants.
Map Ref: S, C4 **OS Grid Ref:** TQ480375

SPet **PETTET'S NURSERY** ⌂ ♿
Poison Cross, Eastry, Sandwich, Kent CT13 0EA
Ⓣ (01304) 613869
Ⓜ 07961 998354
Ⓕ (01304) 613869
Ⓔ terry@pettetsnursery.fsnet.co.uk
Ⓦ www.pettetsnursery.co.uk
Contact: T & E H P Pettet
Opening Times: 0900-1700 daily Mar-Jun. 1000-1600 Jul-Oct weekdays only.
Credit Cards: None
Specialities: *Clematis*, herbaceous perennials, pelargoniums, fuchsias.
Map Ref: S, C6

SPhx **PHOENIX PERENNIAL PLANTS** ⌂ ♿
Paice Lane, Medstead, Alton, Hampshire GU34 5PR
Ⓣ (01420) 560695
Ⓕ (01420) 563640
Ⓔ marina@phoenixperennialplants.co.uk
Ⓦ www.phoenixperennialplants.co.uk
Contact: Marina Christopher
Opening Times: 1100-1700 Fri & Sat 25th Mar-22nd Oct 2011. Other times by appt. only.

Cat. Cost: 4 × 1st class.
Credit Cards: All major credit/debit cards
Specialities: Perennials, many uncommon. *Achillea*, *Eryngium*, hardy chrysanthemums, *Monarda*, *Phlox*, *Sanguisorba*, *Thalictrum*, *Verbascum*, centaureas, bulbs, prairie plants, grasses, especially *Molinia* & late-flowering perennials.
Notes: Co-located with Select Seeds SSss. Also sells wholesale.
Map Ref: S, C2 **OS Grid Ref:** SU657362

SPin **John and Lynsey's Plants** ♿
2 Hillside Cottages, Trampers Lane, North Boarhunt, Fareham, Hampshire PO17 6DA
Ⓣ (01329) 832786
Contact: Mrs Lynsey Pink
Opening Times: By appt. only. Open under NGS.
Cat. Cost: None issued.
Credit Cards: None
Specialities: Mainly *Salvia* with a wide range of other unusual perennials. Stock is only available in small quantities but we are happy to try & propagate anything that we have. Nat. Collection of species *Salvia*.
Map Ref: S, D2 **OS Grid Ref:** SU603109

SPlb **Plantbase** ⊠ ⛺ € ♿
Sleepers Stile Road, Cousley Wood, Wadhurst, East Sussex TN5 6QX
Ⓣ (01892) 785599
Ⓜ 07967 601064
Ⓔ graham@plantbase.freeserve.co.uk
Ⓦ www.plantbase.co.uk
Contact: Graham Blunt
Opening Times: 1000-1700, 7 days all year (appt. advisable).
Min Mail Order UK: Nmc
Min Mail Order EU: Nmc
Cat. Cost: Online only.
Credit Cards: All major credit/debit cards
Specialities: Wide range of alpines, perennials, shrubs, climbers, waterside plants, herbs, Australasian, South African & South American plants in particular. Some available in small quantities only.
Map Ref: S, C5

SPoG **The Potted Garden Nursery** ♿
Ashford Road, Bearsted, Maidstone, Kent ME14 4NH
Ⓣ (01622) 737801
Ⓦ www.thepottedgarden.co.uk
Contact: Any staff member
Opening Times: 0900-1730 (dusk in winter) 7 days. Xmas/New Year period opening times on website or answerphone.
Credit Cards: All major credit/debit cards
Notes: Mail order not available.
Map Ref: S, C5 **OS Grid Ref:** TQ810550

SPol **Pollie's Perennials and Daylily Nursery** ⊠ € ♿
Lodore, Mount Pleasant Lane, Sway, Lymington, Hampshire SO41 8LS
Ⓣ (01590) 682577
Ⓕ (01590) 682577
Ⓔ terry@maasz.fsnet.co.uk
Ⓦ www.polliesdaylilies.co.uk
Contact: Pollie Maasz
Opening Times: 1000-1730 w/ends & 1400-1730 Mon-Fri during the daylily season, late-May to mid-Aug. Other times by appt. only.
Min Mail Order UK: Nmc
Min Mail Order EU: £20.00
Cat. Cost: 2 × 1st class.
Credit Cards: None
Specialities: *Hemerocallis*, also less commonly available hardy perennials. Stock available in small quantities only. Nat. Collection of Spider & Unusual Form *Hemerocallis*. 1400+ different cvs can be viewed, mid Jun-mid Sep.
Notes: Mail order, daylilies only.
Map Ref: S, D2

SPop **Pops Plants** ⊠ ✈ ⛺ €
Pops Cottage, Barford Lane, Downton, Salisbury, Wiltshire SP5 3PZ
Ⓣ (01725) 511421
Ⓔ mail@popsplants.com
Ⓦ www.popsplants.com
Contact: Lesley Roberts
Opening Times: By appt. only, please.
Min Mail Order UK: 5 plants.
Min Mail Order EU: 5 plants.
Cat. Cost: £2.00
Specialities: *Primula auricula*. Some varieties in ltd. numbers. Nat. Collection of Show, Alpine, Double & Striped Auriculas.
Notes: Credit cards accepted online only. Min. mail order outside EU, 10 plants.

SPtl **Petals for Plants** ♿
Burwash Road, Broad Oak, Heathfield, East Sussex TN21 8XG
Ⓣ (01435) 884111
Ⓔ pauleast@petalsforplants.co.uk
Ⓦ www.petalsforplants.co.uk
Contact: Paul East

KEY
⊠ Mail order to UK or EU — ⛺ Delivers to shows
✈ Exports beyond EU — € Euro accepted
♿ Accessible by wheelchair — ◆ See Display advertisement

S

Opening Times: 0900-1730 Mon-Sat, 1015-1630 Sun (summer). 0900-1700 Mon-Sat, 1015-1630 Sun (winter).
Credit Cards: All, except American Express
Specialities: Shrubs, roses, perennials, fruit & ornamental trees, conifers, acers & climbers.
Map Ref: S, C4 **OS Grid Ref:** TQ6021

SReu **G Reuthe Ltd** ⊠
Crown Point Nursery, Sevenoaks Road, Ightham, Nr Sevenoaks, Kent TN15 0HB
Ⓣ (01732) 865614
Ⓕ (01732) 862166
Ⓔ reuthe@hotmail.co.uk
Contact: C & P Tomlin
Opening Times: 0900-1600 Thu-Sat. Closed Jan, Jul & Aug.
Min Mail Order UK: £30.00 + p&p
Min Mail Order EU: £500.00
Cat. Cost: £2.50
Credit Cards: Visa, Access
Specialities: Rhododendrons & azaleas, trees, shrubs & climbers.
Notes: Mail order certain plants only to EU.
Map Ref: S, C4

SRGP **Rosie's Garden Plants** ⊠ ⊠ ⌂
Fieldview Cottage, Pratling Street, Aylesford, Kent ME20 7DG
Ⓣ (01622) 715777
Ⓜ 07740 696277
Ⓕ (01622) 715777
Ⓔ jcaviolet@aol.com
Ⓦ www.rosiesgardenplants.biz
Contact: J C Aviolet
Opening Times: Not open. Mail order only.
Min Mail Order UK: Nmc
Min Mail Order EU: Nmc
Cat. Cost: Online only.
Specialities: Hardy *Geranium*, *Buddleja* & *Aster*. 'Named' herbaceous & shrubs. Roses.
Notes: Check web for dates of shows, talks & Farmers Markets.

SRiv **River Garden Nurseries** ⊠ ⌂ €
Troutbeck, Otford, Sevenoaks, Kent TN14 5PH
Ⓣ (01959) 525588
Ⓕ (01959) 525810
Ⓔ box@river-garden.co.uk
Ⓦ www.river-garden.co.uk
Contact: Jenny Alban Davies
Opening Times: By appt. only.
Min Mail Order UK: £10.00 + p&p
Min Mail Order EU: £50.00 + p&p
Cat. Cost: 2 × 1st class.
Credit Cards: All major credit/debit cards
Specialities: *Buxus* species, cultivars & *Buxus* hedging. *Buxus* topiary.
Notes: Also sells wholesale.
Map Ref: S, C4 **OS Grid Ref:** TQ523593

SRkn **Rapkyns Nursery** ⊠ ⌂ ♿
Street End Lane, Broad Oak, Heathfield, East Sussex TN21 8UB
Ⓣ (01825) 830065
Ⓜ 07771 916933
Ⓕ (01825) 830065
Ⓔ rapkyns@homecall.co.uk
Ⓦ www.rapkynsnursery.co.uk
Contact: Steven & Fiona Moore
Opening Times: 1000-1700 Tue, Thu & Fri, Mar-Oct incl.
Min Mail Order UK: Nmc
Min Mail Order EU: Nmc
Cat. Cost: 2 × 1st class or online.
Credit Cards: None
Specialities: Unusual shrubs, perennials & climbers. Asters, Campanulas, *Ceanothus*, geraniums, lavenders, *Clematis*, penstemons & grasses. New collections of *Phormium*, *Crocosmia*, *Anemone*, *Heuchera*, *Heucherella*, *Echinacea*, *Phlox*, *Coreopsis*, *Helleborus* & *Kniphofia*. Extensive range of salvias.
Notes: Nursery next door to Scotsford Farm, TN21 8UB. Mail order Sep-Apr incl. Also sells wholesale.
Map Ref: S, C4 **OS Grid Ref:** TQ604248

SRms **Rumsey Gardens** ⊠ ♿ ◆
117 Drift Road, Clanfield, Waterlooville, Hampshire PO8 0PD
Ⓣ (023) 9259 3367
Ⓔ info@rumsey-gardens.co.uk
Ⓦ www.rumsey-gardens.co.uk
Contact: Mrs M A Giles
Opening Times: 0900-1700 Mon-Sat & 1000-1600 Sun & B/hols. Closed Sun Nov-Feb.
Min Mail Order UK: £15.00
Cat. Cost: Online only.
Credit Cards: Visa, MasterCard, Switch
Specialities: Wide general range. Herbaceous, alpines, heathers & ferns. Nat. & International Collection of *Cotoneaster*.
Map Ref: S, D2

SRot **Rotherview Nursery** ⊠ ⌂ € ♿
Ivy House Lane, Three Oaks, Hastings, East Sussex TN35 4NP
Ⓣ (01424) 756228
Ⓔ rotherview@btinternet.com
Ⓦ www.rotherview.com
Contact: Ray & Wendy Bates

Opening Times: 1000-1700 Mar-Oct, 1000-1530 Nov-Feb, 7 days.
Min Mail Order UK: Nmc
Min Mail Order EU: Nmc
Cat. Cost: 6 × 1st class.
Credit Cards: All major credit/debit cards
Specialities: Alpines.
Notes: Nursery is on same site as Coghurst Camellias. Also sells wholesale.
Map Ref: S, D5

SSea **SEALE NURSERIES** ♿
Seale Lane, Seale, Farnham, Surrey
GU10 1LD
Ⓣ (01252) 782410
Ⓔ catherine@sealenurseries.demon.co.uk
Ⓦ www.sealenurseries.co.uk
Contact: David & Catherine May
Opening Times: 1000-1600 Tue-Sat incl. Other times by appt. Closed 25th Dec-mid Jan.
Cat. Cost: None issued.
Credit Cards: Visa, Access, Delta, MasterCard
Specialities: Roses & *Pelargonium*. Some varieties in short supply, please phone first.
Map Ref: S, C3 **OS Grid Ref:** SU887477

SSpi **SPINNERS GARDEN** ♿
School Lane, Boldre, Lymington, Hampshire
SO41 5QE
Ⓣ (01590) 675488
Ⓜ 07545 432090
Ⓔ info@spinnersgarden.co.uk
Ⓦ www.spinnersgarden.co.uk
Contact: Andrew Roberts
Opening Times: 1000-1700 Mon-Sat, Mar-Oct. By appt. only Nov, Dec, Jan & Feb.
Cat. Cost: Sae for plant list.
Credit Cards: All major credit/debit cards
Specialities: Less common trees & shrubs esp. *Acer*, *Magnolia*, species & lacecap *Hydrangea*.

SSss **SELECT SEEDS** ⊠ ♿
Paice Lane, Medstead, Nr Alton, Hampshire
GU34 5PR
Ⓣ (01420) 560695
Ⓕ (01420) 563640
Ⓔ marina@phoenixperennialplants.co.uk
Contact: Marina Christopher
Opening Times: Not open. Mail order only.
Min Mail Order UK: £10.00
Cat. Cost: 3 × 1st class.
Credit Cards: All major credit/debit cards
Specialities: Seeds. *Aconitum*, *Eryngium*, *Thalictrum*, *Sanguisorba* & *Angelica*.
Notes: Only sells seed by mail order. Credit cards not accepted by phone. Co-located with Phoenix Perennial Plants SPhx.
Map Ref: S, C2 **OS Grid Ref:** SU657362

SSta **STARBOROUGH NURSERY** ⊠ ♿
Starborough Road, Marsh Green, Edenbridge, Kent
TN8 5RB
Ⓣ (01732) 865614
Ⓕ (01732) 862166
Ⓔ starborough@hotmail.co.uk
Contact: C & P Tomlin
Opening Times: 0900-1600 Thu, Fri & Sat. Closed Jan, Jul & Aug.
Min Mail Order UK: £30.00 + p&p
Min Mail Order EU: Certain plants only to EU.
Cat. Cost: £2.50
Credit Cards: Visa, Access
Specialities: Rare and unusual shrubs esp. *Daphne*, *Acer*, *Cercis*, rhododendrons & azaleas, *Magnolia* & *Nyssa*.

SSvw **SOUTHVIEW NURSERIES** ⊠
Chequers Lane, Eversley Cross, Hook, Hampshire
RG27 0NT
Ⓣ (0118) 9732206
Ⓔ Mark@Trenear.freeserve.co.uk
Ⓦ www.southviewnurseries.co.uk
Contact: Mark & Elaine Trenear
Opening Times: By appt. Apr-Jun only.
Min Mail Order UK: Nmc
Cat. Cost: Free.
Credit Cards: None
Specialities: Unusual hardy plants. Nat. Collection of Old Pinks. Good selection of hardy chrysanthemums, asters, geraniums & other perennials.
Notes: Orders by prior arrangement only. Talks given to garden societies & groups.
Map Ref: S, C3 **OS Grid Ref:** SU795612

STes **TEST VALLEY NURSERY** ⊠
Stockbridge Road, Timsbury, Romsey, Hampshire
SO51 0NG
Ⓣ (01794) 368881
Ⓔ george@testvalleynursery.co.uk
Ⓦ www.testvalleynursery.co.uk
Contact: George Benn
Opening Times: Not open. Mail order only.
Min Mail Order UK: Nmc
Specialities: Large range of herbaceous perennials, incl. unusual & new varieties. Some varieties available in small quantities only. Phone first to avoid disappointment.
Map Ref: S, C2

KEY
⊠ Mail order to UK or EU — Delivers to shows
Exports beyond EU — € Euro accepted
♿ Accessible by wheelchair — ◆ See Display advertisement

STrG **Terrace Gardener** ✉ €
8 Foxbush, Hildenborough, Kent TN11 9HT
Ⓣ (01732) 832762
Ⓔ johan@terracegardener.com
Ⓦ www.terracegardener.co.uk
Contact: Mr J Hall
Opening Times: Not open. Mail order only, incl. online & by phone. Telephone orders 0800-1700 Mon-Fri.
Min Mail Order UK: Nmc
Cat. Cost: Free.
Credit Cards: All major credit/debit cards
Specialities: Mediterranean trees & plants. Container gardening. Architectural & hardy exotics.

SUsu **Usual & Unusual Plants** €
Onslow House, Magham Down, Hailsham, East Sussex BN27 1PL
Ⓣ (01323) 840967
Ⓔ jennie@uuplants.co.uk
Ⓦ www.uuplants.co.uk
Contact: Jennie Maillard
Opening Times: 0930-1730 Wed-Sat, 17th Mar-16th Oct. Other times can be arranged but strictly by appt. only.
Cat. Cost: £2.00 + sae or online.
Credit Cards: None
Specialities: Small quantities of a wide variety of unusual garden-worthy perennials esp. *Agapanthus*, *Echinacea*, *Erysimum*, *Euphorbia*, *Geum*, hardy *Geranium*, *Salvia*, *Sanguisorba*, *Sedum*, *Thalictrum* & grasses.
Map Ref: S, D4 **OS Grid Ref:** TQ607113

S

SVic **Victoriana Nursery Gardens** ✉
Challock, Ashford, Kent TN25 4DG
Ⓣ (01233) 740529
Ⓕ 0203 292 1529
Ⓔ For email, use contact form on website.
Ⓦ www.victoriananursery.co.uk
Contact: Serena Shirley
Opening Times: 0930-1630 (or dusk if sooner) Mon-Fri, 1030-1500 (or dusk if sooner) Sat.
Min Mail Order UK: £1.95
Cat. Cost: Free by post or online.
Credit Cards: All major credit/debit cards
Specialities: Heritage & unusual vegetable plants, seeds, fruit trees & bushes. Also 600+ varieties of *Fuchsia*.
Notes: Also sells wholesale.
Map Ref: S, C5 **OS Grid Ref:** TR018501

SWal **Wallace Plants**
Lewes Road Nursery, Lewes Road (B2124), Laughton, East Sussex BN8 6BN
Ⓣ (01323) 811729
Ⓔ plants@wallace-plants.co.uk
Ⓦ www.wallace-plants.co.uk
Contact: Simon Wallace
Opening Times: 1000-1800 Mar-Sep, 1000-1600 Oct-Feb. 7 days, incl. B/hols.
Cat. Cost: 2 × 1st class for availability list.
Credit Cards: None
Specialities: Ornamental grasses, hebes, herbaceous/perennials, shrubs, salvias, herbs, cacti & choice, rare & unusual plants.
Map Ref: S, D4 **OS Grid Ref:** TQ513126

SWat **Water Meadow Nursery** ✉
Cheriton, Nr Alresford, Hampshire SO24 0QB
Ⓣ (01962) 771895
Ⓔ plantaholic@onetel.com
Ⓦ www.plantaholic.co.uk
Contact: Mrs Sandy Worth
Opening Times: 1000-1700 Wed-Sat, Mar-Jul. 1000-1700 or dusk Fri & Sat, Aug-Oct. Due to staff costs, please phone first.
Min Mail Order UK: £10.00 + p&p
Min Mail Order EU: £50.00 + p&p
Cat. Cost: Full catalogue online only. 2 × 1st class for individual plant lists, please indicate with application.
Credit Cards: All major credit/debit cards
Specialities: Water lilies, extensive water garden plants, unusual herbaceous perennials, aromatic herbs & wildflowers. New Super Poppy Range. Nat. Collection of *Papaver orientale* Group & the Re-blooming *Papaver* Super Poppy Series.
Notes: Mail order by 24 or 48 hour courier service only. Also sells wholesale.
Map Ref: S, C2

SWCr **Wych Cross Nurseries** ✉
Wych Cross, Forest Row, East Sussex RH18 5JW
Ⓣ (01342) 822705
Ⓕ (01342) 828246
Ⓔ jp@wychcross.co.uk
Ⓦ www.wychcross.co.uk
Contact: J Paisley
Opening Times: 0900-1730 Mon-Sat.
Min Mail Order UK: Nmc
Cat. Cost: Free.
Credit Cards: All major credit/debit cards
Specialities: Roses.
Map Ref: S, C4 **OS Grid Ref:** TQ420320

SWhi **John Hall Plants Ltd** ✉ €
Whitehall Nursery, Red Lane (Off Churt Road), Headley Down, Hampshire GU35 8SR
Ⓣ (01428) 715505
Ⓜ 07714 344327

Ⓔ info@johnhallplants.com
Ⓦ www.johnhallplants.com
Contact: John Hall
Opening Times: 0900-1630 Mon-Fri, 0900-1300 Sat, by appt. only.
Min Mail Order UK: Nmc
Min Mail Order EU: Nmc
Cat. Cost: By email only.
Credit Cards: None
Specialities: *Erica* and *Calluna*.
Notes: Also sells wholesale.
Map Ref: S, C3 **OS Grid Ref:** SU837371

SWvt **WOLVERTON PLANTS LTD** € ♿ ◆
Wolverton Common, Tadley, Hampshire RG26 5RU
Ⓣ (01635) 298453
Ⓕ (01635) 299075
Ⓔ Julian@wolvertonplants.co.uk
Ⓦ www.wolvertonplants.co.uk
Contact: Julian Jones
Opening Times: 0900-1800 (or dusk Nov-Feb), 7 days. Closed Xmas/New Year.
Cat. Cost: Online only.
Credit Cards: All major credit/debit cards
Specialities: Wide range of herbaceous perennials & shrubs grown on a commercial scale for the public.
Notes: Also sells wholesale. Horticultural club visits welcome by prior arrangement.
Map Ref: S, C2 **OS Grid Ref:** SU555589

WALES AND THE WEST

WAba **ABACUS NURSERIES** ⊠
Drummau Road, Skewen, Neath, West Glamorgan SA10 6NW
Ⓣ (01792) 817994
Ⓔ plants@abacus-nurseries.co.uk
Ⓦ www.abacus-nurseries.co.uk
Contact: David Hill
Opening Times: Not open to the public. Collection by arrangement.
Min Mail Order UK: Nmc
Cat. Cost: 2 × 2nd class.
Credit Cards: None
Specialities: *Dahlia*.

WAbb **ABBEY DORE COURT GARDEN** € ♿
Abbey Dore Court, Abbey Dore, Herefordshire, HR2 0AD
Ⓣ (01981) 240419
Ⓕ (01981) 240419
Ⓦ www.abbeydorecourt.co.uk
Contact: Mrs C Ward
Opening Times: Garden & nursery open Apr-Sep any day. A prior phone call is essential if coming any distance.
Cat. Cost: None issued.
Credit Cards: None
Specialities: Mainly hardy perennials, many unusual, which may be seen growing in the garden. *Astrantia*, *Crocosmia*, *Helleborus*, *Paeonia*, *Pulmonaria* & *Sedum*.
Map Ref: W, C4 **OS Grid Ref:** SO388308

WAbe **ABERCONWY NURSERY** 🏠
Graig, Glan Conwy, Colwyn Bay, Conwy LL28 5TL
Ⓣ (01492) 580875
Contact: Keith & Tim Lever
Opening Times: 1000-1600 Tue-Sun Mar-Sep incl.
Cat. Cost: 2 × 2nd class.
Credit Cards: Visa, MasterCard
Specialities: Alpines, including specialist varieties, esp. gentians, dionysias, dwarf *Dianthus*, *Primula*, *Saxifraga* & dwarf ericaceous plants. Some choice shrubs & woodland plants incl. smaller ferns.
Map Ref: W, A3 **OS Grid Ref:** SH799744

WAln **L A ALLEN** ⊠
Windy Ridge, Llandrindod Wells, Powys LD1 5NY
Ⓔ leslie.allen@mypostoffice.co.uk
Contact: Les Allen
Opening Times: By prior appt.
Min Mail Order UK: Nmc
Min Mail Order EU: Nmc
Cat. Cost: 6 × 1st class.
Credit Cards: None
Specialities: All sections of *Primula auricula*. Type: alpine auricula, show edged, show self, doubles, show stripes. Surplus plants from private collection so available in small quantities. Occasionally only 1 or 2 available of some cvs.
Notes: Also sells wholesale.

WAul **AULDEN FARM** ⊠
Aulden, Leominster, Herefordshire HR6 0JT
Ⓣ (01568) 720129
Ⓔ pf@auldenfarm.co.uk
Ⓦ www.auldenfarm.co.uk
Contact: Alun & Jill Whitehead
Opening Times: 1000-1700 Tue & Thu Apr-Aug. Thu only in Sep. Other times by appt. Please phone.
Min Mail Order UK: Nmc
Min Mail Order EU: £20.00

KEY
⊠ Mail order to UK or EU 🏠 Delivers to shows
✈ Exports beyond EU € Euro accepted
♿ Accessible by wheelchair ◆ See Display advertisement

Cat. Cost: 2 × 1st class.
Credit Cards: Paypal
Specialities: Hardy herbaceous perennials, with a special interest in *Hemerocallis* & *Iris*. Nat. Collection of Siberian *Iris*.
Notes: Mail order available for small quantities. Garden & nursery open for NGS, see website for details. Groups welcome. Talks given.
Map Ref: W, C4 **OS Grid Ref:** SO462548

WBla **BLACK MOUNTAIN AURICULAS** ⊠ ⌂ € ♿
Whitegrove Nurseries, Fferm Gelliwen, Llanedi, Pontardulais, Swansea, West Glamorgan SA4 0FR
Ⓣ (01269) 832509
Ⓜ 07967 488782
Ⓕ (01269) 832509
Ⓔ whitegrovenurseries@tiscali.co.uk
Contact: Richard Williams
Opening Times: By prior appt. only.
Min Mail Order UK: Nmc
Min Mail Order EU: £50
Cat. Cost: 2 x 1st class.
Credit Cards: None
Specialities: *Primula auricula*. Many cultivars available in very small quantities only.
Map Ref: W, D3 **OS Grid Ref:** SN573083

WBor **BORDERVALE PLANTS** ⊠ ⌂ ♿
Nantyderi, Sandy Lane, Ystradowen, Cowbridge, Vale of Glamorgan CF71 7SX
Ⓣ (01446) 774036
Ⓔ lonytwod@googlemail.com
Contact: Claire E Jenkins
Opening Times: 1000-1700 Fri-Sun & B/hols Mar-early Oct. Other times please phone.
Min Mail Order UK: £20.00 + p&p
Cat. Cost: 3 × 1st class.
Credit Cards: None
Specialities: Unusual herbaceous perennials, trees & shrubs, as well as cottage garden plants, many displayed in the 2-acre garden.
Notes: Mail order available for smaller items, subject to season. Garden open May-Sep when nursery open. Also open for NGS. See website for details.
Map Ref: W, D3 **OS Grid Ref:** ST022776

WBou **BOUTS COTTAGE NURSERIES** ⊠ ⌂ €
Bouts Lane, Inkberrow, Worcestershire WR7 4HP
Ⓣ (01386) 792923
Ⓦ www.boutsviolas.co.uk
Contact: M & S Roberts
Opening Times: Strictly by appt. only.
Min Mail Order UK: Nmc
Min Mail Order EU: Nmc
Cat. Cost: 1st class sae.
Credit Cards: None
Specialities: *Viola*.

WBrk **BROCKAMIN PLANTS** ⌂ ♿
Brockamin, Old Hills, Callow End, Worcestershire WR2 4TQ
Ⓣ (01905) 830370
Ⓔ dickstonebrockamin@tinyworld.co.uk
Contact: Margaret Stone
Opening Times: By appt. only.
Cat. Cost: Free.
Credit Cards: None
Specialities: Nat. Collections of *Aster novae-angliae*, *Erigeron* cvs, *Geranium sanguineum*, *G. macrorrhizum* & *G. × cantabrigiense*. Plants available in small quantities only.
Map Ref: W, C5 **OS Grid Ref:** SO830488

WBuc **BUCKNELL NURSERIES** ⊠
Bucknell, Shropshire SY7 0EL
Ⓣ (01547) 530606
Ⓕ (01547) 530699
Ⓔ nickcoull@yahoo.co.uk
Contact: A N Coull
Opening Times: 0800-1700 Mon-Fri & 1000-1300 Sat.
Min Mail Order UK: Nmc
Cat. Cost: Free.
Credit Cards: All major credit/debit cards
Specialities: Bare-rooted hedging conifers & forest trees.
Notes: Also sells wholesale.

WCAu **CLAIRE AUSTIN HARDY PLANTS** ⊠ €
Edgebolton, Shawbury, Shrewsbury, Shropshire SY4 4EL
Ⓣ (01939) 251173
Ⓕ (01939) 251311
Ⓔ enquiries@claireaustin-hardyplants.co.uk
Ⓦ www.claireaustin-hardyplants.co.uk
Contact: Claire Austin
Opening Times: Open during Jun when iris field is in flower. See website for details.
Min Mail Order UK: Nmc
Min Mail Order EU: Nmc
Cat. Cost: UK free; Europe €7.00
Credit Cards: MasterCard, Visa, Switch
Specialities: *Paeonia*, *Iris*, *Hemerocallis* & hardy plants. Nat. Collections of Bearded *Iris* & Hybrid Herbaceous *Paeonia*.
Map Ref: W, B4

WCFE **CHARLES F ELLIS** ⊠ €
Oak Piece Nurseries, Stanton, Nr Broadway, Worcestershire WR12 7NQ
Ⓣ (01386) 584077
Ⓕ (01386) 584491

Ⓔ ellisplants@cooptel.net
Ⓦ www.ellisplants.co.uk
Contact: Charles Ellis
Opening Times: 1000-1600 7 days 1st Apr-30th Sep. Other times by appt.
Min Mail Order UK: Nmc
Cat. Cost: None issued.
Credit Cards: None
Specialities: Wide range of shrubs, conifers & climbers, some of them unusual. Some available in small quantities only.
Map Ref: W, C5

WChG **Chennels Gate Gardens & Nursery** ♿
Eardisley, Herefordshire HR3 6LT
Ⓣ (01544) 327288
Contact: Mark Dawson
Opening Times: 1000-1700 7 days Mar-Oct.
Cat. Cost: None issued.
Credit Cards: None
Specialities: Interesting & unusual cottage garden plants, grasses & shrubs.

WCks **Cooks Garden Centre** ⊠ ⌂ € ♿
26 Worcester Road, Stourport-on-Severn, Worcestershire DY13 9PB
Ⓣ (01299) 826169
Ⓜ (01299) 824441
Ⓔ Cooksgardencentre@yahoo.com
Ⓦ Cooks-garden-centre.co.uk
Contact: Paul Cook
Opening Times: 0900-1800 Mon-Sun.
Min Mail Order UK: Nmc
Credit Cards: All major credit/debit cards
Specialities: General range.
Notes: Also sells wholesale.
Map Ref: W, C5

WCol **Colesbourne Gardens** ⌂ ♿
Estate Office, Colesbourne, Cheltenham, Gloucestershire GL53 9NP
Ⓣ (01242) 870264
Ⓕ (01242) 870541
Ⓔ info@colesbournegardens.org.uk
Ⓦ www.colesbournegardens.org.uk
Contact: John Grimshaw
Opening Times: 1300-1600 w/ends in Feb/Mar for Colesbourne Park Snowdrop Open Days. See website for details.
Cat. Cost: Availability list published online 1st Dec.
Credit Cards: None
Specialities: *Galanthus*, pot-grown from dormant bulbs planted in autumn, often in small quantities only.
Notes: Plants may be reserved for collection.
Map Ref: W, C5 **OS Grid Ref:** SO9983513461

WCot **Cotswold Garden Flowers** ⊠ ⌂ €
Sands Lane, Badsey, Evesham, Worcestershire WR11 7EZ
Ⓣ nursery: (01386) 833849 or mail order: (01386) 422829
Ⓜ 07812 833849
Ⓕ nursery: (01386) 49844
Ⓔ info@cgf.net
Ⓦ www.cgf.net
Contact: Bob Brown
Opening Times: 0900-1730 Mon-Fri, 1000-1730 Sat & Sun Mar-Sep. 0900-1630 Mon-Fri, w/ends by appt. only Oct-Feb.
Min Mail Order UK: Nmc
Min Mail Order EU: Nmc
Cat. Cost: £1.50 or 6 × 1st class.
Credit Cards: MasterCard, Access, Visa, Switch
Specialities: A very wide range of easy & unusual perennials.
Notes: Ltd wheelchair access. Also sells wholesale.
Map Ref: W, C5 **OS Grid Ref:** SP077426

WCre **Crescent Plants** ⊠ ♿
Stoney Cross, Marden, Hereford, Herefordshire HR1 3EW
Ⓣ (01432) 880262
Ⓕ (01432) 880262
Ⓔ crescent@btinternet.com
Ⓦ www.auriculas.co.uk
Contact: June Poole
Opening Times: Open by appt. only. Essential to phone first.
Min Mail Order UK: Nmc
Min Mail Order EU: Nmc
Cat. Cost: Free.
Credit Cards: Paypal
Specialities: Named varieties of *Primula auricula* incl. show, alpine, double, striped & border types.
Notes: Payment by Paypal via website, cheque with order or invoice. Orders dispatched post free.
Map Ref: W, C4 **OS Grid Ref:** SO525477

WCru **Crûg Farm Plants** ⊠ ⌂ ♿
Griffith's Crossing, Caernarfon, Gwynedd LL55 1TU
Ⓣ (01248) 670232
Ⓔ mailorder@crug-farm.co.uk
Ⓦ www.mailorder.crug-farm.co.uk
Contact: B and S Wynn-Jones

KEY
⊠ Mail order to UK or EU ⌂ Delivers to shows
✈ Exports beyond EU € Euro accepted
♿ Accessible by wheelchair ◆ See Display advertisement

W

Opening Times: 1000-1700 Thu-Sat, last Thu in Mar to 3rd Sat in Sep, incl. Fri B/hol. Or all year Mon-Fri by appt.
Min Mail Order UK: Nmc
Min Mail Order EU: Nmc
Cat. Cost: 5 × 2nd class or online.
Credit Cards: All major credit/debit cards
Specialities: Unusual & rare inc. trees, shrubs, herbaceous & bulbous, mostly self-collected new introductions from the Far East & the Americas. Rare woody & climbers esp. *Acer, Araliaceae, Carpinus, Hydrangeaceae* & *Magnolia* with many other extraordinary introductions. Shade plants esp. *Convallariaceae, Liliaceae, Ranunculaceae* & *Saxifragaceae*. Many supplied bare rooted. Nat. Collections of *Coriaria, Paris* & *Polygonatum*.
Notes: Delivery by overnight carrier for UK & Ireland. Courier for rest of EU.
Map Ref: W, A2 **OS Grid Ref:** SH509652

W

WDib **Dibley's Nurseries** ⊠ ⌂ € ♿ ◆
Llanelidan, Ruthin, Denbighshire
LL15 2LG
Ⓣ (01978) 790677
Ⓕ (01978) 790668
Ⓔ sales@dibleys.com
Ⓦ www.dibleys.com
Contact: R Dibley
Opening Times: 1000-1700 7 days, Apr-Aug. 1000-1700 Mon-Fri, Mar, Sep & Oct.
Min Mail Order UK: Nmc
Min Mail Order EU: Nmc
Cat. Cost: Free.
Credit Cards: Visa, Access, Switch, Electron, Solo
Specialities: *Streptocarpus, Columnea, Solenostemon, Saintpaulia* & other gesneriads & *Begonia*. Nat. Collection of *Streptocarpus*.
Notes: Also sells wholesale.
Map Ref: W, A3

WEve **Evergreen Conifer Centre** ⊠ ♿ ◆
Tenbury Road, Rock, Nr Kidderminster, Worcestershire DY14 9RB
Ⓣ (01299) 266581
Ⓔ brian@evergreen-conifers.co.uk
Ⓦ www.evergreen-conifers.co.uk
Contact: Brian Warrington
Opening Times: 0900-1630 Tue-Sat (closed Sun & Mon). Please phone before travelling some distance.
Min Mail Order UK: Nmc
Cat. Cost: 4 × 1st class.
Credit Cards: All major credit/debit cards
Specialities: Acers. Dwarf, ornamental, rare & specimen conifers. Hedging conifers. Ornamental trees & heathers.
Notes: Mail order for dwarf conifers only.
Map Ref: W, C4 **OS Grid Ref:** SO731737

WFar **Farmyard Nurseries** ⊠ ♿
Dol Llan Road, Llandysul, Carmarthenshire
SA44 4RL
Ⓣ (01559) 363389
Ⓕ (01559) 362200
Ⓔ richard@farmyardnurseries.co.uk
Ⓦ www.farmyardnurseries.co.uk
Contact: Richard Bramley
Opening Times: 1000-1700 7 days excl. Xmas, Boxing & New Year's Day.
Min Mail Order UK: Nmc
Min Mail Order EU: Nmc
Cat. Cost: 4 × 1st class.
Credit Cards: Visa, Switch, MasterCard
Specialities: Excellent general range esp. *Helleborus, Hosta, Tricyrtis* & *Schizostylis*, plus shrubs, trees, climbers, alpines & esp. herbaceous. Nat. Collections of *Tricyrtis* & *Primula sieboldii*.
Notes: Also sells wholesale.
Map Ref: W, C2 **OS Grid Ref:** SN421406

WFib **Fibrex Nurseries Ltd** ⊠ ✈ ⌂ ♿
Honeybourne Road, Pebworth, Stratford-on-Avon, Warwickshire
CV37 8XP
Ⓣ (01789) 720788
Ⓕ (01789) 721162
Ⓔ sales@fibrex.co.uk
Ⓦ www.fibrex.co.uk
Contact: U Key-Davis & R L Godard-Key
Opening Times: 0900-1700 Mon-Fri, 1st Mar-31st Aug. 0900-1600 Mon-Fri 1st Sep-28th Feb. 1030-1600 Sat & Sun 2nd Apr-31st Jul. Closed last 2 weeks Dec & 1st week Jan. Closed Easter Sun & Aug B/hol Mon.
Min Mail Order UK: £10.00 + p&p
Min Mail Order EU: £20.00 + p&p
Cat. Cost: 3 × 1st class.
Credit Cards: Switch, MasterCard, Visa, Maestro
Specialities: *Hedera*, ferns, *Pelargonium*. Nat. Collections of *Pelargonium* & *Hedera*. Plant collections subject to time of year, please check by phone.
Notes: Also sells wholesale.
Map Ref: W, C5 **OS Grid Ref:** SP133458

WGob **The Gobbett Nursery** ⊠
Farlow, Kidderminster, Worcestershire
DY14 8TD
Ⓣ (01746) 718647
Ⓕ (01746) 718647
Ⓔ christine.link@lineone.net

Ⓦ www.thegobbettnursery.co.uk
Contact: C H Link
Opening Times: 1030-1700, Mon-Sat.
Min Mail Order UK: £10.00
Min Mail Order EU: £50.00
Cat. Cost: 3 × 1st class.
Credit Cards: None
Specialities: *Syringa, Magnolia, Camellia* & *Cornus*. Some varieties available in small quantities only.
Map Ref: W, B4 **OS Grid Ref:** SO648811

WGor **Gordon's Nursery** ⊠ ♠ ♿
1 Cefnpennar Cottages, Cefnpennar, Mountain Ash, Mid-Glamorgan CF45 4EE
Ⓣ (01443) 474593
Ⓕ (01443) 475835
Ⓔ sales@gordonsnursery.co.uk
Ⓦ www.gordonsnursery.co.uk
Contact: D A Gordon
Opening Times: 1000-1800 7 days Mar-Jun. 1000-1700 7 days Jul-Oct. 1100-1600 weekends only Nov & Feb. Closed Dec-Jan.
Min Mail Order UK: Nmc
Cat. Cost: 3 × 1st class.
Credit Cards: All major credit/debit cards
Specialities: Shrubs, perennials, alpines & dwarf conifers. Some plants available in small quantities only.
Notes: Mail order only available in some cases, please check for conditions in catalogue.
Map Ref: W, D3 **OS Grid Ref:** SO037012

WGrn **Green's Leaves** ⊠ ♠ ♿
36 Ford House Road, Newent, Gloucestershire GL18 1LQ
Ⓣ (01531) 820154
Ⓜ 07890 413036
Ⓔ r.paul.green@hotmail.co.uk
Contact: Paul Green
Opening Times: By appt. only. Please phone to arrange.
Min Mail Order UK: £10.00 + p&p
Cat. Cost: 4 × 2nd class.
Credit Cards: None
Specialities: Ornamental grasses, sedges & phormiums. Increasing range of rare & choice shrubs, also some perennials.
Notes: Also sells wholesale.
Map Ref: W, C4 **OS Grid Ref:** SO732273

WGwG **Gwynfor Growers** ⊠ ♠
Gwynfor, Pontgarreg, Llangranog, Llandysul, Ceredigion SA44 6AU
Ⓣ (01239) 654151
Ⓔ info@gwynfor.co.uk
Ⓦ www.gwynfor.co.uk
Contact: Steve & Angie Hipkin
Opening Times: 1000 to 2000 or sunset if earlier, Wed, Thu & Sun, all year round.
Min Mail Order UK: Nmc
Cat. Cost: PDF list available by email.
Credit Cards: Paypal
Specialities: Welsh fruit trees. *Rosmarinus*. Classic & contemporary plants to intrigue & delight plantsmen & garden designers alike. Some plants available in small quantities only. Rarities propagated to order.
Notes: Plants also available at local farmers' markets, plant fairs & some NGS Open Gardens.
Map Ref: W, C2 **OS Grid Ref:** SN331536

WHal **Hall Farm Nursery** ⊠ ♠ €
Vicarage Lane, Kinnerley, Nr Oswestry, Shropshire SY10 8DH
Ⓣ (01691) 682135
Ⓕ (01691) 682135
Ⓔ info@hallfarmnursery.co.uk
Ⓦ www.hallfarmnursery.co.uk
Contact: Christine & Nick Ffoulkes-Jones
Opening Times: 1000-1700 Tue-Sat 1st Mar-29th Oct 2011.
Min Mail Order UK: £20.00
Cat. Cost: Online only.
Credit Cards: Visa, MasterCard, Electron, Maestro
Specialities: Unusual herbaceous plants, grasses, bog plants, late-flowering perennials, foliage plants, woodland plants, scree alpine plants.
Notes: Nursery partially accessible for wheelchairs.
Map Ref: W, B4 **OS Grid Ref:** SJ333209

WHar **Harley Nursery** ⊠ ♿
Harley, Shrewsbury, Shropshire SY5 6LN
Ⓣ (01952) 510241
Ⓕ (01952) 510570
Ⓔ plants@harleynursery.co.uk
Ⓦ www.harleynursery.co.uk
Contact: Nick Murphy
Opening Times: 0900-1730 Mon & Thu-Sat (closed Tue & Wed), 1000-1600 Sun & B/hols. Winter hours 0830-1630 Mon & Thu-Sat (closed Tue & Wed), 1000-1600 Sun & B/hols.
Min Mail Order UK: Nmc
Cat. Cost: 2 × 1st class.
Credit Cards: All major credit/debit cards

KEY
⊠ Mail order to UK or EU ♠ Delivers to shows
✈ Exports beyond EU € Euro accepted
♿ Accessible by wheelchair ◆ See Display advertisement

W

Specialities: Wide range of ornamental & fruit trees & fruit bushes. Own-grown shrubs, climbers, wide range of hedging plants. Top fruit propagated to order.
Map Ref: W, B4

WHCr **HERGEST CROFT GARDENS**
Kington, Herefordshire HR5 3EG
Ⓣ (01544) 230160
Ⓜ 07968 435627
Ⓕ (01544) 232031
Ⓔ gardens@hergest.co.uk
Ⓦ www.hergest.co.uk
Contact: Stephen Lloyd
Opening Times: 1200-1730, 7 days, Apr-Oct.
Cat. Cost: None issued.
Credit Cards: All major credit/debit cards
Specialities: *Acer*, *Betula* & unusual woody plants.
Notes: Limited wheelchair access.

WHer **THE HERB GARDEN & HISTORICAL PLANT NURSERY** ⊠
Ty Capel Pensarn, Pentre Berw, Anglesey, Gwynedd LL60 6LG
Ⓣ (01248) 422208 or (01545) 580893
Ⓜ 07751 583958
Ⓕ (01248) 422208
Ⓔ corinnetremaine@gmail.com
Ⓦ www.HistoricalPlants.co.uk
Contact: Corinne & David Tremaine-Stevenson
Opening Times: By appt. only.
Min Mail Order UK: £15.00 + p&p
Min Mail Order EU: £50.00 + p&p sterling only.
Cat. Cost: Online, or £3.00 by post in the spring.
Credit Cards: None
Specialities: Rarer herbs, rare natives & wild flowers; rare & unusual & historical perennials & old roses.
Map Ref: W, A2

WHfH **HERBS FOR HEALING** ⊠ € ♿
Barnsley Herb Garden, Barnsley, Nr Cirencester, Gloucestershire GL7 5EE
Ⓜ 07773 687493
Ⓔ herbs@herbsforhealing.net
Ⓦ www.herbsforhealing.net
Contact: Davina Wynne-Jones
Opening Times: 1000-1500 Wed, plus Fri afternoons.
Min Mail Order UK: Nmc
Credit Cards: Paypal
Specialities: Medicinal & some culinary herbs. Display garden.
Notes: Courses and workshops on use of herbs. Sells at local farmers markets. Nursery in Clapton's Lane, Barnsley, behind Barnsley House Hotel. See web for directions.
Map Ref: W, D5 **OS Grid Ref:** SP048177

WHil **HILLVIEW HARDY PLANTS** ⊠ ✈ ⌂ € ♿
(off B4176), Worfield, Nr Bridgnorth, Shropshire WV15 5NT
Ⓣ (01746) 716454
Ⓜ 07974 391608
Ⓕ (01746) 716454
Ⓔ hillview@themutual.net
Ⓦ www.hillviewhardyplants.com
Contact: Ingrid, John & Sarah Millington
Opening Times: 0900-1700 Mon-Sat Mar-mid Oct. At other times, please phone first.
Min Mail Order UK: £10.00 + p&p
Min Mail Order EU: £10.00 + p&p
Cat. Cost: 4 × 2nd class.
Credit Cards: All major credit/debit cards
Specialities: Choice herbaceous perennials incl. *Acanthus* & *Acanthaceae*, *Albuca*, *Aquilegia*, auricula, *Primula*, *Canna*, *Crocosmia*, *Eucomis*, *Ixia*, South African bulbs. Nat. Collections of *Acanthus* & *Albuca*.
Notes: Also sells wholesale.
Map Ref: W, B4 **OS Grid Ref:** SO772969

WHlf **HAYLOFT PLANTS** ⊠ ◆
Manor Farm, Pensham, Pershore, Worcestershire WR10 3HB
Ⓣ (01386) 554440 or (01386) 562999
Ⓕ (01386) 553833
Ⓔ info@hayloftplants.co.uk
Ⓦ www.hayloftplants.co.uk
Contact: Yvonne Walker
Opening Times: Not open. Mail order only.
Min Mail Order UK: Nmc
Min Mail Order EU: Nmc
Cat. Cost: Free.
Credit Cards: All major credit/debit cards

WHoo **HOO HOUSE NURSERY** € ◆
Hoo House, Gloucester Road, Tewkesbury, Gloucestershire GL20 7DA
Ⓣ (01684) 293389
Ⓕ (01684) 293389
Ⓔ nursery@hoohouse.co.uk
Ⓦ www.hoohouse.co.uk
Contact: Robin & Julie Ritchie
Opening Times: 1000-1700 Mon-Sat, 1100-1700 Sun.
Cat. Cost: 3 × 1st class.
Credit Cards: All major credit/debit cards
Specialities: Wide range of herbaceous & alpines incl. *Aster*, *Cyclamen*, *Geranium*, *Penstemon* & many later-flowering varieties.

Nat. Collections of *Platycodon* & *Gentiana asclepiadea* cvs.
Notes: Partially accessible for wheelchairs. Also sells wholesale.
Map Ref: W, C5 **OS Grid Ref:** SO893293

WHor **HORTICULTURAL SALES** ⊠ € ◆
Upper Brockington, Berrington Street, Bodenham, Herefordshire HR1 3HT
Ⓣ (01568) 797747
Ⓜ 07966 635005
Ⓕ (01568) 797013
Ⓔ pdavies@hortsales.fsnet.co.uk
Contact: Peter Davies
Opening Times: By appt. only.
Min Mail Order UK: Nmc
Min Mail Order EU: Nmc
Cat. Cost: Free but available by email only.
Credit Cards: None
Specialities: *Acer*, *Pinus* & grafted conifers, plus wide selection of less commonly grown shrubs, available in small quantities only.
Notes: Offers plant finding service. Also sells wholesale, 35 years experience in trade.

WHrl **HARRELLS HARDY PLANTS** ⊠
(Office) 15 Coxlea Close, Evesham, Worcestershire WR11 4JS
Ⓣ (01386) 443077
Ⓜ 07799 577120 or 07733 446606
Ⓔ mail@harrellshardyplants.co.uk
Ⓦ www.harrellshardyplants.co.uk
Contact: Liz Nicklin & Kate Phillips
Opening Times: 1000-1200 Sun Mar-Nov. Other times by appt. Please phone.
Min Mail Order UK: Nmc
Cat. Cost: 4 × 2nd class.
Credit Cards: None
Specialities: Display gardens showcase wide range of hardy perennials, esp. *Hemerocallis* & grasses.
Notes: Nursery located off Rudge Rd, Evesham. Please phone for directions or see catalogue. Partial wheelchair access. Mail order Nov-Mar only.
Map Ref: W, C5 **OS Grid Ref:** SP033443

WIce **ICE ALPINES** ⊠ ♿
Lyehead, Bewdley, Worcestershire DY12 2UW
Ⓣ (01299) 269219
Ⓕ (01562) 510003
Ⓔ icealpines@gmail.com
Ⓦ www.Icealpines.co.uk
Contact: Mark Lagomarsino
Opening Times: Mail order. Open by appt. only.
Min Mail Order UK: Nmc
Min Mail Order EU: £18
Credit Cards: Paypal
Specialities: British grown alpine & rockery plants.

WIvy **IVYCROFT PLANTS** ⊠ € ♿
Upper Ivington, Leominster, Herefordshire HR6 0JN
Ⓣ (01568) 720344
Ⓔ ivycroft@homecall.co.uk
Ⓦ www.ivycroftgarden.co.uk
Contact: Roger Norman
Opening Times: 0900-1600 Thu, Feb & Apr-Sep. Other times by appt., please phone.
Min Mail Order UK: Nmc
Min Mail Order EU: Nmc
Cat. Cost: Sae for specialist lists.
Credit Cards: None
Specialities: *Cyclamen*, *Galanthus*, *Salix*, alpines, herbaceous & ferns.
Notes: Mail order for *Galanthus* & *Salix* only.
Map Ref: W, C4 **OS Grid Ref:** SO464562

WJas **PAUL JASPER TREES** ⊠ €
(Office) The Lighthouse, Bridge Street, Leominster, Herefordshire HR6 8DX
Ⓕ (01568) 616499 for orders.
Ⓔ enquiries@jaspertrees.co.uk
Ⓦ www.jaspertrees.co.uk
Contact: Paul Jasper
Opening Times: Not open. Mail order only.
Min Mail Order UK: £40.00 + p&p
Cat. Cost: Online only.
Credit Cards: None
Specialities: Full range of fruit & ornamental trees. Over 100 modern and traditional fruit tree varieties plus 100 ornamental tree varieties, all direct from the grower. Many unusual varieties of *Malus domestica* & *Prunus*.
Notes: Regular catalogue updates & notes on website. Also sells wholesale.
Map Ref: W, C4 **OS Grid Ref:** SO495595

WJek **JEKKA'S HERB FARM** ⊠ ⛺ ♿
Rose Cottage, Shellards Lane, Alveston, Bristol, South Gloucestershire BS35 3SY
Ⓣ (01454) 418878
Ⓕ (01454) 424907
Ⓔ sales@jekkasherbfarm.com
Ⓦ www.jekkasherbfarm.com
Contact: Jekka McVicar
Opening Times: 4 times a year. Please check website for dates.

KEY
⊠ Mail order to UK or EU ⛺ Delivers to shows
✈ Exports beyond EU € Euro accepted
♿ Accessible by wheelchair ◆ See Display advertisement

Min Mail Order UK: £15 plants
Min Mail Order EU: Seeds only to the EU.
Cat. Cost: 4 × 1st class.
Credit Cards: Visa, MasterCard, Delta, Maestro
Specialities: Culinary, medicinal, aromatic, decorative herbs. Soil Association licensed G5869.
Map Ref: W, D4

WJPR **JPR Environmental** ⊠
(Office) Unit 2, Breadstone Business Centre, Breadstone, Berkeley, Gloucestershire GL13 9HF
Ⓣ (01453) 811537
Ⓕ (01453) 810646
Ⓔ enquiries@jprenvironmental.co.uk
Ⓦ www.jprwillow.co.uk
Contact: John Robinthwaite
Opening Times: Mail order only. 0900-1700.
Min Mail Order UK: £6.00
Credit Cards: All, except American Express
Specialities: *Salix.*
Notes: Also sells wholesale.

W

WJun **Jungle Giants** ⊠ ☒ € ♿
Ferney, Onibury, Craven Arms, Shropshire SY7 9BJ
Ⓣ (01584) 856200
Ⓕ (01584) 856663
Ⓔ bamboo@junglegiants.co.uk
Ⓦ www.junglegiants.co.uk
Contact: Michael Brisbane
Opening Times: 7 days. By appt. only please.
Min Mail Order UK: £25.00 + p&p
Min Mail Order EU: £100.00 + p&p
Cat. Cost: Online only.
Credit Cards: Access, MasterCard, Visa
Specialities: Bamboos.
Notes: Also sells wholesale.
Map Ref: W, C4 **OS Grid Ref:** SO430779

WKif **Kiftsgate Court Gardens** ♿
Kiftsgate Court, Chipping Camden, Gloucestershire GL55 6LN
Ⓣ (01386) 438777
Ⓕ (01386) 438777
Ⓔ anne@kiftsgate.co.uk
Ⓦ www.kiftsgate.co.uk
Contact: Mrs J Chambers
Opening Times: 1200-1800 Sat-Wed, May, Jun & Jul. 1400-1800 Sat-Wed, Aug. 1400-1800 Sun, Mon & Wed, Apr & Sep.
Cat. Cost: None issued.
Credit Cards: All, except American Express
Specialities: Small range of unusual plants.
Map Ref: W, C5 **OS Grid Ref:** SP170430

WLav **The Lavender Garden** ⊠ ⌂ €
Ashcroft Nurseries, Nr Ozleworth, Kingscote, Tetbury, Gloucestershire GL8 8YF
Ⓣ (01453) 860356 or 549286
Ⓜ 07837 582943
Ⓔ Andrew007Bullock@aol.com
Ⓦ www.TheLavenderG.co.uk
Contact: Andrew Bullock
Opening Times: 1100-1700 Sat & Sun. Weekdays variable, please phone. 1st Nov-1st Mar by appt. only.
Min Mail Order UK: £10.00 + p&p
Min Mail Order EU: £20.00 + p&p
Cat. Cost: 2 × 1st class.
Credit Cards: All major credit/debit cards
Specialities: *Lavandula, Buddleja,* plants to attract butterflies. Herbs, wildflowers. Nat. Collection of *Buddleja.*
Notes: Also sells wholesale.
Map Ref: W, D5 **OS Grid Ref:** ST798948

WMAq **Merebrook Water Plants** ⊠
Kingfisher Barn, Merebrook Farm, Hanley Swan, Worcestershire WR8 0DX
Ⓣ (01684) 310950
Ⓜ 07876 777066
Ⓔ enquiries@pondplants.co.uk
Ⓦ www.pondplants.co.uk
Contact: Roger Kings & Biddi Kings
Opening Times: Not open. Mail order only.
Min Mail Order UK: Nmc
Min Mail Order EU: £25.00
Cat. Cost: Online only.
Credit Cards: All major credit/debit cards
Specialities: *Nymphaea,* Louisiana irises & other aquatic plants. International Waterlily & Water Gardening Soc. accredited collection.

WMnd **Mynd Hardy Plants** ♿
Delbury Hall Estate, Diddlebury, Craven Arms, Shropshire SY7 9DH
Ⓣ (01584) 841222
Ⓔ myndhardyplants@aol.com
Ⓦ www.myndplants.co.uk
Contact: Mark Zenick
Opening Times: 1300-1700 Wed-Fri, 1000-1700 Sat, 26th Mar-17th Sep. 1300-1700 B/Hol Mons. 1300-1700 Sun May-Jul. Other times, phone for appt.
Cat. Cost: 4 × 2nd class.
Credit Cards: All major credit/debit cards
Specialities: Herbaceous plants, specialising in American bred, British grown, *Hemerocallis.* Home to New Hope Garden's *Hemerocallis* plants.
Notes: Also sells wholesale.
Map Ref: W, B4 **OS Grid Ref:** SO510852

WMoo **MOORLAND COTTAGE PLANTS** ⊠ ♿
Rhyd-y-Groes, Brynberian,
Crymych, Pembrokeshire
SA41 3TT
Ⓣ (01239) 891363
Ⓦ www.moorlandcottageplants.co.uk
Contact: Jennifer Matthews
Opening Times: 1030-1730 daily excl. Wed 1st Mar-30th Sep.
Min Mail Order UK: See cat. for details.
Cat. Cost: 4 × 1st class.
Credit Cards: None
Specialities: Traditional & unusual hardy perennials. Many garden-worthy rarities. Cottage garden plants, ferns & many shade plants, moisture lovers, ornamental grasses & bamboos, colourful ground cover.
Notes: Display garden open for NGS from mid-May.
Map Ref: W, C2 **OS Grid Ref:** SN091343

WMou **MOUNT PLEASANT TREES**
Rockhampton, Berkeley, Gloucestershire
GL13 9DU
Ⓣ (01454) 260348
Ⓔ info@mountpleasanttrees.com
Ⓦ www.mountpleasanttrees.com
Contact: Tom Locke & Elizabeth Murphy
Opening Times: By appt. only.
Cat. Cost: Free.
Credit Cards: All major credit/debit cards
Specialities: Wide range of trees for forestry, hedging, woodlands & gardens esp. *Populus, Salix, Tilia* & *Quercus*.
Notes: Also sells wholesale.
Map Ref: W, D4 **OS Grid Ref:** ST654929

WNew **NEWBRIDGE NURSERY** ⊠ ♿
Crundale, Haverfordwest, Pembrokeshire
SA62 4EJ
Ⓣ (01437) 731678
Ⓕ (01437) 731678
Ⓔ newbridgenursery@btinternet.com
Ⓦ www.newbridgeplantcentre.co.uk
Contact: Phil & Jane Davies
Opening Times: 1000-1730 daily throughout year.
Min Mail Order UK: Nmc
Cat. Cost: 2 × 1st class.
Credit Cards: All major credit/debit cards
Specialities: Wide range of herbaceous perennials & alpines from the common to the more unusual. Also a selection of coastal & acid-loving shrubs.
Notes: Credit cards not accepted for mail order. Plants also sold at Haverfordwest Farmers Market.
Map Ref: W, D2 **OS Grid Ref:** SM991196

WNHG **NEW HOPE GARDENS** ⊠ ♿
The Old Chapel, Cefn Einion,
Nr Bishops Castle, Shropshire
SY9 5LF
Ⓣ Office: (01588) 630750 or Nursery: (01584) 841222
Ⓔ Newhopegardensmz@aol.com
Ⓦ www.newhopegardens.com
Contact: Mark Zenick
Opening Times: 1300-1700 Wed-Fri, 1000-1700 Sat, 26th Mar-17th Sep. 1300-1700 B/hol Mons during season. 1300-1700 Sun, May-Jul. Other times phone nursery for appt. Daylily Open W/ends 2nd/3rd, 9th/10th, 16th/17th, 23rd/24th Jul 2011.
Min Mail Order UK: Nmc
Min Mail Order EU: Nmc
Cat. Cost: Online only. Plant list on request.
Credit Cards: All major credit/debit cards
Specialities: American bred, British grown, *Hemerocallis*. Ships bare-rooted plants.
Map Ref: W, B4

WOld **OLD COURT NURSERIES** ⊠
Colwall, Nr Malvern, Worcestershire
WR13 6QE
Ⓣ (01684) 540416
Ⓔ paulpicton@btinternet.com
Ⓦ www.autumnasters.co.uk
Contact: Paul, Meriel or Helen Picton
Opening Times: 1430-1700 Wed-Fri, May-Aug. 1200-1700 Wed-Sun, Aug. 1100-1700 7 days, 1st week Sep-2nd week Oct. Also by appt. May to Oct.
Min Mail Order UK: Nmc
Min Mail Order EU: Nmc
Credit Cards: None
Specialities: Nat. Collection of Michaelmas Daisies. Herbaceous perennials.
Notes: Mail order for *Aster* only. Display garden open Aug-Oct.
Map Ref: W, C4 **OS Grid Ref:** SO759430

WOut **OUT OF THE COMMON WAY** ⊠ ⌂ €
(Office) Penhyddgan, Boduan,
Pwllheli, Gwynedd
LL53 8YH
Ⓣ office: (01758) 721577 or nursery: (01407) 720431
Ⓔ ziggymen22@tesco.net
Contact: Joanna Davidson (nursery) Margaret Mason (office & mail order)

KEY
⊠ Mail order to UK or EU ⌂ Delivers to shows
✈ Exports beyond EU € Euro accepted
♿ Accessible by wheelchair ◆ See Display advertisement

W

Opening Times: By arrangement.
Min Mail Order UK: Nmc
Min Mail Order EU: Nmc
Cat. Cost: A5 sae letter rate postage.
Credit Cards: None
Specialities: *Labiates*, esp. *Nepeta* & *Salvia. Aster*, *Geranium* & *Crocosmia.* Native plants. Some plants propagated in small quantities only. Will propagate salvias to order.
Notes: Nursery is at Pandy Treban, Bryngwran, Anglesey. Partially accessible for wheelchairs.
Map Ref: W, A2 **OS Grid Ref:** SH370778

WPat **Chris Pattison** ⊠ € ♿
Brookend, Pendock, Gloucestershire
GL19 3PL
Ⓣ (01531) 650480
Ⓕ (01531) 650480
Ⓔ cp@chris-pattison.co.uk
Ⓦ www.chris-pattison.co.uk
Contact: Chris Pattison
Opening Times: 0900-1700 Mon-Fri. W/ends by appt. only.
Min Mail Order UK: £10.00 +p&p
Cat. Cost: 3 × 1st class.
Credit Cards: None
Specialities: Choice rare shrubs & alpines. Grafted stock esp. Japanese maples & liquidambars. Wide range of *Viburnum* & dwarf/miniature trees & shrubs suitable for bonsai or rockery.
Notes: Mail order Nov-Feb only. Also sells wholesale.
Map Ref: W, C5 **OS Grid Ref:** SO781327

WPer **Perhill Nurseries** ⊠ € ♿
Worcester Road, Great Witley, Worcestershire
WR6 6JT
Ⓣ (01299) 896329
Ⓕ (01299) 896990
Ⓔ perhillp@btconnect.com
Ⓦ www.perhillplants.co.uk
Contact: Duncan Straw
Opening Times: 0900-1700 most weekdays but please phone first if travelling any distance. Closed weekends.
Min Mail Order UK: Nmc
Min Mail Order EU: £10.00
Cat. Cost: 6 × 2nd class.
Credit Cards: All major credit/debit cards
Specialities: 2000+ varieties of rare, unusual alpines & herbaceous perennials incl. *Penstemon*, *Campanula*, *Salvia*, *Thymus*, herbs, *Veronica*.
Notes: Also sells wholesale. Coach parties welcome.
Map Ref: W, C4 **OS Grid Ref:** SO763656

WPGP **Pan-Global Plants** ♿
The Walled Garden, Frampton Court, Frampton-on-Severn, Gloucestershire
GL2 7EX
Ⓣ (01452) 741641
Ⓜ 07801 275138
Ⓔ info@panglobalplants.com
Ⓦ www.panglobalplants.com
Contact: Nick Macer
Opening Times: 1100-1700 Wed-Sun 1st Feb-31st Oct. Also B/hols. Closed 2nd Sun in Sep. Winter months by appt., please phone first.
Cat. Cost: 6 × 1st class.
Credit Cards: Maestro, MasterCard, Visa, Solo, Delta
Specialities: A plantsman's nursery offering a very wide selection of rare & desirable trees, shrubs, herbaceous, bamboos, exotics, climbers, ferns etc. Specialities incl. *Magnolia*, *Hydrangea*, *Bamboo* & *Agavaceae*.
Map Ref: W, D5 **OS Grid Ref:** SO750080

WPnn **The Perennial Nursery** ⊠
Rhosygilwen, Llanrhian Road, St Davids, Haverfordwest, Pembrokeshire SA62 6DB
Ⓣ (01437) 721954
Ⓦ www.droughttolerantplants.co.uk
Contact: Mrs Philipa Symons
Opening Times: 1030-1630 Mar-Oct. Closed Sun & Mon.
Min Mail Order UK: Nmc
Min Mail Order EU: Nmc
Cat. Cost: Online only.
Credit Cards: Visa, MasterCard
Specialities: *Rosmarinus*, *Lampranthus*, wind & drought-tolerant plants.
Notes: Also sells wholesale.
Map Ref: W, C1 **OS Grid Ref:** SM775292

WPnP **Penlan Perennials** ⊠ €
Wern Rhos, Newchapel, Boncath, Pembrokeshire SA37 0EN
Ⓣ (01239) 842260
Ⓜ 07857 675312
Ⓕ (01239) 842260
Ⓔ info@penlanperennials.co.uk
Ⓦ www.penlanperennials.co.uk
Contact: Richard Cain
Opening Times: Mail order only. Open for collection of orders only.
Min Mail Order UK: Nmc
Min Mail Order EU: Nmc
Cat. Cost: Online, or sae for CD-ROM.
Credit Cards: All major credit/debit cards
Specialities: Aquatic, marginal & bog plants. Shade-loving & woodland perennials, ferns & hardy geraniums, all grown peat-free.

Notes: Mail order all year, next day delivery. Secure online web ordering. Nursery has relocated so please note new phone number (above). Also sells wholesale.

WPtf **Pantyfod Garden Nursery** ⊠
Llandewi Brefi, Tregaron, Ceredigion
SY25 6PE
Ⓣ (01570) 493564
Ⓔ sales@pantyfodgarden.co.uk
Ⓦ www.pantyfodgarden.co.uk
Contact: Susan Rowe
Opening Times: Mail order only. Not open to visitors. Garden occasionally open under the National Gardens Scheme, when plants are offered for sale. Please check with NGS for Open Days.
Min Mail Order UK: Nmc
Min Mail Order EU: Nmc
Cat. Cost: Online only.
Credit Cards: Paypal
Specialities: Unusual hardy perennials, hardy geraniums, black plants, woodland plants, grasses, plants for moist soil. All plants grown largely peat-free. Many plants available in small quantities.
Notes: Stock changes throughout the year. See website for regular updates or phone/email. Email to enquire about plants not listed on website.
Map Ref: W, C3 **OS Grid Ref:** SN654540

WRHF **Red House Farm** ♿
Flying Horse Lane, Bradley Green,
Nr Redditch, Worcestershire B96 6QT
Ⓣ (01527) 821269
Ⓕ (01527) 821674
Ⓔ redhousenursery@googlemail.com
Ⓦ www.redhousefarmgardenandnursery.co.uk
Contact: Mrs Maureen Weaver
Opening Times: 0900-1700 Mon-Sat all year. 1000-1700 Sun & B/hols.
Cat. Cost: 2 × 1st class.
Credit Cards: None
Specialities: Cottage garden perennials.
Map Ref: W, C5 **OS Grid Ref:** SO986623

WSFF **Saith Ffynnon Wildlife Plants** ⊠ € ♿
Whitford, Holywell, Flintshire CH8 9EQ
Ⓣ (01352) 711198
Ⓕ (01352) 716777
Ⓔ jan@7wells.org
Ⓦ www.7wells.co.uk
Contact: Jan Miller
Opening Times: By appt. only.
Min Mail Order UK: Nmc
Min Mail Order EU: Nmc
Cat. Cost: 2 × 1st class (list only) or full catalogue online.
Credit Cards: All major credit/debit cards
Specialities: Plants and seeds to attract butterflies and moths. Natural dye plants. Nat. Collection of *Eupatorium*. Stock available in small quantities unless ordered well in advance.
Notes: Percentage of profits go to Butterfly Conservation. Also sells wholesale. Credit cards accepted via website only.

WSHC **Stone House Cottage Nurseries** ♿
Stone, Nr Kidderminster, Worcestershire
DY10 4BG
Ⓣ (01562) 69902
Ⓔ louisa@shcn.co.uk
Ⓦ www.shcn.co.uk
Contact: L N Arbuthnott
Opening Times: 1000-1700 Wed-Sat. By appt. only mid Sep-mid Mar.
Cat. Cost: Sae.
Credit Cards: None
Specialities: Small general range esp. wall shrubs, climbers & unusual plants.
Map Ref: W, C5 **OS Grid Ref:** SO863750

WShi **Shipton Bulbs** ⊠ ⌂ €
Y Felin, Henllan Amgoed, Whitland,
Carmarthenshire SA34 0SL
Ⓣ (01994) 240125
Ⓕ (01994) 241180
Ⓔ bluebell@zoo.co.uk
Ⓦ www.bluebellbulbs.co.uk
Contact: John Shipton & Aelfwyn Shipton
Opening Times: By appt. only.
Min Mail Order UK: Nmc
Min Mail Order EU: Nmc
Cat. Cost: Sae.
Credit Cards: All major credit/debit cards
Specialities: Native British bulbs. Bulbs & plants for naturalising.
Map Ref: W, D2 **OS Grid Ref:** SN188207

WSpi **Spinneywell Nursery** ⊠ ⌂
Spinneywell Farm, Waterlane, Oakridge,
Stroud, Gloucestershire GL6 7PH
Ⓣ (01452) 770092
Ⓜ 07986 887158
Ⓕ (01452) 770151
Ⓔ wendy.spinneywell@virgin.net
Ⓦ www.spinneywellplants.co.uk
Contact: Wendy Asher

KEY
⊠ Mail order to UK or EU
⌂ Delivers to shows
Exports beyond EU
€ Euro accepted
♿ Accessible by wheelchair
◆ See Display advertisement

Opening Times: 0900-1600 Mon-Fri, Apr-Sep. 1000-1500 Mon-Fri, Oct-Mar.
Min Mail Order UK: £10.00 + p&p
Min Mail Order EU: £30.00 + p&p
Cat. Cost: Online only.
Credit Cards: All major credit/debit cards
Specialities: *Buxus*, *Taxus* & unusual herbaceous & shrubs. Hellebores, euphorbias, *Ceanothus*, hardy geraniums.
Notes: Plant sourcing service available. Mail order only after Jul 2011. Also sells wholesale.
Map Ref: W, D5 **OS Grid Ref:** SO921044

WSSs **Shropshire Sarracenias** ⊠ ✈ ⌂ € ♿
5 Field Close, Malinslee, Telford, Shropshire TF4 2EH
Ⓣ (01952) 501598
Ⓔ mike@carnivorousplants.uk.com
Ⓦ www.carnivorousplants.uk.com
Contact: Mike King
Opening Times: By appt. only.
Min Mail Order UK: Nmc
Min Mail Order EU: Nmc
Cat. Cost: 2 × 1st class.
Credit Cards: Paypal
Specialities: *Sarracenia. Dionaea muscipula* & forms. Some stock available in small quantities only. Nat. Collections of *Sarracenia* & *Dionaea*.
Map Ref: W, B4 **OS Grid Ref:** SJ689085

WSuV **Sunnybank Vine Nursery (National Vine Collection)** ⊠ ✈
Cwm Barn, King Street, Ewyas Harold, Rowlestone, Herefordshire HR2 OEE
Ⓣ (01981) 240256
Ⓔ Sarah@sunnybankvines.co.uk
Ⓦ www.sunnybankvines.co.uk
Contact: Sarah Bell
Opening Times: Not open. Mail order only.
Min Mail Order UK: £10.00 incl. p&p
Min Mail Order EU: £15.00 incl. p&p
Cat. Cost: Online only.
Credit Cards: None
Specialities: Vines. Nat. Collection of *Vitis vinifera* (hardy, incl. dessert & wine). 70 varieties available as rooted plants, the entire Collection usually available as bare wood cuttings for own propagation.
Notes: EU sales by arrangement.

WTan **Tan-y-Llyn Nurseries** ⊠
Meifod, Powys SY22 6YB
Ⓣ (01938) 500370
Ⓔ info@tanyllyn-nursery.co.uk
Ⓦ www.tanyllyn-nursery.co.uk
Contact: Callum Johnston
Opening Times: 1000-1700 Tue-Sat Mar-Jun and at other times by appt.
Min Mail Order UK: Nmc
Cat. Cost: 2 × 1st class or online.
Credit Cards: Paypal
Specialities: Herbs, alpines, perennials.
Map Ref: W, B3 **OS Grid Ref:** SJ167125

WTcb **T-Cubed Plants** ⊠ ⌂ ♿
Wall End Nursery, Wall End Barn, Stoke Prior, Herefordshire HR6 0ND
Ⓣ (01568) 760152
Ⓜ 07775 001287
Ⓔ t3plants@aol.com
Ⓦ www.t3plants.co.uk
Contact: Eric Turner & Leila Jackson
Opening Times: 1000-1500 Mon-Fri, Apr-Oct. Other times by appt.
Min Mail Order UK: Nmc
Min Mail Order EU: Nmc
Cat. Cost: 3 × 1st class.
Specialities: *Abutilon*, *Salvia*, *Rudbeckia*, *Sanguisorba*, *Persicaria* & *Thalictrum*. Many shown by genus in display beds.
Notes: Open for group visits & talks. Evening visits for horticultural groups by prior arrangement. See website for special events. Also sells wholesale.
Map Ref: W, C4 **OS Grid Ref:** SO524566

WThu **Thuya Alpine Nursery** ⊠ ⌂
Glebelands, Hartpury, Gloucestershire GL19 3BW
Ⓣ (01452) 700548
Contact: S W Bond
Opening Times: 1000-dusk Sat & B/hols. 1100-dusk Sun, Weekdays appt. advised.
Min Mail Order UK: £4.00 + p&p
Min Mail Order EU: £10.00 + p&p
Cat. Cost: 4 × 2nd class.
Credit Cards: None
Specialities: Wide and changing range including rarities, available in smallish numbers.
Notes: Partially accessible for wheelchair users. Will deliver plants to AGS shows.
Map Ref: W, C5

WTin **Tinpenny Plants** ⊠
Smithfield Cottage, The Green, Bishops Norton, Gloucestershire GL2 9LP
Ⓣ (01452) 731013
Ⓔ elaine@lime.ws
Ⓦ www.tinpenny.plus.com
Contact: Elaine Horton
Opening Times: By appt. all year round. Email for details.
Min Mail Order UK: Nmc
Cat. Cost: None issued.

Credit Cards: None
Specialities: Wide range of hardy garden-worthy plants esp. *Helleborus*, *Iris* & *Sempervivum*. Small nursery will propagate to order rare plants from own stock. Small quantities only of some plants.

WTou **Touchwood Plants** ⊠ 🗷
4 Clyne Valley Cottages, Killay, Swansea, West Glamorgan SA2 7DU
Ⓣ (01792) 522443
Ⓔ Carrie.Thomas@ntlworld.com
Ⓦ www.touchwoodplants.co.uk
Contact: Carrie Thomas
Opening Times: Most reasonable days/times. Please phone first.
Min Mail Order UK: Nmc
Min Mail Order EU: Nmc
Cat. Cost: 1 × 1st class large sae.
Credit Cards: All major credit/debit cards
Specialities: Seeds & plants. Nat. Collection of *Aquilegia vulgaris* cvs & hybrids. Plant stocks held in small quantities. Main stock is seed. Garden & *Aquilegia* Collection open.
Notes: Plants sent bare-rooted at relevant times of the year. Beyond the UK only seeds exported. Credit cards accepted online only.
Map Ref: W, D3 **OS Grid Ref:** SS600924

WTul **National Collection of Tulbaghia** ⊠
Llety Moel, Rhos-y-Garth, Llanilar, Nr Aberystwyth, Ceredigion SY23 4SG
Ⓣ (01974) 241505
Ⓜ 07891 333656
Ⓔ liz.powney@btinternet.com
Contact: Elizabeth Powney
Opening Times: Open by appt. only.
Min Mail Order UK: Nmc
Min Mail Order EU: Nmc
Cat. Cost: None issued.
Credit Cards: None
Specialities: Nat. Collection of *Tulbaghia*. Plants sold to support the Collection. Available in small quantities only.

WViv **Viv Marsh Postal Plants** ⊠
Walford Heath, Shrewsbury, Shropshire SY4 2HT
Ⓣ (01939) 291475
Ⓔ mail@postalplants.co.uk
Ⓦ www.postalplants.co.uk
Contact: Mr Viv Marsh
Opening Times: Selected w/ends in spring & autumn. Please phone for details. Other times by appt. only.
Min Mail Order UK: £33.00 plant value
Min Mail Order EU: £33.00 plant value
Cat. Cost: Free.
Credit Cards: All major credit/debit cards
Specialities: *Specialists in Alstroemeria* & *Lathyrus*. Nat. Collection of *Alstroemeria* applied for.
Notes: Wheelchair access with assistance. No disabled toilet.
Map Ref: W, B4 **OS Grid Ref:** SJ446198

WWau **Waun Nurseries** ⊠ ⌂
Rhydlewis, Llandysul, Ceredigion SA44 5PS
Ⓣ (01239) 851359
Ⓔ sales@waunnurseries.co.uk
Ⓦ www.waunnurseries.co.uk
Contact: A Matthews
Opening Times: 1000-1600 Thu & Fri. Other times by appt. only
Min Mail Order UK: Nmc
Cat. Cost: Online only.
Credit Cards: All major credit/debit cards
Specialities: *Prunus laurocerasus*, *Photinia* & *Eucalyptus*. Some stock available in small quantities only.
Notes: Mail order for plants up to max. size 2 ltr pots only. Also sells wholesale.
Map Ref: W, C2

WWEG **World's End Garden Nursery** ⊠ ◆
Moseley Road, Hallow, Worcester, Worcestershire WR2 6NJ
Ⓣ (01905) 640977
Ⓕ (01905) 641373
Ⓔ info@worldsendgarden.co.uk
Ⓦ www.worldsendgarden.co.uk
Contact: Kristina & Robin Pearce
Opening Times: Open by appt. only.
Min Mail Order UK: £20.00
Min Mail Order EU: £20.00
Cat. Cost: Online only.
Credit Cards: All major credit/debit cards
Specialities: Wide range of herbaceous perennials, hardy ferns & ornamental grasses. Especially *Hosta*, *Geum*, *Leucantheum*, *Helenium*.
Notes: Also sells wholesale.
Map Ref: W, C5 **OS Grid Ref:** SO815597

WWFP **Whitehall Farmhouse Plants** ⊠ ⌂
Sevenhampton, Cheltenham, Gloucestershire GL54 5TL
Ⓣ (01242) 820772
Ⓜ 07711 021034
Ⓕ (01242) 821226

KEY
⊠ Mail order to UK or EU ⌂ Delivers to shows
🗷 Exports beyond EU € Euro accepted
♿ Accessible by wheelchair ◆ See Display advertisement

W

Ⓔ info@wfplants.co.uk
Ⓦ www.wfplants.co.uk
Contact: Victoria Logue
Opening Times: By appt. only.
Min Mail Order UK: Nmc
Cat. Cost: 2 × 1st class.
Credit Cards: None
Specialities: A small nursery producing a range of interesting & easy hardy perennials for the garden. Some plants held in small quantities only.
Map Ref: W, C5 **OS Grid Ref:** SP018229

WWFS **Welsh Fruit Stocks** ⊠
Bryngwyn, Kington, Herefordshire HR5 3QZ
Ⓣ (01497) 851209
Ⓔ sian@welshfruitstocks.co.uk
Ⓦ www.welshfruitstocks.co.uk
Contact: Sîan Fromant
Opening Times: By prior appt. only. Mail order only.
Min Mail Order UK: Nmc
Cat. Cost: Sae.
Credit Cards: All major credit/debit cards
Specialities: Soft fruit.
Notes: Credit cards accepted for online orders only. Also sells wholesale.

W

WWlt **Wollerton Old Hall Garden** ♿
Wollerton, Market Drayton, Shropshire TF9 3NA
Ⓣ (01630) 685760
Ⓔ info@wollertonoldhallgarden.com
Ⓦ www.wollertonoldhallgarden.com
Contact: Mr John Jenkins
Opening Times: 1200-1700 Fri, Sun & B/hols Easter-end Sep.
Cat. Cost: None issued.
Credit Cards: All, except American Express
Specialities: Perennials, hardy & half-hardy.
Map Ref: W, B4 **OS Grid Ref:** SJ624296

Abroad

XBlo **Table Bay View Nursery** ⊠ ☒ €
(Office) 60 Molteno Road, Oranjezicht, Cape Town 8001, South Africa
Ⓣ (27) (0)21 683 5108
Ⓕ (27) (0)21 683 5108
Ⓔ info@tablebayviewnursery.co.za
Contact: Terence Bloch
Opening Times: Mail order only. No personal callers.
Min Mail Order UK: £15.00 + p&p
Min Mail Order EU: £15.00
Cat. Cost: £3.40 (postal order)
Credit Cards: None
Specialities: Tropical & sub-tropical ornamental & fruiting plants. Self-harvested seed, predominently from our own inventory of mother stock plants.
Notes: Due to high local bank charges can no longer accept foreign bank cheques only undated postal orders.

XDel **Pépinière Delphwood** ⊠ ☒ ⌂ € ♿
La Forêterie, 16500 Manot, Charentes, France
Ⓣ (33) (0)5 4571 4451
Ⓜ (33) 61085 1187
Ⓕ (33) (0)5 4571 4451
Ⓔ delphwood@orange.fr
Ⓦ www.delphwoodhibiscus.eu
Contact: Robert Justice-Leeson
Opening Times: 1200-1900, 7 days.
Min Mail Order UK: Nmc
Min Mail Order EU: Nmc
Credit Cards: All major credit/debit cards
Specialities: Hardy herbaceous perennial *Hibiscus*.
Notes: Botanic park open to the public (no charge). Mail order autumn-spring. Also sells wholesale.

XEll **Ellebore** ⊠ ⌂ €
La Chamotière, 61 360 Saint-Jouin-de-Blavou, France
Ⓣ (33) (0)2 3383 3772
Ⓜ (33) 6802 28674
Ⓕ (33) (0)2 3383 3773
Ⓔ pepiniere.ellebore@orange.fr
Ⓦ www.pepiniere-ellebore.fr
Contact: Nadine Albouy & Christian Geoffroy
Opening Times: 1000-1800 Wed-Sat, mid-Feb to late Jun & Sep-Dec. 1500-1800 Thu, Fri & Sat, Jul, Aug & Jan to mid-Feb.
Min Mail Order UK: Nmc
Min Mail Order EU: Nmc
Cat. Cost: Free.
Credit Cards: All major credit/debit cards
Specialities: *Helleborus*. Bulbs. *Clematis*.
Notes: Also sells wholesale.

XFro **Frosch Exclusive Perennials** ⊠ ☒ €
Ziegelstadelweg 5, D-83623 Dietramszell-Lochen, Germany
Ⓣ (49) (0)172 842 2050
Ⓕ (49) 8027 904 9975
Ⓔ info@cypripedium.de
Ⓦ www.cypripedium.de
Contact: Michael Weinert
Opening Times: Not open. Mail order only. Orders taken between 0700-2200 hours.
Min Mail Order UK: £350.00 + p&p
Min Mail Order EU: £350.00 + p&p
Cat. Cost: Online only.

Credit Cards: None
Specialities: *Cypripedium* hybrids. Hardy orchids.
Notes: Also sells wholesale.

XLum **Lumen Plantes Vivaces** ⊠ ✈ ⌂ €
Les Coutets, 24100 Creysse-Bergerac, Occitania, France
Ⓣ (33) (0)5 5357 6215
Ⓕ (33) (0)5 5358 5488
Ⓔ lumenviva@aol.com
Ⓦ www.lumen.fr
Contact: Michel Lumen
Opening Times: 0900-1200 & 1300-1630 Mon-Thu, 0900-1200 & 1300-1530 Fri. Closed Sat, Sun & B/hols. 0900-1200 & 1300-1830 Mon-Sat, Mar-Jun.
Min Mail Order UK: Nmc
Min Mail Order EU: Nmc
Cat. Cost: Online only.
Credit Cards: Visa, MasterCard
Specialities: Hardy perennials. French Nat. Collection of *Miscanthus*.
Notes: Also sells wholesale.
OS Grid Ref: 44° 51' 43.29 N, 0° 32' 32.11 E

XPde **Pépinière de l'Île** ⊠ ✈ ⌂ €
Keranroux, 22870, Ile de Brehat, France
Ⓣ 33 (0)2 96 200384
Ⓜ 0686 128609
Ⓕ 33 (0)2 96 200384
Ⓔ contact@pepiniere-brehat.com
Ⓦ www.pepiniere-brehat.com
Contact: Laurence Blasco & Charles Blasco
Opening Times: 1400-1800 spring & summer. Other times by appt. incl. Aug.
Min Mail Order UK: Nmc
Min Mail Order EU: Nmc
Cat. Cost: €6.00
Credit Cards: None
Specialities: *Agapanthus* & *Echium*. Plants from South Africa, Madeira, Canary Islands & New Zealand.

XSen **Les Senteurs Du Quercy** ⊠ € ♿
Mas de Fraysse, Escamps, Lot, 46230 France
Ⓣ (33) (0)5 652 10167
Ⓔ melie.fred@aliceadsl.fr
Ⓦ www.senteursduquercy.com
Contact: Frédéric Prévot
Opening Times: 1400-1800 spring & summer (excl. Aug). Other times, incl. Aug by appt.
Min Mail Order UK: Nmc
Min Mail Order EU: Nmc
Cat. Cost: €5.00
Specialities: *Salvia*, *Iris*, *Phlomis*, *Teucrium*, *Lavandula* and drought tolerant plants. French Nat. Coll. of *Salvia* species.

X

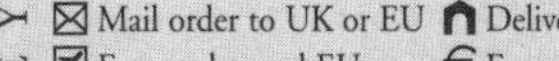

KEY
⊠ Mail order to UK or EU ⌂ Delivers to shows
✈ Exports beyond EU € Euro accepted
♿ Accessible by wheelchair ◆ See Display advertisement

Nursery Index by Name

Nurseries that are included in the *RHS Plant Finder* for the first time this year (or have been reintroduced) are marked in **bold type**. Full details of the nurseries will be found in **Nursery Details by Code** on page 842. For a key to the geographical codes, see the start of **Nurseries.**

Buckingham Nurseries	LBuc
Buckland Plants	**GBuc**
Bucknell Nurseries	WBuc
Burncoose Nurseries	CBcs
Burnham Nurseries	CBur
Cacti & Succulents	SCac
Cairnsmore Nursery	GCai
Cally Gardens	GCal
Cambridge Garden Plants	ECGP
Camellia Grove Nursery	SCam
Canna Man	**SCan**
Cants of Colchester Ltd	ECnt
Caradoc Doy	CDoy
Caths Garden Plants	NCGa
Chapel Farm House Nursery	CCha
Charleshurst Farm Nursery	SChF
Chase Plants (formerly Meadows Nursery)	CCse
Beth Chatto Gardens Ltd, The	ECha
Chennels Gate Gardens & Nursery	WChG
Chew Valley Trees	CCVT
Chiltern Seeds	NChl
Chipchase Castle Nursery	NChi
Choice Landscapes	ECho
Chrysanthemums Direct	MCms
Churcher, John	SChr
Churchtown Carnivores	NChu
Cider Apple Trees	CCAT
Clay Lane Nursery	LCla
Coblands Nursery	**SCob**
James Cocker & Sons	GCoc
Coghurst Camellias	SCog
Colesbourne Gardens	**WCol**
Constantine Garden Nursery (formerly Fir Tree Farm)	CCon
Cooks Garden Centre	**WCks**
Cool Temperate	MCoo
Cooling's Nurseries Ltd	SCoo
Coton Manor Garden	MCot
Cotswold Garden Flowers	WCot
Cottage Garden Nursery	LCtg
Cottage Garden Plants	NCot
Cottage Nurseries	ECtt
County Park Nursery	ECou
Craigieburn Garden	GCra
Creake Plant Centre	ECre
Crescent Plants	WCre
Crin Gardens	MCri
Crocosmia Gardens, The	**ECrc**
Croft 16 Daffodils	GCro
Crofters Nurseries	SCrf
Cromar Nursery	SCmr
Cross Common Nursery	CCCN
Croston Cactus	NCro
Crown Nursery	ECrN
Crûg Farm Plants	WCru
Culm View Nursery	CCVN
D K Plants	MDKP
D'Arcy & Everest	EDAr
Daisy Roots	**LDai**
P de Jager & Sons Ltd	SDeJ
Derek Lloyd Dean	LDea
Deelish Garden Centre	IDee
Desert to Jungle	CDTJ
Desirable Plants	CDes
Devon Croft Nursery	MDev
Dibley's Nurseries	WDib
Dickson Nurseries Ltd	IDic
Different Plants	EDif
Dobies of Devon	CDob
Dove Cottage Nursery & Garden	NDov
Downderry Nursery	SDow
Drointon Nurseries	NDro
Duchy of Cornwall	CDoC
Dulford Nurseries	CDul
Jack Dunckley's Birchfield Nursery	SBfd
Dysons Nurseries	SDys
East Northdown Farm Nursery	SEND
Edrom Nurseries	GEdr
Edulis	LEdu
Eggleston Hall Gardens	NEgg
Ellebore	XEll
Charles F Ellis	WCFE
Elsworth Herbs	CEls
Elworthy Cottage Plants	CElw
English Woodlands	SEWo
Entwood Farm Plants	CEnt
Equatorial Plant Co.	NEqu
Essex Carnivorous Plants	EECP
Evergreen Conifer Centre	WEve
Exclusive Plants (incorporating Pine Lodge Gardens & Nursery)	CPLG
Exotic Garden Company, The	EExo
Fairweather's Garden Centre	SFai
Family Trees	SFam
Farmyard Nurseries	WFar
Fern Nursery, The	EFer
Fernwood Nursery	CWil
Fibrex Nurseries Ltd	WFib
Field House Nursery	MFie
Field of Blooms	IFoB
Fir Trees Pelargonium Nursery	NFir
Firgrove Plants	SFgr
Flora Exotica	EFEx
Flower Bower, The	CFwr
Fly Trap Plants, The	EFly
Forest Edge Nurseries	**CFst**
Frogswell Nursery	IFro
Frosch Exclusive Perennials	XFro
Garden Blooms	NGBl
Garden House Nursery	NGdn
Garden House Enterprises	CGHE
Garden Plants	SGar
Gardeners Boutique (formerly Plants of Special Interest)	NGBo
Glendoick Gardens Ltd	**GGGa**
Gobbett Nursery, The	WGob

Name	Code
Goldbrook Plants	EGol
Golden Hill Nurseries	SGol
Gordon's Nursery	WGor
Gortkelly Castle Nursery & Arboretum	IGor
Gosbrook Pelargoniums	MGbk
Goscote Nurseries Ltd	MGos
Grange Farm Plants	EGFP
Grasslands Nursery	**MGrl**
Grayson, Peter (Sweet Pea Seedsman)	MPet
Great Dixter Nurseries	SDix
Great Western Gladiolus Nursery, The	CGrW
Green Garden Herbs	EGHP
Green, Mary	NMyG
Green's Leaves	WGrn
Griffin, D	**EGri**
C W Groves & Son Ltd	CGro
Gwynfor Growers	WGwG
Habitat Aid Ltd.	CHab
Hall Farm Nursery	WHal
John Hall Plants Ltd	SWhi
Halls of Heddon	NHal
Hardy Exotics	CHEx
Hardy's Cottage Garden Plants	SHar
Harley Nursery	WHar
Harlow Carr Plant Centre (RHS)	**NRHS**
Harperley Hall Farm Nurseries	**NHpl**
Harrells Hardy Plants	WHrl
Hart Canna	**SHaC**
Hartside Nursery Garden	NHar
Harveys Garden Plants	**EHrv**
Hawthornes Nursery, The	NHaw
Hayloft Plants	WHlf
Heaselands Garden Nursery	SHea
Henry Street Nursery	LStr
Herb Garden & Historical Plant Nursery, The	WHer
Herb Nursery, The	MHer
Herbary, The	CHby
Herbs for Healing	WHfH
Hergest Croft Gardens	WHCr
Herterton House Garden Nursery	NHer
Herts Hellebores	LHel
Heucheraholics	SHeu
Hewitt-Cooper Carnivorous Plants	CHew
Hidden Valley Gardens	CHVG
Hidden Valley Nursery	CHid
High Garden Nurseries	CHGN
Highdown Nursery	SHDw
Hill House Nursery & Gardens	CHll
Hillier Garden Centres	**SHil**
Hillview Hardy Plants	WHil
Himalayan Garden Co., The	NHim
Himalayan Gardens Ltd.	**GHim**
Hoecroft Plants	EHoe
Holden Clough Nursery Ltd.	NHol
Home Plants	SHom
Homestead Plants	MHom
Honeysome Aquatic Nursery	EHon
Hoo House Nursery	WHoo
Hooksgreen Herbs Ltd	**MHoo**
Hopleys Plants Ltd	LHop
Horticultural Sales	**WHor**
Hoyland Plant Centre	NHoy
Kevin Hughes Plants	SKHP
Hull Farm	EHul
Hydrangea Haven	SHyH
Ice Alpines	**WIce**
Iden Croft Herbs	SIde
Iris Garden, The	CIri
Iris of Sissinghurst	SIri
Irisesonline	EIri
Ivycroft Plants	WIvy
JPR Environmental	WJPR
Jackson's Nurseries	MJac
Jasmine Cottage Gardens	CJas
Paul Jasper Trees	WJas
Jekka's Herb Farm	WJek
Jo's Garden Enterprise	GJos
John and Lynsey's Plants	SPin
Jungle Giants	WJun
Junker's Nursery Ltd. (formerly P M A Plant Specialities)	CJun
Keepers Nursery	SKee
Kelways	CKel
Kent Street Nurseries	SKen
Kenwith Nursery (Gordon Haddow)	CKen
Kevock Garden Plants	GKev
Kiftsgate Court Gardens	WKif
Kilmurry Nursery	IKil
Kinlochlaich Garden Plant Centre	GKin
Knoll Gardens	CKno
L.B. Plants	NLBP
L W Plants	LLWP
Lakka Bulbs	CLak
Landford Trees	CLnd
Landlife Wildflowers Ltd	NLan
Landscape Plants	SLPl
Laneside Hardy Orchid Nursery	NLAp
Langthorns Plantery	ELan
Larch Cottage Nurseries	NLar
Larkspur Nursery	ELar
Laurel Farm Herbs	ELau
Laurels Nursery, The	SLau
Lavender Garden, The	WLav
Layham Garden Centre & Nursery	SLay
Lea Rhododendron Gardens Ltd	MLea
Lime Cross Nursery	SLim
Linn Botanic Gardens	GLin
Little Brook Fuchsias	SLBF
Little Heath Farm (UK)	LLHF
C S Lockyer (Fuchsias)	CLoc
Loder Plants	SLdr
Logie Steading Plants	GLog
Long Acre Plants	CLAP
Long House Plants	ELon
Longcombe Nursery and Garden Centre	CLng

Waterperry Gardens Ltd	MWat
Waterside Nursery	MWts
Waun Nurseries	WWau
Wayside Aquatics	**EWay**
Weasdale Nurseries Ltd.	NWea
Welsh Fruit Stocks	WWFS
West Acre Gardens	EWes
West Somerset Garden Centre	CWSG
Westcountry Nurseries	CWCL
Westonbirt Plants	LWst
Westshores Nurseries	NWsh
Jill White	EJWh
White Veil Fuchsias	CWVF
Whitehall Farmhouse Plants	WWFP
Whitehill Farm Nursery	MWhi
Whitelea Nursery	MWht
Wibble Farm Nurseries	CWib
Winchester Growers Ltd	**CWGr**
Windrush Willow	CWiW
Wisley Plant Centre (RHS)	LRHS
Witton, D S	NWit
Wollerton Old Hall Garden	WWlt
Wolverton Plants Ltd	SWvt
Wonder Tree, The	CWon
Woodlands	EWld
Woottens Plants	EWoo
World's End Garden Nursery	WWEG
Nigel Wright Rhododendrons	CWri
Wych Cross Nurseries	SWCr
Yaffles	LYaf
Yorkshire Lavender	**NYoL**

SPECIALIST NURSERIES

Nurseries have classified themselves under the following headings where they *exclusively* or *predominantly* supply this range of plants. Plant groups are set out in alphabetical order. Refer to **Nursery Details by Code** on page 842 for details of the nurseries whose codes are listed under the plant group which interests you. See page 839 for a fuller explanation.

ACID-LOVING PLANTS

CBcs, CFst, CMac, CMen, CWCL, CWri, ECho, EECP, EFly, GGGa, IBlr, IPen, ITim, IVic, LMil, MFie, MGos, MLea, MMuc, MPnt, MSnd, NHar, NHim, NLar, SCam, SCog, SFai, SHea, SLdr, SReu, SRot, WAbe, WThu

ALPINE/ROCK PLANTS

CEls, CWat, CWil, CWon, ECho, EDAr, EHoe, EPot, GAgs, GEdr, GHim, GKev, IBal, IPen, ITim, LAma, LWst, MCri, NHar, NHpl, NMen, NMin, NNth, NRya, NSla, NYoL, SCog, SPop, SRot, WAbe, WAln, WBla, WCre, WGor, WHoo, WIce, WSpi, WThu, WTul

AQUATIC PLANTS

CBen, CRow, CWat, EHon, EWay, LPBA, MSKA, MWts, SWat, WMAq, WPnP

BAMBOOS

CAgr, CDTJ, CEnt, CPHo, ENBC, ERod, ETod, GBin, IMou, MBrN, MDev, MMoz, MMuc, MWhi, MWht, NGdn, NHim, SBig, WJun, WPGP

BRITISH WILD FLOWERS

CArn, CHab, CHby, CRea, GPoy, MHer, NBir, NLan, NLAp, NMin, NMir, NYoL, SWat, WHer, WHfH, WJek, WLav, WSFF, WShi

BULBOUS PLANTS

CAvo, CBro, CGrW, CLak, CPne, CQua, CRea, CTca, CWCL, ECho, EPot, ERCP, GCro, GHim, GKev, IBlr, LAma, LWst, MCri, MSSP, NHoy, NHpl, NMin, SDeJ, WCol, WShi, WTul, XEll

CACTUS AND SUCCULENTS

CAbb, CFwr, CPhi, CTrC, EAmu, EGri, EShb, LToo, NCro, NOaD, SCac, SChr, WPGP

CARNIVOROUS PLANTS

CHew, CSWC, EECP, EFEx, EFly, NChu, WSSs

CHALK-LOVING PLANTS

CBot, CSev, CSpe, EGFP, LSRN, NLan, SAll, SEND, SGar, SHar, SKHP, SMrs, SSss, SUsu, XEll

CLIMBERS

CCon, CLng, CRHN, CSPN, CTri, CWCL, CWGN, ELan, ETho, LSRN, MBlu, MGos, MOWG, MSwo, NSti, NTay, SKHP, SLau, SMDP, WCru, WFib, WSHC, XEll

COASTAL PLANTS

CCCN, CPne, CTrC, IBal, ISsi, IVic, NHoy, SBod, SChr, SEND, SGar, SMea, WPnn

CONIFERS

CKen, CMac, CMen, EHul, MBlu, MPkF, NLar, SBig, SLim, WEve, WGor, WMou, WThu

CONSERVATORY PLANTS

CBcs, CCCN, CEls, CFwr, CHll, CLak, CRHN, CSpe, EABi, EBak, EOHP, EShb, EUJe, IFro, LToo, MBPg, MOWG, MREP, NChu, NFir, SPlb, WSFF, WTcb, XBlo

DROUGHT-TOLERANT PLANTS

CBot, CKno, CPne, CWil, ECGP, ECha, EGri, EHoe, ETod, LLWP, MBPg, MPnt, NFir, NHoy, NMRc, SAll, SDow, SEND, SPhx, SPlb, SUsu, WFib, WHil, WPnn, XLum, XSen

FERNS

CBty, CDTJ, CKel, CLAP, EFer, ELan, EShb, GBin, GEdr, IBal, IMou, ISha, LPBA, LTen, MMoz, NMyG, SApp, SRot, WAbe, WFib, WMoo, WPnP, WSpi, WWEG

FRUIT

CAgr, CCAT, CTho, CTri, ECrN, EPom, EUJe, GPri, GTwe, LBuc, LEdu, MCoo, SCmr, SCrf, SEWo, SFam, SKee, SVic, WBuc, WHar, WJas, WWFS

Grasses

CKno, EHoe, EPPr, GBin, GCal, IFoB, IMou, LEdu, LLWP, MBel, MBrN, MMoz, MNrw, MWhi, NGdn, NMRc, NOak, NWsh, SApp, SBea, SHDw, SMea, SMHy, SPhx, SSss, SUsu, SWal, WGrn, WHal, WMoo, WWEG, XLum

Hedging

CCVT, CSil, CTho, CTrC, CTri, EBtc, ECrN, ERom, ISsi, LBuc, LTen, MSwo, SDow, SEWo, SLay, SRiv, SVic, WBuc, WEve, WHar, WLav, WMou

Herbs

CArn, CHby, CSev, CWan, EGHP, ELau, ENfk, EOHP, GPoy, LEdu, LLWP, MHer, MHoo, NBir, NYoL, SDow, SHDw, SVic, SWal, SWat, WHfH, WJek, WLav

Marginal/Bog Plants

CBen, CLAP, CMHG, CWat, EECP, EFly, EHon, GKev, IPen, IVic, MMuc, MWts, NBir, NChu, NCot, NMRc, WHal, WMAq, WMoo, WPnP, WShi

Orchids

CBur, CLAP, EFEx, GEdr, LAma, LWst, LYaf, NEqu, NLAp, WHer, XFro

Organic

CBgR, CHby, CTuc, CWon, GPoy, LEdu, LLWP, LTen, MBel, MCri, NHoy, NOak, NWad, SPav, SPol, WGwG, WJek, WPnP, WSFF, WShi, WWFS

Ornamental trees

CBcs, CBty, CCVT, CDul, CJun, CMac, CMCN, CMen, CSto, CTho, CTri, CWon, EBtc, ECrN, EGFP, ELan, ERod, ERom, LBuc, LMaj, LMil, LTen, MBlu, MGos, MPkF, MSwo, NLar, SBir, SCrf, SEWo, SKHP, SLau, SLay, SLim, WBuc, WCru, WEve, WHar, WHCr, WJas, WMou, WPGP, XLum

Palms

CPHo, EAmu, EGri, MREP, SBig, SChr

Peat Free

CBgR, CBot, CCse, CCVN, CElw, CHby, CLAP, CMea, CPHo, CPom, CRHN, CSam, CSev, CTho, CTsd, EBla, ECrN, ELau, EMal, EPts, IBlr, LEdu, LLWP, MBel, MBNS, MCri, MLHP, MMoz, MWhi, NBid, NLan, NNth, NOak, SAll, SBch, SBfd, SCan, SPad, SPav, STes, WCAu, WCru, WGwG, WHoo, WJek, WPnP, WSFF, WShi, WSpi, WTcb, XEll

Period Plants

CArn, CKel, CQua, CSev, CSil, CWGr, EBtc, ESgI, MPnt, SAll, SPop, WAln, WHer, WSpi

Propagate to Order

CCCN, CCon, CCse, CEls, CElw, CFst, CLAP, CMac, CMen, CPHo, CPne, CSev, CTsd, CWGr, CWon, CWVF, ECho, ECrN, EECP, EGFP, EHoe, ENfk, EOHP, EPri, ERhR, ERod, EShb, GBuc, GKev, GQue, IBal, IFro, IMou, IPPN, IRar, LBMP, LEdu, LLWP, LMil, MDev, MLHP, MMoz, MMuc, MNrw, MOWG, MPnt, MRav, NChi, NCot, NHoy, NNth, NRya, NYoL, SAga, SBch, SCam, SChr, SCrf, SEND, SFam, SGar, SHDw, SHyH, SLdr, SPhx, SPin, SPol, SRGP, SSea, STes, SUsu, SWat, WAln, WCAu, WCru, WFib, WGwG, WHer, WHil, WJek, WLav, WMoo, WOld, WPat, WPnP, WSFF, WSpi, WSSs, WTcb, WTin, XBlo, XLum

Roses

CGro, CKel, CPou, ECnt, ESty, GCoc, IDic, LShp, LSRN, LStr, MAus, SFam, SLay, SRGP, SSea, SWCr

Seed

CBot, CDob, CHby, CHVG, CKno, CRea, CSpe, CSut, CTuc, EGHP, GPoy, MFie, MPet, NChl, NEqu, NLan, NRob, SSss, WHil, WJek, WSFF, WTou, XBlo

Specimen-size Plants

CCVT, CFst, CJun, CKel, CPhi, CPHo, CPne, CSWC, CWon, EAmu, EBtc, ECrN, EHoe, EHul, ELau, ENfk, ERom, ETod, EUJe, GGGa, IMou, LEdu, LMaj, LMil, LTen, LTop, MDev, MGos, MLea, MMuc, MOWG, MPhe, MPnt, MREP, MWht, NCro, NGBo, NHoy, NLAp, NNth, SBfd, SBig, SCam, SCrf, SEND, SEWo, SFai, SGol, SHyH, SLdr, SReu, SSta, SWat, WCru, WEve, WJek, WPat, WSpi, WTcb

Topiary

ERom, ETod, LTop, MREP, SRiv

Tropical

CCCN, CCon, CDTJ, CFwr, CPHo, EAmu, EUJe, GHim, ISsi, LToo, MOWG, MREP, SBst, SHaC, SPlb, WCru, WHil, WTcb, XBlo

INDEX MAP

The maps on the following pages show the approximate location of the nurseries whose details are listed in this directory.

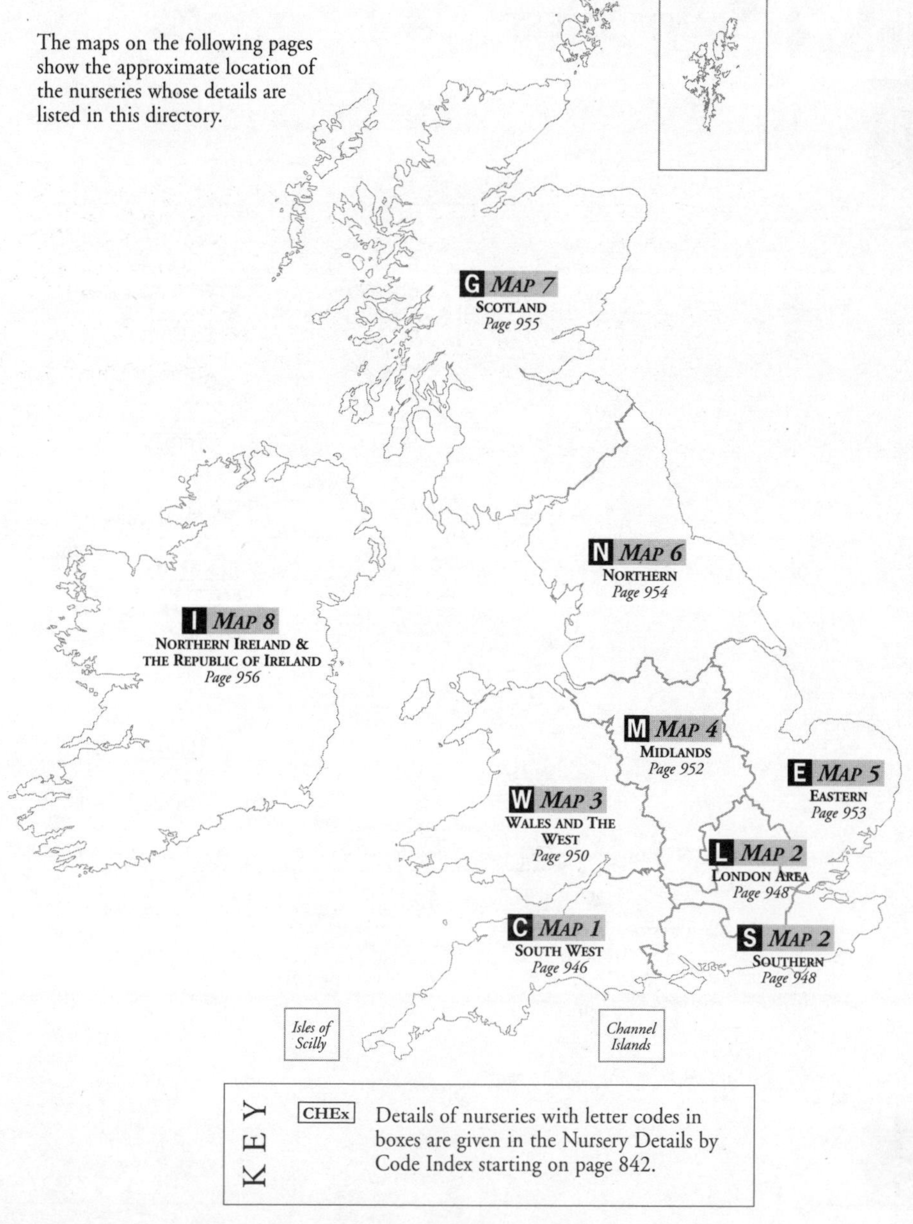

KEY

CHEx — Details of nurseries with letter codes in boxes are given in the Nursery Details by Code Index starting on page 842.

C
MAP ONE
SOUTH WEST
1
2
3
A
B
C
D
Llanelli
M4
Neath
Swansea
Port Talbot
Bridgend
CSil
Ilfracombe
Combe Martin
CMHG
Barnstaple
Bideford
CAni
CHid
CWCL
CKen
CWri
CPne
A377
CYeo
Bude
CWil
A39
CCha
CPbn
Okehampton
CSto
Launceston
CBre
CRow
Tavistock
Newton Abbot
CBct
Wadebridge
CTca
CGHE
CHll
A38
CLng
Bodmin
Liskeard
CTsd
CDoC
CMam
Newquay
CPrp
Plymouth
A30
CPLG
CHVG
CPou
CRHN
St Austell
Truro
St Ives
Redruth
CHEx
Camborne
CBcS
CTrC
Penzance
Helston
Falmouth
COlW
CCon
CQua
CCCN
1
2
3

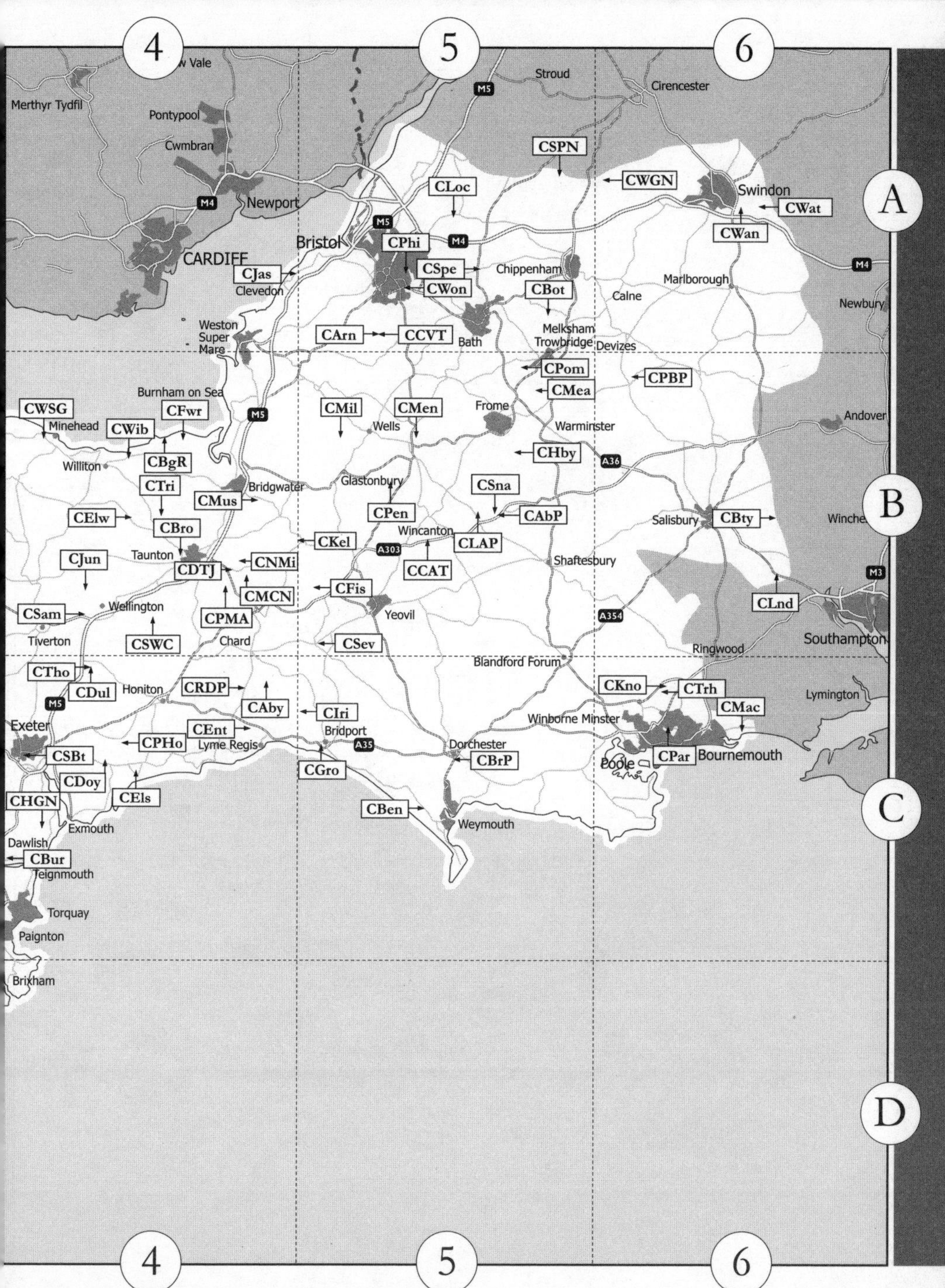
4
5
6
A
B
C
D
Merthyr Tydfil
Pontypool
Cwmbran
Newport
CARDIFF
M4
M5
Stroud
Cirencester
CSPN
CWGN
CLoc
Swindon
CWat
CWan
Bristol
CPhi
CSpe
CWon
Chippenham
CBot
CJas
Clevedon
Marlborough
Calne
Newbury
Weston Super Mare
CArn
CCVT
Bath
Melksham
Trowbridge
Devizes
CPom
CMea
CPBP
Burnham on Sea
CWSG
CFwr
CMil
CMen
Frome
Minehead
CWib
Wells
Warminster
Andover
Williton
CBgR
CHby
A36
CTri
Bridgwater
Glastonbury
CSna
CMus
CElw
CPen
CAbP
Salisbury
CBty
CBro
CKel
Wincanton
CLAP
A303
Taunton
CJun
CDTJ
CNMi
CCAT
Shaftesbury
M3
CMCN
CFis
CLnd
CSam
Wellington
CPMA
Yeovil
A354
Southampton
Tiverton
CSWC
Chard
CSev
Ringwood
Blandford Forum
CTho
CDul
Honiton
CRDP
CKno
CTrh
Lymington
CAby
CIri
CMac
Exeter
CEnt
Winborne Minster
CPHo
Lyme Regis
Bridport
CSBt
A35
Dorchester
CPar
Bournemouth
CDoy
CGro
CBrP
Poole
CHGN
CEls
Exmouth
CBen
Weymouth
Dawlish
CBur
Teignmouth
Torquay
Paignton
Brixham

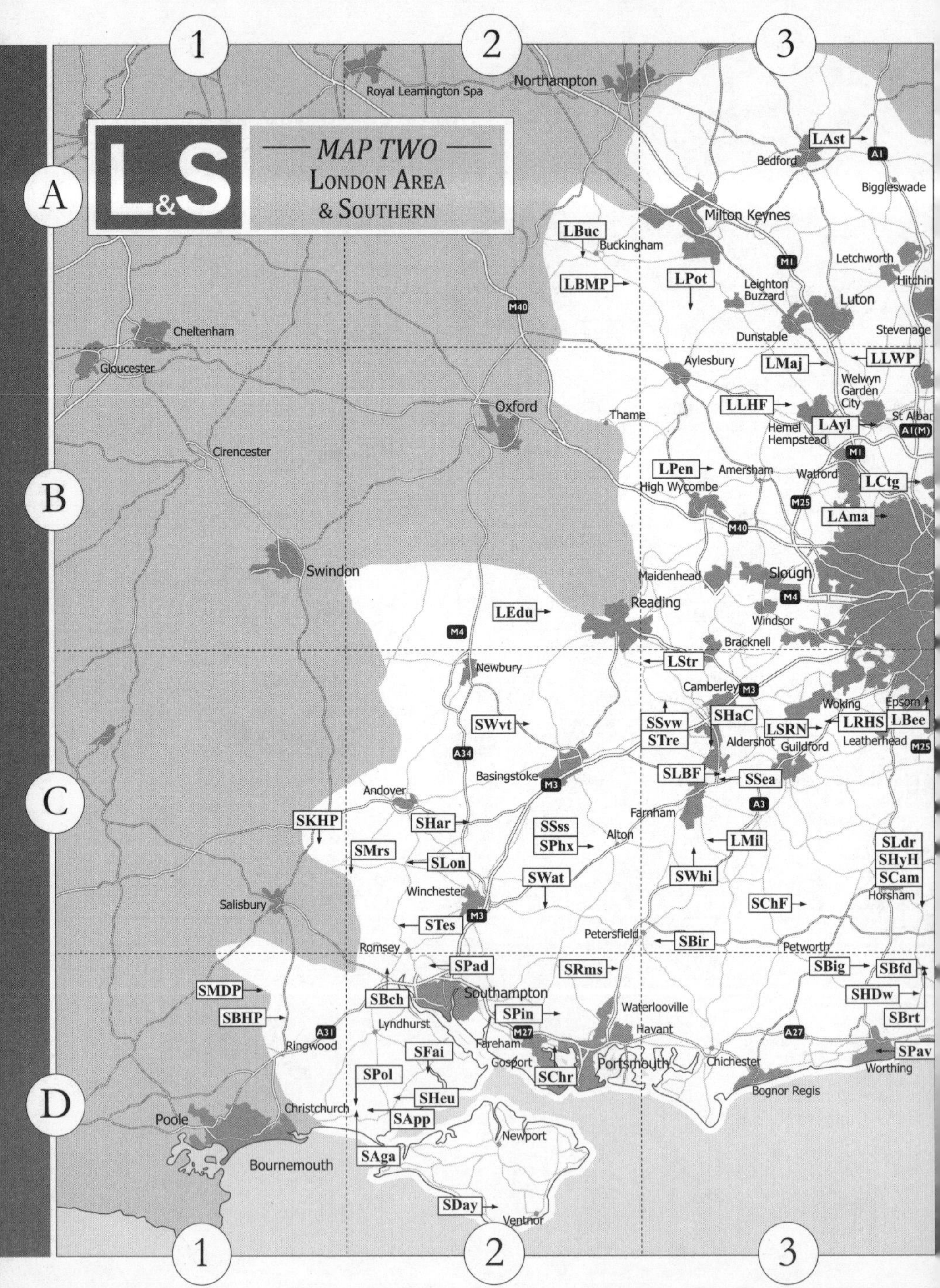
L&S
MAP TWO
London Area
& Southern
1
2
3
A
B
C
D
Royal Leamington Spa
Northampton
Bedford
LAst
A1
Biggleswade
Milton Keynes
LBuc
Buckingham
LBMP
LPot
Leighton
Buzzard
M1
Letchworth
Hitchin
Luton
M40
Cheltenham
Gloucester
Dunstable
Stevenage
Aylesbury
LMaj
LLWP
Welwyn
Garden
City
Oxford
Thame
LLHF
Hemel
Hempstead
LAyl
St Albans
A1(M)
Cirencester
LPen
Amersham
High Wycombe
Watford
LCtg
M25
LAma
M40
Swindon
Maidenhead
Slough
M4
Reading
LEdu
M4
Windsor
Bracknell
Newbury
LStr
Camberley
M3
SSvw
STre
SHaC
Woking
LSRN
LRHS
Epsom
LBee
SWvt
Aldershot
Guildford
Leatherhead
M25
A34
Basingstoke
M3
SLBF
SSea
Andover
A3
SKHP
SHar
Farnham
SSss
SPhx
Alton
LMil
SLdr
SHyH
SCam
SMrs
SLon
SWat
SWhi
Horsham
Winchester
SChF
Salisbury
M3
STes
Petersfield
SBir
Romsey
Petworth
SPad
SRms
SBig
SBfd
SMDP
SBch
Southampton
SHDw
SBHP
SPin
Waterlooville
SBrt
A31
Lyndhurst
M27
Havant
A27
Ringwood
SFai
Fareham
Gosport
Portsmouth
Chichester
SPav
Worthing
SPol
SChr
Bognor Regis
SHeu
Christchurch
SApp
Poole
Newport
SAga
Bournemouth
SDay
Ventnor

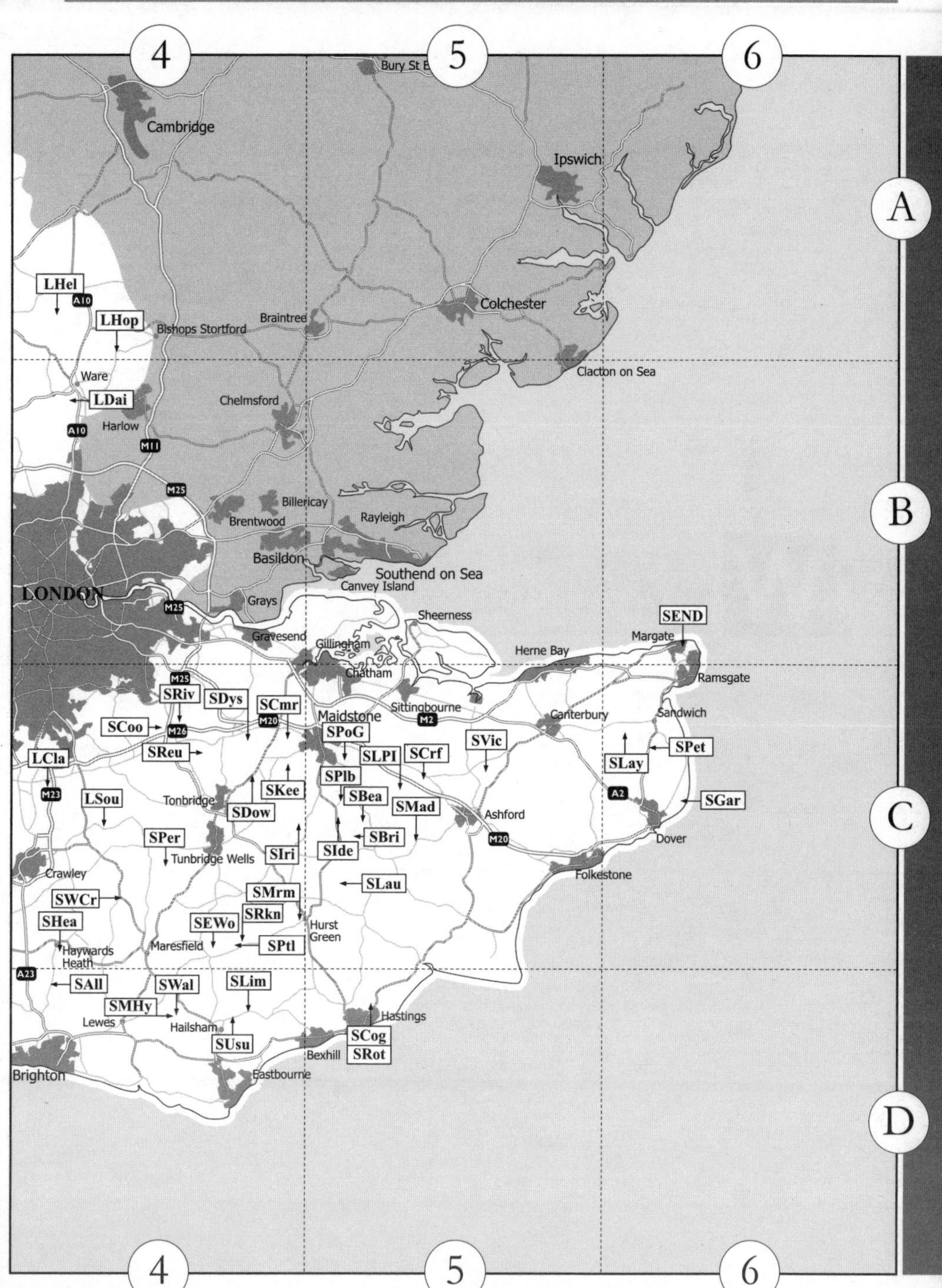
4
5
6
A
B
C
D
Bury St E
Cambridge
Ipswich
Colchester
Braintree
Bishops Stortford
Clacton on Sea
Ware
Chelmsford
Harlow
Billericay
Brentwood
Rayleigh
Basildon
Southend on Sea
Canvey Island
LONDON
Grays
Sheerness
Gravesend
Gillingham
Chatham
Herne Bay
Margate
Ramsgate
Sittingbourne
Maidstone
Canterbury
Sandwich
Tonbridge
Ashford
Dover
Tunbridge Wells
Folkestone
Crawley
Hurst Green
Haywards Heath
Maresfield
Lewes
Hailsham
Hastings
Bexhill
Brighton
Eastbourne
A10
M11
M25
M20
M26
M2
M23
A2
A23
LHel
LHop
LDai
SEND
SRiv
SDys
SCmr
SCoo
SPoG
SReu
SLPI
SCrf
SVic
SPet
SLay
LCla
SPlb
SKee
SBea
SMad
SGar
LSou
SDow
SBri
SPer
SIri
SIde
SLau
SMrm
SWCr
SRkn
SHea
SEWo
SPtl
SAll
SWal
SLim
SMHy
SUsu
SCog
SRot

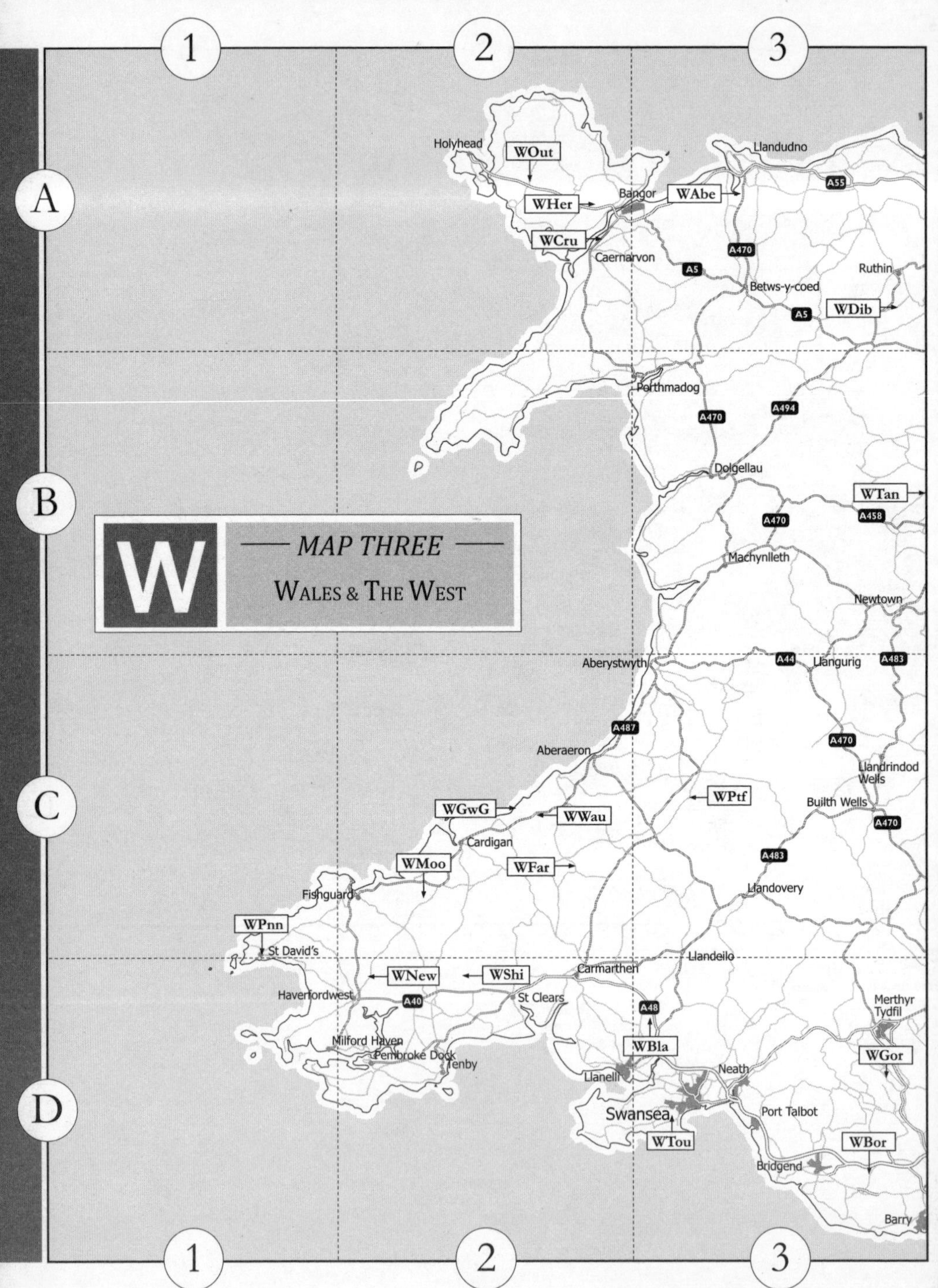
1
2
3
A
B
C
D
W
MAP THREE
WALES & THE WEST
Holyhead
WOut
Llandudno
A55
WHer
Bangor
WAbe
WCru
Caernarvon
A5
A470
Ruthin
Betws-y-coed
WDib
A5
Porthmadog
A470
A494
Dolgellau
WTan
A470
A458
Machynlleth
Newtown
Aberystwyth
A44
Llangurig
A483
A487
A470
Aberaeron
Llandrindod Wells
WPtf
Builth Wells
WGwG
WWau
A470
Cardigan
A483
WMoo
WFar
Fishguard
Llandovery
WPnn
St David's
Llandeilo
WNew
WShi
Carmarthen
Haverfordwest
A40
St Clears
A48
Merthyr Tydfil
Milford Haven
Pembroke Dock
Tenby
WBla
WGor
Llanelli
Neath
Swansea
Port Talbot
WTou
WBor
Bridgend
Barry

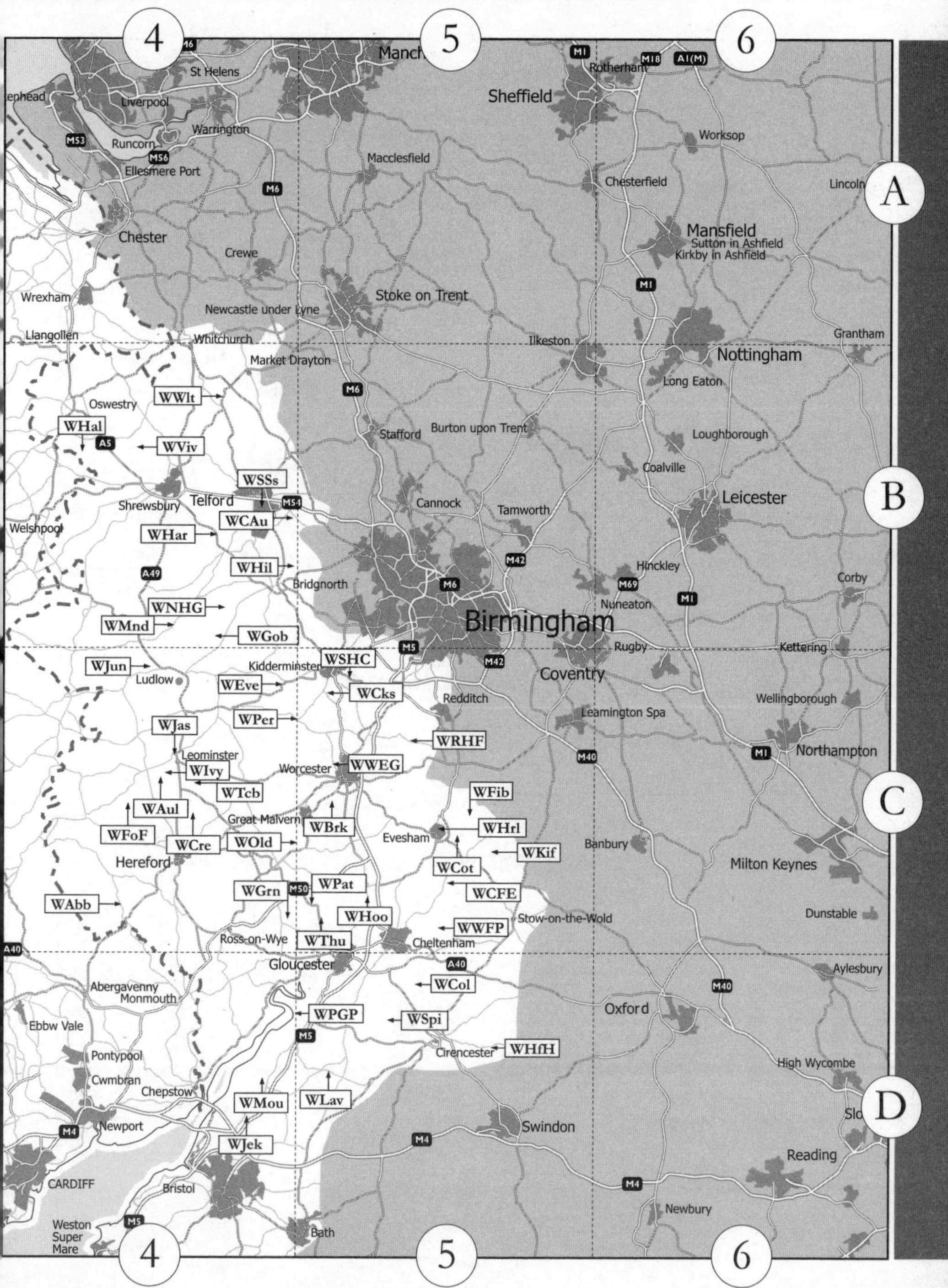
4
5
6
A
B
C
D
Manch
St Helens
Liverpool
Warrington
Runcorn
Ellesmere Port
Chester
Crewe
Wrexham
Llangollen
Whitchurch
Newcastle under Lyne
Stoke on Trent
Macclesfield
Sheffield
Rotherham
Worksop
Chesterfield
Lincoln
Mansfield
Sutton in Ashfield
Kirkby in Ashfield
Ilkeston
Nottingham
Long Eaton
Grantham
Market Drayton
Oswestry
Stafford
Burton upon Trent
Loughborough
Coalville
Leicester
Telford
Shrewsbury
Welshpool
Cannock
Tamworth
Hinckley
Corby
Bridgnorth
Nuneaton
Birmingham
Rugby
Kettering
Kidderminster
Ludlow
Coventry
Redditch
Leamington Spa
Wellingborough
Leominster
Worcester
Northampton
Great Malvern
Evesham
Banbury
Hereford
Milton Keynes
Stow-on-the-Wold
Dunstable
Ross-on-Wye
Cheltenham
Gloucester
Aylesbury
Abergavenny
Monmouth
Oxford
Ebbw Vale
Cirencester
Pontypool
High Wycombe
Cwmbran
Chepstow
Newport
Swindon
Reading
CARDIFF
Bristol
Newbury
Weston
Super
Mare
Bath
M6
M1
M18
A1(M)
M53
M56
M54
M42
M69
M5
M50
M40
A5
A49
A40
M4
WWlt
WHal
WViv
WSSs
WCAu
WHar
WHil
WNHG
WMnd
WGob
WJun
WSHC
WEve
WCks
WPer
WJas
WRHF
WIvy
WWEG
WTcb
WAul
WFib
WFoF
WBrk
WHrl
WCre
WOld
WKif
WCot
WGrn
WPat
WCFE
WAbb
WHoo
WWFP
WThu
WCol
WPGP
WSpi
WHfH
WMou
WLav
WJek

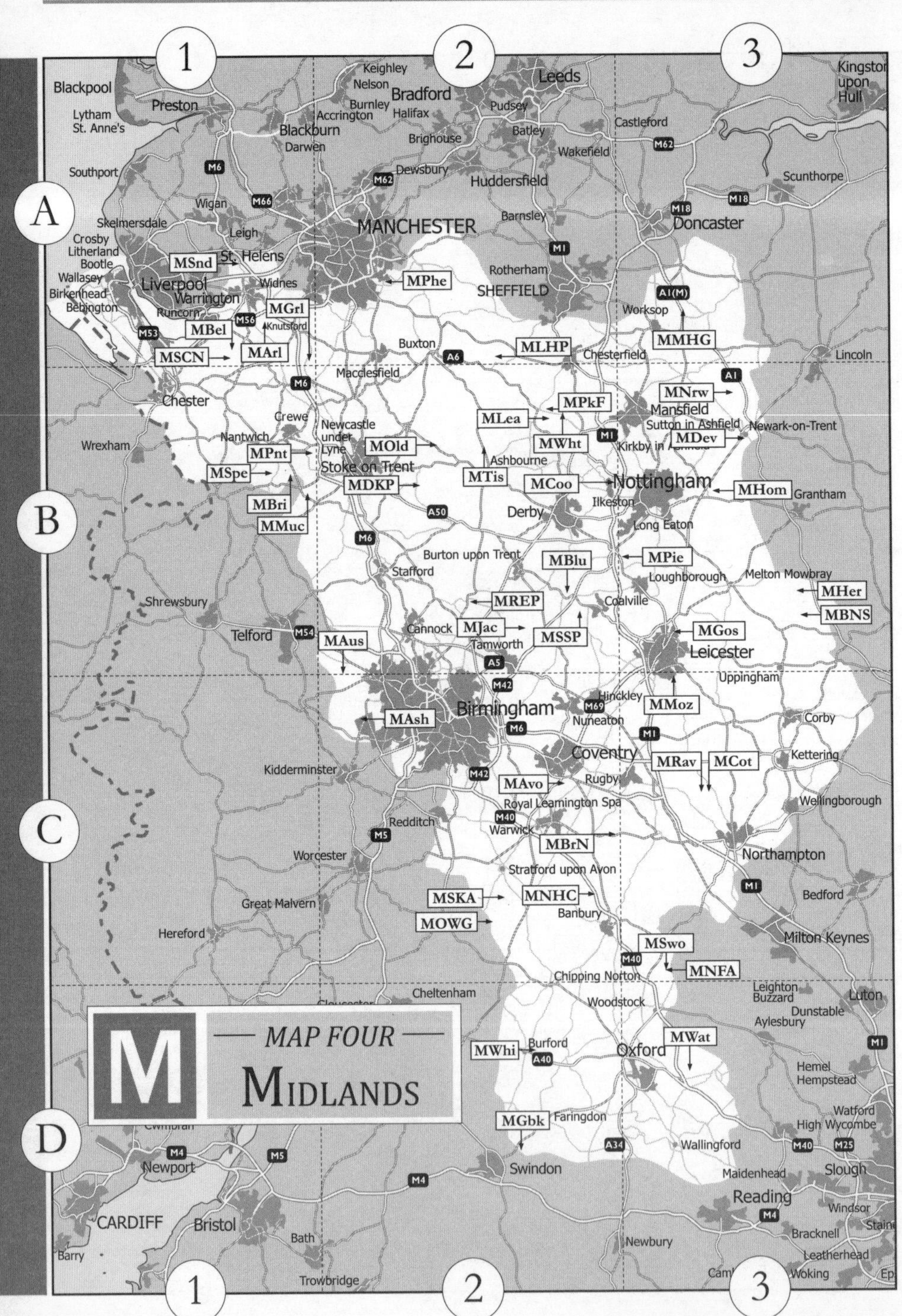
1
2
3
A
B
C
D
MAP FOUR
M
MIDLANDS
Blackpool
Preston
Lytham St. Anne's
Keighley
Nelson
Burnley
Accrington
Blackburn
Darwen
Bradford
Halifax
Brighouse
Leeds
Pudsey
Batley
Castleford
Kingston upon Hull
Wakefield
Dewsbury
Huddersfield
Southport
Scunthorpe
Wigan
Skelmersdale
Leigh
MANCHESTER
Barnsley
Doncaster
Crosby
Litherland
Bootle
Wallasey
Birkenhead
Bebington
Liverpool
St. Helens
Widnes
Warrington
Runcorn
Knutsford
Rotherham
SHEFFIELD
Worksop
Buxton
Chesterfield
Lincoln
Macclesfield
Chester
Crewe
Nantwich
Newcastle under Lyne
Stoke on Trent
Mansfield
Sutton in Ashfield
Kirkby in Ashfield
Newark-on-Trent
Wrexham
Ashbourne
Nottingham
Ilkeston
Grantham
Derby
Long Eaton
Burton upon Trent
Stafford
Loughborough
Melton Mowbray
Shrewsbury
Coalville
Telford
Cannock
Tamworth
Leicester
Uppingham
Hinckley
Birmingham
Nuneaton
Corby
Coventry
Kettering
Kidderminster
Rugby
Royal Leamington Spa
Wellingborough
Redditch
Warwick
Worcester
Northampton
Stratford upon Avon
Great Malvern
Banbury
Bedford
Hereford
Milton Keynes
Chipping Norton
Cheltenham
Woodstock
Leighton Buzzard
Luton
Dunstable
Aylesbury
Burford
Oxford
Hemel Hempstead
Faringdon
Watford
High Wycombe
Newport
Wallingford
Swindon
Maidenhead
Slough
Reading
CARDIFF
Bristol
Bath
Windsor
Bracknell
Barry
Newbury
Leatherhead
Trowbridge
Woking
MSnd
MPhe
MGrl
MBel
MArl
MSCN
MLHP
MMHG
MNrw
MPkF
MLea
MWht
MDev
MPnt
MOld
MSpe
MDKP
MTis
MCoo
MHom
MBri
MMuc
MBlu
MPie
MREP
MHer
MBNS
MJac
MSSP
MAus
MGos
MMoz
MAsh
MRav
MCot
MAvo
MBrN
MSKA
MNHC
MOWG
MSwo
MNFA
MWhi
MWat
MGbk
M6
M62
M66
M18
M1
A1(M)
M56
M53
A6
A1
A50
M54
A5
M42
M69
M6
M40
M5
A40
A34
M4
M25

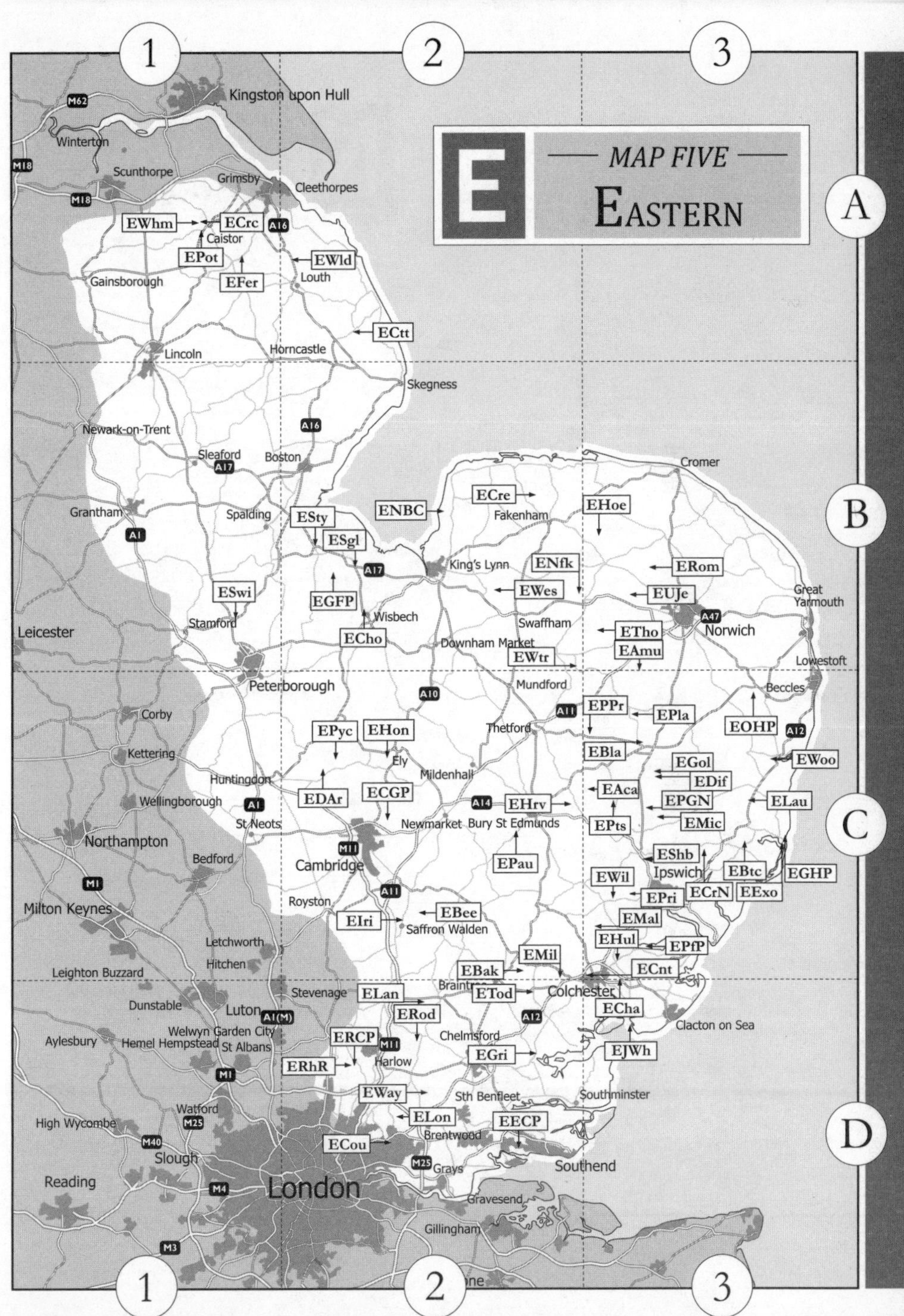
E
MAP FIVE
EASTERN
1
2
3
A
B
C
D
Kingston upon Hull
Winterton
Scunthorpe
Grimsby
Cleethorpes
EWhm
ECrc
Caistor
EPot
EFer
EWld
Louth
Gainsborough
ECtt
Lincoln
Horncastle
Skegness
Newark-on-Trent
Sleaford
Boston
Grantham
Spalding
ESty
ESgl
ENBC
ECre
Fakenham
EHoe
Cromer
King's Lynn
ENfk
ERom
EWes
EUJe
Great Yarmouth
ESwi
EGFP
Wisbech
Stamford
Swaffham
ETho
Norwich
Leicester
ECho
Downham Market
EAmu
EWtr
Lowestoft
Peterborough
Mundford
Beccles
EPPr
EPla
Corby
Thetford
EOHP
EPyc
EHon
Kettering
EBla
EWoo
Ely
EGol
EDif
Huntingdon
Mildenhall
EDAr
ECGP
EAca
EPGN
ELau
Wellingborough
EHrv
St Neots
Newmarket
Bury St Edmunds
EPts
EMic
Northampton
EPau
EShb
Bedford
Cambridge
Ipswich
EBtc
EGHP
EWil
ECrN
EExo
EPri
Milton Keynes
Royston
EBee
EIri
Saffron Walden
EMal
Letchworth
EHul
EPfP
Hitchen
EMil
EBak
ECnt
Leighton Buzzard
Colchester
Stevenage
ELan
ETod
Dunstable
Luton
ECha
ERod
Welwyn Garden City
Aylesbury
Hemel Hempstead
St Albans
ERCP
Chelmsford
Clacton on Sea
EJWh
ERhR
Harlow
EGri
EWay
Watford
Sth Benfleet
Southminster
High Wycombe
ELon
EECP
Brentwood
ECou
Slough
Grays
Southend
Reading
London
Gravesend
Gillingham
M62
M18
A16
A17
A1
A47
A10
A11
A12
A14
M11
M1
A1(M)
M25
M40
M4
M3

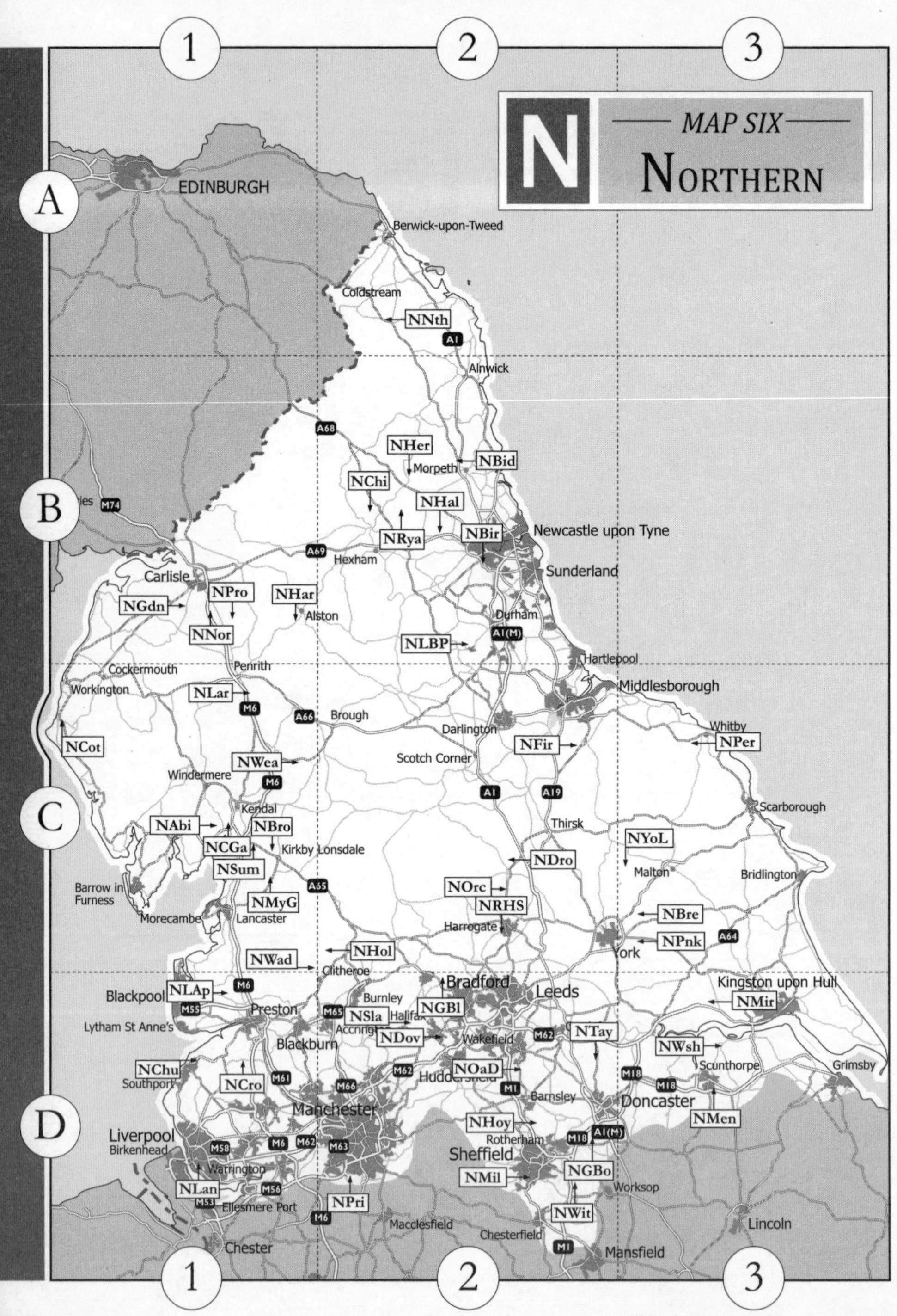
N
MAP SIX
NORTHERN
1
2
3
A
B
C
D
EDINBURGH
Berwick-upon-Tweed
Coldstream
NNth
A1
Alnwick
A68
NHer
Morpeth
NBid
NChi
NHal
NRya
NBir
Newcastle upon Tyne
M74
A69
Hexham
Sunderland
Carlisle
NPro
NHar
NGdn
Alston
Durham
NNor
NLBP
A1(M)
Hartlepool
Cockermouth
Penrith
Middlesborough
Workington
NLar
M6
A66
Brough
Darlington
Whitby
NFir
NPer
NCot
Scotch Corner
NWea
Windermere
A19
Scarborough
Kendal
Thirsk
NAbi
NBro
NYoL
NCGa
Kirkby Lonsdale
NDro
NSum
Malton
Bridlington
Barrow in Furness
A65
NOrc
NMyG
NRHS
Morecambe
Lancaster
NBre
Harrogate
NPnk
A64
York
NHol
NWad
Clitheroe
Kingston upon Hull
Bradford
Blackpool
NLAp
Leeds
NMir
Burnley
M55
Preston
M65
NSla
NGBl
Halifax
Lytham St Anne's
Accrington
NTay
NDov
Wakefield
M62
Blackburn
NWsh
NChu
Scunthorpe
Grimsby
Southport
NCro
M61
M66
NOaD
M18
Huddersfield
M1
Barnsley
Doncaster
Manchester
NHoy
NMen
Liverpool
Birkenhead
M58
M63
Rotherham
Sheffield
Warrington
NGBo
NMil
NLan
M56
Worksop
M53
Ellesmere Port
NPri
NWit
Macclesfield
Chesterfield
Lincoln
Chester
Mansfield

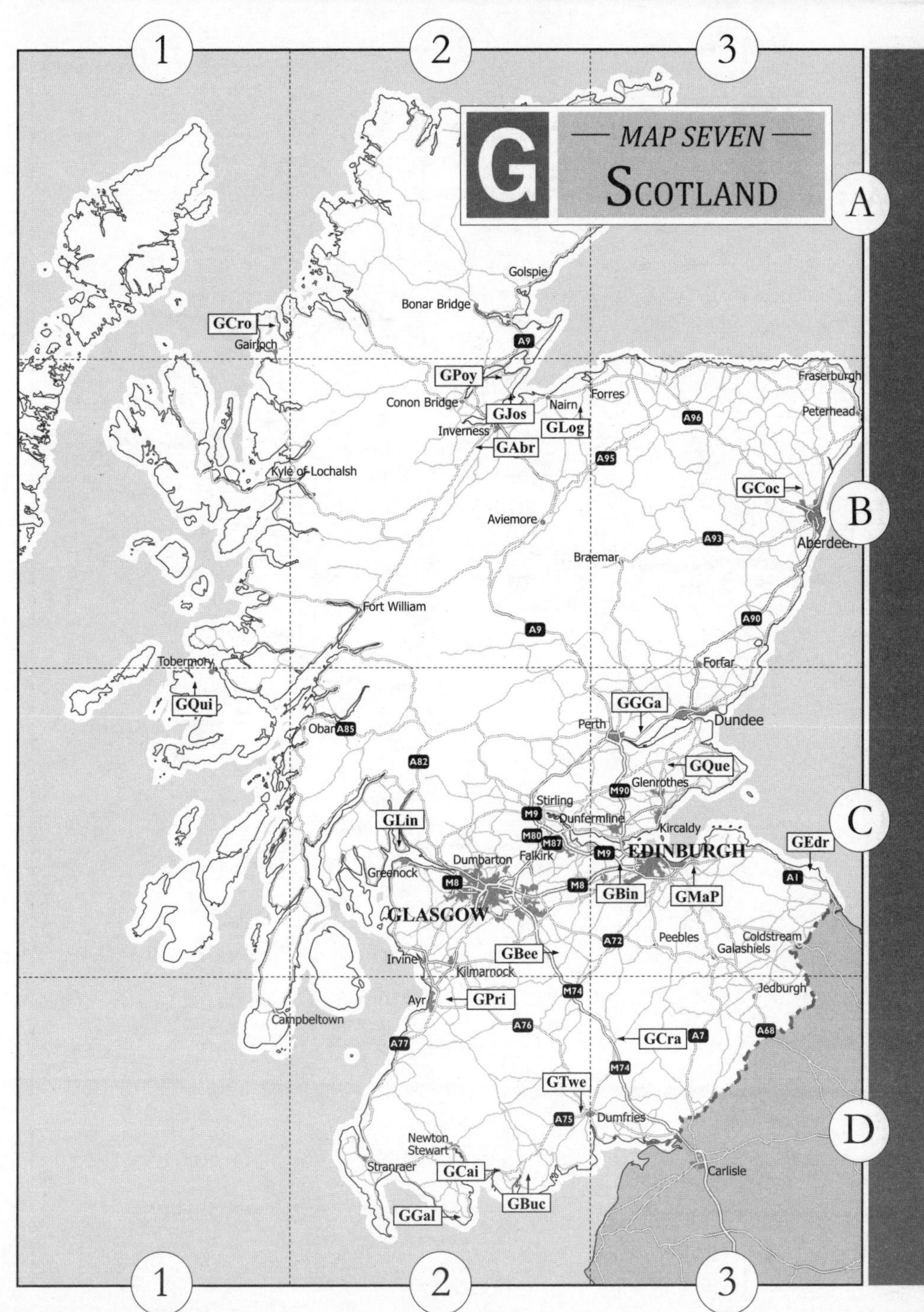
G
— MAP SEVEN —
SCOTLAND
1
2
3
A
B
C
D
Golspie
Bonar Bridge
GCro
Gairloch
A9
GPoy
Conon Bridge
GJos
Nairn
Forres
GLog
Inverness
GAbr
Fraserburgh
Peterhead
A96
A95
Kyle of Lochalsh
GCoc
Aviemore
A93
Aberdeen
Braemar
Fort William
A9
A90
Tobermory
GQui
Forfar
GGGa
Perth
Dundee
Oban
A85
A82
GQue
Glenrothes
M90
Stirling
M9
Dunfermline
GLin
Kircaldy
M80
M87
GEdr
Dumbarton
Falkirk
M9
EDINBURGH
Greenock
M8
A1
M8
GBin
GMaP
GLASGOW
Peebles
Coldstream
Galashiels
A72
GBee
Irvine
Kilmarnock
Jedburgh
M74
Ayr
GPri
Campbeltown
A76
GCra
A7
A68
A77
M74
GTwe
A75
Dumfries
Newton Stewart
Stranraer
GCai
Carlisle
GBuc
GGal

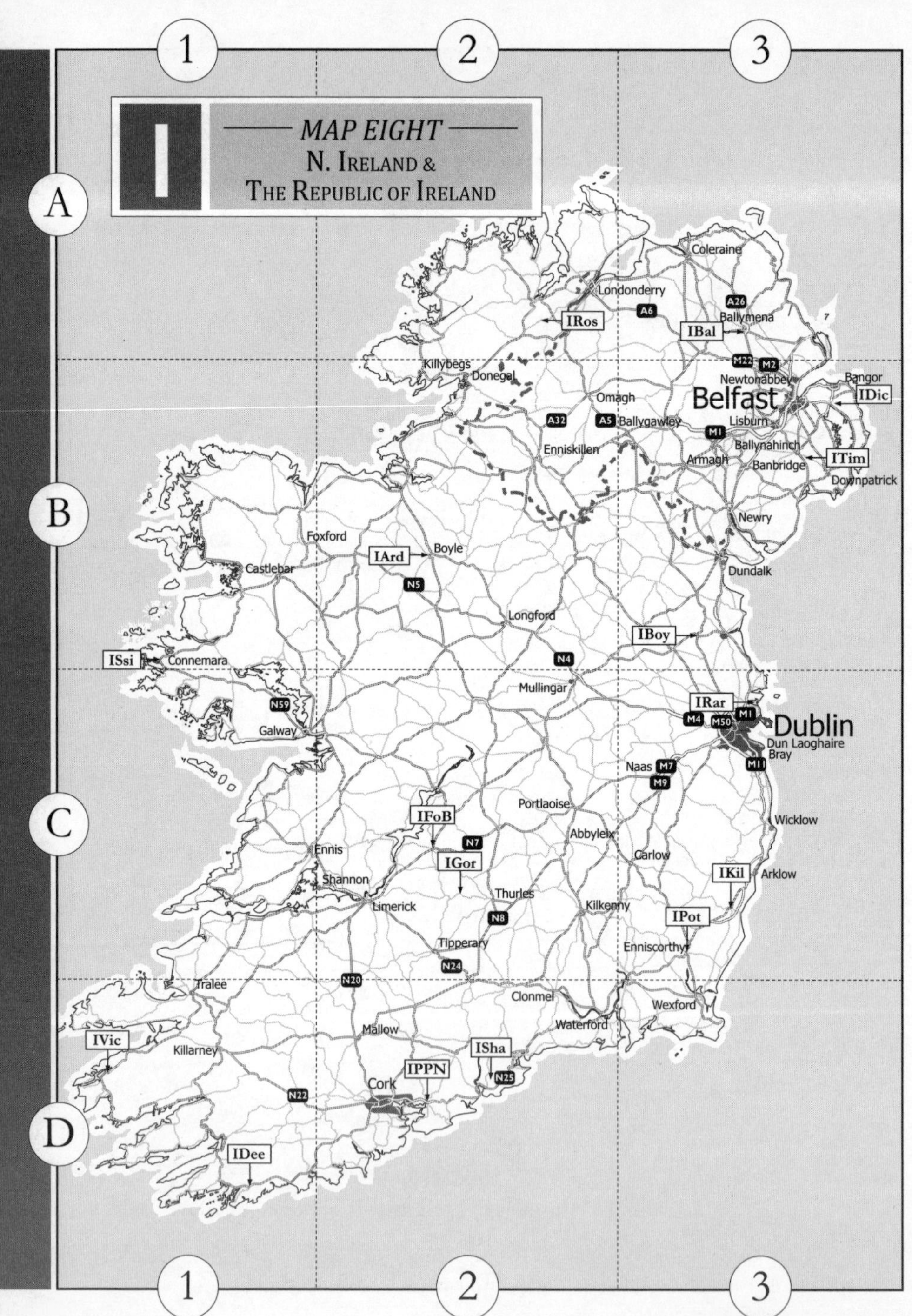
1
2
3
A
B
C
D
I
MAP EIGHT
N. Ireland &
The Republic of Ireland
Coleraine
Londonderry
A6
A26
IRos
Ballymena
IBal
Killybegs
Donegal
M22
M2
Newtonabbey
Bangor
Belfast
IDic
Omagh
A32
A5
Ballygawley
Lisburn
M1
Enniskillen
Ballynahinch
Armagh
Banbridge
ITim
Downpatrick
Newry
Foxford
IArd
Boyle
Castlebar
N5
Dundalk
Longford
IBoy
ISsi
Connemara
N4
Mullingar
IRar
M1
M4
M50
Dublin
N59
Galway
Dun Laoghaire
Bray
Naas
M7
M11
M9
Portlaoise
IFoB
Wicklow
Abbyleix
N7
Ennis
IGor
Carlow
IKil
Arklow
Shannon
Thurles
Limerick
Kilkenny
N8
IPot
Tipperary
Enniscorthy
N24
N20
Tralee
Clonmel
Wexford
Waterford
Mallow
IVic
Killarney
ISha
IPPN
N25
Cork
N22
IDee

RHS Show Awards 2010

RHS Plant Finder nurseries that were awarded RHS medals at four major RHS Shows in 2010.

Chelsea Gold

Jacques Amand International
Claire Austin Hardy Plants
David Austin Roses Ltd
Avon Bulbs
Burncoose Nurseries
Chrysanthemums Direct
Dibley's Nurseries
Fernwood Nursery
Hall Farm Nursery
Hardy's Cottage Garden Plants
Hewitt-Cooper Carnivorous Plants
Hillier Garden Centres
Kelways
Knoll Gardens
Mallet Court Nursery
Mendip Bonsai Studio
Plantagogo.com
Rhodes & Rockliffe
Thorncroft Clematis
Westcountry Nurseries
Winchester Growers Ltd

Chelsea Silver-Gilt

Broadleigh Gardens
Culm View Nursery
D'Arcy & Everest
Downderry Nursery
Harveys Garden Plants
Heucheraholics (as Solva Plants)
Hoyland Plant Centre
Potash Nursery
Rotherview Nursery

Chelsea Silver

Fibrex Nurseries Ltd
Oak Tree Nursery
Pennard Plants **(Lindley Silver)**
W Robinson & Sons Ltd
Tendercare Nurseries Ltd
Topiary Arts
Waterside Nursery

Chelsea Bronze

Botanic Nursery, The
Mickfield Hostas
Primrose Bank

Hampton Court Gold

Jacques Amand International (& Most Creative Exhibit in Floral Marquee)
Avon Bulbs
Caths Garden Plants
Chrysanthemums Direct
Culm View Nursery
Derek Lloyd Dean
Desert to Jungle
Dibley's Nurseries (2 awards & Chelsea Plant of the Year Award)
Downderry Nursery
Fibrex Nurseries Ltd (2 awards)
Fir Trees Pelargonium Nursery
Hardy's Cottage Garden Plants
Hart Canna
Harveys Garden Plants
Hewitt-Cooper Carnivorous Plants
Hoyland Plant Centre
C S Lockyer (Fuchsias)
Mallet Court Nursery
Marshall's Malmaisons
Mendip Bonsai Studio
The Old Walled Garden
Dave Parkinson Plants
Plantagogo.com
Potash Nursery
Taylors Clematis Nursery
Waterside Nursery
Winchester Growers Ltd

Hampton Court Silver-Gilt

David Austin Roses Ltd
Big Plant Nursery
Brookfield Plants

Burncoose Nurseries
Daisy Roots
Downderry Nursery (**Lindley Silver-Gilt**)
Essex Carnivorous Plants (**Lindley Silver-Gilt**)
Heucheraholics
Holden Clough Nursery Ltd.
Hooksgreen Herbs Ltd
Hopleys Plants Ltd
Hoyland Plant Centre
Kelways
Mickfield Hostas (**Lindley Silver-Gilt**)
Oak Tree Nursery
Primrose Bank
Rotherview Nursery
South West Carnivorous Plants
Todd's Botanics
Water Meadow Nursery (**Lindley Silver-Gilt**)

Hampton Court Silver

Burnham Nurseries
Cooks Garden Centre
Field House Nursery (**Lindley Silver**)
Harperley Hall Farm Nurseries
Hillview Hardy Plants (**Lindley Silver**)
Pine Cottage Plants
Seale Nurseries
Squire's Garden Centres
Style Roses

Hampton Court Bronze

Bentley Plants
Botanic Nursery, The
Field House Nursery (**Lindley Bronze**)
Pennard Plants
Plantbase

Tatton Gold

Caths Garden Plants
Chrysanthemums Direct
Culm View Nursery
Dibley's Nurseries
Fibrex Nurseries Ltd
Fir Trees Pelargonium Nursery
Hall Farm Nursery
Harperley Hall Farm Nurseries
Hartside Nursery Garden
Dave Parkinson Plants (& Best Exhibit in Floral Marquee)
Potash Nursery
Waterside Nursery

Tatton Silver-Gilt

Brookfield Plants
Brownthwaite Hardy Plants
Desert to Jungle
Dibley's Nurseries
Mary Green
Heucheraholics
Holden Clough Ltd
Hooksgreen Herbs Ltd
Hoyland Plant Centre
Morton Nurseries Ltd
Plantagogo.com
Primrose Bank
W Robinson & Sons Ltd (**Lindley Silver-Gilt**)
Slack Top Nurseries
Taylors Clematis Nursery

Tatton Silver

Broadleigh Gardens
Cairnsmore Nursery
Hardy's Cottage Garden Plants
Oak Tree Nursery
Pennard Plants

Tatton Bronze

Jacques Amand International
Botanic Nursery, The
Cooks Garden Centre

Geranium 'Rozanne'

big plant
nursery

NORFOLK HERBS
Blackberry Farm, Dillington, Dereham, NR19 2QD
01362 860812
info@norfolkherbs.co.uk
Specialist growers of culinary, medicinal and aromatic herb plants for your garden, patio or window ledge
Herbs, Scented Pelargoniums Bay Trees, Terracotta and Mail Order Plants
Open: April to Aug. Mon to Sat, 9am to 5pm.
Sundays, 10am to 4pm
Please view our website for all other opening times and directions.
www.norfolkherbs.co.uk
www.homescentherbs.co.uk

TOPIARY

THE ROMANTIC GARDEN NURSERY

SWANNINGTON
NORWICH
NORFOLK
NR9 5NW
Tel: 01603 261488
Fax: 01603 864231

Specialist nursery with topiary of all shapes and sizes. Field grown Box and Yew from 20cm to 2m high. Large selection of specimen size trees and shrubs available.

Delivery all over the UK.

4 x 1st CLASS STAMPS FOR CATALOGUE

email: enquiries@romantic-garden-nursery.co.uk
www.romantic-garden-nursery.co.uk

Discover

Beechcroft

NURSERIES & GARDEN CENTRE

***- The Nursery with the* GROW HOW!**

Probably the widest range of plants in the Midlands — huge range of seasonal plants, trees and shrubs, raised in our own nursery.

Many unusual and 'hard to find' plants

Well stocked garden and gift shop

Open 7 days a week, all year round

TEL: 01562 710358
FAX: 01562 710507
E-mail: mail@beechcroft.com

Madeley Road, Madeley Heath
Belbroughton, Stourbridge
West Midlands, DY9 9XA

- just 4 minutes from M5 Junction 4

www.beechcroft.com

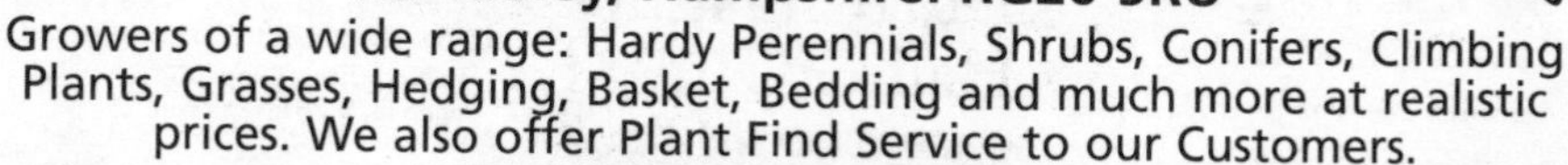

Open 7 days 9am-6pm Winter 9am - Dusk
Wolverton Plants
We Accept all Major Credit Cards

HTA

HTA

INDEX OF ADVERTISERS

The HARDY PLANT SOCIETY

Inspiring interest in hardy perennial garden plants

Membership Application 2011

Annual Subscription

- Subscriptions are renewable annually on 1 January.
- Subscriptions of members joining after 1 October are valid until the end of the following year.
- Overseas members are requested to pay in pounds sterling by International Money Order or by credit/debit Card. An optional charge of £10.00 is made for airmail postage outside Western Europe of all literature, if preferred.

Please use BLOCK CAPITALS and send this form with your payment to the Administrator or alternatively you can telephone the Administrator with details of your credit/debit Card.

Please tick the type of membership required and if airmail postage option required:

☐ Single £17.00 per year (one member)

☐ Joint £19.00 per year (two members at the same address)

☐ Airmail postage £10.00 per year (optional for members outside Western Europe only)

NAME(S) .... / ....

ADDRESS ....

.... POSTCODE ....

TELEPHONE .... MOBILE ....

EMAIL ....

Payment Option 1: I enclose ◯ cheque* ◯ postal order* payable to **The Hardy Plant Society** for £.................. in pounds sterling ONLY please. *(* indicate cheque or postal order as appropriate)*

(Please also write your address on reverse of cheque/postal order)

Payment Option 2: Please debit my credit/debit card by the sum of £..................

CARD NUMBER ☐☐☐☐ ☐☐☐☐ ☐☐☐☐ ☐☐☐☐

EXPIRY DATE ☐☐ / ☐☐ SECURITY CODE *(last three digits)* ☐☐☐

(MM) *(YY)*

Name as printed on card ....

Signature .... Date ....

Send this completed form (or a photocopy) with payment to:

The Administrator, Pam Adams, The Hardy Plant Society, Little Orchard, Great Comberton, Pershore, WR10 3DP

Tel: 01386 710 317 Email: admin@hardy-plant.org.uk

The Hardy Plant Society is a Registered Charity, number 208080 RHS PF/2011-12

THE NATIONAL PLANT COLLECTIONS®

Plant Heritage

Patron: HRH The Prince of Wales

The Lost Garden of Britain

We have a long history of gardening, plant collecting and breeding in the British Isles so our gardens contain an amazing diversity of plants. Due to the imperatives of marketing and fashion, the desire for 'new' varieties and the practicalities of bulk cultivation, many plants unique to British gardens have been lost. This diversity is important as a genetic resource for the future and as a cultural link to the past.

What is Plant Heritage?

The mission of Plant Heritage is to conserve, document and make available this resource for the benefit of horticulture, education and science. The main conservation vehicle is the National Plant Collection® scheme where individuals or organisations undertake to preserve a group of related plants in trust for the future. Our 40 local groups across Britain support the administration of the scheme, the collection holders and propagate rare plants; working to promote the conservation of cultivated plants.

Who are the National Plant Collection® Holders?

Collection holders come from every sector of horticulture, amateur and professional. Almost half of the existing 660 National Collections are in private ownership and include allotments, back gardens and large estates. 121 collections are found in nurseries, which range from large commercial concerns to the
all specialist grower. 57 local authorities are
olved in the scheme, including Sir Harold Hillier
rdens & Arboretum (Hampshire County Council)
d Leeds City Council. Universities, agricultural
leges, schools, arboreta and botanic gardens all
d to the diversity, and there are also a number of
lections on properties belonging to English
ritage, The National Trust and The National
st for Scotland.

Please see Membership Application Form

What do Collection Holders do?

Collection holders subscribe to the scheme's ideals and stringent regulations. As well as protecting the living plants in their chosen group, they also work on areas including education, scientific research and nomenclature, with the common aim of conserving cultivated plants.

How can you Help Plant Heritage?

You can play your part in supporting plant conservation by becoming a member of Plant Heritage. Regular journals will keep you informed of how your support is helping to save our plant biodiversity. Through your local group you can play a more active role in plant conservation working with collection holders, attending talks, plant sales, local horticultural shows and nursery visits.

How to Join:

Please contact
Membership
Plant Heritage
12 Home Farm, Loseley Park
Guildford
Surrey
GU3 1HS

Tel: (01483) 447540
Fax: (01483) 458933
E-mail: membership@plantheritage.org.uk
Website: www.plantheritage.com

t Heritage seeks to conserve, document, promote and make available Britain and Ireland's rich ersity of garden plants for the benefit of everyone through horticulture, education and science'